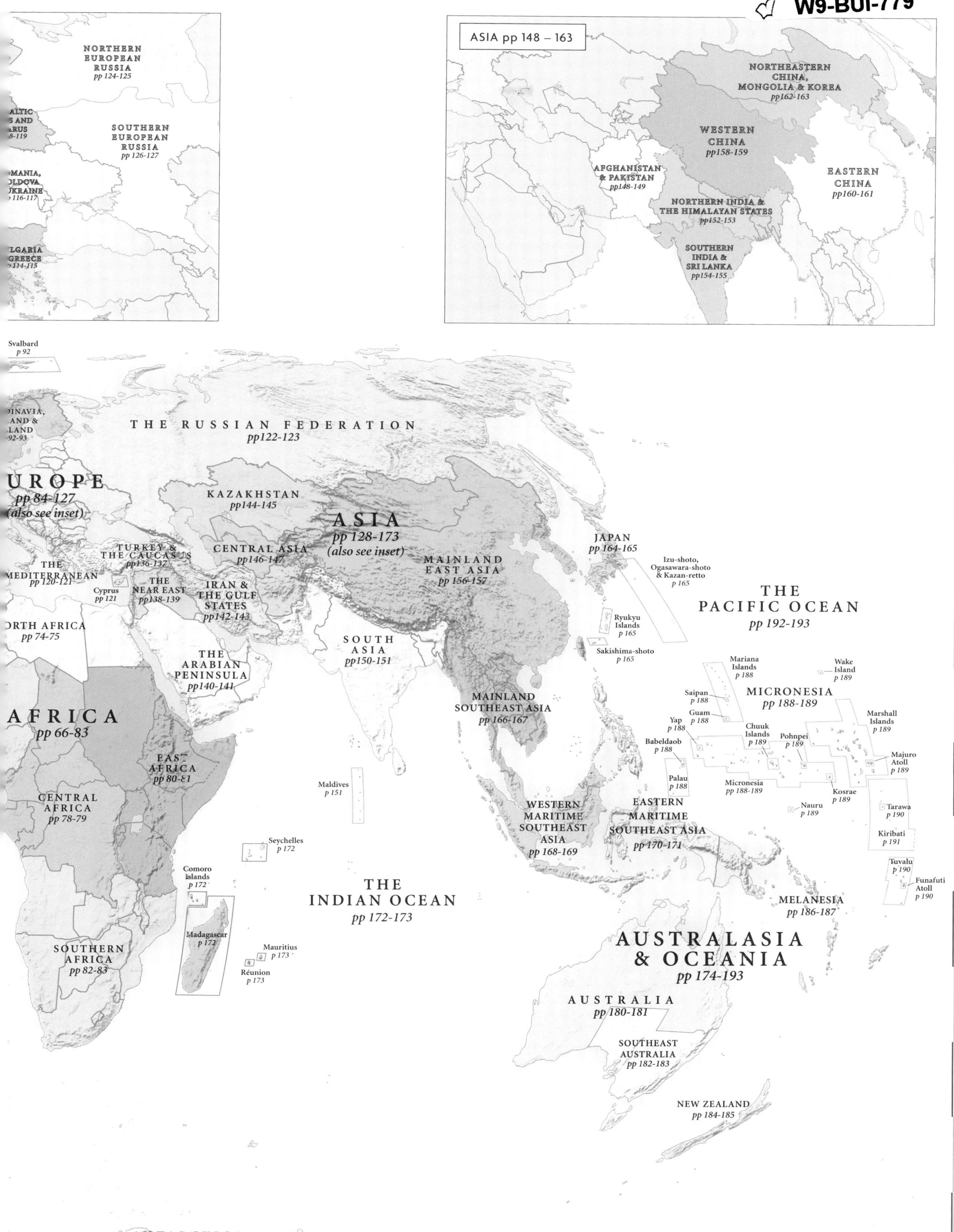

NORTHERN EUROPEAN RUSSIA
pp 124-125
SOUTHERN EUROPEAN RUSSIA
pp 126-127
ASIA pp 148 – 163
NORTHEASTERN CHINA, MONGOLIA & KOREA
pp162-163
WESTERN CHINA
pp158-159
AFGHANISTAN & PAKISTAN
pp148-149
EASTERN CHINA
pp160-161
NORTHERN INDIA & THE HIMALAYAN STATES
pp152-153
SOUTHERN INDIA & SRI LANKA
pp154-155
Svalbard
p 92
THE RUSSIAN FEDERATION
pp122-123
pp 84-127
(also see inset)
KAZAKHSTAN
pp144-145
ASIA
pp 128-173
(also see inset)
CENTRAL ASIA
pp146-147
JAPAN
pp 164-165
Izu-shoto, Ogasawara-shoto & Kazan-retto
p 165
MAINLAND EAST ASIA
pp 156-157
Cyprus
p 121
THE NEAR EAST
pp138-139
IRAN & THE GULF STATES
pp142-143
Ryukyu Islands
p 165
THE PACIFIC OCEAN
pp 192-193
Sakishima-shoto
p 165
SOUTH ASIA
pp150-151
THE ARABIAN PENINSULA
pp140-141
Mariana Islands
p 188
Wake Island
p 189
Saipan
p 188
MICRONESIA
pp 188-189
Guam
p 188
MAINLAND SOUTHEAST ASIA
pp 166-167
Yap
p 188
Chuuk Islands
p 189
Pohnpei
p 189
Marshall Islands
p 189
Babeldaob
p 188
Majuro Atoll
p 189
AFRICA
pp 66-83
Palau
p 188
Micronesia
pp 188-189
Kosrae
p 189
Maldives
p 151
CENTRAL AFRICA
pp 78-79
WESTERN MARITIME SOUTHEAST ASIA
pp 168-169
EASTERN MARITIME SOUTHEAST ASIA
pp 170-171
Nauru
p 189
Tarawa
p 190
Kiribati
p 191
Seychelles
p 172
Comoro Islands
p 172
Tuvalu
p 190
Funafuti Atoll
p 190
THE INDIAN OCEAN
pp 172-173
MELANESIA
pp 186-187
Madagascar
p 172
AUSTRALASIA & OCEANIA
pp 174-193
SOUTHERN AFRICA
pp 82-83
Mauritius
p 173
Réunion
p 173
AUSTRALIA
pp 180-181
SOUTHEAST AUSTRALIA
pp 182-183
NEW ZEALAND
pp 184-185
ANTARCTICA
pp 194-195

CONCISE
ATLAS
OF THE WORLD

CONCISE

ATLAS

OF THE WORLD

London • New York • Munich • Melbourne • Delhi

LONDON, NEW YORK, MELBOURNE, MUNICH, DELHI

FOR THE FOURTH EDITION

Publishing Director Jonathan Metcalf **Managing Cartographers** David Roberts • Simon Mumford **Art Director** Bryn Walls
Managing Editor Debra Wolter **Designers** Nimbus Design, Langworth, UK • Giraffe, London, UK • Yak El-Droubie
Cartographers Roger Bullen • DEMAP, Strathdale, Australia • Paul Eames • Encompass Graphics Ltd, Brighton, UK • Ed Merritt • Rob Stokes • Iorwerth Watkins
Jacket Designers Lee Ellwood • Duncan Turner **Systems Co-ordinator** Philip Rowles

General Geographical Consultants

Physical Geography Denys Brunsden, Emeritus Professor, Department of Geography, King's College, London
Human Geography Professor J Malcolm Wagstaff, Department of Geography, University of Southampton
Place Names Caroline Burgess, Permanent Committee on Geographical Names, London
Boundaries International Boundaries Research Unit, Mountjoy Research Centre, University of Durham

Digital Mapping Consultants

DK Cartopia developed by George Galfalvi and XMap Ltd, London
Professor Jan-Peter Muller, Department of Photogrammetry and Surveying, University College, London
Cover globes, planets and information on the Solar System provided by Philip Eales and Kevin Tildsley, Planetary Visions Ltd, London

Regional Consultants

North America Dr David Green, Department of Geography, King's College, London • Jim Walsh, Head of Reference, Wessell Library, Tufts University, Medford, Massachussetts
South America Dr David Preston, School of Geography, University of Leeds **Europe** Dr Edward M Yates, formerly of the Department of Geography, King's College, London
Africa Dr Philip Amis, Development Administration Group, University of Birmingham • Dr Ieuan Ll Griffiths, Department of Geography, University of Sussex
Dr Tony Binns, Department of Geography, University of Sussex
Central Asia Dr David Turnock, Department of Geography, University of Leicester **South and East Asia** Dr Jonathan Rigg, Department of Geography, University of Durham
Australasia and Oceania Dr Robert Allison, Department of Geography, University of Durham

Acknowledgements

Digital terrain data created by Eros Data Center, Sioux Falls, South Dakota, USA. Processed by GVS Images Inc, California, USA and Planetary Visions Ltd, London, UK
Cambridge International Reference on Current Affairs (CIRCA), Cambridge, UK • Digitization by Robertson Research International, Swanley, UK • Peter Clark
British Isles maps generated from a dataset supplied by Map Marketing Ltd/European Map Graphics Ltd in combination with DK Cartopia copyright data

DORLING KINDERSLEY CARTOGRAPHY

Editor-in-Chief Andrew Heritage **Managing Cartographer** David Roberts **Senior Cartographic Editor** Roger Bullen
Editorial Direction Louise Cavanagh **Database Manager** Simon Lewis **Art Direction** Chez Picthall

Cartographers
Pamela Alford • James Anderson • Caroline Bowie • Dale Buckton • Tony Chambers • Jan Clark • Bob Croser • Martin Darlison • Damien Demaj • Claire Ellam • Sally Gable
Jeremy Hepworth • Geraldine Horner • Chris Jackson • Christine Johnston • Julia Lunn • Michael Martin • Ed Merritt • James Mills-Hicks • Simon Mumford • John Plumer
John Scott • Ann Stephenson • Gail Townsley • Julie Turner • Sarah Vaughan • Jane Voss • Scott Wallace • Iorwerth Watkins • Bryony Webb • Alan Whitaker • Peter Winfield

Digital Maps Created in DK Cartopia by
Tom Coulson • Thomas Robertshaw
Philip Rowles • Rob Stokes

Managing Editor
Lisa Thomas

Editors
Thomas Heath • Wim Jenkins • Jane Oliver
Siobhan Ryan • Elizabeth Wyse

Editorial Research
Helen Dangerfield • Andrew Rebeiro-Hargrave

Additional Editorial Assistance
Debra Clapson • Robert Damon • Ailsa Heritage
Constance Novis • Jayne Parsons • Chris Whitwell

Placenames Database Team
Natalie Clarkson • Ruth Duxbury • Caroline Falce • John Featherstone • Dan Gardiner
Ciárán Hynes • Margaret Hynes • Helen Rudkin • Margaret Stevenson • Annie Wilson

Senior Managing Art Editor
Philip Lord

Designers
Scott David • Carol Ann Davis • David Douglas • Rhonda Fisher
Karen Gregory • Nicola Liddiard • Paul Williams

Illustrations
Ciárán Hughes • Advanced Illustration, Congleton, UK

Picture Research
Melissa Albany • James Clarke • Anna Lord
Christine Rista • Sarah Moule • Louise Thomas

Production
Linda Dare

First published in the United States in 2001 as the DK Concise Atlas of the World by DK Publishing, 375 Hudson Street, New York 10014

Second Edition 2003. Reprinted with revisions 2004. Third Edition 2005. Fourth Edition 2008

Reprographics by MDP Ltd, Wiltshire, UK
Printed and bound by Star Standard, Singapore

See our complete catalog at www.dk.com

Library of Congress Cataloging-in-Publication Data

DK Concise atlas of the World - - 1st American ed. 2001
p. cm.
"Copyright 2001 Dorling Kindersley Limited" - - Verso t.p.
Includes geographical glossary and index-gazetteers.
ISBN-13: 978-0-7566-3346-2
1.Atlases. I.DK Publishing,Inc. II. Dorling Kindersley Limited
G1021 D625 2000
912 - - DC21

Introduction

For many, the outstanding legacy of the twentieth century was the way in which the Earth shrank. As we enter the third millennium, it is increasingly important for us to have a clear vision of the World in which we live. The human population has increased fourfold since 1900. The last scraps of *terra incognita* – the polar regions and ocean depths – have been penetrated and mapped. New regions have been colonized, and previously hostile realms claimed for habitation. The advent of aviation technology and mass tourism allows many of us to travel further, faster, and more frequently than ever before. In doing so we are given a bird's-eye view of the Earth's surface denied to our forebears.

At the same time, the amount of information about our world has grown enormously. Telecommunications can span the greatest distances in fractions of a second: our multimedia environment hurls uninterrupted streams of data at us, on the printed page, through the airwaves, and across our television and computer screens; events from all corners of the globe reach us instantaneously, and are witnessed as they unfold. Our sense of stability and certainty has been eroded; instead, we are aware that the World is in a constant state of flux and change. Natural disasters, man-made cataclysms, and conflicts between nations remind us daily of the enormity and fragility of our domain. The events of September 11, 2001, threw into a very stark relief the levels of ignorance and inaccessibility that exist when trying to "know" or "understand" our planet and its many cultures.

The current crisis in our "global" culture has made the need greater than ever before for everyone to possess an atlas. The *DK Concise Atlas of the World* has been conceived to meet this need. At its core, like all atlases, it seeks to define where places are, to describe their main characteristics, and to locate them in relation to other places. Every attempt has been made to make the information on the maps as clear and accessible as possible. In addition, each page of the atlas provides a wealth of further information, bringing the maps to life. Using photographs, diagrams, "at-a-glance" maps, introductory texts and captions, the atlas builds up a detailed portait of those features – cultural, political, economic, and geomorphological – which make each region unique, and which are also the main agents of change.

This Fourth Edition of the *DK Concise Atlas of the World* incorporates thousands of revisions and updates affecting every map and every page, and reflects many of the geo-political developments which continue to alter the shape of our world. The *DK Concise Atlas of the World* has been created to bring all these benefits to a new audience, in a handy format and at an affordable price.

CONTENTS

Introduction v

Contents ..... vi–vii

How to use this Atlas ..... viii–ix

THE WORLD

The solar system ..... x–xi

The physical world ..... xii–xiii

Structure of the Earth ..... xiv–xv

Shaping the landscape ..... xvi–xvii

The world's oceans ..... xviii–xix

The global climate ..... xx–xxi

Life on Earth ..... xxii–xxiii

Population and settlement ..... xxiv–xxv

The economic system ..... xxvi–xxvii

The political world ..... xxviii–xxix

States and boundaries ..... xxx–xxxi

International disputes xxxii

ATLAS OF THE WORLD

North America

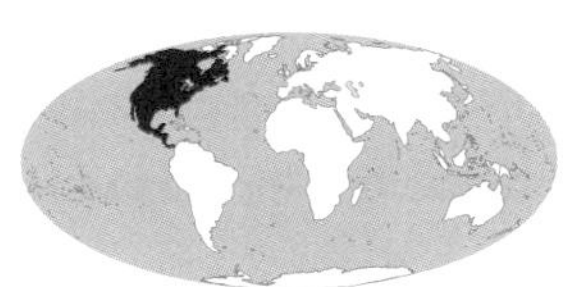

NORTH AMERICA 1

PHYSICAL NORTH AMERICA 2–3

POLITICAL NORTH AMERICA 4–5

NORTH AMERICAN RESOURCES 6–7

Canada 8–9

Canada: Western Provinces 10–11
Alberta, British Columbia, Manitoba, Saskatchewan, Yukon

Canada: Eastern Provinces 12–13
New Brunswick, Newfoundland & Labrador, Nova Scotia, Ontario, Prince Edward Island, Québec, St Pierre & Miquelon

Southeastern Canada 14–15
Southern Ontario, Southern Québec

United States of America 16–17

USA: Northeastern States 18–19
Connecticut, Maine, Massachussetts, New Hampshire, New Jersey, New York, Pennsylvania, Rhode Island, Vermont

USA: Mid-Eastern States 20–21
Delaware, District of Columbia, Kentucky, Maryland, North Carolina, South Carolina, Tennessee, Virginia, West Virginia

USA: Southern States 22–23
Alabama, Florida, Georgia, Louisiana, Mississippi

USA: Texas 24–25

USA: South Midwestern States 26–27
Arkansas, Kansas, Missouri, Oklahoma

USA: Upper Plains States 28–29
Iowa, Minnesota, Nebraska, North Dakota, South Dakota

USA: Great Lakes States 30–31
Illinois, Indiana, Michigan, Ohio, Wisconsin

USA: North Mountain States 32–33
Idaho, Montana, Oregon, Washington, Wyoming

USA: California & Nevada 34–35

USA: South Mountain States 36–37
Arizona, Colorado, New Mexico, Utah

USA: Hawai'i & Alaska 38–39

Mexico 40–41

Central America 42–43
Belize, Costa Rica, El Salvador, Guatemala, Honduras, Nicaragua, Panama

The Caribbean 44–45
Anguilla, Antigua & Barbuda, Aruba, Bahamas, Barbados, British Virgin Islands, Cayman Islands, Cuba, Dominica, Dominican Republic, Grenada, Guadeloupe, Haiti, Jamaica, Martinique, Montserrat, Navassa Island, Netherlands Antilles, Puerto Rico, St Kitts & Nevis, St Lucia, St Vincent & the Grenadines, Trinidad & Tobago, Turks & Caicos Islands, Virgin Islands (US)

South America

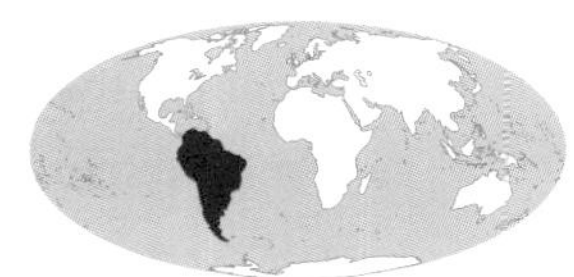

SOUTH AMERICA 46–47

PHYSICAL SOUTH AMERICA 48–49

POLITICAL SOUTH AMERICA 50–51

SOUTH AMERICAN RESOURCES 52–53

Northern South America 54–55
Colombia, French Guiana, Guyana Suriname, Venezuela

Western South America 56–57
Bolivia, Ecuador, Peru

Brazil 58–59

Eastern South America 60–61
Southeast Brazil, Northeast Argentina, Uruguay

Southern South America 62–63
Argentina, Chile, Paraguay

The Atlantic Ocean 64–65

Africa

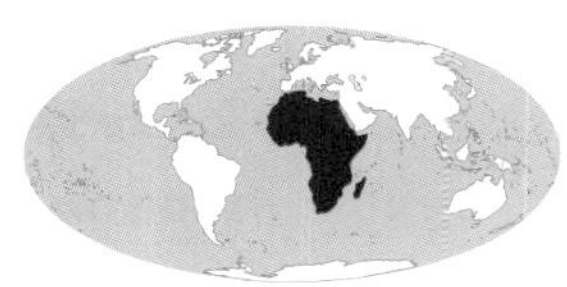

AFRICA 66–67

PHYSICAL AFRICA 68–69

POLITICAL AFRICA 70–71

AFRICAN RESOURCES 72–73

North Africa 74–75
Algeria, Egypt, Libya, Morocco, Tunisia, Western Sahara

West Africa 76–77
Benin, Burkina, Cape Verde, Gambia, Ghana, Guinea, Guinea-Bissau, Ivory Coast, Liberia, Mali, Mauritania, Niger, Nigeria, Senegal, Sierra Leone, Togo

Central Africa 78–79
Cameroon, Central African Republic, Chad, Congo, Dem. Rep. Congo, Equatorial Guinea, Gabon, Sao Tome & Principe

East Africa 80–81
Burundi, Djibouti, Eritrea, Ethiopia, Kenya, Rwanda, Somalia, Sudan, Tanzania, Uganda

Southern Africa 82–83
Angola, Botswana, Lesotho, Malawi, Mozambique, Namibia, South Africa, Swaziland, Zambia, Zimbabwe

Europe

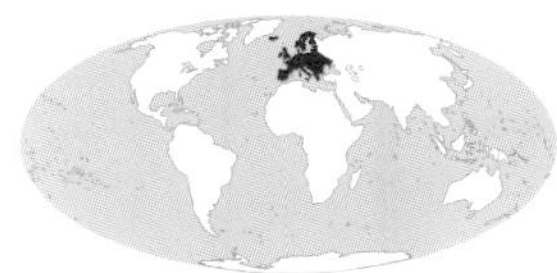

EUROPE ... 84–85

PHYSICAL EUROPE ... 86–87

POLITICAL EUROPE ... 88–89

EUROPEAN RESOURCES ... 90–91

Scandinavia, Finland & Iceland ... 92–93
Denmark, Finland, Iceland, Norway, Svalbard, Sweden

Southern Scandinavia ... 94–95
Denmark, Faeroe Islands, Southern Norway, Southern Sweden

The British Isles ... 96–97
Channel Islands, Ireland, Isle of Man, United Kingdom

The Low Countries ... 98–99
Belgium, Luxembourg, Netherlands

Germany ... 100–101

France ... 102–103
France, Monaco

The Iberian Peninsula ... 104–105
Andorra, Gibraltar, Portugal, Spain

The Italian Peninsula ... 106–107
Italy, San Marino, Vatican City

The Alpine States ... 108–109
Austria, Liechtenstein, Slovenia, Switzerland

Central Europe ... 110–111
Czech Republic, Hungary, Poland, Slovakia

Southeast Europe ... 112–113
Albania, Bosnia & Herzegovina, Croatia, Macedonia, Montenegro, Serbia

Bulgaria & Greece ... 114–115
(including European Turkey)

Romania, Moldova & Ukraine ... 116–117

The Baltic States & Belarus ... 118–119
Belarus, Estonia, Latvia, Lithuania, Kaliningrad

The Mediterranean ... 120–121

The Russian Federation ... 122–123

Northern European Russia ... 124–125

Southern European Russia ... 126–127

Asia

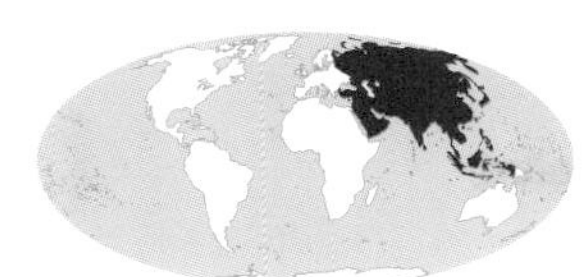

ASIA ... 128–129

PHYSICAL ASIA ... 130–131

POLITICAL ASIA ... 132–133

ASIAN RESOURCES ... 134–135

Turkey & the Caucasus ... 136–137
Armenia, Azerbaijan, Georgia, Turkey

The Near East ... 138–139
Iraq, Israel, Jordan, Lebanon, Syria

The Arabian Peninsula ... 140–141
Bahrain, Kuwait, Oman, Qatar, Saudi Arabia, United Arab Emirates, Yemen

Iran & the Gulf States ... 142–143
Bahrain, Iran, Kuwait, Qatar, United Arab Emirates

Kazakhstan ... 144–145

Central Asia ... 146–147
Kyrgyzstan, Tajikistan, Turkmenistan, Uzbekistan

Afghanistan & Pakistan ... 148–149

South Asia ... 150–151
Bangladesh, Bhutan, India, Maldives, Nepal, Pakistan, Sri Lanka

Northern India & the Himalayan States ... 152–153
Bangladesh, Bhutan, Nepal, Northern India

Southern India & Sri Lanka ... 154–155

Mainland East Asia ... 156–157
China, Mongolia, North Korea, South Korea, Taiwan

Western China ... 158–159

Eastern China ... 160–161
Eastern China, Taiwan

Northeastern China, Mongolia & Korea ... 162–163
Mongolia, Northeastern China, North Korea, South Korea

Japan ... 164–165

Mainland Southeast Asia ... 166–167
Cambodia, Laos, Myanmar, Paracel Islands, Thailand, Vietnam

Western Maritime Southeast Asia ... 168–169
Brunei, Indonesia, Malaysia, Singapore

Eastern Maritime Southeast Asia ... 170–171
East Timor, Indonesia, Philippines

The Indian Ocean ... 172–173

Australasia & Oceania

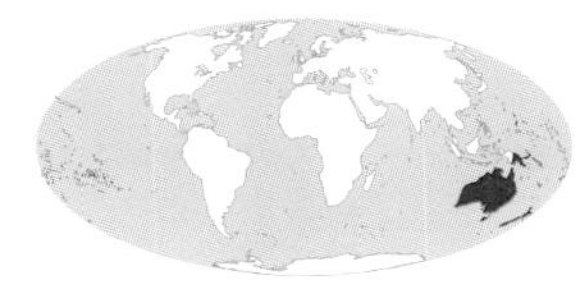

AUSTRALASIA & OCEANIA ... 174–175

POLITICAL AUSTRALASIA & OCEANIA ... 176–177

AUSTRALASIAN & OCEANIAN RESOURCES ... 178–179

Australia ... 180–181

Southeast Australia ... 182–183
New South Wales, South Australia, Tasmania, Victoria

New Zealand ... 184–185

Melanesia ... 186–187
Fiji, New Caledonia, Papua New Guinea, Solomon Islands, Vanuatu

Micronesia ... 188–189
Guam, Marshall Islands, Micronesia, Nauru, Northern Mariana Islands, Palau, Wake Island

Polynesia ... 190–191
Cook Islands, Easter Island, French Polynesia, Kiribati, Niue, Pitcairn Islands, Tokelau, Tuvalu, Wallis & Futuna

The Pacific Ocean ... 192–193

Antarctica ... 194–195

The Arctic ... 196–197

INDEX–GAZETTEER

Geographical comparisons ... 198–199

Countries of the world including The time zones ... 200–207

Geographical glossary ... 208–210

Geographical names ... 211

Index ... 212–349

Acknowledgements ... 350

Key to maps

Regional

Physical features

elevation

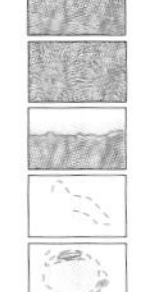

- 6000m / 19,686ft
- 4000m / 13,124ft
- 3000m / 9843ft
- 2000m / 6562ft
- 1000m / 3281ft
- 500m / 1640ft
- 250m / 820ft
- 100m / 328ft
- sea level
- below sea level

- ▲ elevation above sea level (mountain height)
- volcano
- ✕ pass
- ▼ elevation below sea level (depression depth)

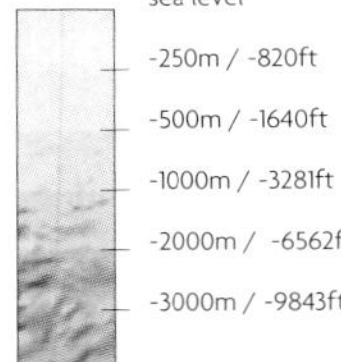

- sand desert
- lava flow
- coastline
- reef
- atoll

sea depth

- sea level
- -250m / -820ft
- -500m / -1640ft
- -1000m / -3281ft
- -2000m / -6562ft
- -3000m / -9843ft

- ▲ seamount / guyot symbol
- ▼ undersea spot depth

Drainage features

- main river
- secondary river
- tertiary river
- minor river
- main seasonal river
- secondary seasonal river
- canal
- waterfall
- rapids
- dam
- perennial lake
- seasonal lake
- perennial salt lake
- seasonal salt lake
- reservoir

- salt flat / salt pan
- marsh / salt marsh
- mangrove
- wadi
- spring / well / waterhole / oasis

Ice features

- ice cap / sheet
- ice shelf
- glacier / snowfield
- summer pack ice limit
- winter pack ice limit

Communications

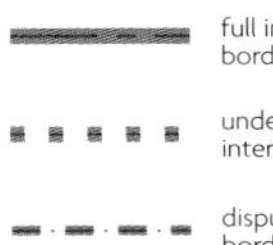

- motorway / highway
- motorway / highway (under construction)
- major road
- minor road
- tunnel (road)
- main line
- minor line
- tunnel (rail)
- ✈ international airport

Borders

- full international border
- undefined international border
- disputed de facto border
- disputed territorial claim border
- indication of country extent (Pacific only)
- indication of dependent territory extent (Pacific only)
- demarcation/ cease fire line
- autonomous / federal region border
- 2nd order internal administrative border
- 3rd order internal administrative border

Settlements

- built up area

settlement population symbols

- more than 5 million
- 1 million to 5 million
- 500,000 to 1 million
- 100,000 to 500,000
- 50,000 to 100,000
- 10,000 to 50,000
- fewer than 10,000
- country/dependent territory capital city
- autonomous / federal region / 2nd order internal administrative centre
- 3rd order internal administrative centre

Miscellaneous features

- ancient wall
- site of interest
- scientific station

Graticule features

- lines of latitude and longitude / Equator
- Tropics / Polar circles
- 45° degrees of longitude / latitude

Typographic key

Physical features

landscape features	*Namib Desert* *Massif Central* *ANDES*
headland	*Nordkapp*
elevation / volcano / pass	Mount Meru 4556 m
drainage features	*Lake Geneva*
rivers / canals spring / well / waterhole / oasis / waterfall / rapids / dam	*Mekong*
ice features	*Vatnajökull*
sea features	*Golfe de Lion* *Andaman Sea* *INDIAN OCEAN*
undersea features	*Barracuda Fracture Zone*

Regions

country	ARMENIA
dependent territory with parent state	NIUE (to NZ)
region outside feature area	ANGOLA
autonomous / federal region	MINAS GERAIS
2nd order internal administrative region	MINSKAYA VOBLASTS'
3rd order internal administrative region	Vaucluse
cultural region	New England

Settlements

capital city	BEIJING
dependent territory capital city	FORT-DE-FRANCE
other settlements	Chicago Adana Tizi Ozou Yonezawa Farnham

Miscellaneous

sites of interest / miscellaneous	Valley of the Kings
Tropics / Polar circles	*Antarctic Circle*

How to use this Atlas

The atlas is organized by continent, moving eastward from the International Date Line. The opening section describes the world's structure, systems, and its main features. The Atlas of the World which follows, is a continent-by-continent guide to today's world, starting with a comprehensive insight into the physical, political, and economic structure of each continent, followed by integrated mapping and descriptions of each region or country.

The world

The introductory section of the Atlas deals with every aspect of the planet, from physical structure to human geography, providing an overall picture of the world we live in. Complex topics such as the landscape of the Earth, climate, oceans, population, and economic patterns are clearly explained with the aid of maps, diagrams drawn from the latest information.

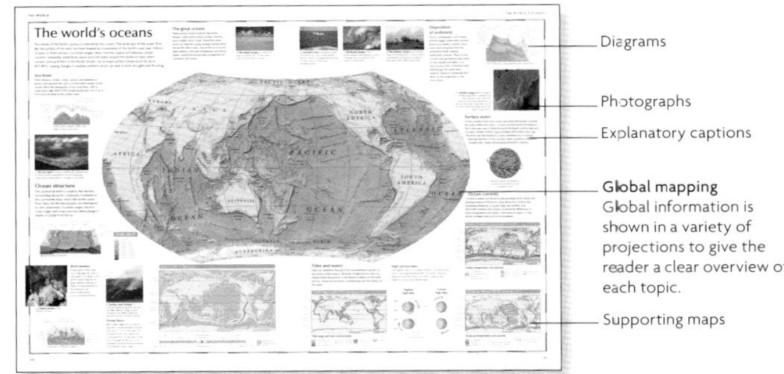

The world's oceans
Diagrams
Photographs
Explanatory captions
Global mapping
Global information is shown in a variety of projections to give the reader a clear overview of each topic.
Supporting maps

The political continent

The political portrait of the continent is a vital reference point for every continental section, showing the position of countries relative to one another, and the relationship between human settlement and geographic location. The complex mosaic of languages spoken in each continent is mapped, as is the effect of communications networks on the pattern of settlement.

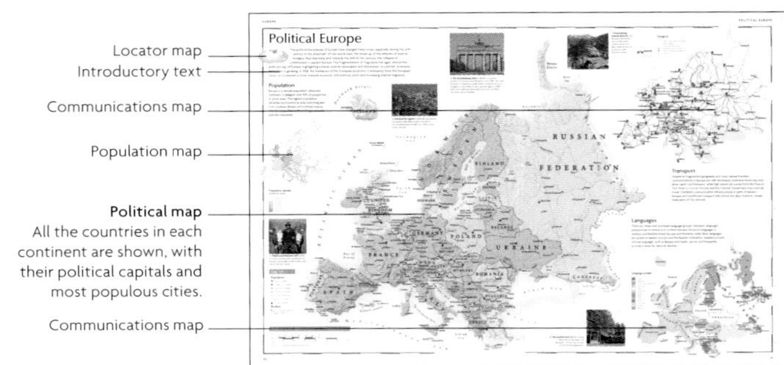

Political Europe
Locator map
Introductory text
Communications map
Population map
Political map
All the countries in each continent are shown, with their political capitals and most populous cities.
Communications map

Continental resources

The Earth's rich natural resources, including oil, gas, minerals, and fertile land, have played a key role in the development of society. These pages show the location of minerals and agricultural resources on each continent, and how they have been instrumental in dictating industrial growth and the varieties of economic activity across the continent.

South American resources
Mineral resources map
Environmental issues map
Land use map
Industry map
Comparative wealth map

The physical continent

The astonishing variety of landforms, and the dramatic forces that created and continue to shape the landscape, are explained in the continental physical spread. Cross-sections, illustrations, and terrain maps highlight the different parts of the continent, showing how nature's forces have produced the landscapes we see today.

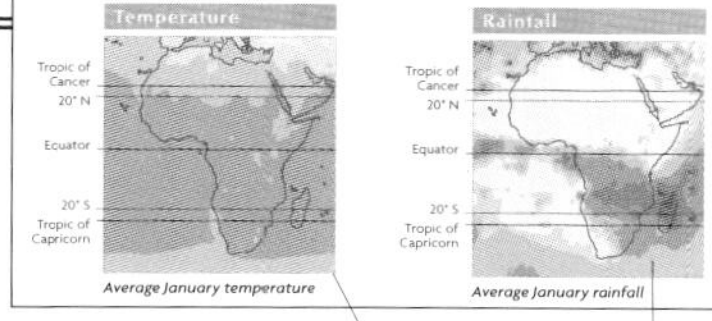

Temperature
Rainfall
Tropic of Cancer 20° N
Equator
20° S
Tropic of Capricorn
Average January temperature
Average January rainfall

Climate charts
Rainfall and temperature charts clearly show the continental patterns of rainfall and temperature.

Climate map
Climatic regions vary across each continent. The map displays the differing climatic regions, as well as daily hours of sunshine at selected weather stations.

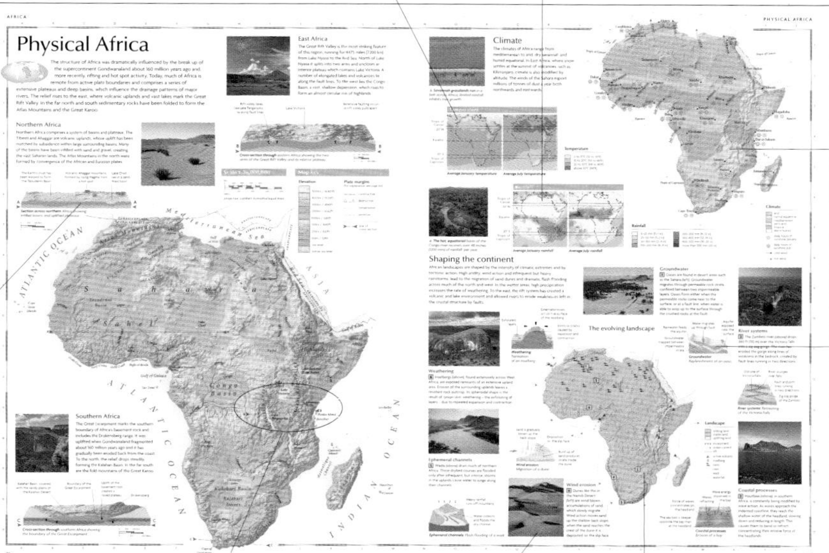

Physical Africa

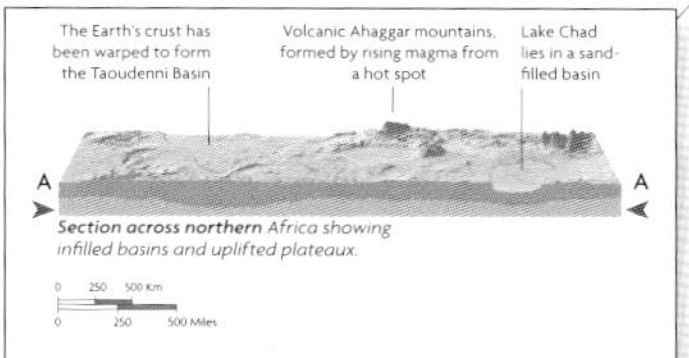

The Earth's crust has been warped to form the Taoudenni Basin
Volcanic Ahaggar mountains, formed by rising magma from a hot spot
Lake Chad lies in a sand-filled basin
A
A
Section across northern Africa showing infilled basins and uplifted plateaux.

Cross-sections
Detailed cross-sections through selected parts of the continent show the underlying geomorphic structure.

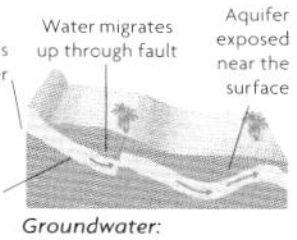

Rainwater feeds the aquifer
Water migrates up through fault
Aquifer exposed near the surface
Groundwater trapped between impermeable strata
Groundwater: Replenishment of an oasis

Landform diagrams
The complex formation of many typical landforms is summarized in these easy-to-understand illustrations.

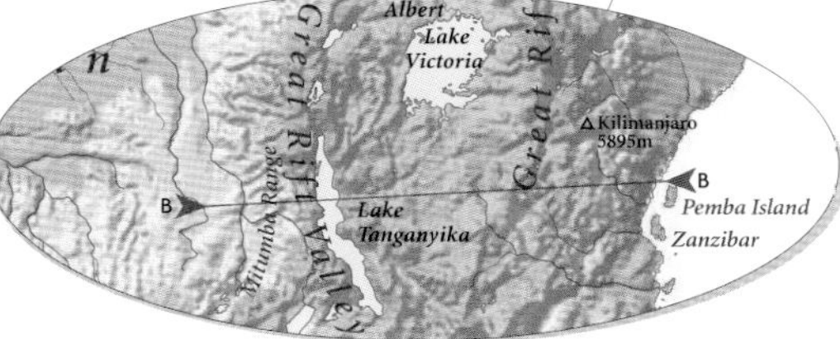

Albert
Lake Victoria
Kilimanjaro 5895m
Pemba Island
Zanzibar
Lake Tanganyika
Great Rift Valley
B
B

Main physical map
Detailed satellite data has been used to create an accurate and visually striking picture of the surface of the continent.

Photographs
A wide range of beautiful photographs bring the world's regions to life.

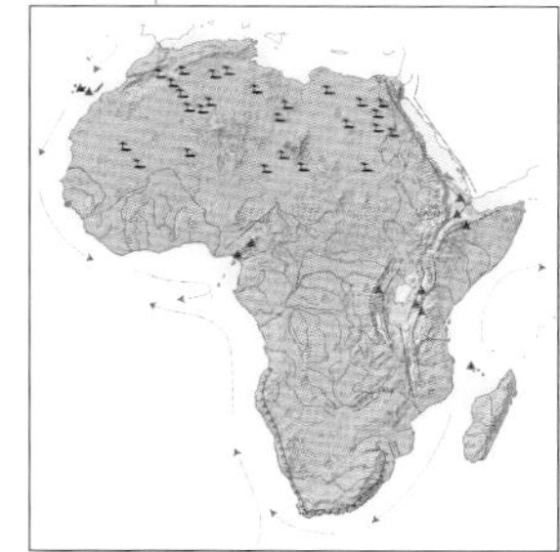

Landscape evolution map
The physical shape of each continent is affected by a variety of forces which continually sculpt and modify the landscape. This map shows the major processes which affect different parts of the continent.

Regional mapping

The main body of the Atlas is a unique regional map set, with detailed information on the terrain, the human geography of the region and its infrastructure. Around the edge of the map, additional "at-a-glance" maps, give an instant picture of regional industry, land use and agriculture. The detailed terrain map (shown in perspective), focuses on the main physical features of the region, and is enhanced by annotated illustrations, and photographs of the physical structure.

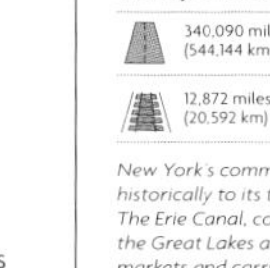

Transportation network
340,090 miles (544,344 km)
4813 miles (7730 km)
12,872 miles (20,592 km)
2108 miles (3389 km)
New York's commercial success is tied historically to its transportation connections. The Erie Canal, completed in 1825, opened up the Great Lakes and the interior to New York's markets and carried a stream of immigrants into the Midwest.

Transportation network
The differing extent of the transport network for each region is shown here, along with key facts about the transportation system.

Regional Locator
This small map shows the location of each country in relation to its continent.

Key to main map
A key to the population symbols and land heights accompanies the main map.

World locator
This locates the continent in which the region is found on a small world map.

Canada
Maine
Vermont
New Hampshire
New York
Massachusetts
Connecticut
Rhode Island
Pennsylvania
New Jersey
Atlantic Ocean

Land use map
This shows the different types of land use which characterize the region, as well as indicating the principal agricultural activities.

USA: NORTHEASTERN STATES
Lake Ontario
Lake Erie
New York
Pennsylvania
Maine
Atlantic Ocean

Map keys
Each supporting map has its own key.

Grid reference
The framing grid provides a location reference for each place listed in the Index.

The urban/rural population divide

urban 83% | rural 17%

0 10 20 30 40 50 60 70 80 90 100

Population density	Total land area
335 people per sq mile (120 people per sq km)	162,258 sq miles (420,232 sq km)

Urban/rural population divide
The proportion of people in the region who live in urban and rural areas, as well as the overall population density and land area are clearly shown in these simple graphics.

Canada
Maine
Vermont
New Hampshire
New York
Massachusetts
Connecticut
Rhode Island
Pennsylvania
New Jersey
Atlantic Ocean

Transportation and industry map
The main industrial areas are mapped, and the most important industrial and economic activities of the region are shown.

Nashua
Winchester
Lowell
Fitchburg
Leominster
Lawrence
Gloucester
Salem
Beverly
Lynn
Massachusetts
Malden
Cambridge
Boston
Bay
Quincy
Weymouth
Worcester
Framingham
Marshfield
Brockton
Plymouth
Provincetown
Providence
Cranston

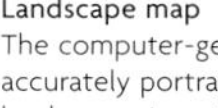

Continuation symbols
These symbols indicate where adjacent maps can be found.

Main regional map
A wealth of information is displayed on the main map, building up a rich portrait of the interaction between the physical landscape and the human and political geography of each region. The key to the regional maps can be found on page viii.

Landscape map
The computer-generated terrain model accurately portrays an oblique view of the landscape. Annotations highlight the most important geographic features of the region.

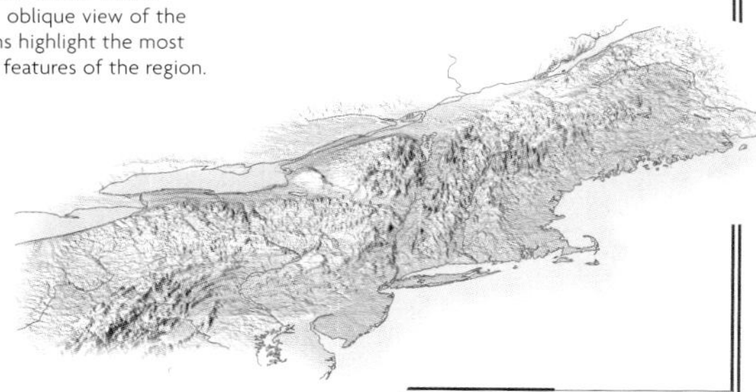

Jupiter

- *Diameter:* 88,846 miles (142,984 km)
- *Mass:* 1,900,000 million million million tons
- *Temperature:* -153°C (extremes not available)
- *Distance from Sun:* 483 million miles (778 million km)
- *Length of day:* 9.84 hours
- *Length of year:* 11.86 earth years
- *Surface gravity:* 1 kg = 2.53 kg

Mars

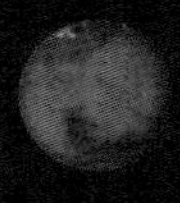

- *Diameter:* 4217 miles (6786 km)
- *Mass:* 642 million million million tons
- *Temperature:* -137 to 37°C
- *Distance from Sun:* 142 million miles (228 million km)
- *Length of day:* 24.623 hours
- *Length of year:* 1.88 earth years
- *Surface gravity:* 1 kg = 0.38 kg

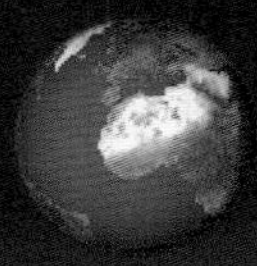

Earth

- *Diameter:* 7926 miles (12,756 km)
- *Mass:* 5976 million million million tons
- *Temperature:* -70 to 55°C
- *Distance from Sun:* 93 million miles (150 million km)
- *Length of day:* 23.92 hours
- *Length of year:* 365.25 earth days
- *Surface gravity:* 1 kg = 1 kg

Venus

- *Diameter:* 7520 miles (12,102 km)
- *Mass:* 4870 million million million tons
- *Temperature:* 457°C (extremes not available)
- *Distance from Sun:* 67 million miles (108 million km)
- *Length of day:* 243.01 earth days
- *Length of year:* 224.7 earth days
- *Surface gravity:* 1 kg = 0.88 kg

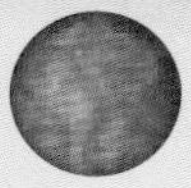

Mercury

- *Diameter:* 3031 miles (4878 km)
- *Mass:* 330 million million million tons
- *Temperature:* -173 to 427°C
- *Distance from Sun:* 36 million miles (58 million km)
- *Length of day:* 58.65 earth days
- *Length of year:* 87.97 earth days
- *Surface gravity:* 1 kg = 0.38 kg

The Solar System

Nine major planets, their satellites, and countless minor planets (asteroids) orbit the Sun to form the Solar System. The Sun, our nearest star, creates energy from nuclear reactions deep within its interior, providing all the light and heat which make life on Earth possible. The Earth is unique in the Solar System in that it supports life: its size, gravitational pull and distance from the Sun have all created the optimum conditions for the evolution of life. The planetary images seen here are composites derived from actual spacecraft images (not shown to scale).

The Sun

- *Diameter:* 864,948 miles (1,392,000 km)
- *Mass:* 1990 million million million million tons

The Sun was formed when a swirling cloud of dust and gas contracted, pulling matter into its center. When the temperature at the center rose to 1,000,000°C, nuclear fusion – the fusing of hydrogen into helium, creating energy – occurred, releasing a constant stream of heat and light.

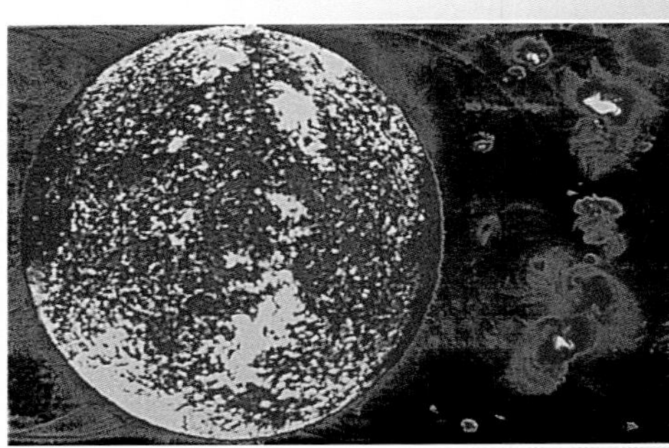

▲ ***Solar flares are*** *sudden bursts of energy from the Sun's surface. They can be 125,000 miles (200,000 km) long.*

The formation of the Solar System

The cloud of dust and gas thrown out by the Sun during its formation cooled to form the Solar System. The smaller planets nearest the Sun are formed of minerals and metals. The outer planets were formed at lower temperatures, and consist of swirling clouds of gases.

The Milankovitch Cycle

The amount of radiation from the Sun which reaches the Earth is affected by variations in the Earth's orbit and the tilt of the Earth's axis, as well as by "wobbles" in the axis. These variations cause three separate cycles, corresponding with the durations of recent ice ages.

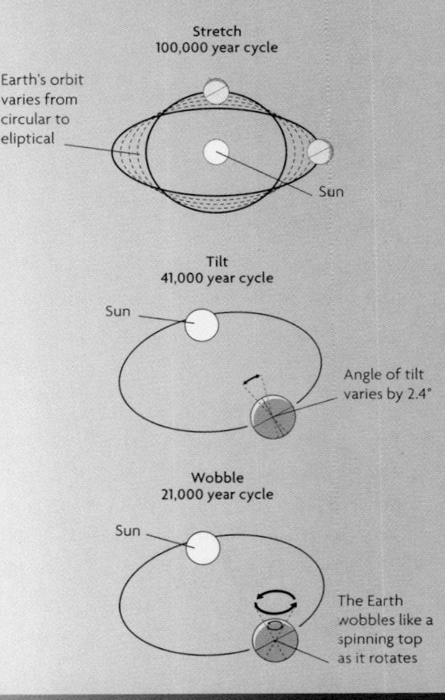
Stretch
100,000 year cycle
Earth's orbit varies from circular to elliptical
Sun
Tilt
41,000 year cycle
Sun
Angle of tilt varies by 2.4°
Wobble
21,000 year cycle
Sun
The Earth wobbles like a spinning top as it rotates

Saturn

- **Diameter:** *74,974 miles (120,660 km)*
- **Mass:** *570,000 million million million tons*
- **Temperature:** *-185°C (extremes not available)*
- **Distance from Sun:** *887 million miles (1427 million km)*
- **Length of day:** *10.23 hours*
- **Length of year:** *29.46 earth years*
- **Surface gravity:** *1 kg = 1.07 kg*

Uranus

- **Diameter:** *31,763 miles (51,118 km)*
- **Mass:** *86,800 million million million tons*
- **Temperature:** *-214°C (extremes not available)*
- **Distance from Sun:** *1783 million miles (2870 million km)*
- **Length of day:** *17.9 hours*
- **Length of year:** *84.01 earth years*
- **Surface gravity:** *1 kg = 0.92 kg*

Neptune

- **Diameter:** *30,775 miles (49,528 km)*
- **Mass:** *102,000 million million million tons*
- **Temperature:** *-225°C (extremes not available)*
- **Distance from Sun:** *2794 million miles (4497 million km)*
- **Length of day:** *19.2 hours*
- **Length of year:** *164.79 earth years*
- **Surface gravity:** *1 kg = 1.18 kg*

Space Debris

Millions of objects, remnants of planetary formation, circle the Sun in a zone lying between Mars and Jupiter: the asteroid belt. Fragments of asteroids break off to form meteoroids, which can reach the Earth's surface. Comets, composed of ice and dust, originated outside our Solar System. Their elliptical orbit brings them close to the Sun and into the inner Solar System.

▲ ***Meteor Crater** in Arizona is 4200 ft (1300 m) wide and 660 ft (200 m) deep. It was formed over 10,000 years ago.*

Possible and actual meteorite craters

Map key

- Possible impact craters
- Meteorite impact craters

▲ ***The orbit of** Halley's Comet brings it close to the Earth every 76 years. It last visited in 1986.*

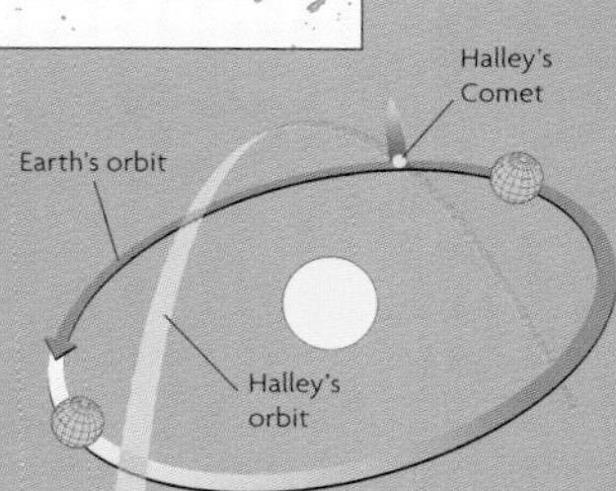
Halley's Comet
Earth's orbit
Halley's orbit

Orbit of Halley's Comet around the Sun

The Earth's Atmosphere

During the early stages of the Earth's formation, ash, lava, carbon dioxide, and water vapor were discharged onto the surface of the planet by constant volcanic eruptions. The water formed the oceans, while carbon dioxide entered the atmosphere or was dissolved in the oceans. Clouds, formed of water droplets, reflected some of the Sun's radiation back into space. The Earth's temperature stabilized and early life forms began to emerge, converting carbon dioxide into life-giving oxygen.

◄ ***It is thought** that the gases that make up the Earth's atmosphere originated deep within the interior, and were released many millions of years ago during intense volcanic actvity, similar to this eruption at Mount St. Helens.*

Pluto

- **Diameter:** *1429 miles (2300 km)*
- **Mass:** *13 million million million tons*
- **Temperature:** *-236°C (extremes not available)*
- **Distance from Sun:** *3666 million miles (5900 million km)*
- **Length of day:** *6.39 hours*
- **Length of year:** *248.54 earth years*
- **Surface gravity:** *1 kg = 0.30 kg*

Order and relative distance from the sun of planets

Sun, Mercury, Venus, Earth, Mars, Jupiter, Saturn, Uranus, Neptune, Pluto

mill. km: 0, 500, 1000, 1500, 2000, 2500, 3000, 3500, 4000, 4500, 5000, 5500, 6000

mill. miles: 0, 500, 1000, 1500, 2000, 2500, 3000, 3500, 4000

The physical world

The Earth's surface is constantly being transformed: it is uplifted, folded, and faulted by tectonic forces; weathered and eroded by wind, water, and ice. Sometimes change is dramatic, the spectacular results of earthquakes or floods. More often it is a slow process lasting millions of years. A physical map of the world represents a snapshot of the ever-evolving architecture of the Earth. This terrain map shows the whole surface of the Earth, both above and below the sea.

The world in section

These cross-sections around the Earth, one in the northern hemisphere; one straddling the Equator, reveal the limited areas of land above sea level in comparison with the extent of the sea floor. The greater erosive effects of weathering by wind and water limit the upward elevation of land above sea level, while the deep oceans retain their dramatic mountain and trench profiles.

Aleutian Trench · Pacific Ocean · Rocky Mountains
60°N · 180° · 150°W · 120°W

Cross-section: Northern hemisphere

Hawaiian Islands
20°N · 10°S · 180° · 150°W · 120°W

Cross-section: Southern hemisphere

Map key

Geographical regions

- ice
- tundra
- needleleaf forest
- broadleaf forest
- cultivated land
- hot desert
- cold desert
- tropical grassland
- tropical rain forest
- mountain
- submarine regions

Scale 1:73,000,000

Km 0 250 500 1000 1500 2000
Miles 0 250 500 1000 1500 2000

projection: Wagner VII

Northern hemisphere

Most of the land on Earth is concentrated in the northern hemisphere, although Europe and North America are the only continents which lie wholly in the north.

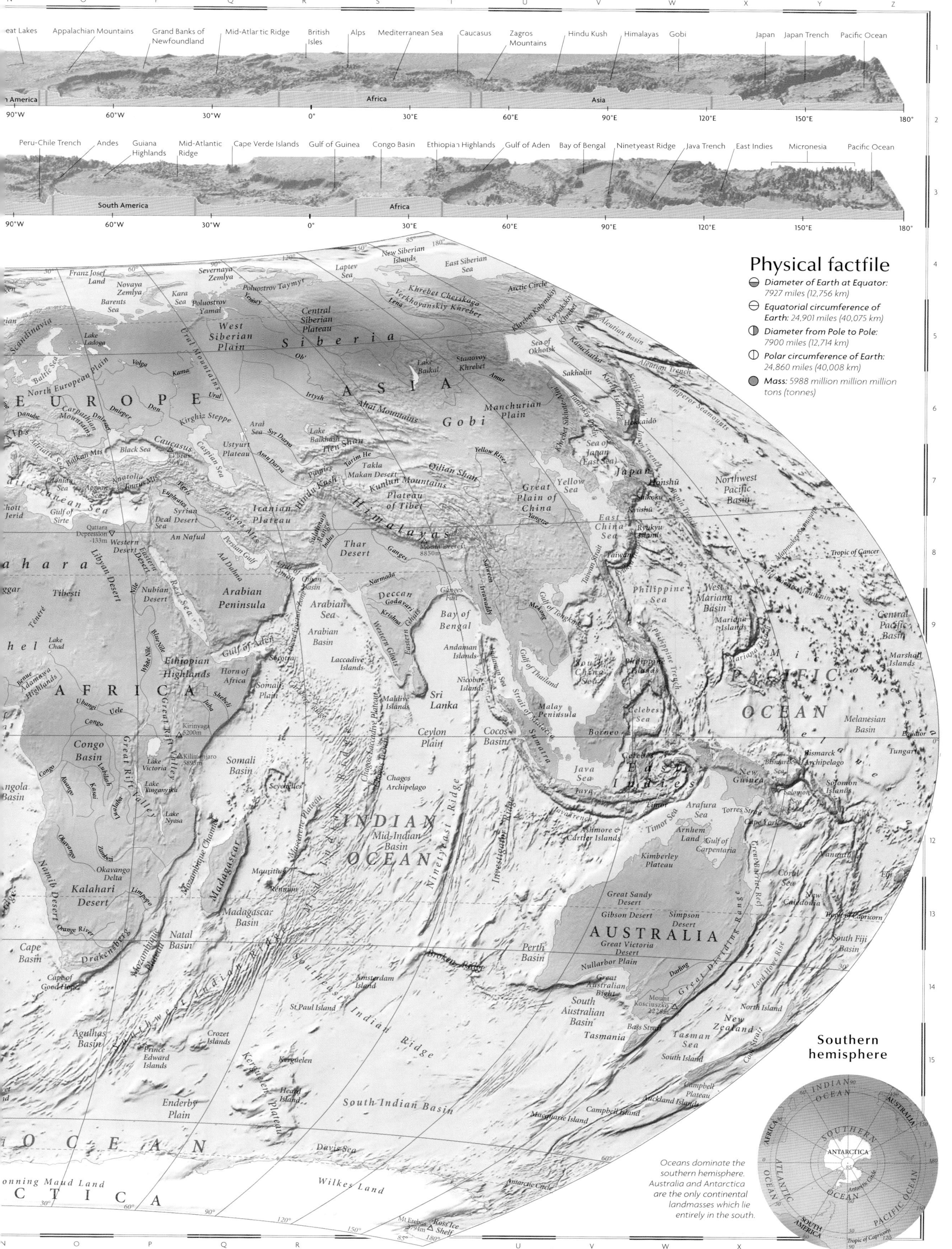

Great Lakes
Appalachian Mountains
Grand Banks of Newfoundland
Mid-Atlantic Ridge
British Isles
Alps
Mediterranean Sea
Caucasus
Zagros Mountains
Hindu Kush
Himalayas
Gobi
Japan
Japan Trench
Pacific Ocean
America
Africa
Asia
90°W
60°W
30°W
0°
30°E
60°E
90°E
120°E
150°E
180°
Peru-Chile Trench
Andes
Guiana Highlands
Mid-Atlantic Ridge
Cape Verde Islands
Gulf of Guinea
Congo Basin
Ethiopian Highlands
Gulf of Aden
Bay of Bengal
Ninetyeast Ridge
Java Trench
East Indies
Micronesia
Pacific Ocean
South America
Africa
EUROPE
ASIA
Siberia
AFRICA
INDIAN OCEAN
PACIFIC OCEAN
AUSTRALIA
East Indies
Micronesia
Melanesia
Franz Josef Land
Novaya Zemlya
Severnaya Zemlya
New Siberian Islands
Laptev Sea
East Siberian Sea
Barents Sea
Kara Sea
Poluostrov Yamal
Poluostrov Taymyr
Central Siberian Plateau
West Siberian Plain
Khrebet Cherskogo
Verkhoyanskiy Khrebet
Arctic Circle
Sea of Okhotsk
Aleutian Basin
Aleutian Trench
Kamchatka
Sakhalin
Stanovoy Khrebet
Lake Baikal
Amur
Lake Ladoga
Scandinavia
Baltic Sea
North European Plain
Volga
Kama
Ural Mountains
Ural
Ob'
Irtysh
Carpathian Mountains
Danube
Dnieper
Dniester
Don
Kirghiz Steppe
Altai Mountains
Gobi
Manchurian Plain
Emperor Seamounts
Kuril Islands
Hokkaidō
Sea of Japan (East Sea)
Honshū
Shikoku
Kyūshū
Japan
Northwest Pacific Basin
Alps
Adriatic Sea
Balkan Mts
Black Sea
Caucasus
Caspian Sea
Aral Sea
Syr Darya
Ustyurt Plateau
Amu Darya
Lake Balkhash
Tien Shan
Pamirs
Tarim He
Takla Makan Desert
Kunlun Mountains
Qilian Shan
Yellow River
Yellow Sea
Great Plain of China
Yangtze
East China Sea
Ryukyu Islands
Taiwan
Taiwan Strait
Plateau of Tibet
Himalayas
Mount Everest 8850m
Hindu Kush
Iranian Plateau
Zagros Mts
Anatolia
Taurus Mts
Aegean Sea
Euphrates
Tigris
Syrian Desert
Dead Sea
An Nafud
Persian Gulf
Gulf of Oman
Ad Dahna
Arabian Peninsula
Mediterranean Sea
Gulf of Sirte
Chott Jerid
Qattara Depression -133m
Western Desert
Eastern Desert
Libyan Desert
Sahara
Tibesti
Nubian Desert
Nile
Red Sea
Sahel
Lake Chad
Blue Nile
White Nile
Ethiopian Highlands
Gulf of Aden
Socotra
Horn of Africa
Somali Plain
Benue
Adamawa Highlands
Ubangi
Uele
Congo
Congo Basin
Great Rift Valley
Kirinyaga 5200m
Kilimanjaro 5895m
Lake Victoria
Lake Tanganyika
Lake Nyasa
Angola Basin
Kasai
Lualaba
Okavango
Zambezi
Okavango Delta
Kalahari Desert
Namib Desert
Limpopo
Orange River
Drakensberg
Cape Basin
Cape of Good Hope
Mozambique Channel
Madagascar
Madagascar Basin
Mozambique Plateau
Natal Basin
Mauritius
Réunion
Somali Basin
Seychelles
Mascarene Plateau
Agulhas Basin
Prince Edward Islands
Crozet Islands
Kerguelen
Kerguelen Plateau
Heard Island
Enderby Plain
Thar Desert
Indus
Ganges
Narmada
Deccan
Godavari
Krishna
Western Ghats
Eastern Ghats
Ganges Fan
Bay of Bengal
Arabian Sea
Arabian Basin
Laccadive Islands
Maldive Islands
Chagos-Laccadive Plateau
Chagos Archipelago
Sri Lanka
Ceylon Plain
Mid-Indian Basin
Mid-Indian Ridge
Ninetyeast Ridge
Investigator Ridge
Andaman Islands
Nicobar Islands
Andaman Sea
Salween
Irrawaddy
Mekong
Gulf of Tongking
Gulf of Thailand
Strait of Malacca
Malay Peninsula
Sumatra
Cocos Basin
South China Sea
Philippine Sea
Philippine Islands
Philippine Trench
Borneo
Celebes Sea
Celebes
Java Sea
Java
Java Trench
Timor
Timor Sea
Arafura Sea
Ashmore & Cartier Islands
Arnhem Land
Gulf of Carpentaria
Cape York
Torres Strait
New Guinea
Bismarck Sea
Bismarck Archipelago
Solomon Sea
Solomon Islands
West Mariana Basin
Mariana Islands
Mariana Trench
Central Pacific Basin
Marshall Islands
Tropic of Cancer
Melanesian Basin
Equator
Tungaru
Vanuatu
Fiji
Coral Sea
New Caledonia
Tropic of Capricorn
South Fiji Basin
Great Barrier Reef
Kimberley Plateau
Great Sandy Desert
Gibson Desert
Simpson Desert
Great Victoria Desert
Nullarbor Plain
Great Australian Bight
Darling
Great Dividing Range
Mount Kosciuszko 2228m
Bass Strait
Tasmania
South Australian Basin
Perth Basin
Broken Ridge
Amsterdam Island
St.Paul Island
Southeast Indian Ridge
Southwest Indian Ridge
South Indian Basin
Lord Howe Rise
North Island
New Zealand
Tasman Sea
South Island
Campbell Plateau
Auckland Islands
Campbell Island
Macquarie Island
Davis Sea
Wilkes Land
Antarctic Circle
Dronning Maud Land
ANTARCTICA
OCEAN
Mt Erebus 3794m
Ross Ice Shelf
Southern hemisphere
INDIAN OCEAN
AUSTRALIA
SOUTHERN OCEAN
ANTARCTICA
AFRICA
ATLANTIC OCEAN
PACIFIC OCEAN
SOUTH AMERICA
Antarctic Circle
Tropic of Capricorn

Physical factfile

- **Diameter of Earth at Equator:** 7927 miles (12,756 km)
- **Equatorial circumference of Earth:** 24,901 miles (40,075 km)
- **Diameter from Pole to Pole:** 7900 miles (12,714 km)
- **Polar circumference of Earth:** 24,860 miles (40,008 km)
- **Mass:** 5988 million million million tons (tonnes)

Oceans dominate the southern hemisphere. Australia and Antarctica are the only continental landmasses which lie entirely in the south.

Structure of the Earth

The Earth as it is today is just the latest phase in a constant process of evolution which has occurred over the past 4.5 billion years. The Earth's continents are neither fixed nor stable; over the course of the Earth's history, propelled by currents rising from the intense heat at its center, the great plates on which they lie have moved, collided, joined together, and separated. These processes continue to mold and transform the surface of the Earth, causing earthquakes and volcanic eruptions and creating oceans, mountain ranges, deep ocean trenches, and island chains.

Inside the Earth

The Earth's hot inner core is made up of solid iron, while the outer core is composed of liquid iron and nickel. The mantle nearest the core is viscous, whereas the rocky upper mantle is fairly rigid. The crust is the rocky outer shell of the Earth. Together, the upper mantle and the crust form the lithosphere.

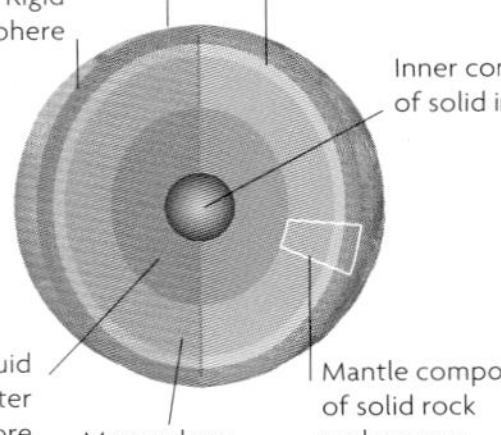

Rocky crust
Viscous asthenosphere
Rigid lithosphere
Inner core of solid iron
Liquid outer core
Mesosphere
Mantle composed of solid rock and magma

The dynamic Earth

The Earth's crust is made up of eight major (and several minor) rigid continental and oceanic tectonic plates, which fit closely together. The positions of the plates are not static. They are constantly moving relative to one another. The type of movement between plates affects the way in which they alter the structure of the Earth. The oldest parts of the plates, known as shields, are the most stable parts of the Earth and little tectonic activity occurs here.

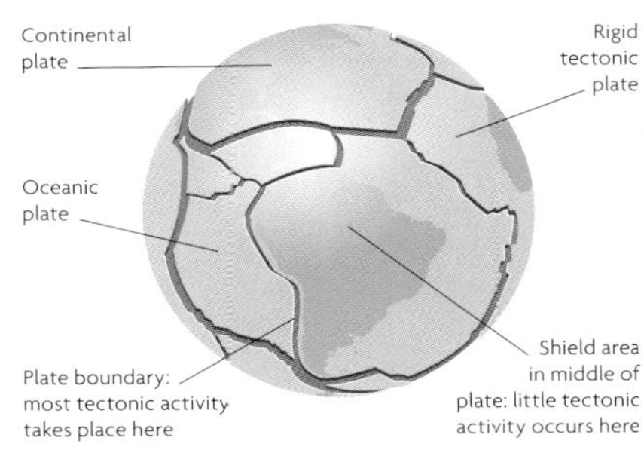

Continental plate
Rigid tectonic plate
Oceanic plate
Plate boundary: most tectonic activity takes place here
Shield area in middle of plate: little tectonic activity occurs here

Inner core
Outer core
Subduction zone
Ocean crust
Movement of plate
Mid-ocean ridge
Lithosphere
Asthenosphere
Mesosphere
Continental crust

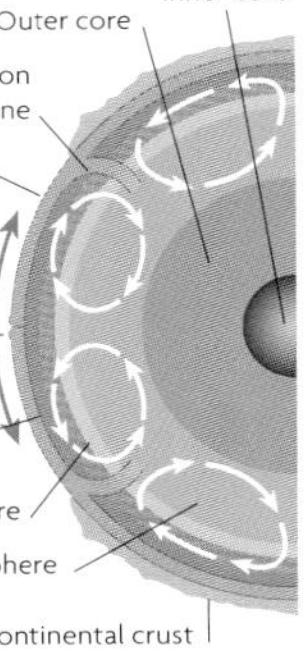

Convection currents

Deep within the Earth, at its inner core, temperatures may exceed 8,100°F (4,500°C). This heat warms rocks in the mesosphere which rise through the partially molten mantle, displacing cooler rocks just below the solid crust, which sink, and are warmed again by the heat of the mantle. This process is continuous, creating convection currents which form the moving force beneath the Earth's crust.

Plate boundaries

The boundaries between the plates are the areas where most tectonic activity takes place. Three types of movement occur at plate boundaries: the plates can either move toward each other, move apart, or slide past each other. The effect this has on the Earth's structure depends on whether the margin is between two continental plates, two oceanic plates, or an oceanic and continental plate.

▲ *The Mid-Atlantic Ridge rises above sea level in Iceland, producing geysers and volcanoes.*

Mid-ocean ridges

Mid-ocean ridges are formed when two adjacent oceanic plates pull apart, allowing magma to force its way up to the surface, which then cools to form solid rock. Vast amounts of volcanic material are discharged at these mid-ocean ridges which can reach heights of 10,000 ft (3000 m).

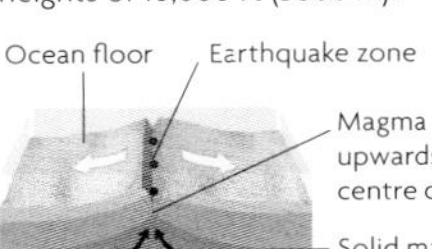

Ocean floor
Earthquake zone
Magma pushed upwards along centre of ridge
Solid mantle

Formation of a mid-ocean ridge

▲ *Mount Pinatubo is an active volcano, lying on the Pacific "Ring of Fire."*

Ocean plates meeting

Oceanic crust is denser and thinner than continental crust; on average it is 3 miles (5 km) thick, while continental crust averages 18–24 miles (30–40 km). When oceanic plates of similar density meet, the crust is contorted as one plate overrides the other, forming deep sea trenches and volcanic island arcs above sea level.

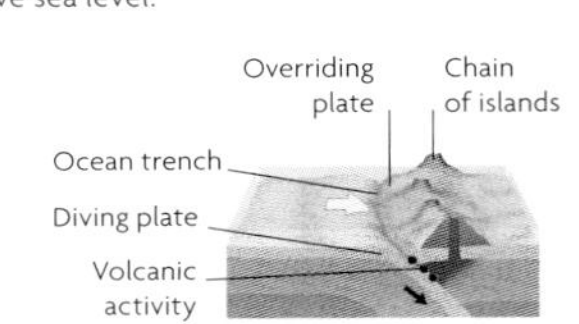

Overriding plate
Chain of islands
Ocean trench
Diving plate
Volcanic activity

Ocean plates meeting to form an island arc

Tectonic activity
uncertain plate boundary
volcanic zone
earthquake zone
hot spot
rift valley

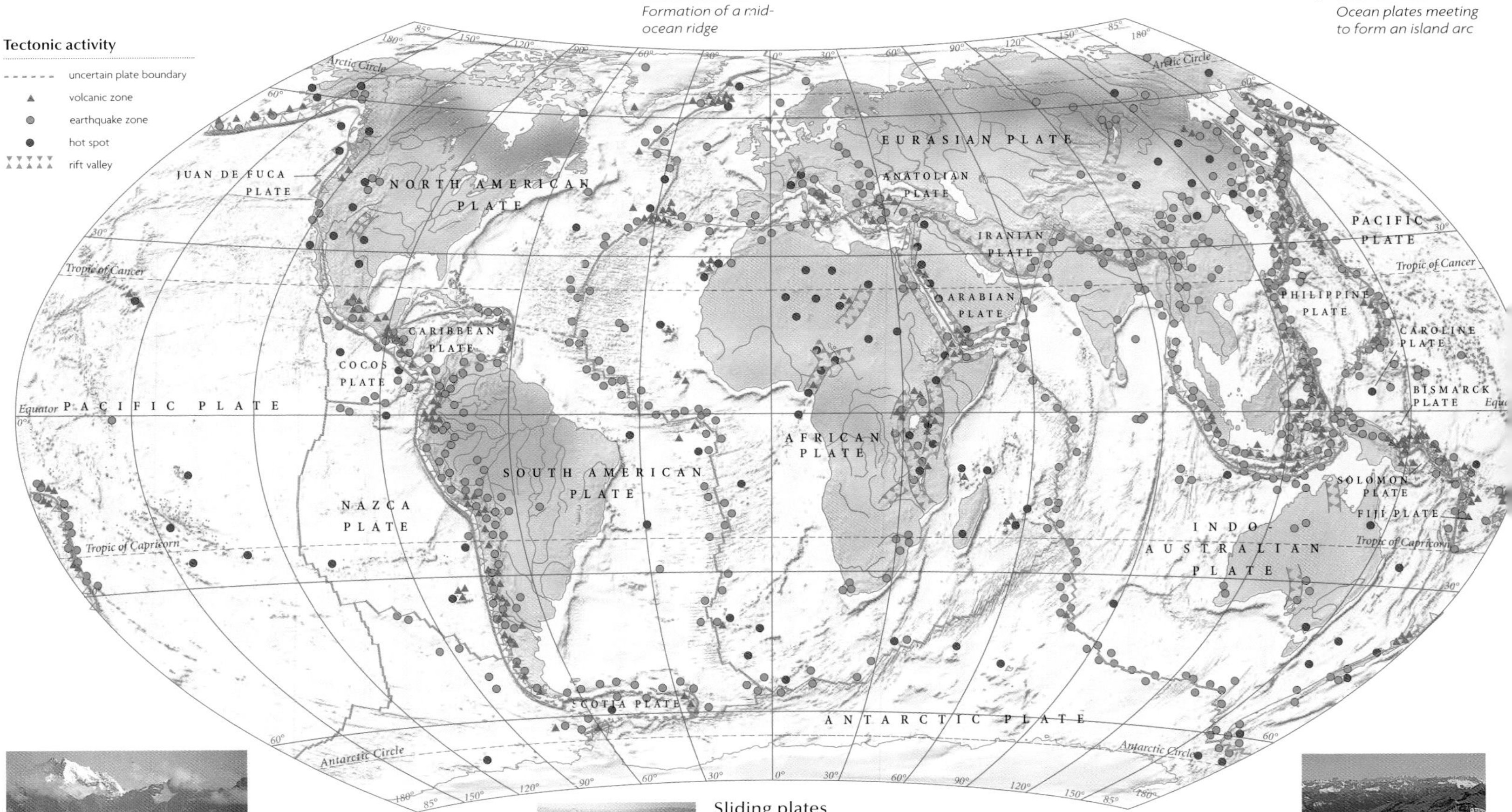

JUAN DE FUCA PLATE
NORTH AMERICAN PLATE
EURASIAN PLATE
ANATOLIAN PLATE
IRANIAN PLATE
ARABIAN PLATE
PACIFIC PLATE
PHILIPPINE PLATE
CAROLINE PLATE
BISMARCK PLATE
CARIBBEAN PLATE
COCOS PLATE
PACIFIC PLATE
AFRICAN PLATE
SOUTH AMERICAN PLATE
NAZCA PLATE
SOLOMON PLATE
FIJI PLATE
INDO-AUSTRALIAN PLATE
SCOTIA PLATE
ANTARCTIC PLATE
Arctic Circle
Tropic of Cancer
Equator
Tropic of Capricorn
Antarctic Circle

◄ *The Andean mountain chain is the typical result of the impact of a diving plate.*

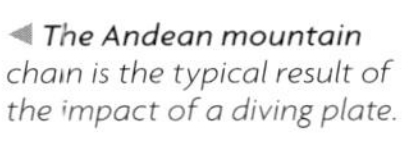

Diving plates

When an oceanic and a continental plate meet, the denser oceanic plate is driven underneath the continental plate, which is crumpled by the collision to form mountain ranges. As the ocean plate plunges downward, it heats up, and molten rock (magma) is forced up to the surface.

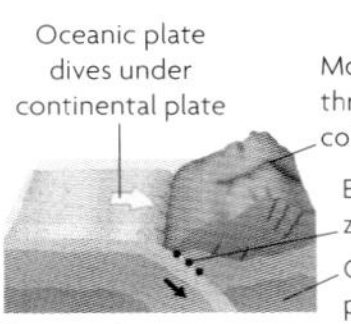

Oceanic plate dives under continental plate
Mountains thrust up by collision
Earthquake zone
Continental plate

Diving plate

▲ *The deep fracture caused by the sliding plates of the San Andreas Fault can be clearly seen in parts of California.*

Sliding plates

When two plates slide past each other, friction is caused along the fault line which divides them. The plates do not move smoothly, and the uneven movement causes earthquakes.

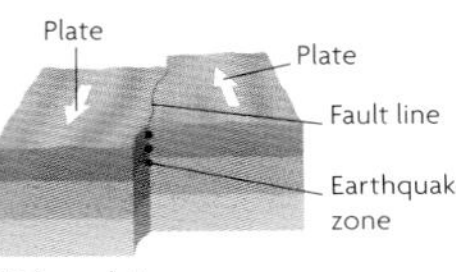

Plate
Plate
Fault line
Earthquake zone

Sliding plates

► *The Alps were formed when the African Plate collided with the Eurasian Plate, about 65 million years ago.*

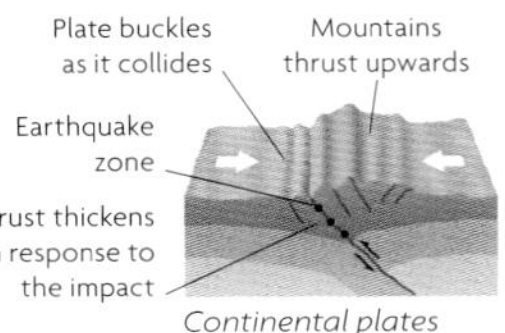

Plate buckles as it collides
Mountains thrust upwards
Earthquake zone
Crust thickens in response to the impact

Continental plates colliding to form a mountain range

Colliding plates

When two continental plates collide, great mountain chains are thrust upward as the crust buckles and folds under the force of the impact.

Continental drift

Although the plates which make up the Earth's crust move only a few inches in a year, over the millions of years of the Earth's history, its continents have moved many thousands of miles, to create new continents, oceans, and mountain chains

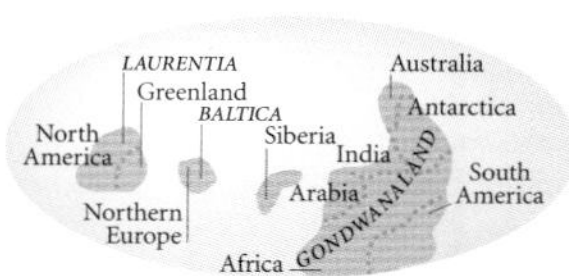
LAURENTIA
Greenland
BALTICA
North America
Siberia
India
Arabia
Northern Europe
Africa
GONDWANALAND
Australia
Antarctica
South America

1: Cambrian period

570–510 million years ago. Most continents are in tropical latitudes. The supercontinent of Gondwanaland reaches the South Pole.

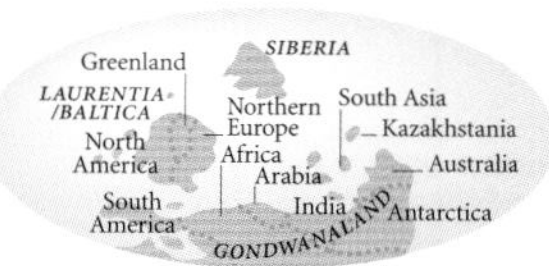
Greenland
SIBERIA
LAURENTIA /BALTICA
North America
Northern Europe
Africa
Arabia
South America
South Asia
Kazakhstania
Australia
India
Antarctica
GONDWANALAND

2: Devonian period

408–362 million years ago. The continents of Gondwanaland and Laurentia are drifting northward.

ANGARALAND
Siberia
LAURENTIA
North America
Greenland
Northern Europe
Northwest China
Australia
Antarctica
South America
Arabia
Africa
GONDWANALAND

3: Carboniferous period

362–290 million years ago. The Earth is dominated by three continents; Laurentia, Angaraland, and Gondwanaland.

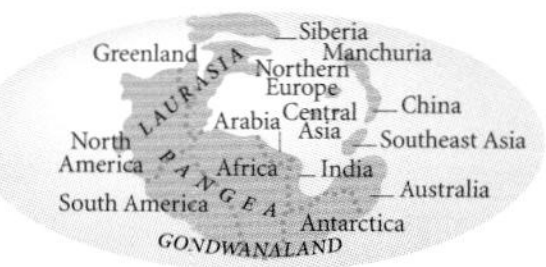
Greenland
Siberia
Manchuria
LAURASIA
Northern Europe
China
Central Asia
Arabia
Southeast Asia
North America
PANGEA
Africa
India
Australia
South America
Antarctica
GONDWANALAND

4: Triassic period

245–208 million years ago. All three major continents have joined to form the super-continent of Pangea.

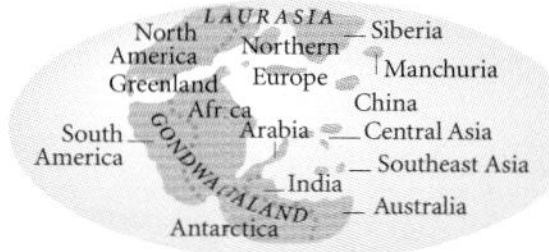
LAURASIA
North America
Northern Europe
Siberia
Greenland
Manchuria
China
Africa
Arabia
Central Asia
South America
Southeast Asia
India
GONDWANALAND
Australia
Antarctica

5: Jurassic period

208–145 million years ago. The super-continent of Pangea begins to break up, causing an overall rise in sea levels.

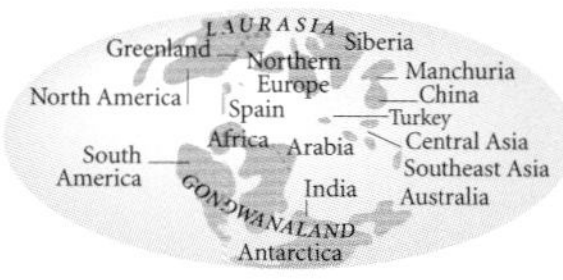
LAURASIA
Greenland
Northern Europe
Siberia
Manchuria
North America
Spain
China
Turkey
Africa
Arabia
Central Asia
South America
Southeast Asia
India
Australia
GONDWANALAND
Antarctica

6: Cretaceous period

145–65 million years ago. Warm, shallow seas cover much of the land: sea levels are about 80 ft (25 m) above present levels.

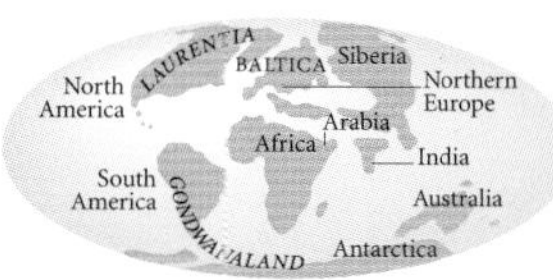
LAURENTIA
BALTICA
Siberia
North America
Northern Europe
Arabia
Africa
India
South America
Australia
GONDWANALAND
Antarctica

7: Tertiary period

65–2 million years ago. Although the world's geography is becoming more recognizable, major events such as the creation of the Himalayan mountain chain, are still to occur during this period.

Continental shields

The centers of the Earth's continents, known as shields, were established between 2500 and 500 million years ago; some contain rocks over three billion years old. They were formed by a series of turbulent events: plate movements, earthquakes, and volcanic eruptions. Since the Pre-Cambrian period, over 570 million years ago, they have experienced little tectonic activity, and today, these flat, low-lying slabs of solidified molten rock form the stable centers of the continents. They are bounded or covered by successive belts of younger sedimentary rock.

Canadian (Laurentian)
Scandinavian (Fenno-Scandian)
Siberian
Korean
Indian
African
Guyana (Venezuelan)
Brazilian
Australian
Antarctic

The Hawaiian island chain

A hot spot lying deep beneath the Pacific Ocean pushes a plume of magma from the Earth's mantle up through the Pacific Plate to form volcanic islands. While the hot spot remains stationary, the plate on which the islands sit is moving slowly. A long chain of islands has been created as the plate passes over the hot spot.

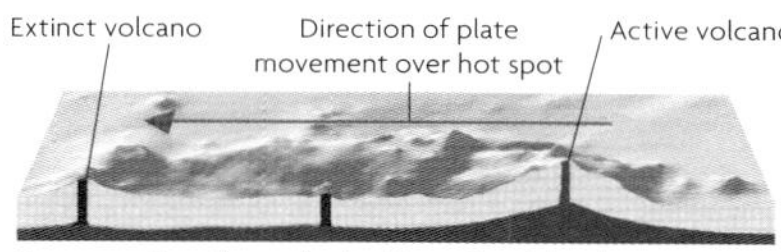
Extinct volcano
Direction of plate movement over hot spot
Active volcano

Cross-section through the Hawaiian Islands

Evolution of the Hawaiian Islands

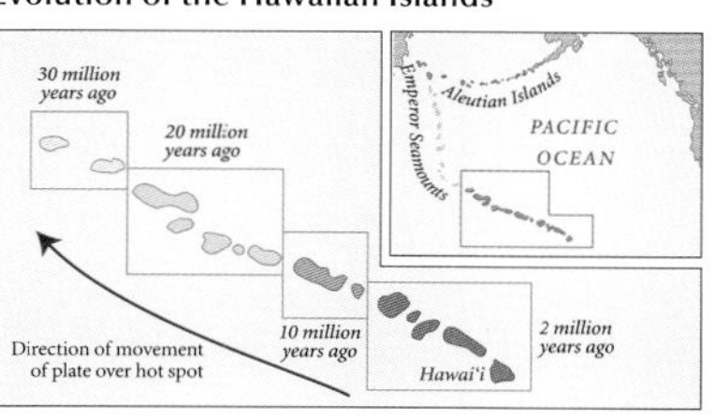
30 million years ago
20 million years ago
10 million years ago
2 million years ago
Direction of movement of plate over hot spot
Hawai'i
Aleutian Islands
Emperor Seamounts
PACIFIC OCEAN

Creation of the Himalayas

Between 10 and 20 million years ago, the Indian subcontinent, part of the ancient continent of Gondwanaland, collided with the continent of Asia. The Indo-Australian Plate continued to move northward, displacing continental crust and uplifting the Himalayas, the world's highest mountain chain.

Movements of India

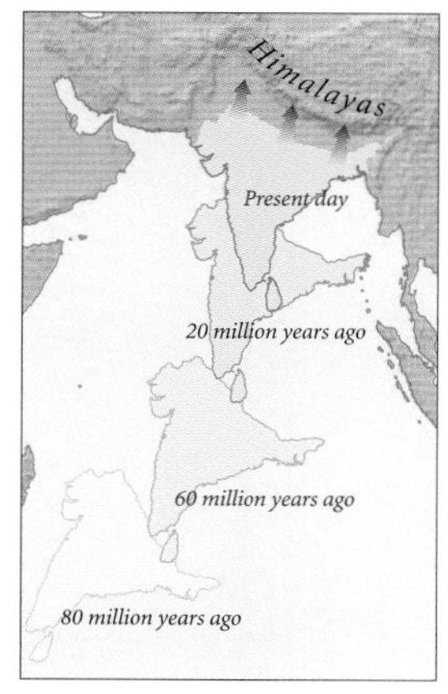
Himalayas
Present day
20 million years ago
60 million years ago
80 million years ago

Force of collision pushes up mountains

Cross-section through the Himalayas

▲ ***The Himalayas were*** *uplifted when the Indian subcontinent collided with Asia.*

The Earth's geology

The Earth's rocks are created in a continual cycle. Exposed rocks are weathered and eroded by wind, water, and chemicals and deposited as sediments. If they pass into the Earth's crust they will be transformed by high temperatures and pressures into metamorphic rocks or they will melt and solidify as igneous rocks.

▲ ***Gneiss formations in*** *Norway's Jotunheimen Mountains.*

Gneiss

1 Gneiss is a metamorphic rock made at great depth during the formation of mountain chains, when intense heat and pressure transform sedimentary or igneous rocks.

◀ ***Basalt columns at*** *Giant's Causeway, Northern Ireland, UK.*

Basalt

2 Basalt is an igneous rock, formed when small quantities of magma lying close to the Earth's surface cool rapidly.

Limestone

3 Limestone is a sedimentary rock, which is formed mainly from the calcite skeletons of marine animals which have been compressed into rock.

▲ ***Limestone hills, Guilin,*** *China.*

Sandstone

8 Sandstones are sedimentary rocks formed mainly in deserts, beaches, and deltas. Desert sandstones are formed of grains of quartz which have been well rounded by wind erosion.

▲ ***Rock stacks*** *of desert sandstone, at Bryce Canyon National Park, Utah, US.*

◀ ***Extrusive igneous rocks*** *are formed during volcanic eruptions, as here in Hawai'i.*

Andesite

7 Andesite is an extrusive igneous rock formed from magma which has solidified on the Earth's crust after a volcanic eruption.

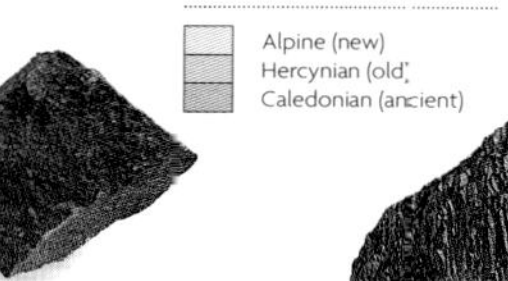

1 2 3 4 5 6 7 8

Geological regions

- continental shield
- sedimentary cover
- coral formation
- igneous rock types

Mountain ranges

- Alpine (new)
- Hercynian (old)
- Caledonian (ancient)

Coral

4 Coral reefs are formed from the skeletons of millions of individual corals.

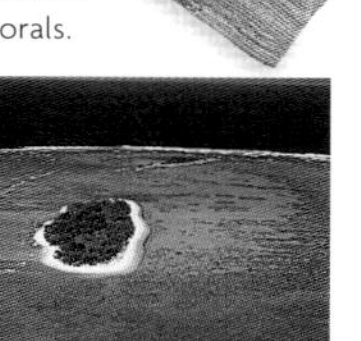

▲ ***Great Barrier Reef,*** *Australia.*

Schist

6 Schist is a metamorphic rock formed during mountain building, when temperature and pressure are comparatively high. Both mudstones and shales reform into schist under these conditions.

▶ ***Schist formations in*** *the Atlas Mountains, northwestern Africa.*

Granite

5 Granite is an intrusive igneous rock formed from magma which has solidified deep within the Earth's crust. The magma cools slowly, producing a coarse-grained rock.

▶ ***Namibia's Namaqualand Plateau*** *is formed of granite.*

Shaping the landscape

The basic material of the Earth's surface is solid rock: valleys, deserts, soil, and sand are all evidence of the powerful agents of weathering, erosion, and deposition which constantly shape and transform the Earth's landscapes. Water, either flowing continually in rivers or seas, or frozen and compacted into solid sheets of ice, has the most clearly visible impact on the Earth's surface. But wind can transport fragments of rock over huge distances and strip away protective layers of vegetation, exposing rock surfaces to the impact of extreme heat and cold.

Coastal water

The world's coastlines are constantly changing; every day, tides deposit, sift and sort sand, and gravel on the shoreline. Over longer periods, powerful wave action erodes cliffs and headlands and carves out bays.

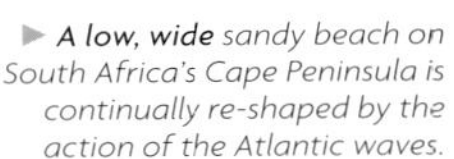

► **A low, wide** sandy beach on South Africa's Cape Peninsula is continually re-shaped by the action of the Atlantic waves.

▲ **The sheer chalk** cliffs at Seven Sisters in southern England are constantly under attack from waves.

Water

Less than 2% of the world's water is on the land, but it is the most powerful agent of landscape change. Water, as rainfall, groundwater, and rivers, can transform landscapes through both erosion and deposition. Eroded material carried by rivers forms the world's most fertile soils.

▲ **Waterfalls such as** the Iguaçu Falls on the border between Argentina and southern Brazil, erode the underlying rock, causing the falls to retreat.

Groundwater

In regions where there are porous rocks such as chalk, water is stored underground in large quantities; these reservoirs of water are known as aquifers. Rain percolates through topsoil into the underlying bedrock, creating an underground store of water. The limit of the saturated zone is called the water table.

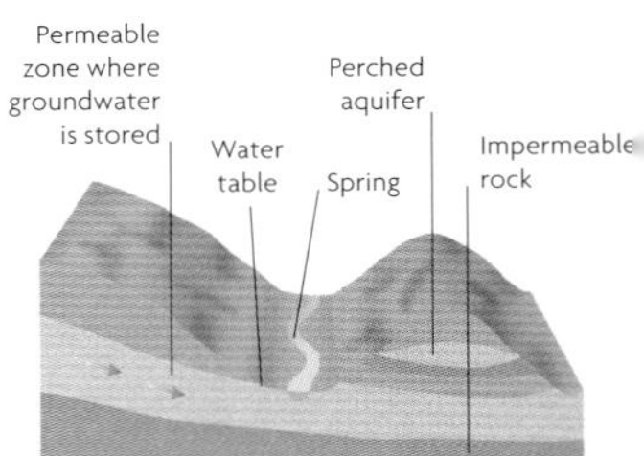
Permeable zone where groundwater is stored
Water table
Spring
Perched aquifer
Impermeable rock

Storage of groundwater in an aquifer

World river systems

drainage basin

World river systems:
Sediment deposited annually per drainage basin

tons per sq mile per year: 9120, 6080, 1520, 760

tonnes per sq km per year: 1600, 400, 200 and less

Rivers

Rivers erode the land by grinding and dissolving rocks and stones. Most erosion occurs in the river's upper course as it flows through highland areas. Rock fragments are moved along the river bed by fast-flowing water and deposited in areas where the river slows down, such as flat plains, or where the river enters seas or lakes.

River valleys

Over long periods of time rivers erode uplands to form characteristic V-shaped valleys with smooth sides.

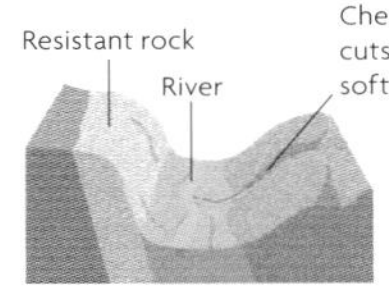
Resistant rock
River
Chemical erosion cuts valley in softer rock

River valley erosion

Deltas

When a river deposits its load of silt and sediment (alluvium) on entering the sea, it may form a delta. As this material accumulates, it chokes the mouth of the river, forcing it to create new channels to reach the sea.

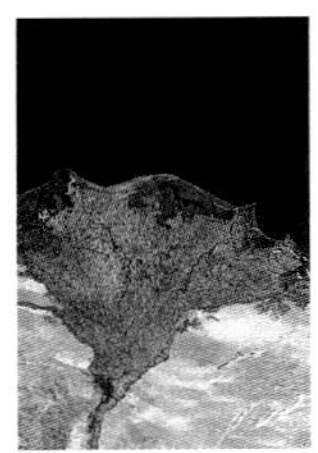

► **The Nile forms** a broad delta as it flows into the Mediterranean.

Drainage basins

The drainage basin is the area of land drained by a major trunk river and its smaller branch rivers or tributaries. Drainage basins are separated from one another by natural boundaries known as watersheds.

Watershed · Major trunk river · Alps · Dolomites · Apennines · Tributary river · Delta · River mouth · Po Valley

The drainage basin of the Po river, northern Italy.

Meanders

In their lower courses, rivers flow slowly. As they flow across the lowlands, they form looping bends called meanders.

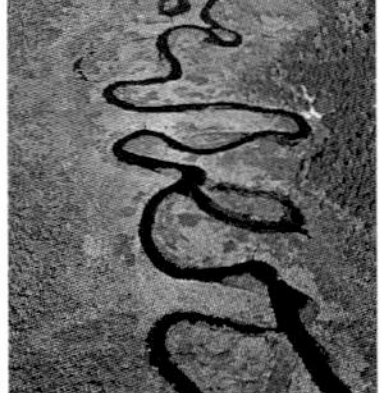

▲ **The Mississippi River** forms meanders as it flows across the southern US.

▲ **The meanders of** Utah's San Juan River have become deeply incised.

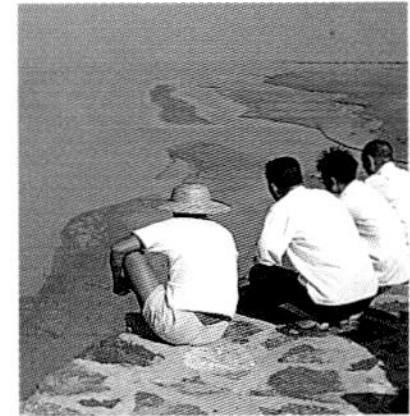

◄ **Mud is deposited** by China's Yellow River in its lower course.

Deposition

When rivers have deposited large quantities of fertile alluvium, they are forced to find new channels through the alluvium deposits, creating braided river systems.

Landslides

Heavy rain and associated flooding on slopes can loosen underlying rocks, which crumble, causing the top layers of rock and soil to slip.

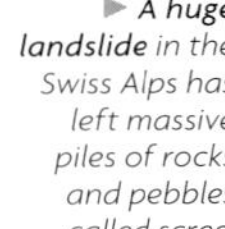

► **A huge landslide** in the Swiss Alps has left massive piles of rocks and pebbles called scree.

▲ **A deep gully** in the French Alps caused by the scouring of upper layers of turf.

Gullies

In areas where soil is thin, rainwater is not effectively absorbed, and may flow overland. The water courses downhill in channels, or gullies, and may lead to rapid erosion of soil.

Ice

During its long history, the Earth has experienced a number of glacial episodes when temperatures were considerably lower than today. During the last Ice Age, 18,000 years ago, ice covered an area three times larger than it does today. Over these periods, the ice has left a remarkable legacy of transformed landscapes.

Glaciers

Glaciers are formed by the compaction of snow into "rivers" of ice. As they move over the landscape, glaciers pick up and carry a load of rocks and boulders which erode the landscape they pass over, and are eventually deposited at the end of the glacier.

▲ ***A massive glacier*** *advancing down a valley in southern Argentina.*

Glacial valleys

Glaciers can erode much more powerfully than rivers. They form steep-sided, flat-bottomed valleys with a typical U-shaped profile. Valleys created by tributary glaciers, whose floors have not been eroded to the same depth as the main glacial valley floor, are called hanging valleys

▲ ***The U-shaped profile*** *and piles of morainic debris are characteristic of a valley once filled by a glacier.*

▲ ***A series of*** *hanging valleys high up in the Chilean Andes.*

▲ ***The profile of*** *the Matterhorn has been formed by three cirques lying "back-to-back."*

Cirques

Cirques are basin-shaped hollows which mark the head of a glaciated valley. Where neighboring cirques meet, they are divided by sharp rock ridges called arêtes. It is these arêtes which give the Matterhorn its characteristic profile.

Fjords

Fjords are ancient glacial valleys flooded by the sea following the end of a period of glaciation. Beneath the water, the valley floor can be 4000 ft (1300 m) deep.

▲ ***A fjord fills*** *a former glacial valley in southern New Zealand.*

Past and present world ice-cover and glacial features

Past and present world ice cover and glacial features

extent of last Ice Age
loess deposits
post-glacial feature
glacial feature
present day ice cover
glacial field

Post-glacial features

When a glacial episode ends, the retreating ice leaves many features. These include depositional ridges called moraines, which may be eroded into low hills known as drumlins; sinuous ridges called eskers; kames, which are rounded hummocks; depressions known as kettle holes; and windblown loess deposits.

Kame terrace
Retreating glacier
Kettle hole
Esker
Drumlin
Braided river
Terminal moraine
Windblown loess
Glacial till
Bedrock

Post-glacial landscape features

Ice shattering

Water drips into fissures in rocks and freezes, expanding as it does so. The pressure weakens the rock, causing it to crack, and eventually to shatter into polygonal patterns.

▲ ***Irregular polygons show*** *through the sedge-grass tundra in the Yukon, Canada.*

Periglaciation

Periglacial areas occur near to the edge of ice sheets. A layer of frozen ground lying just beneath the surface of the land is known as permafrost. When the surface melts in the summer, the water is unable to drain into the frozen ground, and so "creeps" downhill, a process known as solifluction.

Wind

Strong winds can transport rock fragments great distances, especially where there is little vegetation to protect the rock. In desert areas, wind picks up loose, unprotected sand particles, carrying them over great distances. This powerfully abrasive debris is blasted at the surface by the wind, eroding the landscape into dramatic shapes.

Prevailing winds and dust trajectories

Prevailing winds
northeast trade / southeast trade
westerly / westerly
polar easterly / polar easterly

Dust trajectories
trajectory of aeolian dust

Hot and cold deserts

Main desert types
hot arid
semi-arid
cold polar

Temperature

Most of the world's deserts are in the tropics. The cold deserts which occur elsewhere are arid because they are a long way from the rain-giving sea. Rock in deserts is exposed because of lack of vegetation and is susceptible to changes in temperature; extremes of heat and cold can cause both cracks and fissures to appear in the rock.

Deposition

The rocky, stony floors of the world's deserts are swept and scoured by strong winds. The smaller, finer particles of sand are shaped into surface ripples, dunes, or sand mountains, which rise to a height of 650 ft (200 m). Dunes usually form single lines, running perpendicular to the direction of the prevailing wind. These long, straight ridges can extend for over 100 miles (160 km).

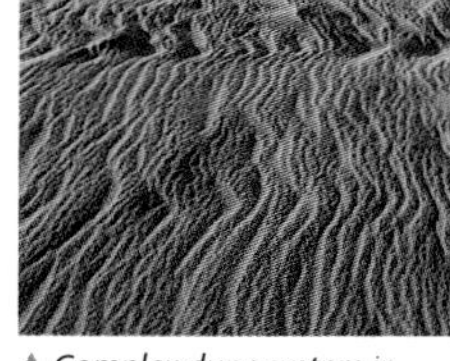

▲ ***Barchan dunes*** *in the Arabian Desert.*

▲ ***Complex dune system*** *in the Sahara.*

Heat

Fierce sun can heat the surface of rock, causing it to expand more rapidly than the cooler, underlying layers. This creates tensions which force the rock to crack or break up. In arid regions, the evaporation of water from rock surfaces dissolves certain minerals within the water, causing salt crystals to form in small openings in the rock. The hard crystals force the openings to widen into cracks and fissures.

Desert abrasion

Abrasion creates a wide range of desert landforms from faceted pebbles and wind ripples in the sand, to large-scale features such as yardangs (low, streamlined ridges), and scoured desert pavements.

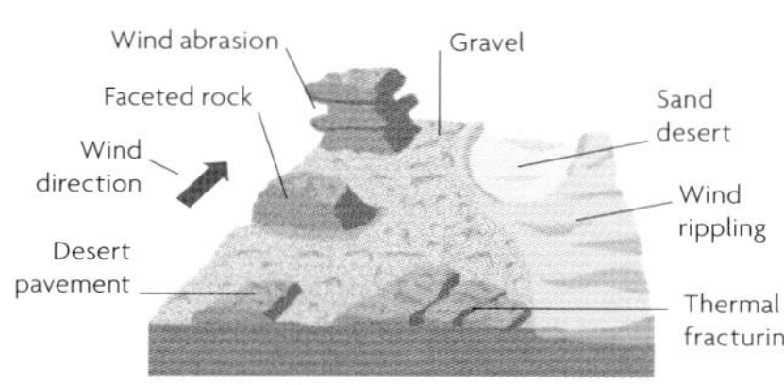
Wind abrasion
Gravel
Faceted rock
Sand desert
Wind direction
Wind rippling
Desert pavement
Thermal fracturing

Features of a desert surface

Dunes

Dunes are shaped by wind direction and sand supply. Where sand supply is limited, crescent-shaped barchan dunes are formed.

Types of dune

Wind direction

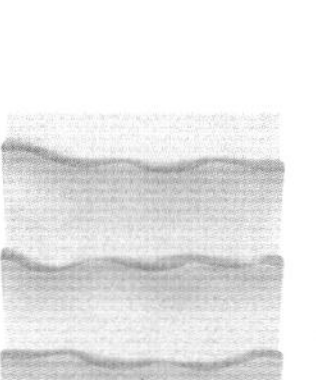

Transverse dune

Barchan dune

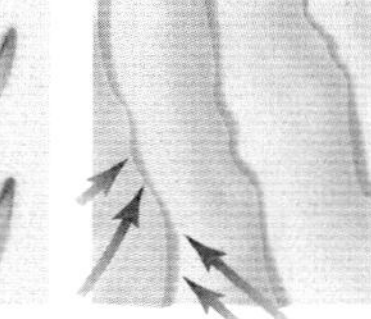

Linear dune

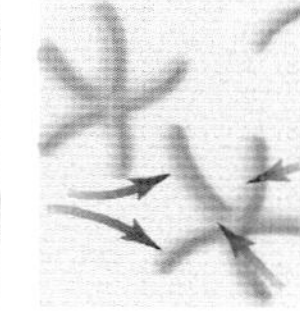

Star dune

▲ ***The cracked and*** *parched floor of Death Valley, California. This is one of the hottest deserts on Earth.*

◀ ***This dry valley*** *at Ellesmere Island in the Canadian Arctic is an example of a cold desert. The cracked floor and scoured slopes are features also found in hot deserts.*

The world's oceans

Two-thirds of the Earth's surface is covered by the oceans. The landscape of the ocean floor, like the surface of the land, has been shaped by movements of the Earth's crust over millions of years to form volcanic mountain ranges, deep trenches, basins, and plateaus. Ocean currents constantly redistribute warm and cold water around the world. A major warm current, such as El Niño in the Pacific Ocean, can increase surface temperature by up to 46°F (8°C), causing changes in weather patterns which can lead to both droughts and flooding.

The great oceans

There are five oceans on Earth: the Pacific, Atlantic, Indian, and Southern oceans, and the much smaller Arctic Ocean. These five ocean basins are relatively young, having evolved within the last 80 million years. One of the most recent plate collisions, between the Eurasian and African plates, created the present-day arrangement of continents and oceans.

▲ *The Indian Ocean accounts for approximately 20% of the total area of the world's oceans.*

Sea level

If the influence of tides, winds, currents, and variations in gravity were ignored, the surface of the Earth's oceans would closely follow the topography of the ocean floor, with an underwater ridge 3000 ft (915 m) high producing a rise of up to 3 ft (1 m) in the level of the surface water.

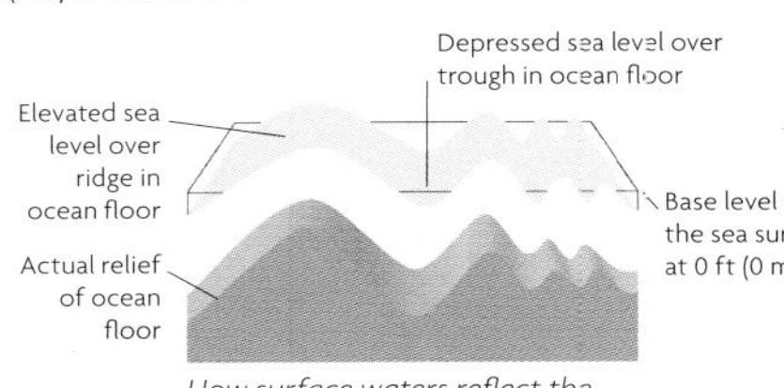
Depressed sea level over trough in ocean floor
Elevated sea level over ridge in ocean floor
Base level of the sea surface at 0 ft (0 m)
Actual relief of ocean floor

How surface waters reflect the relief of the ocean floor

▲ ***The low relief** of many small Pacific islands such as these atolls at Huahine in French Polynesia makes them vulnerable to changes in sea level.*

Ocean structure

The continental shelf is a shallow, flat seabed surrounding the Earth's continents. It extends to the continental slope, which falls to the ocean floor. Here, the flat abyssal plains are interrupted by vast, underwater mountain ranges, the mid-ocean ridges, and ocean trenches which plunge to depths of 35,828 ft (10,920 m).

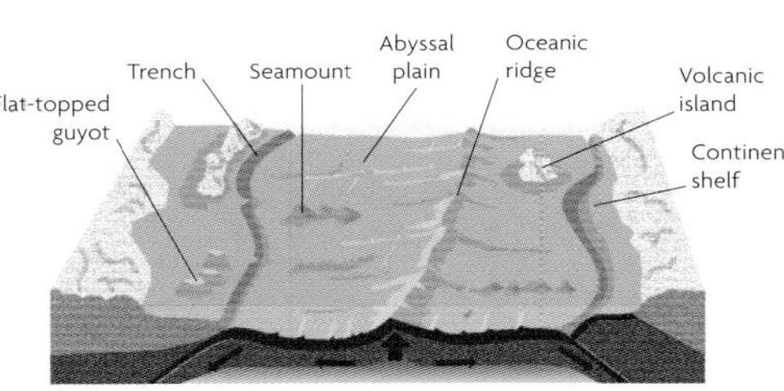
Trench
Seamount
Abyssal plain
Oceanic ridge
Volcanic island
Flat-topped guyot
Continental shelf

Typical sea-floor features

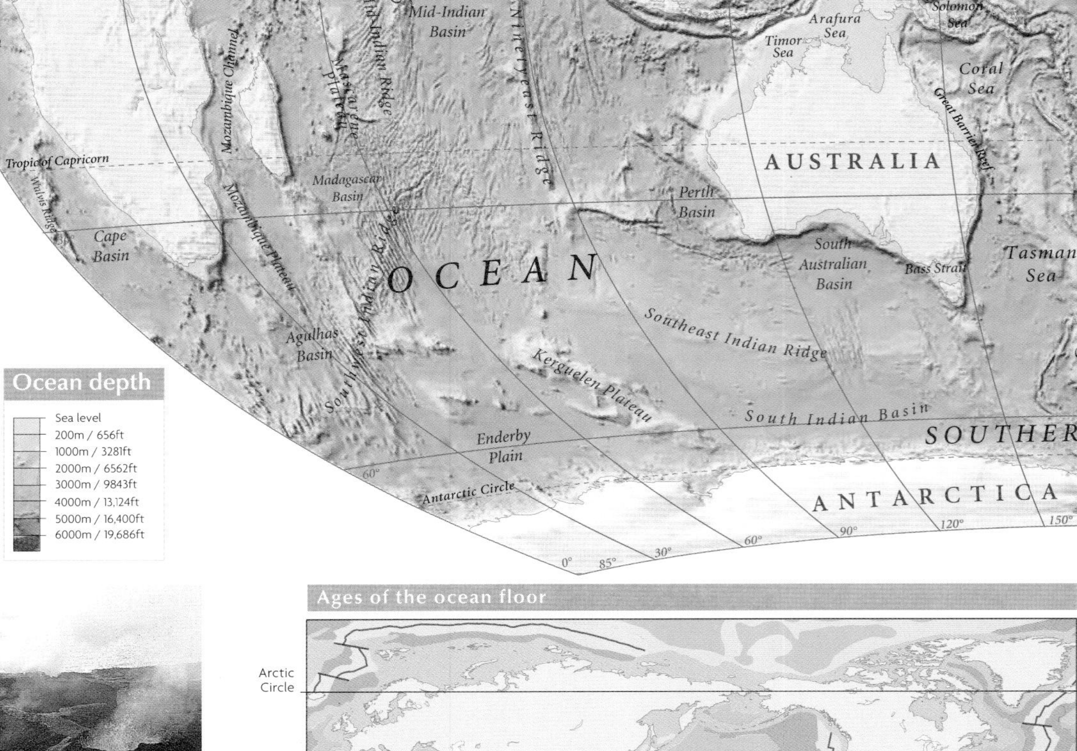
EUROPE
ASIA
AFRICA
AUSTRALIA
ANTARCTICA
INDIAN OCEAN
SOUTHERN
Arctic Circle
Tropic of Cancer
Equator
Tropic of Capricorn
Antarctic Circle
Barents Sea
Kara Sea
Laptev Sea
North Sea
Baltic Sea
Black Sea
Caspian Sea
Mediterranean Sea
Red Sea
Persian Gulf
Arabian Sea
Bay of Bengal
Gulf of Thailand
South China Sea
Sunda Shelf
Strait of Malacca
Celebes Sea
Philippine Sea
Sea of Okhotsk
Sea of Japan (East Sea)
Yellow Sea
East China Sea
Northwest Pacific Basin
Gulf of Guinea
Angola Basin
Cape Basin
Somali Basin
Mozambique Channel
Madagascar Basin
Mid-Indian Basin
Mid-Indian Ridge
Ninetyeast Ridge
Agulhas Basin
Kerguelen Plateau
Enderby Plain
Southeast Indian Ridge
South Indian Basin
Perth Basin
South Australian Basin
Bass Strait
Tasman Sea
Coral Sea
Arafura Sea
Timor Sea
Melanesian Basin
Ocean depth
Sea level
200m / 656ft
1000m / 3281ft
2000m / 6562ft
3000m / 9843ft
4000m / 13,124ft
5000m / 16,400ft
6000m / 19,686ft

Black smokers

These vents in the ocean floor disgorge hot, sulfur-rich water from deep in the Earth's crust. Despite the great depths, a variety of lifeforms have adapted to the chemical-rich environment which surrounds black smokers.

▲ ***A black smoker** in the Atlantic Ocean.*

Chimney
Plume of hot mineral laden water
Water percolates into the sea floor
Ocean floor
Water heated by hot basalt

Formation of black smokers

▲ ***Surtsey, near Iceland,** is a volcanic island lying directly over the Mid-Atlantic Ridge. It was formed in the 1960s following intense volcanic activity nearby.*

Ocean floors

Mid-ocean ridges are formed by lava which erupts beneath the sea and cools to form solid rock. This process mirrors the creation of volcanoes from cooled lava on the land. The ages of sea floor rocks increase in parallel bands outward from central ocean ridges.

Ages of the ocean floor

Arctic Circle
Tropic of Cancer
Equator
Tropic of Capricorn
Antarctic Circle

Jurassic | Cretaceous | Tertiary (Paleogene) | Quaternary | Cretaceous | Jurassic

208 million years old | 145 | 65 | 23 | 0 | 23 | 65 | 145 | 208 million years old

Tertiary (Neogene)

Age uncertain
Continental shelf and island arcs

▲ ***Currents in the** Southern Ocean are driven by some of the world's fiercest winds, including the Roaring Forties, Furious Fifties, and Shrieking Sixties.*

▲ ***The Pacific Ocean** is the world's largest and deepest ocean, covering over one-third of the surface of the Earth.*

▲ ***The Atlantic Ocean** was formed when the landmasses of the eastern and western hemispheres began to drift apart 180 million years ago.*

Deposition of sediment

Storms, earthquakes, and volcanic activity trigger underwater currents known as turbidity currents which scour sand and gravel from the continental shelf, creating underwater canyons. These strong currents pick up material deposited at river mouths and deltas, and carry it across the continental shelf and through the underwater canyons, where it is eventually laid down on the ocean floor in the form of fans.

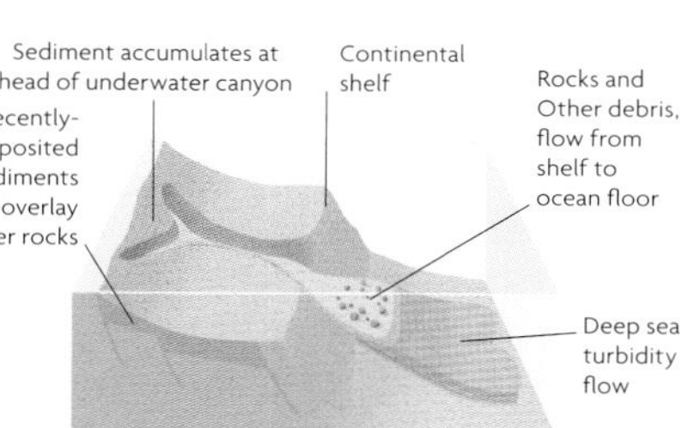
Sediment accumulates at head of underwater canyon
Continental shelf
Rocks and Other debris, flow from shelf to ocean floor
Recently-deposited sediments overlay older rocks
Deep sea turbidity flow

How sediment is deposited on the ocean floor

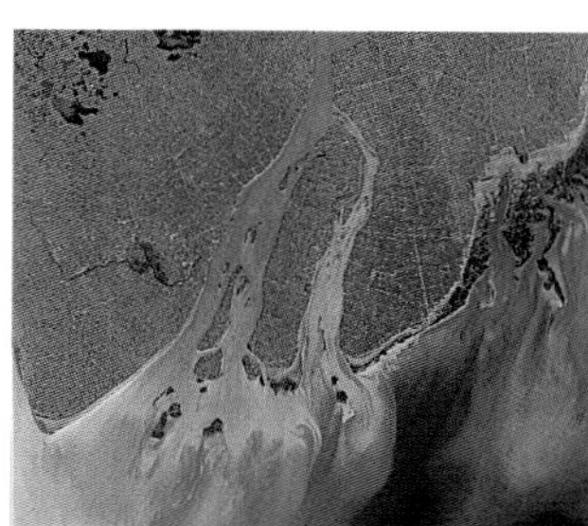

▶ ***Satellite image of** the Yangtze (Chang Jiang) Delta, in which the land appears red. The river deposits immense quantities of silt into the East China Sea, much of which will eventually reach the deep ocean floor.*

Surface water

Ocean currents move warm water away from the Equator toward the poles, while cold water is, in turn, moved towards the Equator. This is the main way in which the Earth distributes surface heat and is a major climatic control. Approximately 4000 million years ago, the Earth was dominated by oceans and there was no land to interrupt the flow of the currents, which would have flowed as straight lines, simply influenced by the Earth's rotation.

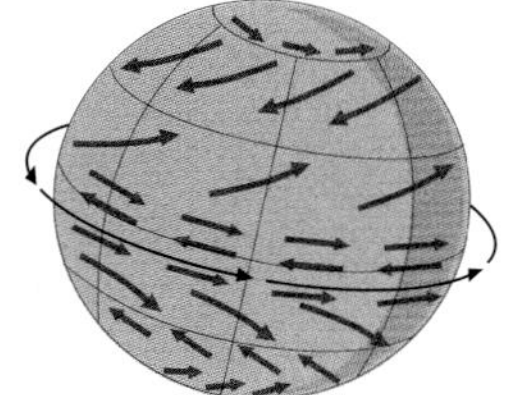

Idealized globe showing the movement of water around a landless Earth.

Ocean currents

Surface currents are driven by the prevailing winds and by the spinning motion of the Earth, which drives the currents into circulating whirlpools,or gyres. Deep sea currents, over 330 ft (100 m) below the surface, are driven by differences in water temperature and salinity, which have an impact on the density of deep water and on its movement.

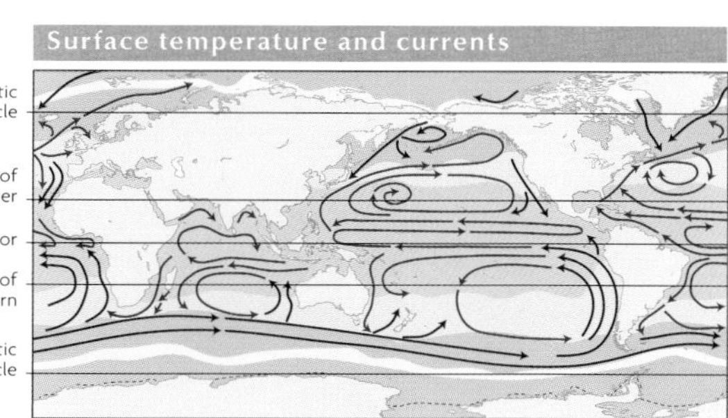
Surface temperature and currents
Arctic Circle
Tropic of Cancer
Equator
Tropic of Capricorn
Antarctic Circle

Surface temperature and currents

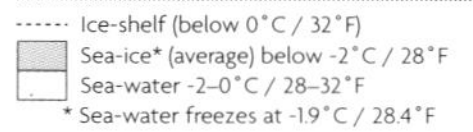
Ice-shelf (below 0°C / 32°F)
Sea-ice* (average) below -2°C / 28°F
Sea-water -2–0°C / 28–32°F
* Sea-water freezes at -1.9°C / 28.4°F
0–10°C / 32–50°F
10–20°C / 50–68°F
20–30°C / 68–86°F

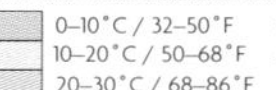
warm current
cold current

Tides and waves

Tides are created by the pull of the Sun and Moon's gravity on the surface of the oceans. The levels of high and low tides are influenced by the position of the Moon in relation to the Earth and Sun. Waves are formed by wind blowing over the surface of the water.

High and low tides

The highest tides occur when the Earth, the Moon and the Sun are aligned *(below left)*. The lowest tides are experienced when the Sun and Moon align at right angles to one another *(below right)*.

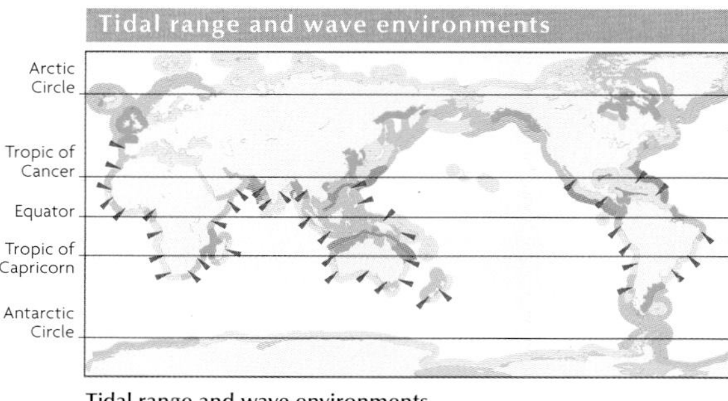
Tidal range and wave environments
Arctic Circle
Tropic of Cancer
Equator
Tropic of Capricorn
Antarctic Circle

Tidal range and wave environments

less than 2m / 7ft
2–4m / 7–13ft
greater than 4m / 13ft
east coast swell
west coast swell
tropical cyclone
storm wave
ice-shelf

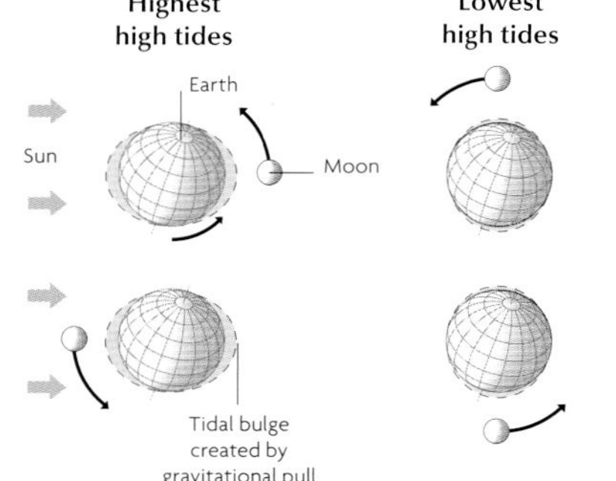
Highest high tides
Lowest high tides
Earth
Sun
Moon
Tidal bulge created by gravitational pull

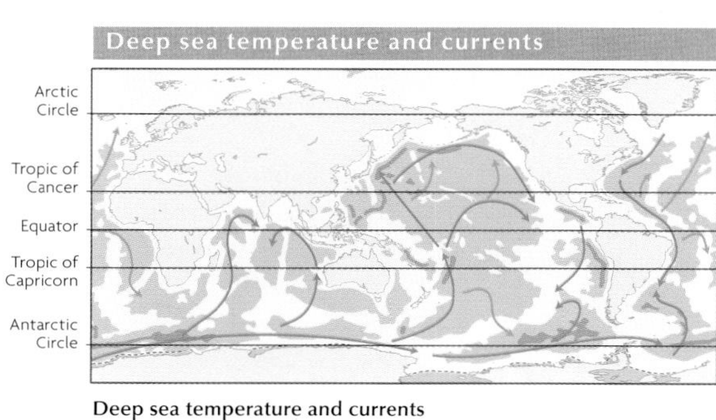
Deep sea temperature and currents
Arctic Circle
Tropic of Cancer
Equator
Tropic of Capricorn
Antarctic Circle

Deep sea temperature and currents

Ice-shelf (below 0°C / 32°F)
Sea-water -2–0°C / 28–32°F (below 5000m / 16,400ft)
Sea-water 0–5°C / 32–41°F (below 4000m / 13,120ft)

Primary currents
Secondary currents

The global climate

The Earth's climatic types consist of stable patterns of weather conditions averaged out over a long period of time. Different climates are categorized according to particular combinations of temperature and humidity. By contrast, weather consists of short-term fluctuations in wind temperature, and humidity conditions. Different climates are determined by latitude, altitude, the prevailing wind, and circulation of ocean currents. Longer-term changes in climate, such as global warming or the onset of ice ages, are punctuated by shorter-term events which comprise the day-to-day weather of a region, such as frontal depressions, hurricanes, and blizzards.

The atmosphere, wind and weather

The Earth's atmosphere has been compared to a giant ocean of air which surrounds the planet. Its circulation patterns are similar to the currents in the oceans and are influenced by three factors; the Earth's orbit around the Sun and rotation about its axis, and variations in the amount of heat radiation received from the Sun. If both heat and moisture were not redistributed between the Equator and the poles, large areas of the Earth would be uninhabitable.

◄ *Heavy fogs, as here in southern England, form as moisture-laden air passes over cold ground.*

Temperature

The world can be divided into three major climatic zones, stretching like large belts across the latitudes: the tropics which are warm; the cold polar regions and the temperate zones which lie between them. Temperatures across the Earth range from above 86°F (30°C) in the deserts to as low as -70°F (-55°C) at the poles. Temperature is also controlled by altitude; because air becomes cooler and less dense the higher it gets, mountainous regions are typically colder than those areas which are at, or close to, sea level.

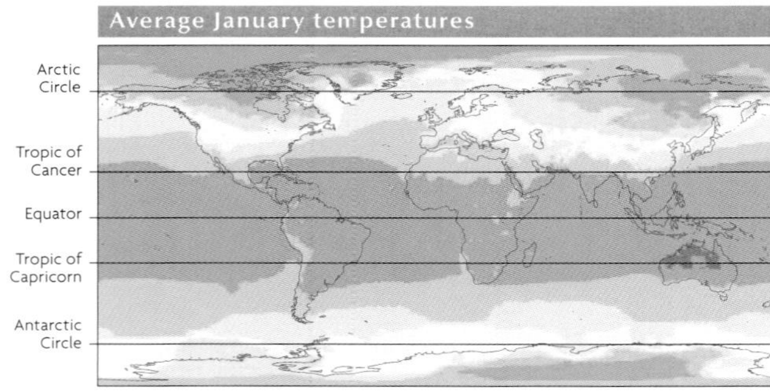
Average January temperatures
Arctic Circle
Tropic of Cancer
Equator
Tropic of Capricorn
Antarctic Circle

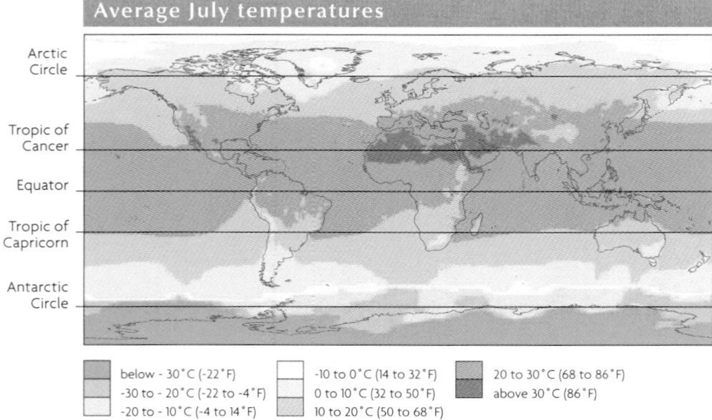
Average July temperatures
Arctic Circle
Tropic of Cancer
Equator
Tropic of Capricorn
Antarctic Circle

below - 30°C (-22°F)
-30 to - 20°C (-22 to -4°F)
-20 to - 10°C (-4 to 14°F)
-10 to 0°C (14 to 32°F)
0 to 10°C (32 to 50°F)
10 to 20°C (50 to 68°F)
20 to 30°C (68 to 86°F)
above 30°C (86°F)

Global air circulation

Air does not simply flow from the Equator to the poles, it circulates in giant cells known as Hadley and Ferrel cells. As air warms it expands, becoming less dense and rising; this creates areas of low pressure. As the air rises it cools and condenses, causing heavy rainfall over the tropics and slight snowfall over the poles. This cool air then sinks, forming high pressure belts. At surface level in the tropics these sinking currents are deflected poleward as the westerlies and toward the equator as the trade winds. At the poles they become the polar easterlies.

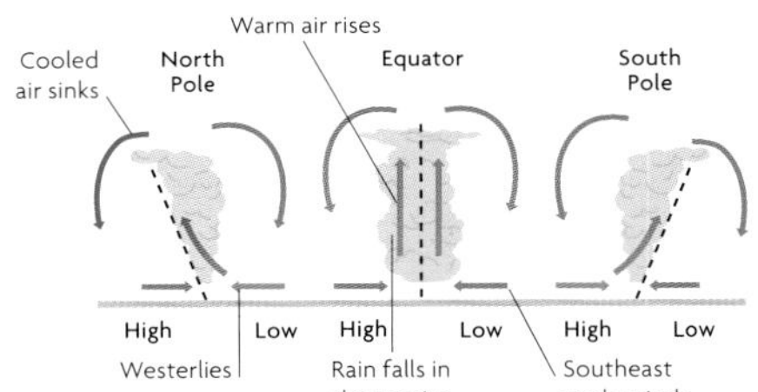
Warm air rises
Cooled air sinks
North Pole
Equator
South Pole
High
Low
Westerlies
High
Low
Rain falls in the tropics
High
Low
Southeast trade winds

▲ ***The Antarctic pack** ice expands its area by almost seven times during the winter as temperatures drop and surrounding seas freeze.*

POLAR
Arctic Circle
January
July
Chinook
January
Alaska Current
WESTERLIES
North Pacific Current
Blizzards
December–March
Labrador Current
North Atlantic Drift
Gulf Stream
WESTERLIES
California Current
Northers January
Tornadoes May–July
Tropic of Cancer
NORTH EAST TRADES
Northern Equatorial Current
North Equatorial Current
NORTH EAST TRADES
Canary Current
Equatorial Counter Current
Doldrums
El Niño
Equator
Doldrums
South Equatorial Current
South Equatorial Current
SOUTH EAST TRADES
El Niño
Peru (Humboldt) Current
Brazil Current
SOUTH EAST TRADES
Tropic of Capricorn
Falkland Current
Pampero
WESTERLIES
West Wind Drift
Antarctic Circle
POLAR

Climatic change

The Earth is currently in a warm phase between ice ages. Warmer temperatures result in higher sea levels as more of the polar ice caps melt. Most of the world's population lives near coasts, so any changes which might cause sea levels to rise, could have a potentially disastrous impact.

▲ ***This ice fair,** painted by Pieter Brueghel the Younger in the 17th century, shows the Little Ice Age which peaked around 300 years ago.*

The greenhouse effect

Gases such as carbon dioxide are known as "greenhouse gases" because they allow shortwave solar radiation to enter the Earth's atmosphere, but help to stop longwave radiation from escaping. This traps heat, raising the Earth's temperature. An excess of these gases, such as that which results from the burning of fossil fuels, helps trap more heat and can lead to global warming.

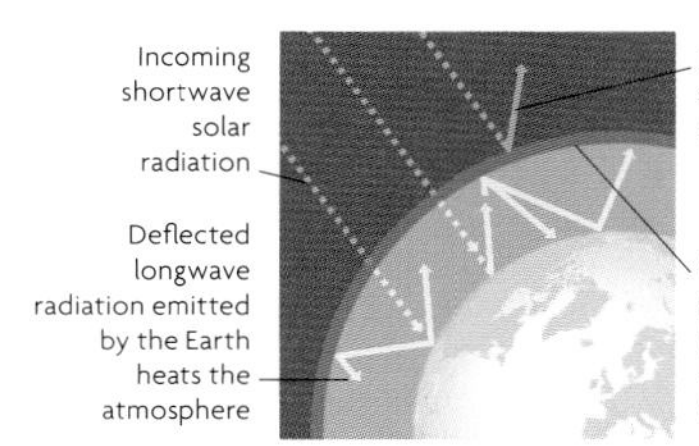
Incoming shortwave solar radiation
Deflected shortwave solar radiation
Deflected longwave radiation emitted by the Earth heats the atmosphere
Greenhouse gases prevent the escape of longwave radiation

◀ *The islands of the Caribbean, Mexico's Gulf coast and the southeastern US are often hit by hurricanes formed far out in the Atlantic.*

Oceanic water circulation

In general, ocean currents parallel the movement of winds across the Earth's surface. Incoming solar energy is greatest at the Equator and least at the poles. So, water in the oceans heats up most at the Equator and flows poleward, cooling as it moves north or south toward the Arctic or Antarctic. The flow is eventually reversed and cold water currents move back toward the Equator. These ocean currents act as a vast system for moving heat from the Equator toward the poles and are a major influence on the distribution of the Earth's climates.

▲ *In marginal climatic zones years of drought can completely dry out the land and transform grassland to desert.*

Map key

Climate zones: ice cap, subarctic, tundra, continental, temperate, warm temperate, mediterranean, semi-arid, arid, hot humid, humid equatorial, tropical

Ocean currents: warm, cold

Prevailing winds: warm, cold

Local winds: warm, cold, June seasonal*

* (seasonal winds which can either be warm or cold)

▲ *The wide range of environments found in the Andes is strongly related to their altitude, which modifies climatic influences. While the peaks are snow-capped, many protected interior valleys are semi-tropical.*

Tilt and rotation

The tilt and rotation of the Earth during its annual orbit largely control the distribution of heat and moisture across its surface, which correspondingly controls its large-scale weather patterns. As the Earth annually rotates around the Sun, half its surface is receiving maximum radiation, creating summer and winter seasons. The angle of the Earth means that on average the tropics receive two and a half times as much heat from the Sun each day as the poles.

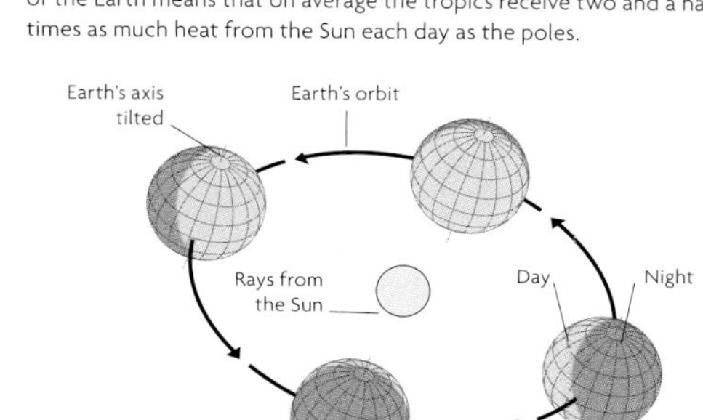
Earth's axis tilted
Earth's orbit
Rays from the Sun
Day
Night

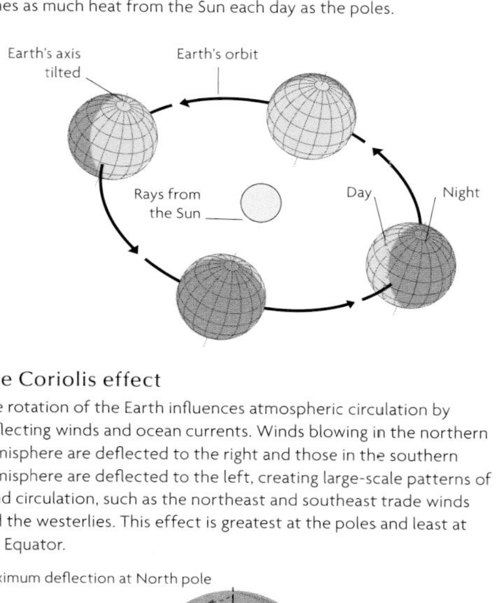

The Coriolis effect

The rotation of the Earth influences atmospheric circulation by deflecting winds and ocean currents. Winds blowing in the northern hemisphere are deflected to the right and those in the southern hemisphere are deflected to the left, creating large-scale patterns of wind circulation, such as the northeast and southeast trade winds and the westerlies. This effect is greatest at the poles and least at the Equator.

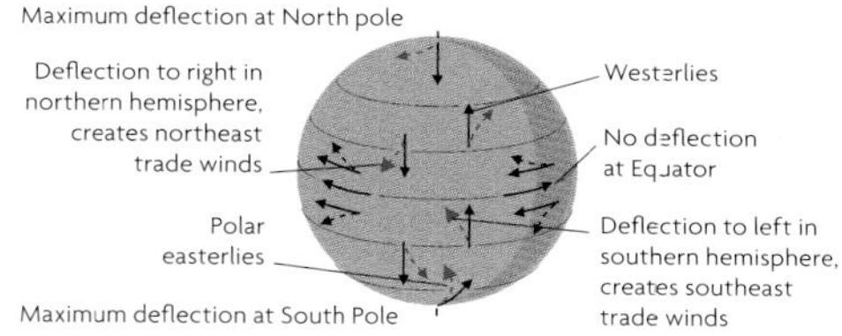
Maximum deflection at North pole
Deflection to right in northern hemisphere, creates northeast trade winds
Westerlies
No deflection at Equator
Polar easterlies
Deflection to left in southern hemisphere, creates southeast trade winds
Maximum deflection at South Pole

Precipitation

When warm air expands, it rises and cools, and the water vapor it carries condenses to form clouds. Heavy, regular rainfall is characteristic of the equatorial region, while the poles are cold and receive only slight snowfall. Tropical regions have marked dry and rainy seasons, while in the temperate regions rainfall is relatively unpredictable.

▲ *Monsoon rains, which affect southern Asia from May to September, are caused by sea winds blowing across the warm land.*

▲ *Heavy tropical rainstorms occur frequently in Papua New Guinea, often causing soil erosion and landslides in cultivated areas.*

Average January rainfall

Average July rainfall

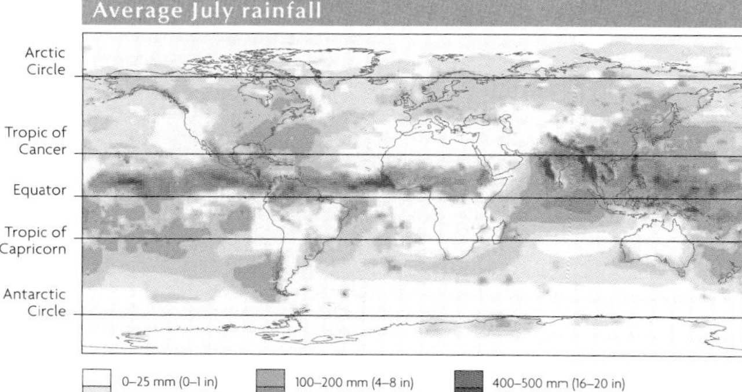
Arctic Circle
Tropic of Cancer
Equator
Tropic of Capricorn
Antarctic Circle
0–25 mm (0–1 in)
25–50 mm (1–2 in)
50–100 mm (2–4 in)
100–200 mm (4–8 in)
200–300 mm (8–12 in)
300–400 mm (12–16 in)
400–500 mm (16–20 in)
above 500 mm (20 in)

▲ *The intensity of some blizzards in Canada and the northern US can give rise to snowdrifts as high as 10 ft (3 m).*

▲ *The Atacama Desert in Chile is one of the driest places on Earth, with an average rainfall of less than 2 inches (50 mm) per year.*

▲ *Violent thunderstorms occur along advancing cold fronts, when cold, dry air masses meet warm, moist air, which rises rapidly, its moisture condensing into thunderclouds. Rain and hail become electrically charged, causing lightning.*

The rainshadow effect

When moist air is forced to rise by mountains, it cools and the water vapor falls as precipitation, either as rain or snow. Only the dry, cold air continues over the mountains, leaving inland areas with little or no rain. This is called the rainshadow effect and is one reason for the existence of the Mojave Desert in California, which lies east of the Coast Ranges.

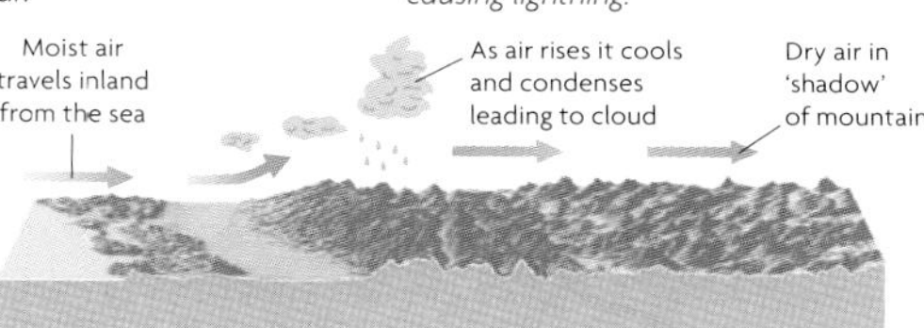
Moist air travels inland from the sea
As air rises it cools and condenses leading to cloud
Dry air in 'shadow' of mountain

The rainshadow effect

Life on Earth

A unique combination of an oxygen-rich atmosphere and plentiful water is the key to life on Earth. Apart from the polar ice caps, there are few areas which have not been colonized by animals or plants over the course of the Earth's history. Plants process sunlight to provide them with their energy, and ultimately all the Earth's animals rely on plants for survival. Because of this reliance, plants are known as primary producers, and the availability of nutrients and temperature of an area is defined as its primary productivity, which affects the quantity and type of animals which are able to live there. This index is affected by climatic factors – cold and aridity restrict the quantity of life, whereas warmth and regular rainfall allow a greater diversity of species.

Biogeographical regions

The Earth can be divided into a series of biogeographical regions, or biomes, ecological communities where certain species of plant and animal coexist within particular climatic conditions. Within these broad classifications, other factors including soil richness, altitude, and human activities such as urbanization, intensive agriculture, and deforestation, affect the local distribution of living species within each biome.

Polar regions

A layer of permanent ice at the Earth's poles covers both seas and land. Very little plant and animal life can exist in these harsh regions.

Tundra

A desolate region, with long, dark freezing winters and short, cold summers. With virtually no soil and large areas of permanently frozen ground known as permafrost, the tundra is largely treeless, though it is briefly clothed by small flowering plants in the summer months.

Needleleaf forests

With milder summers than the tundra and less wind, these areas are able to support large forests of coniferous trees.

Broadleaf forests

Much of the northern hemisphere was once covered by deciduous forests, which occurred in areas with marked seasonal variations. Most deciduous forests have been cleared for human settlement.

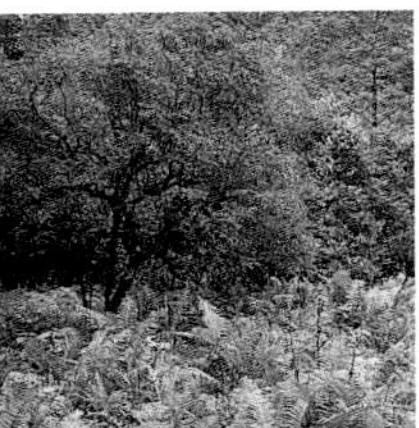

Temperate rain forests

In warmer wetter areas, such as southern China, temperate deciduous forests are replaced by evergreen forest.

Deserts

Deserts are areas with negligible rainfall. Most hot deserts lie within the tropics; cold deserts are dry because of their distance from the moisture-providing sea.

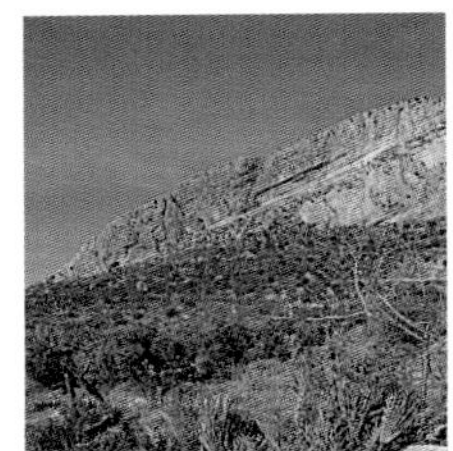

Mediterranean

Hot, dry summers and short winters typify these areas, which were once covered by evergreen shrubs and woodland, but have now been cleared by humans for agriculture.

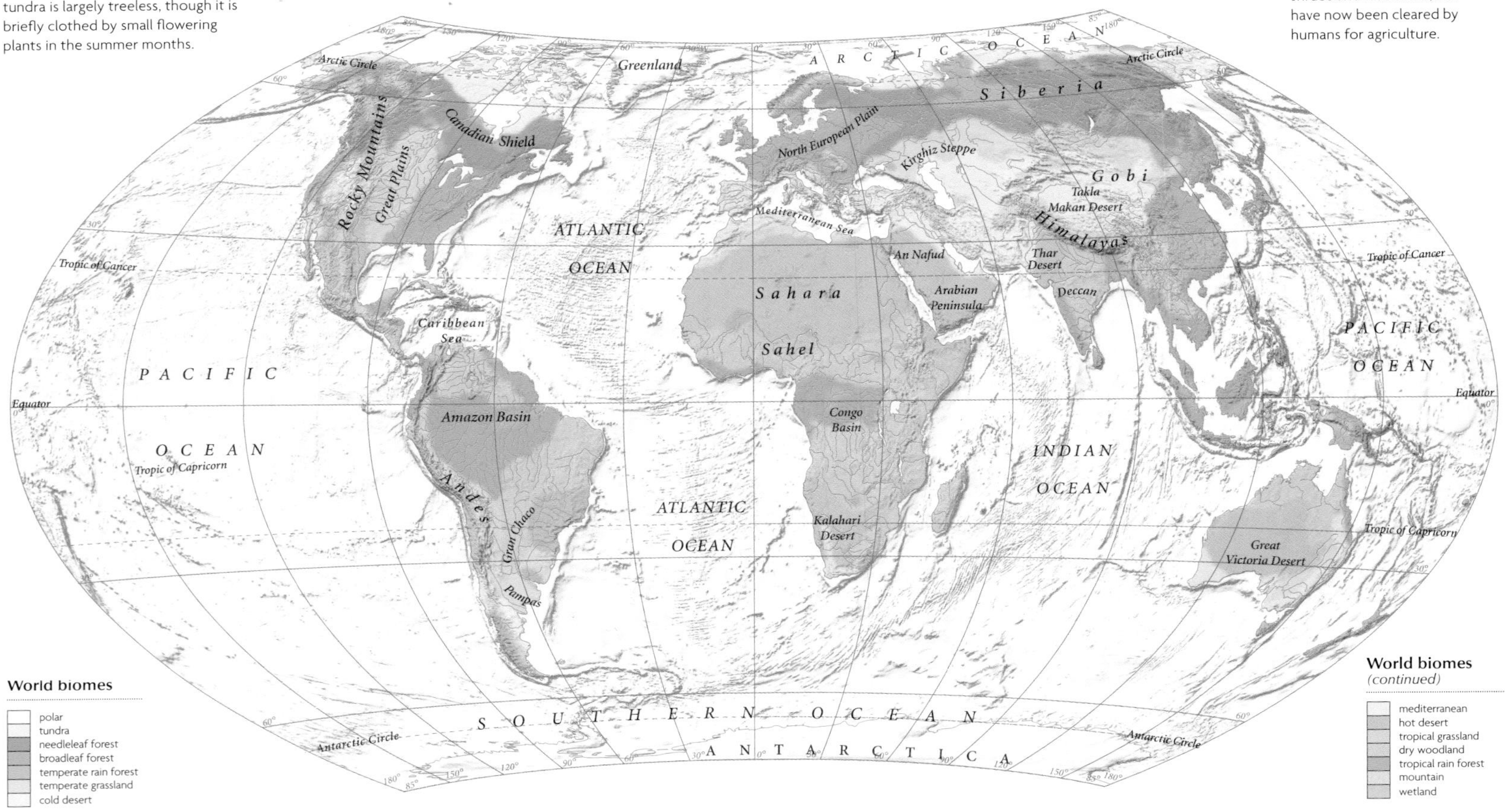

Arctic Circle
Greenland
A R C T I C O C E A N
Siberia
Rocky Mountains
Great Plains
Canadian Shield
North European Plain
Kirghiz Steppe
Gobi
Takla Makan Desert
Himalayas
Mediterranean Sea
An Nafud
Thar Desert
Arabian Peninsula
Deccan
Tropic of Cancer
ATLANTIC OCEAN
Sahara
Sahel
Caribbean Sea
PACIFIC OCEAN
Equator
Amazon Basin
Congo Basin
INDIAN OCEAN
Tropic of Capricorn
Andes
Gran Chaco
Pampas
Kalahari Desert
Great Victoria Desert
SOUTHERN OCEAN
Antarctic Circle
ANTARCTICA

World biomes

- polar
- tundra
- needleleaf forest
- broadleaf forest
- temperate rain forest
- temperate grassland
- cold desert

World biomes *(continued)*

- mediterranean
- hot desert
- tropical grassland
- dry woodland
- tropical rain forest
- mountain
- wetland

Tropical and temperate grasslands

The major grassland areas are found in the centers of the larger continental landmasses. In Africa's tropical savannah regions, seasonal rainfall alternates with drought. Temperate grasslands, also known as steppes and prairies are found in the northern hemisphere, and in South America, where they are known as the pampas.

Dry woodlands

Trees and shrubs, adapted to dry conditions, grow widely spaced from one another, interspersed by savannah grasslands.

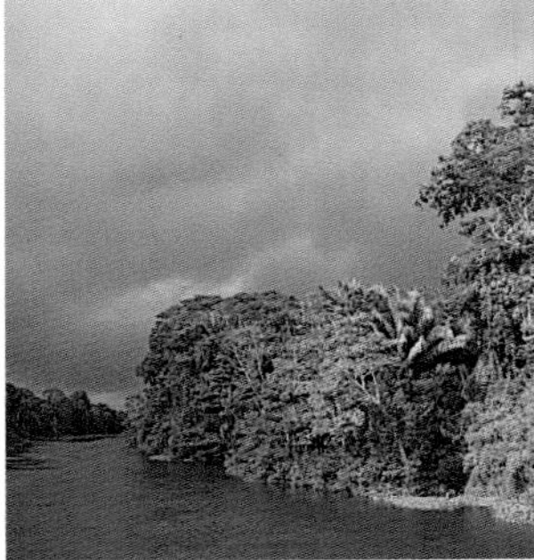

Tropical rain forests

Characterized by year-round warmth and high rainfall, tropical rain forests contain the highest diversity of plant and animal species on Earth.

Mountains

Though the lower slopes of mountains may be thickly forested, only ground-hugging shrubs and other vegetation will grow above the tree line which varies according to both altitude and latitude.

Wetlands

Rarely lying above sea level, wetlands are marshes, swamps, and tidal flats. Some, with their moist, fertile soils, are rich feeding grounds for fish and breeding grounds for birds. Others have little soil structure and are too acidic to support much plant and animal life.

Biodiversity

The number of plant and animal species, and the range of genetic diversity within the populations of each species, make up the Earth's biodiversity. The plants and animals which are endemic to a region – that is, those which are found nowhere else in the world – are also important in determining levels of biodiversity. Human settlement and intervention have encroached on many areas of the world once rich in endemic plant and animal species. Increasing international efforts are being made to monitor and conserve the biodiversity of the Earth's remaining wild places.

Animal adaptation

The degree of an animal's adaptability to different climates and conditions is extremely important in ensuring its success as a species. Many animals, particularly the largest mammals, are becoming restricted to ever-smaller regions as human development and modern agricultural practices reduce their natural habitats. In contrast, humans have been responsible – both deliberately and accidentally – for the spread of some of the world's most successful species. Many of these introduced species are now more numerous than the indigenous animal populations.

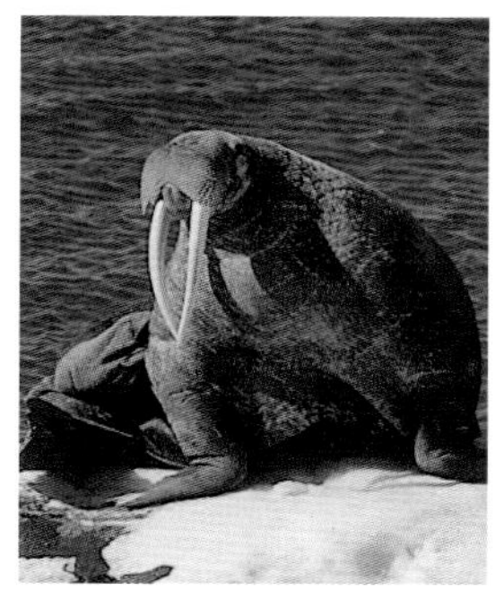

Polar animals

The frozen wastes of the polar regions are able to support only a small range of species which derive their nutritional requirements from the sea. Animals such as the walrus *(left)* have developed insulating fat, stocky limbs, and double-layered coats to enable them to survive in the freezing conditions.

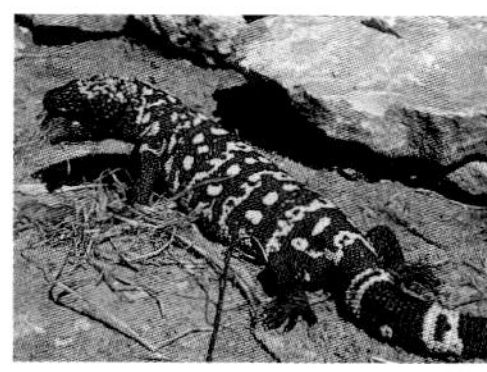

Desert animals

Many animals which live in the extreme heat and aridity of the deserts are able to survive for days and even months with very little food or water. Their bodies are adapted to lose heat quickly and to store fat and water. The Gila monster *(above)* stores fat in its tail.

Diversity of animal species

Number of animal species per country

- more than 2000
- 1000–1999
- 700–999
- 400–699
- 200–399
- 100–199
- 0–99
- data not available

Marine biodiversity

The oceans support a huge variety of different species, from the world's largest mammals like whales and dolphins down to the tiniest plankton. The greatest diversities occur in the warmer seas of continental shelves, where plants are easily able to photosynthesize, and around coral reefs, where complex ecosystems are found. On the ocean floor, nematodes can exist at a depth of more than 10,000 ft (3000 m) below sea level.

Amazon rain forest

The vast Amazon Basin is home to the world's greatest variety of animal species. Animals are adapted to live at many different levels from the treetops to the tangled undergrowth which lies beneath the canopy. The sloth *(below)* hangs upside down in the branches. Its fur grows from its stomach to its back to enable water to run off quickly.

High altitudes

Few animals exist in the rarefied atmosphere of the highest mountains. However, birds of prey such as eagles and vultures *(above)*, with their superb eyesight can soar as high as 23,000 ft (7000 m) to scan for prey below.

Urban animals

The growth of cities has reduced the amount of habitat available to many species. A number of animals are now moving closer into urban areas to scavenge from the detritus of the modern city *(left)*. Rodents, particularly rats and mice, have existed in cities for thousands of years, and many insects, especially moths, quickly develop new coloring to provide them with camouflage.

Endemic species

Isolated areas such as Australia and the island of Madagascar, have the greatest range of endemic species. In Australia, these include marsupials such as the kangaroo *(below)*, which carry their young in pouches on their bodies. Destruction of habitat, pollution, hunting, and predators introduced by humans, are threatening this unique biodiversity.

Plant adaptation

Environmental conditions, particularly climate, soil type, and the extent of competition with other organisms, influence the development of plants into a number of distinctive forms. Similar conditions in quite different parts of the world create similar adaptations in the plants, which may then be modified by other, local, factors specific to the region.

Cold conditions

In areas where temperatures rarely rise above freezing, plants such as lichens *(left)* and mosses grow densely, close to the ground.

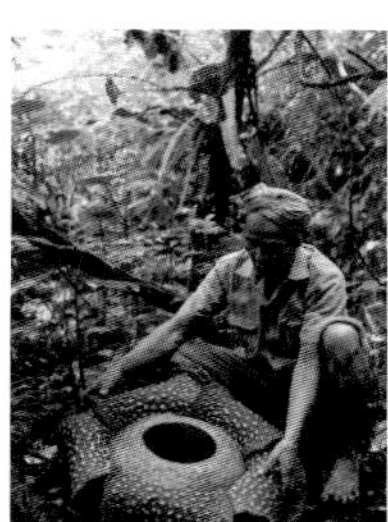

Rain forests

Most of the world's largest and oldest plants are found in rain forests; warmth and heavy rainfall provide ideal conditions for vast plants like the world's largest flower, the rafflesia *(left)*.

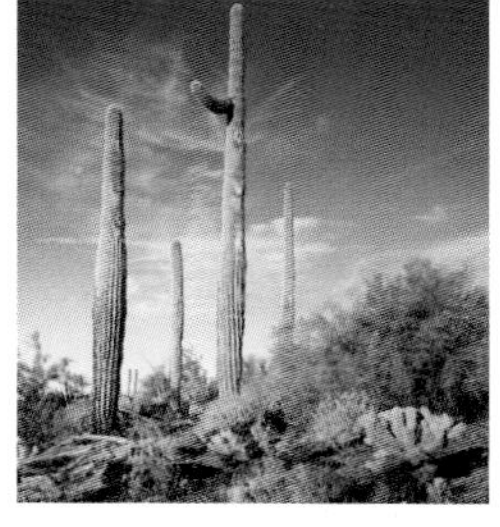

Hot, dry conditions

Arid conditions lead to the development of plants whose surface area has been reduced to a minimum to reduce water loss. In cacti *(above)*, which can survive without water for months, leaves are minimal or not present at all.

Ancient plants

Some of the world's most primitive plants still exist today, including algae, cycads, and many ferns *(above)*, reflecting the success with which they have adapted to changing conditions.

Resisting predators

A great variety of plants have developed devices including spines *(above)*, poisons, stinging hairs, and an unpleasant taste or smell to deter animal predators.

Diversity of plant species

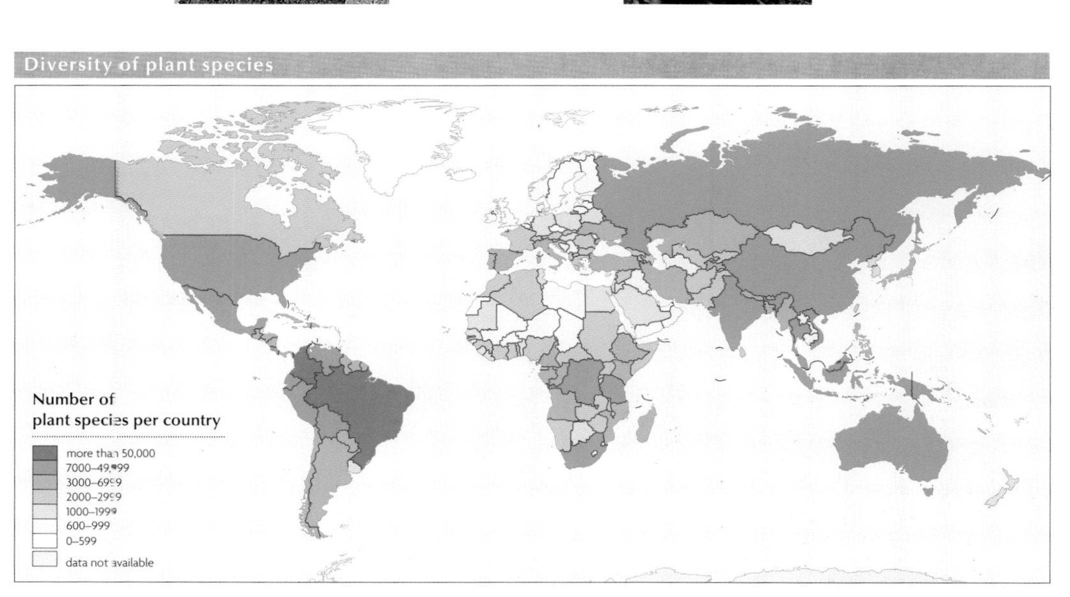
Number of plant species per country
more than 50,000
7000–49,999
3000–6999
2000–2999
1000–1999
600–999
0–599
data not available

Weeds

Weeds such as bindweed *(above)* are fast-growing, easily dispersed, and tolerant of a number of different environments, enabling them to quickly colonize suitable habitats. They are among the most adaptable of all plants.

Population and settlement

The Earth's population is projected to rise from its current level of about 6.5 billion to reach some 10 billion by 2025. The global distribution of this rapidly growing population is very uneven, and is dictated by climate, terrain, and natural and economic resources. The great majority of the Earth's people live in coastal zones, and along river valleys. Deserts cover over 20% of the Earth's surface, but support less than 5% of the world's population. It is estimated that over half of the world's population live in cities – most of them in Asia – as a result of mass migration from rural areas in search of jobs. Many of these people live in the so-called "megacities," some with populations as great as 40 million.

Patterns of settlement

The past 200 years have seen the most radical shift in world population patterns in recorded history.

Nomadic life

All the world's peoples were hunter-gatherers 10,000 years ago. Today nomads, who live by following available food resources, account for less than 0.0001% of the world's population. They are mainly pastoral herders, moving their livestock from place to place in search of grazing land.

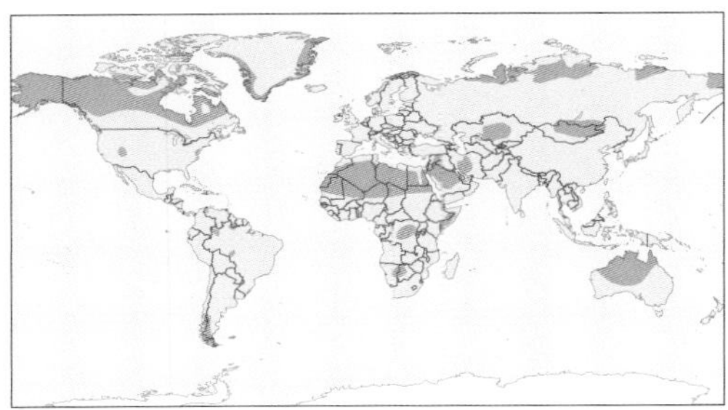

Nomadic population

Nomadic population area

The growth of cities

In 1900 there were only 14 cities in the world with populations of more than a million, mostly in the northern hemisphere. Today, as more and more people in the developing world migrate to towns and cities, there are over 30 cities whose population exceeds 5 million, and around 440 "million-cities."

Million-cities in 1900

Million-cities in 1900

• Cities over 1 million population

Million-cities in 2005

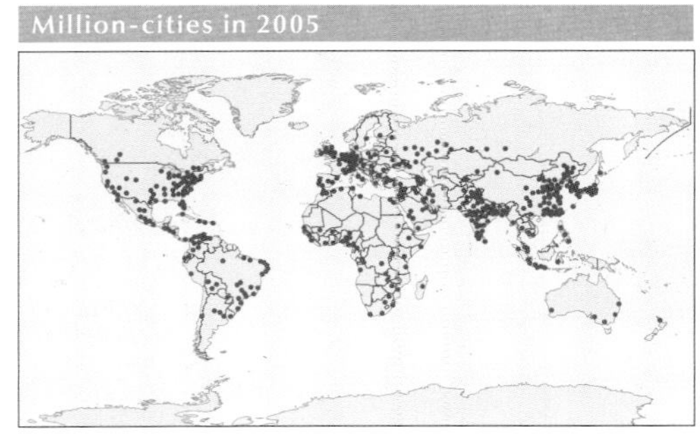

Million-cities in 2005

• Cities over 1 million population

North America

The eastern and western seaboards of the US, with huge expanses of interconnected cities, towns, and suburbs, are vast, densely-populated megalopolises. Central America and the Caribbean also have high population densities. Yet, away from the coasts and in the wildernesses of northern Canada the land is very sparsely settled.

▲ *Vancouver on Canada's west coast, grew up as a port city. In recent years it has attracted many Asian immigrants, particularly from the Pacific Rim.*

▲ ***North America's central** plains, the continent's agricultural heartland, are thinly populated and highly productive.*

Europe

With its temperate climate, and rich mineral and natural resources, Europe is generally very densely settled. The continent acts as a magnet for economic migrants from the developing world, and immigration is now widely restricted. Birthrates in Europe are generally low, and in some countries, such as Germany, the populations have stabilized at zero growth, with a fast-growing elderly population.

▲ ***Many European cities,** like Siena, once reflected the "ideal" size for human settlements. Modern technological advances have enabled them to grow far beyond the original walls.*

▲ ***Within the densely-populated** Netherlands the reclamation of coastal wetlands is vital to provide much-needed land for agriculture and settlement.*

Population density (inhabitants per sq km)

- More than 200
- 101–200
- 51–100
- 21–50
- 11–20
- 6–10
- 1–5
- Less than 1

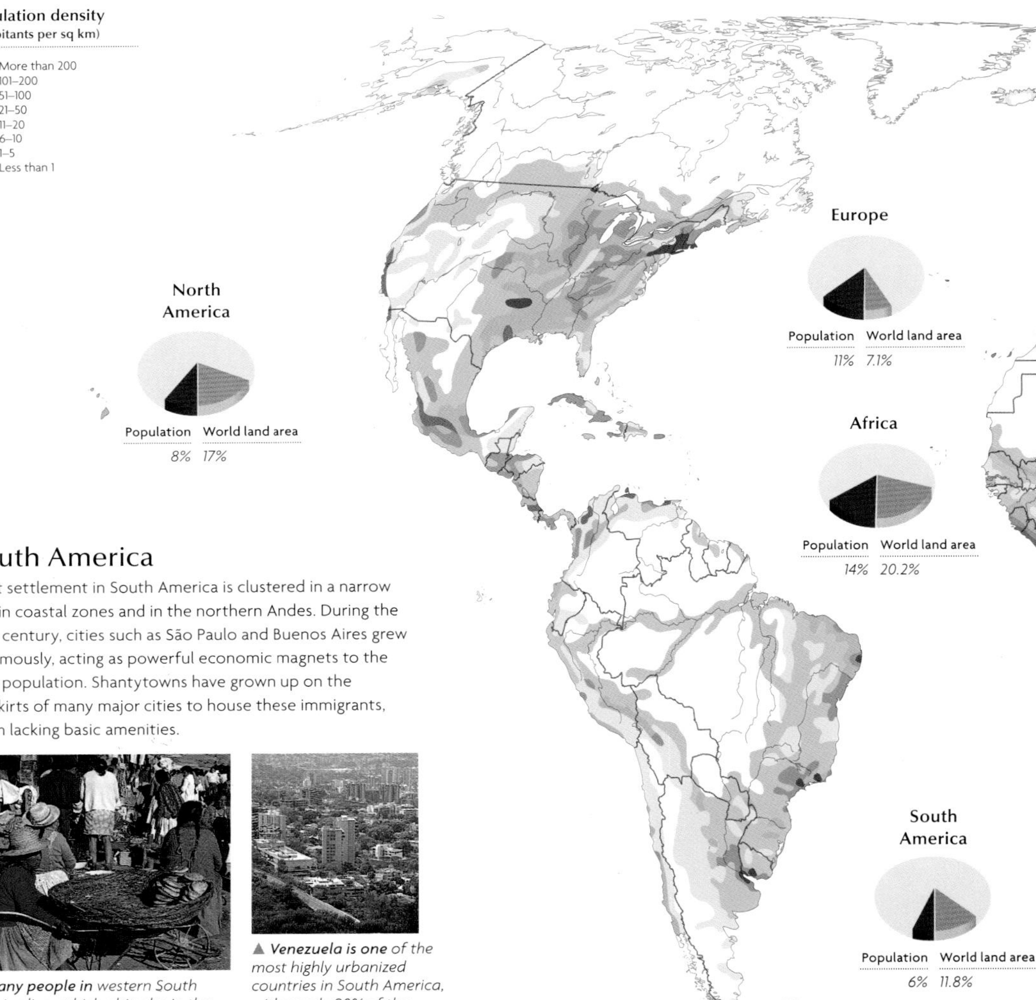
North America
Population 8%
World land area 17%
Europe
Population 11%
World land area 7.1%
Africa
Population 14%
World land area 20.2%
South America
Population 6%
World land area 11.8%

South America

Most settlement in South America is clustered in a narrow belt in coastal zones and in the northern Andes. During the 20th century, cities such as São Paulo and Buenos Aires grew enormously, acting as powerful economic magnets to the rural population. Shantytowns have grown up on the outskirts of many major cities to house these immigrants, often lacking basic amenities.

▲ ***Many people in** western South America live at high altitudes in the Andes, both in cities and in villages such as this one in Bolivia.*

▲ ***Venezuela is one** of the most highly urbanized countries in South America, with nearly 90% of the population living in cities such as Caracas.*

Africa

The arid climate of much of Africa means that settlement of the continent is sparse, focusing in coastal areas and fertile regions such as the Nile Valley. Africa still has a high proportion of nomadic agriculturalists, although many are now becoming settled, and the population is predominantly rural.

▲ ***Cities such as** Nairobi (above), Cairo, and Johannesburg have grown rapidly in recent years, although only Cairo has a significant population on a global scale.*

▲ ***Traditional lifestyles and** homes persist across much of Africa, which has a higher proportion of rural or village-based population than any other continent.*

Asia

Most Asian settlement originally centered around the great river valleys such as the Indus, the Ganges, and the Yangtze. Today, almost 60% of the world's population lives in Asia, many in burgeoning cities – particularly in the economically-buoyant Pacific Rim countries. Even rural population densities are high in many countries; practices such as terracing in Southeast Asia making the most of the available land.

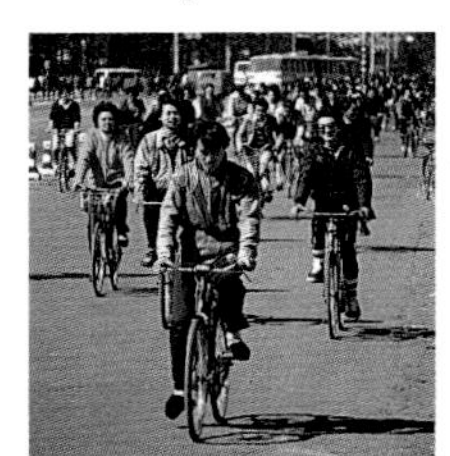

▲ ***Many of China's** cities are now vast urban areas with populations of more than 5 million people.*

▲ ***This stilt village** in Bangladesh is built to resist the regular flooding. Pressure on land, even in rural areas, forces many people to live in marginal areas.*

Population structures

Population pyramids are an effective means of showing the age structures of different countries, and highlighting changing trends in population growth and decline. The typical pyramid for a country with a growing, youthful population, is broad-based *(left)*, reflecting a high birth rate and a far larger number of young rather than elderly people. In contrast, countries with populations whose numbers are stabilizing have a more balanced distribution of people in each age band, and may even have lower numbers of people in the youngest age ranges, indicating both a high life expectancy, and that the population is now barely replacing itself *(right)*. The Russian Federation *(centre)* shows a marked decline in population due to a combination of a high death rate and low birth rate. The government has taken steps to reverse this trend by providing improved child support and health care. Immigration is also seen as vital to help sustain the population.

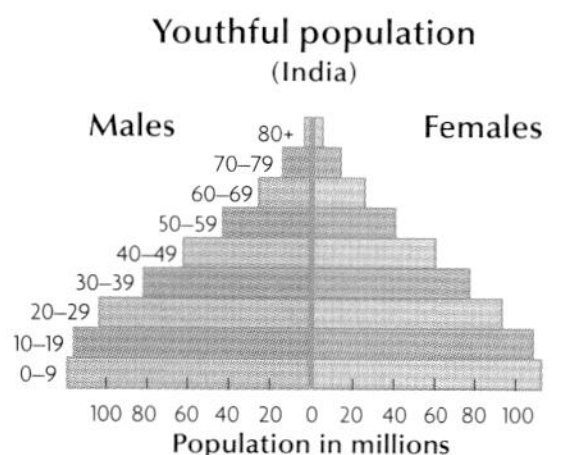
Youthful population
(India)
Males
Females
80+
70–79
60–69
50–59
40–49
30–39
20–29
10–19
0–9
100 80 60 40 20 0 20 40 60 80 100
Population in millions

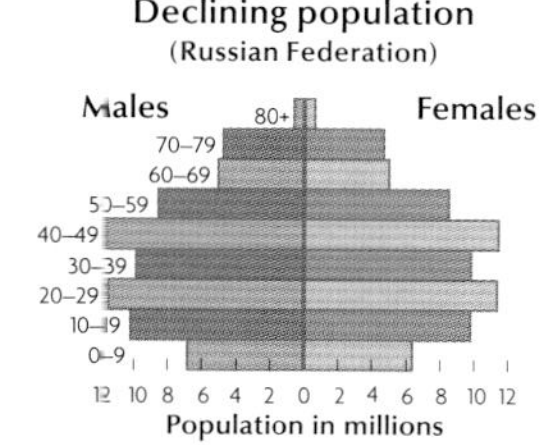
Declining population
(Russian Federation)
Males
Females
80+
70–79
60–69
50–59
40–49
30–39
20–29
10–19
0–9
12 10 8 6 4 2 0 2 4 6 8 10 12
Population in millions

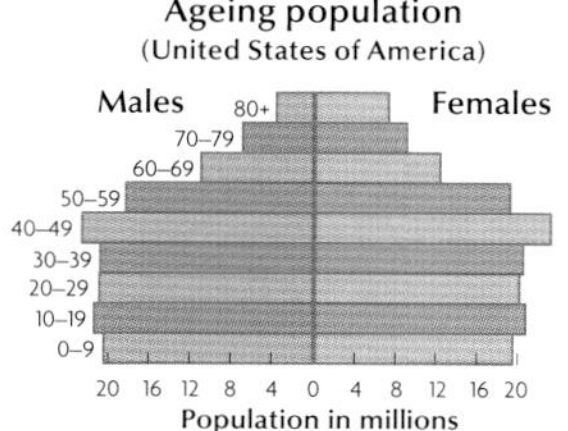
Ageing population
(United States of America)
Males
Females
80+
70–79
60–69
50–59
40–49
30–39
20–29
10–19
0–9
20 16 12 8 4 0 4 8 12 16 20
Population in millions

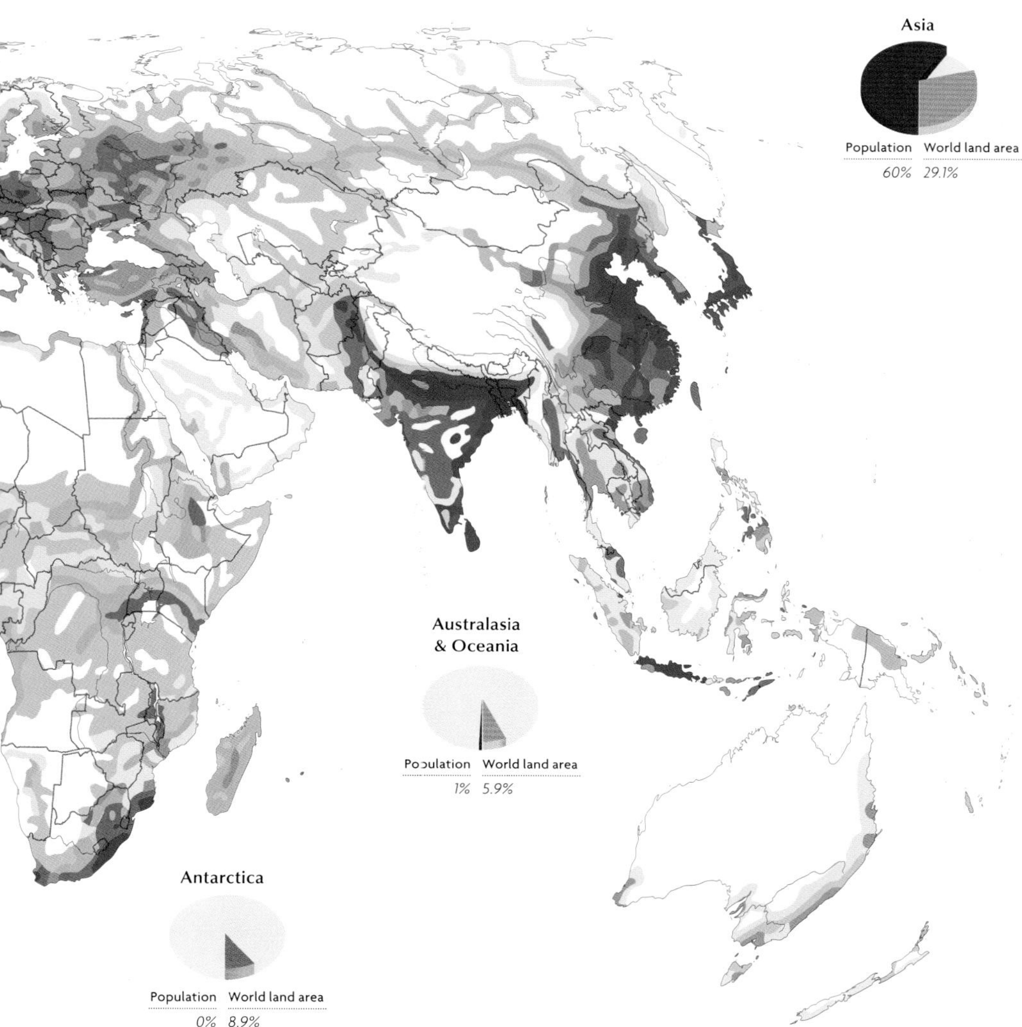
Asia
Population
World land area
60%
29.1%
Australasia & Oceania
Population
World land area
1%
5.9%
Antarctica
Population
World land area
0%
8.9%

Australasia and Oceania

This is the world's most sparsely settled region. The peoples of Australia and New Zealand live mainly in the coastal cities, with only scattered settlements in the arid interior. The Pacific islands can only support limited populations because of their remoteness and lack of resources.

▶ ***Brisbane, on*** *Australia's Gold Coast is the most rapidly expanding city in the country. The great majority of Australia's population lives in cities near the coasts.*

◀ ***The remote highlands*** *of Papua New Guinea are home to a wide variety of peoples, many of whom still subsist by traditional hunting and gathering.*

Average world birth rates

Birthrates are much higher in Africa, Asia, and South America than in Europe and North America. Increased affluence and easy access to contraception are both factors which can lead to a significant decline in a country's birthrate.

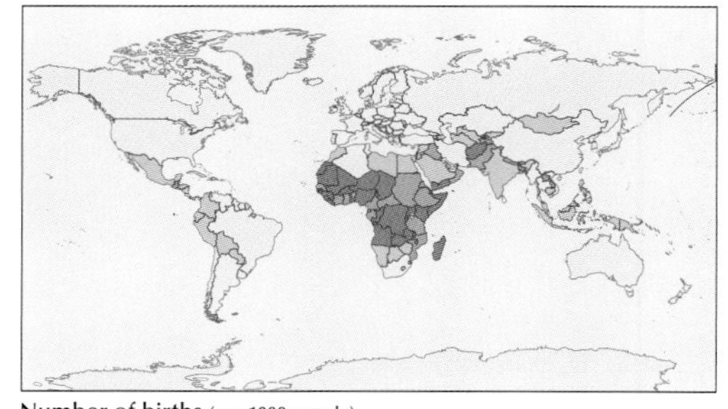

Number of births (per 1000 people)

above 40 · 30–39 · 20–29 · below 20 · data not available

Population growth

Improvements in food supply and advances in medicine have both played a major role in the remarkable growth in global population, which has increased five-fold over the last 150 years. Food supplies have risen with the mechanization of agriculture and improvements in crop yields. Better nutrition, together with higher standards of public health and sanitation, have led to increased longevity and higher birthrates.

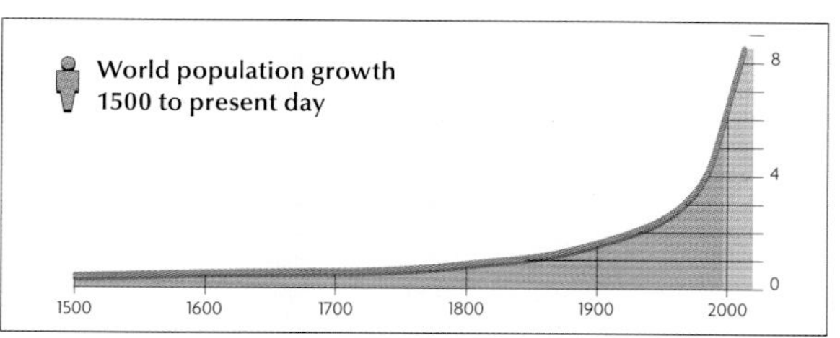
World population growth
1500 to present day
8
4
0
1500
1600
1700
1800
1900
2000

World nutrition

Two-thirds of the world's food supply is consumed by the industrialized nations, many of which have a daily calorific intake far higher than is necessary for their populations to maintain a healthy body weight. In contrast, in the developing world, about 800 million people do not have enough food to meet their basic nutritional needs.

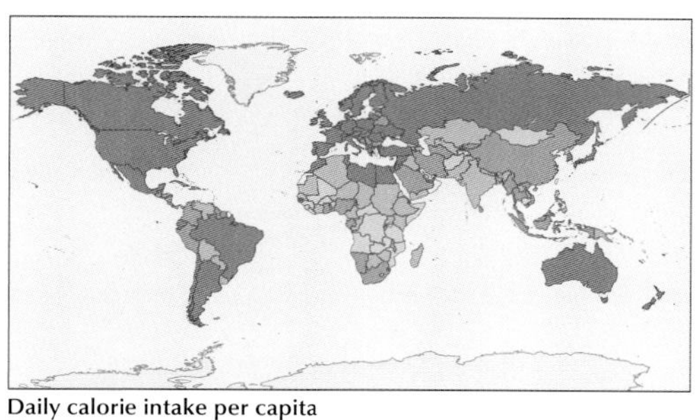

Daily calorie intake per capita

above 3000 · 2500–2999 · 2000–2499 · below 2000 · data not available

World life expectancy

Improved public health and living standards have greatly increased life expectancy in the developed world, where people can now expect to live twice as long as they did 100 years ago. In many of the world's poorest nations, inadequate nutrition and disease, means that the average life expectancy still does not exceed 45 years.

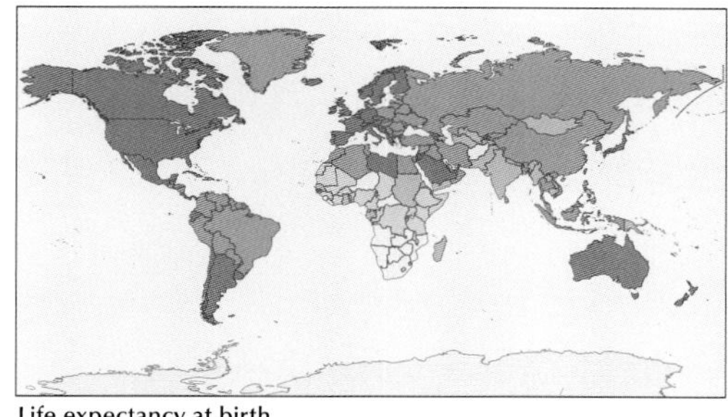

Life expectancy at birth

above 75 years · 65–74 years · 55–64 years · 45–54 years · below 44 years · data not available

World infant mortality

In parts of the developing world infant mortality rates are still high; access to medical services such as immunization, adequate nutrition, and the promotion of breast-feeding have been important in combating infant mortality.

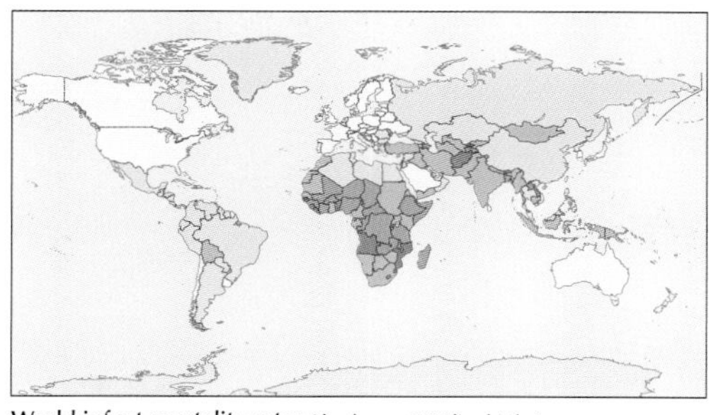

World infant mortality rates (deaths per 1000 live births)

above 125 · 75–124 · 35–74 · 15–34 · below 15 · data not available

The economic system

The wealthy countries of the developed world, with their aggressive, market-led economies and their access to productive new technologies and international markets, dominate the world economic system. At the other extreme, many of the countries of the developing world are locked in a cycle of national debt, rising populations, and unemployment. The state-managed economies of the former communist bloc began to be dismantled during the 1990s, and China is emerging as a major economic power following decades of isolation.

Trade blocs

EU / CACM — NAFTA / SADC — ASEAN / ECOWAS — LAIA / CEEAC

Trade blocs

International trade blocs are formed when groups of countries, often already enjoying close military and political ties, join together to offer mutually preferential terms of trade for both imports and exports. Increasingly, global trade is dominated by three main blocs: the EU, NAFTA, and ASEAN. They are supplanting older trade blocs such as the Commonwealth, a legacy of colonialism.

International trade flows

World trade acts as a stimulus to national economies, encouraging growth. Over the last three decades, as heavy industries have declined services – banking, insurance, tourism, airlines, and shipping – have taken an increasingly large share of world trade. Manufactured articles now account for nearly two-thirds of world trade; raw materials and food make up less than a quarter of the total.

Shipping

Ships carry 80% of international cargo, and extensive container ports, where cargo is stored, are vital links in the international transportation network.

Coke is it!

Multinationals

Multinational companies are increasingly penetrating inaccessible markets. The reach of many American commodities is now global.

Primary products

Many countries, particularly in the Caribbean and Africa, are still reliant on primary products such as rubber and coffee, which makes them vulnerable to fluctuating prices.

Service industries

Service industries such as banking, tourism and insurance were the fastest-growing industrial sector in the last half of the 20th century. Lloyds of London is the center of the world insurance market.

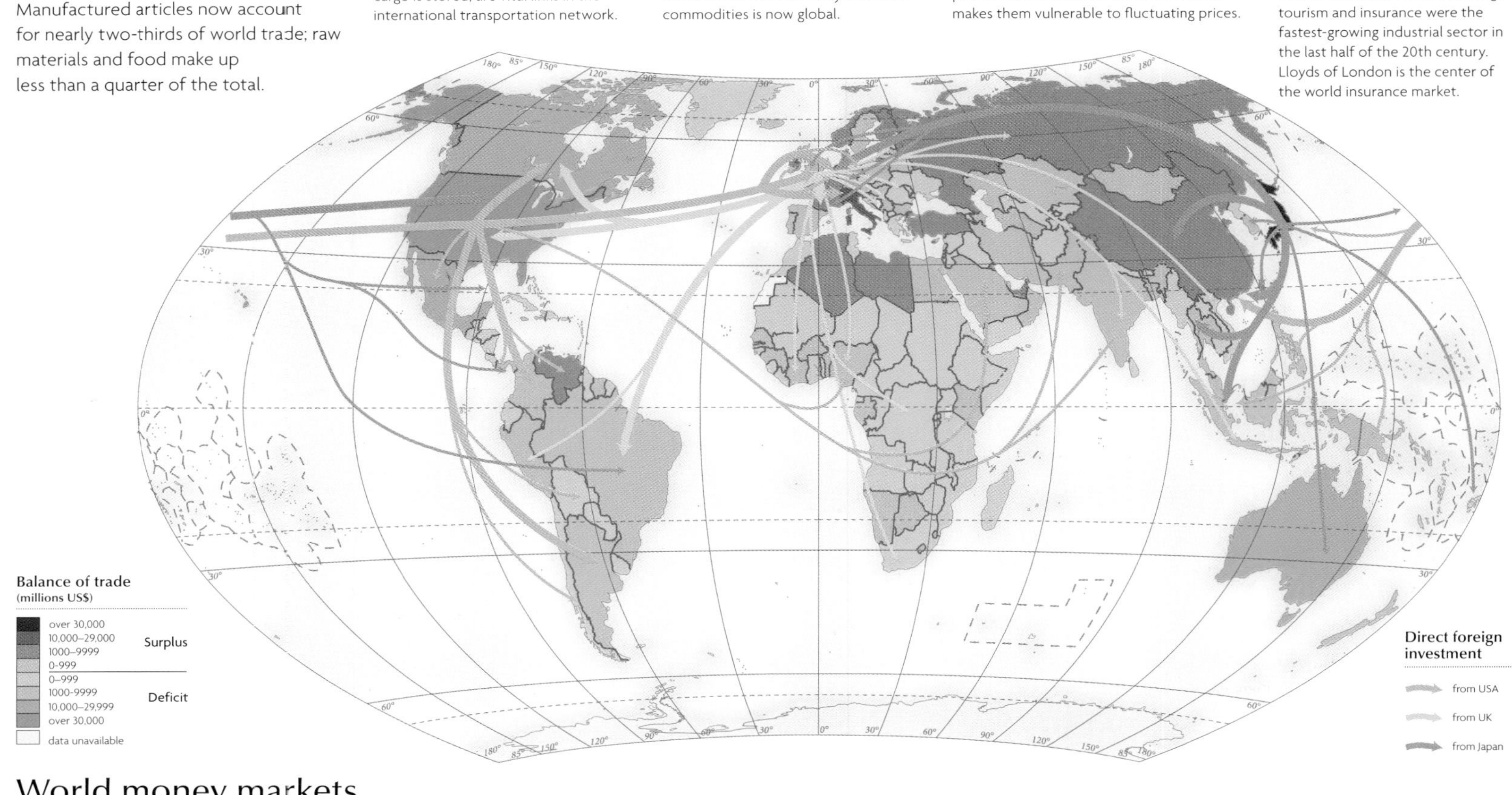
Balance of trade
(millions US$)
Surplus
over 30,000
10,000–29,000
1000–9999
0–999
Deficit
0–999
1000–9999
10,000–29,999
over 30,000
data unavailable
Direct foreign investment
from USA
from UK
from Japan

World money markets

The financial world has traditionally been dominated by three major centers – Tokyo, New York, and London, which house the headquarters of stock exchanges, multinational corporations and international banks. Their geographic location means that, at any one time in a 24-hour day, one major market is open for trading in shares, currencies, and commodities. Since the late 1980s, technological advances have enabled transactions between financial centers to occur at ever-greater speed, and new markets have sprung up throughout the world.

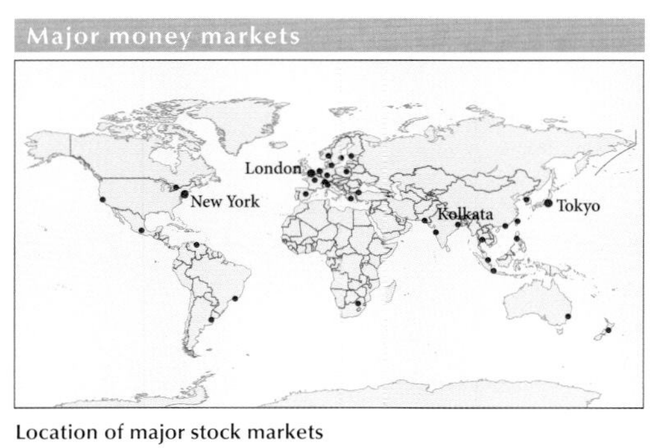
Major money markets
London
New York
Kolkata
Tokyo
Location of major stock markets
Major stock markets

▲ *The Tokyo Stock Market crashed in 1990, leading to a slow-down in the growth of the world's most powerful economy, and a refocusing on economic policy away from export-led growth and toward the domestic market.*

New stock markets

New stock markets are now opening in many parts of the world, where economies have recently emerged from state controls. In Moscow and Beijing, and several countries in eastern Europe, newly-opened stock exchanges reflect the transition to market-driven economies.

▲ ***Dealers at the** Kolkata Stock Market. The Indian economy has been opened up to foreign investment and many multinationals now have bases there.*

The developing world

International trade in capital and currency is dominated by the rich nations of the northern hemisphere. In parts of Africa and Asia, where exports of any sort are extremely limited, home-produced commodities are simply sold in local markets.

▲ ***Markets have thrived** in communist Vietnam since the introduction of a liberal economic policy.*

World wealth disparity

A global assessment of Gross Domestic Product (GDP) by nation reveals great disparities. The developed world, with only a quarter of the world's population, has 80% of the world's manufacturing income. Civil war, conflict, and political instability further undermine the economic self-sufficiency of many of the world's poorest nations.

Urban sprawl

Cities are expanding all over the developing world, attracting economic migrants in search of work and opportunities. In cities such as Rio de Janeiro, housing has not kept pace with the population explosion, and squalid shanty towns *(favelas)* rub shoulders with middle-class housing.

▲ ***The favelas of** Rio de Janeiro sprawl over the hills surrounding the city.*

▲ ***Cities such as** Detroit have been badly hit by the decline in heavy industry.*

Urban decay

Although the US still dominates the global economy, it faces deficits in both the federal budget and the balance of trade. Vast discrepancies in personal wealth, high levels of unemployment, and the dismantling of welfare provisions throughout the 1980s have led to severe deprivation in several of the inner cities of North America's industrial heartland.

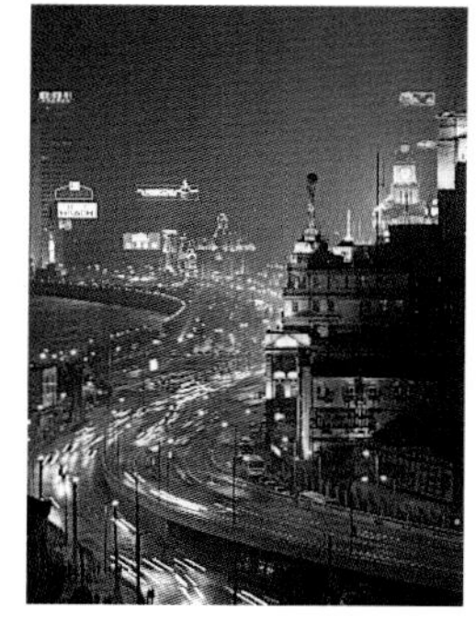

◀ ***Foreign investment has** encouraged new infrastructure development in cities like Shanghai.*

Booming cities

Since the 1980s the Chinese government has set up special industrial zones, such as Shanghai, where foreign investment is encouraged through tax incentives. Migrants from rural China pour into these regions in search of work, creating "boomtown" economies.

Comparative world wealth

World economies - average GDP per capita (US$)

- above 20,000
- 5000–20,000
- 2000–5000
- below 2000
- data unavailable

Economic "tigers"

The economic "tigers" of the Pacific Rim – China, Singapore, and South Korea – have grown faster than Europe and the US over the last decade. Their export- and service-led economies have benefited from stable government, low labor costs, and foreign investment.

▲ ***Hong Kong, with** its fine natural harbour, is one of the most important ports in Asia.*

Agricultural economies

In parts of the developing world, people survive by subsistence farming – only growing enough food for themselves and their families. With no surplus product, they are unable to exchange goods for currency, the only means of escaping the poverty trap. In other countries, farmers have been encouraged to concentrate on growing a single crop for the export market. This reliance on cash crops leaves farmers vulnerable to crop failure and to changes in the market price of the crop.

▲ ***The Ugandan uplands** are fertile, but poor infrastructure hampers the export of cash crops.*

▲ ***A shopping arcade** in Paris displays a great profusion of luxury goods.*

The affluent West

The capital cities of many countries in the developed world are showcases for consumer goods, reflecting the increasing importance of the service sector, and particularly the retail sector, in the world economy. The idea of shopping as a leisure activity is unique to the western world. Luxury goods and services attract visitors, who in turn generate tourist revenue.

Tourism

In 2004, there were over 700 million tourists worldwide. Tourism is now the world's biggest single industry, employing over 130 million people, though frequently in low-paid unskilled jobs. While tourists are increasingly exploring inaccessible and less-developed regions of the world, the benefits of the industry are not always felt at a local level. There are also worries about the environmental impact of tourism, as the world's last wildernesses increasingly become tourist attractions.

▲ ***Botswana's Okavango Delta** is an area rich in wildlife. Tourists go on safaris to the region, but the impact of tourism is controlled.*

Money flows

Foreign investment in the developing world during the 1970s led to a global financial crisis in the 1980s, when many countries were unable to meet their debt repayments. The International Monetary Fund (IMF) was forced to reschedule the debts and, in some cases, write them off completely. Within the developing world, austerity programs have been initiated to cope with the debt, leading in turn to high unemployment and galloping inflation. In many parts of Africa, stricken economies are now dependent on international aid.

◀ ***In rural Southeast Asia,** babies are given medical checks by UNICEF as part of a global aid program sponsored by the UN.*

Tourist arrivals

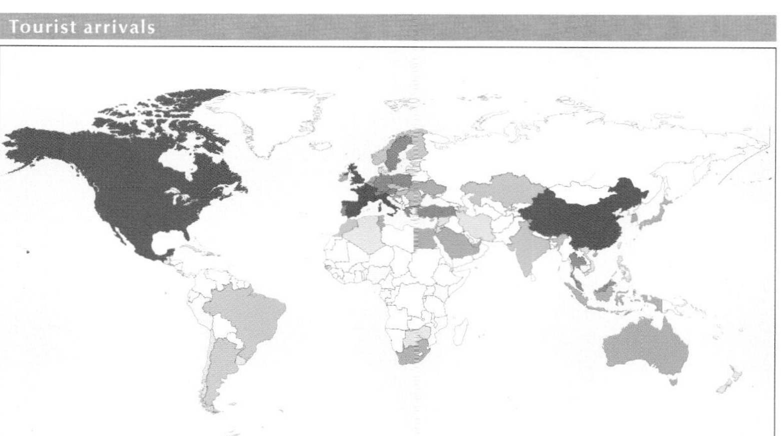

Tourist arrivals

- over 20 million
- 10–20 million
- 5–10 million
- 2.5–5 million
- 1–2.5 million
- 700,000–999,000
- under 700,000
- data unavailable

International debt

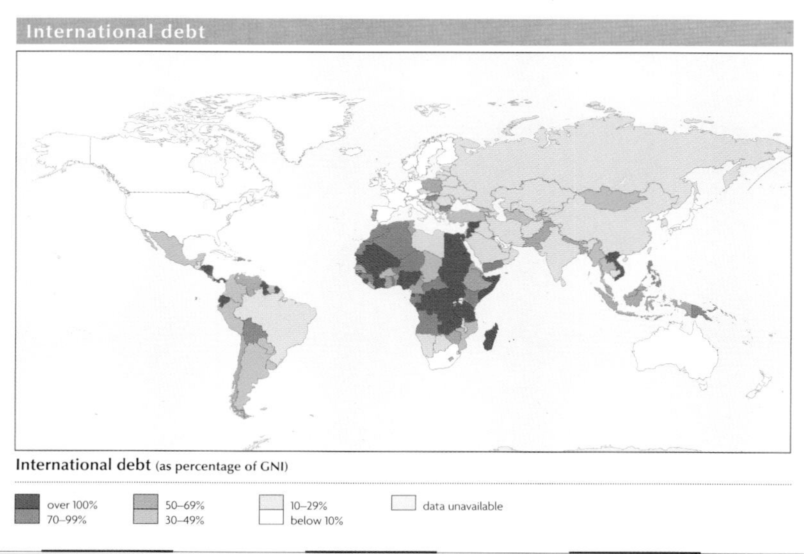

International debt (as percentage of GNI)

- over 100%
- 70–99%
- 50–69%
- 30–49%
- 10–29%
- below 10%
- data unavailable

The political world

There are 194 independent countries in the world today. With the exception of Antarctica, where territorial claims have been deferred by international treaty, every land area of the Earth's surface either belongs to, or is claimed by, one country or another. The largest country in the world is the Russian Federation, the smallest is Vatican City. Some 60 overseas dependent territories remain, administered variously by France, Australia, Denmark, New Zealand, Norway, Portugal, the UK, the US, and the Netherlands.

International borders

The map shows three main types of boundary between states. Full borders represent internationally agreed and recognized territorial boundaries. Undefined borders exist where no fixed boundary between states has been demarcated; the boundaries indicated in this way show approximate areas of sovereignty. A disputed border is indicated where a *de facto* territorial boundary exists, which is not agreed or is subject to arbitration.

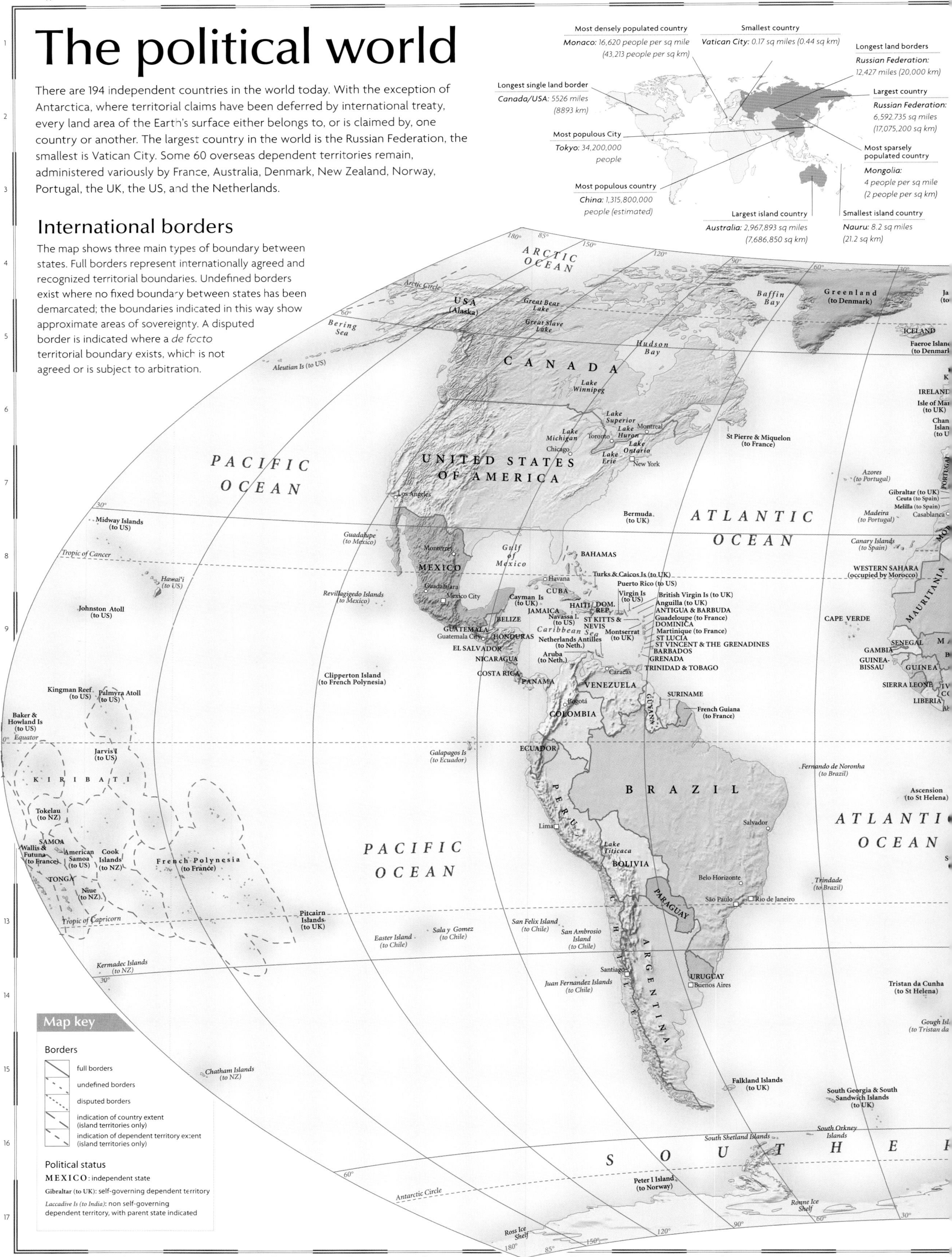

Most densely populated country
Monaco: 16,620 people per sq mile (43,213 people per sq km)
Smallest country
Vatican City: 0.17 sq miles (0.44 sq km)
Longest land borders
Russian Federation: 12,427 miles (20,000 km)
Longest single land border
Canada/USA: 5526 miles (8893 km)
Largest country
Russian Federation: 6,592,735 sq miles (17,075,200 sq km)
Most populous City
Tokyo: 34,200,000 people
Most sparsely populated country
Mongolia: 4 people per sq mile (2 people per sq km)
Most populous country
China: 1,315,800,000 people (estimated)
Largest island country
Australia: 2,967,893 sq miles (7,686,850 sq km)
Smallest island country
Nauru: 8.2 sq miles (21.2 sq km)
ARCTIC OCEAN
Arctic Circle
USA (Alaska)
Bering Sea
Aleutian Is (to US)
Great Bear Lake
Great Slave Lake
Baffin Bay
Greenland (to Denmark)
ICELAND
Faeroe Islands (to Denmark)
Hudson Bay
CANADA
Lake Winnipeg
Lake Superior
Lake Michigan
Lake Huron
Lake Ontario
Lake Erie
Montreal
Toronto
Chicago
New York
IRELAND
Isle of Man (to UK)
St Pierre & Miquelon (to France)
UNITED STATES OF AMERICA
Los Angeles
PACIFIC OCEAN
Azores (to Portugal)
Gibraltar (to UK)
Ceuta (to Spain)
Melilla (to Spain)
Casablanca
Madeira (to Portugal)
Midway Islands (to US)
Bermuda (to UK)
ATLANTIC OCEAN
Guadalupe (to Mexico)
Canary Islands (to Spain)
Tropic of Cancer
Monterrey
Gulf of Mexico
BAHAMAS
MEXICO
Hawai'i (to US)
Turks & Caicos Is (to UK)
Havana
Puerto Rico (to US)
WESTERN SAHARA (occupied by Morocco)
Guadalajara
CUBA
Virgin Is (to US)
British Virgin Is (to UK)
Revillagigedo Islands (to Mexico)
Mexico City
Cayman Is (to UK)
HAITI
DOM. REP.
Anguilla (to UK)
ANTIGUA & BARBUDA
MAURITANIA
Johnston Atoll (to US)
JAMAICA
Navassa I. (to US)
ST KITTS & NEVIS
Guadeloupe (to France)
DOMINICA
BELIZE
CAPE VERDE
Caribbean Sea
Montserrat (to UK)
Martinique (to France)
ST LUCIA
GUATEMALA
Guatemala City
HONDURAS
Netherlands Antilles (to Neth.)
ST VINCENT & THE GRENADINES
BARBADOS
EL SALVADOR
GAMBIA
SENEGAL
Aruba (to Neth.)
GRENADA
NICARAGUA
TRINIDAD & TOBAGO
GUINEA-BISSAU
GUINEA
Clipperton Island (to French Polynesia)
COSTA RICA
Caracas
PANAMA
VENEZUELA
SIERRA LEONE
LIBERIA
Kingman Reef (to US)
Palmyra Atoll (to US)
SURINAME
Bogotá
GUYANA
French Guiana (to France)
Baker & Howland Is (to US)
COLOMBIA
Equator
Galapagos Is (to Ecuador)
ECUADOR
Jarvis I (to US)
Fernando de Noronha (to Brazil)
KIRIBATI
BRAZIL
Ascension (to St Helena)
Tokelau (to NZ)
PERU
Lima
Salvador
SAMOA
Wallis & Futuna (to France)
American Samoa (to US)
Cook Islands (to NZ)
French Polynesia (to France)
Lake Titicaca
BOLIVIA
TONGA
Niue (to NZ)
Belo Horizonte
Trindade (to Brazil)
São Paulo
Rio de Janeiro
PARAGUAY
Pitcairn Islands (to UK)
Tropic of Capricorn
San Felix Island (to Chile)
Easter Island (to Chile)
Sala y Gomez (to Chile)
San Ambrosio Island (to Chile)
CHILE
ARGENTINA
Kermadec Islands (to NZ)
Santiago
URUGUAY
Buenos Aires
Juan Fernandez Islands (to Chile)
Tristan da Cunha (to St Helena)
Gough Isl. (to Tristan da
Map key
Borders
full borders
undefined borders
disputed borders
indication of country extent (island territories only)
indication of dependent territory extent (island territories only)
Political status
MEXICO: independent state
Gibraltar (to UK): self-governing dependent territory
Laccadive Is (to India): non self-governing dependent territory, with parent state indicated
Chatham Islands (to NZ)
Falkland Islands (to UK)
South Georgia & South Sandwich Islands (to UK)
South Shetland Islands
South Orkney Islands
SOUTHERN
Peter I Island (to Norway)
Antarctic Circle
Ronne Ice Shelf
Ross Ice Shelf

The world in 1914

The early years of the 20th century saw the mainly European colonial empires reaching their greatest extents by 1914. Two world wars inaugurated their disintegration, but even in 1950 there were only 82 independent countries. Since then, over 100 have gained their independence, culminating in the breakup of the Soviet Union and former Yugoslavia in the early 1990s.

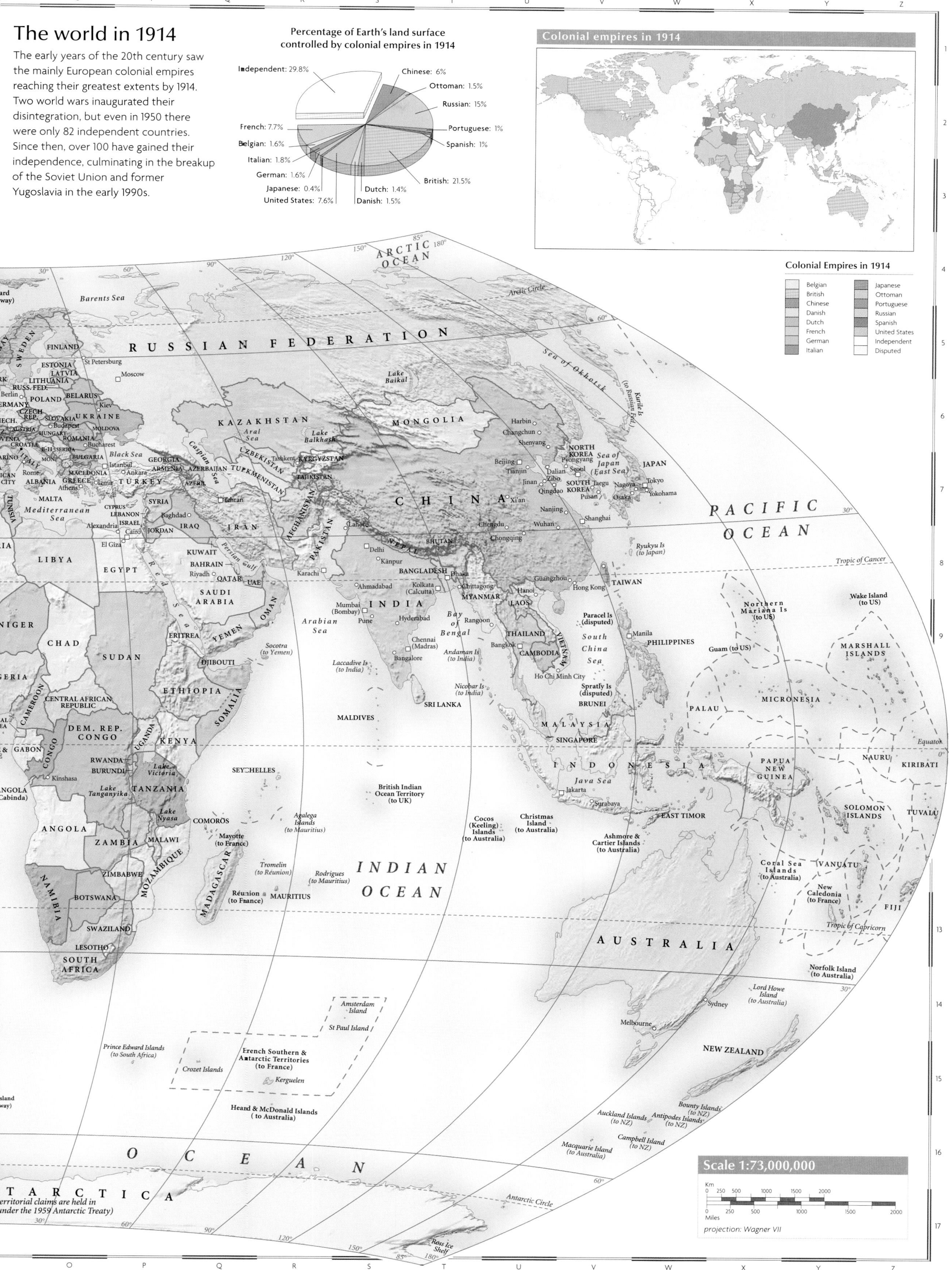

Percentage of Earth's land surface controlled by colonial empires in 1914
Independent: 29.8%
Chinese: 6%
Ottoman: 1.5%
Russian: 15%
French: 7.7%
Portuguese: 1%
Belgian: 1.6%
Spanish: 1%
Italian: 1.8%
German: 1.6%
Japanese: 0.4%
United States: 7.6%
Dutch: 1.4%
Danish: 1.5%
British: 21.5%
Colonial empires in 1914
Colonial Empires in 1914
Belgian
British
Chinese
Danish
Dutch
French
German
Italian
Japanese
Ottoman
Portuguese
Russian
Spanish
United States
Independent
Disputed
ARCTIC OCEAN
Barents Sea
Arctic Circle
RUSSIAN FEDERATION
FINLAND
SWEDEN
St Petersburg
ESTONIA
LATVIA
LITHUANIA
RUSS. FED.
Moscow
BELARUS
POLAND
Berlin
Kiev
CZECH REP.
SLOVAKIA
UKRAINE
MOLDOVA
Budapest
HUNGARY
ROMANIA
Bucharest
CROATIA
BULGARIA
Black Sea
Istanbul
Ankara
MACEDONIA
Rome
ALBANIA
GREECE
Athens
Izmir
TURKEY
MALTA
Mediterranean Sea
CYPRUS
LEBANON
ISRAEL
Alexandria
Cairo
JORDAN
SYRIA
Baghdad
IRAQ
GEORGIA
ARMENIA
AZERBAIJAN
Caspian Sea
Tehran
IRAN
KAZAKHSTAN
Aral Sea
Lake Balkhash
UZBEKISTAN
TURKMENISTAN
Tashkent
KYRGYZSTAN
TAJIKISTAN
AFGHANISTAN
PAKISTAN
Lahore
Delhi
Kanpur
NEPAL
BHUTAN
BANGLADESH
Dhaka
Karachi
Ahmadabad
Kolkata (Calcutta)
Chittagong
Mumbai (Bombay)
INDIA
Pune
Hyderabad
Arabian Sea
Bay of Bengal
Chennai (Madras)
Bangalore
SRI LANKA
MALDIVES
Laccadive Is (to India)
Andaman Is (to India)
Nicobar Is (to India)
LIBYA
EGYPT
El Giza
KUWAIT
BAHRAIN
Riyadh
QATAR
UAE
SAUDI ARABIA
OMAN
YEMEN
Persian Gulf
Red Sea
Socotra (to Yemen)
ERITREA
DJIBOUTI
ETHIOPIA
SOMALIA
NIGER
CHAD
SUDAN
CENTRAL AFRICAN REPUBLIC
CAMEROON
DEM. REP. CONGO
CONGO
GABON
UGANDA
KENYA
RWANDA
BURUNDI
Lake Victoria
Kinshasa
TANZANIA
Lake Tanganyika
Lake Nyasa
ANGOLA (Cabinda)
ANGOLA
ZAMBIA
MALAWI
COMOROS
Mayotte (to France)
MOZAMBIQUE
ZIMBABWE
NAMIBIA
BOTSWANA
MADAGASCAR
SWAZILAND
LESOTHO
SOUTH AFRICA
SEYCHELLES
Agalega Islands (to Mauritius)
British Indian Ocean Territory (to UK)
Tromelin (to Réunion)
Rodrigues (to Mauritius)
Réunion (to France)
MAURITIUS
INDIAN OCEAN
Lake Baikal
MONGOLIA
Harbin
Changchun
Shenyang
Beijing
Tianjin
Dalian
Zibo
Jinan
Qingdao
Xi'an
CHINA
Nanjing
Wuhan
Shanghai
Chengdu
Chongqing
Guangzhou
Hong Kong
TAIWAN
NORTH KOREA
Pyongyang
Seoul
SOUTH KOREA
Taegu
Pusan
Sea of Japan (East Sea)
JAPAN
Nagoya
Tokyo
Yokohama
Osaka
Sea of Okhotsk
Kuril Is (to Russian Fed.)
Ryukyu Is (to Japan)
MYANMAR
Hanoi
LAOS
Rangoon
THAILAND
Bangkok
CAMBODIA
VIETNAM
Ho Chi Minh City
Paracel Is (disputed)
South China Sea
Spratly Is (disputed)
Manila
PHILIPPINES
BRUNEI
MALAYSIA
SINGAPORE
INDONESIA
Java Sea
Jakarta
Surabaya
EAST TIMOR
Cocos (Keeling) Islands (to Australia)
Christmas Island (to Australia)
Ashmore & Cartier Islands (to Australia)
PACIFIC OCEAN
Tropic of Cancer
Northern Mariana Is (to US)
Wake Island (to US)
Guam (to US)
MARSHALL ISLANDS
PALAU
MICRONESIA
Equator
PAPUA NEW GUINEA
NAURU
KIRIBATI
SOLOMON ISLANDS
TUVALU
Coral Sea Islands (to Australia)
VANUATU
New Caledonia (to France)
FIJI
Tropic of Capricorn
AUSTRALIA
Norfolk Island (to Australia)
Lord Howe Island (to Australia)
Sydney
Melbourne
NEW ZEALAND
Bounty Islands (to NZ)
Auckland Islands (to NZ)
Antipodes Islands (to NZ)
Campbell Island (to NZ)
Macquarie Island (to Australia)
Amsterdam Island
St Paul Island
Prince Edward Islands (to South Africa)
French Southern & Antarctic Territories (to France)
Crozet Islands
Kerguelen
Heard & McDonald Islands (to Australia)
OCEAN
ANTARCTICA
territorial claims are held in under the 1959 Antarctic Treaty)
Antarctic Circle
Ross Ice Shelf
Scale 1:73,000,000
Km
0 250 500 1000 1500 2000
Miles
0 250 500 1000 1500 2000
projection: Wagner VII

States and boundaries

There are over 190 sovereign states in the world today; in 1950 there were only 82. Over the last half-century national self-determination has been a driving force for many states with a history of colonialism and oppression. As more borders have been added to the world map, the number of international border disputes has increased.

In many cases, where the impetus toward independence has been religious or ethnic, disputes with minority groups have also caused violent internal conflict. While many newly-formed states have moved peacefully toward independence, successfully establishing government by multiparty democracy, dictatorship by military regime or individual despot is often the result of the internal power-struggles which characterize the early stages in the lives of new nations.

The nature of politics

Democracy is a broad term: it can range from the ideal of multiparty elections and fair representation to, in countries such as Singapore, a thin disguise for single-party rule. In despotic regimes, on the other hand, a single, often personal authority has total power; institutions such as parliament and the military are mere instruments of the dictator.

◀ **The stars and** stripes of the US flag are a potent symbol of the country's status as a federal democracy.

The changing world map

Decolonization

In 1950, large areas of the world remained under the control of a handful of European countries (*page xxviii*). The process of decolonization had begun in Asia, where, following the Second World War, much of southern and southeastern Asia sought and achieved self-determination. In the 1960s, a host of African states achieved independence, so that by 1965, most of the larger tracts of the European overseas empires had been substantially eroded. The final major stage in decolonization came with the breakup of the Soviet Union and the Eastern bloc after 1990. The process continues today as the last toeholds of European colonialism, often tiny island nations, press increasingly for independence.

▲ **Icons of communism,** including statues of former leaders such as Lenin and Stalin, were destroyed when the Soviet bloc was dismantled in 1989, creating several new nations.

▲ **Iran has been** one of the modern world's few true theocracies; Islam has an impact on every aspect of political life.

▲ **North Korea is** an independent communist republic. Power is concentrated in the hands of Kim Jong Il.

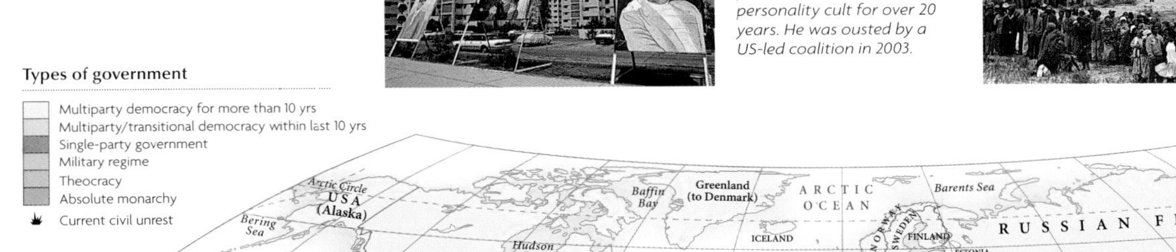

◀ **Saddam Hussein former** autocratic leader of Iraq, promoted an extreme personality cult for over 20 years. He was ousted by a US-led coalition in 2003.

◀ **South Africa became** a democracy in 1994, when elections ended over a century of white minority rule.

New nations 1945–1965

New nations 1965–present

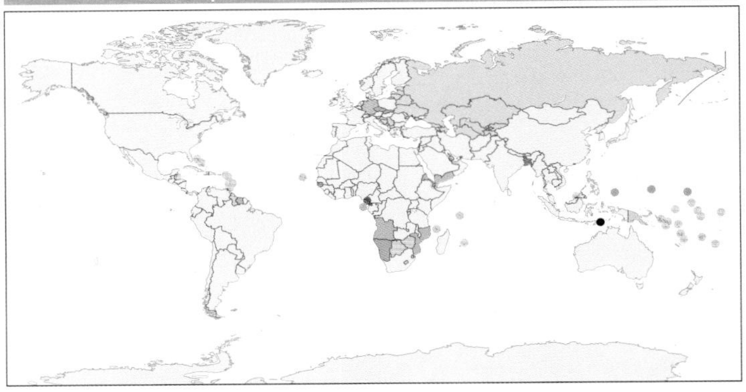

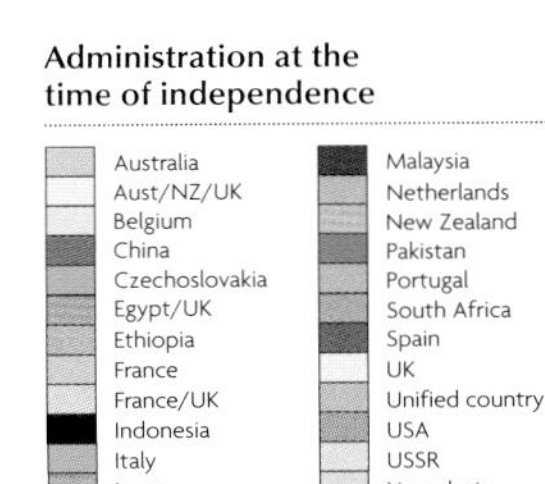

Administration at the time of independence

- Australia
- Aust/NZ/UK
- Belgium
- China
- Czechoslovakia
- Egypt/UK
- Ethiopia
- France
- France/UK
- Indonesia
- Italy
- Japan
- Malaysia
- Netherlands
- New Zealand
- Pakistan
- Portugal
- South Africa
- Spain
- UK
- Unified country
- USA
- USSR
- Yugoslavia

▲ **In Brunei the** Sultan has ruled by decree since 1962; power is closely tied to the royal family. The Sultan's brothers are responsible for finance and foreign affairs.

Types of government

- Multiparty democracy for more than 10 yrs
- Multiparty/transitional democracy within last 10 yrs
- Single-party government
- Military regime
- Theocracy
- Absolute monarchy
- Current civil unrest

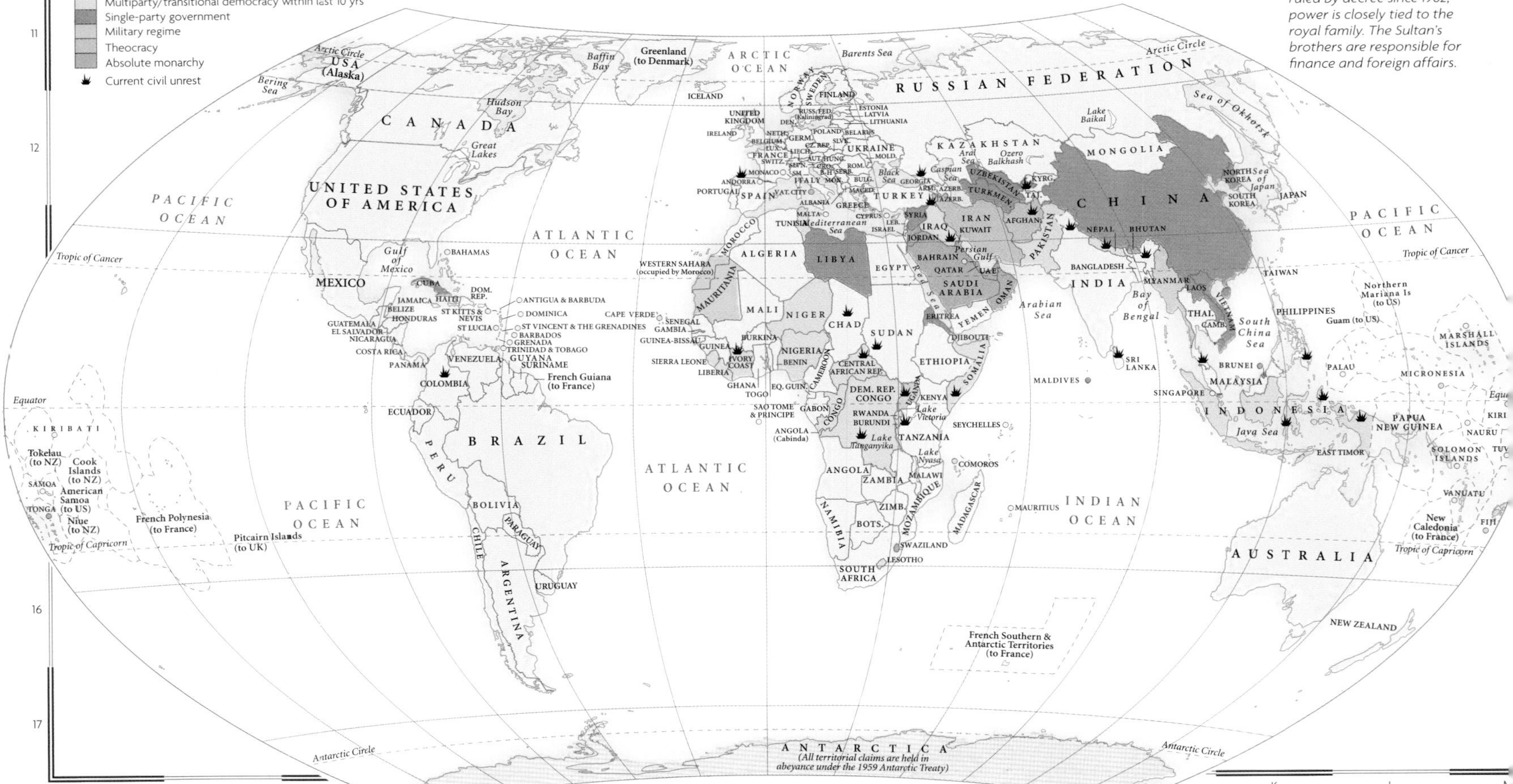

ARCTIC OCEAN
RUSSIAN FEDERATION
CANADA
UNITED STATES OF AMERICA
PACIFIC OCEAN
ATLANTIC OCEAN
MEXICO
BRAZIL
CHINA
INDIA
MONGOLIA
KAZAKHSTAN
ALGERIA
LIBYA
EGYPT
SAUDI ARABIA
IRAN
SUDAN
ETHIOPIA
INDIAN OCEAN
INDONESIA
AUSTRALIA
ARGENTINA
ANTARCTICA
(All territorial claims are held in abeyance under the 1959 Antarctic Treaty)
NEW ZEALAND
French Southern & Antarctic Territories (to France)
Greenland (to Denmark)
French Guiana (to France)
French Polynesia (to France)
Pitcairn Islands (to UK)
Tropic of Cancer
Tropic of Capricorn
Arctic Circle
Antarctic Circle
Equator

Lines on the map

The determination of international boundaries can use a variety of criteria. Many of the borders between older states follow physical boundaries; some mirror religious and ethnic differences; others are the legacy of complex histories of conflict and colonialism, while others have been imposed by international agreements or arbitration.

Post-colonial borders

When the European colonial empires in Africa were dismantled during the second half of the 20th century, the outlines of the new African states mirrored colonial boundaries. These boundaries had been drawn up by colonial administrators, often based on inadequate geographical knowledge. Such arbitrary boundaries were imposed on people of different languages, racial groups, religions, and customs. This confused legacy often led to civil and international war.

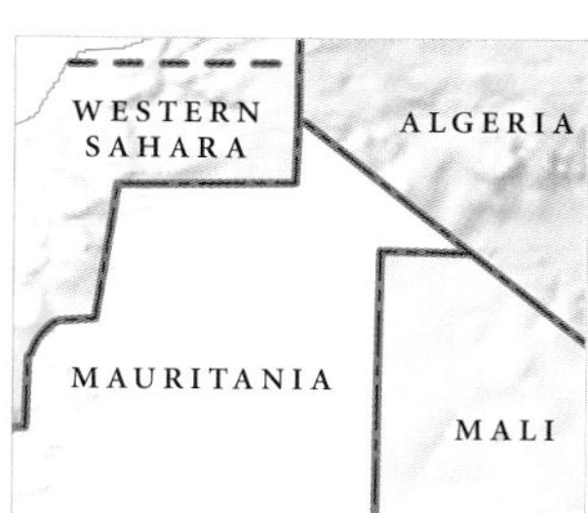
WESTERN SAHARA
ALGERIA
MAURITANIA
MALI

▲ **The conflict that** has plagued many African countries since independence has caused millions of people to become refugees.

Physical borders

Many of the world's countries are divided by physical borders: lakes, rivers, mountains. The demarcation of such boundaries can, however, lead to disputes. Control of waterways, water supplies, and fisheries are frequent causes of international friction.

Enclaves

The shifting political map over the course of history has frequently led to anomalous situations. Parts of national territories may become isolated by territorial agreement, forming an enclave. The West German part of the city of Berlin, which until 1989 lay a hundred miles (160km) within East German territory, was a famous example

Baltic Sea
ESTONIA
RUSSIAN FEDERATION
LATVIA
LITHUANIA
RUSS. FED. (Kaliningrad)
POLAND
BELARUS

Antarctica

When Antarctic exploration began a century ago, seven nations, Australia, Argentina, Britain, Chile, France, New Zealand, and Norway, laid claim to the new territory. In 1961 the Antarctic Treaty, now signed by 45 nations, agreed to hold all territorial claims in abeyance.

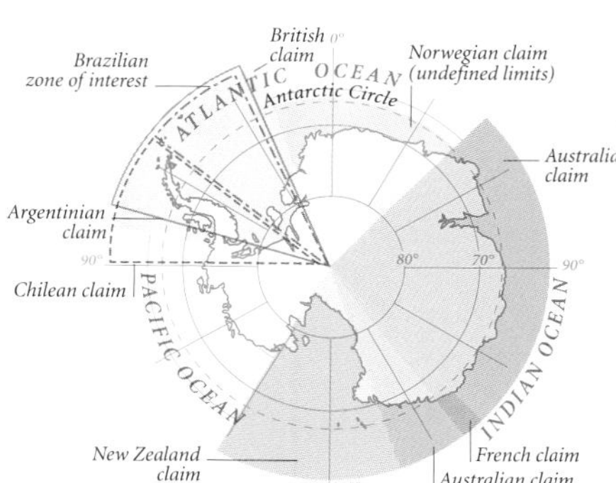
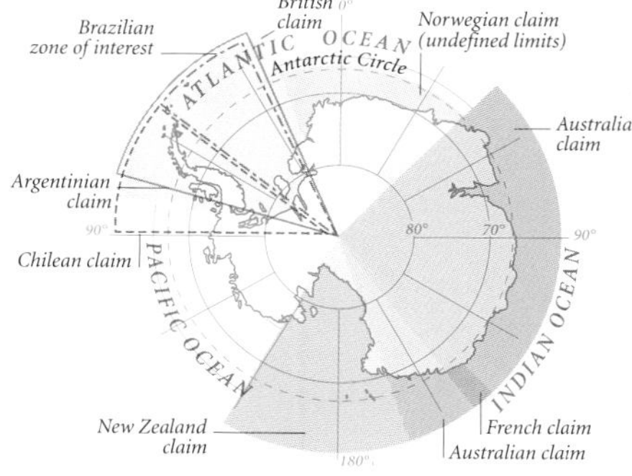
Brazilian zone of interest
British claim
Norwegian claim (undefined limits)
ATLANTIC OCEAN
Antarctic Circle
Australian claim
Argentinian claim
Chilean claim
PACIFIC OCEAN
INDIAN OCEAN
New Zealand claim
French claim
Australian claim

World boundaries

Dates from which current boundaries have existed

- 1990–present
- 1965–1989
- 1945–1965
- 1915–1945
- 1850–1914
- 1800–1849
- Pre-1800

▲ **Since the independence** of Lithuania and Belarus, the peoples of the Russian enclave of Kaliningrad have become physically isolated.

Geometric borders

Straight lines and lines of longitude and latitude have occasionally been used to determine international boundaries; and indeed the world's second longest continuous international boundary, between Canada and the USA follows the 49th Parallel for over one-third of its course. Many Canadian, American, and Australian internal administrative boundaries are similarly determined using a geometric solution.

CANADA
49th Parallel
UNITED STATES OF AMERICA

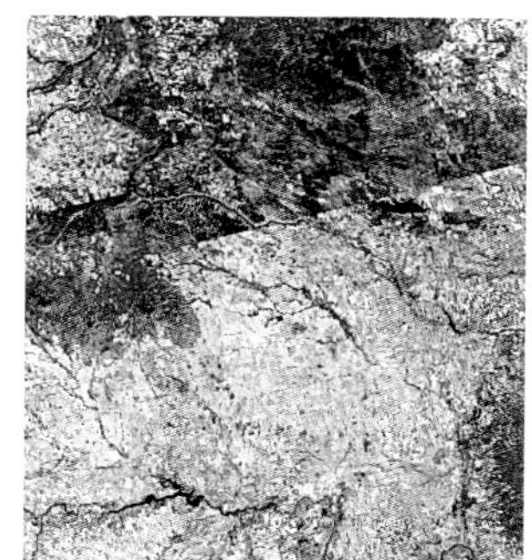

▲ **Different farming techniques** in Canada and the US clearly mark the course of the international boundary in this satellite map.

Lake borders

Countries which lie next to lakes usually fix their borders in the middle of the lake. Unusually the Lake Nyasa border between Malawi and Tanzania runs along Tanzania's shore.

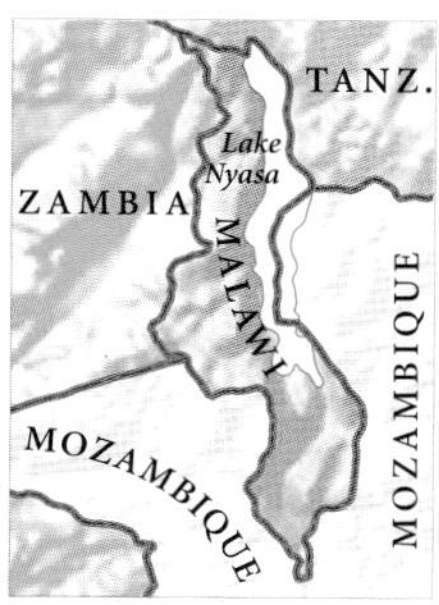
TANZ.
Lake Nyasa
ZAMBIA
MALAWI
MOZAMBIQUE
MOZAMBIQUE

▲ **Complicated agreements between** colonial powers led to the awkward division of Lake Nyasa.

River borders

Rivers alone account for one-sixth of the world's borders. Many great rivers form boundaries between a number of countries. Changes in a river's course and interruptions of its natural flow can lead to disputes, particularly in areas where water is scarce. The center of the river's course is the nominal boundary line.

GERMANY
Danube
UKRAINE
SLOVAKIA
AUSTRIA
HUNGARY
ROMANIA
CROATIA
SERBIA
Danube
BULGARIA

▲ **The Danube forms** all or part of the border between nine European nations.

Mountain borders

Mountain ranges form natural barriers and are the basis for many major borders, particularly in Europe and Asia. The watershed is the conventional boundary demarcation line, but its accurate determination is often problematic.

FRANCE
Pyrenees
ANDORRA
SPAIN

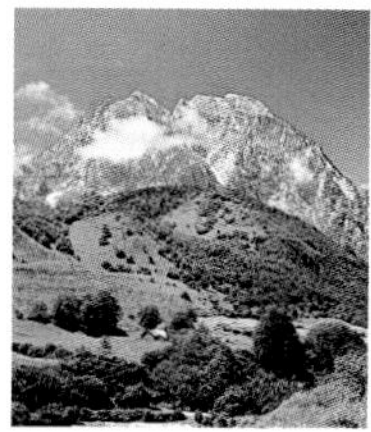

▲ **The Pyrenees form** a natural mountain border between France and Spain.

Shifting boundaries – Poland

Borders between countries can change dramatically over time. The nations of eastern Europe have been particularly affected by changing boundaries. Poland is an example of a country whose boundaries have changed so significantly that it has literally moved around Europe. At the start of the 16th century, Poland was the largest nation in Europe. Between 1772 and 1795, it was absorbed into Prussia, Austria, and Russia, and it effectively ceased to exist. After the First World War, Poland became an independent country once more, but its borders changed again after the Second World War following invasions by both Soviet Russia and Nazi Germany.

Moscow
POLAND
Warsaw
Kiev

▲ **In 1634, Poland** was the largest nation in Europe, its eastern boundary reaching toward Moscow.

Moscow
RUSSIA
PRUSSIA
Warsaw
Kiev
AUSTRIA

▲ **From 1772–1795, Poland** was gradually partitioned between Austria, Russia, and Prussia. Its eastern boundary receded by over 100 miles (160 km).

Moscow
POLAND
Warsaw
Kiev

▲ **Following the First World War,** Poland was reinstated as an independent state, but it was less than half the size it had been in 1634.

Moscow
POLAND
Warsaw
Kiev

▲ **After the Second World War,** the Baltic Sea border was extended westward, but much of the eastern territory was annexed by Russia.

International disputes

There are more than 60 disputed borders or territories in the world today. Although many of these disputes can be settled by peaceful negotiation, some areas have become a focus for international conflict. Ethnic tensions have been a major source of territorial disagreement throughout history, as has the ownership of, and access to, valuable natural resources. The turmoil of the postcolonial era in many parts of Africa is partly a result of the 19th century "carve-up" of the continent, which created potential for conflict by drawing often arbitrary lines through linguistic and cultural areas.

North and South Korea

Since 1953, the *de facto* border between North and South Korea has been a cease-fire line which straddles the 38th Parallel and is designated as a demilitarized zone. Both countries have heavy fortifications and troop concentrations behind this zone.

CHINA
NORTH KOREA
Sea of Japan
PYONGYANG
SEOUL
SOUTH KOREA
Yellow Sea

▲ *Heavy fortifications on the border between North and South Korea.*

FREEDOM FOR CY

▲ *The so-called 'green line' divides Cyprus into Greek and Turkish sectors.*

Cyprus

Cyprus was partitioned in 1974, following an invasion by Turkish troops. The south is now the Greek Cypriot Republic of Cyprus, while the self-proclaimed Turkish Republic of Northern Cyprus is recognized only by Turkey.

TURKISH REPUBLIC OF NORTHERN CYPRUS (recognized only by Turkey)
Mediterranean Sea
Kyrenia Mountains
Karpasia
NICOSIA
CYPRUS
Troodos
UK Sovereign Base Area
Larnaka
UK Sovereign Base Area
Lemesós (Limassol)
Mediterranean Sea

Jammu and Kashmir

Disputes over Jammu and Kashmir have caused three serious wars between India and Pakistan since 1947. Pakistan wishes to annex the largely Muslim territory, while India refuses to cede any territory or to hold a referendum, and also lays claim to the entire territory. Most international maps show the "line of control" agreed in 1972 as the *de facto* border. In addition, India has territorial disputes with neighboring China. The situation is further complicated by a Kashmiri independence movement, active since the late 1980s.

▲ *Indian army troops maintain their positions in the mountainous terrain of northern Kashmir.*

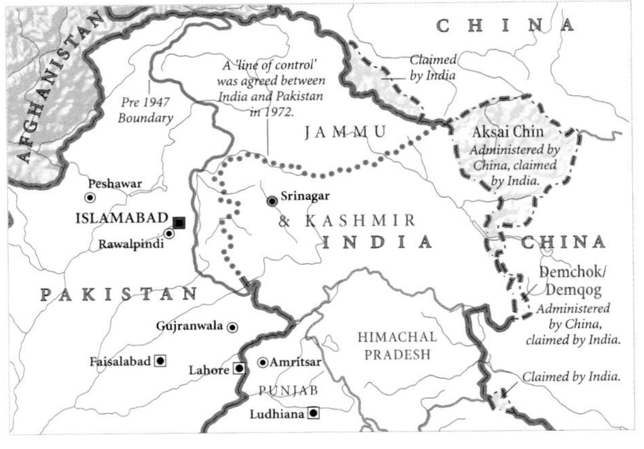
AFGHANISTAN
CHINA
Pre 1947 Boundary
A 'line of control' was agreed between India and Pakistan in 1972.
Claimed by India
JAMMU
Aksai Chin
Administered by China, claimed by India.
Peshawar
ISLAMABAD
Rawalpindi
Srinagar
& KASHMIR
INDIA
CHINA
PAKISTAN
Demchok/ Demqog
Administered by China, claimed by India.
Gujranwala
HIMACHAL PRADESH
Faisalabad
Lahore
Amritsar
Claimed by India.
PUNJAB
Ludhiana

Conflicts and international disputes

Countries contributing troops to coalition force in Iraq
Major active territorial or border disputes
Countries involved in internal conflict
Active territorial or border disputes and internal conflict

RUSSIAN FEDERATION
UNITED STATES OF AMERICA
KAZAKHSTAN
MONGOLIA
CHINA
INDIA
AUSTRALIA
JAPAN
NORTH KOREA
SOUTH KOREA
Kurile Islands
Aksai Chin
Demchok
Jammu and Kashmir
Arunachal Pradesh
Senkaku Islands
TAIWAN
Paracel Islands
PHILIPPINES
Spratly Islands
MALAYSIA
INDONESIA
SRI LANKA
NEPAL
PAKISTAN
AFGHANISTAN
UZBEKISTAN
Chechnya
GEORG.
ARM.
AZERB.
TURKEY
CYPRUS
SYRIA
IRAQ
ISRAEL
Golan Heights
EGYPT
GREECE
SPAIN
Gibraltar
Ceuta
Melilla
MOROCCO
WESTERN SAHARA
CHAD
SUDAN
ERITREA
ETHIOPIA
SOMALIA
NIGERIA
C.A.R.
DEM. REP. CONGO
UGANDA
KENYA
BURUNDI
IVORY COAST
ESTONIA
LATVIA
LITHUANIA
DENMARK
UNITED KINGDOM
NETH.
POLAND
CZ.REP.
SLVK.
ITALY
ROM.
BULG.
MACEDONIA
ALB.
NORWAY
CUBA
Guantanamo Bay
EL SALVADOR
VENEZUELA
GUYANA
SURINAME
French Guiana
COLOMBIA
ARGENTINA
Falkland Islands

The Falkland Islands

The British dependent territory of the Falkland Islands was invaded by Argentina in 1982, sparking a full-scale war with the UK. In 1995, the UK and Argentina reached an agreement on the exploitation of oil reserves around the islands.

◄ *British warships in Falkland Sound during the 1982 war with Argentina.*

Jenin
Tulkarm
Qalqiliya
Nablus
WEST BANK
ISRAEL
Jordan
Auja et Tahta
Nu'eima
Jericho
Ramallah
JERUSALEM
JORDAN
Bethlehem
Hebron (Israel retains 15% control)
Dead Sea
Palestinian control
Mixed control
Israeli settlement block
Israeli settlement
Palestinian settlement
West Bank fence

Israel

Israel was created in 1948 following the 1947 UN Resolution (147) on Palestine. Until 1979 Israel had no borders, only cease-fire lines from a series of wars in 1948, 1967, and 1973. Treaties with Egypt in 1979 and Jordan in 1994 led to these borders being defined and agreed. Negotiations over Israeli settlements and Palestinian self-government seen little effective progress since 2000.

LEBANON
Mediterranean Sea
SYRIA
GOLAN HEIGHTS
WEST BANK
GAZA STRIP
ISRAEL
JORDAN
EGYPT

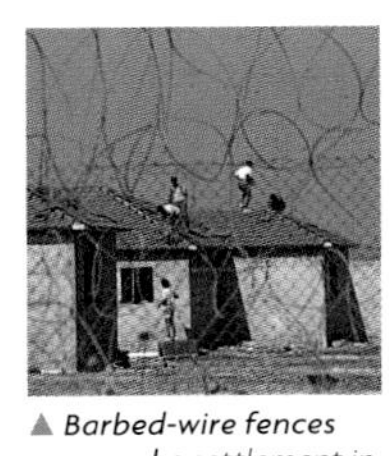

▲ *Barbed-wire fences surround a settlement in the Golan Heights.*

Former Yugoslavia

Following the disintegration in 1991 of the communist state of Yugoslavia, the breakaway states of Croatia and Bosnia and Herzegovina came into conflict with the "parent" state (consisting of Serbia and Montenegro). Warfare focused on ethnic and territorial ambitions in Bosnia. The tenuous Dayton Accord of 1995 sought to recognize the post-1990 borders, whilst providing for ethnic partition and required international peace-keeping troops to maintain the terms of the peace.

CROATIA
Sava
Bihać
Brčko
Banja Luka
Tuzla
Jajce
BOSNIA &
Srebrenica
HERZEGOVINA
Drina
SERBIA
Gornji Vakuf
Split
SARAJEVO
Goražde
Mostar
Adriatic Sea
Dubrovnik
MONTENEGRO
Republika Srpska
Federacija Bosna i Hercegovina

▲ *Most claimant states have small military garrisons on the Spratly Islands.*

The Spratly Islands

The site of potential oil and natural gas reserves, the Spratly Islands in the South China Sea have been claimed by China, Vietnam, Taiwan, Malaysia, and the Philippines since the Japanese gave up a wartime claim in 1951.

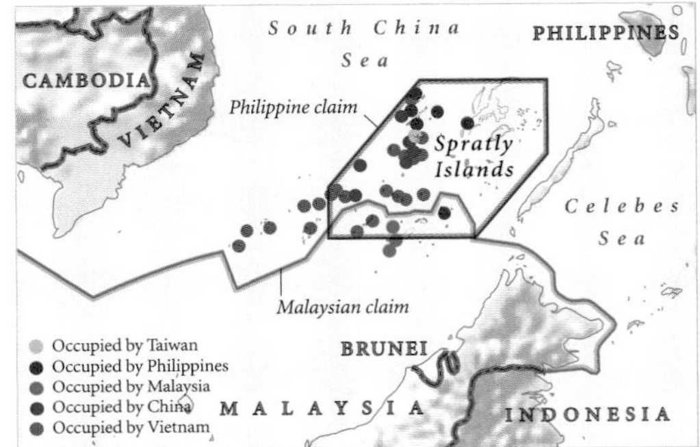
South China Sea
PHILIPPINES
CAMBODIA
VIETNAM
Philippine claim
Spratly Islands
Celebes Sea
Malaysian claim
BRUNEI
Occupied by Taiwan
Occupied by Philippines
Occupied by Malaysia
Occupied by China
Occupied by Vietnam
MALAYSIA
INDONESIA

ATLAS
OF THE WORLD

THE MAPS IN THIS ATLAS ARE ARRANGED CONTINENT BY CONTINENT, STARTING FROM THE INTERNATIONAL DATE LINE, AND MOVING EASTWARD. THE MAPS PROVIDE A UNIQUE VIEW OF TODAY'S WORLD, COMBINING TRADITIONAL CARTOGRAPHIC TECHNIQUES WITH THE LATEST REMOTE-SENSED AND DIGITAL TECHNOLOGY.

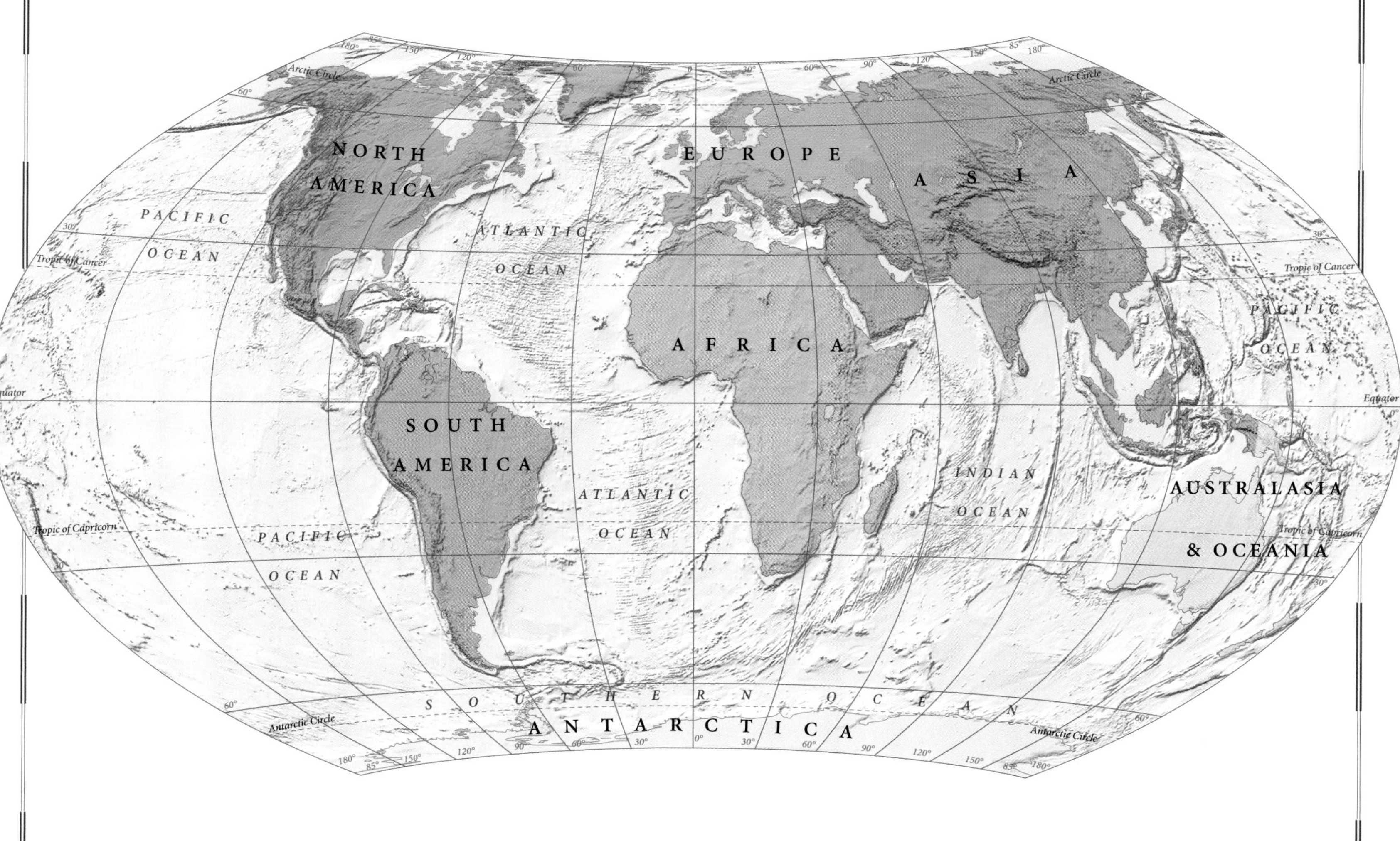

NORTH AMERICA
EUROPE
ASIA
PACIFIC OCEAN
ATLANTIC OCEAN
AFRICA
SOUTH AMERICA
INDIAN OCEAN
ATLANTIC OCEAN
PACIFIC OCEAN
PACIFIC OCEAN
AUSTRALASIA & OCEANIA
SOUTHERN OCEAN
ANTARCTICA
Arctic Circle
Tropic of Cancer
Equator
Tropic of Capricorn
Antarctic Circle

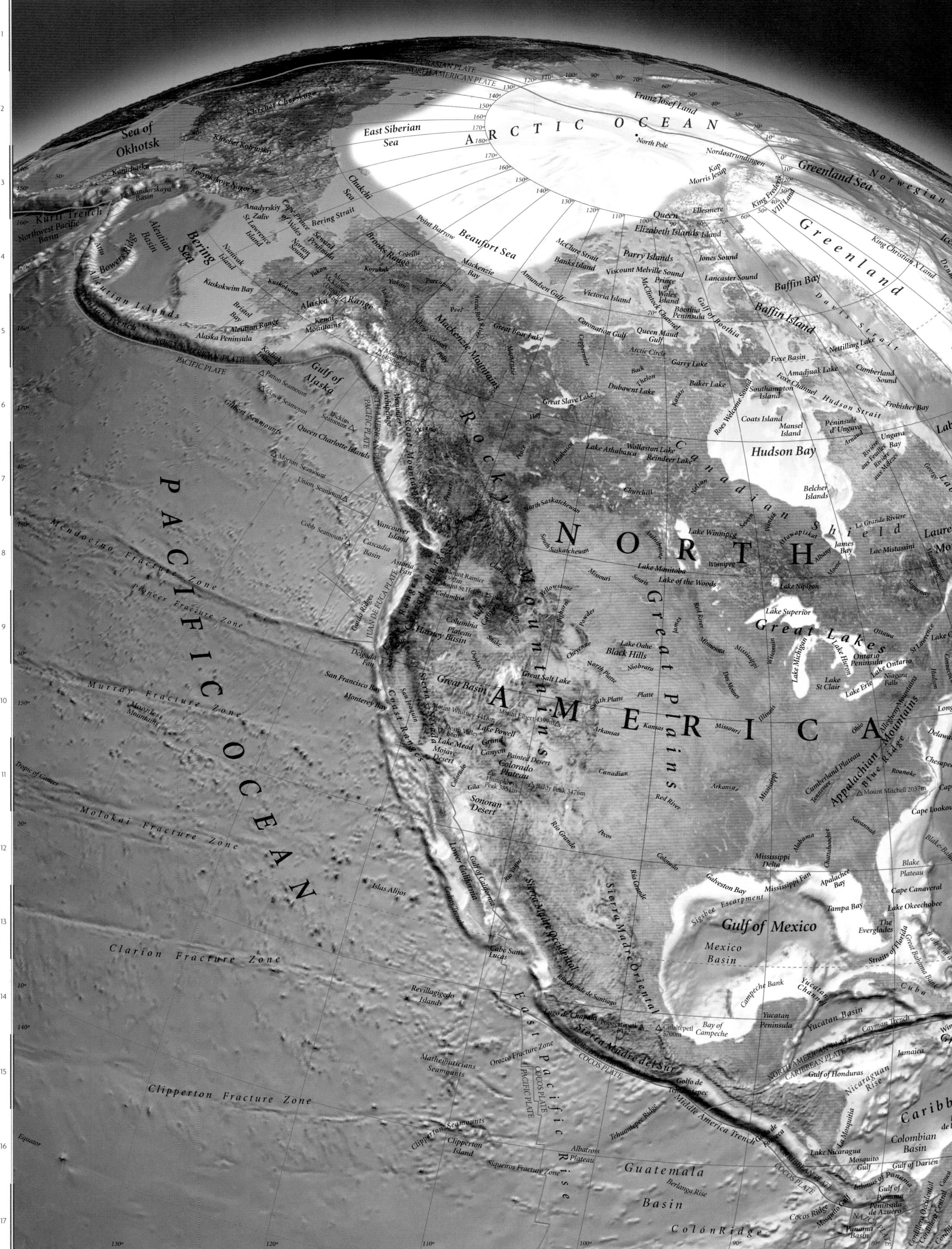

ARCTIC OCEAN
North Pole
Franz Josef Land
East Siberian Sea
Sea of Okhotsk
Chukchi Sea
Bering Strait
Bering Sea
Beaufort Sea
Greenland Sea
Greenland
Norwegian
Nordøstrundingen
Kap Morris Jesup
Queen Elizabeth Islands
Ellesmere Island
King Frederik VIII Land
King Christian X Land
Parry Islands
Jones Sound
Lancaster Sound
Baffin Bay
Baffin Island
Davis Strait
Banks Island
McClure Strait
Viscount Melville Sound
Prince of Wales Island
Victoria Island
Amundsen Gulf
Gulf of Boothia
Boothia Peninsula
McClintock Channel
Coronation Gulf
Queen Maud Gulf
Arctic Circle
Garry Lake
Baker Lake
Dubawnt Lake
Great Bear Lake
Great Slave Lake
Foxe Basin
Foxe Channel
Amadjuak Lake
Nettilling Lake
Cumberland Sound
Frobisher Bay
Hudson Strait
Southampton Island
Coats Island
Mansel Island
Roes Welcome Sound
Hudson Bay
Péninsule d'Ungava
Ungava Bay
Belcher Islands
James Bay
Lake Athabasca
Wollaston Lake
Reindeer Lake
Churchill
Canadian Shield
Lake Winnipeg
Lake Manitoba
Lake of the Woods
Lake Nipigon
Lac Mistassini
La Grande Rivière
Lake Superior
Great Lakes
Lake Michigan
Lake Huron
Lake St Clair
Lake Erie
Lake Ontario
Niagara Falls
Ontario Peninsula
NORTH AMERICA
Rocky Mountains
Mackenzie Mountains
Great Plains
Black Hills
Yellowstone
Great Salt Lake
Great Basin
Harney Basin
Columbia Plateau
Mount Rainier
Mount Whitney 4418m
Mount Elbert 4399m
Lake Powell
Lake Mead
Grand Canyon
Mojave Desert
Painted Desert
Colorado Plateau
Humphreys Peak 3851m
Baldy Peak 3476m
Sonoran Desert
Appalachian Mountains
Allegheny Mountains
Blue Ridge
Cumberland Plateau
Mount Mitchell 2037m
Cape Lookout
Mississippi Delta
Mississippi Fan
Galveston Bay
Apalachee Bay
Tampa Bay
Cape Canaveral
Lake Okeechobee
The Everglades
Straits of Florida
Blake Plateau
Sigsbee Escarpment
Gulf of Mexico
Mexico Basin
Campeche Bank
Yucatan Channel
Yucatan Peninsula
Yucatan Basin
Bay of Campeche
Cayman Trench
Cuba
Jamaica
Gulf of Honduras
Nicaraguan Rise
Lake Nicaragua
Mosquito Gulf
Colombian Basin
Gulf of Darién
Isthmus of Panama
Gulf of Panama
Panama Basin
Sierra Madre Occidental
Sierra Madre Oriental
Sierra Madre del Sur
Lago de Chapala
Popocatépetl
Citlaltépetl 5700m
Golfo de Tehuantepec
Golfo de Fonseca
Middle America Trench
Tehuantepec Ridge
Gulf of California
Lower California
Cabo San Lucas
Islas Alijos
Revillagigedo Islands
East Pacific Rise
Orozco Fracture Zone
Mathematicians Seamounts
Clipperton Seamounts
Clipperton Island
Clipperton Fracture Zone
Clarion Fracture Zone
Siqueiros Fracture Zone
Albatross Plateau
Guatemala Basin
Berlanga Rise
Cocos Ridge
Colón Ridge
COCOS PLATE
PACIFIC PLATE
CARIBBEAN PLATE
NORTH AMERICAN PLATE
NAZCA PLATE
EURASIAN PLATE
JUAN DE FUCA PLATE
PACIFIC OCEAN
Molokai Fracture Zone
Murray Fracture Zone
Moonless Mountains
Pioneer Fracture Zone
Mendocino Fracture Zone
Gorda Ridges
Cascadia Basin
Astoria Fan
Delgada Fan
San Francisco Bay
Monterey Bay
Coast Ranges
Cascade Range
Sierra Nevada
Coast Mountains
Vancouver Island
Cobb Seamount
Union Seamount
Morton Seamount
Queen Charlotte Islands
Dickins Seamount
Gilbert Seamounts
Patton Seamount
Gulf of Alaska
Kodiak Island
Alaska Peninsula
Alaska Range
Aleutian Range
Kenai Mountains
Brooks Range
Kuskokwim Bay
Bristol Bay
Nunivak Island
St Lawrence Island
Norton Sound
Seward Peninsula
Point Barrow
Aleutian Islands
Aleutian Trench
Aleutian Basin
Bowers Ridge
Kuril Trench
Northwest Pacific Basin
Kamchatka
Anadyrskiy Zaliv
Tropic of Cancer
Equator

North America

North America is the world's third largest continent with a total area of 9,358,340 sq miles (24,238,000 sq km) including Greenland and the Caribbean islands. It lies wholly within the Northern Hemisphere.

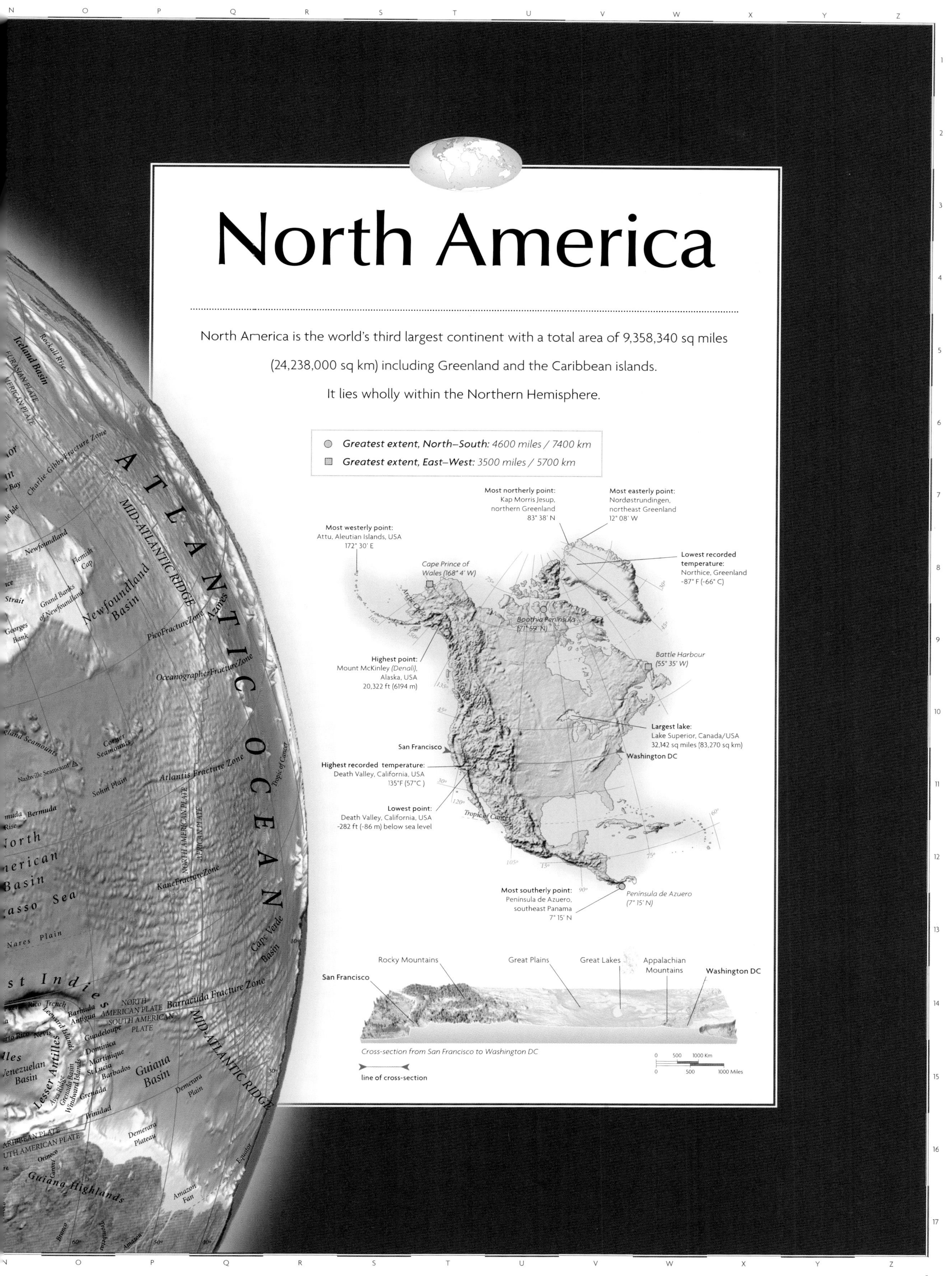

Greatest extent, North–South: 4600 miles / 7400 km
Greatest extent, East–West: 3500 miles / 5700 km
Most northerly point: Kap Morris Jesup, northern Greenland 83° 38′ N
Most easterly point: Nordøstrundingen, northeast Greenland 12° 08′ W
Most westerly point: Attu, Aleutian Islands, USA 172° 30′ E
Cape Prince of Wales (168° 4′ W)
Lowest recorded temperature: Northice, Greenland -87° F (-66° C)
Boothia Peninsula (71° 59′ N)
Highest point: Mount McKinley (Denali), Alaska, USA 20,322 ft (6194 m)
Battle Harbour (55° 35′ W)
Largest lake: Lake Superior, Canada/USA 32,142 sq miles (83,270 sq km)
San Francisco
Washington DC
Highest recorded temperature: Death Valley, California, USA 135°F (57°C)
Lowest point: Death Valley, California, USA -282 ft (-86 m) below sea level
Tropic of Cancer
Most southerly point: Peninsula de Azuero, southeast Panama 7° 15′ N
Peninsula de Azuero (7° 15′ N)
Rocky Mountains
Great Plains
Great Lakes
Appalachian Mountains
San Francisco
Washington DC
Cross-section from San Francisco to Washington DC
line of cross-section
0 500 1000 Km
0 500 1000 Miles
ATLANTIC OCEAN
MID-ATLANTIC RIDGE
Newfoundland Basin
Iceland Basin
Rockall Rise
Charlie-Gibbs Fracture Zone
Azores
Oceanographer Fracture Zone
Atlantis Fracture Zone
Kane Fracture Zone
Barracuda Fracture Zone
NORTH AMERICAN PLATE
AFRICAN PLATE
SOUTH AMERICAN PLATE
Cape Verde Basin
Guiana Basin
Demerara Plain
Demerara Plateau
Amazon Fan
Guiana Highlands
Lesser Antilles
Sohm Plain
Corner Seamounts
Nares Plain
Tropic of Cancer
Equator

Physical North America

The North American continent can be divided into a number of major structural areas: the Western Cordillera, the Canadian Shield, the Great Plains, and Central Lowlands, and the Appalachians. Other smaller regions include the Gulf Atlantic Coastal Plain which borders the southern coast of North America from the southern Appalachians to the Great Plains. This area includes the expanding Mississippi Delta. A chain of volcanic islands, running in an arc around the margin of the Caribbean Plate, lie to the east of the Gulf of Mexico.

The Western Cordillera

About 80 million years ago the Pacific and North American plates collided, uplifting the Western Cordillera. This consists of the Aleutian, Coast, Cascade, and Sierra Nevada mountains, and the inland Rocky Mountains. These run parallel from the Arctic to Mexico

The weight of the ice sheet, 1.8 miles (3 km) thick, has depressed the land to 0.6 miles (1 km) below sea level

▲ *This computer-generated view shows the ice-covered island of Greenland without its ice cap.*

Volcanic rock

Strata have been thrust eastward along fault lines

The Rocky Mountain Trench is the longest linear fault on the continent

B B

***Cross-section through the** Western Cordillera showing direction of mountain building.* ⟶

0 50 100 Km
0 50 100 Miles

The Canadian Shield

Spanning northern Canada and Greenland, this geologically stable plain forms the heart of the continent, containing rocks more than two billion years old. A long history of weathering and repeated glaciation has scoured the region, leaving flat plains, gentle hummocks, numerous small basins and lakes, and the bays and islands of the Arctic

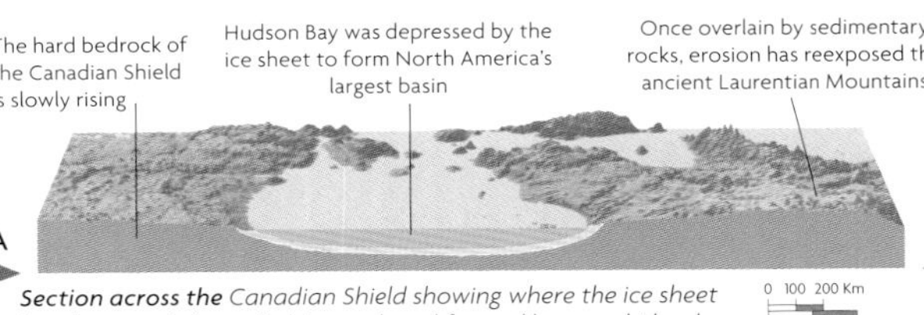
The hard bedrock of the Canadian Shield is slowly rising
Hudson Bay was depressed by the ice sheet to form North America's largest basin
Once overlain by sedimentary rocks, erosion has reexposed the ancient Laurentian Mountains
A
A

***Section across the** Canadian Shield showing where the ice sheet has depressed the underlying rock and formed bays and islands.*

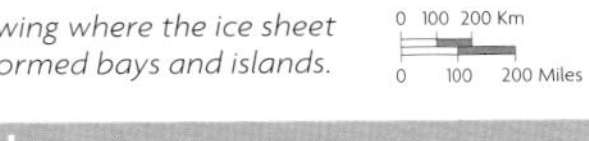
0 100 200 Km
0 100 200 Miles

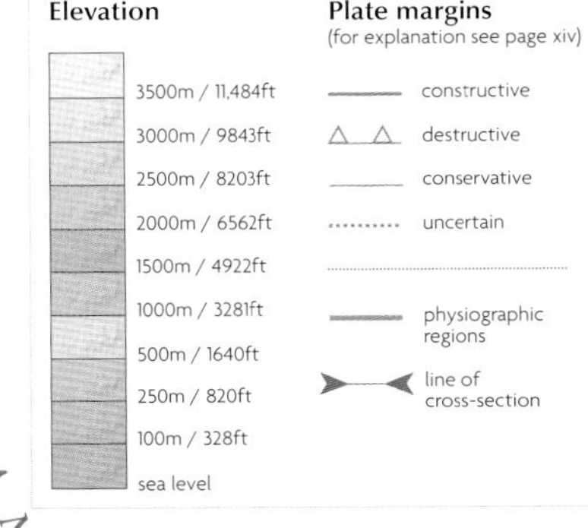
Map key
Elevation
3500m / 11,484ft
3000m / 9843ft
2500m / 8203ft
2000m / 6562ft
1500m / 4922ft
1000m / 3281ft
500m / 1640ft
250m / 820ft
100m / 328ft
sea level
Plate margins
(for explanation see page xiv)
constructive
destructive
conservative
uncertain
physiographic regions
line of cross-section

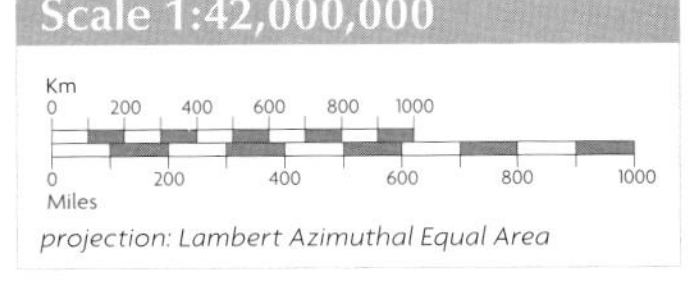
Scale 1:42,000,000
Km 0 200 400 600 800 1000
0 200 400 600 800 1000 Miles
projection: Lambert Azimuthal Equal Area

Greenland · Baffin Bay · Baffin Island · Davis Strait · Foxe Basin · Hudson Strait · Labrador Sea · Hudson Bay · Labrador · Laurentian Mountains · Newfoundland · ATLANTIC OCEAN · Beaufort Sea · Bering Sea · Aleutian Islands · Aleutian Range · Alaska Range · Mount McKinley 6194m · Brooks Range · Mackenzie Delta · Mackenzie Mountains · Mackenzie · Great Bear Lake · Great Slave Lake · Lake Athabasca · Reindeer Lake · Lake Winnipeg · Lake Manitoba · CANADIAN SHIELD · CENTRAL LOWLANDS · GREAT PLAINS · WESTERN CORDILLERA · ROCKY MOUNTAINS · Gulf of Alaska · NORTH AMERICAN PLATE · PACIFIC PLATE · Coast Mountains · Cascade Range · Mount Rainier 4392m · Mount St Helens 2549m · Great Basin · Great Salt Lake · Colorado · Colorado Plateau · Grand Canyon · Sierra Nevada · San Joaquin · San Andreas Fault · Death Valley · Mojave Desert · Sonoran Desert · Lower California · Gulf of California · Sierra Madre Occidental · Sierra Madre Oriental · Sierra Madre del Sur · Volcán Pico de Orizaba 5700m · Rio Grande · Missouri · Arkansas · Mississippi · Ohio · Lake Superior · Lake Michigan · Lake Huron · Lake Erie · Lake Ontario · Great Lakes · St Lawrence · Nova Scotia · Cape Cod · Appalachian Mountains · APPALACHIANS · GULF ATLANTIC COASTAL PLAIN · Mississippi Delta · Gulf of Mexico · Yucatan Peninsula · West Indies · Greater Antilles · Lesser Antilles · Caribbean Sea · Lake Nicaragua · Isthmus of Panama · NORTH AMERICAN PLATE · CARIBBEAN PLATE · COCOS PLATE · SOUTH AMERICAN PLATE · SOUTH AMERICA · PACIFIC OCEAN · ASIA · Bering Strait

The Great Plains & Central Lowlands

Deposits left by retreating glaciers and rivers have made this vast flat area very fertile. In the north this is the result of glaciation, with deposits up to one mile (1.7 km) thick, covering the basement rock. To the south and west, the massive Missouri/Mississippi river system has for centuries deposited silt across the plains, creating broad, flat floodplains and deltas.

Sedimentary layers overlay domed basement rock

Upland rivers drain south toward the Mississippi Basin

Confluence of the Missouri and Mississippi Rivers

D D

***Section across the** Great Plains and Central Lowlands showing river systems and structure.*

0 200 400 Km
0 200 400 Miles

The Appalachians

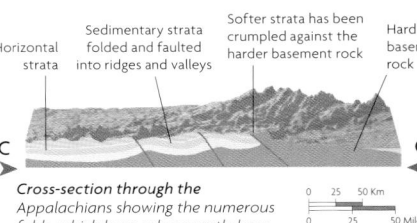

The Appalachian Mountains, uplifted about 400 million years ago, are some of the oldest in the world. They have been lowered and rounded by erosion and now slope gently toward the Atlantic across a broad coastal plain.

Horizontal strata

Sedimentary strata folded and faulted into ridges and valleys

Softer strata has been crumpled against the harder basement rock

Hard basement rock

C C

***Cross-section through the** Appalachians showing the numerous folds, which have subsequently been weathered to create a rounded relief.*

0 25 50 Km
0 25 50 Miles

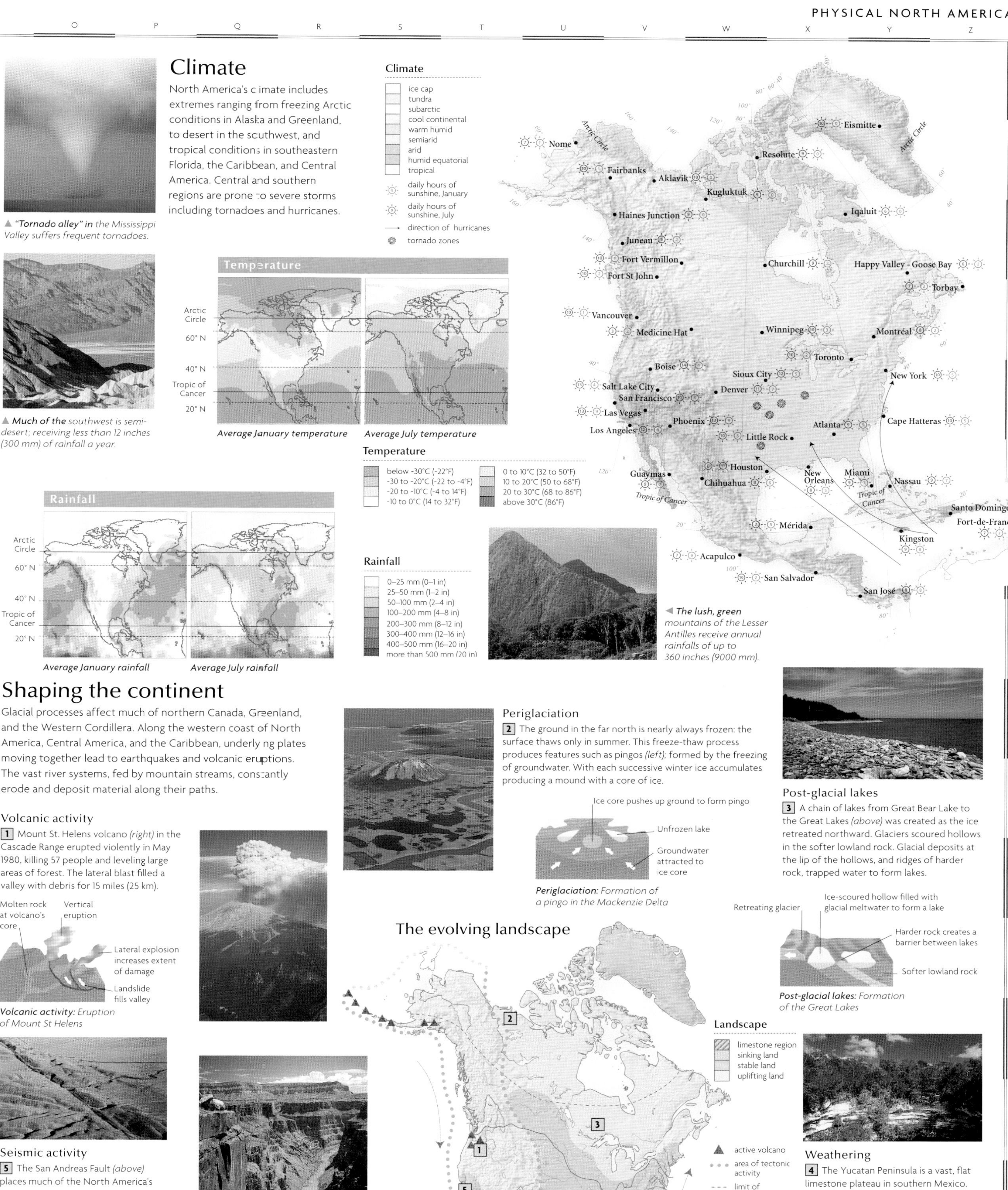
Climate
ice cap
tundra
subarctic
cool continental
warm humid
semiarid
arid
humid equatorial
tropical
daily hours of sunshine, January
daily hours of sunshine, July
direction of hurricanes
tornado zones
Temperature
Arctic Circle
60° N
40° N
Tropic of Cancer
20° N
below -30°C (-22°F)
-30 to -20°C (-22 to -4°F)
-20 to -10°C (-4 to 14°F)
-10 to 0°C (14 to 32°F)
0 to 10°C (32 to 50°F)
10 to 20°C (50 to 68°F)
20 to 30°C (68 to 86°F)
above 30°C (86°F)
Rainfall
0–25 mm (0–1 in)
25–50 mm (1–2 in)
50–100 mm (2–4 in)
100–200 mm (4–8 in)
200–300 mm (8–12 in)
300–400 mm (12–16 in)
400–500 mm (16–20 in)
more than 500 mm (20 in)
Arctic Circle
Tropic of Cancer
Eismitte
Nome
Resolute
Fairbanks
Aklavik
Kugluktuk
Haines Junction
Iqaluit
Juneau
Fort Vermillon
Churchill
Happy Valley - Goose Bay
Fort St John
Torbay
Vancouver
Medicine Hat
Winnipeg
Montréal
Toronto
Boise
Sioux City
New York
Salt Lake City
Denver
San Francisco
Las Vegas
Phoenix
Cape Hatteras
Los Angeles
Atlanta
Little Rock
Houston
Guaymas
New Orleans
Miami
Nassau
Chihuahua
Santo Domingo
Fort-de-France
Mérida
Kingston
Acapulco
San Salvador
San José

Climate

North America's climate includes extremes ranging from freezing Arctic conditions in Alaska and Greenland, to desert in the southwest, and tropical conditions in southeastern Florida, the Caribbean, and Central America. Central and southern regions are prone to severe storms including tornadoes and hurricanes.

▲ *"Tornado alley" in the Mississippi Valley suffers frequent tornadoes.*

▲ *Much of the southwest is semi-desert; receiving less than 12 inches (300 mm) of rainfall a year.*

Average January temperature *Average July temperature*

Average January rainfall *Average July rainfall*

◄ *The lush, green mountains of the Lesser Antilles receive annual rainfalls of up to 360 inches (9000 mm).*

Shaping the continent

Glacial processes affect much of northern Canada, Greenland, and the Western Cordillera. Along the western coast of North America, Central America, and the Caribbean, underlying plates moving together lead to earthquakes and volcanic eruptions. The vast river systems, fed by mountain streams, constantly erode and deposit material along their paths.

Volcanic activity

1 Mount St. Helens volcano *(right)* in the Cascade Range erupted violently in May 1980, killing 57 people and leveling large areas of forest. The lateral blast filled a valley with debris for 15 miles (25 km).

Molten rock at volcano's core
Vertical eruption
Lateral explosion increases extent of damage
Landslide fills valley

Volcanic activity: *Eruption of Mount St Helens*

Periglaciation

2 The ground in the far north is nearly always frozen: the surface thaws only in summer. This freeze-thaw process produces features such as pingos *(left)*; formed by the freezing of groundwater. With each successive winter ice accumulates producing a mound with a core of ice.

Ice core pushes up ground to form pingo
Unfrozen lake
Groundwater attracted to ice core

Periglaciation: *Formation of a pingo in the Mackenzie Delta*

Post-glacial lakes

3 A chain of lakes from Great Bear Lake to the Great Lakes *(above)* was created as the ice retreated northward. Glaciers scoured hollows in the softer lowland rock. Glacial deposits at the lip of the hollows, and ridges of harder rock, trapped water to form lakes.

Retreating glacier
Ice-scoured hollow filled with glacial meltwater to form a lake
Harder rock creates a barrier between lakes
Softer lowland rock

Post-glacial lakes: *Formation of the Great Lakes*

The evolving landscape

Landscape
limestone region
sinking land
stable land
uplifting land
active volcano
area of tectonic activity
limit of permafrost
maximum limit of glaciation
ocean current
1
2
3
4
5
6

Seismic activity

5 The San Andreas Fault *(above)* places much of the North America's west coast under constant threat from earthquakes. It is caused by the Pacific Plate grinding past the North American Plate at a faster rate, though in the same direction.

Pacific Plate
San Andreas Fault
Fault is caused by faster movement of Pacific Plate
North American Plate

Seismic activity: *Action of the San Andreas Fault*

River erosion

6 The Grand Canyon *(above)* in the Colorado Plateau was created by the downward erosion of the Colorado River, combined with the gradual uplift of the plateau, over the past 30 million years. The contours of the canyon formed as the softer rock layers eroded into gentle slopes, and the hard rock layers into cliffs. The depth varies from 3855–6560 ft (1175–2000 m).

Soft rock is easily eroded into gentle slopes
Hard rock resists erosion
Colorado River cuts down through rock

River Erosion: *Formation of the Grand Canyon*

Weathering

4 The Yucatan Peninsula is a vast, flat limestone plateau in southern Mexico. Weathering action from both rainwater and underground streams has enlarged fractures in the rock to form caves and hollows, called sinkholes *(above)*.

Porous limestone plateau
Rainwater erodes porous rock forming sinkholes
Sea level
Underground stream further erodes rock

Weathering: *Water erosion on the Yucatan Peninsula*

Political North America

Democracy is well established in some parts of the continent but is a recent phenomenon in others. The economically dominant nations of Canada and the US have a long democratic tradition but elsewhere, notably in the countries of Central America, political turmoil has been more common. In Nicaragua and Haiti, harsh dictatorships have only recently been superseded by democratically elected governments. North America's largest countries, Canada, Mexico, and the US have federal state systems, sharing political power between national and state governments. The US has intervened militarily on several occasions in Central America and the Caribbean to protect its strategic interests.

Transportation

In the 19th century, railroads opened up the North American continent. Air transportation is now more common for long distance passenger travel, although railroads are still extensively used for bulk freight transportation. Waterways like the Mississippi River are important for the transportation of bulk materials, and the Panama Canal is a vital link between the Pacific and Atlantic Oceans. In the 20th century, road transportation increased massively, with the introduction of cheap, mass-produced motor cars and extensive highway construction.

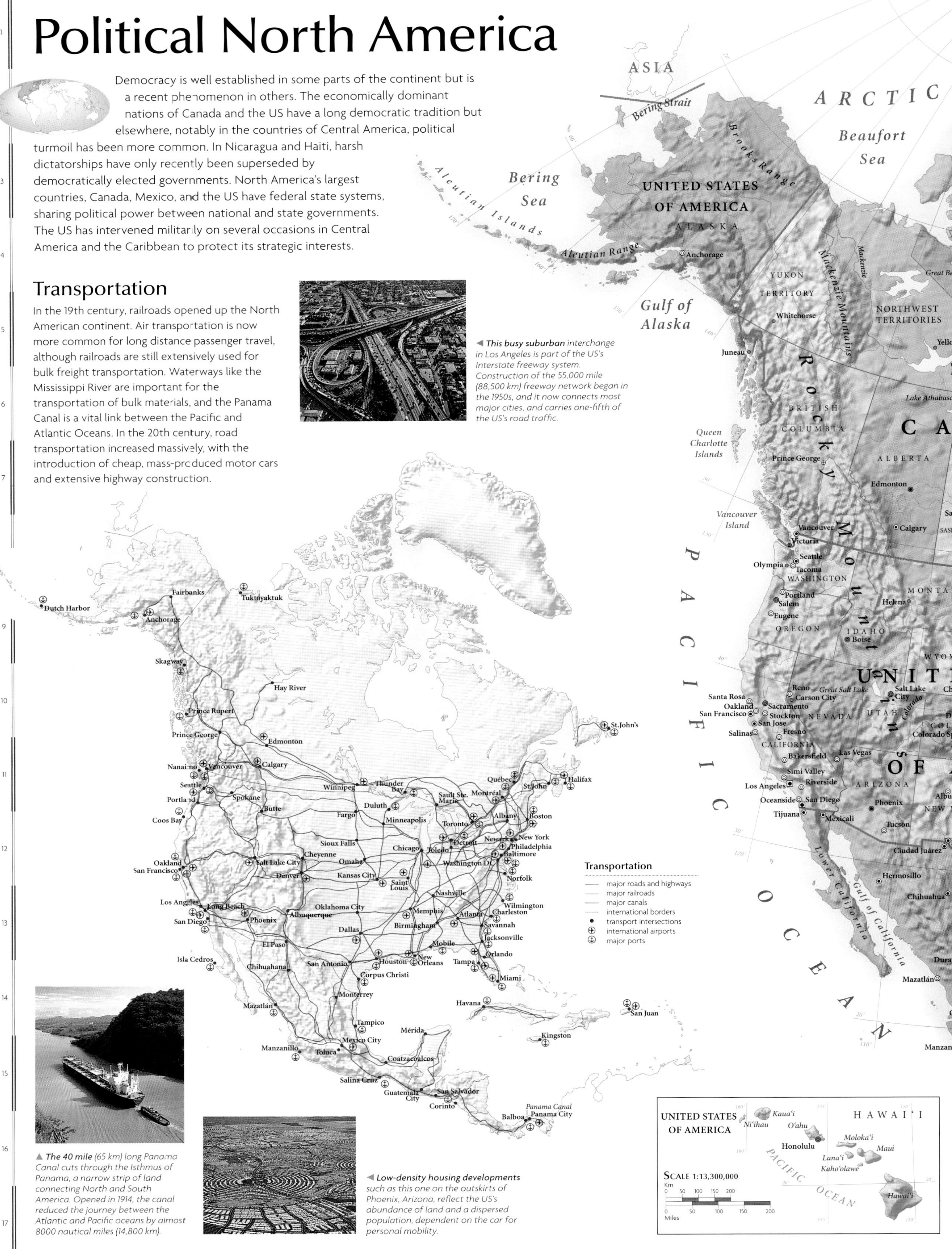

ASIA
Bering Strait
ARCTIC
Beaufort Sea
Brooks Range
Bering Sea
Aleutian Islands
UNITED STATES OF AMERICA
ALASKA
Aleutian Range
Anchorage
Gulf of Alaska
YUKON TERRITORY
Whitehorse
Mackenzie Mountains
NORTHWEST TERRITORIES
Juneau
Queen Charlotte Islands
BRITISH COLUMBIA
Rocky Mountains
Prince George
ALBERTA
Edmonton
Calgary
Lake Athabasca
Vancouver Island
Vancouver
Victoria
Seattle
Olympia
Tacoma
WASHINGTON
PACIFIC OCEAN
Portland
Salem
Eugene
OREGON
Helena
IDAHO
Boise
Reno
Carson City
Great Salt Lake
Salt Lake City
Santa Rosa
Oakland
San Francisco
Sacramento
Stockton
San Jose
Salinas
Fresno
NEVADA
UTAH
CALIFORNIA
Bakersfield
Las Vegas
Simi Valley
Los Angeles
Riverside
Oceanside
San Diego
Tijuana
Mexicali
ARIZONA
Phoenix
Tucson
Ciudad Juárez
Hermosillo
Chihuahua
Lower California
Gulf of California
Mazatlán
Manzanillo
Transportation
major roads and highways
major railroads
major canals
international borders
transport intersections
international airports
major ports
UNITED STATES OF AMERICA
HAWAI'I
Kaua'i
Ni'ihau
O'ahu
Honolulu
Moloka'i
Maui
Lana'i
Kaho'olawe
Hawai'i
PACIFIC OCEAN
SCALE 1:13,300,000

◀ This busy suburban interchange in Los Angeles is part of the US's Interstate freeway system. Construction of the 55,000 mile (88,500 km) freeway network began in the 1950s, and it now connects most major cities, and carries one-fifth of the US's road traffic.

▲ The 40 mile (65 km) long Panama Canal cuts through the Isthmus of Panama, a narrow strip of land connecting North and South America. Opened in 1914, the canal reduced the journey between the Atlantic and Pacific oceans by almost 8000 nautical miles (14,800 km).

◀ Low-density housing developments such as this one on the outskirts of Phoenix, Arizona, reflect the US's abundance of land and a dispersed population, dependent on the car for personal mobility.

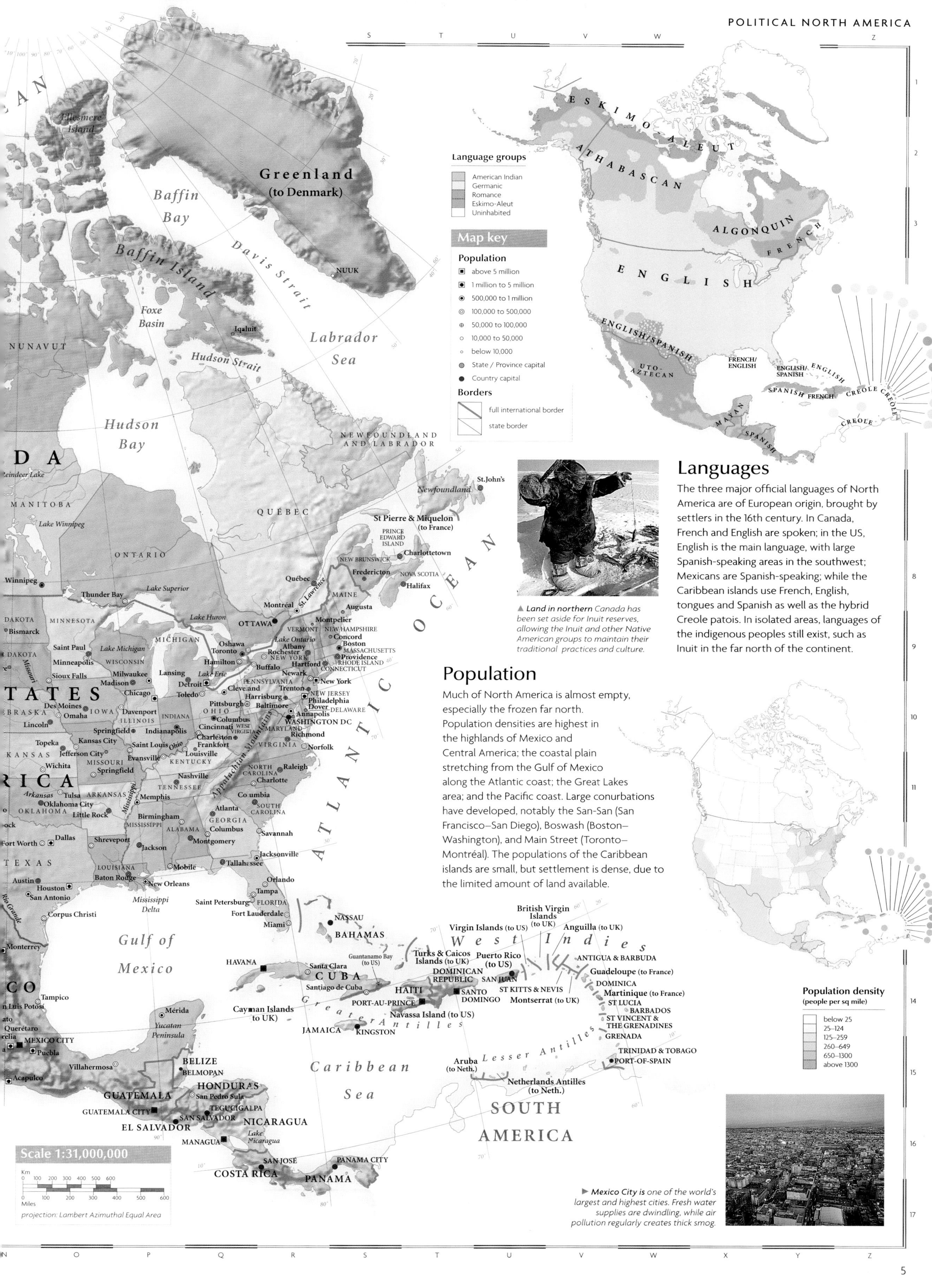
Greenland
(to Denmark)
Baffin Bay
Baffin Island
Davis Strait
NUUK
Foxe Basin
Iqaluit
NUNAVUT
Hudson Strait
Labrador Sea
Hudson Bay
NEWFOUNDLAND AND LABRADOR
Newfoundland
St.John's
QUEBEC
MANITOBA
Lake Winnipeg
ONTARIO
St Pierre & Miquelon (to France)
PRINCE EDWARD ISLAND
Charlottetown
NEW BRUNSWICK
Fredericton
NOVA SCOTIA
Halifax
Québec
Winnipeg
Thunder Bay
Lake Superior
Montréal
OTTAWA
MAINE
Augusta
Lake Huron
Montpelier
VERMONT
NEW HAMPSHIRE
Concord
Lake Ontario
Boston
MASSACHUSETTS
Albany
Rochester
Providence
RHODE ISLAND
NEW YORK
Hartford
CONNECTICUT
Toronto
Oshawa
Hamilton
Buffalo
MICHIGAN
Lake Michigan
Saint Paul
Minneapolis
WISCONSIN
Milwaukee
Lansing
Lake Erie
Detroit
Madison
Sioux Falls
Newark
New York
PENNSYLVANIA
Cleveland
Trenton
NEW JERSEY
Philadelphia
Harrisburg
Baltimore
Dover
DELAWARE
Annapolis
WASHINGTON DC
Chicago
Toledo
Pittsburgh
OHIO
Des Moines
IOWA
Davenport
Omaha
ILLINOIS
INDIANA
Columbus
Lincoln
Springfield
Indianapolis
Cincinnati
WEST VIRGINIA
MARYLAND
Richmond
Charleston
Topeka
Kansas City
Saint Louis
Frankfort
VIRGINIA
Norfolk
KANSAS
Jefferson City
Louisville
Evansville
KENTUCKY
Wichita
MISSOURI
Springfield
NORTH CAROLINA
Raleigh
Nashville
Charlotte
TENNESSEE
Appalachian Mountains
Arkansas
Tulsa
ARKANSAS
Memphis
Columbia
Oklahoma City
OKLAHOMA
Little Rock
SOUTH CAROLINA
Atlanta
Birmingham
GEORGIA
MISSISSIPPI
ALABAMA
Columbus
Savannah
Dallas
Fort Worth
Shreveport
Jackson
Montgomery
Jacksonville
TEXAS
LOUISIANA
Mobile
Tallahassee
Baton Rouge
Austin
Houston
New Orleans
Orlando
San Antonio
Mississippi Delta
Tampa
Saint Petersburg
FLORIDA
Fort Lauderdale
Corpus Christi
Miami
Gulf of Mexico
ATLANTIC OCEAN
NASSAU
BAHAMAS
HAVANA
Santa Clara
CUBA
Guantanamo Bay (to US)
Santiago de Cuba
Turks & Caicos Islands (to UK)
DOMINICAN REPUBLIC
HAITI
PORT-AU-PRINCE
SANTO DOMINGO
Puerto Rico (to US)
SAN JUAN
Virgin Islands (to US)
British Virgin Islands (to UK)
Anguilla (to UK)
West Indies
ANTIGUA & BARBUDA
Guadeloupe (to France)
ST KITTS & NEVIS
Montserrat (to UK)
DOMINICA
Martinique (to France)
ST LUCIA
BARBADOS
ST VINCENT & THE GRENADINES
GRENADA
TRINIDAD & TOBAGO
PORT-OF-SPAIN
Cayman Islands (to UK)
Navassa Island (to US)
Greater Antilles
JAMAICA
KINGSTON
Lesser Antilles
Aruba (to Neth.)
Netherlands Antilles (to Neth.)
Caribbean Sea
SOUTH AMERICA
Monterrey
Tampico
Mérida
Yucatan Peninsula
MEXICO CITY
Puebla
Acapulco
Villahermosa
BELIZE
BELMOPAN
GUATEMALA
GUATEMALA CITY
HONDURAS
San Pedro Sula
TEGUCIGALPA
SAN SALVADOR
EL SALVADOR
NICARAGUA
Lake Nicaragua
MANAGUA
SAN JOSÉ
COSTA RICA
PANAMA CITY
PANAMA
Scale 1:31,000,000
Km 0 100 200 300 400 500 600
Miles 0 100 200 300 400 500 600
projection: Lambert Azimuthal Equal Area
Language groups
American Indian
Germanic
Romance
Eskimo-Aleut
Uninhabited
ESKIMO-ALEUT
ATHABASCAN
ALGONQUIN
FRENCH
ENGLISH
ENGLISH/SPANISH
UTO-AZTECAN
FRENCH/ENGLISH
ENGLISH/SPANISH
ENGLISH
SPANISH
FRENCH
CREOLE
CREOLE
CREOLE
MAYAN
SPANISH
Map key
Population
above 5 million
1 million to 5 million
500,000 to 1 million
100,000 to 500,000
50,000 to 100,000
10,000 to 50,000
below 10,000
State / Province capital
Country capital
Borders
full international border
state border
Population density (people per sq mile)
below 25
25–124
125–259
260–649
650–1300
above 1300

▲ *Land in northern* Canada has been set aside for Inuit reserves, allowing the Inuit and other Native American groups to maintain their traditional practices and culture.

Languages

The three major official languages of North America are of European origin, brought by settlers in the 16th century. In Canada, French and English are spoken; in the US, English is the main language, with large Spanish-speaking areas in the southwest; Mexicans are Spanish-speaking; while the Caribbean islands use French, English, tongues and Spanish as well as the hybrid Creole patois. In isolated areas, languages of the indigenous peoples still exist, such as Inuit in the far north of the continent.

Population

Much of North America is almost empty, especially the frozen far north. Population densities are highest in the highlands of Mexico and Central America; the coastal plain stretching from the Gulf of Mexico along the Atlantic coast; the Great Lakes area; and the Pacific coast. Large conurbations have developed, notably the San-San (San Francisco–San Diego), Boswash (Boston–Washington), and Main Street (Toronto–Montréal). The populations of the Caribbean islands are small, but settlement is dense, due to the limited amount of land available.

▶ *Mexico City* is one of the world's largest and highest cities. Fresh water supplies are dwindling, while air pollution regularly creates thick smog.

North American resources

The two northern countries of Canada and the US are richly endowed with natural resources that have helped to fuel economic development. The US is the world's largest economy, although today it is facing stiff competition from the Far East. Mexico has relied on oil revenues but there are hopes that the North American Free Trade Agreement (NAFTA), will encourage trade growth with Canada and the US. The poorer countries of Central America and the Caribbean depend largely on cash crops and tourism.

Industry

The modern, industrialized economies of the US and Canada contrast sharply with those of Mexico, Central America, and the Caribbean. Manufacturing is especially important in the US; vehicle production is concentrated around the Great Lakes, while electronic and hi-tech industries are increasingly found in the western and southern states. Mexico depends on oil exports and assembly work, taking advantage of cheap labor. Many Central American and Caribbean countries rely heavily on agricultural exports.

◀ *After its purchase from Russia in 1867, Alaska's frozen lands were largely ignored by the US. Oil reserves similar in magnitude to those in eastern Texas were discovered in Prudhoe Bay, Alaska in 1968. Freezing temperatures and a fragile environment hamper oil extraction.*

Standard of living

The US and Canada have one of the highest overall standards of living in the world. However, many people still live in poverty, especially in urban ghettos and some rural areas. Central America and the Caribbean are markedly poorer than their wealthier northern neighbors. Haiti is the poorest country in the western hemisphere.

Standard of living
(UN human development index)

high

low

▲ *Fish such as cod, flounder and plaice are caught in the Grand Banks, off the Newfoundland coast, and processed in many North Atlantic coastal settlements.*

▲ *South of San Francisco, "Silicon Valley" is both a national and international center for hi-tech industries, electronic industries, and research institutions.*

▲ *Multinational companies rely on cheap labor and tax benefits to assemble vehicles in Mexican factories.*

▲ *The health of the Wall Street stock market in New York is the standard measure of the state of the world's economy.*

Industry

- aerospace
- brewing
- car/vehicle manufacture
- chemicals
- defense
- electronics
- engineering
- film industry
- finance
- food processing
- hi-tech industry
- iron & steel
- pharmaceuticals
- printing & publishing
- research & development
- shipbuilding
- sugar processing
- textiles
- timber processing
- tobacco processing
- coal
- oil
- gas
- industrial cities
- major industrial areas

GNI per capita (US$)

- below 1999
- 2000–4999
- 5000–9999
- 10,000–19,999
- 20,000–24,999
- above 25,000

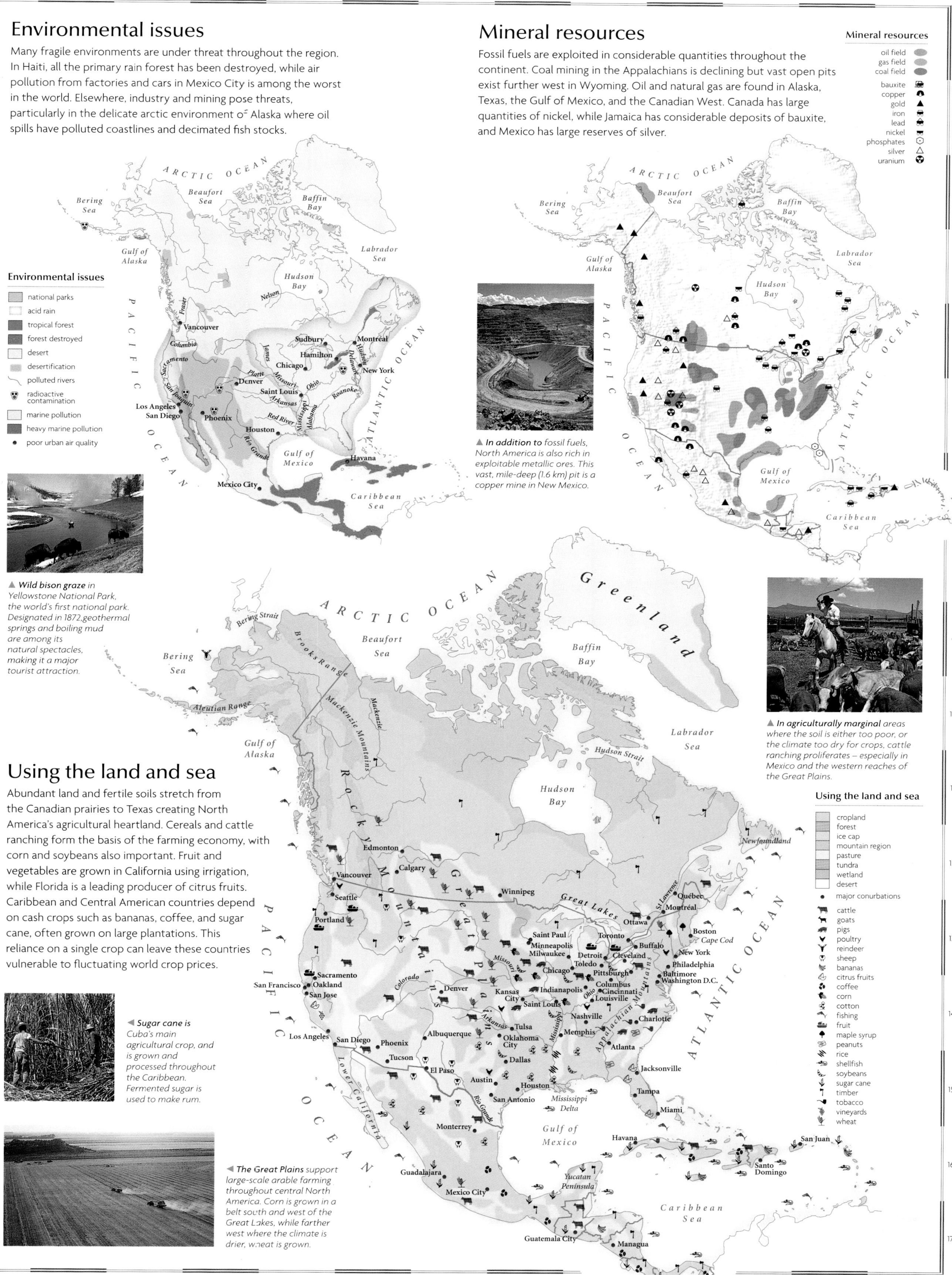
Environmental issues
national parks
acid rain
tropical forest
forest destroyed
desert
desertification
polluted rivers
radioactive contamination
marine pollution
heavy marine pollution
poor urban air quality
Mineral resources
oil field
gas field
coal field
bauxite
copper
gold
iron
lead
nickel
phosphates
silver
uranium
Using the land and sea
cropland
forest
ice cap
mountain region
pasture
tundra
wetland
desert
major conurbations
cattle
goats
pigs
poultry
reindeer
sheep
bananas
citrus fruits
coffee
corn
cotton
fishing
fruit
maple syrup
peanuts
rice
shellfish
soybeans
sugar cane
timber
tobacco
vineyards
wheat

Environmental issues

Many fragile environments are under threat throughout the region. In Haiti, all the primary rain forest has been destroyed, while air pollution from factories and cars in Mexico City is among the worst in the world. Elsewhere, industry and mining pose threats, particularly in the delicate arctic environment of Alaska where oil spills have polluted coastlines and decimated fish stocks.

▲ *Wild bison graze in* Yellowstone National Park, the world's first national park. Designated in 1872,geothermal springs and boiling mud are among its natural spectacles, making it a major tourist attraction.

Mineral resources

Fossil fuels are exploited in considerable quantities throughout the continent. Coal mining in the Appalachians is declining but vast open pits exist further west in Wyoming. Oil and natural gas are found in Alaska, Texas, the Gulf of Mexico, and the Canadian West. Canada has large quantities of nickel, while Jamaica has considerable deposits of bauxite, and Mexico has large reserves of silver.

▲ *In addition to* fossil fuels, North America is also rich in exploitable metallic ores. This vast, mile-deep (1.6 km) pit is a copper mine in New Mexico.

Using the land and sea

Abundant land and fertile soils stretch from the Canadian prairies to Texas creating North America's agricultural heartland. Cereals and cattle ranching form the basis of the farming economy, with corn and soybeans also important. Fruit and vegetables are grown in California using irrigation, while Florida is a leading producer of citrus fruits. Caribbean and Central American countries depend on cash crops such as bananas, coffee, and sugar cane, often grown on large plantations. This reliance on a single crop can leave these countries vulnerable to fluctuating world crop prices.

▲ *In agriculturally marginal* areas where the soil is either too poor, or the climate too dry for crops, cattle ranching proliferates – especially in Mexico and the western reaches of the Great Plains.

◀ *Sugar cane is* Cuba's main agricultural crop, and is grown and processed throughout the Caribbean. Fermented sugar is used to make rum.

◀ *The Great Plains* support large-scale arable farming throughout central North America. Corn is grown in a belt south and west of the Great Lakes, while farther west where the climate is drier, wheat is grown.

Canada

Canada is the second largest country in the world, and with only about one-tenth of its land area inhabited, it is one of the most sparsely populated. Canada became a confederation in 1867, though Newfoundland did not join until 1949. As a founding member of the UN and of the Commonwealth, Canada has played an important role in international affairs. A constitutional crisis, focusing on the French-speaking Québécois, and Inuit, and Native American land rights, dominated politics in the 1990s. In 1999, part of the Northwest Territories, Nunavut, became a self-governing homeland for the Inuit.

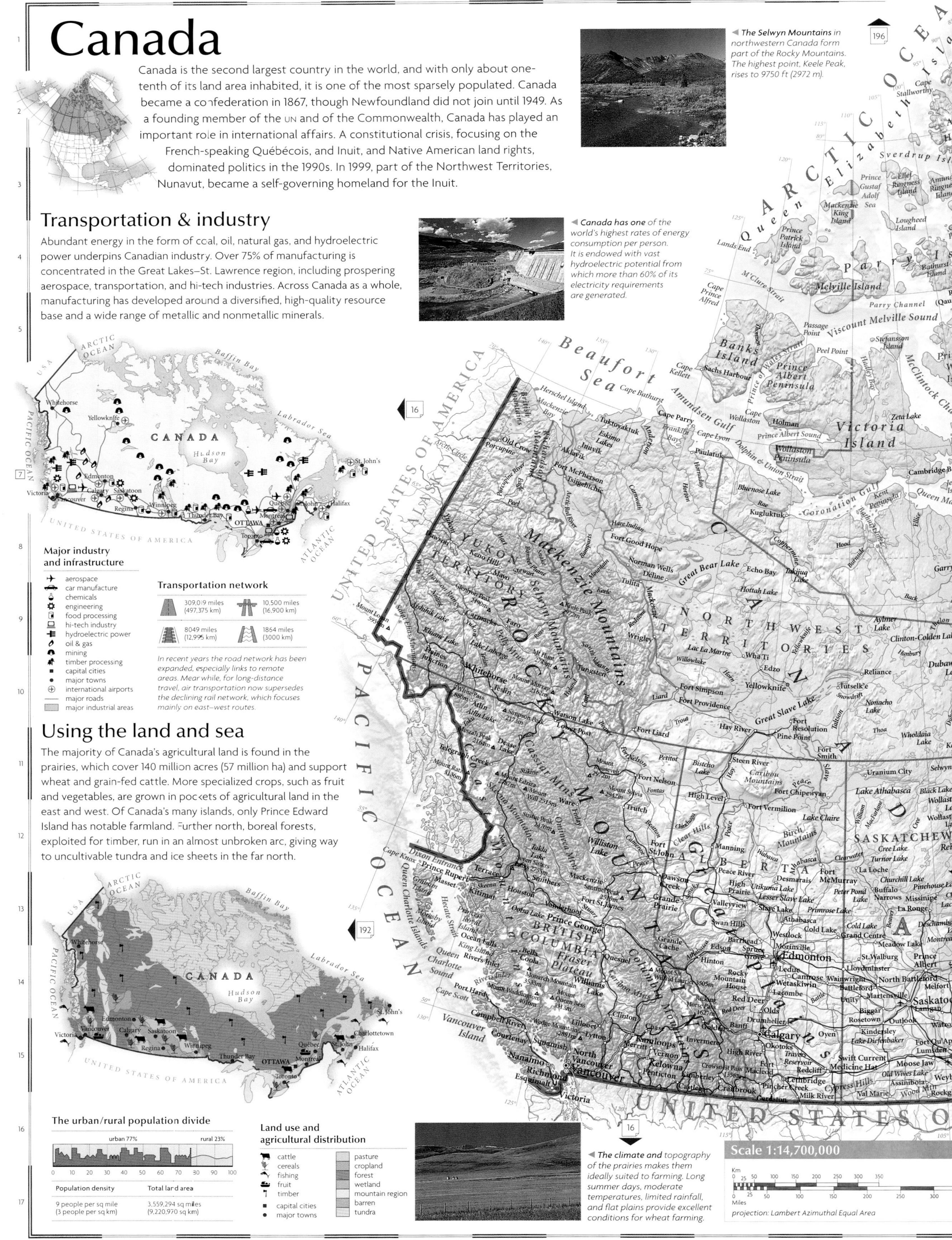

◄ *The Selwyn Mountains in northwestern Canada form part of the Rocky Mountains. The highest point, Keele Peak, rises to 9750 ft (2972 m).*

Transportation & industry

Abundant energy in the form of coal, oil, natural gas, and hydroelectric power underpins Canadian industry. Over 75% of manufacturing is concentrated in the Great Lakes–St. Lawrence region, including prospering aerospace, transportation, and hi-tech industries. Across Canada as a whole, manufacturing has developed around a diversified, high-quality resource base and a wide range of metallic and nonmetallic minerals.

◄ *Canada has one of the world's highest rates of energy consumption per person. It is endowed with vast hydroelectric potential from which more than 60% of its electricity requirements are generated.*

Major industry and infrastructure

- aerospace
- car manufacture
- chemicals
- engineering
- food processing
- hi-tech industry
- hydroelectric power
- oil & gas
- mining
- timber processing
- capital cities
- major towns
- international airports
- major roads
- major industrial areas

Transportation network

309,019 miles (497,375 km)	10,500 miles (16,900 km)
8049 miles (12,995 km)	1864 miles (3000 km)

In recent years the road network has been expanded, especially links to remote areas. Meanwhile, for long-distance travel, air transportation now supersedes the declining rail network, which focuses mainly on east–west routes.

Using the land and sea

The majority of Canada's agricultural land is found in the prairies, which cover 140 million acres (57 million ha) and support wheat and grain-fed cattle. More specialized crops, such as fruit and vegetables, are grown in pockets of agricultural land in the east and west. Of Canada's many islands, only Prince Edward Island has notable farmland. Further north, boreal forests, exploited for timber, run in an almost unbroken arc, giving way to uncultivable tundra and ice sheets in the far north.

The urban/rural population divide

urban 77% — rural 23%

Population density	Total land area
9 people per sq mile (3 people per sq km)	3,559,294 sq miles (9,220,970 sq km)

Land use and agricultural distribution

- cattle
- cereals
- fishing
- fruit
- timber
- capital cities
- major towns
- pasture
- cropland
- forest
- wetland
- mountain region
- barren
- tundra

◄ *The climate and topography of the prairies makes them ideally suited to farming. Long summer days, moderate temperatures, limited rainfall, and flat plains provide excellent conditions for wheat farming.*

Scale 1:14,700,000

projection: Lambert Azimuthal Equal Area

196
16
192
16

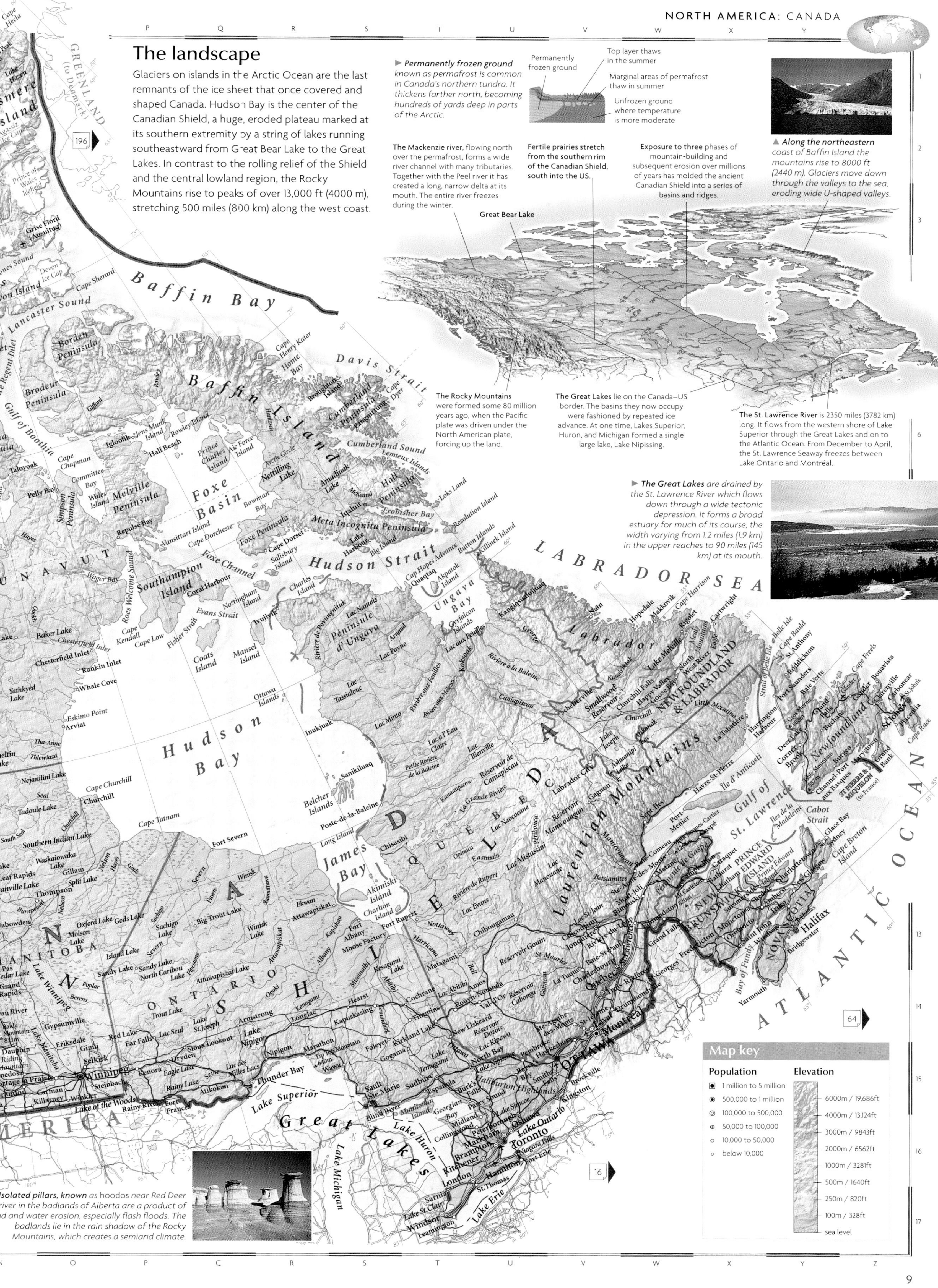
Permanently frozen ground
Top layer thaws in the summer
Marginal areas of permafrost thaw in summer
Unfrozen ground where temperature is more moderate
Great Bear Lake
Baffin Bay
Davis Strait
Baffin Island
Foxe Basin
Hudson Strait
LABRADOR SEA
Hudson Bay
James Bay
NEWFOUNDLAND & LABRADOR
QUÉBEC
ONTARIO
Laurentian Mountains
Gulf of St. Lawrence
ATLANTIC OCEAN
Lake Superior
Great Lakes
Lake Huron
Lake Ontario
Lake Erie
Lake Michigan
Lake Winnipeg
NOVA SCOTIA
NEW BRUNSWICK
PRINCE EDWARD ISLAND
Montréal
OTTAWA
Québec
Toronto
Halifax
Winnipeg
Map key
Population
1 million to 5 million
500,000 to 1 million
100,000 to 500,000
50,000 to 100,000
10,000 to 50,000
below 10,000
Elevation
6000m / 19,686ft
4000m / 13,124ft
3000m / 9843ft
2000m / 6562ft
1000m / 3281ft
500m / 1640ft
250m / 820ft
100m / 328ft
sea level

The landscape

Glaciers on islands in the Arctic Ocean are the last remnants of the ice sheet that once covered and shaped Canada. Hudson Bay is the center of the Canadian Shield, a huge, eroded plateau marked at its southern extremity by a string of lakes running southeastward from Great Bear Lake to the Great Lakes. In contrast to the rolling relief of the Shield and the central lowland region, the Rocky Mountains rise to peaks of over 13,000 ft (4000 m), stretching 500 miles (800 km) along the west coast.

► *Permanently frozen ground known as permafrost is common in Canada's northern tundra. It thickens farther north, becoming hundreds of yards deep in parts of the Arctic.*

The Mackenzie river, flowing north over the permafrost, forms a wide river channel with many tributaries. Together with the Peel river it has created a long, narrow delta at its mouth. The entire river freezes during the winter.

Fertile prairies stretch from the southern rim of the Canadian Shield, south into the US.

Exposure to three phases of mountain-building and subsequent erosion over millions of years has molded the ancient Canadian Shield into a series of basins and ridges.

▲ *Along the northeastern coast of Baffin Island the mountains rise to 8000 ft (2440 m). Glaciers move down through the valleys to the sea, eroding wide U-shaped valleys.*

The Rocky Mountains were formed some 80 million years ago, when the Pacific plate was driven under the North American plate, forcing up the land.

The Great Lakes lie on the Canada–US border. The basins they now occupy were fashioned by repeated ice advance. At one time, Lakes Superior, Huron, and Michigan formed a single large lake, Lake Nipissing.

The St. Lawrence River is 2350 miles (3782 km) long. It flows from the western shore of Lake Superior through the Great Lakes and on to the Atlantic Ocean. From December to April, the St. Lawrence Seaway freezes between Lake Ontario and Montréal.

► *The Great Lakes are drained by the St. Lawrence River which flows down through a wide tectonic depression. It forms a broad estuary for much of its course, the width varying from 1.2 miles (1.9 km) in the upper reaches to 90 miles (145 km) at its mouth.*

***Isolated pillars, known** as hoodoos near Red Deer river in the badlands of Alberta are a product of wind and water erosion, especially flash floods. The badlands lie in the rain shadow of the Rocky Mountains, which creates a semiarid climate.*

196

64

16

Canada:
WESTERN PROVINCES

Alberta, British Columbia, Manitoba, Saskatchewan, Yukon Territory

The mountains of the west coast, incorporating British Columbia and the Yukon Territory, descend into the vast, flat prairies of Alberta, Saskatchewan, and Manitoba. The empty lands and fertile soils of the prairie provinces attracted migrants, and the descendants of early European immigrants still make up a large proportion of the population. The mechanization of agriculture has reduced the need for labor, and rural population densities remain low. The majority of the people live within 100 miles (160 km) of the southern Canada–US border, and in British Columbia, one of the leading Canadian provinces in terms of economic wealth. The Yukon Territory, in the far north, remains a relatively unspoiled wilderness, containing large, untapped mineral reserves. This province has a significant population of Native American people, many of whom maintain a traditional lifestyle.

16

Using the land and sea

Wheat farming is the economic mainstay of Alberta, Manitoba, and Saskatchewan, which contain 82% of farmland in Canada. Cattle are also raised on the prairies. Forestry and fishing are the most prominent resource-based industries in British Columbia. Despite the mountainous terrain, fruit and specialized grains can be grown in the Okanagan and Fraser valleys.

Land use and agricultural distribution

- cattle
- cereals
- fishing
- fruit
- timber
- major towns
- pasture
- cropland
- forest
- wetland
- barren
- tundra

The urban/rural population divide

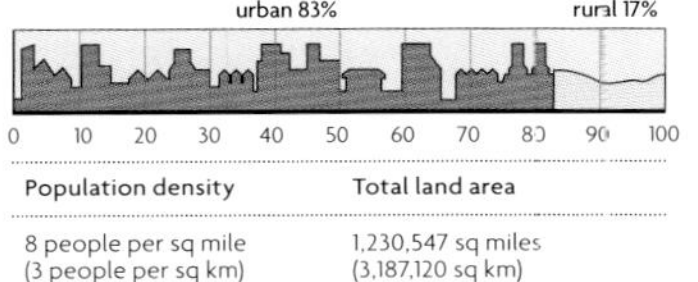
urban 83%
rural 17%
0
10
20
30
40
50
60
70
80
90
100

Population density	Total land area
8 people per sq mile (3 people per sq km)	1,230,547 sq miles (3,187,120 sq km)

Large, highly mechanized and often very specialized farms, requiring huge investment but little labor, characterize modern farming in the prairies.

Transportation & industry

The western provinces contain a wealth of mineral resources. Alberta holds the bulk of Canada's fossil fuels; the other provinces contain reserves of metallic ores, such as zinc, lead, and silver. Isolation from markets has slowed the development of manufacturing, restricting it to the large cities like Vancouver, Winnipeg, and Calgary. Hydroelectric power is widely exploited, although there is increasing concern about potential ecological damage.

Major industry and infrastructure

- aerospace
- chemicals
- coal
- engineering
- food processing
- hydroelectric power
- mining
- oil & gas
- timber processing
- major towns
- international airports
- major roads
- major industrial areas

Transportation network

- 82,438 miles (135,145 km)
- 6459 miles (10,401 km)
- 24,041 miles (38,694 km)
- None

The transportation network of the western provinces is dominated by east–west routes that weave through mountain passes and spread across the plains. Access to some northern areas is restricted to air travel.

192

Much of the Yukon Territory is uninhabited tundra. Industry is based on the extraction of mineral resources, and to a lesser extent, on the scattered forests of the south.

The Fraser River valley is a major area of settlement in British Columbia. Railroads cross the Rocky Mountains via this valley.

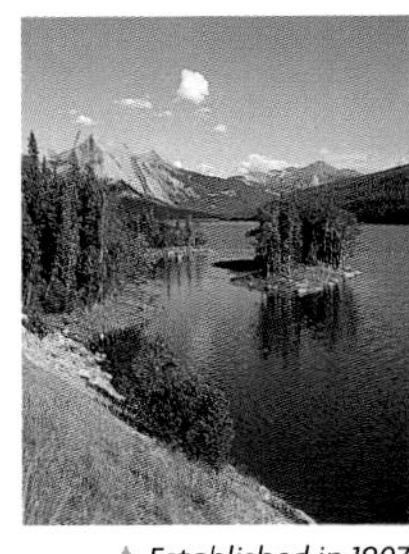

Established in 1907, Jasper National Park lies in the heart of the Rocky Mountains. It is noted for its spectacular alpine scenery and contains part of the large Columbia Icefield.

The landscape

The massive Rocky Mountains form a continental divide between rivers flowing eastward and westward. The interior plains lie east of the mountains, stretching from the Arctic Circle south into the US. Covered with glacial deposits from the last Ice Age, these are interspersed with hilly regions and long, steep escarpments.

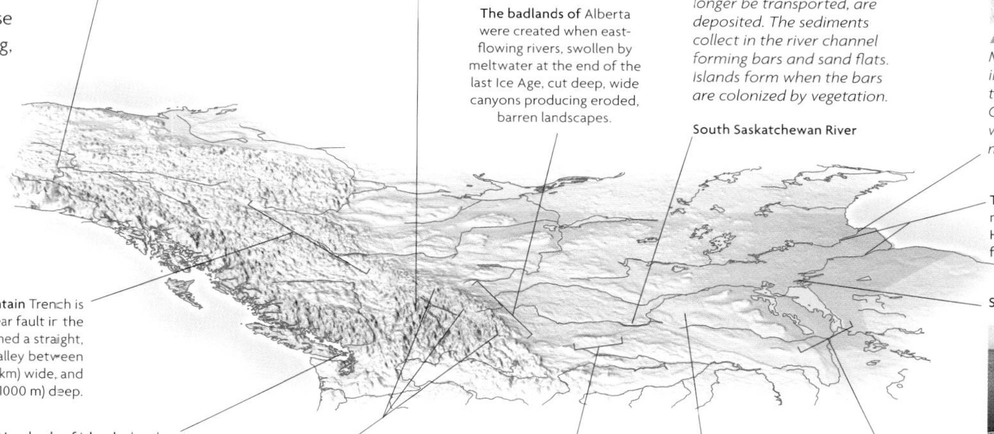

Mount Logan rises 19,551 ft (5959 m). It is the highest peak in Canada.

The Columbia Icefield in the Rocky Mountains is the source of two major rivers, the Athabasca and the North Saskatchewan.

Vegetated island

River flow is diverted by deposited sediments

Bar

Sand flat

▲ ***Braided rivers are*** *shallow and fast-flowing. The interlaced branches are formed when excess sediments, which can no longer be transported, are deposited. The sediments collect in the river channel forming bars and sand flats. Islands form when the bars are colonized by vegetation.*

▲ ***Across the tundra*** *of northern Manitoba, widespread permafrost inhibits water from permeating the soil. This causes rivers like the Churchill to flow in many channels, which can be frozen for up to six months during the winter.*

The badlands of Alberta were created when east-flowing rivers, swollen by meltwater at the end of the last Ice Age, cut deep, wide canyons producing eroded, barren landscapes.

South Saskatchewan River

The Nelson and Churchill rivers drain northward across the Canadian Shield to Hudson Bay. The shield covers three-fifths of Saskatchewan.

Setting Lake

The Rocky Mountain Trench is the longest linear fault in the world. It has formed a straight, flat-bottomed valley between 2–9 miles (4–15 km) wide, and up to 3280 ft (1000 m) deep.

Hundreds of islands dot the fjord-indented coast of British Columbia; the largest is Vancouver Island.

Three major passes cut through the Rocky Mountains: Yellowhead, Kicking Horse, and Crowsnest. They are all used as transportation routes through the mountains.

The Cypress Hills rise to 4806 ft (1465 m) above the surrounding plain. Having escaped the last glaciation they contain unique plant and animal life. The silvery lupine, bunchberry, and lodgepole pine all grow in the cool, moist climate of the hills.

The Alberta and Saskatchewan plains bear strong testament to past glaciations. The Assiniboine, Saskatchewan and Qu'Appelle rivers occupy flat-bottomed, steep-sided valleys eroded during the last Ice Age by glacial meltwater.

▲ ***Ancient granite outcrops,*** *part of the Canadian Shield, rise above the surface of Setting Lake, which was initially formed by meltwater from the last Ice Age.*

The lowlands of Manitoba are a basin that once held the vast post-glacial Lake Agassiz, remnants of which include Lake Winnipeg, Lake Winnipegosis, and Lake Manitoba.

Map key

Population

- 500,000 to 1 million
- 100,000 to 500,000
- 50,000 to 100,000
- 10,000 to 50,000
- below 10,000

Elevation

- 6000m / 19,686ft
- 4000m / 13,124ft
- 3000m / 9843ft
- 2000m / 6562ft
- 1000m / 3281ft
- 500m / 1640ft
- 250m / 820ft
- 100m / 328ft
- sea level

Scale 1:8,250,000

Km 0 25 50 100 150 200 250

Miles 0 25 50 100 150 200 250

projection: Lambert Conformal Conic

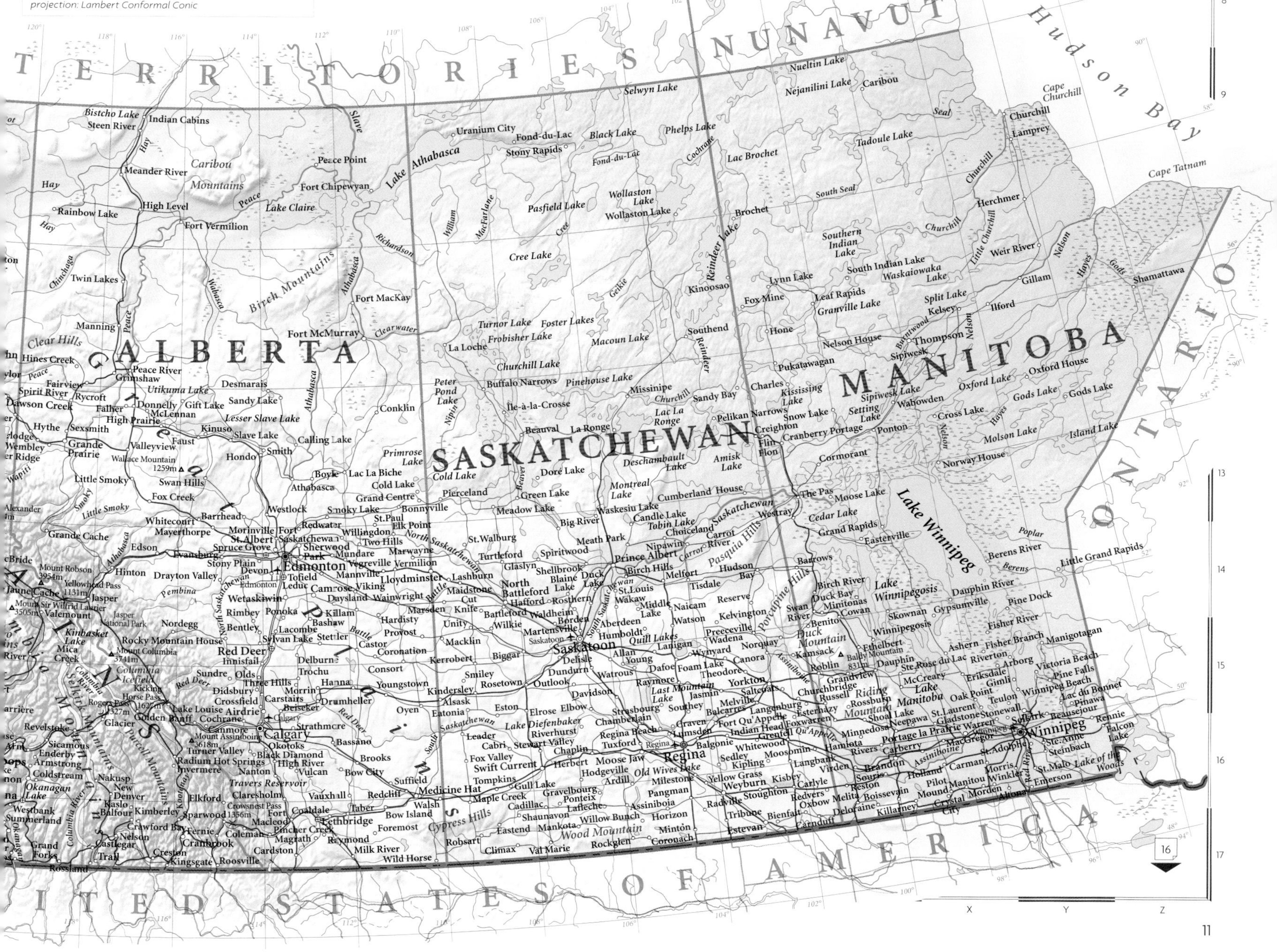

16

Canada: EASTERN PROVINCES

New Brunswick, Newfoundland & Labrador, Nova Scotia, Ontario, Prince Edward Island, Québec, *St Pierre & Miquelon (to France)*

Colonized by both the English and the French during the 16th century, Canada's eastern provinces are still marked by their dual influences. They contain the last fragment of once-sizeable French territories, the islands of St. Pierre and Miquelon. French remains Canada's second official language and Québec's first language. The population of the eastern provinces is highly concentrated in the south, especially along the border with the US. A recent decline in fishing in the Atlantic provinces has encouraged a steady flow of westerly migration to more prosperous regions. The north, around Hudson Bay, remains snow-covered for most of the year and the indigenous Inuit people make up the bulk of its sparse population.

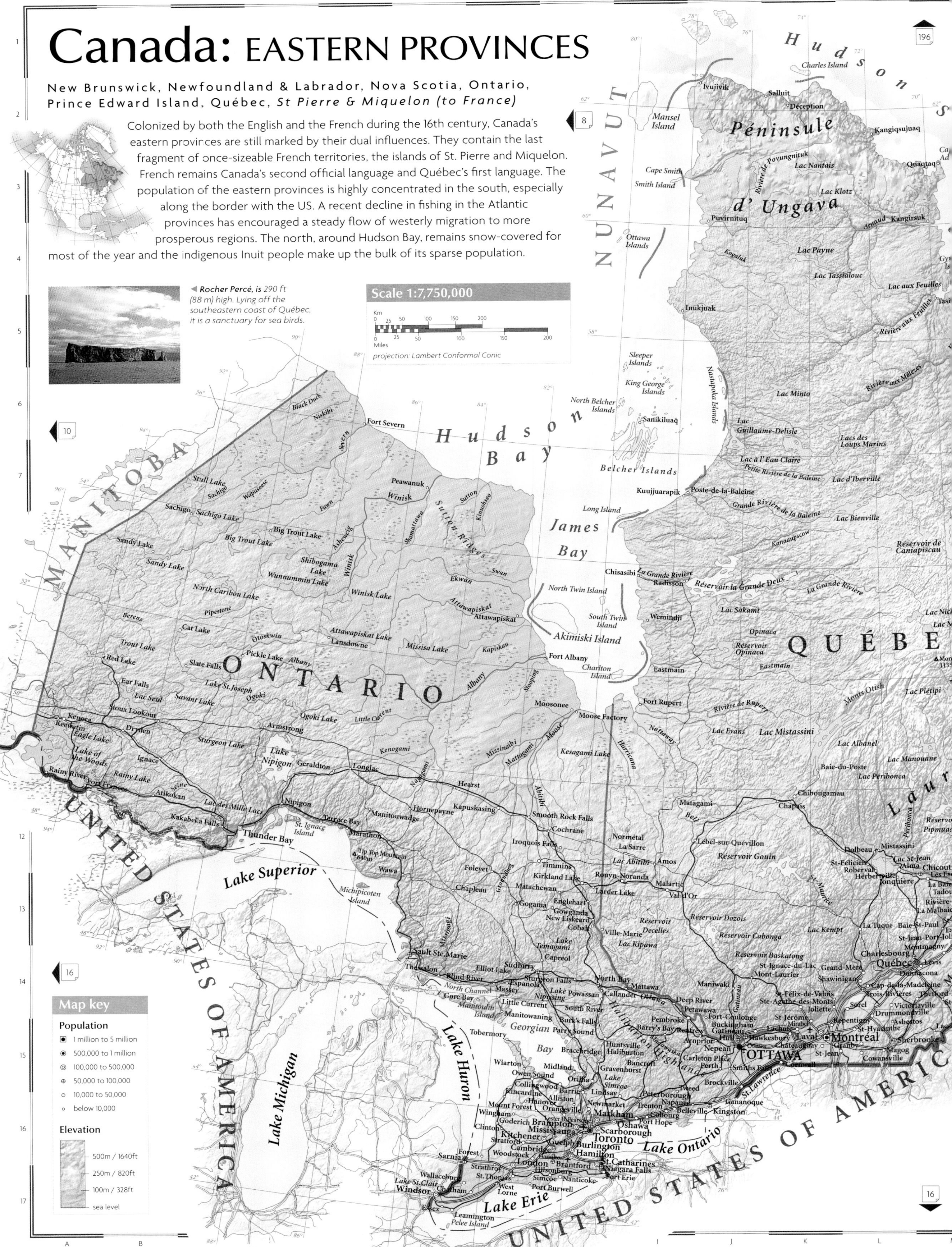

◀ Rocher Percé, is 290 ft (88 m) high. Lying off the southeastern coast of Québec, it is a sanctuary for sea birds.
Scale 1:7,750,000
Km 0 25 50 100 150 200
Miles 0 25 50 100 150 200
projection: Lambert Conformal Conic
Map key
Population
1 million to 5 million
500,000 to 1 million
100,000 to 500,000
50,000 to 100,000
10,000 to 50,000
below 10,000
Elevation
500m / 1640ft
250m / 820ft
100m / 328ft
sea level
196
8
10
16
16
NUNAVUT
MANITOBA
ONTARIO
QUÉBEC
UNITED STATES OF AMERICA
Hudson Bay
Hudson Strait
James Bay
Péninsule d' Ungava
Lake Superior
Lake Michigan
Lake Huron
Georgian Bay
Lake Erie
Lake Ontario
OTTAWA
Montréal
Québec
Toronto
Thunder Bay
Sault Ste. Marie
Sudbury
North Bay
Timmins
Kingston
Hamilton
London
Windsor
Kitchener
Sherbrooke
Akimiski Island
Belcher Islands
Mansel Island
Charles Island
Fort Severn
Fort Albany
Moosonee
Moose Factory
Kuujjuarapik
Chisasibi
Lac Mistassini
Réservoir Gouin
Lake Nipigon
Lake of the Woods
Rainy River
Kenora
Red Lake
Sandy Lake
Big Trout Lake
Attawapiskat
Hearst
Kapuskasing
Cochrane
Rouyn-Noranda
Val-d'Or
Chibougamau
Ivujivik
Salluit
Kangiqsujuaq
Puvirnituq
Inukjuak
Kangirsuk
Quaqtaq

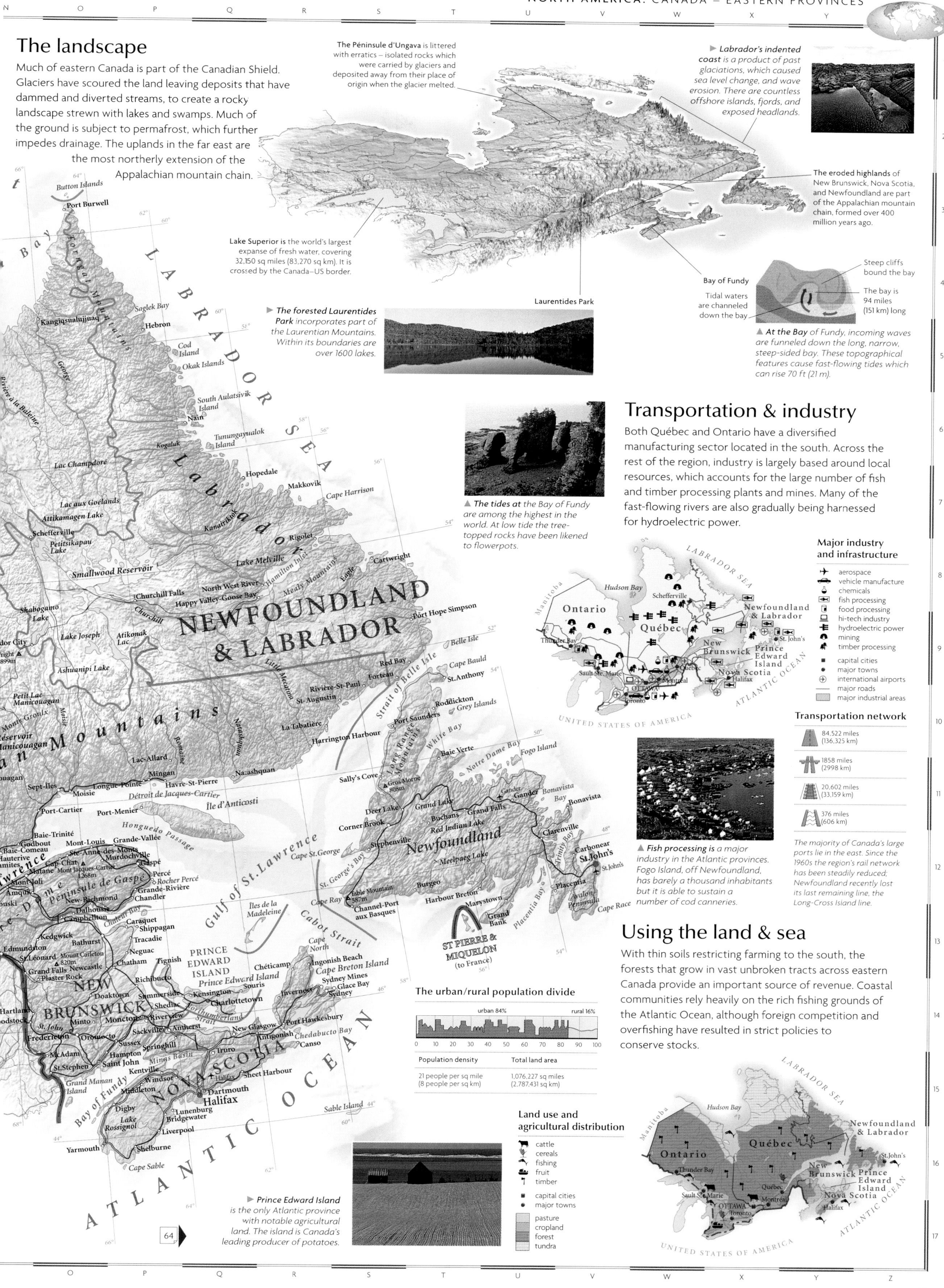
The landscape
Much of eastern Canada is part of the Canadian Shield. Glaciers have scoured the land leaving deposits that have dammed and diverted streams, to create a rocky landscape strewn with lakes and swamps. Much of the ground is subject to permafrost, which further impedes drainage. The uplands in the far east are the most northerly extension of the Appalachian mountain chain.
The Péninsule d'Ungava is littered with erratics – isolated rocks which were carried by glaciers and deposited away from their place of origin when the glacier melted.
Labrador's indented coast is a product of past glaciations, which caused sea level change, and wave erosion. There are countless offshore islands, fjords, and exposed headlands.
The eroded highlands of New Brunswick, Nova Scotia, and Newfoundland are part of the Appalachian mountain chain, formed over 400 million years ago.
Lake Superior is the world's largest expanse of fresh water, covering 32,150 sq miles (83,270 sq km). It is crossed by the Canada–US border.
Bay of Fundy
Laurentides Park
Steep cliffs bound the bay
The bay is 94 miles (151 km) long
Tidal waters are channeled down the bay
At the Bay of Fundy, incoming waves are funneled down the long, narrow, steep-sided bay. These topographical features cause fast-flowing tides which can rise 70 ft (21 m).
The forested Laurentides Park incorporates part of the Laurentian Mountains. Within its boundaries are over 1600 lakes.
The tides at the Bay of Fundy are among the highest in the world. At low tide the tree-topped rocks have been likened to flowerpots.
Transportation & industry
Both Québec and Ontario have a diversified manufacturing sector located in the south. Across the rest of the region, industry is largely based around local resources, which accounts for the large number of fish and timber processing plants and mines. Many of the fast-flowing rivers are also gradually being harnessed for hydroelectric power.
Major industry and infrastructure
aerospace
vehicle manufacture
chemicals
fish processing
food processing
hi-tech industry
hydroelectric power
mining
timber processing
capital cities
major towns
international airports
major roads
major industrial areas
Transportation network
84,522 miles (136,325 km)
1858 miles (2998 km)
20,602 miles (33,159 km)
376 miles (606 km)
The majority of Canada's large ports lie in the east. Since the 1960s the region's rail network has been steadily reduced; Newfoundland recently lost its last remaining line, the Long-Cross Island line.
Fish processing is a major industry in the Atlantic provinces. Fogo Island, off Newfoundland, has barely a thousand inhabitants but it is able to sustain a number of cod canneries.
Using the land & sea
With thin soils restricting farming to the south, the forests that grow in vast unbroken tracts across eastern Canada provide an important source of revenue. Coastal communities rely heavily on the rich fishing grounds of the Atlantic Ocean, although foreign competition and overfishing have resulted in strict policies to conserve stocks.
The urban/rural population divide
urban 84%
rural 16%
0 10 20 30 40 50 60 70 80 90 100
Population density
21 people per sq mile (8 people per sq km)
Total land area
1,076,227 sq miles (2,787,431 sq km)
Land use and agricultural distribution
cattle
cereals
fishing
fruit
timber
capital cities
major towns
pasture
cropland
forest
tundra
Prince Edward Island is the only Atlantic province with notable agricultural land. The island is Canada's leading producer of potatoes.
NEWFOUNDLAND & LABRADOR
LABRADOR SEA
Labrador
Gulf of St. Lawrence
NEW BRUNSWICK
NOVA SCOTIA
PRINCE EDWARD ISLAND
ATLANTIC OCEAN
ST PIERRE & MIQUELON (to France)
Newfoundland
Ontario
Québec
Hudson Bay
UNITED STATES OF AMERICA
64

Southeastern Canada

Southern Ontario, Southern Québec

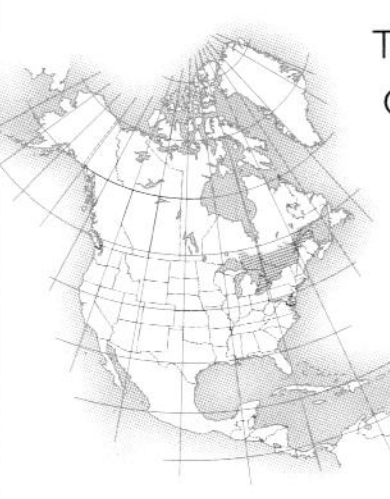

The southern parts of Québec and Ontario form the economic heart of Canada. The two provinces are divided by their language and culture; in Québec, French is the main language, whereas English is spoken in Ontario. Separatist sentiment in Québec has led to a provincial referendum on the question of a sovereignty association with Canada. The region contains Canada's capital, Ottawa and its two largest cities: Toronto, the center of commerce and Montréal, the cultural and administrative heart of French Canada.

▲ *The port at* Montréal *is situated on the St. Lawrence Seaway. A network of 16 locks allows oceangoing vessels access to routes once plied by fur-trappers and early settlers.*

Transportation & industry

The cities of southern Québec and Ontario, and their hinterlands, form the heart of Canadian manufacturing industry. Toronto is Canada's leading financial center, and Ontario's motor and aerospace industries have developed around the city. A major center for nickel mining lies to the north of Toronto. Most of Québec's industry is located in Montréal, the oldest port in North America. Chemicals, paper manufacture, and the construction of transportation equipment are leading industrial activities.

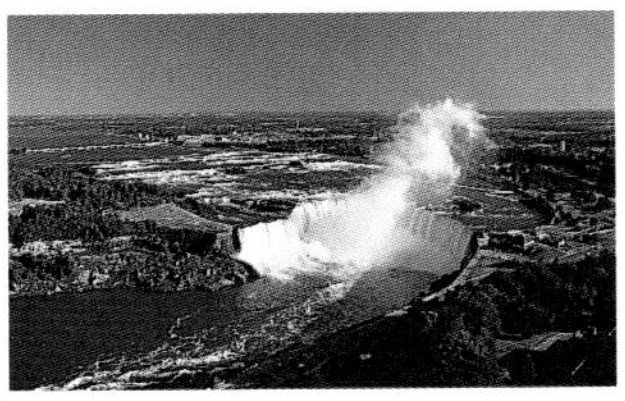

▶ **Niagara Falls lies** *on the border between Canada and the US. It comprises a system of two falls: American Falls, in New York, is separated from Horseshoe Falls in Ontario, by Goat Island. Horseshoe Falls, seen here, plunges 184 ft (56 m) and is 2500 ft (762 m) wide.*

Major industry and infrastructure

- car manufacture
- chemicals
- engineering
- finance
- food processing
- hi-tech industry
- mining
- iron & steel
- textiles
- paper industry
- timber processing
- capital cities
- major towns
- international airports
- major roads
- major industrial areas

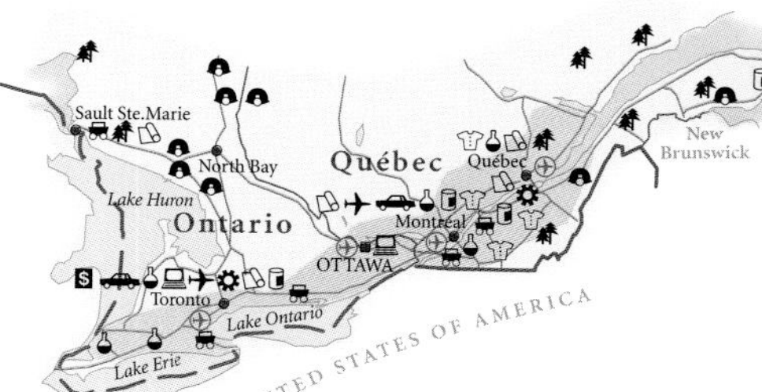
Sault Ste.Marie
North Bay
Québec
Québec
Lake Huron
Ontario
Montréal
OTTAWA
Toronto
Lake Ontario
Lake Erie
New Brunswick
UNITED STATES OF AMERICA

Transportation network

The opening of the St. Lawrence Seaway in 1959 finally allowed oceangoing ships (up to 24,000 tons [tonnes]) access to the interior of Canada, creating a vital trading route.

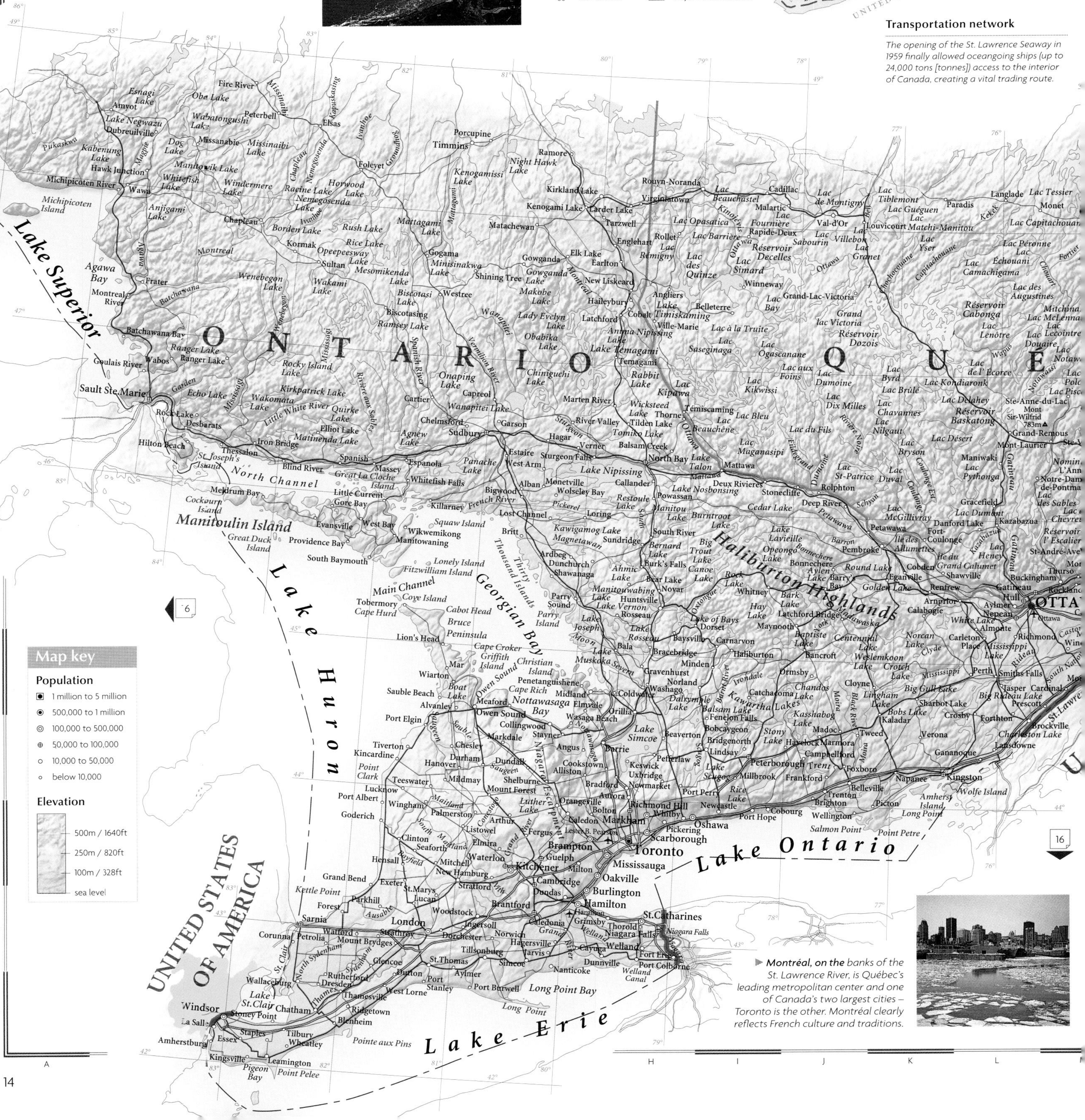

Map key

Population

- 1 million to 5 million
- 500,000 to 1 million
- 100,000 to 500,000
- 50,000 to 100,000
- 10,000 to 50,000
- below 10,000

Elevation

- 500m / 1640ft
- 250m / 820ft
- 100m / 328ft
- sea level

6

16

▶ **Montréal,** *on the banks of the St. Lawrence River, is Québec's leading metropolitan center and one of Canada's two largest cities – Toronto is the other. Montréal clearly reflects French culture and traditions.*

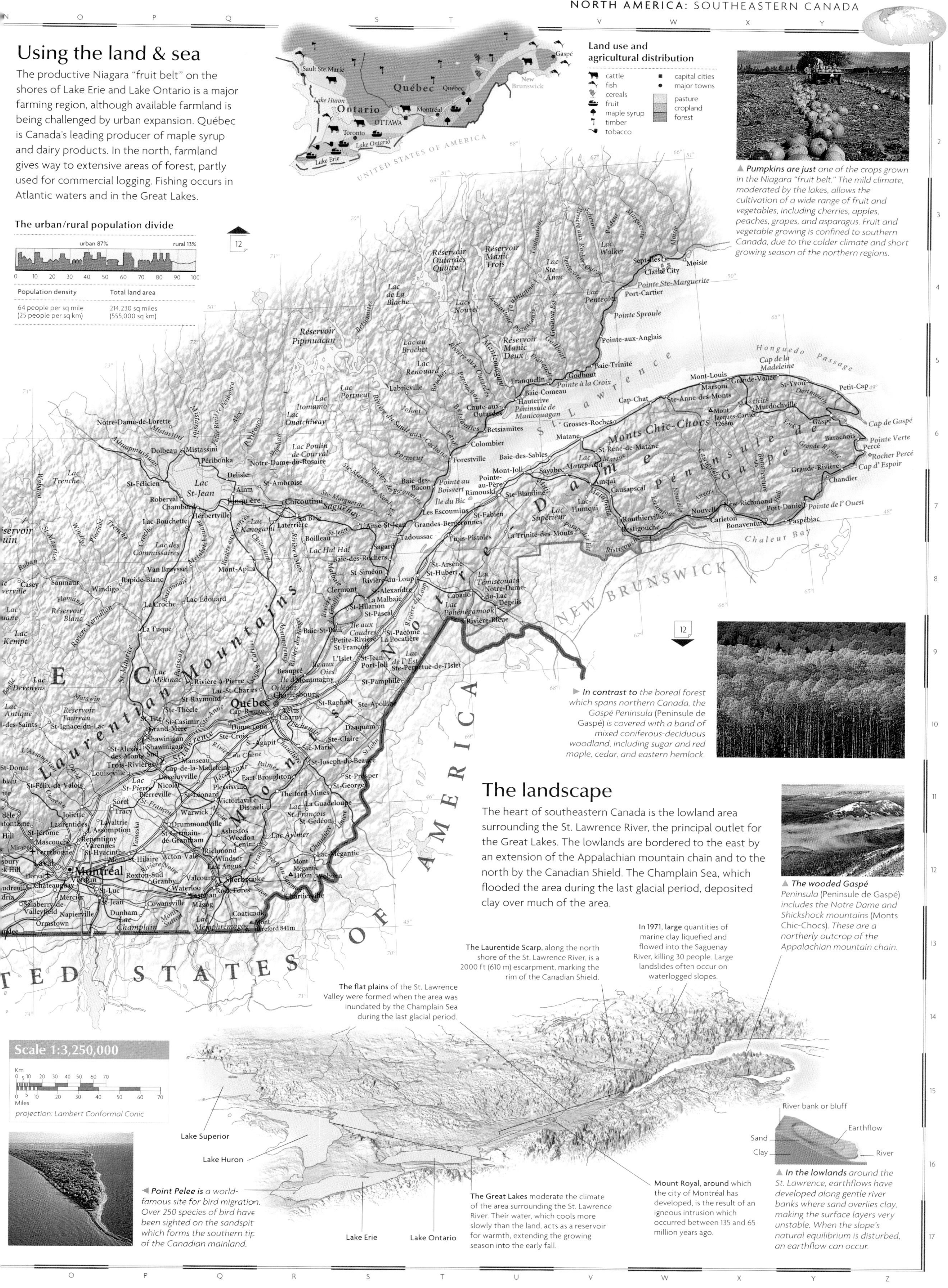

Land use and agricultural distribution
cattle
fish
cereals
fruit
maple syrup
timber
tobacco
capital cities
major towns
pasture
cropland
forest
Québec
Ontario
OTTAWA
Montréal
Toronto
Sault Ste. Marie
Lake Huron
Lake Ontario
Lake Erie
New Brunswick
Gaspé
UNITED STATES OF AMERICA
Laurentian Mountains
Monts Notre Dame
Monts Chic-Chocs
Péninsule de Gaspé
St Lawrence
NEW BRUNSWICK
UNITED STATES OF AMERICA
Honguedo Passage
Chaleur Bay
Lac St-Jean
Québec
Montréal
Scale 1:3,250,000
Km
Miles
projection: Lambert Conformal Conic
River bank or bluff
Earthflow
Sand
Clay
River
Lake Superior
Lake Huron
Lake Erie
Lake Ontario

Using the land & sea

The productive Niagara "fruit belt" on the shores of Lake Erie and Lake Ontario is a major farming region, although available farmland is being challenged by urban expansion. Québec is Canada's leading producer of maple syrup and dairy products. In the north, farmland gives way to extensive areas of forest, partly used for commercial logging. Fishing occurs in Atlantic waters and in the Great Lakes.

The urban/rural population divide

urban 87% | rural 13%

Population density	Total land area
64 people per sq mile (25 people per sq km)	214,230 sq miles (555,000 sq km)

▲ *Pumpkins are just one of the crops grown in the Niagara "fruit belt." The mild climate, moderated by the lakes, allows the cultivation of a wide range of fruit and vegetables, including cherries, apples, peaches, grapes, and asparagus. Fruit and vegetable growing is confined to southern Canada, due to the colder climate and short growing season of the northern regions.*

▶ *In contrast to the boreal forest which spans northern Canada, the Gaspé Peninsula (Peninsule de Gaspé) is covered with a band of mixed coniferous-deciduous woodland, including sugar and red maple, cedar, and eastern hemlock.*

The landscape

The heart of southeastern Canada is the lowland area surrounding the St. Lawrence River, the principal outlet for the Great Lakes. The lowlands are bordered to the east by an extension of the Appalachian mountain chain and to the north by the Canadian Shield. The Champlain Sea, which flooded the area during the last glacial period, deposited clay over much of the area.

▲ *The wooded Gaspé Peninsula (Peninsule de Gaspé) includes the Notre Dame and Shickshock mountains (Monts Chic-Chocs). These are a northerly outcrop of the Appalachian mountain chain.*

The Laurentide Scarp, along the north shore of the St. Lawrence River, is a 2000 ft (610 m) escarpment, marking the rim of the Canadian Shield.

In 1971, large quantities of marine clay liquefied and flowed into the Saguenay River, killing 30 people. Large landslides often occur on waterlogged slopes.

The flat plains of the St. Lawrence Valley were formed when the area was inundated by the Champlain Sea during the last glacial period.

◀ *Point Pelee is a world-famous site for bird migration. Over 250 species of bird have been sighted on the sandspit which forms the southern tip of the Canadian mainland.*

The Great Lakes moderate the climate of the area surrounding the St. Lawrence River. Their water, which cools more slowly than the land, acts as a reservoir for warmth, extending the growing season into the early fall.

Mount Royal, around which the city of Montréal has developed, is the result of an igneous intrusion which occurred between 135 and 65 million years ago.

▲ *In the lowlands around the St. Lawrence, earthflows have developed along gentle river banks where sand overlies clay, making the surface layers very unstable. When the slope's natural equilibrium is disturbed, an earthflow can occur.*

The United States of America

COTERMINOUS US (FOR ALASKA AND HAWAII SEE PAGES 38-39)

The US's progression from frontier territory to economic and political superpower has taken less than 200 years. The 48 coterminous states, along with the outlying states of Alaska and Hawaii, are part of a federal union, held together by the guiding principles of the US Constitution, which embodies the ideals of democracy and liberty for all. Abundant fertile land and a rich resource base fueled and sustained US economic development. With the spread of agriculture and the growth of trade and industry came the need for a larger workforce, which was supplied by millions of immigrants, many seeking an escape from poverty and political or religious persecution. Immigration continues today, particularly from Central America and Asia.

▲ ***Washington D.C. was*** *established as the nation's capital in 1790. It is home to the sea of national government, on Capitol Hill, as well as the President's official residence, the White House.*

▶ ***The clear waters*** *of Niaga Falls cascade 190 ft (58 m) into th gorge below. It is one of Americ most famous spectacles and leading tourist attraction. The fa are slowly receding and the gor may one day stretch from La Ontario to Lake Er*

▲ ***Mount Rainier is*** *a dormant volcano in the Cascade Range, Washington. This 14,090 ft (4392 m) peak is flanked by the most extensive glacier outside Alaska.*

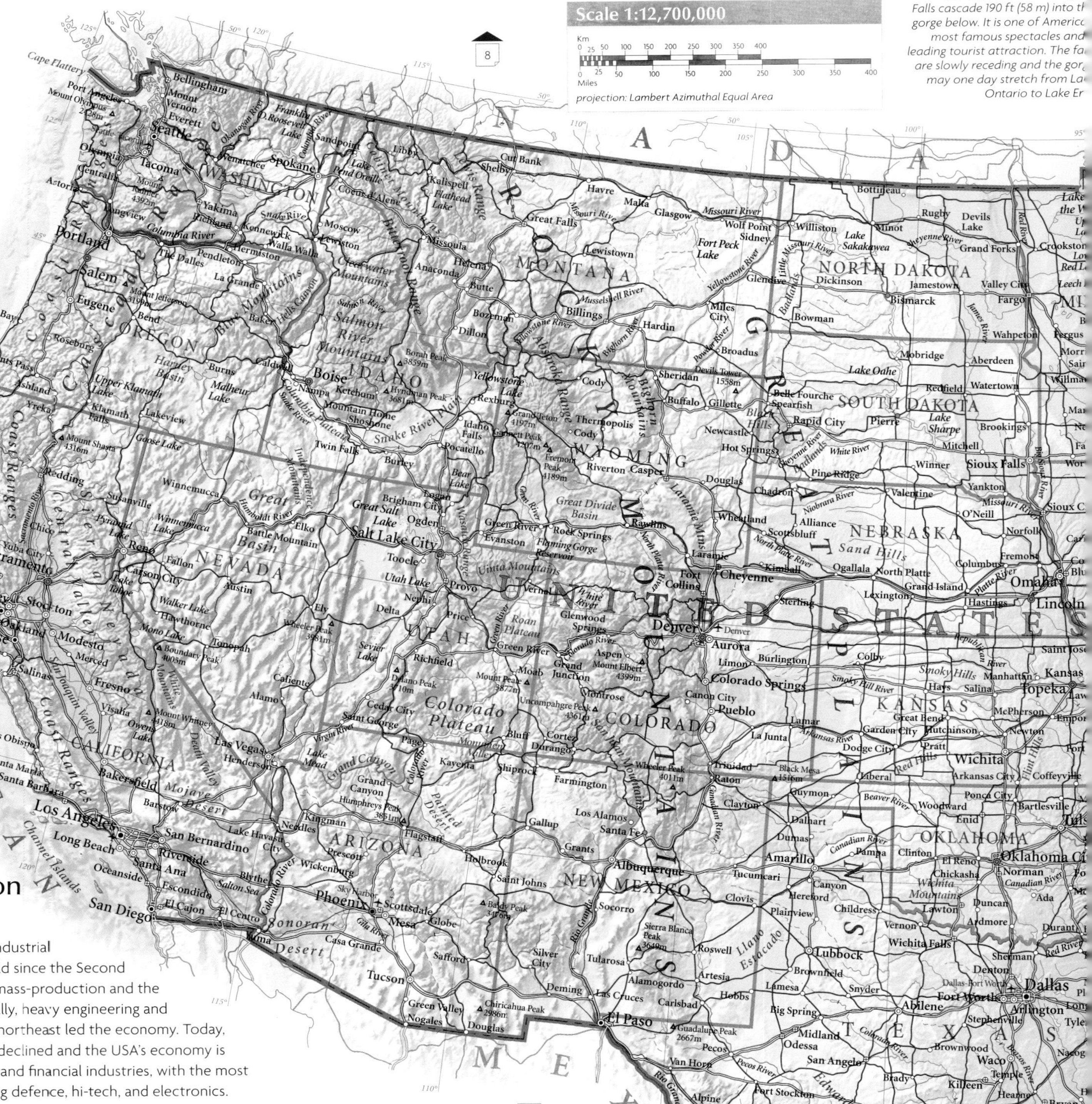

Scale 1:12,700,000

Km 0 25 50 100 150 200 250 300 350 400

Miles 0 25 50 100 150 200 250 300 350 400

projection: Lambert Azimuthal Equal Area

8

192

40

Transportation & industry

The USA has been the industrial powerhouse of the world since the Second World War, pioneering mass-production and the consumer lifestyle. Initially, heavy engineering and manufacturing in the northeast led the economy. Today, heavy industry has declined and the USA's economy is driven by service and financial industries, with the most important being defence, hi-tech, and electronics.

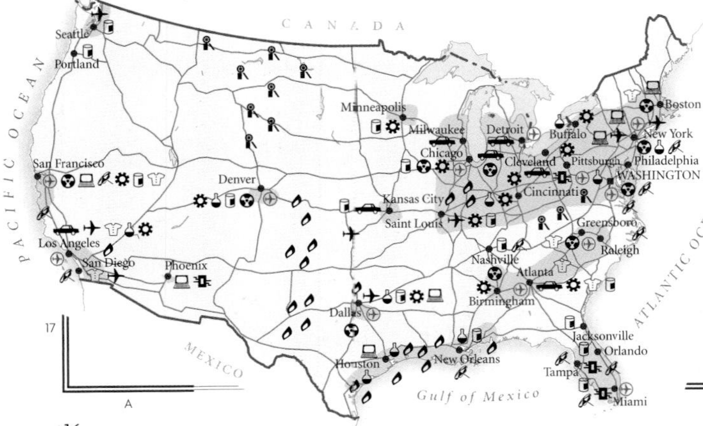

Transportation network

3,875,040 miles (6,240,000 km)

52,388 miles (84,361 km)

148,308 miles (235,238 km)

25,467 miles (41,009 km)

Transportation in the US is dominated by the car which, with the extensive Interstate Highway system, allows great personal mobility. Today, internal air flights between major cities provide the most rapid cross-country travel.

Major industry and infrastructure

- aerospace
- car manufacture
- chemicals
- coal
- electronics
- engineering
- food processing
- hi-tech industry
- oil & gas
- research & development
- textiles
- tourism
- capital cities
- major towns
- international airports
- major roads
- major industrial areas

The landscape

The high, rugged mountain ranges of the west are about 80 million years old, geologically young compared to the old, eroded, Appalachian mountain chain, which dates from when North America and Europe were joined together as part of the supercontinent Pangaea, 400 million years ago. In contrast, the Great Plains and Mississippi Basin have a low relief and fertile soils.

Mount Rainier

Great Plains

The Great Lakes

Niagara Falls

Death Valley, California, 282 ft (86 m) below sea level, is the lowest point in the western hemisphere and one of the hottest places on Earth. Temperatures of 190° F (88° C) have been recorded here.

Monument Valley's striking sandstone spires and pillars *(buttes)* have been formed by the action of wind, water, heat, and cold.

The deep gullies of South Dakota's badlands are created by periodic, torrential rainfall, which erodes the soft soils and rocks. Their form has been greatly affected by changes in land use.

Most of the US is drained by the great Mississippi River system. At its mouth, where levées are breached, floodwaters are carried to the swamps through a series of channels. This region is known as the bayou.

Barrier beaches, bars and spits are typical of the Atlantic coast. These sand formations around Cape Hatteras stretch along the coast for 200 miles (320 km).

The Great Smoky Mountains, part of the ancient Appalachian mountain chain, formed a natural barrier to early settlers attempting to penetrate the country's interior.

The Everglades are a vast area of sawgrass swamp covering 4000 sq miles (10,300 sq km) of southern Florida.

◄ ***Devils Tower,** in Wyoming is a 1280 ft (390 m) intrusion of basalt rock, which cooled to form octagonal pillars. In 1906 it became the first US National Monument.*

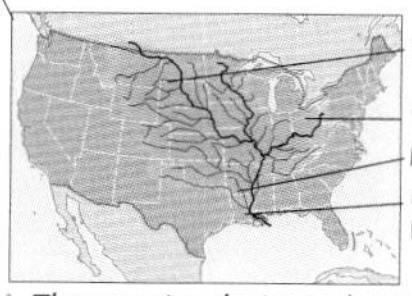

Missouri River

Ohio River

Mississippi River

Mississippi Delta

▲ ***The massive drainage** basin of the Mississippi covers 1,250,000 sq miles (3,200,000 sq km). It includes all areas drained by the Mississippi and its chief tributaries, the Missouri and Ohio Rivers, and drains the entire region from the Appalachians to the Rockies.*

Map key

Population

- above 5 million
- 1 million to 5 million
- 500,000 to 1 million
- 100,000 to 500,000
- 50,000 to 100,000
- 10,000 to 50,000
- below 10,000

Elevation

- 4000m / 13,124ft
- 3000m / 9843ft
- 2000m / 6562ft
- 1000m / 3281ft
- 500m / 1640ft
- 250m / 820ft
- 100m / 328ft
- sea level

8

64

64

Using the land and sea

Over half of the US is used for agriculture, typified by the large cereal grain farms and cattle ranches of the Great Plains and Midwest prairie regions. Although wheat and corn are still primary crops, a diverse range of fruits and vegetables are grown in the fertile areas, particularly near the east and west coasts. Despite the abundance of cultivable land, inadequate soil management has resulted in a third of the topsoil being lost through wind and water erosion.

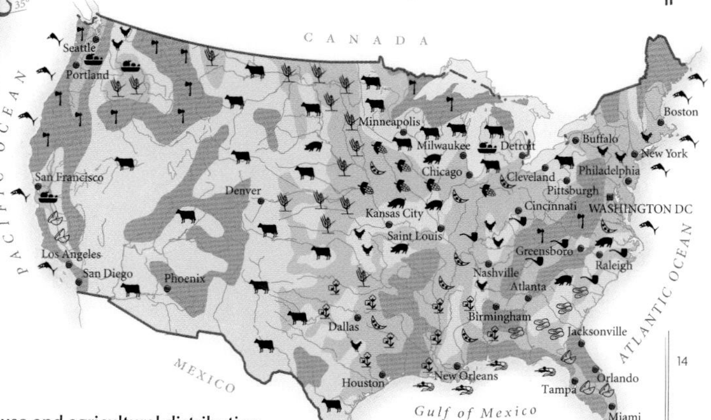

Land use and agricultural distribution

- cattle
- pigs
- poultry
- citrus fruits
- cotton
- fishing
- fruit
- corn
- peanuts
- shellfish
- soybeans
- timber
- tobacco
- wheat

- capital cities
- major towns

- pasture
- cropland
- forest
- wetland
- desert
- mountain region

The urban/rural population divide

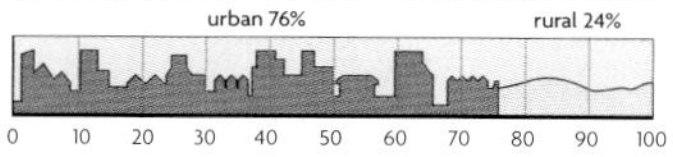

urban 76% | rural 24%

0 10 20 30 40 50 60 70 80 90 100

Population density	Total land area
98 people per sq mile (38 people per sq km)	2,959,045 sq miles (7,663,631 sq km)

► *Fakahatchee Strand is part of the extensive subtropical swamps in the Florida Everglades. The swamps support a wide variety of animal life, including many rare birds, fish, alligators, and crocodiles.*

◄ ***Farming** on the Great Plains and in the Midwest is characterized by large-scale, mechanized wheat farms.*

USA: NORTHEASTERN STATES

Connecticut, Maine, Massachusetts, New Hampshire, New Jersey, New York, Pennsylvania, Rhode Island, Vermont

The indented coast and vast woodlands of the northeastern states were the original core area for European expansion. The rustic character of New England prevails after nearly four centuries, while the great cities of the Atlantic seaboard have formed an almost continuous urban region. Over 20 million immigrants entered New York from 1855 to 1924 and the northeast became the industrial center of the US. After the decline of mining and heavy manufacturing, economic dynamism has been restored with the growth of hi-tech and service industries.

▲ *Chelsea in Vermont, surrounded by trees in their fall foliage. Tourism and agriculture dominate the economy of this self-consciously rural state, where no town exceeds 30,000 people.*

Map key

Population

- above 5 million
- 1 million to 5 million
- 500,000 to 1 million
- 100,000 to 500,000
- 50,000 to 100,000
- 10,000 to 50,000
- below 10,000

Elevation

- 1000m / 3281ft
- 500m / 1640ft
- 250m / 820ft
- 100m / 328ft
- sea level

Transportation network

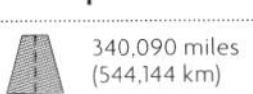

340,090 miles (544,144 km)	4813 miles (7700 km)
12,872 miles (20,592 km)	2108 miles (3389 km)

New York's commercial success is tied historically to its transportation connections. The Erie Canal, completed in 1825, opened up the Great Lakes and the interior to New York's markets and carried a stream of immigrants into the Midwest.

Transportation & industry

The principal seaboard cities grew up on trade and manufacturing. They are now global centers of commerce and corporate administration, dominating the regional economy. Research and development facilities support an expanding electronics and communications sector throughout the region. Pharmaceutical and chemical industries are important in New Jersey and Pennsylvania.

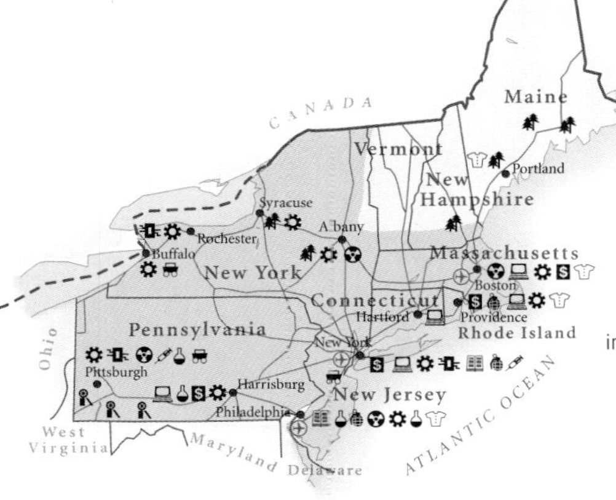
CANADA
Maine
Portland
Vermont
New Hampshire
Syracuse
Albany
Rochester
Buffalo
New York
Massachusetts
Boston
Connecticut
Hartford
Providence
Rhode Island
Pennsylvania
Ohio
Pittsburgh
Harrisburg
New York
New Jersey
Philadelphia
West Virginia
Maryland
Delaware
ATLANTIC OCEAN

Major industry and infrastructure

- chemicals
- coal
- defense
- electronics
- engineering
- finance
- hi-tech industry
- iron & steel
- pharmaceuticals
- printing & publishing
- research & development
- textiles
- timber processing
- major towns
- international airports
- major roads
- major industrial area

CANADA
Lake Ontario
Saint Lawrence River
Thousand Islands
Rochester
Syracuse
Buffalo
Niagara Falls
Adirondack Mountains
Lake Champlain
Lake Erie

NEW YORK
Finger Lakes
Catskill Mountains
Albany
Binghamton
Erie
Appalachian Mountains

PENNSYLVANIA
Pittsburgh
Harrisburg
Philadelphia
New York
NEW JERSEY
Trenton
WEST VIRGINIA
MARYLAND
DELAWARE
ATLANTIC OCEAN

14
32
64
20
22

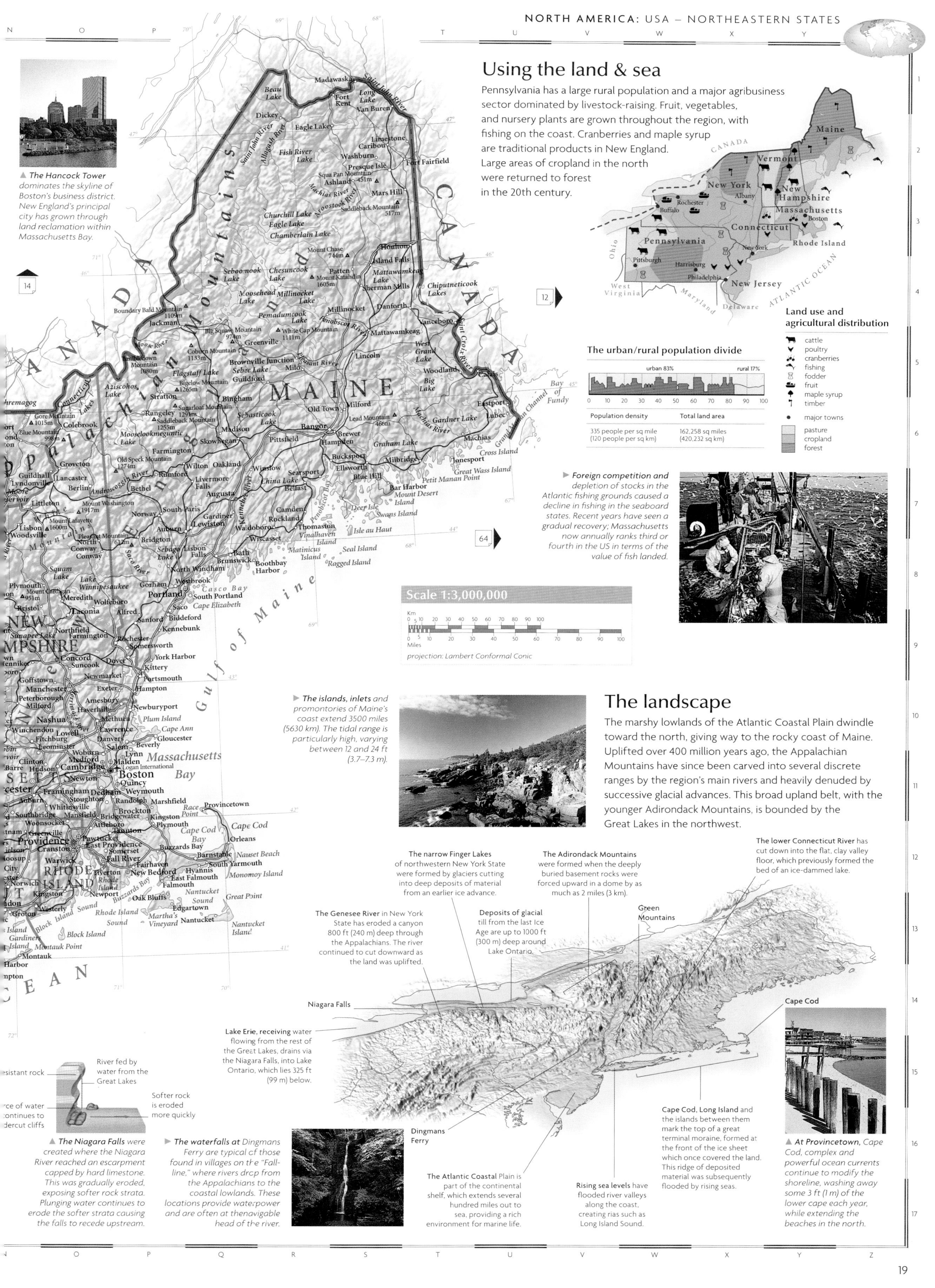

MAINE
CANADA
Gulf of Maine
Massachusetts Bay
Cape Cod Bay
Bay of Fundy
Scale 1:3,000,000
projection: Lambert Conformal Conic
The urban/rural population divide
urban 83%
rural 17%
Population density
335 people per sq mile (120 people per sq km)
Total land area
162,258 sq miles (420,232 sq km)
Land use and agricultural distribution
cattle
poultry
cranberries
fishing
fodder
fruit
maple syrup
timber
major towns
pasture
cropland
forest
Niagara Falls
Green Mountains
Cape Cod
Dingmans Ferry
River fed by water from the Great Lakes
Softer rock is eroded more quickly

▲ **The Hancock Tower** dominates the skyline of Boston's business district. New England's principal city has grown through land reclamation within Massachusetts Bay.

Using the land & sea

Pennsylvania has a large rural population and a major agribusiness sector dominated by livestock-raising. Fruit, vegetables, and nursery plants are grown throughout the region, with fishing on the coast. Cranberries and maple syrup are traditional products in New England. Large areas of cropland in the north were returned to forest in the 20th century.

▶ **Foreign competition and** depletion of stocks in the Atlantic fishing grounds caused a decline in fishing in the seaboard states. Recent years have seen a gradual recovery; Massachusetts now annually ranks third or fourth in the US in terms of the value of fish landed.

▶ **The islands, inlets** and promontories of Maine's coast extend 3500 miles (5630 km). The tidal range is particularly high, varying between 12 and 24 ft (3.7–7.3 m).

The landscape

The marshy lowlands of the Atlantic Coastal Plain dwindle toward the north, giving way to the rocky coast of Maine. Uplifted over 400 million years ago, the Appalachian Mountains have since been carved into several discrete ranges by the region's main rivers and heavily denuded by successive glacial advances. This broad upland belt, with the younger Adirondack Mountains, is bounded by the Great Lakes in the northwest.

The narrow Finger Lakes of northwestern New York State were formed by glaciers cutting into deep deposits of material from an earlier ice advance.

The Adirondack Mountains were formed when the deeply buried basement rocks were forced upward in a dome by as much as 2 miles (3 km).

The lower Connecticut River has cut down into the flat, clay valley floor, which previously formed the bed of an ice-dammed lake.

The Genesee River in New York State has eroded a canyon 800 ft (240 m) deep through the Appalachians. The river continued to cut downward as the land was uplifted.

Deposits of glacial till from the last Ice Age are up to 1000 ft (300 m) deep around Lake Ontario.

Lake Erie, receiving water flowing from the rest of the Great Lakes, drains via the Niagara Falls, into Lake Ontario, which lies 325 ft (99 m) below.

Cape Cod, Long Island and the islands between them mark the top of a great terminal moraine, formed at the front of the ice sheet which once covered the land. This ridge of deposited material was subsequently flooded by rising seas.

The Atlantic Coastal Plain is part of the continental shelf, which extends several hundred miles out to sea, providing a rich environment for marine life.

Rising sea levels have flooded river valleys along the coast, creating rias such as Long Island Sound.

▲ **The Niagara Falls** were created where the Niagara River reached an escarpment capped by hard limestone. This was gradually eroded, exposing softer rock strata. Plunging water continues to erode the softer strata causing the falls to recede upstream.

▶ **The waterfalls at** Dingmans Ferry are typical of those found in villages on the "Fall-line," where rivers drop from the Appalachians to the coastal lowlands. These locations provide waterpower and are often at the navigable head of the river.

▲ **At Provincetown,** Cape Cod, complex and powerful ocean currents continue to modify the shoreline, washing away some 3 ft (1 m) of the lower cape each year, while extending the beaches in the north.

USA: MID-EASTERN STATES

Delaware, District of Columbia, Kentucky, Maryland, North Carolina, South Carolina, Tennessee, Virginia, West Virginia

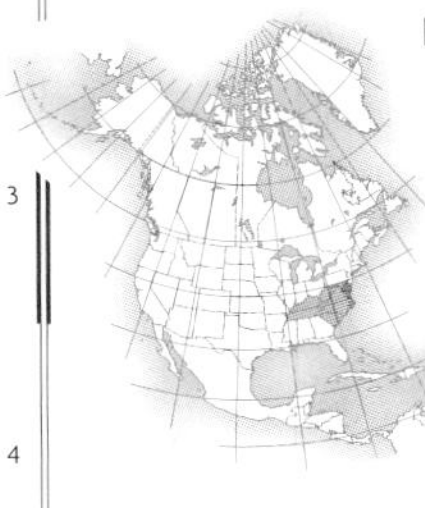

Key events in American history took place in this diverse region, which became the front line between the North and the South during the Civil War of the 1860s. Strong regional contrasts exist between the fertile coastal plains, the isolated upcountry of the Appalachian Mountains, and the cotton-growing areas of the Mississippi lowlands to the west. While coal mining, a traditional industry in the Appalachians, has declined in recent years leaving much rural poverty, service industries elsewhere have increased, especially in Washington DC, the nation's capital.

Map key

Population

- 500,000 to 1 million
- 100,000 to 500,000
- 50,000 to 100,000
- 10,000 to 50,000
- below 10,000

Elevation

- 6000m / 19,686ft
- 4000m / 13,124ft
- 3000m / 9843ft
- 2000m / 6562ft
- 1000m / 3281ft
- 500m / 1640ft
- 250m / 820ft
- 100m / 328ft
- sea level

Scale 1:3,250,000

projection: Lambert Conformal Conic

▲ *The Bluegrass region of Kentucky centers on the town of Lexington. This exceptionally fertile rolling plain is well known for its thoroughbred horse-breeding ranches.*

Transportation & industry

In the urbanized northeast, manufacturing remains important, alongside a burgeoning service sector. North Carolina is a major center for industrial research and development. Traditional industries include Tennessee whiskey and textiles in South Carolina. The decline of open-pit coal mining in the Appalachians has been hastened by environmental controls, although adventure-tourism is a flourishing new industry.

Major industry and infrastructure

- adventure-tourism
- car manufacture
- coal
- electronics
- engineering
- finance
- food processing
- hi-tech industry
- mining
- research & development
- textiles
- capital cities
- major towns
- international airports
- major roads
- major industrial areas

Transportation network

452,218 miles (723,548 km)	5737 miles (8267 km)
18,336 miles (29,503 km)	4404 miles (7081 km)

Tennessee's rivers are part of an important inland bulk transportation network. Memphis connects with New Orleans in the south, and with cities as distant as Minneapolis, Sioux City, Chicago, and Pittsburgh, via the Mississippi and its tributaries.

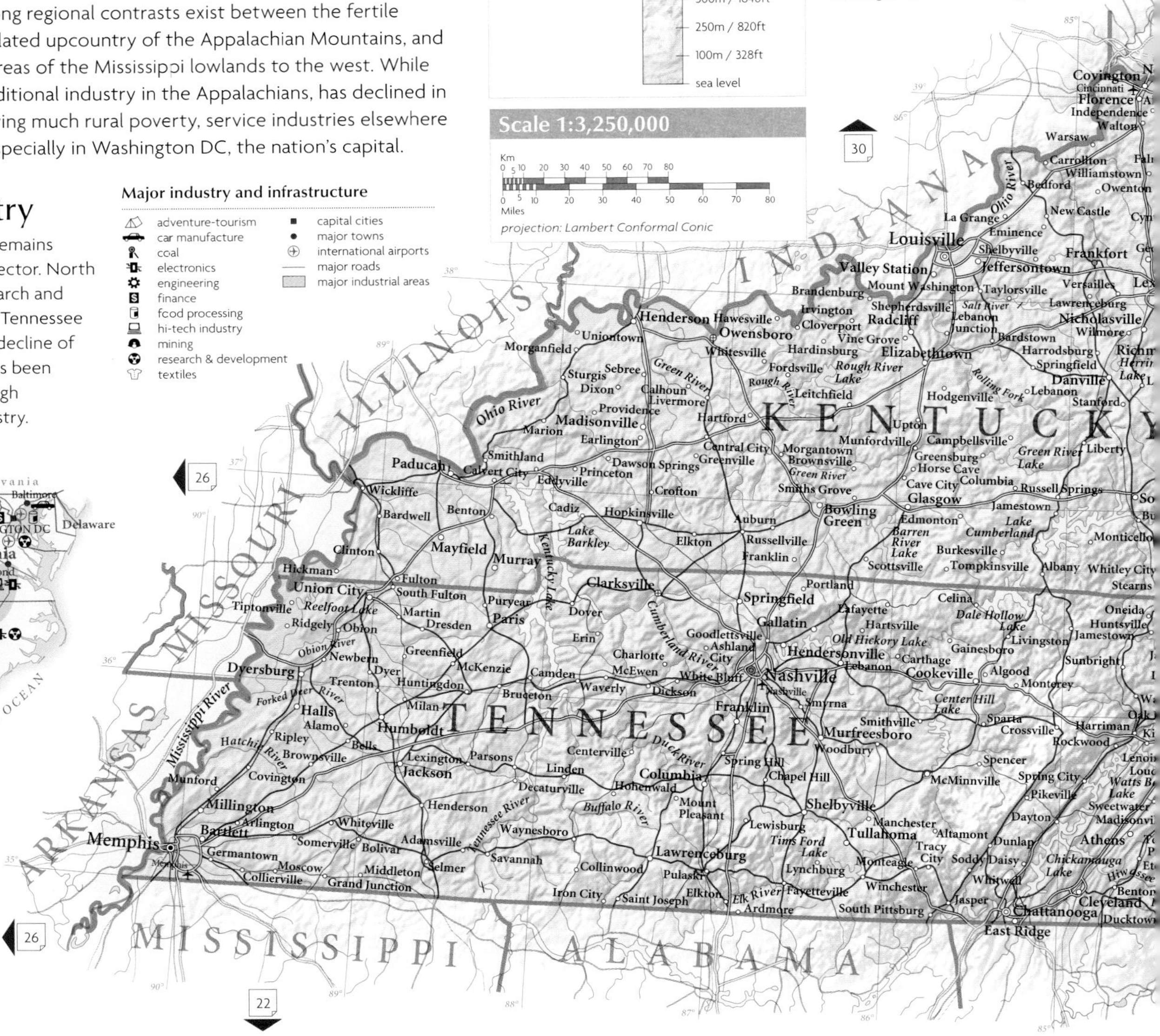

The landscape

The eastern tributaries of the Mississippi drain the interior lowlands. The Cumberland Plateau and the parallel ranges of the Appalachians have been successively uplifted and eroded over time, with the eastern side reduced to a series of foothills known as the Piedmont. The broad coastal plain gradually falls away into salt marshes, lagoons, and offshore bars, broken by flooded estuaries along the shores of the Atlantic.

Natural Bridge in eastern Kentucky is an arch 78 ft (26 m) long and 65 ft (20 m) high. It has been shaped from resistant sandstone by gradual weathering processes, which removed the softer rock lying underneath.

The Allegheny Mountains form the northwestern edge of the Appalachian mountain chain. Continuous folding has formed rich seams of bituminous coal.

◀ *Farmland on the eastern shores of Chesapeake Bay is sustained by artificial drainage. The area also provides refuge for a variety of waterfowl.*

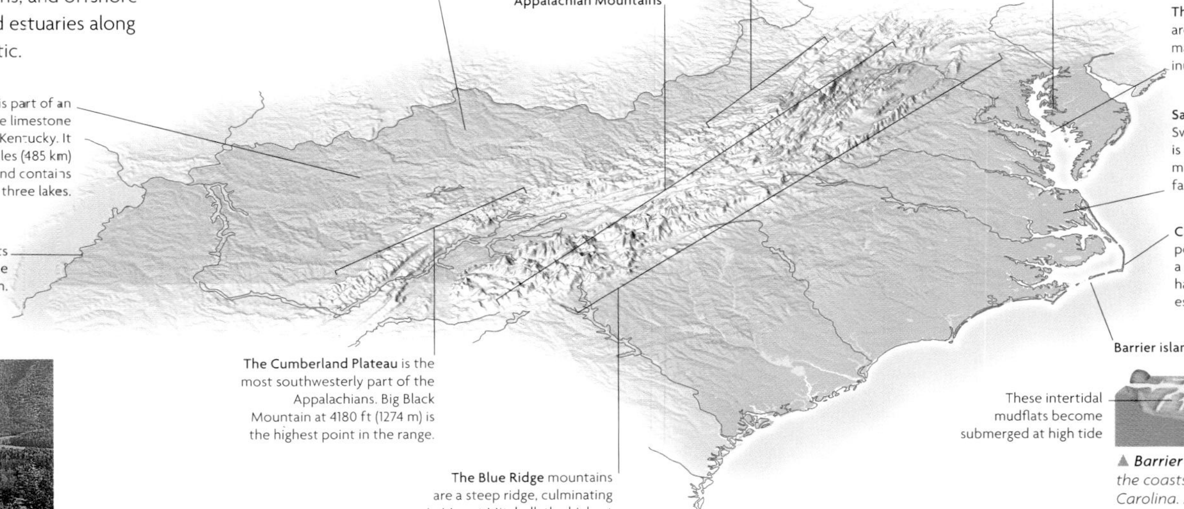

Appalachian Mountains

The many inlets of Chesapeake Bay are the flooded tributaries of the main river valley, which have been inundated by rising sea levels.

The Mammoth Cave is part of an extensive cave system in the limestone region of southwestern Kentucky. It stretches for over 300 miles (485 km) on five different levels and contains three rivers and three lakes.

Salt marshes such as Great Dismal Swamp, develop where the coast is sheltered. Vast areas of such marshland have been reclaimed for farmland and settlement.

The Mississippi River and its tributary the Ohio River form the western border of the region.

Cape Hatteras is the easternmost point of an offshore barrier island, a wave-deposited sand-bar which has become permanent, establishing its own vegetation.

The Cumberland Plateau is the most southwesterly part of the Appalachians. Big Black Mountain at 4180 ft (1274 m) is the highest point in the range.

Barrier islands

These intertidal mudflats become submerged at high tide

Tidal inlet

Barrier island

The Blue Ridge mountains are a steep ridge, culminating in Mount Mitchell, the highest point in the Appalachians, at 6684 ft (2037 m).

◀ *The Great Smoky Mountains form the western escarpment of the Appalachians. The region is heavily forested, with over 130 species of tree.*

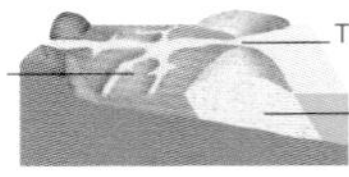

▲ *Barrier islands are common along the coasts of North and South Carolina. As sea levels rise, wave action builds up ridges of sand and pebbles parallel to the coast, separated by lagoons or intertidal mud flats, which are flooded at high tide.*

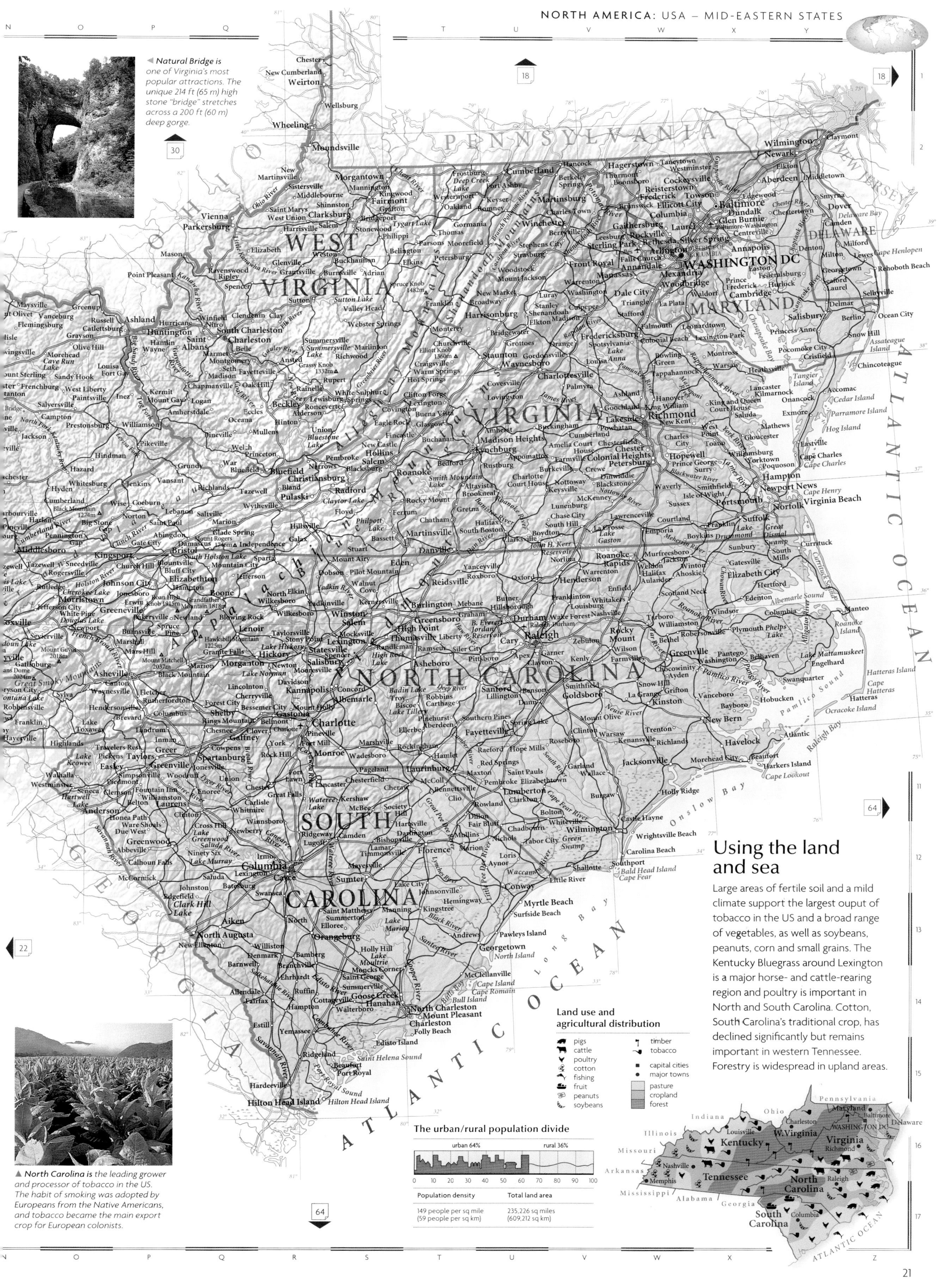
PENNSYLVANIA
OHIO
WEST VIRGINIA
VIRGINIA
MARYLAND
DELAWARE
NEW JERSEY
WASHINGTON DC
NORTH CAROLINA
SOUTH CAROLINA
GEORGIA
ATLANTIC OCEAN
Land use and agricultural distribution
pigs
cattle
poultry
cotton
fishing
fruit
peanuts
soybeans
timber
tobacco
capital cities
major towns
pasture
cropland
forest
The urban/rural population divide
urban 64%
rural 36%
0 10 20 30 40 50 60 70 80 90 100
Population density
149 people per sq mile
(59 people per sq km)
Total land area
235,226 sq miles
(609,212 sq km)

◀ *Natural Bridge is one of Virginia's most popular attractions. The unique 214 ft (65 m) high stone "bridge" stretches across a 200 ft (60 m) deep gorge.*

▲ *North Carolina is the leading grower and processor of tobacco in the US. The habit of smoking was adopted by Europeans from the Native Americans, and tobacco became the main export crop for European colonists.*

Using the land and sea

Large areas of fertile soil and a mild climate support the largest ouput of tobacco in the US and a broad range of vegetables, as well as soybeans, peanuts, corn and small grains. The Kentucky Bluegrass around Lexington is a major horse- and cattle-rearing region and poultry is important in North and South Carolina. Cotton, South Carolina's traditional crop, has declined significantly but remains important in western Tennessee. Forestry is widespread in upland areas.

USA: SOUTHERN STATES

Alabama, Florida, Georgia, Louisiana, Mississippi

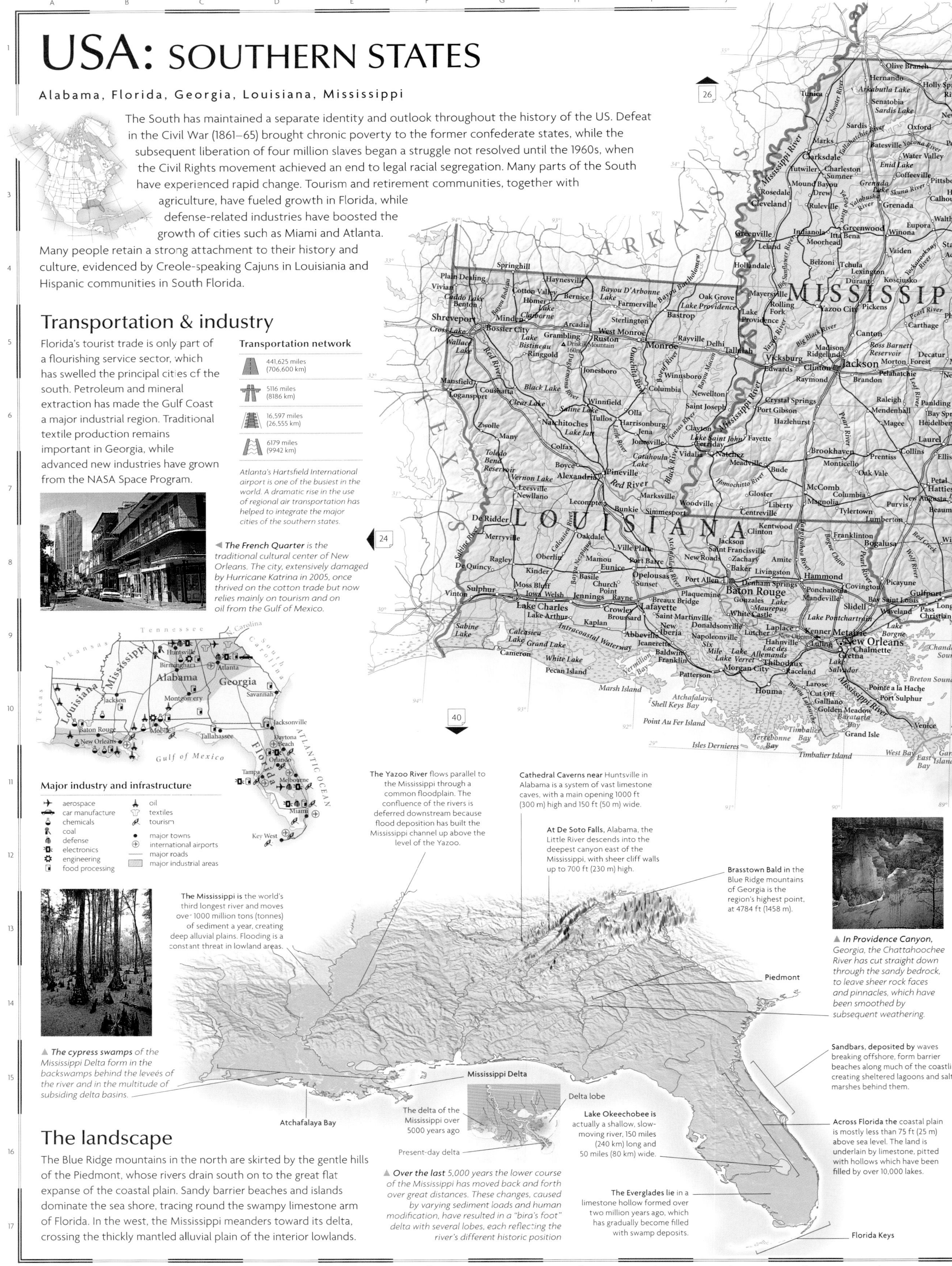

The South has maintained a separate identity and outlook throughout the history of the US. Defeat in the Civil War (1861–65) brought chronic poverty to the former confederate states, while the subsequent liberation of four million slaves began a struggle not resolved until the 1960s, when the Civil Rights movement achieved an end to legal racial segregation. Many parts of the South have experienced rapid change. Tourism and retirement communities, together with agriculture, have fueled growth in Florida, while defense-related industries have boosted the growth of cities such as Miami and Atlanta. Many people retain a strong attachment to their history and culture, evidenced by Creole-speaking Cajuns in Louisiana and Hispanic communities in South Florida.

26

24

40

Transportation & industry

Florida's tourist trade is only part of a flourishing service sector, which has swelled the principal cities of the south. Petroleum and mineral extraction has made the Gulf Coast a major industrial region. Traditional textile production remains important in Georgia, while advanced new industries have grown from the NASA Space Program.

Transportation network

- 441,625 miles (706,600 km)
- 5116 miles (8186 km)
- 16,597 miles (26,555 km)
- 6179 miles (9942 km)

Atlanta's Hartsfield International airport is one of the busiest in the world. A dramatic rise in the use of regional air transportation has helped to integrate the major cities of the southern states.

◀ ***The French Quarter** is the traditional cultural center of New Orleans. The city, extensively damaged by Hurricane Katrina in 2005, once thrived on the cotton trade but now relies mainly on tourism and on oil from the Gulf of Mexico.*

Major industry and infrastructure

- aerospace
- car manufacture
- chemicals
- coal
- defense
- electronics
- engineering
- food processing
- oil
- textiles
- tourism
- major towns
- international airports
- major roads
- major industrial areas

The Yazoo River flows parallel to the Mississippi through a common floodplain. The confluence of the rivers is deferred downstream because flood deposition has built the Mississippi channel up above the level of the Yazoo.

Cathedral Caverns near Huntsville in Alabama is a system of vast limestone caves, with a main opening 1000 ft (300 m) high and 150 ft (50 m) wide.

At De Soto Falls, Alabama, the Little River descends into the deepest canyon east of the Mississippi, with sheer cliff walls up to 700 ft (230 m) high.

Brasstown Bald in the Blue Ridge mountains of Georgia is the region's highest point, at 4784 ft (1458 m).

▲ ***In Providence Canyon**, Georgia, the Chattahoochee River has cut straight down through the sandy bedrock, to leave sheer rock faces and pinnacles, which have been smoothed by subsequent weathering.*

The Mississippi is the world's third longest river and moves over 1000 million tons (tonnes) of sediment a year, creating deep alluvial plains. Flooding is a constant threat in lowland areas.

Piedmont

▲ ***The cypress swamps** of the Mississippi Delta form in the backswamps behind the levees of the river and in the multitude of subsiding delta basins.*

Sandbars, deposited by waves breaking offshore, form barrier beaches along much of the coastline, creating sheltered lagoons and salt marshes behind them.

Mississippi Delta

Delta lobe

Atchafalaya Bay

The delta of the Mississippi over 5000 years ago

Present-day delta

Lake Okeechobee is actually a shallow, slow-moving river, 150 miles (240 km) long and 50 miles (80 km) wide.

Across Florida the coastal plain is mostly less than 75 ft (25 m) above sea level. The land is underlain by limestone, pitted with hollows which have been filled by over 10,000 lakes.

▲ ***Over the last** 5,000 years the lower course of the Mississippi has moved back and forth over great distances. These changes, caused by varying sediment loads and human modification, have resulted in a "bird's foot" delta with several lobes, each reflecting the river's different historic position*

The Everglades lie in a limestone hollow formed over two million years ago, which has gradually become filled with swamp deposits.

Florida Keys

The landscape

The Blue Ridge mountains in the north are skirted by the gentle hills of the Piedmont, whose rivers drain south on to the great flat expanse of the coastal plain. Sandy barrier beaches and islands dominate the sea shore, tracing round the swampy limestone arm of Florida. In the west, the Mississippi meanders toward its delta, crossing the thickly mantled alluvial plain of the interior lowlands.

Scale 1:4,000,000

Km 0 10 20 40 60 80 100

Miles 0 10 20 40 60 80 100

projection: Lambert Conformal Conic

Map key

Population

- 500,000 to 1 million
- 100,000 to 500,000
- 50,000 to 100,000
- 10,000 to 50,000
- below 10,000

Elevation

- 4000m / 13,124ft
- 3000m / 9843ft
- 2000m / 6562ft
- 1000m / 3281ft
- 500m / 1640ft
- 250m / 820ft
- 100m / 328ft
- sea level

▲ Mangrove swamps and islets merge across Whitewater Bay, in the Everglades National Park. Alligators, crocodiles, endangered aquatic mammals such as manatees, and a great variety of birds inhabit the subtropical sanctuary.

◄ New Orleans was devastated by Hurricane Katrina in August 2005. Around 1200 lives were lost across the region. Florida and the Gulf coast are prone to hurricanes every fall.

Using the land & sea

In recent years a wide variety of cash crops has been grown in lands once dominated by cotton. The semitropical Florida climate has made it a world leader in the growing of citrus fruit. Georgia has a similar reputation for peanuts; elsewhere soybeans, sugar cane, poultry, and cattle are important. Fishing takes place in Atlantic and Gulf waters, with shellfishing in the shallow Louisiana "bayou".

The urban/rural population divide

urban 72% rural 28%

0 10 20 30 40 50 60 70 80 90 100

Population density	Total land area
149 people per sq mile (57 people per sq km)	253,046 sq miles (655,364 sq km)

▲ Cotton production, once an economic mainstay, has fallen by more than 50% since 1900. Soil erosion, pests, and new farming techniques have shifted cotton farming west toward Texas and California.

Land use and agricultural distribution

- cattle
- pigs
- poultry
- citrus
- cotton
- fishing
- peanuts
- shellfish
- soybeans
- sugar cane
- timber
- major towns
- pasture
- cropland
- forest
- wetland

► Duck Key is one of the chain of limestone and coral islands that form the Florida Keys. The Overseas Highway, completed in 1938, extends 100 miles (160 km) from the mainland to Key West along causeways and bridges.

USA: Texas

First explored by Spaniards moving north from Mexico in search of gold, Texas was controlled by Spain and then by Mexico, before becoming an independent republic in 1836, and joining the Union of States in 1845. During the 19th century, many migrants who came to Texas raised cattle on the abundant land; in the 20th century, they were joined by prospectors attracted by the promise of oil riches. Today, although natural resources, especially oil, still form the basis of its wealth, the diversified Texan economy includes thriving hi-tech and financial industries. The major urban centers, home to 80% of the population, lie in the south and east, and include Houston, the "oil-city," and Dallas–Fort Worth. Hispanic influences remain strong, especially in southern and western Texas.

▲ ***Dallas was founded*** *in 1841 as a prairie trading post and its development was stimulated by the arrival of railroads. Cotton and then oil funded the town's early growth. Today, the modern, high rise skyline of Dallas reflects the city's position as a leading center of banking, insurance, and the petroleum industry in the southwest.*

36

Using the land

Cotton production and livestock-raising, particularly cattle, dominate farming, although crop failures and the demands of local markets have led to some diversification. Following the introduction of modern farming techniques, cotton production spread out from the east to the plains of western Texas. Cattle ranches are widespread, while sheep and goats are raised on the dry Edwards Plateau.

Land use and agricultural distribution

cattle
goats
sheep
cereals
cotton
major towns
pasture
cropland
forest
barren

The urban/rural population divide

urban 80% | rural 20%

0 10 20 30 40 50 60 70 80 90 100

Population density	Total land area
84 people per sq mile (33 people per sq km)	261,797 sq miles (678,028 sq km)

▲ ***The huge cattle*** *ranches of Texas developed during the 19th century when land was plentiful and could be acquired cheaply. Today, more cattle and sheep are raised in Texas than in any other state.*

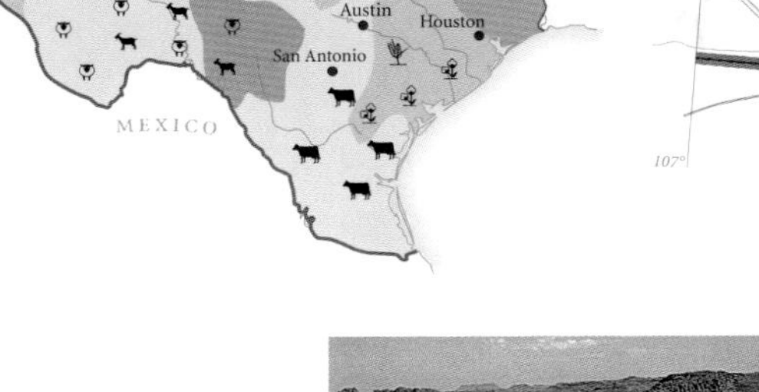
Amarillo
Oklahoma
Arkansas
New Mexico
El Paso
Dallas
Louisiana
Texas
Austin
Houston
San Antonio
MEXICO

The landscape

Texas is made up of a series of massive steps descending from the mountains and high plains of the west and northwest to the coastal lowlands in the southeast. Many of the state's borders are delineated by water. The Rio Grande flows from the Rocky Mountains to the Gulf of Mexico, marking the border with Mexico.

▲ ***Cap Rock Escarpment*** *juts out from the plains, running 200 miles (320 km) from north to south. Its height varies from 300 ft (90 m) rising to sheer cliffs up to 1000 ft (300 m).*

40

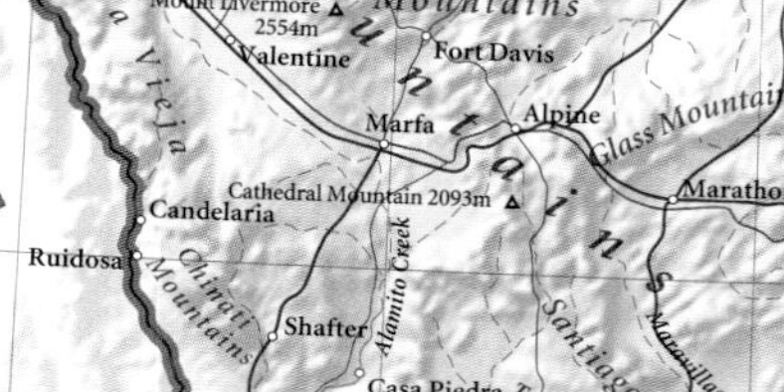

The Llano Estacado or Staked Plain in northern Texas is known for its harsh environment. In the north, freezing winds carrying ice and snow sweep down from the Rocky Mountains. To the south, sandstorms frequently blow up, scouring anything in their paths. Flash floods, in the wide, flat riverbeds that remain dry for most of the year, are another hazard.

The Red River flows for 1300 miles (2090 km), marking most of the northern border of Texas. A dam and reservoir along its course provide vital irrigation and hydroelectric power to the surrounding area.

The Guadalupe Mountains lie in the southern Rocky Mountains. They incorporate Guadalupe Peak, the highest in Texas, rising 8749 ft (2667 m).

Sabine River

Extensive forests of pine and cypress grow in the eastern corner of the coastal lowlands where the average rainfall is 45 inches (1145 mm) a year. This is higher than the rest of the state and over twice the average in the west.

The Rio Grande flows from the Rocky Mountains through semi-arid land, supporting sparse vegetation. The river actually shrinks along its course, losing more water through evaporation and seepage than it gains from its tributaries and rainfall.

In the coastal lowlands of southeastern Texas the Earth's crust is warping, causing the land to subside and allowing the sea to invade. Around Galveston, the rate of downward tilting is 6 inches (15 cm) per year. Erosion of the coast is also exacerbated by hurricanes.

Big Bend National Park

Edwards Plateau is a limestone outcrop. It is part of the Great Plains, bounded to the southeast by the Balcones Escarpment, which marks the southerly limit of the plains.

Oil deposits

Oil trapped by fault

Oil deposits migrate through reservoir rocks such as shale

Oil accumulates beneath impermeable cap rock

Impermeable rock strata

Salt dome

▲ ***Oil deposits are*** *found beneath much of Texas. They collect as oil migrates upward through porous layers of rock until it is trapped, either by a cap of rock above a salt dome, or by a fault line which exposes impermeable rock through which the oil cannot rise.*

◄ ***Flowing through*** *1500 ft (450 m) high gorges, the shallow, muddy Rio Grande makes a 90° bend. This marks the southern border of Big Bend National Park, and gives it its name. The area is a mixture of forested mountains, deserts, and canyons.*

Padre Island

Laguna Madre in southern Texas has been almost completely cut off from the sea by Padre Island. This sand bank was created by wave action, carrying and depositing material along the coast. The process is known as longshore drift.

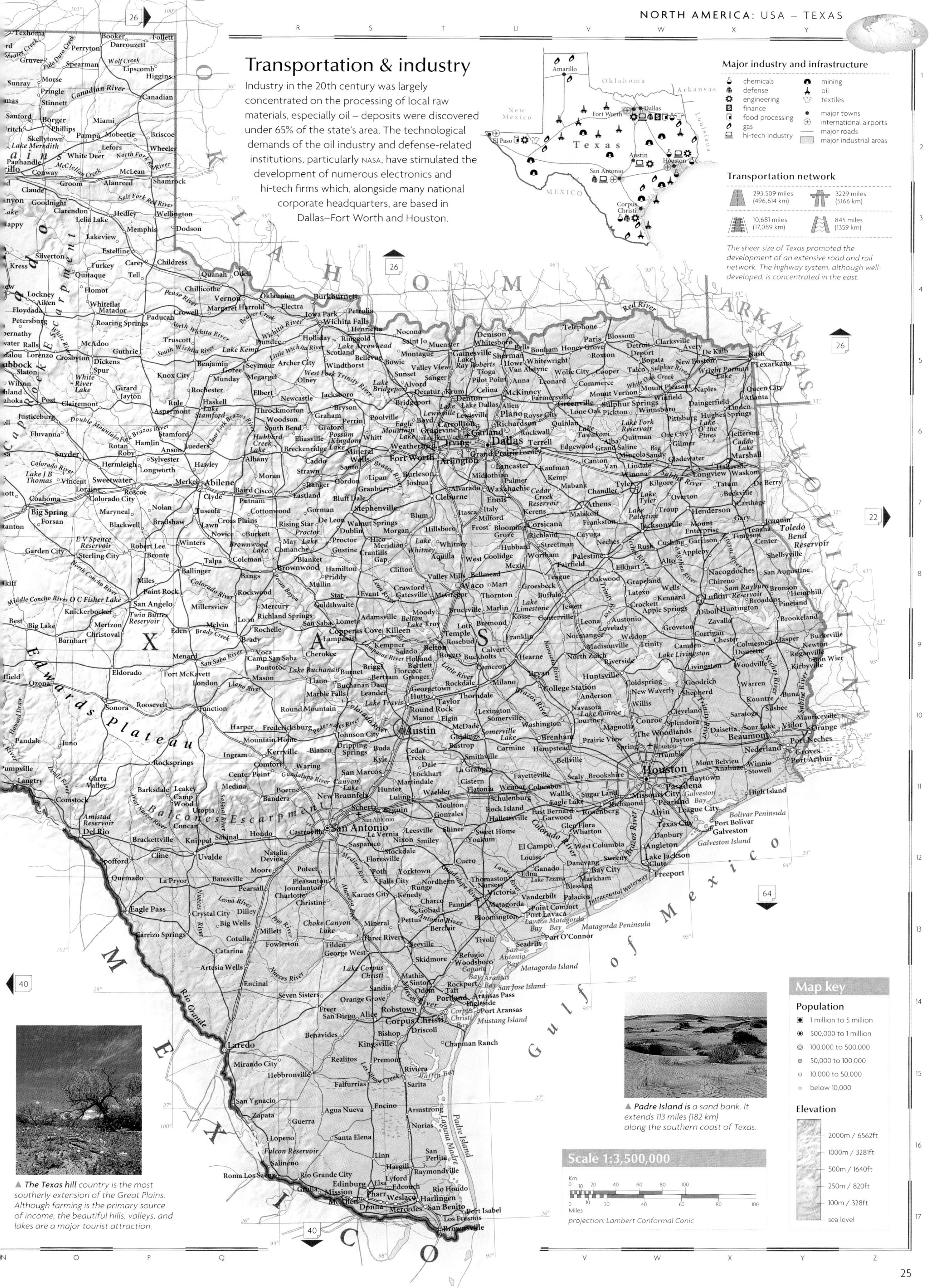
Transportation & industry
Industry in the 20th century was largely concentrated on the processing of local raw materials, especially oil – deposits were discovered under 65% of the state's area. The technological demands of the oil industry and defense-related institutions, particularly NASA, have stimulated the development of numerous electronics and hi-tech firms which, alongside many national corporate headquarters, are based in Dallas–Fort Worth and Houston.
Major industry and infrastructure
chemicals
defense
engineering
finance
food processing
gas
hi-tech industry
mining
oil
textiles
major towns
international airports
major roads
major industrial areas
Transportation network
293,509 miles (496,614 km)
3229 miles (5166 km)
10,681 miles (17,089 km)
845 miles (1359 km)
The sheer size of Texas promoted the development of an extensive road and rail network. The highway system, although well-developed, is concentrated in the east.
Map key
Population
1 million to 5 million
500,000 to 1 million
100,000 to 500,000
50,000 to 100,000
10,000 to 50,000
below 10,000
Elevation
2000m / 6562ft
1000m / 3281ft
500m / 1640ft
250m / 820ft
100m / 328ft
sea level
Scale 1:3,500,000
projection: Lambert Conformal Conic
Gulf of Mexico
OKLAHOMA
ARKANSAS
LOUISIANA
MEXICO
TEXAS
Edwards Plateau
Balcones Escarpment
Caprock Escarpment
Dallas
Fort Worth
Houston
Austin
San Antonio
Corpus Christi
El Paso
Amarillo

▲ Padre Island is a sand bank. It extends 113 miles (182 km) along the southern coast of Texas.

▲ The Texas hill country is the most southerly extension of the Great Plains. Although farming is the primary source of income, the beautiful hills, valleys, and lakes are a major tourist attraction.

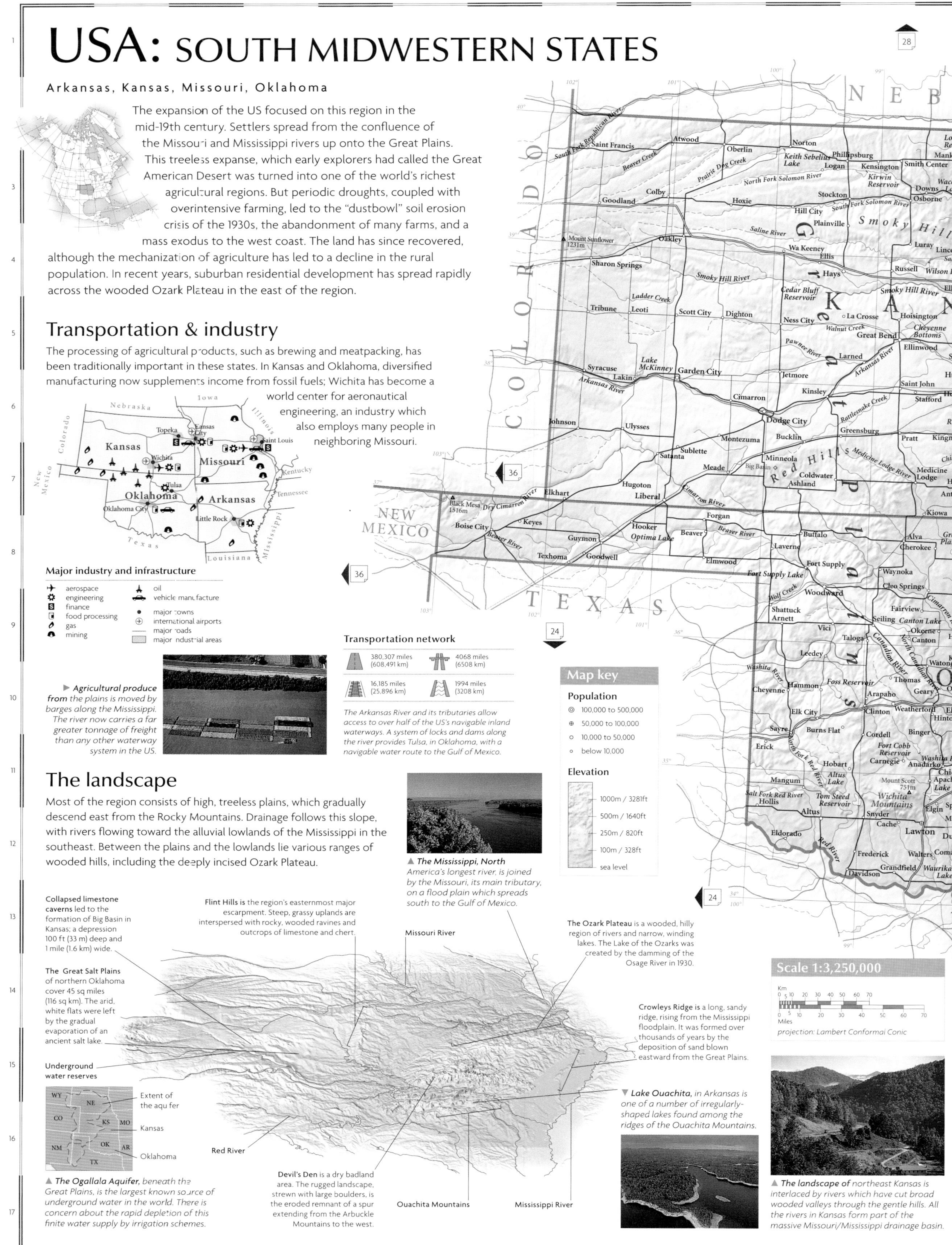

USA: SOUTH MIDWESTERN STATES

Arkansas, Kansas, Missouri, Oklahoma

The expansion of the US focused on this region in the mid-19th century. Settlers spread from the confluence of the Missouri and Mississippi rivers up onto the Great Plains. This treeless expanse, which early explorers had called the Great American Desert was turned into one of the world's richest agricultural regions. But periodic droughts, coupled with overintensive farming, led to the "dustbowl" soil erosion crisis of the 1930s, the abandonment of many farms, and a mass exodus to the west coast. The land has since recovered, although the mechanization of agriculture has led to a decline in the rural population. In recent years, suburban residential development has spread rapidly across the wooded Ozark Plateau in the east of the region.

Transportation & industry

The processing of agricultural products, such as brewing and meatpacking, has been traditionally important in these states. In Kansas and Oklahoma, diversified manufacturing now supplements income from fossil fuels; Wichita has become a world center for aeronautical engineering, an industry which also employs many people in neighboring Missouri.

Major industry and infrastructure

- aerospace
- engineering
- finance
- food processing
- gas
- mining
- oil
- vehicle manufacture
- major towns
- international airports
- major roads
- major industrial areas

▶ ***Agricultural produce** from the plains is moved by barges along the Mississippi. The river now carries a far greater tonnage of freight than any other waterway system in the US.*

Transportation network

380,307 miles (608,491 km)	4068 miles (6508 km)
16,185 miles (25,896 km)	1994 miles (3208 km)

The Arkansas River and its tributaries allow access to over half of the US's navigable inland waterways. A system of locks and dams along the river provides Tulsa, in Oklahoma, with a navigable water route to the Gulf of Mexico.

Map key

Population

- 100,000 to 500,000
- 50,000 to 100,000
- 10,000 to 50,000
- below 10,000

Elevation

- 1000m / 3281ft
- 500m / 1640ft
- 250m / 820ft
- 100m / 328ft
- sea level

Scale 1:3,250,000

projection: Lambert Conformal Conic

The landscape

Most of the region consists of high, treeless plains, which gradually descend east from the Rocky Mountains. Drainage follows this slope, with rivers flowing toward the alluvial lowlands of the Mississippi in the southeast. Between the plains and the lowlands lie various ranges of wooded hills, including the deeply incised Ozark Plateau.

▲ ***The Mississippi**, North America's longest river, is joined by the Missouri, its main tributary, on a flood plain which spreads south to the Gulf of Mexico.*

Collapsed limestone caverns led to the formation of Big Basin in Kansas; a depression 100 ft (33 m) deep and 1 mile (1.6 km) wide.

Flint Hills is the region's easternmost major escarpment. Steep, grassy uplands are interspersed with rocky, wooded ravines and outcrops of limestone and chert.

Missouri River

The Ozark Plateau is a wooded, hilly region of rivers and narrow, winding lakes. The Lake of the Ozarks was created by the damming of the Osage River in 1930.

The Great Salt Plains of northern Oklahoma cover 45 sq miles (116 sq km). The arid, white flats were left by the gradual evaporation of an ancient salt lake.

Crowleys Ridge is a long, sandy ridge, rising from the Mississippi floodplain. It was formed over thousands of years by the deposition of sand blown eastward from the Great Plains.

Underground water reserves

Extent of the aquifer

Kansas

Oklahoma

▼ ***Lake Ouachita**, in Arkansas is one of a number of irregularly-shaped lakes found among the ridges of the Ouachita Mountains.*

Red River

Devil's Den is a dry badland area. The rugged landscape, strewn with large boulders, is the eroded remnant of a spur extending from the Arbuckle Mountains to the west.

Ouachita Mountains

Mississippi River

▲ ***The Ogallala Aquifer**, beneath the Great Plains, is the largest known source of underground water in the world. There is concern about the rapid depletion of this finite water supply by irrigation schemes.*

▲ ***The landscape of** northeast Kansas is interlaced by rivers which have cut broad wooded valleys through the gentle hills. All the rivers in Kansas form part of the massive Missouri/Mississippi drainage basin.*

IOWA
MISSOURI
ILLINOIS
KANSAS
OKLAHOMA
ARKANSAS
TEXAS
LOUISIANA
MISSISSIPPI
TENNESSEE
KENTUCKY
Ozark Plateau
Ouachita Mountains
Boston Mountains
Mississippi River
Missouri River
Kansas City
Saint Louis
Jefferson City
Topeka
Tulsa
Oklahoma City
Little Rock
Springfield
Land use and agricultural distribution
cattle
poultry
cereals
corn
cotton
fodder
rice
soybeans
major towns
pasture
cropland
forest
Nebraska
Iowa
Illinois
Colorado
Kansas
Missouri
Kentucky
New Mexico
Oklahoma
Arkansas
Tennessee
Texas
Louisiana
Mississippi
Kansas City
Topeka
Saint Louis
Wichita
Tulsa
Oklahoma City
Little Rock
The urban/rural population divide
urban 65%
rural 35%
0 10 20 30 40 50 60 70 80 90 100
Population density
54 people per sq mile (21 people per sq km)
Total land area
271,436 sq miles (702,992 sq km)

▶ **Gateway Arch,** *in Saint Louis, Missouri, is 634 ft (192 m) high. The huge steel arch symbolizes the city's historic role as the "Gateway to the West".*

Using the land

The problems of a harsh continental climate, with severe winters and hot, dry summers, are partially offset by the rich soils of the plains. Kansas is a major cereal crop producer, ranking first in US production of wheat and sorghum. Rainfall increases toward the east, favoring the cultivation of soybeans, cotton, and rice, with corn concentrated in Missouri. Huge herds of cattle are raised in Oklahoma, Kansas, and Missouri.

▲ **A combine harvester** *works the land on the great plains. A hundred years ago this region, also known as the prairies – the French word for pasture – was covered with tall, wild grasses.*

USA: UPPER PLAINS STATES

Iowa, Minnesota, Nebraska, North Dakota, South Dakota

Lying at the very heart of the North American continent, much of this region was acquired from France as part of the Louisiana Purchase in 1803. The area was largely bypassed by the early waves of westward migrants. When Europeans did settle, during the 19th century, they displaced the Native Americans who lived on the plains. The settlers planted arable crops and raised cattle on the immensely fertile prairie land, founding an agrarian tradition which flourishes today. Most of this region remains rural; of the five states, only in Minnesota has there been significant diversification away from agriculture and resource-based industries into the hi-tech and service sectors.

Using the land

The popular image of these states as agricultural is entirely justified; prairies stretch uninterrupted across most of the area. Croplands fall into two regions: the wheat belt of the plains, and the corn belt of the central US. Cash crops, such as soybeans, are grown to supplement incomes. Livestock, particularly pigs and cattle, are raised throughout this region.

The urban/rural population divide

urban 64% rural 36%

0 10 20 30 40 50 60 70 80 90 100

Population density	Total land area
31 people per sq mile (12 people per sq km)	357,212 sq miles (925,143 sq km)

► *Dark, fertile prairie soils in the southeast provide Minnesota's most productive farmland. Hot, humid summers create a long growing season for corn cultivation.*

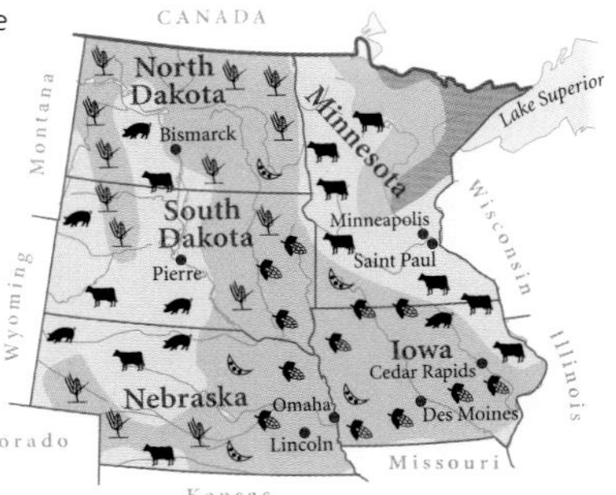

CANADA
North Dakota
Bismarck
Minnesota
Lake Superior
South Dakota
Pierre
Minneapolis
Saint Paul
Iowa
Cedar Rapids
Des Moines
Nebraska
Omaha
Lincoln
Montana
Wyoming
Wisconsin
Illinois
Colorado
Kansas
Missouri

Land use and agricultural distribution

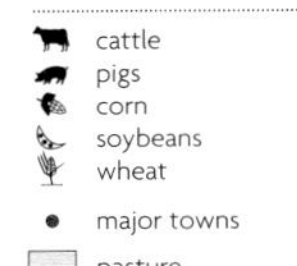

cattle
pigs
corn
soybeans
wheat
major towns
pasture
cropland
forest
wetland

Transportation & industry

Food processing and the production of farm machinery are supported by the large agricultural sector. Mineral exploitation is also an important activity: gold is mined in the ore-rich Black Hills of South Dakota, and both North Dakota and Nebraska are emerging as major petroleum producers.

► *Water erosion along the Little Missouri River has carried away sedimentary deposits, creating rugged landscapes known as badlands.*

Transportation network

504,522 miles (807,235 km)
3422 miles (5475 km)
16,940 miles (27,104 km)
683 miles (1098 km)

Nebraska's central location has made it an important transportation artery for east–west traffic. Minnesota's road network radiates out from the hub of the twin cities, Minneapolis–Saint Paul.

CANADA, North Dakota, Bismarck, Fargo, Minnesota, Duluth, Lake Superior, South Dakota, Pierre, Sioux Falls, Minneapolis, Saint Paul, Iowa, Cedar Rapids, Des Moines, Nebraska, Omaha, Lincoln, Montana, Wyoming, Wisconsin, Illinois, Colorado, Kansas, Missouri

Major industry and infrastructure

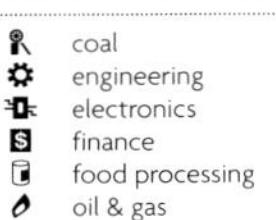

coal
engineering
electronics
finance
food processing
oil & gas
mining
major towns
international airports
major roads
major industrial areas

The landscape

These states straddle the Great Plains and the lowlands of the central US, with Minnesota lying in a transition zone between the eastern forests and the prairies. The region was shaped by repeated ice advances and retreats, leaving a flat relief, broken only by the numerous lakes and broad river networks that drain the prairies.

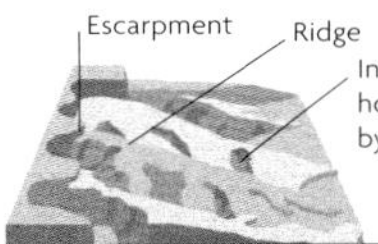

Escarpment
Ridge
In permeable strata hollows are formed by small mudslides
Water flowing into gullies erodes back the escarpment

▲ ***Badlands are formed** by stormwater run-off. This flows down the impermeable strata of the escarpment and saturates the permeable strata, leading to mudslides and the formation of gullies.*

▲ ***In the badlands** of North and South Dakota, horizontal layers of sandstone have been eroded by rivers, leaving a landscape of narrow gullies, sharp crests and pinnacles.*

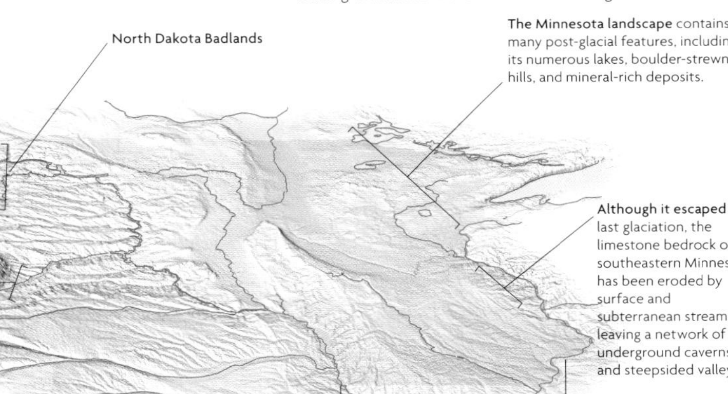

North Dakota Badlands
South Dakota Badlands
Missouri River
Mississippi River

The Minnesota landscape contains many post-glacial features, including its numerous lakes, boulder-strewn hills, and mineral-rich deposits.

Although it escaped the last glaciation, the limestone bedrock of southeastern Minnesota has been eroded by surface and subterranean streams, leaving a network of underground caverns and steepsided valleys.

▲ ***Chimney Rock is** a remnant of an ancient land surface, eroded by the North Platte River. The tip of its spire stands 500 ft (150 m) above the plain.*

◄ ***In northeastern Iowa,** the Mississippi and its tributaries have deeply incised the underlying bedrock creating a hilly terrain, with bluffs standing 300 ft (90 m) above the valley.*

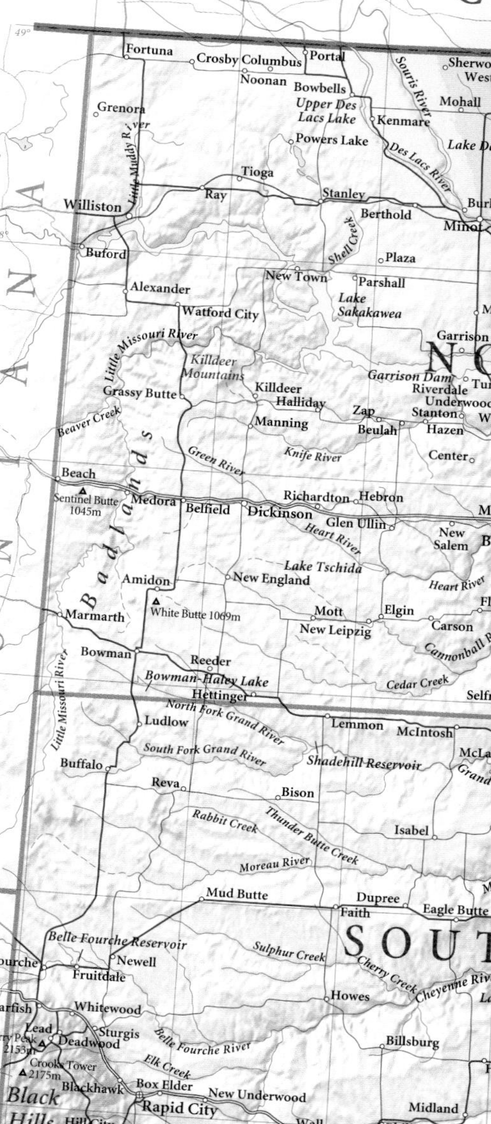

MONTANA
WYOMING
COLORADO
Fortuna
Crosby
Columbus
Portal
Noonan
Bowbells
Upper Des Lacs Lake
Kenmare
Grenora
Powers Lake
Tioga
Ray
Stanley
Berthold
Williston
Buford
New Town
Parshall
Lake Sakakawea
Alexander
Watford City
Killdeer Mountains
Killdeer
Halliday
Grassy Butte
Manning
Beach
Sentinel Butte 1045m
Medora
Belfield
Dickinson
Richardton
Hebron
Glen Ullin
Amidon
New England
White Butte 1069m
Marmarth
Mott
New Leipzig
Elgin
Bowman
Reeder
Bowman-Haley Lake
Hettinger
Lemmon
Ludlow
Buffalo
Reva
Bison
Isabel
Mud Butte
Dupree
Faith
Eagle Butte
Belle Fourche Reservoir
Belle Fourche
Newell
Fruitdale
Spearfish
Whitewood
Lead
Deadwood
Sturgis
Black Hills
Box Elder
Rapid City
New Underwood
Harney Peak 2207m
Mount Rushmore 1745m
Hill City
Hermosa
Custer
Wall
Philip
Midland
Kadoka
Interior
Pringle
Hot Springs
Angostura Reservoir
Edgemont
Oelrichs
Pine Ridge
Batesland
Martin
Merriman
Gordon
Chadron
Rushville
Hay Springs
Harrison
Crawford
Box Butte Reservoir
Niobrara River
Hemingford
Alliance
Lakeside
Hyannis
Mitchell
Scottsbluff
Gering
Bayard
Bridgeport
Harrisburg
Sand Hills
Arthur
Oshkosh
Lake C. W. McConaughy
Kimball
Sidney
Chappell
Ogallala
Sutherland
South Platte River
North Platte River
Grant
Imperial
Hayes Center
Enders Reservoir
Benkelman
Trenton
32

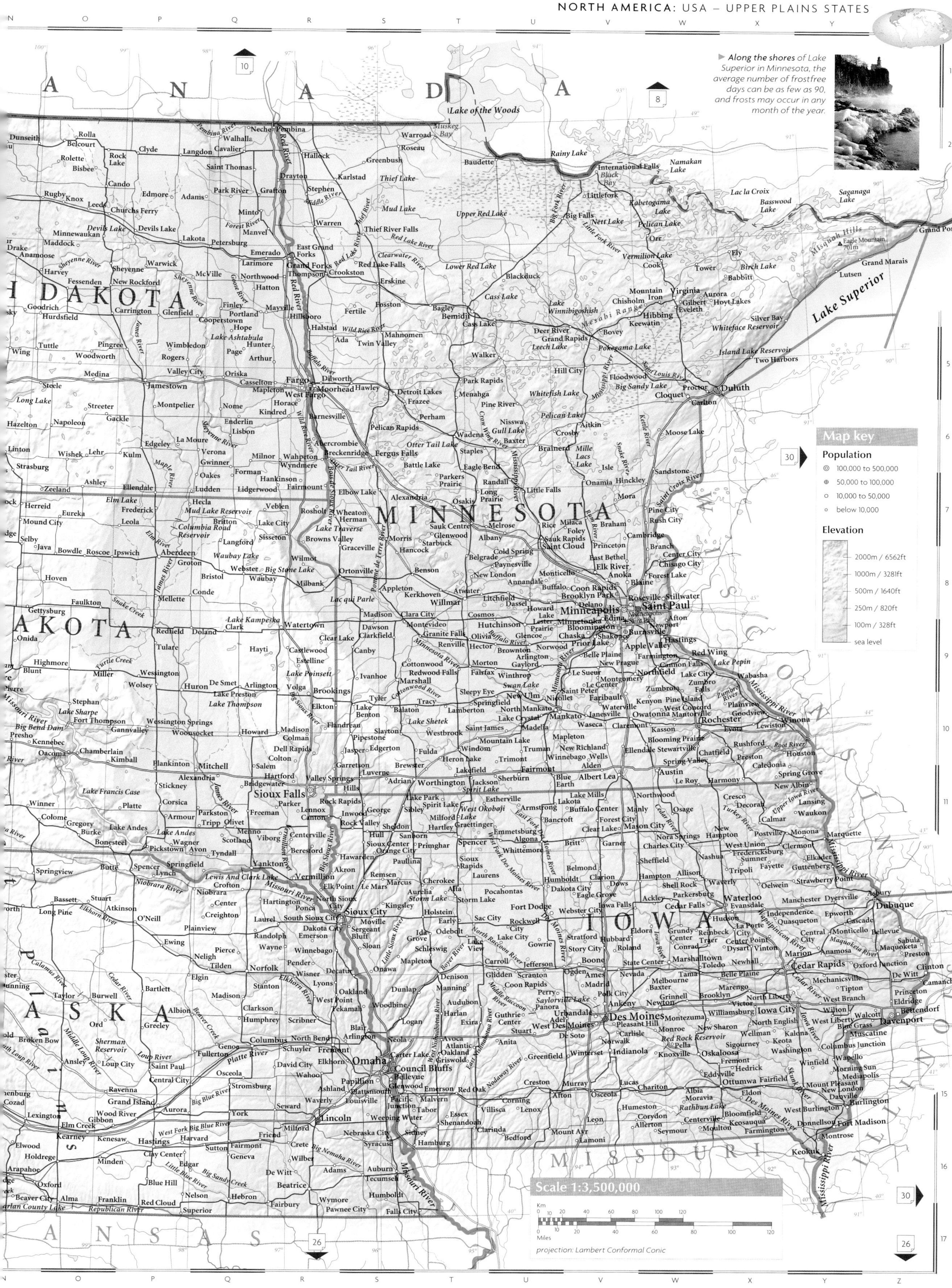

Along the shores of Lake Superior in Minnesota, the average number of frostfree days can be as few as 90, and frosts may occur in any month of the year.

Map key

Population

- 100,000 to 500,000
- 50,000 to 100,000
- 10,000 to 50,000
- below 10,000

Elevation

- 2000m / 6562ft
- 1000m / 3281ft
- 500m / 1640ft
- 250m / 820ft
- 100m / 328ft
- sea level

Scale 1:3,500,000

projection: Lambert Conformal Conic

MINNESOTA

IOWA

USA: GREAT LAKES STATES

Illinois, Indiana, Michigan, Ohio, Wisconsin

The states bordering the Great Lakes developed rapidly in the second half of the 19th century as a result of improvements in communications: railroads to the west and waterways to the south and east. Fertile land and good links with growing eastern seaboard c ties encouraged the development of agriculture and food processing. Migrants from Europe and other parts of the US flooded into the region and for much of the 20th century the region's economy boomed. However, in recent years heavy industry has declined, earning the region the unwanted label the "Rustbelt."

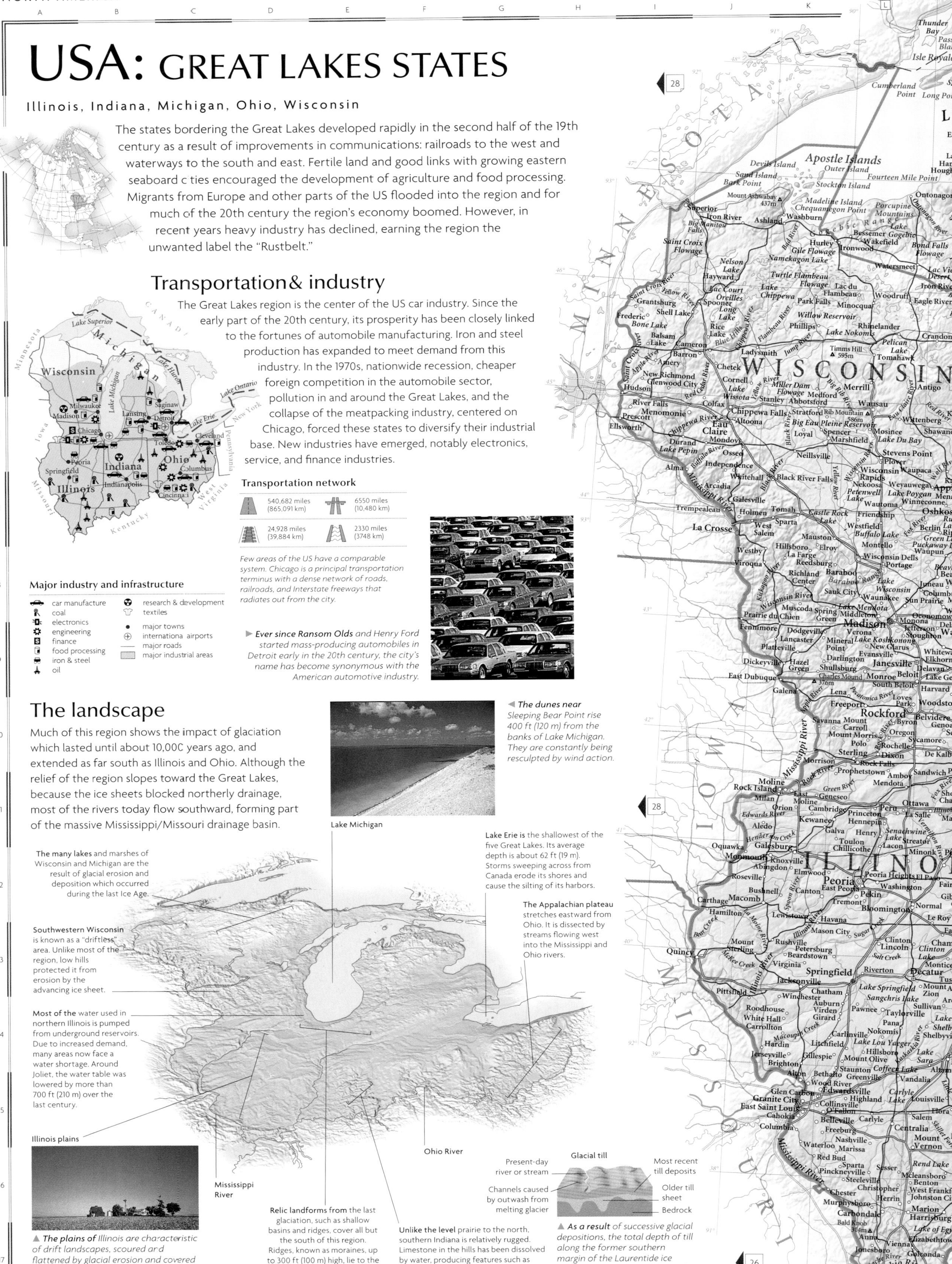

Transportation& industry

The Great Lakes region is the center of the US car industry. Since the early part of the 20th century, its prosperity has been closely linked to the fortunes of automobile manufacturing. Iron and steel production has expanded to meet demand from this industry. In the 1970s, nationwide recession, cheaper foreign competition in the automobile sector, pollution in and around the Great Lakes, and the collapse of the meatpacking industry, centered on Chicago, forced these states to diversify their industrial base. New industries have emerged, notably electronics, service, and finance industries.

Transportation network

540,682 miles (865,091 km)	6550 miles (10,480 km)
24,928 miles (39,884 km)	2330 miles (3748 km)

Few areas of the US have a comparable system. Chicago is a principal transportation terminus with a dense network of roads, railroads, and Interstate freeways that radiates out from the city.

Major industry and infrastructure

- car manufacture
- coal
- electronics
- engineering
- finance
- food processing
- iron & steel
- oil
- research & development
- textiles
- major towns
- international airports
- major roads
- major industrial areas

▶ ***Ever since Ransom Olds** and Henry Ford started mass-producing automobiles in Detroit early in the 20th century, the city's name has become synonymous with the American automotive industry.*

The landscape

Much of this region shows the impact of glaciation which lasted until about 10,000 years ago, and extended as far south as Illinois and Ohio. Although the relief of the region slopes toward the Great Lakes, because the ice sheets blocked northerly drainage, most of the rivers today flow southward, forming part of the massive Mississippi/Missouri drainage basin.

◀ ***The dunes near** Sleeping Bear Point rise 400 ft (120 m) from the banks of Lake Michigan. They are constantly being resculpted by wind action.*

Lake Michigan

The many lakes and marshes of Wisconsin and Michigan are the result of glacial erosion and deposition which occurred during the last Ice Age.

Lake Erie is the shallowest of the five Great Lakes. Its average depth is about 62 ft (19 m). Storms sweeping across from Canada erode its shores and cause the silting of its harbors.

Southwestern Wisconsin is known as a "driftless" area. Unlike most of the region, low hills protected it from erosion by the advancing ice sheet.

The Appalachian plateau stretches eastward from Ohio. It is dissected by streams flowing west into the Mississippi and Ohio rivers.

Most of the water used in northern Illinois is pumped from underground reservoirs. Due to increased demand, many areas now face a water shortage. Around Joliet, the water table was lowered by more than 700 ft (210 m) over the last century.

Illinois plains

Mississippi River

Ohio River

Relic landforms from the last glaciation, such as shallow basins and ridges, cover all but the south of this region. Ridges, known as moraines, up to 300 ft (100 m) high, lie to the south of Lake Michigan.

Unlike the level prairie to the north, southern Indiana is relatively rugged. Limestone in the hills has been dissolved by water, producing features such as sinkholes and underground caves.

▲ ***The plains of** Illinois are characteristic of drift landscapes, scoured and flattened by glacial erosion and covered with fertile glacial deposits.*

Glacial till

Present-day river or stream

Channels caused by outwash from melting glacier

Most recent till deposits

Older till sheet

Bedrock

▲ ***As a result** of successive glacial depositions, the total depth of till along the former southern margin of the Laurentide ice sheet can exceed 1300 ft (400 m).*

MINNESOTA
WISCONSIN
ILLINOIS
IOWA
MISSOURI
Lake Superior
Apostle Islands
Madison
Rockford
Peoria
Springfield
La Crosse
Mississippi River
Wisconsin
Michigan
Indiana
Ohio
Illinois

28
28
26

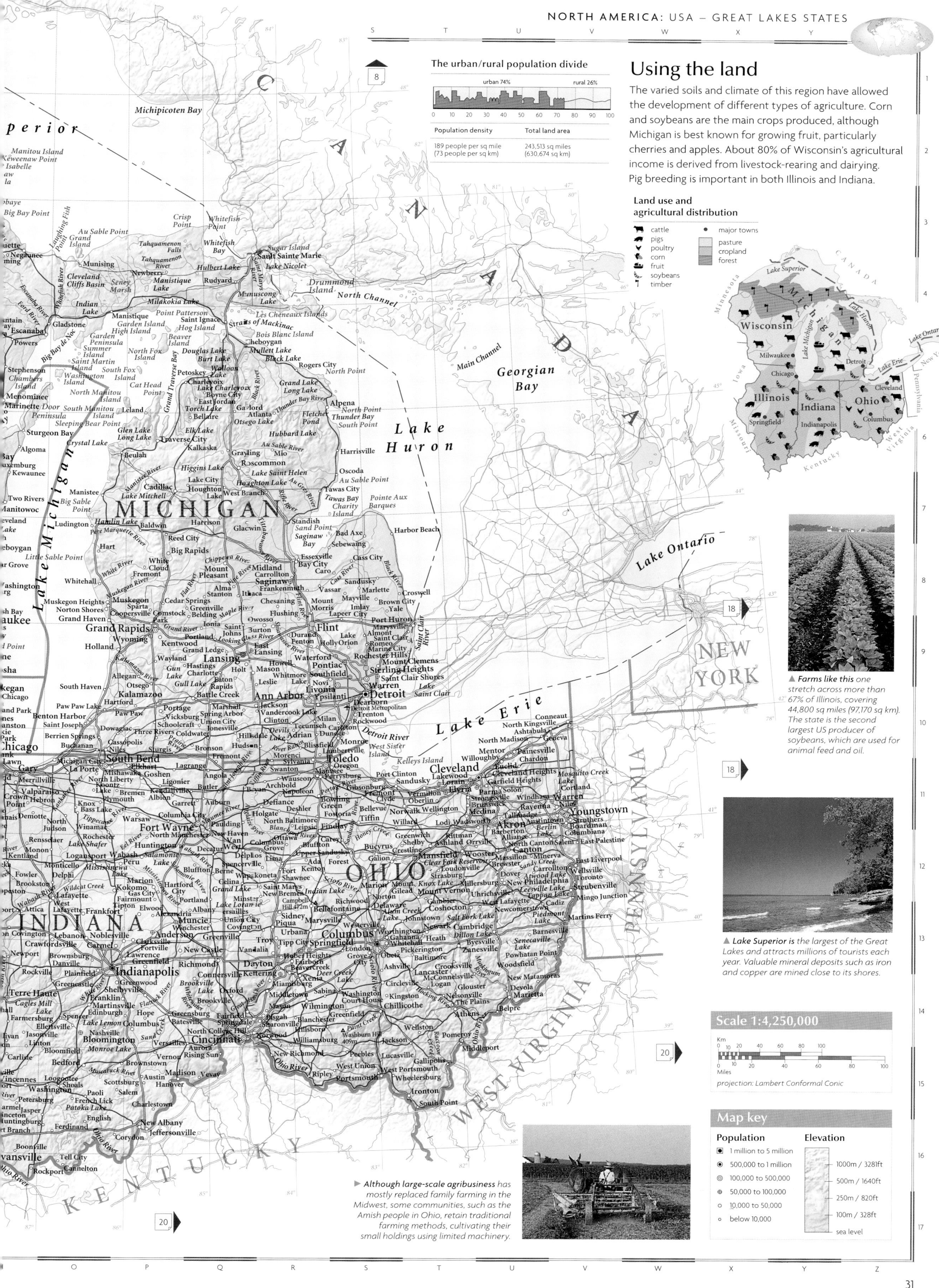
Lake Superior
Lake Michigan
Lake Huron
Lake Erie
Lake Ontario
Georgian Bay
MICHIGAN
INDIANA
OHIO
NEW YORK
PENNSYLVANIA
WEST VIRGINIA
KENTUCKY
CANADA
Detroit
Chicago
Cleveland
Indianapolis
Columbus
Toledo
Grand Rapids
Lansing
Flint
Fort Wayne
Cincinnati
Dayton

The urban/rural population divide

urban 74% rural 26%

Population density	Total land area
189 people per sq mile (73 people per sq km)	243,513 sq miles (630,674 sq km)

Using the land

The varied soils and climate of this region have allowed the development of different types of agriculture. Corn and soybeans are the main crops produced, although Michigan is best known for growing fruit, particularly cherries and apples. About 80% of Wisconsin's agricultural income is derived from livestock-rearing and dairying. Pig breeding is important in both Illinois and Indiana.

Land use and agricultural distribution

cattle, pigs, poultry, corn, fruit, soybeans, timber, major towns, pasture, cropland, forest

▲ Farms like this one stretch across more than 67% of Illinois, covering 44,800 sq miles (97,170 sq km). The state is the second largest US producer of soybeans, which are used for animal feed and oil.

▲ Lake Superior is the largest of the Great Lakes and attracts millions of tourists each year. Valuable mineral deposits such as iron and copper are mined close to its shores.

► Although large-scale agribusiness has mostly replaced family farming in the Midwest, some communities, such as the Amish people in Ohio, retain traditional farming methods, cultivating their small holdings using limited machinery.

Scale 1:4,250,000

projection: Lambert Conformal Conic

Map key

Population
- 1 million to 5 million
- 500,000 to 1 million
- 100,000 to 500,000
- 50,000 to 100,000
- 10,000 to 50,000
- below 10,000

Elevation
- 1000m / 3281ft
- 500m / 1640ft
- 250m / 820ft
- 100m / 328ft
- sea level

USA: NORTH MOUNTAIN STATES

Idaho, Montana, Oregon, Washington, Wyoming

The remoteness of the northwestern states, coupled with the rugged landscape, ensured that this was one of the last areas settled by Europeans in the 19th century. Fur-trappers and gold-prospectors followed the Snake River westward as it wound its way through the Rocky Mountains. The states of the northwest have pioneered many conservationist policies, with the first US National Park opened at Yellowstone in 1872. More recently, the Cascades and Rocky Mountains have become havens for adventure tourism. The mountains still serve to isolate the western seaboard from the rest of the continent. This isolation has encouraged West Coast cities to expand their trade links with countries of the Pacific Rim.

▲ *The Snake River has cut down into the basalt of the Columbia Basin to form Hells Canyon, the deepest in the US, with cliffs up to 7900 ft (2408 m) high.*

Map key

Population
- 500,000 to 1 million
- 100,000 to 500,000
- 50,000 to 100,000
- 10,000 to 50,000
- below 10,000

Elevation
- 4000m / 13,124ft
- 3000m / 9843ft
- 2000m / 6562ft
- 1000m / 3281ft
- 500m / 1640ft
- 250m / 820ft
- 100m / 328ft
- sea level

Scale 1:4,250,000

projection: Lambert Conformal Conic

► *Fine-textured, volcanic soils in the hilly Palouse region of eastern Washington are susceptible to erosion.*

Using the land

Wheat farming in the east gives way to cattle ranching as rainfall decreases. Irrigated farming in the Snake River valley produces large yields of potatoes and other vegetables. Dairying and fruit-growing take place in the wet western lowlands between the mountain ranges.

The urban/rural population divide

urban 74% — rural 26%

Population density	Total land area
26 people per sq mile (10 people per sq km)	487,970 sq miles (1,263,716 sq km)

Land use and agricultural distribution

- cattle
- poultry
- cereals
- fruit
- potatoes
- timber
- major towns
- pasture
- cropland
- forest

Transportation & industry

Minerals and timber are extremely important in this region. Uranium, precious metals, copper, and coal are all mined, the latter in vast open-cast pits in Wyoming; oil and natural gas are extracted further north. Manufacturing, notably related to the aerospace and electronics industries, is important in western cities.

CANADA
PACIFIC OCEAN
Seattle
Tacoma
Spokane
Washington
Lewiston
Great Falls
Helena
Montana
Billings
Pasco
Portland
Salem
Eugene
Oregon
Boise
Idaho
Pocatello
Twin Falls
Casper
Wyoming
Cheyenne
North Dakota
South Dakota
Nebraska
California
Nevada
Utah
Colorado

Transportation network

- 347,857 miles (556,571 km)
- 4200 miles (6720 km)
- 12,354 miles (19,766 km)
- 1108 miles (1782 km)

The Union Pacific Railroad has been in service across Wyoming since 1867. The route through the Rocky Mountains is now shared with the Interstate 80, a major east–west highway.

Major industry and infrastructure

- adventure tourism
- aerospace
- coal
- chemicals
- electronics
- food processing
- mining
- oil & gas
- timber processing
- major towns
- international airports
- major roads
- major industrial areas

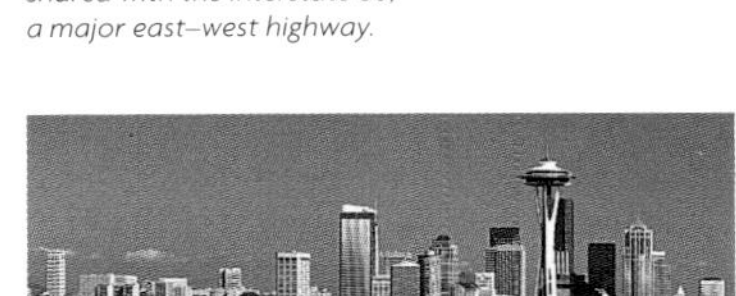

◄ *Seattle lies in one of Puget Sound's many inlets. The city receives oil and other resources from Alaska, and benefits from expanding trade across the Pacific.*

◄ *Crater Lake, Oregon, is 6 miles (10 km) wide and 1800 ft (600 m) deep. It marks the site of a volcanic cone, which collapsed after an eruption within the last 7000 years.*

The landscape

The Rocky Mountains are flanked by lower parallel ranges, which spread onto the Great Plains in the east and surmount the broad lava plateau which extends westward. The Cascade Range divides the Columbia Basin from the coastlands, where the low areas around Puget Sound are broken by the steep, volcanic Olympic Mountains and the wooded hills of the Coast Ranges.

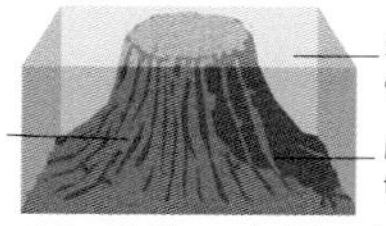

Molten rock cools, forming parallel columns

Surrounding strata eroded away

Molten rock wells up from the Earth's core

▲ *Devil's Tower in Wyoming is an igneous intrusion, formed below the Earth's surface. Molten rock intruded through cracks in the overlying strata and cooled. Over time, the softer rock layers have been eroded away, leaving only the tower standing.*

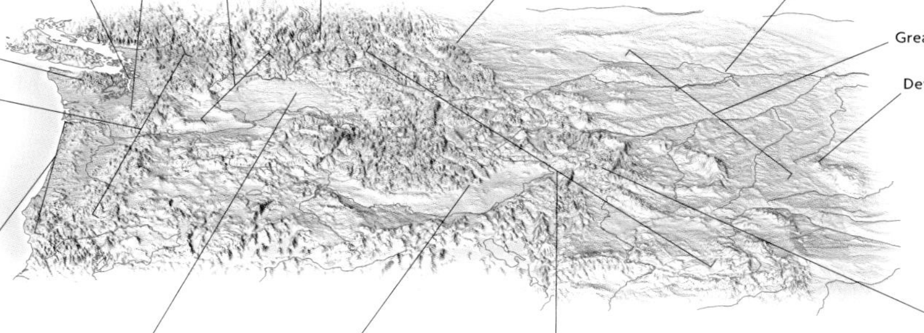

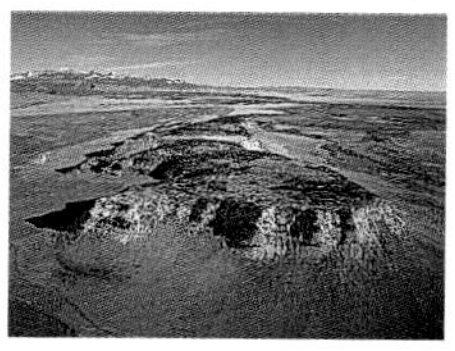

Glacial valleys on the seaward side of the Olympic Mountains receive about 142 inches (3600 mm) of rain per year, supporting the only true rain forest of the northern hemisphere.

Puget Sound

Mount St. Helens erupted in 1980, killing 57 people and devastating a huge area.

Columbia Basin

Grand Coulee and the lesser *coulées* (ravines) were cut by cataclysmic floods, from the release of an ice-dammed lake, at the end of the last Ice Age.

The Continental Divide, or watershed, crosses the Lewis Range. From here, rivers flow east to Hudson Bay, south to the Gulf of Mexico and west to the Pacific Ocean.

▶ ***Piney Buttes** are the remnants of an older, higher land surface gradually weathered and eroded into isolated outcrops with flat tops and steep sides.*

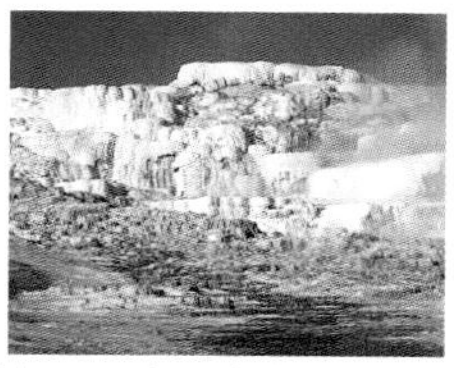

Great Plains

Devil's Tower

The Cascades are glacially scoured volcanic mountains, the highest of which is Mount Rainier, a dormant volcano at 14,409 ft (4392 m).

Coast Ranges

The plateaus of the Columbia and Snake rivers represent one of the world's largest accumulations of lava. Over 5 million years ago, successive flows of molten basalt buried the existing land surface by up to 450 ft (150 m).

The contorted rock shapes at "Craters of the Moon" National Monument in Idaho were left 2000 years ago by the sporadic upwelling of viscous lava from fissures in the basalt plateau.

Rocky Mountains

▲ ***Water from the** hot springs in Yellowstone National Park deposits minerals as it cools in rock pools. Long periods of deposition have created these rock terraces.*

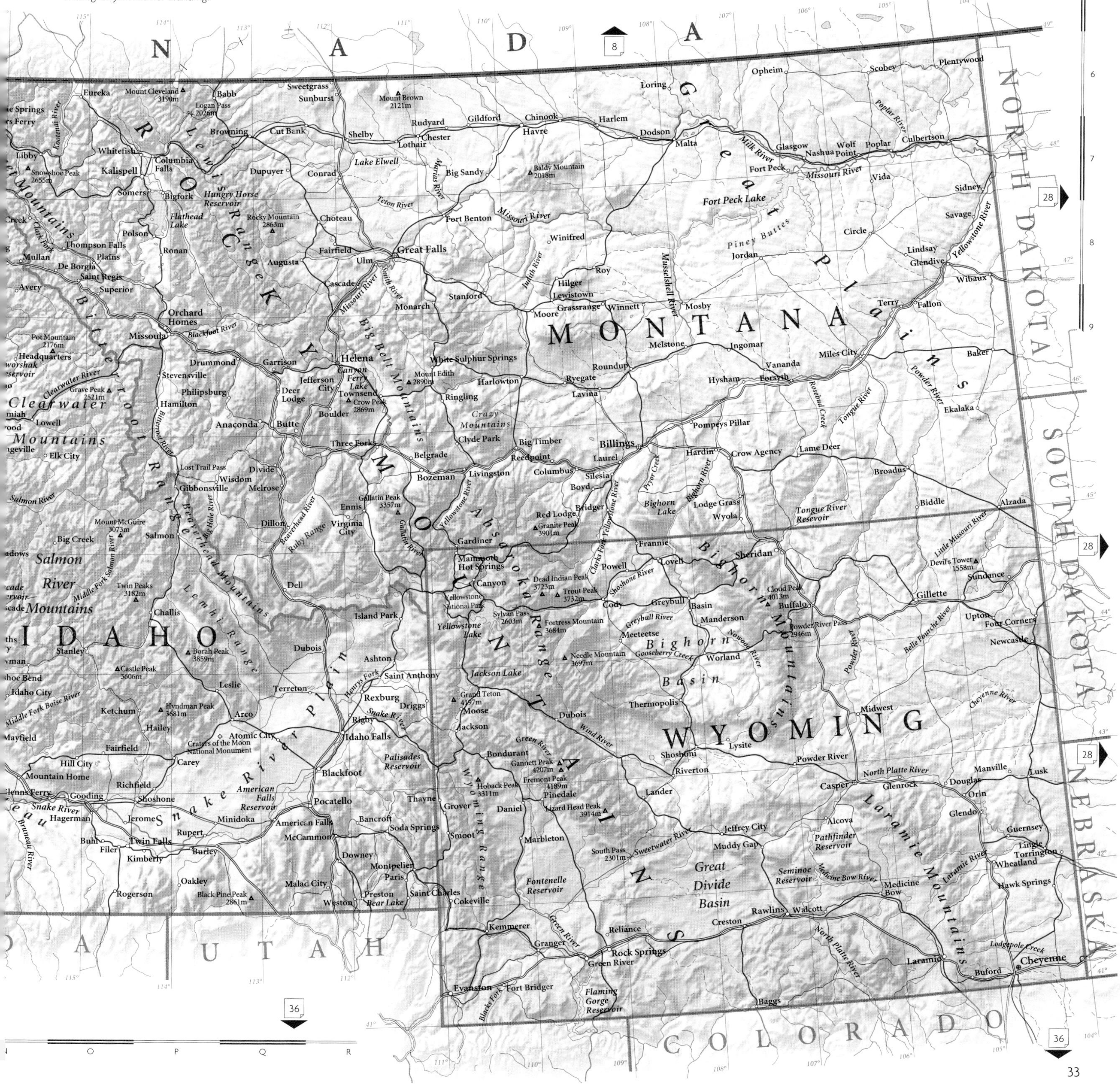

CANADA
NORTH DAKOTA
SOUTH DAKOTA
NEBRASKA
COLORADO
UTAH
IDAHO
MONTANA
WYOMING
ROCKY MOUNTAINS
Great Plains
Lewis Range
Bitterroot Range
Clearwater Mountains
Salmon River Mountains
Lemhi Range
Big Belt Mountains
Absaroka Range
Bighorn Mountains
Bighorn Basin
Wind River Range
Wyoming Range
Laramie Mountains
Great Divide Basin
Snake River Plain
Crazy Mountains
Ruby Range
Helena
Great Falls
Missoula
Billings
Bozeman
Butte
Cheyenne
Casper
Idaho Falls
Pocatello
Twin Falls
Yellowstone National Park
Yellowstone Lake
Jackson Lake
Fort Peck Lake
Missouri River
Yellowstone River
Snake River
Piney Buttes
Devil's Tower 1558m
Gannett Peak 4207m
Grand Teton 4197m
Granite Peak 3901m
Cloud Peak 4013m
Borah Peak 3859m

USA: CALIFORNIA & NEVADA

The Gold Rush of 1849 attracted the first major wave of European settlers to the West Coast. The pleasant climate, beautiful scenery, and dynamic economy continue to attract immigrants – despite the ever-present danger of earthquakes – and California has become the US's most populous state. The overwhelmingly urban population is concentrated in the vast conurbations of Los Angeles, San Francisco, and San Diego; new immigrants include people from South Korea, the Philippines, Vietnam, and Mexico. Nevada's arid lands were initially exploited for minerals; in recent years, revenue from mining has been superseded by income from the tourist and gambling centers of Las Vegas and Reno.

Map key

Population

- 1 million to 5 million
- 500,000 to 1 million
- 100,000 to 500,000
- 50,000 to 100,000
- 10,000 to 50,000
- below 10,000

Elevation

- 4000m / 13,124ft
- 3000m / 9843ft
- 2000m / 6562ft
- 1000m / 3281ft
- 500m / 1640ft
- 250m / 820ft
- 100m / 328ft
- sea level

Scale 1:3,250,000

Km 0 5 10 20 30 40 50 60 70 80

Miles 0 5 10 20 30 40 50 60 70 80

projection: Lambert Conformal Conic

Transportation & industry

Nevada's rich mineral reserves ushered in a period of mining wealth which has now been replaced by revenue generated from gambling. California supports a broad set of activities including defense-related industries and research and development facilities. "Silicon Valley," near San Francisco, is a world leading center for microelectronics, while tourism and the Los Angeles film industry also generate large incomes.

DUNES
OASIS
CASINO

Gambling was legalized in Nevada in 1931. Las Vegas has since become the center of this multimillion dollar industry.

Oregon
Idaho
Nevada
Utah
Reno
Carson City
Ely
Sacramento
Oakland
San Francisco
San Jose
California
Las Vegas
Bakersfield
Arizona
Los Angeles
San Diego
PACIFIC OCEAN
MEXICO

Major industry and infrastructure

- aerospace
- car manufacture
- defense
- film industry
- finance
- food processing
- gambling
- hi-tech industry
- mining
- pharmaceuticals
- research & development
- textiles
- tourism
- major towns
- international airports
- major roads
- major industrial areas

Transportation network

211,459 miles (338,334 km)	2944 miles (4710 km)
7822 miles (12,595 km)	190 miles (360 km)

In California, the motor vehicle is a vital part of daily life, and an extensive freeway system runs throughout the state, cementing its position as the most important mode of transport.

The General Sherman sequoia tree in Sequoia National Park is around 2500 years old and at 275 ft (84 m) is one of the largest living things on earth.

192

The landscape

The broad Central Valley divides California's coastal mountains from the Sierra Nevada. The San Andreas Fault, running beneath much of the state, is the site of frequent earth tremors and sometimes more serious earthquakes. East of the Sierra Nevada, the landscape is characterized by the basin and range topography with stony deserts and many salt lakes.

Rising molten rock causes stretching of the Earth's crust

Extensive cracking (faulting) uplifted a series of ridges

As ridges are eroded they fill intervening valleys with sediments

Molten rock (magma) welling up to form a dome in the Earth's interior, causes the brittle surface rocks to stretch and crack. Some areas were uplifted to form mountains (ranges), while others sunk to form flat valleys (basins).

Most of California's agriculture is confined to the fertile and extensively irrigated Central Valley, running between the Coast Ranges and the Sierra Nevada. It incorporates the San Joaquin and Sacramento valleys.

The dramatic granitic rock formations of Half Dome and El Capitan, and the verdant coniferous forests, attract millions of visitors annually to Yosemite National Park in the Sierra Nevada.

Sierra Nevada

The Great Basin dominates most of Nevada's topography containing large open basins, punctuated by eroded features such as *buttes* and *mesas*. River flow tends to be seasonal, dependent upon spring showers and winter snow melt.

Wheeler Peak is home to some of the world's oldest trees, bristlecone pines, which live for up to 5000 years.

When the Hoover Dam across the Colorado River was completed in 1936, it created Lake Mead, one of the largest artificial lakes in the world, extending for 115 miles (285 km) upstream.

The San Andreas Fault is a transverse fault which extends for 650 miles (1050 km) through California. Major earthquakes occur when the land either side of the fault moves at different rates. San Francisco was devastated by an earthquake in 1906.

Death Valley

Named by migrating settlers in 1849, Death Valley is the driest, hottest place in North America, as well as being the lowest point on land in the western hemisphere, at 282 ft (86 m) below sea level.

The sparsely populated Mojave Desert receives less than 8 inches (200 mm) of rainfall a year. It is used extensively for weapons-testing and military purposes.

The Salton Sea was created accidentally between 1905 and 1907 when an irrigation channel from the Colorado River broke out of its banks and formed this salty 300 sq mile (777 sq km), landlocked lake.

Amargosa Desert

The Sierra Nevada create a "rainshadow," preventing rain from reaching much of Nevada. Pacific air masses, passing over the mountains, are stripped of their moisture.

Using the land

California is the leading agricultural producer in the US, although low rainfall makes irrigation essential. The long growing season and abundant sunshine allow many crops to be grown in the fertile Central Valley including grapes, citrus fruits, vegetables, and cotton. Almost 17 million acres (6.8 million hectares) of California's forests are used commercially. Nevada's arid climate and poor soil are largely unsuitable for agriculture; 85% of its land is state owned and large areas are used for underground testing of nuclear weapons.

Land use and agricultural distribution

- cattle
- citrus fruits
- fruit
- irrigation
- timber
- vineyards
- major towns
- pasture
- cropland
- forest
- desert

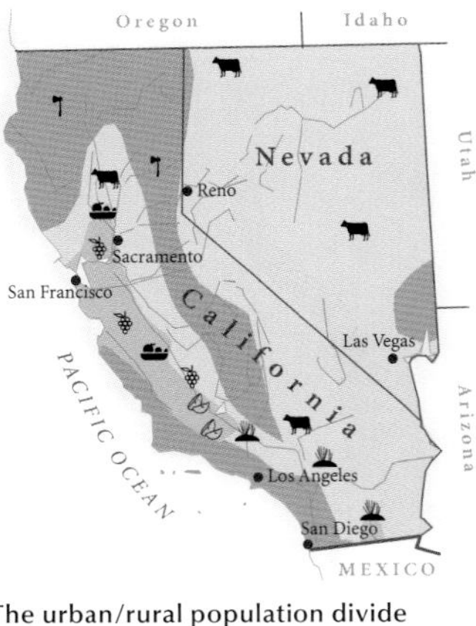
Oregon
Idaho
Nevada
Reno
Utah
Sacramento
San Francisco
California
Las Vegas
Arizona
PACIFIC OCEAN
Los Angeles
San Diego
MEXICO

Without considerable irrigation, this fertile valley at Palm Springs would still be part of the Sonoran Desert. California's farmers account for about 80% of the state's total water usage.

The urban/rural population divide

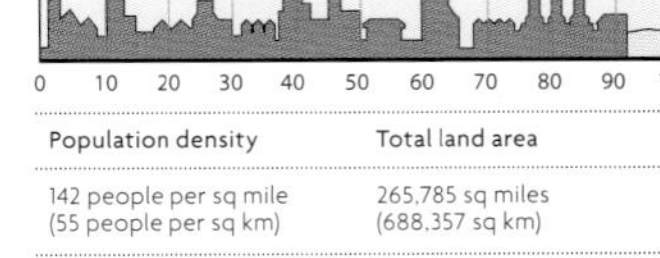
urban 92%
rural 8%
0 10 20 30 40 50 60 70 80 90 100

Population density	Total land area
142 people per sq mile (55 people per sq km)	265,785 sq miles (688,357 sq km)

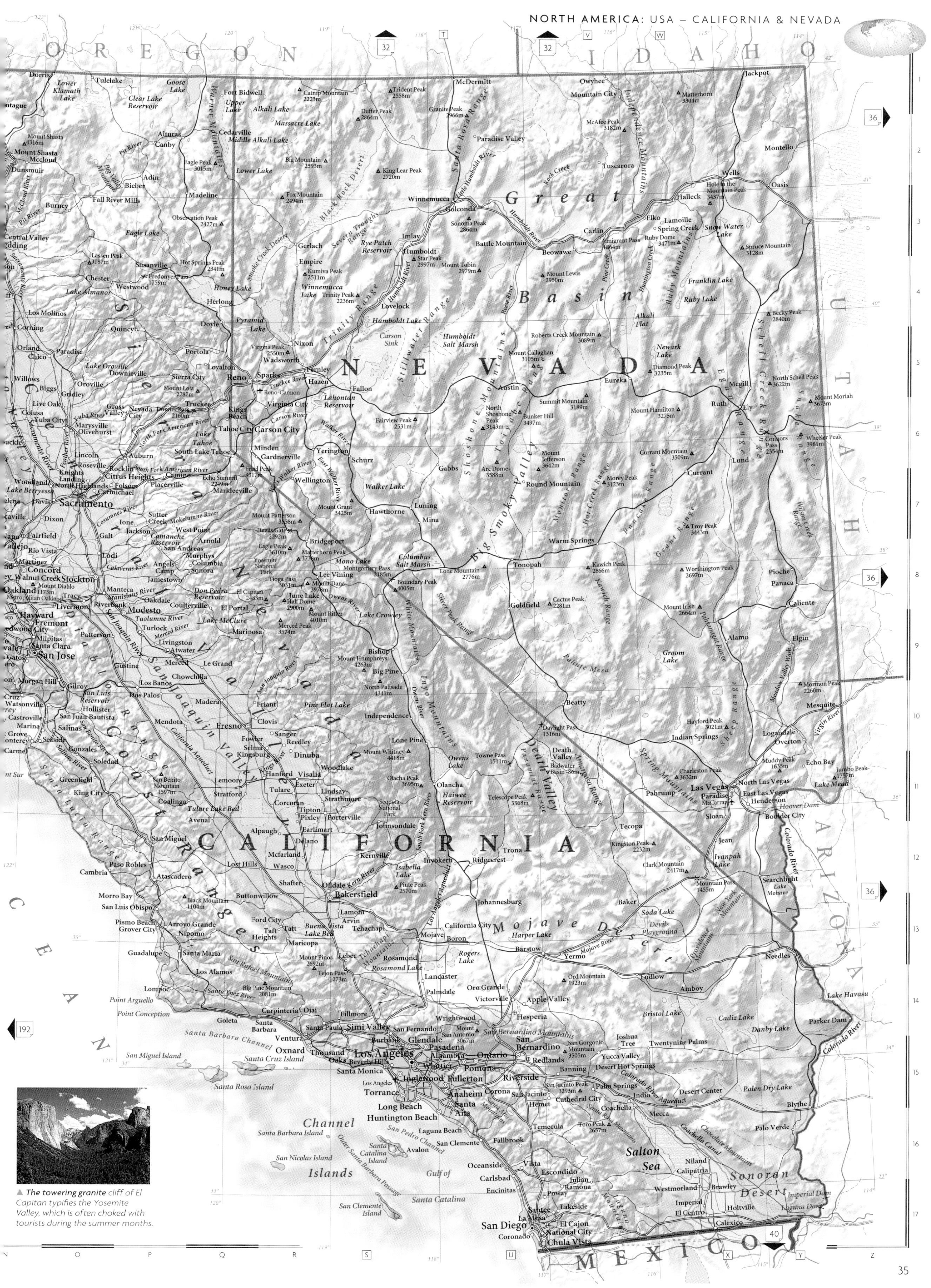
OREGON
IDAHO
UTAH
ARIZONA
MEXICO
NEVADA
CALIFORNIA
Great Basin
OCEAN
Mojave Desert
Sonoran Desert
Death Valley
Salton Sea
Channel Islands
Gulf of Santa Catalina
Santa Barbara Channel
Sierra Nevada
Coast Ranges
San Joaquin Valley
Sacramento Valley
Lake Tahoe
Lake Mead
Mono Lake
Las Vegas
Reno
Carson City
Sacramento
San Francisco
Oakland
San Jose
Stockton
Modesto
Fresno
Bakersfield
Los Angeles
San Diego
San Bernardino
Riverside
Long Beach
Anaheim
Santa Barbara
Oxnard
Palm Springs
Barstow
Needles
Elko
Ely
Winnemucca
Tonopah
Henderson
Mount Whitney 4418m
Mount Shasta 4316m
Lassen Peak 3187m
Boundary Peak 4005m
North Palisade 4341m
Wheeler Peak 3981m
El Capitan 2307m
Half Dome 2900m
Yosemite National Park
Sequoia National Park
Colorado River
Humboldt River
Owens River
Tehachapi Mountains
San Rafael Mountains
Ruby Mountains
Spring Mountains
Sonora Peak 2864m
32
36
36
36
40
192

▲ The towering granite cliff of El Capitan typifies the Yosemite Valley, which is often choked with tourists during the summer months.

USA: SOUTH MOUNTAIN STATES

Arizona, Colorado, New Mexico, Utah

This arid region, characterized by expansive plateaus and spectacular canyons is home to several distinct peoples. The ruins of cliff dwellings built a thousand years ago by the Anasazi people still exist today, and native Americans own one-third of the land in Arizona. Spanish and Mexican conquest and settlement left a hispanic presence which is strongest in New Mexico. The Mormons, who came to the Great Salt Lake seeking religious freedom in 1847, were among the earliest Anglo-American settlers and now make up over 70% of Utah's population. The region's mineral wealth drove rapid development in the 20th century, yet the constraints of a fragile environment, including widespread water shortages, may limit prospects for growth.

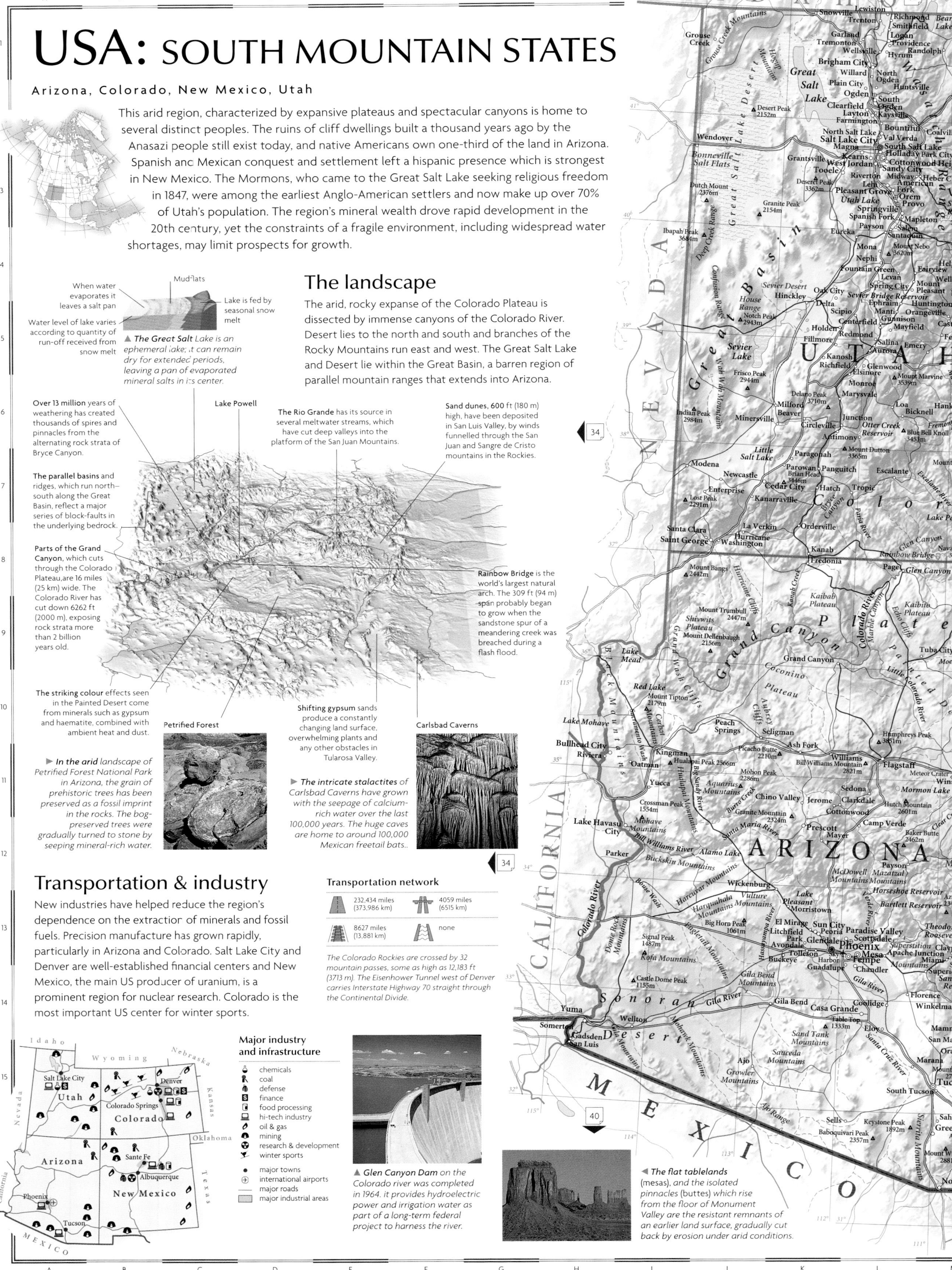

Mudflats
When water evaporates it leaves a salt pan
Lake is fed by seasonal snow melt
Water level of lake varies according to quantity of run-off received from snow melt
Lake Powell
Over 13 million years of weathering has created thousands of spires and pinnacles from the alternating rock strata of Bryce Canyon.
The Rio Grande has its source in several meltwater streams, which have cut deep valleys into the platform of the San Juan Mountains.
Sand dunes, 600 ft (180 m) high, have been deposited in San Luis Valley, by winds funnelled through the San Juan and Sangre de Cristo mountains in the Rockies.
The parallel basins and ridges, which run north–south along the Great Basin, reflect a major series of block-faults in the underlying bedrock.
Parts of the Grand Canyon, which cuts through the Colorado Plateau, are 16 miles (25 km) wide. The Colorado River has cut down 6262 ft (2000 m), exposing rock strata more than 2 billion years old.
Rainbow Bridge is the world's largest natural arch. The 309 ft (94 m) span probably began to grow when the sandstone spur of a meandering creek was breached during a flash flood.
The striking colour effects seen in the Painted Desert come from minerals such as gypsum and haematite, combined with ambient heat and dust.
Petrified Forest
Shifting gypsum sands produce a constantly changing land surface, overwhelming plants and any other obstacles in Tularosa Valley.
Carlsbad Caverns
Transportation network
232,434 miles (373,986 km)
4059 miles (6515 km)
8627 miles (13,881 km)
none
Major industry and infrastructure
chemicals
coal
defense
finance
food processing
hi-tech industry
oil & gas
mining
research & development
winter sports
major towns
international airports
major roads
major industrial areas
Idaho
Wyoming
Nebraska
Salt Lake City
Denver
Utah
Colorado Springs
Colorado
Kansas
Nevada
Oklahoma
Arizona
Santa Fe
Albuquerque
New Mexico
Texas
California
Phoenix
Tucson
MEXICO
IDAHO
NEVADA
UTAH
ARIZONA
CALIFORNIA
MEXICO
Great Salt Lake
Great Basin
Great Salt Lake Desert
Grand Canyon
Colorado Plateau
Painted Desert
Sonoran Desert
Salt Lake City
Provo
Ogden
Flagstaff
Phoenix
Mesa
Tempe
Yuma
Colorado River

▲ *The Great Salt Lake is an ephemeral lake; it can remain dry for extended periods, leaving a pan of evaporated mineral salts in its center.*

► *In the arid landscape of Petrified Forest National Park in Arizona, the grain of prehistoric trees has been preserved as a fossil imprint in the rocks. The bog-preserved trees were gradually turned to stone by seeping mineral-rich water.*

► *The intricate stalactites of Carlsbad Caverns have grown with the seepage of calcium-rich water over the last 100,000 years. The huge caves are home to around 100,000 Mexican freetail bats..*

The landscape

The arid, rocky expanse of the Colorado Plateau is dissected by immense canyons of the Colorado River. Desert lies to the north and south and branches of the Rocky Mountains run east and west. The Great Salt Lake and Desert lie within the Great Basin, a barren region of parallel mountain ranges that extends into Arizona.

Transportation & industry

New industries have helped reduce the region's dependence on the extraction of minerals and fossil fuels. Precision manufacture has grown rapidly, particularly in Arizona and Colorado. Salt Lake City and Denver are well-established financial centers and New Mexico, the main US producer of uranium, is a prominent region for nuclear research. Colorado is the most important US center for winter sports.

The Colorado Rockies are crossed by 32 mountain passes, some as high as 12,183 ft (3713 m). The Eisenhower Tunnel west of Denver carries Interstate Highway 70 straight through the Continental Divide.

▲ *Glen Canyon Dam on the Colorado river was completed in 1964. it provides hydroelectric power and irrigation water as part of a long-term federal project to harness the river.*

◄ *The flat tablelands (mesas), and the isolated pinnacles (buttes) which rise from the floor of Monument Valley are the resistant remnants of an earlier land surface, gradually cut back by erosion under arid conditions.*

32 34 40

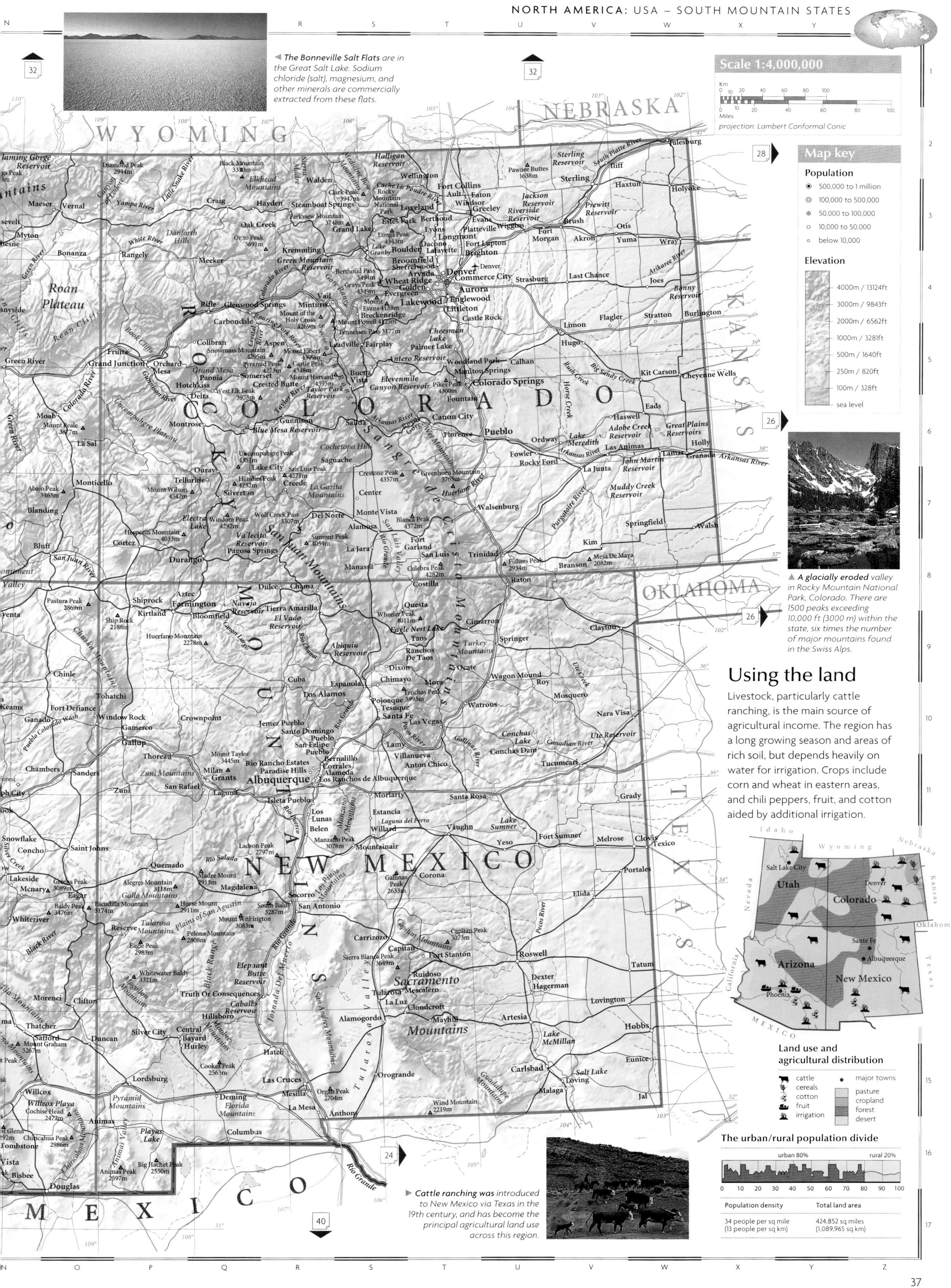
Scale 1:4,000,000
Km
Miles
projection: Lambert Conformal Conic
Map key
Population
500,000 to 1 million
100,000 to 500,000
50,000 to 100,000
10,000 to 50,000
below 10,000
Elevation
4000m / 13124ft
3000m / 9843ft
2000m / 6562ft
1000m / 3281ft
500m / 1640ft
250m / 820ft
100m / 328ft
sea level
WYOMING
NEBRASKA
KANSAS
OKLAHOMA
TEXAS
COLORADO
NEW MEXICO
MEXICO
ROCKY MOUNTAINS
Land use and agricultural distribution
cattle
cereals
cotton
fruit
irrigation
major towns
pasture
cropland
forest
desert
The urban/rural population divide
urban 80%
rural 20%
Population density
34 people per sq mile
(13 people per sq km)
Total land area
424,852 sq miles
(1,089,965 sq km)

◀ *The Bonneville Salt Flats are in the Great Salt Lake. Sodium chloride (salt), magnesium, and other minerals are commercially extracted from these flats.*

▲ *A glacially eroded valley in Rocky Mountain National Park, Colorado. There are 1500 peaks exceeding 10,000 ft (3000 m) within the state, six times the number of major mountains found in the Swiss Alps.*

Using the land

Livestock, particularly cattle ranching, is the main source of agricultural income. The region has a long growing season and areas of rich soil, but depends heavily on water for irrigation. Crops include corn and wheat in eastern areas, and chili peppers, fruit, and cotton aided by additional irrigation.

▶ *Cattle ranching was introduced to New Mexico via Texas in the 19th century, and has become the principal agricultural land use across this region.*

USA: HAWAI'I

The 122 islands of the Hawaiian archipelago – which are part of Polynesia – are the peaks of the world's largest volcanoes. They rise approximately 6 miles (9.7 km) from the floor of the Pacific Ocean. The largest, the island of Hawai'i, remains highly active. Hawai'i became the US's 50th state in 1959. A tradition of receiving immigrant workers is reflected in the islands' ethnic diversity, with peoples drawn from around the rim of the Pacific. Only 9% of the current population are native Polynesians.

▲ *The island of* Moloka'i *is formed from volcanic rock. Mature sand dunes cover the rocks in coastal areas.*

Transportation & industry

Tourism dominates the economy, with over 90% of the population employed in services. The naval base at Pearl Harbor is also a major source of employment. Industry is concentrated on the island of O'ahu and relies mostly on imported materials, while agricultural produce is processed locally.

Transportation network

Roads	4102 miles (6600 km)	Railways	none
Airports	43 miles (69 km)	Waterways	none

Hawai'i relies on ocean-surface transportation. Honolulu is the main focus of this network, bringing foreign trade and the markets of mainland US to Hawai'i's outer islands

◀ *Haleakala's extinct volcanic crater is the world's largest. The giant caldera, containing many secondary cones, is 2000 ft (600 m) deep and 20 miles (32 km) in circumference.*

Major industry and infrastructure

- food processing
- military base
- textiles
- tourism
- major towns
- international airports
- major roads
- major industrial areas

Ni'ihau, Kaua'i, O'ahu, Honolulu, Moloka'i, Lāna'i, Kaho'olawe, Maui, Hawai'i, Hilo, Hawai'i, PACIFIC OCEAN

Using the land & sea

The ice-free coastline of Alaska provides access to salmon fisheries and more than 129 million acres (52.2 million ha) of forest. Most of Alaska is uncultivable, and around 90% of food is imported. Barley, hay, and hothouse products are grown around Anchorage, where dairy farming is also concentrated.

The urban/rural population divide

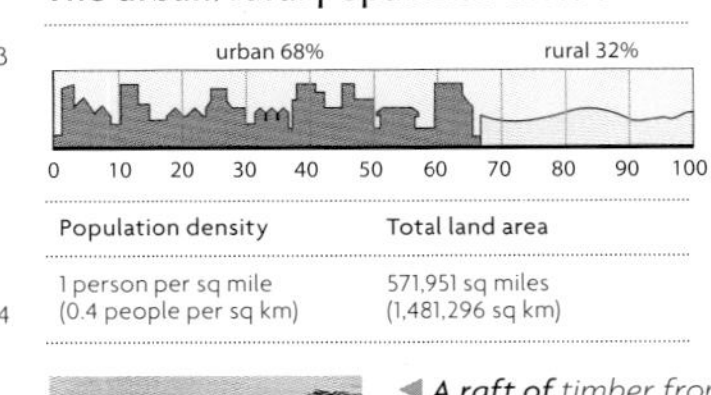
urban 68%
rural 32%
0 10 20 30 40 50 60 70 80 90 100

Population density	Total land area
1 person per sq mile (0.4 people per sq km)	571,951 sq miles (1,481,296 sq km)

◀ *A raft of timber from the Tongass forest is hauled by a tug, bound for the pulp mills of the Alaskan coast between Juneau and Ketchikan.*

CHUKCHI SEA
RUSSIAN FEDERATION
Bering Strait
BERING SEA
Arctic Circle
Cape Lisburne
Point Hope
Shishmaref
Little Diomede Island
Cape Prince of Wales
Brooks Mountain 883m
Brevig Mission
Port Clarence
Teller
Cape Douglas
Cape Rodney
Nome
Cape Nome
Northwest Cape
Gambell
Savoonga
Saint Lawrence Island
Southwest Cape
Camp Kulowiye
Northeast Cape
Southeast Cape
Emmonak
Alakanuk
Sheldons Point
Scammon Bay
Hooper Bay
Chevak
Hall Island
Glory of Russia Cape
Saint Matthew Island
Upright Cape
Pinnacle Island
Cape Mohican
Mekoryuk
Nunivak Island
Roberts Mountain 510m
Cape Mendenhall
Tanunak
Newtok
Kipnuk
Saint Paul Island
Saint Paul
Pribilof Islands
Saint George Island
Saint George

122
192

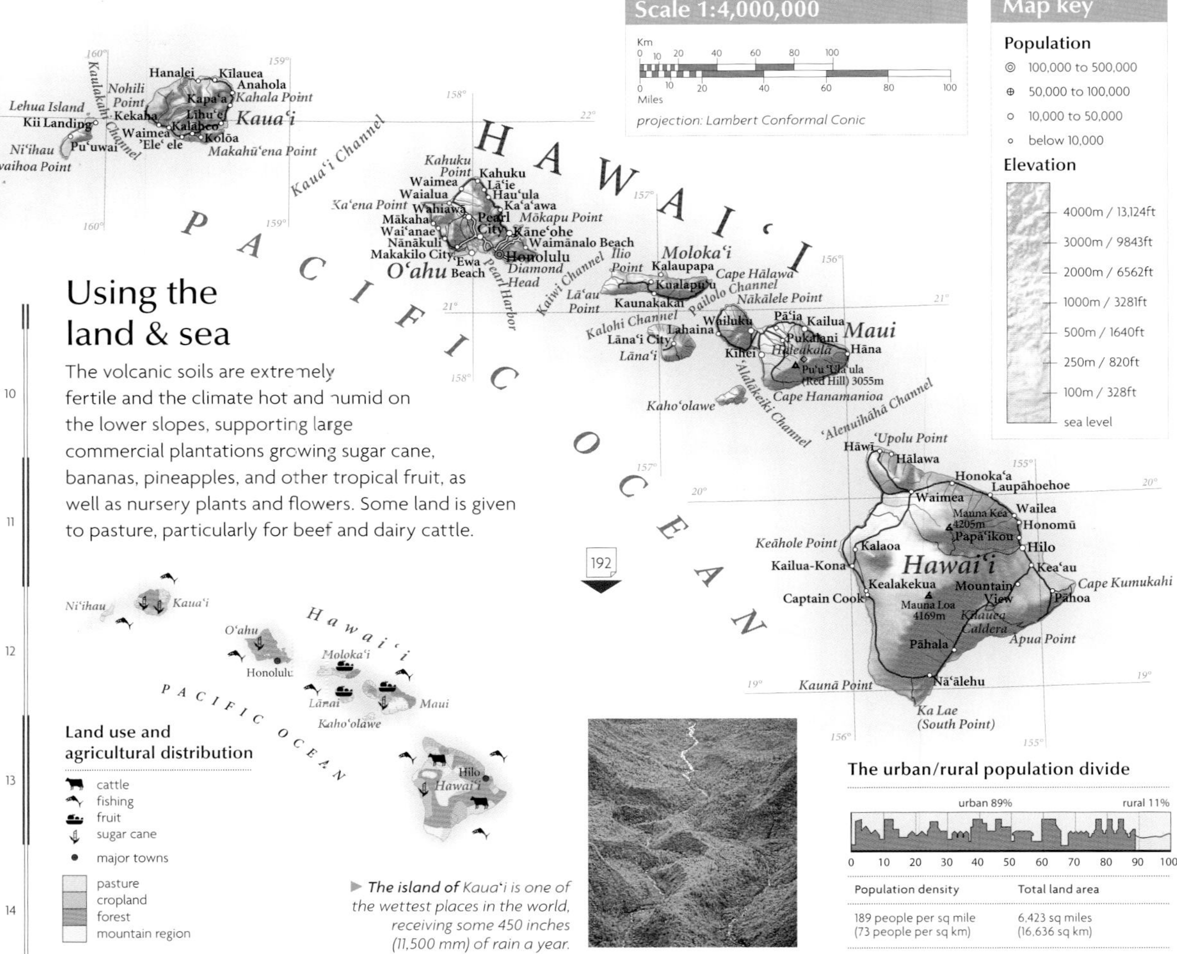
HAWAI'I
PACIFIC OCEAN
Kaua'i
Ni'ihau
Lehua Island
Kii Landing
Pu'uwai
Kawaihoa Point
Hanalei
Kīlauea
Anahola
Kahala Point
Nohili Point
Kekaha
Waimea
Kapa'a
Lihu'e
Kalaheo
Kōloa
'Ele'ele
Makahū'ena Point
Kaulakahi Channel
Kaua'i Channel
Kahuku Point
Kahuku
Lā'ie
Hau'ula
Ka'a'awa
Ka'ena Point
Waimea
Waialua
Wahiawā
Mōkapu Point
Kāne'ohe
Waimānalo Beach
Pearl City
Honolulu
Diamond Head
O'ahu
Ewa Beach
Pearl Harbor
Kaiwi Channel
Moloka'i
Kalaupapa
Kaunakakai
Cape Hālawa
Pailolo Channel
Lā'au Point
Kalohi Channel
Lāna'i City
Lāna'i
Lahaina
Wailuku
Kahului
Pā'ia
Kīhei
Pukalani
Haleakala
Maui
Hāna
Nākālele Point
Pu'u 'Ula'ula (Red Hill) 3055m
Kaho'olawe
Cape Hanamanioa
'Alenuihāhā Channel
'Upolu Point
Hāwī
Hālawa
Honoka'a
Laupāhoehoe
Waimea
Mauna Kea 4205m
Papa'ikou
Wailea
Honomū
Hilo
Keāhole Point
Kalaoa
Kailua-Kona
Hawai'i
Kea'au
Cape Kumukahi
Captain Cook
Kealakekua
Mountain View
Pāhoa
Mauna Loa 4169m
Kīlauea Caldera
Pāhala
Apua Point
Kaunā Point
Nā'ālehu
Ka Lae (South Point)

Scale 1:4,000,000

projection: Lambert Conformal Conic

Map key

Population

- 100,000 to 500,000
- 50,000 to 100,000
- 10,000 to 50,000
- below 10,000

Elevation

- 4000m / 13,124ft
- 3000m / 9843ft
- 2000m / 6562ft
- 1000m / 3281ft
- 500m / 1640ft
- 250m / 820ft
- 100m / 328ft
- sea level

Using the land & sea

The volcanic soils are extremely fertile and the climate hot and humid on the lower slopes, supporting large commercial plantations growing sugar cane, bananas, pineapples, and other tropical fruit, as well as nursery plants and flowers. Some land is given to pasture, particularly for beef and dairy cattle.

Land use and agricultural distribution

- cattle
- fishing
- fruit
- sugar cane
- major towns
- pasture
- cropland
- forest
- mountain region

Ni'ihau, Kaua'i, O'ahu, Honolulu, Moloka'i, Lāna'i, Kaho'olawe, Maui, Hawai'i, Hilo, Hawai'i, PACIFIC OCEAN

▶ *The island of* Kaua'i *is one of the wettest places in the world, receiving some 450 inches (11,500 mm) of rain a year.*

The urban/rural population divide

urban 89% | rural 11%

Population density	Total land area
189 people per sq mile (73 people per sq km)	6,423 sq miles (16,636 sq km)

Map key

Population

- 100,000 to 500,000
- 50,000 to 100,000
- 10,000 to 50,000
- below 10,000

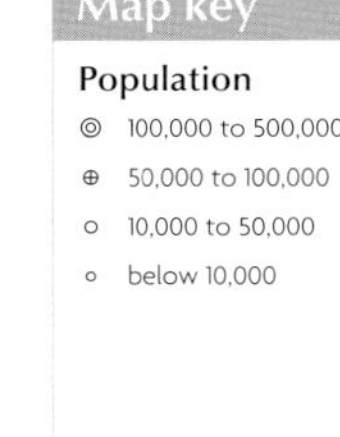

Elevation

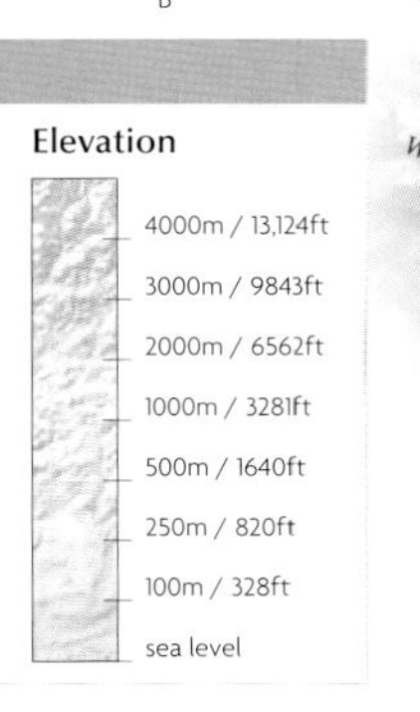
4000m / 13,124ft
3000m / 9843ft
2000m / 6562ft
1000m / 3281ft
500m / 1640ft
250m / 820ft
100m / 328ft
sea level

Aleutian Islands
PACIFIC OCEAN
Near Islands
Cape Wrangell
Attu Island
Attu
Agattu Strait
Shemya Island
Agattu Island
Krugloi Point
Cape Sabak
Buldir Island
Kiska Island
Vega Point
Rat Islands
Rat Island
Amchitka Island
Segula Island
Little Sitkin Island
Semisopochnoi Island
Anvil Peak 1221m
Amchitka Pass
Gareloi Island
Tanaga Island
Tanaga Volcano 1806m
Delarof Islands
Cape Sasmik
Kanaga Island
Kanaga Volcano 1307m
Great Sitkin Island
Adak Island
Kagalaska Island
Andreanof Islands
Atka Island
Atka
Seguam Island
Amlia Island
Seguam Pass
Amukta Pass
Yunaska Island
Carlisle Island
Amukta Island
Herbert Island
Islands of Four Mountains
Umnak Island
Nikolski
Fox Islands
Unalaska Island
Dutch Harbor
Makushin Volcano 2036m
Akutan Island
Akutan
Akun Island
Unimak Pass
Pogromni Volcano 2857m
Shishaldin Volcano 2857m
Unimak Island
Tigalda Island
Avatanak Island
Krenitzin Is

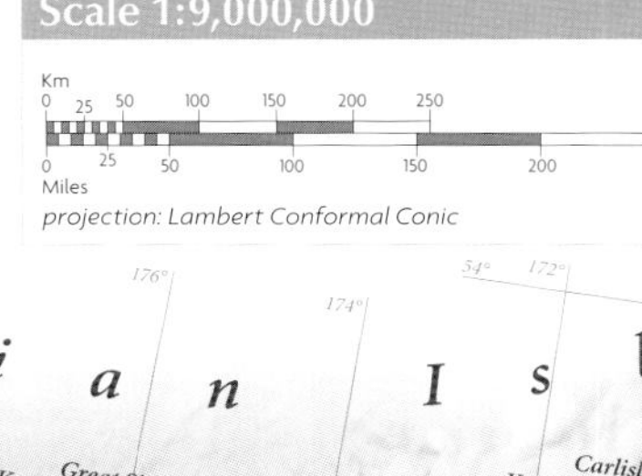
Scale 1:9,000,000
projection: Lambert Conformal Conic

Land use and agricultural distribution

- fishing
- reindeer
- fruit
- major towns
- forest
- barren
- tundra

USA: ALASKA

Almost 650,000 people live in Alaska, a wilderness of ice, forest, mountains, and plains, purchased from Russia in 1867 and twice the size of Texas. The discovery of large oil reserves has brought prosperity to the US's "last frontier," while advancing the need to preserve natural habitats and the traditional livelihoods of indigenous peoples, such as the Aleuts and Inupiaq.

196

The landscape

The mountains of the Pacific coast culminate in the heavily glaciated Alaska Range and extend west, to the Alaska Peninsula and the great volcanic arc of the Aleutian Islands. The interior plains are drained by the Yukon River and bounded by the bare, jagged peaks of the Brooks Range to the north.

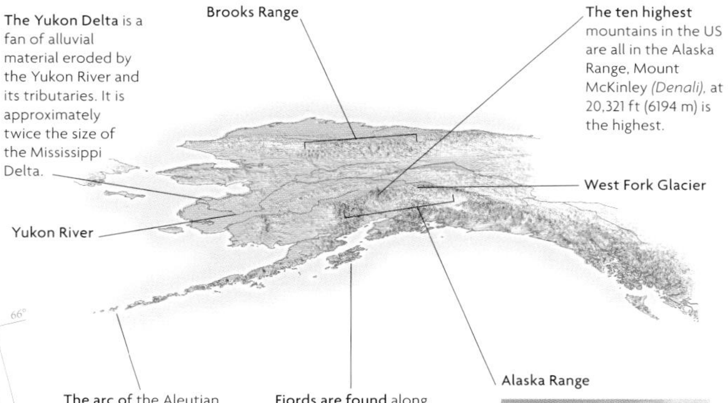

The Yukon Delta is a fan of alluvial material eroded by the Yukon River and its tributaries. It is approximately twice the size of the Mississippi Delta.

Brooks Range

The ten highest mountains in the US are all in the Alaska Range. Mount McKinley *(Denali)*, at 20,321 ft (6194 m) is the highest.

West Fork Glacier

Yukon River

The arc of the Aleutian Islands marks the boundary between the Eurasian and Pacific tectonic plates.

Fjords are found along the coast where valleys, deeply excavated by large glaciers, were inundated by rising seas.

Alaska Range

▲ *By August, the Alaska Range is covered with autumnal tundra vegetation.*

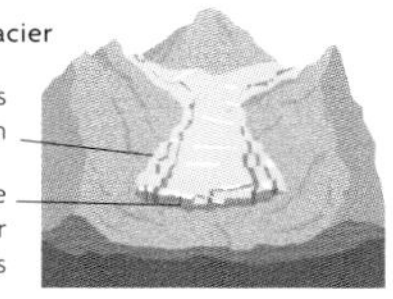

8

West Fork Glacier

The surging ice mass shears along the glacier margin

Deep crevasses divide the front of the surging glacier into large ice blocks

▲ ***Surging glaciers make** rapid and dramatic advances, normally after periods of snow accumulation. West Fork Glacier in the Susitna River Basin traveled 2.5 miles (4 km) in 1987.*

ARCTIC OCEAN

BEAUFORT SEA

ALASKA

Brooks Range

CANADA

Gulf of Alaska

Alexander Archipelago

Bristol Bay

Alaska Peninsula

Transportation & industry

Large areas of Alaska are undeveloped, and much of the existing infrastructure is a legacy of Cold War military investment. Mineral ores, including gold, have been mined for over a century, but the oil business now dominates the economy. Processing industries such as paper-pulp mills supply Japan and other markets on the Pacific Rim.

192

192

Transportation network

- 13,524 miles (21,760 km)
- 49 miles (78 km)
- 482 miles (772 km)
- none

Over 40 million gallons (182 million litres) of oil are pumped through the Trans-Alaska Pipeline every day. The oil takes six days to travel the 789 miles (1262 km) from Prudhoe Bay to Valdez.

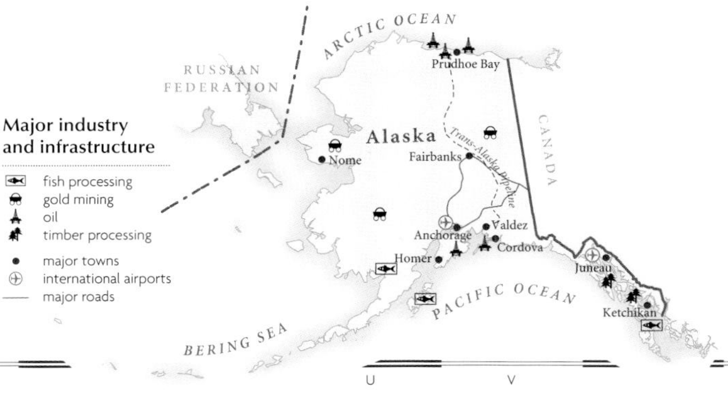

Major industry and infrastructure

- fish processing
- gold mining
- oil
- timber processing
- major towns
- international airports
- major roads

▲ ***The Trans-Alaska Pipeline** has carried crude oil from Prudhoe Bay since 1977. The oilfield is the US's largest and is estimated to be equal in size to the biggest oilfields of the Persian Gulf.*

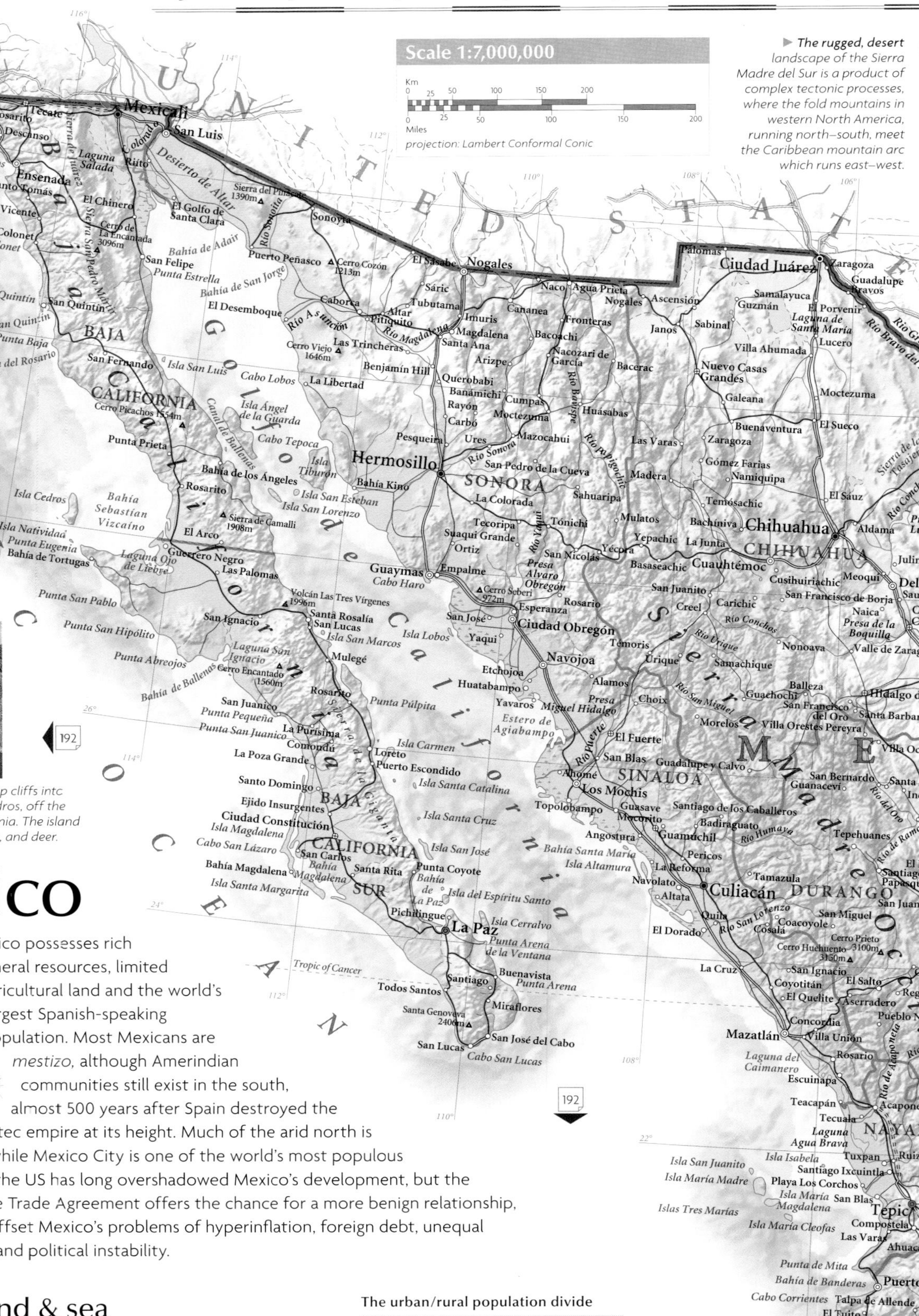

Scale 1:7,000,000

projection: Lambert Conformal Conic

▶ ***The rugged, desert*** *landscape of the Sierra Madre del Sur is a product of complex tectonic processes, where the fold mountains in western North America, running north–south, meet the Caribbean mountain arc which runs east–west.*

▲ ***Wave action has*** *cut steep cliffs into the igneous rocks of Isla Cedros, off the Pacific coast of Baja California. The island is home to sea lions, reptiles, and deer.*

Mexico

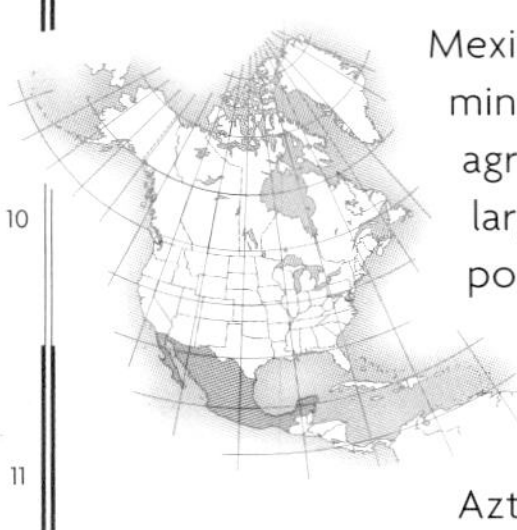

Mexico possesses rich mineral resources, limited agricultural land and the world's largest Spanish-speaking population. Most Mexicans are *mestizo*, although Amerindian communities still exist in the south, almost 500 years after Spain destroyed the Aztec empire at its height. Much of the arid north is sparsely inhabited, while Mexico City is one of the world's most populous cities. Conflict with the US has long overshadowed Mexico's development, but the North American Free Trade Agreement offers the chance for a more benign relationship, which may help to offset Mexico's problems of hyperinflation, foreign debt, unequal wealth distribution, and political instability.

Using the land & sea

Corn occupies much of the cultivated area. Commercial plantations of coffee, sugar, vanilla, and cotton are found along the Gulf coastal plain and in irrigated parts of the arid north, which is otherwise used for extensive ranching. Fishing is important, particularly shellfish for export. A soaring population has created the need for grain imports since 1980.

The urban/rural population divide

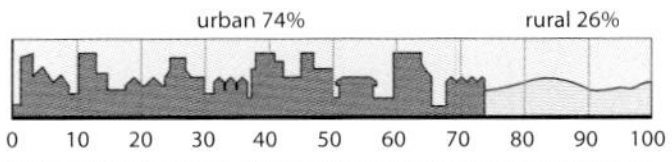

urban 74% | rural 26%

0 10 20 30 40 50 60 70 80 90 100

Population density	Total land area
140 people per sq mile (54 people per sq km)	755,865 sq miles (1,958,200 sq km)

Land use and agricultural distribution

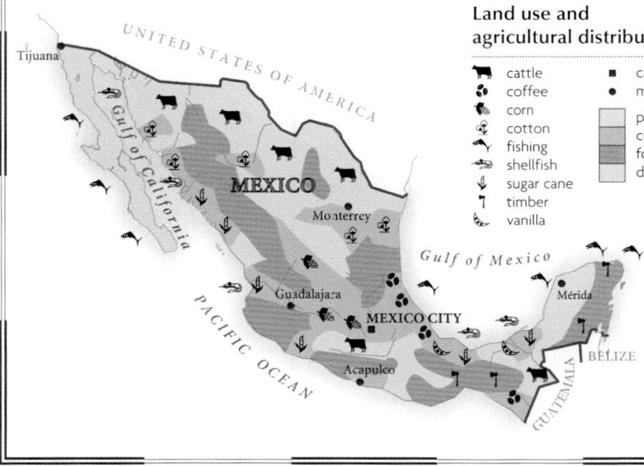

cattle, coffee, corn, cotton, fishing, shellfish, sugar cane, timber, vanilla

capital cities, major towns

pasture, cropland, forest, desert

▶ ***Coffee beans spread*** *out to dry in the sun. Coffee, grown mainly on the Gulf coastal plain, is Mexico's most valuable export crop.*

Map key

Mexico: Administrative regions

Distrito Federal

Population

- above 5 million
- 1 million to 5 million
- 500,000 to 1 million
- 100,000 to 500,000
- 50,000 to 100,000
- 10,000 to 50,000
- below 10,000

Elevation

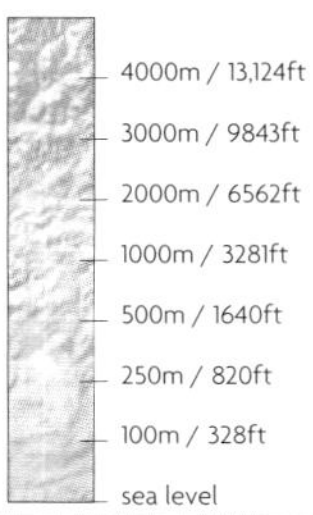

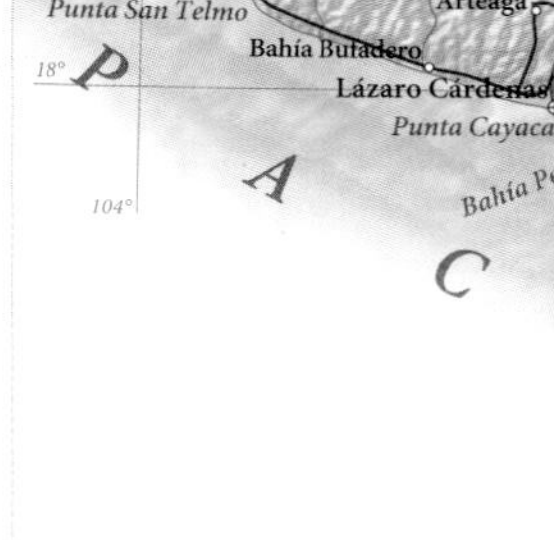
4000m / 13,124ft
3000m / 9843ft
2000m / 6562ft
1000m / 3281ft
500m / 1640ft
250m / 820ft
100m / 328ft
sea level

southward from
...stal plains by the
. The two ranges
...ively,
...ing
The long, narrow, extremely arid peninsula of Baja (lower) California is an elongated granite block, separated from the mainland by the flooded rift valley of the Gulf of California (Golfo de California).
Wave action has constructed sand bars which shelter lagoons along the shore of the Gulf coastal plain.
The dormant cone of Volcán Pico de Orizaba is, at 18,700 ft (5700 m), the highest peak in Mexico. In North America, only Mount McKinley and Mount Logan are taller.
Sierra Madre Oriental
Rio Grande
The heavily-forested Isthmus of Tehuantepec (Istmo de Tehuantepec) is a graben; a low-lying trough created by downward movement of the bedrock between two fault lines.
Sierra Madre Occidental
Gulf of California
Direction of plate movement
Gulf of California
Edge of continental crust
Spreading oceanic ridge
Río Balsas
Popocatépetl
The unstable, earthquake-prone, upland basin around Mexico City was once a region of shallow lakes. Flood control measures and domestic consumption over the last four centuries have caused the virtual disappearance of this surface water.
The highlands of Chiapas are a series of horsts, blocks of land thrust upward between two fault lines. Volcanic cones have developed where lava has flowed out from the faults.
UNITED STATES OF AMERICA
MEXICO
Gulf of California
Gulf of Mexico
PACIFIC OCEAN
BELIZE
GUATEMALA
Major industry and infrastructure
brewing
car manufacture
chemicals
electronics
fish processing
maquiladoras
mining
oil & gas
textiles
capital cities
major towns
international airports
major roads
major industrial areas
Transportation network
67,564 miles (108,746 km)
3994 miles (6429 km)
16,561 miles (26,656 km)
1801 miles (2900 km)
Fast, modern highways or autopistas now link Mexico City with Toluca, Puebla and other satellite cities, yet distant centers like Chihuahua are still served by narrow roads and an outdated railroad network.
Bahía de Campeche
Yucatan Channel
Yucatan Peninsula
Golfo de Tehuantepec
Sierra Madre del Sur
Sierra Madre Oriental
PACIFIC OCEAN

▲ *Tropical rainforest abounds in the Yucatan Peninsula, a broad, low limestone shelf. Rivers are rare due to the porous nature of limestone, so the forest is mostly fed by streams and underground water.*

▲ *The Gulf of California* (Golfo de California) *began to open out about 4 million years ago as a result of rifting and plate displacement along transform faults.*

▲ *Popocatépetl is a dormant volcano, part of the Pacific "Ring of Fire." The crater is over half a mile (1 km) wide.*

Transportation & industry

Oil and gas on the Gulf coast are Mexico's main sources of export income. Metal mining has declined but the country remains a leading global producer of silver. Manufacturing is heavily concentrated around the metropolitan area of Mexico City, while the duty-free movement of goods in the US border region, under the *Maquiladora* (twin plant) scheme, has created new hi-tech and service growth centers.

▲ *A stone figure reclines by the Temple of Warriors, within the Mayan city of Chichén-Itzá. The Maya civilization flourished across the Yucatan Peninsula between 200 and 900 AD.*

16
58
42
42

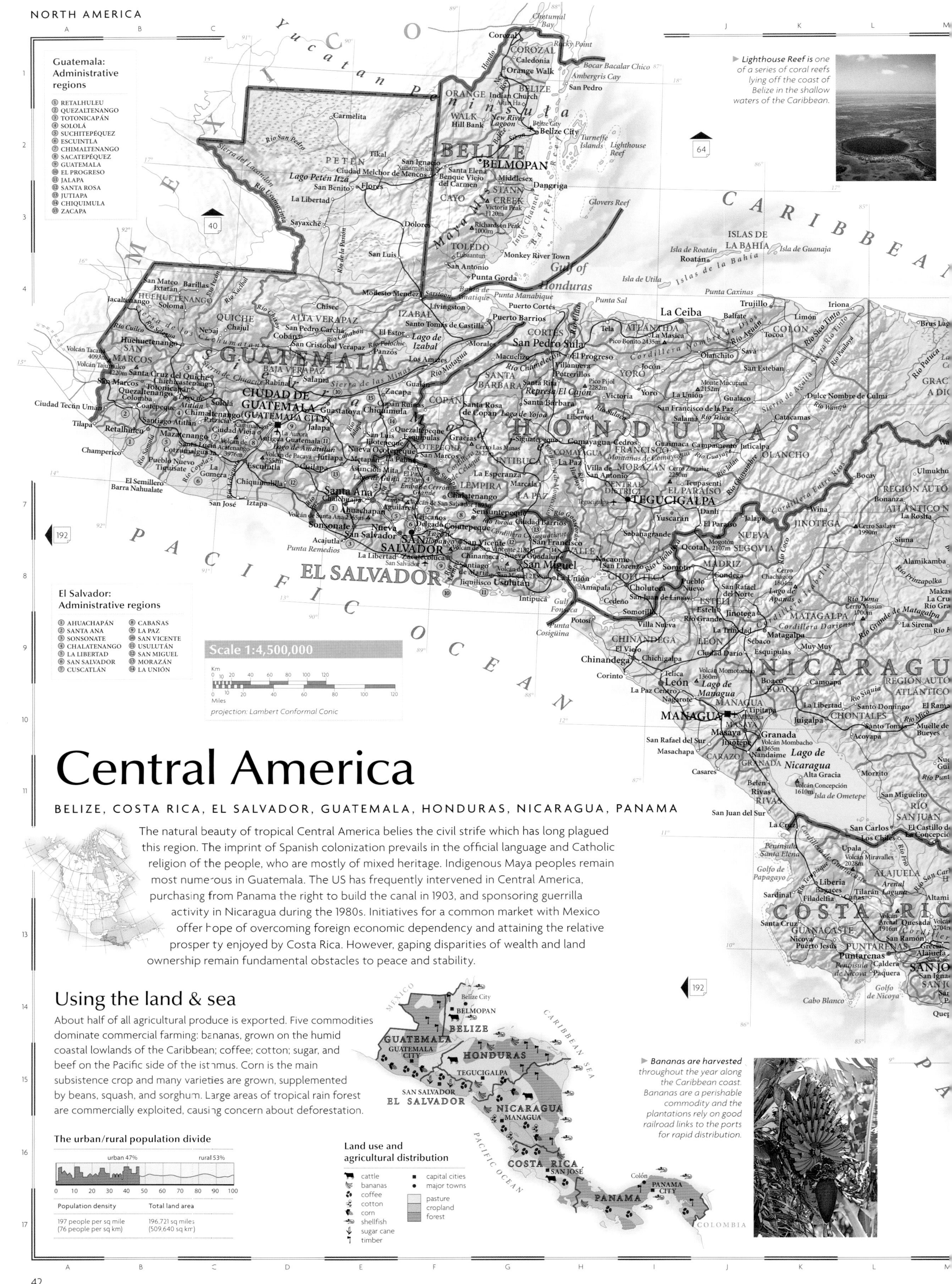

Guatemala: Administrative regions
1 RETALHULEU
2 QUEZALTENANGO
3 TOTONICAPÁN
4 SOLOLÁ
5 SUCHITEPÉQUEZ
6 ESCUINTLA
7 CHIMALTENANGO
8 SACATEPÉQUEZ
9 GUATEMALA
10 EL PROGRESO
11 JALAPA
12 SANTA ROSA
13 JUTIAPA
14 CHIQUIMULA
15 ZACAPA
El Salvador: Administrative regions
1 AHUACHAPÁN
2 SANTA ANA
3 SONSONATE
4 CHALATENANGO
5 LA LIBERTAD
6 SAN SALVADOR
7 CUSCATLÁN
8 CABAÑAS
9 LA PAZ
10 SAN VICENTE
11 USULUTÁN
12 SAN MIGUEL
13 MORAZÁN
14 LA UNIÓN
Scale 1:4,500,000
projection: Lambert Conformal Conic
MEXICO
Yucatan Peninsula
BELIZE
BELMOPAN
Belize City
GUATEMALA
CIUDAD DE GUATEMALA (GUATEMALA CITY)
HONDURAS
TEGUCIGALPA
EL SALVADOR
SAN SALVADOR
NICARAGUA
MANAGUA
COSTA RICA
SAN JOSÉ
CARIBBEAN
PACIFIC OCEAN
Gulf of Honduras
Lago de Nicaragua
Lighthouse Reef

64
40
192
192

Lighthouse Reef is one of a series of coral reefs lying off the coast of Belize in the shallow waters of the Caribbean.

Central America

BELIZE, COSTA RICA, EL SALVADOR, GUATEMALA, HONDURAS, NICARAGUA, PANAMA

The natural beauty of tropical Central America belies the civil strife which has long plagued this region. The imprint of Spanish colonization prevails in the official language and Catholic religion of the people, who are mostly of mixed heritage. Indigenous Maya peoples remain most numerous in Guatemala. The US has frequently intervened in Central America, purchasing from Panama the right to build the canal in 1903, and sponsoring guerrilla activity in Nicaragua during the 1980s. Initiatives for a common market with Mexico offer hope of overcoming foreign economic dependency and attaining the relative prosperity enjoyed by Costa Rica. However, gaping disparities of wealth and land ownership remain fundamental obstacles to peace and stability.

Using the land & sea

About half of all agricultural produce is exported. Five commodities dominate commercial farming: bananas, grown on the humid coastal lowlands of the Caribbean; coffee; cotton; sugar, and beef on the Pacific side of the isthmus. Corn is the main subsistence crop and many varieties are grown, supplemented by beans, squash, and sorghum. Large areas of tropical rain forest are commercially exploited, causing concern about deforestation.

The urban/rural population divide

urban 47% — rural 53%

Population density	Total land area
197 people per sq mile (76 people per sq km)	196,721 sq miles (509,640 sq km)

Land use and agricultural distribution

cattle, bananas, coffee, cotton, corn, shellfish, sugar cane, timber, capital cities, major towns, pasture, cropland, forest

Bananas are harvested throughout the year along the Caribbean coast. Bananas are a perishable commodity and the plantations rely on good railroad links to the ports for rapid distribution.

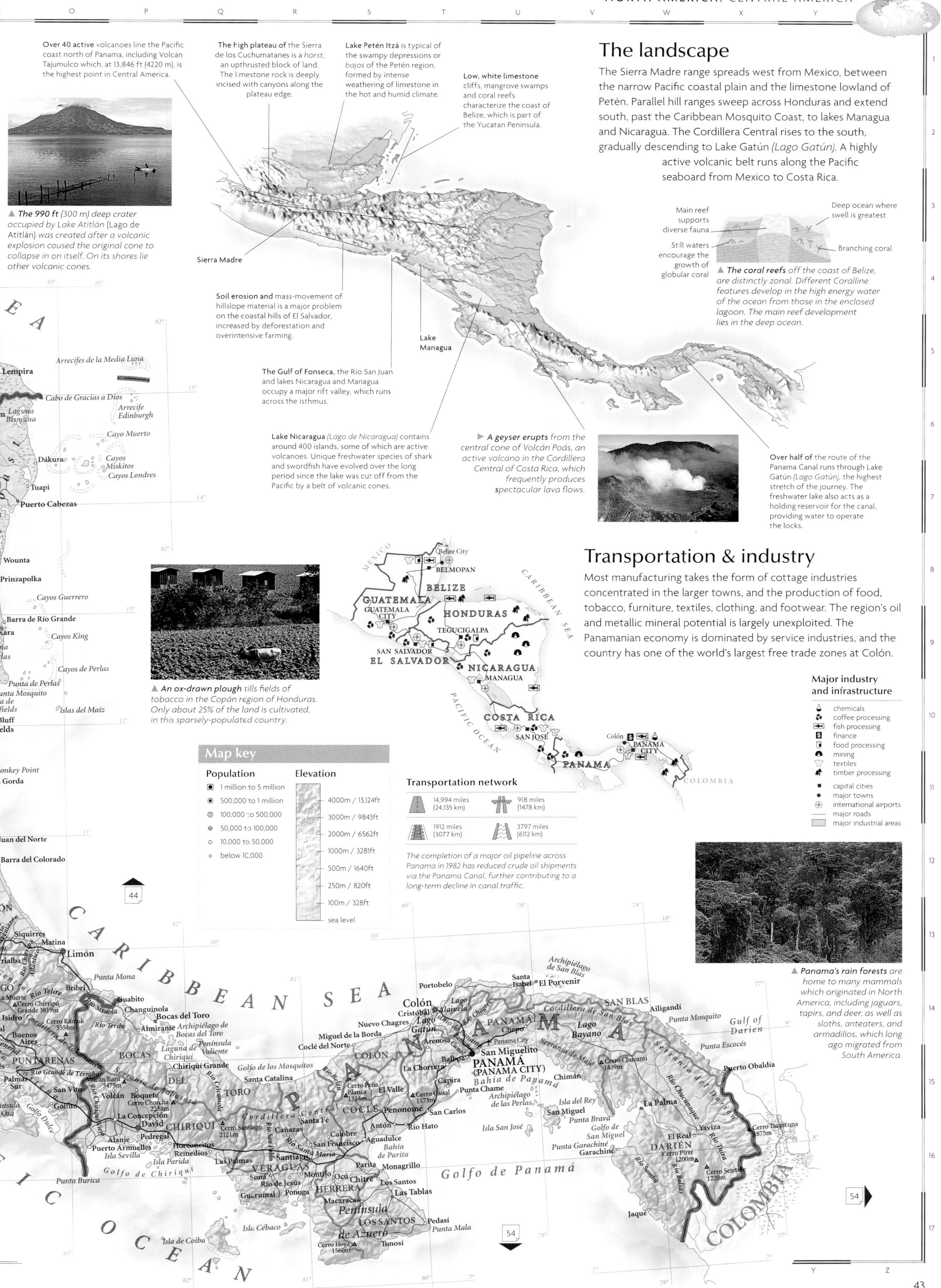

The landscape
The Sierra Madre range spreads west from Mexico, between the narrow Pacific coastal plain and the limestone lowland of Petén. Parallel hill ranges sweep across Honduras and extend south, past the Caribbean Mosquito Coast, to lakes Managua and Nicaragua. The Cordillera Central rises to the south, gradually descending to Lake Gatún (Lago Gatún). A highly active volcanic belt runs along the Pacific seaboard from Mexico to Costa Rica.
Over 40 active volcanoes line the Pacific coast north of Panama, including Volcán Tajumulco which, at 13,846 ft (4220 m), is the highest point in Central America.
The high plateau of the Sierra de los Cuchumatanes is a horst, an upthrusted block of land. The limestone rock is deeply incised with canyons along the plateau edge.
Lake Petén Itzá is typical of the swampy depressions or bajos of the Petén region, formed by intense weathering of limestone in the hot and humid climate.
Low, white limestone cliffs, mangrove swamps and coral reefs characterize the coast of Belize, which is part of the Yucatan Peninsula.
The 990 ft (300 m) deep crater occupied by Lake Atitlán (Lago de Atitlán) was created after a volcanic explosion caused the original cone to collapse in on itself. On its shores lie other volcanic cones.
Sierra Madre
Soil erosion and mass-movement of hillslope material is a major problem on the coastal hills of El Salvador, increased by deforestation and overintensive farming.
Lake Managua
The Gulf of Fonseca, the Río San Juan and lakes Nicaragua and Managua occupy a major rift valley, which runs across the isthmus.
Lake Nicaragua (Lago de Nicaragua) contains around 400 islands, some of which are active volcanoes. Unique freshwater species of shark and swordfish have evolved over the long period since the lake was cut off from the Pacific by a belt of volcanic cones.
A geyser erupts from the central cone of Volcán Poás, an active volcano in the Cordillera Central of Costa Rica, which frequently produces spectacular lava flows.
Over half of the route of the Panama Canal runs through Lake Gatún (Lago Gatún), the highest stretch of the journey. The freshwater lake also acts as a holding reservoir for the canal, providing water to operate the locks.
Main reef supports diverse fauna
Still waters encourage the growth of globular coral
Deep ocean where swell is greatest
Branching coral
The coral reefs off the coast of Belize, are distinctly zonal. Different Coralline features develop in the high energy water of the ocean from those in the enclosed lagoon. The main reef development lies in the deep ocean.
Transportation & industry
Most manufacturing takes the form of cottage industries concentrated in the larger towns, and the production of food, tobacco, furniture, textiles, clothing, and footwear. The region's oil and metallic mineral potential is largely unexploited. The Panamanian economy is dominated by service industries, and the country has one of the world's largest free trade zones at Colón.
An ox-drawn plough tills fields of tobacco in the Copán region of Honduras. Only about 25% of the land is cultivated, in this sparsely-populated country.
MEXICO
Belize City
BELMOPAN
BELIZE
GUATEMALA
GUATEMALA CITY
HONDURAS
TEGUCIGALPA
SAN SALVADOR
EL SALVADOR
NICARAGUA
MANAGUA
COSTA RICA
SAN JOSÉ
PANAMA
Colón
PANAMA CITY
COLOMBIA
CARIBBEAN SEA
PACIFIC OCEAN
Major industry and infrastructure
chemicals
coffee processing
fish processing
finance
food processing
mining
textiles
timber processing
capital cities
major towns
international airports
major roads
major industrial areas
Transportation network
14,994 miles (24,135 km)
918 miles (1478 km)
1912 miles (3077 km)
3797 miles (6112 km)
The completion of a major oil pipeline across Panama in 1982 has reduced crude oil shipments via the Panama Canal, further contributing to a long-term decline in canal traffic.
Map key
Population
1 million to 5 million
500,000 to 1 million
100,000 to 500,000
50,000 to 100,000
10,000 to 50,000
below 10,000
Elevation
4000m / 13,124ft
3000m / 9843ft
2000m / 6562ft
1000m / 3281ft
500m / 1640ft
250m / 820ft
100m / 328ft
sea level
Panama's rain forests are home to many mammals which originated in North America, including jaguars, tapirs, and deer, as well as sloths, anteaters, and armadillos, which long ago migrated from South America.
CARIBBEAN SEA
PACIFIC OCEAN
PANAMA
Golfo de Panamá
Gulf of Darien
Golfo de Chiriquí
Golfo de los Mosquitos
Península de Azuero
Archipiélago de San Blas
Archipiélago de las Perlas
Archipiélago de Bocas del Toro
Isla de Coiba
Isla Cébaco
Isla del Rey
Isla San José
Colón
Portobelo
Limón
Bocas del Toro
David
Santiago
Chitré
Las Tablas
San Miguelito
PANAMÁ (PANAMA CITY)
La Chorrera
La Palma
Puerto Obaldía
Jaqué
Yaviza
Cerro Tacarcuna 1875m
Cerro Pirre 1200m
Cerro Hoya 1560m
Volcán Barú 3475m
Arrecifes de la Media Luna
Cabo de Gracias a Dios
Cayos Miskitos
Cayos Londres
Puerto Cabezas
Cayos King
Cayos de Perlas
Islas del Maíz
Monkey Point
San Juan del Norte
Barra del Colorado
COLOMBIA
44
54

◀ The Caribbean's virgin rain forest, seen here in Jamaica, is increasingly at risk from agricultural, industrial and tourist development. On some islands, the rain forest has virtually disappeared.

▲ The large bar which lies submerged in front of Marina Cay in the British Virgin Islands, has been built up by waves, depositing a bank of sand which partially encloses the islet.

Scale 1:6,000,000

projection: Lambert Conformal Conic

The Caribbean

BAHAMAS, GREATER ANTILLES, LESSER ANTILLES

The islands known as the West Indies form a great arc which trails eastward from the Gulf of Mexico almost to Venezuela, enclosing the Caribbean Sea. During the period of European colonization, which began in the 16th century, Britain, France, Spain, and the Netherlands struggled for control of the area. Some countries remained politically tied to their colonial rulers until late in the 20th century, and most islands' economies still bear the legacy of the plantation system. A diverse mix of peoples, with roots drawn from Africa, East Asia, and Europe replaced the original Amerindian population, creating a unique and remarkably homogeneous culture, reflected in the various Creole languages and musical forms such as reggae and calypso.

Using the land & sea

Agriculture has long been the basis of most Caribbean economies. Much agricultural land is set aside for cash crops such as sugar, spices, citrus fruits, bananas, and cocoa, which are grown for export. Diversification is being encouraged to reduce the islands' reliance on imported grain and vulnerability to price fluctuations.

▶ Market traders in St. George's, the capital of Grenada, sell a wide variety of fresh fruit and vegetables. The island is known particularly for its spices and is the world's second-largest producer of nutmeg after Indonesia.

The urban/rural population divide

urban 65% — rural 35%

Population density	Total land area
435 people per sq mile (168 people per sq km)	88,396 sq miles (229,005 sq km)

Land use and agricultural distribution

cattle, bananas, coffee, fishing, shellfish, sugar cane, tobacco, major towns, pasture, cropland, forest

Map key

Population

- 1 million to 5 million
- 500,000 to 1 million
- 100,000 to 500,000
- 50,000 to 100,000
- 10,000 to 50,000
- below 10,000

Elevation

- 3000m / 9843ft
- 2000m / 6562ft
- 1000m / 3281ft
- 500m / 1640ft
- 250m / 820ft
- 100m / 328ft
- sea level

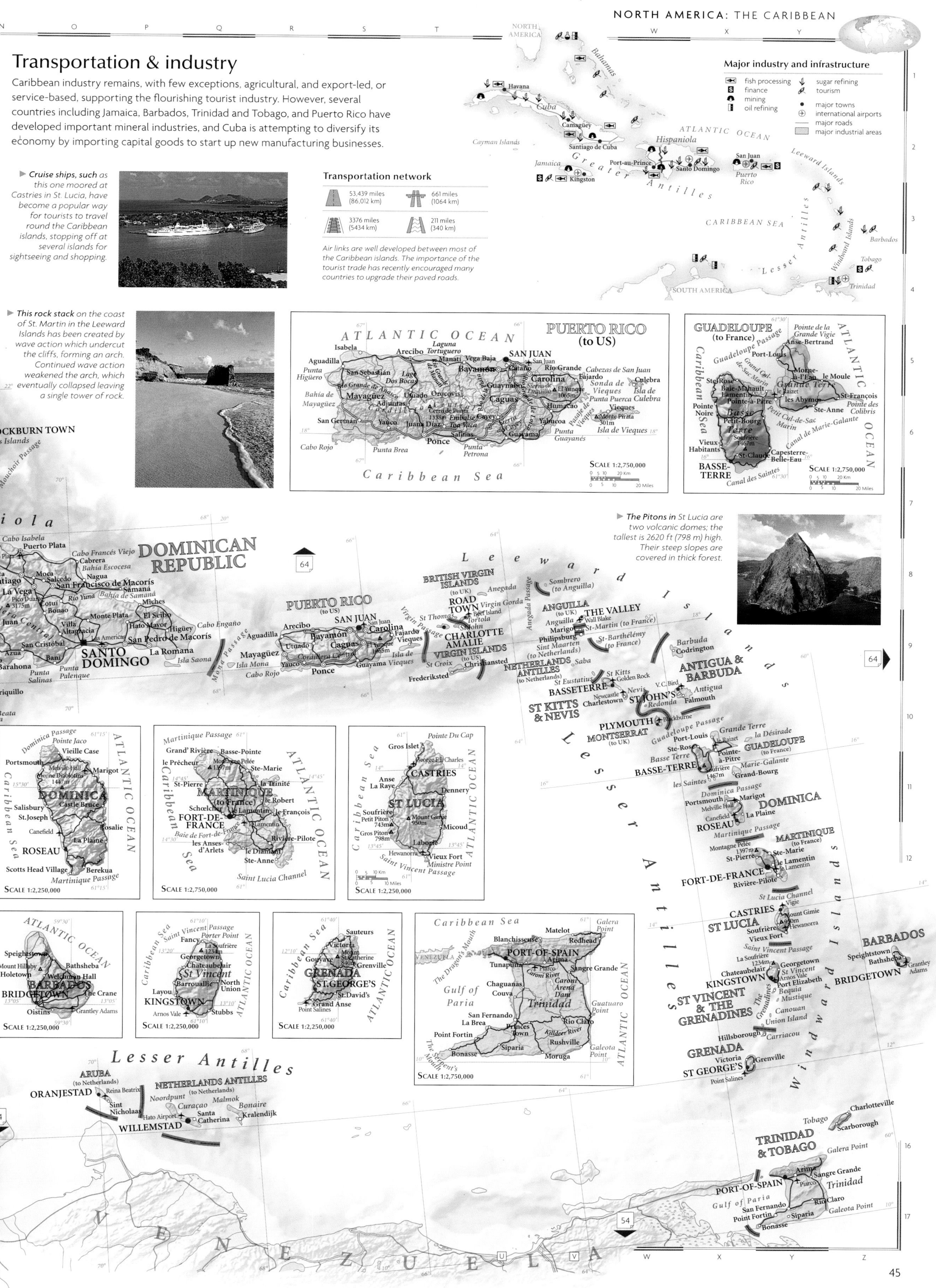
Major industry and infrastructure
fish processing
finance
mining
oil refining
sugar refining
tourism
major towns
international airports
major roads
major industrial areas
Transportation network
53,439 miles (86,012 km)
661 miles (1064 km)
3376 miles (5434 km)
211 miles (340 km)
Air links are well developed between most of the Caribbean islands. The importance of the tourist trade has recently encouraged many countries to upgrade their paved roads.
ATLANTIC OCEAN
CARIBBEAN SEA
Havana
Cuba
Camagüey
Santiago de Cuba
Cayman Islands
Jamaica
Kingston
Greater Antilles
Hispaniola
Port-au-Prince
Santo Domingo
San Juan
Puerto Rico
Bahamas
Leeward Islands
Lesser Antilles
Windward Islands
Barbados
Tobago
Trinidad
SOUTH AMERICA
PUERTO RICO (to US)
Caribbean Sea
GUADELOUPE (to France)
DOMINICAN REPUBLIC
SANTO DOMINGO
BRITISH VIRGIN ISLANDS (to UK)
ROAD TOWN
ANGUILLA (to UK)
THE VALLEY
CHARLOTTE AMALIE
VIRGIN ISLANDS (to US)
NETHERLANDS ANTILLES (to Netherlands)
ST KITTS & NEVIS
BASSETERRE
ANTIGUA & BARBUDA
ST JOHN'S
PLYMOUTH
MONTSERRAT (to UK)
BASSE-TERRE
DOMINICA
ROSEAU
MARTINIQUE (to France)
FORT-DE-FRANCE
ST LUCIA
CASTRIES
ST VINCENT & THE GRENADINES
KINGSTOWN
BARBADOS
BRIDGETOWN
GRENADA
ST GEORGE'S
TRINIDAD & TOBAGO
PORT-OF-SPAIN
ARUBA (to Netherlands)
ORANJESTAD
NETHERLANDS ANTILLES (to Netherlands)
WILLEMSTAD
Lesser Antilles
VENEZUELA
SCALE 1:2,750,000
SCALE 1:2,250,000

Transportation & industry

Caribbean industry remains, with few exceptions, agricultural, and export-led, or service-based, supporting the flourishing tourist industry. However, several countries including Jamaica, Barbados, Trinidad and Tobago, and Puerto Rico have developed important mineral industries, and Cuba is attempting to diversify its economy by importing capital goods to start up new manufacturing businesses.

▶ *Cruise ships, such as this one moored at Castries in St. Lucia, have become a popular way for tourists to travel round the Caribbean islands, stopping off at several islands for sightseeing and shopping.*

▶ *This rock stack on the coast of St. Martin in the Leeward Islands has been created by wave action which undercut the cliffs, forming an arch. Continued wave action weakened the arch, which eventually collapsed leaving a single tower of rock.*

▶ *The Pitons in St Lucia are two volcanic domes; the tallest is 2620 ft (798 m) high. Their steep slopes are covered in thick forest.*

South America

Reaching from the humid tropics down into the cold south Atlantic, South America has an area of 6,886,000 sq miles (17,835,000 sq km). There are 12 separate countries, with the largest, Brazil, covering almost half the continent.

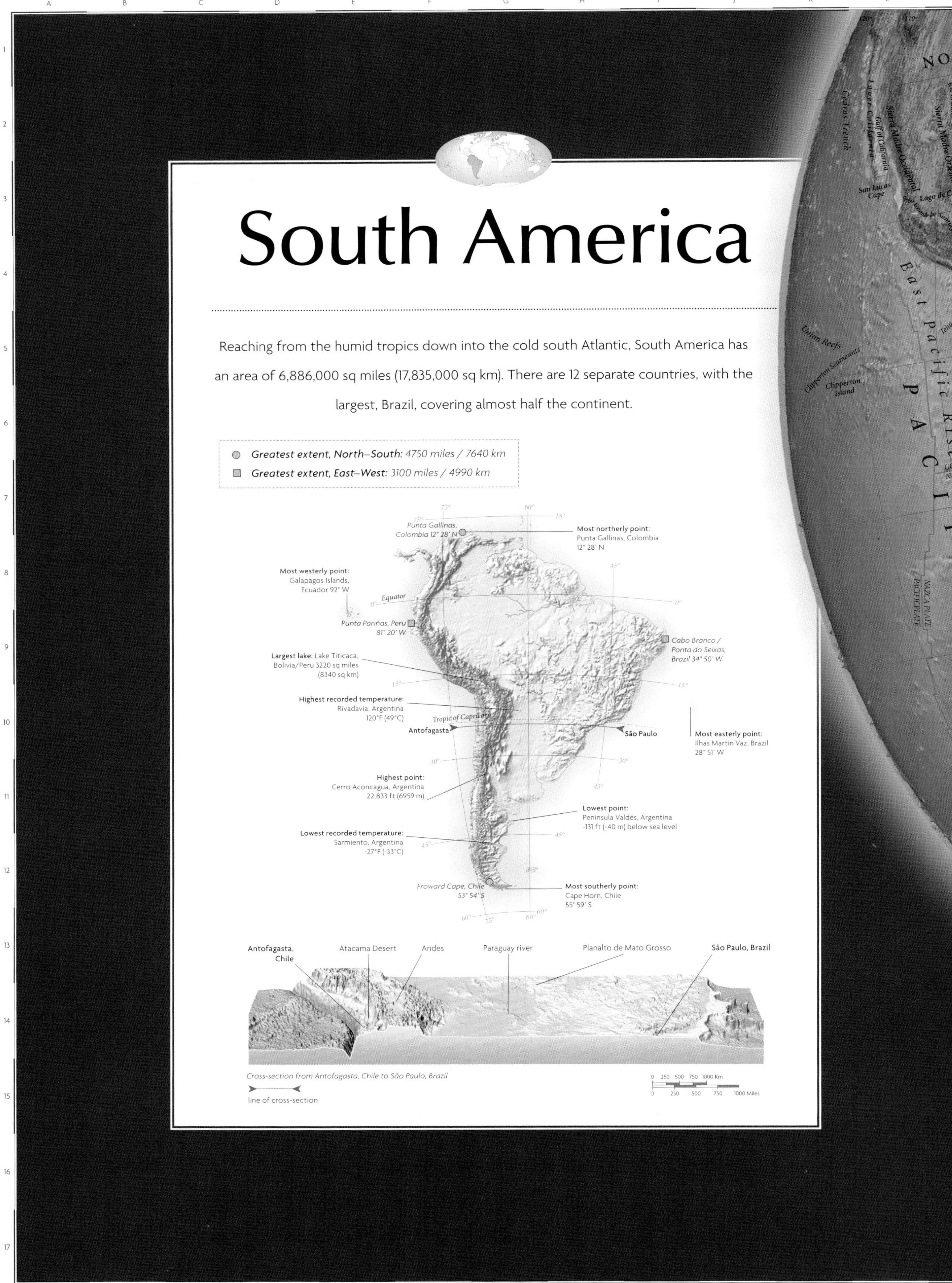

Greatest extent, North–South: 4750 miles / 7640 km
Greatest extent, East–West: 3100 miles / 4990 km
Punta Gallinas, Colombia 12° 28' N
Most northerly point: Punta Gallinas, Colombia 12° 28' N
Most westerly point: Galapagos Islands, Ecuador 92° W
Equator
Punta Pariñas, Peru 81° 20' W
Cabo Branco / Ponta do Seixas, Brazil 34° 50' W
Largest lake: Lake Titicaca, Bolivia/Peru 3220 sq miles (8340 sq km)
Highest recorded temperature: Rivadavia, Argentina 120°F (49°C)
Tropic of Capricorn
Antofagasta
São Paulo
Most easterly point: Ilhas Martin Vaz, Brazil 28° 51' W
Highest point: Cerro Aconcagua, Argentina 22,833 ft (6959 m)
Lowest point: Peninsula Valdés, Argentina -131 ft (-40 m) below sea level
Lowest recorded temperature: Sarmiento, Argentina -27°F (-33°C)
Froward Cape, Chile 53° 54' S
Most southerly point: Cape Horn, Chile 55° 59' S
Antofagasta, Chile
Atacama Desert
Andes
Paraguay river
Planalto de Mato Grosso
São Paulo, Brazil
0 250 500 750 1000 Km
0 250 500 750 1000 Miles
NOR
Rio Grande
Sierra Madre Oriental
Sierra Madre Occidental
Gulf of California
Lower California
Cedros Trench
San Lucas Cape
Lago de Chapala
East Pacific Rise
Union Reefs
Clipperton Seamounts
Clipperton Island
PACIFI
NAZCA PLATE
PACIFIC PLATE

Cross-section from Antofagasta, Chile to São Paulo, Brazil

line of cross-section

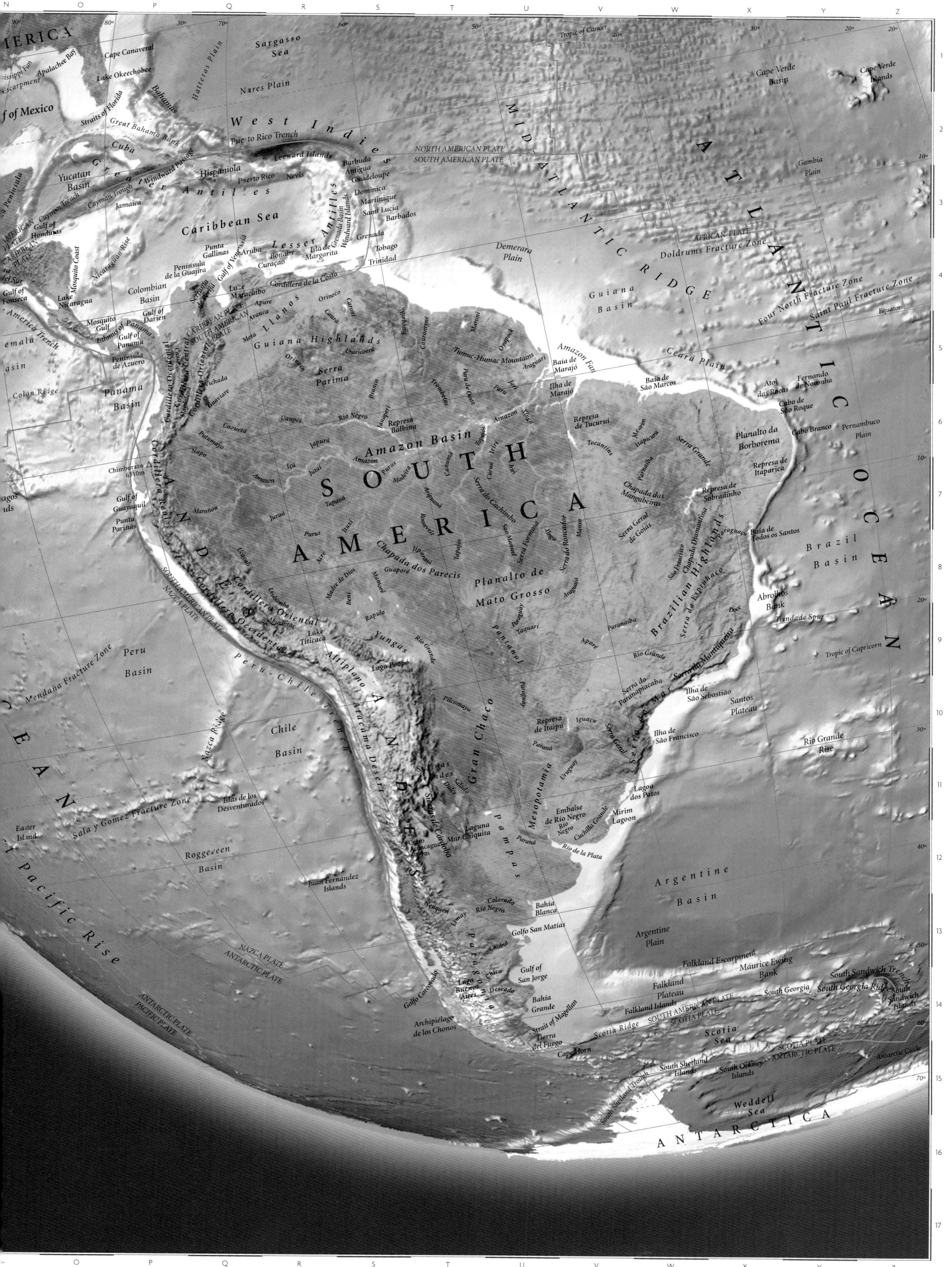
SOUTH AMERICA
ATLANTIC OCEAN
West Indies
Caribbean Sea
Sargasso Sea
MID-ATLANTIC RIDGE
ANDES
Amazon Basin
Guiana Highlands
Brazilian Highlands
Planalto de Mato Grosso
Gran Chaco
Pampas
Patagonia
ANTARCTICA
Weddell Sea
Scotia Sea
Argentine Basin
Brazil Basin
Guiana Basin
Peru Basin
Chile Basin
Peru-Chile Trench
Pacific Rise
Falkland Plateau
Cape Verde Islands
Tropic of Cancer
Tropic of Capricorn
Equator
Antarctic Circle

Physical South America

Three major physiographic regions characterize South America. The oldest, the ancient Brazilian Shield and the smaller Guyana and Patagonian shields, form the stable core of the continent. Stretching along the entire west coast are the younger Andean fold mountains with many summits rising to 20,000 ft (6100 m). These two diverse regions are separated by a number of sedimentary basins carrying South America's large river systems to the sea. These include the massive Amazon Basin and the basin of the Gran Chaco.

The Amazon Basin and Guyana Shield

The Amazon river occupies a large depression in the Earth's crust, formed by the uplift of the Andes. It is covered by thick volcanic deposits and layers of alluvium – these have been laid down by the Amazon's many tributaries. To the north is the smaller Guyana Shield.

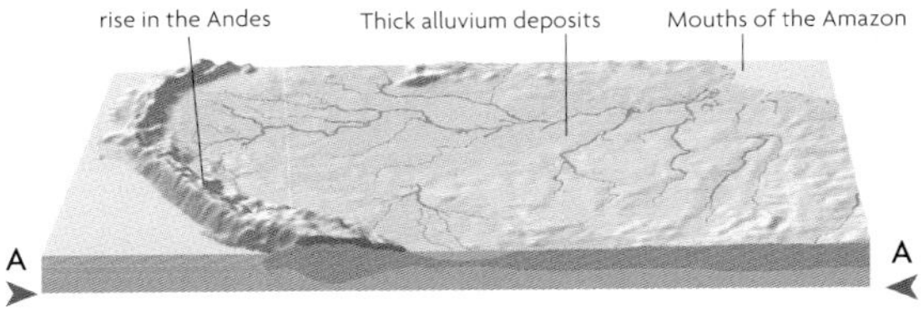

Section across northern South America showing Amazon Basin and its drainage pattern.

Scale 1:30,500,000

projection: Lambert Azimuthal Equal Area

The Andean Uplands

The Andean Uplands run along the west coast of South America. They are being uplifted as the Nazca Plate is subducted beneath the South American Plate. They contain some of the world's largest volcanoes, such as Cotopaxi, and Lake Titicaca which occupies a dormant site. The far south has many large ice-sheets and a fragmented coastline.

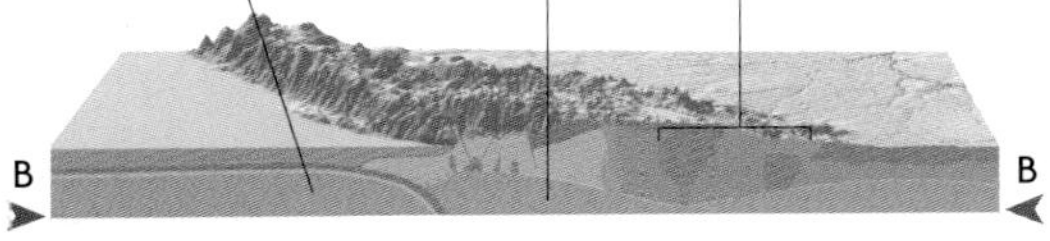

Cross-section through the Andes showing the subduction of the Nazca Plate beneath the South American Plate.

The Brazilian Shield and Gran Chaco

The immense Brazilian Shield underlies more than one-third of South America. It is pitted with numerous volcanic intrusions, and a large basaltic plateau exists between the Paraná river and the Atlantic Ocean. The flat Gran Chaco lies to the west of the shield, covered by sedimentary deposits eroded from the Andes, and transported by South America's mighty rivers.

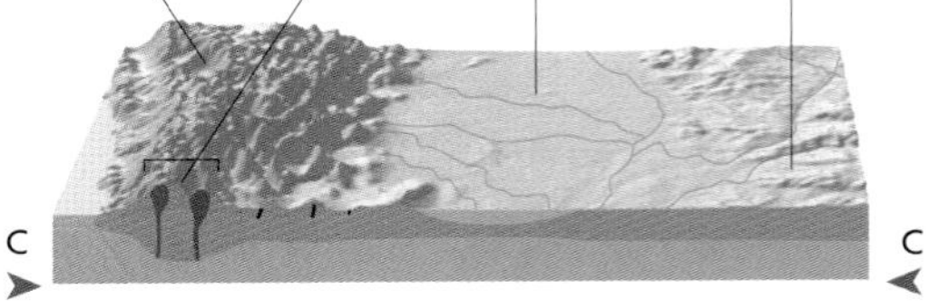

Section across central South America showing the flat basin of the Gran Chaco and the ancient Brazilian Shield.

Map key

Elevation

6000m / 19,686ft
4000m / 13,124ft
3000m / 9843ft
2000m / 6562ft
1500m / 4922ft
1000m / 3281ft
500m / 1640ft
250m / 820ft
100m / 328ft
sea level

Plate margins (for explanation see page xiv)

constructive
destructive
conservative
uncertain

physiographic regions
line of cross-section

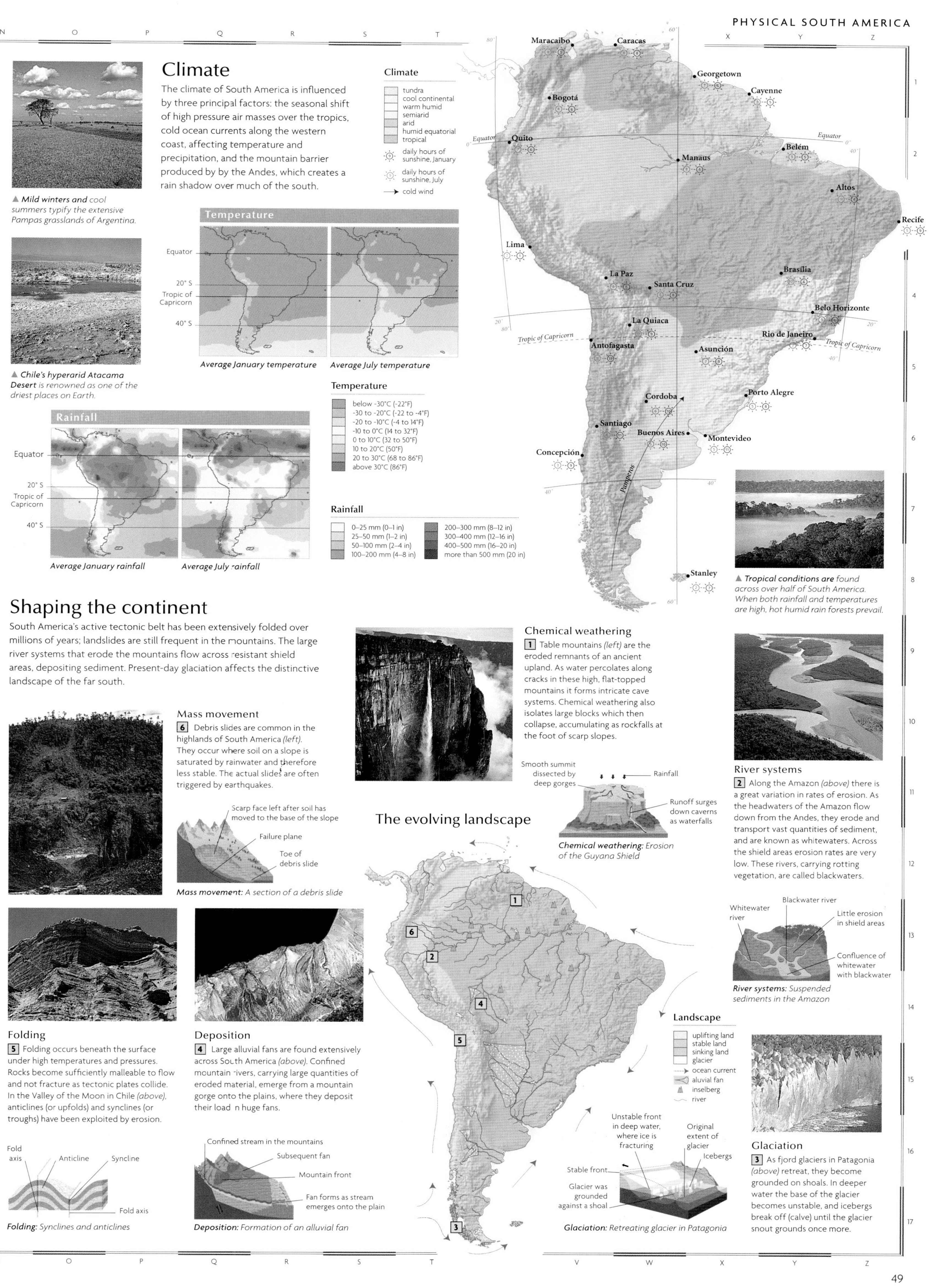

Climate
tundra
cool continental
warm humid
semiarid
arid
humid equatorial
tropical
daily hours of sunshine, January
daily hours of sunshine, July
cold wind
Maracaibo
Caracas
Georgetown
Cayenne
Bogotá
Quito
Equator
Belém
Manaus
Altos
Recife
Lima
Brasília
La Paz
Santa Cruz
Belo Horizonte
La Quiaca
Tropic of Capricorn
Rio de Janeiro
Antofagasta
Asunción
Porto Alegre
Cordoba
Santiago
Buenos Aires
Montevideo
Concepción
Pamperos
Stanley
Temperature
Equator
20° S
Tropic of Capricorn
40° S
Temperature
below -30°C (-22°F)
-30 to -20°C (-22 to -4°F)
-20 to -10°C (-4 to 14°F)
-10 to 0°C (14 to 32°F)
0 to 10°C (32 to 50°F)
10 to 20°C (50°F)
20 to 30°C (68 to 86°F)
above 30°C (86°F)
Rainfall
Rainfall
0–25 mm (0–1 in)
25–50 mm (1–2 in)
50–100 mm (2–4 in)
100–200 mm (4–8 in)
200–300 mm (8–12 in)
300–400 mm (12–16 in)
400–500 mm (16–20 in)
more than 500 mm (20 in)
Smooth summit dissected by deep gorges
Rainfall
Runoff surges down caverns as waterfalls
Scarp face left after soil has moved to the base of the slope
Failure plane
Toe of debris slide
Whitewater river
Blackwater river
Little erosion in shield areas
Confluence of whitewater with blackwater
Landscape
uplifting land
stable land
sinking land
glacier
ocean current
aluvial fan
inselberg
river
Fold axis
Anticline
Syncline
Fold axis
Confined stream in the mountains
Subsequent fan
Mountain front
Fan forms as stream emerges onto the plain
Unstable front in deep water, where ice is fracturing
Original extent of glacier
Icebergs
Stable front
Glacier was grounded against a shoal

Climate

The climate of South America is influenced by three principal factors: the seasonal shift of high pressure air masses over the tropics, cold ocean currents along the western coast, affecting temperature and precipitation, and the mountain barrier produced by by the Andes, which creates a rain shadow over much of the south.

▲ *Mild winters and cool summers typify the extensive Pampas grasslands of Argentina.*

▲ *Chile's hyperarid Atacama Desert is renowned as one of the driest places on Earth.*

Average January temperature

Average July temperature

Average January rainfall

Average July rainfall

▲ *Tropical conditions are found across over half of South America. When both rainfall and temperatures are high, hot humid rain forests prevail.*

Shaping the continent

South America's active tectonic belt has been extensively folded over millions of years; landslides are still frequent in the mountains. The large river systems that erode the mountains flow across resistant shield areas, depositing sediment. Present-day glaciation affects the distinctive landscape of the far south.

Chemical weathering

1 Table mountains *(left)* are the eroded remnants of an ancient upland. As water percolates along cracks in these high, flat-topped mountains it forms intricate cave systems. Chemical weathering also isolates large blocks which then collapse, accumulating as rockfalls at the foot of scarp slopes.

***Chemical weathering:** Erosion of the Guyana Shield*

Mass movement

6 Debris slides are common in the highlands of South America *(left)*. They occur where soil on a slope is saturated by rainwater and therefore less stable. The actual slides are often triggered by earthquakes.

***Mass movement:** A section of a debris slide*

River systems

2 Along the Amazon *(above)* there is a great variation in rates of erosion. As the headwaters of the Amazon flow down from the Andes, they erode and transport vast quantities of sediment, and are known as whitewaters. Across the shield areas erosion rates are very low. These rivers, carrying rotting vegetation, are called blackwaters.

***River systems:** Suspended sediments in the Amazon*

The evolving landscape

Folding

5 Folding occurs beneath the surface under high temperatures and pressures. Rocks become sufficiently malleable to flow and not fracture as tectonic plates collide. In the Valley of the Moon in Chile *(above)*, anticlines (or upfolds) and synclines (or troughs) have been exploited by erosion.

***Folding:** Synclines and anticlines*

Deposition

4 Large alluvial fans are found extensively across South America *(above)*. Confined mountain rivers, carrying large quantities of eroded material, emerge from a mountain gorge onto the plains, where they deposit their load in huge fans.

***Deposition:** Formation of an alluvial fan*

Glaciation

3 As fjord glaciers in Patagonia *(above)* retreat, they become grounded on shoals. In deeper water the base of the glacier becomes unstable, and icebergs break off (calve) until the glacier snout grounds once more.

***Glaciation:** Retreating glacier in Patagonia*

Political South America

Modern South America's political boundaries have their origins in the territorial endeavors of explorers during the 16th century, who claimed almost the entire continent for Portugal and Spain. The Portuguese land in the east later evolved into the federal state of Brazil, while the Spanish vice-royalties eventually emerged as separate independent nation-states in the early 19th century. South America's growing population has become increasingly urbanized, with the growth of coastal cities into large conurbations like Rio de Janeiro and Buenos Aires. In Brazil, Argentina, Chile, and Uruguay, a succession of military dictatorships has given way to fragile, but strengthening, democracies.

◀ ***Europe retains a*** *small foothold in South America. Kourou in French Guiana was the site chosen by the European Space Agency to launch the Ariane rocket. As a result of its status as a French overseas department, French Guiana is actually part of the European Union.*

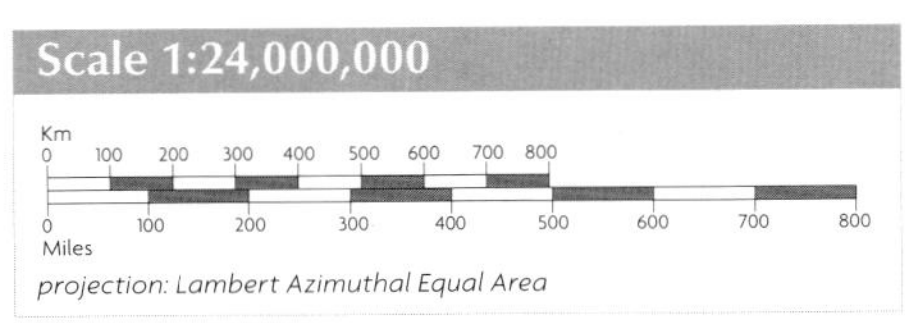
Scale 1:24,000,000
Km
0 100 200 300 400 500 600 700 800
0 100 200 300 400 500 600 700 800
Miles
projection: Lambert Azimuthal Equal Area

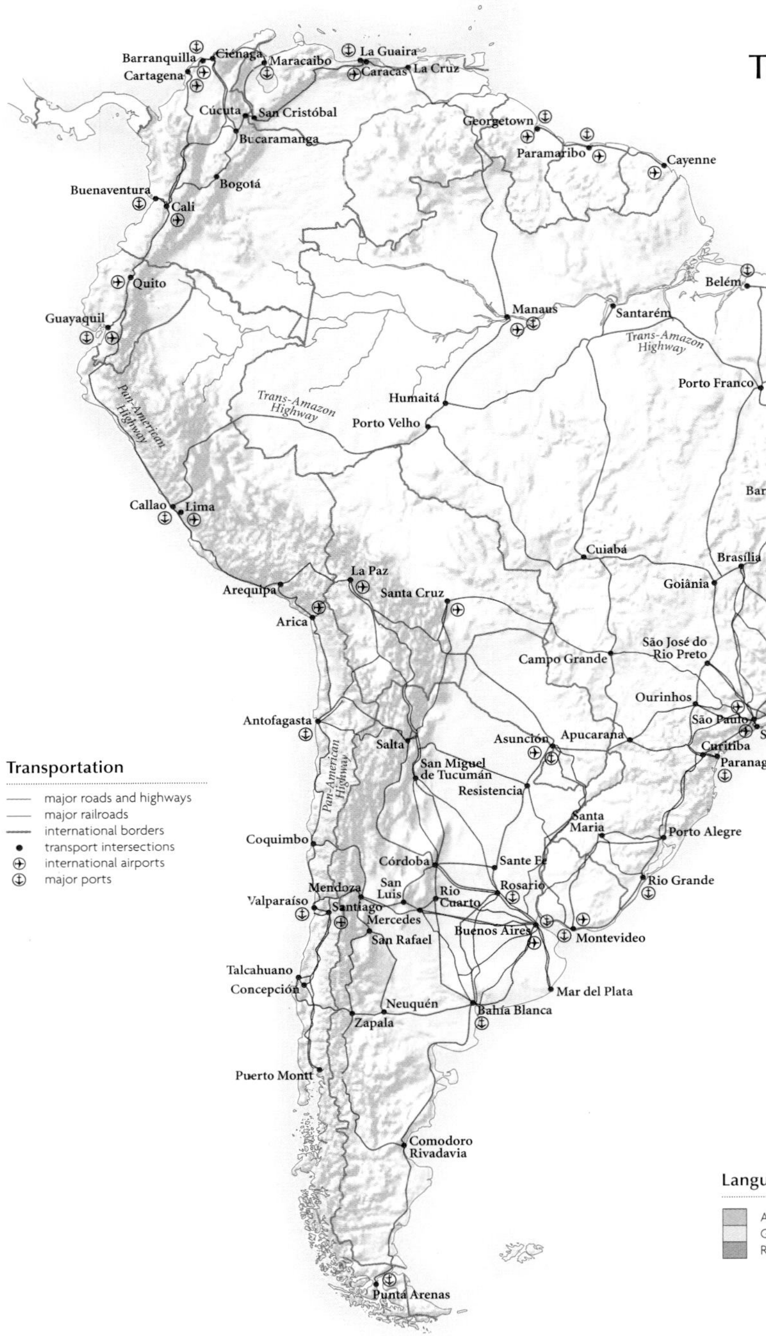

Transportation

Most major road and rail routes are confined to the coastal regions by the forbidding natural barriers of the Andes mountains and the Amazon Basin. Few major cross-continental routes exist, although Buenos Aires serves as a transportation center for the main rail links to La Paz and Valparaíso, while the construction of the Trans-Amazon and Pan-American Highways have made direct road travel possible from Recife to Lima and from Puerto Montt up the coast into central America. A new waterway project is proposed to transform the River Paraguay into a major shipping route, although it involves considerable wetland destruction.

Transportation

- major roads and highways
- major railroads
- international borders
- transport intersections
- international airports
- major ports

▶ *South America's most extensive rail network is centered on the Argentinian capital, Buenos Aires. The construction of new rail lines ouward from this important port, allowed the colonization of the Pampas lands for agriculture.*

Languages

Prior to European exploration in the 16th century, a diverse range of indigenous languages were spoken across the continent. With the arrival of Iberian settlers, Spanish became the dominant language, with Portuguese spoken in Brazil, and Native American languages such as Quechua and Guaraní, becoming concentrated in the continental interior. Today this pattern persists, although successive European colonization has led to Dutch being spoken in Suriname, English in Guyana, and French in French Guiana, while in large urban areas, Japanese and Chinese are increasingly common.

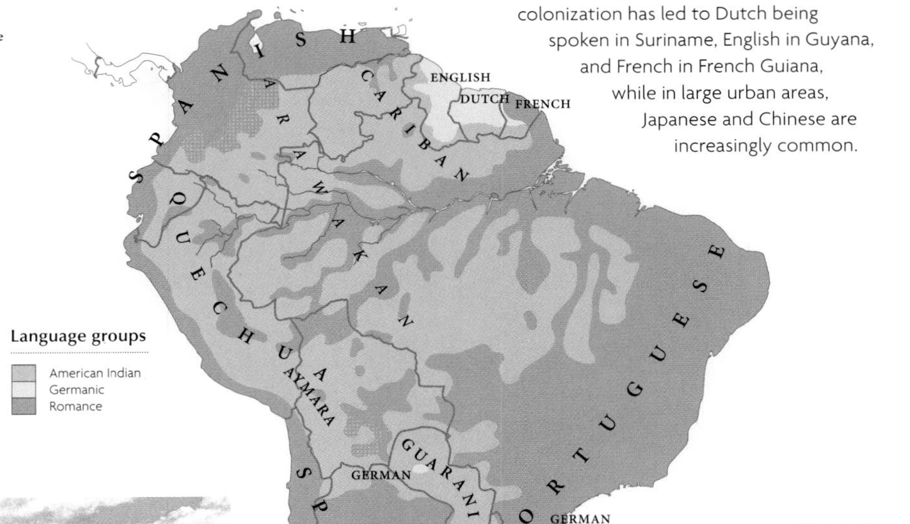

Language groups

- American Indian
- Germanic
- Romance

▶ ***Chile's main port,*** *Valparaíso, is a vital national shipping center, in addition to playing a key role in the growing trade with Pacific nations. The country's awkward, elongated shape means that sea transportation is frequently used for internal travel and communications in Chile.*

▲ ***Indigenous South American*** *lifestyles have not been totally submerged by European cultures and languages. The continental interior, and particularly the Amazon Basin, is still home to many different ethnic peoples.*

▶ ***Lima's magnificent*** *cathedral reflects South America's colonial past with its unmistakably Spanish style. In July 1821, Peru became the last Spanish colony on the mainland to declare independence.*

In April 1960, Brazil's government began the move from Rio de Janeiro to Brasília, a futuristic new city built in the sparsely populated interior. Brasília is now the federal capital of Brazil.

Rapid urbanization was a feature of most South American countries in the latter half of the 20th century. In many cases, this unchecked growth has led to the development of sprawling slums, lacking adequate water and sewerage facilities.

Map key

Population

- above 5 million
- 1 million to 5 million
- 500,000 to 1 million
- 100,000 to 500,000
- 50,000 to 100,000
- 10,000 to 50,000
- below 10,000
- Country capital
- State capital

Borders

- full international border
- disputed de facto border
- disputed territorial claim border
- state border

Perched high in the Andes like many of the cities in western South America, La Paz, Bolivia is the world's highest capital city at over 11,500 ft (3500 m).

Population

Almost half of South America's population lives in Brazil but, due to the large uninhabited expanses of the Amazon Basin, its overall population density is much lower than in other countries. During the 20th century the most important population trend was the movement from rural to urban areas, giving rise to great population concentrations in large cities like São Paulo, Rio de Janeiro, Caracas, Lima, Bogotá, and Buenos Aires.

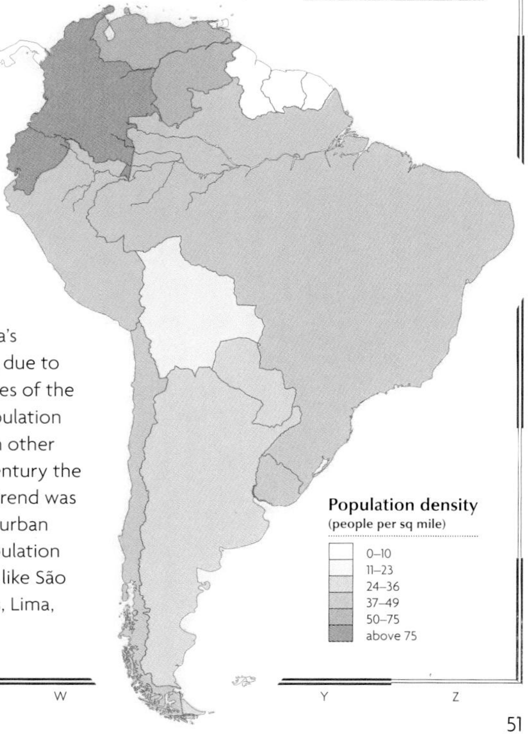

Population density (people per sq mile)

- 0–10
- 11–23
- 24–36
- 37–49
- 50–75
- above 75

South American resources

Agriculture still provides the largest single form of employment in South America, although rural unemployment and poverty continue to drive people towards the huge coastal cities in search of jobs and opportunities. Mineral and fuel resources, although substantial, are distributed unevenly; few countries have both fossil fuels and minerals. To break industrial dependence on raw materials, boost manufacturing, and improve infrastructure, governments borrowed heavily from the World Bank in the 1960s and 1970s. This led to the accumulation of massive debts which are unlikely ever to be repaid. Today, Brazil dominates the continent's economic output, followed by Argentina. Recently, the less-developed western side of South America has benefited due to its geographical position; for example Chile is increasingly exporting raw materials to Japan.

◀ *Ciudad Guayana is a planned industrial complex in eastern Venezuela, built as an iron and steel center to exploit the nearby iron ore reserves.*

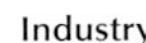

Industry

- aerospace
- brewing
- car/vehicle manufacture
- chemicals
- electronics
- engineering
- finance
- fish processing
- food processing
- hi-tech industry
- iron & steel
- meat processing
- metal refining
- narcotics
- pharmaceuticals
- printing & publishing
- shipbuilding
- sugar processing
- textiles
- timber processing
- tobacco processing
- wine
- oil
- gas
- industrial cities
- major industrial areas

▲ *The cold Peru Current flows north from the Antarctic along the Pacific coast of Peru, providing rich nutrients for one of the world's largest fishing grounds. However, overexploitation has severely reduced Peru's anchovy catch.*

Standard of living

Wealth disparities throughout the continent create a wide gulf between affluent landowners and those afflicted by chronic poverty in inner city slums. The illicit production of cocaine, and the hugely influential drug barons who control its distribution, contribute to the violent disorder and corruption which affect northwestern South America, destabilizing local governments and economies.

Standard of living
(UN human development index)

- low
- high

GNI per capita (US$)

- below 999
- 1000–1999
- 2000–2999
- 3000–3999
- 4000–4999
- above 5000

▶ *Both Argentina and Chile are now exploring the southernmost tip of the continent in search of oil. Here in Punta Arenas, a drilling rig is being prepared for exploratory drilling in the Strait of Magellan.*

Industry

Argentina and Brazil are South America's most industrialized countries and São Paulo is the continent's leading industrial center. Long-term government investment in Brazilian industry has encouraged a diverse industrial base; engineering, steel production, food processing, textile manufacture, and chemicals predominate. The illegal production of cocaine is economically significant in the Andean countries of Colombia and Bolivia. In Venezuela, the oil-dominated economy has left the country vulnerable to world oil price fluctuations. Food processing and mineral exploitation are common throughout the less industrially developed parts of the continent, including Bolivia, Chile, Ecuador, and Peru.

Environmental issues

The Amazon Basin is one of the last great wilderness areas left on Earth. The tropical rain forests which grow there are a valuable genetic resource, containing innumerable unique plants and animals. The forests are increasingly under threat from new and expanding settlements and "slash-and-burn" farming techniques, which clear land for the raising of beef cattle, causing land degradation and soil erosion.

▲ ***Clouds of smoke*** *billow from the burning Amazon rainforest. Over 11,500 sq miles (30,000 sq km) of virgin rainforest are being cleared annually, destroying an ancient, irreplaceable, natural resource and biodiverse habitat.*

Environmental issues

- national parks
- tropical forest
- forest destroyed
- desert
- desertification
- polluted rivers
- marine pollution
- heavy marine pollution
- poor urban air quality

Mineral resources

Over a quarter of the world's known copper reserves are found at the Chuquicamata mine in northern Chile, and other metallic minerals such as tin are found along the length of the Andes. The discovery of oil and gas at Venezuela's Lake Maracaibo in 1917 turned the country into one of the world's leading oil producers. In contrast, South America is virtually devoid of coal, the only significant deposit being on the peninsula of Guajira in Colombia.

◀ ***Copper is Chile's*** *largest export, most of which is mined at Chuquicamata. Along the length of the Andes, metallic minerals like copper and tin are found in abundance, formed by the excessive pressures and heat involved in mountain-building.*

Mineral resources

- oil field
- gas field
- coal field
- bauxite
- copper
- diamonds
- gold
- iron
- lead
- silver
- tin

Using the land and sea

Many foods now common worldwide originated in South America. These include the potato, tomato, squash, and cassava. Today, large herds of beef cattle roam the temperate grasslands of the Pampas, supporting an extensive meatpacking trade in Argentina, Uruguay and Paraguay. Corn is grown as a staple crop across the continent and coffee is grown as a cash crop in Brazil and Colombia. Coca plants grown in Bolivia, Peru, and Colombia provide most of the world's cocaine. Fish and shellfish are caught off the western coast, especially anchovies off Peru, shrimps off Ecuador and pilchards off Chile.

◀ ***South America, and*** *Brazil in particular, now leads the world in coffee production, mainly growing Coffea Arabica in large plantations. Coffee beans are harvested, roasted and brewed to produce the world's second most popular drink, after tea.*

◀ ***The Pampas region*** *of southeast South America is characterized by extensive, flat plains, and populated by cattle and ranchers (gauchos). Argentina is a major world producer of beef, much of which is exported to the US for use in hamburgers.*

◀ ***High in the Andes,*** *hardy alpacas graze on the barren land. Alpacas are thought to have been domesticated by the Incas, whose nobility wore robes made from their wool. Today, they are still reared and prized for their soft, warm fleeces.*

Using the land and sea

- barren land
- cropland
- desert
- forest
- mountain region
- pasture
- major conurbations
- cattle
- pigs
- sheep
- bananas
- corn
- citrus fruits
- cocoa
- cotton
- coffee
- fishing
- oil palms
- peanuts
- rubber
- shellfish
- soybeans
- sugar cane
- vineyards
- wheat

Northern South America

COLOMBIA, GUYANA, SURINAME, VENEZUELA, French Guiana (to France)

Fringed by the Pacific and Atlantic oceans and the Caribbean Sea, South America's northern region has a rich range of natural resources, some exploited for centuries by colonial powers including the Spanish, French, Dutch, and British, others still to be fully explored. The prospects for further economic development in Colombia, Guyana, and Suriname are blighted by drug-related violence and political instability. Venezuela, despite huge incomes from its oil reserves, remains less developed in other industrial sectors. French Guiana is an overseas *département* of France, now seeking greater autonomy. Most of the major population centers, such as Bogotá, have grown up in the temperate conditions of the high Andes or, like Caracas, at strategic points along the Caribbean coast.

▶ *Flowers grown in* Colombia are exported all over the world, and include fine carnations and roses. Here, workers are cutting roses which have been grown in plastic greenhouses.

Map key

Population

- ▣ 1 million to 5 million
- ◉ 500,000 to 1 million
- ◎ 100,000 to 500,000
- ⊕ 50,000 to 100,000
- ○ 10,000 to 50,000
- ○ below 10,000

Elevation

- 4000m / 13,124ft
- 3000m / 9843ft
- 2000m / 6562ft
- 1000m / 3281ft
- 500m / 1640ft
- 250m / 820ft
- 100m / 328ft
- sea level

42

192

56

▲ *Large open squares* like the Plaza de Bolívar in Bogotá are characteristic of many cities founded by the Spanish.

◀ *Scattered farms and villages have grown up on the gentle slopes of this Colombian river valley, utilizing the fertile soils for farming.*

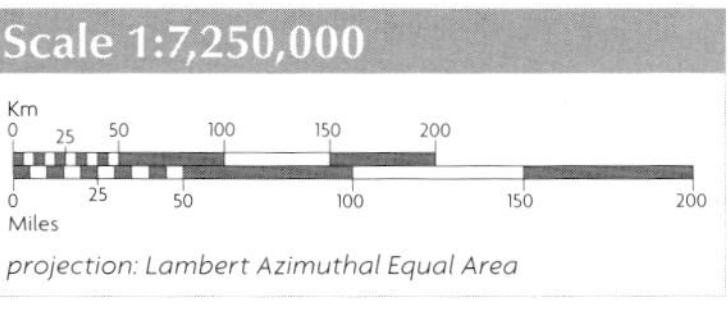

Scale 1:7,250,000
Km
0 25 50 100 150 200
Miles
0 25 50 100 150 200
projection: Lambert Azimuthal Equal Area

56

58

▲ *The Orinoco river* flows from its source in the southern Guiana Highlands to form a broad delta on Venezuela's Atlantic coast. One of its distributary channels opens into a wide bay called the Serpent's Mouth.

Transportation & industry

Many mineral resources are mined in Colombia, including fuels, gold, and precious and semiprecious stones. Revenues from coffee and exports of illegal narcotics are crucial to the economy. Venezuela's major economic activity is the oil industry around Lake Maracaibo *(Lago de Maracaibo)*. Sugar and bauxite are exported from Guyana and Suriname.

Transportation network

31,720 miles (51,054 km)	
3411 miles (5490 km)	
2448 miles (3940 km)	
22,429 miles (36,100 km)	

Rivers are an important means of transportation in Colombia; many are extensively navigable. The Pan-American Highway runs through Colombia. In Venezuela, much infrastructure investment is linked to the oil industry.

Major industry and infrastructure

- chemicals
- finance
- food processing
- iron & steel
- narcotics
- mining
- oil
- oil refining
- pharmaceuticals
- textiles
- timber processing
- capital cities
- major towns
- international airports
- major roads
- major industrial areas

▲ *Vast oil reserves around Lake Maracaibo (Lago de Maracaibo) form the focus of Venezuelan industry. Incomes from oil are used to invest in other industries and in the development of infrastructure.*

Using the land

The Andean basins support cereals and potatoes. Livestock graze at higher altitudes and on the drier tropical grasslands known as the *llanos;* hardy goats are reared in scrubland areas. Grown at higher elevations, coffee is an important cash crop, as is cotton, sugar cane, bananas, citrus fruits, cocoa, and rice, farmed on the Caribbean lowlands. Coca is the most widely grown narcotic plant, with heroin poppies grown in Colombia and marijuana in lowland areas throughout the region.

The urban/rural population divide

urban 80% — rural 20%

Population density	Total land area
78 people per sq mile (30 people per sq km)	1,111,317 sq miles (2,879,060 sq km)

Land use and agricultural distribution

- cattle
- goats
- bananas
- cereals
- coffee
- cotton
- sugar cane
- capital cities
- major towns
- pasture
- cropland
- forest
- wetlands
- mountain region

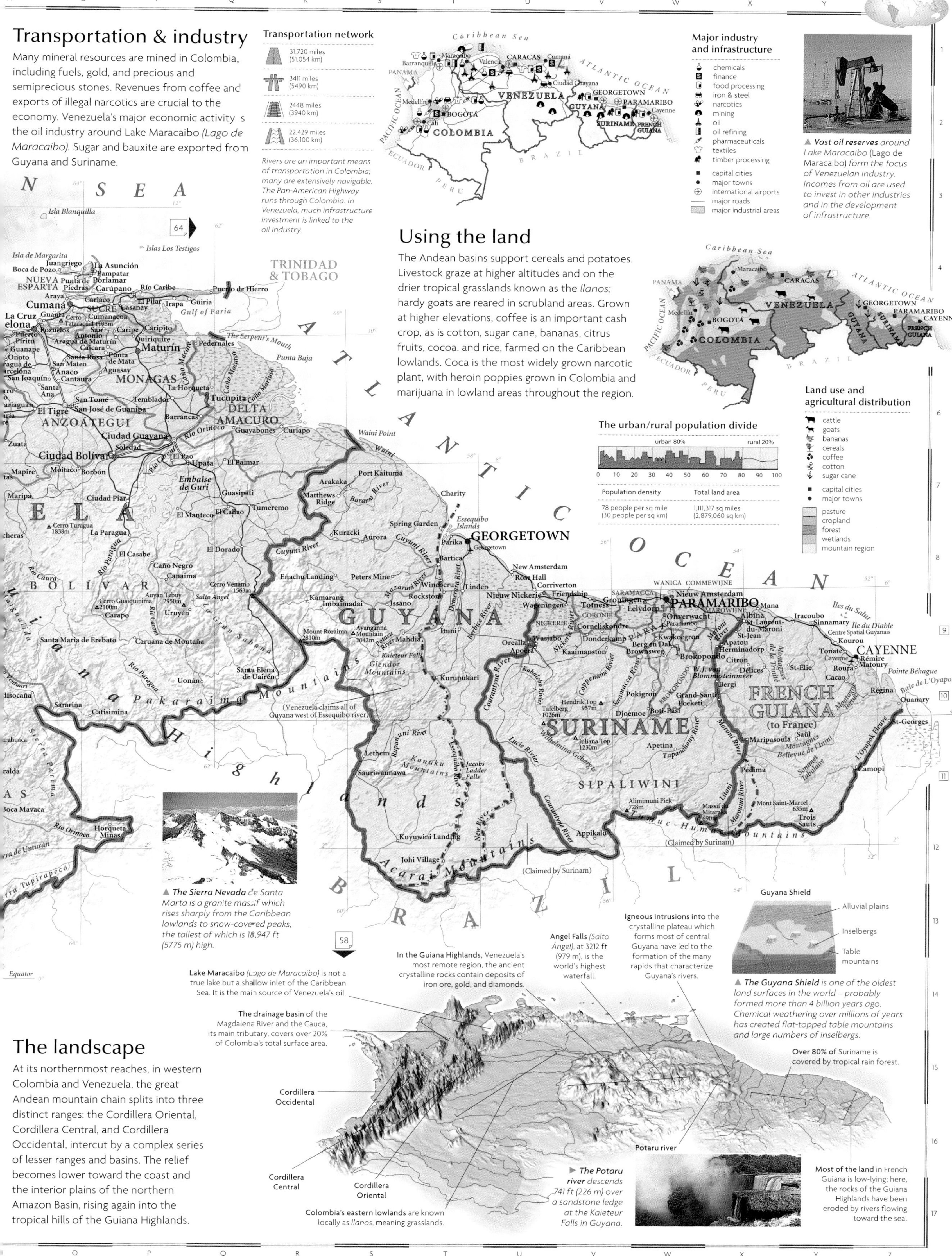

Caribbean Sea
ATLANTIC OCEAN
PACIFIC OCEAN
CARACAS
BOGOTA
GEORGETOWN
PARAMARIBO
CAYENNE
VENEZUELA
COLOMBIA
GUYANA
SURINAME
FRENCH GUIANA (to France)
BRAZIL
ECUADOR
PERU
PANAMA
TRINIDAD & TOBAGO
Guiana Highlands
Pakaraima Mountains
Acarai Mountains
Tumuc-Humac Mountains
(Venezuela claims all of Guyana west of Essequibo river)
(Claimed by Surinam)
Guyana Shield
Alluvial plains
Inselbergs
Table mountains
Cordillera Occidental
Cordillera Central
Cordillera Oriental
Potaru river

▲ *The Sierra Nevada de Santa Marta is a granite massif which rises sharply from the Caribbean lowlands to snow-covered peaks, the tallest of which is 18,947 ft (5775 m) high.*

64

58

▲ *The Guyana Shield is one of the oldest land surfaces in the world – probably formed more than 4 billion years ago. Chemical weathering over millions of years has created flat-topped table mountains and large numbers of inselbergs.*

The landscape

At its northernmost reaches, in western Colombia and Venezuela, the great Andean mountain chain splits into three distinct ranges: the Cordillera Oriental, Cordillera Central, and Cordillera Occidental, intercut by a complex series of lesser ranges and basins. The relief becomes lower toward the coast and the interior plains of the northern Amazon Basin, rising again into the tropical hills of the Guiana Highlands.

Lake Maracaibo (*Lago de Maracaibo*) is not a true lake but a shallow inlet of the Caribbean Sea. It is the main source of Venezuela's oil.

The drainage basin of the Magdalena River and the Cauca, its main tributary, covers over 20% of Colombia's total surface area.

In the Guiana Highlands, Venezuela's most remote region, the ancient crystalline rocks contain deposits of iron ore, gold, and diamonds.

Angel Falls *(Salto Ángel)*, at 3212 ft (979 m), is the world's highest waterfall.

Igneous intrusions into the crystalline plateau which forms most of central Guyana have led to the formation of the many rapids that characterize Guyana's rivers.

Over 80% of Suriname is covered by tropical rain forest.

Colombia's eastern lowlands are known locally as *llanos*, meaning grasslands.

► *The Potaru river descends 741 ft (226 m) over a sandstone ledge at the Kaieteur Falls in Guyana.*

Most of the land in French Guiana is low-lying; here, the rocks of the Guiana Highlands have been eroded by rivers flowing toward the sea.

Western South America

BOLIVIA, ECUADOR, PERU

The three states of Western South America share a similar geography and recent history. Dominated by the Inca empire until Spanish conquest in the 16th century, they achieved independence from Spain in the early 19th century. The precipitous terrain of the Andes presents severe difficulties for overland transportation and continues to be a barrier to national unity and stability. Although Ecuador is now a relatively stable democracy, the military is highly influential in Peru and Bolivia, while the drug trade and associated corruption discourages external aid and economic progress. Wealth and power are still largely concentrated in the hands of a small elite of families, who attained their position during the Spanish colonial period. Energy resources and political recognition for the indigenous peoples are becoming increasingly important issues, particularly in Bolivia.

The landscape

Bolivia, Peru, and Ecuador each possess a high Andean mountain region and an eastern region consisting of tropical lowlands and the Andean slope leading down to them. Toward the south of the region, the mountains widen to form the high plateau of the Altiplano. Peru and Ecuador also have fertile, lowland coastal plains. A wide variety of environments include *selva* (tropical rain forest), *montaña* (mountain forest), and grassland.

Cotopaxi is the world's highest active volcano, with a peak 19,347 ft (5897 m) high. A massive eruption in 1877 caused a mudflow which destroyed everything in its path for 150 miles (240 km).

Much of eastern Ecuador is covered by the tropical rain forest of the Amazon Basin.

Fast-flowing tributaries of the Amazon, which rise in the Andes, run eastward through the front ranges to reach the tropical lowlands. They cut valleys so deep that tropical environments can be found extending well into mountainous areas.

The coastal floodplains are the source of Ecuador's richest soils, enabling the cultivation of a wide range of crops.

Rolling hills and level plains typify the *montaña* and *selva* region, which makes up more than 65% of Peru.

The Bolivian *oriente* covers more than two-thirds of the country. It includes *llanos* – low alluvial plains, massive swamps, flooded bottomlands, savannah grassland, and tropical forests.

The steepness of the Andean slopes means that avalanches and debris flows are an ever-present danger. A landslide starting from Nevado Huascarán in Peru in 1970 killed 20,000 people in 2.5 minutes when it engulfed an inhabited valley.

The Peruvian Andes are relatively young mountains which are continually being uplifted, making the area very unstable, with frequent earthquakes. The transportation difficulties that they present continue to form a barrier to national unity.

The Altiplano is a flat, high plateau lying between the Cordillera Oriental and the Cordillera Occidental at a height of up to 12,500 ft (3800 m). At its margins lie many spurs and alluvial fans.

Lake Titicaca

▲ ***Lake Titicaca, which*** *forms part of the border between Peru and Bolivia, is the largest lake in South America and the highest significant body of water in the world at an altitude of 12,507 ft (3812 m).*

Bolivian Andes

▲ ***Nevado de Illampu*** *and Nevado de Ancohuma, at 21,275 ft (6485 m) and 21,490 ft (6550 m) respectively, form Illampu, the highest mountain in the Bolivian Andes.*

Eruption column

Falling ash

Lava flows

Subduction zone

Magma chamber

Zone of magma generation

▲ ***There are many*** *large and active volcanoes in the Andes. Magma generated in the heart of the volcano erupts in a huge cloud of ash. Ashfall deposits are common throughout the Andes and the rock produced is known as andesite. This is rapidly soaked by heavy rain, causing massive debris flows.*

▶ ***Ecuador's capital city,*** *Quito, lies high in the Andes, nestling between snowcapped peaks. At 9350 ft (2850 m), Quito is the second highest capital in the world – La Paz in Bolivia is the highest.*

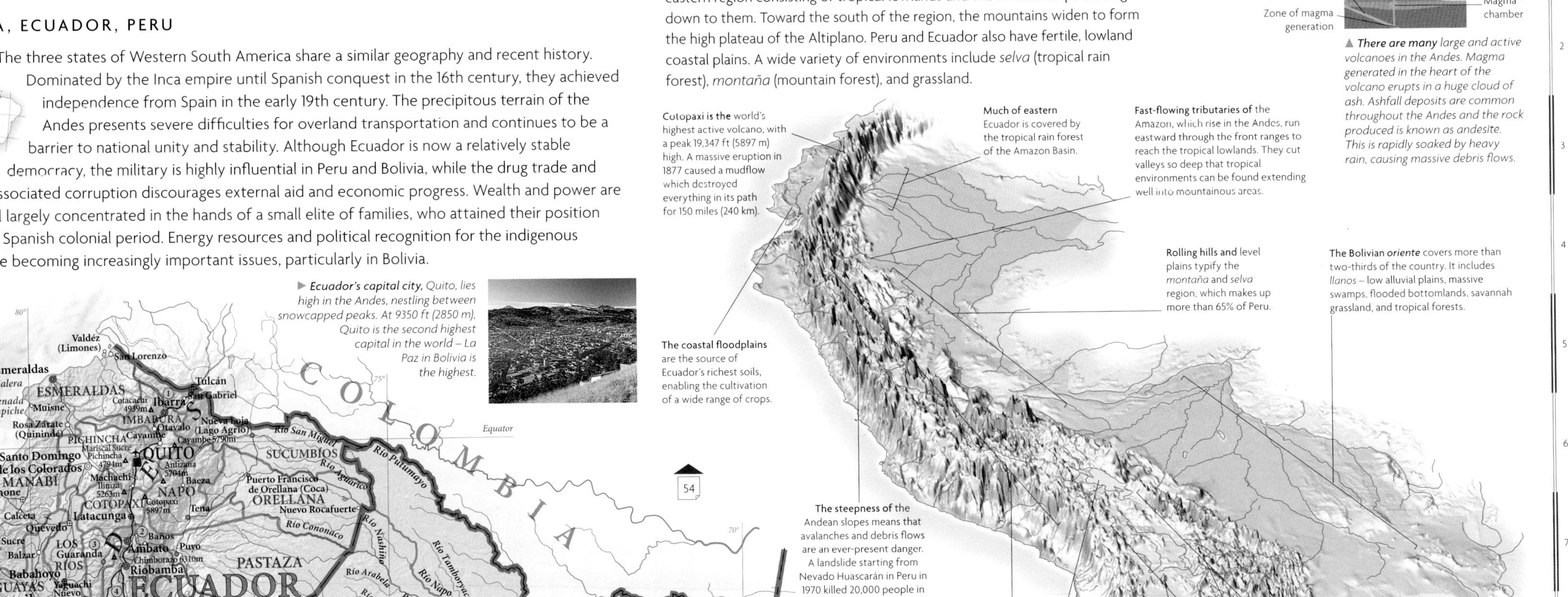
COLOMBIA
ECUADOR
BRAZIL
PERU
QUITO
Guayaquil
Iquitos
Esmeraldas
Manta
Cuenca
Machala
Loja
Piura
Chiclayo
Trujillo
Chimbote
Pucallpa
LORETO
PASTAZA
AMAZONAS
CAJAMARCA
SAN MARTÍN
HUÁNUCO
LA LIBERTAD
LAMBAYEQUE
PIURA
TUMBES
Amazon
Río Napo
Río Putumayo
Río Marañón
Río Ucayali
Golfo de Guayaquil
Equator

192

54

58

Ecuador: Administrative regions

1. CARCHI
2. TUNGURAHUA
3. BOLÍVAR
4. CHIMBORAZO

Map key

Population	Elevation
▣ above 5 million	6000m / 19,686ft
◙ 1 million to 5 million	4000m / 13,124ft
◉ 500,000 to 1 million	3000m / 9843ft
◎ 100,000 to 500,000	2000m / 6562ft
⊕ 50,000 to 100,000	1000m / 3281ft
○ 10,000 to 50,000	500m / 1640ft
∘ below 10,000	250m / 820ft
	100m / 328ft
	sea level

Scale 1:8,500,000

Km 0 25 50 100 150 200 250 300

Miles 0 25 50 100 150 200 250 300

projection: Lambert Azimuthal Equal Area

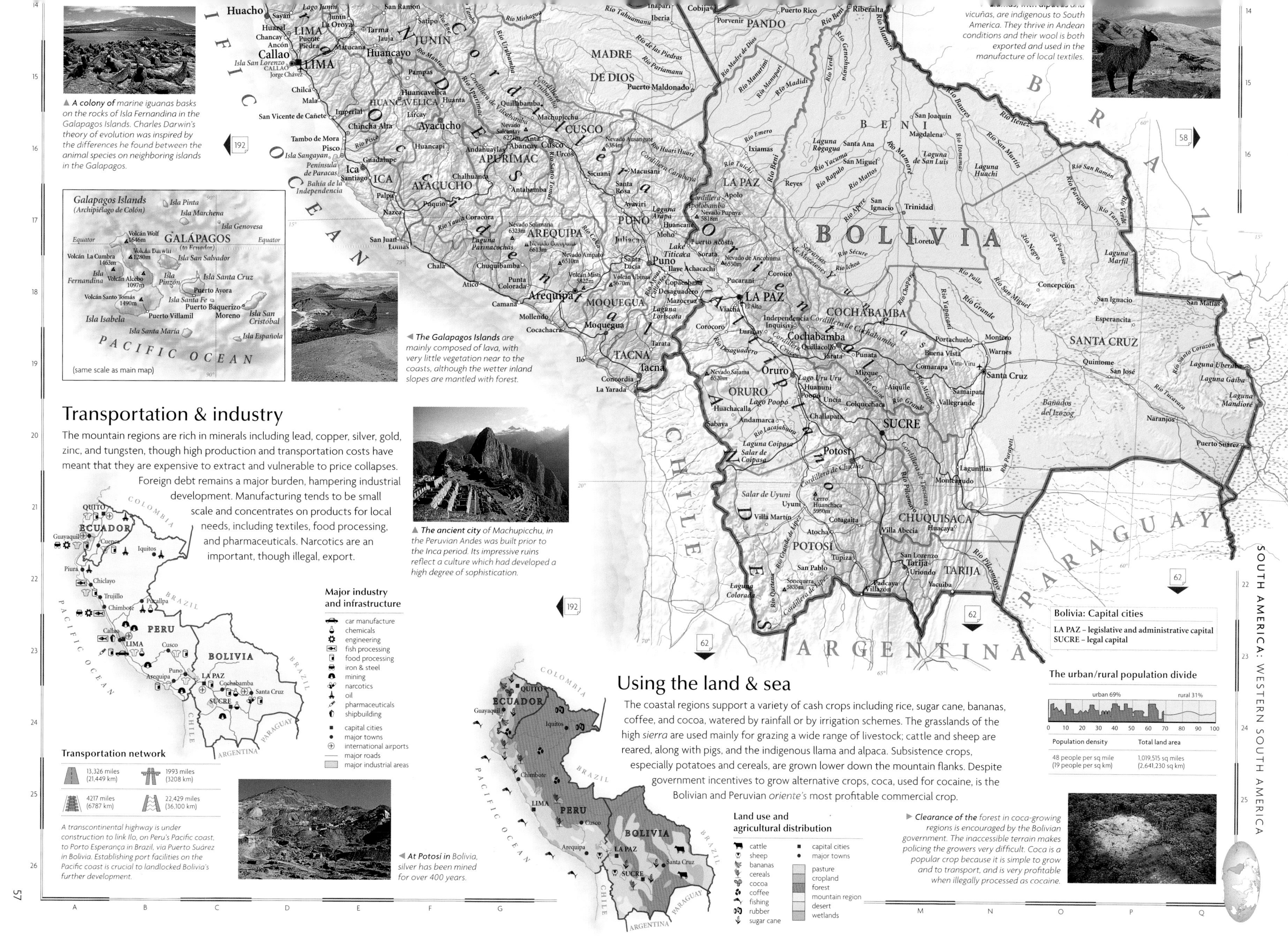
BOLIVIA
BRAZIL
PARAGUAY
ARGENTINA
CHILE
PACIFIC OCEAN
PANDO
BENI
LA PAZ
COCHABAMBA
SANTA CRUZ
ORURO
POTOSÍ
CHUQUISACA
TARIJA
SUCRE
Cordillera Oriental
Cordillera Occidental
Altiplano
ANDES
MADRE DE DIOS
CUSCO
PUNO
AREQUIPA
MOQUEGUA
TACNA
APURÍMAC
AYACUCHO
HUANCAVELICA
JUNÍN
LIMA
ICA
Galapagos Islands
(Archipiélago de Colón)
GALÁPAGOS
(same scale as main map)

vicuñas, are indigenous to South America. They thrive in Andean conditions and their wool is both exported and used in the manufacture of local textiles.

▲ **A colony of** marine iguanas basks on the rocks of Isla Fernandina in the Galapagos Islands. Charles Darwin's theory of evolution was inspired by the differences he found between the animal species on neighboring islands in the Galapagos.

◀ **The Galapagos Islands** are mainly composed of lava, with very little vegetation near to the coasts, although the wetter inland slopes are mantled with forest.

Transportation & industry

The mountain regions are rich in minerals including lead, copper, silver, gold, zinc, and tungsten, though high production and transportation costs have meant that they are expensive to extract and vulnerable to price collapses. Foreign debt remains a major burden, hampering industrial development. Manufacturing tends to be small scale and concentrates on products for local needs, including textiles, food processing, and pharmaceuticals. Narcotics are an important, though illegal, export.

▲ **The ancient city** of Machupicchu, in the Peruvian Andes was built prior to the Inca period. Its impressive ruins reflect a culture which had developed a high degree of sophistication.

Major industry and infrastructure

- car manufacture
- chemicals
- engineering
- fish processing
- food processing
- iron & steel
- mining
- narcotics
- oil
- pharmaceuticals
- shipbuilding
- capital cities
- major towns
- international airports
- major roads
- major industrial areas

Transportation network

13,326 miles (21,449 km)	1993 miles (3208 km)
4217 miles (6787 km)	22,429 miles (36,100 km)

A transcontinental highway is under construction to link Ilo, on Peru's Pacific coast, to Porto Esperança in Brazil, via Puerto Suárez in Bolivia. Establishing port facilities on the Pacific coast is crucial to landlocked Bolivia's further development.

◀ **At Potosí in** Bolivia, silver has been mined for over 400 years.

Using the land & sea

The coastal regions support a variety of cash crops including rice, sugar cane, bananas, coffee, and cocoa, watered by rainfall or by irrigation schemes. The grasslands of the high *sierra* are used mainly for grazing a wide range of livestock; cattle and sheep are reared, along with pigs, and the indigenous llama and alpaca. Subsistence crops, especially potatoes and cereals, are grown lower down the mountain flanks. Despite government incentives to grow alternative crops, coca, used for cocaine, is the Bolivian and Peruvian *oriente's* most profitable commercial crop.

Land use and agricultural distribution

- cattle
- sheep
- bananas
- cereals
- cocoa
- coffee
- fishing
- rubber
- sugar cane
- capital cities
- major towns
- pasture
- cropland
- forest
- mountain region
- desert
- wetlands

▶ **Clearance of the** forest in coca-growing regions is encouraged by the Bolivian government. The inaccessible terrain makes policing the growers very difficult. Coca is a popular crop because it is simple to grow and to transport, and is very profitable when illegally processed as cocaine.

Bolivia: Capital cities

LA PAZ – legislative and administrative capital
SUCRE – legal capital

The urban/rural population divide

urban 69% — rural 31%

Population density	Total land area
48 people per sq mile (19 people per sq km)	1,019,515 sq miles (2,641,230 sq km)

Brazil

Brazil is the largest country in South America, with a population of 179 million – greater than the combined total for the whole of the rest of the continent. The 26 states which make up the federal republic of Brazil are administered from the purpose-built capital, Brasília. Tropical rain forest, covering more than one-third of the country, contains rich natural resources, but great tracts are sacrificed to agriculture, industry and urban expansion on a daily basis. Most of Brazil's multiethnic population now live in cities, some of which are vast areas of urban sprawl; São Paulo is one of the world's biggest conurbations, with more than 19 million inhabitants. Although prosperity is a reality for some, many people still live in great poverty, and mounting foreign debts continue to damage Brazil's prospects of economic advancement.

Using the land

Brazil has immense natural resources, including minerals and hardwoods, many of which are found in the fragile rain forest. Brazil is the world's leading coffee grower and a major producer of livestock, sugar, and orange juice concentrate. Soybeans for animal feed, particularly for poultry feed, have become the country's most significant crop.

The urban/rural population divide

urban 78% | rural 22%

Population density	Total land area
55 people per sq mile (21 people per sq km)	3,286,472 sq miles (8,511,970 sq km)

Land use and agricultural distribution

cattle, pigs, sheep, citrus fruits, coffee, cotton, soybeans, sugar cane, timber, capital cities, major towns, pasture, cropland, forest

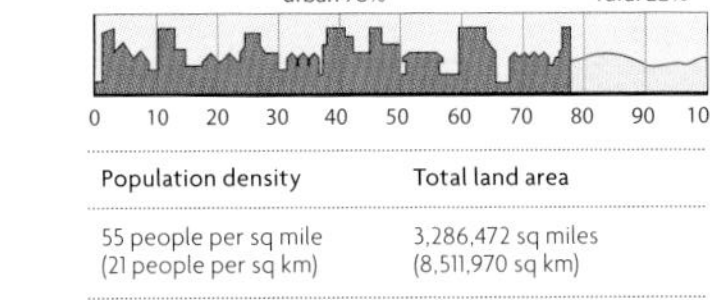

▶ *The fecundity of parts of Brazil's rain forest results from exceptionally high levels of rainfall and the quantities of silt deposited by the Amazon river system.*

The landscape

The Amazon Basin, containing the largest area of tropical rain forest on Earth, covers nearly half of Brazil. It is bordered by two shield areas: in the south by the Brazilian Highlands, and in the north by the Guiana Highlands. The east coast is dominated by a great escarpment which runs for 1600 miles (2565 km).

Brazil's highest mountain is the Pico da Neblina which was only discovered in 1962. It is 9888 ft (3014 m) high.

The floodplains which border the Amazon river are made up of a variety of different features including shallow lakes and swamps, mangrove forests in the tidal delta area, and fertile levées on river banks and point bars.

The Amazon Basin is the largest river basin in the world. The Amazon river and over a thousand tributaries drain an area of 2,375,000 sq miles (6,150,000 sq km) and carry one-fifth of the world's fresh water out to sea.

Guiana Highlands

Pantanal wetlands

The ancient Brazilian Highlands have a varied topography. Their plateaus, hills, and deep valleys are bordered by highly-eroded mountains containing important mineral deposits. They are drained by three great river systems, the Amazon, the Paraguay–Paraná, and the São Francisco.

The São Francisco Basin has a climate unique in Brazil. Known as the "drought polygon," it has almost no rain during the dry season, leading to regular disastrous droughts.

The northeastern scrublands are known as the *caatinga*, a virtually impenetrable thorny woodland, sometimes intermixed with cacti where water is scarce.

The famous Sugar Loaf Mountain (*Pão de Açúcar*) which overlooks Rio de Janeiro is a fine example of a volcanic plug a domed core of solidified lava left after the slopes of the original volcano have eroded away.

Deep natural harbors such as Baia de Guanabara were created where the steep slopes of the Serra da Mantiqueira plunge directly into the ocean.

▶ *The Pantanal region in the south of Brazil is an extension of the Gran Chaco plain. The swamps and marshes of this area are renowned for their beauty, and abundant and unique wildlife, including wildfowl and these caimans, a type of crocodile.*

◀ *The Iguaçu river surges over the spectacular Iguaçu Falls* (Saltos do Iguaçu) *toward the Paraná river. Falls like these are increasingly under pressure from large-scale hydroelectric projects such as that at Itaipú.*

Hillslope gullying

Rainfall; Direction of growth; Overland water flow; Water seeps through hillslope; Gully

◀ *Large-scale gullies are common in Brazil, particularly on hillslopes from which vegetation has been removed. Gullies grow headwards (up the slope), aided by a combination of erosion through water seepage and rainwater runoff.*

Map key

Population	Elevation
above 5 million	3000m / 9843ft
1 million to 5 million	2000m / 6562ft
500,000 to 1 million	1000m / 3281ft
100,000 to 500,000	500m / 1640ft
50,000 to 100,000	250m / 820ft
10,000 to 50,000	100m / 328ft
below 10,000	sea level

54
54
64
54
56

Scale 1:14,250,000
Km 0 25 50 100 150 200 250 300 350 400
Miles 0 25 50 100 150 200 250 300 350 400
projection: Lambert Azimuthal Equal Area
BRAZIL
PERU
BOLIVIA
PARAGUAY
ARGENTINA
URUGUAY
ATLANTIC OCEAN
ACRE
RONDÔNIA
MATO GROSSO
MATO GROSSO DO SUL
TOCANTINS
GOIÁS
DISTRITO FEDERAL
BRASÍLIA
MINAS GERAIS
BAHIA
PIAUÍ
SÃO PAULO
PARANÁ
SANTA CATARINA
RIO GRANDE DO SUL
RIO DE JANEIRO
ESPÍRITO SANTO
SERGIPE
ALAGOAS
PERNAMBUCO
PARAÍBA
RIO GRANDE DO NORTE
Planalto de Mato Grosso
Planalto Central
(Brazilian Highlands)
Pantanal
Espigão Mestre
Chapada dos Parecis
Serra do Cachimbo
Serra Formosa
Serra do Roncador
Tropic of Capricorn
Porto Velho
Rio Branco
Cuiabá
Campo Grande
Goiânia
Palmas do Tocantins
Belo Horizonte
Rio de Janeiro
São Paulo
Curitiba
Florianópolis
Porto Alegre
Salvador
Aracaju
Maceió
Recife
João Pessoa
Natal
Vitória
Major industry and infrastructure
car manufacture
chemicals
electronics
finance
food processing
iron & steel
mining
oil
printing & publishing
textiles
timber processing
tourism
capital cities
major towns
international airports
major roads
major industrial areas
Transportation network
101,893 miles (164,000 km)
3293 miles (5300 km)
18,889 miles (30,403 km)
31,065 miles (50,000 km)

Transportation & industry

Brazilian industry is diverse and well developed, in part as a result of past government incentives, including the prohibition of imports. Industries which have benefited include car manufacture, petrochemicals, and microelectronics. Textiles, clothing, and footwear are among Brazil's most successful exports. The country's services and tourism sectors are also expanding rapidly.

An extensive new road network is being built to link Brazil's main centers. Investment is needed to update the antiquated railroad system. In São Paulo, the subway system is being extended to accommodate the expanding population.

*▶ **Brazil's urban population** has grown by over 6% per year since the mid-1970s – at current population levels a rate of nearly 6 million people annually. In Rio de Janeiro prosperous neighborhoods exist alongside over 450 shantytowns or favelas, some of which house as many as 250,000 people.*

*▶ **A gaucho** in traditional costume herds beef cattle on the grasslands of the Rio Grande do Sul in southern Brazil.*

*◀ **Picinguaba Beach lies** in Serra do Mar State Park in São Paulo state. São Paulo's beaches stretch for 386 miles (622 km) along the Atlantic coast.*

Eastern South America

URUGUAY, NORTHEAST ARGENTINA, SOUTHEAST BRAZIL

The vast conurbations of Rio de Janeiro, São Paulo, and Buenos Aires form the core of South America's highly-urbanized eastern region. São Paulo state, with over 40 million inhabitants, is among the world's 20 most powerful economies, and São Paulo is the fastest growing city on the continent. Rio de Janeiro and Buenos Aires, transformed in the last hundred years from port cities to great metropolitan areas each with more than 10 million inhabitants, typify the unstructured growth and wealth disparities of South America's great cities. In Uruguay, over two fifths of the population lives in the capital, Montevideo, which faces Buenos Aires across the Plate River *(Río de la Plata)*. Immigration from the countryside has created severe pressure on the urban infrastructure, particularly on available housing, leading to a profusion of crowded shanty settlements *(favelas* or *barrios)*.

Using the land

Most of Uruguay and the Pampas of northern Argentina are devoted to the rearing of livestock, especially cattle and sheep, which are central to both countries' economies. Soybeans, first produced in Brazil's Rio Grande do Sul, are now more widely grown for large-scale export, as are cereals, sugar cane, and grapes. Subsistence crops, including potatoes, corn and sugar beets, are grown on the remaining arable land.

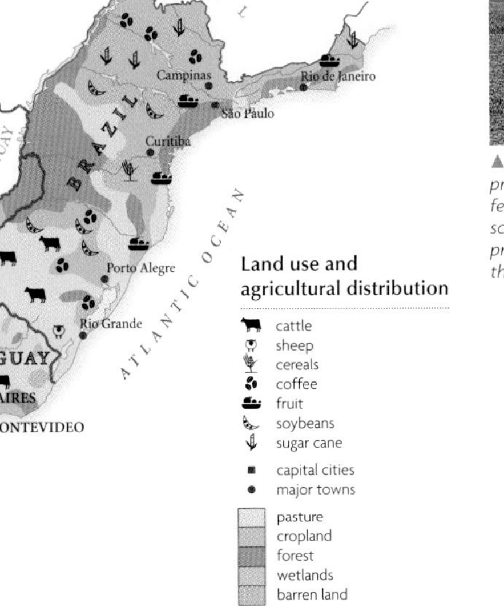

Land use and agricultural distribution

- cattle
- sheep
- cereals
- coffee
- fruit
- soybeans
- sugar cane
- capital cities
- major towns
- pasture
- cropland
- forest
- wetlands
- barren land

◀ ***The rolling grasslands*** *of Uruguay are ideally suited to the rearing of cattle, which are concentrated in great herds throughout the region.*

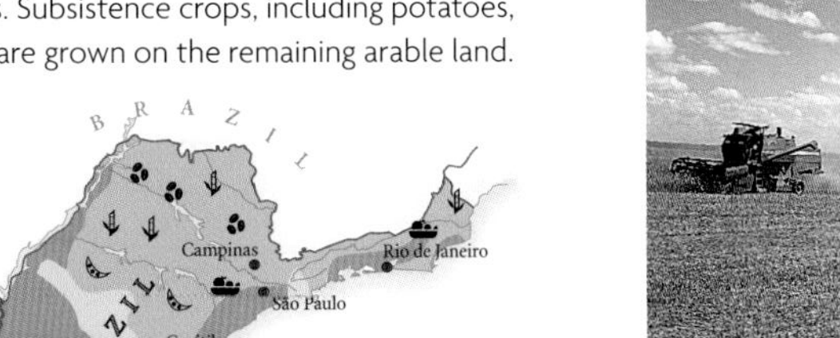

▲ ***Soybeans are harvested****, pressed, and processed into soycake, which is used as animal feed. The cake is fed mainly to chickens on large-scale factory farms, and the growth in soy production has been an important factor in the expansion of the Brazilian poultry trade.*

Transportation & industry

Southeast Brazil is home to much of the important motor and capital goods industry, largely based around São Paulo; iron and steel production is also concentrated in this region. Uruguay's economy continues to be based mainly on the export of livestock products including meat and leather goods. Buenos Aires is Argentina's chief port, and the region has a varied and sophisticated economic base including service-based industries such as finance and publishing, as well as primary processing.

Major industry and infrastructure

- car manufacture
- chemicals
- engineering
- finance
- food processing
- iron & steel
- meat processing
- printing & publishing
- shipbuilding
- textiles
- timber processing
- capital cities
- major towns
- international airports
- major roads
- major industrial areas

Transportation network

Throughout the region, road networks need to be expanded to cope with urban development. Plans are underway to build a bridge over the Plate River (Rio de la Plata) to link Colonia and Buenos Aires.

Scale 1:7,000,000

projection: Lambert Azimuthal Equal Area

Map key

Population

- above 5 million
- 1 million to 5 million
- 500,000 to 1 million
- 100,000 to 500,000
- 50,000 to 100,000
- 10,000 to 50,000
- below 10,000

Elevation

- 2000m / 6562ft
- 1000m / 3281ft
- 500m / 1640ft
- 250m / 820ft
- 100m / 328ft
- sea level

▲ ***The Itaipú dam*** *on the Paraná river is one of the largest hydroelectric projects in the world, jointly financed by Brazil and Paraguay.*

▶ ***Rio de Janeiro's*** *annual carnival, Mardi Gras, which ushers in the start of Lent, is an extravagant five-day parade through the city, characterized by fantastically decorated floats, exuberant*

58

62

64

The landscape

The southern reaches of the Brazilian Highlands follow the Atlantic coast to form low, rolling hills in the northeast of Uruguay. Much of South America's mid-eastern region and all of Uruguay has a gentle relief with land rarely rising above 300 ft (100 m). Argentina's northeast comprises two main regions: a long, narrow lowland known as Mesopotamia; and part of the Pampas grasslands.

▲ ***In 1900, Buenos Aires** was a modest port city with a population of less than 1 million. Today, more than 12 million people live in the city and its environs.*

◀ ***Tall lines of** palm trees edge the savannah landscape of Mesopotamia in northeastern Argentina.*

Tracing the edge of São Paulo state, the Paraná river drains the Brazilian Highlands, finally reaching the sea at the Plate River (*Río de la Plata*). Along with the Paraguay river, it is at the center of a controversial scheme to turn the largely unnavigable route into a great shipping canal.

The state of Rio Grande do Sul contains some of Brazil's most fertile soils. The weathered rocks produce *terra rossa*, a reddish-purple soil renowned for the rich coffee it produces.

In winter, polar air masses and the cyclonic storms associated with them, can bring heavy rain, frosts, and even snow, as far north as São Paulo.

Mesopotamia is a narrow depression, no more than 180 miles (290 km) wide, which lies between the Paraná and Uruguay rivers, stretching more than 1000 miles (1603 km) south from the Brazilian Shield to the Pampas.

Paraná river

The Serra do Mar runs along the Atlantic coast toward Porto Alegre. South of this, the land slopes away to become lower and more level in Uruguay.

The Argentinian Pampas lie to the south of the River Plate (*Río de la Plata*), meeting southern Mesopotamia in the north and the Atlantic Ocean to the east. They are covered by deposits of silt, alluvium and volcanic ash.

▶ ***A number of** large inland tidal lakes fringe the Atlantic coastlines of Uruguay and southeastern Brazil.*

Coastal lagoons

Freshwater river

River delta

Sand barrier formed from sandy silts eroded in the Pampas region

Sand bar builds in parallel to the shoreline

Saltwater

▲ ***The Atlantic coast** of Uruguay and southern Brazil has many large lagoons. Long-term lagoons are formed when sea levels change; 6000 years ago, the sea level near Buenos Aires was 6.5 ft (2 m) higher than it is today. More temporary lagoons are enclosed by spits and sandbars, created by the drifting of sand and sediment in parallel with the shoreline.*

Low plateaux and hills, like the Cuchilla Grande, dominate the landscape of Uruguay, which lies in a transitional zone between the humid Pampas of Argentina and the hilly uplands of Brazil.

The River Plate (*Río de la Plata*) is a great estuary formed at the confluence of the Paraná and Uruguay rivers near Nueva Palmira.

◀ ***Montevideo became the** capital of Uruguay following independence in 1828. The focus for Uruguayan industry and trade, it is also a popular destination for tourists from other South American countries.*

Southern South America

ARGENTINA, CHILE, PARAGUAY

South America's cone-shaped southern region is shared by Argentina and Chile, two overwhelmingly urbanized nations whose populations live mainly in or around the capital cities, Buenos Aires and Santiago. The people are largely *mestizo* or of European origin; in the early 20th century Argentina absorbed waves of new European immigrants, many from Italy and Germany. Paraguay is far less urbanized than its neighbors, with a homogeneous population of mixed Spanish and Guaraní origin, who retain their Indian roots through the Guaraní language. Though most Paraguayans live in the southeast, near Asunción, the indigenous Indians live in the sparsely populated Gran Chaco. The Gran Chaco is also home to some of Argentina's minority indigenous peoples, who otherwise live mainly in Andean regions. Chile's estimated 800,000 Mapauche Indians live almost exclusively in the south.

Transportation & industry

Food processing and agricultural exports remain a fundamental part of Argentina's economy. The growth of manufacturing is regularly hampered by hyper-inflation and massive foreign debts. The world's most important copper producer and one of the top twenty gold producers, Chile also has a thriving wine and grape industry. Most Paraguayan exports involve primary processing, although domestic goods are produced for home markets.

▲ ***Chuquicamata copper mine,*** *lies on a desert plateau near Calama in the Andes of northern Chile. It is the world's largest open-pit copper mine.*

▲ ***Boiling water*** *and steam emerge from a volcanic vent, one of the Tatio geysers which lie at the foot of Cerro de Tocorpuri near Chile's border with Bolivia.*

▶ ***Floodwaters cover*** *the land in the Gran Chaco, partly submerging its vegetation of fan palms and hyacinths.*

Major industry and infrastructure

- chemicals
- engineering
- food processing
- meat processing
- mining
- oil
- textiles
- timber processing
- capital cities
- major towns
- international airports
- major roads
- major industrial areas

Transportation network

55,062 miles (93,453 km)	3038 miles (4889 km)
26,811 miles (43,153 km)	9180 miles (14,775 km)

Argentina's state transportation system is under-going privatization, though the outmoded rail network requires updating. Paraguay requires foreign investment to upgrade its roads and railroads. Essential internal air routes, especially across the Andes, are well developed in all three countries.

Map key

Population

- 1 million to 5 million
- 500,000 to 1 million
- 100,000 to 500,000
- 50,000 to 100,000
- 10,000 to 50,000
- below 10,000

Elevation

- 6000m / 19,686ft
- 4000m / 13,124ft
- 3000m / 9843ft
- 2000m / 6562ft
- 1000m / 3281ft
- 500m / 1640ft
- 250m / 820ft
- 100m / 328ft

56

58

The landscape

The Andes run from north to south, forming a precipitous natural border between Chile and Argentina. East of the Andes are the scrublands of the Gran Chaco and the plains of the Pampas, which extend northward toward Paraguay. In the far southwest, Chile's indented Pacific coastline has many features typical of areas which have been affected by glaciation.

▲ *The Atacama Desert* (Desierto de Atacama) *in Chile is one of the driest places on Earth where some areas have never recorded any rain. It contains a number of salt lakes.*

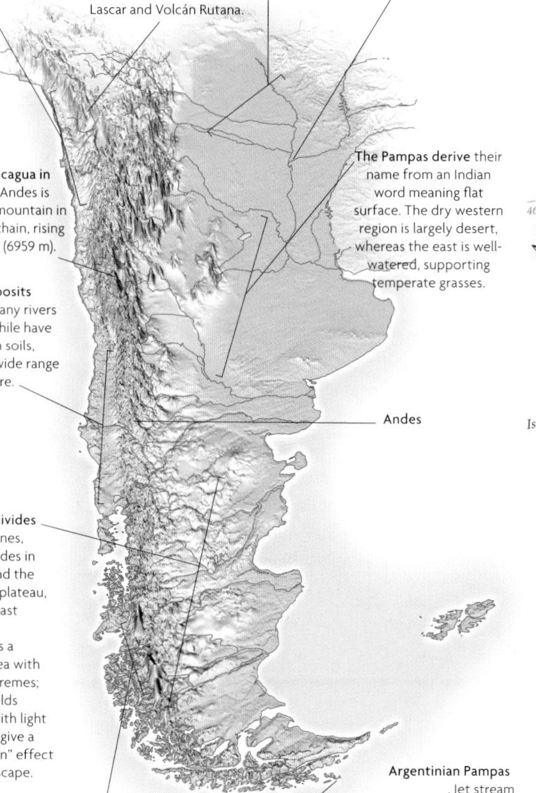

The Gran Chaco combines poor drainage, extremely hot temperatures and thorn-infested scrub to make it one of South America's most inhospitable regions.

Landlocked Paraguay relies on its river system for access to the sea and to produce hydroelectric power. The most important river system is the Paraguay–Paraná which provides links into neighboring countries including Brazil, Uruguay, and Argentina.

Most of the highest mountains in Chile's northern Andes are volcanoes like Volcán Lascar and Volcán Rutana.

The Pampas derive their name from an Indian word meaning flat surface. The dry western region is largely desert, whereas the east is well-watered, supporting temperate grasses.

Cerro Aconcagua in the central Andes is the tallest mountain in the whole chain, rising to 22,834 ft (6959 m).

Alluvial deposits from the many rivers in central Chile have created rich soils, ideal for a wide range of agriculture.

Andes

Patagonia divides into two zones, with the Andes in the west, and the lower main plateau, extending east toward the Atlantic. It is a desolate area with climatic extremes; dark lava fields scattered with light bunchgrass give a "leopard skin" effect to the landscape.

The Patagonian ice sheet is the world's third largest ice field, covering 6560 sq miles (17,000 sq km). Patagonia also contains many typical features from past glaciations. These include glacial lakes, U-shaped valleys, fjords, and deep-cut channels.

Cape Horn is the most southerly point of South America. The severity of the "Roaring Forties" winds makes the Horn one of the world's most treacherous shipping regions.

Argentinian Pampas

Jet stream

Rainfall

Windblown particles

Ice-capped Andes are source of loess

Thick layer of loess sediments

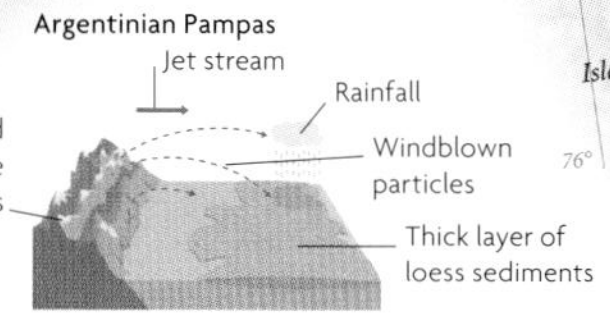

▲ ***A thick, fertile layer** of loess lies in the basin underlying the Argentinian Pampas. It has been laid down following successive periods of glaciation. The minute loess particles are transported as dust and deposited by a downward air motion, or following rainfall.*

192

64

▲ ***Great blocks of** ice break away from the jagged blue peaks of these ice mountains to form icebergs off the coast of Patagonia, Argentina's most southerly region.*

Using the land & sea

The rich plains of the Pampas support massive herds of cattle, producing meat, milk, and hides essential to the domestic and export markets of both Argentina and Paraguay. Wheat and fruit are Argentina's other major agricultural products. A wide range of soft fruits, citrus fruits, and more specialized crops such as walnuts, and grapes for wine and the table, are grown in Chile's fertile Central Valley, while the landscape to the south is dominated by forestry, mainly growing commercial radiata pine. Paraguay is self-sufficient in wheat and other staples. Cotton, coffee, tobacco, and oil sources such as soybeans, are the major export crops.

The urban/rural population divide

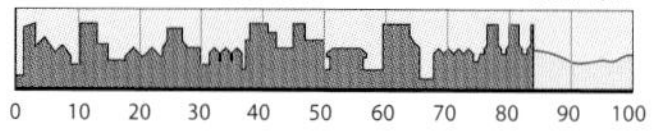

urban 84% — rural 16%

0 10 20 30 40 50 60 70 80 90 100

Population density	Total land area
40 people per sq mile (15 people per sq km)	1,498,757 sq miles (3,882,790 sq km)

Land use and agricultural distribution

cattle, sheep, cereals, fruit, grapes, timber, fishing

capital cities, major towns

pasture, cropland, forest, barren land, mountain region, desert

Scale 1:9,750,000

projection: Lambert Azimuthal Equal Area

▲ ***Charred tree stumps** surround a cattle enclosure on the island of Tierra del Fuego in southern Argentina. Forest clearance to provide grazing land for cattle is of major environmental concern.*

The Atlantic Ocean

The Atlantic is the youngest of the world's oceans, formed about 180 million years ago when the landmasses of the eastern and western hemispheres separated. Its underwater topography is dominated by the Mid-Atlantic Ridge, a huge mountain system running north to south along the center of the ocean. Although most of the ridge's peaks lie below the sea, some emerge as volcanic islands, like Iceland and the Azores. The Atlantic contains a wealth of resources, including substantial oil and gas reserves and rich fishing grounds. Until the 1950s, the north Atlantic was the world's busiest shipping route; cheaper air transportation and alternative routes have shifted patterns of world trade.

▲ ***Surtsey near Iceland,*** *lies on the Mid-Atlantic Ridge. The island was formed in 1963 following a volcanic eruption caused by sea-floor spreading.*

Resources

Development of the oil and gas reserves in the Atlantic began in the 1940s around the Gulf of Mexico. Since then other areas have been exploited, including the North Sea, the west coast of Africa and the area east of Newfoundland and Nova Scotia. There is also extensive mining of sand, gravel, and shell deposits by the US and UK. For centuries, the north Atlantic's fishing grounds have been utilized more heavily than other oceans, leading to a serious decline in many fish stocks.

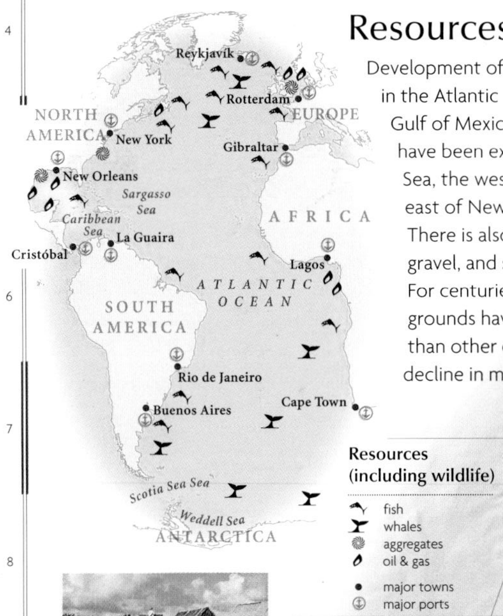

Resources (including wildlife)

- fish
- whales
- aggregates
- oil & gas
- major towns
- major ports

▲ ***Fishing in the*** *seas around northwestern Europe dates back over 1500 years. The high nutrient content of the seas makes them ideal breeding grounds for many species of fish.*

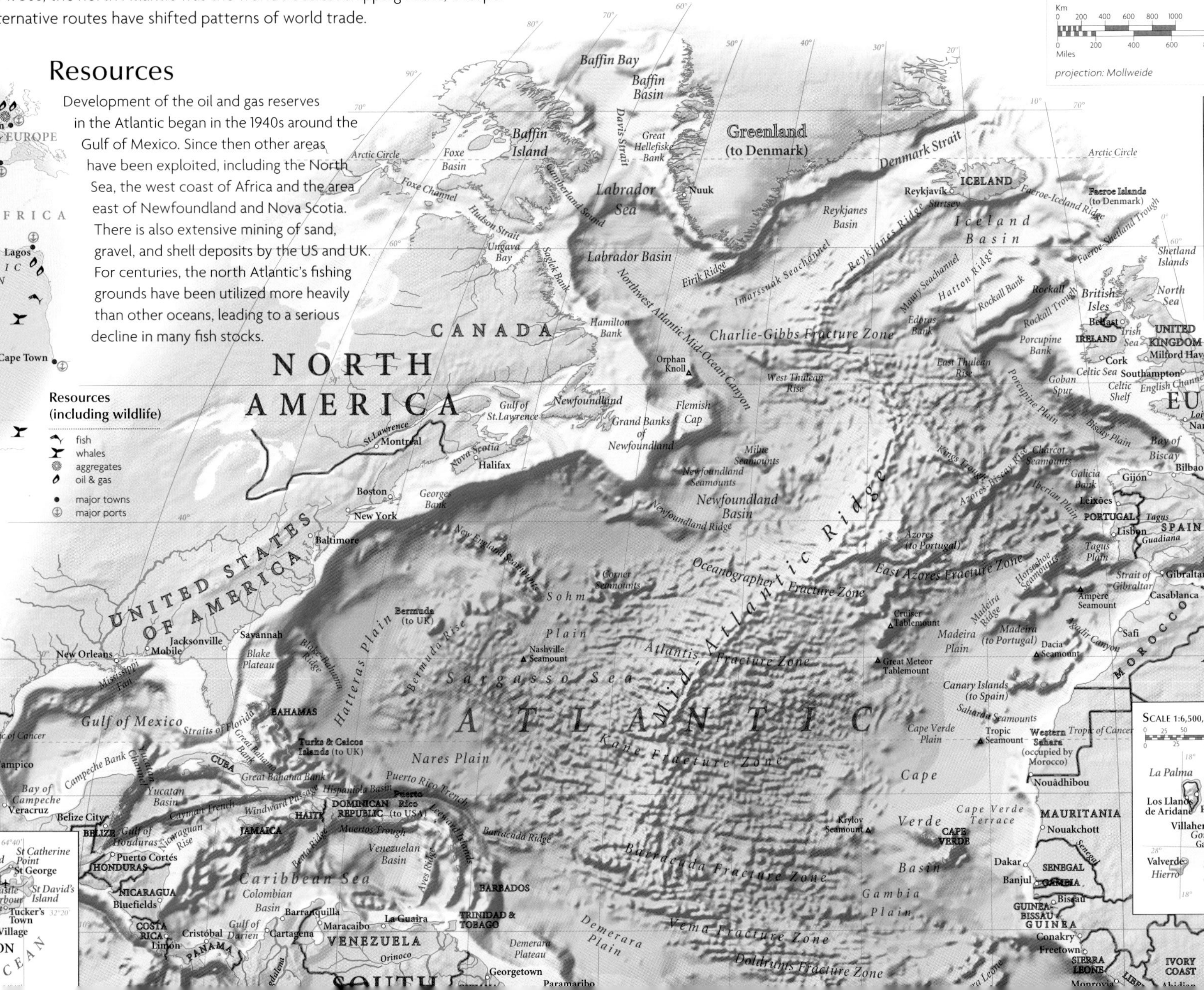

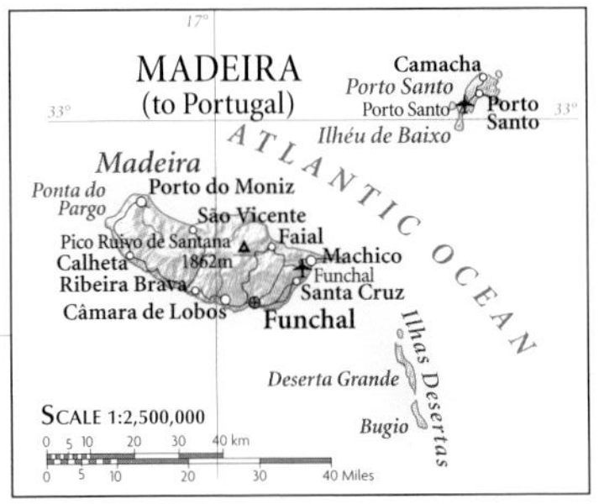

Scale 1:48,000,000

projection: Mollweide

▲ ***On January 5*** *1993, the oil tanker Braer ran aground in the Shetland Islands, spilling 83,660 tons (85,000 tonnes) of light crude oil into the ocean, devastating the local marine ecosystem.*

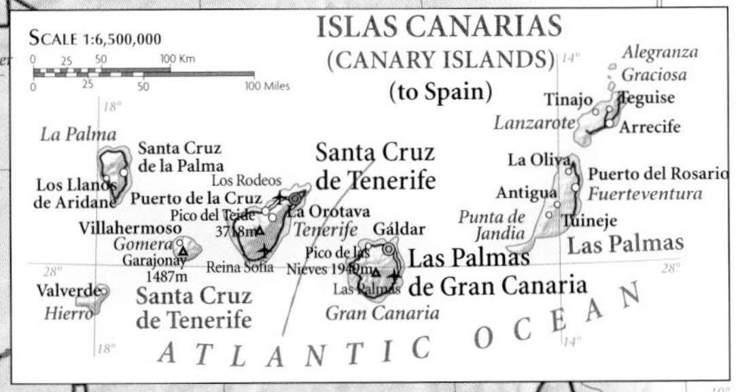

AZORES (to Portugal)

MADEIRA (to Portugal)

ISLAS CANARIAS (CANARY ISLANDS) (to Spain)

BERMUDA (to UK)

The landscape

The floor of the Atlantic is spreading by about one inch (2.5 cm) a year. The South American and African plates are moving apart drawing molten rock up from the Earth's core. The Mid-Atlantic Ridge lies along the boundary of the two plates, forming the world's longest mountain range and dividing the Atlantic floor into two parallel troughs. These troughs are subdivided into numerous smaller basins by transform faults. Most of the oceanic islands in the Atlantic are volcanic in origin; either part of the Mid-Atlantic Ridge or the Caribbean arc.

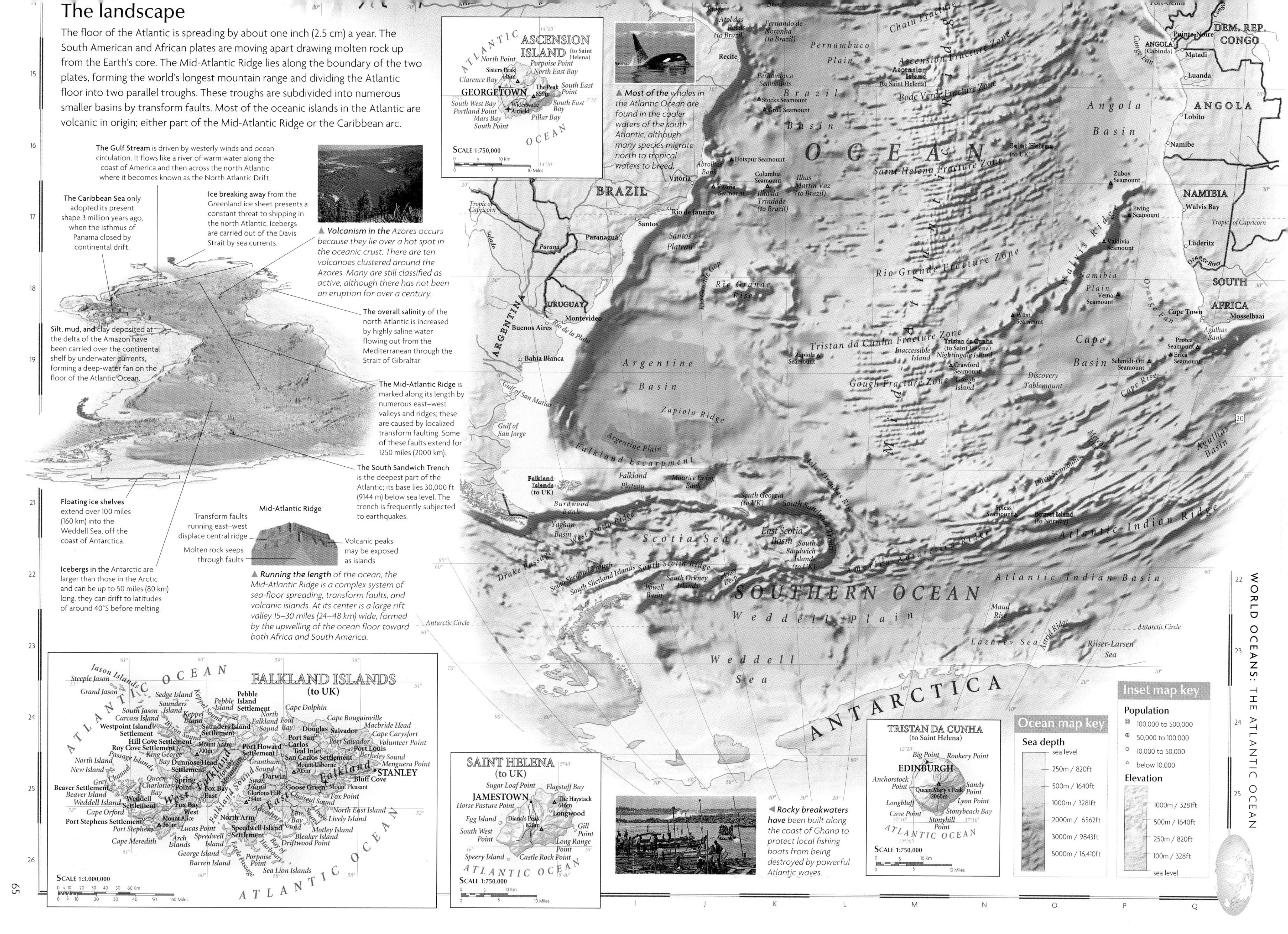

ATLANTIC OCEAN
SOUTHERN OCEAN
ANTARCTICA
BRAZIL
ARGENTINA
URUGUAY
ANGOLA
NAMIBIA
SOUTH AFRICA
DEM. REP. CONGO
Argentine Basin
Brazil Basin
Angola Basin
Cape Basin
Scotia Sea
Weddell Sea
Weddell Plain
Atlantic-Indian Basin
Atlantic-Indian Ridge
Walvis Ridge
Rio Grande Rise
Falkland Escarpment
South Sandwich Trench
Drake Passage
Lazarev Sea
Riiser-Larsen Sea
Antarctic Circle
Tropic of Capricorn
ASCENSION ISLAND (to Saint Helena)
GEORGETOWN
SCALE 1:750,000
SAINT HELENA (to UK)
JAMESTOWN
SCALE 1:750,000
TRISTAN DA CUNHA (to Saint Helena)
EDINBURGH
SCALE 1:750,000
FALKLAND ISLANDS (to UK)
STANLEY
SCALE 1:3,000,000
Mid-Atlantic Ridge
Transform faults running east–west displace central ridge
Molten rock seeps through faults
Volcanic peaks may be exposed as islands

The Gulf Stream is driven by westerly winds and ocean circulation. It flows like a river of warm water along the coast of America and then across the north Atlantic where it becomes known as the North Atlantic Drift.

The Caribbean Sea only adopted its present shape 3 million years ago, when the Isthmus of Panama closed by continental drift.

Ice breaking away from the Greenland ice sheet presents a constant threat to shipping in the north Atlantic. Icebergs are carried out of the Davis Strait by sea currents.

▲ ***Volcanism in the** Azores occurs because they lie over a hot spot in the oceanic crust. There are ten volcanoes clustered around the Azores. Many are still classified as active, although there has not been an eruption for over a century.*

Silt, mud, and clay deposited at the delta of the Amazon have been carried over the continental shelf by underwater currents, forming a deep-water fan on the floor of the Atlantic Ocean.

The overall salinity of the north Atlantic is increased by highly saline water flowing out from the Mediterranean through the Strait of Gibraltar.

The Mid-Atlantic Ridge is marked along its length by numerous east–west valleys and ridges; these are caused by localized transform faulting. Some of these faults extend for 1250 miles (2000 km).

The South Sandwich Trench is the deepest part of the Atlantic; its base lies 30,000 ft (9144 m) below sea level. The trench is frequently subjected to earthquakes.

Floating ice shelves extend over 100 miles (160 km) into the Weddell Sea, off the coast of Antarctica.

Icebergs in the Antarctic are larger than those in the Arctic and can be up to 50 miles (80 km) long. they can drift to latitudes of around 40°S before melting.

▲ ***Running the length** of the ocean, the Mid-Atlantic Ridge is a complex system of sea-floor spreading, transform faults, and volcanic islands. At its center is a large rift valley 15–30 miles (24–48 km) wide, formed by the upwelling of the ocean floor toward both Africa and South America.*

▲ ***Most of the** whales in the Atlantic Ocean are found in the cooler waters of the south Atlantic, although many species migrate north to tropical waters to breed.*

◀ ***Rocky breakwaters** have been built along the coast of Ghana to protect local fishing boats from being destroyed by powerful Atlantic waves.*

Ocean map key

Sea depth
- sea level
- 250m / 820ft
- 500m / 1640ft
- 1000m / 3281ft
- 2000m / 6562ft
- 3000m / 9843ft
- 5000m / 16,410ft

Inset map key

Population
- ◎ 100,000 to 500,000
- ⊕ 50,000 to 100,000
- ○ 10,000 to 50,000
- ○ below 10,000

Elevation
- 1000m / 328ft
- 500m / 1640ft
- 250m / 820ft
- 100m / 328ft
- sea level

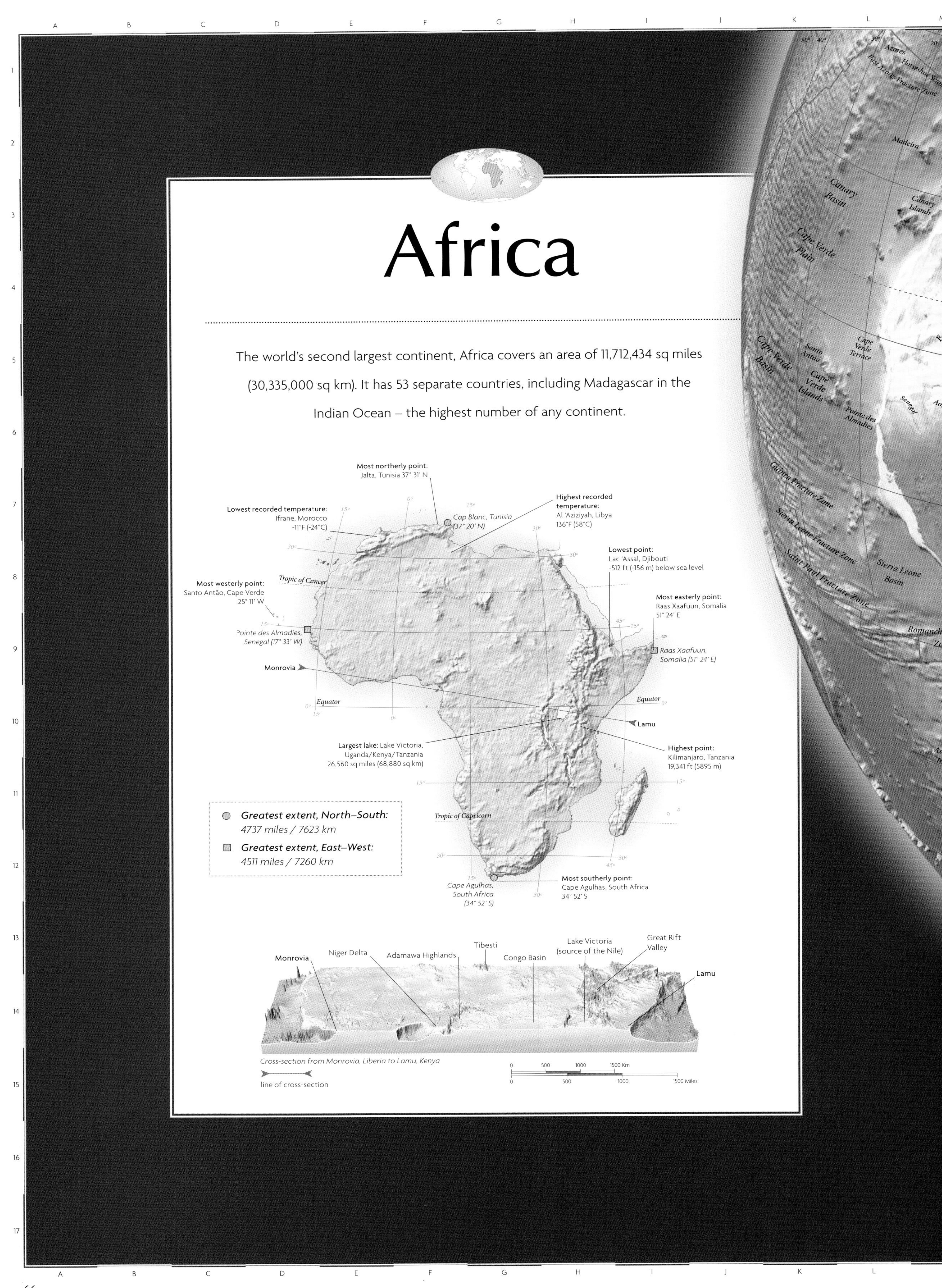
Africa
The world's second largest continent, Africa covers an area of 11,712,434 sq miles (30,335,000 sq km). It has 53 separate countries, including Madagascar in the Indian Ocean – the highest number of any continent.
Most northerly point: Jalta, Tunisia 37° 31' N
Cap Blanc, Tunisia (37° 20' N)
Lowest recorded temperature: Ifrane, Morocco -11°F (-24°C)
Highest recorded temperature: Al 'Aziziyah, Libya 136°F (58°C)
Lowest point: Lac 'Assal, Djibouti -512 ft (-156 m) below sea level
Most westerly point: Santo Antão, Cape Verde 25° 11' W
Pointe des Almadies, Senegal (17° 33' W)
Most easterly point: Raas Xaafuun, Somalia 51° 24' E
Raas Xaafuun, Somalia (51° 24' E)
Monrovia
Tropic of Cancer
Equator
Lamu
Largest lake: Lake Victoria, Uganda/Kenya/Tanzania 26,560 sq miles (68,880 sq km)
Highest point: Kilimanjaro, Tanzania 19,341 ft (5895 m)
Tropic of Capricorn
Greatest extent, North–South: 4737 miles / 7623 km
Greatest extent, East–West: 4511 miles / 7260 km
Cape Agulhas, South Africa (34° 52' S)
Most southerly point: Cape Agulhas, South Africa 34° 52' S
Monrovia
Niger Delta
Adamawa Highlands
Tibesti
Congo Basin
Lake Victoria (source of the Nile)
Great Rift Valley
Lamu
Cross-section from Monrovia, Liberia to Lamu, Kenya
line of cross-section
0 500 1000 1500 Km
0 500 1000 1500 Miles
Azores
Horseshoe Seamounts
East Azores Fracture Zone
Madeira
Canary Basin
Canary Islands
Cape Verde Plain
Cape Verde Basin
Santo Antão
Cape Verde Terrace
Cape Verde Islands
Pointe des Almadies
Senegal
Guinea Fracture Zone
Sierra Leone Fracture Zone
Saint Paul Fracture Zone
Sierra Leone Basin
Romanche

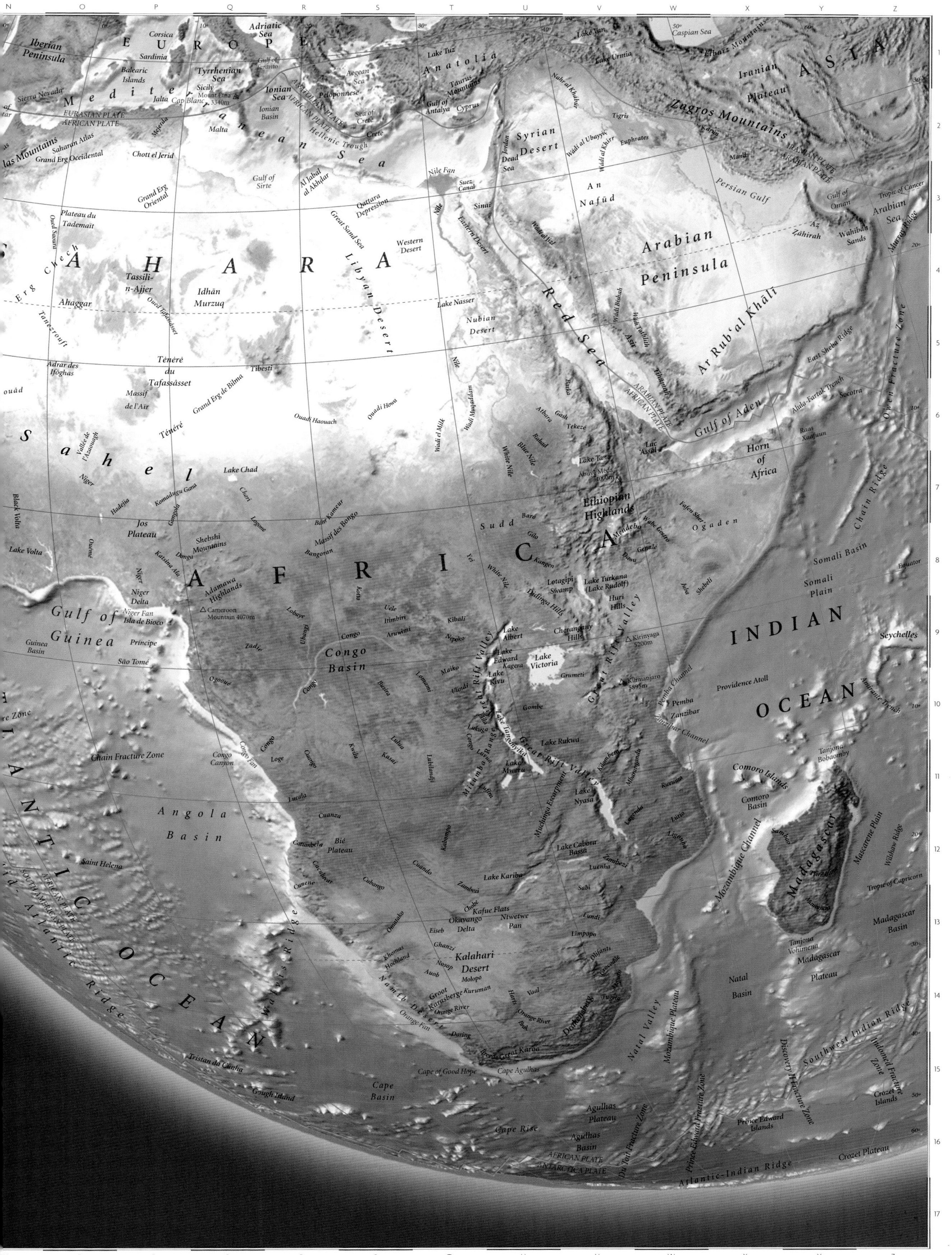
N O P Q R S T U V W X Y Z
1 2 3 4 5 6 7 8 9 10 11 12 13 14 15 16 17
EUROPE
Iberian Peninsula
Corsica
Sardinia
Balearic Islands
Adriatic Sea
Tyrrhenian Sea
Sicily
Mount Etna 3340m
Jalta
Cap Blanc
Sierra Nevada
Mediterranean Sea
EURASIAN PLATE
AFRICAN PLATE
Ionian Sea
Ionian Basin
Malta
Aegean Sea
Peloponnese
Sea of Crete
Crete
Hellenic Trough
ANATOLIAN PLATE
AFRICAN PLATE
Anatolia
Lake Tuz
Taurus Mountains
Gulf of Antalya
Cyprus
Lake Van
Lake Urmia
Caspian Sea
Elburz Mountains
Iranian Plateau
ASIA
Zagros Mountains
IRANIAN PLATE
ARABIAN PLATE
Tigris
Euphrates
Saharan Atlas
Atlas Mountains
Grand Erg Occidental
Chott el Jerid
Gulf of Sirte
Grand Erg Oriental
Al Jabal al Akhdar
Qattara Depression
Great Sand Sea
Nile Fan
Suez Canal
Sinai
Jordan
Dead Sea
Syrian Desert
Wadi al Ubayyiḍ
An Nafūd
Persian Gulf
Gulf of Oman
Tropic of Cancer
Arabian Sea
Az Zāhirah
Wahibah Sands
Plateau du Tademaït
SAHARA
Tassili-n-Ajjer
Idhān Murzuq
Libyan Desert
Western Desert
Eastern Desert
Nile
Lake Nasser
Nubian Desert
Red Sea
Arabian Peninsula
Ar Rubʿ al Khālī
Ahaggar
Tanezrouft
Erg Chech
Adrar des Ifôghas
Ténéré du Tafassâsset
Tibesti
Massif de l'Aïr
Grand Erg de Bilma
Ténéré
Ouadi Haouach
Ouadi Howa
Wadi al Milk
Wadi Muqaddam
ARABIAN PLATE
AFRICAN PLATE
Gulf of Aden
East Sheba Ridge
Alula-Fartak Trench
Socotra
Owen Fracture Zone
Raas Xaafuun
Horn of Africa
Sahel
Lake Chad
Niger
Komadugu Gana
Chari
Atbara
Blue Nile
White Nile
Lake Tana
Lac Assal
Ethiopian Highlands
Ogaden
Sudd
Baro
Gilo
Kangen
Mendebo
Genale
Shebeli
Juba
Black Volta
Lake Volta
Jos Plateau
Shebshi Mountains
Bangoran
Massif des Bongo
AFRICA
Niger Delta
Adamawa Highlands
Lake Turkana (Lake Rudolf)
Lotagipi Swamp
Huri Hills
Chain Ridge
Somali Basin
Somali Plain
Equator
INDIAN OCEAN
Seychelles
Gulf of Guinea
Niger Fan
Isla de Bioco
Cameroon Mountain 4070m
Guinea Basin
Príncipe
São Tomé
Congo Basin
Congo
Ubangi
Lake Albert
Lake Edward
Lake Kivu
Lake Victoria
Kirinyaga 5200m
Kilimanjaro 5895m
Great Rift Valley
Western Rift Valley
Pemba
Zanzibar
Providence Atoll
Amirante Trench
Lake Tanganyika
Lake Rukwa
Lake Mweru
Mitumba Range
Chain Fracture Zone
Congo Canyon
Congo Fan
Angola Basin
Lake Nyasa
Muchinga Escarpment
Comoro Islands
Comoro Basin
Tanjona Bobaomby
Madagascar
Mozambique Channel
Mascarene Plain
Bié Plateau
Cuanza
Saint Helena
Lake Kariba
Lake Cabora Bassa
Zambezi
Okavango Delta
Kafue Flats
Ntwetwe Pan
Kalahari Desert
Limpopo
Tropic of Capricorn
Madagascar Basin
Madagascar Plateau
Tanjona Vohimena
Namib Desert
Orange River
Orange Fan
Great Karoo
Drakensberg
Natal Valley
Mozambique Plateau
Natal Basin
Walvis Ridge
ATLANTIC OCEAN
Mid-Atlantic Ridge
Tristan da Cunha
Gough Island
Cape of Good Hope
Cape Agulhas
Cape Basin
Cape Rise
Agulhas Plateau
Agulhas Basin
AFRICAN PLATE
ANTARCTICA PLATE
Du Toit Fracture Zone
Prince Edward Fracture Zone
Discovery II Fracture Zone
Prince Edward Islands
Southwest Indian Ridge
Indomed Fracture Zone
Crozet Islands
Crozet Plateau
Atlantic-Indian Ridge

Physical Africa

The structure of Africa was dramatically influenced by the break up of the supercontinent Gondwanaland about 160 million years ago and, more recently, rifting and hot spot activity. Today, much of Africa is remote from active plate boundaries and comprises a series of extensive plateaus and deep basins, which influence the drainage patterns of major rivers. The relief rises to the east, where volcanic uplands and vast lakes mark the Great Rift Valley. In the far north and south sedimentary rocks have been folded to form the Atlas Mountains and the Great Karoo.

East Africa

The Great Rift Valley is the most striking feature of this region, running for 4475 miles (7200 km) from Lake Nyasa to the Red Sea. North of Lake Nyasa it splits into two arms and encloses an interior plateau which contains Lake Victoria. A number of elongated lakes and volcanoes lie along the fault lines. To the west lies the Congo Basin, a vast, shallow depression, which rises to form an almost circular rim of highlands.

Rift valley lakes, like Lake Tanganyika, lie along fault lines

Lake Victoria

Extensive faulting occurs as rift valley pulls apart

***Cross-section through** eastern Africa showing the two arms of the Great Rift Valley and its interior plateau.*

Northern Africa

Northern Africa comprises a system of basins and plateaus. The Tibesti and Ahaggar are volcanic uplands, whose uplift has been matched by subsidence within large surrounding basins. Many of the basins have been infilled with sand and gravel, creating the vast Saharan lands. The Atlas Mountains in the north were formed by convergence of the African and Eurasian plates.

The Earth's crust has been warped to form the Taoudenni Basin

Volcanic Ahaggar mountains, formed by rising magma from a hot spot

Lake Chad lies in a sand-filled basin

***Section across northern** Africa showing infilled basins and uplifted plateaus.*

Scale 1:40,000,000

projection: Lambert Azimuthal Equal Area

Map key

Elevation

- 5000m / 16,405ft
- 4000m / 13,124ft
- 3000m / 9843ft
- 2000m / 6562ft
- 1000m / 3281ft
- 500m / 1640ft
- 250m / 820ft
- 100m / 328ft
- sea level
- below sea level

Plate margins (for explanation see page xiv)

- constructive
- destructive
- conservative
- uncertain
- line of cross-section

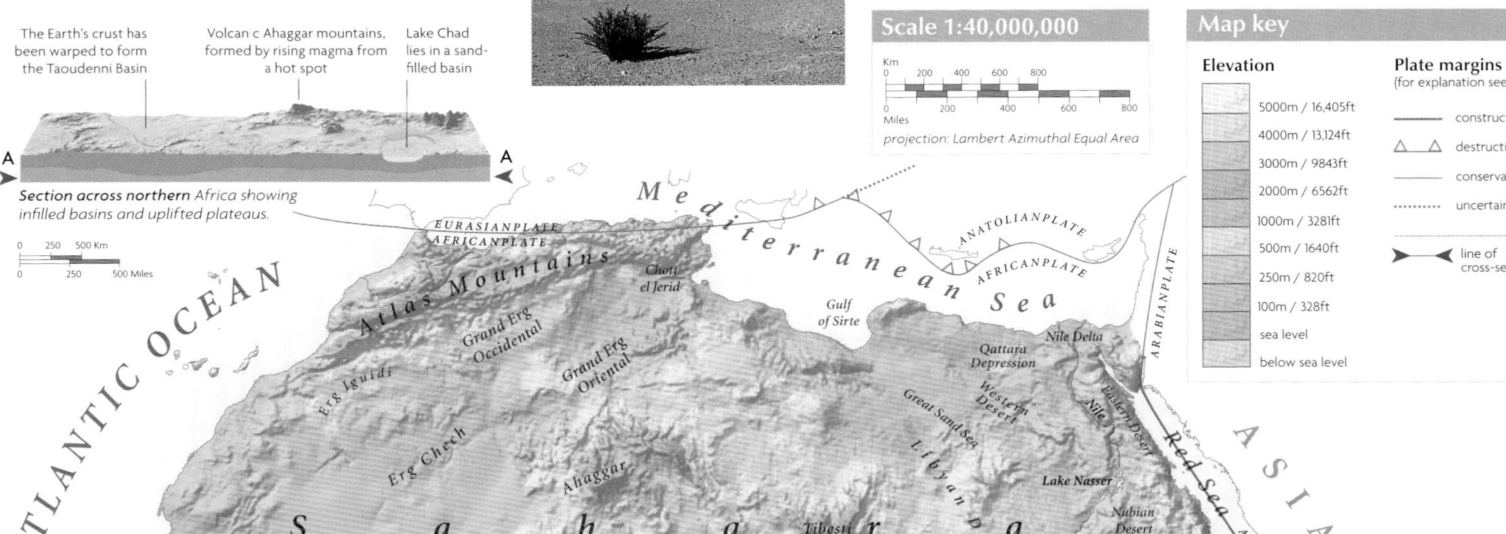
Mediterranean Sea
EURASIAN PLATE
AFRICAN PLATE
ANATOLIAN PLATE
ARABIAN PLATE
Atlas Mountains
Chott el Jerid
Gulf of Sirte
Grand Erg Occidental
Grand Erg Oriental
Erg Iguidi
Erg Chech
Ahaggar
Sahara
Tibesti
Qattara Depression
Nile Delta
Western Desert
Great Sand Sea
Libyan Desert
Eastern Desert
Nile
Red Sea
Lake Nasser
Nubian Desert
ASIA
ATLANTIC OCEAN
Cape Verde Islands
Taoudenni Basin
Senegal
Niger
Massif de l'Aïr
Ténéré
Lake Chad
Sahel
Blue Nile
White Nile
Lake Tana
Gulf of Aden
Horn of Africa
Ethiopian Highlands

Southern Africa

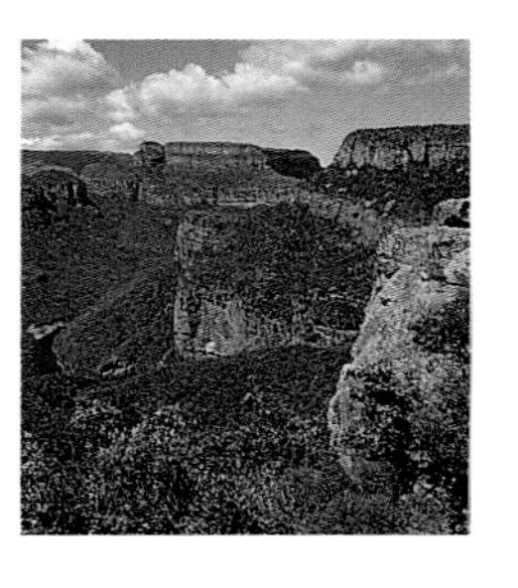

The Great Escarpment marks the southern boundary of Africa's basement rock and includes the Drakensberg range. It was uplifted when Gondwanaland fragmented about 160 million years ago and it has gradually been eroded back from the coast. To the north, the relief drops steadily, forming the Kalahari Basin. In the far south are the fold mountains of the Great Karoo.

Kalahari Basin, covered with the sandy plains of the Kalahari Desert

Boundary of the Great Escarpment

Uplift of the basement rock created a raised plateau

Drakensberg

***Cross-section through** southern Africa showing the boundary of the Great Escarpment.*

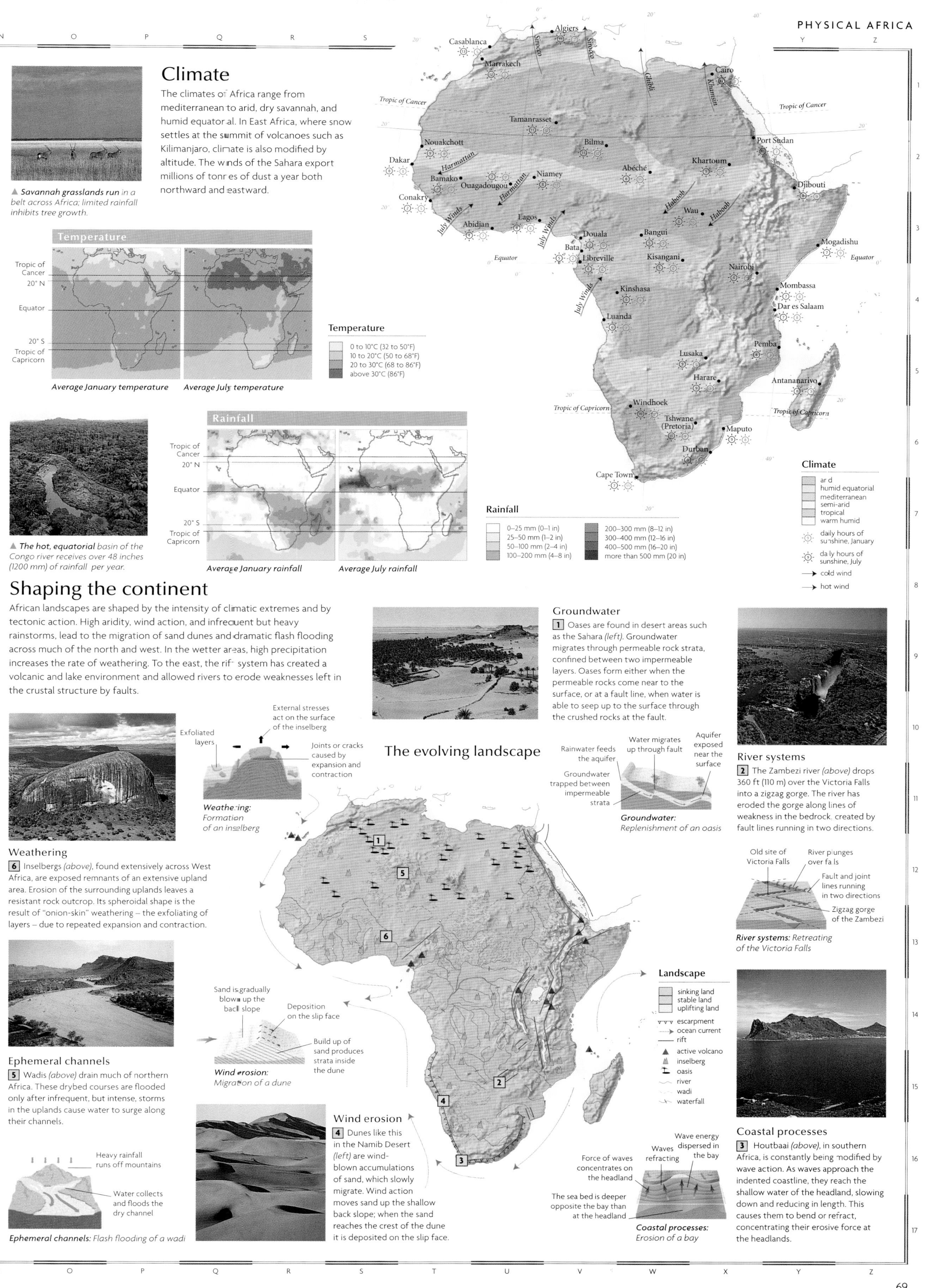

Climate

The climates of Africa range from mediterranean to arid, dry savannah, and humid equatorial. In East Africa, where snow settles at the summit of volcanoes such as Kilimanjaro, climate is also modified by altitude. The winds of the Sahara export millions of tonnes of dust a year both northward and eastward.

▲ *Savannah grasslands run in a belt across Africa; limited rainfall inhibits tree growth.*

Temperature
Tropic of Cancer
20° N
Equator
20° S
Tropic of Capricorn
Temperature
0 to 10°C (32 to 50°F)
10 to 20°C (50 to 68°F)
20 to 30°C (68 to 86°F)
above 30°C (86°F)

Average January temperature   *Average July temperature*

Rainfall
Tropic of Cancer
20° N
Equator
20° S
Tropic of Capricorn
Rainfall
0–25 mm (0–1 in)
25–50 mm (1–2 in)
50–100 mm (2–4 in)
100–200 mm (4–8 in)
200–300 mm (8–12 in)
300–400 mm (12–16 in)
400–500 mm (16–20 in)
more than 500 mm (20 in)

Average January rainfall   *Average July rainfall*

▲ *The hot, equatorial basin of the Congo river receives over 48 inches (1200 mm) of rainfall per year.*

Algiers
Casablanca
Marrakech
Sirocco
Ghibli
Khamsin
Cairo
Tropic of Cancer
Tamanrasset
Nouakchott
Bilma
Port Sudan
Dakar
Harmattan
Khartoum
Abéché
Bamako
Ouagadougou
Niamey
Djibouti
Conakry
July Winds
Haboob
Wau
Abidjan
Lagos
Bangui
Douala
Mogadishu
Bata
Libreville
Kisangani
Equator
Nairobi
Kinshasa
Mombassa
Dar es Salaam
Luanda
Pemba
Lusaka
Harare
Antananarivo
Tropic of Capricorn
Windhoek
Tshwane (Pretoria)
Maputo
Durban
Cape Town
Climate
arid
humid equatorial
mediterranean
semi-arid
tropical
warm humid
daily hours of sunshine, January
daily hours of sunshine, July
cold wind
hot wind

Shaping the continent

African landscapes are shaped by the intensity of climatic extremes and by tectonic action. High aridity, wind action, and infrequent but heavy rainstorms, lead to the migration of sand dunes and dramatic flash flooding across much of the north and west. In the wetter areas, high precipitation increases the rate of weathering. To the east, the rift system has created a volcanic and lake environment and allowed rivers to erode weaknesses left in the crustal structure by faults.

Groundwater

1 Oases are found in desert areas such as the Sahara *(left)*. Groundwater migrates through permeable rock strata, confined between two impermeable layers. Oases form either when the permeable rocks come near to the surface, or at a fault line, when water is able to seep up to the surface through the crushed rocks at the fault.

Rainwater feeds the aquifer
Water migrates up through fault
Aquifer exposed near the surface
Groundwater trapped between impermeable strata

***Groundwater:** Replenishment of an oasis*

River systems

2 The Zambezi river *(above)* drops 360 ft (110 m) over the Victoria Falls into a zigzag gorge. The river has eroded the gorge along lines of weakness in the bedrock, created by fault lines running in two directions.

Old site of Victoria Falls
River plunges over falls
Fault and joint lines running in two directions
Zigzag gorge of the Zambezi

***River systems:** Retreating of the Victoria Falls*

The evolving landscape

Exfoliated layers
External stresses act on the surface of the inselberg
Joints or cracks caused by expansion and contraction

***Weathering:** Formation of an inselberg*

Weathering

6 Inselbergs *(above)*, found extensively across West Africa, are exposed remnants of an extensive upland area. Erosion of the surrounding uplands leaves a resistant rock outcrop. Its spheroidal shape is the result of "onion-skin" weathering – the exfoliating of layers – due to repeated expansion and contraction.

Ephemeral channels

5 Wadis *(above)* drain much of northern Africa. These drybed courses are flooded only after infrequent, but intense, storms in the uplands cause water to surge along their channels.

Heavy rainfall runs off mountains
Water collects and floods the dry channel

***Ephemeral channels:** Flash flooding of a wadi*

Sand is gradually blown up the back slope
Deposition on the slip face
Build up of sand produces strata inside the dune
1
5
6
2
4
3
Landscape
sinking land
stable land
uplifting land
escarpment
ocean current
rift
active volcano
inselberg
oasis
river
wadi
waterfall

***Wind erosion:** Migration of a dune*

Wind erosion

4 Dunes like this in the Namib Desert *(left)* are wind-blown accumulations of sand, which slowly migrate. Wind action moves sand up the shallow back slope; when the sand reaches the crest of the dune it is deposited on the slip face.

Force of waves concentrates on the headland
Waves refracting
Wave energy dispersed in the bay
The sea bed is deeper opposite the bay than at the headland

***Coastal processes:** Erosion of a bay*

Coastal processes

3 Houtbaai *(above)*, in southern Africa, is constantly being modified by wave action. As waves approach the indented coastline, they reach the shallow water of the headland, slowing down and reducing in length. This causes them to bend or refract, concentrating their erosive force at the headlands.

Political Africa

The political map of modern Africa only emerged following the end of the Second World War. Over the next half-century, all of the countries formerly controlled by European powers gained independence from their colonial rulers – only Liberia and Ethiopia were never colonized. The postcolonial era has not been an easy period for many countries, but there have been moves toward multiparty democracy across much of the continent. In South Africa, democratic elections replaced the internationally-condemned apartheid system only in 1994. Other countries have still to find political stability; corruption in government, and ethnic tensions are serious problems. National infrastructures, based on the colonial transportation systems built to exploit Africa's resources, are often inappropriate for independent economic development.

Languages

Three major world languages act as *lingua francas* across the African continent: Arabic in North Africa; English in southern and eastern Africa and Nigeria; and French in Central and West Africa, and in Madagascar. A huge number of African languages are spoken as well – over 2000 have been recorded, with more than 400 in Nigeria alone – reflecting the continuing importance of traditional cultures and values. In the north of the continent, the extensive use of Arabic reflects Middle Eastern influences while Bantu is widely-spoken across much of southern Africa.

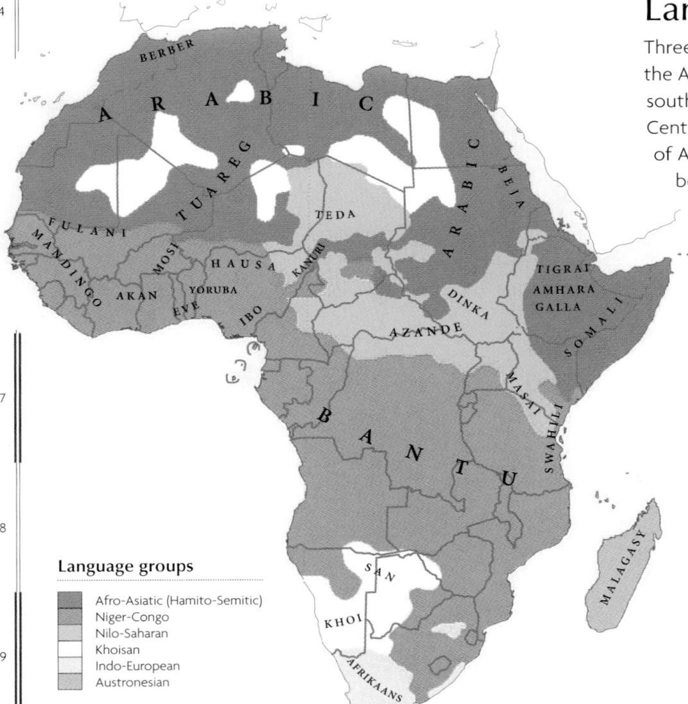
BERBER
ARABIC
TUAREG
TEDA
ARABIC
BEJA
FULANI
MANDINGO
MOSI
HAUSA
KANURI
AKAN
YORUBA
EWE
IBO
DINKA
TIGRAI
AMHARA
GALLA
SOMALI
AZANDE
MASAI
SWAHILI
BANTU
MALAGASY
SAN
KHOI
AFRIKAANS
Language groups
Afro-Asiatic (Hamito-Semitic)
Niger-Congo
Nilo-Saharan
Khoisan
Indo-European
Austronesian

Official African languages

French
English
Arabic
Portuguese
Swahili
Amharic
Spanish
French/English
French/Arabic
French/Malagasy
English/Swahili
Arabic/Somali

▲ *Islamic influences are evident throughout North Africa. The Great Mosque at Kairouan, Tunisia, is Africa's holiest Islamic place.*

▲ ***In northeastern Nigeria,*** *people speak Kanuri – a dialect of the Nilo-Saharan language group.*

Madeira (to Portugal)
MOROCCO
Canary Islands (to Spain)
LAÂYOUNE
Western Sahara (Occupied by Morocco)
Tropic of Cancer
MAURITANIA
NOUAKCHOTT
CAPE VERDE
PRAIA
SENEGAL
DAKAR
Kaolack
BANJUL
GAMBIA
GUINEA-BISSAU
BISSAU
BAMAKO
GUINEA
CONAKRY
Koidu
FREETOWN
SIERRA LEONE
MONROVIA
LIBERIA
YAMOUSSOUKRO

Transportation

African railroads were built to aid the exploitation of natural resources, and most offer passage only from the interior to the coastal cities, leaving large parts of the continent untouched – five landlocked countries have no railroads at all. The Congo, Nile, and Niger river networks offer limited access to land within the continental interior, but have a number of waterfalls and cataracts which prevent navigation from the sea. Many roads were developed in the 1960s and 1970s, but economic difficulties are making the maintenance and expansion of the networks difficult.

► ***South Africa has*** *the largest concentration of railroads in Africa. Over 20,000 miles (32,000 km) of routes have been built since 1870.*

▲ ***Traditional means of*** *transportation, such as the camel, are still widely used across the less accessible parts of Africa.*

◄ ***The Congo river,*** *though not suitable for river transportation along its entire length, forms a vital link for people and goods in its navigable inland reaches.*

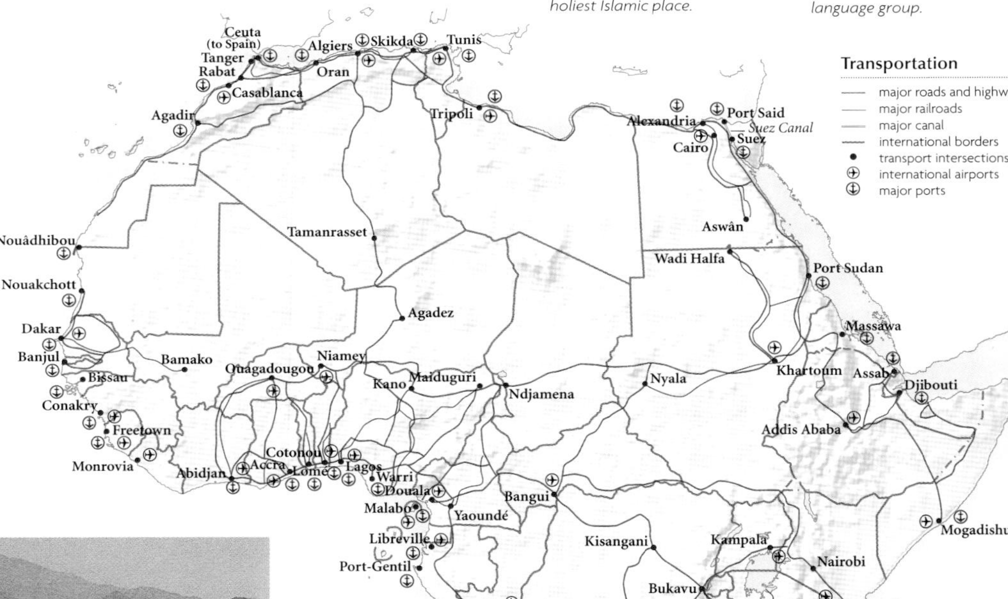
Ceuta (to Spain)
Tanger
Rabat
Casablanca
Algiers
Oran
Skikda
Tunis
Tripoli
Agadir
Alexandria
Port Said
Suez Canal
Suez
Cairo
Aswân
Tamanrasset
Nouâdhibou
Nouakchott
Wadi Halfa
Port Sudan
Agadez
Massawa
Dakar
Banjul
Bissau
Bamako
Ouagadougou
Niamey
Kano
Maiduguri
Ndjamena
Nyala
Khartoum
Assab
Djibouti
Conakry
Freetown
Monrovia
Abidjan
Accra
Lomé
Cotonou
Lagos
Warri
Douala
Malabo
Yaoundé
Bangui
Addis Ababa
Mogadishu
Libreville
Port-Gentil
Kisangani
Kampala
Nairobi
Bukavu
Brazzaville
Kinshasa
Pointe-Noire
Matadi
Kananga
Kalemie
Mombasa
Dodoma
Dar es Salaam
Mbeya
Luanda
Lobito
Lubumbashi
Namibe
Lusaka
Nampula
Livingstone
Harare
Tsumeb
Bulawayo
Beira
Antananarivo
Toamasina
Windhoek
Walvis Bay
Tshwane (Pretoria)
Johannesburg
Maputo
Keetmanshoop
Durban
Cape Town
Port Elizabeth
Transportation
major roads and highways
major railroads
major canal
international borders
transport intersections
international airports
major ports

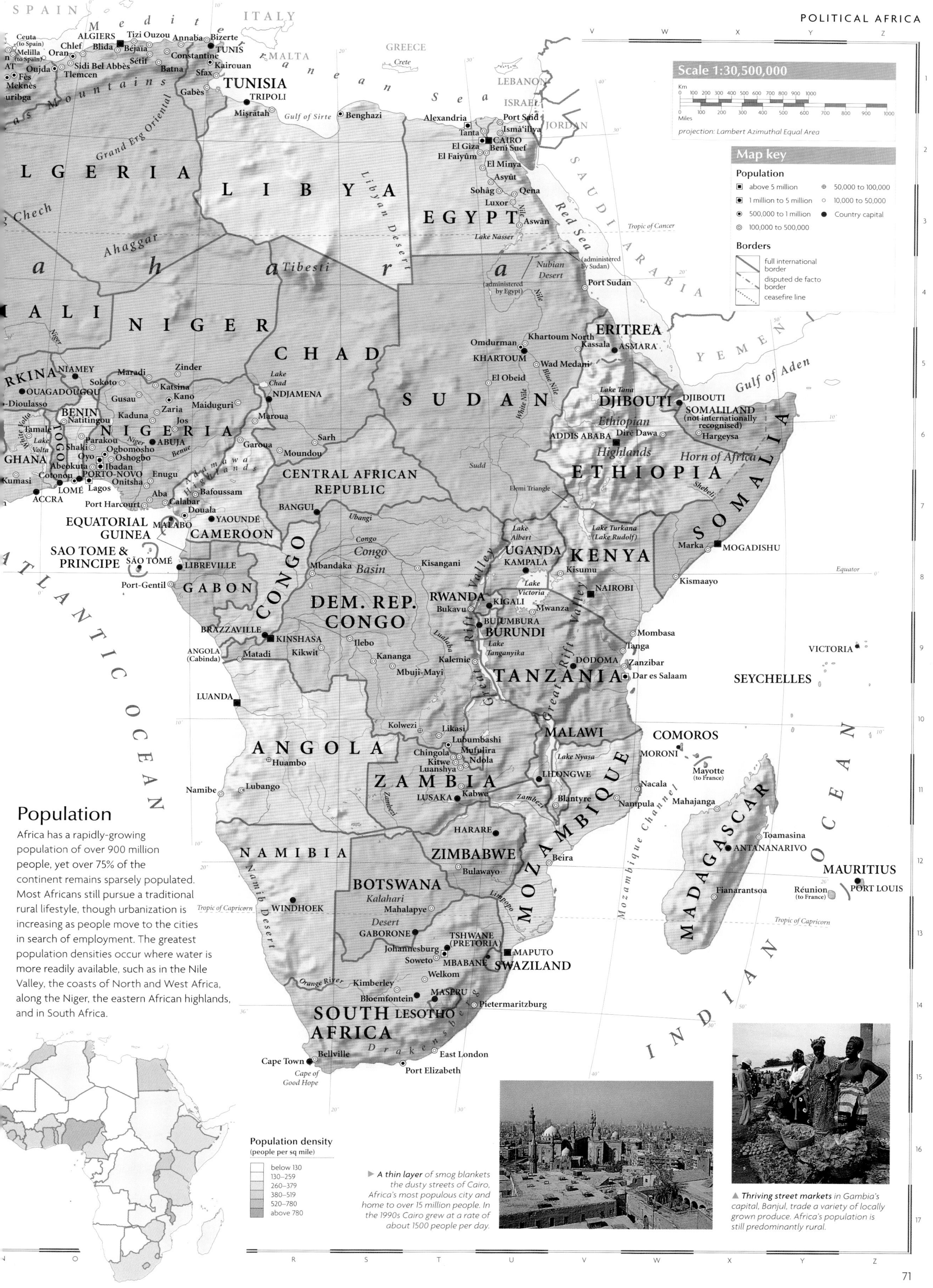
Scale 1:30,500,000
Km
0 100 200 300 400 500 600 700 800 900 1000
Miles
projection: Lambert Azimuthal Equal Area
Map key
Population
above 5 million
1 million to 5 million
500,000 to 1 million
100,000 to 500,000
50,000 to 100,000
10,000 to 50,000
Country capital
Borders
full international border
disputed de facto border
ceasefire line
SPAIN
ITALY
GREECE
MALTA
Crete
LEBANON
ISRAEL
JORDAN
SAUDI ARABIA
YEMEN
Mediterranean Sea
Ceuta (to Spain)
Melilla (to Spain)
ALGIERS
Tizi Ouzou
Annaba
Bizerte
TUNIS
Chlef
Blida
Bejaïa
Constantine
Oran
Sétif
Kairouan
Oujda
Sidi Bel Abbès
Batna
Sfax
Fès
Tlemcen
Meknès
Gabès
TUNISIA
TRIPOLI
Mişratah
Gulf of Sirte
Benghazi
Alexandria
Port Said
Tanta
Ismâ'ilîya
CAIRO
El Giza
Beni Suef
El Faiyûm
El Minya
Asyût
Sohâg
Qena
Luxor
Aswân
Lake Nasser
EGYPT
Red Sea
Tropic of Cancer
(administered by Sudan)
(administered by Egypt)
Nubian Desert
Port Sudan
ALGERIA
LIBYA
Grand Erg Oriental
Libyan Desert
Ahaggar
Tibesti
Sahara
MALI
NIGER
CHAD
SUDAN
ERITREA
ASMARA
Kassala
Khartoum North
Omdurman
KHARTOUM
Wad Medani
El Obeid
Blue Nile
White Nile
Nile
Lake Tana
DJIBOUTI
SOMALILAND (not internationally recognised)
Hargeysa
Gulf of Aden
ADDIS ABABA
Dire Dawa
Ethiopian Highlands
Horn of Africa
ETHIOPIA
SOMALIA
Shebeli
Elemi Triangle
Sudd
BURKINA
NIAMEY
Maradi
Zinder
OUAGADOUGOU
Sokoto
Katsina
Kano
Bobo-Dioulasso
Gusau
Maiduguri
Lake Chad
NDJAMENA
BENIN
Natitingou
Kaduna
Zaria
Jos
Maroua
TOGO
Tamale
NIGERIA
Lake Volta
Parakou
ABUJA
Garoua
Sarh
Moundou
Shaki
Ogbomosho
Benue
Oyo
Oshogbo
GHANA
Abeokuta
Ibadan
Adamawa Highlands
Kumasi
PORTO-NOVO
Enugu
Cotonou
Onitsha
LOMÉ
Lagos
ACCRA
Aba
Bafoussam
Port Harcourt
Calabar
Douala
CENTRAL AFRICAN REPUBLIC
BANGUI
Ubangi
EQUATORIAL GUINEA
MALABO
YAOUNDÉ
CAMEROON
SAO TOME & PRINCIPE
SÃO TOMÉ
LIBREVILLE
GABON
Port-Gentil
CONGO
Congo
Congo Basin
Mbandaka
Kisangani
DEM. REP. CONGO
Lake Albert
UGANDA
KAMPALA
KENYA
Lake Turkana (Lake Rudolf)
Marka
MOGADISHU
Kisumu
Lake Victoria
NAIROBI
Equator
Kismaayo
RWANDA
KIGALI
Bukavu
Mwanza
BUJUMBURA
BURUNDI
Mombasa
Tanga
BRAZZAVILLE
KINSHASA
Kikwit
Ilebo
ANGOLA (Cabinda)
Matadi
Kananga
Lualaba
Lake Tanganyika
Kalemie
DODOMA
Zanzibar
Dar es Salaam
Mbuji-Mayi
TANZANIA
Great Rift Valley
VICTORIA
SEYCHELLES
LUANDA
ATLANTIC OCEAN
Kolwezi
Likasi
Lubumbashi
MALAWI
COMOROS
MORONI
Mayotte (to France)
ANGOLA
Huambo
Chingola
Mufulira
Kitwe
Ndola
Luanshya
Lake Nyasa
LILONGWE
Nacala
ZAMBIA
Zambezi
LUSAKA
Kabwe
Blantyre
Nampula
Mahajanga
Namibe
Lubango
MOZAMBIQUE
Mozambique Channel
HARARE
MADAGASCAR
Toamasina
ANTANANARIVO
NAMIBIA
ZIMBABWE
Beira
Bulawayo
MAURITIUS
PORT LOUIS
Réunion (to France)
Fianarantsoa
Namib Desert
BOTSWANA
Kalahari Desert
Limpopo
Tropic of Capricorn
WINDHOEK
Mahalapye
GABORONE
TSHWANE (PRETORIA)
Johannesburg
MAPUTO
Soweto
MBABANE
SWAZILAND
Welkom
Orange River
Kimberley
Bloemfontein
MASERU
Pietermaritzburg
SOUTH AFRICA
LESOTHO
Drakensberg
East London
Cape Town
Bellville
Port Elizabeth
Cape of Good Hope
INDIAN OCEAN

Population

Africa has a rapidly-growing population of over 900 million people, yet over 75% of the continent remains sparsely populated. Most Africans still pursue a traditional rural lifestyle, though urbanization is increasing as people move to the cities in search of employment. The greatest population densities occur where water is more readily available, such as in the Nile Valley, the coasts of North and West Africa, along the Niger, the eastern African highlands, and in South Africa.

Population density
(people per sq mile)

- below 130
- 130–259
- 260–379
- 380–519
- 520–780
- above 780

▶ *A thin layer of smog blankets the dusty streets of Cairo, Africa's most populous city and home to over 15 million people. In the 1990s Cairo grew at a rate of about 1500 people per day.*

▲ *Thriving street markets in Gambia's capital, Banjul, trade a variety of locally grown produce. Africa's population is still predominantly rural.*

African resources

The economies of most African countries are dominated by subsistence and cash crop agriculture, with limited industrialization. Manufacturing is largely confined to South Africa. Many countries depend on a single resource, such as copper or gold, or a cash crop, such as coffee, for export income, which can leave them vulnerable to fluctuations in world commodity prices. In order to diversify their economies and develop a wider industrial base, investment from overseas is being actively sought by many African governments.

Industry

Many African industries concentrate on the extraction and processing of raw materials. These include the oil industry, food processing, mining, and textile production. South Africa accounts for over half of the continent's industrial output with much of the remainder coming from the countries along the northern coast. Over 60% of Africa's workforce is employed in agriculture.

The unspoiled natural splendor of wildlife reserves, like the Serengeti National Park in Tanzania, attract tourists to Africa from around the globe. The tourist industry in Kenya and Tanzania is particularly well developed, where it accounts for almost 10% of GNI.

Standard of living

Since the 1960s most countries in Africa have seen significant improvements in life expectancy, healthcare, and education. However, 28 of the 30 most deprived countries in the world are African, and the continent as a whole lies well behind the rest of the world in terms of meeting many basic human needs.

Standard of living
(UN human development index)

high

low

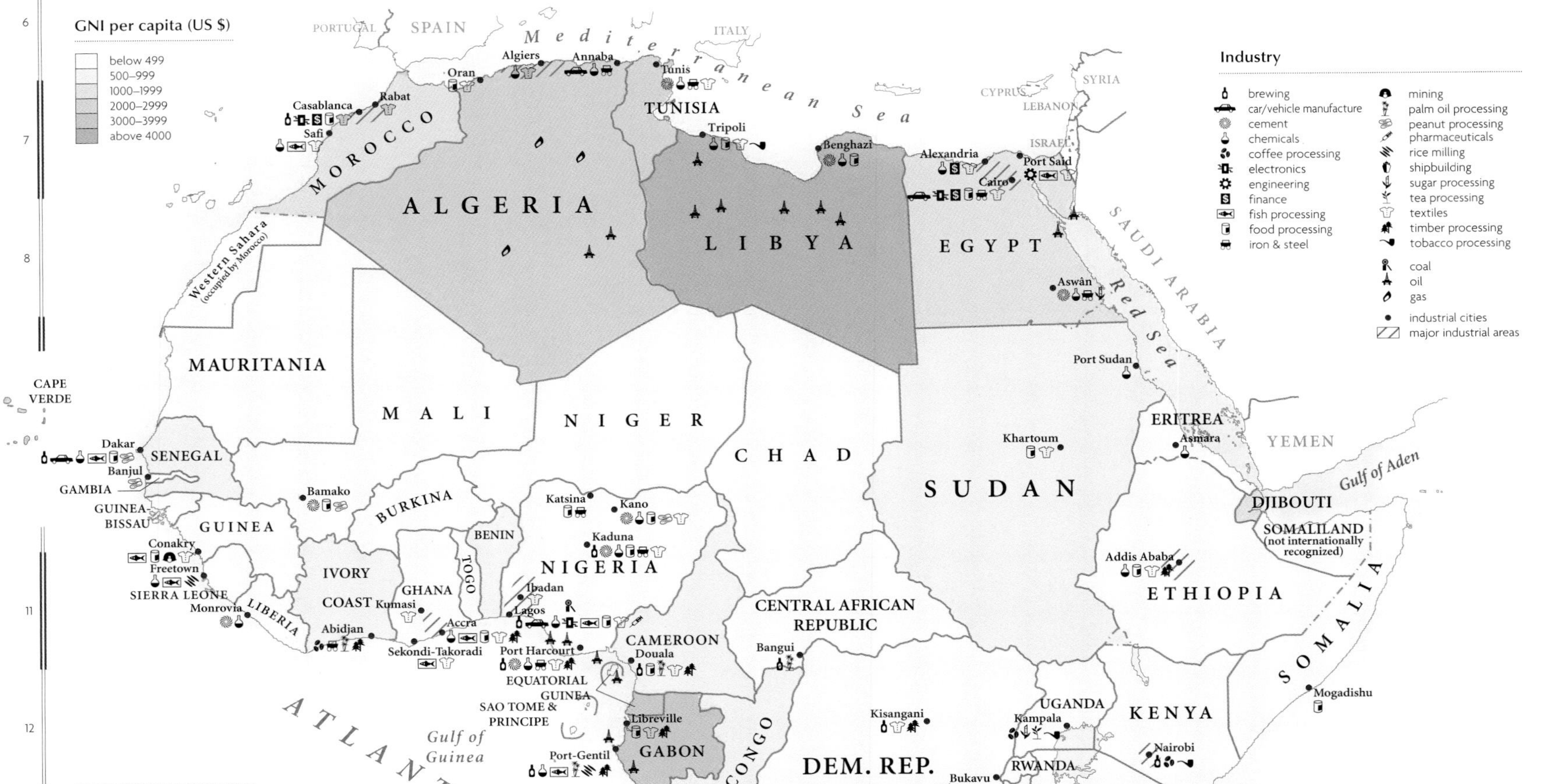

GNI per capita (US $)

- below 499
- 500–999
- 1000–1999
- 2000–2999
- 3000–3999
- above 4000

Industry

- brewing
- car/vehicle manufacture
- cement
- chemicals
- coffee processing
- electronics
- engineering
- finance
- fish processing
- food processing
- iron & steel
- mining
- palm oil processing
- peanut processing
- pharmaceuticals
- rice milling
- shipbuilding
- sugar processing
- tea processing
- textiles
- timber processing
- tobacco processing
- coal
- oil
- gas
- industrial cities
- major industrial areas

PORTUGAL SPAIN ITALY CYPRUS SYRIA LEBANON ISRAEL Mediterranean Sea

MOROCCO ALGERIA TUNISIA LIBYA EGYPT Western Sahara (occupied by Morocco) MAURITANIA MALI NIGER CHAD SUDAN ERITREA DJIBOUTI SOMALILAND (not internationally recognized) ETHIOPIA SOMALIA CAPE VERDE SENEGAL GAMBIA GUINEA-BISSAU GUINEA SIERRA LEONE LIBERIA IVORY COAST BURKINA GHANA TOGO BENIN NIGERIA CAMEROON CENTRAL AFRICAN REPUBLIC EQUATORIAL GUINEA SAO TOME & PRINCIPE GABON CONGO DEM. REP. CONGO UGANDA KENYA RWANDA BURUNDI TANZANIA SEYCHELLES ANGOLA ZAMBIA MALAWI COMOROS Mayotte (to France) MOZAMBIQUE ZIMBABWE NAMIBIA BOTSWANA MADAGASCAR MAURITIUS Réunion (to France) SOUTH AFRICA SWAZILAND LESOTHO

SAUDI ARABIA Red Sea YEMEN Gulf of Aden ATLANTIC OCEAN Gulf of Guinea INDIAN OCEAN Mozambique Channel

Casablanca Rabat Safi Oran Algiers Annaba Tunis Tripoli Benghazi Alexandria Cairo Port Said Aswân Port Sudan Khartoum Asmara Addis Ababa Dakar Banjul Bamako Conakry Freetown Monrovia Abidjan Kumasi Sekondi-Takoradi Accra Lagos Ibadan Katsina Kano Kaduna Port Harcourt Douala Bangui Libreville Port-Gentil Brazzaville Pointe-Noire Kinshasa Kisangani Kampala Nairobi Mogadishu Mombasa Bukavu Kananga Dodoma Zanzibar Dar es Salaam Luanda Lobito Lubumbashi Ndola Lusaka Blantyre Harare Kwekwe Bulawayo Beira Antananarivo Walvis Bay Windhoek Tshwane (Pretoria) Johannesburg Maputo Kimberley Durban East London Port Elizabeth Cape Town

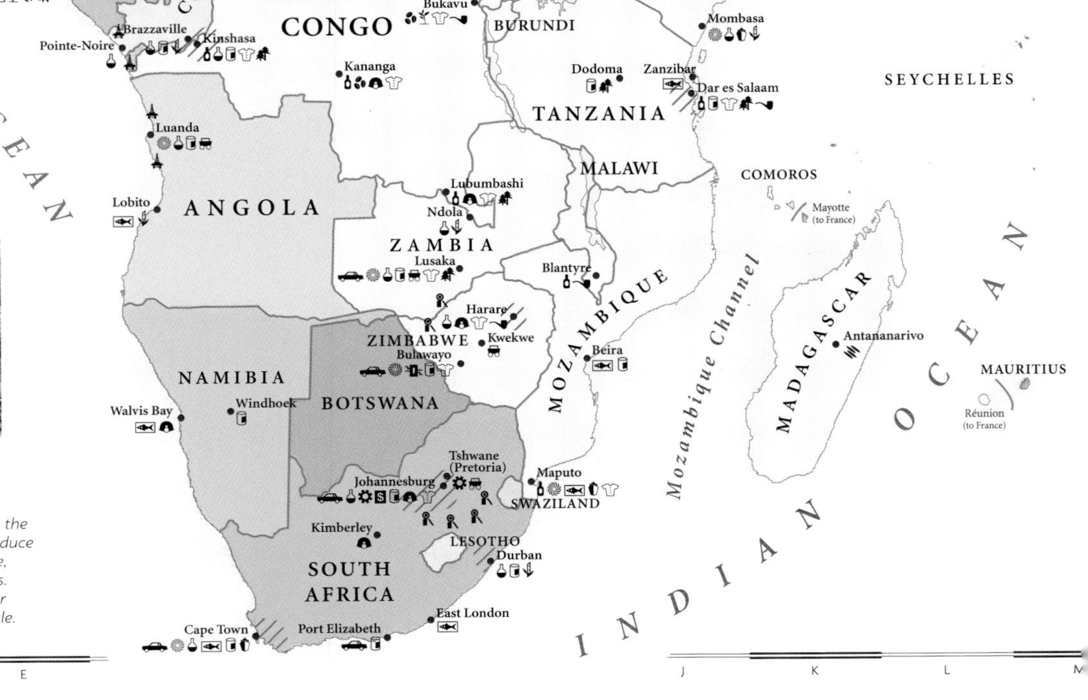

The discovery of oil in the swampy Niger Delta during the 1960s made Nigeria one of Africa's richer nations. As world oil prices fell in the 1980s, the Nigerian economy faltered.

Exotic rugs and brightly colored textiles are sold in a street market along the banks of the river Nile in Luxor, Egypt.

The Rössing uranium mines in Namibia are one of the largest in the world. Canada and Australia produce over half the world's uranium ore, used to fuel nuclear power plants. Elsewhere, South Africa and Niger also mine uranium on a large scale.

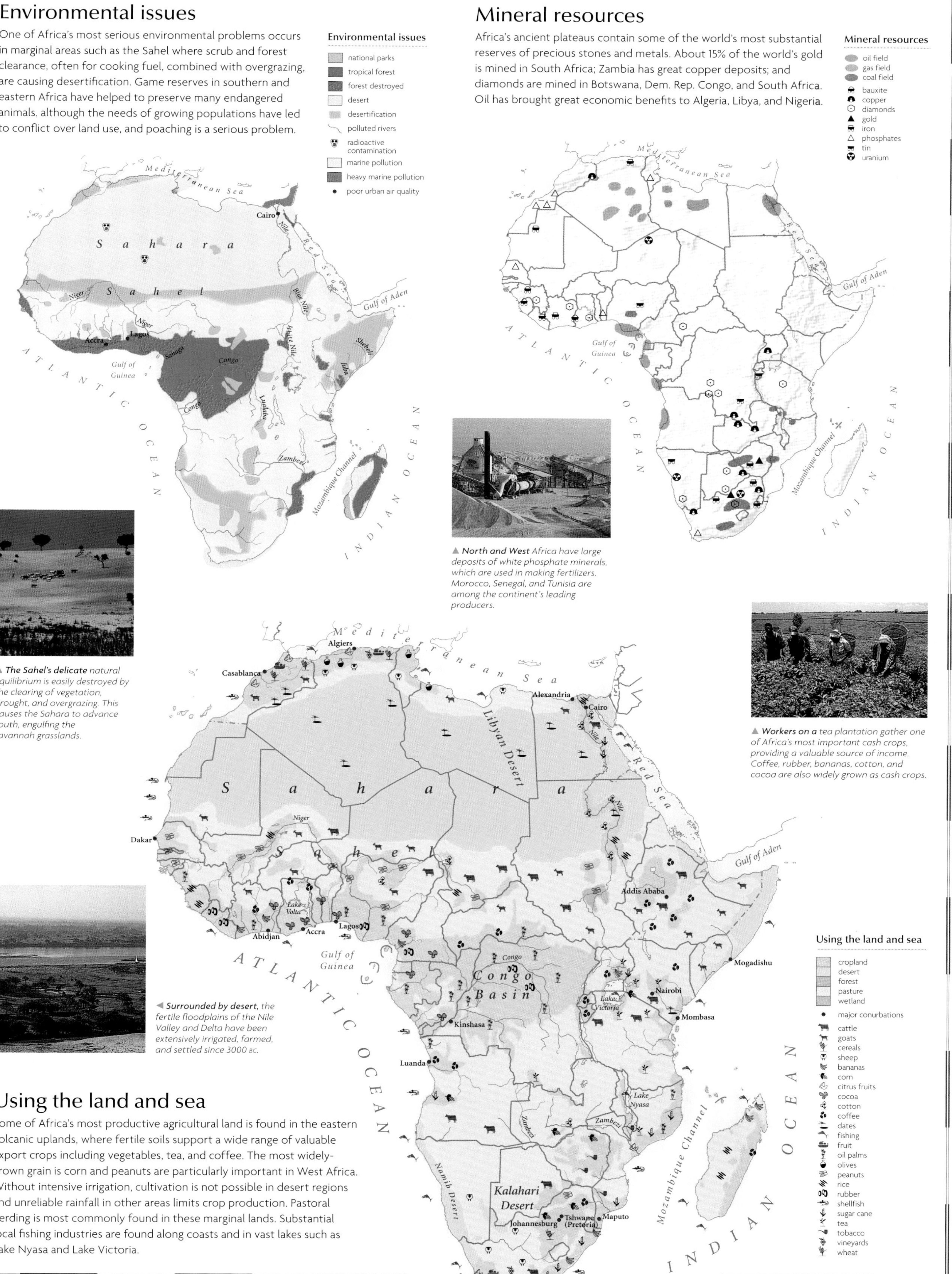
Environmental issues
national parks
tropical forest
forest destroyed
desert
desertification
polluted rivers
radioactive contamination
marine pollution
heavy marine pollution
poor urban air quality
Mineral resources
oil field
gas field
coal field
bauxite
copper
diamonds
gold
iron
phosphates
tin
uranium
Using the land and sea
cropland
desert
forest
pasture
wetland
major conurbations
cattle
goats
cereals
sheep
bananas
corn
citrus fruits
cocoa
cotton
coffee
dates
fishing
fruit
oil palms
olives
peanuts
rice
rubber
shellfish
sugar cane
tea
tobacco
vineyards
wheat
Mediterranean Sea
Sahara
Sahel
Cairo
Accra
Lagos
Gulf of Guinea
Gulf of Aden
Red Sea
Atlantic Ocean
Indian Ocean
Mozambique Channel
Algiers
Casablanca
Alexandria
Libyan Desert
Dakar
Abidjan
Lake Volta
Addis Ababa
Mogadishu
Congo Basin
Nairobi
Lake Victoria
Mombasa
Kinshasa
Luanda
Lake Nyasa
Namib Desert
Kalahari Desert
Johannesburg
Tshwane (Pretoria)
Maputo
Cape Town

Environmental issues

One of Africa's most serious environmental problems occurs in marginal areas such as the Sahel where scrub and forest clearance, often for cooking fuel, combined with overgrazing, are causing desertification. Game reserves in southern and eastern Africa have helped to preserve many endangered animals, although the needs of growing populations have led to conflict over land use, and poaching is a serious problem.

▲ *The Sahel's delicate natural equilibrium is easily destroyed by the clearing of vegetation, drought, and overgrazing. This causes the Sahara to advance south, engulfing the savannah grasslands.*

Mineral resources

Africa's ancient plateaus contain some of the world's most substantial reserves of precious stones and metals. About 15% of the world's gold is mined in South Africa; Zambia has great copper deposits; and diamonds are mined in Botswana, Dem. Rep. Congo, and South Africa. Oil has brought great economic benefits to Algeria, Libya, and Nigeria.

▲ *North and West Africa have large deposits of white phosphate minerals, which are used in making fertilizers. Morocco, Senegal, and Tunisia are among the continent's leading producers.*

▲ *Workers on a tea plantation gather one of Africa's most important cash crops, providing a valuable source of income. Coffee, rubber, bananas, cotton, and cocoa are also widely grown as cash crops.*

◄ *Surrounded by desert, the fertile floodplains of the Nile Valley and Delta have been extensively irrigated, farmed, and settled since 3000 BC.*

Using the land and sea

Some of Africa's most productive agricultural land is found in the eastern volcanic uplands, where fertile soils support a wide range of valuable export crops including vegetables, tea, and coffee. The most widely-grown grain is corn and peanuts are particularly important in West Africa. Without intensive irrigation, cultivation is not possible in desert regions and unreliable rainfall in other areas limits crop production. Pastoral herding is most commonly found in these marginal lands. Substantial local fishing industries are found along coasts and in vast lakes such as Lake Nyasa and Lake Victoria.

North Africa

ALGERIA, EGYPT, LIBYA, MOROCCO, TUNISIA, WESTERN SAHARA

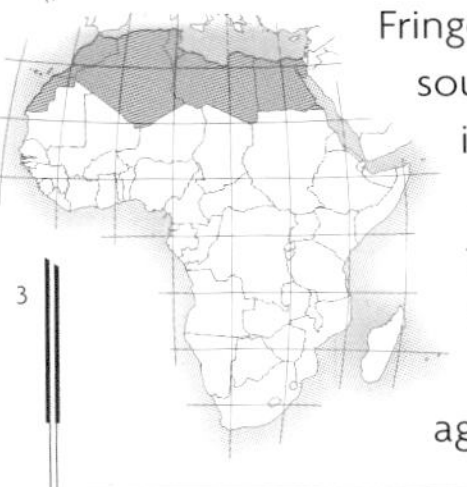

Fringed by the Mediterranean along the northern coast and by the arid Sahara in the south, North Africa reflects the influence of many invaders, both European and, most importantly, Arab, giving the region an almost universal Islamic flavor and a common Arabic language. The countries lying to the west of Egypt are often referred to as the Maghreb, an Arabic term for "west." Today, Morocco and Tunisia exploit their culture and landscape for tourism, while rich oil and gas deposits aid development in Libya and Algeria, despite political turmoil. Egypt, with its fertile, Nile-watered agricultural land and varied industrial base, is the most populous nation.

▲ *These rock piles in Algeria's Ahaggar mountains are the result of weathering caused by extremes of temperature. Great cracks or joints appear in the rocks, which are then worn and smoothed by the wind.*

The landscape

The Atlas Mountains, which extend across much of Morocco, northern Algeria, and Tunisia, are part of the fold mountain system which also runs through much of southern Europe. They recede to the south and east, becoming a steppe landscape before meeting the Sahara desert which covers more than 90% of the region. The sediments of the Sahara overlie an ancient plateau of crystalline rock, some of which is more than four billion years old.

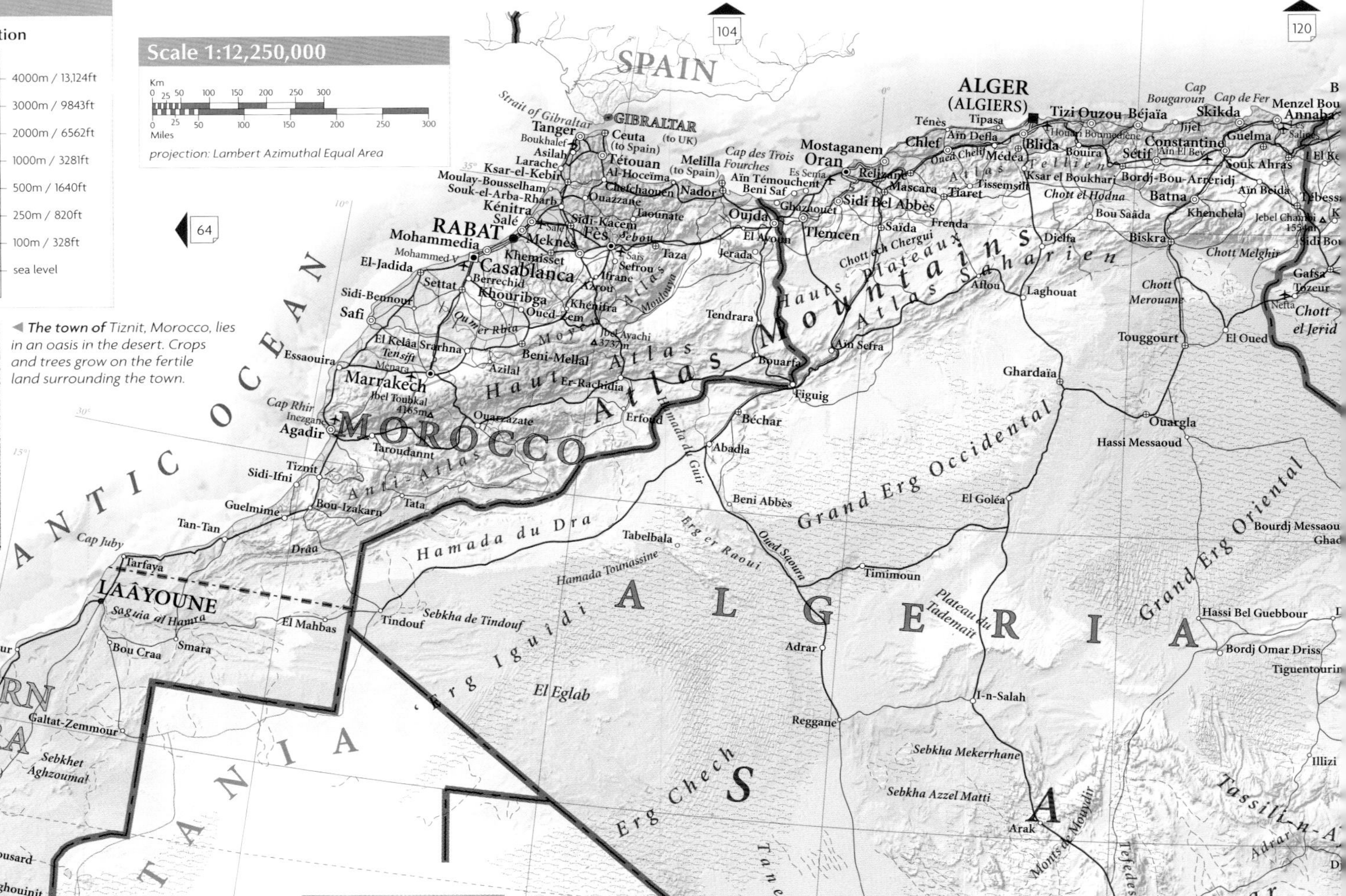

Map key

Population
- ■ above 5 million
- ▣ 1 million to 5 million
- ◉ 500,000 to 1 million
- ◎ 100,000 to 500,000
- ⊕ 50,000 to 100,000
- ○ 10,000 to 50,000
- ∘ below 10,000

Elevation
- 4000m / 13,124ft
- 3000m / 9843ft
- 2000m / 6562ft
- 1000m / 3281ft
- 500m / 1640ft
- 250m / 820ft
- 100m / 328ft
- sea level

Scale 1:12,250,000

Km 0 25 50 100 150 200 250 300

Miles 0 25 50 100 150 200 250 300

projection: Lambert Azimuthal Equal Area

◀ *The town of Tiznit, Morocco, lies in an oasis in the desert. Crops and trees grow on the fertile land surrounding the town.*

▶ *The Grand Erg Occidental is one of Algeria's great Saharan sand seas. Wind force and direction determines the nature of landforms such as the linear or seif dunes in the foreground.*

104
120
64
76
76

Using the land & sea

Sheltered valleys in the Atlas Mountains, the Nile Valley and Delta, and the Mediterranean coast are the main sources of good farming land. A wide variety of valuable crops including cereals, rice, and cotton, and woods such as cedar and cork, are grown. Typical Mediterranean crops such as olives, figs, dates, and citrus fruits also thrive in these areas. The Nile Valley is particularly fertile, and most of Egypt's population lives close to the river. Elsewhere, irrigation is essential to improve crop yields on the desert margins.

Land use and agricultural distribution
- goats
- sheep
- cereals
- citrus fruits
- cork
- cotton
- dates
- fishing
- olives
- vineyards
- capital cities
- major towns
- pasture
- cropland
- forest
- desert

The urban/rural population divide

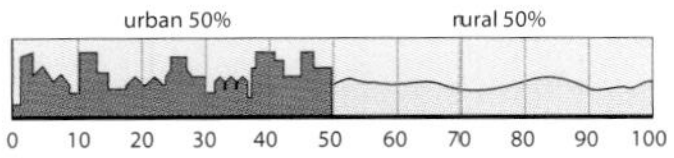

urban 50% | rural 50%

0 10 20 30 40 50 60 70 80 90 100

Population density	Total land area
65 people per sq mile (25 people per sq km)	2,215,020 sq miles (5,738,394 sq km)

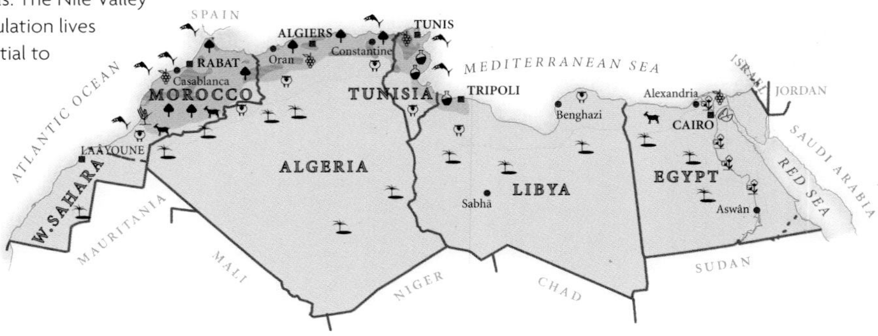

▲ *Many North African nomads, such as the Bedouin, maintain a traditional pastoral lifestyle on the desert fringes, moving their herds of sheep, goats, and camels from place to place – crossing country borders in order to find sufficient grazing land.*

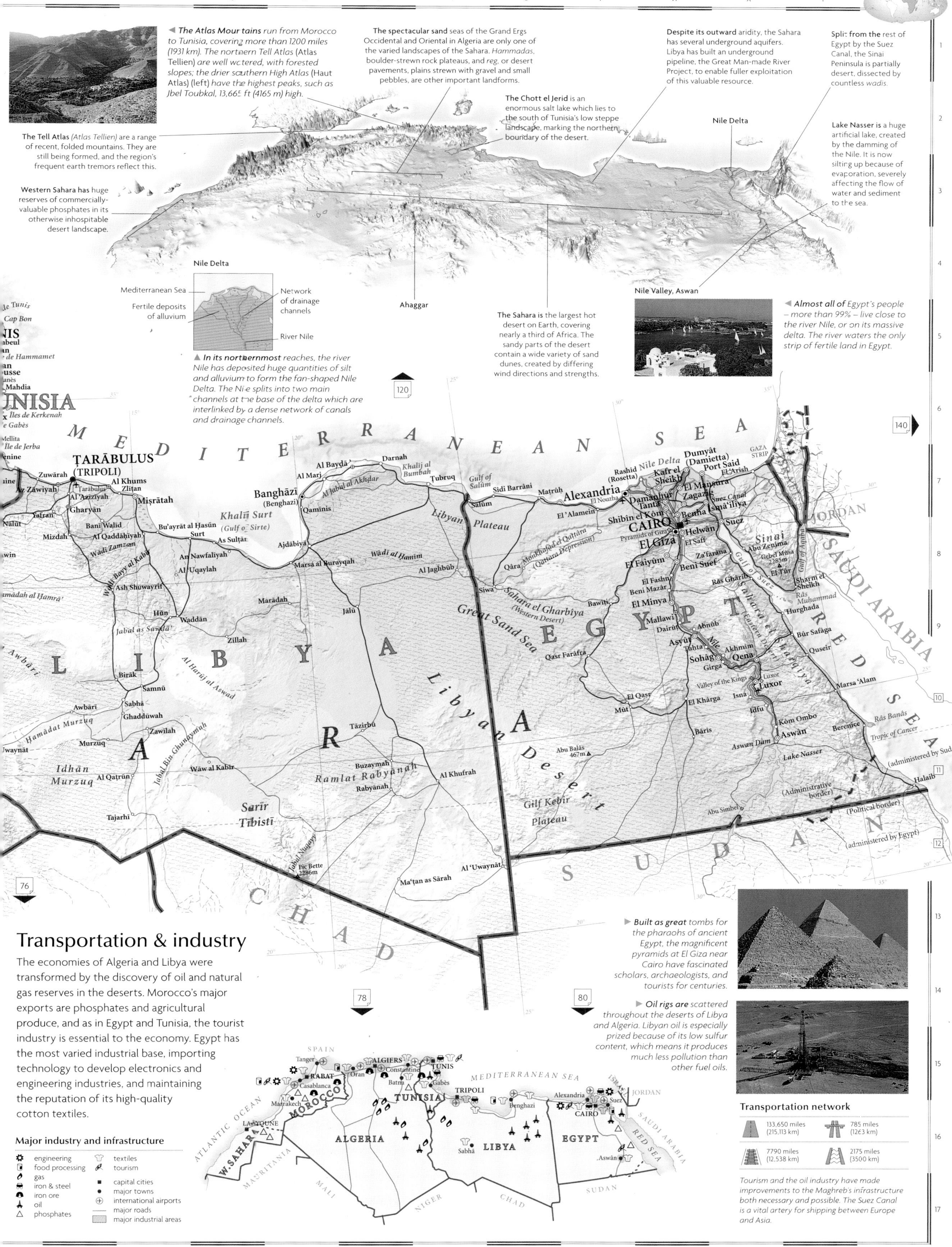

The Tell Atlas (Atlas Tellien) are a range of recent, folded mountains. They are still being formed, and the region's frequent earth tremors reflect this.
Western Sahara has huge reserves of commercially-valuable phosphates in its otherwise inhospitable desert landscape.
The spectacular sand seas of the Grand Ergs Occidental and Oriental in Algeria are only one of the varied landscapes of the Sahara. Hammadas, boulder-strewn rock plateaus, and reg, or desert pavements, plains strewn with gravel and small pebbles, are other important landforms.
The Chott el Jerid is an enormous salt lake which lies to the south of Tunisia's low steppe landscape, marking the northern boundary of the desert.
Despite its outward aridity, the Sahara has several underground aquifers. Libya has built an underground pipeline, the Great Man-made River Project, to enable fuller exploitation of this valuable resource.
Split from the rest of Egypt by the Suez Canal, the Sinai Peninsula is partially desert, dissected by countless wadis.
Lake Nasser is a huge artificial lake, created by the damming of the Nile. It is now silting up because of evaporation, severely affecting the flow of water and sediment to the sea.
Nile Delta
Ahaggar
The Sahara is the largest hot desert on Earth, covering nearly a third of Africa. The sandy parts of the desert contain a wide variety of sand dunes, created by differing wind directions and strengths.
Nile Valley, Aswan
Mediterranean Sea
Fertile deposits of alluvium
Network of drainage channels
River Nile
MEDITERRANEAN SEA
LIBYA
EGYPT
SAHARA
TUNISIA
ṬARĀBULUS (TRIPOLI)
Banghāzī (Benghazi)
Alexandria
CAIRO
El Giza
Port Said
Suez
Luxor
Aswân
Lake Nasser
Libyan Desert
Great Sand Sea
Gilf Kebir Plateau
Sinai
RED SEA
SAUDI ARABIA
JORDAN
SUDAN
CHAD
Tropic of Cancer

▲ The Atlas Mountains run from Morocco to Tunisia, covering more than 1200 miles (1931 km). The northern Tell Atlas (Atlas Tellien) are well watered, with forested slopes; the drier southern High Atlas (Haut Atlas) (left) have the highest peaks, such as Jbel Toubkal, 13,665 ft (4165 m) high.

▲ In its northernmost reaches, the river Nile has deposited huge quantities of silt and alluvium to form the fan-shaped Nile Delta. The Nile splits into two main channels at the base of the delta which are interlinked by a dense network of canals and drainage channels.

◄ Almost all of Egypt's people – more than 99% – live close to the river Nile, or on its massive delta. The river waters the only strip of fertile land in Egypt.

► Built as great tombs for the pharaohs of ancient Egypt, the magnificent pyramids at El Giza near Cairo have fascinated scholars, archaeologists, and tourists for centuries.

► Oil rigs are scattered throughout the deserts of Libya and Algeria. Libyan oil is especially prized because of its low sulfur content, which means it produces much less pollution than other fuel oils.

Transportation & industry

The economies of Algeria and Libya were transformed by the discovery of oil and natural gas reserves in the deserts. Morocco's major exports are phosphates and agricultural produce, and as in Egypt and Tunisia, the tourist industry is essential to the economy. Egypt has the most varied industrial base, importing technology to develop electronics and engineering industries, and maintaining the reputation of its high-quality cotton textiles.

Major industry and infrastructure

engineering, food processing, gas, iron & steel, iron ore, oil, phosphates, textiles, tourism, capital cities, major towns, international airports, major roads, major industrial areas

Transportation network

133,650 miles (215,113 km)
785 miles (1263 km)
7790 miles (12,538 km)
2175 miles (3500 km)

Tourism and the oil industry have made improvements to the Maghreb's infrastructure both necessary and possible. The Suez Canal is a vital artery for shipping between Europe and Asia.

West Africa

BENIN, BURKINA, CAPE VERDE, GAMBIA, GHANA, GUINEA, GUINEA-BISSAU, IVORY COAST, LIBERIA, MALI, MAURITANIA, NIGER, NIGERIA, SENEGAL, SIERRA LEONE, TOGO

West Africa is an immensely diverse region, encompassing the desert landscapes and mainly Muslim populations of the southern Saharan countries, and the tropical rain forests of the more humid south, with a great variety of local languages and cultures. The rich natural resources and accessibility of the area were quickly exploited by Europeans; most of the Africans taken by slave traders came from this region, causing serious depopulation. The very different influences of West Africa's leading colonial powers, Britain and France, remain today, reflected in the languages and institutions of the countries they once governed.

▶ *The dry scrub of the Sahel is only suitable for grazing herd animals like these cattle in Mali.*

Scale 1:10,000,000

Km 0 25 50 100 150 200 250

Miles 0 25 50 100 150 200 250

projection: Lambert Azimuthal Equal Area

Transportation & industry

Abundant natural resources including oil and metallic minerals are found in much of West Africa, although investment is required for their further exploitation. Nigeria experienced an oil boom during the 1970s but subsequent growth has been sporadic. Most industry in other countries has a primary basis, including mining, logging, and food processing.

Transportation network

62,154 miles (100,038 km)		1037 miles (1669 km)	
6752 miles (10,867 km)		10,192 miles (16,405 km)	

The road and rail systems are most developed near the coasts. Some of the landlocked countries remain disadvantaged by the difficulty of access to ports, and their poor road networks.

MOROCCO
W. SAHARA
ALGERIA
LIBYA
MAURITANIA
NOUAKCHOTT
MALI
NIGER
CHAD
DAKAR
SENEGAL
BANJUL
GAMBIA
BISSAU
GUINEA-BISSAU
GUINEA
CONAKRY
FREETOWN
SIERRA LEONE
MONROVIA
LIBERIA
BAMAKO
BURKINA
OUAGADOUGOU
NIAMEY
Kano
NIGERIA
ABUJA
IVORY COAST
GHANA
TOGO
BENIN
ACCRA
LOME
PORTO-NOVO
Lagos
Ibadan
Port Harcourt
YAMOUSSOUKRO
CAMEROON
ATLANTIC OCEAN

Major industry and infrastructure

- chemicals
- cotton spinning
- food processing
- mining
- oil
- palm oil processing
- peanut processing
- textiles
- vehicle manufacture
- capital cities
- major towns
- international airports
- major roads
- major industrial areas

Map key

Population

- 1 million to 5 million
- 500,000 to 1 million
- 100,000 to 500,000
- 50,000 to 100,000
- 10,000 to 50,000
- below 10,000

Elevation

- 2000m / 6562ft
- 1000m / 3281ft
- 500m / 1640ft
- 250m / 820ft
- 100m / 328ft
- sea level

CAPE VERDE

Santo Antão, Pombas, Ilhas de Barlavento, Mindelo, São Vicente, Ribeira Brava, Pedra Lume, Amílcar Cabral, Sal, São Nicolau, Boa Vista, João Barrosa, ATLANTIC OCEAN, Tarrafal, Maio, Fogo, São Filipe, Santiago, PRAIA, Ilhas de Sotavento

(same scale as main map)

◀ *The southern regions of West Africa still contain great swathes of tropical rainforest, including some of the world's most prized hardwood trees, such as mahogany and iroko.*

Using the land & sea

The humid southern regions are most suitable for cultivation; in these areas, cash crops such as coffee, cotton, cocoa, and rubber are grown in large quantities. Peanuts (groundnuts) are grown throughout West Africa. In the north, advancing desertification has made the Sahel increasingly unviable for cultivation, and pastoral farming is more common. Great herds of sheep, cattle, and goats are grazed on the savannah grasses, and fishing is important in coastal and delta areas.

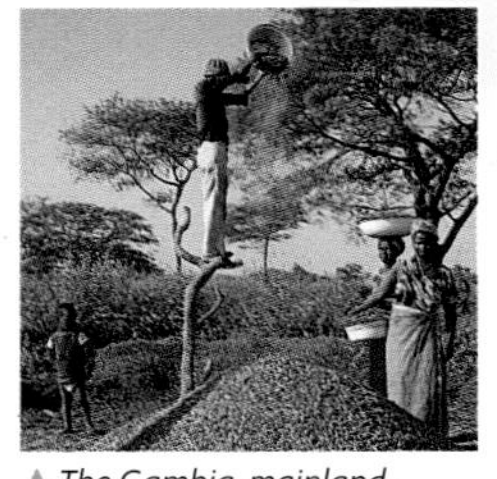

▲ *The Gambia, mainland Africa's smallest country, produces great quantities of peanuts. Winnowing is used to separate the nuts from their stalks.*

MOROCCO
W. SAHARA
ALGERIA
LIBYA
SAHARA
MAURITANIA
NOUAKCHOTT
MALI
NIGER
CHAD
DAKAR
SENEGAL
BANJUL
GAMBIA
BISSAU
GUINEA-BISSAU
GUINEA
CONAKRY
FREETOWN
SIERRA LEONE
MONROVIA
LIBERIA
BAMAKO
BURKINA
OUAGADOUGOU
NIAMEY
NIGERIA
ABUJA
IVORY COAST
GHANA
TOGO
BENIN
ACCRA
LOME
PORTO-NOVO
Lagos
YAMOUSSOUKRO
CAMEROON
ATLANTIC OCEAN

Land use and agricultural distribution

- goats
- sheep
- cocoa
- coffee
- cotton
- oil palms
- peanuts
- rubber
- shellfish
- capital cities
- major towns
- pasture
- cropland
- forest
- desert

The urban/rural population divide

urban 36% — rural 64%

0 10 20 30 40 50 60 70 80 90 100

Population density	Total land area
104 people per sq mile (40 people per sq km)	2,337,137 sq miles (6,054,760 sq km)

WESTERN SAHARA (occupied by Morocco)

MAURITANIA

SENEGAL

GAMBIA

GUINEA-BISSAU

GUINEA

SIERRA LEONE

LIBERIA

ATLANTIC OCEAN

The landscape

There are two major topographical areas in West Africa: the northern deserts are part of the Saharan region which stretches across the whole continent; the grasslands of the Sahel and the southern Guinea coast are part of Africa's central plateau. The landscape is generally low, rarely rising above 1500 ft (457 m) and consists mainly of plains, broken by an occasional high plateau or mountain range.

▲ *Inselbergs, found across the Sahel, are isolated hills, or outcrops, formed where the surrounding plain has eroded away, leaving only the more resistant remnants of the original plateau.*

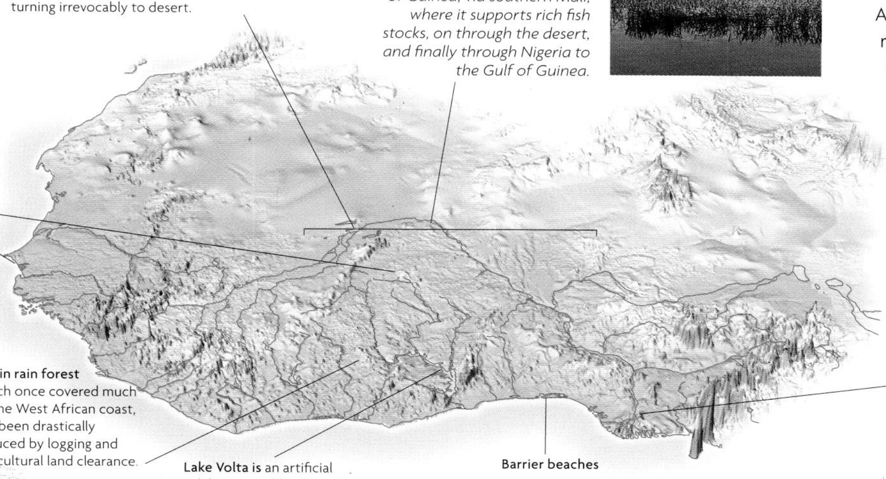

The dry grasslands of the Sahel border the southern reaches of the Sahara. Overgrazing, drought, and the cutting down of trees for firewood, means that much of the Sahel is turning irrevocably to desert.

► ***The Niger river*** *flows for 2600 miles (4181 km) from Fouta Djallon, on the plateau of Guinea, via southern Mali, where it supports rich fish stocks, on through the desert, and finally through Nigeria to the Gulf of Guinea.*

Two types of coastline characterize West Africa. Swampy, muddy coasts, colonized by mangroves occur on river deltas and where ocean currents are weak, like the coast of Senegal. Sandy beaches, with barrier ridges and lagoons, form where currents are stronger.

Virgin rain forest which once covered much of the West African coast, has been drastically reduced by logging and agricultural land clearance.

Lake Volta is an artificial lake, created by the damming of the Volta river. It links the drier northern areas with the coast and is intended to provide fresh water for drinking, fisheries, and irrigation.

Barrier beaches

Fluvial deposits
Lagoon
River dammed by barrier beach
Barrier beach
Estuarine deposits

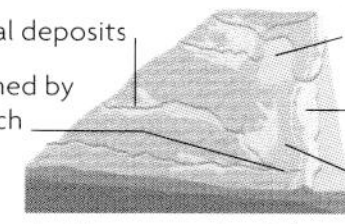

▲ *Along much of the West African coast, barrier beaches have built up and dammed river mouths, forming fluvial and estuarine plains.*

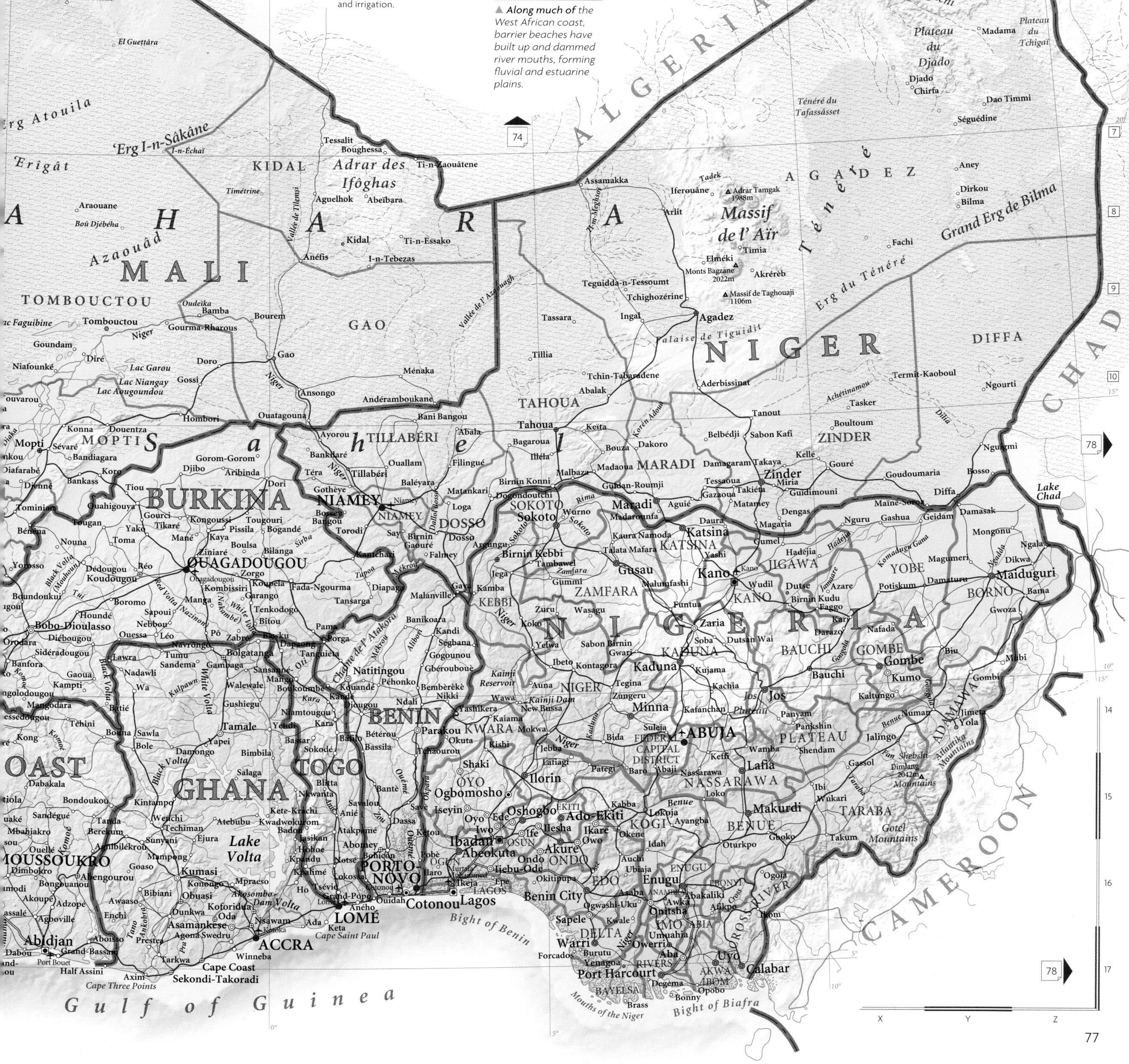

As it nears the Gulf of Guinea, the Niger forks into many strands. When the river floods, alluvium is deposited over a wide area. This creates fertile soils, able to support both crops and livestock.

Central Africa

CAMEROON, CENTRAL AFRICAN REPUBLIC, CHAD, CONGO, DEM. REP. CONGO, EQUATORIAL GUINEA, GABON, SAO TOME & PRINCIPE

The great rain forest basin of the Congo river embraces most of remote Central Africa. The interior was largely unknown to Europeans until late in the 19th century, when its tribal kingdoms were split – principally between France and Belgium – with Sao Tome and Principe the lone Portuguese territory, and Equatorial Guinea controlled by Spain. Open democracy and regional economic integration are important goals for these nations – several of which have only recently emerged from restrictive regimes – and investment is needed to improve transportation infrastructures. Many of the small, but fast-growing and increasingly urban population, speak French, the regional *lingua franca*, along with several hundred Pygmy, Bantu, and Sudanic dialects.

The landscape

Lake Chad lies in a desert basin bounded by the volcanic Tibesti mountains in the north, plateaus in the east and, in the south, the broad watershed of the Congo basin. The vast circular depression of the Congo is isolated from the coastal plain by the granite Massif du Chaillu. To the northwest, the volcanoes and fold mountains of the Cameroon Ridge *(Dorsale Camerounaise)* extend as islands into the Gulf of Guinea. The high fold mountains fringing the east of the Congo Basin fall steeply to the lakes of the Great Rift Valley.

◀ *A plug of resistant lava, at the southwestern end of the Cameroon Ridge (Dorsale Camerounaise), is all that remains of an eroded volcano.*

The volcanic massif of Cameroon Mountain occupies an area which remains volcanically active.

Gulf of Guinea

Massif du Chaillu

Lake Chad is the remnant of an inland sea, which once occupied much of the surrounding basin. A series of droughts since the 1970s has reduced the area of this shallow freshwater lake to about 1000 sq miles (2599 sq km).

The lakelike expansion of the Congo river at Stanley Pool is the lowest point of the interior basin, although the river still descends more than 1000 ft (300 m) to reach the sea.

Rich mineral deposits in the "Copper Belt" of Dem. Rep. Congo were formed under intense heat and pressure when the ancient African Shield was uplifted to form the region's mountains.

The Tibesti mountains are the highest in the Sahara. They were pushed up by the movement of the African Plate over a hot spot, which first formed the northern Ahaggar mountains and is now thought to lie under the Great Rift Valley.

The Congo river is second only to the Amazon in the volume of water it carries, and in the size of its drainage basin.

Lake Tanganyika, the world's second deepest lake, is the largest of a series of linear "ribbon" lakes occupying a trench within the Great Rift Valley.

Broad, shallow basin

Waterfalls and cataracts

Submarine canyon

▲ *The Congo river flows sluggishly through the rain forest of the interior basin. Toward the coast, the river drops steeply in a series of waterfalls and cataracts. At this point, the erosional power of the river becomes so great that it has formed a deep submarine canyon offshore.*

▲ *Virgin tropical rain forest covers the Ruwenzori range on the borders of Dem. Rep. Congo and Uganda.*

▲ *The vast sandflats surrounding Lake Chad were once covered by water. Changing climatic patterns caused the lake to shrink, and desert now covers much of its previous area.*

Transportation & industry

Large reserves of valuable minerals are found in Central Africa: copper, cobalt, zinc, and diamonds are mined in Dem. Rep. Congo and manganese in Gabon. Congo, Cameroon, Gabon, and Equatorial Guinea have oil deposits and oil has also been recently discovered in Chad. Goods such as palm oil and rubber are processed for export.

▲ *The ancient rocks of Dem. Rep. Congo hold immense and varied mineral reserves. This open pit copper mine is at Kolwezi in the far south.*

LIBYA
CHAD
NDJAMENA
SUDAN
NIGER
NIGERIA
CAMEROON
CENTRAL AFRICAN REPUBLIC
BANGUI
Douala
MALABO
YAOUNDE
EQ. GUINEA
LIBREVILLE
SAO TOME & PRINCIPE
Port-Gentil
GABON
BRAZZAVILLE
CONGO
KINSHASA
DEM. REP. CONGO
Kisangani
Bukavu
Kananga
UGANDA
RWANDA
BURUNDI
TANZANIA
ANGOLA (CABINDA)
ANGOLA
ATLANTIC OCEAN
Kolwezi
Lubumbashi
ZAMBIA

Major industry and infrastructure

- brewing
- chemicals
- cobalt
- copper
- diamonds
- food processing
- manganese
- oil
- palm oil processing
- textiles
- tin
- capital cities
- major towns
- international airports
- major roads
- major industrial areas

Transportation network

102,747 miles (165,774 km)	37 miles (60 km)
3985 miles (6414 km)	14,110 miles (22,710 km)

The Trans-Gabon railroad, which began operating in 1987, has opened up new sources of timber and manganese. Elsewhere, much investment is needed to update and improve road, rail, and water transportation.

74

76

Map key

Population

- 1 million to 5 million
- 500,000 to 1 million
- 100,000 to 500,000
- 50,000 to 100,000
- 10,000 to 50,000
- below 10,000

Elevation

- 4000m / 13,124ft
- 3000m / 9843ft
- 2000m / 6562ft
- 1000m / 3281ft
- 500m / 1640ft
- 250m / 820ft
- 100m / 328ft
- sea level

Scale 1:10,500,000

Km 0 25 50 100 150 200 250

Miles 0 25 50 100 150 200 250

projection: Lambert Azimuthal Equal Area

CENTRAL AFRICAN REPUBLIC
CAMEROON
EQUATORIAL GUINEA
SAO TOME & PRINCIPE
GABON
CONGO
DEM. REP. CONGO
ANGOLA
ANGOLA (CABINDA)
ZAMBIA
TANZANIA
UGANDA
RWANDA
BURUNDI
ATLANTIC OCEAN
Gulf of Guinea
Bight of Biafra
Equator
Lake Tanganyika
Lake Albert
Lake Edward
Lake Kivu
Lake Mweru
BANGUI
YAOUNDÉ
MALABO
LIBREVILLE
SÃO TOMÉ
BRAZZAVILLE
KINSHASA
Douala
Port-Gentil
Pointe-Noire
Mbandaka
Kisangani
Kananga
Mbuji-Mayi
Lubumbashi
Bukavu
Goma
Bandundu
Matadi
Kindu
Kalemie
Kamina
Likasi
Kolwezi
Berbérati
Bambari
Bouar
Bozoum
Ouesso
Dolisie
Franceville
Lambaréné
Bafoussam
Bamenda
Congo Basin
Monts Mitumba
Great Rift Valley

▲ **The great Congo** river forms part of the border between Congo and Dem. Rep. Congo. The river is fast-flowing, and a series of falls and rapids means that it is only partly navigable.

Using the land

Cash crops for export include cocoa, coffee, and rubber. Shifting cultivation is widely practiced, and plantains are the staple food of the equatorial region, grown with yam and taro. Cassava, guinea corn (sorghum), and millet are the main subsistence crops in savannah areas. Cattle farming is limited to areas free of tsetse fly, and fish from the interior rivers are an important protein source.

Land use and agricultural distribution

cattle
cocoa
coffee
cotton
palms
peanuts
rubber
timber
capital cities
major towns
pasture
cropland
forest
desert

▲ **High-quality timber is** floated to Port-Gentil, Gabon, via the Ogooué river. Timber provides important export revenue for several countries, although there has been concern about the uncontrolled logging of rare tropical woods.

The urban/rural population divide

urban 33% | rural 67%

0 10 20 30 40 50 60 70 80 90 100

Population density	Total land area
43 people per sq mile (17 people per sq km)	2,023,939 sq miles (5,243,364 sq km)

East Africa

BURUNDI, DJIBOUTI, ERITREA, ETHIOPIA, KENYA, RWANDA, SOMALIA, SUDAN, TANZANIA, UGANDA

The countries of East Africa divide into two distinct cultural regions. Sudan and the "Horn" nations have been influenced by the Middle East; Ethiopia was the home of one of the earliest Christian civilizations, and Sudan reflects both Muslim and Christian influences. The southern countries share a closer cultural affinity with other sub-Saharan nations. Some of Africa's most densely populated countries lie in this region, and the needs of a growing number of people have put pressure on marginal lands and fragile environments. Although most East African economies remain strongly agricultural, Kenya has developed a varied industrial base.

The landscape

East Africa's most significant landscape feature is the Great Rift Valley, which formed during the most recent phase of continental movement when the rigid basement rocks cracked and buckled. Great blocks of land were raised and lowered, creating huge flat-bottomed valleys and steep escarpments, sometimes covered by volcanic extrusions in highland areas.

◀ *This dome at Gonder, in Ethiopia, is a volcanic intrusion, formed when molten rock pushed up the surface of the Earth and then solidified, leaving an outcrop of igneous rock.*

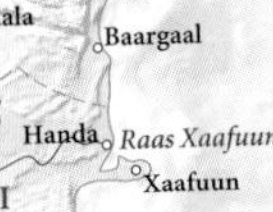

Ephemeral lake forms at far edge of slope
Central block slopes towards main fault
Boundary fault

▲ ***The eastern arm** of the Great Rift Valley is gradually being pulled apart; however the forces on one side are greater than the other causing the land to slope. This affects regional drainage which migrates down the slope.*

Much of northern Sudan is covered by desert. However, in the tropical wetlands of the southern Sudd region, annual rainfall can sometimes exceed 40 inches (1000 mm).

The tiny countries of Rwanda and Burundi are mainly mountainous, with large areas of inaccessible tropical rain forest.

Lake Tanganyika lies 8202 ft (2500 m) above sea level. It has a depth of nearly 4700 ft (1435 m). The lake traces the valley floor for some 400 miles (644 km) of the western arm of the Great Rift Valley.

Lake Victoria occupies a vast basin between the two arms of the Great Rift Valley. It is the world's second largest lake in terms of surface area, extending 26,560 sq miles (68,880 sq km). The lake contains numerous islands and coral reefs.

A vast plateau lies between the eastern and western rift valleys in Kenya, Uganda, and western Tanzania. It has been leveled by long periods of erosion to form a peneplain, but is dotted with inselbergs – outcrops of more resistant rocks.

Lava flows on uplifted areas either side of the eastern branch of the Great Rift Valley gave the Ethiopian Highlands – a series of high, wide plateaus – their distinctive rounded appearance and fertile soils.

Kilimanjaro

▲ ***An extinct volcano**, Kilimanjaro is Africa's highest mountain, rising 19,340 ft (5895 m). Once famed for its snow-capped peak, this has almost competely melted due to changing climatic conditions.*

▶ ***The Kassala region** in eastern Sudan is watered by the Atbara River, an important tributary of the Nile. Most of the population is engaged in agriculture, growing cotton and cereals.*

74

78

140

Map key
Population
1 million to 5 million
500,000 to 1 million
100,000 to 500,000
50,000 to 100,000
10,000 to 50,000
below 10,000
Elevation
4000m / 13,124ft
3000m / 9843ft
2000m / 6562ft
1000m / 3281ft
500m / 1640ft
250m / 820ft
100m / 328ft
sea level
Scale 1:10,500,000
projection: Lambert Azimuthal Equal Area
Major industry and infrastructure
chemicals
cement
coffee processing
frankincense
hydroelectric power
sisal processing
sugar refining
tea processing
textiles
wildlife reserves
capital cities
major towns
international airports
major roads
major industrial areas
Transportation network
102,421 miles (164,929 km)
Trans-East African Highway
7068 miles (11,381 km)
2837 miles (4568 km)
Land use and agricultural distribution
cattle
goats
sheep
coffee
cotton
sugar cane
sisal
tea
timber
capital cities
major towns
pasture
cropland
forest
wetland
desert
The urban/rural population divide
urban 19%
rural 81%
Population density
83 people per sq mile (32 people per sq km)
Total land area
2,413,758 sq miles (6,253,259 sq km)
KENYA
UGANDA
TANZANIA
SOMALIA
ETHIOPIA
RWANDA
BURUNDI
Lake Victoria
Lake Tanganyika
Lake Nyasa
NAIROBI
KAMPALA
DODOMA
MUQDISHO (MOGADISHU)
Dar es Salaam
Mombasa
INDIAN OCEAN

Transportation & industry

Most exports from this region consist of raw materials which have undergone primary processing. These include cotton, sugar, tea, sisal, and coffee. Fast-flowing rivers in the highlands generate hydroelectric power, which has great future potential. The appeal of Kenya's wildlife and beaches has made tourism a crucial part of the economy.

◄ *The great Ngorongoro Crater in Tanzania is an immense relic of past volcanic activity. Other examples are found throughout Kenya and Tanzania.*

▲ ***The magnificent National Parks** of Kenya and Tanzania provide essential refuges for many of Africa's rarest animals. Tourism brings in much-needed cash to sustain these important conservation projects.*

The landlocked nations suffer economically from their restricted access to the coast and from underdeveloped infrastructures. Kenya and Tanzania are investing in new transportation links.

Using the land

The Lake Victoria basin and rich volcanic soils of the Kenyan, Tanzanian, and Ugandan uplands support subsistence crops and cash crops, such as coffee, tea, cotton, sugar cane, and a variety of high-quality vegetables. Where rainfall is too variable for cultivation, pastoralism predominates. In the most arid regions camels are common; elsewhere large herds of cattle, sheep, and goats are raised. Tsetse fly infestation limits human settlement and agriculture in much of this region.

▲ ***This flat valley** floor in Burundi is crisscrossed by irrigation channels which provide a constant source of water for the coffee grown here.*

Southern Africa

ANGOLA, BOTSWANA, LESOTHO, MALAWI, MOZAMBIQUE, NAMIBIA, SOUTH AFRICA, SWAZILAND, ZAMBIA, ZIMBABWE

Africa's vast southern plateau has been a contested homeland for disparate peoples for many centuries. The European incursion began with the slave trade and quickened in the 19th century, when the discovery of enormous mineral wealth secured South Africa's regional economic dominance. The struggle against white minority rule led to strife in Namibia, Zimbabwe, and the former Portuguese territories of Angola and Mozambique. South Africa's notorious apartheid laws, which denied basic human rights to more than 75% of the people, led to the state being internationally ostracized until 1994, when the first fully democratic elections inaugurated a new era of racial justice.

Transportation & industry

South Africa, the world's largest exporter of gold, has a varied economy which generates about 75% of the region's income and draws migrant labor from neighboring states. Angola exports petroleum; Botswana and Namibia rely on diamond mining; and Zambia is seeking to diversify its economy to compensate for declining copper reserves.

◀ *Almost all new mining ventures in Zimbabwe are now subject to government control. This mine at Bindura in northeastern Zimbabwe produces nickel, one of the country's top three minerals in terms of economic value.*

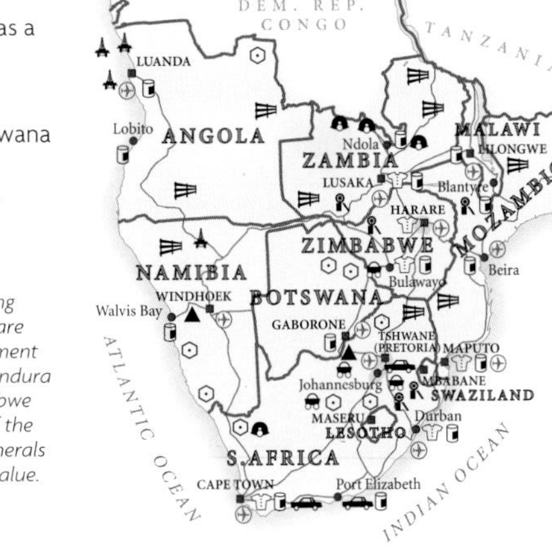

Major industry and infrastructure

- car manufacture
- coal
- copper
- diamonds
- food processing
- gold
- oil
- textiles
- uranium
- wildlife reserves
- capital cities
- major towns
- international airports
- major roads
- major industrial areas

The landscape

Most of southern Africa rests on a concave plateau comprising the Kalahari basin and a mountainous fringe, skirted by a coastal plain which widens out in Mozambique. The plateau extends north, toward the Planalto de Bié in Angola, the Congo Basin and the lake-filled troughs of the Great Rift Valley. The eastern region is drained by the Zambezi and Limpopo rivers, and the Orange is the major western river.

Thousands of years of evaporating water have produced the Etosha Pan, one of the largest salt flats in the world. Lake and river sediments in the area indicate that the region was once less arid.

The Okavango/Cubango River flows from the Planalto de Bié to the swamplands of the Okavango Delta, one of the world's largest inland deltas, where it divides into countless distributary channels, feeding out into the desert.

At Victoria Falls, the Zambezi river has cut a spectacular gorge taking advantage of large joints in the basalt, which were first formed as the lava cooled and contracted.

▶ *The fast-flowing Zambezi river cuts a deep, wide channel as it flows along the Zimbabwe/Zambia border.*

Lake Nyasa occupies one of the deep troughs of the Great Rift Valley, where the land has been displaced downward by as much as 3000 ft (920 m).

Planalto de Bié

Khorixas, Namibia

Namib Desert

Great Rift Valley

Limpopo river

Bushveld intrusion

▲ *Finger Rock, near Khorixas, Namibia is a remnant of a former land surface, which has been denuded by erosion over the last 5 million years. These occasional stacks of partially weathered rocks interrupt the plains of the dry southern interior.*

The Kalahari desert is the largest continuous sand surface in the world. Iron oxide gives a distinctive red color to the windblown sand, which, in eastern areas covers the bedrock by over 200 ft (60 m).

Volcanic lava, over 250 million years old, caps the peaks of the Drakensberg range, which lie on the mountainous rim of southern Africa's interior plateau.

The Orange River, one of the longest in Africa, rises in Lesotho and is the only major river in the south which flows westward, rather than to the east coast.

The mountains of the Little Karoo are composed of sedimentary rocks which have been substantially folded and faulted.

Broad, flat-topped mountains characterize the Great Karoo, which have been cut from level rock strata under extremely arid conditions.

Transportation network

84,213 miles (135,609 km)		746 miles (1202 km)	
23,208 miles (37,372 km)		3815 miles (6144 km)	

Southern Africa's Cape-gauge rail network is by far the largest in the continent. About two-thirds of the 20,000 mile (32,000 km) system lies within South Africa. Lines such as the Harare–Bulawayo route have become corridors for industrial growth.

▲ *Following a series of droughts, this baobab tree in Zimbabwe now stands alone in a field once filled by sugar cane. The thick trunk and small leaves of the baobab help it to conserve water, enabling it to survive even in drought conditions.*

Scale 1:10,500,000

Km 0 25 50 100 150 200 250 300

Miles 0 25 50 100 150 200 250 300

projection: Lambert Azimuthal Equal Area

Bushveld intrusion

Gabbro and peridotite
Granite
Magnetite
Chromite
Platinum minerals

▲ *The Bushveld intrusion lies on South Africa's high "veld." Molten magma intruded into the Earth's crust creating a saucer-shaped feature, more than 180 miles (300 km) across, containing regular layers of precious minerals, overlain by a dome of granite.*

Map key

Population

- 1 million to 5 million
- 500,000 to 1 million
- 100,000 to 500,000
- 50,000 to 100,000
- 10,000 to 50,000
- below 10,000

Elevation

- 3000m / 9843ft
- 2000m / 6562ft
- 1000m / 3281ft
- 500m / 1640ft
- 250m / 820ft
- 100m / 328ft
- sea level

South Africa: Capital cities

TSHWANE (PRETORIA) – administrative capital
CAPE TOWN – legislative capital
BLOEMFONTEIN – judicial capital

78

80

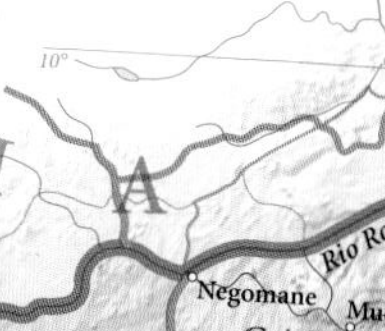

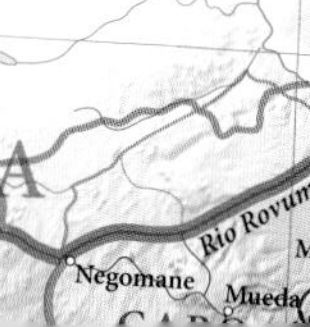
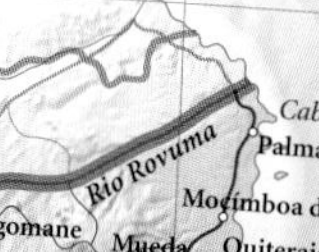
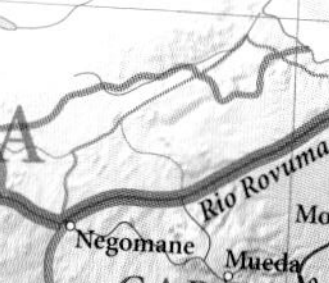

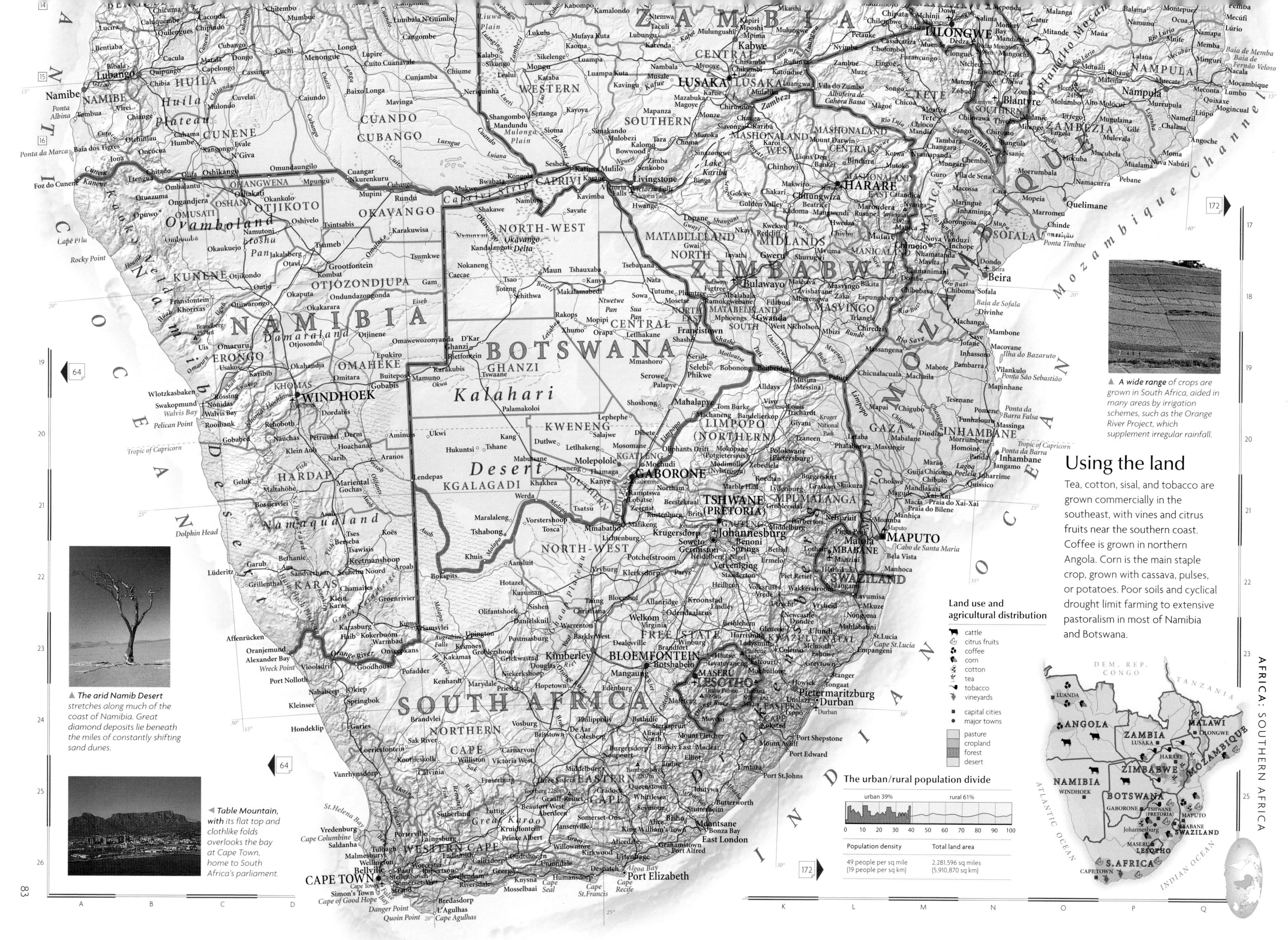
ZAMBIA
NAMIBIA
BOTSWANA
ZIMBABWE
MOZAMBIQUE
SOUTH AFRICA
LESOTHO
SWAZILAND
Kalahari Desert
Namib Desert
INDIAN OCEAN
ATLANTIC OCEAN
Mozambique Channel
LUSAKA
HARARE
WINDHOEK
GABORONE
TSHWANE (PRETORIA)
MAPUTO
MBABANE
MASERU
BLOEMFONTEIN
CAPE TOWN
Johannesburg
Durban
Port Elizabeth
Bulawayo
Beira
Land use and agricultural distribution
cattle
citrus fruits
coffee
corn
cotton
tea
tobacco
vineyards
capital cities
major towns
pasture
cropland
forest
desert
The urban/rural population divide
urban 39%
rural 61%
Population density
49 people per sq mile (19 people per sq km)
Total land area
2,281,596 sq miles (5,910,870 sq km)

▲ **A wide range** *of crops are grown in South Africa, aided in many areas by irrigation schemes, such as the Orange River Project, which supplement irregular rainfall.*

Using the land

Tea, cotton, sisal, and tobacco are grown commercially in the southeast, with vines and citrus fruits near the southern coast. Coffee is grown in northern Angola. Corn is the main staple crop, grown with cassava, pulses, or potatoes. Poor soils and cyclical drought limit farming to extensive pastoralism in most of Namibia and Botswana.

▲ **The arid Namib Desert** *stretches along much of the coast of Namibia. Great diamond deposits lie beneath the miles of constantly shifting sand dunes.*

◀ **Table Mountain,** *with its flat top and clothlike folds overlooks the bay at Cape Town, home to South Africa's parliament.*

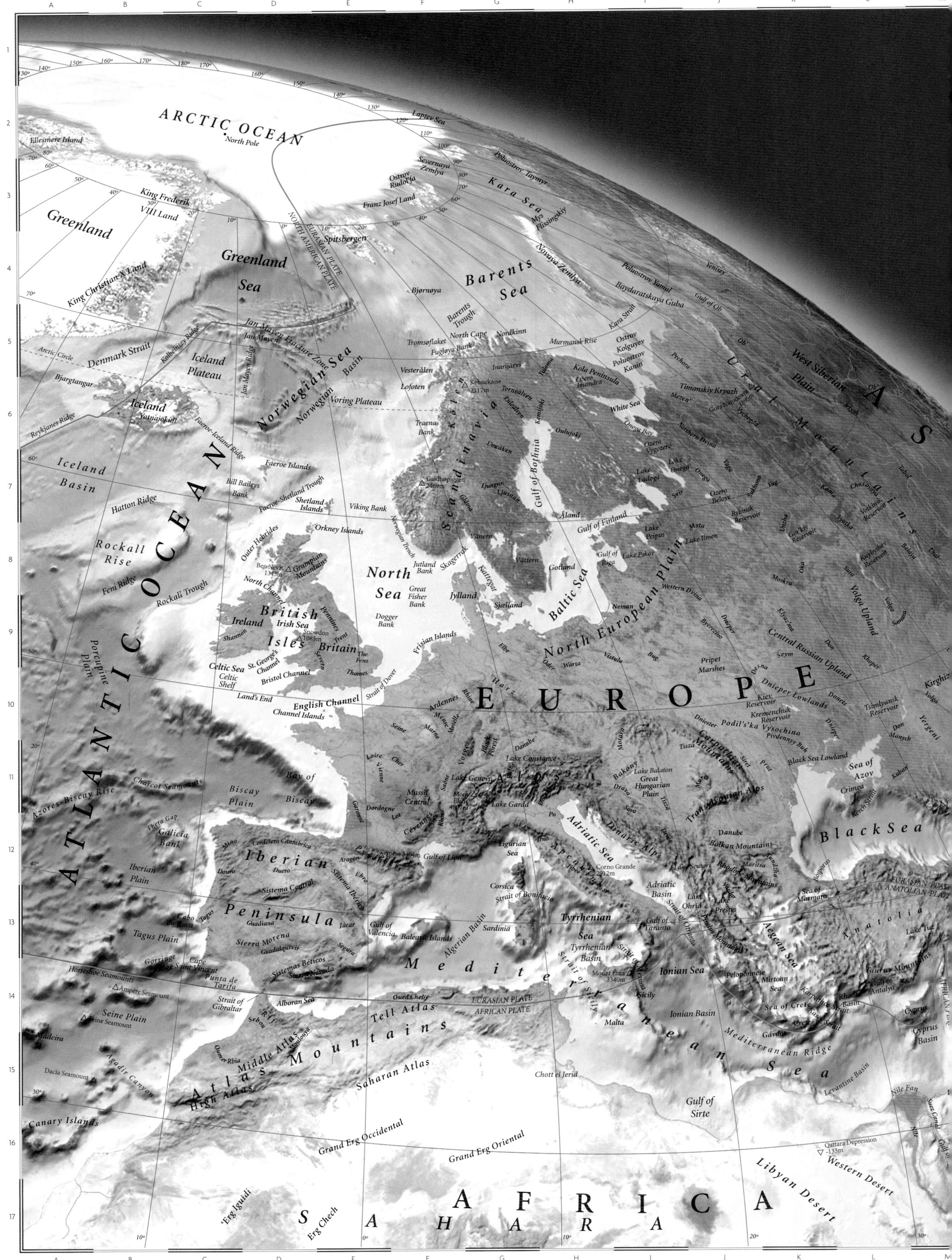

ARCTIC OCEAN
North Pole
Ellesmere Island
Laptev Sea
Severnaya Zemlya
Ostrov Rudol'fa
Franz Josef Land
Poluostrov Taymyr
Kara Sea
Mys Zhelaniya
King Frederik VIII Land
Greenland
Greenland Sea
NORTH AMERICAN PLATE
EURASIAN PLATE
Spitsbergen
Novaya Zemlya
King Christian X Land
Barents Sea
Bjørnøya
Barents Trough
Poluostrov Yamal
Baydaratskaya Guba
Gulf of Ob
Yenisey
Jan Mayen Fracture Zone
Jan Mayen
Kolbeinsey Ridge
Denmark Strait
Arctic Circle
Iceland Plateau
Jan Mayen Ridge
Norwegian Sea
Norwegian Basin
Voring Plateau
Tromsøflaket
North Cape
Nordkinn
Fugløya Bank
Murmansk Rise
Kara Strait
Ostrov Kolguyev
Poluostrov Kanin
Pechora
Ob'
West Siberian Plain
Ural Mountains
ASIA
Vesterålen
Lofoten
Inarijärvi
Kebnekaise 2117m
Torneälven
Kola Peninsula
Ozero Imandra
Timanskiy Kryazh
Mezen'
White Sea
Bjargtangar
Iceland
Vatnajökull
Reykjanes Ridge
Faeroe-Iceland Ridge
Traena Bank
Kølen
Scandinavia
Umeälven
Oulujoki
Onega Bay
Northern Dvina
Ozero Vygozero
Lake Onega
Iceland Basin
Faeroe Islands
Bill Baileys Bank
Faeroe-Shetland Trough
Shetland Islands
Galdhøpiggen 2469m
Ljungan
Gulf of Bothnia
Lake Ladoga
Svir
Ozero Beloye
Rybinsk Reservoir
Tobol
Chusovaya
Kama
Votkinsk Reservoir
Hatton Ridge
ATLANTIC OCEAN
Viking Bank
Norwegian Trench
Glåma
Åland
Gulf of Finland
Lake Peipus
Msta
Lake Ilmen
Orkney Islands
Outer Hebrides
Rockall Rise
Ben Nevis 1343m
Grampian Mountains
North Sea
Jutland Bank
Skagerrak
Vänern
Vättern
Kattegat
Gotland
Gulf of Riga
Lake Pskov
Oka
Moskva
Volga Upland
Feni Ridge
Rockall Trough
North Channel
Great Fisher Bank
Jylland
Sjælland
Baltic Sea
Western Dvina
North European Plain
British Isles
Ireland
Irish Sea
Snowdon 1085m
Pennines
Trent
Great Britain
Dogger Bank
Frisian Islands
Neman
Dnieper
Central Russian Upland
Porcupine Plain
Shannon
St. George's Channel
Severn
The Fens
Thames
Elbe
Oder
Warta
Vistula
Bug
Pripet Marshes
Desna
Seym
Don
Khoper
Celtic Sea
Celtic Shelf
Bristol Channel
Strait of Dover
Harz
EUROPE
Land's End
English Channel
Channel Islands
Ardennes
Rhine
Meuse
Moselle
Kiev Reservoir
Dnieper Lowlands
Kremenchuk Reservoir
Donets
Tsimlyansk Reservoir
Dniester
Podil's'ka Vysochina
Pivdennyy Buh
Seine
Marne
Black Forest
Danube
Carpathian Mountains
Lake Constance
Loire
Vienne
Cher
Vosges
Tisza
Siret
Prut
Black Sea Lowland
Sea of Azov
Crimea
Kerch Strait
Manych
Charcot Seamounts
Bay of Biscay
Biscay Plain
Massif Central
Lake Geneva
Alps
Mont Blanc 4807m
Lake Garda
Lake Balaton
Great Hungarian Plain
Bakony
Drava
Sava
Transylvanian Alps
Azores-Biscay Rise
Dordogne
Lot
Garonne
Cévennes
Rhône
Po
Adriatic Sea
Dinaric Alps
Danube
Black Sea
Theta Gap
Galicia Bank
Miño
Cordillera Cantábrica
Pyrenees
Aneto 3404m
Gulf of Lion
Ligurian Sea
Arno
Apennines
Tiber
Corno Grande 2912m
Balkan Mountains
Maritsa
Rhodope Mountains
Lake Scutari
Bosporus
Sea of Marmara
EURASIAN PLATE
ANATOLIAN PLATE
Iberian Plain
Iberian Peninsula
Douro
Duero
Aragón
Ebro
Sistema Central
Sistema Ibérico
Corsica
Strait of Bonifacio
Adriatic Basin
Strait of Otranto
Lake Ohrid
Lake Prespa
Cabo da Roca
Tagus
Guadiana
Júcar
Gulf of Valencia
Balearic Islands
Algerian Basin
Sardinia
Tyrrhenian Sea
Tyrrhenian Basin
Gulf of Taranto
Pindus Mountains
Aegean Sea
Anatolia
Lake Tuz
Tagus Plain
Sierra Morena
Guadalquivir
Segura
Mediterranean Sea
Strait of Messina
Gorringe Ridge
Cape Saint Vincent
Sistemas Béticos
Sierra Nevada
Horseshoe Seamounts
Punta de Tarifa
Mount Etna 3340m
Ionian Sea
Peloponnese
Mirtoan Sea
Taurus Mountains
Gulf of Antalya
Ampère Seamount
Strait of Gibraltar
Alboran Sea
Oued Chelif
EURASIAN PLATE
AFRICAN PLATE
Sicily
Strait of Sicily
Sea of Crete
Karpathos Strait
Kasos Strait
Rhodes Basin
Cyprus
Seine Plain
Seine Seamount
Rif
Sebou
Tell Atlas
Malta
Ionian Basin
Gávdos
Cyprus Basin
Madeira
Oumer Rbia
Moulouya
Middle Atlas
Atlas Mountains
Mediterranean Ridge
Agadir Canyon
Dacia Seamount
High Atlas
Saharan Atlas
Chott el Jerid
Levantine Basin
Nile Fan
Gulf of Sirte
Suez Canal
Canary Islands
Grand Erg Occidental
Grand Erg Oriental
Qattara Depression -133m
Western Desert
Nile
Libyan Desert
AFRICA
SAHARA
'Erg Iguidi
Erg Chech

Europe

Europe is the world's second smallest continent, covering 4,053,309 sq miles (10,498,000 sq km). It comprises 45 separate countries, including Turkey and the Russian Federation, although the greater parts of these nations lie in Asia.

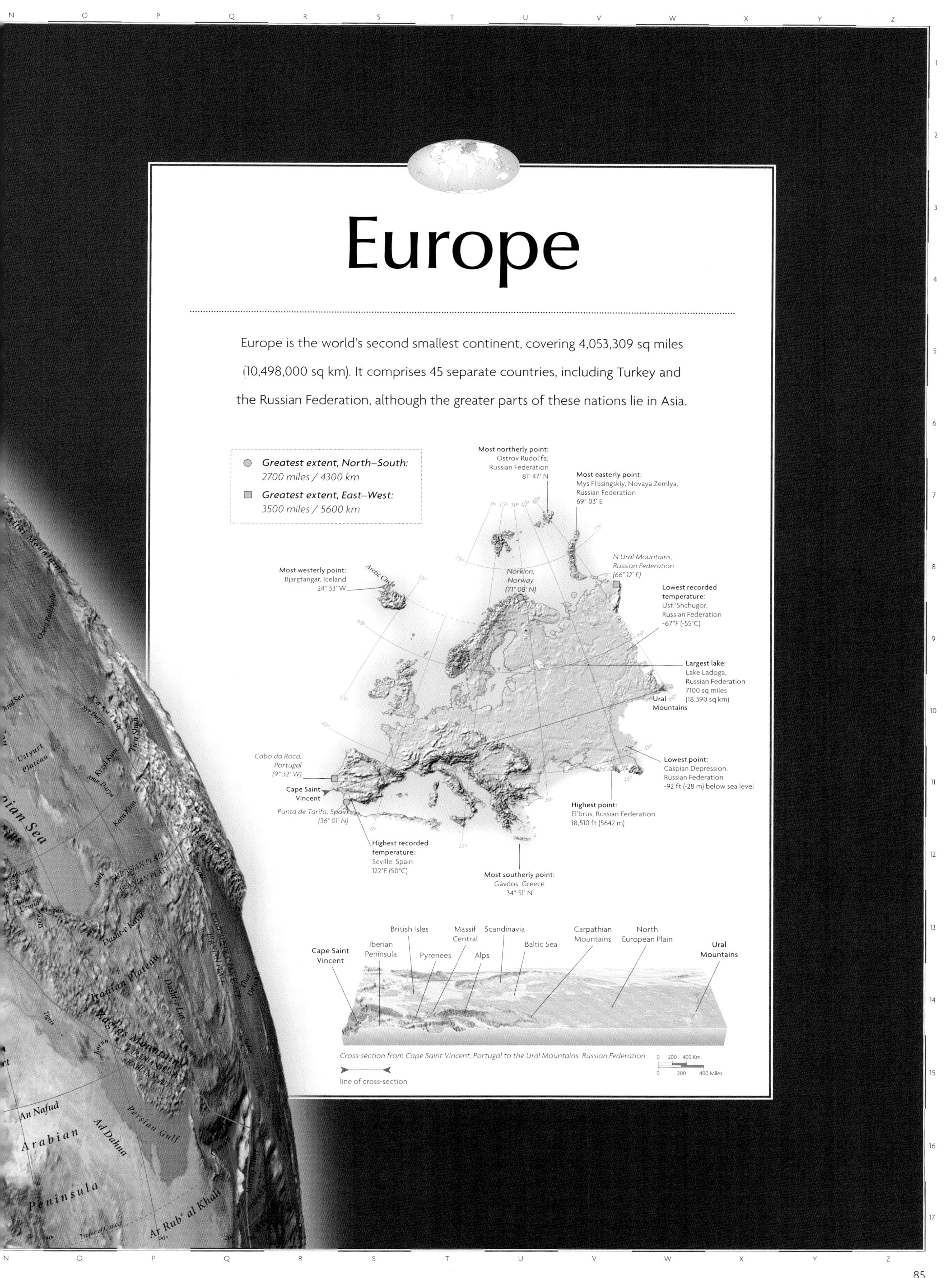

Greatest extent, North–South: 2700 miles / 4300 km
Greatest extent, East–West: 3500 miles / 5600 km
Most northerly point: Ostrov Rudol'fa, Russian Federation 81° 47' N
Most easterly point: Mys Flissingskiy, Novaya Zemlya, Russian Federation 69° 03' E
N Ural Mountains, Russian Federation (66° 12' E)
Most westerly point: Bjargtangar, Iceland 24° 33' W
Arctic Circle
Norkinn, Norway (71° 08' N)
Lowest recorded temperature: Ust 'Shchugor, Russian Federation -67°F (-55°C)
Largest lake: Lake Ladoga, Russian Federation 7100 sq miles (18,390 sq km)
Ural Mountains
Cabo da Roca, Portugal (9° 32' W)
Cape Saint Vincent
Punta de Tarifa, Spain (36° 01' N)
Lowest point: Caspian Depression, Russian Federation -92 ft (-28 m) below sea level
Highest point: El'brus, Russian Federation 18,510 ft (5642 m)
Highest recorded temperature: Seville, Spain 122°F (50°C)
Most southerly point: Gávdos, Greece 34° 51' N
Cape Saint Vincent
Iberian Peninsula
British Isles
Pyrenees
Massif Central
Alps
Scandinavia
Baltic Sea
Carpathian Mountains
North European Plain
Ural Mountains
Cross-section from Cape Saint Vincent, Portugal to the Ural Mountains, Russian Federation
0 200 400 Km
0 200 400 Miles
line of cross-section
Aral Sea
Ustyurt Plateau
Tien Shan
Kyzyl Kum
Kara Kum
Iranian Plateau
Dasht-e Kavir
Dasht-e Lut
Zagros Mountains
Tigris
An Nafud
Arabian Peninsula
Ad Dahna
Persian Gulf
Ar Rub' al Khali
Tropic of Cancer

Physical Europe

The physical diversity of Europe belies its relatively small size. To the northwest and south it is enclosed by mountains. The older, rounded Atlantic Highlands of Scandinavia and the British Isles lie to the north and the younger, rugged peaks of the Alpine Uplands to the south. In between lies the North European Plain, stretching 2485 miles (4000 km) from The Fens in England to the Ural Mountains in Russia. South of the plain lies a series of gently folded sedimentary rocks separated by ancient plateaus, known as massifs.

The North European Plain

Rising less than 1000 ft (300 m) above sea level, the North European Plain strongly reflects past glaciation. Ridges of both coarse moraine and finer, windblown deposits have accumulated over much of the region. The ice sheet also diverted a number of river channels from their original courses.

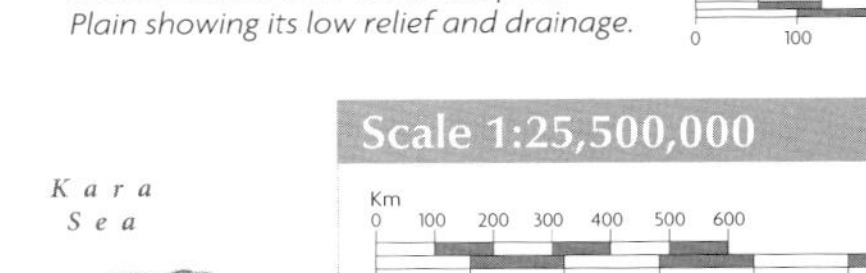

Glacial lakes
Rivers were diverted from their original course by the ice sheet
A layer of glacial sediments covers the North European Plain
B
B
0 100 200 Km
0 100 200 Miles

Section across the North European Plain showing its low relief and drainage.

The Atlantic Highlands

The Atlantic Highlands were formed by compression against the Scandinavian Shield during the Caledonian mountain-building period over 500 million years ago. The highlands were once part of a continuous mountain chain, now divided by the North Sea and a submerged rift valley.

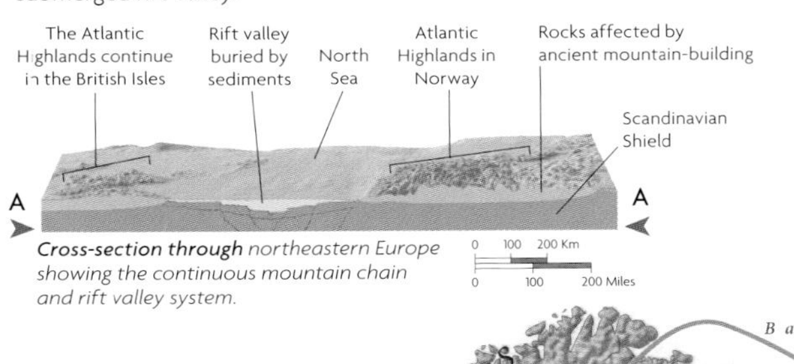

The Atlantic Highlands continue in the British Isles
Rift valley buried by sediments
North Sea
Atlantic Highlands in Norway
Rocks affected by ancient mountain-building
Scandinavian Shield
A
A
0 100 200 Km
0 100 200 Miles

Cross-section through northeastern Europe showing the continuous mountain chain and rift valley system.

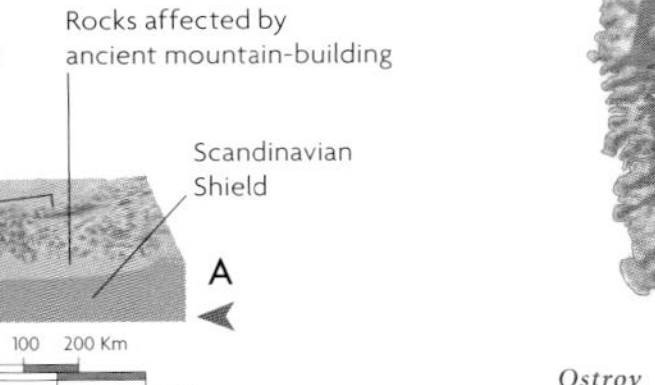

Scale 1:25,500,000

Km 0 100 200 300 400 500 600

Miles 0 100 200 300 400 600

projection: Lambert Azimuthal Equal Area

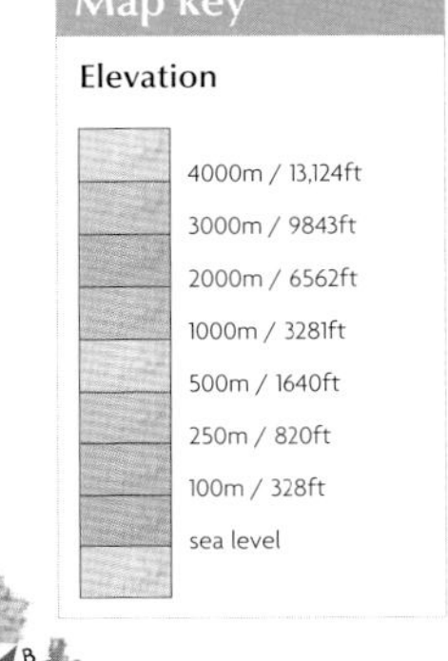

Map key
Elevation
4000m / 13,124ft
3000m / 9843ft
2000m / 6562ft
1000m / 3281ft
500m / 1640ft
250m / 820ft
100m / 328ft
sea level

Plate margins
(for explanation see page xiv)

- constructive
- destructive
- conservative
- uncertain
- physiographic regions
- line of cross-section

Iceland
NORTH AMERICAN PLATE
EURASIAN PLATE
Norwegian Sea
ATLANTIC OCEAN
Faeroe Islands
Shetland Islands
Outer Hebrides
British Isles
Ireland
Shannon
Britain
The Fens
Thames
English Channel
ATLANTIC HIGHLANDS
SCANDINAVIAN SHIELD
Kölen
Gulf of Bothnia
Vänern
Vättern
North Sea
Jylland
Baltic Sea
Gulf of Riga
Novaya Zemlya
Kara Sea
Ostrov Kolguyev
Barents Sea
Kola Peninsula
White Sea
Northern Dvina
Lake Onega
Lake Ladoga
Ural Mountains
Western Dvina
NORTH EUROPEAN PLAIN
Central Russian Upland
Volga Uplands
Volga
Elbe
Vistula
Oder
Rhine
Harz
Ardennes
Seine
Loire
PLATEAUX AND LOWLANDS
Bay of Biscay
Massif Central
Garonne
Rhône
Douro
Iberian Peninsula
Pyrenees
Ebro
Guadalquivir
ALPINE UPLANDS
Alps
Mt Blanc 4807m
Po
Corsica
Sardinia
Balearic Islands
Apennines
Vesuvius 1171m
Tyrrhenian Sea
Sicily
Etna 3263m
Malta
Danube
Carpathian Mountains
Great Hungarian Plain
Dinaric Alps
Adriatic Sea
Balkan Mountains
Dnieper
Dniester
Don
Sea of Azov
Crimea
Caspian Sea
Caucasus
Elbrus 5642m
Black Sea
ASIA
EURASIAN PLATE
ANATOLIAN PLATE
AFRICAN PLATE
Peloponnese
Aegean Sea
Ionian Sea
Crete
Mediterranean Sea

The plateaus and lowlands

The uplifted plateaus or massifs of southern central Europe are the result of long-term erosion, later followed by uplift. They are the source areas of many of the rivers which drain Europe's lowlands. In some of the higher reaches, fractures have enabled igneous rocks from deep in the Earth to reach the surface.

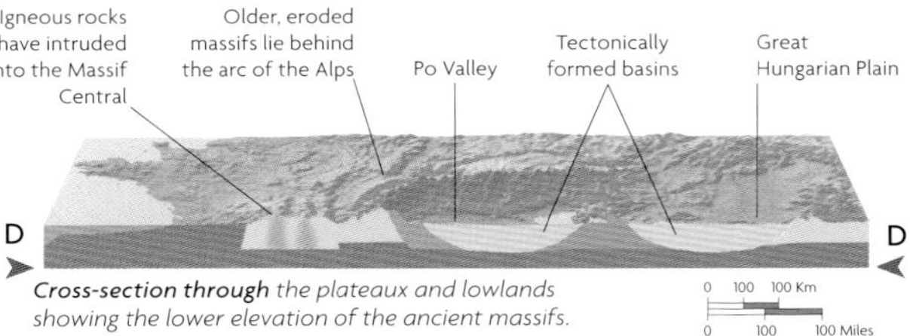

Igneous rocks have intruded into the Massif Central
Older, eroded massifs lie behind the arc of the Alps
Po Valley
Tectonically formed basins
Great Hungarian Plain
D
D
0 100 100 Km
0 100 100 Miles

Cross-section through the plateaux and lowlands showing the lower elevation of the ancient massifs.

The Alpine Uplands

The collision of the African and European continents, which began about 65 million years ago, folded and then uplifted a series of mountain ranges running across southern Europe and into Asia. Two major lines of folding can be traced: one includes the Pyrenees, the Alps, and the Carpathian Mountains; the other incorporates the Apennines and the Dinaric Alps.

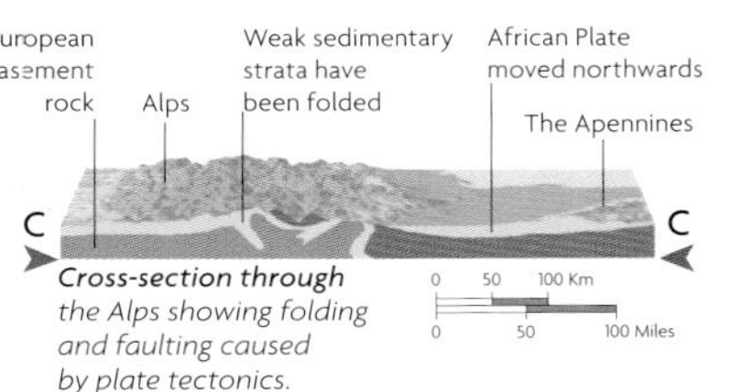

European basement rock
Alps
Weak sedimentary strata have been folded
African Plate moved northwards
The Apennines
C
C
0 50 100 Km
0 50 100 Miles

Cross-section through the Alps showing folding and faulting caused by plate tectonics.

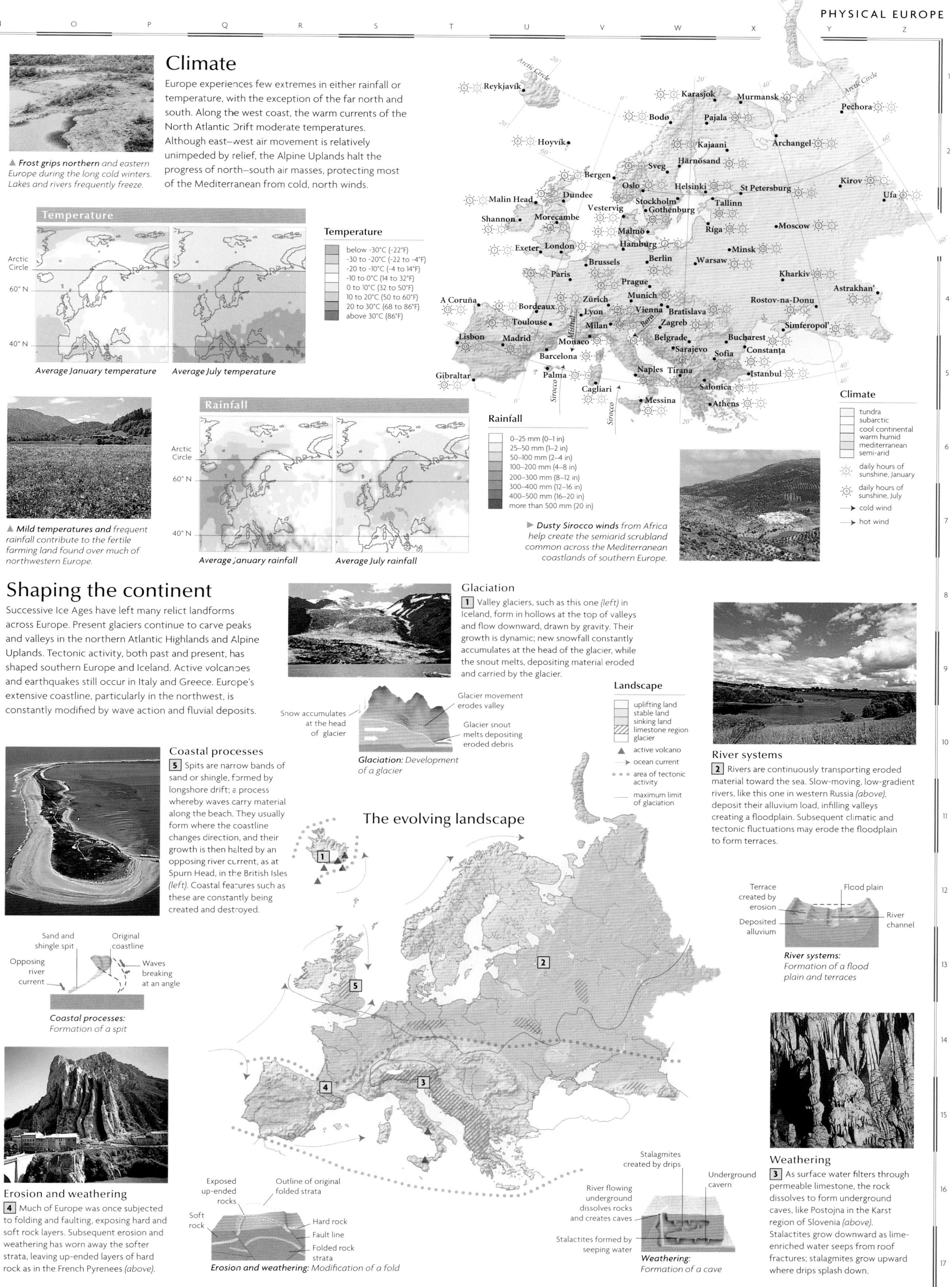

Climate

Europe experiences few extremes in either rainfall or temperature, with the exception of the far north and south. Along the west coast, the warm currents of the North Atlantic Drift moderate temperatures. Although east–west air movement is relatively unimpeded by relief, the Alpine Uplands halt the progress of north–south air masses, protecting most of the Mediterranean from cold, north winds.

▲ *Frost grips northern* and eastern Europe during the long cold winters. Lakes and rivers frequently freeze.

Temperature
Arctic Circle
60° N
40° N
Temperature
below -30°C (-22°F)
-30 to -20°C (-22 to -4°F)
-20 to -10°C (-4 to 14°F)
-10 to 0°C (14 to 32°F)
0 to 10°C (32 to 50°F)
10 to 20°C (50 to 68°F)
20 to 30°C (68 to 86°F)
above 30°C (86°F)

Average January temperature *Average July temperature*

▲ *Mild temperatures and* frequent rainfall contribute to the fertile farming land found over much of northwestern Europe.

Rainfall
Arctic Circle
60° N
40° N
Rainfall
0–25 mm (0–1 in)
25–50 mm (1–2 in)
50–100 mm (2–4 in)
100–200 mm (4–8 in)
200–300 mm (8–12 in)
300–400 mm (12–16 in)
400–500 mm (16–20 in)
more than 500 mm (20 in)

Average January rainfall *Average July rainfall*

Reykjavík
Hoyvík
Karasjok
Murmansk
Bodø
Pajala
Pechora
Kajaani
Archangel
Härnösand
Bergen
Sveg
Oslo
Helsinki
St Petersburg
Kirov
Ufa
Malin Head
Dundee
Stockholm
Tallinn
Vestervig
Gothenburg
Shannon
Morecambe
Riga
Moscow
Malmö
Exeter
London
Hamburg
Minsk
Berlin
Brussels
Warsaw
Paris
Prague
Kharkiv
Astrakhan'
Munich
A Coruña
Bordeaux
Zürich
Vienna
Bratislava
Rostov-na-Donu
Lyon
Toulouse
Milan
Zagreb
Simferopol'
Lisbon
Madrid
Monaco
Belgrade
Bucharest
Sarajevo
Sofia
Constanța
Barcelona
Gibraltar
Palma
Naples
Tirana
Istanbul
Cagliari
Salonica
Messina
Athens
Mistral
Bora
Sirocco
Arctic Circle
Climate
tundra
subarctic
cool continental
warm humid
mediterranean
semi-arid
daily hours of sunshine, January
daily hours of sunshine, July
cold wind
hot wind

▶ *Dusty Sirocco winds* from Africa help create the semiarid scrubland common across the Mediterranean coastlands of southern Europe.

Shaping the continent

Successive Ice Ages have left many relict landforms across Europe. Present glaciers continue to carve peaks and valleys in the northern Atlantic Highlands and Alpine Uplands. Tectonic activity, both past and present, has shaped southern Europe and Iceland. Active volcanoes and earthquakes still occur in Italy and Greece. Europe's extensive coastline, particularly in the northwest, is constantly modified by wave action and fluvial deposits.

Glaciation

1 Valley glaciers, such as this one *(left)* in Iceland, form in hollows at the top of valleys and flow downward, drawn by gravity. Their growth is dynamic; new snowfall constantly accumulates at the head of the glacier, while the snout melts, depositing material eroded and carried by the glacier.

Snow accumulates at the head of glacier
Glacier movement erodes valley
Glacier snout melts depositing eroded debris

Glaciation: *Development of a glacier*

River systems

2 Rivers are continuously transporting eroded material toward the sea. Slow-moving, low-gradient rivers, like this one in western Russia *(above)*, deposit their alluvium load, infilling valleys creating a floodplain. Subsequent climatic and tectonic fluctuations may erode the floodplain to form terraces.

Terrace created by erosion
Flood plain
Deposited alluvium
River channel

River systems: *Formation of a flood plain and terraces*

Coastal processes

5 Spits are narrow bands of sand or shingle, formed by longshore drift; a process whereby waves carry material along the beach. They usually form where the coastline changes direction, and their growth is then halted by an opposing river current, as at Spurn Head, in the British Isles *(left)*. Coastal features such as these are constantly being created and destroyed.

Sand and shingle spit
Original coastline
Opposing river current
Waves breaking at an angle

Coastal processes: *Formation of a spit*

The evolving landscape

Landscape
uplifting land
stable land
sinking land
limestone region
glacier
active volcano
ocean current
area of tectonic activity
maximum limit of glaciation
1
2
3
4
5

Erosion and weathering

4 Much of Europe was once subjected to folding and faulting, exposing hard and soft rock layers. Subsequent erosion and weathering has worn away the softer strata, leaving up-ended layers of hard rock as in the French Pyrenees *(above)*.

Exposed up-ended rocks
Outline of original folded strata
Soft rock
Hard rock
Fault line
Folded rock strata

Erosion and weathering: *Modification of a fold*

Stalagmites created by drips
Underground cavern
River flowing underground dissolves rocks and creates caves
Stalactites formed by seeping water

Weathering: *Formation of a cave*

Weathering

3 As surface water filters through permeable limestone, the rock dissolves to form underground caves, like Postojna in the Karst region of Slovenia *(above)*. Stalactites grow downward as lime-enriched water seeps from roof fractures; stalagmites grow upward where drips splash down.

Political Europe

The political boundaries of Europe have changed many times, especially during the 20th century in the aftermath of two world wars, the breakup of the empires of Austria-Hungary, Nazi Germany and, toward the end of the century, the collapse of communism in eastern Europe. The fragmentation of Yugoslavia has again altered the political map of Europe, highlighting a trend toward nationalism and devolution. In contrast, economic federalism is growing. In 1958, the formation of the European Economic Community (now the European Union or EU) started a move toward economic and political union and increasing internal migration.

▲ ***The Brandenburg Gate*** *in Berlin is a potent symbol of German reunification. From 1961, the road beneath it ended in a wall, built to stop the flow of refugees to the West. It was opened again in 1989 when the wall was destroyed and East and West Germany were reunited.*

Population

Europe is a densely populated, urbanized continent; in Belgium over 90% of people live in urban areas. The highest population densities are found in an area stretching east from southern Britain and northern France, into Germany. The northern fringes are only sparsely populated.

Denmark Strait
REYKJAVÍK
ICELAND
Arctic Circle

▲ ***Demand for space*** *in densely populated European cities like London has led to the development of high-rise offices and urban sprawl.*

Population density
(people per sq mile)

- below 130
- 130–259
- 260–379
- 380–519
- 520–780
- above 780

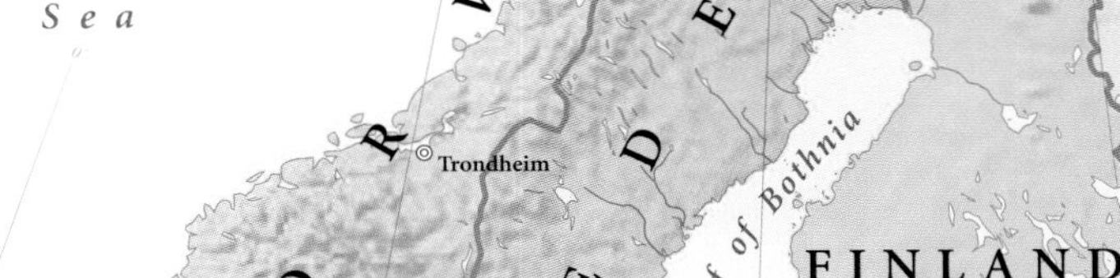
NORWAY
SWEDEN
FINLAND
Gulf of Bothnia
ESTONIA
LATVIA
LITHUANIA

ATLANTIC OCEAN
North Sea
UNITED KINGDOM
IRELAND
DENMARK
NETH.
GERMANY
POLAND

FRANCE
Bay of Biscay
SWITZERLAND
AUSTRIA

CZECH REPUBLIC
SLOVAKIA
HUNGARY
ROMANIA

CROATIA
BOS. & HERZ.
SERBIA
BULGARIA
MONTENEGRO
ALBANIA
GREECE

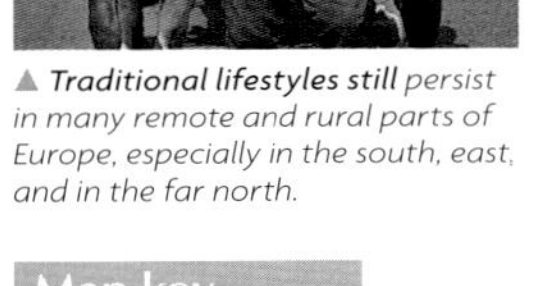

▲ ***Traditional lifestyles still*** *persist in many remote and rural parts of Europe, especially in the south, east, and in the far north.*

Map key

Population

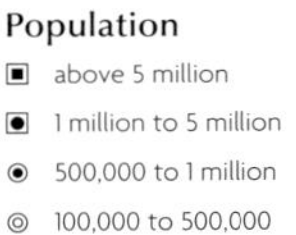

- ▣ above 5 million
- ◘ 1 million to 5 million
- ◉ 500,000 to 1 million
- ◎ 100,000 to 500,000
- ⊕ 50,000 to 100,000
- ○ 10,000 to 50,000
- ● Country capital

Borders

- full international border

Pyrenees
ANDORRA

SPAIN
PORTUGAL
ITALY
Mediterranean Sea
Tyrrhenian Sea
Ionian Sea

Scale 1:17,250,000

Km 0 100 200 300 400 500 600 700

Miles 0 100 200 300 400 500 600 700

projection: Lambert Azimuthal Equal Area

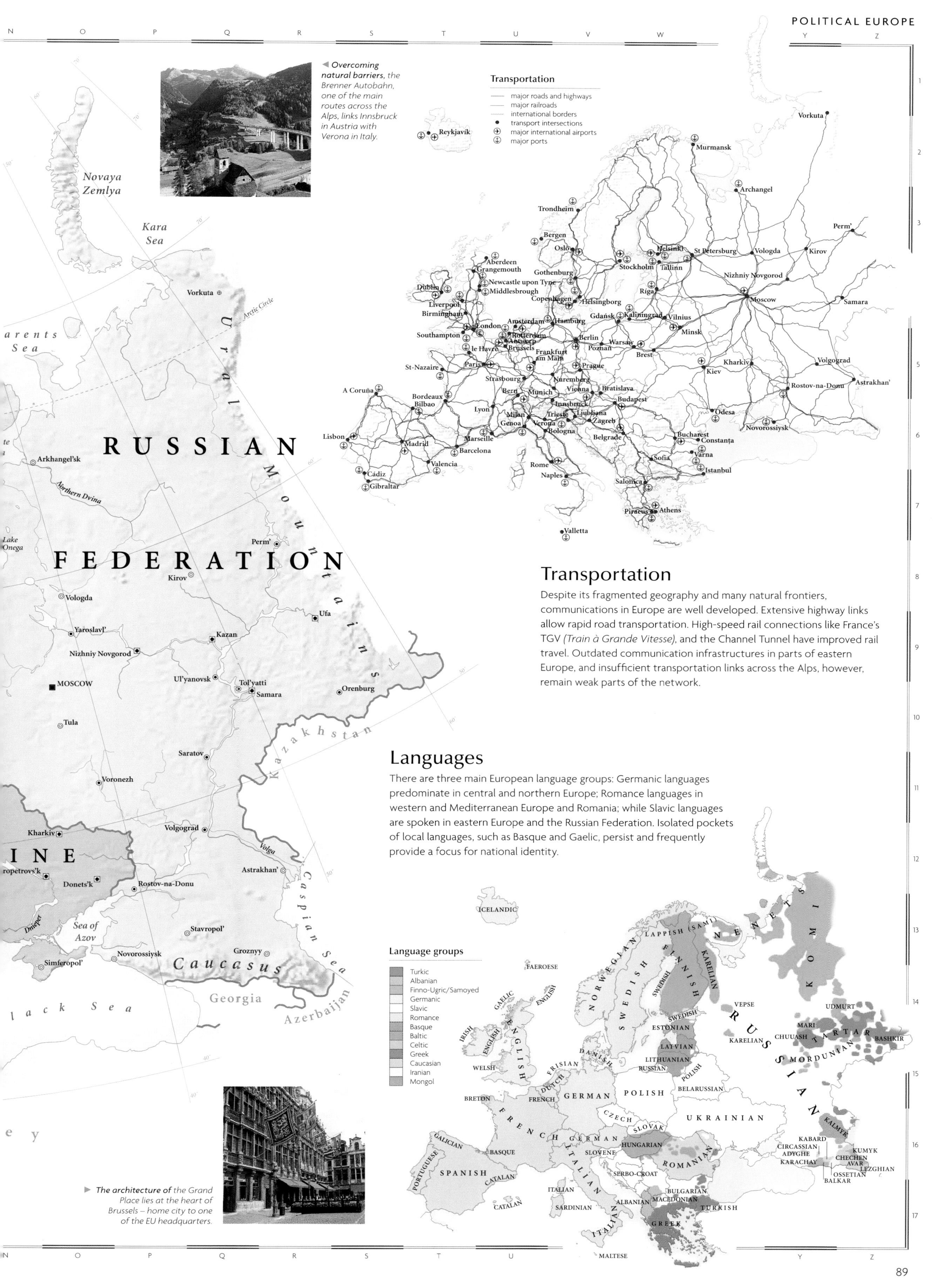
Novaya Zemlya
Kara Sea
Barents Sea
RUSSIAN FEDERATION
Ural Mountains
Kazakhstan
Caspian Sea
Caucasus
Georgia
Azerbaijan
Black Sea
Sea of Azov
Transportation
major roads and highways
major railroads
international borders
transport intersections
major international airports
major ports
Language groups
Turkic
Albanian
Finno-Ugric/Samoyed
Germanic
Slavic
Romance
Basque
Baltic
Celtic
Greek
Caucasian
Iranian
Mongol

◄ *Overcoming natural barriers,* the Brenner Autobahn, one of the main routes across the Alps, links Innsbruck in Austria with Verona in Italy.

Transportation

Despite its fragmented geography and many natural frontiers, communications in Europe are well developed. Extensive highway links allow rapid road transportation. High-speed rail connections like France's TGV *(Train à Grande Vitesse)*, and the Channel Tunnel have improved rail travel. Outdated communication infrastructures in parts of eastern Europe, and insufficient transportation links across the Alps, however, remain weak parts of the network.

Languages

There are three main European language groups: Germanic languages predominate in central and northern Europe; Romance languages in western and Mediterranean Europe and Romania; while Slavic languages are spoken in eastern Europe and the Russian Federation. Isolated pockets of local languages, such as Basque and Gaelic, persist and frequently provide a focus for national identity.

► *The architecture of* the Grand Place lies at the heart of Brussels – home city to one of the EU headquarters.

European resources

Europe's large tracts of fertile, accessible land, combined with its generally temperate climate, have allowed a greater percentage of land to be used for agricultural purposes than in any other continent. Extensive coal and iron ore deposits were used to create steel and manufacturing industries during the 19th and 20th centuries. Today, although natural resources have been widely exploited, and heavy industry is of declining importance, the growth of hi-tech and service industries has enabled Europe to maintain its wealth.

Industry

Europe's wealth was generated by the rise of industry and colonial exploitation during the 19th century. The mining of abundant natural resources made Europe the industrial center of the world. Adaptation has been essential in the changing world economy, and a move to service-based industries has been widespread except in eastern Europe, where heavy industry still dominates.

▲ ***Countries like Hungary** are still struggling to modernize inefficient factories left over from extensive, centrally-planned industrialization during the communist era.*

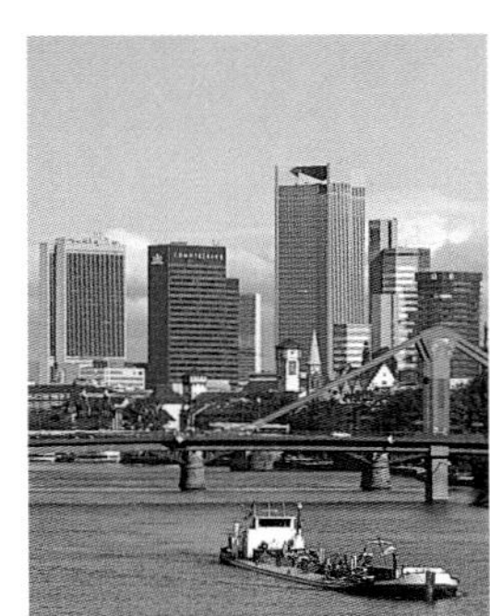

◄ ***Frankfurt am Main** is an example of a modern service-based city. The skyline is dominated by headquarters from the worlds of banking and commerce.*

▲ ***Other power sources** are becoming more attractive as fossil fuels run out; 16% of Europe's electricity is now provided by hydroelectric power.*

Standard of living

Living standards in western Europe are among the highest in the world, although there is a growing sector of homeless, jobless people. Eastern Europeans have lower overall standards of living – a legacy of stagnated economies.

Standard of living
(UN human development index)

- low
- high
- data not available

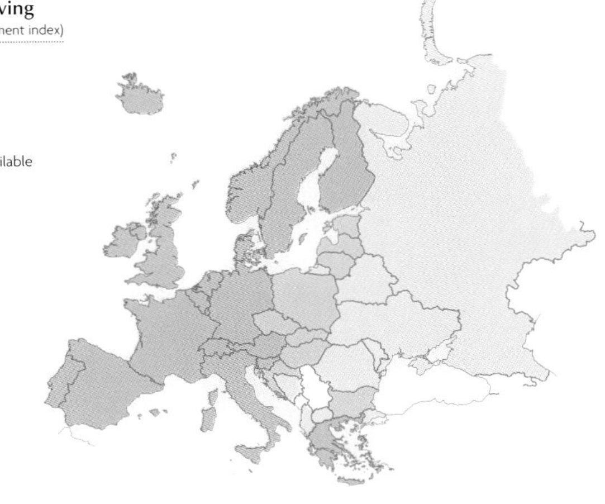

► ***Skiing brings millions** of tourists to the slopes each year, which means that even unproductive, marginal land is used to create wealth in the French, Swiss, Italian, and Austrian Alps.*

ATLANTIC OCEAN · Norwegian Sea · North Sea · Barents Sea · Baltic Sea · Gulf of Bothnia · Bay of Biscay · Mediterranean Sea · Tyrrhenian Sea · Adriatic Sea · Ionian Sea · Aegean Sea · Black Sea · Caspian Sea

ICELAND · IRELAND · UNITED KINGDOM · NORWAY · SWEDEN · FINLAND · DENMARK · ESTONIA · LATVIA · LITHUANIA · RUSS. FED. (Kaliningrad) · BELARUS · POLAND · NETH. · BELG. · LUX. · GERMANY · CZECH REP. · SLOVAKIA · AUSTRIA · SWITZ. · LIECH. · HUNGARY · ROMANIA · MOLDOVA · UKRAINE · RUSSIAN FEDERATION · KAZAKHSTAN · GEORGIA · AZERBAIJAN · FRANCE · ANDORRA · MONACO · SPAIN · PORTUGAL · ITALY · SAN MARINO · VATICAN CITY · SLVN. · CROATIA · BOSNIA & HERZ. · SERBIA · MONT. · ALBANIA · MACED. · BULGARIA · GREECE · TURKEY · MALTA · MOROCCO

Faeroe Islands (to Denmark) · Isle of Man (to UK) · Channel Islands (to UK) · Gibraltar (to UK) · Ceuta (to Spain) · Melilla (to Spain) · Balearic Islands · Corsica · Sardinia · Sicily · Crete · Novaya Zemlya · Ostrov Kolguyev

Reykjavík · Glasgow · Belfast · Dublin · Newcastle upon Tyne · Liverpool · Manchester · Birmingham · Cardiff · London · Trondheim · Bergen · Oslo · Stockholm · Gothenburg · Malmö · Copenhagen · Turku · Helsinki · Tallinn · Riga · Vilnius · Murmansk · Archangel · St Petersburg · Cherepovets · Yaroslavl' · Ivanovo · Nizhniy Novgorod · Kazan' · Perm' · Ufa · Moscow · Ryazan' · Tula · Tol'yatti · Samara · Saratov · Voronezh · Kursk · Volgograd · Kharkiv · Donets'k · Dnipropetrovs'k · Kryvyy Rih · Rostov-na-Donu · Kiev · Minsk · Gdańsk · Poznań · Łódź · Warsaw · Katowice · Kraków · Hamburg · Berlin · Amsterdam · Rotterdam · Essen · Antwerp · Brussels · Liège · Lille · Cologne · Leipzig · Dresden · Frankfurt am Main · Prague · Metz · Strasbourg · Stuttgart · Munich · Linz · Vienna · Bratislava · Budapest · Zürich · Rouen · Paris · Nantes · Bordeaux · Lyon · Toulouse · Marseille · A Coruña · Bilbao · Porto · Lisbon · Madrid · Barcelona · Seville · Turin · Milan · Venice · Genoa · Bologna · Rome · Naples · Taranto · Palermo · Zagreb · Belgrade · Sofia · Ploeşti · Bucharest · Constanța · Varna · Odesa · Istanbul · Salonica · Piraeus · Athens

GNI per capita (US $)

- below 1999
- 2000–4999
- 5000–9999
- 10,000–19,999
- 20,000–24,999
- above 25,000

Industry

- aerospace
- brewing
- car/vehicle manufacture
- chemicals
- defense
- electronics
- engineering
- finance
- food processing
- hi-tech industry
- iron & steel
- pharmaceuticals
- printing & publishing
- shipbuilding
- textiles
- timber processing
- wine
- coal
- oil
- gas
- industrial cities
- major industrial areas

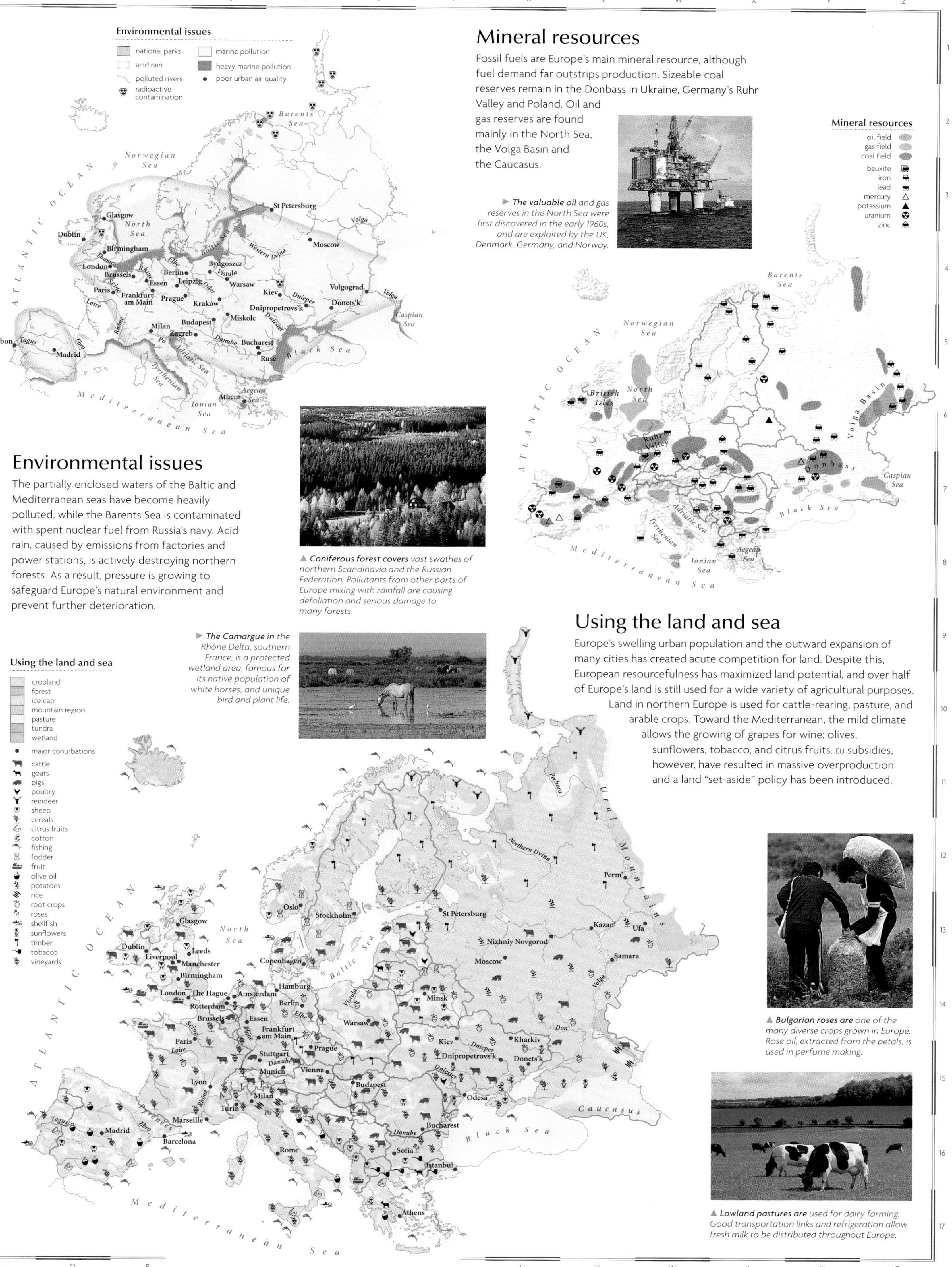

Environmental issues
national parks
acid rain
polluted rivers
radioactive contamination
marine pollution
heavy marine pollution
poor urban air quality
Mineral resources
oil field
gas field
coal field
bauxite
iron
lead
mercury
potassium
uranium
zinc
Using the land and sea
cropland
forest
ice cap
mountain region
pasture
tundra
wetland
major conurbations
cattle
goats
pigs
poultry
reindeer
sheep
cereals
citrus fruits
cotton
fishing
fodder
fruit
olive oil
potatoes
rice
root crops
roses
shellfish
sunflowers
timber
tobacco
vineyards

Mineral resources

Fossil fuels are Europe's main mineral resource, although fuel demand far outstrips production. Sizeable coal reserves remain in the Donbass in Ukraine, Germany's Ruhr Valley and Poland. Oil and gas reserves are found mainly in the North Sea, the Volga Basin and the Caucasus.

▶ *The valuable oil and gas reserves in the North Sea were first discovered in the early 1960s, and are exploited by the UK, Denmark, Germany, and Norway.*

Environmental issues

The partially enclosed waters of the Baltic and Mediterranean seas have become heavily polluted, while the Barents Sea is contaminated with spent nuclear fuel from Russia's navy. Acid rain, caused by emissions from factories and power stations, is actively destroying northern forests. As a result, pressure is growing to safeguard Europe's natural environment and prevent further deterioration.

▲ *Coniferous forest covers vast swathes of northern Scandinavia and the Russian Federation. Pollutants from other parts of Europe mixing with rainfall are causing defoliation and serious damage to many forests.*

▶ *The Camargue in the Rhône Delta, southern France, is a protected wetland area famous for its native population of white horses, and unique bird and plant life.*

Using the land and sea

Europe's swelling urban population and the outward expansion of many cities has created acute competition for land. Despite this, European resourcefulness has maximized land potential, and over half of Europe's land is still used for a wide variety of agricultural purposes.

Land in northern Europe is used for cattle-rearing, pasture, and arable crops. Toward the Mediterranean, the mild climate allows the growing of grapes for wine; olives, sunflowers, tobacco, and citrus fruits. EU subsidies, however, have resulted in massive overproduction and a land "set-aside" policy has been introduced.

▲ *Bulgarian roses are one of the many diverse crops grown in Europe. Rose oil, extracted from the petals, is used in perfume making.*

▲ *Lowland pastures are used for dairy farming. Good transportation links and refrigeration allow fresh milk to be distributed throughout Europe.*

Scandinavia, Finland & Iceland

DENMARK, NORWAY, SWEDEN, FINLAND, ICELAND

Jutting into the Arctic Circle, this northern swath of Europe has some of the continent's harshest environments, but benefits from great reserves of oil, gas, and natural evergreen forests. While most early settlers came from the south, migrants to Finland came from the east, giving it a distinct language and culture. Since the late 19th century, the Scandinavian states have developed strong egalitarian traditions. Today, their welfare benefits systems are among the most extensive in the world, and standards of living are high. The Lapps, or Sami, maintain their traditional lifestyle in the northern regions of Norway, Sweden, and Finland.

The landscape

Glaciers up to 10,000 ft (3000 m) deep covered most of Scandinavia and Finland during the last Ice Age. The effects of glaciation mark the entire landscape, from the mountains to the lowlands, across the tundra landscape of Lapland, and the lake districts of Sweden and Finland.

(same scale as main map)

SCALE 1:9,000,000

projection: Lambert Conformal Conic

Using the land & sea

The cold climate, short growing season, poorly developed soil, steep slopes, and exposure to high winds across northern regions means that most agriculture is concentrated, with the population, in the south. Most of Finland and much of Norway and Sweden are covered by dense forests of pine, spruce, and birch, which supply the timber industries.

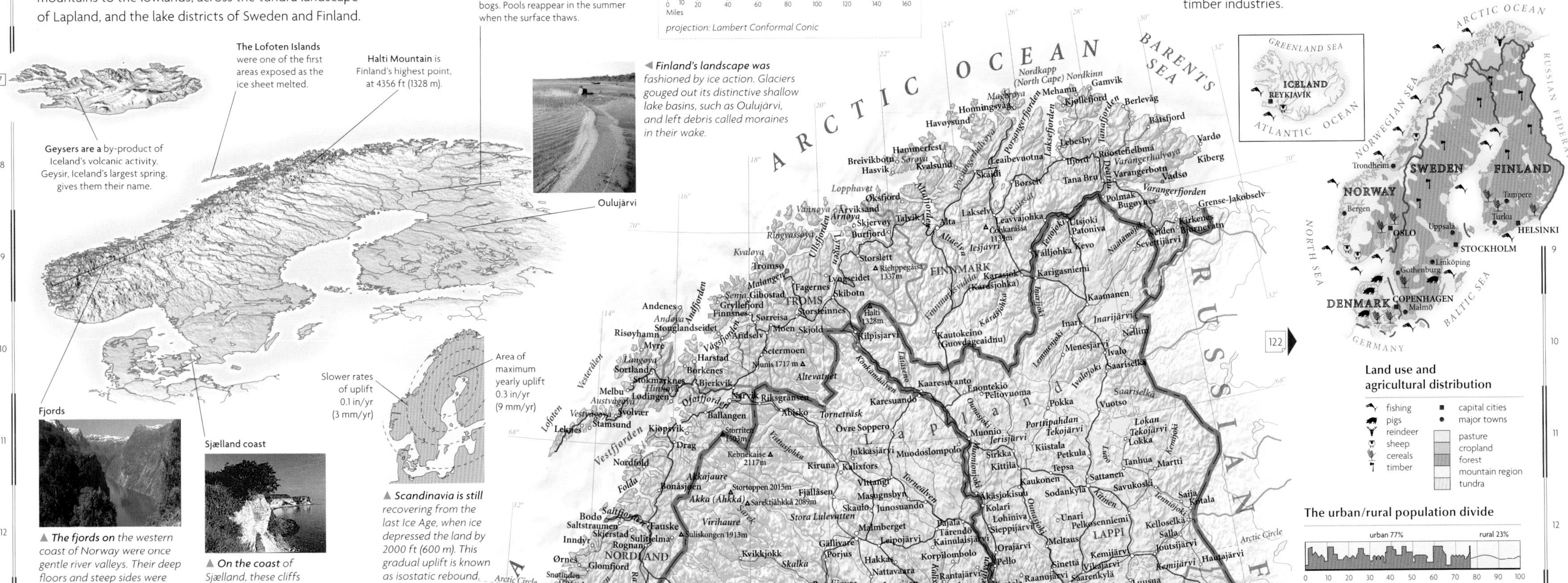
Scale 1:5,500,000
projection: Lambert Conformal Conic
ARCTIC OCEAN
BARENTS SEA
RUSSIAN FEDERATION
Land use and agricultural distribution
fishing
pigs
reindeer
sheep
cereals
timber
capital cities
major towns
pasture
cropland
forest
mountain region
tundra
The urban/rural population divide
urban 77%
rural 23%
Population density
51 people per sq mile
Total land area
473,970 sq miles
Area of maximum yearly uplift 0.3 in/yr (9 mm/yr)
Slower rates of uplift 0.1 in/yr (3 mm/yr)
Oulujärvi
Fjords
Sjælland coast
122

The Lofoten Islands were one of the first areas exposed as the ice sheet melted.

Halti Mountain is Finland's highest point, at 4356 ft (1328 m).

Lapland, north of the Arctic Circle, is an area of undulating fells and plains known as tundra. The subsoil is permanently frozen and therefore impermeable. There are many peat bogs. Pools reappear in the summer when the surface thaws.

Geysers are a by-product of Iceland's volcanic activity. Geysir, Iceland's largest spring, gives them their name.

◀ *Finland's landscape was fashioned by ice action. Glaciers gouged out its distinctive shallow lake basins, such as Oulujärvi, and left debris called moraines in their wake.*

▲ *Scandinavia is still recovering from the last Ice Age, when ice depressed the land by 2000 ft (600 m). This gradual uplift is known as isostatic rebound.*

▲ *The fjords on the western coast of Norway were once gentle river valleys. Their deep floors and steep sides were carved out by glaciers during the last Ice Age, and they were later flooded by the sea.*

▲ *On the coast of Sjælland, these cliffs have been eroded by the sea, exposing layers of chalk and limestone.*

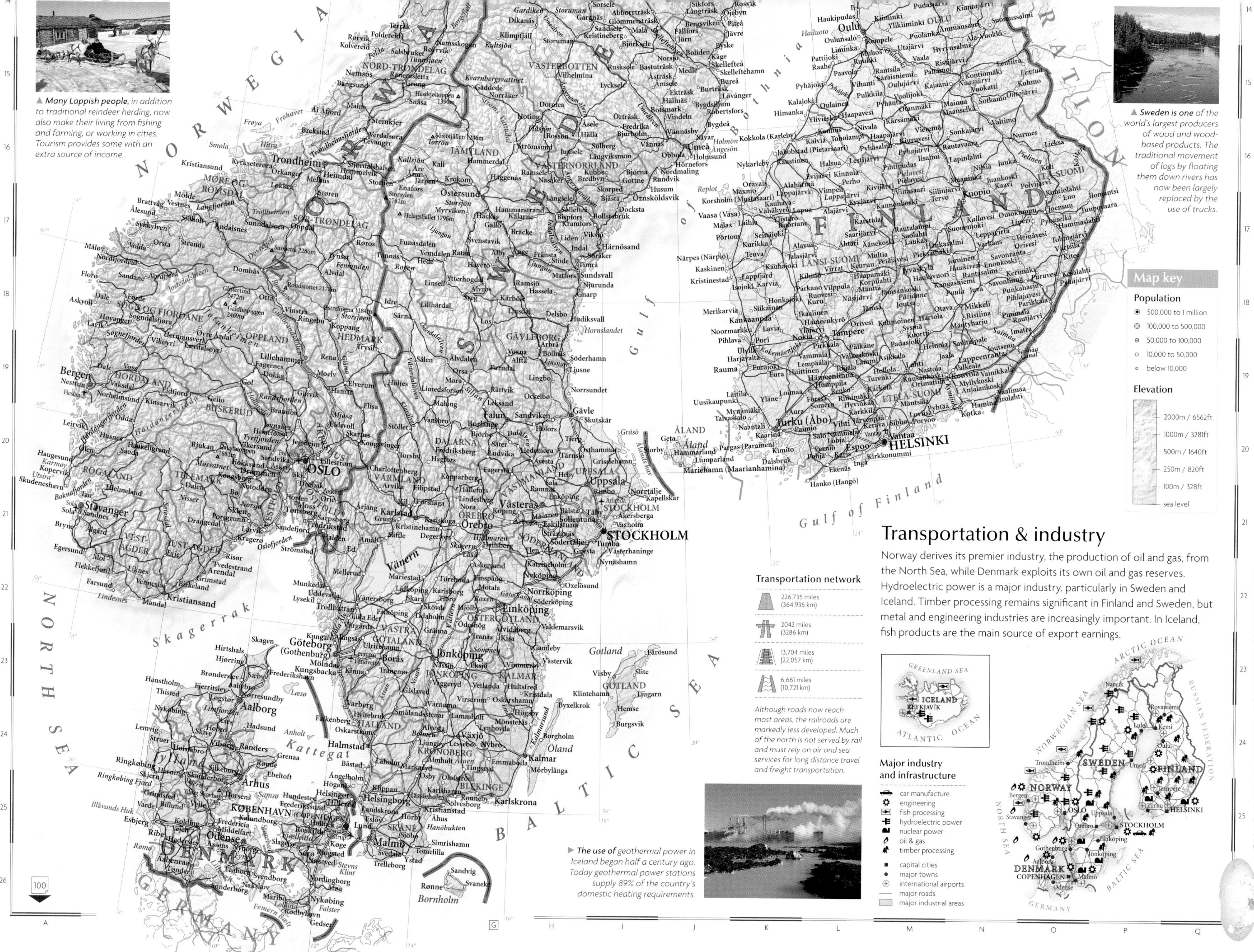
NORWEGIAN SEA
NORTH SEA
Skagerrak
Kattegat
BALTIC SEA
Gulf of Bothnia
Gulf of Finland
NORWAY
SWEDEN
FINLAND
DENMARK
GERMANY
RUSSIAN FEDERATION
OSLO
STOCKHOLM
HELSINKI
KØBENHAVN (COPENHAGEN)
ÅLAND
Gotland
Öland
Bornholm
Jylland
Vänern
Bergen
Stavanger
Trondheim
Göteborg (Gothenburg)
Malmö
Uppsala
Turku (Åbo)
Tampere
Oulu
Aalborg
Århus
Odense

▲ **Many Lappish people,** *in addition to traditional reindeer herding, now also make their living from fishing and farming, or working in cities. Tourism provides some with an extra source of income.*

▲ **Sweden is one** *of the world's largest producers of wood and wood-based products. The traditional movement of logs by floating them down rivers has now been largely replaced by the use of trucks.*

Map key

Population

- 500,000 to 1 million
- 100,000 to 500,000
- 50,000 to 100,000
- 10,000 to 50,000
- below 10,000

Elevation

- 2000m / 6562ft
- 1000m / 3281ft
- 500m / 1640ft
- 250m / 820ft
- 100m / 328ft
- sea level

Transportation & industry

Norway derives its premier industry, the production of oil and gas, from the North Sea, while Denmark exploits its own oil and gas reserves. Hydroelectric power is a major industry, particularly in Sweden and Iceland. Timber processing remains significant in Finland and Sweden, but metal and engineering industries are increasingly important. In Iceland, fish products are the main source of export earnings.

Transportation network

- 226,735 miles (364,936 km)
- 2042 miles (3286 km)
- 13,704 miles (22,057 km)
- 6,661 miles (10,721 km)

Although roads now reach most areas, the railroads are markedly less developed. Much of the north is not served by rail and must rely on air and sea services for long distance travel and freight transportation.

▶ *The use of geothermal power in Iceland began half a century ago. Today geothermal power stations supply 89% of the country's domestic heating requirements.*

Major industry and infrastructure

- car manufacture
- engineering
- fish processing
- hydroelectric power
- nuclear power
- oil & gas
- timber processing
- capital cities
- major towns
- international airports
- major roads
- major industrial areas

GREENLAND SEA
ICELAND
REYKJAVIK
ATLANTIC OCEAN
ARCTIC OCEAN
NORWEGIAN SEA
NORTH SEA
BALTIC SEA
RUSSIAN FEDERATION
NORWAY
SWEDEN
FINLAND
DENMARK
GERMANY
OSLO
STOCKHOLM
HELSINKI
COPENHAGEN

100

Southern Scandinavia

SOUTHERN NORWAY, SOUTHERN SWEDEN, DENMARK

Scandinavia's economic and political hub is the more habitable and accessible southern region. Many of the area's major cities are on the southern coasts, including Oslo and Stockholm, the capitals of Norway and Sweden. In Denmark, most of the population and the capital, Copenhagen, are located on its many islands. A cultural unity links the three Scandinavian countries. Their main languages, Danish, Swedish, and Norwegian, are mutually intelligible, and they all retain their monarchies, although the parliaments have legislative control.

Using the land

Agriculture in southern Scandinavia is highly mechanized although farms are small. Denmark is the most intensively farmed country and its western pastureland is used mainly for pig farming. Cereal crops including wheat, barley, and oats, predominate in eastern Denmark and in the far south of Sweden. Southern Norway, and Sweden have large tracts of forest which are exploited for logging.

The urban/rural population divide

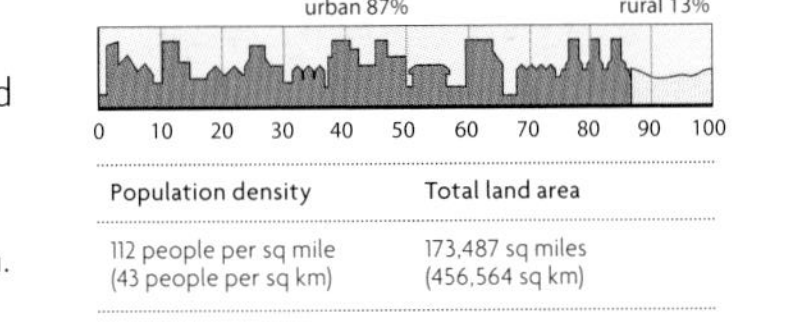
urban 87%
rural 13%
0 10 20 30 40 50 60 70 80 90 100

Population density	Total land area
112 people per sq mile (43 people per sq km)	173,487 sq miles (456,564 sq km)

Land use and agricultural distribution

cattle, pigs, sheep, cereals, fodder, root crops, timber; capital cities, major towns; pasture, cropland, forest, mountain region

NORWAY · SWEDEN · DENMARK · NORWEGIAN SEA · NORTH SEA · BALTIC SEA · GERMANY · Trondheim · Bergen · OSLO · Uppsala · Örebro · STOCKHOLM · Linköping · Gothenburg · Aalborg · COPENHAGEN · Odense · Malmö

▲ In Norway winters are longer and colder inland than in coastal areas, where the warm current of the North Atlantic Drift moderates the climate.

The landscape

Southern Scandinavia, with the exception of Norway, has a flatter terrain than the rest of the region. Denmark and southern Sweden are both extensions of the North European Plain. In this area, because of glacial deposition rather than erosion, the soils are deeper and more fertile.

Acid rain, caused by industrial pollution carried north from elsewhere in Europe, harms plant and animal life in Scandinavian forests and lakes. The region's surface rocks lack lime to neutralize the acid, so making the problem more serious.

Olden

◀ *In the past, glaciers such as this one in Olden, Norway, were much larger. Today, many are retreating to yield the spectacular glacial scenery.*

The peak of Glittertind in the Jotunheimen mountains is 8110 ft (2472 m) high.

Distinctive low ridges, called eskers, are found across southern Sweden. They are formed from sand and gravel deposits left by retreating glaciers.

▲ ***Limestone pillars eroded*** *by the sea dot the coast of Gotland and surrounding islands.*

The lakes of southern Sweden remain from a period when the land was completely flooded. As the ice which covered the area melted, the land rose, leaving lakes in shallow, ice-scoured depressions. Sweden has over 90,000 lakes.

Denmark's flat and fertile soils are formed on glacial deposits between 100–160 ft (30–50 m) deep.

Vänern in Sweden is the largest lake in Scandinavia. It covers an area of 2080 sq miles (5390 sq km).

Sognefjorden

Erosion by glaciers deepened existing river valleys · Sea level · When the ice retreated the valley was flooded by the sea · Old valley floor

▲ ***Sognefjorden is the*** *deepest of Norway's many fjords. It drops to 4291 ft (1308 m) below sea level.*

96 · 92 · 92

Scale 1:3,250,000

projection: Lambert Conformal Conic

Map key

Population: 500,000 to 1 million · 100,000 to 500,000 · 50,000 to 100,000 · 10,000 to 50,000 · below 10,000

Elevation: 2000m / 6562ft · 1000m / 3281ft · 500m / 1640ft · 250m / 820ft · 100m / 328ft · sea level

NORWEGIAN SEA · NORD-TRØNDELAG · SØR-TRØNDELAG · MØRE OG ROMSDAL · SOGN OG FJORDANE · OPPLAND · HEDMARK · JÄMTLAND · VÄSTERNORRLAND · GÄVLEBORG · Gulf of Bothnia · Trondheim

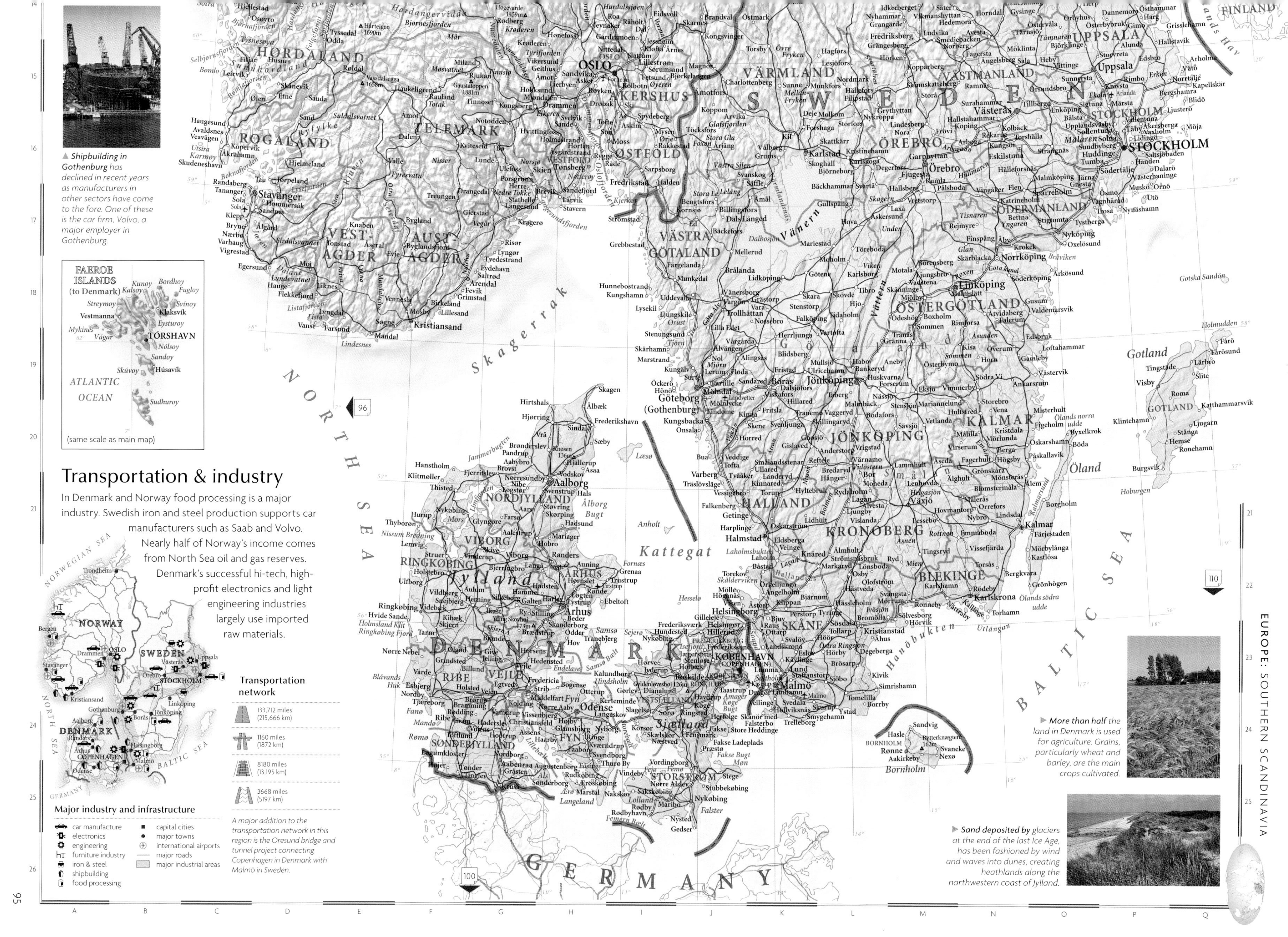
NORWAY
SWEDEN
DENMARK
GERMANY
FINLAND
NORTH SEA
BALTIC SEA
Skagerrak
Kattegat
Hanöbukten
Ålands Hav
HORDALAND
ROGALAND
TELEMARK
VEST-AGDER
AUST-AGDER
ØSTFOLD
AKERSHUS
VÄRMLAND
VÄSTMANLAND
UPPSALA
STOCKHOLM
ÖREBRO
SÖDERMANLAND
ÖSTERGÖTLAND
VÄSTRA GÖTALAND
JÖNKÖPING
KALMAR
HALLAND
KRONOBERG
BLEKINGE
SKÅNE
NORDJYLLAND
VIBORG
RINGKØBING
ÅRHUS
VEJLE
RIBE
SØNDERJYLLAND
FYN
STORSTRØM
Jylland
Sjælland
Gotland
Öland
Bornholm
Vänern
Vättern
OSLO
STOCKHOLM
KØBENHAVN (COPENHAGEN)
Göteborg (Gothenburg)
Malmö
Aalborg
Århus
Odense
Kristiansand
Stavanger
96
100
110
FAEROE ISLANDS (to Denmark)
TÓRSHAVN
ATLANTIC OCEAN
(same scale as main map)

▲ **Shipbuilding in** Gothenburg has declined in recent years as manufacturers in other sectors have come to the fore. One of these is the car firm, Volvo, a major employer in Gothenburg.

Transportation & industry

In Denmark and Norway food processing is a major industry. Swedish iron and steel production supports car manufacturers such as Saab and Volvo. Nearly half of Norway's income comes from North Sea oil and gas reserves. Denmark's successful hi-tech, high-profit electronics and light engineering industries largely use imported raw materials.

Transportation network

- 133,712 miles (215,666 km)
- 1160 miles (1872 km)
- 8180 miles (13,195 km)
- 3668 miles (5197 km)

A major addition to the transportation network in this region is the Oresund bridge and tunnel project connecting Copenhagen in Denmark with Malmö in Sweden.

Major industry and infrastructure

- car manufacture
- electronics
- engineering
- furniture industry
- iron & steel
- shipbuilding
- food processing
- capital cities
- major towns
- international airports
- major roads
- major industrial areas

▶ **More than half** the land in Denmark is used for agriculture. Grains, particularly wheat and barley, are the main crops cultivated.

▶ **Sand deposited by** glaciers at the end of the last Ice Age, has been fashioned by wind and waves into dunes, creating heathlands along the northwestern coast of Jylland.

The British Isles

UNITED KINGDOM, IRELAND

The British Isles have for centuries played a central role in European and world history. England, Wales, Scotland, and Northern Ireland together form the United Kingdom (UK), while the southern portion of Ireland is an independent country, self-governing since 1921. Although England has tended to be the politically and economically dominant partner in the UK, the Scots, Welsh, and Irish maintain independent cultures, distinct national identities and languages. Southeastern England is the most densely populated part of this crowded region, with over eight million people living in and around the London area.

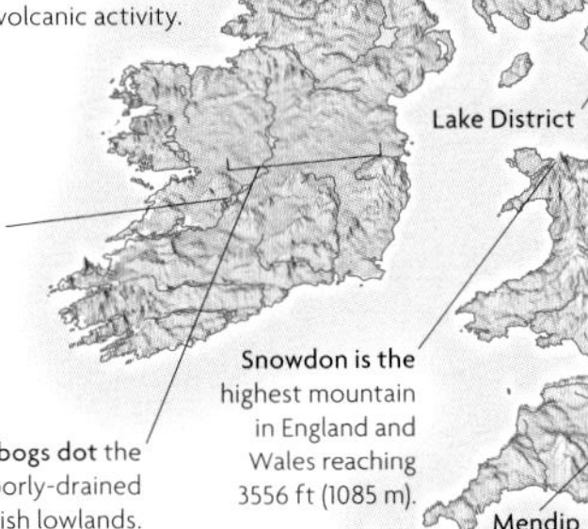

▲ *The valley of* Glen Coe *in the Scottish Highlands is a U-shaped valley, typical of the north and west of the British Isles, where glaciers shaped much of the landscape.*

Transportation & industry

The British Isles' industrial base was founded primarily on coal, iron, and textiles, based largely in the north. Today, the most productive sectors include hi-tech industries clustered mainly in southeastern England, chemicals, finance, and the service sector, particularly tourism.

Major industry and infrastructure

- car manufacture
- chemicals
- engineering
- hi-tech industry
- iron & steel
- tourism
- capital cities
- major towns
- international airports
- major roads
- major industrial areas

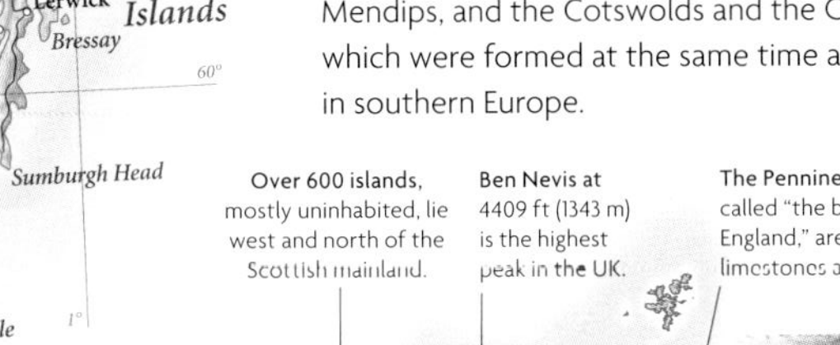
ATLANTIC OCEAN
NORTH SEA
Aberdeen
Dundee
Edinburgh
Glasgow
UNITED KINGDOM
Newcastle upon Tyne
Belfast
Leeds
Liverpool
Manchester
IRELAND
DUBLIN
Nottingham
Birmingham
Norwich
Cork
Oxford
Cardiff
Bristol
LONDON
English Channel

Transportation network

285,947 miles (460,240 km)	2023 miles (3578 km)
11,825 miles (19,032km)	3976 miles (6400 km)

The UK's congested roads have become a major focus of environmental concern in recent years. No longer an island, the UK was finally linked to continental Europe by the Channel Tunnel in 1994.

◄ *Clew Bay in western Ireland, is characteristic of the heavily indented west coast, where deep wide-mouthed bays separate the mountains of Mayo, Donegal, and Kerry as they thrust out into the Atlantic Ocean.*

Shetland Islands
Herma Ness
Unst
Yell
Fetlar
Hillswick
St Magnus Bay
Sullom Voe
Out Skerries
Whalsay
Papa Stour
Mainland
Lerwick
Bressay
Foula
Scalloway
West Burra
Fitful Head
Sumburgh Head
Fair Isle
Orkney Islands
North Ronaldsay
Papa Westray
Westray
Sanday
Rousay
Eday
Stronsay
Shapinsay
Stromness
Kirkwall
Hoy
Scapa Flow
Burray
St Margaret's Hope
South Ronaldsay
Pentland Firth
Duncansby Head
John o'Groats
Dunnet Head
Thurso
Sule Skerry
Stack Skerry
North Rona
Sula Sgeir
Cape Wrath
Durness
Strathy Point
Tongue
Halkirk
Caithness
Noss Head
Wick
Ben Hope 927m
Ben Klibreck 721m
Kinbrace
Helmsdale
Brora
Golspie
Dornoch
Tain
Dornoch Firth
Tarbat Ness
Moray Firth
Lossiemouth
Elgin
Macduff
Banff
Kinnaird Head
Fraserburgh
Peterhead
Buchan Ness
Butt of Lewis
Port of Ness
Carloway
Stornoway
Isle of Lewis
Broad Bay
Eye Peninsula
Eddrachillis Bay
Lochinver
Enard Bay
Ullapool
The Minch
Harris
Tarbert
Scarp
Taransay
Pabbay
Sound of Harris
Shiant Islands
The Little Minch
North Uist
Lochmaddy
Benbecula
Monach Islands
South Uist
Lochboisdale
Eriskay
Barra
Barra Head
Flannan Isles
St Kilda
Sea of the Hebrides
Uig
Portree
Isle of Skye
Raasay
Inner Sound
Loch Torridon
Loch Maree
Kyle of Lochalsh
Stromeferry
Broadford
Canna
Rhum
Eigg
Muck
Mallaig
Loch Morar
Point of Ardnamurchan
Coll
Tobermory
Tiree
Isle of Mull
Ben More 966m
Iona
Oban
Firth of Lorn
Colonsay
Jura
Islay
Port Askaig
Port Ellen
Gigha Island
Lochgilphead
Tarbert
Inveraray
Loch Awe
Loch Fyne
Isle of Bute
Rothesay
Brodick
Greenock
Helensburgh
Dumbarton
Clydebank
Glasgow
Paisley
Motherwell
East Kilbride
Kilmarnock
Irvine
Hamilton
Wishaw
Lanark
Airdrie
Coatbridge
Cumbernauld
Livingston
Falkirk
Grangemouth
Stirling
Loch Lomond
Callander
Loch Katrine
Ben More 1174m
Ben Lawers 1214m
Loch Tay
Aberfeldy
Pitlochry
Loch Rannoch
Loch Ericht
Crieff
Perth
Kinross
Alloa
Dunfermline
Edinburgh
Kirkcaldy
Glenrothes
Cupar
St Andrews
Fife Ness
Firth of Forth
North Berwick
Haddington
Dundee
Firth of Tay
Carnoustie
Arbroath
Forfar
Brechin
Montrose
Kirriemuir
Blairgowrie
Braemar
Lochnagar 1154m
Ben Macdui 1309m
Cairn Gorm 1245m
Cairngorm Mountains
Grampian Mountains
Ben Nevis 1343m
Fort William
Loch Shiel
Glen Coe
Ballachulish
Fort Augustus
Loch Lochy
Glen Mor
Loch Ness
Carn Eige 1182m
Inverness
Grantown-on-Spey
Aviemore
Monadhliath Mountains
Nairn
Forres
Cromarty
Dingwall
Invergordon
Beauly
Beinn Dearg 1084m
Lairg
Loch Shin
Oykel
North West Highlands
Sutherland
Ross and Cromarty
Huntly
Keith
Buckie
Turriff
Ellon
Inverurie
Aberdeen
Girdle Ness
Stonehaven
Banchory
Aberdeen
Kincardine
Angus
SCOTLAND
St Abb's Head
Eyemouth
Berwick-upon-Tweed
Holy Island
Duns
Coldstream
Kelso
Newtown St Boswells
Galashiels
Peebles
East Lothian
Midlothian
Berwick
Outer Hebrides
Inner Hebrides
ATLANTIC OCEAN
64
92

The landscape

Rugged uplands dominate the landscape of Scotland, Wales, and northern England. All the peaks in the British Isles over 4000 ft (1219 m) lie in highland Scotland. Lowland England rises into several ranges of rolling hills, including the older Mendips, and the Cotswolds and the Chilterns, which were formed at the same time as the Alps in southern Europe.

Over 600 islands, mostly uninhabited, lie west and north of the Scottish mainland.
Ben Nevis at 4409 ft (1343 m) is the highest peak in the UK.
The Pennines, sometimes called "the backbone of England," are formed of limestones and grits.
The lowlands of Scotland, drained by the Tay, Forth, and Clyde rivers, are centered on a rift valley. The region contains valuable coal reserves.
Thousands of hexagonal basalt columns form Giant's Causeway on the north coast of Antrim. These were created by volcanic activity.
Lake District
The British Isles have no large-scale river systems. The Shannon is the longest, at 230 miles (370 km).
Peat bogs dot the poorly-drained Irish lowlands.
Snowdon is the highest mountain in England and Wales reaching 3556 ft (1085 m).
Mendip Hills
Chiltern Hills
The Fens are a low-lying area reclaimed from the sea.
The Cotswold Hills are characterized by a series of limestone ridges overlooking clay vales.
Durdle Door
Black Ven, Lyme Regis

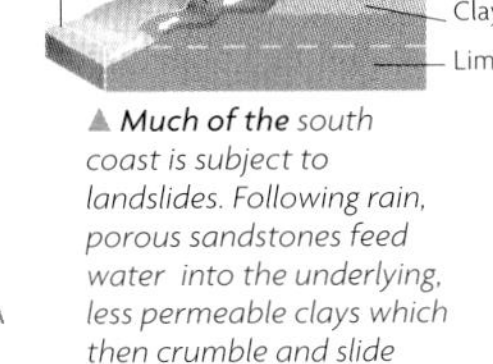

▲ *Ullswater in the Lake District fills a deep valley formed by glacial erosion.*

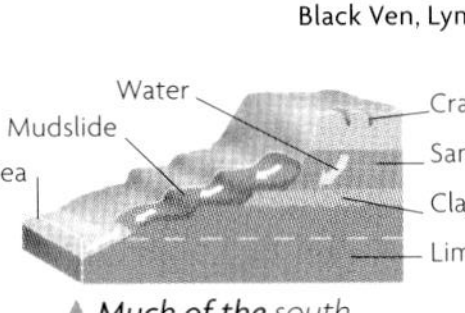

◄ *Dartmoor, studded with tors, is an exposed part of a vast granite dome, formed when molten rock intruded into the Earth's crust.*

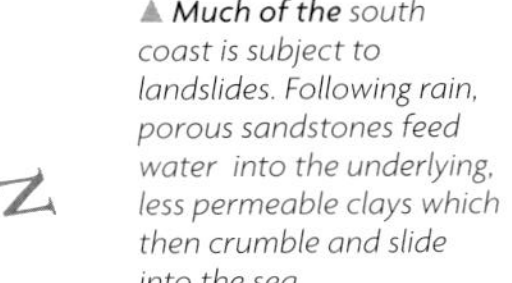

▲ *Coastal erosion around the British Isles forms striking features such as this limestone arch, Durdle Door in Dorset.*

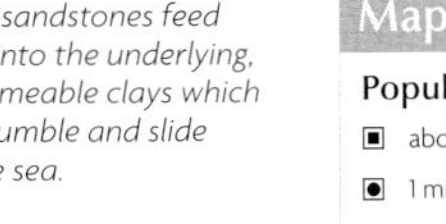
Water
Mudslide
Sea
Cracks
Sandstone
Clay
Limestone

▲ *Much of the south coast is subject to landslides. Following rain, porous sandstones feed water into the underlying, less permeable clays which then crumble and slide into the sea.*

Map key

Population	Elevation
above 5 million	1000m / 3281ft
1 million to 5 million	500m / 1640ft
500,000 to 1 million	250m / 820ft
100,000 to 500,000	100m / 328ft
50,000 to 100,000	sea level
10,000 to 50,000	
below 10,000	

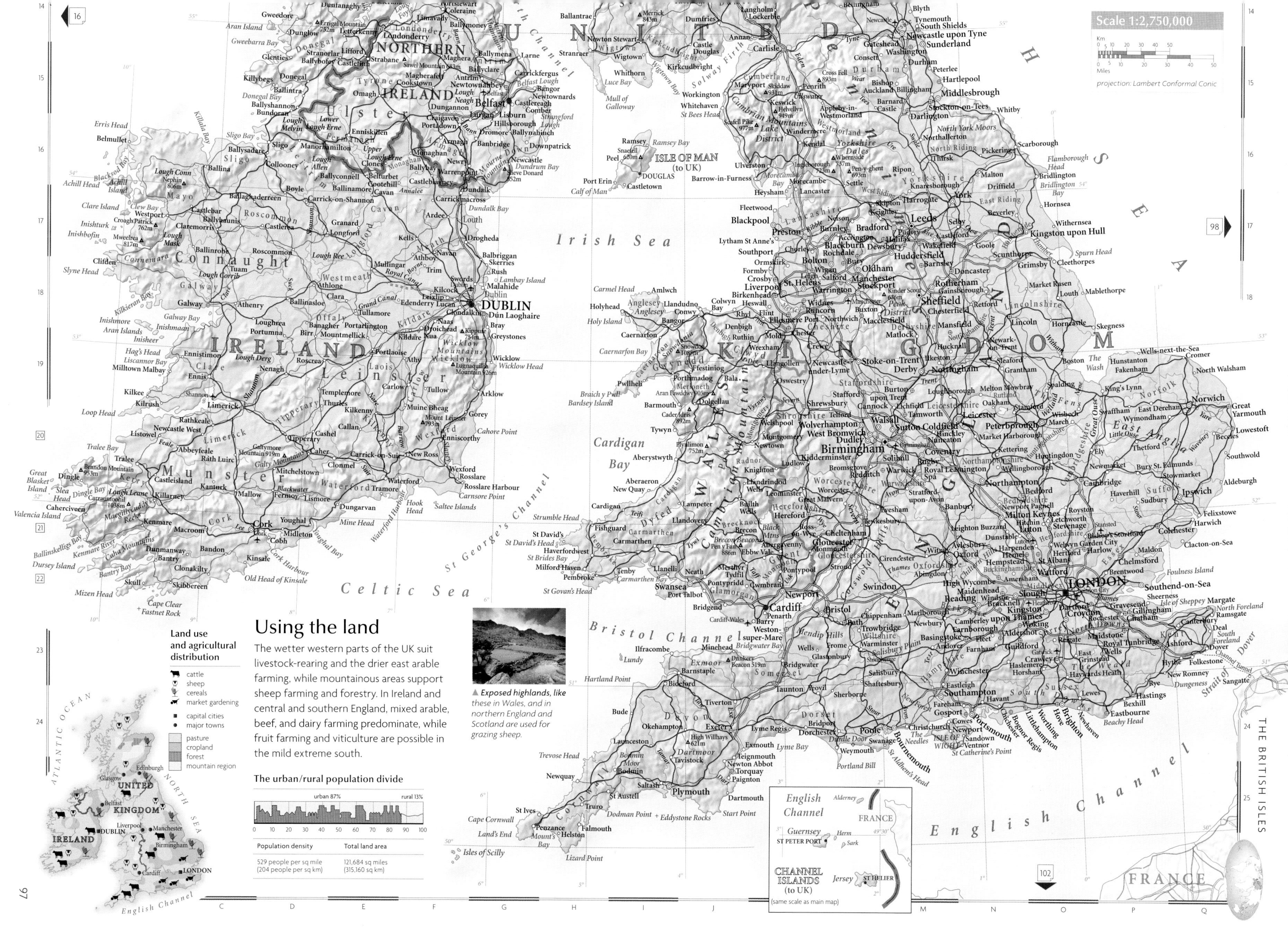
Scale 1:2,750,000
projection: Lambert Conformal Conic
Irish Sea
Celtic Sea
St George's Channel
Bristol Channel
English Channel
North Sea
IRELAND
UNITED KINGDOM
NORTHERN IRELAND
ISLE OF MAN (to UK)
CHANNEL ISLANDS (to UK)
(same scale as main map)
FRANCE
DUBLIN
LONDON
Belfast
Cardiff
Birmingham
Manchester
Liverpool
Leeds
Bristol
Edinburgh
Glasgow

Using the land

The wetter western parts of the UK suit livestock-rearing and the drier east arable farming, while mountainous areas support sheep farming and forestry. In Ireland and central and southern England, mixed arable, beef, and dairy farming predominate, while fruit farming and viticulture are possible in the mild extreme south.

▲ *Exposed highlands, like these in Wales, and in northern England and Scotland are used for grazing sheep.*

The urban/rural population divide

urban 87% | rural 13%

Population density	Total land area
529 people per sq mile (204 people per sq km)	121,684 sq miles (315,160 sq km)

Land use and agricultural distribution

- cattle
- sheep
- cereals
- market gardening
- capital cities
- major towns
- pasture
- cropland
- forest
- mountain region

The Low Countries

BELGIUM, LUXEMBOURG, NETHERLANDS

One of northwestern Europe's strategic crossroads, the Low Countries are united by a common history in which they have often been a battleground in European wars. For over a thousand years they were ruled by foreign powers. Even after they achieved independence, the three countries maintained close links, later forming the world's first totally free labor and goods market, the Benelux Economic Union, which became the core of the European Community (now the European Union or EU). These states have remained at the forefront of wider European cooperation; Brussels, The Hague, and Luxembourg are hosts to major institutions of the EU.

The landscape

The main geographical regions of the Netherlands are the northern glacial heathlands, the low-lying lands of the Rhine and Maas/Meuse, the reclaimed polders, and the dune coast and islands. Belgium includes part of the Ardennes, together with the coalfields on its northern flanks, and the fertile Flanders plain.

Schoorl

◀ *Heathlands, like these at Schoorl, are found along the coast of the Netherlands. Much of the coast was breached by the sea in the 5th century, creating its distinctive inlets and islands.*

Dune system

Sea

Polder

Drainage ditch

▲ *Extensive sand dune systems along the coast have prevented flooding of the land. Behind the dunes, marshy land is drained to form polders, usable land suitable for agriculture.*

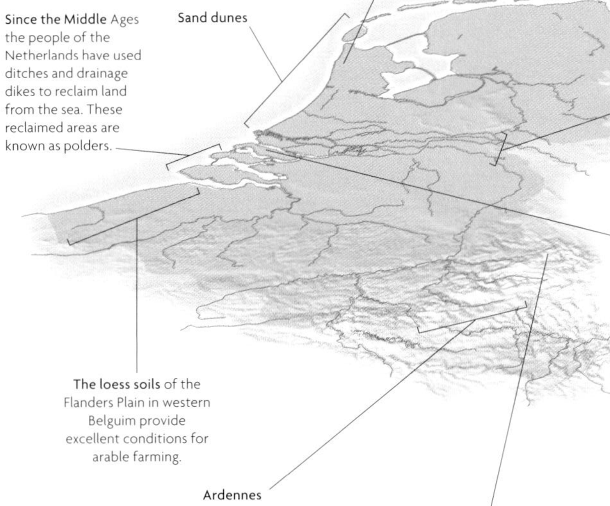

▲ *One-third of the Netherlands lies below sea level and flooding is a constant threat. Barrages have been built across the mouths of many rivers to contain floodwaters.*

Since the Middle Ages the people of the Netherlands have used ditches and drainage dikes to reclaim land from the sea. These reclaimed areas are known as polders.

Sand dunes

The parallel valleys of the Maas/Meuse and Rhine rivers were created when the Rhine was deflected from its previous course by the ice sheet which formed during the last Ice Age.

Silts and sands eroded by the Rhine throughout its course are deposited to form a delta on the west coast of the Netherlands.

The loess soils of the Flanders Plain in western Belgium provide excellent conditions for arable farming.

Ardennes

▶ *Uplifted and folded 220 million years ago, the Ardennes have since been reduced to relatively level plateaus, then sharply incised by rivers such as the Maas/Meuse.*

Hautes Fagnes is the highest part of Belgium. The bogs and streams in this upland region result from high rainfall and low temperatures.

Major industry and infrastructure

- aerospace
- finance
- engineering
- hi-tech industry
- pharmaceuticals
- textiles
- capital cities
- major towns
- international airports
- major roads
- major industrial areas

NETHERLANDS AMSTERDAM THE HAGUE Rotterdam Utrecht Enschede Nijmegen Eindhoven Breda Antwerp Brugge Ghent Kortrijk BRUSSELS Maastricht BELGIUM Liège Charleroi LUXEMBOURG LUXEMBOURG Differdange Groningen NORTH SEA GERMANY FRANCE

Transportation & industry

In the western Netherlands, a massive, sprawling industrialized zone encompasses many new hi-tech and service industries. Belgium's central region has emerged as the country's light manufacturing and services center. Luxembourg city is home to more than 160 banks and the European headquarters of many international companies.

Transportation network

140,588 miles (226,281 km)	2565 miles (4129 km)	4099 miles (6598 km)	4134 miles (6653 km)

The Low Countries hold a key position on the North Sea, containing Europe's two largest ports, Rotterdam and Antwerp, which are connected to a comprehensive system of inland waterways.

100

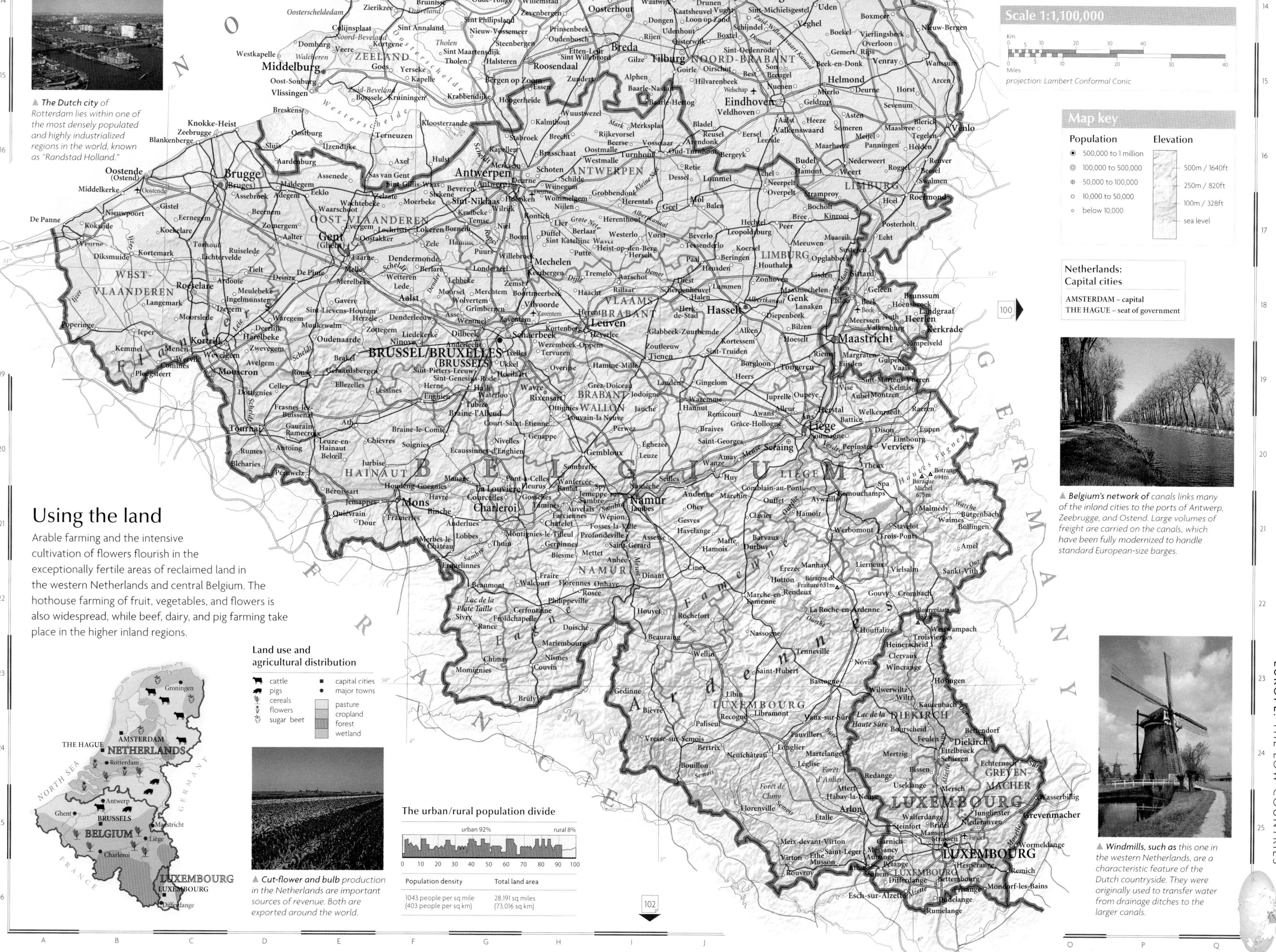
Scale 1:1,100,000
Km 0 5 10 20 30 40
Miles 0 5 10 20 30 40
projection: Lambert Conformal Conic
Map key
Population
500,000 to 1 million
100,000 to 500,000
50,000 to 100,000
10,000 to 50,000
below 10,000
Elevation
500m / 1640ft
250m / 820ft
100m / 328ft
sea level
Netherlands: Capital cities
AMSTERDAM – capital
THE HAGUE – seat of government
BELGIUM
LUXEMBOURG
GERMANY
FRANCE
NORTH SEA
BRUSSEL/BRUXELLES (BRUSSELS)
Antwerpen (Antwerp)
Gent (Ghent)
Brugge (Bruges)
Oostende (Ostend)
Liège
Namur
Charleroi
Mons
Leuven
Hasselt
Maastricht
Eindhoven
Breda
Tilburg
Middelburg
Arlon
Diekirch
Grevenmacher
LUXEMBOURG
Land use and agricultural distribution
cattle
pigs
cereals
flowers
sugar beet
capital cities
major towns
pasture
cropland
forest
wetland
The urban/rural population divide
urban 92%
rural 8%
Population density
1043 people per sq mile (403 people per sq km)
Total land area
28,191 sq miles (73,016 sq km)

▲ **The Dutch city** of Rotterdam lies within one of the most densely populated and highly industrialized regions in the world, known as "Randstad Holland."

▲ **Belgium's network of** canals links many of the inland cities to the ports of Antwerp, Zeebrugge, and Ostend. Large volumes of freight are carried on the canals, which have been fully modernized to handle standard European-size barges.

▲ **Windmills, such as** this one in the western Netherlands, are a characteristic feature of the Dutch countryside. They were originally used to transfer water from drainage ditches to the larger canals.

Using the land

Arable farming and the intensive cultivation of flowers flourish in the exceptionally fertile areas of reclaimed land in the western Netherlands and central Belgium. The hothouse farming of fruit, vegetables, and flowers is also widespread, while beef, dairy, and pig farming take place in the higher inland regions.

▲ **Cut-flower and bulb** production in the Netherlands are important sources of revenue. Both are exported around the world.

100
102

Germany

Despite the devastation of its industry and infrastructure during the Second World War and its separation from eastern Germany during the Cold War, West Germany made a rapid recovery in the following generation to become Europe's most formidable economic power. When the Berlin Wall was dismantled in 1989, the two halves of Germany were politically united for the first time in 40 years. Complete social and economic unity remain a longer term goal, as East German industry and society adapt to a free market. Germany has been a key player in the creation of the European Union (EU) and in moves toward a single European currency.

The landscape

The plains of northern Germany, the volcanic plateaus and mountains of the central uplands, and the Bavarian Alps are the three principal geographic regions in Germany. North to south the land rises steadily from barely 300 ft (90 m) in the plains to 6500 ft (2000 m) in the Bavarian Alps, which are a small but distinct region in the far south.

The heathlands of northern Germany are covered by glacial deposits of sandy outwash soil which makes them largely infertile. They support only sheep and solitary trees.

Lüneburg Heath (*Lüneburger Heide*)

Müritz lake covers 45 sq miles (117 sq km), but is only 108 ft (33 m) deep. It lies in a shallow valley formed by meltwater flowing out from a retreating ice sheet. These valleys are known as *Urstromtäler*.

Much of the landscape of northern Germany has been shaped by glaciation. During the last Ice Age, the ice sheet advanced as far the northern slopes of the central uplands.

Fault lines
Rhine
Downfaulted block

Part of the floor of the Rhine Rift Valley was let down between two parallel faults in the Earth's crust.

The Rhine is Germany's principal waterway and one of Europe's longest rivers, flowing 820 miles (1320 km).

Rhine Rift Valley

Zugspitze, the highest peak in Germany at 9719 ft (2962 m), was formed during the Alpine mountain-building period, 30 million years ago.

The Danube rises in the Black Forest (*Schwarzwald*) and flows east, across a wide valley, on its course to the Black Sea.

The Harz Mountains were formed 300 million years ago. They are block-faulted mountains, formed when a section of the Earth's crust was thrust up between two faults.

Elbe river

The Elbe flows in wide meanders across the north German plain to the North Sea. At its mouth it is 10 miles (16 km) wide.

Using the land

Germany has a large, efficient agricultural sector, and produces more than three-quarters of its own food. The major crops grown are cereals and sugar beet on the more fertile soils, and root crops, rye, oats, and fodder on the poorer soils of the northern plains and central uplands. Southern Germany is also a principal producer of high quality wines. Vineyards cover the slopes surrounding the Rhine and its tributaries.

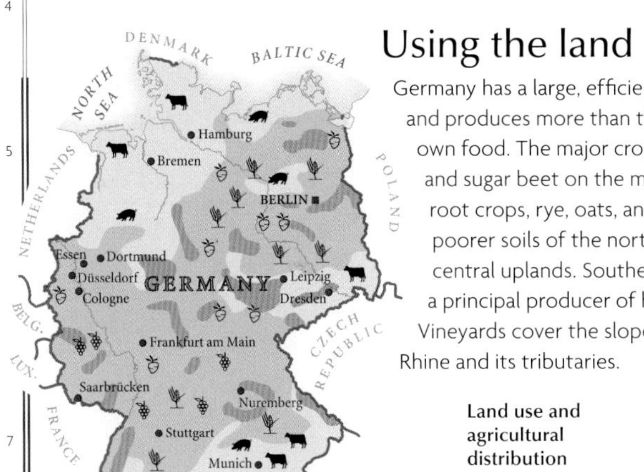
DENMARK
BALTIC SEA
NORTH SEA
NETHERLANDS
POLAND
BELG.
LUX.
FRANCE
SWITZ.
AUSTRIA
CZECH REPUBLIC
GERMANY
Hamburg
Bremen
BERLIN
Essen
Dortmund
Düsseldorf
Cologne
Leipzig
Dresden
Frankfurt am Main
Saarbrücken
Nuremberg
Stuttgart
Munich

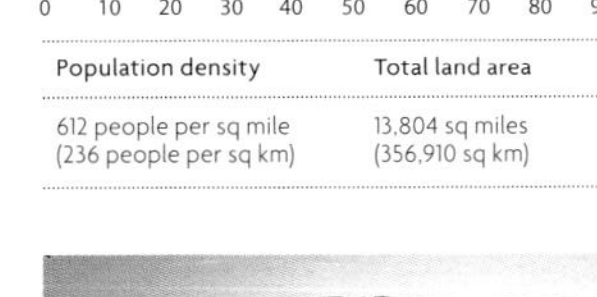
Land use and agricultural distribution
cattle
pigs
cereals
sugar beet
vineyards
capital cities
major towns
pasture
cropland
forest

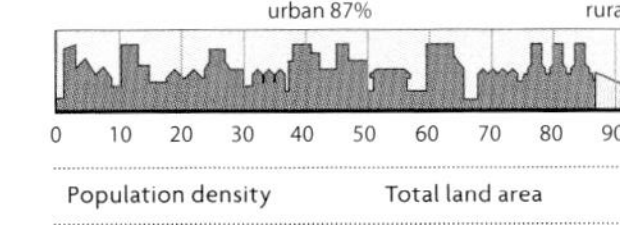

The urban/rural population divide

urban 87% rural 13%

0 10 20 30 40 50 60 70 80 90 100

Population density	Total land area
612 people per sq mile (236 people per sq km)	13,804 sq miles (356,910 sq km)

The Moselle river flows through the Rhine State Uplands (Rheinisches Schiefergebirge). *During a period of uplift, preexisting river meanders were deeply incised, to form its present dramatic contours.*

Scale 1:2,500,000

Km 0 5 10 20 30 40 50 60 70
Miles 0 5 10 20 30 40 50 60 70

projection: Lambert Conformal Conic

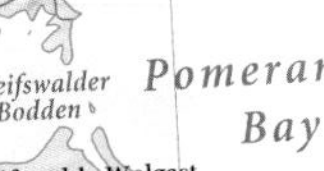
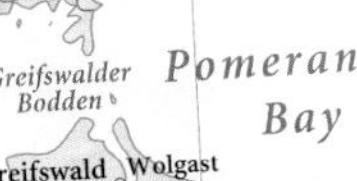

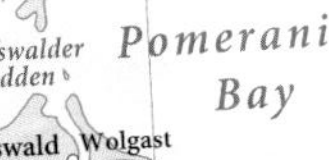
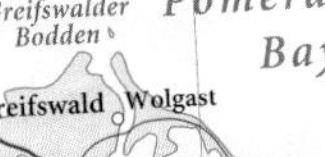

92
96
98
110

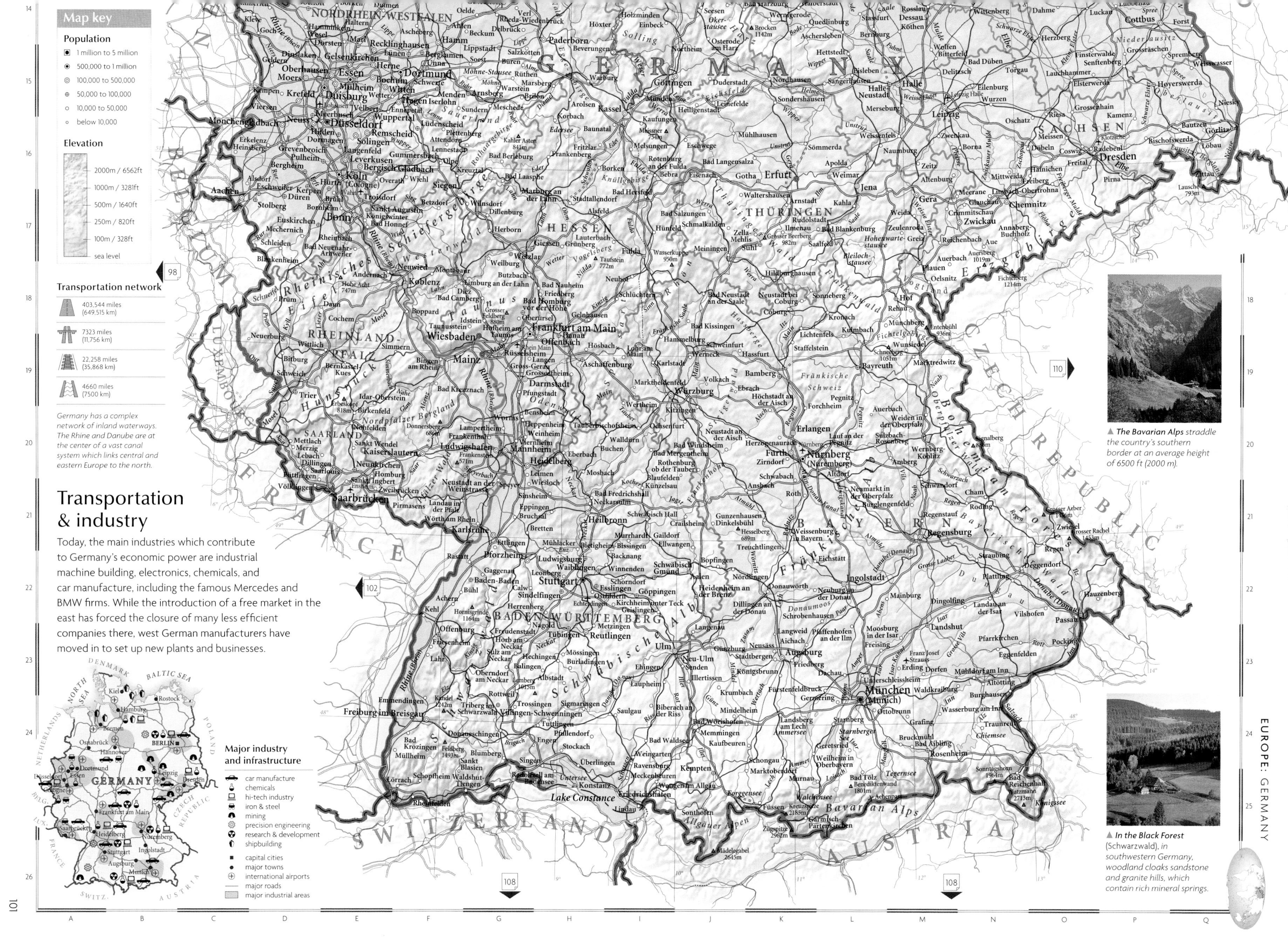
Map key
Population
1 million to 5 million
500,000 to 1 million
100,000 to 500,000
50,000 to 100,000
10,000 to 50,000
below 10,000
Elevation
2000m / 6562ft
1000m / 3281ft
500m / 1640ft
250m / 820ft
100m / 328ft
sea level
Transportation network
403,544 miles (649,515 km)
7323 miles (11,756 km)
22,258 miles (35,868 km)
4660 miles (7500 km)
Germany has a complex network of inland waterways. The Rhine and Danube are at the center of a vast canal system which links central and eastern Europe to the north.
GERMANY
NORDRHEIN-WESTFALEN
HESSEN
THÜRINGEN
SACHSEN
RHEINLAND-PFALZ
SAARLAND
BADEN-WÜRTTEMBERG
BAYERN
BELGIUM
LUXEMBOURG
FRANCE
SWITZERLAND
AUSTRIA
CZECH REPUBLIC
98
102
108
108
110
Major industry and infrastructure
car manufacture
chemicals
hi-tech industry
iron & steel
mining
precision engineering
research & development
shipbuilding
capital cities
major towns
international airports
major roads
major industrial areas

Transportation & industry

Today, the main industries which contribute to Germany's economic power are industrial machine building, electronics, chemicals, and car manufacture, including the famous Mercedes and BMW firms. While the introduction of a free market in the east has forced the closure of many less efficient companies there, west German manufacturers have moved in to set up new plants and businesses.

▲ *The Bavarian Alps straddle the country's southern border at an average height of 6500 ft (2000 m).*

▲ *In the Black Forest* (Schwarzwald), *in southwestern Germany, woodland cloaks sandstone and granite hills, which contain rich mineral springs.*

France

FRANCE, MONACO

Europe's second largest nation and the founder of modern Republican government, France is a major center of culture and fashion, and a leading producer of both agricultural and industrial goods. It has played a leading role in European events for centuries, and remains a key player in the push toward European unity. The Paris Basin is the most highly populated area; Île de France is home to over 11 million people. Large parts of France remain thinly populated, particularly the mountainous Massif Central, Pyrenees, and southern Alps.

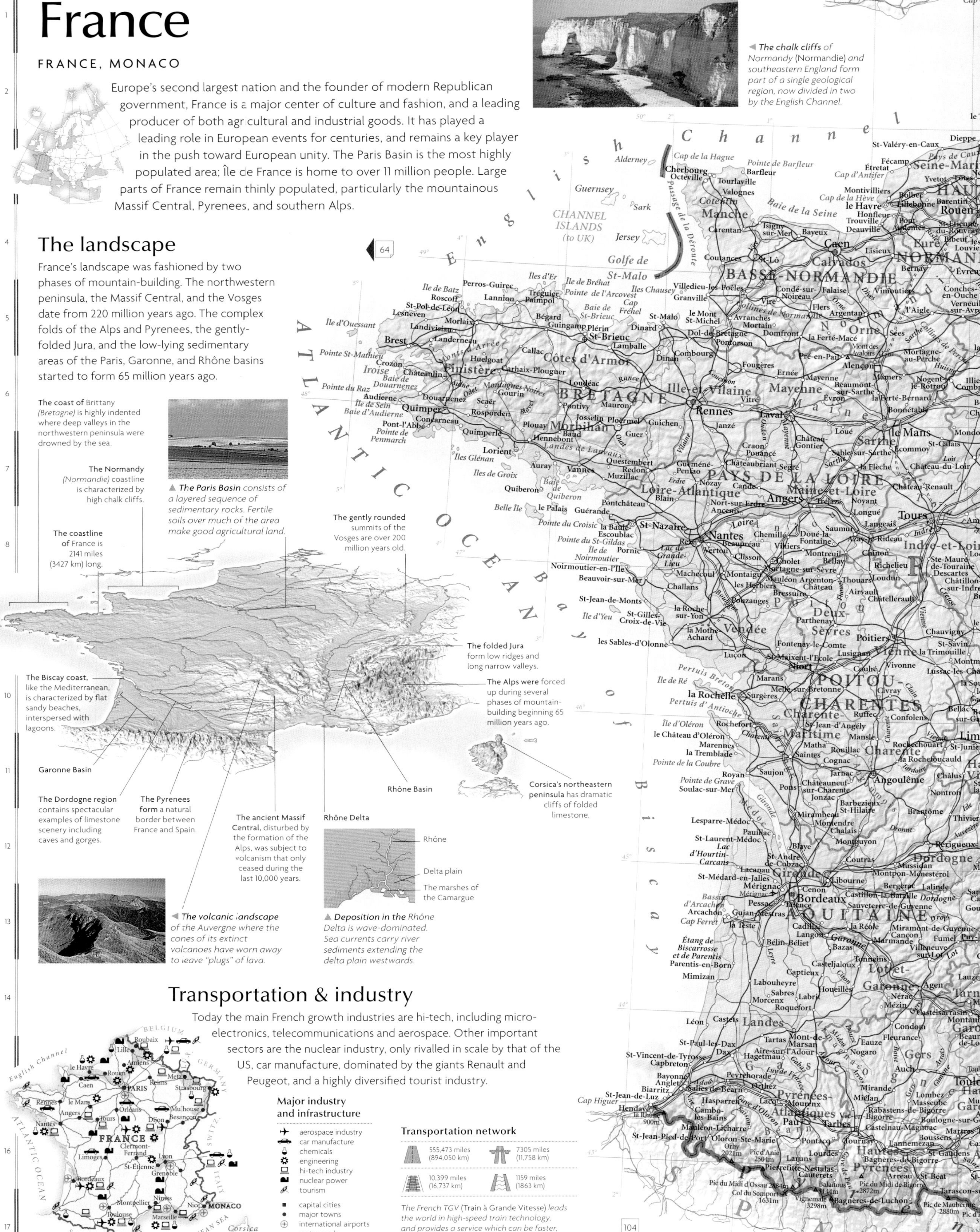
English Channel
CHANNEL ISLANDS (to UK)
Alderney
Guernsey
Sark
Jersey
Golfe de St-Malo
ATLANTIC OCEAN
Bay of Biscay
BASSE-NORMANDIE
BRETAGNE
PAYS DE LA LOIRE
POITOU-CHARENTES
AQUITAINE
Cherbourg
Caen
Brest
Rennes
Nantes
Angers
Tours
Poitiers
la Rochelle
Bordeaux
Pau
Rhône
Delta plain
The marshes of the Camargue
BELGIUM
GERMANY
SWITZ.
ITALY
SPAIN
MEDITERRANEAN SEA
FRANCE
MONACO
Corsica
PARIS
Major industry and infrastructure
aerospace industry
car manufacture
chemicals
engineering
hi-tech industry
nuclear power
tourism
capital cities
major towns
international airports
major roads
major industrial areas
Transportation network
555,473 miles (894,050 km)
7305 miles (11,758 km)
10,399 miles (16,737 km)
1159 miles (1863 km)

The chalk cliffs of Normandy (Normandie) and southeastern England form part of a single geological region, now divided in two by the English Channel.

The landscape

France's landscape was fashioned by two phases of mountain-building. The northwestern peninsula, the Massif Central, and the Vosges date from 220 million years ago. The complex folds of the Alps and Pyrenees, the gently-folded Jura, and the low-lying sedimentary areas of the Paris, Garonne, and Rhône basins started to form 65 million years ago.

The coast of Brittany *(Bretagne)* is highly indented where deep valleys in the northwestern peninsula were drowned by the sea.

The Normandy *(Normandie)* coastline is characterized by high chalk cliffs.

The coastline of France is 2141 miles (3427 km) long.

The Paris Basin consists of a layered sequence of sedimentary rocks. Fertile soils over much of the area make good agricultural land.

The gently rounded summits of the Vosges are over 200 million years old.

The folded Jura form low ridges and long narrow valleys.

The Alps were forced up during several phases of mountain-building beginning 65 million years ago.

The Biscay coast, like the Mediterranean, is characterized by flat sandy beaches, interspersed with lagoons.

Garonne Basin

The Dordogne region contains spectacular examples of limestone scenery including caves and gorges.

The Pyrenees form a natural border between France and Spain.

The ancient Massif Central, disturbed by the formation of the Alps, was subject to volcanism that only ceased during the last 10,000 years.

Rhône Basin

Corsica's northeastern peninsula has dramatic cliffs of folded limestone.

Rhône Delta

The volcanic landscape of the Auvergne where the cones of its extinct volcanoes have worn away to leave "plugs" of lava.

Deposition in the Rhône Delta is wave-dominated. Sea currents carry river sediments extending the delta plain westwards.

Transportation & industry

Today the main French growth industries are hi-tech, including micro-electronics, telecommunications and aerospace. Other important sectors are the nuclear industry, only rivalled in scale by that of the US, car manufacture, dominated by the giants Renault and Peugeot, and a highly diversified tourist industry.

The French TGV (Train à Grande Vitesse) leads the world in high-speed train technology, and provides a service which can be faster, door-to-door, than air travel.

64

104

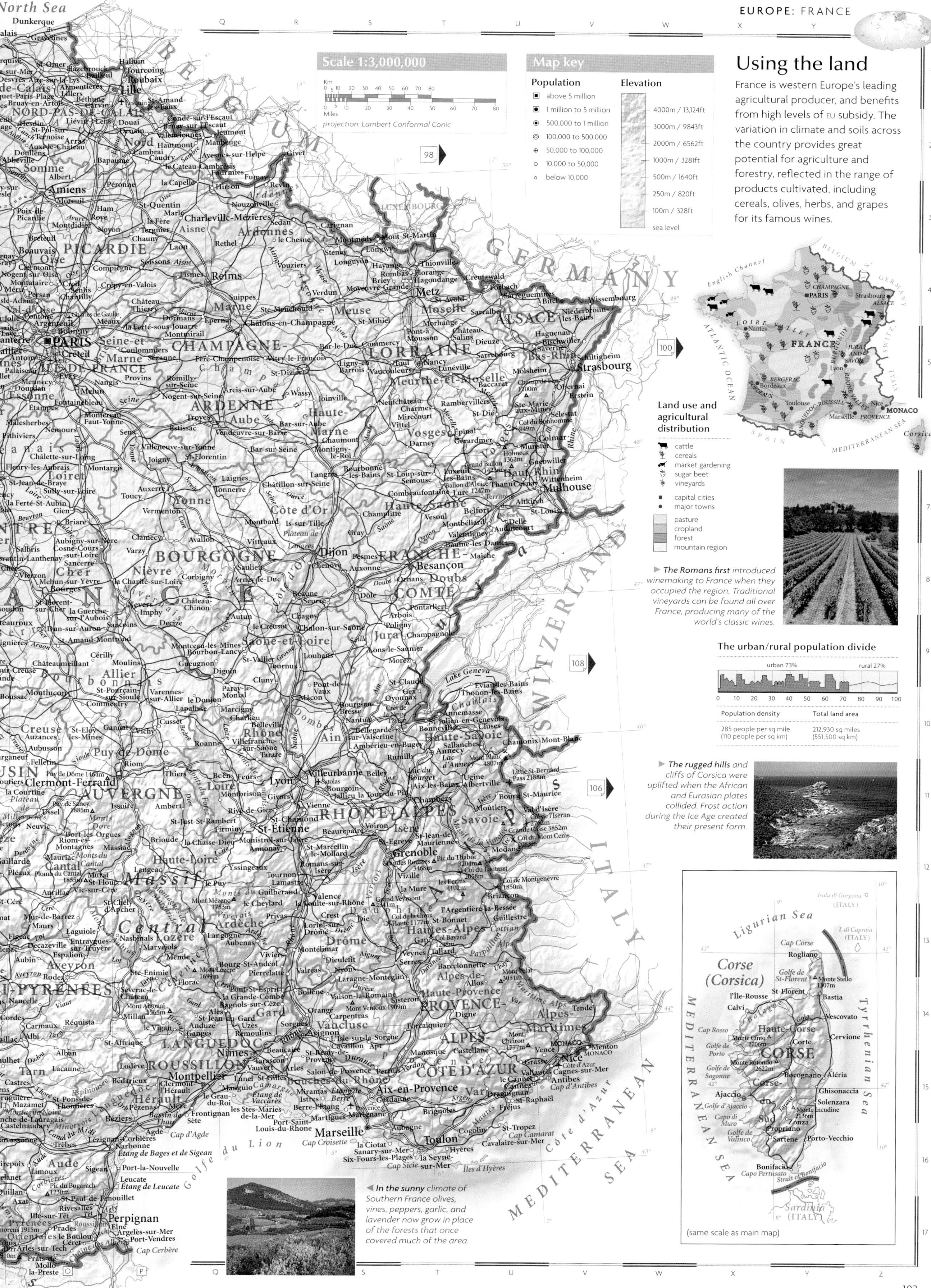
Scale 1:3,000,000
Km
Miles
projection: Lambert Conformal Conic
Map key
Population
above 5 million
1 million to 5 million
500,000 to 1 million
100,000 to 500,000
50,000 to 100,000
10,000 to 50,000
below 10,000
Elevation
4000m / 13,124ft
3000m / 9843ft
2000m / 6562ft
1000m / 3281ft
500m / 1640ft
250m / 820ft
100m / 328ft
sea level
Land use and agricultural distribution
cattle
cereals
market gardening
sugar beet
vineyards
capital cities
major towns
pasture
cropland
forest
mountain region
The urban/rural population divide
urban 73%
rural 27%
Population density
285 people per sq mile (110 people per sq km)
Total land area
212,930 sq miles (551,500 sq km)
Corse (Corsica)
(same scale as main map)

Using the land

France is western Europe's leading agricultural producer, and benefits from high levels of EU subsidy. The variation in climate and soils across the country provides great potential for agriculture and forestry, reflected in the range of products cultivated, including cereals, olives, herbs, and grapes for its famous wines.

▶ *The Romans first introduced winemaking to France when they occupied the region. Traditional vineyards can be found all over France, producing many of the world's classic wines.*

▶ *The rugged hills and cliffs of Corsica were uplifted when the African and Eurasian plates collided. Frost action during the Ice Age created their present form.*

◀ *In the sunny climate of Southern France olives, vines, peppers, garlic, and lavender now grow in place of the forests that once covered much of the area.*

The Iberian peninsula

ANDORRA, GIBRALTAR, PORTUGAL, SPAIN (Azores, Canary Islands, Madeira on p.64)

The Iberian peninsula is separated from the rest of Europe by the Pyrenees, and at its most southerly point is only 5 miles (8 km) from North Africa. The location of Iberia has been central to its diverse history. The Greeks, Carthaginians, Romans, Visigoths, and most recently the Moors, invaded Iberia at various times. For much of the 20th century, both Spain and Portugal were governed by right-wing dictators. Since the establishment of democratic governments in the mid-1970s, modernization has been rapid and both countries are now among the most popular of European holiday destinations.

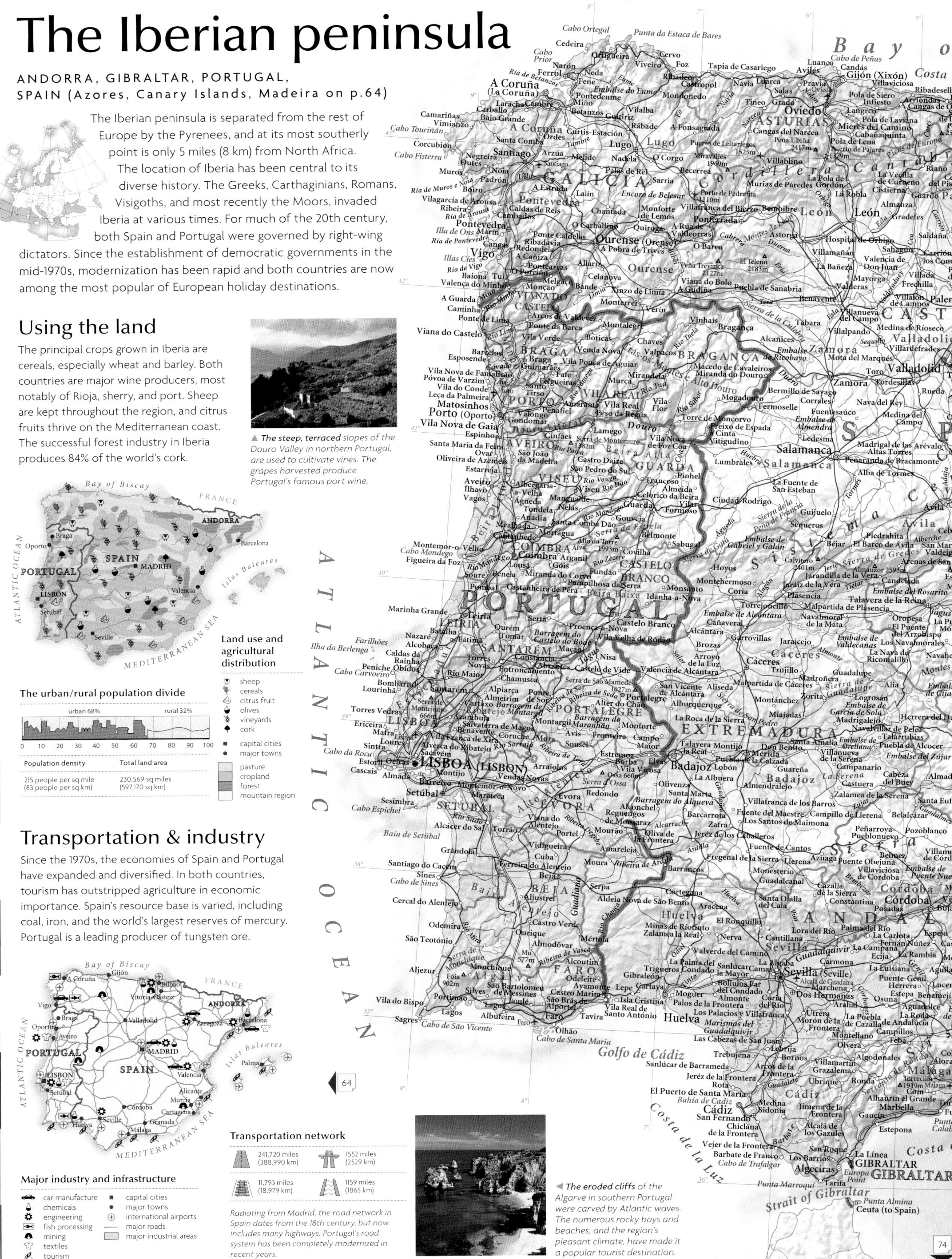

Bay of Biscay
ATLANTIC OCEAN
PORTUGAL
GALICIA
ASTURIAS
Cordillera Cantábrica
Sistema Central
EXTREMADURA
ANDALUCÍA
Golfo de Cádiz
Costa de la Luz
Strait of Gibraltar
GIBRALTAR
MOROCCO
Ceuta (to Spain)
Lisboa (Lisbon)
Porto (Oporto)
Sevilla (Seville)
Salamanca
Valladolid

Using the land

The principal crops grown in Iberia are cereals, especially wheat and barley. Both countries are major wine producers, most notably of Rioja, sherry, and port. Sheep are kept throughout the region, and citrus fruits thrive on the Mediterranean coast. The successful forest industry in Iberia produces 84% of the world's cork.

▲ *The steep, terraced slopes of the Douro Valley in northern Portugal, are used to cultivate vines. The grapes harvested produce Portugal's famous port wine.*

Land use and agricultural distribution

- sheep
- cereals
- citrus fruit
- olives
- vineyards
- cork
- capital cities
- major towns
- pasture
- cropland
- forest
- mountain region

The urban/rural population divide

urban 68% — rural 32%

0 10 20 30 40 50 60 70 80 90 100

Population density	Total land area
215 people per sq mile (83 people per sq km)	230,569 sq miles (597,170 sq km)

Transportation & industry

Since the 1970s, the economies of Spain and Portugal have expanded and diversified. In both countries, tourism has outstripped agriculture in economic importance. Spain's resource base is varied, including coal, iron, and the world's largest reserves of mercury. Portugal is a leading producer of tungsten ore.

Major industry and infrastructure

- car manufacture
- chemicals
- engineering
- fish processing
- mining
- textiles
- tourism
- capital cities
- major towns
- international airports
- major roads
- major industrial areas

Transportation network

241,720 miles (388,990 km)	1552 miles (2529 km)	11,793 miles (18,979 km)	1159 miles (1865 km)

Radiating from Madrid, the road network in Spain dates from the 18th century, but now includes many highways. Portugal's road system has been completely modernized in recent years.

◄ *The eroded cliffs of the Algarve in southern Portugal were carved by Atlantic waves. The numerous rocky bays and beaches, and the region's pleasant climate, have made it a popular tourist destination.*

64

74

102

▶ *The climate in northwestern Spain is milder in both summer and winter than in the rest of the country, creating a verdant environment, more commonly associated with northwestern Europe.*

Map key

Population

- 1 million to 5 million
- 500,000 to 1 million
- 100,000 to 500,000
- 50,000 to 100,000
- 10,000 to 50,000
- below 10,000

Elevation

- 3000m / 9843ft
- 2000m / 6562ft
- 1000m / 3281ft
- 500m / 1640ft
- 250m / 820ft
- 100m / 328ft
- sea level

Scale 1:3,000,000

Km 0 5 10 20 30 40 50 60 70 80

Miles 0 5 10 20 30 40 50 60 70 80

projection: Lambert Conformal Conic

The landscape

A vast plateau, the Meseta dominates the centre of the peninsula, enclosed by the Cordillera Cantábrica to the north and the Sierra Morena to the south. It is drained by three major rivers, the Douro/Duero, the Tagus, and the Guadalquivir. The peninsula experiences great variations in climate and rainfall, both regionally and locally.

▲ *The Pyrenees form Iberia's northeastern boundary, running for 270 miles (440 km), dividing the peninsula from the rest of Europe.*

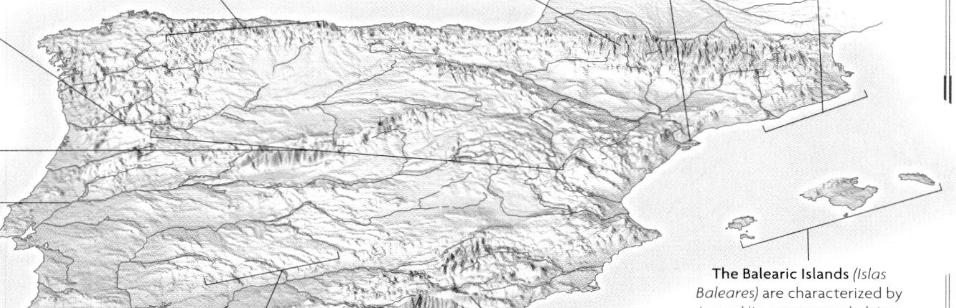

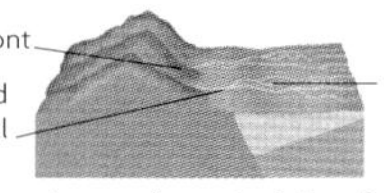

The Ebro river has formed the peninsula's largest delta. Recently, sediment flows have been seriously disturbed by nearby reservoirs.

On the northeastern coast sea level changes are evident from wave-cut beaches which rise up to 200 ft (60 m) above the present sea level.

Cordillera Cantábrica

Douro/Duero river

The Meseta plateau averages 1970 ft (600 m) in height and is now largely dry and treeless.

Tagus River

The Balearic Islands *(Islas Baleares)* are characterized by jagged limestones and plains.

Mountain front

Weathered material

Pediment

▲ *Pediments are characteristic of semiarid lands across Iberia. A pediment is a flat, low-lying, eroded platform, cut into the bedrock. Weathered material is transported by streams and deposited in broad fan shapes on the pediment..*

The Guadalquivir river brings vital irrigation water to the plains, and like many of Iberia's rivers, is prone to flooding.

Sierra Morena

The Sierra Nevada in southern Spain contain Iberia's highest peak, Mulhacén, which rises 11,418 ft (3481 m).

▶ *In the Sierra de los Filabres deforestation and overgrazing, which cause soil erosion, have created semidesert badlands.*

The Italian peninsula

ITALY, SAN MARINO, VATICAN CITY

The Italian peninsula is a land of great contrasts. Until unification in 1861, Italy was a collection of independent states, whose competitiveness during the Renaissance resulted in the architectural and artistic magnificence of cities such as Rome, Florence, and Venice. The majority of Italy's population and economic activity is concentrated in the north, centered on the sophisticated industrial city of Milan. Southern Italy, the *Mezzogiorno*, has a harsh terrain, and remains far less developed than the north. Attempts to attract industry and investment in the south are frequently deterred by the entrenched network of organized crime and corruption.

The landscape

The mainly mountainous and hilly Italian peninsula took its present form following a collision between the African and Eurasian tectonic plates. The Alps in the northwest rise to a high point of 15,772 ft (4807 m) at Mont Blanc *(Monte Bianco)* on the French border, while the Apennines *(Appennino)* form a rugged backbone, running along the entire length of the country.

▶ *The island of Sardinia is an ancient land mass, an uplifted section of very old igneous rocks. Its rugged mountainous regions provide pasture for sheep and goats, while its valleys support some agriculture.*

Costa Smeralda

Mont Blanc *(Monte Bianco)*

▲ ***The Dolomites** (Alpi Dolomitiche) are formed of thick limestones, overlying weaker marine strata. They have distinctive serrated peaks and many massive landslides occur.*

The distinctive square shape of the Gulf of Taranto *(Golfo di Taranto)* was defined by numerous block faults. Earthquakes are common in this region.

The Po Valley once formed part of the Adriatic Sea. Sediments of gravel, sand, and clay washed down from the Alps gradually filling the bay and forming a broad, cultivable plain.

The Apennines *(Appennino)* are the source of most of Italy's rivers. They run 823 miles (1324 km) down the length of the peninsula.

The Pontine Marshes *(Agro Pontino)* are bounded by low sand hills which prevent natural drainage.

Vesuvius *(Vesuvio)*

Sardinia is the second largest island in the Mediterranean Sea. The highest point is Punta La Marmora at 6017 ft (1834 m).

The southwestern tip of Sicily lies 95 miles (152 km) from the north African mainland and is part of the same geological region.

The Strait of Messina *(Stretto di Messina)* is between 2 and 12 miles (3–19 km) wide, and is a rich fishing ground.

Sicily is the largest island in the Mediterranean at 9926 sq miles (25,708 sq km).

Vesuvius *(Vesuvio)*

Monte Somma

Old crater

Present-day crater has developed within the old crater of Monte Somma

▲ ***There have been** four volcanoes on the site of Vesuvius since volcanic activity began here more than 10,000 years ago.*

Using the land

Italy produces 95% of its own food. The best farming land is in the Po Valley in northern Italy, where soft wheat and rice are grown. Irrigation is essential to agriculture in much of the south. Italy is a major producer and exporter of citrus fruits, olives, tomatoes, and wine.

The urban/rural population divide

urban 67% | rural 33%

0 10 20 30 40 50 60 70 80 90 100

Population density	Total land area
506 people per sq mile (195 people per sq km)	116,320 sq miles (301,270 sq km)

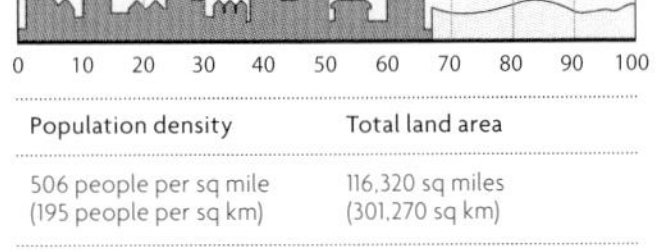

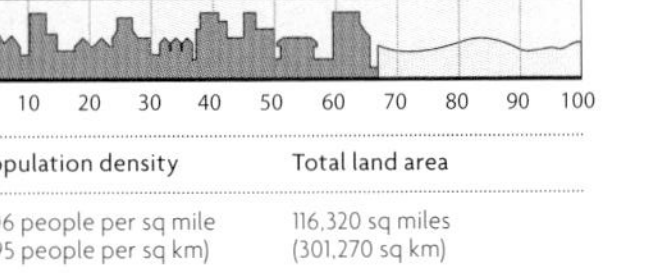

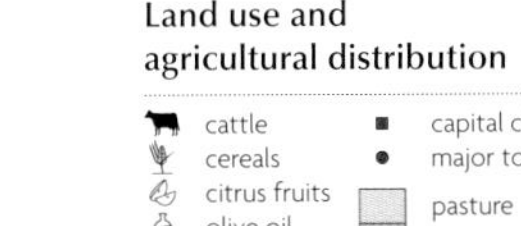

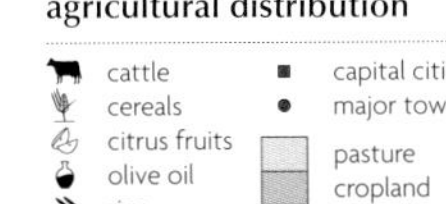

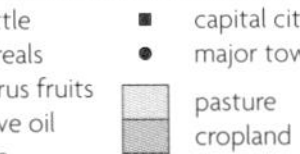

Land use and agricultural distribution

- cattle
- cereals
- citrus fruits
- olive oil
- rice
- capital cities
- major towns
- pasture
- cropland
- forest

Scale 1:2,750,000

projection: Lambert Conformal Conic

108
108
108
112
120
102

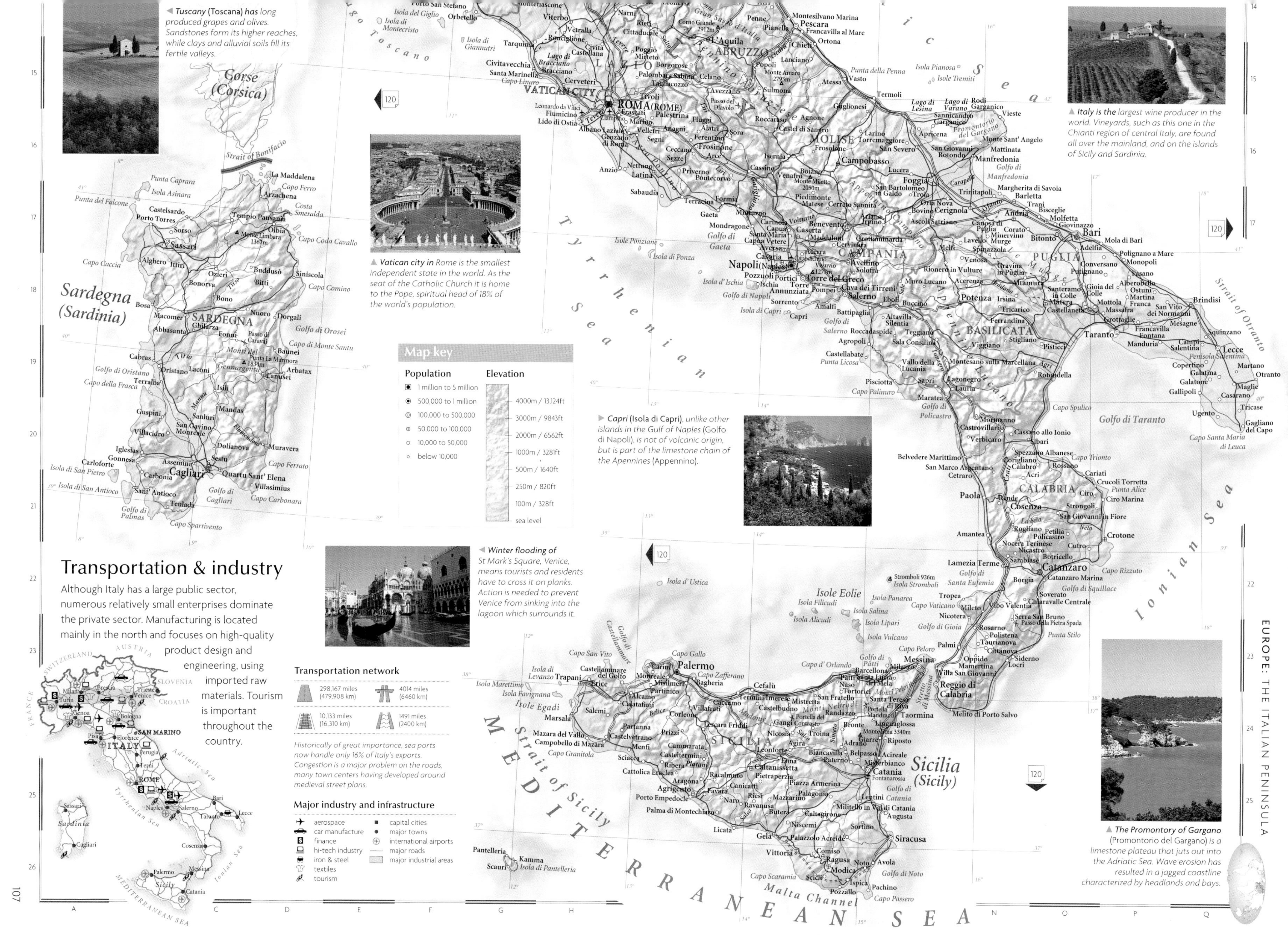

Tyrrhenian Sea
Ionian Sea
MEDITERRANEAN SEA
Strait of Sicily
Strait of Otranto
Strait of Bonifacio
Malta Channel
Golfo di Taranto
Sardegna (Sardinia)
Corse (Corsica)
Sicilia (Sicily)
ROMA (ROME)
VATICAN CITY
Napoli (Naples)
ABRUZZO
MOLISE
CAMPANIA
PUGLIA
BASILICATA
CALABRIA
SARDEGNA
SICILIA
Isole Eolie
Isole Egadi
Palermo
Cagliari
Bari
Taranto
Catanzaro
Messina
Catania
Siracusa

◀ **Tuscany** (Toscana) **has** long produced grapes and olives. Sandstones form its higher reaches, while clays and alluvial soils fill its fertile valleys.

▲ **Vatican city in** Rome is the smallest independent state in the world. As the seat of the Catholic Church it is home to the Pope, spiritual head of 18% of the world's population.

▲ **Italy is the** largest wine producer in the world. Vineyards, such as this one in the Chianti region of central Italy, are found all over the mainland, and on the islands of Sicily and Sardinia.

Map key

Population

- 1 million to 5 million
- 500,000 to 1 million
- 100,000 to 500,000
- 50,000 to 100,000
- 10,000 to 50,000
- below 10,000

Elevation

- 4000m / 13,124ft
- 3000m / 9843ft
- 2000m / 6562ft
- 1000m / 3281ft
- 500m / 1640ft
- 250m / 820ft
- 100m / 328ft
- sea level

▶ **Capri** (Isola di Capri), unlike other islands in the Gulf of Naples (Golfo di Napoli), is not of volcanic origin, but is part of the limestone chain of the Apennines (Appennino).

Transportation & industry

Although Italy has a large public sector, numerous relatively small enterprises dominate the private sector. Manufacturing is located mainly in the north and focuses on high-quality product design and engineering, using imported raw materials. Tourism is important throughout the country.

◀ **Winter flooding of** St Mark's Square, Venice, means tourists and residents have to cross it on planks. Action is needed to prevent Venice from sinking into the lagoon which surrounds it.

Transportation network

- 298,167 miles (479,908 km)
- 4014 miles (6460 km)
- 10,133 miles (16,310 km)
- 1491 miles (2400 km)

Historically of great importance, sea ports now handle only 16% of Italy's exports. Congestion is a major problem on the roads, many town centers having developed around medieval street plans.

Major industry and infrastructure

- aerospace
- car manufacture
- finance
- hi-tech industry
- iron & steel
- textiles
- tourism
- capital cities
- major towns
- international airports
- major roads
- major industrial areas

▲ **The Promontory of Gargano** (Promontorio del Gargano) is a limestone plateau that juts out into the Adriatic Sea. Wave erosion has resulted in a jagged coastline characterized by headlands and bays.

The Alpine states

AUSTRIA, LIECHTENSTEIN, SLOVENIA, SWITZERLAND

The Alpine countries of Austria, Switzerland, Liechtenstein, and Slovenia form a narrow strip across western Europe's geographical core, lying on the main north–south trading routes across the Alps. Switzerland, politically neutral since 1815, is an important international meeting place and houses one of the headquarters of the United Nations, it only became a member in 2002. Austria, once at the heart of the great Habsburg Empire has been a fully independent nation since 1955, and maintains a deserved reputation as an international center of culture. Slovenia declared independence from the former Yugoslavia in 1991 and despite initial economic hardship, is now starting to achieve the prosperity enjoyed by its Alpine neighbors.

Using the land

The Alpine region's mountainous terrain discourages cultivation over much of the land area. The primary agricultural activity is the raising of dairy and beef cattle on the pasture land of the lower mountain slopes. Austria is self-supporting in grains, and crops such as wheat, barley, and grapes are grown on the east Austrian lowlands. Woodlands are more prevalent in the eastern Alps; both Austria and Slovenia have large tracts of forest.

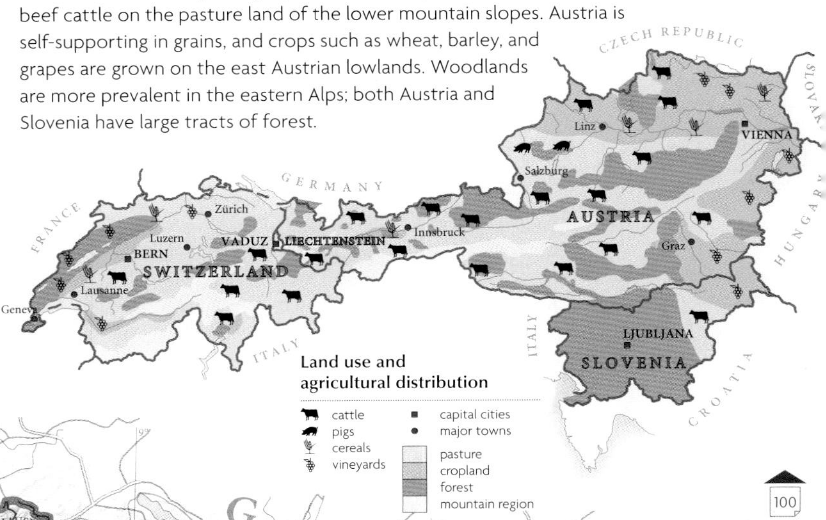

Land use and agricultural distribution

cattle
pigs
cereals
vineyards
capital cities
major towns
pasture
cropland
forest
mountain region

The Matterhorn, on the Swiss-Italian border, is one of the highest mountains in the Alps, at 14,692 ft (4478 m). The term "horn" refers to its distinctive peak, formed by three glaciers eroding hollows, known as cirques, in each of its sides.

The landscape

The Alps occupy three-fifths of Switzerland, most of southern Austria and the northwest of Slovenia. They were formed by the collision of the African and Eurasian tectonic plates, which began 65 million years ago. Their complex geology is reflected in the differing heights and rock types of the various ranges. The Rhine flows along Liechtenstein's border with Switzerland, creating a broad floodplain in the north and west of Liechtenstein. In the far northeast and east are a number of lowland regions, including the Vienna Basin, Burgenland, and the plain of the Danube. Slovenia's major rivers largely flow across the lower eastern regions; in the west, the rivers flow underground through the limestone Karst region.

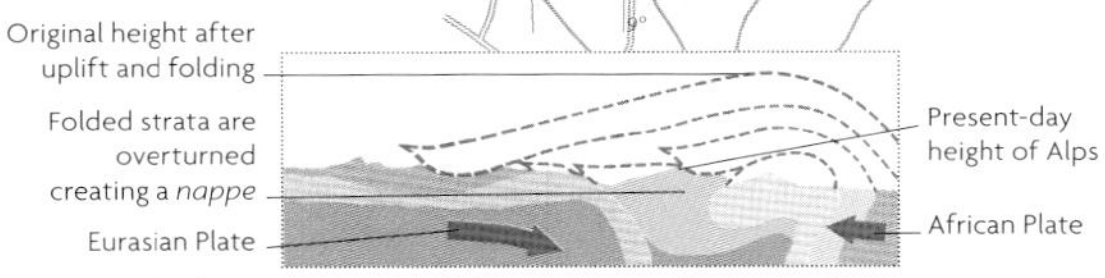

Original height after uplift and folding
Folded strata are overturned creating a *nappe*
Eurasian Plate
Present-day height of Alps
African Plate

The convergence of the African and Eurasian plates compressed and folded huge masses of rock strata. As the plates continued to move together, the folded strata were overturned, creating complex nappes. Much of the rock strata has since been eroded, resulting in the current topography of the Alps.

Constricted as it cuts through ridges in the Alps, the Danube meanders across the lowlands, where uplift combined with river erosion has deepened meanders.

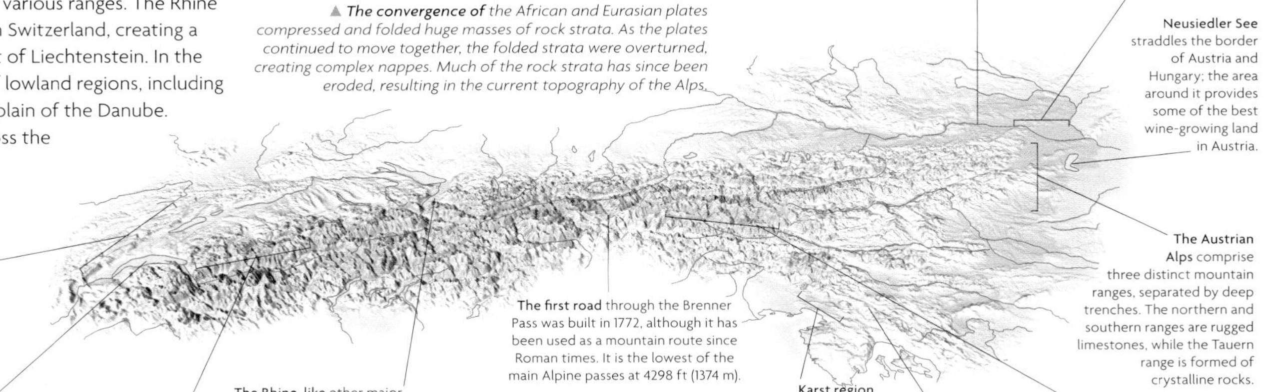

The Vienna Basin lies mainly below 390 ft (120 m). It gradually subsided and filled with sediment as the Alps were uplifted.

Neusiedler See straddles the border of Austria and Hungary; the area around it provides some of the best wine-growing land in Austria.

The Austrian Alps comprise three distinct mountain ranges, separated by deep trenches. The northern and southern ranges are rugged limestones, while the Tauern range is formed of crystalline rocks.

The mountains of the Jura form a natural border between Switzerland and France. Their marine limestones date from over 200 million years ago. When the Alps were formed the Jura were folded into a series of parallel ridges and troughs.

The first road through the Brenner Pass was built in 1772, although it has been used as a mountain route since Roman times. It is the lowest of the main Alpine passes at 4298 ft (1374 m).

Karst region

Tectonic activity has resulted in dramatic changes in land height over very short distances. Lake Geneva, lying at 1221 ft (372 m) is only 43 miles (70 km) away from the 15,772 ft (4807 m) peak of Mont Blanc, on the France–Italy border.

The Bernese Alps (*Berner Alpen*) contain the Aletsch, which at 15 miles (24 km) is the longest Alpine glacier.

The Rhine, like other major Alpine rivers, follows a broad, flat trough between the mountains. Along part of its course, the Rhine forms the boundary between Switzerland and Liechtenstein.

The deep, blue lakes of the Karst region are part of a drainage network which runs largely underground through this limestone area.

The limestone cave system at Postojna extends for more than 10 miles (16 km) and includes caverns reaching 125 ft (40 m) in height and width.

The Tauern range in the central Austrian Alps contains the highest mountain in Austria, the towering Grossglockner, rising 12,461 ft (3798 m).

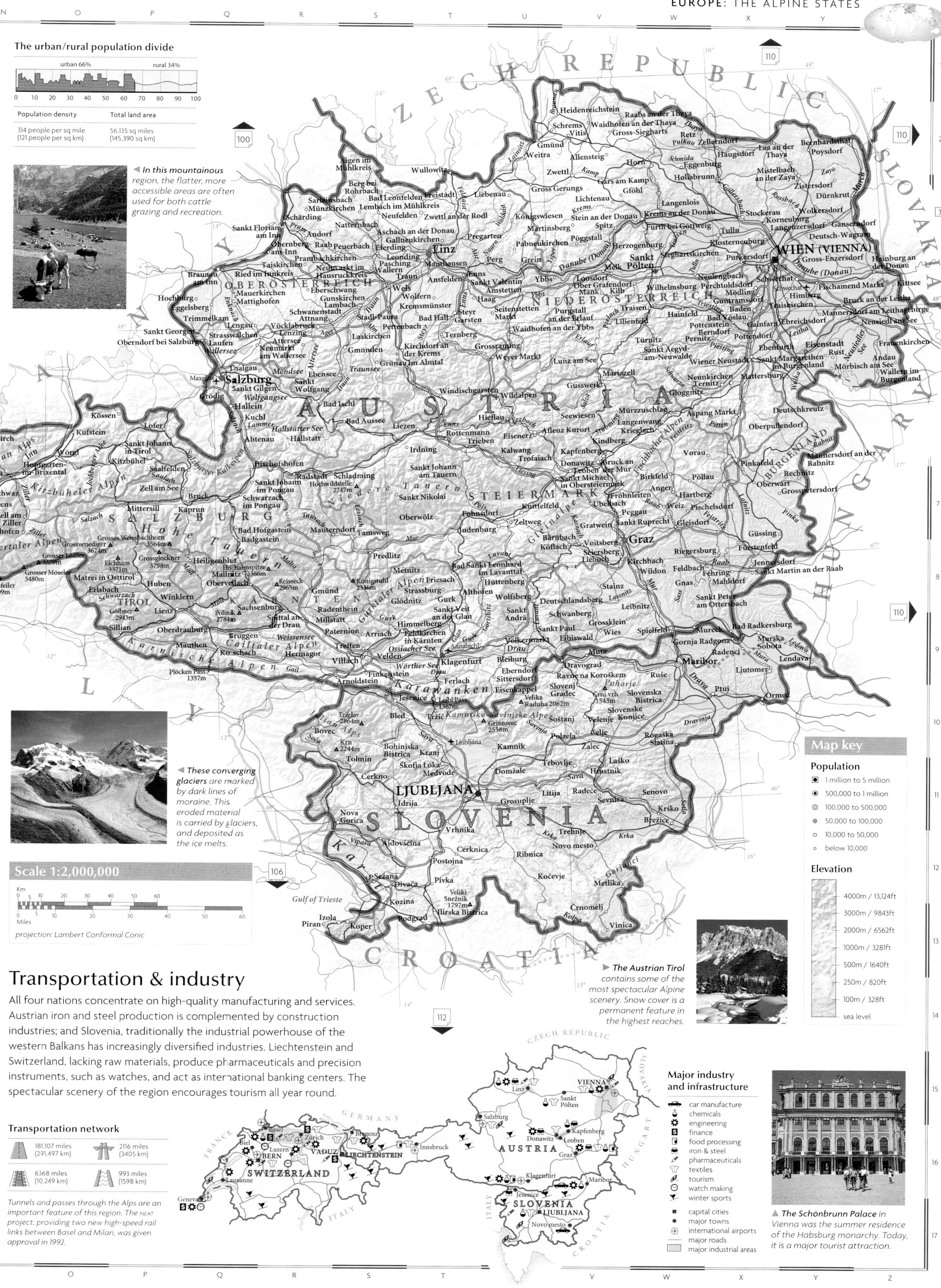

CZECH REPUBLIC
SLOVAKIA
HUNGARY
CROATIA
ITALY
AUSTRIA
SLOVENIA
WIEN (VIENNA)
LJUBLJANA
Linz
Salzburg
Graz
Klagenfurt
Maribor
OBERÖSTERREICH
NIEDERÖSTERREICH
STEIERMARK
SALZBURG
TIROL
KÄRNTEN
BURGENLAND
Hohe Tauern
Niedere Tauern
Karawanken
Julian Alps
Gulf of Trieste
Danube (Donau)
Drau
Mur
Sava

The urban/rural population divide

urban 66% — rural 34%

Population density	Total land area
314 people per sq mile (121 people per sq km)	56,135 sq miles (145,390 sq km)

◄ *In this mountainous region, the flatter, more accessible areas are often used for both cattle grazing and recreation.*

◄ *These converging glaciers are marked by dark lines of moraine. This eroded material is carried by glaciers, and deposited as the ice melts.*

Scale 1:2,000,000

projection: Lambert Conformal Conic

► *The Austrian Tirol contains some of the most spectacular Alpine scenery. Snow cover is a permanent feature in the highest reaches.*

Map key

Population
- 1 million to 5 million
- 500,000 to 1 million
- 100,000 to 500,000
- 50,000 to 100,000
- 10,000 to 50,000
- below 10,000

Elevation
- 4000m / 13,124ft
- 3000m / 9843ft
- 2000m / 6562ft
- 1000m / 3281ft
- 500m / 1640ft
- 250m / 820ft
- 100m / 328ft
- sea level

Transportation & industry

All four nations concentrate on high-quality manufacturing and services. Austrian iron and steel production is complemented by construction industries; and Slovenia, traditionally the industrial powerhouse of the western Balkans has increasingly diversified industries. Liechtenstein and Switzerland, lacking raw materials, produce pharmaceuticals and precision instruments, such as watches, and act as international banking centers. The spectacular scenery of the region encourages tourism all year round.

Transportation network

181,107 miles (291,497 km)	2116 miles (3405 km)
6368 miles (10,249 km)	993 miles (1598 km)

Tunnels and passes through the Alps are an important feature of this region. The NEAT project, providing two new high-speed rail links between Basel and Milan, was given approval in 1992.

Major industry and infrastructure

- car manufacture
- chemicals
- engineering
- finance
- food processing
- iron & steel
- pharmaceuticals
- textiles
- tourism
- watch making
- winter sports
- capital cities
- major towns
- international airports
- major roads
- major industrial areas

▲ *The Schönbrunn Palace in Vienna was the summer residence of the Habsburg monarchy. Today, it is a major tourist attraction.*

Central Europe

CZECH REPUBLIC, HUNGARY, POLAND, SLOVAKIA

When Slovakia and the Czech Republic became separate countries in 1993, they joined Hungary and Poland in a new role as independent nation states, following centuries of shifting boundaries and imperial strife. This turbulent history bequeathed the region a rich cultural heritage, shared through the works of its many great writers and composers, and celebrated in the vibrant historic capitals of Prague, Budapest, and Warsaw. Having shaken off years of Soviet domination in 1989, these states are confronting the challenge of winning commercial investment to modernize outmoded industries as they integrate their economies with those of the European Union.

The landscape

The forested Carpathian Mountains, uplifted with the Alps, lie southeast of the older Bohemian Massif, which contains the Sudeten and Krusné Hory *(Erzgebirge)* ranges. They divide the fertile plains of the Danube to the south and the Vistula *(Wisla)*, which flows north across vast expanses of glacial deposits into the Baltic Sea.

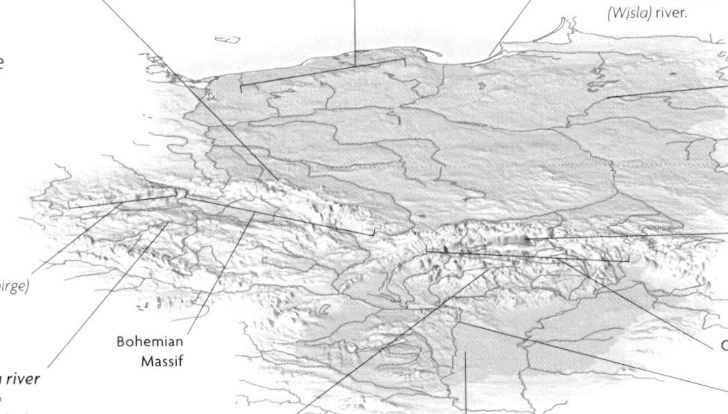

Hot mineral springs occur where geothermally heated water wells up through faults and fractures in the rocks of the Sudeten Mountains.

Pomerania is a sandy coastal region of glacially-formed lakes stretching west from the Vistula *(Wisla)*.

Longshore currents moving east along the Baltic coast have built a 40 mile (65 km) spit composed of material from the Vistula *(Wisla)* river.

▲ ***The Biebrza river** has left meanders and oxbow lakes as it flows across low-lying ground.*

Gerlachovsky Stit,in the Tatra Mountains, is Slovakia's highest mountain, at 8711ft (2655 m).

Krusné Hory *(Erzgebirge)*

Bohemian Massif

Carpathian Mountains

Danube river

◀ ***The Berounka river** cuts through the precipitous wooded landscape of the Bohemian Massif, banked by a broad floodplain.*

The Slovak Ore Mountains *(Slovenské Rudohorie)* are noted for their mineral resources, including high-grade iron ore.

The Great Hungarian Plain formed by the floodplain of the Danube is a mixture of steppe and cultivated land, covering nearly half of Hungary's total area.

Bluff
Direction of flow
Slip-off slope

▲ ***Meanders form as** rivers flow across plains at a low gradient. A steep cliff or bluff, forms on the outside curve, and a gentler slip-off slope on the inside bend.*

Transportation & industry

Heavy industry has dominated postwar life in Central Europe. Poland has large coal reserves, having inherited the Silesian coalfield from Germany after the Second World War, allowing the export of large quantities of coal, along with other minerals. Hungary specializes in consumer goods and services, while Slovakia's industrial base is still relatively small. The Czech Republic's traditional glassworks and breweries bring some stability to its precarious Soviet-built manufacturing sector.

Major industry and infrastructure

car manufacture
chemicals
engineering
food processing
mining
shipbuilding
tourism

capital cities
major towns
international airports
major roads
major industrial areas

Transportation network

213,997 miles (344,600 km)
817 miles (1315 km)
27,479 miles (44,249 km)
3784 miles (6094 km)

The huge growth of tourism and business has prompted major investment in the transportation infrastructure, with new roadbuilding schemes within and between the main cities of the region.

▲ ***Budapest, the capital** of Hungary, straddles the Danube. It comprises the historic towns of Buda, on the west bank, and Pest, which contains the Parliament Building, seen here on the far bank.*

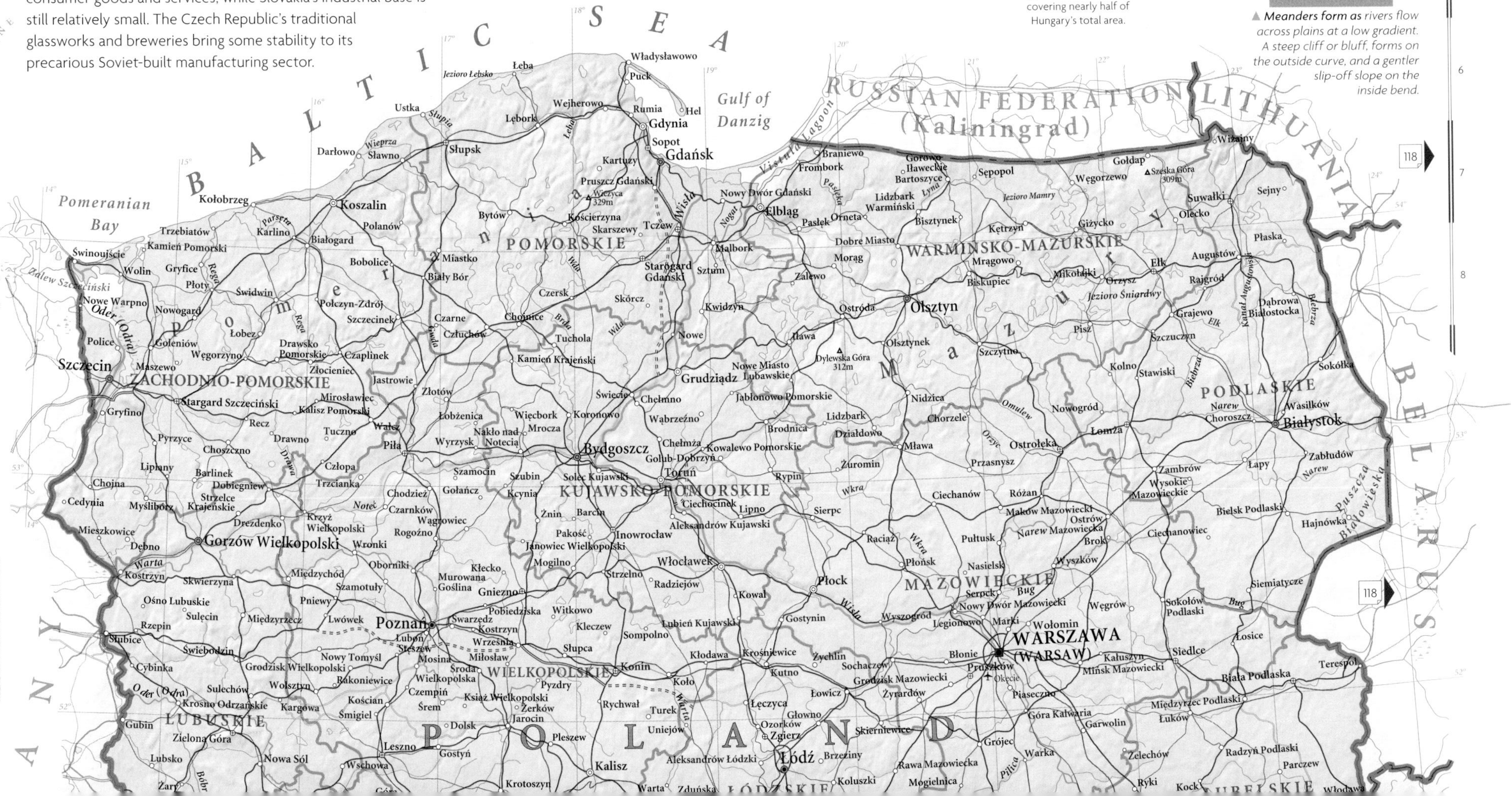

118
118

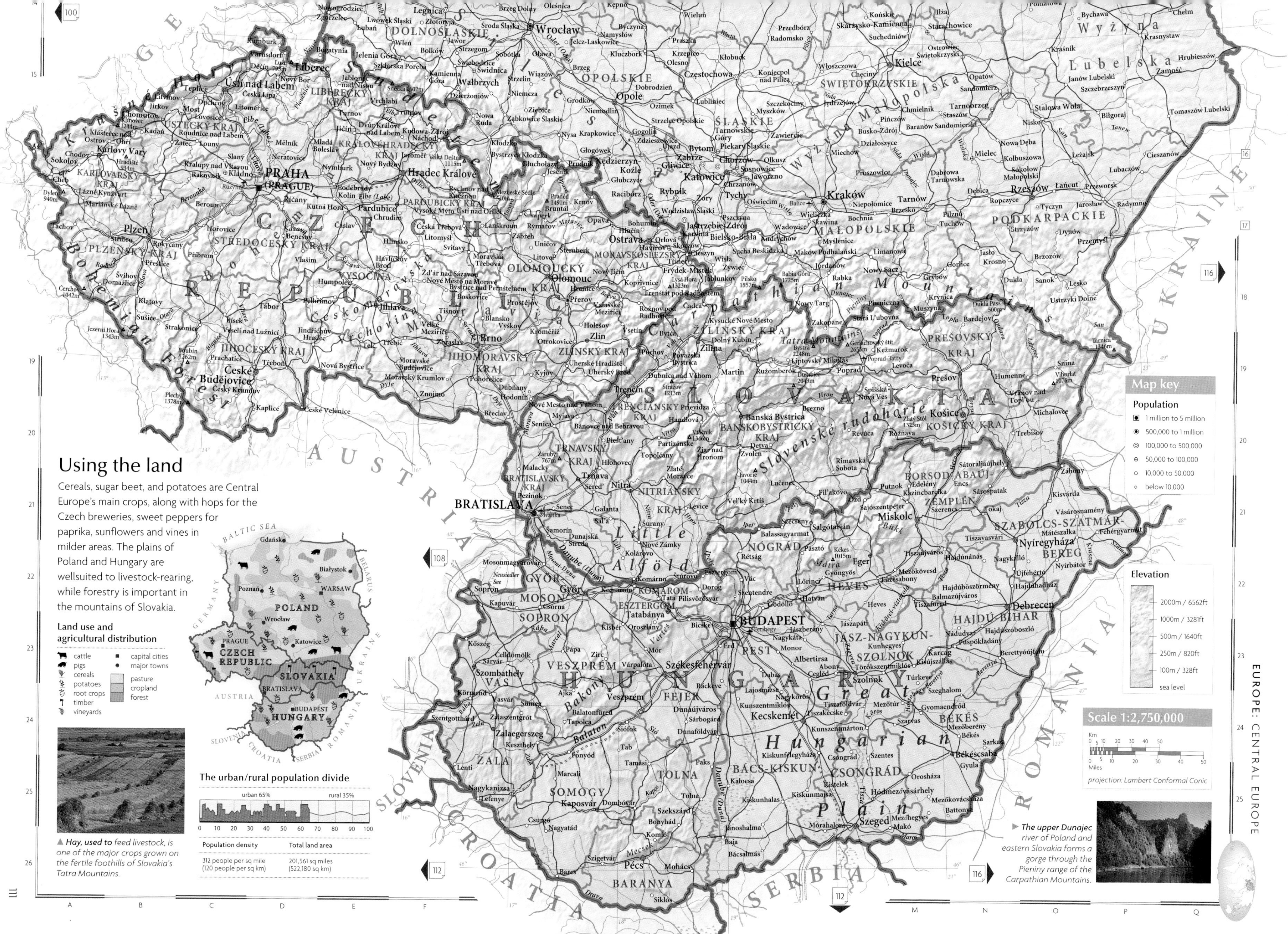
CZECH REPUBLIC
SLOVAKIA
HUNGARY
AUSTRIA
UKRAINE
ROMANIA
SERBIA
CROATIA
SLOVENIA
GERMANY
PRAHA (PRAGUE)
BRATISLAVA
BUDAPEST
Map key
Population
1 million to 5 million
500,000 to 1 million
100,000 to 500,000
50,000 to 100,000
10,000 to 50,000
below 10,000
Elevation
2000m / 6562ft
1000m / 3281ft
500m / 1640ft
250m / 820ft
100m / 328ft
sea level
Scale 1:2,750,000
projection: Lambert Conformal Conic

Using the land

Cereals, sugar beet, and potatoes are Central Europe's main crops, along with hops for the Czech breweries, sweet peppers for paprika, sunflowers and vines in milder areas. The plains of Poland and Hungary are wellsuited to livestock-rearing, while forestry is important in the mountains of Slovakia.

Land use and agricultural distribution
cattle
pigs
cereals
potatoes
root crops
timber
vineyards
capital cities
major towns
pasture
cropland
forest
BALTIC SEA
POLAND
CZECH REPUBLIC
SLOVAKIA
HUNGARY
The urban/rural population divide
urban 65%
rural 35%
Population density
312 people per sq mile (120 people per sq km)
Total land area
201,561 sq miles (522,180 sq km)

▲ **Hay, used to** feed livestock, is one of the major crops grown on the fertile foothills of Slovakia's Tatra Mountains.

▶ **The upper Dunajec** river of Poland and eastern Slovakia forms a gorge through the Pieniny range of the Carpathian Mountains.

Southeast Europe

ALBANIA, BOSNIA & HERZEGOVINA, CROATIA, MACEDONIA, MONTENEGRO, SERBIA

For 46 years the federation of Yugoslavia held together the most diverse ethnic region in Europe, along the picturesque mountain hinterland of the Dalmatian coast. Economic collapse resulted in internal tensions. In the early 1990s, civil war broke out in both Croatia and Bosnia as the ethnic populations struggled to establish their own exclusive territories. Peace was only restored by the UN after NATO launched air strikes in 1995. Montenegro voted to split from Serbia in 2006 while the future for the province of Kosovo, whose attempts to gain autonomy in 1998 were crushed by the Serbian government, is still unresolved. Neighboring Albania is slowly improving its fragile economy but remains one of Europe's poorest nations.

▲ **Hot, dry summers** *and mild winters offer excellent conditions for viticulture in Montenegro. The precipitous Dinaric Alps have kept this region relatively isolated for centuries.*

Scale 1:2,750,000

projection: Lambert Conformal Conic

The landscape

The Tisza, Sava, and Drava Rivers drain the broad northern lowland, meeting the Danube after it crosses the Hungarian border. In the west, the Dinaric Alps divide the Adriatic Sea from the interior. Mainland valleys and elongated islands run parallel to the steep Dalmatian *(Dalmacija)* coastline, following alternating bands of resistant limestone.

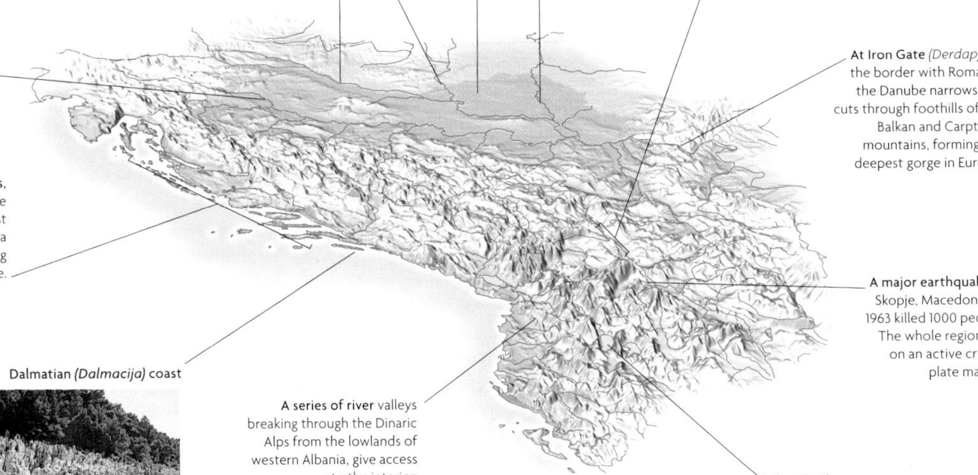

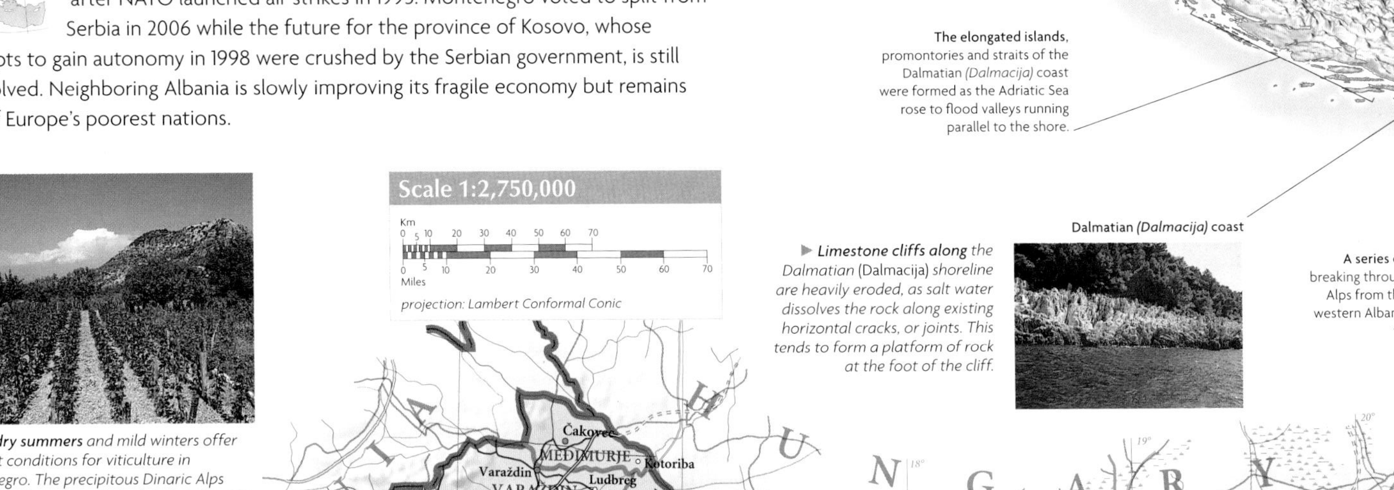

Sava river
Drava river
Tisza river
At least 70% of the fresh water in the western Balkans drains eastward into theBlack Sea, mostly via the Danube *(Dunav)*.
The river floodplains of the Pannonian Basin are flanked by terraces of gravel and wind-blown glacial deposits known as loess.
At Iron Gate *(Derdap)*, on the border with Romania, the Danube narrows and cuts through foothills of the Balkan and Carpthian mountains, forming the deepest gorge in Europe.
The elongated islands, promontories and straits of the Dalmatian *(Dalmacija)* coast were formed as the Adriatic Sea rose to flood valleys running parallel to the shore.
Dalmatian *(Dalmacija)* coast
A major earthquake at Skopje, Macedonia, in 1963 killed 1000 people. The whole region lies on an active crustal plate margin.
A series of river valleys breaking through the Dinaric Alps from the lowlands of western Albania, give access to the interior.
Lake Ohrid

Poljes in the Kosovo region

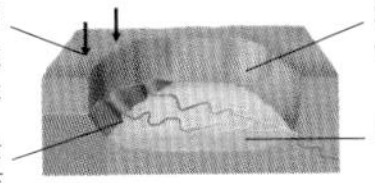

Underground drainage along joints in the rock

Spring at foot of cliff

Sheer limestone walls enclose all sides

Flat *polje* floor

▲ **Rain and underground** *water dissolve limestone along massive vertical joints (cracks). This creates* poljes: *depressions several miles across with steep walls and broad, flat floors.*

▶ **Limestone cliffs along** *the Dalmatian* (Dalmacija) *shoreline are heavily eroded, as salt water dissolves the rock along existing horizontal cracks, or joints. This tends to form a platform of rock at the foot of the cliff.*

▲ **Lake Ohrid borders** *Albania and Macedonia. Ohrid is the deepest lake in the western Balkans, reaching depths of 938 ft (286 m).*

108
110
116
120
114

MONTENEGRO
KOSOVO
MACEDONIA
ALBANIA
PODGORICA
SKOPJE
TIRANË (TIRANA)
DUBROVNIK-NERETVA
Adriatic Sea
Strait of Otranto
GREECE
BULGARIA
114

The historic center of Mostar in southern Bosnia, with its famous 16th-century Turkish bridge, was destroyed by shelling during 1993. The town was formerly the capital of Herzegovina.

Transportation & industry

Processing industries based on the region's wealth of mineral reserves predominate in Albania and Macedonia. In other regions, industrial plants have been commandeered, if not destroyed in the war and mineral extraction has severely declined. The fast-flowing rivers found throughout the Dinaric Alps are exploited to generate hydroelectric power.

Major industry and infrastructure

- aluminum refining
- car manufacture
- chemicals
- engineering
- food processing
- hydroelectric power
- mining
- shipbuilding
- textiles
- timber processing
- capital cities
- major towns
- international airports
- major roads

Transportation network

46,996 miles (75,642 km)		685 miles (1103 km)	
5413 miles (8713 km)		879 miles (1415 km)	

The war has resulted in the destruction or disintegration of infrastructure for transportation, communications, and power supply, though this is now in the process of recovery.

Industrial processing plants were established throughout Albania by the Hoxha regime, which collapsed in 1992. They remain incongruous among the villages of one of Europe's most conservative rural societies.

The ancient Croatian port of Dubrovnik was one of the former Yugoslavia's most popular tourist resorts and an important point of access to the sea along the Dalmatian (Dalmacija) coast. Shelling of the old city by Serb forces in 1991 provoked international condemnation.

Using the land

Crops of wheat, maize, sugar beet, vegetables, and fruit are widely grown. The hilly terrain is suited to forestry and livestock farming. The mild, Mediterranean climate of the coastal regions provides ideal conditions for growing vines and olives. Albania's largely agricultural economy has been adversely affected by the recent dismantling of state farms.

Sweet red peppers are dried in the sun, ready to make paprika. Macedonia's economy is mainly agricultural and its fertile soils support a broad range of crops.

Land use and agricultural distribution

- pigs
- sheep
- cereals
- fruit
- olives
- sugar beet
- timber
- tobacco
- vineyards
- capital cities
- major towns
- pasture
- cropland
- forest
- mountain region

The urban/rural population divide

urban 51% — rural 49%

Population density	Total land area
240 people per sq mile (93 people per sq km)	95,038 sq miles (246,278 sq km)

The Tara river is one of Montenegro's major rivers. It flows into the Danube via the Drina and Sava rivers. Along its course the Tara has eroded spectacular gorges up to 3280 ft (1000 m) deep.

Map key

Population

- 1 million to 5 million
- 500,000 to 1 million
- 100,000 to 500,000
- 50,000 to 100,000
- 10,000 to 50,000
- below 10,000

Elevation

- 2000m / 6562ft
- 1000m / 3281ft
- 500m / 1640ft
- 250m / 820ft
- 100m / 328ft
- sea level

Bulgaria & Greece

Including EUROPEAN TURKEY

Greece is renowned as the original hearth of western civilization. The rugged terrain and numerous islands have profoundly affected its development, creating a strong agricultural and maritime tradition. In the past 50 years, this formerly rural society has rapidly urbanized, with one third of the population now living in the capital, Athens, and in the northern city of Salonica. Bulgaria, dominated for centuries by the Ottoman Turks, became part of the eastern bloc after the Second World War, only slowly emerging from Soviet influence in 1989. Moves toward democracy led to some instability in Bulgaria and Greece, now outweighed by the challenge of integration with the European Union.

Transportation & industry

Soviet investment introduced heavy industry into Bulgaria, and the processing of agricultural produce, such as tobacco, is important throughout the country. Both countries have substantial shipyards and Greece has one of the world's largest merchant fleets. Many small craft workshops, producing textiles and processed foods, are clustered around Greek cities. The service and construction sectors have profited from the successful tourist industry.

Major industry and infrastructure

- chemicals
- engineering
- food processing
- shipbuilding
- textiles
- tourism
- capital cities
- major towns
- international airports
- major roads
- major industrial areas

112

Transportation network

- 103,930 miles (167,630 km)
- 345 miles (557 km)
- 4346 miles (6995 km)
- 294 miles (474 km)

Bulgaria's railroads require investment to revive an outdated infrastructure. In Greece, despite a developing road network, ferry-boats remain the most effective form of transportation in many areas.

▲ ***A towering pinnacle** at Metéora in central Greece is home to the monastery of Roussanou. The 24 rock towers which dominate the plain of Thessaly (Thessalía) are remnants of an old plateau. Long-term weathering along fissures in the rock has worn away the rest of the plateau.*

The landscape

Bulgaria's Balkan mountains divide the Danubian Plain *(Dunavska Ravnina)* and Maritsa Basin, meeting the Black Sea in the east along sandy beaches. The steep Rhodope Mountains form a natural barrier with Greece, while the younger Pindus form a rugged central spine which descends into the Aegean Sea to give a vast archipelago of over 2000 islands, the largest of which is Crete.

Mount Olympus is the mythical home of the Greek Gods and, at 9570 ft (2917 m), is the highest mountain in Greece.

Limestone rocks exposed by erosion of metamorphic rocks

Mount Olympus

Ancient metamorphic rock, formed miles below the surface

Younger limestones created in shallow seas

▲ ***Mount Olympus** is a composite of rocks formed by two major tectonic events. First the older metamorphic rocks were thrust over the limestones, then two million years ago regional warping and subsequent erosion, reexposed the limestone.*

The Peloponnese consist of several mountainous peninsulas, linked to the mainland by the Isthmus of Corinth. The Corinth Canal *(Dioryga Korinthou)*, built in 1893, cuts through the isthmus, linking the Aegean and Ionian Seas.

Corinth Canal *(Dioryga Korinthou)*

Rhodope Mountains

The Danube, Europe's second longest river, forms most of Bulgaria's northern border. The Danubian plain *(Dunavska Ravnina)*, extending from the southern bank, is extremely fertile.

Balkan Mountains

Maritsa Basin

Pindus Mountains

The islands of Crete, Kythira, Karpathos, and Rhodes are part of an arc which bends southeastward from the Peloponnese, forming the southern boundary of the Aegean.

Kythira

Crete

Karpathos

Rhodes

▲ ***The Arda river** cuts through the Rhodope Mountains in rugged, rocky gorges.*

▲ ***Layers of black** volcanic ash still cover the island of Santorini. This volcano last erupted 3500 years ago, but still shows signs of volcanic activity.*

ROMANIA
SERBIA
MACEDONIA
BULGARIA
TURKEY
BLACK SEA
Scale 1:2,750,000
projection: Lambert Conformal Conic
SOFIYA
Plovdiv
Varna
Burgas
Ruse
Stara Zagora
Pleven
Istanbul

116

112

Using the land & sea

The fertile plains of Bulgaria support cattle, fruit, vegetables, tobacco, and cereal cultivation, while also providing traditional industries with grapes for wine, sunflowers for oil, and roses for perfume. Over half of Greece is barren upland. Citrus fruit, olives, and tobacco are widely exported, yet much of rural life is still characterized by subsistence cropping and goat herding.

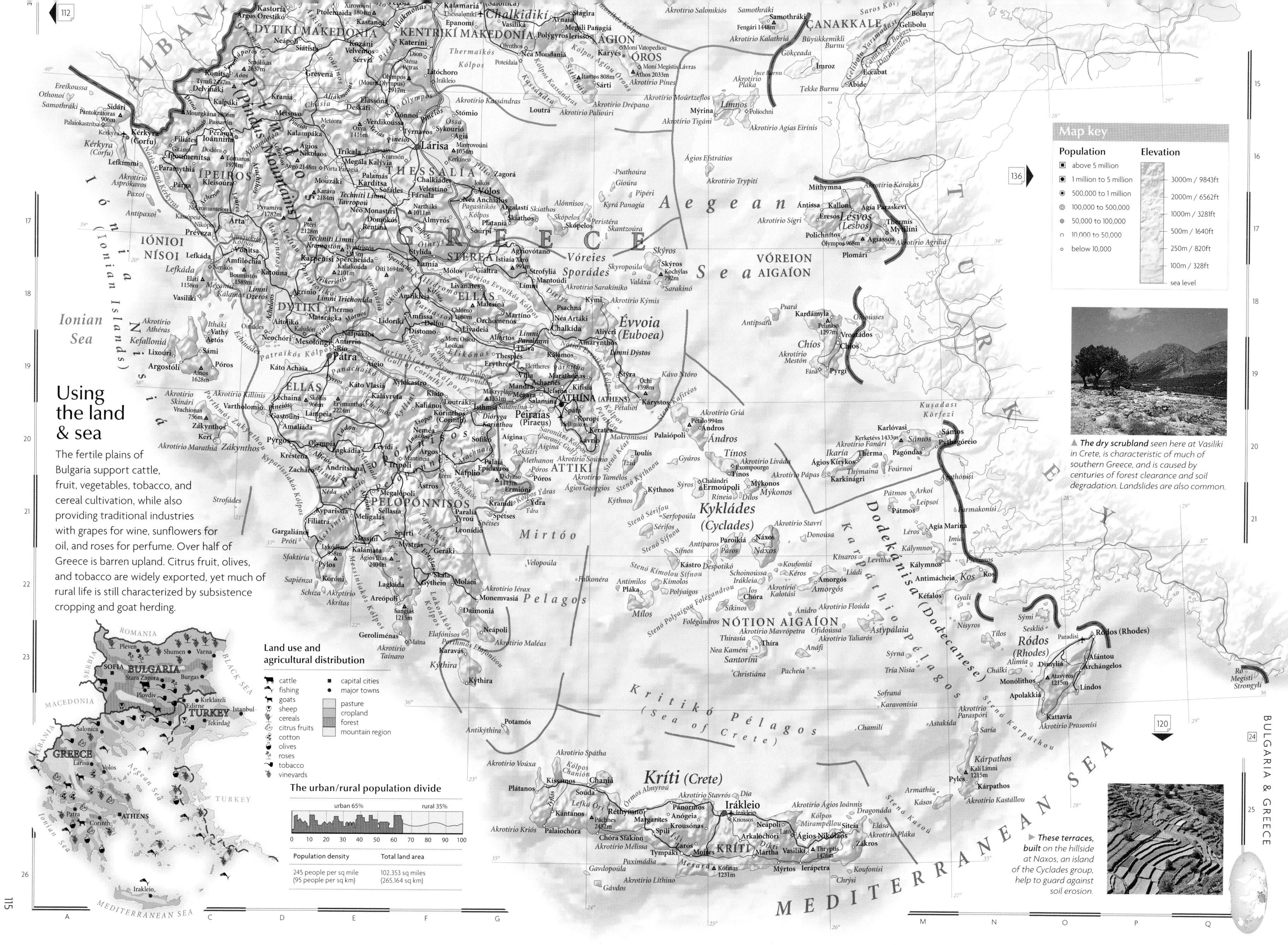
Map key
Population
above 5 million
1 million to 5 million
500,000 to 1 million
100,000 to 500,000
50,000 to 100,000
10,000 to 50,000
below 10,000
Elevation
3000m / 9843ft
2000m / 6562ft
1000m / 3281ft
500m / 1640ft
250m / 820ft
100m / 328ft
sea level
Land use and agricultural distribution
cattle
fishing
goats
sheep
cereals
citrus fruits
cotton
olives
roses
tobacco
vineyards
capital cities
major towns
pasture
cropland
forest
mountain region
The urban/rural population divide
urban 65%
rural 35%
0 10 20 30 40 50 60 70 80 90 100
Population density
245 people per sq mile (95 people per sq km)
Total land area
102,353 sq miles (265,164 sq km)
GREECE
BULGARIA
TURKEY
ALBANIA
Ionian Sea
Aegean Sea
MEDITERRANEAN SEA
Kríti (Crete)
Kykládes (Cyclades)
Dodekánisa (Dodecanese)
Pelopónnisos
Píndos (Pindus Mountains)
Athína (Athens)
Iónioi Nísoi (Ionian Islands)
Kritikó Pélagos (Sea of Crete)
Mirtóo Pelagos
Karpáthio Pélagos
Vóreion Aigaíon
Nótion Aigaíon

▲ **The dry scrubland** seen here at Vasilikí in Crete, is characteristic of much of southern Greece, and is caused by centuries of forest clearance and soil degradation. Landslides are also common.

▶ **These terraces,** built on the hillside at Naxos, an island of the Cyclades group, help to guard against soil erosion.

112 136 120 24

Romania, Moldova & Ukraine

The industrial, social, and cultural make-up of Romania and the former Soviet states of Moldova and Ukraine still bear the imprint of their communist past. As part of the USSR, Ukraine was a leading agricultural, industrial, and energy producer. These industries, like those in Moldova and Romania, are now being reoriented more firmly toward western markets. As a result of shifting borders, and Soviet policy actively encouraging Russian immigration into other Soviet states like Ukraine and Moldova, all three countries now contain large numbers of foreign nationals. Moldovans and Romanians are still close in terms of language and culture, although Moldova is striving to remain an independent nation.

BELARUS
POLAND
SLOVAKIA
HUNGARY
SERBIA
BULGARIA
ROMANIA
UKRAINE
MOLDOVA
Pripet Marshes
VOLYNS'KA OBLAST'
RIVNENS'KA OBLAST'
L'VIVS'KA OBLAST'
TERNOPIL'S'KA OBLAST'
KHMEL'NYTS'KA OBLAST'
IVANO-FRANKIVS'KA OBLAST'
ZAKARPATS'KA OBLAST'
CHERNIVETS'KA OBLAST'
Carpathian Mountains
Transylvania
Carpații Meridionali
L'viv
Luts'k
Rivne
Ternopil'
Khmel'nyts'kyy
Ivano-Frankivs'k
Uzhhorod
Chernivtsi
Satu Mare
Baia Mare
Suceava
Botoșani
Iași
Oradea
Cluj-Napoca
Târgu Mureș
Bistrița
Piatra-Neamț
Bacău
Arad
Timișoara
Alba Iulia
Sibiu
Brașov
Galați
Brăila
Buzău
Ploiești
Târgoviște
Pitești
Craiova
Drobeta-Turnu Severin
Reșița
Deva
Râmnicu Vâlcea
Slatina
Alexandria
Giurgiu
Călărași
Slobozia
Focșani
BUCUREȘTI (BUCHAREST)
Danube (Dunărea)

110
110
112
114

Using the land

The fertile black soils of Ukraine, often called "the breadbasket of Europe," have enabled the cultivation of a variety of cereals and vegetables, which are widely exported. Romania and Moldova also grow cereals, sunflowers, and vegetables, and are noted for the quality of their wines.

The fertile lands and tolerant climate of Moldova are ideally suited to growing grapes for wine.

Land use and agricultural distribution

- cattle
- pigs
- poultry
- sheep
- cereals
- cotton
- sugar beet
- sunflowers
- vineyards
- capital cities
- major towns
- pasture
- cropland
- forest
- wetland

The urban/rural population divide

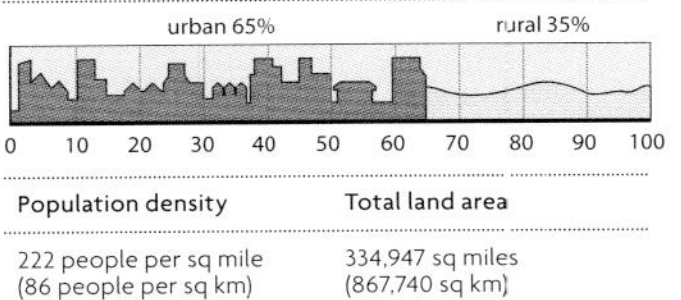

urban 65%
rural 35%
0
10
20
30
40
50
60
70
80
90
100

Population density	Total land area
222 people per sq mile (86 people per sq km)	334,947 sq miles (867,740 sq km)

Glacial lakes are found throughout the Transylvanian Alps (Carpatii Meridionali), although the mountains no longer have any permanent snow cover.

Transportation & industry

Heavy industry using local raw materials characterizes much of this region. The industrial heartland of Ukraine, specializing in metal and machine-building industries, is based around its vast mineral reserves in the Donbass region. In Moldova, food processing draws on produce from its agricultural sector. Romanian industry relies both on local raw materials and imported iron, steel, and oil.

BELARUS
RUSSIAN FEDERATION
POLAND
SLOVAKIA
HUNGARY
SERBIA
BULGARIA
BLACK SEA
UKRAINE
MOLDOVA
ROMANIA
Luts'k
L'viv
KIEV
Kharkiv
Kremenchuk
Dnipropetrovs'k
Donbass
Donets'k
Kryvyy Rih
Chernivtsi
Bălți
CHIȘINĂU
Odesa
Simferopol'
Cluj-Napoca
Timișoara
Brașov
Galați
BUCHAREST

Major industry and infrastructure

- car manufacture
- chemicals
- coal
- engineering
- food processing
- mining
- oil & gas
- textiles
- tourism
- capital cities
- major towns
- international airports
- major roads
- major industrial areas

Transportation network

170,707 miles (274,757 km)	1170 miles (1883 km)
21,474 miles (34,563 km)	4130 miles (6647 km)

Increased industrialization has necessitated the upgrading of road and rail networks in all three countries. Modernization has tended to focus only on major cities and industrial areas.

During the 1960s and 1970s, many industries, like this carbon factory, developed using the mineral resources on the flanks of the Transylvanian Alps (Carpatii Meridionali).

Scale 1:3,500,000

Km 0 5 10 20 30 40 50 60 70 80 90 100

Miles 0 5 10 20 30 40 50 60 70 80 90 100

projection: Lambert Conformal Conic

Map key

Population

- 1 million to 5 million
- 500,000 to 1 million
- 100,000 to 500,000
- 50,000 to 100,000
- 10,000 to 50,000
- below 10,000

Elevation

- 2000m / 6562ft
- 1000m / 3281ft
- 500m / 1640ft
- 250m / 820ft
- 100m / 328ft
- sea level

118
122
126
120

Old glaciated valley

Water has eroded a new post-glacial valley

▲ ***Balkas are common** throughout Ukraine. They are large U-shaped valleys, formed during the last Ice Age, which contain narrower, deep valleys. These were incised by a sudden flow of water, following an icemelt.*

▲ ***The Swallow's Nest** castle at Yalta is one of many tourist resorts on the Crimean (Krym) coast, dubbed the "Russian Riviera."*

The landscape

Vast flat lowlands and gently rolling hills cover most of southeastern Europe. In the southwest, the Carpathian Mountains form a gentle arc. To the south of the Carpathian Mountains lies the Danube Plain, across which the Danube river flows to the Black Sea. To the north and east, the hills of Moldova level out into low plains, running east to the steppes of Ukraine.

► ***Divided into crystalline** massifs, the southern arm of the Carpathian Mountains, the Transylvanian Alps (Carpatii Meridionali), extend 170 miles (274 km) across southwestern Romania.*

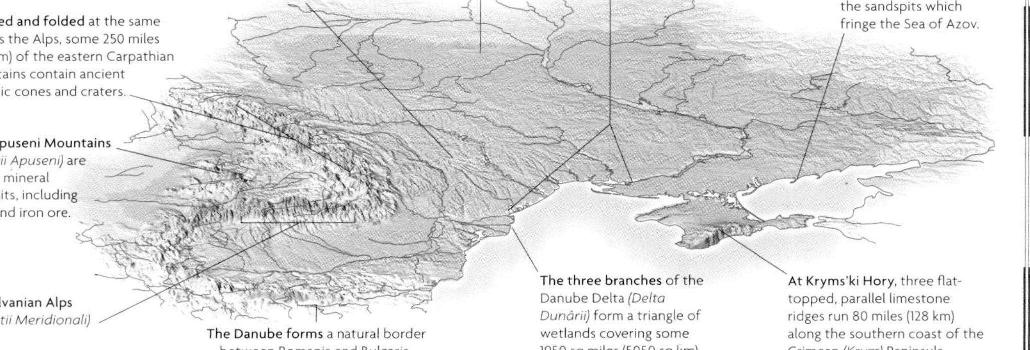

Steppe landscape covers two-thirds of Ukraine. These flat, treeless grasslands extend from central Europe to central Asia.

Most of the major rivers in southeastern Europe, like the Danube, the Dniester, and Dnieper flow south and east to the Black Sea.

The Codrii Hills dominate the landscape of central Moldova; they are intersected by deep, flat valleys and ravines.

Counterclockwise currents have created the sandspits which fringe the Sea of Azov.

Uplifted and folded at the same time as the Alps, some 250 miles (400 km) of the eastern Carpathian Mountains contain ancient volcanic cones and craters.

The Apuseni Mountains *(Muntii Apuseni)* are rich in mineral deposits, including gold and iron ore.

Transylvanian Alps *(Carpatii Meridionali)*

The Danube forms a natural border between Romania and Bulgaria.

The three branches of the Danube Delta *(Delta Dunării)* form a triangle of wetlands covering some 1950 sq miles (5050 sq km).

At Kryms'ki Hory, three flat-topped, parallel limestone ridges run 80 miles (128 km) along the southern coast of the Crimean *(Krym)* Peninsula.

The Baltic states & Belarus

BELARUS, ESTONIA, LATVIA, LITHUANIA, Kaliningrad

Occupying Europe's main corridor to Russia, the four distinct cultures of Estonia, Latvia, Lithuania, and Belarus share a history of struggle for nationhood against the interests of more powerful neighbors. As the first republics to declare their independence from the Soviet Union in 1990–91, the Baltic states of Estonia, Latvia, and Lithuania sought an economic role in the EU, while reaffirming their European cultural roots through the church and a strong musical tradition. Meanwhile, Belarus has shown economic and political allegiance to Russia by joining the Commonwealth of Independent States.

Gulf of Finland
Narva Bay
Gulf of Riga
Irbe Strait
BALTIC SEA
RUSSIAN FEDERATION
ESTONIA
LATVIA
LITHUANIA
TALLINN
RĪGA
Tartu
Pärnu
Narva
Lake Peipus
Lake Pskov
Saaremaa
HIIUMAA
Vidzeme
Augstiene
Liepāja
Ventspils
Klaipėda
Šiauliai
Panevėžys
Daugavpils
Jelgava
Vitsyebsk
Navapolatsk
Polatsk
VITSYEBSKAYA
Western Dvina (Daugava)
Land use and agricultural distribution
cattle
pigs
cereals
flax
potatoes
timber
capital cities
major towns
pasture
cropland
forest
wetland
RUSS.FED.
BELARUS
MINSK
VILNIUS
POLAND
UKRAINE

▲ **The seaport of** Riga is Latvia's capital and the center of economic and cultural life. With a 32% Russian minority in Latvia, language and the right to national citizenship are key issues.

Using the land

Across the four nations cattle and pig farming are widespread, together with diverse arable crops, including flax for making linen, potatoes used to produce vodka, cereals, and other vegetables. Almost a third of the land is forested; demand for timber has increased the importance of forest management.

The urban/rural population divide

urban 69% — rural 31%

Population density	Total land area
122 people per sq mile (47 people per sq km)	145,006 sq miles (375,656 sq km)

▶ **A pine forest** in northern Belarus. Conifers in the north give way to hardwood forest farther south. Timber mills are supplied with logs floated along the country's many navigable waterways.

▲ **The Western Dvina** river provides hydroelectric power and, during the summer months, access to the Baltic Sea. The lower course of the river freezes from December to April.

122

Map key

Population

- 1 million to 5 million
- 500,000 to 1 million
- 100,000 to 500,000
- 50,000 to 100,000
- 10,000 to 50,000
- below 10,000

Elevation

- 250m / 820ft
- 100m / 328ft
- sea level

122

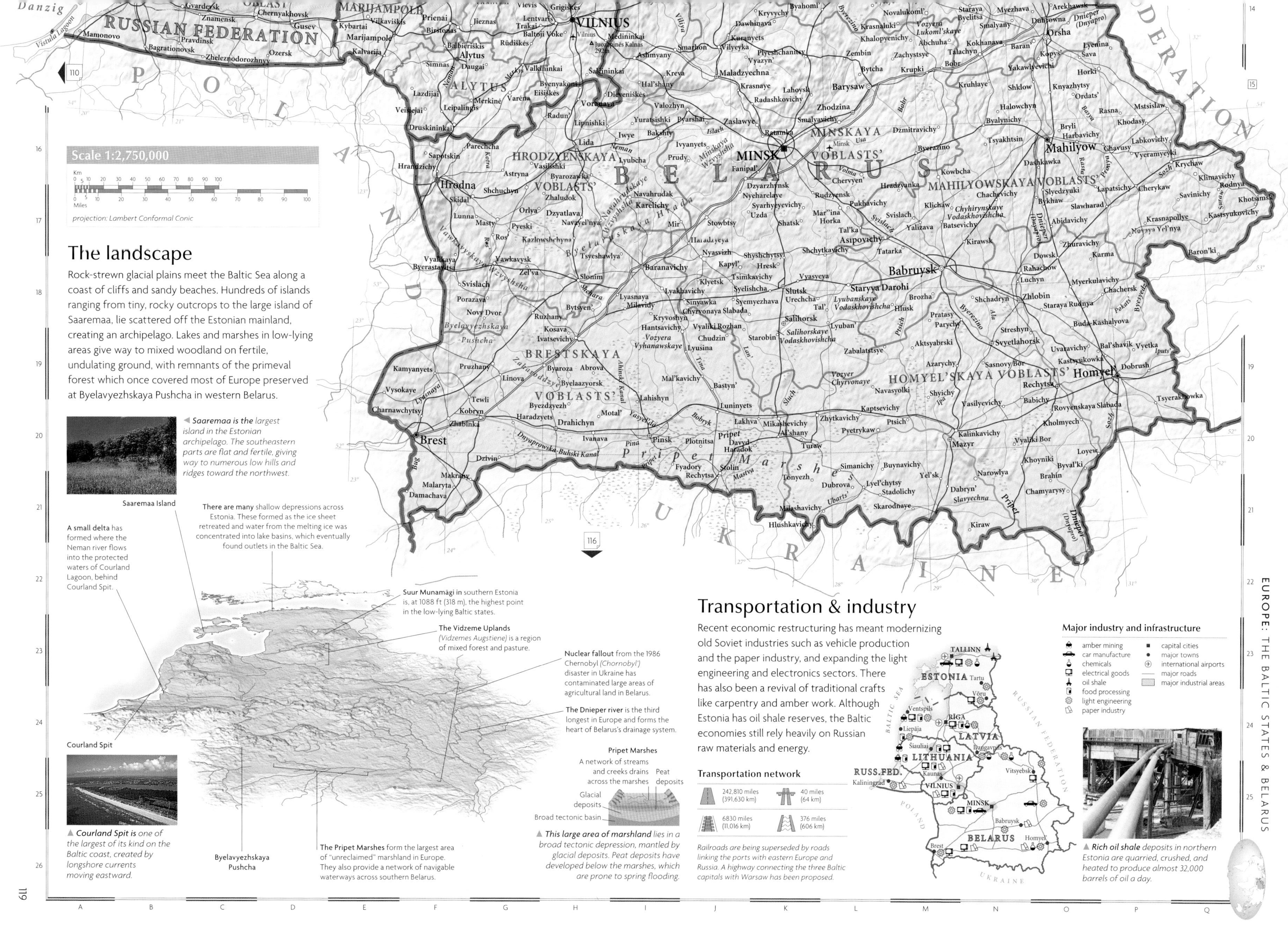

Scale 1:2,750,000
projection: Lambert Conformal Conic
RUSSIAN FEDERATION
POLAND
BELARUS
UKRAINE
MINSK
VILNIUS
HRODZYENSKAYA VOBLASTS'
MINSKAYA VOBLASTS'
MAHILYOWSKAYA VOBLASTS'
BRESTSKAYA VOBLASTS'
HOMYEL'SKAYA VOBLASTS'
Pripet Marshes
Suur Munamägi in southern Estonia is, at 1088 ft (318 m), the highest point in the low-lying Baltic states.
The Vidzeme Uplands (Vidzemes Augstiene) is a region of mixed forest and pasture.
There are many shallow depressions across Estonia. These formed as the ice sheet retreated and water from the melting ice was concentrated into lake basins, which eventually found outlets in the Baltic Sea.
A small delta has formed where the Neman river flows into the protected waters of Courland Lagoon, behind Courland Spit.
Nuclear fallout from the 1986 Chernobyl (Chornobyl') disaster in Ukraine has contaminated large areas of agricultural land in Belarus.
The Dnieper river is the third longest in Europe and forms the heart of Belarus's drainage system.
The Pripet Marshes form the largest area of "unreclaimed" marshland in Europe. They also provide a network of navigable waterways across southern Belarus.
Courland Spit
Byelavyezhskaya Pushcha
Pripet Marshes
A network of streams and creeks drains across the marshes
Peat deposits
Glacial deposits
Broad tectonic basin
Major industry and infrastructure
amber mining
car manufacture
chemicals
electrical goods
oil shale
food processing
light engineering
paper industry
capital cities
major towns
international airports
major roads
major industrial areas
Transportation network
242,810 miles (391,630 km)
40 miles (64 km)
6830 miles (11,016 km)
376 miles (606 km)

The landscape

Rock-strewn glacial plains meet the Baltic Sea along a coast of cliffs and sandy beaches. Hundreds of islands ranging from tiny, rocky outcrops to the large island of Saaremaa, lie scattered off the Estonian mainland, creating an archipelago. Lakes and marshes in low-lying areas give way to mixed woodland on fertile, undulating ground, with remnants of the primeval forest which once covered most of Europe preserved at Byelavyezhskaya Pushcha in western Belarus.

◀ *Saaremaa is the largest island in the Estonian archipelago. The southeastern parts are flat and fertile, giving way to numerous low hills and ridges toward the northwest.*

Saaremaa Island

▲ *Courland Spit is one of the largest of its kind on the Baltic coast, created by longshore currents moving eastward.*

▲ *This large area of marshland lies in a broad tectonic depression, mantled by glacial deposits. Peat deposits have developed below the marshes, which are prone to spring flooding.*

Transportation & industry

Recent economic restructuring has meant modernizing old Soviet industries such as vehicle production and the paper industry, and expanding the light engineering and electronics sectors. There has also been a revival of traditional crafts like carpentry and amber work. Although Estonia has oil shale reserves, the Baltic economies still rely heavily on Russian raw materials and energy.

Railroads are being superseded by roads linking the ports with eastern Europe and Russia. A highway connecting the three Baltic capitals with Warsaw has been proposed.

▲ *Rich oil shale deposits in northern Estonia are quarried, crushed, and heated to produce almost 32,000 barrels of oil a day.*

The Mediterranean

The Mediterranean Sea stretches over 2500 miles (4000 km) east to west, separating Europe from Africa. At its westernmost point it is connected to the Atlantic Ocean through the Strait of Gibraltar. In the east, the Suez canal, opened in 1869, gives passage to the Indian Ocean. In the northeast, linked by the Sea of Marmara, lies the Black Sea. The Mediterranean is bordered by almost 30 states and territories, and more than 100 million people live on its shores and islands. Throughout history, the Mediterranean has been a focal area for many great empires and civilizations, reflected in the variety of cultures found on its shores. Since the 1960s, development along the southern coast of Europe has expanded rapidly to accommodate increasing numbers of tourists and to enable the exploitation of oil and gas reserves. This has resulted in rising levels of pollution, threatening the future of the sea.

▲ *Monte Carlo is just one of the luxurious resorts scattered along the Riviera, which stretches along the coast from Cannes in France to La Spezia in Italy. The region's mild winters and hot summers have attracted wealthy tourists since the early 19th century.*

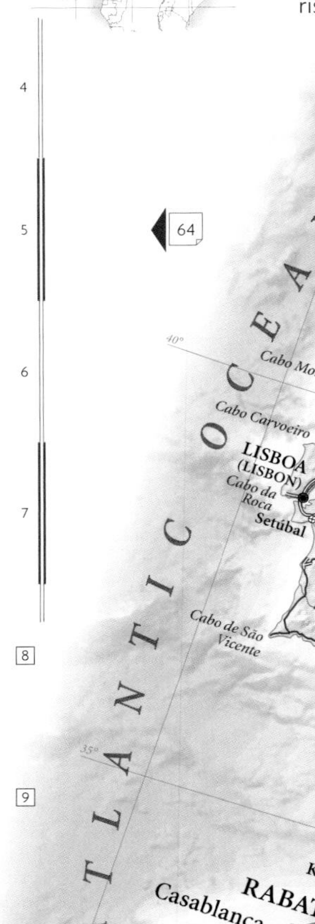

Cabo Fisterra
64
ATLANTIC OCEAN
Cabo Mondego
Cabo Carvoeiro
LISBOA
(LISBON)
Cabo da Roca
Setúbal
Cabo de São Vicente
Casablanca

The landscape

The Mediterranean Sea is almost totally landlocked, joined to the Atlantic Ocean through the Strait of Gibraltar, which is only 8 miles (13 km) wide. Lying on an active plate margin, sea floor movements have formed a variety of basins, troughs, and ridges. A submarine ridge running from Tunisia to the island of Sicily divides the Mediterranean into two distinct basins. The western basin is characterized by broad, smooth abyssal (or ocean) plains. In contrast, the eastern basin is dominated by a large ridge system, running east to west.

The narrow Strait of Gibraltar inhibits water exchange between the Mediterranean Sea and the Atlantic Ocean, producing a high degree of salinity and a low tidal range within the Mediterranean. The lack of tides has encouraged the build-up of pollutants in many semienclosed bays.

Main surface current

Dense currents sink below surface

Denser, more saline currents flow back to Atlantic

▲ *Because the Mediterranean is almost enclosed by land, its circulation is quite different to the oceans. There is one major current which flows in from the Atlantic and moves east. Currents flowing back to the Atlantic are denser and flow below the main current.*

Industrial pollution flowing from the Dnieper and Danube rivers has destroyed a large proportion of the fish population that used to inhabit the upper layers of the Black Sea.

The Ionian Basin is the deepest in the Mediterranean, reaching depths of 16,800 ft (5121 m).

The edge of the Eurasian Plate is edged by a continental shelf. In the Mediterranean Sea this is widest at the Ebro Fan where it extends 60 miles (96 km).

Oxygen in the Black Sea dissolved only in its upp[er] layers; at depths below 230–300 ft (70–100 m) th[e] sea is "dead" and can support no lifeforms other than specially adapted bacteria.

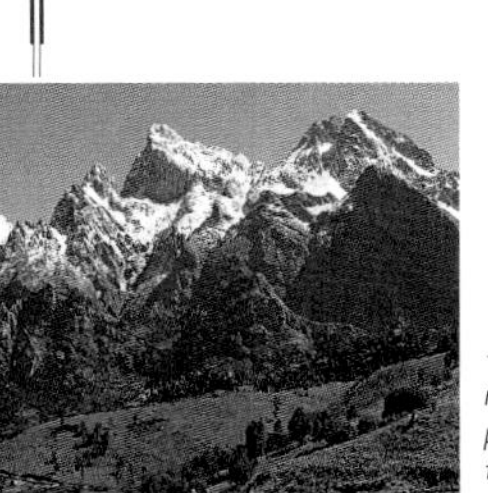

◀ *The Atlas Mountains are a range of fold mountains that lie in Morocco and Algeria. They run parallel to the Mediterranean, forming a topographical and climatic divide between the Mediterranean coast and the western Sahara.*

An arc of active submarine, island and mainland volcanoes, including Etna and Vesuvius, lie in and around southern Italy. The area is also susceptible to earthquakes and landslides.

Nutrient flows into the eastern Mediterranean, and sediment flows to the Nile Delta have been severely lowered by the building of the Aswan Dam across the Nile in Egypt. This is causing the delta to shrink.

The Suez Canal, opened in 1[869,] extends 100 miles (160 km) f[rom] Port Said to the Gulf of Sue[z].

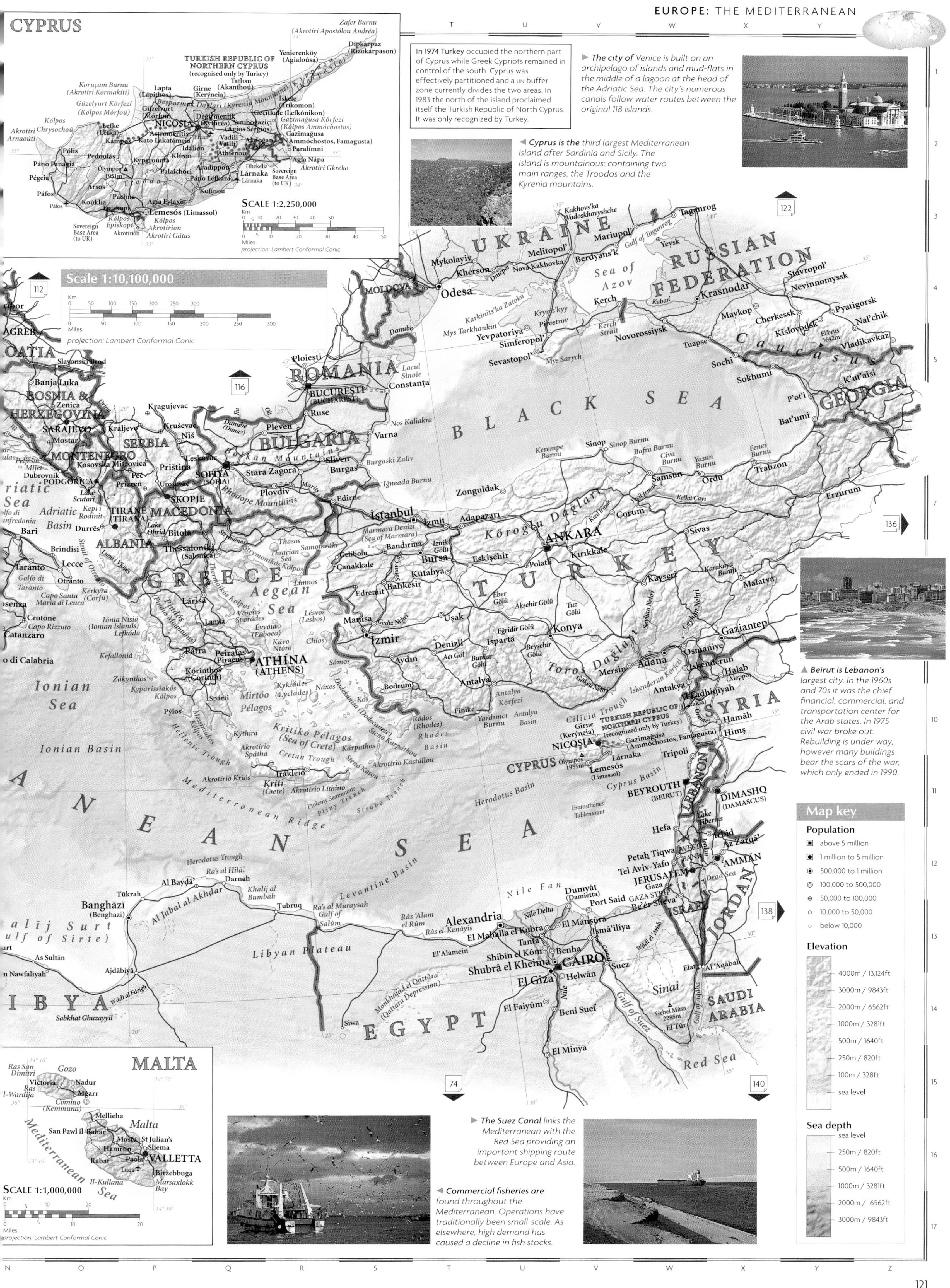
CYPRUS
TURKISH REPUBLIC OF NORTHERN CYPRUS (recognised only by Turkey)
NICOSIA (Lefkosia)
Lemesós (Limassol)
Lárnaka
Gazimağusa (Ammóchostos, Famagusta)
SCALE 1:2,250,000
projection: Lambert Conformal Conic
Scale 1:10,100,000
projection: Lambert Conformal Conic
UKRAINE
RUSSIAN FEDERATION
MOLDOVA
ROMANIA
BULGARIA
SERBIA
MONTENEGRO
BOSNIA & HERZEGOVINA
MACEDONIA
ALBANIA
GREECE
TURKEY
GEORGIA
SYRIA
LEBANON
ISRAEL
JORDAN
CYPRUS
SAUDI ARABIA
EGYPT
LIBYA
BLACK SEA
Sea of Azov
Aegean Sea
Ionian Sea
MEDITERRANEAN SEA
Red Sea
BUCUREȘTI (BUCHAREST)
SOFIYA (SOFIA)
SKOPJE
TIRANË (TIRANA)
ATHÍNA (ATHENS)
ANKARA
İstanbul
BEYROUTH (BEIRUT)
DIMASHQ (DAMASCUS)
JERUSALEM
'AMMĀN
CAIRO
Alexandria
MALTA
VALLETTA
SCALE 1:1,000,000
projection: Lambert Conformal Conic
Map key
Population
above 5 million
1 million to 5 million
500,000 to 1 million
100,000 to 500,000
50,000 to 100,000
10,000 to 50,000
below 10,000
Elevation
4000m / 13,124ft
3000m / 9843ft
2000m / 6562ft
1000m / 3281ft
500m / 1640ft
250m / 820ft
100m / 328ft
sea level
Sea depth
sea level
250m / 820ft
500m / 1640ft
1000m / 3281ft
2000m / 6562ft
3000m / 9843ft

In 1974 Turkey occupied the northern part of Cyprus while Greek Cypriots remained in control of the south. Cyprus was effectively partitioned and a UN buffer zone currently divides the two areas. In 1983 the north of the island proclaimed itself the Turkish Republic of North Cyprus. It was only recognized by Turkey.

► *The city of Venice is built on an archipelago of islands and mud-flats in the middle of a lagoon at the head of the Adriatic Sea. The city's numerous canals follow water routes between the original 118 islands.*

◄ *Cyprus is the third largest Mediterranean island after Sardinia and Sicily. The island is mountainous; containing two main ranges, the Troodos and the Kyrenia mountains.*

▲ *Beirut is Lebanon's largest city. In the 1960s and 70s it was the chief financial, commercial, and transportation center for the Arab states. In 1975 civil war broke out. Rebuilding is under way, however many buildings bear the scars of the war, which only ended in 1990.*

► *The Suez Canal links the Mediterranean with the Red Sea providing an important shipping route between Europe and Asia.*

◄ *Commercial fisheries are found throughout the Mediterranean. Operations have traditionally been small-scale. As elsewhere, high demand has caused a decline in fish stocks.*

The Russian Federation

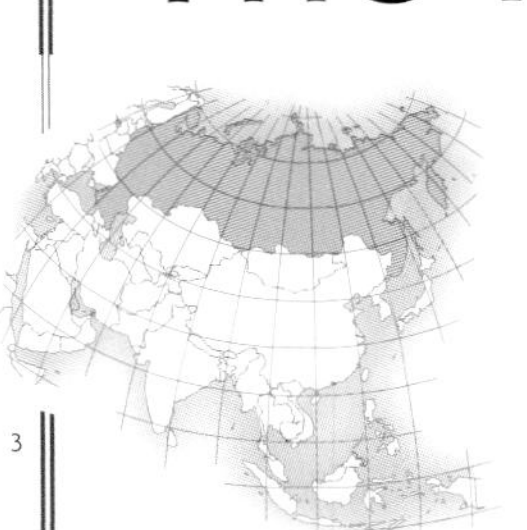

The Cold War era of global relations was concluded in 1991 with the formal dissolution of the Soviet Union. The Russian Federation declared its separate sovereignty from the foundering communist empire following independence declarations from a number of former Soviet republics. As the leading member of the Commonwealth of Independent States, the Russian Federation has a central role in the development of post-Soviet Eurasia. Crossing 11 time zones, the Russian Federation is almost twice the size of the US, and with more than 150 ethnic minorities and 21 autonomous republics, regionalist dissent within its own territory remains a danger.

▶ *Summer beds of moss and lichen scatter a 90% surface cover of ice across the islands of Franz Josef Land (Zemlya Frantsa-Iosifa), the northernmost land in the eastern hemisphere.*

THE RUSSIAN FEDERATION: ADMINISTRATIVE REGIONS

124-125

126-127

The administrative area names in European Russia have been omitted west of the Ural Mountains. Please refer to pages 124–125 and 126–127 where these areas are shown at a larger scale.

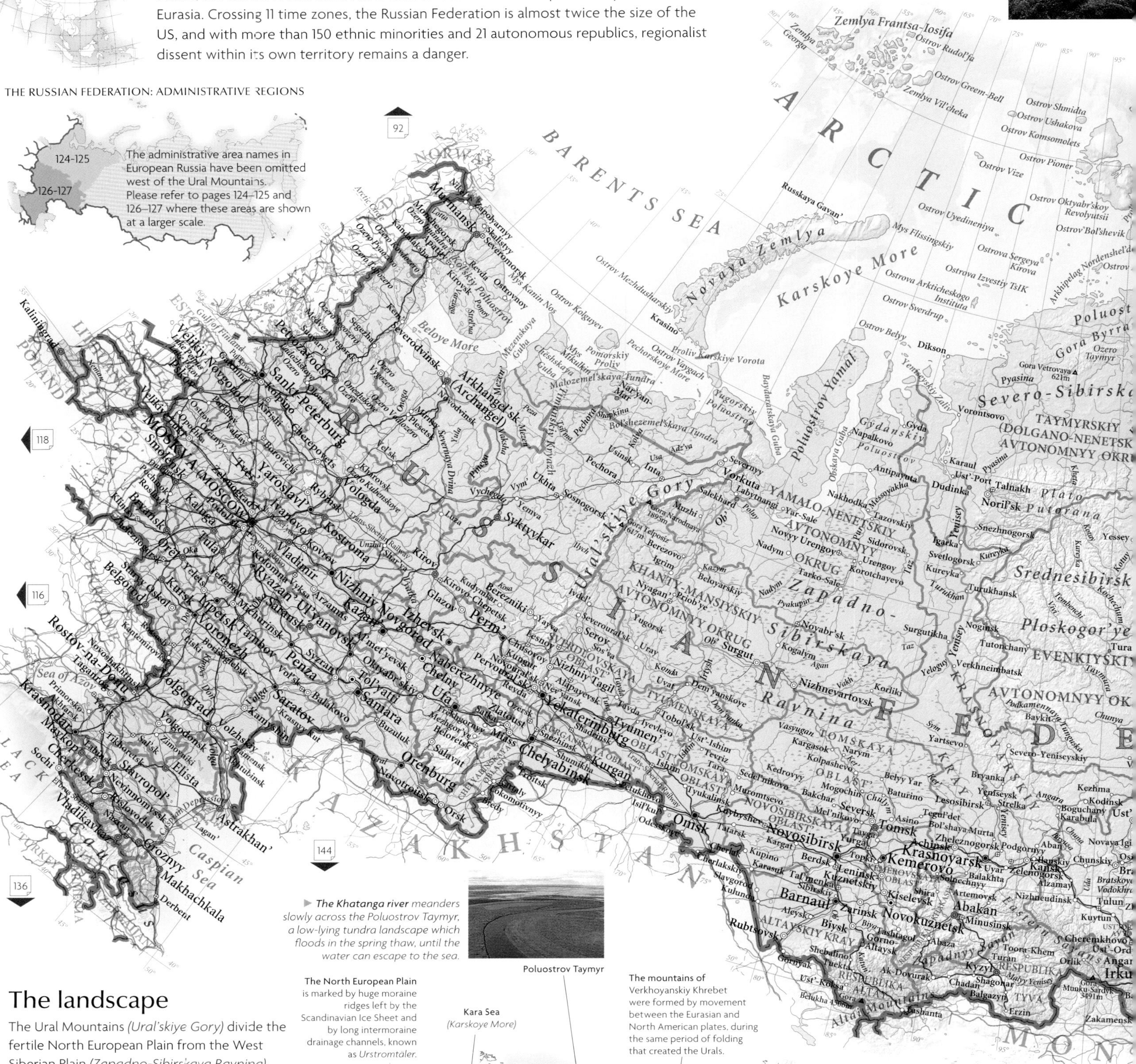

▶ *The Khatanga river meanders slowly across the Poluostrov Taymyr, a low-lying tundra landscape which floods in the spring thaw, until the water can escape to the sea.*

The landscape

The Ural Mountains *(Ural'skiye Gory)* divide the fertile North European Plain from the West Siberian Plain *(Zapadno-Sibirskaya Ravnina)*, the world's largest area of flat ground, crossed by giant rivers flowing north to the Kara Sea *(Karskoye More)*. The land rises to the Central Siberian Plateau *(Srednesibirskoye Ploskogor'ye)* and becomes more mountainous to the southeast. These immense topographic regions intersect with latitudinal vegetation bands. The tundra of the extreme north gives way to a vast area of coniferous woodland, which is known as *taiga*, larger than the Amazon rain forest. This belt turns to mixed forest and then steppe grasslands toward the south.

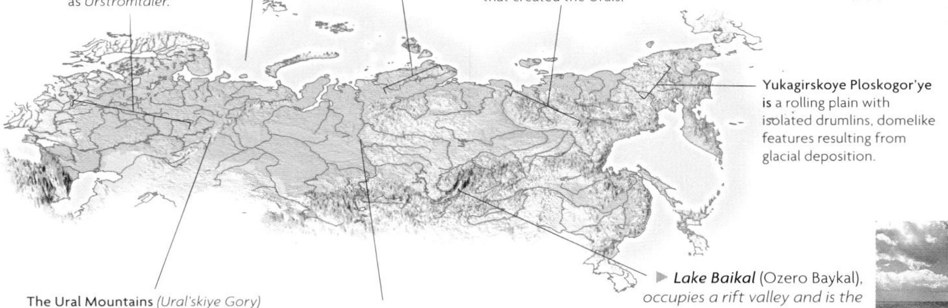

The North European Plain is marked by huge moraine ridges left by the Scandinavian Ice Sheet and by long intermoraine drainage channels, known as *Urstromtaler*.

Kara Sea *(Karskoye More)*

Poluostrov Taymyr

The mountains of Verkhoyanskiy Khrebet were formed by movement between the Eurasian and North American plates, during the same period of folding that created the Urals.

Yukagirskoye Ploskogor'ye is a rolling plain with isolated drumlins, domelike features resulting from glacial deposition.

The Ural Mountains *(Ural'skiye Gory)* extend 1550 miles (2500 km). They were formed over 280 million years ago, folded as the East European and Siberian plates moved closer together.

The Yenisey is one of the world's longest rivers, and also among the most languid, dropping only 500 ft (152 m) over 1200 miles (2000 km).

▶ **Lake Baikal** (Ozero Baykal), *occupies a rift valley and is the world's deepest lake, over 1 mile (1.6 km) in depth. It is fed by over 300 rivers and drained by just one, the Angara.*

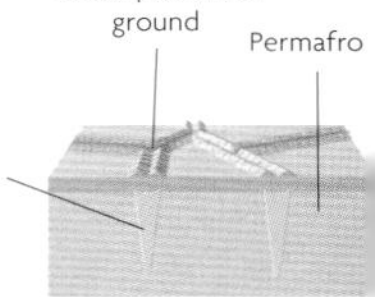

Polygon shapes create patterned ground

Permafro

Permanent ice wedges up to 16 ft (5 m) deep

▲ **Patterned ground is** *permafrost feature fou extensively across nort Russia. Seasonal contr of the permafrost crea polygonal cracks, whic filled by ice wedges.*

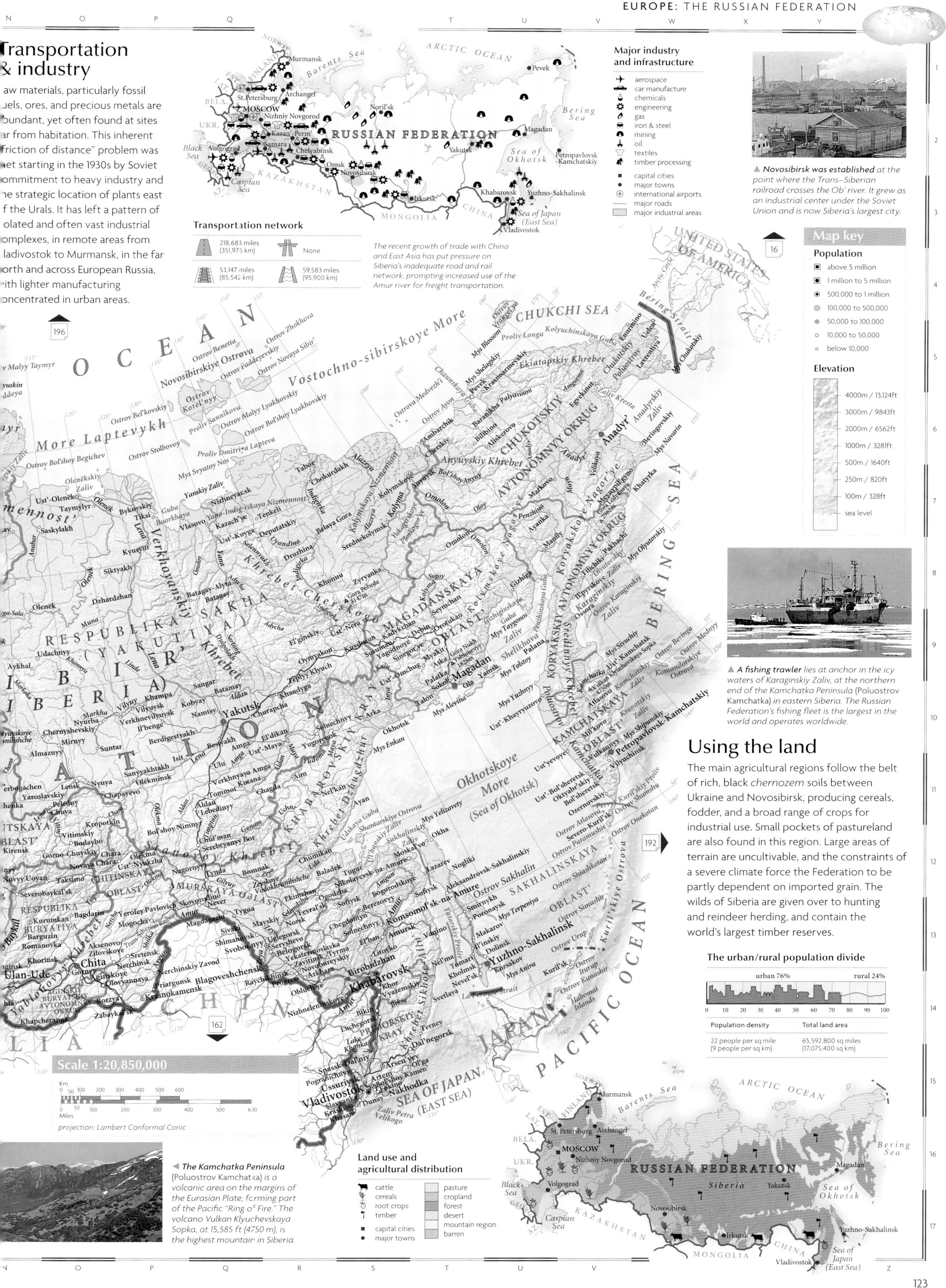

Major industry and infrastructure
aerospace
car manufacture
chemicals
engineering
gas
iron & steel
mining
oil
textiles
timber processing
capital cities
major towns
international airports
major roads
major industrial areas
RUSSIAN FEDERATION
Transportation network
218,683 miles (351,975 km)
None
53,147 miles (85,542 km)
59,583 miles (95,900 km)
Map key
Population
above 5 million
1 million to 5 million
500,000 to 1 million
100,000 to 500,000
50,000 to 100,000
10,000 to 50,000
below 10,000
Elevation
4000m / 13,124ft
3000m / 9843ft
2000m / 6562ft
1000m / 3281ft
500m / 1640ft
250m / 820ft
100m / 328ft
sea level
Scale 1:20,850,000
projection: Lambert Conformal Conic
The urban/rural population divide
urban 76%
rural 24%
Population density
22 people per sq mile (9 people per sq km)
Total land area
65,592,800 sq miles (17,075,400 sq km)
Land use and agricultural distribution
cattle
cereals
root crops
timber
capital cities
major towns
pasture
cropland
forest
desert
mountain region
barren

ransportation & industry

aw materials, particularly fossil uels, ores, and precious metals are bundant, yet often found at sites ar from habitation. This inherent friction of distance" problem was et starting in the 1930s by Soviet ommitment to heavy industry and he strategic location of plants east f the Urals. It has left a pattern of olated and often vast industrial omplexes, in remote areas from ladivostok to Murmansk, in the far orth and across European Russia, ith lighter manufacturing oncentrated in urban areas.

The recent growth of trade with China and East Asia has put pressure on Siberia's inadequate road and rail network, prompting increased use of the Amur river for freight transportation.

▲ ***Novosibirsk was established*** *at the point where the Trans-Siberian railroad crosses the Ob' river. It grew as an industrial center under the Soviet Union and is now Siberia's largest city.*

▲ ***A fishing trawler*** *lies at anchor in the icy waters of Karaginskiy Zaliv, at the northern end of the Kamchatka Peninsula (Poluostrov Kamchatka) in eastern Siberia. The Russian Federation's fishing fleet is the largest in the world and operates worldwide.*

Using the land

The main agricultural regions follow the belt of rich, black *chernozem* soils between Ukraine and Novosibirsk, producing cereals, fodder, and a broad range of crops for industrial use. Small pockets of pastureland are also found in this region. Large areas of terrain are uncultivable, and the constraints of a severe climate force the Federation to be partly dependent on imported grain. The wilds of Siberia are given over to hunting and reindeer herding, and contain the world's largest timber reserves.

◄ ***The Kamchatka Peninsula*** (Poluostrov Kamchatka) *is a volcanic area on the margins of the Eurasian Plate, forming part of the Pacific "Ring of Fire." The volcano Vulkan Klyuchevskaya Sopka, at 15,585 ft (4750 m), is the highest mountain in Siberia.*

Northern European Russia

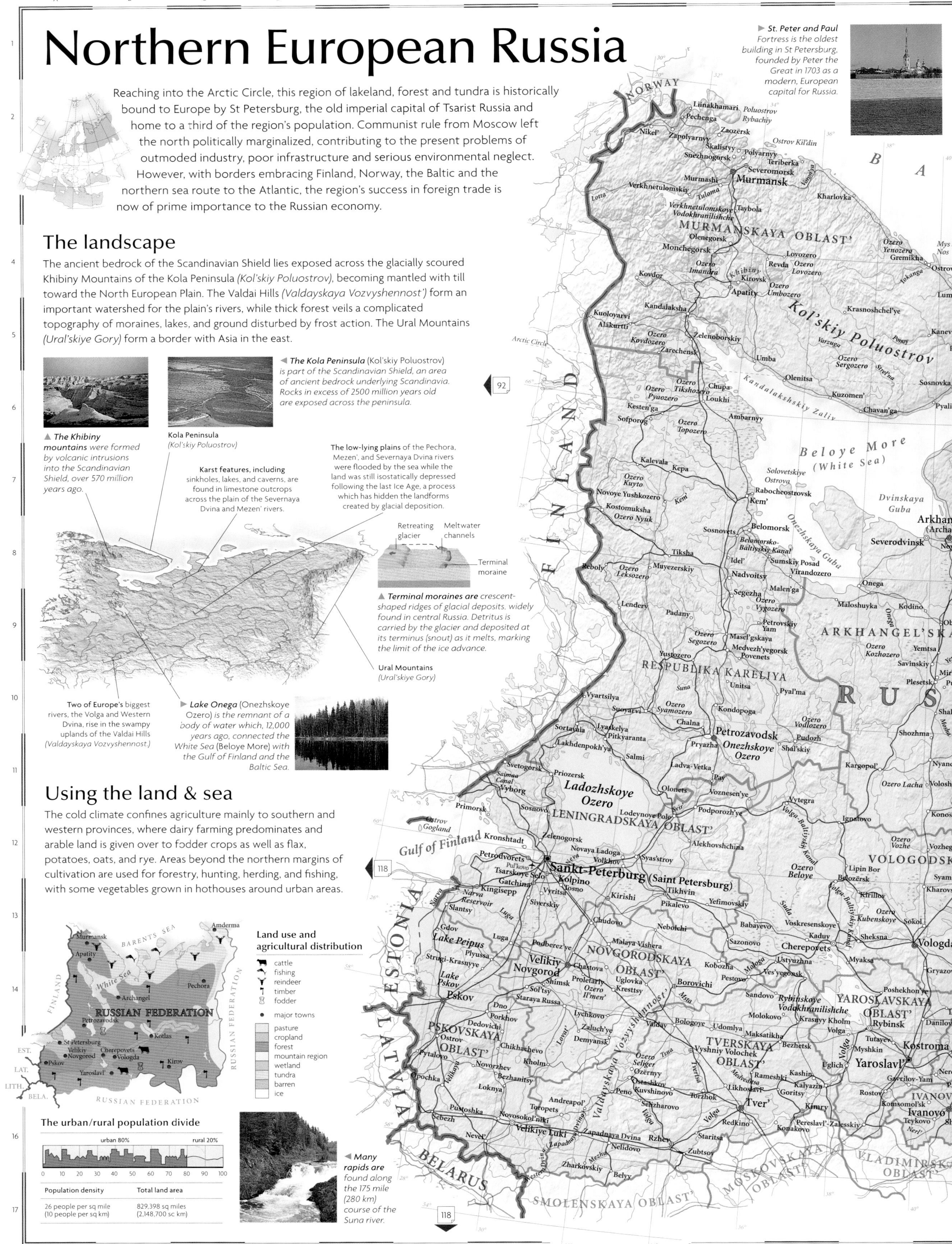

NORWAY
FINLAND
ESTONIA
LATVIA
BELARUS
Beloye More (White Sea)
Kol'skiy Poluostrov
Kandalakshskiy Zaliv
Onezhskaya Guba
Dvinskaya Guba
Gulf of Finland
Arctic Circle
MURMANSKAYA OBLAST'
RESPUBLIKA KARELIYA
ARKHANGEL'SKAYA
LENINGRADSKAYA OBLAST'
NOVGORODSKAYA OBLAST'
PSKOVSKAYA OBLAST'
TVERSKAYA OBLAST'
VOLOGODSKAYA
YAROSLAVSKAYA OBLAST'
SMOLENSKAYA OBLAST'
MOSKOVSKAYA OBLAST'
VLADIMIRSKAYA OBLAST'
Murmansk
Severomorsk
Monchegorsk
Kirovsk
Apatity
Kandalaksha
Kem'
Belomorsk
Segezha
Kondopoga
Petrozavodsk
Ladozhskoye Ozero
Onezhskoye Ozero
Vyborg
Kronshtadt
Sankt-Peterburg (Saint Petersburg)
Kolpino
Gatchina
Kingisepp
Tikhvin
Kirishi
Lake Peipus
Pskov
Velikiy Novgorod
Valdayskaya Vozvyshennost'
Tver'
Rybinsk
Yaroslavl'
Kostroma
Vologda
Cherepovets
Severodvinsk
Velikiye Luki
Rybinskoye Vodokhranilishche

Reaching into the Arctic Circle, this region of lakeland, forest and tundra is historically bound to Europe by St Petersburg, the old imperial capital of Tsarist Russia and home to a third of the region's population. Communist rule from Moscow left the north politically marginalized, contributing to the present problems of outmoded industry, poor infrastructure and serious environmental neglect. However, with borders embracing Finland, Norway, the Baltic and the northern sea route to the Atlantic, the region's success in foreign trade is now of prime importance to the Russian economy.

▶ *St. Peter and Paul Fortress is the oldest building in St Petersburg, founded by Peter the Great in 1703 as a modern, European capital for Russia.*

The landscape

The ancient bedrock of the Scandinavian Shield lies exposed across the glacially scoured Khibiny Mountains of the Kola Peninsula *(Kol'skiy Poluostrov)*, becoming mantled with till toward the North European Plain. The Valdai Hills *(Valdayskaya Vozvyshennost')* form an important watershed for the plain's rivers, while thick forest veils a complicated topography of moraines, lakes, and ground disturbed by frost action. The Ural Mountains *(Ural'skiye Gory)* form a border with Asia in the east.

▲ **The Khibiny mountains** *were formed by volcanic intrusions into the Scandinavian Shield, over 570 million years ago.*

◀ **The Kola Peninsula** (Kol'skiy Poluostrov) *is part of the Scandinavian Shield, an area of ancient bedrock underlying Scandinavia. Rocks in excess of 2500 million years old are exposed across the peninsula.*

Kola Peninsula *(Kol'skiy Poluostrov)*

Karst features, including sinkholes, lakes, and caverns, are found in limestone outcrops across the plain of the Severnaya Dvina and Mezen' rivers.

The low-lying plains of the Pechora, Mezen', and Severnaya Dvina rivers were flooded by the sea while the land was still isostatically depressed following the last Ice Age, a process which has hidden the landforms created by glacial deposition.

Retreating glacier — Meltwater channels — Terminal moraine

▲ **Terminal moraines are** *crescent-shaped ridges of glacial deposits, widely found in central Russia. Detritus is carried by the glacier and deposited at its terminus (snout) as it melts, marking the limit of the ice advance.*

Ural Mountains *(Ural'skiye Gory)*

Two of Europe's biggest rivers, the Volga and Western Dvina, rise in the swampy uplands of the Valdai Hills *(Valdayskaya Vozvyshennost.)*

▶ **Lake Onega** (Onezhskoye Ozero) *is the remnant of a body of water which, 12,000 years ago, connected the White Sea (Beloye More) with the Gulf of Finland and the Baltic Sea.*

Using the land & sea

The cold climate confines agriculture mainly to southern and western provinces, where dairy farming predominates and arable land is given over to fodder crops as well as flax, potatoes, oats, and rye. Areas beyond the northern margins of cultivation are used for forestry, hunting, herding, and fishing, with some vegetables grown in hothouses around urban areas.

Land use and agricultural distribution

- cattle
- fishing
- reindeer
- timber
- fodder
- major towns
- pasture
- cropland
- forest
- mountain region
- wetland
- tundra
- barren
- ice

The urban/rural population divide

urban 80% — rural 20%

0 10 20 30 40 50 60 70 80 90 100

Population density	Total land area
26 people per sq mile (10 people per sq km)	829,398 sq miles (2,148,700 sc km)

◀ *Many rapids are found along the 175 mile (280 km) course of the Suna river.*

Scale 1:6,000,000
Km
Miles
projection: Lambert Conformal Conic
Map key
Population
1 million to 5 million
500,000 to 1 million
100,000 to 500,000
50,000 to 100,000
10,000 to 50,000
below 10,000
Elevation
1000m / 3281ft
500m / 1640ft
250m / 820ft
100m / 328ft
sea level
Major industry and infrastructure
chemicals
coal
defence
engineering
food processing
hydro-electric power
mining
oil & gas
textiles
timber processing
major towns
international airports
major roads
major industrial areas
Transportation network
53,700 miles (85,920 km)
None
10,300 miles (16,572 km)
12,500 miles (20,000 km)
RUSSIAN FEDERATION
BARENTS SEA
White Sea
FINLAND
EST.
LAT.
LITH.
BELA.
Murmansk
Apatity
Archangel
Petrozavodsk
St Petersburg
Velikiy Novgorod
Pskov
Cherepovets
Vologda
Yaroslavl'
Kotlas
Kirov
Pechora
Amderma
NENETSKIY AVTONOMNYY OKRUG
RESPUBLIKA KOMI
PERMSKAYA OBLAST'
KIROVSKAYA OBLAST'
UDMURTSKAYA RESPUBLIKA
NIZHEGORODSKAYA OBLAST'
RESPUBLIKA MARIY EL
RESPUBLIKA TATARSTAN
RESPUBLIKA BASHKORTOSTAN
YAMALO-NENETSKIY AVTONOMNYY OKRUG
KHANTY-MANSIYSKIY AVTONOMNYY OKRUG
SVERDLOVSKAYA OBLAST'
Ural'skiye Gory
Timanskiy Kryazh
Bol'shezemel'skaya Tundra
Malozemel'skaya Tundra
Severnyye Uvaly
Ostrov Kolguyev
Ostrov Vaygach
Yugorskiy Poluostrov
Cheshskaya Guba
Pechorskaya Guba
Nar'yan-Mar
Vorkuta
Inta
Ukhta
Syktyvkar
Kotlas
Kirov
Perm'
Solikamsk
Berezniki

◀ *The Ural Mountains* (Ural'skiye Gory) *form the traditional boundary between Europe and Asia. Elevations rarely exceed 6000 ft (1830 m). The region is extremely barren in the far northern latitudes.*

Transportation & industry

The ports of St. Petersburg, Murmansk, and Archangel serve a regional economy led by large-scale resource extraction. Nickel, iron ore, and apatite are mined in the Kola Peninsula *(Kol'skiy Poluostrov)*, and fossil fuels in the Pechora Basin. Paper production is central to Archangel's vast timber industry, while St. Petersburg, drawing on ample labor, has become a major manufacturing center.

Railroads linking remote industrial centers with the region's ports are the principal means of supply, although the impressive system of canals, linking natural waterways, is used for freight haulage during the summer.

▶ *Ice forces the port at St. Petersburg to close in winter, yet Murmansk, on the Barents Sea, remains open, its waters prevented from freezing by warmer ocean currents extending from the North Atlantic Drift.*

► **Kaliningrad has been** *a Russian enclave since 1945. The port is an important center for the Russian Federation's Baltic fishing fleet.*

◄ **St Basil's Cathedral,** *completed in 1561, stands in Moscow's Red Square next to the Kremlin; the original fortified stronghold of the city.*

Southern European Russia

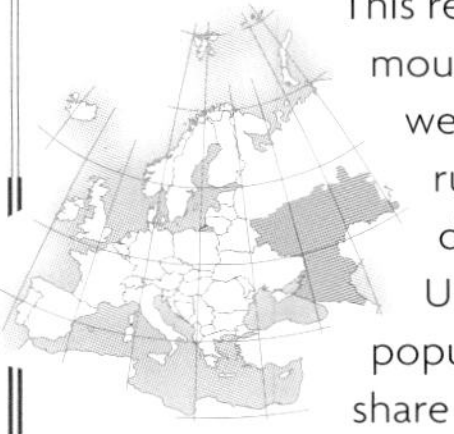

This region, divided from Asia by desert, seas, and mountains, has exerted a powerful influence both east and west since the 13th century. Over 70 years of Communist rule produced a highly urbanized, industrial society dominated by Moscow, which was the capital of the Soviet Union until 1991. Almost two-thirds of the Russian Federation's population live in this core area, with a relatively high per capita share of its wealth. However, the rapid growth of a market economy has caused great social upheaval, with rising crime and political instability.

The landscape

Ancient folds in the deep sedimentary strata of the North European Plain have created a sequence of high and low regions. The Central Russian Upland *(Srednerusskaya Vozvyshennost')* in the west is deeply incised by rivers draining into the lowland of the Oka and Don rivers. In the east the Volga, Europe's longest river, flows south to the Caspian Sea, dividing the Volga Uplands *(Privolzhskaya Vozvyshennost')* from the foothills of the Ural Mountains *(Ural'skiye Gory)*. The Caucasus mountains and the Black Sea form a natural border to the southwest.

▲ **A plantation of** *Scots pine helps consolidate the loose sandy soils of the Meshchera Lowland* (Meshcherskaya Nizina)*, which lies on the bed of an old glacial lake.*

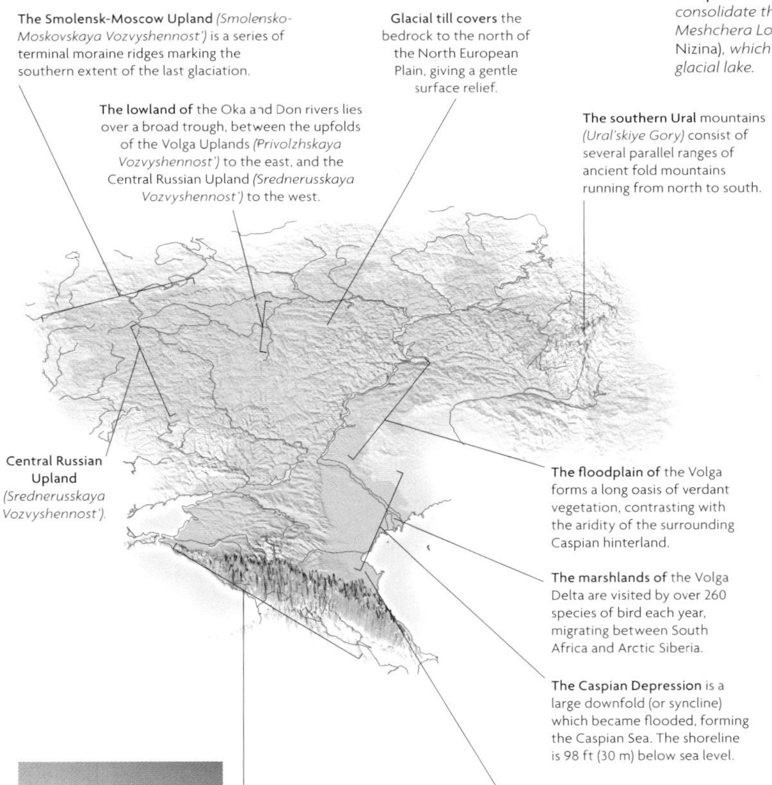

The Smolensk-Moscow Upland *(Smolensko-Moskovskaya Vozvyshennost')* is a series of terminal moraine ridges marking the southern extent of the last glaciation.

Glacial till covers the bedrock to the north of the North European Plain, giving a gentle surface relief.

The lowland of the Oka and Don rivers lies over a broad trough, between the upfolds of the Volga Uplands *(Privolzhskaya Vozvyshennost')* to the east, and the Central Russian Upland *(Srednerusskaya Vozvyshennost')* to the west.

The southern Ural mountains *(Ural'skiye Gory)* consist of several parallel ranges of ancient fold mountains running from north to south.

Central Russian Upland *(Srednerusskaya Vozvyshennost')*.

The floodplain of the Volga forms a long oasis of verdant vegetation, contrasting with the aridity of the surrounding Caspian hinterland.

The marshlands of the Volga Delta are visited by over 260 species of bird each year, migrating between South Africa and Arctic Siberia.

The Caspian Depression is a large downfold (or syncline) which became flooded, forming the Caspian Sea. The shoreline is 98 ft (30 m) below sea level.

Drifting sand occupies large areas of the south, forming dunes up to 50 ft (15 m) high.

◄ **The Caucasus mountains** *run from the Black Sea to the Caspian Sea. They include El'brus which, at 18,511 ft (5642 m), is the highest point in Europe. It is still uplifting at a rate of 0.4 inches (10 mm) per year.*

Salt dome

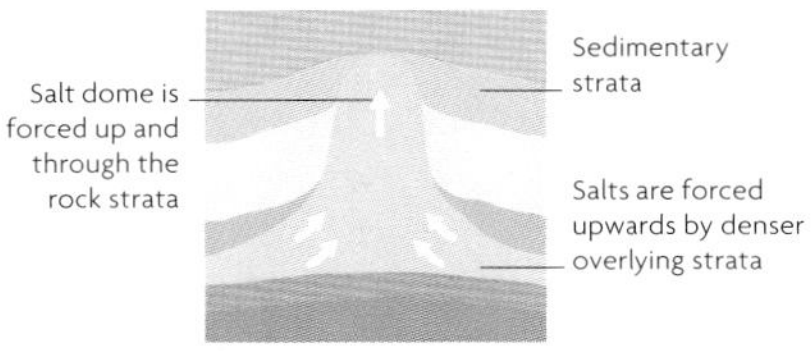

Salt dome is forced up and through the rock strata

Sedimentary strata

Salts are forced upwards by denser overlying strata

▲ **Salt domes, rounded** *hills up to 500 ft (150 m) high, are produced as less dense rock salts are displaced under the extreme pressure of denser, overlying strata and forced up toward the surface creating domes. They are widespread in the Caspian Depression.*

Scale 1:6,000,000
Km 0 10 20 40 60 80 100 120 140
Miles 0 10 20 40 60 80 100 120 140
projection: Lambert Conformal Conic
Map key
Population
above 5 million
1 million to 5 million
500,000 to 1 million
100,000 to 500,000
50,000 to 100,000
10,000 to 50,000
below 10,000
Elevation
4000m / 13,124ft
3000m / 9843ft
2000m / 6562ft
1000m / 3281ft
500m / 1640ft
250m / 820ft
100m / 328ft
sea level
KOSTROMSKAYA OBLAST'
KIROVSKAYA OBLAST'
PERMSKAYA OBLAST'
SVERDLOVSKAYA OBLAST'
CHELYABINSKAYA OBLAST'
NIZHEGORODSKAYA OBLAST'
UDMURTSKAYA RESPUBLIKA
RESPUBLIKA MARIY EL
CHAVASH RESPUBLIKI
RESPUBLIKA TATARSTAN
RESPUBLIKA MORDOVIYA
ULYANOVSKAYA OBLAST'
RESPUBLIKA BASHKORTOSTAN
PENZENSKAYA OBLAST'
SAMARSKAYA OBLAST'
ORENBURGSKAYA OBLAST'
SARATOVSKAYA OBLAST'
VOLGOGRADSKAYA OBLAST'
ASTRAKHANSKAYA OBLAST'
RESPUBLIKA KALMYKIYA
STAVROPOL'SKIY KRAY
CHECHENSKAYA RESPUBLIKA
RESPUBLIKA DAGESTAN
RUSSIAN FEDERATION
KAZAKHSTAN
GEORGIA
AZERBAIJAN
Caspian Sea
Caspian Depression
Ural'skiye Gory
Kuybyshevskoye Vodokhranilishche
Volgogradskoye Vodokhranilishche
Tsimlyanskoye Vodokhranilishche
Saratovskoye Vodokhranilishche
Nizhnekamskoye Vodokhranilishche
Nizhniy Novgorod
Kazan'
Izhevsk
Samara
Ufa
Orenburg
Saratov
Volgograd
Astrakhan'
Penza
Saransk
Ul'yanovsk
Tol'yatti
Cheboksary
Yoshkar-Ola
Naberezhnyye Chelny
Elista
Makhachkala
Groznyy
Vladikavkaz
Orsk
136
144

Using the land

In the cold, humid north and in the southern Urals *(Ural'skiye Gory)*, small grains, potatoes, and flax are commonly rotated with legumes which support livestock farming. The rich *chernozem* (or black earth) areas support diverse crops such as sugar beet, hemp, sunflowers, millet, and vegetables. Further south, aridity restricts husbandry to extensive grazing, with intensive fruit and rice cultivation along the oasis of the Volga.

The urban/rural population divide

urban 71% — rural 29%

0 10 20 30 40 50 60 70 80 90 100

Population density	Total land area
119 people per sq mile (46 people per sq km)	705,916 sq miles (1,828,800 sq km)

Land use and agricultural distribution

sheep, flax, potatoes, rice, sunflowers, sugar beet, timber

capital cities, major towns

pasture, cropland, forest, wetland, mountain region, tundra

RUSSIAN FEDERATION
BELARUS
MOSCOW
Nizhniy Novgorod
Ufa
Samara
Voronezh
RUSSIAN FEDERATION
UKRAINE
KAZAKHSTAN
Rostov-na-Donu
Sea of Azov
Astrakhan'
Caspian Sea
BLACK SEA
GEORGIA
Groznyy
AZERB.

Transportation & industry

Manufacturing is largely based around Moscow and the Volga region, which became a major industrial area during the Second World War. Both Moscow and Nizhniy Novgorod are centers of skilled labor for light manufacturing and engineering. Most of Russia's main chemical plants are located along the Volga, and one of the world's largest car factories was recently opened in Tol'yatti. Processing and machine construction plants use oil, gas, and hydroelectric power from the Volga Basin and metallic minerals from the Urals *(Ural'skiye Gory)* and Kursk.

◀ ***Industrial plants are*** *massed along the Volga. Environmental stress from decades of unbridled industrial development has prompted widespread concern about pollution levels.*

Transportation network

250,000 miles (402,000 km)	None
28,000 miles (44,800 km)	16,300 miles (26,080 km)

Seventy private and national flag airlines have been created from the reorganization of the state airline Aeroflot, which maintained the world's largest fleet of aircraft during the Soviet era.

Major industry and infrastructure

aerospace, car manufacture, chemicals, defense, electronics, engineering, gas, mining, oil, textiles

capital cities, major towns, international airports, major roads, major industrial areas

RUSSIAN FEDERATION
BELARUS
MOSCOW
Nizhniy Novgorod
Kazan'
Ufa
Tula
Ryazan'
Ul'yanovsk
Bryansk
Penza
Tol'yatti
Samara
Kursk
Voronezh
Saratov
Belgorod
Orsk
RUSSIAN FEDERATION
UKRAINE
KAZAKHSTAN
Volgograd
Rostov-na-Donu
Sea of Azov
Astrakhan'
Stavropol'
Caspian Sea
BLACK SEA
GEORGIA
Groznyy
AZERB.

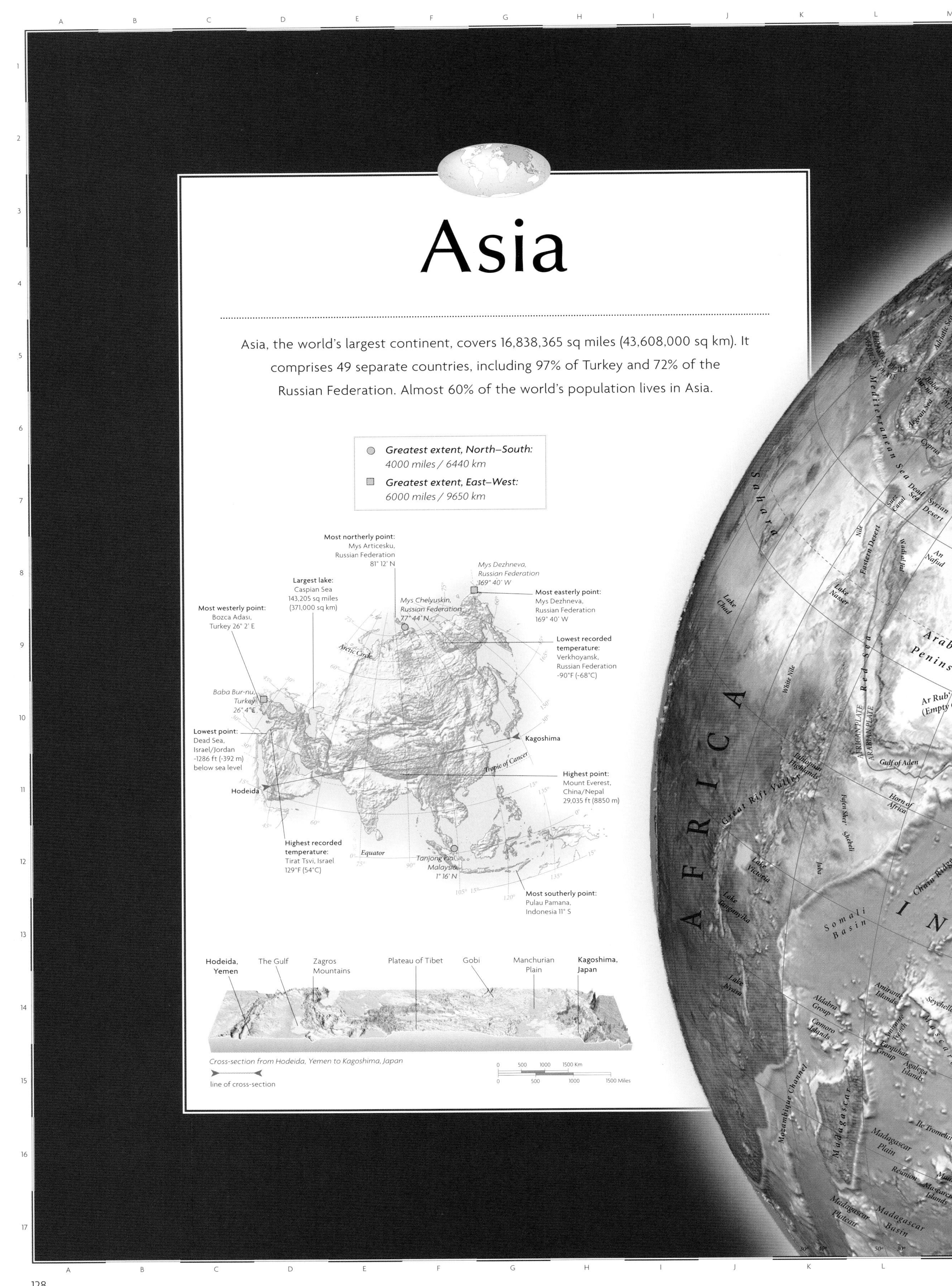

Asia
Asia, the world's largest continent, covers 16,838,365 sq miles (43,608,000 sq km). It comprises 49 separate countries, including 97% of Turkey and 72% of the Russian Federation. Almost 60% of the world's population lives in Asia.
Greatest extent, North–South: 4000 miles / 6440 km
Greatest extent, East–West: 6000 miles / 9650 km
Most northerly point: Mys Articesku, Russian Federation 81° 12' N
Mys Dezhneva, Russian Federation 169° 40' W
Largest lake: Caspian Sea 143,205 sq miles (371,000 sq km)
Most westerly point: Bozca Adası, Turkey 26° 2' E
Mys Chelyuskin, Russian Federation 77° 44' N
Most easterly point: Mys Dezhneva, Russian Federation 169° 40' W
Lowest recorded temperature: Verkhoyansk, Russian Federation -90°F (-68°C)
Arctic Circle
Baba Bur-nu, Turkey 26° 4' E
Lowest point: Dead Sea, Israel/Jordan -1286 ft (-392 m) below sea level
Kagoshima
Tropic of Cancer
Highest point: Mount Everest, China/Nepal 29,035 ft (8850 m)
Hodeida
Highest recorded temperature: Tirat Tsvi, Israel 129°F (54°C)
Equator
Tanjong Piai, Malaysia 1° 16' N
Most southerly point: Pulau Pamana, Indonesia 11° S
Hodeida, Yemen
The Gulf
Zagros Mountains
Plateau of Tibet
Gobi
Manchurian Plain
Kagoshima, Japan
Cross-section from Hodeida, Yemen to Kagoshima, Japan
line of cross-section
0 500 1000 1500 Km
0 500 1000 1500 Miles
AFRICA
Sahara
Mediterranean Sea
Aegean Sea
Cyprus
Suez Canal
Dead Sea
Syrian Desert
An Nafud
Nile
Eastern Desert
Lake Nasser
Lake Chad
Red Sea
Arabian Peninsula
White Nile
Ar Rub' al Khali (Empty Quarter)
AFRICAN PLATE
ARABIAN PLATE
Gulf of Aden
Ethiopian Highlands
Great Rift Valley
Horn of Africa
Shebeli
Juba
Lake Victoria
Lake Tanganyika
Somali Basin
Chain Ridge
Lake Nyasa
Aldabra Group
Comoro Islands
Amirante Islands
Seychelles
Farquhar Group
Agalega Islands
Mozambique Channel
Madagascar
Madagascar Plain
Île Tromelin
Réunion
Mascarene Islands
Madagascar Plateau
Madagascar Basin

ARCTIC OCEAN
North Pole
NORTH AMERICAN PLATE
EURASIAN PLATE
Norwegian Sea
Scandinavia
North Sea
Barents Sea
Franz Josef Land
Novaya Zemlya
Kara Sea
Severnaya Zemlya
Mys Chelyuskin
Laptev Sea
New Siberian Islands
East Siberian Sea
Bering Strait
Chukot Range
Bering Sea
Baltic Sea
Gulf of Bothnia
Gulf of Finland
North European Plain
Central Russian Upland
Ural Mountains
Poluostrov Taymyr
North Siberian Lowland
Putorana Mountains
Central Siberian Plateau
Verkhoyanskiy Khrebet
Khrebet Cherskogo
Kolyma Range
Koryak Range
West Siberian Plain
Siberia
Sea of Okhotsk
Kamchatka
Caspian Depression
Caucasus
Caspian Sea
Aral Sea
Ustyurt Plateau
Kirghiz Steppe
Lake Balkhash
Turan Lowland
Kara Kum
Lake Baikal
Sayanskiy Khrebet
Stanovoy Khrebet
Altai Mountains
ASIA
Tien Shan
Dzungaria
Plateau of Mongolia
Gobi
Great Khingan Range
Manchurian Plain
EUROPE
Elburz Mountains
EURASIAN PLATE
IRANIAN PLATE
Great Salt Desert
Zagros Mountains
Iranian Plateau
Kuh-e Fuladi 5143m
Hindu Kush
Pamirs
Karakoram Range
Takla Makan Desert
Tarim Basin
Kunlun Mountains
Plateau of Tibet
Altun Shan
Qilian Shan
Nan Shan
Ordos Desert
Sea of Japan (East Sea)
Yellow Sea
Korea Bay
Bo Hai
Great Plain of China
Himalayas
Annapurna 8091m
Mount Everest 8850m
Thar Desert
Punjab Plains
Rigestan
Sulaiman Range
Gulf of Oman
Gulf of Kachchh
Arabian Sea
Arabian Basin
ARABIAN PLATE
INDO-AUSTRALIAN PLATE
Vindhya Range
Satpura Range
Ajanta Range
Deccan
Western Ghats
Eastern Ghats
Malabar Coast
Coromandel Coast
Gulf of Khambhat
Mouths of the Ganges
Bay of Bengal
Khasi Hills
Patkai Range
Arakan Yoma
East China Sea
Taiwan Strait
Taiwan
Hainan Strait
Hainan
Gulf of Tongking
Luzon Strait
Philippine Sea
PHILIPPINE PLATE
PACIFIC OCEAN
Japan
Honshu
Hokkaido
Kyushu
Shikoku
Kurile Islands
Ryukyu Islands
Tropic of Cancer
Lakshadweep
Laccadive Islands
Cape Comorin
Gulf of Mannar
Sri Lanka
Maldives
INDIAN OCEAN
Chagos-Laccadive Plateau
Ceylon Plain
Chagos Trench
Mid-Indian Basin
Ninetyeast Ridge
Andaman Islands
Andaman Sea
Nicobar Islands
Gulf of Martaban
Gulf of Thailand
Isthmus of Kra
South China Sea
South China Basin
Mouths of the Mekong
Philippines
Luzon
Mindoro
Palawan
Sulu Sea
Mindanao
Celebes Sea
Philippine Trench
Malay Peninsula
Strait of Malacca
Sumatra
Sunda Shelf
Borneo
Gunung Kinabalu 4094m
Greater Sunda Islands
Gunung Kerinci 3806m
Java Sea
East Indies
Makassar Strait
Celebes
Moluccas
Banda Sea
New Guinea
Lesser Sunda Islands
Java Trench
Sunda Trough
Timor Trough
Arafura Sea
Torres Strait
Cocos Basin
Cocos Islands
Christmas Island
Investigator Ridge
Ninetyeast Ridge
AUSTRALIA
Equator

Physical Asia

The structure of Asia can be divided into two distinct regions. The landscape of northern Asia consists of old mountain chains, shields, plateaus, and basins, like the Ural Mountains in the west and the Central Siberian Plateau to the east. To the south of this region, are a series of plateaus and basins, including the vast Plateau of Tibet and the Tarim Basin. In contrast, the landscapes of southern Asia are much younger, formed by tectonic activity beginning about 65 million years ago, leading to an almost continuous mountain chain running from Europe, across much of Asia, and culminating in the mighty Himalayan mountain belt, formed when the Indo-Australian Plate collided with the Eurasian Plate. They are still being uplifted today. North of the mountains lies a belt of deserts, including the Gobi and the Takla Makan. In the far south, tectonic activity has formed narrow island arcs, extending over 4000 miles (7000 km). To the west lies the Arabian Shield, once part of the African Plate. As it was rifted apart from Africa, the Arabian Plate collided with the Eurasian Plate, uplifting the Zagros Mountains.

Coastal Lowlands and Island Arcs

The coastal plains that fringe Southeast Asia contain many large delta systems, caused by high levels of rainfall and erosion of the Himalayas, the Plateau of Tibet, and relict loess deposits. To the south is an extensive island archipelago, lying on the drowned Sunda Shelf. Most of these islands are volcanic in origin, caused by the subduction of the Indo-Australian Plate beneath the Eurasian Plate.

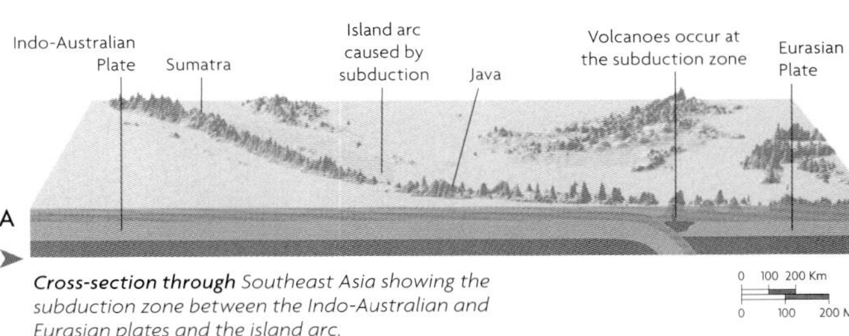
Indo-Australian Plate
Sumatra
Island arc caused by subduction
Java
Volcanoes occur at the subduction zone
Eurasian Plate
A

Cross-section through Southeast Asia showing the subduction zone between the Indo-Australian and Eurasian plates and the island arc.

The Indian Shield and Himalayan System

The large shield area beneath the Indian subcontinent is between 2.5 and 3.5 billion years old. As the floor of the southern Indian Ocean spread, it pushed the Indian Shield north. This was eventually driven beneath the Plateau of Tibet. This process closed up the ancient Tethys Sea and uplifted the world's highest mountain chain, the Himalayas. Much of the uplifted rock strata was from the seabed of the Tethys Sea, partly accounting for the weakness of the rocks and the high levels of erosion found in the Himalayas.

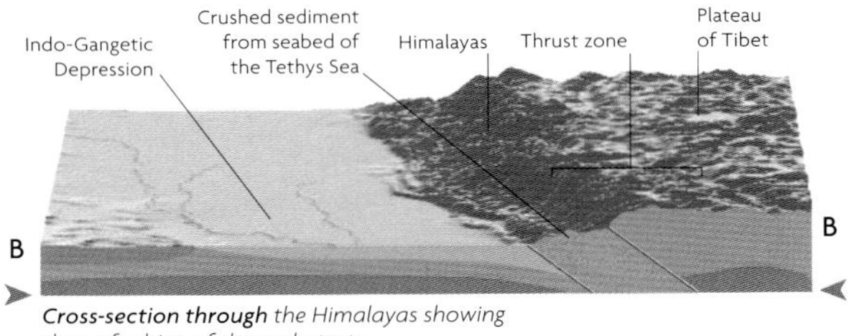

Indo-Gangetic Depression · Crushed sediment from seabed of the Tethys Sea · Himalayas · Thrust zone · Plateau of Tibet

Cross-section through the Himalayas showing thrust faulting of the rock strata.

East Asian Plains and Uplands

Several, small, isolated shield areas, such as the Shandong Peninsula, are found in east Asia. Between these stable shield areas, large river systems like the Yangtze and the Yellow River have deposited thick layers of sediment, forming extensive alluvial plains. The largest of these is the Great Plain of China, the relief of which does not rise above 300 ft (100 m).

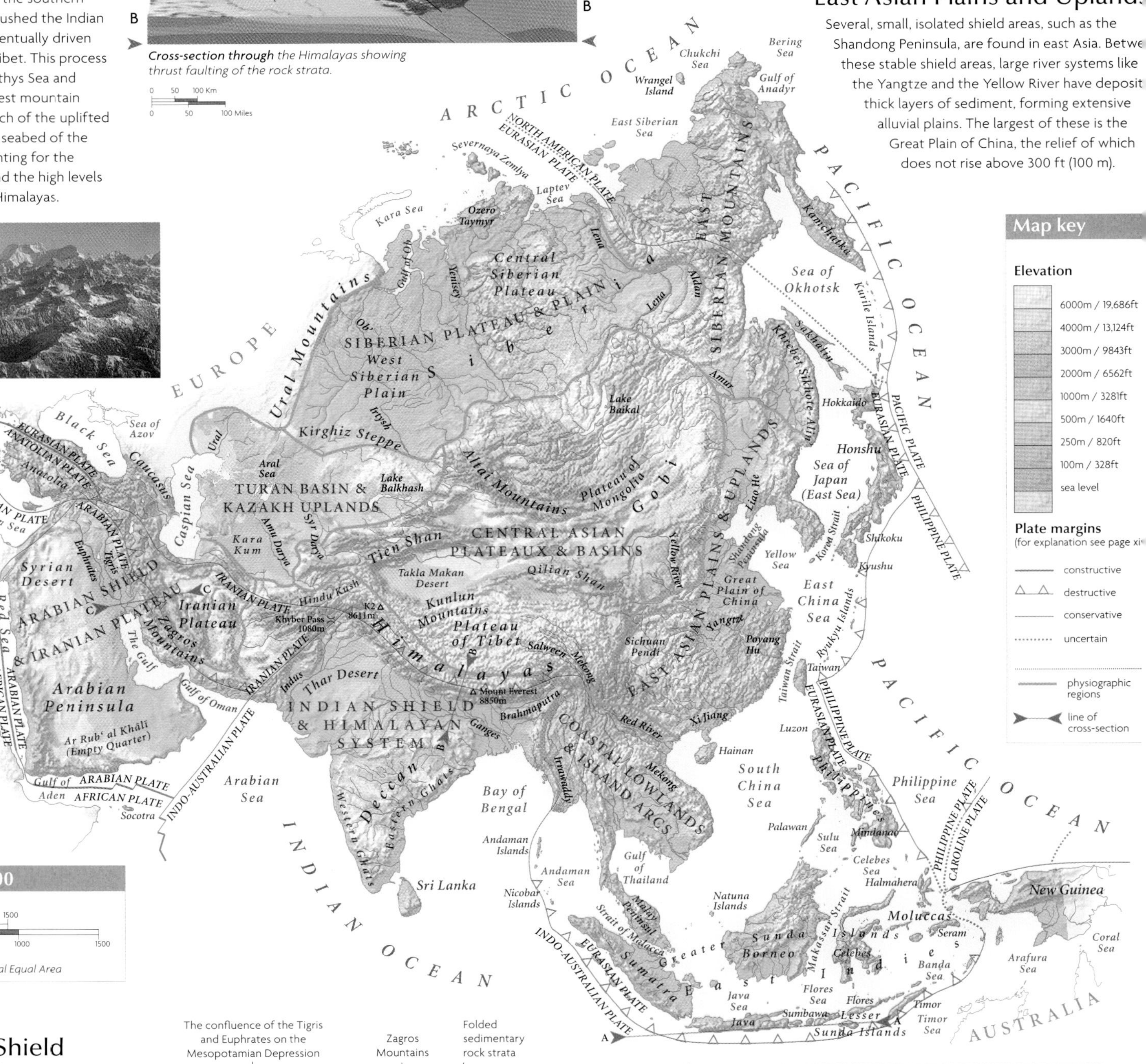

Map key

Elevation: 6000m / 19,686ft; 4000m / 13,124ft; 3000m / 9843ft; 2000m / 6562ft; 1000m / 3281ft; 500m / 1640ft; 250m / 820ft; 100m / 328ft; sea level

Plate margins (for explanation see page xi): constructive; destructive; conservative; uncertain

physiographic regions; line of cross-section

Scale 1:63,000,000

projection: Lambert Azimuthal Equal Area

The Arabian Shield and Iranian Plateau

Approximately five million years ago, rifting of the continental crust split the Arabian Plate from the African Plate and flooded the Red Sea. As this rift spread, the Arabian Plate collided with the Eurasian Plate, transforming part of the Tethys seabed into the Zagros Mountains which run northwest-southeast across western Iran.

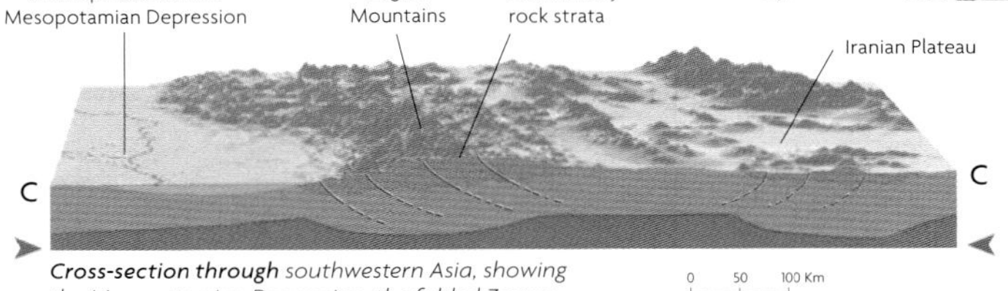

The confluence of the Tigris and Euphrates on the Mesopotamian Depression · Zagros Mountains · Folded sedimentary rock strata · Iranian Plateau

Cross-section through southwestern Asia, showing the Mesopotamian Depression, the folded Zagros Mountains and the Iranian Plateau.

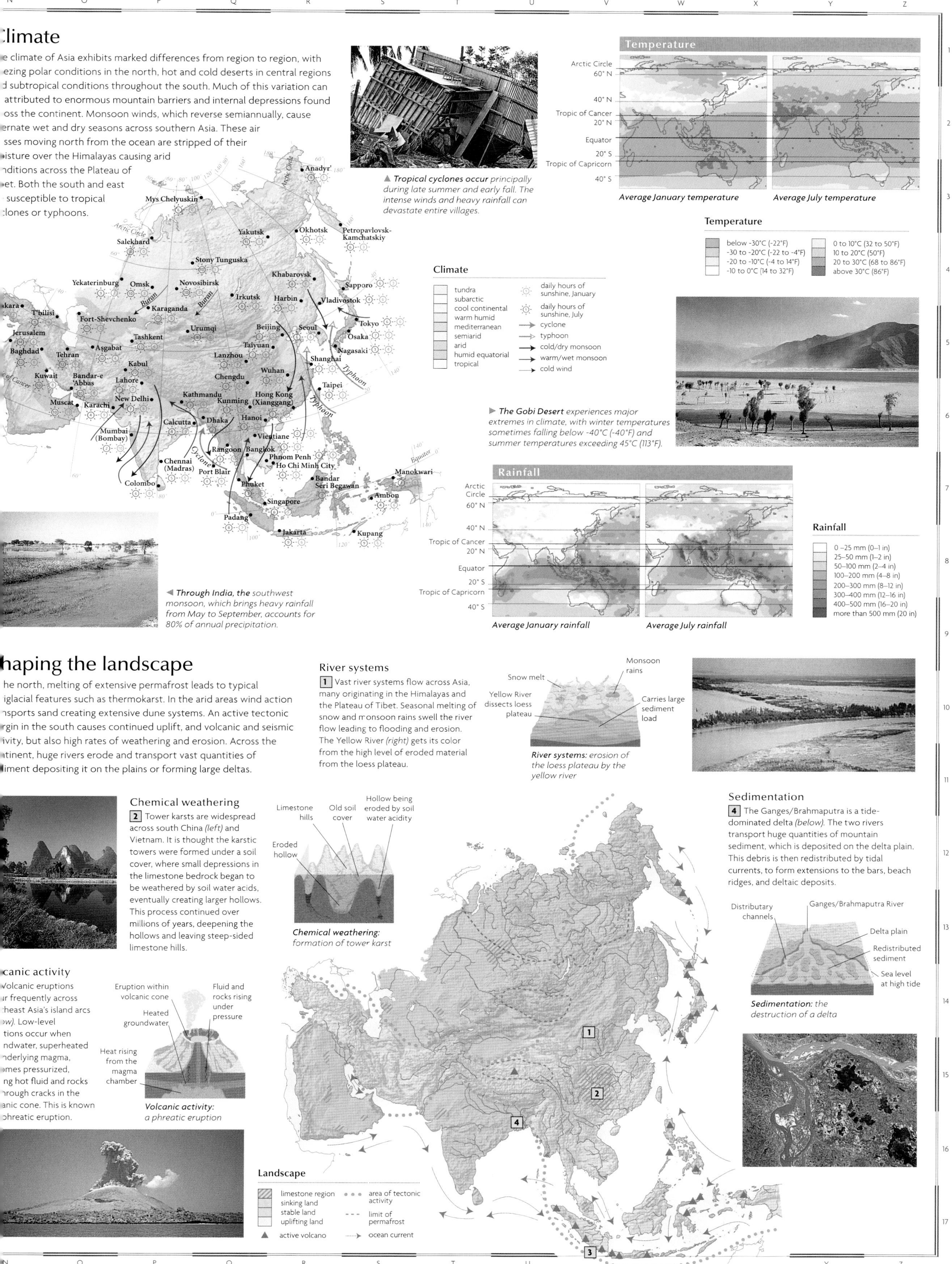

:limate

e climate of Asia exhibits marked differences from region to region, with ezing polar conditions in the north, hot and cold deserts in central regions d subtropical conditions throughout the south. Much of this variation can attributed to enormous mountain barriers and internal depressions found oss the continent. Monsoon winds, which reverse semiannually, cause ernate wet and dry seasons across southern Asia. These air sses moving north from the ocean are stripped of their isture over the Himalayas causing arid nditions across the Plateau of et. Both the south and east susceptible to tropical :lones or typhoons.

Climate
tundra
subarctic
cool continental
warm humid
mediterranean
semiarid
arid
humid equatorial
tropical
daily hours of sunshine, January
daily hours of sunshine, July
cyclone
typhoon
cold/dry monsoon
warm/wet monsoon
cold wind
Anadyr'
Mys Chelyuskin
Salekhard
Yakutsk
Okhotsk
Petropavlovsk-Kamchatskiy
Stony Tunguska
Khabarovsk
Yekaterinburg
Omsk
Novosibirsk
Irkutsk
Harbin
Sapporo
Vladivostok
Karaganda
Tokyo
Fort-Shevchenko
Urumqi
Beijing
Seoul
Osaka
Jerusalem
Tashkent
Taiyuan
Nagasaki
Baghdad
Tehran
Asgabat
Lanzhou
Shanghai
Typhoon
Kabul
Wuhan
Kuwait
Bandar-e 'Abbas
Lahore
Chengdu
Taipei
Kathmandu
Kunming
Hong Kong (Xianggang)
Muscat
Karachi
New Delhi
Hanoi
Calcutta
Dhaka
Mumbai (Bombay)
Vientiane
Rangoon
Bangkok
Cyclone
Phnom Penh
Ho Chi Minh City
Chennai (Madras)
Port Blair
Manokwari
Bandar Seri Begawan
Colombo
Phuket
Ambon
Singapore
Padang
Jakarta
Kupang

▲ *Tropical cyclones occur principally during late summer and early fall. The intense winds and heavy rainfall can devastate entire villages.*

Temperature
Arctic Circle 60° N
40° N
Tropic of Cancer 20° N
Equator
20° S
Tropic of Capricorn
40° S
Average January temperature
Average July temperature
Temperature
below -30°C (-22°F)
-30 to -20°C (-22 to -4°F)
-20 to -10°C (-4 to 14°F)
-10 to 0°C (14 to 32°F)
0 to 10°C (32 to 50°F)
10 to 20°C (50°F)
20 to 30°C (68 to 86°F)
above 30°C (86°F)

► *The Gobi Desert experiences major extremes in climate, with winter temperatures sometimes falling below -40°C (-40°F) and summer temperatures exceeding 45°C (113°F).*

Rainfall
Arctic Circle 60° N
40° N
Tropic of Cancer 20° N
Equator
20° S
Tropic of Capricorn
40° S
Average January rainfall
Average July rainfall
Rainfall
0–25 mm (0–1 in)
25–50 mm (1–2 in)
50–100 mm (2–4 in)
100–200 mm (4–8 in)
200–300 mm (8–12 in)
300–400 mm (12–16 in)
400–500 mm (16–20 in)
more than 500 mm (20 in)

◄ *Through India, the southwest monsoon, which brings heavy rainfall from May to September, accounts for 80% of annual precipitation.*

haping the landscape

he north, melting of extensive permafrost leads to typical iglacial features such as thermokarst. In the arid areas wind action nsports sand creating extensive dune systems. An active tectonic rgin in the south causes continued uplift, and volcanic and seismic ivity, but also high rates of weathering and erosion. Across the ntinent, huge rivers erode and transport vast quantities of iment depositing it on the plains or forming large deltas.

River systems

1 Vast river systems flow across Asia, many originating in the Himalayas and the Plateau of Tibet. Seasonal melting of snow and monsoon rains swell the river flow leading to flooding and erosion. The Yellow River *(right)* gets its color from the high level of eroded material from the loess plateau.

Snow melt
Monsoon rains
Yellow River dissects loess plateau
Carries large sediment load

***River systems:** erosion of the loess plateau by the yellow river*

Chemical weathering

2 Tower karsts are widespread across south China *(left)* and Vietnam. It is thought the karstic towers were formed under a soil cover, where small depressions in the limestone bedrock began to be weathered by soil water acids, eventually creating larger hollows. This process continued over millions of years, deepening the hollows and leaving steep-sided limestone hills.

Limestone hills
Old soil cover
Hollow being eroded by soil water acidity
Eroded hollow

***Chemical weathering:** formation of tower karst*

canic activity

Volcanic eruptions ir frequently across heast Asia's island arcs w). Low-level tions occur when ndwater, superheated nderlying magma, mes pressurized, ng hot fluid and rocks rough cracks in the anic cone. This is known hreatic eruption.

Eruption within volcanic cone
Fluid and rocks rising under pressure
Heated groundwater
Heat rising from the magma chamber

***Volcanic activity:** a phreatic eruption*

Sedimentation

4 The Ganges/Brahmaputra is a tide-dominated delta *(below)*. The two rivers transport huge quantities of mountain sediment, which is deposited on the delta plain. This debris is then redistributed by tidal currents, to form extensions to the bars, beach ridges, and deltaic deposits.

Distributary channels
Ganges/Brahmaputra River
Delta plain
Redistributed sediment
Sea level at high tide

***Sedimentation:** the destruction of a delta*

Landscape
limestone region
sinking land
stable land
uplifting land
active volcano
area of tectonic activity
limit of permafrost
ocean current
1
2
3
4

Political Asia

Asia is the world's largest continent, encompassing many different and discrete realms, from the desert Arab lands of the southwest to the subtropical archipelago of Indonesia; from the vast barren wastes of Siberia to the fertile river valleys of China and South Asia, seats of some of the world's most ancient civilizations. The collapse of the Soviet Union has fragmented the north of the continent into the Siberian portion of the Russian Federation, and the new republics of Central Asia. Strong religious traditions heavily influence the politics of South and Southwest Asia. Hindu and Muslim rivalries threaten to upset the political equilibrium in South Asia where India – in terms of population – remains the world's largest democracy. Communist China another population giant, is reasserting its position as a world and political power, while on its doorstep, the economically progressive and dynamic Pacific Rim countries, led by Japan, continue to assert their worldwide economic force.

Population density
(people per sq mile)

- below 25
- 25–124
- 125–259
- 260–649
- 650–10,400
- above 10,400

Population

Some of the world's most populous and least populous regions are in Asia. The plains of eastern China, the Ganges river plains in India, Japan, and the Indonesian island of Java, all have very high population densities; by contrast parts of Siberia and the Plateau of Tibet are virtually uninhabited. China has the world's greatest population – 20% of the globe's total – while India, with the second largest, is likely to overtake China within 30 years.

◀ ***Over 13 million** people bustle through Kolkata's maze of crowded, narrow streets. Population densities in India's largest city reach almost 85,000 per sq mile (33,000 per sq km).*

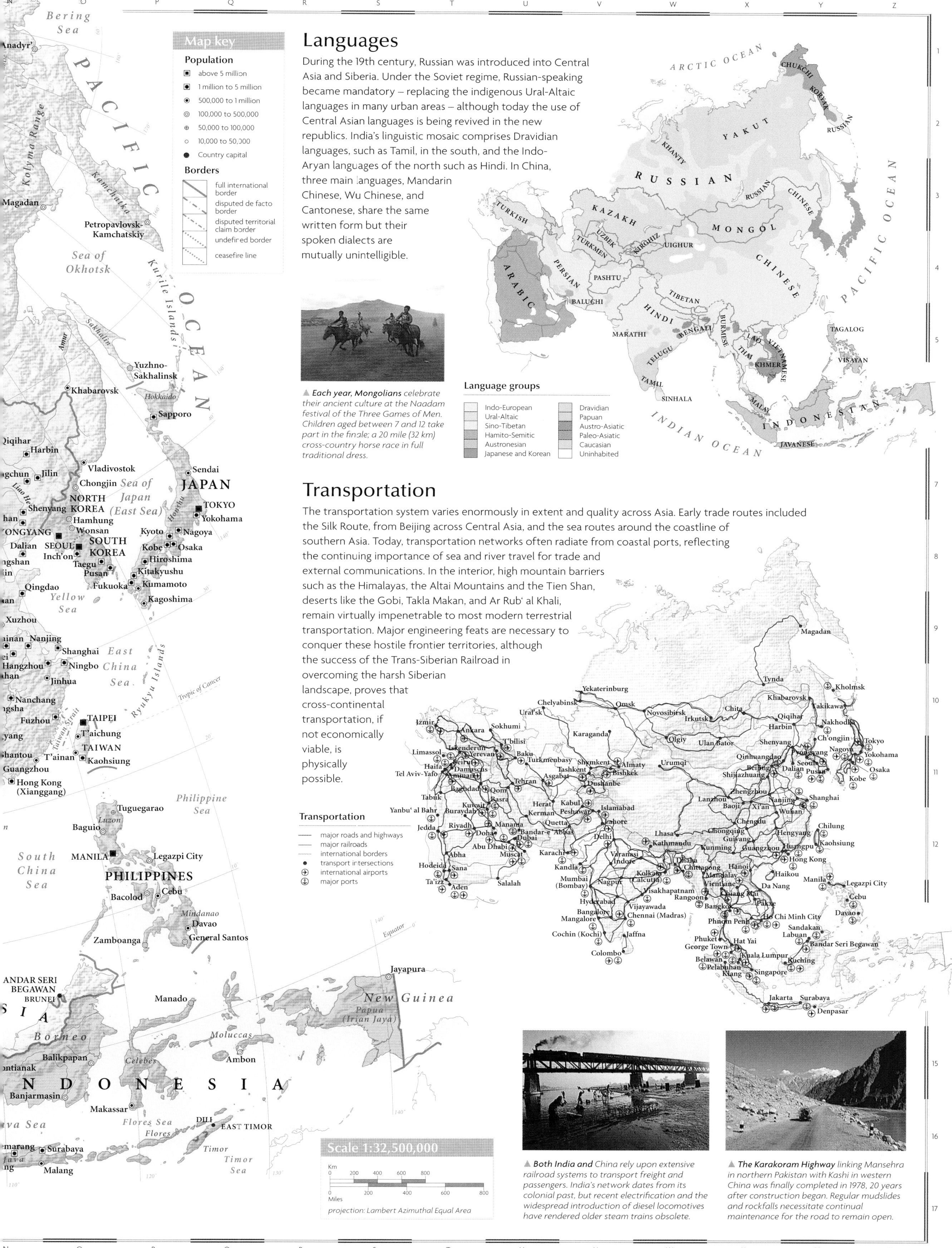
Map key
Population
above 5 million
1 million to 5 million
500,000 to 1 million
100,000 to 500,000
50,000 to 100,000
10,000 to 50,000
Country capital
Borders
full international border
disputed de facto border
disputed territorial claim border
undefined border
ceasefire line
Language groups
Indo-European
Ural-Altaic
Sino-Tibetan
Hamito-Semitic
Austronesian
Japanese and Korean
Dravidian
Papuan
Austro-Asiatic
Paleo-Asiatic
Caucasian
Uninhabited
Transportation
major roads and highways
major railroads
international borders
transport intersections
international airports
major ports
Scale 1:32,500,000
projection: Lambert Azimuthal Equal Area

Languages

During the 19th century, Russian was introduced into Central Asia and Siberia. Under the Soviet regime, Russian-speaking became mandatory – replacing the indigenous Ural-Altaic languages in many urban areas – although today the use of Central Asian languages is being revived in the new republics. India's linguistic mosaic comprises Dravidian languages, such as Tamil, in the south, and the Indo-Aryan languages of the north such as Hindi. In China, three main languages, Mandarin Chinese, Wu Chinese, and Cantonese, share the same written form but their spoken dialects are mutually unintelligible.

▲ *Each year, Mongolians celebrate their ancient culture at the Naadam festival of the Three Games of Men. Children aged between 7 and 12 take part in the finale; a 20 mile (32 km) cross-country horse race in full traditional dress.*

Transportation

The transportation system varies enormously in extent and quality across Asia. Early trade routes included the Silk Route, from Beijing across Central Asia, and the sea routes around the coastline of southern Asia. Today, transportation networks often radiate from coastal ports, reflecting the continuing importance of sea and river travel for trade and external communications. In the interior, high mountain barriers such as the Himalayas, the Altai Mountains and the Tien Shan, deserts like the Gobi, Takla Makan, and Ar Rub' al Khali, remain virtually impenetrable to most modern terrestrial transportation. Major engineering feats are necessary to conquer these hostile frontier territories, although the success of the Trans-Siberian Railroad in overcoming the harsh Siberian landscape, proves that cross-continental transportation, if not economically viable, is physically possible.

▲ ***Both India and*** *China rely upon extensive railroad systems to transport freight and passengers. India's network dates from its colonial past, but recent electrification and the widespread introduction of diesel locomotives have rendered older steam trains obsolete.*

▲ ***The Karakoram Highway*** *linking Mansehra in northern Pakistan with Kashi in western China was finally completed in 1978, 20 years after construction began. Regular mudslides and rockfalls necessitate continual maintenance for the road to remain open.*

Asian resources

Although agriculture remains the economic mainstay of most Asian countries, the number of people employed in agriculture has steadily declined, as new industries have been developed during the past 30 years. China, Indonesia, Malaysia, Thailand, and Turkey have all experienced far-reaching structural change in their economies, while the breakup of the Soviet Union has created a new economic challenge in the Central Asian republics. The countries of The Persian Gulf illustrate the rapid transformation from rural nomadism to modern, urban society which oil wealth has brought to parts of the continent. Asia's most economically dynamic countries, Japan, Singapore, South Korea, and Taiwan, fringe the Pacific Ocean and are known as the Pacific Rim. In contrast, other Southeast Asian countries like Laos and Cambodia remain both economically and industrially underdeveloped.

Industry

East Asian industry leads the continent in both productivity and efficiency; electronics, hi-tech industries, car manufacture, and shipbuilding are important. The so-called economic "tigers" of the Pacific Rim are Japan, South Korea, and Taiwan and in recent years China has rediscovered its potential as an economic superpower. Heavy industries such as engineering, chemicals, and steel typify the industrial complexes along the corridor created by the Trans-Siberian Railroad, the Fergana Valley in Central Asia, and also much of the huge industrial plain of east China. The discovery of oil in the Persian Gulf has brought immense wealth to countries that previously relied on subsistence agriculture on marginal desert land.

Standard of living

Despite Japan's high standards of living, and Southwest Asia's oil-derived wealth, immense disparities exist across the continent. Afghanistan remains one of the world's most underdeveloped nations, as do the mountain states of Nepal and Bhutan. Further rapid population growth is exacerbating poverty and overcrowding in many parts of India and Bangladesh.

Standard of living
(UN human development index)

- low
- high

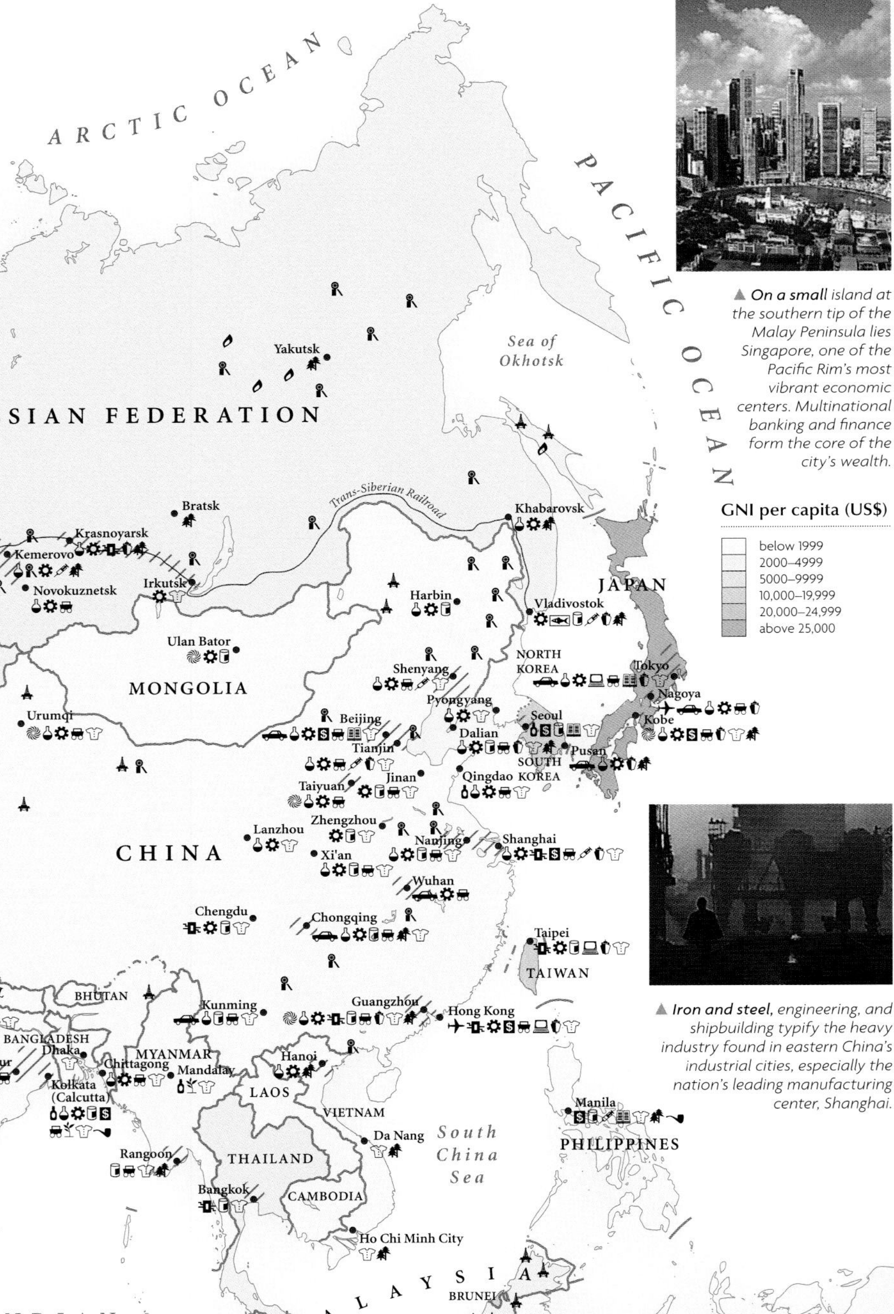

Industry
aerospace
brewing
car/vehicle manufacture
cement
chemicals
electronics
engineering
finance
fish processing
food processing
hi-tech industry
iron & steel
pharmaceuticals
printing & publishing
shipbuilding
sugar processing
tea processing
textiles
timber processing
tobacco processing
coal
oil
gas
industrial cities
major industrial areas
GNI per capita (US$)
below 1999
2000–4999
5000–9999
10,000–19,999
20,000–24,999
above 25,000
ARCTIC OCEAN
PACIFIC OCEAN
INDIAN OCEAN
Sea of Okhotsk
RUSSIAN FEDERATION
KAZAKHSTAN
MONGOLIA
CHINA
JAPAN
NORTH KOREA
SOUTH KOREA
TAIWAN
PHILIPPINES
VIETNAM
LAOS
THAILAND
CAMBODIA
MYANMAR
MALAYSIA
BRUNEI
SINGAPORE
INDONESIA
EAST TIMOR
INDIA
SRI LANKA
BANGLADESH
NEPAL
BHUTAN
PAKISTAN
AFGHANISTAN
IRAN
IRAQ
SAUDI ARABIA
YEMEN
OMAN
UAE
QATAR
BAHRAIN
KUWAIT
JORDAN
ISRAEL
LEBANON
SYRIA
CYPRUS
TURKEY
GEORGIA
ARMENIA
AZERB.
TURKMENISTAN
UZBEKISTAN
KYRGYZSTAN
TAJIKISTAN
Aral Sea
Caspian Sea
Red Sea
Persian Gulf
Gulf of Oman
Gulf of Aden
Arabian Sea
South China Sea
Trans-Siberian Railway
Trans-Siberian Railroad
Yekaterinburg
Chelyabinsk
Magnitogorsk
Omsk
Novosibirsk
Kemerovo
Krasnoyarsk
Novokuznetsk
Bratsk
Irkutsk
Yakutsk
Khabarovsk
Vladivostok
Karaganda
Almaty
Tashkent
Farghona
Dushanbe
Asgabat
Urumqi
Ulan Bator
Harbin
Shenyang
Pyongyang
Beijing
Tianjin
Dalian
Seoul
Pusan
Tokyo
Nagoya
Kobe
Jinan
Qingdao
Taiyuan
Zhengzhou
Lanzhou
Xi'an
Nanjing
Shanghai
Wuhan
Chengdu
Chongqing
Taipei
Kunming
Guangzhou
Hong Kong
Hanoi
Da Nang
Manila
Ho Chi Minh City
Bangkok
Rangoon
Kuala Lumpur
Singapore
Jakarta
Surabaya
Istanbul
Izmir
Ankara
Tbilisi
Yerevan
Baku
Beirut
Damascus
Tel Aviv-Yafo
Amman
Kirkuk
Baghdad
Tehran
Isfahan
Basra
Kuwait
Ad Damman
Riyadh
Jedda
Abu Dhabi
Dubai
Rawalpindi
Lahore
Karachi
Delhi
Kanpur
Ahmadabad
Indore
Jamshedpur
Dhaka
Chittagong
Mandalay
Kolkata (Calcutta)
Nagpur
Mumbai (Bombay)
Bangalore
Chennai (Madras)

▲ **On a small** island at the southern tip of the Malay Peninsula lies Singapore, one of the Pacific Rim's most vibrant economic centers. Multinational banking and finance form the core of the city's wealth.

▲ **Iron and steel**, engineering, and shipbuilding typify the heavy industry found in eastern China's industrial cities, especially the nation's leading manufacturing center, Shanghai.

◀ **Traditional industries are** still crucial to many rural economies across Asia. Here, on the Vietnamese coast, salt has been extracted from seawater by evaporation and is being loaded into a van to take to market.

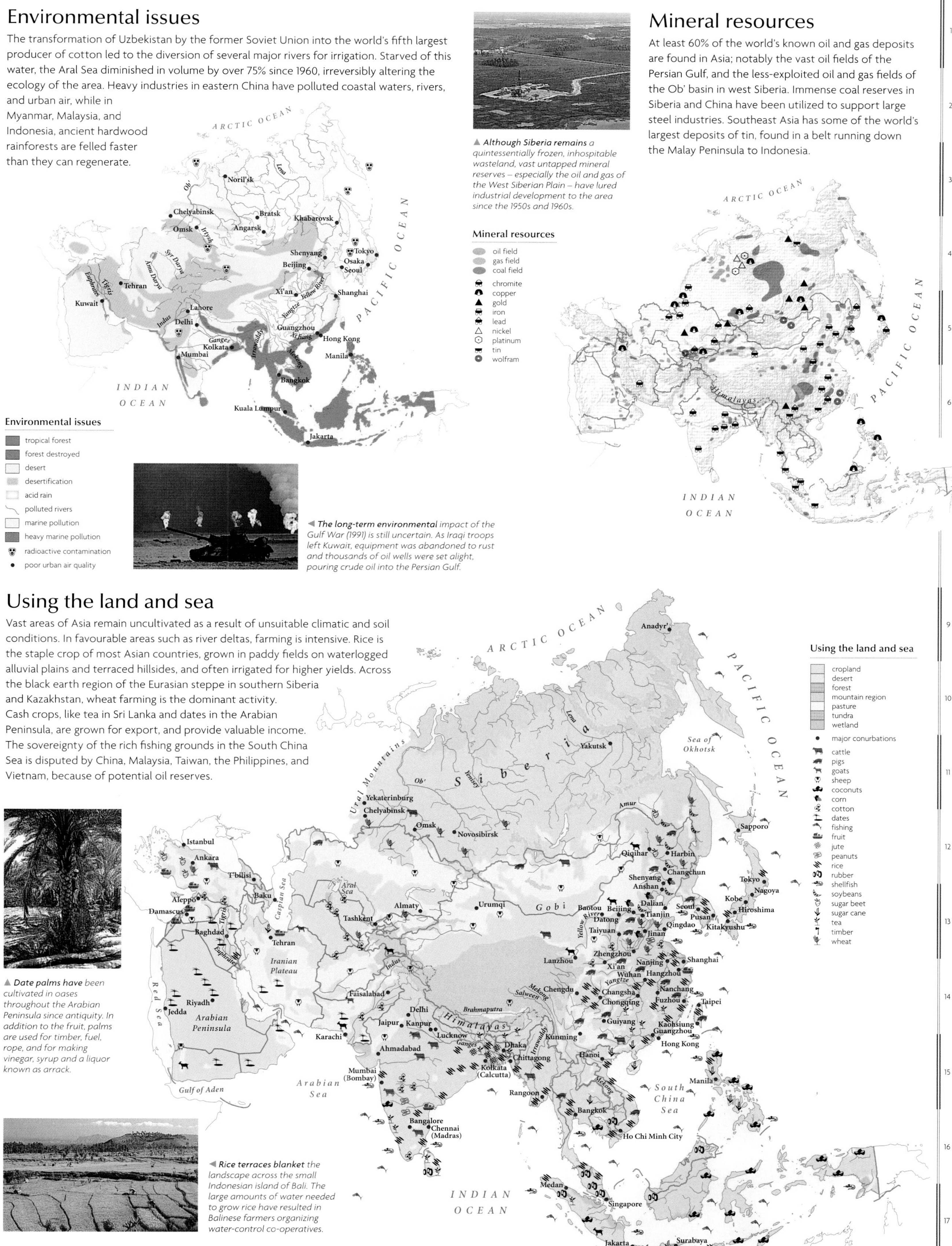
Environmental issues
tropical forest
forest destroyed
desert
desertification
acid rain
polluted rivers
marine pollution
heavy marine pollution
radioactive contamination
poor urban air quality
Mineral resources
oil field
gas field
coal field
chromite
copper
gold
iron
lead
nickel
platinum
tin
wolfram
Using the land and sea
cropland
desert
forest
mountain region
pasture
tundra
wetland
major conurbations
cattle
pigs
goats
sheep
coconuts
corn
cotton
dates
fishing
fruit
jute
peanuts
rice
rubber
shellfish
soybeans
sugar beet
sugar cane
tea
timber
wheat
ARCTIC OCEAN
PACIFIC OCEAN
INDIAN OCEAN
Siberia
Himalayas
Gobi
Arabian Peninsula
Iranian Plateau
Arabian Sea
South China Sea
Sea of Okhotsk
Gulf of Aden
Red Sea
Caspian Sea
Aral Sea
Ural Mountains

Environmental issues

The transformation of Uzbekistan by the former Soviet Union into the world's fifth largest producer of cotton led to the diversion of several major rivers for irrigation. Starved of this water, the Aral Sea diminished in volume by over 75% since 1960, irreversibly altering the ecology of the area. Heavy industries in eastern China have polluted coastal waters, rivers, and urban air, while in Myanmar, Malaysia, and Indonesia, ancient hardwood rainforests are felled faster than they can regenerate.

▲ *Although Siberia remains a quintessentially frozen, inhospitable wasteland, vast untapped mineral reserves – especially the oil and gas of the West Siberian Plain – have lured industrial development to the area since the 1950s and 1960s.*

◄ *The long-term environmental impact of the Gulf War (1991) is still uncertain. As Iraqi troops left Kuwait, equipment was abandoned to rust and thousands of oil wells were set alight, pouring crude oil into the Persian Gulf.*

Mineral resources

At least 60% of the world's known oil and gas deposits are found in Asia; notably the vast oil fields of the Persian Gulf, and the less-exploited oil and gas fields of the Ob' basin in west Siberia. Immense coal reserves in Siberia and China have been utilized to support large steel industries. Southeast Asia has some of the world's largest deposits of tin, found in a belt running down the Malay Peninsula to Indonesia.

Using the land and sea

Vast areas of Asia remain uncultivated as a result of unsuitable climatic and soil conditions. In favourable areas such as river deltas, farming is intensive. Rice is the staple crop of most Asian countries, grown in paddy fields on waterlogged alluvial plains and terraced hillsides, and often irrigated for higher yields. Across the black earth region of the Eurasian steppe in southern Siberia and Kazakhstan, wheat farming is the dominant activity. Cash crops, like tea in Sri Lanka and dates in the Arabian Peninsula, are grown for export, and provide valuable income. The sovereignty of the rich fishing grounds in the South China Sea is disputed by China, Malaysia, Taiwan, the Philippines, and Vietnam, because of potential oil reserves.

▲ *Date palms have been cultivated in oases throughout the Arabian Peninsula since antiquity. In addition to the fruit, palms are used for timber, fuel, rope, and for making vinegar, syrup and a liquor known as arrack.*

◄ *Rice terraces blanket the landscape across the small Indonesian island of Bali. The large amounts of water needed to grow rice have resulted in Balinese farmers organizing water-control co-operatives.*

Turkey & the Caucasus

ARMENIA, AZERBAIJAN, GEORGIA, TURKEY

This region occupies the fragmented junction between Europe, Asia, and the Russian Federation. Sunni Islam provides a common identity for the secular state of Turkey, which the revered leader Kemal Atatürk established from the remnants of the Ottoman Empire after the First World War. Turkey has a broad resource base and expanding trade links with Europe, but the east is relatively undeveloped and strife between the state and a large Kurdish minority has yet to be resolved. Georgia is similarly challenged by ethnic separatism, while the Christian state of Armenia and the mainly Muslim and oil-rich Azerbaijan are locked in conflict over the territory of Nagorno-Karabakh.

Transportation & industry

Turkey leads the region's well diversified economy. Petrochemicals, textiles, engineering, and food processing are the main industries. Azerbaijan is able to export oil, while the other states rely heavily on hydroelectric power and imported fuel. Georgia produces precision machinery. War and earthquake damage have devastated Armenia's infrastructure.

▲ *Azerbaijan has substantial oil reserves, located in and around the Caspian Sea. They were some of the earliest oilfields in the world to be exploited.*

BLACK SEA
RUSSIAN FEDERATION
CASPIAN SEA
GEORGIA
T'BILISI
ARMENIA
YEREVAN
AZERBAIJAN
BAKU
TURKEY
ANKARA
Istanbul
Izmit
Bursa
Izmir
Konya
Antalya
Adana
Gaziantep
Iskenderun
Diyarbakır
Erzurum
Sivas
Kayseri
Samsun
MEDITERRANEAN SEA
SYRIA
IRAQ
IRAN
GREECE
BULGARIA

Major industry and infrastructure

- carpet weaving
- cement
- chemicals
- coal
- engineering
- food processing
- oil
- textiles
- tourism
- vehicle manufacture
- capital cities
- major towns
- international airports
- major roads
- major industrial areas

Transportation network

- 114,867 miles (184,882 km)
- 5778 miles (9300 km)
- 8120 miles (13,069 km)
- 745 miles (1200 km)

Physical and political barriers have severely limited communications between Armenia, Georgia and Azerbaijan. Turkey has a relatively well-developed transportation network.

Using the land & sea

Turkey is largely self-sufficient in food. The irrigated Black Sea coastlands have the world's highest yields of hazelnuts. Tobacco, cotton, sultanas, tea, and figs are the region's main cash crops and a great range of fruit and vegetables are grown. Wine grapes are among the labor-intensive crops which allow full use of limited agricultural land in the Caucasus. Sturgeon fishing is particularly important in Azerbaijan.

BLACK SEA
RUSSIAN FEDERATION
CASPIAN SEA
GEORGIA
T'BILISI
ARMENIA
YEREVAN
AZERBAIJAN
BAKU
TURKEY
ANKARA
Istanbul
Samsun
Izmir
Konya
Antalya
Adana
Diyarbakır
MEDITERRANEAN SEA
SYRIA
IRAQ
IRAN
GREECE
BULGARIA

Land use and agricultural distribution

- cattle
- goats
- cotton
- fishing
- fruit
- hazelnuts
- olives
- sugar beet
- tobacco
- vineyards
- capital cities
- major towns
- pasture
- cropland
- forest

The urban/rural population divide

urban 72% | rural 28%

0 10 20 30 40 50 60 70 80 90 100

Population density	Total land area
238 people per sq mile (92 people per sq km)	368,912 sq miles (955,730 sq km)

▲ *For many centuries, Istanbul has held tremendous strategic importance as a crucial gateway between Europe and Asia. Founded by the Greeks as Byzantium, the city became the center of the East Roman Empire and was known as Constantinople to the Romans. From the 15th century onward the city became the center of the great Ottoman Empire.*

BULGARIA
GREECE
BLACK SEA
Aegean Sea
MEDITERRANEAN SEA
Marmara Denizi (Sea of Marmara)
Edirne
İstanbul
İzmit
Bursa
Çanakkale
Balıkesir
İzmir
Manisa
Aydın
Denizli
Muğla
Antalya
Isparta
Burdur
Afyon
Kütahya
Eskişehir
Bilecik
Zonguldak
Bolu
ANKARA
Kırıkkale
Çankırı
Kastamonu
Sinop
Samsun
Amasya
Çorum
Tokat
Sivas
Yozgat
Kırşehir
Nevşehir
Aksaray
Kayseri
Niğde
Konya
Karaman
Mersin
Tarsus
Adana
Osmaniye
Gaziantep
İskenderun
Antakya
Tuz Gölü
Anadolu
Toros Dağları

114

120

The landscape

The deeply eroded hills and salty basins of the Anatolian Plateau are bordered by several mountain ranges along the Black Sea coast, and the limestone Taurus Mountains *(Toros Daglari)* in the south. A lowland trough divides the Caucasus and the Lesser Caucasus, which form a formidable barrier of peaks in the north.

Limestone weathering in the Anatolian Plateau
Eroded gully
High plateau
Layers of tephra
Remnant landforms
Anatolian Plateau
Pamukkale
Map key
Population
above 5 million
1 million to 5 million
500,000 to 1 million
100,000 to 500,000
50,000 to 100,000
10,000 to 50,000
below 10,000
Elevation
4000m / 13,124ft
3000m / 9843ft
2000m / 6562ft
1000m / 3281ft
500m / 1640ft
250m / 820ft
100m / 328ft
sea level
RUSSIAN FEDERATION
GEORGIA
ARMENIA
AZERBAIJAN
IRAN
IRAQ
SYRIA
Caspian Sea
T'BILISI
YEREVAN
BAKI (Baku)
Sokhumi
Bat'umi
K'ut'aisi
Trabzon
Erzurum
Gyumri
Vanadzor
Gäncä
Sumqayit
Van Gölü
Diyarbakir
Malatya
Elazig
Sanliurfa
Mardin
Batman
Van
Kazbek 5047m
Scale 1:4,500,000
projection: Lambert Conformal Conic

▲ **In central Turkey,** rainwater has chemically weathered away numerous layers of limestone, leaving isolated outcrops and pinnacles and deep eroded gullies.

▶ ***The Caucasus are*** *fold mountains, which formed around the same time as the Taurus Mountains (Toros Daglari) around 65 million years ago and have since been modified by volcanic eruptions.*

▲ ***The white rock terraces*** *at Pamukkale in western Turkey were formed when underground water, heated by volcanic activity, dissolved minerals in the rocks. When the water reached the surface and evaporated the minerals were left behind in these extraordinary formations.*

The straits of the Bosporus and the Dardanelles, respectively linking the Black and Mediterranean seas with the Sea of Marmara, formed after the last Ice Age when a rising sea level caused these former river valleys to be flooded.

Many of the rivers crossing the Anatolian Plateau never reach the sea, but drain into salt marshes and shallow salt lakes such as Lake Tuz *(Tuz Golu)*, where much of the water is lost to evaporation.

Lava has flowed over large areas of the Lesser Caucasus within the last five million years, producing extensive basalt plateaus.

The earthquake that struck Armenia in 1988 killed over 55,000 people and devastated the country's infrastructure.

The volcanic cone of Mount Ararat is the highest peak in Turkey, with an altitude of 16,853 ft (5137 m).

Long, parallel mountain ranges run from east to west into the Aegean Sea, which has risen since the last Ice Age to form a drowned coastline of numerous islands and extended inlets.

The folded peaks of the Taurus Mountains *(Toros Daglari)* were formed 60–65 million years ago, at the same time as the Alps. The rock is mainly limestone, with deep caves, gorges, and underground rivers.

The Cilician Gates *(Gulek Bogazi)*, a major pass through the Taurus Mountains *(Toros Daglari)*, is the point where streams flow from the interior plateau onto the lowland of Adana.

Thick, temperate forest veils the seaward slopes of the Kaçkar Daglari. The southern slopes, which lie in a rainshadow, are dry and barren.

The granite massif near Surami divides the lowlands of Georgia from the oil-rich basin of Azerbaijan's Kura river, which has built a large delta into the Caspian Sea.

The shallow, saline Lake Van *(Van Gölü)* is the largest lake in Turkey. Dry terraces mark a previous shoreline 181 ft (55 m) above the present water level.

▶ ***Since the 6th century bc,*** *the pinnacles and caves of east-central Anatolia have been utilized as dwellings. Many are still inhabited today.*

▲ ***The fisheries*** *of Azerbaijan are noted for their hauls of sturgeon, and the Caspian Sea accounts for 80% of the world's total catch. However, stocks are now under serious threat due to overfishing.*

▲ ***Traditional steam baths*** *are found throughout the region, and are used for socializing as well as for bathing.*

The Near East

IRAQ, ISRAEL, JORDAN, LEBANON, SYRIA

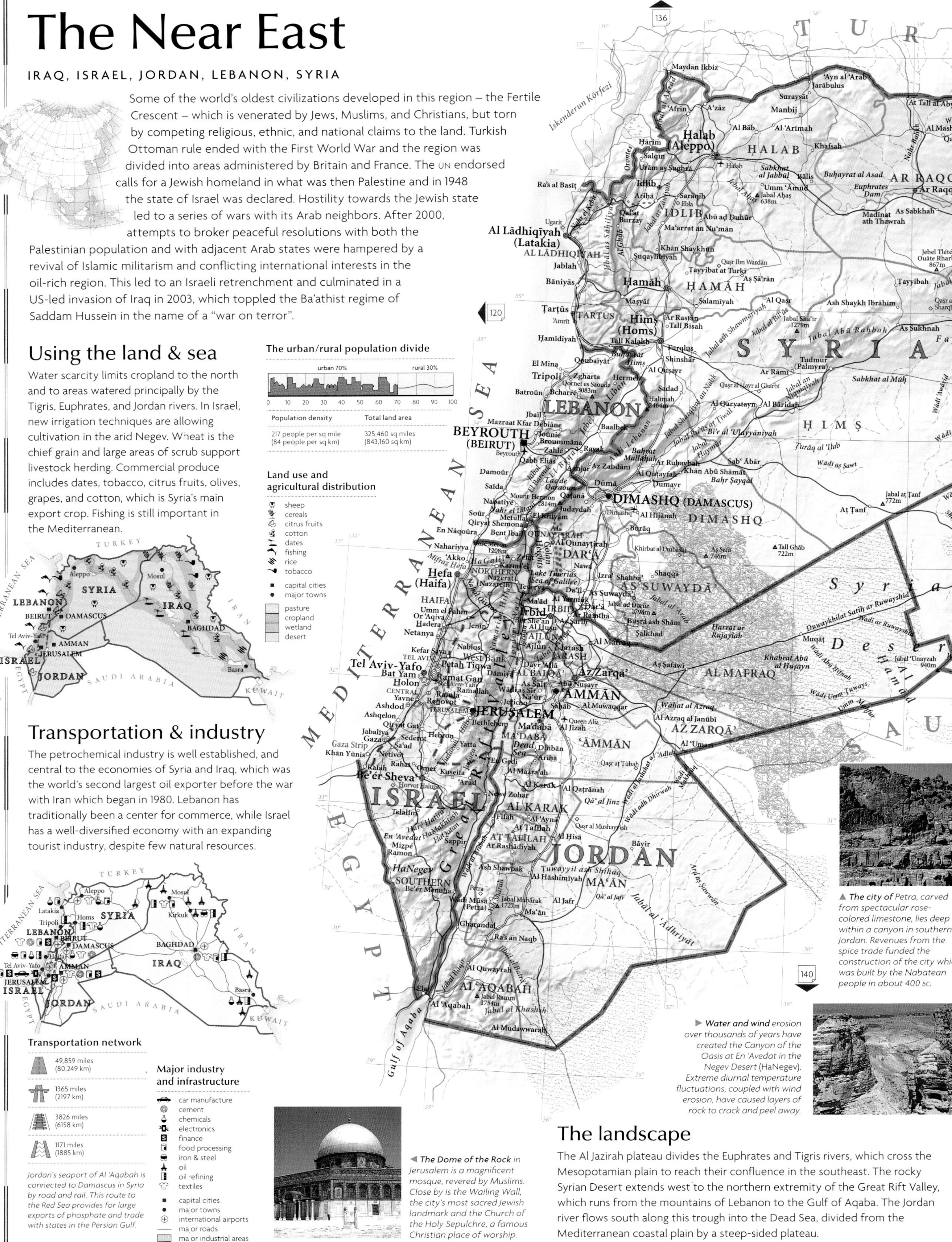

TURKEY
SYRIA
LEBANON
ISRAEL
JORDAN
EGYPT
SAUDI ARABIA
MEDITERRANEAN SEA
Gulf of Aqaba
Halab (Aleppo)
Al Lādhiqīyah (Latakia)
Ḥamāh
Ḥimṣ (Homs)
Ṭarṭūs
Tripoli
BEYROUTH (BEIRUT)
DIMASHQ (DAMASCUS)
Hefa (Haifa)
Tel Aviv-Yafo
JERUSALEM
'AMMĀN
Az Zarqā'
Irbid
Be'ér Sheva
Elat
Al 'Aqabah
Ar Raqqah
Syrian Desert
Dead Sea
Great Rift Valley
136
120
140

Some of the world's oldest civilizations developed in this region – the Fertile Crescent – which is venerated by Jews, Muslims, and Christians, but torn by competing religious, ethnic, and national claims to the land. Turkish Ottoman rule ended with the First World War and the region was divided into areas administered by Britain and France. The UN endorsed calls for a Jewish homeland in what was then Palestine and in 1948 the state of Israel was declared. Hostility towards the Jewish state led to a series of wars with its Arab neighbors. After 2000, attempts to broker peaceful resolutions with both the Palestinian population and with adjacent Arab states were hampered by a revival of Islamic militarism and conflicting international interests in the oil-rich region. This led to an Israeli retrenchment and culminated in a US-led invasion of Iraq in 2003, which toppled the Ba'athist regime of Saddam Hussein in the name of a "war on terror".

Using the land & sea

Water scarcity limits cropland to the north and to areas watered principally by the Tigris, Euphrates, and Jordan rivers. In Israel, new irrigation techniques are allowing cultivation in the arid Negev. Wheat is the chief grain and large areas of scrub support livestock herding. Commercial produce includes dates, tobacco, citrus fruits, olives, grapes, and cotton, which is Syria's main export crop. Fishing is still important in the Mediterranean.

The urban/rural population divide

urban 70% | rural 30%

0 10 20 30 40 50 60 70 80 90 100

Population density	Total land area
217 people per sq mile (84 people per sq km)	325,460 sq miles (843,160 sq km)

Land use and agricultural distribution

- sheep
- cereals
- citrus fruits
- cotton
- dates
- fishing
- rice
- tobacco
- capital cities
- major towns
- pasture
- cropland
- wetland
- desert

Transportation & industry

The petrochemical industry is well established, and central to the economies of Syria and Iraq, which was the world's second largest oil exporter before the war with Iran which began in 1980. Lebanon has traditionally been a center for commerce, while Israel has a well-diversified economy with an expanding tourist industry, despite few natural resources.

Transportation network

- 49,859 miles (80,249 km)
- 1365 miles (2197 km)
- 3826 miles (6158 km)
- 1171 miles (1885 km)

Jordan's seaport of Al 'Aqabah is connected to Damascus in Syria by road and rail. This route to the Red Sea provides for large exports of phosphate and trade with states in the Persian Gulf.

Major industry and infrastructure

- car manufacture
- cement
- chemicals
- electronics
- finance
- food processing
- iron & steel
- oil
- oil refining
- textiles
- capital cities
- major towns
- international airports
- major roads
- major industrial areas

◀ ***The Dome of the Rock*** *in Jerusalem is a magnificent mosque, revered by Muslims. Close by is the Wailing Wall, the city's most sacred Jewish landmark and the Church of the Holy Sepulchre, a famous Christian place of worship.*

▲ ***The city of*** *Petra, carved from spectacular rose-colored limestone, lies deep within a canyon in southern Jordan. Revenues from the spice trade funded the construction of the city which was built by the Nabatean people in about 400 BC.*

▶ ***Water and wind*** *erosion over thousands of years have created the Canyon of the Oasis at En 'Avedat in the Negev Desert (HaNegev). Extreme diurnal temperature fluctuations, coupled with wind erosion, have caused layers of rock to crack and peel away.*

The landscape

The Al Jazirah plateau divides the Euphrates and Tigris rivers, which cross the Mesopotamian plain to reach their confluence in the southeast. The rocky Syrian Desert extends west to the northern extremity of the Great Rift Valley, which runs from the mountains of Lebanon to the Gulf of Aqaba. The Jordan river flows south along this trough into the Dead Sea, divided from the Mediterranean coastal plain by a steep-sided plateau.

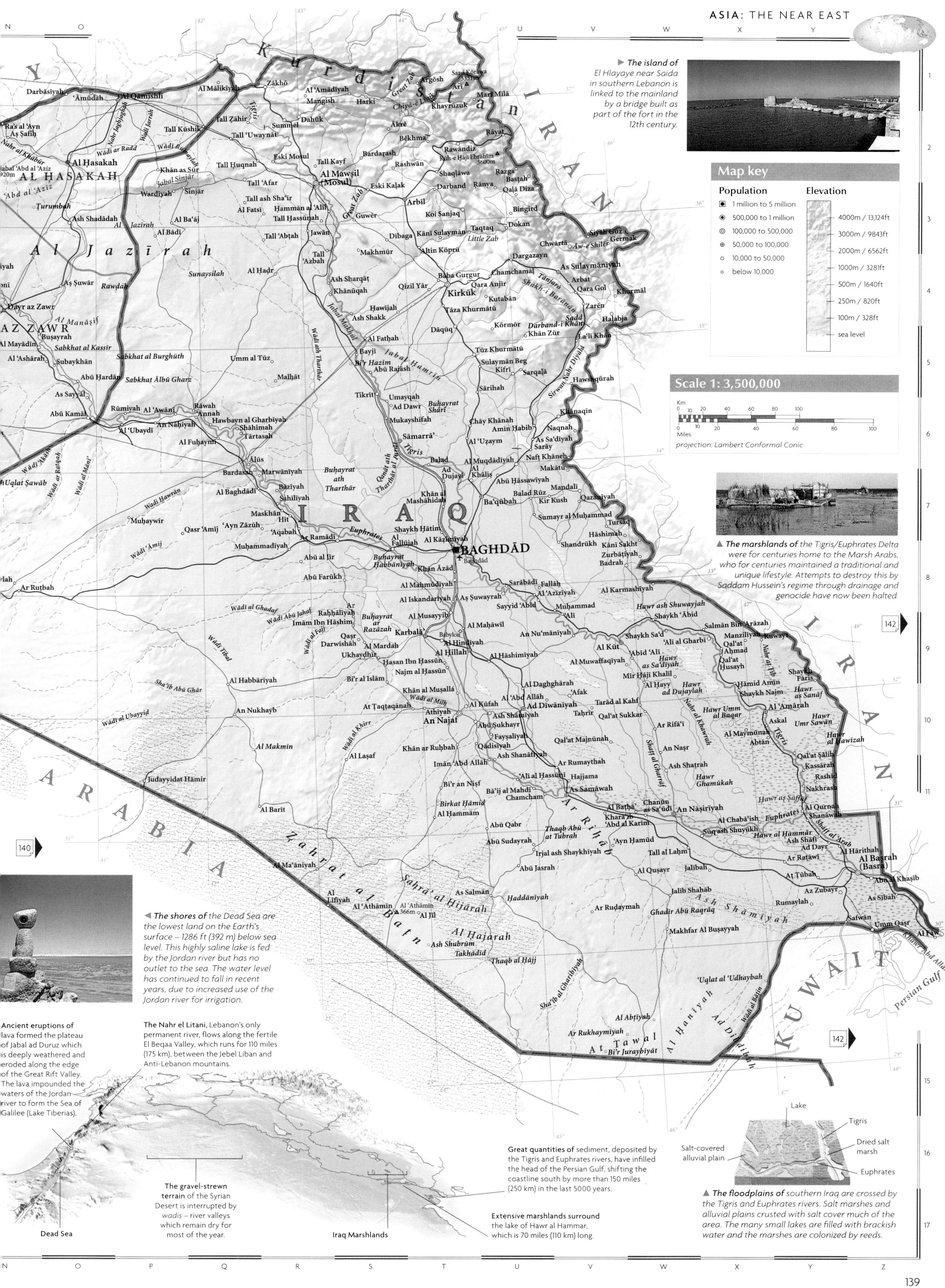
Map key
Population
1 million to 5 million
500,000 to 1 million
100,000 to 500,000
50,000 to 100,000
10,000 to 50,000
below 10,000
Elevation
4000m / 13,124ft
3000m / 9843ft
2000m / 6562ft
1000m / 3281ft
500m / 1640ft
250m / 820ft
100m / 328ft
sea level
Scale 1: 3,500,000
projection: Lambert Conformal Conic
IRAQ
BAGHDĀD
IRAN
KUWAIT
ARABIA
Kurdistan
Al Jazīrah
Persian Gulf
Euphrates
Tigris
Lake
Tigris
Dried salt marsh
Salt-covered alluvial plain
Euphrates
Dead Sea
Iraq Marshlands

▶ **The island of** El Hlayaye near Saida in southern Lebanon is linked to the mainland by a bridge built as part of the fort in the 12th century.

▲ **The marshlands of** the Tigris/Euphrates Delta were for centuries home to the Marsh Arabs, who for centuries maintained a traditional and unique lifestyle. Attempts to destroy this by Saddam Hussein's regime through drainage and genocide have now been halted.

◀ **The shores of** the Dead Sea are the lowest land on the Earth's surface – 1286 ft (392 m) below sea level. This highly saline lake is fed by the Jordan river but has no outlet to the sea. The water level has continued to fall in recent years, due to increased use of the Jordan river for irrigation.

Ancient eruptions of lava formed the plateau of Jabal ad Duruz which is deeply weathered and eroded along the edge of the Great Rift Valley. The lava impounded the waters of the Jordan river to form the Sea of Galilee (Lake Tiberias).

The Nahr el Litani, Lebanon's only permanent river, flows along the fertile El Beqaa Valley, which runs for 110 miles (175 km), between the Jebel Liban and Anti-Lebanon mountains.

The gravel-strewn terrain of the Syrian Desert is interrupted by *wadis* – river valleys which remain dry for most of the year.

Great quantities of sediment, deposited by the Tigris and Euphrates rivers, have infilled the head of the Persian Gulf, shifting the coastline south by more than 150 miles (250 km) in the last 5000 years.

Extensive marshlands surround the lake of Hawr al Hammar, which is 70 miles (110 km) long.

▲ **The floodplains of** southern Iraq are crossed by the Tigris and Euphrates rivers. Salt marshes and alluvial plains crusted with salt cover much of the area. The many small lakes are filled with brackish water and the marshes are colonized by reeds.

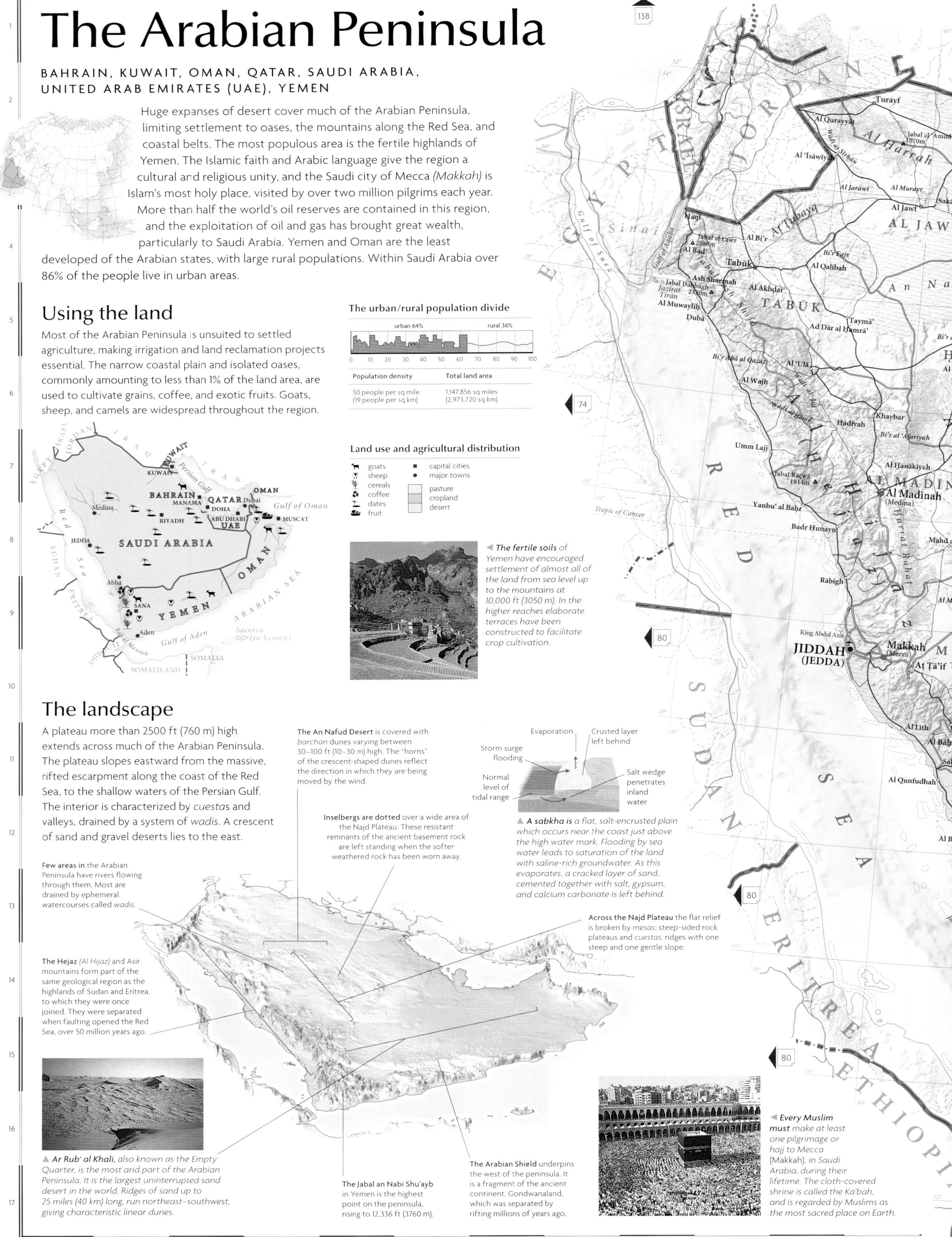

The Arabian Peninsula

BAHRAIN, KUWAIT, OMAN, QATAR, SAUDI ARABIA, UNITED ARAB EMIRATES (UAE), YEMEN

Huge expanses of desert cover much of the Arabian Peninsula, limiting settlement to oases, the mountains along the Red Sea, and coastal belts. The most populous area is the fertile highlands of Yemen. The Islamic faith and Arabic language give the region a cultural and religious unity, and the Saudi city of Mecca *(Makkah)* is Islam's most holy place, visited by over two million pilgrims each year. More than half the world's oil reserves are contained in this region, and the exploitation of oil and gas has brought great wealth, particularly to Saudi Arabia. Yemen and Oman are the least developed of the Arabian states, with large rural populations. Within Saudi Arabia over 86% of the people live in urban areas.

Using the land

Most of the Arabian Peninsula is unsuited to settled agriculture, making irrigation and land reclamation projects essential. The narrow coastal plain and isolated oases, commonly amounting to less than 1% of the land area, are used to cultivate grains, coffee, and exotic fruits. Goats, sheep, and camels are widespread throughout the region.

The urban/rural population divide

urban 64% — rural 36%

0 10 20 30 40 50 60 70 80 90 100

Population density	Total land area
50 people per sq mile (19 people per sq km)	1,147,856 sq miles (2,973,720 sq km)

Land use and agricultural distribution

goats, sheep, cereals, coffee, dates, fruit; capital cities, major towns; pasture, cropland, desert

◄ *The fertile soils of Yemen have encouraged settlement of almost all of the land from sea level up to the mountains at 10,000 ft (3050 m). In the higher reaches elaborate terraces have been constructed to facilitate crop cultivation.*

The landscape

A plateau more than 2500 ft (760 m) high extends across much of the Arabian Peninsula. The plateau slopes eastward from the massive, rifted escarpment along the coast of the Red Sea, to the shallow waters of the Persian Gulf. The interior is characterized by *cuestas* and valleys, drained by a system of *wadis*. A crescent of sand and gravel deserts lies to the east.

The An Nafud Desert is covered with *barchan* dunes varying between 30–100 ft (10–30 m) high. The "horns" of the crescent-shaped dunes reflect the direction in which they are being moved by the wind.

Inselbergs are dotted over a wide area of the Najd Plateau. These resistant remnants of the ancient basement rock are left standing when the softer weathered rock has been worn away.

Evaporation / Crusted layer left behind / Storm surge flooding / Normal level of tidal range / Salt wedge penetrates inland water

▲ *A sabkha is a flat, salt-encrusted plain which occurs near the coast just above the high water mark. Flooding by sea water leads to saturation of the land with saline-rich groundwater. As this evaporates, a cracked layer of sand, cemented together with salt, gypsum, and calcium carbonate is left behind.*

Few areas in the Arabian Peninsula have rivers flowing through them. Most are drained by ephemeral watercourses called *wadis*.

Across the Najd Plateau the flat relief is broken by *mesas*; steep-sided rock plateaus and *cuestas*; ridges with one steep and one gentle slope.

The Hejaz *(Al Hijaz)* and Asir mountains form part of the same geological region as the highlands of Sudan and Eritrea, to which they were once joined. They were separated when faulting opened the Red Sea, over 50 million years ago.

▲ *Ar Rub' al Khali, also known as the Empty Quarter, is the most arid part of the Arabian Peninsula. It is the largest uninterrupted sand desert in the world. Ridges of sand up to 25 miles (40 km) long, run northeast–southwest, giving characteristic linear dunes.*

The Jabal an Nabi Shu'ayb in Yemen is the highest point on the peninsula, rising to 12,336 ft (3760 m).

The Arabian Shield underpins the west of the peninsula. It is a fragment of the ancient continent, Gondwanaland, which was separated by rifting millions of years ago.

◄ *Every Muslim must make at least one pilgrimage or hajj to Mecca (Makkah), in Saudi Arabia, during their lifetime. The cloth-covered shrine is called the Ka'bah, and is regarded by Muslims as the most sacred place on Earth.*

138

◄ Saudi Arabia contains the world's largest oil reserves, lying mainly along the Persian Gulf coast. Each day the region produces around 10 million barrels of oil. Here, in the desert, excess oil is being burnt off.

Transportation & industry

The extraction and refining of oil and gas are the major industrial activities in the Arabian Peninsula. The region also has an active construction sector, with many Arab cities reflecting the wealth generated by the oil industry. The service sector is dominated by financial and technical institutions, which, like the construction sector, mainly serve the oil industry. Traditional handicrafts such as carpet-weaving are found in rural areas.

Transportation network

- 44,832 miles (72,159 km)
- 673 miles (1083 km)
- 670 miles (1078 km)
- none

Internal surface transportation is poorly developed across the peninsula. Along the coast, commercial routes have developed, but connections between bordering states rely on major airports.

Major industry and infrastructure

cement	capital cities
chemicals	major towns
iron & steel	international airports
oil	major roads
oil refining	major industrial areas
food processing	

142

► Seasonal watercourses or wadis drain much of the interior of the Arabian Peninsula. Although they remain dry for much of the year, they are prone to flash floods after heavy rains.

Map key

Population

- 1 million to 5 million
- 500,000 to 1 million
- 100,000 to 500,000
- 50,000 to 100,000
- 10,000 to 50,000
- below 10,000

Elevation

- 3000m / 9843ft
- 2000m / 6562ft
- 1000m / 3281ft
- 500m / 1640ft
- 250m / 820ft
- 100m / 328ft
- sea level

Scale 1:8,250,000

Km 0 25 50 100 150 200 250

Miles 0 25 50 100 150 200 250

projection: Lambert Conformal Conic

80

Iran & the Gulf states

BAHRAIN, IRAN, KUWAIT, QATAR, UNITED ARAB EMIRATES (UAE)

The discovery of oil in the Persian Gulf in the 1930s brought great wealth to the surrounding states. The revenue was largely used to modernize industry and infrastructure, initiating great social change in these formerly agrarian countries. Today, over 90% of the people in the Gulf states live in urban areas, and foreign nationals make up a sizeable proportion of the population in Kuwait, Qatar, and the United Arab Emirates. The importance of control of the oil reserves has led to a number of territorial disputes, including most recently the Iran–Iraq War (1980-88) and the First Gulf War (1991). Islam is practiced almost exclusively throughout the region and two distinct strands are found; Sunni Muslims in Qatar, Kuwait, and UAE, and Shi'a Muslims in Iran and Bahrain. In 1979 Iran became the world's largest theocracy.

136
138

The landscape

The land rises steeply from the fragmented coastal lowlands bordering the Persian Gulf, to reach Iran's interior plateau, bounded by heavily eroded mountain chains. An unstable plate boundary runs northwest to southeast across Iran causing frequent earthquakes. On the sandy west coast of the Persian Gulf, the relief is generally flat, with patches of salt marsh. Bahrain consists of two groups of islands, which are mostly small and rocky.

Pyroclastic layers
Lava flow
Lava flow layers

▲ *Qolleh-ye Damavand in the Elburz Mountains is a composite volcano. It comprises layers of lava and pyroclasts fragmentary rocks which accumulate on the slopes of the volcano after being ejected into the air.*

▲ *Marine sediments from deep beneath the ancient Tethys Sea have been uplifted to form the Elburz Mountains, which stretch along the shores of the Caspian Sea, northern Iran.*

Lava and ash from previous volcanic activity covers a 200 mile (320 km) stretch from the border with Azerbaijan to the Caspian Sea.

Iran's two mountain chains, the Zagros and Elburz, were uplifted at the same time as the Alps in Europe, when the African Plate collided with the Eurasian Plate.

Caspian Sea

Qolleh-ye Damavand

Dominated by a vast, semi-arid interior plateau, most of Iran lies above 1640 ft (500 m). The region is poorly drained with many of its basins remaining dry for months at a time.

The fierce Shamal wind affects much of this region. Every summer it blows dust south from the flood plains of the Tigris and Euphrates, reducing visibility to such an extent that Kuwait International Airport is frequently forced to close.

The Dasht-e Lut

Autumn winds blowing across the Persian Gulf can reach speeds of up to 95 mph (150 kmph) causing severe storms, squalls, and waterspouts.

Prolific springs tapping artesian water make cultivation possible across the north of Bahrain's main island. This provides a sharp contrast to the sandy plains in the south and west.

The oilfields of the Persian Gulf are formed from marine shale deposits lying in sedimentary basins at the margins of the Zagros Mountains.

Numerous islands lie along the southern coast of the Persian Gulf. Some of these are salt domes, created when less dense salts were displaced and forced up to the surface by denser, overlying strata.

◀ *The Dasht-e Lut covers a large portion of eastern Iran with its dry, wind-eroded plain of scattered sandstone pillars and salty depressions. During the summer, temperatures soar, making it one of the world's hottest, driest places.*

140

Using the land & sea

Along the coast of the Caspian Sea, desalinated water allows fruits and vegetables to be produced, although water shortages and desert soils still limit farming. Sheep are the most important livestock raised in Iran and commercial forests cover the northwest of the country. Shrimp stocks were decimated by pollution during the Gulf War, but fishing remains important for domestic and export markets.

◀ *All of the Gulf states have commercial fishing fleets. Before the discovery of oil, fishing was the region's leading industry.*

Land use and agricultural distribution

goats, sheep, cereals, citrus fruits, cotton, dates, fishing, timber
capital cities, major towns
pasture, cropland, forest, desert, wetland

The urban/rural population divide

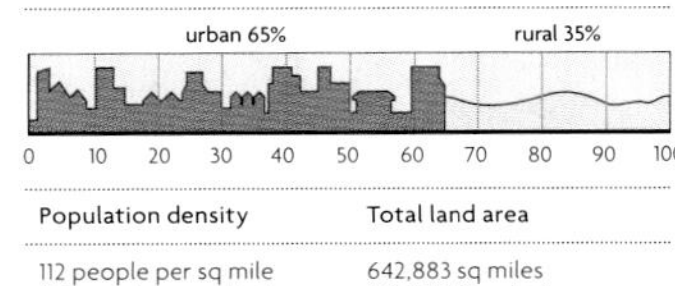

urban 65%
rural 35%
0 10 20 30 40 50 60 70 80 90 100

Population density	Total land area
112 people per sq mile (43 people per sq km)	642,883 sq miles (1,665,500 sq km)

◀ *The Kuwait Towers in the center of Kuwait are symbols of the vast wealth oil has brought to the country. Before 1960, the city had only one main street and was surrounded by a mud wall.*

◀ *Many volcanoes lie in Iran's 1200 mile (1930 km) volcanic belt, including the country's highest peak, the now-extinct Qolleh-ye Damavand at 18,600 ft (5671 m).*

▶ *Extensive oil and gas exploitation in the Gulf region has allowed the economic transformation of the Gulf states. Consequently, many of these states have a hugely improved per capita income compared to the 1960's.*

Transportation & industry

Both onshore and offshore oil reserves are exploited throughout the region. Kuwait not only extracts but also refines 80% of its oil. Bahrain has diversified its economy to become the main commercial and financial center in the Persian Gulf. Iran produces a wide range of products: textile mills are widespread and carpet weaving is an important export industry.

Major industry and infrastructure

- carpet manufacture
- chemicals
- finance
- food processing
- oil
- oil refining
- textiles
- capital city
- major towns
- international airports
- major roads
- major industrial areas

Transportation network

- 63,543 miles (102,274 km)
- 884 miles (1423 km)
- 3822 miles (6151 km)
- 562 miles (904 km)

Major towns and neighboring countries are linked by adequate road networks, although rural areas are less well served. Bahrain is linked to the mainland by a 15 mile (25 km) long causeway.

Map key

Population

- above 5 million
- 1 million to 5 million
- 500,000 to 1 million
- 100,000 to 500,000
- 50,000 to 100,000
- 10,000 to 50,000
- below 10,000

Elevation

- 4000m / 13,124ft
- 3000m / 9843ft
- 2000m / 6562ft
- 1000m / 3281ft
- 500m / 1640ft
- 250m / 820ft
- 100m / 328ft
- sea level

Scale 1:6,000,000

projection: Lambert Conformal Conic

146

148

Kazakhstan

Abundant natural resources lie in the immense steppe grasslands, deserts, and central plateau of the former Soviet republic of Kazakhstan. An intensive program of industrial and agricultural development to exploit these resources during the Soviet era resulted in catastrophic industrial pollution, including fallout from nuclear testing and the shrinkage of the Aral Sea. Since independence, the government has encouraged foreign investment and liberalized the economy to promote growth. The adoption of Kazakh as the national language is intended to encourage a new sense of national identity in a state where living conditions for the majority remain harsh, both in cramped urban centers and impoverished rural areas.

Transportation & industry

The single most important industry in Kazakhstan is mining, based around extensive oil deposits near the Caspian Sea, the world's largest chromium mine, and vast reserves of iron ore. Recent foreign investment has helped to develop industries including food processing and steel manufacture, and to expand the exploitation of mineral resources. The Russian space program is still based at Baykonyr, near Kyzylorda in central Kazakhstan.

RUSSIAN FEDERATION
Petropavlovsk
Pavlodar
Rudnyy
Ural'sk
ASTANA
Temirtau
Karaganda
Semipalatinsk
Ust'Kamenogorsk
Aktobe
KAZAKHSTAN
Atyrau
Zhezkazgan
Aktau
Caspian Sea
Aral Sea
Kyzylorda
Taldykorgan
Almaty
Taraz
Shymkent
UZBEKISTAN
KYRGYZSTAN
TURKMENISTAN
CHINA

Major industry and infrastructure

- chemicals
- engineering
- fish processing
- food processing
- iron & steel
- metallurgy
- mining
- oil
- capital cities
- major towns
- international airports
- major roads
- major industrial areas

Transportation network

- 48,263 miles (77,680 km)
- none
- 8483 miles (13,660 km)
- 3900 miles (2423 km)

Industrial areas in the north and east are well-connected to Russia. Air and rail links with Germany and China have been established through foreign investment. Better access to Baltic ports is being sought.

An open-pit coal mine in Kazakhstan. Foreign investment is being actively sought by the Kazakh government in order to fully exploit the potential of the country's rich mineral reserves.

Using the land & sea

The rearing of large herds of sheep and goats on the steppe grasslands forms the core of Kazakh agriculture. Arable cultivation and cotton-growing in pasture and desert areas was encouraged during the Soviet era, but relative yields are low. The heavy use of fertilizers and the diversion of natural water sources for irrigation has degraded much of the land.

The urban/rural population divide

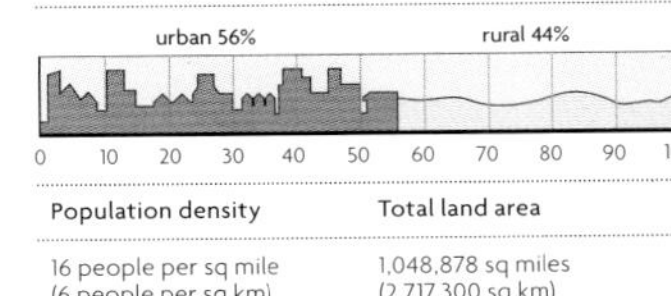

urban 56%
rural 44%
0 10 20 30 40 50 60 70 80 90 100

Population density	Total land area
16 people per sq mile (6 people per sq km)	1,048,878 sq miles (2,717,300 sq km)

Land use and agricultural distribution

- cattle
- goats
- sheep
- cotton
- fishing
- wheat
- capital cities
- major towns
- pasture
- cropland
- forest
- mountain region
- desert

RUSSIAN FEDERATION
Uralsk
Rudnyy
ASTANA
Ust'Kamenogorsk
Semipalatinsk
Karaganda
Atyrau
KAZAKHSTAN
Aktau
Aral Sea
Kyzylorda
Taldykorgan
Almaty
Shymkent
UZBEKISTAN
KYRGYZSTAN
TURKMENISTAN
CHINA
Caspian Sea

The nomadic peoples who moved their herds around the steppe grasslands are now largely settled, although echoes of their traditional lifestyle, in particular their superb riding skills, remain.

RUSSIA
Ural'sk
Kamenka
Zachagansk
Fedorovka
Burlin
Aksay
Chingirlau
Algabas
Ozero Shalkar
Chapayev
Lubenka
Zhympity
Kaztalovka
ZAPADNYY KAZAKHSTAN
Yesensay
Zhalpaktal
Zhanibek
Urda
Novaya Kazanka
Kaldygayty
Aktobe (Aktyubinsk)
Martuk
Khobda
Akzhar
Khromtau
Alga
Kandyagash
Zhuryn
Shubarkuduk
Uil
Miyaly
Ryn-Peski
Kulagino
Inderborskiy
Karabau
Caspian Depression
ATYRAU
Makhambet
Makat
Dossor
Akkystau
Atyrau
Ganyushkino
Sagiz
Emba
AKTYUBINSK
Gory Mugodzhary
Zharkamys
Komsomol'skiy
Kul'sary
Koschagyl
Karaton
Gryada Shirkala
Plato Shagyray
Peski Bol'shiye Barsuki
Shalkar
Boranku
Sarykamys
Severnyy Chink Ustyurta
Caspian Sea
Zaliv Komsomolets
Sor Mertvyy Kultuk
Ostrov Kulaly
Mys Tyub-Karagan
Fort-Shevchenko
Mangyshlakskiy Zaliv
Shebir
Beyneu
Turush
Sor Kaydak
Tauchik
Shetpe
Zharmysh
Say-Utës
Aktau
Plato Mangyshlak
MANGISTAU
Zhetybay
Zhanaozen
Kuryk
Ustyurt Plateau
UZBEKISTAN
TURKMENISTAN
Karabalyk
Nadezhdinka
Fedorovka
Ozërnoye
Kostanay
Rudnyy
Tobol
Lisakovsk
Denisovka
Zhitikara
KOSTANAY
Turgayskaya Stolovaya Strana
Zhailma
Komsomol'skoye
Karabutak
Ozero Kyzylkol'
Irgiz
Peski Priaral'skiye Karakumy
Saksaul'skiy
Aral'sk
Zaliv Tushchybas
Ayteke Bi
Kazalinsk
Maylybas
Baykonyr Space Launch Centre
Syr Darya
KYZYLORDA
Ostrov Vozrozhdeniya
Aral Sea
Uyaly
Turanskaya Nizmennost'

122
122
146
146

Map key

Population

- 1 million to 5 million
- 500,000 to 1 million
- 100,000 to 500,000
- 50,000 to 100,000
- 10,000 to 50,000
- below 10,000

Elevation

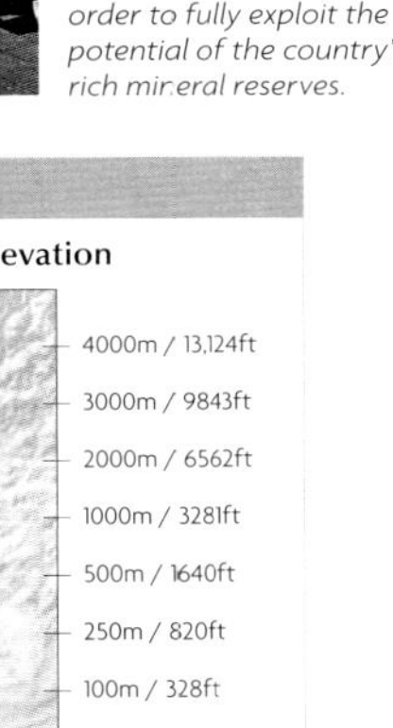

4000m / 13,124ft
3000m / 9843ft
2000m / 6562ft
1000m / 3281ft
500m / 1640ft
250m / 820ft
100m / 328ft
sea level

Scale 1:7,000,000

Km 0 25 50 100 150 200 250
Miles 0 25 50 100 150 200 250

projection: Lambert Conformal Conic

The landscape

Stretching more than 1250 miles (2000 km) from the Caspian Sea in the west to China in the east, more than 40% of Kazakhstan is covered by steppe grasslands which give way to barren desert in the south. The land rises eastward towards the mineral-rich central plateau, to form the Altai Mounta ns.

1960 1996 2010

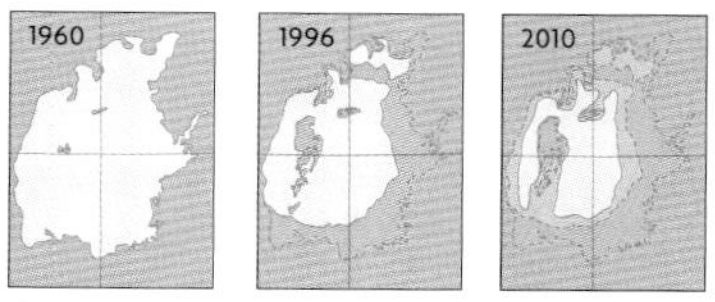

▲ *Since 1960, the Aral Sea has shrunk by 75%, become extremely saline, and lost all but five of its once-abundant fish species. Factors in this ecological disaster include the excessive use of fertilizers, defoliants and the diversion of its main source rivers for the irrigation of desert lands.*

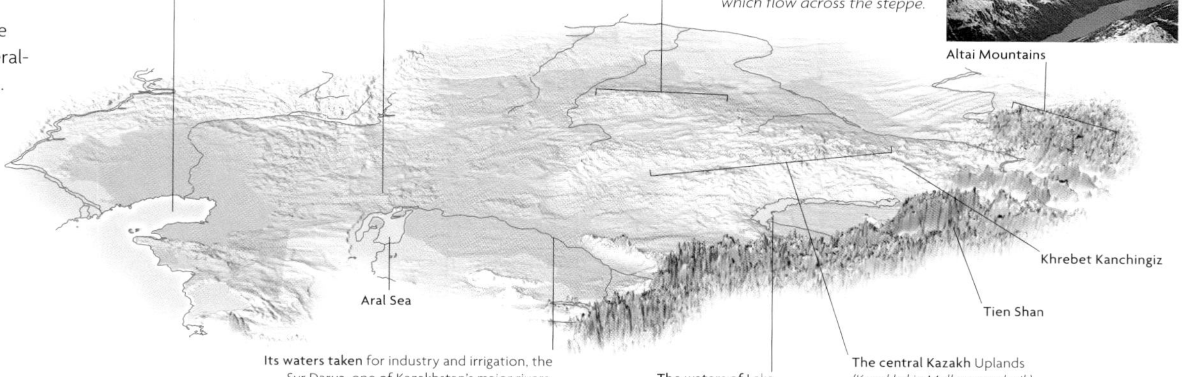

The Caspian Sea is the largest body of inland water in the world.

The desert of Peski Bol'shiye Barsuki is mainly sandy, displaying a number of classic dune formations. Groundwater supports a small amount of vegetation.

A large number of salt lakes fill depressions in the rolling uplands of central Kazakhstan.

► ***The Altai Mountains*** *lie on Kazakhstan's eastern borders with China and the Russian Federation. Cold and largely barren, they are the source of many of the rivers which flow across the steppe.*

Altai Mountains

Khrebet Kanchingiz

Tien Shan

Aral Sea

Its waters taken for industry and irrigation, the Syr Darya, one of Kazakhstan's major rivers, now barely reaches the Aral Sea which it used to fill. Like many Kazakh rivers it has been heavily polluted with chemicals and its flow has been restricted by up to 60%.

The waters of Lake Balkhash *(Ozero Balkhash)*, unlike those of the Aral Sea, are still able to support a fishing industry.

The central Kazakh Uplands *(Kazakhskiy Melkosopochnik)* contain much of the country's mineral riches. The landscape is largely flat with occasional rocky outcrops and hillocks.

► ***Immense stretches*** *of steppe grasslands characterize much of the Kazakh landscape. These lowland areas have been used for arable cultivation in recent years, although problems with irrigation have meant that much of the land is being allowed to revert to its natural vegetation and pastoral usage.*

122

156

146

▲ ***Rows of pine*** *trees edge this valley near Almaty. The snow-covered slopes in the background are used for skiing.*

Central Asia

KYRGYZSTAN, TAJIKISTAN, TURKMENISTAN, UZBEKISTAN

The four republics that declared independence in 1991 were created in the early years of the Soviet Union, promoting ethnic divisions in a region whose common focus, since the 8th century, has been Islam. Traditional rural, nomadic ways of life have survived the Soviet era, while the benefits of modern industry and grand irrigation schemes have resulted in severe pollution in the delicate, arid environment of the steppe, particularly in Uzbekistan. Many ethnic minority groups are scattered among the four republics, with isolated communities in the mountains of Kyrgyzstan. The current Islamic revival has brought hope of greater regional unity, in spite of religious factionalism which, in 1992, plunged Tajikistan into civil war.

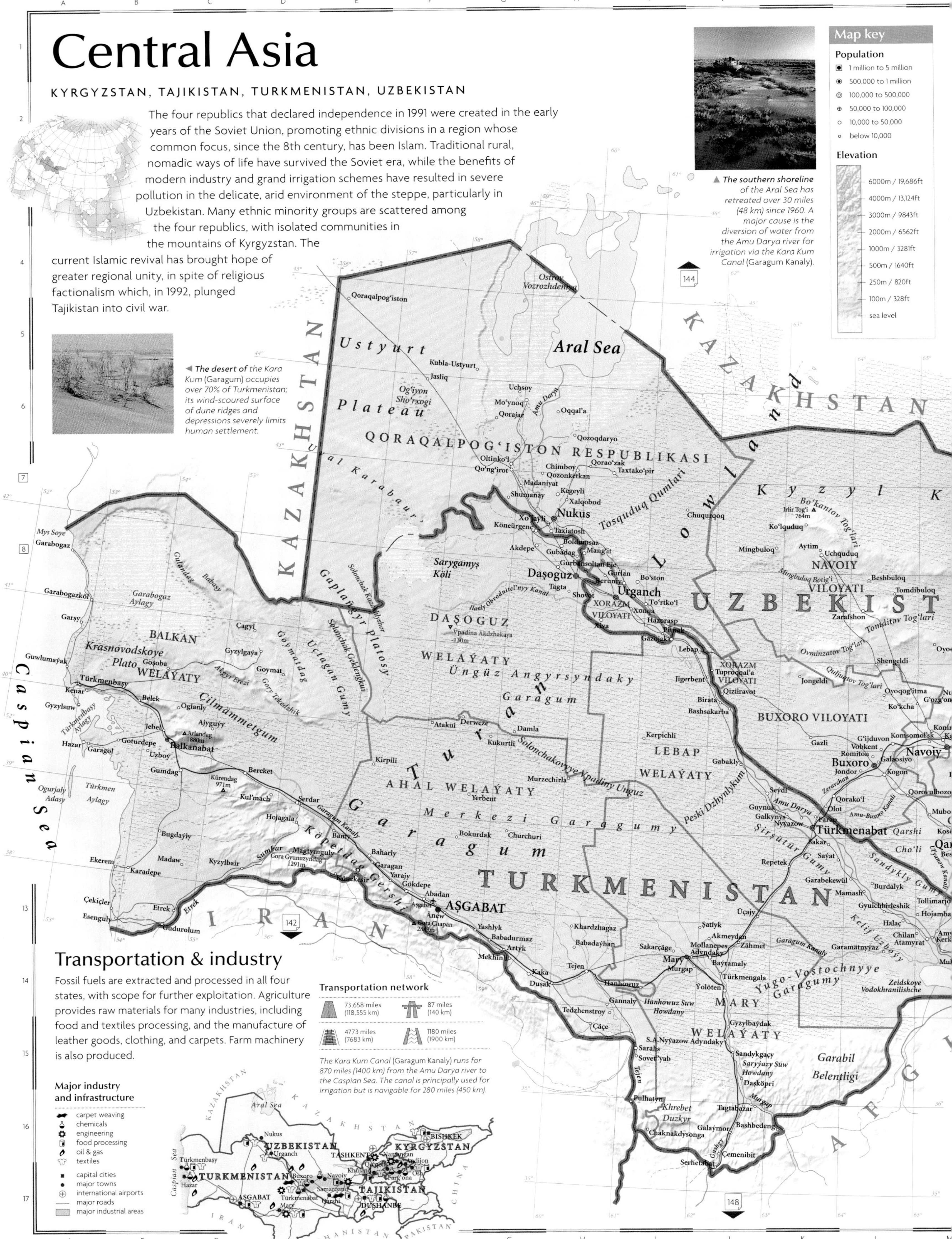
Map key
Population
1 million to 5 million
500,000 to 1 million
100,000 to 500,000
50,000 to 100,000
10,000 to 50,000
below 10,000
Elevation
6000m / 19,686ft
4000m / 13,124ft
3000m / 9843ft
2000m / 6562ft
1000m / 3281ft
500m / 1640ft
250m / 820ft
100m / 328ft
sea level
Aral Sea
KAZAKHSTAN
UZBEKISTAN
TURKMENISTAN
IRAN
Caspian Sea
Ustyurt Plateau
QORAQALPOG'ISTON RESPUBLIKASI
Turan Lowland
Kyzyl Kum
NAVOIY VILOYATI
BUXORO VILOYATI
XORAZM VILOYATI
DAŞOGUZ WELAÝATY
BALKAN WELAÝATY
AHAL WELAÝATY
LEBAP WELAÝATY
MARY WELAÝATY
Garagum
Nukus
Daşoguz
Urganch
Buxoro
Navoiy
Türkmenabat
Türkmenbaşy
Balkanabat
AŞGABAT
Mary
Transportation network
73,658 miles (118,555 km)
87 miles (140 km)
4773 miles (7683 km)
1180 miles (1900 km)
Major industry and infrastructure
carpet weaving
chemicals
engineering
food processing
oil & gas
textiles
capital cities
major towns
international airports
major roads
major industrial areas

▲ The southern shoreline of the Aral Sea has retreated over 30 miles (48 km) since 1960. A major cause is the diversion of water from the Amu Darya river for irrigation via the Kara Kum Canal (Garagum Kanaly).

◄ The desert of the Kara Kum (Garagum) occupies over 70% of Turkmenistan; its wind-scoured surface of dune ridges and depressions severely limits human settlement.

Transportation & industry

Fossil fuels are extracted and processed in all four states, with scope for further exploitation. Agriculture provides raw materials for many industries, including food and textiles processing, and the manufacture of leather goods, clothing, and carpets. Farm machinery is also produced.

The Kara Kum Canal (Garagum Kanaly) runs for 870 miles (1400 km) from the Amu Darya river to the Caspian Sea. The canal is principally used for irrigation but is navigable for 280 miles (450 km).

The landscape

The great Tien Shan and Pamir ranges meet in a succession of high mountain chains. These mountains encircle the fertile Fergana Valley and reach west into the desert of the Kyzyl Kum, dividing the Syr Darya and Amu Darya rivers. Sandy steppeland extends to the shores of the Caspian Sea, with the desert of the Kara Kum *(Garagum)* in the south. The Amu Darya drains into the Aral Sea in the north.

The Amu Darya is the only river in Central Asia with a sufficient volume of water to cross the desert of the Kara Kum *(Garagum)* from the Pamirs to the Aral Sea, where it forms a delta largely vegetated by scrub grasses.

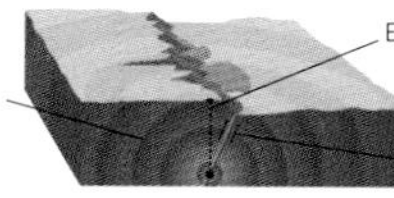

Shock waves travel through ground

Epicenter

Fault

▲ ***In the heavily*** *fractured and faulted mountain region, earthquakes are common, caused by the sudden release of tension along active fault lines.*

◀ ***Bare mountains provide*** *a stark background to the croplands along the Naryn river in Kyrgyzstan. Irrigation is essential for cultivation in this dry region.*

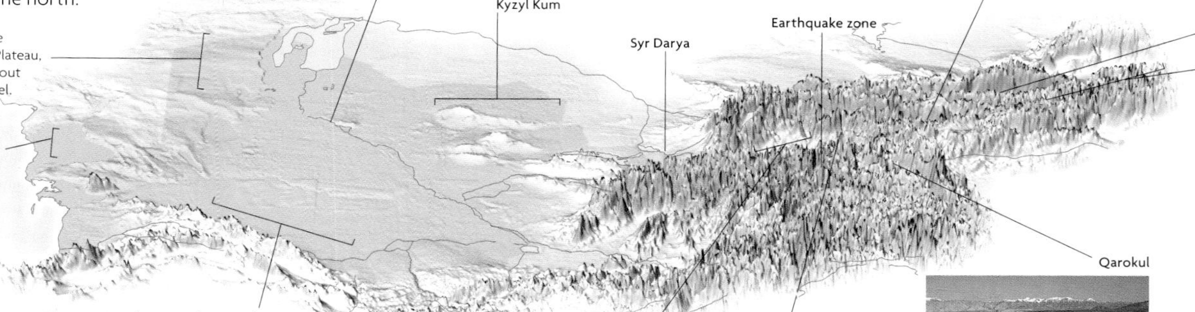

Naryn river

Ozero Issyk-Kul' lies at an altitude of 5193 ft (1584 m). The lake remains ice-free throughout the year, due to the slight salinity of the water.

Kyzyl Kum

Earthquake zone

Syr Darya

Tien Shan

Salt marshes fill many of the depressions in the Ustyurt Plateau, a barren, rocky tableland about 650 ft (200 m) above sea level.

Some of the world's largest deposits of marine salts are found in Garabogaz Aylagy. This shallow, saline gulf has an average depth of only 33 ft (10 m), and a very high evaporation rate, producing the salty deposits.

▲ ***The Tien Shan*** *extend from China in the east, reaching heights over 24,400 ft (7439 m) and branching into many parallel ranges in the west.*

Qarokul

The Kara Kum *(Garagum)* is one of the world's largest expanses of sand. Wind action has created a terrain of shifting, crescent-shaped sand dunes known as barchans.

A series of major rock faults has created the Fergana Valley, a deep depression surrounded by high mountains. Water from the Syr Darya river and from underground sources supports intensive agriculture, despite minimal rainfall.

Mount Communism *(Qullai Kommunizm)*, in the northern Pamirs, was so named for being the highest point in the former Soviet Union, rising to 24,590 ft (7495 m).

◀ ***Nestling high in*** *the Pamir range, and fed by glacial meltwater, Qarokul is the largest of the lakes in this region.*

Scale 1:4,750,000

Km 0 10 20 40 60 80 100 120

Miles 0 10 20 40 60 80 100 120

projection: Lambert Conformal Conic

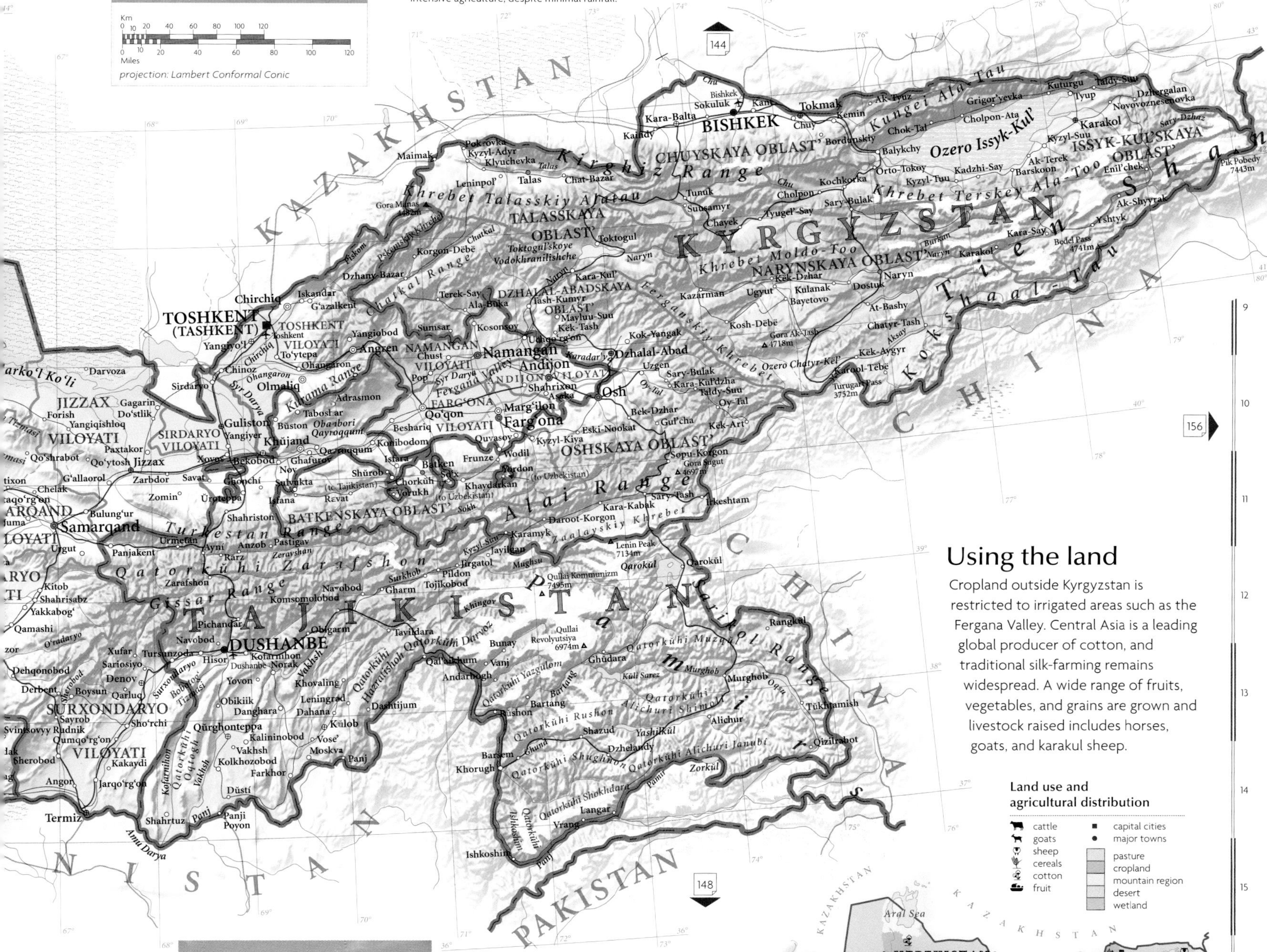

144

156

148

Using the land

Cropland outside Kyrgyzstan is restricted to irrigated areas such as the Fergana Valley. Central Asia is a leading global producer of cotton, and traditional silk-farming remains widespread. A wide range of fruits, vegetables, and grains are grown and livestock raised includes horses, goats, and karakul sheep.

Land use and agricultural distribution

- cattle
- goats
- sheep
- cereals
- cotton
- fruit
- capital cities
- major towns
- pasture
- cropland
- mountain region
- desert
- wetland

▶ ***Plentiful sunshine,*** *rich soils and massive irrigation schemes have made Uzbekistan the world's fifth largest cotton producer, although water shortages now prevent any further expansion of irrigated land.*

The urban/rural population divide

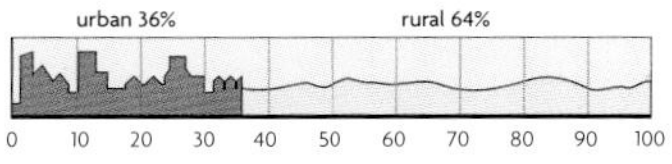

urban 36% | rural 64%

0 10 20 30 40 50 60 70 80 90 100

Population density	Total land area
88 people per sq mile (34 people per sq km)	492,961 sq miles (1,277,100 sq km)

Afghanistan & Pakistan

Pakistan was created by the partition of British India in 1947, becoming the western arm of a new Islamic state for Indian Muslims; the eastern sector, in Bengal, seceded to become the separate country of Bangladesh in 1971. Over half of Pakistan's 158 million people live in the Punjab, at the fertile head of the great Indus Basin. The river sustains a national economy based on irrigated agriculture, including cotton for the vital textiles industry. Afghanistan, a mountainous, landlocked country, with an ancient and independent culture, has been wracked by war since 1979. Factional strife escalated into an international conflict in late 2001, as US-led troops ousted the militant and fundamentally Islamist *taliban* regime as part of their "war on terror."

◀ ***The town of*** *Bamian lies high inthe Hindu Kush west of Kabul. Between the 2nd and 5th centuries two huge statues of Buddha were carved into the nearby rock,the largest of which stood 125 ft (38 m) high. The statues were destroyed by the taliban regime in March 2001.*

Transportation & industry

Pakistan is highly dependent on the cotton textiles industry, although diversified manufacture is expanding around cities such as Karachi and Lahore. Afghanistan's limited industry is based mainly on the processing of agricultural raw materials and includes traditional crafts such as carpet weaving.

Major industry and infrastructure

- carpet weaving
- chemicals
- engineering
- finance
- food processing
- iron & steel
- oil & gas
- textiles
- capital cities
- major towns
- international airports
- major roads
- major industrial areas

Transportation network

- 96,154 miles (154,763 km)
- 211 miles (340 km)
- 4852 miles (7814 km)
- 745 miles (1200 km)

The Karakoram Highway was completed after 20 years of construction in 1978. It breaches the Himalayan mountain barrier providing a commercial motor route linking lowland Pakistan and China.

▶ ***The Karakoram Highway*** *is one of the highest major roads in the world. It took over 24,000 workers almost 20 years to complete.*

The landscape

Afghanistan's topography is dominated by the mountains of the Hindu Kush, which spread south and west into numerous mountain spurs. The dry plateau of southwestern Afghanistan extends into Pakistan and the hills which overlook the great Indus Basin. In northern Pakistan the Hindu Kush, Himalayan, and Karakoram ranges meet to form one of the world's highest mountain regions.

◀ ***The Hunza river*** *rises in the northern Karakoram Range, running for 120 miles (193 km) before joining the Gilgit river.*

▶ ***The arid Hindu Kush*** *makes much of Afghanistan uninhabitable, with over 50% of the land lying above 6500 ft (2000 m).*

Hunza river

The plains and foothills which extend from the northern slopes of the Hindu Kush are part of the great grassy steppe lands of Central Asia.

Hindu Kush

K2 (Mount Godwin Austen), in the Karakoram Range, is the second highest mountain in the world, at an altitude of 28,251 ft (8611 m).

Frequent earthquakes mean that mountain-building processes are continuing in this region, as the Indo-Australian Plate drifts northward, colliding with the Eurasian Plate.

Some of the largest glaciers outside the polar regions are found in the Karakoram Range, including Siachen Glacier *(Siachen Muztagh)*, which is 40 miles (72 km) long.

Himalayas

The soils of the Punjab plain are nourished by enormous quantities of sediment, carried from the Himalayas by the five tributaries of the Indus river.

Mountain chains running southwest from the Hindu Kush into Pakistan form a barrier to the humid winds which blow from the Indian Ocean, creating arid conditions across southern Afghanistan.

The Indus Basin is part of the Indus-Ganges lowland, a vast depression which has been filled with layers of sediment over the last 50 million years. These deposits are estimated to be over 16,400 ft (5000 m) deep.

The Indus Delta is prone to heavy flooding and high levels of salinity. It remains a largely uncultivated wilderness area.

Glacis covered by coarse-grained sediment

Sediments washed down from mountains accumulate on glacis slopes

Bedrock

Fine sediments deposited on salt flats are removed by wind erosion.

▲ ***Glacis are gentle,*** *debris-covered slopes which lead into saltflats or deserts. They typically occur at the base of mountains in arid regions such as Afghanistan.*

Scale 1:5,000,000

projection: Lambert Conformal Conic

146

142

142

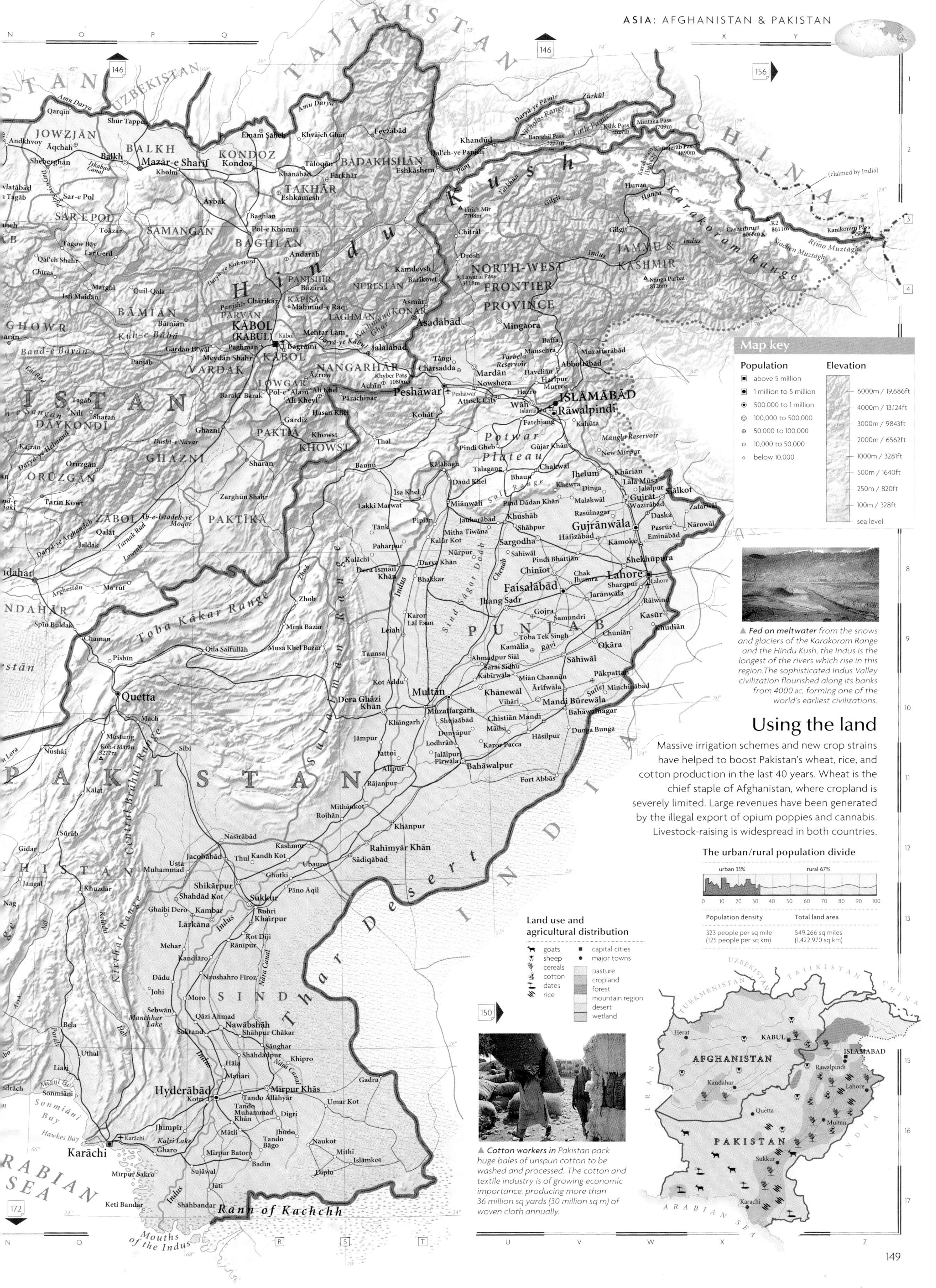
Map key
Population
above 5 million
1 million to 5 million
500,000 to 1 million
100,000 to 500,000
50,000 to 100,000
10,000 to 50,000
below 10,000
Elevation
6000m / 19,686ft
4000m / 13,124ft
3000m / 9843ft
2000m / 6562ft
1000m / 3281ft
500m / 1640ft
250m / 820ft
100m / 328ft
sea level
The urban/rural population divide
urban 33%
rural 67%
0 10 20 30 40 50 60 70 80 90 100
Population density
323 people per sq mile (125 people per sq km)
Total land area
549,266 sq miles (1,422,970 sq km)
Land use and agricultural distribution
goats
sheep
cereals
cotton
dates
rice
capital cities
major towns
pasture
cropland
forest
mountain region
desert
wetland
AFGHANISTAN
PAKISTAN
TAJIKISTAN
UZBEKISTAN
TURKMENISTAN
CHINA
INDIA
IRAN
ARABIAN SEA
KABUL
ISLAMABAD
Herat
Kandahar
Quetta
Rawalpindi
Lahore
Multan
Sukkur
Karachi
Hindu Kush
Karakoram Range
Thar Desert
Toba Kākar Range
Sulaimān Range
Kīrthar Range
Central Brāhui Range
Potwar Plateau
Rann of Kachchh
Mouths of the Indus
NORTH-WEST FRONTIER PROVINCE
JAMMU & KASHMIR
PUNJAB
SIND
ISLĀMĀBĀD
Rāwalpindi
Peshāwar
KĀBOL (KABUL)
Karāchi
Hyderābād
Faisalābād
Gujrānwāla
Multān
Quetta
Mazār-e Sharīf
K2 8611m
Nanga Parbat 8126m
Tirich Mir 7708m
(claimed by India)
146
156
150
172

▲ **Fed on meltwater** from the snows and glaciers of the Karakoram Range and the Hindu Kush, the Indus is the longest of the rivers which rise in this region. The sophisticated Indus Valley civilization flourished along its banks from 4000 BC, forming one of the world's earliest civilizations.

Using the land

Massive irrigation schemes and new crop strains have helped to boost Pakistan's wheat, rice, and cotton production in the last 40 years. Wheat is the chief staple of Afghanistan, where cropland is severely limited. Large revenues have been generated by the illegal export of opium poppies and cannabis. Livestock-raising is widespread in both countries.

▲ **Cotton workers in** Pakistan pack huge bales of unspun cotton to be washed and processed. The cotton and textile industry is of growing economic importance, producing more than 36 million sq yards (30 million sq m) of woven cloth annually.

South Asia

BANGLADESH, BHUTAN, INDIA, MALDIVES, NEPAL, PAKISTAN, SRI LANKA

More than one-fifth of the world's population lives in the south Asian subcontinent. Great cultural diversity has come from a long succession of foreign invaders, including Hindu Aryans, Islamic Moguls, and the British, whose empire incorporated the princely states of the Maharajas and extended to the borders of Nepal and Bhutan in the Himalayas. Independent since 1947, India is the world's largest democracy, and at the current rate of growth, may overtake China as the world's most populous country during the 21st century. There are points of tension in the region over claims for independence by the Sikhs in the Indian Punjab and the Tamil separatists in Sri Lanka, and the long-standing dispute with Pakistan over Jammu and Kashmir in the north.

◀ *The towering Karakoram and Hindu Kush ranges, formed at the same time as the Himalayas, dominate Pakistan's northern borders. K2 on the border of northern Pakistan is the second highest mountain on Earth, at 28,251 ft (8611 m).*

The landscape

South Asia is effectively isolated from the rest of Asia by desert along the western flank of Pakistan, and a continuous wall of mountains, dominated by the Himalayas, to the north and east. The great basins of the Indus and Ganges separate this mountain fringe from the rolling plateau of the Indian peninsula, which is bordered by a line of coastal hills, the Eastern and Western Ghats.

The Indus river flows more than 1970 miles (3180 km) from southwestern Tibet to its mouth on the Arabian Sea. It has an estimated catchment area of 450,000 sq miles (1,165,500 sq km).

The coast of western Pakistan is a staircase of folded rock strata caused by successive periods of rapid uplift.

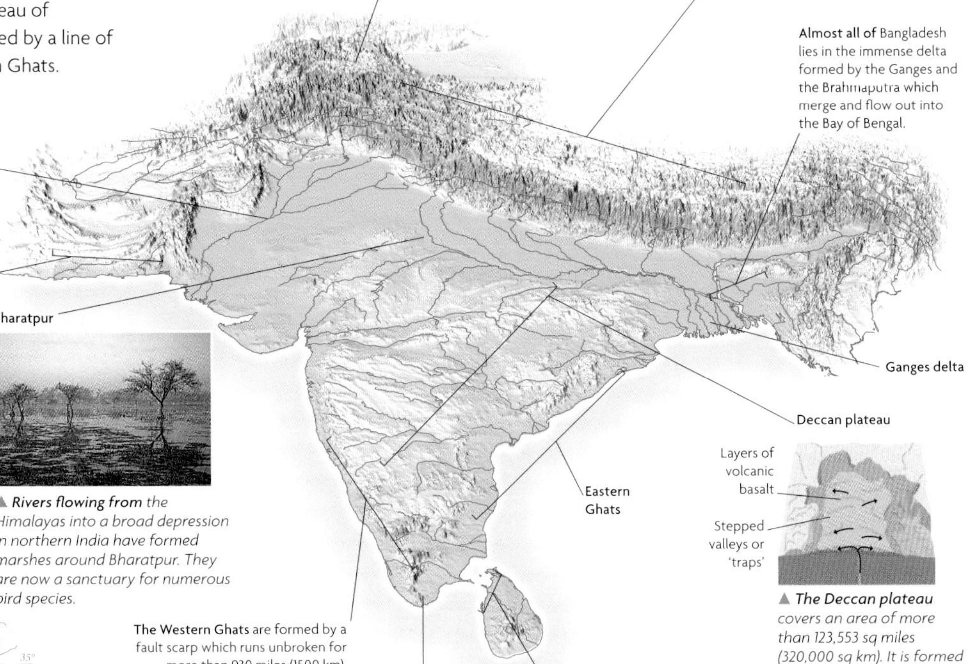

◀ ***The Indus valley*** *near Skardu in northern Pakistan has been partially infilled by great quantities of eroded sediment. Most of this is carried from the region's bare slopes by swollen rivers during the spring thaw and mass movement activity.*

The Himalayas are the highest and most extensive mountain system in the world. They were formed when the Indo-Australian Plate collided with the Eurasian Plate about 40 million years ago, thrusting up huge masses of land and creating a "ripple" effect, which formed lesser mountain ranges in Tibet and Southeast Asia. Mount Everest is the world's tallest mountain at 29,035 ft (8850 m).

Almost all of Bangladesh lies in the immense delta formed by the Ganges and the Brahmaputra which merge and flow out into the Bay of Bengal.

Bharatpur

Ganges delta

Deccan plateau

Eastern Ghats

Layers of volcanic basalt

Stepped valleys or 'traps'

▲ ***Rivers flowing from*** *the Himalayas into a broad depression in northern India have formed marshes around Bharatpur. They are now a sanctuary for numerous bird species.*

The Western Ghats are formed by a fault scarp which runs unbroken for more than 930 miles (1500 km). They reach their highest point at the southern Cardamom Hills.

Trivandrum in southern India normally receives the first of the monsoon rains, which are essential to south Asian agriculture and moderate the extreme summer heat. The monsoon then moves northward over a period of about two months.

Coastal deposition has formed many typical features along the western coast of Sri Lanka. These include spits and bars, sometimes enclosing lagoons.

▲ ***The Deccan plateau*** *covers an area of more than 123,553 sq miles (320,000 sq km). It is formed of deep layers of volcanic basalt, reaching thicknesses of more than 9800 ft (3000 m) toward the coast. Distinctive stepped valleys cut in the basalt plateau by rivers are known as "traps."*

146 148 156 156 156 142

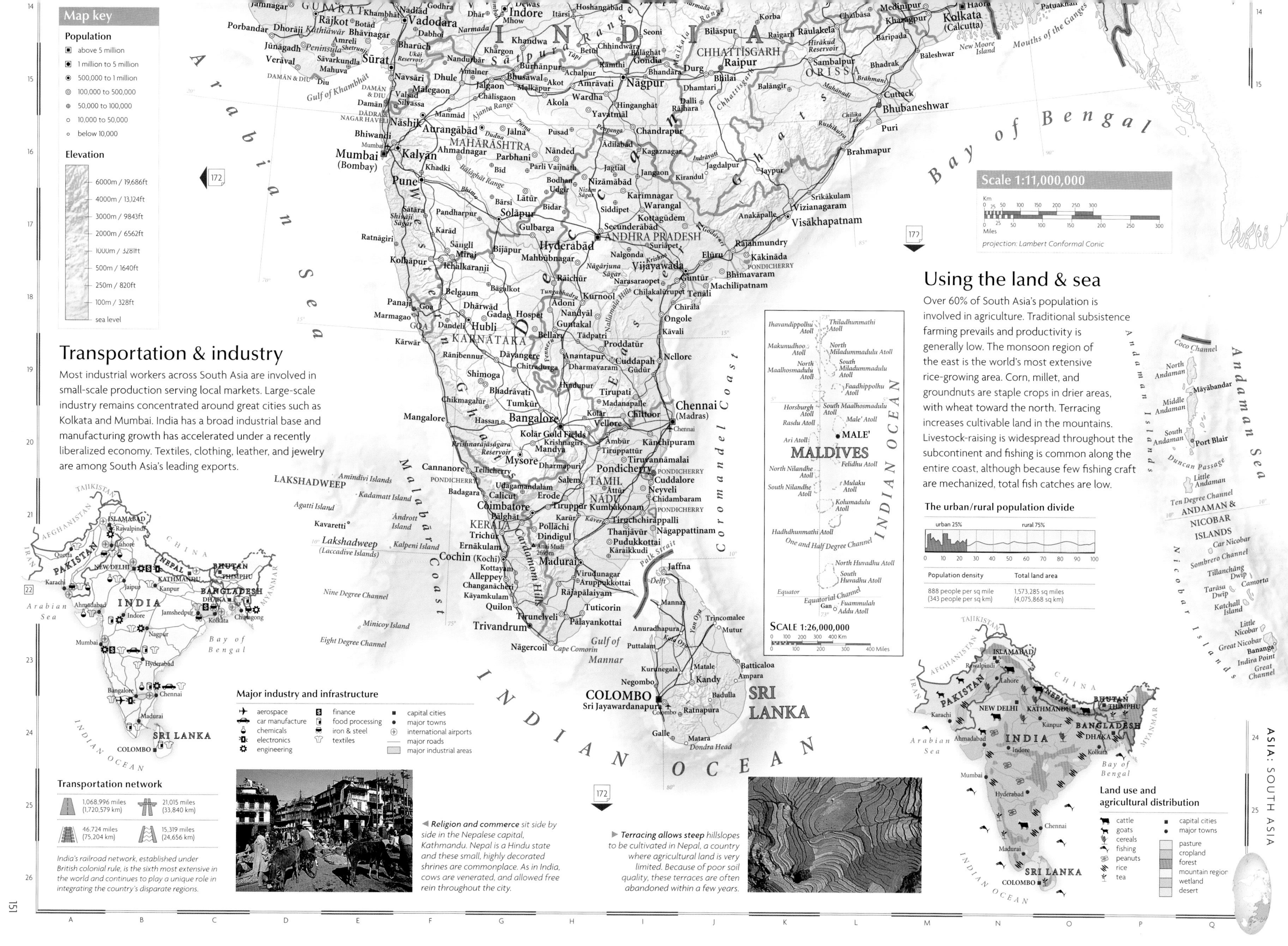
Map key
Population
above 5 million
1 million to 5 million
500,000 to 1 million
100,000 to 500,000
50,000 to 100,000
10,000 to 50,000
below 10,000
Elevation
6000m / 19,686ft
4000m / 13,124ft
3000m / 9843ft
2000m / 6562ft
1000m / 3281ft
500m / 1640ft
250m / 820ft
100m / 328ft
sea level
Scale 1:11,000,000
projection: Lambert Conformal Conic
Arabian Sea
Bay of Bengal
INDIAN OCEAN
INDIA
SRI LANKA
MALDIVES
LAKSHADWEEP
ANDAMAN & NICOBAR ISLANDS
Andaman Sea
SCALE 1:26,000,000
Major industry and infrastructure
aerospace
car manufacture
chemicals
electronics
engineering
finance
food processing
iron & steel
textiles
capital cities
major towns
international airports
major roads
major industrial areas
Transportation network
1,068,996 miles (1,720,579 km)
21,015 miles (33,840 km)
46,724 miles (75,204 km)
15,319 miles (24,656 km)
The urban/rural population divide
urban 25%
rural 75%
Population density
888 people per sq mile (343 people per sq km)
Total land area
1,573,285 sq miles (4,075,868 sq km)
Land use and agricultural distribution
cattle
goats
cereals
fishing
peanuts
rice
tea
capital cities
major towns
pasture
cropland
forest
mountain region
wetland
desert

Transportation & industry

Most industrial workers across South Asia are involved in small-scale production serving local markets. Large-scale industry remains concentrated around great cities such as Kolkata and Mumbai. India has a broad industrial base and manufacturing growth has accelerated under a recently liberalized economy. Textiles, clothing, leather, and jewelry are among South Asia's leading exports.

India's railroad network, established under British colonial rule, is the sixth most extensive in the world and continues to play a unique role in integrating the country's disparate regions.

◀ *Religion and commerce* sit side by side in the Nepalese capital, Kathmandu. Nepal is a Hindu state and these small, highly decorated shrines are commonplace. As in India, cows are venerated, and allowed free rein throughout the city.

Using the land & sea

Over 60% of South Asia's population is involved in agriculture. Traditional subsistence farming prevails and productivity is generally low. The monsoon region of the east is the world's most extensive rice-growing area. Corn, millet, and groundnuts are staple crops in drier areas, with wheat toward the north. Terracing increases cultivable land in the mountains. Livestock-raising is widespread throughout the subcontinent and fishing is common along the entire coast, although because few fishing craft are mechanized, total fish catches are low.

▶ *Terracing allows steep* hillslopes to be cultivated in Nepal, a country where agricultural land is very limited. Because of poor soil quality, these terraces are often abandoned within a few years.

172

Northern India & the Himalayan states

BANGLADESH, BHUTAN, NEPAL, Arunachal Pradesh, Assam, Bihar, Chandigarh, Delhi, Haryana, Himachal Pradesh, Jammu & Kashmir, Jharkhand, Manipur, Meghalaya, Mizoram, Nagaland, Punjab, Rajasthan, Sikkim, Tripura, Uttaranchal, Uttar Pradesh, West Bengal

The Ganges and Brahmaputra river basins and the massive mountain barrier of the Himalayas define this region's landscape and have served to reinforce potent cultural and religious differences among its people. Hinduism pervades most aspects of national life and is a growing political force within India, a secular country which also encompasses the center of Sikhism at Amritsar and the world's largest Muslim minority. Nepal is a crowded mountain state, which faces severe ecological problems from deforestation, while the tiny Himalayan Buddhist kingdom of Bhutan is emerging from long-term isolation, to welcome selected visitors. The Muslim state of Bangladesh, formerly East Pakistan, is one of the world's most densely populated countries and one of the poorest, with more than 145 million people living largely on the massive Ganges/Brahmaputra delta. Many Bangladeshis live under threat of repeated, catastrophic floods.

◄ ***The Golden Temple** in Amritsar, the most sacred shrine of the Sikh religion, was the scene of violent clashes between Sikh separatists and government forces in 1984.*

Scale 1:6,500,000

Km: 0 10 20 40 60 80 100 120 140 160 180 200

Miles: 0 10 20 40 60 80 100 120 140 160 180 200

projection: Lambert Conformal Conic

148

156

154

Map key

Population

- 1 million to 5 million
- 500,000 to 1 million
- 100,000 to 500,000
- 50,000 to 100,000
- 10,000 to 50,000
- below 10,000

Elevation

- 6000m / 19,686ft
- 4000m / 13,124ft
- 3000m / 9843ft
- 2000m / 6562ft
- 1000m / 3281ft
- 500m / 1640ft
- 250m / 820ft
- 100m / 328ft
- sea level

Transportation & industry

Textiles, engineering, chemicals, and electronics are leading industries in north India. The plateau of Chota Nagpur provides ore for iron and steel production in the major industrial region northeast of Kolkata. Bangladesh processes jute and Nepal has a small manufacturing sector based on agricultural produce, while Bhutan's limited industry is concentrated in the southern lowland area.

Major industry and infrastructure

- adventure tourism
- car manufacture
- chemicals
- coal
- electronics
- engineering
- finance
- food processing
- iron & steel
- jute processing
- oil
- tea processing
- textiles
- capital cities
- major towns
- international airports
- major roads
- major industrial areas

Transportation network

Over 60% of Bangladesh's internal trade is carried by boat. The country has a very disjointed land transportation network, with no bridges over the Brahmaputra and few road crossings on the Ganges river.

The landscape

Most of the region is drained by the Ganges river, which meets the Brahmaputra in Bangladesh to form an immense delta before flowing into the Bay of Bengal. The Himalayas extend eastward over 1500 miles (2400 km), from the parallel ranges running through Jammu and Kashmir. The Thar Desert occupies the southwest.

▸ *The Fir Panjal Range in southwestern Kashmir rises to elevations of 12,500 ft (3810 m). Despite the freezing conditions, settlements and extensive pastures are found above the tree line.*

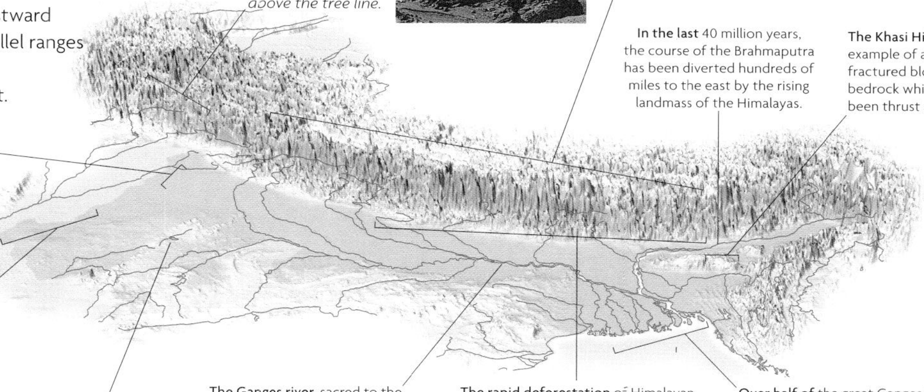

The northern ranges of the Himalayas contain the highest mountains in the world, with average heights of more than 23,000 ft (7000 m) and many peaks higher than 26,000 ft (8000 m).

▲ ***The summit of** Machhapuchhre rises to 22,942 ft (6993 m). It is also known as the "Fish's Tail" because of its distinctive peak.*

In the last 40 million years, the course of the Brahmaputra has been diverted hundreds of miles to the east by the rising landmass of the Himalayas.

The Khasi Hills are an example of a *horst*, a fractured block of bedrock which has been thrust upward.

The Indian Punjab lies mainly to the west of the Ganges watershed and its rivers flow into the Indus. Control of this water resource has been a source of great friction with neighboring Pakistan.

The border between India and Pakistan runs through the Thar Desert, an area of sandy seif dunes 50–100 ft (15–30 m) in height. Fossils found in the desert indicate that the dunes, stabilized by vegetation, have been in their current position for about 3000 years.

Sambhar Salt Lake in Rajasthan is India's largest lake. Unlike most of the Himalayan lakes which are glacial in origin – formed in ice-scoured basins or as the result of depositional damming – it is an ephemeral salt lake filled periodically by flash flooding.

The Ganges river, sacred to the Hindu people, drains a vast lowland area at the base of the Himalayas. The northern plains are covered by sandy deposits, broken by mud banks formed when the river floods.

The rapid deforestation of Himalayan valleys has led to acute soil erosion and increased rates of rainwater runoff, both cited as possible causes of the worsening floods downstream in the Ganges/Brahmaputra delta, although natural rates are high and may be the real cause.

Over half of the great Ganges/Brahmaputra delta floods each year during the monsoon as rivers, swollen by meltwater from the Himalayas and by excess rainwater, break their banks and fertilize the land with nutrient-rich sediment.

Debris slides in the middle Himalayas

Soil blocks
Slide plain
Debris fans at base of slope

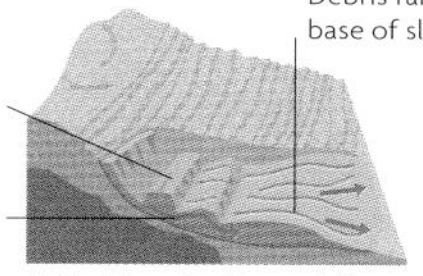

▲ ***Soil loss in** the middle Himalayas has largely been attributed to debris slides, where large blocks of soil are mobilized by saturation along a slide plane. Once mobile, the soil slides down the slope, gaining speed and thinning to form a fan at the base of the slope.*

Using the land

Grain production dominates land use. Rice is most widely grown in the east. Irrigation and new crop strains have dramatically increased yields in the Punjab, a major wheat-producing area. River floodplains are intensively farmed and livestock herding is widespread, particularly in Bhutan. Regional crops include jute in Bangladesh, tea in Assam, cardamom in Sikkim, and saffron in Kashmir.

The urban/rural population divide

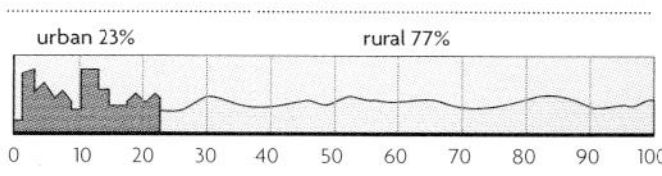

urban 23% | rural 77%

0 10 20 30 40 50 60 70 80 90 100

Population density	Total land area
993 people per sq mile (384 people per sq km)	665,104 sq miles (1,723,068 sq km)

▲ ***An adverse climate,** steep slopes, and poor soils limit crop cultivation in Bhutan, which is a largely agrarian economy. Rice, corn, and wheat are the main staples, although orchards are being established as the soil and climate suit this type of farming.*

Land use and agricultural distribution

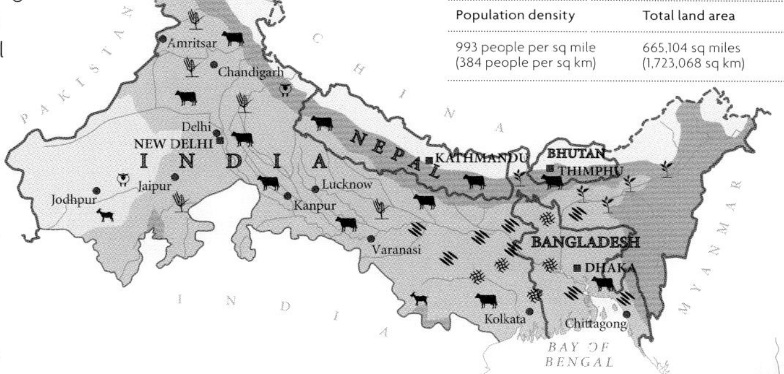

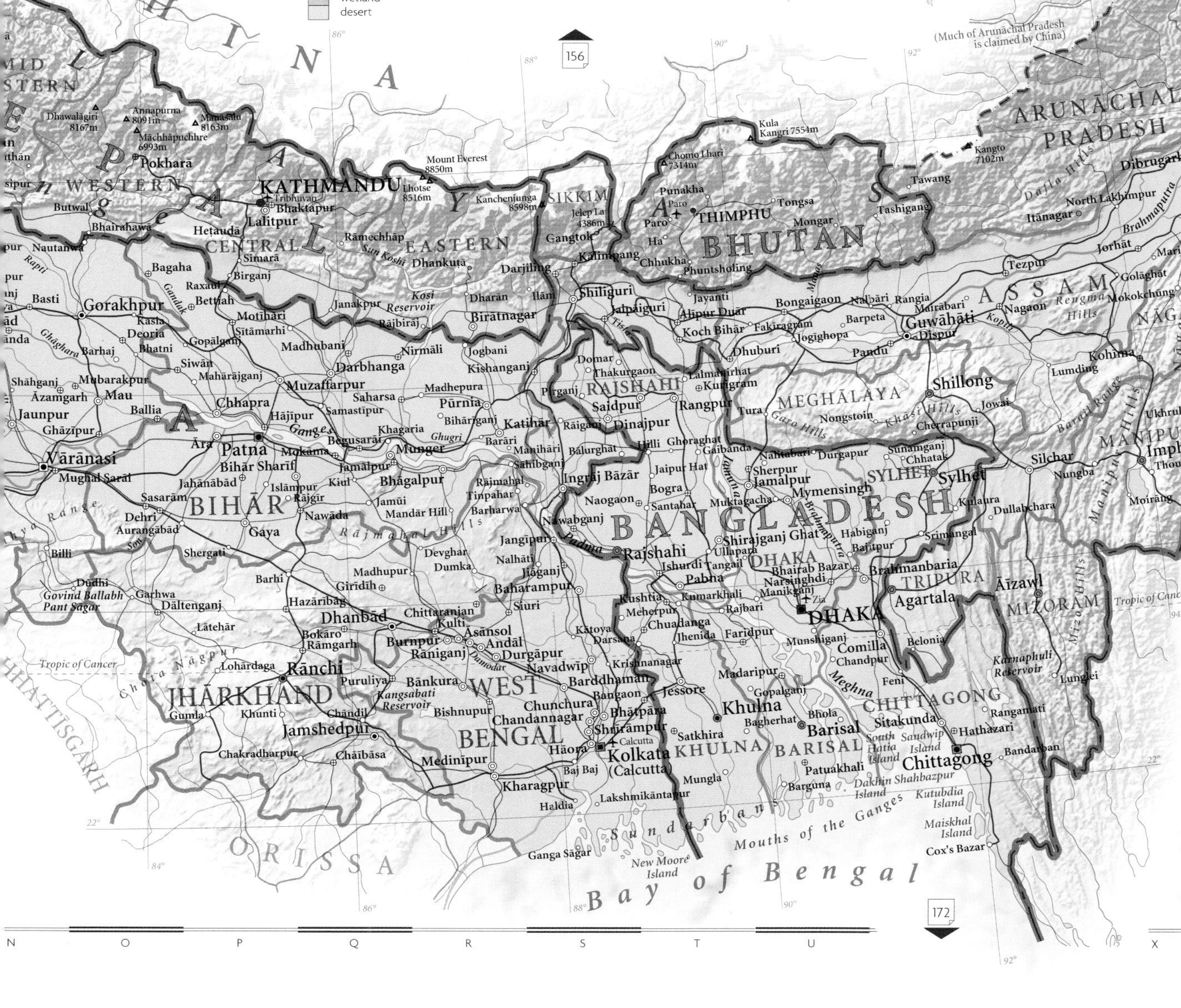

- cattle
- goats
- sheep
- cereals
- jute
- rice
- tea
- capital cities
- major towns
- pasture
- cropland
- forest
- mountain region
- wetland
- desert

156

166

172

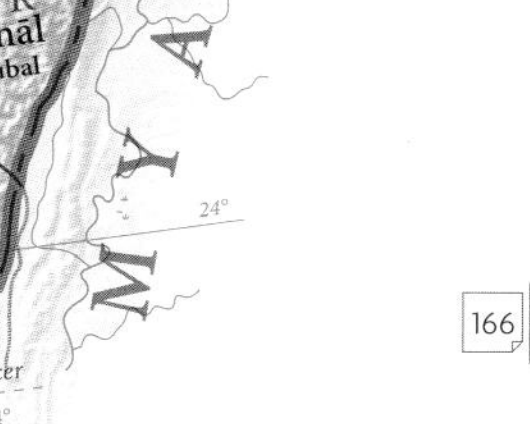

▲ ***Flooded streets in** Dhaka, Bangladesh are a testament to the region's vulnerability to flooding. In 1988 alone, 75% of the country was flooded, leaving thousands of people dead and over 25 million homeless.*

Southern India & Sri Lanka

SRI LANKA, Andhra Pradesh, Chhattisgarh, Dadra & Nagar Haveli, Daman & Diu, Goa, Gujarat, Karnataka, Kerala, Lakshadweep, Madhya Pradesh, Maharashtra, Orissa, Pondicherry, Tamil Nadu

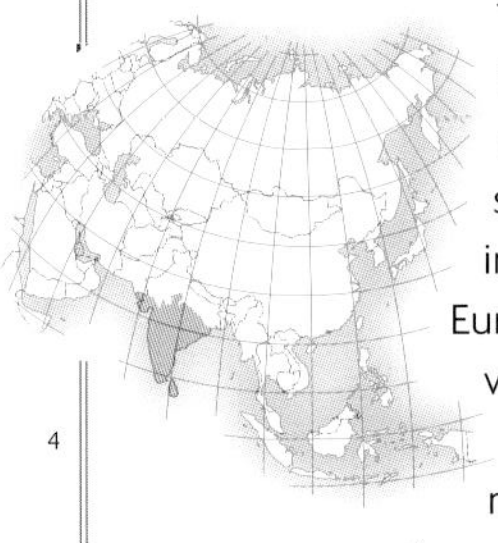

The unique and highly independent southern states reflect the diverse and decentralized nature of India, which has fourteen official languages. The southern half of the peninsula lay beyond the reach of early invaders from the north and retained the distinct and ancient culture of Dravidian peoples such as the Tamils, whose language is spoken in preference to Hindi throughout southern India. The interior plateau of southern India is less densely populated than the coastal lowlands, where the European colonial imprint is strongest. Urban and industrial growth is accelerating, but southern India's vast population remains predominantly rural. The island of Sri Lanka has two distinct cultural groups; the mainly Buddhist Sinhalese majority, and the Tamil minority whose struggle for a homeland in the northeast has led to prolonged civil war.

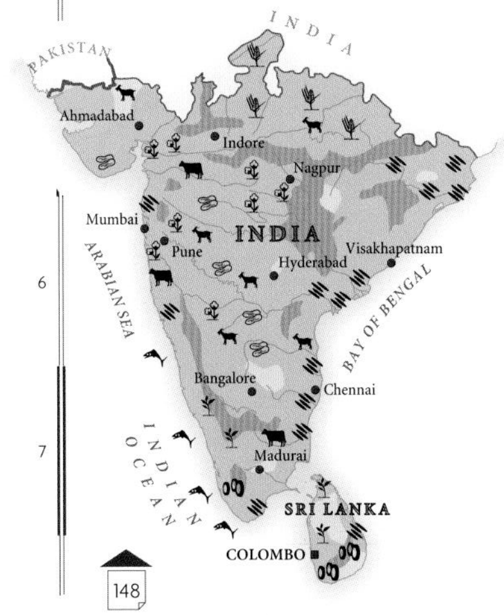

Using the land and sea

Rice is the main staple in the east, in Sri Lanka and along the humid Malabar Coast. Peanuts are grown on the Deccan plateau, with wheat, corn, and chickpeas, toward the north. Sri Lanka is a leading exporter of tea, coconuts and rubber. Cotton plantations supply local mills around Nagpur and Mumbai. Fishing supports many communities in Kerala and the Laccadive Islands.

Land use and agricultural distribution

cattle, goats, cereals, cotton, fishing, peanuts, rice, rubber, tea, capital cities, major towns, pasture, cropland, forest, wetland

The urban/rural population divide

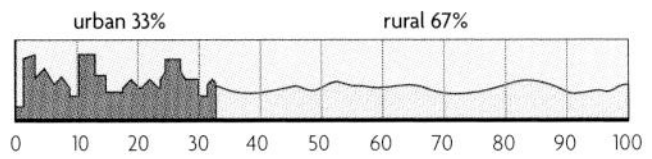

urban 33% — rural 67%

Population density	Total land area
730 people per sq mile (282 people per sq km)	698,295 sq miles (1,809,054 sq km)

The landscape

The undulating Deccan plateau underlies most of southern India; it slopes gently down toward the east and is largely enclosed by the Ghats coastal hill ranges. The Western Ghats run continuously along the Arabian Sea coast, while the Eastern Ghats are interrupted by rivers which follow the slope of the plateau and flow across broad lowlands into the Bay of Bengal. The plateaus and basins of Sri Lanka's central highlands are surrounded by a broad plain.

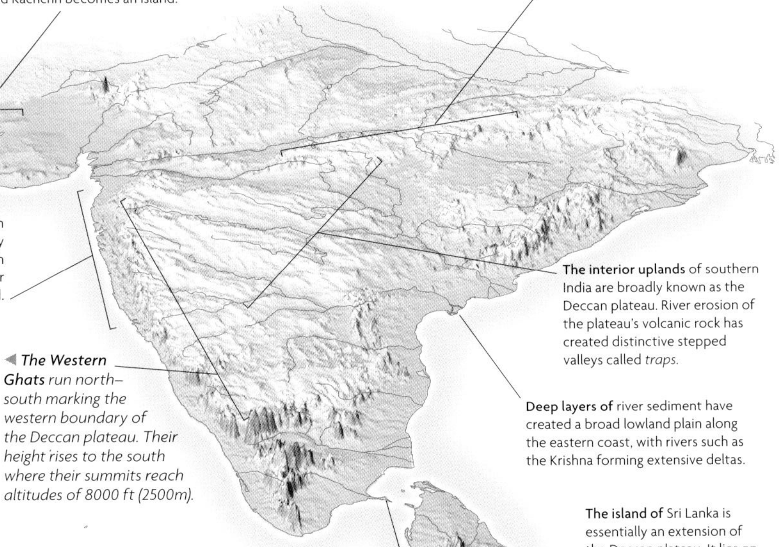

Along the northern boundary of the Deccan plateau, old basement rocks are interspersed with younger sedimentary strata. This creates spectacular scarplands, cut by numerous waterfalls along the softer sedimentary strata.

The Rann of Kachchh tidal marshes encircle the low-lying Kachchh peninsula. For several months during the rainy season the water level of the marshes rises and Kachchh becomes an island.

The Konkan coast, which runs between Daman and Goa, is characterized by rocky headlands, and bays with crescent-shaped beaches. Flooded river valleys known as *rias* extend inland.

The interior uplands of southern India are broadly known as the Deccan plateau. River erosion of the plateau's volcanic rock has created distinctive stepped valleys called *traps*.

The Western Ghats run north–south marking the western boundary of the Deccan plateau. Their height rises to the south where their summits reach altitudes of 8000 ft (2500m).

Deep layers of river sediment have created a broad lowland plain along the eastern coast, with rivers such as the Krishna forming extensive deltas.

The island of Sri Lanka is essentially an extension of the Deccan plateau. It lies on the Indian continental shelf and is composed of the same hard, crystalline rocks.

Adam's Bridge

Relict of ancient tombolo; Adam's Bridge; Ocean currents cause sediment build up; Sri Lanka

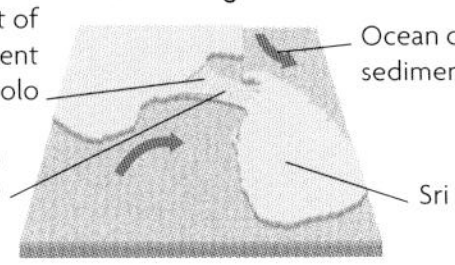

Adam's Bridge (Rama's Bridge) is a chain of sandy shoals lying about 4 ft (1.2 m) under the sea between India and Sri Lanka. They once formed the world's longest tombolo, or land bridge, before the sea level began to rise several thousand years ago.

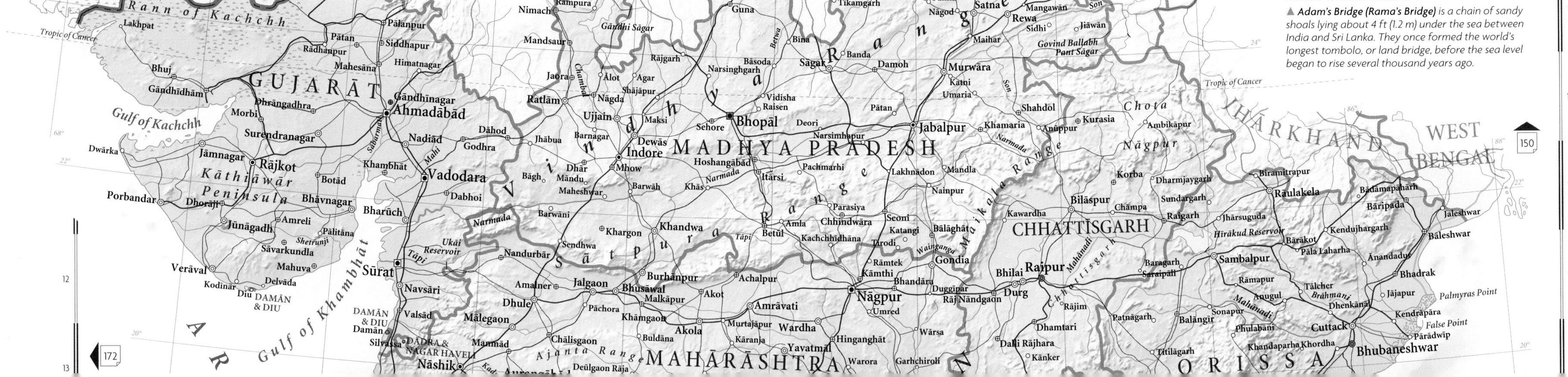

Map key

Population

- above 5 million
- 1 million to 5 million
- 500,000 to 1 million
- 100,000 to 500,000
- 50,000 to 100,000
- 10,000 to 50,000
- below 10,000

Elevation

- 2000m / 6562ft
- 1000m / 3281ft
- 500m / 1640ft
- 250m / 820ft
- 100m / 328ft
- sea level

▲ ***Sea pencils thrive*** *on the coral reefs around the coast of the Laccadive Islands and Sri Lanka. The reefs support an amazing diversity of marine life, but are increasingly under threat from growing coastal populations.*

▲ ***Local fisheries around*** *Sri Lanka afford great potential for exploitation. However, many fishermen living on the coastal fringes saw their livelihoods destroyed by the devastating effects of the Asian tsunami in 2004.*

Scale 1:7,000,000

Km 0 25 50 100 150 200

Miles 0 25 50 100 150 200

projection: Lambert Conformal Conic

▲ ***The great triumphal*** *arch of Charminar, built in 1591, epitomizes the fine Islamic architecture which the Moghuls brought from the north to Hyderabad, the capital of Andhra Pradesh.*

Transportation & industry

South India has a broad industrial base, with three leading regions. Around Mumbai, Bangalore, and Ahmadabad, cotton mills and chemical plants make use of cheap hydroelectric power generated in the Western Ghats. Light engineering and textiles are well established to the south and west of Chennai. Sri Lanka's industry is based mainly on the processing of agricultural products.

Major industry and infrastructure

- aerospace
- car manufacture
- chemicals
- electronics
- engineering
- food processing
- iron & steel
- pharmaceuticals
- printing & publishing
- shipbuilding
- tea processing
- textiles
- tobacco processing
- capital cities
- major towns
- international airports
- major roads
- major industrial areas

Transportation network

India's hard-surfaced road network has grown almost tenfold since independence, yet many villages are still only accessible on foot, even in densely populated rural areas.

▶ ***Mumbai is one*** *of the largest and most densely populated cities in the world. It is the center of India's textile trade and has important finance and commerce sectors.*

172

Mainland East Asia

CHINA, MONGOLIA, NORTH KOREA, SOUTH KOREA, TAIWAN

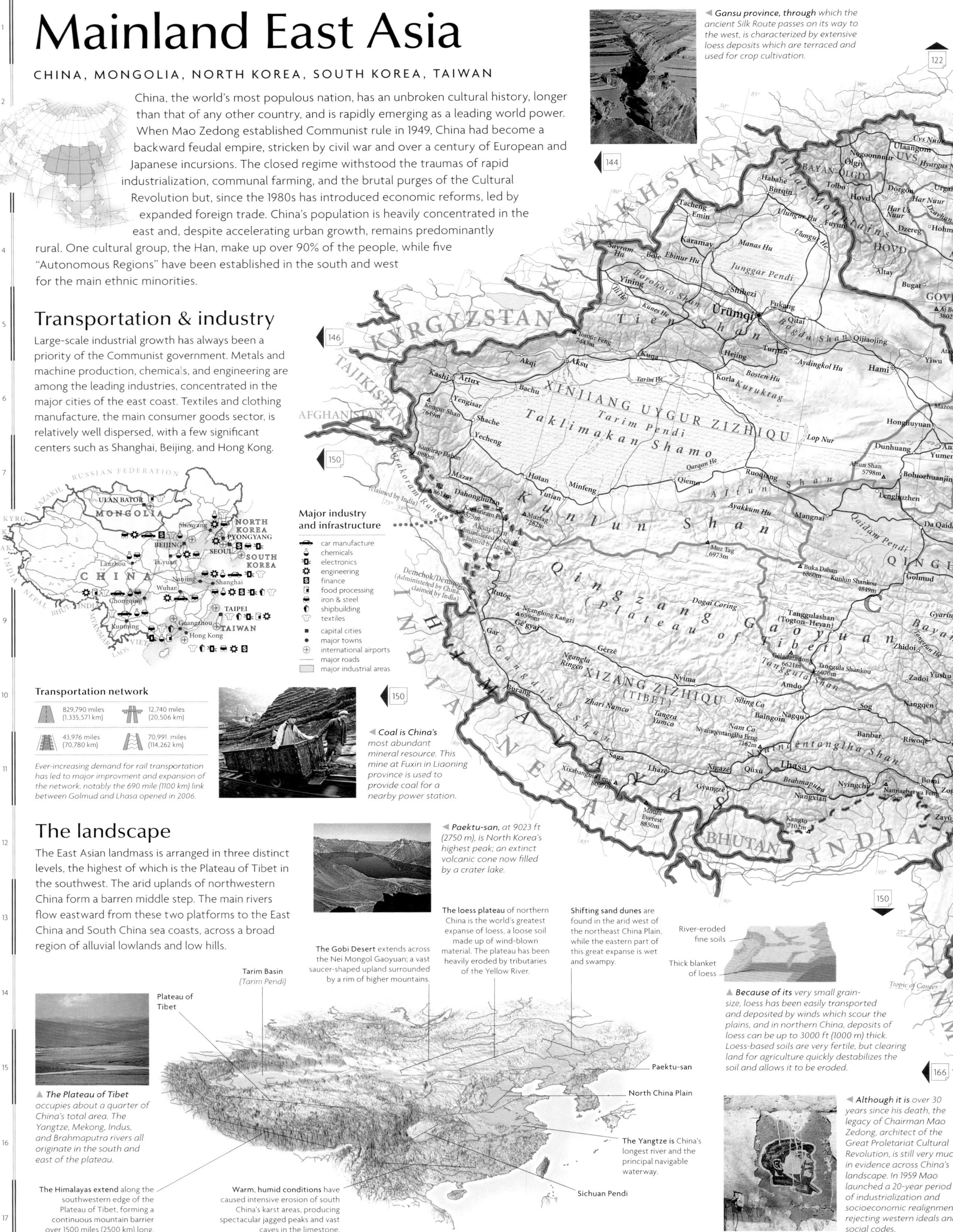

China, the world's most populous nation, has an unbroken cultural history, longer than that of any other country, and is rapidly emerging as a leading world power. When Mao Zedong established Communist rule in 1949, China had become a backward feudal empire, stricken by civil war and over a century of European and Japanese incursions. The closed regime withstood the traumas of rapid industrialization, communal farming, and the brutal purges of the Cultural Revolution but, since the 1980s has introduced economic reforms, led by expanded foreign trade. China's population is heavily concentrated in the east and, despite accelerating urban growth, remains predominantly rural. One cultural group, the Han, make up over 90% of the people, while five "Autonomous Regions" have been established in the south and west for the main ethnic minorities.

Transportation & industry

Large-scale industrial growth has always been a priority of the Communist government. Metals and machine production, chemicals, and engineering are among the leading industries, concentrated in the major cities of the east coast. Textiles and clothing manufacture, the main consumer goods sector, is relatively well dispersed, with a few significant centers such as Shanghai, Beijing, and Hong Kong.

RUSSIAN FEDERATION
ULAN BATOR
MONGOLIA
NORTH KOREA
PYONGYANG
SOUTH KOREA
SEOUL
BEIJING
Shenyang
Lanzhou
Taiyuan
CHINA
Nanjing
Shanghai
Wuhan
Chongqing
TAIPEI
TAIWAN
Kunming
Guangzhou
Hong Kong
Major industry and infrastructure
car manufacture
chemicals
electronics
engineering
finance
food processing
iron & steel
shipbuilding
textiles
capital cities
major towns
international airports
major roads
major industrial areas

Transportation network

829,790 miles (1,335,571 km)		12,740 miles (20,506 km)	
43,976 miles (70,780 km)		70,991 miles (114,262 km)	

Ever-increasing demand for rail transportation has led to major improvment and expansion of the network, notably the 690 mile (1100 km) link between Golmud and Lhasa opened in 2006.

◀ ***Coal is China's** most abundant mineral resource. This mine at Fuxin in Liaoning province is used to provide coal for a nearby power station.*

◀ ***Gansu province, through** which the ancient Silk Route passes on its way to the west, is characterized by extensive loess deposits which are terraced and used for crop cultivation.*

The landscape

The East Asian landmass is arranged in three distinct levels, the highest of which is the Plateau of Tibet in the southwest. The arid uplands of northwestern China form a barren middle step. The main rivers flow eastward from these two platforms to the East China and South China sea coasts, across a broad region of alluvial lowlands and low hills.

◀ ***Paektu-san,** at 9023 ft (2750 m), is North Korea's highest peak; an extinct volcanic cone now filled by a crater lake.*

Plateau of Tibet
Tarim Basin (Tarim Pendi)
Paektu-san
North China Plain
Sichuan Pendi
River-eroded fine soils
Thick blanket of loess

The Gobi Desert extends across the Nei Mongol Gaoyuan; a vast saucer-shaped upland surrounded by a rim of higher mountains.

The loess plateau of northern China is the world's greatest expanse of loess, a loose soil made up of wind-blown material. The plateau has been heavily eroded by tributaries of the Yellow River.

Shifting sand dunes are found in the arid west of the northeast China Plain, while the eastern part of this great expanse is wet and swampy.

The Yangtze is China's longest river and the principal navigable waterway.

The Himalayas extend along the southwestern edge of the Plateau of Tibet, forming a continuous mountain barrier over 1500 miles (2500 km) long.

Warm, humid conditions have caused intensive erosion of south China's karst areas, producing spectacular jagged peaks and vast caves in the limestone.

▲ ***The Plateau of Tibet** occupies about a quarter of China's total area. The Yangtze, Mekong, Indus, and Brahmaputra rivers all originate in the south and east of the plateau.*

▲ ***Because of its** very small grain-size, loess has been easily transported and deposited by winds which scour the plains, and in northern China, deposits of loess can be up to 3000 ft (1000 m) thick. Loess-based soils are very fertile, but clearing land for agriculture quickly destabilizes the soil and allows it to be eroded.*

◀ ***Although it is** over 30 years since his death, the legacy of Chairman Mao Zedong, architect of the Great Proletariat Cultural Revolution, is still very much in evidence across China's landscape. In 1959 Mao launched a 20-year period of industrialization and socioeconomic realignment, rejecting western ideals and social codes.*

122 144 146 150 150 150 166

Scale 1:14,000,000
projection: Lambert Conformal Conic
Map key
Population
above 5 million
1 million to 5 million
500,000 to 1 million
100,000 to 500,000
50,000 to 100,000
10,000 to 50,000
below 10,000
Elevation
6000m / 19,686ft
4000m / 13,124ft
3000m / 9843ft
2000m / 6562ft
1000m / 3281ft
500m / 1640ft
250m / 820ft
100m / 328ft
sea level
RUSSIAN FEDERATION
MONGOLIA
ULAANBAATAR (ULAN BATOR)
NORTH KOREA
P'YÖNGYANG
SOUTH KOREA
SOUL (SEOUL)
SEA OF JAPAN (EAST SEA)
Yellow Sea
EAST CHINA SEA
SOUTH CHINA SEA
TAIWAN
T'AIPEI
BEIJING (PEKING)
VIETNAM
LAOS
Hong Kong (Xianggang)
Macao (Aomen)
Land use and agricultural distribution
pigs
sheep
corn
cotton
fishing
fruit
rice
sugar cane
soybeans
capital cities
major towns
pasture
cropland
forest
mountain region
The urban/rural population divide
urban 32%
rural 68%
0 10 20 30 40 50 60 70 80 90 100
Population density
325 people per sq mile (125 people per sq km)
Total land area
4,288,672 sq miles (11,110,550 sq km)

Using the land & sea

Around 90% of China is unsuitable for cultivation, being either climatically or topographically adverse, or lacking sufficiently fertile soils. Most of the west is used for nomadic herding, while farmland is concentrated in the eastern monsoon region, with rice grown in the tropical and subtropical south. Cereals and soybeans predominate as rainfall and temperatures decline further north.

◀ *The Great Wall of China remains one of the world's largest-ever construction projects, and is so vast that it is visible from space. Sections were added as late as 1640 and it runs for over 4000 miles (6400 km) from the Yellow Sea to Central Asia.*

Western China

Gansu, Ningxia, Qinghai, Tibet, Xinjiang

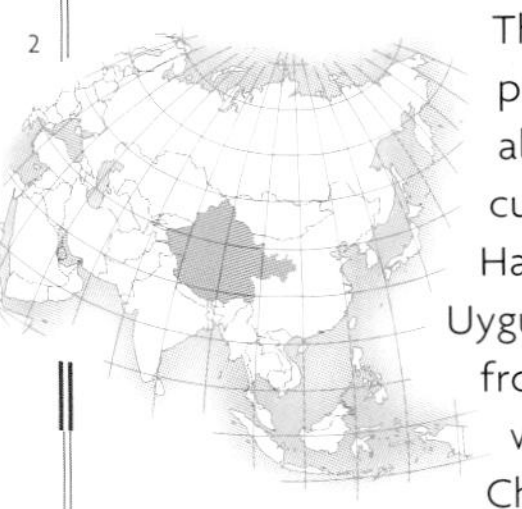

The plateaus and basins of China's dry, desolate western domain are sparsely populated and largely undeveloped, although they have rich mineral reserves; they also form a critical buffer zone for China, in a geographically important and culturally sensitive part of the Asian continent. Across most of the west, the Han Chinese are outnumbered by a range of cultural groups, including the Uygur, the largest group of the various seminomadic Muslim peoples from Central Asia. The remote, inhospitable Plateau of Tibet is the world's coldest and highest plateau. It has been occupied by the Chinese since 1950. Tibet is one of western China's five "Autonomous Regions," but its reclusive Buddhist culture has been systematically undermined by the Chinese government.

Map key

Population

- 1 million to 5 million
- 500,000 to 1 million
- 100,000 to 500,000
- 50,000 to 100,000
- 10,000 to 50,000
- below 10,000

Elevation

- 6000m / 19,686ft
- 4000m / 13,124ft
- 3000m / 9843ft
- 2000m / 6562ft
- 1000m / 3281ft
- 500m / 1640ft
- 250m / 820ft
- 100m / 328ft
- sea level

Scale 1:7,750,000

Km 0 25 50 100 150 200

Miles 0 25 50 100 150 200

projection: Lambert Conformal Conic

▲ ***The Lhasa He*** *is one of the many rivers that drain the vast Plateau of Tibet. From its source in the Nyainqêntanglha Shan range and fed by the spring meltwater, it eventually joins the upper Brahmaputra 40 miles (65 km) southwest of Lhasa.*

Using the land

Agriculture is constrained by the cold, dry climate and lack of fertile soils in the region, although irrigation and glasshouse farming are increasing agricultural potential. Large quantities of fruit, like melons and grapes, are grown at the oases of Hami and Turpan in Xinjiang, and new irrigation schemes have greatly increased cotton and wheat production in the Tarim Basin *(Tarim Pendi)*. Most of the great area of Tibet and Qinghai is devoted to pastoralism. Sheep are the principal livestock.

Land use and agricultural distribution

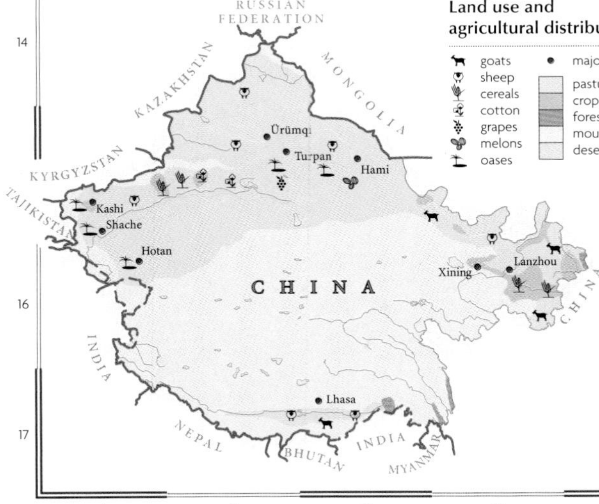

- goats
- sheep
- cereals
- cotton
- grapes
- melons
- oases
- major towns
- pasture
- cropland
- forest
- mountain region
- desert

◀ ***The Potala Palace,*** *in Tibet's capital, Lhasa, was the former residence of the Dalai Lama, Tibetan Buddhism's spiritual leader. Tibet remains only sparsely populated; forming over 20% of China's landmass, it supports fewer than 1% of its population.*

The landscape

The Himalayas mark the southwestern edge of the Plateau of Tibet, an extreme mountain wilderness which occupies nearly a quarter of China's total area. A large structural depression, the Qaidam Pendi, lies at its northeastern edge. The Kunlun mountain chain isolates the plateau from the desert to the north, where the Tien Shan range forms a spur between the Tarim Basin *(Tarim Pendi)* and Dzungarian Basin *(Junggar Pendi)*.

The Tien Shan reach elevations of over 24,419 ft (7435 m) and have permanent ice fields, from which large glaciers extend.

Dzungarian Basin *(Junggar Pendi)*

▶ ***The Bogda Shan,** an eastward arm of the Tien Shan range, rise high above the Turpan Depression* (Turpan Pendi).

The Turpan Depression *(Turpan Pendi)* is the lowest and hottest place in China. Temperatures can exceed 117°F (47°C) around the lake of Aydingkol Hu, which lies 505 ft (154 m) below sea level.

Northwestern China is largely a region of internal drainage. The Tarim He flows only as far as Lop Nur, where its water is lost by evapotranspiration from the lake and land surface.

A vast glacial lake filled much of the Tarim Basin *(Tarim Pendi)* during the last Ice Age. This area is now occupied by the Takla Makan Desert *(Taklimakan Shamo)*. A remnant of the lake, Lop Nur, forms the eastern margin, where it is fed by the Tarim He.

Sand dunes cover western parts of the the basin of Qaidam Pendi. Strong winds frequently carry the sands east, threatening the agricultural areas around the lake of Qinghai Hu.

◀ ***The terrain of** the Plateau of Tibet consists of mountain peaks and open plateaus, dotted with brackish lakes. These are probably remnants of the Tethys Sea, which covered the area before it was uplifted following the collision of the Indo-Australian and Eurasian plates.*

Mount Everest is the world's highest peak, at 29,035 ft (8850 m). The summit marks the border between China and Nepal.

Tarim Basin *(Tarim Pendi)*

Oases at edge of basin

Barchan sand dunes in Takla Makan Desert *(Taklimakan Shamo)*

Lop Nur

▲ ***The Tarim Basin** (Tarim Pendi) has no permanent rivers. Rainfall from the surrounding Plateau of Tibet and Tien Shan ranges drains into the basin's sand and gravel floor.*

▲ ***From its source,** high in eastern Qinghai, the Yellow River starts on a 3395 mile (5464 km) journey to the Yellow Sea.*

Transportation & industry

Oil extraction at Yumen and in the Dzungarian and Qaidam basins has led to the growth of the petrochemical industry and a range of heavy manufacturing plants in the cities of Lanzhou and Urumqi. Tibet, and most of Xinjiang, have little industry beyond traditional handicrafts, especially textiles at Hotan and Kashi, located along the ancient Silk Route. Nuclear and space-research testing are carried out at Lop Nur in Xinjiang.

Transportation network

The construction of roads connecting Lhasa in Tibet with Sichuan, Qinghai, and Xinjiang was achieved in the 1950s, in spite of the extreme physical conditions of the Plateau of Tibet.

Major industry and infrastructure

- agribusiness
- chemicals
- coal
- engineering
- food processing
- iron & steel
- nuclear testing
- oil
- textiles
- major towns
- major roads
- major industrial areas

Eastern China

TAIWAN, Anhui, Beijing, Chongqing, Fujian, Guangdong, Guangxi, Guizhou, Hainan, Hebei, Henan, Hubei, Hunan, Jiangsu, Jiangxi, Shaanxi, Shandong, Shanghai, Shanxi, Sichuan, Tianjin, Yunnan, Zhejiang

The east is China's heartland. Massive industrial development since 1949 has transformed much of the densely populated rural landscape, in a region still prone to flooding and drought. Over 30 cities have populations of over a million, including the giant metropolis of Shanghai and the capital Beijing, which has been China's cultural and political center since the 13th century. The ethnically diverse southwest and the oil-rich interior provinces of Sichuan and Shaanxi have largely missed out on the remarkable economic growth occurring in designated free-trade areas along the coasts of the South and East China seas. The republic of Taiwan was established in 1949 by Chinese nationalists ousted from the mainland by the victorious Communist forces. Taiwan now has one of the strongest economies in the world but its sovereignty is not recognized by China. Hong Kong provides a major international trade link for China; a 99-year "lease" period of British control was concluded in 1997.

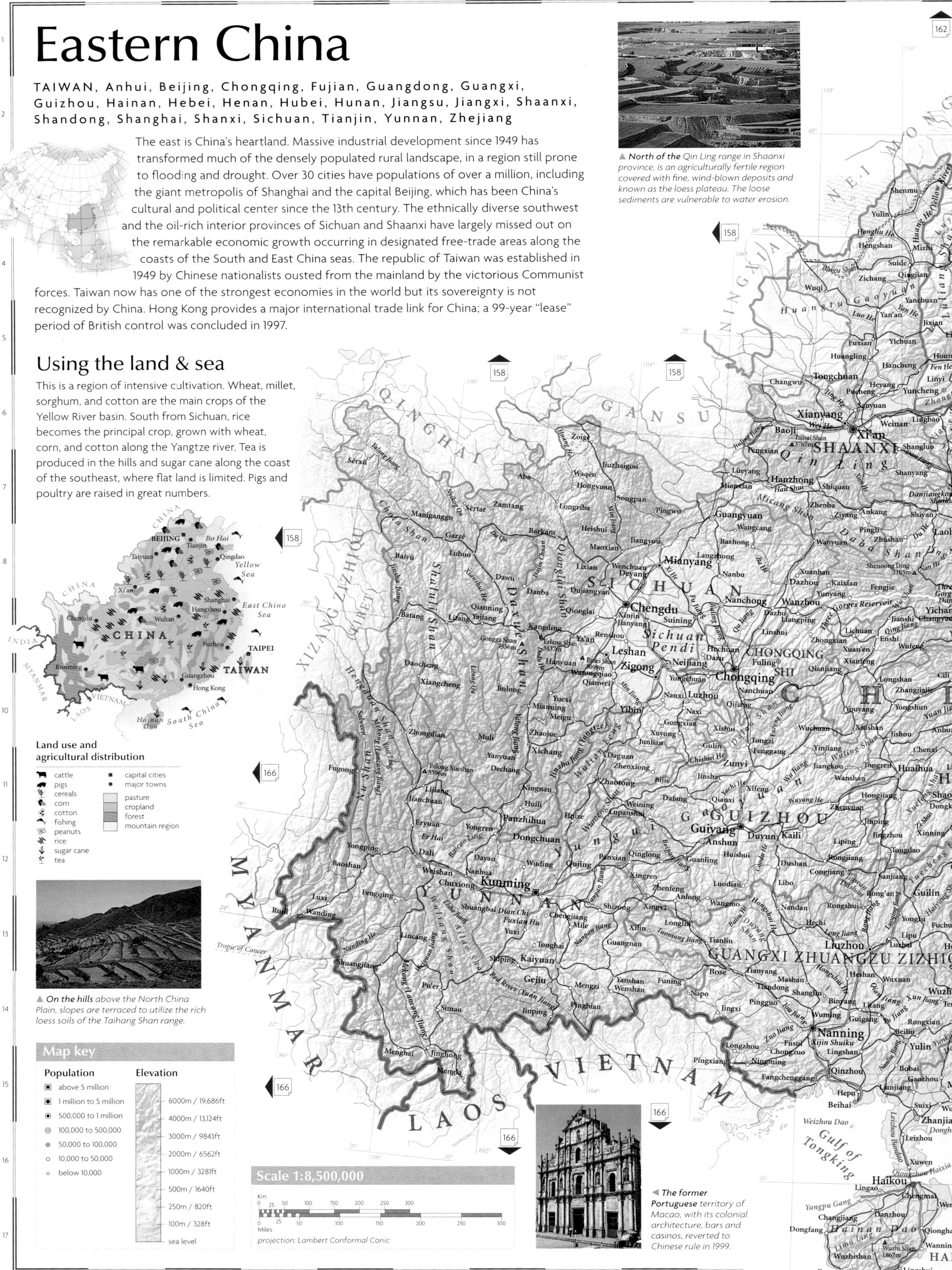

QINGHAI
GANSU
NINGXIA
SICHUAN
SHAANXI
GUIZHOU
YUNNAN
GUANGXI ZHUANGZU ZIZHIQU
CHONGQING SHI
XIZANG ZIZHIQU (TIBET)
MYANMAR
LAOS
VIETNAM
Gulf of Tongking
Hainan Dao
Chengdu
Chongqing
Kunming
Guiyang
Nanning
Xi'an
Haikou
Mianyang
Lanzhou
Panzhihua
Zigong
Leshan
Yibin
Zunyi
Liuzhou
Zhanjiang
Qin Ling
Daba Shan
Sichuan Pendi
Yunnan
Tropic of Cancer
158
162
166

▲ North of the Qin Ling range in Shaanxi province, is an agriculturally fertile region covered with fine, wind-blown deposits and known as the loess plateau. The loose sediments are vulnerable to water erosion.

Using the land & sea

This is a region of intensive cultivation. Wheat, millet, sorghum, and cotton are the main crops of the Yellow River basin. South from Sichuan, rice becomes the principal crop, grown with wheat, corn, and cotton along the Yangtze river. Tea is produced in the hills and sugar cane along the coast of the southeast, where flat land is limited. Pigs and poultry are raised in great numbers.

CHINA
BEIJING
Tianjin
Bo Hai
Taiyuan
Qingdao
Yellow Sea
Xi'an
Shanghai
Hangzhou
East China Sea
Wuhan
Chengdu
CHINA
INDIA
MYANMAR
Fuzhou
TAIPEI
TAIWAN
Kunming
Guangzhou
Hong Kong
VIETNAM
LAOS
Hainan Dao
South China Sea

Land use and agricultural distribution

- cattle
- pigs
- cereals
- corn
- cotton
- fishing
- peanuts
- rice
- sugar cane
- tea
- capital cities
- major towns
- pasture
- cropland
- forest
- mountain region

▲ *On the hills* above the North China Plain, slopes are terraced to utilize the rich loess soils of the Taihang Shan range.

Map key

Population

- above 5 million
- 1 million to 5 million
- 500,000 to 1 million
- 100,000 to 500,000
- 50,000 to 100,000
- 10,000 to 50,000
- below 10,000

Elevation

- 6000m / 19,686ft
- 4000m / 13,124ft
- 3000m / 9843ft
- 2000m / 6562ft
- 1000m / 3281ft
- 500m / 1640ft
- 250m / 820ft
- 100m / 328ft
- sea level

Scale 1:8,500,000

Km 0 25 50 100 150 200 250 300
Miles 0 25 50 100 150 200 250 300

projection: Lambert Conformal Conic

◀ *The former Portuguese* territory of Macao, with its colonial architecture, bars and casinos, reverted to Chinese rule in 1999.

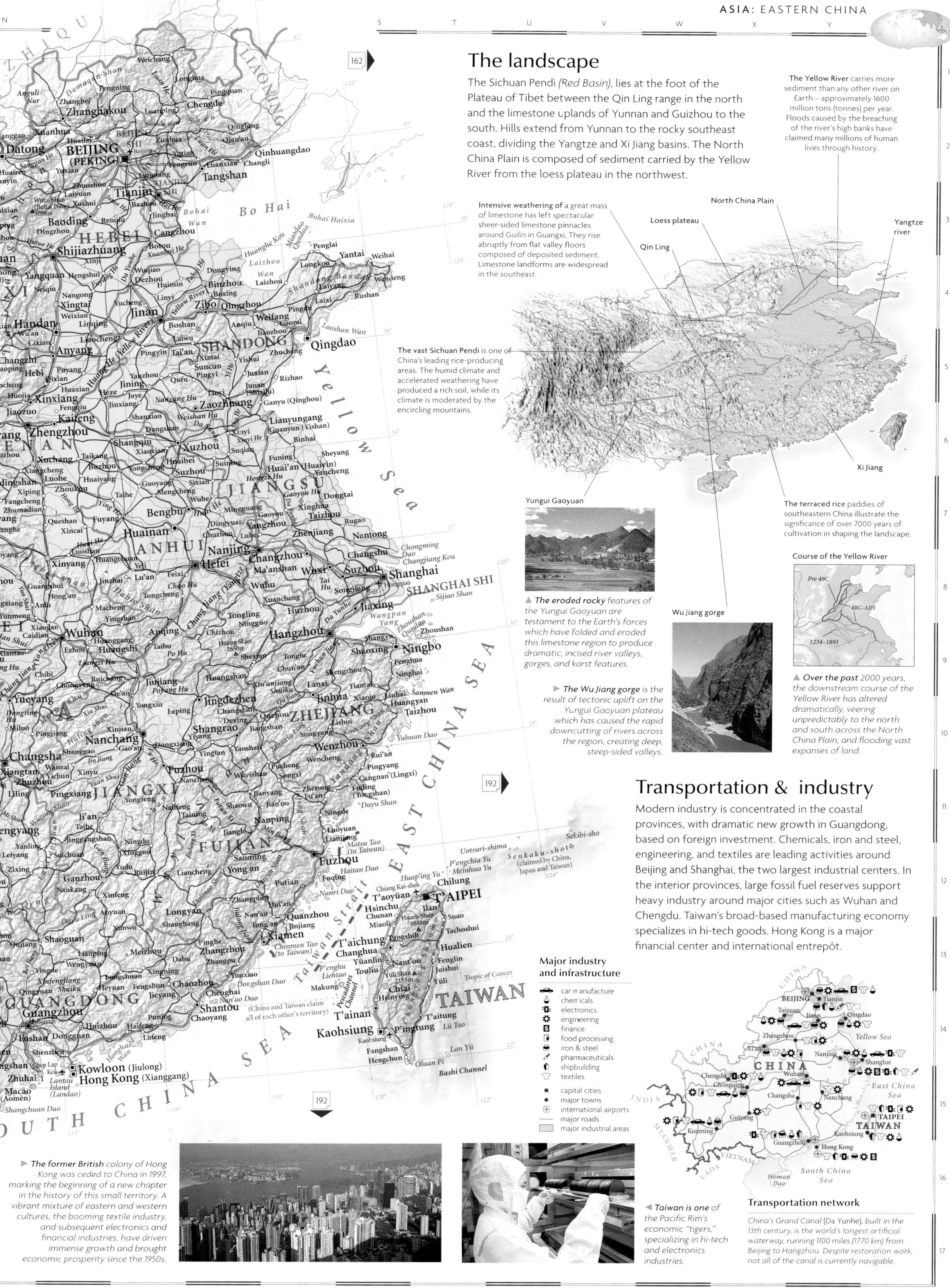

The landscape

The Sichuan Pendi *(Red Basin)*, lies at the foot of the Plateau of Tibet between the Qin Ling range in the north and the limestone uplands of Yunnan and Guizhou to the south. Hills extend from Yunnan to the rocky southeast coast, dividing the Yangtze and Xi Jiang basins. The North China Plain is composed of sediment carried by the Yellow River from the loess plateau in the northwest.

The Yellow River carries more sediment than any other river on Earth – approximately 1600 million tons (tonnes) per year. Floods caused by the breaching of the river's high banks have claimed many millions of human lives through history.

Intensive weathering of a great mass of limestone has left spectacular sheer-sided limestone pinnacles around Guilin in Guangxi. They rise abruptly from flat valley floors composed of deposited sediment. Limestone landforms are widespread in the southeast.

North China Plain
Loess plateau
Qin Ling
Yangtze river
Xi Jiang
Yungui Gaoyuan
Wu Jiang gorge

The vast Sichuan Pendi is one of China's leading rice-producing areas. The humid climate and accelerated weathering have produced a rich soil, while its climate is moderated by the encircling mountains.

The terraced rice paddies of southeastern China illustrate the significance of over 7000 years of cultivation in shaping the landscape.

▲ *The eroded rocky features of the Yungui Gaoyuan are testament to the Earth's forces which have folded and eroded this limestone region to produce dramatic, incised river valleys, gorges, and karst features.*

► *The Wu Jiang gorge is the result of tectonic uplift on the Yungui Gaoyuan plateau which has caused the rapid downcutting of rivers across the region, creating deep, steep-sided valleys.*

Course of the Yellow River

Pre 4BC
4BC–AD11
1234–1891

▲ *Over the past 2000 years, the downstream course of the Yellow River has altered dramatically, veering unpredictably to the north and south across the North China Plain, and flooding vast expanses of land.*

Transportation & industry

Modern industry is concentrated in the coastal provinces, with dramatic new growth in Guangdong, based on foreign investment. Chemicals, iron and steel, engineering, and textiles are leading activities around Beijing and Shanghai, the two largest industrial centers. In the interior provinces, large fossil fuel reserves support heavy industry around major cities such as Wuhan and Chengdu. Taiwan's broad-based manufacturing economy specializes in hi-tech goods. Hong Kong is a major financial center and international entrepôt.

Major industry and infrastructure

car manufacture
chemicals
electronics
engineering
finance
food processing
iron & steel
pharmaceuticals
shipbuilding
textiles
capital cities
major towns
international airports
major roads
major industrial areas

► *The former British colony of Hong Kong was ceded to China in 1997, marking the beginning of a new chapter in the history of this small territory. A vibrant mixture of eastern and western cultures, the booming textile industry, and subsequent electronics and financial industries, have driven immense growth and brought economic prosperity since the 1950s.*

◄ *Taiwan is one of the Pacific Rim's economic "tigers," specializing in hi-tech and electronics industries.*

Transportation network

China's Grand Canal (Da Yunhe), built in the 13th century, is the world's longest artificial waterway, running 1100 miles (1770 km) from Beijing to Hangzhou. Despite restoration work, not all of the canal is currently navigable.

Northeastern China, Mongolia & Korea

MONGOLIA, NORTH KOREA, SOUTH KOREA, Heilongjiang, Inner Mongolia, Jilin, Liaoning

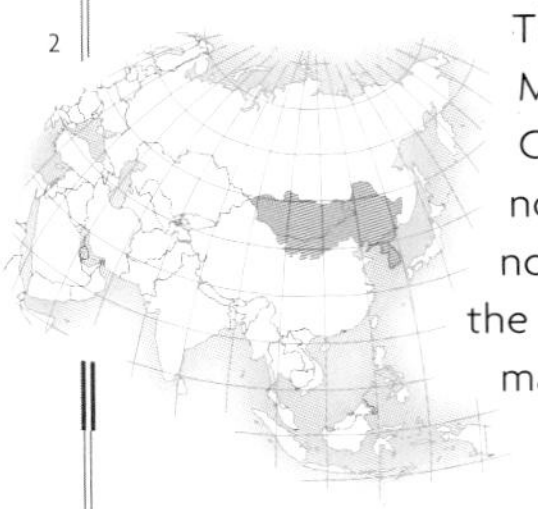

This northerly region has been a domain of shifting borders and competing colonial powers for centuries. Mongolia was the heartland of Chinghiz Khan's vast Mongol empire in the 13th century, while northeastern China was home to the Manchus, China's last ruling dynasty (1644–1911). The mineral and forest wealth of the northeast helped make this China's principal region of heavy industry, although the outdated state factories now face decline. South Korea's state-led market economy has grown dramatically and Seoul is now one of the world's largest cities. The austere communist regime of North Korea has isolated itself from the expanding markets of the Pacific Rim and faces continuing economic stagnation.

▲ *The Eurasian steppe stretches from the mouth of the Danube in Europe, to Mongolia. In Mongolia, nomadic people have lived in felt huts called yurts or gers, for thousands of years.*

Map key

Population

- above 5 million
- 1 million to 5 million
- 500,000 to 1 million
- 100,000 to 500,000
- 50,000 to 100,000
- 10,000 to 50,000
- below 10,000

Elevation

- 4000m / 13,124ft
- 3000m / 9843ft
- 2000m / 6562ft
- 1000m / 3281ft
- 500m / 1640ft
- 250m / 820ft
- 100m / 328ft
- sea level

Scale 1:7,750,000

Km 0 25 50 100 150 200

Miles 0 25 50 100 150 200

projection: Lambert Conformal Conic

RUSSIAN FEDERATION

MONGOLIA

XINJIANG UYGUR ZIZHIQU

GANSU

NINGXIA

NEI MONGOL

ULAANBAATAR (ULAN BATOR)

The landscape

The great North China Plain is largely enclosed by mountain ranges including the Great and Lesser Khingan Ranges *(Da Hinggan Ling* and *Xiao Hinggan Ling)* in the north, and the Changbai Shan, which extend south into the rugged peninsula of Korea. The broad steppeland plateau of Nei Mongol Gaoyuan borders the southeastern edge of the great cold desert of the Gobi which extends west across the southern reaches of Mongolia. In northwest Mongolia the Altai Mountains and various lesser ranges are interspersed with lakeland basins.

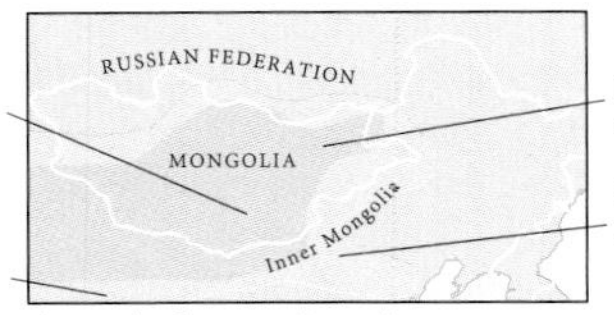

RUSSIAN FEDERATION
MONGOLIA
Inner Mongolia
Gobi
Semiarid zone
Desert zone
Ordos Desert (Mu Us Shadi)

▲ *Much of Mongolia and Inner Mongolia is a vast desert area. To the south and east, a semiarid region extends into China proper.*

▲ *The Gobi desert stretches from Central Asia, through Mongolia and into China. Bare rock surfaces, rather than sand dunes, typify the cold desert landscape of the Gobi.*

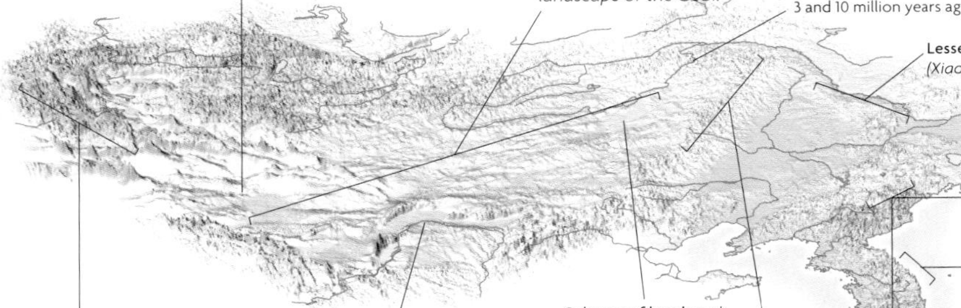

Tributaries of the Amur river follow U-shaped valleys through the Great Khingan Range *(Da Hinggan Ling)*. These were cut by ice-age glaciers between 3 and 10 million years ago.

Lesser Khingan Range *(Xiao Hinggan Ling)*

Changbai Shan

T'aebaek-sanmaek

The Altai Mountains are the highest and longest of the mountain ranges that extend into Mongolia from the northwest. These mountains provide one of the last refuges for the endangered snow leopard.

The Yellow River sweeps north around the Ordos Desert *(Mu Us Shadi)*, bringing water to an otherwise barren region.

Columns of basalt rock protrude in occasional clusters from the flat surface of the eastern Gobi. Their regular, six-sided form was produced when the rock cooled and contracted from its molten state.

Great Khingan Range *(Da Hinggan Ling)*

A crater lake occupies the 9023 ft (2750 m) snowy summit of the extinct volcano Paektu-san, the highest peak in the mountains of the Changbai Shan.

◄ *The wooded mountain range of T'aebaek-sanmaek forms the backbone of the Korean peninsula, running north–south along the eastern coastline.*

Transportation & industry

North Korea's centrally-planned economy is strongly oriented toward heavy industry, while South Korea has a broad manufacturing base which includes textiles, steel, electronics, and one of the world's largest shipbuilding industries. Mongolia and Inner Mongolia's great mineral resource potential is largely undeveloped. The heavy industrial region around Shenyang produces iron, steel, chemicals, and cement on a massive scale.

▲ *Ulan Bator, the Mongolian capital bears many of the hallmarks of Soviet-style central planning, the result of economic and industrial assistance from the Soviet Union following Mongolian independence in 1921.*

Transportation network

Liaoning has China's most comprehensive railroad network, the legacy of the Japanese occupation of Manchuria in the 20th century. The railroads are used primarily for freight transportation.

Major industry and infrastructure

car manufacture
chemicals
coal
electronics
engineering
finance
food processing
iron & steel
pharmaceuticals
shipbuilding
textiles
capital cities
major towns
international airports
major roads
major industrial areas

▶ *While North Korea has remained politically and economically isolated from the rest of the world, South Korea has enjoyed immense economic growth. It has benefited considerably from US economic aid in the aftermath of the Korean war of 1950–1953.*

Using the land & sea

Mongolia and Inner Mongolia rely heavily on livestock farming, with only about 1% of the land area cultivated. Northeastern China produces wheat, corn, soybeans, and sugar beet. The cool climate limits the range of crops and large upland areas of the northeast remain forested. Rice is the staple food of North and South Korea. The latter has become a leading ocean-fishing nation.

Land use and agricultural distribution

goats
pigs
sheep
corn
fishing
rice
soybeans
sugar beet
wheat
capital cities
major towns
pasture
cropland
forest
mountain region
desert

Japan

In the years since the end of the Second World War, Japan has become the world's most dynamic industrial nation. The country comprises a string of over 4000 islands which lie in a great northeast to southwest arc in the northwest Pacific. Four major islands: Hokkaido, Honshu, Shikoku, and Kyushu are home to the great majority of Japan's population of 128 million people, although the mountainous terrain of the central region means that most cities are situated on the coast. A densely populated industrial belt stretches along much of Honshu's southern coast, including Japan's crowded capital, Tokyo. Alongside its spectacular economic growth and the increasing westernization of its cities, Japan still maintains a highly individual culture, reflected in its traditional food, formal behavioral codes, unique Shinto religion, and a deep reverence for the emperor.

Using the land and sea

Although only about 11% of Japan is suitable for cultivation, substantial government support, a favorable climate and intensive farming methods enable the country to be virtually self-sufficient in rice producti Northern Hokkaido, the largest and most productive farming region, has an open terrain and climate similar to that of the American Midwest, and produces over half of Japan's cereal requirements. Farmers are being encouraged to diversify by growing fruit, vegetables, and wheat, as well as raising livestock.

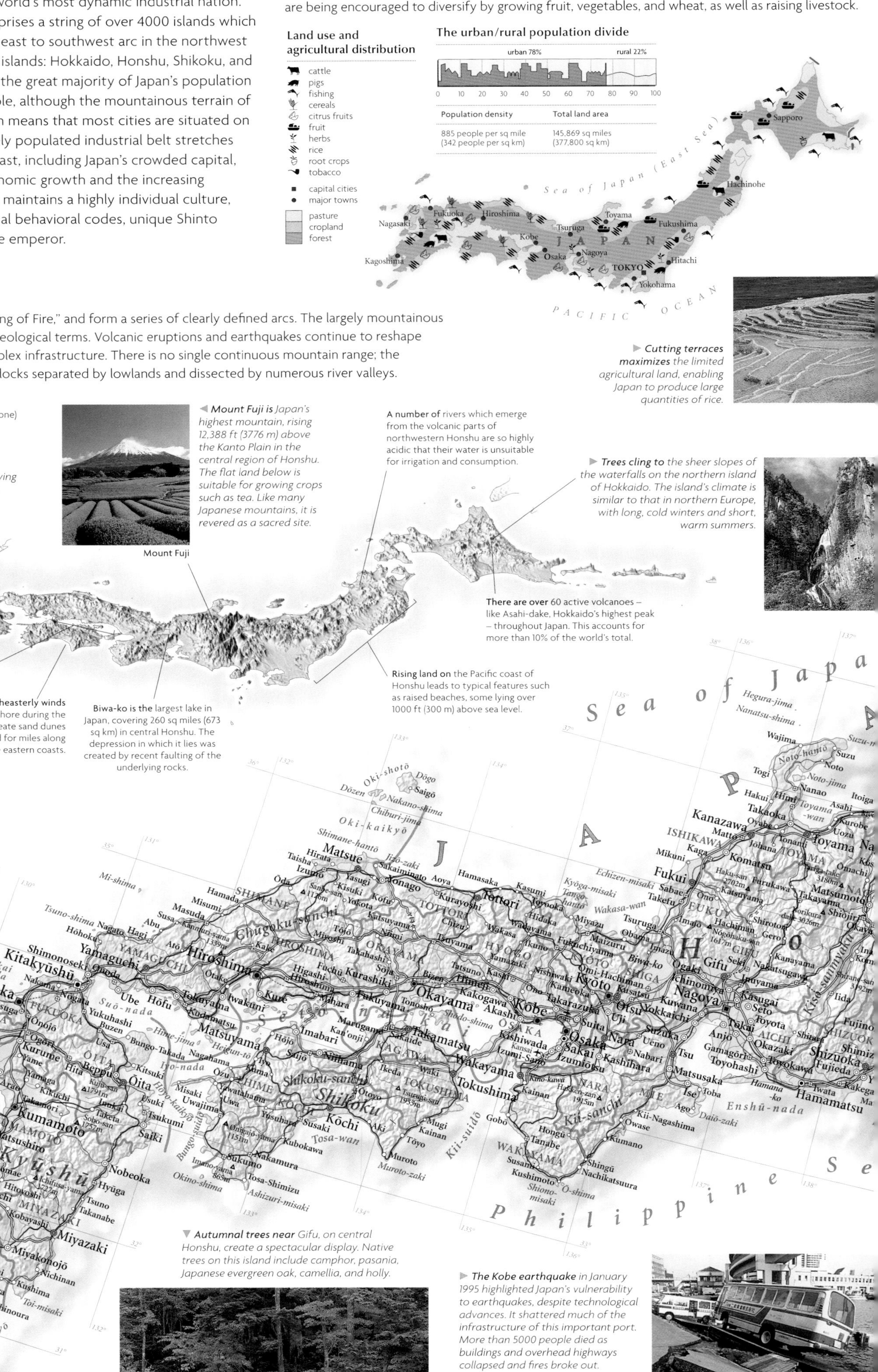

Land use and agricultural distribution
cattle
pigs
fishing
cereals
citrus fruits
fruit
herbs
rice
root crops
tobacco
capital cities
major towns
pasture
cropland
forest
The urban/rural population divide
urban 78%
rural 22%
0 10 20 30 40 50 60 70 80 90 100
Population density
885 people per sq mile (342 people per sq km)
Total land area
145,869 sq miles (377,800 sq km)
Sea of Japan (East Sea)
PACIFIC OCEAN
JAPAN
Sapporo
Hachinohe
Fukuoka
Hiroshima
Nagasaki
Kagoshima
Kobe
Osaka
Nagoya
Tsuruga
Toyama
Fukushima
Hitachi
TOKYO
Yokohama
Sea of Japan (East Sea)
Japan Trench (subduction zone)
Active volcanic island
Mount Fuji
Sea of Japan
East China Sea
Philippine Sea
Korea Strait

▶ **Cutting terraces** *maximizes the limited agricultural land, enabling Japan to produce large quantities of rice.*

The landscape

The islands of Japan lie on the Pacific "Ring of Fire," and form a series of clearly defined arcs. The largely mountainous landscape was formed very recently in geological terms. Volcanic eruptions and earthquakes continue to reshape the terrain and shake the country's complex infrastructure. There is no single continuous mountain range; the mountains divide into many small land blocks separated by lowlands and dissected by numerous river valleys.

▲ ***Japan is part*** *of an arc of volcanic islands, formed by the Pacific Plate diving under the Eurasian Plate. This process generates intense stress which is periodically released as earthquakes.*

◀ ***Mount Fuji is*** *Japan's highest mountain, rising 12,388 ft (3776 m) above the Kanto Plain in the central region of Honshu. The flat land below is suitable for growing crops such as tea. Like many Japanese mountains, it is revered as a sacred site.*

A number of rivers which emerge from the volcanic parts of northwestern Honshu are so highly acidic that their water is unsuitable for irrigation and consumption.

▶ ***Trees cling to*** *the sheer slopes of the waterfalls on the northern island of Hokkaido. The island's climate is similar to that in northern Europe, with long, cold winters and short, warm summers.*

In much of Kyushu the coast is subsiding, giving a highly indented coastline. In some places, former hilltops are barely visible above the current sea level.

There are over 60 active volcanoes – like Asahi-dake, Hokkaido's highest peak – throughout Japan. This accounts for more than 10% of the world's total.

Rising land on the Pacific coast of Honshu leads to typical features such as raised beaches, some lying over 1000 ft (300 m) above sea level.

The Inland Sea *(Seto-naikai)* has resulted from the depression of faulted blocks which has allowed sea water to invade the region between northern Shikoku and western Honshu.

Strong southeasterly winds blowing onshore during the winter create sand dunes which extend for miles along the eastern coasts.

Biwa-ko is the largest lake in Japan, covering 260 sq miles (673 sq km) in central Honshu. The depression in which it lies was created by recent faulting of the underlying rocks.

157

▼ ***Autumnal trees near*** *Gifu, on central Honshu, create a spectacular display. Native trees on this island include camphor, pasania, Japanese evergreen oak, camellia, and holly.*

▶ ***The Kobe earthquake*** *in January 1995 highlighted Japan's vulnerability to earthquakes, despite technological advances. It shattered much of the infrastructure of this important port. More than 5000 people died as buildings and overhead highways collapsed and fires broke out.*

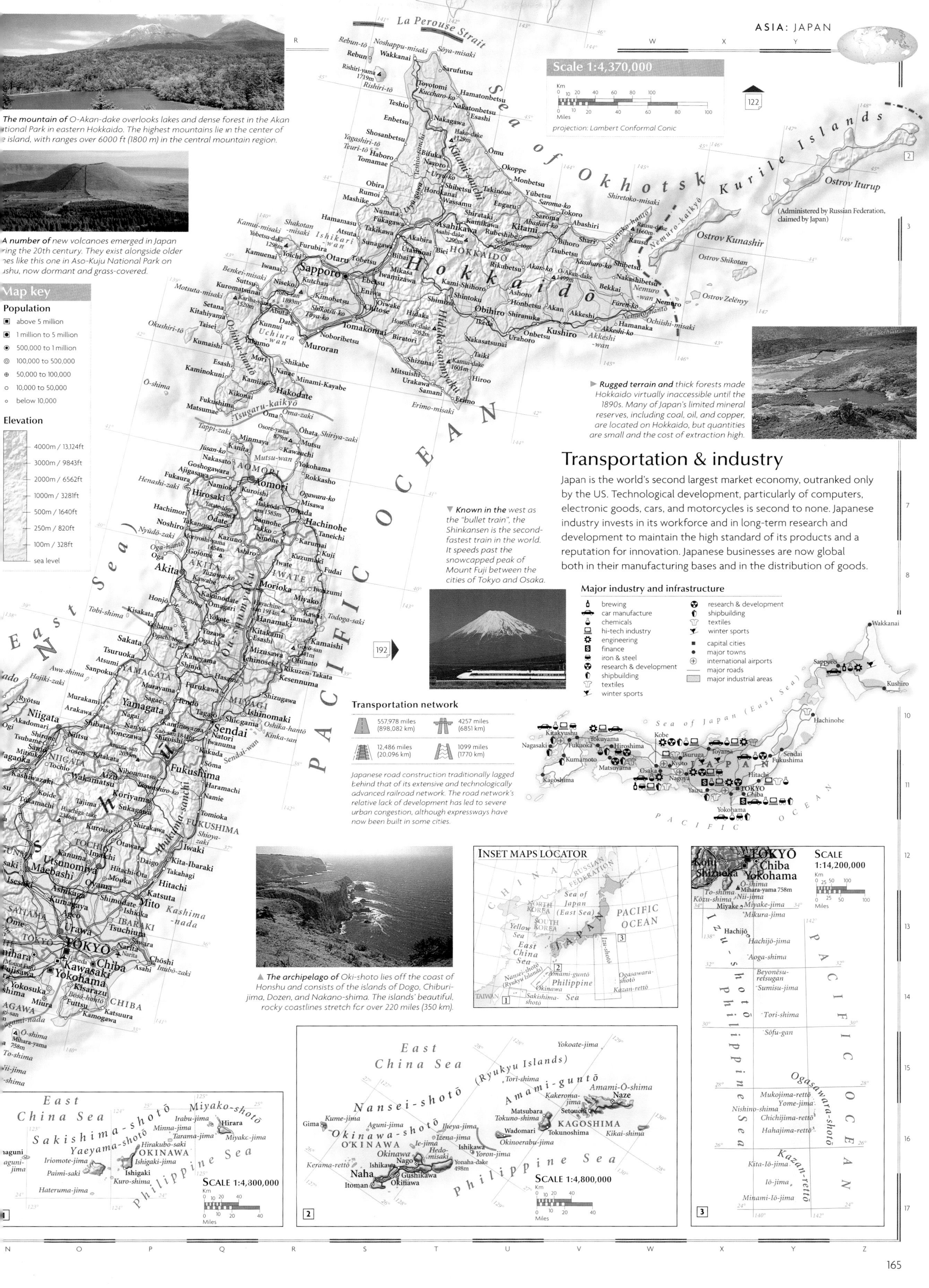
Scale 1:4,370,000
projection: Lambert Conformal Conic
Map key
Population
above 5 million
1 million to 5 million
500,000 to 1 million
100,000 to 500,000
50,000 to 100,000
10,000 to 50,000
below 10,000
Elevation
4000m / 13,124ft
3000m / 9843ft
2000m / 6562ft
1000m / 3281ft
500m / 1640ft
250m / 820ft
100m / 328ft
sea level
Sea of Okhotsk
Kurile Islands
(Administered by Russian Federation, claimed by Japan)
Hokkaidō
PACIFIC OCEAN
East Sea (Sea of Japan)
Major industry and infrastructure
brewing
car manufacture
chemicals
hi-tech industry
engineering
finance
iron & steel
research & development
shipbuilding
textiles
winter sports
capital cities
major towns
international airports
major roads
major industrial areas
Transportation network
557,978 miles (898,082 km)
4257 miles (6851 km)
12,486 miles (20,096 km)
1099 miles (1770 km)
INSET MAPS LOCATOR
SCALE 1:14,200,000
SCALE 1:4,300,000
SCALE 1:4,800,000
East China Sea
Philippine Sea
Nansei-shotō (Ryukyu Islands)
Sakishima-shotō
Ogasawara-shotō
Izu-shotō

The mountain of O-Akan-dake overlooks lakes and dense forest in the Akan National Park in eastern Hokkaido. The highest mountains lie in the center of the island, with ranges over 6000 ft (1800 m) in the central mountain region.

A number of new volcanoes emerged in Japan during the 20th century. They exist alongside older ones like this one in Aso-Kuju National Park on Kyushu, now dormant and grass-covered.

Rugged terrain and thick forests made Hokkaido virtually inaccessible until the 1890s. Many of Japan's limited mineral reserves, including coal, oil, and copper, are located on Hokkaido, but quantities are small and the cost of extraction high.

Transportation & industry

Japan is the world's second largest market economy, outranked only by the US. Technological development, particularly of computers, electronic goods, cars, and motorcycles is second to none. Japanese industry invests in its workforce and in long-term research and development to maintain the high standard of its products and a reputation for innovation. Japanese businesses are now global both in their manufacturing bases and in the distribution of goods.

Known in the west as the "bullet train", the Shinkansen is the second-fastest train in the world. It speeds past the snowcapped peak of Mount Fuji between the cities of Tokyo and Osaka.

Japanese road construction traditionally lagged behind that of its extensive and technologically advanced railroad network. The road network's relative lack of development has led to severe urban congestion, although expressways have now been built in some cities.

The archipelago of Oki-shoto lies off the coast of Honshu and consists of the islands of Dogo, Chiburi-jima, Dozen, and Nakano-shima. The islands' beautiful, rocky coastlines stretch for over 220 miles (350 km).

Mainland Southeast Asia

CAMBODIA, LAOS, MYANMAR, THAILAND, VIETNAM

Thickly forested mountains, intercut by the broad valleys of five great rivers characterize the landscape of Southeast Asia's mainland countries. Agriculture remains the main activity for much of the population, which is concentrated in the river flood plains and deltas. Linked ethnic and cultural roots give the region a distinct identity. Most people on the mainland are Theravada Buddhists, and the Philippines is the only predominantly Christian country in Southeast Asia. Foreign intervention began in the 16th century with the opening of the spice trade; Cambodia, Laos and Vietnam were French colonies until the end of the Second World War, Myanmar was under British control. Only Thailand was never colonized. Today, Thailand is poised to play a leading role in the economic development of the Pacific Rim, and Laos and Vietnam have begun to mend the devastation of the Vietnam War, and to develop their economies. With continuing political instability and a shattered infrastructure, Cambodia faces an uncertain future, while Burma is seeking investment and the ending of its long isolation from the world community.

Myanmar: Capital cities

YANGON – capital
PYINMANA – administrative capital

▲ *The Irrawaddy river is Myanmar's vital central artery, watering the ricefields and providing a rich source of fish, as well as an important transport link, particularly for local traffic.*

The landscape

A series of mountain ranges runs north–south through the mainland, formed as the result of the collision between the Eurasian Plate and the Indian subcontinent, which created the Himalayas. They are interspersed by the valleys of a number of great rivers. On their passage to the sea these rivers have deposited sediment, forming huge, fertile flood plains and deltas.

The coastline of the Isthmus of Kra

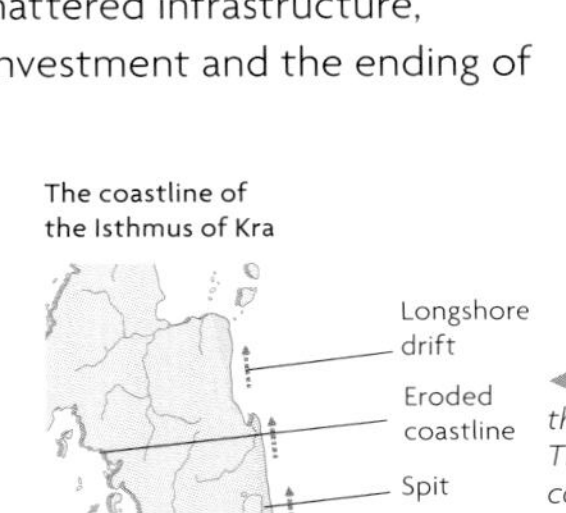
Longshore drift
Eroded coastline
Spit
Lagoon
Wave attack

◄ *The east and west coasts of the Isthmus of Kra differ greatly. The tectonically uplifting west coast is exposed to the harsh south-westerly monsoon and is heavily eroded. On the east coast, longshore currents produce depositional features such as spits and lagoons.*

Mountains dominate the Laotian landscape with more than 90% of the land lying more than 600 ft (180 m) above sea level. The mountains of the Chaîne Annamitique form the country's eastern border.

Hkakabo Razi is the highest point in mainland Southeast Asia. It rises 19,300 ft (5885 m) at the border between China and Myanmar.

The Red River delta in northern Vietnam is fringed to the north by steep-sided, round-topped limestone hills, typical of karst scenery.

The Irrawaddy river runs virtually north–south, draining the plains of northern Myanmar. The Irrawaddy delta is the country's main rice-growing area.

Salween River

Isthmus of Kra

Malay Peninsula

▲ *The coast of the Isthmus of Kra, in southeast Thailand has many small, precipitous islands like these, formed by chemical erosion on limestone, which is weathered along vertical cracks. The humidity of the climate in Southeast Asia increases the rate of weathering.*

◄ *The fast-flowing waters of the Mekong river cascade over this waterfall in Champasak province in Laos. The force of the water erodes rocks at the base of the fall.*

Tonle Sap, a freshwater lake, drains into the Mekong delta via the Mekong river. It is the largest lake in Southeast Asia.

The Mekong river flows through southern China and Myanmar, then for much of its length forms the border between Laos and Thailand, flowing through Cambodia before terminating in a vast delta on the southern Vietnamese coast.

Using the land and sea

The fertile flood plains of rivers such as the Mekong and Salween, and the humid climate, enable the production of rice throughout the region. Cambodia, Laos, and Myanmar still have substantial forests, producing hardwoods such as teak and rosewood. Cash crops include tropical fruits such as coconuts, bananas and pineapples, rubber, oil palm, sugar cane and the jute substitute, kenaf. Pigs and cattle are the main livestock raised. Large quantities of marine and freshwater fish are caught throughout the region.

▲ *Commercial logging – still widespread in Myanmar – has now been stopped in Thailand because of over-exploitation of the tropical rainforest.*

The urban/rural population divide

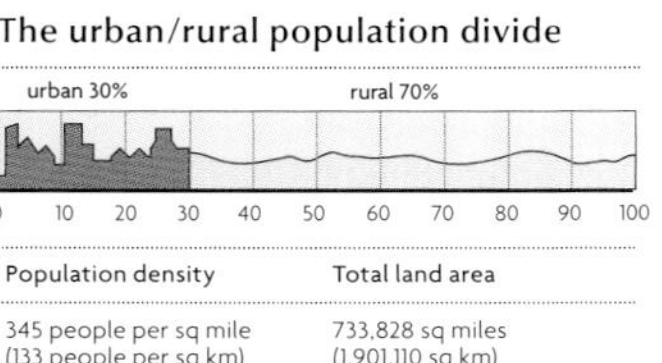
urban 30%
rural 70%
0 10 20 30 40 50 60 70 80 90 100

Population density	Total land area
345 people per sq mile (133 people per sq km)	733,828 sq miles (1,901,110 sq km)

Land use and agricultural distribution

- cattle
- pigs
- bananas
- coconuts
- fishing
- oil palms
- rice
- rubber
- sugar cane
- timber
- capital cities
- major towns
- pasture
- cropland
- forest
- wetland

152 172 168

Transportation & industry

Industrial manufacturing has become increasingly important in Thailand and Vietnam in recent years. The assembling of component-based electrical and electronic goods is becoming more common throughout this region, with foreign companies benefiting from low labour costs and the upgrading of technology. The economies of Myanmar and Cambodia are still based on agricultural produce and the processing of raw materials. Tin is the region's most important metal, and nickel, copper and chromite are also mined, although the quantities produced are not significant on a global scale. Thailand's successful tourist industry is the country's highest earner of foreign exchange.

Transportation network

82,958 miles (133,524 km)	267 miles (430 km)
7500 miles (12,071 km)	28,585 miles (46,008 km)

Transportation development has concentrated on the building of road networks. Water and sea transport remain important, although air links have improved, particularly in Thailand and the Philippines.

Major industry and infrastructure

- chemicals
- electronics
- engineering
- finance
- food processing
- iron & steel
- oil & gas
- mining
- shipbuilding
- textiles
- timber processing
- capital cities
- major towns
- international airports
- major roads
- major industrial areas

► ***Opium poppies are** destroyed under army supervision in Thailand. This action is part of a government-sponsored initiative to reduce the trade in drugs such as heroin, which is derived from these plants. Drug trafficking is a major problem throughout the region; the area is known as the "Golden Triangle", and Laos is the third-largest producer of opium poppies in the world.*

The Paracel Islands are a strategically sensitive island group, disputed by several surrounding countries. The Paracels are claimed by China, Taiwan and Vietnam, though only China has actually occupied them.

▼ ***The city of** Hue in central Vietnam was the country's capital under the 13 emperors of the Nguyen dynasty from 1802 to 1945. It is the site of a number of religious monuments, including the Thien-Mu Pagoda.*

Map key

Population

- above 5 million
- 1 million to 5 million
- 500,000 to 1 million
- 100,000 to 500,000
- 50,000 to 100,000
- 10,000 to 50,000
- below 10,000

Elevation

- 4000m / 13,124ft
- 3000m / 9843ft
- 2000m / 6562ft
- 1000m / 3281ft
- 500m / 1640ft
- 250m / 820ft
- 100m / 328ft
- sea level

Scale 1:8,611,000

Km 0 25 50 100 150 200
Miles 0 25 50 100 150 200

projection: Lambert Conformal Conic

160
160
170
168

Western Maritime Southeast Asia

BRUNEI, INDONESIA, MALAYSIA, SINGAPORE

The world's largest archipelago, Indonesia's myriad islands stretch 3100 miles (5000 km) eastwards across the Pacific, from the Malay Peninsula to western New Guinea. Only about 1500 of the 13,677 islands are inhabited and the huge, predominently Muslim population is unevenly distributed, with some two-thirds crowded onto the western islands of Java, Madura, and Bali. The national government is trying to resettle large numbers of people from these islands to other parts of the country to reduce population pressure there. Malaysia, split between the mainland and the east Malaysian states of Sabah and Sarawak on Borneo, has a diverse population, as well as a fast-growing economy, although the pace of its development is still far outstripped by that of Singapore. This small island nation is the financial and commercial capital of Southeast Asia. The Sultanate of Brunei in northern Borneo, one of the world's last princely states, has an extremely high standard of living, based on its oil revenues.

The landscape

Indonesia's western islands are characterized by rugged volcanic mountains cloaked with dense tropical forest, which slope down to coastal plains covered by thick alluvial swamps. The Sunda Shelf, an extension of the Eurasian Plate, lies between Java, Bali, Sumatra, and Borneo. These islands' mountains rise from a base below the sea, and they were once joined together by dry land, which has since been submerged by rising sea levels.

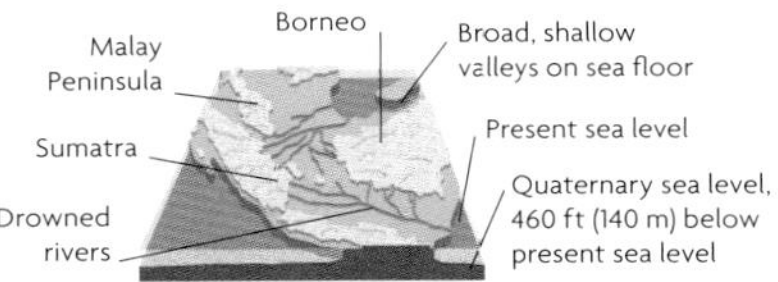

Borneo
Malay Peninsula
Sumatra
Drowned rivers
Broad, shallow valleys on sea floor
Present sea level
Quaternary sea level, 460 ft (140 m) below present sea level

▲ *The Sunda Shelf underlies this whole region. It is one of the largest submarine shelves in the world, covering an area of 714,285 sq miles (1,850,000 sq km). During the early Quaternary period, when sea levels were lower, the shelf was exposed.*

◄ *Danau (lake) Toba in Sumatra fills an enormous caldera 18 miles (30 km) wide and 62 miles (100 km) long – the largest in the world. It was formed through a combination of volcanic action and tectonic activity.*

Malay Peninsula has a rugged east coast, but the west coast, fronting the Strait of Malacca, has many sheltered beaches and bays. The two coasts are divided by the Banjaran Titiwangsa, which run the length of the peninsula.

Gunung Kinabalu is the highest peak in Malaysia, rising 13,455 ft (4101 m).

◄ *The river of Sungai Mahakam cuts through the central highlands of Borneo, the third largest island in the world, with a total area of 290,000 sq miles (757,050 sq km). Although mountainous, Borneo is one of the most stable of the Indonesian islands, with little volcanic activity.*

The island of Krakatau *(Pulau Rakata)*, lying between Sumatra and Java, was all but destroyed in 1883, when the volcano erupted. The release of gas and dust into the atmosphere disrupted cloud cover and global weather patterns for several years.

Gunung Semeru

Indonesia has more than 220 volcanoes, most of which are still active. They are strung out along the island arc from Sumatra through the Lesser Sunda Islands, into the Moluccas and Celebes.

Transportation & industry

Singapore has a thriving economy based on international trade and finance. Annual trade through the port is among the highest of any in the world. Indonesia's western islands still depend on natural resources, particularly petroleum, gas, and wood, although the economy is rapidly diversifying with manufactured exports including garments, consumer electronics, and footwear. A high-profile aircraft industry has developed in Bandung on Java. Malaysia has a fast-growing and varied manufacturing sector, although oil, gas, and timber remain important resource-based industries.

► *Ranks of gleaming skyscrapers, new motorways and infrastructure construction reflect the investment which is pouring into Southeast Asian cities like the Malaysian capital, Kuala Lumpur. Traditional housing and markets still exist amidst the new developments. Many of the city's inhabitants subsist at a level far removed from the prosperity implied by its outward modernity.*

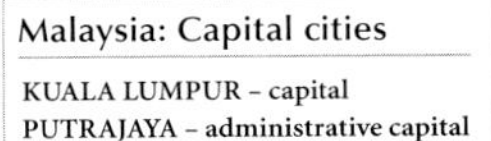

Malaysia: Capital cities
KUALA LUMPUR – capital
PUTRAJAYA – administrative capital

THAILAND
Kota Bharu
Kuala Terengganu
Alor Setar
George Town
Ipoh
Kuantan
KUALA LUMPUR
PUTRAJAYA
Seremban
Melaka
Johor Bahru
SINGAPORE
Tanjungpinang
Pekanbaru
Strait of Malacca
Bandaaceh
Medan
Pematangsiantar
Tebingtinggi
Padang
Jambi
Palembang
Bengkulu
BENGKULU
SUMATERA UTARA
SUMATERA BARAT
Gunungsitoli
Pulau Nias
Pulau Siberut
Kepulauan Mentawai
Selat Mentawai
Pulau Enggano
INDIAN OCEAN
Equator

166
172
172

Using the land and sea

Rice is the most important arable crop in Indonesia and Malaysia, and both countries manage to meet almost all of their domestic demand. Malaysian rubber accounts for 25% of world production and is the main cash crop, grown on plantations and small farms, along with oil palms and copra. Timber is exported from both Malaysia and Indonesia. Modern agricultural techniques enable Singapore to produce fruits and vegetables despite a shortage of suitable land.

▶ Spiral cuts in the bark of this rubber palm show where it has been tapped. Sophisticated 'cloning' techniques mean that trees which produce consistently high quantities of rubber can be easily reproduced.

Transportation network

165,272 miles (266,010 km)

958 miles (1,542 km)

5,061 miles (8,146 km)

18,070 miles (29,084 km)

Singapore's metro system, completed in 1991, is among the most efficient in the world. Malaysia has several fast, modern highways and most roads are paved. Indonesia's many islands make improvement of the shipping infrastructure a priority.

Major industry and infrastructure

- aerospace
- copra processing
- chemicals
- electronics
- engineering
- finance
- food processing
- iron & steel
- oil
- ship building
- timber processing
- textiles
- capital cities
- major towns
- international airports
- major roads
- major industrial areas

Land use and agricultural distribution

- coconuts
- fishing
- oil palms
- rice
- rubber
- shellfish
- sugar cane
- timber
- capital cities
- major towns
- pasture
- cropland
- forest
- wetland

The urban/rural population divide

urban 44% | rural 56%

0 10 20 30 40 50 60 70 80 90 100

Population density	Total land area
297 people per sq mile (115 people per sq km)	828,356 sq miles (2,146,000 sq km)

▼ This tiny island near Kota Kinabalu, in Sabah, eastern Malaysia, is a part of a designated national park. Thickly forested, it is surrounded by broad, sandy beaches and shallow inland seas.

▲ The volcano of Gunung Semeru in eastern Java lies on the Pacific "Ring of Fire". It is part of the ancient Tennegger volcano and remains highly active.

Scale 1:8,750,000

Km 0 25 50 100 150 200

Miles 0 25 50 100 150 200

projection: Mercator

Map key

Population

- above 5 million
- 1 million to 5 million
- 500,000 to 1 million
- 100,000 to 500,000
- 50,000 to 100,000
- 10,000 to 50,000
- below 10,000

Elevation

- 4000m / 13,124ft
- 3000m / 9843ft
- 2000m / 6562ft
- 1000m / 3281ft
- 500m / 1640ft
- 250m / 820ft
- 100m / 328ft
- sea level

166
170

Eastern Maritime Southeast Asia

EAST TIMOR, INDONESIA, PHILIPPINES

The Philippines takes its name from Philip II of Spain who was king when the islands were colonized during the 16th century. Almost 400 years of Spanish, and later US, rule have left their mark on the country's culture; English is widely spoken and over 90% of the population is Christian. The Philippines' economy is agriculturally based – inadequate infrastructure and electrical power shortages have so far hampered faster industrial growth. Indonesia's eastern islands are less economically developed than the rest of the country. Papua (Irian Jaya), which constitutes the western portion of New Guinea, is one of the world's last great wildernesses. East Timor is the newest independent state in the world, gaining full autonomy in 2002.

▲ *The traditional boat-shaped houses of the Toraja people in Sulawesi. Although now Christian, the Toraja still practice the animist traditions and rituals of their ancestors. They are famous for their elaborate funeral ceremonies and burial sites in cliffside caves.*

The landscape

Located on the Pacific "Ring of Fire" the Philippines' 7100 islands are subject to frequent earthquakes and volcanic activity. Their terrain is largely mountainous, with narrow coastal plains and interior valleys and plains. Luzon and Mindanao are by far the largest islands and comprise roughly 66% of the country's area. Indonesia's eastern islands are mountainous and dotted with volcanoes, both active and dormant.

▶ *Lake Taal on the Philippines island of Luzon lies within the crater of an immense volcano that erupted twice in the 20th century, first in 1911 and again in 1965, causing the deaths of more than 3200 people.*

The Spratly Islands are a strategically sensitive island group, disputed by several surrounding countries. The Spratlys are claimed by China, Taiwan, Vietnam, Malaysia and the Philippines and are particularly important as they lie on oil and gas deposits.

Mindanao has five mountain ranges many of which have large numbers of active volcanoes. Lying just west of the Philippines Trench, which forms the boundary between the colliding Philippine and Eurasian plates, the entire island chain is subject to earthquakes and volcanic activity.

The 1000 islands of the Moluccas are the fabled Spice Islands of history, whose produce attracted traders from around the globe. Most of the northern and central Moluccas have dense vegetation and rugged mountainous interiors where elevations often exceed 3000 feet (9144 m).

▲ *Bohol in the southern Philippines is famous for its so-called "chocolate hills". There are more than 1000 of these regular mounds on the island. The hills are limestone in origin, the smoothed remains of an earlier cycle of erosion. Their brown appearance in the dry season gives them their name.*

The four-pronged island of Celebes is the product of complex tectonic activity which ruptured and then reattached small fragments of the Earth's crust to form the island's many peninsulas.

Coral islands such as Timor in eastern Indonesia show evidence of very recent and dramatic movements of the Earth's plates. Reefs in Timor have risen by as much as 4000 ft (1300 m) in the last million years.

The Pegunungan Jayawijaya range in central Papua (Irian Jaya) contains the world's highest range of limestone mountains, some with peaks more than 16,400 ft (5000 m) high. Heavy rainfall and high temperatures, which promote rapid weathering, have led to the creation of large underground caves and river systems such as the river of Sungai Baliem.

SOUTH CHINA SEA
SPRATLY ISLANDS (disputed)
MALAYSIA
KALIMANTAN TIMUR
Equator
KALIMANTAN SELATAN
Java Sea
NUSA TENGGARA
Mataram

168

Using the land and sea

Indonesia's eastern islands are less intensively cultivated than those in the west. Coconuts, coffee and spices such as cloves and nutmeg are the major commercial crops while rice, corn and soya beans are grown for local consumption. The Philippines' rich, fertile soils support year-round production of a wide range of crops. The country is one of the world's largest producers of coconuts and a major exporter of coconut products, including one-third of the world's copra. Although much of the arable land is given over to rice and corn, the main staple food crops, tropical fruits such as bananas, pineapples and mangos, and sugar cane are also grown for export.

◀ *The terracing of land to restrict soil erosion and create flat surfaces for agriculture is a common practice throughout Southeast Asia, particularly where land is scarce. These terraces are on Luzon in the Philippines.*

Land use and agricultural distribution

coconuts; fishing; rice; rubber; shellfish; sugar cane; capital cities; major towns; pasture; cropland; forest; wetland

The urban/rural population divide

urban 45% / rural 55%

Population density	Total land area
258 people per sq mile (160 people per sq km)	654,771 sq miles (1,053,755 sq km)

▲ *More than two-thirds of Papua's (Irian Jaya) land area is heavily forested and the population of around 1.5 million live mainly in isolated tribal groups using more than 80 distinct languages.*

Transportation & industry

The Philippines' economy is primarily a mixture of agriculture and light industry. The manufacturing sector is still developing; many factories are licensees of foreign companies producing finished goods for export. Mining is also important – the country's chromite, nickel and copper deposits are among the largest in the world. Agriculture is the main activity in eastern Indonesia. Most industry has a primary basis, including logging, food-processing and mining. Nickel, the most important metal, is produced on Sulawesi, in Papua (Irian Jaya), and in the Moluccas.

Transportation network

- 16,652 miles (26,800 km)
- None
- 500 miles (805 km)
- 8704 miles (14,008 km)

Sulawesi has some good roads, but on Papua (Irian Jaya) and the Moluccas there are few road interconnections between major settled areas. Water and sea transport remain important although air links have improved in the Philippines.

Major industry and infrastructure

- copra processing
- chemicals
- finance
- food processing
- mining
- oil
- timber processing
- textiles
- capital cities
- major towns
- international airports
- major roads
- major industrial areas

Manila is the *Philippines' chief port and transport centre, and the focus of the country's commercial, industrial and cultural activities. Much of the city lies below sea level, and it suffers from floods during the rainy summer season.*

Map key

Population

- above 5 million
- 1 million to 5 million
- 500,000 to 1 million
- 100,000 to 500,000
- 50,000 to 100,000
- 10,000 to 50,000
- below 10,000

Elevation

- 4000m / 13,124ft
- 3000m / 9843ft
- 2000m / 6562ft
- 1000m / 3281ft
- 500m / 1640ft
- 250m / 820ft
- 100m / 328ft
- sea level

Scale 1:,11,800,000

Km 0 50 100 200 300 400

Miles 0 50 100 200 300 400

projection: Mercator

The Indian Ocean

Despite being the smallest of the three major oceans, the evolution of the Indian Ocean was the most complex. The ocean basin was formed during the breakup of the supercontinent Gondwanaland, when the Indian subcontinent moved northeast, Africa moved west, and Australia separated from Antarctica. Like the Pacific Ocean, the warm waters of the Indian Ocean are punctuated by coral atolls and islands. About one-fifth of the world's population – over a billion people – live on its shores. In 2004, over 290,000 died and millions more were left homeless after a tsunami devastated large stretches of the ocean's coastline.

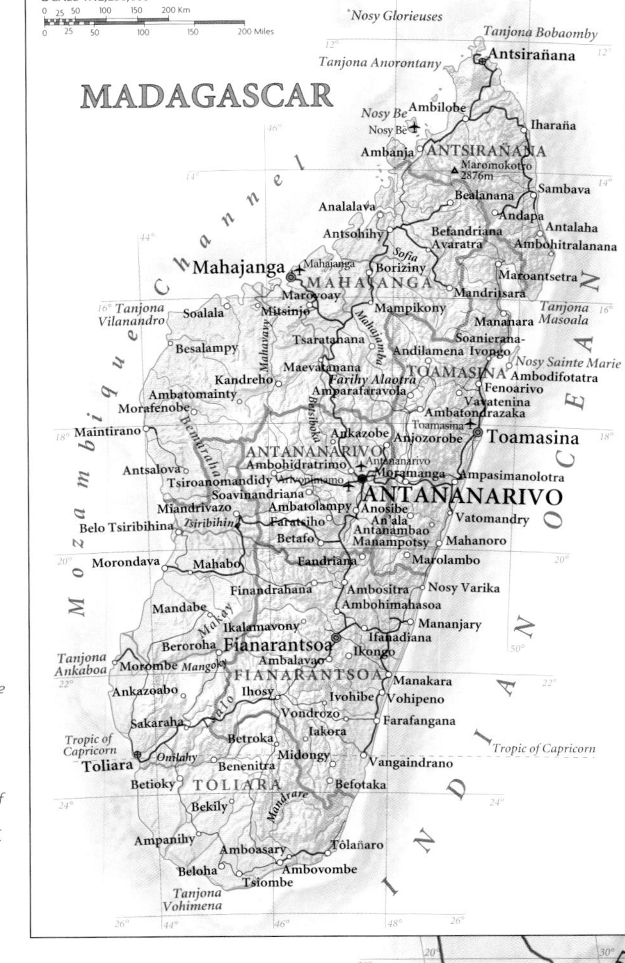

SCALE 1:12,250,000
MADAGASCAR
Nosy Glorieuses
Tanjona Bobaomby
Antsirañana
Tanjona Anorontany
Ambilobe
Nosy Be
Iharaña
Ambanja
ANTSIRAÑANA
Maromokotro 2876m
Sambava
Bealanana
Andapa
Antalaha
Analalava
Antsohihy
Befandriana
Avaratra
Ambohitralanana
Mahajanga
MAHAJANGA
Sofia
Boriziny
Marovoay
Maroantsetra
Mandritsara
Mampikony
Tanjona Masoala
Mitsinjo
Tanjona Vilanandro
Soalala
Tsaratanana
Mananara
Soanierana-Ivongo
Besalampy
Andilamena
Nosy Sainte Marie
Kandreho
Maevatanana
Fariby Alaotra
TOAMASINA
Ambodifotatra
Fenoarivo
Ampasindava
Ambatomainty
Amparafaravola
Vavatenina
Morafenobe
Ambatondrazaka
Maintirano
Ankazobe
Anjozorobe
Toamasina
ANTANANARIVO
Antsalova
Tsiroanomandidy
Moramanga
Ampasimanolotra
Soavinandriana
ANTANANARIVO
Miandrivazo
Ambatolampy
Anosibe
Belo Tsiribihina
Faratsiho
An'ala
Vatomandry
Betafo
Antanambao
Manampotsy
Mahanoro
Morondava
Mahabo
Eandriana
Marolambo
Mandabe
Fianandrahana
Ambositra
Ambohimahasoa
Nosy Varika
Ikalamavony
Mananjary
Beroroha
Fianarantsoa
Ifanadiana
Tanjona Ankaboa
Morombe
Mangoky
Ambalavao
Ikongo
FIANARANTSOA
Manakara
Ankazoabo
Ihosy
Ivohibe
Vohipeno
Sakaraha
Vondrozo
Farafangana
Iakora
Tropic of Capricorn
Toliara
Betroka
Benenitra
Midongy
Vangaindrano
Betioky
TOLIARA
Befotaka
Bekily
Ampanihy
Tôlañaro
Amboasary
Beloha
Ambovombe
Tsiombe
Tanjona Vohimena
Mozambique Channel
INDIAN OCEAN

The landscape

The Indian Ocean began forming about 150 million years ago, but in its present form it is relatively young, only about 36 million years old. Along the three subterranean mountain chains of its mid-ocean ridge the seafloor is still spreading. The Indian Ocean has fewer trenches than other oceans and only a narrow continental shelf around most of its surrounding land.

Sediments come from Ganges/Brahmaputra river system

Submarine canyons transport sediment to fan – some of these are more than 1500 miles (2500 km) long

Sri Lanka

▲ **The Ganges Fan** *is one of the world's largest submarine accumulations of sediment, extending far beyond Sri Lanka. It is fed by the Ganges/Brahmaputra river system, whose sediment is carried through a network of underwater canyons at the edge of the continental shelf.*

The mid-oceanic ridge runs from the Arabian Sea. It diverges east of Madagascar. One arm runs southwest to join the Mid-Atlantic Ridge, the other branches southeast, joining the Pacific-Antarctic Ridge, southeast of Tasmania.

The Ninetyeast Ridge takes its name from the line of longitude it follows. It is the world's longest and straightest under-sea ridge.

Two of the world's largest rivers flow into the Indian Ocean; the Indus and the Ganges/Brahmaputra. Both have deposited enormous fans of sediment.

Indus River

► *A large proportion of the coast of Thailand, on the Isthmus of Kra, is stabilized by mangrove thickets. They act as an important breeding ground for wildlife.*

The Java Trench is the world's longest, it runs 1600 miles (2570 km) from the southwest of Java, but is only 50 miles (80 km) wide.

The relief of Madagascar rises from a low-lying coastal strip in the east, to the central plateau. The plateau is also a major watershed separating Madagascar's three main river basins.

► ***The central group*** *of the Seychelles are mountainous, granite islands. They have a narrow coastal belt and lush, tropical vegetation cloaks the highlands.*

The Kerguelen Islands in the Southern Ocean were created by a hot spot in the Earth's crust. The islands were formed in succession as the Antarctic Plate moved slowly over the hot spot.

The circulation in the northern Indian Ocean is controlled by the monsoon winds. Biannually these winds reverse their pattern, causing a reversal in the surface currents and alternative high and low pressure conditions over Asia and Australia.

Resources

Many of the small islands in the Indian Ocean rely exclusively on tuna-fishing and tourism to maintain their economies. Most fisheries are artisanal, although large-scale tuna-fishing does take place in the Seychelles, Mauritius and the western Indian Ocean. Other resources include oil in the Persian Gulf, pearls in the Red Sea, and tin from deposits off the shores of Myanmar, Thailand, and Indonesia.

Suez, Kuwait, ASIA, Mumbai, Rangoon, Arabian Sea, Bay of Bengal, South China Sea, Singapore, AFRICA, Mombasa, Java Sea, INDIAN OCEAN, Timor Sea, Toamasina, AUSTRALIA, Fremantle, SOUTHERN OCEAN, ANTARCTICA

Resources (including wildlife)

- fish
- penguins
- shellfish
- whales
- oil & gas
- tin deposits
- tourism
- major towns
- major ports

► ***The recent use*** *of large dragnets for tuna-fishing has not only threatened the livelihoods of many small-scale fisheries, but also caused widespread environmental concern about the potential impact on other marine species.*

SCALE 1:5,000,000

Grande Comore, Mitsamiouli, Saondzou 1087m, Hahaya, Mbéni, MORONI, Koimbani, Le Kartala 2361m, Mitsoudjé, Foumbouni, Dembéni, INDIAN OCEAN, COMOROS, Anjouan, Ouani, Mohéli, Moutsamudou, Domoni, Miringoni, Fomboni, Sima, Nioumachoua, Ouanani, Moya, Mramani, MAYOTTE (to France), Mozambique Channel, Comoro Islands, Dzaoudzi, Pamandzi, MAMOUDZOU, Bandrélé

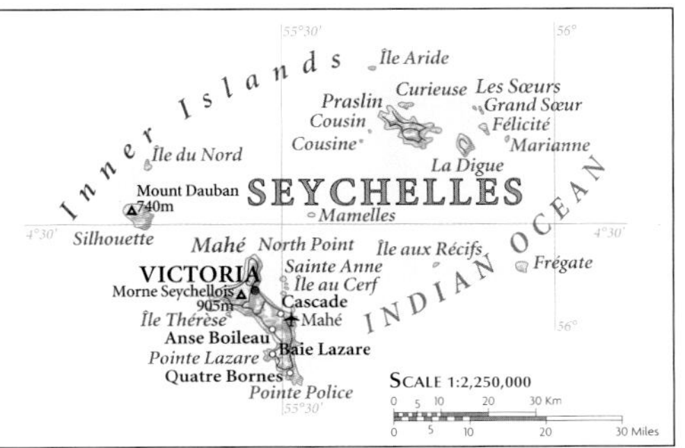

Inner Islands
Île Aride
Curieuse
Les Sœurs
Praslin
Grand Sœur
Cousin
Félicité
Cousine
Marianne
Île du Nord
La Digue
Mount Dauban 740m
SEYCHELLES
Mamelles
Silhouette
Mahé
North Point
Île aux Récifs
Frégate
VICTORIA
Sainte Anne
Île au Cerf
Morne Seychellois 905m
Cascade
Île Thérèse
Mahé
INDIAN OCEAN
Anse Boileau
Baie Lazare
Pointe Lazare
Quatre Bornes
Pointe Police
SCALE 1:2,250,000

▲ ***Coral reefs support*** *an enormous diversity of animal and plant life. Many species of tropical fish, like these squirrel fish, live and feed around the profusion of reefs and atolls in the Indian Ocean.*

Scale 1:47,000,000
Km 0 200 400 600 800 1000
Miles 0 200 400 600 800 1000
projection: Mollweide
ASIA
IRAN
Bandar-e 'Abbās
Persian Gulf
OMAN
Doha
Abu Dhabi
Dubai
UAE
Gwadar
Gulf of Oman
Mina' Qābūs
PAKISTAN
Karāchi
Indus
Ganges
Brahmaputra
BANGLADESH
Dhaka
Chittagong
Kolkata (Calcutta)
INDIA
Bhavnagar
Narmada
Mumbai (Bombay)
Godavari
Krishna
Visākhapatnam
Mangalore
Chennai (Madras)
Cochin
Tuticorin
Colombo
Trincomalee
Sri Lanka
SRI LANKA
Laccadive Islands (to India)
MALDIVES
MYANMAR
Irrawaddy
Salween
Rangoon
Mekong
CHINA
LAOS
VIETNAM
THAILAND
CAMBODIA
Gulf of Tongking
Gulf of Thailand
Bay of Bengal
Ganges Fan
Andaman Islands (to India)
Andaman Sea
Andaman Basin
Nicobar Islands (to India)
Bedawan
Strait of Malacca
Klang
Singapore
MALAYSIA
Sumatra
Borneo
INDONESIA
Java Sea
Java
Bali
Sumbawa
Lombok Basin
Pulau Sumba
Timor
Savu
EAST TIMOR
Java Trench
Java Ridge
Celebes
Celebes Sea
Sulu Sea
Makassar Strait
Molucca Sea
Ceram Sea
Banda Sea
New Guinea
Arafura Sea
Timor Trough
Timor Sea
Joseph Bonaparte Gulf
Darwin
Gulf of Carpentaria
Wyndham
King Sound
Broome
Sahul Shelf
Ashmore & Cartier Islands (to Australia)
Christmas Island (to Australia)
Roo Rise
North Australian Basin
Rowley Shoals
Gascoyne Plain
Exmouth Plateau
Port Hedland
Cuvier Basin
Cuvier Plateau
Shark Bay
Geraldton
AUSTRALIA
Tropic of Capricorn
Fremantle
Bunbury
Albany
Perth Basin
Naturaliste Plateau
Great Australian Bight
Spencer Gulf
Port Augusta
Darling
Murray
Adelaide
Kangaroo Island
Melbourne
King Island
Bass Strait
Tasmania
Tasman Plateau
South Australian Basin
South Australian Plain
East China Sea
Ryukyu Islands
TAIWAN
Tropic of Cancer
PHILIPPINES
Philippine Sea
South China Sea
Equator
Arabian Sea
Arabian Basin
Indus Fan
Murray Ridge
Owen Fracture Zone
Socotra (to Yemen)
Sālālah
Carlsberg Ridge
Chain Ridge
Mid-Indian Ridge
Laccadive Plateau
Chagos Laccadive Plateau
Chagos Trench
Chagos Archipelago
Diego Garcia
British Indian Ocean Territory (to UK)
Ceylon Plain
Mid-Indian Basin
Ninetyeast Ridge
Cocos Basin
Cocos Islands (to Australia)
Investigator Ridge
Wharton Basin
Wallaby Plateau
Batavia Seamount
Gulden Draak Seamount
East Indiaman Ridge
Broken Ridge
Diamantina Fracture Zone
Naturaliste Fracture Zone
Seychelles Bank
Mahé
Mascarene Plateau
Saya de Malha Bank
Agalega Islands (to Mauritius)
Mascarene Basin
Nazareth Bank
Cargados Carajos Bank
Rodrigues (to Mauritius)
MAURITIUS
Mascarene Islands
Réunion (to France)
Madagascar Basin
Argo Fracture Zone
Egeria Fracture Zone
INDIAN OCEAN
Southwest Indian Ridge
Crozet Basin
Crozet Plateau
Crozet Islands
Amsterdam Fracture Zone
Amsterdam Island
St. Paul Island
French Southern & Antarctic Territories (to France)
Kerguelen
Kerguelen Plateau
Heard & McDonald Islands (to Australia)
Lena Tablemount
Banzare Seamounts
Southeast Indian Ridge
SOUTHERN OCEAN
South Indian Basin
Antarctic Circle
Prydz Bay
ANTARCTICA
RÉUNION (to France)
Scale 1:2,250,000
ST-DENIS
Ste-Marie
Le Port
Ste-Suzanne
St-André
St-Paul
St-Benoit
Salazie
Pointe des Aigrettes
St-Gilles-les-Bains
Piton des Neiges 3070m
Trois-Bassins
St-Leu
Cilaos
La Plaine-des-Palmistes
Ste-Rose
Pointe au Sel
Piton de la Fournaise 2632m
Le Tampon
St-Louis
St-Pierre
Point de la Rivière St-Etienne
Pointe de la Table
St-Joseph
St-Philippe
INDIAN OCEAN
Ocean map key
Sea Depth
sea level
250m / 820ft
500m / 1640ft
1000m / 3281ft
2000m / 6562ft
3000m / 9843ft
Inset map key
Population
500,000 to 1 million
100,000 to 500,000
50,000 to 100,000
10,000 to 50,000
below 10,000
Elevation
3000m / 9843ft
2000m / 6562ft
1000m / 3281ft
500m / 1640ft
250m / 820ft
100m / 328ft
sea level
MAURITIUS
Round Island
Flat Island
Gunner's Quoin
Canonniers Point
Île D'Ambre
Triolet
Pamplemousses
Goodlands
PORT LOUIS
Rivière du Rempart
Beau Bassin
Rose Hill
Centre de Flacq
Quatre Bornes
Bel Air
Mont du Rempart
Vacoas
Tamarin
Curepipe
Piton de la Petite Rivière Noire 828m
Rose Belle
Mahebourg
Pointe Sud Ouest
Chemin Grenier
Souillac
Ramgoolam
Scale 1:2,250,000
INDIAN OCEAN

◀ The steeper eastern side of Madagascar is drained by numerous short, fast-flowing rivers. In contrast, larger, more languid rivers flow across the west. Both erode huge quantities of Madagascar's reddish soil.

▶ There are over 1300 small coral islands in the Maldives, but only about 200 are inhabited. They are based around an ancient submerged volcanic mountain range and all the islands are low-lying, none rising more than 6 ft (1.8 m) above sea level.

▲ The island of Mauritius is volcanic in origin. Its central plateau is bounded by mountains which may once have formed the rim of a volcanic crater.

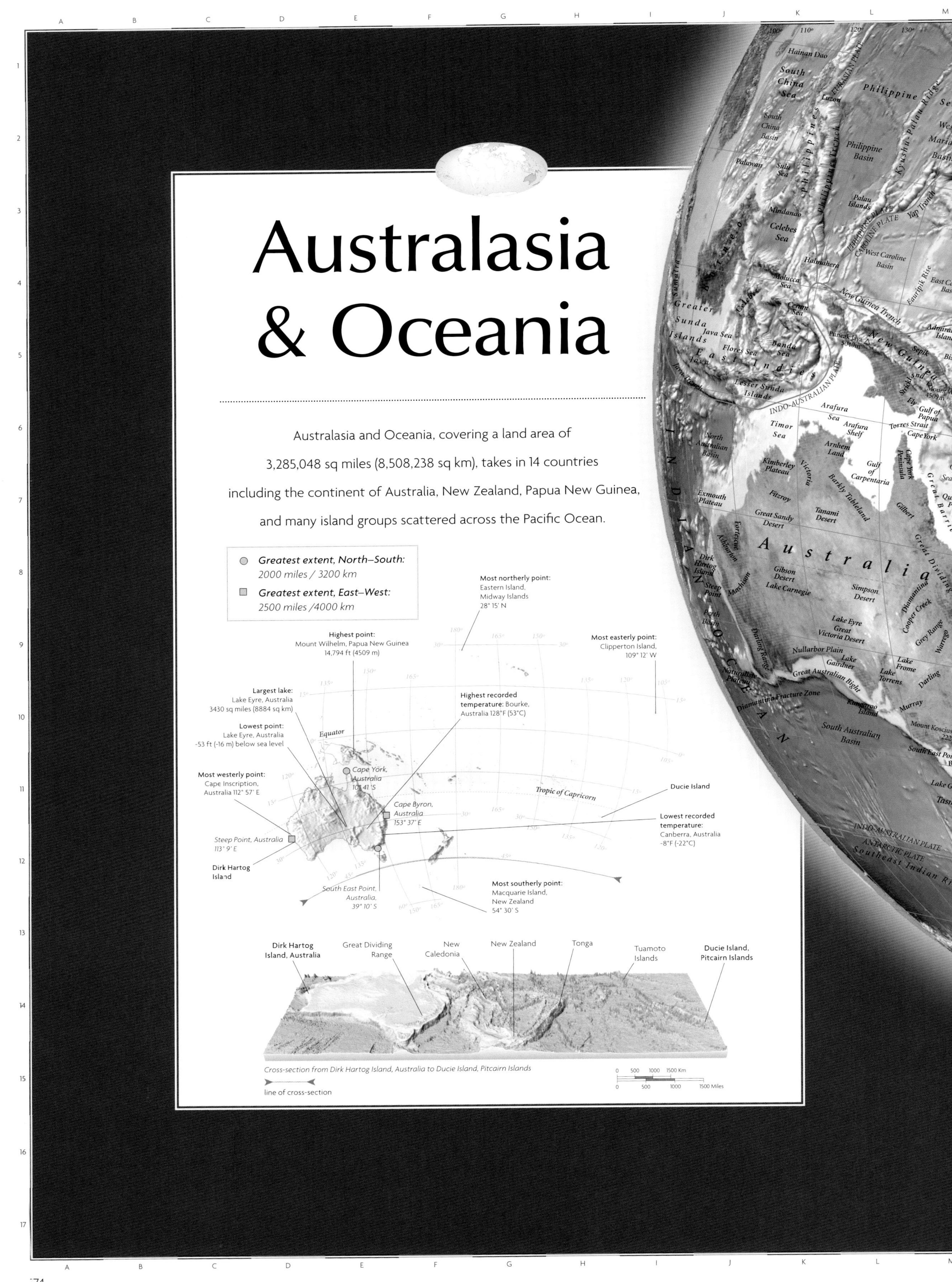

Australasia & Oceania
Australasia and Oceania, covering a land area of 3,285,048 sq miles (8,508,238 sq km), takes in 14 countries including the continent of Australia, New Zealand, Papua New Guinea, and many island groups scattered across the Pacific Ocean.
Greatest extent, North–South: 2000 miles / 3200 km
Greatest extent, East–West: 2500 miles /4000 km
Most northerly point: Eastern Island, Midway Islands 28° 15' N
Highest point: Mount Wilhelm, Papua New Guinea 14,794 ft (4509 m)
Most easterly point: Clipperton Island, 109° 12' W
Largest lake: Lake Eyre, Australia 3430 sq miles (8884 sq km)
Highest recorded temperature: Bourke, Australia 128°F (53°C)
Lowest point: Lake Eyre, Australia -53 ft (-16 m) below sea level
Equator
Most westerly point: Cape Inscription, Australia 112° 57' E
Cape York, Australia 10° 41' S
Cape Byron, Australia 153° 37' E
Tropic of Capricorn
Ducie Island
Lowest recorded temperature: Canberra, Australia -8°F (-22°C)
Steep Point, Australia 113° 9' E
Dirk Hartog Island
South East Point, Australia, 39° 10' S
Most southerly point: Macquarie Island, New Zealand 54° 30' S
Dirk Hartog Island, Australia
Great Dividing Range
New Caledonia
New Zealand
Tonga
Tuamoto Islands
Ducie Island, Pitcairn Islands
Cross-section from Dirk Hartog Island, Australia to Ducie Island, Pitcairn Islands
line of cross-section
0 500 1000 1500 Km
0 500 1000 1500 Miles
Hainan Dao
South China Sea
Philippine Sea
Philippine Basin
Celebes Sea
Greater Sunda Islands
Java Sea
Flores Sea
Banda Sea
Lesser Sunda Islands
Arafura Sea
Timor Sea
Gulf of Carpentaria
Great Sandy Desert
Tanami Desert
Australia
Gibson Desert
Lake Carnegie
Simpson Desert
Great Victoria Desert
Nullarbor Plain
Great Australian Bight
Kangaroo Island
South Australian Basin
INDIAN OCEAN
New Guinea

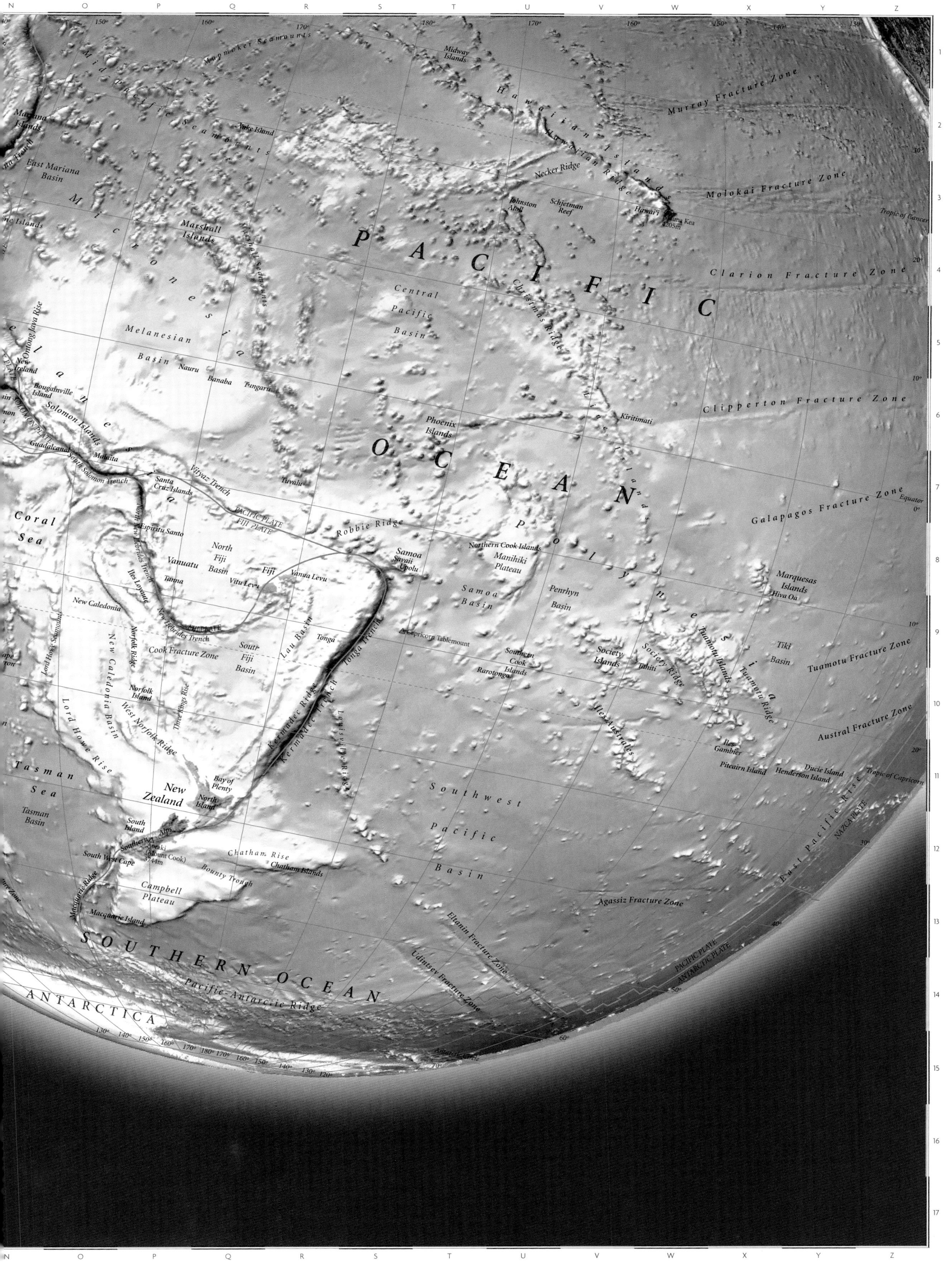
PACIFIC OCEAN
SOUTHERN OCEAN
ANTARCTICA
Midway Islands
Hawaiian Islands
Hawaiian Ridge
Murray Fracture Zone
Molokai Fracture Zone
Clarion Fracture Zone
Clipperton Fracture Zone
Galapagos Fracture Zone
Tuamotu Fracture Zone
Austral Fracture Zone
Agassiz Fracture Zone
Eltanin Fracture Zone
Udintsev Fracture Zone
Mid-Pacific Seamounts
Marshall Seamounts
Mariana Islands
East Mariana Basin
Micronesia
Melanesia
Polynesia
Marshall Islands
Wake Island
Necker Ridge
Johnston Atoll
Schjetman Reef
Hawai'i
Mauna Kea
Central Pacific Basin
Christmas Ridge
Line Islands
Melanesian Basin
Nauru
Banaba
Tungaru
Ontong Java Rise
New Ireland
Bougainville Island
Solomon Islands
Guadalcanal
Malaita
South Solomon Trench
Vityaz Trench
Santa Cruz Islands
Phoenix Islands
Kiritimati
Tuvalu
Coral Sea
Espiritu Santo
North New Hebrides Trench
Vanuatu
Tanna
North Fiji Basin
Fiji
Vanua Levu
Viti Levu
Robbie Ridge
Samoa
Savaii
Upolu
Northern Cook Islands
Manihiki Plateau
Samoa Basin
Penrhyn Basin
Marquesas Islands
Hiva Oa
Iles Loyauté
New Caledonia
New Hebrides Trench
Cook Fracture Zone
South Fiji Basin
Lau Basin
Tonga
Tonga Trench
Capricorn Tablemount
Southern Cook Islands
Rarotonga
Society Islands
Tahiti
Society Ridge
Tuamotu Islands
Tuamotu Ridge
Tiki Basin
Lord Howe Seamounts
Norfolk Ridge
New Caledonia Basin
Norfolk Island
West Norfolk Ridge
Three Kings Rise
Kermadec Ridge
Kermadec Trench
Louisville Ridge
Iles Australes
Iles Gambier
Pitcairn Island
Henderson Island
Ducie Island
Tropic of Cancer
Equator
Tropic of Capricorn
Lord Howe Rise
Tasman Sea
Tasman Basin
New Zealand
Bay of Plenty
North Island
South Island
Southern Alps
Aoraki (Mount Cook) 3744m
South West Cape
Chatham Rise
Chatham Islands
Bounty Trough
Campbell Plateau
Macquarie Ridge
Macquarie Island
Southwest Pacific Basin
East Pacific Rise
Pacific-Antarctic Ridge
PACIFIC PLATE
FIJI PLATE
ANTARCTIC PLATE
NAZCA PLATE
Antarctic Circle

Political Australasia & Oceania

Vast expanses of ocean separate this geographically fragmented realm, characterized more by each country's isolation than by any political unity. Australia's and New Zealand's traditional ties with the United Kingdom, as members of the Commonwealth, are now being called into question as Australasian and Oceanian nations are increasingly looking to forge new relationships with neighboring Asian countries like Japan. External influences have featured strongly in the politics of the Pacific Islands; the various territories of Micronesia were largely under US control until the late 1980s, and France, New Zealand, the US, and the UK still have territories under colonial rule in Polynesia. Nuclear weapons-testing by Western superpowers was widespread during the Cold War period, but has now been discontinued.

◄ *Western Australia's mineral* wealth has transformed its state capital, Perth, into one of Australia's major cities. Perth is one of the world's most isolated cities – over 2500 miles (4000 km) from the population centers of the eastern seaboard.

Scale 1:35,500,000

projection: Lambert Azimuthal Equal Area

Population

Density of settlement in the region is generally low. Australia is one of the least densely populated countries on Earth with over 80% of its population living within 25 miles (40 km) of the coast – mostly in the southeast of the country. New Zealand, and the island groups of Melanesia, Micronesia, and Polynesia, are much more densely populated, although many of the smaller islands remain uninhabited.

Population density (people per sq mile)

- below 10
- 10-62
- 63-130
- 131-259
- 260-519
- 520-780
- above 780

▲ *The myriad of* small coral islands that are scattered across the Pacific Ocean are often uninhabited, as they offer little shelter from the weather, often no fresh water, and only limited food supplies.

◄ *The planes of* the Australian Royal Flying Doctor Service are able to cover large expanses of barren land quickly, bringing medical treatment to the most inaccessible and far-flung places.

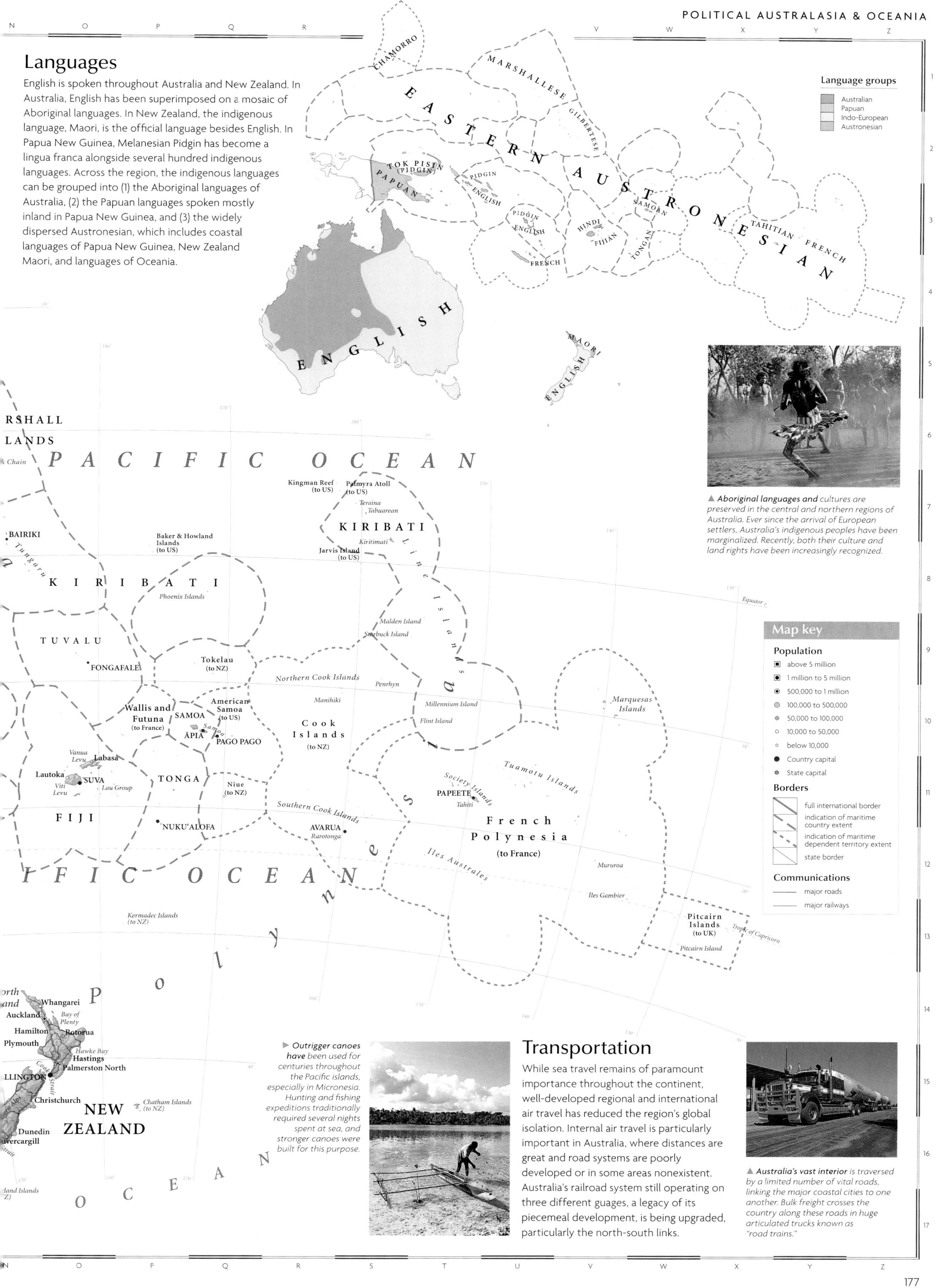

Languages

English is spoken throughout Australia and New Zealand. In Australia, English has been superimposed on a mosaic of Aboriginal languages. In New Zealand, the indigenous language, Maori, is the official language besides English. In Papua New Guinea, Melanesian Pidgin has become a lingua franca alongside several hundred indigenous languages. Across the region, the indigenous languages can be grouped into (1) the Aboriginal languages of Australia, (2) the Papuan languages spoken mostly inland in Papua New Guinea, and (3) the widely dispersed Austronesian, which includes coastal languages of Papua New Guinea, New Zealand Maori, and languages of Oceania.

Language groups
Australian
Papuan
Indo-European
Austronesian
CHAMORRO
MARSHALLESE
GILBERTESE
EASTERN AUSTRONESIAN
TOK PISIN (PIDGIN)
PAPUAN
PIDGIN ENGLISH
SAMOAN
HINDI
FIJIAN
TONGAN
TAHITIAN
FRENCH
ENGLISH
MAORI
PACIFIC OCEAN
Kingman Reef (to US)
Palmyra Atoll (to US)
Teraina
Tabuaerean
KIRIBATI
Kiritimati
Jarvis Island (to US)
Line Islands
BAIRIKI
Baker & Howland Islands (to US)
Tungaru
Phoenix Islands
TUVALU
FONGAFALE
Tokelau (to NZ)
Malden Island
Starbuck Island
Northern Cook Islands
Penrhyn
Manihiki
Millennium Island
Flint Island
Marquesas Islands
Wallis and Futuna (to France)
SAMOA
American Samoa (to US)
APIA
PAGO PAGO
Cook Islands (to NZ)
Vanua Levu
Labasa
Lautoka
SUVA
Viti Levu
Lau Group
TONGA
Niue (to NZ)
Tuamotu Islands
Society Islands
PAPEETE
Tahiti
FIJI
NUKU'ALOFA
Southern Cook Islands
AVARUA
Rarotonga
French Polynesia (to France)
Iles Australes
Mururoa
Iles Gambier
Pitcairn Islands (to UK)
Pitcairn Island
Tropic of Capricorn
Equator
Kermadec Islands (to NZ)
POLYNESIA
Whangarei
Auckland
Bay of Plenty
Hamilton
Rotorua
Plymouth
Hawke Bay
Hastings
Palmerston North
WELLINGTON
Cook Strait
Christchurch
NEW ZEALAND
Chatham Islands (to NZ)
Dunedin
Invercargill
OCEAN

▲ *Aboriginal languages and cultures are preserved in the central and northern regions of Australia. Ever since the arrival of European settlers, Australia's indigenous peoples have been marginalized. Recently, both their culture and land rights have been increasingly recognized.*

Map key

Population

- above 5 million
- 1 million to 5 million
- 500,000 to 1 million
- 100,000 to 500,000
- 50,000 to 100,000
- 10,000 to 50,000
- below 10,000
- Country capital
- State capital

Borders

- full international border
- indication of maritime country extent
- indication of maritime dependent territory extent
- state border

Communications

- major roads
- major railways

▶ ***Outrigger canoes have** been used for centuries throughout the Pacific islands, especially in Micronesia. Hunting and fishing expeditions traditionally required several nights spent at sea, and stronger canoes were built for this purpose.*

Transportation

While sea travel remains of paramount importance throughout the continent, well-developed regional and international air travel has reduced the region's global isolation. Internal air travel is particularly important in Australia, where distances are great and road systems are poorly developed or in some areas nonexistent. Australia's railroad system still operating on three different guages, a legacy of its piecemeal development, is being upgraded, particularly the north-south links.

▲ ***Australia's vast interior** is traversed by a limited number of vital roads, linking the major coastal cities to one another. Bulk freight crosses the country along these roads in huge articulated trucks known as "road trains."*

Australasian & Oceanian resources

Natural resources are of major economic importance throughout Australasia and Oceania. Australia in particular is a major world exporter of raw materials such as coal, iron ore, and bauxite, while New Zealand's agricultural economy is dominated by sheep-raising. Trade with western Europe has declined significantly in the last 20 years, and the Pacific Rim countries of Southeast Asia are now the main trading partners, as well as a source of new settlers to the region. Australasia and Oceania's greatest resources are its climate and environment; tourism increasingly provides a vital source of income for the whole continent.

▲ ***The largely unpolluted** waters of the Pacific Ocean support rich and varied marine life, much of which is farmed commercially. Here, oysters are gathered for market off the coast of New Zealand's South Island.*

Northern Mariana Islands (to US)
Saipan
Guam (to US)
MICRO
PALAU

▶ ***Huge flocks of** sheep are a common sight in New Zealand, where they outnumber people by 12 to 1. New Zealand is one of the world's largest exporters of wool and frozen lamb.*

Standard of living

In marked contrast to its neighbor, Australia, with one of the world's highest life expectancies and standards of living, Papua New Guinea is one of the world's least developed countries. In addition, high population growth and urbanization rates throughout the Pacific islands contribute to overcrowding. In Australia and New Zealand, the Aboriginal and Maori people have been isolated, although recently their traditional land ownership rights have begun to be legally recognized in an effort to ease their social and economic isolation, and to improve living standards.

Standard of living
(UN human development index)
low
high
figures unavailable

PAPUA
NEW GUINE
New Guinea
Port Mo
Arafura Sea
Torres Strait
Timor Sea
Darwin
Gulf of Carpentaria
Great Barrie
Townsville
INDIAN OCEAN
AUSTRALIA
Adelaide
Perth

Environmental issues

The prospect of rising sea levels poses a threat to many low-lying islands in the Pacific. The testing of nuclear weapons, once common throughout the region, was finally discontinued in 1996. Australia's ecological balance has been irreversibly altered by the introduction of alien species. Although it has the world's largest underground water reserve, the Great Artesian Basin, the availability of fresh water in Australia remains critical. Periodic droughts combined with overgrazing lead to desertification and increase the risk of devastating bush fires, and occasional flash floods.

Eniwetak Atoll
Bikini Atoll
SOUTHER
Malden Island
Fangataufa
Coral Sea
PACIFIC OCEAN
INDIAN OCEAN
Mackenzie
Darling
Murray
Murchison
Sydney
Tasman Sea

Environmental issues

- national parks
- tropical forest
- forest destroyed
- desert
- desertification
- polluted rivers
- radioactive contamination
- marine pollution
- heavy marine pollution
- poor urban air quality

▲ ***In 1946 Bikini Atoll,** in the Marshall Islands, was chosen as the site for Operation Crossroads – investigating the effects of atomic bombs upon naval vessels. Further nuclear tests continued until the early 1990s. The long-term environmental effects are unknown.*

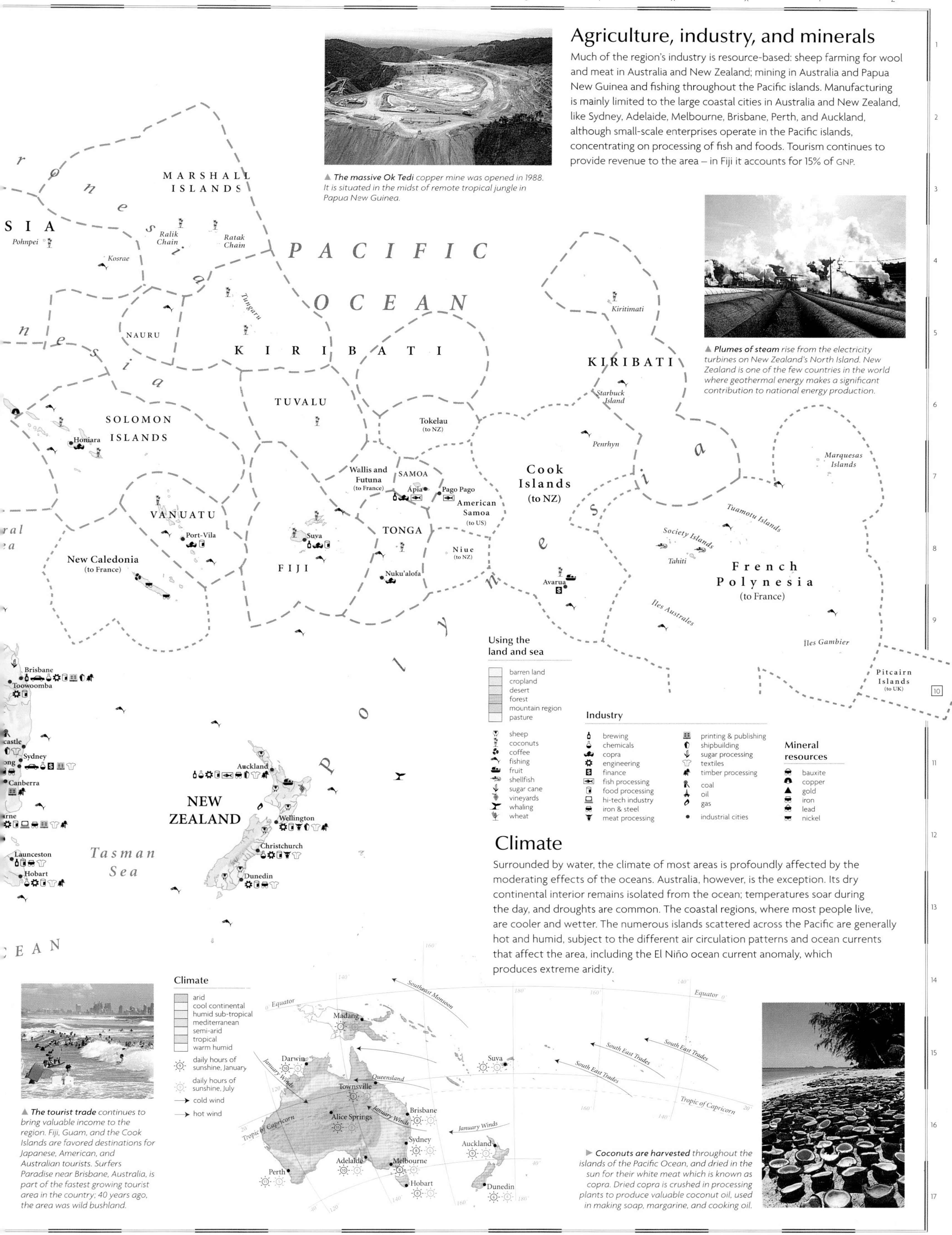
MARSHALL ISLANDS
Ralik Chain
Ratak Chain
Pohnpei
Kosrae
PACIFIC OCEAN
NAURU
KIRIBATI
Tungaru
Kiritimati
Starbuck Island
TUVALU
SOLOMON ISLANDS
Honiara
Tokelau (to NZ)
Penrhyn
Wallis and Futuna (to France)
SAMOA
Apia
Pago Pago
American Samoa (to US)
Cook Islands (to NZ)
Marquesas Islands
Tuamotu Islands
Society Islands
Tahiti
VANUATU
Port-Vila
Suva
FIJI
TONGA
Niue (to NZ)
Nuku'alofa
New Caledonia (to France)
Avarua
French Polynesia (to France)
Iles Australes
Iles Gambier
Pitcairn Islands (to UK)
Brisbane
Toowoomba
Sydney
Canberra
Launceston
Hobart
Tasman Sea
Auckland
NEW ZEALAND
Wellington
Christchurch
Dunedin
Using the land and sea
barren land
cropland
desert
forest
mountain region
pasture
sheep
coconuts
coffee
fishing
fruit
shellfish
sugar cane
vineyards
whaling
wheat
Industry
brewing
chemicals
copra
engineering
finance
fish processing
food processing
hi-tech industry
iron & steel
meat processing
printing & publishing
shipbuilding
sugar processing
textiles
timber processing
coal
oil
gas
industrial cities
Mineral resources
bauxite
copper
gold
iron
lead
nickel
Climate
arid
cool continental
humid sub-tropical
mediterranean
semi-arid
tropical
warm humid
daily hours of sunshine, January
daily hours of sunshine, July
cold wind
hot wind
Equator
Southeast Monsoon
South East Trades
January Winds
Tropic of Capricorn
Madang
Darwin
Queensland
Townsville
Alice Springs
Perth
Adelaide
Melbourne
Hobart
Auckland
Dunedin

Agriculture, industry, and minerals

Much of the region's industry is resource-based: sheep farming for wool and meat in Australia and New Zealand; mining in Australia and Papua New Guinea and fishing throughout the Pacific islands. Manufacturing is mainly limited to the large coastal cities in Australia and New Zealand, like Sydney, Adelaide, Melbourne, Brisbane, Perth, and Auckland, although small-scale enterprises operate in the Pacific islands, concentrating on processing of fish and foods. Tourism continues to provide revenue to the area – in Fiji it accounts for 15% of GNP.

▲ *The massive Ok Tedi copper mine was opened in 1988. It is situated in the midst of remote tropical jungle in Papua New Guinea.*

▲ *Plumes of steam rise from the electricity turbines on New Zealand's North Island. New Zealand is one of the few countries in the world where geothermal energy makes a significant contribution to national energy production.*

Climate

Surrounded by water, the climate of most areas is profoundly affected by the moderating effects of the oceans. Australia, however, is the exception. Its dry continental interior remains isolated from the ocean; temperatures soar during the day, and droughts are common. The coastal regions, where most people live, are cooler and wetter. The numerous islands scattered across the Pacific are generally hot and humid, subject to the different air circulation patterns and ocean currents that affect the area, including the El Niño ocean current anomaly, which produces extreme aridity.

▲ *The tourist trade continues to bring valuable income to the region. Fiji, Guam, and the Cook Islands are favored destinations for Japanese, American, and Australian tourists. Surfers Paradise near Brisbane, Australia, is part of the fastest growing tourist area in the country; 40 years ago, the area was wild bushland.*

▶ *Coconuts are harvested throughout the islands of the Pacific Ocean, and dried in the sun for their white meat which is known as copra. Dried copra is crushed in processing plants to produce valuable coconut oil, used in making soap, margarine, and cooking oil.*

Australia

Australia is the world's smallest continent, a stable landmass lying between the Indian and Pacific oceans. Previously home to its aboriginal peoples only, since the end of the 18th century immigration has transformed the face of the country. Initially settlers came mainly from western Europe, particularly the UK, and for years Australia remained wedded to its British colonial past. More recent immigrants have come from eastern Europe, and from Asian countries such as Japan, South Korea, and Indonesia. Australia is now forging strong trading links with these "Pacific Rim" countries and its economic future seems to lie with Asia and the Americas, rather than Europe, its traditional partner.

◀ **Uluru (Ayers Rock),** *the world's largest free-standing rock, is a massive outcrop of red sandstone in Australia's desert center. Wind and sandstorms have ground the rock into the smooth curves seen here. Uluru is revered as a sacred site by many aboriginal peoples.*

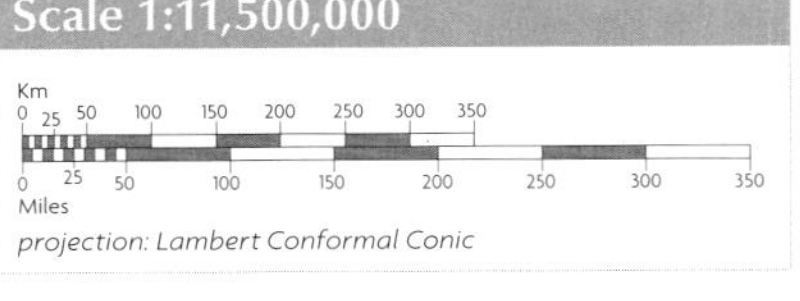
Scale 1:11,500,000
Km
0 25 50 100 150 200 250 300 350
0 25 50 100 150 200 250 300 350
Miles
projection: Lambert Conformal Conic

Map key

Population
1 million to 5 million
500,000 to 1 million
100,000 to 500,000
50,000 to 100,000
10,000 to 50,000
below 10,000

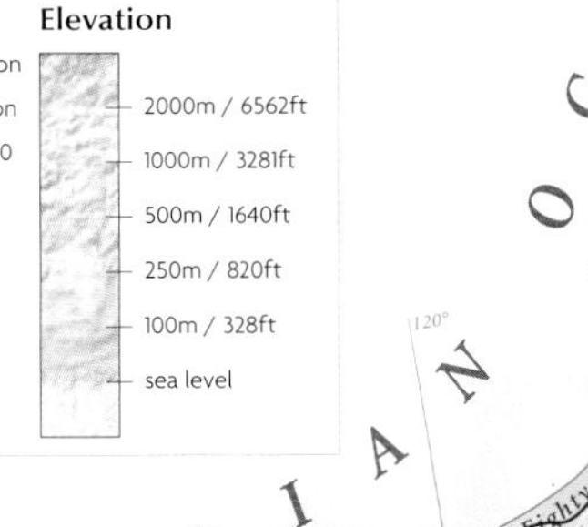
Elevation
2000m / 6562ft
1000m / 3281ft
500m / 1640ft
250m / 820ft
100m / 328ft
sea level

Using the land

Over 104 million sheep are dispersed in vast herds around the country, contributing to a major export industry. Cattle-ranching is important, particularly in the west. Wheat, and grapes for Australia's wine industry, are grown mainly in the south. Much of the country is desert, unsuitable for agriculture unless irrigation is used.

The urban/rural population divide

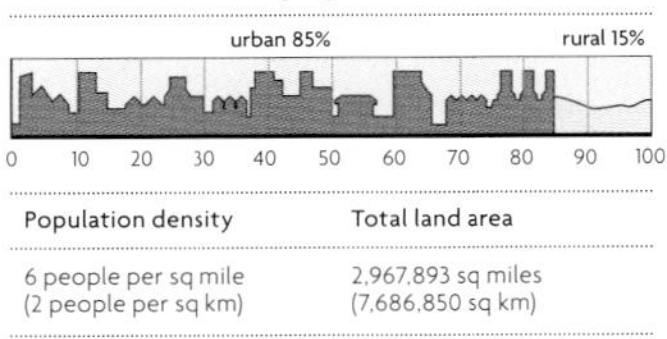
urban 85%
rural 15%
0 10 20 30 40 50 60 70 80 90 100

Population density	Total land area
6 people per sq mile (2 people per sq km)	2,967,893 sq miles (7,686,850 sq km)

Land use and agricultural distribution

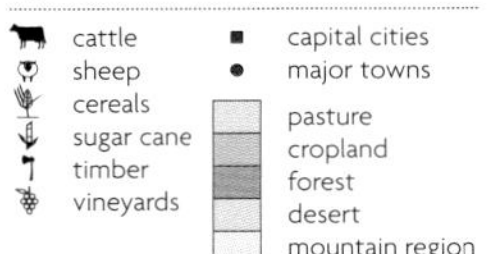
cattle
sheep
cereals
sugar cane
timber
vineyards
capital cities
major towns
pasture
cropland
forest
desert
mountain region

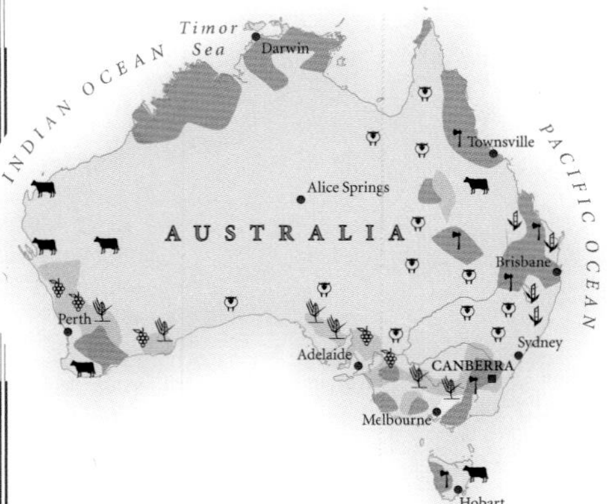
Timor Sea
Darwin
INDIAN OCEAN
PACIFIC OCEAN
Townsville
Alice Springs
AUSTRALIA
Brisbane
Perth
Sydney
Adelaide
CANBERRA
Melbourne
Hobart

▲ *Lines of ripening vines stretch for miles in Barossa Valley, a major wine-growing region near Adelaide.*

The landscape

Australia consists of many eroded plateaus, lying firmly in the middle of the Indo-Australian Plate. It is the world's flattest continent, and the driest, after Antarctica. The coasts tend to be more hilly and fertile, especially in the east. The mountains of the Great Dividing Range form a natural barrier between the eastern coastal areas and the flat, dry plains and desert regions of the Australian "outback."

▲ *The Great Barrier Reef is the world's largest area of coral islands and reefs. It runs for about 1240 miles (2000 km) along the Queensland coast.*

▲ *The Pinnacles are a series of rugged sandstone pillars. Their strange shapes have been formed by water and wind erosion.*

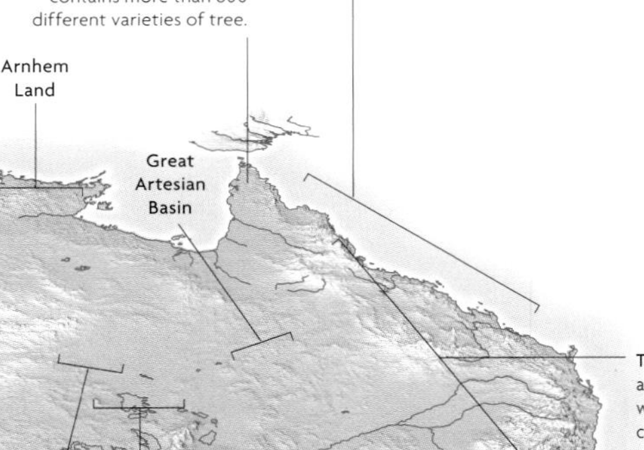
The ancient Kimberley Plateau is the source of some of Australia's richest mineral deposits, including diamonds.
Uluru (Ayers Rock)
Arnhem Land
The tropical rain forest of the Cape York Peninsula contains more than 600 different varieties of tree.
Great Artesian Basin
The Great Dividing Range forms a watershed between east- and west-flowing rivers. Erosion has created deep valleys, gorges, and waterfalls where rivers tumble over escarpments on their way to the sea.
Australian Alps
Tasmania has the same geological structure as the Australian Alps. During the last period of glaciation, 18,000 years ago, sea levels were some 300 ft (100 m) lower and it was joined to the mainland.
The Lake Eyre basin, lying 51 ft (16 m) below sea level, is one of the largest inland drainage systems in the world, covering an area of more than 500,000 sq miles (1,300,000 sq km).
The Simpson Desert has a number of large salt pans, created by the evaporation of past rivers and now sourced by seasonal rains. Some are crusted with gypsum, but most are covered by common salt crystals.
More than half of Australia rests on a uniform shield over 600 million years old. It is one of the Earth's original geological plates.
The Nullarbor Plain is a low-lying limestone plateau which is so flat that the Trans-Australian Railway runs through it in a straight line for more than 300 miles (483 km).

154

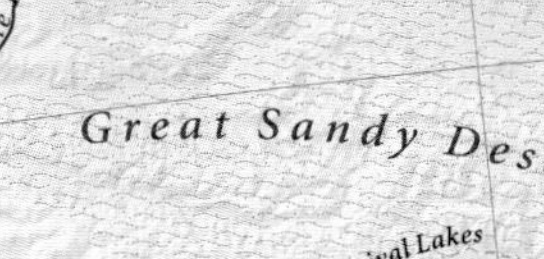

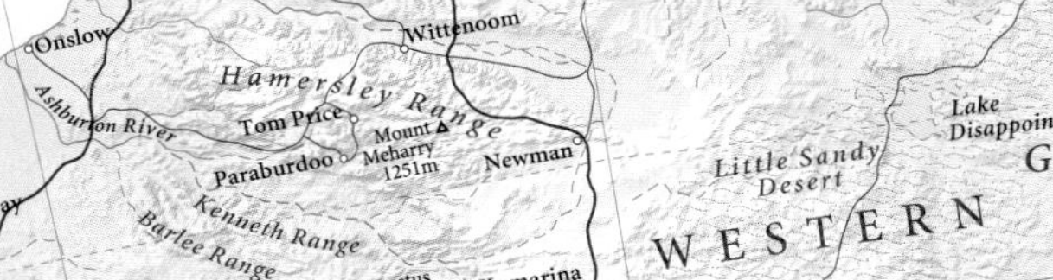

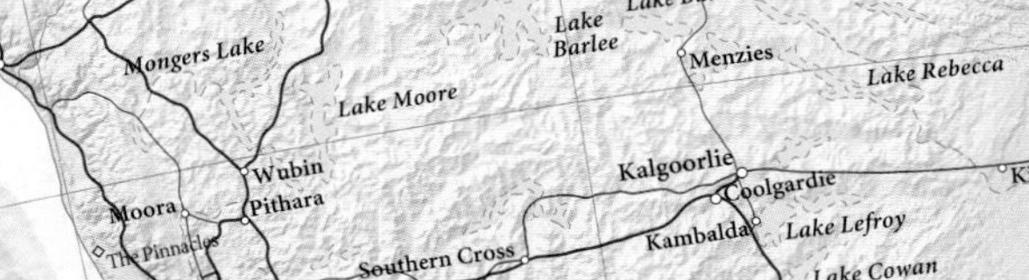

Great Artesian Basin

Rainwater replenishes aquifer

Aquifers from which artesian water is obtained

Underground water movements

Lake Eyre

▲ *The Great Artesian Basin underlies nearly 20% of the total area of Australia, providing a valuable store of underground water, essential to Australian agriculture. The ephemeral rivers which drain the northern part of the basin have highly braided courses and, in consequence, the area is known as "channel country."*

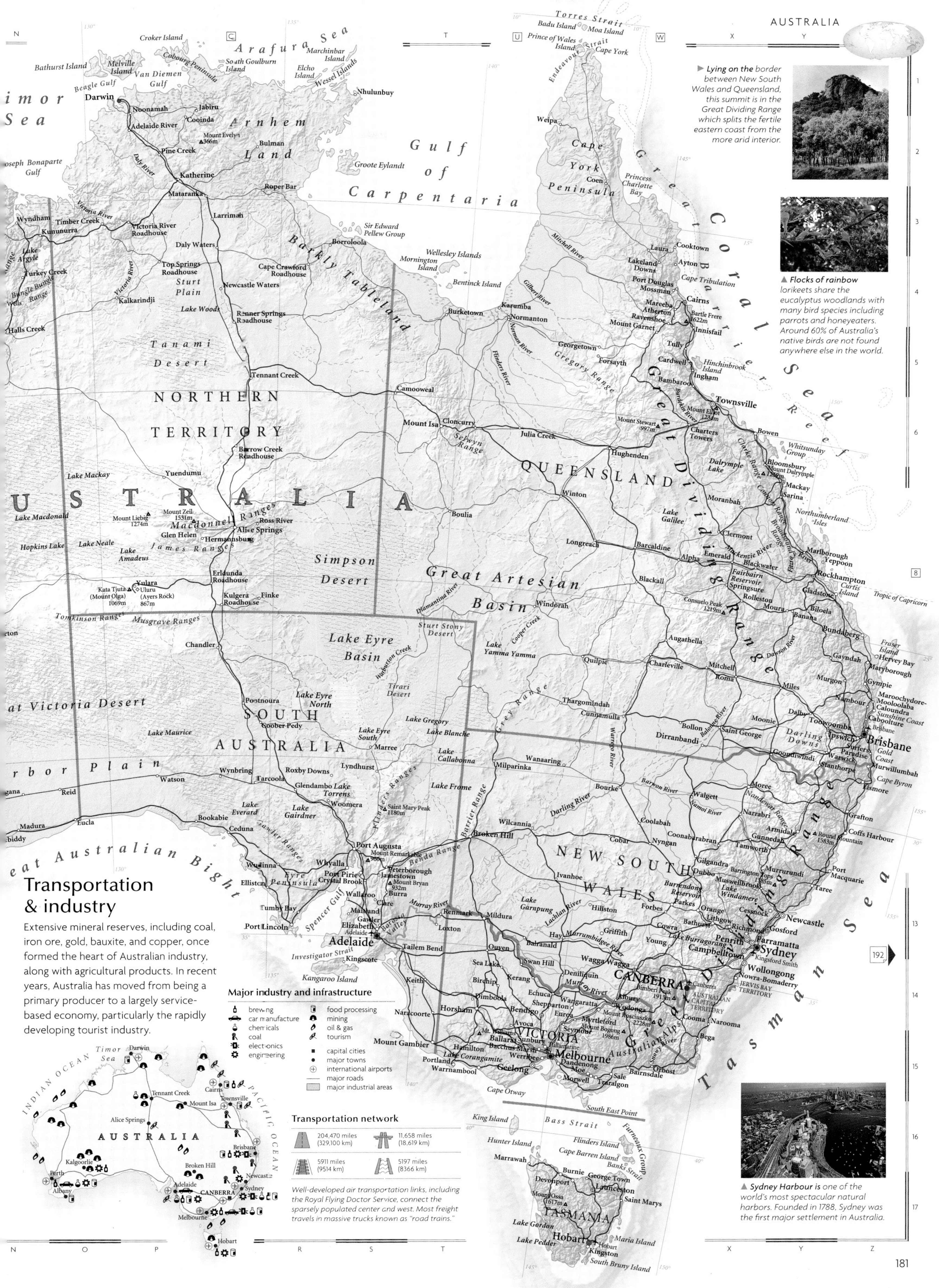
Arafura Sea
Timor Sea
Gulf of Carpentaria
Coral Sea
Tasman Sea
Great Australian Bight
Torres Strait
Bass Strait
Great Barrier Reef
Tropic of Capricorn
NORTHERN TERRITORY
QUEENSLAND
SOUTH AUSTRALIA
NEW SOUTH WALES
VICTORIA
TASMANIA
AUSTRALIAN CAPITAL TERRITORY
JERVIS BAY TERRITORY
AUSTRALIA
Arnhem Land
Cape York Peninsula
Barkly Tableland
Tanami Desert
Sturt Plain
Simpson Desert
Great Artesian Basin
Lake Eyre Basin
Great Victoria Desert
Nullarbor Plain
Great Dividing Range
Australian Alps
Macdonnell Ranges
James Ranges
Musgrave Ranges
Flinders Ranges
Gawler Ranges
Darwin
Katherine
Tennant Creek
Alice Springs
Uluru (Ayers Rock) 867m
Kata Tjuta (Mount Olga) 1069m
Mount Isa
Cairns
Townsville
Rockhampton
Brisbane
Gold Coast
Sydney
Newcastle
Wollongong
CANBERRA
Melbourne
Geelong
Adelaide
Port Augusta
Hobart
Launceston
Mount Kosciuszko 2228m
Bartle Frere 1622m
Kangaroo Island
Fraser Island
Groote Eylandt
Melville Island
Bathurst Island

Transportation & industry

Extensive mineral reserves, including coal, iron ore, gold, bauxite, and copper, once formed the heart of Australian industry, along with agricultural products. In recent years, Australia has moved from being a primary producer to a largely service-based economy, particularly the rapidly developing tourist industry.

Major industry and infrastructure

- brewing
- car manufacture
- chemicals
- coal
- electronics
- engineering
- food processing
- mining
- oil & gas
- tourism
- capital cities
- major towns
- international airports
- major roads
- major industrial areas

Transportation network

204,470 miles (329,100 km)	11,658 miles (18,619 km)
5911 miles (9514 km)	5197 miles (8366 km)

Well-developed air transportation links, including the Royal Flying Doctor Service, connect the sparsely populated center and west. Most freight travels in massive trucks known as "road trains."

▶ *Lying on the border between New South Wales and Queensland, this summit is in the Great Dividing Range which splits the fertile eastern coast from the more arid interior.*

▲ *Flocks of rainbow lorikeets share the eucalyptus woodlands with many bird species including parrots and honeyeaters. Around 60% of Australia's native birds are not found anywhere else in the world.*

▲ *Sydney Harbour is one of the world's most spectacular natural harbors. Founded in 1788, Sydney was the first major settlement in Australia.*

192

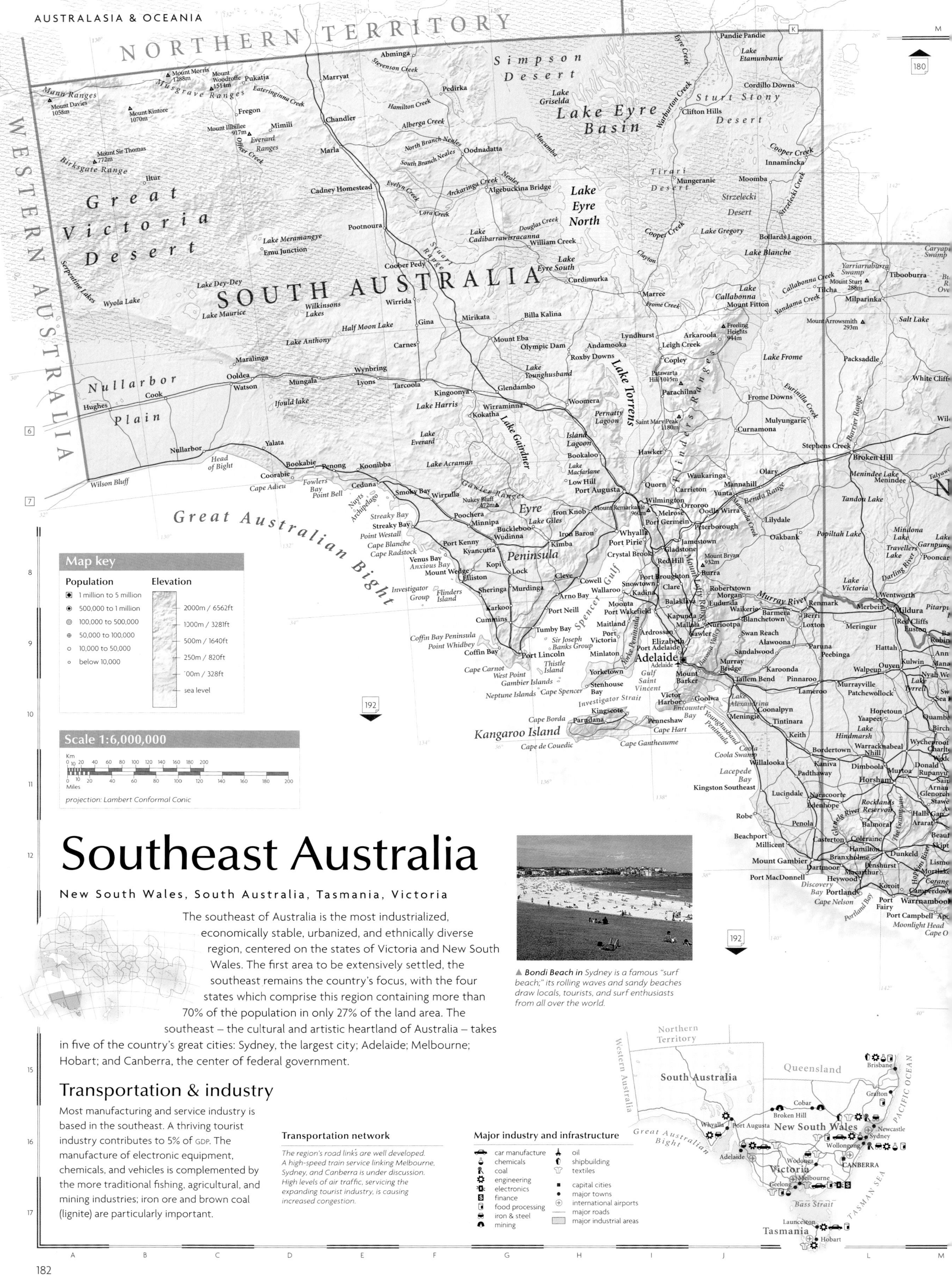
NORTHERN TERRITORY
WESTERN AUSTRALIA
SOUTH AUSTRALIA
Great Victoria Desert
Nullarbor Plain
Great Australian Bight
Simpson Desert
Lake Eyre Basin
Sturt Stony Desert
Lake Eyre North
Lake Torrens
Eyre Peninsula
Kangaroo Island
Adelaide
Map key
Population
1 million to 5 million
500,000 to 1 million
100,000 to 500,000
50,000 to 100,000
10,000 to 50,000
below 10,000
Elevation
2000m / 6562ft
1000m / 3281ft
500m / 1640ft
250m / 820ft
100m / 328ft
sea level
Scale 1:6,000,000
projection: Lambert Conformal Conic

Southeast Australia

New South Wales, South Australia, Tasmania, Victoria

The southeast of Australia is the most industrialized, economically stable, urbanized, and ethnically diverse region, centered on the states of Victoria and New South Wales. The first area to be extensively settled, the southeast remains the country's focus, with the four states which comprise this region containing more than 70% of the population in only 27% of the land area. The southeast – the cultural and artistic heartland of Australia – takes in five of the country's great cities: Sydney, the largest city; Adelaide; Melbourne; Hobart; and Canberra, the center of federal government.

▲ *Bondi Beach in Sydney is a famous "surf beach;" its rolling waves and sandy beaches draw locals, tourists, and surf enthusiasts from all over the world.*

Transportation & industry

Most manufacturing and service industry is based in the southeast. A thriving tourist industry contributes to 5% of GDP. The manufacture of electronic equipment, chemicals, and vehicles is complemented by the more traditional fishing, agricultural, and mining industries; iron ore and brown coal (lignite) are particularly important.

Transportation network

The region's road links are well developed. A high-speed train service linking Melbourne, Sydney, and Canberra is under discussion. High levels of air traffic, servicing the expanding tourist industry, is causing increased congestion.

Major industry and infrastructure

car manufacture
chemicals
coal
engineering
electronics
finance
food processing
iron & steel
mining
oil
shipbuilding
textiles
capital cities
major towns
international airports
major roads
major industrial areas
Northern Territory
Western Australia
South Australia
Queensland
New South Wales
Victoria
Tasmania
Great Australian Bight
Bass Strait
TASMAN SEA
PACIFIC OCEAN
CANBERRA
Adelaide
Melbourne
Sydney
Hobart
Brisbane

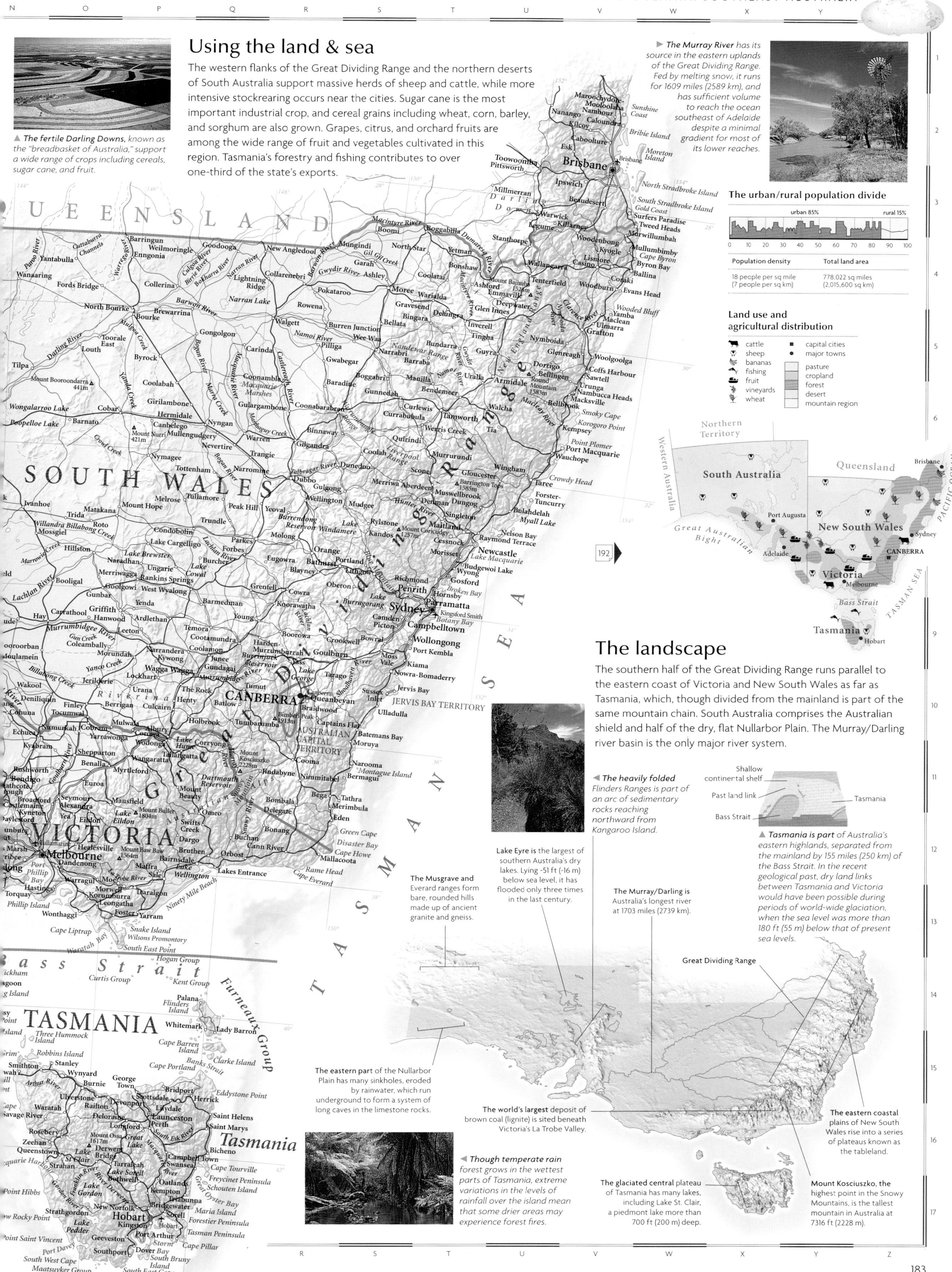

The urban/rural population divide
urban 85%
rural 15%
Population density
18 people per sq mile (7 people per sq km)
Total land area
778,022 sq miles (2,015,600 sq km)
Land use and agricultural distribution
cattle
sheep
bananas
fishing
fruit
vineyards
wheat
capital cities
major towns
pasture
cropland
forest
desert
mountain region
Shallow continental shelf
Past land link
Tasmania
Bass Strait
Great Dividing Range

Using the land & sea

The western flanks of the Great Dividing Range and the northern deserts of South Australia support massive herds of sheep and cattle, while more intensive stockrearing occurs near the cities. Sugar cane is the most important industrial crop, and cereal grains including wheat, corn, barley, and sorghum are also grown. Grapes, citrus, and orchard fruits are among the wide range of fruit and vegetables cultivated in this region. Tasmania's forestry and fishing contributes to over one-third of the state's exports.

▲ *The fertile Darling Downs, known as the "breadbasket of Australia," support a wide range of crops including cereals, sugar cane, and fruit.*

▶ *The Murray River has its source in the eastern uplands of the Great Dividing Range. Fed by melting snow, it runs for 1609 miles (2589 km), and has sufficient volume to reach the ocean southeast of Adelaide despite a minimal gradient for most of its lower reaches.*

192

The landscape

The southern half of the Great Dividing Range runs parallel to the eastern coast of Victoria and New South Wales as far as Tasmania, which, though divided from the mainland is part of the same mountain chain. South Australia comprises the Australian shield and half of the dry, flat Nullarbor Plain. The Murray/Darling river basin is the only major river system.

◀ *The heavily folded Flinders Ranges is part of an arc of sedimentary rocks reaching northward from Kangaroo Island.*

▲ *Tasmania is part of Australia's eastern highlands, separated from the mainland by 155 miles (250 km) of the Bass Strait. In the recent geological past, dry land links between Tasmania and Victoria would have been possible during periods of world-wide glaciation, when the sea level was more than 180 ft (55 m) below that of present sea levels.*

Lake Eyre is the largest of southern Australia's dry lakes. Lying -51 ft (-16 m) below sea level, it has flooded only three times in the last century.

The Musgrave and Everard ranges form bare, rounded hills made up of ancient granite and gneiss.

The Murray/Darling is Australia's longest river at 1703 miles (2739 km).

The eastern part of the Nullarbor Plain has many sinkholes, eroded by rainwater, which run underground to form a system of long caves in the limestone rocks.

The world's largest deposit of brown coal (lignite) is sited beneath Victoria's La Trobe Valley.

The eastern coastal plains of New South Wales rise into a series of plateaus known as the tableland.

◀ *Though temperate rain forest grows in the wettest parts of Tasmania, extreme variations in the levels of rainfall over the island mean that some drier areas may experience forest fires.*

The glaciated central plateau of Tasmania has many lakes, including Lake St. Clair, a piedmont lake more than 700 ft (200 m) deep.

Mount Kosciuszko, the highest point in the Snowy Mountains, is the tallest mountain in Australia at 7316 ft (2228 m).

New Zealand

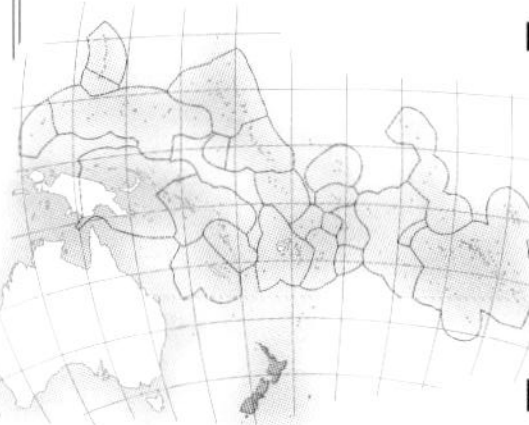

Lying 1500 miles east-southeast of Australia, New Zealand was originally settled by the Maori people of Polynesia. It was visited by Europeans for the first time only as recently as the 1770s. The islands' rugged topography means that most settlement has concentrated in coastal areas. People of European origin make up about 70% of the population of 4 million, following immigration which began in the 1920s. Many recent settlers have come from Asia, including India and China, and a number of the Pacific islands. The Maori now make up a minority of less than half a million. Their ancient claims to at least half of national territory, however, are gaining increasing legal credence.

The landscape

New Zealand comprises two large islands and many scattered smaller islands. On South Island the Alpine Fault marks the boundary between the Pacific and Indo-Australian plates. Tectonic activity has strongly influenced the formation of the Southern Alps, snowcapped mountains with several peaks over 9800 ft (3000 m). North Island has a lower and less extensive mountain region, containing forested hills, a central volcanic plateau, and downlands.

Mountain-building in the Southern Alps

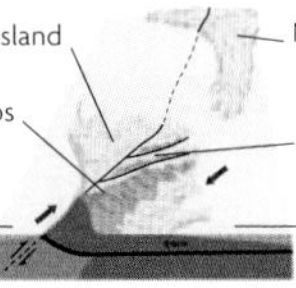

South Island
North Island
Southern Alps
Alpine Fault
Indo-Australian Plate
Pacific Plate

▲ ***The Southern Alps** have been formed by "slip" faulting. The Indo-Australian and Pacific plates run in opposite directions along the Alpine Fault. Although they slide past each other, they are also being thrust over one another, causing the continental crust of the Pacific Plate to be uplifted to form the Alps.*

◀ ***The Northland region** is characterized by many coastal inlets. These are lined by mangrove swamps, signaling the change to a subtropical climate in the far north of the island.*

◀ ***The Rotorua and** Taupo valleys have some of the largest and most spectacular thermal springs in New Zealand. These occur when superheated groundwater rises to the surface through joints in the rocks.*

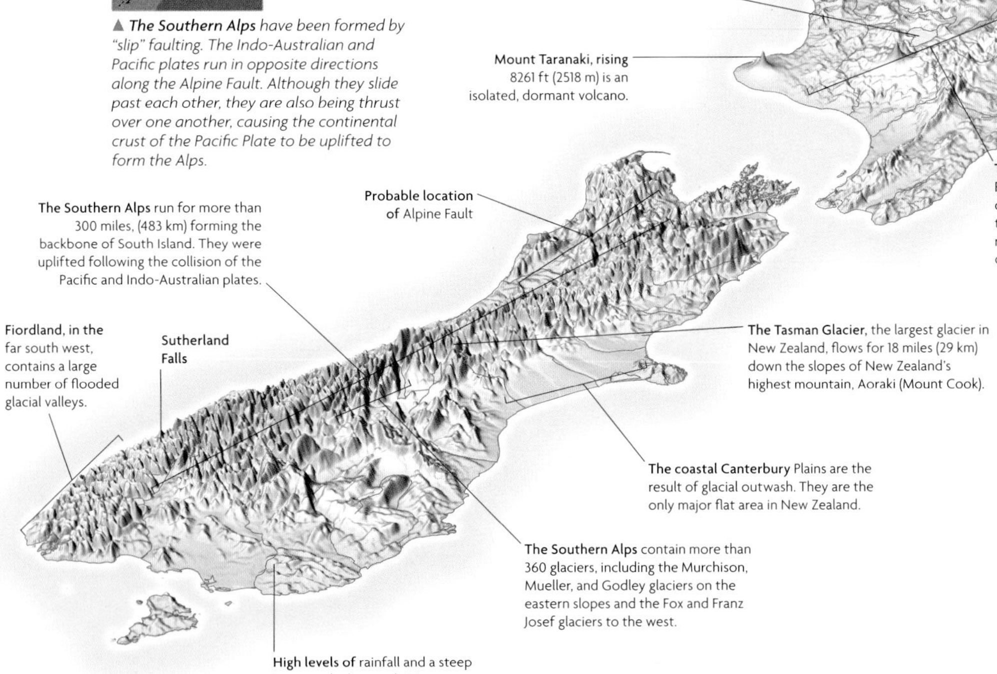

Northland

Rotorua

Lake Taupo is New Zealand's largest inland lake. It occupies the crater of an extinct volcano.

Mount Taranaki, rising 8261 ft (2518 m) is an isolated, dormant volcano.

The boundary between the Indo-Australian Plate and the Pacific Plate runs through the center of North Island, leading to many typical volcanic features. The plateau which rises from the slopes of Lake Taupo contains a string of active volcanoes.

Probable location of Alpine Fault

The Southern Alps run for more than 300 miles, (483 km) forming the backbone of South Island. They were uplifted following the collision of the Pacific and Indo-Australian plates.

Fiordland, in the far south west, contains a large number of flooded glacial valleys.

Sutherland Falls

The Tasman Glacier, the largest glacier in New Zealand, flows for 18 miles (29 km) down the slopes of New Zealand's highest mountain, Aoraki (Mount Cook).

The coastal Canterbury Plains are the result of glacial outwash. They are the only major flat area in New Zealand.

The Southern Alps contain more than 360 glaciers, including the Murchison, Mueller, and Godley glaciers on the eastern slopes and the Fox and Franz Josef glaciers to the west.

High levels of rainfall and a steep topography has made New Zealand's rivers swift-running. In the southern reaches of both islands, rivers such as the Mokoreta form broad, braided streams.

▶ ***Clouds of steam** rise from White Island, an active, offshore volcano lying in the Bay of Plenty, off the northern coast of North Island.*

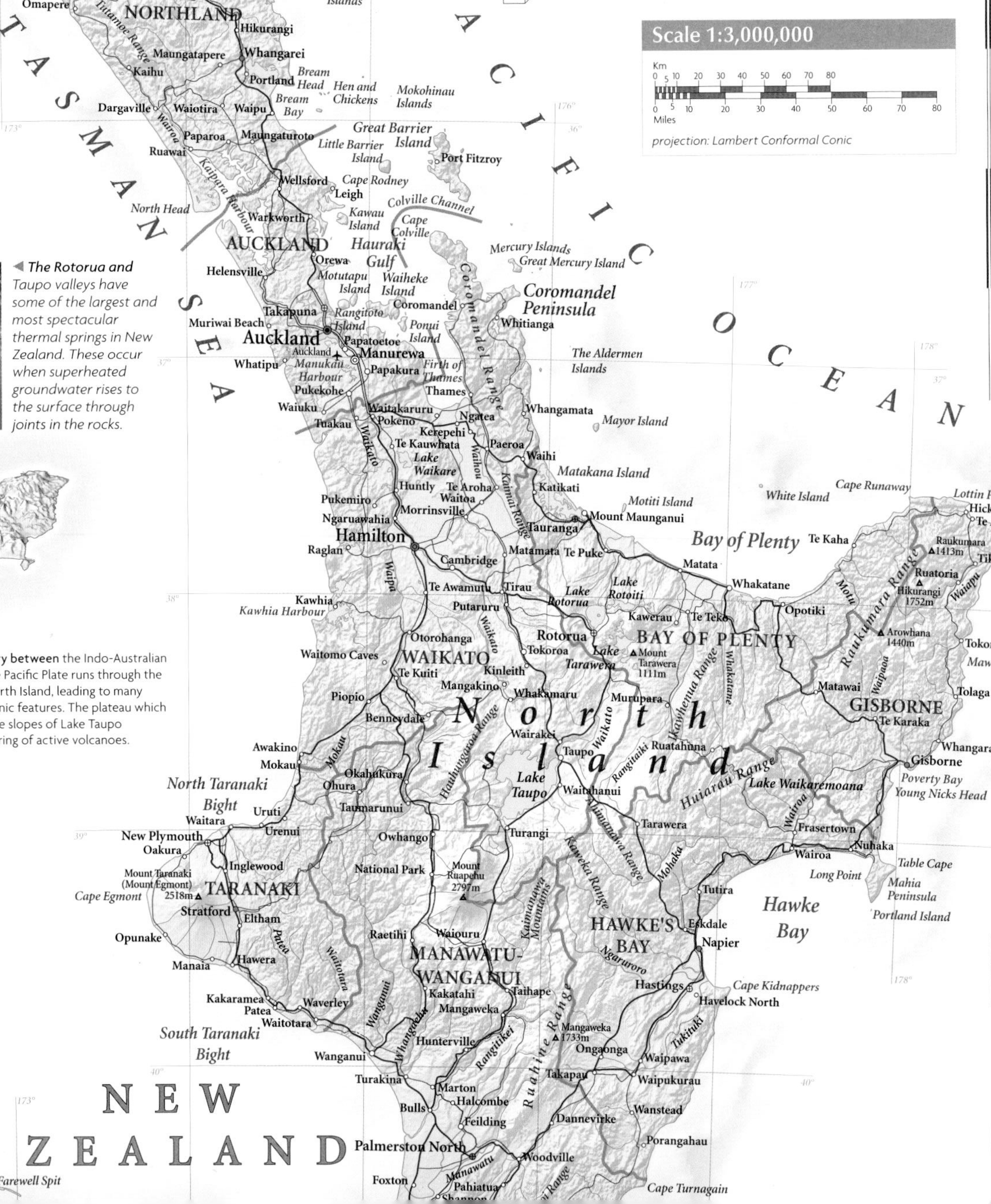

Scale 1:3,000,000

projection: Lambert Conformal Conic

192

PACIFIC OCEAN

TASMAN SEA

NEW ZEALAND

North Island

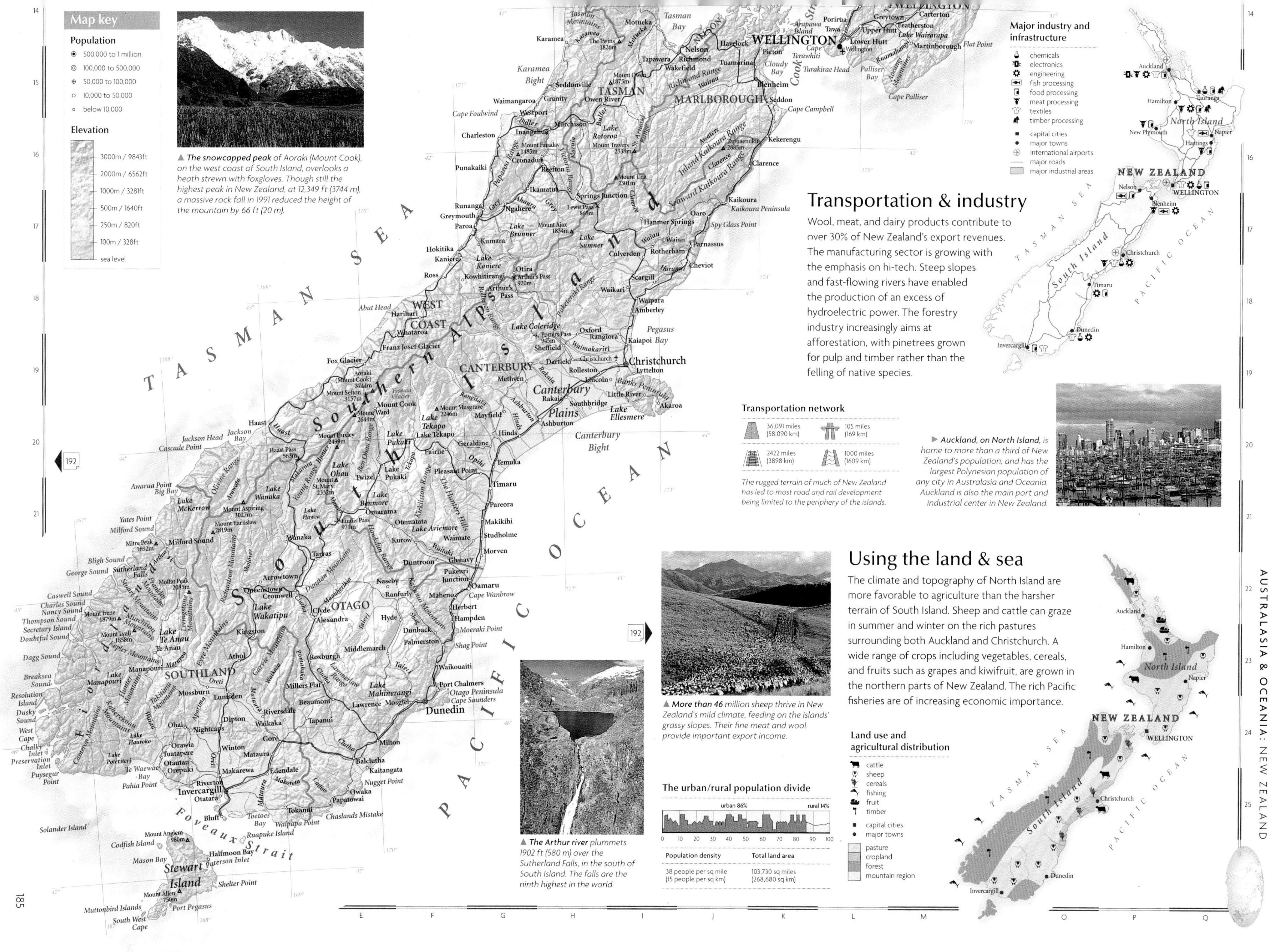
Map key
Population
500,000 to 1 million
100,000 to 500,000
50,000 to 100,000
10,000 to 50,000
below 10,000
Elevation
3000m / 9843ft
2000m / 6562ft
1000m / 3281ft
500m / 1640ft
250m / 820ft
100m / 328ft
sea level
TASMAN SEA
PACIFIC OCEAN
South Island
Southern Alps
Fiordland
WELLINGTON
Christchurch
Dunedin
Invercargill
Stewart Island
Foveaux Strait
Canterbury Plains
Canterbury Bight
CANTERBURY
WEST COAST
OTAGO
SOUTHLAND
TASMAN
MARLBOROUGH
NELSON
Major industry and infrastructure
chemicals
electronics
engineering
fish processing
food processing
meat processing
textiles
timber processing
capital cities
major towns
international airports
major roads
major industrial areas
NEW ZEALAND
North Island
Transportation network
36,091 miles (58,090 km)
105 miles (169 km)
2422 miles (3898 km)
1000 miles (1609 km)
Land use and agricultural distribution
cattle
sheep
cereals
fishing
fruit
timber
capital cities
major towns
pasture
cropland
forest
mountain region
The urban/rural population divide
urban 86%
rural 14%
0 10 20 30 40 50 60 70 80 90 100
Population density
38 people per sq mile (15 people per sq km)
Total land area
103,730 sq miles (268,680 sq km)

▲ **The snowcapped peak** *of Aoraki (Mount Cook), on the west coast of South Island, overlooks a heath strewn with foxgloves. Though still the highest peak in New Zealand, at 12,349 ft (3744 m), a massive rock fall in 1991 reduced the height of the mountain by 66 ft (20 m).*

Transportation & industry

Wool, meat, and dairy products contribute to over 30% of New Zealand's export revenues. The manufacturing sector is growing with the emphasis on hi-tech. Steep slopes and fast-flowing rivers have enabled the production of an excess of hydroelectric power. The forestry industry increasingly aims at afforestation, with pinetrees grown for pulp and timber rather than the felling of native species.

The rugged terrain of much of New Zealand has led to most road and rail development being limited to the periphery of the islands.

▶ **Auckland, on North Island,** *is home to more than a third of New Zealand's population, and has the largest Polynesian population of any city in Australasia and Oceania. Auckland is also the main port and industrial center in New Zealand.*

Using the land & sea

The climate and topography of North Island are more favorable to agriculture than the harsher terrain of South Island. Sheep and cattle can graze in summer and winter on the rich pastures surrounding both Auckland and Christchurch. A wide range of crops including vegetables, cereals, and fruits such as grapes and kiwifruit, are grown in the northern parts of New Zealand. The rich Pacific fisheries are of increasing economic importance.

▲ **The Arthur river** *plummets 1902 ft (580 m) over the Sutherland Falls, in the south of South Island. The falls are the ninth highest in the world.*

▲ **More than 46** *million sheep thrive in New Zealand's mild climate, feeding on the islands' grassy slopes. Their fine meat and wool provide important export income.*

192

Melanesia

FIJI, New Caledonia *(to France)*, PAPUA NEW GUINEA, SOLOMON ISLANDS, VANUATU

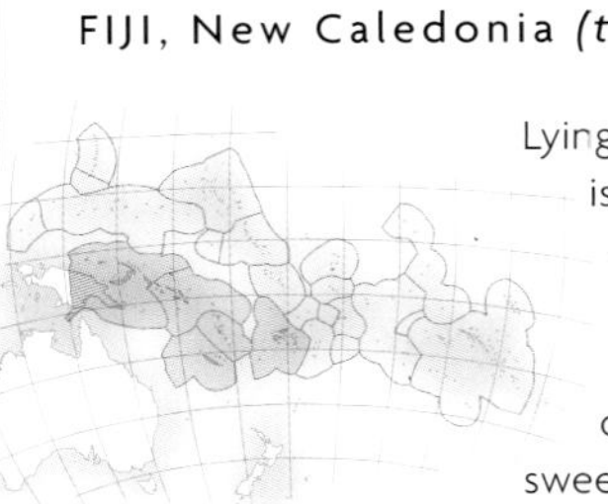

Lying in the southwest Pacific Ocean, northeast of Australia and south of the Equator, the islands of Melanesia form one of the three geographic divisions (along with Polynesia and Micronesia) of Oceania. Melanesia's name derives from the Greek melas, "black", and *nesoi*, "islands". Most of the larger islands are volcanic in origin. The smaller islands tend to be coral atolls and are mainly uninhabited. Rugged mountains, covered by dense rainforest, take up most of the land area. Melanesian's cultivate yams, taro, and sweet potatoes for local consumption and live in small, usually dispersed, homesteads.

▲ ***Huli tribesmen from** Southern Highlands Province in Papua New Guinea parade in ceremonial dress, their powdered wigs decorated with exotic plumage and their faces and bodies painted with coloured pigments.*

Map key

Population
- ◎ 100,000 to 500,000
- ⊕ 50,000 to 100,000
- ○ 10,000 to 50,000
- ○ below 10,000

Elevation

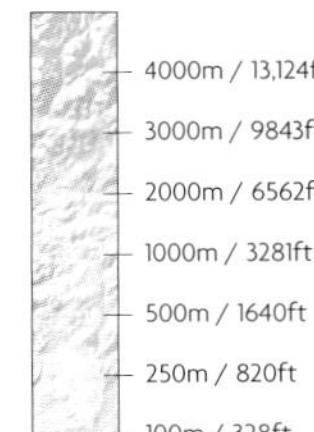

4000m / 13,124ft
3000m / 9843ft
2000m / 6562ft
1000m / 3281ft
500m / 1640ft
250m / 820ft
100m / 328ft
sea level

168
192
180

◀ ***Lying close to** the banks of the Sepik river in northern Papua New Guinea, this building is known as the Spirit House. It is constructed from leaves and twigs, ornately woven and trimmed into geometric patterns. The house is decorated with a mask and topped by a carved statue.*

Transportation & Industry

The processing of natural resources generates significant export revenue for the countries of Melanesia. The region relies mainly on copra, tuna and timber exports, with some production of cocoa and palm oil. The islands have substantial mineral resources including the world's largest copper reserves on Bougainville Island; gold, and potential oil and natural gas. Tourism has become the fastest growing sector in most of the countries' economies.

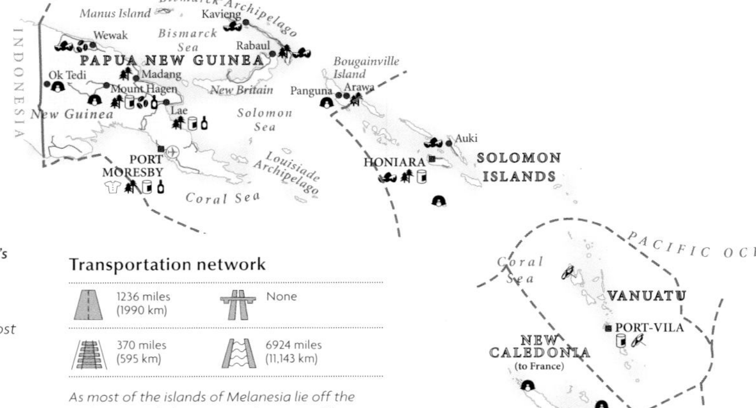

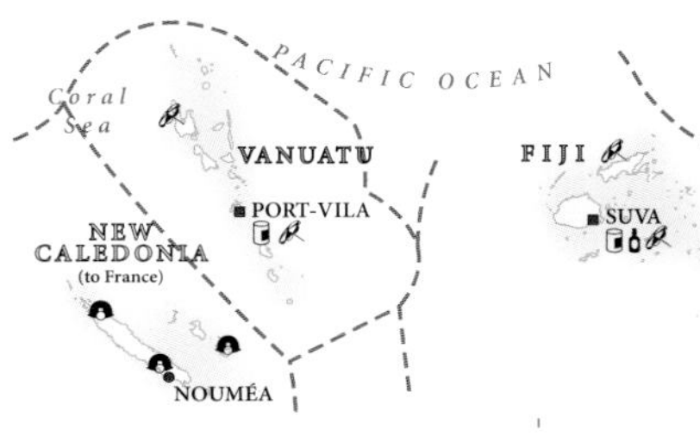

PACIFIC OCEAN
PAPUA NEW GUINEA
SOLOMON ISLANDS
VANUATU
FIJI
NEW CALEDONIA (to France)
PORT MORESBY
HONIARA
PORT-VILA
SUVA
NOUMÉA
Coral Sea

▲ ***On one of** Vanuatu's many islands, beach houses stand at the water's edge, surrounded by coconut palms and other tropical vegetation. The unspoilt beaches and tranquillity of its islands are drawing ever-larger numbers of tourists to Vanuatu.*

◀ ***On New Caledonia's** main island, relatively high interior plateaux descend to coastal plains. Nickel is the most important mineral resource, but the hills also harbor metallic deposits including chrome, cobalt, iron, gold, silver, and copper.*

Transportation network

1236 miles (1990 km)	None
370 miles (595 km)	6924 miles (11,143 km)

As most of the islands of Melanesia lie off the major sea and air routes, services to and from the rest of the world are infrequent. Transportation by road on rugged terrain is difficult and expensive.

Major industry and infrastructure
- beverages
- coffee processing
- copra processing
- food processing
- mining
- textiles
- timber processing
- tourism
- capital cities
- major towns
- international airports
- major roads

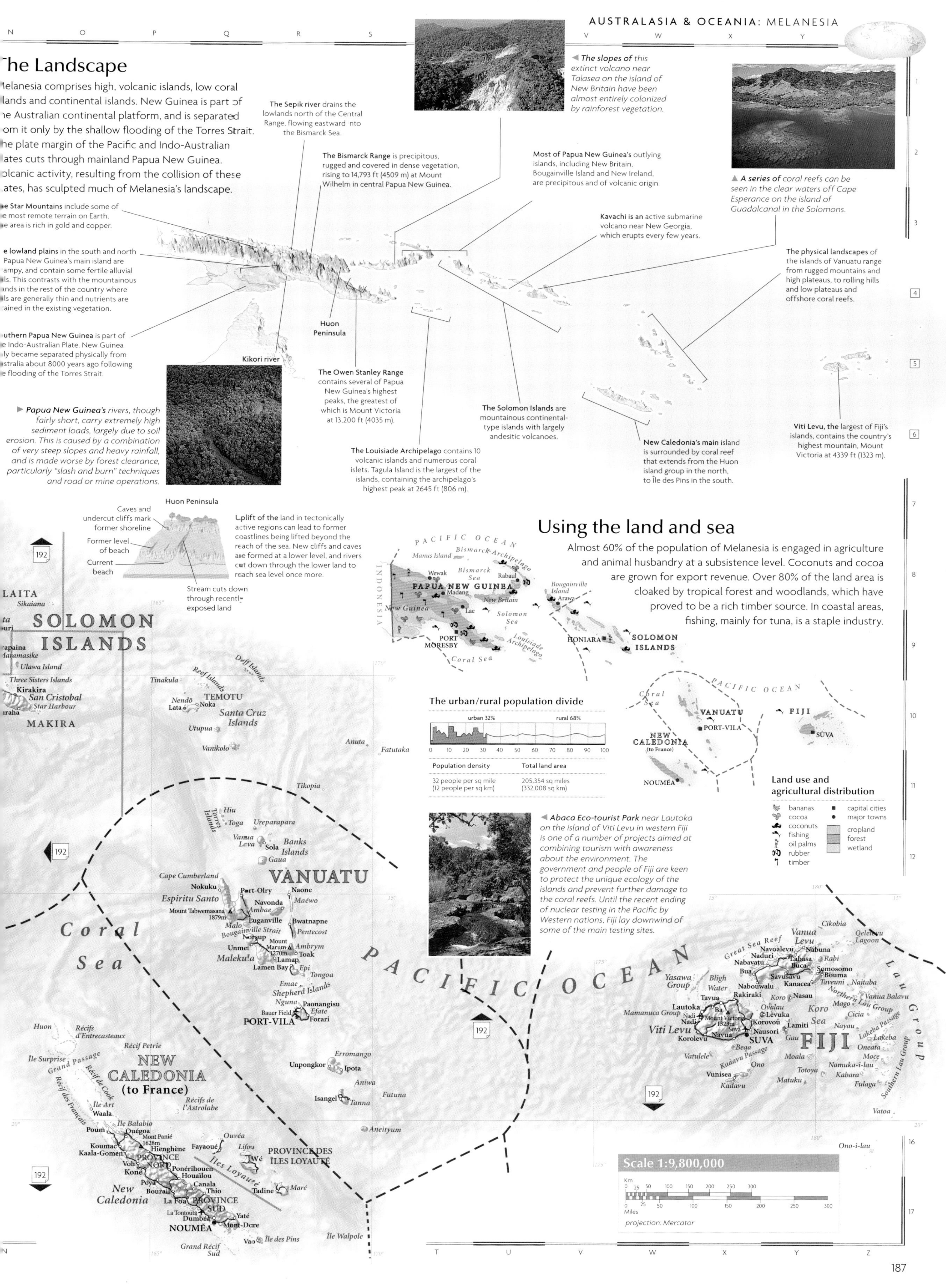
he Landscape
lelanesia comprises high, volcanic islands, low coral
lands and continental islands. New Guinea is part of
he Australian continental platform, and is separated
om it only by the shallow flooding of the Torres Strait.
he plate margin of the Pacific and Indo-Australian
ates cuts through mainland Papua New Guinea.
olcanic activity, resulting from the collision of these
ates, has sculpted much of Melanesia's landscape.
The Sepik river drains the lowlands north of the Central Range, flowing eastward into the Bismarck Sea.
The Bismarck Range is precipitous, rugged and covered in dense vegetation, rising to 14,793 ft (4509 m) at Mount Wilhelm in central Papua New Guinea.
Most of Papua New Guinea's outlying islands, including New Britain, Bougainville Island and New Ireland, are precipitous and of volcanic origin.
The slopes of this extinct volcano near Talasea on the island of New Britain have been almost entirely colonized by rainforest vegetation.
A series of coral reefs can be seen in the clear waters off Cape Esperance on the island of Guadalcanal in the Solomons.
e Star Mountains include some of e most remote terrain on Earth. e area is rich in gold and copper.
e lowland plains in the south and north Papua New Guinea's main island are ampy, and contain some fertile alluvial ils. This contrasts with the mountainous ands in the rest of the country where ils are generally thin and nutrients are ained in the existing vegetation.
Kavachi is an active submarine volcano near New Georgia, which erupts every few years.
The physical landscapes of the islands of Vanuatu range from rugged mountains and high plateaus, to rolling hills and low plateaus and offshore coral reefs.
uthern Papua New Guinea is part of e Indo-Australian Plate. New Guinea ly became separated physically from stralia about 8000 years ago following e flooding of the Torres Strait.
Huon Peninsula
Kikori river
The Owen Stanley Range contains several of Papua New Guinea's highest peaks, the greatest of which is Mount Victoria at 13,200 ft (4035 m).
The Solomon Islands are mountainous continental-type islands with largely andesitic volcanoes.
Viti Levu, the largest of Fiji's islands, contains the country's highest mountain, Mount Victoria at 4339 ft (1323 m).
Papua New Guinea's rivers, though fairly short, carry extremely high sediment loads, largely due to soil erosion. This is caused by a combination of very steep slopes and heavy rainfall, and is made worse by forest clearance, particularly "slash and burn" techniques and road or mine operations.
The Louisiade Archipelago contains 10 volcanic islands and numerous coral islets. Tagula Island is the largest of the islands, containing the archipelago's highest peak at 2645 ft (806 m).
New Caledonia's main island is surrounded by coral reef that extends from the Huon island group in the north, to Île des Pins in the south.
Huon Peninsula
Caves and undercut cliffs mark former shoreline
Former level of beach
Current beach
Stream cuts down through recently exposed land
Uplift of the land in tectonically active regions can lead to former coastlines being lifted beyond the reach of the sea. New cliffs and caves are formed at a lower level, and rivers cut down through the lower land to reach sea level once more.
Using the land and sea
Almost 60% of the population of Melanesia is engaged in agriculture and animal husbandry at a subsistence level. Coconuts and cocoa are grown for export revenue. Over 80% of the land area is cloaked by tropical forest and woodlands, which have proved to be a rich timber source. In coastal areas, fishing, mainly for tuna, is a staple industry.
PACIFIC OCEAN
PAPUA NEW GUINEA
PORT MORESBY
SOLOMON ISLANDS
HONIARA
VANUATU
PORT-VILA
FIJI
SUVA
NEW CALEDONIA (to France)
NOUMÉA
The urban/rural population divide
urban 32%
rural 68%
Population density
32 people per sq mile (12 people per sq km)
Total land area
205,354 sq miles (332,008 sq km)
Land use and agricultural distribution
bananas
cocoa
coconuts
fishing
oil palms
rubber
timber
capital cities
major towns
cropland
forest
wetland
Abaca Eco-tourist Park near Lautoka on the island of Viti Levu in western Fiji is one of a number of projects aimed at combining tourism with awareness about the environment. The government and people of Fiji are keen to protect the unique ecology of the islands and prevent further damage to the coral reefs. Until the recent ending of nuclear testing in the Pacific by Western nations, Fiji lay downwind of some of the main testing sites.
SOLOMON ISLANDS
VANUATU
NEW CALEDONIA (to France)
FIJI
Coral Sea
PACIFIC OCEAN
Scale 1:9,800,000
projection: Mercator
192

Micronesia

MARSHALL ISLANDS, MICRONESIA, NAURU, PALAU,
Guam, Northern Mariana Islands, Wake Island

The Micronesian islands lie in the western reaches of the Pacific Ocean and are all part of the same volcanic zone. The Federated States of Micronesia is the largest group, with more than 600 atolls and forested volcanic islands in an area of more than 1120 sq miles (2900 sq km). Micronesia is a mixture of former colonies, overseas territories, and dependencies. Most of the region still relies on aid and subsidies to sustain economies limited by resources, isolation, and an emigrating population, drawn to New Zealand and Australia by the attractions of a western lifestyle.

Palau

Palau is an archipelago of over 200 islands, only eight of which are inhabited. It was the last remaining UN trust territory in the Pacific, controlled by the US until 1994, when it became independent. The economy operates on a subsistence level, with coconuts and cassava the principal crops. Fishing licenses and tourism provide foreign currency.

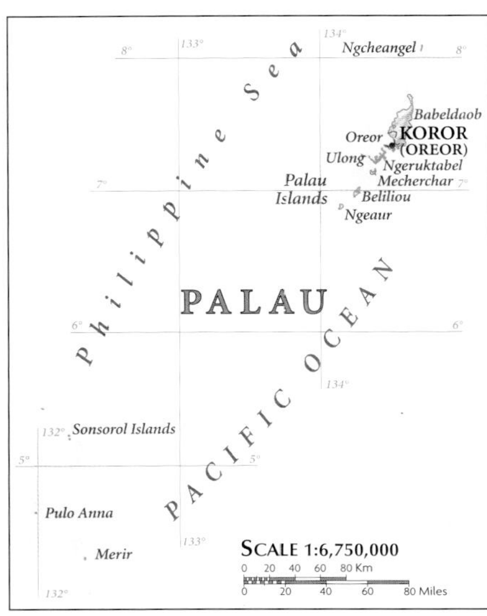

Philippine Sea
Ngcheangel
Babeldaob
Oreor
KOROR (OREOR)
Ulong
Ngeruktabel
Palau Islands
Mecherchar
Beliliou
Ngeaur
PALAU
PACIFIC OCEAN
Sonsorol Islands
Pulo Anna
Merir
SCALE 1:6,750,000
0 20 40 60 80 Km
0 20 40 60 80 Miles

SCALE 1:825,000
0 2.5 5 10 Km
0 2.5 5 10 Miles
Philippine Sea
Ngaregur
Ollei
Aiwokako Passage
Chol
Ngardmau Bay
Chelab
Ulimang
Ngetbong
Kgkeklau
Ngermechau
Imeong
West Passage
Namai Bay
Babeldaob
Ibobang
Melekeok
Ngchemiangel
Ngerkeai
Komebail Lagoon
Namekakl Passage
Arakabesan
Ngetkip
Airai
KOROR (OREOR)
Oikuul
Oreor
PACIFIC OCEAN

Guam *(to US)*

Lying at the southern end of the Mariana Islands, Guam is an important US military base and tourist destination. Social and political life is dominated by the indigenous Chamorro, who make up just under half the population, although the increasing prevalence of western culture threatens Guam's traditional social stability.

◀ *The tranquility of these coastal lagoons, at Inarajan in southern Guam, belies the fact that the island lies in a region where typhoons are common.*

Northern Mariana Islands *(to US)*

A US Commonwealth territory, the Northern Marianas comprise the whole of the Mariana archipelago except for Guam. The islands retain their close links with the US and continue to receive American aid. Tourism, though bringing in much-needed revenue, has speeded the decline of the traditional subsistence economy. Most of the population lives on Saipan.

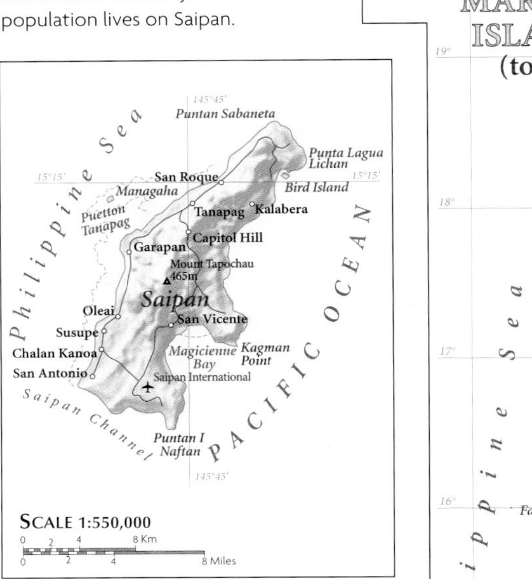

Philippine Sea
Puntan Sabaneta
Punta Lagua Lichan
San Roque
Managaha
Bird Island
Puetton Tanapag
Tanapag
Kalabera
Garapan
Capitol Hill
Mount Tapochau 465m
Saipan
Oleai
San Vicente
Susupe
Chalan Kanoa
Magicienne Bay
Kagman Point
San Antonio
Saipan International
Saipan Channel
Puntan I Naftan
PACIFIC OCEAN
SCALE 1:550,000
0 2 4 8 Km
0 2 4 8 Miles

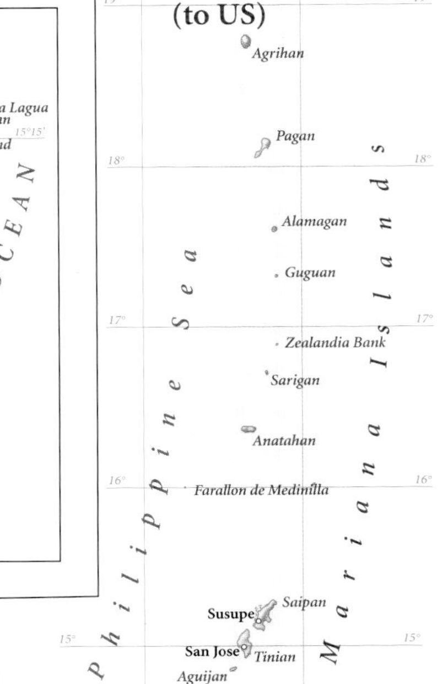

Farallon de Pajaros
Supply Reef
PACIFIC OCEAN
Maug Islands
Asuncion Island
NORTHERN MARIANA ISLANDS (to US)
Agrihan
Pagan
Alamagan
Guguan
Zealandia Bank
Sarigan
Anatahan
Farallon de Medinilla
Philippine Sea
Mariana Islands
Saipan
Susupe
San Jose
Tinian
Aguijan

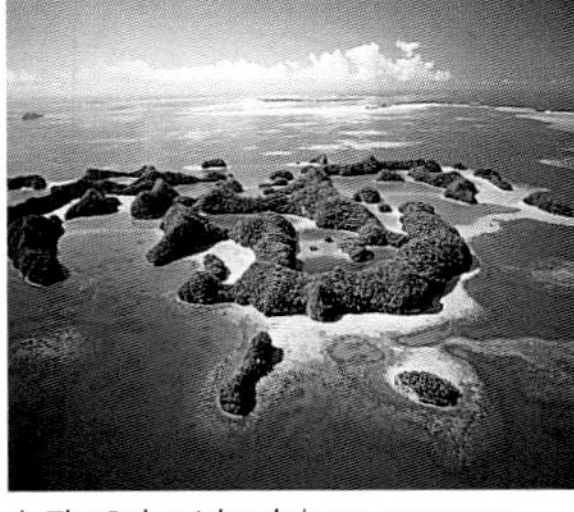

▲ *The Palau Islands have numerous hidden lakes and lagoons. These sustain their own ecosystems which have developed in isolation. This has produced adaptations in the animals and plants that are often unique to each lake.*

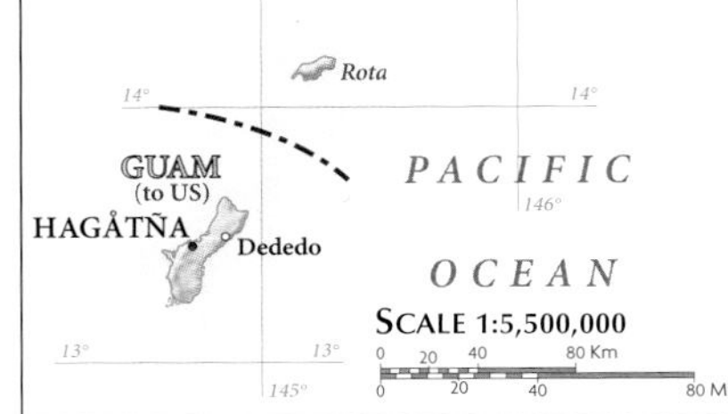

Rota
GUAM (to US)
HAGÅTÑA
Dededo
PACIFIC OCEAN
SCALE 1:5,500,000
0 20 40 80 Km
0 20 40 80 Miles

Micronesia

A mixture of high volcanic islands and low-lying coral atolls, the Federated States of Micronesia include all the Caroline Islands except Palau. Pohnpei, Kosrae, Chuuk, and Yap are the four main island cluster states, each of which has its own language, with English remaining the official language. Nearly half the population is concentrated on Pohnpei, the largest island. Independent since 1986, the islands continue to receive considerable aid from the US which supplements an economy based primarily on fishing and copra processing.

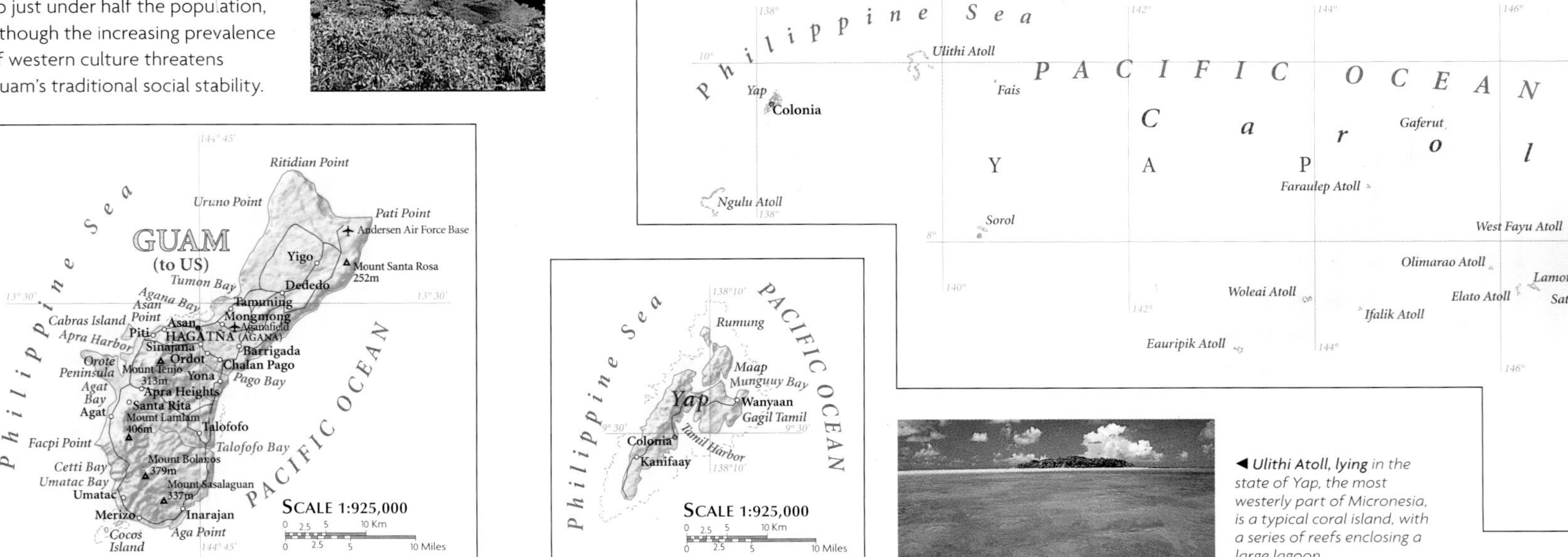

Philippine Sea
Ulithi Atoll
Fais
PACIFIC OCEAN
Yap
Colonia
CAROLINE
YAP
Gaferut
Faraulep Atoll
Ngulu Atoll
Sorol
West Fayu Atoll
Olimarao Atoll
Lamotrek
Woleai Atoll
Elato Atoll
Satawal
Ifalik Atoll
Eauripik Atoll
Ritidian Point
Uruno Point
Pati Point
Andersen Air Force Base
GUAM (to US)
Tumon Bay
Yigo
Dededo
Mount Santa Rosa 252m
Agana Bay
Tamuning
Cabras Island
Asan Point
Asan
Mongmong
Apra Harbor
Piti
HAGÅTÑA (AGANA)
Sinajana
Orote Peninsula
Ordot
Barrigada
Mount Tenjo 313m
Chalan Pago
Agat Bay
Yona
Pago Bay
Agat
Apra Heights
Santa Rita
Mount Lamlam 406m
Talofofo
Facpi Point
Talofofo Bay
Mount Bolanos 379m
Cetti Bay
Umatac Bay
Mount Sasalaguan 337m
Umatac
Merizo
Inarajan
Cocos Island
Aga Point
Philippine Sea
PACIFIC OCEAN
SCALE 1:925,000
0 2.5 5 10 Km
0 2.5 5 10 Miles
Rumung
Maap
Munguuy Bay
Yap
Wanyaan
Gagil Tamil
Tamil Harbor
Colonia
Kanifaay
SCALE 1:925,000
0 2.5 5 10 Km
0 2.5 5 10 Miles

◀ *Ulithi Atoll, lying in the state of Yap, the most westerly part of Micronesia, is a typical coral island, with a series of reefs enclosing a large lagoon.*

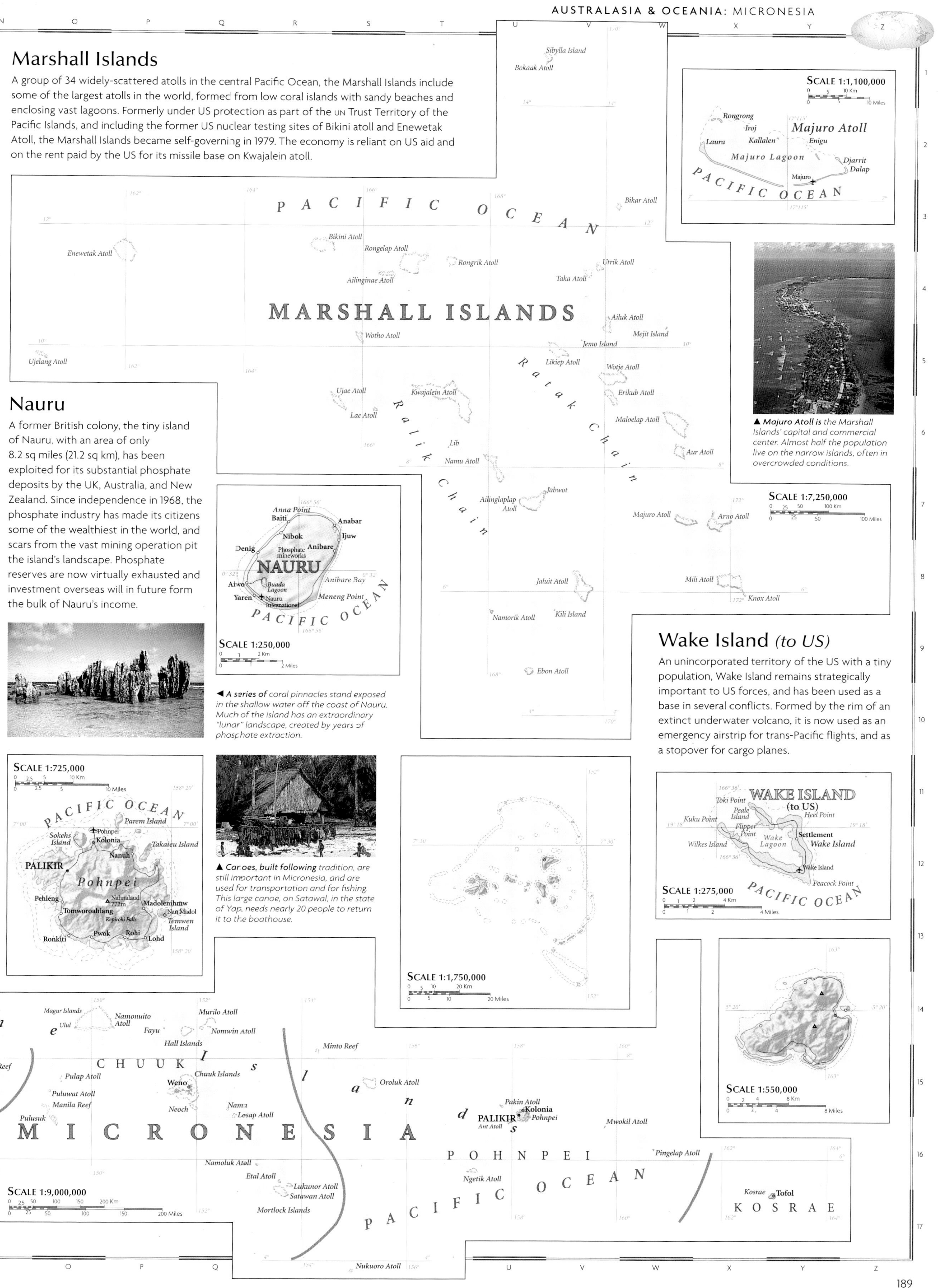

Sibylla Island
Bokaak Atoll
SCALE 1:1,100,000
Rongrong
Iroj
Majuro Atoll
Laura
Kallalen
Enigu
Majuro Lagoon
Djarrit
Dalap
Majuro
PACIFIC OCEAN
PACIFIC OCEAN
Bikar Atoll
Bikini Atoll
Rongelap Atoll
Enewetak Atoll
Rongrik Atoll
Utrik Atoll
Ailinginae Atoll
Taka Atoll
MARSHALL ISLANDS
Ailuk Atoll
Mejit Island
Wotho Atoll
Jemo Island
Ujelang Atoll
Likiep Atoll
Wotje Atoll
Ratak Chain
Ujae Atoll
Kwajalein Atoll
Erikub Atoll
Lae Atoll
Ralik Chain
Maloelap Atoll
Lib
Aur Atoll
Namu Atoll
Jabwot
Ailinglaplap Atoll
SCALE 1:7,250,000
Majuro Atoll
Arno Atoll
Jaluit Atoll
Mili Atoll
Knox Atoll
Namorik Atoll
Kili Island
Ebon Atoll
Anna Point
Baiti
Anabar
Nibok
Ijuw
Denig
Phosphate mineworks
Anibare
NAURU
Aiwo
Buada Lagoon
Anibare Bay
Yaren
Nauru International
Meneng Point
PACIFIC OCEAN
SCALE 1:250,000
SCALE 1:725,000
PACIFIC OCEAN
Parem Island
Pohnpei
Kolonia
Sokehs Island
Takaieu Island
Nanuh
PALIKIR
Pohnpei
Pehleng
Nahnalaud 772m
Madolenihmw
Tomworoahlang
Kepirohi Falls
Nan Madol
Temwen Island
Pwok
Rohi
Ronkiti
Lohd
SCALE 1:1,750,000
WAKE ISLAND (to US)
Toki Point
Peale Island
Kuku Point
Heel Point
Flipper Point
Wake Lagoon
Settlement
Wilkes Island
Wake Island
Peacock Point
SCALE 1:275,000
PACIFIC OCEAN
SCALE 1:550,000
Magur Islands
Namonuito Atoll
Murilo Atoll
Ulul
Fayu
Nomwin Atoll
Hall Islands
Minto Reef
CHUUK
Chuuk Islands
Pulap Atoll
Weno
Oroluk Atoll
Puluwat Atoll
Manila Reef
Neoch
Nama
Losap Atoll
Pakin Atoll
Kolonia
PALIKIR
Pohnpei
Ant Atoll
Mwokil Atoll
Pulusuk
MICRONESIA
Islands
POHNPEI
Pingelap Atoll
Namoluk Atoll
Etal Atoll
Ngetik Atoll
Lukunor Atoll
Satawan Atoll
Kosrae
Tofol
SCALE 1:9,000,000
Mortlock Islands
PACIFIC OCEAN
KOSRAE
Nukuoro Atoll

Marshall Islands

A group of 34 widely-scattered atolls in the central Pacific Ocean, the Marshall Islands include some of the largest atolls in the world, formed from low coral islands with sandy beaches and enclosing vast lagoons. Formerly under US protection as part of the UN Trust Territory of the Pacific Islands, and including the former US nuclear testing sites of Bikini atoll and Enewetak Atoll, the Marshall Islands became self-governing in 1979. The economy is reliant on US aid and on the rent paid by the US for its missile base on Kwajalein atoll.

▲ *Majuro Atoll is the Marshall Islands' capital and commercial center. Almost half the population live on the narrow islands, often in overcrowded conditions.*

Nauru

A former British colony, the tiny island of Nauru, with an area of only 8.2 sq miles (21.2 sq km), has been exploited for its substantial phosphate deposits by the UK, Australia, and New Zealand. Since independence in 1968, the phosphate industry has made its citizens some of the wealthiest in the world, and scars from the vast mining operation pit the island's landscape. Phosphate reserves are now virtually exhausted and investment overseas will in future form the bulk of Nauru's income.

◀ *A series of coral pinnacles stand exposed in the shallow water off the coast of Nauru. Much of the island has an extraordinary "lunar" landscape, created by years of phosphate extraction.*

▲ *Canoes, built following tradition, are still important in Micronesia, and are used for transportation and for fishing. This large canoe, on Satawal, in the state of Yap, needs nearly 20 people to return it to the boathouse.*

Wake Island *(to US)*

An unincorporated territory of the US with a tiny population, Wake Island remains strategically important to US forces, and has been used as a base in several conflicts. Formed by the rim of an extinct underwater volcano, it is now used as an emergency airstrip for trans-Pacific flights, and as a stopover for cargo planes.

Polynesia

KIRIBATI, TUVALU, Cook Islands, Easter Island, French Polynesia, Niue, Pitcairn Islands, Tokelau, Wallis & Futuna

The numerous island groups of Polynesia lie to the east of Australia, scattered over a vast area in the south Pacific. The islands are a mixture of low-lying coral atolls, some of which enclose lagoons, and the tips of great underwater volcanoes. The populations on the islands are small, and most people are of Polynesian origin, as are the Maori of New Zealand. Local economies remain simple, relying mainly on subsistence crops, mineral deposits, many now exhausted, fishing, and tourism.

Kiribati

A former British colony, Kiribati became independent in 1979. Banaba's phosphate deposits ran out in 1980, following decades of exploitation by the British. Economic development remains slow and most agriculture is at a subsistence level, though coconuts provide export income, and underwater agriculture is being developed.

PACIFIC OCEAN
Iku
Buariki
Taratai
Abaokoro
Marenanuka
Nabeina
Tabiteuea
Tarawa
Bikeman
Bonriki
Bikenebu
Betio
Eita
Tarawa
BAIRIKI
Banraeaba
SCALE 1:1,100,000
0 5 10 Km
0 5 10 Miles

▶ *With the exception of Banaba all the islands in Kiribati's three groups are low-lying, coral atolls. This aerial view shows the sparsely vegetated islands, intercut by many small lagoons.*

Tuvalu

A chain of nine coral atolls, 360 miles (579 km) long with a land area of just over 9 sq miles (23 sq km), Tuvalu is one of the world's smallest and most isolated states. As the Ellice Islands, Tuvalu was linked to the Gilbert Islands (now part of Kiribati) as a British colony until independence in 1978. Politically and socially conservative, Tuvaluans live by fishing and subsistence farming.

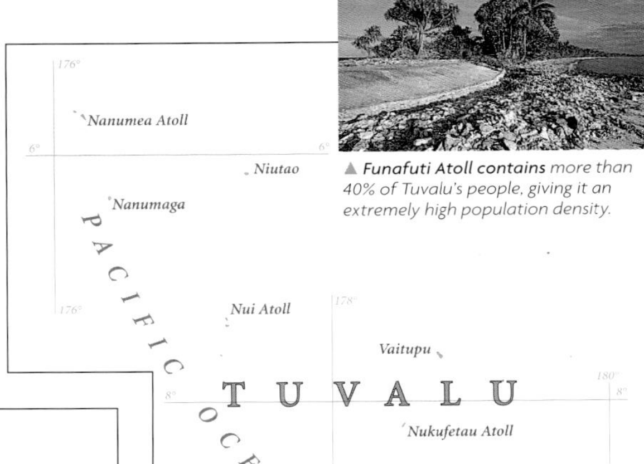
Nanumea Atoll
Niutao
Nanumaga
PACIFIC

▲ ***Funafuti Atoll contains** more than 40% of Tuvalu's people, giving it an extremely high population density.*

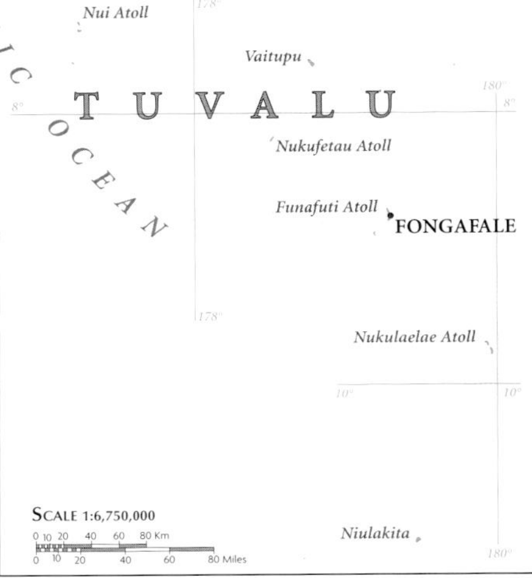
Nui Atoll
Vaitupu
TUVALU
OCEAN
Nukufetau Atoll
Funafuti Atoll
FONGAFALE
Nukulaelae Atoll
Niulakita
SCALE 1:6,750,000

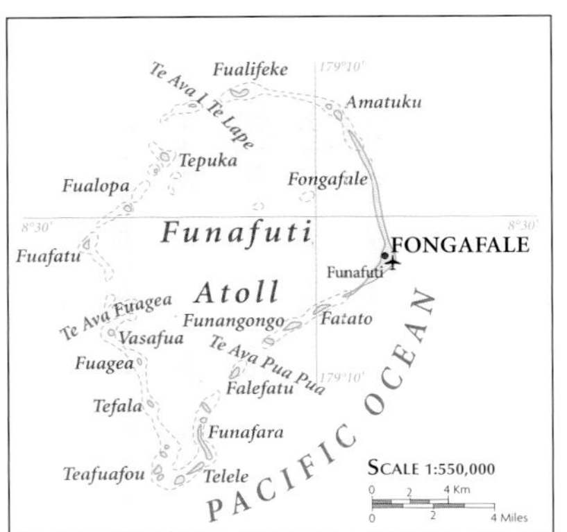
Fualifeke
Te Ava I Te Lape
Amatuku
Tepuka
Fongafale
Fualopa
Funafuti
FONGAFALE
Fuafatu
Atoll
Funafuti
Te Ava Fuagea
Funangongo
Fatato
Vasafua
Fuagea
Te Ava Pua Pua
Falefatu
Tefala
Funafara
Teafuafou
Telele
PACIFIC OCEAN
SCALE 1:550,000

Tokelau *(to New Zealand)*

A low-lying coral atoll, Tokelau is a dependent territory of New Zealand with few natural resources. Although a 1990 cyclone destroyed crops and infrastructure, a tuna cannery and the sale of fishing licenses have raised revenue and a catamaran link between the islands has increased their tourism potential. Tokelau's small size and economic weakness makes independence from New Zealand unlikely.

▲ ***Fishermen cast their** nets to catch small fish in the shallow waters off Atafu Atoll, the most westerly island in Tokelau.*

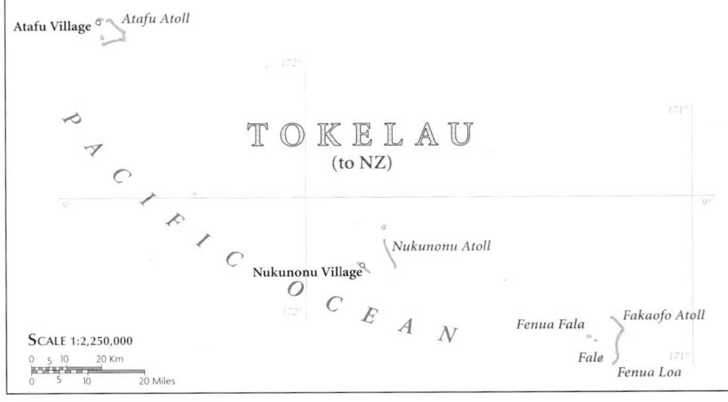
Atafu Village
Atafu Atoll
TOKELAU
(to NZ)
PACIFIC OCEAN
Nukunonu Atoll
Nukunonu Village
Fenua Fala
Fakaofo Atoll
Fale
Fenua Loa
SCALE 1:2,250,000

Wallis & Futuna
(to France)

In contrast to other French overseas territories in the south Pacific, the inhabitants of Wallis and Futuna have shown little desire for greater autonomy. A subsistence economy produces a variety of tropical crops, while foreign currency remittances come from expatriates and from the sale of licenses to Japanese and Korean fishing fleets.

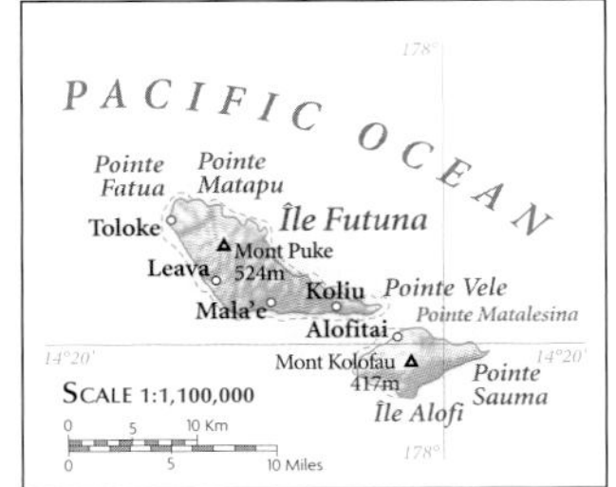
PACIFIC OCEAN
Pointe Fatua
Pointe Matapu
Île Futuna
Toloke
Mont Puke 524m
Leava
Kolia
Pointe Vele
Pointe Matalesina
Mala'e
Alofitai
Mont Kolofau 417m
Pointe Sauma
Île Alofi
SCALE 1:1,100,000

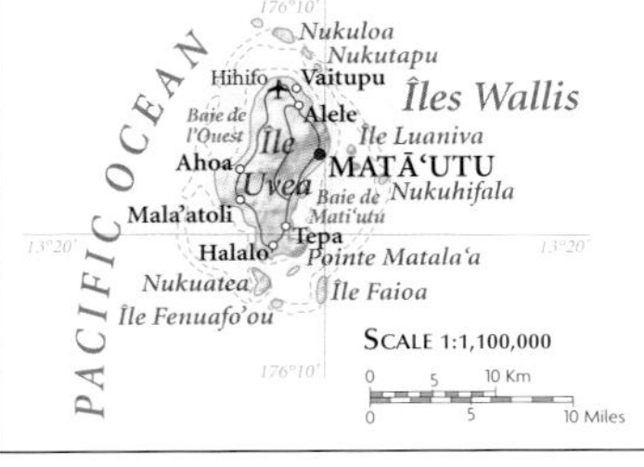
Nukuloa
Nukutapu
Hihifo
Vaitupu
Îles Wallis
Baie de l'Ouest
Alele
Île Luaniva
Ahoa
Île Uvea
MATĀ'UTU
Baie de Mati'utu
Nukuhifala
Mala'atoli
Tepa
Halalo
Pointe Matala'a
Nukuatea
Île Faioa
Île Fenuafo'ou
PACIFIC OCEAN
SCALE 1:1,100,000

Cook Islands *(to New Zealand)*

A mixture of coral atolls and volcanic peaks, the Cook Islands achieved self-government in 1965 but exist in free association with New Zealand. A diverse economy includes pearl and giant clam farming, and an ostrich farm, plus tourism and banking. A 1991 friendship treaty with France provides for French surveillance of territorial waters.

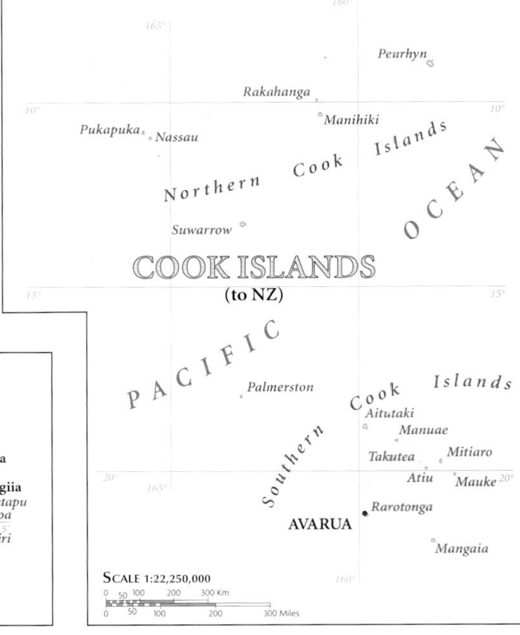
Peurhyn
Rakahanga
Manihiki
Pukapuka
Nassau
Northern Cook Islands
Suwarrow
OCEAN
COOK ISLANDS
(to NZ)
PACIFIC
Palmerston
Southern Cook Islands
Aitutaki
Manuae
Takutea
Mitiaro
Atiu
Mauke
Rarotonga
AVARUA
Mangaia
SCALE 1:22,250,000

Niue *(to New Zealand)*

Niue, the world's largest coral island, is self-governing but exists in free association with New Zealand. Tropical fruits are grown for local consumption; tourism and the sale of postage stamps provide foreign currency. The lack of local job prospects has led more than 10,000 Niueans to emigrate to New Zealand, which has now invested heavily in Niue's economy in the hope of reversing this trend.

▲ ***Palm trees fringe** the white sands of a beach on Aitutaki in the Southern Cook Islands, where tourism is of increasing economic importance.*

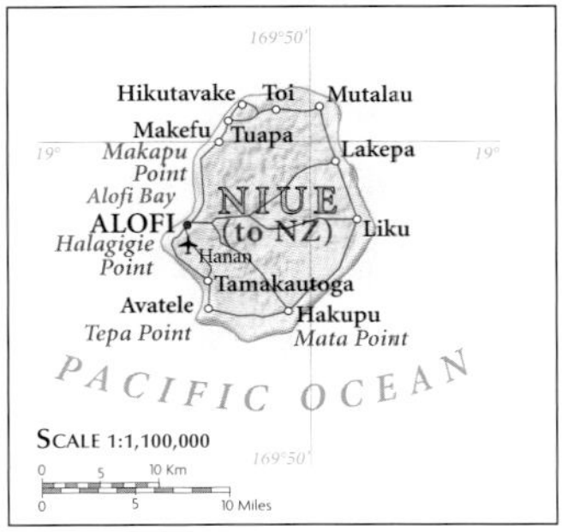
Hikutavake
Toi
Mutalau
Makefu
Tuapa
Makapu Point
Lakepa
Alofi Bay
ALOFI
NIUE
(to NZ)
Liku
Halagigie Point
Hanan
Tamakautoga
Avatele
Hakupu
Tepa Point
Mata Point
PACIFIC OCEAN
SCALE 1:1,100,000

▲ ***Waves have cut** back the original coastline, exposing a sandy beach, near Mutalau in the northeast corner of Niue.*

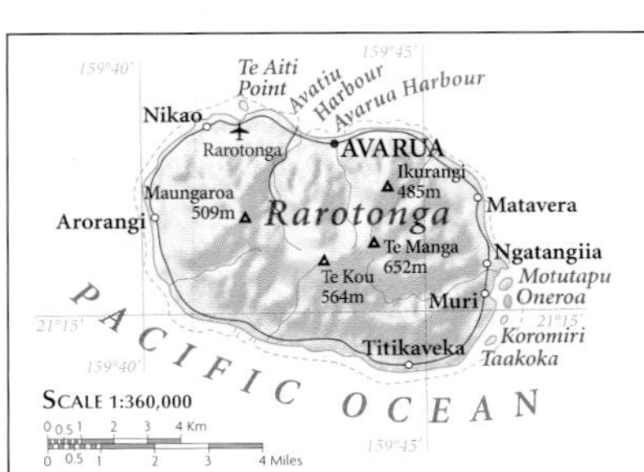
Te Aiti Point
Avatiu Harbour
Avarua Harbour
Nikao
Rarotonga
AVARUA
Ikurangi 485m
Maungaroa 509m
Rarotonga
Matavera
Arorangi
Te Manga 652m
Te Kou 564m
Ngatangiia
Motutapu
Muri
Oneroa
Titikaveka
Koromiri
Taakoka
PACIFIC OCEAN
SCALE 1:360,000

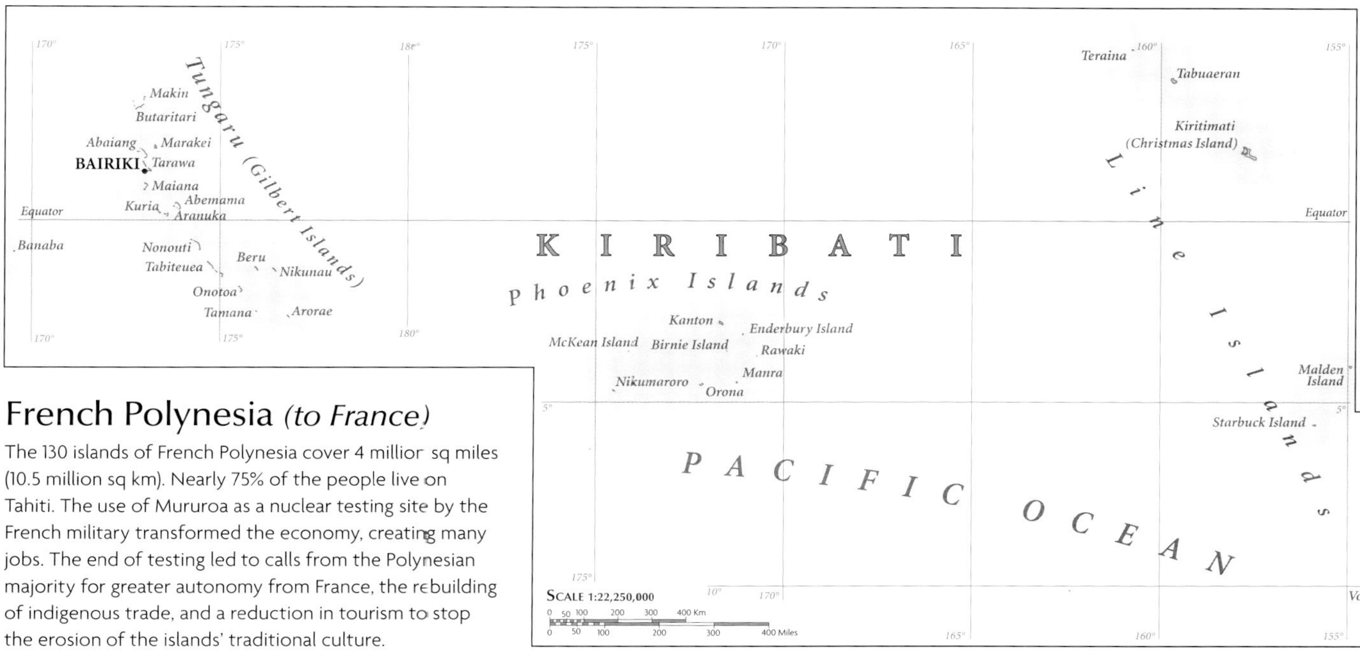

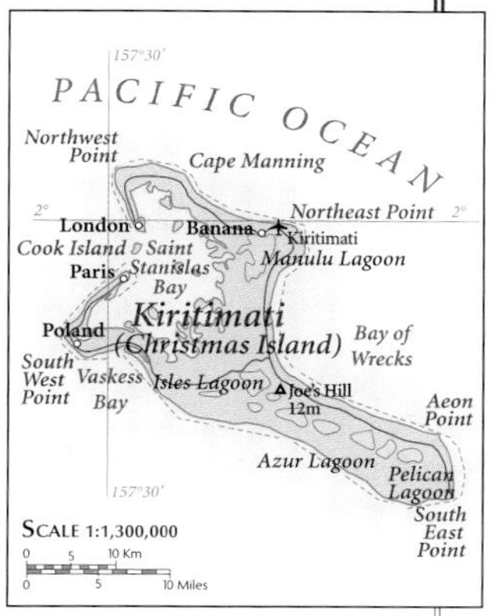

French Polynesia *(to France)*

The 130 islands of French Polynesia cover 4 million sq miles (10.5 million sq km). Nearly 75% of the people live on Tahiti. The use of Mururoa as a nuclear testing site by the French military transformed the economy, creating many jobs. The end of testing led to calls from the Polynesian majority for greater autonomy from France, the rebuilding of indigenous trade, and a reduction in tourism to stop the erosion of the islands' traditional culture.

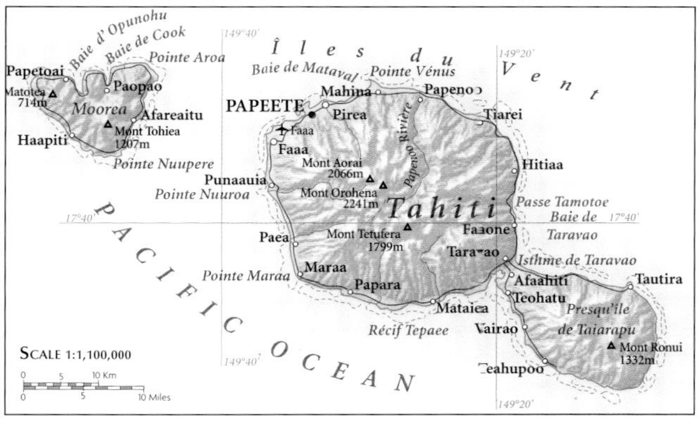

◀ *The traditional Tahitian welcome for visitors, who are greeted by parties of canoes, has become a major tourist attraction.*

Pitcairn Islands *(to UK)*

Britain's most isolated dependency, Pitcairn Island was first populated by mutineers from the HMS *Bounty* in 1790. Emigration is further depleting the already limited gene pool of the island's inhabitants, with associated social and health problems. Barter, fishing, and subsistence farming form the basis of the economy although postage stamp sales provide foreign currency earnings, and offshore mineral exploitation may boost the economy in future.

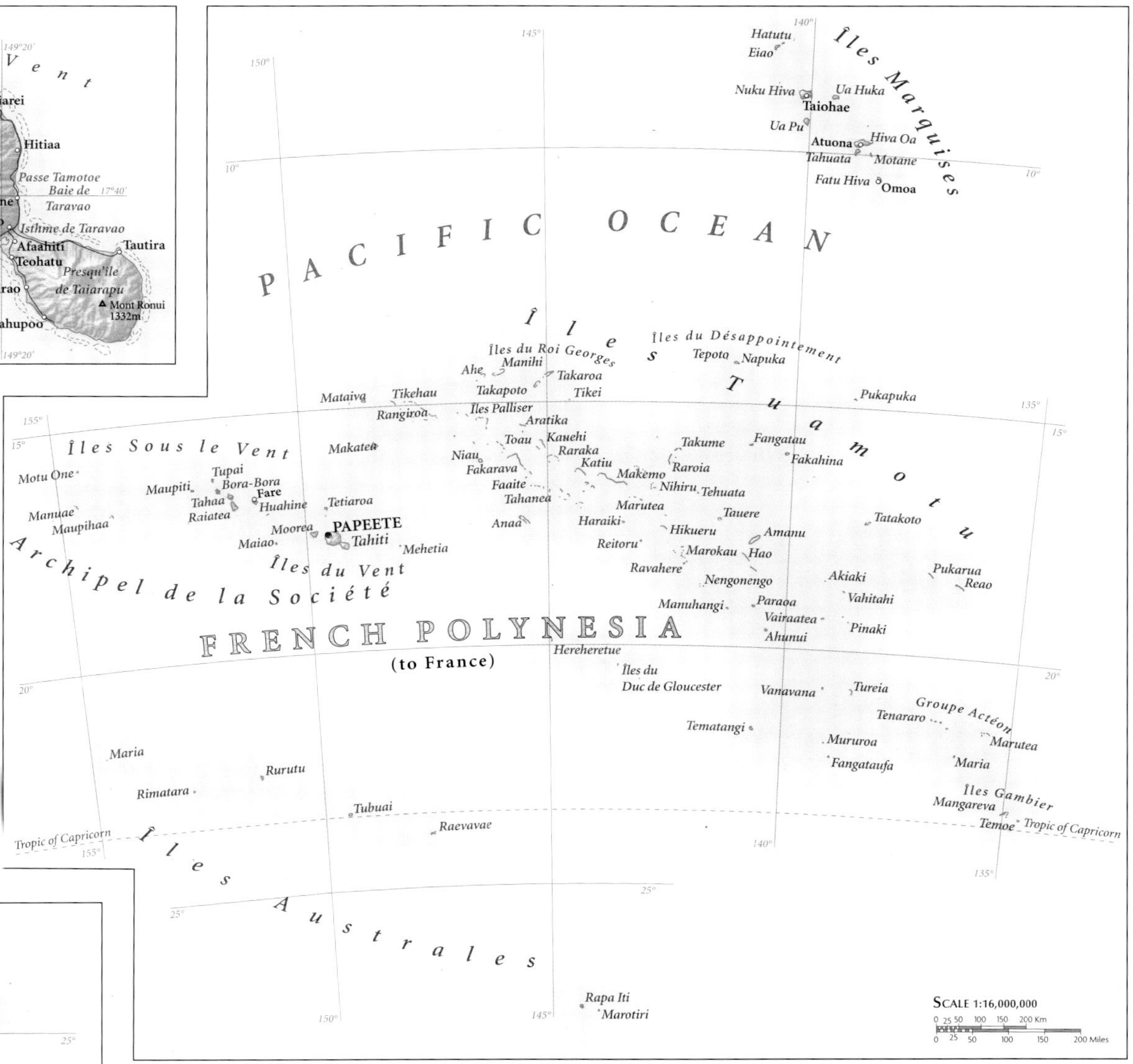

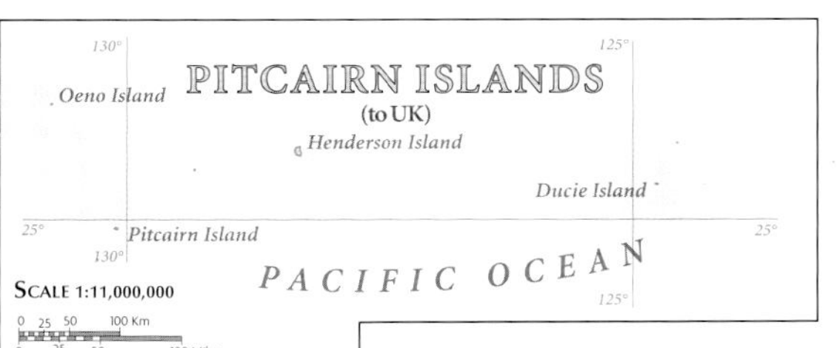
PITCAIRN ISLANDS
(to UK)
Oeno Island
Henderson Island
Ducie Island
Pitcairn Island
PACIFIC OCEAN
SCALE 1:11,000,000

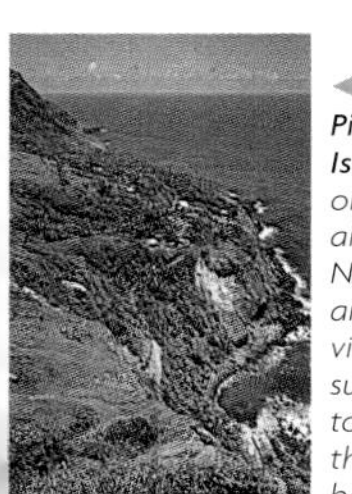

◀ *The Pitcairn Islanders rely on regular airdrops from New Zealand and periodic visits by supply vessels to provide them with basic commodities.*

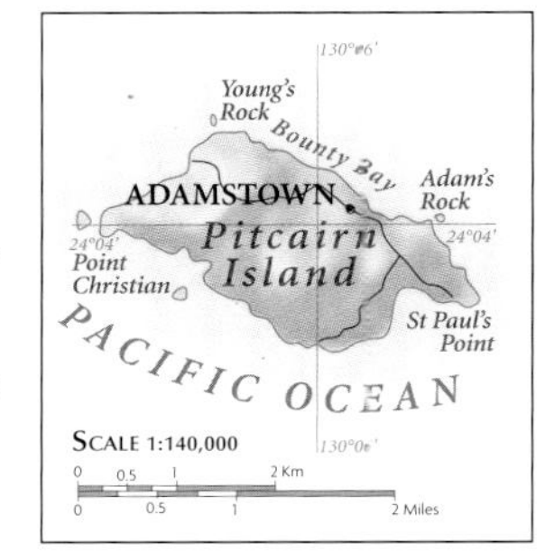
Young's Rock
Bounty Bay
ADAMSTOWN
Adam's Rock
Pitcairn Island
Point Christian
St Paul's Point
PACIFIC OCEAN
SCALE 1:140,000

Easter Island *(to Chile)*

One of the most easterly islands in Polynesia, Easter Island *(Isla de Pascua)* – also known as Rapa Nui, is part of Chile. The mainly Polynesian inhabitants support themselves by farming, which is mainly of a subsistence nature, and includes cattle rearing and crops such as sugar cane, bananas, corn, gourds, and potatoes. In recent years, tourism has become the most important source of income and the island sustains a small commercial airport.

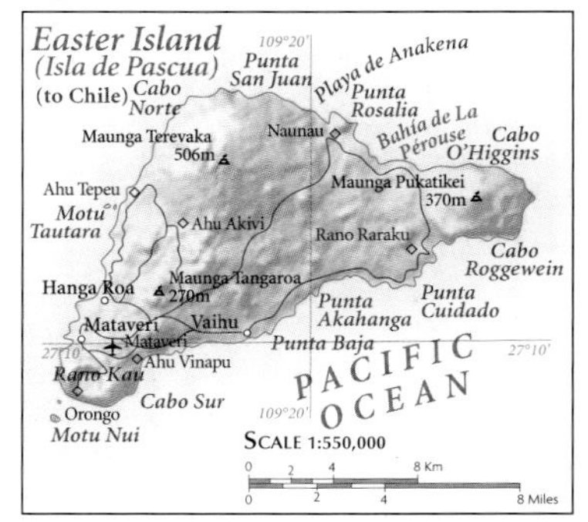
Easter Island
(Isla de Pascua)
(to Chile)
Cabo Norte
Punta San Juan
Playa de Anakena
Punta Rosalia
Bahía de La Pérouse
Cabo O'Higgins
Maunga Terevaka 506m
Naunau
Maunga Pukatikei 370m
Ahu Tepeu
Motu Tautara
Ahu Akivi
Rano Raraku
Cabo Roggewein
Hanga Roa
Maunga Tangaroa 270m
Mataveri
Vaihu
Punta Akahanga
Punta Cuidado
Ahu Vinapu
Punta Baja
Rano Kau
Orongo
Motu Nui
Cabo Sur
PACIFIC OCEAN
SCALE 1:550,000

▲ ***The Naunau**, a series of huge stone statues overlook Playa de Anakena, on Easter Island. Carved from a soft volcanic rock, they were erected between 400 and 900 years ago.*

The Pacific Ocean

The Pacific is the world's largest and deepest ocean. It is nearly twice the area of the Atlantic and contains almost three times as much water. The ocean is dotted with islands and surrounded by some of the world's most populous states; over half the world's population lives on its shores. The Pacific is bordered by active plate margins known as the "Ring of Fire," causing earthquakes and tsunamis, and creating volcanic islands and subterranean mountain chains. The largest underwater mountains break the surface as island arcs. The fisheries of the Pacific are some of the most productive in the world and provide a vital resource for many of the Pacific islands. Since the Second World War there has been a shift in trading patterns, with a considerable growth in trade between the US and the countries of the Pacific Rim.

The Ring of Fire

The active plate margins surrounding the Pacific have created numerous land and island volcanoes along its border. The actual basin of the Pacific is made up of a number of separate tectonic plates which move away from each other, colliding with other plates. When they collide, the oceanic plates, being thinner, are forced beneath the thicker continental plates, forming deep ocean trenches and high ridges. These collision zones are known as subduction zones and are characterized by intense seismic and volcanic activity.

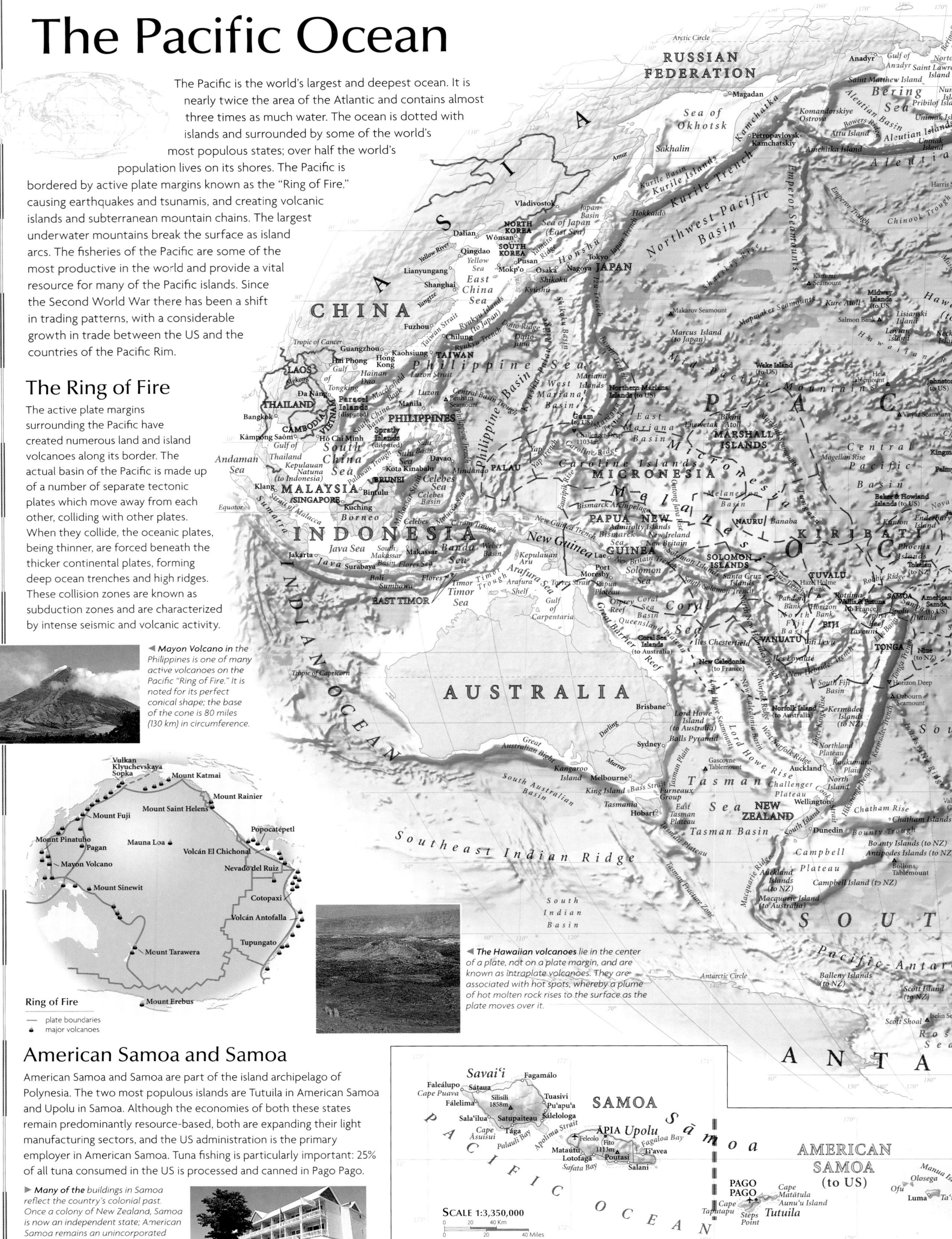

RUSSIAN FEDERATION
ASIA
CHINA
INDONESIA
AUSTRALIA
PACIFIC OCEAN
INDIAN OCEAN
JAPAN
PHILIPPINES
MICRONESIA
MARSHALL ISLANDS
PAPUA NEW GUINEA
SOLOMON ISLANDS
VANUATU
FIJI
TONGA
TUVALU
KIRIBATI
NEW ZEALAND
EAST TIMOR
MALAYSIA
SINGAPORE
BRUNEI
THAILAND
CAMBODIA
VIETNAM
LAOS
TAIWAN
PALAU
Sea of Okhotsk
Bering Sea
Sea of Japan (East Sea)
East China Sea
Philippine Sea
South China Sea
Coral Sea
Tasman Sea
Northwest Pacific Basin
Central Pacific Basin
Southeast Indian Ridge
South Indian Basin
Ring of Fire
plate boundaries
major volcanoes
Mount Katmai
Mount Rainier
Mount Saint Helens
Mount Fuji
Mount Pinatubo
Mayon Volcano
Mauna Loa
Popocatépetl
Volcán El Chichonal
Nevado del Ruiz
Cotopaxi
Volcán Antofalla
Tupungato
Mount Tarawera
Mount Erebus
SAMOA
AMERICAN SAMOA (to US)
Savai'i
Upolu
Tutuila
APIA
PAGO PAGO
PACIFIC OCEAN
SCALE 1:3,350,000

◀ *Mayon Volcano in the Philippines is one of many active volcanoes on the Pacific "Ring of Fire." It is noted for its perfect conical shape; the base of the cone is 80 miles (130 km) in circumference.*

◀ ***The Hawaiian volcanoes** lie in the center of a plate, not on a plate margin, and are known as intraplate volcanoes. They are associated with hot spots, whereby a plume of hot molten rock rises to the surface as the plate moves over it.*

American Samoa and Samoa

American Samoa and Samoa are part of the island archipelago of Polynesia. The two most populous islands are Tutuila in American Samoa and Upolu in Samoa. Although the economies of both these states remain predominantly resource-based, both are expanding their light manufacturing sectors, and the US administration is the primary employer in American Samoa. Tuna fishing is particularly important: 25% of all tuna consumed in the US is processed and canned in Pago Pago.

▶ ***Many of the** buildings in Samoa reflect the country's colonial past. Once a colony of New Zealand, Samoa is now an independent state; American Samoa remains an unincorporated territory of the United States.*

The Landscape

Although it is still the largest ocean, the basin of the Pacific has been gradually decreasing in size due to the movement of the Indo-Australian Plate. The oldest parts are about 135 million years old. The eastern border of the Pacific is characterized by a continuous mountain chain running the length of the North and South American continents. The eastern basin has a low, uninterrupted relief, at depths averaging 15,000 ft (4570 m). In contrast, the western Pacific is scattered with island arcs and bounded by a series of deep ocean trenches. An almost continuous chain of volcanoes surrounds the ocean and an active mid-ocean ridge runs northeast–southwest.

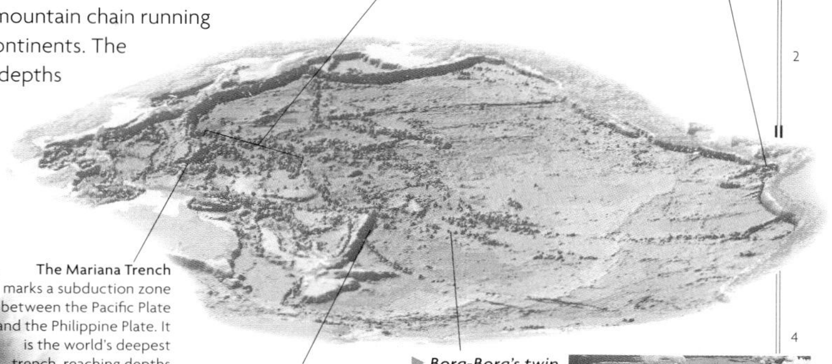

Micronesia consists of numerous small, oceanic islands in the western Pacific. The Micronesian islands are all oceanic in origin, rising directly up from the ocean floor.

The Peru–Chile Trench is the longest trench in the Pacific, extending 3660 miles (5900 km), and following the line of the Andes mountain range down the west coast of South America.

The Mariana Trench marks a subduction zone between the Pacific Plate and the Philippine Plate. It is the world's deepest trench, reaching depths of 36,201 ft (11,034 m).

The Tonga Trench lies north of New Zealand's North Island. The trench reaches average depths of 34,448 ft (10,500 m), which is more than twice the average depth of the ocean.

▶ ***Bora-Bora's twin mountain*** *peaks are the remnants of an ancient volcano, now surrounded by a large lagoon, fringed with coral.*

Scale 1:67,500,000

projection: Mollweide

Map key

Population: below 10,000

Elevation: 1000m / 3281ft; 500m / 1640ft; 250m / 820ft; 100m / 328ft; sea level

Sea Depth: sea level; 250m / 820ft; 500m / 1640ft; 1000m / 3281ft; 2000m / 6562ft; 3000m / 9843ft; 5000m / 16,410ft

▶ ***Wave action has*** *eroded this shoreline near Port Campbell in southeastern Australia leaving isolated pinnacles of rock cut off from the main coastline. They are known as the "Twelve Apostles."*

Tonga

The Kingdom of Tonga lies in the southwest Pacific, about 2000 miles (3000 km) off the east coast of Australia. It comprises 169 islands of which only 36 are permanently inhabited. The majority of the population live on the largest island, Tongatapu. There are only three sizeable towns and the main commercial center is the capital Nuku'alofa. Tonga's economy is based mainly on agriculture; coconuts, bananas, and vanilla are grown as cash crops for export. Although there is some light manufacturing, growing land shortages have forced increased migration to New Zealand and Australia.

◀ ***Coral reefs and*** *atolls are found throughout the warm waters of the south Pacific. Reefs build up from the skeletons of millions of coral polyps – tiny sea creatures that cling to the reef and secrete calcium carbonate around their bodies, forming a hard protective skeleton.*

▼ ***The islands of*** *Tonga fall into two belts; those in the east are low, coral islands, while those in the west are high and volcanic. Four of the islands still contain active volcanoes. The mountainous, western islands are covered with verdant tropical vegetation.*

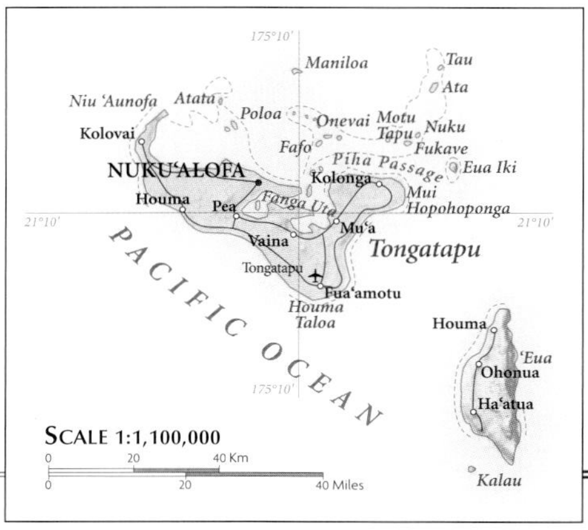

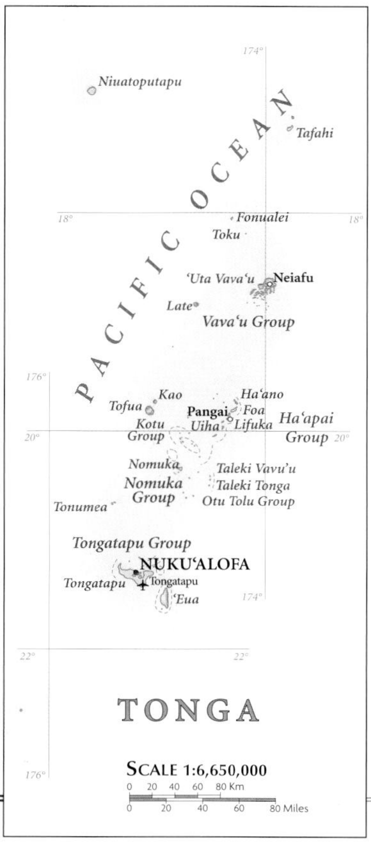

SCALE 1:1,100,000

TONGA

SCALE 1:6,650,000

Antarctica

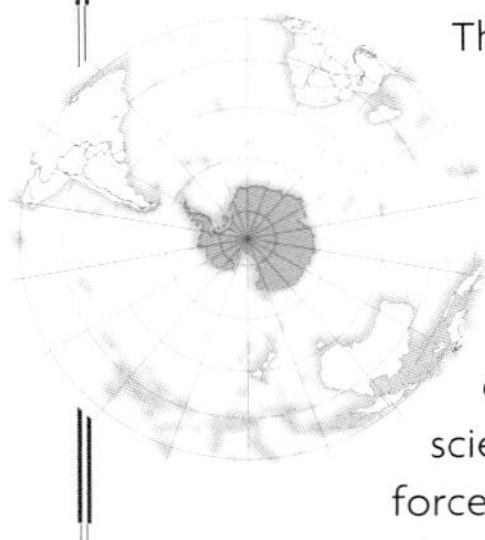

The ice-covered continent of Antarctica, which is the Earth's most southerly region, has drawn explorers and entrepreneurs seeking challenge and riches in its wintry lands for over 200 years. The extreme climate has deterred any large-scale settlement of the continent, and though commercial hunters built outposts in the past, habitation is now limited to scientific bases. The Antarctic Treaty, which came into force in 1961, provides for international governance and scientific cooperation in place of potential territorial conflict.

Resources

Many ore minerals, including iron and gold, are found in the Antarctic, and there are also coal reserves in the Transantarctic Mountains. The severe conditions and environmental importance of the region mean that exploitation of potential mineral resources is both uneconomic and undesirable. The unique wildlife and landscape draw a small number of tourists annually.

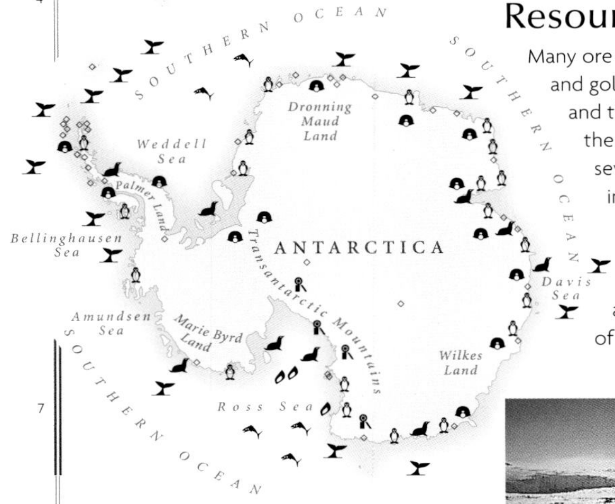

Resources (including wildlife)

- coal
- fish
- minerals
- oil & gas
- penguins
- seals
- whales
- polar research base

◀ *Most settlements in Antarctica are research bases such as this one at Rothera on Adelaide Island, although there is a small Chilean settlement on King George Island.*

The landscape

There are two distinct parts to Antarctica: Lesser Antarctica, a series of ice-covered, mountainous islands, joined together by the ice; and the high plateau of Greater Antarctica. The Ross Sea and the Weddell Sea are outliers of the Southern Ocean – deep bays partially covered by thick ice shelves.

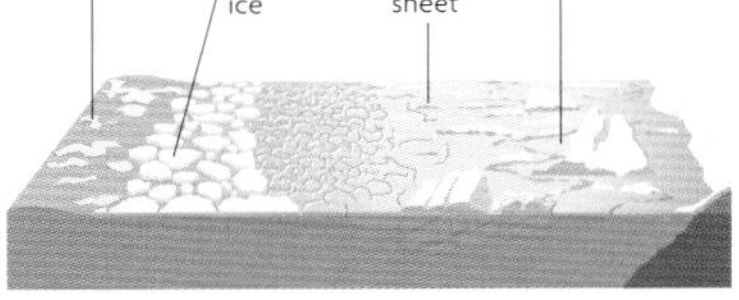

Grease ice · Pancake ice · Sea-ice sheet · Ice floe

▲ *Pack ice forms out at sea in freezing temperatures. At the outer limits, grease ice congeals on the surface of the ocean. This is then spun around by wind and waves into irregular "pancakes," freezing and breaking up several times before bonding together again to form sea-ice sheets, which finally cement into enormous ice floes.*

◀ *On Elephant Island, the coast is edged by glaciers, although the land is not permanently covered by ice.*

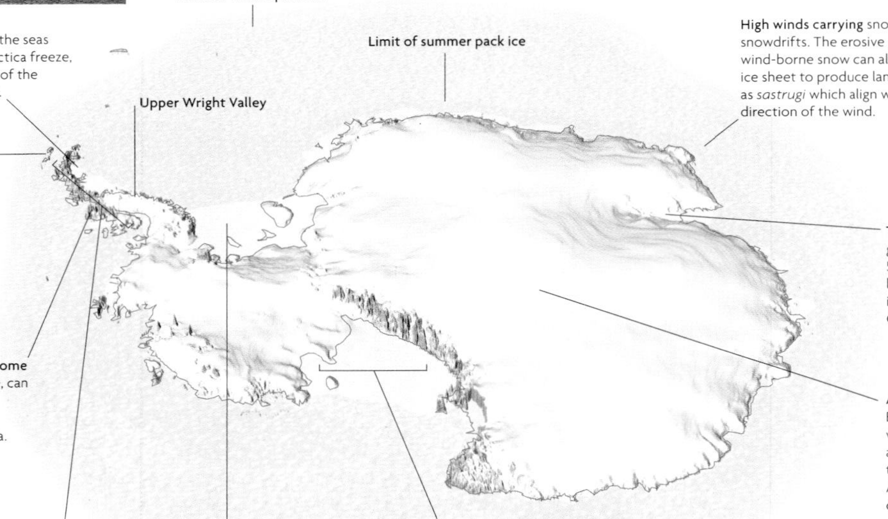

Limit of winter pack ice

Limit of summer pack ice

Upper Wright Valley

Elephant Island

During the winter the seas surrounding Antarctica freeze, increasing the size of the continent by 100%.

High winds carrying snow form huge snowdrifts. The erosive power of the wind-borne snow can also sculpt the ice sheet to produce landforms known as *sastrugi* which align with the direction of the wind.

The Lambert Glacier is the largest glacier system in the world, up to 50 miles (80 km) wide at its seaward limit, and reaching 180 miles (300 km) into the interior by way of the Prince Charles Mountains.

Many volcanoes, some of them still active, can be found in the mountains of the Antarctic Peninsula.

Antarctica is the highest continent on Earth, because of the great thickness of ice which overlays the land. In places the ice alone can each up to 15,700 ft (4800 m) thick. Much of the basement rock of west Antarctica lies below sea level, pushed down by the weight of the ice.

The mountainous Antarctic Peninsula is formed of rocks 65–225 million years old, overlain by more recent rocks and glacial deposits. It is connected to the Andes in South America by a submarine ridge.

Nearly half – 44% – of the Antarctic coastline is bounded by ice shelves, like the Ronne Ice Shelf, which float on the Ocean. These are joined to the inland ice sheet by dome-shaped ice "rises."

More than 30% of Antarctic ice is contained in the Ross Ice Shelf.

◀ *The barren, flat-bottomed Upper Wright Valley was once filled by a glacier, but is now dry, strewn with boulders and pebbles. In some dry valleys, there has been no rain for over 2 million years.*

▲ *Large colonies of seabirds live in the extremely harsh Antarctic climate. The Emperor penguins seen here, the smaller Adélie penguin, the Antarctic petrel, and the South Polar skua are the only birds that breed exclusively on the continent.*

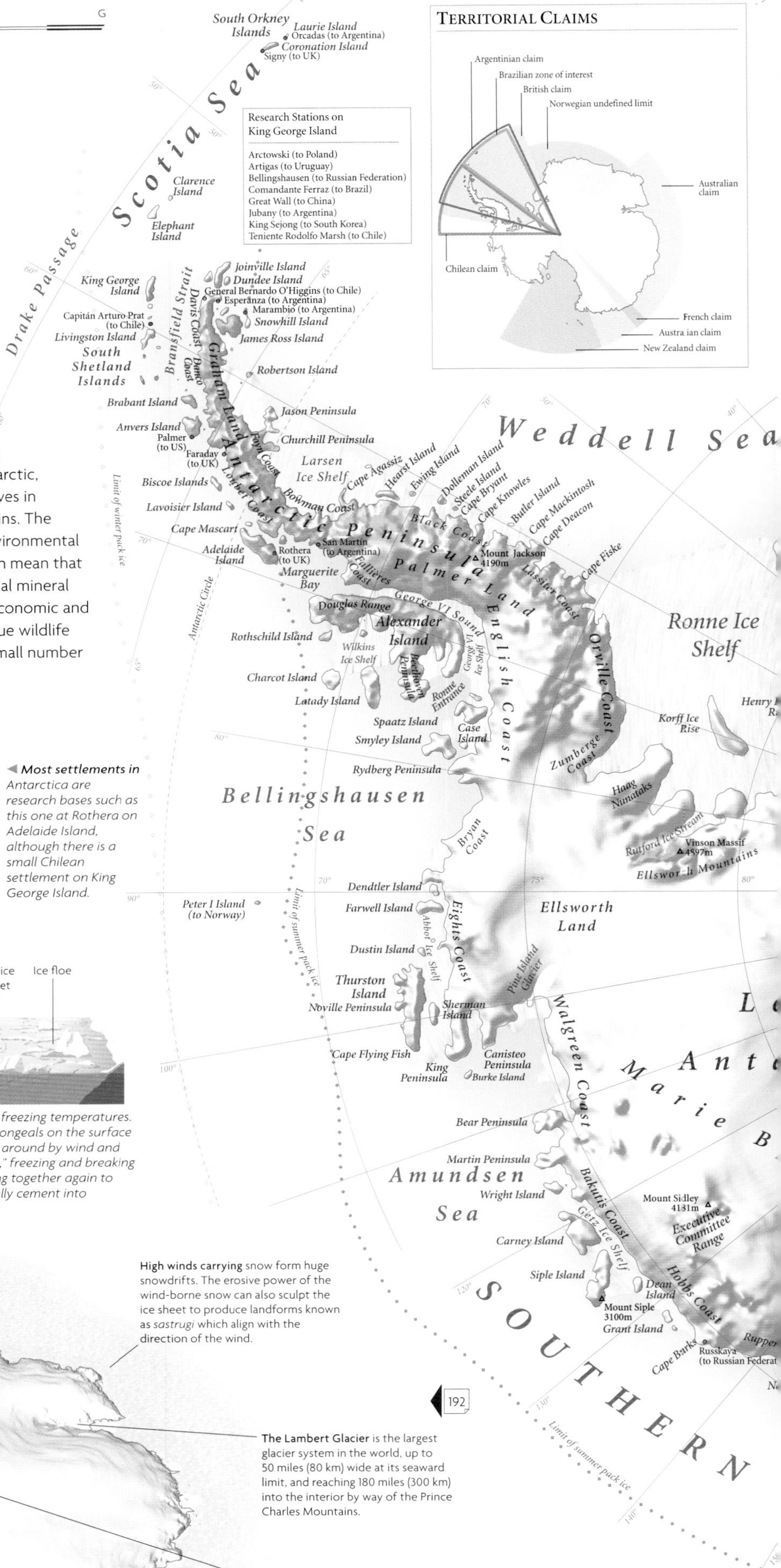

Territorial Claims

- Argentinian claim
- Brazilian zone of interest
- British claim
- Norwegian undefined limit
- Australian claim
- Chilean claim
- French claim
- Australian claim
- New Zealand claim

Research Stations on King George Island

- Arctowski (to Poland)
- Artigas (to Uruguay)
- Bellingshausen (to Russian Federation)
- Comandante Ferraz (to Brazil)
- Great Wall (to China)
- Jubany (to Argentina)
- King Sejong (to South Korea)
- Teniente Rodolfo Marsh (to Chile)

192

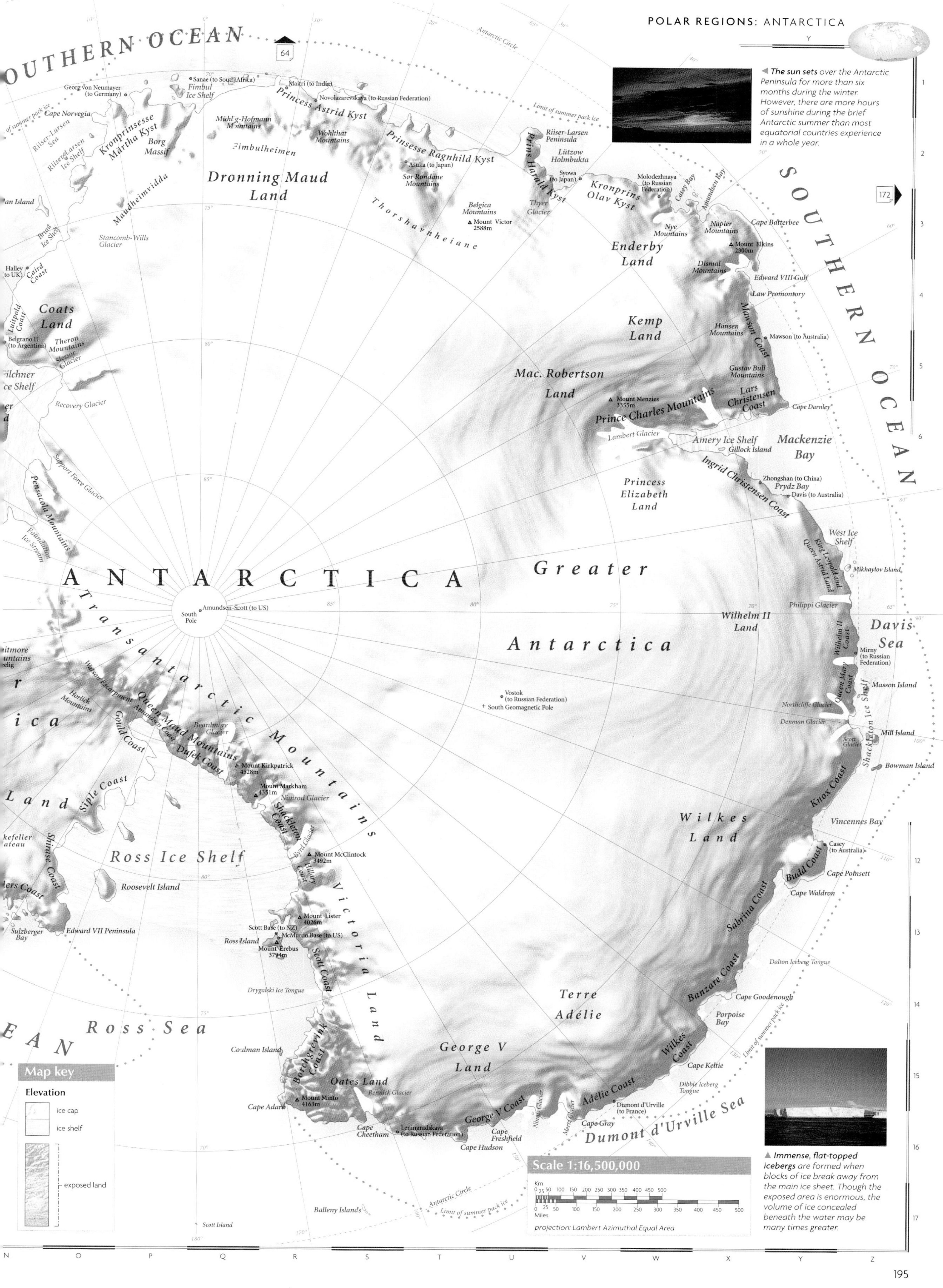
SOUTHERN OCEAN
64
Georg von Neumayer (to Germany)
Sanae (to South Africa)
Fimbul Ice Shelf
Maitri (to India)
Princess Astrid Kyst
Novolazarevskaya (to Russian Federation)
Cape Norvegia
Riiser-Larsen Sea
Riiser-Larsen Ice Shelf
Kronprinsesse Märtha Kyst
Borg Massif
Mühlig-Hofmann Mountains
Fimbulheimen
Wohlthat Mountains
Prinsesse Ragnhild Kyst
Limit of summer pack ice
Riiser-Larsen Peninsula
Lützow Holmbukta
Prins Harald Kyst
Syowa (to Japan)
Asuka (to Japan)
Sør Rondane Mountains
Dronning Maud Land
Maudheimvidda
Thorshavnheiane
Belgica Mountains
Mount Victor 2588m
Thyer Glacier
Kronprins Olav Kyst
Molodezhnaya (to Russian Federation)
Casey Bay
Amundsen Bay
172
SOUTHERN OCEAN
Brunt Ice Shelf
Stancomb-Wills Glacier
Halley (to UK)
Caird Coast
Nye Mountains
Napier Mountains
Cape Batterbee
Mount Elkins 2300m
Enderby Land
Dismal Mountains
Edward VIII Gulf
Law Promontory
Coats Land
Luitpold Coast
Belgrano II (to Argentina)
Theron Mountains
Slessor Glacier
Kemp Land
Hansen Mountains
Mawson Coast
Mawson (to Australia)
Filchner Ice Shelf
Recovery Glacier
Mac. Robertson Land
Gustav Bull Mountains
Lars Christensen Coast
Mount Menzies 3355m
Prince Charles Mountains
Cape Darnley
Lambert Glacier
Amery Ice Shelf
Gillock Island
Mackenzie Bay
Support Force Glacier
Pensacola Mountains
Foundation Ice Stream
Princess Elizabeth Land
Ingrid Christensen Coast
Zhongshan (to China)
Prydz Bay
Davis (to Australia)
West Ice Shelf
King Leopold and Queen Astrid Land
Mikhaylov Island
ANTARCTICA
Greater Antarctica
South Pole
Amundsen-Scott (to US)
Philippi Glacier
Wilhelm II Land
Davis Sea
Wilhelm II Coast
Mirny (to Russian Federation)
Transantarctic Mountains
Whitmore Mountains
Horlick Mountains
Watson Escarpment
Queen Maud Mountains
Amundsen Coast
Gould Coast
Beardmore Glacier
Dufek Coast
Vostok (to Russian Federation)
South Geomagnetic Pole
Queen Mary Coast
Masson Island
Northcliffe Glacier
Denman Glacier
Shackleton Ice Shelf
Mill Island
Scott Glacier
Bowman Island
Mount Kirkpatrick 4528m
Mount Markham 4351m
Nimrod Glacier
Shackleton Coast
Siple Coast
Knox Coast
Vincennes Bay
Wilkes Land
Rockefeller Plateau
Ross Ice Shelf
Byrd Glacier
Mount McClintock 3492m
Hillary Coast
Casey (to Australia)
Budd Coast
Cape Poinsett
Cape Waldron
Shirase Coast
Saunders Coast
Roosevelt Island
Victoria Land
Sulzberger Bay
Edward VII Peninsula
Mount Lister 4026m
Scott Base (to NZ)
McMurdo Base (to US)
Ross Island
Mount Erebus 3794m
Sabrina Coast
Dalton Iceberg Tongue
Scott Coast
Drygalski Ice Tongue
Banzare Coast
Terre Adélie
Cape Goodenough
Porpoise Bay
Ross Sea
Coulman Island
Borchgrevink Coast
George V Land
Wilkes Coast
Oates Land
Rennick Glacier
Cape Keltie
Dibble Iceberg Tongue
Mount Minto 4163m
Cape Adare
Adélie Coast
Ninnis Glacier
Mertz Glacier
Dumont d'Urville (to France)
Cape Gray
George V Coast
Dumont d'Urville Sea
Cape Cheetham
Leningradskaya (to Russian Federation)
Cape Freshfield
Cape Hudson
Antarctic Circle
Balleny Islands
Scott Island
Map key
Elevation
ice cap
ice shelf
exposed land
Scale 1:16,500,000
Km
0 25 50 100 150 200 250 300 350 400 450 500
Miles
0 25 50 100 150 200 250 300 350 400 450 500
projection: Lambert Azimuthal Equal Area

The sun sets over the Antarctic Peninsula for more than six months during the winter. However, there are more hours of sunshine during the brief Antarctic summer than most equatorial countries experience in a whole year.

Immense, flat-topped icebergs are formed when blocks of ice break away from the main ice sheet. Though the exposed area is enormous, the volume of ice concealed beneath the water may be many times greater.

The Arctic

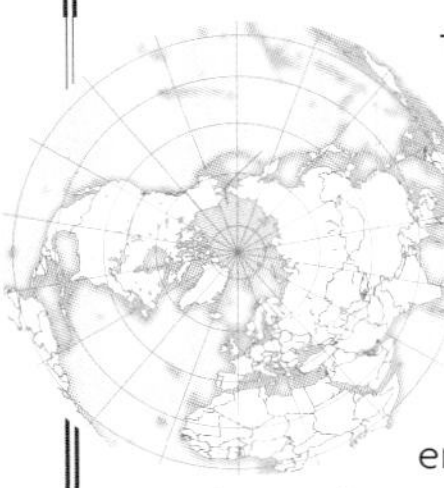

Three continents, Asia, North America, and Europe, reach into the Arctic Circle at their northernmost limits, almost entirely encircling the Arctic Ocean. Despite the region's extraordinarily harsh climate, it has been inhabited for thousands of years by peoples such as the European Lapps, the Russian Nenet, and the North American Inuit, who draw a living from fishing, herding, and hunting. More recently, particularly in the Russian Arctic, opportunities to exploit oil and other mineral reserves have encouraged immigration. Pollution of the Arctic's unique ecology and damage to the traditional lifestyles of many native peoples have been the unfortunate results of this activity, and international cooperation is needed to safeguard the future of the region.

Map key

Population

- above 5 million
- 1 million to 5 million
- 500,000 to 1 million
- 100,000 to 500,000
- 50,000 to 100,000
- 10,000 to 50,000
- below 10,000

Sea Depth

sea level
250m / 820ft
500m / 1640ft
1000m / 3281ft
2000m / 6562ft
3000m / 9843ft

Scale 1:23,500,000

Km 0 100 200 300 400 500 600
Miles 0 100 200 300 400 500 600

projection: Lambert Azimuthal Equal Area

▲ *Windblown snow etches deep patterns in the ice sheet known as sastrugi. They align with the direction of the wind*

Resources

Large quantities of coal, oil, and natural gas are to be found in the basins of the Arctic Ocean, and in northern Canada, Alaska, and the Russian Federation. The cost and difficulty of extraction and, more recently, awareness of damage to the environment, have limited exploitation to coastal regions. The unfrozen waters have stocks of fish including cod, flounder, and haddock. Quotas have now been put in place to restrict the number of fish caught annually. Reindeer are herded in large numbers by many of the native Arctic peoples. Most grain and vegetables are imported from elsewhere.

Bering Sea
NORTH AMERICA
ASIA
ARCTIC OCEAN
Inuvik
Tiksi
Noril'sk
Qaanaaq
Murmansk
Reykjavík
ATLANTIC OCEAN
EUROPE

▲ **Icebreakers are ships** *with specially strengthened hulls, designed to break a path through the ice. They are used to keep important routes open during the winter, when falling temperatures cause much of the Arctic Ocean to freeze over.*

Resources

- coal
- fish
- mining
- oil & gas
- radioactive contamination
- major towns
- major ports

The landscape

The Arctic Ocean comprises two large ocean basins divided by three submarine ridges, the greatest of which, the Lomonosov Ridge, is a huge underwater mountain range which has an average height of more than 10,000 ft (3000 m). The lands which encircle the Arctic Ocean are underlain by great shield areas of ancient rocks, which were heavily glaciated during the last Ice Age.

◀ *Icebergs are constantly broken up and reshaped by wind and the oceans. This flat-topped iceberg has been undercut, leaving a craggy ice cliff.*

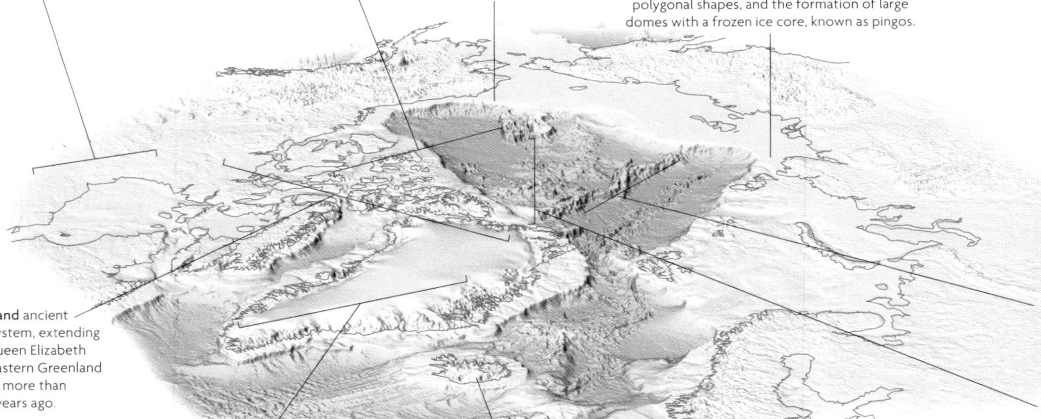

The Canadian Shield underlies almost all of the Canadian Arctic. It is a very stable plateau of ancient rock, now covered by glacial lakes and sediment, which supports tundra vegetation.

The Arctic Ocean is the world's smallest ocean with a total area of 5,440,000 sq miles (15,100,000 sq km).

At a latitude of more than 75° N, the Arctic Ocean is almost permanently covered by pack ice, though high winds and the movement of the seas may cause the ice to crack and break up.

In the more southerly reaches of the Arctic, like Siberia, much of the land is covered by permafrost. In the summer, higher temperatures warm the frozen ground, causing a number of typical phenomena. These include solifluction, the fast downhill movement of top soil layers; freeze/thaw activity, which patterns the ground into regular polygonal shapes, and the formation of large domes with a frozen ice core, known as pingos.

A complex and ancient mountain system, extending from the Queen Elizabeth Islands to eastern Greenland was formed more than 245 million years ago.

Lomonosov Ridge

Arctic ice shelf

◀ **Much of Greenland** *is covered by a massive ice sheet more than 650,000 sq miles (1,683,400 sq km) in extent. The weight of the ice has depressed the central land area to form a basin lying more than 1000 ft (300 m) below sea level. Only at the edges of the island is bare rock visible.*

Iceland has five major glaciers, sustained by heavy snowfall. Parts of the ice cap cover active volcanoes, such as Bárdharbunga, which periodically erupt causing the melted ice to form a great lake at the glacier margins.

Ice sheet
Iceberg
Crevasses occur at the edge of the ice sheet
Sea water melts the edge of the ice sheet

▲ **At the boundary** *of the Arctic ice shelves, sea water flows under the ice causing melting and forming crevasses on the surface. This eventually weakens blocks of ice which break away as icebergs. This process is known as calving.*

CANADA
NORTH AMERICA
Great Bear Lake
Great Slave Lake
Kugluktuk
Bathurst Inlet
Cambridge Bay
Queen Maud Gulf
Back
Nelson
Churchill
Hudson Bay
Southampton Island
Coats Island
Repulse Bay
Melville Peninsula
Mansel Island
Foxe Basin
Prince Charles Island
Ivujivik
Inukjuak
Hudson Strait
Lake Harbour
Baffin Isl
Ungava Bay
Cape Chidley
Cumberland Sound
Frobisher Bay
Davis Str
Nain
Labrador Sea
Maniit
NUUK
Paamiut
Ivittu
Labrador Basin
Qaqortoq
Nanortalik
Nunap Isua (Kap Farvel)
Eirik Ridge
ATLAN

192
8
8
64

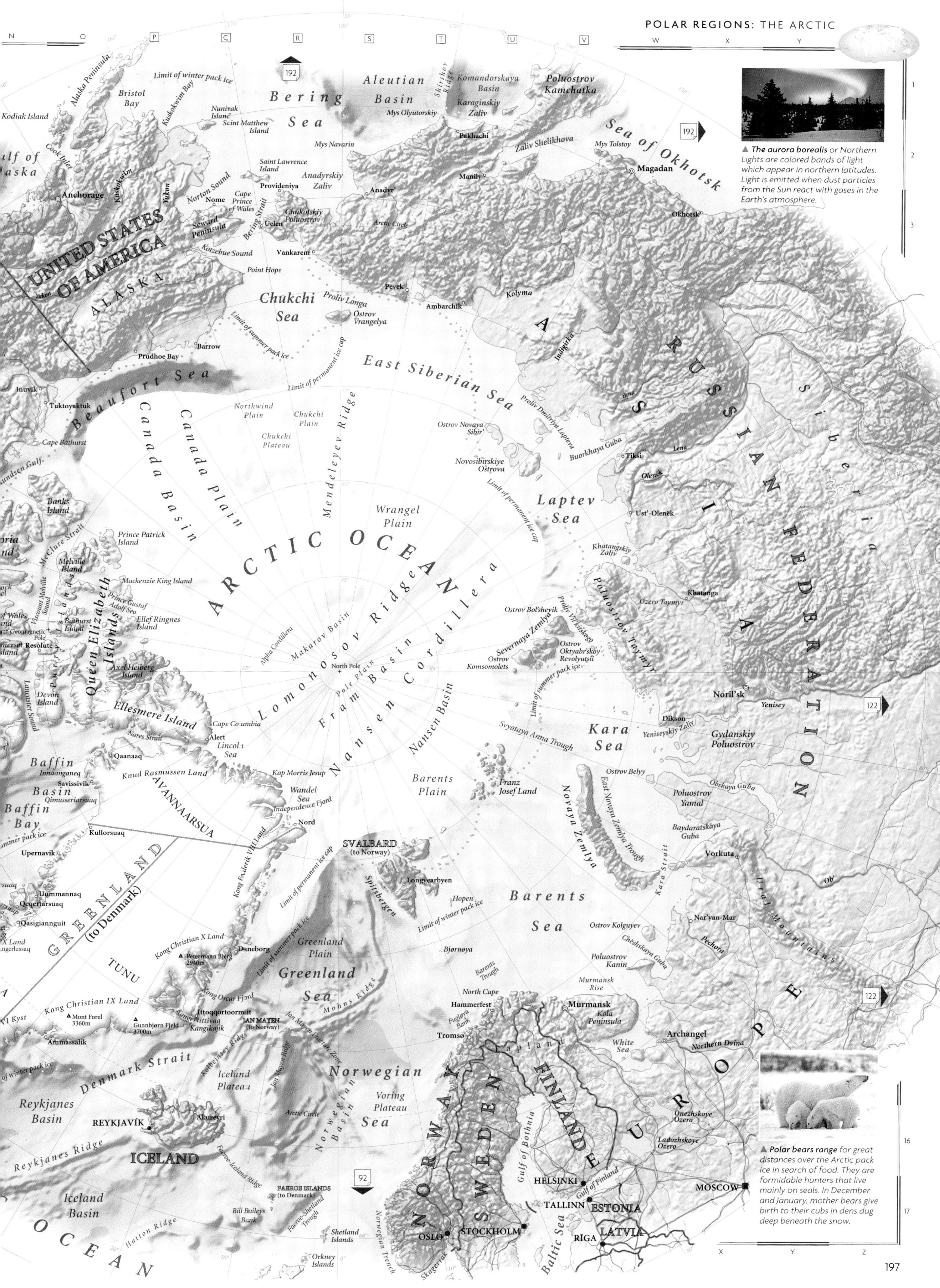

▲ **The aurora borealis** or Northern Lights are colored bands of light which appear in northern latitudes. Light is emitted when dust particles from the Sun react with gases in the Earth's atmosphere.

▲ **Polar bears range** for great distances over the Arctic pack ice in search of food. They are formidable hunters that live mainly on seals. In December and January, mother bears give birth to their cubs in dens dug deep beneath the snow.

Geographical comparisons

Largest countries

Russian Federation	6,592,735 sq miles	(17,075,200 sq km)
Canada	3,851,788 sq miles	(9,976,140 sq km)
USA	3,717,792 sq miles	(9,629,091 sq km)
China	3,705,386 sq miles	(9,596,960 sq km)
Brazil	3,286,470 sq miles	(8,511,965 sq km)
Australia	2,967,893 sq miles	(7,686,850 sq km)
India	1,269,339 sq miles	(3,287,590 sq km)
Argentina	1,068,296 sq miles	(2,766,890 sq km)
Kazakhstan	1,049,150 sq miles	(2,717,300 sq km)
Sudan	967,493 sq miles	(2,505,815 sq km)

Smallest countries

Vatican City	0.17 sq miles	(0.44 sq km)
Monaco	0.75 sq miles	(1.95 sq km)
Nauru	8.2 sq miles	(21.2 sq km)
Tuvalu	10 sq miles	(26 sq km)
San Marino	24 sq miles	(61 sq km)
Liechtenstein	62 sq miles	(160 sq km)
Marshall Islands	70 sq miles	(181 sq km)
St. Kitts & Nevis	101 sq miles	(261 sq km)
Maldives	116 sq miles	(300 sq km)
Malta	124 sq miles	(320 sq km)

Largest islands

To the nearest 1000 – or 100,000 for the largest

Greenland	849,400 sq miles	(2,200,000 sq km)
New Guinea	312,000 sq miles	(808,000 sq km)
Borneo	292,222 sq miles	(757,050 sq km)
Madagascar	229,300 sq miles	(594,000 sq km)
Sumatra	202,300 sq miles	(524,000 sq km)
Baffin Island	183,800 sq miles	(476,000 sq km)
Honshu	88,800 sq miles	(230,000 sq km)
Britain	88,700 sq miles	(229,800 sq km)
Victoria Island	81,900 sq miles	(212,000 sq km)
Ellesmere Island	75,700 sq miles	(196,000 sq km)

Richest countries

GNI per capita, in US$

Luxembourg	56,230
Norway	52,030
Liechtenstein	50,000
Switzerland	48,230
USA	41,400
Denmark	40,650
Iceland	38,620
Japan	37,810
Sweden	35,770
Ireland	34,280

Poorest countries

GNI per capita, in US$

Burundi	90
Ethiopia	110
Liberia	110
Congo, Dem. Rep.	120
Somalia	120
Guinea-Bissau	160
Malawi	170
Eritrea	180
Sierra Leone	200
Rwanda	220
Afghanistan	222
Niger	230

Most populous countries

China	1,315,800,000
India	1,103,400,000
USA	298,200,000
Indonesia	222,800,000
Brazil	186,400,000
Cameroon	163,000,000
Pakistan	157,900,000
Russian Federation	143,200,000
Bangladesh	141,800,000
Nigeria	131,500,000

Least populous countries

Vatican City	921
Tuvalu	11,636
Nauru	13,048
Palau	20,303
San Marino	28,880
Monaco	32,409
Liechtenstein	33,717
St Kitts & Nevis	38,958
Marshall Islands	59,071
Antigua & Barbuda	68,722
Dominica	69,029
Andorra	70,549

Most densely populated countries

Monaco	43,212 people per sq mile	(16,620 per sq km)
Singapore	18,220 people per sq mile	(7049 per sq km)
Vatican City	5418 people per sq mile	(2093 per sq km)
Malta	3242 people per sq mile	(1256 per sq km)
Maldives	2836 people per sq mile	(1097 per sq km)
Bangledesh	2743 people per sq mile	(1059 per sq km)
Bahrain	2663 people per sq mile	(1030 per sq km)
China	1838 people per sq mile	(710 per sq km)
Mauritius	1671 people per sq mile	(645 per sq km)
Barbados	1627 people per sq mile	(628 per sq km)

Most sparsely populated countries

Mongolia	4 people per sq mile	(2 per sq km)
Namibia	6 people per sq mile	(2 per sq km)
Australia	7 people per sq mile	(3 per sq km)
Mauritania	8 people per sq mile	(3 per sq km)
Suriname	8 people per sq mile	(3 per sq km)
Botswana	8 people per sq mile	(3 per sq km)
Iceland	8 people per sq mile	(3 per sq km)
Canada	9 people per sq mile	(4 per sq km)
Libya	9 people per sq mile	(4 per sq km)
Guyana	10 people per sq mile	(4 per sq km)

Most widely spoken languages

1. Chinese (Mandarin)	6. Arabic
2. English	7. Bengali
3. Hindi	8. Portuguese
4. Spanish	9. Malay-Indonesian
5. Russian	10. French

Largest conurbations

	Population
Tokyo	34,200,000
Mexico City	22,800,000
Seoul	22,300,000
New York	21,900,000
São Paulo	20,200,000
Mumbai	19,850,000
Delhi	19,700,000
Shanghai	18,150,000
Los Angeles	18,000,000
Osaka	16,800,000
Jakarta	16,550,000
Kolkata	15,650,000
Cairo	15,600,000
Manila	14,950,000
Karachi	14,300,000
Moscow	13,750,000
Buenos Aires	13,450,000
Dacca	13,250,000
Rio de Janeiro	12,150,000
Beijing	12,100,000
London	12,000,000
Tehran	11,850,000
Istanbul	11,500,000
Lagos	11,100,000
Shenzhen	10,700,000

Countries with the most land borders

14: China	(Afghanistan, Bhutan, India, Kazakhstan, Kyrgyzstan, Laos, Mongolia, Myanmar, Nepal, North Korea, Pakistan, Russian Federation, Tajikistan, Vietnam)
14: Russian Federation	(Azerbaijan, Belarus, China, Estonia, Finland, Georgia, Kazakhstan, Latvia, Lithuania, Mongolia, North Korea, Norway, Poland, Ukraine)
10: Brazil	(Argentina, Bolivia, Colombia, French Guiana, Guyana, Paraguay, Peru, Suriname, Uruguay, Venezuela)
9: Congo, Dem. Rep.	(Angola, Burundi, Central African Republic, Congo, Rwanda, Sudan, Tanzania, Uganda, Zambia)
9: Germany	(Austria, Belgium, Czech Republic, Denmark, France, Luxembourg, Netherlands, Poland, Switzerland)
9: Sudan	(Central African Republic, Chad, Dem. Rep.Congo, Egypt, Eritrea, Ethiopia, Kenya, Libya, Uganda)
8: Austria	(Czech Republic, Germany, Hungary, Italy, Liechtenstein, Slovakia, Slovenia, Switzerland)
8: France	(Andorra, Belgium, Germany, Italy, Luxembourg, Monaco, Spain, Switzerland)
8: Tanzania	(Burundi, Dem. Rep.Congo, Kenya, Malawi, Mozambique, Rwanda, Uganda, Zambia)
8: Turkey	(Armenia, Azerbaijan, Bulgaria, Georgia, Greece, Iran, Iraq, Syria)
8: Zambia	(Angola, Botswana, Dem. Rep.Congo, Malawi, Mozambique, Namibia, Tanzania, Zimbabwe)

Longest rivers

Nile (NE Africa)	4160 miles	(6695 km)
Amazon (South America)	4049 miles	(6516 km)
Yangtze (China)	3915 miles	(6299 km)
Mississippi/Missouri (USA)	3710 miles	(5969 km)
Ob'-Irtysh (Russian Federation)	3461 miles	(5570 km)
Yellow River (China)	3395 miles	(5464 km)
Congo (Central Africa)	2900 miles	(4667 km)
Mekong (Southeast Asia)	2749 miles	(4425 km)
Lena (Russian Federation)	2734 miles	(4400 km)
Mackenzie (Canada)	2640 miles	(4250 km)
Yenisey (Russian Federation)	2541 miles	(4090km)

Highest mountains

Height above sea level

Everest	29,035 ft	(8850 m)
K2	28,253 ft	(8611 m)
Kanchenjunga I	28,210 ft	(8598 m)
Makalu I	27,767 ft	(8463 m)
Cho Oyu	26,907 ft	(8201 m)
Dhaulagiri I	26,796 ft	(8167 m)
Manaslu I	26,783 ft	(8163 m)
Nanga Parbat I	26,661 ft	(8126 m)
Annapurna I	26,547 ft	(8091 m)
Gasherbrum I	26,471 ft	(8068 m)

Largest bodies of inland water

With area and depth

Caspian Sea	143,243 sq miles (371,000 sq km)	3215 ft (980 m)
Lake Superior	31,151 sq miles (83,270 sq km)	1289 ft (393 m)
Lake Victoria	26,828 sq miles (69,484 sq km)	328 ft (100 m)
Lake Huron	23,436 sq miles (60,700 sq km)	751 ft (229 m)
Lake Michigan	22,402 sq miles (58,020 sq km)	922 ft (281 m)
Lake Tanganyika	12,703 sq miles (32,900 sq km)	4700 ft (1435 m)
Great Bear Lake	12,274 sq miles (31,790 sq km)	1047 ft (319 m)
Lake Baikal	11,776 sq miles (30,500 sq km)	5712 ft (1741 m)
Great Slave Lake	10,981 sq miles (28,440 sq km)	459 ft (140 m)
Lake Erie	9,915 sq miles (25,680 sq km)	197 ft (60 m)

Deepest ocean features

Challenger Deep, Mariana Trench (Pacific)	36,201 ft	(11,034 m)
Vityaz III Depth, Tonga Trench (Pacific)	35,704 ft	(10,882 m)
Vityaz Depth, Kurile-Kamchatka Trench (Pacific)	34,588 ft	(10,542 m)
Cape Johnson Deep, Philippine Trench (Pacific)	34,441 ft	(10,497 m)
Kermadec Trench (Pacific)	32,964 ft	(10,047 m)
Ramapo Deep, Japan Trench (Pacific)	32,758 ft	(9984 m)
Milwaukee Deep, Puerto Rico Trench (Atlantic)	30,185 ft	(9200 m)
Argo Deep, Torres Trench (Pacific)	30,070 ft	(9165 m)
Meteor Depth, South Sandwich Trench (Atlantic)	30,000 ft	(9144 m)
Planet Deep, New Britain Trench (Pacific)	29,988 ft	(9140 m)

Greatest waterfalls

Mean flow of water

Boyoma (Congo)	600,400 cu. ft/sec	(17,000 cu.m/sec)
Khône (Laos/Cambodia)	410,000 cu. ft/sec	(11,600 cu.m/sec)
Niagara (USA/Canada)	195,000 cu. ft/sec	(5500 cu.m/sec)
Grande (Uruguay)	160,000 cu. ft/sec	(4500 cu.m/sec)
Paulo Afonso (Brazil)	100,000 cu. ft/sec	(2800 cu.m/sec)
Urubupunga (Brazil)	97,000 cu. ft/sec	(2750 cu.m/sec)
Iguaçu (Argentina/Brazil)	62,000 cu. ft/sec	(1700 cu.m/sec)
Maribondo (Brazil)	53,000 cu. ft/sec	(1500 cu.m/sec)
Victoria (Zimbabwe)	39,000 cu. ft/sec	(1100 cu.m/sec)
Kabalega (Uganda)	42,000 cu. ft/sec	(1200 cu.m/sec)
Churchill (Canada)	35,000 cu. ft/sec	(1000 cu.m/sec)
Cauvery (India)	33,000 cu. ft/sec	(900 cu.m/sec)

Highest waterfalls

* Indicates that the total height is a single leap

Angel (Venezuela)	3212 ft	(979 m)
Tugela (South Africa)	3110 ft	(948 m)
Utigard (Norway)	2625 ft	(800 m)
Mongefossen (Norway)	2539 ft	(774 m)
Mtarazi (Zimbabwe)	2500 ft	(762 m)
Yosemite (USA)	2425 ft	(739 m)
Ostre Mardola Foss (Norway)	2156 ft	(657 m)
Tyssestrengane (Norway)	2119 ft	(646 m)
***Cuquenan** (Venezuela)	2001 ft	(610 m)
Sutherland (New Zealand)	1903 ft	(580 m)
***Kjellfossen** (Norway)	1841 ft	(561 m)

Largest deserts

NB – Most of Antarctica is a polar desert, with only 50mm of precipitation annually

Sahara	3,450,000 sq miles	(9,065,000 sq km)
Gobi	500,000 sq miles	(1,295,000 sq km)
Ar Rub al Khali	289,600 sq miles	(750,000 sq km)
Great Victorian	249,800 sq miles	(647,000 sq km)
Sonoran	120,000 sq miles	(311,000 sq km)
Kalahari	120,000 sq miles	(310,800 sq km)
Kara Kum	115,800 sq miles	(300,000 sq km)
Takla Makan	100,400 sq miles	(260,000 sq km)
Namib	52,100 sq miles	(135,000 sq km)
Thar	33,670 sq miles	(130,000 sq km)

Hottest inhabited places

Djibouti (Djibouti)	86° F	(30 °C)
Timbouctou (Mali)	84.7° F	(29.3 °C)
Tirunelveli (India)		
Tuticorin (India)		
Nellore (India)	84.5° F	(29.2 °C)
Santa Marta (Colombia)		
Aden (Yemen)	84° F	(28.9 °C)
Madurai (India)		
Niamey (Niger)		
Hodeida (Yemen)	83.8° F	(28.8 °C)
Ouagadougou (Burkina)		
Thanjavur (India)		
Tiruchchirappalli (India)		

Driest inhabited places

Aswân (Egypt)	0.02 in	(0.5 mm)
Luxor (Egypt)	0.03 in	(0.7 mm)
Arica (Chile)	0.04 in	(1.1 mm)
Ica (Peru)	0.1 in	(2.3 mm)
Antofagasta (Chile)	0.2 in	(4.9 mm)
El Minya (Egypt)	0.2 in	(5.1 mm)
Asyût (Egypt)	0.2 in	(5.2 mm)
Callao (Peru)	0.5 in	(12.0 mm)
Trujillo (Peru)	0.55 in	(14.0 mm)
El Faiyûm (Egypt)	0.8 in	(19.0 mm)

Wettest inhabited places

Buenaventura (Colombia)	265 in	(6743 mm)
Monrovia (Liberia)	202 in	(5131 mm)
Pago Pago (American Samoa)	196 in	(4990 mm)
Moulmein (Myanmar)	191 in	(4852 mm)
Lae (Papua New Guinea)	183 in	(4645 mm)
Baguio (Luzon Island, Philippines)	180 in	(4573 mm)
Sylhet (Bangladesh)	176 in	(4457 mm)
Padang (Sumatra, Indonesia)	166 in	(4225 mm)
Bogor (Java, Indonesia)	166 in	(4225 mm)
Conakry (Guinea)	171 in	(4341 mm)

The time zones

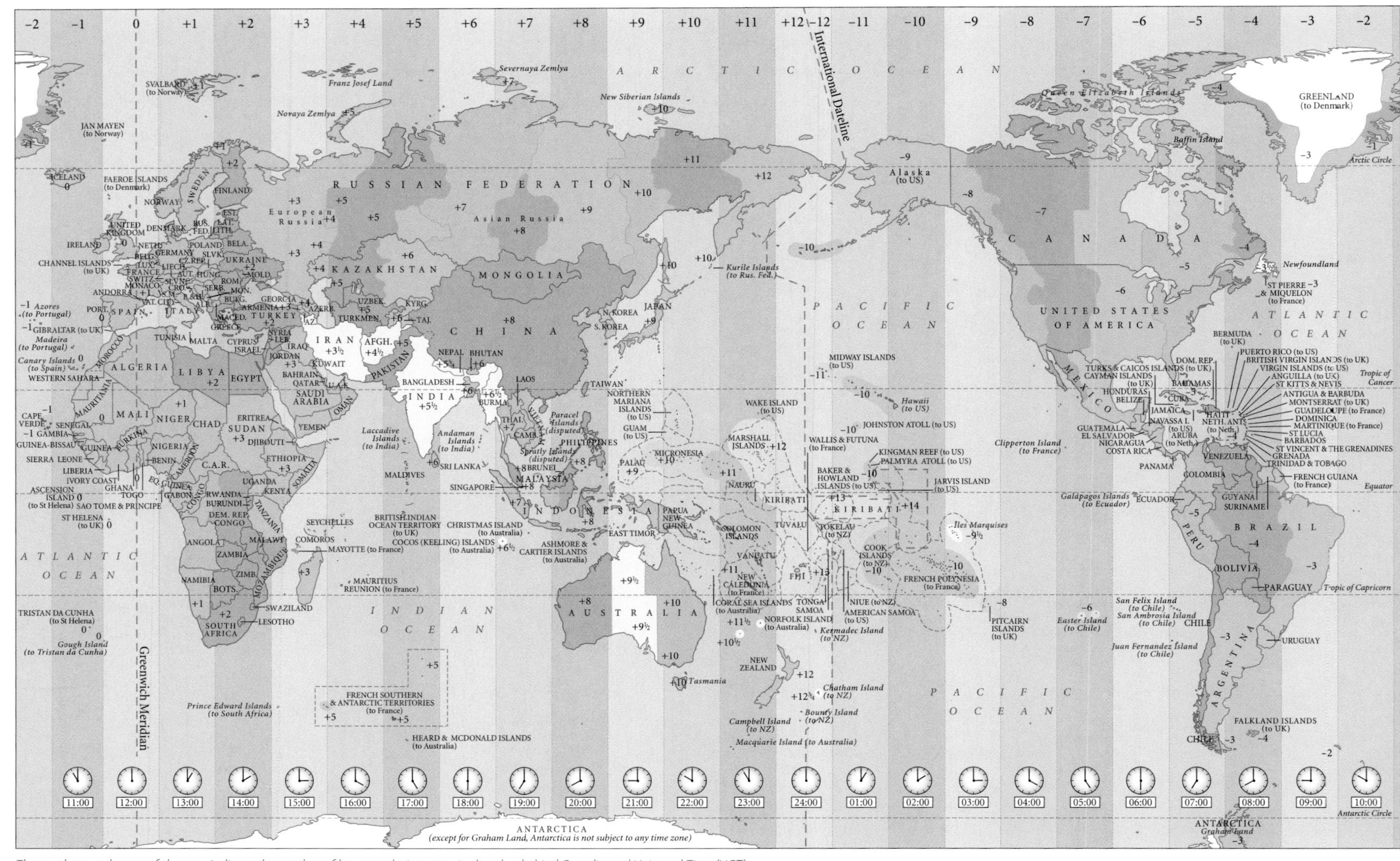
-2 -1 0 +1 +2 +3 +4 +5 +6 +7 +8 +9 +10 +11 +12 -12 -11 -10 -9 -8 -7 -6 -5 -4 -3 -2
International Dateline
Greenwich Meridian
ARCTIC OCEAN
RUSSIAN FEDERATION
European Russia
Asian Russia
KAZAKHSTAN
MONGOLIA
CHINA
IRAN
INDIA
ALGERIA
LIBYA
EGYPT
MALI
NIGER
CHAD
SUDAN
AUSTRALIA
NEW ZEALAND
CANADA
UNITED STATES OF AMERICA
Alaska (to US)
MEXICO
BRAZIL
BOLIVIA
PERU
ARGENTINA
CHILE
GREENLAND (to Denmark)
PACIFIC OCEAN
ATLANTIC OCEAN
INDIAN OCEAN
ANTARCTICA (except for Graham Land, Antarctica is not subject to any time zone)
11:00 12:00 13:00 14:00 15:00 16:00 17:00 18:00 19:00 20:00 21:00 22:00 23:00 24:00 01:00 02:00 03:00 04:00 05:00 06:00 07:00 08:00 09:00 10:00

The numbers at the top of the map indicate the number of hours each time zone is ahead or behind Coordinated Universal Time (UCT).
The clocks and 24-hour times given at the bottom of the map show the time in each time zone when it is 12:00 hours noon UCT.

Time zones

Because Earth is a rotating sphere, the Sun shines on only half of its surface at any one time. Thus, it is simultaneously morning, evening, and nighttime in different parts of the world. Because of these disparities, each country or part of a country adheres to a local time. A region of Earth's surface within which a single local time is used is called a time zone. The world is divided into 24 time zones by means of 24 standard meridians of longitude, each 15° apart. Time is measured in each zone as so many hours ahead or behind Coordinated Universal Time (UCT). Countries, or parts of countries, falling in the vicinity of each zone adopt its time as shown on the map above. Thus, when it is 12:00 noon UCT in London, it will 2:00 pm in Zambia.

Standard Time

Standard time is the official local time in a particular country or part of a country. It is defined by the time zone or zones associated with that country or region. Although time zones are arranged roughly in longitudinal bands, in many places the borders of a zone do not fall exactly on longitudinal meridians, as can be seen on the map (above), but are determined by geographical factors or by borders between countries or parts of countries. Most countries have just one time zone and one standard time, but some large countries (such as the US, Canada, and Russia) are split between several time zones, so standard time varies across those countries. For example, the coterminous United States straddles four time zones and so has four standard times, called the Eastern, Central, Mountain, and Pacific standard times. China is unusual in that just one standard time is used for the whole country, even though it extends across 60° of longitude from west to east.

Coordinated Universal Time

Coordinated Universal Time (UTC) is a reference by which the local time in each time zone is set. For example, Australian Western Standard Time (the local time in Western Australia) is set 8 hours ahead of UTC (it is UTC+8), whereas Eastern Standard Time in the United States is set 5 hours behind UTC (it is UTC-5). UTC is a successor to, and closely approximates, Greenwich Mean Time (GMT). However, UTC is based on an atomic clock, whereas GMT is determined by the Sun's position in the sky relative to the 0° longitudinal meridian, which runs through Greenwich, UK.

The International Dateline

The International Dateline is an imaginary line from pole to pole that roughly corresponds to the 180° longitudinal meridian, forming an arbitrary marker between calendar days. The dateline is needed because of the use of local times around the world rather than a single universal time. When moving from west to east across the dateline, travelers have to set their watches back one day. Those traveling in the opposite direction, from east to west, must add a day. Wide variations from the 180° longitude occur through the Bering Strait—to avoid dividing Siberia into two separate calendar days—and in the Pacific Ocean—to allow certain islands the same calendar day as New Zealand. Changes were made to the International Dateline in 1995 that made Millennium Island (formerly Caroline Island) in Kiribati the first land area to witness the beginning of the year 2000.

Daylight saving time

Daylight saving is a summertime adjustment to the local time in a country or region, designed to cause a higher proportion of its citizens' waking hours to pass during daylight. To follow the system, timepieces are advanced by an hour on a pre-decided date in spring and reverted back in the fall.

Countries of the World

There are currently 194 independent countries in the world – more than at any previous time – and 59 dependencies. Antarctica is the only land area on Earth that is not officially part of, and does not belong to, any single country.

In 1950, the world comprised 82 countries. In the decades following, many more states came into being as they achieved independence from their former colonial rulers. Most recent additions were caused by the breakup of the former Soviet Union in 1991, and the former Yugoslavia in 1992, which swelled the ranks of independent states. In May 2006 Montenegro voted to split from Serbia, making it the latest country to gain independence.

Country factfile key

Formation Date of independence / date current borders were established

Population Total population / population density – based on total *land* area / percentage of urban-based population

Languages An asterisk (*) denotes the official language(s)

Calorie consumption Average number of calories consumed daily per person

AFGHANISTAN
Central Asia

Official name Islamic State of Afghanistan
Formation 1919 / 1919
Capital Kabul
Population 29.9 million / 119 people per sq mile (46 people per sq km) / 22%
Total area 250,000 sq miles (647,500 sq km)
Languages Pashtu*, Tajik, Dari, Farsi, Uzbek, Turkmen
Religions Sunni Muslim 84%, Shi'a Muslim 15%, Other 1%
Ethnic mix Pashtun 38%, Tajik 25%, Hazara 19%, Uzbek and Turkmen 15%, Other 3%
Government Transitional regime
Currency New afghani = 100 puls
Literacy rate 36%
Calorie consumption 1539 calories

ALBANIA
Southeast Europe

Official name Republic of Albania
Formation 1912 / 1921
Capital Tirana
Population 3.1 million / 293 people per sq mile (113 people per sq km) / 42%
Total area 11,100 sq miles (28,748 sq km)
Languages Albanian*, Greek
Religions Sunni Muslim 70%, Orthodox Christian 20%, Roman Catholic 10%
Ethnic mix Albanian 93%, Greek 5%, Other 2%
Government Parliamentary system
Currency Lek = 100 qindarka (qintars)
Literacy rate 99%
Calorie consumption 2848 calories

ALGERIA
North Africa

Official name People's Democratic Republic of Algeria
Formation 1962 / 1962
Capital Algiers
Population 32.9 million / 36 people per sq mile (14 people per sq km) / 60%
Total area 919,590 sq miles (2,381,740 sq km)
Languages Arabic, Tamazight (Kabyle, Shawia, Tamashek), French
Religions Sunni Muslim 99%, Christian and Jewish 1%
Ethnic mix Arab 75%, Berber 24%, European and Jewish 1%
Government Presidential system
Currency Algerian dinar = 100 centimes
Literacy rate 70%
Calorie consumption 3022 calories

ANDORRA
Southwest Europe

Official name Principality of Andorra
Formation 1278 / 1278
Capital Andorra la Vella
Population 70,549 / 392 people per sq mile (152 people per sq km) / 63%
Total area 181 sq miles (468 sq km)
Languages Spanish, Catalan, French, Portuguese
Religions Roman Catholic 94%, Other 6%
Ethnic mix Spanish 46%, Andorran 28%, Other 18%, French 8%
Government Parliamentary system
Currency Euro = 100 cents
Literacy rate 99%
Calorie consumption Not available

ANGOLA
Southern Africa

Official name Republic of Angola
Formation 1975 / 1975
Capital Luanda
Population 15.9 million / 33 people per sq mile (13 people per sq km) / 34%
Total area 481,351 sq miles (1,246,700 sq km)
Languages Portuguese*, Umbundu, Kimbundu, Kikongo
Religions Roman Catholic 50%, Other 30%, Protestant 20%
Ethnic mix Ovimbundu 37%, Other 25%, Kimbundu 25%, Bakongo 13%
Government Presidential system
Currency Readjusted kwanza = 100 lwei
Literacy rate 67%
Calorie consumption 2083 calories

ANTIGUA & BARBUDA
West Indies

Official name Antigua and Barbuda
Formation 1981 / 1981
Capital St. John's
Population 68,722 / 404 people per sq mile (156 people per sq km) / 37%
Total area 170 sq miles (442 sq km)
Languages English, English patois
Religions Anglican 45%, Other Protestant 42%, Roman Catholic 10%, Other 2%, Rastafarian 1%
Ethnic mix Black African 95%, Other 5%
Government Parliamentary system
Currency Eastern Caribbean dollar = 100 cents
Literacy rate 86%
Calorie consumption 2349 calories

ARGENTINA
South America

Official name Republic of Argentina
Formation 1816 / 1816
Capital Buenos Aires
Population 38.7 million / 37 people per sq mile (14 people per sq km) / 90%
Total area 1,068,296 sq miles (2,766,890 sq km)
Languages Spanish*, Italian, Amerindian languages
Religions Roman Catholic 90%, Other 6%, Protestant 2%, Jewish 2%
Ethnic mix Indo-European 83%, Mestizo 14%, Jewish 2%, Amerindian 1%
Government Presidential system
Currency new Argentine peso = 100 centavos
Literacy rate 97%
Calorie consumption 2992 calories

ARMENIA
Southwest Asia

Official name Republic of Armenia
Formation 1991 / 1991
Capital Yerevan
Population 3 million / 261 people per sq mile (101 people per sq km) / 70%
Total area 11,506 sq miles (29,800 sq km)
Languages Armenian*, Azeri, Russian
Religions Armenian Apostolic Church (Orthodox) 94%, Other 6%
Ethnic mix Armenian 93%, Azeri 3%, Other 2%, Russian 2%
Government Presidential system
Currency Dram = 100 luma
Literacy rate 99%
Calorie consumption 2268 calories

AUSTRALIA
Australasia & Oceania

Official name Commonwealth of Australia
Formation 1901 / 1901
Capital Canberra
Population 20.2 million / 7 people per sq mile (3 people per sq km) / 85%
Total area 2,967,893 sq miles (7,686,850 sq km)
Languages English*, Italian, Cantonese, Greek, Arabic, Vietnamese, Aboriginal languages
Religions Roman Catholic 26%, Anglican 24%, Other 23%, Nonreligious 13%, United Church 8%, Other Protestant 6%
Ethnic mix European 92%, Asian 5%, Aboriginal and other 3%
Government Parliamentary system
Currency Australian dollar = 100 cents
Literacy rate 99%
Calorie consumption 3054 calories

AUSTRIA
Central Europe

Official name Republic of Austria
Formation 1918 / 1919
Capital Vienna
Population 8.2 million / 257 people per sq mile (99 people per sq km) / 65%
Total area 32,378 sq miles (83,858 sq km)
Languages German*, Croatian, Slovenian, Hungarian (Magyar)
Religions Roman Catholic 78%, Nonreligious 9%, Other (including Jewish and Muslim) 8%, Protestant 5%
Ethnic mix Austrian 93%, Croat, Slovene, and Hungarian 6%, Other 1%
Government Parliamentary system
Currency Euro = 100 cents
Literacy rate 99%
Calorie consumption 3673 calories

AZERBAIJAN
Southwest Asia

Official name Republic of Azerbaijan
Formation 1991 / 1991
Capital Baku
Population 8.4 million / 251 people per sq mile (97 people per sq km) / 57%
Total area 33,436 sq miles (86,600 sq km)
Languages Azeri, Russian
Religions Shi'a Muslim 68%, Sunni Muslim 26%, Russian Orthodox 3%, Armenian Apostolic Church (Orthodox) 2%, Other 1%
Ethnic mix Azeri 90%, Dagestani 3%, Russian 3%, Other 2%, Armenian 2%
Government Presidential system
Currency Manat = 100 gopik
Literacy rate 99%
Calorie consumption 2575 calories

BAHAMAS
West Indies

Official name Commonwealth of the Bahamas
Formation 1973 / 1973
Capital Nassau
Population 323,000 / 84 people per sq mile (32 people per sq km) / 89%
Total area 5382 sq miles (13,940 sq km)
Languages English*, English Creole, French Creole
Religions Baptist 32%, Anglican 20%, Roman Catholic 19%, Other 17%, Methodist 6%, Church of God 6%
Ethnic mix Black African 85%, Other 15%
Government Parliamentary system
Currency Bahamian dollar = 100 cents
Literacy rate 96%
Calorie consumption 2755 calories

BAHRAIN
Southwest Asia

Official name Kingdom of Bahrain
Formation 1971 / 1971
Capital Manama
Population 727,000 / 2663 people per sq mile (1030 people per sq km) / 97%
Total area 239 sq miles (620 sq km)
Languages Arabic*
Religions Muslim (mainly Shi'a) 99%, Other 1%
Ethnic mix Bahraini 70%, Iranian, Indian, and Pakistani 24%, Other Arab 4%, European 2%
Government Monarchy
Currency Bahraini dinar = 1000 fils
Literacy rate 88%
Calorie consumption Not available

BANGLADESH
South Asia

Official name People's Republic of Bangladesh
Formation 1971 / 1971
Capital Dhaka
Population 142 million / 2743 people per sq mile (1059 people per sq km) / 25%
Total area 55,598 sq miles (144,000 sq km)
Languages Bengali*, Urdu, Chakma, Marma (Magh), Garo, Khasi, Santhali, Tripuri, Mro
Religions Muslim (mainly Sunni) 87%, Hindu 12%, Other 1%
Ethnic mix Bengali 98%, Other 2%
Government Parliamentary system
Currency Taka = 100 poisha
Literacy rate 41%
Calorie consumption 2205 calories

BARBADOS
West Indies

Official name Barbados
Formation 1966 / 1966
Capital Bridgetown
Population 270,000 / 1627 people per sq mile (628 people per sq km) / 50%
Total area 166 sq miles (430 sq km)
Languages English*, Bajan (Barbadian English)
Religions Anglican 40%, Other 24%, Nonreligious 17%, Pentecostal 8%, Methodist 7%, Roman Catholic 4%
Ethnic mix Black African 90%, Other 10%
Government Parliamentary system
Currency Barbados dollar = 100 cents
Literacy rate 99%
Calorie consumption 3091 calories

BELARUS
Eastern Europe

Official name Republic of Belarus
Formation 1991 / 1991
Capital Minsk
Population 9.8 million / 122 people per sq mile (47 people per sq km) / 71%
Total area 80,154 sq miles (207,600 sq km)
Languages Belarussian*, Russian
Religions Orthodox Christian 60%, Other 32%, Roman Catholic 8%
Ethnic mix Belarussian 78%, Russian 13%, Polish 4%, Ukrainian 3%, Other 2%
Government Presidential system
Currency Belarussian rouble = 100 kopeks
Literacy rate 99%
Calorie consumption 3000 calories

BELGIUM
Northwest Europe

Official name Kingdom of Belgium
Formation 1830 / 1919
Capital Brussels
Population 10.4 million / 821 people per sq mile (317 people per sq km) / 97%
Total area 11,780 sq miles (30,510 sq km)
Languages Dutch*, French*, German
Religions Roman Catholic 88%, Other 10%, Muslim 2%
Ethnic mix Fleming 58%, Walloon 33%, Other 6%, Italian 2%, Moroccan 1%
Government Parliamentary system
Currency Euro = 100 cents
Literacy rate 99%
Calorie consumption 3584 calories

BELIZE
Central America

Official name Belize
Formation 1981 / 1981
Capital Belmopan
Population 270,000 / 31 people per sq mile (12 people per sq km) / 54%
Total area 8867 sq miles (22,966 sq km)
Languages English*, English Creole, Spanish, Mayan, Garifuna (Carib)
Religions Roman Catholic 62%, Other 13%, Anglican 12%, Methodist 6%, Mennonite 4%, Seventh-day Adventist 3%
Ethnic mix Mestizo 44%, Creole 30%, Maya 11%, Garifuna 7%, Other 4%, Asian Indian 4%
Government Parliamentary system
Currency Belizean dollar = 100 cents
Literacy rate 77%
Calorie consumption 2869 calories

BENIN
West Africa

Official name Republic of Benin
Formation 1960 / 1960
Capital Porto-Novo
Population 8.4 million / 197 people per sq mile (76 people per sq km) / 42%
Total area 43,483 sq miles (112,620 sq km)
Languages French*, Fon, Bariba, Yoruba, Adja, Houeda, Somba
Religions Voodoo 50%, Muslim 30%, Christian 20%
Ethnic mix Fon 47%, Other 31%, Adja 12%, Bariba 10%
Government Presidential system
Currency CFA franc = 100 centimes
Literacy rate 34%
Calorie consumption 2548 calories

BHUTAN
South Asia

Official name Kingdom of Bhutan
Formation 1656 / 1865
Capital Thimphu
Population 2.2 million / 121 people per sq mile (47 people per sq km) / 7%
Total area 18,147 sq miles (47,000 sq km)
Languages Dzongkha*, Nepali, Assamese
Religions Mahayana Buddhist 70%, Hindu 24%, Other 6%
Ethnic mix Bhute 50%, Other 25%, Nepalese 25%
Government Monarchy
Currency Ngultrum = 100 chetrum
Literacy rate 47%
Calorie consumption Not available

BOLIVIA
South America

Official name Republic of Bolivia
Formation 1825 /1938
Capital La Paz (administrative); Sucre (judicial)
Population 9.2 million / 22 people per sq mile (8 people per sq km) / 63%
Total area 424,162 sq miles (1,098,580 sq km)
Languages Aymara*, Quechua*, Spanish*
Religions Roman Catholic 93%, Other 7%
Ethnic mix Quechua 37%, Aymara 32%, Mixed race 13%, European 10%, Other 8%
Government Presidential system
Currency Boliviano = 100 centavos
Literacy rate 87%
Calorie consumption 2235 calories

BOSNIA & HERZEGOVINA
Southeast Europe

Official name Bosnia and Herzegovina
Formation 1992 / 1992
Capital Sarajevo
Population 3.9 million / 198 people per sq mile (76 people per sq km) / 43%
Total area 19,741 sq miles (51,129 sq km)
Languages Serbo-Croat*
Religions Muslim (mainly Sunni) 40%, Orthodox Christian 31%, Roman Catholic 15%, Other 10%, Protestant 4%
Ethnic mix Bosniak 48%, Serb 38%, Croat 14%
Government Parliamentary system
Currency Marka = 100 pfeninga
Literacy rate 95%
Calorie consumption 2894 calories

BOTSWANA
Southern Africa

Official name Republic of Botswana
Formation 1966 / 1966
Capital Gaborone
Population 1.8 million / 8 people per sq mile (3 people per sq km) / 50%
Total area 231,803 sq miles (600,370 sq km)
Languages English*, Setswana, Shona, San, Khoikhoi, isiNdebele
Religions Traditional beliefs 50%, Christian (mainly Protestant) 30%, Other (including Muslim) 20%
Ethnic mix Tswana 98%, Other 2%
Government Presidential system
Currency Pula = 100 thebe
Literacy rate 79%
Calorie consumption 2151 calories

BRAZIL
South America

Official name Federative Republic of Brazil
Formation 1822 / 1828
Capital Brasília
Population 186 million / 57 people per sq mile (22 people per sq km) / 81%
Total area 3,286,470 sq miles (8,511,965 sq km)
Languages Portuguese*, German, Italian, Spanish, Polish, Japanese, Amerindian languages
Religions Roman Catholic 74%, Protestant 15%, Atheist 7%, Other 4%
Ethnic mix Black 53%, Mixed race 40%, White 6%, Other 1%
Government Presidential system
Currency Real = 100 centavos
Literacy rate 88%
Calorie consumption 3049 calories

BRUNEI
Southeast Asia

Official name Sultanate of Brunei
Formation 1984 / 1984
Capital Bandar Seri Begawan
Population 374,000 / 184 people per sq mile (71 people per sq km) / 72%
Total area 2228 sq miles (5770 sq km)
Languages Malay*, English, Chinese
Religions Muslim (mainly Sunni) 66%, Buddhist 14%, Other 10%, Christian 10%
Ethnic mix Malay 67%, Chinese 16%, Other 11%, Indigenous 6%
Government Monarchy
Currency Brunei dollar = 100 cents
Literacy rate 93%
Calorie consumption 2855 calories

BULGARIA
Southeast Europe

Official name Republic of Bulgaria
Formation 1908 / 1947
Capital Sofia
Population 7.7 million / 180 people per sq mile (70 people per sq km) / 70%
Total area 42,822 sq miles (110,910 sq km)
Languages Bulgarian*, Turkish, Romani
Religions Orthodox Christian 83%, Muslim 12%, Other 4%, Roman Catholic 1%
Ethnic mix Bulgarian 84%, Turkish 9%, Roma 5%, Other 2%
Government Parliamentary system
Currency Lev = 100 stotinki
Literacy rate 98%
Calorie consumption 2848 calories

BURKINA
West Africa

Official name Burkina Faso
Formation 1960 / 1960
Capital Ouagadougou
Population 13.2 million / 125 people per sq mile (48 people per sq km) / 19%
Total area 105,869 sq miles (274,200 sq km)
Languages French*, Mossi, Fulani, Tuareg, Dyula, Songhai
Religions Muslim 55%, Traditional beliefs 35%, Roman Catholic 9%, Other Christian 1%
Ethnic mix Other 50%, Mossi 50%
Government Presidential system
Currency CFA franc = 100 centimes
Literacy rate 13%
Calorie consumption 2462 calories

BURUNDI
Central Africa

Official name Republic of Burundi
Formation 1962 / 1962
Capital Bujumbura
Population 7.5 million / 757 people per sq mile (292 people per sq km) / 9%
Total area 10,745 sq miles (27,830 sq km)
Languages Kirundi*, French*, Kiswahili
Religions Christian 60%, Traditional beliefs 39%, Muslim 1%
Ethnic mix Hutu 85%, Tutsi 14%, Twa 1%
Government Presidential system
Currency Burundi franc = 100 centimes
Literacy rate 59%
Calorie consumption 1649 calories

CAMBODIA
Southeast Asia

Official name Kingdom of Cambodia
Formation 1953 / 1953
Capital Phnom Penh
Population 14.1 million / 207 people per sq mile (80 people per sq km) / 16%
Total area 69,900 sq miles (181,040 sq km)
Languages Khmer*, French, Chinese, Vietnamese, Cham
Religions Buddhist 93%, Muslim 6%, Christian 1%
Ethnic mix Khmer 90%, Other 5%, Vietnamese 4%, Chinese 1%
Government Parliamentary system
Currency Riel = 100 sen
Literacy rate 74%
Calorie consumption 2046 calories

CAMEROON
Central Africa

Official name Republic of Cameroon
Formation 1960 / 1961
Capital Yaoundé
Population 16.3 million / 907 people per sq mile (350 people per sq km) / 49%
Total area 183,567 sq miles (475,400 sq km)
Languages English*, French*, Bamileke, Fang, Fulani
Religions Roman Catholic 35%, Traditional beliefs 25%, Muslim 22%, Protestant 18%
Ethnic mix Cameroon highlanders 31%, Other 21%, Equatorial Bantu 19%, Kirdi 11%, Fulani 10%, Northwestern Bantu 8%
Government Presidential system
Currency CFA franc = 100 centimes
Literacy rate 68%
Calorie consumption 2273 calories

CANADA
North America

Official name Canada
Formation 1867 / 1949
Capital Ottawa
Population 32.3 million / 9 people per sq mile (4 people per sq km) / 77%
Total area 3,851,788 sq miles (9,976,140 sq km)
Languages English*, French*, Chinese, Italian, German, Ukrainian, Inuktitut, Cree
Religions Roman Catholic 44%, Protestant 29%, Other and nonreligious 27%
Ethnic mix British origin 44%, French origin 25%, Other European 20%, Other 11%
Government Parliamentary system
Currency Canadian dollar = 100 cents
Literacy rate 99%
Calorie consumption 3589 calories

CAPE VERDE
Atlantic Ocean

Official name Republic of Cape Verde
Formation 1975
Capital Praia
Population 507,000 / 326 people per sq mile (126 people per sq km) / 62%
Total area 1557 sq miles (4033 sq km)
Languages Portuguese*, Portuguese Creole
Religions Roman Catholic 97%, Other 2%, Protestant (Church of the Nazarene) 1%
Ethnic mix Mestiço 60%, African 30%, Other 10%
Government Mixed presidential–parliamentary system
Currency Cape Verde escudo = 100 centavos
Literacy rate 76%
Calorie consumption 3243 calories

CENTRAL AFRICAN REPUBLIC
Central Africa

Official name Central African Republic
Formation 1960 / 1960
Capital Bangui
Population 4 million / 17 people per sq mile (6 people per sq km) / 41%
Total area 240,534 sq miles (622,984 sq km)
Languages Sango, Banda, Gbaya, French
Religions Traditional beliefs 60%, Christian (mainly Roman Catholic) 35%, Muslim 5%
Ethnic mix Baya 34%, Banda 27%, Mandjia 21%, Sara 10%, Other 8%
Government Presidential system
Currency CFA franc = 100 centimes
Literacy rate 49%
Calorie consumption 1980 calories

CHAD
Central Africa

Official name Republic of Chad
Formation 1960 / 1960
Capital N'Djamena
Population 9.7 million / 20 people per sq mile (8 people per sq km) / 24%
Total area 495,752 sq miles (1,284,000 sq km)
Languages French, Sara, Arabic, Maba
Religions Muslim 55%, Traditional beliefs 35%, Christian 10%
Ethnic mix Nomads (Tuareg and Toubou) 38%, Sara 30%, Other 17%, Arab 15%
Government Presidential system
Currency CFA franc = 100 centimes
Literacy rate 26%
Calorie consumption 2114 calories

CHILE
South America

Official name Republic of Chile
Formation 1818 / 1883
Capital Santiago
Population 16.3 million / 56 people per sq mile (22 people per sq km) / 86%
Total area 292,258 sq miles (756,950 sq km)
Languages Spanish*, Amerindian languages
Religions Roman Catholic 80%, Other and nonreligious 20%
Ethnic mix Mixed race and European 90%, Amerindian 10%
Government Presidential system
Currency Chilean peso = 100 centavos
Literacy rate 96%
Calorie consumption 2863 calories

CHINA
East Asia

Official name People's Republic of China
Formation 960 / 1999
Capital Beijing
Population 1.32 billion / 365 people per sq mile (141 people per sq km) / 32%
Total area 3,705,386 sq miles (9,596,960 sq km)
Languages Mandarin*, Wu, Cantonese, Hsiang, Min, Hakka, Kan
Religions Nonreligious 59%, Traditional beliefs 20%, Other 13%, Buddhist 6%, Muslim 2%
Ethnic mix Han 92%, Other 6%, Hui 1%, Zhuang 1%
Government One-party state
Currency Renminbi (known as yuan) = 10 jiao
Literacy rate 91%
Calorie consumption 2951 calories

COLOMBIA
South America

Official name Republic of Colombia
Formation 1819 / 1903
Capital Bogotá
Population 45.6 million / 114 people per sq mile (44 people per sq km) / 74%
Total area 439,733 sq miles (1,138,910 sq km)
Languages Spanish*, Wayuu, Páez, and other Amerindian languages
Religions Roman Catholic 95%, Other 5%
Ethnic mix Mestizo 58%, White 20%, European–African 14%, African 4%, African–Amerindian 3%, Amerindian 1%
Government Presidential system
Currency Colombian peso = 100 centavos
Literacy rate 94%
Calorie consumption 2585 calories

COMOROS
Indian Ocean

Official name Union of the Comoros
Formation 1975 / 1975
Capital Moroni
Population 798,000 / 927 people per sq mile (358 people per sq km) / 33%
Total area 838 sq miles (2170 sq km)
Languages Arabic*, Comoran, French
Religions Muslim (mainly Sunni) 98%, Other 1%, Roman Catholic 1%
Ethnic mix Comoran 97%, Other 3%
Government Presidential system
Currency Comoros franc = 100 centimes
Literacy rate 56%
Calorie consumption 1754 calories

CONGO
Central Africa

Official name Republic of the Congo
Formation 1960 / 1960
Capital Brazzaville
Population 4 million / 30 people per sq mile (12 people per sq km) / 63%
Total area 132,046 sq miles (342,000 sq km)
Languages French*, Kongo, Teke, Lingala
Religions Traditional beliefs 50%, Roman Catholic 25%, Protestant 23%, Muslim 2%
Ethnic mix Bakongo 48%, Sangha 20%, Teke 17%, Mbochi 12%, Other 3%
Government Presidential system
Currency CFA franc = 100 centimes
Literacy rate 83%
Calorie consumption 2162 calories

CONGO, DEM. REP.
Central Africa

Official name Democratic Republic of the Congo
Formation 1960 / 1960
Capital Kinshasa
Population 57.5 million / 66 people per sq mile (25 people per sq km) / 30%
Total area 905,563 sq miles (2,345,410 sq km)
Languages French*, Kiswahili, Tshiluba, Kikongo, Lingala
Religions Roman Catholic 50%, Protestant 20%, Traditional beliefs and other 10%, Muslim 10%, Kimbanguist 10%
Ethnic mix Other 55%, Bantu and Hamitic 45%
Government Transitional regime
Currency Congolese franc = 100 centimes
Literacy rate 65%
Calorie consumption 1599 calories

COSTA RICA
Central America

Official name Republic of Costa Rica
Formation 1838 / 1838
Capital San José
Population 4.3 million / 218 people per sq mile (84 people per sq km) / 52%
Total area 19,730 sq miles (51,100 sq km)
Languages Spanish*, English Creole, Bribri, Cabecar
Religions Roman Catholic 76%, Other (including Protestant) 24%
Ethnic mix Mestizo and European 96%, Black 2%, Chinese 1%, Amerindian 1%
Government Presidential system
Currency Costa Rican colón = 100 centimos
Literacy rate 96%
Calorie consumption 2876 calories

CROATIA
Southeast Europe

Official name Republic of Croatia
Formation 1991 / 1991
Capital Zagreb
Population 4.6 million / 211 people per sq mile (81 people per sq km) / 58%
Total area 21,831 sq miles (56,542 sq km)
Languages Croatian*
Religions Roman Catholic 88%, Other 7%, Orthodox Christian 4%, Muslim 1%
Ethnic mix Croat 90%, Other 5%, Serb 4%, Bosniak 1%
Government Parliamentary system
Currency Kuna = 100 lipas
Literacy rate 98%
Calorie consumption 2799 calories

CUBA
West Indies

Official name Republic of Cuba
Formation 1902 / 1902
Capital Havana
Population 11.3 million / 264 people per sq mile (102 people per sq km) / 75%
Total area 42,803 sq miles (110,860 sq km)
Languages Spanish*
Religions Nonreligious 49%, Roman Catholic 40%, Atheist 6%, Other 4%, Protestant 1%
Ethnic mix White 66%, European–African 22%, Black 12%
Government One-party state
Currency Cuban peso = 100 centavos
Literacy rate 97%
Calorie consumption 3152 calories

CYPRUS
Southeast Europe

Official name Republic of Cyprus
Formation 1960 / 1960
Capital Nicosia
Population 835,000 / 234 people per sq mile (90 people per sq km) / 57%
Total area 3571 sq miles (9250 sq km)
Languages Greek, Turkish
Religions Orthodox Christian 78%, Muslim 18%, Other 4%
Ethnic mix Greek 85%, Turkish 12%, Other 3%
Government Presidential system
Currency Cyprus pound (Turkish lira in TRNC) = 100 cents (Cyprus pound); 100 kurus (Turkish lira)
Literacy rate 97%
Calorie consumption 3255 calories

CZECH REPUBLIC
Central Europe

Official name Czech Republic
Formation 1993 / 1993
Capital Prague
Population 10.2 million / 335 people per sq mile (129 people per sq km) / 75%
Total area 30,450 sq miles (78,866 sq km)
Languages Czech*, Slovak, Hungarian (Magyar)
Religions Roman Catholic 39%, Atheist 38%, Other 18%, Protestant 3%, Hussite 2%
Ethnic mix Czech 81%, Moravian 13%, Slovak 6%
Government Parliamentary system
Currency Czech koruna = 100 haleru
Literacy rate 99%
Calorie consumption 3171 calories

DENMARK
Northern Europe

Official name Kingdom of Denmark
Formation AD 950 / 1945
Capital Copenhagen
Population 5.4 million / 330 people per sq mile (127 people per sq km) / 85%
Total area 16,639 sq miles (43,094 sq km)
Languages Danish*
Religions Evangelical Lutheran 89%, Other 10%, Roman Catholic 1%
Ethnic mix Danish 96%, Other (including Scandinavian and Turkish) 3%, Faeroese and Inuit 1%
Government Parliamentary system
Currency Danish krone = 100 øre
Literacy rate 99%
Calorie consumption 3439 calories

DJIBOUTI
East Africa

Official name Republic of Djibouti
Formation 1977 / 1977
Capital Djibouti
Population 793,000 / 89 people per sq mile (34 people per sq km) / 83%
Total area 8494 sq miles (22,000 sq km)
Languages French*, Arabic*, Somali, Afar
Religions Muslim (mainly Sunni) 94%, Christian 6%
Ethnic mix Issa 60%, Afar 35%, Other 5%
Government Presidential system
Currency Djibouti franc = 100 centimes
Literacy rate 66%
Calorie consumption 2220 calories

DOMINICA
West Indies

Official name Commonwealth of Dominica
Formation 1978 / 1978
Capital Roseau
Population 69,029 / 238 people per sq mile (92 people per sq km) / 71%
Total area 291 sq miles (754 sq km)
Languages English*, French Creole
Religions Roman Catholic 77%, Protestant 15%, Other 8%
Ethnic mix Black 91%, Mixed race 6%, Carib 2%, Other 1%
Government Parliamentary system
Currency Eastern Caribbean dollar = 100 cents
Literacy rate 88%
Calorie consumption 2763 calories

DOMINICAN REPUBLIC
West Indies

Official name Dominican Republic
Formation 1865 / 1865
Capital Santo Domingo
Population 8.9 million / 476 people per sq mile (184 people per sq km) / 65%
Total area 18,679 sq miles (48,380 sq km)
Languages Spanish*, French Creole
Religions Roman Catholic 92%, Other and nonreligious 8%
Ethnic mix Mixed race 75%, White 15%, Black 10%
Government Presidential system
Currency Dominican Republic peso = 100 centavos
Literacy rate 88%
Calorie consumption 2347 calories

EAST TIMOR
Southeast Asia

Official name Democratic Republic of Timor-Leste
Formation 2002 / 2002
Capital Dili
Population 947,000 / 168 people per sq mile (65 people per sq km) / 8%
Total area 5756 sq miles (14,874 sq km)
Languages Tetum (Portuguese/Austronesian), Bahasa Indonesia, and Portuguese
Religions Roman Catholic 95%, Other 5%
Ethnic mix Papuan groups approx 85%, Indonesian approx 13%, Chinese 2%
Government Parliamentary system
Currency US dollar = 100 cents
Literacy rate 59%
Calorie consumption 2806 calories

ECUADOR
South America

Official name Republic of Ecuador
Formation 1830 / 1941
Capital Quito
Population 13.2 million / 123 people per sq mile (48 people per sq km) / 65%
Total area 109,483 sq miles (283,560 sq km)
Languages Spanish*, Quechua*, other Amerindian languages
Religions Roman Catholic 93%, Protestant, Jewish, and other 7%
Ethnic mix Mestizo 55%, Amerindian 25%, White 10%, Black 10%
Government Presidential system
Currency US dollar = 100 cents
Literacy rate 91%
Calorie consumption 2754 calories

EGYPT
North Africa

Official name Arab Republic of Egypt
Formation 1936 / 1982
Capital Cairo
Population 74 million / 193 people per sq mile (74 people per sq km) / 45%
Total area 386,660 sq miles (1,001,450 sq km)
Languages Arabic*, French, English, Berber
Religions Muslim (mainly Sunni) 94%, Coptic Christian and other 6%
Ethnic mix Eastern Hamitic 90%, Nubian, Armenian, and Greek 10%
Government Presidential system
Currency Egyptian pound = 100 piastres
Literacy rate 56%
Calorie consumption 3338 calories

EL SALVADOR
Central America

Official name Republic of El Salvador
Formation 1841 / 1841
Capital San Salvador
Population 6.9 million / 862 people per sq mile (333 people per sq km) / 47%
Total area 8124 sq miles (21,040 sq km)
Languages Spanish*
Religions Roman Catholic 80%, Evangelical 18%, Other 2%
Ethnic mix Mestizo 94%, Amerindian 5%, White 1%
Government Presidential system
Currency Salvadorean colón & US dollar = 100 centavos (colón); 100 cents (US dollar)
Literacy rate 80%
Calorie consumption 2584 calories

EQUATORIAL GUINEA
Central Africa

Official name Republic of Equatorial Guinea
Formation 1968 / 1968
Capital Malabo
Population 504,000 / 47 people per sq mile (18 people per sq km) / 48%
Total area 10,830 sq miles (28,051 sq km)
Languages Spanish*, Fang, Bubi
Religions Roman Catholic 90%, Other 10%
Ethnic mix Fang 85%, Other 11%, Bubi 4%
Government Presidential system
Currency CFA franc = 100 centimes
Literacy rate 84%
Calorie consumption Not available

ERITREA
East Africa

Official name State of Eritrea
Formation 1993 / 2002
Capital Asmara
Population 4.4 million / 97 people per sq mile (37 people per sq km) / 19%
Total area 46,842 sq miles (121,320 sq km)
Languages Arabic*, Tigrinya*, English, Tigre, Afar, Bilen, Kunama, Nara, Saho, Hadareb
Religions Christian 45%, Muslim 45%, Other 10%
Ethnic mix Tigray 50%, Tigray and Kunama 40%, Afar 4%, Other 3%, Saho 3%
Government Transitional regime
Currency Nakfa = 100 cents
Literacy rate 57%
Calorie consumption 1513 calories

ESTONIA
Northeast Europe

Official name Republic of Estonia
Formation 1991 / 1991
Capital Tallinn
Population 1.3 million / 75 people per sq mile (29 people per sq km) / 69%
Total area 17,462 sq miles (45,226 sq km)
Languages Estonian*, Russian
Religions Evangelical Lutheran 56%, Orthodox Christian 25%, Other 19%
Ethnic mix Estonian 62%, Russian 30%, Other 8%
Government Parliamentary system
Currency Kroon = 100 senti
Literacy rate 99%
Calorie consumption 3002 calories

ETHIOPIA
East Africa

Official name Federal Democratic Republic of Ethiopia
Formation 1896 / 2002
Capital Addis Ababa
Population 77.4 million / 181 people per sq mile (70 people per sq km) / 18%
Total area 435,184 sq miles (1,127,127 sq km)
Languages Amharic*, Tigrinya, Galla, Sidamo, Somali, English, Arabic
Religions Orthodox Christian 40%, Muslim 40%, Traditional beliefs 15%, Other 5%
Ethnic mix Oromo 40%, Amhara 25%, Other 14%, Sidamo 9%, Berta 6%, Somali 6%
Government Parliamentary system
Currency Ethiopian birr = 100 cents
Literacy rate 42%
Calorie consumption 1857 calories

FIJI
Australasia & Oceania

Official name Republic of the Fiji Islands
Formation 1970 / 1970
Capital Suva
Population 848,000 / 120 people per sq mile (46 people per sq km) / 49%
Total area 7054 sq miles (18,270 sq km)
Languages English*, Fijian*, Hindi, Urdu, Tamil, Telugu
Religions Hindu 38%, Methodist 37%, Roman Catholic 9%, Other 8%, Muslim 8%
Ethnic mix Melanesian 48%, Indian 46%, Other 6%
Government Parliamentary system
Currency Fiji dollar = 100 cents
Literacy rate 93%
Calorie consumption 2894 calories

FINLAND
Northern Europe

Official name Republic of Finland
Formation 1917 / 1947
Capital Helsinki
Population 5.2 million / 44 people per sq mile (17 people per sq km) / 67%
Total area 130,127 sq miles (337,030 sq km)
Languages Finnish*, Swedish*, Sámi
Religions Evangelical Lutheran 89%, Orthodox Christian 1%, Roman Catholic 1%, Other 9%
Ethnic mix Finnish 93%, Other (including Sámi) 7%
Government Parliamentary system
Currency Euro = 100 cents
Literacy rate 99%
Calorie consumption 3100 calories

FRANCE
Western Europe

Official name French Republic
Formation 987 / 1919
Capital Paris
Population 60.5 million / 285 people per sq mile (110 people per sq km) / 76%
Total area 211,208 sq miles (547,030 sq km)
Languages French*, Provençal, German, Breton, Catalan, Basque
Religions Roman Catholic 88%, Muslim 8%, Protestant 2%, Buddhist 1%, Jewish 1%
Ethnic mix French 90%, North African (mainly Algerian) 6%, German (Alsace) 2%, Other 2%
Government Mixed presidential–parliamentary system
Currency Euro = 100 cents
Literacy rate 99%
Calorie consumption 3654 calories

GABON
Central Africa

Official name Gabonese Republic
Formation 1960 / 1960
Capital Libreville
Population 1.4 million / 14 people per sq mile (5 people per sq km) / 81%
Total area 103,346 sq miles (267,667 sq km)
Languages French*,Fang, Punu, Sira, Nzebi, Mpongwe
Religions Christian (mainly Roman Catholic) 55%, Traditional beliefs 40%, Other 4%, Muslim 1%
Ethnic mix Fang 35%, Other Bantu 29%, Eshira 25%, European and other African 9%, French 2%
Government Presidential system
Currency CFA franc = 100 centimes
Literacy rate 71%
Calorie consumption 2637 calories

GAMBIA
West Africa

Official name Republic of the Gambia
Formation 1965 / 1965
Capital Banjul
Population 1.5 million / 389 people per sq mile (150 people per sq km) / 33%
Total area 4363 sq miles (11,300 sq km)
Languages English*, Mandinka, Fulani, Wolof, Jola, Soninke
Religions Sunni Muslim 90%, Christian 9%, Traditional beliefs 1%
Ethnic mix Mandinka 42%, Fulani 18%, Wolof 16%, Jola 10%, Serahuli 9%, Other 5%
Government Presidential system
Currency Dalasi = 100 butut
Literacy rate 38%
Calorie consumption 2273 calories

GEORGIA
Southwest Asia

Official name Georgia
Formation 1991 / 1991
Capital Tbilisi
Population 4.5 million / 167 people per sq mile (65 people per sq km) / 61%
Total area 26,911 sq miles (69,700 sq km)
Languages Georgian*, Russian, Azeri, Armenian, Mingrelian, Ossetian, Abkhazian
Religions Georgian Orthodox 65%, Muslim 11%, Russian Orthodox 10%, Armenian Orthodox 8%, Other 6%
Ethnic mix Georgian 70%, Armenian 8%, Russian 5%, Azeri 6%, Ossetian 3%, Other 7%
Government Presidential system
Currency Lari = 100 tetri
Literacy rate 99%
Calorie consumption 2354 calories

GERMANY
Northern Europe

Official name Federal Republic of Germany
Formation 1871 / 1990
Capital Berlin
Population 82.7 million / 613 people per sq mile (237 people per sq km) / 88%
Total area 137,846 sq miles (357,021 sq km)
Languages German*, Turkish
Religions Protestant 34%, Roman Catholic 33%, Other 30%, Muslim 3%
Ethnic mix German 92%, Other 3%, Other European 3%, Turkish 2%
Government Parliamentary system
Currency Euro = 100 cents
Literacy rate 99%
Calorie consumption 3496 calories

GHANA
West Africa

Official name Republic of Ghana
Formation 1957 / 1957
Capital Accra
Population 22.1 million / 249 people per sq mile (96 people per sq km) / 38%
Total area 92,100 sq miles (238,540 sq km)
Languages Twi, Fanti, Ewe, Ga, Adangbe, Gurma, Dagomba (Dagbani)
Religions Christian 69%, Muslim 16%, Traditional beliefs 9%, Other 6%
Ethnic mix Ashanti and Fanti 52%, Moshi-Dagomba 15%, Ewe 12%, Other 11%, Ga and Ga-adanbe 8%, Yoruba 1%
Government Presidential system
Currency Cedi = 100 pesewas
Literacy rate 54%
Calorie consumption 2667 calories

GREECE
Southeast Europe

Official name Hellenic Republic
Formation 1829 / 1947
Capital Athens
Population 11.1 million / 220 people per sq mile (85 people per sq km) / 60%
Total area 50,942 sq miles (131,940 sq km)
Languages Greek*, Turkish, Macedonian, Albanian
Religions Orthodox Christian 98%, Other 1%, Muslim 1%
Ethnic mix Greek 98%, Other 2%
Government Parliamentary system
Currency Euro = 100 cents
Literacy rate 91%
Calorie consumption 3721 calories

GRENADA
West Indies

Official name Grenada
Formation 1974 / 1974
Capital St. George's
Population 89,502 / 683 people per sq mile (263 people per sq km) / 38%
Total area 131 sq miles (340 sq km)
Languages English*, English Creole
Religions Roman Catholic 68%, Anglican 17%, Other 15%
Ethnic mix Black African 82%, Mulatto (mixed race) 13%, East Indian 3%, Other 2%
Government Parliamentary system
Currency Eastern Caribbean dollar = 100 cents
Literacy rate 96%
Calorie consumption 2932 calories

GUATEMALA
Central America

Official name Republic of Guatemala
Formation 1838 / 1838
Capital Guatemala City
Population 12.6 million / 301 people per sq mile (116 people per sq km) / 40%
Total area 42,042 sq miles (108,890 sq km)
Languages Spanish*, Quiché, Mam, Cakchiquel, Kekchi
Religions Roman Catholic 65%, Protestant 33%, Other and nonreligious 2%
Ethnic mix Amerindian 60%, Mestizo 30%, Other 10%
Government Presidential system
Currency Quetzal = 100 centavos
Literacy rate 69%
Calorie consumption 2219 calories

GUINEA
West Africa

Official name Republic of Guinea
Formation 1958 / 1958
Capital Conakry
Population 9.4 million / 99 people per sq mile (38 people per sq km) / 33%
Total area 94,925 sq miles (245,857 sq km)
Languages French*, Fulani, Malinke, Soussou
Religions Muslim 65%, Traditional beliefs 33%, Christian 2%
Ethnic mix Fulani 30%, Malinke 30%, Soussou 15%, Kissi 10%, Other tribes 10%, Other 5%
Government Presidential system
Currency Guinea franc = 100 centimes
Literacy rate 41%
Calorie consumption 2409 calories

GUINEA-BISSAU
West Africa

Official name Republic of Guinea-Bissau
Formation 1974 / 1974
Capital Bissau
Population 1.6 million / 147 people per sq mile (57 people per sq km) / 24%
Total area 13,946 sq miles (36,120 sq km)
Languages Portuguese*, Balante, Fulani, Malinke, Portuguese Creole
Religions Traditional beliefs 52%, Muslim 40%, Christian 8%
Ethnic mix Other tribes 31%, Balante 25%, Fula 20%, Mandinka 12%, Mandyako 11%, Other 1%
Government Presidential system
Currency CFA franc = 100 centimes
Literacy rate 40%
Calorie consumption 2024 calories

GUYANA
South America

Official name Cooperative Republic of Guyana
Formation 1966 / 1966
Capital Georgetown
Population 751,000 / 10 people per sq mile (4 people per sq km) / 38%
Total area 83,000 sq miles (214,970 sq km)
Languages English*, Hindi, Tamil, Amerindian languages, English Creole
Religions Christian 57%, Hindu 33%, Muslim 9%, Other 1%
Ethnic mix East Indian 52%, Black African 38%, Other 4%, Amerindian 4%, European and Chinese 2%
Government Presidential system
Currency Guyanese dollar = 100 cents
Literacy rate 97%
Calorie consumption 2692 calories

HAITI
West Indies

Official name Republic of Haiti
Formation 1804 / 1844
Capital Port-au-Prince
Population 8.5 million / 799 people per sq mile (308 people per sq km) / 36%
Total area 10,714 sq miles (27,750 sq km)
Languages French Creole*, French*
Religions Roman Catholic 80%, Protestant 16%, Other (including Voodoo) 3%, Nonreligious 1%
Ethnic mix Black African 95%, Mulatto (mixed race) and European 5%
Government Transitional regime
Currency Gourde = 100 centimes
Literacy rate 52%
Calorie consumption 2086 calories

HONDURAS
Central America

Official name Republic of Honduras
Formation 1838 / 1838
Capital Tegucigalpa
Population 7.2 million / 167 people per sq mile (64 people per sq km) / 53%
Total area 43,278 sq miles (112,090 sq km)
Languages Spanish*, Garifuna (Carib), English Creole
Religions Roman Catholic 97%, Protestant 3%
Ethnic mix Mestizo 90%, Black African 5%, Amerindian 4%, White 1%
Government Presidential system
Currency Lempira = 100 centavos
Literacy rate 80%
Calorie consumption 2356 calories

HUNGARY
Central Europe

Official name Republic of Hungary
Formation 1918 / 1947
Capital Budapest
Population 10.1 million / 283 people per sq mile (109 people per sq km) / 64%
Total area 35,919 sq miles (93,030 sq km)
Languages Hungarian (Magyar)*
Religions Roman Catholic 52%, Calvinist 16%, Other 15%, Nonreligious 14%, Lutheran 3%
Ethnic mix Magyar 90%, Other 7%, Roma 2%, German 1%
Government Parliamentary system
Currency Forint = 100 fillér
Literacy rate 99%
Calorie consumption 3483 calories

ICELAND
Northwest Europe

Official name Republic of Iceland
Formation 1944 / 1944
Capital Reykjavik
Population 295,000 / 8 people per sq mile (3 people per sq km) / 93%
Total area 39,768 sq miles (103,000 sq km)
Languages Icelandic*
Religions Evangelical Lutheran 93%, Nonreligious 6%, Other (mostly Christian) 1%
Ethnic mix Icelandic 94%, Other 5%, Danish 1%
Government Parliamentary system
Currency Icelandic króna = 100 aurar
Literacy rate 99%
Calorie consumption 3249 calories

INDIA
South Asia

Official name Republic of India
Formation 1947 / 1947
Capital New Delhi
Population 1.1 billion / 961 people per sq mile (371 people per sq km) / 28%
Total area 1,269,338 sq miles (3,287,590 sq km)
Languages Hindi*, English*, Bengali, Marathi, Telugu, Tamil, Bihari, Gujarati, Kanarese, Urdu
Religions Hindu 83%, Muslim 11%, Christian 2%, Sikh 2%, Other 1%, Buddhist 1%
Ethnic mix Indo-Aryan 72%, Dravidian 25%, Mongoloid and other 3%
Government Parliamentary system
Currency Indian rupee = 100 paise
Literacy rate 61%
Calorie consumption 2459 calories

INDONESIA
Southeast Asia

Official name Republic of Indonesia
Formation 1949 / 1999
Capital Jakarta
Population 223 million / 321 people per sq mile (124 people per sq km) / 41%
Total area 741,096 sq miles (1,919,440 sq km)
Languages Bahasa Indonesia*, Javanese, Sundanese, Madurese, Dutch
Religions Sunni Muslim 87%, Protestant 6%, Roman Catholic 3%, Hindu 2%, Other 2%
Ethnic mix Javanese 45%, Sundanese 14%, Coastal Malays 8%, Madurese 8%, Other 25%
Government Presidential system
Currency Rupiah = 100 sen
Literacy rate 88%
Calorie consumption 2904 calories

IRAN
Southwest Asia

Official name Islamic Republic of Iran
Formation 1502 / 1990
Capital Tehran
Population 69.5 million / 110 people per sq mile (42 people per sq km) / 62%
Total area 636,293 sq miles (1,648,000 sq km)
Languages Farsi*, Azeri, Luri, Gilaki, Mazanderani, Kurdish, Turkmen, Arabic, Baluchi
Religions Shi'a Muslim 93%, Sunni Muslim 6%, Other 1%
Ethnic mix Persian 50%, Azari 24%, Other 10%, Kurdish 8%, Lur and Bakhtiari 8%
Government Islamic theocracy
Currency Iranian rial = 100 dinars
Literacy rate 77%
Calorie consumption 3085 calories

IRAQ
Southwest Asia

Official name Republic of Iraq
Formation 1932 / 1990
Capital Baghdad
Population 28.8 million / 171 people per sq mile (66 people per sq km) / 77%
Total area 168,753 sq miles (437,072 sq km)
Languages Arabic*, Kurdish, Turkic languages, Armenian, Assyrian
Religions Shi'a Muslim 60%, Sunni Muslim 35%, Other (including Christian) 5%
Ethnic mix Arab 80%, Kurdish 15%, Turkmen 3%, Other 2%
Government Transitional regime
Currency New Iraqi dinar = 1000 fils
Literacy rate 40%
Calorie consumption 2197 calories

IRELAND
Northwest Europe

Official name Ireland
Formation 1922 / 1922
Capital Dublin
Population 4.1 million / 154 people per sq mile (60 people per sq km) / 59%
Total area 27,135 sq miles (70,280 sq km)
Languages English*, Irish Gaelic*
Religions Roman Catholic 88%, Other and nonreligious 9%, Anglican 3%
Ethnic mix Irish 93%, Other 4%, British 3%
Government Parliamentary system
Currency Euro = 100 cents
Literacy rate 99%
Calorie consumption 3656 calories

ISRAEL
Southwest Asia

Official name State of Israel
Formation 1948 / 1994
Capital Jerusalem (not internationally recognized)
Population 6.7 million / 854 people per sq mile (330 people per sq km) / 91%
Total area 8019 sq miles (20,770 sq km)
Languages Hebrew*, Arabic, Yiddish, German, Russian, Polish, Romanian, Persian
Religions Jewish 80%, Muslim (mainly Sunni) 16%, Druze and other 2%, Christian 2%
Ethnic mix Jewish 80%, Other (mostly Arab) 20%
Government Parliamentary system
Currency Shekel = 100 agorot
Literacy rate 97%
Calorie consumption 3666 calories

ITALY
Southern Europe

Official name Italian Republic
Formation 1861 / 1947
Capital Rome
Population 58.1 million / 512 people per sq mile (198 people per sq km) / 67%
Total area 116,305 sq miles (301,230 sq km)
Languages Italian*, German, French, Rhaeto-Romanic, Sardinian
Religions Roman Catholic 85%, Other and nonreligious 13%, Muslim 2%
Ethnic mix Italian 94%, Other 4%, Sardinian 2%
Government Parliamentary system
Currency Euro = 100 cents
Literacy rate 99%
Calorie consumption 3671 calories

IVORY COAST
West Africa

Official name Republic of Côte d'Ivoire
Formation 1960 / 1960
Capital Yamoussoukro
Population 18.2 million / 148 people per sq mile (57 people per sq km) / 46%
Total area 124,502 sq miles (322,460 sq km)
Languages French*, Akan, Kru, Voltaic
Religions Muslim 38%, Traditional beliefs 25%, Roman Catholic 25%, Protestant 6%, Other 6%
Ethnic mix Baoulé 23%, Other 19%, Bété 18%, Senufo 15%, Agni-Ashanti 14%, Mandinka 11%
Government Presidential system
Currency CFA franc = 100 centimes
Literacy rate 48%
Calorie consumption 2631 calories

JAMAICA
West Indies

Official name Jamaica
Formation 1962 / 1962
Capital Kingston
Population 2.7 million / 646 people per sq mile (249 people per sq km) / 56%
Total area 4243 sq miles (10,990 sq km)
Languages English*, English Creole
Religions Other and nonreligious 45%, Other Protestant 20%, Church of God 18%, Baptist 10%, Anglican 7%
Ethnic mix Black African 75%, Mulatto (mixed race) 13%, European and Chinese 11%, East Indian 1%
Government Parliamentary system
Currency Jamaican dollar = 100 cents
Literacy rate 88%
Calorie consumption 2685 calories

JAPAN
East Asia

Official name Japan
Formation 1590 / 1972
Capital Tokyo
Population 128 million / 881 people per sq mile (340 people per sq km) / 79%
Total area 145,882 sq miles (377,835 sq km)
Languages Japanese, Korean, Chinese
Religions Shinto and Buddhist 76%, Buddhist 16%, Other (including Christian) 8%
Ethnic mix Japanese 99%, Other (mainly Korean) 1%
Government Parliamentary system
Currency Yen = 100 sen
Literacy rate 99%
Calorie consumption 2761 calories

JORDAN
Southwest Asia

Official name Hashemite Kingdom of Jordan
Formation 1946 / 1967
Capital Amman
Population 5.6 million / 163 people per sq mile (63 people per sq km) / 74%
Total area 35,637 sq miles (92,300 sq km)
Languages Arabic*
Religions Muslim (mainly Sunni) 92%, Other (mostly Christian) 8%
Ethnic mix Arab 98%, Circassian 1%, Armenian 1%
Government Monarchy
Currency Jordanian dinar = 1000 fils
Literacy rate 90%
Calorie consumption 2673 calories

KAZAKHSTAN
Central Asia

Official name Republic of Kazakhstan
Formation 1991 / 1991
Capital Astana
Population 14.8 million / 14 people per sq mile (5 people per sq km) / 56%
Total area 1,049,150 sq miles (2,717,300 sq km)
Languages Kazakh*, Russian*, Ukrainian, Tatar, German, Uzbek, Uighur
Religions Muslim (mainly Sunni) 47%, Orthodox Christian 44%, Other 9%
Ethnic mix Kazakh 53%, Russian 30%, Other 9% Ukrainian 4%, Tatar 2%, German 2%
Government Presidential system
Currency Tenge = 100 tiyn
Literacy rate 99%
Calorie consumption 2677 calories

KENYA
East Africa

Official name Republic of Kenya
Formation 1963 / 1963
Capital Nairobi
Population 34.3 million / 157 people per sq mile (60 people per sq km) / 33%
Total area 224,961 sq miles (582,650 sq km)
Languages Kiswahili*, English*, Kikuyu, Luo, Kalenjin, Kamba
Religions Christian 60%, Traditional beliefs 25%, Other 9%, Muslim 6%
Ethnic mix Other 30%, Kikuyu 21%, Luhya 14% Luo 13%, Kalenjin 11%, Kamba 11%
Government Presidential system
Currency Kenya shilling = 100 cents
Literacy rate 74%
Calorie consumption 2090 calories

KIRIBATI
Australasia & Oceania

Official name Republic of Kiribati
Formation 1979 / 1979
Capital Bairiki (Tarawa Atoll)
Population 103,092 / 376 people per sq mile (145 people per sq km) / 36%
Total area 277 sq miles (717 sq km)
Languages English*, Kiribati
Religions Roman Catholic 53%, Kiribati Protestant Church 39%, Other 8%
Ethnic mix Micronesian 96%, Other 4%
Government Nonparty system
Currency Australian dollar = 100 cents
Literacy rate 99%
Calorie consumption 2859 calories

KUWAIT
Southwest Asia

Official name State of Kuwait
Formation 1961 / 1961
Capital Kuwait City
Population 2.7 million / 392 people per sq mile (152 people per sq km) / 98%
Total area 6880 sq miles (17,820 sq km)
Languages Arabic*, English
Religions Sunni Muslim 45%, Shi'a Muslim 40%, Christian, Hindu, and other 15%
Ethnic mix Kuwaiti 45%, Other Arab 35%, South Asian 9%, Other 7%, Iranian 4%
Government Monarchy
Currency Kuwaiti dinar = 1000 fils
Literacy rate 83%
Calorie consumption 3010 calories

KYRGYZSTAN
Central Asia

Official name Kyrgyz Republic
Formation 1991 / 1991
Capital Bishkek
Population 5.3 million / 69 people per sq mile (27 people per sq km) / 33%
Total area 76,641 sq miles (198,500 sq km)
Languages Kyrgyz*, Russian*, Uzbek, Tatar, Ukrainian
Religions Muslim (mainly Sunni) 70%, Orthodox Christian 30%
Ethnic mix Kyrgyz 57%, Russian 19%, Uzbek 13%, Other 7%, Tatar 2%, Ukrainian 2%
Government Presidential system
Currency Som = 100 tyyn
Literacy rate 99%
Calorie consumption 2999 calories

LAOS
Southeast Asia

Official name Lao People's Democratic Republic
Formation 1953 / 1953
Capital Vientiane
Population 5.9 million / 66 people per sq mile (26 people per sq km) / 24%
Total area 91,428 sq miles (236,800 sq km)
Languages Lao*, Mon-Khmer, Yao, Vietnamese, Chinese, French
Religions Buddhist 85%, Other (including animist) 15%
Ethnic mix Lao Loum 66%, Lao Theung 30%, Other 2%, Lao Soung 2%
Government One-party state
Currency New kip = 100 at
Literacy rate 69%
Calorie consumption 2312 calories

LATVIA
Northeast Europe

Official name Republic of Latvia
Formation 1991 / 1991
Capital Riga
Population 2.3 million / 92 people per sq mile (36 people per sq km) / 69%
Total area 24,938 sq miles (64,589 sq km)
Languages Latvian*, Russian
Religions Lutheran 55%, Roman Catholic 24%, Other 12%, Orthodox Christian 9%
Ethnic mix Latvian 57%, Russian 32%, Belarussian 4%, Ukrainian 3%, Polish 2%, Other 2%
Government Parliamentary system
Currency Lats = 100 santims
Literacy rate 99%
Calorie consumption 2938 calories

LEBANON
Southwest Asia

Official name Republic of Lebanon
Formation 1941 / 1941
Capital Beirut
Population 3.6 million / 911 people per sq mile (352 people per sq km) / 90%
Total area 4015 sq miles (10,400 sq km)
Languages Arabic*, French, Armenian, Assyrian
Religions Muslim 70%, Christian 30%
Ethnic mix Arab 94%, Armenian 4%, Other 2%
Government Parliamentary system
Currency Lebanese pound = 100 piastres
Literacy rate 87%
Calorie consumption 3196 calories

LESOTHO
Southern Africa

Official name Kingdom of Lesotho
Formation 1966 / 1966
Capital Maseru
Population 1.8 million / 154 people per sq mile (59 people per sq km) / 28%
Total area 11,720 sq miles (30,355 sq km)
Languages English*, Sesotho*, isiZulu
Religions Christian 90%, Traditional beliefs 10%
Ethnic mix Sotho 97%, European and Asian 3%
Government Parliamentary system
Currency Loti = 100 lisente
Literacy rate 81%
Calorie consumption 2638 calories

LIBERIA
West Africa

Official name Republic of Liberia
Formation 1847 / 1847
Capital Monrovia
Population 3.3 million / 89 people per sq mile (34 people per sq km) / 45%
Total area 43,000 sq miles (111,370 sq km)
Languages English*, Kpelle, Vai, Bassa, Kru, Grebo, Kissi, Gola, Loma
Religions Christian 68%, Traditional beliefs 18%, Muslim 14%
Ethnic mix Indigenous tribes (16 main groups) 95%, Americo-Liberians 5%
Government Transitional regime
Currency Liberian dollar = 100 cents
Literacy rate 58%
Calorie consumption 1900 calories

LIBYA
North Africa

Official name Great Socialist People's Libyan Arab Jamahariyah
Formation 1951 / 1951
Capital Tripoli
Population 5.9 million / 9 people per sq mile (3 people per sq km) / 88%
Total area 679,358 sq miles (1,759,540 sq km)
Languages Arabic*, Tuareg
Religions Muslim (mainly Sunni) 97%, Other 3%
Ethnic mix Arab and Berber 95%, Other 5%
Government One-party state
Currency Libyan dinar = 1000 dirhams
Literacy rate 82%
Calorie consumption 3320 calories

LIECHTENSTEIN
Central Europe

Official name Principality of Liechtenstein
Formation 1719 / 1719
Capital Vaduz
Population 33,717 / 544 people per sq mile (211 people per sq km) / 21%
Total area 62 sq miles (160 sq km)
Languages German*, Alemannish dialect, Italian
Religions Roman Catholic 81%, Other 12%, Protestant 7%
Ethnic mix Liechtensteiner 62%, Foreign residents 38%
Government Parliamentary system
Currency Swiss franc = 100 rappen/centimes
Literacy rate 99%
Calorie consumption Not available

LITHUANIA
Northeast Europe

Official name Republic of Lithuania
Formation 1991 / 1991
Capital Vilnius
Population 3.4 million / 135 people per sq mile (52 people per sq km) / 68%
Total area 25,174 sq miles (65,200 sq km)
Languages Lithuanian*, Russian
Religions Roman Catholic 83%, Other 12%, Protestant 5%
Ethnic mix Lithuanian 80%, Russian 9%, Polish 7%, Other 2%, Belarussian 2%
Government Parliamentary system
Currency Litas (euro is also legal tender) = 100 centu
Literacy rate 99%
Calorie consumption 3324 calories

LUXEMBOURG
Northwest Europe

Official name Grand Duchy of Luxembourg
Formation 1867 / 1867
Capital Luxembourg-Ville
Population 465,000 / 466 people per sq mile (180 people per sq km) / 92%
Total area 998 sq miles (2586 sq km)
Languages Luxembourgish*, German*, French*
Religions Roman Catholic 97%, Protestant, Orthodox Christian, and Jewish 3%
Ethnic mix Luxembourger 73%, Foreign residents 27%
Government Parliamentary system
Currency Euro = 100 cents
Literacy rate 99%
Calorie consumption 3701 calories

MACEDONIA
Southeast Europe

Official name Republic of Macedonia
Formation 1991 / 1991
Capital Skopje
Population 2 million / 201 people per sq mile (78 people per sq km) / 62%
Total area 9781 sq miles (25,333 sq km)
Languages Macedonian, Albanian, Serbo-Croat
Religions Orthodox Christian 59%, Muslim 26%, Other 10%, Roman Catholic 4%, Protestant 1%
Ethnic mix Macedonian 64%, Albanian 25%, Turkish 4%, Roma 3%, Other 2%, Serb 2%
Government Mixed presidential–parliamentary system
Currency Macedonian denar = 100 deni
Literacy rate 96%
Calorie consumption 2655 calories

MADAGASCAR
Indian Ocean

Official name Republic of Madagascar
Formation 1960 / 1960
Capital Antananarivo
Population 18.6 million / 83 people per sq mile (32 people per sq km) / 30%
Total area 226,656 sq miles (587,040 sq km)
Languages Malagasy*, French*
Religions Traditional beliefs 52%, Christian (mainly Roman Catholic) 41%, Muslim 7%
Ethnic mix Other Malay 46%, Merina 26%, Betsimisaraka 15%, Betsileo 12%, Other 1%
Government Presidential system
Currency Ariary = 5 iraimbilanja
Literacy rate 71%
Calorie consumption 2005 calories

MALAWI
Southern Africa

Official name Republic of Malawi
Formation 1964 / 1964
Capital Lilongwe
Population 12.9 million / 355 people per sq mile (137 people per sq km) / 25%
Total area 45,745 sq miles (118,480 sq km)
Languages English*, Chewa*, Lomwe, Yao, Ngoni
Religions Protestant 55%, Roman Catholic 20%, Muslim 20%, Traditional beliefs 5%
Ethnic mix Bantu 99%, Other 1%
Government Presidential system
Currency Malawi kwacha = 100 tambala
Literacy rate 64%
Calorie consumption 2155 calories

MALAYSIA
Southeast Asia

Official name Federation of Malaysia
Formation 1963 / 1965
Capital Kuala Lumpur; Putrajaya (administrative)
Population 25.3 million / 199 people per sq mile (77 people per sq km) / 57%
Total area 127,316 sq miles (329,750 sq km)
Languages Malay*, Chinese*, Bahasa Malaysia, Tamil, English
Religions Muslim (mainly Sunni) 53%, Buddhist 19%, Chinese faiths 12%, Other 7%, Christian 7%, Traditional beliefs 2%
Ethnic mix Malay 48%, Chinese 29%, Indigenous tribes 12%, Indian 6%, Other 5%
Government Parliamentary system
Currency Ringgit = 100 sen
Literacy rate 89%
Calorie consumption 2881 calories

MALDIVES
Indian Ocean

Official name Republic of Maldives
Formation 1965 / 1965
Capital Male'
Population 329,000 / 2836 people per sq mile (1097 people per sq km) / 30%
Total area 116 sq miles (300 sq km)
Languages Dhivehi (Maldivian)*, Sinhala, Tamil, Arabic
Religions Sunni Muslim 100%
Ethnic mix Arab–Sinhalese–Malay 100%
Government Nonparty system
Currency Rufiyaa = 100 lari
Literacy rate 97%
Calorie consumption 2548 calories

MALI
West Africa

Official name Republic of Mali
Formation 1960 / 1960
Capital Bamako
Population 13.5 million / 29 people per sq mile (11 people per sq km) / 30%
Total area 478,764 sq miles (1,240,000 sq km)
Languages French*, Bambara, Fulani, Senufo, Soninke
Religions Muslim (mainly Sunni) 80%, Traditional beliefs 18%, Christian 1%, Other 1%
Ethnic mix Bambara 32%, Other 26%, Fulani 14%, Senufo 12%, Soninka 9%, Tuareg 7%
Government Presidential system
Currency CFA franc = 100 centimes
Literacy rate 19%
Calorie consumption 2174 calories

MALTA
Southern Europe

Official name Republic of Malta
Formation 1964 / 1964
Capital Valletta
Population 402,000 / 3242 people per sq mile (1256 people per sq km) / 91%
Total area 122 sq miles (316 sq km)
Languages Maltese*, English
Religions Roman Catholic 98%, Other and nonreligious 2%
Ethnic mix Maltese 96%, Other 4%
Government Parliamentary system
Currency Maltese lira = 100 cents
Literacy rate 88%
Calorie consumption 3587 calories

MARSHALL ISLANDS
Australasia & Oceania

Official name Republic of the Marshall Islands
Formation 1986 / 1986
Capital Majuro
Population 59,071 / 844 people per sq mile (326 people per sq km) / 69%
Total area 70 sq miles (181 sq km)
Languages Marshallese*, English*, Japanese, German
Religions Protestant 90%, Roman Catholic 8%, Other 2%
Ethnic mix Micronesian 97%, Other 3%
Government Presidential system
Currency US dollar = 100 cents
Literacy rate 91%
Calorie consumption Not available

MAURITANIA
West Africa

Official name Islamic Republic of Mauritania
Formation 1960 / 1960
Capital Nouakchott
Population 3.1 million / 8 people per sq mile (3 people per sq km) / 58%
Total area 397,953 sq miles (1,030,700 sq km)
Languages French*, Hassaniyah Arabic, Wolof
Religions Sunni Muslim 100%
Ethnic mix Maure 81%, Wolof 7%, Tukolor 5%, Other 4%, Soninka 3%
Government Transitional regime
Currency Ouguiya = 5 khoums
Literacy rate 51%
Calorie consumption 2772 calories

MAURITIUS
Indian Ocean

Official name Republic of Mauritius
Formation 1968 / 1968
Capital Port Louis
Population 1.2 million / 1671 people per sq mile (645 people per sq km) / 41%
Total area 718 sq miles (1860 sq km)
Languages English*, French Creole, Hindi, Urdu, Tamil, Chinese, French
Religions Hindu 52%, Roman Catholic 26%, Muslim 17%, Other 3%, Protestant 2%
Ethnic mix Indo-Mauritian 68%, Creole 27%, Sino-Mauritian 3%, Franco-Mauritian 2%
Government Parliamentary system
Currency Mauritian rupee = 100 cents
Literacy rate 84%
Calorie consumption 2955 calories

MEXICO
North America

Official name United Mexican States
Formation 1836 / 1848
Capital Mexico City
Population 107 million / 145 people per sq mile (56 people per sq km) / 74%
Total area 761,602 sq miles (1,972,550 sq km)
Languages Spanish*, Nahuatl, Mayan, Zapotec, Mixtec, Otomi, Totonac, Tzotzil, Tzeltal
Religions Roman Catholic 88%, Other 7%, Protestant 5%
Ethnic mix Mestizo 60%, Amerindian 30%, European 9%, Other 1%
Government Presidential system
Currency Mexican peso = 100 centavos
Literacy rate 90%
Calorie consumption 3145 calories

MICRONESIA
Australasia & Oceania

Official name Federated States of Micronesia
Formation 1986 / 1986
Capital Palikir (Pohnpei Island)
Population 108,105 / 399 people per sq mile (154 people per sq km) / 28%
Total area 271 sq miles (702 sq km)
Languages Trukese, Pohnpeian, Mortlockese, Kosraean, English
Religions Roman Catholic 50%, Protestant 48%, Other 2%
Ethnic mix Micronesian 100%
Government Nonparty system
Currency US dollar = 100 cents
Literacy rate 81%
Calorie consumption Not available

MOLDOVA
Southeast Europe

Official name Republic of Moldova
Formation 1991 / 1991
Capital Chisinau
Population 4.2 million / 323 people per sq mile (125 people per sq km) / 46%
Total area 13,067 sq miles (33,843 sq km)
Languages Moldovan*, Ukrainian, Russian
Religions Orthodox Christian 98%, Jewish 2%
Ethnic mix Moldovan 65%, Ukrainian 14%, Russian 13%, Other 4%, Gagauz 4%
Government Parliamentary system
Currency Moldovan leu = 100 bani
Literacy rate 96%
Calorie consumption 2806 calories

MONACO
Southern Europe

Official name Principality of Monaco
Formation 1861 / 1861
Capital Monaco-Ville
Population 32,409 / 43212 people per sq mile (16620 people per sq km) / 100%
Total area 0.75 sq miles (1.95 sq km)
Languages French*, Italian, Monégasque, English
Religions Roman Catholic 89%, Protestant 6%, Other 5%
Ethnic mix French 47%, Other 20% Monégasque 17%, Italian 16%
Government Monarchy
Currency Euro = 100 cents
Literacy rate 99%
Calorie consumption Not available

MONGOLIA
East Asia

Official name Mongolia
Formation 1924 / 1924
Capital Ulan Bator
Population 2.6 million / 4 people per sq mile (2 people per sq km) / 64%
Total area 604,247 sq miles (1,565,000 sq km)
Languages Khalkha Mongolian*, Kazakh, Chinese, Russian
Religions Tibetan Buddhist 96%, Muslim 4%
Ethnic mix Mongol 90%, Kazakh 4%, Other 2%, Chinese 2%, Russian 2%
Government Mixed presidential–parliamentary system
Currency Tugrik (tögrög) = 100 möngö
Literacy rate 98%
Calorie consumption 2249 calories

MONTENEGRO
Europe

Official name Republic of Montenegro
Formation 2006 / 2006
Capital Podgorica
Population 620,145 / 116 people per sq mile (45 people per sq km) / 62%
Total area 5,332 sq miles (13,812 sq km)
Languages Montenegrin, Serbian, Albanian
Religions Orthodox Christian 74%, Muslim 18%, Roman Catholic 4%, Other 4%
Ethnic mix Montenegrin 43%, Serb 32%, Bosniak 8%, Albanian 5%, Other 12%
Government Parliamentary system
Currency Euro = 100 cents
Literacy rate 98%
Calorie consumption Not available

MOROCCO
North Africa

Official name Kingdom of Morocco
Formation 1956 / 1956
Capital Rabat
Population 31.5 million / 183 people per sq mile (71 people per sq km) / 56%
Total area 172,316 sq miles (446,300 sq km)
Languages Arabic*, Tamazight (Berber), French, Spanish
Religions Muslim (mainly Sunni) 99%, Other (mostly Christian) 1%
Ethnic mix Arab 70%, Berber 29%, European 1%
Government Monarchy
Currency Moroccan dirham = 100 centimes
Literacy rate 51%
Calorie consumption 3052 calories

MOZAMBIQUE
Southern Africa

Official name Republic of Mozambique
Formation 1975 / 1975
Capital Maputo
Population 19.8 million / 65 people per sq mile (25 people per sq km) / 40%
Total area 309,494 sq miles (801,590 sq km)
Languages Portuguese*, Makua, Xitsonga, Sena, Lomwe
Religions Traditional beliefs 56%, Christian 30%, Muslim 14%
Ethnic mix Makua Lomwe 47%, Tsonga 23%, Malawi 12%, Shona 11%, Yao 4%, Other 3%
Government Presidential system
Currency Metical = 100 centavos
Literacy rate 47%
Calorie consumption 2079 calories

MYANMAR (BURMA)
Southeast Asia

Official name Union of Myanmar
Formation 1948 / 1948
Capital Rangoon (Yangon), Pyinmana
Population 50.5 million / 199 people per sq mile (77 people per sq km) / 28%
Total area 261,969 sq miles (678,500 sq km)
Languages Burmese*, Shan, Karen, Rakhine, Chin, Yangbye, Kachin, Mon
Religions Buddhist 87%, Christian 6%, Muslim 4%, Other 2%, Hindu 1%
Ethnic mix Burman (Bamah) 68%, Other 13%, Shan 9%, Karen 6%, Rakhine 4%
Government Military-based regime
Currency Kyat = 100 pyas
Literacy rate 90%
Calorie consumption 2937 calories

NAMIBIA
Southern Africa

Official name Republic of Namibia
Formation 1990 / 1994
Capital Windhoek
Population 2 million / 6 people per sq mile (2 people per sq km) / 31%
Total area 318,694 sq miles (825,418 sq km)
Languages English*, Ovambo, Kavango, Bergdama, German, Afrikaans
Religions Christian 90%, Traditional beliefs 10%
Ethnic mix Ovambo 50%, Other tribes 16%, Kavango 9%, Other 9%, Damara 8%, Herero 8%
Government Presidential system
Currency Namibian dollar = 100 cents
Literacy rate 85%
Calorie consumption 2278 calories

NAURU
Australasia & Oceania

Official name Republic of Nauru
Formation 1968 / 1968
Capital None
Population 13,048 / 1611 people per sq mile (621 people per sq km) / 100%
Total area 8.1 sq miles (21 sq km)
Languages Nauruan*, Kiribati, Chinese, Tuvaluan, English
Religions Nauruan Congregational Church 60%, Roman Catholic 35%, Other 5%
Ethnic mix Nauruan 62%, Other Pacific islanders 25%, Chinese and Vietnamese 8%, European 5%
Government Parliamentary system
Currency Australian dollar = 100 cents
Literacy rate 95%
Calorie consumption Not available

NEPAL
South Asia

Official name Kingdom of Nepal
Formation 1769 / 1769
Capital Kathmandu
Population 27.1 million / 513 people per sq mile (198 people per sq km) / 12%
Total area 54,363 sq miles (140,800 sq km)
Languages Nepali*, Maithili, Bhojpuri
Religions Hindu 90%, Buddhist 5%, Muslim 3%, Other (including Christian) 2%
Ethnic mix Nepalese 52%, Other 19%, Maithili 11%, Tibeto-Burmese 10%, Bhojpuri 8%
Government Monarchy
Currency Nepalese rupee = 100 paise
Literacy rate 49%
Calorie consumption 2453 calories

NETHERLANDS
Northwest Europe

Official name Kingdom of the Netherlands
Formation 1648 / 1839
Capital Amsterdam; The Hague (administrative)
Population 16.3 million / 1245 people per sq mile (481 people per sq km) / 89%
Total area 16,033 sq miles (41,526 sq km)
Languages Dutch*, Frisian
Religions Roman Catholic 36%, Other 34%, Protestant 27%, Muslim 3%
Ethnic mix Dutch 82%, Other 12%, Surinamese 2%, Turkish 2%, Moroccan 2%
Government Parliamentary system
Currency Euro = 100 cents
Literacy rate 99%
Calorie consumption 3362 calories

NEW ZEALAND
Australasia & Oceania

Official name New Zealand
Formation 1947 / 1947
Capital Wellington
Population 4 million / 39 people per sq mile (15 people per sq km) / 86%
Total area 103,737 sq miles (268,680 sq km)
Languages English*, Maori
Religions Anglican 24%, Other 22%, Presbyterian 18%, Nonreligious 16%, Roman Catholic 15%, Methodist 5%
Ethnic mix European 77%, Maori 12%, Other immigrant 6%, Pacific islanders 5%
Government Parliamentary system
Currency New Zealand dollar = 100 cents
Literacy rate 99%
Calorie consumption 3219 calories

NICARAGUA
Central America

Official name Republic of Nicaragua
Formation 1838 / 1838
Capital Managua
Population 5.5 million / 120 people per sq mile (46 people per sq km) / 65%
Total area 49,998 sq miles (129,494 sq km)
Languages Spanish*, English Creole, Miskito
Religions Roman Catholic 80%, Protestant Evangelical 17%, Other 3%
Ethnic mix Mestizo 69%, White 14%, Black 8%, Amerindian 5%, Zambo 4%
Government Presidential system
Currency Córdoba oro = 100 centavos
Literacy rate 77%
Calorie consumption 2298 calories

NIGER
West Africa

Official name Republic of Niger
Formation 1960 / 1960
Capital Niamey
Population 14 million / 29 people per sq mile (11 people per sq km) / 21%
Total area 489,188 sq miles (1,267,000 sq km)
Languages French*, Hausa, Djerma, Fulani, Tuareg, Teda
Religions Muslim 85%, Traditional beliefs 14%, Other (including Christian) 1%
Ethnic mix Hausa 54%, Djerma and Songhai 21%, Fulani 10%, Tuareg 9%, Other 6%
Government Presidential system
Currency CFA franc = 100 centimes
Literacy rate 14%
Calorie consumption 2130 calories

NIGERIA
West Africa

Official name Federal Republic of Nigeria
Formation 1960 / 1961
Capital Abuja
Population 132 million / 374 people per sq mile (144 people per sq km) / 44%
Total area 356,667 sq miles (923,768 sq km)
Languages English*, Hausa, Yoruba, Ibo
Religions Muslim 50%, Christian 40%, Traditional beliefs 10%
Ethnic mix Other 29%, Hausa 21%, Yoruba 21%, Ibo 18%, Fulani 11%
Government Presidential system
Currency Naira = 100 kobo
Literacy rate 67%
Calorie consumption 2726 calories

NORTH KOREA
East Asia

Official name Democratic People's Republic of Korea
Formation 1948 / 1953
Capital Pyongyang
Population 22.5 million / 484 people per sq mile (187 people per sq km) / 60%
Total area 46,540 sq miles (120,540 sq km)
Languages Korean*
Religions Atheist 100%
Ethnic mix Korean 100%
Government One-party state
Currency North Korean won = 100 chon
Literacy rate 99%
Calorie consumption 2142 calories

NORWAY
Northern Europe

Official name Kingdom of Norway
Formation 1905 / 1905
Capital Oslo
Population 4.6 million / 39 people per sq mile (15 people per sq km) / 76%
Total area 125,181 sq miles (324,220 sq km)
Languages Norwegian* (Bokmål "book language" and Nynorsk "new Norsk"), Sámi
Religions Evangelical Lutheran 89%, Other and nonreligious 10%, Roman Catholic 1%
Ethnic mix Norwegian 93%, Other 6%, Sámi 1%
Government Parliamentary system
Currency Norwegian krone = 100 øre
Literacy rate 99%
Calorie consumption 3484 calories

OMAN
Southwest Asia

Official name Sultanate of Oman
Formation 1951 / 1951
Capital Muscat
Population 2.6 million / 32 people per sq mile (12 people per sq km) / 84%
Total area 82,031 sq miles (212,460 sq km)
Languages Arabic*, Baluchi, Farsi, Hindi, Punjabi
Religions Ibadi Muslim 75%, Other Muslim and Hindu 25%
Ethnic mix Arab 88%, Baluchi 4%, Persian 3%, Indian and Pakistani 3%, African 2%
Government Monarchy
Currency Omani rial = 1000 baizas
Literacy rate 74%
Calorie consumption Not available

PAKISTAN
South Asia

Official name Islamic Republic of Pakistan
Formation 1947 / 1971
Capital Islamabad
Population 158 million / 531 people per sq mile (205 people per sq km) / 37%
Total area 310,401 sq miles (803,940 sq km)
Languages Urdu*, Baluchi, Brahui, Pashtu, Punjabi, Sindhi
Religions Sunni Muslim 77%, Shi'a Muslim 20%, Hindu 2%, Christian 1%
Ethnic mix Punjabi 56%, Pathan (Pashtun) 15%, Sindhi 14%, Mohajir 7%, Other 4%, Baluchi 4%
Government Presidential system
Currency Pakistani rupee = 100 paisa
Literacy rate 49%
Calorie consumption 2419 calories

PALAU
Australasia & Oceania

Official name Republic of Palau
Formation 1994 / 1994
Capital Koror
Population 20,303 / 104 people per sq mile (40 people per sq km) / 70%
Total area 177 sq miles (458 sq km)
Languages Palauan, English, Japanese, Angaur, Tobi, Sonsorolese
Religions Christian 66%, Modekngei 34%
Ethnic mix Micronesian 87%, Filipino 8%, Chinese and other Asian 5%
Government Nonparty system
Currency US dollar = 100 cents
Literacy rate 98%
Calorie consumption Not available

PANAMA
Central America

Official name Republic of Panama
Formation 1903 / 1903
Capital Panama City
Population 3.2 million / 109 people per sq mile (42 people per sq km) / 56%
Total area 30,193 sq miles (78,200 sq km)
Languages Spanish*, English Creole, Amerindian languages, Chibchan languages
Religions Roman Catholic 86%, Other 8%, Protestant 6%
Ethnic mix Mestizo 60%, White 14%, Black 12%, Amerindian 8%, Asian 4%, Other 2%
Government Presidential system
Currency Balboa = 100 centesimos
Literacy rate 92%
Calorie consumption 2272 calories

PAPUA NEW GUINEA
Australasia & Oceania

Official name Independent State of Papua New Guinea
Formation 1975 / 1975
Capital Port Moresby
Population 5.9 million / 34 people per sq mile (13 people per sq km) / 17%
Total area 178,703 sq miles (462,840 sq km)
Languages Pidgin English*, Papuan*, English, Motu, 750 (est.) native languages
Religions Protestant 60%, Roman Catholic 37%, Other 3%
Ethnic mix Melanesian and mixed race 100%
Government Parliamentary system
Currency Kina = 100 toeas
Literacy rate 57%
Calorie consumption 2193 calories

PARAGUAY
South America

Official name Republic of Paraguay
Formation 1811 / 1938
Capital Asunción
Population 6.2 million / 40 people per sq mile (16 people per sq km) / 56%
Total area 157,046 sq miles (406,750 sq km)
Languages Guarani*, Spanish*, German
Religions Roman Catholic 96%, Protestant (including Mennonite) 4%
Ethnic mix Mestizo 90%, Other 8%, Amerindian 2%
Government Presidential system
Currency Guaraní = 100 centimos
Literacy rate 92%
Calorie consumption 2565 calories

PERU
South America

Official name Republic of Peru
Formation 1824 / 1941
Capital Lima
Population 28 million / 57 people per sq mile (22 people per sq km) / 73%
Total area 496,223 sq miles (1,285,200 sq km)
Languages Spanish*, Quechua*, Aymara*
Religions Roman Catholic 95%, Other 5%
Ethnic mix Amerindian 50%, Mestizo 40%, White 7%, Other 3%
Government Presidential system
Currency New sol = 100 centimos
Literacy rate 88%
Calorie consumption 2571 calories

PHILIPPINES
Southwest Asia

Official name Republic of the Philippines
Formation 1946 / 1946
Capital Manila
Population 83.1 million / 722 people per sq mile (279 people per sq km) / 59%
Total area 115,830 sq miles (300,000 sq km)
Languages Filipino*, English*, Tagalog, Cebuano, Ilocano, Hiligaynon, many other local languages
Religions Roman Catholic 83%, Protestant 9%, Muslim 5%, Other (including Buddhist) 3%
Ethnic mix Malay 95%, Other 3%, Chinese 2%
Government Presidential system
Currency Philippine peso = 100 centavos
Literacy rate 93%
Calorie consumption 2379 calories

POLAND
Northern Europe

Official name Republic of Poland
Formation 1918 / 1945
Capital Warsaw
Population 38.5 million / 328 people per sq mile (126 people per sq km) / 66%
Total area 120,728 sq miles (312,685 sq km)
Languages Polish*
Religions Roman Catholic 93%, Other and nonreligious 5%, Orthodox Christian 2%
Ethnic mix Polish 97%, Other 2%, Silesian 1%
Government Parliamentary system
Currency Zloty = 100 groszy
Literacy rate 99%
Calorie consumption 3374 calories

PORTUGAL
Southwest Europe

Official name Republic of Portugal
Formation 1139 / 1640
Capital Lisbon
Population 10.5 million / 296 people per sq mile (114 people per sq km) / 64%
Total area 35,672 sq miles (92,391 sq km)
Languages Portuguese
Religions Roman Catholic 97%, Other 2%, Protestant 1%
Ethnic mix Portuguese 98%, African and other 2%
Government Parliamentary system
Currency Euro = 100 cents
Literacy rate 93%
Calorie consumption 3741 calories

QATAR
Southwest Asia

Official name State of Qatar
Formation 1971 / 1971
Capital Doha
Population 813,000 / 191 people per sq mile (74 people per sq km) / 93%
Total area 4416 sq miles (11,437 sq km)
Languages Arabic*
Religions Muslim (mainly Sunni) 95%, Other 5%
Ethnic mix Arab 40%, Indian 18%, Pakistani 18%, Other 14%, Iranian 10%
Government Monarchy
Currency Qatar riyal = 100 dirhams
Literacy rate 89%
Calorie consumption Not available

ROMANIA
Southest Europe

Official name Romania
Formation 1878 / 1947
Capital Bucharest
Population 21.7 million / 244 people per sq mile (94 people per sq km) / 56%
Total area 91,699 sq miles (237,500 sq km)
Languages Romanian*, Hungarian (Magyar), Romani, German
Religions Romanian Orthodox 87%, Roman Catholic 5%, Protestant 4%, Other 2%, Greek Orthodox 1%, Greek Catholic (Uniate) 1%
Ethnic mix Romanian 89%, Magyar 7%, Roma 3%, Other 1%
Government Presidential system
Currency Romanian leu = 100 bani
Literacy rate 97%
Calorie consumption 3455 calories

RUSSIAN FEDERATION
Europe / Asia

Official name Russian Federation
Formation 1480 / 1991
Capital Moscow
Population 143 million / 22 people per sq mile (8 people per sq km) / 78%
Total area 6,592,735 sq miles (17,075,200 sq km)
Languages Russian*, Tatar, Ukrainian, Chavash, various other national languages
Religions Orthodox Christian 75%, Other 15%, Muslim 10%
Ethnic mix Russian 82%, Other 10%, Tatar 4%, Ukrainian 3%, Chavash 1%
Government Presidential system
Currency Russian rouble = 100 kopeks
Literacy rate 99%
Calorie consumption 3072 calories

RWANDA
Central Africa

Official name Republic of Rwanda
Formation 1962 / 1962
Capital Kigali
Population 9 million / 934 people per sq mile (361 people per sq km) / 6%
Total area 10,169 sq miles (26,338 sq km)
Languages Kinyarwanda*, French*, Kiswahili, English
Religions Roman Catholic 56%, Traditional beliefs 25%, Muslim 10%, Protestant 9%
Ethnic mix Hutu 90%, Tutsi 9%, Other (including Twa) 1%
Government Presidential system
Currency Rwanda franc = 100 centimes
Literacy rate 64%
Calorie consumption 2084 calories

SAINT KITTS & NEVIS
West Indies

Official name Federation of Saint Christopher and Nevis
Formation 1983 / 1983
Capital Basseterre
Population 38,958 / 280 people per sq mile (108 people per sq km) / 34%
Total area 101 sq miles (261 sq km)
Languages English*, English Creole
Religions Anglican 33%, Methodist 29%, Other 22%, Moravian 9%, Roman Catholic 7%
Ethnic mix Black 94%, Mixed race 3%, Other and Amerindian 2%, White 1%
Government Parliamentary system
Currency Eastern Caribbean dollar = 100 cents
Literacy rate 98%
Calorie consumption 2609 calories

SAINT LUCIA
West Indies

Official name Saint Lucia
Formation 1979 / 1979
Capital Castries
Population 166,312 / 705 people per sq mile (273 people per sq km) / 38%
Total area 239 sq miles (620 sq km)
Languages English*, French Creole
Religions Roman Catholic 90%, Other 10%
Ethnic mix Black 90%, Mulatto (mixed race) 6%, Asian 3%, White 1%
Government Parliamentary system
Currency Eastern Caribbean dollar = 100 cents
Literacy rate 90%
Calorie consumption 2988 calories

SAINT VINCENT & THE GRENADINES

West Indies

Official name Saint Vincent and the Grenadines
Formation 1979 / 1979
Capital Kingstown
Population 117,534 / 897 people per sq mile (346 people per sq km) / 55%
Total area 150 sq miles (389 sq km)
Languages English*, English Creole
Religions Anglican 47%, Methodist 28%, Roman Catholic 13%, Other 12%
Ethnic mix Black 66%, Mulatto (mixed race) 19%, Asian 6%, Other 5%, White 4%
Government Parliamentary system
Currency Eastern Caribbean dollar = 100 cents
Literacy rate 88%
Calorie consumption 2599 calories

SAMOA

Australasia & Oceania

Official name Independent State of Samoa
Formation 1962 / 1962
Capital Apia
Population 185,000 / 169 people per sq mile (65 people per sq km) / 22%
Total area 1104 sq miles (2860 sq km)
Languages Samoan*, English*
Religions Christian 99%, Other 1%
Ethnic mix Polynesian 90%, Euronesian 9%, Other 1%
Government Parliamentary system
Currency Tala = 100 sene
Literacy rate 99%
Calorie consumption 2945 calories

SAN MARINO

Southern Europe

Official name Republic of San Marino
Formation 1631 / 1631
Capital San Marino
Population 28,880 / 1203 people per sq mile (473 people per sq km) / 94%
Total area 23.6 sq miles (61 sq km)
Languages Italian*
Religions Roman Catholic 93%, Other and nonreligious 7%
Ethnic mix Sammarinese 80%, Italian 19%, Other 1%
Government Parliamentary system
Currency Euro = 100 cents
Literacy rate 99%
Calorie consumption Not available

SÃO TOMÉ & PRÍNCIPE

West Africa

Official name Democratic Republic of São Tomé and Príncipe
Formation 1975 / 1975
Capital São Tomé
Population 187,410 / 505 people per sq mile (195 people per sq km) / 47%
Total area 386 sq miles (1001 sq km)
Languages Portuguese*, Portuguese Creole
Religions Roman Catholic 84%, Other 16%
Ethnic mix Black 90%, Portuguese and Creole 10%
Government Presidential system
Currency Dobra = 100 centimos
Literacy rate 83%
Calorie consumption 2460 calories

SAUDI ARABIA

Southwest Asia

Official name Kingdom of Saudi Arabia
Formation 1932 / 1932
Capital Riyadh; Jiddah (administrative)
Population 24.6 million / 30 people per sc mile (12 people per sq km) / 86%
Total area 756,981 sq miles (1,960,582 sq km)
Languages Arabic*
Religions Sunni Muslim 85%, Shi'a Muslim 15%
Ethnic mix Arab 90%, Afro-Asian 10%
Government Monarchy
Currency Saudi riyal = 100 halalat
Literacy rate 79%
Calorie consumption 2844 calories

SENEGAL

West Africa

Official name Republic of Senegal
Formation 1960 / 1960
Capital Dakar
Population 11.7 million / 157 people per sq mile (61 people per sq km) / 47%
Total area 75,749 sq miles (196,190 sq km)
Languages French*, Diola, Mandinka, Malinke, Pulaar, Serer, Soninke, Wolof
Religions Sunni Muslim 90%, Christian (mainly Roman Catholic) 5%, Traditional beliefs 5%
Ethnic mix Wolof 43%, Toucouleur 24%, Serer 15%, Other 11%, Diola 4%, Malinke 3%
Government Presidential system
Currency CFA franc = 100 centimes
Literacy rate 39%
Calorie consumption 2279 calories

SERBIA

Europe

Official name Republic of Serbia
Formation 2006 /2006
Capital Belgrade
Population 9.7 million / 290 people per sq mile (112 people per sq km) / 52%
Total area 34,116 sq miles (88,361 sq km)
Languages Serbo-Croat*, Albanian, Hungarian
Religions Orthodox Christian 85%, Muslim 6%, Other 6%, Roman Catholic 3%
Ethnic mix Serb 66%, Albanian 19%, Hungarian 4%, Bosniak 2%, Other 9%
Government Parliamentary system
Currency Dinar (Serbia) = 100 para
Literacy rate 98%
Calorie consumption Not available

SEYCHELLES

Indian Ocean

Official name Republic of Seychelles
Formation 1976 / 1976
Capital Victoria
Population 81,188 / 781 people per sq mile (301 people per sq km) / 64%
Total area 176 sq miles (455 sq km)
Languages French Creole*, English, French
Religions Roman Catholic 90%, Anglican 8%, Other (including Muslim) 2%
Ethnic mix Creole 89%, Indian 5%, Other 4%, Chinese 2%
Government Presidential system
Currency Seychelles rupee = 100 cents
Literacy rate 92%
Calorie consumption 2465 calories

SIERRA LEONE

West Africa

Official name Republic of Sierra Leone
Formation 1961 / 1961
Capital Freetown
Population 5.5 million / 199 people per sq mile (77 people per sq km) / 37%
Total area 27,698 sq miles (71,740 sq km)
Languages English*, Mende, Temne, Krio
Religions Muslim 30%, Traditional beliefs 30%, Other 30%, Christian 10%
Ethnic mix Mende 35%, Temne 32%, Other 21%, Limba 8%, Kuranko 4%
Government Presidential system
Currency Leone = 100 cents
Literacy rate 30%
Calorie consumption 1936 calories

SINGAPORE

Southeast Asia

Official name Republic of Singapore
Formation 1965 / 1965
Capital Singapore
Population 4.3 million / 18220 people per sq mile (7049 people per sq km) / 100%
Total area 250 sq miles (648 sq km)
Languages English*, Malay*, Mandarin*, Tamil*
Religions Buddhist 55%, Taoist 22%, Muslim 16%, Hindu, Christian, and Sikh 7%
Ethnic mix Chinese 77%, Malay 14%, Indian 8%, Other 1%
Government Parliamentary system
Currency Singapore dollar = 100 cents
Literacy rate 93%
Calorie consumption Not available

SLOVAKIA

Central Europe

Official name Slovak Republic
Formation 1993 / 1993
Capital Bratislava
Population 5.4 million / 285 people per sq mile (110 people per sq km) / 57%
Total area 18,859 sq miles (48,845 sq km)
Languages Slovak*, Hungarian (Magyar), Czech
Religions Roman Catholic 60%, Other 18%, Atheist 10%, Protestant 8%, Orthodox Christian 4%
Ethnic mix Slovak 85%, Magyar 11%, Other 2%, Roma 1%, Czech 1%
Government Parliamentary system
Currency Slovak koruna = 100 halierov
Literacy rate 99%
Calorie consumption 2889 calories

SLOVENIA

Central Europe

Official name Republic of Slovenia
Formation 1991 / 1991
Capital Ljubljana
Population 2 million / 256 people per sq mile (99 people per sq km) / 50%
Total area 7820 sq miles (20,253 sq km)
Languages Slovene*, Serbo-Croat
Religions Roman Catholic 96%, Other 3%, Muslim 1%
Ethnic mix Slovene 83%, Other 12%, Serb 2%, Croat 2%, Bosniak 1%
Government Parliamentary system
Currency Tolar = 100 stotinov
Literacy rate 99%
Calorie consumption 3001 calories

SOLOMON ISLANDS

Australasia & Oceania

Official name Solomon Islands
Formation 1978 / 1978
Capital Honiara
Population 478,000 / 44 people per sq mile (17 people per sq km) / 20%
Total area 10,985 sq miles (28,450 sq km)
Languages English*, Melanesian Pidgin, Pidgin English
Religions Anglican 34%, Roman Catholic 19%, Methodist 11%, Seventh-day Adventist 10%, South Seas Evangelical Church 17%, Other 9%
Ethnic mix Melanesian 94%, Polynesian 4%, Other 2%
Government Parliamentary system
Currency Solomon Islands dollar = 100 cents
Literacy rate 77%
Calorie consumption 2265 calories

SOMALIA

East Africa

Official name Somalia
Formation 1960 / 1960
Capital Mogadishu
Population 8.2 million / 34 people per sq mile (13 people per sq km) / 28%
Total area 246,199 sq miles (637,657 sq km)
Languages Somali*, Arabic*, English, Italian
Religions Sunni Muslim 98%, Christian 2%
Ethnic mix Somali 85%, Other 15%
Government Transitional regime
Currency Somali shilling = 100 centesimi
Literacy rate 24%
Calorie consumption 1628 calories

SOUTH AFRICA

Southern Africa

Official name Republic of South Africa
Formation 1934 / 1994
Capital Pretoria; Cape Town; Bloemfontein
Population 47.4 million / 101 people per sq mile (39 people per sq km) / 55%
Total area 471,008 sq miles (1,219,912 sq km)
Languages English, isiZulu, isiXhosa, Afrikaans, Sepedi, Setswana, Sesotho, Xitsonga, siSwati, Tshivenda, isiNdebele
Religions Christian 68%, Traditional beliefs and animist 29%, Muslim 2%, Hindu 1%
Ethnic mix Black 79%, White 10%, Colored 9%, Asian 2%
Government Presidential system
Currency Rand = 100 cents
Literacy rate 82%
Calorie consumption 2956 calories

SOUTH KOREA

East Asia

Official name Republic of Korea
Formation 1948 / 1953
Capital Seoul
Population 47.8 million / 1254 people per sq mile (484 people per sq km) / 82%
Total area 38,023 sq miles (98,480 sq km)
Languages Korean*
Religions Mahayana Buddhist 47%, Protestant 38%, Roman Catholic 11%, Confucianist 3%, Other 1%
Ethnic mix Korean 100%
Government Presidential system
Currency South Korean won = 100 chon
Literacy rate 98%
Calorie consumption 3058 calories

SPAIN

Southeast Europe

Official name Kingdom of Spain
Formation 1492 / 1713
Capital Madrid
Population 43.1 million / 224 people per sq mile (86 people per sq km) / 78%
Total area 194,896 sq miles (504,782 sq km)
Languages Spanish*, Catalan*, Galician*, Basque*
Religions Roman Catholic 96%, Other 4%
Ethnic mix Castilian Spanish 72%, Catalan 17%, Galician 6%, Basque 2%, Other 2%, Roma 1%
Government Parliamentary system
Currency Euro = 100 cents
Literacy rate 98%
Calorie consumption 3371 calories

SRI LANKA

South Asia

Official name Democratic Socialist Republic of Sri Lanka
Formation 1948 / 1948
Capital Colombo
Population 20.7 million / 828 people per sq mile (320 people per sq km) / 24%
Total area 25,332 sq miles (65,610 sq km)
Languages Sinhala, Tamil, Sinhala-Tamil, English
Religions Buddhist 69%, Hindu 15%, Muslim 8%, Christian 8%
Ethnic mix Sinhalese 74%, Tamil 18%, Moor 7%, Burgher, Malay, and Veddha 1%
Government Mixed presidential–parliamentary system
Currency Sri Lanka rupee = 100 cents
Literacy rate 90%
Calorie consumption 2385 calories

SUDAN

East Africa

Official name Republic of the Sudan
Formation 1956 / 1956
Capital Khartoum
Population 36.2 million / 37 people per sq mile (14 people per sq km) / 36%
Total area 967,493 sq miles (2,505,810 sq km)
Languages Arabic*, Dinka, Nuer, Nubian, Beja, Zande, Bari, Fur, Shilluk, Lotuko
Religions Muslim (mainly Sunni) 70%, Traditional beliefs 20%, Christian 9%, Other 1%
Ethnic mix Other Black 52%, Arab 40%, Dinka and Beja 7%, Other 1%
Government Presidential system
Currency Sudanese pound or dinar = 100 piastres
Literacy rate 59%
Calorie consumption 2228 calories

SURINAME

South America

Official name Republic of Suriname
Formation 1975 / 1975
Capital Paramaribo
Population 499,000 / 8 people per sq mile (3 people per sq km) / 74%
Total area 63,039 sq miles (163,270 sq km)
Languages Dutch*, Sranan (Creole), Javanese, Sarnami Hindi, Saramaccan, Chinese, Carib
Religions Hindu 27%, Protestant 25%, Roman Catholic 23%, Muslim 20%, Traditional beliefs 5%
Ethnic mix Creole 34%, South Asian 34%, Javanese 18%, Black 9%, Other 5%
Government Parliamentary system
Currency Suriname dollar (guilder until 2004) = 100 cents
Literacy rate 88%
Calorie consumption 2652 calories

SWAZILAND

Southern Africa

Official name Kingdom of Swaziland
Formation 1968 / 1968
Capital Mbabane
Population 1 million / 151 people per sq mile (58 people per sq km) / 26%
Total area 6704 sq miles (17,363 sq km)
Languages English*, siSwati*, isiZulu, Xitsonga
Religions Christian 60%, Traditional beliefs 40%
Ethnic mix Swazi 97%, Other 3%
Government Monarchy
Currency Lilangeni = 100 cents
Literacy rate 79%
Calorie consumption 2322 calories

SWEDEN

Northern Europe

Official name Kingdom of Sweden
Formation 1523 / 1905
Capital Stockholm
Population 9 million / 57 people per sq mile (22 people per sq km) / 83%
Total area 173,731 sq miles (449,964 sq km)
Languages Swedish*, Finnish, Sámi
Religions Evangelical Lutheran 82%, Other 13%, Roman Catholic 2%, Muslim 2%, Orthodox Christian 1%
Ethnic mix Swedish 88%, Foreign-born or first-generation immigrant 10%, Finnish and Sámi 2%
Government Parliamentary system
Currency Swedish krona = 100 ore
Literacy rate 99%
Calorie consumption 3185 calories

SWITZERLAND

Central Europe

Official name Swiss Confederation
Formation 1291 / 1857
Capital Bern
Population 7.3 million / 475 people per sq mile (184 people per sq km) / 68%
Total area 15,942 sq miles (41,290 sq km)
Languages German*, French*, Italian*, Romansch*, Swiss-German
Religions Roman Catholic 46%, Protestant 40%, Other and nonreligious 12%, Muslim 2%
Ethnic mix German 65%, French 18%, Italian 10%, Other 6%, Romansch 1%
Government Parliamentary system
Currency Swiss franc = 100 rappen/centimes
Literacy rate 99%
Calorie consumption 3526 calories

SYRIA

Southwest Asia

Official name Syrian Arab Republic
Formation 1941 / 1967
Capital Damascus
Population 19 million / 267 people per sq mile (103 people per sq km) / 55%
Total area 71,498 sq miles (184,180 sq km)
Languages Arabic*, French, Kurdish, Armenian, Circassian, Turkic languages, Assyrian, Aramaic
Religions Sunni Muslim 74%, Other Muslim 16%, Christian 10%
Ethnic mix Arab 89%, Kurdish 6%, Other 3%, Armenian, Turkmen, and Circassian 2%
Government One-party state
Currency Syrian pound = 100 piasters
Literacy rate 83%
Calorie consumption 3038 calories

TAIWAN

East Asia

Official name Republic of China (ROC)
Formation 1949 / 1949
Capital Taipei
Population 22.9 million / 1838 people per sq mile (710 people per sq km) / 69%
Total area 13,892 sq miles (35,980 sq km)
Languages Amoy Chinese, Mandarin Chinese, Hakka Chinese
Religions Buddhist, Confucianist, and Taoist 93%, Christian 5%, Other 2%
Ethnic mix Han (pre-20th-century migration) 84%, Han (20th-century migration) 14%, Aboriginal 2%
Government Presidential system
Currency Taiwan dollar = 100 cents
Literacy rate 97%
Calorie consumption Not available

TAJIKISTAN

Central Asia

Official name Republic of Tajikistan
Formation 1991 / 1991
Capital Dushanbe
Population 6.5 million / 118 people per sq mile (45 people per sq km) / 28%
Total area 55,251 sq miles (143,100 sq km)
Languages Tajik*, Uzbek, Russian
Religions Sunni Muslim 80%, Other 15%, Shi'a Muslim 5%
Ethnic mix Tajik 62%, Uzbek 24%, Russian 8%, Other 4%, Tatar 1%, Kyrgyz 1%
Government Presidential system
Currency Somoni = 100 diram
Literacy rate 99%
Calorie consumption 1828 calories

TANZANIA

East Africa

Official name United Republic of Tanzania
Formation 1964 / 1964
Capital Dodoma
Population 38.3 million / 112 people per sq mile (43 people per sq km) / 33%
Total area 364,898 sq miles (945,087 sq km)
Languages English*, Kiswahili*, Sukuma, Chagga, Nyamwezi, Hehe, Makonde, Yao, Sandawe
Religions Muslim 33%, Christian 33%, Traditional beliefs 30%, Other 4%
Ethnic mix Native African (over 120 tribes) 99%, European and Asian 1%
Government Presidential system
Currency Tanzanian shilling = 100 cents
Literacy rate 69%
Calorie consumption 1975 calories

THAILAND

Southeastern Asia

Official name Kingdom of Thailand
Formation 1238 / 1907
Capital Bangkok
Population 64.2 million / 325 people per sq mile (126 people per sq km) / 22%
Total area 198,455 sq miles (514,000 sq km)
Languages Thai*, Chinese, Malay, Khmer, Mon, Karen, Miao
Religions Buddhist 95%, Muslim 4% Other (including Christian) 1%
Ethnic mix Thai 83%, Chinese 12%, Malay 3%, Khmer and Other 2%
Government Parliamentary system
Currency Baht = 100 stang
Literacy rate 93%
Calorie consumption 2467 calories

TOGO

Western Africa

Official name Republic of Togo
Formation 1960 / 1960
Capital Lomé
Population 6.1 million / 290 people per sq mile (112 people per sq km) / 33%
Total area 21,924 sq miles (56,785 sq km)
Languages French*, Ewe, Kabye, Gurma
Religions Traditional beliefs 50%, Christian 35%, Muslim 15%
Ethnic mix Ewe 46%, Kabye 27%, Other African 26%, European 1%
Government Presidential system
Currency CFA franc = 100 centimes
Literacy rate 53%
Calorie consumption 2345 calories

TONGA

Australasia & Oceania

Official name Kingdom of Tonga
Formation 1970 / 1970
Capital Nuku'alofa
Population 112,422 / 404 people per sq mile (156 people per sq km) / 43%
Total area 289 sq miles (748 sq km)
Languages Tongan*, English
Religions Free Wesleyan 41%, Roman Catholic 16%, Church of Jesus Christ of Latter-day Saints 14%, Free Church of Tonga 12%, Other 17%
Ethnic mix Polynesian 99%, Other 1%
Government Monarchy
Currency Pa'anga (Tongan dollar) = 100 seniti
Literacy rate 99%
Calorie consumption Not available

TRINIDAD & TOBAGO
West Indies

Official name Republic of Trinidad and Tobago
Formation 1962 / 1962
Capital Port-of-Spain
Population 1.3 million / 656 people per sq mile (253 people per sq km) / 74%
Total area 1980 sq miles (5128 sq km)
Languages English*, English Creole, Hindi, French, Spanish
Religions Christian 60%, Hindu 24%, Other and nonreligious 9%, Muslim 7%
Ethnic mix East Indian 40%, Black 40%, Mixed race 19%, White and Chinese 1%
Government Parliamentary system
Currency Trinidad and Tobago dollar = 100 cents
Literacy rate 99%
Calorie consumption 2732 calories

TUNISIA
North Africa

Official name Republic of Tunisia
Formation 1956 / 1956
Capital Tunis
Population 10.1 million / 168 people per sq mile (65 people per sq km) / 68%
Total area 63,169 sq miles (163,610 sq km)
Languages Arabic*, French
Religions Muslim (mainly Sunni) 98%, Christian 1%, Jewish 1%
Ethnic mix Arab and Berber 98%, Jewish 1%, European 1%
Government Presidential system
Currency Tunisian dinar = 1000 millimes
Literacy rate 74%
Calorie consumption 3238 calories

TURKEY
Asia / Europe

Official name Republic of Turkey
Formation 1923 / 1939
Capital Ankara
Population 73.2 million / 246 people per sq mile (95 people per sq km) / 75%
Total area 301,382 sq miles (780,580 sq km)
Languages Turkish*, Kurdish, Arabic, Circassian, Armenian, Greek, Georgian, Ladino
Religions Muslim (mainly Sunni) 99%, Other 1%
Ethnic mix Turkish 70%, Kurdish 20%, Other 8%, Arab 2%
Government Parliamentary system
Currency new Turkish lira = 100 kurus
Literacy rate 88%
Calorie consumption 3357 calories

TURKMENISTAN
Central Asia

Official name Turkmenistan
Formation 1991 / 1991
Capital Ashgabat
Population 4.8 million / 25 people per sq mile (10 people per sq km) / 45%
Total area 188,455 sq miles (488,100 sq km)
Languages Turkmen*, Uzbek, Russian, Kazakh, Tatar
Religions Sunni Muslim 87%, Orthodox Christian 11%, Other 2%
Ethnic mix Turkmen 77%, Uzbek 9%, Russian 7%, Other 4%, Kazakh 2%, Tatar 1%
Government One-party state
Currency Manat = 100 tenga
Literacy rate 99%
Calorie consumption 2742 calories

TUVALU
Australasia & Oceania

Official name Tuvalu
Formation 1978 / 1978
Capital Fongafale, on Funafuti Atoll
Population 11,636 / 1164 people per sq mile (448 people per sq km) / 45%
Total area 10 sq miles (26 sq km)
Languages Tuvaluan, Kiribati, English
Religions Church of Tuvalu 97%, Other 1%, Baha'i 1%, Seventh-day Adventist 1%
Ethnic mix Polynesian 96%, Other 4%
Government Nonparty system
Currency Australian dollar and Tuvaluan dollar = 100 cents
Literacy rate 98%
Calorie consumption Not available

UGANDA
East Africa

Official name Republic of Uganda
Formation 1962 / 1962
Capital Kampala
Population 28.8 million / 374 people per sq mile (144 people per sq km) / 14%
Total area 91,135 sq miles (236,040 sq km)
Languages English*, Luganda, Nkole, Chiga, Lango, Acholi, Teso, Lugbara
Religions Roman Catholic 38%, Protestant 33%, Traditional beliefs 13%, Muslim (mainly Sunni) 8%, Other 8%
Ethnic mix Bantu tribes 50%, Other 45%, Sudanese 5%
Government Nonparty system
Currency New Uganda shilling = 100 cents
Literacy rate 69%
Calorie consumption 2410 calories

UKRAINE
Eastern Europe

Official name Ukraine
Formation 1991 / 1991
Capital Kiev
Population 46.5 million / 199 people per sq mile (77 people per sq km) / 68%
Total area 223,089 sq miles (603,700 sq km)
Languages Ukrainian*, Russian, Tatar
Religions Christian (mainly Orthodox) 95%, Other 4%, Jewish 1%
Ethnic mix Ukrainian 73%, Russian 22%, Other 4%, Jewish 1%
Government Presidential system
Currency Hryvna = 100 kopiykas
Literacy rate 99%
Calorie consumption 3054 calories

UNITED ARAB EMIRATES
Southwest Asia

Official name United Arab Emirates
Formation 1971 / 1972
Capital Abu Dhabi
Population 4.5 million / 139 people per sq mile (54 people per sq km) / 86%
Total area 32,000 sq miles (82,880 sq km)
Languages Arabic*, Farsi, Indian and Pakistani languages, English
Religions Muslim (mainly Sunni) 96%, Christian, Hindu, and other 4%
Ethnic mix Asian 60%, Emirian 25%, Other Arab 12%, European 3%
Government Monarchy
Currency UAE dirham = 100 fils
Literacy rate 77%
Calorie consumption 3225 calories

UNITED KINGDOM
Northwest Europe

Official name United Kingdom of Great Britain and Northern Ireland
Formation 1707 / 1922
Capital London
Population 59.7 million / 640 people per sq mile (247 people per sq km) / 90%
Total area 94,525 sq miles (244,820 sq km)
Languages English*, Welsh, Scottish Gaelic
Religions Anglican 45%, Roman Catholic 9%, Presbyterian 4%, Other 42%
Ethnic mix English 80%, Scottish 9%, West Indian, Asian, and other 5%, Northern Irish 3%, Welsh 3%
Government Parliamentary system
Currency Pound sterling = 100 pence
Literacy rate 99%
Calorie consumption 3412 calories

UNITED STATES
North America

Official name United States of America
Formation 1776 / 1959
Capital Washington D.C.
Population 298 million / 84 people per sq mile (33 people per sq km) / 77%
Total area 3,717,792 sq miles (9,626,091 sq km)
Languages English*, Spanish, Chinese, French, German, Tagalog, Vietnamese, Italian, Korean, Russian, Polish
Religions Protestant 52%, Roman Catholic 25%, Muslim 2%, Jewish 2%, Other 19%
Ethnic mix White 69%, Hispanic 13%, Black American/African 13%, Asian 4%, Native American 1%
Government Presidential system
Currency US dollar = 100 cents
Literacy rate 99%
Calorie consumption 3774 calories

URUGUAY
South America

Official name Eastern Republic of Uruguay
Formation 1828 / 1828
Capital Montevideo
Population 3.5 million / 52 people per sq mile (20 people per sq km) / 91%
Total area 68,039 sq miles (176,220 sq km)
Languages Spanish*
Religions Roman Catholic 66%, Other and nonreligious 30%, Jewish 2%, Protestant 2%
Ethnic mix White 90%, Mestizo 6%, Black 4%
Government Presidential system
Currency Uruguayan peso = 100 centésimos
Literacy rate 98%
Calorie consumption 2828 calories

UZBEKISTAN
Central Asia

Official name Republic of Uzbekistan
Formation 1991 / 1991
Capital Tashkent
Population 26.6 million / 154 people per sq mile (59 people per sq km) / 37%
Total area 172,741 sq miles (447,400 sq km)
Languages Uzbek*, Russian, Tajik, Kazakh
Religions Sunni Muslim 88%, Orthodox Christian 9%, Other 3%
Ethnic mix Uzbek 71%, Other 12%, Russian 8%, Tajik 5%, Kazakh 4%
Government Presidential system
Currency Som = 100 tiyin
Literacy rate 99%
Calorie consumption 2241 calories

VANUATU
Australasia & Oceania

Official name Republic of Vanuatu
Formation 1980 / 1980
Capital Port Vila
Population 211,000 / 45 people per sq mile (17 people per sq km) / 20%
Total area 4710 sq miles (12,200 sq km)
Languages Bislama* (Melanesian pidgin), English*, French*, other indigenous languages
Religions Presbyterian 37%, Other 19%, Anglican 15%, Roman Catholic 15%, Traditional beliefs 8%, Seventh-day Adventist 6%
Ethnic mix Melanesian 94%, Other 3%, Polynesian 3%
Government Parliamentary system
Currency Vatu = 100 centimes
Literacy rate 74%
Calorie consumption 2587 calories

VATICAN CITY
Southern Europe

Official name State of the Vatican City
Formation 1929 / 1929
Capital Vatican City
Population 921 / 5418 people per sq mile (2093 people per sq km) / 100%
Total area 0.17 sq miles (0.44 sq km)
Languages Italian*, Latin*
Religions Roman Catholic 100%
Ethnic mix The current pope is German. Cardinals are from many nationalities, but Italians form the largest group. Most of the resident lay persons are Italian.
Government Papal state
Currency Euro = 100 cents
Literacy rate 99%
Calorie consumption Not available

VENEZUELA
South America

Official name Bolivarian Republic of Venezuela
Formation 1830 / 1830
Capital Caracas
Population 26.7 million / 78 people per sq mile (30 people per sq km) / 87%
Total area 352,143 sq miles (912,050 sq km)
Languages Spanish*, Amerindian languages
Religions Roman Catholic 89%, Protestant and other 11%
Ethnic mix Mestizo 69%, White 20%, Black 9%, Amerindian 2%
Government Presidential system
Currency Bolivar = 100 centimos
Literacy rate 93%
Calorie consumption 2336 calories

VIETNAM
Southeast Asia

Official name Socialist Republic of Vietnam
Formation 1976 / 1976
Capital Hanoi
Population 84.2 million / 670 people per sq mile (259 people per sq km) / 20%
Total area 127,243 sq miles (329,560 sq km)
Languages Vietnamese*, Chinese, Thai, Khmer, Muong, Nung, Miao, Yao, Jarai
Religions Buddhist 55%, Other and nonreligious 38%, Christian (mainly Roman Catholic) 7%
Ethnic mix Vietnamese 88%, Other 6%, Chinese 4%, Thai 2%
Government One-party state
Currency Dông = 10 hao = 100 xu
Literacy rate 90%
Calorie consumption 2566 calories

YEMEN
Southwest Asia

Official name Republic of Yemen
Formation 1990 / 1990
Capital Sana
Population 21 million / 97 people per sq mile (37 people per sq km) / 25%
Total area 203,849 sq miles (527,970 sq km)
Languages Arabic*
Religions Sunni Muslim 55%, Shi'a Muslim 42%, Christian, Hindu, and Jewish 3%
Ethnic mix Arab 95%, Afro-Arab 3%, Indian, Somali, and European 2%
Government Presidential system
Currency Yemeni rial = 100 sene
Literacy rate 49%
Calorie consumption 2038 calories

ZAMBIA
Southern Africa

Official name Republic of Zambia
Formation 1964 / 1964
Capital Lusaka
Population 11.7 million / 41 people per sq mile (16 people per sq km) / 45%
Total area 290,584 sq miles (752,614 sq km)
Languages English*, Bemba, Tonga, Nyanja, Lozi, Lala-Bisa, Nsenga
Religions Christian 63%, Traditional beliefs 36%, Muslim and Hindu 1%
Ethnic mix Bemba 34%, Other African 26%, Tonga 16%, Nyanja 14%, Lozi 9%, European 1%
Government Presidential system
Currency Zambian kwacha = 100 ngwee
Literacy rate 68%
Calorie consumption 1927 calories

ZIMBABWE
Southern Africa

Official name Republic of Zimbabwe
Formation 1980 / 1980
Capital Harare
Population 13 million / 87 people per sq mile (34 people per sq km) / 35%
Total area 150,803 sq miles (390,580 sq km)
Languages English*, Shona, isiNdebele
Religions Syncretic (Christian/traditional beliefs) 50%, Christian 25%, Traditional beliefs 24%, Other (including Muslim) 1%
Ethnic mix Shona 71%, Ndebele 16%, Other African 11%, White 1%, Asian 1%
Government Presidential system
Currency Zimbabwe dollar = 100 cents
Literacy rate 90%
Calorie consumption 1943 calories

GLOSSARY

This glossary lists all geographical, technical, and foreign language terms that appear in the text, followed by a brief definition of the term. Any acronyms used in the text are also listed in full. Terms in italics are for cross-reference and indicate that the word is separately defined in the glossary.

A

Aboriginal The original (*indigenous*) inhabitants of a country or continent. Especially used with reference to Australia.

Abyssal plain A broad *plain* found in the depths of the ocean, more than 10,000 ft (3,000 m) below sea level.

Acid rain Rain, sleet, snow, or mist which has absorbed waste gases from fossil-fueled power stations and vehicle exhausts, becoming more acid. It causes severe environmental damage.

Adaptation The gradual evolution of plants and animals so that they become better suited to survive and reproduce in their *environment*.

Afforestation The planting of new forest in areas that were once forested but have been cleared.

Agribusiness A term applied to activities such as the growing of crops, rearing of animals, or the manufacture of farm machinery, which eventually leads to the supply of agricultural produce at market.

Air mass A huge, homogeneous mass of air, within which horizontal patterns of temperature and *humidity* are consistent. Air masses are separated by *fronts*.

Alliance An agreement between two or more states, to work together to achieve common purposes.

Alluvial fan A large fan-shaped deposit of fine sediments deposited by a river as it emerges from a narrow, mountain valley onto a broad, open *plain*.

Alluvium Material deposited by rivers. Nowadays usually only applied to finer particles of silt and clay.

Alpine Mountain *environment*, between the *treeline* and the level of permanent snow cover.

Alpine mountains Ranges of mountains formed between 30 and 65 million years ago, by *folding*, in western and central Europe.

Amerindian A term applied to people *indigenous* to North, Central, and South America.

Animal husbandry The business of rearing animals.

Antarctic circle The parallel which lies at *latitude* of 66° 32' S.

Anticline A geological *fold* that forms an arch shape, curving upward in the rock *strata*.

Anticyclone An area of relatively high atmospheric pressure.

Aquaculture Collective term for the farming of produce derived from the sea, including fish-farming, the cultivation of shellfish, and plants such as seaweed.

Aquifer A body of rock that can absorb water. Also applied to any rock strata that have sufficient porosity to yield *groundwater* through wells or springs.

Arable Land which has been plowed and is being used, or is suitable, for growing crops.

Archipelago A group or chain of islands.

Arctic Circle The parallel that lies at a *latitude* of 66° 32' N.

Arête A thin, jagged mountain ridge that divides two adjacent *cirques*, found in regions where *glaciation* has occurred.

Arid Dry. An area of low rainfall, where the rate of *evaporation* may be greater than that of *precipitation*. Often defined as those areas that receive less than one inch (25 mm) of rain a year. In these areas only drought-resistant plants can survive.

Artesian well A naturally occurring source of underground water, stored in an *aquifer*.

Artisanal Small-scale, manual operation, such as fishing, using little or no machinery.

ASEAN Association of Southeast Asian Nations. Established in 1967 to promote economic, social, and cultural cooperation. Its members include Brunei, Indonesia, Malaysia, Philippines, Singapore, and Thailand.

Aseismic A region where *earthquake* activity has ceased.

Asteroid A minor planet circling the Sun, mainly between the orbits of Mars and Jupiter.

Asthenosphere A zone of hot, partially melted rock, which underlies the *lithosphere*, within the Earth's *crust*.

Atmosphere The envelope of odorless, colorless and tasteless gases surrounding the Earth, consisting of *oxygen* (23%), *nitrogen* (75%), argon (1%), *carbon dioxide* (0.03%), as well as tiny proportions of other gases.

Atmospheric pressure The pressure created by the action of gravity on the gases surrounding the Earth.

Atoll A ring-shaped island or *coral reef* often enclosing a *lagoon* of sea water.

Avalanche The rapid movement of a mass of snow and ice down a steep slope. Similar movements of other materials are described as *rock avalanches* or *landslides* and *sand avalanches*.

B

Badlands A landscape that has been heavily eroded and dissected by rainwater, and which has little or no vegetation.

Back slope The gentler windward slope of a sand *dune* or gentler slope of a *cuesta*.

Bajos An *alluvial fan* deposited by a river at the base of mountains and hills that encircle *desert* areas.

Bar, coastal An offshore strip of sand or shingle, either above or below the water. Usually parallel to the shore but sometimes crescent-shaped or at an oblique angle.

Barchan A crescent-shaped sand *dune*, formed where wind direction is very consistent. The horns of the crescent point downwind and where there is enough sand the barchan is mobile.

Barrio A Spanish term for the shantytowns – settlements of shacks – that are clustered around many South and Central American cities (*see also* *Favela*).

Basalt Dark, fine-grained *igneous rock* that is formed near the Earth's surface from fast-cooling *lava*.

Base level The level below which flowing water cannot erode the land.

Basement rock A mass of ancient rock often of *PreCambrian age*, covered by a layer of more recent *sedimentary rocks*. Commonly associated with *shield* areas.

Beach Lake or sea shore where waves break and there is an accumulation of loose sand, mud, gravel, or pebbles.

Bedrock Solid, consolidated and relatively unweathered rock, found on the surface of the land or just below a layer of soil or *weathered* rock.

Biodiversity The quantity of animal or plant species in a given area.

Biomass The total mass of organic matter – plants and animals – in a given area. It is usually measured in kilogrammes per square meter. Plant biomass is proportionally greater than that of animals, except in cities.

Biosphere The zone just above and below the Earth's surface, where all plants and animals live.

Blizzard A severe windstorm with snow and sleet. Visibility is often severely restricted.

Bluff The steep bank of a *meander*, formed by the erosive action of a river.

Boreal forest Tracts of mainly coniferous forest found in northern *latitudes*.

Breccia A type of rock composed of sharp fragments, cemented by a fine-grained material such as clay.

Butte An isolated, flat-topped hill with steep or vertical sides, buttes are the eroded remnants of a former land surface

C

Caatinga Portuguese (Brazilian) term for thorny woodland growing in areas of pale granitic soils.

CACM Central American Common Market. Established in 1960 to further economic ties between its members, which are Costa Rica, El Salvador, Guatemala, Honduras, and Nicaragua.

Calcite Hexagonal crystals of calcium carbonate.

Caldera A huge volcanic vent, often containing a number of smaller vents, and sometimes a crater lake.

Carbon cycle The transfer of carbon to and from the *atmosphere*. This occurs on land through *photosynthesis*. In the sea, *carbon dioxide* is absorbed, some returning to the air and some taken up into the bodies of sea creatures.

Carbon dioxide A colorless, odorless gas (CO_2) that makes up 0.03% of the *atmosphere*.

Carbonation The process whereby rocks are broken down by carbonic acid. Carbon dioxide in the air dissolves in rainwater, forming carbonic acid. *Limestone* terrain can be rapidly eaten away.

Cash crop A single crop grown specifically for export sale, rather than for local use. Typical examples include coffee, tea, and citrus fruits.

Cassava A type of grain meal, used to produce tapioca. A staple crop in many parts of Africa.

Castle kopje Hill or rock outcrop, especially in southern Africa, where steep sides, and a summit composed of blocks, give a castle-like appearance.

Cataracts A series of stepped waterfalls created as a river flows over a band of hard, resistant rock.

Causeway A raised route through marshland or a body of water.

CEEAC Economic Community of Central African States. Established in 1983 to promote regional cooperation and if possible, establish a common market between 16 Central African nations.

Chemical weathering The chemical reactions leading to the decomposition of rocks. Types of chemical weathering include *carbonation*, *hydrolysis*, and *oxidation*.

Chernozem A fertile soil, also known as "black earth" consisting of a layer of dark topsoil, rich in decaying vegetation, overlying a lighter chalky layer.

Cirque Armchair-shaped basin, found in mountain regions, with a steep back, or rear, wall and a raised rock lip, often containing a lake (or *tarn*). The cirque floor has been eroded by a *glacier*, while the back wall is eroded both by the *glacier* and by *weathering*.

Climate The average weather conditions in a given area over a period of years, sometimes defined as 30 years or more.

Cold War A period of hostile relations between the US and the Soviet Union and their allies after the Second World War.

Composite volcano Also known as a strato-volcano, the volcanic cone is composed of alternating deposits of *lava* and *pyroclastic* material.

Compound A substance made up of *elements* chemically combined in a consistent way.

Condensation The process whereby a gas changes into a liquid. For example, water vapor in the *atmosphere* condenses around tiny airborne particles to form droplets of water.

Confluence The point at which two rivers meet.

Conglomerate Rock composed of large, water-worn or rounded pebbles, held together by a natural cement.

Coniferous forest A forest type containing trees which are generally, but not necessarily, *evergreen* and have slender, needlelike leaves. Coniferous trees reproduce by means of seeds contained in a cone.

Continental drift The theory that the continents of today are fragments of one or more prehistoric *supercontinents* which have moved across the Earth's surface, creating ocean basins. The theory has been superseded by a more sophisticated one – *plate tectonics*.

Continental shelf An area of the continental crust, below sea level, which slopes gently. It is separated from the deep ocean by a much more steeply inclined *continental slope*.

Continental slope A steep slope running from the edge of the *continental shelf* to the ocean floor.

Conurbation A vast metropolitan area created by the expansion of towns and cities into a virtually continuous urban area.

Cool continental A rainy *climate* with warm summers [warmest month below 76°F (22°C)] and often severe winters [coldest month below 32°F (0°C)].

Copra The dried, white kernel of a coconut, from which coconut oil is extracted.

Coral reef An underwater barrier created by colonies of the coral polyp. Polyps secrete a protective skeleton of calcium carbonate, and reefs develop as live polyps build on the skeletons of dead generations.

Core The center of the Earth, consisting of a dense mass of iron and nickel. It is thought that the outer core is molten or liquid, and that the hot inner core is solid due to extremely high pressures.

Coriolis effect A deflecting force caused by the rotation of the Earth. In the northern hemisphere a body, such as an *air mass* or ocean current, is deflected to the right, and in the southern hemisphere to the left. This prevents winds from blowing straight from areas of high to low pressure.

Coulées A US / Canadian term for a ravine formed by river *erosion*.

Craton A large block of the Earth's *crust* which has remained stable for a long period of *geological time*. It is made up of ancient *shield* rocks.

Cretaceous A period of *geological time* beginning about 145 million years ago and lasting until about 65 million years ago.

Crevasse A deep crack in a *glacier*.

Crust The hard, thin outer shell of the Earth. The crust floats on the *mantle*, which is softer and more dense. Under the oceans (oceanic crust) the crust is 3.7–6.8 miles (6–11 km) thick. Continental crust averages 18–24 miles (30–40 km).

Crystalline rock Rocks formed when molten *magma* crystallizes (*igneous rocks*) or when heat or pressure cause re-crystallization (*metamorphic rocks*). Crystalline rocks are distinct from *sedimentary rocks*.

Cuesta A hill which rises into a steep slope on one side but has a gentler gradient on its other slope.

Cyclone An area of low *atmospheric pressure*, occurring where the air is warm and relatively low in density, causing low level winds to spiral. *Hurricanes* and *typhoons* are tropical cyclones.

D

De facto
1 Government or other activity that takes place, or exists in actuality if not by right.
2 A border, which exists in practice, but which is not officially recognized by all the countries it adjoins.

Deciduous forest A forest of trees that shed their leaves annually at a particular time or season. In *temperate* climates the fall of leaves occurs in the autumn. Some *coniferous* trees, such as the larch, are deciduous. Deciduous vegetation contrasts with *evergreen*, which keeps its leaves for more than a year.

Defoliant Chemical spray used to remove foliage (leaves) from trees.

Deforestation The act of cutting down and clearing large areas of forest for human activities, such as agricultural land or urban development.

Delta Low-lying, fan-shaped area at a river mouth, formed by the *deposition* of successive layers of *sediment*. Slowing as it enters the sea, a river deposits sediment and may, as a result, split into numerous smaller channels, known as *distributaries*.

Denudation The combined effect of *weathering*, *erosion*, and *mass movement*, which, over long periods, exposes underlying rocks.

Deposition The laying down of material that has accumulated:
(1) after being *eroded* and then transported by physical forces such as wind, ice, or water;
(2) as organic remains, such as coal and coral;
(3) as the result of *evaporation* and chemical *precipitation*.

Depression
1 In climatic terms it is a large low pressure system.
2 A complex *fold*, producing a large valley, which incorporates both a *syncline* and an *anticline*.

Desert An *arid* region of low rainfall, with little vegetation or animal life, which is adapted to the dry conditions. The term is now applied not only to hot tropical and subtropical regions, but to arid areas of the continental interiors and to the ice deserts of the *Arctic* and *Antarctic*.

Desertification The gradual extension of *desert* conditions in *arid* or *semiarid* regions, as a result of climatic change or human activity, such as over-grazing and *deforestation*.

Despot A ruler with absolute power. Despots are often associated with oppressive regimes.

Detritus Piles of rock deposited by an erosive agent such as a river or *glacier*.

Distributary A minor branch of a river, which does not rejoin the main stream, common at *deltas*.

Diurnal Daily, something that occurs each day. Diurnal temperature refers to the variation in temperature over the course of a full day and night.

Divide A US term describing the area of high ground separating two *drainage basins*.

Donga A steep-sided *gully*, resulting from *erosion* by a river or by floods.

Dormant A term used to describe a *volcano* which is not currently erupting. They differ from extinct volcanoes as dormant volcanoes are still considered likely to erupt in the future.

Drainage basin The area drained by a single river system, its boundary is marked by a *watershed* or *divide*.

Drought A long period of continuously low rainfall.

Drumlin A long, streamlined hillock composed of material deposited by a *glacier*. They often occur in groups known as swarms.

Dune A mound or ridge of sand, shaped, and often moved, by the wind. They are found in hot *deserts* and on low-lying coasts where onshore winds blow across sandy beaches.

Dyke A wall constructed in low-lying areas to contain floodwaters or protect from high tides.

E

Earthflow The rapid movement of soil and other loose surface material down a slope, when saturated by water. Similar to a mudflow but not as fast-flowing, due to a lower percentage of water.

Earthquake Sudden movements of the Earth's *crust*, causing the ground to shake. Frequently occurring at *tectonic plate* margins. The shock, or series of shocks, spreads out from an *epicenter*.

EC The European Community (*see* EU).

Ecosystem A system of living organisms – plants and animals – interacting with their *environment*.

ECOWAS Economic Community of West African States. Established in 1975, it incorporates 16 West African states and aims to promote closer regional and economic cooperation.

Element
1 A constituent of the *climate* – *precipitation*, *humidity*, temperature, *atmospheric pressure*, or wind.
2 A substance that cannot be separated into simpler substances by chemical means.

El Niño A climatic phenomenon, the El Niño effect occurs about 14 times each century and leads to major shifts in global air circulation. It is associated with unusually warm currents off the coasts of Peru, Ecuador and Chile. The anomaly can last for up to two years.

Environment The conditions created by the surroundings (both natural and artificial) within which an organism lives. In human geography the word includes the surrounding economic, cultural, and social conditions.

Eon (aeon) Traditionally a long, but indefinite, period of *geological time*.

Ephemeral A nonpermanent feature, often used in connection with seasonal rivers or lakes in dry areas.

Epicenter The point on the Earth's surface directly above the underground origin – or focus – of an *earthquake*.

Equator The line of *latitude* which lies equidistant between the North and South Poles.

Erg An extensive area of sand *dunes*, particularly in the Sahara Desert.

Erosion The processes which wear away the surface of the land. *Glaciers*, wind, rivers, waves, and currents all carry debris which causes *erosion*. Some definitions also include *mass movement* due to gravity as an agent of erosion.

Escarpment A steep slope at the margin of a level, upland surface. In a landscape created by *folding*, escarpments (or scarps) frequently lie behind a more gentle backward slope.

Esker A narrow, winding ridge of sand and gravel deposited by streams of water flowing beneath or at the edge of a *glacier*.

Erratic A rock transported by a *glacier* and deposited some distance from its place of origin.

Eustacy A world-wide fall or rise in ocean levels.

EU The European Union. Established in 1965, it was formerly known as the EEC (European Economic Community) and then the EC (European Community). Its members are Austria, Belgium, Denmark, Finland, France, Germany, Greece, Ireland, Italy, Luxembourg, Netherlands, Portugal, Spain, Sweden, and UK. It seeks to establish an integrated European common market and eventual federation.

Evaporation The process whereby a liquid or solid is turned into a gas or vapor. Also refers to the diffusion of water vapor into the *atmosphere* from exposed water surfaces such as lakes and seas.

Evapotranspiration The loss of moisture from the Earth's surface through a combination of *evaporation*, and *transpiration* from the leaves of plants.

Evergreen Plants with long-lasting leaves, which are not shed annually or seasonally.

Exfoliation A kind of *weathering* whereby scalelike flakes of rock are peeled or broken off by the development of salt crystals in water within the rocks. *Groundwater*, which contains dissolved salts, seeps to the surface and evaporates, precipitating a film of salt crystals, which expands causing fine cracks. As these grow, flakes of rock break off.

Extrusive rock *Igneous* rock formed when molten material (*magma*) pours forth at the Earth's surface and cools rapidly. It usually has a glassy texture.

F

Factionalism The actions of one or more minority political group acting against the interests of the majority government.

Fault A fracture or crack in rock, where strains (*tectonic* movement) have caused blocks to move, vertically or laterally, relative to each other.

Fauna Collective name for the animals of a particular period of time, or region.

Favela Brazilian term for the shantytowns or temporary huts that have grown up around the edge of many South and Central American cities.

Ferrel cell A component in the global pattern of air circulation, which rises in the colder *latitudes* (60° N and S) and descends in warmer *latitudes* (30° N and S). The Ferrel cell forms part of the world's three-cell air circulation pattern, with the *Hadley* and Polar cells.

Fissure A deep crack in a rock or a *glacier*.

Fjord A deep, narrow inlet, created when the sea inundates the *U-shaped valley* created by a *glacier*.

Flash flood A sudden, short-lived rise in the water level of a river or stream, or surge of water down a dry river channel, or *wadi*, caused by heavy rainfall.

Flax A plant used to make linen.

Floodplain The broad, flat part of a river valley, adjacent to the river itself, formed by *sediment* deposited during flooding.

Flora The collective name for the plants of a particular period of time or region.

Flow The movement of a river within its banks, particularly in terms of the speed and volume of water.

Fold A bend in the rock *strata* of the Earth's *crust*, resulting from compression.

Fossil The remains, or traces,of a dead organism preserved in the Earth's *crust*.

Fossil dune A *dune* formed in a once-*arid* region which is now wetter. *Dunes* normally move with the wind, but in these cases vegetation makes them stable.

Fossil fuel Fuel – coal, natural gas or oil – composed of the fossilized remains of plants and animals.

Front The boundary between two *air masses*, which contrast sharply in temperature and *humidity*.

Frontal depression An area of low pressure caused by rising warm air. They are generally 600–1,200 miles (1,000–2,000 km) in diameter. Within *depressions* there are both warm and cold fronts.

Frost shattering A form of *weathering* where water freezes in cracks, causing expansion. As temperatures fluctuate and the ice melts and refreezes, it eventually causes the rocks to shatter and fragments of rock to break off.

G

Gaucho South American term for a stock herder or cowboy who works on the grassy *plains* of Paraguay, Uruguay, and Argentina.

Geological timescale The chronology of the Earth's history as revealed in its rocks. Geological time is divided into a number of periods: *eon*, era, period, epoch, age, and chron (the shortest). These units are not of uniform length.

Geosyncline A concave fold (*syncline*) or large depression in the Earth's *crust*, extending hundreds of miles. This basin contains a deep layer of sediment, especially at its center, from the land masses around it.

Geothermal energy Heat derived from hot rocks within the Earth's *crust* and resulting in hot springs, steam, or hot rocks at the surface. The energy is generated by rock movements, and from the breakdown of radioactive elements occurring under intense pressure.

GDP Gross Domestic Product. The total value of goods and services produced by a country excluding income from foreign countries.

Geyser A jet of steam and hot water that intermittently erupts from vents in the ground in areas that are, or were, *volcanic*. Some geysers occasionally reach heights of 196 ft (60 m).

Ghetto An area of a city or region occupied by an overwhelming majority of people from one racial or religious group, who may be subject to persecution or containment.

Glaciation The growth of *glaciers* and *ice sheets*, and their impact on the landscape.

Glacier A body of ice moving downslope under the influence of gravity and consisting of compacted and frozen snow. A glacier is distinct from an *ice sheet*, which is wider and less confined by features of the landscape.

Glacio-eustacy A world-wide change in the level of the oceans, caused when the formation of *ice sheets* takes up water or when their melting returns water to the ocean. The formation of ice sheets in the *Pleistocene* epoch, for example, caused sea level to drop by about 320 ft (100-m).

Glaciofluvial To do with glacial *meltwater*, the landforms it creates and its processes; *erosion*, transportation, and *deposition*. Glaciofluvial effects are more powerful and rapid where they occur within or beneath the *glacier*, rather than beyond its edge.

Glacis A gentle slope or *pediment*.

Global warming An increase in the average temperature of the Earth. At present the *greenhouse effect* is thought to contribute to this.

GNP Gross National Product. The total value of goods and services produced by a country.

Gondwanaland The *supercontinent* thought to have existed over 200 million years ago in the southern hemisphere. Gondwanaland is believed to have comprised today's Africa, Madagascar, Australia, parts of South America, *Antarctica*, and the Indian subcontinent.

Graben A block of rock let down between two parallel *faults*. Where the graben occurs within a valley, the structure is known as a *rift valley*.

Grease ice Slicks of ice which form in *Antarctic* seas, when ice crystals are bonded together by wind and wave action.

Greenhouse effect A change in the temperature of the *atmosphere*. Short-wave solar radiation travels through the *atmosphere* unimpeded to the Earth's surface, whereas outgoing, long-wave terrestrial radiation is absorbed by materials that reradiate it back to the Earth. Radiation trapped in this way, by water vapor, carbon dioxide, and other "greenhouse gases," keeps the Earth warm. As more *carbon dioxide* is released into the atmosphere by the burning of *fossil fuels*, the greenhouse effect may cause a global increase in temperature.

Groundwater Water that has seeped into the pores, cavities, and cracks of rocks or into soil and water held in an *aquifer*.

Gully A deep, narrow channel eroded in the landscape by *ephemeral* streams.

Guyot A small, flat-topped submarine mountain, formed as a result of subsidence which occurs during *sea-floor spreading*.

Gypsum A soft mineral *compound* (hydrated calcium sulphate), used as the basis of many forms of plaster, including plaster of Paris.

H

Hadley cell A large-scale component in the global pattern of air circulation. Warm air rises over the *Equator* and blows at high altitude toward the poles, sinking in subtropical regions (30° N and 30° S) and creating high pressure. The air then flows at the surface toward the *Equator* in the form of trade winds. There is one cell in each hemisphere. Named after G. Hadley, who published his theory in 1735.

Hamada An Arabic word for a plateau of bare rock in a *desert*.

Hanging valley A tributary valley that ends suddenly, high above the bed of the main valley. The effect is found where the main valley has been more deeply eroded by a *glacier*, than has the tributary valley. A stream in a hanging valley will descend to the floor of the main valley as a waterfall or *cataract*.

Headwards The action of a river eroding back upstream, as opposed to the normal process of downstream *erosion*. Headwards erosion is often associated with *gullying*.

Hoodos Pinnacles of rock that have been worn away by *weathering* in *semiarid* regions.

Horst A block of the Earth's *crust* which has been left upstanding by the sinking of adjoining blocks along fault lines.

Hot spot A region of the Earth's *crust* where high thermal activity occurs, often leading to volcanic eruptions. Hot spots often occur far from plate boundaries, but their movement is associated with *plate tectonics*.

Humid equatorial Rainy *climate* with no winter, where the coolest month is generally above 64°F (18°C).

Humidity The relative amount of moisture held in the Earth's *atmosphere*.

Hurricane
1 A tropical *cyclone* occurring in the Caribbean and western North Atlantic.
2 A wind of more than 55 knots (75 kmph).

Hydroelectric power Energy produced by harnessing the rapid movement of water down steep mountain slopes to drive turbines to generate electricity.

Hydrolysis The chemical breakdown of rocks in reaction with water, forming new compounds.

I

Ice Age A period in the Earth's history when surface temperatures in the temperate *latitudes* were much lower and *ice sheets* expanded considerably. There have been *ice ages* from *Pre-Cambrian* times onward. The most recent began two million years ago and ended 10,000 years ago.

Ice cap A permanent dome of ice in highland areas. The term ice cap is often seen as distinct from *ice sheet*, which denotes a much wider covering of ice; and is also used refer to the very extensive polar and Greenland ice caps.

Ice floe A large, flat mass of ice floating free on the ocean surface. It is usually formed after the break-up of winter ice by heavy storms.

Ice sheet A continuous, very thick layer of ice and snow. The term is usually used of ice masses which are continental in extent.

Ice shelf A floating mass of ice attached to the edge of a coast. The seaward edge is usually a sheer cliff up to 100 ft (30-m) high.

Ice wedge Massive blocks of ice up to 6.5-ft (2-m) wide at the top and extending 32-ft (10-m) deep. They are found in cracks in *polygonally-patterned* ground in *periglacial* regions.

Iceberg A large mass of ice in a lake or a sea, which has broken off from a floating *ice sheet* (an *ice shelf*) or from a *glacier*.

Igneous rock Rock formed when molten material, *magma*, from the hot, lower layers of the Earth's *crust*, cools, solidifies, and crystallizes, either within the Earths *crust* (*intrusive*) or on the surface (*extrusive*).

IMF International Monetary Fund. Established in 1944 as a UN agency, it contains 182 members around the world and is concerned with world monetary stability and economic development.

Incised meander A *meander* where the river, following its original course, cuts deeply into *bedrock*. This may occur when a mature, meandering river begins to erode its bed much more vigorously after the surrounding land has been uplifted.

Indigenous People, plants, or animals native to a particular region.

Infrastructure The communications and services – roads, railroads, and telecommunications – necessary for the functioning of a country or region.

Inselberg An isolated, steep-sided hill, rising from a low *plain* in *semiarid* and *savannah* landscapes. Inselbergs are usually composed of a rock, such as granite, which resists *erosion*.

Interglacial A period of global *climate*, between two *ice ages*, when temperatures rise and *ice sheets* and *glaciers* retreat.

Intraplate volcano A *volcano* which lies in the centre of one of the Earth's *tectonic plates*, rather than, as is more common, at its edge. They are thought to have been formed by a *hot spot*.

Intrusion (intrusive igneous rock) Rock formed when molten material, *magma*, penetrates existing rocks below the Earth's surface before cooling and solidifying. These rocks cool more slowly than extrusive rock and therefore tend to have coarser grains.

Irrigation The artificial supply of agricultural water to dry areas, often involving the creation of canals and the diversion of natural watercourses.

Island arc A curved chain of islands. Typically, such an arc fringes an ocean trench, formed at the margin between two *tectonic plates*. As one plate overrides another, *earthquakes* and volcanic activity are common and the islands themselves are often volcanic cones.

Isostacy The state of equilibrium that the Earth's *crust* maintains as its lighter and heavier parts float on the denser underlying mantle.

Isthmus A narrow strip of land connecting two larger landmasses or islands.

J

Jet stream A narrow belt of westerly winds in the *troposphere*, at altitudes above 39,000 ft (12,000 m). Jet streams tend to blow more strongly in winter and include: the subtropical jet stream; the *polar* front jet stream in mid-*latitudes*; the *Arctic* jet stream; and the polar-night jet stream.

Joint A crack in a rock, formed where blocks of rock have not shifted relative to each other, as is the case with a *fault*. Joints are created by *folding*; by shrinkage in *igneous rock* as it cools or *sedimentary rock* as it dries out; and by the release of pressure in a rock mass when overlying materials are removed by *erosion*.

Jute A plant fiber used to make coarse ropes, sacks, and matting.

K

Kame A mound of stratified sand and gravel with steep sides, deposited in a *crevasse* by *meltwater* running over a *glacier*. When the ice retreats, this forms an undulating terrain of hummocks.

Karst A barren *limestone* landscape created by carbonic acid in streams and rainwater, in areas where *limestone* is close to the surface. Typical features include caverns, towerlike hills, *sinkholes*, and flat limestone pavements.

Kettle hole A round hollow formed in a glacial deposit by a detached block of glacial ice, which later melted. They can fill with water to form kettle-lakes.

L

Lagoon A shallow stretch of coastal salt-water behind a partial barrier such as a sandbank or *coral reef*. Lagoon is also used to describe the water encircled by an *atoll*.

LAIA Latin American Integration Association. Established in 1980, its members are Argentina, Bolivia, Brazil, Chile, Colombia, Ecuador, Mexico, Paraguay, Peru, Uruguay, and Venezuala. It aims to promote economic cooperation between member states.

Landslide The sudden downslope movement of a mass of rock or earth on a slope, caused either by heavy rain; the impact of waves; an *earthquake* or human activity.

Laterite A hard red deposit left by *chemical weathering* in tropical conditions, and consisting mainly of oxides of iron and aluminium.

Latitude The angular distance from the *Equator*, to a given point on the Earth's surface. Imaginary lines of *latitude* running parallel to the Equator encircle the Earth, and are measured in degrees north or south of the Equator. The Equator is 0°, the poles 90° South and North respectively. Also called parallels.

Laurasia In the theory of *continental drift*, the northern part of the great *supercontinent* of *Pangaea*. Laurasia is said to consist of N America, Greenland and all of Eurasia north of the Indian subcontinent.

Lava The molten rock, *magma*, which erupts onto the Earth's surface through a *volcano*, or through a *fault* or crack in the Earth's *crust*. Lava refers to the rock both in its molten and in its later, solidified form.

Leaching The process whereby water dissolves minerals and moves them down through layers of soil or rock.

Levée A raised bank alongside the channel of a river. Levées are either human-made or formed in times of flood when the river overflows its channel, slows and deposits much of its *sediment* load.

Lichen An organism which is the symbiotic product of an algae and a fungus. Lichens form in tight crusts on stones and trees, and are resistant to extreme cold. They are often found in tundra regions.

Lignite Low-grade coal, also known as brown coal. Found in large deposits in eastern Europe.

Limestone A porous *sedimentary* rock formed from carbonate materials.

Lingua franca The language adopted as the common language between speakers whose native languages are different. This is common in former colonial states.

Lithosphere The rigid upper layer of the Earth, comprising the *crust* and the upper part of the *mantle*.

Llanos Vast grassland *plains* of northern South America.

Loess Fine-grained, yellow deposits of unstratified silts and sands. Loess is believed to be wind-carried *sediment* created in the last *Ice Age*. Some deposits may later have been redistributed by rivers. Loess-derived soils are of high quality, fertile, and easy to work.

Longitude A division of the Earth which pinpoints how far east or west a given place is from the Prime Meridian (0°) which runs through the Royal Observatory at Greenwich, England (UK). Imaginary lines of longitude are drawn around the world from pole to pole. The world is divided into 360 degrees.

Longshore drift The movement of sand and silt along the coast, carried by waves hitting the beach at an angle.

M

Magma Underground, molten rock, which is very hot and highly charged with gas. It is generated at great pressure, at depths 10 miles (16 km) or more below the Earth's surface. It can issue as *lava* at the Earth's surface or, more often, solidify below the surface as *intrusive igneous rock*.

Mantle The layer of the Earth between the *crust* and the *core*. It is about 1,800 miles (2,900-km) thick. The uppermost layer of the mantle is the soft, 125-mile (200 km) thick *asthenosphere* on which the more rigid *lithosphere* floats.

Maquiladoras Factories on the Mexico side of the Mexico/US border, that are allowed to import raw materials and components duty-free and use low-cost labor to assemble the goods, finally exporting them for sale in the US.

Market gardening The intensive growing of fruit and vegetables close to large local markets.

Mass movement Downslope movement of weathered materials such as rock, often helped by rainfall or glacial *meltwater*. Mass movement may be a gradual process or rapid, as in a *landslide* or rockfall.

Massif A single very large mountain or an area of mountains with uniform characteristics and clearly-defined boundaries.

Meander A looplike bend in a river, which is found typically in the lower, mature reaches of a river but can form wherever the valley is wide and the slope gentle.

Mediterranean climate A temperate *climate* of hot, dry summers and warm, damp winters. This is typical of the western fringes of the world's continents in the warm temperate regions between *latitudes* of 30° and 40° (north and south).

Meltwater Water resulting from the melting of a *glacier* or *ice sheet*.

Mesa A broad, flat-topped hill, characteristic of *arid* regions.

Mesosphere A layer of the Earth's *atmosphere*, between the *stratosphere* and the *thermosphere*. Extending from about 25–50 miles (40–80 km) above the surface of the Earth.

Mestizo A person of mixed *Amerindian* and European origin.

Metallurgy The refining and working of metals.

Metamorphic rocks Rocks that have been altered from their original form, in terms of texture, composition, and structure by intense heat, pressure, or by the introduction of new chemical substances – or a combination of more than one of these.

Meteor A body of rock, metal or other material, that travels through space at great speeds. Meteors are visible as they enter the Earth's *atmosphere* as shooting stars and fireballs.

Meteorite The remains of a *meteor* that has fallen to Earth.

Meteoroid A *meteor* that is still traveling in space, outside the Earth's *atmosphere*.

Mezzogiorno A term applied to the southern portion of Italy.

Milankovitch hypothesis A theory suggesting that there are a series of cycles that slightly alter the Earth's position when rotating about the Sun. The cycles identified all affect the amount of *radiation* the Earth receives at different *latitudes*. The theory is seen as a key factor in the cause of *ice ages*.

Millet A grain-crop, forming part of the staple diet in much of Africa.

Mistral A strong, dry, cold northerly or north-westerly wind, which blows from the Massif Central of France to the Mediterranean Sea. It is common in winter and its cold blasts can cause crop damage in the Rhône Delta, in France.

Mohorovicic discontinuity (Moho) The structural divide at the margin between the Earth's *crust* and the *mantle*. On average it is 20 miles (35-km) below the continents and 6-miles (10 km) below the oceans. The different densities of the *crust* and the mantle cause *earthquake* waves to accelerate at this point.

Monarchy A form of government in which the head of state is a single hereditary monarch. The monarch may be a mere figurehead, or may retain significant authority.

Monsoon A wind that changes direction biannually. The change is caused by the reversal of pressure over landmasses and the adjacent oceans. Because the inflowing moist winds bring rain, the term monsoon is also used to refer to the rains themselves. The term is derived from and most commonly refers to the seasonal winds of south and east Asia.

Montaña Mountain areas along the west coast of South America.

Moraine Debris, transported and deposited by a *glacier* or *ice sheet* in unstratified, mixed, piles of rock, boulders, pebbles, and clay.

Mountain-building The formation of *fold* mountains by tectonic activity. Also known as orogeny, mountain-building often occurs on the margin where two *tectonic plates* collide. The periods when most mountain-building occurred are known as orogenic phases and lasted many millions of years.

Mudflow An *avalanche* of mud that occurs when a mass of soil is drenched by rain or melting snow. It is a type of *mass movement*, faster than an *earthflow* because it is lubricated by water.

N

Nappe A mass of rocks which has been overfolded by repeated thrust *faulting*.

NAFTA The North American Free Trade Association. Established in 1994 between Canada, Mexico, and the US to set up a free-trade zone.

NASA The North American Space Agency. It is a government body, established in 1958 to develop manned and unmanned space programs.

NATO The North Atlantic Treaty Organization. Established in 1949 to promote mutual defense and cooperation between its members, which are Belgium, Canada, Czech Republic, Denmark, France, Germany, Greece, Iceland, Italy, Luxembourg, the Netherlands, Norway, Portugal, Poland, Spain, Turkey, UK, and US.

Nitrogen The odorless, colorless gas that makes up 78% of the atmosphere. Within the soil, it is a vital nutrient for plants.

Nomads (nomadic) Wandering communities that move around in search of suitable pasture for their herds of animals.

Nuclear fusion A technique used to create a new nucleus by the merging of two lighter ones, resulting in the release of large quantities of energy.

O

Oasis A fertile area in the midst of a *desert*, usually watered by an underground *aquifer*.

Oceanic ridge A mid-ocean ridge formed, according to the theory of *plate tectonics*, when plates drift apart and hot *magma* pours through to form new oceanic *crust*.

Oligarchy The government of a state by a small, exclusive group of people – such as an elite class or a family group.

Onion-skin weathering The *weathering* away or *exfoliation* of a rock or outcrop by the peeling off of surface layers.

Oriente A flatter region lying to the east of the Andes in South America.

Outwash plain *Glaciofluvial* material (typically clay, sand, and gravel) carried beyond an ice sheet by *meltwater* streams, forming a broad, flat deposit.

Oxbow lake A crescent-shaped lake formed on a river *floodplain* when a river erodes the outside bend of a *meander*, making the neck of the *meander* narrower until the river cuts across the neck. The meander is cut off and is dammed off with sediment, creating an oxbow lake. Also known as a cut-off or mortlake.

Oxidation A form of *chemical weathering* where *oxygen* dissolved in water reacts with minerals in rocks – particularly iron – to form oxides. Oxidation causes brown or yellow staining on rocks, and eventually leads to the break down of the rock.

Oxygen A colorless, odorless gas which is one of the main constituents of the Earth's *atmosphere* and is essential to life on Earth.

Ozone layer A layer of enriched *oxygen* (O_3) within the stratosphere, mostly between 18–50 miles (30–80 km) above the Earth's surface. It is vital to the existence of life on Earth because it absorbs harmful shortwave ultraviolet radiation, while allowing beneficial longer wave ultraviolet radiation to penetrate to the Earth's surface.

P

Pacific Rim The name given to the economically-dynamic countries bordering the Pacific Ocean.

Pack ice Ice masses more than 10 ft (3-m) thick that form on the sea surface and are not attached to a landmass.

Pancake ice Thin discs of ice, up to 8 ft (2.4 m) wide which form when slicks of *grease ice* are tossed together by winds and stormy seas.

Pangaea In the theory of continental drift, Pangaea is the original great land mass which, about 190 million years ago, began to split into Gondwanaland in the south and Laurasia in the north, separated by the Tethys Sea.

Pastoralism Grazing of livestock– usually sheep, goats, or cattle. Pastoralists in many drier areas have traditionally been *nomadic*.

Parallel *see Latitude.*

Peat Ancient, partially-decomposed vegetation found in wet, boggy conditions where there is little *oxygen*. It is the first stage in the development of coal and is often dried for use as fuel. It is also used to improve soil quality.

Pediment A gently-sloping ramp of *bedrock* below a steeper slope, often found at mountain edges in *desert* areas, but also in other climatic zones. Pediments may include depositional elements such as *alluvial fans*.

Peninsula A thin strip of land surrounded on three of its sides by water. Large examples include Florida and Korea.

Per capita Latin term meaning "for each person."

Periglacial Regions on the edges of *ice sheets* or *glaciers* or, more commonly, cold regions experiencing intense frost action, *permafrost* or both. Periglacial climates bring long, freezing winters and short, mild summers.

Permafrost Permanently frozen ground, typical of *Arctic* regions. Although a layer of soil above the permafrost melts in summer, the melted water does not drain through the permafrost.

Permeable rocks Rocks through which water can seep, because they are either porous or cracked.

Pharmaceuticals The manufacture of medicinal drugs.

Phreatic eruption A volcanic eruption which occurs when *lava* combines with *groundwater*, superheating the water and causing a sudden emission of steam at the surface.

Physical weathering (mechanical weathering) The breakdown of rocks by physical, as opposed to chemical, processes. Examples include: changes in pressure or temperature; the effect of windblown sand; the pressure of growing salt crystals in cracks within rock; and the expansion and contraction of water within rock as it freezes and thaws.

Pingo A dome of earth with a core of ice, found in *tundra* regions. Pingos are formed either when *groundwater* freezes and expands, pushing up the land surface, or when trapped, freezing water in a lake expands and pushes up lake *sediments* to form the pingo dome.

Placer A belt of mineral-bearing rock *strata* lying at or close to the Earth's surface, from which minerals can be easily extracted.

Plain A flat, level region of land, often relatively low-lying.

Plateau A highland tract of flat land.

Plate *see Tectonic plates.*

Plate tectonics The study of *tectonic plates*, that helps to explain *continental drift*, mountain formation and volcanic activity. The movement of tectonic plates may be explained by the currents of rock rising and falling from within the Earth's *mantle*, as it heats up and then cools. The boundaries of the plates are known as plate margins and most mountains, *earthquakes*, and *volcanoes* occur at these margins. Constructive margins are moving apart; destructive margins are crunching together and conservative margins are sliding past one another.

Pleistocene A period of *geological time* spanning from about 5.2 million years ago to 1.6 million years ago.

Plutonic rock *Igneous* rocks found deep below the surface. They are coarse-grained because they cooled and solidified slowly.

Polar The zones within the *Arctic* and *Antarctic* circles.

Polje A long, broad *depression* found in *karst* (*limestone*) regions.

Polygonal patterning Typical ground patterning, found in areas where the soil is subject to severe frost action, often in *periglacial* regions.

Porosity A measure of how much water can be held within a rock or a soil. Porosity is measured as the percentage of holes or pores in a material, compared to its total volume. For example, the porosity of slate is less than 1%, whereas that of gravel is 25–35%.

Prairies Originally a French word for grassy *plains* with few or no trees.

Pre-Cambrian The earliest period of *geological time* dating from over 570-million years ago.

Precipitation The fall of moisture from the *atmosphere* onto the surface of the Earth, whether as dew, hail, rain, sleet, or snow.

Pyramidal peak A steep, isolated mountain summit, formed when the back walls of three or more *cirques* are cut back and move toward each other. The cliffs around such a horned peak, or horn, are divided by sharp *arêtes*. The Matterhorn in the Swiss Alps is an example.

Pyroclasts Fragments of rock ejected during volcanic eruptions.

Q

Quaternary The current period of *geological time*, which started about 1.6-million years ago.

R

Radiation The emission of energy in the form of particles or waves. Radiation from the sun includes heat, light, ultraviolet rays, gamma rays, and X-rays. Only some of the solar energy radiated into space reaches the Earth.

Rainforest Dense forests in tropical zones with high rainfall, temperature and *humidity*. Strictly, the term applies to the equatorial rain forest in tropical lowlands with constant rainfall and no seasonal change. The Congo and Amazon basins are examples. The term is applied more loosely to lush forest in other climates. Within rain forests organic life is dense and varied: at least 40% of all plant and animal species are found here and there may be as many as 100 tree species per hectare.

Rainshadow An area which experiences low rainfall, because of its position on the leeward side of a mountain range.

Reg A large area of stony *desert*, where tightly-packed gravel lies on top of clayey sand. A reg is formed where the wind blows away the finer sand.

Remote-sensing Method of obtaining information about the *environment* using unmanned equipment, such as a satellite, that relays the information to a point where it is collected and used.

Resistance The capacity of a rock to resist *denudation*, by processes such as *weathering* and *erosion*.

Ria A flooded *V-shaped river valley* or estuary, flooded by a rise in sea level (*eustacy*) or sinking land. It is shorter than a *fjord* and gets deeper as it meets the sea.

Rift valley A long, narrow depression in the Earth's *crust*, formed by the sinking of rocks between two *faults*.

River channel The trough which contains a river and is molded by the flow of water within it.

Roche moutonée A rock found in a glaciated valley. The side facing the flow of the *glacier* has been smoothed and rounded, while the other side has been left more rugged because the *glacier*, as it flows over it, has plucked out frozen fragments and carried them away.

Runoff Water draining from a land surface by flowing across it.

S

Sabkha The floor of an isolated *depression* that occurs in an *arid environment* – usually covered by salt deposits and devoid of vegetation.

SADC Southern African Development Community. Established in 1992 to promote economic integration between its member states, which are Angola, Botswana, Lesotho, Malawi, Mauritius, Mozambique, Namibia, South Africa, Swaziland, Tanzania, Zambia, and Zimbabwe.

Salt plug A rounded hill produced by the upward doming of rock *strata* caused by the movement of salt or other evaporite deposits under intense pressure.

Sastrugi Ice ridges formed by wind action. They lie parallel to the direction of the wind.

Savannah Open grassland found between the zone of *deserts*, and that of tropical *rain forests* in the tropics and subtropics. Scattered trees and shrubs are found in some kinds of savannah. A savannah *climate* usually has wet and dry seasons.

Scarp *see Escarpment.*

Scree Piles of rock fragments beneath a cliff or rock face, caused by mechanical *weathering*, especially *frost shattering*, where the expansion and contraction of freezing and thawing water within the rock, gradually breaks it up.

Sea-floor spreading The process whereby *tectonic plates* move apart, allowing hot *magma* to erupt and solidify. This forms a new sea floor and, ultimately, widens the ocean.

Seamount An isolated, submarine mountain or hill, probably of volcanic origin.

Season A period of time linked to regular changes in the weather, especially the intensity of solar *radiation*.

Sediment Grains of rock transported and deposited by rivers, sea, ice, or wind.

Sedimentary rocks Rocks formed from the debris of preexisting rocks or of organic material. They are found in many *environments* – on the ocean floor, on beaches, rivers, and *deserts*. Organically-formed sedimentary rocks include coal and chalk. Other sedimentary rocks, such as flint, are formed by chemical processes. Most of these rocks contain *fossils*, which can be used to date them.

Seif A sand *dune* which lies parallel to the direction of the prevailing wind. Seifs form steep-sided ridges, sometimes extending for miles.

Seismic activity Movement within the Earth, such as an *earthquake* or *tremor*.

Selva A region of wet forest found in the Amazon Basin.

Semiarid, semidesert The *climate* and landscape which lies between *savannah* and *desert* or between savannah and a *mediterranean* climate. In semiarid conditions there is a little more moisture than in a true *desert*; and more patches of drought-resistant vegetation can survive.

Shale (marine shale) A compacted *sedimentary rock*, with fine-grained particles. Marine shale is formed on the seabed. Fuel such as oil may be extracted from it.

Sheetwash Water that runs downhill in thin sheets without forming channels. It can cause *sheet erosion*.

Sheet erosion The washing away of soil by a thin film or sheet of water, known as *sheetwash*.

Shield A vast stable block of the Earth's *crust*, which has experienced little or no *mountain-building*.

Sierra The Spanish word for mountains.

Sinkhole A circular *depression* in a *limestone* region. They are formed by the collapse of an underground cave system or the *chemical weathering* of the *limestone*.

Sisal A plant-fiber used to make matting.

Slash and burn A farming technique involving the cutting down and burning of scrub forest, to create agricultural land. After a number of seasons this land is abandoned and the process is repeated. This practice is common in Africa and South America.

Slip face The steep leeward side of a sand *dune* or slope. Opposite side to a *back slope*.

Soil A thin layer of rock particles mixed with the remains of dead plants and animals. This occurs naturally on the surface of the Earth and provides a medium for plants to grow.

Soil creep The very gradual downslope movement of rock debris and soil, under the influence of gravity. This is a type of *mass movement*.

Soil erosion The wearing away of soil more quickly than it is replaced by natural processes. Soil can be carried away by wind as well as by water. Human activities, such as over-grazing and the clearing of land for farming, accelerate the process in many areas.

Solar energy Energy derived from the Sun. Solar energy is converted into other forms of energy. For example, the wind and waves, as well as the creation of plant material in photosynthesis, depend on solar energy.

Solifluction A kind of *soil creep*, where water in the surface layer has saturated the soil and rock debris which slips slowly downhill. It often happens where frozen top-layer deposits thaw, leaving frozen layers below them.

Sorghum A type of grass found in South America, similar to sugar cane. When refined it is used to make molasses.

Spit A thin linear deposit of sand or shingle extending from the sea shore. Spits are formed as angled waves shift sand along the beach, eventually extending a ridge of sand beyond a change in the angle of the coast. Spits are common where the coastline bends, especially at estuaries.

Squash A type of edible gourd.

Stack A tall, isolated pillar of rock near a coastline, created as wave action erodes away the adjacent rock.

Stalactite A tapering cylinder of mineral deposit, hanging from the roof of a cave in a *karst* area. It is formed by calcium carbonate, dissolved in water, which drips through the roof of a *limestone* cavern.

Stalagmite A cone of calcium carbonate, similar to a *stalactite*, rising from the floor of a *limestone* cavern and formed when drops of water fall from the roof of a *limestone* cave. If the water has dripped from a *stalactite* above the stalagmite, the two may join to form a continuous pillar.

Staple crop The main crop on which a country is economically and or physically reliant. For example, the major crop grown for large-scale local consumption in South Asia is rice.

Steppe Large areas of dry grassland in the northern hemisphere – particularly found in southeast Europe and central Asia.

Strata The plural of stratum, a distinct, virtually horizontal layer of deposited material, lying parallel to other layers.

Stratosphere A layer of the *atmosphere*, above the *troposphere*, extending from about 7–30 miles (11–50 km) above the Earth's surface. In the lower part of the stratosphere, the temperature is relatively stable and there is little moisture.

Strike-slip fault Occurs where plates move sideways past each other and blocks of rocks move horizontally in relation to each other, not up or down as in normal *faults*.

Subduction zone A region where two *tectonic plates* collide, forcing one beneath the other. Typically, a dense oceanic plate dips below a lighter continental plate, melting in the heat of the *asthenosphere*. This is why the zone is also called a destructive margin (*see Plate tectonics*). These zones are characterized by *earthquakes*, volcanoes, *mountain-building*, and the development of oceanic trenches and *island arcs*.

Submarine canyon A steep-sided valley, that extends along the *continental shelf* to the ocean floor. Often formed by *turbidity currents*.

Submarine fan Deposits of silt and *alluvium*, carried by large rivers forming great fan-shaped deposits on the ocean floor.

Subsistence agriculture An agricultural practice in which enough food is produced to support the farmer and his dependents, but not providing any surplus to generate an income.

Subtropical A term applied loosely to *climates* which are nearly tropical or tropical for a part of the year – areas north or south of the *tropics* but outside the *temperate zone*.

Supercontinent A large continent that breaks up to form smaller continents or that forms when smaller continents merge. In the theory of *continental drift*, the supercontinents are *Pangaea*, *Gondwanaland*, and *Laurasia*.

Sustainable development An approach to development, especially applied to economies across the world which exploit natural resources without destroying them or the *environment*.

Syncline A basin-shaped downfold in rock *strata*, created when the *strata* are compressed, for example where *tectonic plates* collide.

T

Tableland A highland area with a flat or gently undulating surface.

Taiga The belt of *coniferous* forest found in the north of Asia and North America. The conifers are adapted to survive low temperatures and long periods of snowfall.

Tarn A Scottish term for a small mountain lake, usually found at the head of a *glacier*.

Tectonic plates Plates, or tectonic plates, are the rigid slabs which form the Earth's outer shell, the *lithosphere*. Eight big plates and several smaller ones have been identified.

Temperate A moderate *climate* without extremes of temperature, typical of the mid-*latitudes* between the *tropics* and the *polar* circles.

Theocracy A state governed by religious laws – today Iran is the world's largest theocracy.

Thermokarst Subsidence created by the thawing of ground ice in *periglacial* areas, creating depressions.

Thermosphere A layer of the Earth's *atmosphere* which lies above the *mesosphere*, about 60–300 miles (100–500 km) above the Earth

Terraces Steps cut into steep slopes to create flat surfaces for cultivating crops. They also help reduce soil *erosion* on unconsolidated slopes. They are most common in heavily-populated parts of Southeast Asia.

Till Unstratified glacial deposits or drift left by a *glacier* or *ice sheet*. Till includes mixtures of clay, sand, gravel, and boulders.

Topography The typical shape and features of a given area such as land height and terrain.

Tombolo A large sand *spit* which attaches part of the mainland to an island.

Tornado A violent, spiraling windstorm, with a center of very low pressure. Wind speeds reach 200 mph (320 kmph) and there is often thunder and heavy rain.

Transform fault In *plate tectonics*, a *fault* of continental scale, occurring where two plates slide past each other, staying close together for example, the San Andreas Fault, USA. The jerky, uneven movement creates *earthquakes* but does not destroy or add to the Earth's *crust*

Transpiration The loss of water vapor through the pores (or stomata) of plants. The process helps to return moisture to the *atmosphere*.

Trap An area of fine-grained *igneous rock* that has been extruded and cooled on the Earth's surface in stages, forming a series of steps or terraces.

Treeline The line beyond which trees cannot grow, dependent on *latitude* and altitude, as well as local factors such as soil.

Tremor A slight *earthquake*.

Trench (oceanic trench) A long, deep trough in the ocean floor, formed, according to the theory of *plate tectonics*, when two plates collide and one dives under the other, creating a *subduction zone*.

Tropics The zone between the *Tropic of Cancer* and the *Tropic of Capricorn* where the *climate* is hot. Tropical climate is also applied to areas rather further north and south of the *Equator* where the climate is similar to that of the true tropics.

Tropic of Cancer A line of *latitude* or imaginary circle round the Earth, lying at 23° 28′ N.

Tropic of Capricorn A line of *latitude* or imaginary circle round the Earth, lying at 23° 28′ S.

Troposphere The lowest layer of the Earth's *atmosphere*. From the surface, it reaches a height of between 4–10 miles (7–16 km). It is the most turbulent zone of the atmosphere and accounts for the generation of most of the world's weather. The layer above it is called the *stratosphere*.

Tsunami A huge wave created by shock waves from an *earthquake* under the sea. Reaching speeds of up to 600 mph (960-kmph), the wave may increase to heights of 50 ft (15 m) on entering coastal waters; and it can cause great damage.

Tundra The treeless *plains* of the *Arctic Circle*, found south of the *polar* region of permanent ice and snow, and north of the belt of *coniferous* forests known as *taiga*. In this region of long, very cold winters, vegetation is usually limited to mosses, *lichens*, sedges, and rushes, although flowers and dwarf shrubs blossom in the brief summer.

Turbidity current An oceanic feature. A turbidity current is a mass of *sediment*-laden water thathas substantial erosive power. Turbidity currents are thought to contribute to the formation of *submarine canyons*.

Typhoon A kind of *hurricane* (or tropical cyclone) bringing violent winds and heavy rain, a typhoon can do great damage. They occur in the South China Sea, especially around the Philippines.

U

U-shaped valley A river valley that has been deepened and widened by a *glacier*. They are characteristically flat-bottomed and steep-sided and generally much deeper than river valleys.

UN United Nations. Established in 1945, it contains 188 nations and aims to maintain international peace and security, and promote cooperation over economic, social, cultural, and humanitarian problems.

UNICEF United Nations Children's Fund. A UN organization set up to promote family and child related programs.

Urstromtäler A German word used to describe *meltwater* channels that flowed along the front edge of the advancing *ice sheet* during the last Ice Age, 18,000–20,000 years ago.

V

V-shaped valley A typical valley eroded by a river in its upper course.

Virgin rain forest Tropical *rain-forest* in its original state, untouched by human activity such as logging, clearance for agriculture, settlement, or roadbuilding.

Viticulture The cultivation of grapes for wine.

Volcano An opening or vent in the Earth's *crust* where molten rock, *magma*, erupts. Volcanoes tend to be conical but may also be a crack in the Earth's surface or a hole blasted through a mountain. The magma is accompanied by other materials such as gas, steam, and fragments of rock, or *pyroclasts*. They tend to occur on destructive or constructive tectonic*plate* margins.

W-Z

Wadi The dry bed left by a torrent of water. Also classified as a *ephemeral* stream, found in *arid* and *semiarid* regions, which are subject to sudden and often severe flash flooding.

Warm humid climate A rainy climate with warm summers and mild winters.

Water cycle The continuous circulation of water between the Earth's surface and the *atmosphere*. The processes include *evaporation* and *transpiration* of moisture into the atmosphere, and its return as *precipitation*, some of which flows into lakes and oceans.

Water table The upper level of *groundwater* saturation in permeable rock *strata*.

Watershed The dividing line between one *drainage basin* – an area where all streams flow into a single river system – and another. In the US, watershed also means the whole drainage basin of a single river system – its catchment area.

Waterspout A rotating column of water in the form of cloud, mist, and spray which form on open water. Often has the appearance of a small *tornado*.

Weathering The decay and breakup of rocks at or near the Earth's surface, caused by water, wind, heat or ice, organic material, or the *atmosphere*. *Physical weathering* includes the effects of frost and temperature changes. Biological weathering includes the effects of plant roots, burrowing animals and the acids produced by animals, especially as they decay after death. *Carbonation* and *hydrolysis* are among many kinds of *chemical weathering*.

Geographical names

he following glossary lists eographical terms occurring n the maps and in main-ntry names in the Index-Gazetteer. These terms may recede, follow or be run ogether with the proper lement of the name; where hey precede it the term is eversed for indexing urposes - thus Poluostrov amal is indexed as Yamal, oluostrov.

Key

Geographical term
Language, Term

A

Danish, Norwegian, River
b *Persian*, River
drar *Berber*, Mountains
gía, Ágios *Greek*, Saint
ir *Indonesian*, River
kra *Greek*, Cape, point
lpen *German*, Alps
lt- *German*, Old
ltiplanicie *Spanish*, Plateau
lve(en) *Swedish*, River
in *Swedish*, River
nse *French*, Bay
qabat *Arabic*, Pass
rchipiélago *Spanish*, Archipelago
rcipelago *Italian*, Archipelago
rquipélago *Portuguese*, Archipelago
rrecife(s) *Spanish*, Reef(s)
ru *Tamil*, River
ugstiene *Latvian*, Upland
ukštuma *Lithuanian*, Upland
ust- *Norwegian*, Eastern
vtonomnyy Okrug *Russian*, Autonomous district
w *Kurdish*, River
yn *Arabic*, Spring, well
youn *Arabic*, Wells

B

aelt *Danish*, Strait
ahía *Spanish*, Bay
ahr *Arabic*, River
aía *Portuguese*, Bay
aie *French*, Bay
añado *Spanish*, Marshy land
andao *Chinese*, Peninsula
anjaran *Malay*, Mountain range
arajı *Turkish*, Dam
arragem *Portuguese*, Reservoir
assin *French*, Basin
atang *Malay*, Stream
einn, Ben *Gaelic*, Mountain
erg *Afrikaans, Norwegian*, Mountain
esar *Indonesian, Malay*, Big
irkat, Birket *Arabic*, Lake, well,
oğazi *Turkish*, Lake
oka *Serbo-Croatian*, Bay
ol'sh-aya, -iye, -oy, -oye *Russian*, Big
otigh(i) *Uzbek*, Depression basin
re(en) *Norwegian*, Glacier
redning *Danish*, Bay
ucht *German*, Bay
ugt(en) *Danish*, Bay
uhayrat *Arabic*, Lake, reservoir
uheiret *Arabic*, Lake
ukit *Malay*, Mountain
ukta *Norwegian*, Bay
ukten *Swedish*, Bay
ulag *Mongolian*, Spring
ulak *Uighur*, Spring
urnu *Turkish*, Cape, point
uraha *Somali*, Mountains

C

abo *Portuguese*, Cape
aka *Tibetan*, Salt lake
anal *Spanish*, Channel
ap *French*, Cape
apo *Italian*, Cape, headland
ascada *Portuguese*, Waterfall
ayo(s) *Spanish*, Islet(s), rock(s)
erro *Spanish*, Mountain
haîne *French*, Mountain range
hapada *Portuguese*, Hills, upland
hau *Cantonese*, Island
hāy *Turkish*, River
hhâk *Cambodian*, Bay
hhu *Tibetan*, River
hŏsuji *Korean*, Reservoir
hott *Arabic*, Depression, salt lake
hŭli *Uzbek*, Grassland, steppe
h'ün-tao *Chinese*, Island group
huŏr Phnum *Cambodian*, Mountains
Ciudad *Spanish*, City, town
Co *Tibetan*, Lake
Colline(s) *French*, Hill(s)
Cordillera *Spanish*, Mountain range
Costa *Spanish*, Coast
Côte *French*, Coast
Coxilha *Portuguese*, Mountains
Cuchilla *Spanish*, Mountains

D

Daban *Mongolian, Uighur*, Pass
Daği *Azerbaijani, Turkish*, Mountain
Dağlari *Azerbaijani, Turkish*, Mountains
-dake *Japanese*, Peak
-dal(en) *Norwegian*, Valley
Danau *Indonesian*, Lake
Dao *Chinese*, Island
Đao *Vietnamese*, Island
Daryā *Persian*, River
Daryācheh *Persian*, Lake
Dasht *Persian*, Desert, plain
Dawḥat *Arabic*, Bay
Denizi *Turkish*, Sea
Dere *Turkish*, Stream
Desierto *Spanish*, Desert
Dili *Azerbaijani*, Spit
-do *Korean*, Island
Dooxo *Somali*, Valley
Düzü *Azerbaijani*, Steppe
-dwīp *Bengali*, Island

E

-eilanden *Dutch*, Islands
Embalse *Spanish*, Reservoir
Ensenada *Spanish*, Bay
Erg *Arabic*, Dunes
Estany *Catalan*, Lake
Estero *Spanish*, Inlet
Estrecho *Spanish*, Strait
Étang *French*, Lagoon, lake
-ey *Icelandic*, Island
Ezero *Bulgarian, Macedonian*, Lake
Ezers *Latvian*, Lake

F

Feng *Chinese*, Peak
Fjord *Danish*, Fjord
-fjord(en) *Danish, Norwegian, Swedish*, fjord
-fjørdhur *Faeroese*, Fjord
Fleuve *French*, River
Fliegu *Maltese*, Channel
-fljór *Icelandic*, River
-flói *Icelandic*, Bay
Forêt *French*, Forest

G

-gan *Japanese*, Rock
-gang *Korean*, River
Ganga *Hindi, Nepali, Sinhala*, River
Gaoyuan *Chinese*, Plateau
Garagumy *Turkmen*, Sands
-gawa *Japanese*, River
Gebel *Arabic*, Mountain
-gebirge *German*, Mountain range
Ghadīr *Arabic*, Well
Ghubbat *Arabic*, Bay
Gjiri *Albanian*, Bay
Gol *Mongolian*, River
Golfe *French*, Gulf
Golfo *Italian, Spanish*, Gulf
Göl(ü) *Turkish*, Lake
Golyam, -a *Bulgarian*, Big
Gora *Russian, Serbo-Croatian*, Mountain
Góra *Polish*, mountain
Gory *Russian*, Mountain
Gryada *Russian*, ridge
Guba *Russian*, Bay
-gundo *Korean*, island group
Gunung *Malay*, Mountain

H

Ḥadd *Arabic*, Spit
-haehyŏp *Korean*, Strait
Haff *German*, Lagoon
Hai *Chinese*, Bay, lake, sea
Haixia *Chinese*, Strait
Hamada *Arabic*, Plateau
Ḥammādat *Arabic*, Plateau
Hāmūn *Persian*, Lake
-hantō *Japanese*, Peninsula
Har, Haré *Hebrew*, Mountain
Ḥarrat *Arabic*, Lava-field
Hav(et) *Danish, Swedish*, Sea
Hawr *Arabic*, Lake
Hāyk' *Amharic*, Lake
He *Chinese*, River
-hegység *Hungarian*, Mountain range
Heide *German*, Heath, moorland
Helodrano *Malagasy*, Bay
Higashi- *Japanese*, East(ern)
Ḥiṣā' *Arabic*, Well
Hka *Burmese*, River
-ho *Korean*, Lake
Hô *Korean*, Reservoir
Holot *Hebrew*, Dunes
Hora *Belarussian, Czech*, Mountain
Hrada *Belarussian*, Mountain, ridge
Hsi *Chinese*, River
Hu *Chinese*, Lake
Huk *Danish*, Point

I

Île(s) *French*, Island(s)
Ilha(s) *Portuguese*, Island(s)
Ilhéu(s) *Portuguese*, Islet(s)
Imeni *Russian*, In the name of
Inish- *Gaelic*, Island
Insel(n) *German*, Island(s)
Irmağı, Irmak *Turkish*, River
Isla(s) *Spanish*, Island(s)
Isola (Isole) *Italian*, Island(s)

J

Jabal *Arabic*, Mountain
Jāl *Arabic*, Ridge
-järv *Estonian*, Lake
-järvi *Finnish*, Lake
Jazā'ir *Arabic*, Islands
Jazīrat *Arabic*, Island
Jazīreh *Persian*, Island
Jebel *Arabic*, Mountain
Jezero *Serbo-Croatian*, Lake
Jezioro *Polish*, Lake
Jiang *Chinese*, River
-jima *Japanese*, Island
Jižní *Czech*, Southern
-jõgi *Estonian*, River
-joki *Finnish*, River
-jökull *Icelandic*, Glacier
Jūn *Arabic*, Bay
Juzur *Arabic*, Islands

K

Kaikyō *Japanese*, Strait
-kaise *Lappish*, Mountain
Kali *Nepali*, River
Kalnas *Lithuanian*, Mountain
Kalns *Latvian*, Mountain
Kang *Chinese*, Harbor
Kangri *Tibetan*, Mountain(s)
Kaôh *Cambodian*, Island
Kapp *Norwegian*, Cape
Káto *Greek*, Lower
Kavīr *Persian*, Desert
K'edi *Georgian*, Mountain range
Kediet *Arabic*, Mountain
Kepi *Albanian*, Cape, point
Kepulauan *Indonesian, Malay*, Island group
Khalig, Khalij *Arabic*, Gulf
Khawr *Arabic*, Inlet
Khola *Nepali*, River
Khrebet *Russian*, Mountain range
Ko *Thai*, Island
-ko *Japanese*, Inlet, lake
Kólpos *Greek*, Bay
-kopf *German*, Peak
Körfäzi *Azerbaijani*, Bay
Körfezi *Turkish*, Bay
Kõrgustik *Estonian*, Upland
Kosa *Russian, Ukrainian*, Spit
Koshi *Nepali*, River
Kou *Chinese*, Rivermouth
Kowtal *Persian*, Pass
Kray *Russian*, Region, territory
Kryazh *Russian*, Ridge
Kuduk *Uighur*, Well
Kūh(hā) *Persian*, Mountain(s)
-kul' *Russian*, Lake
Kŭl(i) *Tajik, Uzbek*, Lake
-kundo *Korean*, Island group
-kysten *Norwegian*, Coast
Kyun *Burmese*, Island

L

Laaq *Somali*, Watercourse
Lac *French*, Lake
Lacul *Romanian*, Lake
Lagh *Somali*, Stream
Lago *Italian, Portuguese, Spanish*, Lake
Lagoa *Portuguese*, Lagoon
Laguna *Italian, Spanish*, Lagoon, lake
Laht *Estonian*, Bay
Laut *Indonesian*, Bay
Lembalemba *Malagasy*, Plateau
Lerr *Armenian*, Mountain
Lerrnashght'a *Armenian*, Mountain range
Les *Czech*, Forest
Lich *Armenian*, Lake
Liehtao *Chinese*, Island group
Liqeni *Albanian*, Lake
Límni *Greek*, Lake
Ling *Chinese*, Mountain range
Llano *Spanish*, Plain, prairie
Lumi *Albanian*, River
Lyman *Ukrainian*, Estuary

M

Madīnat *Arabic*, City, town
Mae Nam *Thai*, River
-mägi *Estonian*, Hill
Maja *Albanian*, Mountain
Mal *Albanian*, Mountains
Mal-aya, -oye, -yy, *Russian*, Small
-man *Korean*, Bay
Mar *Spanish*, Lake
Marios *Lithuanian*, Lake
Massif *French*, Mountains
Meer *German*, Lake
-meer *Dutch*, Lake
Melkosopochnik *Russian*, Plain
-meri *Estonian*, Sea
Mifraz *Hebrew*, Bay
Minami- *Japanese*, South(ern)
-misaki *Japanese*, Cape, point
Monkhafad *Arabic*, Depression
Montagne(s) *French*, Mountain(s)
Montañas *Spanish*, Mountains
Mont(s) *French*, Mountain(s)
Monte *Italian, Portuguese*, Mountain
More *Russian*, Sea
Mörön *Mongolian*, River
Mys *Russian*, Cape, point

N

-nada *Japanese*, Open stretch of water
Nagor'ye *Russian*, Upland
Naḥal *Hebrew*, River
Nahr *Arabic*, River
Nam *Laotian*, River
Namakzār *Persian*, Salt desert
Né-a, -on, -os *Greek*, New
Nedre- *Norwegian*, Lower
-neem *Estonian*, Cape, point
Nehri *Turkish*, River
-nes *Norwegian*, Cape, point
Nevado *Spanish*, Mountain (snow-capped)
Nieder- *German*, Lower
Nishi- *Japanese*, West(ern)
-nísi *Greek*, Island
Nisoi *Greek*, Islands
Nizhn-eye, -iy, -iye, -yaya *Russian*, Lower
Nizmennost' *Russian*, Lowland, plain
Nord *Danish, French, German*, North
Norte *Portuguese, Spanish*, North
Nos *Bulgarian*, Point, spit
Nosy *Malagasy*, Island
Nov-a, -i, *Bulgarian, Serbo-Croatian*, New
Nov-aya, -o, -oye, -yy, -yye *Russian*, New
Now-a, -e, -y *Polish*, New
Nur *Mongolian*, Lake
Nuruu *Mongolian*, Mountains
Nuur *Mongolian*, Lake
Nyzovyna *Ukrainian*, Lowland, plain

O

-ø *Danish*, Island
Ober- *German*, Upper
Oblast' *Russian*, Province
Órmos *Greek*, Bay
Orol(i) *Uzbek*, Island
Øster- *Norwegian*, Eastern
Ostrov(a) *Russian*, Island(s)
Otok *Serbo-Croatian*, Island
Oued *Arabic*, Watercourse
-oy *Faeroese*, Island
-øy(a) *Norwegian*, Island
Oya *Sinhala*, River
Ozero *Russian, Ukrainian*, Lake

P

Passo *Italian*, Pass
Pegunungan *Indonesian, Malay*, Mountain range
Pélagos *Greek*, Sea
Pendi *Chinese*, Basin
Penisola *Italian*, Peninsula
Pertuis *French*, Strait
Peski *Russian*, Sands
Phanom *Thai*, Mountain
Phou *Laotian*, Mountain
Pi *Chinese*, Point
Pic *Catalan, French*, Peak
Pico *Portuguese, Spanish*, Peak
-piggen *Danish*, Peak
Pik *Russian*, Peak
Pivostriv *Ukrainian*, Peninsula
Planalto *Portuguese*, Plateau
Planina, Planini *Bulgarian, Macedonian, Serbo-Croatian*, Mountain range
Plato *Russian*, Plateau
Ploskogor'ye *Russian*, Upland
Poluostrov *Russian*, Peninsula
Ponta *Portuguese*, Point
Porthmós *Greek*, Strait
Pótamos *Greek*, River
Presa *Spanish*, Dam
Prokhod *Bulgarian*, Pass
Proliv *Russian*, Strait
Pulau *Indonesian, Malay*, Island
Pulu *Malay*, Island
Punta *Spanish*, Point
Pushcha *Belorussian*, Forest
Puszcza *Polish*, Forest

Q

Qā' *Arabic*, Depression
Qalamat *Arabic*, Well
Qatorkŭh(i) *Tajik*, Mountain
Qiuling *Chinese*, Hills
Qolleh *Persian*, Mountain
Qu *Tibetan*, Stream
Quan *Chinese*, Well
Qulla(i) *Tajik*, Peak
Qundao *Chinese*, Island group

R

Raas *Somali*, Cape
-rags *Latvian*, Cape
Ramlat *Arabic*, Sands
Ra's *Arabic*, Cape, headland, point
Ravnina *Bulgarian, Russian*, Plain
Récif *French*, Reef
Recife *Portuguese*, Reef
Reka *Bulgarian*, River
Represa (Rep.) *Portuguese, Spanish*, Reservoir
Reshteh *Persian*, Mountain range
Respublika *Russian*, Republic, first-order administrative division
Respublika(si) *Uzbek*, Republic, first-order administrative division
-retsugan *Japanese*, Chain of rocks
-rettō *Japanese*, Island chain
Riacho *Spanish*, Stream
Riban' *Malagasy*, Mountains
Rio *Portuguese*, River
Río *Spanish*, River
Riu *Catalan*, River
Rivier *Dutch*, River
Rivière *French*, River
Rowd *Pashtu*, River
Rt *Serbo-Croatian*, Point
Rūd *Persian*, River
Rūdkhāneh *Persian*, River
Rudohorie *Slovak*, Mountains
Ruisseau *French*, Stream

S

-saar *Estonian*, Island
-saari *Finnish*, Island
Sabkhat *Arabic*, Salt marsh
Sāgar(a) *Hindi*, Lake, reservoir
Ṣaḥrā' *Arabic*, Desert
Saint, Sainte *French*, Saint
Salar *Spanish*, Salt-pan
Salto *Portuguese, Spanish*, Waterfall
Samudra *Sinhala*, Reservoir
-san *Japanese, Korean*, Mountain
-sanchi *Japanese*, Mountains
-sandur *Icelandic*, Beach
Sankt *German, Swedish*, Saint
-sanmaek *Korean*, Mountain range
-sanmyaku *Japanese*, Mountain range
San, Santa, Santo *Italian, Portuguese, Spanish*, Saint
São *Portuguese*, Saint
Sarīr *Arabic*, Desert
Sebkha, Sebkhet *Arabic*, Depression, salt marsh
Sedlo *Czech*, Pass
See *German*, Lake
Selat *Indonesian*, Strait
Selatan *Indonesian*, Southern
-selkä *Finnish*, Lake, ridge
Selseleh *Persian*, Mountain range
Serra *Portuguese*, Mountain
Serranía *Spanish*, Mountain
-seto *Japanese*, Channel, strait
Sever-naya, -noye, -nyy, -o *Russian*, Northern
Sha'īb *Arabic*, Watercourse
Shākh *Kurdish*, Mountain
Shamo *Chinese*, Desert
Shan *Chinese*, Mountain(s)
Shankou *Chinese*, Pass
Shanmo *Chinese*, Mountain range
Shaṭṭ *Arabic*, Distributary
Shet' *Amharic*, River
Shi *Chinese*, Municipality
-shima *Japanese*, Island
Shiqqat *Arabic*, Depression
-shotō *Japanese*, Group of islands
Shuiku *Chinese*, Reservoir
Shŭrkhog(i) *Uzbek*, Salt marsh
Sierra *Spanish*, Mountains
Sint *Dutch*, Saint
-sjø(en) *Norwegian*, Lake
-sjön *Swedish*, Lake
Solonchak *Russian*, Salt lake
Solonchakovyye Vpadiny *Russian*, Salt basin, wetlands
Son *Vietnamese*, Mountain
Sông *Vietnamese*, River
Sør- *Norwegian*, Southern
-spitze *German*, Peak
Star-á, -é *Czech*, Old
Star-aya, -oye, -yy, -yye *Russian*, Old
Stenó *Greek*, Strait
Step' *Russian*, Steppe
Štít *Slovak*, Peak
Stœng *Cambodian*, River
Stolovaya Strana *Russian*, Plateau
Stredné *Slovak*, Middle
Střední *Czech*, Middle
Stretto *Italian*, Strait
Su Anbari *Azerbaijani*, Reservoir
-suidō *Japanese*, Channel, strait
Sund *Swedish*, Sound, strait
Sungai *Indonesian, Malay*, River
Suu *Turkish*, River

T

Tal *Mongolian*, Plain
Tandavan' *Malagasy*, Mountain range
Tangorombohitr' *Malagasy*, Mountain massif
Tanjung *Indonesian, Malay*, Cape, point
Tao *Chinese*, Island
Ṭaraq *Arabic*, Hills
Tassili *Berber*, Mountain, plateau
Tau *Russian*, Mountain(s)
Taungdan *Burmese*, Mountain range
Techníti Límni *Greek*, Reservoir
Tekojärvi *Finnish*, Reservoir
Teluk *Indonesian, Malay*, Bay
Tengah *Indonesian*, Middle
Terara *Amharic*, Mountain
Timur *Indonesian*, Eastern
-tind(an) *Norwegian*, Peak
Tizma(si) *Uzbek*, Mountain range, ridge
-tō *Japanese*, island
Tog *Somali*, Valley
-tōge *Japanese*, pass
Togh(i) *Uzbek*, mountain
Tônlé *Cambodian*, Lake
Top *Dutch*, Peak
-tunturi *Finnish*, Mountain
Ṭurāq *Arabic*, hills
Tur'at *Arabic*, Channel

U

Udde(n) *Swedish*, Cape, point
'Uqlat *Arabic*, Well
Utara *Indonesian*, Northern
Uul *Mongolian*, Mountains

V

Väin *Estonian*, Strait
Vallée *French*, Valley
-vatn *Icelandic*, Lake
-vatnet *Norwegian*, Lake
Velayat *Turkmen*, Province
-vesi *Finnish*, Lake
Vestre- *Norwegian*, Western
-vidda *Norwegian*, Plateau
-vík *Icelandic*, Bay
-viken *Swedish*, Bay, inlet
Vinh *Vietnamese*, Bay
Víztárloló *Hungarian*, Reservoir
Vodaskhovishcha *Belarussian*, Reservoir
Vodokhranilishche (Vdkhr.) *Russian*, Reservoir
Vodoskhovyshche (Vdskh.) *Ukrainian*, Reservoir
Volcán *Spanish*, Volcano
Vostochn-o, yy *Russian*, Eastern
Vozvyshennost' *Russian*, Upland, plateau
Vozyera *Belarussian*, Lake
Vpadina *Russian*, Depression
Vrchovina *Czech*, Mountains
Vrha *Macedonian*, Peak
Vychodné *Slovak*, Eastern
Vysochyna *Ukrainian*, Upland
Vysočina *Czech*, Upland

W

Waadi *Somali*, Watercourse
Wādī *Arabic* Watercourse
Wāḥat, Wâhat *Arabic*, Oasis
Wald *German*, Forest
Wan *Chinese*, Bay
Way *Indonesian*, River
Webi *Somali*, River
Wenz *Amharic*, River
Wiloyat(i) *Uzbek*, Province
Wyżyna *Polish*, Upland
Wzgórza *Polish*, Upland
Wzvyshsha *Belarussian*, Upland

X

Xé *Laotian*, River
Xi *Chinese*, Stream

Y

-yama *Japanese*, Mountain
Yanchi *Chinese*, Salt lake
Yang *Chinese*, Bay
Yanhu *Chinese*, Salt lake
Yarımadası *Azerbaijani, Turkish*, Peninsula
Yaylası *Turkish*, Plateau
Yazovir *Bulgarian*, Reservoir
Yoma *Burmese*, Mountains
Ytre- *Norwegian*, Outer
Yü *Chinese*, Island
Yunhe *Chinese*, Canal
Yuzhn-o, -yy *Russian*, Southern

Z

-zaki *Japanese*, Cape, point
Zaliv *Bulgarian, Russian*, Bay
-zan *Japanese*, Mountain
Zangbo *Tibetan*, River
Zapadn-aya, -o, -yy *Russian*, Western
Západné *Slovak*, Western
Západní *Czech*, Western
Zatoka *Polish, Ukrainian*, Bay
-zee *Dutch*, Sea
Zemlya *Russian*, Earth, land
Zizhiqu *Chinese*, Autonomous region

Index

This index lists all the placenames and features shown on the regional and continental maps in this Atlas. Placenames are referenced to the largest scale map on which they appear. The policy followed throughout the Atlas is to use the local spelling or local name at regional level; commonly-used English language names may occasionally be added (in parentheses) where this is an aid to identification e.g. Firenze (Florence). English names, where they exist, have been used for all international features e.g. oceans and country names; they are also used on the continental maps and in the introductory World section; these are then fully cross-referenced to the local names found on the regional maps. The index also contains commonly-found alternative names and variant spellings, which are also fully cross-referenced.

All main entry names are those of settlements unless otherwise indicated by the use of italicized definitions or representative symbols, which are keyed at the foot of each page.

Glossary of Abbreviations

This glossary provides a comprehensive guide to the abbreviations used in this Atlas, and in the Index.

A

abbrev. abbreviated
AD Anno Domini
Afr. Afrikaans
Alb. Albanian
Amh. Amharic
anc. ancient
approx. approximately
Ar. Arabic
Arm. Armenian
ASEAN Association of South East Asian Nations
ASSR Autonomous Soviet Socialist Republic
Aust. Australian
Az. Azerbaijani
Azerb. Azerbaijan

B

Basq. Basque
BC before Christ
Bel. Belarussian
Ben. Bengali
Ber. Berber
B-H Bosnia-Herzegovina
bn billion (one thousand million)
BP British Petroleum
Bret. Breton
Brit. British
Bul. Bulgarian
Bur. Burmese

C

C central
C. Cape
°C degrees Centigrade
CACM Central America Common Market
Cam. Cambodian
Cant. Cantonese
CAR Central African Republic
Cast. Castilian
Cat. Catalan
CEEAC Central America Common Market
Chin. Chinese
CIS Commonwealth of Independent States
cm centimetre(s)
Cro. Croat
Cz. Czech
Czech Rep. Czech Republic

D

Dan. Danish
Div. Divehi
Dom. Rep. Dominican Republic
Dut. Dutch

E

E east
EC *see* EU
EEC *see* EU
ECOWAS Economic Community of West African States
ECU European Currency Unit
EMS European Monetary System
Eng. English
est estimated
Est. Estonian
EU European Union (previously European Community [EC], European Economic Community [EEC])

F

°F degrees Fahrenheit
Faer. Faeroese
Fij. Fijian
Fin. Finnish
Fr. French
Fris. Frisian
ft foot/feet
FYROM Former Yugoslav Republic of Macedonia

G

g gram(s)
Gael. Gaelic
Gal. Galician
GDP Gross Domestic Product (the total value of goods and services produced by a country excluding income from foreign countries)
Geor. Georgian
Ger. German
Gk Greek
GNP Gross National Product (the total value of goods and services produced by a country)

H

Heb. Hebrew
HEP hydro-electric power
Hind. Hindi
hist. historical
Hung. Hungarian

I

I. Island
Icel. Icelandic
in inch(es)
In. Inuit (Eskimo)
Ind. Indonesian
Intl International
Ir. Irish
Is Islands
It. Italian

J

Jap. Japanese

K

Kaz. Kazakh
kg kilogram(s)
Kir. Kirghiz
km kilometre(s)
km² square kilometre (singular)
Kor. Korean
Kurd. Kurdish

L

L. Lake
LAIA Latin American Integration Association
Lao. Laotian
Lapp. Lappish
Lat. Latin
Latv. Latvian
Liech. Liechtenstein
Lith. Lithuanian
Lux. Luxembourg

M

m million/metre(s)
Mac. Macedonian
Maced. Macedonia
Mal. Malay
Malg. Malagasy
Malt. Maltese
mi. mile(s)
Mong. Mongolian
Mt. Mountain **Mts** Mountains

N

N north
NAFTA North American Free Trade Agreement
Nep. Nepali
Neth. Netherlands
Nic. Nicaraguan
Nor. Norwegian
NZ New Zealand

P

Pash. Pashtu
PNG Papua New Guinea
Pol. Polish
Poly. Polynesian
Port. Portuguese
prev. previously

R

Rep. Republic
Res. Reservoir
Rmsch Romansch
Rom. Romanian
Rus. Russian
Russ. Fed. Russian Federation

S

S south
SADC Southern Africa Development Community
SCr. Serbo-Croatian
Sinh. Sinhala
Slvk Slovak
Slvn. Slovene
Som. Somali
Sp. Spanish
St., St Saint
Strs Straits
Swa. Swahili
Swe. Swedish
Switz. Switzerland

T

Taj. Tajik
Th. Thai
Thai. Thailand
Tib. Tibetan
Turk. Turkish
Turkm. Turkmenistan

U

UAE United Arab Emirates
Uigh. Uighur
UK United Kingdom
Ukr. Ukrainian
UN United Nations
Urd. Urdu
US/USA United States of America
USSR Union of Soviet Socialist Republics
Uzb. Uzbek

V

var. variant
Vdkhr. Vodokhranilishche (Russian for reservoir)
Vdskh. Vodoskhovyshche (Ukrainian for reservoir)
Vtn. Vietnamese

W

W west
Wel. Welsh

Y

Yugo. Yugoslavia

1

25 de Mayo *see* Veinticinco de Mayo
137 *Y13* **26 Bakı Komissarı** ***Rus.*** Imeni 26 Bakinskikh Komissarov. SE Azerbaijan
26 Baku Komissarlary Adyndaky *see* Uzboý
10 *M16* **100 Mile House** ***var.*** Hundred Mile House. British Columbia, SW Canada

A

Aa *see* Gauja
95 *G24* **Aabenraa** ***var.*** Åbenrå, ***Ger.*** Apenrade. Sønderjylland, SW Denmark
95 *G20* **Aabybro** ***var.*** Åbybro. Nordjylland, N Denmark
101 *C16* **Aachen** ***Dut.*** Aken, ***Fr.*** Aix-la-Chapelle; ***anc.*** Aquae Grani, Aquisgranum. Nordrhein-Westfalen, W Germany
Aaiún *see* Laâyoune
95 *M24* **Aakirkeby** ***var.*** Åkirkeby. Bornholm, E Denmark
95 *G20* **Aalborg** ***var.*** Ålborg, Ålborg-Nørresundby; ***anc.*** Alburgum. Nordjylland, N Denmark
Aalborg Bugt *see* Ålborg Bugt
101 *J21* **Aalen** Baden-Württemberg, S Germany
95 *G21* **Aalestrup** ***var.*** Ålestrup. Viborg, NW Denmark
98 *I11* **Aalsmeer** Noord-Holland, C Netherlands
99 *F18* **Aalst** ***Fr.*** Alost. Oost-Vlaanderen, C Belgium
99 *K18* **Aalst** ***Fr.*** Alost. Noord-Brabant, S Netherlands
98 *O12* **Aalten** Gelderland, E Netherlands
99 *D17* **Aalter** Oost-Vlaanderen, NW Belgium
Aanaar *see* Inari
Aanaarjävri *see* Inarijärvi
93 *M17* **Äänekoski** Länsi-Soumi, W Finland
138 *H7* **Aanjar** ***var.*** ʻAnjar. C Lebanon
83 *G21* **Aansluit** Northern Cape, N South Africa
Aar *see* Aare
108 *F7* **Aarau** Aargau, N Switzerland
108 *D8* **Aarberg** Bern, W Switzerland
99 *D16* **Aardenburg** Zeeland, SW Netherlands
108 *D8* **Aare** ***var.*** Aar. ≈ W Switzerland
108 *F7* **Aargau** ***Fr.*** Argovie. ◐ *canton* N Switzerland
Aarhus *see* Århus
Aarlen *see* Arlon
95 *G21* **Aars** ***var.*** Års. Nordjylland, N Denmark
99 *I17* **Aarschot** Vlaams Brabant, C Belgium
Aassi, Nahr el *see* Orontes
Aat *see* Ath
160 *G7* **Aba** ***prev.*** Ngawa. Sichuan, C China
79 *P16* **Aba** Orientale, NE Dem. Rep. Congo
77 *V17* **Aba** Abia, S Nigeria
140 *J6* **Abā al Qazāz, Bi'r** *well* NW Saudi Arabia
Abā as Suʻūd *see* Najrān
59 *G14* **Abacaxis, Rio** ≈ NW Brazil
Abaco Island *see* Great Abaco/Little Abaco
Abaco Island *see* Great Abaco, Bahamas
142 *K10* **Ābādān** Khūzestān, SW Iran
146 *F13* **Abadan** ***prev.*** Bezmein, ***Rus.*** Byuzmeyin. Ahal Welaýaty, C Turkmenistan
143 *O10* **Ābādeh** Fārs, C Iran
74 *H8* **Abadla** W Algeria
59 *M20* **Abaeté** Minas Gerais, SE Brazil
Abag Qi *see* Xin Hot
62 *P7* **Abaí** Caazapá, S Paraguay
Abai *see* Blue Nile
191 *O2* **Abaiang** ***var.*** Apia; ***prev.*** Charlotte Island. *atoll* Tungaru, W Kiribati
Abaj *see* Abay
77 *U15* **Abaji** Federal Capital District, C Nigeria
37 *O7* **Abajo Peak** ▲ Utah, W USA
77 *V16* **Abakaliki** Ebonyi, SE Nigeria
122 *K13* **Abakan** Respublika Khakasiya, S Russian Federation
77 *S11* **Abala** Tillabéri, SW Niger
77 *U11* **Abalak** Tahoua, C Niger
119 *N14* **Abalyanka** ***Rus.*** Obolyanka. ≈ N Belarus
122 *L12* **Aban** Krasnoyarskiy Kray, S Russian Federation
143 *P9* **Āb Anbār-e Kān Sorkh** Yazd, C Iran
57 *G16* **Abancay** Apurímac, SE Peru
190 *H2* **Abaokoro** *atoll* Tungaru, W Kiribati
Abariringa *see* Kanton
143 *P10* **Abarkū** Yazd, C Iran
165 *V3* **Abashiri** ***var.*** Abasiri. Hokkaidō, NE Japan
165 *U3* **Abashiri-ko** ◎ Hokkaidō, NE Japan
Abasiri *see* Abashiri
41 *P10* **Abasolo** Tamaulipas, C Mexico
186 *F9* **Abau** Central, S Papua New Guinea
145 *R10* **Abay** ***var.*** Abaj. Karaganda, C Kazakhstan
81 *I15* **Ābaya Hāyk'** ***Eng.*** Lake Margherita, ***It.*** Abbaia. ◎ SW Ethiopia
Ābay Wenz *see* Blue Nile
122 *K13* **Abaza** Respublika Khakasiya, S Russian Federation
Abbaia *see* Ābaya Hāyk'
143 *Q13* **Āb Bārīk** Fārs, S Iran
107 *C18* **Abbasanta** Sardegna, Italy, C Mediterranean Sea
Abbatis Villa *see* Abbeville
30 *M3* **Abbaye, Point** *headland* Michigan, N USA
Abbazia *see* Opatija
Abbé, Lake *see* Abhe, Lake
103 *N2* **Abbeville** ***anc.*** Abbatis Villa. Somme, N France
23 *R7* **Abbeville** Alabama, S USA
23 *U6* **Abbeville** Georgia, SE USA
22 *I9* **Abbeville** Louisiana, S USA
21 *P12* **Abbeville** South Carolina, SE USA
97 *B20* **Abbeyfeale** ***Ir.*** Mainistir na Féile. SW Ireland
106 *D8* **Abbiategrasso** Lombardia, NW Italy
93 *I14* **Abborrträsk** Norrbotten, N Sweden
194 *J9* **Abbot Ice Shelf** *ice shelf* Antarctica
10 *M17* **Abbotsford** British Columbia, SW Canada
30 *K6* **Abbotsford** Wisconsin, N USA
149 *U5* **Abbottābād** North-West Frontier Province, NW Pakistan
119 *M14* **Abchuha** ***Rus.*** Obchuga. Minskaya Voblasts', NW Belarus
98 *I10* **Abcoude** Utrecht, C Netherlands
139 *N2* **ʻAbd al ʻAzīz, Jabal** ▲▲ NE Syria
141 *U17* **ʻAbd al Kūrī** *island* SE Yemen
139 *Z13* **ʻAbd Allāh, Khawr** *bay* Iraq/Kuwait
127 *U6* **Abdulino** Orenburgskaya Oblast', W Russian Federation
78 *J10* **Abéché** ***var.*** Abécher, Abeshr. Ouaddaï, SE Chad
Abécher *see* Abéché
143 *S8* **Āb-e Garm va Sard** Yazd, E Iran
77 *R8* **Abeïbara** Kidal, NE Mali
105 *P5* **Abejar** Castilla-León, N Spain
54 *E9* **Abejorral** Antioquia, W Colombia
Abela *see* Ávila
Abellinum *see* Avellino
92 *Q2* **Abeløya** *island* Kong Karls Land, E Svalbard
80 *I13* **Ābeltī** Oromo, C Ethiopia
191 *O2* **Abemama** ***var.*** Apamama; ***prev.*** Roger Simpson Island. *atoll* Tungaru, W Kiribati
171 *Y15* **Abemaree** ***var.*** Abermarre. Papua, E Indonesia
77 *O16* **Abengourou** E Ivory Coast
Åbenrå *see* Aabenraa
101 *L22* **Abens** ≈ SE Germany
77 *S16* **Abeokuta** Ogun, SW Nigeria
97 *I20* **Aberaeron** SW Wales, UK
Aberbrothock *see* Arbroath
Abercorn *see* Mbala
29 *R6* **Abercrombie** North Dakota, N USA
183 *T7* **Aberdeen** New South Wales, SE Australia
9 *T15* **Aberdeen** Saskatchewan, S Canada
83 *H25* **Aberdeen** Eastern Cape, S South Africa
96 *L9* **Aberdeen** ***anc.*** Devana. NE Scotland, UK
21 *X2* **Aberdeen** Maryland, NE USA
23 *N3* **Aberdeen** Mississippi, S USA
21 *T10* **Aberdeen** North Carolina, SE USA
29 *P8* **Aberdeen** South Dakota, N USA
32 *F8* **Aberdeen** Washington, NW USA
96 *K9* **Aberdeen** *cultural region* NE Scotland, UK
8 *L8* **Aberdeen Lake** ◎ Nunavut, NE Canada
96 *J10* **Aberfeldy** C Scotland, UK
97 *K21* **Abergavenny** ***anc.*** Gobannium. SE Wales, UK
Abergwaun *see* Fishguard
Abermarre *see* Abemaree
25 *N5* **Abernathy** Texas, SW USA
Abersee *see* Wolfgangsee
Abertawe *see* Swansea
Aberteifi *see* Cardigan
32 *I15* **Abert, Lake** ◎ Oregon, NW USA
97 *I20* **Aberystwyth** W Wales, UK
Abeshr *see* Abéché
Ábeskovvu *see* Abisko
106 *F10* **Abetone** Toscana, C Italy
125 *V5* **Abez'** Respublika Komi, NW Russian Federation
142 *M5* **Āb Garm** Qazvin, N Iran
141 *N12* **Abhā** ʻAsīr, SW Saudi Arabia
142 *M5* **Abhar** Zanjān, NW Iran
Abhé Bad/Ābhē Bid Hāyk' *see* Abhe, Lake
80 *K12* **Abhe, Lake** ***var.*** Lake Abbé, ***Amh.*** Ābhē Bid Hāyk', ***Som.*** Abhé Bad. ◎ Djibouti/Ethiopia
77 *V17* **Abia** ◐ *state* SE Nigeria
139 *V9* **ʻAbīd ʻAlī** E Iraq
119 *O17* **Abidavichy** ***Rus.*** Obidovichi. Mahilyowskaya Voblasts', E Belarus
115 *L15* **Abide** Çanakkale, NW Turkey
77 *N17* **Abidjan** S Ivory Coast
Āb-i-Istāda *see* Īstādeh-ye Moqor, Āb-e-
27 *N4* **Abilene** Kansas, C USA
25 *Q7* **Abilene** Texas, SW USA
Abindonia *see* Abingdon
97 *M21* **Abingdon** ***anc.*** Abindonia. S England, UK
30 *K12* **Abingdon** Illinois, N USA
21 *P8* **Abingdon** Virginia, NE USA
Abingdon *see* Pinta, Isla
18 *J15* **Abington** Pennsylvania, NE USA
126 *K14* **Abinsk** Krasnodarskiy Kray, SW Russian Federation
37 *R9* **Abiquiu Reservoir** ⊡ New Mexico, SW USA
Āb-i-safed *see* Sefīd, Darya-ye
92 *I10* **Abisko** ***Lapp.*** Ábeskovvu. Norrbotten, N Sweden
12 *G12* **Abitibi** ≈ Ontario, S Canada
12 *H12* **Abitibi, Lac** ◎ Ontario/Québec, S Canada
80 *J10* **Ābīy Ādī** Tigray, N Ethiopia
118 *H6* **Abja-Paluoja** Viljandimaa, S Estonia
137 *Q8* **Abkhazia** ◐ *autonomous republic* NW Georgia
182 *F1* **Abminga** South Australia
75 *W9* **Abnûb** C Egypt
Åbo *see* Turku
152 *G9* **Abohar** Punjab, N India
77 *O17* **Aboisso** SE Ivory Coast
78 *H5* **Abo, Massif d'** ▲▲ NW Chad
77 *R16* **Abomey** S Benin
79 *F16* **Abong Mbang** Est, SE Cameroon
111 *L23* **Abony** Pest, C Hungary
78 *J11* **Abou-Déïa** Salamat, SE Chad
Aboudouhour *see* Abū aḍ Ḍuhūr
Abou Kémal *see* Abū Kamāl
Abou Simbel *see* Abu Simbel
137 *T12* **Abovyan** C Armenia
141 *P15* **Abrād, Wādī** *seasonal river* W Yemen
Abraham Bay *see* The Carlton
104 *G10* **Abrantes** ***var.*** Abrántes. Santarém, C Portugal
62 *J4* **Abra Pampa** Jujuy, N Argentina
Abrashlare *see* Brezovo
54 *G7* **Abrego** Norte de Santander, N Colombia
Abrene *see* Pytalovo
40 *C7* **Abreojos, Punta** *headland* W Mexico
65 *J16* **Abrolhos Bank** *undersea feature* W Atlantic Ocean
119 *H19* **Abrova** ***Rus.*** Obrovo. Brestskaya Voblasts', SW Belarus
116 *G11* **Abrud** ***Ger.*** Gross-Schlatten, ***Hung.*** Abrudbánya. Alba, SW Romania
Abrudbánya *see* Abrud
118 *E6* **Abruka** *island* SW Estonia
107 *J15* **Abruzzese, Appennino** ▲▲ C Italy
107 *J14* **Abruzzo** ◐ *region* C Italy
141 *N14* **ʻAbs** ***var.*** Sūq ʻAbs. W Yemen
33 *T12* **Absaroka Range** ▲▲ Montana/Wyoming, NW USA
137 *Z11* **Abşeron Yarımadası** ***Rus.*** Apsheronskiy Poluostrov. *peninsula* E Azerbaijan
143 *N6* **Āb Shīrīn** Eşfahān, C Iran
139 *X10* **Abtān** SE Iraq
109 *R6* **Abtenau** Salzburg, NW Austria
152 *E14* **Ābu** Rājasthān, N India
164 *E12* **Abu** Yamaguchi, Honshū, SW Japan
138 *I4* **Abū aḍ Ḍuhūr** ***Fr.*** Aboudouhour. Idlib, NW Syria
143 *P17* **Abū al Abyaḍ** *island* C United Arab Emirates
138 *K10* **Abū al Ḥuṣayn, Khabrat** ◎ N Jordan
139 *R8* **Abū al Jīr** C Iraq
139 *Y12* **Abū al Khaṣīb** ***var.*** Abul Khasib. SE Iraq
139 *U12* **Abū at Tubrah, Thaqb** *well* S Iraq
75 *V11* **Abu Balâs** ▲ SW Egypt
Abu Dhabi *see* Abū Ẓaby
139 *R8* **Abū Farūkh** C Iraq
80 *C12* **Abu Gabra** Southern Darfur, W Sudan
139 *P10* **Abū Ghār, Shaʻīb** *dry watercourse* S Iraq
80 *G7* **Abu Hamed** River Nile, N Sudan
139 *O5* **Abū Ḥardān** ***var.*** Hajîne. Dayr az Zawr, E Syria
139 *T7* **Abū Ḥāssawīyah** E Iraq
138 *K10* **Abū Ḥifnah, Wādī** *dry watercourse* N Jordan
77 *V15* **Abuja** ● (Nigeria) Federal Capital District, C Nigeria
139 *R9* **Abū Jahaf, Wādī** *dry watercourse* C Iraq
56 *F12* **Abujao, Río** ≈ E Peru
139 *U12* **Abū Jasrah** S Iraq
139 *O6* **Abū Kamāl** ***Fr.*** Abou Kémal. Dayr az Zawr, E Syria
165 *P12* **Abukuma-sanchi** ▲▲ Honshū, C Japan
Abula *see* Ávila
Abul Khasib *see* Abū al Khaṣīb
79 *K16* **Abumombazi** ***var.*** Abumonbazi. Equateur, N Dem. Rep. Congo
Abumonbazi *see* Abumombazi
59 *D15* **Abunã** Rondônia, W Brazil
56 *K13* **Abunã, Rio** ***var.*** Río Abuná. ≈ Bolivia/Brazil
138 *G10* **Abū Nuṣayr** ***var.*** Abu Nuseir. ʻAmmān, W Jordan
Abu Nuseir *see* Abū Nuṣayr
139 *T12* **Abū Qabr** S Iraq
138 *K5* **Abū Raḥbah, Jabal** ▲▲ C Syria
139 *S5* **Abū Rajāsh** N Iraq
139 *W13* **Abū Raqrāq, Ghadīr** *well* S Iraq
152 *E14* **Ābu Road** Rājasthān, N India
80 *I6* **Abu Shagara, Ras** *headland* NE Sudan
75 *W12* **Abu Simbel** ***var.*** Abou Simbel, Abū Sunbul. *ancient monument* S Egypt
139 *U12* **Abū Sudayrah** S Iraq
139 *T10* **Abū Şukhayr** S Iraq
Abū Sunbul *see* Abu Simbel
185 *E18* **Abut Head** *headland* South Island, New Zealand
80 *E9* **Abu ʻUrug** Northern Kordofan, C Sudan
80 *K12* **Ābuyē Mēda** ▲ C Ethiopia
80 *D11* **Abu Zabad** Western Kordofan, C Sudan
Abū Ẓabī *see* Abū Ẓaby
143 *P16* **Abū Ẓaby** ***var.*** Abū Ẓabī, ***Eng.*** Abu Dhabi. ● (United Arab Emirates) Abū Ẓaby, C United Arab Emirates
75 *X8* **Abu Zenîma** E Egypt
95 *N17* **Åby** Östergötland, S Sweden
Abyaḍ, Al Baḥr al *see* White Nile
Åbybro *see* Aabybro
80 *D13* **Abyei** Western Kordofan, S Sudan
Abyla *see* Ávila
Abymes *see* les Abymes
Abyssinia *see* Ethiopia
Açâba *see* Assaba
54 *F11* **Acacias** Meta, C Colombia
58 *L13* **Açailandia** Maranhão, E Brazil
Acaill *see* Achill Island
42 *E8* **Acajutla** Sonsonate, W El Salvador
79 *D17* **Acalayong** SW Equatorial Guinea
41 *N13* **Acámbaro** Guanajuato, C Mexico
54 *C6* **Acandí** Chocó, NW Colombia
104 *H4* **A Cañiza** ***var.*** La Cañiza. Galicia, NW Spain
40 *J11* **Acaponeta** Nayarit, C Mexico
40 *J11* **Acaponeta, Río de** ≈ C Mexico

◆ Country
● Country Capital
◇ Dependent Territory
○ Dependent Territory Capital
◐ Administrative Regions
✈ International Airport
▲ Mountain
▲▲ Mountain Range
Volcano
≈ River
◎ Lake
⊡ Reservoir

41 O16 **Acapulco** *var.* Acapulco de Juárez. Guerrero, S Mexico
Acapulco de Juárez *see* Acapulco
55 T13 **Acarai Mountains** *Sp.* Serra Acaraí. ▲▲ Brazil/Guyana
Acaraí, Serra *see* Acarai Mountains
58 O13 **Acaraú** Ceará, NE Brazil
54 J6 **Acarigua** Portuguesa, N Venezuela
42 C6 **Acatenango, Volcán de** ▲ S Guatemala
41 Q15 **Acatlán** *var.* Acatlán de Osorio. Puebla, S Mexico
Acatlán de Osorio *see* Acatlán
41 S15 **Acayucan** *var.* Acayucán. Veracruz-Llave, E Mexico
Accho *see* 'Akko
21 Y5 **Accomac** Virginia, NE USA
77 Q17 **Accra** ● (Ghana)SE Ghana
97 L17 **Accrington** NW England, UK
61 B19 **Acebal** Santa Fe, C Argentina
168 H8 **Aceh** *off.* Daerah Istimewa Aceh, *var.* Acheen, Achin, Atchin, Atjeh. ◐ autonomous district NW Indonesia
107 M18 **Acerenza** Basilicata, S Italy
107 K17 **Acerra** *anc.* Acerrae. Campania, S Italy
Acerrae *see* Acerra
57 J17 **Achacachi** La Paz, W Bolivia
54 K7 **Achaguas** Apure, C Venezuela
154 H12 **Achalpur** *prev.* Elichpur, Ellichpur. Mahārāshtra, C India
61 F18 **Achar** Tacuarembó, C Uruguay
115 H19 **Acharnés** *var.* Aharnes; *prev.* Akharnaí. Attikí, C Greece
Ach'asar Lerr *see* Achkasar
Acheen *see* Aceh
99 K15 **Achel** Limburg, NE Belgium
115 D16 **Achelóos** *var.* Akhelóös, Aspropótamos; *anc.* Achelous. ~ W Greece
Achelous *see* Achelóos
163 W8 **Acheng** Heilongjiang, NE China
109 N6 **Achenkirch** Tirol, W Austria
101 L24 **Achenpass** pass Austria/Germany
109 N7 **Achensee** ◎ W Austria
101 F22 **Achern** Baden-Württemberg, SW Germany
115 C15 **Acherón** ~ W Greece
77 W11 **Achétinamou** ~ S Niger
152 J12 **Achhnera** Uttar Pradesh, N India
42 C7 **Achiguate, Río** ~ S Guatemala
97 A16 **Achill Head** *Ir.* Ceann Acla. headland W Ireland
97 A16 **Achill Island** *Ir.* Acaill. island W Ireland
100 H11 **Achim** Niedersachsen, NW Germany
149 S5 **Achin** Nangarhār, E Afghanistan
Achin *see* Aceh
122 K12 **Achinsk** Krasnoyarskiy Kray, S Russian Federation
162 E5 **Achit Nuur** ◎ NW Mongolia
137 T11 **Achkasar** *Arm.* Ach'asar Lerr. ▲ Armenia/Georgia
126 K13 **Achuyevo** Krasnodarskiy Kray, SW Russian Federation
81 F16 **Achwa** *var.* Aswa. ~ N Uganda
136 E15 **Acıgöl** salt lake SW Turkey
107 L24 **Acireale** Sicilia, Italy, C Mediterranean Sea
Aciris *see* Agri
25 N7 **Ackerly** Texas, SW USA
22 M4 **Ackerman** Mississippi, S USA
29 W13 **Ackley** Iowa, C USA
44 J5 **Acklins Island** island SE Bahamas
Acla, Ceann *see* Achill Head
62 H11 **Aconcagua, Cerro** ▲ W Argentina
Açores/Açores, Arquipélago dos/Açores, Ilhas dos *see* Azores
104 H2 **A Coruña** *Cast.* La Coruña, *Eng.* Corunna; *anc.* Caronium. Galicia, NW Spain
104 G2 **A Coruña** *Cast.* La Coruña. ◐ province Galicia, NW Spain
42 L10 **Acoyapa** Chontales, S Nicaragua
106 H13 **Acquapendente** Lazio, C Italy
106 J13 **Acquasanta Terme** Marche, C Italy
106 I13 **Acquasparta** Lazio, C Italy
106 C9 **Acqui Terme** Piemonte, NW Italy
Acrae *see* Palazzola Acreide
182 F7 **Acraman, Lake** salt lake South Australia
59 A15 **Acre** *off.* Estado do Acre. ◐ state W Brazil
Acre *see* 'Akko
Acre, Estado do *see* Acre
59 C16 **Acre, Rio** ~ W Brazil
107 N20 **Acri** Calabria, SW Italy
Acte *see* Ágion Óros
191 Y12 **Actéon, Groupe** island group Îles Tuamotu, SE French Polynesia
15 P12 **Acton-Vale** Québec, SE Canada
41 P13 **Actopan** *var.* Actopán. Hidalgo, C Mexico
Actopán *see* Actopan
59 P14 **Açu** *var.* Assu. Rio Grande do Norte, E Brazil
Acunum Acusio *see* Montélimar
77 Q17 **Ada** SE Ghana
112 L8 **Ada** Vojvodina, N Serbia
29 R5 **Ada** Minnesota, N USA
31 R12 **Ada** Ohio, N USA
27 O12 **Ada** Oklahoma, C USA
162 L8 **Adaatsag** *var.* Tavin. Dundgovĭ, C Mongolia
Ada Bazar *see* Adapazarı
40 D3 **Adair, Bahía de** bay NW Mexico
104 M7 **Adaja** ~ N Spain
38 H17 **Adak Island** island Aleutian Islands, Alaska, USA
Adalia *see* Antalya
Adalia, Gulf of *see* Antalya Körfezi
141 X9 **Adam** N Oman
Adama *see* Nazrēt
60 I8 **Adamantina** São Paulo, S Brazil
79 E14 **Adamaoua** *Eng.* Adamawa. ◐ province N Cameroon
68 F11 **Adamaoua, Massif d'** *Eng.* Adamawa Highlands. plateau NW Cameroon
77 Y14 **Adamawa** ◐ state E Nigeria
Adamawa *see* Adamaoua
Adamawa Highlands *see* Adamaoua, Massif d'
106 F6 **Adamello** ▲ N Italy
81 J14 **Ādami Tulu** Oromo, C Ethiopia
63 M23 **Adam, Mount** *var.* Monte Independencia. ▲ West Falkland, Falkland Islands
29 R16 **Adams** Nebraska, C USA
18 I8 **Adams** New York, NE USA
29 Q3 **Adams** North Dakota, N USA
155 I23 **Adam's Bridge** chain of shoals NW Sri Lanka
32 H10 **Adams, Mount** ▲ Washington, NW USA
Adam's Peak *see* Sri Pada
191 R16 **Adam's Rock** island Pitcairn Island, Pitcairn Islands
191 P16 **Adamstown** ○ (Pitcairn Islands)Pitcairn Island, Pitcairn Islands
20 G10 **Adamsville** Tennessee, S USA
25 S9 **Adamsville** Texas, SW USA
141 O17 **'Adan** *Eng.* Aden. SW Yemen
136 K16 **Adana** *var.* Seyhan. Adana, S Turkey
136 K16 **Adana** *var.* Seyhan. ◐ province S Turkey
Adâncata *see* Horlivka
169 V12 **Adang, Teluk** bay Borneo, C Indonesia
136 F11 **Adapazarı** *prev.* Ada Bazar. Sakarya, NW Turkey
80 H8 **Adarama** River Nile, NE Sudan
195 Q16 **Adare, Cape** cape Antarctica
106 E6 **Adda** *anc.* Addua. ~ N Italy
80 A13 **Adda** ~ W Sudan
143 Q17 **Aḍ Ḍab'īyah** Abū Ẓaby, C United Arab Emirates
143 O18 **Aḍ Ḍafrah** desert S United Arab Emirates
141 Q6 **Ad Dahnā'** desert E Saudi Arabia
74 A11 **Ad Dakhla** *var.* Dakhla. SW Western Sahara
Ad Dalanj *see* Dilling
Ad Damar *see* Ed Damer
Ad Damazīn *see* Ed Damazin
Ad Dāmir *see* Ed Damer
173 N2 **Ad Dammām** desert NE Saudi Arabia
141 R6 **Ad Dammān** *var.* Dammām. Ash Sharqīyah, NE Saudi Arabia
Ad Dāmūr *see* Damoûr
140 K5 **Ad Dār al Ḩamrā'** Tabūk, NW Saudi Arabia
140 M13 **Ad Darb** Jīzān, SW Saudi Arabia
141 O8 **Ad Dawādimī** Ar Riyāḍ, C Saudi Arabia
143 N16 **Ad Dawḩah** *Eng.* Doha. ● (Qatar) C Qatar
143 N16 **Ad Dawḩah** *Eng.* Doha. ✈ C Qatar
139 S6 **Ad Dawr** N Iraq
139 Y12 **Ad Dayr** *var.* Dayr, Shahbān. E Iraq
Addi Arkay *see* Ādī Ārk'ay
139 X15 **Ad Dibdibah** physical region Iraq/Kuwait
Aḍ Ḍiffah *see* Libyan Plateau
Addis Ababa *see* Ādīs Ābeba
Addison *see* Webster Springs
139 U10 **Ad Dīwānīyah** *var.* Diwaniyah. C Iraq
Addoa *see* Adda
151 K22 **Addu Atoll** atoll S Maldives
Ad Dujail *see* Ad Dujayl
139 T7 **Ad Dujayl** *var.* Ad Dujail. N Iraq
Ad Duwaym/Ad Duwēm *see* Ed Dueim
99 D16 **Adegem** Oost-Vlaanderen, NW Belgium
23 U7 **Adel** Georgia, SE USA
29 U14 **Adel** Iowa, C USA
182 I9 **Adelaide** state capital South Australia
44 H2 **Adelaide** New Providence, N Bahamas
182 I9 **Adelaide** ✈ South Australia
194 H6 **Adelaide Island** island Antarctica
181 P2 **Adelaide River** Northern Territory, N Australia
76 M10 **'Adel Bagrou** Hodh ech Chargui, SE Mauritania
186 D6 **Adelbert Range** ▲▲ N Papua New Guinea
180 K3 **Adele Island** island Western Australia
107 O17 **Adelfia** Puglia, SE Italy
195 V16 **Adélie Coast** physical region Antarctica
195 V14 **Adélie, Terre** physical region Antarctica
Adelnau *see* Odolanów
Adelsberg *see* Postojna
Aden *see* 'Adan
Aden *see* Khormaksar
141 Q17 **Aden, Gulf of** gulf SW Arabian Sea
77 V10 **Aderbissinat** Agadez, C Niger
Adhaim *see* Al 'Uẓaym
143 R16 **Adh Dhayd** *var.* Al Dhaid. Ash Shāriqah, NE United Arab Emirates
140 M4 **'Adhfā'** spring/well NW Saudi Arabia
138 I13 **'Ādhriyāt, Jabāl al** ▲▲ S Jordan
80 I10 **Ādī Ārk'ay** *var.* Addi Arkay. Amhara, N Ethiopia
182 C7 **Adieu, Cape** headland South Australia
106 H8 **Adige** *Ger.* Etsch. ~ N Italy
80 J10 **Ādīgrat** Tigray, N Ethiopia
154 I13 **Ādilābād** *var.* Ādilābād. Andhra Pradesh, C India
Ādilābād *see* Ādilābād
35 P2 **Adin** California, W USA
171 V14 **Adi, Pulau** island E Indonesia
18 K8 **Adirondack Mountains** ▲▲ New York, NE USA
80 J13 **Ādīs Ābeba** *Eng.* Addis Ababa. ● (Ethiopia) Ādīs Ābeba, C Ethiopia
80 J13 **Ādīs Ābeba** ✈ Ādīs Ābeba, C Ethiopia
80 I11 **Ādīs Zemen** Amhara, N Ethiopia
Adi Ugri *see* Mendefera
137 N15 **Adıyaman** Adıyaman, SE Turkey
137 N15 **Adıyaman** ◐ province S Turkey
116 L11 **Adjud** Vrancea, E Romania
45 T6 **Adjuntas** C Puerto Rico
Adjuntas, Presa de las *see* Vicente Guerrero, Presa
Ādkup *see* Erikub Atoll
126 L15 **Adler** Krasnodarskiy Kray, SW Russian Federation
Adler *see* Orlice
108 G7 **Adliswil** Zürich, NW Switzerland
32 G7 **Admiralty Inlet** inlet Washington, NW USA
39 X13 **Admiralty Island** island Alexander Archipelago, Alaska, USA
186 E5 **Admiralty Islands** island group N Papua New Guinea
136 B14 **Adnan Menderes** ✈ (İzmir) İzmir, W Turkey
37 V6 **Adobe Creek Reservoir** ▣ Colorado, C USA
77 T16 **Ado-Ekiti** Ekiti, SW Nigeria
Adola *see* Kibre Mengist
61 C23 **Adolfo González Chaues** Buenos Aires, E Argentina
155 H17 **Ādoni** Andhra Pradesh, C India
102 K15 **Adour** *anc.* Aturus. ~ SW France
Adowa *see* Ādwa
105 O15 **Adra** Andalucía, S Spain
107 L24 **Adrano** Sicilia, Italy, C Mediterranean Sea
74 I9 **Adrar** C Algeria
76 K7 **Adrar** ◐ region C Mauritania
74 L11 **Adrar** ▲▲ SE Algeria
74 A12 **Adrar Souttouf** ▲▲ SW Western Sahara
Adrasman *see* Adrasmon
147 Q10 **Adrasmon** *Rus.* Adrasman. NW Tajikistan
78 K10 **Adré** Ouaddaï, E Chad
106 H9 **Adria** *anc.* Atria, Hadria, Hatria. Veneto, NE Italy
31 R10 **Adrian** Michigan, N USA
29 S11 **Adrian** Minnesota, N USA
27 R5 **Adrian** Missouri, C USA
24 M2 **Adrian** Texas, SW USA
21 S4 **Adrian** West Virginia, NE USA
Adrianople/Adrianopolis *see* Edirne
121 P7 **Adriatic Basin** undersea feature Adriatic Sea, N Mediterranean Sea
Adriatico, Mare *see* Adriatic Sea
106 L13 **Adriatic Sea** *Alb.* Deti Adriatik, *It.* Mare Adriatico, *SCr.* Jadransko More, *Slvn.* Jadransko Morje. sea N Mediterranean Sea
Adriatik, Deti *see* Adriatic Sea
Adua *see* Ādwa
Aduana del Sásabe *see* El Sásabe
79 O17 **Adusa** Orientale, NE Dem. Rep. Congo
118 J13 **Adutiškis** Vilnius, E Lithuania
27 Y7 **Advance** Missouri, C USA
65 D25 **Adventure Sound** bay East Falkland, Falkland Islands
80 J10 **Ādwa** *var.* Adowa, *It.* Adua. Tigray, N Ethiopia
123 Q8 **Adycha** ~ NE Russian Federation
126 L14 **Adygeya, Respublika** ◐ autonomous republic SW Russian Federation
Adzhikui *see* Ajyguýy
77 N17 **Adzopé** SE Ivory Coast
125 U4 **Adz'va** ~ NW Russian Federation
125 U5 **Adz'vavom** Respublika Komi, NW Russian Federation
Ædua *see* Autun
115 K19 **Aegean Islands** island group Greece/Turkey
Aegean North *see* Vóreion Aigaíon
115 I17 **Aegean Sea** *Gk.* Aigaíon Pelagos, Aigaío Pélagos, *Turk.* Ege Denizi. sea NE Mediterranean Sea
Aegean South *see* Nótion Aigaíon
118 H3 **Aegviidu** *Ger.* Charlottenhof. Harjumaa, NW Estonia
Aegyptus *see* Egypt
Aelana *see* Al 'Aqabah
Aelok *see* Ailuk Atoll
Aelōninae *see* Ailinginae Atoll
Aelōnlaplap *see* Ailinglaplap Atoll
Æmilia *see* Emilia-Romagna
Æmilianum *see* Millau
Aemona *see* Ljubljana
Aenaria *see* Ischia
Aeolian Islands *see* Eolie, Isole
191 Z3 **Aeon Point** headland Kiritimati, NE Kiribati
95 G24 **Ærø** *Ger.* Arrö. island C Denmark
95 H24 **Ærøskøbing** Fyn, C Denmark
Æsernia *see* Isernia
104 G3 **A Estrada** Galicia, NW Spain
115 C18 **Aetós** Itháki, Iónioi Nísoi, Greece, C Mediterranean Sea
191 Q8 **Afaahiti** Tahiti, W French Polynesia
139 U10 **'Afak** C Iraq
Afanasjevo *see* Afanas'yevo
125 T14 **Afanas'yevo** *var.* Afanasjevo. Kirovskaya Oblast', NW Russian Federation
Afándou *see* Afántou
115 O23 **Afántou** *var.* Afándou. Ródos, Dodekánisa, Greece, Aegean Sea
80 K11 **Āfar** ◐ region NE Ethiopia
Afar Depression *see* Danakil Desert
191 O7 **Afareaitu** Moorea, W French Polynesia
140 L7 **'Afarīyah, Bi'r al** well NW Saudi Arabia
Afars et des Issas, Territoire Français des *see* Djibouti
83 D22 **Affenrücken** Karas, SW Namibia
Afghānestān, Dowlat-e Eslāmī-ye *see* Afghanistan
148 M6 **Afghanistan** *off.* Islamic State of Afghanistan, *Per.* Dowlat-e Eslāmī-ye Afghānestān; *prev.* Republic of Afghanistan. ◆ islamic state C Asia
Afghanistan, Islamic State of *see* Afghanistan
Afghanistan, Republic of *see* Afghanistan
Afgoi *see* Afgooye
81 N17 **Afgooye** *It.* Afgoi. Shabeellaha Hoose, S Somalia
141 N8 **'Afīf** Ar Riyāḍ, C Saudi Arabia
77 V17 **Afikpo** Ebonyi, S Nigeria
Afiun Karahissar *see* Afyon
Åfjord *see* Åi Åfjord
109 V6 **Aflenz Kurort** Steiermark, E Austria
74 J6 **Aflou** N Algeria
81 L18 **Afmadow** Jubbada Hoose, S Somalia
39 Q14 **Afognak Island** island Alaska, USA
104 J2 **A Fonsagrada** Galicia, NW Spain
186 E9 **Afore** Northern, S Papua New Guinea
59 O15 **Afrânio** Pernambuco, E Brazil
66-67 **Africa** continent
68 L11 **Africa, Horn of** physical region Ethiopia/Somalia
172 K11 **Africana Seamount** undersea feature SW Indian Ocean
86 A14 **African Plate** tectonic plate
138 I2 **'Afrīn** Ḩalab, N Syria
136 M15 **Afşin** Kahramanmaraş, C Turkey
98 J7 **Afsluitdijk** dam N Netherlands
29 U15 **Afton** Iowa, C USA
29 W9 **Afton** Minnesota, N USA
27 R8 **Afton** Oklahoma, C USA
136 F14 **Afyon** *prev.* Afyonkarahisar. Afyon, W Turkey
136 F14 **Afyon** *var.* Afiun Karahissar, Afyonkarahisar. ◐ province W Turkey
Afyonkarahisar *see* Afyon
Agadès *see* Agadez
77 V10 **Agadez** *prev.* Agadès. Agadez, C Niger
77 W8 **Agadez** ◐ department N Niger
74 E8 **Agadir** SW Morocco
64 M9 **Agadir Canyon** undersea feature SE Atlantic Ocean
145 R12 **Agadyr'** Karaganda, C Kazakhstan
173 O7 **Agalega Islands** island group N Mauritius
42 K6 **Agalta, Sierra de** ▲▲ E Honduras
122 I10 **Agan** ~ C Russian Federation
Agana/Agaña *see* Hagåtña
188 B15 **Agana Bay** bay NW Guam
188 C16 **Agana Field** ✈ (Agana) C Guam
171 Kk13 **Agano-gawa** ~ Honshū, C Japan
188 B17 **Aga Point** headland S Guam
154 G9 **Agar** Madhya Pradesh, C India
81 I14 **Āgaro** Oromo, C Ethiopia
153 V15 **Agartala** state capital Tripura, NE India
194 I5 **Agassiz, Cape** headland Antarctica
175 V13 **Agassiz Fracture Zone** fracture zone S Pacific Ocean
188 B16 **Agat** W Guam
188 B16 **Agat Bay** bay W Guam
145 P13 **Agat, Gory** hill C Kazakhstan
Agatha *see* Agde
115 M20 **Agathónisi** island Dodekánisa, Greece, Aegean Sea
171 X14 **Agats** Papua, E Indonesia
155 C21 **Agatti Island** island Lakshadweep, India, N Indian Ocean
38 D16 **Agattu Island** island Aleutian Islands, Alaska, USA
38 D16 **Agattu Strait** strait Aleutian Islands, Alaska, USA
14 B8 **Agawa** ~ Ontario, S Canada
14 B8 **Agawa Bay** lake bay Ontario, S Canada
77 N17 **Agboville** SE Ivory Coast
137 V12 **Ağdam** *Rus.* Agdam. SW Azerbaijan
Agdam *see* Ağdam
103 P16 **Agde** *anc.* Agatha. Hérault, S France
103 P16 **Agde, Cap d'** cape S France
Agedabia *see* Ajdābiyā
102 L14 **Agen** *anc.* Aginnum. Lot-et-Garonne, SW France
Agendicum *see* Sens
165 O13 **Ageo** Saitama, Honshū, S Japan
109 R5 **Ager** ~ N Austria
Agere Hiywet *see* Hägere Hiywet
108 G8 **Ägerisee** ◎ W Switzerland
142 M10 **Āghā Jārī** Khūzestān, SW Iran
39 P15 **Aghiyuk Island** island Alaska, USA
74 B12 **Aghouinit** SE Western Sahara
Aghri Dagh *see* Büyükağrı Dağı
74 B10 **Aghzoumal, Sebkhet** *var.* Sebjet Agsumal. salt lake E Western Sahara
115 F15 **Agiá** *var.* Ayiá. Thessalía, C Greece
40 G7 **Agiabampo, Estero de** estuary NW Mexico
121 P3 **Agía Fýlaxis** *var.* Ayia Phyla. S Cyprus
Agialoúsa *see* Yenierenköy
115 M21 **Agía Marína** Léros, Dodekánisa, Greece, Aegean Sea
121 Q2 **Agía Nápa** *var.* Ayia Napa. E Cyprus
115 L16 **Agía Paraskeví** Lésvos, E Greece
115 J15 **Agías Eirínis, Akrotírio** headland Límnos, E Greece
Agiasós *see* Agiassós
115 L17 **Agiassós** *var.* Agiasós, Ayiásos, Ayiássos. Lésvos, E Greece
Aginnum *see* Agen
123 O14 **Aginskiy Buryatskiy Avtonomnyy Okrug** ◐ autonomous district S Russian Federation
123 O14 **Aginskoye** Aginskiy Buryatskiy Avtonomnyy Okrug, S Russian Federation
115 I14 **Ágion Óros** *Eng.* Mount Athos. ◐ monastic republic NE Greece
115 H14 **Ágion Óros** *var.* Akte, Aktí; *anc.* Acte. peninsula NE Greece
114 D13 **Ágios Achílleios** religious building Dytikí Makedonía, N Greece
115 J16 **Ágios Efstrátios** *var.* Áyios Evstrátios, Hagios Evstrátios. island E Greece
115 H20 **Ágios Geórgios** island Kykládes, Greece, Aegean Sea
115 E21 **Ágios Ilías** ▲ S Greece
115 K25 **Ágios Ioannis, Akrotírio** headland Kríti, Greece, E Mediterranean Sea
115 L20 **Ágios Kírykos** *var.* Áyios Kírikos. Ikaría, Dodekánisa, Greece, Aegean Sea
115 K25 **Ágios Nikólaos** *var.* Áyios Nikólaos. Kríti, Greece, E Mediterranean Sea
115 D16 **Ágios Nikolaos** Thessalía, C Greece
115 H14 **Agíou Órous, Kólpos** gulf N Greece
107 K24 **Agira** *anc.* Agyrium. Sicilia, Italy, C Mediterranean Sea
115 G20 **Agkístri** island S Greece
114 G12 **Agkístro** *var.* Angistro. ▲ NE Greece
103 O17 **Agly** ~ S France
Agnetheln *see* Agnita
14 E10 **Agnew Lake** ◎ Ontario, S Canada
77 O16 **Agnibilékrou** E Ivory Coast
116 I11 **Agnita** *Ger.* Agnetheln, *Hung.* Szentágota. Sibiu, SW Romania
107 K15 **Agnone** Molise, C Italy
164 K14 **Ago** Mie, Honshū, SW Japan
106 C8 **Agogna** ~ N Italy
Agoitz *see* Agoiz
105 R3 **Agoiz** *var.* Agoitz, Aoiz. Navarra, N Spain
77 P17 **Agona Swedru** *var.* Swedru. SE Ghana
Agordat *see* Akurdet
Agosta *see* Augusta
103 N15 **Agout** ~ S France
152 J12 **Āgra** Uttar Pradesh, N India
Agra and Oudh, United Provinces of *see* Uttar Pradesh
Agram *see* Zagreb
105 U5 **Agramunt** Cataluña, NE Spain
105 Q5 **Agreda** Castilla-León, N Spain
137 S13 **Ağrı** *var.* Karaköse; *prev.* Karakılısse. Ağrı, NE Turkey
137 S13 **Ağrı** ◐ province NE Turkey
107 N19 **Agri** *anc.* Aciris. ~ S Italy
Agri Dagi *see* Büyükağrı Dağı
107 J24 **Agrigento** *Gk.* Akragas; *prev.* Girgenti. Sicilia, Italy, C Mediterranean Sea
188 K4 **Agrihan** island N Northern Mariana Islands
115 L17 **Agriliá, Akrotírio** *prev.* Ákra Maléas. cape Lésvos, E Greece
115 D18 **Agrínio** *prev.* Agrinion. Dytikí Ellás, W Greece
Agrinion *see* Agrínio
115 G17 **Agriovótano** Évvoia, C Greece
107 L18 **Agropoli** Campania, S Italy
127 T3 **Agryz** Udmurtskaya Respublika, NW Russian Federation
137 U11 **Ağstafa** *Rus.* Akstafa. NW Azerbaijan
137 X11 **Ağsu** *Rus.* Akhsu. C Azerbaijan
Agsumal, Sebjet *see* Aghzoumal, Sebkhet
40 J11 **Agua Brava, Laguna** lagoon W Mexico
54 F7 **Aguachica** Cesar, N Colombia
59 J20 **Água Clara** Mato Grosso do Sul, SW Brazil
44 D5 **Aguada de Pasajeros** Cienfuegos, C Cuba
54 J5 **Aguada Grande** Lara, N Venezuela
45 S5 **Aguadilla** W Puerto Rico
43 S16 **Aguadulce** Coclé, S Panama
104 L14 **Aguadulce** Andalucía, S Spain
41 O8 **Agualeguas** Nuevo León, NE Mexico
40 L9 **Aguanaval, Río** ~ C Mexico
42 J5 **Aguán, Río** ~ N Honduras
25 R16 **Agua Nueva** Texas, SW USA
60 J8 **Aguapeí, Rio** ~ S Brazil
61 E14 **Aguapey, Río** ~ NE Argentina
40 G3 **Agua Prieta** Sonora, NW Mexico
104 G5 **A Guarda** *var.* A Guardia, Laguardia, La Guardia. Galicia, NW Spain
A Guardia *see* A Guarda
56 E6 **Aguarico, Río** ~ Ecuador/Peru
55 O6 **Aguasay** Monagas, NE Venezuela
40 M12 **Aguascalientes** Aguascalientes, C Mexico
40 L12 **Aguascalientes** ◐ state C Mexico
57 I18 **Aguas Calientes, Río** ~ S Peru
105 R7 **Aguasvivas** ~ NE Spain
60 J7 **Agua Vermelha, Represa de** ▣ S Brazil
56 E12 **Aguaytía** Ucayali, C Peru
104 I5 **A Gudiña** *var.* La Gudiña. Galicia, NW Spain
104 G7 **Águeda** Aveiro, N Portugal
104 J8 **Águeda** ~ Portugal/Spain
77 Q8 **Aguelhok** Kidal, NE Mali
77 V12 **Aguié** Maradi, S Niger
188 K8 **Aguijan** island S Northern Mariana Islands
104 M14 **Aguilar** *var.* Aguilar de la Frontera. Andalucía, S Spain
104 M3 **Aguilar de Campóo** Castilla-León, N Spain
Aguilar de la Frontera *see* Aguilar
42 F7 **Aguilares** San Salvador, C El Salvador
105 Q14 **Águilas** Murcia, SE Spain
40 L15 **Aguililla** Michoacán de Ocampo, SW Mexico
Agulhas *see* L'Agulhas
172 J11 **Agulhas Bank** undersea feature SW Indian Ocean
172 K11 **Agulhas Basin** undersea feature SW Indian Ocean
83 F26 **Agulhas, Cape** *Afr.* Kaap Agulhas. headland SW South Africa
Agulhas, Kaap *see* Agulhas, Cape
60 O9 **Agulhas Negras, Pico das** ▲ SE Brazil
172 K11 **Agulhas Plateau** undersea feature SW Indian Ocean
165 S16 **Aguni-jima** island Nansei-shotō, SW Japan
Agurain *see* Salvatierra
54 G5 **Agustín Codazzi** *var.* Codazzi. Cesar, N Colombia
Agyrium *see* Agira
74 L12 **Ahaggar** high plateau region SE Algeria
146 E12 **Ahal Welaýaty** *Rus.* Akhalskiy Velayat. ◐ province C Turkmenistan
142 K2 **Ahar** Āzarbāyjān-e Sharqī, NW Iran
Aharnes *see* Acharnés
138 J3 **Aḩaş, Jabal** ▲ NW Syria
138 J3 **Aḩaş, Jebal** ▲ W Syria
185 G16 **Ahaura** ~ South Island, New Zealand
100 E13 **Ahaus** Nordrhein-Westfalen, NW Germany
191 U9 **Ahe** atoll Îles Tuamotu, C French Polynesia
184 N10 **Ahimanawa Range** ▲▲ North Island, New Zealand
119 I19 **Ahinski Kanal** *Rus.* Oginskiy Kanal. canal SW Belarus
186 G10 **Ahioma** SE Papua New Guinea
184 I2 **Ahipara** Northland, North Island, New Zealand
184 I2 **Ahipara Bay** bay SE Tasman Sea
Áhkká *see* Akka
39 N13 **Ahklun Mountains** ▲▲ Alaska, USA
137 R14 **Ahlat** Bitlis, E Turkey
101 F14 **Ahlen** Nordrhein-Westfalen, W Germany
154 D10 **Ahmadābād** *var.* Ahmedabad. Gujarāt, W India
143 R10 **Ahmadābād** Kermān, C Iran
Ahmadi *see* Al Aḩmadī
Ahmad Khel *see* Ḩasan Khēl
155 F14 **Ahmadnagar** *var.* Ahmednagar. Mahārāshtra, W India
149 T9 **Ahmadpur Siāl** Punjab, E Pakistan
77 N5 **Aḩmar, 'Erg el** desert N Mali
80 K13 **Ahmar Mountains** ▲▲ C Ethiopia
Ahmedabad *see* Ahmadābād
Ahmednagar *see* Ahmadnagar
114 N12 **Ahmetbey** Kırklareli, NW Turkey
14 H12 **Ahmic Lake** ◎ Ontario, S Canada
190 G12 **Ahoa** Île Uvea, E Wallis and Futuna
40 G8 **Ahomé** Sinaloa, C Mexico
21 X8 **Ahoskie** North Carolina, SE USA
101 D17 **Ahr** ~ W Germany
143 N12 **Ahram** *var.* Ahrom. Būshehr, S Iran
100 J9 **Ahrensburg** Schleswig-Holstein, N Germany
Ahrom *see* Ahram
93 L17 **Ähtäri** Länsi-Suomi, W Finland
40 K12 **Ahuacatlán** Nayarit, C Mexico
42 E7 **Ahuachapán** Ahuachapán, W El Salvador
42 A9 **Ahuachapán** ◐ department W El Salvador
191 V16 **Ahu Akivi** *var.* Siete Moai. ancient monument Easter Island, Chile, E Pacific Ocean
191 W11 **Ahunui** atoll Îles Tuamotu, C French Polynesia
185 E20 **Ahuriri** ~ South Island, New Zealand
95 L22 **Åhus** Skåne, S Sweden
Ahu Tahira *see* Ahu Vinapu
191 V16 **Ahu Tepeu** ancient monument Easter Island, Chile, E Pacific Ocean
191 V17 **Ahu Vinapu** *var.* Ahu Tahira. ancient monument Easter Island, Chile, E Pacific Ocean
142 L9 **Ahvāz** *var.* Ahwāz; *prev.* Nāsiri. Khūzestān, SW Iran
Ahvenanmaa *see* Åland
141 Q16 **Ahwar** SW Yemen
Ahwāz *see* Ahvāz
94 H7 **Åi Åfjord** *var.* Åfjord, Årnes. Sør-Trøndelag, C Norway
Aibak *see* Āybak
101 K22 **Aichach** Bayern, SE Germany
164 L14 **Aichi** *off.* Aichi-ken, *var.* Aiti. ◐ prefecture Honshū, SW Japan
Aichi-ken *see* Aichi
Aïdin *see* Aydın
Aidussina *see* Ajdovščina
Aifir, Clochán an *see* Giant's Causeway
Aigaíon Pelagos/Aigaío Pélagos *see* Aegean Sea
109 S3 **Aigen im Mühlkreis** Oberösterreich, N Austria
115 G20 **Aígina** *var.* Aiyina, Egina. Aígina, C Greece
115 G20 **Aígina** island S Greece

◆ Country
● Country Capital
◇ Dependent Territory
○ Dependent Territory Capital
◐ Administrative Regions
✈ International Airport
▲ Mountain
▲▲ Mountain Range
▲ Volcano
~ River
◎ Lake
▣ Reservoir

115 E18 **Aígio** *var.* Egio; *prev.* Aíyion. Dytikí Ellás, S Greece
108 C10 **Aigle** Vaud, SW Switzerland
103 P14 **Aigoual, Mont** ▲ S France
173 O16 **Aigrettes, Pointe des** *headland* W Réunion
61 G19 **Aiguá** *var.* Aigua. Maldonado, S Uruguay
Aigua *see* Aiguá
103 S13 **Aigues** ≈ SE France
103 N10 **Aigurande** Indre, C France
Ai-hun *see* Heihe
163 N10 **Aikawa** Niigata, Sado, C Japan
21 Q13 **Aiken** South Carolina, SE USA
25 N4 **Aiken** Texas, SW USA
160 F13 **Ailao Shan** ▲▲ SW China
43 W14 **Ailigandí** San Blas, NE Panama
189 R4 **Ailinginae Atoll** *var.* Aelōninae. *atoll* Ralik Chain, SW Marshall Islands
189 T7 **Ailinglaplap Atoll** *var.* Aelōnlaplap. *atoll* Ralik Chain, S Marshall Islands
Aillionn, Loch *see* Allen, Lough
96 H13 **Ailsa Craig** *island* SW Scotland, UK
189 V5 **Ailuk Atoll** *var.* Aelok. *atoll* Ratak Chain, NE Marshall Islands
123 R11 **Aim** Khabarovskiy Kray, E Russian Federation
103 R11 **Ain** ◐ *department* E France
103 S10 **Ain** ≈ E France
118 G7 **Ainaži** *Est.* Heinaste, *Ger.* Hainasch. Limbaži, N Latvia
74 L6 **Aïn Beida** NE Algeria
76 K4 **'Aïn Ben Tili** Tiris Zemmour, N Mauritania
74 J5 **Aïn Defla** *var.* Aïn Eddefla. N Algeria
Aïn Eddefla *see* Aïn Defla
74 L5 **Ain El Bey** ✈ (Constantine) NE Algeria
115 C19 **Aínos** ▲ Kefallinía, Iónioi Nísoi, Greece, C Mediterranean Sea
105 T4 **Ainsa** Aragón, NE Spain
74 I7 **Aïn Sefra** NW Algeria
29 N13 **Ainsworth** Nebraska, C USA
Aintab *see* Gaziantep
74 H5 **Aïn Témouchent** N Algeria
186 C6 **Aiome** Madang, N Papua New Guinea
Aïoun el Atrous/Aïoun el Atroûss *see* 'Ayoûn el 'Atroûs
54 E11 **Aipe** Huila, C Colombia
56 D9 **Aipena, Río** ≈ N Peru
57 L19 **Aiquile** Cochabamba, C Bolivia
Aïr *see* Aïr, Massif de l'
188 E10 **Airai** Babeldaob, C Palau
188 E10 **Airai** ✈ (Oreor) Babeldaob, N Palau
168 I11 **Airbangis** Sumatera, NW Indonesia
9 Q16 **Airdrie** Alberta, SW Canada
96 I12 **Airdrie** S Scotland, UK
Air du Azbine *see* Aïr, Massif de l'
97 M17 **Aire** ≈ N England, UK
102 K15 **Aire-sur-l'Adour** Landes, SW France
103 O1 **Aire-sur-la-Lys** Pas-de-Calais, N France
9 Q6 **Air Force Island** *island* Baffin Island, Nunavut, NE Canada
169 Q13 **Airhitam, Teluk** *bay* Borneo, C Indonesia
171 Q11 **Airmadidi** Sulawesi, N Indonesia
77 V8 **Aïr, Massif de l'** *var.* Aïr, Air du Azbine, Asben. ▲▲ NC Niger
108 G10 **Airolo** Ticino, S Switzerland
102 K9 **Airvault** Deux-Sèvres, W France
101 K19 **Aisch** ≈ S Germany
63 G20 **Aisén** *off.* Región Aisén del General Carlos Ibañez del Campo, *var.* Aysen. ◐ *region* S Chile
Aisén del General Carlos Ibañez del Campo, Región *see* Aisén
10 H7 **Aishihik Lake** ◎ Yukon Territory, W Canada
103 P3 **Aisne** ◐ *department* N France
103 R4 **Aisne** ≈ NE France
109 T4 **Aist** ≈ N Austria
114 K13 **Aisými** Anatolikí Makedonía kai Thráki, NE Greece
105 S11 **Aitana** ▲ E Spain
186 B5 **Aitape** *var.* Eitape. Sandaun, NW Papua New Guinea
Aiti *see* Aichi
29 V6 **Aitkin** Minnesota, N USA
115 D18 **Aitolikó** *var.* Etoliko; *prev.* Aitolikón. Dytikí Ellás, C Greece
Aitolikón *see* Aitolikó
190 L15 **Aitutaki** *island* S Cook Islands
116 H11 **Aiud** *Ger.* Strassburg, *Hung.* Nagyenyed; *prev.* Engeten. Alba, SW Romania
118 I9 **Aiviekste** ≈ C Latvia
189 Q8 **Aiwo** SW Nauru
188 E8 **Aiwokako Passage** *passage* Babeldaob, N Palau
Aix *see* Aix-en-Provence
103 S15 **Aix-en-Provence** *var.* Aix; *anc.* Aquae Sextiae. Bouches-du-Rhône, SE France
Aix-la-Chapelle *see* Aachen
103 T11 **Aix-les-Bains** Savoie, E France
186 A6 **Aiyang, Mount** ▲ NW Papua New Guinea
Aíyina *see* Aígina
Aíyion *see* Aígio
153 W15 **Āīzawl** *state capital* Mizoram, NE India
118 H9 **Aizkraukle** Aizkraukle, S Latvia
118 C9 **Aizpute** Liepāja, W Latvia
165 O11 **Aizu-Wakamatsu** *var.* Aizuwakamatu. Fukushima, Honshū, C Japan
Aizuwakamatu *see* Aizu-Wakamatsu
103 X15 **Ajaccio** Corse, France, C Mediterranean Sea
103 X15 **Ajaccio, Golfe d'** *gulf* Corse, France, C Mediterranean Sea
41 Q15 **Ajalpán** Puebla, S Mexico
154 F13 **Ajanta Range** ▲▲ C India
137 R10 **Ajaria** ◐ *autonomous republic* SW Georgia
Ajastan *see* Armenia
93 G14 **Ajaureforsen** Västerbotten, N Sweden
185 H17 **Ajax, Mount** ▲ South Island, New Zealand
162 F9 **Aj Bogd Uul** ▲ SW Mongolia
75 R8 **Ajdābiyā** *var.* Agedabia, Ajdābiyah. NE Libya
Ajdābiyah *see* Ajdābiyā
109 S12 **Ajdovščina** *Ger.* Haidenschaft, *It.* Aidussina. W Slovenia
165 Q7 **Ajigasawa** Aomori, Honshū, C Japan
Ajjinena *see* El Geneina
111 H23 **Ajka** Veszprém, W Hungary
138 G9 **'Ajlūn** Irbid, N Jordan
138 H9 **'Ajlūn, Jabal** ▲▲ W Jordan
Ájluokta *see* Drag
143 R15 **'Ajmān** *var.* Ajman, 'Ujmān. 'Ajmān, NE United Arab Emirates
Ajman *see* 'Ajmān
152 G12 **Ajmer** *var.* Ajmere. Rājasthān, N India
Ajmere *see* Ajmer
Ajnabulak *see* Aynabulak
36 J15 **Ajo** Arizona, SW USA
105 N2 **Ajo, Cabo de** *cape* N Spain
36 J16 **Ajo Range** ▲▲ Arizona, SW USA
146 C14 **Ajyguýy** *Rus.* Adzhikui. Balkan Welaýaty, W Turkmenistan
Akaba *see* Al 'Aqabah
165 T3 **Akabira** Hokkaidō, NE Japan
165 N10 **Akadomari** Niigata, Sado, C Japan
81 E20 **Akagera** *var.* Kagera. ≈ Rwanda/Tanzania *see also* Kagera
191 W16 **Akahanga, Punta** *headland* Easter Island, Chile, E Pacific Ocean
80 J13 **Āk'ak'i** Oromo, C Ethiopia
155 G15 **Akalkot** Mahārāshtra, W India
Akamagaseki *see* Shimonoseki
165 U4 **Akan** Hokkaidō, NE Japan
165 U4 **Akan-ko** ◎ Hokkaidō, NE Japan
Akanthoú *see* Tatlısu
185 I19 **Akaroa** Canterbury, South Island, New Zealand
80 E6 **Akasha** Northern, N Sudan
164 I13 **Akashi** *var.* Akasi. Hyōgo, Honshū, SW Japan
139 N7 **'Akāsh, Wādī** *var.* Wādī 'Ukash. *dry watercourse* W Iraq
Akasi *see* Akashi
92 K11 **Äkäsjokisuu** Lappi, N Finland
137 S11 **Akbaba Dağı** ▲ Armenia/Turkey
Akbük Limanı *see* Güllük Körfezi
127 V8 **Akbulak** Orenburgskaya Oblast', W Russian Federation
137 O11 **Akçaabat** Trabzon, NE Turkey
137 N15 **Akçadağ** Malatya, C Turkey
136 G11 **Akçakoca** Düzce, NW Turkey
Akchakaya, Vpadina *see* Akdzhakaya, Vpadina
76 H7 **Akchâr** *desert* W Mauritania
145 S12 **Akchatau** *Kaz.* Aqshataū. Karaganda, C Kazakhstan
136 L13 **Akdağlar** ▲▲ C Turkey
136 E17 **Ak Dağları** ▲▲ SW Turkey
136 K13 **Akdağmadeni** Yozgat, C Turkey
146 G8 **Akdepe** *prev.* Ak-Tepe, Leninsk, *Turkm.* Lenin. Daşoguz Welaýat, N Turkmenistan
Ak-Dere *see* Byala
121 P2 **Akdoğan** *Gk.* Lýsi. C Cyprus
122 J14 **Ak-Dovurak** Respublika Tyva, S Russian Federation
146 F9 **Akdzhakaya, Vpadina** *var.* Vpadina Akchakaya. *depression* N Turkmenistan
171 S11 **Akelamo** Pulau Halmahera, E Indonesia
Aken *see* Aachen
Akermanceaster *see* Bath
95 P15 **Åkersberga** Stockholm, C Sweden
95 H15 **Akershus** ◐ *county* S Norway
79 L16 **Aketi** Orientale, N Dem. Rep. Congo
146 C10 **Akgyr Erezi** *Rus.* Gryada Akkyr. *hill range* NW Turkmenistan
Akhalskiy Velayat *see* Ahal Welaýaty
137 S10 **Akhalts'ikhe** SW Georgia
Akhangaran *see* Ohangaron
Akharnaí *see* Acharnés
75 R7 **Akhḑar, Al Jabal al** *hill range* NE Libya
Akhelóös *see* Achelóos
39 Q15 **Akhiok** Kodiak Island, Alaska, USA
136 C13 **Akhisar** Manisa, W Turkey
75 X10 **Akhmîm** *anc.* Panopolis. C Egypt
152 H6 **Akhnūr** Jammu and Kashmir, NW India
Akhsu *see* Ağsu
127 P11 **Akhtuba** ≈ SW Russian Federation
127 P11 **Akhtubinsk** Astrakhanskaya Oblast', SW Russian Federation
Akhtyrka *see* Okhtyrka
164 H14 **Aki** Kōchi, Shikoku, SW Japan
39 N12 **Akiachak** Alaska, USA
39 N12 **Akiak** Alaska, USA
191 X11 **Akiaki** *atoll* Îles Tuamotu, E French Polynesia
12 H9 **Akimiski Island** *island* Nunavut, C Canada
136 K17 **Akıncı Burnu** *headland* S Turkey
Akıncılar *see* Selçuk
117 U10 **Akinovka** Zaporiz'ka Oblast', S Ukraine
Åkirkeby *see* Aakirkeby
165 P8 **Akita** Akita, Honshū, C Japan
165 Q8 **Akita** *off.* Akita-ken. ◐ *prefecture* Honshū, C Japan
Akita-ken *see* Akita
76 H8 **Akjoujt** *prev.* Fort-Repoux. Inchiri, W Mauritania
92 H11 **Akka** *Lapp.* Áhkká. ▲ N Sweden
92 H11 **Akkajaure** ◎ N Sweden
Akkala *see* Oqqal'a
155 L25 **Akkaraipattu** Eastern Province, E Sri Lanka
145 P13 **Akkense** Karaganda, C Kazakhstan
Akkerman *see* Bilhorod-Dnistrovs'kyy
127 W8 **Akkermanovka** Orenburgskaya Oblast', W Russian Federation
165 V4 **Akkeshi** Hokkaidō, NE Japan
165 V4 **Akkeshi-ko** ◎ Hokkaidō, NE Japan
165 V5 **Akkeshi-wan** *bay* NW Pacific Ocean
138 F8 **'Akko** *Eng.* Acre, *Fr.* Saint-Jean-d'Acre, *Bibl.* Accho, Ptolemaïs. Northern, N Israel
145 Q8 **Akkol'** *Kaz.* Aqköl; *prev.* Alekseyevka, *Kaz.* Alekseevka. Akmola, C Kazakhstan
145 T14 **Akkol'** *Kaz.* Aqköl. Almaty, SE Kazakhstan
145 Q16 **Akkol'** *Kaz.* Aqköl. Zhambyl, C Kazakhstan
144 M11 **Akkol', Ozero** *prev.* Ozero Zhaman-Akkol. ◎ C Kazakhstan
98 L6 **Akkrum** Friesland, N Netherlands
145 U8 **Akku** *prev.* Lebyazh'ye. Pavlodar, NE Kazakhstan
144 F12 **Akkystau** *Kaz.* Aqqystaū. Atyrau, SW Kazakhstan
8 G6 **Aklavik** Northwest Territories, NW Canada
Akmeņrags *see* Akmenrags
118 B9 **Akmenrags** *prev.* Akmeņrags. *headland* W Latvia
158 E9 **Akmeqit** Xinjiang Uygur Zizhiqu, NW China
146 J14 **Akmeydan** Mary Welaýaty, C Turkmenistan
145 P9 **Akmola** *off.* Akmolinskaya Oblast', *Kaz.* Aqmola Oblysy; *prev.* Tselinogradskaya Oblast. ◐ *province* C Kazakhstan
Akmola *see* Astana
Akmolinsk *see* Astana
Akmolinskaya Oblast' *see* Akmola
Aknavásár *see* Târgu Ocna
118 I11 **Aknīste** Jēkabpils, S Latvia
81 G14 **Akobo** Jonglei, SE Sudan
81 G14 **Akobo** *var.* Ākobowenz. ≈ Ethiopia/Sudan
Ākobowenz *see* Akobo
154 H12 **Akola** Mahārāshtra, C India
Akordat *see* Akurdet
77 Q16 **Akosombo Dam** *dam* SE Ghana
154 H12 **Akot** Mahārāshtra, C India
77 N16 **Akoupé** SE Ivory Coast
12 M3 **Akpatok Island** *island* Nunavut, E Canada
158 G7 **Akqi** Xinjiang Uygur Zizhiqu, NW China
138 I2 **Akrād, Jabal al** ▲▲ N Syria
Akragas *see* Agrigento
92 H3 **Akranes** Vesturland, W Iceland
139 S2 **Ākrē** *Ar.* 'Aqrah. N Iraq
95 C16 **Åkrehamn** Rogaland, S Norway
77 V9 **Akrérèb** Agadez, C Niger
115 D22 **Akrítas, Akrotírio** *cape* S Greece
37 V3 **Akron** Colorado, C USA
29 R12 **Akron** Iowa, C USA
31 U12 **Akron** Ohio, N USA
Akrotiri *see* Akrotírion
Akrotiri Bay *see* Akrotírion, Kólpos
Ákrotirio Kafiréas *see* Ntóro, Kávo
121 P3 **Akrotírion** *var.* Akrotiri. *UK air base* S Cyprus
121 P3 **Akrotírion, Kólpos** *var.* Akrotiri Bay. *bay* S Cyprus
Akrotírio Salonikós *see* Salonikiós, Akrotírio
Akrotírio Spánta *see* Spátha, Akrotírio
121 O3 **Akrotiri Sovereign Base Area** *UK military installation* S Cyprus
158 F11 **Aksai Chin** *Chin.* Aksayqin. *disputed region* China/India
Aksaj *see* Aksay
136 I15 **Aksaray** Aksaray, C Turkey
136 I15 **Aksaray** ◐ *province* C Turkey
144 G8 **Aksay** *var.* Aksaj, *Kaz.* Aqsay. Zapadnyy Kazakhstan, NW Kazakhstan
127 O11 **Aksay** Volgogradskaya Oblast', SW Russian Federation
147 W10 **Ak-say** *var.* Toxkan He. ≈ China/Kyrgyzstan
Aksay/Aksay Kazakzu Zizhixian *see* Boluozhuanjing/Hongliuwan
Aksayqin *see* Aksai Chin
158 G11 **Aksayqin Hu** ◎ NW China
136 G14 **Akşehir** Konya, W Turkey
136 G14 **Akşehir Gölü** ◎ C Turkey
136 G16 **Akseki** Antalya, SW Turkey
123 P13 **Aksenovo-Zilovskoye** Chitinskaya Oblast', S Russian Federation
145 V11 **Akshatau, Khrebet** ▲▲ E Kazakhstan
147 Y8 **Ak-Shyyrak** Issyk-Kul'skaya Oblast', E Kyrgyzstan
Akstafa *see* Ağstafa
158 H7 **Aksu** Xinjiang Uygur Zizhiqu, NW China
145 R8 **Aksu** *Kaz.* Aqsū. Akmola, N Kazakhstan
145 W13 **Aksu** *Kaz.* Aqsū. Almaty, SE Kazakhstan
145 T8 **Aksu** *var.* Jermak, *Kaz.* Ermak, *prev* Yermak. Pavlodar, NE Kazakhstan
145 V13 **Aksu** *Kaz.* Aqsū. ≈ SE Kazakhstan
145 X11 **Aksuat** *Kaz.* Aqsūat. Vostochnyy Kazakhstan, E Kazakhstan
145 Y11 **Aksuat** *Kaz.* Aqsūat. Vostochnyy Kazakhstan, SE Kazakhstan
127 S4 **Aksubayevo** Respublika Tatarstan, W Russian Federation
158 H7 **Aksu He** *Rus.* Sary-Dzhaz. ≈ China/Kyrgyzstan *see also* Sary-Dzhaz
Aksu He *see* Sary-Dzhaz
80 J10 **Āksum** Tigray, N Ethiopia
145 O12 **Aktas** *Kaz.* Aqtas. Karaganda, C Kazakhstan
Aktash *see* Oqtosh
147 V9 **Ak-Tash, Gora** ▲ C Kyrgyzstan
145 R10 **Aktau** *Kaz.* Aqtaū. Karaganda, C Kazakhstan
144 E11 **Aktau** *Kaz.* Aqtaū; *prev.* Shevchenko. Mangistau, W Kazakhstan
Aktau, Khrebet *see* Oqtogh, Qatorkŭhi, Tajikistan
Aktau, Khrebet *see* Oqtow Tizmasi, Uzbekistan
Akte *see* Ágion Óros
Ak-Tepe *see* Akdepe
147 X7 **Ak-Terek** Issyk-Kul'skaya Oblast', E Kyrgyzstan
Aktí *see* Ágion Óros
Aktjubinsk/Aktyubinsk *see* Aktobe
158 E8 **Akto** Xinjiang Uygur Zizhiqu, NW China
144 I10 **Aktobe** *Kaz.* Aqtöbe; *prev.* Aktjubinsk. Aktyubinsk, NW Kazakhstan
145 V12 **Aktogay** *Kaz.* Aqtoghay. Vostochnyy Kazakhstan, E Kazakhstan
119 M18 **Aktsyabrski** *Rus.* Oktyabr'skiy; *prev.* Karpilovka. Homyel'skaya Voblasts', SE Belarus
144 H11 **Aktyubinsk** *off.* Aktyubinskaya Oblast', *Kaz.* Aqtöbe Oblysy. ◐ *province* W Kazakhstan
Aktyubinskaya Oblast' *see* Aktyubinsk
147 W7 **Ak-Tyuz** *var.* Aktyuz. Chuyskaya Oblast', N Kyrgyzstan
Aktyuz *see* Ak-Tyuz
79 J17 **Akula** Equateur, NW Dem. Rep. Congo
164 C15 **Akune** Kagoshima, Kyūshū, SW Japan
38 L16 **Akun Island** *island* Aleutian Islands, Alaska, USA
80 J9 **Akurdet** *var.* Agordat, Akordat. C Eritrea
77 T16 **Akure** Ondo, SW Nigeria
92 J2 **Akureyri** Nordhurland Eystra, N Iceland
38 L17 **Akutan** Akutan Island, Alaska, USA
38 K17 **Akutan Island** *island* Aleutian Islands, Alaska, USA
77 V17 **Akwa Ibom** ◐ *state* SE Nigeria
Akyab *see* Sittwe
127 W7 **Ak"yar** Respublika Bashkortostan, W Russian Federation
144 J10 **Akzhar** *prev.* Novorossiyskiy, Novorossiyskoye. Aktyubinsk, NW Kazakhstan
145 Y11 **Akzhar** *Kaz.* Aqzhar. Vostochnyy Kazakhstan, E Kazakhstan
94 F13 **Ål** Buskerud, S Norway
119 N18 **Ala** *Rus.* Ola. ≈ SE Belarus
20 H11 **Alabama** *off.* State of Alabama, *also known as* Camellia State, Heart of Dixie, The Cotton State, Yellowhammer State. ◐ *state* S USA
23 P6 **Alabama River** ≈ Alabama, S USA
23 P4 **Alabaster** Alabama, S USA
139 U10 **Al 'Abd Allāh** *var.* Al Abdullah. S Iraq
Al Abdullah *see* Al 'Abd Allāh
139 W14 **Al Abṭīyah** *well* S Iraq
147 S9 **Ala-Buka** Dzhalal-Abadskaya Oblast', W Kyrgyzstan
136 J12 **Alaca** Çorum, N Turkey
136 K10 **Alaçam** Samsun, N Turkey
Alacant *see* Alicante
23 V9 **Alachua** Florida, SE USA
137 S13 **Aladağlar** ▲▲ W Turkey
136 K15 **Ala Dağları** ▲▲ C Turkey
162 I5 **Alag-Erdene** *var.* Manhan. Hövsgöl, N Mongolia
127 O16 **Alagir** Respublika Severnaya Osetiya, SW Russian Federation
106 B6 **Alagna Valsesia** Valle d'Aosta, NW Italy
103 P12 **Alagnon** ≈ C France
59 P16 **Alagoas** *off.* Estado de Alagoas. ◐ *state* E Brazil
Alagoas, Estado de *see* Alagoas
59 P17 **Alagoinhas** Bahia, E Brazil
105 R5 **Alagón** Aragón, NE Spain
104 J9 **Alagón** ≈ W Spain
93 K16 **Alahärmä** Länsi-Soumi, W Finland
al Ahdar *see* Al Akhḑar
Álaheaieatnu *see* Altaelva
142 K12 **Al Aḩmadī** *var.* Ahmadi. E Kuwait
Al Ain *see* Al 'Ayn
105 Z8 **Alaior** *prev.* Alayor. Menorca, Spain, W Mediterranean Sea
147 T11 **Alai Range** *Rus.* Alayskiy Khrebet. ▲▲ Kyrgyzstan/Tajikistan
Alais *see* Alès
141 X11 **Al 'Ajā'iz** E Oman
141 X11 **Al 'Ajā'iz** *oasis* SE Oman
93 L16 **Alajärvi** Länsi-Soumi, W Finland
118 K4 **Alajõe** Ida-Virumaa, NE Estonia
42 M13 **Alajuela** Alajuela, C Costa Rica
42 L12 **Alajuela** *off.* Provincia de Alajuela. ◐ *province* N Costa Rica
43 T14 **Alajuela, Lago** ◎ C Panama
Alajuela, Provincia de *see* Alajuela
38 M11 **Alakanuk** Alaska, USA
140 K5 **Al Akhḑar** *var.* al Ahdar. Tabūk, NW Saudi Arabia
Alaköl *see* Alakol', Ozero
145 X13 **Alakol', Ozero** *Kaz.* Alaköl. ◎ SE Kazakhstan
124 I5 **Alakurtti** Murmanskaya Oblast', NW Russian Federation
38 F10 **Alalākeiki Channel** *var.* Alalakeiki Channel. *channel* Hawaii, USA, C Pacific Ocean
Al 'Alamayn *see* El 'Alamein
139 R1 **Al 'Amādīyah** N Iraq
188 K5 **Alamagan** *island* C Northern Mariana Islands
139 X10 **Al 'Amārah** *var.* Amara. E Iraq
80 J11 **Ālamat'ā** Tigray, N Ethiopia
37 R11 **Alameda** New Mexico, SW USA
121 T13 **'Alam el Rûm, Râs** *headland* N Egypt
Alamícamba *see* Alamikamba
42 M8 **Alamikamba** *var.* Alamícamba. Región Autónoma Atlántico Norte, NE Nicaragua
24 K11 **Alamito Creek** ≈ Texas, SW USA
40 M8 **Alamitos, Sierra de los** ▲ NE Mexico
41 Q12 **Álamo** Veracruz-Llave, C Mexico
35 X9 **Alamo** Nevada, W USA
20 F9 **Alamo** Tennessee, S USA
37 S14 **Alamogordo** New Mexico, SW USA
36 J12 **Alamo Lake** ⊡ Arizona, SW USA
40 H7 **Alamos** Sonora, NW Mexico
37 S7 **Alamosa** Colorado, C USA
93 J20 **Åland** *var.* Aland Islands, *Fin.* Ahvenanmaa. ◐ *province* SW Finland
93 J19 **Åland** *Fin.* Ahvenanmaa. *island* SW Finland
88 K9 **Åland** *var.* Aland Islands, *Fin.* Ahvenanmaa. *island group* SW Finland
Aland Islands *see* Åland
Aland Sea *see* Ålands Hav
95 Q14 **Ålands Hav** *var.* Aland Sea. *strait* Baltic Sea/Gulf of Bothnia
43 P16 **Alanje** Chiriquí, SW Panama
25 O2 **Alanreed** Texas, SW USA
136 G17 **Alanya** Antalya, S Turkey
23 U7 **Alapaha River** ≈ Florida/Georgia, SE USA
122 G10 **Alapayevsk** Sverdlovskaya Oblast', C Russian Federation
Alappuzha *see* Alleppey
138 F14 **Al 'Aqabah** *var.* Akaba, Aqaba, 'Aqaba; *anc.* Aelana, Elath. Al 'Aqabah, SW Jordan
138 G14 **Al 'Aqabah** *off.* Muḩāfaz̧at Al 'Aqabah. ◐ *governorate* SW Jordan
Al 'Arabīyah as Su'ūdīyah *see* Saudi Arabia
al Araïch *see* Larache
105 Q10 **Alarcón** Castilla-La Mancha, C Spain
105 Q9 **Alarcón, Embalse de** ⊡ C Spain
138 J2 **Al 'Arīmah** *Fr.* Arime. Ḩalab, N Syria
Al 'Arīsh *see* El 'Arîsh
141 P6 **Al Arṭāwīyah** Ar Riyāḑ, N Saudi Arabia
Alasca, Golfo de *see* Alaska, Gulf of
136 D14 **Alaşehir** Manisa, W Turkey
139 N5 **Al 'Ashārah** *var.* Ashara. Dayr az Zawr, E Syria
Al Ashkhara *see* Al Ashkharah
141 Z9 **Al Ashkharah** *var.* Al Ashkhara. NE Oman
AlAsimah *see* 'Ammān
39 P8 **Alaska** *off.* State of Alaska, *also known as* Land of the Midnight Sun, The Last Frontier, Seward's Folly; *prev.* Russian America. ◐ *state* NW USA
39 T13 **Alaska, Gulf of** *var.* Golfo de Alasca. *gulf* Canada/USA
39 O15 **Alaska Peninsula** *peninsula* Alaska, USA
39 Q11 **Alaska Range** ▲▲ Alaska, USA
Al-Asnam *see* Chlef
106 B10 **Alassio** Liguria, NW Italy
137 Y12 **Älät** *Rus.* Alyat; *prev.* Alyaty-Pristan'. SE Azerbaijan
Alat *see* Olot
139 S13 **Al 'Athāmīn** S Iraq
39 P7 **Alatna River** ≈ Alaska, USA
107 J15 **Alatri** Lazio, C Italy
Alattio *see* Alta
127 P5 **Alatyr'** Chavash Respubliki, W Russian Federation
56 C7 **Alausí** Chimborazo, C Ecuador
105 O3 **Álava** *Basq.* Araba. ◐ *province* País Vasco, N Spain
137 T11 **Alaverdi** N Armenia
Alavo *see* Alavus
93 N14 **Ala-Vuokki** Oulu, E Finland
93 K17 **Alavus** *Swe.* Alavo. Länsi-Soumi, W Finland
Al 'Awābī *see* Awābī
139 P6 **Al 'Awānī** W Iraq
Al Awaynāt *see* Al 'Uwaynāt
182 K9 **Alawoona** South Australia
Alaykel'/Alay-Kuu *see* Këk-Art
143 R17 **Al 'Ayn** *var.* Al Ain. Abū Z̧aby, E United Arab Emirates
143 R17 **Al 'Ayn** *var.* Al Ain. ✈ Abū Z̧aby, E United Arab Emirates
138 G12 **Al 'Aynā** Al Karak, W Jordan
Alayor *see* Alaior
Alayskiy Khrebet *see* Alai Range
123 S6 **Alazeya** ≈ NE Russian Federation
139 U8 **Al 'Azīzīyah** *var.* Aziziya. E Iraq
120 M12 **Al 'Azīzīyah** NW Libya
138 I10 **Al Azraq al Janūbī** Az Zarqā', N Jordan
106 B9 **Alba** *anc.* Alba Pompeia. Piemonte, NW Italy
25 V6 **Alba** Texas, SW USA
116 G11 **Alba** ◐ *county* W Romania
139 P3 **Al Ba'āj** N Iraq
138 J2 **Al Bāb** Ḩalab, N Syria
116 G10 **Albac** *Hung.* Fehérvölgy; *prev.* Álbák. Alba, SW Romania
105 Q11 **Albacete** Castilla-La Mancha, C Spain
105 P11 **Albacete** ◐ *province* Castilla-La Mancha, C Spain
140 I4 **Al Bad'** Tabūk, NW Saudi Arabia
104 L7 **Alba de Tormes** Castilla-León, N Spain
139 P3 **Al Bādī** N Iraq
141 V8 **Al Badī'ah** ✈ (Abū Z̧aby) Abū Z̧aby, C United Arab Emirates
143 P17 **Al Badī'ah** *var.* Al Bedei'ah. *spring/well* C United Arab Emirates
95 H19 **Ålbæk** Nordjylland, N Denmark
139 Q7 **Al Baghdādī** *var.* Khān al Baghdādī. SW Iraq
Al Bāha *see* Al Bāḩah
140 M11 **Al Bāḩah** *var.* Al Bāha. Al BāḨah, SW Saudi Arabia
140 M11 **Al Bāḩah** *var.* Minţaqat al Bāḩah. ◐ *province* W Saudi Arabia
Al Baḩrayn *see* Bahrain
105 S11 **Albaida** País Valenciano, E Spain
116 H11 **Alba Iulia** *Ger.* Weissenburg, *Hung.* Gyulafehérvár; *prev.* Bălgrad, Karlsburg, Károly-Fehérvár. Alba, W Romania
Álbák *see* Albac
138 G10 **Al Balqā'** *off.* Muḩāfaz̧at al Balqā', *var.* Balqā'. ◐ *governorate* NW Jordan
14 F11 **Alban** Ontario, S Canada
103 O15 **Alban** Tarn, S France
12 K11 **Albanel, Lac** ◎ Québec, SE Canada
113 L20 **Albania** *off.* Republic of Albania, *Alb.* Republika e Shqipqërisë, Shqipëria; *prev.* People's Socialist Republic of Albania. ◆ *republic* SE Europe
Albania *see* Aubagne
Albania, People's Socialist Republic of *see* Albania
Albania, Republic of *see* Albania
107 H15 **Albano Laziaie** Lazio, C Italy
180 J14 **Albany** Western Australia
23 S7 **Albany** Georgia, SE USA
31 P13 **Albany** Indiana, N USA
20 L8 **Albany** Kentucky, S USA
29 U7 **Albany** Minnesota, N USA
27 R2 **Albany** Missouri, C USA
18 L10 **Albany** *state capital* New York, NE USA
32 G12 **Albany** Oregon, NW USA
25 Q6 **Albany** Texas, SW USA
12 F10 **Albany** ≈ Ontario, S Canada
Alba Pompeia *see* Alba
Alba Regia *see* Székesfehérvár
138 J6 **Al Bāridah** *var.* Bāridah. Ḩimş, C Syria
139 Q11 **Al Barīt** S Iraq
105 R8 **Albarracín** Aragón, NE Spain
139 Y12 **Al Başrah** *Eng.* Basra, *hist.* Busra, Bussora. SE Iraq
139 V11 **Al Baṭḩā'** SE Iraq
141 X8 **Al Bāṭinah** *var.* Batinah. *coastal region* N Oman
0 H16 **Albatross Plateau** *undersea feature* E Pacific Ocean
Al Batrūn *see* Batroûn
121 Q12 **Al Bayḑā'** *var.* Beida. NE Libya
141 P16 **Al Bayḑā'** *var.* Al Beida. SW Yemen
Al Bedei'ah *see* Al Badī'ah
Al Beida *see* Al Bayḑā'
21 S10 **Albemarle** *var.* Albermarle. North Carolina, SE USA
Albemarle Island *see* Isabela, Isla
21 N8 **Albemarle Sound** *inlet* W Atlantic Ocean
106 B10 **Albenga** Liguria, NW Italy
104 L8 **Alberche** ≈ C Spain
103 O17 **Albères, Chaîne des** *var.* les Albères, Montes Albères. ▲▲ France/Spain
Albères, Montes *see* Albères, Chaîne des
182 F2 **Alberga Creek** *seasonal river* South Australia
104 G7 **Albergaria-a-Velha** Aveiro, N Portugal
105 S10 **Alberic** País Valenciano, E Spain
Albermarle *see* Albemarle
107 P18 **Alberobello** Puglia, SE Italy
108 J7 **Alberschwende** Vorarlberg, W Austria
103 O3 **Albert** Somme, N France
9 O12 **Alberta** ◐ *province* SW Canada
Albert Edward Nyanza *see* Edward, Lake
61 C20 **Alberti** Buenos Aires, E Argentina
111 K23 **Albertirsa** Pest, C Hungary
99 I16 **Albertkanaal** *canal* N Belgium
79 P17 **Albert, Lake** *var.* Albert Nyanza, Lac Mobutu Sese Seko. ◎ Uganda/Dem. Rep. Congo
29 V11 **Albert Lea** Minnesota, N USA
81 F16 **Albert Nile** ≈ NW Uganda
Albert Nyanza *see* Albert, Lake
103 T11 **Albertville** Savoie, E France
23 Q2 **Albertville** Alabama, S USA
Albertville *see* Kalemie
103 N15 **Albi** *anc.* Albiga. Tarn, S France
29 W15 **Albia** Iowa, C USA
Albiga *see* Albi
55 X9 **Albina** Marowijne, NE Suriname
83 A15 **Albina, Ponta** *headland* SW Angola
30 M16 **Albion** Illinois, N USA
31 P11 **Albion** Indiana, N USA
29 P14 **Albion** Nebraska, C USA
18 E9 **Albion** New York, NE USA
18 B12 **Albion** Pennsylvania, NE USA
Al Biqā' *see* El Beqaa
140 J4 **Al Bi'r** *var.* Bi'r Ibn Hirmās. Tabūk, NW Saudi Arabia
140 M12 **Al Birk** Makkah, SW Saudi Arabia
141 Q9 **Al Biyāḑ** *desert* C Saudi Arabia
98 H13 **Alblasserdam** Zuid-Holland, SW Netherlands
Albocácer *see* Albocàsser
105 T8 **Albocàsser** *Cast.* Albocácer. País Valenciano, E Spain
Albona *see* Labin
105 O17 **Alborán, Isla de** *island* S Spain
Alborán, Mar de *see* Alboran Sea
105 N17 **Alboran Sea** *Sp.* Mar de Alborán. *sea* SW Mediterranean Sea
Ålborg *see* Aalborg
95 H21 **Ålborg Bugt** *var.* Aalborg Bugt. *bay* N Denmark
Ålborg-Nørresundby *see* Aalborg
143 O5 **Alborz, Reshteh-ye Kūhhā-ye** *Eng.* Elburz Mountains. ▲▲ N Iran
105 Q14 **Albox** Andalucía, S Spain
101 H23 **Albstadt** Baden-Württemberg, SW Germany
104 G14 **Albufeira** Beja, S Portugal
139 P5 **Ālbū Gharz, Sabkhat** ◎ W Iraq
105 O15 **Albuñol** Andalucía, S Spain
37 Q11 **Albuquerque** New Mexico, SW USA
141 W8 **Al Buraymī** *var.* Buraimi. N Oman

◆ Country ● Country Capital ◇ Dependent Territory ○ Dependent Territory Capital ◐ Administrative Regions ✈ International Airport ▲ Mountain ▲▲ Mountain Range Volcano ≈ River ◎ Lake ⊡ Reservoir

143 R17 **Al Buraymī** var. Buraimi. spring/well Oman/United Arab Emirates
Al Burayqah see Marsá al Burayqah
Alburgum see Aalborg
104 I10 **Alburquerque** Extremadura, W Spain
181 V14 **Albury** New South Wales, SE Australia
141 T14 **Al Buzūn** SE Yemen
93 G17 **Alby** Västernorrland, C Sweden
Albyn, Glen see Mor, Glen
104 G12 **Alcácer do Sal** Setúbal, W Portugal
Alcalá de Chisvert/Alcalá de Chivert see Alcalà de Xivert
104 K14 **Alcalá de Guadaira** Andalucía, S Spain
105 O8 **Alcalá de Henares** Ar. Alkal'a; anc. Complutum. Madrid, C Spain
104 K16 **Alcalá de los Gazules** Andalucía, S Spain
105 T8 **Alcalà de Xivert** var. Alcalá de Chisvert, Cast. Alcalá de Chivert. País Valenciano, E Spain
105 N14 **Alcalá La Real** Andalucía, S Spain
107 I23 **Alcamo** Sicilia, Italy, C Mediterranean Sea
105 T4 **Alcanadre** ≈ NE Spain
105 T8 **Alcanar** Cataluña, NE Spain
104 J5 **Alcañices** Castilla-León, N Spain
105 T7 **Alcañiz** Aragón, NE Spain
104 I9 **Alcántara** Extremadura, W Spain
104 J9 **Alcántara, Embalse de** ⊠ W Spain
105 R13 **Alcantarilla** Murcia, SE Spain
105 P11 **Alcaraz** Castilla-La Mancha, C Spain
105 P12 **Alcaraz, Sierra de** ⛰ C Spain
104 I12 **Alcarrache** ≈ SW Spain
105 T6 **Alcarràs** Cataluña, NE Spain
105 N14 **Alcaudete** Andalucía, S Spain
Alcázar see Ksar-el-Kebir
105 O10 **Alcázar de San Juan** anc. Alce. Castilla-La Mancha, C Spain
Alcazarquivir see Ksar-el-Kebir
Alce see Alcázar de San Juan
57 B17 **Alcebo, Volcán** 🌋 Galapagos Islands, Ecuador, E Pacific Ocean
139 X12 **Al Chabā'ish** var. Al Kaba'ish. SE Iraq
117 Y7 **Alchevs'k** prev. Kommunarsk, Voroshilovsk. Luhans'ka Oblast', E Ukraine
Alcira see Alzira
21 N9 **Alcoa** Tennessee, S USA
104 F9 **Alcobaça** Leiria, C Portugal
105 N8 **Alcobendas** Madrid, C Spain
Alcoi see Alcoy
105 P7 **Alcolea del Pinar** Castilla-La Mancha, C Spain
104 I11 **Alconchel** Extremadura, W Spain
Alcora see L'Alcora
105 N8 **Alcorcón** Madrid, C Spain
105 S7 **Alcorisa** Aragón, NE Spain
61 B19 **Alcorta** Santa Fe, C Argentina
104 H14 **Alcoutim** Faro, S Portugal
33 W15 **Alcova** Wyoming, C USA
105 S11 **Alcoy** Cat. Alcoi. País Valenciano, E Spain
105 Y9 **Alcúdia** Mallorca, Spain, W Mediterranean Sea
105 Y9 **Alcúdia, Badia d'** bay Mallorca, Spain, W Mediterranean Sea
172 M7 **Aldabra Group** island group SW Seychelles
139 U10 **Al Daghghārah** C Iraq
40 J5 **Aldama** Chihuahua, N Mexico
41 P11 **Aldama** Tamaulipas, C Mexico
123 Q11 **Aldan** Respublika Sakha (Yakutiya), NE Russian Federation
123 Q10 **Aldan** ≈ NE Russian Federation
Aldar see Aldarhaan
al Dar al Baida see Rabat
162 G7 **Aldarhaan** var. Aldar. Dzavhan, W Mongolia
97 Q20 **Aldeburgh** E England, UK
105 P5 **Aldehuela de Calatañazor** Castilla-León, N Spain
Aldeia Nova see Aldeia Nova de São Bento
104 H13 **Aldeia Nova de São Bento** var. Aldeia Nova. Beja, S Portugal
29 V11 **Alden** Minnesota, N USA
184 N6 **Aldermen Islands, The** island group N New Zealand
97 L25 **Alderney** island Channel Islands
97 N22 **Aldershot** S England, UK
21 R6 **Alderson** West Virginia, NE USA
Al Dhaid see Adh Dhayd
30 J11 **Aledo** Illinois, N USA
76 H9 **Aleg** Brakna, SW Mauritania
64 Q10 **Alegranza** island Islas Canarias, Spain, NE Atlantic Ocean
37 P12 **Alegres Mountain** ▲ New Mexico, SW USA
61 F15 **Alegrete** Rio Grande do Sul, S Brazil
61 C16 **Alejandra** Santa Fe, C Argentina
193 T11 **Alejandro Selkirk, Isla** island Islas Juan Fernández, Chile, E Pacific Ocean
124 I12 **Alekhovshchina** Leningradskaya Oblast', NW Russian Federation
39 O13 **Aleknagik** Alaska, USA
Aleksandriya see Oleksandriya
Aleksandropol' see Gyumri
126 L3 **Aleksandrov** Vladimirskaya Oblast', W Russian Federation
113 N14 **Aleksandrovac** Serbia, C Serbia
127 R9 **Aleksandrov Gay** Saratovskaya Oblast', W Russian Federation
127 U6 **Aleksandrovka** Orenburgskaya Oblast', W Russian Federation
Aleksandrovka see Oleksandrivka
114 J8 **Aleksandrovo** Lovech, N Bulgaria
125 V13 **Aleksandrovsk** Permskaya Oblast', NW Russian Federation
Aleksandrovsk see Zaporizhzhya
127 N14 **Aleksandrovskoye** Stavropol'skiy Kray, SW Russian Federation
123 T12 **Aleksandrovsk-Sakhalinskiy** Ostrov Sakhalin, Sakhalinskaya Oblast', SE Russian Federation
110 J10 **Aleksandrów Kujawski** Kujawskio-pormorskie, C Poland
110 K12 **Aleksandrów Łódzki** Łódzkie, C Poland
Alekseevka see Alekseyevka, Akmola, Kazakhstan
Alekseevka see Akkol', Akmola, Kazakhstan
Alekseevka see Terekty
Alekseevka see Terekty
145 P7 **Alekseyevka** Kaz. Alekseevka. Akmola, N Kazakhstan
126 L9 **Alekseyevka** Belgorodskaya, W Russian Federation
127 S7 **Alekseyevka** Samarskaya Oblast', W Russian Federation
Alekseyevka see Akkol'
Alekseyevka Terekty, Vostochnyy Kazakhstan, Kazakhstan
127 R4 **Alekseyevskoye** Respublika Tatarstan, W Russian Federation
126 K5 **Aleksin** Tul'skaya Oblast', W Russian Federation
113 O14 **Aleksinac** Serbia, SE Serbia
190 G11 **Alele** Île Uvea, E Wallis and Futuna
95 N20 **Ålem** Kalmar, S Sweden
102 L6 **Alençon** Orne, N France
58 I12 **Alenquer** Pará, NE Brazil
38 G10 **'Alenuihaha Channel** var Alenuihaha Channel. channel Hawaii, USA, C Pacific Ocean
Alep/Aleppo see Ḥalab
Aleppo see Ḥalab
103 Y15 **Aléria** Corse, France, C Mediterranean Sea
197 Q11 **Alert** Ellesmere Island, Nunavut, N Canada
103 Q14 **Alès** prev. Alais. Gard, S France
116 G9 **Aleşd** Hung. Élesd. Bihor, SW Romania
106 C9 **Alessandria** Fr. Alexandrie. Piemonte, N Italy
Ålestrup see Aalestrup
94 D9 **Ålesund** Møre og Romsdal, S Norway
108 E10 **Aletschhorn** ▲ SW Switzerland
197 S1 **Aleutian Basin** undersea feature Bering Sea
38 H17 **Aleutian Islands** island group Alaska, USA
39 P14 **Aleutian Range** ⛰ Alaska, USA
0 B5 **Aleutian Trench** undersea feature S Bering Sea
123 T10 **Alevina, Mys** cape E Russian Federation
15 Q6 **Alex** ≈ Québec, SE Canada
28 J3 **Alexander** North Dakota, N USA
39 W14 **Alexander Archipelago** island group Alaska, USA
Alexanderbaai see Alexander Bay
83 D23 **Alexander Bay** Afr. Alexanderbaai. Northern Cape, W South Africa
23 Q5 **Alexander City** Alabama, S USA
194 J6 **Alexander Island** island Antarctica
Alexander Range see Kirghiz Range
183 O12 **Alexandra** Victoria, SE Australia
185 D22 **Alexandra** Otago, South Island, New Zealand
115 F14 **Alexándreia** var. Alexándria. Kentrikí Makedonía, N Greece
Alexandretta see İskenderun
Alexandretta, Gulf of see İskenderun Körfezi
15 N13 **Alexandria** Ontario, SE Canada
121 U13 **Alexandria** Ar. Al Iskandarīyah. N Egypt
44 J12 **Alexandria** C Jamaica
116 J15 **Alexandria** Teleorman, S Romania
31 P13 **Alexandria** Indiana, N USA
20 M4 **Alexandria** Kentucky, S USA
22 H7 **Alexandria** Louisiana, S USA
29 T7 **Alexandria** Minnesota, N USA
29 Q11 **Alexandria** South Dakota, N USA
21 W4 **Alexandria** Virginia, NE USA
Alexándria see Alexándreia
18 I7 **Alexandria Bay** New York, NE USA
Alexandrie see Alessandria
182 J10 **Alexandrina, Lake** ◎ South Australia
114 K13 **Alexandroúpoli** var. Alexandroúpolis, Turk. Dedeagaç, Dedeagach. Anatolikí Makedonía kai Thráki, NE Greece
Alexandroúpolis see Alexandroúpoli
10 L15 **Alexis Creek** British Columbia, SW Canada
122 I13 **Aleysk** Altayskiy Kray, S Russian Federation
139 S8 **Al Fallūjah** var. Falluja. C Iraq
105 R8 **Alfambra** ≈ E Spain
Al Faqa see Faq'
141 R15 **Al Farḍah** C Yemen
105 Q4 **Alfaro** La Rioja, N Spain
105 U5 **Alfarràs** Cataluña, NE Spain
Al Fāshir see El Fasher
Al Fashn see El Fashn
114 M7 **Alfatar** Silistra, NE Bulgaria
139 S5 **Al Fatḥah** C Iraq
139 Q3 **Al Fatsī** N Iraq
139 Z13 **Al Fāw** var. Fao. SE Iraq
Al Fayyūm see El Faiyûm
115 D20 **Alfeiós** prev. Alfiós; anc. Alpheius, Alpheus. ≈ S Greece
100 I13 **Alfeld** Niedersachsen, C Germany
Alfiós see Alfeiós
Alföld see Great Hungarian Plain
94 C11 **Ålfotbreen** glacier S Norway
19 P9 **Alfred** Maine, NE USA
18 F11 **Alfred** New York, NE USA
61 K14 **Alfredo Vagner** Santa Catarina, S Brazil
94 M12 **Alfta** Gävleborg, C Sweden
140 K12 **Al Fuḥayḥīl** var. Fahaheel. SE Kuwait
139 Q6 **Al Fuḥaymī** C Iraq
143 S16 **Al Fujayrah** Eng. Fujairah. Al Fujayrah, NE United Arab Emirates
143 S16 **Al Fujayrah** Eng. Fujairah. ✈ Al Fujayrah, NE United Arab Emirates
Al-Furāt see Euphrates
144 I10 **Alga** Kaz. Algha. Aktyubinsk, NW Kazakhstan
144 G9 **Algabas** Zapadnyy Kazakhstan, NW Kazakhstan
95 C17 **Ålgård** Rogaland, S Norway
104 G14 **Algarve** cultural region S Portugal
182 G3 **Algebuckina Bridge** South Australia
104 K16 **Algeciras** Andalucía, SW Spain
105 S10 **Algemesí** País Valenciano, E Spain
Al-Genain see El Geneina
120 F9 **Alger** var. Algiers, El Djazaïr, Al Jazair. ● (Algeria) N Algeria
74 H9 **Algeria** off. Democratic and Popular Republic of Algeria. ◆ republic N Africa
Algeria, Democratic and Popular Republic of see Algeria
120 J8 **Algerian Basin** var. Balearic Plain. undersea feature W Mediterranean Sea
Algha see Alga
138 I4 **Al Ghāb** ◎ NW Syria
141 X10 **Al Ghābah** var. Ghaba. C Oman
141 U14 **Al Ghayḍah** E Yemen
140 M6 **Al Ghazālah** Ḥā'il, NW Saudi Arabia
107 B17 **Alghero** Sardegna, Italy, C Mediterranean Sea
95 M20 **Älghult** Kronoberg, S Sweden
Al Ghurdaqah see Hurghada
Algiers see Alger
105 S10 **Alginet** País Valenciano, E Spain
83 I26 **Algoa Bay** bay S South Africa
104 L15 **Algodonales** Andalucía, S Spain
105 N9 **Algodor** ≈ C Spain
Al Golea see El Goléa
31 N6 **Algoma** Wisconsin, N USA
29 U12 **Algona** Iowa, C USA
20 L8 **Algood** Tennessee, S USA
105 O2 **Algorta** País Vasco, N Spain
61 E18 **Algorta** Río Negro, W Uruguay
Al Haba see Haba
139 Q10 **Al Habbārīyah** S Iraq
Al Hadhar see Al Ḥaḍr
139 Q4 **Al Ḥaḍr** var. Al Hadhar; anc. Hatra. NW Iraq
139 T13 **Al Ḥajarah** desert S Iraq
141 W8 **Al Ḥajar al Gharbī** ⛰ N Oman
141 Y8 **Al Ḥajar ash Sharqī** ⛰ NE Oman
141 R15 **Al Ḥajarayn** C Yemen
138 L10 **Al Ḥamād** desert Jordan/Saudi Arabia
Al Hamad see Syrian Desert
75 N9 **Al Ḥamādah al Ḥamrā'** var. Al Ḥamrā'. desert NW Libya
105 N15 **Alhama de Granada** Andalucía, S Spain
105 R13 **Alhama de Murcia** Murcia, SE Spain
35 T15 **Alhambra** California, W USA
139 T12 **Al Ḥammām** S Iraq
141 X8 **Al Ḥamrā'** NE Oman
Al Ḥamrā' see Al Ḥamādah al Ḥamrā'
141 O6 **Al Ḥamūdīyah** spring/well N Saudi Arabia
140 M7 **Al Ḥanākīyah** Al Madīnah, W Saudi Arabia
139 W14 **Al Ḥanīyah** escarpment Iraq/Saudi Arabia
139 Y12 **Al Hārithah** SE Iraq
140 L3 **Al Ḥarrah** desert NW Saudi Arabia
75 Q10 **Al Harūj al Aswad** desert C Libya
Al Hasaifin see Al Ḥusayfīn
139 N2 **Al Ḥasakah** var. Al Hasijah, El Haseke, Fr. Hassetché. Al Ḥasakah, NE Syria
139 O2 **Al Ḥasakah** off. Muḥāfaẓat al Ḥasakah, var. Al Hasakah, Āl Hasakah, Hasakah, Hassakeh. ⬖ governorate NE Syria
Al Hasakah see 'Āmūdah
Al Hasakah see Al Ḥasakah
139 T9 **Al Hāshimīyah** C Iraq
138 G13 **Al Hāshimīyah** Ma'ān, S Jordan
104 M15 **Alhaurín el Grande** Andalucía, S Spain
141 Q16 **Al Ḥawrā** S Yemen
139 V10 **Al Ḥayy** var. Kut al Hai, Kūt al Ḥayy. E Iraq
141 U11 **Al Ḥibāk** desert E Saudi Arabia
138 H8 **Al Hījānah** var. Hejanah, Hijanah. Dimashq, W Syria
140 K7 **Al Ḥijāz** Eng. Hejaz. coastal and highland region NW Saudi Arabia
Al Hilbeh see 'Ulayyānīyah, Bi'r al
139 T9 **Al Ḥillah** var. Hilla. C Iraq
139 T9 **Al Hindīyah** var. Hindiya. C Iraq
138 G12 **Al Ḥisā** Aṭ Ṭafīlah, W Jordan
74 G5 **Al-Hoceïma** var. al Hoceima, Al-Hoceima, Alhucemas; prev. Villa Sanjurjo. N Morocco
Alhucemas see Al-Hoceïma
105 N17 **Alhucemas, Peñon de** island group S Spain
141 N15 **Al Ḥudaydah** Eng. Hodeida. W Yemen
141 N15 **Al Ḥudaydah** var. Hodeida. ✈ W Yemen
140 M4 **Al Ḥudūd ash Shamālīyah** var. Minṭaqat al Ḥudūd ash Shamālīyah, Eng. Northern Border Region. ⬖ province N Saudi Arabia
141 S7 **Al Hufūf** var. Hofuf. Ash Sharqīyah, NE Saudi Arabia
al-Hurma see Al Khurmah
141 X7 **Al Ḥusayfīn** var. Al Hasaifin. N Oman
138 G9 **Al Ḥuṣn** var. Husn. Irbid, N Jordan
139 U9 **'Alī** E Iraq
104 L10 **Alia** Extremadura, W Spain
143 P9 **'Alīābād** Yazd, C Iran
'Alīābad see Qā'emshahr
105 S7 **Aliaga** Aragón, NE Spain
136 B13 **Aliağa** İzmir, W Turkey
Aliákmon see Aliákmonas
115 F14 **Aliákmonas** prev. Aliákmon; anc. Haliacmon. ≈ N Greece
139 W9 **'Alī al Gharbī** E Iraq
139 U11 **'Alī al Ḥassūnī** S Iraq
115 G18 **Alíartos** Stereá Ellás, C Greece
137 Y12 **Āli-Bayramli** Rus. Ali-Bayramly. SE Azerbaijan
Ali-Bayramly see Āli-Bayramli
114 P12 **Alibey Barajī** ⊠ NW Turkey
77 S13 **Alibori** ≈ N Benin
112 M10 **Alibunar** Vojvodina, NE Serbia
105 S12 **Alicante** Cat. Alacant, Lat. Lucentum. País Valenciano, SE Spain
105 S12 **Alicante** ⬖ province País Valenciano, SE Spain
105 S12 **Alicante** ✈ Murcia, E Spain
83 I25 **Alice** Eastern Cape, S South Africa
25 S14 **Alice** Texas, SW USA
83 I25 **Alicedale** Eastern Cape, S South Africa
65 B25 **Alice, Mount** hill West Falkland, Falkland Islands
107 P20 **Alice, Punta** headland S Italy
181 Q7 **Alice Springs** Northern Territory, C Australia
23 N4 **Aliceville** Alabama, S USA
147 U13 **Alichur** SE Tajikistan
147 U14 **Alichuri Janubí, Qatorkŭhi** Rus. Yuzhno-Alichurskiy Khrebet. ⛰ SE Tajikistan
147 U13 **Alichuri Shimolí, Qatorkŭhi** Rus. Severo-Alichurskiy Khrebet. ⛰ SE Tajikistan
107 K22 **Alicudi, Isola** island Isole Eolie, S Italy
152 J11 **Aligarh** Uttar Pradesh, N India
142 M7 **Alīgūdarz** Lorestān, W Iran
163 U5 **Alihe** var. Oroqen Zizhiqi. Nei Mongol Zizhiqu, N China
0 F12 **Alijos, Islas** islets California, SW USA
149 R6 **'Alī Kbel** Pash. 'Alī Khēl. Paktīkā, E Afghanistan
Ali Khel see 'Alī Kheyl, Paktīā, Afghanistan
'Alī Khēl see 'Ali Kbel, Paktīkā, Afghanistan
149 R6 **'Alī Kheyl** var. Ali Khel, Jajī. Paktīā, SE Afghanistan
141 V17 **Al Ikhwān** island group SE Yemen
Aliki see Alykí
79 H19 **Alima** ≈ C Congo
Al Imārāt al 'Arabīyah al Muttaḥidah see United Arab Emirates
115 N23 **Alimía** island Dodekánisa, Greece, Aegean Sea
55 V12 **Alimimuni Piek** ▲ S Suriname
79 K15 **Alindao** Basse-Kotto, S Central African Republic
95 J18 **Alingsås** Västra Götaland, S Sweden
81 K18 **Alinjugul** spring/well E Kenya
149 S11 **Alīpur** Punjab, E Pakistan
153 T12 **Alīpur Duār** West Bengal, NE India
18 B14 **Aliquippa** Pennsylvania, NE USA
80 L12 **'Ali Sabieh** var. 'Alī Sabīḥ. S Djibouti
'Alī Sabīḥ see 'Ali Sabieh
140 K3 **Al 'Īsāwīyah** Al Jawf, NW Saudi Arabia
104 J10 **Aliseda** Extremadura, W Spain
139 T8 **Al Iskandarīyah** C Iraq
Al Iskandarīyah see Alexandria
123 T6 **Aliskerovo** Chukotskiy Avtonomnyy Okrug, NE Russian Federation
114 H13 **Alistráti** Kentrikí Makedonía, NE Greece
39 P15 **Alitak Bay** bay Kodiak Island, Alaska, USA
Al Ittiḥād see Madīnat ash Sha'b
115 H18 **Alivéri** var. Alivérion. Évvoia, C Greece
Alivérion see Alivéri
Aliwal-Noord see Aliwal North
83 I24 **Aliwal North** Afr. Aliwal-Noord. Eastern Cape, SE South Africa
121 Q13 **Al Jabal al Akhḍar** ⛰ NE Libya
138 H13 **Al Jafr** Ma'ān, S Jordan
75 T8 **Al Jaghbūb** NE Libya
142 K11 **Al Jahrā'** var. Al Jahrah, Jahra. C Kuwait
Al Jahrah see Al Jahrā'
Al Jamāhīrīyah al 'Arabīyah al Lībīyah ash Sha'bīyah al Ishtirākīy see Libya
140 K3 **Al Jarāwī** spring/well NW Saudi Arabia
141 X11 **Al Jawārah** oasis SE Oman
140 L3 **Al Jawf** off. Jauf. Al Jawf, NW Saudi Arabia
140 L4 **Al Jawf** var. Minṭaqat al Jawf. ⬖ province N Saudi Arabia
Al Jawlān see Golan Heights
Al Jazair see Alger
139 N4 **Al Jazīrah** physical region Iraq/Syria
104 F14 **Aljezur** Faro, S Portugal
139 S13 **Al Jīl** S Iraq
138 G11 **Al Jīzah** var. Jiza. 'Ammān, N Jordan
Al Jīzah see El Gîza
Al Jubail see Al Jubayl
141 S6 **Al Jubayl** var. Al Jubail. Ash Sharqīyah, NE Saudi Arabia
141 T10 **Al Juḥaysh, Qalamat** well SE Saudi Arabia
143 N15 **Al Jumaylīyah** N Qatar
Al Junaynah see El Geneina
104 G13 **Aljustrel** Beja, S Portugal
Al Kaba'ish see Al Chabā'ish
Al-Kadhimain see Al Kāẓimīyah
Al Kāf see El Kef
Alkal'a see Alcalá de Henares
35 W4 **Alkali Flat** salt flat Nevada, W USA
35 Q1 **Alkali Lake** ◎ Nevada, W USA
141 Z9 **Al Kāmil** NE Oman
138 G11 **Al Karak** var. El Kerak, Karak, Kerak; anc. Kir Moab, Kir of Moab. Al Karak, W Jordan
138 G12 **Al Karak** off. Muḥāfaẓat al Karak. ⬖ governorate W Jordan
139 W8 **Al Karmashīyah** E Iraq
Al-Kashaniya see Al Qash'ānīyah
Al-Kasr al-Kebir see Ksar-el-Kebir
139 T8 **Al Kāẓimīyah** var. Al-Kadhimain, Kadhimain. C Iraq
99 J18 **Alken** Limburg, NE Belgium
141 X8 **Al Khābūrah** var. Khabura. N Oman
Al Khalīl see Hebron
139 T7 **Al Khāliṣ** C Iraq
Al Khaluf see Khalūf
Al Khārijah see El Khârga
141 Q8 **Al Kharj** Ar Riyāḍ, C Saudi Arabia
141 W6 **Al Khaṣab** var. Khasab. N Oman
Al Khaur see Al Khawr
143 N15 **Al Khawr** var. Al Khaur, Al Khor. N Qatar
142 K12 **Al Khīrān** var. Al Khiran. SE Kuwait
141 W9 **Al Khīrān** spring/well NW Oman
Al Khiyām see El Khiyam
Al-Khobar see Al Khubar
Al Khor see Al Khawr
141 S6 **Al Khubar** var. Al-Khobar. Ash Sharqīyah, NE Saudi Arabia
75 T11 **Al Khufrah** SE Libya
120 M12 **Al Khums** var. Homs, Khoms, Khums. NW Libya
141 R15 **Al Khuraybah** C Yemen
140 M9 **Al Khurmah** var. al-Hurma. Makkah, W Saudi Arabia
141 V9 **Al Kidan** desert NE Saudi Arabia
127 V4 **Alkino-2** Respublika Bashkortostan, W Russian Federation
98 H9 **Alkmaar** Noord-Holland, NW Netherlands
139 T10 **Al Kūfah** var. Kufa. S Iraq
141 T10 **Al Kursū'** desert E Saudi Arabia
139 V9 **Al Kūt** var. Kūt al 'Amārah, Kut al Imara. E Iraq
Al-Kuwait see Al Kuwayt
Al Kuwayr see Guwēr
142 K11 **Al Kuwayt** var. Al-Kuwait, Eng. Kuwait, Kuwait City; prev. Qurein. ● (Kuwait) E Kuwait
142 K11 **Al Kuwayt** ✈ C Kuwait
115 G19 **Alkyonidón, Kólpos** gulf C Greece
141 N4 **Al Labbah** physical region N Saudi Arabia
138 G4 **Al Lādhiqīyah** Eng. Latakia, Fr. Lattaquié; anc. Laodicea, Laodicea ad Mare. Al Lādhiqīyah, W Syria
138 H4 **Al Lādhiqīyah** off. Muḥāfaẓat al Ļādhiqīyah, var. Al Lathqiyah, Latakia, Lattakia. ⬖ governorate W Syria
19 R2 **Allagash River** ≈ Maine, NE USA
152 M13 **Allahābād** Uttar Pradesh, N India
143 S3 **Allāh Dāgh, Reshteh-ye** ⛰ NE Iran
39 Q8 **Allakaket** Alaska, USA
9 T15 **Allan** Saskatchewan, S Canada
166 L6 **Allanmyo** Magwe, C Myanmar (Burma)
83 I22 **Allanridge** Free State, C South Africa
104 H4 **Allariz** Galicia, NW Spain
139 R11 **Al Laṣaf** var. Al Lussuf. S Iraq
Al Lathqiyah see Al Lādhiqīyah
23 S2 **Allatoona Lake** ⊠ Georgia, SE USA
83 J19 **Alldays** Limpopo, NE South Africa
Alle see Łyna
31 P10 **Allegan** Michigan, N USA
18 E14 **Allegheny Mountains** ⛰ NE USA
18 E12 **Allegheny Plateau** ⛰ New York/Pennsylvania, NE USA
18 D11 **Allegheny Reservoir** ⊠ New York/Pennsylvania, NE USA
18 E12 **Allegheny River** ≈ New York/Pennsylvania, NE USA
22 K9 **Allemands, Lac des** ◎ Louisiana, S USA
25 U6 **Allen** Texas, SW USA
21 R14 **Allendale** South Carolina, SE USA
41 N6 **Allende** Coahuila de Zaragoza, NE Mexico
41 O9 **Allende** Nuevo León, NE Mexico
97 D16 **Allen, Lough** Ir. Loch Aillionn. ◎ NW Ireland
185 B26 **Allen, Mount** ▲ Stewart Island, Southland, SW New Zealand
109 V2 **Allensteig** Niederösterreich, N Austria
Allenstein see Olsztyn
18 I14 **Allentown** Pennsylvania, NE USA
155 G23 **Alleppey** var. Alappuzha; prev. Alleppi. Kerala, SW India
Alleppi see Alleppey
100 J12 **Aller** ≈ NW Germany
29 V16 **Allerton** Iowa, C USA
99 K19 **Alleur** Liège, E Belgium
101 J25 **Allgäuer Alpen** ⛰ Austria/Germany
28 J13 **Alliance** Nebraska, C USA
31 U12 **Alliance** Ohio, N USA
103 O10 **Allier** ⬖ department N France
139 R13 **Al Līfīyah** S Iraq
44 J13 **Alligator Pond** C Jamaica
21 Y9 **Alligator River** ≈ North Carolina, SE USA
29 W12 **Allison** Iowa, C USA
14 G14 **Alliston** Ontario, S Canada
140 L11 **Al Līth** Makkah, SW Saudi Arabia
Al Liwā' see Līwā
96 J12 **Alloa** C Scotland, UK
103 U14 **Allos** Alpes-de-Haute-Provence, SE France
108 D6 **Allschwil** Basel-Land, NW Switzerland
Al Lubnān see Lebanon
141 N14 **Al Luḥayyah** W Yemen
14 K12 **Allumettes, Île des** island Québec, SE Canada
Al Lussuf see Al Laṣaf
109 S5 **Alm** ≈ N Austria
15 Q7 **Alma** Québec, SE Canada
27 S10 **Alma** Arkansas, C USA
23 V7 **Alma** Georgia, SE USA
27 P4 **Alma** Kansas, C USA
31 Q8 **Alma** Michigan, N USA
29 O17 **Alma** Nebraska, C USA
30 I7 **Alma** Wisconsin, N USA
139 R12 **Al Ma'ānīyah** S Iraq
Alma-Ata see Almaty
Alma-Atinskaya Oblast' see Almaty
Almacellas see Almacelles
105 T5 **Almacelles** var. Almacellas. Cataluña, NE Spain
104 F11 **Almada** Setúbal, W Portugal
104 L11 **Almadén** Castilla-La Mancha, C Spain
66 L6 **Almadies, Pointe des** headland W Senegal
140 L7 **Al Madīnah** Eng. Medina. Al Madīnah, W Saudi Arabia
140 L7 **Al Madīnah** off. Minṭaqat al Madīnah. ⬖ province W Saudi Arabia
138 H9 **Al Mafraq** var. Mafraq. Al Mafraq, N Jordan
138 J10 **Al Mafraq** off. Muḥāfaẓat al Mafraq. ⬖ governorate NW Jordan
141 R15 **Al Maghārim** C Yemen
105 N11 **Almagro** Castilla-La Mancha, C Spain
Al Maḥallah al Kubrá see El Mahalla el Kubra
139 T9 **Al Maḥāwīl** var. Khān al Maḥāwīl. C Iraq
Al Mahdiyah see Mahdia
139 T8 **Al Maḥmūdīyah** var. Mahmudiya. C Iraq
141 T14 **Al Mahrah** ⛰ E Yemen
141 P7 **Al Majma'ah** Ar Riyāḍ, C Saudi Arabia
139 Q11 **Al Makmīn** well S Iraq
139 Q1 **Al Mālikīyah** var. Malkiye. Al Ḥasakah, N Syria
Almalyk see Olmaliq
Al Mamlakah see Morocco
Al Mamlaka al Urduniya al Hashemiyah see Jordan
143 Q18 **Al Manādir** var. Al Manadir. desert Oman/United Arab Emirates
142 L15 **Al Manāmah** Eng. Manama. ● (Bahrain) N Bahrain
139 O5 **Al Manāṣif** ⛰ E Syria
35 O4 **Almanor, Lake** ⊠ California, W USA
105 R11 **Almansa** Castilla-La Mancha, C Spain
Al Manṣūrah see El Manṣûra
104 L3 **Almanza** Castilla-León, N Spain
104 L8 **Almanzor** ▲ W Spain
105 P14 **Almanzora** ≈ SE Spain
139 S9 **Al Mardah** C Iraq
Al-Mariyya see Almeria
75 R7 **Al Marj** var. Barka, It. Barce. NE Libya
138 L2 **Al Mashrafah** Ar Raqqah, N Syria
141 X8 **Al Maṣna'ah** var. Al Muṣana'a. NE Oman
Almassora see Almazora
Almatinskaya Oblast' see Almaty
145 U15 **Almaty** var. Alma-Ata. Almaty, SE Kazakhstan
145 S14 **Almaty** off. Almatinskaya Oblast', Kaz. Almaty Oblysy; prev. Alma-Atinskaya Oblast'. ⬖ province SE Kazakhstan
145 U15 **Almaty** ✈ Almaty, SE Kazakhstan
Almaty Oblysy see Almaty
al-Mawailih see Al Muwayliḥ
139 R3 **Al Mawṣil** Eng. Mosul. N Iraq
139 N5 **Al Mayādīn** var. Mayadin, Fr. Meyadine. Dayr az Zawr, E Syria
139 X10 **Al Maymūnah** var. Maimuna. SE Iraq
141 N5 **Al Mayyāh** Ḥā'il, N Saudi Arabia
Al Ma'zam see Al Ma'zim
105 P6 **Almazán** Castilla-León, N Spain
141 W8 **Al Ma'zim** var. Al Ma'zam. NW Oman
123 N11 **Almaznyy** Respublika Sakha (Yakutiya), NE Russian Federation
105 T9 **Almazora** Cat Almassora. País Valenciano, E Spain
Al Mazra' see Al Mazra'ah
138 G11 **Al Mazra'ah** var. Al Mazra', Mazra'a. Al Karak, W Jordan
101 G15 **Alme** ≈ W Germany
104 I7 **Almeida** Guarda, N Portugal
104 G10 **Almeirim** Santarém, C Portugal
98 O10 **Almelo** Overijssel, E Netherlands
105 S9 **Almenara** País Valenciano, E Spain
105 P12 **Almenaras** ▲ S Spain

◆ Country
● Country Capital
◇ Dependent Territory
○ Dependent Territory Capital
⬖ Administrative Regions
✈ International Airport
▲ Mountain
⛰ Mountain Range
🌋 Volcano
≈ River
◎ Lake
⊠ Reservoir

105 P5 **Almenar de Soria** Castilla-León, N Spain
104 J6 **Almendra, Embalse de** ⊠ Castilla-León, NW Spain
104 J11 **Almendralejo** Extremadura, W Spain
98 J10 **Almere** var. Almere-stad. Flevoland, C Netherlands
98 J10 **Almere-Buiten** Flevoland, C Netherlands
98 J10 **Almere-Haven** Flevoland, C Netherlands
Almere-stad see Almere
105 P15 **Almería** Ar. Al-Mariyya; anc. Unci, Lat. Portus Magnus. Andalucía, S Spain
105 P14 **Almería** ◐ province Andalucía, S Spain
105 P15 **Almería, Golfo de** gulf S Spain
127 S5 **Al'met'yevsk** Respublika Tatarstan, W Russian Federation
95 L21 **Älmhult** Kronoberg, S Sweden
141 U9 **Al Miḩrāḑ** desert NE Saudi Arabia
Al Mīnā' see El Mina
104 L17 **Almina, Punta** headland Ceuta, Spain, N Africa
Al Minyā see El Minya
Al Miqdādīyah see Al Muqdādīyah
43 P14 **Almirante** Bocas del Toro, NW Panama
Almirós see Almyrós
140 M9 **Al Mislaḩ** spring/well W Saudi Arabia
Almissa see Omiš
104 G13 **Almodôvar** var. Almodóvar. Beja, S Portugal
104 M11 **Almodóvar del Campo** Castilla-La Mancha, C Spain
105 Q9 **Almodóvar del Pinar** Castilla-La Mancha, C Spain
31 S9 **Almont** Michigan, N USA
14 L13 **Almonte** Ontario, SE Canada
104 J14 **Almonte** Andalucía, S Spain
104 K9 **Almonte** ~ W Spain
152 K9 **Almora** Uttaranchal, N India
104 M8 **Almorox** Castilla-La Mancha, C Spain
141 S7 **Al Mubarraz** Ash Sharqīyah, E Saudi Arabia
Al Muḑaibī see Al Muḑaybī
138 G15 **Al Mudawwarah** Ma'ān, SW Jordan
141 Y9 **Al Muḑaybī** var. Al Muḑaibī. NE Oman
Almudébar see Almudévar
105 S5 **Almudévar** var. Almudébar. Aragón, NE Spain
141 S15 **Al Mukallā** var. Mukalla. SE Yemen
141 N16 **Al Mukhā** Eng. Mocha. SW Yemen
105 N15 **Almuñécar** Andalucía, S Spain
139 U7 **Al Muqdādīyah** var. Al Miqdādīyah. C Iraq
140 L3 **Al Murayr** spring/well NW Saudi Arabia
136 M12 **Almus** Tokat, N Turkey
Al Muşana'a see Al Maşna'ah
139 T9 **Al Musayyib** var. Musaiyib. C Iraq
139 V9 **Al Muwaffaqīyah** S Iraq
138 H10 **Al Muwaqqar** var. El Muwaqqar. 'Ammān, W Jordan
140 J5 **Al Muwayliḩ** var. al-Mawailih. Tabūk, NW Saudi Arabia
115 F17 **Almyrós** var. Almirós. Thessalía, C Greece
115 I24 **Almyroú, Órmos** bay Kríti, Greece, E Mediterranean Sea
Al Nūwfalīyah see An Nawfalīyah
96 L13 **Alnwick** N England, UK
Al Obayyid see El Obeid
Al Odaid see Al 'Udayd
190 B16 **Alofi** ○ (Niue) W Niue
190 A16 **Alofi Bay** bay W Niue, C Pacific Ocean
190 E13 **Alofi, Île** island S Wallis and Futuna
190 E13 **Alofitai** Île Alofi, W Wallis and Futuna
Aloha State see Hawai'i
118 G7 **Aloja** Limbaži, N Latvia
153 X10 **Along** Arunāchel Pradesh, NE India
115 H16 **Alónnisos** island Vóreioi Sporádes, Greece, Aegean Sea
104 M15 **Álora** Andalucía, S Spain
171 Q16 **Alor, Kepulauan** island group E Indonesia
171 Q16 **Alor, Pulau** prev. Ombai. island Kepulauan Alor, E Indonesia
171 O16 **Alor, Selat** strait Flores Sea/Savu Sea
168 I7 **Alor Setar** var. Alor Star, Alur Setar. Kedah, Peninsular Malaysia
Alor Star see Alor Setar
Alost see Aalst
Alost see Aalst
154 F9 **Ālot** Madhya Pradesh, C India
186 G10 **Alotau** Milne Bay, SE Papua New Guinea
171 Y16 **Alotip** Papua, E Indonesia
Al Oued see El Oued
35 R12 **Alpaugh** California, W USA
Alpen see Alps
31 R6 **Alpena** Michigan, N USA
Alpes see Alps
103 S14 **Alpes-de-Haute-Provence** ◐ department SE France
103 U14 **Alpes-Maritimes** ◐ department SE France
181 W8 **Alpha** Queensland, E Australia
197 R9 **Alpha Cordillera** var. Alpha Ridge. undersea feature Arctic Ocean
Alpha Ridge see Alpha Cordillera
Alpheius see Alfeiós
99 I15 **Alphen** Noord-Brabant, S Netherlands
Alphen see Alphen aan den Rijn
98 H11 **Alphen aan den Rijn** var. Alphen. Zuid-Holland, C Netherlands
Alpheus see Alfeiós
Alpi see Alps
104 G10 **Alpiarça** Santarém, C Portugal
24 K10 **Alpine** Texas, SW USA
108 F8 **Alpnach** Unterwalden, W Switzerland
108 D11 **Alps** Fr. Alpes, Ger. Alpen, It. Alpi. ▲▲ C Europe
141 W8 **Al Qābil** var. Qabil. N Oman
Al Qaḑārif see Gedaref
75 P8 **Al Qaddāḩīyah** N Libya
Al Qāhirah see Cairo
140 K4 **Al Qalībah** Tabūk, NW Saudi Arabia
139 O1 **Al Qāmishlī** var. Kamishli, Qamishly. Al Ḩasakah, NE Syria
138 I6 **Al Qaryatayn** var. Qaryatayn, Fr. Qariateïne. Ḩimş, C Syria
142 K11 **Al Qash'ānīyah** var. Al-Kashaniya. NE Kuwait
141 N7 **Al Qaşīm** var. Mintaqat Qaşim, Qassim. ◐ province C Saudi Arabia
138 J5 **Al Qaşr** Ḩimş, C Syria
Al Qaşr see El Qaşr
Al Qaşrayn see Kasserine
141 S6 **Al Qaţīf** Ash Sharqīyah, NE Saudi Arabia
138 G11 **Al Qaţrānah** var. El Qatrani, Qatrana. Al Karak, W Jordan
75 P11 **Al Qaţrūn** SW Libya
Al Qayrawān see Kairouan
Al-Qsar al-Kbir see Ksar-el-Kebir
Al Qubayyāt see Qoubaïyât
Al Quds/Al Quds ash Sharīf see Jerusalem
104 H12 **Alqueva, Barragem do** ⊠ Portugal/Spain
138 G8 **Al Qunayţirah** var. El Kuneitra, El Quneitra, Kuneitra, Qunaytra. Al Qunayţirah, SW Syria
138 G8 **Al Qunayţirah** off. Muḩāfaẓat al Qunayţirah, var. El Q'unayţirah, Qunayţirah, Fr. Kuneitra. ◐ governorate SW Syria
140 M11 **Al Qunfudhah** Makkah, SW Saudi Arabia
140 K2 **Al Qurayyāt** Al Jawf, NW Saudi Arabia
139 Y11 **Al Qurnah** var. Kurna. SE Iraq
139 V12 **Al Quşayr** S Iraq
138 I6 **Al Quşayr** var. El Quseir, Quşayr, Fr. Kousseir. Ḩimş, W Syria
Al Quşayr see Quseir
138 H7 **Al Quţayfah** var. Quţayfah, Qutayfe, Quteife, Fr. Kouteifé. Dimashq, W Syria
141 P8 **Al Quwayīyah** Ar Riyāḑ, C Saudi Arabia
Al Quwayr see Guwēr
138 F14 **Al Quwayrah** var. El Quweira. Al 'Aqabah, SW Jordan
Al Rayyan see Ar Rayyān
Al Ruweis see Ar Ruways
95 G24 **Als** Ger. Alsen. island SW Denmark
103 U5 **Alsace** Ger. Elsass; anc. Alsatia. ◐ region NE France
9 R16 **Alsask** Saskatchewan, S Canada
Alsasua see Altsasu
Alsatia see Alsace
101 C16 **Alsdorf** Nordrhein-Westfalen, W Germany
10 G8 **Alsek** ~ Canada/USA
Alsen see Als
101 F19 **Alsenz** ~ W Germany
101 H17 **Alsfeld** Hessen, C Germany
119 K20 **Al'shany** Rus. Ol'shany. Brestskaya Voblasts', SW Belarus
Alsókubin see Dolný Kubín
118 C9 **Alsunga** Kuldīga, W Latvia
Alt see Olt
92 K9 **Alta** Fin. Alattio. Finnmark, N Norway
29 T12 **Alta** Iowa, C USA
108 I7 **Altach** Vorarlberg, W Austria
92 K9 **Altaelva** Lapp. Álaheaieatnu. ~ N Norway
92 J8 **Altafjorden** fjord NE Norwegian Sea
62 K10 **Alta Gracia** Córdoba, C Argentina
42 K11 **Alta Gracia** Rivas, SW Nicaragua
54 H4 **Altagracia** Zulia, NW Venezuela
54 M5 **Altagracia de Orituco** Guárico, N Venezuela
Altai see Altai Mountains
Altai see Altai Mountains
129 T7 **Altai Mountains** var. Altai. ▲▲ C Asia
129 T7 **Altai Mountains** var. Altai, Chin. Altay Shan, Rus. Altay. ▲▲ Asia/Europe
23 V6 **Altamaha River** ~ Georgia, SE USA
58 J13 **Altamira** Pará, NE Brazil
54 D12 **Altamira** Huila, S Colombia
42 M13 **Altamira** Alajuela, N Costa Rica
41 Q11 **Altamira** Tamaulipas, C Mexico
30 L15 **Altamont** Illinois, N USA
27 Q7 **Altamont** Kansas, C USA
32 H16 **Altamont** Oregon, NW USA
20 K10 **Altamont** Tennessee, S USA
23 X11 **Altamonte Springs** Florida, SE USA
107 O17 **Altamura** anc. Lupatia. Puglia, SE Italy
40 H9 **Altamura, Isla** island C Mexico
Altan see Erdenehayrhan
Altanbulag see Bayanhayrhan
Altanbulag see Bayanhayrhan
163 Q7 **Altan Emel** var. Xin Barag Youqi. Nei Mongol Zizhiqu, N China
Altan-Ovoo see Tsenher
163 N9 **Altanshiree** var. Chamdmanī. Dornigovĭ, SE Mongolia
Altanteel see Dzereg
162 D5 **Altantsögts** var. Tsagaantüngi. Bayan-Ölgiy, NW Mongolia
40 F3 **Altar** Sonora, NW Mexico
40 D2 **Altar, Desierto de** var. Sonoran Desert. desert Mexico/USA see also Sonoran Desert
Altar, Desierto de see Sonoran Desert
105 Q8 **Altas, Sierra** ▲ N Spain
40 H9 **Altata** Sinaloa, C Mexico
42 D4 **Alta Verapaz** off. Departamento de Alta Verapaz. ◐ department C Guatemala
Alta Verapaz, Departamento de see Alta Verapaz
107 L18 **Altavilla Silentia** Campania, S Italy
21 T7 **Altavista** Virginia, NE USA
158 L2 **Altay** Xinjiang Uygur Zizhiqu, NW China
162 D6 **Altay** var. Chihertey. Bayan-Ölgiy, W Mongolia
162 F9 **Altay** var. Bayan-Ovoo. Govi-Altay, SW Mongolia
162 F9 **Altay** var. Bayan-Ovoo. Govi-Altay, SW Mongolia
162 G8 **Altay** prev. Yösönbulag. Govi-Altay, W Mongolia
162 E8 **Altay** var. Bor-Udzüür. Hovd, W Mongolia
162 E8 **Altay** var. Bor-Udzüür. Hovd, W Mongolia
Altay Altai Mountains, Asia/Europe
Altay see Bayantes, Mongolia
122 J14 **Altay, Respublika** var. Gornyy Altay; prev. Gorno-Altayskaya Respublika. ◐ autonomous republic S Russian Federation
Altay Shan see Altai Mountains
123 I13 **Altayskiy Kray** ◐ territory S Russian Federation
Altbetsche see Bečej
101 L20 **Altdorf** Bayern, SE Germany
108 G8 **Altdorf** var. Altorf. Uri, C Switzerland
105 T11 **Altea** País Valenciano, E Spain
100 L10 **Alte Elde** ~ N Germany
101 M16 **Altenburg** Thüringen, E Germany
Altenburg see Bucureşti, Romania
Altenburg Baia de Criş, Romania
100 P12 **Alte Oder** ~ NE Germany
104 H10 **Alter do Chão** Portalegre, C Portugal
Āltesjávri see Altevatnet
92 I10 **Altevatnet** Lapp. Āltesjávri. ◎ N Norway
27 V12 **Altheimer** Arkansas, C USA
109 T9 **Althofen** Kärnten, S Austria
114 H7 **Altimir** Vratsa, NW Bulgaria
136 K11 **Altınkaya Barajı** ⊠ N Turkey
139 S3 **Altin Köprü** var. Altun Kupri. N Iraq
136 E13 **Altıntaş** Kütahya, W Turkey
57 K18 **Altiplano** physical region W South America
Altkanischa see Kanjiža
103 U7 **Altkirch** Haut-Rhin, NE France
Altlublau see Stará L'ubovňa
100 L12 **Altmark** cultural region N Germany
Altmoldowa see Moldova Veche
25 W8 **Alto** Texas, SW USA
104 H11 **Alto Alentejo** physical region S Portugal
59 I19 **Alto Araguaia** Mato Grosso, C Brazil
58 L12 **Alto Bonito** Pará, NE Brazil
83 O15 **Alto Molócuè** Zambézia, NE Mozambique
30 K15 **Alton** Illinois, N USA
27 W8 **Alton** Missouri, C USA
9 X17 **Altona** Manitoba, S Canada
18 E14 **Altoona** Pennsylvania, NE USA
30 J6 **Altoona** Wisconsin, N USA
62 N3 **Alto Paraguay** off. Departamento del Alto Paraguay. ◐ department N Paraguay
Alto Paraguay, Departamento del see Alto Paraguay
59 L17 **Alto Paraíso de Goiás** Goiás, S Brazil
62 P6 **Alto Paraná** off. Departamento del Alto Paraná. ◐ department E Paraguay
Alto Paraná see Paraná
Alto Paraná, Departamento del see Alto Paraná
59 L15 **Alto Parnaíba** Maranhão, E Brazil
56 H13 **Alto Purús, Río** ~ E Peru
Altorf see Altdorf
63 H19 **Alto Río Senguer** var. Alto Río Senguerr. Chubut, S Argentina
Alto Río Senguerr see Alto Río Senguer
41 Q13 **Altotonga** Veracruz-Llave, E Mexico
101 N23 **Altötting** Bayern, SE Germany
Altpasua see Stara Pazova
Altraga see Bayandzürh
105 P3 **Altsasu** Cast. Alsasua. Navarra, N Spain
Alt-Schwanenburg see Gulbene
Altsohl see Zvolen
108 I7 **Altstätten** Sankt Gallen, NE Switzerland
42 G1 **Altun Ha** ruins Belize, N Belize
Altun Kupri see Altin Köprü
158 D8 **Altun Shan** ▲ C China
158 L9 **Altun Shan** var. Altyn Tagh. ▲▲ NW China
35 P2 **Alturas** California, W USA
26 K12 **Altus** Oklahoma, C USA
26 K11 **Altus Lake** ⊠ Oklahoma, C USA
Altvater see Praděd
Altyn Tagh see Altun Shan
Alu see Shortland Island
al-'Ubaila see Al 'Ubaylah
139 O6 **Al 'Ubaydī** W Iraq
141 T9 **Al 'Ubaylah** var. al-'Ubaila. Ash Sharqīyah, E Saudi Arabia
141 T9 **Al 'Ubaylah** spring/well E Saudi Arabia
Al Ubayyiḑ see El Obeid
141 T7 **Al 'Udayd** var. Al Odaid. Abū Ẓaby, W United Arab Emirates
118 J8 **Alūksne** Ger. Marienburg. Alūksne, NE Latvia
140 K6 **Al 'Ulā** Al Madīnah, NW Saudi Arabia
173 N4 **Alula-Fartak Trench** var. Illaue Fartak Trench. undersea feature W Indian Ocean
138 I11 **Al 'Umarī** 'Ammān, E Jordan
31 S13 **Alum Creek Lake** ⊠ Ohio, N USA
63 H15 **Aluminé** Neuquén, C Argentina
95 O14 **Alunda** Uppsala, C Sweden
117 T14 **Alupka** Respublika Krym, S Ukraine
75 P8 **Al 'Uqaylah** N Libya
Al Uqşur see Luxor
Al Urdunn see Jordan
168 J9 **Alur Panal** bay Sumatera, W Indonesia
Alur Setar see Alor Setar
141 V10 **Al 'Urūq al Mu'tariḑah** salt lake SE Saudi Arabia
139 Q7 **Ālūs** C Iraq
117 T13 **Alushta** Respublika Krym, S Ukraine
75 N11 **Al 'Uwaynāt** var. Al Awaynāt. SW Libya
75 U12 **Al Awaynāt** SE Libya
139 T6 **Al 'Uẓaym** var. Adhaim. E Iraq
26 L8 **Alva** Oklahoma, C USA
104 H8 **Alva** ~ N Portugal
95 J18 **Alvängen** Västra Götaland, S Sweden
14 F14 **Alvanley** Ontario, S Canada
41 S14 **Alvarado** Veracruz-Llave, E Mexico
25 T7 **Alvarado** Texas, SW USA
58 D13 **Alvarães** Amazonas, NW Brazil
40 G6 **Álvaro Obregón, Presa** ⊠ W Mexico
94 H10 **Alvdal** Hedmark, S Norway
94 K12 **Älvdalen** Dalarna, C Sweden
61 E15 **Alvear** Corrientes, NE Argentina
104 F10 **Alverca do Ribatejo** Lisboa, C Portugal
95 L20 **Alvesta** Kronoberg, S Sweden
25 W12 **Alvin** Texas, SW USA
94 O13 **Älvkarleby** Uppsala, C Sweden
25 S5 **Alvord** Texas, SW USA
93 G18 **Älvros** Jämtland, C Sweden
92 J13 **Älvsbyn** Norrbotten, N Sweden
142 K12 **Al Wafrā'** SE Kuwait
140 J6 **Al Wajh** Tabūk, NW Saudi Arabia
143 N16 **Al Wakrah** var. Wakra. C Qatar
138 M8 **al Walaj, Sha'īb** dry watercourse W Iraq
152 I11 **Alwar** Rājasthān, N India
141 Q5 **Al Wari'ah** Ash Sharqīyah, N Saudi Arabia
155 G22 **Alwaye** Kerala, SW India
Alxa Zuoqi see Bayan Hot
Alxa Zuoqi see Bayan Hot
Alx Youqi see Ehen Hudag
Al Yaman see Yemen
138 G9 **Al Yarmūk** Irbid, N Jordan
Alyat/Alyaty-Pristan' see Älät
115 I14 **Alykí** var. Aliki. Thásos, N Greece
119 F14 **Alytus** Pol. Olita. Alytus, S Lithuania
119 F15 **Alytus** ◐ province S Lithuania
101 N23 **Alz** ~ SE Germany
33 Y11 **Alzada** Montana, NW USA
122 L12 **Alzamay** Irkutskaya Oblast', S Russian Federation
99 M25 **Alzette** ~ S Luxembourg
105 S10 **Alzira** var. Alcira; anc. Saetabicula, Suero. País Valenciano, E Spain
Al Zubair see Az Zubayr
181 O8 **Amadeus, Lake** seasonal lake Northern Territory, C Australia
81 E15 **Amadi** Western Equatoria, SW Sudan
9 R7 **Amadjuak Lake** ◎ Baffin Island, Nunavut, N Canada
95 J23 **Amager** island E Denmark
165 N14 **Amagi-san** ▲ Honshū, S Japan
171 S13 **Amahai** var. Masohi. Pulau Seram, E Indonesia
38 M16 **Amak Island** island Alaska, USA
164 B14 **Amakusa-nada** gulf Kyūshū, SW Japan
95 J16 **Åmål** Västra Götaland, S Sweden
54 E8 **Amalfi** Antioquia, N Colombia
107 L18 **Amalfi** Campania, S Italy
115 D19 **Amaliáda** var. Amaliás. Dytikí Ellás, S Greece
Amaliás see Amaliáda
154 F12 **Amalner** Mahārāshtra, C India
171 W14 **Amamapare** Papua, E Indonesia
59 H21 **Amambaí, Serra de** var. Cordillera de Amambay, Serra de Amambay. ▲ Brazil/Paraguay see also Amambay, Cordillera de
62 P4 **Amambay** off. Departamento del Amambay. ◐ department E Paraguay
62 P5 **Amambay, Cordillera de** var. Serra de Amambaí, Serra de Amambay. ▲ Brazil/Paraguay see also Amambaí, Serra de
Amambay, Departamento del see Amambay
Amambay, Serra de see Amambaí, Serra de/Amambay, Cordillera de
165 U16 **Amami-guntō** island group SW Japan
165 V15 **Amami-Ō-shima** island S Japan
186 A5 **Amanab** Sandaun, NW Papua New Guinea
106 J13 **Amandola** Marche, C Italy
107 N21 **Amantea** Calabria, SW Italy
191 W10 **Amanu** island Îles Tuamotu, C French Polynesia
58 J10 **Amapá** Amapá, NE Brazil
58 J11 **Amapá** off. Estado de Amapá; prev. Território de Amapá. ◐ state NE Brazil
Amapá, Estado de see Amapá
42 H8 **Amapala** Valle, S Honduras
Amapá, Território de see Amapá
Amara see Al 'Amārah
104 H6 **Amarante** Porto, N Portugal
166 M5 **Amarapura** Mandalay, C Myanmar (Burma)
Amardalay see Delgertsogt
Amardalay see Delgertsogt
104 I12 **Amareleja** Beja, S Portugal
35 V11 **Amargosa Range** ▲▲ California, W USA
25 N2 **Amarillo** Texas, SW USA
Amarinthos see Amárynthos
107 K15 **Amaro, Monte** ▲ C Italy
115 H18 **Amárynthos** var. Amarinthos. Évvoia, C Greece
Amasia see Amasya
136 K12 **Amasya** anc. Amasia. Amasya, N Turkey
136 K11 **Amasya** ◐ province N Turkey
42 F4 **Amatique, Bahía de** bay Gulf of Honduras, W Caribbean Sea
42 D6 **Amatitlán, Lago de** ◎ S Guatemala
107 J14 **Amatrice** Lazio, C Italy
190 C8 **Amatuku** atoll C Tuvalu
99 J20 **Amay** Liège, E Belgium
48 F7 **Amazon** Sp. Amazonas. ~ Brazil/Peru
59 C14 **Amazonas** off. Estado do Amazonas. ◐ state N Brazil
54 G15 **Amazonas** off. Comisaria del Amazonas. ◐ province SE Colombia
56 C10 **Amazonas** off. Departamento de Amazonas. ◐ department N Peru
54 M12 **Amazonas** off. Territorio Amazonas. ◐ federal territory S Venezuela
Amazonas see Amazon
Amazonas, Comisaria del see Amazonas
Amazonas, Departamento de see Amazonas
Amazonas, Estado do see Amazonas
Amazonas, Territorio see Amazonas
48 F7 **Amazon Basin** basin N South America
47 V5 **Amazon Fan** undersea feature W Atlantic Ocean
58 K11 **Amazon, Mouths of the** delta NE Brazil
187 R13 **Ambae** var. Aoba, Omba. island C Vanuatu
152 I9 **Ambāla** Haryāna, NW India
155 J26 **Ambalangoda** Southern Province, SW Sri Lanka
155 K26 **Ambalantota** Southern Province, S Sri Lanka
172 I6 **Ambalavao** Fianarantsoa, C Madagascar
54 E10 **Ambalema** Tolima, C Colombia
79 E17 **Ambam** Sud, S Cameroon
172 J2 **Ambanja** Antsiranana, N Madagascar
123 T6 **Ambarchik** Respublika Sakha (Yakutiya), NE Russian Federation
62 K9 **Ambargasta, Salinas de** salt lake C Argentina
124 J6 **Ambarnyy** Respublika Kareliya, NW Russian Federation
56 C7 **Ambato** Tungurahua, C Ecuador
172 I5 **Ambatolampy** Antananarivo, C Madagascar
172 H4 **Ambatomainty** Mahajanga, W Madagascar
172 J4 **Ambatondrazaka** Toamasina, C Madagascar
101 L20 **Amberg** var. Amberg in der Oberpfalz. Bayern, SE Germany
Amberg in der Oberpfalz see Amberg
42 H1 **Ambergris Cay** island NE Belize
103 S11 **Ambérieu-en-Bugey** Ain, E France
185 I18 **Amberley** Canterbury, South Island, New Zealand
103 P11 **Ambert** Puy-de-Dôme, C France
Ambianum see Amiens
76 J11 **Ambidédi** Kayes, SW Mali
154 M10 **Ambikāpur** Chhattīsgarh, C India
172 J2 **Ambilobe** Antsiranana, N Madagascar
39 O7 **Ambler** Alaska, USA
Amblève see Amel
Ambo see Hägere Hiywet
172 I8 **Amboasary** Toliara, S Madagascar
172 J4 **Ambodifotatra** var. Ambodifototra. Toamasina, E Madagascar
Amboenten see Ambunten
172 I5 **Ambohidratrimo** Antananarivo, C Madagascar
172 I6 **Ambohimahasoa** Fianarantsoa, SE Madagascar
172 K3 **Ambohitralanana** Antsiranana, NE Madagascar
Amboina see Ambon
102 M8 **Amboise** Indre-et-Loire, C France
171 S13 **Ambon** prev. Amboina, Amboyna. Pulau Ambon, E Indonesia
171 S13 **Ambon, Pulau** island E Indonesia
81 I20 **Amboseli, Lake** ◎ Kenya/Tanzania
172 I6 **Ambositra** Fianarantsoa, SE Madagascar
172 I8 **Ambovombe** Toliara, S Madagascar
35 W14 **Amboy** California, W USA
30 L11 **Amboy** Illinois, N USA
Amboyna see Ambon
Ambracia see Árta
Ambre, Cap d' see Bobaomby, Tanjona
18 B14 **Ambridge** Pennsylvania, NE USA
Ambrim see Ambrym
82 A11 **Ambriz** Bengo, NW Angola
Ambrizete see N'Zeto
187 R13 **Ambrym** var. Ambrim. island C Vanuatu
169 T16 **Ambunten** prev. Amboenten. Pulau Madura, E Indonesia
186 B6 **Ambunti** East Sepik, NW Papua New Guinea
155 I20 **Āmbūr** Tamil Nādu, SE India
38 E17 **Amchitka Island** island Aleutian Islands, Alaska, USA
38 F17 **Amchitka Pass** strait Aleutian Islands, Alaska, USA
141 R15 **'Amd** C Yemen
78 J10 **Am Dam** Ouaddaï, E Chad
171 U16 **Amdassa** Pulau Yamdena, E Indonesia
125 U1 **Amderma** Nenetskiy Avtonomnyy Okrug, NW Russian Federation
159 N14 **Amdo** Xizang Zizhiqu, W China
40 K13 **Ameca** Jalisco, SW Mexico
41 P14 **Amecameca** var. Amecameca de Juárez. México, C Mexico
Amecameca de Juárez see Amecameca
61 A20 **Ameghino** Buenos Aires, E Argentina
99 M21 **Amel** Fr. Amblève. Liège, E Belgium
98 K4 **Ameland** Fris. It Amelân. island Waddeneilanden, N Netherlands
Amelân, It see Ameland
107 H14 **Amelia** Umbria, C Italy
21 V6 **Amelia Court House** Virginia, NE USA
23 W8 **Amelia Island** island Florida, SE USA
18 L12 **Amenia** New York, NE USA
America see United States of America
65 M21 **America-Antarctica Ridge** undersea feature S Atlantic Ocean
America in Miniature see Maryland
60 L9 **Americana** São Paulo, S Brazil
33 Q15 **American Falls** Idaho, NW USA
33 Q15 **American Falls Reservoir** ⊠ Idaho, NW USA
36 L3 **American Fork** Utah, W USA
192 K16 **American Samoa** ◇ US unincorporated territory W Polynesia
23 S6 **Americus** Georgia, SE USA
98 K12 **Amerongen** Utrecht, C Netherlands
98 K11 **Amersfoort** Utrecht, C Netherlands
97 N21 **Amersham** SE England, UK
30 I5 **Amery** Wisconsin, N USA
195 W6 **Amery Ice Shelf** ice shelf Antarctica
29 V13 **Ames** Iowa, C USA
19 P10 **Amesbury** Massachusetts, NE USA
Amestratus see Mistretta
115 F18 **Amfíkleia** var. Amfíklia. Stereá Ellás, C Greece
Amfíklia see Amfíkleia
115 D17 **Amfilochía** var. Amfilokhía. Dytikí Ellás, C Greece
Amfilokhía see Amfilochía
114 H13 **Amfípoli** anc. Amphipolis. site of ancient city Kentrikí Makedonía, NE Greece
115 F18 **Ámfissa** Stereá Ellás, C Greece
123 Q10 **Amga** Respublika Sakha (Yakutiya), NE Russian Federation
123 Q11 **Amga** ~ NE Russian Federation
163 R7 **Amgalang** var. Xin Barag Zuoqi. Nei Mongol Zizhiqu, N China
123 V5 **Amguema** ~ NE Russian Federation
123 S12 **Amgun'** ~ SE Russian Federation
80 J12 **Amhara** ◐ region N Ethiopia
13 P15 **Amherst** Nova Scotia, SE Canada
18 M11 **Amherst** Massachusetts, NE USA
18 D10 **Amherst** New York, NE USA
24 M4 **Amherst** Texas, SW USA
21 U6 **Amherst** Virginia, NE USA
Amherst see Kyaikkami
14 C18 **Amherstburg** Ontario, S Canada
21 Q6 **Amherstdale** West Virginia, NE USA
14 K15 **Amherst Island** island Ontario, SE Canada
Amida see Diyarbakır
28 J6 **Amidon** North Dakota, N USA
103 O3 **Amiens** anc. Ambianum, Samarobriva. Somme, N France
139 P8 **'Āmij, Wādī** var. Wadi 'Amīq. dry watercourse W Iraq
136 L17 **Amik Ovası** ◎ S Turkey
76 E9 **Amilcar Cabral** ✈ Sal, NE Cape Verde
Amilḩayt, Wādī see Umm al Ḩayt, Wādī
Amindaion/Amindeo see Amýntaio
155 C21 **Amīndīvi Islands** island group Lakshadweep, India, N Indian Ocean
139 U6 **Amin Habib** E Iraq
83 E20 **Aminuis** Omaheke, E Namibia
'Amīq, Wadi see 'Āmij, Wādī
142 J7 **Amīrābād** Īlām, NW Iran
Amirante Bank see Amirante Ridge
173 N6 **Amirante Basin** undersea feature W Indian Ocean
173 N6 **Amirante Islands** var. Amirantes Group. island group C Seychelles
173 N7 **Amirante Ridge** var. Amirante Bank. undersea feature W Indian Ocean
Amirantes Group see Amirante Islands
173 N7 **Amirante Trench** undersea feature W Indian Ocean
9 U13 **Amisk Lake** ◎ Saskatchewan, C Canada
Amistad, Presa de la see Amistad Reservoir
25 O12 **Amistad Reservoir** var. Presa de la Amistad. ⊠ Mexico/USA
Amisus see Samsun
22 K8 **Amite** var. Amite City. Louisiana, S USA
Amite City see Amite
27 T12 **Amity** Arkansas, C USA
154 H11 **Amla** prev. Amulla. Madhya Pradesh, C India
38 I17 **Amlia Island** island Aleutian Islands, Alaska, USA
97 I18 **Amlwch** NW Wales, UK
Ammaia see Portalegre
138 H10 **'Ammān** var. Amman; anc. Philadelphia, Bibl. Rabbah Ammon, Rabbath Ammon. ● (Jordan) 'Ammān, NW Jordan
138 H10 **'Ammān** off. Muḩāfaẓat 'Ammān; prev. Al 'Āşimah. ◐ governorate NW Jordan
'Ammān, Muḩāfaẓat see 'Ammān
93 N14 **Ämmänsaari** Oulu, E Finland

◆ Country ● Country Capital ◇ Dependent Territory ○ Dependent Territory Capital ◐ Administrative Regions ✈ International Airport ▲ Mountain ▲▲ Mountain Range Volcano ~ River ◎ Lake ⊠ Reservoir

92 H13 **Ammarnäs** Västerbotten, N Sweden
197 O15 **Ammassalik** *var.* Angmagssalik. Tunu, S Greenland
101 K24 **Ammer** ≈ SE Germany
101 K24 **Ammersee** ◎ SE Germany
98 J13 **Ammerzoden** Gelderland, C Netherlands
Ammóchostos *see* Gazimağusa
Ammóchostos, Kólpos *see* Gazimağusa Körfezi
Amnok-kang *see* Yalu
Amoea *see* Portalegre
Amoentai *see* Amuntai
Amoerang *see* Amurang
143 O4 **Āmol** *var.* Amul. Māzandarān, N Iran
115 K21 **Amorgós** Amorgós, Kykládes, Greece, Aegean Sea
115 K22 **Amorgós** *island* Kykládes, Greece, Aegean Sea
23 N3 **Amory** Mississippi, S USA
12 I13 **Amos** Québec, SE Canada
95 G15 **Åmot** Buskerud, S Norway
95 E15 **Åmot** Telemark, S Norway
95 J15 **Åmotfors** Värmland, C Sweden
76 L10 **Amourj** Hodh ech Chargui, SE Mauritania
Amoy *see* Xiamen
172 H7 **Ampanihy** Toliara, SW Madagascar
155 L25 **Ampara** *var.* Amparai. Eastern Province, E Sri Lanka
172 J4 **Amparafaravola** Toamasina, E Madagascar
Amparai *see* Ampara
60 M9 **Amparo** São Paulo, S Brazil
172 J5 **Ampasimanolotra** Toamasina, E Madagascar
57 H17 **Ampato, Nevado** ▲ S Peru
101 L23 **Amper** ≈ SE Germany
64 M9 **Ampère Seamount** *undersea feature* E Atlantic Ocean
Amphipolis *see* Amfípoli
167 X10 **Amphitrite Group** *island group* N Paracel Islands
171 T16 **Amplawas** *var.* Emplawas. Pulau Babar, E Indonesia
105 U7 **Amposta** Cataluña, NE Spain
15 V7 **Amqui** Québec, SE Canada
141 O14 **'Amrān** W Yemen
Amraoti *see* Amrāvati
154 H12 **Amrāvati** *prev.* Amraoti. Mahārāshtra, C India
154 C11 **Amreli** Gujarāt, W India
108 H6 **Amriswil** Thurgau, NE Switzerland
138 H5 **'Amrīt** *ruins* Tarṭūs, W Syria
152 H7 **Amritsar** Punjab, N India
152 J10 **Amroha** Uttar Pradesh, N India
100 G7 **Amrum** *island* NW Germany
93 I15 **Åmsele** Västerbotten, N Sweden
98 I10 **Amstelveen** Noord-Holland, C Netherlands
98 I10 **Amsterdam** ● (Netherlands) Noord-Holland, C Netherlands
18 K10 **Amsterdam** New York, NE USA
173 Q11 **Amsterdam Fracture Zone** *tectonic feature* S Indian Ocean
173 R11 **Amsterdam Island** *island* NE French Southern and Antarctic Territories
109 U4 **Amstetten** Niederösterreich, N Austria
78 J11 **Am Timan** Salamat, SE Chad
146 L12 **Amu-Buxoro Kanali** *var.* Aral-Bukhorskiy Kanal. *canal* C Uzbekistan
139 O1 **'Āmūdah** *var.* Amude. Al Ḥasakah, N Syria
147 O15 **Amu Darya** *Rus.* Amudar'ya, *Taj.* Dar"yoi Amu, *Turkm.* Amyderya, *Uzb.* Amudaryo; *anc.* Oxus. ≈ C Asia
Amu-Dar'ya *see* Amyderya
Amudar'ya/Amudaryo/Amu, Dar"yoi *see* Amu Darya
Amude *see* 'Āmūdah
140 L3 **'Amūd, Jabal al** ▲ NW Saudi Arabia
38 J17 **Amukta Island** *island* Aleutian Islands, Alaska, USA
38 I17 **Amukta Pass** *strait* Aleutian Islands, Alaska, USA
Amul *see* Āmol
Amulla *see* Amla
Amundsen Basin *see* Fram Basin
195 X3 **Amundsen Bay** *bay* Antarctica
195 P10 **Amundsen Coast** *physical region* Antarctica
8 I6 **Amundsen Gulf** *gulf* Northwest Territories, N Canada
193 O14 **Amundsen Plain** *undersea feature* S Pacific Ocean
195 Q9 **Amundsen-Scott** *US research station* Antarctica
194 J11 **Amundsen Sea** *sea* S Pacific Ocean
94 M12 **Amungen** ◎ C Sweden
169 U13 **Amuntai** *prev.* Amoentai. Borneo, C Indonesia
129 W6 **Amur** *Chin.* Heilong Jiang. ≈ China/Russian Federation
171 Q11 **Amurang** *prev.* Amoerang. Sulawesi, C Indonesia
105 O3 **Amurrio** País Vasco, N Spain
123 S13 **Amursk** Khabarovskiy Kray, SE Russian Federation
123 Q12 **Amurskaya Oblast'** ◈ *province* SE Russian Federation
80 G7 **'Amur, Wadi** ≈ NE Sudan
115 C17 **Amvrakikós Kólpos** *gulf* W Greece
Amvrosiyevka *see* Amvrosiyivka
117 X8 **Amvrosiyivka** *Rus.* Amvrosiyevka. Donets'ka Oblast', SE Ukraine
146 M14 **Amyderya** *Rus.* Amu-Dar'ya. Lebap Welaýaty, NE Turkmenistan
Amyderya *see* Amu Darya
114 E13 **Amýntaio** *var.* Amindeo; *prev.* Amíndaion. Dytikí Makedonía, N Greece
14 B6 **Amyot** Ontario, S Canada
191 U10 **Anaa** *atoll* Îles Tuamotu, C French Polynesia
Anabanoea *see* Anabanua
171 N14 **Anabanua** *prev.* Anabanoea. Sulawesi, C Indonesia
189 R8 **Anabar** NE Nauru
123 N8 **Anabar** ≈ NE Russian Federation
An Abhainn Mhór *see* Blackwater
55 O6 **Anaco** Anzoátegui, NE Venezuela
33 Q10 **Anaconda** Montana, NW USA
32 H7 **Anacortes** Washington, NW USA
26 M11 **Anadarko** Oklahoma, C USA
114 N12 **Ana Dere** ≈ NW Turkey
104 G8 **Anadia** Aveiro, N Portugal
Anadolu Dağlarī *see* Doğu Karadeniz Dağları
123 V6 **Anadyr'** Chukotskiy Avtonomnyy Okrug, NE Russian Federation
123 V6 **Anadyr'** ≈ NE Russian Federation
Anadyr, Gulf of *see* Anadyrskiy Zaliv
129 X4 **Anadyrskiy Khrebet** *var.* Chukot Range. ▲▲ NE Russian Federation
123 W6 **Anadyrskiy Zaliv** *Eng.* Gulf of Anadyr. *gulf* NE Russian Federation
115 K22 **Anáfi** *anc.* Anaphe. *island* Kykládes, Greece, Aegean Sea
107 J15 **Anagni** Lazio, C Italy
'Ānah *see* 'Annah
35 T15 **Anaheim** California, W USA
10 L15 **Anahim Lake** British Columbia, SW Canada
38 B8 **Anahola** Kaua'i, Hawai'i, USA, C Pacific Ocean
41 O7 **Anáhuac** Nuevo León, NE Mexico
25 X11 **Anahuac** Texas, SW USA
155 G22 **Anai Mudi** ▲ S India
Anaiza *see* 'Unayzah
155 M15 **Anakāpalle** Andhra Pradesh, E India
191 W15 **Anakena, Playa de** *beach* Easter Island, Chile, E Pacific Ocean
39 Q7 **Anaktuvuk Pass** Alaska, USA
39 Q6 **Anaktuvuk River** ≈ Alaska, USA
172 J3 **Analalava** Mahajanga, NW Madagascar
44 F6 **Ana Maria, Golfo de** *gulf* N Caribbean Sea
Anambas Islands *see* Anambas, Kepulauan
169 N8 **Anambas, Kepulauan** *var.* Anambas Islands. *island group* W Indonesia
77 U17 **Anambra** ◈ *state* SE Nigeria
29 N4 **Anamoose** North Dakota, N USA
29 Y13 **Anamosa** Iowa, C USA
136 H17 **Anamur** Mersin, S Turkey
136 H17 **Anamur Burnu** *headland* S Turkey
154 O12 **Ānandadur** Orissa, E India
155 H18 **Anantapur** Andhra Pradesh, S India
152 H5 **Anantnāg** *var.* Islamabad. Jammu and Kashmir, NW India
Ananyev *see* Anan'yiv
117 O9 **Anan'yiv** *Rus.* Ananyev. Odes'ka Oblast', SW Ukraine
126 J14 **Anapa** Krasnodarskiy Kray, SW Russian Federation
Anaphe *see* Anáfi
59 K18 **Anápolis** Goiás, C Brazil
143 R10 **Anār** Kermān, C Iran
Anár *see* Inari
143 P7 **Anārak** Eşfahān, C Iran
Anar Dara *see* Anār Darreh
148 J7 **Anār Darreh** *var.* Anar Dara. Farāh, W Afghanistan
Anárjohka *see* Inarijoki
23 X9 **Anastasia Island** *island* Florida, SE USA
188 K7 **Anatahan** *island* C Northern Mariana Islands
128 M6 **Anatolia** *plateau* C Turkey
86 F14 **Anatolian Plate** *tectonic feature* Asia/Europe
114 H13 **Anatolikí Makedonía kai Thráki** *Eng.* Macedonia East and Thrace. ◈ *region* NE Greece
Anatom *see* Aneityum
62 L8 **Añatuya** Santiago del Estero, N Argentina
An Baile Meánach *see* Ballymena
An Bhearú *see* Barrow
An Bhóinn *see* Boyne
An Blascaod Mór *see* Great Blasket Island
An Cabhán *see* Cavan
An Caisleán Nua *see* Newcastle
An Caisleán Riabhach *see* Castlerea, Ireland
An Caisleán Riabhach *see* Castlereagh
56 C13 **Ancash** *off.* Departamento de Ancash. ◈ *department* W Peru
Ancash, Departamento de *see* Ancash
An Cathair *see* Caher
102 J8 **Ancenis** Loire-Atlantique, NW France
An Chanáil Ríoga *see* Royal Canal
An Cheacha *see* Caha Mountains
39 R11 **Anchorage** Alaska, USA
39 R12 **Anchorage** ✈ Alaska, USA
39 Q13 **Anchor Point** Alaska, USA
An Chorr Chríochach *see* Cookstown
65 M24 **Anchorstack Point** *headland* W Tristan da Cunha
An Clár *see* Clare
An Clochán *see* Clifden
An Clochán Liath *see* Dunglow
23 U12 **Anclote Keys** *island group* Florida, SE USA
An Cóbh *see* Cobh
57 J17 **Ancohuma, Nevado de** ▲ W Bolivia
An Comar *see* Comber
57 D14 **Ancón** Lima, W Peru
106 J12 **Ancona** Marche, C Italy
Ancuabe *see* Ancuabi
82 Q13 **Ancuabi** *var.* Ancuabe. Cabo Delgado, NE Mozambique
63 F17 **Ancud** *prev.* San Carlos de Ancud. Los Lagos, S Chile
63 G17 **Ancud, Golfo de** *gulf* S Chile
Ancyra *see* Ankara
163 V8 **Anda** Heilongjiang, NE China
57 G16 **Andahuaylas** Apurímac, S Peru
An Daingean *see* Dingle
153 R15 **Andāl** West Bengal, NE India
94 E9 **Åndalsnes** Møre og Romsdal, S Norway
104 K13 **Andalucía** *Eng.* Andalusia. ◈ *autonomous community* S Spain
23 P7 **Andalusia** Alabama, S USA
Andalusia *see* Andalucía
151 Q21 **Andaman and Nicobar Islands** *var.* Andamans and Nicobars. ◈ *union territory* India, NE Indian Ocean
173 T4 **Andaman Basin** *undersea feature* NE Indian Ocean
151 P19 **Andaman Islands** *island group* India, NE Indian Ocean
Andamans and Nicobars *see* Andaman and Nicobar Islands
173 T4 **Andaman Sea** *sea* NE Indian Ocean
57 K19 **Andamarca** Oruro, C Bolivia
182 H5 **Andamooka** South Australia
141 Y9 **'Andām, Wādī** *seasonal river* NE Oman
172 J3 **Andapa** Antsirañana, NE Madagascar
149 R4 **Andarāb** *var.* Banow. Baghlān, NE Afghanistan
Andarbag *see* Andarbogh
147 S13 **Andarbogh** *Rus.* Andarbag, Anderbak. S Tajikistan
109 Z5 **Andau** Burgenland, E Austria
108 I10 **Andeer** Graubünden, S Switzerland
92 H9 **Andenes** Nordland, C Norway
99 J20 **Andenne** Namur, SE Belgium
77 S11 **Andéramboukane** Gao, E Mali
Anderbak *see* Andarbogh
99 G18 **Anderlecht** Brussels, C Belgium
99 G21 **Anderlues** Hainaut, S Belgium
108 G9 **Andermatt** Uri, C Switzerland
101 E17 **Andernach** *anc.* Antunnacum. Rheinland-Pfalz, SW Germany
188 D15 **Andersen Air Force Base** *air base* NE Guam
39 R9 **Anderson** Alaska, USA
35 N4 **Anderson** California, W USA
31 P13 **Anderson** Indiana, N USA
27 R8 **Anderson** Missouri, C USA
21 P11 **Anderson** South Carolina, SE USA
25 V10 **Anderson** Texas, SW USA
95 K20 **Anderstorp** Jönköping, S Sweden
54 D9 **Andes** Antioquia, W Colombia
47 P7 **Andes** ▲▲ W South America
29 P12 **Andes, Lake** ◎ South Dakota, N USA
92 H9 **Andfjorden** *fjord* E Norwegian Sea
155 H16 **Andhra Pradesh** ◈ *state* E India
98 J8 **Andijk** Noord-Holland, NW Netherlands
147 S10 **Andijon** *Rus.* Andizhan. Andijon Viloyati, E Uzbekistan
147 S10 **Andijon Viloyati** *Rus.* Andizhanskaya Oblast'. ◈ *province* E Uzbekistan
Andikíthira *see* Antikýthira
172 J4 **Andilamena** Toamasina, C Madagascar
142 L8 **Andīmeshk** *var.* Andimishk; *prev.* Salehābād. Khūzestān, SW Iran
Andimishk *see* Andīmeshk
Andipáros *see* Antíparos
Andipaxi *see* Antípaxoi
Andípsara *see* Antípsara
136 L16 **Andīrīn** Kahramanmaraş, S Turkey
158 J8 **Andirlangar** Xinjiang Uygur Zizhiqu, NW China
Andírrion *see* Antírrio
Ándissa *see* Ántissa
Andizhan *see* Andijon
Andizhanskaya Oblast' *see* Andijon Viloyati
149 N2 **Andkhvoy** Fāryāb, N Afghanistan
105 Q2 **Andoain** País Vasco, N Spain
163 Y15 **Andong** *Jap.* Antō. E South Korea
109 R4 **Andorf** Oberösterreich, N Austria
105 S7 **Andorra** Aragón, NE Spain
105 V4 **Andorra** *off.* Principality of Andorra, *Cat.* Valls d'Andorra, *Fr.* Vallée d'Andorre. ◆ *monarchy* SW Europe
Andorra *see* Andorra la Vella
105 V4 **Andorra la Vella** *var.* Andorra, *Fr.* Andorre la Vielle, *Sp.* Andorra la Vieja. ● (Andorra) C Andorra
Andorra la Vieja *see* Andorra la Vella
Andorra, Principality of *see* Andorra
Andorra, Valls d'/Andorra, Vallée d' *see* Andorra
Andorre la Vielle *see* Andorra la Vella
97 M22 **Andover** S England, UK
27 N6 **Andover** Kansas, C USA
92 G10 **Andøya** *island* C Norway
60 I8 **Andradina** São Paulo, S Brazil
105 X9 **Andratx** Mallorca, Spain, W Mediterranean Sea
39 N10 **Andreafsky River** ≈ Alaska, USA
38 H17 **Andreanof Islands** *island group* Aleutian Islands, Alaska, USA
124 H16 **Andreapol'** Tverskaya Oblast', W Russian Federation
Andreas, Cape *see* Zafer Burnu
Andreevka *see* Kabanbay
21 N10 **Andrews** North Carolina, SE USA
21 T13 **Andrews** South Carolina, SE USA
24 M7 **Andrews** Texas, SW USA
173 N5 **Andrew Tablemount** *var.* Gora Andryu. *undersea feature* W Indian Ocean
Andreyevka *see* Kabanbay
107 N17 **Andria** Puglia, SE Italy
113 K16 **Andrijevica** E Montenegro
115 E20 **Andrítsaina** Pelopónnisos, S Greece
An Droichead Nua *see* Newbridge
Andropov *see* Rybinsk
115 J19 **Ándros** Ándros, Kykládes, Greece, Aegean Sea
115 J20 **Ándros** *island* Kykládes, Greece, Aegean Sea
19 O7 **Androscoggin River** ≈ Maine/New Hampshire, NE USA
44 F3 **Andros Island** *island* NW Bahamas
127 R7 **Androsovka** Samarskaya Oblast', W Russian Federation
44 G3 **Andros Town** Andros Island, NW Bahamas
155 D21 **Āndrott Island** *island* Lakshadweep, India, N Indian Ocean
117 N5 **Andrushivka** Zhytomyrs'ka Oblast', N Ukraine
111 K17 **Andrychów** Małopolskie, S Poland
Andryu, Gora *see* Andrew Tablemount
92 I10 **Andselv** Troms, N Norway
79 O17 **Andudu** Orientale, NE Dem. Rep. Congo
105 N13 **Andújar** *anc.* Illiturgis. Andalucía, SW Spain
82 C12 **Andulo** Bié, W Angola
103 Q14 **Anduze** Gard, S France
An Earagail *see* Errigal Mountain
95 L19 **Aneby** Jönköping, S Sweden
Anécho *see* Aného
77 Q9 **Anéfis** Kidal, NE Mali
45 U8 **Anegada** *island* NE British Virgin Islands
61 B25 **Anegada, Bahía** *bay* E Argentina
45 U9 **Anegada Passage** *passage* Anguilla/British Virgin Islands
77 R17 **Aného** *var.* Anécho; *prev.* Petit-Popo. S Togo
197 D17 **Aneityum** *var.* Anatom; *prev.* Kéamu. *island* S Vanuatu
117 N10 **Anenii Noi** *Rus.* Novyye Aneny. C Moldova
186 F7 **Anepmete** New Britain, E Papua New Guinea
105 U4 **Aneto** ▲ NE Spain
146 F13 **Änew** *Rus.* Annau. Ahal Welaýaty, C Turkmenistan
Änewetak *see* Enewetak Atoll
77 Y8 **Aney** Agadez, NE Niger
An Fheoir *see* Nore
122 L12 **Angara** ≈ C Russian Federation
122 M13 **Angarsk** Irkutskaya Oblast', S Russian Federation
Angaur *see* Ngeaur
93 G17 **Ånge** Västernorrland, C Sweden
Angel *see* Úhlava
40 D4 **Ángel de la Guarda, Isla** *island* NW Mexico
171 O3 **Angeles** *off.* Angeles City. Luzon, N Philippines
Angeles City *see* Angeles
Angel Falls *see* Ángel, Salto
95 J22 **Ängelholm** Skåne, S Sweden
61 A17 **Angélica** Santa Fe, C Argentina
25 W8 **Angelina River** ≈ Texas, SW USA
55 Q9 **Ángel, Salto** *Eng.* Angel Falls. *waterfall* E Venezuela
95 M15 **Ängelsberg** Västmanland, C Sweden
35 P8 **Angels Camp** California, W USA
109 W7 **Anger** Steiermark, SE Austria
Angerapp *see* Ozersk
Angerburg *see* Węgorzewo
93 H15 **Ångermanälven** ≈ N Sweden
100 P11 **Angermünde** Brandenburg, NE Germany
102 K7 **Angers** *anc.* Juliomagus. Maine-et-Loire, NW France
15 W7 **Angers** ≈ Québec, SE Canada
93 J16 **Ängesön** *island* N Sweden
Angistro *see* Ágkistro
114 H13 **Angítis** ≈ NE Greece
167 R13 **Ângk Tasaôm** *prev.* Angtassom. Takêv, S Cambodia
185 C25 **Anglem, Mount** ▲ Stewart Island, Southland, SW New Zealand
97 I18 **Anglesey** *cultural region* NW Wales, UK
97 I18 **Anglesey** *island* NW Wales, UK
102 I15 **Anglet** Pyrénées-Atlantiques, SW France
25 W12 **Angleton** Texas, SW USA
Anglia *see* England
14 H9 **Angliers** Québec, SE Canada
Anglo-Egyptian Sudan *see* Sudan
Angmagssalik *see* Ammassalik
167 Q7 **Ang Nam Ngum** ◎ C Laos
79 N16 **Ango** Orientale, N Dem. Rep. Congo
83 Q15 **Angoche** Nampula, E Mozambique
63 G14 **Angol** Araucanía, C Chile
31 Q11 **Angola** Indiana, N USA
82 A9 **Angola** *off.* Republic of Angola; *prev.* People's Republic of Angola, Portuguese West Africa. ◆ *republic* SW Africa
65 P15 **Angola Basin** *undersea feature* E Atlantic Ocean
Angola, People's Republic of *see* Angola
Angola, Republic of *see* Angola
39 X13 **Angoon** Admiralty Island, Alaska, USA
147 O14 **Angor** Surkhondaryo Viloyati, S Uzbekistan
Angora *see* Ankara
186 C6 **Angoram** East Sepik, NW Papua New Guinea
40 H8 **Angostura** Sinaloa, C Mexico
Angostura *see* Ciudad Bolívar
41 U17 **Angostura, Presa de la** ⊠ SE Mexico
28 J11 **Angostura Reservoir** ⊠ South Dakota, N USA
102 L11 **Angoulême** *anc.* Iculisma. Charente, W France
102 K11 **Angoumois** *cultural region* W France
64 O2 **Angra do Heroísmo** Terceira, Azores, Portugal, NE Atlantic Ocean
60 O10 **Angra dos Reis** Rio de Janeiro, SE Brazil
Angra Pequena *see* Lüderitz
147 Q10 **Angren** Toshkent Viloyati, E Uzbekistan
Angtassom *see* Ângk Tasaôm
167 O10 **Ang Thong** *var.* Angthong. Ang Thong, C Thailand
Angthong *see* Ang Thong
79 M16 **Angu** Orientale, N Dem. Rep. Congo
105 S5 **Angües** Aragón, NE Spain
45 U9 **Anguilla** ◇ *UK dependent territory* E West Indies
45 V9 **Anguilla** *island* E West Indies
44 F4 **Anguilla Cays** *islets* SW Bahamas
Angul *see* Anugul
161 N1 **Anguli Nur** ◎ E China
79 O18 **Angumu** Orientale, E Dem. Rep. Congo
14 G14 **Angus** Ontario, S Canada
96 J10 **Angus** *cultural region* E Scotland, UK
59 K19 **Anhangüera** Goiás, S Brazil
99 I21 **Anhée** Namur, S Belgium
95 I21 **Anholt** *island* C Denmark
160 M11 **Anhua** *var.* Dongping. Hunan, S China
161 P8 **Anhui** *var.* Anhui Sheng, Anhwei, Wan. ◈ *province* E China
AnhuiSheng/Anhwei Wan *see* Anhui
39 O11 **Aniak** Alaska, USA
39 O12 **Aniak River** ≈ Alaska, USA
An Iarmhí *see* Westmeath
189 R8 **Anibare** E Nauru
189 R8 **Anibare Bay** *bay* E Nauru, W Pacific Ocean
Anicium *see* le Puy
115 K22 **Ánidro** *island* Kykládes, Greece, Aegean Sea
77 R15 **Anié** C Togo
77 Q15 **Anié** ≈ C Togo
102 J16 **Anie, Pic d'** ▲ SW France
127 Y7 **Anikhovka** Orenburgskaya Oblast', W Russian Federation
14 G9 **Anima Nipissing Lake** ◎ Ontario, S Canada
37 O16 **Animas** New Mexico, SW USA
37 P16 **Animas Peak** ▲ New Mexico, SW USA
37 P16 **Animas Valley** *valley* New Mexico, SW USA
116 F13 **Anina** *Ger.* Steierdorf, *Hung.* Stájerlakanina; *prev.* Ştaierdorf-Anina, Steierdorf-Anina, Steyerlak-Anina. Caraş-Severin, SW Romania
29 U14 **Anita** Iowa, C USA
123 U14 **Aniva, Mys** *cape* Ostrov Sakhalin, SE Russian Federation
187 S15 **Aniwa** *island* S Vanuatu
93 M19 **Anjalankoski** Etelä-Suomi, S Finland
'Anjar *see* Aanjar
Anjiangying *see* Luanping
14 B8 **Anjigami Lake** ◎ Ontario, S Canada
164 K14 **Anjō** *var.* Anzyô. Aichi, Honshū, SW Japan
102 J8 **Anjou** *cultural region* NW France
172 I13 **Anjouan** *var.* Nzwani, Johanna Island. *island* SE Comoros
172 J4 **Anjozorobe** Antananarivo, C Madagascar
163 W13 **Anju** W North Korea
98 M5 **Anjum** *Fris.* Eanjum. Friesland, N Netherlands
172 G6 **Ankaboa, Tanjona** *headland* W Madagascar
160 L7 **Ankang** *prev.* Xing'an. Shaanxi, C China
136 I12 **Ankara** *prev.* Angora; *anc.* Ancyra. ● (Turkey) Ankara, C Turkey
136 H12 **Ankara** ◈ *province* C Turkey
95 N19 **Ankarsrum** Kalmar, S Sweden
172 H6 **Ankazoabo** Toliara, SW Madagascar
172 I4 **Ankazobe** Antananarivo, C Madagascar
29 V14 **Ankeny** Iowa, C USA
167 V11 **An Khê** Gia Lai, C Vietnam
100 O9 **Anklam** Mecklenburg-Vorpommern, NE Germany
80 K13 **Ānkober** Amhara, N Ethiopia
77 O17 **Ankobra** ≈ S Ghana
79 N22 **Ankoro** Katanga, SE Dem. Rep. Congo
99 L24 **Anlier, Forêt d'** *forest* SE Belgium
160 I13 **Anlong** Guizhou, S China
An Longfort *see* Longford
167 R11 **Ânlong Vêng** Siĕmréab, NW Cambodia
An Lorgain *see* Lurgan
161 N8 **Anlu** Hubei, C China
An Mhí *see* Meath
An Mhuir Cheilteach *see* Celtic Sea
An Muileann gCearr *see* Mullingar
93 F16 **Ånn** Jämtland, C Sweden
126 M8 **Anna** Voronezhskaya Oblast', W Russian Federation
30 L17 **Anna** Illinois, N USA
25 U5 **Anna** Texas, SW USA
74 L5 **Annaba** *prev.* Bône. NE Algeria
An Nabatīyah at Taḥtā *see* Nabatîyé
101 N17 **Annaberg-Buchholz** Sachsen, E Germany
109 T9 **Annabichl** ✈ (Klagenfurt) Kärnten, S Austria
140 M5 **An Nafūd** *desert* NW Saudi Arabia
139 P6 **'Annah** *var.* 'Ānah. NW Iraq
139 P6 **An Nāḥiyah** W Iraq
139 T10 **An Najaf** *var.* Najaf. S Iraq
21 V5 **Anna, Lake** ⊠ Virginia, NE USA
97 F16 **Annalee** ≈ N Ireland
167 S9 **Annamitique, Chaîne** ▲▲ C Laos
97 J14 **Annan** S Scotland, UK
29 U8 **Annandale** Minnesota, N USA
21 W4 **Annandale** Virginia, NE USA
189 Q7 **Anna Point** *headland* N Nauru
21 X3 **Annapolis** *state capital* Maryland, NE USA
188 A10 **Anna, Pulo** *island* S Palau
153 O10 **Annapurna** ▲ C Nepal
An Nāqūrah *see* En Nâqoûra
31 R10 **Ann Arbor** Michigan, N USA
An Nás *see* Naas
139 W12 **An Nāṣirīyah** *var.* Nasiriya. SE Iraq
139 W11 **An Naṣr** E Iraq
Annau *see* Änew
121 O13 **An Nawfalīyah** *var.* Al Nūwfalīyah. N Libya
19 P10 **Ann, Cape** *headland* Massachusetts, NE USA
180 I10 **Annean, Lake** ◎ Western Australia
Anneciacum *see* Annecy
103 T11 **Annecy** *anc.* Anneciacum. Haute-Savoie, E France
103 T11 **Annecy, Lac d'** ◎ E France
103 T10 **Annemasse** Haute-Savoie, E France
39 Z14 **Annette Island** *island* Alexander Archipelago, Alaska, USA
An Nhon *see* Binh Đinh
An Nīl al Abyaḍ *see* White Nile
An Nīl al Azraq *see* Blue Nile
23 Q3 **Anniston** Alabama, S USA
79 A19 **Annobón** *island* W Equatorial Guinea
103 R12 **Annonay** Ardèche, E France
44 K12 **Annotto Bay** C Jamaica
141 R5 **An Nu'ayrīyah** *var.* Narīya. Ash Sharqīyah, NE Saudi Arabia
182 M9 **Annuello** Victoria, SE Australia
139 Q10 **An Nukhayb** S Iraq
139 U9 **An Nu'mānīyah** E Iraq
Áno Arkhánai *see* Archánes
115 J25 **Anógeia** *cont.* Anogia, *var.* Anóyia. Kríti, Greece, E Mediterranean Sea
Anogia *see* Anógeia
29 V8 **Anoka** Minnesota, N USA
An Ómaigh *see* Omagh
172 I1 **Anorontany, Tanjona** *headland* N Madagascar
172 J5 **Anosibe An'Ala** Toamasina, E Madagascar
Anóyia *see* Anógeia
An Pointe *see* Warrenpoint
161 P9 **Anqing** Anhui, E China
161 Q5 **Anqiu** Shandong, E China
An Ráth *see* Ráthluirc
An Ribhéar *see* Kenmare River
An Ros *see* Rush
99 K19 **Ans** Liège, E Belgium
Anşāb *see* Nişāb
171 W12 **Ansas** Papua, E Indonesia
101 J20 **Ansbach** Bayern, SE Germany
An Sciobairín *see* Skibbereen
An Scoil *see* Skull
An Seancheann *see* Old Head of Kinsale
45 Y5 **Anse-Bertrand** Grande Terre, N Guadeloupe
172 H17 **Anse Boileau** Mahé, NE Seychelles
45 S11 **Anse La Raye** NW Saint Lucia
54 D9 **Anserma** Caldas, W Colombia
109 T4 **Ansfelden** Oberösterreich, N Austria
163 U12 **Anshan** Liaoning, NE China
160 J12 **Anshun** Guizhou, S China
61 F17 **Ansina** Tacuarembó, C Uruguay
29 O15 **Ansley** Nebraska, C USA
25 P6 **Anson** Texas, SW USA
77 Q10 **Ansongo** Gao, E Mali
An Srath Bán *see* Strabane
21 R5 **Ansted** West Virginia, NE USA
171 Y13 **Ansudu** Papua, E Indonesia
57 G15 **Anta** Cusco, S Peru
57 G16 **Antabamba** Apurímac, C Peru
Antafalva *see* Kovačica
136 L17 **Antakya** *anc.* Antioch, Antiochia. Hatay, S Turkey
172 K3 **Antalaha** Antsirañana, NE Madagascar
136 F17 **Antalya** *prev.* Adalia; *anc.* Attaleia, *Bibl.* Attalia. Antalya, SW Turkey
136 F17 **Antalya** ◈ *province* SW Turkey
136 F16 **Antalya** ✈ Antalya, SW Turkey
121 U10 **Antalya Basin** *undersea feature* E Mediterranean Sea
Antalya, Gulf of *see* Antalya Körfezi
136 F16 **Antalya Körfezi** *var.* Gulf of Adalia, *Eng.* Gulf of Antalya. *gulf* SW Turkey
172 J5 **Antanambao Manampotsy** Toamasina, E Madagascar
172 I5 **Antananarivo** *prev.* Tananarive. ● (Madagascar) Antananarivo, C Madagascar
172 I4 **Antananarivo** ◈ *province* C Madagascar
172 J5 **Antananarivo** ✈ Antananarivo, C Madagascar

◆ Country
● Country Capital
◇ Dependent Territory
○ Dependent Territory Capital
◈ Administrative Regions
✈ International Airport
▲ Mountain
▲▲ Mountain Range
Volcano
≈ River
◎ Lake
⊠ Reservoir

An tAonach *see* Nenagh
194-195 **Antarctica** *continent*
194 *I5* **Antarctic Peninsula** *peninsula* Antarctica
61 *J15* **Antas, Rio das** ≈ S Brazil
189 *U16* **Ant Atoll** *atoll* Caroline Islands, E Micronesia
An Teampall Mór *see* Templemore
Antep *see* Gaziantep
104 *M15* **Antequera** *anc.* Anticaria, Antiquaria. Andalucía, S Spain
Antequera *see* Oaxaca
37 *S5* **Antero Reservoir** ⊠ Colorado, C USA
26 *M7* **Anthony** Kansas, C USA
37 *R16* **Anthony** New Mexico, SW USA
182 *D5* **Anthony, Lake** *salt lake* South Australia
74 *E8* **Anti-Atlas** ▲▲ SW Morocco
103 *U15* **Antibes** *anc.* Antipolis. Alpes-Maritimes, SE France
103 *U15* **Antibes, Cap d'** *headland* SE France
Anticaria *see* Antequera
13 *Q11* **Anticosti, Île d'** *Eng.* Anticosti Island. *island* Québec, E Canada
Anticosti Island *see* Anticosti, Île d'
102 *K3* **Antifer, Cap d'** *headland* N France
30 *L6* **Antigo** Wisconsin, N USA
13 *Q15* **Antigonish** Nova Scotia, SE Canada
64 *P11* **Antigua** Fuerteventura, Islas Canarias, NE Atlantic Ocean
45 *X10* **Antigua** *island* S Antigua and Barbuda, Leeward Islands
Antigua *see* Antigua Guatemala
45 *W9* **Antigua and Barbuda** ◆ *island state* E West Indies
42 *C6* **Antigua Guatemala** *var.* Antigua. Sacatepéquez, SW Guatemala
41 *P11* **Antiguo Morelos** *var.* Antiguo-Morelos. Tamaulipas, C Mexico
115 *F19* **Antíkyras, Kólpos** *gulf* C Greece
115 *G24* **Antikýthira** *var.* Andikíthira. *island* S Greece
138 *I7* **Anti-Lebanon** *var.* Jebel esh Sharqi, *Ar.* Al Jabal ash Sharqi, *Fr.* Anti-Liban. ▲▲ Lebanon/Syria
Anti-Liban *see* Anti-Lebanon
115 *M22* **Antimácheia** Kos, Dodekánisa, Greece
115 *I22* **Antímilos** *island* Kykládes, Greece, Aegean Sea
36 *L6* **Antimony** Utah, W USA
An tInbhear Mór *see* Arklow
30 *M10* **Antioch** Illinois, N USA
Antioch *see* Antakya
102 *I10* **Antioche, Pertuis d'** *inlet* W France
Antiochia *see* Antakya
54 *D8* **Antioquia** Antioquia, C Colombia
54 *E8* **Antioquia** *off.* Departamento de Antioquia. ◐ *province* C Colombia
Antioquia, Departamento de *see* Antioquia
115 *J21* **Antíparos** *var.* Andipáros. *island* Kykládes, Greece, Aegean Sea
115 *B17* **Antípaxoi** *var.* Andipaxi. *island* Iónioi Nísoi, Greece, C Mediterranean Sea
122 *J8* **Antipayuta** Yamalo-Nenetskiy Avtonomnyy Okrug, N Russian Federation
192 *L12* **Antipodes Islands** *island group* S New Zealand
Antipolis *see* Antibes
115 *J18* **Antípsara** *var.* Andípsara. *island* E Greece
Antiquaria *see* Antequera
15 *N10* **Antique, Lac** ◎ Québec, SE Canada
115 *E18* **Antírrio** *var.* Andírrion. Dytikí Ellás, C Greece
115 *K16* **Ántissa** *var.* Ándissa. Lésvos, E Greece
An tIúr *see* Newry
Antivari *see* Bar
56 *C6* **Antizana** ▲ N Ecuador
27 *Q13* **Antlers** Oklahoma, C USA
93 *J14* **Antnäs** Norrbotten, N Sweden
Antö *see* Andong
62 *G5* **Antofagasta** Antofagasta, N Chile
62 *G6* **Antofagasta** *off.* Región de Antofagasta. ◐ *region* N Chile
Antofagasta, Región de *see* Antofagasta
62 *I7* **Antofalla, Salar de** *salt lake* NW Argentina
99 *D20* **Antoing** Hainaut, SW Belgium
43 *S16* **Antón** Coclé, C Panama
24 *M5* **Anton** Texas, SW USA
37 *T11* **Anton Chico** New Mexico, SW USA
60 *K12* **Antonina** Paraná, S Brazil
103 *O5* **Antony** Hauts-de-Seine, N France
Antratsit *see* Antratsyt
117 *Y8* **Antratsyt** *Rus.* Antratsit. Luhans'ka Oblast', E Ukraine
97 *G15* **Antrim** *Ir.* Aontroim. NE Northern Ireland, UK
97 *G14* **Antrim** *Ir.* Aontroim. *cultural region* NE Northern Ireland, UK
97 *G14* **Antrim Mountains** ▲▲ NE Northern Ireland, UK
172 *H5* **Antsalova** Mahajanga, W Madagascar
Antserana *see* Antsirañana
An tSionainn *see* Shannon
172 *J2* **Antsirañana** *var.* Antserana; *prev.* Antsirane, Diégo-Suarez. Antsirañana, N Madagascar
172 *J2* **Antsirañana** ◐ *province* N Madagascar
Antsirane *see* Antsirañana
An tSiúir *see* Suir
118 *I7* **Antsla** *Ger.* Anzen. Võrumaa, SE Estonia
An tSláine *see* Slaney
172 *J3* **Antsohihy** Mahajanga, NW Madagascar
63 *G14* **Antuco, Volcán** Ѧ C Chile
169 *W10* **Antu, Gunung** ▲ Borneo, N Indonesia
An Tullach *see* Tullow
An-tung *see* Dandong
Antunnacum *see* Andernach
Antwerp *see* Antwerpen
99 *G16* **Antwerpen** *Eng.* Antwerp, *Fr.* Anvers. Antwerpen, N Belgium
99 *H16* **Antwerpen** *Eng.* Antwerp. ◐ *province* N Belgium
An Uaimh *see* Navan
154 *N12* **Anugul** *var.* Angul. Orissa, E India
152 *F9* **Anūpgarh** Rājasthān, NW India
154 *K10* **Anūppur** Madhya Pradesh, C India
155 *K24* **Anuradhapura** North Central Province, C Sri Lanka
Anvers *see* Antwerpen
194 *G4* **Anvers Island** *island* Antarctica
39 *N11* **Anvik** Alaska, USA
39 *N10* **Anvik River** ≈ Alaska, USA
38 *F17* **Anvil Peak** ▲ Semisopochnoi Island, Alaska, USA
159 *P7* **Anxi** *var.* Yuanquan. Gansu, N China
182 *F8* **Anxious Bay** *bay* South Australia
161 *O5* **Anyang** Henan, C China
159 *S11* **A'nyêmaqên Shan** ▲▲ C China
118 *H12* **Anykščiai** Utena, E Lithuania
161 *P13* **Anyuan** *var.* Xinshan. Jiangxi, S China
123 *T7* **Anyuysk** Chukotskiy Avtonomnyy Okrug, NE Russian Federation
123 *T7* **Anyuyskiy Khrebet** ▲▲ NE Russian Federation
54 *D8* **Anza** Antioquia, C Colombia
Anzen *see* Antsla
107 *I16* **Anzio** Lazio, C Italy
55 *O6* **Anzoátegui** *off.* Estado Anzoátegui. ◐ *state* NE Venezuela
Anzoátegui, Estado *see* Anzoátegui
147 *P12* **Anzob** W Tajikistan
Anzyô *see* Anjō
Aoba *see* Ambae
165 *X13* **Aoga-shima** *island* Izu-shotō, SE Japan
Aohan Qi *see* Xinhui
Aoiz *see* Agoiz
186 *M9* **Aola** *var.* Tenaghau. Guadalcanal, C Solomon Islands
166 *M15* **Ao Luk Nua** Krabi, SW Thailand
Aomen *see* Macao
172 *N8* **Aomori** Aomori, Honshū, C Japan
172 *N8* **Aomori** *off.* Aomori-ken. ◐ *prefecture* Honshū, C Japan
Aomori-ken *see* Aomori
Aontroim *see* Antrim
115 *C15* **Aóos** *var.* Vijosa, Vijosë, *Alb.* Lumi i Vjosës. ≈ Albania/Greece *see also* Vjosës, Lumi i
Aóos *see* Vjosës, Lumi i
191 *Q7* **Aorai, Mont** Ѧ Tahiti, W French Polynesia
185 *E19* **Aoraki** *prev.* Aorangi, Mount Cook. ▲ South Island, New Zealand
167 *R13* **Aôral, Phnum** *prev.* Phnom Aural. ▲ W Cambodia
Aorangi *see* Aoraki
185 *L15* **Aorangi Mountains** ▲▲ North Island, New Zealand
184 *H13* **Aorere** ≈ South Island, New Zealand
106 *A7* **Aosta** *anc.* Augusta Praetoria. Valle d'Aosta, NW Italy
77 *O11* **Aougoundou, Lac** ◎ S Mali
76 *K9* **Aoukâr** *var.* Aouker. *plateau* C Mauritania
78 *J13* **Aouk, Bahr** ≈ Central African Republic/Chad
Aouker *see* Aoukâr
74 *B11* **Aousard** SE Western Sahara
164 *H12* **Aoya** Tottori, Honshū, SW Japan
Aoyang *see* Shanggao
78 *H5* **Aozou** Borkou-Ennedi-Tibesti, N Chad
26 *M11* **Apache** Oklahoma, C USA
36 *L14* **Apache Junction** Arizona, SW USA
24 *J9* **Apache Mountains** ▲▲ Texas, SW USA
36 *M16* **Apache Peak** ▲ Arizona, SW USA
116 *H10* **Apahida** Cluj, NW Romania
23 *T9* **Apalachee Bay** *bay* Florida, SE USA
23 *T3* **Apalachee River** ≈ Georgia, SE USA
23 *S10* **Apalachicola** Florida, SE USA
23 *S10* **Apalachicola Bay** *bay* Florida, SE USA
23 *R9* **Apalachicola River** ≈ Florida, SE USA
Apam *see* Apan
Apamama *see* Abemama
41 *P14* **Apan** *var.* Apam. Hidalgo, C Mexico
42 *J8* **Apanás, Lago de** ◎ NW Nicaragua
54 *H14* **Apaporis, Río** ≈ Brazil/Colombia
185 *C23* **Aparima** ≈ South Island, New Zealand
171 *O1* **Aparri** Luzon, N Philippines
112 *J9* **Apatin** Vojvodina, NW Serbia
124 *J4* **Apatity** Murmanskaya Oblast', NW Russian Federation
55 *X9* **Apatou** NW French Guiana
40 *M14* **Apatzingán** *var.* Apatzingán de la Constitución. Michoacán de Ocampo, SW Mexico
Apatzingán de la Constitución *see* Apatzingán
171 *X12* **Apauwar** Papua, E Indonesia
Apaxtla *see* Apaxtla de Castrejón
41 *O15* **Apaxtla de Castrejón** *var.* Apaxtla. Guerrero, S Mexico
118 *J7* **Ape** Alūksne, NE Latvia
98 *L11* **Apeldoorn** Gelderland, E Netherlands
Apennines *see* Appennino
Apenrade *see* Aabenraa
57 *L17* **Apere, Río** ≈ C Bolivia
55 *W11* **Apetina** Sipaliwini, SE Suriname
21 *U9* **Apex** North Carolina, SE USA
79 *M16* **Api** Orientale, N Dem. Rep. Congo
152 *M9* **Api** ▲ NW Nepal
192 *H16* **Āpia** ● (Samoa) Upolu, SE Samoa
Apia *see* Abaiang
60 *K11* **Apiaí** São Paulo, S Brazil
170 *M16* **Api, Gunung** ▲ Pulau Sangeang, S Indonesia
187 *N9* **Apio** Maramasike Island, N Solomon Islands
41 *O15* **Apipilulco** Guerrero, S Mexico
41 *P14* **Apizaco** Tlaxcala, S Mexico
104 *I4* **A Pobla de Trives** *Cast.* Puebla de Trives. Galicia, NW Spain
55 *U9* **Apoera** Sipaliwini, NW Suriname
115 *O23* **Apolakkiá** Ródos, Dodekánisa, Greece, Aegean Sea
101 *L16* **Apolda** Thüringen, C Germany
192 *H16* **Apolima Strait** *strait* C Pacific Ocean
182 *M13* **Apollo Bay** Victoria, SE Australia
Apollonia *see* Sozopol
57 *J16* **Apolo** La Paz, W Bolivia
57 *J16* **Apolobamba, Cordillera** ▲▲ Bolivia/Peru
171 *Q8* **Apo, Mount** Ѧ Mindanao, S Philippines
23 *W11* **Apopka** Florida, SE USA
23 *W11* **Apopka, Lake** ◎ Florida, SE USA
59 *J19* **Aporé, Rio** ≈ SW Brazil
30 *K2* **Apostle Islands** *island group* Wisconsin, N USA
Apostolas Andreas, Cape *see* Zafer Burnu
61 *F14* **Apóstoles** Misiones, NE Argentina
Apostólou Andréa, Akrotíri *see* Zafer Burnu
117 *S9* **Apostolove** *Rus.* Apostolovo. Dnipropetrovs'ka Oblast', E Ukraine
Apostolovo *see* Apostolove
17 *S10* **Appalachian Mountains** ▲▲ E USA
95 *K14* **Äppelbo** Dalarna, C Sweden
98 *N7* **Appelscha** *Fris.* Appelskea. Friesland, N Netherlands
Appelskea *see* Appelscha
106 *G11* **Appennino** *Eng.* Apennines. ▲▲ Italy/San Marino
107 *L17* **Appennino Napoletano** ▲▲ C Italy
108 *I7* **Appenzell** Appenzell, NW Switzerland
108 *H7* **Appenzell** ◐ *canton* NE Switzerland
55 *V12* **Appikalo** Sipaliwini, S Suriname
98 *O5* **Appingedam** Groningen, NE Netherlands
25 *X8* **Appleby** Texas, SW USA
97 *L15* **Appleby-in-Westmorland** Cumbria, NW England, UK
30 *K10* **Apple River** ≈ Illinois, N USA
30 *I5* **Apple River** ≈ Wisconsin, N USA
25 *W9* **Apple Springs** Texas, SW USA
29 *S8* **Appleton** Minnesota, N USA
30 *M7* **Appleton** Wisconsin, N USA
27 *S5* **Appleton City** Missouri, C USA
35 *U14* **Apple Valley** California, W USA
29 *V9* **Apple Valley** Minnesota, N USA
21 *U6* **Appomattox** Virginia, NE USA
188 *B16* **Apra Harbour** *harbor* W Guam
188 *B16* **Apra Heights** W Guam
106 *F6* **Aprica, Passo dell'** *pass* N Italy
107 *M15* **Apricena** *anc.* Hadria Picena. Puglia, SE Italy
126 *L14* **Apsheronsk** Krasnodarskiy Kray, SW Russian Federation
Apsheronskiy Poluostrov *see* Abşeron Yarımadası
103 *S15* **Apt** *anc.* Apta Julia. Vaucluse, SE France
Apta Julia *see* Apt
38 *H12* **'Āpua Point** *var.* Apua Point. *headland* Hawai'i, USA, C Pacific Ocean
60 *I10* **Apucarana** Paraná, S Brazil
Apulia *see* Puglia
54 *K8* **Apure** *off.* Estado Apure. ◐ *state* C Venezuela
Apure, Estado *see* Apure
54 *J7* **Apure, Río** ≈ W Venezuela
57 *F16* **Apurímac** *off.* Departamento de Apurímac. ◐ *department* C Peru
Apurímac, Departamento de *see* Apurímac
57 *F15* **Apurímac, Río** ≈ S Peru
116 *G10* **Apuseni, Munţii** ▲▲ W Romania
Aqaba/'Aqaba *see* Al 'Aqabah
138 *F15* **Aqaba, Gulf of** *var.* Gulf of Elat, *Ar.* Khalīj al 'Aqabah; *anc.* Sinus Aelaniticus. *gulf* NE Red Sea
139 *R7* **'Aqabah** C Iraq
'Aqabah, Khalīj al *see* Aqaba, Gulf of
149 *O2* **Āqchah** *var.* Āqcheh. Jowzjān, N Afghanistan
Āqcheh *see* Āqchah
Aqköl *see* Akkol'
Aqmola *see* Astana
Aqmola Oblysy *see* Akmola
158 *L10* **Aqqikkol Hu** ◎ NW China
Aqqystaū *see* Akkystau
'Aqrah *see* Ākrē
Aqsay *see* Aksay
Aqshataū *see* Akchatau
Aqsū *see* Aksu
Aqsūat *see* Aksuat
Aqtas *see* Aktas
Aqtaū *see* Aktau
Aqtöbe *see* Aktobe
Aqtöbe Oblysy *see* Aktyubinsk
Aqtoghay *see* Aktogay
Aquae Augustae *see* Dax
Aquae Calidae *see* Bath
Aquae Flaviae *see* Chaves
Aquae Grani *see* Aachen
Aquae Panoniae *see* Baden
Aquae Sextiae *see* Aix-en-Provence
Aquae Solis *see* Bath
Aquae Tarbelicae *see* Dax
36 *J11* **Aquarius Mountains** ▲▲ Arizona, SW USA
62 *O5* **Aquidabán, Río** ≈ E Paraguay
59 *H20* **Aquidauana** Mato Grosso do Sul, S Brazil
40 *L15* **Aquila** Michoacán de Ocampo, S Mexico
Aquila/Aquila degli Abruzzi *see* L'Aquila
25 *T8* **Aquilla** Texas, SW USA
44 *L9* **Aquin** S Haiti
Aquisgranum *see* Aachen
102 *J13* **Aquitaine** ◐ *region* SW France
Aqzhar *see* Akzhar
153 *P13* **Āra** *prev.* Arrah. Bihār, N India
105 *S4* **Ara** ≈ NE Spain
23 *P2* **Arab** Alabama, S USA
Araba *see* Álava
138 *G12* **'Arabah, Wādī al** *Heb.* Ha'Arava. ◐ *dry watercourse* Israel/Jordan
117 *U12* **Arabats'ka Strilka, Kosa** *spit* S Ukraine
117 *U12* **Arabats'ka Zatoka** *gulf* S Ukraine
'Arab, Baḩr al *see* Arab, Bahr el
80 *C12* **Arab, Bahr el** *var.* Baḩr al 'Arab. ≈ S Sudan
56 *E7* **Arabela, Río** ≈ N Peru
173 *O4* **Arabian Basin** *undersea feature* N Arabian Sea
Arabian Desert *see* Sahara el Sharqîya
141 *N9* **Arabian Peninsula** *peninsula* SW Asia
85 *P15* **Arabian Plate** *tectonic feature* Africa/Asia/Europe
141 *W14* **Arabian Sea** *sea* NW Indian Ocean
Arabicus, Sinus *see* Red Sea
Khalīj al 'Arabī *see* Gulf, The
Arabistan *see* Khūzestān
'Arabīyah as Su'ūdīyah, Al Mamlakah al *see* Saudi Arabia
'Arabīyah Jumhūrīyah, Mişr al *see* Egypt
138 *I9* **'Arab, Jabal al** ▲▲ S Syria
Arab Republic of Egypt *see* Egypt
139 *Y12* **'Arab, Shaţţ al** *Eng.* Shatt al Arab, *Per.* Arvand Rūd. ≈ Iran/Iraq
136 *I11* **Araç** Kastamonu, N Turkey
59 *P16* **Aracaju** *state capital* Sergipe, E Brazil
54 *F5* **Aracataca** Magdalena, N Colombia
58 *P13* **Aracati** Ceará, E Brazil
60 *J8* **Araçatuba** São Paulo, S Brazil
136 *I11* **Araç Çayı** ≈ N Turkey
104 *J13* **Aracena** Andalucía, S Spain
115 *F20* **Arachnaío** ▲▲ S Greece
115 *D16* **Árachthos** *var.* Arta, *prev.* Árakhthos; *anc.* Arachthus. ≈ W Greece
Arachthus *see* Árachthos
59 *N19* **Araçuaí** Minas Gerais, SE Brazil
138 *F11* **'Arad** Southern, S Israel
116 *F11* **Arad** Arad, W Romania
116 *F11* **Arad** ◐ *county* W Romania
78 *J9* **Arada** Biltine, NE Chad
143 *P18* **'Arādah** Abū Ẓaby, S United Arab Emirates
Aradhippou *see* Aradippou
121 *Q3* **Aradíppou** *var.* Aradhippou. SE Cyprus
174 *K6* **Arafura Sea** *Ind.* Laut Arafuru. *sea* W Pacific Ocean
174 *L6* **Arafura Shelf** *undersea feature* C Arafura Sea
Arafuru, Laut *see* Arafura Sea
59 *J18* **Aragarças** Goiás, C Brazil
Aragats, Gora *see* Aragats Lerr
137 *T12* **Aragats Lerr** *Rus.* Gora Aragats. ▲ W Armenia
32 *E14* **Arago, Cape** *headland* Oregon, NW USA
105 *R6* **Aragón** ◐ *autonomous community* E Spain
105 *Q4* **Aragón** ≈ NE Spain
107 *J24* **Aragona** Sicilia, Italy, C Mediterranean Sea
105 *Q7* **Aragoncillo** ▲ C Spain
54 *L5* **Aragua** *off.* Estado Aragua. ◐ *state* N Venezuela
55 *N6* **Aragua de Barcelona** Anzoátegui, NE Venezuela
55 *O5* **Aragua de Maturín** Monagas, NE Venezuela
Aragua, Estado *see* Aragua
59 *K15* **Araguaia, Río** *var.* Araguaya. ≈ C Brazil
59 *K19* **Araguari** Minas Gerais, SE Brazil
58 *J11* **Araguari, Rio** ≈ SW Brazil
Araguaya *see* Araguaia, Río
104 *K14* **Arahal** Andalucía, S Spain
165 *N11* **Arai** Niigata, Honshū, C Japan
Árainn *see* Inishmore
Árainn Mhór *see* Aran Island
Ara Jovis *see* Aranjuez
74 *J11* **Arak** C Algeria
171 *Y15* **Arak** Papua, E Indonesia
142 *M7* **Arāk** *prev.* Sultānābād. Markazī, W Iran
188 *D10* **Arakabesan** *island* Palau Islands, N Palau
55 *S7* **Arakaka** NW Guyana
166 *K6* **Arakan State** *var.* Rakhine State. ◐ *state* W Myanmar (Burma)
166 *K5* **Arakan Yoma** ▲▲ W Myanmar (Burma)
165 *O10* **Arakawa** Niigata, Honshū, C Japan
Árakhthos *see* Árachthos
Araks/Arak's *see* Aras
158 *H7* **Aral** Xinjiang Uygur Zizhiqu, NW China
Aral *see* Aralsk, Kazakhstan
Aral *see* Vose', Tajikistan
Aral-Bukhorskiy Kanal *see* Amu-Buxoro Kanali
137 *T12* **Aralık** Iğdır, E Turkey
146 *H5* **Aral Sea** *Kaz.* Aral Tengizi, *Rus.* Aral'skoye More, *Uzb.* Orol Dengizi. *inland sea* Kazakhstan/Uzbekistan
144 *L13* **Aral'sk** *Kaz.* Aral. Kzylorda, SW Kazakhstan
Aral'skoye More/Aral Tengizi *see* Aral Sea
41 *O10* **Aramberri** Nuevo León, NE Mexico
186 *B8* **Aramia** ≈ SW Papua New Guinea
143 *N6* **Ārān** *var.* Golārā. Eşfahān, C Iran
105 *N5* **Aranda de Duero** Castilla-León, N Spain
112 *M12* **Arandelovac** *prev.* Arandjelovac. Serbia, C Serbia
Arandjelovac *see* Arandelovac
97 *J19* **Aran Fawddwy** ▲ NW Wales, UK
97 *C14* **Aran Island** *Ir.* Árainn Mhór. *island* NW Ireland
97 *A18* **Aran Islands** *island group* W Ireland
105 *N9* **Aranjuez** *anc.* Ara Jovis. Madrid, C Spain
83 *E20* **Aranos** Hardap, SE Namibia
25 *U14* **Aransas Bay** *inlet* Texas, SW USA
25 *T14* **Aransas Pass** Texas, SW USA
191 *O3* **Aranuka** *prev.* Nanouki. *atoll* Tungaru, W Kiribati
167 *Q11* **Aranyaprathet** Prachin Buri, S Thailand
Aranyosasztal *see* Zlatý Stôl
Aranyosgyéres *see* Câmpia Turzii
Aranyosmarót *see* Zlaté Moravce
164 *C14* **Arao** Kumamoto, Kyūshū, SW Japan
77 *O8* **Araouane** Tombouctou, N Mali
26 *L10* **Arapaho** Oklahoma, C USA
29 *N16* **Arapahoe** Nebraska, C USA
57 *I16* **Arapa, Laguna** ◎ SE Peru
185 *K14* **Arapawa Island** *island* C New Zealand
61 *E17* **Arapey Grande, Río** ≈ N Uruguay
59 *P16* **Arapiraca** Alagoas, E Brazil
140 *M3* **'Ar'ar** Al Ḩudūd ash Shamālīyah, NW Saudi Arabia
54 *G15* **Araracuara** Caquetá, S Colombia
61 *K15* **Araranguá** Santa Catarina, S Brazil
60 *L8* **Araraquara** São Paulo, S Brazil
59 *O13* **Araras** Ceará, E Brazil
58 *I14* **Araras** Pará, N Brazil
60 *L9* **Araras** São Paulo, S Brazil
60 *H11* **Araras, Serra das** ▲▲ S Brazil
137 *U12* **Ararat** S Armenia
182 *M12* **Ararat** Victoria, SE Australia
Ararat, Mount *see* Büyükağrı Dağı
140 *M3* **'Ar'ar, Wādī** *wadi* Iraq/Saudi Arabia
129 *N7* **Aras** *Arm.* Arak's, *Az.* Araz Nehri, *Per.* Rūd-e Aras, *Rus.* Araks; *prev.* Araxes. ≈ SW Asia
105 *R9* **Aras de Alpuente** País Valenciano, E Spain
137 *S13* **Aras Güneyi Dağları** ▲▲ NE Turkey
Aras, Rūd-e *see* Aras
191 *U9* **Aratika** *atoll* Îles Tuamotu, C French Polynesia
Aratürük *see* Yiwu
54 *I8* **Arauca** Arauca, NE Colombia
54 *I8* **Arauca** *off.* Intendencia de Arauca. ◐ *province* NE Colombia
Arauca, Intendencia de *see* Arauca
63 *G15* **Araucanía** *off.* Región de la Araucanía. ◐ *region* C Chile
Araucanía, Región de la *see* Araucanía
54 *L7* **Arauca, Río** ≈ Colombia/Venezuela
63 *F14* **Arauco** Bío Bío, C Chile
63 *F14* **Arauco, Golfo de** *gulf* S Chile
54 *H8* **Arauquita** Arauca, C Colombia
Arausio *see* Orange
152 *F13* **Arāvali Range** ▲▲ N India
186 *J7* **Arawa** Bougainville Island, NE Papua New Guinea
185 *C20* **Arawata** ≈ South Island, New Zealand
186 *F7* **Arawe Islands** *island group* E Papua New Guinea
59 *L20* **Araxá** Minas Gerais, SE Brazil
Araxes *see* Aras
55 *O5* **Araya** Sucre, N Venezuela
Araz Nehri *see* Aras
105 *R4* **Arba** ≈ N Spain
81 *I15* **Ārba Minch'** Southern, S Ethiopia
139 *U4* **Arbat** NE Iraq
107 *D19* **Arbatax** Sardegna, Italy, C Mediterranean Sea
Arbe *see* Rab
Arbela *see* Arbīl
139 *S3* **Arbīl** *var.* Erbil, Irbīl, *Kurd.* Hawlēr; *anc.* Arbela. N Iraq
95 *M16* **Arboga** Västmanland, C Sweden
95 *M16* **Arbogaån** ≈ C Sweden
103 *S9* **Arbois** Jura, E France
54 *D6* **Arboletes** Antioquia, NW Colombia
9 *X15* **Arborg** Manitoba, S Canada
94 *N12* **Arbrå** Gävleborg, C Sweden
96 *K10* **Arbroath** *anc.* Aberbrothock. E Scotland, UK
35 *N6* **Arbuckle** California, W USA
27 *N12* **Arbuckle Mountains** ▲▲ Oklahoma, C USA
162 *I5* **Arbulag** *var.* Mandal. Hövsgöl, N Mongolia
Arbuzinka *see* Arbyzynka
117 *Q8* **Arbyzynka** *Rus.* Arbuzinka. Mykolayivs'ka Oblast', S Ukraine
103 *U12* **Arc** ≈ E France
102 *J13* **Arcachon** Gironde, SW France
102 *J13* **Arcachon, Bassin d'** *inlet* SW France
18 *E10* **Arcade** New York, NE USA
23 *W14* **Arcadia** Florida, SE USA
22 *H5* **Arcadia** Louisiana, S USA
30 *J7* **Arcadia** Wisconsin, N USA
Arcae Remorum *see* Châlons-en-Champagne
44 *L9* **Arcahaie** C Haiti
34 *K3* **Arcata** California, W USA
35 *U6* **Arc Dome** ▲ Nevada, W USA
107 *J16* **Arce** Lazio, C Italy
41 *O15* **Arcelia** Guerrero, S Mexico
99 *M15* **Arcen** Limburg, SE Netherlands
115 *J25* **Archánes** *var.* Áno Arkhánai, Epáno Archánes; *prev.* Epáno Arkhánai. Kríti, Greece, E Mediterranean Sea
Archangel *see* Arkhangel'sk
Archangel Bay *see* Chëshskaya Guba
115 *O23* **Archángelos** *var.* Arhangelos, Arkhángelos. Ródos, Dodekánisa, Greece, Aegean Sea
114 *F7* **Archar** ≈ NW Bulgaria
31 *R11* **Archbold** Ohio, N USA
105 *R12* **Archena** Murcia, SE Spain
25 *R5* **Archer City** Texas, SW USA
104 *M14* **Archidona** Andalucía, S Spain
65 *B25* **Arch Islands** *island group* SW Falkland Islands
106 *G13* **Arcidosso** Toscana, C Italy
103 *Q5* **Arcis-sur-Aube** Aube, N France
182 *F3* **Arckaringa Creek** *seasonal river* South Australia
106 *G7* **Arco** Trentino-Alto Adige, N Italy
33 *Q14* **Arco** Idaho, NW USA
30 *M14* **Arcola** Illinois, N USA
105 *P6* **Arcos de Jalón** Castilla-León, N Spain
104 *K15* **Arcos de la Frontera** Andalucía, S Spain
104 *G5* **Arcos de Valdevez** Viana do Castelo, N Portugal
59 *P15* **Arcoverde** Pernambuco, E Brazil
102 *H5* **Arcovest, Pointe de l'** *headland* NW France
Arctic Mid Oceanic Ridge *see* Nansen Cordillera
197 *R8* **Arctic Ocean** *ocean*
8 *G7* **Arctic Red River** ≈ Northwest Territories/Yukon Territory, NW Canada
Arctic Red River *see* Tsiigehtchic
39 *S6* **Arctic Village** Alaska, USA
194 *H1* **Arctowski** *Polish research station* South Shetland Islands, Antarctica
114 *I12* **Arda** *var.* Ardhas, *Gk* Ardas. ≈ Bulgaria/Greece *see also* Ardas
Arda *see* Ardas
142 *L2* **Ardabīl** *var.* Ardebil. Ardabīl, NW Iran
142 *L2* **Ardabīl** *off.* Ostān-e Ardabīl. ◐ *province* NW Iran
Ardabīl, Ostān-e *see* Ardabīl
137 *R11* **Ardahan** Ardahan, NE Turkey
137 *S11* **Ardahan** ◐ *province* Ardahan, Turkey Asia
143 *P8* **Ardakān** Yazd, C Iran
94 *E12* **Årdalstangen** Sogn Og Fjordane, S Norway
137 *R11* **Ardanuç** Artvin, NE Turkey
114 *L12* **Ardas** *var.* Ardhas, *Bul.* Arda. ≈ Bulgaria/Greece *see also* Arda
Ardas *see* Arda
138 *I13* **Ard aş Şawwān** *var.* Ardh es Suwwān. *plain* S Jordan
127 *P5* **Ardatov** Respublika Mordoviya, W Russian Federation
14 *G12* **Ardbeg** Ontario, S Canada
Ardeal *see* Transylvania
Ardebil *see* Ardabīl
103 *Q13* **Ardèche** ◐ *department* E France
103 *Q13* **Ardèche** ≈ C France
97 *F17* **Ardee** *Ir.* Baile Átha Fhirdhia. Louth, NE Ireland
103 *Q3* **Ardennes** ◐ *department* NE France
99 *J23* **Ardennes** *physical region* Belgium/France
137 *Q11* **Ardeşen** Rize, NE Turkey
143 *O7* **Ardestān** *var.* Ardistan. Eşfahān, C Iran
108 *J9* **Ardez** Graubünden, SE Switzerland
Ardhas *see* Arda/Ardas
Ardh es Suwwān *see* Ard aş Şawwān
Ardila *see* Ardila, Ribeira de
104 *I12* **Ardila, Ribeira de** *Sp.* Ardilla. ≈ Portugal/Spain *see also* Ardilla
Ardila, Ribeira de *see* Ardilla
9 *T17* **Ardill** Saskatchewan, S Canada
104 *I12* **Ardilla** *Port.* Ribeira de Ardila. ≈ Portugal/Spain *see also* Ardila, Ribeira de
40 *M11* **Ardilla, Cerro la** ▲ C Mexico
114 *J12* **Ardino** Kŭrdzhali, S Bulgaria
Ardistan *see* Ardestān
183 *P9* **Ardlethan** New South Wales, SE Australia
Ard Mhacha *see* Armagh
23 *P1* **Ardmore** Alabama, S USA
27 *N13* **Ardmore** Oklahoma, C USA
20 *J10* **Ardmore** Tennessee, S USA
96 *G10* **Ardnamurchan, Point of** *headland* N Scotland, UK
Árdni *see* Arnøya
99 *C17* **Ardooie** West-Vlaanderen, W Belgium
182 *I9* **Ardrossan** South Australia
116 *H9* **Ardusat** *Hung.* Erdőszáda. Maramureş, N Romania
93 *F16* **Åre** Jämtland, C Sweden
79 *P16* **Arebi** Orientale, NE Dem. Rep. Congo
45 *T5* **Arecibo** C Puerto Rico
171 *V13* **Aredo** Papua, E Indonesia
59 *P14* **Areia Branca** Rio Grande do Norte, E Brazil
119 *O14* **Arekhawsk** *Rus.* Orekhovsk. Vitsyebskaya Voblasts', N Belarus
Arel *see* Arlon
Arelas/Arelate *see* Arles
Arenal, Embalse de *see* Arenal Laguna
42 *L12* **Arenal Laguna** *var.* Embalse de Arenal. ◎ NW Costa Rica
42 *L13* **Arenal, Volcán** Ѧ NW Costa Rica
34 *K6* **Arena, Point** *headland* California, W USA
59 *H17* **Arenápolis** Mato Grosso, W Brazil
40 *G10* **Arena, Punta** *headland* W Mexico
104 *L8* **Arenas de San Pedro** Castilla-León, N Spain

◆ Country
● Country Capital
◇ Dependent Territory
○ Dependent Territory Capital
◐ Administrative Regions
✈ International Airport
▲ Mountain
▲▲ Mountain Range
Ѧ Volcano
≈ River
◎ Lake
⊠ Reservoir

63 I24 **Arenas, Punta de** headland S Argentina
61 B20 **Arenaza** Buenos Aires, E Argentina
95 F17 **Arendal** Aust-Agder, S Norway
99 J16 **Arendonk** Antwerpen, N Belgium
43 T15 **Arenosa** Panamá, N Panama
Arensburg see Kuressaare
105 W5 **Arenys de Mar** Cataluña, NE Spain
106 C9 **Arenzano** Liguria, NW Italy
115 F22 **Areópoli** prev. Areópolis. Pelopónnisos, S Greece
Areópolis see Areópoli
57 H18 **Arequipa** Arequipa, SE Peru
57 G17 **Arequipa** off. Departamento de Arequipa. ◐ department Arequia SW Peru
Arequipa, Departamento de see Arequipa
61 B19 **Arequito** Santa Fe, C Argentina
104 M7 **Arévalo** Castilla-León, N Spain
106 H12 **Arezzo** anc. Arretium. Toscana, C Italy
105 Q4 **Arga** N Spain
Argaeus see Erciyes Daği
115 G17 **Argalastí** Thessalía, C Greece
105 O10 **Argamasilla de Alba** Castilla-La Mancha, C Spain
158 L8 **Argan** Xinjiang Uygur Zizhiqu, NW China
105 O8 **Arganda** Madrid, C Spain
104 H8 **Arganil** Coimbra, N Portugal
171 P6 **Argao** Cebu, C Philippines
153 V15 **Argartala** Tripura, NE India
123 N9 **Arga-Sala** Respublika Sakha (Yakutiya),NE Russian Federation
103 P17 **Argelès-sur-Mer** Pyrénées-Orientales, S France
103 T15 **Argens** SE France
106 H9 **Argenta** Emilia-Romagna, N Italy
102 K5 **Argentan** Orne, N France
103 N12 **Argentat** Corrèze, C France
106 A9 **Argentera** Piemonte, NE Italy
103 N5 **Argenteuil** Val-d'Oise, N France
62 K13 **Argentina** off. Republic of Argentina. ◆ republic S South America
Argentina Basin see Argentine Basin
Argentina, Republic of see Argentina
Argentine Abyssal Plain see Argentine Plain
65 I19 **Argentine Basin** var. Argentina Basin. undersea feature SW Atlantic Ocean
65 I20 **Argentine Plain** var. Argentine Abyssal Plain. undersea feature SW Atlantic Ocean
Argentine Rise see Falkland Plateau
63 H22 **Argentino, Lago** ◎ S Argentina
102 K8 **Argenton-Château** Deux-Sèvres, W France
102 M9 **Argenton-sur-Creuse** Indre, C France
Argentoratum see Strasbourg
116 I12 **Argeş** ◐ county S Romania
116 K14 **Argeş** S Romania
149 O8 **Arghandāb, Daryā-ye** SE Afghanistan
Arghastān see Arghestān
149 O8 **Arghestān** Pash. Arghastān. SE Afghanistan
Argirocastro see Gjirokastër
80 E7 **Argo** Northern, N Sudan
173 P7 **Argo Fracture Zone** tectonic feature C Indian Ocean
115 F20 **Argolikós Kólpos** gulf S Greece
103 R4 **Argonne** physical region NE France
115 F20 **Árgos** Pelopónnisos, S Greece
139 S1 **Argōsh** N Iraq
115 D14 **Árgos Orestikó** Dytikí Makedonía, N Greece
115 B19 **Argostóli** var. Argostólion. Kefallonía, Iónia Nisiá, Greece, C Mediterranean Sea
Argostólion see Argostóli
Argovie see Aargau
35 O14 **Arguello, Point** headland California, W USA
127 P16 **Argun** Chechenskaya Respublika, SW Russian Federation
157 T2 **Argun** Chin. Ergun He, Rus. Argun'. China/Russian Federation
77 T12 **Argungu** Kebbi, NW Nigeria
Arguut see Guchin-Us
181 N3 **Argyle, Lake** salt lake Western Australia
96 G12 **Argyll** cultural region W Scotland, UK
Argyrokastron see Gjirokastër
162 I7 **Arhangay** ◐ province C Mongolia
Arhangelos see Archángelos
95 P14 **Arholma** Stockholm, C Sweden
95 G22 **Århus** var. Aarhus. Århus, C Denmark
95 G22 **Århus** ◐ county C Denmark
139 T1 **Ārī** E Iraq
Aria see Herāt
83 F22 **Ariamsvlei** Karas, SE Namibia
107 L17 **Ariano Irpino** Campania, S Italy
54 F11 **Ariari, Río** C Colombia
151 K19 **Ari Atoll** atoll C Maldives
77 P11 **Aribinda** N Burkina
62 G2 **Arica** hist. San Marcos de Arica. Tarapacá, N Chile
54 H16 **Arica** Amazonas, S Colombia
62 G2 **Arica** ✕ Tarapacá, N Chile
114 E13 **Aridaía** var. Aridea, Aridhaía. Dytikí Makedonía, N Greece
Aridea see Aridaía
172 I15 **Aride, Île** island Inner Islands, NE Seychelles
Aridhaía see Aridaía
103 N17 **Ariège** ◐ department S France
102 M16 **Ariège** var. la Riege. Andorra/France
116 H11 **Arieș** W Romania
149 U10 **Ārifwāla** Punjab, E Pakistan
Ariguaní see El Difícil
138 G11 **Arīḥā** Al Karak, W Jordan
138 I3 **Arīḥā** var. Arīhā. Idlib, W Syria
Arīhā see Arīḥā
Arīḥā see Jericho
37 W4 **Arikaree River** Colorado/Nebraska, C USA
112 L13 **Arilje** Serbia, W Serbia
45 U14 **Arima** Trinidad, Trinidad and Tobago
Arime see Al 'Arīmah
Ariminum see Rimini
59 H16 **Arinos, Rio** W Brazil
40 M14 **Ario de Rosales** var. Ario de Rosáles. Michoacán de Ocampo, SW Mexico
Ario de Rosáles see Ario de Rosales
118 F12 **Ariogala** Kaunas, C Lithuania
47 T7 **Aripuanã** W Brazil
59 E15 **Ariquemes** Rondônia, W Brazil
121 W13 **'Arish, Wâdi el** NE Egypt
54 K6 **Arismendi** Barinas, C Venezuela
10 J14 **Aristazabal Island** island SW Canada
60 F13 **Aristóbulo del Valle** Misiones, NE Argentina
172 I5 **Arivonimamo** ✕ (Antananarivo) Antananarivo, C Madagascar
Arixang see Wenquan
105 Q6 **Ariza** Aragón, NE Spain
62 I6 **Arizaro, Salar de** salt lake NW Argentina
105 O2 **Arizgoiti** var Basauri. País Vasco, N Spain
62 K13 **Arizona** San Luis, C Argentina
36 J12 **Arizona** off. State of Arizona, also known as Copper State, Grand Canyon State. ◐ state SW USA
40 G4 **Arizpe** Sonora, NW Mexico
95 J16 **Årjäng** Värmland, C Sweden
143 P8 **Arjenān** Yazd, C Iran
92 I13 **Arjeplog** Norrbotten, N Sweden
54 E5 **Arjona** Bolívar, N Colombia
105 N13 **Arjona** Andalucía, S Spain
123 S10 **Arka** Khabarovskiy Kray, E Russian Federation
22 L2 **Arkabutla Lake** ⊠ Mississippi, S USA
127 O7 **Arkadak** Saratovskaya Oblast', W Russian Federation
27 T13 **Arkadelphia** Arkansas, C USA
115 J25 **Arkalochóri** ; prev. Arkalokhórion. Kríti, Greece, E Mediterranean Sea
Arkalohori/Arkalokhórion see Arkalochóri
145 O10 **Arkalyk** Kaz. Arqalyq. Kostanay, N Kazakhstan
27 U10 **Arkansas** off. State of Arkansas, also known as The Land of Opportunity. ◐ state S USA
27 W14 **Arkansas City** Arkansas, C USA
27 O7 **Arkansas City** Kansas, C USA
16 K11 **Arkansas River** C USA
182 J5 **Arkaroola** South Australia
Arkhángelos see Archángelos
124 L8 **Arkhangel'sk** Eng. Archangel. Arkhangel'skaya Oblast', NW Russian Federation
124 L9 **Arkhangel'skaya Oblast'** ◐ province NW Russian Federation
127 O14 **Arkhangel'skoye** Stavropol'skiy Kray, SW Russian Federation
123 R14 **Arkhara** Amurskaya Oblast', S Russian Federation
97 G19 **Arklow** Ir. An tInbhear Mór. SE Ireland
115 M20 **Arkoí** island Dodekánisa, Greece, Aegean Sea
27 R11 **Arkoma** Oklahoma, C USA
100 O7 **Arkona, Kap** cape NE Germany
95 N17 **Arkösund** Östergötland, S Sweden
122 J6 **Arkticheskogo Instituta, Ostrova** island N Russian Federation
95 O15 **Arlanda** ✕ (Stockholm) Stockholm, C Sweden
146 C11 **Arlandag** Rus. Gora Arlan. ▲ W Turkmenistan
Arlan, Gora see Arlandag
105 O5 **Arlanza** N Spain
105 N5 **Arlanzón** N Spain
103 R15 **Arles** var. Arles-sur-Rhône; anc. Arelas, Arelate. Bouches-du-Rhône, SE France
Arles-sur-Rhône see Arles
103 O17 **Arles-sur-Tech** Pyrénées-Orientales, S France
29 U9 **Arlington** Minnesota, N USA
29 R15 **Arlington** Nebraska, C USA
32 J11 **Arlington** Oregon, NW USA
29 R10 **Arlington** South Dakota, N USA
20 E10 **Arlington** Tennessee, S USA
25 T6 **Arlington** Texas, SW USA
21 W4 **Arlington** Virginia, NE USA
32 H7 **Arlington** Washington, NW USA
30 M10 **Arlington Heights** Illinois, N USA
77 U8 **Arlit** Agadez, C Niger
99 L24 **Arlon** Dut. Aarlen, Ger. Arel, Lat. Orolaunum. Luxembourg, SE Belgium
27 R7 **Arma** Kansas, C USA
97 F16 **Armagh** Ir. Ard Mhacha. S Northern Ireland, UK
97 F16 **Armagh** cultural region S Northern Ireland, UK
102 K15 **Armagnac** cultural region S France
103 Q7 **Armançon** C France
60 K10 **Armando Laydner, Represa** ⊠ S Brazil
115 M24 **Armathía** island SE Greece
137 T12 **Armavir** prev. Hoktemberyan, Rus. Oktemberyan. SW Armenia
126 M14 **Armavir** Krasnodarskiy Kray, SW Russian Federation
54 E10 **Armenia** Quindío, W Colombia
137 T12 **Armenia** off. Republic of Armenia, var. Ajastan, Arm. Hayastani Hanrapetut'yun; prev. Armenian Soviet Socialist Republic. ◆ republic SW Asia
Armenian Soviet Socialist Republic see Armenia
Armenia, Republic of see Armenia
Armenierstadt see Gherla
103 O1 **Armentières** Nord, N France
40 K14 **Armería** Colima, SW Mexico
183 T5 **Armidale** New South Wales, SE Australia
29 P11 **Armour** South Dakota, N USA
61 B18 **Armstrong** Santa Fe, C Argentina
9 N16 **Armstrong** British Columbia, SW Canada
12 D11 **Armstrong** Ontario, S Canada
29 U11 **Armstrong** Iowa, C USA
25 S16 **Armstrong** Texas, SW USA
117 S11 **Armyans'k** Rus. Armyansk. Respublika Krym, S Ukraine
115 H14 **Arnaía** Cont. Arnea. Kentrikí Makedonía, N Greece
121 N2 **Arnaoúti, Akrotíri** var. Arnaoútis, Cape Arnaouti. cape W Cyprus
Arnaoútis, Cape/Arnaoútis see Arnaoúti, Akrotíri
12 L4 **Arnaud** Québec, E Canada
103 Q8 **Arnay-le-Duc** Côte d'Or, C France
Arnea see Arnaía
105 Q4 **Arnedo** La Rioja, N Spain
95 I14 **Årnes** Akershus, S Norway
26 K9 **Arnett** Oklahoma, C USA
98 L12 **Arnhem** Gelderland, SE Netherlands
181 Q2 **Arnhem Land** physical region Northern Territory, N Australia
106 F11 **Arno** C Italy
Arno see Arno Atoll
189 W7 **Arno Atoll** var. Arno. atoll Ratak Chain, NE Marshall Islands
182 H8 **Arno Bay** South Australia
35 Q8 **Arnold** California, W USA
27 X5 **Arnold** Missouri, C USA
29 N15 **Arnold** Nebraska, C USA
109 R10 **Arnoldstein** Slvn. Pod Klošter. Kärnten, S Austria
103 N9 **Arnon** C France
45 P14 **Arnos Vale** ✕ (Kingstown) Saint Vincent, SE Saint Vincent and the Grenadines
92 I8 **Arnøya** Lapp. Árdni. island N Norway
14 L12 **Arnprior** Ontario, SE Canada
101 G15 **Arnsberg** Nordrhein-Westfalen, W Germany
101 K16 **Arnstadt** Thüringen, C Germany
Arnswalde see Choszczno
54 K5 **Aroa** Yaracuy, N Venezuela
83 E21 **Aroab** Karas, SE Namibia
Ároania see Chelmós
191 O5 **Aroa, Pointe** headland Moorea, W French Polynesia
Aroe Islands see Aru, Kepulauan
101 H15 **Arolsen** Niedersachsen, C Germany
106 C7 **Arona** Piemonte, NE Italy
19 R3 **Aroostook River** Canada/USA
Arop Island see Long Island
38 M12 **Aropuk Lake** ◎ Alaska, USA
191 P4 **Arorae** atoll Tungaru, W Kiribati
190 G16 **Arorangi** Rarotonga, S Cook Islands
108 I9 **Arosa** Graubünden, S Switzerland
104 F4 **Arousa, Ría de** estuary E Atlantic Ocean
184 P8 **Arowhana** ▲ North Island, New Zealand
137 V12 **Arp'a** Az. Arpaçay. Armenia/Azerbaijan
137 S11 **Arpaçay** Kars, NE Turkey
Arpaçay see Arp'a
Arqalyq see Arkalyk
149 N14 **Arra** SW Pakistan
Arrabona see Győr
Arrah see Āra
Ar Rahad see Er Rahad
139 R9 **Ar Raḥḥālīyah** C Iraq
60 Q10 **Arraial do Cabo** Rio de Janeiro, SE Brazil
104 H11 **Arraiolos** Évora, S Portugal
139 R8 **Ar Ramādī** var. Ramadi, Rumadiya. SW Iraq
138 J6 **Ar Rāmī** Ḥimṣ, C Syria
Ar Rams see Rams
138 H9 **Ar Ramthā** var. Ramtha. Irbid, N Jordan
96 H13 **Arran, Isle of** island SW Scotland, UK
138 L3 **Ar Raqqah** var. Rakka; anc. Nicephorium. Ar Raqqah, N Syria
138 L3 **Ar Raqqah** off. Muḥāfaẓat al Raqqah, var. Raqqah, Fr. Rakka. ◐ governorate N Syria
103 O2 **Arras** anc. Nemetocenna. Pas-de-Calais, N France
105 P3 **Arrasate** Cast. Mondragón. País Vasco, N Spain
138 G12 **Ar Rashādīyah** Aṭ ṭafilah, W Jordan
138 I5 **Ar Rastān** var. Rastâne. Ḥimṣ, W Syria
139 X12 **Ar Raṭāwī** E Iraq
102 L15 **Arrats** S France
141 N16 **Ar Rawḍah** Makkah, S Saudi Arabia
141 Q15 **Ar Rawḍah** S Yemen
142 K11 **Ar Rawḍatayn** var. Raudhatain. N Kuwait
143 N16 **Ar Rayyān** var. Al Rayyan. C Qatar
102 L17 **Arreau** Hautes-Pyrénées, S France
64 Q11 **Arrecife** var. Arrecife de Lanzarote, Puerto Arrecife. Lanzarote, Islas Canarias, NE Atlantic Ocean
Arrecife de Lanzarote see Arrecife
43 P6 **Arrecife Edinburgh** reef NE Nicaragua
61 C19 **Arrecifes** Buenos Aires, E Argentina
102 F6 **Arrée, Monts d'** NW France
Ar Refā'ī see Ar Rifā'ī
Arretium see Arezzo
Arriaca see Guadalajara
109 S9 **Arriach** Kärnten, S Austria
41 T16 **Arriaga** Chiapas, SE Mexico
41 N12 **Arriaga** San Luis Potosí, C Mexico
139 W10 **Ar Rifā'ī** var. Ar Refā'ī. SE Iraq
139 V12 **Ar Riḥāb** salt flat S Iraq
104 L2 **Arriondas** Asturias, N Spain
141 Q7 **Ar Riyāḍ** Eng. Riyadh. ● (Saudi Arabia) Ar Riyāḍ, C Saudi Arabia
141 O8 **Ar Riyāḍ** off. Minṭaqat ar Riyāḍ. ◐ province C Saudi Arabia
141 S15 **Ar Riyān** S Yemen
Arrō see Ærø
61 H18 **Arroio Grande** Rio Grande do Sul, S Brazil
102 K15 **Arros** S France
103 Q9 **Arroux** C France
25 R5 **Arrowhead, Lake** ⊠ Texas, SW USA
182 L5 **Arrowsmith, Mount** hill New South Wales, SE Australia
185 D21 **Arrowtown** Otago, South Island, New Zealand
61 D17 **Arroyo Barú** Entre Ríos, E Argentina
104 J10 **Arroyo de la Luz** Extremadura, W Spain
63 J16 **Arroyo de la Ventana** Río Negro, SE Argentina
35 P13 **Arroyo Grande** California, W USA
Ar Ru'ays see Ar Ruways
141 R11 **Ar Rub 'al Khālī** Eng. Empty Quarter, Great Sandy Desert. desert SW Asia
139 V13 **Ar Rudaymah** S Iraq
61 A16 **Arrufó** Santa Fe, C Argentina
138 I7 **Ar Ruḥaybah** var. Ruhaybeh, Fr. Rouhaïbé. Dimashq, W Syria
139 V15 **Ar Rukhaymīyah** well S Iraq
139 U11 **Ar Rumaythah** var. Rumaitha. S Iraq
141 X8 **Ar Rustāq** var. Rostak, Rustaq. N Oman
139 N8 **Ar Ruṭbah** var. Rutba. SW Iraq
140 M3 **Ar Rūthīyah** spring/well NW Saudi Arabia
ar-Ruwaida see Ar Ruwayḍah
141 O8 **Ar Ruwayḍah** var. Ar-Ruwaida. Jīzān, C Saudi Arabia
143 N15 **Ar Ruways** var. Al Ruweis, Ar Ru'ays, Ruwais. N Qatar
143 O17 **Ar Ruways** var. Ar Ru'ays. Abū Ẓaby, W United Arab Emirates
Ārs see Aars
Arsanias see Murat Nehri
123 S15 **Arsen'yev** Primorskiy Kray, SE Russian Federation
155 G19 **Arsikere** Karnātaka, W India
127 R3 **Arsk** Respublika Tatarstan, W Russian Federation
94 N10 **Årskogen** Gävleborg, C Sweden
121 O3 **Ársos** C Cyprus
94 N13 **Årsunda** Gävleborg, C Sweden
115 C17 **Árta** anc. Ambracia. Ípeiros, W Greece
105 Y9 **Artà** Mallorca, Spain, W Mediterranean Sea
Arta see Árachthos
137 T12 **Artashat** S Armenia
40 M15 **Arteaga** Michoacán de Ocampo, SW Mexico
123 S15 **Artem** Primorskiy Kray, SE Russian Federation
44 C4 **Artemisa** La Habana, W Cuba
117 W7 **Artemivs'k** Donets'ka Oblast', E Ukraine
122 K13 **Artemovsk** Krasnoyarskiy Kray, S Russian Federation
105 U5 **Artesa de Segre** Cataluña, NE Spain
37 U14 **Artesia** New Mexico, SW USA
25 Q14 **Artesia Wells** Texas, SW USA
108 G8 **Arth** Schwyz, C Switzerland
14 F15 **Arthur** Ontario, S Canada
30 M14 **Arthur** Illinois, N USA
28 L14 **Arthur** Nebraska, C USA
29 Q5 **Arthur** North Dakota, N USA
185 B21 **Arthur** South Island, New Zealand
18 B13 **Arthur, Lake** ⊠ Pennsylvania, NE USA
183 N15 **Arthur River** Tasmania, SE Australia
185 G18 **Arthur's Pass** Canterbury, South Island, New Zealand
185 G17 **Arthur's Pass** pass South Island, New Zealand
44 I3 **Arthur's Town** Cat Island, C Bahamas
44 M9 **Artibonite, Rivière de l'** C Haiti
61 E16 **Artigas** prev. San Eugenio, San Eugenio del Cuareim. Artigas, N Uruguay
61 E16 **Artigas** ◐ department N Uruguay
194 H1 **Artigas** Uruguayan research station Antarctica
137 T11 **Art'ik** W Armenia
187 O16 **Art, Île** island Îles Belep, W New Caledonia
103 O2 **Artois** cultural region N France
136 L12 **Artova** Tokat, N Turkey
105 Y9 **Artrutx, Cap d'** var. Cabo Dartuch. cape Menorca, Spain, W Mediterranean Sea
Artsiz see Artsyz
117 N11 **Artsyz** Rus. Artsiz. Odes'ka Oblast', SW Ukraine
158 E7 **Artux** Xinjiang Uygur Zizhiqu, NW China
137 R11 **Artvin** Artvin, NE Turkey
137 R11 **Artvin** ◐ province NE Turkey
146 G14 **Artyk** Ahal Welaýaty, C Turkmenistan
79 Q16 **Aru** Orientale, NE Dem. Rep. Congo
81 E17 **Arua** NW Uganda
104 I4 **A Rúa de Valdeorras** var. La Rúa. Galicia, NW Spain
Aruângua see Luangwa
45 O15 **Aruba** var. Oruba. ◇ Dutch autonomous region S West Indies
47 Q4 **Aruba** island Aruba, Lesser Antilles
Aru Islands see Aru, Kepulauan
171 W15 **Aru, Kepulauan** Eng. Aru Islands; prev. Aroe Islands. island group E Indonesia
153 W10 **Arunāchal Pradesh** prev. North East Frontier Agency, North East Frontier Agency of Assam. ◐ state NE India
Arun Qi see Naji
155 H23 **Aruppukkottai** Tamil Nādu, SE India
81 I20 **Arusha** Arusha, N Tanzania
81 I21 **Arusha** ◐ region E Tanzania
81 I20 **Arusha** ✕ Arusha, N Tanzania
54 C9 **Arusí, Punta** headland NW Colombia
155 J23 **Aruvi Aru** NW Sri Lanka
79 M17 **Aruwimi** var. Ituri (upper course). NE Dem. Rep. Congo
Árva see Orava
37 T4 **Arvada** Colorado, C USA
Arvand Rūd see 'Arab, Shaṭṭ al
162 J8 **Arvayheer** Övörhangay, C Mongolia
9 O10 **Arviat** prev. Eskimo Point. Nunavut, C Canada
93 I14 **Arvidsjaur** Norrbotten, N Sweden
95 J15 **Arvika** Värmland, C Sweden
92 J8 **Årviksand** Troms, N Norway
35 S13 **Arvin** California, W USA
163 S8 **Arxan** Nei Mongol Zizhiqu, N China
145 P7 **Arykbalyk** Kaz. Aryqbalyq. Severnyy Kazakhstan, N Kazakhstan
Aryqbalyq see Arykbalyk
145 P17 **Arys'** Kaz. Arys. Yuzhnyy Kazakhstan, S Kazakhstan
Arys see Arys'
Arys see Orzysz
Arys Köli see Arys, Ozero
145 O14 **Arys, Ozero** Kaz. Arys Köli. ◎ C Kazakhstan
107 D16 **Arzachena** Sardegna, Italy, C Mediterranean Sea
127 O4 **Arzamas** Nizhegorodskaya Oblast', W Russian Federation
141 V13 **Arzāt** S Oman
104 H3 **Arzúa** Galicia, NW Spain
111 A16 **Aš** Ger. Asch. Karlovarský Kraj, W Czech Republic
95 H15 **Ås** Akershus, S Norway
Åsa see Asaa
95 H20 **Asaa** var. Åsa. Nordjylland, N Denmark
83 E21 **Asab** Karas, S Namibia
77 U16 **Asaba** Delta, S Nigeria
149 S4 **Asadābād** var. Asadābād; prev. Chaghasarāy. Konar, E Afghanistan
Asadābād see Asadābād
138 K3 **Asad, Buḥayrat al** ◎ N Syria
63 H20 **Asador, Pampa del** plain S Argentina
165 P14 **Asahi** Chiba, Honshū, S Japan
164 M11 **Asahi** Toyama, Honshū, SW Japan
165 T13 **Asahi-dake** ▲ Hokkaidō, N Japan
165 T3 **Asahikawa** Hokkaidō, N Japan
147 S10 **Asaka** Rus. Assake; prev. Leninsk. Andijon Viloyati, E Uzbekistan
77 P17 **Asamankese** SE Ghana
188 B15 **Asan** W Guam
188 B15 **Asan Point** headland W Guam
153 R15 **Āsānsol** West Bengal, NE India
80 K12 **Āsayita** Afar, NE Ethiopia
171 T12 **Asbakin** Papua, E Indonesia
Asben see Aïr, Massif de l'
15 Q12 **Asbestos** Québec, SE Canada
29 Y13 **Asbury** Iowa, C USA
18 K15 **Asbury Park** New Jersey, NE USA
41 Z12 **Ascención, Bahiá de la** bay NW Caribbean Sea
40 I3 **Ascensión** Chihuahua, N Mexico
65 M14 **Ascension Fracture Zone** tectonic feature C Atlantic Ocean
65 G14 **Ascension Island** ◇ dependency of St.Helena C Atlantic Ocean
65 N16 **Ascension Island** island C Atlantic Ocean
Asch see Aš
109 S3 **Aschach an der Donau** Oberösterreich, N Austria
101 H18 **Aschaffenburg** Bayern, SW Germany
101 F14 **Ascheberg** Nordrhein-Westfalen, W Germany
101 L14 **Aschersleben** Sachsen-Anhalt, C Germany
106 G12 **Asciano** Toscana, C Italy
106 J13 **Ascoli Piceno** anc. Asculum Picenum. Marche, C Italy
107 M17 **Ascoli Satriano** anc. Asculub, Ausculum Apulum. Puglia, SE Italy
108 G11 **Ascona** Ticino, S Switzerland
Asculub see Ascoli Satriano
Asculum Picenum see Ascoli Piceno
80 L11 **Aseb** var. Assab, Amh. Āseb. SE Eritrea
95 M20 **Åseda** Kronoberg, S Sweden
127 T6 **Asekeyevo** Orenburgskaya Oblast', W Russian Federation
81 J14 **Āsela** var. Asella, Aselle, Asselle. Oromo, C Ethiopia
93 H15 **Åsele** Västerbotten, N Sweden
Asella/Aselle see Āsela
94 K12 **Åsen** Dalarna, C Sweden
114 J11 **Asenovgrad** prev. Stanimaka. Plovdiv, C Bulgaria
171 O13 **Asera** Sulawesi, C Indonesia
95 E17 **Åseral** Vest-Agder, S Norway
118 J3 **Aseri** var. Asserien, Ger. Asserin. Ida-Virumaa, NE Estonia
40 J10 **Aserradero** Durango, W Mexico
146 F13 **Aşgabat** prev. Ashgabat, Ashkhabad, Poltoratsk. ● (Turkmenistan) Ahal Welaýaty, C Turkmenistan
146 F13 **Aşgabat** ✕ Ahal Welaýaty, C Turkmenistan
95 H16 **Åsgårdstrand** Vestfold, S Norway
Ashara see Al 'Ashārah
23 T6 **Ashburn** Georgia, SE USA
185 G19 **Ashburton** Canterbury, South Island, New Zealand
185 G19 **Ashburton** South Island, New Zealand
180 H8 **Ashburton River** Western Australia
145 V10 **Ashchysu** E Kazakhstan
10 M16 **Ashcroft** British Columbia, SW Canada
138 E10 **Ashdod** anc. Azotos, Lat. Azotus. Central, W Israel
27 S14 **Ashdown** Arkansas, C USA
21 T9 **Asheboro** North Carolina, SE USA
9 X15 **Ashern** Manitoba, S Canada
21 P10 **Asheville** North Carolina, SE USA
12 E8 **Asheweig** Ontario, C Canada
27 V9 **Ash Flat** Arkansas, C USA
183 T4 **Ashford** New South Wales, SE Australia
97 P22 **Ashford** SE England, UK
36 K11 **Ash Fork** Arizona, SW USA
Ashgabat see Aşgabat
27 T7 **Ash Grove** Missouri, C USA
165 O12 **Ashikaga** var. Asikaga. Tochigi, Honshū, S Japan
165 Q8 **Ashiro** Iwate, Honshū, C Japan
164 F15 **Ashizuri-misaki** Shikoku, SW Japan
Ashkelon see Ashqelon
Ashkhabad see Aşgabat
23 Q4 **Ashland** Alabama, S USA
26 K7 **Ashland** Kansas, C USA
21 P5 **Ashland** Kentucky, S USA
19 S2 **Ashland** Maine, NE USA
22 M1 **Ashland** Mississippi, S USA
27 U4 **Ashland** Missouri, C USA
29 S15 **Ashland** Nebraska, C USA
31 T12 **Ashland** Ohio, N USA
32 G15 **Ashland** Oregon, NW USA
21 W6 **Ashland** Virginia, NE USA
30 K3 **Ashland** Wisconsin, N USA
20 I8 **Ashland City** Tennessee, S USA
183 S4 **Ashley** New South Wales, SE Australia
29 O7 **Ashley** North Dakota, N USA
173 W7 **Ashmore and Cartier Islands** ◇ Australian external territory E Indian Ocean
119 I14 **Ashmyany** Rus. Oshmyany. Hrodzyenskaya Voblasts', W Belarus
18 K12 **Ashokan Reservoir** ⊠ New York, NE USA
165 U4 **Ashoro** Hokkaidō, NE Japan
138 E10 **Ashqelon** var. Ashkelon. Southern, C Israel
Ashraf see Behshahr
139 O3 **Ash Shadādah** var. Ash Shaddādah, Jisr ash Shadadi, Shaddādī, Shedadi, Tell Shedadi. Al Ḥasakah, NE Syria
Ash Shaddādah see Ash Shadādah
139 Y12 **Ash Shāfī** E Iraq
139 R4 **Ash Shakk** var. Shaykh. C Iraq
Ash Shām see Dimashq
Ash Shām/Ash Shām see Dimashq
139 T10 **Ash Shāmīyah** var. Shamiya. C Iraq
139 Y13 **Ash Shāmīyah** var. Al Bādiyah al Janūbīyah. desert S Iraq
139 T11 **Ash Shanāfīyah** var. Ash Shināfīyah. S Iraq
138 G13 **Ash Sharāh** var. Esh Sharā. ▲ W Jordan
143 R16 **Ash Shāriqah** Eng. Sharjah. Ash Shāriqah, NE United Arab Emirates
143 R16 **Ash Shāriqah** var. Sharjah. ✕ Ash Shāriqah, NE United Arab Emirates
140 I4 **Ash Sharmah** var. Šarma. Tabūk, NW Saudi Arabia
139 R4 **Ash Sharqāṭ** NW Iraq
141 S10 **Ash Sharqīyah** off. Al Minṭaqah ash Sharqīyah, Eng. Eastern Region. ◐ province E Saudi Arabia
Ash Sharqīyah see Al 'Ubaylah
139 W11 **Ash Shaṭrah** var. Shatra. SE Iraq
138 G13 **Ash Shawbak** Ma'ān, W Jordan
138 L5 **Ash Shaykh Ibrāhīm** Ḥimṣ, C Syria
141 O17 **Ash Shaykh 'Uthmān** SW Yemen
141 S15 **Ash Shiḥr** SE Yemen
Ash Shināfīyah see Ash Shanāfīyah
141 V12 **Ash Shişar** var. Shisur. SW Oman
139 S13 **Ash Shubrūm** well S Iraq
141 R10 **Ash Shuqqān** desert E Saudi Arabia
75 O9 **Ash Shuwayrif** var. Ash Shwayrif. N Libya
Ash Shwayrif see Ash Shuwayrif
31 U10 **Ashtabula** Ohio, N USA
29 Q5 **Ashtabula, Lake** ⊠ North Dakota, N USA
137 T12 **Ashtarak** W Armenia
142 M6 **Āshtīān** var. Āshtiyān. Markazī, W Iran
Āshtiyān see Āshtīān
33 R13 **Ashton** Idaho, NW USA
13 O10 **Ashuanipi Lake** ◎ Newfoundland and Labrador, E Canada
15 P6 **Ashuapmushuan** Québec, SE Canada
23 Q3 **Ashville** Alabama, S USA
31 S14 **Ashville** Ohio, N USA
30 K3 **Ashwabay, Mount** hill Wisconsin, N USA

◆ Country
● Country Capital
◇ Dependent Territory
○ Dependent Territory Capital
◐ Administrative Regions
✕ International Airport
▲ Mountain
▲ Mountain Range
Volcano
River
◎ Lake
⊠ Reservoir

128-129 **Asia** *continent*
171 T11 **Asia, Kepulauan** *island group* E Indonesia
154 N13 **Āsika** Orissa, E India
Asikaga *see* Ashikaga
93 M18 **Asikkala** *var.* Vääksy. Etelä-Suomi, S Finland
74 G5 **Asilah** N Morocco
'Aṣī, Nahr al *see* Orontes
107 B16 **Asinara, Isola** *island* W Italy
122 J12 **Asino** Tomskaya Oblast', C Russian Federation
119 O14 **Asintorf** *Rus.* Osintorf. Vitsyebskaya Voblasts', N Belarus
119 L17 **Asipovichy** *Rus.* Osipovichi. Mahilyowskaya Voblasts', C Belarus
141 N12 **'Asīr** *off.* Minṭaqat 'Asīr. ◐ *province* SW Saudi Arabia
140 M11 **'Asīr** *Eng.* Asir. ▲▲ SW Saudi Arabia
'Asīr, Minṭaqat *see* 'Asīr
139 X10 **Askal** E Iraq
137 P13 **Aşkale** Erzurum, NE Turkey
117 T11 **Askaniya-Nova** Khersons'ka Oblast', S Ukraine
95 H15 **Asker** Akershus, S Norway
95 L17 **Askersund** Örebro, C Sweden
Askī Kalak *see* Eski Kaļak
95 I15 **Askim** Østfold, S Norway
127 V3 **Askino** Respublika Bashkortostan, W Russian Federation
115 D14 **Áskio** ▲▲ N Greece
152 L9 **Askot** Uttaranchal, N India
94 C12 **Askvoll** Sogn Og Fjordane, S Norway
136 A13 **Aslan Burnu** *headland* W Turkey
136 L16 **Aslantaş Barajı** ⊠ S Turkey
149 S4 **Asmār** *var.* Bar Kunar. Kunar, E Afghanistan
80 I9 **Asmara** *Amh.* Āsmera. ● (Eritrea) C Eritrea
Āsmera *see* Asmara
95 L21 **Åsnen** ◎ S Sweden
115 F19 **Asopós** ⇝ S Greece
171 W13 **Asori** Papua, E Indonesia
80 G12 **Āsosa** Benishangul, W Ethiopia
32 M10 **Asotin** Washington, NW USA
Aspadana *see* Eşfahān
Aspang *see* Aspang Markt
109 X6 **Aspang Markt** *var.* Aspang. Niederösterreich, E Austria
105 S12 **Aspe** País Valenciano, E Spain
37 R5 **Aspen** Colorado, C USA
25 P6 **Aspermont** Texas, SW USA
Asphaltites, Lacus *see* Dead Sea
Aspinwall *see* Colón
185 C20 **Aspiring, Mount** ▲ South Island, New Zealand
115 B16 **Asprókavos, Ákrotírio** *headland* Kérkyra, Iónioi Nísoi, Greece, C Mediterranean Sea
Aspropótamos *see* Achelóos
Assab *see* Aseb
76 J10 **Assaba** *var.* Açâba. ◐ *region* S Mauritania
138 L4 **As Sabkhah** *var.* Sabkha. Ar Raqqah, NE Syria
139 U6 **As Sa'dīyah** E Iraq
138 I8 **Aş Şafā** ▲ S Syria
138 I10 **Aş Şafāwī** Al Mafraq, N Jordan
Aş Şaff *see* El Şaff
139 N2 **Aş Şafīḩ** Al Ḩasakah, N Syria
Aş Şaḩrā' al Gharbīyah *see* Sahara el Gharbîya
Aş Şaḩrā' ash Sharqīyah *see* Sahara el Sharqîya
Assake *see* Asaka
As Salamīyah *see* Salamīyah
141 Q4 **As Sālimī** *var.* Salemy. SW Kuwait
67 W7 **'Assal, Lac** ◎ C Djibouti
As Sallūm *see* Salûm
139 T13 **As Salmān** S Iraq
138 G10 **As Salṭ** *var.* Salt. Al Balqā', NW Jordan
142 M16 **As Salwā** *var.* Salwa, Salwah. S Qatar
153 V12 **Assam** ◐ *state* NE India
Assamaka *see* Assamakka
77 T8 **Assamakka** *var.* Assamaka. Agadez, NW Niger
139 U11 **As Samāwah** *var.* Samawa. S Iraq
As Saqia al Hamra *see* Saguia al Hamra
138 J4 **Aş Şā'rān** Ḩamāh, C Syria
138 G9 **Aş Şarīḩ** Irbid, N Jordan
21 Z5 **Assateague Island** *island* Maryland, NE USA
139 O6 **As Sayyāl** *var.* Sayyāl. Dayr az Zawr, E Syria
99 G18 **Asse** Vlaams Brabant, C Belgium
99 D16 **Assebroek** West-Vlaanderen, NW Belgium
Asselle *see* Āsela
107 C20 **Assemini** Sardegna, Italy, C Mediterranean Sea
98 N7 **Assen** Drenthe, NE Netherlands
99 E16 **Assenede** Oost-Vlaanderen, NW Belgium
95 G24 **Assens** Fyn, C Denmark
Asserien/Asserin *see* Aseri
99 I21 **Assesse** Namur, SE Belgium
141 Y8 **As Sīb** *var.* Seeb. NE Oman
139 Z13 **As Sībah** *var.* Sibah. SE Iraq
9 T17 **Assiniboia** Saskatchewan, S Canada
11 V15 **Assiniboine** ⇝ Manitoba, S Canada
9 P16 **Assiniboine, Mount** ▲ Alberta/British Columbia, SW Canada
Assiout *see* Asyût
60 J9 **Assis** São Paulo, S Brazil
106 I13 **Assisi** Umbria, C Italy
Assiut *see* Asyût
Assling *see* Jesenice
Assouan *see* Aswân
Assu *see* Açu
Assuan *see* Aswân
142 K12 **Aş Şubayḩīyah** *var.* Subiyah. S Kuwait
141 R16 **As Sufāl** S Yemen
138 L5 **As Sukhnah** *var.* Sukhne, *Fr.* Soukhné. Ḩimş, C Syria
139 U4 **As Sulaymānīyah** *var.* Sulaimaniya, *Kurd.* Slêmānī. NE Iraq
141 P11 **As Sulayyil** Ar Riyāḑ, S Saudi Arabia
121 O13 **As Sulṭān** N Libya
141 Q5 **Aş Şummān** *desert* N Saudi Arabia
141 Q16 **Aş Şurrah** SW Yemen
139 N4 **Aş Şuwār** *var.* Şuwār. Dayr az Zawr, E Syria
138 H9 **As Suwaydā'** *var.* El Suweida, Es Suweida, Suweida, *Fr.* Soueida. As Suwaydā', SW Syria
138 H9 **As Suwaydā'** *off.* Muḩāfaẓat as Suwaydā', *var.* As Suwaydā, Suwaydā, Suweida. ◐ *governorate* S Syria
141 Z9 **As Suwayḩ** NE Oman
141 X8 **As Suwayq** *var.* Suwaik. N Oman
139 T8 **Aş Şuwayrah** *var.* Suwaira. E Iraq
As Suways *see* Suez
Asta Colonia *see* Asti
Astacus *see* İzmit
115 M23 **Astakída** *island* SE Greece
145 Q9 **Astana** *prev.* Akmola, Akmolinsk, Tselinograd, Aqmola. ● (Kazakhstan) Akmola, N Kazakhstan
142 M3 **Āstāneh** Gīlān, NW Iran
Asta Pompeia *see* Asti
137 Y14 **Astara** S Azerbaijan
Astarabad *see* Gorgān
99 L15 **Asten** Noord-Brabant, SE Netherlands
Asterābād *see* Gorgān
106 C8 **Asti** *anc.* Asta Colonia, Asta Pompeia, Hasta Colonia, Hasta Pompeia. Piemonte, NW Italy
Astigi *see* Ecija
Astipálaia *see* Astypálaia
148 L16 **Astola Island** *island* SW Pakistan
152 H4 **Astor** Jammu and Kashmir, NW India
104 K4 **Astorga** *anc.* Asturica Augusta. Castilla-León, N Spain
32 F10 **Astoria** Oregon, NW USA
0 F8 **Astoria Fan** *undersea feature* E Pacific Ocean
95 J22 **Åstorp** Skåne, S Sweden
Astrabad *see* Gorgān
127 Q13 **Astrakhan'** Astrakhanskaya Oblast', SW Russian Federation
Astrakhan-Bazar *see* Cälilabad
127 Q11 **Astrakhanskaya Oblast'** ◐ *province* SW Russian Federation
93 J15 **Åsträsk** Västerbotten, N Sweden
Astrida *see* Butare
65 O22 **Astrid Ridge** *undersea feature* S Atlantic Ocean
187 P15 **Astrolabe, Récifs de l'** *reef* C New Caledonia
121 P2 **Astromerítis** N Cyprus
115 F20 **Ástros** Pelopónnisos, S Greece
119 G16 **Astryna** *Rus.* Ostryna. Hrodzyenskaya Voblasts', W Belarus
104 J2 **Asturias** ◐ *autonomous community* NW Spain
Asturias *see* Oviedo
Asturica Augusta *see* Astorga
115 L22 **Astypálaia** *var.* Astipálaia, *It.* Stampalia. *island* Kykládes, Greece, Aegean Sea
192 G16 **Āsuisui, Cape** *cape* Savai'i, W Samoa
195 S2 **Asuka** *Japanese research station* Antarctica
62 O6 **Asunción** ● (Paraguay) Central, S Paraguay
62 O6 **Asunción** ✕ Central, S Paraguay
188 K3 **Asuncion Island** *island* N Northern Mariana Islands
42 E6 **Asunción Mita** Jutiapa, SE Guatemala
Asunción Nochixtlán *see* Nochixtlán
40 E3 **Asunción, Río** ⇝ NW Mexico
95 M18 **Åsunden** ◎ S Sweden
118 K11 **Asvyeya** *Rus.* Osveya. Vitsyebskaya Voblasts', N Belarus
Aswa *see* Achwa
75 X11 **Aswân** *var.* Assouan, Assuan; *anc.* Syene. SE Egypt
75 X11 **Aswân High Dam** *dam* SE Egypt
75 W9 **Asyût** *var.* Assiout, Assiut, Siut; *anc.* Lycopolis. C Egypt
193 W15 **Ata** *island* Tongatapu Group, SW Tonga
62 G8 **Atacama** *off.* Región de Atacama. ◐ *region* C Chile
Atacama Desert *see* Atacama, Desierto de
62 H4 **Atacama, Desierto de** *Eng.* Atacama Desert. *desert* N Chile
62 I6 **Atacama, Puna de** ▲▲ NW Argentina
Atacama, Región de *see* Atacama
62 I5 **Atacama, Salar de** *salt lake* N Chile
54 E11 **Ataco** Tolima, C Colombia
190 H8 **Atafu Atoll** *island* NW Tokelau
190 H8 **Atafu Village** Atafu Atoll, NW Tokelau
74 K12 **Atakor** ▲▲ SE Algeria
77 R14 **Atakora, Chaîne de l'** *var.* Atakora Mountains. ▲▲ N Benin
Atakora Mountains *see* Atakora, Chaîne de l'
77 R16 **Atakpamé** C Togo
146 F11 **Atakui** Ahal Welaýaty, C Turkmenistan
58 B13 **Atalaia do Norte** Amazonas, N Brazil
146 M14 **Atamyrat** *prev.* Kerki. Lebap Welaýaty, E Turkmenistan
76 I7 **Aṭâr** Adrar, W Mauritania
162 G10 **Atas Bogd** ▲ SW Mongolia
35 P12 **Atascadero** California, W USA
25 S13 **Atascosa River** ⇝ Texas, SW USA
145 R11 **Atasu** Karaganda, C Kazakhstan
145 R12 **Atasu** ⇝ Karaganda, C Kazakhstan
193 V15 **Atata** *island* Tongatapu Group, S Tonga
136 H10 **Atatürk** ✕ (İstanbul) İstanbul, NW Turkey
137 N16 **Atatürk Barajı** ⊠ S Turkey
115 O23 **Atavýros** *prev* Attavyros. Ródos, Dodekánisa, Aegean Sea
115 O23 **Atavýros** *prev.* Attávyros. ▲ Ródos, Dodekánisa, Greece, Aegean Sea
Atax *see* Aude
80 G8 **Atbara** *var.* 'Aṭbārah. River Nile, NE Sudan
80 H8 **Atbara** *var.* Nahr 'Aṭbarah. ⇝ Eritrea/Sudan
'Aṭbārah/'Aṭbarah, Nahr *see* Atbara
145 P9 **Atbasar** Akmola, N Kazakhstan
At-Bashi *see* At-Bashy
147 W9 **At-Bashy** *var.* At-Bashi. Narynskaya Oblast', C Kyrgyzstan
22 I10 **Atchafalaya Bay** *bay* Louisiana, S USA
22 I8 **Atchafalaya River** ⇝ Louisiana, S USA
Atchin *see* Aceh
27 Q3 **Atchison** Kansas, C USA
77 P16 **Atebubu** C Ghana
105 Q6 **Ateca** Aragón, NE Spain
40 K11 **Atengo, Río** ⇝ C Mexico
Aternum *see* Pescara
107 K15 **Atessa** Abruzzo, C Italy
Ateste *see* Este
99 E19 **Ath** *var.* Aat. Hainaut, SW Belgium
9 Q13 **Athabasca** Alberta, SW Canada
9 Q12 **Athabasca** *var.* Athabaska. ⇝ Alberta, SW Canada
9 R10 **Athabasca, Lake** ◎ Alberta/Saskatchewan, SW Canada
Athabaska *see* Athabasca
115 C16 **Athamánon** ▲▲ C Greece
97 F17 **Athboy** *Ir.* Baile Átha Buí. E Ireland
Athenae *see* Athína
97 C18 **Athenry** *Ir.* Baile Átha an Rí. W Ireland
23 P2 **Athens** Alabama, S USA
23 T3 **Athens** Georgia, SE USA
31 T14 **Athens** Ohio, N USA
20 M10 **Athens** Tennessee, S USA
25 V7 **Athens** Texas, SW USA
Athens *see* Athína
115 B18 **Athéras, Akrotírio** *cape* Kefallonía, Iónia Nisiá, Greece, C Mediterranean Sea
181 W4 **Atherton** Queensland, NE Australia
81 I19 **Athi** ⇝ S Kenya
121 Q2 **Athíenou** SE Cyprus
115 H19 **Athína** *Eng.* Athens, *prev.* Athínai; *anc.* Athenae. ● (Greece) Attikí, C Greece
Athínai *see* Athína
139 S10 **Athīyah** C Iraq
97 D18 **Athlone** *Ir.* Baile Átha Luain. C Ireland
155 F16 **Athni** Karnātaka, W India
185 C23 **Athol** Southland, South Island, New Zealand
19 N11 **Athol** Massachusetts, NE USA
115 I15 **Áthos** ▲ NE Greece
Athos, Mount *see* Ágion Óros
Ath Thawrah *see* Madīnat ath Thawrah
141 P5 **Ath Thumāmī** *spring/well* N Saudi Arabia
99 L25 **Athus** Luxembourg, SE Belgium
97 E19 **Athy** *Ir.* Baile Átha Í. C Ireland
78 I10 **Ati** Batha, C Chad
81 F16 **Atiak** NW Uganda
57 G17 **Atico** Arequipa, SW Peru
105 O6 **Atienza** Castilla-La Mancha, C Spain
39 Q6 **Atigun Pass** *pass* Alaska, USA
12 B12 **Atikokan** Ontario, S Canada
13 O9 **Atikonak Lac** ◎ Newfoundland and Labrador, E Canada
42 C6 **Atitlán, Lago de** ◎ W Guatemala
190 L16 **Atiu** *island* S Cook Islands
Atjeh *see* Aceh
123 T9 **Atka** Magadanskaya Oblast', E Russian Federation
38 H17 **Atka** Atka Island, Alaska, USA
38 H17 **Atka Island** *island* Aleutian Islands, Alaska, USA
127 O7 **Atkarsk** Saratovskaya Oblast', W Russian Federation
27 U11 **Atkins** Arkansas, C USA
29 O13 **Atkinson** Nebraska, C USA
171 T12 **Atkri** Papua, E Indonesia
41 O13 **Atlacomulco** *var.* Atlacomulco de Fabela. México, C Mexico
Atlacomulco de Fabela *see* Atlacomulco
23 S3 **Atlanta** *state capital* Georgia, SE USA
31 R6 **Atlanta** Michigan, N USA
25 X6 **Atlanta** Texas, SW USA
29 T15 **Atlantic** Iowa, C USA
21 Y10 **Atlantic** North Carolina, SE USA
23 W8 **Atlantic Beach** Florida, SE USA
18 J17 **Atlantic City** New Jersey, NE USA
172 L14 **Atlantic-Indian Basin** *undersea feature* SW Indian Ocean
172 K13 **Atlantic-Indian Ridge** *undersea feature* SW Indian Ocean
54 E4 **Atlántico** *off.* Departamento del Atlántico. ◐ *province* NW Colombia
64-65 **Atlantic Ocean** *ocean*
Atlántico, Departamento del *see* Atlántico
42 K7 **Atlántico Norte, Región Autónoma** *prev.* Zelaya Norte. ◐ *autonomous region* NE Nicaragua
42 L10 **Atlántico Sur, Región Autónoma** *prev.* Zelaya Sur. ◐ *autonomous region* SE Nicaragua
42 I5 **Atlántida** ◐ *department* N Honduras
77 Y15 **Atlantika Mountains** ▲▲ E Nigeria
64 J10 **Atlantis Fracture Zone** *tectonic feature* NW Atlantic Ocean
74 H7 **Atlas Mountains** ▲▲ NW Africa
123 V11 **Atlasova, Ostrov** *island* SE Russian Federation
123 V10 **Atlasovo** Kamchatskaya Oblast', E Russian Federation
120 G11 **Atlas Saharien** *var.* Saharan Atlas. ▲▲ Algeria/Morocco
Atlas, Tell *see* Atlas Tellien
120 H10 **Atlas Tellien** *Eng.* Tell Atlas. ▲▲ N Algeria
10 I9 **Atlin** British Columbia, W Canada
10 I9 **Atlin Lake** ◎ British Columbia, W Canada
41 P14 **Atlixco** Puebla, S Mexico
94 B11 **Atløyna** *island* S Norway
155 I17 **Ātmakūr** Andhra Pradesh, C India
23 O8 **Atmore** Alabama, S USA
101 J20 **Atmühl** ⇝ S Germany
94 H11 **Atna** ⇝ S Norway
164 E13 **Atō** Yamaguchi, Honshū, SW Japan
57 L21 **Atocha** Potosí, S Bolivia
27 P12 **Atoka** Oklahoma, C USA
27 O12 **Atoka Lake** *var.* Atoka Reservoir. ⊠ Oklahoma, C USA
Atoka Reservoir *see* Atoka Lake
33 Q14 **Atomic City** Idaho, NW USA
40 L10 **Atotonilco** Zacatecas, C Mexico
Atotonilco *see* Atotonilco el Alto
40 M13 **Atotonilco el Alto** *var.* Atotonilco. Jalisco, SW Mexico
77 N7 **Atouila, 'Erg** *desert* N Mali
41 N16 **Atoyac** *var.* Atoyac de Alvarez. Guerrero, S Mexico
Atoyac de Alvarez *see* Atoyac
41 P15 **Atoyac, Río** ⇝ S Mexico
39 O5 **Atqasuk** Alaska, USA
Atrak/Atrak, Rūd-e *see* Etrek
95 J20 **Ätran** ⇝ S Sweden
54 C7 **Atrato, Río** ⇝ NW Colombia
Atrek *see* Etrek
107 K14 **Atri** Abruzzi, C Italy
Atria *see* Adria
165 P9 **Atsumi** Yamagata, Honshū, C Japan
165 S3 **Atsuta** Hokkaidō, NE Japan
143 Q17 **Aṭ Ṭaff** *desert* C United Arab Emirates
138 G12 **Aṭ Ṭafīlah** *var.* Et Tafila, Tafila. At Ṭafilah, W Jordan
138 G12 **Aṭ Ṭafīlah** *off.* Muḩāfaẓat aṭ Ṭafīlah. ◐ *governorate* W Jordan
140 L10 **Aṭ Ṭā'if** Makkah, W Saudi Arabia
Attaleia/Attalia *see* Antalya
23 Q3 **Attalla** Alabama, S USA
138 L2 **At Tall al Abyaḑ** *var.* Tall al Abyaḑ, Tell Abyad, *Fr.* Tell Abiad. Ar Raqqah, N Syria
138 L7 **At Tanf** Ḩimş, S Syria
Attapu *see* Samakhixai
139 S10 **At Taqtaqānah** C Iraq
Attávyros *see* Atavýros
Attavyros *see* Atavýros
139 V15 **At Tawal** *desert* Iraq/Saudi Arabia
12 G9 **Attawapiskat** Ontario, C Canada
12 F9 **Attawapiskat** ⇝ Ontario, S Canada
12 D9 **Attawapiskat Lake** ◎ Ontario, C Canada
At Taybé *see* Ţayyibah
101 F16 **Attendorn** Nordrhein-Westfalen, W Germany
109 R5 **Attersee** Salzburg, NW Austria
109 R5 **Attersee** ◎ N Austria
99 L24 **Attert** Luxembourg, SE Belgium
138 M4 **At Tibnī** *var.* Tibnī. Dayr az Zawr, NE Syria
31 N13 **Attica** Indiana, N USA
18 E10 **Attica** New York, NE USA
Attica *see* Attikí
13 N7 **Attikamagen Lake** ◎ Newfoundland and Labrador, E Canada
115 H20 **Attikí** *Eng.* Attica. ◐ *region* C Greece
19 O12 **Attleboro** Massachusetts, NE USA
109 R5 **Attnang** Oberösterreich, N Austria
149 U6 **Attock City** Punjab, E Pakistan
Attopeu *see* Samakhixai
25 X8 **Attoyac River** ⇝ Texas, SW USA
38 D16 **Attu** Attu Island, Alaska, USA
139 Y12 **Aṭ Ṭūbah** E Iraq
140 K4 **Aṭ Ṭubayq** *plain* Jordan/Saudi Arabia
38 C16 **Attu Island** *island* Aleutian Islands, Alaska, USA
155 I21 **Āttūr** Tamil Nādu, SE India
Aṭ Ṭūr *see* El Ṭûr
141 N17 **At Turbah** SW Yemen
62 I12 **Atuel, Río** ⇝ C Argentina
191 X7 **Atuona** Hiva Oa, NE French Polynesia
Aturus *see* Adour
95 M18 **Åtvidaberg** Östergötland, S Sweden
35 P9 **Atwater** California, W USA
29 T8 **Atwater** Minnesota, N USA
26 I2 **Atwood** Kansas, C USA
31 U12 **Atwood Lake** ⊠ Ohio, N USA
127 P5 **Atyashevo** Respublika Mordoviya, W Russian Federation
144 F12 **Atyrau** *prev.* Gur'yev. Atyrau, W Kazakhstan
144 E11 **Atyrau** *off.* Atyrauskaya Oblast', *var.Kaz.* Atyraū Oblysy; *prev.* Gur'yevskaya Oblast'. ◐ *province* W Kazakhstan
Atyraū Oblysy/Atyrauskaya Oblast' *see* Atyrau
Atyrauskaya Oblast' *see* Atyrau
108 J7 **Au** Vorarlberg, NW Austria
186 B4 **Aua Island** *island* NW Papua New Guinea
103 S16 **Aubagne** *anc.* Albania. Bouches-du-Rhône, SE France
99 L25 **Aubange** Luxembourg, SE Belgium
103 Q6 **Aube** ◐ *department* N France
103 R6 **Aube** ⇝ N France
99 L19 **Aubel** Liège, E Belgium
103 Q13 **Aubenas** Ardèche, E France
103 O8 **Aubigny-sur-Nère** Cher, C France
103 O13 **Aubin** Aveyron, S France
103 O13 **Aubrac, Monts d'** ▲▲ S France
36 J10 **Aubrey Cliffs** *cliff* Arizona, SW USA
23 R5 **Auburn** Alabama, S USA
35 P6 **Auburn** California, W USA
30 K14 **Auburn** Illinois, N USA
31 Q11 **Auburn** Indiana, N USA
20 J7 **Auburn** Kentucky, S USA
19 P8 **Auburn** Maine, NE USA
19 N11 **Auburn** Massachusetts, NE USA
29 S16 **Auburn** Nebraska, C USA
18 H10 **Auburn** New York, NE USA
32 H8 **Auburn** Washington, NW USA
103 N11 **Aubusson** Creuse, C France
118 E10 **Auce** *Ger.* Autz. Dobele, SW Latvia
102 L15 **Auch** *Lat.* Augusta Auscorum, Elimberrum. Gers, S France
77 U16 **Auchi** Edo, S Nigeria
23 T9 **Aucilla River** ⇝ Florida/Georgia, SE USA
184 L6 **Auckland** Auckland, North Island, New Zealand
184 K5 **Auckland** *off.* Auckland Region. ◐ *region* North Island, New Zealand
184 L6 **Auckland** ✕ Auckland, North Island, New Zealand
192 J12 **Auckland Islands** *island group* S New Zealand
Auckland Region *see* Auckland
103 O16 **Aude** ◐ *department* S France
103 N16 **Aude** *anc.* Atax. ⇝ S France
Audenarde *see* Oudenaarde
Audern *see* Audru
102 E6 **Audierne** Finistère, NW France
102 E6 **Audierne, Baie d'** *bay* NW France
103 U7 **Audincourt** Doubs, E France
118 G5 **Audru** *Ger.* Audern. Pärnumaa, SW Estonia
29 T14 **Audubon** Iowa, C USA
101 N17 **Aue** Sachsen, E Germany
100 H12 **Aue** ⇝ NW Germany
100 L9 **Auerbach** Bayern, SE Germany
101 M17 **Auerbach** Sachsen, E Germany
108 I10 **Auererrhein** ⇝ SW Switzerland
101 N17 **Auersberg** ▲ E Germany
181 W9 **Augathella** Queensland, E Australia
31 Q12 **Auglaize River** ⇝ Ohio, N USA
83 F22 **Augrabies Falls** *waterfall* W South Africa
31 R7 **Au Gres River** ⇝ Michigan, N USA
Augsbourg *see* Augsburg
101 K22 **Augsburg** *Fr.* Augsbourg; *anc.* Augusta Vindelicorum. Bayern, S Germany
180 I14 **Augusta** Western Australia
107 L25 **Augusta** *It.* Agosta. Sicilia, Italy, C Mediterranean Sea
27 W11 **Augusta** Arkansas, C USA
23 V3 **Augusta** Georgia, SE USA
27 O6 **Augusta** Kansas, C USA
19 Q7 **Augusta** *state capital* Maine, NE USA
33 Q8 **Augusta** Montana, NW USA
Augusta *see* London
Augusta Auscorum *see* Auch
Augusta Emerita *see* Mérida
Augusta Praetoria *see* Aosta
Augusta Suessionum *see* Soissons
Augusta Trajana *see* Stara Zagora
Augusta Treverorum *see* Trier
Augusta Vangionum *see* Worms
Augusta Vindelicorum *see* Augsburg
95 G24 **Augustenborg** *Ger.* Augustenburg. Sønderjylland, SW Denmark
Augustenburg *see* Augustenborg
39 Q13 **Augustine Island** *island* Alaska, USA
14 L9 **Augustines, Lac des** ◎ Québec, SE Canada
Augustobona Tricassium *see* Troyes
Augustodunum *see* Autun
Augustodurum *see* Bayeux
Augustoritum Lemovicensium *see* Limoges
110 O8 **Augustów** *Rus.* Avgustov. Podlaskie, NE Poland
Augustow Canal *see* Augustowski, Kanał
110 O8 **Augustowski, Kanał** *Eng.* Augustow Canal, *Rus.* Avgustovskiy Kanal. *canal* NE Poland
180 I9 **Augustus, Mount** ▲ Western Australia
186 M9 **Auki** Malaita, N Solomon Islands
21 W8 **Aulander** North Carolina, SE USA
180 L7 **Auld, Lake** *salt lake* C Western Australia
Aulie Ata/Auliye-Ata *see* Taraz
144 M8 **Auliyekol'** *prev.* Semiozernoye. Kostanay, N Kazakhstan
106 E10 **Aulla** Toscana, C Italy
102 F6 **Aulne** ⇝ NW France
Aulong *see* Ulong
37 T3 **Ault** Colorado, C USA
95 F22 **Aulum** *var* avlum. Ringkøbing, C Denmark
103 N3 **Aumale** Seine-Maritime, N France
Auminzatau, Gory *see* Ovminzatovo Tog'lari
Auminzatau, Gory *see* Ovminzatovo Tog'lari
77 T14 **Auna** Niger, W Nigeria
95 H21 **Auning** Århus, C Denmark
192 K17 **Aunu'u Island** *island* W American Samoa
83 E20 **Auob** *var.* Oup. ⇝ Namibia/South Africa
93 K19 **Aura** Länsi-Soumi, SW Finland
109 R5 **Aurach** ⇝ N Austria
Aural, Phnom *see* Aôral, Phnum
153 O14 **Aurangābād** Bihār, N India
154 F13 **Aurangābād** Mahārāshtra, C India
189 V7 **Aur Atoll** *atoll* E Marshall Islands
102 G7 **Auray** Morbihan, NW France
94 G13 **Aurdal** Oppland, S Norway
94 F8 **Aure** Møre og Romsdal, S Norway
29 T12 **Aurelia** Iowa, C USA
Aurelia Aquensis *see* Baden-Baden
Aurelianum *see* Orléans
120 J10 **Aurès, Massif de l'** ▲▲ NE Algeria
100 F10 **Aurich** Niedersachsen, NW Germany
103 O13 **Aurillac** Cantal, C France
Aurine, Alpi *see* Zillertaler Alpen
Aurium *see* Ourense
14 H15 **Aurora** Ontario, S Canada
55 S8 **Aurora** NW Guyana
37 T4 **Aurora** Colorado, C USA
30 M11 **Aurora** Illinois, N USA
31 Q15 **Aurora** Indiana, N USA
29 W4 **Aurora** Minnesota, N USA
27 S8 **Aurora** Missouri, C USA
29 P16 **Aurora** Nebraska, C USA
36 J5 **Aurora** Utah, W USA
Aurora *see* San Francisco, Philippines
Aurora *see* Maéwo, Vanuatu
94 F10 **Aursjøen** ◎ S Norway
94 I9 **Aursunden** ◎ S Norway
83 D21 **Aus** Karas, SW Namibia
Ausa *see* Vic
14 E16 **Ausable** ⇝ Ontario, S Canada
31 O3 **Au Sable Point** *headland* Michigan, N USA
31 S7 **Au Sable Point** *headland* Michigan, N USA
31 R6 **Au Sable River** ⇝ Michigan, N USA
57 H16 **Ausangate, Nevado** ▲ C Peru
Auschwitz *see* Oświęcim
Ausculum Apulum *see* Ascoli Satriano
105 Q4 **Ausejo** La Rioja, N Spain
Aussig *see* Ústí nad Labem
95 F17 **Aust-Agder** ◐ *county* S Norway
92 P2 **Austfonna** *glacier* NE Svalbard
31 P15 **Austin** Indiana, N USA
29 W11 **Austin** Minnesota, N USA
35 U5 **Austin** Nevada, W USA
25 S10 **Austin** *state capital* Texas, SW USA
180 J10 **Austin, Lake** *salt lake* Western Australia
31 V11 **Austintown** Ohio, N USA
25 V9 **Austonio** Texas, SW USA
Australes, Archipel des *see* Australes, Îles
Australes et Antarctiques Françaises, Terres *see* French Southern and Antarctic Territories
191 T14 **Australes, Îles** *var.* Archipel des Australes, Îles Tubuai, Tubuai Islands, *Eng.* Austral Islands. *island group* SW French Polynesia
175 Y11 **Austral Fracture Zone** *tectonic feature* S Pacific Ocean
174 M8 **Australia** *continent*
181 O7 **Australia** *off.* Commonwealth of Australia. ◆ *commonwealth republic*
Australia, Commonwealth of *see* Australia
183 Q12 **Australian Alps** ▲▲ SE Australia
183 R11 **Australian Capital Territory** *prev.* Federal Capital Territory. ◐ *territory* SE Australia
Australie, Bassin Nord de l' *see* North Australian Basin
Austral Islands *see* Australes, Îles
Austrava *see* Ostrov
109 T6 **Austria** *off.* Republic of Austria, *Ger.* Österreich. ◆ *republic* C Europe
Austria, Republic of *see* Austria
92 K3 **Austurland** ◐ *region* SE Iceland
92 G10 **Austvågøya** *island* C Norway
58 G13 **Autazes** Amazonas, N Brazil
102 M16 **Auterive** Haute-Garonne, S France
Autesiodorum *see* Auxerre
103 N2 **Authie** ⇝ N France
Autissiodorum *see* Auxerre
40 K14 **Autlán** *var.* Autlán de Navarro. Jalisco, SW Mexico
Autlán de Navarro *see* Autlán
Autricum *see* Chartres
103 Q9 **Autun** *anc.* Ædua, Augustodunum. Saône-et-Loire, C France
Autz *see* Auce
99 H20 **Auvelais** Namur, S Belgium
103 P11 **Auvergne** ◐ *region* C France
102 M12 **Auvézère** ⇝ W France
103 P7 **Auxerre** *anc.* Autesiodorum, Autissiodorum. Yonne, C France
103 N2 **Auxi-le-Château** Pas-de-Calais, N France
103 S8 **Auxonne** Côte d'Or, C France
55 P9 **Auyan Tebuy** ▲ SE Venezuela
103 O10 **Auzances** Creuse, C France
27 U8 **Ava** Missouri, C USA
142 M5 **Āvaj** Qazvin, N Iran
95 C15 **Avaldsnes** Rogaland, S Norway
103 Q8 **Avallon** Yonne, C France
102 K6 **Avaloirs, Mont des** ▲ NW France
35 S16 **Avalon** Santa Catalina Island, California, W USA
18 J17 **Avalon** New Jersey, NE USA
13 V13 **Avalon Peninsula** *peninsula* Newfoundland and Labrador, E Canada
197 Q11 **Avannaarsua** ◐ *province* N Greenland
60 K10 **Avaré** São Paulo, S Brazil
Avaricum *see* Bourges
190 H16 **Avarua** ○ (Cook Islands) Rarotonga, S Cook Islands
190 H16 **Avarua Harbour** *harbor* Rarotonga, S Cook Islands

◆ Country
● Country Capital
◇ Dependent Territory
○ Dependent Territory Capital
◐ Administrative Regions
✕ International Airport
▲ Mountain
▲▲ Mountain Range
Volcano
⇝ River
◎ Lake
⊠ Reservoir

Avasfelsőfalu *see* Negrești-Oaș
38 *L17* **Avatanak Island** *island* Aleutian Islands, Alaska, USA
190 *B16* **Avatele** S Niue
190 *H16* **Avatiu** Rarotonga, S Cook Islands
190 *H15* **Avatiu Harbour** *harbor* Rarotonga, S Cook Islands
Avdeyevka *see* Avdiyivka
114 *J13* **Ávdira** Anatolikí Makedonía kai Thráki, NE Greece
117 *X8* **Avdiyivka** *Rus.* Avdeyevka. Donets'ka Oblast', SE Ukraine
Avdzaga *see* Gurvanbulag
Avdzaga *see* Gurvanbulag
104 *G6* **Ave** ≈ N Portugal
104 *G7* **Aveiro** *anc.* Talabriga. Aveiro, W Portugal
104 *G7* **Aveiro** ◈ *district* N Portugal
Avela *see* Ávila
99 *D18* **Avelgem** West-Vlaanderen, W Belgium
61 *D20* **Avellaneda** Buenos Aires, E Argentina
107 *L17* **Avellino** *anc.* Abellinum. Campania, S Italy
35 *Q12* **Avenal** California, W USA
Avenio *see* Avignon
94 *E8* **Averoya** *island* S Norway
107 *K17* **Aversa** Campania, S Italy
33 *N9* **Avery** Idaho, NW USA
25 *W5* **Avery** Texas, SW USA
Aves, Islas de *see* Las Aves, Islas
Avesnes *see* Avesnes-sur-Helpe
103 *Q2* **Avesnes-sur-Helpe** *var.* Avesnes. Nord, N France
64 *G12* **Aves Ridge** *undersea feature* SE Caribbean Sea
95 *M14* **Avesta** Dalarna, C Sweden
103 *O14* **Aveyron** ◈ *department* S France
103 *N14* **Aveyron** ≈ S France
107 *J15* **Avezzano** Abruzzo, C Italy
115 *D16* **Avgó** ▲ C Greece
Avgustov *see* Augustów
Avgustovskiy Kanal *see* Augustowski, Kanał
96 *J9* **Aviemore** N Scotland, UK
185 *F21* **Aviemore, Lake** ◎ South Island, New Zealand
103 *R15* **Avignon** *anc.* Avenio. Vaucluse, SE France
104 *M7* **Ávila** *var.* Avila; *anc.* Abela, Abula, Abyla, Avela. Castilla-León, C Spain
104 *L8* **Ávila** ◈ *province* Castilla-León, C Spain
104 *K2* **Avilés** Asturias, NW Spain
118 *J4* **Avinurme** *Ger.* Awwinorm. Ida-Virumaa, NE Estonia
104 *H10* **Avis** Portalegre, C Portugal
avlum *see* Aulum
182 *M11* **Avoca** Victoria, SE Australia
29 *T14* **Avoca** Iowa, C USA
182 *M11* **Avoca River** ≈ Victoria, SE Australia
107 *L25* **Avola** Sicilia, Italy, C Mediterranean Sea
18 *F10* **Avon** New York, NE USA
29 *P12* **Avon** South Dakota, N USA
97 *M23* **Avon** ≈ S England, UK
97 *L20* **Avon** ≈ C England, UK
36 *K13* **Avondale** Arizona, SW USA
23 *X13* **Avon Park** Florida, SE USA
102 *J5* **Avranches** Manche, N France
103 *O3* **Avre** ≈ N France
Avveel *see* Ivalojoki
186 *M6* **Avuavu** *var.* Kolotambu. Guadalcanal, C Solomon Islands
Avveel *see* Ivalo
Avvil *see* Ivalo
77 *O17* **Awaaso** *var.* Awaso. SW Ghana
141 *X8* **Awābī** *var.* Al 'Awābī. NE Oman
184 *L9* **Awakino** Waikato, North Island, New Zealand
142 *M15* **'Awālī** C Bahrain
99 *K19* **Awans** Liège, E Belgium
184 *I2* **Awanui** Northland, North Island, New Zealand
148 *M14* **Awārān** Baluchistān, SW Pakistan
81 *K16* **Awara Plain** *plain* NE Kenya
80 *M13* **Āwarē** Somali, E Ethiopia
138 *M6* **'Awāriḍ, Wādī** *dry watercourse* E Syria
185 *B20* **Awarua Point** *headland* South Island, New Zealand
81 *J14* **Āwasa** Southern, S Ethiopia
80 *K13* **Āwash** Afar, NE Ethiopia
80 *K12* **Āwash** *var.* Hawash. ≈ C Ethiopia
Awaso *see* Awaaso
158 *H7* **Awat** Xinjiang Uygur Zizhiqu, NW China
185 *J15* **Awatere** ≈ South Island, New Zealand
75 *O10* **Awbārī** SW Libya
75 *N9* **Awbāri, Idhān** *var.* Edeyen d'Oubari. *desert* Algeria/Libya
80 *M12* **Awdal** *off* Gobolka Awdal. ◈ N Somalia
80 *C13* **Aweil** Northern Bahr el Ghazal, SW Sudan
96 *H11* **Awe, Loch** ◎ W Scotland, UK
77 *U16* **Awka** Anambra, SW Nigeria
39 *O6* **Awuna River** ≈ Alaska, USA
Awwinorm *see* Avinurme
Ax *see* Dax
Axarfjördhur *see* Öxarfjördhur
103 *N17* **Axat** Aude, S France
99 *F16* **Axel** Zeeland, SW Netherlands
197 *P9* **Axel Heiberg Island** *var.* Axel Heiburg. *island* Nunavut, N Canada
Axel Heiburg *see* Axel Heiberg Island
77 *O17* **Axim** S Ghana
114 *F13* **Axiós** *var.* Vardar. ≈ Greece/FYR Macedonia *see also* Vardar
Axiós *see* Vardar
103 *N17* **Ax-les-Thermes** Ariège, S France
120 *D11* **Ayachi, Jbel** ▲ C Morocco
61 *D22* **Ayacucho** Buenos Aires, E Argentina
57 *F15* **Ayacucho** Ayacucho, S Peru
57 *E16* **Ayacucho** *off.* Departamento de Ayacucho. ◈ *department* SW Peru
Ayacucho, Departamento de *see* Ayacucho
145 *W11* **Ayagoz** *var.* Ayaguz, *Kaz.* Ayaköz; *prev.* Sergiopol. Vostochnyy Kazakhstan, E Kazakhstan
113 *V12* **Ayagoz** *var.* Ayaguz, *Kaz.* Ayakoz. ≈ E Kazakhstan
Ayaguz *see* Ayagoz
Ayakagytma *see* Oyoqog'itma
Ayakkuduk *see* Oyoqquduq
158 *L10* **Ayakkum Hu** ◎ NW China
Ayakoz *see* Ayagoz
Ayaköz *see* Ayagoz
104 *H14* **Ayamonte** Andalucía, S Spain
123 *S11* **Ayan** Khabarovskiy Kray, E Russian Federation
136 *J10* **Ayancık** Sinop, N Turkey
55 *S9* **Ayanganna Mountain** ▲ C Guyana
77 *U16* **Ayangba** Kogi, C Nigeria
123 *U7* **Ayanka** Koryakskiy Avtonomnyy Okrug, E Russian Federation
54 *E7* **Ayapel** Córdoba, NW Colombia
136 *H12* **Ayaş** Ankara, N Turkey
57 *I16* **Ayaviri** Puno, S Peru
149 *P3* **Āybak** *var.* Aibak, Haibak; *prev.* Samangān. Samangān, NE Afghanistan
147 *N10* **Aydarko'l Ko'li** *Rus.* Ozero Aydarkul'. ◎ C Uzbekistan
Aydarkul', Ozero *see* Aydarko'l Ko'li
21 *W10* **Ayden** North Carolina, SE USA
136 *C15* **Aydın** *var.* Aïdin; *anc.* Tralles Aydin. Aydın, SW Turkey
136 *C15* **Aydın** *var.* Aïdin. ◈ *province* SW Turkey
136 *I17* **Aydıncık** Mersin, S Turkey
136 *C15* **Aydın Dağları** ▲▲ W Turkey
158 *L6* **Aydingkol Hu** ◎ NW China
127 *X7* **Aydyrlinskiy** Orenburgskaya Oblast', W Russian Federation
105 *S4* **Ayerbe** Aragón, NE Spain
Ayers Rock *see* Uluru
Ayeyarwady *see* Irrawaddy
Ayiá *see* Agiá
Ayia Napa *see* Agía Nápa
Ayia Phyla *see* Agía Fýlaxis
Ayiásos/Ayiássos *see* Agiassós
Áyios Evstrátios *see* Ágios Efstrátios
Áyios Kírikos *see* Ágios Kírykos
Áyios Nikólaos *see* Ágios Nikólaos
80 *I11* **Āykel** Amhara, N Ethiopia
123 *N9* **Aykhal** Respublika Sakha (Yakutiya), NE Russian Federation
14 *J12* **Aylen Lake** ◎ Ontario, SE Canada
97 *N21* **Aylesbury** SE England, UK
105 *O6* **Ayllón** Castilla-León, N Spain
14 *F17* **Aylmer** Ontario, S Canada
14 *L12* **Aylmer** Québec, SE Canada
15 *R12* **Aylmer, Lac** ◎ Québec, SE Canada
8 *L9* **Aylmer Lake** ◎ Northwest Territories, NW Canada
145 *V14* **Aynabulak** *cont.* Ajnabulak. Almaty, SE Kazakhstan
138 *K2* **'Ayn al 'Arab** Ḥalab, N Syria
Aynayn *see* 'Aynīn
139 *V12* **'Ayn Ḥamūd** S Iraq
147 *P12* **Ayní** *prev.* Varzimanor Ayni. W Tajikistan
140 *M10* **'Aynīn** *var.* Aynayn. *spring/well* SW Saudi Arabia
21 *U12* **Aynor** South Carolina, SE USA
139 *Q7* **'Ayn Zāzūh** C Iraq
153 *N12* **Ayodhya** Uttar Pradesh, N India
123 *S6* **Ayon, Ostrov** *island* NE Russian Federation
105 *R11* **Ayora** País Valenciano, E Spain
77 *Q11* **Ayorou** Tillabéri, W Niger
79 *E16* **Ayos** Centre, S Cameroon
76 *L5* **'Ayoûn 'Abd el Mâlek** *well* N Mauritania
76 *K10* **'Ayoûn el 'Atroûs** *var.* Aïoun el Atrous, Aïoun el Atroûss. Hodh el Gharbi, SE Mauritania
96 *I13* **Ayr** W Scotland, UK
96 *I13* **Ayr** ≈ W Scotland, UK
96 *I13* **Ayrshire** *cultural region* SW Scotland, UK
Aysen *see* Aisén
80 *L12* **Āysha** Somali, E Ethiopia
144 *L14* **Ayteke Bi** *Kaz.* Zhangaqazaly; *prev.* Novokazalinsk. Kzylorda, SW Kazakhstan
146 *K8* **Aytim** Nawoiy Viloyati, N Uzbekistan
181 *W4* **Ayton** Queensland, NE Australia
114 *M9* **Aytos** Burgas, E Bulgaria
171 *T11* **Ayu, Kepulauan** *island group* E Indonesia
A Yun Pa *see* Cheo Reo
169 *V11* **Ayu, Tanjung** *cape* Borneo, N Indonesia
41 *P16* **Ayutlá** *var.* Ayutla de los Libres. Guerrero, S Mexico
40 *K13* **Ayutla** Jalisco, C Mexico
Ayutla de los Libres *see* Ayutlá
167 *O11* **Ayutthaya** *var.* Phra Nakhon Si Ayutthaya. Phra Nakhon Si Ayutthaya, C Thailand
136 *B13* **Ayvalik** Balıkesir, W Turkey
99 *L20* **Aywaille** Liège, E Belgium
141 *R13* **'Aywat aṣ Ṣay'ar, Wādī** *seasonal river* N Yemen
Azaffal *see* Azeffâl
105 *T9* **Azahar, Costa del** *coastal region* E Spain
105 *S6* **Azaila** Aragón, NE Spain
104 *F10* **Azambuja** Lisboa, C Portugal
153 *N13* **Āzamgarh** Uttar Pradesh, N India
77 *O9* **Azaouâd** *desert* C Mali
77 *S10* **Azaouagh, Vallée de l'** *var.* Azaouak. ≈ W Niger
Azaouak *see* Azaouagh, Vallée de l'
61 *F14* **Azara** Misiones, NE Argentina
Azaran *see* Hashtrūd
Azärbaycan/Azärbaycan Respublikasī *see* Azerbaijan
Āzārbāyjān-e Bākhtarı *see* Āzārbāyjān-e Gharbī
142 *I4* **Āzārbāyjān-e Gharbī** *off.* Ostān-e Āzārbāyjān-e Gharbī, *Eng.* West Azerbaijan; *prev.* Āzārbāyjān-e Bākhtarı. NW Iran
Āzārbāyjān-e Gharbī, Ostān-e *see* Āzārbāyjān-e Gharbī
Azarbayjan-e Khavari *see* Āzārbāyjān-e Sharqī
Āzārbāyjān-e Khāvarī *see* Āzārbāyjān-e Sharqī
142 *J3* **Āzārbāyjān-e Sharqī** *off* Ostān-e Azarbāyjān-e Sharqī, *Eng* East Azerbaijan; *prev.* Azarbayjan-e Khavari. ◈ *province*
142 *J3* **Āzārbāyjān-e Sharqī** *off.* Ostān-e Āzārbāyjān-e Sharqī, *Eng.* East Azerbaijan; *prev.* Āzārbāyjān-e Khāvarī. ◈ *province* NW Iran
Āzārbāyjān-e Sharqī, Ostān-e *see* Āzārbāyjān-e Sharqī
77 *W13* **Azare** Bauchi, N Nigeria
119 *M19* **Azarychy** *Rus.* Ozarichi. Homyel'skaya Voblasts', SE Belarus
102 *L8* **Azay-le-Rideau** Indre-et-Loire, C France
138 *I2* **A'zāz** Ḥalab, NW Syria
76 *H7* **Azeffâl** *var.* Azaffal. *desert* Mauritania/Western Sahara
137 *V12* **Azerbaijan** *off.* Azerbaijani Republic, *Az.* Azärbaycan, Azärbaycan Respublikasī; *prev.* Azerbaijan SSR. ◆ *republic* SE Asia
Azerbaijani Republic *see* Azerbaijan
Azerbaijan SSR *see* Azerbaijan
145 *T7* **Azhbulat, Ozero** ◎ NE Kazakhstan
74 *F7* **Azilal** C Morocco
Azimabad *see* Patna
19 *O6* **Aziscohos Lake** ⊠ Maine, NE USA
Azizbekov *see* Vayk'
Azizie *see* Telish
Aziziya *see* Al 'Azīzīyah
127 *T4* **Aznakayevo** Respublika Tatarstan, W Russian Federation
56 *C8* **Azogues** Cañar, S Ecuador
64 *N2* **Azores** *var.* Açores, Ilhas dos Açores, *Port.* Arquipélago dos Açores. *island group* Portugal, NE Atlantic Ocean
64 *L8* **Azores-Biscay Rise** *undersea feature* E Atlantic Ocean
Azotos/Azotus *see* Ashdod
78 *K11* **Azoum, Bahr** *seasonal river* SE Chad
126 *L12* **Azov** Rostovskaya Oblast', SW Russian Federation
126 *J13* **Azov, Sea of** *Rus.* Azovskoye More, *Ukr.* Azovs'ke More. *sea* NE Black Sea
Azovs'ke More/Azovskoye More *see* Azov, Sea of
138 *I10* **Azraq, Wāḥat al** *oasis* N Jordan
Āzro *see* Āzrow
74 *G6* **Azrou** C Morocco
149 *R5* **Āzrow** *var.* Āzro. Lowgar, E Afghanistan
37 *P8* **Aztec** New Mexico, SW USA
36 *M13* **Aztec Peak** ▲ Arizona, SW USA
45 *N9* **Azua** *var.* Azua de Compostela. S Dominican Republic
Azua de Compostela *see* Azua
104 *K12* **Azuaga** Extremadura, W Spain
56 *B8* **Azuay** ◈ *province* W Ecuador
164 *C13* **Azuchi-Ō-shima** *island* SW Japan
105 *O11* **Azuer** ≈ C Spain
43 *S17* **Azuero, Península de** *peninsula* S Panama
62 *I6* **Azufre, Volcán** *var.* Volcán Lastarria. ⛰ N Chile
116 *J12* **Azuga** Prahova, SE Romania
61 *C22* **Azul** Buenos Aires, E Argentina
62 *I8* **Azul, Cerro** ▲ NW Argentina
56 *E12* **Azul, Cordillera** ▲▲ C Peru
165 *P11* **Azuma-san** ▲ Honshū, C Japan
103 *V15* **Azur, Côte d'** *coastal region* SE France
191 *Z3* **Azur Lagoon** ◎ Kiritimati, E Kiribati
'Azza *see* Gaza
Az Zāb al Kabīr *see* Great Zab
138 *H7* **Az Zabdānī** *var.* Zabadani. Dimashq, W Syria
141 *W8* **Aẓ Ẓāhirah** *desert* NW Oman
141 *S6* **Aẓ Ẓahrān** *Eng.* Dhahran. Ash Sharqīyah, NE Saudi Arabia
141 *R6* **Aẓ Ẓahrān al Khubar** *var.* Dhahran Al Khobar. ✈ Ash Sharqīyah, NE Saudi Arabia
Az Zaqāzīq *see* Zagazig
138 *H10* **Az Zarqā'** *var.* Zarqa. Az Zarqā', NW Jordan
138 *I11* **Az Zarqā'** *off.* Muḥāfazat az Zarqā', *var.* Zarqa. ◈ *governorate* N Jordan
75 *O7* **Az Zāwiyah** *var.* Zawia. NW Libya
141 *N15* **Az Zaydīyah** W Yemen
74 *I11* **Azzel Matti, Sebkha** *var.* Sebkra Azz el Matti. *salt flat* C Algeria
141 *P6* **Az Zilfī** Ar Riyāḍ, N Saudi Arabia
139 *Y13* **Az Zubayr** *var.* Al Zubair. SE Iraq
Az Zuqur *see* Jabal Zuuqar, Jazīrat

B

187 *X15* **Ba** *prev.* Mba. Viti Levu, W Fiji
Ba *see* Da Răng, Sông
171 *P17* **Baa** Pulau Rote, C Indonesia
138 *H7* **Baalbek** *var.* Ba'labakk; *anc.* Heliopolis. E Lebanon
108 *G8* **Baar** Zug, N Switzerland
81 *L17* **Baardheere** *var.* Bardere, *It.* Bardera. Gedo, SW Somalia
80 *Q12* **Baargaal** Bari, NE Somalia
99 *I15* **Baarle-Hertog** Antwerpen, N Belgium
99 *I15* **Baarle-Nassau** Noord-Brabant, N Belgium
98 *J11* **Baarn** Utrecht, C Netherlands
162 *H9* **Baatsagaan** *var.* Bayansayr. Bayanhongor, C Mongolia
114 *D13* **Baba** *var.* Buševa, *Gk.* Varnoús. ▲▲ FYR Macedonia/Greece
76 *H10* **Bababé** Brakna, W Mauritania
136 *G10* **Baba Burnu** *headland* NW Turkey
117 *N13* **Babadag** Tulcea, SE Romania
137 *X10* **Babadağ Dağı** ▲ NE Azerbaijan
146 *H14* **Babadaýhan** *Rus.* Babadaykhan; *prev.* Kirovsk. Ahal Welaýaty, C Turkmenistan
Babadaykhan *see* Babadaýhan
146 *G14* **Babadurmaz** Ahal Welaýaty, C Turkmenistan
114 *M12* **Babaeski** Kırklareli, NW Turkey
139 *T4* **Bāba Gurgur** N Iraq
56 *B7* **Babahoyo** *prev.* Bodegas. Los Ríos, C Ecuador
149 *P5* **Bābā, Kūh-e** ▲▲ C Afghanistan
171 *N12* **Babana** Sulawesi, C Indonesia
Babao *see* Qilian
171 *Q12* **Babar, Kepulauan** *island group* E Indonesia
171 *T12* **Babar, Pulau** *island* Kepulauan Babar, E Indonesia
152 *G4* **Bābāsar Pass** *pass* India/Pakistan
Babashy, Gory *see* Babaşy
146 *C9* **Babaşy** *Rus.* Gory Babashy. ▲▲ W Turkmenistan
168 *M13* **Babat** Sumatera, W Indonesia
81 *H21* **Babati** Manyara, NE Tanzania
124 *J13* **Babayevo** Vologodskaya Oblast', NW Russian Federation
127 *Q15* **Babayurt** Respublika Dagestan, SW Russian Federation
33 *P6* **Babb** Montana, NW USA
29 *X4* **Babbitt** Minnesota, N USA
188 *E9* **Babeldaob** *var.* Babeldaop, Babelthuap. *island* N Palau
Babeldaop *see* Babeldaob
141 *N17* **Bab el Mandeb** *strait* Gulf of Aden/Red Sea
Babelthuap *see* Babeldaob
111 *K17* **Babia Góra** *var.* Babia Hora. ▲ Poland/Slovakia
Babia Hora *see* Babia Góra
Babian Jiang *see* Black River
Babichi *see* Babichy
119 *N19* **Babichy** *Rus.* Babichi. Homyel'skaya Voblasts', SE Belarus
112 *I10* **Babina Greda** Vukovar-Srijem, E Croatia
10 *K13* **Babine Lake** ◎ British Columbia, SW Canada
143 *O4* **Bābol** *var.* Babul, Balfrush, Barfrush; *prev.* Barfurush. Māzandarān, N Iran
143 *O4* **Bābolsar** *var.* Babulsar; *prev.* Meshed-i-Sar. Māzandarān, N Iran
36 *L16* **Baboquivari Peak** ▲ Arizona, SW USA
79 *G15* **Baboua** Nana-Mambéré, W Central African Republic
119 *M17* **Babruysk** *Rus.* Bobruysk. Mahilyowskaya Voblasts', E Belarus
Babu *see* Hezhou
Babul *see* Bābol
Babulsar *see* Bābolsar
113 *O19* **Babuna** ▲▲ C FYR Macedonia
113 *O19* **Babuna** ≈ C FYR Macedonia
148 *K7* **Bābūs, Dasht-e** *Pash.* Bebas, Dasht-i. ▲▲ W Afghanistan
171 *O1* **Babuyan Channel** *channel* N Philippines
171 *O1* **Babuyan Island** *island* N Philippines
139 *T9* **Babylon** *site of ancient city* C Iraq
112 *J9* **Bač** *Ger.* Batsch. Vojvodina, NW Serbia
58 *M13* **Bacabal** Maranhão, E Brazil
41 *Y14* **Bacalar** Quintana Roo, SE Mexico
41 *Y14* **Bacalar Chico, Boca** *strait* SE Mexico
171 *Q12* **Bacan, Kepulauan** *island group* E Indonesia
171 *S12* **Bacan, Pulau** *prev.* Batjan. *island* Maluku, E Indonesia
116 *L10* **Bacău** *Hung.* Bákó. Bacău, NE Romania
116 *K11* **Bacău** ◈ *county* E Romania
Băc Bô, Vinh *see* Tongking, Gulf of
167 *T5* **Băc Can** *var* Bach Thong. Băc Thai, N Vietnam
103 *T5* **Baccarat** Meurthe-et-Moselle, NE France
183 *N12* **Bacchus Marsh** Victoria, SE Australia
40 *H4* **Bacerac** Sonora, NW Mexico
116 *L10* **Băcești** Vaslui, E Romania
167 *T6* **Băc Giang** Ha Băc, N Vietnam
54 *I5* **Bachaquero** Zulia, NW Venezuela
Bacher *see* Pohorje
118 *M13* **Bacheykava** *Rus.* Bocheykovo. Vitsyebskaya Voblasts', N Belarus
40 *I5* **Bachíniva** Chihuahua, N Mexico
Bach Thong *see* Băc Can
158 *G8* **Bachu** Xinjiang Uygur Zizhiqu, NW China
9 *N8* **Back** ≈ Nunavut, N Canada
112 *K10* **Bačka Palanka** *prev.* Palanka. Serbia, NW Serbia
112 *K8* **Bačka Topola** *Hung.* Topolya; *prev. Hung.* Bácstopolya. Vojvodina, N Serbia
95 *J17* **Bäckefors** Västra Götaland, S Sweden
Bäckermühle Schulzenmühle *see* Żywiec
95 *L16* **Bäckhammar** Värmland, C Sweden
112 *K9* **Bački Petrovac** *Hung.* Petrőcz; *prev.* Petrovac, Petrovácz. Vojvodina, NW Serbia
101 *I21* **Backnang** Baden-Württemberg, SW Germany
167 *S15* **Bac Liêu** *var.* Vinh Loi. Minh Hai, S Vietnam
167 *T6* **Băc Ninh** Ha Băc, N Vietnam
40 *G4* **Bacoachi** Sonora, NW Mexico
171 *P6* **Bacolod** *off.* Bacolod City. Negros, C Philippines
Bacolod City *see* Bacolod
171 *O4* **Baco, Mount** ▲ Mindoro, N Philippines
111 *K25* **Bácsalmás** Bács-Kiskun, S Hungary
Bácsjózseffalva *see* Žednik
111 *J24* **Bács-Kiskun** *off.* Bács-Kiskun Megye. ◈ *county* S Hungary
Bács-Kiskun Megye *see* Bács-Kiskun
Bácsszenttamás *see* Srbobran
Bácstopolya *see* Bačka Topola
Bactra *see* Balkh
Bada *see* Xilin
155 *F21* **Badagara** Kerala, SW India
101 *M24* **Bad Aibling** Bayern, SE Germany
162 *I13* **Badain Jaran Shamo** *desert* N China
104 *I11* **Badajoz** *anc.* Pax Augusta. Extremadura, W Spain
104 *J11* **Badajoz** ◈ *province* Extremadura, W Spain
149 *S2* **Badakhshān** ◈ *province* NE Afghanistan
105 *W6* **Badalona** *anc.* Baetulo. Cataluña, E Spain
154 *O11* **Bādāmapāhārh** Orissa, E India
152 *K8* **Badarīnāth** ▲ N India
169 *O10* **Badas, Kepulauan** *island group* W Indonesia
109 *S6* **Bad Aussee** Salzburg, E Austria
31 *S8* **Bad Axe** Michigan, N USA
101 *G16* **Bad Berleburg** Nordrhein-Westfalen, W Germany
101 *L17* **Bad Blankenburg** Thüringen, C Germany
Bad Borseck *see* Borsec
101 *G18* **Bad Camberg** Hessen, W Germany
100 *L8* **Bad Doberan** Mecklenburg-Vorpommern, N Germany
101 *N14* **Bad Düben** Sachsen, E Germany
109 *X4* **Baden** *var.* Baden bei Wien; *anc.* Aquae Panoniae, Thermae Pannonicae. Niederösterreich, NE Austria
108 *F9* **Baden** Aargau, N Switzerland
101 *G21* **Baden-Baden** *anc.* Aurelia Aquensis. Baden-Württemberg, SW Germany
Baden bei Wien *see* Baden
101 *G22* **Baden-Württemberg** *Fr.* Bade-Wurtemberg. ◈ *state* SW Germany
112 *A10* **Baderna** Istra, NW Croatia
Bade-Wurtemberg *see* Baden-Württemberg
101 *H20* **Bad Fredrichshall** Baden-Württemberg, S Germany
100 *P11* **Bad Freienwalde** Brandenburg, NE Germany
109 *Q8* **Badgastein** *var.* Gastein. Salzburg, NW Austria
Badger State *see* Wisconsin
148 *L4* **Bādghīs** ◈ *province* NW Afghanistan
109 *T5* **Bad Hall** Oberösterreich, N Austria
101 *J14* **Bad Harzburg** Niedersachsen, C Germany
101 *I16* **Bad Hersfeld** Hessen, C Germany
98 *I10* **Badhoevedorp** Noord-Holland, C Netherlands
109 *Q8* **Bad Hofgastein** Salzburg, NW Austria
Bad Homburg *see* Bad Homburg vor der Höhe
101 *G18* **Bad Homburg vor der Höhe** *var.* Bad Homburg. Hessen, W Germany
101 *E17* **Bad Honnef** Nordrhein-Westfalen, W Germany
149 *Q17* **Badīn** Sind, SE Pakistan
21 *S10* **Badin Lake** ⊠ North Carolina, SE USA
40 *I8* **Badiraguato** Sinaloa, C Mexico
109 *R6* **Bad Ischl** Oberösterreich, N Austria
Badjawa *see* Bajawa
Badje-Sohppar *see* Övre Soppero
101 *J18* **Bad Kissingen** Bayern, SE Germany
Bad Königswart *see* Lázně Kynžvart
101 *F19* **Bad Kreuznach** Rheinland-Pfalz, SW Germany
101 *F24* **Bad Krozingen** Baden-Württemberg, SW Germany
101 *G16* **Bad Laasphe** Nordrhein-Westfalen, W Germany
28 *J6* **Badlands** *physical region* North Dakota, N USA
101 *K16* **Bad Langensalza** Thüringen, C Germany
109 *T3* **Bad Leonfelden** Oberösterreich, N Austria
101 *I20* **Bad Mergentheim** Baden-Württemberg, SW Germany
101 *H17* **Bad Nauheim** Hessen, W Germany
101 *E17* **Bad Neuenahr-Arhweiler** Rheinland-Pfalz, W Germany
Bad Neustadt *see* Bad Neustadt an der Saale
101 *J18* **Bad Neustadt an der Saale** *var.* Bad Neustadt. Berlin, C Germany
Badnur *see* Betūl
100 *H13* **Bad Oeynhausen** Nordrhein-Westfalen, NW Germany
100 *J9* **Bad Oldesloe** Schleswig-Holstein, N Germany
77 *Q16* **Badou** C Togo
Bad Polzin *see* Połczyn-Zdrój
100 *H13* **Bad Pyrmont** Niedersachsen, C Germany
109 *X9* **Bad Radkersburg** Steiermark, SE Austria
139 *V8* **Badrah** E Iraq
Badrah *see* Tarialan
101 *N24* **Bad Reichenhall** Bayern, SE Germany
140 *K8* **Badr Ḥunayn** Al Madīnah, W Saudi Arabia
28 *M10* **Bad River** ≈ South Dakota, N USA
30 *K4* **Bad River** ≈ Wisconsin, N USA
100 *H13* **Bad Salzuflen** Nordrhein-Westfalen, NW Germany
101 *J16* **Bad Salzungen** Thüringen, C Germany
109 *V8* **Bad Sankt Leonhard im Lavanttal** Kärnten, S Austria
100 *K9* **Bad Schwartau** Schleswig-Holstein, N Germany
101 *L24* **Bad Tölz** Bayern, SE Germany
181 *U1* **Badu Island** *island* Queensland, NE Australia
155 *K25* **Badulla** Uva Province, C Sri Lanka
109 *X5* **Bad Vöslau** Niederösterreich, NE Austria
101 *I24* **Bad Waldsee** Baden-Württemberg, S Germany
35 *U11* **Badwater Basin** *depression* California, W USA
101 *J20* **Bad Windsheim** Bayern, C Germany
101 *J23* **Bad Wörishofen** Bayern, S Germany
100 *G10* **Bad Zwischenahn** Niedersachsen, NW Germany
104 *M13* **Baena** Andalucía, S Spain
Baeterrae/Baeterrae Septimanorum *see* Béziers
Baetic Cordillera/Baetic Mountains *see* Béticos, Sistemas
Baetulo *see* Badalona
57 *K18* **Baeza** Napo, NE Ecuador
105 *N13* **Baeza** Andalucía, S Spain
79 *D15* **Bafang** Ouest, W Cameroon
76 *H12* **Bafatá** C Guinea-Bissau
149 *U5* **Baffa** North-West Frontier Province, NW Pakistan
197 *O11* **Baffin Basin** *undersea feature* N Labrador Sea
197 *N12* **Baffin Bay** *bay* Canada/Greenland
25 *T15* **Baffin Bay** *inlet* Texas, SW USA
196 *M12* **Baffin Island** *island* Nunavut, NE Canada
79 *E15* **Bafia** Centre, C Cameroon
77 *R14* **Bafilo** NE Togo
76 *J12* **Bafing** ≈ W Africa
76 *J12* **Bafoulabé** Kayes, W Mali
79 *D15* **Bafoussam** Ouest, W Cameroon
143 *R9* **Bāfq** Yazd, C Iran
136 *L10* **Bafra** Samsun, N Turkey
136 *L10* **Bafra Burnu** *headland* N Turkey
143 *S12* **Bāft** Kermān, S Iran
79 *N18* **Bafwabalinga** Orientale, NE Dem. Rep. Congo
79 *N18* **Bafwaboli** Orientale, NE Dem. Rep. Congo
79 *N17* **Bafwasende** Orientale, NE Dem. Rep. Congo
42 *K13* **Bagaces** Guanacaste, NW Costa Rica
153 *O12* **Bagaha** Bihār, N India
155 *F16* **Bāgalkot** Karnātaka, W India
81 *J22* **Bagamoyo** Pwani, E Tanzania
Bagan Datok *see* Bagan Datuk
168 *J8* **Bagan Datuk** *var.* Bagan Datok. Perak, Peninsular Malaysia
171 *R7* **Baganga** Mindanao, S Philippines
168 *J9* **Bagansiapiapi** *var.* Pasirpangarayan. Sumatera, W Indonesia
162 *M8* **Baganuur** *var* Nüürst. Töv, C Mongolia
Bagaria *see* Bagheria
77 *T11* **Bagaroua** Tahoua, W Niger
79 *I20* **Bagata** Bandundu, W Dem. Rep. Congo
Bagdad *see* Baghdād
123 *O13* **Bagdarin** Respublika Buryatiya, S Russian Federation
61 *G17* **Bagé** Rio Grande do Sul, S Brazil
Bagenalstown *see* Muine Bheag
Bagerhat *see* Bagherhat
103 *P16* **Bages et de Sigean, Étang de** ◎ S France
33 *W17* **Baggs** Wyoming, C USA
154 *F11* **Bāgh** Madhya Pradesh, C India
139 *T8* **Baghdād** *var.* Bagdad, *Eng.* Baghdad. ● (Iraq) C Iraq
139 *T8* **Baghdād** ✈ C Iraq
Baghdad *see* Baghdād
153 *T16* **Bagherhat** *var.* Bagerhat. Khulna, S Bangladesh
107 *J23* **Bagheria** *var.* Bagaria. Sicilia, Italy, C Mediterranean Sea
143 *S10* **Bāghīn** Kermān, C Iran
149 *Q3* **Baghlān** Baghlān, NE Afghanistan
149 *Q3* **Baghlān** *var.* Bāghlān. ◈ *province* NE Afghanistan
Bāghlān *see* Baghlān
148 *M7* **Bāghrān** Helmand, S Afghanistan
29 *T4* **Bagley** Minnesota, N USA
106 *H10* **Bagnacavallo** Emilia-Romagna, C Italy
102 *K16* **Bagnères-de-Bigorre** Hautes-Pyrénées, S France
102 *L17* **Bagnères-de-Luchon** Hautes-Pyrénées, S France
106 *F11* **Bagni di Lucca** Toscana, C Italy
106 *H11* **Bagno di Romagna** Emilia-Romagna, C Italy
103 *R14* **Bagnols-sur-Cèze** Gard, S France
162 *M14* **Bag Nur** ◎ N China
171 *P6* **Bago** *off.* Bago City. Negros, C Philippines
Bago *see* Pegu
Bago City *see* Bago

76 M13 **Bagoé** ≈ Ivory Coast/Mali
Bagrāmē see Bagrāmī
149 R5 **Bagrāmī** var. Bagrāmē. Kābōl, E Afghanistan
119 B14 **Bagrationovsk** Ger. Preussisch Eylau. Kaliningradskaya Oblast', W Russian Federation
Bagrax see Bohu
Bagrax Hu see Bosten Hu
56 C10 **Bagua** Amazonas, NE Peru
171 O2 **Baguio** off. Baguio City. Luzon, N Philippines
Baguio City see Baguio
77 V9 **Bagzane, Monts** ▲ N Niger
Bāḩah, Minţaqat al see Al Bāḩah
Bahama Islands see Bahamas
44 H3 **Bahamas** off. Commonwealth of the Bahamas. ◆ island state N West Indies
0 L13 **Bahamas** var. Bahama Islands. island group N West Indies
Bahamas, Commonwealth of the see Bahamas
153 S15 **Baharampur** prev. Berhampore. West Bengal, NE India
146 E12 **Baharly** var. Bäherden, Rus. Bakharden; prev. Bakherden. Ahal Welaýaty, C Turkmenistan
149 U10 **Bahāwalnagar** Punjab, E Pakistan
149 T11 **Bahāwalpur** Punjab, E Pakistan
136 L16 **Bahçe** Osmaniye, S Turkey
160 J8 **Ba He** ≈ C China
Bäherden see Baharly
59 N16 **Bahia** off. Estado da Bahia. ◈ state E Brazil
61 B24 **Bahía Blanca** Buenos Aires, E Argentina
40 L15 **Bahía Bufadero** Michoacán de Ocampo, SW Mexico
63 J19 **Bahía Bustamante** Chubut, SE Argentina
40 D5 **Bahía de los Ángeles** Baja California, NW Mexico
40 C6 **Bahía de Tortugas** Baja California Sur, W Mexico
Bahia, Estado da see Bahia
42 J4 **Bahía, Islas de la** Eng. Bay Islands. island group N Honduras
40 E5 **Bahía Kino** Sonora, NW Mexico
40 E9 **Bahía Magdalena** var. Puerto Magdalena. Baja California Sur, W Mexico
54 C8 **Bahía Solano** var. Ciudad Mutis, Solano. Chocó, W Colombia
80 I11 **Bahir Dar** var. Bahr Dar, Bahrdar Giyorgis. Amhara, N Ethiopia
141 X8 **Bahlā'** var. Bahlah, Bahlat. NW Oman
Bāhla see Bālān
Bahlah/Bahlat see Bahlā'
152 M11 **Bahraich** Uttar Pradesh, N India
143 M14 **Bahrain** off. State of Bahrain, Dawlat al Bahrayn, Ar. Al Baḩrayn, prev. Bahrein; anc. Tylos, Tyros. ◆ monarchy SW Asia
142 M14 **Bahrain** ✖ C Bahrain
142 M15 **Bahrain, Gulf of** gulf Persian Gulf, NW Arabian Sea
Bahrain, State of see Bahrain
138 I7 **Baḩrat Mallāḩah** ◎ W Syria
Bahrayn, Dawlat al see Bahrain
Bahr Dar/Bahrdar Giyorgis see Bahir Dar
Bahrein see Bahrain
Bahr el, Azraq see Blue Nile
81 E16 **Bahr el Gabel** ◈ state S Sudan
80 E13 **Bahr ez Zaref** ≈ C Sudan
67 R8 **Bahr Kameur** ≈ N Central African Republic
Bahr Tabariya, Sea of see Tiberias, Lake
143 W15 **Bāhū Kalāt** Sīstān va Balūchestān, SE Iran
118 N13 **Bahushewsk** Rus. Bogushëvsk. Vitsyebskaya Voblasts', NE Belarus
Bai see Tagow Bāy
116 G13 **Baia de Aramă** Mehedinţi, SW Romania
116 G11 **Baia de Criş** Ger. Altenburg, Hung. Körösbánya. Hunedoara, SW Romania
83 A16 **Baia dos Tigres** Namibe, SW Angola
82 A13 **Baia Farta** Benguela, W Angola
116 H9 **Baia Mare** Ger. Frauenbach, Hung. Nagybánya; prev. Neustadt. Maramureş, NW Romania
116 H8 **Baia Sprie** Ger. Mittelstadt, Hung. Felsőbánya. Maramureş, NW Romania
78 G13 **Baïbokoum** Logone-Oriental, SW Chad
160 F12 **Baicao Ling** ▲▲ SW China
163 U9 **Baicheng** var. Pai-ch'eng; prev. T'aon-an. Jilin, NE China
158 I6 **Baicheng** var. Bay. Xinjiang Uygur Zizhiqu, NW China
116 J13 **Băicoi** Prahova, SE Romania
Baidoa see Baydhabo
15 U6 **Baie-Comeau** Québec, SE Canada
15 T7 **Baie-des-Bacon** Québec, SE Canada
15 S8 **Baie-des-Rochers** Québec, SE Canada
15 U6 **Baie-des-Sables** Québec, SE Canada
12 K11 **Baie-du-Poste** Québec, SE Canada
172 H17 **Baie Lazare** Mahé, NE Seychelles
45 Y5 **Baie-Mahault** Basse Terre, C Guadeloupe
15 R9 **Baie-St-Paul** Québec, SE Canada
15 V5 **Baie-Trinité** Québec, SE Canada
13 T11 **Baie Verte** Newfoundland and Labrador, SE Canada
Baiguan see Shangyu
Baihe see Erdaobaihe
139 U11 **Bā'ij al Mahdī** S Iraq
Baiji see Bayjī
Baikal, Lake see Baykal, Ozero
Bailādila see Kirandul
Baile an Chaistil see Ballycastle
Baile an Róba see Ballinrobe
Baile an tSratha see Ballintra
Baile Átha an Rí see Athenry
Baile Átha Buí see Athboy
Baile Átha Cliath see Dublin
Baile Átha Fhirdhia see Ardee
Baile Átha Í see Athy
Baile Átha Luain see Athlone
Baile Átha Troim see Trim
Baile Brigín see Balbriggan
Baile Easa Dara see Ballysadare
116 I13 **Băile Govora** Vâlcea, SW Romania
116 F13 **Băile Herculane** Ger. Herkulesbad, Hung. Herkulesfürdő. Caraş-Severin, SW Romania
Baile Locha Riach see Loughrea
Baile Mhistéala see Mitchelstown
Baile Monaidh see Ballymoney
105 N12 **Bailén** Andalucía, S Spain
Baile na hInse see Ballynahinch
Baile na Lorgan see Castleblayney
Baile na Mainistreach see Newtownabbey
Baile Nua na hArda see Newtownards
116 I12 **Băile Olăneşti** Vâlcea, SW Romania
116 H14 **Băileşti** Dolj, SW Romania
163 N12 **Bailingmiao** var. Darhan Muminggan Lianheqi. Nei Mongol Zizhiqu, N China
58 K11 **Bailique, Ilha** island NE Brazil
103 O1 **Bailleul** Nord, N France
78 H12 **Ba Illi** Chari-Baguirmi, SW Chad
159 V12 **Bailong Jiang** ≈ C China
82 C13 **Bailundo** Port. Vila Teixeira da Silva. Huambo, C Angola
159 T13 **Baima** var. Sêraitang. Qinghai, C China
Baima see Baxoi
186 C8 **Baimuru** Gulf, S Papua New Guinea
158 M16 **Bainang** Xizang Zizhiqu, W China
23 S8 **Bainbridge** Georgia, SE USA
171 O17 **Baing** Pulau Sumba, SE Indonesia
158 M14 **Baingoin** Xizang Zizhiqu, W China
104 G2 **Baio Grande** Galicia, NW Spain
104 G4 **Baiona** Galicia, NW Spain
163 V7 **Baiquan** Heilongjiang, NE China
Bā'ir see Bāyir
158 I11 **Bairab Co** ◎ W China
25 Q7 **Baird** Texas, SW USA
39 N7 **Baird Mountains** ▲▲ Alaska, USA
Baireuth see Bayreuth
190 H3 **Bairiki** ● (Kiribati) Tarawa, NW Kiribati
Bairin Youqi see Daban
Bairin Zuoqi see Lindong
145 P17 **Bairkum** Kaz. Bayyrqum. Yuzhnyy Kazakhstan, S Kazakhstan
183 P12 **Bairnsdale** Victoria, SE Australia
171 P6 **Bais** Negros, S Philippines
102 L15 **Baïse** var. Baise. ≈ S France
Baise see Baïse
163 W11 **Baishan** prev. Hunjiang. Jilin, NE China
Baishan see Mashan
118 F12 **Baisogala** Šiauliai, C Lithuania
189 Q7 **Baiti** N Nauru
Baitou Shan see Paektu-san
104 G13 **Baixo Alentejo** physical region S Portugal
64 P5 **Baixo, Ilhéu de** island Madeira, Portugal, NE Atlantic Ocean
83 E15 **Baixo Longa** Cuando Cubango, SE Angola
159 V10 **Baiyin** Gansu, C China
160 E8 **Baiyü** var. Jianshe. Sichuan, C China
161 N14 **Baiyun** ✖ (Guangzhou) Guangdong, S China
160 K4 **Baiyu Shan** ▲▲ C China
111 J25 **Baja** Bács-Kiskun, S Hungary
40 C4 **Baja California** ◈ state NW Mexico
40 C4 **Baja California** Eng. Lower California. peninsula NW Mexico
40 E9 **Baja California Sur** ◈ state W Mexico
Bājah see Béja
Bajan see Bayan
191 V16 **Baja, Punta** headland Easter Island, Chile, E Pacific Ocean
40 B4 **Baja, Punta** headland NW Mexico
55 R5 **Baja, Punta** headland NE Venezuela
42 D5 **Baja Verapaz** off. Departamento de Baja Verapaz. ◈ department C Guatemala
Baja Verapaz, Departamento de see Baja Verapaz
171 N16 **Bajawa** prev. Badjawa. Flores, S Indonesia
153 S16 **Baj Baj** prev. Budge-Budge. West Bengal, E India
141 N15 **Bājil** W Yemen
183 U4 **Bajimba, Mount** ▲ New South Wales, SE Australia
112 K13 **Bajina Bašta** Serbia, W Serbia
153 U14 **Bajitpur** Dhaka, E Bangladesh
112 K8 **Bajmok** Vojvodina, NW Serbia
Bajo Boquete see Boquete
113 L17 **Bajram Curri** Kukës, N Albania
79 J14 **Bakala** Ouaka, C Central African Republic
127 T4 **Bakaly** Respublika Bashkortostan, W Russian Federation
Bakan see Shimonoseki
145 U14 **Bakanas** Kaz. Baqanas. Almaty, SE Kazakhstan
145 V12 **Bakanas** Kaz. Baqanas. ≈ E Kazakhstan
149 R4 **Bākārak** Panjshīr, NE Afghanistan
145 U14 **Bakbakty** Kaz. Baqbaqty. Almaty, SE Kazakhstan
122 J12 **Bakchar** Tomskaya Oblast', C Russian Federation
76 I11 **Bakel** E Senegal
35 W13 **Baker** California, W USA
22 J8 **Baker** Louisiana, S USA
33 Y9 **Baker** Montana, NW USA
32 L12 **Baker** Oregon, NW USA
192 L7 **Baker and Howland Islands** ◇ US unincorporated territory W Polynesia
36 L12 **Baker Butte** ▲ Arizona, SW USA
39 X15 **Baker Island** island Alexander Archipelago, Alaska, USA
9 N9 **Baker Lake** Nunavut, N Canada
9 N9 **Baker Lake** ◎ Nunavut, N Canada
32 H6 **Baker, Mount** ▲ Washington, NW USA
35 R13 **Bakersfield** California, W USA
24 M9 **Bakersfield** Texas, SW USA
21 P9 **Bakersville** North Carolina, SE USA
Bākhābī see Bū Khābī
Bakharden see Baharly
Bakhardok see Bokurdak
143 U5 **Bākharz, Kuhhā-ye** ▲▲ NE Iran
152 D13 **Bākhāsar** Rājasthān, NW India
Bakhchisaray see Bakhchysaray
117 T13 **Bakhchysaray** Rus. Bakhchisaray. Respublika Krym, S Ukraine
Bakherden see Baharly
117 R3 **Bakhmach** Chernihivs'ka Oblast', N Ukraine
Bākhtarān see Kermānshāh
143 Q11 **Bakhtegān, Daryācheh-ye** ◎ C Iran
145 X12 **Bakhty** Vostochnyy Kazakhstan, E Kazakhstan
137 Z11 **Bakı** Eng. Baku. ● (Azerbaijan) E Azerbaijan
80 M12 **Baki** Awdal, N Somalia
137 Z11 **Bakı** ✖ E Azerbaijan
136 C13 **Bakır Çayı** ≈ W Turkey
92 L1 **Bakkafjördhur** Austurland, NE Iceland
92 L1 **Bakkaflói** sea area W Norwegian Sea
81 I15 **Bako** Southern, S Ethiopia
76 L15 **Bako** NW Ivory Coast
Bákó see Bacău
111 H23 **Bakony** Eng. Bakony Mountains, Ger. Bakonywald. ▲▲ W Hungary
Bakony Mountains/ Bakonywald see Bakony
81 M16 **Bakool** off. Gobolka Bakool. ◈ region W Somalia
Bakool, Gobolka see Bakool
79 L15 **Bakouma** Mbomou, SE Central African Republic
127 N15 **Baksan** Kabardino-Balkarskaya Respublika, SW Russian Federation
119 I16 **Bakshty** Hrodzyenskaya Voblasts', W Belarus
Baku see Bakı
194 K12 **Bakutis Coast** physical region Antarctica
Bakwanga see Mbuji-Mayi
145 O15 **Bakyrly** Yuzhnyy Kazakhstan, S Kazakhstan
14 H13 **Bala** Ontario, S Canada
136 I13 **Balâ** Ankara, C Turkey
97 J19 **Bala** NW Wales, UK
170 L7 **Balabac Island** island W Philippines
Balabac, Selat see Balabac Strait
169 V5 **Balabac Strait** var. Selat Balabac. strait Malaysia/Philippines
Ba'labakk see Baalbek
187 P16 **Balabio, Île** island Province Nord, W New Caledonia
116 I14 **Balaci** Teleorman, S Romania
139 S7 **Balad** N Iraq
123 R12 **Baladek** Khabarovskiy Kray, SE Russian Federation
139 U7 **Balad Rūz** E Iraq
154 J11 **Bālāghāt** Madhya Pradesh, C India
155 F14 **Bālāghāt Range** ▲▲ W India
103 X14 **Balagne** physical region Corse, France, C Mediterranean Sea
105 U5 **Balaguer** Cataluña, NE Spain
105 S3 **Balaïtous** var. Pic de Balaïtous. ▲ France/Spain
Balaitous, Pic de see Balaïtous
Bálák see Ballangen
127 O3 **Balakhna** Nizhegorodskaya Oblast', W Russian Federation
122 L12 **Balakhta** Krasnoyarskiy Kray, S Russian Federation
182 I9 **Balaklava** South Australia
Balakleya see Balakliya
117 V6 **Balakliya** Rus. Balakleya. Kharkivs'ka Oblast', E Ukraine
127 Q7 **Balakovo** Saratovskaya Oblast', W Russian Federation
83 P14 **Balama** Cabo Delgado, N Mozambique
169 U6 **Balambangan, Pulau** island East Malaysia
148 L3 **Bālā Morghāb** Laghmān, NW Afghanistan
152 E11 **Bālān** prev. Bāhla. Rājasthān, NW India
116 J10 **Bălan** Hung. Balánbánya. Harghita, C Romania
Balánbánya see Bălan
171 O3 **Balanga** Luzon, N Philippines
154 M12 **Balāngīr** prev. Bolangir. Orissa, E India
127 N8 **Balashov** Saratovskaya Oblast', W Russian Federation
Balasore see Bāleshwar
111 K21 **Balassagyarmat** Nógrád, N Hungary
29 S10 **Balaton** Minnesota, N USA
111 H24 **Balaton** var. Lake Balaton, Ger. Plattensee. ◎ W Hungary
111 I23 **Balatonfüred** var. Füred. Veszprém, W Hungary
Balaton, Lake see Balaton
116 I11 **Bălăuşeri** Ger. Bladenmarkt, Hung. Balavásár. Mureş, C Romania
Balavásár see Bălăuşeri
105 Q11 **Balazote** Castilla-La Mancha, C Spain
Balázsfalva see Blaj
119 F14 **Balbieriškis** Kaunas, S Lithuania
186 J7 **Balbi, Mount** ▲ Bougainville Island, NE Papua New Guinea
58 F11 **Balbina, Represa** ⊠ NW Brazil
43 T15 **Balboa** Panamá, C Panama
97 G17 **Balbriggan** Ir. Baile Brigín. E Ireland
Balbunar see Kubrat
81 N17 **Balcad** Shabeellaha Dhexe, C Somalia
61 D23 **Balcarce** Buenos Aires, E Argentina
9 U16 **Balcarres** Saskatchewan, S Canada
114 O8 **Balchik** Dobrich, NE Bulgaria
185 E24 **Balclutha** Otago, South Island, New Zealand
25 Q12 **Balcones Escarpment** escarpment Texas, SW USA
18 F14 **Bald Eagle Creek** ≈ Pennsylvania, NE USA
Baldenburg see Biały Bór
21 V12 **Bald Head Island** island North Carolina, SE USA
27 W10 **Bald Knob** Arkansas, C USA
30 K17 **Bald Knob** hill Illinois, N USA
Baldohn see Baldone
118 G9 **Baldone** Ger. Baldohn. Rīga, W Latvia
22 I9 **Baldwin** Louisiana, S USA
31 P7 **Baldwin** Michigan, N USA
27 Q4 **Baldwin City** Kansas, C USA
39 N8 **Baldwin Peninsula** headland Alaska, USA
18 H9 **Baldwinsville** New York, NE USA
23 N2 **Baldwyn** Mississippi, S USA
9 W15 **Baldy Mountain** ▲ Manitoba, S Canada
33 T7 **Baldy Mountain** ▲ Montana, NW USA
37 O13 **Baldy Peak** ▲ Arizona, SW USA
Bâle see Basel
Balearic Plain see Algerian Basin
Baleares see Illes Baleares
105 X11 **Baleares, Islas** Eng. Balearic Islands. island group Spain, W Mediterranean Sea
Baleares Major see Mallorca
Balearic Islands see Baleares, Islas
Balearis Minor see Menorca
169 S9 **Baleh, Batang** ≈ East Malaysia
12 I8 **Baleine, Grande Rivière de la** ≈ Québec, E Canada
12 K7 **Baleine, Petite Rivière de la** ≈ Québec, SE Canada
12 K7 **Baleine, Petite Rivière de la** ≈ Québec, SE Canada
13 N6 **Baleine, Rivière à la** ≈ Québec, E Canada
99 J16 **Balen** Antwerpen, N Belgium
171 O3 **Baler** Luzon, N Philippines
154 P11 **Bāleshwar** prev. Balasore. Orissa, E India
77 S12 **Baléyara** Tillabéri, W Niger
127 T1 **Balezino** Udmurtskaya Respublika, NW Russian Federation
42 J4 **Balfate** Colón, N Honduras
9 O17 **Balfour** British Columbia, SW Canada
29 N3 **Balfour** North Dakota, N USA
Balfrush see Bābol
122 L14 **Balgazyn** Respublika Tyva, S Russian Federation
9 U16 **Balgonie** Saskatchewan, S Canada
Bălgrad see Alba Iulia
81 J19 **Balguda** spring/well S Kenya
158 K6 **Balguntay** Xinjiang Uygur Zizhiqu, NW China
141 R16 **Baljḩāf** S Yemen
152 F13 **Bāli** Rājasthān, N India
169 U17 **Bali** ◈ province S Indonesia
169 T17 **Bali** island C Indonesia
111 K16 **Balice** ✖ (Kraków) Małopolskie, S Poland
171 Y14 **Baliem, Sungai** ≈ Papua, E Indonesia
136 C12 **Balıkesir** Balıkesir, W Turkey
136 C12 **Balıkesir** ◈ province NW Turkey
138 L3 **Balīkh, Nahr** ≈ N Syria
169 V12 **Balikpapan** Borneo, C Indonesia
Bali Laut see Bali Sea
171 N9 **Balimbing** Tawitawi, SW Philippines
186 B8 **Balimo** Western, SW Papua New Guinea
Bálinc see Balinţ
101 H23 **Balingen** Baden-Württemberg, SW Germany
116 F11 **Balinţ** Hung. Bálinc. Timiş, W Romania
171 O1 **Balintang Channel** channel N Philippines
138 K3 **Bālis** Ḩalab, N Syria
169 T16 **Bali Sea** Ind Bali Laut. sea C Indonesia
98 K7 **Balk** Friesland, N Netherlands
146 B11 **Balkanabat** Rus. Nebitdag. Balkan Welaýaty, W Turkmenistan
121 R6 **Balkan Mountains** Bul./SCr. Stara Planina. ▲▲ Bulgaria/Serbia
Balkanskiy Welayat see Balkan Welaýaty
146 B9 **Balkan Welaýaty** Rus. Balkanskiy Velayat. ◈ province W Turkmenistan
145 P8 **Balkashino** Akmola, N Kazakhstan
149 O2 **Balkh** anc. Bactra. Balkh, N Afghanistan
149 P2 **Balkh** ◈ province N Afghanistan
145 T13 **Balkhash** Kaz. Balqash. Karaganda, SE Kazakhstan
Balkhash, Lake see Balkhash, Ozero
145 T13 **Balkhash, Ozero** Eng. Lake Balkhash, Kaz. Balqash. ◎ SE Kazakhstan
Balla Balla see Mbalabala
96 H10 **Ballachulish** N Scotland, UK
180 M12 **Balladonia** Western Australia
97 C16 **Ballaghaderreen** Ir. Bealach an Doirín. C Ireland
92 H10 **Ballangen** Lapp. Bálák. Nordland, NW Norway
97 H14 **Ballantrae** W Scotland, UK
183 N12 **Ballarat** Victoria, SE Australia
180 K11 **Ballard, Lake** salt lake Western Australia
Ballari see Bellary
76 L11 **Ballé** Koulikoro, W Mali
40 D7 **Ballenas, Bahía de** bay W Mexico
40 D5 **Ballenas, Canal de** channel NW Mexico
195 R17 **Balleny Islands** island group Antarctica
40 J7 **Balleza** var. San Pablo Balleza. Chihuahua, N Mexico
114 M13 **Ballı** Tekirdağ, NW Turkey
153 O13 **Ballia** Uttar Pradesh, N India
183 V4 **Ballina** New South Wales, SE Australia
97 C16 **Ballina** Ir. Béal an Átha. W Ireland
97 D16 **Ballinamore** Ir. Béal an Átha Móir. NW Ireland
97 D18 **Ballinasloe** Ir. Béal Átha na Sluaighe. W Ireland
25 P8 **Ballinger** Texas, SW USA
97 C17 **Ballinrobe** Ir. Baile an Róba. W Ireland
97 A21 **Ballinskelligs Bay** Ir. Bá na Scealg. inlet SW Ireland
97 D15 **Ballintra** Ir. Baile an tSratha. NW Ireland
103 T7 **Ballon d'Alsace** ▲ NE France
Ballon de Guebwiller see Grand Ballon
113 K21 **Ballsh** var. Ballshi. Fier, SW Albania
Ballshi see Ballsh
98 K4 **Ballum** Friesland, N Netherlands
97 F16 **Ballybay** Ir. Béal Átha Beithe. N Ireland
97 E14 **Ballybofey** Ir. Bealach Féich. NW Ireland
97 G14 **Ballycastle** Ir. Baile an Chaistil. N Northern Ireland, UK
97 G15 **Ballyclare** Ir. Bealach Cláir. E Northern Ireland, UK
97 E16 **Ballyconnell** Ir. Béal Átha Conaill. N Ireland
97 C17 **Ballyhaunis** Ir. Beál Átha hAmhnais. W Ireland
97 G14 **Ballymena** Ir. An Baile Meánach. NE Northern Ireland, UK
97 F14 **Ballymoney** Ir. Baile Monaidh. NE Northern Ireland, UK
97 G15 **Ballynahinch** Ir. Baile na hInse. SE Northern Ireland, UK
97 D16 **Ballysadare** Ir. Baile Easa Dara. NW Ireland
97 D15 **Ballyshannon** Ir. Béal Átha Seanaidh. NW Ireland
63 H19 **Balmaceda** Aisén, S Chile
63 G23 **Balmaceda, Cerro** ▲ S Chile
111 N22 **Balmazújváros** Hajdú-Bihar, E Hungary
108 E10 **Balmhorn** ▲ SW Switzerland
182 L12 **Balmoral** Victoria, SE Australia
24 K9 **Balmorhea** Texas, SW USA
Balneario Claromecó see Claromecó
Balochistān see Baluchistān
82 B13 **Balombo** Port. Norton de Matos, Vila Norton de Matos. Benguela, W Angola
82 B13 **Balombo** ≈ W Angola
181 X10 **Balonne River** ≈ Queensland, E Australia
152 E13 **Bālotra** Rājasthān, N India
145 V14 **Balpyk Bi** prev. Kirovskiy, Kaz. Kirov. Almaty, SE Kazakhstan
Balqā'/Balqā', Muḩāfaẓat al see Al Balqā'
Balqash see Balkhash, Ozero
Balqash see Balkhash
152 M12 **Balrāmpur** Uttar Pradesh, N India
182 M9 **Balranald** New South Wales, SE Australia
116 H14 **Balş** Olt, S Romania
14 H11 **Balsam Creek** Ontario, S Canada
30 I5 **Balsam Lake** Wisconsin, N USA
14 I14 **Balsam Lake** ◎ Ontario, SE Canada
59 M14 **Balsas** Maranhão, E Brazil
41 M15 **Balsas, Río** var. Río Mexcala. ≈ S Mexico
43 W16 **Balsas, Río** ≈ SE Panama
119 O18 **Bal'shavik** Rus. Bol'shevik. Homyel'skaya Voblasts', SE Belarus
95 O15 **Bålsta** Uppsala, C Sweden
108 E7 **Balsthal** Solothurn, NW Switzerland
117 O8 **Balta** Odes'ka Oblast', SW Ukraine
105 N5 **Baltanás** Castilla-León, N Spain
61 E16 **Baltasar Brum** Artigas, N Uruguay
116 M9 **Bălţi** Rus. Bel'tsy. N Moldova
Baltic Port see Paldiski
118 B10 **Baltic Sea** Ger. Ostee, Rus. Baltiskoye More. sea N Europe
21 X3 **Baltimore** Maryland, NE USA
31 T13 **Baltimore** Ohio, N USA
21 X3 **Baltimore-Washington** ✖ Maryland, E USA
Baltischport/Baltiski see Paldiski
Baltiskoye More see Baltic Sea
119 A14 **Baltiysk** Ger. Pillau. Kaliningradskaya Oblast', W Russian Federation
Baltkrievija see Belarus
119 H14 **Baltoji Voke** Vilnius, SE Lithuania
Balūchestān va Sīstān see Sīstān va Balūchestān
148 M12 **Baluchistān** var. Balochistān, Beluchistan. ◈ province SW Pakistan
171 P5 **Balud** Masbate, N Philippines
169 T9 **Balui, Batang** ≈ East Malaysia
153 S13 **Bālurghat** West Bengal, NE India
118 J8 **Balvi** Balvi, NE Latvia
147 W7 **Balykchy** Kir. Ysyk-Köl; prev. Issyk-Kul', Rybach'ye. Issyk-Kul'skaya Oblast', NE Kyrgyzstan
56 B7 **Balzar** Guayas, W Ecuador
108 I8 **Balzers** S Liechtenstein
143 T12 **Bam** Kermān, SE Iran
77 Y13 **Bama** Borno, NE Nigeria
76 L12 **Bamako** ● (Mali) Capital District, SW Mali
77 P10 **Bamba** Gao, C Mali
42 M8 **Bambana, Río** ≈ NE Nicaragua
79 J15 **Bambari** Ouaka, C Central African Republic
181 W5 **Bambaroo** Queensland, NE Australia
101 K19 **Bamberg** Bayern, SE Germany
21 R14 **Bamberg** South Carolina, SE USA
79 M16 **Bambesa** Orientale, N Dem. Rep. Congo
76 G11 **Bambey** W Senegal
79 H16 **Bambio** Sangha-Mbaéré, SW Central African Republic
83 I24 **Bamboesberge** ▲ S South Africa
79 D14 **Bamenda** Nord-Ouest, W Cameroon
10 K17 **Bamfield** Vancouver Island, British Columbia, SW Canada
Bami see Bamy
149 P4 **Bāmīān** var. Bāmiān. Bāmīān, NE Afghanistan
149 O4 **Bāmīān** ◈ province C Afghanistan
79 J14 **Bamingui** Bamingui-Bangoran, C Central African Republic
78 J13 **Bamingui** ≈ N Central African Republic
78 J13 **Bamingui-Bangoran** ◈ prefecture N Central African Republic
143 V13 **Bampūr** Sīstān va Balūchestān, SE Iran
186 C8 **Bamu** ≈ SW Papua New Guinea
146 E12 **Bamy** Rus. Bami. Ahal Welaýaty, C Turkmenistan
Bán see Bánovce nad Bebravou
81 N17 **Banaadir** off. Gobolka Banaadir. ◈ region S Somalia
Banaadir, Gobolka see Banaadir
191 N3 **Banaba** var. Ocean Island. island Tungaru, W Kiribati
59 O14 **Banabuiú, Açude** ⊠ NE Brazil
57 O19 **Bañados del Izozog** salt lake SE Bolivia
97 D18 **Banagher** Ir. Beannchar. C Ireland
79 M17 **Banalia** Orientale, N Dem. Rep. Congo
76 L12 **Banamba** Koulikoro, W Mali
40 G4 **Banámichi** Sonora, NW Mexico
181 Y9 **Banana** Queensland, E Australia
191 Z2 **Banana** prev. Main Camp. Kiritimati, E Kiribati
59 K16 **Bananal, Ilha do** island C Brazil
23 Y12 **Banana River** lagoon Florida, SE USA
151 Q22 **Bananga** Andaman and Nicobar Islands, India, NE Indian Ocean
Banaras see Vārānasi
114 N13 **Banarlı** Tekirdağ, NW Turkey
152 H12 **Banās** ≈ N India
75 Z11 **Banâs, Râs** cape E Egypt
112 N10 **Banatski Karlovac** Vojvodina, NE Serbia
141 P16 **Banā, Wādī** dry watercourse SW Yemen
136 E14 **Banaz** Uşak, W Turkey
136 E14 **Banaz Çayı** ≈ W Turkey
159 P14 **Banbar** var. Coka. Xizang Zizhiqu, W China
97 G15 **Banbridge** Ir. Droichead na Banna. SE Northern Ireland, UK
Ban Bua Yai see Bua Yai
97 M21 **Banbury** S England, UK
167 O7 **Ban Chiang Dao** Chiang Mai, NW Thailand
96 K9 **Banchory** NE Scotland, UK
14 J13 **Bancroft** Ontario, SE Canada
33 R15 **Bancroft** Idaho, NW USA
29 U11 **Bancroft** Iowa, C USA
154 I9 **Bānda** Madhya Pradesh, C India
152 L13 **Bānda** Uttar Pradesh, N India
168 F7 **Bandaaceh** var. Banda Atjeh; prev. Koetaradja, Kutaradja, Kutaraja. Sumatera, W Indonesia
Banda Atjeh see Bandaaceh
171 S14 **Banda, Kepulauan** island group E Indonesia
Banda, Laut see Banda Sea
77 N17 **Bandama** var. Bandama Fleuve. ≈ S Ivory Coast
77 N15 **Bandama Blanc** ≈ C Ivory Coast
Bandama Fleuve see Bandama
Bandar 'Abbās see Bandar-e 'Abbās
153 W16 **Bandarban** Chittagong, SE Bangladesh
80 Q13 **Bandarbeyla** var. Bender Beila, Bender Beyla. Bari, NE Somalia
143 R14 **Bandar-e 'Abbās** var. Bandar 'Abbās; prev. Gombroon. Hormozgān, S Iran
142 M3 **Bandar-e Anzalī** Gīlān, NW Iran
143 N12 **Bandar-e Būshehr** var. Būshehr, Eng. Bushire. Būshehr, S Iran
142 M11 **Bandar-e Gonāveh** var. Ganāveh; prev. Gonāveh. Būshehr, SW Iran
143 T15 **Bandar-e Jāsk** Hormozgān, SE Iran
143 S15 **Bandar-e Kangān** var Kangān. Būshehr, S Iran
143 R14 **Bandar-e Khamīr** Hormozgān, S Iran
143 Q14 **Bandar-e Langeh** var. Bandar-e Lengeh, Lingeh. Hormozgān, S Iran
Bandar-e Lengeh see Bandar-e Langeh

◆ Country
● Country Capital
◇ Dependent Territory
○ Dependent Territory Capital
◈ Administrative Regions
✖ International Airport
▲ Mountain
▲▲ Mountain Range
△ Volcano
≈ River
◎ Lake
⊠ Reservoir

142 L10 **Bandar-e Māhshahr** var. Māh-Shahr; prev. Bandar-e Ma'shūr. Khūzestān, SW Iran
Bandar-e Ma'shūr see Bandar-e Māhshahr
143 O14 **Bandar-e Nakhīlū** Hormozgān, S Iran
Bandar-e Shāh see Bandar-e Torkaman
143 P4 **Bandar-e Torkaman** var. Bandar-e Torkeman, Bandar-e Torkman; prev. Bandar-e Shāh. Golestán, N Iran
Bandar-e Torkeman/ Bandar-e Torkman see Bandar-e Torkaman
Bandar Kassim see Boosaaso
168 M15 **Bandar Lampung** var. Bandarlampung, Tanjungkarang-Telukbetung; prev. Tandjoengkarang, Tanjungkarang, Teloekbetoeng, Telukbetung. Sumatera, W Indonesia
Bandarlampung see Bandar Lampung
Bandar Maharani see Muar
Bandar Masulipatnam see Machilipatnam
Bandar Penggaram see Batu Pahat
169 T7 **Bandar Seri Begawan** prev. Brunei Town. ● (Brunei) N Brunei
169 T7 **Bandar Seri Begawan** ✈ N Brunei
171 R15 **Banda Sea** var. Laut Banda. sea E Indonesia
104 H5 **Bande** Galicia, NW Spain
59 G15 **Bandeirantes** Mato Grosso, W Brazil
59 N20 **Bandeira, Pico da** ▲ SE Brazil
83 K19 **Bandelierkop** Limpopo, NE South Africa
62 L8 **Bandera** Santiago del Estero, N Argentina
25 Q11 **Bandera** Texas, SW USA
40 J13 **Banderas, Bahía de** bay W Mexico
77 O11 **Bandiagara** Mopti, C Mali
152 I12 **Bāndīkūi** Rājasthān, N India
136 C11 **Bandırma** var. Penderma. Balıkesir, NW Turkey
Bandjarmasin see Banjarmasin
Bandoeng see Bandung
97 C21 **Bandon** Ir. Droicheadna Bandan. SW Ireland
32 E14 **Bandon** Oregon, NW USA
167 R8 **Ban Dong Bang** Nong Khai, E Thailand
167 Q6 **Ban Donkon** Oudômxai, N Laos
172 J14 **Bandrélé** SE Mayotte
79 H20 **Bandundu** prev. Banningville. Bandundu, W Dem. Rep. Congo
79 I21 **Bandundu** off. Région de Bandundu. ◐ region W Dem. Rep. Congo
Bandundu, Région de see Bandundu
169 O16 **Bandung** prev. Bandoeng. Jawa, C Indonesia
116 L15 **Băneasa** Constanța, SW Romania
142 J4 **Bāneh** Kordestān, N Iran
44 I7 **Banes** Holguín, E Cuba
9 P16 **Banff** Alberta, SW Canada
96 K8 **Banff** NE Scotland, UK
96 K8 **Banff** cultural region NE Scotland, UK
Bánffyhunyad see Huedin
77 N14 **Banfora** SW Burkina
155 H19 **Bangalore** state capital Karnātaka, S India
153 S16 **Bangaon** West Bengal, NE India
79 L15 **Bangassou** Mbomou, SE Central African Republic
186 D7 **Bangeta, Mount** ▲ C Papua New Guinea
171 P12 **Banggai, Kepulauan** island group C Indonesia
171 Q12 **Banggai, Pulau** island Kepulauan Banggai, N Indonesia
171 X13 **Banggelapa** Papua, E Indonesia
Banggi see Banggi, Pulau
169 V6 **Banggi, Pulau** var. Banggi. island East Malaysia
121 P13 **Banghāzī** Eng. Bengazi, Benghazi, It. Bengasi. NE Libya
Bang Hieng see Xé Banghiang
169 O13 **Bangka-Belitung** off. Propinsi Bangka-Belitung. ◐ province W Indonesia
Propinsi Bangka-Belitung see Bangka-Belitung
169 P11 **Bangkai, Tanjung** var. Bankai. cape Borneo, N Indonesia
169 S16 **Bangkalan** Pulau Madura, C Indonesia
169 N12 **Bangka, Pulau** island W Indonesia
169 N13 **Bangka, Selat** strait Sumatera, W Indonesia
169 N13 **Bangka, Selat** var. Selat Likupang. strait Sulawesi, N Indonesia
168 J11 **Bangkinang** Sumatera, W Indonesia
168 K12 **Bangko** Sumatera, W Indonesia
Bangkok see Krung Thep
Bangkok, Bight of see Krung Thep, Ao
153 T14 **Bangladesh** off. People's Republic of Bangladesh; prev. East Pakistan. ◆ republic S Asia
Bangladesh, People's Republic of see Bangladesh
167 V13 **Ba Ngoi** Khanh Hoa, S Vietnam
152 K5 **Bangong Co** var. Pangong Tso. ◎ China/India see also Pangong Tso
Bangong Co see Pangong Tso
97 I18 **Bangor** NW Wales, UK
97 G15 **Bangor** Ir. Beannchar. E Northern Ireland, UK
19 R6 **Bangor** Maine, NE USA
18 I14 **Bangor** Pennsylvania, NE USA
67 R8 **Bangoran** ≈ S Central African Republic
Bang Phra see Trat
Bang Pla Soi see Chon Buri
25 Q8 **Bangs** Texas, SW USA
167 N13 **Bang Saphan** var. Bang Saphan Yai. Prachuap Khiri Khan, SW Thailand
Bang Saphan Yai see Bang Saphan
36 I8 **Bangs, Mount** ▲ Arizona, SW USA
93 E15 **Bangsund** Nord-Trøndelag, C Norway
171 O2 **Bangued** Luzon, N Philippines
79 I15 **Bangui** ● (Central African Republic) Ombella-Mpoko, SW Central African Republic
79 I15 **Bangui** ✈ Ombella-Mpoko, SW Central African Republic
83 N16 **Bangula** Southern, S Malawi
Bangwaketse see Southern
82 K12 **Bangweulu, Lake** var. Lake Bengweulu. ◎ N Zambia
Banhā see Benha
Ban Hat Yai see Hat Yai
167 Q7 **Ban Hin Heup** Viangchan, C Laos
Ban Houayxay/Ban Houei Sai see Houayxay
167 O12 **Ban Hua Hin** var. Hua Hin. Prachuap Khiri Khan, SW Thailand
79 L14 **Bani** Haute-Kotto, E Central African Republic
45 O9 **Baní** S Dominican Republic
77 N12 **Bani** ≈ S Mali
Banias see Bāniyās
77 S11 **Bani Bangou** Tillabéri, SW Niger
76 M12 **Banifing** var. Ngorolaka. ≈ Burkina/Mali
77 R13 **Banikoara** N Benin
Banī Mazār see Beni Mazâr
114 K8 **Baniski Lom** ≈ N Bulgaria
21 U7 **Banister River** ≈ Virginia, NE USA
Banī Suwayf see Beni Suef
75 O8 **Banī Walīd** NW Libya
138 H5 **Bāniyās** var. Banias, Baniyas, Paneas. Ṭarṭūs, W Syria
113 K14 **Banja** Serbia, W Serbia
Banjak, Kepulauan see Banyak, Kepulauan
112 J12 **Banja Koviljača** Serbia, W Serbia
112 G11 **Banja Luka** ◐ Republika Srpska, NW Bosnia and Herzegovina
169 T13 **Banjarmasin** prev. Bandjarmasin. Borneo, C Indonesia
76 F11 **Banjul** prev. Bathurst. ● (Gambia) W Gambia
76 F11 **Banjul** ✈ W Gambia
Bank see Bankä
137 Y13 **Bankä** Rus. Bank. SE Azerbaijan
167 S11 **Ban Kadian** var. Ban Kadiene. Champasak, S Laos
Ban Kadiene see Ban Kadian
Bankai see Bangkai, Tanjung
166 M14 **Ban Kam Phuam** Phangnga, SW Thailand
Ban Kantang see Kantang
77 O11 **Bankass** Mopti, S Mali
95 L19 **Bankeryd** Jönköping, S Sweden
83 K16 **Banket** Mashonaland West, N Zimbabwe
167 T11 **Ban Khamphô** Attapu, S Laos
23 O4 **Bankhead Lake** ⊠ Alabama, S USA
77 Q11 **Bankilaré** Tillabéri, SW Niger
Banks, Îles see Banks Islands
10 I14 **Banks Island** island British Columbia, SW Canada
187 R12 **Banks Islands** Fr. Îles Banks. island group N Vanuatu
23 U8 **Banks Lake** ◎ Georgia, SE USA
32 K8 **Banks Lake** ⊠ Washington, NW USA
185 I19 **Banks Peninsula** peninsula South Island, New Zealand
183 Q15 **Banks Strait** strait SW Tasman Sea
Ban Kui Nua see Kui Buri
153 R16 **Bānkura** West Bengal, NE India
167 S8 **Ban Lakxao** var. Lak Sao. Bolikhamxai, C Laos
167 O16 **Ban Lam Phai** Songkhla, SW Thailand
Ban Mae Sot see Mae Sot
Ban Mae Suai see Mae Suai
Ban Mak Khaeng see Udon Thani
166 M3 **Banmauk** Sagaing, N Myanmar (Burma)
Banmo see Bhamo
167 T10 **Ban Mun-Houamuang** S Laos
97 F14 **Bann** var. Lower Bann, Upper Bann. ≈ N Northern Ireland, UK
167 S10 **Ban Nadou** Salavan, S Laos
167 S9 **Ban Nakala** Savannakhét, S Laos
167 Q8 **Ban Nakha** Viangchan, C Laos
167 S9 **Ban Nakham** Khammouan, S Laos
167 P7 **Ban Namoun** Xaignabouli, N Laos
167 O17 **Ban Nang Sata** Yala, SW Thailand
167 N15 **Ban Na San** Surat Thani, SW Thailand
167 R7 **Ban Nasi** Xiangkhoang, N Laos
44 I3 **Bannerman Town** Eleuthera Island, C Bahamas
35 V15 **Banning** California, W USA
Banningville see Bandundu
167 S11 **Ban Nongsim** Champasak, S Laos
149 S7 **Bannu** prev. Edwardesabad. North-West Frontier Province, NW Pakistan
Bañolas see Banyoles
56 C7 **Baños** Tungurahua, C Ecuador
Bánovce see Bánovce nad Bebravou
111 I19 **Bánovce nad Bebravou** var. Bánovce, Hung. Bán. Trenčiansky Kraj, W Slovakia
112 I12 **Banovići** ◐ Federacija Bosna I Hercegovina, E Bosnia and Herzegovina
Banow see Andarāb
Ban Pak Phanang see Pak Phanang
167 O7 **Ban Pan Nua** Lampang, NW Thailand
167 Q9 **Ban Phai** Khon Kaen, E Thailand
167 T9 **Ban Phou A Douk** Khammouan, C Laos
167 Q8 **Ban Phu** Uthai Thani, W Thailand
167 O11 **Ban Pong** Ratchaburi, W Thailand
190 I3 **Banraeaba** Tarawa, W Kiribati
167 N10 **Ban Sai Yok** Kanchanaburi, W Thailand
Ban Sattahip/Ban Sattahipp see Sattahip
Ban Sichon see Sichon
Ban Si Racha see Siracha
111 J19 **Banská Bystrica** Ger. Neusohl, Hung. Besztercebánya. Banskobystrický Kraj, C Slovakia
111 K20 **Banskobystrický Kraj** ◐ region C Slovakia
167 R8 **Ban Sôppheung** Bolikhamxai, C Laos
Ban Sop Prap see Sop Prap
152 G15 **Bānswāra** Rājasthān, N India
167 N15 **Ban Ta Khun** Surat Thani, SW Thailand
Ban Takua Pa see Takua Pa
167 S8 **Ban Talak** Khammouan, C Laos
77 R15 **Bantè** W Benin
167 N16 **Banten** off. Propinsi Banten. ◐ province W Indonesia
Propinsi Banten see Banten
167 Q8 **Ban Thabôk** Bolikhamxai, C Laos
167 T9 **Ban Tôp** Savannakhét, S Laos
97 B21 **Bantry** Ir. Beanntraí. Cork, SW Ireland
97 A21 **Bantry Bay** Ir. Bá Bheanntraí. bay SW Ireland
155 F19 **Bantvāl** var. Bantwāl. Karnātaka, E India
Bantwāl see Bantvāl
114 N9 **Banya** Burgas, E Bulgaria
168 G10 **Banyak, Kepulauan** prev. Kepulauan Banjak. island group NW Indonesia
105 U8 **Banya, La** headland E Spain
79 E14 **Banyo** Adamaoua, NW Cameroon
105 X4 **Banyoles** var. Bañolas. Cataluña, NE Spain
167 N16 **Ban Yong Sata** Trang, SW Thailand
195 X14 **Banzare Coast** physical region Antarctica
173 Q14 **Banzare Seamounts** undersea feature Indian Ocean
Banzart see Bizerte
163 Q12 **Baochang** var. Taibus Qi. Nei Mongol Zizhiqu, N China
161 O3 **Baoding** var. Pao-ting; prev. Tsingyuan. Hebei, E China
Baoebaoe see Baubau
Baoi, Oileán see Dursey Island
160 J6 **Baoji** var. Pao-chi, Paoki. Shaanxi, C China
163 U9 **Baokang** var. Hoqin Zuoyi Zhongji. Nei Mongol Zizhiqu, N China
186 L8 **Baolo** Santa Isabel, N Solomon Islands
167 U13 **Bao Lôc** Lâm Đông, S Vietnam
163 Z7 **Baoqing** Heilongjiang, NE China
Baoqing see Shaoyang
79 H15 **Baoro** Nana-Mambéré, W Central African Republic
160 E12 **Baoshan** var. Pao-shan. Yunnan, SW China
163 N13 **Baotou** var. Pao-t'ou, Paotow. Nei Mongol Zizhiqu, N China
76 K12 **Baoulé** ≈ W Mali
76 L14 **Baoulé** ≈ S Mali
Bao Yèn see Phô Rang
103 O2 **Bapaume** Pas-de-Calais, N France
14 J13 **Baptiste Lake** ◎ Ontario, SE Canada
Bapu see Meigu
Baqanas see Bakanas
Baqbaqty see Bakbakty
159 P14 **Baqên** var. Dartang. Xizang Zizhiqu, W China
138 F14 **Bāqir, Jabal** ▲▲ S Jordan
139 T7 **Ba'qūbah** var. Qubba. C Iraq
62 H5 **Baquedano** Antofagasta, N Chile
Baquerizo Moreno see Puerto Baquerizo Moreno
113 J18 **Bar** It. Antivari. S Montenegro
116 M6 **Bar** Vinnyts'ka Oblast', C Ukraine
80 E10 **Bara** Northern Kordofan, C Sudan
81 M18 **Baraawe** It. Brava. Shabeellaha Hoose, S Somalia
152 M12 **Bāra Banki** Uttar Pradesh, N India
30 L8 **Baraboo** Wisconsin, N USA
30 K8 **Baraboo Range** hill range Wisconsin, N USA
Baracaldo see San Vicente de Barakaldo
15 Y6 **Barachois** Québec, SE Canada
44 J7 **Baracoa** Guantánamo, E Cuba
61 C19 **Baradero** Buenos Aires, E Argentina
183 R6 **Baradine** New South Wales, SE Australia
Baraf Daja Islands see Damar, Kepulauan
154 M12 **Baragarh** Orissa, E India
81 I17 **Baragoi** Rift Valley, W Kenya
45 N9 **Barahona** SW Dominican Republic
153 W13 **Barail Range** ▲▲ NE India
80 I9 **Baraka** var. Barka, Ar. Khawr Barakah. seasonal river Eritrea/Sudan
80 G10 **Barakat** Gezira, C Sudan
Barakī see Barakī Barak
149 Q6 **Barakī Barak** var. Barakī, Baraki Rajan. Lowgar, E Afghanistan
Baraki Rajan see Barakī Barak
154 N11 **Bārākot** Orissa, E India
55 S7 **Barama River** ≈ N Guyana
155 E14 **Bārāmati** Mahārāshtra, W India
152 H5 **Bārāmūla** Jammu and Kashmir, NW India
119 N14 **Baran'** Vitsyebskaya Voblasts', NE Belarus
152 I14 **Bārān** Rājasthān, N India
139 U4 **Barānān, Shākh-i** ▲▲ E Iraq
119 I17 **Baranavichy** Pol. Baranowicze, Rus. Baranovichi. Brestskaya Voblasts', SW Belarus
123 T6 **Baranikha** Chukotskiy Avtonomnyy Okrug, NE Russian Federation
116 M4 **Baranivka** Zhytomyrs'ka Oblast', N Ukraine
39 W14 **Baranof Island** island Alexander Archipelago, Alaska, USA
Baranovichi/Baranowicze see Baranavichy
111 N15 **Baranów Sandomierski** Podkarpackie, SE Poland
111 I26 **Baranya** off. Baranya Megye. ◐ county S Hungary
Baranya Megye see Baranya
153 R13 **Barāri** Bihār, NE India
22 L10 **Barataria Bay** bay Louisiana, S USA
Barat Daya, Kepulauan see Damar, Kepulauan
118 L12 **Baravukha** Rus. Borovukha. Vitsyebskaya Voblasts', N Belarus
54 E11 **Baraya** Huila, C Colombia
59 M21 **Barbacena** Minas Gerais, SE Brazil
54 B13 **Barbacoas** Nariño, SW Colombia
54 L6 **Barbacoas** Aragua, N Venezuela
45 Z13 **Barbados** ◆ island state SE West Indies
47 S3 **Barbados** island Barbados
105 U11 **Barbaria, Cap de** var. Cabo de Berbería. cape Formentera, E Spain
114 N13 **Barbaros** Tekirdağ, NW Turkey
74 A11 **Barbas, Cap** headland S Western Sahara
105 T5 **Barbastro** Aragón, NE Spain
104 K16 **Barbate** ≈ SW Spain
104 K16 **Barbate de Franco** Andalucía, S Spain
83 K21 **Barberton** Mpumalanga, NE South Africa
31 U12 **Barberton** Ohio, N USA
102 K12 **Barbezieux-St-Hilaire** Charente, W France
54 G9 **Barbosa** Boyaca, C Colombia
21 N7 **Barbourville** Kentucky, S USA
45 W9 **Barbuda** island N Antigua and Barbuda
181 W8 **Barcaldine** Queensland, E Australia
Barcarozsnyó see Râşnov
104 I11 **Barcarrota** Extremadura, W Spain
Barcău see Berettyó
Barce see Al Marj
107 L23 **Barcellona** var. Barcellona Pozzo di Gotto. Sicilia, Italy, C Mediterranean Sea
Barcellona Pozzo di Gotto see Barcellona
105 W6 **Barcelona** anc. Barcino, Barcinona. Cataluña, E Spain
55 N5 **Barcelona** Anzoátegui, NE Venezuela
105 S5 **Barcelona** ◐ province Cataluña, NE Spain
105 W6 **Barcelona** ✈ Cataluña, E Spain
103 U14 **Barcelonnette** Alpes-de-Haute-Provence, SE France
58 E12 **Barcelos** Amazonas, N Brazil
104 G5 **Barcelos** Braga, N Portugal
110 I10 **Barcin** Ger. Bartschin. Kujawski-pomorskie, C Poland
Barcino/Barcinona see Barcelona
Barcoo see Cooper Creek
111 H26 **Barcs** Somogy, SW Hungary
137 W11 **Bärdä** Rus. Barda. C Azerbaijan
Barda see Bärdä
78 H5 **Bardaï** Borkou-Ennedi-Tibesti, N Chad
139 R2 **Bardaraṣh** N Iraq
139 Q7 **Bardasah** SW Iraq
153 S16 **Barddhamān** West Bengal, NE India
111 N18 **Bardejov** Ger. Bartfeld, Hung. Bártfa. Presovský Kraj, E Slovakia
105 R4 **Bárdenas Reales** physical region N Spain
Bardera/Bardere see Baardheere
Bardesīr see Bardsīr
92 K3 **Bardharbunga** ▲ C Iceland
Bardhë, Drini i see Beli Drim
106 E9 **Bardi** Emilia-Romagna, C Italy
106 A8 **Bardonecchia** Piemonte, W Italy
97 H19 **Bardsey Island** island NW Wales, UK
143 S11 **Bardsīr** var. Bardesīr, Mashīz. Kermān, C Iran
20 L6 **Bardstown** Kentucky, S USA
Barduli see Barletta
20 G7 **Bardwell** Kentucky, S USA
152 K11 **Bareilly** var. Bareli. Uttar Pradesh, N India
Bareli see Bareilly
98 H13 **Barendrecht** Zuid-Holland, SW Netherlands
102 M3 **Barentin** Seine-Maritime, N France
92 N3 **Barentsburg** Spitsbergen, W Svalbard
Barentsevo More/Barents Havet see Barents Sea
92 O3 **Barentsøya** island E Svalbard
197 T11 **Barents Plain** undersea feature N Barents Sea
125 P3 **Barents Sea** Nor. Barents Havet, Rus. Barentsevo More. sea Arctic Ocean
197 U14 **Barents Trough** undersea feature SW Barents Sea
80 I9 **Barentu** W Eritrea
102 J3 **Barfleur** Manche, N France
102 J3 **Barfleur, Pointe de** headland N France
Barfrush/Barfurush see Bābol
158 H14 **Barga** Xizang Zizhiqu, W China
105 N9 **Bargas** Castilla-La Mancha, C Spain
81 J15 **Bargē** Southern, S Ethiopia
106 A9 **Barge** Piemonte, NE Italy
153 U16 **Barguna** Barisal, S Bangladesh
Bărguşad see Vorotan
123 N13 **Barguzin** Respublika Buryatiya, S Russian Federation
153 O13 **Barhaj** Uttar Pradesh, N India
183 N10 **Barham** New South Wales, SE Australia
152 J12 **Barhan** Uttar Pradesh, N India
19 S7 **Bar Harbor** Mount Desert Island, Maine, NE USA
153 R14 **Barharwa** Jhārkhand, NE India
153 P15 **Barhi** Jhārkhand, N India
107 O17 **Bari** var. Bari delle Puglie; anc. Barium. Puglia, SE Italy
80 P12 **Bari** Off. Gobolka Bari. ◐ region NE Somalia
167 T14 **Ba Ria** var. Châu Thanh. Ba Ria-Vung Tau, S Vietnam
Bāridah see Al Bāridah
Bari delle Puglie see Bari
Bari, Gobolka see Bari
Barikot see Barīkowṭ
149 T4 **Barīkowṭ** var. Barikot. Konar, NE Afghanistan
42 C4 **Barillas** var. Santa Cruz Barillas. Huehuetenango, NW Guatemala
54 J6 **Barinas** Barinas, W Venezuela
54 I7 **Barinas** off. Estado Barinas; prev. Zamora. ◐ state C Venezuela
Barinas, Estado see Barinas
54 I6 **Barinitas** Barinas, NW Venezuela
154 P11 **Bāripada** Orissa, E India
60 K9 **Bariri** São Paulo, S Brazil
75 W11 **Bârîs** S Egypt
152 G14 **Bari Sādri** Rājasthān, N India
153 U16 **Barisal** Barisal, S Bangladesh
153 U16 **Barisal** ◐ division S Bangladesh
168 I10 **Barisan, Pegunungan** ▲▲ Sumatera, W Indonesia
169 T12 **Barito, Sungai** ≈ Borneo, C Indonesia
Barium see Bari
Bårjås see Porjus
Barka see Baraka
Barka see Al Marj
160 H8 **Barkam** Sichuan, C China
118 J9 **Barkava** Madona, C Latvia
10 M15 **Barkerville** British Columbia, SW Canada
14 J12 **Bark Lake** ◎ Ontario, SE Canada
20 H7 **Barkley, Lake** ⊠ Kentucky/Tennessee, S USA
10 K17 **Barkley Sound** inlet British Columbia, W Canada
83 J24 **Barkly East** Afr. Barkly-Oos. Eastern Cape, SE South Africa
Barkly-Oos see Barkly East
181 S4 **Barkly Tableland** plateau Northern Territory/Queensland, N Australia
Barkly-Wes see Barkly West
83 H22 **Barkly West** Afr. Barkly-Wes. Northern Cape, N South Africa
159 O5 **Barkol** var. Barkol Kazak Zizhixian. Xinjiang Uygur Zizhiqu, NW China
159 O5 **Barkol Hu** ◎ NW China
Barkol Kazak Zizhixian see Barkol
30 J3 **Bark Point** headland Wisconsin, N USA
25 P11 **Barksdale** Texas, SW USA
Bar Kunar see Asmār
116 L11 **Bârlad** prev. Birlad. Vaslui, E Romania
116 M11 **Bârlad** prev. Bîrlad. ≈ E Romania
76 D9 **Barlavento, Ilhas de** var. Windward Islands. island group N Cape Verde
103 R5 **Bar-le-Duc** var. Bar-sur-Ornain. Meuse, NE France
180 K11 **Barlee, Lake** ◎ Western Australia
180 H8 **Barlee Range** ▲▲ Western Australia
107 N16 **Barletta** anc. Barduli. Puglia, SE Italy
110 E10 **Barlinek** Ger. Berlinchen. Zachodnio-pomorskie, NW Poland
27 S11 **Barling** Arkansas, C USA
171 U12 **Barma** Papua, E Indonesia
183 Q9 **Barmedman** New South Wales, SE Australia
Barmen-Elberfeld see Wuppertal
152 D12 **Bārmer** Rājasthān, NW India
182 K9 **Barmera** South Australia
97 I19 **Barmouth** NW Wales, UK
154 F10 **Barnagar** Madhya Pradesh, C India
152 H9 **Barnāla** Punjab, NW India
97 L15 **Barnard Castle** N England, UK
183 O6 **Barnato** New South Wales, SE Australia
112 I13 **Barnaul** Altayskiy Kray, C Russian Federation
109 V8 **Bärnbach** Steiermark, SE Austria
18 K16 **Barnegat** New Jersey, NE USA
23 S4 **Barnesville** Georgia, SE USA
29 R6 **Barnesville** Minnesota, N USA
31 U13 **Barnesville** Ohio, N USA
98 K11 **Barneveld** var. Barnveld. Gelderland, C Netherlands
25 O9 **Barnhart** Texas, SW USA
27 P8 **Barnsdall** Oklahoma, C USA
97 M17 **Barnsley** N England, UK
19 Q12 **Barnstable** Massachusetts, NE USA
97 I23 **Barnstaple** SW England, UK
Barnveld see Barneveld
21 Q14 **Barnwell** South Carolina, SE USA
77 U15 **Baro** Niger, C Nigeria
67 U8 **Baro** var. Baro Wenz. ≈ Ethiopia/Sudan
Baro see Baro Wenz
Baroda see Vadodara
149 U2 **Baroghil Pass** var. Kowtal-e Barowghīl. pass Afghanistan/Pakistan
119 Q17 **Baron'ki** Rus. Boron'ki. Mahilyowskaya Voblasts', E Belarus
182 J9 **Barossa Valley** valley South Australia
Baroui see Salisbury
81 H14 **Baro Wenz** var. Baro, Nahr Barū. ≈ Ethiopia/Sudan
Baro Wenz see Baro
Barowghīl, Kowtal-e see Baroghil Pass
153 U12 **Barpeta** Assam, NE India
31 S7 **Barques, Pointe Aux** headland Michigan, N USA
54 I5 **Barquisimeto** Lara, NW Venezuela
59 N16 **Barra** Bahia, E Brazil
96 E9 **Barra** island NW Scotland, UK
183 T5 **Barraba** New South Wales, SE Australia
60 L9 **Barra Bonita** São Paulo, S Brazil
64 J12 **Barracuda Fracture Zone** var. Fifteen Twenty Fracture Zone. tectonic feature SW Atlantic Ocean
64 G11 **Barracuda Ridge** undersea feature N Atlantic Ocean
43 N12 **Barra del Colorado** Limón, NE Costa Rica
43 N9 **Barra de Río Grande** Región Autónoma Atlántico Sur, E Nicaragua
82 A11 **Barra do Cuanza** Luanda, NW Angola
60 O9 **Barra do Piraí** Rio de Janeiro, SE Brazil
61 D16 **Barra do Quaraí** Rio Grande do Sul, SE Brazil
59 G14 **Barra do São Manuel** Pará, N Brazil
83 N19 **Barra Falsa, Ponta da** headland S Mozambique
96 E10 **Barra Head** headland NW Scotland, UK
60 O9 **Barra Mansa** Rio de Janeiro, SE Brazil
57 D14 **Barranca** Lima, W Peru
54 F8 **Barrancabermeja** Santander, N Colombia
54 H4 **Barrancas** La Guajira, N Colombia
54 J6 **Barrancas** Barinas, NW Venezuela
55 Q6 **Barrancas** Monagas, NE Venezuela
54 F6 **Barranco de Loba** Bolívar, N Colombia
104 I12 **Barrancos** Beja, S Portugal
62 N7 **Barranqueras** Chaco, N Argentina
54 E4 **Barranquilla** Atlántico, N Colombia
83 N20 **Barra, Ponta da** headland S Mozambique
105 P11 **Barrax** Castilla-La Mancha, C Spain
19 N11 **Barre** Massachusetts, NE USA
18 M7 **Barre** Vermont, NE USA
59 M17 **Barreiras** Bahia, E Brazil
104 F11 **Barreiro** Setúbal, W Portugal
65 C26 **Barren Island** island S Falkland Islands
20 K7 **Barren River Lake** ⊠ Kentucky, S USA
60 L7 **Barretos** São Paulo, S Brazil
9 P14 **Barrhead** Alberta, SW Canada
14 G14 **Barrie** Ontario, S Canada
9 N16 **Barrière** British Columbia, SW Canada
14 H8 **Barrière, Lac** ◎ Québec, SE Canada
182 L6 **Barrier Range** hill range New South Wales, SE Australia
42 G3 **Barrier Reef** reef E Belize
188 C16 **Barrigada** C Guam
Barrington Island see Santa Fe, Isla
183 T7 **Barrington Tops** ▲ New South Wales, SE Australia
183 O4 **Barringun** New South Wales, SE Australia
59 K18 **Barro Alto** Goiás, S Brazil
59 N14 **Barro Duro** Piauí, NE Brazil
30 J5 **Barron** Wisconsin, N USA
14 J12 **Barron** ≈ Ontario, SE Canada
61 H15 **Barros Cassal** Rio Grande do Sul, S Brazil
45 P14 **Barrouallie** Saint Vincent, W Saint Vincent and the Grenadines
39 O4 **Barrow** Alaska, USA
97 E20 **Barrow** Ir. An Bhearú. ≈ SE Ireland
181 Q6 **Barrow Creek Roadhouse** Northern Territory, N Australia
97 J16 **Barrow-in-Furness** NW England, UK
180 G7 **Barrow Island** island Western Australia
39 O4 **Barrow, Point** headland Alaska, USA
9 V14 **Barrows** Manitoba, S Canada
97 J22 **Barry** S Wales, UK
14 J12 **Barry's Bay** Ontario, SE Canada
144 K14 **Barsakel'mes, Ostrov** island SW Kazakhstan
Baršć Łužyca see Forst
147 S14 **Barsem** S Tajikistan
145 V11 **Barshatas** Vostochnyy Kazakhstan, E Kazakhstan
155 F14 **Bārsi** Mahārāshtra, W India
100 I13 **Barsinghausen** Niedersachsen, C Germany

◆ Country ● Country Capital ◇ Dependent Territory ○ Dependent Territory Capital ◐ Administrative Regions ✈ International Airport ▲ Mountain ▲▲ Mountain Range Volcano ≈ River ◎ Lake ⊠ Reservoir

147 X8 **Barskoon** Issyk-Kul'skaya Oblast', E Kyrgyzstan
100 F10 **Barssel** Niedersachsen, NW Germany
35 U14 **Barstow** California, W USA
24 L8 **Barstow** Texas, SW USA
103 R6 **Bar-sur-Aube** Aube, NE France
Bar-sur-Ornain see Bar-le-Duc
103 Q6 **Bar-sur-Seine** Aube, N France
147 S13 **Bartang** S Tajikistan
147 T13 **Bartang** ≈ SE Tajikistan
Bartenstein see Bartoszyce
Bártfa/Bartfeld see Bardejov
100 N7 **Barth** Mecklenburg-Vorpommern, NE Germany
27 W13 **Bartholomew, Bayou** ≈ Arkansas/Louisiana, S USA
55 T8 **Bartica** N Guyana
136 H10 **Bartın** Bartın, NW Turkey
136 H10 **Bartın** ◈ *province* NW Turkey
181 W4 **Bartle Frere** ▲ Queensland, E Australia
27 P8 **Bartlesville** Oklahoma, C USA
29 P14 **Bartlett** Nebraska, C USA
20 E10 **Bartlett** Tennessee, S USA
25 T9 **Bartlett** Texas, SW USA
36 L13 **Bartlett Reservoir** ▣ Arizona, SW USA
19 N6 **Barton** Vermont, NE USA
110 L7 **Bartoszyce** *Ger.* Bartenstein. Warmińsko-mazurskie, NE Poland
23 W12 **Bartow** Florida, SE USA
Bartschin see Barcin
168 J10 **Barumun, Sungai** ≈ Sumatera, W Indonesia
Barū, Nahr see Baro Wenz
169 S17 **Barung, Nusa** *island* S Indonesia
168 H9 **Barus** Sumatera, NW Indonesia
162 I9 **Baruunbayan-Ulaan** *var.* Höövör. Övörhangay, C Mongolia
Baruunsuu see Tsogttsetsiy
Baruunsuu see Tsogttsetsiy
163 P8 **Baruun-Urt** Sühbaatar, E Mongolia
43 P15 **Barú, Volcán** *var.* Volcán de Chiriquí. ⋀ W Panama
99 K21 **Barvaux** Luxembourg, SE Belgium
42 M13 **Barva, Volcán** ⋀ NW Costa Rica
117 W6 **Barvinkove** Kharkivs'ka Oblast', E Ukraine
154 G11 **Barwāh** Madhya Pradesh, C India
Bärwalde Neumark see Mieszkowice
154 F11 **Barwāni** Madhya Pradesh, C India
183 P5 **Barwon River** ≈ New South Wales, SE Australia
119 L15 **Barysaw** *Rus.* Borisov. Minskaya Voblasts', NE Belarus
127 Q6 **Barysh** Ul'yanovskaya Oblast', W Russian Federation
117 Q4 **Baryshivka** Kyyivs'ka Oblast', N Ukraine
79 J17 **Basankusu** Equateur, NW Dem. Rep. Congo
117 N11 **Basarabeasca** *Rus.* Bessarabka. SE Moldova
116 M14 **Basarabi** Constanţa, SW Romania
40 H6 **Basaseachic** Chihuahua, NW Mexico
Basauri see Arizgoiti
61 D18 **Basavilbaso** Entre Ríos, E Argentina
79 F21 **Bas-Congo** *off.* Région du Bas-Congo; *prev.* Bas-Zaïre. ◈ *region* SW Dem. Rep. Congo
Bas-Zaïre, Région du see Bas-Congo
108 E6 **Basel** *Eng.* Basle, *Fr.* Bâle. Basel-Stadt, NW Switzerland
108 E7 **Basel** *Eng.* Basle, *Fr.* Bâle. ◈ *canton* NW Switzerland
143 T14 **Bashākerd, Kūhhā-ye** ▲▲ SE Iran
9 Q15 **Bashaw** Alberta, SW Canada
146 K16 **Bashbedeng** Mary Welaýaty, S Turkmenistan
83 J24 **Bashee** ≈ S South Africa
161 T15 **Bashi Channel** *Chin.* Pa-shih Hai-hsia. *channel* Philippines/Taiwan
Bashkiria see Bashkortostan, Respublika
122 F11 **Bashkortostan, Respublika** *prev.* Bashkiria. ◈ *autonomous republic* W Russian Federation
127 N6 **Bashmakovo** Penzenskaya Oblast', W Russian Federation
146 J10 **Bashsakarba** Lebap Welaýaty, NE Turkmenistan
117 R9 **Bashtanka** Mykolayivs'ka Oblast', S Ukraine
22 H8 **Basile** Louisiana, S USA
107 M18 **Basilicata** ◈ *region* S Italy
33 V13 **Basin** Wyoming, C USA
97 N22 **Basingstoke** S England, UK
143 U8 **Başīran** Khorāsān-e Janūbī, E Iran
112 B10 **Baška** *It.* Bescanuova. Primorje-Gorski Kotar, NW Croatia
137 T15 **Başkale** Van, SE Turkey
14 L10 **Baskatong, Réservoir** ▣ Québec, SE Canada
137 O14 **Baskil** Elazığ, E Turkey
Basle see Basel
154 H9 **Bāsoda** Madhya Pradesh, C India
79 L17 **Basoko** Orientale, N Dem. Rep. Congo
Basque Country, The see País Vasco
Basra see Al Başrah
103 U5 **Bas-Rhin** ◈ *department* NE France
Bassam see Grand-Bassam
9 Q16 **Bassano** Alberta, SW Canada
106 H7 **Bassano del Grappa** Veneto, NE Italy
77 Q15 **Bassar** *var.* Bassari. NW Togo
Bassari see Bassar
172 L9 **Bassas da India** *island group* W Madagascar
108 D7 **Bassecourt** Jura, W Switzerland
166 K8 **Bassein** *var.* Pathein. Irrawaddy, SW Myanmar (Burma)
79 J15 **Basse-Kotto** ◈ *prefecture* S Central African Republic
105 V5 **Bassella** Cataluña, NE Spain
102 J5 **Basse-Normandie** *Eng.* Lower Normandy. ◈ *region* N France
45 Q11 **Basse-Pointe** N Martinique
76 H12 **Basse Santa Su** E Gambia
Basse-Saxe see Niedersachsen
45 X6 **Basse-Terre** ○ (Guadeloupe) Basse Terre, SW Guadeloupe
45 V10 **Basseterre** ● (Saint Kitts and Nevis) Saint Kitts, Saint Kitts and Nevis
45 X6 **Basse Terre** *island* W Guadeloupe
29 O13 **Bassett** Nebraska, C USA
21 S7 **Bassett** Virginia, NE USA
37 N15 **Bassett Peak** ▲ Arizona, SW USA
76 M10 **Bassikounou** Hodh ech Chargui, SE Mauritania
77 R15 **Bassila** W Benin
Bass, Îlots de see Marotiri
31 O11 **Bass Lake** Indiana, N USA
183 O14 **Bass Strait** *strait* SE Australia
100 H11 **Bassum** Niedersachsen, NW Germany
29 X3 **Basswood Lake** ◎ Canada/USA
95 J21 **Båstad** Skåne, S Sweden
139 U2 **Basţah** E Iraq
153 N12 **Basti** Uttar Pradesh, N India
103 X14 **Bastia** Corse, France, C Mediterranean Sea
99 L23 **Bastogne** Luxembourg, SE Belgium
22 I5 **Bastrop** Louisiana, S USA
25 T11 **Bastrop** Texas, SW USA
93 J15 **Bastuträsk** Västerbotten, N Sweden
119 J19 **Bastyn'** *Rus.* Bostyn'. Brestskaya Voblasts', SW Belarus
Basuo see Dongfang
Basutoland see Lesotho
119 O15 **Basya** ≈ E Belarus
117 V8 **Basyl'kivka** Dnipropetrovs'ka Oblast', E Ukraine
Bas-Zaïre see Bas-Congo
79 D17 **Bata** NW Equatorial Guinea
79 D17 **Bata** ✈ S Equatorial Guinea
Batae Coritanorum see Leicester
123 Q8 **Batagay** Respublika Sakha (Yakutiya), NE Russian Federation
123 P8 **Batagay-Alyta** Respublika Sakha (Yakutiya), NE Russian Federation
112 L10 **Batajnica** Vojvodina, N Serbia
136 H15 **Bataklĭk Gölü** ◎ S Turkey
114 H11 **Batak, Yazovir** ▣ SW Bulgaria
152 H7 **Batāla** Punjab, N India
104 F9 **Batalha** Leiria, C Portugal
79 N17 **Batama** Orientale, NE Dem. Rep. Congo
123 Q10 **Batamay** Respublika Sakha (Yakutiya), NE Russian Federation
160 F9 **Batang** *var.* Bazhong. Sichuan, C China
79 I14 **Batangafo** Ouham, NW Central African Republic
171 P8 **Batangas** *off.* Batangas City. Luzon, N Philippines
Batangas City see Batangas
Bătania see Battonya
171 Q10 **Batan Islands** *island group* N Philippines
60 L8 **Batatais** São Paulo, S Brazil
18 E10 **Batavia** New York, NE USA
Batavia see Jakarta
173 T9 **Batavia Seamount** *undersea feature* E Indian Ocean
126 L12 **Bataysk** Rostovskaya Oblast', SW Russian Federation
14 B9 **Batchawana** ≈ Ontario, S Canada
14 B9 **Batchawana Bay** Ontario, S Canada
167 Q12 **Bătdâmbâng** *prev.* Battambang. Bătdâmbâng, NW Cambodia
79 G20 **Batéké, Plateaux** *plateau* S Congo
183 S11 **Batemans Bay** New South Wales, SE Australia
21 Q13 **Batesburg** South Carolina, SE USA
28 K12 **Batesland** South Dakota, N USA
27 V10 **Batesville** Arkansas, C USA
31 Q14 **Batesville** Indiana, N USA
22 L2 **Batesville** Mississippi, S USA
25 Q13 **Batesville** Texas, SW USA
44 L13 **Bath** E Jamaica
97 L22 **Bath** *hist.* Akermanceaster; *anc.* Aquae Calidae, Aquae Solis. SW England, UK
19 Q8 **Bath** Maine, NE USA
18 F11 **Bath** New York, NE USA
Bath see Berkeley Springs
78 I10 **Batha** *off.* Préfecture du Batha. ◈ *prefecture* C Chad
78 I10 **Batha** *seasonal river* C Chad
Batha, Préfecture du see Batha
141 Y8 **Baṭḥā', Wādī al** *dry watercourse* NE Oman
152 H9 **Bathinda** Punjab, NW India
98 M11 **Bathmen** Overijssel, E Netherlands
45 Z14 **Bathsheba** E Barbados
183 R8 **Bathurst** New South Wales, SE Australia
13 O13 **Bathurst** New Brunswick, SE Canada
Bathurst see Banjul
8 H6 **Bathurst, Cape** *headland* Northwest Territories, NW Canada
196 L8 **Bathurst Inlet** Nunavut, N Canada
196 L8 **Bathurst Inlet** *inlet* Nunavut, N Canada
181 N1 **Bathurst Island** *island* Northern Territory, N Australia
197 O9 **Bathurst Island** *island* Parry Islands, Nunavut, N Canada
77 O14 **Batié** SW Burkina
Batinah see Al Bāṭinah
141 Y9 **Bāṭin, Wādī al** *dry watercourse* SW Asia
15 P9 **Batiscan** ≈ Québec, SE Canada
136 F16 **Batı Toroslar** ▲▲ SW Turkey
Batjan see Bacan, Pulau
147 R11 **Batken** Batenskaya Oblast', SW Kyrgyzstan
Batken Oblasty see Batkenskaya Oblast'
147 Q11 **Batkenskaya Oblast'** *Kir.* Batken Oblasty. ◈ *province* SW Kyrgyzstan
Batlle y Ordóñez see José Batlle y Ordóñez
183 Q10 **Batlow** New South Wales, SE Australia
137 Q15 **Batman** *var.* İluh. Batman, SE Turkey
137 Q15 **Batman** ◈ *province* SE Turkey
74 L6 **Batna** NE Algeria
163 O7 **Batnorov** *var.* Dundbürd. Hentiy, E Mongolia
Batoe see Batu, Kepulauan
162 K7 **Bat-Öldziy** *var.* Övt. Övörhangay, C Mongolia
Bat-Öldziyt see Dzaamar
22 J8 **Baton Rouge** *state capital* Louisiana, S USA
79 G15 **Batouri** Est, E Cameroon
138 G14 **Batrā', Jibāl al** ▲▲ S Jordan
138 G6 **Batroûn** *var.* Al Batrūn. N Lebanon
Batsch see Bač
Batsevichi see Batsevichy
119 M17 **Batsevichy** *Rus.* Batsevichi. Mahilyowskaya Voblasts', E Belarus
92 M7 **Båtsfjord** Finnmark, N Norway
163 N7 **Batshireet** *var.* Eg, Hentiy. ◈ *province* N Mongolia
162 L7 **Batsümber** *var.* Mandal. Töv, C Mongolia
Battambang see Bătdâmbâng
195 X3 **Batterbee, Cape** *headland* Antarctica
155 L24 **Batticaloa** Eastern Province, E Sri Lanka
99 L19 **Battice** Liège, E Belgium
107 L18 **Battipaglia** Campania, S Italy
9 R15 **Battle** ≈ Alberta/Saskatchewan, SW Canada
Battle Born State see Nevada
31 Q10 **Battle Creek** Michigan, N USA
27 T7 **Battlefield** Missouri, C USA
9 S15 **Battleford** Saskatchewan, S Canada
29 S6 **Battle Lake** Minnesota, N USA
35 U3 **Battle Mountain** Nevada, W USA
111 M25 **Battonya** *Rom.* Bătania. Békés, SE Hungary
162 J7 **Battsengel** *var.* Jargalant. Arhangay, C Mongolia
168 D11 **Batu, Kepulauan** *prev.* Batoe. *island group* W Indonesia
137 Q10 **Bat'umi** W Georgia
168 K10 **Batu Pahat** *prev.* Bandar Penggaram. Johor, Peninsular Malaysia
171 O12 **Baturebe** Sulawesi, N Indonesia
122 J12 **Baturino** Tomskaya Oblast', C Russian Federation
117 R3 **Baturyn** Chernihivs'ka Oblast', N Ukraine
138 F10 **Bat Yam** Tel Aviv, C Israel
127 Q4 **Batyrevo** Chuvashskaya Respublika, W Russian Federation
Batys Qazaqstan Oblysy see Zapadnyy Kazakhstan
102 F5 **Batz, Île de** *island* NW France
169 Q10 **Bau** Sarawak, East Malaysia
171 N2 **Bauang** Luzon, N Philippines
171 P14 **Baubau** *var.* Baoebaoe. Pulau Buton, C Indonesia
77 W14 **Bauchi** Bauchi, NE Nigeria
77 W14 **Bauchi** ◈ *state* C Nigeria
102 H7 **Baud** Morbihan, NW France
29 T2 **Baudette** Minnesota, N USA
193 S9 **Bauer Basin** *undersea feature* E Pacific Ocean
187 R14 **Bauer Field** *var.* Port Vila. ✈ (Port-Vila) Éfaté, C Vanuatu
13 T9 **Bauld, Cape** *cape* Newfoundland and Labrador, E Canada
103 T8 **Baume-les-Dames** Doubs, E France
101 I15 **Baunatal** Hessen, C Germany
107 D18 **Baunei** Sardegna, Italy, C Mediterranean Sea
57 M15 **Baures, Río** ≈ N Bolivia
60 K9 **Bauru** São Paulo, S Brazil
Baushar see Bawshar
118 G10 **Bauska** *Ger.* Bauske. Bauska, S Latvia
Bauske see Bauska
101 Q15 **Bautzen** *Lus.* Budyšin. Sachsen, E Germany
145 Q16 **Bauyrzhan Momyshuly** *Kaz.* Baŭyrzhan Momyshuly; *prev.* Burnoye. Zhambyl, S Kazakhstan
Bauzanum see Bolzano
Bavaria see Bayern
109 N7 **Bavarian Alps** *Ger.* Bayrische Alpen. ▲▲ Austria/Germany
Bavière see Bayern
40 H4 **Bavispe, Río** ≈ NW Mexico
127 T5 **Bavly** Respublika Tatarstan, W Russian Federation
169 P13 **Bawal, Pulau** *island* N Indonesia
169 T12 **Bawan** Borneo, C Indonesia
183 O12 **Baw Baw, Mount** ▲ Victoria, SE Australia
169 S15 **Bawean, Pulau** *island* S Indonesia
75 V9 **Bawīṭī** N Egypt
77 Q13 **Bawku** N Ghana
167 N7 **Bawlakè** Kayah State, C Myanmar (Burma)
169 H11 **Bawo Ofuloa** Pulau Tanahmasa, W Indonesia
141 Y8 **Bawshar** *var.* Baushar. NE Oman
Ba Xian see Bazhou
158 M8 **Baxkorgan** Xinjiang Uygur Zizhiqu, W China
23 V6 **Baxley** Georgia, SE USA
159 R15 **Baxoi** *var.* Baima. Xizang Zizhiqu, W China
29 W14 **Baxter** Iowa, C USA
29 U6 **Baxter** Minnesota, N USA
27 R8 **Baxter Springs** Kansas, C USA
81 M17 **Bay** *off.* Gobolka Bay. ◈ *region* SW Somalia
Bay see Baicheng
44 H7 **Bayamo** Granma, E Cuba
45 U5 **Bayamón** E Puerto Rico
163 W8 **Bayan** Heilongjiang, NE China
170 L16 **Bayan** *prev.* Bajan. Pulau Lombok, C Indonesia
162 M8 **Bayan** *var.* Maanĭt. Töv, C Mongolia
Bayan see Hölönbuyr
Bayan Hölönbuyr, Dornod, Mongolia
Bayan see Ihhet
Bayan Ihhet, Dornogovĭ, Mongolia
Bayan see Bayan-Uul, Govĭ-Altay, Mongolia
Bayan see Bayanhutag, Hentiy, Mongolia
Bayan see Bürentogtoh, Hövsgol, Mongolia
152 I12 **Bayāna** Rājasthān, N India
149 N5 **Bāyān, Band-e** ▲▲ C Afghanistan
162 H8 **Bayanbulag** Bayanhongor, C Mongolia
Bayanbulag see Ömnödelger
Bayanbulag see Ömnödelgar
158 J5 **Bayanbulak** Xinjiang Uygur Zizhiqu, W China
162 L7 **Bayanchandmanĭ** *var.* Ihsüüj. Töv, C Mongolia
162 J11 **Bayandalay** *var.* Dalay. Ömnögovĭ, S Mongolia
163 O9 **Bayandelger** *var.* Shireet. Sühbaatar, SE Mongolia
162 I5 **Bayandzürh** *var.* Altraga. Hövsgöl, N Mongolia
Bayan Gol see Dengkou
Bayangol see Bugat
162 I9 **Bayangovĭ** *var.* Örgön. Bayanhongor, C Mongolia
159 R12 **Bayan Har Shan** *var.* Bayan Khar. ▲▲ C China
162 G6 **Bayanhayrhan** Dzavhan, N Mongolia
162 G6 **Bayanhayrhan** *var* Altanbulag. Dzavhan, N Mongolia
162 I8 **Bayanhongor** Bayanhongor, C Mongolia
162 H9 **Bayanhongor** ◈ *province* C Mongolia
162 K14 **Bayan Hot** *var.* Alxa Zuoqi. Nei Mongol Zizhiqu, N China
162 K14 **Bayan Hot** *var.* Alxa Zuoqi. Nei Mongol Zizhiqu, N China
163 O8 **Bayanhutag** *var.* Bayan. Hentiy, C Mongolia
163 T9 **Bayan Huxu** *var.* Horqin Zuoyi Zhongqi. Nei Mongol Zizhiqu, N China
Bayan Khar see Bayan Har Shan
168 J7 **Bayan Lepas** ✈ (George Town) Pinang, Peninsular Malaysia
162 I10 **Bayanlig** *var.* Hatansuudal. Bayanhongor, C Mongolia
162 K13 **Bayan Mod** Nei Mongol Zizhiqu, N China
163 N8 **Bayanmönh** *var.* Ulaan-Ereg. Hentiy, E Mongolia
Bayan Nuru see Xar Burd
162 E5 **Bayannuur** *var.* Tsul-Ulaan. Bayan-Ölgiy, W Mongolia
163 N12 **Bayan Obo** Nei Mongol Zizhiqu, N China
43 V15 **Bayano, Lago** ◎ E Panama
162 C5 **Bayan-Ölgiy** ◈ *province* NW Mongolia
162 H9 **Bayan-Öndör** *var.* Bulgan. Bayanhongor, C Mongolia
162 H9 **Bayan-Öndör** *var.* Bulgan. Bayanhongor, C Mongolia
162 K8 **Bayan-Öndör** *var.* Bulgan. Övörhangay, C Mongolia
162 K8 **Bayan-Öndör** *var.* Bumbat. Övörhangay, C Mongolia
162 L8 **Bayan-Önjüül** *var.* Ihhayrhan. Töv, C Mongolia
163 O7 **Bayan-Ovoo** *var.* Javhlant. Hentiy, E Mongolia
162 L11 **Bayan-Ovoo** *var.* Ergenetsogt. Ömnögovĭ, S Mongolia
162 L11 **Bayan-Ovoo** *var.* Erdenetsogt. Ömnögovĭ, S Mongolia
Bayan-Ovoo see Altay
Bayan-Ovoo see Altay
Bayansayr see Baatsagaan
159 Q9 **Bayan Shan** ▲ C China
162 J9 **Bayanteeg** Övörhangay, C Mongolia
162 G5 **Bayantes** *var.* Altay. Dzavhan, N Mongolia
Bayantöhöm see Büren
162 M8 **Bayantsagaan** *var.* Dzogsool. Töv, C Mongolia
163 P7 **Bayantümen** *var.* Tsagaanders. Dornod, NE Mongolia
Bayan-Uhaa see Ih-Uul
163 R10 **Bayan Ul** *var.* Xi Ujimqin Qi. Nei Mongol Zizhiqu, N China
Bayan-Ulaan see Dzüünbayan-Ulaan
Bayan-Ulaan see Dzüünbayan-Ulaan
163 O7 **Bayan-Uul** *var.* Javarthushuu. Dornod, NE Mongolia
162 F7 **Bayan-Uul** *var.* Bayan. Govĭ-Altay, W Mongolia
162 M8 **Bayanuur** *var.* Tsul-Ulaan. Töv, C Mongolia
28 J14 **Bayard** Nebraska, C USA
37 P15 **Bayard** New Mexico, SW USA
103 T13 **Bayard, Col** *pass* SE France
Bayasgalant see Mönhhaan
136 J12 **Bayat** Çorum, N Turkey
171 P6 **Bayawan** Negros, C Philippines
143 R10 **Bayāz** Kermān, C Iran
171 Q6 **Baybay** Leyte, C Philippines
21 X10 **Bayboro** North Carolina, SE USA
137 P12 **Bayburt** Bayburt, NE Turkey
137 P12 **Bayburt** ◈ *province* NE Turkey
31 R8 **Bay City** Michigan, N USA
25 V12 **Bay City** Texas, SW USA
Baydarata Bay see Baydaratskaya Guba
122 J7 **Baydaratskaya Guba** *var.* Baydarata Bay. *bay* N Russian Federation
81 M16 **Baydhabo** *var.* Baydhowa, Isha Baydhabo, *It.* Baidoa. Bay, SW Somalia
Baydhowa see Baydhabo
101 N21 **Bayerischer Wald** ▲▲ SE Germany
101 K21 **Bayern** *Eng.* Bavaria, *Fr.* Bavière. ◈ *state* SE Germany
147 V9 **Bayetovo** Narynskaya Oblast', C Kyrgyzstan
102 K4 **Bayeux** *anc.* Augustodurum. Calvados, N France
14 E15 **Bayfield** ≈ Ontario, S Canada
145 O15 **Baygakum** *Kaz.* Bäygequm. Kzylorda, S Kazakhstan
Bäygequm see Baygakum
136 C14 **Bayındır** İzmir, SW Turkey
138 H12 **Bāyir** *var.* Bā'ir. Ma'ān, S Jordan
Bay Islands see Bahía, Islas de la
139 R5 **Bayjī** *var.* Baiji. N Iraq
Baykadam see Saudakent
123 N13 **Baykal, Ozero** *Eng.* Lake Baikal. ◎ S Russian Federation
123 M14 **Baykal'sk** Irkutskaya Oblast', S Russian Federation
137 R15 **Baykan** Siirt, SE Turkey
123 L11 **Baykit** Evenkiyskiy Avtonomnyy Okrug, C Russian Federation
145 N12 **Baykonur** *var.* Baykonyr. Karaganda, C Kazakhstan
Baykonur see Baykonyr
144 M14 **Baykonyr** *var* Baykonur, *Kaz* Bayqongyr; *prev.* Leninsk. Kyzylorda, S Kazakhstan
Baykonyr see Baykonur
158 E7 **Baykurt** Xinjiang Uygur Zizhiqu, W China
14 I9 **Bay, Lac** ◎ Québec, SE Canada
127 W6 **Baymak** Respublika Bashkortostan, W Russian Federation
23 O8 **Bay Minette** Alabama, S USA
143 O17 **Baynūnah** *desert* W United Arab Emirates
184 O8 **Bay of Plenty** *off.* Bay of Plenty Region. ◈ *region* North Island, New Zealand
Bay of Plenty Region see Bay of Plenty
191 Z3 **Bay of Wrecks** *bay* Kiritimati, E Kiribati
Bayonnaise Rocks see Beyonēsu-retsugan
102 I15 **Bayonne** *anc.* Lapurdum. Pyrénées-Atlantiques, SW France
22 H4 **Bayou D'Arbonne Lake** ▣ Louisiana, S USA
23 N9 **Bayou La Batre** Alabama, S USA
Bayou State see Mississippi
Bayqadam see Saudakent
Bayqongyr see Baykonyr
Bayram-Ali see Bayramaly
146 J14 **Baýramaly** *var.* Bayramaly; *prev.* Bayram-Ali. Mary Welaýaty, S Turkmenistan
101 L19 **Bayreuth** *var.* Baireuth. Bayern, SE Germany
Bayrische Alpen see Bavarian Alps
Bayrūt see Beyrouth
22 L9 **Bay Saint Louis** Mississippi, S USA
Baysān see Bet She'an
Bayshint see Öndörshireet
14 H13 **Bays, Lake of** ◎ Ontario, S Canada
22 M6 **Bay Springs** Mississippi, S USA
Bay State see Massachusetts
Baysun see Boysun
14 H13 **Baysville** Ontario, S Canada
141 N15 **Bayt al Faqīh** W Yemen
158 M4 **Baytik Shan** ▲▲ China/Mongolia
Bayt Laḥm see Bethlehem
25 W11 **Baytown** Texas, SW USA
169 V11 **Bayur, Tanjung** *cape* Borneo, N Indonesia
121 N14 **Bayy al Kabīr, Wādī** *dry watercourse* NW Libya
Bayyrqum see Bairkum
105 P14 **Baza** Andalucía, S Spain
137 X10 **Bazardüzü Dağı** *Rus.* Gora Bazardyuzyu. ▲ N Azerbaijan
Bazardyuzyu, Gora see Bazardüzü Dağı
Bazargic see Dobrich
83 N18 **Bazaruto, Ilha do** *island* SE Mozambique
102 K14 **Bazas** Gironde, SW France
105 O14 **Baza, Sierra de** ▲▲ S Spain
160 J8 **Bazhong** *var* Bazhou. Sichuan, C China
Bazhong see Batang
161 P3 **Bazhou** , Ba Xian. Hebei, E China
Bazhou see Bazhong
14 M9 **Bazin** ≈ Québec, SE Canada
Bazin see Pezinok
139 Q7 **Bāzīyah** C Iraq
138 H6 **Bcharré** *var.* Bcharreh, Bsharrī, Bsherri. NE Lebanon
Bcharreh see Bcharré
28 J5 **Beach** North Dakota, N USA
182 K12 **Beachport** South Australia
97 O23 **Beachy Head** *headland* SE England, UK
18 K13 **Beacon** New York, NE USA
63 J25 **Beagle Channel** *channel* Argentina/Chile
181 O1 **Beagle Gulf** *gulf* Northern Territory, N Australia
Bealach an Doirín see Ballaghaderreen
Bealach Cláir see Ballyclare
Bealach Féich see Ballybofey
172 J3 **Bealanana** Mahajanga, NE Madagascar
Béal an Átha see Ballina
Béal an Átha Móir see Ballinamore
Béal an Mhuirhead see Belmullet
Béal Átha Beithe see Ballybay
Béal Átha Conaill see Ballyconnell
Beál Átha hAmhnais see Ballyhaunis
Béal Átha na Sluaighe see Ballinasloe
Béal Átha Seanaidh see Ballyshannon
Bealdovuopmi see Peltovuoma
Béal Feirste see Belfast
Béal Tairbirt see Belturbet
Beanna Boirche see Mourne Mountains
Beannchar see Banagher, Ireland
Beannchar see Bangor, Northern Ireland, UK
Beanntraí see Bantry
Bearalváhki see Berlevåg
23 N2 **Bear Creek** ≈ Alabama/Mississippi, S USA
30 J13 **Bear Creek** ≈ Illinois, N USA
27 U13 **Bearden** Arkansas, C USA
195 Q10 **Beardmore Glacier** *glacier* Antarctica
30 K13 **Beardstown** Illinois, N USA
28 L14 **Bear Hill** ▲ Nebraska, C USA
Bear Island see Bjørnøya
14 H12 **Bear Lake** Ontario, S Canada
36 M1 **Bear Lake** ◎ Idaho/Utah, NW USA
39 U11 **Bear, Mount** ▲ Alaska, USA
102 J16 **Béarn** *cultural region* SW France
194 J11 **Bear Peninsula** *peninsula* Antarctica
152 I7 **Beās** ≈ India/Pakistan
105 P3 **Beasain** País Vasco, N Spain
105 O12 **Beas de Segura** Andalucía, S Spain
45 N10 **Beata, Cabo** *headland* SW Dominican Republic
45 N10 **Beata, Isla** *island* SW Dominican Republic
64 F11 **Beata Ridge** *undersea feature* N Caribbean Sea
29 R17 **Beatrice** Nebraska, C USA
83 L16 **Beatrice** Mashonaland East, NE Zimbabwe
9 N11 **Beatton** ≈ British Columbia, W Canada
9 N11 **Beatton River** British Columbia, W Canada
35 V10 **Beatty** Nevada, W USA
21 N6 **Beattyville** Kentucky, S USA
173 X16 **Beau Bassin** W Mauritius
103 R15 **Beaucaire** Gard, S France
14 I8 **Beauchastel, Lac** ◎ Québec, SE Canada
14 I10 **Beauchêne, Lac** ◎ Québec, SE Canada
183 V3 **Beaudesert** Queensland, E Australia
182 M12 **Beaufort** Victoria, SE Australia
21 X11 **Beaufort** North Carolina, SE USA
21 R15 **Beaufort** South Carolina, SE USA
38 M11 **Beaufort Sea** *sea* Arctic Ocean
Beaufort-Wes see Beaufort West
83 G25 **Beaufort West** *Afr.* Beaufort-Wes. Western Cape, SW South Africa
103 N7 **Beaugency** Loiret, C France
19 R1 **Beau Lake** ▣ Maine, NE USA
96 I8 **Beauly** N Scotland, UK
99 G21 **Beaumont** Hainaut, S Belgium
185 E23 **Beaumont** Otago, South Island, New Zealand
22 M7 **Beaumont** Mississippi, S USA
25 X10 **Beaumont** Texas, SW USA
102 M15 **Beaumont-de-Lomagne** Tarn-et-Garonne, S France
102 L6 **Beaumont-sur-Sarthe** Sarthe, NW France
103 R8 **Beaune** Côte d'Or, C France
15 R9 **Beaupré** Québec, SE Canada
102 J8 **Beaupréau** Maine-et-Loire, NW France
99 I22 **Beauraing** Namur, SE Belgium
103 R12 **Beaurepaire** Isère, E France
9 Y16 **Beausejour** Manitoba, S Canada
103 N4 **Beauvais** *anc.* Bellovacum, Caesaromagus. Oise, N France
9 S13 **Beauval** Saskatchewan, C Canada
102 I9 **Beauvoir-sur-Mer** Vendée, NW France
39 R8 **Beaver** Alaska, USA
26 J8 **Beaver** Oklahoma, C USA
18 B14 **Beaver** Pennsylvania, NE USA
36 K6 **Beaver** Utah, W USA
10 L9 **Beaver** ≈ British Columbia/Yukon Territory, W Canada
9 S13 **Beaver** ≈ Saskatchewan, C Canada
29 N17 **Beaver City** Nebraska, C USA
10 G6 **Beaver Creek** Yukon Territory, W Canada
31 R14 **Beavercreek** Ohio, N USA
39 S8 **Beaver Creek** ≈ Alaska, USA
26 H3 **Beaver Creek** ≈ Kansas/Nebraska, C USA
28 J5 **Beaver Creek** ≈ Montana/North Dakota, N USA
29 Q14 **Beaver Creek** ≈ Nebraska, C USA
25 Q4 **Beaver Creek** ≈ Texas, SW USA
30 M8 **Beaver Dam** Wisconsin, N USA
30 M8 **Beaver Dam Lake** ◎ Wisconsin, N USA
18 B14 **Beaver Falls** Pennsylvania, NE USA
33 P12 **Beaverhead Mountains** ▲▲ Idaho/Montana, NW USA
33 Q12 **Beaverhead River** ≈ Montana, NW USA
65 A25 **Beaver Island** *island* W Falkland Islands
31 P5 **Beaver Island** *island* Michigan, N USA
27 S9 **Beaver Lake** ▣ Arkansas, C USA
9 N13 **Beaverlodge** Alberta, W Canada
18 I8 **Beaver River** ≈ New York, NE USA
26 J8 **Beaver River** ≈ Oklahoma, C USA
18 B13 **Beaver River** ≈ Pennsylvania, NE USA
65 A25 **Beaver Settlement** Beaver Island, W Falkland Islands
Beaver State see Oregon
14 H14 **Beaverton** Ontario, S Canada
32 G11 **Beaverton** Oregon, NW USA
152 G12 **Beāwar** Rājasthān, N India
Bebas, Dasht-i see Bābūs, Dasht-e
60 L8 **Bebedouro** São Paulo, S Brazil
101 I16 **Bebra** Hessen, C Germany
41 W12 **Becal** Campeche, SE Mexico
15 Q11 **Bécancour** ≈ Québec, SE Canada
97 Q19 **Beccles** E England, UK
112 L9 **Bečej** *Ger.* Altbetsche. *Hung.* Óbecse, Rácz-Becse; *prev.* Magyar-Becse, Stari Bečej. Vojvodina, N Serbia
104 I3 **Becerréa** Galicia, NW Spain
74 H7 **Béchar** *prev.* Colomb-Béchar. W Algeria
39 O14 **Becharof Lake** ◎ Alaska, USA

◆ Country ◇ Dependent Territory ◈ Administrative Regions ▲ Mountain ⋀ Volcano ◎ Lake
● Country Capital ○ Dependent Territory Capital ✈ International Airport ▲▲ Mountain Range ≈ River ▣ Reservoir

116 H15 **Bechet** *var.* Bechetu. Dolj, SW Romania
Bechetu *see* Bechet
21 R6 **Beckley** West Virginia, NE USA
101 G14 **Beckum** Nordrhein-Westfalen, W Germany
25 X7 **Beckville** Texas, SW USA
35 X4 **Becky Peak** ▲ Nevada, W USA
116 I9 **Beclean** *Hung.* Bethlen; *prev.* Betlen. Bistriţa-Năsăud, N Romania
Bécs *see* Wien
111 H18 **Bečva** *Ger.* Betschau, *Pol.* Beczwa. ~ E Czech Republic
Beczwa *see* Bečva
103 P15 **Bédarieux** Hérault, S France
120 B10 **Beddouza, Cap** *headland* W Morocco
80 I13 **Bedelē** Oromo, C Ethiopia
147 Y8 **Bedel Pass** *Rus.* Pereval Bedel. *pass* China/Kyrgyzstan
Bedel, Pereval *see* Bedel Pass
95 H22 **Beder** Århus, C Denmark
97 N20 **Bedford** E England, UK
31 O15 **Bedford** Indiana, N USA
29 U16 **Bedford** Iowa, C USA
20 L4 **Bedford** Kentucky, S USA
18 D15 **Bedford** Pennsylvania, NE USA
21 T6 **Bedford** Virginia, NE USA
97 N20 **Bedfordshire** *cultural region* E England, UK
127 N5 **Bednodem'yanovsk** Penzenskaya Oblast', W Russian Federation
98 N5 **Bedum** Groningen, NE Netherlands
27 V11 **Beebe** Arkansas, C USA
Beechy Group *see* Chichijima-rettō
45 T9 **Beef Island** ✈ (Road Town)Tortola, E British Virgin Islands
Beehive State *see* Utah
99 L18 **Beek** Limburg, SE Netherlands
99 L18 **Beek** ✈ (Maastricht) Limburg, SE Netherlands
99 K14 **Beek-en-Donk** Noord-Brabant, S Netherlands
138 F13 **Be'ér Menuḥa** *var* Be'er Menukha. Southern, S Israel
Be'erMenukha *see* Be'ér Menuḥa
99 D16 **Beernem** West-Vlaanderen, NW Belgium
99 I16 **Beerse** Antwerpen, N Belgium
Beersheba *see* Be'ér Sheva'
138 E11 **Be'ér Sheva'** *var.* Beersheba, *Ar.* Bir es Saba. Southern, S Israel
98 J13 **Beesd** Gelderland, C Netherlands
99 M16 **Beesel** Limburg, SE Netherlands
83 J21 **Beestekraal** North-West, N South Africa
194 J7 **Beethoven Peninsula** *peninsula* Alexander Island, Antarctica
Beetstersweach *see* Beetsterzwaag
98 M6 **Beetsterzwaag** *Fris.* Beetstersweach. Friesland, N Netherlands
25 S13 **Beeville** Texas, SW USA
79 J18 **Befale** Equateur, NW Dem. Rep. Congo
Befandriana *see* Befandriana Avaratra
172 J3 **Befandriana Avaratra** *var.* Befandriana, Befandriana Nord. Mahajanga, NW Madagascar
Befandriana Nord *see* Befandriana Avaratra
79 K18 **Befori** Equateur, N Dem. Rep. Congo
172 I7 **Befotaka** Fianarantsoa, S Madagascar
183 R11 **Bega** New South Wales, SE Australia
102 G5 **Bégard** Côtes d'Armor, NW France
112 M9 **Begejski Kanal** *canal* Vojvodina, NE Serbia
94 G13 **Begna** ~ S Norway
Begoml' *see* Byahoml'
Begovat *see* Bekobod
153 Q13 **Begusarai** Bihār, NE India
143 R9 **Behābād** Yazd, C Iran
Behagle *see* Laï
55 Z10 **Béhague, Pointe** *headland* E French Guiana
Behar *see* Bihār
142 M10 **Behbahān** *var.* Behbehān. Khūzestān, SW Iran
Behbehān *see* Behbahān
44 G3 **Behring Point** Andros Island, W Bahamas
143 P4 **Behshahr** *prev.* Ashraf. Māzandarān, N Iran
163 V6 **Bei'an** Heilongjiang, NE China
Beibunar *see* Sredishte
Beibu Wan *see* Tongking, Gulf of
Beida *see* Al Bayḍā'
80 H13 **Beigi** Oromo, C Ethiopia
160 L16 **Beihai** Guangxi Zhuangzu Zizhiqu, S China
159 Q10 **Bei Hulsan Hu** ◎ C China
161 N13 **Bei Jiang** ~ S China
161 O2 **Beijing** *var.* Pei-ching, *Eng.* Peking; *prev.* Pei-p'ing. ● Beijing Shi, E China
161 P2 **Beijing** ✈ Beijing Shi, E China
Beijing *see* Beijing Shi, China
161 O2 **Beijing Shi** *var.* Beijing, Jing, Pei-ching, *Eng.* Peking; *prev.* Pei-p'ing. ◈ *municipality* E China
76 G8 **Beïla** Trarza, W Mauritania
98 N7 **Beilen** Drenthe, NE Netherlands
160 L15 **Beiliu** *var* Lingcheng. Guangxi Zhuangzu Zizhiqu, S China
159 O12 **Beilu He** ~ W China
Beilul *see* Beylul
163 U12 **Beining** *prev.* Beizhen. Liaoning, NE China
96 H8 **Beinn Dearg** ▲ N Scotland, UK
Beinn MacDuibh *see* Ben Macdui
160 I12 **Beipan Jiang** ~ S China
163 T12 **Beipiao** Liaoning, NE China
83 N17 **Beira** Sofala, C Mozambique
83 N17 **Beira** ✈ Sofala, C Mozambique
104 I7 **Beira Alta** *former province* N Portugal
104 H9 **Beira Baixa** *former province* C Portugal
104 G8 **Beira Litoral** *former province* N Portugal
Beirut *see* Beyrouth
Beisän *see* Bet She'an
9 Q16 **Beiseker** Alberta, SW Canada
Beitai Ding *see* Wutai Shan
83 K19 **Beitbridge** Matabeleland South, S Zimbabwe
116 G10 **Beiuş** *Hung.* Belényes. Bihor, NW Romania
Beizhen *see* Beining
104 H12 **Beja** *anc.* Pax Julia. Beja, SE Portugal
74 M5 **Béja** *var.* Bājah. N Tunisia
104 G13 **Beja** ◈ *district* S Portugal
120 I9 **Béjaïa** *var.* Bejaïa, *Fr.* Bougie; *anc.* Saldae. NE Algeria
Bejaïa *see* Béjaïa
104 K8 **Béjar** Castilla-León, N Spain
Bejraburi *see* Phetchaburi
Bekaa Valley *see* El Beqaa
Bekabad *see* Bekobod
Békás *see* Bicaz
169 O15 **Bekasi** Jawa, C Indonesia
Bek-Budi *see* Qarshi
Bekdaş/Bekdash *see* Garabogaz
147 T10 **Bek-Dzhar** Oshskaya Oblast', SW Kyrgyzstan
111 N24 **Békés** *Rom.* Bichiş. Békés, SE Hungary
111 M24 **Békés** *off.* Békés Megye. ◈ *county* SE Hungary
111 M24 **Békéscsaba** *Rom.* Bichiş-Ciaba. Békés, SE Hungary
Békés Megye *see* Békés
139 S2 **Bēkhma** E Iraq
172 H7 **Bekily** Toliara, S Madagascar
165 W4 **Bekkai** Hokkaidō, NE Japan
147 Q11 **Bekobod** *Rus.* Bekabad; *prev.* Begovat. Toshkent Viloyati, E Uzbekistan
127 O7 **Bekovo** Penzenskaya Oblast', W Russian Federation
Bel *see* Beliu
152 M13 **Bela** Uttar Pradesh, N India
149 N15 **Bela** Baluchistān, SW Pakistan
79 F15 **Bélabo** Est, C Cameroon
112 N10 **Bela Crkva** *Ger.* Weisskirchen, *Hung.* Fehértemplom. Vojvodina, W Serbia
173 Y16 **Bel Air** *var.* Rivière Sèche. E Mauritius
104 L12 **Belalcázar** Andalucía, S Spain
113 P15 **Bela Palanka** Serbia, SE Serbia
119 H16 **Belarus** *off.* Republic of Belarus, *var.* Belorussia, *Latv.* Baltkrievija; *prev.* Belorussian SSR, *Rus.* Belorusskaya SSR. ◆ *republic* E Europe
Belarus, Republic of *see* Belarus
Belau *see* Palau
59 H21 **Bela Vista** Mato Grosso do Sul, SW Brazil
83 L21 **Bela Vista** Maputo, S Mozambique
168 I8 **Belawan** Sumatera, W Indonesia
Běla Woda *see* Weisswasser
127 U4 **Belaya** ~ W Russian Federation
123 R7 **Belaya Gora** Respublika Sakha (Yakutiya), NE Russian Federation
126 M11 **Belaya Kalitiva** Rostovskaya Oblast', SW Russian Federation
125 R14 **Belaya Kholunitsa** Kirovskaya Oblast', NW Russian Federation
Belaya Tserkov' *see* Bila Tserkva
77 V11 **Belbédji** Zinder, S Niger
110 K13 **Bełchatów** *var.* Bełchatow. Łódzski, C Poland
Bełchatow *see* Bełchatów
Belcher, Îles *see* Belcher Islands
12 H7 **Belcher Islands** *Fr.* Îles Belcher. *island group* Nunavut, SE Canada
105 S6 **Belchite** Aragón, NE Spain
29 O2 **Belcourt** North Dakota, N USA
31 P9 **Belding** Michigan, N USA
127 U5 **Belebey** Respublika Bashkortostan, W Russian Federation
81 N16 **Beledweyne** *var.* Belet Huen, *It.* Belet Uen. Hiiraan, C Somalia
146 B10 **Belek** Balkan Welaýaty, W Turkmenistan
58 L12 **Belém** *var.* Pará. *state capital* Pará, N Brazil
65 I14 **Belém Ridge** *undersea feature* C Atlantic Ocean
62 I7 **Belén** Catamarca, NW Argentina
54 G9 **Belén** Boyacá, C Colombia
42 J11 **Belén** Rivas, SW Nicaragua
62 O5 **Belén** Concepción, C Paraguay
61 D16 **Belén** Salto, N Uruguay
37 R12 **Belen** New Mexico, SW USA
61 D20 **Belén de Escobar** Buenos Aires, E Argentina
114 J7 **Belene** Pleven, N Bulgaria
114 J7 **Belene, Ostrov** *island* N Bulgaria
43 R15 **Belén, Río** ~ C Panama
Belényes *see* Beiuş
Embalse de Belesar *see* Belesar, Encoro de
104 H3 **Belesar, Encoro de** *Sp.* Embalse de Belesar. ▣ NW Spain
Belet Huen/Belet Uen *see* Beledweyne
126 J5 **Belëv** Tul'skaya Oblast', W Russian Federation
19 R7 **Belfast** Maine, NE USA
97 G15 **Belfast** *Ir.* Béal Feirste. ◐ E Northern Ireland, UK
97 G15 **Belfast** ✈ E Northern Ireland, UK
97 G15 **Belfast Lough** *Ir.* Loch Lao. *inlet* E Northern Ireland, UK
28 K5 **Belfield** North Dakota, N USA
103 U7 **Belfort** Territoire-de-Belfort, E France
Belgard *see* Białogard
155 E17 **Belgaum** Karnātaka, W India
Belgian Congo *see* Congo (Democratic Republic of)
195 T3 **Belgica Mountains** ▲▲ Antarctica
België/Belgique *see* Belgium
99 F20 **Belgium** *off.* Kingdom of Belgium, *Dut.* België, *Fr.* Belgique. ◆ *monarchy* NW Europe
Belgium, Kingdom of *see* Belgium
126 J8 **Belgorod** Belgorodskaya Oblast', W Russian Federation
Belgorod-Dnestrovskiy *see* Bilhorod-Dnistrovs'kyy
126 J8 **Belgorodskaya Oblast'** ◈ *province* W Russian Federation
Belgrad *see* Beograd
29 T8 **Belgrade** Minnesota, N USA
33 S11 **Belgrade** Montana, NW USA
Belgrade *see* Beograd
Belgrano, Cabo *see* Meredith, Cape
195 N5 **Belgrano II** *Argentinian research station* Antarctica
21 X9 **Belhaven** North Carolina, SE USA
107 I23 **Belice** *anc.* Hypsas. ~ Sicilia, Italy, C Mediterranean Sea
Belice *see* Belize/Belize City
113 M16 **Beli Drim** *Alb.* Drini i Bardhë. ~ Albania/Serbia
Beligrad *see* Berat
188 C8 **Beliliou** *prev.* Peleliu. *island* S Palau
114 L8 **Beli Lom, Yazovir** ▣ NE Bulgaria
112 I8 **Beli Manastir** *Hung.* Pélmonostor; *prev.* Monostor. Osijek-Baranja, NE Croatia
102 J13 **Bélin-Béliet** Gironde, SW France
79 F17 **Bélinga** Ogooué-Ivindo, NE Gabon
21 S4 **Belington** West Virginia, NE USA
127 O6 **Belinskiy** Penzenskaya Oblast', W Russian Federation
169 N12 **Belinyu** Pulau Bangka, W Indonesia
169 O13 **Belitung, Pulau** *island* W Indonesia
116 F10 **Beliu** *Hung.* Bel. Arad, W Romania
114 I9 **Beli Vit** ~ NW Bulgaria
42 G2 **Belize** *Sp.* Belice; *prev.* British Honduras, Colony of Belize. ◆ *commonwealth republic* Central America
42 F2 **Belize** *Sp.* Belice. ◈ *district* NE Belize
42 G2 **Belize** ~ Belize/Guatemala
Belize *see* Belize City
42 G2 **Belize City** *var.* Belize, *Sp.* Belice. Belize, NE Belize
42 G2 **Belize City** ✈ Belize, NE Belize
Belize, Colony of *see* Belize
Beljak *see* Villach
39 N16 **Belkofski** Alaska, USA
123 O6 **Bel'kovskiy, Ostrov** *island* Novosibirskiye Ostrova, NE Russian Federation
14 J8 **Bell** ~ Québec, SE Canada
10 J15 **Bella Bella** British Columbia, SW Canada
102 M10 **Bellac** Haute-Vienne, C France
10 K15 **Bella Coola** British Columbia, SW Canada
106 D6 **Bellagio** Lombardia, N Italy
31 P6 **Bellaire** Michigan, N USA
106 D6 **Bellano** Lombardia, N Italy
155 G17 **Bellary** *var.* Ballari. Karnātaka, S India
183 S5 **Bellata** New South Wales, SE Australia
61 D16 **Bella Unión** Artigas, N Uruguay
61 C14 **Bella Vista** Corrientes, NE Argentina
62 J7 **Bella Vista** Tucumán, N Argentina
62 P4 **Bella Vista** Amambay, C Paraguay
56 B10 **Bellavista** Cajamarca, N Peru
56 D11 **Bellavista** San Martín, N Peru
183 U6 **Bellbrook** New South Wales, SE Australia
27 V5 **Belle** Missouri, C USA
21 Q5 **Belle** West Virginia, NE USA
31 R13 **Bellefontaine** Ohio, N USA
18 F14 **Bellefonte** Pennsylvania, NE USA
28 J9 **Belle Fourche** South Dakota, N USA
28 J9 **Belle Fourche Reservoir** ▣ South Dakota, N USA
28 K9 **Belle Fourche River** ~ South Dakota/Wyoming, N USA
103 S10 **Bellegarde-sur-Valserine** Ain, E France
23 Y14 **Belle Glade** Florida, SE USA
102 G8 **Belle Île** *island* NW France
13 T9 **Belle Isle** *island* Belle Isle, Newfoundland and Labrador, E Canada
13 S10 **Belle Isle, Strait of** *strait* Newfoundland and Labrador, E Canada
Bellenz *see* Bellinzona
29 W14 **Belle Plaine** Iowa, C USA
29 V9 **Belle Plaine** Minnesota, N USA
14 I9 **Belleterre** Québec, SE Canada
14 J15 **Belleville** Ontario, SE Canada
103 R10 **Belleville** Rhône, E France
30 K15 **Belleville** Illinois, N USA
27 N3 **Belleville** Kansas, C USA
29 Z15 **Bellevue** Iowa, C USA
29 S15 **Bellevue** Nebraska, C USA
31 S11 **Bellevue** Ohio, N USA
25 S5 **Bellevue** Texas, SW USA
32 H8 **Bellevue** Washington, NW USA
55 Y11 **Bellevue de l'Inini, Montagnes** ▲▲ S French Guiana
103 S11 **Belley** Ain, E France
Bellin *see* Kangirsuk
183 V6 **Bellingen** New South Wales, SE Australia
97 L14 **Bellingham** N England, UK
32 H6 **Bellingham** Washington, NW USA
Belling Hausen Mulde *see* Southeast Pacific Basin
194 H2 **Bellingshausen** *Russian research station* South Shetland Islands, Antarctica
Bellingshausen *see* Motu One
Bellingshausen Abyssal Plain *see* Bellingshausen Plain
196 R14 **Bellingshausen Plain** *var.* Bellingshausen Abyssal Plain. *undersea feature* SE Pacific Ocean
194 I8 **Bellingshausen Sea** *sea* Antarctica
98 P6 **Bellingwolde** Groningen, NE Netherlands
108 H11 **Bellinzona** *Ger.* Bellenz. Ticino, S Switzerland
25 T8 **Bellmead** Texas, SW USA
54 E8 **Bello** Antioquia, W Colombia
61 B21 **Bellocq** Buenos Aires, E Argentina
Bello Horizonte *see* Belo Horizonte
186 L10 **Bellona** *var.* Mungiki. *island* S Solomon Islands
Bellovacum *see* Beauvais
182 D7 **Bell, Point** *headland* South Australia
20 F9 **Bells** Tennessee, S USA
25 U5 **Bells** Texas, SW USA
92 N3 **Bellsund** *inlet* SW Svalbard
106 H6 **Belluno** Veneto, NE Italy
62 L11 **Bell Ville** Córdoba, C Argentina
83 E26 **Bellville** Western Cape, SW South Africa
25 U11 **Bellville** Texas, SW USA
104 L12 **Belmez** Andalucía, S Spain
29 V12 **Belmond** Iowa, C USA
18 E11 **Belmont** New York, NE USA
21 R10 **Belmont** North Carolina, SE USA
59 O18 **Belmonte** Bahia, E Brazil
104 I8 **Belmonte** Castelo Branco, C Portugal
105 P10 **Belmonte** Castilla-La Mancha, C Spain
42 G2 **Belmopan** ● (Belize) Cayo, C Belize
97 B16 **Belmullet** *Ir.* Béal an Mhuirhead. Mayo, W Ireland
99 E20 **Belœil** Hainaut, SW Belgium
123 R13 **Belogorsk** Amurskaya Oblast', SE Russian Federation
Belogorsk *see* Bilohirs'k
114 F7 **Belogradchik** Vidin, NW Bulgaria
172 H8 **Beloha** Toliara, S Madagascar
59 M20 **Belo Horizonte** *prev.* Bello Horizonte. *state capital* Minas Gerais, SE Brazil
26 M3 **Beloit** Kansas, C USA
30 L9 **Beloit** Wisconsin, N USA
Belokorovichi *see* Bilokorovychi
124 J8 **Belomorsk** Respublika Kareliya, NW Russian Federation
124 J8 **Belomorsko-Baltiyskiy Kanal** *Eng.* White Sea-Baltic Canal, White Sea Canal. *canal* NW Russian Federation
153 V15 **Belonia** Tripura, NE India
Beloozersk *see* Byelaazyorsk
Belopol'ye *see* Bilopillya
105 O4 **Belorado** Castilla-León, N Spain
126 L14 **Belorechensk** Krasnodarskiy Kray, SW Russian Federation
127 W5 **Beloretsk** Respublika Bashkortostan, W Russian Federation
Belorussia/Belorussian SSR *see* Belarus
Belorusskaya Gryada *see* Byelaruskaya Hrada
Belorusskaya SSR *see* Belarus
Beloshchel'ye *see* Nar'yan-Mar
114 N8 **Beloslav** Varna, E Bulgaria
Belostok *see* Białystok
Belo-sur-Tsiribihina *see* Belo Tsiribihina
172 H5 **Belo Tsiribihina** *var.* Belo-sur-Tsiribihina. Toliara, W Madagascar
Belovár *see* Bjelovar
Belovezhskaya, Pushcha *see* Białowieska, Puszcza/Byelavyezhskaya, Pushcha
114 H10 **Belovo** Pazardzhik, C Bulgaria
Belovodsk *see* Bilovods'k
122 H9 **Beloyarskiy** Khanty-Mansiyskiy Avtonomnyy Okrug, N Russian Federation
124 K7 **Beloye More** *Eng.* White Sea. *sea* NW Russian Federation
124 K13 **Beloye, Ozero** ◎ NW Russian Federation
114 J10 **Belozem** Plovdiv, C Bulgaria
124 K13 **Belozërsk** Vologodskaya Oblast', NW Russian Federation
108 D8 **Belp** Bern, W Switzerland
108 D8 **Belp** ✈ (Bern) Bern, C Switzerland
107 L24 **Belpasso** Sicilia, Italy, C Mediterranean Sea
31 U14 **Belpre** Ohio, N USA
98 M8 **Belterwijde** ◎ N Netherlands
27 R4 **Belton** Missouri, C USA
21 P11 **Belton** South Carolina, SE USA
25 T9 **Belton** Texas, SW USA
25 S9 **Belton Lake** ▣ Texas, SW USA
Bel'tsy *see* Bălţi
97 E16 **Belturbet** *Ir.* Béal Tairbirt. Cavan, N Ireland
Beluchistan *see* Baluchistān
145 Z9 **Belukha, Gora** ▲ Kazakhstan/Russian Federation
107 M20 **Belvedere Marittimo** Calabria, SW Italy
30 L10 **Belvidere** Illinois, N USA
18 J14 **Belvidere** New Jersey, NE USA
Bely *see* Belyy
127 V8 **Belyayevka** Orenburgskaya Oblast', W Russian Federation
Belynichi *see* Byalynichy
124 H17 **Belyy** *var.* Bely, Beyj. Tverskaya Oblast', W Russian Federation
126 I6 **Belyye Berega** Bryanskaya Oblast', W Russian Federation
122 J6 **Belyy, Ostrov** *island* N Russian Federation
122 J11 **Belyy Yar** Tomskaya Oblast', C Russian Federation
100 N13 **Belzig** Brandenburg, NE Germany
22 K4 **Belzoni** Mississippi, S USA
172 H4 **Bemaraha** *var.* Plateau du Bemaraha. ▲▲ W Madagascar
Bemaraha, Plateau du *see* Bemaraha
82 B10 **Bembe** Uíge, NW Angola
77 S14 **Bembèrèkè** *var.* Bimbéréké. N Benin
104 K12 **Bembézar** ~ SW Spain
104 J3 **Bembibre** Castilla-León, N Spain
29 T4 **Bemidji** Minnesota, N USA
98 L12 **Bemmel** Gelderland, SE Netherlands
171 T13 **Bemu** Pulau Seram, E Indonesia
Benāb *see* Bonāb
105 T5 **Benabarre** *var.* Benavarn. Aragón, NE Spain
Benaco *see* Garda, Lago di
79 L20 **Bena-Dibele** Kasai Oriental, C Dem. Rep. Congo
105 R9 **Benageber, Embalse de** ▣ E Spain
183 O11 **Benalla** Victoria, SE Australia
104 M14 **Benamejí** Andalucía, S Spain
Benares *see* Vārānasi
Benavarn *see* Benabarre
104 F10 **Benavente** Santarém, C Portugal
104 K5 **Benavente** Castilla-León, N Spain
25 S15 **Benavides** Texas, SW USA
96 F8 **Benbecula** *island* NW Scotland, UK
Bencovazzo *see* Benkovac
32 H13 **Bend** Oregon, NW USA
182 K7 **Benda Range** ▲▲ South Australia
183 T6 **Bendemeer** New South Wales, SE Australia
Bender *see* Tighina
Bender Beila/Bender Beyla *see* Bandarbeyla
Bender Cassim *see* Bender Cassim/Bender Qaasim
Bendery *see* Tighina
183 N11 **Bendigo** Victoria, SE Australia
118 E10 **Bēne** Dobele, SW Latvia
98 K13 **Beneden-Leeuwen** Gelderland, C Netherlands
101 L24 **Benediktenwand** ▲ S Germany
Benemérita de San Cristóbal *see* San Cristóbal
77 N12 **Bénéna** Ségou, S Mali
172 I7 **Benenitra** Toliara, S Madagascar
Beneschau *see* Benešov
Beneški Zaliv *see* Venice, Gulf of
111 D17 **Benešov** *Ger.* Beneschau. Středočeský Kraj, W Czech Republic
123 Q5 **Benetta, Ostrov** *island* Novosibirskiye Ostrova, NE Russian Federation
107 L17 **Benevento** *anc.* Beneventum, Malventum. Campania, S Italy
Beneventum *see* Benevento
173 S3 **Bengal, Bay of** *bay* N Indian Ocean
79 M17 **Bengamisa** Orientale, N Dem. Rep. Congo
Bengasi *see* Banghāzī
Bengazi *see* Banghāzī
161 P7 **Bengbu** *var.* Peng-pu. Anhui, E China
32 L9 **Benge** Washington, NW USA
Benghazi *see* Banghāzī
168 K10 **Bengkalis** Pulau Bengkalis, W Indonesia
168 K10 **Bengkalis, Pulau** *island* W Indonesia
169 Q10 **Bengkayang** Borneo, C Indonesia
Bengkoeloe *see* Bengkulu
168 K14 **Bengkulu** *prev.* Bengkoeloe, Benkoelen, Benkulen. Sumatera, W Indonesia
168 K13 **Bengkulu** *off.* Propinsi Bengkulu; *prev.* Bengkoeloe, Benkoelen, Benkulen. ◈ *province* W Indonesia
Bengkulu, Propinsi *see* Bengkulu
82 A11 **Bengo** ◈ *province* W Angola
95 J16 **Bengtsfors** Västra Götaland, S Sweden
82 B13 **Benguela** *var.* Benguella. Benguela, W Angola
83 A14 **Benguela** ◈ *province* W Angola
Benguella *see* Benguela
Bengweulu, Lake *see* Bangweulu, Lake
121 V13 **Benha** *var.* Banhā. N Egypt
192 F6 **Benham Seamount** *undersea feature* W Philippine Sea
96 H6 **Ben Hope** ▲ N Scotland, UK
79 P18 **Beni** Nord Kivu, NE Dem. Rep. Congo
57 L15 **Beni** *var.* El Beni. ◈ *department* N Bolivia
74 H8 **Beni Abbès** W Algeria
105 T8 **Benicarló** País Valenciano, E Spain
105 T9 **Benicasim** *cat* Benicàssim. País Valenciano, E Spain
Benicàssim *see* Benicasim
105 T12 **Benidorm** País Valenciano, SE Spain
75 W9 **Beni Mazâr** *var.* Banī Mazār. C Egypt
121 C11 **Beni-Mellal** C Morocco
77 R14 **Benin** *off.* Republic of Benin; *prev.* Dahomey. ◆ *republic* W Africa
77 S17 **Benin, Bight of** *gulf* W Africa
77 U16 **Benin City** Edo, SW Nigeria
Benin, Republic of *see* Benin
57 K16 **Beni, Río** ~ N Bolivia
120 F10 **Beni Saf** *var.* Beni-Saf. NW Algeria
Beni-Saf *see* Beni Saf
80 H12 **Benishangul** ◈ *region* W Ethiopia
105 T11 **Benissa** País Valenciano, E Spain
121 V14 **Beni Suef** *var.* Banī Suwayf. N Egypt
9 V15 **Benito** Manitoba, S Canada
Benito *see* Uolo, Río
61 C23 **Benito Juárez** Buenos Aires, E Argentina
41 P14 **Benito Juárez Internacional** ✈ (México) México, S Mexico
25 P5 **Benjamin** Texas, SW USA
58 B13 **Benjamin Constant** Amazonas, N Brazil
40 F4 **Benjamín Hill** Sonora, NW Mexico
63 F19 **Benjamín, Isla** *island* Archipiélago de los Chonos, S Chile
164 Q4 **Benkei-misaki** *headland* Hokkaidō, NE Japan
28 L17 **Benkelman** Nebraska, C USA
96 I7 **Ben Klibreck** ▲ N Scotland, UK
Benkoelen *see* Bengkulu
Benkoelen/Bengkoeloe *see* Bengkulu
112 D13 **Benkovac** *It.* Bencovazzo. Zadar, SW Croatia
Benkulen *see* Bengkulu
96 I11 **Ben Lawers** ▲ C Scotland, UK
96 J9 **Ben Macdui** *var.* Beinn MacDuibh. ▲ C Scotland, UK
96 G11 **Ben More** ▲ W Scotland, UK
96 I11 **Ben More** ▲ C Scotland, UK
96 H7 **Ben More Assynt** ▲ N Scotland, UK
185 E20 **Benmore, Lake** ◎ South Island, New Zealand
98 L12 **Bennekom** Gelderland, SE Netherlands
21 T11 **Bennettsville** South Carolina, SE USA
96 H10 **Ben Nevis** ▲ N Scotland, UK
184 M9 **Benneydale** Waikato, North Island, New Zealand
Bennichab *see* Bennichchâb
76 H8 **Bennichchâb** *var.* Bennichab. Inchiri, W Mauritania
18 L10 **Bennington** Vermont, NE USA
185 E20 **Ben Ohau Range** ▲▲ South Island, New Zealand
83 J21 **Benoni** Gauteng, NE South Africa
172 J2 **Be, Nosy** *var.* Nossi-Bé. *island* NW Madagascar
Bénoué *see* Benue
42 F2 **Benque Viejo del Carmen** Cayo, W Belize
101 G19 **Bensheim** Hessen, W Germany
37 N16 **Benson** Arizona, SW USA
29 S8 **Benson** Minnesota, N USA
21 U10 **Benson** North Carolina, SE USA
171 N15 **Benteng** Pulau Selayar, C Indonesia
83 A14 **Bentiaba** Namibe, SW Angola
181 T4 **Bentinck Island** *island* Wellesley Islands, Queensland, N Australia
80 E13 **Bentiu** Wahda, S Sudan
138 G8 **Bent Jbaïl** *var.* Bint Jubayl. S Lebanon
9 Q15 **Bentley** Alberta, SW Canada
61 I15 **Bento Gonçalves** Rio Grande do Sul, S Brazil
27 U12 **Benton** Arkansas, C USA
30 L16 **Benton** Illinois, N USA
20 H7 **Benton** Kentucky, S USA
22 G5 **Benton** Louisiana, S USA
27 Y7 **Benton** Missouri, C USA
20 M10 **Benton** Tennessee, S USA
31 O10 **Benton Harbor** Michigan, N USA
27 S9 **Bentonville** Arkansas, C USA
77 V16 **Benue** ◈ *state* SE Nigeria
78 F13 **Benue** *Fr.* Bénoué. ~ Cameroon/Nigeria
163 V12 **Benxi** *prev.* Pen-ch'i, Penhsihu, Penki. Liaoning, NE China
112 K10 **Beočin** Vojvodina, N Serbia
Beodericsworth *see* Bury St Edmunds
112 M11 **Beograd** *Eng.* Belgrade, *Ger.* Belgrad; *anc.* Singidunum. ● (Serbia) Serbia, N Serbia
112 L11 **Beograd** *Eng.* Belgrade. ✈ Serbia, N Serbia
112 L11 **Beograd** ✈ Serbia, Serbia and Montenegro
76 M16 **Béoumi** C Ivory Coast
35 V3 **Beowawe** Nevada, W USA
164 E14 **Beppu** Ōita, Kyūshū, SW Japan
187 X15 **Beqa** *prev.* Mbengga. *island* W Fiji
45 Y14 **Bequia** *island* C Saint Vincent and the Grenadines
113 L16 **Berane** *prev.* Ivangrad. E Montenegro
113 L21 **Berat** *var.* Berati, *SCr.* Beligrad. Berat, C Albania
113 L21 **Berat** ◈ *district* C Albania
Berătău *see* Berettyó
Berati *see* Berat
Beraun *see* Berounka, Czech Republic
Beraun *see* Beroun, Czech Republic
171 U13 **Berau, Teluk** *var.* MacCluer Gulf. *bay* Papua, E Indonesia
80 G8 **Berber** River Nile, NE Sudan
80 N12 **Berbera** Sahil, NW Somalia
79 H16 **Berbérati** Mambéré-Kadéï, SW Central African Republic
Berberia, Cabo de *see* Barbaria, Cap de
55 T9 **Berbice River** ~ NE Guyana
Berchid *see* Berrechid
103 N2 **Berck-Plage** Pas-de-Calais, N France
25 T13 **Berclair** Texas, SW USA
117 W10 **Berda** ~ SE Ukraine
Berdichev *see* Berdychiv
123 P10 **Berdigestyakh** Respublika Sakha (Yakutiya), NE Russian Federation
122 J12 **Berdsk** Novosibirskaya Oblast', C Russian Federation

◆ Country
● Country Capital
◇ Dependent Territory
○ Dependent Territory Capital
◈ Administrative Regions
✈ International Airport
▲ Mountain
▲▲ Mountain Range
Volcano
~ River
◎ Lake
▣ Reservoir

117 W10 **Berdyans'k** *Rus.* Berdyansk; *prev.* Osipenko. Zaporiz'ka Oblast', SE Ukraine
117 W10 **Berdyans'ka Kosa** *spit* SE Ukraine
117 V10 **Berdyans'ka Zatoka** *gulf* S Ukraine
117 N5 **Berdychiv** *Rus.* Berdichev. Zhytomyrs'ka Oblast', N Ukraine
20 M6 **Berea** Kentucky, S USA
Beregovo/Beregszász *see* Berehove
116 G8 **Berehove** *Cz.* Berehovo, *Hung.* Beregszász, *Rus.* Beregovo. Zakarpats'ka Oblast', W Ukraine
Berehovo *see* Berehove
186 D9 **Bereina** Central, S Papua New Guinea
146 C11 **Bereket** *prev. Rus.* Gazandzhyk, Kazandzhik, *Turkm.* Gazanjyk. Balkan Welaýaty, W Turkmenistan
45 O12 **Berekua** S Dominica
77 O16 **Berekum** W Ghana
75 Y11 **Berenice** *var.* Minâ Baranîs. SE Egypt
9 O14 **Berens** ≈ Manitoba/Ontario, C Canada
9 X14 **Berens River** Manitoba, C Canada
29 R12 **Beresford** South Dakota, N USA
116 J4 **Berestechko** Volyns'ka Oblast', NW Ukraine
116 M11 **Bereşti** Galaţi, E Romania
117 U6 **Berestova** ≈ E Ukraine
Beretău *see* Berettyó
111 N23 **Berettyó** *Rom.* Barcău; *prev.* Berătău, Beretău. ≈ Hungary/Romania
111 N23 **Berettyóújfalu** Hajdú-Bihar, E Hungary
Berëza/Bereza Kartuska *see* Byaroza
117 Q4 **Berezan'** Kyyivs'ka Oblast', N Ukraine
117 Q10 **Berezanka** Mykolayivs'ka Oblast', S Ukraine
116 J6 **Berezhany** *Pol.* Brzeżany. Ternopil's'ka Oblast', W Ukraine
Berezina *see* Byerezino
Berezino *see* Byerazino
117 P10 **Berezivka** *Rus.* Berezovka. Odes'ka Oblast', SW Ukraine
117 Q2 **Berezna** Chernihivs'ka Oblast', NE Ukraine
116 L3 **Berezne** Rivnens'ka Oblast', NW Ukraine
117 R9 **Bereznehuvate** Mykolayivs'ka Oblast', S Ukraine
125 N10 **Bereznik** Arkhangel'skaya Oblast', NW Russian Federation
125 U13 **Berezniki** Permskaya Oblast', NW Russian Federation
Berëzovka *see* Byarozawka, Belarus
Berezovka *see* Berezivka, Ukraine
122 H9 **Berezovo** Khanty-Mansiyskiy Avtonomnyy Okrug, N Russian Federation
127 O9 **Berezovskaya** Volgogradskaya Oblast', SW Russian Federation
123 S13 **Berezovyy** Khabarovskiy Kray, E Russian Federation
83 E25 **Berg** ≈ W South Africa
Berg *see* Berg bei Rohrbach
105 V4 **Berga** Cataluña, NE Spain
95 N20 **Berga** Kalmar, S Sweden
136 B13 **Bergama** İzmir, W Turkey
106 E7 **Bergamo** *anc.* Bergomum. Lombardia, N Italy
105 P3 **Bergara** País Vasco, N Spain
109 S3 **Berg bei Rohrbach** *var.* Berg. Oberösterreich, N Austria
100 O6 **Bergen** Mecklenburg-Vorpommern, NE Germany
101 I11 **Bergen** Niedersachsen, NW Germany
98 H8 **Bergen** Noord-Holland, NW Netherlands
94 C13 **Bergen** Hordaland, S Norway
Bergen *see* Mons
55 W9 **Berg en Dal** Brokopondo, C Suriname
99 G15 **Bergen op Zoom** Noord-Brabant, S Netherlands
102 L13 **Bergerac** Dordogne, SW France
99 J16 **Bergeyk** Noord-Brabant, S Netherlands
101 D16 **Bergheim** Nordrhein-Westfalen, W Germany
55 X10 **Bergi** Sipaliwini, E Suriname
101 E16 **Bergisch Gladbach** Nordrhein-Westfalen, W Germany
101 F14 **Bergkamen** Nordrhein-Westfalen, W Germany
95 N21 **Bergkvara** Kalmar, S Sweden
Bergomum *see* Bergamo
98 K13 **Bergse Maas** ≈ S Netherlands
95 P15 **Bergshamra** Stockholm, C Sweden
94 N10 **Bergsjö** Gävleborg, C Sweden
93 J14 **Bergsviken** Norrbotten, N Sweden
98 L6 **Bergum** *Fris.* Burgum. Friesland, N Netherlands
98 M6 **Bergumer Meer** ◎ N Netherlands
94 N12 **Bergviken** ◎ C Sweden
168 M11 **Berhala, Selat** *strait* Sumatera, W Indonesia
Berhampore *see* Baharampur
99 J17 **Beringen** Limburg, NE Belgium
39 T12 **Bering Glacier** *glacier* Alaska, USA
Beringov Proliv *see* Bering Strait
192 L2 **Bering Sea** *sea* N Pacific Ocean
38 L9 **Bering Strait** *Rus.* Beringov Proliv. *strait* Bering Sea/ Chukchi Sea
Berislav *see* Beryslav
105 O15 **Berja** Andalucía, S Spain
94 H9 **Berkåk** Sør-Trøndelag, S Norway
98 N11 **Berkel** ≈ Germany/Netherlands
35 N8 **Berkeley** California, W USA
65 E24 **Berkeley Sound** *sound* NE Falkland Islands
21 V2 **Berkeley Springs** *var.* Bath. West Virginia, NE USA
195 N6 **Berkner Island** *island* Antarctica
114 G8 **Berkovitsa** Montana, NW Bulgaria
97 M22 **Berkshire** *former county* S England, UK
99 H17 **Berlaar** Antwerpen, N Belgium
Berlanga *see* Berlanga de Duero
105 P6 **Berlanga de Duero** *var.* Berlanga. Castilla-León, N Spain
0 I16 **Berlanga Rise** *undersea feature* E Pacific Ocean
99 F17 **Berlare** Oost-Vlaanderen, NW Belgium
104 E9 **Berlenga, Ilha da** *island* C Portugal
92 M7 **Berlevåg** *Lapp.* Bearalváhki. Finnmark, N Norway
100 O12 **Berlin** ● Berlin, NE Germany
21 Z4 **Berlin** Maryland, NE USA
19 O7 **Berlin** New Hampshire, NE USA
18 D16 **Berlin** Pennsylvania, NE USA
30 L7 **Berlin** Wisconsin, N USA
100 O12 **Berlin** ◈ *state* NE Germany
Berlinchen *see* Barlinek
31 U12 **Berlin Lake** ⊠ Ohio, N USA
183 R11 **Bermagui** New South Wales, SE Australia
40 L8 **Bermejillo** Durango, C Mexico
62 L5 **Bermejo, Río** ≈ N Argentina
62 I10 **Bermejo, Río** ≈ W Argentina
62 M6 **Bermejo (viejo), Río** ≈ N Argentina
105 P2 **Bermeo** País Vasco, N Spain
104 K6 **Bermillo de Sayago** Castilla-León, N Spain
106 E6 **Bermina, Pizzo** *Rmsch.* Piz Bernina. ▲ Italy/Switzerland *see also* Bermina, Piz
Bermina, Pizzo *see* Bernina, Piz
64 A12 **Bermuda** *var.* Bermuda Islands, Bermudas; *prev.* Somers Islands. ◇ *UK crown colony* NW Atlantic Ocean
1 N11 **Bermuda** *var.* Great Bermuda, Long Island, Main Island. *island* Bermuda
Bermuda Islands *see* Bermuda
Bermuda-New England Seamount Arc *see* New England Seamounts
1 N11 **Bermuda Rise** *undersea feature* C Sargasso Sea
Bermudas *see* Bermuda
108 D8 **Bern** *Fr.* Berne. ● (Switzerland) Bern, W Switzerland
108 D9 **Bern** *Fr.* Berne. ◈ *canton* W Switzerland
37 R11 **Bernalillo** New Mexico, SW USA
14 H12 **Bernard Lake** ◎ Ontario, S Canada
61 B18 **Bernardo de Irigoyen** Santa Fe, NE Argentina
18 J14 **Bernardsville** New Jersey, NE USA
63 K14 **Bernasconi** La Pampa, C Argentina
100 O12 **Bernau** Brandenburg, NE Germany
102 L4 **Bernay** Eure, N France
101 L14 **Bernburg** Sachsen-Anhalt, C Germany
109 X5 **Berndorf** Niederösterreich, NE Austria
31 Q12 **Berne** Indiana, N USA
Berne *see* Bern
108 D10 **Berner Alpen** *var.* Berner Oberland, *Eng.* Bernese Oberland. ▲▲ SW Switzerland
Berner Oberland/Bernese Oberland *see* Berner Alpen
109 Y2 **Bernhardsthal** Niederösterreich, N Austria
22 H4 **Bernice** Louisiana, S USA
27 Y8 **Bernie** Missouri, C USA
180 G9 **Bernier Island** *island* Western Australia
Bernina Pass *see* Bernina, Passo del
108 J10 **Bernina, Passo del** *Eng.* Bernina Pass. *pass* SE Switzerland
108 J10 **Bernina, Piz** *It.* Pizzo Bernina. ▲ Italy/Switzerland *see also* Bermina, Pizzo
Bernina, Piz *see* Bermina, Pizzo
99 E20 **Bérnissart** Hainaut, SW Belgium
101 E18 **Bernkastel-Kues** Rheinland-Pfalz, W Germany
Beroea *see* Ḩalab
172 H6 **Beroroha** Toliara, SW Madagascar
Béroubouay *see* Gbéroubouè
111 C17 **Beroun** *Ger.* Beraun. Středočeský Kraj, W Czech Republic
111 C16 **Berounka** *Ger.* Beraun. ≈ W Czech Republic
113 Q18 **Berovo** E FYR Macedonia
74 F6 **Berrechid** *var.* Berchid. W Morocco
103 R15 **Berre, Étang de** ◎ SE France
103 S15 **Berre-l'Étang** Bouches-du-Rhône, SE France
182 K9 **Berri** South Australia
31 O10 **Berrien Springs** Michigan, N USA
183 O10 **Berrigan** New South Wales, SE Australia
103 N9 **Berry** *cultural region* C France
35 N7 **Berryessa, Lake** ◎ California, W USA
44 G2 **Berry Islands** *island group* N Bahamas
27 T9 **Berryville** Arkansas, C USA
21 V3 **Berryville** Virginia, NE USA
83 D21 **Berseba** Karas, S Namibia
117 O8 **Bershad'** Vinnyts'ka Oblast', C Ukraine
28 L3 **Berthold** North Dakota, N USA
37 T3 **Berthoud** Colorado, C USA
37 S4 **Berthoud Pass** *pass* Colorado, C USA
79 F15 **Bertoua** Est, E Cameroon
25 S10 **Bertram** Texas, SW USA
63 G22 **Bertrand, Cerro** ▲ S Argentina
99 J23 **Bertrix** Luxembourg, SE Belgium
191 P3 **Beru** *var.* Peru. *atoll* Tungaru, W Kiribati
Beruni *see* Beruniy
146 I9 **Beruniy** *var.* Biruni, *Rus.* Beruni. Qoraqalpog'iston Respublikasi, W Uzbekistan
58 F13 **Beruri** Amazonas, NW Brazil
18 H14 **Berwick** Pennsylvania, NE USA
96 K12 **Berwick** *cultural region* SE Scotland, UK
96 L12 **Berwick-upon-Tweed** N England, UK
117 S10 **Beryslav** *Rus.* Berislav. Khersons'ka Oblast', S Ukraine
Berytus *see* Beyrouth
172 H4 **Besalampy** Mahajanga, W Madagascar
103 T8 **Besançon** *anc.* Besontium, Vesontio. Doubs, E France
103 P10 **Besbre** ≈ C France
Bescanuova *see* Baška
Besdan *see* Bezdan
Besed' *see* Byesyedz'
147 R10 **Beshariq** *Rus.* Besharyk; *prev.* Kirovo. Farg'ona Viloyati, E Uzbekistan
Besharyk *see* Beshariq
146 L9 **Beshbuloq** *Rus.* Beshulak. Navoiy Viloyati, N Uzbekistan
Beshenkovichi *see* Byeshankovichy
146 M13 **Beshkent** Qashqadaryo Viloyati, S Uzbekistan
Beshulak *see* Beshbuloq
112 L10 **Beška** Vojvodina, N Serbia
Beskra *see* Biskra
127 O16 **Beslan** Respublika Severnaya Osetiya, SW Russian Federation
113 P16 **Besna Kobila** ▲ SE Serbia
137 N16 **Besni** Adıyaman, S Turkey
Besontium *see* Besançon
121 Q2 **Beşparmak Dağları** *Eng.* Kyrenia Mountains. ▲▲ N Cyprus
Bessarabka *see* Basarabeasca
92 O2 **Bessels, Kapp** *headland* C Svalbard
23 P4 **Bessemer** Alabama, S USA
30 K3 **Bessemer** Michigan, N USA
21 Q10 **Bessemer City** North Carolina, SE USA
102 M10 **Bessines-sur-Gartempe** Haute-Vienne, C France
99 K15 **Best** Noord-Brabant, S Netherlands
25 N9 **Best** Texas, SW USA
125 O11 **Bestuzhevo** Arkhangel'skaya Oblast', NW Russian Federation
123 M11 **Bestyakh** Respublika Sakha (Yakutiya), NE Russian Federation
Beszterce *see* Bistriţa
Besztercebánya *see* Banská Bystrica
172 I5 **Betafo** Antananarivo, C Madagascar
104 H2 **Betanzos** Galicia, NW Spain
104 G2 **Betanzos, Ría de** *estuary* NW Spain
79 G15 **Bétaré Oya** Est, E Cameroon
105 S9 **Bétera** País Valenciano, E Spain
77 R15 **Bétérou** C Benin
83 K21 **Bethal** Mpumalanga, NE South Africa
30 K15 **Bethalto** Illinois, N USA
83 D21 **Bethanie** *var.* Bethanien, Bethany. Karas, S Namibia
Bethanien *see* Bethanie
27 S2 **Bethany** Missouri, C USA
27 N10 **Bethany** Oklahoma, C USA
Bethany *see* Bethanie
39 N12 **Bethel** Alaska, USA
19 P7 **Bethel** Maine, NE USA
21 W9 **Bethel** North Carolina, SE USA
18 B15 **Bethel Park** Pennsylvania, NE USA
21 W3 **Bethesda** Maryland, NE USA
83 J22 **Bethlehem** Free State, C South Africa
18 I14 **Bethlehem** Pennsylvania, NE USA
138 F10 **Bethlehem** *Ar.* Bayt Laḩm, *Heb.* Bet Leḩem. C West Bank
Bethlen *see* Beclean
83 I24 **Bethulie** Free State, C South Africa
103 O1 **Béthune** Pas-de-Calais, N France
102 M3 **Béthune** ≈ N France
104 M14 **Béticos, Sistemas** *var.* Sistema Penibético, *Eng.* Baetic Cordillera, Baetic Mountains. ▲▲ S Spain
54 I6 **Betijoque** Trujillo, NW Venezuela
59 M20 **Betim** Minas Gerais, SE Brazil
190 H3 **Betio** Tarawa, W Kiribati
172 H7 **Betioky** Toliara, S Madagascar
Bet Leḩem *see* Bethlehem
Betlen *see* Beclean
167 O17 **Betong** Yala, SW Thailand
79 I16 **Bétou** La Likouala, N Congo
145 P14 **Betpak-Dala** *Kaz.* Betpaqdala. *plateau* S Kazakhstan
Betpaqdala *see* Betpak-Dala
172 H7 **Betroka** Toliara, S Madagascar
Betschau *see* Bečva
138 G9 **Bet She'an** *Ar.* Baysān, Beisān; *anc.* Scythopolis. Northern, N Israel
15 T6 **Betsiamites** Québec, SE Canada
15 T6 **Betsiamites** ≈ Québec, SE Canada
172 I4 **Betsiboka** ≈ N Madagascar
99 M25 **Bettembourg** Luxembourg, S Luxembourg
99 M23 **Bettendorf** Diekirch, NE Luxembourg
29 Z14 **Bettendorf** Iowa, C USA
75 R13 **Bette, Pic** *var.* Bikkū Bitti, *It.* Picco Bette. ▲ S Libya
Bette, Picco *see* Bette, Pic
153 P12 **Bettiah** Bihār, N India
39 Q7 **Bettles** Alaska, USA
95 N17 **Bettna** Södermanland, C Sweden
154 H11 **Betūl** *prev.* Badnur. Madhya Pradesh, C India
154 H9 **Betwa** ≈ C India
101 F16 **Betzdorf** Rheinland-Pfalz, W Germany
82 C9 **Béu** Uíge, NW Angola
31 P6 **Beulah** Michigan, N USA
28 L5 **Beulah** North Dakota, N USA
98 M8 **Beulakerwijde** ◎ N Netherlands
98 L13 **Beuningen** Gelderland, SE Netherlands
Beuthen *see* Bytom
103 N7 **Beuvron** ≈ C France
99 F16 **Beveren** Oost-Vlaanderen, N Belgium
21 T9 **B. Everett Jordan Reservoir** *var.* Jordan Lake. ⊠ North Carolina, SE USA
97 N17 **Beverley** E England, UK
Beverley *see* Beverly
99 J17 **Beverlo** Limburg, NE Belgium
19 P11 **Beverly** Massachusetts, NE USA
32 J9 **Beverly** *var.* Beverley. Washington, NW USA
35 S15 **Beverly Hills** California, W USA
101 I14 **Beverungen** Nordrhein-Westfalen, C Germany
98 H9 **Beverwijk** Noord-Holland, W Netherlands
108 C10 **Bex** Vaud, W Switzerland
97 P23 **Bexhill** *var.* Bexhill-on-Sea. SE England, UK
Bexhill-on-Sea *see* Bexhill
136 E17 **Bey Dağları** ▲▲ SW Turkey
Beyj *see* Belyy
136 E10 **Beykoz** İstanbul, NW Turkey
76 K15 **Beyla** SE Guinea
137 X12 **Beyläqan** *prev.* Zhdanov. SW Azerbaijan
80 L10 **Beylul** *var.* Beilul. SE Eritrea
144 H14 **Beyneu** *Kaz.* Beyneū. Mangistau, SW Kazakhstan
Beyneū *see* Beyneu
165 X14 **Beyonēsu-retsugan** *Eng.* Bayonnaise Rocks. *island group* SE Japan
136 G12 **Beypazarı** Ankara, NW Turkey
155 F21 **Beypore** Kerala, SW India
138 G7 **Beyrouth** *var.* Bayrūt, *Eng.* Beirut; *anc.* Berytus. ● (Lebanon) W Lebanon
138 G7 **Beyrouth** ✈ W Lebanon
136 G15 **Beyşehir** Konya, SW Turkey
136 G15 **Beyşehir Gölü** ◎ C Turkey
108 J7 **Bezau** Vorarlberg, NW Austria
112 J8 **Bezdan** *Ger.* Besdan, *Hung.* Bezdán. Vojvodina, NW Serbia
Bezdezh *see* Byezdzyezh
124 G15 **Bezhanitsy** Pskovskaya Oblast', W Russian Federation
124 K15 **Bezhetsk** Tverskaya Oblast', W Russian Federation
103 P16 **Béziers** *anc.* Baeterrae, Baeterrae Septimanorum, Julia Beterrae. Hérault, S France
Bezmein *see* Abadan
Bezwada *see* Vijayawāda
154 P12 **Bhadrak** *var.* Bhadrakh. Orissa, E India
Bhadrakh *see* Bhadrak
155 F19 **Bhadra Reservoir** ⊠ SW India
155 F18 **Bhadrāvati** Karnātaka, SW India
153 R14 **Bhāgalpur** Bihār, NE India
Bhairab *see* Bhairab Bazar
153 U14 **Bhairab Bazar** *var.* Bhairab. Dhaka, C Bangladesh
153 O11 **Bhairahawā** Western, S Nepal
149 S8 **Bhakkar** Punjab, E Pakistan
153 P11 **Bhaktapur** Central, C Nepal
167 N3 **Bhamo** *var.* Banmo. Kachin State, N Myanmar (Burma)
Bhāmragad *see* Bhāmragarh
154 K13 **Bhāmragarh** *var.* Bhāmragad. Mahārāshtra, C India
154 J12 **Bhandāra** Mahārāshtra, C India
Bhārat *see* India
152 J12 **Bharatpur** *prev.* Bhurtpore. Rājasthān, N India
154 D11 **Bharūch** Gujarāt, W India
155 E18 **Bhatkal** Karnātaka, W India
153 O13 **Bhatni** *var.* Bhatni Junction. Uttar Pradesh, N India
Bhatni Junction *see* Bhatni
153 S16 **Bhātpāra** West Bengal, NE India
149 U7 **Bhaun** Punjab, E Pakistan
Bhaunagar *see* Bhāvnagar
154 M13 **Bhavānīpātna** Orissa, E India
155 H21 **Bhavānīsāgar Reservoir** ⊠ S India
154 D11 **Bhāvnagar** *prev.* Bhaunagar. Gujarāt, W India
Bheanntraí, Bá *see* Bantry Bay
Bheara, Béal an *see* Gweebarra Bay
154 K12 **Bhilai** Chhattīsgarh, C India
152 G13 **Bhīlwāra** Rājasthān, N India
155 E14 **Bhīma** ≈ S India
155 K16 **Bhīmavaram** Andhra Pradesh, E India
154 I7 **Bhind** Madhya Pradesh, C India
152 E13 **Bhīnmāl** Rājasthān, N India
Bhir *see* Bīd
154 D13 **Bhiwandi** Mahārāshtra, W India
152 H10 **Bhiwāni** Haryāna, N India
152 L13 **Bhognīpur** Uttar Pradesh, N India
153 U16 **Bhola** Barisal, S Bangladesh
154 H10 **Bhopāl** *state capital* Madhya Pradesh, C India
155 J14 **Bhopālpatnam** Chhattīsgarh, C India
155 E14 **Bhor** Mahārāshtra, W India
154 O12 **Bhubaneshwar** *prev.* Bhubaneswar, Bhuvaneshwar. *state capital* Orissa, E India
Bhubaneswar *see* Bhubaneshwar
154 B9 **Bhuj** Gujarāt, W India
Bhuket *see* Phuket
Bhurtpore *see* Bharatpur
Bhusaval *see* Bhusāwal
154 G12 **Bhusāwal** *prev.* Bhusaval. Mahārāshtra, C India
153 T12 **Bhutan** *off.* Kingdom of Bhutan, *var.* Druk-yul. ◆ *monarchy* S Asia
Bhutan, Kingdom of *see* Bhutan
Bhuvaneshwar *see* Bhubaneshwar
143 T15 **Bīābān, Kūh-e** ▲▲ S Iran
77 V18 **Biafra, Bight of** *var.* Bight of Bonny. *bay* W Africa
171 W12 **Biak** Papua, E Indonesia
171 W12 **Biak, Pulau** *island* E Indonesia
110 P12 **Biała Podlaska** LubelskieE Poland
110 F7 **Białogard** *Ger.* Belgard. Zachodnio-pomorskie, NW Poland
110 P10 **Białowieska, Puszcza** *Bel.* Byelavyezhskaya Pushcha, *Rus.* Belovezhskaya Pushcha. *physical region* Belarus/Poland *see also* Byelavyezhskaya, Pushcha
Białowieska, Puszcza *see* Byelavyezhskaya Pushcha
110 G8 **Biały Bór** *Ger.* Baldenburg. Zachodnio-pomorskie, NW Poland
110 P9 **Białystok** *Rus.* Belostok, Bielostok. Podlaskie, NE Poland
107 L24 **Biancavilla** *prev.* Inessa. Sicilia, Italy, C Mediterranean Sea
Bianco, Monte *see* Blanc, Mont
Bianjing *see* Xunke
76 L15 **Biankouma** W Ivory Coast
167 R7 **Bia, Phou** *var.* Pou Bia. ▲ C Laos
Bia, Pou *see* Bia, Phou
143 R5 **Bīārjmand** Semnān, N Iran
105 P4 **Biarra** ≈ NE Spain
102 I15 **Biarritz** Pyrénées-Atlantiques, SW France
108 H10 **Biasca** Ticino, S Switzerland
61 E17 **Biassini** Salto, N Uruguay
Biasteri *see* Laguardia
165 S3 **Bibai** Hokkaidō, NE Japan
83 B15 **Bibala** *Port.* Vila Arriaga. Namibe, SW Angola
104 I4 **Bibéi** ≈ NW Spain
Biberach *see* Biberach an der Riss
101 I23 **Biberach an der Riss** *var.* Biberach, *Ger.* Biberach an der Riß. Baden-Württemberg, S Germany
108 E7 **Biberist** Solothurn, NW Switzerland
77 O16 **Bibiani** SW Ghana
112 C13 **Bibinje** Zadar, SW Croatia
Biblical Gebal *see* Jbaïl
116 I5 **Bibrka** *Pol.* Bóbrka, *Rus.* Bobrka. L'vivs'ka Oblast', NW Ukraine
117 N10 **Bic** ≈ S Moldova
113 M18 **Bicaj** Kukës, NE Albania
116 K10 **Bicaz** *Hung.* Békás. Neamţ, NE Romania
183 Q16 **Bicheno** Tasmania, SE Australia
Bichiş *see* Békés
Bichiş-Ciaba *see* Békéscsaba
Bichitra *see* Phichit
137 P8 **Bichvint'a** *Rus.* Pitsunda. NW Georgia
15 T7 **Bic, Île du** *island* Québec, SE Canada
32 J10 **Bickleton** Washington, NW USA
36 L6 **Bicknell** Utah, W USA
171 S11 **Bicoli** Pulau Halmahera, E Indonesia
111 J22 **Bicske** Fejér, C Hungary
155 F14 **Bīd** *prev.* Bhir. Mahārāshtra, W India
77 U15 **Bida** Niger, C Nigeria
155 H15 **Bīdar** Karnātaka, C India
141 Y8 **Bidbid** NE Oman
19 P9 **Biddeford** Maine, NE USA
98 L9 **Biddinghuizen** Flevoland, C Netherlands
33 X11 **Biddle** Montana, NW USA
97 J23 **Bideford** SW England, UK
82 D13 **Bié** ◈ *province* C Angola
35 O2 **Bieber** California, W USA
110 O9 **Biebrza** ≈ NE Poland
165 T3 **Biei** Hokkaidō, NE Japan
108 D8 **Biel** *Fr.* Bienne. Bern, W Switzerland
100 G13 **Bielefeld** Nordrhein-Westfalen, NW Germany
108 D8 **Bieler See** *Fr.* Lac de Bienne. ◎ W Switzerland
Bielitz/Bielitz-Biala *see* Bielsko-Biała
106 C7 **Biella** Piemonte, N Italy
Bielostok *see* Białystok
111 J17 **Bielsko-Biała** *Ger.* Bielitz, Bielitz-Biala. Śląskie, S Poland
110 P10 **Bielsk Podlaski** Białystok, E Poland
Bien Bien *see* Điện Biên
Biên Đông *see* South China Sea
9 V17 **Bienfait** Saskatchewan, S Canada
167 T14 **Biên Hoa** Đông Nai, S Vietnam
Bienne *see* Biel
Bienne, Lac de *see* Bieler See
12 K8 **Bienville, Lac** ◎ Québec, C Canada
82 D13 **Bié, Planalto do** *var.* Bié Plateau. *plateau* C Angola
Bié Plateau *see* Bié, Planalto do
108 B9 **Bière** Vaud, W Switzerland
98 O4 **Bierum** Groningen, NE Netherlands
98 I13 **Biesbos** *var.* Biesbosch. *wetland* S Netherlands
Biesbosch *see* Biesbos
99 H21 **Biesme** Namur, S Belgium
101 H21 **Bietigheim-Bissingen** Baden-Württemberg, SW Germany
99 I23 **Bièvre** Namur, SE Belgium
79 D18 **Bifoun** Moyen-Ogooué, NW Gabon
165 T2 **Bifuka** Hokkaidō, NE Japan
136 C11 **Biga** Çanakkale, NW Turkey
136 C13 **Bigadiç** Balıkesir, W Turkey
26 J7 **Big Basin** *basin* Kansas, C USA
185 B20 **Big Bay** *bay* South Island, New Zealand
31 O5 **Big Bay de Noc** ◎ Michigan, N USA
31 N3 **Big Bay Point** *headland* Michigan, N USA
33 R10 **Big Belt Mountains** ▲▲ Montana, NW USA
29 N10 **Big Bend Dam** *dam* South Dakota, N USA
24 K12 **Big Bend National Park** *national park* Texas, S USA
22 K5 **Big Black River** ≈ Mississippi, S USA
27 O3 **Big Blue River** ≈ Kansas/ Nebraska, C USA
24 M10 **Big Canyon** ≈ Texas, SW USA
33 N12 **Big Creek** Idaho, NW USA
23 N8 **Big Creek Lake** ⊠ Alabama, S USA
23 X15 **Big Cypress Swamp** *wetland* Florida, SE USA
39 S9 **Big Delta** Alaska, USA
30 K6 **Big Eau Pleine Reservoir** ⊠ Wisconsin, N USA
19 P5 **Bigelow Mountain** ▲ Maine, NE USA
162 G9 **Biger** *var* Jargalant. Govĭ-Altay, W Mongolia
29 U3 **Big Falls** Minnesota, N USA
33 P8 **Bigfork** Montana, NW USA
29 U3 **Big Fork River** ≈ Minnesota, N USA
9 S15 **Biggar** Saskatchewan, S Canada
180 L3 **Bigge Island** *island* Western Australia
35 O5 **Biggs** California, W USA
32 I11 **Biggs** Oregon, NW USA
14 K13 **Big Gull Lake** ◎ Ontario, SE Canada
37 P16 **Big Hachet Peak** ▲ New Mexico, SW USA
33 P11 **Big Hole River** ≈ Montana, NW USA
33 V13 **Bighorn Basin** *basin* Wyoming, C USA
33 U11 **Bighorn Lake** ◎ Montana/ Wyoming, N USA
33 W13 **Bighorn Mountains** ▲▲ Wyoming, C USA
36 J13 **Big Horn Peak** ▲ Arizona, SW USA
33 V11 **Bighorn River** ≈ Montana/ Wyoming, NW USA
9 S7 **Big Island** *island* Nunavut, NE Canada
39 O16 **Big Koniuji Island** *island* Shumagin Islands, Alaska, USA
25 N9 **Big Lake** Texas, SW USA
19 T5 **Big Lake** ◎ Maine, NE USA
30 I3 **Big Manitou Falls** *waterfall* Wisconsin, N USA
35 R2 **Big Mountain** ▲ Nevada, W USA
108 G10 **Bignasco** Ticino, S Switzerland
29 R16 **Big Nemaha River** ≈ Nebraska, C USA
76 G12 **Bignona** SW Senegal
Bigorra *see* Tarbes
Bigosovo *see* Bihosava
35 S10 **Big Pine** California, W USA
35 Q14 **Big Pine Mountain** ▲ California, W USA
27 V6 **Big Piney Creek** ≈ Missouri, C USA
65 M24 **Big Point** *headland* N Tristan da Cunha
31 P8 **Big Rapids** Michigan, N USA
30 K6 **Big Rib River** ≈ Wisconsin, N USA
14 L14 **Big Rideau Lake** ◎ Ontario, SE Canada
9 T14 **Big River** Saskatchewan, C Canada
27 X5 **Big River** ≈ Missouri, C USA
31 N7 **Big Sable Point** *headland* Michigan, N USA
33 S7 **Big Sandy** Montana, NW USA
25 W6 **Big Sandy** Texas, SW USA
37 V5 **Big Sandy Creek** ≈ Colorado, C USA
29 Q16 **Big Sandy Creek** ≈ Nebraska, C USA
29 V5 **Big Sandy Lake** ◎ Minnesota, N USA
36 J11 **Big Sandy River** ≈ Arizona, SW USA
21 P5 **Big Sandy River** ≈ S USA
23 V6 **Big Satilla Creek** ≈ Georgia, SE USA
29 R12 **Big Sioux River** ≈ Iowa/ South Dakota, N USA
35 U7 **Big Smoky Valley** *valley* Nevada, W USA
25 N7 **Big Spring** Texas, SW USA
19 Q5 **Big Squaw Mountain** ▲ Maine, NE USA
21 O7 **Big Stone Gap** Virginia, NE USA
29 Q8 **Big Stone Lake** ◎ Minnesota/ South Dakota, N USA
22 K4 **Big Sunflower River** ≈ Mississippi, S USA
33 T11 **Big Timber** Montana, NW USA
12 D8 **Big Trout Lake** Ontario, C Canada
14 I12 **Big Trout Lake** ◎ Ontario, SE Canada
35 O2 **Big Valley Mountains** ▲▲ California, W USA
25 Q13 **Big Wells** Texas, SW USA
14 F11 **Bigwood** Ontario, S Canada
112 D11 **Bihać** ◈ NW Bosnia and Herzegovina
153 P14 **Bihār** *prev.* Behar. ◈ *state* N India
Bihār *see* Bihār Sharīf
81 F20 **Biharamulo** Kagera, NW Tanzania
153 R13 **Bihāriganj** Bihār, NE India
153 P14 **Bihār Sharīf** *var.* Bihār. Bihār, N India
116 F10 **Bihor** ◈ *county* NW Romania
165 V3 **Bihoro** Hokkaidō, NE Japan
118 K11 **Bihosava** *Rus.* Bigosovo. Vitsyebskaya Voblasts', NW Belarus
Bijagos Archipelago *see* Bijagós, Arquipélago dos
76 G13 **Bijagós, Arquipélago dos** *var.* Bijagos Archipelago. *island group* W Guinea-Bissau
155 F16 **Bijāpur** Karnātaka, C India
142 K5 **Bījār** Kordestān, W Iran
112 J11 **Bijeljina** ◈ Republika Srpska, NE Bosnia and Herzegovina
113 K15 **Bijelo Polje** E Montenegro
160 E11 **Bijiang** Yunnan, SW China
160 I11 **Bijie** Guizhou, S China
152 J10 **Bijnor** Uttar Pradesh, N India
152 F11 **Bīkāner** Rājasthān, NW India
189 V3 **Bikar Atoll** *var.* Pikaar. *atoll* Ratak Chain, N Marshall Islands
190 H3 **Bikeman** *atoll* Tungaru, W Kiribati
190 I3 **Bikenebu** Tarawa, W Kiribati
123 S14 **Bikin** Khabarovskiy Kray, SE Russian Federation

◆ Country ● Country Capital ◇ Dependent Territory ○ Dependent Territory Capital ◈ Administrative Regions ✈ International Airport ▲ Mountain ▲▲ Mountain Range ⩘ Volcano ≈ River ◎ Lake ⊠ Reservoir

123 S14 **Bikin** ≈ SE Russian Federation
189 R3 **Bikini Atoll** *var.* Pikinni. *atoll* Ralik Chain, NW Marshall Islands
83 L17 **Bikita** Masvingo, E Zimbabwe
Bikkû Bittî *see* Bette, Pic
79 I19 **Bikoro** Equateur, W Dem. Rep. Congo
141 Z9 **Bilād Banī Bū 'Alī** NE Oman
141 Z9 **Bilād Banī Bū Ḥasan** NE Oman
141 X9 **Bilād Manaḥ** *var.* Manaḥ. NE Oman
77 Q12 **Bilanga** C Burkina
152 F12 **Bilāra** Rājasthān, N India
152 K10 **Bilāri** Uttar Pradesh, N India
138 J5 **Bil'ās, Jabal al** ▲▲ C Syria
154 L11 **Bilāspur** Chhattīsgarh, C India
152 I8 **Bilāspur** Himāchal Pradesh, N India
168 J9 **Bila, Sungai** ≈ Sumatera, W Indonesia
137 Y13 **Biläsuvar** *Rus.* Bilyasuvar; *prev.* Pushkino. SE Azerbaijan
117 O5 **Bila Tserkva** *Rus.* Belaya Tserkov'. Kyyivs'ka Oblast', N Ukraine
167 N11 **Bilauktaung Range** *var.* Thanintari Taungdan. ▲▲ Myanmar (Burma)/ Thailand
105 O2 **Bilbao** *Basq.* Bilbo. País Vasco, N Spain
Bilbo *see* Bilbao
92 H2 **Bíldudalur** Vestfirdhir, NW Iceland
113 I16 **Bileća** ◈ Republika Srpska, S Bosnia and Herzegovina
136 E12 **Bilecik** Bilecik, NW Turkey
136 F12 **Bilecik** ◈ *province* NW Turkey
116 E11 **Biled** *Ger.* Billed, *Hung.* Billéd. Timiș, W Romania
111 O15 **Biłgoraj** Lubelskie, E Poland
117 P11 **Bilhorod-Dnistrovs'kyy** *Rus.* Belgorod-Dnestrovskiy, *Rom.* Cetatea Albă, *prev.* Akkerman; *anc.* Tyras. Odes'ka Oblast', SW Ukraine
79 M16 **Bili** Orientale, N Dem. Rep. Congo
123 T6 **Bilibino** Chukotskiy Avtonomnyy Okrug, NE Russian Federation
166 M8 **Bilin** Mon State, S Myanmar (Burma)
113 N21 **Bilisht** *var.* Bilishti. Korçë, SE Albania
Bilishti *see* Bilisht
183 N10 **Billabong Creek** *var.* Moulamein Creek. *seasonal river* New South Wales, SE Australia
182 G4 **Billa Kalina** South Australia
197 Q17 **Bill Baileys Bank** *undersea feature* N Atlantic Ocean
Billed/Billéd *see* Biled
153 N14 **Billi** Uttar Pradesh, N India
97 M15 **Billingham** N England, UK
33 U11 **Billings** Montana, NW USA
95 J16 **Billingsfors** Västra Götaland, S Sweden
Bill of Cape Clear, The *see* Clear, Cape
28 L9 **Billsburg** South Dakota, N USA
95 F23 **Billund** Ribe, W Denmark
36 L11 **Bill Williams Mountain** ▲ Arizona, SW USA
36 I12 **Bill Williams River** ≈ Arizona, SW USA
77 Y8 **Bilma** Agadez, NE Niger
77 Y8 **Bilma, Grand Erg de** *desert* NE Niger
181 Y9 **Biloela** Queensland, E Australia
112 G8 **Bilo Gora** ▲▲ N Croatia
117 U13 **Bilohirs'k** *Rus.* Belogorsk; *prev.* Karasubazar. Respublika Krym, S Ukraine
116 M3 **Bilokorovychi** *Rus.* Belokorovichi. Zhytomyrs'ka Oblast', N Ukraine
117 X5 **Bilokurakine** Luhans'ka Oblast', E Ukraine
117 T3 **Bilopillya** *Rus.* Belopol'ye. Sums'ka Oblast', NE Ukraine
117 Y6 **Bilovods'k** *Rus.* Belovodsk. Luhans'ka Oblast', E Ukraine
22 M9 **Biloxi** Mississippi, S USA
117 R10 **Bilozerka** Khersons'ka Oblast', S Ukraine
117 W7 **Bilozers'ke** Donets'ka Oblast', E Ukraine
98 J11 **Bilthoven** Utrecht, C Netherlands
78 K9 **Biltine** Biltine, E Chad
78 J9 **Biltine** *off.* Préfecture de Biltine. ◈ *prefecture* E Chad
Biltine, Préfecture de *see* Biltine
Bilüü *see* Ulaanhus
Bilwi *see* Puerto Cabezas
Bilyasuvar *see* Biläsuvar
117 O11 **Bilyayivka** Odes'ka Oblast', SW Ukraine
99 K18 **Bilzen** Limburg, NE Belgium
Bimbéréké *see* Bembèrèkè
183 R10 **Bimberi Peak** ▲ New South Wales, SE Australia
77 Q15 **Bimbila** E Ghana
79 I15 **Bimbo** Ombella-Mpoko, SW Central African Republic
44 F2 **Bimini Islands** *island group* W Bahamas
154 I9 **Bīna** Madhya Pradesh, C India
143 T4 **Bīnālūd, Kūh-e** ▲▲ NE Iran
99 F20 **Binche** Hainaut, S Belgium
Bindloe Island *see* Marchena, Isla
83 L16 **Bindura** Mashonaland Central, NE Zimbabwe
105 T5 **Binefar** Aragón, NE Spain
83 J16 **Binga** Matabeleland North, W Zimbabwe
183 T5 **Bingara** New South Wales, SE Australia
101 F18 **Bingen am Rhein** Rheinland-Pfalz, SW Germany
26 M11 **Binger** Oklahoma, C USA
Bingerau *see* Węgrów
Bin Ghalfān, Jazā'ir *see* Ḥalāniyāt, Juzur al
19 Q6 **Bingham** Maine, NE USA
18 H11 **Binghamton** New York, NE USA
Bin Ghanīmah, Jabal *see* Bin Ghunaymah, Jabal
75 P11 **Bin Ghunaymah, Jabal** *var.* Jabal Bin Ghanīmah. ▲▲ C Libya
139 U3 **Bingird** NE Iraq
Bingmei *see* Congjiang
137 P14 **Bingöl** Bingöl, E Turkey
137 P14 **Bingöl** ◈ *province* E Turkey
161 R6 **Binhai** *var.* Dongkan. Jiangsu, E China
167 V11 **Binh Đinh** *var.* An Nhon. Binh Đinh, C Vietnam
167 U10 **Binh Sơn** *var.* Châu Ô. Quang Ngai, C Vietnam
Binimani *see* Bintimani
168 I8 **Binjai** Sumatera, W Indonesia
183 R6 **Binnaway** New South Wales, SE Australia
108 E6 **Binningen** Basel-Land, NW Switzerland
168 J8 **Bintang, Banjaran** ▲▲ Peninsular Malaysia
168 M10 **Bintan, Pulau** *island* Kepulauan Riau, W Indonesia
76 J14 **Bintimani** *var.* Binimani. ▲ NE Sierra Leone
Bint Jubayl *see* Bent Jbaïl
169 S9 **Bintulu** Sarawak, East Malaysia
169 S9 **Bintuni** *prev.* Steenkool. Papua, E Indonesia
163 W8 **Binxian** Heilongjiang, NE China
160 K14 **Binyang** *var.* Binzhou. Guangxi Zhuangzu Zizhiqu, S China
161 Q4 **Binzhou** Shandong, E China
Binzhou *see* Binyang
63 G14 **Bío Bío** *var.* Región del Bío Bío. ◈ *region* C Chile
Bío Bío, Región del *see* Bío Bío
63 G14 **Bío Bío, Río** ≈ C Chile
79 C16 **Bioco, Isla de** *var.* Bioko, *Eng.* Fernando Po, *Sp.* Fernando Póo; *prev.* Macías Nguema Biyogo. *island* NW Equatorial Guinea
112 D13 **Biograd na Moru** *It.* Zaravecchia. Zadar, SW Croatia
Bioko *see* Bioco, Isla de
113 F14 **Biokovo** ▲▲ S Croatia
Biorra *see* Birr
Bipontium *see* Zweibrücken
143 W13 **Bīrag, Kūh-e** ▲▲ SE Iran
75 O10 **Birāk** *var.* Brak. C Libya
139 S10 **Bi'r al Islām** C Iraq
154 N11 **Biramitrapur** Orissa, E India
139 T11 **Bi'r an Nişf** S Iraq
78 L12 **Birao** Vakaga, NE Central African Republic
146 J10 **Birata** *Rus.* Darganata, Dargan-Ata. Lebap Welaýaty, NE Turkmenistan
158 M6 **Biratar Bulak** *well* NW China
153 R12 **Birātnagar** Eastern, SE Nepal
165 R5 **Biratori** Hokkaidō, NE Japan
39 S8 **Birch Creek** Alaska, USA
38 M11 **Birch Creek** ≈ Alaska, USA
9 T14 **Birch Hills** Saskatchewan, S Canada
182 M10 **Birchip** Victoria, SE Australia
29 X4 **Birch Lake** ◎ Minnesota, N USA
9 Q11 **Birch Mountains** ▲▲ Alberta, W Canada
9 V15 **Birch River** Manitoba, S Canada
44 H12 **Birchs Hill** *hill* W Jamaica
39 R11 **Birchwood** Alaska, USA
188 I5 **Bird Island** *island* S Northern Mariana Islands
137 N16 **Birecik** Şanlıurfa, S Turkey
152 M10 **Birendranagar** *var.* Surkhet. Mid Western, W Nepal
Bir es Saba *see* Be'ér Sheva'
74 A12 **Bir-Gandouz** SW Western Sahara
153 P12 **Birganj** Central, C Nepal
81 B14 **Biri** ≈ W Sudan
Bi'r Ibn Hirmās *see* Al Bi'r
143 U8 **Bīrjand** Khorāsān-e Janūbī, E Iran
139 T11 **Birkat Ḥāmid** *well* S Iraq
95 F18 **Birkeland** Aust-Agder, S Norway
101 E19 **Birkenfeld** Rheinland-Pfalz, SW Germany
97 K18 **Birkenhead** NW England, UK
109 W7 **Birkfeld** Steiermark, SE Austria
182 A2 **Birksgate Range** ▲▲ South Australia
Birlad *see* Bârlad
97 K20 **Birmingham** C England, UK
23 P4 **Birmingham** Alabama, S USA
97 M20 **Birmingham** ✕ C England, UK
Bir Moghrein *see* Bîr Mogreïn
76 J4 **Bîr Mogreïn** *var.* Bir Moghrein; *prev.* Fort-Trinquet. Tiris Zemmour, N Mauritania
191 S4 **Birnie Island** *atoll* Phoenix Islands, C Kiribati
77 S12 **Birnin Gaouré** *var.* Birni-Ngaouré. Dosso, SW Niger
Birni-Ngaouré *see* Birnin Gaouré
77 S12 **Birnin Kebbi** Kebbi, NW Nigeria
77 T12 **Birnin Konni** *var.* Birni-Nkonni. Tahoua, SW Niger
Birni-Nkonni *see* Birnin Konni
77 W13 **Birnin Kudu** Jigawa, N Nigeria
123 S16 **Birobidzhan** Yevreyskaya Avtonomnaya Oblast', SE Russian Federation
97 D18 **Birr** *var.* Parsonstown, *Ir.* Biorra. C Ireland
183 P4 **Birrie River** ≈ New South Wales/Queensland, SE Australia
108 D7 **Birse** ≈ NW Switzerland
Birsen *see* Biržai
108 E6 **Birsfelden** Basel-Land, NW Switzerland
127 U4 **Birsk** Respublika Bashkortostan, W Russian Federation
119 F14 **Birštonas** Kaunas, C Lithuania
159 P14 **Biru** Xinjiang Uygur Zizhiqu, W China
Biruni *see* Beruniy
122 L12 **Biryusa** ≈ C Russian Federation
122 L12 **Biryusinsk** Irkutskaya Oblast', C Russian Federation
118 G10 **Biržai** *Ger.* Birsen. Panevėžys, NE Lithuania
121 P16 **Birżebbuġa** SE Malta
Bisanthe *see* Tekirdağ
171 R12 **Bisa, Pulau** *island* Maluku, E Indonesia
37 N17 **Bisbee** Arizona, SW USA
29 O2 **Bisbee** North Dakota, N USA
Biscaia, Baía de *see* Biscay, Bay of
102 I13 **Biscarrosse et de Parentis, Étang de** ◎ SW France
104 M1 **Biscay, Bay of** *Sp.* Golfo de Vizcaya, *Port.* Baía de Biscaia. *bay* France/Spain
23 Z16 **Biscayne Bay** *bay* Florida, SE USA
64 M7 **Biscay Plain** *undersea feature* SE Bay of Biscay
107 N17 **Bisceglie** Puglia, SE Italy
Bischoflack *see* Škofja Loka
Bischofsburg *see* Biskupiec
109 Q7 **Bischofshofen** Salzburg, NW Austria
101 P15 **Bischofswerda** Sachsen, E Germany
103 V5 **Bischwiller** Bas-Rhin, NE France
21 T10 **Biscoe** North Carolina, SE USA
194 G5 **Biscoe Islands** *island group* Antarctica
14 E9 **Biscotasi Lake** ◎ Ontario, S Canada
14 E9 **Biscotasing** Ontario, S Canada
54 J6 **Biscucuy** Portuguesa, NW Venezuela
114 K11 **Biser** Khaskovo, S Bulgaria
113 D15 **Biševo** *It.* Busi. *island* SW Croatia
141 N12 **Bishah, Wādī** *dry watercourse* C Saudi Arabia
147 U7 **Bishkek** *var.* Pishpek; *prev.* Frunze. ● (Kyrgyzstan) Chuyskaya Oblast', N Kyrgyzstan
147 U7 **Bishkek** ✕ Chuyskaya Oblast', N Kyrgyzstan
153 R16 **Bishnupur** West Bengal, NE India
83 J25 **Bisho** Eastern Cape, S South Africa
35 S9 **Bishop** California, W USA
25 S15 **Bishop** Texas, SW USA
97 L15 **Bishop Auckland** N England, UK
Bishop's Lynn *see* King's Lynn
97 O21 **Bishop's Stortford** E England, UK
21 S12 **Bishopville** South Carolina, SE USA
138 M5 **Bishrī, Jabal** ▲▲ E Syria
163 U4 **Bishui** Heilongjiang, NE China
81 G17 **Bisina, Lake** *prev.* Lake Salisbury. ◎ E Uganda
Biskara *see* Biskra
74 L6 **Biskra** *var.* Beskra, Biskara. NE Algeria
110 M8 **Biskupiec** *Ger.* Bischofsburg. Warmińsko-Mazurskie, NE Poland
171 R7 **Bislig** Mindanao, S Philippines
27 X6 **Bismarck** Missouri, C USA
28 M5 **Bismarck** *state capital* North Dakota, N USA
186 D5 **Bismarck Archipelago** *island group* NE Papua New Guinea
129 Z16 **Bismarck Plate** *tectonic feature* W Pacific Ocean
186 D7 **Bismarck Range** ▲▲ N Papua New Guinea
186 E6 **Bismarck Sea** *sea* W Pacific Ocean
137 P15 **Bismil** Dıyarbakır, SE Turkey
43 N6 **Bismuna, Laguna** *lagoon* NE Nicaragua
Bisnulok *see* Phitsanulok
171 R10 **Bisoa, Tanjung** *headland* Pulau Halmahera, N Indonesia
28 K7 **Bison** South Dakota, N USA
93 H17 **Bispfors** Jämtland, C Sweden
76 G13 **Bissau** ● (Guinea-Bissau) W Guinea-Bissau
76 G13 **Bissau** ✕ W Guinea-Bissau
99 M24 **Bissen** Luxembourg, C Luxembourg
Bissojohka *see* Børselv
76 G12 **Bissorā** W Guinea-Bissau
9 O10 **Bistcho Lake** ◎ Alberta, W Canada
22 G5 **Bistineau, Lake** ⊠ Louisiana, S USA
Bistrica *see* Ilirska Bistrica
116 I9 **Bistrița** *Ger.* Bistritz, *Hung.* Beszterce; *prev.* Nösen. Bistrița-Năsăud, N Romania
116 K10 **Bistrița** *Ger.* Bistritz. ≈ NE Romania
116 I9 **Bistrița-Năsăud** ◈ *county* N Romania
Bistritz *see* Bistrița
Bistritz ober Pernstein *see* Bystřice nad Pernštejnem
152 L11 **Biswān** Uttar Pradesh, N India
110 M7 **Bisztynek** Warmińsko-Mazurskie, NE Poland
79 E17 **Bitam** Woleu-Ntem, N Gabon
101 D18 **Bitburg** Rheinland-Pfalz, SW Germany
103 U4 **Bitche** Moselle, NE France
78 I11 **Bitkine** Guéra, C Chad
137 R15 **Bitlis** Bitlis, SE Turkey
137 R14 **Bitlis** ◈ *province* E Turkey
Bitoeng *see* Bitung
113 N20 **Bitola** *Turk.* Monastir; *prev.* Bitolj. S FYR Macedonia
Bitolj *see* Bitola
107 O17 **Bitonto** *anc.* Butuntum. Puglia, SE Italy
77 Q13 **Bitou** *var.* Bittou. SE Burkina
155 C20 **Bitra Island** *island* Lakshadweep, India, N Indian Ocean
101 M14 **Bitterfeld** Sachsen-Anhalt, E Germany
32 O9 **Bitterroot Range** ▲▲ Idaho/ Montana, NW USA
33 P10 **Bitterroot River** ≈ Montana, NW USA
107 D18 **Bitti** Sardegna, Italy, C Mediterranean Sea
Bittou *see* Bitou
171 Q11 **Bitung** *prev.* Bitoeng. Sulawesi, C Indonesia
60 I12 **Bituruna** Paraná, S Brazil
77 Y13 **Biu** Borno, E Nigeria
Biumba *see* Byumba
164 J13 **Biwa-ko** ◎ Honshū, SW Japan
171 X14 **Biwarlaut** Papua, E Indonesia
27 P10 **Bixby** Oklahoma, C USA
122 J13 **Biya** ≈ S Russian Federation
122 J13 **Biysk** Altayskiy Kray, S Russian Federation
164 H13 **Bizen** Okayama, Honshū, SW Japan
Bizerta *see* Bizerte
120 K10 **Bizerte** *Ar.* Banzart, *Eng.* Bizerta. N Tunisia
Bizkaia *see* Vizcaya
92 G2 **Bjargtangar** *headland* W Iceland
Bjärnå *see* Perniö
95 K22 **Bjärnum** Skåne, S Sweden
93 I16 **Bjästa** Västernorrland, C Sweden
113 I14 **Bjelašnica** ▲ SE Bosnia and Herzegovina
112 C10 **Bjelolasica** ▲ NW Croatia
112 F8 **Bjelovar** *Hung.* Belovár. Bjelovar-Bilogora, N Croatia
112 F8 **Bjelovar-Bilogora** *off.* Bjelovarsko-Bilogorska Županija. ◈ *province* NE Croatia
Bjelovarsko-Bilogorska Županija *see* Bjelovar-Bilogora
92 H10 **Bjerkvik** Nordland, C Norway
95 G21 **Bjerringbro** Viborg, NW Denmark
Bjeshkët e Namuna *see* North Albanian Alps
95 L14 **Björbo** Dalarna, C Sweden
95 I15 **Bjørkelangen** Akershus, S Norway
95 O14 **Björklinge** Uppsala, C Sweden
93 I14 **Björksele** Västerbotten, N Sweden
93 I16 **Björna** Västernorrland, C Sweden
95 C14 **Bjørnafjorden** *fjord* S Norway
95 L16 **Björneborg** Värmland, C Sweden
Björneborg *see* Pori
95 E14 **Bjornesfjorden** ◎ S Norway
92 M9 **Bjørnevatn** Finnmark, N Norway
197 T13 **Bjørnøya** *Eng.* Bear Island. *island* N Norway
93 I15 **Bjurholm** Västerbotten, N Sweden
95 J22 **Bjuv** Skåne, S Sweden
76 M12 **Bla** Ségou, W Mali
181 W8 **Blackall** Queensland, E Australia
29 V2 **Black Bay** *lake bay* Minnesota, N USA
27 N9 **Black Bear Creek** ≈ Oklahoma, C USA
97 K17 **Blackburn** NW England, UK
45 W10 **Blackburne** ✕ (Plymouth) E Montserrat
39 T11 **Blackburn, Mount** ▲ Alaska, USA
35 N5 **Black Butte Lake** ⊠ California, W USA
194 J5 **Black Coast** *physical region* Antarctica
9 Q16 **Black Diamond** Alberta, SW Canada
18 K11 **Black Dome** ▲ New York, NE USA
113 L18 **Black Drin** *Alb.* Lumi i Drinit të Zi, *SCr.* Crni Drim. ≈ Albania/FYR Macedonia
29 U4 **Blackduck** Minnesota, N USA
12 D6 **Black Duck** ≈ Ontario, C Canada
33 R14 **Blackfoot** Idaho, NW USA
33 P9 **Blackfoot River** ≈ Montana, NW USA
Black Forest *see* Schwarzwald
28 J10 **Blackhawk** South Dakota, N USA
28 I10 **Black Hills** ▲▲ South Dakota/ Wyoming, N USA
9 T10 **Black Lake** ◎ Saskatchewan, C Canada
22 G6 **Black Lake** ⊠ Louisiana, S USA
31 Q5 **Black Lake** ◎ Michigan, N USA
18 I7 **Black Lake** ◎ New York, NE USA
26 F7 **Black Mesa** ▲ Oklahoma, C USA
21 P10 **Black Mountain** North Carolina, SE USA
35 P13 **Black Mountain** ▲ California, W USA
37 Q2 **Black Mountain** ▲ Colorado, C USA
96 K1 **Black Mountains** ▲▲ SE Wales, UK
36 H10 **Black Mountains** ▲▲ Arizona, SW USA
21 O7 **Black Mountains** ▲ Kentucky, E USA
33 Q16 **Black Pine Peak** ▲ Idaho, NW USA
97 K17 **Blackpool** NW England, UK
37 Q14 **Black Range** ▲▲ New Mexico, SW USA
44 I12 **Black River** W Jamaica
14 J14 **Black River** ≈ Ontario, SE Canada
129 U12 **Black River** *Chin.* Babian Jiang, Lixian Jiang, *Fr.* Rivière Noire, *Vtn.* Sông Đa. ≈ China/Vietnam
44 I12 **Black River** ≈ W Jamaica
39 T7 **Black River** ≈ Alaska, USA
37 N13 **Black River** ≈ Arizona, SW USA
27 X7 **Black River** ≈ Arkansas/ Missouri, C USA
22 I7 **Black River** ≈ Louisiana, S USA
31 S8 **Black River** ≈ Michigan, N USA
31 Q5 **Black River** ≈ Michigan, N USA
18 I8 **Black River** ≈ New York, NE USA
21 T13 **Black River** ≈ South Carolina, SE USA
30 J7 **Black River** ≈ Wisconsin, N USA
30 J7 **Black River Falls** Wisconsin, N USA
35 R3 **Black Rock Desert** *desert* Nevada, W USA
Black Sand Desert *see* Garagum
21 S7 **Blacksburg** Virginia, NE USA
136 H10 **Black Sea** *var.* Euxine Sea, *Bul.* Cherno More, *Rom.* Marea Neagră, *Rus.* Chernoye More, *Turk.* Karadeniz, *Ukr.* Chorne More. *sea* Asia/Europe
117 Q10 **Black Sea Lowland** *Ukr.* Prychornomor'ska Nyzovyna. *depression* SE Europe
33 S17 **Blacks Fork** ≈ Wyoming, C USA
23 V7 **Blackshear** Georgia, SE USA
23 S6 **Blackshear, Lake** ⊠ Georgia, SE USA
97 A16 **Blacksod Bay** *Ir.* Cuan an Fhóid Duibh. *inlet* W Ireland
21 V7 **Blackstone** Virginia, NE USA
77 O14 **Black Volta** *var.* Borongo, Mouhoun, Moun Hou, *Fr.* Volta Noire. ≈ W Africa
23 O5 **Black Warrior River** ≈ Alabama, S USA
181 X8 **Blackwater** Queensland, E Australia
97 D20 **Blackwater** *Ir.* An Abhainn Mhór. ≈ S Ireland
27 T4 **Blackwater River** ≈ Missouri, C USA
21 W7 **Blackwater River** ≈ Virginia, NE USA
Blackwater State *see* Nebraska
27 N8 **Blackwell** Oklahoma, C USA
25 P7 **Blackwell** Texas, SW USA
99 J15 **Bladel** Noord-Brabant, S Netherlands
Bladenmarkt *see* Bălăușeri
114 G11 **Blagoevgrad** *prev.* Gorna Dzhumaya. Blagoevgrad, W Bulgaria
114 G11 **Blagoevgrad** ◈ *province* SW Bulgaria
123 Q14 **Blagoveshchensk** Amurskaya Oblast', SE Russian Federation
127 V4 **Blagoveshchensk** Respublika Bashkortostan, W Russian Federation
102 I7 **Blain** Loire-Atlantique, NW France
29 V8 **Blaine** Minnesota, N USA
32 H6 **Blaine** Washington, NW USA
9 T15 **Blaine Lake** Saskatchewan, S Canada
29 S14 **Blair** Nebraska, C USA
96 J10 **Blairgowrie** C Scotland, UK
18 C15 **Blairsville** Pennsylvania, NE USA
116 H11 **Blaj** *Ger.* Blasendorf, *Hung.* Balázsfalva. Alba, SW Romania
64 F9 **Blake-Bahama Ridge** *undersea feature* W Atlantic Ocean
23 S7 **Blakely** Georgia, SE USA
64 E10 **Blake Plateau** *var.* Blake Terrace. *undersea feature* W Atlantic Ocean
30 M1 **Blake Point** *headland* Michigan, N USA
Blake Terrace *see* Blake Plateau
61 B24 **Blanca, Bahía** *bay* E Argentina
56 C12 **Blanca, Cordillera** ▲▲ W Peru
105 T12 **Blanca, Costa** *physical region* SE Spain
37 S7 **Blanca Peak** ▲ Colorado, C USA
24 I9 **Blanca, Sierra** ▲ Texas, SW USA
120 K9 **Blanc, Cap** *headland* N Tunisia
Blanc, Cap *see* Nouâdhibou, Râs
31 R12 **Blanchard River** ≈ Ohio, N USA
182 E8 **Blanche, Cape** *headland* South Australia
182 J4 **Blanche, Lake** ◎ South Australia
31 R14 **Blanchester** Ohio, N USA
182 J9 **Blanchetown** South Australia
45 U13 **Blanchisseuse** Trinidad, Trinidad and Tobago
103 T11 **Blanc, Mont** *It.* Monte Bianco. ▲ France/Italy
25 R11 **Blanco** Texas, SW USA
42 K14 **Blanco, Cabo** *headland* NW Costa Rica
32 D14 **Blanco, Cape** *headland* Oregon, NW USA
62 H10 **Blanco, Río** ≈ W Argentina
56 F10 **Blanco, Río** ≈ NE Peru
15 O9 **Blanc, Réservoir** ⊠ Québec, SE Canada
21 R7 **Bland** Virginia, NE USA
92 I2 **Blanda** ≈ N Iceland
37 O7 **Blanding** Utah, W USA
105 X5 **Blanes** Cataluña, NE Spain
103 N3 **Blangy-sur-Bresle** Seine-Maritime, N France
111 C18 **Blanice** *Ger.* Blanitz. ≈ SE Czech Republic
Blanitz *see* Blanice
99 C16 **Blankenberge** West-Vlaanderen, NW Belgium
101 D17 **Blankenheim** Nordrhein-Westfalen, W Germany
25 R8 **Blanket** Texas, SW USA
55 O3 **Blanquilla, Isla** *var.* La Blanquilla. *island* N Venezuela
Blanquilla, La *see* Blanquilla, Isla.
61 F18 **Blanquillo** Durazno, C Uruguay
111 G18 **Blansko** *Ger.* Blanz. Jihomoravský Kraj, SE Czech Republic
83 N15 **Blantyre** *var.* Blantyre-Limbe. Southern, S Malawi
83 N15 **Blantyre** ✕ Southern, S Malawi
Blantyre-Limbe *see* Blantyre
Blanz *see* Blansko
98 J10 **Blaricum** Noord-Holland, C Netherlands
Blasendorf *see* Blaj
Blatnitsa *see* Durankulak
113 F15 **Blato** *It.* Blatta. Dubrovnik-Neretva, S Croatia
Blatta *see* Blato
108 E10 **Blatten** Valais, SW Switzerland
101 J20 **Blaufelden** Baden-Württemberg, SW Germany
95 E23 **Blåvands Huk** *headland* W Denmark
102 G6 **Blavet** ≈ NW France
102 J12 **Blaye** Gironde, SW France
183 R8 **Blayney** New South Wales, SE Australia
65 D25 **Bleaker Island** *island* SE Falkland Islands
109 T10 **Bled** *Ger.* Veldes. NW Slovenia
99 D20 **Bléharies** Hainaut, SW Belgium
109 U9 **Bleiburg** *Slvn.* Pliberk. Kärnten, S Austria
101 L17 **Bleiloch-stausee** ⊠ C Germany
98 H12 **Bleiswijk** Zuid-Holland, W Netherlands
95 L22 **Blekinge** ◈ *county* S Sweden
14 D17 **Blenheim** Ontario, S Canada
185 K15 **Blenheim** Marlborough, South Island, New Zealand
99 M15 **Blerick** Limburg, SE Netherlands
Blesae *see* Blois
25 V13 **Blessing** Texas, SW USA
14 I10 **Bleu, Lac** ◎ Québec, SE Canada
Blibba *see* Blitta
120 H10 **Blida** *var.* El Boulaïda, El Boulaïda. N Algeria
95 P15 **Blidö** Stockholm, C Sweden
95 K18 **Blidsberg** Västra Götaland, S Sweden
185 A21 **Bligh Sound** *sound* South Island, New Zealand
187 X14 **Bligh Water** *strait* NW Fiji
14 D11 **Blind River** Ontario, S Canada
31 R11 **Blissfield** Michigan, N USA
77 R15 **Blitta** *prev.* Blibba. C Togo
19 O13 **Block Island** *island* Rhode Island, NE USA
19 O13 **Block Island Sound** *sound* Rhode Island, NE USA
98 H10 **Bloemendaal** Noord-Holland, W Netherlands
83 H23 **Bloemfontein** *var.* Mangaung. ● (South Africa-judicial capital) Free State, C South Africa
83 I22 **Bloemhof** North-West, NW South Africa
102 M7 **Blois** *anc.* Blesae. Loir-et-Cher, C France
98 L8 **Blokzijl** Overijssel, N Netherlands
95 N20 **Blomstermåla** Kalmar, S Sweden
92 I2 **Blönduós** Nordhurland Vestra, N Iceland
110 L11 **Błonie** Mazowieckie, C Poland
97 C14 **Bloody Foreland** *Ir.* Cnoc Fola. *headland* NW Ireland
31 N15 **Bloomfield** Indiana, N USA
29 X16 **Bloomfield** Iowa, C USA
27 Y8 **Bloomfield** Missouri, C USA
37 P9 **Bloomfield** New Mexico, SW USA
25 U7 **Blooming Grove** Texas, SW USA
29 W10 **Blooming Prairie** Minnesota, N USA
30 L13 **Bloomington** Illinois, N USA
31 O15 **Bloomington** Indiana, N USA
29 V9 **Bloomington** Minnesota, N USA
25 U13 **Bloomington** Texas, SW USA
18 H14 **Bloomsburg** Pennsylvania, NE USA
181 X7 **Bloomsbury** Queensland, NE Australia
169 R16 **Blora** Jawa, C Indonesia
18 G12 **Blossburg** Pennsylvania, NE USA
25 V5 **Blossom** Texas, SW USA
123 T5 **Blossom, Mys** *cape* Ostrov Vrangelya, NE Russian Federation
23 R8 **Blountstown** Florida, SE USA
21 P8 **Blountville** Tennessee, S USA
21 Q9 **Blowing Rock** North Carolina, SE USA
108 J8 **Bludenz** Vorarlberg, W Austria
36 L6 **Blue Bell Knoll** ▲ Utah, W USA
23 Y12 **Blue Cypress Lake** ◎ Florida, SE USA
29 U11 **Blue Earth** Minnesota, N USA
21 Q7 **Bluefield** Virginia, NE USA
21 R7 **Bluefield** West Virginia, NE USA
43 N10 **Bluefields** Región Autónoma Atlántico Sur, SE Nicaragua
43 N10 **Bluefields, Bahía de** *bay* W Caribbean Sea
29 Z14 **Blue Grass** Iowa, C USA
Bluegrass State *see* Kentucky
Blue Hen State *see* Delaware
19 S7 **Blue Hill** Maine, NE USA
29 P16 **Blue Hill** Nebraska, C USA
30 J5 **Blue Hills** *hill range* Wisconsin, N USA
34 L3 **Blue Lake** California, W USA
Blue Law State *see* Connecticut
37 Q6 **Blue Mesa Reservoir** ⊠ Colorado, C USA
27 S12 **Blue Mountain** ▲ Arkansas, C USA
19 O6 **Blue Mountain** ▲ New Hampshire, NE USA
18 K8 **Blue Mountain** ▲ New York, NE USA
18 H15 **Blue Mountain** *ridge* Pennsylvania, NE USA

◆ Country ◇ Dependent Territory ◈ Administrative Regions ▲ Mountain ⋀ Volcano ◎ Lake
● Country Capital ○ Dependent Territory Capital ✕ International Airport ▲▲ Mountain Range ≈ River ⊠ Reservoir

44 H10 **Blue Mountain Peak** ▲ E Jamaica
183 S8 **Blue Mountains** ▲▲ New South Wales, SE Australia
32 L11 **Blue Mountains** ▲▲ Oregon/Washington, NW USA
80 G12 **Blue Nile** ◈ *state* E Sudan
80 H12 **Blue Nile** *var.* Abai, Bahr el, Azraq, *Amh.* Äbay Wenz, *Ar.* An Nīl al Azraq. ↝ Ethiopia/Sudan
8 J7 **Bluenose Lake** ◎ Nunavut, NW Canada
27 O3 **Blue Rapids** Kansas, C USA
23 S1 **Blue Ridge** Georgia, SE USA
17 S11 **Blue Ridge** *var.* Blue Ridge Mountains. ▲▲ North Carolina/Virginia, USA
23 S1 **Blue Ridge Lake** ⊠ Georgia, SE USA
Blue Ridge Mountains *see* Blue Ridge
9 N15 **Blue River** British Columbia, SW Canada
27 O12 **Blue River** ↝ Oklahoma, C USA
27 R4 **Blue Springs** Missouri, C USA
21 R6 **Bluestone Lake** ⊠ West Virginia, NE USA
185 C25 **Bluff** Southland, South Island, New Zealand
37 O8 **Bluff** Utah, W USA
21 P8 **Bluff City** Tennessee, S USA
65 E24 **Bluff Cove** East Falkland, Falkland Islands
25 S7 **Bluff Dale** Texas, SW USA
183 N15 **Bluff Hill Point** *headland* Tasmania, SE Australia
31 Q12 **Bluffton** Indiana, N USA
31 R12 **Bluffton** Ohio, N USA
25 T7 **Blum** Texas, SW USA
101 G24 **Blumberg** Baden-Württemberg, SW Germany
60 K13 **Blumenau** Santa Catarina, S Brazil
29 N9 **Blunt** South Dakota, N USA
32 H15 **Bly** Oregon, NW USA
39 R13 **Blying Sound** *sound* Alaska, USA
97 M14 **Blyth** N England, UK
35 Y16 **Blythe** California, W USA
27 Y9 **Blytheville** Arkansas, C USA
117 V7 **Blyznyuky** Kharkivs'ka Oblast', E Ukraine
95 G16 **Bø** Telemark, S Norway
76 I15 **Bo** S Sierra Leone
171 O4 **Boac** Marinduque, N Philippines
42 K10 **Boaco** Boaco, S Nicaragua
42 J10 **Boaco** ◈ *department* C Nicaragua
79 I15 **Boali** Ombella-Mpoko, SW Central African Republic
Boalsert *see* Bolsward
31 V12 **Boardman** Ohio, N USA
32 J11 **Boardman** Oregon, NW USA
14 F13 **Boat Lake** ◎ Ontario, S Canada
58 F10 **Boa Vista** *state capital* Roraima, NW Brazil
76 D9 **Boa Vista** *island* Ilhas de Barlavento, E Cape Verde
23 Q2 **Boaz** Alabama, S USA
160 L15 **Bobai** Guangxi Zhuangzu Zizhiqu, S China
172 J1 **Bobaomby, Tanjona** *Fr.* Cap d'Ambre. *headland* N Madagascar
155 M14 **Bobbili** Andhra Pradesh, E India
106 D9 **Bobbio** Emilia-Romagna, C Italy
14 I14 **Bobcaygeon** Ontario, SE Canada
Bober *see* Bóbr
103 O5 **Bobigny** Seine-St-Denis, N France
77 N13 **Bobo-Dioulasso** SW Burkina
110 G8 **Bobolice** *Ger.* Bublitz. Zachodnio-pomorskie, NW Poland
83 J19 **Bobonong** Central, E Botswana
171 R11 **Bobopayo** Pulau Halmahera, E Indonesia
114 G10 **Bobovdol** Kyustendil, W Bulgaria
119 M15 **Bobr** Minskaya Voblasts', NW Belarus
119 M15 **Bobr** ↝ C Belarus
111 E14 **Bóbr** *Eng.* Bobrawa, *Ger.* Bober. ↝ SW Poland
Bobrawa *see* Bóbr
Bobrik *see* Bobryk
Bobrinets *see* Bobrynets'
Bobrka/Bóbrka *see* Bibrka
126 L8 **Bobrov** Voronezhskaya Oblast', W Russian Federation
117 Q4 **Bobrovytsya** Chernihivs'ka Oblast', N Ukraine
Bobruysk *see* Babruysk
119 J19 **Bobryk** *Rus.* Bobrik. ↝ SW Belarus
117 Q8 **Bobrynets'** *Rus.* Bobrinets. Kirovohrads'ka Oblast', C Ukraine
14 K14 **Bobs Lake** ◎ Ontario, SE Canada
54 I6 **Bobures** Zulia, NW Venezuela
42 H1 **Boca Bacalar Chico** *headland* N Belize
112 G11 **Bočac** ◈ Republika Srpska, NW Bosnia and Herzegovina
41 R14 **Boca del Río** Veracruz-Llave, S Mexico
55 O4 **Boca de Pozo** Nueva Esparta, NE Venezuela
59 C15 **Boca do Acre** Amazonas, N Brazil
55 N12 **Boca Mavaca** Amazonas, S Venezuela
79 G14 **Bocaranga** Ouham-Pendé, W Central African Republic
23 Z15 **Boca Raton** Florida, SE USA
43 P14 **Bocas del Toro** Bocas del Toro, NW Panama
43 P15 **Bocas del Toro** *off.* Provincia de Bocas del Toro. ◈ *province* NW Panama
43 P15 **Bocas del Toro, Archipiélago de** *island group* NW Panama
Bocas del Toro, Provincia de *see* Bocas del Toro
42 L7 **Bocay** Jinotega, N Nicaragua
105 N6 **Boceguillas** Castilla-León, N Spain
Bocheykovo *see* Bacheykava
111 L17 **Bochnia** Małopolskie, SE Poland
99 K16 **Bocholt** Limburg, NE Belgium
101 D14 **Bocholt** Nordrhein-Westfalen, W Germany
101 E15 **Bochum** Nordrhein-Westfalen, W Germany
103 Y15 **Bocognano** Corse, France, C Mediterranean Sea
54 I6 **Boconó** Trujillo, NW Venezuela
116 F12 **Bocşa** *Ger.* Bokschen, *Hung.* Boksánbánya. Caraş-Severin, SW Romania
79 H15 **Boda** Lobaye, SW Central African Republic
94 L12 **Boda** Dalarna, C Sweden
95 O20 **Böda** Kalmar, S Sweden
95 L19 **Bodafors** Jönköping, S Sweden
123 O12 **Bodaybo** Irkutskaya Oblast', E Russian Federation
22 G5 **Bodcau, Bayou** *var.* Bodcau Creek. ↝ Louisiana, S USA
Bodcau Creek *see* Bodcau, Bayou
44 D8 **Bodden Town** *var.* Boddentown. Grand Cayman, SW Cayman Islands
Boddentown *see* Bodden Town
101 K14 **Bode** ↝ C Germany
34 L7 **Bodega Head** *headland* California, W USA
Bodegas *see* Babahoyo
98 H11 **Bodegraven** Zuid-Holland, C Netherlands
78 H8 **Bodélé** *depression* W Chad
92 J13 **Boden** Norrbotten, N Sweden
Bodensee *see* Constance, Lake, C Europe
65 M15 **Bode Verde Fracture Zone** *tectonic feature* E Atlantic Ocean
155 H14 **Bodhan** Andhra Pradesh, C India
Bodī *see* Jinst
155 H22 **Bodināyakkanūr** Tamil Nādu, SE India
108 H10 **Bodio** Ticino, S Switzerland
Bodjonegoro *see* Bojonegoro
97 I24 **Bodmin** SW England, UK
97 I24 **Bodmin Moor** *moorland* SW England, UK
92 G12 **Bodø** Nordland, C Norway
59 H20 **Bodoquena, Serra da** ▲▲ SW Brazil
136 B16 **Bodrum** Muğla, SW Turkey
Bodzafordulő *see* Intorsura Buzăului
99 L14 **Boekel** Noord-Brabant, SE Netherlands
Boeloekoemba *see* Bulukumba
103 Q11 **Boën** Loire, E France
79 K18 **Boende** Equateur, C Dem. Rep. Congo
25 R11 **Boerne** Texas, SW USA
Boeroe *see* Buru, Pulau
Boetoeng *see* Buton, Pulau
22 I5 **Boeuf River** ↝ Arkansas/Louisiana, S USA
76 H14 **Boffa** Guinée-Maritime, W Guinea
Bó Finne, Inis *see* Inishbofin
Boga *see* Bogë
166 L9 **Bogale** Irrawaddy, SW Myanmar (Burma)
22 L8 **Bogalusa** Louisiana, S USA
77 Q12 **Bogandé** C Burkina
79 I15 **Bogangolo** Ombella-Mpoko, C Central African Republic
183 Q7 **Bogan River** ↝ New South Wales, SE Australia
25 W5 **Bogata** Texas, SW USA
111 D14 **Bogatynia** *Ger.* Reichenau. Dolnośląskie, SW Poland
136 K13 **Boğazlıyan** Yozgat, C Turkey
79 J17 **Bogbonga** Equateur, NW Dem. Rep. Congo
158 J14 **Bogcang Zangbo** ↝ W China
162 I9 **Bogd** *var.* Horiult. Bayanhongor, C Mongolia
162 J10 **Bogd** *var.* Hovd. Övörhangay, C Mongolia
158 L5 **Bogda Feng** ▲ NW China
114 I9 **Bogdan** ▲ C Bulgaria
113 Q20 **Bogdanci** SE FYR Macedonia
158 M5 **Bogda Shan** *var.* Po-ko-to Shan. ▲▲ NW China
113 K17 **Bogë** *var.* Boga. Shkodër, N Albania
Bogendorf *see* Łuków
95 G23 **Bogense** Fyn, C Denmark
183 T3 **Boggabilla** New South Wales, SE Australia
183 S6 **Boggabri** New South Wales, SE Australia
186 D6 **Bogia** Madang, N Papua New Guinea
97 N23 **Bognor Regis** SE England, UK
Bogodukhov *see* Bohodukhiv
181 V15 **Bogong, Mount** ▲ Victoria, SE Australia
169 O16 **Bogor** *Dut.* Buitenzorg. Jawa, C Indonesia
126 L5 **Bogoroditsk** Tul'skaya Oblast', W Russian Federation
127 O3 **Bogorodsk** Nizhegorodskaya Oblast', W Russian Federation
Bogorodskoje *see* Bogorodskoye
123 S12 **Bogorodskoye** Khabarovskiy Kray, SE Russian Federation
125 R15 **Bogorodskoye** *var.* Bogorodskoje. Kirovskaya Oblast', NW Russian Federation
54 F10 **Bogotá** *prev.* Santa Fe, Santa Fe de Bogotá. ● (Colombia) Cundinamarca, C Colombia
153 T14 **Bogra** Rajshahi, N Bangladesh
Bogschan *see* Boldu
122 L12 **Boguchany** Krasnoyarskiy Kray, C Russian Federation
126 M9 **Boguchar** Voronezhskaya Oblast', W Russian Federation
76 H10 **Bogué** Brakna, SW Mauritania
22 K8 **Bogue Chitto** ↝ Louisiana/Mississippi, S USA
Bogushëvsk *see* Bahushewsk
Boguslav *see* Bohuslav
44 K12 **Bog Walk** C Jamaica
161 Q3 **Bo Hai** *var.* Gulf of Chihli. *gulf* NE China
161 R3 **Bohai Haixia** *strait* NE China
161 Q3 **Bohai Wan** *bay* NE China
111 C17 **Bohemia** *Cz.* Čechy, *Ger.* Böhmen. *cultural and historical region* W Czech Republic
111 B18 **Bohemian Forest** *Cz.* Ceský Les, Šumava, *Ger.* Böhmerwald. ▲▲ C Europe
Bohemian-Moravian Highlands *see* Českomoravská Vrchovina
77 R16 **Bohicon** S Benin
109 S11 **Bohinjska Bistrica** *Ger.* Wocheiner Feistritz. NW Slovenia
Bohkká *see* Pokka
Böhmen *see* Bohemia
Böhmerwald *see* Bohemian Forest
Böhmisch-Krumau *see* Český Krumlov
Böhmisch-Leipa *see* Česká Lípa
Böhmisch-Mährische Höhe *see* Českomoravská Vrchovina
Böhmisch-Trübau *see* Česká Třebová
117 U5 **Bohodukhiv** *Rus.* Bogodukhov. Kharkivs'ka Oblast', E Ukraine
171 Q6 **Bohol** *island* C Philippines
171 Q7 **Bohol Sea** *var.* Mindanao Sea. *sea* S Philippines
116 I7 **Bohorodchany** Ivano-Frankivs'ka Oblast', W Ukraine
Böhöt *see* Öndörshil
158 K6 **Bohu** *var.* Bagrax. Xinjiang Uygur Zizhiqu, NW China
111 I17 **Bohumín** *Ger.* Oderberg; *prev.* Neuoderberg, Nový Bohumín. Moravskoslezský Kraj, E Czech Republic
117 P6 **Bohuslav** *Rus.* Boguslav. Kyyivs'ka Oblast', N Ukraine
58 F11 **Boiaçu** Roraima, N Brazil
107 K16 **Boiano** Molise, C Italy
15 R8 **Boilleau** Québec, SE Canada
59 O17 **Boipeba, Ilha de** *island* SE Brazil
104 G3 **Boiro** Galicia, NW Spain
31 Q5 **Bois Blanc Island** *island* Michigan, N USA
29 R7 **Bois de Sioux River** ↝ Minnesota, N USA
33 N14 **Boise** *var.* Boise City. *state capital* Idaho, NW USA
26 G8 **Boise City** Oklahoma, C USA
Boise City *see* Boise
33 N14 **Boise River, Middle Fork** ↝ Idaho, NW USA
Bois, Lac des *see* Woods, Lake of the
Bois-le-Duc *see* 's-Hertogenbosch
9 W17 **Boissevain** Manitoba, S Canada
15 T7 **Boisvert, Pointe au** *headland* Québec, SE Canada
100 K10 **Boizenburg** Mecklenburg-Vorpommern, N Germany
Bojador *see* Boujdour
113 K18 **Bojana** *Alb.* Bunë. ↝ Albania/Montenegro *see also* Bunë
Bojana *see* Bunë
143 S3 **Bojnūrd** *var.* Bujnurd. Khorāsān-e Shemālī, N Iran
169 R16 **Bojonegoro** *prev.* Bodjonegoro. Jawa, C Indonesia
189 T1 **Bokaak Atoll** *var.* Bokak, Taongi. *atoll* Ratak Chain, NE Marshall Islands
Bokak *see* Bokaak Atoll
146 K6 **Bo'kantov Tog'lari** *Rus* Gory Bukantau. N Uzbekistan
146 K8 **Bo'kantov Tog'lari** *Rus.* Gory Bukantau. ▲ N Uzbekistan
153 Q15 **Bokāro** Jhārkhand, N India
79 I18 **Bokatola** Equateur, NW Dem. Rep. Congo
76 H13 **Boké** W Guinea
Bokhara *see* Buxoro
183 Q4 **Bokharra River** ↝ New South Wales/Queensland, SE Australia
95 C16 **Boknafjorden** *fjord* S Norway
78 H11 **Bokoro** Chari-Baguirmi, W Chad
79 K19 **Bokota** Equateur, NW Dem. Rep. Congo
167 N13 **Bokpyin** Tenasserim, S Myanmar (Burma)
Boksánbánya/Bokschen *see* Bocşa
83 F21 **Bokspits** Kgalagadi, SW Botswana
79 K18 **Bokungu** Equateur, C Dem. Rep. Congo
146 F12 **Bokurdak** *Rus.* Bakhardok. Ahal Welaýaty, C Turkmenistan
78 G10 **Bol** Lac, W Chad
76 G13 **Bolama** SW Guinea-Bissau
Bolangir *see* Balāngīr
Bolanos *see* Bolaños, Mount, Guam
Bolaños *see* Bolaños de Calatrava, Spain
105 N11 **Bolaños de Calatrava** *var.* Bolaños. Castilla-La Mancha, C Spain
188 B17 **Bolanos, Mount** *var.* Bolanos. ▲ S Guam
40 L12 **Bolaños, Río** ↝ C Mexico
115 M14 **Bolayır** Çanakkale, NW Turkey
102 L3 **Bolbec** Seine-Maritime, N France
116 L13 **Boldu** *var.* Bogschan. Buzău, SE Romania
146 H8 **Boldumsaz** *prev.* Kalinin, Kalininsk, Porsy. Daşoguz Welaýaty, N Turkmenistan
158 I4 **Bole** *var.* Bortala. Xinjiang Uygur Zizhiqu, NW China
77 O15 **Bole** NW Ghana
79 J19 **Boleko** Equateur, W Dem. Rep. Congo
111 E14 **Bolesławiec** *Ger.* Bunzlau. Dolnośląskie, SW Poland
127 R4 **Bolgar** *prev.* Kuybyshev. Respublika Tatarstan, W Russian Federation
77 P14 **Bolgatanga** N Ghana
Bolgrad *see* Bolhrad
117 N12 **Bolhrad** *Rus.* Bolgrad. Odes'ka Oblast', SW Ukraine
163 Y8 **Boli** Heilongjiang, NE China
79 I19 **Bolia** Bandundu, W Dem. Rep. Congo
93 J14 **Boliden** Västerbotten, N Sweden
171 T13 **Bolifar** Pulau Seram, E Indonesia
171 N2 **Bolinao** Luzon, N Philippines
54 C12 **Bolívar** Cauca, SW Colombia
27 T6 **Bolivar** Missouri, C USA
20 F10 **Bolivar** Tennessee, S USA
54 F7 **Bolívar** *off.* Departmento de Bolívar. ◈ *province* N Colombia
56 A13 **Bolívar** ◈ *province* C Ecuador
55 N9 **Bolívar** *off.* Estado Bolívar. ◈ *state* SE Venezuela
Bolívar, Departmento de *see* Bolívar
Bolívar, Estado *see* Bolívar
25 X12 **Bolivar Peninsula** *headland* Texas, SW USA
54 I6 **Bolívar, Pico** ▲ W Venezuela
57 K17 **Bolivia** *off.* Republic of Bolivia. ◆ *republic* W South America
Bolivia, Republic of *see* Bolivia
112 O13 **Boljevac** Serbia, E Serbia
Bolkenhain *see* Bolków
126 J5 **Bolkhov** Orlovskaya Oblast', W Russian Federation
111 F14 **Bolków** *Ger.* Bolkenhain. Dolnośląskie, SW Poland
182 K3 **Bollards Lagoon** South Australia
103 R14 **Bollène** Vaucluse, SE France
94 N12 **Bollnäs** Gävleborg, C Sweden
181 W10 **Bollon** Queensland, C Australia
192 L12 **Bollons Tablemount** *undersea feature* S Pacific Ocean
93 H17 **Bollstabruk** Västernorrland, C Sweden
Bolluilos de Par del Condado *see* Bollullos Par del Condado
104 J14 **Bollullos Par del Condado** *var.* Bolluilos de Par del Condado. Andalucía, S Spain
95 K21 **Bolmen** ◎ S Sweden
137 T10 **Bolnisi** S Georgia
79 H19 **Bolobo** Bandundu, W Dem. Rep. Congo
106 G10 **Bologna** Emilia-Romagna, N Italy
124 I15 **Bologoye** Tverskaya Oblast', W Russian Federation
79 J18 **Bolomba** Equateur, NW Dem. Rep. Congo
41 X13 **Bolonchén de Rejón** *var.* Bolonchén de Rejón. Campeche, SE Mexico
114 J13 **Boloústra, Ákrotírio** *cape* NE Greece
167 L8 **Bolovens, Plateau des** *plateau* S Laos
106 H13 **Bolsena** Lazio, C Italy
107 G14 **Bolsena, Lago di** ◎ C Italy
126 B3 **Bol'shakovo** *Ger.* Kreuzingen; *prev.* Gross-Skaisgirren. Kaliningradskaya Oblast', W Russian Federation
Bol'shaya Berëstovitsa *see* Vyalikaya Byerastavitsa
127 S7 **Bol'shaya Chernigovka** Samarskaya Oblast', W Russian Federation
127 S7 **Bol'shaya Glushitsa** Samarskaya Oblast', W Russian Federation
144 H9 **Bol'shaya Khobda** *Kaz.* Ülkenqobda. ↝ Kazakhstan/Russian Federation
126 M12 **Bol'shaya Martynovka** Rostovskaya Oblast', SW Russian Federation
122 K12 **Bol'shaya Murta** Krasnoyarskiy Kray, C Russian Federation
125 V4 **Bol'shaya Rogovaya** ↝ NW Russian Federation
125 U7 **Bol'shaya Synya** ↝ NW Russian Federation
145 V9 **Bol'shaya Vladimirovka** Vostochnyy Kazakhstan, E Kazakhstan
123 V11 **Bol'sheretsk** Kamchatskaya Oblast', E Russian Federation
127 W3 **Bol'sheust'ikinskoye** Respublika Bashkortostan, W Russian Federation
Bol'shevik *see* Bal'shavik
122 L5 **Bol'shevik, Ostrov** *island* Severnaya Zemlya, N Russian Federation
125 U4 **Bol'shezemel'skaya Tundra** *physical region* NW Russian Federation
144 J13 **Bol'shiye Barsuki, Peski** *desert* SW Kazakhstan
123 T7 **Bol'shoy Anyuy** ↝ NE Russian Federation
123 N7 **Bol'shoy Begichev, Ostrov** *island* NE Russian Federation
123 S15 **Bol'shoye Kamen'** Primorskiy Kray, SE Russian Federation
127 O4 **Bol'shoye Murashkino** Nizhegorodskaya Oblast', W Russian Federation
127 W4 **Bol'shoy Iremel'** ▲ W Russian Federation
127 R7 **Bol'shoy Irgiz** ↝ W Russian Federation
123 Q6 **Bol'shoy Lyakhovskiy, Ostrov** *island* NE Russian Federation
123 Q11 **Bol'shoy Nimnyr** Respublika Sakha (Yakutiya), NE Russian Federation
Bol'shoy Rozhan *see* Vyaliki Rozhan
144 E10 **Bol'shoy Uzen'** *Kaz.* Ülkenözen. ↝ Kazakhstan/Russian Federation
40 K6 **Bolson de Mapimi** ▲▲ NW Mexico
98 K6 **Bolsward** *Fris.* Boalsert. Friesland, N Netherlands
105 T4 **Boltaña** Aragón, NE Spain
14 G15 **Bolton** Ontario, S Canada
97 K17 **Bolton** *prev.* Bolton-le-Moors. NW England, UK
21 V12 **Bolton** North Carolina, SE USA
Bolton-le-Moors *see* Bolton
136 G11 **Bolu** Bolu, NW Turkey
136 G11 **Bolu** ◈ *province* NW Turkey
186 G9 **Bolubolu** Goodenough Island, S Papua New Guinea
92 H1 **Bolungarvík** Vestfirdhir, NW Iceland
159 O10 **Boluntay** Qinghai, W China
159 P8 **Boluozhuanjing**, Aksay Kazakzu Zizhixian. Gansu, N China
136 F14 **Bolvadin** Afyon, W Turkey
114 M10 **Bolyarovo** *prev.* Pashkeni. Yambol, E Bulgaria
106 G6 **Bolzano** *Ger.* Bozen; *anc.* Bauzanum. Trentino-Alto Adige, N Italy
79 F22 **Boma** Bas-Congo, W Dem. Rep. Congo
183 R12 **Bombala** New South Wales, SE Australia
104 F10 **Bombarral** Leiria, C Portugal
Bombay *see* Mumbai
171 U13 **Bomberai, Semenanjung** *cape* Papua, E Indonesia
81 F18 **Bombo** S Uganda
162 I8 **Bömbögör** *var.* Dzadgay. Bayanhongor, C Mongolia
79 I17 **Bomboma** Equateur, NW Dem. Rep. Congo
59 I14 **Bom Futuro** Pará, N Brazil
159 Q15 **Bomi** *var.* Bowo, Zhamo. Xizang Zizhiqu, W China
79 N17 **Bomili** Orientale, NE Dem. Rep. Congo
59 N17 **Bom Jesus da Lapa** Bahia, E Brazil
60 Q8 **Bom Jesus do Itabapoana** Rio de Janeiro, SE Brazil
95 C15 **Bømlafjorden** *fjord* S Norway
95 B15 **Bømlo** *island* S Norway
12 Q12 **Bomnak** Amurskaya Oblast', SE Russian Federation
79 I17 **Bomongo** Equateur, NW Dem. Rep. Congo
61 K14 **Bom Retiro** Santa Catarina, S Brazil
79 L15 **Bomu** *var.* Mbomou, Mbomu, M'Bomu. ↝ Central African Republic/Dem. Rep. Congo
142 J3 **Bonāb** *var.* Benāb, Bunab. Āzarbāyjān-e Sharqī, N Iran
45 Q16 **Bonaire** *island* E Netherlands Antilles
39 U11 **Bona, Mount** ▲ Alaska, USA
183 Q17 **Bonang** Victoria, SE Australia
42 L7 **Bonanza** Región Autónoma Atlántico Norte, NE Nicaragua
37 O4 **Bonanza** Utah, W USA
45 O8 **Bonao** C Dominican Republic
180 L3 **Bonaparte Archipelago** *island group* Western Australia
32 K6 **Bonaparte, Mount** ▲ Washington, NW USA
39 N11 **Bonasila Dome** ▲ Alaska, USA
92 H11 **Bonnåsjøen** Nordland, C Norway
45 T15 **Bonasse** Trinidad, Trinidad and Tobago
15 X7 **Bonaventure** Québec, SE Canada
15 X7 **Bonaventure** ↝ Québec, SE Canada
13 V11 **Bonavista** Newfoundland, Newfoundland and Labrador, SE Canada
13 U11 **Bonavista Bay** *inlet* NW Atlantic Ocean
79 E19 **Bonda** Ogooué-Lolo, C Gabon
127 N6 **Bondari** Tambovskaya Oblast', W Russian Federation
106 G9 **Bondeno** Emilia-Romagna, C Italy
30 L4 **Bond Falls Flowage** ◎ Michigan, N USA
79 L16 **Bondo** Orientale, N Dem. Rep. Congo
171 N17 **Bondokodi** Pulau Sumba, S Indonesia
77 O15 **Bondoukou** E Ivory Coast
Bondoukui/Bondoukuy *see* Boundoukui
169 T17 **Bondowoso** Jawa, C Indonesia
33 S14 **Bondurant** Wyoming, C USA
Bône *see* Annaba
Bone *see* Watampone
30 I5 **Bone Lake** ◎ Wisconsin, N USA
171 P14 **Bonelipu** Pulau Buton, C Indonesia
171 O15 **Bonerate, Kepulauan** *var.* Macan. *island group* C Indonesia
29 O12 **Bonesteel** South Dakota, N USA
62 I8 **Bonete, Cerro** ▲ N Argentina
171 O14 **Bone, Teluk** *bay* Sulawesi, C Indonesia
108 D6 **Bonfol** Jura, NW Switzerland
153 U12 **Bongaigaon** Assam, NE India
79 K17 **Bongandanga** Equateur, NW Dem. Rep. Congo
78 L13 **Bongo, Massif des** *var.* Chaîne des Mongos. ▲▲ NE Central African Republic
78 G12 **Bongor** Mayo-Kébbi, SW Chad
77 N16 **Bongouanou** E Ivory Coast
167 V11 **Bồng Sơn** *var.* Hoai Nhơn. Binh Đinh, C Vietnam
25 U5 **Bonham** Texas, SW USA
Bonhard *see* Bonyhád
103 U6 **Bonhomme, Col du** *pass* NE France
103 Y16 **Bonifacio** Corse, France, C Mediterranean Sea
Bonifacio, Bocche de/Bonifacio, Bouches de *see* Bonifacio, Strait of
103 Y16 **Bonifacio, Strait of** *Fr.* Bouches de Bonifacio, *It.* Bocche di Bonifacio. *strait* C Mediterranean Sea
23 Q8 **Bonifay** Florida, SE USA
Bonin Islands *see* Ogasawara-shotō
192 H5 **Bonin Trench** *undersea feature* NW Pacific Ocean
23 W15 **Bonita Springs** Florida, SE USA
42 I5 **Bonito, Pico** ▲ N Honduras
101 E17 **Bonn** Nordrhein-Westfalen, W Germany
14 J12 **Bonnechere** Ontario, SE Canada
14 J12 **Bonnechere** ↝ Ontario, SE Canada
33 N7 **Bonners Ferry** Idaho, NW USA
27 R4 **Bonner Springs** Kansas, C USA
102 L6 **Bonnétable** Sarthe, NW France
27 X6 **Bonne Terre** Missouri, C USA
10 J5 **Bonnet Plume** ↝ Yukon Territory, NW Canada
102 M6 **Bonneval** Eure-et-Loir, C France
103 T10 **Bonneville** Haute-Savoie, E France
36 J3 **Bonneville Salt Flats** *salt flat* Utah, W USA
77 U18 **Bonny** Rivers, S Nigeria
Bonny, Bight of *see* Biafra, Bight of
37 W4 **Bonny Reservoir** ⊠ Colorado, C USA
9 R14 **Bonnyville** Alberta, SW Canada
107 C18 **Bono** Sardegna, Italy, C Mediterranean Sea
Bononia *see* Vidin, Bulgaria
Bononia *see* Boulogne-sur-Mer, France
107 B18 **Bonorva** Sardegna, Italy, C Mediterranean Sea
30 M15 **Bonpas Creek** ↝ Illinois, N USA
190 I3 **Bonriki** Tarawa, W Kiribati
183 T4 **Bonshaw** New South Wales, SE Australia
76 I16 **Bonthe** SW Sierra Leone
171 N2 **Bontoc** Luzon, N Philippines
25 Y9 **Bon Wier** Texas, SW USA
111 J25 **Bonyhád** *Ger.* Bonhard. Tolna, S Hungary
Bonzabaai *see* Bonza Bay
83 J25 **Bonza Bay** *Afr.* Bonzabaai. Eastern Cape, S South Africa
182 D7 **Bookabie** South Australia
182 H6 **Bookaloo** South Australia
37 P5 **Book Cliffs** *cliff* Colorado/Utah, W USA
25 P1 **Booker** Texas, SW USA
76 K15 **Boola** SE Guinea
183 O8 **Booligal** New South Wales, SE Australia
99 G17 **Boom** Antwerpen, N Belgium
43 N6 **Boom** *var.* Boon. Región Autónoma Atlántico Norte, NE Nicaragua
183 S3 **Boomi** New South Wales, SE Australia
Boon *see* Boom
29 V13 **Boone** Iowa, C USA
21 Q8 **Boone** North Carolina, SE USA
27 S11 **Booneville** Arkansas, C USA
20 N6 **Booneville** Kentucky, S USA
23 N2 **Booneville** Mississippi, S USA
21 V3 **Boonsboro** Maryland, NE USA
162 H9 **Böön Tsagaan Nuur** ◎ S Mongolia
34 L6 **Boonville** California, W USA
31 N16 **Boonville** Indiana, N USA
27 U4 **Boonville** Missouri, C USA
18 I9 **Boonville** New York, NE USA
80 M12 **Booramo** Awdal, NW Somalia
183 O6 **Booroondarra, Mount** *hill* New South Wales, SE Australia
183 N9 **Booroorban** New South Wales, SE Australia
183 R9 **Boorowa** New South Wales, SE Australia
99 H17 **Boortmeerbeek** Vlaams Brabant, C Belgium
80 P11 **Boosaaso** *var.* Bandar Kassim, Bender Qaasim, Bosaso, *It.* Bender Cassim. Bari, N Somalia
19 Q8 **Boothbay Harbor** Maine, NE USA
Boothia Felix *see* Boothia Peninsula
9 N6 **Boothia, Gulf of** *gulf* Nunavut, NE Canada
8 M6 **Boothia Peninsula** *prev.* Boothia Felix. *peninsula* Nunavut, NE Canada
79 E18 **Booué** Ogooué-Ivindo, NE Gabon
101 J21 **Bopfingen** Baden-Württemberg, S Germany
101 F18 **Boppard** Rheinland-Pfalz, W Germany
62 M4 **Boquerón** *off.* Departamento de Boquerón. ◈ *department* W Paraguay
Boquerón, Departamento de *see* Boquerón
43 P15 **Boquete** *var.* Bajo Boquete. Chiriquí, W Panama
40 J6 **Boquilla, Presa de la** ⊠ N Mexico
40 L5 **Boquillas** *var.* Boquillas del Carmen. Coahuila de Zaragoza, NE Mexico
Boquillas del Carmen *see* Boquillas
112 P12 **Bor** Serbia, E Serbia
81 F15 **Bor** Jonglei, S Sudan
95 L20 **Bor** Jönköping, S Sweden
136 J15 **Bor** Niğde, S Turkey
191 S10 **Bora-Bora** *island* Îles Sous le Vent, W French Polynesia
167 Q9 **Borabu** Maha Sarakham, E Thailand
33 P13 **Borah Peak** ▲ Idaho, NW USA
145 U16 **Boralday** *prev.* Burunday. Almaty, SE Kazakhstan
144 G13 **Borankul** *prev.* Opornyy. Mangistau, SW Kazakhstan
95 J19 **Borås** Västra Götaland, S Sweden
143 N11 **Borāzjān** *var.* Borazjān. Būshehr, S Iran
Borazjān *see* Borāzjān
58 G13 **Borba** Amazonas, N Brazil
104 H11 **Borba** Évora, S Portugal
Borbetomagus *see* Worms
55 O7 **Borbón** Bolívar, E Venezuela
59 Q15 **Borborema, Planalto da** *plateau* NE Brazil
116 M14 **Borcea, Braţul** ↝ S Romania
Borchalo *see* Marneuli
195 R15 **Borchgrevink Coast** *physical region* Antarctica
137 Q11 **Borçka** Artvin, NE Turkey
98 N11 **Borculo** Gelderland, E Netherlands
182 G10 **Borda, Cape** *headland* South Australia
102 K13 **Bordeaux** *anc.* Burdigala. Gironde, SW France
9 T15 **Borden** Saskatchewan, S Canada
14 D8 **Borden Lake** ◎ Ontario, S Canada
9 N4 **Borden Peninsula** *peninsula* Baffin Island, Nunavut, NE Canada

182 K11 **Bordertown** South Australia
92 H2 **Bordheyri** Vestfirdhir, NW Iceland
95 B18 **Bordhoy** Dan. Bordø. island NE Faeroe Islands
106 B11 **Bordighera** Liguria, NW Italy
74 K5 **Bordj-Bou-Arreridj** var. Bordj Bou Arreridj, Bordj Bou Arréridj. N Algeria
74 L10 **Bordj Omar Driss** E Algeria
143 N13 **Bord Khūn** Hormozgān, S Iran
Bordø see Bordhoy
147 V7 **Bordunskiy** Chuyskaya Oblast', N Kyrgyzstan
95 M17 **Borensberg** Östergötland, S Sweden
Borgå see Porvoo
92 L2 **Borgarfjördhur** Austurland, NE Iceland
92 H3 **Borgarnes** Vesturland, W Iceland
93 G14 **Børgefjelt** ⛰ C Norway
98 O7 **Borger** Drenthe, NE Netherlands
25 N2 **Borger** Texas, SW USA
95 N20 **Borgholm** Kalmar, S Sweden
107 N22 **Borgia** Calabria, SW Italy
99 J18 **Borgloon** Limburg, NE Belgium
195 P2 **Borg Massif** ⛰ Antarctica
22 L9 **Borgne, Lake** ◎ Louisiana, S USA
106 C7 **Borgomanero** Piemonte, NE Italy
106 G10 **Borgo Panigale** ✈ (Bologna) Emilia-Romagna, N Italy
107 J15 **Borgorose** Lazio, C Italy
106 A9 **Borgo San Dalmazzo** Piemonte, NE Italy
106 G11 **Borgo San Lorenzo** Toscana, C Italy
106 C7 **Borgosesia** Piemonte, NE Italy
106 E9 **Borgo Val di Taro** Emilia-Romagna, C Italy
106 G6 **Borgo Valsugana** Trentino-Alto Adige, N Italy
Borhoyn Tal see Dzamïn-Üüd
167 R8 **Borikhan** var. Borikhane. Bolikhamxai, C Laos
Borikhane see Borikhan
Borislav see Boryslav
127 N8 **Borisoglebsk** Voronezhskaya Oblast', W Russian Federation
Borisov see Barysaw
Borisovgrad see Pŭrvomay
Borispol' see Boryspil'
172 I3 **Boriziny** Mahajanga, NW Madagascar
105 Q5 **Borja** Aragón, NE Spain
Borjas Blancas see Les Borges Blanques
137 S10 **Borjomi** Rus. Borzhomi. C Georgia
118 L12 **Borkavichy** Rus. Borkovichi. Vitsyebskaya Voblasts', N Belarus
101 H16 **Borken** Hessen, C Germany
101 E14 **Borken** Nordrhein-Westfalen, W Germany
92 H10 **Borkenes** Troms, N Norway
78 H7 **Borkou-Ennedi-Tibesti** off. Préfecture du Borkou-Ennedi-Tibesti. ◈ prefecture N Chad
Borkou-Ennedi-Tibesti, Préfecture du see Borkou-Ennedi-Tibesti
Borkovichi see Borkavichy
100 E9 **Borkum** island NW Germany
81 K17 **Bor, Lagh** var. Lak Bor. dry watercourse NE Kenya
Bor, Lak see Bor, Lagh
95 M14 **Borlänge** Dalarna, C Sweden
106 C9 **Bormida** ≈ NW Italy
106 F6 **Bormio** Lombardia, N Italy
101 M16 **Borna** Sachsen, E Germany
98 O10 **Borne** Overijssel, E Netherlands
99 F17 **Bornem** Antwerpen, N Belgium
169 S10 **Borneo** island Brunei/Indonesia/Malaysia
101 E16 **Bornheim** Nordrhein-Westfalen, W Germany
95 L24 **Bornholm** ◈ county E Denmark
95 L24 **Bornholm** island E Denmark
77 Y13 **Borno** ◈ state NE Nigeria
104 K15 **Bornos** Andalucía, S Spain
162 L7 **Bornuur** Töv, C Mongolia
117 O4 **Borodyanka** Kyyivs'ka Oblast', N Ukraine
158 I5 **Borohoro Shan** ⛰ NW China
77 O13 **Boromo** SW Burkina
35 T13 **Boron** California, W USA
Borongo see Black Volta
Boron'ki see Baron'ki
Borosjenő see Ineu
Borossebes see Sebiş
76 L15 **Borotou** NW Ivory Coast
117 W6 **Borova** Kharkivs'ka Oblast', E Ukraine
114 H8 **Borovan** Vratsa, NW Bulgaria
124 I14 **Borovichi** Novgorodskaya Oblast', W Russian Federation
Borovlje see Ferlach
112 J9 **Borovo** Vukovar-Srijem, NE Croatia
145 Q7 **Borovoye** Kaz. Būrabay. Akmola, N Kazakhstan
126 K4 **Borovsk** Kaluzhskaya Oblast', W Russian Federation
145 N7 **Borovskoy** Kostanay, N Kazakhstan
Borovukha see Baravukha
95 L23 **Borrby** Skåne, S Sweden
181 R3 **Borroloola** Northern Territory, N Australia
116 F9 **Borşa** Bihor, NW Romania
116 I9 **Borşa** Hung. Borsa. Maramureş, N Romania
116 J10 **Borsec** Ger. Bad Borseck, Hung. Borszék. Harghita, C Romania
92 K8 **Børselv** Lapp. Bissojohka. Finnmark, N Norway
113 L23 **Borsh** var. Borshi. Vlorë, S Albania
Borshchev see Borshchiv
116 K7 **Borshchiv** Pol. Borszczów, Rus. Borshchev. Ternopil's'ka Oblast', W Ukraine
Borshi see Borsh
111 L20 **Borsod-Abaúj-Zemplén** off. Borsod-Abaúj-Zemplén Megye. ◈ county NE Hungary
Borsod-Abaúj-Zemplén Megye see Borsod-Abaúj-Zemplén
99 E15 **Borssele** Zeeland, SW Netherlands
Borszczów see Borshchiv
Borszék see Borsec
Bortala see Bole
103 O12 **Bort-les-Orgues** Corrèze, C France
Bor u České Lípy see Nový Bor
Bor-Udzüür see Altay
Bor-Udzüür see Altay
143 N9 **Borūjen** Chahār Maḩall va Bakhtiārī, C Iran
142 L7 **Borūjerd** var. Burujird. Lorestān, W Iran
116 H6 **Boryslav** Pol. Borysław, Rus. Borislav. L'vivs'ka Oblast', NW Ukraine
Borysław see Boryslav
117 P4 **Boryspil'** Rus. Borispol'. Kyyivs'ka Oblast', N Ukraine
117 P4 **Boryspil'** Rus. Borispol'. ✈ (Kyyiv) Kyyivs'ka Oblast', N Ukraine
Borzhomi see Borjomi
117 R3 **Borzna** Chernihivs'ka Oblast', NE Ukraine
123 O14 **Borzya** Chitinskaya Oblast', S Russian Federation
107 B18 **Bosa** Sardegna, Italy, C Mediterranean Sea
112 F10 **Bosanska Dubica** var. Kozarska Dubica. ◈ Republika Srpska, NW Bosnia and Herzegovina
112 G10 **Bosanska Gradiška** var. Gradiška. ◈ Republika Srpska, N Bosnia and Herzegovina
112 F10 **Bosanska Kostajnica** var. Srpska Kostajnica. ◈ Republika Srpska, NW Bosnia and Herzegovina
112 E11 **Bosanska Krupa** var. Krupa, Krupa na Uni. ◈ Federacij Bosna I Hercegovina, NW Bosnia and Herzegovina
112 H10 **Bosanski Brod** var. Srpski Brod. ◈ Republika Srpska, N Bosnia and Herzegovina
112 E10 **Bosanski Novi** var. Novi Grad. ◈ Republika Srpska, NW Bosnia and Herzegovina
112 E11 **Bosanski Petrovac** var. Petrovac. ◈ Federacija Bosna I Hercegovina, NW Bosnia and Herzegovina
112 I10 **Bosanski Šamac** var. Šamac. ◈ Republika Srpska, N Bosnia and Herzegovina
112 E12 **Bosansko Grahovo** var. Grahovo, Hrvatsko Grahovi. ◈ Federacija Bosna I Hercegovina, W Bosnia and Herzegovina
Bosaso see Boosaaso
186 B7 **Bosavi, Mount** ▲ W Papua New Guinea
160 J14 **Bose** Guangxi Zhuangzu Zizhiqu, S China
161 Q5 **Boshan** Shandong, E China
113 P16 **Bosilegrad** prev. Bosiljgrad. Serbia, SE Serbia
Bosiljgrad see Bosilegrad
Bösing see Pezinok
Boskovichi see Borkavichy
98 H12 **Boskoop** Zuid-Holland, C Netherlands
111 G18 **Boskovice** Ger. Boskowitz. Jihomoravský Kraj, SE Czech Republic
Boskowitz see Boskovice
112 I10 **Bosna** ≈ N Bosnia and Herzegovina
113 G14 **Bosna I Hercegovina, Federacija** ◈ republic Bosnia and Herzegovina
112 H12 **Bosnia and Herzegovina** off. Republic of Bosnia and Herzegovina. ◆ republic SE Europe
Bosnia and Herzegovina, Republic of see Bosnia and Herzegovina
79 J16 **Bosobolo** Equateur, NW Dem. Rep. Congo
165 O14 **Bōsō-hantō** peninsula Honshū, S Japan
Bosora see Buşrá ash Shām
Bosphorus/Bosporus see İstanbul Boğazı
Bosporus Cimmerius see Kerch Strait
Bosporus Thracius see İstanbul Boğazı
Bosra see Buşrá ash Shām
79 H14 **Bossangoa** Ouham, C Central African Republic
Bossé Bangou see Bossey Bangou
79 I15 **Bossembélé** Ombella-Mpoko, C Central African Republic
79 H15 **Bossentélé** Ouham-Pendé, W Central African Republic
77 R12 **Bossey Bangou** var. Bossé Bangou. Tillabéri, SW Niger
22 G5 **Bossier City** Louisiana, S USA
83 D20 **Bossiesvlei** Hardap, S Namibia
77 Y11 **Bosso** Diffa, SE Niger
61 F15 **Bossoroca** Rio Grande do Sul, S Brazil
158 J10 **Bostan** Xinjiang Uygur Zizhiqu, W China
142 K3 **Bostānābād** Āžarbāyjān-e Sharqī, N Iran
158 K6 **Bosten Hu** var. Bagrax Hu. ◎ NW China
97 O18 **Boston** prev. St.Botolph's Town. E England, UK
19 O11 **Boston** state capital Massachusetts, NE USA
146 I9 **Bo'ston** Rus. Bustan. Qoraqalpog'iston Respublikasi, W Uzbekistan
10 M17 **Boston Bar** British Columbia, SW Canada
27 T10 **Boston Mountains** ⛰ Arkansas, C USA
15 P8 **Bostonnais** ≈ Québec, SE Canada
Bostyn' see Bastyn'
112 J10 **Bosut** ≈ E Croatia
154 C11 **Botād** Gujarāt, W India
183 T9 **Botany Bay** inlet New South Wales, SE Australia
83 G18 **Boteti** var. Botletle. ≈ N Botswana
114 J9 **Botev** ▲ C Bulgaria
114 H9 **Botevgrad** prev. Orkhaniye. Sofiya, W Bulgaria
93 J16 **Bothnia, Gulf of** Fin. Pohjanlahti, Swe. Bottniska Viken. gulf N Baltic Sea
183 P17 **Bothwell** Tasmania, SE Australia
104 H5 **Boticas** Vila Real, N Portugal
55 W10 **Boti-Pasi** Sipaliwini, C Suriname
Botletle see Boteti
127 P16 **Botlikh** Chechenskaya Respublika, SW Russian Federation
117 N10 **Botna** ≈ E Moldova
147 P12 **Botogot', Tizmasi** Rus. Khrebet Babatag. ⛰ Tajikistan/Uzbekistan
116 I9 **Botoşani** Hung. Botosány. Botoşani, NE Romania
116 K8 **Botoşani** ◈ county NE Romania
Botosány see Botoşani
161 P4 **Botou** prev. Bozhen. Hebei, E China
99 M20 **Botrange** ▲ E Belgium
107 O21 **Botricello** Calabria, SW Italy
83 I23 **Botshabelo** Free State, C South Africa
93 J15 **Botsmark** Västerbotten, N Sweden
83 G19 **Botswana** off. Republic of Botswana. ◆ republic S Africa
Botswana, Republic of see Botswana
29 N2 **Bottineau** North Dakota, N USA
Bottniska Viken see Bothnia, Gulf of
60 L9 **Botucatu** São Paulo, S Brazil
76 M16 **Bouaflé** C Ivory Coast
76 N16 **Bouaké** var. Bwake. C Ivory Coast
79 G14 **Bouar** Nana-Mambéré, W Central African Republic
74 H7 **Bouarfa** NE Morocco
111 B19 **Boubín** ▲ SW Czech Republic
79 I14 **Bouca** Ouham, W Central African Republic
15 T5 **Boucher** ≈ Québec, SE Canada
103 R15 **Bouches-du-Rhône** ◈ department SE France
74 C9 **Bou Craa** var. Bu Craa. NW Western Sahara
77 O9 **Boû Djébéha** oasis C Mali
108 C8 **Boudry** Neuchâtel, W Switzerland
180 L2 **Bougainville, Cape** cape Western Australia
65 E24 **Bougainville, Cape** headland East Falkland, Falkland Islands
Bougainville, Détroit de see Bougainville Strait
186 J7 **Bougainville Island** island NE Papua New Guinea
186 I8 **Bougainville Strait** strait N Solomon Islands
187 Q13 **Bougainville Strait** Fr. Détroit de Bougainville. strait C Vanuatu
120 I9 **Bougaroun, Cap** headland NE Algeria
77 R8 **Boughessa** Kidal, NE Mali
Bougie see Béjaïa
76 L13 **Bougouni** Sikasso, SW Mali
99 J24 **Bouillon** Luxembourg, SE Belgium
74 K5 **Bouira** var. Bouïra. N Algeria
74 D8 **Bou-Izakarn** SW Morocco
74 B9 **Boujdour** var. Bojador. W Western Sahara
74 G5 **Boukhalef** ✈ (Tanger) N Morocco
Boukombé see Boukoumbé
77 R14 **Boukoumbé** var. Boukombé. C Benin
76 G6 **Boû Lanouâr** Dakhlet Nouâdhibou, W Mauritania
37 T4 **Boulder** Colorado, C USA
33 R10 **Boulder** Montana, NW USA
35 X12 **Boulder City** Nevada, W USA
181 T7 **Boulia** Queensland, C Australia
15 N10 **Boullé** ≈ Québec, SE Canada
102 J9 **Boulogne** ≈ NW France
Boulogne see Boulogne-sur-Mer
102 L16 **Boulogne-sur-Gesse** Haute-Garonne, S France
103 N1 **Boulogne-sur-Mer** var. Boulogne; anc. Bononia, Gesoriacum, Gessoriacum. Pas-de-Calais, N France
77 Q12 **Boulsa** C Burkina
77 W11 **Boultoum** Zinder, C Niger
187 Y14 **Bouma** Taveuni, N Fiji
79 G16 **Boumba** ≈ SE Cameroon
76 J9 **Boûmdeïd** var. Boumdeït. Assaba, S Mauritania
Boumdeït see Boûmdeïd
115 C17 **Boumistós** ▲ W Greece
77 O15 **Bouna** NE Ivory Coast
19 P4 **Boundary Bald Mountain** ▲ Maine, NE USA
35 S8 **Boundary Peak** ▲ Nevada, W USA
76 M14 **Boundiali** N Ivory Coast
79 G19 **Boundji** Cuvette, C Congo
77 O13 **Boundoukui** var. Bondoukui, Bondoukuy. W Burkina
36 L2 **Bountiful** Utah, W USA
Bounty Basin see Bounty Trough
191 Q16 **Bounty Bay** bay Pitcairn Island, C Pacific Ocean
192 L12 **Bounty Islands** island group S New Zealand
175 Q13 **Bounty Trough** var. Bounty Basin. undersea feature S Pacific Ocean
187 P17 **Bourail** Province Sud, C New Caledonia
27 V5 **Bourbeuse River** ≈ Missouri, C USA
103 Q9 **Bourbon-Lancy** Saône-et-Loire, C France
31 N11 **Bourbonnais** Illinois, N USA
103 O10 **Bourbonnais** cultural region C France
103 S7 **Bourbonne-les-Bains** Haute-Marne, N France
Bourbon Vendée see la Roche-sur-Yon
74 M8 **Bourdj Messaouda** E Algeria
77 Q10 **Bourem** Gao, C Mali
Bourg see Bourg-en-Bresse
103 N11 **Bourganeuf** Creuse, C France
Bourgas see Burgas
Bourge-en-Bresse see Bourg-en-Bresse
103 S10 **Bourg-en-Bresse** var. Bourg, Bourge-en-Bresse. Ain, E France
103 O8 **Bourges** anc. Avaricum. Cher, C France
103 T11 **Bourget, Lac du** ◎ E France
103 P8 **Bourgogne** Eng. Burgundy. ◈ region E France
103 S11 **Bourgoin-Jallieu** Isère, E France
103 R14 **Bourg-St-Andéol** Ardèche, E France
103 U11 **Bourg-St-Maurice** Savoie, E France
108 C11 **Bourg St. Pierre** Valais, SW Switzerland
76 H8 **Boû Rjeimât** well W Mauritania
183 P5 **Bourke** New South Wales, SE Australia
97 M24 **Bournemouth** S England, UK
99 M23 **Bourscheid** Diekirch, NE Luxembourg
74 K6 **Bou Saâda** var. Bou Saada. N Algeria
36 I13 **Bouse Wash** ≈ Arizona, SW USA
103 N10 **Boussac** Creuse, C France
102 M16 **Boussens** Haute-Garonne, S France
78 H12 **Bousso** prev. Fort-Bretonnet. Chari-Baguirmi, S Chad
76 H9 **Boutilimit** Trarza, SW Mauritania
65 D21 **Bouvet Island** ◇ Norwegian dependency S Atlantic Ocean
77 U11 **Bouza** Tahoua, SW Niger
109 R10 **Bovec** Ger. Flitsch, It. Plezzo. NW Slovenia
98 J8 **Bovenkarspel** Noord-Holland, NW Netherlands
29 V5 **Bovey** Minnesota, N USA
32 M9 **Bovill** Idaho, NW USA
24 L4 **Bovina** Texas, SW USA
107 M17 **Bovino** Puglia, SE Italy
61 C17 **Bovril** Entre Ríos, E Argentina
28 L2 **Bowbells** North Dakota, N USA
9 Q16 **Bow City** Alberta, SW Canada
29 O8 **Bowdle** South Dakota, N USA
181 X6 **Bowen** Queensland, NE Australia
192 L2 **Bowers Ridge** undersea feature S Bering Sea
25 S5 **Bowie** Texas, SW USA
9 R17 **Bow Island** Alberta, SW Canada
Bowkān see Būkān
20 J7 **Bowling Green** Kentucky, S USA
27 V3 **Bowling Green** Missouri, C USA
31 R11 **Bowling Green** Ohio, N USA
21 W5 **Bowling Green** Virginia, NE USA
28 J6 **Bowman** North Dakota, N USA
9 Q7 **Bowman Bay** bay NW Atlantic Ocean
194 I5 **Bowman Coast** physical region Antarctica
28 J7 **Bowman-Haley Lake** ▣ North Dakota, N USA
195 Z11 **Bowman Island** island Antarctica
Bowo see Bomi
183 S9 **Bowral** New South Wales, SE Australia
186 E8 **Bowutu Mountains** ⛰ C Papua New Guinea
83 I16 **Bowwood** Southern, S Zambia
28 I12 **Box Butte Reservoir** ▣ Nebraska, C USA
28 J10 **Box Elder** South Dakota, N USA
95 M18 **Boxholm** Östergötland, S Sweden
Bo Xian/Boxian see Bozhou
161 Q4 **Boxing** Shandong, E China
99 L14 **Boxmeer** Noord-Brabant, SE Netherlands
99 J14 **Boxtel** Noord-Brabant, S Netherlands
136 J10 **Boyabat** Sinop, N Turkey
54 F9 **Boyacá** off. Departamento de Boyacá. ◈ province C Colombia
Boyacá, Departamento de see Boyacá
117 O4 **Boyarka** Kyyivs'ka Oblast', N Ukraine
22 H7 **Boyce** Louisiana, S USA
33 U11 **Boyd** Montana, NW USA
25 S6 **Boyd** Texas, SW USA
21 V8 **Boydton** Virginia, NE USA
Boyer Ahmadī va Kohkīlūyeh see Kohgīlūyeh va Būyer Aḩmad
29 T13 **Boyer River** ≈ Iowa, C USA
21 W8 **Boykins** Virginia, NE USA
9 Q13 **Boyle** Alberta, SW Canada
97 D16 **Boyle** Ir. Mainistirna Búille. C Ireland
97 F17 **Boyne** Ir. An Bhóinn. ≈ E Ireland
31 Q5 **Boyne City** Michigan, N USA
23 Z14 **Boynton Beach** Florida, SE USA
147 O13 **Boysun** Rus. Baysun. Surkhondaryo Viloyati, S Uzbekistan
Bozau see Întorsura Buzăului
136 B12 **Bozcaada** Island Çanakkale, NW Turkey
136 C14 **Boz Dağları** ⛰ W Turkey
33 S11 **Bozeman** Montana, NW USA
Bozen see Bolzano
79 J16 **Bozene** Equateur, NW Dem. Rep. Congo
Bozhen see Botou
161 P7 **Bozhou** var. Boxian, Bo Xian. Anhui, E China
136 H16 **Bozkır** Konya, S Turkey
136 K13 **Bozok Yaylasī** plateau C Turkey
79 H14 **Bozoum** Ouham-Pendé, W Central African Republic
137 N16 **Bozova** Sanlıurfa, S Turkey
Bozrah see Buşrá ash Shām
136 E12 **Bozüyük** Bilecik, NW Turkey
106 B9 **Bra** Piemonte, NW Italy
194 G4 **Brabant Island** island Antarctica
99 I20 **Brabant Walloon** ◈ province C Belgium
113 F15 **Brač** var. Brach, It. Brazza; anc. Brattia. island S Croatia
Bracara Augusta see Braga
107 H15 **Bracciano** Lazio, C Italy
107 H14 **Bracciano, Lago di** ◎ C Italy
14 H13 **Bracebridge** Ontario, S Canada
Brach see Brač
93 G17 **Bräcke** Jämtland, C Sweden
25 P12 **Brackettville** Texas, SW USA
97 N22 **Bracknell** S England, UK
61 K14 **Braço do Norte** Santa Catarina, S Brazil
116 G11 **Brad** Hung. Brád. Hunedoara, SW Romania
107 N18 **Bradano** ≈ S Italy
23 V13 **Bradenton** Florida, SE USA
14 H14 **Bradford** Ontario, S Canada
97 L17 **Bradford** N England, UK
27 W10 **Bradford** Arkansas, C USA
18 D12 **Bradford** Pennsylvania, NE USA
27 T15 **Bradley** Arkansas, C USA
25 P7 **Bradshaw** Texas, SW USA
25 Q9 **Brady** Texas, SW USA
25 Q9 **Brady Creek** ≈ Texas, SW USA
95 G22 **Brædstrup** Vejle, C Denmark
96 J10 **Braemar** NE Scotland, UK
116 K8 **Brăeşti** Botoşani, NW Romania
104 G5 **Braga** anc. Bracara Augusta. Braga, NW Portugal
104 G5 **Braga** ◈ district N Portugal
116 J15 **Bragadiru** Teleorman, S Romania
61 C20 **Bragado** Buenos Aires, E Argentina
104 J5 **Bragança** Eng. Braganza; anc. Julio Briga. Bragança, NE Portugal
104 I5 **Bragança** ◈ district N Portugal
60 N9 **Bragança Paulista** São Paulo, S Brazil
Braganza see Bragança
Bragin see Brahin
29 V7 **Braham** Minnesota, N USA
Brahe see Brda
Brahestad see Raahe
119 O20 **Brahin** Rus. Bragin. Homyel'skaya Voblasts', SE Belarus
153 U15 **Brahmanbaria** Chittagong, E Bangladesh
154 O12 **Brāhmani** ≈ E India
154 N13 **Brahmapur** Orissa, E India
129 S10 **Brahmaputra** var. Padma, Tsangpo, Ben. Jamuna, Chin. Yarlung Zangbo Jiang, Ind. Bramaputra, Dihang, Siang. ≈ S Asia
97 H19 **Braich y Pwll** headland NW Wales, UK
183 R10 **Braidwood** New South Wales, SE Australia
30 M11 **Braidwood** Illinois, N USA
116 M13 **Brăila** Brăila, E Romania
116 L13 **Brăila** ◈ county SE Romania
99 G19 **Braine-l'Alleud** Brabant Walloon, C Belgium
99 F19 **Braine-le-Comte** Hainaut, SW Belgium
29 U6 **Brainerd** Minnesota, N USA
99 J19 **Braives** Liège, E Belgium
83 H23 **Brak** ≈ C South Africa
Brak see Birāk
99 E18 **Brakel** Oost-Vlaanderen, SW Belgium
98 J13 **Brakel** Gelderland, C Netherlands
76 H9 **Brakna** ◈ region S Mauritania
95 J17 **Brålanda** Västra Götaland, S Sweden
Bramaputra see Brahmaputra
95 F23 **Bramming** Ribe, W Denmark
14 G15 **Brampton** Ontario, S Canada
100 F12 **Bramsche** Niedersachsen, NW Germany
116 J12 **Bran** Ger. Törzburg, Hung. Törcsvár. Braşov, S Romania
29 W8 **Branch** Minnesota, N USA
21 R14 **Branchville** South Carolina, SE USA
47 Y6 **Branco, Cabo** headland E Brazil
58 F11 **Branco, Rio** ≈ N Brazil
108 J8 **Brand** Vorarlberg, W Austria
83 B18 **Brandberg** ▲ NW Namibia
95 H14 **Brandbu** Oppland, S Norway
95 F22 **Brande** Ringkøbing, W Denmark
Brandebourg see Brandenburg
100 M12 **Brandenburg** var. Brandenburg an der Havel. Brandenburg, NE Germany
20 K5 **Brandenburg** Kentucky, S USA
100 N12 **Brandenburg** off. Freie und Hansestadt Hamburg, Fr. Brandebourg. ◈ state NE Germany
Brandenburg an der Havel see Brandenburg
83 I23 **Brandfort** Free State, C South Africa
9 W16 **Brandon** Manitoba, S Canada
23 V12 **Brandon** Florida, SE USA
22 L6 **Brandon** Mississippi, S USA
97 A20 **Brandon Mountain** Ir. Cnoc Bréanainn. ▲ SW Ireland
Brandsen see Coronel Brandsen
95 I14 **Brandval** Hedmark, S Norway
83 F24 **Brandvlei** Northern Cape, W South Africa
23 U9 **Branford** Florida, SE USA
110 K7 **Braniewo** Ger. Braunsberg. Warmińsko-mazurskie, N Poland
194 H3 **Bransfield Strait** strait Antarctica
37 U8 **Branson** Colorado, C USA
27 T8 **Branson** Missouri, C USA
14 G16 **Brantford** Ontario, S Canada
102 L12 **Brantôme** Dordogne, SW France
182 L12 **Branxholme** Victoria, SE Australia
Brasil see Brazil
59 C16 **Brasiléia** Acre, W Brazil
59 K18 **Brasília** ● (Brazil) Distrito Federal, C Brazil
Brasil, República Federativa do see Brazil
Braslav see Braslaw
118 J12 **Braslaw** Pol. Brasław, Rus. Braslav. Vitsyebskaya Voblasts', N Belarus
116 J12 **Braşov** Ger. Kronstadt, Hung. Brassó; prev. Oraşul Stalin. Braşov, C Romania
116 I12 **Braşov** ◈ county C Romania
77 U18 **Brass** Bayelsa, S Nigeria
99 H16 **Brasschaat** var. Brasschaet. Antwerpen, N Belgium
Brasschaet see Brasschaat
169 V8 **Brassey, Banjaran** var. Brassey Range. ⛰ East Malaysia
Brassey Range see Brassey, Banjaran
Brassó see Braşov
23 T1 **Brasstown Bald** ▲ Georgia, SE USA
113 K22 **Brataj** Vlorë, SW Albania
114 J10 **Bratan** var. Morozov. ▲ C Bulgaria
111 F21 **Bratislava** Ger. Pressburg, Hung. Pozsony. ● (Slovakia) Bratislavský Kraj, W Slovakia
111 H21 **Bratislavský Kraj** ◈ region W Slovakia
114 H10 **Bratiya** ▲ C Bulgaria
122 M12 **Bratsk** Irkutskaya Oblast', C Russian Federation
117 Q8 **Brats'ke** Mykolayivs'ka Oblast', S Ukraine
122 M13 **Bratskoye Vodokhranilishche** Eng. Bratsk Reservoir. ▣ S Russian Federation
Bratsk Reservoir see Bratskoye Vodokhranilishche
Brattia see Brač
94 D9 **Brattvåg** Møre og Romsdal, S Norway
112 K12 **Bratunac** ◈ Republika Srpska, E Bosnia and Herzegovina
114 J10 **Bratya Daskalovi** prev. Grozdovo. Stara Zagora, C Bulgaria
109 U2 **Braunau** ≈ N Austria
Braunau see Braunau am Inn
109 Q4 **Braunau am Inn** var. Braunau. Oberösterreich, N Austria
Braunsberg see Braniewo
100 J13 **Braunschweig** Eng./Fr. Brunswick. Niedersachsen, N Germany
Brava see Baraawe
105 Y6 **Brava, Costa** coastal region NE Spain
43 V16 **Brava, Punta** headland E Panama
95 N17 **Bråviken** inlet S Sweden
56 B10 **Bravo, Cerro** ▲ N Peru
Bravo del Norte, Río/Bravo, Río see Grande, Rio
35 X17 **Brawley** California, W USA
97 G18 **Bray** Ir. Bré. E Ireland
59 G16 **Brazil** off. Federative Republic of Brazil, Port. República Federativa do Brasil, Sp. Brasil; prev. United States of Brazil. ◆ federal republic South America
65 K15 **Brazil Basin** var. Brazilian Basin, Brazil'skaya Kotlovina. undersea feature W Atlantic Ocean
Brazil, Federative Republic of see Brazil
Brazilian Basin see Brazil Basin
Brazilian Highlands see Central, Planalto
Brazil'skaya Kotlovina see Brazil Basin
Brazil, United States of see Brazil
25 U10 **Brazos River** ≈ Texas, SW USA
Brazza see Brač
79 G21 **Brazzaville** ● (Congo) Capital District, S Congo
79 G21 **Brazzaville** ✈ Le Pool, S Congo
112 J11 **Brčko** ◈ Republika Srpska, NE Bosnia and Herzegovina
110 H8 **Brda** Ger. Brahe. ≈ N Poland
Bré see Bray
185 A23 **Breaksea Sound** sound South Island, New Zealand
184 L4 **Bream Bay** bay North Island, New Zealand
184 L4 **Bream Head** headland North Island, New Zealand
Bréanainn, Cnoc see Brandon Mountain
45 S6 **Brea, Punta** headland W Puerto Rico
22 I9 **Breaux Bridge** Louisiana, S USA
116 J13 **Breaza** Prahova, SE Romania
169 P16 **Brebes** Jawa, C Indonesia
96 K10 **Brechin** E Scotland, UK
99 H15 **Brecht** Antwerpen, N Belgium
37 S4 **Breckenridge** Colorado, C USA
29 R6 **Breckenridge** Minnesota, N USA
25 R6 **Breckenridge** Texas, SW USA
97 J21 **Brecknock** cultural region SE Wales, UK
63 G25 **Brecknock, Península** headland S Chile
111 G19 **Břeclav** Ger. Lundenburg. Jihomoravský Kraj, SE Czech Republic
97 J21 **Brecon** E Wales, UK
97 J21 **Brecon Beacons** ⛰ S Wales, UK
99 I14 **Breda** Noord-Brabant, S Netherlands
95 K20 **Bredaryd** Jönköping, S Sweden

◆ Country
● Country Capital
◇ Dependent Territory
○ Dependent Territory Capital
◈ Administrative Regions
✈ International Airport
▲ Mountain
⛰ Mountain Range
⋀ Volcano
≈ River
◎ Lake
▣ Reservoir

83 F26 **Bredasdorp** Western Cape, SW South Africa
93 H16 **Bredbyn** Västernorrland, N Sweden
122 F11 **Bredy** Chelyabinskaya Oblast', C Russian Federation
99 K17 **Bree** Limburg, NE Belgium
67 T15 **Breede** ≈ S South Africa
98 I7 **Breezand** Noord-Holland, NW Netherlands
113 P18 **Bregalnica** ≈ E FYR Macedonia
108 I6 **Bregenz** *anc.* Brigantium. Vorarlberg, W Austria
108 J7 **Bregenzer Wald** ⛰ W Austria
114 F6 **Bregovo** Vidin, NW Bulgaria
102 H5 **Bréhat, Île de** *island* NW France
92 H2 **Breidhafjördhur** *bay* W Iceland
92 L3 **Breidhdalsvík** Austurland, E Iceland
108 H9 **Breil** *Ger.* Brigels. Graubünden, S Switzerland
92 J8 **Breivikbotn** Finnmark, N Norway
94 I9 **Brekken** Sør-Trøndelag, S Norway
94 G7 **Brekstad** Sør-Trøndelag, S Norway
94 B10 **Bremangerlandet** *island* S Norway
Brême *see* Bremen
100 H11 **Bremen** *Fr.* Brême. Bremen, NW Germany
23 R3 **Bremen** Georgia, SE USA
31 O11 **Bremen** Indiana, N USA
100 H10 **Bremen** *off.* Freie Hansestadt Bremen, *Fr.* Brême. ◈ *state* N Germany
100 G9 **Bremerhaven** Bremen, NW Germany
Bremersdorp *see* Manzini
32 G8 **Bremerton** Washington, NW USA
100 H10 **Bremervörde** Niedersachsen, NW Germany
25 U9 **Bremond** Texas, SW USA
25 U10 **Brenham** Texas, SW USA
108 M8 **Brenner** Tirol, W Austria
Brenner, Col du/Brennero, Passo del *see* Brenner Pass
108 M8 **Brenner Pass** *var.* Brenner Sattel, *Fr.* Col du Brenner, *Ger.* Brennerpass, *It.* Passo del Brennero. *pass* Austria/Italy
Brennerpass *see* Brenner Pass
Brenner Sattel *see* Brenner Pass
108 G10 **Brenno** ≈ SW Switzerland
106 F7 **Breno** Lombardia, N Italy
23 O5 **Brent** Alabama, S USA
106 H7 **Brenta** ≈ NE Italy
97 P21 **Brentwood** E England, UK
18 L14 **Brentwood** Long Island, New York, NE USA
106 F7 **Brescia** *anc.* Brixia. Lombardia, N Italy
99 D15 **Breskens** Zeeland, SW Netherlands
Breslau *see* Wrocław
106 H5 **Bressanone** *Ger.* Brixen. Trentino-Alto Adige, N Italy
96 M2 **Bressay** *island* NE Scotland, UK
102 K9 **Bressuire** Deux-Sèvres, W France
119 F20 **Brest** *Pol.* Brześć nad Bugiem, *Rus.* Brest-Litovsk; *prev.* Brześć Litewski. Brestskaya Voblasts', SW Belarus
102 F5 **Brest** Finistère, NW France
Brest-Litovsk *see* Brest
112 A10 **Brestova** Istra, NW Croatia
Brestskaya Oblast' *see* Brestskaya Voblasts'
119 G19 **Brestskaya Voblasts'** *prev.Rus.* Brestskaya Oblast'. ◈ *province* SW Belarus
102 G6 **Bretagne** *Eng.* Brittany, *Lat.* Britannia Minor. ◈ *region* NW France
116 G12 **Bretea-Română** *Hung.* Oláhbrettye; *prev.* Bretea-Romînă. Hunedoara, W Romania
Bretea-Romînă *see* Bretea-Română
103 O3 **Breteuil** Oise, N France
102 I10 **Breton, Pertuis** *inlet* W France
22 L10 **Breton Sound** *sound* Louisiana, S USA
184 K2 **Brett, Cape** *headland* North Island, New Zealand
101 G21 **Bretten** Baden-Württemberg, SW Germany
99 K15 **Breugel** Noord-Brabant, S Netherlands
106 B6 **Breuil-Cervinia** *It.* Cervinia. Valle d'Aosta, NW Italy
98 I11 **Breukelen** Utrecht, C Netherlands
21 P10 **Brevard** North Carolina, SE USA
38 L9 **Brevig Mission** Alaska, USA
95 G16 **Brevik** Telemark, S Norway
183 P5 **Brewarrina** New South Wales, SE Australia
19 R6 **Brewer** Maine, NE USA
29 T11 **Brewster** Minnesota, N USA
29 N14 **Brewster** Nebraska, C USA
31 U12 **Brewster** Ohio, N USA
Brewster, Kap *see* Kangikajik
183 O8 **Brewster, Lake** ◎ New South Wales, SE Australia
23 P7 **Brewton** Alabama, S USA
Brezhnev *see* Naberezhnyye Chelny
109 W12 **Brežice** *Ger.* Rann. E Slovenia
114 G9 **Breznik** Pernik, W Bulgaria
111 K19 **Brezno** *Ger.* Bries, Briesen, *Hung.* Breznóbánya; *prev.* Brezno nad Hronom. Banskobystrický Kraj, C Slovakia
Breznóbánya/Brezno nad Hronom *see* Brezno
116 I12 **Brezoi** Vâlcea, SW Romania
114 J10 **Brezovo** *prev.* Abrashlare. Plovdiv, C Bulgaria
79 K14 **Bria** Haute-Kotto, C Central African Republic
103 U13 **Briançon** *anc.* Brigantio. Hautes-Alpes, SE France
36 K7 **Brian Head** ▲ Utah, W USA
103 O7 **Briare** Loiret, C France
183 V2 **Bribie Island** *island* Queensland, E Australia
43 O14 **Bribrí** Limón, E Costa Rica
116 L8 **Briceni** *var.* Brinceni, *Rus.* Brichany. N Moldova
Bricgstow *see* Bristol
Brichany *see* Briceni
99 M24 **Bridel** Luxembourg, C Luxembourg
97 J22 **Bridgend** S Wales, UK
14 I14 **Bridgenorth** Ontario, SE Canada
23 Q1 **Bridgeport** Alabama, S USA
35 R8 **Bridgeport** California, W USA
18 L13 **Bridgeport** Connecticut, NE USA
31 N15 **Bridgeport** Illinois, N USA
28 J14 **Bridgeport** Nebraska, C USA
25 S6 **Bridgeport** Texas, SW USA
21 S3 **Bridgeport** West Virginia, NE USA
25 S5 **Bridgeport, Lake** ⊠ Texas, SW USA
33 U11 **Bridger** Montana, NW USA
18 J17 **Bridgeton** New Jersey, NE USA
180 J14 **Bridgetown** Western Australia
45 Y14 **Bridgetown** ● (Barbados) SW Barbados
183 P17 **Bridgewater** Tasmania, SE Australia
13 P16 **Bridgewater** Nova Scotia, SE Canada
19 P12 **Bridgewater** Massachusetts, NE USA
29 Q11 **Bridgewater** South Dakota, N USA
21 U5 **Bridgewater** Virginia, NE USA
19 P8 **Bridgton** Maine, NE USA
97 K23 **Bridgwater** SW England, UK
97 K22 **Bridgwater Bay** *bay* SW England, UK
97 O16 **Bridlington** E England, UK
97 O16 **Bridlington Bay** *bay* E England, UK
183 P15 **Bridport** Tasmania, SE Australia
97 K24 **Bridport** S England, UK
103 O5 **Brie** *cultural region* N France
Brieg *see* Brzeg
Briel *see* Brielle
98 G12 **Brielle** *var.* Briel, Bril, *Eng.* The Brill. Zuid-Holland, SW Netherlands
108 E9 **Brienz** Bern, C Switzerland
108 E9 **Brienzer See** ◎ SW Switzerland
Bries/Briesen *see* Brezno
Brietzig *see* Brzesko
103 S4 **Briey** Meurthe-et-Moselle, NE France
108 E10 **Brig** *Fr.* Brigue, *It.* Briga. Valais, SW Switzerland
Briga *see* Brig
101 G24 **Brigach** ≈ S Germany
18 K17 **Brigantine** New Jersey, NE USA
Brigantio *see* Briançon
Brigantium *see* Bregenz
Brigels *see* Breil
25 S9 **Briggs** Texas, SW USA
36 L1 **Brigham City** Utah, W USA
14 J15 **Brighton** Ontario, SE Canada
97 O23 **Brighton** SE England, UK
37 T4 **Brighton** Colorado, C USA
30 K15 **Brighton** Illinois, N USA
103 T16 **Brignoles** Var, SE France
Brigue *see* Brig
105 O7 **Brihuega** Castilla-La Mancha, C Spain
112 A10 **Brijuni** *It.* Brioni. *island group* NW Croatia
76 G12 **Brikama** W Gambia
Bril *see* Brielle
Brill, The *see* Brielle
101 G15 **Brilon** Nordrhein-Westfalen, W Germany
Brinceni *see* Briceni
107 Q18 **Brindisi** *anc.* Brundisium, Brundusium. Puglia, SE Italy
27 W11 **Brinkley** Arkansas, C USA
Brioni *see* Brijuni
103 P12 **Brioude** *anc.* Brivas. Haute-Loire, C France
Briovera *see* St-Lô
183 U2 **Brisbane** *state capital* Queensland, E Australia
183 V2 **Brisbane** ✈ Queensland, E Australia
25 P2 **Briscoe** Texas, SW USA
106 H10 **Brisighella** Emilia-Romagna, C Italy
108 G11 **Brissago** Ticino, S Switzerland
97 K22 **Bristol** *anc.* Bricgstow. SW England, UK
18 M12 **Bristol** Connecticut, NE USA
23 R9 **Bristol** Florida, SE USA
19 N9 **Bristol** New Hampshire, NE USA
29 Q8 **Bristol** South Dakota, N USA
21 P8 **Bristol** Tennessee, S USA
18 M8 **Bristol** Vermont, NE USA
39 N14 **Bristol Bay** *bay* Alaska, USA
97 I22 **Bristol Channel** *inlet* England/Wales, UK
35 W14 **Bristol Lake** ◎ California, W USA
27 P10 **Bristow** Oklahoma, C USA
86 C10 **Britain** *var.* Great Britain. *island* UK
Britannia Minor *see* Bretagne
10 L12 **British Columbia** *Fr.* Colombie-Britannique. ◈ *province* SW Canada
British Guiana *see* Guyana
British Honduras *see* Belize
173 Q7 **British Indian Ocean Territory** ◇ *UK dependent territory* C Indian Ocean
86 B9 **British Isles** *island group* NW Europe
10 I1 **British Mountains** ⛰ Yukon Territory, NW Canada
British North Borneo *see* Sabah
British Solomon Islands Protectorate *see* Solomon Islands
45 S8 **British Virgin Islands** *var.* Virgin Islands. ◇ *UK dependent territory* E West Indies
83 J21 **Brits** North-West, N South Africa
83 H24 **Britstown** Northern Cape, W South Africa
14 F12 **Britt** Ontario, S Canada
29 V12 **Britt** Iowa, C USA
Brittany *see* Bretagne
29 Q7 **Britton** South Dakota, N USA
Briva Curretia *see* Brive-la-Gaillarde
Briva Isarae *see* Pontoise
Brivas *see* Brioude
Brive *see* Brive-la-Gaillarde
102 M12 **Brive-la-Gaillarde** *prev.* Brive; *anc.* Briva Curretia. Corrèze, C France
105 O4 **Briviesca** Castilla-León, N Spain
Brixen *see* Bressanone
Brixia *see* Brescia
145 S15 **Brlik** *var.* Novotroickoje, Novotroitskoye. Zhambyl, SE Kazakhstan
Brněnský Kraj *see* Jihomoravský Kraj
111 G18 **Brno** *Ger.* Brünn. Jihomoravský Kraj, SE Czech Republic
96 G7 **Broad Bay** *bay* NW Scotland, UK
25 X8 **Broaddus** Texas, SW USA
183 O12 **Broadford** Victoria, SE Australia
96 G9 **Broadford** N Scotland, UK
96 J13 **Broad Law** ▲ S Scotland, UK
23 U3 **Broad River** ≈ Georgia, SE USA
21 N8 **Broad River** ≈ North Carolina/South Carolina, SE USA
181 Y8 **Broadsound Range** ⛰ Queensland, E Australia
33 X11 **Broadus** Montana, NW USA
21 U4 **Broadway** Virginia, NE USA
118 E9 **Brocēni** Saldus, SW Latvia
9 U11 **Brochet** Manitoba, C Canada
9 U10 **Brochet, Lac** ◎ Manitoba, C Canada
15 S5 **Brochet, Lac au** ◎ Québec, SE Canada
101 K14 **Brocken** ▲ C Germany
19 O12 **Brockton** Massachusetts, NE USA
14 L14 **Brockville** Ontario, SE Canada
18 D13 **Brockway** Pennsylvania, NE USA
Brod/Bród *see* Slavonski Brod
9 N5 **Brodeur Peninsula** *peninsula* Baffin Island, Nunavut, NE Canada
96 H13 **Brodick** W Scotland, UK
Brod na Savi *see* Slavonski Brod
110 K9 **Brodnica** *Ger.* Buddenbrock. Kujawski-pomorskie, C Poland
112 G10 **Brod-Posavina** *off.* Brodsko-Posavska Županija. ◈ *province* NE Croatia
Brodsko-Posavska Županija *see* Brod-Posavina
116 J5 **Brody** L'vivs'ka Oblast', NW Ukraine
98 I10 **Broek-in-Waterland** Noord-Holland, C Netherlands
32 L13 **Brogan** Oregon, NW USA
110 N10 **Brok** Mazowieckie, C Poland
27 P9 **Broken Arrow** Oklahoma, C USA
183 T9 **Broken Bay** *bay* New South Wales, SE Australia
29 N15 **Broken Bow** Nebraska, C USA
27 R13 **Broken Bow** Oklahoma, C USA
27 R12 **Broken Bow Lake** ⊠ Oklahoma, C USA
182 L6 **Broken Hill** New South Wales, SE Australia
173 S10 **Broken Ridge** *undersea feature* S Indian Ocean
186 C6 **Broken Water Bay** *bay* W Bismarck Sea
55 W10 **Brokopondo** Brokopondo, NE Suriname
55 W10 **Brokopondo** ◈ *district* C Suriname
Bromberg *see* Bydgoszcz
95 L22 **Bromölla** Skåne, S Sweden
97 L20 **Bromsgrove** W England, UK
95 G20 **Brønderslev** Nordjylland, N Denmark
106 D8 **Broni** Lombardia, N Italy
10 K11 **Bronlund Peak** ▲ British Columbia, W Canada
93 F14 **Brønnøysund** Nordland, C Norway
23 V10 **Bronson** Florida, SE USA
31 Q11 **Bronson** Michigan, N USA
25 X8 **Bronson** Texas, SW USA
107 L24 **Bronte** Sicilia, Italy, C Mediterranean Sea
25 P8 **Bronte** Texas, SW USA
25 Y9 **Brookeland** Texas, SW USA
170 M7 **Brooke's Point** Palawan, W Philippines
27 T3 **Brookfield** Missouri, C USA
22 K7 **Brookhaven** Mississippi, S USA
32 E16 **Brookings** Oregon, NW USA
29 R10 **Brookings** South Dakota, N USA
29 W14 **Brooklyn** Iowa, C USA
29 U8 **Brooklyn Park** Minnesota, N USA
21 U7 **Brookneal** Virginia, NE USA
9 R16 **Brooks** Alberta, SW Canada
25 V11 **Brookshire** Texas, SW USA
38 L8 **Brooks Mountain** ▲ Alaska, USA
38 M11 **Brooks Range** ⛰ Alaska, USA
31 O12 **Brookston** Indiana, N USA
23 V11 **Brooksville** Florida, SE USA
23 N4 **Brooksville** Mississippi, S USA
180 J13 **Brookton** Western Australia
31 Q14 **Brookville** Indiana, N USA
18 D13 **Brookville** Pennsylvania, NE USA
31 Q14 **Brookville Lake** ⊠ Indiana, N USA
180 K5 **Broome** Western Australia
37 S4 **Broomfield** Colorado, C USA
Broos *see* Orăștie
96 J7 **Brora** N Scotland, UK
96 I7 **Brora** ≈ N Scotland, UK
95 F23 **Brørup** Ribe, W Denmark
95 L23 **Brösarp** Skåne, S Sweden
116 J9 **Broșteni** Suceava, NE Romania
102 M6 **Brou** Eure-et-Loir, C France
Broucsella *see* Brussel/Bruxelles
Broughton Bay *see* Tongjosŏn-man
9 R5 **Broughton Island** Nunavut, NE Canada
138 G7 **Broummâna** C Lebanon
22 I9 **Broussard** Louisiana, S USA
98 E13 **Brouwersdam** *dam* SW Netherlands
98 E13 **Brouwershaven** Zeeland, SW Netherlands
117 P4 **Brovary** Kyyivs'ka Oblast', N Ukraine
95 G20 **Brovst** Nordjylland, N Denmark
31 S8 **Brown City** Michigan, N USA
24 M6 **Brownfield** Texas, SW USA
33 Q7 **Browning** Montana, NW USA
33 R6 **Brown, Mount** ▲ Montana, NW USA
0 M9 **Browns Bank** *undersea feature* NW Atlantic Ocean
31 O14 **Brownsburg** Indiana, N USA
18 J16 **Browns Mills** New Jersey, NE USA
44 J12 **Browns Town** C Jamaica
31 P15 **Brownstown** Indiana, N USA
29 R8 **Browns Valley** Minnesota, N USA
20 K7 **Brownsville** Kentucky, S USA
20 F9 **Brownsville** Tennessee, S USA
25 T17 **Brownsville** Texas, SW USA
55 W10 **Brownsweg** Brokopondo, C Suriname
29 U9 **Brownton** Minnesota, N USA
19 R5 **Brownville Junction** Maine, NE USA
25 R8 **Brownwood** Texas, SW USA
25 R8 **Brownwood Lake** ⊠ Texas, SW USA
104 I9 **Brozas** Extremadura, W Spain
119 M18 **Brozha** Mahilyowskaya Voblasts', E Belarus
103 O2 **Bruay-en-Artois** Pas-de-Calais, N France
103 P2 **Bruay-sur-l'Escaut** Nord, N France
14 F13 **Bruce Peninsula** *peninsula* Ontario, S Canada
20 H9 **Bruceton** Tennessee, S USA
25 T9 **Bruceville** Texas, SW USA
101 G21 **Bruchsal** Baden-Württemberg, SW Germany
109 Q7 **Bruck** Salzburg, NW Austria
Bruck *see* Bruck an der Mur
109 Y4 **Bruck an der Leitha** Niederösterreich, NE Austria
109 V7 **Bruck an der Mur** *var.* Bruck. Steiermark, C Austria
101 M24 **Bruckmühl** Bayern, SE Germany
168 E7 **Brueuh, Pulau** *island* NW Indonesia
Bruges *see* Brugge
108 F6 **Brugg** Aargau, NW Switzerland
99 C16 **Brugge** *Fr.* Bruges. West-Vlaanderen, NW Belgium
109 R9 **Bruggen** Kärnten, S Austria
101 E16 **Brühl** Nordrhein-Westfalen, W Germany
99 F14 **Bruinisse** Zeeland, SW Netherlands
169 R9 **Bruit, Pulau** *island* East Malaysia
14 K10 **Brûlé, Lac** ◎ Québec, SE Canada
30 M4 **Brule River** ≈ Michigan/Wisconsin, N USA
99 H23 **Brûly** Namur, S Belgium
59 N17 **Brumado** Bahia, E Brazil
98 M11 **Brummen** Gelderland, E Netherlands
94 H13 **Brumunddal** Hedmark, S Norway
23 Q6 **Brundidge** Alabama, S USA
Brundisium/Brundusium *see* Brindisi
33 N15 **Bruneau River** ≈ Idaho, NW USA
Bruneck *see* Brunico
169 T8 **Brunei** *off.* Sultanate of Brunei, *Mal.* Negara Brunei Darussalam. ◆ *monarchy* SE Asia
169 T7 **Brunei Bay** *var.* Teluk Brunei. *bay* N Brunei
Brunei, Sultanate of *see* Brunei
Brunei, Teluk *see* Brunei Bay
Brunei Town *see* Bandar Seri Begawan
106 H5 **Brunico** *Ger.* Bruneck. Trentino-Alto Adige, N Italy
Brünn *see* Brno
185 G17 **Brunner, Lake** ◎ South Island, New Zealand
99 M18 **Brunssum** Limburg, SE Netherlands
23 W7 **Brunswick** Georgia, SE USA
19 Q8 **Brunswick** Maine, NE USA
21 V3 **Brunswick** Maryland, NE USA
27 T3 **Brunswick** Missouri, C USA
31 T11 **Brunswick** Ohio, N USA
Brunswick *see* Braunschweig
63 H24 **Brunswick, Península** *headland* S Chile
111 H17 **Bruntál** *Ger.* Freudenthal. Moravskoslezský Kraj, E Czech Republic
195 N3 **Brunt Ice Shelf** *ice shelf* Antarctica
Brusa *see* Bursa
37 U3 **Brush** Colorado, C USA
42 M5 **Brus Laguna** Gracias a Dios, E Honduras
60 K13 **Brusque** Santa Catarina, S Brazil
Brussa *see* Bursa
99 E18 **Brussel** *var.* Brussels, *Fr.* Bruxelles, *Ger.* Brüssel; *anc.* Broucsella. ● (Belgium) Brussels, C Belgium *see also* Bruxelles
Brüssel *see* Brussel/Bruxelles
Brussel/Brussels *see* Brussel/Bruxelles
Brussels Brussel/Bruxelles
117 O5 **Brusyliv** Zhytomyrs'ka Oblast', N Ukraine
183 Q12 **Bruthen** Victoria, SE Australia
Bruttium *see* Calabria
Brüx *see* Most
99 E18 **Bruxelles** *var.* Brussels, *Dut.* Brussel, *Ger.* Brüssel; *anc.* Broucsella. ● Brussels, C Belgium *see also* Brussel
Bruxelles *see* Brussel
54 J7 **Bruzual** Apure, W Venezuela
31 Q11 **Bryan** Ohio, N USA
25 U10 **Bryan** Texas, SW USA
194 J4 **Bryan Coast** *physical region* Antarctica
122 L11 **Bryanka** Krasnoyarskiy Kray, C Russian Federation
117 Y7 **Bryanka** Luhans'ka Oblast', E Ukraine
182 J8 **Bryan, Mount** ▲ South Australia
126 I6 **Bryansk** Bryanskaya Oblast', W Russian Federation
126 H6 **Bryanskaya Oblast'** ◈ *province* W Russian Federation
194 J5 **Bryant, Cape** *headland* Antarctica
27 U8 **Bryant Creek** ≈ Missouri, C USA
36 K8 **Bryce Canyon** *canyon* Utah, W USA
119 O15 **Bryli** *Rus.* Bryli. Mahilyowskaya Voblasts', E Belarus
95 C17 **Bryne** Rogaland, S Norway
25 R6 **Bryson** Texas, SW USA
21 N10 **Bryson City** North Carolina, SE USA
14 K11 **Bryson, Lac** ◎ Québec, SE Canada
126 K13 **Bryukhovetskaya** Krasnodarskiy Kray, SW Russian Federation
111 H15 **Brzeg** *Ger.* Brieg; *anc.* Civitas Altae Ripae. Opolskie, S Poland
111 G14 **Brzeg Dolny** *Ger.* Dyhernfurth. Dolnośląskie, SW Poland
Brześć Litewski/Brześć nad Bugiem *see* Brest
111 L17 **Brzesko** *Ger.* Brietzig. Małopolskie, SE Poland
Brzeżany *see* Berezhany
110 K12 **Brzeziny** Łódzkie, C Poland
Brzostowica Wielka *see* Vyalikaya Byerastavitsa
111 O17 **Brzozów** Podkarpackie, SE Poland
Bsharrī/Bsherri *see* Bcharré
187 X14 **Bua** Vanua Levu, N Fiji
95 J20 **Bua** Halland, S Sweden
82 M13 **Bua** ≈ C Malawi
Bua *see* Čiovo
81 L18 **Bu'aale** *It.* Buale. Jubbada Dhexe, SW Somalia
Buache, Mount *see* Mutunte, Mount
189 Q8 **Buada Lagoon** *lagoon* Nauru, C Pacific Ocean
186 M8 **Buala** Santa Isabel, E Solomon Islands
Buale *see* Bu'aale
190 H1 **Buariki** *atoll* Tungaru, W Kiribati
167 Q10 **Bua Yai** *var.* Ban Bua Yai. Nakhon Ratchasima, E Thailand
75 P8 **Bu'ayrāt al Ḩasūn** *var.* Buwayrāt al Hasūn. C Libya
76 H13 **Buba** S Guinea-Bissau
171 P11 **Bubaa** Sulawesi, N Indonesia
81 D20 **Bubanza** NW Burundi
83 K18 **Bubi** *prev.* Bubye. ≈ S Zimbabwe
142 L11 **Būbīyan, Jazīrat** *island* E Kuwait
Bublitz *see* Bobolice
Bubye *see* Bubi
187 Y13 **Buca** *prev.* Mbutha. Vanua Levu, N Fiji
136 F16 **Bucak** Burdur, SW Turkey
54 G8 **Bucaramanga** Santander, N Colombia
107 M18 **Buccino** Campania, S Italy
116 K9 **Bucecea** Botoșani, NE Romania
116 J6 **Buchach** *Pol.* Buczacz. Ternopil's'ka Oblast', W Ukraine
183 Q12 **Buchan** Victoria, SE Australia
76 J17 **Buchanan** *prev.* Grand Bassa. SW Liberia
23 R3 **Buchanan** Georgia, SE USA
31 O11 **Buchanan** Michigan, N USA
21 T6 **Buchanan** Virginia, NE USA
25 R10 **Buchanan Dam** Texas, SW USA
25 R10 **Buchanan, Lake** ⊠ Texas, SW USA
96 L8 **Buchan Ness** *headland* NE Scotland, UK
13 T12 **Buchans** Newfoundland and Labrador, SE Canada
Bucharest *see* București
101 H20 **Buchen** Baden-Württemberg, SW Germany
100 I10 **Buchholz in der Nordheide** Niedersachsen, NW Germany
108 F7 **Buchs** Aargau, N Switzerland
108 I8 **Buchs** Sankt Gallen, NE Switzerland
100 H13 **Bückeburg** Niedersachsen, NW Germany
36 K14 **Buckeye** Arizona, SW USA
Buckeye State *see* Ohio
21 S4 **Buckhannon** West Virginia, NE USA
25 T9 **Buckholts** Texas, SW USA
96 K8 **Buckie** NE Scotland, UK
14 M12 **Buckingham** Québec, SE Canada
21 U6 **Buckingham** Virginia, NE USA
97 N21 **Buckinghamshire** *cultural region* SE England, UK
39 N8 **Buckland** Alaska, USA
182 G7 **Buckleboo** South Australia
26 K7 **Bucklin** Kansas, C USA
27 T3 **Bucklin** Missouri, C USA
36 I12 **Buckskin Mountains** ⛰ Arizona, SW USA
19 R7 **Bucksport** Maine, NE USA
82 A9 **Buco Zau** Cabinda, NW Angola
Bu Craa *see* Bou Craa
116 K14 **București** *Eng.* Bucharest, *Ger.* Bukarest, *prev.* Altenburg; *anc.* Cetatea Damboviței. ● (Romania) București, S Romania
31 S12 **Bucyrus** Ohio, N USA
Buczacz *see* Buchach
94 E9 **Bud** Møre og Romsdal, S Norway
25 S11 **Buda** Texas, SW USA
119 O18 **Buda-Kashalyova** *Rus.* Buda-Koshelëvo. Homyel'skaya Voblasts', SE Belarus
Buda-Koshelëvo *see* Buda-Kashalyova
166 L4 **Budalin** Sagaing, C Myanmar (Burma)
111 J22 **Budapest** *off.* Budapest Főváros, *SCr.* Budimpešta. ● (Hungary) Pest, N Hungary
Budapest Főváros *see* Budapest
152 K11 **Budaun** Uttar Pradesh, N India
141 O9 **Budayyi'ah** *oasis* C Saudi Arabia
195 Y12 **Budd Coast** *physical region* Antarctica
Buddenbrock *see* Brodnica
107 C17 **Budduso** Sardegna, Italy, C Mediterranean Sea
97 I23 **Bude** SW England, UK
22 J7 **Bude** Mississippi, S USA
Budějovický Kraj *see* Jihočeský Kraj
99 K16 **Budel** Noord-Brabant, SE Netherlands
100 I8 **Büdelsdorf** Schleswig-Holstein, N Germany
127 O14 **Budënnovsk** Stavropol'skiy Kray, SW Russian Federation
116 K14 **Budești** Călărași, SE Romania
Budge-Budge *see* Baj Baj
Budgewoi *see* Budgewoi Lake
183 T8 **Budgewoi Lake** *var.* Budgewoi. New South Wales, SE Australia
92 I2 **Búdhardalur** Vesturland, W Iceland
Budimpešta *see* Budapest
79 J16 **Budjala** Equateur, NW Dem. Rep. Congo
106 G10 **Budrio** Emilia-Romagna, C Italy
Budslav *see* Budslaw
119 K14 **Budslaw** *Rus.* Budslav. Minskaya Voblasts', N Belarus
Budua *see* Budva
169 R9 **Budu, Tanjung** *cape* East Malaysia
113 J17 **Budva** *It.* Budua. W Montenegro
Budweis *see* České Budějovice
Budyšin *see* Bautzen
79 D16 **Buea** Sud-Ouest, SW Cameroon
103 S13 **Buëch** ≈ SE France
18 J17 **Buena** New Jersey, NE USA
62 K12 **Buena Esperanza** San Luis, C Argentina
54 C11 **Buenaventura** Valle del Cauca, W Colombia
40 I4 **Buenaventura** Chihuahua, N Mexico
57 M18 **Buena Vista** Santa Cruz, C Bolivia
40 G10 **Buenavista** Baja California Sur, W Mexico
37 S5 **Buena Vista** Colorado, C USA
23 S5 **Buena Vista** Georgia, SE USA
21 T6 **Buena Vista** Virginia, NE USA
44 F5 **Buena Vista, Bahia de** *bay* N Cuba
35 R13 **Buena Vista Lake Bed** ◎ California, W USA
105 P8 **Buendía, Embalse de** ⊠ C Spain
63 F16 **Bueno, Río** ≈ S Chile
62 N12 **Buenos Aires** *hist.* Santa Maria del Buen Aire. ● (Argentina) Buenos Aires, E Argentina
43 O15 **Buenos Aires** Puntarenas, SE Costa Rica
61 C20 **Buenos Aires** *off.* Provincia de Buenos Aires. ◈ *province* E Argentina
63 H19 **Buenos Aires, Lago** *var.* Lago General Carrera. ◎ Argentina/Chile
Buenos Aires, Provincia de *see* Buenos Aires
54 C13 **Buesaco** Nariño, SW Colombia
29 U8 **Buffalo** Minnesota, N USA
26 T6 **Buffalo** Missouri, C USA
18 D10 **Buffalo** New York, NE USA
27 K8 **Buffalo** Oklahoma, C USA
28 J7 **Buffalo** South Dakota, N USA
25 V8 **Buffalo** Texas, SW USA
33 W12 **Buffalo** Wyoming, C USA
29 U11 **Buffalo Center** Iowa, C USA
24 M3 **Buffalo Lake** ⊠ Texas, SW USA
30 K7 **Buffalo Lake** ⊠ Wisconsin, N USA
9 S12 **Buffalo Narrows** Saskatchewan, C Canada
27 U9 **Buffalo River** ≈ Arkansas, C USA
29 R5 **Buffalo River** ≈ Minnesota, N USA
20 I10 **Buffalo River** ≈ Tennessee, S USA
30 J6 **Buffalo River** ≈ Wisconsin, N USA
44 L12 **Buff Bay** E Jamaica
23 T3 **Buford** Georgia, SE USA
28 J3 **Buford** North Dakota, N USA
33 Y17 **Buford** Wyoming, C USA
116 J14 **Buftea** Ilfov, S Romania
84 I9 **Bug** *Bel.* Zakhodni Buh, *Eng.* Western Bug, *Rus.* Zapadnyy Bug, *Ukr.* Zakhidnyy Buh. ≈ E Europe
54 D11 **Buga** Valle del Cauca, W Colombia
Buga *see* Dörvöljin
103 O17 **Bugarach, Pic du** ▲ S France
162 F8 **Bugat** *var.* Bayangol. Govĭ-Altay, SW Mongolia
146 B12 **Bugdaýly** *Rus.* Bugdayly. Balkan Welaýaty, W Turkmenistan
Bugdayly *see* Bugdaýly
Buggs Island Lake *see* John H. Kerr Reservoir
Bughotu *see* Santa Isabel
171 O14 **Bugingkalo** Sulawesi, C Indonesia
64 P6 **Bugio** *island* Madeira, Portugal, NE Atlantic Ocean
92 M8 **Bugøynes** Finnmark, N Norway
125 Q3 **Bugrino** Nenetskiy Avtonomnyy Okrug, NW Russian Federation
127 T5 **Bugul'ma** Respublika Tatarstan, W Russian Federation
Bügür *see* Luntai
127 T6 **Buguruslan** Orenburgskaya Oblast', W Russian Federation
159 R9 **Buh He** ≈ C China
101 F22 **Bühl** Baden-Württemberg, SW Germany
33 O15 **Buhl** Idaho, NW USA

◆ Country ● Country Capital ◇ Dependent Territory ○ Dependent Territory Capital ◈ Administrative Regions ✈ International Airport ▲ Mountain ⛰ Mountain Range ▲ Volcano ≈ River ◎ Lake ⊠ Reservoir

116 *K10* **Buhuşi** Bacău, E Romania
Buie d'Istria *see* Buje
97 *J20* **Builth Wells** E Wales, UK
186 *J8* **Buin** Bougainville Island, NE Papua New Guinea
108 *J9* **Buin, Piz** ▲ Austria/Switzerland
127 *Q4* **Buinsk** Chuvashskaya Respublika, W Russian Federation
127 *Q4* **Buinsk** Respublika Tatarstan, W Russian Federation
163 *R8* **Buir Nur** *Mong.* Buyr Nuur. ◎ China/Mongolia *see also* Buyr Nuur
Buir Nur *see* Buyr Nuur
98 *M5* **Buitenpost** *Fris.* Bûtenpost. Friesland, N Netherlands
Buitenzorg *see* Bogor
83 *F19* **Buitepos** Omaheke, E Namibia
105 *N7* **Buitrago del Lozoya** Madrid, C Spain
Buj *see* Buy
104 *M13* **Bujalance** Andalucía, S Spain
113 *O17* **Bujanovac** Kosovo, SE Serbia
105 *S6* **Bujaraloz** Aragón, NE Spain
112 *A9* **Buje** *It.* Buie d'Istria. Istra, NW Croatia
Bujnurd *see* Bojnūrd
81 *D21* **Bujumbura** *prev.* Usumbura. ● (Burundi) W Burundi
81 *D20* **Bujumbura** ✈ W Burundi
159 *N11* **Buka Daban** *var.* Bukadaban Feng. ▲ C China
Bukadaban Feng *see* Buka Daban
186 *J6* **Buka Island** *island* NE Papua New Guinea
81 *F18* **Bukakata** S Uganda
79 *N24* **Bukama** Katanga, SE Dem. Rep. Congo
142 *J4* **Būkān** *var.* Bowkān. Āzarbāyjān-e Gharbī, NW Iran
Bukantau, Gory *see* Bo'kantov Tog'lari
Bukantau, Gory *see* Bo'kantov Tog'lari
Bukarest *see* Bucureşti
79 *O19* **Bukavu** *prev.* Costermansville. Sud Kivu, E Dem. Rep. Congo
81 *F21* **Bukene** Tabora, NW Tanzania
141 *W8* **Bū Khābī** *var.* Bakhābī. NW Oman
Bukhara *see* Buxoro
Bukharskaya Oblast' *see* Buxoro Viloyati
168 *M14* **Bukitkemuning** Sumatera, W Indonesia
168 *I11* **Bukittinggi** *prev.* Fort de Kock. Sumatera, W Indonesia
111 *L21* **Bükk** ▲▲ NE Hungary
81 *F19* **Bukoba** Kagera, NW Tanzania
113 *N20* **Bukovo** S FYR Macedonia
108 *G6* **Bülach** Zürich, NW Switzerland
Bülaevo *see* Bulayevo
Bulag *see* Tünel, Hövsgöl, Mongolia
Bulag *see* Möngönmorīt, Töv, Mongolia
Bulagiyn Denj *see* Bulgan
183 *U7* **Bulahdelah** New South Wales, SE Australia
171 *P4* **Bulan** Luzon, N Philippines
137 *N11* **Bulancak** Giresun, N Turkey
152 *J10* **Bulandshahr** Uttar Pradesh, N India
137 *R14* **Bulanık** Muş, E Turkey
127 *V7* **Bulanovo** Orenburgskaya Oblast', W Russian Federation
83 *J17* **Bulawayo** *var.* Buluwayo. Bulawayo, SW Zimbabwe
83 *J17* **Bulawayo** ✈ Matabeleland North, SW Zimbabwe
145 *Q6* **Bulayevo** *Kaz.* Bülaevo. Severnyy Kazakhstan, N Kazakhstan
136 *D15* **Buldan** Denizli, SW Turkey
154 *G12* **Buldāna** Mahārāshtra, C India
38 *E16* **Buldir Island** *island* Aleutian Islands, Alaska, USA
Buldur *see* Burdur
162 *I8* **Bulgan** *var.* Bulagiyn Denj. Arhangay, C Mongolia
162 *D7* **Bulgan** *var.* Jargalant. Bayan-Ölgiy, W Mongolia
162 *K6* **Bulgan** Bulgan, N Mongolia
162 *F7* **Bulgan** *var.* Bürenhayrhan. Hovd, W Mongolia
162 *J10* **Bulgan** Ömnögovĭ, S Mongolia
162 *J7* **Bulgan** ◈ *province* N Mongolia
Bulgan Bayan-Öndör, Bayanhongor, Mongolia
Bulgan Bayan-Öndör, W China
Bulgan *see* Bayan-Öndör
Bulgan *see* Darvi, Hovd, Mongolia
Bulgan Tsagaan-Üür, Hövsgöl, Mongolia
Bulgan *see* Bayan-Öndör
114 *H10* **Bulgaria** *off.* Republic of Bulgaria, *Bul.* Bŭlgariya; *prev.* People's Republic of Bulgaria. ◆ *republic* SE Europe
Bulgaria, People's Republic of *see* Bulgaria
Bulgaria, Republic of *see* Bulgaria
Bŭlgariya *see* Bulgaria
114 *L9* **Bŭlgarka** ▲ E Bulgaria
171 *S11* **Buli** Pulau Halmahera, E Indonesia
171 *S11* **Buli, Teluk** *bay* Pulau Halmahera, E Indonesia
160 *J13* **Buliu He** ~ S China
Bullange *see* Büllingen
Bulla, Ostrov *see* Xärä Zirä Adası
104 *M11* **Bullaque** ~ C Spain
105 *Q13* **Bullas** Murcia, SE Spain
80 *M12* **Bullaxaar** Woqooyi Galbeed, NW Somalia
108 *C9* **Bulle** Fribourg, SW Switzerland
185 *G15* **Buller** ~ South Island, New Zealand
183 *P12* **Buller, Mount** ▲ Victoria, SE Australia
36 *H11* **Bullhead City** Arizona, SW USA
99 *N21* **Büllingen** *Fr.* Bullange. Liège, E Belgium
Bullion State *see* Missouri
21 *T14* **Bull Island** *island* South Carolina, SE USA
182 *M4* **Bulloo River Overflow** *wetland* New South Wales, SE Australia
184 *M12* **Bulls** Manawatu-Wanganui, North Island, New Zealand
21 *T14* **Bulls Bay** *bay* South Carolina, SE USA
27 *U9* **Bull Shoals Lake** ⊠ Arkansas/Missouri, C USA
181 *Q2* **Bulman** Northern Territory, N Australia
162 *I6* **Bulnayn Nuruu** ▲▲ N Mongolia
171 *O11* **Bulowa, Gunung** ▲ Sulawesi, N Indonesia
Bulqiza *see* Bulqizë
113 *L19* **Bulqizë** *var.* Bulqiza. Dibër, C Albania
Bulsar *see* Valsād
171 *N14* **Bulukumba** *prev.* Boeloekoemba. Sulawesi, C Indonesia
79 *I21* **Bulungu** Bandundu, SW Dem. Rep. Congo
147 *O11* **Bulung'ur** *Rus.* Bulungur; *prev.* Krasnogvardeysk. Samarqand Viloyati, C Uzbekistan
Bulungur *see* Bulung'ur
Buluwayo *see* Bulawayo
79 *K17* **Bumba** Equateur, N Dem. Rep. Congo
121 *R12* **Bumbah, Khalīj al** *gulf* N Libya
Bumbat *see* Bayan-Öndör
81 *F19* **Bumbire Island** *island* N Tanzania
169 *V8* **Bum Bun, Pulau** *island* East Malaysia
81 *J17* **Buna** North Eastern, NE Kenya
25 *Y10* **Buna** Texas, SW USA
Bunab *see* Bonāb
Bunai *see* M'bunai
147 *S13* **Bunay** S Tajikistan
180 *I13* **Bunbury** Western Australia
97 *E14* **Buncrana** *Ir.* Bun Cranncha. NW Ireland
Bun Cranncha *see* Buncrana
181 *Z9* **Bundaberg** Queensland, E Australia
183 *T5* **Bundarra** New South Wales, SE Australia
100 *G13* **Bünde** Nordrhein-Westfalen, NW Germany
152 *H13* **Būndi** Rājasthān, N India
Bun Dobhráin *see* Bundoran
97 *D15* **Bundoran** *Ir.* Bun Dobhráin. NW Ireland
113 *K18* **Bunë** *SCr.* Bojana. ~ Albania/Montenegro *see also* Bojana
Bunë *see* Bojana
171 *Q8* **Bunga** ~ Mindanao, S Philippines
168 *I12* **Bungalaut, Selat** *strait* W Indonesia
167 *R8* **Bung Kan** Nong Khai, E Thailand
181 *N4* **Bungle Bungle Range** ▲▲ Western Australia
82 *C10* **Bungo** Uíge, NW Angola
81 *G18* **Bungoma** Western, W Kenya
164 *F15* **Bungo-suidō** *strait* SW Japan
164 *E14* **Bungo-Takada** Ōita, Kyūshū, SW Japan
100 *K8* **Bungsberg** *hill* N Germany
Bungur *see* Bunyu
79 *P17* **Bunia** Orientale, NE Dem. Rep. Congo
35 *U6* **Bunker Hill** ▲ Nevada, W USA
22 *I7* **Bunkie** Louisiana, S USA
23 *X10* **Bunnell** Florida, SE USA
105 *S10* **Buñol** País Valenciano, E Spain
98 *K11* **Bunschoten** Utrecht, C Netherlands
136 *K14* **Bünyan** Kayseri, C Turkey
169 *W8* **Bunyu** *var.* Bungur. Borneo, N Indonesia
169 *W8* **Bunyu, Pulau** *island* N Indonesia
Bunzlau *see* Bolesławiec
Buoddobohki *see* Patoniva
123 *P7* **Buorkhaya Guba** *bay* N Russian Federation
171 *Z15* **Bupul** Papua, E Indonesia
81 *K19* **Bura** Coast, SE Kenya
80 *P12* **Buraan** Bari, N Somalia
Būrābay *see* Borovoye
Buraida *see* Buraydah
Buraimi *see* Al Buraymī
145 *Y11* **Buran** Vostochnyy Kazakhstan, E Kazakhstan
158 *G15* **Burang** Xizang Zizhiqu, W China
Burao *see* Burco
138 *H8* **Burāq** Dar'ā, S Syria
141 *O6* **Buraydah** *var.* Buraida. Al Qaşim, N Saudi Arabia
35 *S15* **Burbank** California, W USA
31 *N11* **Burbank** Illinois, N USA
183 *Q8* **Burcher** New South Wales, SE Australia
80 *N13* **Burco** *var.* Burao, Bur'o. Togdheer, NW Somalia
162 *K8* **Bürd** *var.* Ongon. Övörhangay, C Mongolia
146 *L13* **Burdalyk** Lebap Welaýaty, E Turkmenistan
181 *W6* **Burdekin River** ~ Queensland, NE Australia
27 *O7* **Burden** Kansas, C USA
Burdigala *see* Bordeaux
136 *E15* **Burdur** *var.* Buldur. Burdur, SW Turkey
136 *E15* **Burdur** *var.* Buldur. ◈ *province* SW Turkey
136 *E15* **Burdur Gölü** *salt lake* SW Turkey
65 *H21* **Burdwood Bank** *undersea feature* SW Atlantic Ocean
80 *I12* **Burē** Āmhara, N Ethiopia
80 *H13* **Burē** Oromo, C Ethiopia
93 *J15* **Bureå** Västerbotten, N Sweden
162 *K7* **Büreghangay** *var.* Darhan. Bulgan, C Mongolia
101 *G14* **Büren** Nordrhein-Westfalen, W Germany
162 *L8* **Büren** *var* Bayantöhöm. Töv, C Mongolia
162 *K6* **Bürengiyn Nuruu** ▲▲ N Mongolia
Bürenhayrhan *see* Bulgan
162 *I6* **Bürentogtoh** *var.* Bayan. Hövsgol, C Mongolia
Būrewāla *see* Mandi Būrewāla
92 *J9* **Burfjord** Troms, N Norway
100 *L13* **Burg** *var.* Burg an der Ihle, Burg bei Magdeburg. Sachsen-Anhalt, C Germany
Burg an der Ihle *see* Burg
114 *N10* **Burgas** *var.* Bourgas. Burgas, E Bulgaria
114 *M10* **Burgas** ◈ *province* E Bulgaria
114 *N9* **Burgas** ✈ Burgas, E Bulgaria
114 *N10* **Burgaski Zaliv** *gulf* E Bulgaria
114 *M10* **Burgasko Ezero** *lagoon* E Bulgaria
21 *V11* **Burgaw** North Carolina, SE USA
Burg bei Magdeburg *see* Burg
108 *E8* **Burgdorf** Bern, NW Switzerland
109 *Y7* **Burgenland** *off.* Land Burgenland. ◈ *state* SE Austria
13 *S13* **Burgeo** Newfoundland, Newfoundland and Labrador, SE Canada
83 *I24* **Burgersdorp** Eastern Cape, SE South Africa
83 *K20* **Burgersfort** Mpumalanga, NE South Africa
101 *N23* **Burghausen** Bayern, SE Germany
139 *O5* **Burghūth, Sabkhat al** ◎ E Syria
101 *M20* **Burglengenfeld** Bayern, SE Germany
41 *P9* **Burgos** Tamaulipas, C Mexico
105 *N4* **Burgos** Castilla-León, N Spain
105 *N4* **Burgos** ◈ *province* Castilla-León, N Spain
Burgstadlberg *see* Hradiště
95 *P20* **Burgsvik** Gotland, SE Sweden
Burgum *see* Bergum
Burgundy *see* Bourgogne
159 *Q11* **Burhan Budai Shan** ▲▲ C China
136 *B12* **Burhaniye** Balıkesir, W Turkey
154 *G12* **Burhānpur** Madhya Pradesh, C India
127 *W7* **Buribay** Respublika Bashkortostan, W Russian Federation
43 *O17* **Burica, Punta** *headland* Costa Rica/Panama
167 *Q10* **Buriram** *var.* Buri Ram, Puriramya. Buri Ram, E Thailand
Buri Ram *see* Buriram
105 *S10* **Burjassot** País Valenciano, E Spain
81 *N16* **Burka Giibi** Hiiraan, C Somalia
147 *X8* **Burkan** ~ E Kyrgyzstan
25 *R4* **Burkburnett** Texas, SW USA
29 *O12* **Burke** South Dakota, N USA
10 *K15* **Burke Channel** *channel* British Columbia, W Canada
194 *J10* **Burke Island** *island* Antarctica
20 *L7* **Burkesville** Kentucky, S USA
181 *T4* **Burketown** Queensland, NE Australia
25 *Q8* **Burkett** Texas, SW USA
25 *Y9* **Burkeville** Texas, SW USA
21 *V7* **Burkeville** Virginia, NE USA
77 *O12* **Burkina** *off.* Burkina Faso; *prev.* Upper Volta. ◆ *republic* W Africa
Burkina Faso *see* Burkina
194 *L13* **Burks, Cape** *headland* Antarctica
14 *H12* **Burk's Falls** Ontario, S Canada
101 *H23* **Burladingen** Baden-Württemberg, S Germany
25 *T7* **Burleson** Texas, SW USA
33 *P15* **Burley** Idaho, NW USA
144 *G8* **Burlin** Zapadnyy Kazakhstan, NW Kazakhstan
14 *G16* **Burlington** Ontario, S Canada
37 *W4* **Burlington** Colorado, C USA
29 *Y15* **Burlington** Iowa, C USA
27 *P5* **Burlington** Kansas, C USA
21 *T9* **Burlington** North Carolina, SE USA
28 *M3* **Burlington** North Dakota, N USA
18 *L7* **Burlington** Vermont, NE USA
30 *M9* **Burlington** Wisconsin, N USA
27 *Q1* **Burlington Junction** Missouri, C USA
10 *L17* **Burnaby** British Columbia, SW Canada
117 *O12* **Burnas, Ozero** ◎ SW Ukraine
25 *S10* **Burnet** Texas, SW USA
35 *O3* **Burney** California, W USA
183 *O16* **Burnie** Tasmania, SE Australia
97 *L17* **Burnley** NW England, UK
Burnoye *see* Bauyrzhan Momyshuly
153 *R15* **Burnpur** West Bengal, NE India
32 *K14* **Burns** Oregon, NW USA
26 *K11* **Burns Flat** Oklahoma, C USA
20 *M7* **Burnside** Kentucky, S USA
8 *K8* **Burnside** ~ Nunavut, NW Canada
32 *L15* **Burns Junction** Oregon, NW USA
10 *L13* **Burns Lake** British Columbia, SW Canada
29 *V9* **Burnsville** Minnesota, N USA
21 *P9* **Burnsville** North Carolina, SE USA
21 *R4* **Burnsville** West Virginia, NE USA
14 *I13* **Burnt River** ~ Ontario, SE Canada
14 *I11* **Burntroot Lake** ◎ Ontario, SE Canada
9 *W12* **Burntwood** ~ Manitoba, C Canada
Bur'o *see* Burco
158 *L2* **Burqin** Xinjiang Uygur Zizhiqu, NW China
182 *J8* **Burra** South Australia
183 *S9* **Burragorang, Lake** ⊠ New South Wales, SE Australia
96 *K5* **Burray** *island* NE Scotland, UK
113 *L19* **Burrel** *var.* Burreli. Dibër, C Albania
Burreli *see* Burrel
183 *R8* **Burrendong Reservoir** ⊠ New South Wales, SE Australia
183 *R5* **Burren Junction** New South Wales, SE Australia
105 *T9* **Burriana** País Valenciano, E Spain
183 *R10* **Burrinjuck Reservoir** ⊠ New South Wales, SE Australia
36 *J12* **Burro Creek** ~ Arizona, SW USA
40 *M5* **Burro, Serranías del** ▲▲ NW Mexico
62 *K7* **Burruyacú** Tucumán, N Argentina
136 *E12* **Bursa** *var.* Brussa, *prev.* Brusa; *anc.* Prusa. Bursa, NW Turkey
136 *D12* **Bursa** *var.* Brussa, Brussa. ◈ *province* NW Turkey
75 *Y9* **Būr Safāga** *var.* Būr Safājah. E Egypt
Būr Safājah *see* Būr Safāga
Būr Sa'īd *see* Port Said
81 *O14* **Bur Tinle** Nugaal, C Somalia
31 *Q5* **Burt Lake** ◎ Michigan, N USA
118 *H7* **Burtnieks** *var.* Burtnieks Ezers. ◎ N Latvia
Burtnieks Ezers *see* Burtnieks
31 *Q9* **Burton** Michigan, N USA
Burton on Trent *see* Burton upon Trent
97 *M19* **Burton upon Trent** *var.* Burton on Trent, Burton-upon-Trent. C England, UK
93 *J15* **Burträsk** Västerbotten, N Sweden
145 *S14* **Burubaytal** *prev.* Burylbaytal. Zhambyl, SE Kazakhstan
Burujird *see* Borūjerd
Burultokay *see* Fuhai
141 *R15* **Burūm** SE Yemen
Burunday *see* Boralday
81 *D21* **Burundi** *off.* Republic of Burundi; *prev.* Kingdom of Burundi, Urundi. ◆ *republic* C Africa
Burundi, Kingdom of *see* Burundi
Burundi, Republic of *see* Burundi
171 *R13* **Buru, Pulau** *prev.* Boeroe. *island* E Indonesia
77 *T17* **Burutu** Delta, S Nigeria
10 *G7* **Burwash Landing** Yukon Territory, W Canada
29 *O14* **Burwell** Nebraska, C USA
97 *L17* **Bury** NW England, UK
123 *N13* **Buryatiya, Respublika** *prev.* Buryatskaya ASSR. ◈ *autonomous republic* S Russian Federation
Buryatskaya ASSR *see* Buryatiya, Respublika
Burylbaytal *see* Burubaytal
117 *S3* **Buryn'** Sums'ka Oblast', NE Ukraine
97 *P20* **Bury St Edmunds** *hist.* Beodericsworth. E England, UK
114 *G8* **Bŭrziya** ~ NW Bulgaria
106 *D9* **Busalla** Liguria, NW Italy
Busan *see* Pusan
139 *N5* **Buşayrah** Dayr az Zawr, E Syria
Buševa *see* Baba
143 *N12* **Būshehr** *off.* Ostān-e Būshehr. ◈ *province* SW Iran
Būshehr/Bushire *see* Bandar-e Būshehr
Būshehr, Ostān-e *see* Būshehr
25 *N2* **Bushland** Texas, SW USA
30 *J12* **Bushnell** Illinois, N USA
Busi *see* Biševo
81 *G18* **Busia** SE Uganda
Busiasch *see* Buziaş
79 *K16* **Businga** Equateur, NW Dem. Rep. Congo
79 *J18* **Busira** ~ NW Dem. Rep. Congo
116 *I5* **Bus'k** *Rus.* Busk. L'vivs'ka Oblast', W Ukraine
95 *E14* **Buskerud** ◈ *county* S Norway
113 *F14* **Buško Jezero** ⊠ SW Bosnia and Herzegovina
111 *M15* **Busko-Zdrój** Świętokrzyskie, C Poland
Busra *see* Al Başrah, Iraq
Buşrá *see* Buşrá ash Shām, Syria
138 *H9* **Buşrá ash Shām** *var.* Bosora, Bosra, Bozrah, Buşrá. Dar'ā, S Syria
180 *I13* **Busselton** Western Australia
81 *C14* **Busseri** ~ W Sudan
106 *E9* **Busseto** Emilia-Romagna, C Italy
106 *A8* **Bussoleno** Piemonte, NE Italy
Bussora *see* Al Başrah
98 *J10* **Bussum** Noord-Holland, C Netherlands
41 *N7* **Bustamante** Nuevo León, NE Mexico
63 *I23* **Bustamante, Punta** *headland* S Argentina
Bustan *see* Bo'ston
116 *J12* **Buşteni** Prahova, SE Romania
106 *D7* **Busto Arsizio** Lombardia, N Italy
147 *Q10* **Bŭston** *Rus.* Buston. NW Tajikistan
100 *H8* **Büsum** Schleswig-Holstein, N Germany
79 *M16* **Buta** Orientale, N Dem. Rep. Congo
81 *E20* **Butare** *prev.* Astrida. S Rwanda
191 *O2* **Butaritari** *atoll* Tungaru, W Kiribati
Butawal *see* Butwal
96 *H13* **Bute** *cultural region* SW Scotland, UK
162 *K6* **Büteeliyn Nuruu** ▲▲ N Mongolia
10 *L16* **Bute Inlet** *fjord* British Columbia, W Canada
96 *H12* **Bute, Island of** *island* SW Scotland, UK
79 *P18* **Butembo** Nord Kivu, NE Dem. Rep. Congo
Bûtenpost *see* Buitenpost
107 *K25* **Butera** Sicilia, Italy, C Mediterranean Sea
99 *M20* **Bütgenbach** Liège, E Belgium
Butha Qi *see* Zalantun
166 *J5* **Buthidaung** Arakan State, W Myanmar (Burma)
61 *I16* **Butiá** Rio Grande do Sul, S Brazil
81 *F17* **Butiaba** NW Uganda
23 *N6* **Butler** Alabama, S USA
23 *S5* **Butler** Georgia, SE USA
31 *Q11* **Butler** Indiana, N USA
27 *R5* **Butler** Missouri, C USA
18 *B14* **Butler** Pennsylvania, NE USA
194 *K5* **Butler Island** *island* Antarctica
21 *U8* **Butner** North Carolina, SE USA
171 *P14* **Buton, Pulau** *var.* Pulau Butung; *prev.* Boetoeng. *island* C Indonesia
Bütow *see* Bytów
113 *L23* **Butrintit, Liqeni i** ◎ S Albania
23 *N3* **Buttahatchee River** ~ Alabama/Mississippi, S USA
33 *Q10* **Butte** Montana, NW USA
29 *O12* **Butte** Nebraska, C USA
168 *J7* **Butterworth** Pinang, Peninsular Malaysia
83 *J25* **Butterworth** *var.* Gcuwa. Eastern Cape, SE South Africa
13 *O3* **Button Islands** *island group* Nunavut, NE Canada
35 *R13* **Buttonwillow** California, W USA
171 *Q7* **Butuan** *off.* Butuan City. Mindanao, S Philippines
Butuan City *see* Butuan
Butung, Pulau *see* Buton, Pulau
Butuntum *see* Bitonto
126 *M8* **Buturlinovka** Voronezhskaya Oblast', W Russian Federation
153 *O11* **Butwal** *var.* Butawal. Western, C Nepal
101 *G17* **Butzbach** Hessen, W Germany
100 *L9* **Bützow** Mecklenburg-Vorpommern, N Germany
80 *N13* **Buuhoodle** Togdheer, N Somalia
81 *N16* **Buulobarde** *var.* Buulo Berde. Hiiraan, C Somalia Africa
Buulo Berde *see* Buulobarde
80 *P12* **Buuraha Cal Miskaat** ▲▲ NE Somalia
81 *L19* **Buur Gaabo** Jubbada Hoose, S Somalia
99 *M22* **Burgplaatz** ▲ N Luxembourg
162 *H8* **Buutsagaan** *var.* Buyant. Bayanhongor, C Mongolia
Buwayrāt al Ḩasūn *see* Bu'ayrāt al Ḩasūn
146 *L11* **Buxoro** *var.* Bokhara, *Rus.* Bukhara. Buxoro Viloyati, C Uzbekistan
146 *J11* **Buxoro Viloyati** *Rus.* Bukharskaya Oblast'. ◈ *province* C Uzbekistan
100 *I10* **Buxtehude** Niedersachsen, NW Germany
97 *L18* **Buxton** C England, UK
124 *M14* **Buy** *var.* Buj. Kostromskaya Oblast', NW Russian Federation
Buyanbat *see* Jargalant
162 *D6* **Buyant** Bayan-Ölgiy, W Mongolia
Buyant *see* Buutsagaan, Bayanhongor, Mongolia
Buyant *see* Galshar
Buyant Otgon, Dzavhan, Mongolia
Buyant *see* Galshar, Hentiy, Mongolia
163 *N10* **Buyant-Uhaa** Dornogovĭ, SE Mongolia
162 *M7* **Buyant Ukha** ✈ (Ulaanbaatar) Töv, N Mongolia
127 *Q16* **Buynaksk** Respublika Dagestan, SW Russian Federation
119 *L20* **Buynavichy** *Rus.* Buynovichi. Homyel'skaya Voblasts', SE Belarus
Buynovichi *see* Buynavichy
76 *L16* **Buyo** SW Ivory Coast
76 *L16* **Buyo, Lac de** ⊠ W Ivory Coast
163 *R7* **Buyr Nuur** *var.* Buir Nur. ◎ China/Mongolia *see also* Buir Nur
Buyr Nuur *see* Buir Nur
137 *T13* **Büyükağrı Dağı** *var.* Aghri Dagh, Agri Dagi, Koh I Noh, Masis, *Eng.* Great Ararat, Mount Ararat. ▲ E Turkey
137 *R15* **Büyük Çayi** ~ NE Turkey
114 *O13* **Büyük Çekmece** Istanbul, NW Turkey
114 *N12* **Büyükkarıştıran** Kırklareli, NW Turkey
115 *L14* **Büyükkemikli Burnu** *cape* NW Turkey
136 *E15* **Büyükmenderes Nehri** ~ SW Turkey
Büyükzap Suyu *see* Great Zab
102 *M9* **Buzançais** Indre, C France
116 *K13* **Buzău** Buzău, SE Romania
116 *K13* **Buzău** ◈ *county* SE Romania
116 *L12* **Buzău** ~ E Romania
75 *S11* **Buzaymah** *var.* Bzīmah. SE Libya
164 *E13* **Buzen** Fukuoka, Kyūshū, SW Japan
116 *F12* **Buziaş** *Ger.* Busiasch, *Hung.* Buziásfürdő; *prev.* Buziás. Timiş, W Romania
Buziás *see* Buziaş
Buziásfürdő *see* Buziaş
83 *M18* **Búzi, Rio** ~ C Mozambique
117 *Q10* **Buz'kyy Lyman** *bay* S Ukraine
145 *O8* **Buzuluk** Akmola, C Kazakhstan
127 *T6* **Buzuluk** Orenburgskaya Oblast', W Russian Federation
127 *N8* **Buzuluk** ~ SW Russian Federation
19 *P12* **Buzzards Bay** Massachusetts, NE USA
19 *P13* **Buzzards Bay** *bay* Massachusetts, NE USA
83 *G16* **Bwabata** Caprivi, NE Namibia
186 *H10* **Bwagaoia** Misima Island, SE Papua New Guinea
Bwake *see* Bouaké
187 *R13* **Bwatnapne** Pentecost, C Vanuatu
119 *K14* **Byahoml'** *Rus.* Begoml'. Vitsyebskaya Voblasts', N Belarus
114 *J8* **Byala** Ruse, N Bulgaria
114 *N9* **Byala** *prev.* Ak-Dere. Varna, E Bulgaria
Byala Reka *see* Erythropótamos
114 *H8* **Byala Slatina** Vratsa, NW Bulgaria
119 *N15* **Byalynichy** *Rus.* Belynichi. Mahilyowskaya Voblasts', E Belarus
Byan Tumen *see* Choybalsan
119 *G19* **Byaroza** *Pol.* Bereza Kartuska, *Rus.* Berëza. Brestskaya Voblasts', SW Belarus
119 *H16* **Byarozawka** *Rus.* Berëzovka. Hrodzyenskaya Voblasts', W Belarus
Bybles *see* Jbail
111 *O14* **Bychawa** Lubelskie, SE Poland
Bychikha *see* Bychykha
118 *N11* **Bychykha** *Rus.* Bychikha. Vitsyebskaya Voblasts', NE Belarus
111 *I14* **Byczyna** *Ger.* Pitschen. Opolskie, S Poland
110 *I10* **Bydgoszcz** *Ger.* Bromberg. Kujawski-pomorskie, C Poland
119 *H19* **Byelaazyorsk** *Rus.* Beloozersk. Brestskaya Voblasts', SW Belarus
119 *I17* **Byelaruskaya Hrada** *Rus.* Belorusskaya Gryada. *ridge* N Belarus
119 *G18* **Byelavyezhskaya Pushcha** *Pol.* Puszcza Białowieska, *Rus.* Belovezhskaya Pushcha. *forest* Belarus/Poland *see also* Białowieska, Puszcza
Byelavyezhskaya, Pushcha *see* Białowieska, Puszcza
119 *H15* **Byenyakoni** *Rus.* Benyakoni. Hrodzyenskaya Voblasts', W Belarus
119 *M16* **Byerazino** *Rus.* Berezino. Minskaya Voblasts', C Belarus
118 *L13* **Byerazino** *Rus.* Berezino. Vitsyebskaya Voblasts', N Belarus
119 *L14* **Byerezino** *Rus.* Berezina. ~ C Belarus
118 *M13* **Byeshankovichy** *Rus.* Beshenkovichi. Vitsyebskaya Voblasts', N Belarus
31 *U13* **Byesville** Ohio, N USA
119 *P18* **Byesyedz'** *Rus.* Besed'. ~ SE Belarus
119 *H19* **Byezdzyezh** *Rus.* Bezdezh. Brestskaya Voblasts', SW Belarus
93 *J15* **Bygdeå** Västerbotten, N Sweden
94 *F12* **Bygdin** ◎ S Norway
93 *J15* **Bygdsiljum** Västerbotten, N Sweden
95 *E17* **Bygland** Aust-Agder, S Norway
95 *E17* **Byglandsfjord** Aust-Agder, S Norway
119 *N16* **Bykhaw** *Rus.* Bykhov. Mahilyowskaya Voblasts', E Belarus
Bykhov *see* Bykhaw
127 *P9* **Bykovo** Volgogradskaya Oblast', SW Russian Federation
123 *P7* **Bykovskiy** Respublika Sakha (Yakutiya), NE Russian Federation
195 *R12* **Byrd Glacier** *glacier* Antarctica
14 *K10* **Byrd, Lac** ◎ Québec, SE Canada
183 *P5* **Byrock** New South Wales, SE Australia
30 *L10* **Byron** Illinois, N USA
183 *V4* **Byron Bay** New South Wales, SE Australia
183 *V4* **Byron, Cape** *cape* New South Wales, E Australia
63 *F21* **Byron, Isla** *island* S Chile
Byron Island *see* Nikunau
65 *B24* **Byron Sound** *sound* NW Falkland Islands
122 *M6* **Byrranga, Gora** ▲▲ N Russian Federation
93 *J14* **Byske** Västerbotten, N Sweden
111 *K18* **Bystrá** ▲ N Slovakia
111 *F18* **Bystřice nad Pernštejnem** *Ger.* Bistritz ober Pernstein. Vysočina, C Czech Republic
Bystrovka *see* Kemin
111 *G16* **Bystrzyca Kłodzka** *Ger.* Habelschwerdt. Wałbrzych, SW Poland
111 *I18* **Bytča** Žilinský Kraj, N Slovakia
119 *L15* **Bytcha** *Rus.* Bytcha. Minskaya Voblasts', NE Belarus
Byten' *see* Bytsyen'
Byteń/Byten' *see* Bytsyen'
111 *J16* **Bytom** *Ger.* Beuthen. Śląskie, S Poland
110 *H7* **Bytów** *Ger.* Bütow. Pomorskie, N Poland
119 *H18* **Bytsyen'** *Pol.* Byteń, *Rus.* Byten'. Brestskaya Voblasts', SW Belarus
81 *E19* **Byumba** *var.* Biumba. N Rwanda
Byuzmeyin *see* Abadan
119 *O20* **Byval'ki** Homyel'skaya Voblasts', SE Belarus
95 *O20* **Byxelkrok** Kalmar, S Sweden
Byzantium *see* İstanbul
Bzīmah *see* Buzaymah

◆ Country
● Country Capital
◇ Dependent Territory
○ Dependent Territory Capital
◈ Administrative Regions
✈ International Airport
▲ Mountain
▲▲ Mountain Range
Volcano
~ River
◎ Lake
⊠ Reservoir

C

62 O6 **Caacupé** Cordillera, S Paraguay
62 P6 **Caaguazú** *off.* Departamento de Caaguazú. ◆ *department* C Paraguay
Caaguazú, Departamento de *see* Caaguazú
82 C13 **Caála** *var.* Kaala, Robert Williams, *Port.* Vila Robert Williams. Huambo, C Angola
62 P7 **Caazapá** Caazapá, S Paraguay
62 P7 **Caazapá** *off.* Departamento de Caazapá. ◆ *department* SE Paraguay
Caazapá, Departamento de *see* Caazapá
81 P15 **Cabaad, Raas** *headland* C Somalia
55 N10 **Cabadisocaña** Amazonas, S Venezuela
44 F5 **Cabaiguán** Sancti Spíritus, C Cuba
Caballeria, Cabo *see* Cavalleria, Cap de
37 Q14 **Caballo Reservoir** ⊠ New Mexico, SW USA
40 L6 **Caballos Mesteños, Llano de los** *plain* N Mexico
104 L2 **Cabañaquinta** Asturias, N Spain
42 B9 **Cabañas** ◆ *department* E El Salvador
171 O3 **Cabanatuan** *off.* Cabanatuan City. Luzon, N Philippines
Cabanatuan City *see* Cabanatuan
15 T8 **Cabano** Québec, SE Canada
104 L11 **Cabeza del Buey** Extremadura, W Spain
45 V5 **Cabezas de San Juan** *headland* E Puerto Rico
105 N2 **Cabezón de la Sal** Cantabria, N Spain
Cabhán *see* Cavan
61 B23 **Cabildo** Buenos Aires, E Argentina
Cabillonum *see* Chalon-sur-Saône
54 H5 **Cabimas** Zulia, NW Venezuela
82 A9 **Cabinda** *var.* Kabinda. Cabinda, NW Angola
82 A9 **Cabinda** *var.* Kabinda. ◆ *province* NW Angola
33 N7 **Cabinet Mountains** ▲ Idaho/Montana, NW USA
83 B11 **Cabiri** Bengo, NW Angola
63 J20 **Cabo Blanco** Santa Cruz, SE Argentina
82 P13 **Cabo Delgado** *off.* Província de Cabo Delgado. ◆ *province* NE Mozambique
14 L9 **Cabonga, Réservoir** ⊠ Québec, SE Canada
27 V7 **Cabool** Missouri, C USA
183 V2 **Caboolture** Queensland, E Australia
Cabora Bassa, Lake *see* Cahora Bassa, Albufeira de
40 F3 **Caborca** Sonora, NW Mexico
Cabo San Lucas *see* San Lucas
27 V11 **Cabot** Arkansas, C USA
14 F12 **Cabot Head** *headland* Ontario, S Canada
13 R13 **Cabot Strait** *strait* E Canada
Cabo Verde, Ilhas do *see* Cape Verde
104 M14 **Cabra** Andalucía, S Spain
107 B19 **Cabras** Sardegna, Italy, C Mediterranean Sea
188 A15 **Cabras Island** *island* W Guam
45 O8 **Cabrera** N Dominican Republic
104 J4 **Cabrera** ~ NW Spain
105 X10 **Cabrera, Illa de** *anc.* Capraria. *island* Islas Baleares, Spain, W Mediterranean Sea
105 Q15 **Cabrera, Sierra** ▲ S Spain
9 S16 **Cabri** Saskatchewan, S Canada
105 R10 **Cabriel** ~ E Spain
54 M7 **Cabruta** Guárico, C Venezuela
171 N2 **Cabugao** Luzon, N Philippines
54 G10 **Cabuyaro** Meta, C Colombia
60 I13 **Caçador** Santa Catarina, S Brazil
42 G8 **Cacaguatique, Cordillera** *var.* Cordillera. ▲ NE El Salvador
112 L13 **Čačak** Serbia, C Serbia
55 Y10 **Cacao** NE French Guiana
61 H16 **Caçapava do Sul** Rio Grande do Sul, S Brazil
21 U3 **Cacapon River** ~ West Virginia, NE USA
107 J23 **Caccamo** Sicilia, Italy, C Mediterranean Sea
107 A17 **Caccia, Capo** *headland* Sardegna, Italy, C Mediterranean Sea
146 H15 **Çäçe** *var.* Chäche, *Rus.* Chaacha. Ahal Welaýaty, S Turkmenistan
59 G18 **Cáceres** Mato Grosso, W Brazil
104 J10 **Cáceres** *Ar.* Qazris. Extremadura, W Spain
104 J9 **Cáceres** ◆ *province* Extremadura, W Spain
Cachacrou *see* Scotts Head Village
61 C21 **Cacharí** Buenos Aires, E Argentina
26 L12 **Cache** Oklahoma, C USA
10 M16 **Cache Creek** British Columbia, SW Canada
35 N6 **Cache Creek** ~ California, W USA
37 S3 **Cache La Poudre River** ~ Colorado, C USA
Cacheo *see* Cacheu
27 W11 **Cache River** ~ Arkansas, C USA
30 L17 **Cache River** ~ Illinois, N USA
76 G12 **Cacheu** *var.* Cacheo. W Guinea-Bissau
59 I15 **Cachimbo** Pará, NE Brazil
59 H15 **Cachimbo, Serra do** ▲ C Brazil
82 D13 **Cachingues** Bié, C Angola
54 G7 **Cáchira** Norte de Santander, N Colombia
61 H16 **Cachoeira do Sul** Rio Grande do Sul, S Brazil
59 O20 **Cachoeiro de Itapemirim** Espírito Santo, SE Brazil
82 E12 **Cacolo** Lunda Sul, NE Angola
83 C14 **Caconda** Huíla, C Angola
82 A9 **Cacongo** Cabinda, NW Angola
35 U9 **Cactus Peak** ▲ Nevada, W USA
82 A11 **Cacuaco** Luanda, NW Angola
83 B14 **Cacula** Huíla, SW Angola
67 R12 **Caculuvar** ~ SW Angola
59 O19 **Caçumba, Ilha** *island* SE Brazil
55 N10 **Cacuri** Amazonas, S Venezuela
81 N17 **Cadale** Shabeellaha Dhexe, E Somalia
105 X4 **Cadaqués** Cataluña, NE Spain
111 J18 **Čadca** *Hung.* Csaca. Žilinský Kraj, N Slovakia
27 P13 **Caddo** Oklahoma, C USA
25 R6 **Caddo** Texas, SW USA
25 X6 **Caddo Lake** ⊠ Louisiana/Texas, SW USA
27 S12 **Caddo Mountains** ▲ Arkansas, C USA
41 O8 **Cadereyta** Nuevo León, NE Mexico
97 J19 **Cader Idris** ▲ NW Wales, UK
182 F3 **Cadibarrawirracanna, Lake** *salt lake* South Australia
14 I7 **Cadillac** Québec, SE Canada
9 T17 **Cadillac** Saskatchewan, S Canada
102 K13 **Cadillac** Gironde, SW France
31 P7 **Cadillac** Michigan, N USA
105 V4 **Cadí, Torre de** ▲ NE Spain
171 P5 **Cadiz** *off.* Cadiz City. Negros, C Philippines
104 J15 **Cádiz** *anc.* Gades, Gadier, Gadir, Gadire. Andalucía, SW Spain
20 H7 **Cadiz** Kentucky, S USA
31 U13 **Cadiz** Ohio, N USA
104 K15 **Cádiz** ◆ *province* Andalucía, SW Spain
104 I15 **Cadiz, Bahía de** *bay* SW Spain
Cadiz City *see* Cadiz
104 H15 **Cádiz, Golfo de** *Eng.* Gulf of Cadiz. *gulf* Portugal/Spain
Cadiz, Gulf of *see* Cádiz, Golfo de
35 X14 **Cadiz Lake** ◎ California, W USA
182 E2 **Cadney Homestead** South Australia
Cadurcum *see* Cahors
83 F17 **Caecae** North-West, NW Botswana
102 K4 **Caen** Calvados, N France
Caene/Caenepolis *see* Qena
Caerdydd *see* Cardiff
Caer Glou *see* Gloucester
Caer Gybi *see* Holyhead
Caerleon *see* Chester
Caer Luel *see* Carlisle
97 I18 **Caernarfon** *var.* Caernarvon, Carnarvon. NW Wales, UK
97 H18 **Caernarfon Bay** *bay* NW Wales, UK
97 I19 **Caernarvon** *cultural region* NW Wales, UK
Caernarvon *see* Caernarfon
Caesaraugusta *see* Zaragoza
Caesarea Mazaca *see* Kayseri
Caesarobriga *see* Talavera de la Reina
Caesarodunum *see* Tours
Caesaromagus *see* Beauvais
Caesena *see* Cesena
59 N17 **Caetité** Bahia, E Brazil
62 J6 **Cafayate** Salta, N Argentina
171 O2 **Cagayan** ~ Luzon, N Philippines
171 Q7 **Cagayan de Oro** *off.* Cagayan de Oro City. Mindanao, S Philippines
Cagayan de Oro City *see* Cagayan de Oro
170 M8 **Cagayan de Tawi Tawi** *island* S Philippines
171 N6 **Cagayan Islands** *island group* C Philippines
31 O14 **Cagles Mill Lake** ⊠ Indiana, N USA
106 I12 **Cagli** Marche, C Italy
107 C20 **Cagliari** *anc.* Caralis. Sardegna, Italy, C Mediterranean Sea
107 C20 **Cagliari, Golfo di** *gulf* Sardegna, Italy, C Mediterranean Sea
103 U15 **Cagnes-sur-Mer** Alpes-Maritimes, SE France
54 L5 **Cagua** Aragua, N Venezuela
171 O1 **Cagua, Mount** ▲ Luzon, N Philippines
54 F13 **Caguán, Río** ~ SW Colombia
45 U6 **Caguas** E Puerto Rico
146 C9 **Çagyl** *Rus.* Chagyl. Balkan Welaýaty, NW Turkmenistan
23 P5 **Cahaba River** ~ Alabama, S USA
42 E5 **Cahabón, Río** ~ C Guatemala
83 B15 **Cahama** Cunene, SW Angola
97 B21 **Caha Mountains** *Ir.* An Cheacha. ▲ SW Ireland
97 D20 **Caher** *Ir.* An Cathair. S Ireland
97 A21 **Caherciveen** *Ir.* Cathair Saidhbhín. SW Ireland
30 K15 **Cahokia** Illinois, N USA
83 L15 **Cahora Bassa, Albufeira de** *var.* Lake Cabora Bassa. ⊠ NW Mozambique
97 G20 **Cahore Point** *Ir.* Rinn Chathóir. *headland* SE Ireland
102 M14 **Cahors** *anc.* Cadurcum. Lot, S France
56 D9 **Cahuapanas, Río** ~ N Peru
116 M12 **Cahul** *Rus.* Kagul. S Moldova
Cahul, Lacul *see* Kahul, Ozero
83 N16 **Caia** Sofala, C Mozambique
59 J19 **Caiapó, Serra do** ▲ C Brazil
44 F5 **Caibarién** Villa Clara, C Cuba
55 O5 **Caicara** Monagas, NE Venezuela
54 L5 **Caicara de Orinoco** Bolívar, C Venezuela
59 P14 **Caicó** Rio Grande do Norte, E Brazil
44 M6 **Caicos Islands** *island group* W Turks and Caicos Islands
44 L5 **Caicos Passage** *strait* Bahamas/Turks and Caicos Islands
161 O9 **Caidian** *prev.* Hanyang. Hubei, C China
Caiffa *see* Hefa
180 M12 **Caiguna** Western Australia
Cailli, Ceann *see* Hag's Head
40 J11 **Caimanero, Laguna del** *var.* Laguna del Camaronero. *lagoon* E Pacific Ocean
117 N10 **Căinari** *Rus.* Kaynary. C Moldova
57 L19 **Caine, Río** ~ C Bolivia
Caiphas *see* Hefa
195 N4 **Caird Coast** *physical region* Antarctica
96 J9 **Cairn Gorm** ▲ C Scotland, UK
96 J9 **Cairngorm Mountains** ▲ C Scotland, UK
39 P12 **Cairn Mountain** ▲ Alaska, USA
181 W4 **Cairns** Queensland, NE Australia
121 V13 **Cairo** *Ar.* Al Qāhirah, *var.* El Qâhira. ● (Egypt) N Egypt
23 T8 **Cairo** Georgia, SE USA
30 L17 **Cairo** Illinois, N USA
75 V8 **Cairo** ✈ C Egypt
Caiseal *see* Cashel
Caisleán an Bharraigh *see* Castlebar
Caisleán na Finne *see* Castlefinn
96 J6 **Caithness** *cultural region* N Scotland, UK
83 D15 **Caiundo** Cuando Cubango, S Angola
56 C11 **Cajamarca** *prev.* Caxamarca. Cajamarca, NW Peru
56 B11 **Cajamarca** *off.* Departamento de Cajamarca. ◆ *department* N Peru
Cajamarca, Departamento de *see* Cajamarca
103 N14 **Cajarc** Lot, S France
42 G6 **Cajón, Represa El** ⊠ NW Honduras
58 N12 **Caju, Ilha do** *island* NE Brazil
159 R10 **Caka Yanhu** ◎ C China
112 E7 **Čakovec** *Ger.* Csakathurn, *Hung.* Csáktornya; *prev. Ger.* Tschakathurn. Medimurje, N Croatia
77 V17 **Calabar** Cross River, S Nigeria
14 K13 **Calabogie** Ontario, SE Canada
54 L6 **Calabozo** Guárico, C Venezuela
107 N20 **Calabria** *anc.* Bruttium. ◆ *region* SW Italy
104 M16 **Calaburra, Punta de** *headland* S Spain
116 G14 **Calafat** Dolj, SW Romania
Calafate *see* El Calafate
105 Q4 **Calahorra** La Rioja, N Spain
103 N1 **Calais** Pas-de-Calais, N France
19 T5 **Calais** Maine, NE USA
Calais, Pas de *see* Dover, Strait of
Calalen *see* Kallalen
62 H4 **Calama** Antofagasta, N Chile
Calamianes *see* Calamian Group
170 M5 **Calamian Group** *var.* Calamianes. *island group* W Philippines
105 R7 **Calamocha** Aragón, NE Spain
29 N14 **Calamus River** ~ Nebraska, C USA
116 G12 **Călan** *Ger.* Kalan, *Hung.* Pusztakalán. Hunedoara, SW Romania
105 S7 **Calanda** Aragón, NE Spain
168 F9 **Calang** Sumatera, W Indonesia
171 N4 **Calapan** Mindoro, N Philippines
Călăras *see* Călărași
116 M9 **Călărași** *var.* Călăras, *Rus.* Kalarash. C Moldova
116 L14 **Călărași** Călărași, SE Romania
116 K14 **Călărași** ◆ *county* SE Romania
54 E10 **Calarca** Quindío, W Colombia
105 Q12 **Calasparra** Murcia, SE Spain
107 I23 **Calatafimi** Sicilia, Italy, C Mediterranean Sea
105 Q6 **Calatayud** Aragón, NE Spain
171 O4 **Calauag** Luzon, N Philippines
35 P8 **Calaveras River** ~ California, W USA
171 N4 **Calavite, Cape** *headland* Mindoro, N Philippines
171 Q8 **Calbayog** *off.* Calbayog City. Samar, C Philippines
Calbayog City *see* Calbayog
22 G9 **Calcasieu Lake** ◎ Louisiana, S USA
22 H8 **Calcasieu River** ~ Louisiana, S USA
56 B6 **Calceta** Manabí, W Ecuador
61 B16 **Calchaquí** Santa Fe, C Argentina
62 J6 **Calchaquí, Río** ~ NW Argentina
58 J10 **Calçoene** Amapá, NE Brazil
153 S16 **Calcutta** ✈ West Bengal, N India
Calcutta *see* Kolkata
54 E9 **Caldas** *off.* Departamento de Caldas. ◆ *province* W Colombia
104 F10 **Caldas da Rainha** Leiria, W Portugal
Caldas, Departamento de *see* Caldas
104 G3 **Caldas de Reis** *var.* Caldas de Reyes. Galicia, NW Spain
Caldas de Reyes *see* Caldas de Reis
58 F13 **Caldeirão** Amazonas, NW Brazil
62 G7 **Caldera** Atacama, N Chile
42 L14 **Caldera** Puntarenas, W Costa Rica
105 N10 **Calderina** ▲ C Spain
137 T13 **Çaldıran** Van, E Turkey
32 M14 **Caldwell** Idaho, NW USA
27 N8 **Caldwell** Kansas, C USA
14 G15 **Caledon** Ontario, S Canada
83 I23 **Caledon** *var.* Mohokare. ~ Lesotho/South Africa
42 G1 **Caledonia** Corozal, N Belize
14 G16 **Caledonia** Ontario, S Canada
29 X11 **Caledonia** Minnesota, N USA
105 X5 **Calella** *var.* Calella de la Costa. Cataluña, NE Spain
Calella de la Costa *see* Calella
23 P4 **Calera** Alabama, S USA
63 I19 **Caleta Olivia** Santa Cruz, SE Argentina
35 X17 **Calexico** California, W USA
97 H16 **Calf of Man** *island* SW Isle of Man
9 Q16 **Calgary** Alberta, SW Canada
9 Q16 **Calgary** ✈ Alberta, SW Canada
37 U5 **Calhan** Colorado, C USA
64 O5 **Calheta** Madeira, Portugal, NE Atlantic Ocean
23 R2 **Calhoun** Georgia, SE USA
20 I6 **Calhoun** Kentucky, S USA
22 M3 **Calhoun City** Mississippi, S USA
21 P12 **Calhoun Falls** South Carolina, SE USA
54 D11 **Cali** Valle del Cauca, W Colombia
27 V9 **Calico Rock** Arkansas, C USA
155 F21 **Calicut** *var.* Kozhikode. Kerala, SW India
35 Y9 **Caliente** Nevada, W USA
27 U5 **California** Missouri, C USA
18 B15 **California** Pennsylvania, NE USA
35 Q12 **California** *off.* State of California, *also known as* El Dorado, The Golden State. ◆ *state* W USA
35 P11 **California Aqueduct** *aqueduct* California, W USA
35 T13 **California City** California, W USA
40 F6 **California, Golfo de** *Eng.* Gulf of California; *prev.* Sea of Cortez. *gulf* W Mexico
California, Gulf of *see* California, Golfo de
137 Y13 **Cälilabad** *Rus.* Dzhalilabad; *prev.* Astrakhan-Bazar. S Azerbaijan
116 I12 **Călimănești** Vâlcea, SW Romania
116 J9 **Călimani, Munții** ▲ N Romania
Calinisc *see* Cupcina
35 X17 **Calipatria** California, W USA
Calisia *see* Kalisz
34 M7 **Calistoga** California, W USA
83 G25 **Calitzdorp** Western Cape, SW South Africa
41 W12 **Calkiní** Campeche, E Mexico
182 K4 **Callabonna Creek** *var.* Tilcha Creek. *seasonal river* New South Wales/South Australia
182 J4 **Callabonna, Lake** ◎ South Australia
102 G5 **Callac** Côtes d'Armor, NW France
35 U5 **Callaghan, Mount** ▲ Nevada, W USA
Callain *see* Callan
97 E19 **Callan** *Ir.* Callain. S Ireland
14 H11 **Callander** Ontario, S Canada
96 I11 **Callander** C Scotland, UK
98 H7 **Callantsoog** Noord-Holland, NW Netherlands
57 D14 **Callao** Callao, W Peru
57 D15 **Callao** *off.* Departamento del Callao. ◆ *constitutional province* W Peru
Callao, Departamento del *see* Callao
56 F11 **Callaria, Río** ~ E Peru
Callatis *see* Mangalia
9 Q13 **Calling Lake** Alberta, W Canada
Callosa de Ensarriá *see* Callosa d'En Sarrià
105 T11 **Callosa d'En Sarrià** *var.* Callosa de Ensarriá. País Valenciano, E Spain
105 S12 **Callosa de Segura** País Valenciano, E Spain
29 X11 **Calmar** Iowa, C USA
Calmar *see* Kalmar
43 R16 **Calobre** Veraguas, C Panama
23 X14 **Caloosahatchee River** ~ Florida, SE USA
183 V2 **Caloundra** Queensland, E Australia
Calp *see* Calpe
105 T11 **Calpe** *Cat.* Calp. País Valenciano, E Spain
41 P14 **Calpulalpan** Tlaxcala, S Mexico
107 K25 **Caltagirone** Sicilia, Italy, C Mediterranean Sea
107 J24 **Caltanissetta** Sicilia, Italy, C Mediterranean Sea
82 E11 **Caluango** Lunda Norte, NE Angola
82 C12 **Calucinga** Bié, W Angola
82 B12 **Calulo** Cuanza Sul, NW Angola
83 B14 **Caluquembe** Huíla, W Angola
80 Q11 **Caluula** Bari, NE Somalia
102 K4 **Calvados** ◆ *department* N France
186 I10 **Calvados Chain, The** *island group* SE Papua New Guinea
25 U9 **Calvert** Texas, SW USA
20 H7 **Calvert City** Kentucky, S USA
103 X14 **Calvi** Corse, France, C Mediterranean Sea
40 L12 **Calvillo** Aguascalientes, C Mexico
83 F24 **Calvinia** Northern Cape, W South Africa
104 K8 **Calvitero** ▲ W Spain
101 G22 **Calw** Baden-Württemberg, SW Germany
Calydon *see* Kalydón
105 N11 **Calzada de Calatrava** Castilla-La Mancha, C Spain
Cama *see* Kama
82 C11 **Camabatela** Cuanza Norte, NW Angola
64 Q5 **Camacha** Porto Santo, Madeira, Portugal, NE Atlantic Ocean
14 L8 **Camachigama, Lac** ◎ Québec, SE Canada
40 M9 **Camacho** Zacatecas, C Mexico
82 D13 **Camacupa** *var.* General Machado, *Port.* Vila General Machado. Bié, C Angola
54 L7 **Camaguán** Guárico, C Venezuela
44 G6 **Camagüey** *prev.* Puerto Príncipe. Camagüey, C Cuba
44 G5 **Camagüey, Archipiélago de** *island group* C Cuba
40 D5 **Camalli, Sierra de** ▲ NW Mexico
57 G18 **Camana** *var.* Camaná. Arequipa, SW Peru
29 Z14 **Camanche** Iowa, C USA
35 P8 **Camanche Reservoir** ⊠ California, W USA
61 I16 **Camaquã** Rio Grande do Sul, S Brazil
61 H16 **Camaquã, Rio** ~ S Brazil
64 P6 **Câmara de Lobos** Madeira, Portugal, NE Atlantic Ocean
103 U16 **Camarat, Cap** *headland* SE France
41 O8 **Camargo** Tamaulipas, C Mexico
103 R15 **Camargue** *physical region* SE France
104 F2 **Camariñas** Galicia, NW Spain
Camaronero, Laguna del *see* Caimanero, Laguna del
63 J18 **Camarones** Chaco, S Argentina
63 J18 **Camarones, Bahía** *bay* S Argentina
104 J14 **Camas** Andalucía, S Spain
167 S15 **Ca Mau** *var.* Quan Long. Minh Hai, S Vietnam
82 E11 **Camaxilo** Lunda Norte, NE Angola
104 G3 **Cambados** Galicia, NW Spain
Cambay, Gulf of *see* Khambhāt, Gulf of
Camberia *see* Chambéry
97 N22 **Camberley** SE England, UK
167 R12 **Cambodia** *off.* Kingdom of Cambodia, *var.* Democratic Kampuchea, Roat Kampuchea, *Cam.* Kampuchea; *prev.* People's Democratic Republic of Kampuchea. ◆ *republic* SE Asia
Cambodia, Kingdom of *see* Cambodia
102 I16 **Cambo-les-Bains** Pyrénées-Atlantiques, SW France
103 P2 **Cambrai** *Flem.* Kambryk, *prev.* Cambray; *anc.* Cameracum. Nord, N France
Cambray *see* Cambrai
104 H2 **Cambre** Galicia, NW Spain
35 O12 **Cambria** California, W USA
97 J20 **Cambrian Mountains** ▲ C Wales, UK
14 G16 **Cambridge** Ontario, S Canada
44 I12 **Cambridge** W Jamaica
184 M8 **Cambridge** Waikato, North Island, New Zealand
97 O20 **Cambridge** *Lat.* Cantabrigia. E England, UK
32 M12 **Cambridge** Idaho, NW USA
30 K11 **Cambridge** Illinois, N USA
21 Y4 **Cambridge** Maryland, NE USA
19 O11 **Cambridge** Massachusetts, NE USA
29 V7 **Cambridge** Minnesota, N USA
29 N16 **Cambridge** Nebraska, C USA
31 U13 **Cambridge** Ohio, NE USA
8 L7 **Cambridge Bay** Victoria Island, Nunavut, NW Canada
97 O20 **Cambridgeshire** *cultural region* E England, UK
105 U6 **Cambrils de Mar** Cataluña, NE Spain
Cambundi-Catembo *see* Nova Gaia
137 N11 **Çam Burnu** *headland* N Turkey
183 S9 **Camden** New South Wales, SE Australia
23 O6 **Camden** Alabama, S USA
27 U14 **Camden** Arkansas, C USA
21 Y3 **Camden** Delaware, NE USA
19 R7 **Camden** Maine, NE USA
18 I16 **Camden** New Jersey, NE USA
18 I9 **Camden** New York, NE USA
21 R12 **Camden** South Carolina, SE USA
20 H8 **Camden** Tennessee, S USA
25 X9 **Camden** Texas, SW USA
39 S5 **Camden Bay** *bay* S Beaufort Sea
27 U6 **Camdenton** Missouri, C USA
Camellia State *see* Alabama
18 M7 **Camels Hump** ▲ Vermont, NE USA
117 N8 **Camenca** *Rus.* Kamenka. N Moldova
Cameracum *see* Cambrai
22 G9 **Cameron** Louisiana, S USA
25 T9 **Cameron** Texas, SW USA
30 J5 **Cameron** Wisconsin, N USA
10 M12 **Cameron** ~ British Columbia, W Canada
185 A24 **Cameron Mountains** ▲ South Island, New Zealand
79 D15 **Cameroon** *off.* Republic of Cameroon, *Fr.* Cameroun. ◆ *republic* W Africa
79 D15 **Cameroon Mountain** ▲ SW Cameroon
Cameroon, Republic of *see* Cameroon
Cameroon Ridge *see* Camerounaise, Dorsale
Cameroun *see* Cameroon
79 E14 **Camerounaise, Dorsale** *Eng.* Cameroon Ridge. *ridge* NW Cameroon
136 B15 **Çamiçi Gölü** ◎ SW Turkey
171 N3 **Camiling** Luzon, N Philippines
23 T7 **Camilla** Georgia, SE USA
104 G5 **Caminha** Viana do Castelo, N Portugal
35 P7 **Camino** California, W USA
107 J24 **Cammarata** Sicilia, Italy, C Mediterranean Sea
42 K10 **Camoapa** Boaco, S Nicaragua
58 O13 **Camocim** Ceará, E Brazil
106 D10 **Camogli** Liguria, NW Italy
181 S5 **Camooweal** Queensland, C Australia
55 Y11 **Camopi** E French Guiana
151 Q22 **Camorta** *island* Nicobar Islands, India, NE Indian Ocean
42 I6 **Campamento** Olancho, C Honduras
61 D19 **Campana** Buenos Aires, E Argentina
63 F21 **Campana, Isla** *island* S Chile
104 K11 **Campanario** Extremadura, W Spain
107 L17 **Campania** *Eng.* Champagne. ◆ *region* S Italy
27 Y8 **Campbell** Missouri, C USA
185 K15 **Campbell, Cape** *headland* South Island, New Zealand
14 J14 **Campbellford** Ontario, SE Canada
31 R13 **Campbell Hill** *hill* Ohio, N USA
192 K13 **Campbell Island** *island* S New Zealand
175 P13 **Campbell Plateau** *undersea feature* SW Pacific Ocean
10 K17 **Campbell River** Vancouver Island, British Columbia, SW Canada
20 L6 **Campbellsville** Kentucky, S USA
13 O13 **Campbellton** New Brunswick, SE Canada
183 S9 **Campbelltown** New South Wales, SE Australia
183 P16 **Campbell Town** Tasmania, SE Australia
96 G13 **Campbeltown** W Scotland, UK
41 W13 **Campeche** Campeche, SE Mexico
41 W14 **Campeche** ◆ *state* SE Mexico
41 T14 **Campeche, Bahía de** *Eng.* Bay of Campeche. *bay* E Mexico
Campeche, Banco de *see* Campeche Bank
64 C11 **Campeche Bank** *Sp.* Banco de Campeche, Sonda de Campeche. *undersea feature* S Gulf of Mexico
Campeche, Bay of *see* Campeche, Bahía de
Campeche, Sonda de *see* Campeche Bank
44 H7 **Campechuela** Granma, E Cuba
182 M13 **Camperdown** Victoria, SE Australia
167 U6 **Câm Pha** Quang Ninh, N Vietnam
116 H10 **Câmpia Turzii** *Ger.* Jerischmarkt, *Hung.* Aranyosgyéres; *prev.* Cîmpia Turzii, Ghiriș, Gyéres. Cluj, NW Romania
104 K12 **Campillo de Llerena** Extremadura, W Spain
104 L15 **Campillos** Andalucía, S Spain
116 J13 **Câmpina** *prev.* Cîmpina. Prahova, SE Romania
59 Q15 **Campina Grande** Paraíba, E Brazil
60 L9 **Campinas** São Paulo, S Brazil
38 L10 **Camp Kulowiye** Saint Lawrence Island, Alaska, USA
79 D17 **Campo** *var.* Kampo. Sud, SW Cameroon
Campo *see* Ntem
59 N15 **Campo Alegre de Lourdes** Bahia, E Brazil
107 L16 **Campobasso** Molise, C Italy
107 H24 **Campobello di Mazara** Sicilia, Italy, C Mediterranean Sea
Campo Criptana *see* Campo de Criptana
105 O10 **Campo de Criptana** *var.* Campo Criptana. Castilla-La Mancha, C Spain
59 I16 **Campo de Diauarum** *var.* Pôsto Diauarum. Mato Grosso, W Brazil
54 E5 **Campo de la Cruz** Atlántico, N Colombia
105 P11 **Campo de Montiel** *physical region* C Spain
Campo dos Goitacazes *see* Campos
60 H12 **Campo Erê** Santa Catarina, S Brazil
62 L7 **Campo Gallo** Santiago del Estero, N Argentina
59 I20 **Campo Grande** *state capital* Mato Grosso do Sul, SW Brazil
60 K12 **Campo Largo** Paraná, S Brazil
58 N13 **Campo Maior** Piauí, E Brazil
104 I10 **Campo Maior** Portalegre, C Portugal
60 H10 **Campo Mourão** Paraná, S Brazil
60 Q9 **Campos** *var.* Campo dos Goitacazes. Rio de Janeiro, SE Brazil
59 L17 **Campos Belos** Goiás, S Brazil
60 N9 **Campos do Jordão** São Paulo, S Brazil
60 I13 **Campos Novos** Santa Catarina, S Brazil
59 O14 **Campos Sales** Ceará, E Brazil
25 Q9 **Camp San Saba** Texas, SW USA
21 N6 **Campton** Kentucky, S USA
116 I13 **Câmpulung** *prev.* Câmpulung-Mușcel, Cîmpulung. Argeș, S Romania
116 J9 **Câmpulung Moldovenesc** *var.* Cîmpulung Moldovenesc, *Ger.* Kimpolung, *Hung.* Hosszúmezjő. Suceava, NE Romania
Câmpulung-Mușcel *see* Câmpulung
Campus Stellae *see* Santiago
36 L12 **Camp Verde** Arizona, SW USA
25 P11 **Camp Wood** Texas, SW USA
167 V13 **Cam Ranh** Khanh Hoa, S Vietnam
9 Q15 **Camrose** Alberta, SW Canada
Camulodunum *see* Colchester
136 B12 **Çan** Çanakkale, NW Turkey
18 L12 **Canaan** Connecticut, NE USA
9 O13 **Canada** ◆ *commonwealth republic* N North America
197 P6 **Canada Basin** *undersea feature* Arctic Ocean
61 B18 **Cañada de Gómez** Santa Fe, C Argentina
197 P6 **Canada Plain** *undersea feature* Arctic Ocean
61 A18 **Cañada Rosquín** Santa Fe, C Argentina
25 P1 **Canadian** Texas, SW USA
16 K12 **Canadian River** ~ SW USA
8 L12 **Canadian Shield** *physical region* Canada
63 I18 **Cañadón Grande, Sierra** ▲ S Argentina
55 P9 **Canaima** Bolívar, SE Venezuela
136 B11 **Çanakkale** *var.* Dardanelli; *prev.* Chanak, Kale Sultanie. Çanakkale, W Turkey
136 B12 **Çanakkale** ◆ *province* NW Turkey
136 B11 **Çanakkale Boğazı** *Eng.* Dardanelles. *strait* NW Turkey
187 Q17 **Canala** Province Nord, C New Caledonia
59 A15 **Canamari** Amazonas, W Brazil
18 G10 **Canandaigua** New York, NE USA
18 F10 **Canandaigua Lake** ◎ New York, NE USA
40 G3 **Cananea** Sonora, NW Mexico
56 B8 **Cañar** ◆ *province* C Ecuador
64 N10 **Canarias, Islas** *Eng.* Canary Islands. ◆ *autonomous community* Islas Canarias, Spain Europe, NE Atlantic Ocean

◆ Country
● Country Capital
◇ Dependent Territory
○ Dependent Territory Capital
◆ Administrative Regions
✈ International Airport
▲ Mountain
▲ Mountain Range
Volcano
~ River
◎ Lake
⊠ Reservoir

Canaries Basin see Canary Basin
44 C6 **Canarreos, Archipiélago de los** island group W Cuba
Canary Islands see Canarias, Islas
66 K3 **Canary Basin** var. Canaries Basin, Monaco Basin. undersea feature E Atlantic Ocean
42 L13 **Cañas** Guanacaste, NW Costa Rica
18 I10 **Canastota** New York, NE USA
40 K9 **Canatlán** Durango, C Mexico
104 J9 **Cañaveral** Extremadura, W Spain
23 Y11 **Canaveral, Cape** headland Florida, SE USA
59 O18 **Canavieiras** Bahia, E Brazil
43 R16 **Cañazas** Veraguas, W Panama
106 H6 **Canazei** Trentino-Alto Adige, N Italy
183 P6 **Canbelego** New South Wales, SE Australia
183 R10 **Canberra** ● (Australia) Australian Capital Territory, SE Australia
183 R10 **Canberra** ✈ Australian Capital Territory, SE Australia
35 P2 **Canby** California, W USA
29 S9 **Canby** Minnesota, N USA
103 N2 **Canche** ~ N France
102 L13 **Cancon** Lot-et-Garonne, SW France
41 Z11 **Cancún** Quintana Roo, SE Mexico
104 K2 **Candás** Asturias, N Spain
102 J7 **Cande** Maine-et-Loire, NW France
41 W14 **Candelaria** Campeche, SE Mexico
24 J11 **Candelaria** Texas, SW USA
41 W15 **Candelaria, Río** ~ Guatemala/Mexico
104 L8 **Candeleda** Castilla-León, N Spain
Candia see Irákleio
41 P8 **Cándido Aguilar** Tamaulipas, C Mexico
39 N8 **Candle** Alaska, USA
9 T14 **Candle Lake** Saskatchewan, C Canada
18 L13 **Candlewood, Lake** ▣ Connecticut, NE USA
29 O3 **Cando** North Dakota, N USA
Canea see Chaniá
45 O12 **Canefield** ✈ (Roseau) SW Dominica
61 F20 **Canelones** prev. Guadalupe. Canelones, S Uruguay
61 E20 **Canelones** ◈ department S Uruguay
Canendiyú see Canindeyú
63 F14 **Cañete** Bío Bío, C Chile
105 Q9 **Cañete** Castilla-La Mancha, C Spain
Cañete see San Vicente de Cañete
27 P8 **Caney** Kansas, C USA
27 P8 **Caney River** ~ Kansas/ Oklahoma, C USA
105 S3 **Canfranc-Estación** Aragón, NE Spain
83 E14 **Cangamba** Port. Vila de Aljustrel. Moxico, E Angola
82 C12 **Cangandala** Malanje, NW Angola
104 G4 **Cangas** Galicia, NW Spain
104 J2 **Cangas del Narcea** Asturias, N Spain
104 L2 **Cangas de Onís** Asturias, N Spain
161 S11 **Cangnan** var. Lingxi. Zhejiang, SE China
82 C10 **Cangola** Uíge, NW Angola
83 E14 **Cangombe** Moxico, E Angola
63 H21 **Cangrejo, Cerro** ▲ S Argentina
61 H17 **Canguçu** Rio Grande do Sul, S Brazil
161 P3 **Cangzhou** Hebei, E China
12 M7 **Caniapiscau** ~ Québec, E Canada
12 M8 **Caniapiscau, Réservoir de** ▣ Québec, C Canada
107 J24 **Canicattì** Sicilia, Italy, C Mediterranean Sea
136 I11 **Canik Dağları** ▲▲ N Turkey
105 P14 **Caniles** Andalucía, S Spain
59 B16 **Canindé** Acre, W Brazil
62 P6 **Canindeyú** var. Canendiyú, Canindiyú. ◈ department E Paraguay
Canindiyú see Canindeyú
194 J10 **Canisteo Peninsula** peninsula Antarctica
18 F11 **Canisteo River** ~ New York, NE USA
40 M10 **Cañitas** var. Cañitas de Felipe Pescador. Zacatecas, C Mexico
Cañitas de Felipe Pescador see Cañitas
105 P15 **Canjáyar** Andalucía, S Spain
136 I12 **Çankırı** var. Chankiri; anc. Gangra, Germanicopolis. Çankırı, N Turkey
136 I11 **Çankiri** var. Chankiri. ◈ province N Turkey
171 P6 **Canlaon Volcano** ⛰ Negros, C Philippines
9 P16 **Canmore** Alberta, SW Canada
96 F9 **Canna** island NW Scotland, UK
155 F20 **Cannanore** var. Kananur, Kannur. Kerala, SW India
31 O17 **Cannelton** Indiana, N USA
103 U15 **Cannes** Alpes-Maritimes, SE France
39 R5 **Canning River** ~ Alaska, USA
106 C6 **Cannobio** Piemonte, NE Italy
97 L19 **Cannock** C England, UK
28 M6 **Cannonball River** ~ North Dakota, N USA
29 W9 **Cannon Falls** Minnesota, N USA
18 I11 **Cannonsville Reservoir** ▣ New York, NE USA
183 R12 **Cann River** Victoria, SE Australia
61 I16 **Canoas** Rio Grande do Sul, S Brazil
61 I14 **Canoas, Rio** ~ S Brazil
14 I12 **Canoe Lake** ◎ Ontario, SE Canada
60 J12 **Canoinhas** Santa Catarina, S Brazil
37 T6 **Canon City** Colorado, C USA
55 P8 **Caño Negro** Bolívar, SE Venezuela
173 X15 **Canonniers Point** headland N Mauritius
23 W6 **Canoochee River** ~ Georgia, SE USA
9 V15 **Canora** Saskatchewan, S Canada
45 Y14 **Canouan** island S Saint Vincent and the Grenadines
13 R15 **Canso** Nova Scotia, SE Canada
104 M3 **Cantabria** ◈ autonomous community N Spain
104 K3 **Cantábrica, Cordillera** ▲▲ N Spain
Cantabrigia see Cambridge
103 O12 **Cantal** ◈ department C France
105 N6 **Cantalejo** Castilla-León, N Spain
103 O12 **Cantal, Monts du** ▲▲ C France
104 G8 **Cantanhede** Coimbra, C Portugal
Cantaño see Cataño
55 O6 **Cantaura** Anzoátegui, NE Venezuela
116 M11 **Cantemir** Rus. Kantemir. S Moldova
97 Q22 **Canterbury** hist. Cantwaraburh; anc. Durovernum, Lat. Cantuaria. SE England, UK
185 F19 **Canterbury** off. Canterbury Region. ◈ region South Island, New Zealand
185 H20 **Canterbury Bight** bight South Island, New Zealand
185 H19 **Canterbury Plains** plain South Island, New Zealand
Canterbury Region see Canterbury
167 S14 **Cần Thơ** Cần Thơ, S Vietnam
104 K13 **Cantillana** Andalucía, S Spain
59 N15 **Canto do Buriti** Piauí, NE Brazil
23 S2 **Canton** Georgia, SE USA
30 K12 **Canton** Illinois, N USA
22 L5 **Canton** Mississippi, S USA
27 V2 **Canton** Missouri, C USA
18 J7 **Canton** New York, NE USA
21 O10 **Canton** North Carolina, SE USA
31 U12 **Canton** Ohio, N USA
26 L9 **Canton** Oklahoma, C USA
18 G12 **Canton** Pennsylvania, NE USA
29 R11 **Canton** South Dakota, N USA
25 V7 **Canton** Texas, SW USA
Canton see Guangzhou
Canton Island see Kanton
26 L9 **Canton Lake** ▣ Oklahoma, C USA
106 D7 **Cantù** Lombardia, N Italy
Cantuaria/Cantwaraburh see Canterbury
39 R10 **Cantwell** Alaska, USA
59 O16 **Canudos** Bahia, E Brazil
47 T7 **Canumã, Rio** ~ N Brazil
Canusium see Puglia, Canosa di
24 G7 **Canutillo** Texas, SW USA
25 N3 **Canyon** Texas, SW USA
33 S12 **Canyon** Wyoming, C USA
32 K13 **Canyon City** Oregon, NW USA
33 R10 **Canyon Ferry Lake** ◎ Montana, NW USA
25 S11 **Canyon Lake** ▣ Texas, SW USA
167 T5 **Cao Bằng** var. Caobang. Cao Bằng, N Vietnam
Caobang see Cao Bằng
160 J12 **Caodu He** ~ S China
167 S14 **Cao Lanh** Đồng Thap, S Vietnam
82 C11 **Caombo** Malanje, NW Angola
Caorach, Cuan na g see Sheep Haven
Caozhou see Heze
171 Q12 **Capalulu** Pulau Mangole, E Indonesia
54 K8 **Capanaparo, Río** ~ Colombia/Venezuela
58 L12 **Capanema** Pará, NE Brazil
60 L10 **Capão Bonito** São Paulo, S Brazil
60 I13 **Capão Doce, Morro do** ▲ S Brazil
54 I4 **Capatárida** Falcón, N Venezuela
102 I15 **Capbreton** Landes, SW France
Cap-Breton, Île du see Cape Breton Island
15 W6 **Cap-Chat** Québec, SE Canada
15 P11 **Cap-de-la-Madeleine** Québec, SE Canada
103 N13 **Capdenac** Aveyron, S France
183 Q15 **Cape Barren Island** island Furneaux Group, Tasmania, SE Australia
65 O18 **Cape Basin** undersea feature S Atlantic Ocean
13 R14 **Cape Breton Island** Fr. Île du Cap-Breton. island Nova Scotia, SE Canada
23 Y11 **Cape Canaveral** Florida, SE USA
21 Y6 **Cape Charles** Virginia, NE USA
77 P17 **Cape Coast** prev. Cape Coast Castle. S Ghana
Cape Coast Castle see Cape Coast
19 Q12 **Cape Cod Bay** bay Massachusetts, NE USA
23 W15 **Cape Coral** Florida, SE USA
181 R4 **Cape Crawford Roadhouse** Northern Territory, N Australia
9 Q7 **Cape Dorset** Baffin Island, Nunavut, NE Canada
21 N8 **Cape Fear River** ~ North Carolina, SE USA
27 Y7 **Cape Girardeau** Missouri, C USA
21 T14 **Cape Island** island South Carolina, SE USA
186 A6 **Capella** ▲ NW Papua New Guinea
98 H12 **Capelle aan den IJssel** Zuid-Holland, SW Netherlands
83 C15 **Capelongo** Huíla, C Angola
18 J17 **Cape May** New Jersey, NE USA
18 J17 **Cape May Court House** New Jersey, NE USA
Cape Palmas see Harper
8 I16 **Cape Parry** Northwest Territories, N Canada
65 P19 **Cape Rise** undersea feature SW Indian Ocean
Cape Saint Jacques see Vung Tau
Capesterre see Capesterre-Belle-Eau
45 Y6 **Capesterre-Belle-Eau** var. Capesterre. Basse Terre, S Guadeloupe
83 D26 **Cape Town** var. Ekapa, Afr. Kaapstad, Kapstad. ● (South Africa-legislative capital) Western Cape, SW South Africa
83 E26 **Cape Town** ✈ Western Cape, SW South Africa
76 D9 **Cape Verde** off. Republic of Cape Verde, Port. Cabo Verde, Ilhas do Cabo Verde. ◆ republic E Atlantic Ocean
64 L11 **Cape Verde Basin** undersea feature E Atlantic Ocean
66 K5 **Cape Verde Islands** island group E Atlantic Ocean
64 L10 **Cape Verde Plain** undersea feature E Atlantic Ocean
Cape Verde Plateau/Cape Verde Rise see Cape Verde Terrace
Cape Verde, Republic of see Cape Verde
64 L11 **Cape Verde Terrace** var. Cape Verde Plateau, Cape Verde Rise. undersea feature E Atlantic Ocean
181 V2 **Cape York Peninsula** peninsula Queensland, N Australia
44 M8 **Cap-Haïtien** var. Le Cap. N Haiti
43 T15 **Capira** Panamá, C Panama
14 K8 **Capitachouane** ~ Québec, SE Canada
14 L8 **Capitachouane, Lac** ◎ Québec, SE Canada
37 T13 **Capitan** New Mexico, SW USA
194 G3 **Capitán Arturo Prat** Chilean research station South Shetland Islands, Antarctica
37 S13 **Capitan Mountains** ▲▲ New Mexico, SW USA
62 M3 **Capitán Pablo Lagerenza** var. Mayor Pablo Lagerenza. Chaco, N Paraguay
37 T13 **Capitan Peak** ▲ New Mexico, SW USA
188 H5 **Capitol Hill** Saipan, S Northern Mariana Islands
60 I9 **Capivara, Represa** ▣ S Brazil
61 J16 **Capivari** Rio Grande do Sul, S Brazil
113 H15 **Čapljina** ◈ S Bosnia and Herzegovina
83 M15 **Capoche** var. Kapoche. ~ Mozambique/Zambia
Capo Delgado, Província de see Cabo Delgado
107 K17 **Capodichino** ✈ (Napoli) Campania, S Italy
Capodistria see Koper
106 E12 **Capraia, Isola di** island Arcipelago Toscano, C Italy
107 B16 **Caprara, Punta** var. Punta dello Scorno. headland Isola Asinara, W Italy
Capraria see Cabrera, Illa de
14 F10 **Capreol** Ontario, S Canada
107 K18 **Capri** Campania, S Italy
175 S9 **Capricorn Tablemount** undersea feature W Pacific Ocean
107 J18 **Capri, Isola di** island S Italy
83 G16 **Caprivi** ◈ district NE Namibia
Caprivi Concession see Caprivi Strip
83 F16 **Caprivi Strip** Ger. Caprivizipfel; prev. Caprivi Concession. cultural region NE Namibia
Caprivizipfel see Caprivi Strip
25 O5 **Cap Rock Escarpment** cliffs Texas, SW USA
15 R10 **Cap-Rouge** Québec, SE Canada
Cap Saint-Jacques see Vung Tau
38 F12 **Captain Cook** Hawai'i, USA, C Pacific Ocean
183 R10 **Captains Flat** New South Wales, SE Australia
102 K14 **Captieux** Gironde, SW France
107 K17 **Capua** Campania, S Italy
54 F14 **Caquetá** off. Departamento del Caquetá. ◈ province S Colombia
Caquetá, Departamento del see Caquetá
54 E13 **Caquetá, Río** var. Rio Japurá, Yapurá. ~ Brazil/Colombia see also Japurá, Rio
Caquetá, Río see Japurá, Rio
CAR see Central African Republic
Cara see Kara
57 I16 **Carabaya, Cordillera** ▲▲ E Peru
54 K5 **Carabobo** off. Estado Carabobo. ◈ state N Venezuela
Carabobo, Estado see Carabobo
116 I14 **Caracal** Olt, S Romania
58 F10 **Caracaraí** Rondônia, W Brazil
54 L5 **Caracas** ● (Venezuela) Distrito Federal, N Venezuela
54 I5 **Carache** Trujillo, N Venezuela
60 N10 **Caraguatatuba** São Paulo, S Brazil
48 I7 **Carajás, Serra dos** ▲▲ N Brazil
Caralis see Cagliari
54 E9 **Caramanta** Antioquia, W Colombia
171 P4 **Caramoan** Catanduanes Island, N Philippines
Caramurat see Mihail Kogălniceanu
116 F12 **Caransebeș** Ger. Karansebesch, Hung. Karánsebes. Caraș-Severin, SW Romania
Carapella see Carapelle
107 M16 **Carapelle** var. Carapella. ~ SE Italy
55 O9 **Carapo** Bolívar, SE Venezuela
13 P13 **Caraquet** New Brunswick, SE Canada
Caras see Caraz
116 F12 **Carașova** Hung. Krassóvár. Caraș-Severin, SW Romania
116 F12 **Caraș-Severin** ◈ county SW Romania
42 M5 **Caratasca, Laguna de** lagoon NE Honduras
58 C13 **Carauari** Amazonas, NW Brazil
Caravaca see Caravaca de la Cruz
105 Q12 **Caravaca de la Cruz** var. Caravaca. Murcia, SE Spain
106 E7 **Caravaggio** Lombardia, N Italy
107 C18 **Caravai, Passo di** pass Sardegna, Italy, C Mediterranean Sea
59 O19 **Caravelas** Bahia, E Brazil
56 C12 **Caraz** var. Caras. Ancash, W Peru
61 H14 **Carazinho** Rio Grande do Sul, S Brazil
42 J11 **Carazo** ◈ department SW Nicaragua
Carballiño see O Carballiño
104 G2 **Carballo** Galicia, NW Spain
9 W16 **Carberry** Manitoba, S Canada
40 F4 **Carbó** Sonora, NW Mexico
107 C20 **Carbonara, Capo** headland Sardegna, Italy, C Mediterranean Sea
37 Q5 **Carbondale** Colorado, C USA
30 L17 **Carbondale** Illinois, N USA
27 Q4 **Carbondale** Kansas, C USA
18 I13 **Carbondale** Pennsylvania, NE USA
13 V12 **Carbonear** Newfoundland, Newfoundland and Labrador, SE Canada
105 Q9 **Carboneras de Guadazaón** var. Carboneras de Guadazón. Castilla-La Mancha, C Spain
Carboneras de Guadazón see Carboneras de Guadazaón
23 O3 **Carbon Hill** Alabama, S USA
107 B20 **Carbonia** var. Carbonia Centro. Sardegna, Italy, C Mediterranean Sea
Carbonia Centro see Carbonia
105 S10 **Carcaixent** País Valenciano, E Spain
Carcaso see Carcassonne
65 B24 **Carcass Island** island NW Falkland Islands
103 O16 **Carcassonne** anc. Carcaso. Aude, S France
105 R12 **Carche** ▲ S Spain
56 A13 **Carchi** ◈ province N Ecuador
10 I8 **Carcross** Yukon Territory, W Canada
Cardamomes, Chaîne des see Krâvanh, Chuŏr Phnum
155 G22 **Cardamom Hills** ▲▲ SW India
Cardamom Mountains see Krâvanh, Chuŏr Phnum
104 M12 **Cardeña** Andalucía, S Spain
44 D4 **Cárdenas** Matanzas, W Cuba
41 O11 **Cárdenas** San Luis Potosí, C Mexico
41 U15 **Cárdenas** Tabasco, SE Mexico
63 H21 **Cardiel, Lago** ◎ S Argentina
97 K22 **Cardiff** Wel. Caerdydd. ◐ S Wales, UK
97 J22 **Cardiff-Wales** ✈ S Wales, UK
97 I21 **Cardigan** Wel. Aberteifi. SW Wales, UK
97 I20 **Cardigan** cultural region W Wales, UK
97 I20 **Cardigan Bay** bay W Wales, UK
19 N8 **Cardigan, Mount** ▲ New Hampshire, NE USA
14 M13 **Cardinal** Ontario, SE Canada
105 V5 **Cardona** Cataluña, NE Spain
61 E19 **Cardona** Soriano, SW Uruguay
105 V4 **Cardoner** ~ NE Spain
9 Q17 **Cardston** Alberta, SW Canada
181 W5 **Cardwell** Queensland, NE Australia
116 G8 **Carei** Ger. Gross-Karol, Karol, Hung. Nagykároly; prev. Careii-Mari. Satu Mare, NW Romania
Careii-Mari see Carei
58 F13 **Careiro** Amazonas, NW Brazil
102 J4 **Carentan** Manche, N France
104 M2 **Cares** ~ N Spain
33 P14 **Carey** Idaho, NW USA
31 S12 **Carey** Ohio, N USA
25 P4 **Carey** Texas, SW USA
180 L11 **Carey, Lake** ◎ Western Australia
173 O8 **Cargados Carajos Bank** undersea feature C Indian Ocean
102 G6 **Carhaix-Plouguer** Finistère, NW France
61 A22 **Carhué** Buenos Aires, E Argentina
55 O5 **Cariaco** Sucre, NE Venezuela
107 O20 **Cariati** Calabria, SW Italy
2 H17 **Caribbean Plate** tectonic feature
44 I11 **Caribbean Sea** sea W Atlantic Ocean
9 N15 **Cariboo Mountains** ▲▲ British Columbia, SW Canada
9 W9 **Caribou** Manitoba, C Canada
19 S2 **Caribou** Maine, NE USA
9 P10 **Caribou Mountains** ▲▲ Alberta, SW Canada
Caribrod see Dimitrovgrad
40 I6 **Carichic** Chihuahua, N Mexico
103 R3 **Carignan** Ardennes, N France
183 Q5 **Carinda** New South Wales, SE Australia
105 R6 **Cariñena** Aragón, NE Spain
107 I23 **Carini** Sicilia, Italy, C Mediterranean Sea
107 K17 **Carinola** Campania, S Italy
Carinthi see Kärnten
55 O5 **Caripe** Monagas, NE Venezuela
55 P5 **Caripito** Monagas, NE Venezuela
15 W7 **Carleton** Québec, SE Canada
31 S10 **Carleton** Michigan, N USA
13 O14 **Carleton, Mount** ▲ New Brunswick, SE Canada
14 L13 **Carleton Place** Ontario, SE Canada
35 V3 **Carlin** Nevada, W USA
30 K14 **Carlinville** Illinois, N USA
97 K14 **Carlisle** anc. Caer Luel, Luguvallium, Luguvallum. NW England, UK
27 V11 **Carlisle** Arkansas, C USA
31 N15 **Carlisle** Indiana, N USA
29 V14 **Carlisle** Iowa, C USA
21 N5 **Carlisle** Kentucky, S USA
18 F15 **Carlisle** Pennsylvania, NE USA
21 Q11 **Carlisle** South Carolina, SE USA
38 J17 **Carlisle Island** island Aleutian Islands, Alaska, USA
27 R7 **Carl Junction** Missouri, C USA
107 A20 **Carloforte** Sardegna, Italy, C Mediterranean Sea
Carlopago see Karlobag
61 B21 **Carlos Casares** Buenos Aires, E Argentina
61 E18 **Carlos Reyles** Durazno, C Uruguay
61 A21 **Carlos Tejedor** Buenos Aires, E Argentina
97 F19 **Carlow** Ir. Ceatharlach. SE Ireland
97 F19 **Carlow** Ir. Cheatharlach. ◈ county SE Ireland
96 F7 **Carloway** NW Scotland, UK
35 U17 **Carlsbad** California, W USA
37 U15 **Carlsbad** New Mexico, SW USA
Carlsbad see Karlovy Vary
129 N13 **Carlsberg Ridge** undersea feature S Arabian Sea
Carlsruhe see Karlsruhe
29 W6 **Carlton** Minnesota, N USA
9 V17 **Carlyle** Saskatchewan, S Canada
30 L15 **Carlyle** Illinois, N USA
30 L15 **Carlyle Lake** ▣ Illinois, N USA
10 H7 **Carmacks** Yukon Territory, W Canada
106 B9 **Carmagnola** Piemonte, NW Italy
9 X16 **Carman** Manitoba, S Canada
Carmana/Carmania see Kermān
97 I21 **Carmarthen** SW Wales, UK
97 I21 **Carmarthen** cultural region SW Wales, UK
97 I22 **Carmarthen Bay** inlet SW Wales, UK
103 N14 **Carmaux** Tarn, S France
35 N11 **Carmel** California, W USA
31 O13 **Carmel** Indiana, N USA
18 L13 **Carmel** New York, NE USA
97 H18 **Carmel Head** headland NW Wales, UK
42 E2 **Carmelita** Petén, N Guatemala
61 D19 **Carmelo** Colonia, SW Uruguay
41 V14 **Carmen** var. Ciudad del Carmen. Campeche, SE Mexico
61 A25 **Carmen de Patagones** Buenos Aires, E Argentina
40 F8 **Carmen, Isla** island W Mexico
40 M5 **Carmen, Sierra del** ▲▲ NW Mexico
30 M16 **Carmi** Illinois, N USA
35 O7 **Carmichael** California, W USA
Carmiel see Karmi'él
25 U11 **Carmine** Texas, SW USA
104 K14 **Carmona** Andalucía, S Spain
Carmona see Uíge
Carnaro see Kvarner
180 G9 **Carnarvon** Western Australia
14 I13 **Carnarvon** Ontario, SE Canada
83 G24 **Carnarvon** Northern Cape, W South Africa
Carnarvon see Caernarfon
180 K9 **Carnarvon Range** ▲▲ Western Australia
Carn Domhnach see Carndonagh
96 E13 **Carndonagh** Ir. Carn Domhnach. NW Ireland
9 V17 **Carnduff** Saskatchewan, S Canada
26 L11 **Carnegie** Oklahoma, C USA
180 L9 **Carnegie, Lake** salt lake Western Australia
193 U8 **Carnegie Ridge** undersea feature E Pacific Ocean
96 H9 **Carn Eige** ▲ N Scotland, UK
182 F5 **Carnes** South Australia
194 J12 **Carney Island** island Antarctica
18 H16 **Carneys Point** New Jersey, NE USA
Carniche, Alpi see Karnische Alpen
151 Q21 **Car Nicobar** island Nicobar Islands, India, NE Indian Ocean
79 H15 **Carnot** Mambéré-Kadéï, W Central African Republic
182 F10 **Carnot, Cape** headland South Australia
96 K11 **Carnoustie** E Scotland, UK
97 F20 **Carnsore Point** Ir. Ceann an Chairn. headland SE Ireland
8 H7 **Carnwath** ~ Northwest Territories, NW Canada
31 R8 **Caro** Michigan, N USA
23 Z15 **Carol City** Florida, SE USA
59 L14 **Carolina** Maranhão, E Brazil
45 U5 **Carolina** E Puerto Rico
21 V12 **Carolina Beach** North Carolina, SE USA
Caroline Island see Millennium Island
189 N15 **Caroline Islands** island group C Micronesia
129 Z14 **Caroline Plate** tectonic feature
192 H7 **Caroline Ridge** undersea feature E Philippine Sea
Carolopois see Châlons-en-Champagne
45 V14 **Caroni Arena Dam** ▣ Trinidad, Trinidad and Tobago
Caronie, Monti see Nebrodi, Monti
55 P7 **Caroní, Río** ~ E Venezuela
45 U14 **Caroni River** ~ Trinidad, Trinidad and Tobago
Caronium see A Coruña
54 J5 **Carora** Lara, N Venezuela
86 F12 **Carpathian Mountains** var. Carpathians, Cz./Pol. Karpaty, Ger. Karpaten. ▲▲ E Europe
Carpathians see Carpathian Mountains
Carpathos/Carpathus see Kárpathos
116 H12 **Carpații Meridionali** var. Alpi Transilvaniei, Carpații Sudici, Eng. South Carpathians, Transylvanian Alps, Ger. Südkarpaten, Transsylvanische Alpen, Hung. Déli-Kárpátok, Erdélyi-Havasok. ▲▲ C Romania
Carpații Sudici see Carpații Meridionali
174 L7 **Carpentaria, Gulf of** gulf N Australia
Carpentoracte see Carpentras
103 R14 **Carpentras** anc. Carpentoracte. Vaucluse, SE France
106 F9 **Carpi** Emilia-Romagna, N Italy
116 E11 **Cărpiniș** Hung. Gyertyámos. Timiș, W Romania
35 R14 **Carpinteria** California, W USA
23 S9 **Carrabelle** Florida, SE USA
Carraig Aonair see Fastnet Rock
Carraig Fhearghais see Carrickfergus
Carraig Mhachaire Rois see Carrickmacross
Carraig na Siúire see Carrick-on-Suir
Carrantual see Carrauntoohil
106 E10 **Carrara** Toscana, C Italy
61 F20 **Carrasco** ✈ (Montevideo) Canelones, S Uruguay
105 P9 **Carrascosa del Campo** Castilla-La Mancha, C Spain
54 H4 **Carrasquero** Zulia, NW Venezuela
183 O9 **Carrathool** New South Wales, SE Australia
Carrauntohil see Carrauntoohil
97 B21 **Carrauntoohil** Ir. Carrantual, Carrauntohil, Corrán Tuathail. ▲ SW Ireland
45 Y15 **Carriacou** island N Grenada
97 G15 **Carrickfergus** Ir. Carraig Fhearghais. NE Northern Ireland, UK
97 F16 **Carrickmacross** Ir. Carraig Mhachaire Rois. N Ireland
97 D16 **Carrick-on-Shannon** Ir. Cora Droma Rúisc. NW Ireland
97 E20 **Carrick-on-Suir** Ir. Carraig na Siúire. S Ireland
182 I7 **Carrieton** South Australia
40 L7 **Carrillo** Chihuahua, N Mexico
29 O4 **Carrington** North Dakota, N USA
104 M4 **Carrión** ~ N Spain
104 M4 **Carrión de los Condes** Castilla-León, N Spain
25 P13 **Carrizo Springs** Texas, SW USA
37 S13 **Carrizozo** New Mexico, SW USA
29 T13 **Carroll** Iowa, C USA
23 N4 **Carrollton** Alabama, S USA
23 R3 **Carrollton** Georgia, SE USA
30 K14 **Carrollton** Illinois, N USA
20 L4 **Carrollton** Kentucky, S USA
31 R8 **Carrollton** Michigan, N USA
27 T3 **Carrollton** Missouri, C USA
31 U12 **Carrollton** Ohio, N USA
25 T6 **Carrollton** Texas, SW USA
9 U14 **Carrot** ~ Saskatchewan, S Canada
9 U14 **Carrot River** Saskatchewan, C Canada
18 J7 **Carry Falls Reservoir** ▣ New York, NE USA
136 L11 **Çarşamba** Samsun, N Turkey
28 L6 **Carson** North Dakota, N USA
35 Q6 **Carson City** state capital Nevada, W USA
35 R6 **Carson River** ~ Nevada, W USA
35 S5 **Carson Sink** salt flat Nevada, W USA
9 Q16 **Carstairs** Alberta, SW Canada
Carstensz, Puntjak see Jaya, Puncak
54 E5 **Cartagena** var. Cartagena de los Indes. Bolívar, NW Colombia
105 R13 **Cartagena** anc. Carthago Nova. Murcia, SE Spain
54 E13 **Cartagena de Chaira** Caquetá, S Colombia
Cartagena de los Indes see Cartagena
54 D10 **Cartago** Valle del Cauca, W Colombia
43 N14 **Cartago** Cartago, C Costa Rica
42 M14 **Cartago** off. Provincia de Cartago. ◈ province C Costa Rica
Cartago, Provincia de see Cartago
25 O11 **Carta Valley** Texas, SW USA
104 F10 **Cartaxo** Santarém, C Portugal
104 I14 **Cartaya** Andalucía, S Spain
Carteret Islands see Tulun Islands
29 S15 **Carter Lake** Iowa, C USA
23 S3 **Cartersville** Georgia, SE USA
185 M14 **Carterton** Wellington, North Island, New Zealand
30 J13 **Carthage** Illinois, N USA
22 L5 **Carthage** Mississippi, S USA
27 R7 **Carthage** Missouri, C USA
18 I8 **Carthage** New York, NE USA

21 T10 **Carthage** North Carolina, SE USA
20 K8 **Carthage** Tennessee, S USA
25 X7 **Carthage** Texas, SW USA
74 M5 **Carthage** ✈ (Tunis) N Tunisia
Carthago Nova see Cartagena
14 E10 **Cartier** Ontario, S Canada
13 S8 **Cartwright** Newfoundland and Labrador, E Canada
55 P9 **Caruana de Montaña** Bolívar, SE Venezuela
59 Q15 **Caruaru** Pernambuco, E Brazil
55 P5 **Carúpano** Sucre, NE Venezuela
Carusbur see Cherbourg
58 M12 **Carutapera** Maranhão, E Brazil
27 Y9 **Caruthersville** Missouri, C USA
103 O1 **Carvin** Pas-de-Calais, N France
58 E12 **Carvoeiro** Amazonas, NW Brazil
104 E10 **Carvoeiro, Cabo** cape C Portugal
21 U9 **Cary** North Carolina, SE USA
182 M3 **Caryapundy Swamp** wetland New South Wales/Queensland, SE Australia
65 E24 **Carysfort, Cape** headland East Falkland, Falkland Islands
74 F6 **Casablanca** Ar. Dar-el-Beida. NW Morocco
60 M8 **Casa Branca** São Paulo, S Brazil
36 L14 **Casa Grande** Arizona, SW USA
106 C8 **Casale Monferrato** Piemonte, NW Italy
106 E8 **Casalpusterlengo** Lombardia, N Italy
54 H10 **Casanare** off. Intendencia de Casanare. ⬖ province C Colombia
Casanare, Intendencia de see Casanare
55 P5 **Casanay** Sucre, NE Venezuela
24 K11 **Casa Piedra** Texas, SW USA
107 Q19 **Casarano** Puglia, SE Italy
42 J11 **Casares** Carazo, W Nicaragua
105 R10 **Casas Ibáñez** Castilla-La Mancha, C Spain
61 I14 **Casca** Rio Grande do Sul, S Brazil
172 I17 **Cascade** Mahé, NE Seychelles
33 N13 **Cascade** Idaho, NW USA
29 Y13 **Cascade** Iowa, C USA
33 R9 **Cascade** Montana, NW USA
185 B20 **Cascade Point** headland South Island, New Zealand
32 G13 **Cascade Range** ▲▲ Oregon/Washington, NW USA
33 N12 **Cascade Reservoir** ⊠ Idaho, NW USA
0 E8 **Cascadia Basin** undersea feature NE Pacific Ocean
104 E11 **Cascais** Lisboa, C Portugal
15 W7 **Cascapédia** ~ Québec, SE Canada
59 I22 **Cascavel** Ceará, E Brazil
60 G11 **Cascavel** Paraná, S Brazil
106 I13 **Cascia** Umbria, C Italy
106 F11 **Cascina** Toscana, C Italy
19 Q8 **Casco Bay** bay Maine, NE USA
194 J7 **Case Island** island Antarctica
106 B8 **Caselle** ✈ (Torino) Piemonte, NW Italy
107 K17 **Caserta** Campania, S Italy
15 N8 **Casey** Québec, SE Canada
30 M14 **Casey** Illinois, N USA
195 Y12 **Casey** Australian research station Antarctica
195 W3 **Casey Bay** bay Antarctica
80 Q11 **Caseyr, Raas** cape NE Somalia
97 D20 **Cashel** Ir. Caiseal. S Ireland
54 G6 **Casigua** Zulia, W Venezuela
61 B19 **Casilda** Santa Fe, C Argentina
Casim see General Toshevo
183 V4 **Casino** New South Wales, SE Australia
Casinum see Cassino
111 E17 **Čáslav** Ger. Tschaslau. Střední Čechy, C Czech Republic
56 C13 **Casma** Ancash, C Peru
167 S7 **Ca, Sông** ~ N Vietnam
107 K17 **Casoria** Campania, S Italy
105 T6 **Caspe** Aragón, NE Spain
33 X15 **Casper** Wyoming, C USA
84 M10 **Caspian Depression** Kaz. Kaspiy Mangy Oypaty, Rus. Prikaspiyskaya Nizmennost'. depression Kazakhstan/Russian Federation
130 D10 **Caspian Sea** Az. Xäzär Dänizi, Kaz. Kaspiy Tengizi, Per. Baḥr-e Khazar, Daryā-ye Khazar, Rus. Kaspiyskoye More. inland sea Asia/Europe
83 L14 **Cassacatiza** Tete, NW Mozambique
Cassai see Kasai
82 F13 **Cassamba** Moxico, E Angola
107 N20 **Cassano allo Ionio** Calabria, SE Italy
31 S8 **Cass City** Michigan, N USA
Cassel see Kassel
14 M13 **Casselman** Ontario, SE Canada
29 R5 **Casselton** North Dakota, N USA
59 M16 **Cássia** var. Santa Rita de Cassia. Bahia, E Brazil
10 J9 **Cassiar** British Columbia, W Canada
10 K10 **Cassiar Mountains** ▲▲ British Columbia, W Canada
83 C15 **Cassinga** Huíla, SW Angola
107 J16 **Cassino** prev. San Germano; anc. Casinum. Lazio, C Italy
29 T4 **Cass Lake** Minnesota, N USA
29 T4 **Cass Lake** ◎ Minnesota, N USA
31 P10 **Cassopolis** Michigan, N USA
31 S8 **Cass River** ~ Michigan, N USA
27 S8 **Cassville** Missouri, C USA
Castamoni see Kastamonu
58 L12 **Castanhal** Pará, NE Brazil
104 G8 **Castanheira de Pêra** Leiria, C Portugal
41 N7 **Castaños** Coahuila de Zaragoza, NE Mexico
108 I10 **Castasegna** Graubünden, SE Switzerland
106 D8 **Casteggio** Lombardia, N Italy
107 K23 **Castelbuono** Sicilia, Italy, C Mediterranean Sea
107 K15 **Castel di Sangro** Abruzzo, C Italy
106 H7 **Castelfranco Veneto** Veneto, NE Italy
102 K14 **Casteljaloux** Lot-et-Garonne, SW France
107 L18 **Castellabate** var. Santa Maria di Castellabate. Campania, S Italy
107 I23 **Castellammare del Golfo** Sicilia, Italy, C Mediterranean Sea
107 H22 **Castellammare, Golfo di** gulf Sicilia, Italy, C Mediterranean Sea
103 U15 **Castellane** Alpes-de-Haute-Provence, SE France
107 O18 **Castellaneta** Puglia, SE Italy
106 E9 **Castel l'Arquato** Emilia-Romagna, C Italy
61 E21 **Castelli** Buenos Aires, E Argentina
Castelló de la Plana see Castellón de la Plana
105 S8 **Castellón** ⬖ province País Valenciano, E Spain
Castellón see Castellón de la Plana
105 T9 **Castellón de la Plana** Cat. Castelló de la Plana, Castellón. País Valenciano, E Spain
105 S7 **Castellote** Aragón, NE Spain
103 N16 **Castelnaudary** Aude, S France
102 L16 **Castelnau-Magnoac** Hautes-Pyrénées, S France
106 F10 **Castelnovo ne' Monti** Emilia-Romagna, C Italy
Castelnuovo see Herceg-Novi
104 H9 **Castelo Branco** Castelo Branco, C Portugal
104 H8 **Castelo Branco** ⬖ district C Portugal
104 I10 **Castelo de Vide** Portalegre, C Portugal
104 G9 **Castelo do Bode, Barragem do** ⊠ C Portugal
106 G10 **Castel San Pietro Terme** Emilia-Romagna, C Italy
107 B17 **Castelsardo** Sardegna, Italy, C Mediterranean Sea
102 M14 **Castelsarrasin** Tarn-et-Garonne, S France
107 I24 **Casteltermini** Sicilia, Italy, C Mediterranean Sea
107 H24 **Castelvetrano** Sicilia, Italy, C Mediterranean Sea
182 L12 **Casterton** Victoria, SE Australia
102 J15 **Castets** Landes, SW France
106 H12 **Castiglione del Lago** Umbria, C Italy
106 F13 **Castiglione della Pescaia** Toscana, C Italy
106 F8 **Castiglione delle Stiviere** Lombardia, N Italy
104 M9 **Castilla-La Mancha** ⬖ autonomous community NE Spain
104 L5 **Castilla-León** var. Castillia y Leon. ⬖ autonomous community NW Spain
105 N10 **Castilla Nueva** cultural region C Spain
105 N6 **Castilla Vieja** cultural region N Spain
Castillia y Leon see Castilla-León
Castillo de Locubim see Castillo de Locubín
105 N14 **Castillo de Locubín** var. Castillo de Locubim. Andalucía, S Spain
102 K13 **Castillon-la-Bataille** Gironde, SW France
63 I19 **Castillo, Pampa del** plain S Argentina
61 G19 **Castillos** Rocha, SE Uruguay
97 B16 **Castlebar** Ir. Caisleán an Bharraigh. W Ireland
97 F16 **Castleblayney** Ir. Baile na Lorgan. N Ireland
45 O11 **Castle Bruce** E Dominica
36 M5 **Castle Dale** Utah, W USA
36 I14 **Castle Dome Peak** ▲ Arizona, SW USA
97 J14 **Castle Douglas** S Scotland, UK
97 E14 **Castlefinn** Ir. Caisleán na Finne. NW Ireland
97 M17 **Castleford** N England, UK
9 O17 **Castlegar** British Columbia, SW Canada
64 B12 **Castle Harbour** inlet Bermuda, NW Atlantic Ocean
21 V12 **Castle Hayne** North Carolina, SE USA
97 B20 **Castleisland** Ir. Oileán Ciarral. SW Ireland
183 N12 **Castlemaine** Victoria, SE Australia
37 R5 **Castle Peak** ▲ Colorado, C USA
33 O13 **Castle Peak** ▲ Idaho, NW USA
184 N13 **Castlepoint** Wellington, North Island, New Zealand
97 D17 **Castlerea** Ir. An Caisleán Riabhach. W Ireland
97 G15 **Castlereagh** Ir. An Caisleán Riabhach. N Northern Ireland, UK
183 R6 **Castlereagh River** ~ New South Wales, SE Australia
37 T5 **Castle Rock** Colorado, C USA
30 K7 **Castle Rock Lake** ⊠ Wisconsin, N USA
65 G25 **Castle Rock Point** headland S Saint Helena
97 I16 **Castletown** SE Isle of Man
29 R9 **Castlewood** South Dakota, N USA
9 R15 **Castor** Alberta, SW Canada
14 M13 **Castor** ~ Ontario, SE Canada
27 X7 **Castor River** ~ Missouri, C USA
Castra Albiensium see Castres
Castra Regina see Regensburg
103 N15 **Castres** anc. Castra Albiensium. Tarn, S France
98 H9 **Castricum** Noord-Holland, W Netherlands
45 S11 **Castries** ● (Saint Lucia) N Saint Lucia
60 J11 **Castro** Paraná, S Brazil
63 F17 **Castro** Los Lagos, W Chile
104 H7 **Castro Daire** Viseu, N Portugal
104 M13 **Castro del Río** Andalucía, S Spain
Castrogiovanni see Enna
104 H14 **Castro Marim** Faro, S Portugal
104 J2 **Castropol** Asturias, N Spain
105 O2 **Castro-Urdiales** var. Castro Urdiales. Cantabria, N Spain
104 G13 **Castro Verde** Beja, S Portugal
107 N19 **Castrovillari** Calabria, SW Italy
35 N10 **Castroville** California, W USA
25 R12 **Castroville** Texas, SW USA
104 K11 **Castuera** Extremadura, W Spain
61 F19 **Casupá** Florida, S Uruguay
185 A22 **Caswell Sound** sound South Island, New Zealand
137 Q13 **Çat** Erzurum, NE Turkey
42 K6 **Catacamas** Olancho, C Honduras
56 A10 **Catacaos** Piura, NW Peru
22 I7 **Catahoula Lake** ◎ Louisiana, S USA
137 S15 **Çatak** Van, SE Turkey
137 S15 **Çatak Çayi** ~ SE Turkey
114 O12 **Çatalca** İstanbul, NW Turkey
114 O12 **Çatalca Yarimadasi** physical region NW Turkey
62 H6 **Catalina** Antofagasta, N Chile
Catalonia see Cataluña
105 U5 **Cataluña** Cat. Catalunya, Eng. Catalonia. ⬖ autonomous community N Spain
Catalunya see Cataluña
62 I7 **Catamarca** off. Provincia de Catamarca. ⬖ province NW Argentina
Catamarca see San Fernando del Valle de Catamarca
Catamarca, Provincia de see Catamarca
83 M16 **Catandica** Manica, C Mozambique
171 P4 **Catanduanes Island** island N Philippines
60 K8 **Catanduva** São Paulo, S Brazil
107 L24 **Catania** Sicilia, Italy, C Mediterranean Sea
107 M24 **Catania, Golfo di** gulf Sicilia, Italy, C Mediterranean Sea
45 U5 **Cataño** var. Cantaño. E Puerto Rico
107 O21 **Catanzaro** Calabria, SW Italy
107 O22 **Catanzaro Marina** var. Marina di Catanzaro. Calabria, S Italy
Marina di Catanzaro see Catanzaro Marina
25 Q14 **Catarina** Texas, SW USA
171 Q5 **Catarman** Samar, C Philippines
105 S10 **Catarroja** País Valenciano, E Spain
21 R11 **Catawba River** ~ North Carolina/South Carolina, SE USA
171 Q5 **Catbalogan** Samar, C Philippines
14 I14 **Catchacoma** Ontario, SE Canada
41 S15 **Catemaco** Veracruz-Llave, SE Mexico
Cathair na Mart see Westport
Cathair Saidhbhín see Cahersiveen
31 P5 **Cat Head Point** headland Michigan, N USA
23 Q2 **Cathedral Caverns** cave Alabama, S USA
35 V16 **Cathedral City** California, W USA
24 K10 **Cathedral Mountain** ▲ Texas, SW USA
32 G10 **Cathlamet** Washington, NW USA
76 G13 **Catió** S Guinea-Bissau
55 O10 **Catisimiña** Bolívar, SE Venezuela
44 J3 **Cat Island** island C Bahamas
12 B9 **Cat Lake** Ontario, S Canada
21 P5 **Catlettsburg** Kentucky, S USA
185 D24 **Catlins** ~ South Island, New Zealand
35 R1 **Catnip Mountain** ▲ Nevada, W USA
41 Z11 **Catoche, Cabo** headland SE Mexico
27 P9 **Catoosa** Oklahoma, C USA
41 N10 **Catorce** San Luis Potosí, C Mexico
63 I14 **Catriel** Río Negro, C Argentina
62 K13 **Catriló** La Pampa, C Argentina
58 F11 **Catrimani** Roraima, N Brazil
58 E10 **Catrimani, Rio** ~ N Brazil
18 K11 **Catskill** New York, NE USA
18 K11 **Catskill Creek** ~ New York, NE USA
18 J11 **Catskill Mountains** ▲▲ New York, NE USA
18 D11 **Cattaraugus Creek** ~ New York, NE USA
Cattaro see Kotor
Cattaro, Bocche di see Kotorska, Boka
107 I24 **Cattolica Eraclea** Sicilia, Italy, C Mediterranean Sea
83 B14 **Catumbela** ~ W Angola
83 N14 **Catur** Niassa, N Mozambique
82 C10 **Cauale** ~ NE Angola
171 O2 **Cauayan** Luzon, N Philippines
54 C12 **Cauca** off. Departamento del Cauca. ⬖ province SW Colombia
47 P5 **Cauca** ~ SE Venezuela
Cauca, Departamento del see Cauca
58 P13 **Caucaia** Ceará, E Brazil
54 E7 **Cauca, Río** ~ N Colombia
54 E7 **Caucasia** Antioquia, NW Colombia
137 Q8 **Caucasus** Rus. Kavkaz. ▲▲ Georgia/Russian Federation
62 I10 **Caucete** San Juan, W Argentina
105 R11 **Caudete** Castilla-La Mancha, C Spain
103 P2 **Caudry** Nord, N France
82 D11 **Caungula** Lunda Norte, NE Angola
62 G13 **Cauquenes** Maule, C Chile
55 N8 **Caura, Río** ~ C Venezuela
15 V7 **Causapscal** Québec, SE Canada
117 N10 **Căuşeni** Rus. Kaushany. E Moldova
102 M14 **Caussade** Tarn-et-Garonne, S France
102 K17 **Cauterets** Hautes-Pyrénées, S France
10 J15 **Caution, Cape** headland British Columbia, SW Canada
44 H7 **Cauto** ~ E Cuba
Cauvery see Kāveri
102 L3 **Caux, Pays de** physical region N France
107 L18 **Cava de' Tirreni** Campania, S Italy
104 G6 **Cávado** ~ N Portugal
Cavaia see Kavajë
103 R15 **Cavaillon** Vaucluse, SE France
103 U16 **Cavalaire-sur-Mer** Var, SE France
106 G6 **Cavalese** Ger. Gablös. Trentino-Alto Adige, N Italy
29 Q2 **Cavalier** North Dakota, N USA
76 L17 **Cavalla** var. Cavally, Cavally Fleuve. ~ Ivory Coast/Liberia
105 Y8 **Cavalleria, Cap de** var. Cabo Caballeria. cape Menorca, Spain, W Mediterranean Sea
184 K2 **Cavalli Islands** island group N New Zealand
Cavally/Cavally Fleuve see Cavalla
97 E16 **Cavan** Ir. Cabhán. N Ireland
97 E16 **Cavan** Ir. An Cabhán. ⬖ county N Ireland
106 H8 **Cavarzere** Veneto, NE Italy
27 W9 **Cave City** Arkansas, C USA
20 K7 **Cave City** Kentucky, S USA
65 M25 **Cave Point** headland S Tristan da Cunha
21 N5 **Cave Run Lake** ⊠ Kentucky, S USA
58 K11 **Caviana de Fora, Ilha** var. Ilha Caviana. island N Brazil
Caviana, Ilha see Caviana de Fora, Ilha
113 I16 **Cavtat** It. Ragusavecchia. Dubrovnik-Neretva, SE Croatia
Cawnpore see Kānpur
Caxamarca see Cajamarca
58 A13 **Caxias** Amazonas, W Brazil
58 N13 **Caxias** Maranhão, E Brazil
61 I15 **Caxias do Sul** Rio Grande do Sul, S Brazil
42 J4 **Caxinas, Punta** headland N Honduras
82 B11 **Caxito** Bengo, NW Angola
136 F14 **Çay** Afyon, W Turkey
40 L15 **Cayacal, Punta** var. Punta Mongrove. headland S Mexico
56 C6 **Cayambe** Pichincha, N Ecuador
56 C6 **Cayambe** ▲ N Ecuador
21 R12 **Cayce** South Carolina, SE USA
55 Y10 **Cayenne** ○ (French Guiana) NE French Guiana
55 Y10 **Cayenne** ✈ NE French Guiana
44 K10 **Cayes** var. Les Cayes. SW Haiti
45 U6 **Cayey** C Puerto Rico
45 U6 **Cayey, Sierra de** ▲▲ E Puerto Rico
103 N14 **Caylus** Tarn-et-Garonne, S France
44 E8 **Cayman Brac** island E Cayman Islands
44 D8 **Cayman Islands** ◇ UK dependent territory W West Indies
64 D11 **Cayman Trench** undersea feature NW Caribbean Sea
47 O3 **Cayman Trough** undersea feature NW Caribbean Sea
80 O13 **Caynabo** Sool, N Somalia
42 F3 **Cayo** ⬖ district SW Belize
Cayo see San Ignacio
43 N9 **Cayos Guerrero** reef E Nicaragua
43 O9 **Cayos King** reef E Nicaragua
44 E4 **Cay Sal** islet SW Bahamas
14 G16 **Cayuga** Ontario, S Canada
25 V8 **Cayuga** Texas, SW USA
18 G10 **Cayuga Lake** ◎ New York, NE USA
104 K13 **Cazalla de la Sierra** Andalucía, S Spain
116 L14 **Căzăneşti** Ialomiţa, SE Romania
102 M16 **Cazères** Haute-Garonne, S France
112 E10 **Cazin** ⬖ Federacija Bosna I Hercegovina, NW Bosnia and Herzegovina
82 G13 **Cazombo** Moxico, E Angola
105 O13 **Cazorla** Andalucía, S Spain
Cazza see Sušac
104 L4 **Cea** ~ NW Spain
Ceadâr-Lunga see Ciadîr-Lunga
Ceanannas see Kells
Ceann Toirc see Kanturk
58 O13 **Ceará** off. Estado do Ceará. ⬖ state C Brazil
Ceará see Fortaleza
Ceara Abyssal Plain see Ceará Plain
Ceará, Estado do see Ceará
59 Q14 **Ceará Mirim** Rio Grande do Norte, E Brazil
64 J13 **Ceará Plain** var. Ceara Abyssal Plain. undersea feature W Atlantic Ocean
64 I13 **Ceará Ridge** undersea feature C Atlantic Ocean
Ceatharlach see Carlow
43 Q17 **Cébaco, Isla** island SW Panama
40 K7 **Ceballos** Durango, C Mexico
61 G19 **Cebollatí** Rocha, E Uruguay
61 G19 **Cebollatí, Río** ~ E Uruguay
105 P5 **Cebollera** ▲ N Spain
104 M8 **Cebreros** Castilla-León, N Spain
171 P6 **Cebu** off. Cebu City. Cebu, C Philippines
171 P6 **Cebu** island C Philippines
Cebu City see Cebu
107 J16 **Ceccano** Lazio, C Italy
Čechy see Bohemia
106 F12 **Cecina** Toscana, C Italy
26 K4 **Cedar Bluff Reservoir** ⊠ Kansas, C USA
30 M8 **Cedarburg** Wisconsin, N USA
36 J7 **Cedar City** Utah, W USA
25 T11 **Cedar Creek** Texas, SW USA
28 L7 **Cedar Creek** ~ North Dakota, N USA
25 U7 **Cedar Creek Reservoir** ⊠ Texas, SW USA
29 W13 **Cedar Falls** Iowa, C USA
31 N8 **Cedar Grove** Wisconsin, N USA
21 Y6 **Cedar Island** island Virginia, NE USA
23 U11 **Cedar Key** Cedar Keys, Florida, SE USA
23 U11 **Cedar Keys** island group Florida, SE USA
9 V14 **Cedar Lake** ◎ Manitoba, C Canada
14 I11 **Cedar Lake** ◎ Ontario, SE Canada
24 M6 **Cedar Lake** ◎ Texas, SW USA
29 X13 **Cedar Rapids** Iowa, C USA
29 X14 **Cedar River** ~ Iowa/Minnesota, C USA
29 O14 **Cedar River** ~ Nebraska, C USA
31 P8 **Cedar Springs** Michigan, N USA
23 R3 **Cedartown** Georgia, SE USA
27 O7 **Cedar Vale** Kansas, C USA
35 Q2 **Cedarville** California, W USA
104 H1 **Cedeira** Galicia, NW Spain
42 H8 **Cedeño** Choluteca, S Honduras
41 N10 **Cedral** San Luis Potosí, C Mexico
42 I6 **Cedros** Francisco Morazán, C Honduras
40 M9 **Cedros** Zacatecas, C Mexico
40 B5 **Cedros, Isla** island W Mexico
193 R5 **Cedros Trench** undersea feature E Pacific Ocean
182 E7 **Ceduna** South Australia
110 D10 **Cedynia** Ger. Zehden. Zachodnio-pomorskie, W Poland
80 P12 **Ceelaayo** Sanaag, N Somalia
81 O16 **Ceel Buur** It. El Bur. Galguduud, C Somalia
81 N15 **Ceel Dheere** var. Ceel Dher, It. El Dere. Galguduud, C Somalia
Ceel Dher see Ceel Dheere
81 P14 **Ceel Xamure** Mudug, E Somalia
80 O12 **Ceerigaabo** var. Erigabo, Erigavo. Sanaag, N Somalia
107 J23 **Cefalù** anc. Cephaloedium. Sicilia, Italy, C Mediterranean Sea
105 N6 **Cega** ~ N Spain
111 K23 **Cegléd** prev. Czegléd. Pest, C Hungary
113 N18 **Čegrane** W FYR Macedonia
105 Q13 **Cehegín** Murcia, SE Spain
136 K12 **Çekerek** Yozgat, N Turkey
146 B13 **Çekiçler** Rus. Chekishlyar, Turkm. Chekichler. Balkan Welaýaty, W Turkmenistan
107 J15 **Celano** Abruzzo, C Italy
104 H4 **Celanova** Galicia, NW Spain
42 F6 **Celaque, Cordillera de** ▲▲ W Honduras
41 N13 **Celaya** Guanajuato, C Mexico
Celebes see Sulawesi
192 F7 **Celebes Basin** undersea feature SE South China Sea
192 F7 **Celebes Sea** Ind. Laut Sulawesi. sea Indonesia/Philippines
41 W12 **Celestún** Yucatán, E Mexico
31 Q12 **Celina** Ohio, N USA
20 L8 **Celina** Tennessee, S USA
25 U5 **Celina** Texas, SW USA
112 G11 **Čelinac Donji** ⬖ Republika Srpska, N Bosnia and Herzegovina
109 V10 **Celje** Ger. Cilli. C Slovenia
111 G23 **Celldömölk** Vas, W Hungary
100 J12 **Celle** var. Zelle. Niedersachsen, N Germany
99 D19 **Celles** Hainaut, SW Belgium
104 I7 **Celorico da Beira** Guarda, N Portugal
Celovec see Klagenfurt
64 M7 **Celtic Sea** Ir. An Mhuir Cheilteach. sea SW British Isles
64 N7 **Celtic Shelf** undersea feature E Atlantic Ocean
114 L13 **Çeltik Gölu** ◎ NW Turkey
146 J17 **Çemenibit** prev. Rus. Chemenibit. Mary Welaýaty, S Turkmenistan
113 M14 **Čemerno** ▲ C Serbia
105 Q12 **Cenajo, Embalse del** ⊠ S Spain
171 V13 **Cenderawasih, Teluk** var. Teluk Irian, Teluk Sarera. bay W Pacific Ocean
105 P4 **Cenicero** La Rioja, N Spain
106 E9 **Ceno** ~ NW Italy
102 K13 **Cenon** Gironde, SW France
14 K13 **Centennial Lake** ◎ Ontario, SE Canada
Centennial State see Colorado
37 S7 **Center** Colorado, C USA
29 Q13 **Center** Nebraska, C USA
28 M5 **Center** North Dakota, N USA
25 X8 **Center** Texas, SW USA
29 W8 **Center City** Minnesota, N USA
36 L5 **Centerfield** Utah, W USA
20 K9 **Center Hill Lake** ⊠ Tennessee, S USA
29 X13 **Center Point** Iowa, C USA
25 R11 **Center Point** Texas, SW USA
29 W16 **Centerville** Iowa, C USA
27 W7 **Centerville** Missouri, C USA
29 R12 **Centerville** South Dakota, N USA
20 I9 **Centerville** Tennessee, S USA
25 V9 **Centerville** Texas, SW USA
40 M5 **Centinela, Picacho del** ▲ NE Mexico
106 G9 **Cento** Emilia-Romagna, N Italy
Centrafricaine, République see Central African Republic
39 S8 **Central** Alaska, USA
37 P15 **Central** New Mexico, SW USA
83 H18 **Central** ⬖ district E Botswana
138 E10 **Central** ⬖ district C Israel
81 I19 **Central** ⬖ province C Kenya
82 M13 **Central** ⬖ region C Malawi
153 P12 **Central** ⬖ zone C Nepal
186 E9 **Central** ⬖ province S Papua New Guinea
63 I21 **Central** ⬖ department C Paraguay
186 E9 **Central** off. Central Province. ⬖ province S Solomon Islands
83 J14 **Central** ⬖ province C Zambia
117 P11 **Central** ✈ (Odesa) Odes'ka Oblast', SW Ukraine
Central see Centre
79 H14 **Central African Republic** var. République Centrafricaine, abbrev. CAR; prev. Ubangi-Shari, Oubangui-Chari, Territoire de l'Oubangui-Chari. ◆ republic C Africa
192 C6 **Central Basin Trough** undersea feature W Pacific Ocean
Central Borneo see Kalimantan Tengah
149 P12 **Central Brāhui Range** ▲▲ W Pakistan
Central Celebes see Sulawesi Tengah
29 Y13 **Central City** Iowa, C USA
20 I6 **Central City** Kentucky, S USA
29 P15 **Central City** Nebraska, C USA
48 D6 **Central, Cordillera** ▲▲ W Bolivia
54 D11 **Central, Cordillera** ▲▲ W Colombia
42 M13 **Central, Cordillera** ▲▲ C Costa Rica
45 N9 **Central, Cordillera** ▲▲ C Dominican Republic
43 R16 **Central, Cordillera** ▲▲ C Panama
45 S6 **Central, Cordillera** ▲▲ Puerto Rico
42 H7 **Central District** var. Tegucigalpa. ⬖ district C Honduras
Central Group see Inner Islands
30 L15 **Centralia** Illinois, N USA
27 U4 **Centralia** Missouri, C USA
32 G9 **Centralia** Washington, NW USA
Central Indian Ridge see Mid-Indian Ridge
Central Java see Jawa Tengah
Central Kalimantan see Kalimantan Tengah
148 L14 **Central Makrān Range** ▲▲ W Pakistan
192 K7 **Central Pacific Basin** undersea feature C Pacific Ocean
59 M19 **Central, Planalto** var. Brazilian Highlands. ▲▲ E Brazil
32 F15 **Central Point** Oregon, NW USA
155 K25 **Central Province** ⬖ province C Sri Lanka
Central Province see Central
Central Provinces and Berar see Madhya Pradesh
186 B6 **Central Range** ▲▲ NW Papua New Guinea
Central Russian Upland see Srednerusskaya Vozvyshennost'
Central Siberian Plateau/Central Siberian Uplands see Srednesibirskoye Ploskogor'ye
104 K8 **Central, Sistema** ▲▲ C Spain
Central Sulawesi see Sulawesi Tengah
35 N3 **Central Valley** California, W USA
35 P8 **Central Valley** valley California, W USA
23 Q3 **Centre** Alabama, S USA
79 E15 **Centre** Eng. Central. ⬖ province C Cameroon
102 M8 **Centre** ⬖ region N France
173 Y16 **Centre de Flacq** E Mauritius
55 Y9 **Centre Spatial Guyanais** space station N French Guiana
23 O5 **Centreville** Alabama, S USA
21 X3 **Centreville** Maryland, NE USA
22 J7 **Centreville** Mississippi, S USA
Centum Cellae see Civitavecchia
160 M14 **Cenxi** Guangxi Zhuangzu Zizhiqu, S China
Ceos see Tziá
Cephaloedium see Cefalù
112 I9 **Čepin** Hung. Csepén. Osijek-Baranja, E Croatia
Ceram see Seram, Pulau
171 R13 **Ceram Sea** Ind. Laut Seram. sea E Indonesia
192 G8 **Ceram Trough** undersea feature W Pacific Ocean
Cerasus see Giresun
36 I10 **Cerbat Mountains** ▲▲ Arizona, SW USA
103 P17 **Cerbère, Cap** headland S France
104 F13 **Cercal do Alentejo** Setúbal, S Portugal
111 A18 **Čerchov** Ger. Czerkow. ▲ W Czech Republic
103 O13 **Cère** ~ C France
61 A16 **Ceres** Santa Fe, C Argentina
59 K18 **Ceres** Goiás, C Brazil
Ceresio see Lugano, Lago di
103 O17 **Céret** Pyrénées-Orientales, S France
54 E6 **Cereté** Córdoba, NW Colombia
172 I17 **Cerf, Île au** island Inner Islands, NE Seychelles
99 G22 **Cerfontaine** Namur, S Belgium
Cergy-Pontoise see Pontoise
107 N16 **Cerignola** Puglia, SE Italy
Cerigo see Kýthira
103 O9 **Cérilly** Allier, C France
136 D10 **Çerkezköy** Tekirdağ, NW Turkey
109 T12 **Cerknica** Ger. Zirknitz. SW Slovenia
109 S11 **Cerkno** W Slovenia
116 F10 **Cermei** Hung. Csermő. Arad, W Romania
137 O15 **Çermik** Dıyarbakır, SE Turkey
112 I10 **Cerna** Vukovar-Srijem, E Croatia
Cernăuţi see Chernivtsi
116 M14 **Cernavodă** Constanţa, SW Romania
103 U7 **Cernay** Haut-Rhin, NE France
Černice see Schwarzach
41 O8 **Cerralvo** Nuevo León, NE Mexico
40 G9 **Cerralvo, Isla** island W Mexico
107 L16 **Cerreto Sannita** Campania, S Italy
113 L20 **Cërrik** var. Cerriku. Elbasan, C Albania
Cerriku see Cërrik

◆ Country
● Country Capital
◇ Dependent Territory
○ Dependent Territory Capital
⬖ Administrative Regions
✈ International Airport
▲ Mountain
▲▲ Mountain Range
Volcano
~ River
◎ Lake
⊠ Reservoir

41 O11 **Cerritos** San Luis Potosí, C Mexico
60 K11 **Cerro Azul** Paraná, S Brazil
61 F18 **Cerro Chato** Treinta y Tres, E Uruguay
61 F19 **Cerro Colorado** Florida, S Uruguay
56 E13 **Cerro de Pasco** Pasco, C Peru
61 G14 **Cêrro Largo** Rio Grande do Sul, S Brazil
61 G18 **Cerro Largo** ◈ *department* NE Uruguay
42 E7 **Cerrón Grande, Embalse** ⊠ N El Salvador
63 I14 **Cerros Colorados, Embalse** ◎ W Argentina
105 V5 **Cervera** Cataluña, NE Spain
104 M3 **Cervera del Pisuerga** Castilla-León, N Spain
105 Q5 **Cervera del Río Alhama** La Rioja, N Spain
107 H15 **Cerveteri** Lazio, C Italy
106 H10 **Cervia** Emilia-Romagna, N Italy
106 J7 **Cervignano del Friuli** Friuli-Venezia Giulia, NE Italy
107 L17 **Cervinara** Campania, S Italy
Cervinia *see* Breuil-Cervinia
106 B6 **Cervino, Monte** *var.* Matterhorn. ▲ Italy/Switzerland *see also* Matterhorn
Cervino, Monte *see* Matterhorn
103 Y14 **Cervione** Corse, France, C Mediterranean Sea
104 I1 **Cervo** Galicia, NW Spain
54 F5 **Cesar** *off.* Departamento del Cesar. ◈ *province* N Colombia
Cesar, Departamento del *see* Cesar
106 H10 **Cesena** *anc.* Caesena. Emilia-Romagna, N Italy
106 I10 **Cesenatico** Emilia-Romagna, N Italy
118 H8 **Cēsis** *Ger.* Wenden. Cēsis, C Latvia
111 D15 **Česká Lípa** *Ger.* Böhmisch-Leipa. Liberecký Kraj, N Czech Republic
Česká Republika *see* Czech Republic
111 F17 **Česká Třebová** *Ger.* Böhmisch-Trübau. Pardubický Kraj, C Czech Republic
111 D19 **České Budějovice** *Ger.* Budweis. Jihočeský Kraj, S Czech Republic
111 D19 **České Velenice** Jihočeský Kraj, S Czech Republic
111 E18 **Českomoravská Vrchovina** *var.* Českomoravská Vysočina, *Eng.* Bohemian-Moravian Highlands, *Ger.* Böhmisch-Mährische Höhe. ▲▲ S Czech Republic
Českomoravská Vysočina *see* Českomoravská Vrchovina
111 C19 **Český Krumlov** *var.* Böhmisch-Krumau, *Ger.* Krummau. Jihočeský Kraj, S Czech Republic
Ceský Les *see* Bohemian Forest
112 F8 **Česma** ≈ N Croatia
136 A14 **Çeşme** İzmir, W Turkey
Cess *see* Cestos
183 T8 **Cessnock** New South Wales, SE Australia
76 K17 **Cestos** *var.* Cess. ≈ S Liberia
118 I9 **Cesvaine** Madona, E Latvia
116 G14 **Cetate** Dolj, SW Romania
Cetatea Albă *see* Bilhorod-Dnistrovs'kyy
Cetatea Damboviţei *see* Bucureşti
113 J17 **Cetinje** *It.* Cettigne. S Montenegro
107 N20 **Cetraro** Calabria, S Italy
Cette *see* Sète
188 A17 **Cetti Bay** *bay* SW Guam
Cettigne *see* Cetinje
104 L17 **Ceuta** *var.* Sebta. Ceuta, Spain, N Africa
88 C16 **Ceuta** *enclave* Spain, N Africa
106 B9 **Ceva** Piemonte, NE Italy
103 P14 **Cévennes** ▲▲ S France
108 G10 **Cevio** Ticino, S Switzerland
136 K16 **Ceyhan** Adana, S Turkey
136 K17 **Ceyhan Nehri** ≈ S Turkey
137 P17 **Ceylanpinar** Şanlıurfa, SE Turkey
Ceylon *see* Sri Lanka
173 R6 **Ceylon Plain** *undersea feature* N Indian Ocean
Ceyre to the Caribs *see* Marie-Galante
103 Q14 **Cèze** ≈ S France
Chaacha *see* Çäçe
127 P6 **Chaadayevka** Penzenskaya Oblast', W Russian Federation
167 O12 **Cha-Am** Phetchaburi, SW Thailand
143 W15 **Chābahār** *var.* Chāh Bahār, Chahbar. Sīstān va Balūchestān, SE Iran
Chabaricha *see* Khabarikha
61 B19 **Chabas** Santa Fe, C Argentina
103 T10 **Chablais** *physical region* E France
61 B20 **Chacabuco** Buenos Aires, E Argentina
42 K8 **Chachagón, Cerro** ▲ N Nicaragua
56 C10 **Chachapoyas** Amazonas, NW Peru
Chäche *see* Çäçe
119 O18 **Chachersk** *Rus.* Chechersk. Homyel'skaya Voblasts', SE Belarus
119 N16 **Chachevichy** *Rus.* Chechevichi. Mahilyowskaya Voblasts', E Belarus
61 B14 **Chaco** *off.* Provincia de Chaco. ◈ *province* NE Argentina
Chaco *see* Gran Chaco
62 M6 **Chaco Austral** *physical region* N Argentina
62 M3 **Chaco Boreal** *physical region* N Paraguay
62 M6 **Chaco Central** *physical region* N Argentina
39 Y15 **Chacon, Cape** *headland* Prince of Wales Island, Alaska, USA
Chaco, Provincia de *see* Chaco
78 H9 **Chad** *off.* Republic of Chad, *Fr.* Tchad. ◆ *republic* C Africa
122 K14 **Chadan** Respublika Tyva, S Russian Federation
21 U12 **Chadbourn** North Carolina, SE USA
83 L14 **Chadiza** Eastern, E Zambia
67 Q7 **Chad, Lake** *Fr.* Lac Tchad. ◎ C Africa
Chad, Republic of *see* Chad
28 J12 **Chadron** Nebraska, C USA
Chadyr-Lunga *see* Ciadîr-Lunga
163 W14 **Chaeryŏng** SW North Korea
105 P17 **Chafarinas, Islas** *island group* S Spain
27 Y7 **Chaffee** Missouri, C USA
148 L12 **Chāgai Hills** *var.* Chāh Gay. ▲▲ Afghanistan/Pakistan
123 Q11 **Chagda** Respublika Sakha (Yakutiya), NE Russian Federation
Chaghasarāy *see* Asadābād
149 N5 **Chaghcharān** *var.* Chakhcharan, Cheghcheran, Qala Āhangarān. Ghowr, C Afghanistan
103 R9 **Chagny** Saône-et-Loire, C France
173 Q7 **Chagos Archipelago** *var.* Oil Islands. *island group* British Indian Ocean Territory
129 O15 **Chagos Bank** *undersea feature* C Indian Ocean
129 O14 **Chagos-Laccadive Plateau** *undersea feature* N Indian Ocean
173 Q7 **Chagos Trench** *undersea feature* N Indian Ocean
43 T14 **Chagres, Río** ≈ C Panama
45 U14 **Chaguanas** Trinidad, Trinidad and Tobago
54 M6 **Chaguaramas** Guárico, N Venezuela
Chagyl *see* Çagyl
Chahārmahāl and Bakhtiyāri *see* Chahār Maḥall va Bakhtīārī
142 M9 **Chahār Maḥall va Bakhtīārī** *off.* Ostān-e Chahār Maḥall va Bakhtīārī, *var.* Chahārmahāl and Bakhtiyāri. ◈ *province* SW Iran
Chahār Maḥall va Bakhtīārī, Ostān-e *see* Chahār Maḥall va Bakhtīārī
Chāh Bahār/Chahbar *see* Chābahār
143 V13 **Chāh Derāz** Sīstān va Balūchestān, SE Iran
Chāh Gay *see* Chāgai Hills
167 P10 **Chai Badan** Lop Buri, C Thailand
153 Q16 **Chāībāsa** Jhārkhand, N India
79 E19 **Chaillu, Massif du** ▲▲ C Gabon
167 O10 **Chai Nat** *var.* Chainat, Jainat, Jayanath. Chai Nat, C Thailand
Chainat *see* Chai Nat
65 M14 **Chain Fracture Zone** *tectonic feature* E Atlantic Ocean
173 N5 **Chain Ridge** *undersea feature* W Indian Ocean
Chairn, Ceann an *see* Carnsore Point
158 L5 **Chaiwopu** Xinjiang Uygur Zizhiqu, W China
167 Q10 **Chaiyaphum** *var.* Jayabum. Chaiyaphum, C Thailand
62 N10 **Chajarí** Entre Ríos, E Argentina
42 C5 **Chajul** Quiché, W Guatemala
83 K16 **Chakari** Mashonaland West, N Zimbabwe
148 J9 **Chakhānsūr** Nīmrūz, SW Afghanistan
Chakhānsūr *see* Nīmrūz
Chakhcharan *see* Chaghcharān
149 V8 **Chak Jhumra** *var.* Jhumra. Punjab, E Pakistan
146 I16 **Chaknakdysonga** Ahal Welaýaty, S Turkmenistan
153 P16 **Chakradharpur** Jhārkhand, N India
152 J8 **Chakrāta** Uttaranchal, N India
149 U7 **Chakwāl** Punjab, NE Pakistan
57 F17 **Chala** Arequipa, SW Peru
102 K12 **Chalais** Charente, W France
108 D10 **Chalais** Valais, SW Switzerland
115 J20 **Chalándri** *var.* Halandri; *prev.* Khalándrion. *prehistoric site* Sýros, Kykládes, Greece, Aegean Sea
188 H6 **Chalan Kanoa** Saipan, S Northern Mariana Islands
188 C16 **Chalan Pago** C Guam
Chalap Dalam/Chalap Dalan *see* Chehel Abdālān, Kūh-e
42 F7 **Chalatenango** Chalatenango, N El Salvador
42 A9 **Chalatenango** ◈ *department* NW El Salvador
83 P15 **Chalaua** Nampula, NE Mozambique
81 I16 **Chalbi Desert** *desert* N Kenya
42 D7 **Chalchuapa** Santa Ana, W El Salvador
Chalcidice *see* Chalkidikí
Chalcis *see* Chalkída
Chālderān *see* Siāh Chashmeh
103 N6 **Châlette-sur-Loing** Loiret, C France
15 X8 **Chaleur Bay** *Fr.* Baie des Chaleurs. *bay* New Brunswick/Québec, E Canada
Chaleurs, Baie des *see* Chaleur Bay
57 G16 **Chalhuanca** Apurímac, S Peru
154 F12 **Chālisgaon** Mahārāshtra, C India
115 N23 **Chálki** *island* Dodekánisa, Greece, Aegean Sea
115 F16 **Chalkiádes** Thessalía, C Greece
115 H18 **Chalkída** *var.* Halkida, *prev.* Khalkís; *anc.* Chalcis. Evvoia, E Greece
115 G14 **Chalkidikí** *var.* Khalkidhikí; *anc.* Chalcidice. *peninsula* NE Greece
185 A24 **Chalky Inlet** *inlet* South Island, New Zealand
39 S7 **Chalkyitsik** Alaska, USA
102 I9 **Challans** Vendée, NW France
57 K19 **Challapata** Oruro, SW Bolivia
192 H6 **Challenger Deep** *undersea feature* W Pacific Ocean
Challenger Deep *see* Mariana Trench
193 S11 **Challenger Fracture Zone** *tectonic feature* SE Pacific Ocean
192 K11 **Challenger Plateau** *undersea feature* E Tasman Sea
33 P13 **Challis** Idaho, NW USA
22 L9 **Chalmette** Louisiana, S USA
124 J11 **Chalna** Respublika Kareliya, NW Russian Federation
103 Q5 **Châlons-en-Champagne** *prev.* Châlons-sur-Marne, *hist.* Arcae Remorum; *anc.* Carolopois. Marne, NE France
Châlons-sur-Marne *see* Châlons-en-Champagne
103 R9 **Chalon-sur-Saône** *anc.* Cabillonum. Saône-et-Loire, C France
Chaltel, Cerro *see* Fitzroy, Monte
102 M11 **Châlus** Haute-Vienne, C France
143 N4 **Chālūs** Māzandarān, N Iran
101 N20 **Cham** Bayern, SE Germany
108 F7 **Cham** Zug, N Switzerland
37 R8 **Chama** New Mexico, SW USA
Cha Mai *see* Thung Song
83 E22 **Chamaites** Karas, S Namibia
149 O9 **Chaman** Baluchistān, SW Pakistan
37 R9 **Chama, Rio** ≈ New Mexico, SW USA
152 I6 **Chamba** Himāchal Pradesh, N India
81 I25 **Chamba** Ruvuma, S Tanzania
150 H12 **Chambal** ≈ C India
9 U16 **Chamberlain** Saskatchewan, S Canada
29 O11 **Chamberlain** South Dakota, N USA
19 R3 **Chamberlain Lake** ◎ Maine, NE USA
39 S5 **Chamberlin, Mount** ▲ Alaska, USA
37 O11 **Chambers** Arizona, SW USA
18 F16 **Chambersburg** Pennsylvania, NE USA
31 N5 **Chambers Island** *island* Wisconsin, N USA
103 T11 **Chambéry** *anc.* Camberia. Savoie, E France
82 L12 **Chambeshi** Northern, NE Zambia
82 L12 **Chambeshi** ≈ NE Zambia
74 M6 **Chambi, Jebel** *var.* Jabal ash Sha'nabī. ▲ W Tunisia
15 Q7 **Chambord** Québec, SE Canada
139 U11 **Chamcham** S Iraq
139 T4 **Chamchamāļ** N Iraq
Chamdmanī *see* Altanshiree
40 J14 **Chamela** Jalisco, SW Mexico
42 G5 **Chamelecón, Río** ≈ NW Honduras
62 J9 **Chamical** La Rioja, C Argentina
115 L23 **Chamilí** *island* Kykládes, Greece, Aegean Sea
167 Q13 **Châmnar** Kaôh Kông, SW Cambodia
152 K9 **Chamoli** Uttaranchal, N India
103 U11 **Chamonix-Mont-Blanc** Haute-Savoie, E France
154 L11 **Chāmpa** Chhattīsgarh, C India
10 H8 **Champagne** Yukon Territory, W Canada
103 Q5 **Champagne** *cultural region* N France
Champagne *see* Campania
103 Q5 **Champagne-Ardenne** ◈ *region* N France
103 S9 **Champagnole** Jura, E France
30 M13 **Champaign** Illinois, N USA
167 S10 **Champasak** Champasak, S Laos
103 U6 **Champ de Feu** ▲ NE France
13 O7 **Champdoré, Lac** ◎ Québec, NE Canada
42 B6 **Champerico** Retalhuleu, SW Guatemala
108 C11 **Champéry** Valais, SW Switzerland
18 L6 **Champlain** New York, NE USA
18 L9 **Champlain Canal** *canal* New York, NE USA
15 P13 **Champlain, Lac** ◎ Québec, Canada/USA *see also* Champlain, Lake
18 L7 **Champlain, Lake** ◎ Canada/USA *see also* Champlain, Lac
103 S7 **Champlitte** Haute-Saône, E France
41 W13 **Champotón** Campeche, SE Mexico
104 G10 **Chamusca** Santarém, C Portugal
119 O20 **Chamyarysy** *Rus.* Chemerisy. Homyel'skaya Voblasts', SE Belarus
127 P5 **Chamzinka** Respublika Mordoviya, W Russian Federation
Chanáil Mhór, An *see* Grand Canal
Chanak *see* Çanakkale
62 G7 **Chañaral** Atacama, N Chile
104 H13 **Chança, Rio** *var.* Chanza. ≈ Portugal/Spain
57 D14 **Chancay** Lima, W Peru
Chan-chiang/Chanchiang *see* Zhanjiang
62 G13 **Chanco** Maule, Chile South America
39 R7 **Chandalar** Alaska, USA
39 R6 **Chandalar River** ≈ Alaska, USA
152 L10 **Chandan Chauki** Uttar Pradesh, N India
153 S16 **Chandannagar** *prev.* Chandernagore. West Bengal, E India
152 K10 **Chandausi** Uttar Pradesh, N India
22 M10 **Chandeleur Islands** *island group* Louisiana, S USA
22 M9 **Chandeleur Sound** *sound* N Gulf of Mexico
Chandernagore *see* Chandannagar
152 I8 **Chandigarh** *state capital* Punjab, N India
153 Q16 **Chāndil** Jhārkhand, NE India
182 D2 **Chandler** South Australia
15 Y7 **Chandler** Québec, SE Canada
36 L14 **Chandler** Arizona, SW USA
27 O10 **Chandler** Oklahoma, C USA
25 V7 **Chandler** Texas, SW USA
39 Q6 **Chandler River** ≈ Alaska, USA
56 H13 **Chandles, Río** ≈ E Peru
163 N9 **Chandmanĭ** Dornogovĭ, SE Mongolia
162 H9 **Chandmanĭ** *var* Talshand. Govĭ-Altayĭ, C Mongolia
162 E7 **Chandmanĭ** *var.* Urdgol. Hovd, W Mongolia
14 J13 **Chandos Lake** ◎ Ontario, SE Canada
153 U15 **Chandpur** Chittagong, C Bangladesh
154 I13 **Chandrapur** Mahārāshtra, C India
83 J15 **Changa** Southern, S Zambia
Chang'an *see* Rong'an
Changan *see* Xi'an
155 G23 **Changanācheri** Kerala, SW India
83 M19 **Changane** ≈ S Mozambique
83 M16 **Changara** Tete, NW Mozambique
163 X11 **Changbai** *var.* Changbai Chosenzu Zizhixian. Jilin, NE China
Changbai Chosenzu Zizhixian *see* Changbai
163 X11 **Changbai Shan** ▲▲ NE China
163 V10 **Changchun** *var.* Ch'angch'un, Ch'ang-ch'un; *prev.* Hsinking. *province capital* Jilin, NE China
Ch'angch'un/Ch'ang-ch'un *see* Changchun
160 M10 **Changde** Hunan, S China
161 S13 **Changhua** *Jap.* Shōka. C Taiwan
168 L10 **Changi** ✈ (Singapore) E Singapore
158 L5 **Changji** Xinjiang Uygur Zizhiqu, NW China
160 L17 **Changjiang** *var.* Changjiang Lizu Zizhixian, Shiliu. Hainan, S China
157 O13 **Chang Jiang** *var.* Yangtze Kiang, *Eng.* Yangtze. ≈ C China
157 R11 **Chang Jiang** *var.* Yangtze Kiang, *Eng.* Yangtze. ≈ C China
161 S8 **Changjiang Kou** *delta* E China
Changjiang Lizu Zizhixian *see* Changjiang
Changkiakow *see* Zhangjiakou
167 F12 **Chang, Ko** *island* S Thailand
161 Q2 **Changli** Hebei, E China
163 V10 **Changling** Jilin, NE China
Changning *see* Xunwu
161 N11 **Changsha** *var.* Ch'angsha, Ch'ang-sha. *province capital* Hunan, S China
Ch'angsha/Ch'ang-sha *see* Changsha
161 Q10 **Changshan** Zhejiang, SE China
163 V14 **Changshan Qundao** *island group* NE China
161 S8 **Changshu** *var.* Ch'ang-shu. Jiangsu, E China
Ch'ang-shu *see* Changshu
163 V11 **Changtu** Liaoning, NE China
43 P14 **Changuinola** Bocas del Toro, NW Panama
159 N9 **Changweiliang** Qinghai, W China
160 K6 **Changwu** *var.* Zhaoren. Shaanxi, C China
163 U13 **Changxing Dao** *island* N China
160 M9 **Changyang** *var.* Longzhouping. Hubei, C China
163 W14 **Changyŏn** SW North Korea
161 N5 **Changzhi** Shanxi, C China
161 R8 **Changzhou** Jiangsu, E China
115 H24 **Chaniá** *var.* Hania, Khaniá, *Eng.* Canea; *anc.* Cydonia. Kríti, Greece, E Mediterranean Sea
62 J5 **Chañi, Nevado de** ▲ NW Argentina
115 H24 **Chanión, Kólpos** *gulf* Kríti, Greece, E Mediterranean Sea
Chankiri *see* Çankırı
30 M11 **Channahon** Illinois, N USA
155 H20 **Channapatna** Karnātaka, E India
97 K26 **Channel Islands** *Fr.* Iles Normandes. *island group* S English Channel
35 R16 **Channel Islands** *island group* California, W USA
13 S13 **Channel-Port aux Basques** Newfoundland, Newfoundland and Labrador, SE Canada
Channel, The *see* English Channel
97 Q23 **Channel Tunnel** *tunnel* France/UK
24 M2 **Channing** Texas, SW USA
Chantabun/Chantaburi *see* Chanthaburi
104 H3 **Chantada** Galicia, NW Spain
167 P12 **Chanthaburi** *var.* Chantabun, Chantaburi. Chantaburi, S Thailand
103 O4 **Chantilly** Oise, N France
139 V12 **Chanūn as Sa'ūdī** S Iraq
27 Q6 **Chanute** Kansas, C USA
Chanza *see* Chança, Rio
Ch'ao-an/Chaochow *see* Chaozhou
161 P8 **Chao Hu** ◎ E China
167 P11 **Chao Phraya, Mae Nam** ≈ C Thailand
Chaor He *see* Qulin Gol
Chaouèn *see* Chefchaouen
161 P14 **Chaoyang** Guangdong, S China
163 T12 **Chaoyang** Liaoning, NE China
Chaoyang *see* Jiayin, Heilongjiang, China
Chaoyang *see* Huinan, Jilin China
161 Q14 **Chaozhou** *var.* Chaoan, Chao'an, Ch'ao-an; *prev.* Chaochow. Guangdong, SE China
58 N13 **Chapadinha** Maranhão, E Brazil
12 K12 **Chapais** Québec, SE Canada
40 L13 **Chapala** Jalisco, SW Mexico
40 L13 **Chapala, Lago de** ◎ C Mexico
146 F13 **Chapan, Gora** ▲ C Turkmenistan
57 M18 **Chapare, Río** ≈ C Bolivia
54 E11 **Chaparral** Tolima, C Colombia
144 F9 **Chapayevo** Zapadnyy Kazakhstan, NW Kazakhstan
123 O11 **Chapayevo** Respublika Sakha (Yakutiya), NE Russian Federation
127 R6 **Chapayevsk** Samarskaya Oblast', W Russian Federation
60 H13 **Chapecó** Santa Catarina, S Brazil
60 I13 **Chapecó, Rio** ≈ S Brazil
20 J9 **Chapel Hill** Tennessee, S USA
44 J12 **Chapelton** C Jamaica
14 C8 **Chapleau** Ontario, SE Canada
14 D7 **Chapleau** ≈ Ontario, S Canada
9 T16 **Chaplin** Saskatchewan, S Canada
126 M6 **Chaplygin** Lipetskaya Oblast', W Russian Federation
117 S11 **Chaplynka** Khersons'ka Oblast', S Ukraine
9 O6 **Chapman, Cape** *headland* Nunavut, NE Canada
25 T15 **Chapman Ranch** Texas, SW USA
Chapman's *see* Okwa
21 P5 **Chapmanville** West Virginia, NE USA
28 K15 **Chappell** Nebraska, C USA
Chapra *see* Chhapra
56 D9 **Chapuli, Río** ≈ N Peru
76 I6 **Châr** *well* N Mauritania
123 P12 **Chara** Chitinskaya Oblast', S Russian Federation
123 O11 **Chara** ≈ C Russian Federation
54 G8 **Charala** Santander, C Colombia
41 N10 **Charcas** San Luis Potosí, C Mexico
25 T13 **Charco** Texas, SW USA
194 H7 **Charcot Island** *island* Antarctica
64 M8 **Charcot Seamounts** *undersea feature* E Atlantic Ocean
Chardara *see* Shardara
145 P17 **Chardarinskoye Vodokhranilishche** ⊠ S Kazakhstan
31 U11 **Chardon** Ohio, N USA
44 K9 **Chardonnières** SW Haiti
Chardzhev *see* Türkmenabat
Chardzhevskaya Oblast *see* Lebap Welaýaty
Chardzhou/Chardzhui *see* Türkmenabat
102 L11 **Charente** ◈ *department* W France
102 J11 **Charente** ≈ W France
102 J10 **Charente-Maritime** ◈ *department* W France
137 U12 **Ch'arents'avan** C Armenia
78 I12 **Chari** *var.* Shari. ≈ Central African Republic/Chad
78 G11 **Chari-Baguirmi** *off.* Préfecture du Chari-Baguirmi. ◈ *prefecture* SW Chad
Chari-Baguirmi, Préfecture du *see* Chari-Baguirmi
149 Q4 **Chārīkār** Parvān, NE Afghanistan
29 V15 **Chariton** Iowa, C USA
27 U3 **Chariton River** ≈ Missouri, C USA
55 T7 **Charity** NW Guyana
31 R7 **Charity Island** *island* Michigan, N USA
Chärjew *see* Türkmenabat
Chärjew Oblasty *see* Lebap Welaýaty
Charkhlik/Charkhliq *see* Ruoqiang
99 G20 **Charleroi** Hainaut, S Belgium
9 V12 **Charles** Manitoba, C Canada
15 R10 **Charlesbourg** Québec, SE Canada
21 Y7 **Charles, Cape** *headland* Virginia, NE USA
29 W12 **Charles City** Iowa, C USA
21 W6 **Charles City** Virginia, NE USA
103 O5 **Charles de Gaulle** ✈ (Paris) Seine-et-Marne, N France
12 K1 **Charles Island** *island* Nunavut, NE Canada
Charles Island *see* Santa María, Isla
30 K9 **Charles Mound** *hill* Illinois, N USA
185 A22 **Charles Sound** *sound* South Island, New Zealand
185 G15 **Charleston** West Coast, South Island, New Zealand
27 S11 **Charleston** Arkansas, C USA
30 M14 **Charleston** Illinois, N USA
22 L3 **Charleston** Mississippi, S USA
27 Z7 **Charleston** Missouri, C USA
21 T15 **Charleston** South Carolina, SE USA
21 Q5 **Charleston** *state capital* West Virginia, NE USA
14 L14 **Charleston Lake** ◎ Ontario, SE Canada
35 W11 **Charleston Peak** ▲ Nevada, W USA
45 W10 **Charlestown** Nevis, Saint Kitts and Nevis
31 P16 **Charlestown** Indiana, N USA
18 M9 **Charlestown** New Hampshire, NE USA
21 V3 **Charles Town** West Virginia, NE USA
181 W9 **Charleville** Queensland, E Australia
103 R3 **Charleville-Mézières** Ardennes, N France
31 P5 **Charlevoix** Michigan, N USA
31 Q6 **Charlevoix, Lake** ◎ Michigan, N USA
39 T9 **Charley River** ≈ Alaska, USA
64 J6 **Charlie-Gibbs Fracture Zone** *tectonic feature* N Atlantic Ocean
103 Q10 **Charlieu** Loire, E France
31 Q9 **Charlotte** Michigan, N USA
21 R10 **Charlotte** North Carolina, SE USA
20 I8 **Charlotte** Tennessee, S USA
25 R13 **Charlotte** Texas, SW USA
21 R10 **Charlotte** ✈ North Carolina, SE USA
45 T9 **Charlotte Amalie** *prev.* Saint Thomas. ○ (Virgin Islands (US)) Saint Thomas, N Virgin Islands (US)
21 U7 **Charlotte Court House** Virginia, NE USA
23 W14 **Charlotte Harbor** *inlet* Florida, SE USA
Charlotte Island *see* Abaiang
95 J15 **Charlottenberg** Värmland, C Sweden
Charlottenhof *see* Aegviidu
21 U5 **Charlottesville** Virginia, NE USA
13 Q14 **Charlottetown** *province capital* Prince Edward Island, Prince Edward Island, SE Canada
Charlotte Town *see* Roseau
Charlotte Town *see* Gouyave
45 Z16 **Charlotteville** Tobago, Trinidad and Tobago
182 M11 **Charlton** Victoria, SE Australia
12 H10 **Charlton Island** *island* Northwest Territories, C Canada
103 T6 **Charmes** Vosges, NE France
119 F19 **Charnawchytsy** *Rus.* Chernavchitsy. Brestskaya Voblasts', SW Belarus
15 R10 **Charny** Québec, SE Canada
149 T5 **Chārsadda** North-West Frontier Province, NW Pakistan
Charshanga/Charshangngy/Charshangy *see* Köýtendag
Charsk *see* Shar
181 V6 **Charters Towers** Queensland, NE Australia
15 R12 **Chartierville** Québec, SE Canada
102 M6 **Chartres** *anc.* Autricum, Civitas Carnutum. Eure-et-Loir, C France
145 W15 **Charyn** *Kaz.* Sharyn. Almaty, SE Kazakhstan
Charyn *see* Sharyn
61 D21 **Chascomús** Buenos Aires, E Argentina
9 N16 **Chase** British Columbia, SW Canada
21 U7 **Chase City** Virginia, NE USA
19 S4 **Chase, Mount** ▲ Maine, NE USA
118 M13 **Chashniki** *Rus.* Chashniki. Vitsyebskaya Voblasts', N Belarus
115 D15 **Chásia** ▲▲ C Greece
29 V9 **Chaska** Minnesota, N USA
185 D25 **Chaslands Mistake** *headland* South Island, New Zealand
125 R11 **Chasovo** Respublika Komi, NW Russian Federation
Chasovo *see* Vazhgort
124 H14 **Chastova** Novgorodskaya Oblast', NW Russian Federation
143 R3 **Chāt** Golestān, N Iran
Chatak *see* Chhatak
Chatang *see* Zhanang
39 R9 **Chatanika** Alaska, USA
39 R9 **Chatanika River** ≈ Alaska, USA
147 T8 **Chat-Bazar** Talasskaya Oblast', NW Kyrgyzstan
45 Y14 **Chateaubelair** Saint Vincent, W Saint Vincent and the Grenadines
102 J7 **Châteaubriant** Loire-Atlantique, NW France
103 Q8 **Château-Chinon** Nièvre, C France
108 C10 **Château d'Oex** Vaud, W Switzerland
102 L7 **Château-du-Loir** Sarthe, NW France
102 M6 **Châteaudun** Eure-et-Loir, C France
102 K7 **Château-Gontier** Mayenne, NW France
15 O13 **Châteauguay** Québec, SE Canada
102 F6 **Châteaulin** Finistère, NW France
103 N9 **Châteaumeillant** Cher, C France
102 K11 **Châteauneuf-sur-Charente** Charente, W France
102 M7 **Château-Renault** Indre-et-Loire, C France
103 N9 **Châteauroux** *prev.* Indreville. Indre, C France
103 T5 **Château-Salins** Moselle, NE France
103 P4 **Château-Thierry** Aisne, N France
99 H21 **Châtelet** Hainaut, S Belgium
Châtelherault *see* Châtellerault
102 L9 **Châtellerault** *var.* Châtelherault. Vienne, W France
29 X10 **Chatfield** Minnesota, N USA
13 O14 **Chatham** New Brunswick, SE Canada
14 D17 **Chatham** Ontario, S Canada
97 P22 **Chatham** SE England, UK
30 K14 **Chatham** Illinois, N USA
21 T7 **Chatham** Virginia, NE USA
63 F22 **Chatham, Isla** *island* S Chile
175 R12 **Chatham Island** *island* Chatham Islands, New Zealand
Chatham Island *see* San Cristóbal, Isla
Chatham Island Rise *see* Chatham Rise
175 R12 **Chatham Islands** *island group* New Zealand, SW Pacific Ocean
175 Q12 **Chatham Rise** *var.* Chatham Island Rise. *undersea feature* S Pacific Ocean
39 X13 **Chatham Strait** *strait* Alaska, USA
Chathóir, Rinn *see* Cahore Point
102 M9 **Châtillon-sur-Indre** Indre, C France
103 Q7 **Châtillon-sur-Seine** Côte d'Or, C France
147 S8 **Chatkal** *Uzb.* Chotqol. ≈ Kyrgyzstan/Uzbekistan
147 R9 **Chatkal Range** *Rus.* Chatkal'skiy Khrebet. ▲▲ Kyrgyzstan/Uzbekistan

◆ Country
● Country Capital
◇ Dependent Territory
○ Dependent Territory Capital
◈ Administrative Regions
✈ International Airport
▲ Mountain
▲▲ Mountain Range
Volcano
≈ River
◎ Lake
⊠ Reservoir

Chatkal'skiy Khrebet see Chatkal Range
23 N7 **Chatom** Alabama, S USA
Chatrapur see Chhatrapur
143 S10 **Chatrūd** Kermān, C Iran
23 S2 **Chatsworth** Georgia, SE USA
Chāttagām see Chittagong
23 S8 **Chattahoochee** Florida, SE USA
23 R8 **Chattahoochee River** ≈ SE USA
20 L10 **Chattanooga** Tennessee, S USA
147 V10 **Chatyr-Kël', Ozero** ◎ C Kyrgyzstan
147 W9 **Chatyr-Tash** Narynskaya Oblast', C Kyrgyzstan
15 R12 **Chaudière** ≈ Québec, SE Canada
167 S14 **Châu Đôc** var. Chauphu, Chau Phu. An Giang, S Vietnam
152 D13 **Chauhtan** prev. Chohtan. Rājasthān, NW India
166 L5 **Chauk** Magwe, W Myanmar (Burma)
103 R6 **Chaumont** prev. Chaumont-en-Bassigny. Haute-Marne, N France
Chaumont-en-Bassigny see Chaumont
123 T5 **Chaunskaya Guba** bay NE Russian Federation
103 P3 **Chauny** Aisne, N France
Châu Ô see Binh Sơn
Chau Phu see Châu Đôc
102 I5 **Chausey, Îles** island group N France
Chausy see Chavusy
18 C11 **Chautauqua Lake** ◎ New York, NE USA
ChâuThanh see Ba Ria
102 L9 **Chauvigny** Vienne, W France
124 L6 **Chavan'ga** Murmanskaya Oblast', NW Russian Federation
14 K10 **Chavannes, Lac** ◎ Québec, SE Canada
Chavantes, Represa de see Xavantes, Represa de
61 D15 **Chavarría** Corrientes, NE Argentina
127 P4 **Chavash Respubliki** var. Chuvashskaya Respublika, Eng. Chuvashia. ⬖ autonomous republic W Russian Federation
104 I5 **Chaves** anc. Aquae Flaviae. Vila Real, N Portugal
Chávez, Isla see Santa Cruz, Isla
82 G13 **Chavuma** North Western, NW Zambia
119 O16 **Chavusy** Rus. Chausy. Mahilyowskaya Voblasts', E Belarus
Chayan see Shayan
147 U8 **Chayek** Narynskaya Oblast', C Kyrgyzstan
139 T6 **Chāy Khānah** E Iraq
125 T16 **Chaykovskiy** Permskaya Oblast', NW Russian Federation
167 T12 **Chbar** Môndól Kiri, E Cambodia
23 Q4 **Cheaha Mountain** ▲ Alabama, S USA
Cheatharlach see Carlow
21 S2 **Cheat River** ≈ NE USA
111 A16 **Cheb** Ger. Eger. Karlovarský Kraj, W Czech Republic
127 Q3 **Cheboksary** Chavash Respubliki, W Russian Federation
31 Q5 **Cheboygan** Michigan, N USA
Chechaouèn see Chefchaouen
Chechenia see Chechenskaya Respublika
127 O15 **Chechenskaya Respublika** Eng. Chechenia, Chechnia, Rus. Chechnya. ⬖ autonomous republic SW Russian Federation
67 N4 **Chech, Erg** desert Algeria/Mali
Chechevichi see Chachevichy
Che-chiang see Zhejiang
Chechnia/Chechnya see Chechenskaya Respublika
163 Y15 **Chech'ŏn** Jap. Teisen. N South Korea
111 L15 **Chęciny** Świętokrzyskie, S Poland
27 Q10 **Checotah** Oklahoma, C USA
13 R15 **Chedabucto Bay** inlet Nova Scotia, E Canada
166 J7 **Cheduba Island** island W Myanmar (Burma)
37 T5 **Cheesman Lake** ⊠ Colorado, C USA
195 S16 **Cheetham, Cape** headland Antarctica
74 G5 **Chefchaouen** var. Chaouèn, Chechaouèn, Sp. Xauen. N Morocco
Chefoo see Yantai
38 M12 **Chefornak** Alaska, USA
123 R13 **Chegdomyn** Khabarovskiy Kray, SE Russian Federation
76 M4 **Chegga** Tiris Zemmour, NE Mauritania
Cheghcheran see Chaghcharān
32 G9 **Chehalis** Washington, NW USA
32 G9 **Chehalis River** ≈ Washington, NW USA
148 M6 **Chehel Abdālān, Kūh-e** var. Chalap Dalam, Pash. Chalap Dalan. ▲▲ C Afghanistan
115 D14 **Cheimadítis, Límni** var. Límni Cheimadítis. ◎ N Greece
Cheimadítis, Límni see Cheimadítis, Límni
103 U15 **Cheiron, Mont** ▲ SE France
163 X17 **Cheju** Jap. Saishū. S South Korea
163 Y17 **Cheju** ✈ S South Korea
163 Y17 **Cheju-do** Jap. Saishū. prev. Quelpart. island S South Korea
163 X17 **Cheju-haehyŏp** strait S South Korea
Chekiang see Zhejiang
Chekichler/Chekishlyar see Çekiçler
188 F8 **Chelab** Babeldaob, N Palau
147 N11 **Chelak** Rus. Chelek. Samarqand Viloyati, C Uzbekistan
32 J7 **Chelan, Lake** ⊠ Washington, NW USA
Chelek see Chelak
Cheleken see Hazar
Chélif/Chéliff see Chelif, Oued
74 J5 **Chelif, Oued** var. Chélif, Chéliff, Chellif, Shellif. ≈ N Algeria
Chelkar see Shalkar
Chelkar Ozero see Shalkar, Ozero
Chellif see Chelif, Oued
111 P14 **Chełm** Rus. Kholm. Lubelskie, SE Poland
110 I9 **Chełmno** Ger. Culm, Kulm. Kujawski-pomorskie, C Poland
115 E19 **Chelmós** var Aroania. ▲▲ S Greece
14 F10 **Chelmsford** Ontario, S Canada
97 P21 **Chelmsford** E England, UK
110 J9 **Chełmża** Ger. Culmsee, Kulmsee. Kujawski-pomorskie, C Poland
27 Q8 **Chelsea** Oklahoma, C USA
18 M8 **Chelsea** Vermont, NE USA
97 L21 **Cheltenham** C England, UK
105 R9 **Chelva** País Valenciano, E Spain
122 G11 **Chelyabinsk** Chelyabinskaya Oblast', C Russian Federation
122 F1 **Chelyabinskaya Oblast'** ⬖ province C Russian Federation
123 N5 **Chelyuskin, Mys** cape N Russian Federation
41 Y12 **Chemax** Yucatán, SE Mexico
83 N16 **Chemba** Sofala, C Mozambique
82 J13 **Chembe** Luapula, NE Zambia
Chemenibit see Çemenibit
Chemerisy see Chamyarysy
116 K7 **Chemerivtsi** Khmel'nyts'ka Oblast', W Ukraine
102 J8 **Chemillé** Maine-et-Loire, NW France
173 X17 **Chemin Grenier** S Mauritius
101 N16 **Chemnitz** prev. Karl-Marx-Stadt. Sachsen, E Germany
Chemulpo see Inch'ŏn
32 H14 **Chemult** Oregon, NW USA
18 G12 **Chemung River** ≈ New York/Pennsylvania, NE USA
149 U8 **Chenāb** ≈ India/Pakistan
39 S9 **Chena Hot Springs** Alaska, USA
18 I11 **Chenango River** ≈ New York, NE USA
168 J7 **Chenderoh, Tasik** ◎ Peninsular Malaysia
15 Q11 **Chêne, Rivière du** ≈ Québec, SE Canada
32 L8 **Cheney** Washington, NW USA
26 M6 **Cheney Reservoir** ⊠ Kansas, C USA
Chengchiatun see Liaoyuan
Ch'eng-chou/Chengchow see Zhengzhou
161 P1 **Chengde** var. Jehol. Hebei, E China
160 I9 **Chengdu** var. Chengtu, Ch'eng-tu. province capital Sichuan, C China
161 Q14 **Chenghai** Guangdong, S China
Chenghsien see Zhengzhou
160 H13 **Chengjiang** Yunnan, SW China
Chengjiang see Taihe
160 L17 **Chengmai** var. Jinjiang. Hainan, S China
Chengtu/Ch'eng-tu see Chengdu
159 W12 **Chengxian** var. Cheng Xiang. Gansu, C China
Cheng Xiang see Chengxian
Chengyang see Juxian
Chengzhong see Ningming
Chenkiang see Zhenjiang
155 J19 **Chennai** prev. Madras. state capital Tamil Nādu, S India
155 J19 **Chennai** ✈ Tamil Nādu, S India
103 R8 **Chenôve** Côte d'Or, C France
Chenstokhov see Częstochowa
160 L11 **Chenxi** var. Chenyang. Hunan, S China
Chen Xian/Chenxian/Chen Xiang see Chenzhou
Chenyang see Chenxi
161 N12 **Chenzhou** var. Chenxian, Chen Xian, Chen Xiang. Hunan, S China
167 U12 **Cheo Reo** var. A Yun Pa. Gia Lai, S Vietnam
114 I11 **Chepelare** Smolyan, S Bulgaria
114 I11 **Chepelarska Reka** ≈ S Bulgaria
56 B11 **Chepén** La Libertad, C Peru
62 J10 **Chepes** La Rioja, C Argentina
161 O15 **Chep Lap Kok** ✈ (Hong Kong) S China
161 O15 **Chep Lap Kok** ✈ S China
43 U14 **Chepo** Panamá, C Panama
Chepping Wycombe see High Wycombe
125 R14 **Cheptsa** ≈ NW Russian Federation
30 K3 **Chequamegon Point** headland Wisconsin, N USA
103 O8 **Cher** ⬖ department C France
102 M8 **Cher** ≈ C France
Cherangani Hills see Cherangany Hills
81 H17 **Cherangany Hills** var. Cherangani Hills. ▲▲ W Kenya
21 S11 **Cheraw** South Carolina, SE USA
102 I3 **Cherbourg** anc. Carusbur. Manche, N France
127 R5 **Cherdakly** Ul'yanovskaya Oblast', W Russian Federation
125 U12 **Cherdyn'** Permskaya Oblast', NW Russian Federation
124 J14 **Cherekha** ≈ W Russian Federation
122 M13 **Cheremkhovo** Irkutskaya Oblast', S Russian Federation
Cheren see Keren
124 K14 **Cherepovets** Vologodskaya Oblast', NW Russian Federation
125 O11 **Cherevkovo** Arkhangel'skaya Oblast', NW Russian Federation
74 I6 **Chergui, Chott ech** salt lake NW Algeria
Cherikov see Cherykaw
117 P6 **Cherkas'ka Oblast'** var. Cherkasy, Rus. Cherkasskaya Oblast'. ⬖ province C Ukraine
Cherkasskaya Oblast' see Cherkas'ka Oblast'
Cherkassy see Cherkasy
117 Q6 **Cherkasy** Rus. Cherkassy. Cherkas'ka Oblast', C Ukraine
Cherkasy see Cherkas'ka Oblast'
126 M15 **Cherkessk** Karachayevo-Cherkesskaya Respublika, SW Russian Federation
122 H12 **Cherlak** Omskaya Oblast', C Russian Federation
122 H12 **Cherlakskiy** Omskaya Oblast', C Russian Federation
125 U13 **Chermoz** Permskaya Oblast', NW Russian Federation
Chernavchitsy see Charnawchytsy
125 T3 **Chernaya** Nenetskiy Avtonomnyy Okrug, NW Russian Federation
125 T4 **Chernaya** ≈ NW Russian Federation
Chernigov see Chernihiv
Chernigovskaya Oblast' see Chernihivs'ka Oblast'
117 Q2 **Chernihiv** Rus. Chernigov. Chernihivs'ka Oblast', NE Ukraine
Chernihiv see Chernihivs'ka Oblast'
117 V9 **Chernihivka** Zaporiz'ka Oblast', SE Ukraine
117 P2 **Chernihivs'ka Oblast'** var. Chernihiv, Rus. Chernigovskaya Oblast'. ⬖ province NE Ukraine
114 I9 **Cherni Osŭm** ≈ N Bulgaria
116 J8 **Chernivets'ka Oblast'** var. Chernivtsi, Rus. Chernovitskaya Oblast'. ⬖ province W Ukraine
114 I9 **Cherni Vit** ≈ NW Bulgaria
114 G10 **Cherni Vrŭkh** ▲ W Bulgaria
116 K8 **Chernivtsi** Ger. Czernowitz, Rom. Cernăuţi, Rus. Chernovtsy. Chernivets'ka Oblast', W Ukraine
116 M7 **Chernivtsi** Vinnyts'ka Oblast', C Ukraine
Chernivtsi see Chernivets'ka Oblast'
Chernobyl' see Chornobyl'
Cherno More see Black Sea
Chernomorskoye see Chornomors'ke
145 T7 **Chernoretskoye** Pavlodar, NE Kazakhstan
Chernovitskaya Oblast' see Chernivets'ka Oblast'
Chernovtsy see Chernivtsi
145 U8 **Chernoye** Pavlodar, NE Kazakhstan
Chernoye More see Black Sea
125 U16 **Chernushka** Permskaya Oblast', NW Russian Federation
117 N4 **Chernyakhiv** Rus. Chernyakhov. Zhytomyrs'ka Oblast', N Ukraine
Chernyakhov see Chernyakhiv
119 C14 **Chernyakhovsk** Ger. Insterburg. Kaliningradskaya Oblast', W Russian Federation
126 K8 **Chernyanka** Belgorodskaya Oblast', W Russian Federation
125 V5 **Chernyshëva, Gryada** ▲▲ NW Russian Federation
144 J14 **Chernyshëva, Zaliv** gulf SW Kazakhstan
123 O10 **Chernyshevskiy** Respublika Sakha (Yakutiya), NE Russian Federation
127 P13 **Chërnyye Zemli** plain SW Russian Federation
Chërnyy Irtysh see Ertix He, China/Kazakhstan
Chërnyy Irtysh see Kara Irtysh, Kazakhstan
127 V7 **Chernyy Otrog** Orenburgskaya Oblast', W Russian Federation
29 T12 **Cherokee** Iowa, C USA
26 M8 **Cherokee** Oklahoma, C USA
25 R9 **Cherokee** Texas, SW USA
21 O8 **Cherokee Lake** ⊠ Tennessee, S USA
Cherokees, Lake O' The see Grand Lake O' The Cherokees
44 H1 **Cherokee Sound** Great Abaco, N Bahamas
153 V13 **Cherrapunji** Meghālaya, NE India
28 L9 **Cherry Creek** ≈ South Dakota, N USA
18 J16 **Cherry Hill** New Jersey, NE USA
27 Q7 **Cherryvale** Kansas, C USA
21 Q10 **Cherryville** North Carolina, SE USA
Cherski Range see Cherskogo, Khrebet
123 T6 **Cherskiy** Respublika Sakha (Yakutiya), NE Russian Federation
123 R8 **Cherskogo, Khrebet** var. Cherski Range. ▲▲ NE Russian Federation
Cherso see Cres
126 L10 **Chertkovo** Rostovskaya Oblast', SW Russian Federation
Cherven' see Chervyen'
114 H8 **Cherven Bryag** Pleven, N Bulgaria
116 M4 **Chervonoarmiys'k** Zhytomyrs'ka Oblast', N Ukraine
Chervonograd see Chervonohrad
116 I4 **Chervonohrad** Rus. Chervonograd. L'vivs'ka Oblast', NW Ukraine
117 W6 **Chervonooskil's'ke Vodoskhovyshche** Rus. Krasnooskol'skoye Vodokhranilishche. ⊠ NE Ukraine
Chervonoye, Ozero see Chyrvonaye, Vozyera
117 S4 **Chervonozavods'ke** Poltavs'ka Oblast', C Ukraine
119 L16 **Chervyen'** Rus. Cherven'. Minskaya Voblasts', C Belarus
119 P16 **Cherykaw** Rus. Cherikov. Mahilyowskaya Voblasts', E Belarus
31 R9 **Chesaning** Michigan, N USA
21 X5 **Chesapeake Bay** inlet NE USA
Chesha Bay see Chëshskaya Guba
Cheshevlya see Tsyeshawlya
97 K18 **Cheshire** cultural region C England, UK
125 P5 **Chëshskaya Guba** var. Archangel Bay, Chesha Bay, Dvina Bay. bay NW Russian Federation
14 F14 **Chesley** Ontario, S Canada
21 Q10 **Chesnee** South Carolina, SE USA
97 K18 **Chester** Wel. Caerleon, hist. Legaceaster, Lat. Deva, Devana Castra. C England, UK
35 O4 **Chester** California, W USA
30 K16 **Chester** Illinois, N USA
33 S7 **Chester** Montana, NW USA
18 I16 **Chester** Pennsylvania, NE USA
21 R1 **Chester** South Carolina, SE USA
25 X9 **Chester** Texas, SW USA
21 W6 **Chester** Virginia, NE USA
21 R11 **Chester** West Virginia, NE USA
97 M18 **Chesterfield** C England, UK
21 S11 **Chesterfield** South Carolina, SE USA
21 W6 **Chesterfield** Virginia, NE USA
192 J9 **Chesterfield, Îles** island group NW New Caledonia
9 O9 **Chesterfield Inlet** Nunavut, NW Canada
9 O9 **Chesterfield Inlet** inlet Nunavut, N Canada
21 Y3 **Chester River** ≈ Delaware/Maryland, NE USA
21 X3 **Chestertown** Maryland, NE USA
19 R4 **Chesuncook Lake** ◎ Maine, NE USA
30 J5 **Chetek** Wisconsin, N USA
13 R14 **Chéticamp** Nova Scotia, SE Canada
27 Q8 **Chetopa** Kansas, C USA
41 Y14 **Chetumal** var. Payo Obispo. Quintana Roo, SE Mexico
Chetumal, Bahia/Chetumal, Bahía de see Chetumal Bay
42 G1 **Chetumal Bay** var. Bahia Chetumal, Bahía de Chetumal. bay Belize/Mexico
10 M13 **Chetwynd** British Columbia, W Canada
38 M11 **Chevak** Alaska, USA
36 M12 **Chevelon Creek** ≈ Arizona, SW USA
185 J17 **Cheviot** Canterbury, South Island, New Zealand
96 L13 **Cheviot Hills** hill range England/Scotland, UK
96 L13 **Cheviot, The** ▲ NE England, UK
14 M11 **Chevreuil, Lac du** ◎ Québec, SE Canada
81 I16 **Ch'ew Bahir** var. Lake Stefanie. ◎ Ethiopia/Kenya
32 L7 **Chewelah** Washington, NW USA
26 K10 **Cheyenne** Oklahoma, C USA
33 Z17 **Cheyenne** state capital Wyoming, C USA
26 L5 **Cheyenne Bottoms** ◎ Kansas, C USA
16 J8 **Cheyenne River** ≈ South Dakota/Wyoming, N USA
37 W5 **Cheyenne Wells** Colorado, C USA
108 C9 **Cheyres** Vaud, W Switzerland
Chezdi-Oşorheiu see Târgu Secuiesc
153 P13 **Chhapra** prev. Chapra. Bihār, N India
153 V13 **Chhatak** var. Chatak. Sylhet, NE Bangladesh
154 J9 **Chhatarpur** Madhya Pradesh, C India
154 N13 **Chhatrapur** prev. Chatrapur. Orissa, E India
154 K12 **Chhattīsgarh** ⬖ state E India
154 L12 **Chhattīsgarh** plain C India
154 I11 **Chhindwāra** Madhya Pradesh, C India
153 T12 **Chhukha** SW Bhutan
161 S14 **Chiai** var. Chia-i, Chiayi, Kiayi, Jiayi, Jap. Kagi. C Taiwan
Chia-i see Chiai
Chia-mu-ssu see Jiamusi
83 B15 **Chiange** Port. Vila de Almoster. Huíla, SW Angola
Chiang-hsi see Jiangxi
161 S12 **Chiang Kai-shek** ✈ (T'aipei) N Taiwan
167 P8 **Chiang Khan** Loei, E Thailand
167 O7 **Chiang Mai** var. Chiangmai, Chiengmai, Kiangmai. Chiang Mai, NW Thailand
167 O7 **Chiang Mai** ✈ Chiang Mai, NW Thailand
Chiangmai see Chiang Mai
167 O6 **Chiang Rai** var. Chianpai, Chienrai, Muang Chiang Rai. Chiang Rai, NW Thailand
Chiang-su see Jiangsu
Chianning/Chian-ning see Nanjing
Chianpai see Chiang Rai
106 G12 **Chianti** cultural region C Italy
Chiapa see Chiapa de Corzo
41 U16 **Chiapa de Corzo** var. Chiapa. Chiapas, SE Mexico
41 V16 **Chiapas** ⬖ state SE Mexico
106 J12 **Chiaravalle** Marche, C Italy
107 N22 **Chiaravalle Centrale** Calabria, SW Italy
106 E7 **Chiari** Lombardia, N Italy
108 H12 **Chiasso** Ticino, S Switzerland
137 S9 **Chiat'ura** C Georgia
41 P15 **Chiautla** var. Chiautla de Tapia. Puebla, S Mexico
Chiautla de Tapia see Chiautla
106 D10 **Chiavari** Liguria, NW Italy
106 E6 **Chiavenna** Lombardia, N Italy
Chiayi see Chiai
Chiazza see Piazza Armerina
165 O14 **Chiba** var. Tiba. Chiba, Honshū, S Japan
165 O13 **Chiba** off. Chiba-ken, var. Tiba. ⬖ prefecture Honshū, S Japan
83 M18 **Chibabava** Sofala, C Mozambique
Chiba-ken see Chiba
161 O10 **Chibi** prev. Puqi. Hubei, C China
83 B15 **Chibia** Port. João de Almeida, Vila João de Almeida. Huíla, SW Angola
83 M18 **Chiboma** Sofala, C Mozambique
82 J12 **Chibondo** Luapula, N Zambia
82 K11 **Chibote** Luapula, NE Zambia
12 K12 **Chibougamau** Québec, SE Canada
164 H11 **Chiburi-jima** island Oki-shotō, SW Japan
83 M20 **Chibuto** Gaza, S Mozambique
31 N11 **Chicago** Illinois, N USA
31 N11 **Chicago Heights** Illinois, N USA
15 W6 **Chic-Chocs, Monts** Eng. Shickshock Mountains. ▲▲ Québec, SE Canada
39 W13 **Chichagof Island** island Alexander Archipelago, Alaska, USA
57 K20 **Chichas, Cordillera de** ▲▲ SW Bolivia
41 X12 **Chichén-Itzá, Ruinas** ruins Yucatán, SE Mexico
97 N23 **Chichester** SE England, UK
42 C5 **Chichicastenango** Quiché, W Guatemala
42 I9 **Chichigalpa** Chinandega, NW Nicaragua
Ch'i-ch'i-ha-erh see Qiqihar
165 X16 **Chichijima-rettō** Eng. Beechy Group. island group SE Japan
54 K4 **Chichiriviche** Falcón, N Venezuela
39 R11 **Chickaloon** Alaska, USA
20 L10 **Chickamauga Lake** ⊠ Tennessee, S USA
23 N7 **Chickasawhay River** ≈ Mississippi, S USA
26 M11 **Chickasha** Oklahoma, C USA
39 T9 **Chicken** Alaska, USA
104 J16 **Chiclana de la Frontera** Andalucía, S Spain
56 B11 **Chiclayo** Lambayeque, NW Peru
35 N5 **Chico** California, W USA
83 L15 **Chicoa** Tete, NW Mozambique
83 M20 **Chicomo** Gaza, S Mozambique
18 M11 **Chicopee** Massachusetts, NE USA
63 I19 **Chico, Río** ≈ SE Argentina
63 I21 **Chico, Río** ≈ S Argentina
27 W14 **Chicot, Lake** ◎ Arkansas, C USA
15 R7 **Chicoutimi** Québec, SE Canada
15 Q8 **Chicoutimi** ≈ Québec, SE Canada
83 L19 **Chicualacuala** Gaza, SW Mozambique
83 B14 **Chicuma** Benguela, C Angola
155 J21 **Chidambaram** Tamil Nādu, SE India
196 K13 **Chidley, Cape** cape Newfoundland and Labrador, E Canada
101 N24 **Chiemsee** ◎ SE Germany
Chiengmai see Chiang Mai
Chienrai see Chiang Rai
106 B8 **Chieri** Piemonte, NW Italy
106 F8 **Chiese** ≈ N Italy
107 K14 **Chieti** var. Teate. Abruzzo, C Italy
99 E19 **Chièvres** Hainaut, SW Belgium
163 S12 **Chifeng** var. Ulanhad. Nei Mongol Zizhiqu, N China
82 F13 **Chifumage** ≈ E Angola
82 M13 **Chifunda** Eastern, NE Zambia
145 S14 **Chiganak** var. Ciganak. Zhambyl, SE Kazakhstan
39 P15 **Chiginagak, Mount** ▲ Alaska, USA
Chigirin see Chyhyryn
41 P13 **Chignahuapan** Puebla, S Mexico
39 O15 **Chignik** Alaska, USA
83 M19 **Chigombe** ≈ S Mozambique
54 D7 **Chigorodó** Antioquia, NW Colombia
83 M19 **Chigubo** Gaza, S Mozambique
Chihertey see Altay
Chih-fu see Yantai
Chihli see Hebei
Chihli, Gulf of see Bo Hai
40 J6 **Chihuahua** Chihuahua, NW Mexico
40 I6 **Chihuahua** ⬖ state N Mexico
145 O15 **Chiili** Kzylorda, S Kazakhstan
26 M7 **Chikaskia River** ≈ Kansas/Oklahoma, C USA
155 H19 **Chik Ballāpur** Karnātaka, W India
124 G15 **Chikhachevo** Pskovskaya Oblast', W Russian Federation
155 F19 **Chikmagalūr** Karnātaka, W India
129 V7 **Chikoy** ≈ C Russian Federation
83 J15 **Chikumbi** Lusaka, C Zambia
82 M13 **Chikwa** Eastern, NE Zambia
Chikwana see Chikwawa
83 N15 **Chikwawa** var. Chikwana. Southern, S Malawi
155 J16 **Chilakalūrupet** Andhra Pradesh, E India
146 L14 **Chilan** Lebap Welaýaty, E Turkmenistan
Chilapa see Chilapa de Alvarez
41 P16 **Chilapa de Alvarez** var. Chilapa. Guerrero, S Mexico
155 J25 **Chilaw** North Western Province, W Sri Lanka
57 D15 **Chilca** Lima, W Peru
23 Q4 **Childersburg** Alabama, S USA
25 P4 **Childress** Texas, SW USA
63 G14 **Chile** off. Republic of Chile. ◆ republic SW South America
47 R10 **Chile Basin** undersea feature E Pacific Ocean
63 F20 **Chile Chico** Aisén, W Chile
62 I9 **Chilecito** La Rioja, NW Argentina
62 H12 **Chilecito** Mendoza, W Argentina
83 L14 **Chilembwe** Eastern, E Zambia
Chile, Republic of see Chile
193 S11 **Chile Rise** undersea feature SE Pacific Ocean
117 N13 **Chilia Braţul** ≈ SE Romania
Chilia-Nouă see Kiliya
145 V15 **Chilik** Almaty, SE Kazakhstan
145 V15 **Chilik** ≈ SE Kazakhstan
154 O13 **Chilika Lake** var. Chilka Lake. ◎ E India
82 J13 **Chililabombwe** Copperbelt, C Zambia
Chi-lin see Jilin
Chilka Lake see Chilika Lake
10 H9 **Chilkoot Pass** pass British Columbia, W Canada
Chill Ala, Cuan see Killala Bay
62 G13 **Chillán** Bío Bío, C Chile
61 C22 **Chillar** Buenos Aires, E Argentina
Chill Chiaráin, Cuan see Kilkieran Bay
30 K12 **Chillicothe** Illinois, N USA
27 S3 **Chillicothe** Missouri, C USA
31 S14 **Chillicothe** Ohio, N USA
25 Q4 **Chillicothe** Texas, SW USA
10 M17 **Chilliwack** British Columbia, SW Canada
Chill Mhantáin, Ceann see Wicklow Head
Chill Mhantáin, Sléibhte see Wicklow Mountains
108 C10 **Chillon** Vaud, W Switzerland
Chil'mamedkum, Peski/Chilmämetgum see Çilmämmetgum
63 F17 **Chiloé, Isla de** var. Isla Grande de Chiloé. island W Chile
32 H15 **Chiloquin** Oregon, NW USA
41 O16 **Chilpancingo** var. Chilpancingo de los Bravos. Guerrero, S Mexico
Chilpancingo de los Bravos see Chilpancingo
97 N21 **Chiltern Hills** hill range S England, UK
30 M7 **Chilton** Wisconsin, N USA
82 F11 **Chiluage** Lunda Sul, NE Angola
82 N12 **Chilumba** prev. Deep Bay. Northern, N Malawi
161 T12 **Chilung** var. Keelung, Jap. Kirun, Kirun'; prev. Sp. Santissima Trinidad. N Taiwan
83 N15 **Chilwa, Lake** var. Lago Chirua, Lake Shirwa. ◎ SE Malawi
167 R10 **Chi, Mae Nam** ≈ E Thailand
42 C6 **Chimaltenango** Chimaltenango, C Guatemala
42 A2 **Chimaltenango** off. Departamento de Chimaltenango. ⬖ department S Guatemala
Chimaltenango, Departamento de see Chimaltenango
43 V15 **Chimán** Panamá, E Panama
83 M17 **Chimanimani** prev. Mandidzudzure, Melsetter. Manicaland, E Zimbabwe
99 G22 **Chimay** Hainaut, S Belgium
37 S10 **Chimayo** New Mexico, SW USA
Chimbay see Chimboy
56 A13 **Chimborazo** ⬖ province C Ecuador
56 C7 **Chimborazo** ⛰ C Ecuador
56 C12 **Chimbote** Ancash, W Peru
146 H7 **Chimboy** Rus. Chimbay. Qoraqalpog'iston Respublikasi, NW Uzbekistan
186 D7 **Chimbu** ⬖ province C Papua New Guinea
54 F6 **Chimichagua** Cesar, N Colombia
Chimishliya see Cimişlia
Chimkent see Shymkent
Chimkentskaya Oblast' see Yuzhnyy Kazakhstan
28 I14 **Chimney Rock** rock Nebraska, C USA
83 M17 **Chimoio** Manica, C Mozambique
82 K11 **Chimpembe** Northern, NE Zambia
41 O8 **China** Nuevo León, NE Mexico
156 M9 **China** off. People's Republic of China, Chin. Chung-hua Jen-min Kung-ho-kuo, Zhonghua Renmin Gongheguo; prev. Chinese Empire. ◆ republic E Asia
19 Q7 **China Lake** ◎ Maine, NE USA
42 F8 **Chinameca** San Miguel, E El Salvador
Chi-nan/Chinan see Jinan
42 H9 **Chinandega** Chinandega, NW Nicaragua
42 H9 **Chinandega** ⬖ department NW Nicaragua
China, People's Republic of see China
China, Republic of see Taiwan
24 J11 **Chinati Mountains** ▲▲ Texas, SW USA
Chinaz see Chinoz
57 E15 **Chincha Alta** Ica, SW Peru
9 N11 **Chinchaga** ≈ Alberta, SW Canada
Chin-chiang see Quanzhou
Chinchilla see Chinchilla de Monte Aragón
105 Q11 **Chinchilla de Monte Aragón** var. Chinchilla. Castilla-La Mancha, C Spain
54 D10 **Chinchiná** Caldas, W Colombia
105 O8 **Chinchón** Madrid, C Spain
41 Z14 **Chinchorro, Banco** island SE Mexico
Chin-chou/Chinchow see Jinzhou
21 Z5 **Chincoteague** Assateague Island, Virginia, NE USA

◆ Country ● Country Capital ◇ Dependent Territory ○ Dependent Territory Capital ⬖ Administrative Regions ✈ International Airport ▲ Mountain ▲▲ Mountain Range ⛰ Volcano ≈ River ◎ Lake ⊠ Reservoir

83 O17 **Chinde** Zambézia, NE Mozambique
163 X17 **Chin-do** *Jap.* Chin-tō. *island* SW South Korea
159 R13 **Chindu** *var.* Chuqung. Qinghai, C China
166 M2 **Chindwin** N Myanmar (Burma)
Chinese Empire *see* China
Chinghai *see* Qinghai, China
Ch'ing Hai *see* Qinghai Hu, China
Chingildi *see* Shengeldi
Chingildi *see* Shengeldi
144 H9 **Chingirlau** *Kaz.* Shyngghyrlaū. Zapadnyy Kazakhstan, W Kazakhstan
82 J13 **Chingola** Copperbelt, C Zambia
Ching-Tao/Ch'ing-tao *see* Qingdao
82 C13 **Chinguar** Huambo, C Angola
76 I7 **Chinguetti** *var.* Chinguetti. Adrar, C Mauritania
163 Z16 **Chinhae** *Jap.* Chinkai. S South Korea
166 K4 **Chin Hills** ▲ W Myanmar (Burma)
83 K16 **Chinhoyi** *prev.* Sinoia. Mashonaland West, N Zimbabwe
Chinhsien *see* Jinzhou
39 Q14 **Chiniak, Cape** *headland* Kodiak Island, Alaska, USA
14 G10 **Chiniguchi Lake** Ontario, S Canada
149 U8 **Chiniot** Punjab, NE Pakistan
163 Y16 **Chinju** *Jap.* Shinshū. S South Korea
Chinkai *see* Chinhae
78 M13 **Chinko** E Central African Republic
37 O9 **Chinle** Arizona, SW USA
161 R13 **Chinmen Tao** *var.* Jinmen Dao, Quemoy. *island* W Taiwan
Chinnchâr *see* Shinshār
Chinnereth *see* Tiberias, Lake
164 C12 **Chino** *var.* Tino. Nagano, Honshū, S Japan
102 L8 **Chinon** Indre-et-Loire, C France
33 T7 **Chinook** Montana, NW USA
Chinook State *see* Washington
192 L4 **Chinook Trough** *undersea feature* N Pacific Ocean
36 K11 **Chino Valley** Arizona, SW USA
147 P10 **Chinoz** *Rus.* Chinaz. Toshkent Viloyati, E Uzbekistan
82 L12 **Chinsali** Northern, NE Zambia
166 K5 **Chin State** ◆ *state* W Myanmar (Burma)
Chinsura *see* Chunchura
Chin-tō *see* Chin-do
54 E6 **Chinú** Córdoba, NW Colombia
99 K24 **Chiny, Forêt de** *forest* SE Belgium
83 M15 **Chioco** Tete, NW Mozambique
106 H8 **Chioggia** *anc.* Fossa Claudia. Veneto, NE Italy
114 H12 **Chionótrypa** ▲ NE Greece
115 L18 **Chíos** *var.* Hios, Khíos, *It.* Scio, *Turk.* Sakiz-Adasi. Chíos, E Greece
115 K18 **Chíos** *var.* Khíos. *island* E Greece
83 M14 **Chipata** *prev.* Fort Jameson. Eastern, E Zambia
83 C14 **Chipindo** Huíla, C Angola
23 R8 **Chipley** Florida, SE USA
155 D15 **Chiplūn** Mahārāshtra, W India
81 H22 **Chipogolo** Dodoma, C Tanzania
23 R8 **Chipola River** Florida, SE USA
97 L22 **Chippenham** S England, UK
30 J6 **Chippewa Falls** Wisconsin, N USA
30 J4 **Chippewa, Lake** Wisconsin, N USA
31 Q8 **Chippewa River** Michigan, N USA
30 I6 **Chippewa River** Wisconsin, N USA
Chipping Wycombe *see* High Wycombe
114 G8 **Chiprovtsi** Montana, NW Bulgaria
19 T4 **Chiputneticook Lakes** *lakes* Canada/USA
56 D13 **Chiquián** Ancash, W Peru
41 Y11 **Chiquilá** Quintana Roo, SE Mexico
42 E6 **Chiquimula** Chiquimula, SE Guatemala
42 A3 **Chiquimula** *off.* Departamento de Chiquimula. ◆ *department* SE Guatemala
Chiquimula, Departamento de *see* Chiquimula
42 D7 **Chiquimulilla** Santa Rosa, S Guatemala
54 F9 **Chiquinquirá** Boyacá, C Colombia
155 J17 **Chīrāla** Andhra Pradesh, E India
149 N4 **Chīras** Ghowr, N Afghanistan
152 H11 **Chirāwa** Rājasthān, N India
Chirchik *see* Chirchiq
147 Q9 **Chirchiq** *Rus.* Chirchik. Toshkent Viloyati, E Uzbekistan
147 P10 **Chirchiq** E Uzbekistan
Chire *see* Shire
83 L18 **Chiredzi** Masvingo, SE Zimbabwe
25 X8 **Chireno** Texas, SW USA
77 X7 **Chirfa** Agadez, NE Niger
37 O16 **Chiricahua Mountains** ▲ Arizona, SW USA
37 O16 **Chiricahua Peak** ▲ Arizona, SW USA
54 F6 **Chiriguaná** Cesar, N Colombia
39 P15 **Chirikof Island** *island* Alaska, USA
43 P16 **Chiriquí** *off.* Provincia de Chiriquí. ◆ *province* SW Panama
43 P17 **Chiriquí, Golfo de** *Eng.* Chiriqui Gulf. *gulf* SW Panama
43 P15 **Chiriquí Grande** Bocas del Toro, W Panama
Chiriqui Gulf *see* Chiriquí, Golfo de
43 P15 **Chiriquí, Laguna de** *lagoon* NW Panama
Chiriquí, Provincia de *see* Chiriquí
43 O16 **Chiriquí Viejo, Río** W Panama
Chiriquí, Volcán de *see* Barú, Volcán
83 N15 **Chiromo** Southern, S Malawi
114 J10 **Chirpan** Stara Zagora, C Bulgaria
43 N14 **Chirripó Atlántico, Río** E Costa Rica
Chirripó, Cerro *see* Chirripó Grande, Cerro
Chirripó del Pacífico, Río *see* Chirripó, Río
43 N14 **Chirripó Grande, Cerro** *var.* Cerro Chirripó. ▲ SE Costa Rica
43 N13 **Chirripó, Río** *var.* Río Chirripó del Pacífico. NE Costa Rica
Chirua, Lago *see* Chilwa, Lake
83 J15 **Chirundu** Southern, S Zambia
29 W8 **Chisago City** Minnesota, N USA
83 J14 **Chisamba** Central, C Zambia
39 T10 **Chisana** Alaska, USA
82 I13 **Chisasa** North Western, NW Zambia
12 I9 **Chisasibi** Québec, C Canada
42 D4 **Chisec** Alta Verapaz, C Guatemala
127 U5 **Chishmy** Respublika Bashkortostan, W Russian Federation
29 V4 **Chisholm** Minnesota, N USA
160 I11 **Chishui He** C China
Chisimaio/Chisimayu *see* Kismaayo
117 N10 **Chişinău** *Rus.* Kishinev. ● (Moldova) C Moldova
117 N10 **Chişinău** ✈ S Moldova
Chişinău-Criş *see* Chişineu-Criş
116 F10 **Chişineu-Criş** *Hung.* Kisjenő; *prev.* Chişinău-Criş. Arad, W Romania
83 K14 **Chisomo** Central, C Zambia
106 A8 **Chisone** NW Italy
24 K12 **Chisos Mountains** ▲ Texas, SW USA
149 U10 **Chishtiān Mandi** Punjab, E Pakistan
39 T10 **Chistochina** Alaska, USA
127 R4 **Chistopol'** Respublika Tatarstan, W Russian Federation
145 O8 **Chistopol'ye** Severnyy Kazakhstan, N Kazakhstan
123 O13 **Chita** Chitinskaya Oblast', S Russian Federation
83 B16 **Chitado** Cunene, SW Angola
Chitaldroog/Chitaldrug *see* Chitradurga
83 C15 **Chitanda** S Angola
Chitangwiza *see* Chitungwiza
82 F10 **Chitato** Lunda Norte, NE Angola
83 C14 **Chitembo** Bié, C Angola
39 T11 **Chitina** Alaska, USA
39 T11 **Chitina River** Alaska, USA
123 O12 **Chitinskaya Oblast'** ◆ *province* S Russian Federation
82 M11 **Chitipa** Northern, NW Malawi
165 S4 **Chitose** *var.* Titose. Hokkaidō, NE Japan
155 G18 **Chitradurga** *prev.* Chitaldroog, Chitaldrug. Karnātaka, W India
149 T3 **Chitrāl** North-West Frontier Province, NW Pakistan
43 S16 **Chitré** Herrera, S Panama
153 V16 **Chittagong** *Ben.* Chāttagām. Chittagong, SE Bangladesh
153 U16 **Chittagong** ◆ *division* E Bangladesh
153 Q15 **Chittaranjan** West Bengal, NE India
152 G14 **Chittaurgarh** Rājasthān, N India
155 I19 **Chittoor** Andhra Pradesh, E India
155 G21 **Chittūr** Kerala, SW India
83 K16 **Chitungwiza** *prev.* Chitangwiza. Mashonaland East, NE Zimbabwe
62 H4 **Chiuchiu** Antofagasta, N Chile
82 F12 **Chiumbe** *var.* Tshiumbe. Angola/Dem. Rep. Congo
83 F15 **Chiume** Moxico, E Angola
82 K13 **Chiundaponde** Northern, NE Zambia
106 H13 **Chiusi** Toscana, C Italy
54 J5 **Chivacoa** Yaracuy, N Venezuela
106 B8 **Chivasso** Piemonte, NW Italy
83 L17 **Chivhu** *prev.* Enkeldoorn. Midlands, C Zimbabwe
61 C20 **Chivilcoy** Buenos Aires, E Argentina
82 N12 **Chiweta** Northern, N Malawi
42 D4 **Chixoy, Río** *var.* Río Negro, Río Salinas. Guatemala/Mexico
82 H13 **Chizela** North Western, NW Zambia
125 O5 **Chizha** Nenetskiy Avtonomnyy Okrug, NW Russian Federation
161 Q9 **Chizhou** *var.* Guichi. Anhui, E China
164 I12 **Chizu** Tottori, Honshū, SW Japan
Chkalov *see* Orenburg
74 J5 **Chlef** *var.* Ech Cheliff, Ech Chleff; *prev.* Al-Asnam, El Asnam, Orléansville. NW Algeria
115 G18 **Chlómo** ▲ C Greece
111 M15 **Chmielnik** Świętokrzyskie, C Poland
167 S11 **Chŏâm Khsant** Preăh Vihéar, N Cambodia
62 G10 **Choapa, Río** *var.* Choapo. C Chile
Choapas *see* Las Choapas
Choapo *see* Choapa, Río
Choarta *see* Chwārtā
67 T13 **Chobe** N Botswana
14 K8 **Chochocouane** Québec, SE Canada
110 E13 **Chocianów** *Ger.* Kotzenan. Dolnośląskie, SW Poland
54 C9 **Chocó** *off.* Departamento del Chocó. ◆ *province* W Colombia
Chocó, Departamento del *see* Chocó
35 X16 **Chocolate Mountains** ▲ California, W USA
21 W9 **Chocowinity** North Carolina, SE USA
27 N10 **Choctaw** Oklahoma, C USA
23 Q8 **Choctawhatchee Bay** *bay* Florida, SE USA
23 Q8 **Choctawhatchee River** Florida, SE USA
Chodau *see* Chodov
163 V14 **Chŏ-do** *island* SW North Korea
Chodorów *see* Khodoriv
111 A16 **Chodov** *Ger.* Chodau. Karlovarský Kraj, W Czech Republic
110 G10 **Chodzież** Wielkopolskie, C Poland
63 J15 **Choele Choel** Río Negro, C Argentina
83 L14 **Chofombo** Tete, NW Mozambique
Chohtan *see* Chauhtan
9 U14 **Choiceland** Saskatchewan, C Canada
186 K8 **Choiseul** *var.* Lauru. *island* NW Solomon Islands
63 M23 **Choiseul Sound** *sound* East Falkland, Falkland Islands
40 H7 **Choix** Sinaloa, C Mexico
110 D10 **Chojna** Zachodnio-pomorskie, W Poland
110 H8 **Chojnice** *Ger.* Konitz. Pomorskie, N Poland
111 F14 **Chojnów** *Ger.* Hainau, Haynau. Dolnośląskie, SW Poland
167 Q10 **Chok Chai** Nakhon Ratchasima, C Thailand
80 I12 **Ch'ok'ē** *var.* Choke Mountains. ▲ NW Ethiopia
25 R13 **Choke Canyon Lake** Texas, SW USA
Choke Mountains *see* Ch'ok'ē
145 T15 **Chokpar** *Kaz.* Shoqpar. Zhambyl, S Kazakhstan
147 W7 **Chok-Tal** *var.* Choktal. Issyk-Kul'skaya Oblast', E Kyrgyzstan
Choktal *see* Chok-Tal
Chókué *see* Chokwè
123 R7 **Chokurdakh** Respublika Sakha (Yakutiya), NE Russian Federation
83 L20 **Chokwè** *var.* Chókué. Gaza, S Mozambique
188 F8 **Chol** Babeldaob, N Palau
160 E8 **Chola Shan** ▲ C China
102 J8 **Cholet** Maine-et-Loire, NW France
63 H17 **Cholila** Chubut, W Argentina
Cholo *see* Thyolo
147 V8 **Cholpon** Narynskaya Oblast', C Kyrgyzstan
147 X7 **Cholpon-Ata** Issyk-Kul'skaya Oblast', E Kyrgyzstan
41 P14 **Cholula** Puebla, S Mexico
42 I8 **Choluteca** Choluteca, S Honduras
42 H8 **Choluteca** ◆ *department* S Honduras
42 G6 **Choluteca, Río** SW Honduras
83 I15 **Choma** Southern, S Zambia
153 T11 **Chomo Lhari** ▲ NW Bhutan
167 N7 **Chom Thong** Chiang Mai, NW Thailand
111 B15 **Chomutov** *Ger.* Komotau. Ústecký Kraj, NW Czech Republic
123 N11 **Chona** C Russian Federation
163 X15 **Ch'ŏnan** *Jap.* Tenan. W South Korea
167 P11 **Chon Buri** *prev.* Bang Pla Soi. Chon Buri, S Thailand
56 B6 **Chone** Manabí, W Ecuador
Chong'an *see* Wuyishan
163 W13 **Ch'ŏngch'ŏn-gang** W North Korea
163 Y11 **Ch'ŏngjin** NE North Korea
163 W13 **Chŏngju** W North Korea
161 S8 **Chongming Dao** *island* E China
160 J10 **Chongqing** *var.* Ch'ung-ching, Ch'ung-ch'ing, Chungking, Pahsien, Tchongking, Yuzhou. Chongqing Shi, C China
Chŏngup *see* Chŏnju
161 O10 **Chongyang** *var.* Tiancheng. Hubei, C China
160 J15 **Chongzuo** Guangxi Zhuangzu Zizhiqu, S China
163 Y16 **Chŏnju** *prev.* Chŏngup, *Jap.* Seiyu. SW South Korea
163 Y15 **Chŏnju** *Jap.* Zenshū. SW South Korea
Chonnacht *see* Connaught
Chonogol *see* Erdenetsagaan
63 F19 **Chonos, Archipiélago de los** *island group* S Chile
42 K10 **Chontales** ◆ *department* S Nicaragua
167 T13 **Chơn Thanh** Sông Be, S Vietnam
158 K17 **Cho Oyu** *var.* Qowowuyag. ▲ China/Nepal
116 G7 **Chop** *Cz.* Čop, *Hung.* Csap. Zakarpats'ka Oblast', W Ukraine
21 Y3 **Choptank River** Maryland, NE USA
115 J22 **Chóra** *prev* Íos. Íos, Kykládes, Greece, Aegean Sea
115 H25 **Chóra Sfakíon** *var.* Sfákia. Kríti, Greece, E Mediterranean Sea
Chorcaí, Cuan *see* Cork Harbour
43 P15 **Chorcha, Cerro** ▲ W Panama
Chorku *see* Chorkŭh
147 R11 **Chorkŭh** *Rus.* Chorku. N Tajikistan
97 K17 **Chorley** NW England, UK
Chorne More *see* Black Sea
117 R5 **Chornobay** Cherkas'ka Oblast', C Ukraine
117 O3 **Chornobyl'** *Rus.* Chernobyl'. Kyyivs'ka Oblast', N Ukraine
117 R12 **Chornomors'ke** *Rus.* Chernomorskoye. Respublika Krym, S Ukraine
117 R4 **Chornukhy** Poltavs'ka Oblast', C Ukraine
Chorokh/Chorokhi *see* Çoruh Nehri
110 O9 **Choroszcz** Podlaskie, NE Poland
116 K6 **Chortkiv** *Rus.* Chortkov. Ternopil's'ka Oblast', W Ukraine
Chortkov *see* Chortkiv
Chorum *see* Çorum
110 M9 **Chorzele** Mazowieckie, C Poland
111 J16 **Chorzów** *Ger.* Königshütte; *prev.* Królewska Huta. Śląskie, S Poland
163 W12 **Ch'osan** N North Korea
Chośebuz *see* Cottbus
Chōsen-kaikyō *see* Korea Strait
164 P14 **Chōshi** *var.* Tyôsi. Chiba, Honshū, S Japan
63 H14 **Chos Malal** Neuquén, W Argentina
Chosŏn-minjujuŭi-inmin-kanghwaguk *see* North Korea
110 E9 **Choszczno** *Ger.* Arnswalde. Zachodnio-pomorskie, NW Poland
153 O15 **Chota Nāgpur** *plateau* N India
33 R8 **Choteau** Montana, NW USA
Chotqol *see* Chatkal
14 M8 **Chouart** Québec, SE Canada
76 I7 **Choûm** Adrar, C Mauritania
27 Q9 **Chouteau** Oklahoma, C USA
21 X8 **Chowan River** North Carolina, SE USA
35 Q10 **Chowchilla** California, W USA
163 Q7 **Choybalsan** *var.* Hulstay Dornod. Dornod, NE Mongolia
163 P7 **Choybalsan** *prev.* Byan Tumen. Dornod, E Mongolia
162 M9 **Choyr** Govĭ Sumber, C Mongolia
185 I19 **Christchurch** Canterbury, South Island, New Zealand
97 M24 **Christchurch** S England, UK
185 I18 **Christchurch** ✈ Canterbury, South Island, New Zealand
44 J12 **Christiana** C Jamaica
83 H22 **Christiana** Free State, C South Africa
115 J23 **Christiána** *var.* Christiani. *island* Kykládes, Greece, Aegean Sea
Christiani *see* Christiána
Christiania *see* Oslo
14 G13 **Christian Island** *island* Ontario, S Canada
191 P16 **Christian, Point** *headland* Pitcairn Island, Pitcairn Islands
38 M11 **Christian River** Alaska, USA
Christiansand *see* Kristiansand
21 S7 **Christiansburg** Virginia, NE USA
95 G23 **Christiansfeld** Sønderjylland, SW Denmark
Christianshåb *see* Qasigiannguit
39 X14 **Christian Sound** *inlet* Alaska, USA
45 T9 **Christiansted** Saint Croix, S Virgin Islands (US)
Christiansund *see* Kristiansund
25 R13 **Christine** Texas, SW USA
173 U7 **Christmas Island** ◇ *Australian external territory* E Indian Ocean
129 T17 **Christmas Island** *island* E Indian Ocean
Christmas Island *see* Kiritimati
192 M7 **Christmas Ridge** *undersea feature* C Pacific Ocean
30 L16 **Christopher** Illinois, N USA
25 P9 **Christoval** Texas, SW USA
111 F17 **Chrudim** Pardubický Kraj, C Czech Republic
115 K25 **Chrýsi** *island* SE Greece
121 N2 **Chrysochoú, Kólpos** *var.* Khrysokhou Bay. *bay* E Mediterranean Sea
114 I13 **Chrysoúpoli** *var.* Hrisoupoli; *prev.* Khrisoúpolis. Anatolikí Makedonía kai Thráki, NE Greece
111 K16 **Chrzanów** *var.* Chrzanow, *Ger.* Zaumgarten. Śląskie, S Poland
129 Q7 **Chu** *Kaz.* Shū. Kazakhstan/Kyrgyzstan
42 C5 **Chuacús, Sierra de** ▲ W Guatemala
153 S15 **Chuadanga** Khulna, W Bangladesh
Chuan *see* Sichuan
Ch'uan-chou *see* Quanzhou
39 O11 **Chuathbaluk** Alaska, USA
Chubek *see* Moskva
63 I17 **Chubut** *off.* Provincia de Chubut. ◆ *province* S Argentina
Chubut, Provincia de *see* Chubut
63 I17 **Chubut, Río** SE Argentina
43 V15 **Chucanti, Cerro** ▲ E Panama
Ch'u-chiang *see* Shaoguan
43 W15 **Chucunaque, Río** E Panama
Chudin *see* Chudzin
116 M5 **Chudniv** Zhytomyrs'ka Oblast', N Ukraine
124 H13 **Chudovo** Novgorodskaya Oblast', W Russian Federation
Chudskoye Ozero *see* Peipus, Lake
119 J18 **Chudzin** *Rus.* Chudin. Brestskaya Voblasts', SW Belarus
39 Q13 **Chugach Islands** *island group* Alaska, USA
39 S11 **Chugach Mountains** ▲ Alaska, USA
164 G12 **Chūgoku-sanchi** ▲ Honshū, SW Japan
Chugqênsumdo *see* Jigzhi
Chuguyev *see* Chuhuyiv
117 V5 **Chuhuyiv** *var.* Chuguyev. Kharkivs'ka Oblast', E Ukraine
61 H19 **Chuí** Rio Grande do Sul, S Brazil
Chuí *see* Chuy
145 S15 **Chu-Iliyskiye Gory** *Kaz.* Shū-Ile Taūlary. ▲ S Kazakhstan
Chukai *see* Cukai
Chukchi Avtonomnyy Okrug *see* Chukotskiy Avtonomnyy Okrug
Chukchi Peninsula *see* Chukotskiy Poluostrov
197 R6 **Chukchi Plain** *undersea feature* Arctic Ocean
197 R6 **Chukchi Plateau** *undersea feature* Arctic Ocean
197 R4 **Chukchi Sea** *Rus.* Chukotskoye More. *sea* Arctic Ocean
125 N14 **Chukhloma** Kostromskaya Oblast', NW Russian Federation
Chukotka *see* Chukotskiy Avtonomnyy Okrug
Chukot Range *see* Anadyrskiy Khrebet
123 V6 **Chukotskiy Avtonomnyy Okrug** *var.* Chukchi Avtonomnyy Okrug, Chukotka. ◆ *autonomous district* NE Russian Federation
123 W5 **Chukotskiy, Mys** *cape* NE Russian Federation
123 V5 **Chukotskiy Poluostrov** *Eng.* Chukchi Peninsula. *peninsula* NE Russian Federation
Chukotskoye More *see* Chukchi Sea
Chukurkak *see* Chuqurqoq
Chulakkurgan *see* Sholakkorgan
35 U17 **Chula Vista** California, W USA
123 Q12 **Chul'man** Respublika Sakha (Yakutiya), NE Russian Federation
56 B9 **Chulucanas** Piura, NW Peru
122 J12 **Chulym** C Russian Federation
152 K6 **Chumar** Jammu and Kashmir, N India
114 K9 **Chumerna** ▲ C Bulgaria
123 R12 **Chumikan** Khabarovskiy Kray, E Russian Federation
167 Q9 **Chum Phae** Khon Kaen, C Thailand
167 N13 **Chumphon** *var.* Jumporn. Chumphon, SW Thailand
167 O9 **Chumsaeng** *var.* Chum Saeng. Nakhon Sawan, C Thailand
Chum Saeng *see* Chumsaeng
122 L12 **Chuna** C Russian Federation
161 R9 **Chun'an** *var.* Qiandaohu; *prev.* Pailing. Zhejiang, SE China
161 S13 **Chunan** N Taiwan
Chuncheng *see* Yangchun
163 Y14 **Ch'unch'ŏn** *Jap.* Shunsen. N South Korea
153 S16 **Chunchura** *prev.* Chinsura. West Bengal, NE India
145 W15 **Chundzha** Almaty, SE Kazakhstan
Ch'ung-ch'ing/Ch'ung-ching *see* Chongqing
Chung-hua Jen-min Kung-ho-kuo *see* China
163 Y15 **Ch'ungju** *Jap.* Chūshū. C South Korea
Chungking *see* Chongqing
161 T14 **Chungyang Shanmo** *Chin.* Taiwan Shan. ▲ C Taiwan
149 V9 **Chūniān** Punjab, E Pakistan
122 L12 **Chunskiy** Irkutskaya Oblast', S Russian Federation
122 M11 **Chunya** C Russian Federation
124 J6 **Chupa** Respublika Kareliya, NW Russian Federation
125 P8 **Chuprovo** Respublika Komi, NW Russian Federation
57 G17 **Chuquibamba** Arequipa, SW Peru
62 H4 **Chuquicamata** Antofagasta, N Chile
57 L21 **Chuquisaca** ◆ *department* S Bolivia
Chuquisaca *see* Sucre
Chuqung *see* Chindu
146 I8 **Chuqurqoq** *Rus.* Chukurkak. Qoraqalpog'iston Respublikasi, NW Uzbekistan
127 T2 **Chur** Udmurtskaya Respublika, NW Russian Federation
108 I9 **Chur** *Fr.* Coire, *It.* Coira, *Rmsch.* Cuera, Quera; *anc.* Curia Rhaetorum. Graubünden, E Switzerland
123 Q10 **Churapcha** Respublika Sakha (Yakutiya), NE Russian Federation
9 V16 **Churchbridge** Saskatchewan, S Canada
21 O8 **Church Hill** Tennessee, S USA
9 X9 **Churchill** Manitoba, C Canada
9 X10 **Churchill** Manitoba/ Saskatchewan, C Canada
13 P9 **Churchill** Newfoundland and Labrador, E Canada
9 Y9 **Churchill, Cape** *headland* Manitoba, C Canada
13 P9 **Churchill Falls** Newfoundland and Labrador, E Canada
9 S12 **Churchill Lake** Saskatchewan, C Canada
19 Q3 **Churchill Lake** Maine, NE USA
194 I5 **Churchill Peninsula** *peninsula* Antarctica
22 H8 **Church Point** Louisiana, S USA
29 O3 **Churchs Ferry** North Dakota, N USA
146 G12 **Churchuri** Ahal Welaýaty, C Turkmenistan
21 T5 **Churchville** Virginia, NE USA
152 G10 **Chūru** Rājasthān, NW India
54 J4 **Churuguara** Falcón, N Venezuela
167 U11 **Chư Sê** Gia Lai, C Vietnam
144 J12 **Chushkakul, Gory** ▲ SW Kazakhstan
Chūshū *see* Ch'ungju
37 O9 **Chuska Mountains** ▲ Arizona/New Mexico, SW USA
Chu, Sông *see* Sam, Nam
125 V14 **Chusovoy** Permskaya Oblast', NW Russian Federation
147 R10 **Chust** Namangan Viloyati, E Uzbekistan
Chust *see* Khust
15 U6 **Chute-aux-Outardes** Québec, SE Canada
117 U5 **Chutove** Poltavs'ka Oblast', C Ukraine
189 O15 **Chuuk** *var.* Truk. ◆ *state* C Micronesia
189 P15 **Chuuk Islands** *var.* Hogoley Islands; *prev.* Truk Islands. *island group* Caroline Islands, C Micronesia
Chuvashia *see* Chuvash Respubliki
Chuvashskaya Respublika *see* Chuvash Respubliki
Chuwārtah *see* Chwārtā
Chu Xian/Chuxian *see* Chuzhou
160 G13 **Chuxiong** Yunnan, SW China
147 V7 **Chuy** Chuyskaya Oblast', N Kyrgyzstan
61 H19 **Chuy** *var.* Chuí. Rocha, E Uruguay
123 O11 **Chuya** Respublika Sakha (Yakutiya), NE Russian Federation
Chüy Oblasty *see* Chuyskaya Oblast'
147 U8 **Chuyskaya Oblast'** *Kir.* Chüy Oblasty. ◆ *province* N Kyrgyzstan
161 Q7 **Chuzhou** *var.* Chuxian, Chu Xian. Anhui, E China
139 U3 **Chwārtā** *var.* Choarta, Chuwārtah. NE Iraq
119 N16 **Chyhirynskaye Vodaskhovishcha** E Belarus
117 R6 **Chyhyryn** *Rus.* Chigirin. Cherkas'ka Oblast', N Ukraine
119 J18 **Chyrvonaya Slabada** *Rus.* Krasnaya Slabada, Krasnaya Sloboda. Minskaya Voblasts', S Belarus
119 J18 **Chyrvonaya Slabada** *Rus.* Krasnaya Slabada, Krasnaya Sloboda. Minskaya Voblasts', S Belarus
119 L19 **Chyrvonaye, Vozyera** *Rus.* Ozero Chervonoye. SE Belarus
117 N11 **Ciadîr-Lunga** *var.* Ceadâr-Lunga, *Rus.* Chadyr-Lunga. S Moldova
169 P16 **Ciamis** *prev.* Tjiamis. Jawa, C Indonesia
107 I16 **Ciampino** ✈ Lazio, C Italy
169 N16 **Cianjur** *prev.* Tjiandjoer. Jawa, C Indonesia
60 H10 **Cianorte** Paraná, S Brazil
Ciarraí *see* Kerry
112 N13 **Ćićevac** Serbia, E Serbia
187 Z14 **Cicia** *prev.* Thithia. *island* Lau Group, E Fiji
105 P4 **Cidacos** N Spain
136 I10 **Cide** Kastamonu, N Turkey
110 L10 **Ciechanów** *prev.* Zichenau. Mazowieckie, C Poland
110 O10 **Ciechanowiec** *Ger.* Rudelstadt. Podlaskie, E Poland
110 J10 **Ciechocinek** Kujawsko-pomorskie, C Poland
44 F6 **Ciego de Ávila** Ciego de Ávila, C Cuba
54 F4 **Ciénaga** Magdalena, N Colombia
54 E6 **Ciénaga de Oro** Córdoba, NW Colombia
44 E5 **Cienfuegos** Cienfuegos, C Cuba
104 F4 **Cíes, Illas** *island group* NW Spain
111 P16 **Cieszanów** Podkarpackie, SE Poland
111 J17 **Cieszyn** *Cz.* Těšín, *Ger.* Teschen. Śląskie, S Poland
105 R12 **Cieza** Murcia, SE Spain
136 F13 **Çifteler** Eskişehir, W Turkey
105 P7 **Cifuentes** Castilla-La Mancha, C Spain
Ciganak *see* Chiganak
105 P9 **Cigüela** C Spain
136 H14 **Cihanbeyli** Konya, C Turkey
136 H14 **Cihanbeyli Yaylası** *plateau* C Turkey
104 L10 **Cíjara, Embalse de** C Spain
169 P16 **Cikalong** Jawa, S Indonesia
169 N16 **Cikawung** Jawa, S Indonesia
187 Y13 **Cikobia** *prev.* Thikombia. *island* N Fiji
169 P17 **Cilacap** *prev.* Tjilatjap. Jawa, C Indonesia
173 O16 **Cilaos** C Réunion
137 S11 **Çıldır** Ardahan, NE Turkey
137 S11 **Çıldır Gölü** NE Turkey
160 M10 **Cili** Hunan, S China
Cilician Gates *see* Gülek Boğazı
121 V10 **Cilicia Trough** *undersea feature* E Mediterranean Sea
Cill Airne *see* Killarney
Cill Chainnigh *see* Kilkenny
Cill Chaoi *see* Kilkee
Cill Choca *see* Kilcock
Cill Dara *see* Kildare
105 N3 **Cilleruelo de Bezana** Castilla-León, N Spain
Cilli *see* Celje
Cill Mhantáin *see* Wicklow
Cill Rois *see* Kilrush
146 C11 **Çilmämmetgum** *Rus.* Peski Chil'mamedkum, *Turkm.* Chilmämetgum. *desert* Balkan Welaýaty, W Turkmenistan
137 Z11 **Çiloy Adası** *Rus.* Ostrov Zhiloy. *island* E Azerbaijan
26 J6 **Cimarron** Kansas, C USA
37 T9 **Cimarron** New Mexico, SW USA
26 M9 **Cimarron River** Kansas/ Oklahoma, C USA
117 N11 **Cimişlia** *Rus.* Chimishliya. S Moldova
Cimpia Turzii *see* Câmpia Turzii
Cîmpina *see* Câmpina
Cîmpulung *see* Câmpulung

◆ Country
● Country Capital
◇ Dependent Territory
○ Dependent Territory Capital
◆ Administrative Regions
✈ International Airport
▲ Mountain
▲ Mountain Range
Volcano
River
Lake
Reservoir

Cîmpulung Moldovenesc see Câmpulung Moldovenesc
137 P15 Çınar Diyarbakır, SE Turkey
54 J8 Cinaruco, Río ≈ Colombia/Venezuela
Cina Selatan, Laut see South China Sea
105 T5 Cinca ≈ NE Spain
112 G13 Cincar ▲ SW Bosnia and Herzegovina
31 Q15 Cincinnati Ohio, N USA
21 M4 Cincinnati ✈ Kentucky, S USA
Cinco de Outubro see Xá-Muteba
136 C15 Çine Aydın, SW Turkey
99 J21 Ciney Namur, SE Belgium
104 H6 Cinfães Viseu, N Portugal
106 J12 Cingoli Marche, C Italy
41 U16 Cintalapa var. Cintalapa de Figueroa. Chiapas, SE Mexico
Cintalapa de Figueroa see Cintalapa
103 X14 Cinto, Monte ▲ Corse, France, C Mediterranean Sea
Cintra see Sintra
105 Q5 Cintruénigo Navarra, N Spain
Cionn tSáile see Kinsale
116 K13 Ciorani Prahova, SE Romania
113 E14 Čiovo It. Bua. island S Croatia
Cipiúr see Kippure
63 I15 Cipolletti Río Negro, C Argentina
120 L7 Circeo, Capo headland C Italy
39 S8 Circle var. Circle City. Alaska, USA
33 X8 Circle Montana, NW USA
Circle City see Circle
31 S14 Circleville Ohio, N USA
36 K6 Circleville Utah, W USA
169 P16 Cirebon prev. Tjirebon. Jawa, S Indonesia
97 L21 Cirencester anc. Corinium, Corinium Dobunorum. C England, UK
Cirkvenica see Crikvenica
107 O20 Ciro Calabria, SW Italy
107 O20 Cirò Marina Calabria, S Italy
102 K14 Ciron ≈ SW France
Cirquenizza see Crikvenica
25 R7 Cisco Texas, SW USA
116 I12 Cisnădie Ger. Heltau, Hung. Nagydisznód. Sibiu, SW Romania
63 G18 Cisnes, Río ≈ S Chile
25 T11 Cistern Texas, SW USA
104 L3 Cistierna Castilla-León, N Spain
Citharista see la Ciotat
Citlaltépetl see Orizaba, Volcán Pico de
55 X10 Citron NW French Guiana
23 N7 Citronelle Alabama, S USA
35 O7 Citrus Heights California, W USA
106 H7 Cittadella Veneto, NE Italy
106 H13 Città della Pieve Umbria, C Italy
106 H12 Città di Castello Umbria, C Italy
107 I14 Cittaducale Lazio, C Italy
107 N22 Cittanova Calabria, SW Italy
Cittavecchia see Stari Grad
116 G10 Ciucea Hung. Csucsa. Cluj, NW Romania
116 M13 Ciucurova Tulcea, SE Romania
Ciudad Acuña see Villa Acuña
41 N15 Ciudad Altamirano Guerrero, S Mexico
42 G7 Ciudad Barrios San Miguel, NE El Salvador
54 I7 Ciudad Bolívar Barinas, NW Venezuela
55 N7 Ciudad Bolívar prev. Angostura. Bolívar, E Venezuela
40 K6 Ciudad Camargo Chihuahua, N Mexico
40 E8 Ciudad Constitución Baja California Sur, W Mexico
Ciudad Cortés see Cortés
41 V17 Ciudad Cuauhtémoc Chiapas, SE Mexico
42 J9 Ciudad Darío var. Dario. Matagalpa, W Nicaragua
Ciudad de Dolores Hidalgo see Dolores Hidalgo
42 C6 Ciudad de Guatemala Eng. Guatemala City; prev. Santiago de los Caballeros. ● (Guatemala) Guatemala, C Guatemala
Ciudad del Carmen see Carmen
62 Q6 Ciudad del Este prev. Cuidad Presidente Stroessner, Presidente Stroessner, Puerto Presidente Stroessner. Alto Paraná, SE Paraguay
62 K5 Ciudad de Libertador General San Martín var. Libertador General San Martín. Jujuy, C Argentina
Ciudad Delicias see Delicias
41 O11 Ciudad del Maíz San Luis Potosí, C Mexico
Ciudad de México see México
54 J7 Ciudad de Nutrias Barinas, NW Venezuela
Ciudad de Panama see Panamá
55 P7 Ciudad Guayana prev. San Tomé de Guayana, Santo Tomé de Guayana. Bolívar, NE Venezuela
40 K14 Ciudad Guzmán Jalisco, SW Mexico
41 V17 Ciudad Hidalgo Chiapas, SE Mexico
41 N14 Ciudad Hidalgo Michoacán de Ocampo, SW Mexico
40 J3 Ciudad Juárez Chihuahua, N Mexico
40 L8 Ciudad Lerdo Durango, C Mexico
41 Q11 Ciudad Madero var. Villa Cecilia. Tamaulipas, C Mexico
41 P11 Ciudad Mante Tamaulipas, C Mexico
42 F2 Ciudad Melchor de Mencos var. Melchor de Mencos. Petén, NE Guatemala
41 P8 Ciudad Miguel Alemán Tamaulipas, C Mexico
Ciudad Mutis see Bahía Solano
40 G6 Ciudad Obregón Sonora, NW Mexico
54 I5 Ciudad Ojeda Zulia, NW Venezuela
55 P7 Ciudad Piar Bolívar, E Venezuela
Ciudad Porfirio Díaz see Piedras Negras
Ciudad Quesada see Quesada
105 N11 Ciudad Real Castilla-La Mancha, C Spain
105 N11 Ciudad Real ◈ province Castilla-La Mancha, C Spain
104 J7 Ciudad-Rodrigo Castilla-León, N Spain
42 A6 Ciudad Tecún Umán San Marcos, SW Guatemala
Ciudad Trujillo see Santo Domingo
41 P12 Ciudad Valles San Luis Potosí, C Mexico
41 O10 Ciudad Victoria Tamaulipas, C Mexico
42 C6 Ciudad Vieja Suchitepéquez, S Guatemala
116 L8 Ciuhuru var. Reuţel. ≈ N Moldova
105 Z8 Ciutadella var. Ciutadella de Menorca. Menorca, Spain, W Mediterranean Sea
Ciutadella Ciutadella de Menorca see Ciutadella
136 L11 Civa Burnu headland N Turkey
106 J7 Cividale del Friuli Friuli-Venezia Giulia, NE Italy
107 H14 Civita Castellana Lazio, C Italy
106 J12 Civitanova Marche Marche, C Italy
Civitas Altae Ripae see Brzeg
Civitas Carnutum see Chartres
Civitas Eburovicum see Évreux
Civitas Nemetum see Speyer
107 G15 Civitavecchia anc. Centum Cellae, Trajani Portus. Lazio, C Italy
102 L10 Civray Vienne, W France
136 E14 Çivril Denizli, W Turkey
161 O5 Cixian Hebei, E China
137 R16 Cizre Şırnak, SE Turkey
35 W16 Coachella California, W USA
35 W16 Coachella Canal canal California, W USA
40 I9 Coacoyole Durango, C Mexico
25 N7 Coahoma Texas, SW USA
10 K8 Coal ≈ Yukon Territory, NW Canada
40 L14 Coalcomán var. Coalcomán de Matamoros. Michoacán de Ocampo, S Mexico
Coalcomán de Matamoros see Coalcomán
39 T8 Coal Creek Alaska, USA
9 Q17 Coaldale Alberta, SW Canada
27 P12 Coalgate Oklahoma, C USA
35 P11 Coalinga California, W USA
10 L9 Coal River British Columbia, W Canada
21 Q6 Coal River ≈ West Virginia, NE USA
36 M2 Coalville Utah, W USA
58 E13 Coari Amazonas, N Brazil
104 I7 Côa, Rio ≈ N Portugal
59 D14 Coari, Rio ≈ NW Brazil
81 J20 Coast ◈ province SE Kenya
Coast see Pwani
10 G12 Coast Mountains Fr. Chaîne Côtière. ▲▲ Canada/USA
16 C7 Coast Ranges ▲▲ W USA
96 I12 Coatbridge S Scotland, UK
42 B6 Coatepeque Quezaltenango, SW Guatemala
18 H16 Coatesville Pennsylvania, NE USA
15 Q13 Coaticook Québec, SE Canada
9 P9 Coats Island island Nunavut, NE Canada
195 O4 Coats Land physical region Antarctica
41 T14 Coatzacoalcos var. Quetzalcoalco; prev. Puerto México. Veracruz-Llave, E Mexico
41 S14 Coatzacoalcos, Río ≈ SE Mexico
116 M15 Cobadin Constanţa, SW Romania
14 H9 Cobalt Ontario, S Canada
42 D5 Cobán Alta Verapaz, C Guatemala
183 O6 Cobar New South Wales, SE Australia
18 F12 Cobb Hill ▲ Pennsylvania, NE USA
0 D8 Cobb Seamount undersea feature E Pacific Ocean
14 K12 Cobden Ontario, SE Canada
97 D21 Cobh Ir. An Cóbh; prev. Cove of Cork, Queenstown. SW Ireland
57 J14 Cobija Pando, NW Bolivia
Coblence/Coblenz see Koblenz
18 J10 Cobleskill New York, NE USA
14 I15 Cobourg Ontario, SE Canada
181 P1 Cobourg Peninsula headland Northern Territory, N Australia
183 O10 Cobram Victoria, SE Australia
82 N13 Cóbuè Niassa, N Mozambique
101 K18 Coburg Bayern, SE Germany
19 Q5 Coburn Mountain ▲ Maine, NE USA
Coca see Puerto Francisco de Orellana
57 H18 Cocachacra Arequipa, SW Peru
59 J17 Cocalinho Mato Grosso, W Brazil
Cocanada see Kākināda
105 S11 Cocentaina País Valenciano, E Spain
57 L18 Cochabamba hist. Oropeza. Cochabamba, C Bolivia
57 K18 Cochabamba ◈ department C Bolivia
57 L18 Cochabamba, Cordillera de ▲▲ C Bolivia
101 E18 Cochem Rheinland-Pfalz, W Germany
37 R6 Cochetopa Hills ▲▲ Colorado, C USA
155 G22 Cochin var. Kochi. Kerala, SW India
44 D5 Cochinos, Bahía de Eng. Bay of Pigs. bay SE Cuba
37 O16 Cochise Head ▲ Arizona, SW USA
23 U5 Cochran Georgia, SE USA
9 P16 Cochrane Alberta, SW Canada
12 G12 Cochrane Ontario, S Canada
63 G20 Cochrane Aisén, S Chile
9 U10 Cochrane ≈ Manitoba/Saskatchewan, C Canada
Cochrane, Lago see Pueyrredón, Lago
Cocibolca see Nicaragua, Lago de
Cockade State see Maryland
44 M6 Cockburn Harbour South Caicos, S Turks and Caicos Islands
14 C11 Cockburn Island island Ontario, S Canada
44 J3 Cockburn Town San Salvador, E Bahamas
21 X2 Cockeysville Maryland, NE USA
181 N12 Cocklebiddy Western Australia
44 I12 Cockpit Country, The physical region W Jamaica
43 S16 Coclé off. Provincia de Coclé. ◈ province C Panama
43 S15 Coclé del Norte Colón, C Panama
Coclé, Provincia de see Coclé
23 Y12 Cocoa Florida, SE USA
23 Y12 Cocoa Beach Florida, SE USA
79 D17 Cocobeach Estuaire, NW Gabon
44 G5 Coco, Cayo island C Cuba
151 Q19 Coco Channel strait Andaman Sea/Bay of Bengal
173 N6 Coco-de-Mer Seamounts undersea feature W Indian Ocean
36 K10 Coconino Plateau plain Arizona, SW USA
43 N6 Coco, Río var. Río Wanki, Segoviao Wangkí. ≈ Honduras/Nicaragua
173 T7 Cocos Basin undersea feature E Indian Ocean
188 B17 Cocos Island island S Guam
Cocos Island Ridge see Cocos Ridge
129 S17 Cocos Islands island group E Indian Ocean
173 T8 Cocos (Keeling) Islands ◇ Australian external territory E Indian Ocean
0 G15 Cocos Plate tectonic feature
193 T7 Cocos Ridge var. Cocos Island Ridge. undersea feature E Pacific Ocean
40 K13 Cocula Jalisco, SW Mexico
107 D17 Coda Cavallo, Capo headland Sardegna, Italy, C Mediterranean Sea
58 E13 Codajás Amazonas, N Brazil
Codazzi see Agustín Codazzi
19 Q12 Cod, Cape headland Massachusetts, NE USA
185 B25 Codfish Island island SW New Zealand
106 H9 Codigoro Emilia-Romagna, N Italy
13 P5 Cod Island island Newfoundland and Labrador, E Canada
116 J12 Codlea Ger. Zeiden, Hung. Feketehalom. Braşov, C Romania
58 M13 Codó Maranhão, E Brazil
106 E8 Codogno Lombardia, N Italy
116 M10 Codrii hill range C Moldova
45 W9 Codrington Barbuda, Antigua and Barbuda
106 J7 Codroipo Friuli-Venezia Giulia, NE Italy
28 M12 Cody Nebraska, C USA
33 U12 Cody Wyoming, C USA
21 P7 Coeburn Virginia, NE USA
54 E10 Coello Tolima, W Colombia
Coemba see Cuemba
181 V2 Coen Queensland, NE Australia
101 E14 Coesfeld Nordrhein-Westfalen, W Germany
32 M8 Coeur d'Alene Idaho, NW USA
32 M8 Coeur d'Alene Lake ▣ Idaho, NW USA
98 O8 Coevorden Drenthe, NE Netherlands
10 H6 Coffee Creek Yukon Territory, W Canada
30 L15 Coffeen Lake ▣ Illinois, N USA
22 L3 Coffeeville Mississippi, S USA
27 Q8 Coffeyville Kansas, C USA
182 G9 Coffin Bay South Australia
182 F9 Coffin Bay Peninsula peninsula South Australia
183 V5 Coffs Harbour New South Wales, SE Australia
105 R10 Cofrentes País Valenciano, E Spain
Cogilnic see Kohyl'nyk
102 K11 Cognac anc. Compniacum. Charente, W France
106 B7 Cogne Valle d'Aosta, NW Italy
103 U16 Cogolin Var, SE France
105 O7 Cogolludo Castilla-La Mancha, C Spain
Cohalm see Rupea
92 K8 Čohkarášša var. Cuokkaraššа. ▲ N Norway
Čohkkiras see Jukkasjärvi
18 F11 Cohocton River ≈ New York, NE USA
18 L10 Cohoes New York, NE USA
183 N10 Cohuna Victoria, SE Australia
43 P17 Coiba, Isla de island SW Panama
63 H23 Coig, Río ≈ S Argentina
63 G19 Coihaique var. Coyhaique. Aisén, S Chile
155 G21 Coimbatore Tamil Nādu, S India
104 G8 Coimbra anc. Conimbria, Conimbriga. Coimbra, W Portugal
104 G8 Coimbra ◈ district N Portugal
104 L15 Coín Andalucía, S Spain
57 J20 Coipasa, Laguna ◎ W Bolivia
57 J20 Coipasa, Salar de salt lake W Bolivia
Coira/Coire see Chur
Coirib, Loch see Corrib, Lough
54 K6 Cojedes off. Estado Cojedes. ◈ state N Venezuela
Cojedes, Estado see Cojedes
42 F7 Cojutepeque Cuscatlán, C El Salvador
Coka see Banbar
33 S16 Cokeville Wyoming, C USA
182 M13 Colac Victoria, SE Australia
59 O20 Colatina Espírito Santo, SE Brazil
27 O13 Colbert Oklahoma, C USA
100 L12 Colbitz-Letzinger Heide heathland N Germany
26 I3 Colby Kansas, C USA
57 H17 Colca, Río ≈ SW Peru
97 P21 Colchester hist. Colneceaste; anc. Camulodunum. E England, UK
19 N13 Colchester Connecticut, NE USA
38 M16 Cold Bay Alaska, USA
9 R14 Cold Lake Alberta, SW Canada
9 R13 Cold Lake ◎ Alberta/Saskatchewan, S Canada
29 U8 Cold Spring Minnesota, N USA
25 W10 Coldspring Texas, SW USA
9 N17 Coldstream British Columbia, SW Canada
96 L13 Coldstream SE Scotland, UK
14 H13 Coldwater Ontario, S Canada
26 K7 Coldwater Kansas, C USA
31 Q10 Coldwater Michigan, N USA
25 N1 Coldwater Creek ≈ Oklahoma/Texas, SW USA
22 K2 Coldwater River ≈ Mississippi, S USA
183 O9 Coleambally New South Wales, SE Australia
19 O6 Colebrook New Hampshire, NE USA
27 T5 Cole Camp Missouri, C USA
39 T6 Coleen River ≈ Alaska, USA
9 P17 Coleman Alberta, SW Canada
25 Q8 Coleman Texas, SW USA
Çölemerik see Hakkâri
83 K22 Colenso KwaZulu/Natal, E South Africa
182 L12 Coleraine Victoria, SE Australia
97 F14 Coleraine Ir. Cúil Raithin. N Northern Ireland, UK
185 G18 Coleridge, Lake ◎ South Island, New Zealand
83 H24 Colesberg Northern Cape, C South Africa
22 H7 Colfax Louisiana, S USA
32 L9 Colfax Washington, NW USA
30 J6 Colfax Wisconsin, N USA
63 I19 Colhué Huapí, Lago ◎ S Argentina
45 Z6 Colibris, Pointe des headland Grande Terre, E Guadeloupe
106 D6 Colico Lombardia, N Italy
99 E14 Colijnsplaat Zeeland, SW Netherlands
40 L14 Colima Colima, S Mexico
40 K14 Colima ◈ state SW Mexico
40 L14 Colima, Nevado de ⛰ C Mexico
59 M14 Colinas Maranhão, E Brazil
96 F10 Coll island W Scotland, UK
105 N7 Collado Villalba var. Villalba. Madrid, C Spain
183 R4 Collarenebri New South Wales, SE Australia
37 P5 Collbran Colorado, C USA
106 G12 Colle di Val d'Elsa Toscana, C Italy
39 R9 College Alaska, USA
32 K10 College Place Washington, NW USA
25 U10 College Station Texas, SW USA
183 P4 Collerina New South Wales, SE Australia
180 I13 Collie Western Australia
180 L4 Collier Bay bay Western Australia
21 F10 Collierville Tennessee, S USA
106 F11 Collina, Passo della pass C Italy
14 G14 Collingwood Ontario, S Canada
184 I13 Collingwood Tasman, South Island, New Zealand
22 L7 Collins Mississippi, S USA
30 K15 Collinsville Illinois, N USA
27 P9 Collinsville Oklahoma, C USA
20 H10 Collinwood Tennessee, S USA
Collipo see Leiria
63 G14 Collipulli Araucanía, C Chile
97 D16 Collooney Ir. Cúil Mhuine. NW Ireland
29 R10 Colman South Dakota, N USA
103 U6 Colmar Ger. Kolmar. Haut-Rhin, NE France
104 M15 Colmenar Andalucía, S Spain
Colmenar see Colmenar de Oreja
105 O9 Colmenar de Oreja var. Colmenar. Madrid, C Spain
105 N7 Colmenar Viejo Madrid, C Spain
25 X9 Colmesneil Texas, SW USA
Cöln see Köln
Colneceaste see Colchester
40 C3 Colnet Baja California, NW Mexico
59 G15 Colniza Mato Grosso, W Brazil
Cologne see Köln
42 B6 Colomba Quezaltenango, SW Guatemala
Colomb-Béchar see Béchar
54 E11 Colombia Huila, C Colombia
54 G10 Colombia off. Republic of Colombia. ◆ republic N South America
64 E12 Colombian Basin undersea feature SW Caribbean Sea
Colombia, Republic of see Colombia
Colombie-Britannique see British Columbia
15 T6 Colombier Québec, SE Canada
155 J25 Colombo ● (Sri Lanka) Western Province, W Sri Lanka
155 J25 Colombo ✈ Western Province, SW Sri Lanka
29 N11 Colome South Dakota, N USA
61 B19 Colón Buenos Aires, E Argentina
61 D18 Colon Entre Ríos, E Argentina
44 D5 Colón Matanzas, C Cuba
43 T14 Colón prev. Aspinwall. Colón, C Panama
42 K5 Colón ◈ department NE Honduras
43 S15 Colón off. Provincia de Colón. ◈ province N Panama
57 A16 Colón, Archipiélago de var. Islas de los Galápagos, Eng. Galapagos Islands, Tortoise Islands. island group Ecuador, E Pacific Ocean
44 K5 Colonel Hill Crooked Island, SE Bahamas
40 B3 Colonet, Cabo headland NW Mexico
188 G14 Colonia Yap, W Micronesia
61 D19 Colonia ◈ department SW Uruguay
Colonia see Kolonia, Micronesia
Colonia see Colonia del Sacramento, Uruguay
Colonia Agrippina see Köln
61 D20 Colonia del Sacramento var. Colonia. Colonia, SW Uruguay
62 L8 Colonia Dora Santiago del Estero, N Argentina
Colonia Julia Fanestris see Fano
21 W5 Colonial Beach Virginia, NE USA
21 V6 Colonial Heights Virginia, NE USA
Colón, Provincia de see Colón
193 S7 Colón Ridge undersea feature E Pacific Ocean
96 F12 Colonsay island W Scotland, UK
57 K22 Colorada, Laguna ◎ SW Bolivia
37 R6 Colorado off. State of Colorado, also known as Centennial State, Silver State. ◈ state C USA
63 H22 Colorado, Cerro ▲ S Argentina
25 O7 Colorado City Texas, SW USA
36 M7 Colorado Plateau plateau W USA
61 A24 Colorado, Río ≈ E Argentina
43 N12 Colorado, Río ≈ NE Costa Rica
Colorado, Río see Colorado River
16 F12 Colorado River var. Río Colorado. ≈ Mexico/USA
16 K14 Colorado River ≈ Texas, SW USA
35 W15 Colorado River Aqueduct aqueduct California, W USA
44 A4 Colorados, Archipiélago de los island group NW Cuba
62 J9 Colorados, Desagües de los ◎ W Argentina
37 T5 Colorado Springs Colorado, C USA
40 L11 Colotlán Jalisco, SW Mexico
57 L19 Colquechaca Potosí, C Bolivia
23 S7 Colquitt Georgia, SE USA
29 R11 Colton South Dakota, N USA
32 M10 Colton Washington, NW USA
35 P8 Columbia California, W USA
30 K16 Columbia Illinois, N USA
20 L7 Columbia Kentucky, S USA
22 I6 Columbia Louisiana, S USA
21 W3 Columbia Maryland, NE USA
22 L7 Columbia Mississippi, S USA
27 U4 Columbia Missouri, C USA
21 Y9 Columbia North Carolina, SE USA
18 G16 Columbia Pennsylvania, NE USA
21 Q12 Columbia state capital South Carolina, SE USA
20 I9 Columbia Tennessee, S USA
0 F9 Columbia ≈ Canada/USA
32 K9 Columbia Basin basin Washington, NW USA
197 Q10 Columbia, Cape headland Ellesmere Island, Nunavut, NE Canada
31 Q12 Columbia City Indiana, N USA
21 W3 Columbia, District of ◈ federal district NE USA
33 P7 Columbia Falls Montana, NW USA
9 O15 Columbia Icefield ice field Alberta/British Columbia, S Canada
9 O15 Columbia, Mount ▲ Alberta/British Columbia, SW Canada
9 N15 Columbia Mountains ▲▲ British Columbia, SW Canada
23 P4 Columbiana Alabama, S USA
31 V12 Columbiana Ohio, N USA
32 M14 Columbia Plateau plateau Idaho/Oregon, NW USA
29 P7 Columbia Road Reservoir ▣ South Dakota, N USA
65 K16 Columbia Seamount undersea feature C Atlantic Ocean
83 D25 Columbine, Cape headland SW South Africa
105 U9 Columbretes, Islas island group E Spain
23 R5 Columbus Georgia, SE USA
31 P14 Columbus Indiana, N USA
27 R7 Columbus Kansas, C USA
23 N4 Columbus Mississippi, S USA
33 U11 Columbus Montana, NW USA
29 Q15 Columbus Nebraska, C USA
37 Q16 Columbus New Mexico, SW USA
21 P10 Columbus North Carolina, SE USA
28 K2 Columbus North Dakota, N USA
31 S13 Columbus state capital Ohio, N USA
25 U11 Columbus Texas, SW USA
30 L8 Columbus Wisconsin, N USA
31 R12 Columbus Grove Ohio, N USA
29 Y15 Columbus Junction Iowa, C USA
44 J3 Columbus Point headland Cat Island, C Bahamas
35 T8 Columbus Salt Marsh salt marsh Nevada, W USA
35 N6 Colusa California, W USA
32 L7 Colville Washington, NW USA
184 M5 Colville, Cape headland North Island, New Zealand
184 M5 Colville Channel channel North Island, New Zealand
39 P6 Colville River ≈ Alaska, USA
97 J18 Colwyn Bay N Wales, UK
106 H9 Comacchio var. Commachio; anc. Comactium. Emilia-Romagna, N Italy
106 H9 Comacchio, Valli di lagoon Adriatic Sea, N Mediterranean Sea
Comactium see Comacchio
41 V17 Comalapa Chiapas, SE Mexico
41 U15 Comalcalco Tabasco, SE Mexico
63 H16 Comallo Río Negro, SW Argentina
26 M12 Comanche Oklahoma, C USA
25 R8 Comanche Texas, SW USA
194 H2 Comandante Ferraz Brazilian research station Antarctica
62 N6 Comandante Fontana Formosa, N Argentina
63 I22 Comandante Luis Peidra Buena Santa Cruz, S Argentina
59 O18 Comandatuba Bahia, SE Brazil
116 K11 Comănești Hung. Kománfalva. Bacău, SW Romania
57 M19 Comarapa Santa Cruz, C Bolivia
116 J13 Comarnic Prahova, SE Romania
42 H6 Comayagua Comayagua, W Honduras
42 H6 Comayagua ◈ department W Honduras
42 I6 Comayagua, Montañas de ▲▲ C Honduras
21 R15 Combahee River ≈ South Carolina, SE USA
62 G10 Combarbalá Coquimbo, C Chile
103 S7 Combeaufontaine Haute-Saône, E France
97 G15 Comber Ir. An Comar. E Northern Ireland, UK
99 K20 Comblain-au-Pont Liège, E Belgium
102 I6 Combourg Ille-et-Vilaine, NW France
44 M9 Comendador prev. Elías Piña. W Dominican Republic
Comer See see Como, Lago di
25 R11 Comfort Texas, SW USA
153 V15 Comilla Ben. Kumillā. Chittagong, E Bangladesh
99 B18 Comines Hainaut, W Belgium
121 O15 Comino Malt. Kemmuna. island C Malta
107 D18 Comino, Capo headland Sardegna, Italy, C Mediterranean Sea
107 K25 Comiso Sicilia, Italy, C Mediterranean Sea
41 V16 Comitán var. Comitán de Domínguez. Chiapas, SE Mexico
Comitán de Domínguez see Comitán
Commachio see Comacchio
Commander Islands see Komandorskiye Ostrova
103 O10 Commentry Allier, C France
23 T2 Commerce Georgia, SE USA
27 R8 Commerce Oklahoma, C USA
25 V5 Commerce Texas, SW USA
37 T4 Commerce City Colorado, C USA
103 S5 Commercy Meuse, NE France
55 W9 Commewijne var. Commewyne. ◈ district NE Suriname
Commewyne see Commewijne
15 P8 Commissaires, Lac des ◎ Québec, SE Canada
64 A12 Commissioner's Point headland W Bermuda
9 O7 Committee Bay bay Nunavut, N Canada
106 D7 Como anc. Comum. Lombardia, N Italy
63 J19 Comodoro Rivadavia Chubut, SE Argentina
106 D6 Como, Lago di var. Lario, Eng. Lake Como, Ger. Comer See. ◎ N Italy
Como, Lake see Como, Lago di
40 E7 Comondú Baja California Sur, W Mexico
116 F12 Comorâște Hung. Komornok. Caraș-Severin, SW Romania
Comores, République Fédérale Islamique des see Comoros
155 G24 Comorin, Cape headland SE India
172 M8 Comoro Basin undersea feature SW Indian Ocean
172 K14 Comoro Islands island group W Indian Ocean
172 H13 Comoros off. Federal Islamic Republic of the Comoros, Fr. République Fédérale Islamique des Comores. ◆ republic W Indian Ocean
Comoros, Federal Islamic Republic of the see Comoros
10 L17 Comox Vancouver Island, British Columbia, SW Canada
103 O4 Compiègne Oise, N France
Complutum see Alcalá de Henares
Compniacum see Cognac
40 K12 Compostela Nayarit, C Mexico
Compostella see Santiago
60 L11 Comprida, Ilha island S Brazil
117 N11 Comrat Rus. Komrat. S Moldova
25 O11 Comstock Texas, SW USA
31 P9 Comstock Park Michigan, N USA
193 N3 Comstock Seamount undersea feature N Pacific Ocean
Comum see Como
159 N17 Cona Xizang Zizhiqu, W China
76 H14 Conakry ● (Guinea) SW Guinea
76 H14 Conakry ✈ SW Guinea
Conamara see Connemara
Conca see Cuenca

◆ Country ● Country Capital ◇ Dependent Territory ○ Dependent Territory Capital ◈ Administrative Regions ✈ International Airport ▲ Mountain ▲▲ Mountain Range ⛰ Volcano ≈ River ◎ Lake ▣ Reservoir

25 Q12 Concan Texas, SW USA
102 F6 Concarneau Finistère, NW France
83 O17 Conceição Sofala, C Mozambique
59 K15 Conceição do Araguaia Pará, NE Brazil
58 F10 Conceição do Maú Roraima, W Brazil
61 D14 Concepción var. Concepcion. Corrientes, NE Argentina
62 J8 Concepción Tucumán, N Argentina
57 O17 Concepción Santa Cruz, E Bolivia
62 G13 Concepción Bío Bío, C Chile
54 E14 Concepción Putumayo, S Colombia
62 O5 Concepción var. Villa Concepción. Concepción, C Paraguay
62 O5 Concepción off. Departamento de Concepción. ◈ department E Paraguay
Concepción see La Concepción
Concepción de la Vega see La Vega
41 N9 Concepción del Oro Zacatecas, C Mexico
61 D18 Concepción del Uruguay Entre Ríos, E Argentina
Concepción, Departamento de see Concepción
42 K11 Concepción, Volcán ⛰ SW Nicaragua
44 J4 Conception Island island C Bahamas
35 P14 Conception, Point headland California, W USA
54 H6 Concha Zulia, W Venezuela
60 L9 Conchas São Paulo, S Brazil
37 U11 Conchas Dam New Mexico, SW USA
37 U10 Conchas Lake ⊠ New Mexico, SW USA
102 M5 Conches-en-Ouche Eure, N France
37 N12 Concho Arizona, SW USA
40 J5 Conchos, Río ≈ NW Mexico
41 O8 Conchos, Río ≈ C Mexico
108 C8 Concise Vaud, W Switzerland
35 N8 Concord California, W USA
19 O9 Concord state capital New Hampshire, NE USA
21 R10 Concord North Carolina, SE USA
61 D17 Concordia Entre Ríos, E Argentina
60 I13 Concórdia Santa Catarina, S Brazil
54 D9 Concordia Antioquia, W Colombia
40 J10 Concordia Sinaloa, C Mexico
57 I19 Concordia Tacna, SW Peru
27 N3 Concordia Kansas, C USA
27 S4 Concordia Missouri, C USA
167 S7 Con Cuông Nghệ An, N Vietnam
167 T15 Côn Đao var. Con Son. island S Vietnam
Condate see Rennes, Ille-et-Vilaine, France
Condate see St-Claude, Jura, France
Condate see Montereau-Faut-Yonne, Seine-St-Denis, France
29 P8 Conde South Dakota, N USA
42 J8 Condega Estelí, NW Nicaragua
103 P2 Condé-sur-l'Escaut Nord, N France
102 K5 Condé-sur-Noireau Calvados, N France
Condivincum see Nantes
183 P8 Condobolin New South Wales, SE Australia
102 L15 Condom Gers, S France
32 J11 Condon Oregon, NW USA
54 D9 Condoto Chocó, W Colombia
23 P7 Conecuh River ≈ Alabama/Florida, SE USA
106 H7 Conegliano Veneto, NE Italy
61 C19 Conesa Buenos Aires, E Argentina
14 F15 Conestogo ≈ Ontario, S Canada
Confluentes see Koblenz
102 L10 Confolens Charente, W France
36 J4 Confusion Range ▲▲ Utah, W USA
62 N6 Confuso, Río ≈ C Paraguay
21 R12 Congaree River ≈ South Carolina, SE USA
Công Hoa Xa Hôi Chu Nghia Viêt Nam see Vietnam
160 K12 Congjiang var. Bingmei. Guizhou, S China
79 G18 Congo off. Republic of the Congo, Fr. Moyen-Congo; prev. Middle Congo. ◆ republic C Africa
79 K19 Congo off. Democratic Republic of Congo; prev. Zaire, Belgian Congo, Congo (Kinshasa). ◆ republic C Africa
67 T11 Congo var. Kongo, Fr. Zaire. ≈ C Africa
Congo see Zaire (province) Angola
68 G12 Congo Basin drainage basin W Dem. Rep. Congo
67 Q11 Congo Canyon var. Congo Seavalley, Congo Submarine Canyon. undersea feature E Atlantic Ocean
Congo Cone see Congo Fan
Congo/Congo (Kinshasa) see Congo (Democratic Republic of)
65 P15 Congo Fan var. Congo Cone. undersea feature E Atlantic Ocean
Congo Seavalley see Congo Canyon
Congo Submarine Canyon see Congo Canyon
Coni see Cuneo
63 H18 Cónico, Cerro ▲ SW Argentina
Conimbria/Conimbriga see Coimbra
Conjeeveram see Kānchīpuram
9 R13 Conklin Alberta, C Canada
24 M1 Conlen Texas, SW USA
Con, Loch see Conn, Lough
Connacht see Connaught
97 B17 Connaught var. Connacht, Ir. Chonnacht, Cúige. province W Ireland
31 V10 Conneaut Ohio, N USA
18 L13 Connecticut off. State of Connecticut, also known as Blue Law State, Constitution State, Land of Steady Habits, Nutmeg State. ◈ state NE USA
19 N8 Connecticut ≈ Canada/USA
19 O6 Connecticut Lakes lakes New Hampshire, NE USA
32 K9 Connell Washington, NW USA
97 B17 Connemara Ir. Conamara. physical region W Ireland
31 Q14 Connersville Indiana, N USA
97 B16 Conn, Lough Ir. Loch Con. ◎ W Ireland
35 X6 Connors Pass pass Nevada, W USA
181 X7 Connors Range ▲▲ Queensland, E Australia
56 E7 Cononaco, Río ≈ E Ecuador
29 W13 Conrad Iowa, C USA
33 R7 Conrad Montana, NW USA
25 W10 Conroe Texas, SW USA
25 V10 Conroe, Lake ⊠ Texas, SW USA
61 C17 Conscripto Bernardi Entre Ríos, E Argentina
59 M20 Conselheiro Lafaiete Minas Gerais, SE Brazil
Consentia see Cosenza
97 L14 Consett N England, UK
44 B5 Consolación del Sur Pinar del Río, W Cuba
Con Son see Côn Đao
9 R15 Consort Alberta, SW Canada
Constance see Konstanz
108 I6 Constance, Lake Ger. Bodensee. ◎ C Europe
104 G9 Constância Santarém, C Portugal
117 N14 Constanța var. Küstendje, Eng. Constanza, Ger. Konstanza, Turk. Küstence. Constanța, SE Romania
116 L14 Constanța ◈ county SE Romania
Constantia see Coutances
Constantia see Konstanz
104 K13 Constantina Andalucía, S Spain
74 L5 Constantine var. Qacentina, Ar. Qoussantina. NE Algeria
39 O14 Constantine, Cape headland Alaska, USA
Constantinople see İstanbul
Constantiola see Oltenișa
Constanz see Konstanz
Constanza see Constanța
62 G13 Constitución Maule, C Chile
61 D17 Constitución Salto, N Uruguay
Constitution State see Connecticut
105 N10 Consuegra Castilla-La Mancha, C Spain
181 X9 Consuelo Peak ▲ Queensland, E Australia
56 E11 Contamana Loreto, N Peru
Contrasto, Colle del see Contrasto, Portella del
107 K23 Contrasto, Portella del var. Colle del Contrasto. pass Sicilia, Italy, C Mediterranean Sea
54 G8 Contratación Santander, C Colombia
102 M8 Contres Loir-et-Cher, C France
107 O17 Conversano Puglia, SE Italy
27 U11 Conway Arkansas, C USA
19 O8 Conway New Hampshire, NE USA
21 U13 Conway South Carolina, SE USA
25 N2 Conway Texas, SW USA
27 U11 Conway, Lake ⊠ Arkansas, C USA
27 N7 Conway Springs Kansas, C USA
97 J18 Conwy N Wales, UK
23 T3 Conyers Georgia, SE USA
Coo see Kos
182 F4 Coober Pedy South Australia
181 P2 Cooinda Northern Territory, N Australia
182 B6 Cook South Australia
29 W4 Cook Minnesota, N USA
191 N6 Cook, Baie de bay Moorea, W French Polynesia
10 J16 Cook, Cape headland Vancouver Island, British Columbia, SW Canada
37 Q15 Cookes Peak ▲ New Mexico, SW USA
20 L8 Cookeville Tennessee, S USA
175 P9 Cook Fracture Zone tectonic feature S Pacific Ocean
Cook, Grand Récif de see Cook, Récif de
39 Q12 Cook Inlet inlet Alaska, USA
191 X2 Cook Island island Line Islands, E Kiribati
190 J14 Cook Islands ◇ territory in free association with New Zealand S Pacific Ocean
Mount Cook see Aoraki
187 O15 Cook, Récif de var. Grand Récif de Cook. reef S New Caledonia
14 G14 Cookstown Ontario, S Canada
97 F15 Cookstown Ir. An Chorr Chríochach. C Northern Ireland, UK
185 K14 Cook Strait var. Raukawa. strait New Zealand
181 W3 Cooktown Queensland, NE Australia
183 P6 Coolabah New South Wales, SE Australia
182 J11 Coola Coola Swamp wetland South Australia
183 S7 Coolah New South Wales, SE Australia
183 P9 Coolamon New South Wales, SE Australia
183 T4 Coolatai New South Wales, SE Australia
180 K12 Coolgardie Western Australia
36 L14 Coolidge Arizona, SW USA
25 U8 Coolidge Texas, SW USA
183 Q11 Cooma New South Wales, SE Australia
Coomassie see Kumasi
183 R6 Coonabarabran New South Wales, SE Australia
182 J10 Coonalpyn South Australia
183 R6 Coonamble New South Wales, SE Australia
Coondapoor see Kundāpura
155 G21 Coonoor Tamil Nādu, SE India
29 U14 Coon Rapids Iowa, C USA
29 V8 Coon Rapids Minnesota, N USA
25 V5 Cooper Texas, SW USA
181 U9 Cooper Creek var. Barcoo, Cooper's Creek. seasonal river Queensland/South Australia
39 R12 Cooper Landing Alaska, USA
21 T14 Cooper River ≈ South Carolina, SE USA
Cooper's Creek see Cooper Creek
44 H1 Coopers Town Great Abaco, N Bahamas
18 J10 Cooperstown New York, NE USA
29 P4 Cooperstown North Dakota, N USA
31 P9 Coopersville Michigan, N USA
182 D7 Coorabie South Australia
23 Q3 Coosa River ≈ Alabama/Georgia, S USA
32 E14 Coos Bay Oregon, NW USA
183 Q9 Cootamundra New South Wales, SE Australia
97 E16 Cootehill Ir. Muinchille. N Ireland
Čop see Chop
57 J17 Copacabana La Paz, W Bolivia
63 H14 Copahué, Volcán ⛰ C Chile
41 U16 Copainalá Chiapas, SE Mexico
32 F8 Copalis Beach Washington, NW USA
42 F6 Copán ◈ department W Honduras
Copán see Copán Ruinas
25 T14 Copano Bay bay NW Gulf of Mexico
42 F6 Copán Ruinas var. Copán. Copán, W Honduras
Copenhagen see København
107 Q19 Copertino Puglia, SE Italy
62 H7 Copiapó Atacama, N Chile
62 G8 Copiapó, Bahía bay N Chile
62 G7 Copiapó, Río ≈ N Chile
114 M12 Çöpköy Edirne, NW Turkey
182 I5 Copley South Australia
106 H9 Copparo Emilia-Romagna, C Italy
55 V10 Coppename Rivier var. Koppename. ≈ C Suriname
25 S9 Copperas Cove Texas, SW USA
82 J13 Copperbelt ◈ province C Zambia
39 S11 Copper Center Alaska, USA
8 K8 Coppermine ≈ Northwest Territories/Nunavut, N Canada
Coppermine see Kugluktuk
39 T11 Copper River ≈ Alaska, USA
Copper State see Arizona
116 I11 Copșa Mică Ger. Kleinkopisch, Hung. Kiskapus. Sibiu, C Romania
158 J14 Coqên Xizang Zizhiqu, W China
Coquilhatville see Mbandaka
32 E14 Coquille Oregon, NW USA
62 G9 Coquimbo Coquimbo, N Chile
62 G9 Coquimbo off. Región de Coquimbo. ◈ region C Chile
Coquimbo, Región de see Coquimbo
116 I15 Corabia Olt, S Romania
57 F17 Coracora Ayacucho, SW Peru
Cora Droma Rúisc see Carrick-on-Shannon
44 K9 Corail SW Haiti
183 V4 Coraki New South Wales, SE Australia
180 G8 Coral Bay Western Australia
23 Y16 Coral Gables Florida, SE USA
9 P8 Coral Harbour Southampton Island, Northwest Territories, NE Canada
192 I9 Coral Sea sea SW Pacific Ocean
174 M7 Coral Sea Basin undersea feature N Coral Sea
192 H9 Coral Sea Islands ◇ Australian external territory SW Pacific Ocean
182 M12 Corangamite, Lake ◎ Victoria, SE Australia
Corantijn Rivier see Courantyne River
18 B14 Coraopolis Pennsylvania, NE USA
107 N17 Corato Puglia, SE Italy
103 O17 Corbières ▲▲ S France
103 P8 Corbigny Nièvre, C France
21 N7 Corbin Kentucky, S USA
104 L14 Corbones ≈ SW Spain
Corcaigh see Cork
35 R11 Corcoran California, W USA
47 T14 Corcovado, Golfo gulf S Chile
63 G18 Corcovado, Volcán ⛰ S Chile
104 F3 Corcubión Galicia, NW Spain
Corcyra Nigra see Korčula
60 Q9 Cordeiro Rio de Janeiro, SE Brazil
23 T6 Cordele Georgia, SE USA
26 L11 Cordell Oklahoma, C USA
103 N14 Cordes Tarn, S France
62 O6 Cordillera off. Departamento de la Cordillera. ◈ department C Paraguay
Cordillera see Cacaguatique, Cordillera
Cordillera, Departamento de la see Cordillera
182 K1 Cordillo Downs South Australia
62 K10 Córdoba Córdoba, C Argentina
41 R14 Córdoba Veracruz-Llave, E Mexico
104 M13 Córdoba var. Cordoba, Eng. Cordova; anc. Corduba. Andalucía, SW Spain
62 K11 Córdoba off. Provincia de Córdoba. ◈ province C Argentina
54 D7 Córdoba off. Departamento de Córdoba. ◈ province NW Colombia
104 L13 Córdoba ◈ province Andalucía, S Spain
Córdoba, Departamento de see Córdoba
Córdoba, Provincia de see Córdoba
62 K10 Córdoba, Sierras de ▲▲ C Argentina
23 O3 Cordova Alabama, S USA
39 S12 Cordova Alaska, USA
Cordova/Cordoba see Córdoba
Corduba see Córdoba
Corentyne River see Courantyne River
Corfu see Kérkyra
104 J9 Coria Extremadura, W Spain
104 J14 Coria del Río Andalucía, S Spain
183 S8 Coricudgy, Mount ▲ New South Wales, SE Australia
107 N20 Corigliano Calabro Calabria, SW Italy
Corinium/Corinium Dobunorum see Cirencester
23 N1 Corinth Mississippi, S USA
Corinth see Kórinthos
Corinth Canal see Dióryga Korinthou
Corinth, Gulf of/Corinthiacus Sinus see Korinthiakós Kólpos
Corinthus see Kórinthos
42 I9 Corinto Chinandega, NW Nicaragua
97 C21 Cork Ir. Corcaigh. S Ireland
97 C21 Cork Ir. Corcaigh. ◈ county SW Ireland
97 C21 Cork ✈ Cork, SW Ireland
97 D21 Cork Harbour Ir. Cuan Chorcaí. inlet SW Ireland
107 I23 Corleone Sicilia, Italy, C Mediterranean Sea
114 N13 Çorlu Tekirdağ, NW Turkey
114 N12 Çorlu Çayı ≈ NW Turkey
Cormaiore see Courmayeur
9 V13 Cormorant Manitoba, C Canada
23 T2 Cornelia Georgia, SE USA
60 J10 Cornélio Procópio Paraná, S Brazil
55 V9 Corneliskondre Sipaliwini, N Suriname
30 J5 Cornell Wisconsin, N USA
13 S12 Corner Brook Newfoundland, Newfoundland and Labrador, E Canada
Corner Rise Seamounts see Corner Seamounts
64 I9 Corner Seamounts var Corner Rise Seamounts. undersea feature NW Atlantic Ocean
116 M9 Cornești Rus. Korneshty. C Moldova
Corneto see Tarquinia
Cornhusker State see Nebraska
27 X8 Corning Arkansas, C USA
35 N5 Corning California, W USA
29 U15 Corning Iowa, C USA
18 G11 Corning New York, NE USA
Corn Islands see Maíz, Islas del
107 J14 Corno Grande ▲ C Italy
15 N13 Cornwall Ontario, SE Canada
97 H25 Cornwall cultural region SW England, UK
97 G25 Cornwall, Cape headland SW England, UK
54 J4 Coro prev. Santa Ana de Coro. Falcón, NW Venezuela
57 J18 Corocoro La Paz, W Bolivia
57 K17 Coroico La Paz, W Bolivia
184 M5 Coromandel Waikato, North Island, New Zealand
155 K20 Coromandel Coast coast E India
184 M5 Coromandel Peninsula peninsula North Island, New Zealand
184 M6 Coromandel Range ▲▲ North Island, New Zealand
171 N5 Coron Busuanga Island, W Philippines
35 T15 Corona California, W USA
37 T12 Corona New Mexico, SW USA
9 U17 Coronach Saskatchewan, S Canada
35 U17 Coronado California, W USA
43 N15 Coronado, Bahía de bay S Costa Rica
9 R15 Coronation Alberta, SW Canada
8 K7 Coronation Gulf gulf Nunavut, N Canada
194 I1 Coronation Island island Antarctica
39 X14 Coronation Island island Alexander Archipelago, Alaska, USA
61 B18 Coronda Santa Fe, C Argentina
63 F14 Coronel Bío Bío, C Chile
61 D20 Coronel Brandsen var. Brandsen. Buenos Aires, E Argentina
62 K4 Coronel Cornejo Salta, N Argentina
61 B24 Coronel Dorrego Buenos Aires, E Argentina
62 P6 Coronel Oviedo Caaguazú, SE Paraguay
61 B23 Coronel Pringles Buenos Aires, E Argentina
61 B23 Coronel Suárez Buenos Aires, E Argentina
61 E22 Coronel Vidal Buenos Aires, E Argentina
55 V9 Coronie ◈ district NW Suriname
57 G17 Coropuna, Nevado ▲ S Peru
Çorovoda see Çorovodë
113 L22 Çorovodë var. Çorovoda. Berat, S Albania
183 P11 Corowa New South Wales, SE Australia
42 G1 Corozal Corozal, N Belize
54 E6 Corozal Sucre, NW Colombia
42 G1 Corozal ◈ district N Belize
25 T14 Corpus Christi Texas, SW USA
25 T14 Corpus Christi Bay inlet Texas, SW USA
25 R14 Corpus Christi, Lake ⊠ Texas, SW USA
63 F16 Corral Los Lagos, C Chile
105 O9 Corral de Almaguer Castilla-La Mancha, C Spain
104 K6 Corrales Castilla-León, N Spain
37 R11 Corrales New Mexico, SW USA
Corrán Tuathail see Carrauntoohil
106 F9 Correggio Emilia-Romagna, C Italy
59 M16 Corrente Piauí, E Brazil
59 I19 Correntes, Rio ≈ SW Brazil
103 N12 Corrèze ◈ department C France
97 C17 Corrib, Lough Ir. Loch Coirib. ◎ W Ireland
61 C14 Corrientes Corrientes, NE Argentina
61 D15 Corrientes off. Provincia de Corrientes. ◈ province NE Argentina
44 A5 Corrientes, Cabo headland W Cuba
40 I13 Corrientes, Cabo headland SW Mexico
Corrientes, Provincia de see Corrientes
61 C16 Corrientes, Río ≈ NE Argentina
56 E8 Corrientes, Río ≈ Ecuador/Peru
25 W9 Corrigan Texas, SW USA
55 U9 Corriverton E Guyana
Corriza see Korçë
183 Q11 Corryong Victoria, SE Australia
103 F2 Corse Eng. Corsica. ◈ region France, C Mediterranean Sea
101 X13 Corse Eng. Corsica. island France, C Mediterranean Sea
103 Y12 Corse, Cap headland Corse, France, C Mediterranean Sea
103 X15 Corse-du-Sud ◈ department Corse, France, C Mediterranean Sea
29 P11 Corsica South Dakota, N USA
Corsica see Corse
25 U7 Corsicana Texas, SW USA
103 Y15 Corte Corse, France, C Mediterranean Sea
63 G16 Corte Alto Los Lagos, S Chile
104 I13 Cortegana Andalucía, S Spain
43 N15 Cortés var. Ciudad Cortés. Puntarenas, SE Costa Rica
42 G5 Cortés ◈ department NW Honduras
37 P8 Cortez Colorado, C USA
Cortez, Sea of see California, Golfo de
106 H6 Cortina d'Ampezzo Veneto, NE Italy
18 H11 Cortland New York, NE USA
31 V11 Cortland Ohio, N USA
106 H12 Cortona Toscana, C Italy
76 H13 Corubal, Rio ≈ E Guinea-Bissau
104 G10 Coruche Santarém, C Portugal
Çoruh see Rize
137 R11 Çoruh Nehri Geor. Chorokh, Rus. Chorokhi. ≈ Georgia/Turkey
136 K12 Çorum var. Chorum. Çorum, N Turkey
136 J12 Çorum var. Chorum. ◈ province N Turkey
59 H19 Corumbá Mato Grosso do Sul, S Brazil
14 D16 Corunna Ontario, S Canada
Corunna see A Coruña
32 F12 Corvallis Oregon, NW USA
64 M1 Corvo var. Ilha do Corvo. island Azores, Portugal, NE Atlantic Ocean
Corvo, Ilha do see Corvo
31 O16 Corydon Indiana, N USA
29 V16 Corydon Iowa, C USA
Cos see Kos
40 I9 Cosalá Sinaloa, C Mexico
41 R15 Cosamaloapan var. Cosamaloapan de Carpio. Veracruz-Llave, E Mexico
Cosamaloapan de Carpio see Cosamaloapan
107 N21 Cosenza anc. Consentia. Calabria, SW Italy
31 T13 Coshocton Ohio, N USA
42 H9 Cosigüina, Punta headland NW Nicaragua
29 T9 Cosmos Minnesota, N USA
103 O8 Cosne-sur-Loire Nièvre, C France
108 B9 Cossonay Vaud, W Switzerland
Cossyra see Pantelleria
47 R4 Costa, Cordillera de la var. Cordillera de Venezuela. ▲▲ N Venezuela
42 K13 Costa Rica off. Republic of Costa Rica. ◆ republic Central America
Costa Rica, Republic of see Costa Rica
43 N15 Costeña, Fila ▲▲ S Costa Rica
Costermansville see Bukavu
116 I14 Costești Argeș, SW Romania
37 S8 Costilla New Mexico, SW USA
35 O7 Cosumnes River ≈ California, W USA
101 O16 Coswig Sachsen, E Germany
101 M14 Coswig Sachsen-Anhalt, E Germany
Cosyra see Pantelleria
171 Q7 Cotabato Mindanao, S Philippines
56 C5 Cotacachi ▲ N Ecuador
57 L21 Cotagaita Potosí, S Bolivia
103 V15 Côte d'Azur prev. Nice. ✈ (Nice) Alpes-Maritimes, SE France
Côte d'Ivoire see Ivory Coast
Côte d'Ivoire, République de la see Ivory Coast
103 R7 Côte d'Or ◈ department E France
103 R8 Côte d'Or cultural region C France
Côte Française des Somalis see Djibouti
102 J4 Cotentin peninsula N France
102 G6 Côtes d'Armor prev. Côtes-du-Nord. ◈ department NW France
Côtes-du-Nord see Côtes d'Armor
Cöthen see Köthen
Côtière, Chaîne see Coast Mountains
40 M13 Cotija var. Cotija de la Paz. Michoacán de Ocampo, SW Mexico
Cotija de la Paz see Cotija
77 R16 Cotonou var. Kotonu. ● S Benin
77 R16 Cotonou ✈ S Benin
56 B6 Cotopaxi prev. León. ◈ province C Ecuador
56 C6 Cotopaxi ⛰ N Ecuador
Cotrone see Crotone
97 L21 Cotswold Hills var. Cotswolds. hill range S England, UK
Cotswolds see Cotswold Hills
32 F13 Cottage Grove Oregon, NW USA
21 S14 Cottageville South Carolina, SE USA
101 P14 Cottbus Lus. Chośebuz; prev. Kottbus. Brandenburg, E Germany
27 U9 Cotter Arkansas, C USA
106 A9 Cottian Alps Fr. Alpes Cottiennes, It. Alpi Cozie. ▲▲ France/Italy
Cottiennes, Alpes see Cottian Alps
Cotton State, The see Alabama
22 G4 Cotton Valley Louisiana, S USA
36 L12 Cottonwood Arizona, SW USA
32 M10 Cottonwood Idaho, NW USA
29 S9 Cottonwood Minnesota, N USA
25 Q7 Cottonwood Texas, SW USA
27 O5 Cottonwood Falls Kansas, C USA
36 L3 Cottonwood Heights Utah, W USA
29 S10 Cottonwood River ≈ Minnesota, N USA
45 O9 Cotuí C Dominican Republic
25 Q13 Cotulla Texas, SW USA
Cotyora see Ordu
102 I11 Coubre, Pointe de la headland W France
18 E12 Coudersport Pennsylvania, NE USA
15 S9 Coudres, Île aux island Québec, SE Canada
182 G11 Couedic, Cape de headland South Australia
Couentrey see Coventry
102 I6 Couesnon ≈ NW France
32 H10 Cougar Washington, NW USA
102 L10 Couhé Vienne, W France
32 K8 Coulee City Washington, NW USA
195 Q15 Coulman Island island Antarctica
103 P5 Coulommiers Seine-et-Marne, N France
14 K11 Coulonge ≈ Québec, SE Canada
14 K11 Coulonge Est ≈ Québec, SE Canada
35 Q9 Coulterville California, W USA
38 M9 Council Alaska, USA
32 M12 Council Idaho, NW USA
29 S15 Council Bluffs Iowa, C USA
27 O5 Council Grove Kansas, C USA
27 O5 Council Grove Lake ⊠ Kansas, C USA
32 G7 Coupeville Washington, NW USA
55 U12 Courantyne River var. Corantijn Rivier, Corentyne River. ≈ Guyana/Suriname
99 G21 Courcelles Hainaut, S Belgium
108 C7 Courgenay Jura, NW Switzerland
126 B2 Courland Lagoon Ger. Kurisches Haff, Rus. Kurskiy Zaliv. lagoon Lithuania/Russian Federation
118 B12 Courland Spit Lith. Kuršių Nerija, Rus. Kurshskaya Kosa. spit Lithuania/Russian Federation
106 A6 Courmayeur prev. Cormaiore. Valle d'Aosta, NW Italy
108 D7 Courroux Jura, NW Switzerland
10 K17 Courtenay Vancouver Island, British Columbia, SW Canada
21 W7 Courtland Virginia, NE USA
25 V10 Courtney Texas, SW USA
30 J4 Court Oreilles, Lac ◎ Wisconsin, N USA
Courtrai see Kortrijk
99 H19 Court-Saint-Étienne Walloon Brabant, C Belgium
22 G6 Coushatta Louisiana, S USA
172 I16 Cousin island Inner Islands, NE Seychelles
172 I16 Cousine island Inner Islands, NE Seychelles
102 J4 Coutances anc. Constantia. Manche, N France
102 K12 Coutras Gironde, SW France
45 U14 Couva Trinidad, Trinidad and Tobago
108 B8 Couvet Neuchâtel, W Switzerland
99 H22 Couvin Namur, S Belgium
116 K12 Covasna Ger. Kowasna, Hung. Kovászna. Covasna, E Romania
116 J11 Covasna ◈ county E Romania
14 E12 Cove Island island Ontario, S Canada
34 M5 Covelo California, W USA
97 M20 Coventry anc. Couentrey. C England, UK
Cove of Cork see Cobh
21 U5 Covesville Virginia, NE USA
104 I8 Covilhã Castelo Branco, E Portugal
23 T3 Covington Georgia, SE USA
31 N13 Covington Indiana, N USA
20 M3 Covington Kentucky, S USA
22 K8 Covington Louisiana, S USA
31 Q13 Covington Ohio, N USA
20 F9 Covington Tennessee, S USA
21 S6 Covington Virginia, NE USA
183 Q8 Cowal, Lake seasonal lake New South Wales, SE Australia
9 W15 Cowan Manitoba, S Canada
18 F12 Cowanesque River ≈ New York/Pennsylvania, NE USA
180 L12 Cowan, Lake ◎ Western Australia
15 P13 Cowansville Québec, SE Canada

◆ Country
● Country Capital
◇ Dependent Territory
○ Dependent Territory Capital
◈ Administrative Regions
✈ International Airport
▲ Mountain
▲▲ Mountain Range
⛰ Volcano
≈ River
◎ Lake
⊠ Reservoir

182 H8 **Cowell** South Australia
97 M23 **Cowes** S England, UK
27 Q10 **Coweta** Oklahoma, C USA
0 D6 **Cowie Seamount** *undersea feature* NE Pacific Ocean
32 G10 **Cowlitz River** ≈ Washington, NW USA
21 Q11 **Cowpens** South Carolina, SE USA
183 R8 **Cowra** New South Wales, SE Australia
Coxen Hole *see* Roatán
59 I19 **Coxim** Mato Grosso do Sul, S Brazil
59 I19 **Coxim, Rio** ≈ SW Brazil
Coxin Hole *see* Roatán
153 V17 **Cox's Bazar** Chittagong, S Bangladesh
76 H14 **Coyah** Conakry, W Guinea
40 K5 **Coyame** Chihuahua, N Mexico
24 L9 **Coyanosa Draw** ≈ Texas, SW USA
Coyhaique *see* Coihaique
42 C7 **Coyolate, Río** ≈ S Guatemala
Coyote State, The *see* South Dakota
40 I10 **Coyotitán** Sinaloa, C Mexico
41 O16 **Coyuca** *var.* Coyuca de Benítez. Guerrero, S Mexico
41 N15 **Coyuca** *var.* Coyuca de Catalán. Guerrero, S Mexico
Coyuca de Benítez/Coyuca de Catalán *see* Coyuca
29 N15 **Cozad** Nebraska, C USA
Cozie, Alpi *see* Cottian Alps
Cozmeni *see* Kitsman'
40 E3 **Cozón, Cerro** ▲ NW Mexico
41 Z12 **Cozumel** Quintana Roo, E Mexico
41 Z12 **Cozumel, Isla** *island* SE Mexico
32 K8 **Crab Creek** ≈ Washington, NW USA
44 H12 **Crab Pond Point** *headland* W Jamaica
Cracovia/Cracow *see* Kraków
83 I25 **Cradock** Eastern Cape, S South Africa
39 Y14 **Craig** Prince of Wales Island, Alaska, USA
37 Q3 **Craig** Colorado, C USA
97 F15 **Craigavon** C Northern Ireland, UK
21 T5 **Craigsville** Virginia, NE USA
101 J21 **Crailsheim** Baden-Württemberg, S Germany
116 H14 **Craiova** Dolj, SW Romania
10 K12 **Cranberry Junction** British Columbia, SW Canada
18 J8 **Cranberry Lake** ◎ New York, NE USA
9 V13 **Cranberry Portage** Manitoba, C Canada
9 P17 **Cranbrook** British Columbia, SW Canada
30 M5 **Crandon** Wisconsin, N USA
32 K14 **Crane** Oregon, NW USA
24 M9 **Crane** Texas, SW USA
Crane *see* The Crane
25 S8 **Cranfills Gap** Texas, SW USA
19 O12 **Cranston** Rhode Island, NE USA
Cranz *see* Zelenogradsk
59 L15 **Craolândia** Tocantins, E Brazil
102 J7 **Craon** Mayenne, NW France
195 V16 **Crary, Cape** *headland* Antarctica
Crasna *see* Kraszna
32 G14 **Crater Lake** ◎ Oregon, NW USA
33 P14 **Craters of the Moon National Monument** *national park* Idaho, NW USA
59 O14 **Crateús** Ceará, E Brazil
Crathis *see* Crati
107 N20 **Crati** *anc.* Crathis. ≈ S Italy
9 U16 **Craven** Saskatchewan, S Canada
54 I8 **Cravo Norte** Arauca, E Colombia
28 J12 **Crawford** Nebraska, C USA
25 T8 **Crawford** Texas, SW USA
9 O17 **Crawford Bay** British Columbia, SW Canada
65 M19 **Crawford Seamount** *undersea feature* S Atlantic Ocean
31 O13 **Crawfordsville** Indiana, N USA
23 S9 **Crawfordville** Florida, SE USA
97 O23 **Crawley** SE England, UK
33 S10 **Crazy Mountains** ▲▲ Montana, NW USA
9 T11 **Cree** ≈ Saskatchewan, C Canada
37 R7 **Creede** Colorado, C USA
40 I6 **Creel** Chihuahua, N Mexico
9 S11 **Cree Lake** ◎ Saskatchewan, C Canada
9 V13 **Creighton** Saskatchewan, C Canada
29 Q13 **Creighton** Nebraska, C USA
103 O4 **Creil** Oise, N France
106 E8 **Crema** Lombardia, N Italy
106 E8 **Cremona** Lombardia, N Italy
Creole State *see* Louisiana
112 M10 **Crepaja** *Hung.* Cserépalja. Vojvodina, N Serbia
103 O4 **Crépy-en-Valois** Oise, N France
112 B10 **Cres** *It.* Cherso. Primorje-Gorski Kotar, NW Croatia
112 A11 **Cres** *It.* Cherso; *anc.* Crexa. *island* W Croatia
32 H14 **Crescent** Oregon, NW USA
34 K1 **Crescent City** California, W USA
23 W10 **Crescent City** Florida, SE USA
167 X10 **Crescent Group** *island group* C Paracel Islands
23 W10 **Crescent Lake** ◎ Florida, SE USA
29 X11 **Cresco** Iowa, C USA
61 B18 **Crespo** Entre Ríos, E Argentina
54 E5 **Crespo** ✈ (Cartagena) Bolívar, NW Colombia
103 R13 **Crest** Drôme, E France
37 R5 **Crested Butte** Colorado, C USA
31 S12 **Crestline** Ohio, N USA
9 O17 **Creston** British Columbia, SW Canada
29 U15 **Creston** Iowa, C USA
33 V16 **Creston** Wyoming, C USA
37 S7 **Crestone Peak** ▲ Colorado, C USA
23 P8 **Crestview** Florida, SE USA
121 R10 **Cretan Trough** *undersea feature* Aegean Sea, C Mediterranean Sea
29 R16 **Crete** Nebraska, C USA
Crete *see* Kríti
103 O5 **Créteil** Val-de-Marne, N France
Crete, Sea of/Creticum, Mare *see* Kritikó Pélagos
105 X4 **Creus, Cap de** *cape* NE Spain
103 N10 **Creuse** ⬖ *department* C France
102 L9 **Creuse** ≈ C France
103 T4 **Creutzwald** Moselle, NE France
105 S12 **Crevillente** País Valenciano, E Spain
97 L18 **Crewe** C England, UK
21 V7 **Crewe** Virginia, NE USA
Crexa *see* Cres
43 Q15 **Cricamola, Río** ≈ NW Panama
61 K14 **Criciúma** Santa Catarina, S Brazil
96 J11 **Crieff** C Scotland, UK
112 B10 **Crikvenica** *It.* Cirquenizza; *prev.* Cirkvenica, Crjkvenica. Primorje-Gorski Kotar, NW Croatia
Crimea/Crimean Oblast *see* Krym, Respublika
101 M16 **Crimmitschau** *var.* Krimmitschau. Sachsen, E Germany
116 G11 **Crişcior** *Hung.* Kristyor. Hunedoara, W Romania
21 Y5 **Crisfield** Maryland, NE USA
31 P3 **Crisp Point** *headland* Michigan, N USA
59 L19 **Cristalina** Goiás, C Brazil
44 J7 **Cristal, Sierra del** ▲▲ E Cuba
43 T14 **Cristóbal** Colón, C Panama
54 F4 **Cristóbal Colón, Pico** ▲ N Colombia
Cristur/Cristuru Săcuiesc *see* Cristuru Secuiesc
116 I11 **Cristuru Secuiesc** *prev.* Cristur, Cristuru Săcuiesc, *Ger.* Kreutz, Sitaş Cristuru, *Hung.* Székelykeresztúr, Szitás-Keresztúr. Harghita, C Romania
116 F10 **Crişul Alb** *var.* Weisse Kreisch, *Ger.* Weisse Körös, *Hung* Fehér-Körös. ≈ Hungary/Romania
116 F10 **Crişul Negru** *Ger.* Schwarze Körös, *Hung.* Fekete-Körös. ≈ Hungary/Romania
116 G10 **Crişul Repede** *var.* Schnelle Kreisch, *Ger.* Schnelle Körös, *Hung.* Sebes-Körös. ≈ Hungary/Romania
117 N10 **Criuleni** *Rus.* Kriulyany. C Moldova
Crivadia Vulcanului *see* Vulcan
Crjkvenica *see* Crikvenica
113 O17 **Crna Gora** ▲▲ FYR Macedonia/Serbia
Crna Gora *see* Montenegro
113 O20 **Crna Reka** ≈ S FYR Macedonia
Crni Drim *see* Black Drin
109 V10 **Crni Vrh** ▲ NE Slovenia
109 V13 **Črnomelj** *Ger.* Tschernembl. SE Slovenia
97 A17 **Croagh Patrick** *Ir.* Cruach Phádraig. ▲ W Ireland
112 D9 **Croatia** *off.* Republic of Croatia, *Ger.* Kroatien, *SCr.* Hrvatska. ◆ *republic* SE Europe
Croatia, Republic of *see* Croatia
Croce, Picco di *see* Wilde Kreuzspitze
15 P8 **Croche** ≈ Québec, SE Canada
169 V7 **Crocker, Banjaran** *var.* Crocker Range. ▲▲ East Malaysia
Crocker Range *see* Crocker, Banjaran
25 V9 **Crockett** Texas, SW USA
67 V14 **Crocodile** *var.* Krokodil. ≈ N South Africa
Crocodile *see* Limpopo
20 I7 **Crofton** Kentucky, S USA
29 Q12 **Crofton** Nebraska, C USA
Croia *see* Krujë
103 R16 **Croisette, Cap** *headland* SE France
102 G8 **Croisic, Pointe du** *headland* NW France
103 S13 **Croix Haute, Col de la** *pass* E France
15 U5 **Croix, Pointe à la** *headland* Québec, SE Canada
14 F13 **Croker, Cape** *headland* Ontario, S Canada
181 P1 **Croker Island** *island* Northern Territory, N Australia
96 I8 **Cromarty** N Scotland, UK
99 M21 **Crombach** Liège, E Belgium
97 Q18 **Cromer** E England, UK
185 D22 **Cromwell** Otago, South Island, New Zealand
185 H16 **Cronadun** West Coast, South Island, New Zealand
39 O11 **Crooked Creek** Alaska, USA
44 K5 **Crooked Island** *island* SE Bahamas
44 J5 **Crooked Island Passage** *channel* SE Bahamas
32 I13 **Crooked River** ≈ Oregon, NW USA
29 R4 **Crookston** Minnesota, N USA
28 I10 **Crooks Tower** ▲ South Dakota, N USA
31 T14 **Crooksville** Ohio, N USA
183 R9 **Crookwell** New South Wales, SE Australia
14 L14 **Crosby** Ontario, SE Canada
97 K17 **Crosby** *var.* Great Crosby. NW England, UK
29 U6 **Crosby** Minnesota, N USA
28 K2 **Crosby** North Dakota, N USA
25 O5 **Crosbyton** Texas, SW USA
77 V16 **Cross** ≈ Cameroon/Nigeria
23 U10 **Cross City** Florida, SE USA
Crossen *see* Krosno Odrzańskie
27 V14 **Crossett** Arkansas, C USA
97 K15 **Cross Fell** ▲ N England, UK
9 P16 **Crossfield** Alberta, SW Canada
21 Q12 **Cross Hill** South Carolina, SE USA
19 U6 **Cross Island** *island* Maine, NE USA
9 X13 **Cross Lake** Manitoba, C Canada
22 F5 **Cross Lake** ⊠ Louisiana, S USA
36 I12 **Crossman Peak** ▲ Arizona, SW USA
25 Q7 **Cross Plains** Texas, SW USA
77 V17 **Cross River** ⬖ *state* SE Nigeria
20 L9 **Crossville** Tennessee, S USA
31 S8 **Croswell** Michigan, N USA
14 K13 **Crotch Lake** ◎ Ontario, SE Canada
Croton/Crotona *see* Crotone
107 O21 **Crotone** *var.* Cotrone; *anc.* Croton, Crotona. Calabria, SW Italy
33 V11 **Crow Agency** Montana, NW USA
183 U7 **Crowdy Head** *headland* New South Wales, SE Australia
25 Q4 **Crowell** Texas, SW USA
183 O6 **Crowl Creek** *seasonal river* New South Wales, SE Australia
22 H9 **Crowley** Louisiana, S USA
35 S9 **Crowley, Lake** ⊠ California, W USA
27 X10 **Crowleys Ridge** *hill range* Arkansas, C USA
31 N11 **Crown Point** Indiana, N USA
37 P10 **Crownpoint** New Mexico, SW USA
33 R10 **Crow Peak** ▲ Montana, NW USA
9 P17 **Crowsnest Pass** *pass* Alberta/British Columbia, SW Canada
29 T6 **Crow Wing River** ≈ Minnesota, N USA
97 O22 **Croydon** SE England, UK
Crozer, Mount *see* Finkol, Mount
173 P11 **Crozet Basin** *undersea feature* S Indian Ocean
173 O12 **Crozet Islands** *island group* French Southern and Antarctic Territories
173 N12 **Crozet Plateau** *var.* Crozet Plateaus. *undersea feature* SW Indian Ocean
Crozet Plateaus *see* Crozet Plateau
102 E6 **Crozon** Finistère, NW France
Cruacha Dubha, Na *see* Macgillycuddy's Reeks
Cruach Phádraig *see* Croagh Patrick
116 M14 **Crucea** Constanţa, SE Romania
44 E5 **Cruces** Cienfuegos, C Cuba
107 O20 **Crucoli Torretta** Calabria, SW Italy
41 P9 **Cruillas** Tamaulipas, C Mexico
64 K9 **Cruiser Tablemount** *undersea feature* E Atlantic Ocean
61 G14 **Cruz Alta** Rio Grande do Sul, S Brazil
44 G8 **Cruz, Cabo** *headland* S Cuba
60 N9 **Cruzeiro** São Paulo, S Brazil
60 H10 **Cruzeiro do Oeste** Paraná, S Brazil
59 A15 **Cruzeiro do Sul** Acre, W Brazil
23 U11 **Crystal Bay** *bay* Florida, SE USA NE Gulf of Mexico Atlantic Ocean
182 I8 **Crystal Brook** South Australia
9 X17 **Crystal City** Manitoba, S Canada
27 X5 **Crystal City** Missouri, C USA
25 P13 **Crystal City** Texas, SW USA
30 M4 **Crystal Falls** Michigan, N USA
23 Q8 **Crystal Lake** Florida, SE USA
31 O6 **Crystal Lake** ◎ Michigan, N USA
23 V11 **Crystal River** Florida, SE USA
37 Q5 **Crystal River** ≈ Colorado, C USA
22 K6 **Crystal Springs** Mississippi, S USA
Csaca *see* Čadca
Csakathurn/Csáktornya *see* Čakovec
Csap *see* Chop
Csepén *see* Čepin
Cserépalja *see* Crepaja
Csermő *see* Cermei
Csíkszereda *see* Miercurea-Ciuc
111 L24 **Csongrád** Csongrád, SE Hungary
111 L24 **Csongrád** *off.* Csongrád Megye. ⬖ *county* SE Hungary
Csongrád Megye *see* Csongrád
111 H22 **Csorna** Győr-Moson-Sopron, NW Hungary
Csucsa *see* Ciucea
111 G25 **Csurgó** Somogy, SW Hungary
Csurog *see* Čurug
55 L5 **Cúa** Miranda, N Venezuela
82 C11 **Cuale** Malanje, NW Angola
67 T12 **Cuando** *var.* Kwando. ≈ S Africa
83 E15 **Cuando Cubango** *var.* Kuando-Kubango. ⬖ *province* SE Angola
83 E16 **Cuangar** Cuando Cubango, S Angola
82 D11 **Cuango** Lunda Norte, NE Angola
82 C10 **Cuango** Uíge, NW Angola
82 C10 **Cuango** *var.* Kwango. ≈ Angola/Dem. Rep. Congo *see also* Kwango
Cuango *see* Kwango
Cuan, Loch *see* Strangford Lough
82 C12 **Cuanza** *var.* Kwanza. ≈ C Angola
82 B11 **Cuanza Norte** *var.* Kuanza Norte. ⬖ *province* NE Angola
82 B12 **Cuanza Sul** *var.* Kuanza Sul. ⬖ *province* NE Angola
61 E16 **Cuareim, Río** *var.* Rio Quaraí. ≈ Brazil/Uruguay *see also* Quaraí, Rio
Cuareim, Río *see* Quaraí, Rio
83 D15 **Cuatir** ≈ S Angola
40 M7 **Cuatro Ciénegas** *var.* Cuatro Ciénegas de Carranza. Coahuila de Zaragoza, NE Mexico
Cuatro Ciénegas de Carranza *see* Cuatro Ciénegas
40 I6 **Cuauhtémoc** Chihuahua, N Mexico
41 P14 **Cuautla** Morelos, S Mexico
104 H12 **Cuba** Beja, S Portugal
27 W6 **Cuba** Missouri, C USA
37 R10 **Cuba** New Mexico, SW USA
44 E6 **Cuba** *off.* Republic of Cuba. ◆ *republic* W West Indies
47 O2 **Cuba** *island* W West Indies
82 B13 **Cubal** Benguela, W Angola
83 C15 **Cubango** *var.* Kuvango, *Port.* Vila Artur de Paiva, Vila da Ponte. Huíla, SW Angola
83 D16 **Cubango** *var.* Kavango, Kavengo, Kubango, Okavango, Okavanggo. ≈ S Africa *see also* Okavango
Cubango *see* Okavango
54 H8 **Cubará** Boyacá, N Colombia
Cuba, Republic of *see* Cuba
136 I12 **Çubuk** Ankara, N Turkey
83 D14 **Cuchi** Cuando Cubango, C Angola
42 C5 **Cuchumatanes, Sierra de los** ▲▲ W Guatemala
Cuculaya, Rio *see* Kukalaya, Rio
82 E12 **Cucumbi** *prev.* Trás-os-Montes. Lunda Sul, NE Angola
54 G7 **Cúcuta** *var.* San José de Cúcuta. Norte de Santander, N Colombia
31 N9 **Cudahy** Wisconsin, N USA
155 J21 **Cuddalore** Tamil Nādu, SE India
155 I18 **Cuddapah** Andhra Pradesh, S India
104 M6 **Cuéllar** Castilla-León, N Spain
82 D13 **Cuemba** *var.* Coemba. Bié, C Angola
56 B8 **Cuenca** Azuay, S Ecuador
105 Q9 **Cuenca** *anc.* Conca. Castilla-La Mancha, C Spain
105 P9 **Cuenca** ⬖ *province* Castilla-La Mancha, C Spain
40 L9 **Cuencamé** *var.* Cuencamé de Ceniceros. Durango, C Mexico
Cuencamé de Ceniceros *see* Cuencamé
105 Q8 **Cuenca, Serranía de** ▲▲ C Spain
Cuera *see* Chur
105 P5 **Cuerda del Pozo, Embalse de la** ⊠ N Spain
41 O14 **Cuernavaca** Morelos, S Mexico
25 T12 **Cuero** Texas, SW USA
44 I7 **Cueto** Holguín, E Cuba
41 Q13 **Cuetzalán** *var.* Cuetzalán del Progreso. Puebla, S Mexico
Cuetzalán del Progreso *see* Cuetzalán
105 Q14 **Cuevas de Almanzora** Andalucía, S Spain
Cuevas de Vinromá *see* Les Coves de Vinromà
116 H12 **Cugir** *Hung.* Kudzsir. Alba, SW Romania
59 H18 **Cuiabá** *prev.* Cuyabá. *state capital* Mato Grosso, SW Brazil
59 H19 **Cuiabá, Rio** ≈ SW Brazil
41 R15 **Cuicatlán** *var.* San Juan Bautista Cuicatlán. Oaxaca, SE Mexico
191 W16 **Cuidado, Punta** *headland* Easter Island, Chile, E Pacific Ocean
Cuidad Presidente Stroessner *see* Ciudad del Este
Cúige *see* Connaught
Cúige Laighean *see* Leinster
Cúige Mumhan *see* Munster
Cuihua *see* Daguan
98 L13 **Cuijck** Noord-Brabant, SE Netherlands
Cúil an tSúdaire *see* Portarlington
42 D7 **Cuilapa** Santa Rosa, S Guatemala
42 B5 **Cuilco, Río** ≈ W Guatemala
Cúil Mhuine *see* Collooney
Cúil Raithin *see* Coleraine
83 C14 **Cuima** Huambo, C Angola
83 E16 **Cuito** *var.* Kwito. ≈ SE Angola
83 E15 **Cuíto Cuanavale** Cuando Cubango, E Angola
41 N14 **Cuitzeo, Lago de** ◎ C Mexico
27 W4 **Cuivre River** ≈ Missouri, C USA
Çuka *see* Çukë
168 L8 **Cukai** *var.* Chukai, Kemaman. Terengganu, Peninsular Malaysia
113 L23 **Çukë** *var.* Çuka. Vlorë, S Albania
Cularo *see* Grenoble
33 Y7 **Culbertson** Montana, NW USA
28 M16 **Culbertson** Nebraska, C USA
183 P10 **Culcairn** New South Wales, SE Australia
45 W5 **Culebra** *var.* Dewey. E Puerto Rico
45 W6 **Culebra, Isla de** *island* E Puerto Rico
37 T8 **Culebra Peak** ▲ Colorado, C USA
104 J5 **Culebra, Sierra de la** ▲▲ NW Spain
98 J12 **Culemborg** Gelderland, C Netherlands
137 V14 **Culfa** *Rus.* Dzhul'fa. SW Azerbaijan
183 P4 **Culgoa River** ≈ New South Wales/Queensland, SE Australia
40 I9 **Culiacán** *var.* Culiacán Rosales, Culiacán-Rosales. Sinaloa, C Mexico
Culiacán-Rosales/Culiacán Rosales *see* Culiacán
105 P14 **Cúllar-Baza** Andalucía, S Spain
105 S10 **Cullera** País Valenciano, E Spain
23 P3 **Cullman** Alabama, S USA
108 B10 **Cully** Vaud, W Switzerland
Culm *see* Chełmno
Culmsee *see* Chełmża
21 V4 **Culpeper** Virginia, NE USA
185 I17 **Culverden** Canterbury, South Island, New Zealand
55 N5 **Cumaná** Sucre, NE Venezuela
55 O5 **Cumanacoa** Sucre, NE Venezuela
54 C13 **Cumbal, Nevado de** *elevation* S Colombia
21 O7 **Cumberland** Kentucky, S USA
21 U2 **Cumberland** Maryland, NE USA
21 V6 **Cumberland** Virginia, NE USA
187 P12 **Cumberland, Cape** *var.* Cape Nahoi. *headland* Espiritu Santo, N Vanuatu
9 V14 **Cumberland House** Saskatchewan, C Canada
23 W8 **Cumberland Island** *island* Georgia, SE USA
20 L7 **Cumberland, Lake** ⊠ Kentucky, S USA
9 R5 **Cumberland Peninsula** *peninsula* Baffin Island, Nunavut, NE Canada
2 N9 **Cumberland Plateau** *plateau* E USA
30 L1 **Cumberland Point** *headland* Michigan, N USA
21 O7 **Cumberland River** ≈ Kentucky/Tennessee, S USA
9 S6 **Cumberland Sound** *inlet* Baffin Island, Nunavut, NE Canada
96 I12 **Cumbernauld** S Scotland, UK
97 K15 **Cumbria** *cultural region* NW England, UK
97 K15 **Cumbrian Mountains** ▲▲ NW England, UK
23 S2 **Cumming** Georgia, SE USA
Cummin in Pommern *see* Kamień Pomorski
182 G9 **Cummins** South Australia
96 I13 **Cumnock** W Scotland, UK
40 G4 **Cumpas** Sonora, NW Mexico
136 H16 **Çumra** Konya, C Turkey
63 G15 **Cunco** Araucanía, C Chile
54 E9 **Cundinamarca** *off.* Departamento de Cundinamarca. ⬖ *province* C Colombia
Cundinamarca, Departamento de *see* Cundinamarca
41 U15 **Cunduacán** Tabasco, SE Mexico
83 C16 **Cunene** ⬖ *province* S Angola
83 A16 **Cunene** *var.* Kunene. ≈ Angola/Namibia *see also* Kunene
Cunene *see* Kunene
106 A9 **Cuneo** *Fr.* Coni. Piemonte, NW Italy
83 E15 **Cunjamba** Cuando Cubango, E Angola
181 V10 **Cunnamulla** Queensland, E Australia
Čunusavvon *see* Junosuando
Cuokkarašša *see* Čohkarášša
106 B7 **Cuorgne** Piemonte, NE Italy
96 K11 **Cupar** E Scotland, UK
116 L8 **Cupcina** *Rus.* Kupchino; *prev.* Calinisc, Kalinisk. N Moldova
54 C8 **Cupica** Chocó, W Colombia
54 C8 **Cupica, Golfo de** *gulf* W Colombia
112 N13 **Ćuprija** Serbia, E Serbia
Cura *see* Villa de Cura
45 P16 **Curaçao** *island* Netherlands Antilles
56 H13 **Curanja, Río** ≈ E Peru
56 F7 **Curaray, Río** ≈ Ecuador/Peru
116 K14 **Curcani** Călăraşi, SE Romania
182 H4 **Curdimurka** South Australia
103 P7 **Cure** ≈ C France
173 Y16 **Curepipe** C Mauritius
55 R6 **Curiapo** Delta Amacuro, NE Venezuela
Curia Rhaetorum *see* Chur
62 G12 **Curicó** Maule, C Chile
Curieta *see* Krk
172 I15 **Curieuse** *island* Inner Islands, NE Seychelles
59 C16 **Curitiba** Acre, W Brazil
60 K12 **Curitiba** *prev.* Curytiba. *state capital* Paraná, S Brazil
60 J13 **Curitibanos** Santa Catarina, S Brazil
183 S6 **Curlewis** New South Wales, SE Australia
182 J6 **Curnamona** South Australia
83 A15 **Curoca** ≈ SW Angola
183 T6 **Currabubula** New South Wales, SE Australia
59 Q14 **Currais Novos** Rio Grande do Norte, E Brazil
35 W7 **Currant** Nevada, W USA
35 W6 **Currant Mountain** ▲ Nevada, W USA
44 H2 **Current** Eleuthera Island, C Bahamas
27 W8 **Current River** ≈ Arkansas/Missouri, C USA
182 M14 **Currie** Tasmania, SE Australia
21 Y8 **Currituck** North Carolina, SE USA
21 Y8 **Currituck Sound** *sound* North Carolina, SE USA
39 R11 **Curry** Alaska, USA
Curtbunar *see* Tervel
116 I13 **Curtea de Argeş** *var.* Curtea-de-Arges. Argeş, S Romania
Curtea-de-Arges *see* Curtea de Argeş
116 E10 **Curtici** *Ger.* Kurtitsch, *Hung.* Kürtös. Arad, W Romania
28 M16 **Curtis** Nebraska, C USA
104 H2 **Curtis-Estación** Galicia, NW Spain
183 O14 **Curtis Group** *island group* Tasmania, SE Australia
181 Y8 **Curtis Island** *island* Queensland, SE Australia
58 K11 **Curuá, Ilha do** *island* NE Brazil
47 U7 **Curuá, Rio** ≈ N Brazil
49 A14 **Curuçá, Rio** ≈ NW Brazil
112 L9 **Čurug** *Hung.* Csurog. Vojvodina, N Serbia
61 D16 **Curuzú Cuatiá** Corrientes, NE Argentina
59 M19 **Curvelo** Minas Gerais, SE Brazil
18 E14 **Curwensville** Pennsylvania, NE USA
30 M3 **Curwood, Mount** ▲ Michigan, N USA
Curytiba *see* Curitiba
Curzola *see* Korčula
42 A10 **Cuscatlán** ⬖ *department* C El Salvador
57 H15 **Cusco** *var.* Cuzco. Cusco, C Peru
57 H15 **Cusco** *off.* Departamento de Cusco, *var.* Cuzco. ⬖ *department* C Peru
Cusco, Departamento de *see* Cusco
27 O9 **Cushing** Oklahoma, C USA
25 W8 **Cushing** Texas, SW USA
40 I6 **Cusihuiriachic** Chihuahua, N Mexico
103 P10 **Cusset** Allier, C France
23 S6 **Cusseta** Georgia, SE USA
28 J10 **Custer** South Dakota, N USA
Cüstrin *see* Kostrzyn
33 Q7 **Cut Bank** Montana, NW USA
Cutch, Gulf of *see* Kachchh, Gulf of
23 S6 **Cuthbert** Georgia, SE USA
9 S15 **Cut Knife** Saskatchewan, S Canada
23 Y16 **Cutler Ridge** Florida, SE USA
22 K10 **Cut Off** Louisiana, S USA
63 I15 **Cutral-Có** Neuquén, C Argentina
107 O21 **Cutro** Calabria, SW Italy
183 O4 **Cuttaburra Channels** *seasonal river* New South Wales, SE Australia
154 O12 **Cuttack** Orissa, E India
83 C15 **Cuvelai** Cunene, SW Angola
79 G18 **Cuvette** *var.* Région de la Cuvette. ⬖ *province* C Congo
Cuvette, Région de la *see* Cuvette
173 V9 **Cuvier Basin** *undersea feature* E Indian Ocean
173 U9 **Cuvier Plateau** *undersea feature* E Indian Ocean
82 B12 **Cuvo** ≈ W Angola
100 H9 **Cuxhaven** Niedersachsen, NW Germany
Cuyabá *see* Cuiabá
Cuyuni, Río *see* Cuyuni River
55 S8 **Cuyuni River** *var.* Río Cuyuni. ≈ Guyana/Venezuela
Cuzco *see* Cusco
97 K22 **Cwmbran** *Wel.* Cwmbrân. SW Wales, UK
Cwmbrân *see* Cwmbran
28 K15 **C. W. McConaughy, Lake** ⊠ Nebraska, C USA
81 D20 **Cyangugu** SW Rwanda
110 D11 **Cybinka** *Ger.* Ziebingen. Lubuskie, W Poland
Cyclades *see* Kykládes
Cydonia *see* Chaniá
Cymru *see* Wales
20 M5 **Cynthiana** Kentucky, S USA
9 S17 **Cypress Hills** ▲▲ Alberta/Saskatchewan, SW Canada
Cypro-Syrian Basin *see* Cyprus Basin
121 U11 **Cyprus** *off.* Republic of Cyprus, *Gk.* Kypros, *Turk.* Kıbrıs, Kıbrıs Cumhuriyeti. ◆ *republic* E Mediterranean Sea
84 L14 **Cyprus** *Gk.* Kypros, *Turk.* Kıbrıs. *island* E Mediterranean Sea
121 W11 **Cyprus Basin** *var.* Cypro-Syrian Basin. *undersea feature* E Mediterranean Sea
Cyprus, Republic of *see* Cyprus
Cythera *see* Kýthira
Cythnos *see* Kýthnos
110 F9 **Czaplinek** *Ger.* Tempelburg. Zachodnio-pomorskie, NW Poland
Czarna Woda *see* Wda
110 G8 **Czarne** Pomorskie, N Poland
110 G10 **Czarnków** Wielkopolskie, C Poland
111 E17 **Czech Republic** *Cz.* Česká Republika. ◆ *republic* C Europe
Czegléd *see* Cegléd
110 G12 **Czempiń** Wielkopolskie, C Poland
Czenstochau *see* Częstochowa
Czerkow *see* Čerchov
Czernowitz *see* Chernivtsi
110 I8 **Czersk** Pomorskie, N Poland
111 J15 **Częstochowa** *Ger.* Czenstochau, Tschenstochau, *Rus.* Chenstokhov. Śląskie, S Poland
110 F10 **Człopa** *Ger.* Schloppe. Zachodnio-pomorskie, NW Poland
110 H8 **Człuchów** *Ger.* Schlochau. Pomorskie, NW Poland

D

163 V9 **Da'an** *var.* Dalai. Jilin, NE China
15 S10 **Daaquam** Québec, SE Canada
Daawo, Webi *see* Dawa Wenz
54 I4 **Dabajuro** Falcón, NW Venezuela
77 N15 **Dabakala** NE Ivory Coast
163 S11 **Daban** *var* Bairin Youqi. Nei Mongol Zizhiqu, N China
111 K23 **Dabas** Pest, C Hungary
160 L8 **Daba Shan** ▲▲ C China
Dabba *see* Daocheng
140 J5 **Dabbāgh, Jabal** ▲ NW Saudi Arabia
54 D8 **Dabeiba** Antioquia, NW Colombia
154 E11 **Dabhoi** Gujarāt, W India
161 P8 **Dabie Shan** ▲▲ C China
76 J13 **Dabola** C Guinea
77 N17 **Dabou** S Ivory Coast
162 M15 **Dabqig** *var.* Uxin Qi. Nei Mongol Zizhiqu, N China
110 P8 **Dąbrowa Białostocka** Podlaskie, NE Poland
111 M16 **Dąbrowa Tarnowska** Małopolskie, S Poland
119 M20 **Dabryn'** *Rus.* Dobryn'. Homyel'skaya Voblasts', SE Belarus
159 P10 **Dabsan Hu** ◎ C China
161 Q13 **Dabu** *var.* Huliao. Guangdong, S China

◆ Country ● Country Capital ◇ Dependent Territory ○ Dependent Territory Capital ⬖ Administrative Regions ✈ International Airport ▲ Mountain ▲▲ Mountain Range Volcano ≈ River ◎ Lake ⊠ Reservoir

116 H15 Dăbuleni Dolj, SW Romania
Dacca see Dhaka
101 L23 Dachau Bayern, SE Germany
Dachuan see Dazhou
Dacia Bank see Dacia Seamount
64 M10 Dacia Seamount var. Dacia Bank. undersea feature E Atlantic Ocean
37 T3 Dacono Colorado, C USA
Đắc Tô see Đak Tô
Dacura see Dákura
23 W12 Dade City Florida, SE USA
152 L10 Ḍaḍeldhurā var. Dandeldhura. Far Western, W Nepal
23 Q5 Dadeville Alabama, S USA
Dadong see Donggang
103 N15 Dadou ~ S France
154 D12 Dādra and Nagar Haveli ◈ union territory W India
149 P14 Dādu Sind, SE Pakistan
167 U11 Da Du Boloc Kon Tum, C Vietnam
160 G9 Dadu He ~ C China
Daegu see Taegu
Daerah Istimewa Aceh see Aceh
171 P4 Daet Luzon, N Philippines
160 I11 Dafang Guizhou, S China
Dafeng see Shanglin
153 W11 Dafla Hills ▲▲ NE India
9 U15 Dafoe Saskatchewan, S Canada
76 G10 Dagana N Senegal
Dagana see Massakory, Chad
Dagana see Dahana, Tajikistan
Dagcagoin see Zoigê
118 K11 Dagda Krāslava, SE Latvia
Dagden see Hiiumaa
Dagden-Sund see Soela Väin
127 P16 Dagestan, Respublika prev. Dagestanskaya ASSR, Eng. Daghestan. ◈ autonomous republic SW Russian Federation
Dagestanskaya ASSR see Dagestan, Respublika
127 R17 Dagestanskiye Ogni Respublika Dagestan, SW Russian Federation
Dagezhen see Fengning
185 A23 Dagg Sound sound South Island, New Zealand
Daghestan see Dagestan, Respublika
141 Y8 Daghmar NE Oman
Dağliq Quarabağ see Nagorno-Karabakh
Dagö see Hiiumaa
54 D11 Dagua Valle del Cauca, W Colombia
160 H11 Daguan var. Cuihua. Yunnan, SW China
171 N3 Dagupan off. Dagupan City. Luzon, N Philippines
Dagupan City see Dagupan
159 N16 Dagzê var. Dêqên. Xizang Zizhiqu, W China
147 Q13 Dahana Rus. Dagana, Dakhana. SW Tajikistan
163 V10 Dahei Shan ▲▲ N China
163 T7 Da Hinggan Ling Eng. Great Khingan Range. ▲▲ NE China
Dahlac Archipelago see Dahlak Archipelago
80 K9 Dahlak Archipelago var. Dahlac Archipelago. island group E Eritrea
23 T2 Dahlonega Georgia, SE USA
101 O14 Dahme Brandenburg, E Germany
100 O13 Dahme ~ E Germany
141 O14 Dahm, Ramlat desert NW Yemen
154 E10 Dāhod prev. Dohad. Gujarāt, W India
Dahomey see Benin
158 G10 Dahongliutan Xinjiang Uygur Zizhiqu, NW China
Dahra see Dara
139 R2 Dahūk var. Dohuk, Kurd. Dihōk. N Iraq
116 J15 Daia Giurgiu, S Romania
165 P12 Daigo Ibaraki, Honshū, S Japan
163 O13 Dai Hai ◎ N China
Daihoku see T'aipei
186 M8 Dai Island island N Solomon Islands
149 O6 Dāikondī ◈ province C Afghanistan
166 M8 Daik-u Pegu, SW Myanmar (Burma)
138 H9 Dā'īl Dar'ā, S Syria
167 U12 Đại Lanh Khanh Hoa, S Vietnam
161 Q13 Daimao Shan ▲▲ SE China
105 N11 Daimiel Castilla-La Mancha, C Spain
115 F22 Daimoniá Pelopónnisos, S Greece
Dainan see T'ainan
25 W6 Daingerfield Texas, SW USA
Daingin, Bá an see Dingle Bay
159 R13 Dainkognubma Xizang Zizhiqu, W China
164 K14 Daiō-zaki headland Honshū, SW Japan
Dairbhre see Valencia Island
61 B22 Daireaux Buenos Aires, E Argentina
Dairen see Dalian
75 W9 Dairûţ var. Dayrūṭ. C Egypt
25 X10 Daisetta Texas, SW USA
192 G5 Daitō-jima island group SW Japan
192 G5 Daitō Ridge undersea feature N Philippine Sea
161 N3 Daixian var. Dai Xian. Shanxi, C China
Dai Xian see Daixian
Daiyue see Shanyin
161 Q12 Daiyun Shan ▲▲ SE China
44 M8 Dajabón NW Dominican Republic
160 G8 Dajin Chuan ~ C China
148 J6 Dak ◎ W Afghanistan
76 F11 Dakar ● (Senegal) W Senegal
76 F11 Dakar ✕ W Senegal
167 U10 Đak Glây Kon Tum, C Vietnam
Dakhana see Dahana
153 U16 Dakhin Shahbazpur Island island S Bangladesh
Dakhla see Ad Dakhla
76 F7 Dakhlet Nouâdhibou ◈ region NW Mauritania
Đak Lap see Kiên Đuc
Đak Nông see Gia Nghia
77 U11 Dakoro Maradi, S Niger
29 U12 Dakota City Iowa, C USA
29 R13 Dakota City Nebraska, C USA
113 M17 Đakovica var. Djakovica, Alb. Gjakovë. Kosovo, S Serbia
112 I10 Đakovo var. Djakovo, Hung. Diakovár. Osijek-Baranja, E Croatia
Dakshin see Deccan
167 U11 Đak Tô var. Đăc Tô. Kon Tum, C Vietnam
43 N7 Dákura var. Dacura. Región Autónoma Atlántico Norte, NE Nicaragua
95 I14 Dal Akershus, S Norway
82 E12 Dala Lunda Sul, E Angola
108 J8 Dalaas Vorarlberg, W Austria
76 I13 Dalaba W Guinea
Dalai see Da'an
162 I12 Dalain Hob var. Ejin Qi. Nei Mongol Zizhiqu, N China
Dalai Nor see Hulun Nur
163 Q11 Dalai Nur salt lake N China
Dala-Jarna see Järna
95 M14 Dalälven ~ C Sweden
136 C16 Dalaman Muğla, SW Turkey
136 C16 Dalaman ✕ Muğla, SW Turkey
136 D16 Dalaman Çayı ~ SW Turkey
162 K11 Dalandzadgad Ömnögovĭ, S Mongolia
95 D17 Dalane physical region S Norway
189 Z2 Dalap-Uliga-Djarrit var. Delap-Uliga-Darrit, D-U-D. island group Ratak Chain, SE Marshall Islands
94 J12 Dalarna prev. Kopparberg. ◈ county C Sweden
94 L13 Dalarna prev. Eng. Dalecarlia. cultural region C Sweden
95 P16 Dalarö Stockholm, C Sweden
167 U13 Đa Lat Lâm Đông, S Vietnam
Dalay see Bayandalay
148 L12 Dālbandin var. Dāl Bandin. Baluchistān, SW Pakistan
Dāl Bandin see Dālbandin
95 J17 Dalbosjön lake bay S Sweden
181 Y10 Dalby Queensland, E Australia
94 D13 Dale Hordaland, S Norway
94 C12 Dale Sogn Og Fjordane, S Norway
32 K12 Dale Oregon, NW USA
25 T11 Dale Texas, SW USA
Dalecarlia see Dalarna
21 W4 Dale City Virginia, NE USA
20 L8 Dale Hollow Lake ⊡ Kentucky/Tennessee, S USA
98 O8 Dalen Drenthe, NE Netherlands
95 E15 Dalen Telemark, S Norway
166 K14 Daletme Chin State, W Myanmar (Burma)
23 Q7 Daleville Alabama, S USA
98 M9 Dalfsen Overijssel, E Netherlands
24 M1 Dalhart Texas, SW USA
13 O13 Dalhousie New Brunswick, SE Canada
152 I6 Dalhousie Himāchal Pradesh, N India
160 F12 Dali var. Xiaguan. Yunnan, SW China
Dali see Idálion
163 U14 Dalian var. Dairen, Dalien, Lüda, Ta-lien, Rus. Dalny. Liaoning, NE China
105 O15 Dalías Andalucía, S Spain
Dalien see Dalian
Dalijan see Delījān
112 J9 Dalj Hung. Dalja. Osijek-Baranja, E Croatia
Dalja see Dalj
32 F12 Dallas Oregon, NW USA
25 U6 Dallas Texas, SW USA
25 T7 Dallas-Fort Worth ✕ Texas, SW USA
154 K12 Dalli Rājhara Chhattīsgarh, C India
39 X15 Dall Island island Alexander Archipelago, Alaska, USA
38 M12 Dall Lake ◎ Alaska, USA
Dállogilli see Korpilombolo
77 S12 Dallol Bosso seasonal river W Niger
141 U7 Dalmā island W United Arab Emirates
113 E14 Dalmacija Eng. Dalmatia, Ger. Dalmatien, It. Dalmazia. cultural region S Croatia
Dalmatia/Dalmatien/Dalmazia see Dalmacija
Dalmatien see Dalmacija
123 S15 Dal'negorsk Primorskiy Kray, SE Russian Federation
Dalny see Dalian
76 M16 Daloa C Ivory Coast
160 J11 Dalou Shan ▲▲ S China
181 X7 Dalrymple Lake ◎ Queensland, E Australia
14 H14 Dalrymple Lake ◎ Ontario, S Canada
181 X7 Dalrymple, Mount ▲ Queensland, E Australia
93 K20 Dalsbruk Fin. Taalintehdas. Länsi-Suomi, W Finland
95 K19 Dalsjöfors Västra Götaland, S Sweden
95 J17 Dals Långed var. Långed. Västra Götaland, S Sweden
153 O15 Dāltenganj prev. Daltonganj. Jhārkhand, N India
23 R2 Dalton Georgia, SE USA
Daltonganj see Dāltenganj
195 X14 Dalton Iceberg Tongue ice feature Antarctica
92 J1 Dalvík Nordhurland Eystra, N Iceland
Dálvvadis see Jokkmokk
35 N8 Daly City California, W USA
181 P2 Daly River ~ Northern Territory, N Australia
181 Q3 Daly Waters Northern Territory, N Australia
119 F20 Damachava var. Damachova, Pol. Domaczewo, Rus. Domachëvo. Brestskaya Voblasts', SW Belarus
Damachova see Damachava
77 W11 Damagaram Takaya Zinder, S Niger
154 D12 Damān Damān and Diu, W India
154 B12 Damān and Diu ◈ union territory W India
75 V7 Damanhûr anc. Hermopolis Parva. N Egypt
161 O1 Damaqun Shan ▲▲ E China
79 I15 Damara Ombella-Mpoko, S Central African Republic
83 D18 Damaraland physical region C Namibia
171 S15 Damar, Kepulauan var. Baraf Daja Islands, Kepulauan Barat Daya. island group C Indonesia
168 J8 Damar Laut Perak, Peninsular Malaysia
171 S15 Damar, Pulau island Maluku, E Indonesia
Damas see Dimashq
77 Y12 Damasak Borno, NE Nigeria
Damasco see Dimashq
21 Q8 Damascus Virginia, NE USA
Damascus see Dimashq
77 X13 Damaturu Yobe, NE Nigeria
171 R9 Damau Pulau Kaburuang, N Indonesia
143 O5 Damāvand, Qolleh-ye ▲ N Iran
82 B10 Damba Uíge, NW Angola
114 M12 Dambaslar Tekirdağ, NW Turkey
116 J13 Dâmbovița prev. Dîmbovița. ◈ county SE Romania
116 J13 Dâmbovița prev. Dîmbovița. ~ S Romania
173 Y15 D'Ambre, Île island NE Mauritius
155 K24 Dambulla Central Province, C Sri Lanka
44 K9 Dame-Marie SW Haiti
44 J9 Dame Marie, Cap headland SW Haiti
143 Q4 Dāmghān Semnān, N Iran
Damietta see Dumyât
138 G10 Dāmiyā Al Balqā', NW Jordan
146 G11 Damla Daşoguz Welaýaty, N Turkmenistan
Dammām see Ad Dammān
100 G12 Damme Niedersachsen, NW Germany
153 R15 Dāmodar ~ NE India
154 J9 Damoh Madhya Pradesh, C India
77 P15 Damongo NW Ghana
138 G7 Damoûr var. Ad Dāmūr. W Lebanon
171 N11 Dampal, Teluk bay Sulawesi, C Indonesia
180 H7 Dampier Western Australia
180 H6 Dampier Archipelago island group Western Australia
141 U14 Damqawt var. Damqut. E Yemen
159 O13 Dam Qu ~ C China
Damqut see Damqawt
167 R13 Dâmrei, Chuŏr Phmun Fr. Chaîne de l'Éléphant. ▲▲ SW Cambodia
108 C7 Damvant Jura, NW Switzerland
Damwâld see Damwoude
98 L5 Damwoude Fris. Damwâld. Friesland, N Netherlands
159 N15 Damxung var. Gongtang. Xizang Zizhiqu, W China
80 K11 Danakil Desert var. Afar Depression, Danakil Plain. desert E Africa
Danakil Plain see Danakil Desert
35 R8 Dana, Mount ▲ California, W USA
76 L16 Danané W Ivory Coast
167 U10 Đă Năng prev. Tourane. Quang Nam-Đa Năng, C Vietnam
160 G9 Danba var. Zhanggu, Tib. Rongzhag. Sichuan, C China
Danborg see Daneborg
18 L13 Danbury Connecticut, NE USA
25 W12 Danbury Texas, SW USA
35 X15 Danby Lake ◎ California, W USA
194 H4 Danco Coast physical region Antarctica
82 B11 Dande ~ N Angola
Dandeldhura see Ḍaḍeldhurā
155 E17 Dandeli Karnātaka, W India
183 O12 Dandenong Victoria, SE Australia
163 V13 Dandong var. Tan-tung; prev. An-tung. Liaoning, NE China
197 Q14 Daneborg var. Danborg. ◈ Tunu, N Greenland
25 V12 Danevang Texas, SW USA
Dānew see Galkynyş
Danfeng see Shizong
14 L12 Danford Lake Québec, SE Canada
19 T4 Danforth Maine, NE USA
37 P3 Danforth Hills ▲▲ Colorado, C USA
Dangara see Danghara
159 V12 Dangchang Gansu, C China
159 P8 Dangchengwan var. Subei, Subei Mongolzu Zizhixian. Gansu, N China
82 B10 Dange Uíge, NW Angola
Dangerous Archipelago see Tuamotu, Îles
83 E26 Danger Point headland SW South Africa
147 Q13 Danghara Rus. Dangara. SW Tajikistan
159 P8 Danghe Nanshan ▲▲ W China
80 I12 Dangila var. Dānglā. Amhara, NW Ethiopia
159 P8 Dangjin Shankou pass N China
Dangla see Tanggula Shan, China
Dang La see Tanggula Shankou, China
Dānglā see Dangila, Ethiopia
Dangme Chu see Manās
153 Y11 Dāngori Assam, NE India
Dang Raek, Phanom/Dangrek, Chaîne des see Dângrêk, Chuŏr Phnum
167 S11 Dângrêk, Chuŏr Phnum var. Phanom Dang Raek, Phanom Dong Rak, Fr. Chaîne des Dangrek. ▲▲ Cambodia/Thailand
42 G3 Dangriga prev. Stann Creek. Stann Creek, E Belize
161 P6 Dangshan Anhui, E China
33 T15 Daniel Wyoming, C USA
83 H22 Daniëlskuil Northern Cape, N South Africa
19 N12 Danielson Connecticut, NE USA
124 M15 Danilov Yaroslavskaya Oblast', W Russian Federation
127 O9 Danilovka Volgogradskaya Oblast', SW Russian Federation
Danish West Indies see Virgin Islands (US)
160 L7 Dan Jiang ~ C China
160 M7 Danjiangkou Shuiku ⊡ C China
141 W8 Ḑank var. Dhank. NW Oman
152 J7 Dankhar Himāchal Pradesh, N India
126 L6 Dankov Lipetskaya Oblast', W Russian Federation
42 J7 Danlí El Paraíso, S Honduras
Danmark see Denmark
Danmarksstraedet see Denmark Strait
95 O14 Dannemora Uppsala, C Sweden
18 L6 Dannemora New York, NE USA
100 K11 Dannenberg Niedersachsen, N Germany
184 N12 Dannevirke Manawatu-Wanganui, North Island, New Zealand
21 U8 Dan River ~ Virginia, NE USA
167 P8 Dan Sai Loei, C Thailand
18 F10 Dansville New York, NE USA
Dantzig see Gdańsk
86 E12 Danube Bul. Dunav, Cz. Dunaj, Ger. Donau, Hung. Duna, Rom. Dunărea. ~ C Europe
Danubian Plain see Dunavska Ravnina
166 L8 Danubyu Irrawaddy, SW Myanmar (Burma)
Danum see Doncaster
19 P11 Danvers Massachusetts, NE USA
27 T11 Danville Arkansas, C USA
31 N13 Danville Illinois, N USA
31 O14 Danville Indiana, N USA
29 Y15 Danville Iowa, C USA
20 M6 Danville Kentucky, S USA
18 G14 Danville Pennsylvania, NE USA
21 T6 Danville Virginia, NE USA
Danxian/Dan Xian see Danzhou
160 L17 Danzhou prev. Danxian, Dan Xian, Nada. Hainan, S China
Danzhou see Yichuan
Danzig see Gdańsk
Danziger Bucht see Danzig, Gulf of
110 J6 Danzig, Gulf of var. Gulf of Gdańsk, Ger. Danziger Bucht, Pol. Zakota Gdańska, Rus. Gdan'skaya Bukhta. gulf N Poland
160 F10 Daocheng var. Jinzhou, Tib. Dabba. Sichuan, C China
Daojiang see Daoxian
Daokou see Huaxian
104 H7 Dão, Rio ~ N Portugal
Daosa see Dausa
77 Y7 Dao Timmi Agadez, NE Niger
160 M13 Daoxian var. Daojiang. Hunan, S China
77 Q14 Dapaong N Togo
23 N8 Daphne Alabama, S USA
171 P7 Dapitan Mindanao, S Philippines
159 P9 Da Qaidam Qinghai, C China
163 V8 Daqing var. Sartu. Heilongjiang, NE China
163 O13 Daqing Shan ▲▲ N China
163 T11 Daqin Tal var. Naiman Qi. Nei Mongol Zizhiqu, N China
Daqm see Duqm
160 G8 Da Qu var. Do Qu. ~ C China
139 T5 Dāqūq var. Tāwūq. N Iraq
76 G10 Dara var. Dahra. NW Senegal
138 H9 Dar'ā var. Der'a, Fr. Déraa. Dar'ā, SW Syria
138 H8 Dar'ā off. Muḩāfaẓat Dar'ā, var. Darā, Der'a, Derrá. ◈ governorate S Syria
Darā see Dar'ā
143 Q12 Dārāb Fārs, S Iran
116 K8 Darabani Botoşani, NW Romania
Daraj see Dirj
Dar'ā, Muḩāfaẓat see Dar'ā
142 M8 Dārān Eşfahān, W Iran
167 U12 Da Răng, Sông var. Ba. ~ S Vietnam
Daraut-Kurgan see Daroot-Korgon
77 W13 Darazo Bauchi, E Nigeria
139 S3 Darband N Iraq
139 V4 Darband-i Khān, Sadd dam NE Iraq
139 N1 Darbāsīyah var. Derbisīye. Al Ḩasakah, N Syria
118 C11 Darbėnai Klaipėda, NW Lithuania
153 Q13 Darbhanga Bihār, N India
38 M9 Darby, Cape headland Alaska, USA
112 I9 Darda Hung. Dárda. Osijek-Baranja, E Croatia
Dárda see Darda
27 T11 Dardanelle Arkansas, C USA
27 S11 Dardanelle, Lake ⊡ Arkansas, C USA
Dardanelles see Çanakkale Boğazı
Dardanelli see Çanakkale
Dardo see Kangding
Dar-el-Beida see Casablanca
136 M14 Darende Malatya, C Turkey
81 J22 Dar es Salaam Dar es Salaam, E Tanzania
81 J22 Dar es Salaam ✕ Pwani, E Tanzania
185 H18 Darfield Canterbury, South Island, New Zealand
106 F7 Darfo Lombardia, N Italy
80 B10 Darfur var. Darfur Massif. cultural region W Sudan
Darfur Massif see Darfur
Darganata/Dargan-Ata see Birata
143 T3 Dargaz var. Darreh Gaz; prev. Moḩammadābād. Khorāsān-Razavī, NE Iran
139 U4 Dargazayn NE Iraq
183 P12 Dargo Victoria, SE Australia
162 L6 Darhan Darhan Uul, N Mongolia
163 N8 Darhan Hentiy, C Mongolia
Darhan see Büreghangay
Darhan Muminggan Lianheqi see Bailingmiao
162 L6 Darhan Uul ◈ province N Mongolia
23 W7 Darien Georgia, SE USA
43 W16 Darién off. Provincia del Darién. ◈ province SE Panama
Darién, Golfo del see Darien, Gulf of
43 X14 Darien, Gulf of Sp. Golfo del Darién. gulf S Caribbean Sea
Darien, Isthmus of see Panama, Istmo de
Darién, Provincia del see Darién
42 K9 Dariense, Cordillera ▲▲ C Nicaragua
43 W15 Darién, Serranía del ▲▲ Colombia/Panama
163 P10 Darīganga var. Ovoot. Sühbaatar, SE Mongolia
Dario see Ciudad Darío
Dariorigum see Vannes
Dariv see Darvi
Darj see Dirj
Darjeeling see Darjiling
153 S12 Darjiling prev. Darjeeling. West Bengal, NE India
Darkehnen see Ozersk
159 S12 Darlag var. Gümai. Qinghai, C China
183 T3 Darling Downs hill range Queensland, E Australia
28 M2 Darling, Lake ⊡ North Dakota, N USA
180 I12 Darling Range ▲▲ Western Australia
182 L8 Darling River ~ New South Wales, SE Australia
97 M15 Darlington N England, UK
21 T12 Darlington South Carolina, SE USA
30 K9 Darlington Wisconsin, N USA
110 G7 Darłowo Zachodnio-pomorskie, NW Poland
101 G19 Darmstadt Hessen, SW Germany
75 S7 Darnah var. Dérna. NE Libya
103 S6 Darney Vosges, NE France
182 M7 Darnick New South Wales, SE Australia
195 Y6 Darnley, Cape cape Antarctica
105 R7 Daroca Aragón, NE Spain
147 S11 Daroot-Korgon var. Daraut-Kurgan. Oshskaya Oblast', SW Kyrgyzstan
61 A23 Darragueira var. Darregueira. Buenos Aires, E Argentina
Darregueira see Darragueira
Darreh Gaz see Dargaz
142 K7 Darreh Shahr var. Darreh-ye Shahr. Īlām, W Iran
Darreh-ye Shahr see Darreh Shahr
32 I7 Darrington Washington, NW USA
25 P1 Darrouzett Texas, SW USA
153 S15 Darsana var. Darshana. Khulna, N Bangladesh
Darshana see Darsana
100 M7 Darss peninsula NE Germany
100 M7 Darsser Ort cape NE Germany
97 J24 Dart ~ SW England, UK
Dartang see Baqên
97 P22 Dartford SE England, UK
182 L12 Dartmoor Victoria, SE Australia
97 I24 Dartmoor moorland SW England, UK
13 Q15 Dartmouth Nova Scotia, SE Canada
97 J24 Dartmouth SW England, UK
15 Y6 Dartmouth ~ Québec, SE Canada
183 Q11 Dartmouth Reservoir ⊡ Victoria, SE Australia
Dartuch, Cabo see Artrutx, Cap d'
186 C9 Daru Western, SW Papua New Guinea
112 G9 Daruvar Hung. Daruvár. Bjelovar-Bilogora, NE Croatia
Daruvár see Daruvar
Darvaza see Derweze, Turkmenistan
Darvaza see Darvoza, Uzbekistan
Darvazskiy Khrebet see Darvoz, Qatorkŭhi
Darvel Bay see Lahad Datu, Teluk
Darvel, Teluk see Lahad Datu, Teluk
162 F8 Darvi var. Dariv. Govĭ-Altay, W Mongolia
162 F7 Darvi var. Bulgan. Hovd, W Mongolia
148 L9 Darvīshān var. Darweshan, Garmser. Helmand, S Afghanistan
147 O10 Darvoza Rus. Darvaza. Jizzax Viloyati, C Uzbekistan
147 R13 Darvoz, Qatorkŭhi Rus. Darvazskiy Khrebet. ▲▲ C Tajikistan
Darweshan see Darvīshān
63 J15 Darwin Río Negro, S Argentina
181 O1 Darwin prev. Palmerston, Port Darwin. territory capital Northern Territory, N Australia
65 D24 Darwin var. Darwin Settlement. East Falkland, Falkland Islands
62 H8 Darwin, Cordillera ▲▲ N Chile
Darwin Settlement see Darwin
57 B17 Darwin, Volcán Ѫ Galapagos Islands, Ecuador, E Pacific Ocean
149 S8 Darya Khān Punjab, E Pakistan
145 O15 Dar'yalyktakyr, Ravnina plain S Kazakhstan
143 T11 Dārzīn Kermān, S Iran
Dashennongjia see Shennong Ding
Dashhowuz see Daşoguz
Dashhowuz Welayaty see Daşoguz Welaýaty
162 K7 Dashinchilen var. Süüj. Bulgan, C Mongolia
119 O16 Dashkawka Rus. Dashkovka. Mahilyowskaya Voblasts', E Belarus
Dashkhovuz see Daşoguz Welaýaty
Dashkhovuzskiy Velayat see Daşoguz Welaýaty
Dashköpri see Daşköpri
Dashkovka see Dashkawka
148 J15 Dasht ~ SW Pakistan
Dasht-i see Bābūs, Dasht-e
Dashtidzhum see Dashtijum
147 R13 Dashtijum Rus. Dashtidzhum. SW Tajikistan
149 W7 Daska Punjab, NE Pakistan
146 J16 Daşköpri var. Dashköpri, Rus. Tashkepri. Mary Welaýaty, S Turkmenistan
146 H8 Daşoguz Rus. Dashkhovuz, Turkm. Dashhowuz; prev. Tashauz. Daşoguz Welaýaty, N Turkmenistan
146 E9 Daşoguz Welaýaty var. Dashhowuz Welayaty, Rus. Dashkhovuz, Dashkhovuzskiy Velayat. ◈ province N Turkmenistan
Đa, Sông see Black River
77 R15 Dassa var. Dassa-Zoumé. S Benin
Dassa-Zoumé see Dassa
29 U8 Dassel Minnesota, N USA
152 H3 Dastegil Sar ▲ N India
136 C16 Datça Muğla, SW Turkey
165 R4 Date Hokkaidō, NE Japan
154 I8 Datia prev. Duttia. Madhya Pradesh, C India
Dåtnejaevrie see Tunnsjøen
159 T10 Datong var. Qiaotou. Qinghai, C China
161 N2 Datong var. Tatung, Ta-t'ung. Shanxi, C China
Datong see Tong'an
159 S8 Datong He ~ C China
159 S9 Datong Shan ▲▲ C China
169 C10 Datu, Tanjung cape Indonesia/Malaysia
Datu, Teluk see Lahad Datu, Teluk
Daua see Dawa Wenz
172 H16 Dauban, Mount ▲ Silhouette, NE Seychelles
149 T7 Dāūd Khel Punjab, E Pakistan
119 G15 Daugai Alytus, S Lithuania
Daugava see Western Dvina
118 J11 Daugavpils Ger. Dünaburg; prev. Rus. Dvinsk. Daugvapils, SE Latvia
Dauka see Dawkah
Daulatabad see Malāyer
101 D18 Daun Rheinland-Pfalz, W Germany
155 E14 Daund prev. Dhond. Mahārāshtra, W India
166 M12 Daung Kyun island S Myanmar (Burma)
9 W15 Dauphin Manitoba, S Canada
103 S13 Dauphiné cultural region E France
23 N9 Dauphin Island island Alabama, S USA
9 X15 Dauphin River Manitoba, S Canada
77 V12 Daura Katsina, N Nigeria
152 H12 Dausa prev. Daosa. Rājasthān, N India
Dauwa see Dawwah
137 Y10 Däväçi Rus. Divichi. NE Azerbaijan
155 F18 Dāvangere Karnātaka, W India
171 Q8 Davao off. Davao City. Mindanao, S Philippines
Davao City see Davao
171 Q8 Davao Gulf gulf Mindanao, S Philippines
15 Q11 Daveluyville Québec, SE Canada
29 Z14 Davenport Iowa, C USA
32 L8 Davenport Washington, NW USA
43 P16 David Chiriquí, W Panama
15 O11 David ~ Québec, SE Canada
29 R15 David City Nebraska, C USA
David-Gorodok see Davyd-Haradok
9 T16 Davidson Saskatchewan, S Canada
21 R10 Davidson North Carolina, SE USA
26 K12 Davidson Oklahoma, C USA
39 S6 Davidson Mountains ▲▲ Alaska, USA
172 M8 Davie Ridge undersea feature W Indian Ocean
182 A1 Davies, Mount ▲ South Australia
35 O7 Davis California, W USA
27 N12 Davis Oklahoma, C USA
195 Y7 Davis Australian research station Antarctica
194 H3 Davis Coast physical region Antarctica
18 C16 Davis, Mount ▲ Pennsylvania, NE USA
24 K9 Davis Mountains ▲▲ Texas, SW USA
195 Z9 Davis Sea sea Antarctica
65 O20 Davis Seamounts undersea feature S Atlantic Ocean
196 M13 Davis Strait strait Baffin Bay/Labrador Sea
127 U5 Davlekanovo Respublika Bashkortostan, W Russian Federation
108 J9 Davos Rmsch. Tavau. Graubünden, E Switzerland
119 J20 Davyd-Haradok Pol. Dawidgródek, Rus. David-Gorodok. Brestskaya Voblasts', SW Belarus
163 U12 Dawa Liaoning, NE China
141 O11 Dawāsir, Wādī ad dry watercourse S Saudi Arabia
81 K15 Dawa Wenz var. Daua, Webi Daawo. ~ E Africa
Dawaymah, Birkat ad see Umm al Baqar, Hawr
Dawei see Tavoy
119 K14 Dawhinava Rus. Dolginovo. Minskaya Voblasts', N Belarus
Dawidgródek see Davyd-Haradok
141 V12 Dawkah var. Dauka. SW Oman
Dawlat Qaṭar see Qatar
24 M3 Dawn Texas, SW USA
Dawo see Maqên
140 M11 Daws Al Bāḩah, SW Saudi Arabia

10 H5 Dawson var. Dawson City. Yukon Territory, NW Canada
23 S6 Dawson Georgia, SE USA
29 S9 Dawson Minnesota, N USA
Dawson City see Dawson
9 N13 Dawson Creek British Columbia, W Canada
10 H7 Dawson Range ▲▲ Yukon Territory, W Canada
181 Y9 Dawson River ⇝ Queensland, E Australia
10 J15 Dawsons Landing British Columbia, SW Canada
20 I7 Dawson Springs Kentucky, S USA
23 S2 Dawsonville Georgia, SE USA
160 G8 Dawu var. Xianshui. Sichuan, C China
Dawu see Maqên
Dawukou see Shizuishan
141 Y10 Dawwah var. Dauwa. W Oman
102 J15 Dax var. Ax; anc. Aquae Augustae, Aquae Tarbelicae. Landes, SW France
Daxian see Dazhou
Daxue see Wencheng
160 G9 Daxue Shan ▲▲ C China
Dayan see Lijiang
160 G12 Dayao var. Jinbi. Yunnan, SW China
Dayishan see Gaoyou
183 N12 Daylesford Victoria, SE Australia
35 U10 Daylight Pass pass California, W USA
61 D17 Daymán, Río ⇝ N Uruguay
Dayong see Zhangjiajie
Dayr see Ad Dayr
138 G10 Dayr 'Allā var. Deir 'Alla. Al Balqā', N Jordan
139 N4 Dayr az Zawr var. Deir ez Zor. Dayr az Zawr, E Syria
138 M5 Dayr az Zawr off. Muḩāfaẓat Dayr az Zawr, var. Dayr Az-Zor. ◆ governorate E Syria
Dayr az Zawr, Muḩāfaẓat see Dayr az Zawr
Dayr Az-Zor see Dayr az Zawr
Dayrūṭ see Dairûṭ
9 Q15 Daysland Alberta, SW Canada
31 R14 Dayton Ohio, N USA
20 L10 Dayton Tennessee, S USA
25 W11 Dayton Texas, SW USA
32 L10 Dayton Washington, NW USA
23 X10 Daytona Beach Florida, SE USA
169 U12 Dayu Borneo, C Indonesia
161 O13 Dayu Ling ▲▲ S China
161 R7 Da Yunhe Eng. Grand Canal. canal E China
161 S11 Dayu Shan island SE China
160 K8 Dazhou prev. Dachuan, Daxian. Sichuan, C China
160 J9 Dazhu var. Zhuyang. Sichuan, C China
160 J9 Dazu var. Longgang. Chongqing Shi, C China
83 H24 De Aar Northern Cape, C South Africa
194 K5 Deacon, Cape headland Antarctica
39 R5 Deadhorse Alaska, USA
33 T12 Dead Indian Peak ▲ Wyoming, C USA
23 R9 Dead Lake ◎ Florida, SE USA
44 J4 Deadman's Cay Long Island, C Bahamas
138 G11 Dead Sea var. Bahret Lut, Lacus Asphaltites, Ar. Al Baḩr al Mayyit, Baḩrat Lūṭ, Heb. Yam HaMelaḩ. salt lake Israel/Jordan
28 J9 Deadwood South Dakota, N USA
97 Q22 Deal SE England, UK
83 I22 Dealesville Free State, C South Africa
161 P10 De'an var. Puting. Jiangxi, S China
62 K9 Deán Funes Córdoba, C Argentina
194 L12 Dean Island island Antarctica
Deanuvuotna see Tanafjorden
31 S10 Dearborn Michigan, N USA
27 R3 Dearborn Missouri, C USA
Deargget see Tārendö
32 K9 Deary Idaho, NW USA
32 M9 Deary Washington, NW USA
10 J10 Dease ⇝ British Columbia, W Canada
10 J10 Dease Lake British Columbia, W Canada
35 U11 Death Valley California, W USA
35 U11 Death Valley valley California, W USA
92 L9 Deatnu Fin. Tenojoki, Nor. Tana. ⇝ Finland/Norway see also Tenojoki
92 M8 Deatnu Fin. Tenojoki, Nor. Tana. ⇝ Finland/Norway
Deatnu Tenojoki
102 L4 Deauville Calvados, N France
117 X7 Debal'tseve Rus. Debal'tsevo. Donets'ka Oblast', SE Ukraine
Debal'tsevo see Debal'tseve
113 M19 Debar Ger. Dibra, Turk. Debre. W FYR Macedonia
39 O9 Debauch Mountain ▲ Alaska, USA
De Behagle see Laï
25 X7 De Berry Texas, SW USA
127 T2 Debesy Udmurtskaya Respublika, NW Russian Federation
111 N16 Dębica Podkarpackie, SE Poland
De Bildt see De Bilt
98 J11 De Bilt var. De Bildt. Utrecht, C Netherlands
123 T9 Debin Magadanskaya Oblast', E Russian Federation
110 N13 Dęblin Rus. Ivangorod. Lubelskie, E Poland
110 D10 Dębno Zachodnio-pomorskie, NW Poland
39 S10 Deborah, Mount ▲ Alaska, USA
33 N8 De Borgia Montana, NW USA
Debra Birhan see Debre Birhan
Debra Marcos see Debre Mark'os
Debra Tabor see Debre Tabor
Debre see Debar
80 J13 Debre Birhan var. Debra Birhan. Amhara, N Ethiopia
111 N22 Debrecen Ger. Debreczin, Rom. Debreţin; prev. Debreczen. Hajdú-Bihar, E Hungary
Debreczen/Debreczin see Debrecen
80 I12 Debre Mark'os var. Debra Marcos. Amhara, N Ethiopia
113 N19 Debrešte SW FYR Macedonia
80 J11 Debre Tabor var. Debra Tabor. Amhara, N Ethiopia
Debreţin see Debrecen
80 J13 Debre Zeyt Oromo, C Ethiopia
113 L16 Dečani Kosovo, S Serbia
23 P2 Decatur Alabama, S USA
23 S3 Decatur Georgia, SE USA
30 L13 Decatur Illinois, N USA
31 Q12 Decatur Indiana, N USA
22 M5 Decatur Mississippi, S USA
29 S14 Decatur Nebraska, C USA
25 S6 Decatur Texas, SW USA
20 H9 Decaturville Tennessee, S USA
103 O13 Decazeville Aveyron, S France
155 H17 Deccan Hind. Dakshin. plateau C India
14 J8 Decelles, Réservoir ▣ Québec, SE Canada
12 K2 Déception Québec, NE Canada
160 G11 Dechang var. Dezhou. Sichuan, C China
111 C15 Děčín Ger. Tetschen. Ústecký Kraj, NW Czech Republic
103 P9 Decize Nièvre, C France
98 I6 De Cocksdorp Noord-Holland, NW Netherlands
29 X11 Decorah Iowa, C USA
Dedeagaç/Dedeagach see Alexandroúpoli
188 C15 Dededo N Guam
98 N9 Dedemsvaart Overijssel, E Netherlands
19 O11 Dedham Massachusetts, NE USA
63 H19 Dedo, Cerro ▲ SW Argentina
77 O13 Dédougou W Burkina
124 G15 Dedovichi Pskovskaya Oblast', W Russian Federation
Dedu see Wudalianchi
155 J24 Deduru Oya ⇝ W Sri Lanka
83 N14 Dedza Central, S Malawi
83 N14 Dedza Mountain ▲ C Malawi
96 K9 Dee ⇝ NE Scotland, UK
97 J19 Dee Wel. Afon Dyfrdwy. ⇝ England/Wales, UK
Deep Bay see Chilumba
21 T3 Deep Creek Lake ▣ Maryland, NE USA
36 J4 Deep Creek Range ▲▲ Utah, W USA
27 P10 Deep Fork ⇝ Oklahoma, C USA
14 J11 Deep River Ontario, SE Canada
21 T10 Deep River ⇝ North Carolina, SE USA
183 U4 Deepwater New South Wales, SE Australia
31 S14 Deer Creek Lake ◎ Ohio, N USA
23 Z15 Deerfield Beach Florida, SE USA
39 N8 Deering Alaska, USA
38 M16 Deer Island island Alaska, USA
19 S7 Deer Isle island Maine, NE USA
13 S11 Deer Lake Newfoundland and Labrador, SE Canada
99 D18 Deerlijk West-Vlaanderen, W Belgium
33 Q10 Deer Lodge Montana, NW USA
32 L8 Deer Park Washington, NW USA
29 U5 Deer River Minnesota, N USA
Deés see Dej
Defeng see Liping
31 R11 Defiance Ohio, N USA
23 Q8 De Funiak Springs Florida, SE USA
95 L23 Degeberga Skåne, S Sweden
104 H12 Degebe, Ribeira ⇝ S Portugal
80 M13 Degeh Bur Somali, E Ethiopia
15 U9 Dégelis Québec, SE Canada
77 U17 Degema Rivers, S Nigeria
95 L16 Degerfors Örebro, C Sweden
193 R14 De Gerlache Seamounts undersea feature SE Pacific Ocean
101 N21 Deggendorf Bayern, SE Germany
80 I11 Degoma Amhara, N Ethiopia
De Gordyk see Gorredijk
27 T12 De Gray Lake ▣ Arkansas, C USA
180 J6 De Grey River ⇝ Western Australia
126 M10 Degtevo Rostovskaya Oblast', SW Russian Federation
143 X13 Dehak Sīstān va Balūchestān, SE Iran
143 R9 Deh 'Alī Kermān, C Iran
Dehbārez see Rūdān
143 P10 Deh Bīd Fārs, C Iran
142 M10 Deh Dasht Kohkīlūyeh va Būyer AḩMad, SW Iran
75 N8 Dehibat SE Tunisia
Dehli see Delhi
142 K8 Dehlorān Īlām, W Iran
147 N13 Dehqonobod Rus. Dekhkanabad. Qashqadaryo Viloyati, S Uzbekistan
152 J9 Dehra Dūn Uttaranchal, N India
153 O14 Dehri Bihār, N India
148 K10 Deh Shū var. Deshu. Helmand, S Afghanistan
163 W9 Dehui Jilin, NE China
99 D17 Deinze Oost-Vlaanderen, NW Belgium
Deir 'Alla see Dayr 'Allā
Deir ez Zor see Dayr az Zawr
Deirgeirt, Loch see Derg, Lough
116 H9 Dej Hung. Dés; prev. Deés. Cluj, NW Romania
95 K15 Deje Värmland, C Sweden
171 Y15 De Jongs, Tanjung headland Papua, SE Indonesia
De Jouwer see Joure
30 M10 De Kalb Illinois, N USA
22 M5 De Kalb Mississippi, S USA
25 W5 De Kalb Texas, SW USA
Dekéleia see Dhekéleia
79 K20 Dekese Kasai Occidental, C Dem. Rep. Congo
Dekhkanabad see Dehqonobod
79 I14 Dékoa Kémo, C Central African Republic
98 H6 De Koog Noord-Holland, NW Netherlands
30 M9 Delafield Wisconsin, N USA
61 C23 De La Garma Buenos Aires, E Argentina
14 K10 Delahey, Lac ◎ Québec, SE Canada
80 E11 Delami Southern Kordofan, C Sudan
23 X11 De Land Florida, SE USA
35 R12 Delano California, W USA
29 V8 Delano Minnesota, N USA
36 K6 Delano Peak ▲ Utah, W USA
Delap-Uliga-Darrit see Dalap-Uliga-Djarrit
148 L7 Delārām Nīmrūz, SW Afghanistan
38 F17 Delarof Islands island group Aleutian Islands, Alaska, USA
30 M9 Delavan Wisconsin, N USA
31 S13 Delaware Ohio, N USA
18 I17 Delaware off. State of Delaware, also known as Blue Hen State, Diamond State, First State. ◆ state NE USA
18 I17 Delaware Bay bay NE USA
24 J8 Delaware Mountains ▲▲ Texas, SW USA
18 I12 Delaware River ⇝ NE USA
27 Q3 Delaware River ⇝ Kansas, C USA
18 J14 Delaware Water Gap valley New Jersey/Pennsylvania, NE USA
101 G14 Delbrück Nordrhein-Westfalen, W Germany
9 Q15 Delburne Alberta, SW Canada
172 M12 Del Cano Rise undersea feature SW Indian Ocean
113 Q18 Delčevo NE FYR Macedonia
Delcommune, Lac see Nzilo, Lac
98 O10 Delden Overijssel, E Netherlands
183 R12 Delegate New South Wales, SE Australia
De Lemmer see Lemmer
108 D7 Delémont Ger. Delsberg. Jura, NW Switzerland
25 R7 De Leon Texas, SW USA
115 F18 Delfoí Stereá Ellás, C Greece
98 G12 Delft Zuid-Holland, W Netherlands
155 J23 Delft island NW Sri Lanka
98 O5 Delfzijl Groningen, NE Netherlands
0 E9 Delgada Fan undersea feature NE Pacific Ocean
42 F7 Delgado San Salvador, SW El Salvador
82 Q12 Delgado, Cabo headland N Mozambique
162 G8 Delger var. Taygan. Govĭ-Altay, C Mongolia
163 O9 Delgereh var. Hongor. Dornogovĭ, SE Mongolia
162 J8 Delgerhaan var. Hujirt. Töv, C Mongolia
162 K9 Delgerhangay var. Hashaat. Dundgovĭ, C Mongolia
162 L9 Delgertsogt var. Amardalay. Dundgovĭ, C Mongolia
162 L9 Delgertsogt var Amardalay. Dundgovĭ, C Mongolia
80 E6 Delgo Northern, N Sudan
159 R10 Delhi var. Delhi. Qinghai, C China
152 I10 Delhi var. Dehli, Hind. Dilli, hist. Shahjahanabad. union territory capital Delhi, N India
22 J5 Delhi Louisiana, S USA
18 J11 Delhi New York, NE USA
152 I10 Delhi ◆ union territory NW India
136 J17 Deli Burnu headland S Turkey
136 J12 Delice Çayı ⇝ C Turkey
55 X10 Délices C French Guiana
40 J6 Delicias var. Ciudad Delicias. Chihuahua, N Mexico
143 N7 Delījān var. Dalijan, Diliján. Markazī, W Iran
112 P12 Deli Jovan ▲▲ E Serbia
Déli-Kárpátok see Carpaţii Meridionali
8 I8 Déljne prev. Fort Franklin. Northwest Territories, NW Canada
Delingha see Delhi
15 Q7 Delisle Québec, SE Canada
9 T15 Delisle Saskatchewan, S Canada
101 M15 Delitzsch Sachsen, E Germany
33 Q12 Dell Montana, NW USA
24 I7 Dell City Texas, SW USA
103 U7 Delle Territoire-de-Belfort, E France
36 J9 Dellenbaugh, Mount ▲ Arizona, SW USA
29 R11 Dell Rapids South Dakota, N USA
21 Y4 Delmar Maryland, NE USA
18 K11 Delmar New York, NE USA
100 G11 Delmenhorst Niedersachsen, NW Germany
112 C9 Delnice Primorje-Gorski Kotar, NW Croatia
37 R7 Del Norte Colorado, C USA
39 N6 De Long Mountains ▲▲ Alaska, USA
183 P16 Deloraine Tasmania, SE Australia
9 W17 Deloraine Manitoba, S Canada
31 O12 Delphi Indiana, N USA
31 Q12 Delphos Ohio, N USA
23 Z15 Delray Beach Florida, SE USA
25 O12 Del Rio Texas, SW USA
Delsberg see Delémont
94 N11 Delsbo Gävleborg, C Sweden
37 P6 Delta Colorado, C USA
36 K5 Delta Utah, W USA
77 T17 Delta ◆ state S Nigeria
55 Q6 Delta Amacuro off. Territorio Delta Amacuro. ◆ federal district NE Venezuela
Delta Amacuro, Territorio see Delta Amacuro
39 S9 Delta Junction Alaska, USA
23 X11 Deltona Florida, SE USA
183 T5 Delungra New South Wales, SE Australia
162 D6 Delüün var. Rashaant. Bayan-Ölgiy, W Mongolia
154 C12 Delvāda Gujarāt, W India
61 B21 Del Valle Buenos Aires, E Argentina
Delvina see Delvinë
115 C15 Delvináki var. Dhelvinákion; prev. Pogónion. Ípeiros, W Greece
113 L23 Delvinë var. Delvina, It. Delvino. Vlorë, S Albania
Delvino see Delvinë
116 I7 Delyatyn Ivano-Frankivs'ka Oblast', W Ukraine
127 U5 Dëma ⇝ W Russian Federation
105 O5 Demanda, Sierra de la ▲▲ W Spain
39 T5 Demarcation Point headland Alaska, USA
79 K21 Demba Kasai Occidental, C Dem. Rep. Congo
172 H13 Dembéni Grande Comore, NW Comoros
79 M15 Dembia Mbomou, SE Central African Republic
Dembidollo see Dembī Dolo
80 H13 Dembī Dolo var. Dembidollo. Oromo, C Ethiopia
152 K6 Demchok China/India
152 L6 Demchok var. Dêmqog. disputed region China/India see also Dêmqog
Demchok see Dêmqog
98 I12 De Meern Utrecht, C Netherlands
99 I17 Demer ⇝ C Belgium
64 H12 Demerara Plain undersea feature W Atlantic Ocean
64 H12 Demerara Plateau undersea feature W Atlantic Ocean
55 T9 Demerara River ⇝ NE Guyana
126 H3 Demidov Smolenskaya Oblast', W Russian Federation
37 Q15 Deming New Mexico, SW USA
32 H6 Deming Washington, NW USA
58 E10 Demini, Rio ⇝ NW Brazil
136 D13 Demirci Manisa, W Turkey
113 P19 Demir Kapija prev. Železna Vrata. SE FYR Macedonia
114 N11 Demirköy Kırklareli, NW Turkey
100 N9 Demmin Mecklenburg-Vorpommern, NE Germany
23 O5 Demopolis Alabama, S USA
31 N11 Demotte Indiana, N USA
158 F13 Dêmqog var. Demchok. China/India
152 L6 Dêmqog var. Demchok. disputed region China/India see also Demchok
Dêmqog see Demchok
Dêmqog see Demchok
171 Y13 Demta Papua, E Indonesia
121 K11 Dem'yanka ⇝ C Russian Federation
124 H15 Demyansk Novgorodskaya Oblast', W Russian Federation
122 H10 Dem'yanskoye Tyumenskaya Oblast', C Russian Federation
103 P2 Denain Nord, N France
39 S10 Denali Alaska, USA
Denali see McKinley, Mount
81 M14 Denan Somali, E Ethiopia
Denau see Denow
97 J18 Denbigh Wel. Dinbych. NE Wales, UK
97 J18 Denbigh cultural region N Wales, UK
98 I6 Den Burg Noord-Holland, NW Netherlands
99 F18 Dender Fr. Dendre. ⇝ W Belgium
99 F18 Denderleeuw Oost-Vlaanderen, NW Belgium
99 F17 Dendermonde Fr. Termonde. Oost-Vlaanderen, NW Belgium
Dendre see Dender
194 I9 Dendtler Island island Antarctica
98 P10 Denekamp Overijssel, E Netherlands
77 W12 Dengas Zinder, S Niger
Dêngkagoin see T'ewo
162 L13 Dengkou var. Bayan Gol. Nei Mongol Zizhiqu, N China
159 Q14 Dêngqên var. Gyamotang. Xizang Zizhiqu, W China
Deng Xian see Dengzhou
160 M7 Dengzhou prev. Deng Xian. Henan, C China
Dengzhou see Penglai
Den Haag see 's-Gravenhage
180 H10 Denham Western Australia
98 N9 Den Ham Overijssel, E Netherlands
44 J12 Denham, Mount ▲ C Jamaica
22 J8 Denham Springs Louisiana, S USA
98 I7 Den Helder Noord-Holland, NW Netherlands
105 T11 Dénia País Valenciano, E Spain
189 Q8 Denig W Nauru
183 N10 Deniliquin New South Wales, SE Australia
29 T14 Denison Iowa, C USA
25 U5 Denison Texas, SW USA
144 L8 Denisovka prev. Ordzhonikidze. Kostanay, N Kazakhstan
136 D15 Denizli Denizli, SW Turkey
136 D15 Denizli ◆ province SW Turkey
Denjong see Sikkim
183 S7 Denman New South Wales, SE Australia
195 Y10 Denman Glacier glacier Antarctica
21 R14 Denmark South Carolina, SE USA
95 G23 Denmark off. Kingdom of Denmark, Dan. Danmark; anc. Hafnia. ◆ monarchy N Europe
Denmark, Kingdom of see Denmark
92 H1 Denmark Strait var. Danmarksstraedet. strait Greenland/Iceland
45 T11 Dennery E Saint Lucia
98 I7 Den Oever Noord-Holland, NW Netherlands
147 O13 Denow Rus. Denau. Surkhondaryo Viloyati, S Uzbekistan
169 U17 Denpasar prev. Paloe. Bali, C Indonesia
116 E12 Denta Timiş, W Romania
21 Y3 Denton Maryland, NE USA
25 T6 Denton Texas, SW USA
186 G9 D'Entrecasteaux Islands island group SE Papua New Guinea
37 T4 Denver state capital Colorado, C USA
37 T4 Denver ✈ Colorado, C USA
24 L6 Denver City Texas, SW USA
152 J9 Deoband Uttar Pradesh, N India
Deoghar see Devghar
154 E13 Deolāli Mahārāshtra, W India
154 I10 Deori Madhya Pradesh, C India
153 O12 Deoria Uttar Pradesh, N India
99 A17 De Panne West-Vlaanderen, W Belgium
Departamento del Quindío see Quindío
Departamento de Narino, see Narino
54 M5 Dependencia Federal off. Territorio Dependencia Federal. ◇ federal dependency N Venezuela
Dependencia Federal, Territorio see Dependencia Federal
30 M7 De Pere Wisconsin, N USA
18 D10 Depew New York, NE USA
99 E17 De Pinte Oost-Vlaanderen, NW Belgium
25 V5 Deport Texas, SW USA
123 Q8 Deputatskiy Respublika Sakha (Yakutiya), NE Russian Federation
Dêqên see Dagzê
27 S13 De Queen Arkansas, S USA
22 G8 De Quincy Louisiana, S USA
81 J20 Dera spring/well S Kenya
Der'a see Dar'ā
Déraa see Dar'ā
Der'a/Derá/Déraa see Dar'ā
149 S10 Dera Ghāzi Khān var. Dera Ghāzikhān. Punjab, C Pakistan
Dera Ghāzikhān see Dera Ghāzi Khān
149 S8 Dera Ismāīl Khān North-West Frontier Province, C Pakistan
113 L16 Deravica ▲ S Serbia
116 L6 Derazhnya Khmel'nyts'ka Oblast', W Ukraine
127 R17 Derbent Respublika Dagestan, SW Russian Federation
147 N13 Derbent Surkhondaryo Viloyati, S Uzbekistan
Derbisīye see Darbāsīyah
79 M15 Derbissaka Mbomou, SE Central African Republic
180 L4 Derby Western Australia
97 M19 Derby C England, UK
27 N7 Derby Kansas, C USA
97 L18 Derbyshire cultural region C England, UK
112 O11 Đerdap physical region E Serbia
Dereli see Gónoi
162 L9 Deren var. Tsant. Dundgovĭ, C Mongolia
171 W13 Derew ⇝ Papua, E Indonesia
127 R8 Dergachi Saratovskaya Oblast', W Russian Federation
Dergachi see Derhachi
97 C19 Derg, Lough Ir. Loch Deirgeirt. ◎ W Ireland
117 V5 Derhachi Rus. Dergachi. Kharkivs'ka Oblast', E Ukraine
22 G8 De Ridder Louisiana, S USA
137 P16 Derik Mardin, SE Turkey
83 E20 Derm Hardap, C Namibia
144 M14 Dermentobe prev. Dyurment'yube. Kzyl-Orda, S Kazakhstan
27 W14 Dermott Arkansas, C USA
Dérna see Darnah
Dernberg, Cape see Dolphin Head
22 J11 Dernieres, Isles island group Louisiana, S USA
102 I4 Déroute, Passage de la strait Channel Islands/France
Derrá see Dar'ā
Derry see Londonderry
Dertona see Tortona
Dertosa see Tortosa
80 H8 Derudeb Red Sea, NE Sudan
112 H10 Derventa ◇ Republika Srpska, N Bosnia and Herzegovina
183 O16 Derwent Bridge Tasmania, SE Australia
183 O17 Derwent, River ⇝ Tasmania, SE Australia
146 F10 Derweze Rus. Darvaza. Ahal Welaýaty, C Turkmenistan
Deržavinsk see Derzhavinsk
145 O9 Derzhavinsk var. Deržavinsk. ◆ Akmola, C Kazakhstan
Dés see Dej
57 J18 Desaguadero Puno, S Peru
57 J18 Desaguadero, Río ⇝ Bolivia/Peru
191 W9 Désappointement, Îles du island group Îles Tuamotu, C French Polynesia
27 W11 Des Arc Arkansas, C USA
14 C10 Desbarats Ontario, S Canada
62 H13 Descabezado Grande, Volcán ▲ C Chile
40 B2 Descanso Baja California, NW Mexico
102 L9 Descartes Indre-et-Loire, C France
9 T13 Deschambault Lake ◎ Saskatchewan, C Canada
Deschnaer Koppe see Velká Deštná
32 I11 Deschutes River ⇝ Oregon, NW USA
80 J12 Desē var. Desse, It. Dessie. Amhara, N Ethiopia
63 I20 Deseado, Río ⇝ S Argentina
106 F8 Desenzano del Garda Lombardia, N Italy
36 K3 Deseret Peak ▲ Utah, W USA
64 P6 Deserta Grande island Madeira, Portugal, NE Atlantic Ocean
64 P6 Desertas, Ilhas island group Madeira, Portugal, NE Atlantic Ocean
35 X16 Desert Center California, W USA
35 V15 Desert Hot Springs California, W USA
14 K10 Désert, Lac ◎ Québec, SE Canada
36 J2 Desert Peak ▲ Utah, W USA
31 R11 Deshler Ohio, N USA
Deshu see Deh Shū
Desiderii Fanum see St-Dizier
106 D7 Desio Lombardia, N Italy
115 E15 Deskáti var. Dheskáti. Dytikí Makedonía, N Greece
28 L2 Des Lacs River ⇝ North Dakota, N USA
27 X6 Desloge Missouri, C USA
9 Q12 Desmarais Alberta, W Canada
29 Q10 De Smet South Dakota, N USA
29 V14 Des Moines state capital Iowa, C USA
17 N9 Des Moines River ⇝ C USA
117 P4 Desna ⇝ Russian Federation/Ukraine
116 G14 Desnăţui ⇝ S Romania
63 F24 Desolación, Isla island S Chile
29 V14 De Soto Iowa, C USA
23 Q4 De Soto Falls waterfall Alabama, S USA
83 I25 Despatch Eastern Cape, S South Africa
105 N12 Despeñaperros, Desfiladero de pass S Spain
31 N10 Des Plaines Illinois, N USA
115 J21 Despotikó island Kykládes, Greece, Aegean Sea
112 N12 Despotovac Serbia, E Serbia
101 M14 Dessau Sachsen-Anhalt, E Germany
Desse see Desē
99 J16 Dessel Antwerpen, N Belgium
Dessie see Desē
Destêrro see Florianópolis
23 P9 Destin Florida, SE USA
Deštná see Velká Deštná
193 T10 Desventurados, Islas de los island group W Chile
103 N1 Desvres Pas-de-Calais, N France
116 E12 Deta Ger. Detta. Timiş, W Romania
101 H14 Detmold Nordrhein-Westfalen, W Germany
31 S10 Detroit Michigan, N USA
25 W5 Detroit Texas, SW USA
31 S10 Detroit ⇝ Canada/USA
29 S6 Detroit Lakes Minnesota, N USA
31 S10 Detroit Metropolitan ✈ Michigan, N USA
Detta see Deta
167 S10 Det Udom Ubon Ratchathani, E Thailand
111 K20 Detva Hung. Gyeva. Bankobýstricky Kraj, C Slovakia
154 G13 Deūlgaon Rāja Mahārāshtra, C India
99 L15 Deurne Noord-Brabant, SE Netherlands
99 H16 Deurne ✈ (Antwerpen) Antwerpen, N Belgium
Deutsch-Brod see Havlíčkův Brod
Deutschendorf see Poprad
Deutsch-Eylau see Iława
109 Y6 Deutschkreutz Burgenland, E Austria
Deutsch Krone see Wałcz
Deutschland/Deutschland, Bundesrepublik see Germany
109 V9 Deutschlandsberg Steiermark, SE Austria
Deutsch-Südwestafrika see Namibia
109 Y3 Deutsch-Wagram Niederösterreich, E Austria
Deux-Ponts see Zweibrücken
14 I11 Deux Rivieres Ontario, SE Canada
102 K9 Deux-Sèvres ◆ department W France
116 G11 Deva Ger. Diemrich, Hung. Déva. Hunedoara, W Romania
Déva see Deva
Deva see Chester
Devana see Aberdeen
Devana Castra see Chester
Devđelija see Gevgelija
136 L12 Deveci Dağları ▲▲ N Turkey
137 P15 Devegeçidi Barajı ▣ SE Turkey
136 K15 Develi Kayseri, C Turkey
98 M11 Deventer Overijssel, E Netherlands
15 O10 Devenyns, Lac ◎ Québec, SE Canada
96 K8 Deveron ⇝ NE Scotland, UK
153 R14 Devghar prev. Deoghar. Jhārkhand, NE India
27 R10 Devil's Den plateau Arkansas, C USA
35 R7 Devils Gate pass California, W USA
30 J2 Devils Island island Apostle Islands, Wisconsin, N USA
Devil's Island see Diable, Île du
29 P3 Devils Lake North Dakota, N USA
31 R10 Devils Lake ◎ Michigan, N USA
29 O3 Devils Lake ◎ North Dakota, N USA
35 W13 Devils Playground desert California, W USA
25 O11 Devils River ⇝ Texas, SW USA
33 Y12 Devils Tower ▲ Wyoming, C USA
114 I11 Devin prev. Dovlen. Smolyan, S Bulgaria
25 R12 Devine Texas, SW USA
152 H13 Devli Rājasthān, N India
Devne see Devnya
114 N8 Devnya prev. Devne. Varna, E Bulgaria
31 U14 Devola Ohio, N USA
Devoll see Devollit, Lumi i
113 M21 Devollit, Lumi i var. Devoll. ⇝ SE Albania
9 Q14 Devon Alberta, SW Canada

◆ Country
● Country Capital
◇ Dependent Territory
○ Dependent Territory Capital
◆ Administrative Regions
✈ International Airport
▲ Mountain
▲▲ Mountain Range
Volcano
⇝ River
◎ Lake
▣ Reservoir

97 I23 Devon cultural region SW England, UK
197 N10 Devon Island prev. North Devon Island. island Parry Islands, Nunavut, NE Canada
183 O16 Devonport Tasmania, SE Australia
136 H11 Devrek Zonguldak, N Turkey
154 G10 Dewās Madhya Pradesh, C India
De Westerein see Zwaagwesteinde
27 P8 Dewey Oklahoma, C USA
Dewey see Culebra
98 M8 De Wijk Drenthe, NE Netherlands
27 W12 De Witt Arkansas, C USA
29 Z14 De Witt Iowa, C USA
29 R16 De Witt Nebraska, C USA
97 M17 Dewsbury N England, UK
161 Q10 Dexing Jiangxi, S China
27 Y8 Dexter Missouri, C USA
37 U14 Dexter New Mexico, SW USA
160 I8 Deyang Sichuan, C China
182 C4 Dey-Dey, Lake salt lake South Australia
143 S7 Deyhūk Yazd, E Iran
Deynau see Galkynyş
142 L8 Dezfūl var. Dizful. Khūzestān, SW Iran
129 X4 Dezhneva, Mys headland NE Russian Federation
161 P4 Dezhou Shandong, E China
Dezhou see Dechang
Dezh Shāhpūr see Marīvān
Dhaalu Atoll see South Nilandhe Atoll
Dhahran see Aẓ Ẓahrān
Dhahran Al Khobar see Aẓ Ẓahrān al Khubar
153 U14 Dhaka prev. Dacca. ● (Bangladesh) Dhaka, C Bangladesh
153 T15 Dhaka ◆ division C Bangladesh
Dhali see Idálion
141 O15 Dhamār W Yemen
154 K12 Dhamtari Chhattīsgarh, C India
153 Q15 Dhanbād Jhārkhand, NE India
152 L10 Dhangaḍhi var. Dhangarhi. Far Western, W Nepal
Dhangarhi see Dhangaḍhi
Dhank see Ḑank
153 R12 Dhankuṭā Eastern, E Nepal
152 I6 Dhaola Dhār ▲▲ NE India
154 F10 Dhār Madhya Pradesh, C India
153 R12 Dharān var. Dharan Bazar. Eastern, E Nepal
Dharan Bazar see Dharān
155 H21 Dhārāpuram Tamil Nādu, SE India
155 H20 Dharmapuri Tamil Nādu, SE India
155 H18 Dharmavaram Andhra Pradesh, E India
154 M11 Dharmjaygarh Chhattīsgarh, C India
Dharmsāla see Dharmshāla
152 I7 Dharmshāla prev. Dharmsāla. Himāchal Pradesh, N India
155 F17 Dhārwād prev. Dharwar. Karnātaka, SW India
Dharwar see Dhārwād
Dhaulagiri see Dhawalāgiri
153 O10 Dhawalāgiri var Dhaulagiri. ▲ C Nepal
81 L18 Dheere Laaq var. Lak Dera, It. Lach Dera. seasonal river Kenya/Somalia
121 Q3 Dhekeleia Sovereign Base Area UK military installation E Cyprus
121 Q3 Dhekéleia Eng. Dhekelia, Gk. Dekéleia. UK air base SE Cyprus
Dhekélia see Dhekéleia
Dhelvinákion see Delviňáki
113 M22 Dhëmbelit, Majae ▲ S Albania
154 O12 Dhenkānāl Orissa, E India
Dheskáti see Deskáti
138 G11 Dhībān Ma'dabā, NW Jordan
Dhidhimótikhon see Didymóteicho
Dhíkti Ori see Díkti
138 I12 Dhirwah, Wādī adh dry watercourse C Jordan
Dhístomon see Dístomo
Dhodhekánisos see Dodekánisa
Dhodhóni see Dodóni
Dhofar see Ẓufār
Dhomokós see Domokós
Dhond see Daund
155 H17 Dhone Andhra Pradesh, C India
154 B11 Dhorāji Gujarāt, W India
Dhráma see Dráma
154 C10 Dhrāngadhra Gujarāt, W India
Dhrepanon, Akrotírio see Drépano, Akrotírio
153 T13 Dhuburi Assam, NE India
154 F12 Dhule prev. Dhulia. Mahārāshtra, C India
Dhulia see Dhule
Dhún Dealgan, Cuan see Dundalk Bay
Dhún Droma, Cuan see Dundrum Bay
Dhún na nGall, Bá see Donegal Bay
Dhū Shaykh see Qazānīyah
80 Q13 Dhuudo Bari, NE Somalia
81 N15 Dhuusa Marreeb var. Dusa Marreb, It. Dusa Mareb. Galguduud, C Somalia
115 J24 Día island SE Greece
55 Y9 Diable, Île du var. Devil's Island. island N French Guiana
15 N12 Diable, Rivière du ~ Québec, SE Canada
35 N8 Diablo, Mount ▲ California, W USA
35 O9 Diablo Range ▲▲ California, W USA
24 I8 Diablo, Sierra ▲▲ Texas, SW USA
45 O11 Diablotins, Morne ▲ N Dominica
77 N11 Diafarabé Mopti, C Mali
77 N11 Diaka ~ SW Mali
Diakovár see Đakovo
76 I12 Dialakoto S Senegal
61 B18 Diamante Entre Ríos, E Argentina
62 I12 Diamante, Río ~ C Argentina
59 M19 Diamantina Minas Gerais, SE Brazil
59 N17 Diamantina, Chapada ▲▲ E Brazil
173 U11 Diamantina Fracture Zone tectonic feature E Indian Ocean
181 T8 Diamantina River ~ Queensland/South Australia
38 D9 Diamond Head headland O'ahu, Hawai'i, USA
37 P2 Diamond Peak ▲ Colorado, C USA
35 W5 Diamond Peak ▲ Nevada, W USA
Diamond State see Delaware
76 J11 Diamou Kayes, SW Mali
95 I23 Dianalund Vestsjælland, C Denmark
65 G25 Diana's Peak ▲ C Saint Helena
160 M16 Dianbai var. Shuidong. Guangdong, S China
160 G13 Dian Chi ◎ SW China
106 B10 Diano Marina Liguria, NW Italy
163 V11 Diaobingshan var. Tiefa. Liaoning, NE China
77 R13 Diapaga E Burkina
Diarbekr see Diyarbakır
107 J15 Diavolo, Passo del pass C Italy
61 B18 Díaz Santa Fe, C Argentina
141 W6 Dibā al Ḩiṣn var. Dibāh, Dibba. Ash Shāriqah, NE United Arab Emirates
139 S3 Dibaga N Iraq
Dibāh see Dibā al Ḩiṣn
79 L22 Dibaya Kasai Occidental, S Dem. Rep. Congo
Dibba see Dibā al Ḩiṣn
195 W15 Dibble Iceberg Tongue ice feature Antarctica
113 L19 Dibër ◆ district E Albania
83 I20 Dibete Central, SE Botswana
Dibio see Dijon
25 W9 Diboll Texas, SW USA
Dibra see Debar
153 X11 Dibrugarh Assam, NE India
54 G4 Dibulla La Guajira, N Colombia
25 O5 Dickens Texas, SW USA
19 R2 Dickey Maine, NE USA
30 K9 Dickeyville Wisconsin, N USA
28 K5 Dickinson North Dakota, N USA
0 E6 Dickins Seamount undersea feature NE Pacific Ocean
27 O13 Dickson Oklahoma, C USA
20 I9 Dickson Tennessee, S USA
Dicle see Tigris
Dicsőszentmárton see Târnăveni
98 M12 Didam Gelderland, E Netherlands
163 Y8 Didao Heilongjiang, NE China
76 L12 Didiéni Koulikoro, W Mali
Didimo see Dídymo
Didimotiho see Didymóteicho
81 K17 Didimtu spring/well NE Kenya
67 U9 Didinga Hills ▲▲ S Sudan
9 Q16 Didsbury Alberta, SW Canada
152 G11 Dīdwāna Rājasthān, N India
115 G20 Dídymo var. Didimo. ▲ S Greece
114 L12 Didymóteicho var. Dhidhimótikhon, Didimotiho. Anatolikí Makedonía kai Thráki, NE Greece
103 S13 Die Drôme, E France
77 O13 Diébougou SW Burkina
Diedenhofen see Thionville
9 S16 Diefenbaker, Lake ⊠ Saskatchewan, S Canada
62 H7 Diego de Almagro Atacama, N Chile
63 F23 Diego de Almagro, Isla island S Chile
61 A20 Diego de Alvear Santa Fe, C Argentina
173 Q7 Diego Garcia island S British Indian Ocean Territory
Diégo-Suarez see Antsirañana
99 M23 Diekirch Diekirch, C Luxembourg
99 L23 Diekirch ◆ district N Luxembourg
76 K11 Diéma Kayes, W Mali
101 H15 Diemel ~ W Germany
98 I10 Diemen Noord-Holland, C Netherlands
Diemrich see Deva
167 R6 Điên Biên var. Bien Bien, Dien Bien Phu. Lai Châu, N Vietnam
Dien Bien Phu see Điên Biên
167 S7 Diên Châu Nghê An, N Vietnam
99 K18 Diepenbeek Limburg, NE Belgium
98 N11 Diepenheim Overijssel, E Netherlands
98 M10 Diepenveen Overijssel, E Netherlands
100 G12 Diepholz Niedersachsen, NW Germany
102 M3 Dieppe Seine-Maritime, N France
98 M12 Dieren Gelderland, E Netherlands
27 S13 Dierks Arkansas, C USA
99 J17 Diest Vlaams Brabant, C Belgium
108 F7 Dietikon Zürich, NW Switzerland
103 R13 Dieulefit Drôme, E France
103 T5 Dieuze Moselle, NE France
119 H15 Dieveniškės Vilnius, SE Lithuania
98 N7 Diever Drenthe, NE Netherlands
101 F17 Diez Rheinland-Pfalz, W Germany
77 Y12 Diffa Diffa, SE Niger
77 Y10 Diffa ◆ department SE Niger
99 L25 Differdange Luxembourg, SW Luxembourg
13 O16 Digby Nova Scotia, SE Canada
26 J5 Dighton Kansas, C USA
Dignano d'Istria see Vodnjan
103 T14 Digne var. Digne-les-Bains. Alpes-de-Haute-Provence, SE France
Digne-les-Bains see Digne
Digoel see Digul, Sungai
103 Q10 Digoin Saône-et-Loire, C France
171 Q8 Digos Mindanao, S Philippines
149 Q16 Digri Sind, SE Pakistan
171 Y14 Digul Barat, Sungai ~ Papua, E Indonesia
171 Y15 Digul, Sungai prev. Digoel. ~ Papua, E Indonesia
171 Z14 Digul Timur, Sungai ~ Papua, E Indonesia
153 X10 Dihāng ~ NE India
Dihang see Brahmaputra
Dihōk see Dahūk
81 L17 Diinsoor Bay, S Somalia
Dijlah see Tigris
99 H17 Dijle ~ C Belgium
103 R8 Dijon anc. Dibio. Côte d'Or, C France
93 H14 Dikanäs Västerbotten, N Sweden
80 L12 Dikhil SW Djibouti
136 B13 Dikili İzmir, W Turkey
99 B17 Diksmuide var. Dixmuide, Fr. Dixmude. West-Vlaanderen, W Belgium
122 K7 Dikson Taymyrskiy (Dolgano-Nenetskiy) Avtonomnyy Okrug, N Russian Federation
115 K25 Díkti var. Dhíkti Ori. ▲▲ Kríti, Greece, E Mediterranean Sea
77 Z13 Dikwa Borno, NE Nigeria
81 J15 Dila Southern, S Ethiopia
99 G18 Dilbeek Vlaams Brabant, C Belgium
171 Q16 Dili var. Dilli, Dilly. ● (East Timor) N East Timor
77 Y11 Dilia var. Dillia. ~ SE Niger
Dilijan see Delījān
167 U13 Di Linh Lâm Đông, S Vietnam
101 G16 Dillenburg Hessen, W Germany
25 Q13 Dilley Texas, SW USA
Dilli see Dili, East Timor
Dilli see Delhi, India
Dillia see Dilia
80 E11 Dilling var. Ad Dalanj. Southern Kordofan, C Sudan
101 D20 Dillingen Saarland, SW Germany
Dillingen see Dillingen an der Donau
101 J22 Dillingen an der Donau var. Dillingen. Bayern, S Germany
39 O13 Dillingham Alaska, USA
33 Q12 Dillon Montana, NW USA
21 T12 Dillon South Carolina, SE USA
31 T13 Dillon Lake ⊠ Ohio, N USA
Dilly see Dili
Dilman see Salmās
79 K24 Dilolo Katanga, S Dem. Rep. Congo
115 J20 Dílos island Kykládes, Greece, Aegean Sea
141 Y11 Ḑil', Ra's aḍ headland E Oman
29 R5 Dilworth Minnesota, N USA
138 H7 Dimashq var. Ash Shām, Esh Sham, Eng. Damascus, Fr. Damas, It. Damasco. ● Dimashq, SW Syria
138 I8 Dimashq off. Muḩāfaẓat Dimashq, var. Damascus, Ar. Ash Sham, Ash Shām, Damasco, Esh Sham, Fr. Damas. ◆ governorate S Syria
138 I7 Dimashq ✈ Dimashq, S Syria
Dimashq, Muḩāfaẓat see Dimashq
79 L21 Dimbelenge Kasai Occidental, C Dem. Rep. Congo
77 N16 Dimbokro E Ivory Coast
182 L11 Dimboola Victoria, SE Australia
Dâmbovița see Dâmbovița
Dimitrov see Dymytrov
114 K11 Dimitrovgrad Khaskovo, S Bulgaria
127 R5 Dimitrovgrad Ul'yanovskaya Oblast', W Russian Federation
113 Q15 Dimitrovgrad prev. Caribrod. Serbia, SE Serbia
Dimitrovo see Pernik
Dimlang see Vogel Peak
24 M3 Dimmitt Texas, SW USA
114 F7 Dimovo Vidin, NW Bulgaria
59 A16 Dimpolis Acre, W Brazil
115 O23 Dimyliá Ródos, Dodekánisa, Greece, Aegean Sea
171 Q6 Dinagat Island island S Philippines
153 S13 Dinajpur Rajshahi, NW Bangladesh
102 I6 Dinan Côtes d'Armor, NW France
99 I21 Dinant Namur, S Belgium
136 E15 Dinar Afyon, SW Turkey
112 F13 Dinara ▲ W Croatia
Dinara see Dinaric Alps
102 I5 Dinard Ille-et-Vilaine, NW France
112 F13 Dinaric Alps var. Dinara. ▲▲ Bosnia and Herzegovina/Croatia
143 N10 Dīnār, Kūh-e ▲ C Iran
Dinbych see Denbigh
155 H22 Dindigul Tamil Nādu, SE India
83 M19 Dindiza Gaza, S Mozambique
79 H21 Dinga Bandundu, SW Dem. Rep. Congo
149 V7 Dinga Punjab, E Pakistan
158 L16 Dinggyê var. Gyangkar. Xizang Zizhiqu, W China
97 A20 Dingle Ir. An Daingean. SW Ireland
97 A20 Dingle Bay Ir. Bá an Daingin. bay SW Ireland
18 I13 Dingmans Ferry Pennsylvania, NE USA
101 N22 Dingolfing Bayern, SE Germany
171 O1 Dingras Luzon, N Philippines
76 J13 Dinguiraye N Guinea
96 I8 Dingwall N Scotland, UK
159 V10 Dingxi Gansu, C China
Ding Xian see Dingzhou
161 Q7 Dingyuan Anhui, E China
161 O3 Dingzhou prev. Ding Xian. Hebei, E China
167 U6 Đinh Lâp Lang Sơn, N Vietnam
167 T13 Đinh Quan var. Tân Phu. Đông Nai, S Vietnam
100 E13 Dinkel ~ Germany/Netherlands
101 J21 Dinkelsbühl Bayern, S Germany
101 D14 Dinslaken Nordrhein-Westfalen, W Germany
35 R11 Dinuba California, W USA
21 W7 Dinwiddie Virginia, NE USA
98 N13 Dinxperlo Gelderland, E Netherlands
Dio see Díon
Diófás see Nucet
76 M12 Dioïla Koulikoro, W Mali
115 F14 Díon var Dio; anc. Dium. site of ancient city Kentrikí Makedonía, N Greece
115 G19 Dióryga Korinthou Eng. Corinth Canal. canal S Greece
76 G12 Diouloulou SW Senegal
77 N11 Dioura Mopti, W Mali
76 G11 Diourbel W Senegal
152 L10 Dipāyal Far Western, W Nepal
121 R1 Dipkarpaz Gk. Rizokarpaso, Rizokárpason. NE Cyprus
149 R17 Diplo Sind, SE Pakistan
171 P7 Dipolog var. Dipolog City. Mindanao, S Philippines
Dipolog City see Dipolog
185 C23 Dipton Southland, South Island, New Zealand
77 O10 Diré Tombouctou, C Mali
80 L13 Dirē Dawa Dirē Dawa, E Ethiopia
Dirfis see Dírfys
115 H18 Dírfys var. Dirfis. ▲▲ Évvoia, C Greece
75 N9 Dirj var. Daraj, Darj. W Libya
180 G10 Dirk Hartog Island island Western Australia
77 Y8 Dirkou Agadez, NE Niger
181 X11 Dirranbandi Queensland, E Australia
81 O16 Dirri Galguduud, C Somalia
Dirschau see Tczew
37 N6 Dirty Devil River ~ Utah, W USA
32 E10 Disappointment, Cape headland Washington, NW USA
180 L8 Disappointment, Lake salt lake Western Australia
183 R12 Disaster Bay bay New South Wales, SE Australia
44 J11 Discovery Bay C Jamaica
182 K13 Discovery Bay inlet SE Australia
67 Y15 Discovery II Fracture Zone tectonic feature SW Indian Ocean
Discovery Seamount/Discovery Seamounts see Discovery Tablemount
65 O19 Discovery Tablemount var. Discovery Seamount, Discovery Seamounts. undersea feature SW Indian Ocean
108 G9 Disentis Rmsch. Mustér. Graubünden, S Switzerland
39 O10 Dishna River ~ Alaska, USA
Disko Bugt see Qeqertarsuup Tunua
195 X4 Dismal Mountains ▲▲ Antarctica
28 M14 Dismal River ~ Nebraska, C USA
Disna see Dzisna
99 L19 Dison Liège, E Belgium
153 V12 Dispur state capital Assam, NE India
15 R11 Disraeli Québec, SE Canada
115 F18 Dístomo prev. Dhístomon. Stereá Ellás, C Greece
59 L18 Distrito Federal Eng. Federal District. ◆ federal district C Brazil
41 P14 Distrito Federal ◆ federal district S Mexico
54 L4 Distrito Federal off. Territorio Distrito Federal. ◆ federal district N Venezuela
Distrito Federal, Territorio see Distrito Federal
116 J10 Ditrău Hung. Ditró. Harghita, C Romania
Ditró see Ditrău
154 B12 Diu Damān and Diu, W India
Dium see Díon
109 S13 Divača SW Slovenia
102 K5 Dives ~ N France
Divichi see Däväçi
33 Q11 Divide Montana, NW USA
Divin see Dzivin
83 N18 Divinhe Sofala, E Mozambique
59 L20 Divinópolis Minas Gerais, SE Brazil
127 N13 Divnoye Stavropol'skiy Kray, SW Russian Federation
76 M17 Divo S Ivory Coast
Divodurum Mediomatricum see Metz
137 N13 Divriği Sivas, C Turkey
Diwaniyah see Ad Dīwānīyah
14 J10 Dix Milles, Lac ◎ Québec, SE Canada
14 M8 Dix Milles, Lac des ◎ Québec, SE Canada
Dixmude/Dixmuide see Diksmuide
35 N7 Dixon California, W USA
30 L10 Dixon Illinois, N USA
20 I6 Dixon Kentucky, S USA
27 V6 Dixon Missouri, C USA
37 S9 Dixon New Mexico, SW USA
39 Y15 Dixon Entrance strait Canada/USA
18 D14 Dixonville Pennsylvania, NE USA
137 T13 Diyadin Ağrı, E Turkey
139 V5 Diyālá, Nahr var. Rudkhaneh-ye Sīrvān, Sirwan. ~ Iran/Iraq see also Sīrvān, Rudkhaneh-ye
Diyālá, Nahr see Sīrvān, Rūdkhāneh-ye
137 P15 Diyarbakır var. Diarbekr; anc. Amida. Diyarbakır, SE Turkey
137 P15 Diyarbakır var. Diarbekr. ◆ province SE Turkey
Dizful see Dezfūl
79 F16 Dja ~ SE Cameroon
Djadié see Zadié
77 X7 Djado Agadez, NE Niger
77 X6 Djado, Plateau du ▲▲ NE Niger
Djailolo see Halmahera, Pulau
Djajapura see Jayapura
Djakarta see Jakarta
Djakovica see Đakovica
Djakovo see Đakovo
79 G20 Djambala Plateaux, C Congo
Djambi see Hari, Batang
Djambi see Jambi
74 M9 Djanet E Algeria
74 M11 Djanet prev. Fort Charlet. SE Algeria
Djaul see Dyaul Island
Djawa see Jawa
Djéblé see Jablah
78 I10 Djédaa Batha, C Chad
74 J6 Djelfa var. El Djelfa. N Algeria
79 M14 Djéma Haut-Mbomou, E Central African Republic
Djember see Jember
Djeneponto see Jeneponto
77 N12 Djenné var. Jenné. Mopti, C Mali
Djérablous see Jarābulus
Djerba see Jerba, Île de
79 F15 Djérem ~ C Cameroon
Djevdjelija see Gevgelija
77 P11 Djibo N Burkina
80 L12 Djibouti var. Jibuti. ● (Djibouti) E Djibouti
80 L12 Djibouti off. Republic of Djibouti, var. Jibuti; prev. French Somaliland, French Territory of the Afars and Issas, Côte Française des Somalis, Fr. Territoire Français des Afars et des Issas. ◆ republic E Africa
80 L12 Djibouti ✈ C Djibouti
Djibouti, Republic of see Djibouti
Djidjel/Djidjelli see Jijel
55 W10 Djoemoe Sipaliwini, C Suriname
Djokjakarta see Yogyakarta
79 K21 Djoku-Punda Kasai Occidental, S Dem. Rep. Congo
79 K18 Djolu Equateur, N Dem. Rep. Congo
Djombang see Jombang
Djorče Petrov see Đorče Petrov
79 F17 Djoua ~ Congo/Gabon
77 R14 Djougou W Benin
79 F16 Djoum Sud, S Cameroon
78 I8 Djourab, Erg du desert N Chad
79 P17 Djugu Orientale, NE Dem. Rep. Congo
Djumbir see Ďumbier
92 L3 Djúpivogur Austurland, SE Iceland
94 L13 Djura Dalarna, C Sweden
Djurdjevac see Đurđevac
83 G18 D'Kar Ghanzi, NW Botswana
197 U6 Dmitriya Lapteva, Proliv strait N Russian Federation
126 J7 Dmitriyev-L'govskiy Kurskaya Oblast', W Russian Federation
Dmitriyevsk see Makiyivka
126 K3 Dmitrov Moskovskaya Oblast', W Russian Federation
Dmitrovichi see Dzmitravichy
126 J6 Dmitrovsk-Orlovskiy Orlovskaya Oblast', W Russian Federation
117 R3 Dmytrivka Chernihivs'ka Oblast', N Ukraine
Dnepr see Dnieper
Dneprodzerzhinsk see Dniprodzerzhyns'k
Dneprodzerzhinskoye Vodokhranilishche see Dniprodzerzhyns'ke Vodoskhovyshche
Dnepropetrovsk see Dnipropetrovs'k
Dnepropetrovskaya Oblast' see Dnipropetrovs'ka Oblast'
Dneprorudnoye see Dniprorudne
Dneprovskiy Liman see Dniprovs'kyy Lyman
Dneprovsko-Bugskiy Kanal see Dnyaprowska-Buhski, Kanal
Dnestr see Dniester
Dnestrovskiy Liman see Dnistrovs'kyy Lyman
86 H11 Dnieper Bel. Dnyapro, Rus. Dnepr, Ukr. Dnipro. ~ E Europe
117 P3 Dnieper Lowland Bel. Prydnyaprowskaya Nizina, Ukr. Prydniprovs'ka Nyzovyna. lowlands Belarus/Ukraine
116 M8 Dniester Rom. Nistru, Rus. Dnestr, Ukr. Dnister; anc. Tyras. ~ Moldova/Ukraine
Dnipro see Dnieper
117 T7 Dniprodzerzhyns'k Rus. Dneprodzerzhinsk; prev. Kamenskoye. Dnipropetrovs'ka Oblast', E Ukraine
117 T7 Dniprodzerzhyns'ke Vodoskhovyshche Rus. Dneprodzerzhinskoye Vodokhranilishche. ⊠ C Ukraine
117 U7 Dnipropetrovs'k Rus. Dnepropetrovsk; prev. Yekaterinoslav. Dnipropetrovs'ka Oblast', E Ukraine
117 U8 Dnipropetrovs'k ✈ Dnipropetrovs'ka Oblast', S Ukraine
Dnipropetrovs'k see Dnipropetrovs'ka Oblast'
117 T7 Dnipropetrovs'ka Oblast' var. Dnipropetrovs'k, Rus. Dnepropetrovskaya Oblast'. ◆ province E Ukraine
117 U9 Dniprorudne Rus. Dneprorudnoye. Zaporiz'ka Oblast', SE Ukraine
117 Q11 Dniprovs'kyy Lyman Rus. Dneprovskiy Liman. bay S Ukraine
Dnister see Dniester
117 O11 Dnistrovs'kyy Lyman Rus. Dnestrovskiy Liman. inlet S Ukraine
124 G14 Dno Pskovskaya Oblast', W Russian Federation
Dnyapro see Dnieper
119 H20 Dnyaprowska-Buhski, Kanal Rus. Dneprovsko-Bugskiy Kanal. canal SW Belarus
13 O14 Doaktown New Brunswick, SE Canada
78 H13 Doba Logone-Oriental, S Chad
118 E9 Dobele Ger. Doblen. Dobele, W Latvia
101 N16 Döbeln Sachsen, E Germany
171 U12 Doberai, Jazirah Dut. Vogelkop. peninsula Papua, E Indonesia
110 F10 Dobiegniew Ger. Lubuskie, Woldenberg Neumark. Lubuskie, W Poland
Doblen see Dobele
81 K18 Dobli spring/well SW Somalia
112 H11 Doboj ◆ Republika Srpska, N Bosnia and Herzegovina
110 L8 Dobre Miasto Ger. Guttstadt. Warmińsko-mazurskie, NE Poland
114 N7 Dobrich Rom. Bazargic; prev. Tolbukhin. Dobrich, NE Bulgaria
114 N7 Dobrich ◆ province NE Bulgaria
126 M8 Dobrinka Lipetskaya Oblast', W Russian Federation
126 M7 Dobrinka Volgogradskaya Oblast', SW Russian Federation
Dobrla Vas see Eberndorf
111 I15 Dobrodzień Ger. Guttentag. Opolskie, S Poland
Dobrogea see Dobruja
117 W7 Dobropillya Rus. Dobropol'ye. Donets'ka Oblast', SE Ukraine
Dobropol'ye see Dobropillya
117 P8 Dobrovelychkivka Kirovohrads'ka Oblast', C Ukraine
Dobrudja/Dobrudzha see Dobruja
114 O7 Dobruja var. Dobrudja, Bul. Dobrudzha, Rom. Dobrogea. physical region Bulgaria/Romania
119 P19 Dobrush Homyel'skaya Voblasts', SE Belarus
125 U14 Dobryanka Permskaya Oblast', NW Russian Federation
117 P2 Dobryanka Chernihivs'ka Oblast', N Ukraine
Dobryn' see Dabryn'
21 R8 Dobson North Carolina, SE USA
59 N20 Doce, Rio ~ SE Brazil
93 I16 Docksta Västernorrland, C Sweden
41 N10 Doctor Arroyo Nuevo León, NE Mexico
62 L4 Doctor Pedro P. Peña Boquerón, W Paraguay
171 S11 Dodaga Pulau Halmahera, E Indonesia
155 G21 Dodda Betta ▲ S India
Dodecanese see Dodekánisa
115 M22 Dodekánisa var. Nóties Sporádes, Eng. Dodecanese; prev. Dhodhekánisos, Dodekanisos. island group SE Greece
Dodekanisos see Dodekánisa
26 J6 Dodge City Kansas, C USA
30 K9 Dodgeville Wisconsin, N USA
97 H25 Dodman Point headland SW England, UK
81 J14 Dodola Oromo, C Ethiopia
81 H22 Dodoma ● (Tanzania) Dodoma, C Tanzania
81 H22 Dodoma ◆ region C Tanzania
115 C16 Dodóni var. Dhodhóni. site of ancient city Ípeiros, W Greece
33 U7 Dodson Montana, NW USA
25 P3 Dodson Texas, SW USA
98 M12 Doesburg Gelderland, E Netherlands
98 N12 Doetinchem Gelderland, E Netherlands
158 L12 Dogai Coring var. Lake Montcalm. ◎ W China
137 N15 Doğanşehir Malatya, C Turkey
84 E9 Dogger Bank undersea feature C North Sea
23 S10 Dog Island island Florida, SE USA
14 C7 Dog Lake ◎ Ontario, S Canada
106 B9 Dogliani Piemonte, NE Italy
164 H11 Dōgo island Oki-shotō, SW Japan
Do Gonbadān see Dow Gonbadān
77 S12 Dogondoutchi Dosso, SW Niger
Dogrular see Pravda
137 T13 Doğubayazıt Ağrı, E Turkey
137 P12 Doğu Karadeniz Dağları var. Anadolu Dağları. ▲▲ NE Turkey
158 K16 Dogxung Zangbo ~ W China
Doha see Ad Dawḩah
Doha see Ad Dawḩah
Dohad see Dāhod
Dohuk see Dahūk
159 N16 Doilungdêqên var. Namka. Xizang Zizhiqu, W China
114 F12 Doïrani, Límni var. Limni Doïranis, Bul. Ezero Doyransko. ◎ N Greece
Doire see Londonderry
99 H22 Doische Namur, S Belgium
59 P17 Dois de Julho ✈ (Salvador) Bahia, NE Brazil
60 H12 Dois Vizinhos Paraná, S Brazil
80 H10 Doka Gedaref, E Sudan
Doka see Kéita, Bahr
139 T3 Dokan var. Dūkān. E Iraq
94 H13 Dokka Oppland, S Norway
98 L5 Dokkum Friesland, N Netherlands
98 L5 Dokkumer Ee ~ N Netherlands
76 K13 Doko Haute-Guinée, NE Guinea
Dokshitsy see Dokshytsy
118 K13 Dokshytsy Rus. Dokshitsy. Vitsyebskaya Voblasts', N Belarus
117 X8 Dokuchayevs'k var. Dokuchayevsk. Donets'ka Oblast', SE Ukraine
Dokuchayevsk see Dokuchayevs'k

◆ Country
● Country Capital
◇ Dependent Territory
○ Dependent Territory Capital
◆ Administrative Regions
✈ International Airport
▲ Mountain
▲▲ Mountain Range
Volcano
~ River
◎ Lake
⊠ Reservoir

Dolak, Pulau *see* Yos Sudarso, Pulau
29 *P9* **Doland** South Dakota, N USA
63 *J18* **Dolavón** Chaco, S Argentina
15 *P6* **Dolbeau** Québec, SE Canada
102 *I5* **Dol-de-Bretagne** Ille-et-Vilaine, NW France
64 *J13* **Doldrums Fracture Zone** *tectonic feature* W Atlantic Ocean
103 *S8* **Dôle** Jura, E France
97 *J19* **Dolgellau** NW Wales, UK
Dolginovo *see* Dawhinava
Dolgi, Ostrov *see* Dolgiy, Ostrov
125 *U2* **Dolgiy, Ostrov** ***var.*** Ostrov Dolgi. *island* NW Russian Federation
162 *J9* **Dölgöön** Övörhangay, C Mongolia
107 *C20* **Dolianova** Sardegna, Italy, C Mediterranean Sea
Dolina *see* Dolyna
123 *T13* **Dolinsk** Ostrov Sakhalin, Sakhalinskaya Oblast', SE Russian Federation
Dolinskaya *see* Dolyns'ka
79 *F21* **Dolisie** ***prev.*** Loubomo. Le Niari, S Congo
116 *G14* **Dolj** ⬖ *county* SW Romania
98 *P5* **Dollard** *bay* NW Germany
194 *J5* **Dolleman Island** *island* Antarctica
114 *I8* **Dolni Dŭbnik** Pleven, N Bulgaria
114 *F8* **Dolni Lom** Vidin, NW Bulgaria
Dolnja Lendava *see* Lendava
114 *K9* **Dolno Panicherevo** ***var.*** Panicherevo. Sliven, C Bulgaria
129 *F14* **Dolnośląskie** ⬖ *province* SW Poland
111 *K18* **Dolný Kubín** ***Hung.*** Alsókubin. Žilinský Kraj, N Slovakia
106 *H8* **Dolo** Veneto, NE Italy
Dolomites/Dolomiti ***see*** Dolomitiche, Alpi
106 *H6* **Dolomitiche, Alpi** ***var.*** Dolomiti, ***Eng.*** Dolomites. ▲▲ NE Italy
Dolonnur *see* Duolun
Doloon *see* Tsogt-Ovoo
61 *E21* **Dolores** Buenos Aires, E Argentina
42 *E3* **Dolores** Petén, N Guatemala
171 *Q5* **Dolores** Samar, C Philippines
105 *S12* **Dolores** País Valenciano, E Spain
61 *D19* **Dolores** Soriano, SW Uruguay
41 *N12* **Dolores Hidalgo** ***var.*** Ciudad de Dolores Hidalgo. Guanajuato, C Mexico
8 *J7* **Dolphin and Union Strait** *strait* Northwest Territories/Nunavut, N Canada
65 *D23* **Dolphin, Cape** *headland* East Falkland, Falkland Islands
44 *H12* **Dolphin Head** *hill* W Jamaica
83 *B21* **Dolphin Head** ***var.*** Cape Dernberg. *headland* SW Namibia
110 *G12* **Dolsk** ***Ger.*** Dolzig. Weilkopolskie, C Poland
167 *S8* **Đô Lương** Nghê An, N Vietnam
116 *I6* **Dolyna** ***Rus.*** Dolina. vano-Frankivs'ka Oblast', W Ukraine
117 *R8* **Dolyns'ka** ***Rus.*** Dolinskaya. Kirovohrads'ka Oblast', S Ukraine
Dolzig *see* Dolsk
Domachëvo/Domaczewo ***see*** Damachava
117 *P9* **Domanivka** Mykolayivs'ka Oblast', S Ukraine
153 *S13* **Domar** Rajshahi, N Bangladesh
108 *I9* **Domat/Ems** Graubünden, SE Switzerland
111 *A18* **Domažlice** ***Ger.*** Taus. Plzeňský Kraj, W Czech Republic
127 *X8* **Dombarovskiy** Orenburgskaya Oblast', W Russian Federation
94 *G10* **Dombås** Oppland, S Norway
83 *M17* **Dombe** Manica, C Mozambique
82 *A13* **Dombe Grande** Benguela, C Angola
103 *R10* **Dombes** *physical region* E France
111 *I25* **Dombóvár** Tolna, S Hungary
99 *D14* **Domburg** Zeeland, SW Netherlands
58 *L13* **Dom Eliseu** Pará, NE Brazil
Domel Island *see* Letsôk-aw Kyun
103 *O11* **Dôme, Puy de** ▲ C France
36 *H13* **Dome Rock Mountains** ▲▲ Arizona, SW USA
Domesnes, Cape ***see*** Kolkasrags
62 *G8* **Domeyko** Atacama, N Chile
62 *H5* **Domeyko, Cordillera** ▲▲ N Chile
102 *K5* **Domfront** Orne, N France
171 *X13* **Dom, Gunung** ▲ Papua, E Indonesia
45 *X11* **Dominica** ***off.*** Commonwealth of Dominica. ◆ *republic* E West Indies
47 *S3* **Dominica** *island* Dominica
Dominica Channel ***see*** Martinique Passage
Dominica, Commonwealth of ***see*** Dominica
43 *N15* **Dominical** Puntarenas, SE Costa Rica
45 *Q8* **Dominican Republic** ◆ *republic* C West Indies
45 *X11* **Dominica Passage** *passage* E Caribbean Sea
99 *K14* **Dommel** ≈ S Netherlands
81 *O14* **Domo** Somali, E Ethiopia
126 *L4* **Domodedovo** ✈ (Moskva) Moskovskaya Oblast', W Russian Federation
106 *C6* **Domodossola** Piemonte, NE Italy
115 *F17* **Domokós** ***var.*** Dhomokós. Stereá Ellás, C Greece
172 *I14* **Domoni** Anjouan, SE Comoros
61 *G16* **Dom Pedrito** Rio Grande do Sul, S Brazil
Dompoe *see* Dompu
170 *M16* **Dompu** ***prev.*** Dompoe. Sumbawa, C Indonesia
Domschale *see* Domžale
62 *H13* **Domuyo, Volcán** ⛰ W Argentina
109 *U11* **Domžale** ***Ger.*** Domschale. C Slovenia
127 *O10* **Don** ***var.*** Duna, Tanais. ≈ SW Russian Federation
96 *K9* **Don** ≈ NE Scotland, UK
182 *M11* **Donald** Victoria, SE Australia
22 *J9* **Donaldsonville** Louisiana, S USA
23 *S8* **Donalsonville** Georgia, SE USA
Donau *see* Danube
101 *G23* **Donaueschingen** Baden-Württemberg, SW Germany
101 *K22* **Donaumoos** *wetland* S Germany
101 *K22* **Donauwörth** Bayern, S Germany
109 *U7* **Donawitz** Steiermark, SE Austria
117 *X7* **Donbass** *industrial region* Russian Federation/Ukraine
104 *K11* **Don Benito** Extremadura, W Spain
97 *M17* **Doncaster** ***anc.*** Danum. N England, UK
44 *K12* **Don Christophers Point** *headland* C Jamaica
55 *V9* **Donderkamp** Sipaliwini, NW Suriname
82 *B12* **Dondo** Cuanza Norte, NW Angola
171 *O12* **Dondo** Sulawesi, N Indonesia
83 *N17* **Dondo** Sofala, C Mozambique
155 *K26* **Dondra Head** *headland* S Sri Lanka
Dondușani *see* Dondușeni
116 *M8* **Dondușeni** ***var.*** Dondușani, ***Rus.*** Dondyushany. N Moldova
Dondyushany *see* Dondușeni
97 *D15* **Donegal** ***Ir.*** Dún na nGall. Donegal, NW Ireland
97 *D14* **Donegal** ***Ir.*** Dún na nGall. ⬖ *county* NW Ireland
97 *C15* **Donegal Bay** ***Ir.*** Bá Dhún na nGall. *bay* NW Ireland
84 *K10* **Donets** ≈ Russian Federation/Ukraine
117 *X8* **Donets'k** ***Rus.*** Donetsk; ***prev.*** Stalino. Donets'ka Oblast', E Ukraine
117 *W8* **Donets'k** ✈ Donets'ka Oblast', E Ukraine
Donets'k *see* Donets'ka Oblast'
117 *W8* **Donets'ka Oblast'** ***var.*** Donets'k, ***Rus.*** Donetskaya Oblast'; ***prev. Rus.*** Stalins'kaya Oblast'. ⬖ *province* SE Ukraine
Donetskaya Oblast' ***see*** Donets'ka Oblast'
67 *P8* **Donga** ≈ Cameroon/Nigeria
157 *O13* **Dongchuan** Yunnan, SW China
99 *I14* **Dongen** Noord-Brabant, S Netherlands
160 *K17* **Dongfang** ***var.*** Basuo. Hainan, S China
163 *Z7* **Dongfanghong** Heilongjiang, NE China
163 *W11* **Dongfeng** Jilin, NE China
Đông Phu *see* Đông Xoai
171 *N12* **Donggala** Sulawesi, C Indonesia
163 *V13* **Donggang** ***var*** Dadong, ***prev*** Donggou. Liaoning, NE China
Donggou *see* Donggang
161 *O14* **Dongguan** Guangdong, S China
167 *T9* **Đông Ha** Quang Tri, C Vietnam
Dong Hai *see* East China Sea
160 *M16* **Donghai Dao** *island* S China
162 *I12* **Dong He** ***Mong.*** Narin Gol. ≈ N China
Donghe *see* Wangcang
167 *T9* **Đông Hơi** Quang Binh, C Vietnam
108 *H10* **Dongio** Ticino, S Switzerland
Dongkan *see* Binhai
160 *L11* **Dongkou** Hunan, S China
Dongliao *see* Liaoyuan
Dong-nai *see* Đông Nai, Sông
167 *U13* **Đông Nai, Sông** ***var.*** Dong-nai, Dong Noi, Donnai. ≈ S Vietnam
161 *N14* **Dongnan Qiuling** *plateau* SE China
163 *Y9* **Dongning** Heilongjiang, NE China
Dong Noi *see* Đông Nai, Sông
83 *C14* **Dongo** Huíla, C Angola
80 *E7* **Dongola** ***var.*** Donqola, Dunqulah. Northern, N Sudan
79 *I17* **Dongou** La Likouala, NE Congo
Dongping *see* Anhua
Dong Rak, Phanom ***see*** Dângrêk, Chuŏr Phnum
161 *Q14* **Dongshan Dao** *island* SE China
Dongsha Qundao ***see*** Tungsha Tao
Dongsheng *see* Ordos
161 *R7* **Dongtai** Jiangsu, E China
161 *N10* **Dongting Hu** ***var.*** Tung-t'ing Hu. ◎ S China
161 *P10* **Dongxiang** ***var.*** Xiaogang. Jiangxi, S China
167 *T13* **Đông Xoai** ***var.*** Đông Phu. Sông Be, S Vietnam
161 *Q4* **Dongying** Shandong, E China
27 *X8* **Doniphan** Missouri, C USA
Donja Łužica ***see*** Niederlausitz
10 *G7* **Donjek** ≈ Yukon Territory, W Canada
112 *E11* **Donji Lapac** Lika-Senj, W Croatia
112 *H8* **Donji Miholjac** Osijek-Baranja, NE Croatia
112 *P12* **Donji Milanovac** Serbia, E Serbia
112 *G12* **Donji Vakuf** ***var.*** Srbobran. ⬖ Federacija Bosna I Hercegovina, C Bosnia and Herzegovina
98 *M6* **Donkerbroek** Friesland, N Netherlands
167 *P11* **Don Muang** ✈ (Krung Thep) Nonthaburi, C Thailand
25 *S17* **Donna** Texas, SW USA
15 *Q10* **Donnacona** Québec, SE Canada
Donnai *see* Đông Nai, Sông
29 *Y16* **Donnellson** Iowa, C USA
9 *O13* **Donnelly** Alberta, W Canada
35 *P6* **Donner Pass** *Pass* California, W USA
101 *F19* **Donnersberg** ▲ W Germany
Donoso *see* Miguel de la Borda
105 *P2* **Donostia-San Sebastián** País Vasco, N Spain
115 *K21* **Donoúsa** *island* Kykládes, Greece, Aegean Sea
Donoússa *see* Donoúsa
35 *P8* **Don Pedro Reservoir** ▣ California, W USA
Donqola *see* Dongola
126 *L5* **Donskoy** Tul'skaya Oblast', W Russian Federation
81 *L16* **Doolow** Somali, E Ethiopia
39 *Q7* **Doonerak, Mount** ▲ Alaska, USA
98 *J12* **Doorn** Utrecht, C Netherlands
Doornik *see* Tournai
31 *N6* **Door Peninsula** *peninsula* Wisconsin, N USA
80 *P13* **Dooxo Nugaaleed** ***var.*** Nogal Valley. *valley* E Somalia
Do Qu *see* Da Qu
106 *B7* **Dora Baltea** ***anc.*** Duria Major. ≈ NW Italy
180 *K7* **Dora, Lake** *salt lake* Western Australia
106 *A8* **Dora Riparia** ***anc.*** Duria Minor. ≈ NW Italy
Dorbiljin *see* Emin
Dorbod/Dorbod Mongolzu Zizhixian *see* Taikang
Dorbod Mongolzu Zizhixian *see* Taikang
113 *N18* **Đorče Petrov** ***var.*** Djorče Petrov, Gorče Petrov. N Macedonia
14 *F16* **Dorchester** Ontario, S Canada
97 *L24* **Dorchester** ***anc.*** Durnovaria. S England, UK
9 *P7* **Dorchester, Cape** *headland* Baffin Island, Nunavut, NE Canada
83 *D19* **Dordabis** Khomas, C Namibia
102 *L12* **Dordogne** ⬖ *department* SW France
103 *N12* **Dordogne** ≈ W France
98 *H13* **Dordrecht** ***var.*** Dordt, Dort. Zuid-Holland, SW Netherlands
Dordt *see* Dordrecht
103 *P11* **Dore** ≈ C France
9 *S13* **Doré Lake** Saskatchewan, C Canada
103 *O12* **Dore, Monts** ▲▲ C France
101 *M23* **Dorfen** Bayern, SE Germany
107 *D18* **Dorgali** Sardegna, Italy, C Mediterranean Sea
159 *N11* **Dorgê Co** ***var.*** Elsen Nur. ◎ C China
159 *N11* **Dorgê Co** ***var.*** Elsen Nur. ◎ C China
162 *E6* **Dörgön** Hovd, W Mongolia
162 *F7* **Dörgön Nuur** ◎ NW Mongolia
77 *Q12* **Dori** N Burkina
83 *E24* **Doring** ≈ S South Africa
101 *E16* **Dormagen** Nordrhein-Westfalen, W Germany
103 *P4* **Dormans** Marne, N France
108 *E6* **Dornach** Solothurn, NW Switzerland
Dorna Watra *see* Vatra Dornei
108 *J7* **Dornbirn** Vorarlberg, W Austria
96 *I7* **Dornoch** N Scotland, UK
96 *J7* **Dornoch Firth** *inlet* N Scotland, UK
163 *P7* **Dornod** ⬖ *province* E Mongolia
163 *N10* **Dornogovĭ** ⬖ *province* SE Mongolia
77 *P10* **Doro** Tombouctou, S Mali
116 *L14* **Dorobanțu** Călărași, S Romania
111 *J22* **Dorog** Komárom-Esztergom, N Hungary
126 *I4* **Dorogobuzh** Smolenskaya Oblast', W Russian Federation
116 *K8* **Dorohoi** Botoșani, NE Romania
93 *H15* **Dorotea** Västerbotten, N Sweden
Dorpat *see* Tartu
180 *G10* **Dorre Island** *island* Western Australia
183 *U5* **Dorrigo** New South Wales, SE Australia
35 *N1* **Dorris** California, W USA
14 *H13* **Dorset** Ontario, SE Canada
97 *K23* **Dorset** *cultural region* S England, UK
101 *E14* **Dorsten** Nordrhein-Westfalen, W Germany
Dort *see* Dordrecht
101 *F15* **Dortmund** Nordrhein-Westfalen, W Germany
100 *F12* **Dortmund-Ems-Kanal** *canal* W Germany
136 *L17* **Dörtyol** Hatay, S Turkey
142 *L7* **Do Rūd** ***var.*** Dow Rūd, Durud. Lorestān, W Iran
79 *O15* **Doruma** Orientale, N Dem. Rep. Congo
15 *O12* **Dorval** ✈ (Montréal) Québec, SE Canada
162 *F7* **Dörvöljin** ***var.*** Buga. Dzavhan, W Mongolia
45 *T5* **Dos Bocas, Lago** ◎ C Puerto Rico
104 *K14* **Dos Hermanas** Andalucía, S Spain
Dospad Dagh *see* Rhodope Mountains
35 *P10* **Dos Palos** California, W USA
114 *I11* **Dospat** Smolyan, S Bulgaria
114 *H11* **Dospat, Yazovir** ▣ SW Bulgaria
100 *M11* **Dosse** ≈ NE Germany
77 *S12* **Dosso** Dosso, SW Niger
77 *S12* **Dosso** ⬖ *department* SW Niger
144 *G12* **Dossor** Atyrau, SW Kazakhstan
147 *O10* **Do'stlik** Jizzakh Viloyati, C Uzbekistan
147 *Q10* **Do'stlik** Jizzax Viloyati, C Uzbekistan
147 *V9* **Dostuk** Narynskaya Oblast', C Kyrgyzstan
145 *X13* **Dostyk** ***prev.*** Druzhba. Almaty, SE Kazakhstan
23 *R7* **Dothan** Alabama, S USA
39 *T9* **Dot Lake** Alaska, USA
118 *F12* **Dotnuva** Kaunas, C Lithuania
99 *D19* **Dottignies** Hainaut, W Belgium
103 *P2* **Douai** ***prev.*** Douay; ***anc.*** Duacum. Nord, N France
14 *L9* **Douaire, Lac** ◎ Québec, SE Canada
79 *D16* **Douala** ***var.*** Duala. Littoral, W Cameroon
79 *D16* **Douala** ✈ Littoral, W Cameroon
102 *F6* **Douarnenez** Finistère, NW France
102 *E6* **Douarnenez, Baie de** *bay* NW France
Douay *see* Douai
25 *O6* **Double Mountain Fork Brazos River** ≈ Texas, SW USA
23 *O3* **Double Springs** Alabama, S USA
103 *T8* **Doubs** ⬖ *department* E France
108 *C8* **Doubs** ≈ France/Switzerland
185 *A22* **Doubtful Sound** *sound* South Island, New Zealand
184 *J2* **Doubtless Bay** *bay* North Island, New Zealand
25 *X9* **Doucette** Texas, SW USA
102 *K8* **Doué-la-Fontaine** Maine-et-Loire, NW France
77 *O11* **Douentza** Mopti, S Mali
38 *L9* **Douglas** East Falkland, Falkland Islands
97 *I16* **Douglas** ○ (Isle of Man) E Isle of Man
83 *H23* **Douglas** Northern Cape, C South Africa
39 *X13* **Douglas** Alexander Archipelago, Alaska, USA
37 *O17* **Douglas** Arizona, SW USA
23 *U7* **Douglas** Georgia, SE USA
33 *Y15* **Douglas** Wyoming, C USA
21 *O7* **Douglas Cape** *headland* Alaska, N USA
10 *J14* **Douglas Channel** *channel* British Columbia, W Canada
182 *G3* **Douglas Creek** *seasonal river* South Australia
31 *P5* **Douglas Lake** ◎ Michigan, N USA
21 *O9* **Douglas Lake** ▣ Tennessee, S USA
39 *Q13* **Douglas, Mount** ▲ Alaska, USA
194 *I6* **Douglas Range** ▲▲ Alexander Island, Antarctica
121 *P9* **Doukáto, Ákra** *headland* Lefkáda, W Greece
103 *O2* **Doullens** Somme, N France
Douma *see* Dūmā
79 *F15* **Doumé** Est, E Cameroon
99 *E21* **Dour** Hainaut , S Belgium
59 *K18* **Dourada, Serra** ▲▲ S Brazil
59 *I21* **Dourados** Mato Grosso do Sul, S Brazil
103 *N5* **Dourdan** Essonne, N France
104 *O6* **Douro** ***Port.*** Duero. ≈ Portugal/Spain
104 *I6* **Douro** ***Sp.*** Duero. ≈ Portugal/Spain ***see also*** Duero
Douro Duero
104 *G6* **Douro Litoral** *former province* N Portugal
Douvres *see* Dover
102 *K15* **Douze** ≈ SW France
183 *P17* **Dover** Tasmania, SE Australia
97 *Q22* **Dover** ***Fr.*** Douvres, ***Lat.*** Dubris Portus. SE England, UK
21 *Y3* **Dover** *state capital* Delaware, NE USA
19 *P9* **Dover** New Hampshire, NE USA
18 *J14* **Dover** New Jersey, NE USA
31 *U12* **Dover** Ohio, N USA
20 *H8* **Dover** Tennessee, S USA
97 *Q23* **Dover, Strait of** ***var.*** Straits of Dover, ***Fr.*** Pas de Calais. *strait* England, UK/France
Dover, Straits of *see* Dover, Strait of
Dovlen *see* Devin
94 *G11* **Dovre** Oppland, S Norway
94 *G10* **Dovrefjell** *plateau* S Norway
Dovsk *see* Dowsk
83 *M14* **Dowa** Central, C Malawi
31 *O10* **Dowagiac** Michigan, N USA
143 *N10* **Dow Gonbadān** ***var.*** Do Gonbadān, Gonbadān. Kohkīlūyeh va Būyer AḤmad, SW Iran
148 *M2* **Dowlatābād** Fāryāb, N Afghanistan
97 *G16* **Down** *cultural region* SE Northern Ireland, UK
33 *R16* **Downey** Idaho, NW USA
35 *P5* **Downieville** California, W USA
97 *G16* **Downpatrick** ***Ir.*** Dún Pádraig. SE Northern Ireland, UK
26 *M3* **Downs** Kansas, C USA
18 *J12* **Downsville** New York, NE USA
Dow Rūd *see* Do Rūd
29 *V12* **Dows** Iowa, C USA
119 *O17* **Dowsk** ***Rus.*** Dovsk. Homyel'skaya Voblasts', SE Belarus
35 *Q4* **Doyle** California, W USA
18 *I15* **Doylestown** Pennsylvania, NE USA
Doyransko, Ezero ***see*** Doïrani, Límni
114 *I8* **Doyrentsi** Lovech, N Bulgaria
164 *G11* **Dōzen** *island* Oki-shotō, SW Japan
14 *K9* **Dozois, Réservoir** ▣ Québec, SE Canada
74 *D9* **Drâa** *seasonal river* S Morocco
Drâa, Hammada du *see* Dra, Hamada du
Drabble *see* José Enrique Rodó
117 *Q5* **Drabiv** Cherkas'ka Oblast', C Ukraine
Drable *see* José Enrique Rodó
103 *S13* **Drac** ≈ E France
Drač/Draç *see* Durrës
60 *I8* **Dracena** São Paulo, S Brazil
98 *M6* **Drachten** Friesland, N Netherlands
92 *H11* **Drag** ***Lapp.*** Ájluokta. Nordland, C Norway
116 *L14* **Dragalina** Călărași, SE Romania
116 *I14* **Draganesti-Olt** Olt, S Romania
116 *J14* **Drăgănești-Vlașca** Teleorman, S Romania
116 *I13* **Drăgășani** Vâlcea, SW Romania
114 *G9* **Dragoman** Sofiya, W Bulgaria
115 *L25* **Dragonáda** *island* SE Greece
Dragonera, Isla *see* Sa Dragonera
45 *T14* **Dragon's Mouths, The** *strait* Trinidad and Tobago/Venezuela
95 *J23* **Dragør** København, E Denmark
114 *F10* **Dragovishitsa** Kysutendil, W Bulgaria
103 *U15* **Draguignan** Var, SE France
74 *E9* **Dra, Hamada du** ***var.*** Hammada du Drâa, Haut Plateau du Dra. *plateau* W Algeria
Dra, Haut Plateau du *see* Dra, Hamada du
119 *H19* **Drahichyn** ***Pol.*** Drohiczyn Poleski, ***Rus.*** Drogichin. Brestskaya Voblasts', SW Belarus
29 *N4* **Drake** North Dakota, N USA
83 *K23* **Drakensberg** ▲▲ Lesotho/South Africa
194 *F3* **Drake Passage** *passage* Atlantic Ocean/Pacific Ocean
114 *L8* **Dralfa** Tŭrgovishte, N Bulgaria
114 *I12* **Dráma** ***var.*** Dhráma. Anatolikí Makedonía kai Thráki, NE Greece
Dramburg *see* Drawsko Pomorskie
95 *H15* **Drammen** Buskerud, S Norway
95 *H15* **Drammensfjorden** *fjord* S Norway
92 *H1* **Drangajökull** ▲ NW Iceland
95 *F16* **Drangedal** Telemark, S Norway
92 *I2* **Drangsnes** Vestfirdhir, NW Iceland
Drann *see* Dravinja
109 *T10* **Drau** ***var.*** Drava, ***Eng.*** Drave, ***Hung.*** Dráva. ≈ C Europe ***see also*** Drava
Drau *see* Drava
84 *I11* **Drava** ***var.*** Drau, ***Eng.*** Drave, ***Hung.*** Dráva. ≈ C Europe ***see also*** Drau
Drava *see* Drau
Dráva/Drave *see* Drau/Drava
109 *W10* **Dravinja** ***Ger.*** Drann. ≈ NE Slovenia
109 *V9* **Dravograd** ***Ger.*** Unterdrauburg; ***prev.*** Spodnji Dravograd. N Slovenia
110 *F10* **Drawa** ≈ NW Poland
110 *F9* **Drawno** Zachodnio-pomorskie, NW Poland
110 *F9* **Drawsko Pomorskie** ***Ger.*** Dramburg. Zachodnio-pomorskie, NW Poland
29 *R3* **Drayton** North Dakota, N USA
9 *P14* **Drayton Valley** Alberta, SW Canada
186 *B6* **Dreikikir** East Sepik, NW Papua New Guinea
Dreikirchen *see* Teiuș
98 *N7* **Drenthe** ⬖ *province* NE Netherlands
115 *H15* **Drépano, Akrotirio** ***var.*** Akrotírio Dhrepanon. *cape* N Greece
Drepanum *see* Trapani
14 *D17* **Dresden** Ontario, S Canada
101 *O16* **Dresden** Sachsen, E Germany
20 *G8* **Dresden** Tennessee, S USA
118 *M11* **Dretun'** ***Rus.*** Dretun'. Vitsyebskaya Voblasts', N Belarus
102 *M5* **Dreux** ***anc.*** Drocae, Durocasses. Eure-et-Loir, C France
94 *I11* **Drevsjø** Hedmark, S Norway
22 *K3* **Drew** Mississippi, S USA
110 *F10* **Drezdenko** ***Ger.*** Driesen. Lubuskie, W Poland
98 *J12* **Driebergen** ***var.*** Driebergen-Rijsenburg. Utrecht, C Netherlands
Driebergen-Rijsenburg ***see*** Driebergen
Driesen *see* Drezdenko
97 *N16* **Driffield** E England, UK
65 *D25* **Driftwood Point** *headland* East Falkland, Falkland Islands
33 *S14* **Driggs** Idaho, NW USA
Drin *see* Drinit, Lumi
112 *K12* **Drina** ≈ Bosnia and Herzegovina/Serbia
Drin, Gulf of *see* Drinit, Gjiri i
113 *K18* **Drinit, Gjiri i** ***var.*** Pellg i Drinit, ***Eng.*** Gulf of Drin. *gulf* NW Albania
113 *L17* **Drinit, Lumi** ***var.*** Drin. ≈ NW Albania
Drinit, Pellg i *see* Drinit, Gjiri i
Drinit të Zi, Lumi i *see* Black Drin
113 *L22* **Dríno** ***var.*** Drino, Drínos Pótamos, ***Alb.*** Lumi i Drinos. ≈ Albania/Greece
Drinos, Lumi i/Drínos Pótamos *see* Dríno
25 *S11* **Dripping Springs** Texas, SW USA
25 *S15* **Driscoll** Texas, SW USA
22 *H5* **Driskill Mountain** ▲ Louisiana, S USA
Drissa *see* Drysa
94 *G10* **Driva** ≈ S Norway
112 *E13* **Drniš** ***It.*** Šibenik-Knin. Šibenik-Knin, S Croatia
95 *H15* **Drøbak** Akershus, S Norway
116 *G13* **Drobeta-Turnu Severin** ***prev.*** Turnu Severin. Mehedinți, SW Romania
Drocae *see* Dreux
116 *M8* **Drochia** ***Rus.*** Drokiya. N Moldova
97 *F17* **Drogheda** ***Ir.*** Droichead Átha. NE Ireland
Drogichin *see* Drahichyn
Drogobych *see* Drohobych
Drohiczyn Poleski ***see*** Drahichyn
116 *H6* **Drohobych** ***Pol.*** Drohobycz, ***Rus.*** Drogobych. L'vivs'ka Oblast', NW Ukraine
Drohobycz *see* Drohobych
Droichead Átha *see* Drogheda
Droicheadna Bandan *see* Bandon
Droichead na Banna ***see*** Banbridge
Droim Mór *see* Dromore
Drokiya *see* Drochia
103 *R13* **Drôme** ⬖ *department* E France
103 *S13* **Drôme** ≈ E France
97 *G15* **Dromore** ***Ir.*** Droim Mór. SE Northern Ireland, UK
106 *A9* **Dronero** Piemonte, NE Italy
102 *L12* **Dronne** ≈ SW France
195 *Q3* **Dronning Maud Land** *physical region* Antarctica
98 *K6* **Dronrijp** ***Fris.*** Dronryp. Friesland, N Netherlands
Dronryp *see* Dronrijp
98 *L9* **Dronten** Flevoland, C Netherlands
Drontheim *see* Trondheim
102 *L13* **Dropt** ≈ SW France
149 *T4* **Drosh** North-West Frontier Province, NW Pakistan
Drossen *see* Ośno Lubuskie
Drug *see* Durg
Drujba *see* Pitnak
118 *I12* **Drūkšiai** ◎ NE Lithuania
Druk-yul *see* Bhutan
9 *Q16* **Drumheller** Alberta, SW Canada
33 *Q10* **Drummond** Montana, NW USA
31 *R4* **Drummond Island** *island* Michigan, N USA
Drummond Island ***see*** Tabiteuea
21 *X7* **Drummond, Lake** ◎ Virginia, NE USA
15 *P12* **Drummondville** Québec, SE Canada
39 *T11* **Drum, Mount** ▲ Alaska, USA
27 *O9* **Drumright** Oklahoma, C USA
99 *J14* **Drunen** Noord-Brabant, S Netherlands
Druskienniki ***see*** Druskininkai
119 *F15* **Druskininkai** ***Pol.*** Druskienniki. Alytus, S Lithuania
98 *K13* **Druten** Gelderland, SE Netherlands
118 *K11* **Druya** Vitsyebskaya Voblasts', NW Belarus
117 *S2* **Druzhba** Sums'ka Oblast', NE Ukraine
Druzhba *see* Dostyk, Kazakhstan
Druzhba *see* Pitnak, Uzbekistan
123 *R7* **Druzhina** Respublika Sakha (Yakutiya), NE Russian Federation
117 *X7* **Druzhkivka** Donets'ka Oblast', E Ukraine
112 *E12* **Drvar** ⬖ Federacija Bosna I Hercegovina, W Bosnia and Herzegovina
113 *G15* **Drvenik** Split-Dalmacija, SE Croatia
114 *K9* **Dryanovo** Gabrovo, N Bulgaria
26 *G7* **Dry Cimarron River** ≈ Kansas/Oklahoma, C USA
12 *B11* **Dryden** Ontario, C Canada
24 *M11* **Dryden** Texas, SW USA
195 *Q14* **Drygalski Ice Tongue** *ice feature* Antarctica
118 *L11* **Drysa** ***Rus.*** Drissa. ≈ N Belarus
23 *V17* **Dry Tortugas** *island* Florida, SE USA
79 *D15* **Dschang** Ouest, W Cameroon
54 *J5* **Duaca** Lara, N Venezuela
Duacum *see* Douai
Duala *see* Douala
45 *N9* **Duarte, Pico** ▲ C Dominican Republic
140 *J5* **Ḍubā** Tabūk, NW Saudi Arabia
Dubai *see* Dubayy
117 *N9* **Dubăsari** ***Rus.*** Dubossary. NE Moldova
117 *N9* **Dubăsari Reservoir** ▣ NE Moldova
8 *M10* **Dubawnt** ≈ Nunavut, NW Canada
8 *L9* **Dubawnt Lake** ◎ Northwest Territories/Nunavut, N Canada
30 *L6* **Du Bay, Lake** ▣ Wisconsin, N USA
141 *U7* **Dubayy** ***Eng.*** Dubai. Dubayy, NE United Arab Emirates
141 *W7* **Dubayy** ***Eng.*** Dubai. ✈ Dubayy, NE United Arab Emirates
183 *R7* **Dubbo** New South Wales, SE Australia
108 *G7* **Dübendorf** Zürich, NW Switzerland
97 *F18* **Dublin** ***Ir.*** Baile Átha Cliath; ***anc.*** Eblana. ● (Ireland) Dublin, E Ireland
23 *U5* **Dublin** Georgia, SE USA
25 *R7* **Dublin** Texas, SW USA
97 *G18* **Dublin** ***Ir.*** Baile Átha Cliath; ***anc.*** Eblana. ⬖ *county* E Ireland
97 *G18* **Dublin Airport** ✈ Dublin, E Ireland
189 *V12* **Dublon** ***var*** Tonoas. *island* Chuuk Islands, C Micronesia
126 *K2* **Dubna** Moskovskaya Oblast', W Russian Federation
111 *G19* **Dubňany** ***Ger.*** Dubnian. Jihomoravský Kraj, SE Czech Republic
Dubnian *see* Dubňany
111 *I19* **Dubnica nad Váhom** ***Hung.*** Máriatölgyes; ***prev.*** Dubnicz. Trenčiansky Kraj, W Slovakia
Dubnicz *see* Dubnica nad Váhom
116 *K4* **Dubno** Rivnens'ka Oblast', NW Ukraine
33 *R13* **Dubois** Idaho, NW USA
18 *D13* **Du Bois** Pennsylvania, NE USA
33 *T14* **Dubois** Wyoming, C USA
Dubossary *see* Dubăsari
127 *O10* **Dubovka** Volgogradskaya Oblast', SW Russian Federation

◆ Country
● Country Capital
◇ Dependent Territory
○ Dependent Territory Capital
⬖ Administrative Regions
✈ International Airport
▲ Mountain
▲▲ Mountain Range
⛰ Volcano
≈ River
◎ Lake
▣ Reservoir

76 H14 **Dubréka** Guinée-Maritime, SW Guinea
14 B7 **Dubreuilville** Ontario, S Canada
Dubris Portus *see* Dover
119 L20 **Dubrova** *Rus.* Dubrova. Homyel'skaya Voblasts', SE Belarus
Dubrovačko-Neretvanska Županija *see* Dubrovnik-Neretva
126 I5 **Dubrovka** Bryanskaya Oblast', W Russian Federation
113 H16 **Dubrovnik** *It.* Ragusa. Dubrovnik-Neretva, SE Croatia
113 I16 **Dubrovnik** ✕ Dubrovnik-Neretva, SE Croatia
113 F16 **Dubrovnik-Neretva** *off.* Dubrovačko-Neretvanska Županija. ⬖ *province* SE Croatia
Dubrovno *see* Dubrowna
116 L2 **Dubrovytsya** Rivnens'ka Oblast', NW Ukraine
119 O14 **Dubrowna** *Rus.* Dubrovno. Vitsyebskaya Voblasts', N Belarus
29 Z13 **Dubuque** Iowa, C USA
118 E12 **Dubysa** ≈ C Lithuania
167 U11 **Đức Cơ** Gia Lai, C Vietnam
191 V12 **Duc de Gloucester, Îles du** *Eng.* Duke of Gloucester Islands. *island group* C French Polynesia
111 C15 **Duchcov** *Ger.* Dux. Ústecký Kraj, NW Czech Republic
37 N3 **Duchesne** Utah, W USA
191 P17 **Ducie Island** *atoll* E Pitcairn Islands
9 W15 **Duck Bay** Manitoba, S Canada
23 X17 **Duck Key** *island* Florida Keys, Florida, SE USA
9 T14 **Duck Lake** Saskatchewan, S Canada
9 V15 **Duck Mountain** ▲▲ Manitoba, S Canada
20 I9 **Duck River** ≈ Tennessee, S USA
20 M10 **Ducktown** Tennessee, S USA
167 U10 **Đức Phô** Quang Ngai, C Vietnam
Đức Tho *see* Lin Camh
167 U13 **Đức Trong** *var.* Liên Nghia. Lâm Đồng, S Vietnam
D-U-D *see* Dalap-Uliga-Djarrit
99 M25 **Dudelange** *var.* Forge du Sud, *Ger.* Dudelingen. Luxembourg, S Luxembourg
Dudelingen *see* Dudelange
101 J15 **Duderstadt** Niedersachsen, C Germany
153 N15 **Dūdhi** Uttar Pradesh, N India
122 K8 **Dudinka** Taymyrskiy (Dolgano-Nenetskiy) Avtonomnyy Okrug, N Russian Federation
97 L20 **Dudley** C England, UK
154 G13 **Dudna** ≈ C India
76 L16 **Duékoué** W Ivory Coast
104 M5 **Dueñas** Castilla-León, N Spain
104 K4 **Duerna** ≈ NW Spain
105 O6 **Duero** *Port.* Douro. ≈ Portugal/Spain *see also* Douro
Duero *see* Douro
Duero *see* Douro
Duesseldorf *see* Düsseldorf
21 P12 **Due West** South Carolina, SE USA
195 P11 **Dufek Coast** *physical region* Antarctica
99 H17 **Duffel** Antwerpen, C Belgium
35 S2 **Duffer Peak** ▲ Nevada, W USA
187 Q9 **Duff Islands** *island group* E Solomon Islands
Dufour, Pizzo/Dufour, Punta *see* Dufour Spitze
108 E12 **Dufour Spitze** *It.* Pizzo Dufour, Punta Dufour. ▲ Italy/Switzerland
112 D9 **Duga Resa** Karlovac, C Croatia
22 H5 **Dugdemona River** ≈ Louisiana, S USA
154 J12 **Duggīpar** Mahārāshtra, C India
112 B13 **Dugi Otok** *var.* Isola Grossa, *It.* Isola Lunga. *island* W Croatia
113 F14 **Dugopolje** Split-Dalmacija, S Croatia
160 L8 **Du He** ≈ C China
54 M11 **Duida, Cerro** *elevation* S Venezuela
Duinekerke *see* Dunkerque
101 E15 **Duisburg** *prev.* Duisburg-Hamborn. Nordrhein-Westfalen, W Germany
Duisburg-Hamborn *see* Duisburg
99 F14 **Duiveland** *island* SW Netherlands
98 M12 **Duiven** Gelderland, E Netherlands
139 W10 **Dujaylah, Hawr ad** ◎ S Iraq
160 H9 **Dujiangyan** *var.* Guanxian, Guan Xian. Sichuan, C China
81 L18 **Dujuuma** Shabeellaha Hoose, S Somalia
Dūkān *see* Dokan
39 Z14 **Duke Island** *island* Alexander Archipelago, Alaska, USA
Dukelský Priesmy/Dukelský Průsmyk *see* Dukla Pass
Duke of Gloucester Islands *see* Duc de Gloucester, Îles du
81 F14 **Duk Faiwil** Jonglei, SE Sudan
141 T7 **Dukhān** C Qatar
Dukhan Heights *see* Dukhān, Jabal
143 N16 **Dukhān, Jabal** *var.* Dukhan Heights. *hill range* S Qatar
127 Q7 **Dukhovnitskoye** Saratovskaya Oblast', W Russian Federation
126 H4 **Dukhovshchina** Smolenskaya Oblast', W Russian Federation
Dukielska, Przełęcz *see* Dukla Pass
111 N17 **Dukla** Podkarpackie, SE Poland
Duklai Hág *see* Dukla Pass
111 N18 **Dukla Pass** *Cz.* Dukelský Průsmyk, *Ger.* Dukla-Pass, *Hung.* Duklai Hág, *Pol.* Przełęcz Dukielska, *Slvk.* Dukelský Priesmy. *pass* Poland/Slovakia
Dukla-Pass *see* Dukla Pass
Dukou *see* Panzhihua
118 I12 **Dūkštas** Utena, E Lithuania
Dulaan *see* Herlenbayan-Ulaan
159 R10 **Dulan** *var.* Qagan Us. Qinghai, C China
37 R8 **Dulce** New Mexico, SW USA
43 N16 **Dulce, Golfo** *gulf* S Costa Rica
Dulce, Golfo *see* Izabal, Lago de
42 K6 **Dulce Nombre de Culmí** Olancho, C Honduras
62 L9 **Dulce, Río** ≈ C Argentina
123 Q9 **Dulgalakh** ≈ NE Russian Federation
114 M8 **Dŭlgopol** Varna, E Bulgaria
153 V14 **Dullabchara** Assam, NE India
20 D3 **Dulles** ✕ (Washington DC)Virginia, NE USA
101 E14 **Dülmen** Nordrhein-Westfalen, W Germany
114 M7 **Dulovo** Silistra, NE Bulgaria
29 W5 **Duluth** Minnesota, N USA
138 H7 **Dūmā** *Fr.* Douma. Dimashq, SW Syria
171 O8 **Dumagasa Point** *headland* Mindanao, S Philippines
171 P6 **Dumaguete** *var.* Dumaguete City. Negros, C Philippines
Dumaguete City *see* Dumaguete
168 J10 **Dumai** Sumatera, W Indonesia
183 T4 **Dumaresq River** ≈ New South Wales/Queensland, SE Australia
27 W13 **Dumas** Arkansas, C USA
25 N1 **Dumas** Texas, SW USA
138 I7 **Ḑumayr** Dimashq, W Syria
96 I12 **Dumbarton** W Scotland, UK
96 I12 **Dumbarton** *cultural region* C Scotland, UK
187 Q17 **Dumbéa** Province Sud, S New Caledonia
111 K19 **Ďumbier** *Ger.* Djumbir, *Hung.* Gyömbér. ▲ C Slovakia
116 I11 **Dumbrăveni** *Ger.* Elisabethstedt, *Hung.* Erzsébetváros; *prev.* Ebesfalva, Eppeschdorf, Ibaşfalău. Sibiu, C Romania
116 L12 **Dumbrăveni** Vrancea, E Romania
97 J14 **Dumfries** S Scotland, UK
97 J14 **Dumfries** *cultural region* SW Scotland, UK
153 R15 **Dumka** Jhārkhand, NE India
Dümmer *see* Dümmersee
100 G12 **Dümmersee** *var.* Dümmer. ◎ NW Germany
14 J11 **Dumoine** ≈ Québec, SE Canada
14 J10 **Dumoine, Lac** ◎ Québec, SE Canada
195 V16 **Dumont d'Urville** *French research station* Antarctica
195 W15 **Dumont d'Urville Sea** *sea* S Pacific Ocean
14 K11 **Dumont, Lac** ◎ Québec, SE Canada
75 W7 **Dumyât** *Eng.* Damietta. N Egypt
Duna *see* Danube, C Europe
Düna *see* Western Dvina
Duna *see* Don, Russian Federation
Dünaburg *see* Daugavpils
111 J24 **Dunaföldvár** Tolna, C Hungary
Dunaj *see* Wien, Austria
Dunaj *see* Danube, C Europe
111 L18 **Dunajec** ≈ S Poland
111 H21 **Dunajská Streda** *Hung.* Dunaszerdahely. Trnavský Kraj, W Slovakia
Dunapentele *see* Dunaújváros
Dunărea *see* Danube
116 M13 **Dunărea Veche, Braţul** ≈ SE Romania
117 N13 **Dunării, Delta** *delta* SE Romania
Dunaszerdahely *see* Dunajská Streda
111 J23 **Dunaújváros** *prev.* Dunapentele, Sztálinváros. Fejér, C Hungary
Dunav *see* Danube
114 J8 **Dunavska Ravnina** *Eng.* Danubian Plain. *lowlands* N Bulgaria
114 G7 **Dunavtsi** Vidin, NW Bulgaria
123 S15 **Dunay** Primorskiy Kray, SE Russian Federation
Dunayevtsy *see* Dunayivtsi
116 L7 **Dunayivtsi** *Rus.* Dunayevtsy. Khmel'nyts'ka Oblast', NW Ukraine
185 F22 **Dunback** Otago, South Island, New Zealand
10 L17 **Duncan** Vancouver Island, British Columbia, SW Canada
37 O15 **Duncan** Arizona, SW USA
26 M12 **Duncan** Oklahoma, C USA
Duncan Island *see* Pinzón, Isla
151 Q20 **Duncan Passage** *strait* Andaman Sea/Bay of Bengal
96 K6 **Duncansby Head** *headland* N Scotland, UK
14 G12 **Dunchurch** Ontario, S Canada
118 D7 **Dundaga** Talsi, NW Latvia
14 G14 **Dundalk** Ontario, S Canada
97 F16 **Dundalk** *Ir.* Dún Dealgan. Louth, NE Ireland
21 X3 **Dundalk** Maryland, NE USA
97 F16 **Dundalk Bay** *Ir.* Cuan Dhún Dealgan. *bay* NE Ireland
14 G16 **Dundas** Ontario, S Canada
180 L12 **Dundas, Lake** *salt lake* Western Australia
Dundbürd *see* Batnorov
Dún Dealgan *see* Dundalk
15 N13 **Dundee** Québec, SE Canada
83 K22 **Dundee** KwaZulu/Natal, E South Africa
96 K11 **Dundee** E Scotland, UK
31 R10 **Dundee** Michigan, N USA
25 R5 **Dundee** Texas, SW USA
194 H3 **Dundee Island** *island* Antarctica
162 L9 **Dundgovĭ** ⬖ *province* C Mongolia
97 G16 **Dundrum Bay** *Ir.* Cuan Dhún Droma. *inlet* NW Irish Sea
9 T15 **Dundurn** Saskatchewan, S Canada
162 J10 **Dund-Us** Hovd, W Mongolia
Dund-Us *see* Hovd
Dund-Us *see* Dund-Us
185 F23 **Dunedin** Otago, South Island, New Zealand
183 R7 **Dunedoo** New South Wales, SE Australia
97 D14 **Dunfanaghy** *Ir.* Dún Fionnachaidh. NW Ireland
96 J12 **Dunfermline** C Scotland, UK
Dún Fionnachaidh *see* Dunfanaghy
149 V10 **Dunga Bunga** Punjab, E Pakistan
97 F15 **Dungannon** *Ir.* Dún Geanainn. C Northern Ireland, UK
Dun Garbháin *see* Dungarvan
152 F15 **Dūngarpur** Rājasthān, N India
97 E21 **Dungarvan** *Ir.* Dun Garbháin. Waterford, S Ireland
101 N21 **Dungau** *cultural region* SE Germany
Dún Geanainn *see* Dungannon
97 P23 **Dungeness** *headland* SE England, UK
63 I23 **Dungeness, Punta** *headland* S Argentina
Dungloe *see* Dunglow
97 D14 **Dunglow** *var.* Dungloe, *Ir.* An Clochán Liath. Donegal, NW Ireland
183 T7 **Dungog** New South Wales, SE Australia
79 O16 **Dungu** Orientale, NE Dem. Rep. Congo
168 L8 **Dungun** *var.* Kuala Dungun. Terengganu, Peninsular Malaysia
80 I6 **Dungûnab** Red Sea, NE Sudan
15 P13 **Dunham** Québec, SE Canada
Dunheved *see* Launceston
Dunholme *see* Durham
163 X10 **Dunhua** Jilin, NE China
159 P8 **Dunhuang** Gansu, N China
182 L12 **Dunkeld** Victoria, SE Australia
103 O1 **Dunkerque** *Eng.* Dunkirk, *Flem.* Duinekerke; *prev.* Dunquerque. Nord, N France
97 K23 **Dunkery Beacon** ▲ SW England, UK
18 C11 **Dunkirk** New York, NE USA
Dunkirk *see* Dunkerque
77 P17 **Dunkwa** SW Ghana
97 G18 **Dún Laoghaire** *Eng.* Dunleary; *prev.* Kingstown. E Ireland
29 S14 **Dunlap** Iowa, C USA
20 L10 **Dunlap** Tennessee, S USA
Dunleary *see* Dún Laoghaire
Dún Mánmhaí *see* Dunmanway
97 B21 **Dunmanway** *Ir.* Dún Mánmhaí. Cork, SW Ireland
18 I13 **Dunmore** Pennsylvania, NE USA
21 U10 **Dunn** North Carolina, SE USA
Dún na nGall *see* Donegal
23 V11 **Dunnellon** Florida, SE USA
96 J6 **Dunnet Head** *headland* N Scotland, UK
29 N14 **Dunning** Nebraska, C USA
65 B24 **Dunnose Head Settlement** West Falkland, Falkland Islands
14 G17 **Dunnville** Ontario, S Canada
Dún Pádraig *see* Downpatrick
Dunquerque *see* Dunkerque
Dunqulah *see* Dongola
96 L12 **Duns** SE Scotland, UK
29 N2 **Dunseith** North Dakota, N USA
35 N2 **Dunsmuir** California, W USA
97 N21 **Dunstable** *Lat.* Durocobrivae. E England, UK
185 D21 **Dunstan Mountains** ▲▲ South Island, New Zealand
103 O9 **Dun-sur-Auron** Cher, C France
185 F21 **Duntroon** Canterbury, South Island, New Zealand
149 T10 **Dunyāpur** Punjab, E Pakistan
163 U5 **Duobukur He** ≈ NE China
163 R12 **Duolun** *var.* Dolonnur. Nei Mongol Zizhiqu, N China
114 G10 **Dupnitsa** *prev.* Marek, Stanke Dimitrov. Kyustendil, W Bulgaria
28 L8 **Dupree** South Dakota, N USA
33 Q7 **Dupuyer** Montana, NW USA
141 Y11 **Duqm** *var.* Daqm. E Oman
63 F23 **Duque de York, Isla** *island* S Chile
181 N4 **Durack Range** ▲▲ Western Australia
136 K10 **Durağan** Sinop, N Turkey
103 S15 **Durance** ≈ SE France
31 R9 **Durand** Michigan, N USA
30 I6 **Durand** Wisconsin, N USA
40 K10 **Durango** *var.* Victoria de Durango. Durango, W Mexico
105 P3 **Durango** País Vasco, N Spain
37 Q8 **Durango** Colorado, C USA
40 J9 **Durango** ⬖ *state* C Mexico
114 O7 **Durankulak** *Rom.* Răcari; *prev.* Blatnitsa, Duranulac. Dobrich, NE Bulgaria
22 L4 **Durant** Mississippi, S USA
27 P13 **Durant** Oklahoma, C USA
Duranulac *see* Durankulak
105 N6 **Duratón** ≈ N Spain
61 E19 **Durazno** *var.* San Pedro de Durazno. Durazno, C Uruguay
61 E19 **Durazno** ⬖ *department* C Uruguay
Durazzo *see* Durrës
83 K23 **Durban** *var.* Port Natal. KwaZulu/Natal, E South Africa
83 K23 **Durban** ✕ KwaZulu/Natal, E South Africa
118 C9 **Durbe** *Ger.* Durben. Liepāja, W Latvia
Durben *see* Durbe
99 K21 **Durbuy** Luxembourg, SE Belgium
105 N15 **Dúrcal** Andalucía, S Spain
112 F8 **Đurđevac** *Ger.* Sankt Georgen, *Hung.* Szentgyörgy; *prev.* Djurdjevac, Gjurgjevac. Koprivnica-Kri»zevci, N Croatia
113 K15 **Đurđevica Tara** N Montenegro
97 L24 **Durdle Door** *natural arch* S England, UK
158 L3 **Düre** Xinjiang Uygur Zizhiqu, W China
101 D16 **Düren** *anc.* Marcodurum. Nordrhein-Westfalen, W Germany
154 K12 **Durg** *prev.* Drug. Chhattīsgarh, C India
153 U13 **Durgapur** Dhaka, N Bangladesh
153 R15 **Durgāpur** West Bengal, NE India
14 F14 **Durham** Ontario, S Canada
97 M14 **Durham** *hist.* Dunholme. N England, UK
21 U9 **Durham** North Carolina, SE USA
97 L15 **Durham** *cultural region* N England, UK
168 J10 **Duri** Sumatera, W Indonesia
Duria Major *see* Dora Baltea
Duria Minor *see* Dora Riparia
Durlas *see* Thurles
141 P8 **Ḑurmā** Ar Riyāḑ, C Saudi Arabia
113 J15 **Durmitor** ▲ N Montenegro
96 H6 **Durness** N Scotland, UK
109 Y3 **Dürnkrut** Niederösterreich, E Austria
Durnovaria *see* Dorchester
Durobrivae *see* Rochester
Durocasses *see* Dreux
Durocobrivae *see* Dunstable
Durocortorum *see* Reims
Durostorum *see* Silistra
Durovernum *see* Canterbury
113 K20 **Durrës** *var.* Durrësi, Dursi, *It.* Durazzo, *SCr.* Drač, *Turk.* Draç. Durrës, W Albania
113 K19 **Durrës** ⬖ *district* W Albania
Durrësi *see* Durrës
97 A21 **Dursey Island** *Ir.* Oileán Baoi. *island* SW Ireland
Dursi *see* Durrës
Duru *see* Wuchuan
Durud *see* Do Rūd
114 P12 **Durusu** İstanbul, NW Turkey
114 O12 **Durusu Gölü** ◎ NW Turkey
138 I9 **Durūz, Jabal ad** ▲ SW Syria
184 K13 **D'Urville Island** *island* C New Zealand
171 X12 **D'Urville, Tanjung** *cape* Papua, E Indonesia
146 H14 **Dushak** *Rus.* Dushak. Ahal Welaýaty, S Turkmenistan
Dusa Mareb/Dusa Marreb *see* Dhuusa Marreeb
118 I11 **Dusetos** Utena, NE Lithuania
Dushak *see* Dushak
160 K12 **Dushan** Guizhou, S China
147 P13 **Dushanbe** *var.* Dyushambe; *prev.* Stalinabad, *Taj.* Stalinobod. ● (Tajikistan) W Tajikistan
147 P13 **Dushanbe** ✕ W Tajikistan
137 T9 **Dushet'i** E Georgia
18 H13 **Dushore** Pennsylvania, NE USA
185 A23 **Dusky Sound** *sound* South Island, New Zealand
101 E15 **Düsseldorf** *var.* Duesseldorf. Nordrhein-Westfalen, W Germany
147 P14 **Dŭsti** *Rus.* Dusti. SW Tajikistan
194 I9 **Dustin Island** *island* Antarctica
Dutch East Indies *see* Indonesia
Dutch Guiana *see* Surinam
38 L17 **Dutch Harbor** Unalaska Island, Alaska, USA
36 J3 **Dutch Mount** ▲ Utah, W USA
Dutch New Guinea *see* Papua
Dutch West Indies *see* Netherlands Antilles
83 H20 **Dutlwe** Kweneng, S Botswana
67 V16 **Du Toit Fracture Zone** *tectonic feature* SW Indian Ocean
125 U8 **Dutovo** Respublika Komi, NW Russian Federation
77 V13 **Dutsan Wai** *var.* Dutsen Wai. Kaduna, C Nigeria
77 W13 **Dutse** Jigawa, N Nigeria
Dutsen Wai *see* Dutsan Wai
Duttia *see* Datia
14 E17 **Dutton** Ontario, S Canada
36 L7 **Dutton, Mount** ▲ Utah, W USA
162 E7 **Duut** Hovd, W Mongolia
14 K11 **Duval, Lac** ◎ Québec, SE Canada
127 W3 **Duvan** Respublika Bashkortostan, W Russian Federation
138 L9 **Duwaykhilat Satīḩ ar Ruwayshid** *seasonal river* SE Jordan
Dux *see* Duchcov
160 J13 **Duyang Shan** ▲▲ S China
167 T14 **Duyên Hai** Tra Vinh, S Vietnam
160 K12 **Duyun** Guizhou, S China
136 G11 **Düzce** Düzce, NW Turkey
136 K14 **Düzce** ⬖ *province* NW Turkey
Duzdab *see* Zāhedān
Duzenkyr, Khrebet *see* Duzkyr, Khrebet
146 I16 **Duzkyr, Khrebet** *prev.* Khrebet Duzenkyr. ▲▲ S Turkmenistan
Dvina Bay *see* Chëshskaya Guba
Dvinsk *see* Daugavpils
124 L7 **Dvinskaya Guba** *bay* NW Russian Federation
112 E10 **Dvor** Sisak-Moslavina, C Croatia
117 W5 **Dvorichna** Kharkivs'ka Oblast', E Ukraine
111 F16 **Dvůr Králové nad Labem** *Ger.* Königinhof an der Elbe. Královéhradecký Kraj, N Czech Republic
154 A10 **Dwārka** Gujarāt, W India
30 M12 **Dwight** Illinois, N USA
98 N8 **Dwingeloo** Drenthe, NE Netherlands
33 N10 **Dworshak Reservoir** ▣ Idaho, NW USA
Dyal *see* Dyaul Island
Dyanev *see* Galkynyş
Dyatlovo *see* Dzyatlava
186 G5 **Dyaul Island** *var.* Djaul, Dyal. *island* NE Papua New Guinea
20 G8 **Dyer** Tennessee, S USA
9 S5 **Dyer, Cape** *headland* Baffin Island, Nunavut, NE Canada
20 F8 **Dyersburg** Tennessee, S USA
29 Y13 **Dyersville** Iowa, C USA
97 I21 **Dyfed** *cultural region* SW Wales, UK
Dyfrdwy, Afon *see* Dee
Dyhernfurth *see* Brzeg Dolny
111 E19 **Dyje** *var.* Thaya. ≈ Austria/Czech Republic *see also* Thaya
Dyje *see* Thaya
117 T5 **Dykanska** Poltavs'ka Oblast', C Ukraine
127 N16 **Dykhtau** ▲ SW Russian Federation
111 A16 **Dyleń** *Ger.* Tillenberg. ▲ NW Czech Republic
110 K9 **Dylewska Góra** ▲ N Poland
117 O4 **Dymer** Kyyivs'ka Oblast', N Ukraine
117 W7 **Dymytrov** *Rus.* Dimitrov. Donets'ka Oblast', SE Ukraine
111 O17 **Dynów** Podkarpackie, SE Poland
29 X13 **Dysart** Iowa, C USA
Dysna *see* Dzisna
115 H18 **Dýstos, Límni** *var.* Limni Dístos. ◎ Évvoia, C Greece
115 D18 **Dytikí Elláda** *Eng.* Greece West. ⬖ *region* C Greece
115 C14 **Dytikí Makedonía** *Eng.* Macedonia West. ⬖ *region* N Greece
Dyurment'yube *see* Dermentobe
127 U4 **Dyurtyuli** Respublika Bashkortostan, W Russian Federation
Dyushambe *see* Dushanbe
162 K7 **Dzaamar** *var.* Bat-Öldziyt. Töv, C Mongolia
Dzaanhushuu *see* Ihtamir
Dza Chu *see* Mekong
Dzadgay *see* Bömbögör
162 H8 **Dzag** Bayanhongor, C Mongolia
Dzalaa *see* Shinejinst
163 O11 **Dzamïn-Üüd** *var.* Borhoyn Tal. Dornogovĭ, SE Mongolia
172 J14 **Dzaoudzi** E Mayotte
Dzaudzhikau *see* Vladikavkaz
162 G7 **Dzavhan** ⬖ *province* NW Mongolia
162 G7 **Dzavhan Gol** ≈ NW Mongolia
162 G6 **Dzavhanmandal** *var.* Nuga. Dzavhan, W Mongolia
Dzegstey *see* Ögiynuur
162 E7 **Dzereg** *var* Altanteel. Hovd, W Mongolia
127 O3 **Dzerzhinsk** Nizhegorodskaya Oblast', W Russian Federation
Dzerzhinsk *see* Dzyarzhynsk Belarus
Dzerzhinsk *see* Dzerzhyns'k
Dzerzhinskiy *see* Nar'yan-Mar
145 W13 **Dzerzhinskoye** *var.* Dzerzhinskoye. Taldykorgan, SE Kazakhstan
Dzerzhinskoye *see* Tokzhaylau
Dzerzhinskoye *see* Dzerzhinskoye
117 X7 **Dzerzhyns'k** *Rus.* Dzerzhinsk. Donets'ka Oblast', SE Ukraine
116 M5 **Dzerzhyns'k** Zhytomyrs'ka Oblast', N Ukraine
Dzhetygara *see* Zhitikara
Dzhailgan *see* Jayilgan
145 N14 **Dzhalagash** *Kaz.* Zhalashash. Kzylorda, S Kazakhstan
147 T10 **Dzhalal-Abad** *Kir.* Jalal-Abad. Dzhalal-Abadskaya Oblast', W Kyrgyzstan
147 S9 **Dzhalal-Abadskaya Oblast'** *Kir.* Jalal-Abad Oblasty. ⬖ *province* W Kyrgyzstan
Dzhalilabad *see* Cälilabad
Dzhambeyty *see* Zhympity
Dzhambulskaya Oblast' *see* Zhambyl
Dzhanibek *see* Zhanibek
Dzhankel'dy *see* Jongeldi
117 T12 **Dzhankoy** Respublika Krym, S Ukraine
145 V14 **Dzhansugurov** *Kaz.* Zhansügirov. Almaty, SE Kazakhstan
147 R9 **Dzhany-Bazar** *var.* Yangibazar. Dzhalal-Abadskaya Oblast', W Kyrgyzstan
Dzhanybek *see* Zhanibek
123 P8 **Dzhardzhan** Respublika Sakha (Yakutiya), NE Russian Federation
Dzharkurgan *see* Jarqo'rg'on
117 S11 **Dzharylhats'ka Zatoka** *gulf* S Ukraine
Dzhayilgan *see* Jayilgan
Dzhebel *see* Jebel
147 T14 **Dzhelandy** SE Tajikistan
147 Y7 **Dzhergalan** *Kir.* Jyrgalan. Issyk-Kul'skaya Oblast', NE Kyrgyzstan
Dzhetygara *see* Zhitikara
Dzhetysay *see* Zhetysay
Dzhezkazgan *see* Zhezkazgan
Dzhigirbent *see* Jigerbent
Dzhirgatal' *see* Jirgatol
Dzhizak *see* Jizzax
Dzhizakskaya Oblast' *see* Jizzax Viloyati
123 P8 **Dzhugdzhur, Khrebet** ▲▲ E Russian Federation
Dzhul'fa *see* Culfa
Dzhuma *see* Juma
145 W14 **Dzhungarskiy Alatau** ▲▲ China/Kazakhstan
144 M14 **Dzhusaly** *Kaz.* Zholsaly. Kzylorda, SW Kazakhstan
146 J12 **Dzhynlykum, Peski** *desert* E Turkmenistan
110 L9 **Działdowo** Warmińsko-Mazurskie, C Poland
111 L16 **Działoszyce** Świętokrzyskie, C Poland
41 X11 **Dzidzantún** Yucatán, E Mexico
111 G15 **Dzierżoniów** *Ger.* Reichenbach. Dolnośląskie, SW Poland
41 X11 **Dzilam de Bravo** Yucatán, E Mexico
118 L12 **Dzisna** *Rus.* Disna. Vitsyebskaya Voblasts', N Belarus
118 K12 **Dzisna** *Lith.* Dysna, *Rus.* Disna. ≈ Belarus/Lithuania
119 G20 **Dzivin** *Rus.* Divin. Brestskaya Voblasts', SW Belarus
119 M15 **Dzmitravichy** *Rus.* Dmitrovichi. Minskaya Voblasts', C Belarus
Dzogsool *see* Bayantsagaan
162 I5 **Dzöölön** *var* Rinchinlhumbe. Hövsgöl, N Mongolia
129 S8 **Dzungaria** *var.* Sungaria, Zungaria. *physical region* W China
Dzungarian Basin *see* Junggar Pendi
Dzür *see* Tes
162 J8 **Dzüünbayan-Ulaan** *var* Bayan-Ulaan. Övörhangay, C Mongolia
162 J8 **Dzüünbayan-Ulaan** *var.* Bayan-Ulaan. Övörhangay, C Mongolia
Dzüünbulag *see* Matad, Dornod, Mongolia
Dzüünbulag *see* Uulbayan, Sühbaatar, Mongolia
162 L8 **Dzuunmod** Töv, C Mongolia
Dzuunmod *see* Ider
Dzüün Soyonï Nuruu *see* Eastern Sayans
Dzüyl *see* Tonhil
Dzvina *see* Western Dvina
119 J16 **Dzyarzhynsk Belarus** *Rus.* Dzerzhinsk; *prev.* Kaydanovo. Minskaya Voblasts', C Belarus
119 H17 **Dzyatlava** *Pol.* Zdzięciół, *Rus.* Dyatlovo. Hrodzyenskaya Voblasts', W Belarus

E

E *see* Hubei
Éadan Doire *see* Edenderry
37 W6 **Eads** Colorado, C USA
37 O13 **Eagar** Arizona, SW USA
39 T8 **Eagle** Alaska, USA
13 S8 **Eagle** ≈ Newfoundland and Labrador, E Canada
10 I3 **Eagle** ≈ Yukon Territory, NW Canada
29 T7 **Eagle Bend** Minnesota, N USA
28 M8 **Eagle Butte** South Dakota, N USA
29 V12 **Eagle Grove** Iowa, C USA
19 R2 **Eagle Lake** Maine, NE USA
25 U11 **Eagle Lake** Texas, SW USA
12 A11 **Eagle Lake** ◎ Ontario, S Canada
35 P3 **Eagle Lake** ◎ California, W USA
19 R3 **Eagle Lake** ◎ Maine, NE USA
29 Y3 **Eagle Mountain** ▲ Minnesota, N USA
25 T6 **Eagle Mountain Lake** ▣ Texas, SW USA
37 S9 **Eagle Nest Lake** ▣ New Mexico, SW USA
25 P13 **Eagle Pass** Texas, SW USA
65 C25 **Eagle Passage** *passage* SW Atlantic Ocean
35 R8 **Eagle Peak** ▲ California, W USA
35 Q2 **Eagle Peak** ▲ California, W USA
37 P13 **Eagle Peak** ▲ New Mexico, SW USA
10 I4 **Eagle Plain** Yukon Territory, NW Canada
32 G15 **Eagle Point** Oregon, NW USA
186 P10 **Eagle Point** *headland* SE Papua New Guinea
38 R11 **Eagle River** Alaska, USA
30 M2 **Eagle River** Michigan, N USA
30 L4 **Eagle River** Wisconsin, N USA
21 S6 **Eagle Rock** Virginia, NE USA
36 J13 **Eagletail Mountains** ▲▲ Arizona, SW USA
167 U12 **Ea Hleo** Đăk Lăk, S Vietnam
167 U12 **Ea Kar** Đăk Lăk, S Vietnam
Eanjum *see* Anjum
Eanodat *see* Enontekiö
12 B10 **Ear Falls** Ontario, C Canada
27 X10 **Earle** Arkansas, C USA
35 R12 **Earlimart** California, W USA
20 I6 **Earlington** Kentucky, S USA
14 H8 **Earlton** Ontario, S Canada
29 T13 **Early** Iowa, C USA
96 J11 **Earn** ≈ N Scotland, UK
185 C21 **Earnslaw, Mount** ▲ South Island, New Zealand
24 M4 **Earth** Texas, SW USA
21 P11 **Easley** South Carolina, SE USA
East *see* Est
East Açores Fracture Zone *see* East Azores Fracture Zone
97 P19 **East Anglia** *physical region* E England, UK
15 Q12 **East Angus** Québec, SE Canada
East Antarctica *see* Greater Antarctica
18 E10 **East Aurora** New York, NE USA
East Australian Basin *see* Tasman Basin
East Azerbaijan *see* Āżarbāyjān-e Sharqī
East Azerbaijan *see* Āżarbāyjān-e Sharqī
64 L9 **East Azores Fracture Zone** *var.* East Açores Fracture Zone. *tectonic feature* E Atlantic Ocean
22 M11 **East Bay** *bay* Louisiana, S USA
25 V11 **East Bernard** Texas, SW USA
29 V8 **East Bethel** Minnesota, N USA
East Borneo *see* Kalimantan Timur
97 P23 **Eastbourne** SE England, UK
15 R11 **East-Broughton** Québec, SE Canada
44 M6 **East Caicos** *island* E Turks and Caicos Islands
184 R7 **East Cape** *headland* North Island, New Zealand
174 M4 **East Caroline Basin** *undersea feature* SW Pacific Ocean
192 P4 **East China Sea** *Chin.* Dong Hai. *sea* W Pacific Ocean
97 P19 **East Dereham** E England, UK
30 J9 **East Dubuque** Illinois, N USA
9 S17 **Eastend** Saskatchewan, S Canada
193 S10 **Easter Fracture Zone** *tectonic feature* E Pacific Ocean
Easter Island *see* Pascua, Isla de

◆ Country
● Country Capital
◇ Dependent Territory
○ Dependent Territory Capital
⬖ Administrative Regions
✕ International Airport
▲ Mountain
▲▲ Mountain Range
Volcano
≈ River
◎ Lake
▣ Reservoir

81 J18 **Eastern** ⬖ province Kenya
153 Q12 **Eastern** ⬖ zone E Nepal
82 L13 **Eastern** ⬖ province E Zambia
83 H24 **Eastern Cape** off. Eastern Cape Province, Afr. Oos-Kaap. ⬖ province SE South Africa
Eastern Cape Province see Eastern Cape
Eastern Desert see Sahara el Sharqîya
81 F15 **Eastern Equatoria** ⬖ state SE Sudan
Eastern Euphrates see Murat Nehri
155 J17 **Eastern Ghats** ▲▲ SE India
186 E7 **Eastern Highlands** ⬖ province C Papua New Guinea
155 K25 **Eastern Province** ⬖ province E Sri Lanka
Eastern Region see Ash Sharqīyah
122 L13 **Eastern Sayans** Mong. Dzüün Soyonï Nuruu, Rus. Vostochnyy Sayan. ▲▲ Mongolia/Russian Federation
Eastern Scheldt see Oosterschelde
Eastern Sierra Madre see Sierra Madre Oriental
Eastern Transvaal see Mpumalanga
9 W14 **Easterville** Manitoba, C Canada
Easterwâlde see Oosterwolde
63 M23 **East Falkland** var. Isla Soledad. island E Falkland Islands
19 P12 **East Falmouth** Massachusetts, NE USA
East Fayu see Fayu
East Flanders see Oost-Vlaanderen
39 S6 **East Fork Chandalar River** ≈ Alaska, USA
29 U12 **East Fork Des Moines River** ≈ Iowa/Minnesota, C USA
East Frisian Islands see Ostfriesische Inseln
18 K10 **East Glenville** New York, NE USA
29 R4 **East Grand Forks** Minnesota, N USA
97 O23 **East Grinstead** SE England, UK
18 M12 **East Hartford** Connecticut, NE USA
18 M13 **East Haven** Connecticut, NE USA
173 T9 **East Indiaman Ridge** undersea feature E Indian Ocean
129 V16 **East Indies** island group SE Asia
East Java see Jawa Timur
31 Q6 **East Jordan** Michigan, N USA
East Kalimantan see Kalimantan Timur
East Kazakhstan see Vostochnyy Kazakhstan
96 I12 **East Kilbride** S Scotland, UK
25 R7 **Eastland** Texas, SW USA
31 Q9 **East Lansing** Michigan, N USA
35 X11 **East Las Vegas** Nevada, W USA
97 M23 **Eastleigh** S England, UK
31 V12 **East Liverpool** Ohio, N USA
83 J25 **East London** Afr. Oos-Londen; prev. Emonti, Port Rex. Eastern Cape, S South Africa
96 K12 **East Lothian** cultural region SE Scotland, UK
12 I10 **Eastmain** Québec, E Canada
12 J10 **Eastmain** ≈ Québec, C Canada
15 P13 **Eastman** Québec, SE Canada
23 U6 **Eastman** Georgia, SE USA
175 O3 **East Mariana Basin** undersea feature W Pacific Ocean
30 K11 **East Moline** Illinois, N USA
186 H7 **East New Britain** ⬖ province E Papua New Guinea
29 T15 **East Nishnabotna River** ≈ Iowa, C USA
197 V12 **East Novaya Zemlya Trough** var. Novaya Zemlya Trough. undersea feature W Kara Sea
East Nusa Tenggara see Nusa Tenggara Timur
21 X4 **Easton** Maryland, NE USA
18 I14 **Easton** Pennsylvania, NE USA
193 R16 **East Pacific Rise** undersea feature E Pacific Ocean
East Pakistan see Bangladesh
31 V12 **East Palestine** Ohio, N USA
30 L12 **East Peoria** Illinois, N USA
23 S3 **East Point** Georgia, SE USA
19 U6 **Eastport** Maine, NE USA
27 Z8 **East Prairie** Missouri, C USA
19 O12 **East Providence** Rhode Island, NE USA
20 L11 **East Ridge** Tennessee, S USA
97 N16 **East Riding** cultural region N England, UK
18 F9 **East Rochester** New York, NE USA
30 K15 **East Saint Louis** Illinois, N USA
65 K21 **East Scotia Basin** undersea feature SE Scotia Sea
129 Y8 **East Sea** var. Sea of Japan, Rus. Yapanskoye More. Sea NW Pacific Ocean see also Japan, Sea of
186 B6 **East Sepik** ⬖ province NW Papua New Guinea
173 N4 **East Sheba Ridge** undersea feature W Arabian Sea
East Siberian Sea see Vostochno-Sibirskoye More
18 I14 **East Stroudsburg** Pennsylvania, NE USA
East Tasmanian Rise/East Tasmania Plateau/East Tasmania Rise see East Tasman Plateau
192 I12 **East Tasman Plateau** var. East Tasmanian Rise, East Tasmania Plateau, East Tasmania Rise. undersea feature SW Tasman Sea
64 L7 **East Thulean Rise** undersea feature N Atlantic Ocean
171 R16 **East Timor** var. Loro Sae; prev. Portuguese Timor, Timor Timur. ◆ country S Indonesia
21 Y6 **Eastville** Virginia, NE USA
35 R7 **East Walker River** ≈ California/Nevada, W USA
182 D1 **Eateringinna Creek** ≈ South Australia
37 T3 **Eaton** Colorado, C USA
15 Q12 **Eaton** ≈ Québec, SE Canada
9 S16 **Eatonia** Saskatchewan, S Canada
31 Q10 **Eaton Rapids** Michigan, N USA
23 U4 **Eatonton** Georgia, SE USA
32 H9 **Eatonville** Washington, NW USA
30 J6 **Eau Claire** Wisconsin, N USA
12 J7 **Eau Claire, Lac à l'** ◎ Québec, SE Canada
Eau Claire, Lac à L' see St. Clair, Lake
30 L6 **Eau Claire River** ≈ Wisconsin, N USA
188 J16 **Eauripik Atoll** atoll Caroline Islands, C Micronesia
192 H7 **Eauripik Rise** undersea feature W Pacific Ocean
102 K15 **Eauze** Gers, S France
41 P11 **Ébano** San Luis Potosí, C Mexico
97 K21 **Ebbw Vale** SE Wales, UK
79 E17 **Ebebiyin** NE Equatorial Guinea
95 H22 **Ebeltoft** Århus, C Denmark
109 X5 **Ebenfurth** Niederösterreich, E Austria
18 D14 **Ebensburg** Pennsylvania, NE USA
109 S5 **Ebensee** Oberösterreich, N Austria
101 H20 **Eberbach** Baden-Württemberg, SW Germany
121 U8 **Eber Gölü** salt lake C Turkey
109 U9 **Eberndorf** Slvn. Dobrla Vas. Kärnten, S Austria
109 R4 **Eberschwang** Oberösterreich, N Austria
100 O11 **Eberswalde-Finow** Brandenburg, E Germany
Ebesfalva see Dumbrăveni
165 T4 **Ebetsu** var. Ebetu. Hokkaidō, NE Japan
Ebetu see Ebetsu
Ebinayon see Evinayong
158 I4 **Ebinur Hu** ◎ NW China
138 I3 **Ebla** Ar. Tell Mardīkh. site of ancient city Idlib, NW Syria
Eblana see Dublin
108 H7 **Ebnat** Sankt Gallen, NE Switzerland
107 L18 **Eboli** Campania, S Italy
79 E16 **Ebolowa** Sud, S Cameroon
79 N21 **Ebombo** Kasai Oriental, C Dem. Rep. Congo
189 T9 **Ebon Atoll** var. Epoon. atoll Ralik Chain, S Marshall Islands
Ebora see Évora
Eboracum see York
Eborodunum see Yverdon
101 J19 **Ebrach** Bayern, C Germany
109 X5 **Ebreichsdorf** Niederösterreich, E Austria
105 S6 **Ebro** ≈ NE Spain
105 N3 **Ebro, Embalse del** ▣ N Spain
120 G7 **Ebro Fan** undersea feature W Mediterranean Sea
Eburacum see York
Ebusus see Ibiza
Ebusus see Eivissa
99 F20 **Écaussinnes-d'Enghien** Hainaut, SW Belgium
Ecbatana see Hamadān
21 Q6 **Eccles** West Virginia, NE USA
115 L14 **Eceabat** Çanakkale, NW Turkey
171 O2 **Echague** Luzon, N Philippines
Ech Cheliff/Ech Chleff see Chlef
Echeng see Ezhou
115 C18 **Echinádes** island group W Greece
114 J12 **Echínos** var. Ehinos, Ekhínos. Anatolikí Makedonía kai Thráki, NE Greece
164 J12 **Echizen-misaki** headland Honshū, SW Japan
Echmiadzin see Vagharshapat
8 J8 **Echo Bay** Northwest Territories, NW Canada
35 Y11 **Echo Bay** Nevada, W USA
36 L9 **Echo Cliffs** cliff Arizona, SW USA
14 C10 **Echo Lake** ◎ Ontario, S Canada
35 Q7 **Echo Summit** ▲ California, W USA
14 L8 **Échouani, Lac** ◎ Québec, SE Canada
99 L17 **Echt** Limburg, SE Netherlands
101 H22 **Echterdingen** ✕ (Stuttgart) Baden-Württemberg, SW Germany
99 N24 **Echternach** Grevenmacher, E Luxembourg
183 N11 **Echuca** Victoria, SE Australia
104 L14 **Ecija** anc. Astigi. Andalucía, SW Spain
Eckengraf see Viesīte
100 I7 **Eckernförde** Schleswig-Holstein, N Germany
100 J7 **Eckernförder Bucht** inlet N Germany
102 L7 **Écommoy** Sarthe, NW France
14 L10 **Écorce, Lac de l'** ◎ Québec, SE Canada
15 Q8 **Écorces, Rivière aux** ≈ Québec, SE Canada
56 C7 **Ecuador** off. Republic of Ecuador. ◆ republic NW South America
Ecuador, Republic of see Ecuador
80 L10 **Ed** var. Edd. SE Eritrea
95 I17 **Ed** Älvsborg, S Sweden
98 I9 **Edam** Noord-Holland, C Netherlands
96 K4 **Eday** island NE Scotland, UK
25 S17 **Edcouch** Texas, SW USA
Edd see Ed
80 C11 **Ed Da'ein** Southern Darfur, W Sudan
80 G11 **Ed Damazin** var. Ad Damazīn. Blue Nile, E Sudan
80 G8 **Ed Damer** var. Ad Dāmir, Ad Damar. River Nile, NE Sudan
80 E8 **Ed Debba** Northern, N Sudan
80 F10 **Ed Dueim** var. Ad Duwaym, Ad Duwēm. White Nile, C Sudan
183 Q16 **Eddystone Point** headland Tasmania, SE Australia
97 I25 **Eddystone Rocks** rocks SW England, UK
29 W15 **Eddyville** Iowa, C USA
20 H7 **Eddyville** Kentucky, S USA
98 L12 **Ede** Gelderland, C Netherlands
77 T16 **Ede** Osun, SW Nigeria
79 D16 **Edéa** Littoral, SW Cameroon
111 M20 **Edelény** Borsod-Abaúj-Zemplén, NE Hungary
183 R12 **Eden** New South Wales, SE Australia
21 T8 **Eden** North Carolina, SE USA
25 P9 **Eden** Texas, SW USA
97 K14 **Eden** ≈ NW England, UK
83 I23 **Edenburg** Free State, C South Africa
185 D24 **Edendale** Southland, South Island, New Zealand
97 E18 **Edenderry** Ir. Éadan Doire. Offaly, C Ireland
182 L11 **Edenhope** Victoria, SE Australia
21 X8 **Edenton** North Carolina, SE USA
101 G16 **Eder** ≈ NW Germany
101 H15 **Edersee** ◎ W Germany
114 E13 **Édessa** var. Édhessa. Kentrikí Makedonía, N Greece
Edessa see Şanlıurfa
Edfu see Idfu
29 P16 **Edgar** Nebraska, C USA
19 P13 **Edgartown** Martha's Vineyard, Massachusetts, NE USA
39 X13 **Edgecumbe, Mount** ▲ Baranof Island, Alaska, USA
21 Q13 **Edgefield** South Carolina, SE USA
29 P6 **Edgeley** North Dakota, N USA
28 I11 **Edgemont** South Dakota, N USA
92 O3 **Edgeøya** island S Svalbard
27 Q4 **Edgerton** Kansas, C USA
29 S10 **Edgerton** Minnesota, N USA
21 X3 **Edgewood** Maryland, NE USA
25 V6 **Edgewood** Texas, SW USA
Édhessa see Édessa
29 V9 **Edina** Minnesota, N USA
27 U2 **Edina** Missouri, C USA
25 S17 **Edinburg** Texas, SW USA
65 M24 **Edinburgh** var. Settlement of Edinburgh. ○ (Tristan da Cunha) NW Tristan da Cunha
96 J12 **Edinburgh** ● S Scotland, UK
31 P14 **Edinburgh** Indiana, N USA
96 J12 **Edinburgh** ✕ S Scotland, UK
116 L8 **Edineţ** var. Edineţi, Rus. Yedintsy. NW Moldova
Edineţi see Edineţ
Edingen see Enghien
136 B9 **Edirne** Eng. Adrianople, anc Adrianopolis, Hadrianopolis. Edirne, NW Turkey
136 B11 **Edirne** ⬖ province NW Turkey
18 K15 **Edison** New Jersey, NE USA
21 S15 **Edisto Island** South Carolina, SE USA
21 R14 **Edisto River** ≈ South Carolina, SE USA
33 S10 **Edith, Mount** ▲ Montana, NW USA
27 N10 **Edmond** Oklahoma, C USA
32 H8 **Edmonds** Washington, NW USA
9 Q14 **Edmonton** province capital Alberta, SW Canada
20 K7 **Edmonton** Kentucky, S USA
9 Q14 **Edmonton** ✕ Alberta, SW Canada
29 P3 **Edmore** North Dakota, N USA
13 N13 **Edmundston** New Brunswick, SE Canada
25 U12 **Edna** Texas, SW USA
39 X14 **Edna Bay** Kosciusko Island, Alaska, USA
77 U16 **Edo** ⬖ state S Nigeria
106 F6 **Edolo** Lombardia, N Italy
64 L6 **Edoras Bank** undersea feature C Atlantic Ocean
96 G7 **Edrachillis Bay** bay NW Scotland, UK
136 B12 **Edremit** Balıkesir, NW Turkey
136 B12 **Edremit Körfezi** gulf NW Turkey
95 P14 **Edsbro** Stockholm, C Sweden
95 N18 **Edsbruk** Kalmar, S Sweden
94 M12 **Edsbyn** Gävleborg, C Sweden
9 O14 **Edson** Alberta, SW Canada
62 K13 **Eduardo Castex** La Pampa, C Argentina
58 F12 **Eduardo Gomes** ✕ (Manaus) Amazonas, NW Brazil
Edwardesabad see Bannu
67 U9 **Edward, Lake** var. Albert Edward Nyanza, Edward Nyanza, Lac Idi Amin, Lake Rutanzige. ◎ Uganda/Dem. Rep. Congo
Edward Nyanza see Edward, Lake
22 K5 **Edwards** Mississippi, S USA
25 O10 **Edwards Plateau** plain Texas, SW USA
30 J11 **Edwards River** ≈ Illinois, N USA
30 K15 **Edwardsville** Illinois, N USA
195 X4 **Edward VIII Gulf** bay Antarctica
195 O13 **Edward VII Peninsula** peninsula Antarctica
10 J11 **Edziza, Mount** ▲ British Columbia, W Canada
23 H16 **Edzo** prev. Rae-Edzo. Northwest Territories, NW Canada
39 N12 **Eek** Alaska, USA
99 D16 **Eeklo** var. Eekloo. Oost-Vlaanderen, NW Belgium
Eekloo see Eeklo
39 N12 **Eek River** ≈ Alaska, USA
98 N6 **Eelde** Drenthe, NE Netherlands
34 L5 **Eel River** ≈ California, W USA
31 P12 **Eel River** ≈ Indiana, N USA
Eems see Ems
98 O4 **Eemshaven** Groningen, NE Netherlands
98 O5 **Eems Kanaal** canal NE Netherlands
98 M11 **Eerbeek** Gelderland, E Netherlands
99 C17 **Eernegem** West-Vlaanderen, W Belgium
99 J15 **Eersel** Noord-Brabant, S Netherlands
Eesti Vabariik see Estonia
187 R14 **Éfaté** var. Efate, Fr. Vaté; prev. Sandwich Island. island C Vanuatu
Efate see Éfaté
109 S4 **Eferding** Oberösterreich, N Austria
30 M15 **Effingham** Illinois, N USA
117 N15 **Eforie-Nord** Constanţa, SE Romania
117 N15 **Eforie Sud** Constanţa, E Romania
Efyrnwy, Afon see Vyrnwy
Eg see Batshireet
107 G23 **Egadi, Isole** island group S Italy
35 X6 **Egan Range** ▲▲ Nevada, W USA
14 K12 **Eganville** Ontario, SE Canada
Ege Denizi see Aegean Sea
39 O14 **Egegik** Alaska, USA
111 L21 **Eger** Ger. Erlau. Heves, NE Hungary
Eger see Cheb
Eger see Ohre
173 P8 **Egeria Fracture Zone** tectonic feature W Indian Ocean
95 C17 **Egersund** Rogaland, S Norway
108 J7 **Egg** Vorarlberg, NW Austria
101 H14 **Egge-gebirge** ▲▲ C Germany
109 Q4 **Eggelsberg** Oberösterreich, N Austria
109 W2 **Eggenburg** Niederösterreich, NE Austria
101 N22 **Eggenfelden** Bayern, SE Germany
18 J17 **Egg Harbor City** New Jersey, NE USA
65 G25 **Egg Island** island W Saint Helena
183 N14 **Egg Lagoon** Tasmania, SE Australia
99 I20 **Éghezèe** Namur, C Belgium
92 L2 **Egilsstadhir** Austurland, E Iceland
Egina see Aígina
Egindibulaq see Yegindybulak
Egio see Aígio
103 N12 **Égletons** Corrèze, C France
98 H9 **Egmond aan Zee** Noord-Holland, NW Netherlands
Egmont see Taranaki, Mount
184 J10 **Egmont, Cape** cape North Island, New Zealand
Egoli see Johannesburg
Eğri Palanka see Kriva Palanka
95 G23 **Egtved** Vejle, C Denmark
123 U5 **Egvekinot** Chukotskiy Avtonomnyy Okrug, NE Russian Federation
75 V9 **Egypt** off. Arab Republic of Egypt, Ar. Jumhūrīyah Miṣr al 'Arabīyah, prev. United Arab Republic; anc. Aegyptus. ◆ republic NE Africa
30 L17 **Egypt, Lake Of** ▣ Illinois, N USA
162 I14 **Ehen Hudag** var Alx Youqi. Nei Mongol Zizhiqu, N China
164 F14 **Ehime** off. Ehime-ken. ⬖ prefecture Shikoku, SW Japan
Ehime-ken see Ehime
101 I23 **Ehingen** Baden-Württemberg, S Germany
Ehinos see Echínos
21 R14 **Ehrhardt** South Carolina, SE USA
108 L7 **Ehrwald** Tirol, W Austria
191 W6 **Eiao** island Îles Marquises, NE French Polynesia
105 P2 **Eibar** País Vasco, N Spain
98 O11 **Eibergen** Gelderland, E Netherlands
109 V9 **Eibiswald** Steiermark, SE Austria
109 P8 **Eichham** ▲ SW Austria
101 J15 **Eichsfeld** hill range C Germany
101 K21 **Eichstätt** Bayern, SE Germany
100 H8 **Eider** ≈ N Germany
94 E13 **Eidfjord** Hordaland, S Norway
94 D13 **Eidfjorden** fjord S Norway
94 F9 **Eidsvåg** Møre og Romsdal, S Norway
95 I14 **Eidsvoll** Akershus, S Norway
92 N2 **Eidsvollfjellet** ▲ NW Svalbard
Eier-Berg see Suur Munamägi
101 D18 **Eifel** plateau W Germany
108 E9 **Eiger** ▲ C Switzerland
96 G10 **Eigg** island W Scotland, UK
155 D24 **Eight Degree Channel** channel India/Maldives
44 G1 **Eight Mile Rock** Grand Bahama Island, N Bahamas
194 J9 **Eights Coast** physical region Antarctica
180 K6 **Eighty Mile Beach** beach Western Australia
99 L18 **Eijsden** Limburg, SE Netherlands
95 G15 **Eikeren** ◎ S Norway
Eil see Eyl
Eilat see Elat
183 O12 **Eildon** Victoria, SE Australia
183 O12 **Eildon, Lake** ◎ Victoria, SE Australia
80 E8 **Eilei** Northern Kordofan, C Sudan
101 N15 **Eilenburg** Sachsen, E Germany
Eil Malk see Mecherchar
94 H13 **Eina** Oppland, S Norway
101 I14 **Einbeck** Niedersachsen, C Germany
99 K15 **Eindhoven** Noord-Brabant, S Netherlands
108 G8 **Einsiedeln** Schwyz, NE Switzerland
Eipel see Ipeľ
Éire see Ireland
Éireann, Muir see Irish Sea
Eirik Outer Ridge see Eirik Ridge
64 I6 **Eirik Ridge** var. Eirik Outer Ridge. undersea feature E Labrador Sea
92 I3 **Eiríksjökull** ▲ C Iceland
59 B14 **Eirunepé** Amazonas, N Brazil
99 L17 **Eisden** Limburg, NE Belgium
83 F18 **Eiseb** ≈ Botswana/Namibia
Eisen see Yŏngch'ŏn
101 J16 **Eisenach** Thüringen, C Germany
Eisenburg see Vasvár
109 U6 **Eisenerz** Steiermark, SE Austria
100 Q13 **Eisenhüttenstadt** Brandenburg, E Germany
109 U10 **Eisenkappel** Slvn. Železna Kapela. Kärnten, S Austria
Eisenmarkt see Hunedoara
109 Y5 **Eisenstadt** Burgenland, E Austria
Eishū see Yŏngju
119 H15 **Eišiškes** Vilnius, SE Lithuania
101 L15 **Eisleben** Sachsen-Anhalt, C Germany
190 I3 **Eita** Tarawa, W Kiribati
Eitape see Aitape
105 V11 **Eivissa** var. Iviza, Cast. Ibiza; anc. Ebusus. Ibiza, Spain, W Mediterranean Sea
Eivissa see Ibiza
105 R4 **Ejea de los Caballeros** Aragón, NE Spain
40 E8 **Ejido Insurgentes** Baja California Sur, W Mexico
Ejin Qi see Dalain Hob
Ejmiadzin/Ejmiatsin see Vagharshapat
77 P16 **Ejura** C Ghana
41 R16 **Ejutla** var. Ejutla de Crespo. Oaxaca, SE Mexico
Ejutla de Crespo see Ejutla
33 Y10 **Ekalaka** Montana, NW USA
Ekapa see Cape Town
Ekaterinodar see Krasnodar
93 L20 **Ekenäs** Fin. Tammisaari. Etelä-Suomi, SW Finland
146 B13 **Ekerem** Rus. Okarem. Balkan Welaýaty, W Turkmenistan
184 M13 **Eketahuna** Manawatu-Wanganui, North Island, New Zealand
Ekhínos see Echínos
Ostan-e Khorāsān-e Shemālī see Khorāsān-e Shemālī
123 U5 **Ekiatapskiy Khrebet** ▲▲ NE Russian Federation
145 T8 **Ekibastuz** Pavlodar, NE Kazakhstan
123 R13 **Ekimchan** Amurskaya Oblast', SE Russian Federation
95 O15 **Ekoln** ◎ C Sweden
80 I7 **Ekowit** Red Sea, NE Sudan
95 L19 **Eksjö** Jönköping, S Sweden
93 I15 **Ekträsk** Västerbotten, N Sweden
39 O13 **Ekuk** Alaska, USA
12 F9 **Ekwan** ≈ Ontario, C Canada
39 O13 **Ekwok** Alaska, USA
166 M6 **Ela** Mandalay, C Myanmar (Burma)
El Aaiun see El Ayoun
81 N15 **Ēl Ābrēd** Somali, E Ethiopia
115 F22 **Elafónisos** island S Greece
115 F22 **Elafonísou, Porthmós** strait S Greece
El-Aïoun see El Ayoun
75 U8 **El 'Alamein** var. Al 'Alamayn. N Egypt
41 Q12 **El Alazán** Veracruz-Llave, C Mexico
57 J18 **El Alto** var. La Paz. ✕ (La Paz) La Paz, W Bolivia
Elam see Īlām
El Amparo see El Amparo de Apure
54 I8 **El Amparo de Apure** var. El Amparo. Apure, C Venezuela
171 R13 **Elara** Pulau Ambelau, E Indonesia
El Araïch/El Araïche see Larache
40 D6 **El Arco** Baja California, NW Mexico
75 X7 **El 'Arîsh** var. Al 'Arīsh. NE Egypt
115 L25 **Elása** island SE Greece
El Asnam see Chlef
Elassón see Elassóna
115 E15 **Elassóna** prev. Elassón. Thessalía, C Greece
105 N2 **El Astillero** Cantabria, N Spain
138 F14 **Elat** var. Eilat, Elath. Southern, S Israel
Elat, Gulf of see Aqaba, Gulf of
Elath see Elat, Israel
Elath see Al 'Aqabah, Jordan
115 C17 **Eláti** ▲ Lefkáda, Iónioi Nísoi, Greece, C Mediterranean Sea
188 L16 **Elato Atoll** atoll Caroline Islands, C Micronesia
80 C7 **El'Atrun** Northern Darfur, NW Sudan
74 H6 **El Ayoun** var. El Aaiun, El-Aïoun, La Youne. NE Morocco
137 N14 **Elâzığ** var. Elâzig, Elâziz. Elâzığ, E Turkey
137 O14 **Elâzığ** var. Elâzig, Elâziz. ⬖ province C Turkey
Elâzîg/Elâzîz see Elâzığ
23 Q7 **Elba** Alabama, S USA
106 E13 **Elba, Isola d'** island Archipelago Toscano, C Italy
123 S13 **El'ban** Khabarovskiy Kray, E Russian Federation
54 F6 **El Banco** Magdalena, N Colombia
El Barco see O Barco
104 L8 **El Barco de Ávila** Castilla-León, N Spain
El Barco de Valdeorras see O Barco
138 H7 **El Barouk, Jabal** ▲▲ C Lebanon
113 L20 **Elbasan** var. Elbasani. Elbasan, C Albania
113 L20 **Elbasan** ⬖ district C Albania
Elbasani see Elbasan
54 K6 **El Baúl** Cojedes, C Venezuela
86 D11 **Elbe** Cz. Labe. ≈ Czech Republic/Germany
100 L13 **Elbe-Havel-Kanal** canal E Germany
100 K9 **Elbe-Lübeck-Kanal** canal N Germany
El Beni see Beni
138 H7 **El Beqaa** var. Al Biqā', Bekaa Valley. valley E Lebanon
25 R6 **Elbert** Texas, SW USA
37 R5 **Elbert, Mount** ▲ Colorado, C USA
23 U3 **Elberton** Georgia, SE USA
100 K11 **Elbe-Seiten-Kanal** canal N Germany
102 M4 **Elbeuf** Seine-Maritime, N France
Elbing see Elbląg
136 M15 **Elbistan** Kahramanmaraş, S Turkey
110 K7 **Elbląg** var. Elbląg, Ger. Elbing. Warmińsko-Mazurskie, NE Poland
43 N10 **El Bluff** Región Autónoma Atlántico Sur, SE Nicaragua
63 H17 **El Bolsón** Río Negro, W Argentina
105 P11 **El Bonillo** Castilla-La Mancha, C Spain
El Bordo see Patía
El Boulaida/El Bouläida see Blida
9 T16 **Elbow** Saskatchewan, S Canada
29 S7 **Elbow Lake** Minnesota, N USA
127 N16 **El'brus** var. Gora El'brus. ▲ SW Russian Federation
El'brus, Gora see El'brus
126 M15 **El'brusskiy** Karachayevo-Cherkesskaya Respublika, SW Russian Federation
81 D14 **El Buhayrat** var. Lakes State. ⬖ state S Sudan
El Bur see Ceel Buur
98 L10 **Elburg** Gelderland, E Netherlands
105 O6 **El Burgo de Osma** Castilla-León, C Spain
Elburz Mountains see Alborz, Reshteh-ye Kūhhā-ye
35 V17 **El Cajon** California, W USA
63 H22 **El Calafate** var. Calafate. Santa Cruz, S Argentina
55 Q8 **El Callao** Bolívar, E Venezuela
25 U12 **El Campo** Texas, SW USA
54 I7 **El Cantón** Barinas, W Venezuela
35 Q8 **El Capitan** ▲ California, W USA
54 H5 **El Carmelo** Zulia, NW Venezuela
62 J5 **El Carmen** Jujuy, NW Argentina
54 E5 **El Carmen de Bolívar** Bolívar, NW Colombia
55 O8 **El Casabe** Bolívar, SE Venezuela
42 M12 **El Castillo de La Concepción** Río San Juan, SE Nicaragua
El Cayo see San Ignacio
35 X17 **El Centro** California, W USA
55 N6 **El Chaparro** Anzoátegui, NE Venezuela
105 S12 **Elche** Cat. Elx; anc. Ilici, Lat. Illicis. País Valenciano, E Spain
105 Q12 **Elche de la Sierra** Castilla-La Mancha, C Spain
41 U15 **El Chichónal, Volcán** ⛰ SE Mexico
40 C2 **El Chinero** Baja California, NW Mexico
181 R1 **Elcho Island** island Wessel Islands, Northern Territory, N Australia
63 H18 **El Corcovado** Chubut, SW Argentina
105 R12 **Elda** País Valenciano, E Spain
100 M10 **Elde** ≈ NE Germany
98 L12 **Elden** Gelderland, E Netherlands
81 J16 **El Der** spring/well S Ethiopia
El Dere see Ceel Dheere
40 E3 **El Desemboque** Sonora, NW Mexico
54 F5 **El Difícil** var. Ariguaní. Magdalena, N Colombia
123 R10 **El'dikan** Respublika Sakha (Yakutiya), NE Russian Federation
El Djazaïr see Alger
El Djelfa see Djelfa
29 X15 **Eldon** Iowa, C USA
27 U5 **Eldon** Missouri, C USA
54 E13 **El Doncello** Caquetá, S Colombia
29 W13 **Eldora** Iowa, C USA
60 G12 **Eldorado** Misiones, NE Argentina
40 I9 **El Dorado** Sinaloa, C Mexico
27 U14 **El Dorado** Arkansas, C USA
30 M17 **Eldorado** Illinois, N USA
27 O6 **El Dorado** Kansas, C USA
26 K12 **Eldorado** Oklahoma, C USA
25 O9 **Eldorado** Texas, SW USA
55 Q8 **El Dorado** Bolívar, E Venezuela
54 F10 **El Dorado** ✕ (Bogotá) Cundinamarca, C Colombia
El Dorado see California
27 O6 **El Dorado Lake** ▣ Kansas, C USA
27 S6 **El Dorado Springs** Missouri, C USA
81 H18 **Eldoret** Rift Valley, W Kenya
29 Z14 **Eldridge** Iowa, C USA
95 J21 **Eldsberga** Halland, S Sweden
25 R4 **Electra** Texas, SW USA
37 Q7 **Electra Lake** ▣ Colorado, C USA
38 B8 **'Ele'ele** var. Eleele. Kaua'i, Hawai'i, USA
Eleele see 'Ele'ele
Elefantes see Olifants
115 H19 **Elefsína** prev. Elevsís. Attikí, C Greece
115 G19 **Eléftheres** anc. Eleutherae. site of ancient city Attikí/Stereá Ellás, C Greece
114 I13 **Elefteroúpoli** prev. Elevtheroúpolis. Anatolikí Makedonía kai Thráki, NE Greece
74 F10 **El Eglab** ▲▲ SW Algeria
118 F10 **Eleja** Jelgava, C Latvia
Elek see Ilek
119 G14 **Elektrėnai** Vilnius, SE Lithuania
126 L3 **Elektrostal'** Moskovskaya Oblast', W Russian Federation
81 H15 **Elemi Triangle** disputed region Kenya/Sudan
54 G16 **El Encanto** Amazonas, S Colombia
37 R14 **Elephant Butte Reservoir** ▣ New Mexico, SW USA
Éléphant, Chaîne de l' see Dâmrei, Chuŏr Phmun
194 G2 **Elephant Island** island South Shetland Islands, Antarctica
Elephant River see Olifants
El Escorial see San Lorenzo de El Escorial
Élesd see Aleşd
114 F11 **Eleshnitsa** ≈ W Bulgaria

◆ Country ◇ Dependent Territory ⬖ Administrative Regions ▲ Mountain ⛰ Volcano ◎ Lake
● Country Capital ○ Dependent Territory Capital ✕ International Airport ▲▲ Mountain Range ≈ River ▣ Reservoir

137 S13 **Eleşkirt** Ağrı, E Turkey
42 F5 **El Estor** Izabal, E Guatemala
Eleutherae see Eléftheres
44 I2 **Eleuthera Island** island N Bahamas
37 S5 **Elevenmile Canyon Reservoir** ⊠ Colorado, C USA
27 W8 **Eleven Point River** ~ Arkansas/Missouri, C USA
Elevsís see Elefsína
Elevtheroúpolis see Eleftheroúpoli
75 W8 **El Faiyûm** var. Al Fayyūm. N Egypt
80 B10 **El Fasher** var. Al Fāshir. Northern Darfur, W Sudan
75 W8 **El Fashn** var. Al Fashn. C Egypt
El Ferrol/El Ferrol del Caudillo see Ferrol
39 W13 **Elfin Cove** Chichagof Island, Alaska, USA
105 W4 **El Fluvià** ~ NE Spain
40 H7 **El Fuerte** Sinaloa, W Mexico
80 D11 **El Fula** Western Kordofan, C Sudan
El Gedaref see Gedaref
80 A10 **El Geneina** var. Ajjinena, Al-Genain, Al Junaynah. Western Darfur, W Sudan
96 J8 **Elgin** NE Scotland, UK
30 M10 **Elgin** Illinois, N USA
29 P14 **Elgin** Nebraska, C USA
35 Y9 **Elgin** Nevada, W USA
28 L6 **Elgin** North Dakota, N USA
26 M12 **Elgin** Oklahoma, C USA
25 T10 **Elgin** Texas, SW USA
123 R9 **El'ginskiy** Respublika Sakha (Yakutiya), NE Russian Federation
75 W8 **El Gîza** var. Al Jīzah, Gîza, Gizeh. N Egypt
74 J8 **El Goléa** var. Al Golea. C Algeria
40 D2 **El Golfo de Santa Clara** Sonora, NW Mexico
81 G18 **Elgon, Mount** ▲ E Uganda
105 T4 **El Grado** Aragón, NE Spain
94 I10 **Elgpiggen** ▲ S Norway
40 L6 **El Guaje, Laguna** ⊠ NE Mexico
54 H6 **El Guayabo** Zulia, W Venezuela
77 O6 **El Guettâra** oasis N Mali
76 J6 **El Ḥammâmi** desert N Mauritania
76 M5 **El Ḥank** cliff N Mauritania
El Haseke see Al Ḥasakah
80 H10 **El Hawata** Gedaref, E Sudan
El Higo see Higos
171 T16 **Eliase** Pulau Selaru, E Indonesia
Elías Piña see Comendador
25 R6 **Eliasville** Texas, SW USA
Elichpur see Achalpur
37 V13 **Elida** New Mexico, SW USA
115 F18 **Elikónas** ▲▲ C Greece
67 T10 **Elila** ~ W Dem. Rep. Congo
39 N9 **Elim** Alaska, USA
Elimberrum see Auch
Eliocroca see Lorca
61 B16 **Elisa** Santa Fe, C Argentina
Elisabethstedt see Dumbrăveni
Élisabethville see Lubumbashi
127 O13 **Elista** Respublika Kalmykiya, SW Russian Federation
182 I9 **Elizabeth** South Australia
21 Q3 **Elizabeth** West Virginia, NE USA
19 Q9 **Elizabeth, Cape** headland Maine, NE USA
21 Y8 **Elizabeth City** North Carolina, SE USA
21 P8 **Elizabethton** Tennessee, S USA
30 M17 **Elizabethtown** Illinois, N USA
20 K6 **Elizabethtown** Kentucky, S USA
18 L7 **Elizabethtown** New York, NE USA
21 U11 **Elizabethtown** North Carolina, SE USA
18 G15 **Elizabethtown** Pennsylvania, NE USA
74 E6 **El-Jadida** prev. Mazagan. W Morocco
El Jafr see Jafr, Qāʻ al
80 F11 **El Jebelein** White Nile, E Sudan
110 N8 **Ełk** Ger. Lyck. Warmińsko-mazurskie, NE Poland
110 O8 **Ełk** ~ NE Poland
29 Y12 **Elkader** Iowa, C USA
80 G9 **El Kamlin** Gezira, C Sudan
33 N11 **Elk City** Idaho, NW USA
26 K10 **Elk City** Oklahoma, C USA
27 P7 **Elk City Lake** ⊠ Kansas, C USA
34 M5 **Elk Creek** California, W USA
28 J10 **Elk Creek** ~ South Dakota, N USA
74 M5 **El Kef** var. Al Kāf, Le Kef. NW Tunisia
74 F7 **El Kelâa Srarhna** var. Kal al Sraghna. C Morocco
El Kerak see Al Karak
9 P17 **Elkford** British Columbia, SW Canada
El Khalil see Hebron
80 E7 **El Khandaq** Northern, N Sudan
75 W10 **El Khârga** var. Al Khārijah. C Egypt
31 P11 **Elkhart** Indiana, N USA
26 H7 **Elkhart** Kansas, C USA
25 V8 **Elkhart** Texas, SW USA
30 M7 **Elkhart Lake** ◎ Wisconsin, N USA
El Khartûm see Khartoum
37 Q3 **Elkhead Mountains** ▲▲ Colorado, C USA
18 I12 **Elk Hill** ▲ Pennsylvania, NE USA
138 G8 **El Khiyam** , var. Al Khiyām. S Lebanon
29 S15 **Elkhorn** Nebraska, C USA
30 M9 **Elkhorn** Wisconsin, N USA
29 R14 **Elkhorn River** ~ Nebraska, C USA
127 O16 **El'khotovo** Respublika Severnaya Osetiya, SW Russian Federation
114 L10 **Elkhovo** prev. Kizilagach. Yambol, E Bulgaria
21 R8 **Elkin** North Carolina, SE USA
21 S4 **Elkins** West Virginia, NE USA
195 X3 **Elkins, Mount** ▲ Antarctica
14 G8 **Elk Lake** Ontario, S Canada
31 P6 **Elk Lake** ◎ Michigan, N USA
18 F12 **Elkland** Pennsylvania, NE USA
35 W3 **Elko** Nevada, W USA
9 R14 **Elk Point** Alberta, SW Canada
29 R12 **Elk Point** South Dakota, N USA
29 V8 **Elk River** Minnesota, N USA
20 J10 **Elk River** ~ Alabama/Tennessee, S USA
21 R4 **Elk River** ~ West Virginia, NE USA
20 I7 **Elkton** Kentucky, S USA
21 Y2 **Elkton** Maryland, NE USA
29 R10 **Elkton** South Dakota, N USA
20 I10 **Elkton** Tennessee, S USA
21 U5 **Elkton** Virginia, NE USA
El Kuneitra see Al Qunayṭirah
81 L15 **El Kure** Somali, E Ethiopia
80 D12 **El Lagowa** Western Kordofan, C Sudan
39 S12 **Ellamar** Alaska, USA
Ellás see Greece
23 S6 **Ellaville** Georgia, SE USA
197 P9 **Ellef Ringnes Island** island Nunavut, N Canada
29 V10 **Ellendale** Minnesota, N USA
29 P7 **Ellendale** North Dakota, N USA
36 M6 **Ellen, Mount** ▲ Utah, W USA
32 I9 **Ellensburg** Washington, NW USA
18 K12 **Ellenville** New York, NE USA
Ellep see Lib
21 T10 **Ellerbe** North Carolina, SE USA
197 P10 **Ellesmere Island** island Queen Elizabeth Islands, Nunavut, N Canada
185 H19 **Ellesmere, Lake** ◎ South Island, New Zealand
97 K18 **Ellesmere Port** C England, UK
31 O14 **Ellettsville** Indiana, N USA
99 E19 **Ellezelles** Hainaut, SW Belgium
8 L7 **Ellice** ~ Nunavut, NE Canada
Ellice Islands see Tuvalu
Ellichpur see Achalpur
21 W3 **Ellicott City** Maryland, NE USA
23 S2 **Ellijay** Georgia, SE USA
27 W7 **Ellington** Missouri, C USA
26 L5 **Ellinwood** Kansas, C USA
83 J24 **Elliot** Eastern Cape, SE South Africa
14 D10 **Elliot Lake** Ontario, S Canada
181 X6 **Elliot, Mount** ▲ Queensland, E Australia
21 T5 **Elliott Knob** ▲ Virginia, NE USA
26 K4 **Ellis** Kansas, C USA
182 F8 **Elliston** South Australia
22 M7 **Ellisville** Mississippi, S USA
105 V5 **El Llobregat** ~ NE Spain
96 L9 **Ellon** NE Scotland, UK
Ellore see Elūru
21 S13 **Elloree** South Carolina, SE USA
26 M4 **Ellsworth** Kansas, C USA
19 S7 **Ellsworth** Maine, NE USA
30 I6 **Ellsworth** Wisconsin, N USA
26 M11 **Ellsworth, Lake** ⊠ Oklahoma, C USA
194 K9 **Ellsworth Land** physical region Antarctica
194 L9 **Ellsworth Mountains** ▲▲ Antarctica
101 J21 **Ellwangen** Baden-Württemberg, S Germany
18 B14 **Ellwood City** Pennsylvania, NE USA
108 H8 **Elm** Glarus, NE Switzerland
32 G9 **Elma** Washington, NW USA
121 V13 **El Maḥalla el Kubra** var. Al Maḥallah al Kubrá, Mahalla el Kubra. N Egypt
74 E9 **El Mahbas** var. Mahbés. SW Western Sahara
63 H17 **El Maitén** Chubut, W Argentina
136 E16 **Elmalı** Antalya, SW Turkey
80 G10 **El Manaqil** Gezira, C Sudan
54 M12 **El Mango** Amazonas, S Venezuela
75 W7 **El Manṣûra** var. Al Manṣūrah, Manṣūra. N Egypt
55 P8 **El Manteco** Bolívar, E Venezuela
29 O16 **Elm Creek** Nebraska, C USA
El Mediyya see Médéa
77 V9 **Elméki** Agadez, C Niger
108 K7 **Elmen** Tirol, W Austria
18 J16 **Elmer** New Jersey, NE USA
138 G6 **El Mina** var. Al Mīnā'. N Lebanon
75 W9 **El Minya** var. Al Minyā, Minya. C Egypt
14 F15 **Elmira** Ontario, S Canada
18 G11 **Elmira** New York, NE USA
36 K13 **El Mirage** Arizona, SW USA
29 O7 **Elm Lake** ⊠ South Dakota, N USA
El Mojân see San Rafael
105 N7 **El Molar** Madrid, C Spain
76 L7 **El Mrâyer** well C Mauritania
76 L5 **El Mreïti** well N Mauritania
76 L8 **El Mreyyé** desert E Mauritania
29 P8 **Elm River** ~ North Dakota/South Dakota, N USA
100 I9 **Elmshorn** Schleswig-Holstein, N Germany
80 D12 **El Muglad** Western Kordofan, C Sudan
El Muwaqqar see Al Muwaqqar
14 G14 **Elmvale** Ontario, S Canada
30 K12 **Elmwood** Illinois, N USA
26 J8 **Elmwood** Oklahoma, C USA
103 P17 **Elne** anc. Illiberis. Pyrénées-Orientales, S France
54 F11 **El Nevado, Cerro** elevation C Colombia
171 N5 **El Nido** Palawan, W Philippines
62 I12 **El Nihuil** Mendoza, W Argentina
75 W7 **El Nouzha** ✈ (Alexandria) N Egypt
80 E10 **El Obeid** var. Al Obayyid, Al Ubayyiḍ. Northern Kordofan, C Sudan
41 O13 **El Oro** México, S Mexico
56 B8 **El Oro** ◐ province SW Ecuador
61 B19 **Elortondo** Santa Fe, C Argentina
54 J8 **Elorza** Apure, C Venezuela
El Ouâdi see El Oued
74 L7 **El Oued** var. Al Oued, El Ouâdi, El Wad. NE Algeria
36 L15 **Eloy** Arizona, SW USA
55 Q7 **El Palmar** Bolívar, E Venezuela
40 K8 **El Palmito** Durango, W Mexico
55 P7 **El Pao** Bolívar, E Venezuela
54 K5 **El Pao** Cojedes, N Venezuela
42 J7 **El Paraíso** El Paraíso, S Honduras
42 I7 **El Paraíso** ◐ department SE Honduras
30 L12 **El Paso** Illinois, N USA
24 G8 **El Paso** Texas, SW USA
24 G8 **El Paso** ✈ Texas, SW USA
105 U7 **El Perello** Cataluña, NE Spain
55 P5 **El Pilar** Sucre, NE Venezuela
42 F7 **El Pital, Cerro** ▲ El Salvador/Honduras
35 Q9 **El Portal** California, W USA
40 J3 **El Porvenir** Chihuahua, N Mexico
43 U14 **El Porvenir** San Blas, N Panama
105 W6 **El Prat de Llobregat** Cataluña, NE Spain
42 H5 **El Progreso** Yoro, NW Honduras
42 A2 **El Progreso** off. Departamento de El Progreso. ◐ department C Guatemala
El Progreso see Guastatoya
El Progreso, Departamento de see El Progreso
104 L9 **El Puente del Arzobispo** Castilla-La Mancha, C Spain
104 J15 **El Puerto de Santa María** Andalucía, S Spain
62 I8 **El Puesto** Catamarca, NW Argentina
El Qâhira see Cairo
75 V10 **El Qaṣr** var. Al Qaṣr. C Egypt
El Qatrani see Al Qaṭrānah
40 I10 **El Quelite** Sinaloa, C Mexico
62 G9 **Elqui, Río** ~ N Chile
El Q'unayṭirah see Al Qunayṭirah
El Quneitra see Al Qunayṭirah
El Quseir see Al Quṣayr
El Quweira see Al Quwayrah
141 O15 **El-Rahaba** ✈ (Ṣan'ā') W Yemen
42 M10 **El Rama** Región Autónoma Atlántico Sur, SE Nicaragua
43 W16 **El Real** var. El Real de Santa María. Darién, SE Panama
El Real de Santa María see El Real
26 M10 **El Reno** Oklahoma, C USA
40 K9 **El Rodeo** Durango, C Mexico
104 J13 **El Ronquillo** Andalucía, S Spain
9 S16 **Elrose** Saskatchewan, S Canada
30 K8 **Elroy** Wisconsin, N USA
25 S17 **Elsa** Texas, SW USA
75 W8 **El Ṣaff** var. Aṣ Ṣaff. N Egypt
40 J10 **El Salto** Durango, C Mexico
42 D8 **El Salvador** off. Republica de El Salvador. ◆ republic Central America
El Salvador, Republica de see El Salvador
54 K7 **El Samán de Apure** Apure, C Venezuela
14 D7 **Elsas** Ontario, S Canada
40 F3 **El Sásabe** var. Aduana del Sásabe. Sonora, NW Mexico
Elsass see Alsace
40 J5 **El Sáuz** Chihuahua, N Mexico
27 W4 **Elsberry** Missouri, C USA
45 P9 **El Seibo** var. Santa Cruz de El Seibo, Santa Cruz del Seibo. E Dominican Republic
42 B7 **El Semillero Barra Nahualate** Escuintla, SW Guatemala
Elsene see Ixelles
Elsen Nur see Dorgê Co
Elsen Nur see Dorgê Co
36 L6 **Elsinore** Utah, W USA
Elsinore see Helsingør
99 L18 **Elsloo** Limburg, SE Netherlands
60 G13 **El Soberbio** Misiones, NE Argentina
55 N6 **El Socorro** Guárico, C Venezuela
54 L6 **El Sombrero** Guárico, N Venezuela
98 L10 **Elspeet** Gelderland, E Netherlands
98 L12 **Elst** Gelderland, E Netherlands
101 O15 **Elsterwerda** Brandenburg, E Germany
40 J4 **El Sueco** Chihuahua, N Mexico
El Suweida see As Suwaydā'
El Suweis see Suez
54 D12 **El Tambo** Cauca, SW Colombia
175 T13 **Eltanin Fracture Zone** tectonic feature SE Pacific Ocean
105 X5 **El Ter** ~ NE Spain
184 K11 **Eltham** Taranaki, North Island, New Zealand
55 O6 **El Tigre** Anzoátegui, NE Venezuela
El Tigrito see San José de Guanipa
54 J5 **El Tocuyo** Lara, N Venezuela
127 Q10 **El'ton** Volgogradskaya Oblast', SW Russian Federation
32 K10 **Eltopia** Washington, NW USA
El Toro see Mare de Déu del Toro
61 A18 **El Trébol** Santa Fe, C Argentina
40 J13 **El Tuito** Jalisco, SW Mexico
75 X8 **El Ṭûr** var. Aṭ Ṭūr. NE Egypt
155 K16 **Elūru** prev. Ellore. Andhra Pradesh, E India
118 H13 **Elva** Ger. Elwa. Tartumaa, SE Estonia
37 R9 **El Vado Reservoir** ⊠ New Mexico, SW USA
43 S15 **El Valle** Coclé, C Panama
104 I11 **Elvas** Portalegre, C Portugal
54 K7 **El Venado** Apure, C Venezuela
105 V6 **El Vendrell** Cataluña, NE Spain
94 I13 **Elverum** Hedmark, S Norway
42 I9 **El Viejo** Chinandega, NW Nicaragua
54 G7 **El Viejo, Cerro** ▲ C Colombia
54 H6 **El Vigía** Mérida, NW Venezuela
105 Q4 **El Villar de Arnedo** La Rioja, N Spain
59 A14 **Elvira** Amazonas, W Brazil
Elwa see Elva
El Wad see El Oued
81 K17 **El Wak** North Eastern, NE Kenya
33 R7 **Elwell, Lake** ⊠ Montana, NW USA
31 P13 **Elwood** Indiana, N USA
27 R3 **Elwood** Kansas, C USA
29 N16 **Elwood** Nebraska, C USA
Elx see Elche
97 O20 **Ely** E England, UK
29 X4 **Ely** Minnesota, N USA
35 X6 **Ely** Nevada, W USA
El Yopal see Yopal
31 T11 **Elyria** Ohio, N USA
45 S9 **El Yunque** ▲ E Puerto Rico
101 F23 **Elz** ~ SW Germany
187 R14 **Emae** island Shepherd Islands, C Vanuatu
118 I5 **Emajõgi** Ger. Embach. ~ SE Estonia
Emāmrūd see Shāhrūd
149 Q2 **Emām Ṣāḥeb** var. Emam Saheb, Hazarat Imam. Kunduz, NE Afghanistan
Emam Saheb see Emām Ṣāḥeb
Emāmshahr see Shāhrūd
95 M20 **Emån** ~ S Sweden
144 J11 **Emba** Kaz. Embi. Aktyubinsk, W Kazakhstan
144 H12 **Emba** Kaz. Zhem. ~ W Kazakhstan
Embach see Emajõgi
62 K5 **Embarcación** Salta, N Argentina
30 M15 **Embarras River** ~ Illinois, N USA
Embi see Emba
81 I19 **Embu** Eastern, C Kenya
100 E10 **Emden** Niedersachsen, NW Germany
160 H9 **Emei Shan** ▲ Sichuan, C China
29 Q4 **Emerado** North Dakota, N USA
181 X8 **Emerald** Queensland, E Australia
Emerald Isle see Montserrat
57 J15 **Emero, Río** ~ W Bolivia
9 Y17 **Emerson** Manitoba, S Canada
29 T15 **Emerson** Iowa, C USA
29 R13 **Emerson** Nebraska, C USA
36 M5 **Emery** Utah, W USA
Emesa see Ḥimṣ
136 E13 **Emet** Kütahya, W Turkey
186 B8 **Emeti** Western, SW Papua New Guinea
35 V3 **Emigrant Pass** pass Nevada, W USA
78 I6 **Emi Koussi** ▲ N Chad
Emilia see Emilia-Romagna
41 V15 **Emiliano Zapata** Chiapas, SE Mexico
106 E9 **Emilia-Romagna** prev. Emilia; anc. Æmilia. ◐ region N Italy
158 J3 **Emin** var. Dorbiljin. Xinjiang Uygur Zizhiqu, NW China
149 W8 **Eminābād** Punjab, E Pakistan
21 L5 **Eminence** Kentucky, S USA
27 W7 **Eminence** Missouri, C USA
114 N9 **Emine, Nos** headland E Bulgaria
158 J3 **Emin He** ~ NW China
186 G4 **Emirau Island** island N Papua New Guinea
136 F13 **Emirdağ** Afyon, W Turkey
95 M21 **Emmaboda** Kalmar, S Sweden
118 E5 **Emmaste** Hiiumaa, W Estonia
18 I15 **Emmaus** Pennsylvania, NE USA
183 U4 **Emmaville** New South Wales, SE Australia
108 E9 **Emme** ~ W Switzerland
98 L8 **Emmeloord** Flevoland, N Netherlands
98 O8 **Emmen** Drenthe, NE Netherlands
108 F8 **Emmen** Luzern, C Switzerland
101 F23 **Emmendingen** Baden-Württemberg, SW Germany
98 P8 **Emmer-Compascuum** Drenthe, NE Netherlands
101 D14 **Emmerich** Nordrhein-Westfalen, W Germany
29 U12 **Emmetsburg** Iowa, C USA
32 M14 **Emmett** Idaho, NW USA
38 M10 **Emmonak** Alaska, USA
Emona see Ljubljana
Emonti see East London
24 L12 **Emory Peak** ▲ Texas, SW USA
40 F6 **Empalme** Sonora, NW Mexico
83 L23 **Empangeni** KwaZulu/Natal, E South Africa
61 C14 **Empedrado** Corrientes, NE Argentina
192 K3 **Emperor Seamounts** undersea feature NW Pacific Ocean
192 L3 **Emperor Trough** undersea feature N Pacific Ocean
35 R4 **Empire** Nevada, W USA
Empire State of the South see Georgia
Emplawas see Amplawas
106 F11 **Empoli** Toscana, C Italy
27 P5 **Emporia** Kansas, C USA
21 W7 **Emporia** Virginia, NE USA
18 E13 **Emporium** Pennsylvania, NE USA
Empty Quarter see Ar Rub 'al Khālī
100 E10 **Ems** Dut. Eems. ~ NW Germany
100 F13 **Emsdetten** Nordrhein-Westfalen, NW Germany
Ems-Hunte Canal see Küstenkanal
100 F10 **Ems-Jade-Kanal** canal NW Germany
100 F11 **Emsland** cultural region NW Germany
182 D3 **Emu Junction** South Australia
163 T3 **Emur He** ~ NE China
55 R8 **Enachu Landing** NW Guyana
93 F16 **Enafors** Jämtland, C Sweden
94 N11 **Enånger** Gävleborg, C Sweden
96 G7 **Enard Bay** bay NW Scotland, UK
Enareträsk see Inarijärvi
171 X14 **Enarotali** Papua, E Indonesia
138 E12 **En 'Avedat** var. En'Avedat. well S Israel
En'Avedat see En 'Avedat
165 T2 **Enbetsu** Hokkaidō, NE Japan
61 H16 **Encantadas, Serra das** ▲▲ S Brazil
40 E7 **Encantado, Cerro** ▲ NW Mexico
62 P7 **Encarnación** Itapúa, S Paraguay
40 M12 **Encarnación de Díaz** Jalisco, SW Mexico
77 O17 **Enchi** SW Ghana
25 Q14 **Encinal** Texas, SW USA
35 U17 **Encinitas** California, W USA
25 S16 **Encino** Texas, SW USA
54 H6 **Encontrados** Zulia, NW Venezuela
182 I10 **Encounter Bay** inlet South Australia
61 F15 **Encruzilhada** Rio Grande do Sul, S Brazil
61 H16 **Encruzilhada do Sul** Rio Grande do Sul, S Brazil
111 M20 **Encs** Borsod-Abaúj-Zemplén, NE Hungary
193 P3 **Endeavour Seamount** undersea feature N Pacific Ocean
181 V1 **Endeavour Strait** strait Queensland, NE Australia
171 O16 **Endeh** Flores, S Indonesia
95 G23 **Endelave** island C Denmark
191 T4 **Enderbury Island** atoll Phoenix Islands, C Kiribati
9 N16 **Enderby** British Columbia, SW Canada
195 W4 **Enderby Land** physical region Antarctica
173 N14 **Enderby Plain** undersea feature S Indian Ocean
29 Q6 **Enderlin** North Dakota, N USA
Endersdorf see Jędrzejów
28 K16 **Enders Reservoir** ⊠ Nebraska, C USA
18 H11 **Endicott** New York, NE USA
39 P7 **Endicott Mountains** ▲▲ Alaska, USA
118 I5 **Endla Raba** wetland C Estonia
117 T9 **Enerhodar** Zaporiz'ka Oblast', SE Ukraine
57 F14 **Ene, Río** ~ C Peru
189 N4 **Enewetak Atoll** var. Ānewetak, Eniwetok. atoll Ralik Chain, W Marshall Islands
114 L13 **Enez** Edirne, NW Turkey
21 W8 **Enfield** North Carolina, SE USA
186 B7 **Enga** ◐ province W Papua New Guinea
45 Q9 **Engaño, Cabo** headland E Dominican Republic
164 U3 **Engaru** Hokkaidō, NE Japan
138 F11 **'En Gedi** Southern, E Israel
108 F9 **Engelberg** Unterwalden, C Switzerland
21 Y9 **Engelhard** North Carolina, SE USA
127 P8 **Engel's** Saratovskaya Oblast', W Russian Federation
101 G24 **Engen** Baden-Württemberg, SW Germany
Engeten see Aiud
168 K15 **Enggano, Pulau** island W Indonesia
80 J8 **Enghershatu** ▲ N Eritrea
99 F19 **Enghien** Dut. Edingen. Hainaut, SW Belgium
27 V12 **England** Arkansas, C USA
97 M20 **England** Lat. Anglia. cultural region England, UK
14 H8 **Englehart** Ontario, S Canada
37 T4 **Englewood** Colorado, C USA
31 O16 **English** Indiana, N USA
39 Q13 **English Bay** Alaska, USA
English Bazar see Ingrāj Bāzār
97 N25 **English Channel** var. The Channel, Fr. la Manche. channel NW Europe
194 J7 **English Coast** physical region Antarctica
105 S11 **Enguera** País Valenciano, E Spain
118 E8 **Engure** Tukums, W Latvia
118 E8 **Engures Ezers** ◎ NW Latvia
137 R9 **Enguri** Rus. Inguri. ~ NW Georgia
Engyum see Gangi
26 M9 **Enid** Oklahoma, C USA
22 L3 **Enid Lake** ⊠ Mississippi, S USA
189 Y2 **Enigu** island Ratak Chain, SE Marshall Islands
Enikale Strait see Kerch Strait
147 Z8 **Enil'chek** Issyk-Kul'skaya Oblast', E Kyrgyzstan
115 F17 **Enipéfs** ~ C Greece
165 S4 **Eniwa** Hokkaidō, NE Japan
Eniwetok see Enewetak Atoll
Enjiang see Yongfeng
Enkeldoorn see Chivhu
98 J8 **Enkhuizen** Noord-Holland, NW Netherlands
109 Q4 **Enknach** ~ N Austria
95 N15 **Enköping** Uppsala, C Sweden
107 K24 **Enna** var. Castrogiovanni, Henna. Sicilia, Italy, C Mediterranean Sea
80 D11 **En Nahud** Western Kordofan, C Sudan
138 F8 **En Nâqoûra** var. An Nāqūrah. SW Lebanon
En Nazira see Nazerat
78 K8 **Ennedi** plateau E Chad
101 E15 **Ennepetal** Nordrhein-Westfalen, W Germany
183 P4 **Enngonia** New South Wales, SE Australia
97 C19 **Ennis** Ir. Inis. Clare, W Ireland
33 R11 **Ennis** Montana, NW USA
25 U7 **Ennis** Texas, SW USA
97 F20 **Enniscorthy** Ir. Inis Córthaidh. Wexford, SE Ireland
97 E15 **Enniskillen** var. Inniskilling, Ir. Inis Ceithleann. SW Northern Ireland, UK
97 B19 **Ennistimon** Ir. Inis Díomáin. Clare, W Ireland
109 T4 **Enns** Oberösterreich, N Austria
109 T4 **Enns** ~ C Austria
93 O16 **Eno** Pohjois-Karjala, SE Finland
24 M5 **Enochs** Texas, SW USA
93 N17 **Enonkoski** Isä-Suomi, E Finland
92 K10 **Enontekiö** Lapp. Eanodat. Lappi, N Finland
21 Q11 **Enoree** South Carolina, SE USA
21 P11 **Enoree River** ~ South Carolina, SE USA
18 M6 **Enosburg Falls** Vermont, NE USA
171 N13 **Enrekang** Sulawesi, C Indonesia
45 N10 **Enriquillo** SW Dominican Republic
45 N9 **Enriquillo, Lago** ◎ SW Dominican Republic
98 L9 **Ens** Flevoland, N Netherlands
98 P11 **Enschede** Overijssel, E Netherlands
40 B2 **Ensenada** Baja California, NW Mexico
101 E20 **Ensheim** ✈ (Saarbrücken) Saarland, W Germany
160 L9 **Enshi** Hubei, C China
164 L14 **Enshū-nada** gulf SW Japan
23 O8 **Ensley** Florida, SE USA
Enso see Svetogorsk
81 F18 **Entebbe** S Uganda
81 F18 **Entebbe** ✈ C Uganda
101 M18 **Entenbühl** ▲ Czech Republic/Germany
98 N10 **Enter** Overijssel, E Netherlands
23 Q7 **Enterprise** Alabama, S USA
32 L11 **Enterprise** Oregon, NW USA
36 J7 **Enterprise** Utah, W USA
32 J8 **Entiat** Washington, NW USA
105 P15 **Entinas, Punta de las** headland S Spain
108 F8 **Entlebuch** Luzern, W Switzerland
108 F8 **Entlebuch** valley C Switzerland
63 I22 **Entrada, Punta** headland S Argentina
103 O13 **Entraygues-sur-Truyère** Aveyron, S France
187 O14 **Entrecasteaux, Récifs d'** reef N New Caledonia
61 C17 **Entre Ríos** off. Provincia de Entre Ríos. ◐ province NE Argentina
42 K7 **Entre Ríos, Cordillera** ▲▲ Honduras/Nicaragua
Entre Ríos, Provincia de see Entre Ríos
104 G9 **Entroncamento** Santarém, C Portugal
77 V16 **Enugu** Enugu, S Nigeria
77 U16 **Enugu** ◐ state SE Nigeria
123 V5 **Enurmino** Chukotskiy Avtonomnyy Okrug, NE Russian Federation
54 E9 **Envigado** Antioquia, W Colombia
59 B15 **Envira** Amazonas, W Brazil
Enyélé see Enyellé
79 I16 **Enyellé** var. Enyélé. La Likouala, NE Congo
101 H21 **Enz** ~ SW Germany
165 N13 **Enzan** Yamanashi, Honshū, S Japan
104 I2 **Eo** ~ NW Spain
Eochaill see Youghal
Eochaille, Cuan see Youghal Bay
107 K22 **Eolie, Isole** var. Isole Lipari, Eng. Aeolian Islands, Lipari Islands. island group S Italy
189 U12 **Eot** island Chuuk, C Micronesia
Epáno Archánes/Epáno Arkhánai see Archánes
115 G14 **Epanomí** Kentrikí Makedonía, N Greece
98 M10 **Epe** Gelderland, E Netherlands
77 S16 **Epe** Lagos, S Nigeria
79 I17 **Epéna** La Likouala, NE Congo
Eperies/Eperjes see Prešov
103 Q4 **Épernay** anc. Sparnacum. Marne, N France
36 L5 **Ephraim** Utah, W USA
18 H15 **Ephrata** Pennsylvania, NE USA
32 J8 **Ephrata** Washington, NW USA
187 R14 **Epi** var. Épi. island C Vanuatu
Épi see Epi
105 R6 **Épila** Aragón, NE Spain
103 T6 **Épinal** Vosges, NE France
Epiphania see Ḥamāh
Epirus see Ípeiros
121 P3 **Episkopi** SW Cyprus
Episkopi Bay see Episkopí, Kólpos
121 P3 **Episkopí, Kólpos** var. Episkopi Bay. bay SE Cyprus
Epitoli see Tshwane
Epoon see Ebon Atoll
Eporedia see Ivrea
Eppeschdorf see Dumbrăveni
101 H21 **Eppingen** Baden-Württemberg, SW Germany
83 E18 **Epukiro** Omaheke, E Namibia
29 Y13 **Epworth** Iowa, C USA
143 O10 **Eqlīd** var. Iqlid. Fārs, C Iran
Equality State see Wyoming
79 J18 **Equateur** off. Région de l' Equateur. ◐ region N Dem. Rep. Congo
Equateur, Région de l' see Equateur
151 K22 **Equatorial Channel** channel S Maldives
79 B17 **Equatorial Guinea** off. Equatorial Guinea, Republic of. ◆ republic C Africa
Equatorial Guinea, Republic of see Equatorial Guinea
121 V11 **Eratosthenes Tablemount** undersea feature E Mediterranean Sea
Erautini see Johannesburg
136 L12 **Erbaa** Tokat, N Turkey
101 E19 **Erbeskopf** ▲ W Germany
Erbil see Arbīl
121 P2 **Ercan** ✈ (Nicosia) N Cyprus
Ercegnovi see Herceg-Novi
137 T14 **Erçek Gölü** ◎ E Turkey
137 S14 **Erciş** Van, E Turkey
136 K14 **Erciyes Daği** anc. Argaeus. ▲ C Turkey
111 J22 **Érd** Ger. Hanselbeck. Pest, C Hungary
163 X11 **Erdaobaihe** prev. Baihe. Jilin, NE China
159 O12 **Erdaogou** Qinghai, W China
163 X11 **Erdao Jiang** ~ NE China

◆ Country
● Country Capital
◇ Dependent Territory
○ Dependent Territory Capital
◐ Administrative Regions
✈ International Airport
▲ Mountain
▲▲ Mountain Range
Volcano
~ River
◎ Lake
⊠ Reservoir

Erdăt-Sângeorz see Sângeorgiu de Pădure
136 C11 **Erdek** Balıkesir, NW Turkey
Erdély see Transylvania
Erdélyi-Havasok see Carpaţii Meridionali
136 J17 **Erdemli** Mersin, S Turkey
163 O10 **Erdene** var. Ulaan-Uul. Dornogovĭ, SE Mongolia
162 H9 **Erdene** var. Sangiyn Dalay. Govĭ-Altay, C Mongolia
162 E6 **Erdenebüren** var. Har-Us. Hovd, W Mongolia
162 K9 **Erdenedalay** var. Sangiyn Dalay. Dundgovĭ, C Mongolia
162 G7 **Erdenehayrhan** var. Altan. Dzavhan, W Mongolia
162 J7 **Erdenemandal** var. Öldziyt. Arhangay, C Mongolia
162 K6 **Erdenet** Orhon, N Mongolia
163 Q9 **Erdenetsagaan** var. Chonogol. Sühbaatar, E Mongolia
162 I8 **Erdenetsogt** Bayanhongor, C Mongolia
Erdenetsogt see Bayan-Ovoo
78 K7 **Erdi** plateau NE Chad
78 L7 **Erdi Ma** desert NE Chad
101 M23 **Erding** Bayern, SE Germany
Erdőszáda see Ardusat
Erdőszentgyörgy see Sângeorgiu de Pădure
102 I7 **Erdre** ≈ NW France
195 R13 **Erebus, Mount** ※ Ross Island, Antarctica
61 H14 **Erechim** Rio Grande do Sul, S Brazil
163 O7 **Ereen Davaanï Nuruu** ▲▲ NE Mongolia
163 Q6 **Ereentsav** Dornod, NE Mongolia
136 I16 **Ereğli** Konya, S Turkey
136 I15 **Eğridir Gölü** ◎ W Turkey
115 A15 **Ereíkoussa** island Iónioi Nísoi, Greece, C Mediterranean Sea
163 O11 **Erenhot** var. Erlian. Nei Mongol Zizhiqu, NE China
104 M6 **Eresma** ≈ N Spain
115 K17 **Eresós** var. Eressós. Lésvos, E Greece
Eressós see Eresós
Ereymentau see Yermentau
99 K21 **Érezée** Luxembourg, SE Belgium
74 G7 **Erfoud** SE Morocco
101 D16 **Erft** ≈ W Germany
101 K16 **Erfurt** Thüringen, C Germany
137 P15 **Ergani** Diyarbakır, SE Turkey
Ergel see Hatanbulag
136 C10 **Ergene Çayi** var. Ergene Irmaği. ≈ NW Turkey
Ergene Irmaği see Ergene Çayi
Ergenetsogt see Bayan-Ovoo
118 I9 **Ērgļi** Madona, C Latvia
78 H11 **Erguig, Bahr** ≈ SW Chad
163 S5 **Ergun** var. Labudalin; prev. Ergun Youqi. Nei Mongol Zizhiqu, N China
Ergun He see Argun
Ergun Youqi see Ergun
Ergun Zuoqi see Genhe
160 F12 **Er Hai** ▣ SW China
104 K4 **Ería** ≈ NW Spain
80 H8 **Eriba** Kassala, NE Sudan
96 I6 **Eriboll, Loch** inlet NW Scotland, UK
65 Q18 **Erica Seamount** undersea feature SW Indian Ocean
107 H23 **Erice** Sicilia, Italy, C Mediterranean Sea
104 E10 **Ericeira** Lisboa, C Portugal
96 H10 **Ericht, Loch** ◎ C Scotland, UK
26 J11 **Erick** Oklahoma, C USA
18 B11 **Erie** Pennsylvania, NE USA
18 E9 **Erie Canal** canal New York, NE USA
Érié, Lac see Erie, Lake
31 T10 **Erie, Lake** Fr. Lac Érié. ◎ Canada/USA
Erigabo see Ceerigaabo
77 N8 **'Erigât** desert N Mali
Erigavo see Ceerigaabo
92 P2 **Erik Eriksenstretet** strait E Svalbard
9 X15 **Eriksdale** Manitoba, S Canada
189 V6 **Erikub Atoll** var. Ādkup. atoll Ratak Chain, C Marshall Islands
102 G4 **Er, Îles d'** Island group NW France
Erimanthos see Erýmanthos
165 T6 **Erimo** Hokkaidō, NE Japan
165 T6 **Erimo-misaki** headland Hokkaidō, NE Japan
20 H8 **Erin** Tennessee, S USA
96 E9 **Eriskay** island NW Scotland, UK
Erithraí see Erythrés
80 I9 **Eritrea** off. State of Eritrea, Ērtra. ◆ transitional government E Africa
Eritrea, State of see Eritrea
Erivan see Yerevan
101 D16 **Erkelenz** Nordrhein-Westfalen, W Germany
95 P15 **Erken** ◎ C Sweden
101 K19 **Erlangen** Bayern, S Germany
160 G9 **Erlang Shan** ▲ C China
Erlau see Eger
109 V5 **Erlauf** ≈ NE Austria
181 Q8 **Erldunda Roadhouse** Northern Territory, N Australia
Erlian see Erenhot
27 T15 **Erling, Lake** ▣ Arkansas, USA
109 O8 **Erlsbach** Tirol, W Austria
Ermak see Aksu
98 K10 **Ermelo** Gelderland, C Netherlands
83 K21 **Ermelo** Mpumalanga, NE South Africa
136 H17 **Ermenek** Karaman, S Turkey
Érmihályfalva see Valea lui Mihai
115 G20 **Ermióni** Pelopónnisos, S Greece
115 J20 **Ermoúpoli** var. Hermoupolis; prev. Ermoúpolis. Sýyros, Kykládes, Greece, Aegean Sea
Ermoúpolis see Ermoúpoli
Ernabella see Pukatja
155 G22 **Ernākulam** Kerala, SW India
102 J6 **Ernée** Mayenne, NW France
61 H14 **Ernestina, Barragem** ▣ S Brazil
54 E4 **Ernesto Cortissoz** ✈ (Barranquilla) Atlántico, N Colombia
155 H21 **Erode** Tamil Nādu, SE India
Eroj see Iroj
83 C19 **Erongo** ◈ district W Namibia
99 F21 **Erquelinnes** Hainaut, S Belgium
74 G7 **Er-Rachidia** var. Ksar al Soule. E Morocco
80 E11 **Er Rahad** var. Ar Rahad. Northern Kordofan, C Sudan
Er Ramle see Ramla
83 O15 **Errego** Zambézia, NE Mozambique
105 Q2 **Errenteria** Cast. Rentería. País Vasco, N Spain
Er Rif/Er Riff see Rif
97 D14 **Errigal Mountain** Ir. An Earagail. ▲ N Ireland
97 A15 **Erris Head** Ir. Ceann Iorrais. headland W Ireland
187 S15 **Erromango** island S Vanuatu
Error Guyot see Error Tablemount
173 O4 **Error Tablemount** var. Error Guyot. undersea feature W Indian Ocean
80 G11 **Er Roseires** Blue Nile, E Sudan
Erseka see Ersekë
113 M22 **Ersekë** var. Erseka, Kolonjë. Korçë, SE Albania
Érsekújvár see Nové Zámky
29 S4 **Erskine** Minnesota, N USA
103 V6 **Erstein** Bas-Rhin, NE France
108 G9 **Erstfeld** Uri, C Switzerland
158 M3 **Ertai** Xinjiang Uygur Zizhiqu, NW China
126 M7 **Ertil'** Voronezhskaya Oblast', W Russian Federation
Ertis see Irtysh, C Asia
Ertis see Irtyshsk, Kazakhstan
158 K2 **Ertix He** Rus. Chërnyy Irtysh. ≈ China/Kazakhstan
Ērtra see Eritrea
21 P9 **Erwin** North Carolina, SE USA
Erydropótamos see Erythropótamos
115 E19 **Erýmanthos** var. Erimanthos. ▲ S Greece
115 G19 **Erythrés** prev. Erithraí. Stereá Ellás, C Greece
114 L12 **Erythropótamos** Bul. Byala Reka, var Erydropótamos. ≈ Bulgaria/Greece
160 F12 **Eryuan** var. Yuhu. Yunnan, SW China
109 U6 **Erzbach** ≈ W Austria
Erzerum see Erzurum
101 N17 **Erzgebirge** Cz. Krušné Hory, Eng. Ore Mountains. ▲ Czech Republic/Germany see also Krušné Hory
Erzgebirge see Krušné Hory
122 L14 **Erzin** Respublika Tyva, S Russian Federation
137 O13 **Erzincan** var. Erzinjan. Erzincan, E Turkey
137 N13 **Erzincan** var. Erzinjan. ◈ province NE Turkey
Erzinjan see Erzincan
Erzsébetváros see Dumbrăveni
137 Q13 **Erzurum** prev. Erzerum. Erzurum, NE Turkey
137 Q12 **Erzurum** prev. Erzerum. ◈ province NE Turkey
186 G9 **Esa'ala** Normanby Island, SE Papua New Guinea
165 T2 **Esashi** Hokkaidō, NE Japan
165 Q9 **Esashi** var. Esasi. Iwate, Honshū, C Japan
165 Q5 **Esasho** Hokkaidō, N Japan
Esasi see Esashi
95 F23 **Esbjerg** Ribe, W Denmark
Esbo see Espoo
36 L7 **Escalante** Utah, W USA
36 M7 **Escalante River** ≈ Utah, W USA
14 L12 **Escalier, Réservoir l'** ▣ Québec, SE Canada
40 K7 **Escalón** Chihuahua, N Mexico
104 M8 **Escalona** Castilla-La Mancha, C Spain
23 O8 **Escambia River** ≈ Florida, SE USA
31 N5 **Escanaba** Michigan, N USA
31 N4 **Escanaba River** ≈ Michigan, N USA
105 R8 **Escandón, Puerto de** pass E Spain
41 W14 **Escárcega** Campeche, SE Mexico
171 O1 **Escarpada Point** headland Luzon, N Philippines
23 N8 **Escatawpa River** ≈ Alabama/Mississippi, S USA
103 P2 **Escaut** ≈ N France
Escaut see Scheldt
99 M25 **Esch-sur-Alzette** Luxembourg, S Luxembourg
101 J15 **Eschwege** Hessen, C Germany
101 D16 **Eschweiler** Nordrhein-Westfalen, W Germany
Esclaves, Grand Lac des see Great Slave Lake
45 O8 **Escocesa, Bahía** bay N Dominican Republic
43 W15 **Escocés, Punta** headland NE Panama
35 U17 **Escondido** California, W USA
42 M10 **Escondido, Río** ≈ SE Nicaragua
15 S7 **Escoumins, Rivière des** ≈ Québec, SE Canada
37 O13 **Escudilla Mountain** ▲ Arizona, SW USA
40 J11 **Escuinapa** var. Escuinapa de Hidalgo. Sinaloa, C Mexico
Escuinapa de Hidalgo see Escuinapa
42 C6 **Escuintla** Escuintla, S Guatemala
41 V17 **Escuintla** Chiapas, SE Mexico
42 A2 **Escuintla** off. Departamento de Escuintla. ◈ department S Guatemala
Escuintla, Departamento de see Escuintla
15 W7 **Escuminac** ≈ Québec, SE Canada
79 D16 **Eséka** Centre, SW Cameroon
136 I12 **Esenboğa** ✈ (Ankara) Ankara, C Turkey
136 D17 **Eşen Çayı** ≈ SW Turkey
146 B13 **Esenguly** Rus. Gasan-Kuli. Balkan Welaýaty, W Turkmenistan
105 T4 **Ésera** ≈ NE Spain
143 N8 **Eşfahān** Eng. Isfahan; anc. Aspadana. Eşfahān, C Iran
143 O7 **Eşfahān** off. Ostān-e Eşfahān. ◈ province C Iran
Eşfahān, Ostān-e see Eşfahān
105 N5 **Esgueva** ≈ N Spain
149 Q3 **Eshkamesh** Takhār, NE Afghanistan
149 T2 **Eshkāshem** Badakhshān, NE Afghanistan
83 L23 **Eshowe** KwaZulu/Natal, E South Africa
143 T5 **'Eshqābād** Khorāsān, NE Iran
Esh Sham see Dimashq
Esh Sharā see Ash Sharāh
Esik see Yesik
Esil see Yesil'
Esil see Ishim, Kazakhstan/Russian Federation
183 V2 **Esk** Queensland, E Australia
184 O11 **Eskdale** Hawke's Bay, North Island, New Zealand
Eski Dzhumaya see Türgovishte
92 L2 **Eskifjördhur** Austurland, E Iceland
139 S3 **Eski Kaļak** var. Askī Kalak, Kalak. N Iraq
95 N16 **Eskilstuna** Södermanland, C Sweden
8 H6 **Eskimo Lakes** ◎ Northwest Territories, NW Canada
9 O10 **Eskimo Point** headland Nunavut, E Canada
Eskimo Point see Arviat
139 Q2 **Eski Mosul** N Iraq
147 T10 **Eski-Nookat** var. Iski-Nauket. Oshskaya Oblast', SW Kyrgyzstan
136 F12 **Eskişehir** var. Eskishehr. Eskişehir, W Turkey
136 F13 **Eskişehir** var. Eski shehr. ◈ province NW Turkey
Eskishehr see Eskişehir
104 K5 **Esla** ≈ NW Spain
142 J6 **Eslāmābād** var. Eslāmābād-e Gharb; prev. Harunabad, Shāhābād. Kermānshāhān, W Iran
Eslāmābād-e Gharb see Eslāmābād
148 J4 **Eslām Qal'eh** Pash. Islam Qala. Herāt, W Afghanistan
95 K23 **Eslöv** Skåne, S Sweden
143 S12 **Esmā'īlābād** Kermān, S Iran
143 U8 **Esmā'īlābād** Khorāsān, E Iran
136 D14 **Eşme** Uşak, W Turkey
44 G6 **Esmeralda** Camagüey, E Cuba
63 F21 **Esmeralda, Isla** island S Chile
56 B5 **Esmeraldas** Esmeraldas, N Ecuador
56 B5 **Esmeraldas** ◈ province NW Ecuador
Esna see Isna
14 B6 **Esnagi Lake** ◎ Ontario, S Canada
143 V14 **Espakeh** Sīstān va Balūchestān, SE Iran
103 O13 **Espalion** Aveyron, S France
España see Spain
14 E11 **Espanola** Ontario, S Canada
37 S10 **Espanola** New Mexico, SW USA
57 C18 **Española, Isla** var. Hood Island. island Galapagos Islands, Ecuador, E Pacific Ocean
104 M13 **Espejo** Andalucía, S Spain
94 C13 **Espeland** Hordaland, S Norway
100 G12 **Espelkamp** Nordrhein-Westfalen, NW Germany
38 M8 **Espenberg, Cape** headland Alaska, USA
180 L13 **Esperance** Western Australia
186 L9 **Esperance, Cape** headland Guadacanal, C Solomon Islands
57 P18 **Esperancita** Santa Cruz, E Bolivia
61 B17 **Esperanza** Santa Fe, C Argentina
40 G6 **Esperanza** Sonora, NW Mexico
24 H9 **Esperanza** Texas, SW USA
194 H3 **Esperanza** Argentinian research station Antarctica
104 E12 **Espichel, Cabo** cape S Portugal
54 E10 **Espinal** Tolima, C Colombia
48 K10 **Espinhaço, Serra do** ▲▲ SE Brazil
104 G6 **Espinho** Aveiro, N Portugal
59 N18 **Espinosa** Minas Gerais, SE Brazil
103 O15 **Espinouse** ▲▲ S France
60 Q8 **Espírito Santo** off. Estado do Espírito Santo. ◈ state E Brazil
Espírito Santo, Estado do see Espírito Santo
187 P13 **Espiritu Santo** var. Santo. island W Vanuatu
41 Z13 **Espíritu Santo, Bahía del** bay SE Mexico
40 F9 **Espíritu Santo, Isla del** island W Mexico
41 Y12 **Espita** Yucatán, SE Mexico
15 Y7 **Espoir, Cap d'** headland Québec, SE Canada
Esponsede/Esponsende see Esposende
93 L20 **Espoo** Swe. Esbo. Etelä-Suomi, S Finland
104 G5 **Esposende** var. Esponsede, Esponsende. Braga, N Portugal
83 M18 **Espungabera** Manica, SW Mozambique
63 H17 **Esquel** Chubut, SW Argentina
10 L17 **Esquimalt** Vancouver Island, British Columbia, SW Canada
61 C16 **Esquina** Corrientes, NE Argentina
42 E6 **Esquipulas** Chiquimula, SE Guatemala
42 K9 **Esquipulas** Matagalpa, C Nicaragua
94 I8 **Essandjøen** ◎ S Norway
74 E7 **Essaouira** prev. Mogador. W Morocco
Esseg see Osijek
Es Semara see Smara
99 G15 **Essen** Antwerpen, N Belgium
101 E15 **Essen** var. Essen an der Ruhr. Nordrhein-Westfalen, W Germany
Essen an der Ruhr see Essen
74 I5 **Es Senia** ✈ (Oran) NW Algeria
55 T8 **Essequibo Islands** island group N Guyana
55 T11 **Essequibo River** ≈ C Guyana
14 C18 **Essex** Ontario, S Canada
29 T16 **Essex** Iowa, C USA
97 P21 **Essex** cultural region E England, UK
31 R8 **Essexville** Michigan, N USA
101 H22 **Esslingen** var. Esslingen am Neckar. Baden-Württemberg, SW Germany
Esslingen am Neckar see Esslingen
103 N6 **Essonne** ◈ department N France
Es Suweida see As Suwaydā'
79 F16 **Est** Eng. East. ◈ province SE Cameroon
104 I1 **Estaca de Bares, Punta da** point NW Spain
24 M5 **Estacado, Llano** plain New Mexico/Texas, SW USA
63 K25 **Estados, Isla de los** prev. Eng. Staten Island. island S Argentina
Estado Vargas see Vargas
143 P12 **Eşţahbān** Fārs, S Iran
14 F11 **Estaire** Ontario, S Canada
59 P16 **Estância** Sergipe, E Brazil
37 S12 **Estancia** New Mexico, SW USA
104 G7 **Estarreja** Aveiro, N Portugal
102 M17 **Estats, Pic d'** Sp. Pico d'Estats. ▲ France/Spain
Estats, Pico d' see Estats, Pic d'
83 K23 **Estcourt** KwaZulu/Natal, E South Africa
106 H8 **Este** anc. Ateste. Veneto, NE Italy
42 J9 **Estelí** Estelí, NW Nicaragua
42 J9 **Estelí** ◈ department NW Nicaragua
105 Q4 **Estella** Bas. Lizarra. Navarra, N Spain
29 R9 **Estelline** South Dakota, N USA
25 P4 **Estelline** Texas, SW USA
104 L14 **Estepa** Andalucía, S Spain
104 L16 **Estepona** Andalucía, S Spain
39 R9 **Ester** Alaska, USA
9 V16 **Esterhazy** Saskatchewan, S Canada
37 S3 **Estes Park** Colorado, C USA
9 V17 **Estevan** Saskatchewan, S Canada
29 T11 **Estherville** Iowa, C USA
21 R15 **Estill** South Carolina, SE USA
103 Q6 **Estissac** Aube, N France
15 T9 **Est, Lac de l'** ◎ Québec, SE Canada
Estland see Estonia
9 S16 **Eston** Saskatchewan, S Canada
118 G5 **Estonia** off. Republic of Estonia, Est. Eesti Vabariik, Ger. Estland, Latv. Igaunija; prev. Estonian SSR, Rus. Estonskaya SSR. ◆ republic NE Europe
Estonian SSR see Estonia
Estonia, Republic of see Estonia
Estonskaya SSR see Estonia
104 E11 **Estoril** Lisboa, W Portugal
59 L14 **Estreito** Maranhão, E Brazil
104 I8 **Estrela, Serra da** ▲▲ C Portugal
40 D3 **Estrella, Punta** headland NW Mexico
104 F10 **Estremadura** cultural and historical region W Portugal
Estremadura see Extremadura
104 H11 **Estremoz** Évora, S Portugal
79 D18 **Estuaire** off. Province de l'Estuaire, var. L'Estuaire. ◈ province NW Gabon
Estuaire, Province de l' see Estuaire
Eszék see Osijek
111 I22 **Esztergom** Ger. Gran; anc. Strigonium. Komárom-Esztergom, N Hungary
152 K11 **Etah** Uttar Pradesh, N India
189 R17 **Etal Atoll** atoll Mortlock Islands, C Micronesia
99 K24 **Étalle** Luxembourg, SE Belgium
103 N6 **Étampes** Essonne, N France
182 J1 **Etamunbanie, Lake** salt lake South Australia
103 N1 **Étaples** Pas-de-Calais, N France
152 K12 **Etāwah** Uttar Pradesh, N India
15 R10 **Etchemin** ≈ Québec, SE Canada
Etchmiadzin see Vagharshapat
40 G7 **Etchojoa** Sonora, NW Mexico
93 L19 **Etelä-Suomi** ◈ province S Finland
83 B16 **Etengua** Kunene, NW Namibia
99 K25 **Éthe** Luxembourg, SE Belgium
9 W15 **Ethelbert** Manitoba, S Canada
80 H12 **Ethiopia** off. Federal Democratic Republic of Ethiopia; prev. Abyssinia, People's Democratic Republic of Ethiopia. ◆ republic E Africa
Ethiopia, Federal Democratic Republic of see Ethiopia
80 I13 **Ethiopian Highlands** var. Ethiopian Plateau. plateau N Ethiopia
Ethiopian Plateau see Ethiopian Highlands
Ethiopia, People's Democratic Republic of see Ethiopia
34 M2 **Etna** California, W USA
18 B14 **Etna** Pennsylvania, NE USA
94 G12 **Etna** ≈ S Norway
107 L24 **Etna, Monte** Eng. Mount Etna. ※ Sicilia, Italy, C Mediterranean Sea
Etna, Mount see Etna, Monte
95 C15 **Etne** Hordaland, S Norway
Etoliko see Aitolikó
39 Y14 **Etolin Island** island Alexander Archipelago, Alaska, USA
38 L12 **Etolin Strait** strait Alaska, USA
83 C17 **Etosha Pan** salt lake N Namibia
79 G18 **Etoumbi** Cuvette Ouest, NW Congo
20 M10 **Etowah** Tennessee, S USA
23 S2 **Etowah River** ≈ Georgia, SE USA
146 B13 **Etrek** var. Gyzyletrek, Rus. Kizyl-Atrek. Balkan Welaýaty, W Turkmenistan
146 C13 **Etrek** Per. Rūd-e Atrak, Rus. Atrak, Atrek. ≈ Iran/Turkmenistan
102 L3 **Étretat** Seine-Maritime, N France
114 H9 **Etropole** Sofiya, W Bulgaria
Etsch see Adige
Et Tafila see Aţ Ţafilah
99 M23 **Ettelbrück** Diekirch, C Luxembourg
189 V12 **Etten** atoll Chuuk Islands, C Micronesia
99 H14 **Etten-Leur** Noord-Brabant, S Netherlands
76 G7 **Et Tîdra** var. Ile Tidra. island Dakhlet Nouâdhibou, NW Mauritania
101 G21 **Ettlingen** Baden-Württemberg, SW Germany
102 M2 **Eu** Seine-Maritime, N France
193 W16 **'Eua** prev. Middleburg Island. island Tongatapu Group, SE Tonga
193 W15 **Eua Iki** island Tongatapu Group, S Tonga
Euboea see Évvoia
181 O12 **Eucla** Western Australia
31 U11 **Euclid** Ohio, N USA
27 W14 **Eudora** Arkansas, C USA
27 Q4 **Eudora** Kansas, C USA
182 J9 **Eudunda** South Australia
23 R6 **Eufaula** Alabama, S USA
27 Q11 **Eufaula** Oklahoma, C USA
27 Q11 **Eufaula Lake** var. Eufaula Reservoir. ▣ Oklahoma, C USA
Eufaula Reservoir see Eufaula Lake
32 F13 **Eugene** Oregon, NW USA
40 B6 **Eugenia, Punta** headland W Mexico
183 Q8 **Eugowra** New South Wales, SE Australia
104 I2 **Eume** ≈ NW Spain
104 H2 **Eume, Embalse do** ▣ NW Spain
Eumolpias see Plovdiv
59 O18 **Eunápolis** Bahia, SE Brazil
22 H8 **Eunice** Louisiana, S USA
37 W15 **Eunice** New Mexico, SW USA
99 M19 **Eupen** Liège, E Belgium
130 B10 **Euphrates** Ar. Al-Furāt, Turk. Firat Nehri. ≈ SW Asia
138 L3 **Euphrates Dam** dam N Syria
22 M4 **Eupora** Mississippi, S USA
93 K19 **Eura** Länsi-Soumi, SW Finland
93 K19 **Eurajoki** Länsi-Soumi, SW Finland
0-1 **Eurasian Plate** tectonic feature
102 L4 **Eure** ◈ department N France
102 M4 **Eure** ≈ N France
102 M6 **Eure-et-Loir** ◈ department C France
34 K3 **Eureka** California, W USA
27 P6 **Eureka** Kansas, C USA
33 O6 **Eureka** Montana, NW USA
35 V5 **Eureka** Nevada, W USA
29 O7 **Eureka** South Dakota, N USA
36 L4 **Eureka** Utah, W USA
32 K10 **Eureka** Washington, NW USA
27 S9 **Eureka Springs** Arkansas, C USA
182 K6 **Eurinilla Creek** seasonal river South Australia
183 O11 **Euroa** Victoria, SE Australia
172 M9 **Europa** island W Madagascar
104 L3 **Europa, Picos de** ▲▲ N Spain
104 L16 **Europa Point** headland S Gibraltar
84-85 **Europe** continent
98 F12 **Europoort** Zuid-Holland, W Netherlands
Euskadi see País Vasco
101 D17 **Euskirchen** Nordrhein-Westfalen, W Germany
23 W11 **Eustis** Florida, SE USA
182 M9 **Euston** New South Wales, SE Australia
23 N5 **Eutaw** Alabama, S USA
100 K8 **Eutin** Schleswig-Holstein, N Germany
10 K14 **Eutsuk Lake** ▣ British Columbia, SW Canada
Euxine Sea see Black Sea
83 C16 **Evale** Cunene, SW Angola
37 T3 **Evans** Colorado, C USA
9 P14 **Evansburg** Alberta, SW Canada
29 X13 **Evansdale** Iowa, C USA
183 V4 **Evans Head** New South Wales, SE Australia
12 J11 **Evans, Lac** ◎ Québec, SE Canada
37 S5 **Evans, Mount** ▲ Colorado, C USA
31 N10 **Evanston** Illinois, N USA
33 S17 **Evanston** Wyoming, C USA
14 D11 **Evansville** Manitoulin Island, Ontario, S Canada
31 N16 **Evansville** Indiana, N USA
30 L9 **Evansville** Wisconsin, N USA
25 S8 **Evant** Texas, SW USA
143 P13 **Evaz** Fārs, S Iran
29 W4 **Eveleth** Minnesota, N USA
182 E3 **Evelyn Creek** seasonal river South Australia
181 Q2 **Evelyn, Mount** ▲ Northern Territory, N Australia
122 K10 **Evenkiyskiy Avtonomnyy Okrug** ◈ autonomous district N Russian Federation
183 R13 **Everard, Cape** headland Victoria, SE Australia
182 F6 **Everard, Lake** salt lake South Australia
182 C2 **Everard Ranges** ▲▲ South Australia
153 R11 **Everest, Mount** Chin. Qomolangma Feng, Nep. Sagarmāthā. ▲ China/Nepal
18 E15 **Everett** Pennsylvania, NE USA
32 H7 **Everett** Washington, NW USA
99 E17 **Evergem** Oost-Vlaanderen, NW Belgium
23 X16 **Everglades City** Florida, SE USA
23 Y16 **Everglades, The** wetland Florida, SE USA
23 P7 **Evergreen** Alabama, S USA
37 T4 **Evergreen** Colorado, C USA
Evergreen State see Washington
97 L21 **Evesham** C England, UK
103 T10 **Évian-les-Bains** Haute-Savoie, E France
93 K16 **Evijärvi** Länsi-Soumi, W Finland
79 D17 **Evinayong** var. Ebinayon, Evinayoung. C Equatorial Guinea
Evinayoung see Evinayong
115 E18 **Évinos** ≈ C Greece
95 E17 **Evje** Aust-Agder, S Norway
Evmolpia see Plovdiv
104 H11 **Évora** anc. Ebora, Lat. Liberalitas Julia. Évora, C Portugal
104 G11 **Évora** ◈ district S Portugal
102 M4 **Évreux** anc. Civitas Eburovicum. Eure, N France
102 K6 **Évron** Mayenne, NW France
114 L13 **Évros** Bul. Maritsa, Turk. Meriç; anc. Hebrus ≈ SE Europe see also Maritsa/Meriç
Évros see Meriç
Évros see Maritsa
115 F21 **Evrótas** ≈ S Greece
103 O5 **Évry** Essonne, N France
25 O8 **E. V. Spence Reservoir** ▣ Texas, SW USA
115 I18 **Évvoia** Lat. Euboea. island C Greece
38 D9 **'Ewa Beach** var. Ewa Beach. O'ahu, Hawai'i, USA
Ewa Beach see 'Ewa Beach
32 L9 **Ewan** Washington, NW USA
44 K12 **Ewarton** C Jamaica
81 J18 **Ewaso Ng'iro** var. Nyiro. ≈ C Kenya
29 P13 **Ewing** Nebraska, C USA
194 J5 **Ewing Island** island Antarctica
65 P17 **Ewing Seamount** undersea feature E Atlantic Ocean
158 L6 **Ewirgol** Xinjiang Uygur Zizhiqu, W China
79 G19 **Ewo** Cuvette, W Congo
27 S3 **Excelsior Springs** Missouri, C USA
97 J23 **Exe** ≈ SW England, UK
194 L12 **Executive Committee Range** ▲▲ Antarctica
14 E16 **Exeter** Ontario, S Canada
97 J24 **Exeter** anc. Isca Damnoniorum. SW England, UK
35 R11 **Exeter** California, W USA
19 P10 **Exeter** New Hampshire, NE USA
Exin see Kcynia
29 T14 **Exira** Iowa, C USA
97 J23 **Exmoor** moorland SW England, UK
21 Y6 **Exmore** Virginia, NE USA
180 G8 **Exmouth** Western Australia
97 J24 **Exmouth** SW England, UK
180 G8 **Exmouth Gulf** gulf Western Australia
173 V8 **Exmouth Plateau** undersea feature E Indian Ocean
115 J20 **Exompourgo** ancient monument Tínos, Kykládes, Greece, Aegean Sea
104 I10 **Extremadura** var. Estremadura. ◈ autonomous community W Spain
78 F12 **Extrême-Nord** Eng. Extreme North. ◈ province N Cameroon
Extreme North see Extrême-Nord
44 I3 **Exuma Cays** islets C Bahamas
44 I3 **Exuma Sound** sound C Bahamas
81 H20 **Eyasi, Lake** ◎ N Tanzania
95 F17 **Eydehavn** Aust-Agder, S Norway
96 L12 **Eyemouth** SE Scotland, UK
96 G7 **Eye Peninsula** peninsula NW Scotland, UK
80 Q13 **Eyl** It. Eil. Nugaal, E Somalia
103 N11 **Eymoutiers** Haute-Vienne, C France
Eyo (lower course) see Uolo, Río
29 X10 **Eyota** Minnesota, N USA
182 H2 **Eyre Basin, Lake** salt lake South Australia
182 I1 **Eyre Creek** seasonal river Northern Territory/South Australia
174 L9 **Eyre, Lake** salt lake South Australia
185 C22 **Eyre Mountains** ▲▲ South Island, New Zealand
182 H3 **Eyre North, Lake** salt lake South Australia
182 G7 **Eyre Peninsula** peninsula South Australia
182 H4 **Eyre South, Lake** salt lake South Australia
95 B18 **Eysturoy** Dan. Østerø. island N Faeroe Islands
61 D20 **Ezeiza** ✈ (Buenos Aires) Buenos Aires, E Argentina
Ezeres see Ezeriş
116 F12 **Ezeriş** Hung. Ezeres. Caraş-Severin, W Romania
161 O9 **Ezhou** prev. Echeng. Hubei, C China
125 R11 **Ezhva** Respublika Komi, NW Russian Federation
136 B12 **Ezine** Çanakkale, NW Turkey
Ezo see Hokkaidō
Ezra/Ezraa see Izra'

F

191 P7 **Faaa** Tahiti, W French Polynesia
191 P7 **Faaa** ✈ (Papeete) Tahiti, W French Polynesia
95 H24 **Faaborg** var. Fåborg. Fyn, C Denmark
151 K19 **Faadhippolhu Atoll** var. Fadiffolu, Lhaviyani Atoll. atoll N Maldives
191 U10 **Faaite** atoll Îles Tuamotu, C French Polynesia
191 Q8 **Faaone** Tahiti, W French Polynesia
24 H8 **Fabens** Texas, SW USA
94 H12 **Fåberg** Oppland, S Norway
Fåborg see Faaborg

◆ Country ● Country Capital ◇ Dependent Territory ○ Dependent Territory Capital ◈ Administrative Regions ✈ International Airport ▲ Mountain ▲▲ Mountain Range ※ Volcano ≈ River ◎ Lake ▣ Reservoir

106 I12 Fabriano Marche, C Italy
145 U16 Fabrichnyy Almaty, SE Kazakhstan
54 F10 Facatativá Cundinamarca, C Colombia
77 X9 Fachi Agadez, C Niger
188 B16 Facpi Point headland W Guam
18 I13 Factoryville Pennsylvania, NE USA
78 K8 Fada Borkou-Ennedi-Tibesti, E Chad
77 Q13 Fada-Ngourma E Burkina
123 N6 Faddeya, Zaliv bay N Russian Federation
123 Q5 Faddeyevskiy, Ostrov island Novosibirskiye Ostrova, NE Russian Federation
141 W12 Fadhī S Oman
Fadiffolu see Faadhippolhu Atoll
106 H10 Faenza anc. Faventia. Emilia-Romagna, N Italy
64 M5 Faeroe-Iceland Ridge undersea feature NW Norwegian Sea
64 M5 Faeroe Islands Dan. Færøerne, Faer. Føroyar. ◇ Danish external territory N Atlantic Ocean
86 C8 Faeroe Islands island group N Atlantic Ocean
Færøerne see Faeroe Islands
64 N6 Faeroe-Shetland Trough undersea feature NE Atlantic Ocean
104 H6 Fafe Braga, N Portugal
80 K13 Fafen Shet' ≈ E Ethiopia
193 V15 Fafo island Tongatapu Group, S Tonga
192 I16 Fagaloa Bay bay Upolu, E Samoa
192 H15 Fagamālo Savai'i, N Samoa
116 I12 Făgăraş Ger. Fogarasch, Hung. Fogaras. Braşov, C Romania
95 M20 Fagerhult Kalmar, S Sweden
94 G13 Fagernes Oppland, S Norway
92 I9 Fagernes Troms, N Norway
95 M14 Fagersta Västmanland, C Sweden
77 W13 Faggo var. Foggo. Bauchi, N Nigeria
Faghman see Fughmah
Fagibina, Lake see Faguibine, Lac
63 J25 Fagnano, Lago ◎ S Argentina
99 G22 Fagne hill range S Belgium
77 N10 Faguibine, Lac var. Lake Fagibina. ◎ NW Mali
Fahaheel see Al Fuḩayḩīl
Fahlun see Falun
143 U12 Fahraj Kermān, SE Iran
64 P5 Faial Madeira, Portugal, NE Atlantic Ocean
64 N2 Faial var. Ilha do Faial. island Azores, Portugal, NE Atlantic Ocean
Faial, Ilha do see Faial
108 G10 Faido Ticino, S Switzerland
Faifo see Hôi An
Failaka Island see Faylakah
190 G12 Faioa, Île island N Wallis and Futuna
181 W8 Fairbairn Reservoir ⊠ Queensland, E Australia
39 R9 Fairbanks Alaska, USA
21 U12 Fair Bluff North Carolina, SE USA
31 R14 Fairborn Ohio, N USA
23 S3 Fairburn Georgia, SE USA
30 M12 Fairbury Illinois, N USA
29 Q17 Fairbury Nebraska, C USA
29 T9 Fairfax Minnesota, N USA
27 O8 Fairfax Oklahoma, C USA
21 R14 Fairfax South Carolina, SE USA
35 N8 Fairfield California, W USA
33 O14 Fairfield Idaho, NW USA
30 M16 Fairfield Illinois, N USA
29 X15 Fairfield Iowa, C USA
33 R8 Fairfield Montana, NW USA
31 Q14 Fairfield Ohio, N USA
25 U8 Fairfield Texas, SW USA
27 T7 Fair Grove Missouri, C USA
19 P12 Fairhaven Massachusetts, NE USA
23 N8 Fairhope Alabama, S USA
96 L4 Fair Isle island NE Scotland, UK
185 F20 Fairlie Canterbury, South Island, New Zealand
29 U11 Fairmont Minnesota, N USA
29 Q16 Fairmont Nebraska, C USA
21 S3 Fairmont West Virginia, NE USA
31 P13 Fairmount Indiana, N USA
18 H10 Fairmount New York, NE USA
29 R7 Fairmount North Dakota, N USA
37 S5 Fairplay Colorado, C USA
18 F9 Fairport New York, NE USA
9 O12 Fairview Alberta, W Canada
26 L9 Fairview Oklahoma, C USA
36 L4 Fairview Utah, W USA
35 T6 Fairview Peak ▲ Nevada, W USA
188 H14 Fais atoll Caroline Islands, W Micronesia
149 U8 Faisalābād prev. Lyallpur. Punjab, NE Pakistan
Faisaliya see Fayşalīyah
28 L8 Faith South Dakota, N USA
153 N12 Faizābād Uttar Pradesh, N India
Faizabad/Faizābād see Feyzābād
45 S9 Fajardo E Puerto Rico
139 R9 Fajj, Wādī al dry watercourse S Iraq
140 K4 Fajr, Bi'r well NW Saudi Arabia
191 W10 Fakahina atoll Îles Tuamotu, C French Polynesia
190 L10 Fakaofo Atoll island SE Tokelau
191 U10 Fakarava atoll Îles Tuamotu, C French Polynesia
127 T2 Fakel Udmurtskaya Respublika, NW Russian Federation
97 P19 Fakenham E England, UK
171 U13 Fakfak Papua, E Indonesia
153 T12 Fakiragram Assam, NE India
114 M10 Fakiyska Reka ≈ SE Bulgaria
95 J24 Fakse Storstrøm, SE Denmark
95 J24 Fakse Bugt bay SE Denmark
95 J24 Fakse Ladeplads Storstrøm, SE Denmark
163 V11 Faku Liaoning, NE China
76 J14 Falaba N Sierra Leone
102 K5 Falaise Calvados, N France
114 H12 Falakró ▲▲ NE Greece
189 T12 Falalu island Chuuk, C Micronesia
166 L4 Falam Chin State, W Myanmar (Burma)
143 N8 Falāvarjān Eşfahān, C Iran
116 M11 Fălciu Vaslui, E Romania
54 I4 Falcón off. Estado Falcón. ◈ state NW Venezuela
106 J12 Falconara Marittima Marche, C Italy
Falcone, Capo del see Falcone, Punta del
107 A16 Falcone, Punta del var. Capo del Falcone. headland Sardegna, Italy, C Mediterranean Sea
Falcón, Estado see Falcón
9 Y16 Falcon Lake Manitoba, S Canada
Falcon Lake see Falcón, Presa/Falcon Reservoir
41 O7 Falcón, Presa var. Falcon Lake, Falcon Reservoir. ⊠ see also Falcon Reservoir
Falcón, Presa see Falcon Reservoir
25 Q16 Falcon Reservoir var. Falcon Lake, Presa Falcón. ⊠ see also Falcón, Presa
Falcon Reservoir see Falcón, Presa
190 L10 Fale island Fakaofo Atoll, SE Tokelau
192 F15 Faleālupo Savai'i, NW Samoa
190 B10 Falefatu island Funafuti Atoll, C Tuvalu
192 G15 Fālelima Savai'i, NW Samoa
95 N18 Falerum Östergötland, S Sweden
Faleshty see Făleşti
116 M9 Făleşti Rus. Faleshty. NW Moldova
25 S15 Falfurrias Texas, SW USA
9 O13 Falher Alberta, W Canada
Falkenau an der Eger see Sokolov
95 J21 Falkenberg Halland, S Sweden
Falkenberg see Niemodlin
Falkenburg in Pommern see Złocieniec
100 N12 Falkensee Brandenburg, NE Germany
96 J12 Falkirk C Scotland, UK
65 I20 Falkland Escarpment undersea feature SW Atlantic Ocean
63 K24 Falkland Islands var. Falklands, Islas Malvinas. ◇ UK dependent territory SW Atlantic Ocean
47 W14 Falkland Islands island group SW Atlantic Ocean
65 I20 Falkland Plateau var. Argentine Rise. undersea feature SW Atlantic Ocean
Falklands see Falkland Islands
63 M23 Falkland Sound var. Estrecho de San Carlos. strait C Falkland Islands
Falknov nad Ohří see Sokolov
115 H21 Falkonéra island S Greece
95 K18 Falköping Västra Götaland, S Sweden
139 U8 Fallāḩ E Iraq
35 U6 Fallbrook California, W USA
189 U12 Falleallej Pass passage Chuuk Islands, C Micronesia
93 J14 Fällfors Västerbotten, N Sweden
194 I6 Fallières Coast physical region Antarctica
100 I11 Fallingbostel Niedersachsen, NW Germany
33 X9 Fallon Montana, NW USA
35 S5 Fallon Nevada, W USA
19 O12 Fall River Massachusetts, NE USA
27 P6 Fall River Lake ⊠ Kansas, C USA
35 O3 Fall River Mills California, W USA
21 W4 Falls Church Virginia, NE USA
29 S17 Falls City Nebraska, C USA
25 S12 Falls City Texas, SW USA
Falluja see Al Fallūjah
77 S12 Falmey Dosso, SW Niger
45 W10 Falmouth Antigua, Antigua and Barbuda
44 J11 Falmouth W Jamaica
97 H25 Falmouth SW England, UK
20 M4 Falmouth Kentucky, S USA
19 P13 Falmouth Massachusetts, NE USA
21 W5 Falmouth Virginia, NE USA
189 U12 Falos island Chuuk, C Micronesia
83 E26 False Bay Afr. Valsbaai. bay SW South Africa
155 K17 False Divi Point headland E India
38 M16 False Pass Unimak Island, Alaska, USA
154 P12 False Point headland E India
105 U6 Falset Cataluña, NE Spain
95 I25 Falster island SE Denmark
116 K9 Fălticeni Hung. Falticsén. Suceava, NE Romania
Falticsén see Fălticeni
94 M13 Falun var. Fahlun. Kopparberg, C Sweden
Famagusta see Gazimağusa
Famagusta Bay see Gazimağusa Körfezi
62 I8 Famatina La Rioja, NW Argentina
99 J21 Famenne physical region SE Belgium
113 D22 Fan var. Fani. ≈ N Albania
77 X15 Fan ≈ E Nigeria
76 M12 Fana Koulikoro, SW Mali
115 K19 Fána ancient harbor Chíos, SE Greece
189 V13 Fanan island Chuuk, C Micronesia
189 U12 Fanapanges island Chuuk, C Micronesia
115 L20 Fanári, Ákrotírio cape Ikaría, Dodekánisa, Greece, Aegean Sea
45 Q13 Fancy Saint Vincent, Saint Vincent and the Grenadines
172 I5 Fandriana Fianarantsoa, SE Madagascar
167 O6 Fang Chiang Mai, NW Thailand
80 E13 Fangak Jonglei, SE Sudan
191 W10 Fangatau atoll Îles Tuamotu, C French Polynesia
191 X12 Fangataufa island Îles Tuamotu, SE French Polynesia
193 V15 Fanga Uta bay S Tonga
161 N7 Fangcheng Henan, C China
Fangcheng see Fangchenggang
160 K15 Fangchenggang var. Fangcheng Gezu Zizhixian; prev. Fangcheng. Guangxi Zhuangzu Zizhiqu, S China
Fangcheng Gezu Zizhixian see Fangchenggang
161 S15 Fangshan S Taiwan
163 X8 Fangzheng Heilongjiang, NE China
Fani see Fan
119 K16 Fanipal' Rus. Fanipol'. Minskaya Voblasts', C Belarus
Fanipol' see Fanipal'
25 T13 Fannin Texas, SW USA
Fanning Island see Tabuaeran
94 G8 Fannrem Sør-Trøndelag, S Norway
106 I11 Fano anc. Colonia Julia Fanestris, Fanum Fortunae. Marche, C Italy
95 E23 Fanø island W Denmark
167 R5 Fan Si Pan ▲ N Vietnam
Fanum Fortunae see Fano
141 W7 Faq' var. Al Faqa. Dubayy, E United Arab Emirates
Farab see Farap
194 H5 Faraday UK research station Antarctica
185 G16 Faraday, Mount ▲ South Island, New Zealand
79 P16 Faradje Orientale, NE Dem. Rep. Congo
Faradofay see Tôlañaro
172 I7 Farafangana Fianarantsoa, SE Madagascar
148 J7 Farāh var. Farah, Fararud. Farāh, W Afghanistan
148 K7 Farāh ◈ province W Afghanistan
148 J7 Farāh Rūd ≈ W Afghanistan
188 K7 Farallon de Medinilla island C Northern Mariana Islands
188 J2 Farallon de Pajaros var. Uracas. island N Northern Mariana Islands
76 J14 Faranah Haute-Guinée, S Guinea
146 K12 Farab Rus. Farab. Lebap Welaýaty, NE Turkmenistan
Fararud see Farāh
140 M13 Farasān, Jazā'ir island group SW Saudi Arabia
172 I5 Faratsiho Antananarivo, C Madagascar
188 K15 Faraulep Atoll atoll Caroline Islands, C Micronesia
99 H20 Farciennes Hainaut, S Belgium
105 O14 Fardes ≈ S Spain
191 S10 Fare Huahine, W French Polynesia
97 M23 Fareham S England, UK
39 P11 Farewell Alaska, USA
184 H13 Farewell, Cape headland South Island, New Zealand
Farewell, Cape see Nunap Isua
184 I13 Farewell Spit spit South Island, New Zealand
95 I17 Färgelanda Älvsborg, S Sweden
Farghona, Wodii/Farghona Valley see Fergana Valley
Farghona Wodiysi see Fergana Valley
23 V8 Fargo Georgia, SE USA
29 R5 Fargo North Dakota, N USA
147 S10 Farg'ona Rus. Fergana; prev. Novyy Margilan. Farg'ona Viloyati, E Uzbekistan
147 R10 Farg'ona Viloyati Rus. Ferganskaya Oblast'. ◈ province E Uzbekistan
29 V10 Faribault Minnesota, N USA
152 J11 Farīdābād Haryāna, N India Asia
152 H8 Farīdkot Punjab, NW India
153 T15 Faridpur Dhaka, C Bangladesh
75 P11 Fārigh, Wādī al ≈ N Libya
172 I4 Farihy Alaotra ◎ C Madagascar
94 M11 Färila Gävleborg, C Sweden
104 E9 Farilhões island C Portugal
76 G12 Farim NW Guinea-Bissau
Farish see Forish
141 T11 Fāris, Qalamat well SE Saudi Arabia
95 N21 Färjestaden Kalmar, S Sweden
149 R2 Farkhār Takhār, NE Afghanistan
147 Q14 Farkhor Rus. Parkhar. SW Tajikistan
116 F12 Fârliug prev. Fîrliug, Hung. Furluk. Caraş-Severin, SW Romania
115 M21 Farmakonísi island Dodekánisa, Greece, Aegean Sea
30 M13 Farmer City Illinois, N USA
31 N14 Farmersburg Indiana, N USA
25 U6 Farmersville Texas, SW USA
22 H5 Farmerville Louisiana, S USA
29 X16 Farmington Iowa, C USA
19 Q6 Farmington Maine, NE USA
29 V9 Farmington Minnesota, N USA
27 X6 Farmington Missouri, C USA
19 O9 Farmington New Hampshire, NE USA
37 P9 Farmington New Mexico, SW USA
36 L2 Farmington Utah, W USA
21 W9 Farmville North Carolina, SE USA
21 U6 Farmville Virginia, NE USA
97 N22 Farnborough S England, UK
97 N22 Farnham S England, UK
10 J7 Faro Yukon Territory, W Canada
104 G14 Faro Faro, S Portugal
95 Q18 Fårö Gotland, SE Sweden
104 G14 Faro ◈ district S Portugal
78 F13 Faro ≈ Cameroon/Nigeria
104 G14 Faro ✈ Faro, S Portugal
Faro, Punta del see Peloro, Capo
95 Q18 Fårösund Gotland, SE Sweden
173 N7 Farquhar Group island group S Seychelles
18 B13 Farrell Pennsylvania, NE USA
152 K11 Farrukhābād Uttar Pradesh, N India
143 P11 Fārs off. Ostān-e Fārs; anc. Persis. ◈ province S Iran
115 F16 Fársala Thessalía, C Greece
143 R4 Farsīān Golestān, N Iran
95 G21 Farsø Nordjylland, N Denmark
Fārs, Ostān-e see Fārs
95 D18 Farsund Vest-Agder, S Norway
141 U14 Fartak, Ra's headland E Yemen
60 H13 Fartura, Serra da ▲▲ S Brazil
Farvel, Kap see Nunap Isua
24 L4 Farwell Texas, SW USA
194 I9 Farwell Island island Antarctica
152 L9 Far Western ◈ zone W Nepal
148 M3 Faryāb ◈ province N Afghanistan
143 P12 Fasā Fārs, S Iran
141 U12 Fasad, Ramlat desert SW Oman
107 P17 Fasano Puglia, SE Italy
92 L3 Fáskrúdhsfjördhur Austurland, E Iceland
117 O5 Fastiv Rus. Fastov. Kyyivs'ka Oblast', NW Ukraine
97 B22 Fastnet Rock Ir. Carraig Aonair. island SW Ireland
Fastov see Fastiv
190 C9 Fatato island Funafuti Atoll, C Tuvalu
152 K12 Fatehgarh Uttar Pradesh, N India
149 U6 Fatehjang Punjab, E Pakistan
152 G11 Fatehpur Rājasthān, N India
152 L13 Fatehpur Uttar Pradesh, N India
126 J7 Fatezh Kurskaya Oblast', W Russian Federation
76 G11 Fatick W Senegal
104 G9 Fátima Santarém, W Portugal
136 M11 Fatsa Ordu, N Turkey
Fatshan see Foshan
190 D12 Fatua, Pointe var. Pointe Nord. headland Île Futuna, S Wallis and Futuna
191 X7 Fatu Hiva island Îles Marquises, NE French Polynesia
Fatunda see Fatundu
79 H21 Fatundu var. Fatunda. Bandundu, W Dem. Rep. Congo
29 O8 Faulkton South Dakota, N USA
116 L13 Făurei prev. Filimon Sîrbu. Brăila, SE Romania
92 G12 Fauske Nordland, C Norway
9 P13 Faust Alberta, W Canada
99 L23 Fauvillers Luxembourg, SE Belgium
107 J24 Favara Sicilia, Italy, C Mediterranean Sea
Faventia see Faenza
107 G23 Favignana, Isola island Isole Egadi, S Italy
12 D8 Fawn ≈ Ontario, SE Canada
Faxa Bay see Faxaflói
92 H3 Faxaflói Eng. Faxa Bay. bay W Iceland
78 I7 Faya prev. Faya-Largeau, Largeau. Borkou-Ennedi-Tibesti, N Chad
Faya-Largeau see Faya
187 Q16 Fayaoué Province des Îles Loyauté, C New Caledonia
138 M5 Fayḑat hill range E Syria
23 O3 Fayette Alabama, S USA
29 X12 Fayette Iowa, C USA
22 J6 Fayette Mississippi, S USA
27 U4 Fayette Missouri, C USA
27 S9 Fayetteville Arkansas, C USA
21 U10 Fayetteville North Carolina, SE USA
20 J10 Fayetteville Tennessee, S USA
25 U11 Fayetteville Texas, SW USA
21 R5 Fayetteville West Virginia, NE USA
141 R4 Faylakah var. Failaka Island. island E Kuwait
139 T10 Fayşalīyah var. Faisaliya. S Iraq
189 P15 Fayu var. East Fayu. island Hall Islands, C Micronesia
152 G8 Fāzilka Punjab, NW India
Fdérick see Fdérik
76 I6 Fdérik var. Fdérick, Fr. Fort Gouraud. Tiris Zemmour, NW Mauritania
Feabhail, Loch see Foyle, Lough
97 B20 Feale ≈ SW Ireland
21 V12 Fear, Cape headland Bald Head Island, North Carolina, SE USA
35 O6 Feather River ≈ California, W USA
185 M14 Featherston Wellington, North Island, New Zealand
102 L3 Fécamp Seine-Maritime, N France
Fédala see Mohammedia
61 D17 Federación Entre Ríos, E Argentina
61 D17 Federal Entre Ríos, E Argentina
77 T15 Federal Capital District ◈ capital territory C Nigeria
Federal Capital Territory see Australian Capital Territory
Federal District see Distrito Federal
21 Y4 Federalsburg Maryland, NE USA
74 M6 Fedjaj, Chott el var. Chott el Fejaj, Shaṭṭ al Fijāj. salt lake C Tunisia
94 B13 Fedje island S Norway
144 M7 Fedorovka Kostanay, N Kazakhstan
127 U6 Fedorovka Respublika Bashkortostan, W Russian Federation
Fëdory see Fyadory
117 U11 Fedotova Kosa spit SE Ukraine
189 V13 Fefan atoll Chuuk Islands, C Micronesia
111 O21 Fehérgyarmat Szabolcs-Szatmár-Bereg, E Hungary
Fehér-Körös see Crişul Alb
Fehértemplom see Bela Crkva
Fehérvölgy see Albac
100 L7 Fehmarn island N Germany
95 H25 Fehmarn Belt Dan. Femern Bælt, Ger. Fehmarnbelt. strait Denmark /Germany see also Femern Bælt
Fehmarnbelt Fehmarn Belt/Femer Bælt
109 X8 Fehring Steiermark, SE Austria
59 B15 Feijó Acre, W Brazil
184 M12 Feilding Manawatu-Wanganui, North Island, New Zealand
Feira see Feira de Santana
59 O17 Feira de Santana var. Feira. Bahia, E Brazil
109 X7 Feistritz ≈ SE Austria
Feistritz see Ilirska Bistrica
161 P8 Feixi var. Shangpai; prev. Shangpaihe. Anhui, E China
Fejaj, Chott el see Fedjaj, Chott el
111 I23 Fejér off. Fejér Megye. ◈ county W Hungary
Fejér Megye see Fejér
95 I24 Fejø island SE Denmark
136 K15 Feke Adana, S Turkey
Feketehalom see Codlea
Fekete-Körös see Crişul Negru
105 Y9 Felanitx Mallorca, Spain, W Mediterranean Sea
109 T3 Feldaist ≈ N Austria
109 W8 Feldbach Steiermark, SE Austria
101 F24 Feldberg ▲ SW Germany
116 J12 Feldioara Ger. Marienburg, Hung. Földvár. Braşov, C Romania
108 I7 Feldkirch anc. Clunia. Vorarlberg, W Austria
109 S9 Feldkirchen in Kärnten Slvn. Trg. Kärnten, S Austria
Félegyháza see Kiskunfélegyháza
192 H16 Feleolo ✈ (Āpia) Upolu, C Samoa
104 H6 Felgueiras Porto, N Portugal
Felicitas Julia see Lisboa
172 J16 Félicité island Inner Islands, NE Seychelles
151 K20 Felidhu Atoll atoll C Maldives
41 Y13 Felipe Carrillo Puerto Quintana Roo, SE Mexico
97 Q21 Felixstowe E England, UK
103 N11 Felletin Creuse, C France
Fellin see Viljandi
Felsőbánya see Baia Sprie
Felsőmuzslya see Mužlja
Felsővisó see Vişeu de Sus
35 N10 Felton California, W USA
106 H7 Feltre Veneto, NE Italy
95 H25 Femer Bælt Dan. Fehmarn Belt, Ger. Fehmarnbelt. strait Denmark/Germany SW Baltic Sea see also Fehmarn Belt
Femern Bælt Fehmarn Belt
95 I24 Femø island SE Denmark
94 I10 Femunden ◎ S Norway
104 H2 Fene Galicia, NW Spain
14 I14 Fenelon Falls Ontario, SE Canada
189 U13 Feneppi atoll Chuuk Islands, C Micronesia
137 O11 Fener Burnu headland N Turkey
115 J14 Fengári ▲ Samothráki, E Greece
163 V13 Fengcheng var. Feng-cheng, Fenghwangcheng. Liaoning, NE China
Feng-cheng see Fengcheng
160 K11 Fenggang var. Longquan. Guizhou, S China
161 S9 Fenghua Zhejiang, SE China
Fenghwangcheng see Fengcheng
Fengjiaba see Wangcang
160 L9 Fengjie var. Yong'an. Sichuan, C China
160 M14 Fengkai var. Jiangkou. Guangdong, S China
161 T13 Fenglin Jap. Hōrin. C Taiwan
161 P1 Fengning prev. Dagezhen. Hebei, E China
160 E13 Fengqing var. Fengshan. Yunnan, SW China
161 O6 Fengqiu Henan, C China
161 Q2 Fengrun Hebei, E China
Fengshan see Luoyuan
Fengshan see Fengqing
163 T4 Fengshui Shan ▲ NE China
161 P14 Fengshun Guangdong, S China
Fengtien see Shenyang, China
Fengtien see Liaoning, China
160 J7 Fengxian var. Feng Xian; prev. Shuangshipu. Shaanxi, C China
Feng Xian see Fengxian
Fengxiang see Luobei
Fengyizhen see Maoxian
163 P13 Fengzhen Nei Mongol Zizhiqu, N China
160 M6 Fen He ≈ C China
153 V15 Feni Chittagong, E Bangladesh
186 I6 Feni Islands island group NE Papua New Guinea
38 H17 Fenimore Pass strait Aleutian Islands, Alaska, USA
84 B9 Feni Ridge undersea feature N Atlantic Ocean
Fennern see Vändra
30 J9 Fennimore Wisconsin, N USA
172 J4 Fenoarivo Toamasina, E Madagascar
95 I24 Fensmark Storstrøm, SE Denmark
97 O19 Fens, The wetland E England, UK
31 R9 Fenton Michigan, N USA
190 K10 Fenua Fala island SE Tokelau
190 F12 Fenuafo'ou, Île island E Wallis and Futuna
190 L10 Fenua Loa island Fakaofo Atoll, E Tokelau
160 M4 Fenyang Shanxi, C China
117 U13 Feodosiya var. Kefe, It. Kaffa; anc. Theodosia. Respublika Krym, S Ukraine
94 I10 Feragen ◎ S Norway
74 L5 Fer, Cap de headland NE Algeria
31 O16 Ferdinand Indiana, N USA
Ferdinand see Montana, Bulgaria
Ferdinand see Mihail Kogălniceanu, Romania
Ferdinandsberg see Oţelu Roşu
143 T7 Ferdows var. Firdaus; prev. Tūn. Khorāsān-Razavī, E Iran
103 Q5 Fère-Champenoise Marne, N France
Ferencz-József Csúcs see Gerlachovský štít
107 J16 Ferentino Lazio, C Italy
114 L13 Féres Anatolikí Makedonía kai Thráki, NE Greece
Fergana see Farg'ona
147 S10 Fergana Valley var. Farghona Valley, Rus. Ferganskaya Dolina, Taj. Wodii Farghona, Uzb. Farghona Wodiysi. basin Tajikistan/Uzbekistan
Ferganskaya Dolina see Fergana Valley
Ferganskaya Oblast' see Farg'ona Viloyati
147 U9 Ferganskiy Khrebet ▲▲ C Kyrgyzstan
14 F15 Fergus Ontario, S Canada
29 S6 Fergus Falls Minnesota, N USA
186 G9 Fergusson Island var. Kaluwawa. island SE Papua New Guinea
111 K22 Ferihegy ✈ (Budapest) Budapest, C Hungary
Ferizaj see Uroševac
77 N14 Ferkessédougou N Ivory Coast
109 T10 Ferlach Slvn. Borovlje. Kärnten, S Austria
97 E16 Fermanagh cultural region SW Northern Ireland, UK
106 J13 Fermo anc. Firmum Picenum. Marche, C Italy
104 J6 Fermoselle Castilla-León, N Spain
97 D20 Fermoy Ir. Mainistir Fhear Maí. SW Ireland
23 W8 Fernandina Beach Amelia Island, Florida, SE USA
57 A17 Fernandina, Isla var. Narborough Island. island Galapagos Islands, Ecuador, E Pacific Ocean
47 Y5 Fernando de Noronha island E Brazil
Fernando Po/Fernando Póo see Bioco, Isla de
60 J7 Fernandópolis São Paulo, S Brazil
104 M13 Fernán Núñez Andalucía, S Spain
83 Q14 Fernão Veloso, Baia de bay NE Mozambique
34 K3 Ferndale California, W USA
32 H6 Ferndale Washington, NW USA
9 P17 Fernie British Columbia, SW Canada
35 R5 Fernley Nevada, W USA
Ferozepore see Firozpur
107 N18 Ferrandina Basilicata, S Italy
106 G9 Ferrara anc. Forum Alieni. Emilia-Romagna, N Italy
120 F9 Ferrat, Cap headland NW Algeria
107 D20 Ferrato, Capo headland Sardegna, Italy, C Mediterranean Sea
104 G12 Ferreira do Alentejo Beja, S Portugal
56 B11 Ferreñafe Lambayeque, W Peru
108 C12 Ferret Valais, SW Switzerland
102 I13 Ferret, Cap headland W France
22 I6 Ferriday Louisiana, S USA
Ferro see Hierro
107 D16 Ferro, Capo headland Sardegna, Italy, C Mediterranean Sea
104 H2 Ferrol var. El Ferrol; prev. El Ferrol del Caudillo. Galicia, NW Spain
56 B12 Ferrol, Península de peninsula W Peru
36 M5 Ferron Utah, W USA
21 S7 Ferrum Virginia, NE USA
23 O8 Ferry Pass Florida, SE USA
Ferryville see Menzel Bourguiba
29 S4 Fertile Minnesota, N USA
Fertő see Neusiedler See
98 L5 Ferwerd Fris. Ferwert. Friesland, N Netherlands
Ferwert see Ferwerd
74 G6 Fès Eng. Fez. N Morocco
79 I22 Feshi Bandundu, SW Dem. Rep. Congo
29 O4 Fessenden North Dakota, N USA
Festenberg see Twardogóra
27 X5 Festus Missouri, C USA
116 M14 Feteşti Ialomiţa, SE Romania
136 D17 Fethiye Muğla, SW Turkey
96 M1 Fetlar island NE Scotland, UK
95 I15 Fetsund Akershus, S Norway
12 L5 Feuilles, Lac aux ◎ Québec, E Canada
12 L5 Feuilles, Rivière aux ≈ Québec, E Canada
99 M23 Feulen Diekirch, C Luxembourg
103 Q11 Feurs Loire, E France
95 F18 Fevik Aust-Agder, S Norway
123 R13 Fevral'sk Amurskaya Oblast', SE Russian Federation
149 S2 Feyzābād var. Faizabad, Faizābād, Feyzābād, Fyzabad. Badakhshān, NE Afghanistan
Feyzābād see Fayzobod
Fez see Fès
97 J19 Ffestiniog NW Wales, UK
Fhóid Duibh, Cuan an see Blacksod Bay
62 I8 Fiambalá Catamarca, NW Argentina
172 I6 Fianarantsoa Fianarantsoa, C Madagascar
172 H6 Fianarantsoa ◈ province SE Madagascar
78 G12 Fianga Mayo-Kébbi, SW Chad
Ficce see Fichē

◆ Country
● Country Capital
◇ Dependent Territory
○ Dependent Territory Capital
◈ Administrative Regions
✈ International Airport
▲ Mountain
▲▲ Mountain Range
Volcano
≈ River
◎ Lake
⊠ Reservoir

80 J12 **Fichê** *It.* Ficce. C Ethiopia
101 N17 **Fichtelberg** ▲ Czech Republic/Germany
101 M18 **Fichtelgebirge** ▲▲ SE Germany
101 M19 **Fichtelnaab** ≈ SE Germany
106 E9 **Fidenza** Emilia-Romagna, N Italy
113 K21 **Fier** *var.* Fieri. Fier, SW Albania
113 K21 **Fier** ◐ *district* W Albania
Fieri *see* Fier
Fierza *see* Fierzë
113 L17 **Fierzë** *var.* Fierza. Shkodër, N Albania
113 L17 **Fierzës, Liqeni i** ◎ N Albania
108 F10 **Fiesch** Valais, SW Switzerland
106 G11 **Fiesole** Toscana, C Italy
138 G12 **Fīfah** Aṭ ṭafīlah, W Jordan
96 K11 **Fife** *var.* Kingdom of Fife. *cultural region* E Scotland, UK
Fife, Kingdom of *see* Fife
96 K11 **Fife Ness** *headland* E Scotland, UK
Fifteen Twenty Fracture Zone *see* Barracuda Fracture Zone
103 N13 **Figeac** Lot, S France
95 N19 **Figeholm** Kalmar, SE Sweden
Figig *see* Figuig
83 J18 **Figtree** Matabeleland South, SW Zimbabwe
104 F8 **Figueira da Foz** Coimbra, W Portugal
105 X4 **Figueres** Cataluña, E Spain
74 H7 **Figuig** *var.* Figig. E Morocco
Fijājj, Shaṭṭ al *see* Fedjaj, Chott el
187 Y15 **Fiji** *off.* Sovereign Democratic Republic of Fiji, *Fij.* Viti. ◆ *republic* SW Pacific Ocean
192 K9 **Fiji** *island group* SW Pacific Ocean
175 Q8 **Fiji Plate** *tectonic feature*
Fiji, Sovereign Democratic Republic of *see* Fiji
105 P14 **Filabres, Sierra de los** ▲▲ SE Spain
83 K18 **Filabusi** Matabeleland South, S Zimbabwe
42 K13 **Filadelfia** Guanacaste, W Costa Rica
111 K20 **Fil'akovo** *Hung.* Fülek. Banskobýstricky Kraj, C Slovakia
195 N5 **Filchner Ice Shelf** *ice shelf* Antarctica
14 J11 **Fildegrand** ≈ Québec, SE Canada
94 E12 **Fillefjell** ▲▲ S Norway
33 O15 **Filer** Idaho, NW USA
Filevo *see* Vŭrbitsa
116 H14 **Filiaşi** Dolj, SW Romania
115 B16 **Filiátes** Ípeiros, W Greece
115 D21 **Filiatrá** Pelopónnisos, S Greece
107 K22 **Filicudi, Isola** *island* Isole Eolie, S Italy
141 Y10 **Filim** E Oman
Filimon Sîrbu *see* Făurei
77 S11 **Filingué** Tillabéri, W Niger
114 K13 **Filiouri** ≈ NE Greece
Filiouri *see* Líssos
114 I13 **Filippoi** *anc.* Philippi. *site of ancient city* Anatolikí Makedonía kai Thráki, NE Greece
95 L15 **Filipstad** Värmland, C Sweden
108 I9 **Filisur** Graubünden, S Switzerland
35 R14 **Fillmore** California, W USA
36 K5 **Fillmore** Utah, W USA
14 J10 **Fils, Lac du** ◎ Québec, SE Canada
136 H11 **Filyos Çayı** ≈ N Turkey
195 Q1 **Fimbul Ice Shelf** *ice shelf* Antarctica
195 Q2 **Fimbutheimen** *physical region* Antarctica
106 G9 **Finale Emilia** Emilia-Romagna, C Italy
106 C10 **Finale Ligure** Liguria, NW Italy
105 P14 **Fiñana** Andalucía, S Spain
172 I6 **Finandrahana** Fianarantsoa, SE Madagascar
21 S6 **Fincastle** Virginia, NE USA
99 M25 **Findel** ✈ (Luxembourg) Luxembourg, C Luxembourg
96 J9 **Findhorn** ≈ N Scotland, UK
31 R12 **Findlay** Ohio, N USA
18 G11 **Finger Lakes** ◎ New York, NE USA
83 L14 **Fingoè** Tete, NW Mozambique
136 E17 **Finike** Antalya, SW Turkey
102 F6 **Finistère** ◐ *department* NW France
186 D7 **Finisterre Range** ▲▲ N Papua New Guinea
181 Q8 **Finke** Northern Territory, N Australia
109 S10 **Finkenstein** Kärnten, S Austria
189 Y15 **Finkol, Mount** *var.* Mount Crozer. ▲ Kosrae, E Micronesia
93 L17 **Finland** *off.* Republic of Finland, *Fin.* Suomen Tasavalta, Suomi. ◆ *republic* N Europe
124 F12 **Finland, Gulf of** *Est.* Soome Laht, *Fin.* Suomenlahti, *Ger.* Finnischer Meerbusen, *Rus.* Finskiy Zaliv, *Swe.* Finska Viken. *gulf* E Baltic Sea
Finland, Republic of *see* Finland
10 L11 **Finlay** ≈ British Columbia, W Canada
183 O10 **Finley** New South Wales, SE Australia
29 Q4 **Finley** North Dakota, N USA
Finnischer Meerbusen *see* Finland, Gulf of
92 K9 **Finnmark** ◐ *county* N Norway
92 K9 **Finnmarksvidda** *physical region* N Norway
92 I9 **Finnsnes** Troms, N Norway
186 E7 **Finschhafen** Morobe, C Papua New Guinea
94 E13 **Finse** Hordaland, S Norway
Finska Viken/Finskiy Zaliv *see* Finland, Gulf of
95 M17 **Finspång** Östergötland, S Sweden
108 F10 **Finsteraarhorn** ▲ Swtizerland
101 O14 **Finsterwalde** Brandenburg, E Germany
185 A23 **Fiordland** *physical region* South Island, New Zealand
106 E9 **Fiorenzuola d'Arda** Emilia-Romagna, C Italy
Firat Nehri *see* Euphrates
Firdaus *see* Ferdows
18 M14 **Fire Island** *island* New York, NE USA
105 G11 **Firenze** *Eng.* Florence; *anc.* Florentia. Toscana, C Italy
106 G10 **Firenzuola** Toscana, C Italy
14 C6 **Fire River** Ontario, S Canada
Firliug *see* Fârliug
61 B19 **Firmat** Santa Fe, C Argentina
103 Q12 **Firminy** Loire, E France
Firmum Picenum *see* Fermo
152 J12 **Fīrozābād** Uttar Pradesh, N India
152 G8 **Fīrozpur** *var.* Ferozepore. Punjab, NW India
First State *see* Delaware
143 O12 **Fīrūzābād** Fārs, S Iran
Fischamend *see* Fischamend Markt
109 Y4 **Fischamend Markt** *var.* Fischamend. Niederösterreich, NE Austria
109 W6 **Fischbacher Alpen** ▲▲ E Austria
Fischhausen *see* Primorsk
83 D21 **Fish** *var.* Vis. ≈ S Namibia
83 F24 **Fish** *Afr.* Vis. ≈ SW South Africa
9 X15 **Fisher Branch** Manitoba, S Canada
9 X15 **Fisher River** Manitoba, S Canada
19 N13 **Fishers Island** *island* New York, NE USA
37 U8 **Fishers Peak** ▲ Colorado, C USA
9 P9 **Fisher Strait** *strait* Nunavut, N Canada
97 H21 **Fishguard** *Wel.* Abergwaun. SW Wales, UK
19 R2 **Fish River Lake** ◎ Maine, NE USA
194 K6 **Fiske, Cape** *headland* Antarctica
103 P4 **Fismes** Marne, N France
104 F3 **Fisterra, Cabo** *cape* NW Spain
19 N11 **Fitchburg** Massachusetts, NE USA
96 L3 **Fitful Head** *headland* NE Scotland, UK
95 C14 **Fitjar** Hordaland, S Norway
192 H16 **Fito** ▲ Upolu, C Samoa
23 U6 **Fitzgerald** Georgia, SE USA
180 M5 **Fitzroy Crossing** Western Australia
63 G21 **Fitzroy, Monte** *var.* Cerro Chaltel. ▲ S Argentina
181 Y8 **Fitzroy River** ≈ Queensland, E Australia
180 L5 **Fitzroy River** ≈ Western Australia
14 E12 **Fitzwilliam Island** *island* Ontario, S Canada
107 J15 **Fiuggi** Lazio, C Italy
Fiume *see* Rijeka
107 H15 **Fiumicino** Lazio, C Italy
Fiumicino *see* Leonardo da Vinci
106 E10 **Fivizzano** Toscana, C Italy
79 O21 **Fizi** Sud Kivu, E Dem. Rep. Congo
Fizuli *see* Füzuli
92 I11 **Fjällåsen** Norrbotten, N Sweden
95 G20 **Fjerritslev** Nordjylland, N Denmark
F.J.S. *see* Franz Josef Strauss
95 L16 **Fjugesta** Örebro, C Sweden
Fladstrand *see* Frederikshavn
37 V5 **Flagler** Colorado, C USA
23 X10 **Flagler Beach** Florida, SE USA
36 L11 **Flagstaff** Arizona, SW USA
65 H24 **Flagstaff Bay** *bay* N Saint Helena, C Atlantic Ocean
19 P5 **Flagstaff Lake** ◎ Maine, NE USA
94 E13 **Flåm** Sogn Og Fjordane, S Norway
15 O8 **Flamand** ≈ Québec, SE Canada
30 J5 **Flambeau River** ≈ Wisconsin, N USA
97 O16 **Flamborough Head** *headland* E England, UK
100 N13 **Fläming** *hill range* NE Germany
16 H8 **Flaming Gorge Reservoir** ⊠ Utah/Wyoming, NW USA
99 B18 **Flanders** *Dut.* Vlaanderen, *Fr.* Flandre. *cultural region* Belgium/France
Flandre *see* Flanders
29 R10 **Flandreau** South Dakota, N USA
96 D6 **Flannan Isles** *island group* NW Scotland, UK
28 M6 **Flasher** North Dakota, N USA
93 G15 **Flåsjön** ◎ N Sweden
39 O11 **Flat** Alaska, USA
92 H1 **Flateyri** Vestfirdhir, NW Iceland
33 P8 **Flathead Lake** ◎ Montana, NW USA
173 Y15 **Flat Island** *island* N Mauritius
25 T11 **Flatonia** Texas, SW USA
185 M14 **Flat Point** *headland* North Island, New Zealand
27 X6 **Flat River** Missouri, C USA
31 P8 **Flat River** ≈ Michigan, N USA
31 P14 **Flatrock River** ≈ Indiana, N USA
32 E6 **Flattery, Cape** *headland* Washington, NW USA
64 B12 **Flatts Village** *var.* The Flatts Village. C Bermuda
108 H7 **Flawil** Sankt Gallen, NE Switzerland
97 N22 **Fleet** S England, UK
97 K16 **Fleetwood** NW England, UK
18 H15 **Fleetwood** Pennsylvania, NE USA
95 D18 **Flekkefjord** Vest-Agder, S Norway
21 N5 **Flemingsburg** Kentucky, S USA
18 J15 **Flemington** New Jersey, NE USA
64 I7 **Flemish Cap** *undersea feature* NW Atlantic Ocean
95 N16 **Flen** Södermanland, C Sweden
100 I6 **Flensburg** Schleswig-Holstein, N Germany
100 J6 **Flensburger Förde** *inlet* Denmark/Germany
102 K5 **Flers** Orne, N France
95 C14 **Flesland** ✈ (Bergen) Hordaland, S Norway
Flessingue *see* Vlissingen
21 P10 **Fletcher** North Carolina, SE USA
31 R6 **Fletcher Pond** ◎ Michigan, N USA
102 L15 **Fleurance** Gers, S France
108 B8 **Fleurier** Neuchâtel, W Switzerland
99 H20 **Fleurus** Hainaut, S Belgium
103 N7 **Fleury-les-Aubrais** Loiret, C France
98 K10 **Flevoland** ◐ *province* C Netherlands
Flickertail State *see* North Dakota
108 H9 **Flims** Glarus, NE Switzerland
182 F8 **Flinders Island** *island* Investigator Group, South Australia
183 P14 **Flinders Island** *island* Furneaux Group, Tasmania, SE Australia
182 I6 **Flinders Ranges** ▲▲ South Australia
181 U5 **Flinders River** ≈ Queensland, NE Australia
9 V13 **Flin Flon** Manitoba, C Canada
97 K18 **Flint** NE Wales, UK
31 R9 **Flint** Michigan, N USA
97 J18 **Flint** *cultural region* NE Wales, UK
27 O7 **Flint Hills** *hill range* Kansas, C USA
191 Y6 **Flint Island** *island* Line Islands, E Kiribati
23 S4 **Flint River** ≈ Georgia, SE USA
31 R9 **Flint River** ≈ Michigan, N USA
189 X12 **Flipper Point** *headland* C Wake Island
94 I13 **Flisa** Hedmark, S Norway
94 J13 **Flisa** ≈ S Norway
122 J5 **Flissingskiy, Mys** *headland* Novaya Zemlya, NW Russian Federation
Flitsch *see* Bovec
105 U6 **Flix** Cataluña, NE Spain
95 J19 **Floda** Älvsborg, S Sweden
101 O16 **Flöha** ≈ E Germany
25 O4 **Flomot** Texas, SW USA
29 V5 **Floodwood** Minnesota, N USA
30 M15 **Flora** Illinois, N USA
103 P14 **Florac** Lozère, S France
23 Q8 **Florala** Alabama, S USA
103 S4 **Florange** Moselle, NE France
Floreana, Isla *see* Santa María, Isla
23 O2 **Florence** Alabama, S USA
36 L14 **Florence** Arizona, SW USA
37 T6 **Florence** Colorado, C USA
27 O5 **Florence** Kansas, C USA
20 M4 **Florence** Kentucky, S USA
32 E13 **Florence** Oregon, NW USA
21 T12 **Florence** South Carolina, SE USA
25 S9 **Florence** Texas, SW USA
Florence *see* Firenze
54 E13 **Florencia** Caquetá, S Colombia
99 H21 **Florennes** Namur, S Belgium
Florentia *see* Firenze
63 J18 **Florentino Ameghino, Embalse** ◎ S Argentina
99 J24 **Florenville** Luxembourg, SE Belgium
42 E3 **Flores** Petén, N Guatemala
61 E19 **Flores** ◐ *department* S Uruguay
171 O16 **Flores** *island* Nusa Tenggara, C Indonesia
64 M1 **Flores** *island* Azores, Portugal, NE Atlantic Ocean
Floreshty *see* Floreşti
Flores, Lago de *see* Petén Itzá, Lago
Flores, Laut *see* Flores Sea
171 N15 **Flores Sea** *Ind.* Laut Flores. *sea* C Indonesia
116 M8 **Floreşti** *Rus.* Floreshty. N Moldova
25 S12 **Floresville** Texas, SW USA
59 N14 **Floriano** Piauí, E Brazil
61 K14 **Florianópolis** *prev.* Destêrro. *state capital* Santa Catarina, S Brazil
44 G6 **Florida** Camagüey, C Cuba
61 F19 **Florida** Florida, S Uruguay
61 F19 **Florida** ◐ *department* S Uruguay
23 U9 **Florida** *off.* State of Florida, *also known as* Peninsular State, Sunshine State. ◐ *state* SE USA
23 Y17 **Florida Bay** *bay* Florida, SE USA
54 G8 **Floridablanca** Santander, N Colombia
23 Y17 **Florida Keys** *island group* Florida, SE USA
37 Q16 **Florida Mountains** ▲▲ New Mexico, SW USA
64 D10 **Florida, Straits of** *strait* Atlantic Ocean/Gulf of Mexico
114 D13 **Flórina** *var.* Phlórina. Dytikí Makedonía, N Greece
27 X4 **Florissant** Missouri, C USA
94 C11 **Florø** Sogn Og Fjordane, S Norway
115 L22 **Floúda, Ákrotírio** *cape* Astypálaia, Kykládes, Greece, Aegean Sea
21 S7 **Floyd** Virginia, NE USA
25 N4 **Floydada** Texas, SW USA
Flüela Wisshorn *see* Weisshorn
98 K7 **Fluessen** ◎ N Netherlands
105 S5 **Flúmen** ≈ NE Spain
107 C20 **Flumendosa** ≈ Sardegna, Italy, C Mediterranean Sea
31 R9 **Flushing** Michigan, N USA
Flushing *see* Vlissingen
25 O6 **Fluvanna** Texas, SW USA
186 B8 **Fly** ≈ Indonesia/Papua New Guinea
194 I10 **Flying Fish, Cape** *cape* Thurston Island, Antarctica
Flylân *see* Vlieland
193 Y15 **Foa** *island* Ha'apai Group, C Tonga
9 U15 **Foam Lake** Saskatchewan, S Canada
113 J14 **Foča** SE Bosnia and Herzegovina
116 L12 **Focşani** Vrancea, E Romania
Fogaras/Fogarasch *see* Făgăraş
107 M16 **Foggia** Puglia, SE Italy
Foggo *see* Faggo
76 D10 **Fogo** *island* Ilhas de Sotavento, SW Cape Verde
13 U11 **Fogo Island** *island* Newfoundland and Labrador, E Canada
109 U7 **Fohnsdorf** Steiermark, SE Austria
100 G7 **Föhr** *island* NW Germany
104 F14 **Fóia** ▲ S Portugal
14 I10 **Foins, Lac aux** ◎ Québec, SE Canada
103 N17 **Foix** Ariège, S France
126 I5 **Fokino** Bryanskaya Oblast', W Russian Federation
123 S15 **Fokino** Primorskiy Kray, W Russian Federation
Fola, Cnoc *see* Bloody Foreland
94 E13 **Folarskardnuten** ▲ S Norway
92 G11 **Folda** *fjord* C Norway
93 F14 **Foldereid** Nord-Trøndelag, C Norway
Földvár *see* Feldioara
115 J22 **Folégandros** *island* Kykládes, Greece, Aegean Sea
23 O9 **Foley** Alabama, S USA
29 U7 **Foley** Minnesota, N USA
14 E7 **Foleyet** Ontario, S Canada
95 D14 **Folgefonni** *glacier* S Norway
106 I13 **Foligno** Umbria, C Italy
97 Q23 **Folkestone** SE England, UK
23 W8 **Folkston** Georgia, SE USA
94 H10 **Folldal** Hedmark, S Norway
25 P1 **Follett** Texas, SW USA
106 F13 **Follonica** Toscana, C Italy
21 T15 **Folly Beach** South Carolina, SE USA
35 O7 **Folsom** California, W USA
116 M12 **Folteşti** Galaţi, E Romania
172 H14 **Fomboni** Mohéli, S Comoros
18 K10 **Fonda** New York, NE USA
9 S10 **Fond-du-Lac** Saskatchewan, C Canada
30 M8 **Fond du Lac** Wisconsin, N USA
9 T10 **Fond-du-Lac** ≈ Saskatchewan, C Canada
190 C9 **Fongafale** *var.* Funafuti. ● (Tuvalu) Funafuti Atoll, SE Tuvalu
190 G8 **Fongafale** *atoll* C Tuvalu
107 C18 **Fonni** Sardegna, Italy, C Mediterranean Sea
189 V12 **Fono** *island* Chuuk, C Micronesia
54 G4 **Fonseca** La Guajira, N Colombia
Fonseca, Golfo de *see* Fonseca, Gulf of
42 H8 **Fonseca, Gulf of** *Sp.* Golfo de Fonseca. *gulf* C Central America
103 O6 **Fontainebleau** Seine-et-Marne, N France
63 G19 **Fontana, Lago** ◎ W Argentina
21 N10 **Fontana Lake** ⊠ North Carolina, SE USA
107 L24 **Fontanarossa** ✈ (Catania) Sicilia, Italy, C Mediterranean Sea
9 N11 **Fontas** ≈ British Columbia, W Canada
58 D12 **Fonte Boa** Amazonas, N Brazil
102 J10 **Fontenay-le-Comte** Vendée, NW France
33 T16 **Fontenelle Reservoir** ⊠ Wyoming, C USA
193 Y14 **Fonualei** *island* Vava'u Group, N Tonga
111 H24 **Fonyód** Somogy, W Hungary
Foochow *see* Fuzhou
39 Q10 **Foraker, Mount** ▲ Alaska, USA
187 R14 **Forari** Éfaté, C Vanuatu
103 U4 **Forbach** Moselle, NE France
183 Q8 **Forbes** New South Wales, SE Australia
77 T17 **Forcados** Delta, S Nigeria
103 S14 **Forcalquier** Alpes-de-Haute-Provence, SE France
101 K19 **Forchheim** Bayern, SE Germany
35 R13 **Ford City** California, W USA
94 D11 **Førde** Sogn Og Fjordane, S Norway
31 N4 **Ford River** ≈ Michigan, N USA
183 O4 **Fords Bridge** New South Wales, SE Australia
20 J6 **Fordsville** Kentucky, S USA
27 U13 **Fordyce** Arkansas, C USA
76 I14 **Forécariah** SW Guinea
197 O14 **Forel, Mont** ▲ SE Greenland
9 R17 **Foremost** Alberta, SW Canada
14 D16 **Forest** Ontario, S Canada
22 L5 **Forest** Mississippi, S USA
31 S12 **Forest** Ohio, N USA
29 V11 **Forest City** Iowa, C USA
21 Q10 **Forest City** North Carolina, SE USA
32 G11 **Forest Grove** Oregon, NW USA
183 P17 **Forestier Peninsula** *peninsula* Tasmania, SE Australia
29 V8 **Forest Lake** Minnesota, N USA
23 S3 **Forest Park** Georgia, SE USA
29 Q3 **Forest River** ≈ North Dakota, N USA
15 T6 **Forestville** Québec, SE Canada
103 Q11 **Forez, Monts du** ▲▲ C France
96 J10 **Forfar** E Scotland, UK
26 J8 **Forgan** Oklahoma, C USA
Forge du Sud *see* Dudelange
101 J24 **Forggensee** ◎ S Germany
147 N10 **Forish** *Rus.* Farish. Jizzax Viloyati, C Uzbekistan
20 F9 **Forked Deer River** ≈ Tennessee, S USA
32 F7 **Forks** Washington, NW USA
92 N2 **Forlandsundet** *sound* W Svalbard
106 H10 **Forlì** *anc.* Forum Livii. Emilia-Romagna, N Italy
29 Q7 **Forman** North Dakota, N USA
97 K17 **Formby** NW England, UK
105 V11 **Formentera** *anc.* Ophiusa, *Lat.* Frumentum. *island* Islas Baleares, Spain, W Mediterranean Sea
Formentor, Cabo de *see* Formentor, Cap de
105 Y9 **Formentor, Cap de** *var.* Cabo de Formentor, Cape Formentor. *cape* Mallorca, Spain, W Mediterranean Sea
Formentor, Cape *see* Formentor, Cap de
107 J16 **Formia** Lazio, C Italy
62 O7 **Formosa** Formosa, NE Argentina
62 M6 **Formosa** *off.* Provincia de Formosa. ◐ *province* NE Argentina
Formosa *see* Taiwan
Formosa/Formo'sa *see* Taiwan
Formosa, Provincia de *see* Formosa
59 I17 **Formosa, Serra** ▲▲ C Brazil
Formosa Strait *see* Taiwan Strait
95 H21 **Fornæs** *headland* C Denmark
95 H15 **Fornebu** ✈ (Oslo) Akershus, S Norway
25 U6 **Forney** Texas, SW USA
106 E9 **Fornovo di Taro** Emilia-Romagna, C Italy
117 T14 **Foros** Respublika Krym, S Ukraine
Føroyar *see* Faeroe Islands
96 J8 **Forres** NE Scotland, UK
27 X11 **Forrest City** Arkansas, C USA
39 Y15 **Forrester Island** *island* Alexander Archipelago, Alaska, USA
25 N7 **Forsan** Texas, SW USA
181 V5 **Forsayth** Queensland, NE Australia
95 L19 **Forserum** Jönköping, S Sweden
95 K15 **Forshaga** Värmland, C Sweden
93 L19 **Forssa** Etelä-Suomi, S Finland
101 Q14 **Forst** *Lus.* Baršć Łužyca. Brandenburg, E Germany
183 U7 **Forster-Tuncurry** New South Wales, SE Australia
23 T4 **Forsyth** Georgia, SE USA
27 T8 **Forsyth** Missouri, C USA
33 W10 **Forsyth** Montana, NW USA
149 U11 **Fort Abbās** Punjab, E Pakistan
12 G10 **Fort Albany** Ontario, C Canada
56 L13 **Fortaleza** Pando, N Bolivia
58 P13 **Fortaleza** *prev.* Ceará. *state capital* Ceará, NE Brazil
59 D16 **Fortaleza** Rondônia, W Brazil
56 C13 **Fortaleza, Río** ≈ W Peru
Fort-Archambault *see* Sarh
21 U3 **Fort Ashby** West Virginia, NE USA
96 I9 **Fort Augustus** N Scotland, UK
Fort-Bayard *see* Zhanjiang
33 S8 **Fort Benton** Montana, NW USA
35 Q1 **Fort Bidwell** California, W USA
34 L5 **Fort Bragg** California, W USA
31 N16 **Fort Branch** Indiana, N USA
Fort-Bretonnet *see* Bousso
33 T17 **Fort Bridger** Wyoming, C USA
Fort-Cappolani *see* Tidjikja
Fort-Carnot *see* Ikongo
Fort Charlet *see* Djanet
Fort-Chimo *see* Kuujjuaq
9 R10 **Fort Chipewyan** Alberta, C Canada
Fort Cobb Lake *see* Fort Cobb Reservoir
26 L11 **Fort Cobb Reservoir** *var.* Fort Cobb Lake. ⊠ Oklahoma, C USA
37 T3 **Fort Collins** Colorado, C USA
14 K12 **Fort-Coulonge** Québec, SE Canada
Fort-Crampel *see* Kaga Bandoro
Fort-Dauphin *see* Tôlañaro
24 K10 **Fort Davis** Texas, SW USA
37 O10 **Fort Defiance** Arizona, SW USA
45 Q12 **Fort-de-France** *prev.* Fort-Royal. ○ (Martinique) W Martinique
45 P12 **Fort-de-France, Baie de** *bay* W Martinique
Fort de Kock *see* Bukittinggi
23 P6 **Fort Deposit** Alabama, S USA
29 U13 **Fort Dodge** Iowa, C USA
13 S10 **Forteau** Québec, E Canada
106 E11 **Forte dei Marmi** Toscana, C Italy
14 H17 **Fort Erie** Ontario, S Canada
180 H7 **Fortescue River** ≈ Western Australia
19 S2 **Fort Fairfield** Maine, NE USA
Fort-Foureau *see* Kousséri
12 A11 **Fort Frances** Ontario, S Canada
Fort Franklin *see* Déljne
23 R7 **Fort Gaines** Georgia, SE USA
37 T8 **Fort Garland** Colorado, C USA
21 P5 **Fort Gay** West Virginia, NE USA
Fort George *see* La Grande Rivière
27 Q10 **Fort Gibson** Oklahoma, C USA
27 Q9 **Fort Gibson Lake** ⊠ Oklahoma, C USA
8 H7 **Fort Good Hope** *var.* Good Hope. Northwest Territories, NW Canada
23 V4 **Fort Gordon** Georgia, SE USA
Fort Gouraud *see* Fdérik
96 I11 **Forth** ≈ C Scotland, UK
Fort Hall *see* Murang'a
24 H8 **Fort Hancock** Texas, SW USA
Fort Hertz *see* Putao
96 K12 **Forth, Firth of** *estuary* E Scotland, UK
14 L14 **Forthton** Ontario, SE Canada
14 M8 **Fortier** ≈ Québec, SE Canada
Fortín General Eugenio Garay *see* General Eugenio A. Garay
Fort Jameson *see* Chipata
Fort Johnston *see* Mangochi
19 R1 **Fort Kent** Maine, NE USA
Fort-Lamy *see* Ndjamena
23 Z15 **Fort Lauderdale** Florida, SE USA
21 R11 **Fort Lawn** South Carolina, SE USA
8 H10 **Fort Liard** *var.* Liard. Northwest Territories, W Canada
44 M8 **Fort-Liberté** NE Haiti
21 N9 **Fort Loudoun Lake** ⊠ Tennessee, S USA
37 T3 **Fort Lupton** Colorado, C USA
9 R12 **Fort MacKay** Alberta, C Canada
9 Q17 **Fort Macleod** *var.* MacLeod. Alberta, SW Canada
29 Y16 **Fort Madison** Iowa, C USA
Fort Manning *see* Mchinji
25 P9 **Fort McKavett** Texas, SW USA
9 R12 **Fort McMurray** Alberta, C Canada
8 G7 **Fort McPherson** *var.* McPherson. Northwest Territories, NW Canada
21 R11 **Fort Mill** South Carolina, SE USA
Fort-Millot *see* Ngouri
37 U3 **Fort Morgan** Colorado, C USA
23 W14 **Fort Myers** Florida, SE USA
23 W15 **Fort Myers Beach** Florida, SE USA
10 M10 **Fort Nelson** British Columbia, W Canada
10 M10 **Fort Nelson** ≈ British Columbia, W Canada
Fort Norman *see* Tulita
23 Q2 **Fort Payne** Alabama, S USA
33 W7 **Fort Peck** Montana, NW USA
33 V8 **Fort Peck Lake** ⊠ Montana, NW USA
23 Y13 **Fort Pierce** Florida, SE USA
29 N10 **Fort Pierre** South Dakota, N USA
81 E18 **Fort Portal** SW Uganda
8 J10 **Fort Providence** *var.* Providence. Northwest Territories, W Canada
9 U16 **Fort Qu'Appelle** Saskatchewan, S Canada
Fort-Repoux *see* Akjoujt
8 K10 **Fort Resolution** *var.* Resolution. Northwest Territories, W Canada
33 T13 **Fortress Mountain** ▲ Wyoming, C USA
Fort Rosebery *see* Mansa
Fort Rousset *see* Owando
Fort-Royal *see* Fort-de-France
12 I10 **Fort Rupert** *prev.* Rupert House. Québec, SE Canada
8 H13 **Fort St. James** British Columbia, SW Canada
9 N12 **Fort St. John** British Columbia, W Canada
Fort Sandeman *see* Zhob
9 Q14 **Fort Saskatchewan** Alberta, SW Canada
27 R6 **Fort Scott** Kansas, C USA
12 E6 **Fort Severn** Ontario, C Canada
31 R12 **Fort Shawnee** Ohio, N USA
144 E14 **Fort-Shevchenko** Mangistau, W Kazakhstan
Fort-Sibut *see* Sibut
8 I10 **Fort Simpson** *var.* Simpson. Northwest Territories, W Canada
8 I10 **Fort Smith** Northwest Territories, W Canada
27 R10 **Fort Smith** Arkansas, C USA
37 T13 **Fort Stanton** New Mexico, SW USA
24 L9 **Fort Stockton** Texas, SW USA
37 U12 **Fort Sumner** New Mexico, SW USA
26 K8 **Fort Supply** Oklahoma, C USA
26 K8 **Fort Supply Lake** ⊠ Oklahoma, C USA
29 O10 **Fort Thompson** South Dakota, N USA
Fort-Trinquet *see* Bir Mogreïn
105 R12 **Fortuna** Murcia, SE Spain
34 K3 **Fortuna** California, W USA
28 J2 **Fortuna** North Dakota, N USA
23 T5 **Fort Valley** Georgia, SE USA
9 P11 **Fort Vermilion** Alberta, W Canada
Fort Victoria *see* Masvingo
31 P13 **Fortville** Indiana, N USA
23 P9 **Fort Walton Beach** Florida, SE USA
31 P12 **Fort Wayne** Indiana, N USA
96 H10 **Fort William** N Scotland, UK
25 T6 **Fort Worth** Texas, SW USA
28 M7 **Fort Yates** North Dakota, N USA
39 S7 **Fort Yukon** Alaska, USA
Forum Alieni *see* Ferrara
Forum Julii *see* Fréjus
Forum Livii *see* Forlì
143 Q15 **Forūr, Jazīreh-ye** *island* S Iran
94 H7 **Fosen** *physical region* S Norway
161 N14 **Foshan** *var.* Fatshan, Fo-shan, Namhoi. Guangdong, S China
Fo-shan *see* Foshan
Fossa Claudia *see* Chioggia
106 B9 **Fossano** Piemonte, NW Italy
99 H21 **Fosses-la-Ville** Namur, S Belgium
32 J12 **Fossil** Oregon, NW USA
Foss Lake *see* Foss Reservoir
106 I11 **Fossombrone** Marche, C Italy
26 K10 **Foss Reservoir** *var.* Foss Lake. ⊠ Oklahoma, C USA
29 S4 **Fosston** Minnesota, N USA
183 O13 **Foster** Victoria, SE Australia
9 T12 **Foster Lakes** ◎ Saskatchewan, C Canada
31 S12 **Fostoria** Ohio, N USA
79 D19 **Fougamou** Ngounié, C Gabon
102 J6 **Fougères** Ille-et-Vilaine, NW France
Fou-hsin *see* Fuxin
27 S14 **Fouke** Arkansas, C USA
96 K2 **Foula** *island* NE Scotland, UK
65 D24 **Foul Bay** *bay* East Falkland, Falkland Islands

97 *P21* **Foulness Island** *island* SE England, UK
185 *F15* **Foulwind, Cape** *headland* South Island, New Zealand
79 *E15* **Foumban** Ouest, NW Cameroon
172 *H13* **Foumbouni** Grande Comore, NW Comoros
195 *N8* **Foundation Ice Stream** *glacier* Antarctica
37 *T6* **Fountain** Colorado, C USA
36 *L4* **Fountain Green** Utah, W USA
21 *P11* **Fountain Inn** South Carolina, SE USA
27 *S11* **Fourche LaFave River** ≈ Arkansas, C USA
33 *Z13* **Four Corners** Wyoming, C USA
103 *Q2* **Fourmies** Nord, N France
38 *J17* **Four Mountains, Islands of** *island group* Aleutian Islands, Alaska, USA
173 *P17* **Fournaise, Piton de la** ▲ SE Réunion
14 *J8* **Fournière, Lac** ◎ Québec, SE Canada
115 *L20* **Foúrnoi** *island* Dodekánisa, Greece, Aegean Sea
64 *K13* **Four North Fracture Zone** *tectonic feature* W Atlantic Ocean
Fouron-Saint-Martin *see* Sint-Martens-Voeren
30 *L3* **Fourteen Mile Point** *headland* Michigan, N USA
Fou-shan *see* Fushun
76 *I13* **Fouta Djallon** *var.* Futa Jallon. ▲▲ W Guinea
185 *C25* **Foveaux Strait** *strait* S New Zealand
35 *Q11* **Fowler** California, W USA
37 *U6* **Fowler** Colorado, C USA
31 *N12* **Fowler** Indiana, N USA
182 *D7* **Fowlers Bay** *bay* South Australia
25 *R13* **Fowlerton** Texas, SW USA
142 *M3* **Fowman** *var.* Fuman, Fumen. Gīlān, NW Iran
65 *C25* **Fox Bay East** West Falkland, Falkland Islands
65 *C25* **Fox Bay West** West Falkland, Falkland Islands
14 *J14* **Foxboro** Ontario, SE Canada
9 *O14* **Fox Creek** Alberta, W Canada
64 *G5* **Foxe Basin** *sea* Nunavut, N Canada
64 *G5* **Foxe Channel** *channel* Nunavut, N Canada
95 *I16* **Foxen** ◎ C Sweden
9 *Q7* **Foxe Peninsula** *peninsula* Baffin Island, Nunavut, NE Canada
185 *E19* **Fox Glacier** West Coast, South Island, New Zealand
38 *L17* **Fox Islands** *island* Aleutian Islands, Alaska, USA
30 *M10* **Fox Lake** Illinois, N USA
9 *V12* **Fox Mine** Manitoba, C Canada
35 *R3* **Fox Mountain** ▲ Nevada, W USA
65 *E25* **Fox Point** *headland* East Falkland, Falkland Islands
30 *M11* **Fox River** ≈ Illinois/ Wisconsin, N USA
30 *L7* **Fox River** ≈ Wisconsin, N USA
184 *L13* **Foxton** Manawatu-Wanganui, North Island, New Zealand
9 *S16* **Fox Valley** Saskatchewan, S Canada
9 *W16* **Foxwarren** Manitoba, S Canada
97 *E14* **Foyle, Lough** *Ir.* Loch Feabhail. *inlet* N Ireland
194 *H5* **Foyn Coast** *physical region* Antarctica
104 *I2* **Foz** Galicia, NW Spain
60 *I12* **Foz do Areia, Represa de** ⊠ S Brazil
59 *A16* **Foz do Breu** Acre, W Brazil
83 *A16* **Foz do Cunene** Namibe, SW Angola
60 *G12* **Foz do Iguaçu** Paraná, S Brazil
58 *C12* **Foz do Mamoriá** Amazonas, NW Brazil
105 *T6* **Fraga** Aragón, NE Spain
44 *F5* **Fragoso, Cayo** *island* C Cuba
61 *G18* **Fraile Muerto** Cerro Largo, NE Uruguay
99 *H21* **Fraire** Namur, S Belgium
99 *L21* **Fraiture, Baraque de** *hill* SE Belgium
Frakštát *see* Hlohovec
197 *S10* **Fram Basin** *var.* Amundsen Basin. *undersea feature* Arctic Ocean
99 *F20* **Frameries** Hainaut, S Belgium
19 *O11* **Framingham** Massachusetts, NE USA
60 *L7* **Franca** São Paulo, S Brazil
187 *O15* **Français, Récif des** *reef* W New Caledonia
107 *K14* **Francavilla al Mare** Abruzzi, C Italy
107 *P18* **Francavilla Fontana** Puglia, SE Italy
102 *M8* **France** *off.* French Republic, *It./Sp.* Francia; *prev.* Gaul, Gaule, *Lat.* Gallia. ◆ *republic* W Europe
45 *O8* **Francés Viejo, Cabo** *headland* NE Dominican Republic
79 *F19* **Franceville** *var.* Massoukou, Masuku. Haut-Ogooué, E Gabon
79 *F19* **Franceville** ✈ Haut-Ogooué, E Gabon
Francfort *see* Frankfurt am Main
103 *T8* **Franche-Comté** ◈ *region* E France
Francia *see* France
29 *O11* **Francis Case, Lake** ⊠ South Dakota, N USA
60 *H12* **Francisco Beltrão** Paraná, S Brazil
Francisco l. Madero *see* Villa Madero
61 *A21* **Francisco Madero** Buenos Aires, E Argentina
42 *H6* **Francisco Morazán** *prev.* Tegucigalpa. ◈ *department* C Honduras
83 *J18* **Francistown** North East, NE Botswana
Franconian Forest *see* Frankenwald
Franconian Jura *see* Fränkische Alb
98 *K6* **Franeker** *Fris.* Frjentsjer. Friesland, N Netherlands
Frankenalb *see* Fränkische Alb
101 *H16* **Frankenberg** Hessen, C Germany
101 *J20* **Frankenhöhe** *hill range* C Germany
31 *R8* **Frankenmuth** Michigan, N USA
101 *F20* **Frankenstein** *hill* W Germany
Frankenstein/Frankenstein in Schlesien *see* Ząbkowice Śląskie
101 *G20* **Frankenthal** Rheinland-Pfalz, W Germany
101 *L18* **Frankenwald** *Eng.* Franconian Forest. ▲▲ C Germany
44 *J12* **Frankfield** C Jamaica
14 *J14* **Frankford** Ontario, SE Canada
31 *O13* **Frankfort** Indiana, N USA
27 *O3* **Frankfort** Kansas, C USA
20 *L5* **Frankfort** *state capital* Kentucky, S USA
Frankfort on the Main *see* Frankfurt am Main
Frankfurt *see* Frankfurt am Main, Germany
Frankfurt *see* Słubice, Poland
101 *G18* **Frankfurt am Main** *var.* Frankfurt, *Fr.* Francfort; *prev. Eng.* Frankfort on the Main. Hessen, SW Germany
100 *Q12* **Frankfurt an der Oder** Brandenburg, E Germany
101 *L21* **Fränkische Alb** *var.* Frankenalb, *Eng.* Franconian Jura. ▲▲ S Germany
101 *I18* **Fränkische Saale** ≈ C Germany
101 *L19* **Fränkische Schweiz** *hill range* C Germany
23 *R4* **Franklin** Georgia, SE USA
31 *P14* **Franklin** Indiana, N USA
20 *J7* **Franklin** Kentucky, S USA
22 *I9* **Franklin** Louisiana, S USA
29 *O17* **Franklin** Nebraska, C USA
21 *N10* **Franklin** North Carolina, SE USA
18 *C13* **Franklin** Pennsylvania, NE USA
20 *J9* **Franklin** Tennessee, S USA
25 *U9* **Franklin** Texas, SW USA
21 *X7* **Franklin** Virginia, NE USA
21 *T4* **Franklin** West Virginia, NE USA
30 *M9* **Franklin** Wisconsin, N USA
8 *I6* **Franklin Bay** *inlet* Northwest Territories, N Canada
32 *K7* **Franklin D. Roosevelt Lake** ⊠ Washington, NW USA
35 *W4* **Franklin Lake** ◎ Nevada, W USA
185 *B22* **Franklin Mountains** ▲▲ South Island, New Zealand
39 *R5* **Franklin Mountains** ▲▲ Alaska, USA
39 *N4* **Franklin, Point** *headland* Alaska, USA
183 *O17* **Franklin River** ≈ Tasmania, SE Australia
22 *K8* **Franklinton** Louisiana, S USA
21 *U9* **Franklinton** North Carolina, SE USA
Frankstadt *see* Frenštát pod Radhoštěm
25 *V7* **Frankston** Texas, SW USA
33 *U12* **Frannie** Wyoming, C USA
15 *U5* **Franquelin** Québec, SE Canada
15 *U5* **Franquelin** ≈ Québec, SE Canada
83 *C18* **Fransfontein** Kunene, NW Namibia
93 *H17* **Fränsta** Västernorrland, C Sweden
122 *J3* **Frantsa-Iosifa, Zemlya** *Eng.* Franz Josef Land. *island group* N Russian Federation
185 *E18* **Franz Josef Glacier** West Coast, South Island, New Zealand
Franz Josef Land *see* Frantsa-Iosifa, Zemlya
Franz-Josef Spitze *see* Gerlachovský štít
101 *L23* **Franz Josef Strauss** *abbrev.* F.J.S.. ✈ (München) Bayern, SE Germany
107 *A19* **Frasca, Capo della** *headland* Sardegna, Italy, C Mediterranean Sea
107 *I15* **Frascati** Lazio, C Italy
9 *N14* **Fraser** ≈ British Columbia, SW Canada
83 *G24* **Fraserburg** Western Cape, SW South Africa
96 *L8* **Fraserburgh** NE Scotland, UK
181 *Z9* **Fraser Island** *var.* Great Sandy Island. *island* Queensland, E Australia
10 *L14* **Fraser Lake** British Columbia, SW Canada
10 *L15* **Fraser Plateau** *plateau* British Columbia, SW Canada
184 *P10* **Frasertown** Hawke's Bay, North Island, New Zealand
99 *E19* **Frasnes-lez-Buissenal** Hainaut, SW Belgium
108 *I7* **Frastanz** Vorarlberg, NW Austria
14 *B8* **Frater** Ontario, S Canada
Frauenbach *see* Baia Mare
Frauenburg *see* Saldus, Latvia
Frauenburg *see* Frombork, Poland
108 *H6* **Frauenfeld** Thurgau, NE Switzerland
109 *Z5* **Frauenkirchen** Burgenland, E Austria
61 *D19* **Fray Bentos** Río Negro, W Uruguay
61 *F19* **Fray Marcos** Florida, S Uruguay
29 *S6* **Frazee** Minnesota, N USA
104 *M5* **Frechilla** Castilla-León, N Spain
30 *I4* **Frederic** Wisconsin, N USA
95 *G23* **Fredericia** Vejle, C Denmark
21 *W3* **Frederick** Maryland, NE USA
26 *L12* **Frederick** Oklahoma, C USA
29 *P7* **Frederick** South Dakota, N USA
29 *X12* **Fredericksburg** Iowa, C USA
25 *R10* **Fredericksburg** Texas, SW USA
21 *W5* **Fredericksburg** Virginia, NE USA
39 *X13* **Frederick Sound** *sound* Alaska, USA
27 *X6* **Fredericktown** Missouri, C USA
60 *H13* **Frederico Westphalen** Rio Grande do Sul, S Brazil
13 *O15* **Fredericton** *province capital* New Brunswick, SE Canada
95 *I22* **Frederiksborg** *off* Frederiksborgs Amt. ◈ *county* E Denmark
Frederiksborgs Amt *see* Frederiksborg
Frederikshåb *see* Paamiut
95 *H19* **Frederikshavn** *prev.* Fladstrand. Nordjylland, N Denmark
95 *J22* **Frederikssund** Frederiksborg, E Denmark
45 *T9* **Frederiksted** Saint Croix, S Virgin Islands (US)
95 *I22* **Frederiksværk** *var.* Frederiksværk og Hanehoved. Frederiksborg, E Denmark
Frederiksværk og Hanehoved *see* Frederiksværk
54 *E9* **Fredonia** Antioquia, W Colombia
36 *K8* **Fredonia** Arizona, SW USA
27 *P7* **Fredonia** Kansas, C USA
18 *C11* **Fredonia** New York, NE USA
35 *P4* **Fredonyer Pass** *pass* California, W USA
93 *I15* **Fredrika** Västerbotten, N Sweden
95 *L14* **Fredriksberg** Dalarna, C Sweden
Fredrikshald *see* Halden
Fredrikshamn *see* Hamina
95 *H16* **Fredrikstad** Østfold, S Norway
30 *K16* **Freeburg** Illinois, N USA
18 *K15* **Freehold** New Jersey, NE USA
18 *H14* **Freeland** Pennsylvania, NE USA
182 *J5* **Freeling Heights** ▲ South Australia
35 *Q7* **Freel Peak** ▲ California, W USA
9 *Z9* **Freels, Cape** *headland* Newfoundland, Newfoundland and Labrador, E Canada
29 *Q11* **Freeman** South Dakota, N USA
44 *G1* **Freeport** Grand Bahama Island, N Bahamas
30 *L10* **Freeport** Illinois, N USA
25 *W12* **Freeport** Texas, SW USA
44 *G1* **Freeport** ✈ Grand Bahama Island, N Bahamas
25 *R14* **Freer** Texas, SW USA
83 *I22* **Free State** *off.* Free State Province; *prev.* Orange Free State, *Afr.* Oranje Vrystaat. ◈ *province* C South Africa
Free State *see* Maryland
Free State Province *see* Free State
76 *G15* **Freetown** ● (Sierra Leone) W Sierra Leone
172 *J16* **Frégate** *island* Inner Islands, NE Seychelles
104 *J12* **Fregenal de la Sierra** Extremadura, W Spain
182 *C2* **Fregon** South Australia
102 *H5* **Fréhel, Cap** *headland* NW France
94 *F8* **Frei** Møre og Romsdal, S Norway
101 *O16* **Freiberg** Sachsen, E Germany
101 *O16* **Freiberger Mulde** ≈ E Germany
Freiburg *see* Freiburg im Breisgau, Germany
Freiburg *see* Fribourg, Switzerland
101 *F23* **Freiburg im Breisgau** *var.* Freiburg, *Fr.* Fribourg-en-Brisgau. Baden-Württemberg, SW Germany
Freiburg in Schlesien *see* Świebodzice
Freie Hansestadt Bremen *see* Bremen
Freie und Hansestadt Hamburg *see* Brandenburg
101 *L22* **Freising** Bayern, SE Germany
109 *T3* **Freistadt** Oberösterreich, N Austria
Freistadtl *see* Hlohovec
101 *O16* **Freital** Sachsen, E Germany
Freiwaldau *see* Jeseník
104 *J6* **Freixo de Espada à Cinta** Bragança, N Portugal
103 *U15* **Fréjus** *anc.* Forum Julii. Var, SE France
180 *I13* **Fremantle** Western Australia
35 *N9* **Fremont** California, W USA
31 *Q11* **Fremont** Indiana, N USA
29 *W15* **Fremont** Iowa, C USA
31 *P8* **Fremont** Michigan, N USA
29 *R15* **Fremont** Nebraska, C USA
31 *S11* **Fremont** Ohio, N USA
33 *T14* **Fremont Peak** ▲ Wyoming, C USA
36 *M6* **Fremont River** ≈ Utah, W USA
21 *O9* **French Broad River** ≈ Tennessee, S USA
21 *N5* **Frenchburg** Kentucky, S USA
18 *C12* **French Creek** ≈ Pennsylvania, NE USA
32 *K15* **Frenchglen** Oregon, NW USA
55 *Y10* **French Guiana** *var.* Guiana, Guyane. ◇ *French overseas department* N South America
French Guinea *see* Guinea
31 *O15* **French Lick** Indiana, N USA
185 *J14* **French Pass** Marlborough, South Island, New Zealand
191 *T11* **French Polynesia** ◇ *French overseas territory* C Polynesia
French Republic *see* France
14 *F11* **French River** ≈ Ontario, S Canada
French Somaliland *see* Djibouti
173 *P12* **French Southern and Antarctic Territories** *Fr.* Terres Australes et Antarctiques Françaises. ◇ *French overseas territory* S Indian Ocean
French Sudan *see* Mali
French Territory of the Afars and Issas *see* Djibouti
French Togoland *see* Togo
74 *J6* **Frenda** NW Algeria
111 *I18* **Frenštát pod Radhoštěm** *Ger.* Frankstadt. Moravskoslezský Kraj, E Czech Republic
76 *M17* **Fresco** S Ivory Coast
195 *U16* **Freshfield, Cape** *headland* Antarctica
40 *L10* **Fresnillo** Zacatecas, C Mexico
Fresnillo de González Echeverría *see* Fresnillo
35 *Q10* **Fresno** California, W USA
Freu, Cabo del *see* Freu, Cap des
105 *Y9* **Freu, Cap des** *var.* Cabo del Freu. *cape* Mallorca, Spain, W Mediterranean Sea
101 *G22* **Freudenstadt** Baden-Württemberg, SW Germany
Freudenthal *see* Bruntál
183 *Q17* **Freycinet Peninsula** *peninsula* Tasmania, SE Australia
76 *H14* **Fria** Guinée-Maritime, W Guinea
83 *A17* **Fria, Cape** *headland* NW Namibia
35 *Q10* **Friant** California, W USA
62 *K8* **Frías** Catamarca, N Argentina
108 *D9* **Fribourg** *Ger.* Freiburg. Fribourg, W Switzerland
108 *C9* **Fribourg** *Ger.* Freiburg. ◈ *canton* W Switzerland
Fribourg-en-Brisgau *see* Freiburg im Breisgau
32 *G7* **Friday Harbor** San Juan Islands, Washington, NW USA
Friedau *see* Ormož
101 *K23* **Friedberg** Bayern, S Germany
101 *H18* **Friedberg** Hessen, W Germany
Friedeberg Neumark *see* Strzelce Krajeńskie
Friedek-Mistek *see* Frýdek-Místek
Friedland *see* Pravdinsk
101 *I24* **Friedrichshafen** Baden-Württemberg, S Germany
Friedrichstadt *see* Jaunjelgava
29 *Q16* **Friend** Nebraska, C USA
Friendly Islands *see* Tonga
55 *V9* **Friendship** Coronie, N Suriname
30 *L7* **Friendship** Wisconsin, N USA
109 *T8* **Friesach** Kärnten, S Austria
Friesche Eilanden *see* Frisian Islands
101 *F22* **Friesenheim** Baden-Württemberg, SW Germany
Friesische Inseln *see* Frisian Islands
98 *K6* **Friesland** ◈ *province* N Netherlands
60 *Q10* **Frio, Cabo** *headland* SE Brazil
24 *M3* **Friona** Texas, SW USA
42 *L12* **Frío, Río** ≈ N Costa Rica
25 *R13* **Frio River** ≈ Texas, SW USA
99 *M25* **Frisange** Luxembourg, S Luxembourg
Frisches Haff *see* Vistula Lagoon
36 *J6* **Frisco Peak** ▲ Utah, W USA
84 *F9* **Frisian Islands** *Dut.* Friesche Eilanden, *Ger.* Friesische Inseln. *island group* N Europe
18 *L12* **Frissell, Mount** ▲ Connecticut, NE USA
95 *J19* **Fristad** Västra Götaland, S Sweden
25 *N2* **Fritch** Texas, SW USA
95 *J19* **Fritsla** Västra Götaland, S Sweden
101 *H16* **Fritzlar** Hessen, C Germany
106 *H6* **Friuli-Venezia Giulia** ◈ *region* NE Italy
Frjentsjer *see* Franeker
196 *L13* **Frobisher Bay** *inlet* Baffin Island, Nunavut, NE Canada
Frobisher Bay *see* Iqaluit
9 *S12* **Frobisher Lake** ◎ Saskatchewan, C Canada
94 *G7* **Frohavet** *sound* C Norway
Frohenbruck *see* Veselí nad Lužnicí
109 *V7* **Frohnleiten** Steiermark, SE Austria
99 *G22* **Froidchapelle** Hainaut, S Belgium
127 *O9* **Frolovo** Volgogradskaya Oblast', SW Russian Federation
110 *K7* **Frombork** *Ger.* Frauenburg. Warmińsko-Mazurkskie, NE Poland
97 *L22* **Frome** SW England, UK
182 *I4* **Frome Creek** *seasonal river* South Australia
182 *J6* **Frome Downs** South Australia
182 *J5* **Frome, Lake** *salt lake* South Australia
Fronicken *see* Wronki
104 *H10* **Fronteira** Portalegre, C Portugal
40 *M7* **Frontera** Coahuila de Zaragoza, NE Mexico
41 *U14* **Frontera** Tabasco, SE Mexico
40 *G3* **Fronteras** Sonora, NW Mexico
103 *Q16* **Frontignan** Hérault, S France
54 *D8* **Frontino** Antioquia, NW Colombia
21 *V4* **Front Royal** Virginia, NE USA
107 *J16* **Frosinone** *anc.* Frusino. Lazio, C Italy
107 *K16* **Frosolone** Molise, C Italy
25 *U7* **Frost** Texas, SW USA
21 *U2* **Frostburg** Maryland, NE USA
23 *X13* **Frostproof** Florida, SE USA
Frostviken *see* Kvarnbergsvattnet
95 *M15* **Frövi** Örebro, C Sweden
94 *F7* **Frøya** *island* W Norway
37 *P5* **Fruita** Colorado, C USA
28 *J9* **Fruitdale** South Dakota, N USA
23 *W11* **Fruitland Park** Florida, SE USA
Frumentum *see* Formentera
147 *S11* **Frunze** Batkenskaya Oblast', SW Kyrgyzstan
Frunze *see* Bishkek
117 *O9* **Frunzivka** Odes'ka Oblast', SW Ukraine
Frusino *see* Frosinone
108 *E9* **Frutigen** Bern, W Switzerland
111 *I17* **Frýdek-Místek** *Ger.* Friedek-Mistek. Moravskoslezský Kraj, E Czech Republic
193 *V16* **Fua'amotu** Tongatapu, S Tonga
190 *A9* **Fuafatu** *island* Funafuti Atoll, C Tuvalu
190 *A9* **Fuagea** *island* Funafuti Atoll, C Tuvalu
190 *B8* **Fualifeke** *atoll* C Tuvalu
190 *A8* **Fualopa** *island* Funafuti Atoll, C Tuvalu
151 *K22* **Fuammulah** *var.* Gnaviyani Atoll. *atoll* S Maldives
161 *R11* **Fu'an** Fujian, SE China
Fu-chien *see* Fujian
Fu-chou *see* Fuzhou
164 *G13* **Fuchū** *var.* Hutyû. Hiroshima, Honshū, SW Japan
160 *M13* **Fuchuan** Guangxi Zhuangzu Zizhiqu, S China
165 *R8* **Fudai** Iwate, Honshū, C Japan
161 *S11* **Fuding** *var* Tongshan. Fujian, SE China
81 *J20* **Fudua** *spring/well* S Kenya
104 *M16* **Fuengirola** Andalucía, S Spain
104 *J12* **Fuente de Cantos** Extremadura, W Spain
104 *J11* **Fuente del Maestre** Extremadura, W Spain
104 *L12* **Fuente Obejuna** Andalucía, S Spain
104 *L6* **Fuentesaúco** Castilla-León, N Spain
62 *O3* **Fuerte Olimpo** *var.* Olimpo. Alto Paraguay, NE Paraguay
40 *H8* **Fuerte, Río** ≈ C Mexico
64 *Q11* **Fuerteventura** *island* Islas Canarias, Spain, NE Atlantic Ocean
141 *S14* **Fughmah** *var.* Faghman, Fugma. C Yemen
92 *M2* **Fuglehuken** *headland* W Svalbard
Fuglø *see* Fugloy
95 *B18* **Fugloy** *Dan.* Fuglø. *island* NE Faeroe Islands
197 *T15* **Fugløya Bank** *undersea feature* E Norwegian Sea
Fugma *see* Fughmah
81 *K16* **Fugugo** *spring/well* NE Kenya
158 *L2* **Fuhai** *var.* Burultokay. Xinjiang Uygur Zizhiqu, NW China
161 *P10* **Fu He** ≈ S China
Fuhkien *see* Fujian
100 *J9* **Fuhlsbüttel** ✈ (Hamburg) Hamburg, N Germany
101 *L14* **Fuhne** ≈ C Germany
Fu-hsin *see* Fuxin
Fujairah *see* Al Fujayrah
164 *M14* **Fuji** *var.* Huzi. Shizuoka, Honshū, S Japan
161 *Q12* **Fujian** *var.* Fu-chien, Fuhkien, Fukien, Min, Fujian Sheng. ◈ *province* SE China
160 *I9* **Fu Jiang** ≈ C China
Fujian Sheng *see* Fujian
164 *M14* **Fujieda** *var.* Huzieda. Shizuoka, Honshū, S Japan
Fuji, Mount/Fujiyama *see* Fuji-san
163 *Y7* **Fujin** Heilongjiang, NE China
164 *M13* **Fujinomiya** *var.* Huzinomiya. Shizuoka, Honshū, S Japan
164 *N13* **Fuji-san** *var.* Fujiyama, *Eng.* Mount Fuji. ▲ Honshū, SE Japan
165 *N14* **Fujisawa** *var.* Huzisawa. Kanagawa, Honshū, S Japan
165 *T3* **Fukagawa** *var.* Hukagawa. Hokkaidō, NE Japan
158 *L5* **Fukang** Xinjiang Uygur Zizhiqu, W China
165 *P7* **Fukaura** Aomori, Honshū, C Japan
193 *W15* **Fukave** *island* Tongatapu Group, S Tonga
Fukien *see* Fujian
164 *J13* **Fukuchiyama** *var.* Hukutiyama. Kyōto, Honshū, SW Japan
164 *A14* **Fukue** *var.* Hukue. Nagasaki, Fukue-jima, SW Japan
164 *A13* **Fukue-jima** *island* Gotō-rettō, SW Japan
164 *K12* **Fukui** *var.* Hukui. Fukui, Honshū, SW Japan
164 *K12* **Fukui** *off.* Fukui-ken, *var.* Hukui. ◈ *prefecture* Honshū, SW Japan
Fukui-ken *see* Fukui
164 *D13* **Fukuoka** *var.* Hukuoka, *hist.* Najima. Fukuoka, Kyūshū, SW Japan
164 *D13* **Fukuoka** *off.* Fukuoka-ken, *var.* Hukuoka. ◈ *prefecture* Kyūshū, SW Japan
Fukuoka-ken *see* Fukuoka
165 *Q6* **Fukushima** Hokkaidō, NE Japan
165 *Q12* **Fukushima** *off.* Fukushima-ken, *var.* Hukusima. ◈ *prefecture* Honshū, C Japan
Fukushima-ken *see* Fukushima
164 *G13* **Fukuyama** *var.* Hukuyama. Hiroshima, Honshū, SW Japan
76 *G13* **Fulacunda** C Guinea-Bissau
129 *P8* **Fūlādī, Kūh-e** ▲ E Afghanistan
187 *Z15* **Fulaga** *island* Lau Group, E Fiji
101 *I17* **Fulda** Hessen, C Germany
29 *S10* **Fulda** Minnesota, N USA
101 *I16* **Fulda** ≈ C Germany
Fülek *see* Fil'akovo
Fulin *see* Hanyuan
160 *K10* **Fuling** Sichuan, C China
35 *T15* **Fullerton** California, SE USA
29 *P15* **Fullerton** Nebraska, C USA
108 *M8* **Fulpmes** Tirol, W Austria
20 *G8* **Fulton** Kentucky, S USA
23 *N2* **Fulton** Mississippi, S USA
27 *V4* **Fulton** Missouri, C USA
18 *H9* **Fulton** New York, NE USA
Fuman/Fumen *see* Fowman
103 *R3* **Fumay** Ardennes, N France
102 *M13* **Fumel** Lot-et-Garonne, SW France
190 *B10* **Funafara** *atoll* C Tuvalu
190 *C9* **Funafuti** ✈ Funafuti Atoll, C Tuvalu
Funafuti *see* Fongafale
190 *F8* **Funafuti Atoll** *atoll* C Tuvalu
Funan *see* Fusui
190 *B9* **Funangongo** *atoll* C Tuvalu
93 *F17* **Funäsdalen** Jämtland, C Sweden
64 *O6* **Funchal** Madeira, Portugal, NE Atlantic Ocean
64 *P5* **Funchal** ✈ Madeira, Portugal, NE Atlantic Ocean
54 *F5* **Fundación** Magdalena, N Colombia
104 *I8* **Fundão** *var.* Fundáo. Castelo Branco, C Portugal
Fundáo *see* Fundão
13 *O16* **Fundy, Bay of** *bay* Canada/USA
Fünen *see* Fyn
54 *C13* **Fúnes** Nariño, SW Colombia
Fünfkirchen *see* Pécs
83 *M19* **Funhalouro** Inhambane, S Mozambique
161 *R6* **Funing** Jiangsu, E China
160 *I14* **Funing** *var.* Xinhua. Yunnan, SW China
160 *M7* **Funiu Shan** ▲▲ C China
77 *U13* **Funtua** Katsina, N Nigeria
161 *R12* **Fuqing** Fujian, SE China
83 *M14* **Furancungo** Tete, NW Mozambique
116 *I15* **Furculești** Teleorman, S Romania
Füred *see* Balatonfüred
165 *W4* **Fūren-ko** ◎ Hokkaidō, NE Japan
143 *R12* **Fūrg** Fārs, S Iran
Furluk *see* Fârliug
Fūrmanov/Furmanovka *see* Moyynkum
Furmanovo *see* Zhalpaktal
59 *L20* **Furnas, Represa de** ⊠ SE Brazil
183 *Q14* **Furneaux Group** *island group* Tasmania, SE Australia
Furnes *see* Veurne
160 *J10* **Furong Jiang** ≈ S China
138 *I5* **Furqlus** Ḩimş, W Syria
100 *F12* **Fürstenau** Niedersachsen, NW Germany
109 *X8* **Fürstenfeld** Steiermark, SE Austria
101 *L23* **Fürstenfeldbruck** Bayern, S Germany
100 *P12* **Fürstenwalde** Brandenburg, NE Germany
101 *K20* **Fürth** Bayern, S Germany
109 *W3* **Furth bei Göttweig** Niederösterreich, NW Austria
165 *R3* **Furubira** Hokkaidō, NE Japan
94 *L12* **Furudal** Dalarna, C Sweden
164 *L12* **Furukawa** Gifu, Honshū, SW Japan
165 *Q10* **Furukawa** *var.* Hurukawa. Miyagi, Honshū, C Japan
54 *F10* **Fusagasugá** Cundinamarca, C Colombia
Fusan *see* Pusan
Fushë-Arëzi/Fushë-Arrësi *see* Fushë-Arrëz
113 *L18* **Fushë-Arrëz** *var.* Fushë-Arëzi, Fushë-Arrësi. Shkodër, N Albania
Fushë-Kruja *see* Fushë-Krujë
113 *K19* **Fushë-Krujë** *var.* Fushë-Kruja. Durrës, C Albania
163 *V12* **Fushun** *var.* Fou-shan, Fu-shun. Liaoning, NE China
Fu-shun *see* Fushun
Fusin *see* Fuxin
108 *G10* **Fusio** Ticino, S Switzerland
163 *X11* **Fusong** Jilin, NE China
101 *K24* **Füssen** Bayern, S Germany
160 *K15* **Fusui** *prev.* Funan. Guangxi Zhuangzu Zizhiqu, S China
Futa Jallon *see* Fouta Djallon
63 *G18* **Futaleufú** Los Lagos, S Chile
112 *K10* **Futog** Vojvodina, NW Serbia
165 *O14* **Futtsu** *var.* Huttu. Chiba, Honshū, S Japan
187 *S15* **Futuna** *island* S Vanuatu
190 *D12* **Futuna, Île** *island* S Wallis and Futuna
161 *Q11* **Futun Xi** ≈ SE China
160 *L5* **Fuxian** *var.* Fu Xian. Shaanxi, C China
Fuxian *see* Wafangdian
Fu Xian *see* Fuxian
160 *G13* **Fuxian Hu** ⊠ SW China
163 *U12* **Fuxin** *var.* Fou-hsin, Fu-hsin, Fusin. Liaoning, NE China
Fuxing *see* Wangmo
161 *P7* **Fuyang** Anhui, E China
161 *O4* **Fuyang He** ≈ E China
163 *U7* **Fuyu** Heilongjiang, NE China
163 *Z6* **Fuyuan** Heilongjiang, NE China
Fuyu/Fu-yü *see* Songyuan
158 *M3* **Fuyun** *var.* Koktokay. Xinjiang Uygur Zizhiqu, NW China
111 *L22* **Füzesabony** Heves, E Hungary
161 *R12* **Fuzhou** *var.* Foochow, Fu-chou. *province capital* Fujian, SE China
137 *W13* **Füzuli** *Rus.* Fizuli. SW Azerbaijan
119 *I20* **Fyadory** *Rus.* Fëdory. Brestskaya Voblasts', SW Belarus
95 *G24* **Fyn** *off.* Fyns Amt, *var.* Fünen. ◈ *county* C Denmark
95 *G23* **Fyn** *Ger.* Fünen. *island* C Denmark
96 *H12* **Fyne, Loch** *inlet* W Scotland, UK
Fyns Amt *see* Fyn
95 *E16* **Fyresvatnet** ◎ S Norway
FYR Macedonia/FYROM *see* Macedonia, FYR
Fyzabad *see* Feyẕābād

G

Gaafu Alifu Atoll *see* North Huvadhu Atoll
81 *O14* **Gaalkacyo** *var.* Galka'yo, *It.* Galcaio. Mudug, C Somalia
146 *J11* **Gabakly** *Rus.* Kabakly. Lebap Welaýaty, NE Turkmenistan
114 *H8* **Gabare** Vratsa, NW Bulgaria
102 *K15* **Gabas** ≈ SW France
Gabasumdo *see* Tongde
35 *T7* **Gabbs** Nevada, W USA
82 *B12* **Gabela** Cuanza Sul, W Angola
Gaberones *see* Gaborone
189 *X14* **Gabert** *island* Caroline Islands, E Micronesia
74 *M7* **Gabès** *var.* Qābis. E Tunisia
74 *M6* **Gabès, Golfe de** *Ar.* Khalīj Qābis. *gulf* E Tunisia
Gablonz an der Neisse *see* Jablonec nad Nisou

◆ Country
● Country Capital
◇ Dependent Territory
○ Dependent Territory Capital
◈ Administrative Regions
✈ International Airport
▲ Mountain
▲▲ Mountain Range
Volcano
≈ River
◎ Lake
⊠ Reservoir

Gablös see Cavalese
79 E18 Gabon off. Gabonese Republic. ◆ republic C Africa
Gabonese Republic see Gabon
83 I20 Gaborone prev. Gaberones. ● (Botswana) South East, SE Botswana
83 I20 Gaborone ✈ South East, SE Botswana
104 K8 Gabriel y Galán, Embalse de ⊡ W Spain
143 U15 Gābrīk, Rūd-e ⛆ SE Iran
114 J9 Gabrovo Gabrovo, N Bulgaria
114 J9 Gabrovo ◆ province N Bulgaria
76 H12 Gabú prev. Nova Lamego. E Guinea-Bissau
29 O6 Gackle North Dakota, N USA
113 I15 Gacko Repulika Srpska, S Bosnia and Herzegovina
155 F17 Gadag Karnātaka, W India
93 G15 Gäddede Jämtland, C Sweden
159 S12 Gadê Qinghai, C China
Gades/Gadier/Gadir/Gadire see Cádiz
105 P15 Gádor, Sierra de ▲ S Spain
149 S15 Gadra Sind, SE Pakistan
23 Q3 Gadsden Alabama, S USA
36 H15 Gadsden Arizona, SW USA
Gadyach see Hadyach
79 H15 Gadzi Mambéré-Kadéï, SW Central African Republic
116 J13 Găeşti Dâmboviţa, S Romania
107 J17 Gaeta Lazio, C Italy
107 J17 Gaeta, Golfo di var. Gulf of Gaeta. gulf C Italy
Gaeta, Gulf of see Gaeta, Golfo di
188 L14 Gaferut atoll Caroline Islands, W Micronesia
21 Q10 Gaffney South Carolina, SE USA
Gäfle see Gävle
Gäfleborg see Gävleborg
74 M6 Gafsa var. Qafşah. W Tunisia
Gafurov see Ghafurov
147 O10 Gagarin Jizzax Viloyati, C Uzbekistan
101 G21 Gaggenau Baden-Württemberg, SW Germany
188 F16 Gagil Tamil var. Gagil-Tomil. island Caroline Islands, W Micronesia
Gagil-Tomil see Gagil Tamil
127 O4 Gagino Nizhegorodskaya Oblast', W Russian Federation
107 Q19 Gagliano del Capo Puglia, SE Italy
94 L13 Gagnef Dalarna, C Sweden
76 M17 Gagnoa C Ivory Coast
13 N10 Gagnon Québec, E Canada
Gago Coutinho see Lumbala N'Guimbo
137 P8 Gagra NW Georgia
31 S13 Gahanna Ohio, N USA
143 R13 Gahkom Hormozgān, S Iran
Gahnpa see Ganta
57 Q19 Gaíba, Laguna ◎ E Bolivia
153 T13 Gaibanda var. Gaibandah. Rajshahi, NW Bangladesh
Gaibandah see Gaibanda
Gaibhlte, Cnoc Mór na n see Galtymore Mountain
109 R9 Gail ⛆ S Austria
101 I21 Gaildorf Baden-Württemberg, S Germany
103 N15 Gaillac var. Gaillac-sur-Tarn. Tarn, S France
Gaillac-sur-Tarn see Gaillac
Gaillimh see Galway
Gaillimhe, Cuan na see Galway Bay
109 Q9 Gailtaler Alpen ▲ S Austria
63 J17 Gaimán Chaco, S Argentina
20 K8 Gainesboro Tennessee, S USA
23 V10 Gainesville Florida, SE USA
23 T2 Gainesville Georgia, SE USA
27 U8 Gainesville Missouri, C USA
25 T5 Gainesville Texas, SW USA
109 X5 Gainfarn Niederösterreich, NE Austria
97 N18 Gainsborough E England, UK
182 G6 Gairdner, Lake salt lake South Australia
Gaissane see Gáissát
92 L8 Gáissát var. Gaissane. ▲ N Norway
43 T15 Gaital, Cerro ▲ C Panama
21 W3 Gaithersburg Maryland, NE USA
163 U13 Gaizhou Liaoning, NE China
Gaizina Kalns see Gaiziņakalns
118 H7 Gaiziņakalns var. Gaizina Kalns. ▲ E Latvia
Gajac see Villeneuve-sur-Lot
39 S10 Gakona Alaska, USA
Galaassiya see Galaosiyo
Galāġil see Jalājil
Galam, Pulau see Gelam, Pulau
62 J6 Galán, Cerro ▲ NW Argentina
111 H21 Galanta Hung. Galánta. Trnavský Kraj, W Slovakia
146 L11 Galaosiyo Rus. Galaassiya. Buxoro Viloyati, C Uzbekistan
57 B17 Galápagos off. Provincia de Galápagos. ◆ province W Ecuador, E Pacific Ocean
193 P8 Galapagos Fracture Zone tectonic feature E Pacific Ocean
Galapagos Islands see Colón, Archipiélago de
Galápagos, Islas de los see Colón, Archipiélago de
Galápagos, Provincia de see Galápagos
193 S9 Galapagos Rise undersea feature E Pacific Ocean
96 K13 Galashiels SE Scotland, UK
116 M12 Galaţi Ger. Galatz. Galaţi, E Romania
116 L12 Galaţi ◆ county E Romania
107 Q19 Galatina Puglia, SE Italy
107 Q19 Galatone Puglia, SE Italy
Galatz see Galaţi
21 R8 Galax Virginia, NE USA
146 J16 Galaýmor Rus. Kala-i-Mor. Mary Welaýaty, S Turkmenistan
Galcaio see Gaalkacyo
64 P11 Gáldar Gran Canaria, Islas Canarias, NE Atlantic Ocean
94 F11 Galdhøpiggen ▲ S Norway
40 I4 Galeana Chihuahua, N Mexico
41 O9 Galeana Nuevo León, NE Mexico
60 P9 Galeão ✈ (Rio de Janeiro) Rio de Janeiro, SE Brazil
171 R10 Galela Pulau Halmahera, E Indonesia
39 O9 Galena Alaska, USA
30 K10 Galena Illinois, N USA
27 R7 Galena Kansas, C USA
27 T8 Galena Missouri, C USA
45 V15 Galeota Point headland Trinidad, Trinidad and Tobago
105 P13 Galera Andalucía, S Spain
45 Y16 Galera Point headland Trinidad, Trinidad and Tobago
56 A5 Galera, Punta headland NW Ecuador
30 K12 Galesburg Illinois, N USA
30 J7 Galesville Wisconsin, N USA
18 F12 Galeton Pennsylvania, NE USA
116 H9 Gâlgău Hung. Galgó; prev. Gilgău. Sălaj, NW Romania
Galgó see Gâlgău
Galgóc see Hlohovec
81 N15 Galguduud off. Gobolka Galguduud. ◆ region E Somalia
Galguduud, Gobolka see Galguduud
137 Q9 Gali W Georgia
125 N14 Galich Kostromskaya Oblast', NW Russian Federation
114 H7 Galiche Vratsa, NW Bulgaria
104 H3 Galicia anc. Gallaecia. ◆ autonomous community NW Spain
64 M8 Galicia Bank undersea feature E Atlantic Ocean
Galilee see HaGalil
181 W7 Galilee, Lake ◎ Queensland, NE Australia
Galilee, Sea of see Tiberias, Lake
106 E11 Galileo Galilei ✈ (Pisa) Toscana, C Italy
31 S12 Galion Ohio, N USA
Galka'yo see Gaalkacyo
146 K12 Galkynyş prev. Rus. Deynau, Dyanev, Turkm. Dänew. Lebap Welaýaty, NE Turkmenistan
80 H11 Gallabat Gedaref, E Sudan
Gallaecia see Galicia
147 O11 G'allaorol Jizzakh Viloyati, C Uzbekistan
147 O11 G'allaorol Jizzax Viloyati, C Uzbekistan
106 C7 Gallarate Lombardia, NW Italy
27 S2 Gallatin Missouri, C USA
20 J8 Gallatin Tennessee, S USA
33 R11 Gallatin Peak ▲ Montana, NW USA
33 R12 Gallatin River ⛆ Montana/Wyoming, NW USA
155 J26 Galle prev. Point de Galle. Southern Province, SW Sri Lanka
105 S5 Gállego ⛆ NE Spain
193 Q8 Gallego Rise undersea feature E Pacific Ocean
Gallegos see Río Gallegos
63 H23 Gallegos, Río ⛆ Argentina/Chile
Gallia see France
22 K10 Galliano Louisiana, S USA
114 G13 Gallikós ⛆ N Greece
37 S12 Gallinas Peak ▲ New Mexico, SW USA
54 H3 Gallinas, Punta headland NE Colombia
37 T11 Gallinas River ⛆ New Mexico, SW USA
107 Q19 Gallipoli Puglia, SE Italy
Gallipoli see Gelibolu
Gallipoli Peninsula see Gelibolu Yarımadası
31 T15 Gallipolis Ohio, N USA
92 J12 Gällivare Lapp. Váhtjer. Norrbotten, N Sweden
109 T4 Gallneukirchen Oberösterreich, N Austria
93 G17 Gällö Jämtland, C Sweden
105 Q7 Gallo ⛆ C Spain
107 I23 Gallo, Capo headland Sicilia, Italy, C Mediterranean Sea
37 P13 Gallo Mountains ▲ New Mexico, SW USA
18 G8 Galloo Island island New York, NE USA
97 H15 Galloway, Mull of headland S Scotland, UK
37 P10 Gallup New Mexico, SW USA
105 R5 Gallur Aragón, NE Spain
Gâlma see Guelma
162 H7 Galshar var. Buyant. Dzavhan, C Mongolia
163 N9 Galshar var. Buyant. Hentiy, C Mongolia
162 I6 Galt var. Ider. Hövsgöl, C Mongolia
35 O8 Galt California, W USA
74 C10 Galtat-Zemmour C Western Sahara
95 G22 Galten Århus, C Denmark
97 D20 Galtymore Mountain Ir. Cnoc Mór na nGaibhlte. ▲ S Ireland
97 D20 Galty Mountains Ir. Na Gaibhlte. ▲ S Ireland
30 K11 Galva Illinois, N USA
25 X12 Galveston Texas, SW USA
25 W11 Galveston Bay inlet Texas, SW USA
25 W12 Galveston Island island Texas, SW USA
61 B18 Gálvez Santa Fe, C Argentina
97 C18 Galway Ir. Gaillimh. Galway, W Ireland
97 B18 Galway Ir. Gaillimh. ◆ county W Ireland
97 B18 Galway Bay Ir. Cuan na Gaillimhe. bay W Ireland
83 F18 Gam Otjozondjupa, NE Namibia
164 L14 Gamagōri Aichi, Honshū, SW Japan
54 F7 Gamarra Cesar, N Colombia
Gámas see Kaamanen
158 L17 Gamba Xizang Zizhiqu, W China
Gamba see Zamtang
77 P14 Gambaga NE Ghana
80 G13 Gambēla W Ethiopia
81 H14 Gambēla ◆ region W Ethiopia
38 K10 Gambell Saint Lawrence Island, Alaska, USA
76 E12 Gambia off. Republic of The Gambia, The Gambia. ◆ republic W Africa
76 I12 Gambia Fr. Gambie. ⛆ W Africa
64 K12 Gambia Plain undersea feature E Atlantic Ocean
Gambia, Republic of The see Gambia
Gambia, The see Gambia
Gambie see Gambia
31 T13 Gambier Ohio, N USA
191 Y13 Gambier, Îles island group E French Polynesia
182 G10 Gambier Islands island group South Australia
79 H19 Gamboma Plateaux, E Congo
79 G16 Gamboula Mambéré-Kadéï, SW Central African Republic
37 P10 Gamerco New Mexico, SW USA
137 V12 Gamiş Dağı ▲ W Azerbaijan
Gamlakarleby see Kokkola
95 N18 Gamleby Kalmar, S Sweden
Gammelstaden see Gammelstaden
93 J14 Gammelstaden var. Gammelstad. Norrbotten, N Sweden
Gammouda see Sidi Bouzid
155 J25 Gampaha Western Province, W Sri Lanka
155 K25 Gampola Central Province, C Sri Lanka
167 S5 Gâm, Sông ⛆ N Vietnam
92 L7 Gamvik Finnmark, N Norway
150 H13 Gan Addu Atoll, C Maldives
Gan see Gansu
Gan see Jiangxi
Ganaane see Juba
37 O10 Ganado Arizona, SW USA
25 U12 Ganado Texas, SW USA
14 L14 Gananoque Ontario, SE Canada
Ganāveh see Bandar-e Gonāveh
137 V11 Gäncä Rus. Gyandzha; prev. Kirovabad, Yelisavetpol. W Azerbaijan
Ganchi see Ghonchí
Gand see Gent
82 B13 Ganda var. Mariano Machado, Port. Vila Mariano Machado. Benguela, W Angola
79 L22 Gandajika Kasai Oriental, S Dem. Rep. Congo
153 O12 Gandak Nep. Nārāyāni. ⛆ India/Nepal
13 U11 Gander Newfoundland, Newfoundland and Labrador, SE Canada
13 U11 Gander ✈ Newfoundland, Newfoundland and Labrador, E Canada
100 G11 Ganderkesee Niedersachsen, NW Germany
105 T7 Gandesa Cataluña, NE Spain
154 B10 Gāndhīdhām Gujarāt, W India
154 D10 Gāndhīnagar state capital Gujarāt, W India
154 F9 Gāndhi Sāgar ◎ C India
105 T11 Gandía País Valenciano, E Spain
159 O10 Gang Qinghai, W China
152 G9 Gangānagar Rājasthān, NW India
152 I12 Gangāpur Rājasthān, N India
153 S17 Ganga Sāgar West Bengal, NE India
Gangavathi see Gangāwati
155 G17 Gangāwati var. Gangavathi. Karnātaka, C India
159 S9 Gangca var. Shaliuhe. Qinghai, C China
158 H14 Gangdisê Shan Eng. Kailas Range. ▲ W China
103 Q15 Ganges Hérault, S France
153 P13 Ganges Ben. Padma. ⛆ Bangladesh/India see also Padma
Ganges Padma
Ganges Cone see Ganges Fan
173 S3 Ganges Fan var. Ganges Cone. undersea feature N Bay of Bengal
153 U17 Ganges, Mouths of the delta Bangladesh/India
107 K23 Gangi anc. Engyum. Sicilia, Italy, C Mediterranean Sea
152 K8 Gangotri Uttaranchal, N India
Gangra see Çankırı
153 S11 Gangtok state capital Sikkim, N India
159 W11 Gangu Gansu, C China
163 U5 Gan He ⛆ NE China
171 S12 Gani Pulau Halmahera, E Indonesia
161 O12 Gan Jiang ⛆ S China
163 U11 Ganjig var Horqin Zuoyi Houqi. Nei Mongol Zizhiqu, N China
146 H15 Gannaly Ahal Welaýaty, S Turkmenistan
163 U7 Gannan Heilongjiang, NE China
103 P10 Gannat Allier, C France
33 T14 Gannett Peak ▲ Wyoming, C USA
29 O10 Gannvalley South Dakota, N USA
Ganqu see Lhünzhub
109 Y3 Gänserndorf Niederösterreich, NE Austria
Gansos, Lago dos see Goose Lake
159 T9 Gansu var. Gan, Gansu Sheng, Kansu. ◆ province N China
Gansu Sheng see Gansu
76 K16 Ganta var. Gahnpa. NE Liberia
182 H11 Gantheaume, Cape headland South Australia
Gantsevichi see Hantsavichy
161 Q6 Ganyu var. Qingkou. Jiangsu, E China
144 D12 Ganyushkino Atyrau, SW Kazakhstan
161 O12 Ganzhou Jiangxi, S China
Ganzhou see Zhangye
77 Q10 Gao Gao, E Mali
77 R10 Gao ◆ region SE Mali
161 O10 Gao'an Jiangxi, S China
Gaocheng see Litang
Gaoleshan see Xianfeng
Gaongjiang see Yudu
161 N5 Gaoping Shanxi, C China
159 S8 Gaotai Gansu, N China
Gaoth Dobhair see Gweedore
77 O14 Gaoua SW Burkina
76 I13 Gaoual N Guinea
Gaoxiong see Kaohsiung
161 R7 Gaoyou var. Dayishan. Jiangsu, E China
161 R7 Gaoyou Hu ◎ E China
160 M15 Gaozhou Guangdong, S China
103 T13 Gap anc. Vapincum. Hautes-Alpes, SE France
146 E9 Gaplaňgyr Platosy Rus. Plato Kaplangky. ridge Turkmenistan/Uzbekistan
158 G13 Gar var. Gar Xincun. Xizang Zizhiqu, W China
Garabekevyul see Garabekewül
146 L13 Garabekewül Rus. Garabekevyul, Karabekaul. Lebap Welaýaty, E Turkmenistan
146 K15 Garabil Belentligi Rus. Vozvyshennost' Karabil'. ▲ S Turkmenistan
146 A8 Garabogaz Rus. Bekdash. Balkan Welaýaty, NW Turkmenistan
146 B9 Garabogaz Aylagy Rus. Zaliv Kara-Bogaz-Gol. bay NW Turkmenistan
146 A9 Garabogazköl Rus. Kara-Bogaz-Gol. Balkan Welaýaty, E Turkmenistan
146 A9 Garabogazköl Rus. Kara-Bogazkol. Balkan Welaýaty, NW Turkmenistan
43 V16 Garachiné Darién, SE Panama
43 V16 Garachiné, Punta headland SE Panama
146 K12 Garagan Rus. Karagan. Ahal Welaýaty, C Turkmenistan
54 G10 Garagoa Boyacá, C Colombia
146 A11 Garagöl' Rus. Karagel'. Balkan Welaýaty, W Turkmenistan
146 F12 Garagum var. Garagumy, Qara Qum, Eng. Black Sand Desert, Kara Kum; prev. Peski Karakumy. desert C Turkmenistan
146 E12 Garagum Kanaly var. Kara Kum Canal, Rus. Karagumskiy Kanal, Karakumskiy Kanal. canal C Turkmenistan
Garagumy see Garagum
183 S4 Garah New South Wales, SE Australia
64 O11 Garajonay ▲ Gomera, Islas Canarias, NE Atlantic Ocean
114 M8 Gara Khitrino Shumen, NE Bulgaria
76 L13 Garalo Sikasso, SW Mali
Garam see Hron
146 L14 Garamätnyýaz Rus. Karamet-Niyaz. Lebap Welaýaty, E Turkmenistan
Garamszentkereszt see Žiar nad Hronom
77 Q13 Garango S Burkina
59 Q15 Garanhuns Pernambuco, E Brazil
188 H5 Garapan Saipan, S Northern Mariana Islands
Gárasavvon see Karesuando
Gárassavon see Kaaresuvanto
78 J13 Garba Bamingui-Bangoran, N Central African Republic
Garba see Jiulong
81 L16 Garbahaarrey It. Garba Harre. Gedo, SW Somalia
Garba Harre see Garbahaarrey
81 J18 Garba Tula Eastern, C Kenya
27 N9 Garber Oklahoma, C USA
34 L4 Garberville California, W USA
Garbo see Lhozhag
100 I12 Garbsen Niedersachsen, N Germany
60 K9 Garça São Paulo, S Brazil
104 L10 García de Solá, Embalse de ⊡ C Spain
103 Q14 Gard ◆ department S France
103 Q14 Gard ⛆ S France
106 F7 Garda, Lago di var. Benaco, Eng. Lake Garda, Ger. Gardasee. ◎ NE Italy
Garda, Lake see Garda, Lago di
Gardan Divāl see Gardan Dīwāl
149 Q5 Gardan Dīwāl var. Gardan Divāl. Vardak, C Afghanistan
103 S15 Gardanne Bouches-du-Rhône, SE France
Gardasee see Garda, Lago di
100 L12 Gardelegen Sachsen-Anhalt, C Germany
14 B10 Garden ⛆ Ontario, S Canada
23 X6 Garden City Georgia, SE USA
26 I6 Garden City Kansas, C USA
27 S5 Garden City Missouri, C USA
25 N8 Garden City Texas, SW USA
23 P3 Gardendale Alabama, S USA
31 P5 Garden Island island Michigan, N USA
22 M11 Garden Island Bay bay Louisiana, S USA
31 O5 Garden Peninsula peninsula Michigan, N USA
The Garden State see New Jersey
95 I14 Gardermoen Akershus, S Norway
Gardeyz/Gardez see Gardīz
93 G14 Gardiken ◎ N Sweden
19 Q7 Gardiner Maine, NE USA
33 S12 Gardiner Montana, NW USA
19 N13 Gardiners Island island New York, NE USA
149 Q6 Gardīz var. Gardeyz, Gardez, Gordiaz. Paktīā, E Afghanistan
Gardner Island see Nikumaroro
19 T6 Gardner Lake ◎ Maine, NE USA
35 Q6 Gardnerville Nevada, W USA
Gardo see Qardho
106 F7 Gardone Val Trompia Lombardia, N Italy
Garegegasnjárga see Karigasniemi
38 F17 Gareloi Island island Aleutian Islands, Alaska, USA
Gares see Puente la Reina
106 B10 Garessio Piemonte, NE Italy
32 M9 Garfield Washington, NW USA
31 U11 Garfield Heights Ohio, N USA
Gargaliani see Gargaliánoi
115 D21 Gargaliánoi var. Gargaliani. Pelopónnisos, S Greece
107 N15 Gargàno, Promontorio del headland SE Italy
108 J8 Gargellen Graubünden, W Switzerland
93 I14 Gargnäs Västerbotten, N Sweden
118 C11 Gargždai Klaipėda, W Lithuania
154 J13 Garhchiroli Mahārāshtra, C India
153 O15 Garhwa Jhārkhand, N India
171 V13 Gariau Papua, E Indonesia
83 E24 Garies Northern Cape, W South Africa
107 K17 Garigliano ⛆ C Italy
81 K19 Garissa Coast, E Kenya
21 V11 Garland North Carolina, SE USA
25 T6 Garland Texas, SW USA
36 L1 Garland Utah, W USA
106 D8 Garlasco Lombardia, N Italy
119 F14 Garliava Kaunas, S Lithuania
Garm see Gharm
142 M9 Garm, Āb-e var. Rūd-e Khersān. ⛆ SW Iran
101 K25 Garmisch-Partenkirchen Bayern, S Germany
143 O5 Garmsār prev. Qishlaq. Semnān, N Iran
Garmser see Darvīshān
29 V12 Garner Iowa, C USA
21 U9 Garner North Carolina, SE USA
27 Q5 Garnett Kansas, C USA
99 M25 Garnich Luxembourg, SW Luxembourg
182 M8 Garnpung, Lake salt lake New South Wales, SE Australia
Garoe see Garoowe
Garoet see Garut
153 U13 Gāro Hills hill range NE India
102 K13 Garonne anc. Garumna. ⛆ S France
80 P13 Garoowe var. Garoe. Nugaal, N Somalia
78 F12 Garoua var. Garua. Nord, N Cameroon
79 G14 Garoua Boulaï Est, E Cameroon
77 O10 Garou, Lac ◎ C Mali
95 L16 Garphyttan Örebro, C Sweden
29 R11 Garretson South Dakota, N USA
31 Q11 Garrett Indiana, N USA
33 Q10 Garrison Montana, NW USA
28 M4 Garrison North Dakota, N USA
25 X8 Garrison Texas, SW USA
28 L4 Garrison Dam dam North Dakota, N USA
104 J9 Garrovillas Extremadura, W Spain
Garrygala see Magtymguly
8 L8 Garry Lake ◎ Nunavut, N Canada
Gars see Gars am Kamp
109 W3 Gars am Kamp var. Gars. Niederösterreich, NE Austria
81 K20 Garsen Coast, S Kenya
Garshy see Garşy
14 F10 Garson Ontario, S Canada
109 T5 Garsten Oberösterreich, N Austria
Gartar see Qianning
102 M10 Gartempe ⛆ C France
Gartog see Markam
Garua see Garoua
83 D21 Garub Karas, SW Namibia
Garumna see Garonne
169 P16 Garut prev. Garoet. Jawa, C Indonesia
185 C20 Garvie Mountains ▲ South Island, New Zealand
110 N12 Garwolin Mazowieckie, E Poland
25 U12 Garwood Texas, SW USA
Gar Xincun see Gar
146 A9 Garşy var. Garshy, Rus. Karshi. Balkan Welaýaty, NW Turkmenistan
31 N11 Gary Indiana, N USA
25 X7 Gary Texas, SW USA
158 G13 Gar Zangbo ⛆ W China
160 F8 Garzê Sichuan, C China
54 E12 Garzón Huila, S Colombia
Gasan-Kuli see Esenguly
31 P13 Gas City Indiana, N USA
102 K15 Gascogne Eng. Gascony. cultural region S France
26 V5 Gasconade River ⛆ Missouri, C USA
Gascony see Gascogne
180 H9 Gascoyne Junction Western Australia
173 V8 Gascoyne Plain undersea feature E Indian Ocean
180 H9 Gascoyne River ⛆ Western Australia
192 J11 Gascoyne Tablemount undersea feature N Tasman Sea
67 U6 Gash var. Nahr al Qāsh. ⛆ W Sudan
149 X3 Gasherbrum ▲ NE Pakistan
Gas Hu see Gas Hure Hu
77 X12 Gashua Yobe, NE Nigeria
159 N9 Gas Hure Hu var. Gas Hu. ◎ C China
186 G7 Gasmata New Britain, E Papua New Guinea
23 V14 Gasparilla Island island Florida, SE USA
169 O13 Gaspar, Selat strait W Indonesia
15 Y6 Gaspé Québec, SE Canada
15 Z6 Gaspé, Cap de headland Québec, SE Canada
15 X6 Gaspé, Péninsule de var. Péninsule de la Gaspésie. peninsula Québec, SE Canada
Gaspésie, Péninsule de la see Gaspé, Péninsule de
77 W15 Gassol Taraba, E Nigeria
Gastein see Badgastein
21 R10 Gastonia North Carolina, SE USA
21 V8 Gaston, Lake ⊡ North Carolina/Virginia, SE USA
115 D19 Gastoúni Dytikí Ellás, S Greece
63 I17 Gastre Chubut, S Argentina
Gat see Ghāt
105 P15 Gata, Cabo de cape S Spain
Gata, Cape see Gátas, Akrotíri
105 T11 Gata de Gorgos País Valenciano, E Spain
116 E12 Gătaia Ger. Gataja, Hung. Gátalja; prev. Gáttája. Timiş, W Romania
Gataja/Gátalja see Gătaia
121 P3 Gátas, Akrotíri var. Cape Gata. cape S Cyprus
104 J8 Gata, Sierra de ▲ W Spain
124 G13 Gatchina Leningradskaya Oblast', NW Russian Federation
21 P8 Gate City Virginia, NE USA
97 M14 Gateshead NE England, UK
21 X8 Gatesville North Carolina, SE USA
25 S8 Gatesville Texas, SW USA
14 L12 Gatineau Québec, SE Canada
14 L11 Gatineau ⛆ Ontario/Québec, SE Canada
21 N9 Gatlinburg Tennessee, S USA
Gatooma see Kadoma
Gáttája see Gătaia
43 T14 Gatún, Lago ⊡ C Panama
59 N14 Gaturiano Piauí, NE Brazil
97 O22 Gatwick ✈ (London) SE England, UK
187 Y14 Gau prev. Ngau. island C Fiji
187 R12 Gaua var. Santa Maria. island Banks Island, N Vanuatu
104 L16 Gaucín Andalucía, S Spain
Gauhāti see Guwāhāti
118 I8 Gauja Ger. Aa. ⛆ Estonia/Latvia
118 I7 Gaujiena Alūksne, NE Latvia
94 H9 Gauldalen valley S Norway
21 R5 Gauley River ⛆ West Virginia, NE USA
Gaul/Gaule see France
99 D19 Gaurain-Ramecroix Hainaut, SW Belgium
95 F15 Gaustatoppen ▲ S Norway
83 J21 Gauteng off. Gauteng Province; prev. Pretoria-Witwatersrand-Vereeniging. ◆ province NE South Africa
Gauteng see Germiston, South Africa
Gauteng see Johannesburg, South Africa
Gauteng Province see Gauteng
137 U11 Gavarr prev. Kamo. C Armenia
143 P14 Gāvbandī Hormozgān, S Iran
115 H25 Gavdopoúla island SE Greece
115 H26 Gávdos island SE Greece
102 K16 Gave de Pau var. Gave-de-Pay. ⛆ SW France
Gave-de-Pay see Gave de Pau
102 J16 Gave d'Oloron ⛆ SW France
99 E18 Gavere Oost-Vlaanderen, NW Belgium
94 N13 Gävle var. Gäfle; prev. Gefle. Gävleborg, C Sweden
94 M11 Gävleborg var. Gäfleborg, Gefleborg. ◆ county C Sweden
94 O13 Gävlebukten bay C Sweden
124 L16 Gavrilov-Yam Yaroslavskaya Oblast', W Russian Federation
182 I9 Gawler South Australia
182 G7 Gawler Ranges hill range South Australia
Gawso see Goaso
162 H11 Gaxun Nur ◎ N China
153 P14 Gaya Bihār, N India
77 S13 Gaya Dosso, SW Niger
Gaya see Kyjov
31 Q6 Gaylord Michigan, N USA
29 U9 Gaylord Minnesota, N USA
181 Y9 Gayndah Queensland, E Australia
125 T12 Gayny Permskaya Oblast', NW Russian Federation
Gaysin see Haysyn
Gayvorno see Hayvoron
138 E11 Gaza Ar. Ghazzah, Heb. 'Azza. NE Gaza Strip
83 L20 Gaza off. Província de Gaza. ◆ province SW Mozambique
Gaz-Achak see Gazojak
147 Q9 G'azalkent Rus. Gazalkent. Toshkent Viloyati, E Uzbekistan
Gazalkent see G'azalkent
Gazandzhyk/Gazanjyk see Bereket
77 V12 Gazaoua Maradi, S Niger
Gaza, Província de see Gaza
138 E11 Gaza Strip Ar. Qita Ghazzah. disputed region SW Asia
Gazgan see G'ozg'on
Gazgan see G'ozg'on
136 M16 Gaziantep var. Gazi Antep; prev. Aintab, Antep. Gaziantep, S Turkey
136 M17 Gaziantep var. Gazi Antep. ◆ province S Turkey
Gazi Antep see Gaziantep
114 M13 Gaziköy Tekirdağ, NW Turkey
121 Q2 Gazimağusa var. Famagusta, Gk. Ammóchostos. E Cyprus
121 Q2 Gazimağusa Körfezi var. Famagusta Bay, Gk. Kólpos Ammóchostos. bay E Cyprus
146 K11 Gazli Buxoro Viloyati, C Uzbekistan
146 I9 Gazojak Rus. Gaz-Achak. Lebap Welaýaty, NE Turkmenistan
79 K15 Gbadolite Equateur, NW Dem. Rep. Congo
76 K16 Gbanga var. Gbarnga. N Liberia
Gbarnga see Gbanga
77 S14 Gbéroubouè var. Béroubouay. N Benin
77 W16 Gboko Benue, S Nigeria
Gcuwa see Butterworth
110 J7 Gdańsk Fr. Dantzig, Ger. Danzig. Pomorskie, N Poland
Gdan'skaya Bukhta/Gdańsk, Gulf of see Danzig, Gulf of
Gdańska, Zatoka see Danzig, Gulf of
Gdingen see Gdynia
124 F13 Gdov Pskovskaya Oblast', W Russian Federation
110 I6 Gdynia Ger. Gdingen. Pomorskie, N Poland
26 M10 Geary Oklahoma, C USA
Geavvú see Kevo

◆ Country ● Country Capital ◇ Dependent Territory ○ Dependent Territory Capital ◆ Administrative Regions ✈ International Airport ▲ Mountain ▲ Mountain Range ⛰ Volcano ⛆ River ◎ Lake ⊡ Reservoir

76 H12 **Gêba, Rio** ≈ C Guinea-Bissau
136 E11 **Gebze** Kocaeli, NW Turkey
80 H10 **Gedaref** *var.* Al Qaḑārif, El Gedaref. Gedaref, E Sudan
80 H10 **Gedaref** ⬖ *state* E Sudan
80 B11 **Gedid Ras el Fil** Southern Darfur, W Sudan
99 I23 **Gedinne** Namur, SE Belgium
136 E13 **Gediz** Kütahya, W Turkey
136 C14 **Gediz Nehri** ≈ W Turkey
81 N14 **Gedlegubē** Somali, E Ethiopia
81 L17 **Gedo** *off.* Gobolka Gedo. ⬖ *region* SW Somalia
Gedo, Gobolka *see* Gedo
95 I25 **Gedser** Storstrøm, SE Denmark
99 I16 **Geel** *var.* Gheel. Antwerpen, N Belgium
183 N13 **Geelong** Victoria, SE Australia
Ge'e'mu *see* Golmud
99 I14 **Geertruidenberg** Noord-Brabant, S Netherlands
100 H10 **Geeste** ≈ NW Germany
100 J10 **Geesthacht** Schleswig-Holstein, N Germany
183 P17 **Geeveston** Tasmania, SE Australia
Gefle *see* Gävle
Gefleborg *see* Gävleborg
158 G13 **Gê'gyai** Xizang Zizhiqu, W China
77 X12 **Geidam** Yobe, NE Nigeria
9 T11 **Geikie** ≈ Saskatchewan, C Canada
94 F13 **Geilo** Buskerud, S Norway
94 E10 **Geiranger** Møre og Romsdal, S Norway
101 I22 **Geislingen** *var.* Geislingen an der Steige. Baden-Württemberg, SW Germany
Geislingen an der Steige *see* Geislingen
81 F20 **Geita** Mwanza, NW Tanzania
95 G15 **Geithus** Buskerud, S Norway
160 H14 **Gejiu** *var.* Kochiu. Yunnan, S China
Gëkdepe *see* Gökdepe
146 E9 **Geklengkui, Solonchak** *var.* Solonchak Goklenkuy. *salt marsh* NW Turkmenistan
81 D14 **Gel** ≈ W Sudan
107 K25 **Gela** *prev.* Terranova di Sicilia. Sicilia, Italy, C Mediterranean Sea
159 N13 **Gêladaindong** ▲ C China
159 N13 **Gêladaindong** ▲ C China
81 N14 **Geladī** SE Ethiopia
169 P13 **Gelam, Pulau** *var.* Pulau Galam. *island* N Indonesia
Gelaozu Miaozu Zhizhixian *see* Wuchuan
98 L11 **Gelderland** *prev. Eng.* Guelders. ⬖ *province* E Netherlands
98 J13 **Geldermalsen** Gelderland, C Netherlands
101 D14 **Geldern** Nordrhein-Westfalen, W Germany
99 K15 **Geldrop** Noord-Brabant, SE Netherlands
99 L17 **Geleen** Limburg, SE Netherlands
126 K14 **Gelendzhik** Krasnodarskiy Kray, SW Russian Federation
Gelib *see* Jilib
136 B11 **Gelibolu** *Eng.* Gallipoli. Çanakkale, NW Turkey
115 L14 **Gelibolu Yarımadası** *Eng.* Gallipoli Peninsula. *peninsula* NW Turkey
81 O14 **Gellinsor** Mudug, C Somalia
101 H18 **Gelnhausen** Hessen, C Germany
101 E14 **Gelsenkirchen** Nordrhein-Westfalen, W Germany
83 C20 **Geluk** Hardap, SW Namibia
99 H20 **Gembloux** Namur, Belgium
79 J16 **Gemena** Equateur, NW Dem. Rep. Congo
99 L14 **Gemert** Noord-Brabant, SE Netherlands
136 E11 **Gemlik** Bursa, NW Turkey
Gem of the Mountains *see* Idaho
106 J6 **Gemona del Friuli** Friuli-Venezia Giulia, NE Italy
Gem State *see* Idaho
Genalē Wenz *see* Juba
169 R10 **Genali, Danau** ◎ Borneo, N Indonesia
99 G19 **Genappe** Walloon Brabant, C Belgium
137 P14 **Genç** Bingöl, E Turkey
Genck *see* Genk
98 M9 **Genemuiden** Overijssel, E Netherlands
63 K14 **General Acha** La Pampa, C Argentina
61 C21 **General Alvear** Buenos Aires, E Argentina
62 I12 **General Alvear** Mendoza, W Argentina
61 B20 **General Arenales** Buenos Aires, E Argentina
61 D21 **General Belgrano** Buenos Aires, E Argentina
194 H3 **General Bernardo O'Higgins** *Chilean research station* Antarctica
41 O8 **General Bravo** Nuevo León, NE Mexico
62 M7 **General Capdevila** Chaco, N Argentina
General Carrera, Lago *see* Buenos Aires, Lago
41 N9 **General Cepeda** Coahuila de Zaragoza, NE Mexico
63 K15 **General Conesa** Río Negro, E Argentina
61 G18 **General Enrique Martínez** Treinta y Tres, E Uruguay
62 L3 **General Eugenio A. Garay** *var.* Fortín General Eugenio Garay; *prev.* Yrendagüé. Nueva Asunción NW Paraguay
61 C18 **General Galarza** Entre Ríos, E Argentina
61 E22 **General Guido** Buenos Aires, E Argentina
General José F.Uriburu *see* Zárate
61 E22 **General Juan Madariaga** Buenos Aires, E Argentina
41 O16 **General Juan N Alvarez** ✈ (Acapulco) Guerrero, S Mexico
61 B22 **General La Madrid** Buenos Aires, E Argentina
61 E21 **General Lavalle** Buenos Aires, E Argentina
General Machado *see* Camacupa
62 I8 **General Manuel Belgrano, Cerro** ▲ W Argentina
41 O8 **General Mariano Escobero** ✈ (Monterrey) Nuevo León, NE Mexico
61 B20 **General O'Brien** Buenos Aires, E Argentina
62 K13 **General Pico** La Pampa, C Argentina
62 M7 **General Pinedo** Chaco, N Argentina
61 B20 **General Pinto** Buenos Aires, E Argentina
61 E22 **General Pirán** Buenos Aires, E Argentina
43 N15 **General, Río** ≈ S Costa Rica
63 I15 **General Roca** Río Negro, C Argentina
171 Q8 **General Santos** *off.* General Santos City. Mindanao, S Philippines
General Santos City *see* General Santos
41 O9 **General Terán** Nuevo León, NE Mexico
114 N7 **General Toshevo** *Rom.* I.G.Duca; *prev.* Casim, Kasimköj. Dobrich, NE Bulgaria
61 B20 **General Viamonte** Buenos Aires, E Argentina
61 A20 **General Villegas** Buenos Aires, E Argentina
Gênes *see* Genova
18 E11 **Genesee River** ≈ New York/Pennsylvania, NE USA
30 K11 **Geneseo** Illinois, N USA
18 F10 **Geneseo** New York, NE USA
57 L14 **Geneshuaya, Río** ≈ N Bolivia
23 Q8 **Geneva** Alabama, S USA
30 M10 **Geneva** Illinois, N USA
29 Q16 **Geneva** Nebraska, C USA
18 G10 **Geneva** New York, NE USA
31 U10 **Geneva** Ohio, NE USA
Geneva *see* Genève
108 B10 **Geneva, Lake** *Fr.* Lac de Genève, Lac Léman, *var.* le Léman, *Ger.* Genfer See. ◎ France/Switzerland
108 A10 **Genève** *Eng.* Geneva, *Ger.* Genf, *It.* Ginevra. Genève, SW Switzerland
108 A11 **Genève** *Eng.* Geneva, *Ger.* Genf, *It.* Ginevra. ⬖ *canton* SW Switzerland
108 A10 **Genève** *var.* Geneva. ✈ Vaud, SW Switzerland
Genève, Lac de *see* Geneva, Lake
Genf *see* Genève
Genfer See *see* Geneva, Lake
163 T5 **Genhe** *prev.* Ergun Zuoqi. Nei Mongol Zizhiqu, N China
163 S5 **Gen He** ≈ NE China
Genichesk *see* Heniches'k
104 L14 **Genil** ≈ S Spain
99 K18 **Genk** *var.* Genck. Limburg, NE Belgium
164 C13 **Genkai-nada** *gulf* Kyūshū, SW Japan
107 C19 **Gennargentu, Monti del** ▲▲ Sardegna, Italy, C Mediterranean Sea
99 M14 **Gennep** Limburg, SE Netherlands
30 M10 **Genoa** Illinois, N USA
29 Q15 **Genoa** Nebraska, C USA
Genoa *see* Genova
Genoa, Gulf of *see* Genova, Golfo di
106 D10 **Genova** *Eng.* Genoa; *anc.* Genua, *Fr.* Gênes. Liguria, NW Italy
106 D10 **Genova, Golfo di** *Eng.* Gulf of Genoa. *gulf* NW Italy
57 C17 **Genovesa, Isla** *var.* Tower Island. *island* Galapagos Islands, Ecuador, E Pacific Ocean
Genshū *see* Wŏnju
99 E17 **Gent** *Eng.* Ghent, *Fr.* Gand. Oost-Vlaanderen, NW Belgium
169 N16 **Genteng** Jawa, C Indonesia
100 M12 **Genthin** Sachsen-Anhalt, E Germany
27 R9 **Gentry** Arkansas, C USA
Genua *see* Genova
107 I15 **Genzano di Roma** Lazio, C Italy
Geokchay *see* Göyçay
Geok-Tepe *see* Gökdepe
122 I3 **Georga, Zemlya** *Eng.* George Land. *island* Zemlya Frantsa-Iosifa, N Russian Federation
83 G26 **George** Western Cape, S South Africa
29 S11 **George** Iowa, C USA
13 O5 **George** ≈ Newfoundland and Labrador/Québec, E Canada
45 T11 **George F L Charles** *prev.* Vigie. ✈ (Castries) NE Saint Lucia
65 C25 **George Island** *island* S Falkland Islands
183 R10 **George, Lake** ◎ New South Wales, SE Australia
81 E18 **George, Lake** ◎ SW Uganda
23 W10 **George, Lake** ◎ Florida, SE USA
18 L8 **George, Lake** ⊠ New York, NE USA
George Land *see* Georga, Zemlya
Georgenburg *see* Jurbarkas
George River *see* Kangiqsualujjuaq
64 G8 **Georges Bank** *undersea feature* W Atlantic Ocean
185 A21 **George Sound** *sound* South Island, New Zealand
65 F15 **Georgetown** ○ (Ascension Island) NW Ascension Island
181 V5 **Georgetown** Queensland, NE Australia
183 P15 **George Town** Tasmania, SE Australia
44 I4 **George Town** Great Exuma Island, C Bahamas
44 D8 **George Town** *var.* Georgetown. ○ (Cayman Islands) Grand Cayman, SW Cayman Islands
76 H12 **Georgetown** E Gambia
55 T8 **Georgetown** ● (Guyana) N Guyana
168 I7 **George Town** *var.* Penang, Pinang. Pinang, Peninsular Malaysia
45 Y14 **Georgetown** Saint Vincent, Saint Vincent and the Grenadines
21 Y4 **Georgetown** Delaware, NE USA
23 R6 **Georgetown** Georgia, SE USA
20 M5 **Georgetown** Kentucky, S USA
21 T13 **Georgetown** South Carolina, SE USA
25 S10 **Georgetown** Texas, SW USA
55 T8 **Georgetown** ✈ N Guyana
Georgetown *see* George Town
195 U16 **George V Coast** *physical region* Antarctica
194 J7 **George VI Ice Shelf** *ice shelf* Antarctica
194 J6 **George VI Sound** *sound* Antarctica
195 T15 **George V Land** *physical region* Antarctica
25 S14 **George West** Texas, SW USA
137 R9 **Georgia** *off.* Republic of Georgia, *Geor.* Sak'art'velo, *Rus.* Gruzinskaya SSR, Gruziya. ◆ *republic* SW Asia
23 S5 **Georgia** *off.* State of Georgia, *also known as* Empire State of the South, Peach State. ⬖ *state* SE USA
14 F12 **Georgian Bay** *lake bay* Ontario, S Canada
Georgia, Republic of *see* Georgia
10 L17 **Georgia, Strait of** *strait* British Columbia, W Canada
Georgi Dimitrov *see* Kostenets
Georgi Dimitrov, Yazovir *see* Koprinka, Yazovir
114 M9 **Georgi Traykov, Yazovir** ⊠ NE Bulgaria
Georgiu-Dezh *see* Liski
145 W10 **Georgiyevka** Semipalatinsk, E Kazakhstan
Georgiyevka *see* Korday
127 N15 **Georgiyevsk** Stavropol'skiy Kray, SW Russian Federation
100 G13 **Georgsmarienhütte** Niedersachsen, NW Germany
195 O1 **Georg von Neumayer** *German research station* Antarctica
101 M16 **Gera** Thüringen, E Germany
101 K16 **Gera** ≈ C Germany
99 E19 **Geraardsbergen** Oost-Vlaanderen, SW Belgium
115 F21 **Geráki** Pelopónnisos, S Greece
27 W5 **Gerald** Missouri, C USA
47 V8 **Geral de Goiás, Serra** ▲▲ E Brazil
185 G20 **Geraldine** Canterbury, South Island, New Zealand
180 H11 **Geraldton** Western Australia
12 E11 **Geraldton** Ontario, S Canada
60 J12 **Geral, Serra** ▲▲ S Brazil
103 U6 **Gérardmer** Vosges, NE France
Gerasa *see* Jarash
Gerdauen *see* Zheleznodorozhnyy
39 Q11 **Gerdine, Mount** ▲ Alaska, USA
136 H11 **Gerede** Bolu, N Turkey
136 H11 **Gerede Çayī** ≈ N Turkey
148 M8 **Gereshk** Helmand, SW Afghanistan
101 L24 **Geretsried** Bayern, S Germany
105 P14 **Gérgal** Andalucía, S Spain
28 I14 **Gering** Nebraska, C USA
35 R3 **Gerlach** Nevada, W USA
Gerlachfalvi Csúcs/Gerlachovka *see* Gerlachovský štít
111 L18 **Gerlachovský štít** *var.* Gerlachovka, *Ger.* Gerlsdorfer Spitze, *Hung.* Gerlachfalvi Csúcs; *prev.* Stalinov Štít, *Ger.* Franz-Josef Spitze, *Hung.* Ferencz-Jósef Csúcs. ▲ N Slovakia
108 E8 **Gerlafingen** Solothurn, NW Switzerland
Gerlsdorfer Spitze *see* Gerlachovský štít
139 V3 **Germak** E Iraq
German East Africa *see* Tanzania
Germanicopolis *see* Çankırı
Germanicum, Mare/German Ocean *see* North Sea
Germanovichi *see* Hyermanavichy
German Southwest Africa *see* Namibia
20 E10 **Germantown** Tennessee, S USA
101 I15 **Germany** *off.* Federal Republic of Germany, Bundesrepublik Deutschland, *Ger.* Deutschland. ◆ *federal republic* N Europe
Germany, Federal Republic of *see* Germany
101 L23 **Germering** Bayern, SE Germany
83 J21 **Germiston** *var.* Gauteng. Gauteng, NE South Africa
Gernika *see* Gernika-Lumo
105 P2 **Gernika-Lumo** *var.* Gernika, Guernica, Guernica y Lumo. País Vasco, N Spain
164 L12 **Gero** Gifu, Honshū, SW Japan
115 F22 **Geroliménas** Pelopónnisos, S Greece
Gerona *see* Girona
99 H21 **Gerpinnes** Hainaut, S Belgium
102 L15 **Gers** ⬖ *department* S France
102 L14 **Gers** ≈ S France
Gerunda *see* Girona
158 I13 **Gêrzê** *var.* Luring. Xizang Zizhiqu, W China
136 K10 **Gerze** Sinop, N Turkey
Gesoriacum *see* Boulogne-sur-Mer
Gessoriacum *see* Boulogne-sur-Mer
99 J21 **Gesves** Namur, SE Belgium
93 J20 **Geta** Åland, SW Finland
105 N8 **Getafe** Madrid, C Spain
95 J21 **Getinge** Halland, S Sweden
18 F16 **Gettysburg** Pennsylvania, NE USA
29 N8 **Gettysburg** South Dakota, N USA
194 K12 **Getz Ice Shelf** *ice shelf* Antarctica
137 S15 **Gevaş** Van, SE Turkey
Gevgeli *see* Gevgelija
113 Q20 **Gevgelija** *var.* Đevđelija, Djevdjelija, *Turk.* Gevgeli. SE Macedonia
103 T10 **Gex** Ain, E France
92 I3 **Geysir** *physical region* SW Iceland
136 F11 **Geyve** Sakarya, NW Turkey
80 G10 **Gezira** ⬖ *state* E Sudan
109 V3 **Gföhl** Niederösterreich, N Austria
83 H22 **Ghaap Plateau** *Afr.* Ghaapplato. *plateau* C South Africa
Ghaapplato *see* Ghaap Plateau
Ghaba *see* Al Ghābah
138 I8 **Ghāb, Tall** ▲ SE Syria
139 Q9 **Ghadaf, Wādī al** *dry watercourse* C Iraq
Ghadamès *see* Ghadāmis
74 M9 **Ghadāmis** *var.* Ghadamès, Rhadames. W Libya
141 Y10 **Ghadan** E Oman
75 O10 **Ghaddūwah** C Libya
147 Q11 **Ghafurov** *Rus.* Gafurov; *prev.* Sovetabad. NW Tajikistan
153 N12 **Ghāghara** ≈ S Asia
149 P13 **Ghaibi Dero** Sind, SE Pakistan
139 Y13 **Ghalat** E Oman
139 W11 **Ghamūkah, Hawr** ◎ S Iraq
77 P15 **Ghana** *off.* Republic of Ghana. ◆ *republic* W Africa
141 X12 **Ghānah** *spring/well* S Oman
Ghanongga *see* Ranongga
Ghansi/Ghansiland *see* Ghanzi
83 F18 **Ghanzi** *var.* Khanzi. Ghanzi, W Botswana
83 G19 **Ghanzi** *var.* Ghansi, Ghansiland, Khanzi. ⬖ *district* C Botswana
67 T14 **Ghanzi** *var.* Knanzi. ≈ Botswana/South Africa
Ghap'an *see* Kapan
138 F13 **Gharandal** Al'Aqabah, SW Jordan
Gharbt, Jabal al *see* Liban, Jebel
74 K7 **Ghardaïa** N Algeria
139 U14 **Gharibīyah, Sha'īb al** ≈ S Iraq
147 R12 **Gharm** *Rus.* Garm. C Tajikistan
149 P17 **Gharo** Sind, SE Pakistan
139 W10 **Gharrāf, Shaṭṭ al** ≈ S Iraq
Gharvān *see* Gharyān
75 O7 **Gharyān** *var.* Gharvān. NW Libya
74 M11 **Ghāt** *var.* Gat. SW Libya
Ghawdex *see* Gozo
141 U8 **Ghayathi** Abū Ẓaby, W United Arab Emirates
Ghazāl, Baḥr al *see* Ghazal, Bahr el
78 H9 **Ghazal, Bahr el** *var.* Soro. *seasonal river* C Chad
80 E13 **Ghazal, Bahr el** *var.* Baḥr al Ghazāl. ≈ S Sudan
74 H6 **Ghazaouet** NW Algeria
152 J10 **Ghāziābād** Uttar Pradesh, N India
153 O13 **Ghāzīpur** Uttar Pradesh, N India
149 Q6 **Ghaznī** *var.* Ghazni. Ghaznī, E Afghanistan
149 P7 **Ghaznī** ⬖ *province* SE Afghanistan
Ghazzah *see* Gaza
Gheel *see* Geel
Ghelizâne *see* Relizane
Ghent *see* Gent
Gheorghe Braţul *see* Sfântu Gheorghe, Braţul
Gheorghe Gheorghiu-Dej *see* Oneşti
116 J10 **Gheorgheni** *prev.* Gheorghieni, Sîn-Miclăuş, *Ger.* Niklasmarkt, *Hung.* Gyergyószentmiklós. Harghita, C Romania
Gheorghieni *see* Gheorgheni
116 H10 **Gherla** *Ger.* Neuschliss, *Hung.* Szamosújvár; *prev.* Armenierstadt. Cluj, NW Romania
Gheweifat *see* Ghuwayfāt
Ghilan *see* Gīlān
107 C18 **Ghilarza** Sardegna, Italy, C Mediterranean Sea
Ghilizane *see* Relizane
Ghimbi *see* Gīmbī
Ghiriş *see* Câmpia Turzii
103 Y15 **Ghisonaccia** Corse, France, C Mediterranean Sea
147 Q11 **Ghonchí** *Rus.* Ganchi. NW Tajikistan
Ghor *see* Ghowr
153 T13 **Ghoraghat** Rajshahi, NW Bangladesh
149 R13 **Ghotki** Sind, SE Pakistan
148 M5 **Ghowr** *var.* Ghor. ⬖ *province* C Afghanistan
147 T13 **Ghŭdara** *var.* Gudara, *Rus.* Kudara. SE Tajikistan
153 R13 **Ghugri** ≈ N India
147 S14 **Ghund** *Rus.* Gunt. ≈ SE Tajikistan
Ghurdaqah *see* Hurghada
148 J5 **Ghūrīān** Herāt, W Afghanistan
141 T8 **Ghuwayfāt** *var.* Gheweifat. Abū Ẓaby, W United Arab Emirates
121 O14 **Ghuzayyil, Sabkhat** *salt lake* N Libya
126 J3 **Ghzatsk** Smolenskaya Oblast', W Russian Federation
115 G17 **Giáltra** Évvoia, C Greece
Giamame *see* Jamaame
167 U13 **Gia Nghia** *var.* Đak Nông. Đắc Lắc, S Vietnam
114 F13 **Giannitsá** *var.* Yiannitsá. Kentrikí Makedonía, N Greece
107 F14 **Giannutri, Isola di** *island* Archipelago Toscano, C Italy
96 F13 **Giant's Causeway** *Ir.* Clochán an Aifir. *lava flow* N Northern Ireland, UK
167 S15 **Gia Rai** Minh Hai, S Vietnam
107 L24 **Giarre** Sicilia, Italy, C Mediterranean Sea
44 I7 **Gibara** Holguín, E Cuba
29 O16 **Gibbon** Nebraska, C USA
32 K11 **Gibbon** Oregon, NW USA
33 P11 **Gibbonsville** Idaho, NW USA
64 A13 **Gibb's Hill** *hill* S Bermuda
92 I9 **Gibostad** Troms, N Norway
104 I14 **Gibraleón** Andalucía, S Spain
104 L16 **Gibraltar** ○ (Gibraltar) S Gibraltar
104 L16 **Gibraltar** ◇ *UK dependent territory* SW Europe
Gibraltar, Détroit de/Gibraltar, Estrecho de *see* Gibraltar, Strait of
104 J17 **Gibraltar, Strait of** *Fr.* Détroit de Gibraltar, *Sp.* Estrecho de Gibraltar. *strait* Atlantic Ocean/Mediterranean Sea
31 S11 **Gibsonburg** Ohio, N USA
30 M13 **Gibson City** Illinois, N USA
180 L8 **Gibson Desert** *desert* Western Australia
10 L17 **Gibsons** British Columbia, SW Canada
149 N12 **Gīdār** Baluchistān, SW Pakistan
155 I17 **Giddalūr** Andhra Pradesh, E India
25 U10 **Giddings** Texas, SW USA
27 Y8 **Gideon** Missouri, C USA
81 I15 **Gīdolē** Southern, S Ethiopia
118 H13 **Giedraičiai** Utena, E Lithuania
103 O7 **Gien** Loiret, C France
101 G17 **Giessen** Hessen, W Germany
98 O6 **Gieten** Drenthe, NE Netherlands
23 Y13 **Gifford** Florida, SE USA
9 O5 **Gifford** ≈ Baffin Island, Nunavut, NE Canada
100 J12 **Gifhorn** Niedersachsen, N Germany
9 P13 **Gift Lake** Alberta, W Canada
164 L13 **Gifu** *var.* Gihu. Gifu, Honshū, SW Japan
164 K13 **Gifu** *off.* Gifu-ken, *var.* Gihu. ⬖ *prefecture* Honshū, SW Japan
Gifu-ken *see* Gifu
126 M13 **Gigant** Rostovskaya Oblast', SW Russian Federation
40 E8 **Giganta, Sierra de la** ▲▲ W Mexico
54 E12 **Gigante** Huila, S Colombia
114 I7 **Gigen** Pleven, N Bulgaria
Giggiga *see* Jijiga
96 G12 **Gigha Island** *island* SW Scotland, UK
107 E14 **Giglio, Isola del** *island* Archipelago Toscano, C Italy
Gihu *see* Gifu
146 L11 **G'ijduvon** *Rus.* Gizhduvon. Buxoro Viloyati, C Uzbekistan
104 L2 **Gijón** *var.* Xixón. Asturias, NW Spain
81 D20 **Gikongoro** SW Rwanda
36 K14 **Gila Bend** Arizona, SW USA
36 J14 **Gila Bend Mountains** ▲▲ Arizona, SW USA
37 N14 **Gila Mountains** ▲▲ Arizona, SW USA
36 I15 **Gila Mountains** ▲▲ Arizona, SW USA
142 M4 **Gīlān** *off.* Ostān-e Gīlān, *var.* Ghilan, Guilan. ⬖ *province* NW Iran
Gilani *see* Gnjilane
Gīlān, Ostān-e *see* Gīlān
36 L14 **Gila River** ≈ Arizona, SW USA
29 W4 **Gilbert** Minnesota, N USA
Gilbert Islands *see* Tungaru
10 L16 **Gilbert, Mount** ▲ British Columbia, SW Canada
181 U4 **Gilbert River** ≈ Queensland, NE Australia
0 C6 **Gilbert Seamounts** *undersea feature* NE Pacific Ocean
33 S7 **Gildford** Montana, NW USA
83 P15 **Gilé** Zambézia, NE Mozambique
30 K4 **Gile Flowage** ◎ Wisconsin, N USA
182 G7 **Giles, Lake** *salt lake* South Australia
75 U12 **Gilf Kebir Plateau** *Ar.* Haḍabat al Jilf al Kabīr. *plateau* SW Egypt
183 R6 **Gilgandra** New South Wales, SE Australia
Gilgău *see* Gâlgău
81 I19 **Gilgil** Rift Valley, SW Kenya
183 S4 **Gil Gil Creek** ≈ New South Wales, SE Australia
149 V3 **Gilgit** Jammu and Kashmir, NE Pakistan
149 V3 **Gilgit** ≈ N Pakistan
9 X11 **Gillam** Manitoba, C Canada
95 J22 **Gilleleje** Frederiksborg, E Denmark
30 K14 **Gillespie** Illinois, N USA
27 W13 **Gillett** Arkansas, C USA
33 X12 **Gillette** Wyoming, C USA
97 P22 **Gillingham** SE England, UK
195 X6 **Gillock Island** *island* Antarctica
173 O16 **Gillot** ✈ (St-Denis) N Réunion
65 H25 **Gill Point** *headland* E Saint Helena
30 M12 **Gilman** Illinois, N USA
25 W6 **Gilmer** Texas, SW USA
Gilolo *see* Halmahera, Pulau
81 G14 **Gīlo Wenz** ≈ SW Ethiopia
35 O10 **Gilroy** California, W USA
123 Q12 **Gilyuy** ≈ SE Russian Federation
99 I14 **Gilze** Noord-Brabant, S Netherlands
165 R16 **Gima** Okinawa, Kume-jima, SW Japan
80 H13 **Gīmbī** *It.* Ghimbi. Oromo, C Ethiopia
45 T12 **Gimie, Mount** ▲ C Saint Lucia
9 X16 **Gimli** Manitoba, S Canada
Gimma *see* Jīma
95 O14 **Gimo** Uppsala, C Sweden
102 L15 **Gimone** ≈ S France
Gimpoe *see* Gimpu
171 N12 **Gimpu** *prev.* Gimpoe. Sulawesi, C Indonesia
182 F5 **Gina** South Australia
Ginevra *see* Genève
99 J19 **Gingelom** Limburg, NE Belgium
180 I12 **Gingin** Western Australia
171 Q7 **Gingoog** Mindanao, S Philippines
81 K14 **Gīnīr** Oromo, C Ethiopia
Giohar *see* Jawhar
107 O17 **Gióia del Colle** Puglia, SE Italy
107 M22 **Gioia, Golfo di** *gulf* S Italy
Giona *see* Gkióna
115 I16 **Gioúra** *island* Vóreioi Sporádes, Greece, Aegean Sea
107 O17 **Giovinazzo** Puglia, SE Italy
Gipeswic *see* Ipswich
Gipuzkoa *see* Guipúzcoa
Giran *see* Ilan
30 K14 **Girard** Illinois, N USA
27 R7 **Girard** Kansas, C USA
25 O6 **Girard** Texas, SW USA
54 E10 **Girardot** Cundinamarca, C Colombia
172 M7 **Giraud Seamount** *undersea feature* SW Indian Ocean
83 A15 **Giraul** ≈ SW Angola
96 L9 **Girdle Ness** *headland* NE Scotland, UK
137 N11 **Giresun** *var.* Kerasunt; *anc.* Cerasus, Pharnacia. Giresun, NE Turkey
137 N12 **Giresun** *var.* Kerasunt. ⬖ *province* NE Turkey
137 N12 **Giresun Dağları** ▲▲ N Turkey
75 X10 **Girga** *var.* Girgeh, Jirjā. C Egypt
Girgeh *see* Girga
Girgenti *see* Agrigento
153 Q15 **Girīdīh** Jhārkhand, NE India
183 P6 **Girilambone** New South Wales, SE Australia
Girin *see* Jilin
121 W10 **Girne** *Gk.* Kerýneia, Kyrenia. N Cyprus
Giron *see* Kiruna
105 X5 **Girona** *var.* Gerona; *anc.* Gerunda. Cataluña, NE Spain
105 W5 **Gerona** ⬖ *province* Cataluña, NE Spain
102 J12 **Gironde** ⬖ *department* SW France
102 J11 **Gironde** *estuary* SW France
105 V5 **Gironella** Cataluña, NE Spain
103 N15 **Girou** ≈ S France
97 H14 **Girvan** W Scotland, UK
24 M9 **Girvin** Texas, SW USA
184 Q9 **Gisborne** Gisborne, North Island, New Zealand
184 P9 **Gisborne** *off.* Gisborne District. ⬖ *unitary authority* North Island, New Zealand
Gisborne District *see* Gisborne
Giseifu *see* Ŭijŏngbu
Gisenye *see* Gisenyi
81 D19 **Gisenyi** *var.* Gisenye. NW Rwanda
95 K20 **Gislaved** Jönköping, S Sweden
103 N4 **Gisors** Eure, N France
Gissar *see* Hisor
147 P12 **Gissar Range** *Rus.* Gissarskiy Khrebet. ▲▲ Tajikistan/Uzbekistan
Gissarskiy Khrebet *see* Gissar Range
99 B16 **Gistel** West-Vlaanderen, W Belgium
108 F9 **Giswil** Unterwalden, C Switzerland
115 B16 **Gitánes** *ancient monument* Ípeiros, W Greece
81 E20 **Gitarama** C Rwanda
81 E20 **Gitega** C Burundi
Githio *see* Gýtheio
108 H11 **Giubiasco** Ticino, S Switzerland
106 K13 **Giulianova** Abruzzi, C Italy
Giulie, Alpi *see* Julian Alps
Giumri *see* Gyumri
116 M13 **Giurgeni** Ialomiţa, SE Romania
116 J15 **Giurgiu** Giurgiu, S Romania
116 J14 **Giurgiu** ⬖ *county* SE Romania
95 F22 **Give** Vejle, C Denmark
103 R2 **Givet** Ardennes, N France
103 R11 **Givors** Rhône, E France
83 K19 **Giyani** Limpopo, NE South Africa
80 I13 **Giyon** Oromo, C Ethiopia
Giza/Gizeh *see* El Giza
75 V8 **Giza, Pyramids of** *ancient monument* N Egypt
Gizhduvon *see* G'ijduvon
123 U8 **Gizhiga** Magadanskaya Oblast', E Russian Federation
123 T9 **Gizhiginskaya Guba** *bay* E Russian Federation
186 K8 **Gizo** Gizo, NW Solomon Islands
110 N7 **Giżycko** Warmińsko-Mazurskie, NE Poland
Gizymałów *see* Hrymayliv
Gjakovë *see* Đakovica
94 F12 **Gjende** ◎ S Norway
95 F17 **Gjerstad** Aust-Agder, S Norway
Gjilan *see* Gnjilane
Gjinokastër *see* Gjirokastër
113 L23 **Gjirokastër** *var.* Gjirokastra; *prev.* Gjinokastër, *Gk.* Argyrokastron, *It.* Argirocastro. Gjirokastër, S Albania
113 L22 **Gjirokastër** ⬖ *district* S Albania
Gjirokastra *see* Gjirokastër
94 H13 **Gjøvik** Oppland, S Norway
113 J22 **Gjuhëzës, Kepi i** *headland* SW Albania
Gjurgjevac *see* Đurđevac
115 E18 **Gkióna** *var.* Giona. ▲▲ C Greece
121 R3 **Gkréko, Akrotíri** *var.* Cape Greco, Pidálion. *cape* E Cyprus
99 I18 **Glabbeek-Zuurbemde** Vlaams Brabant, C Belgium
13 R14 **Glace Bay** Cape Breton Island, Nova Scotia, SE Canada
9 O16 **Glacier** British Columbia, SW Canada
39 W12 **Glacier Bay** *inlet* Alaska, USA
32 I7 **Glacier Peak** ▲ Washington, NW USA
21 Q7 **Glade Spring** Virginia, NE USA
43 W7 **Gladewater** Texas, SW USA
181 Y8 **Gladstone** Queensland, E Australia
182 I8 **Gladstone** South Australia
9 X16 **Gladstone** Manitoba, S Canada
31 O5 **Gladstone** Michigan, N USA
27 R4 **Gladstone** Missouri, C USA
31 Q7 **Gladwin** Michigan, N USA
95 J15 **Glafsfjorden** ◎ C Sweden
92 H2 **Glåma** *physical region* NW Iceland
94 I12 **Glåma** *var.* Glommen. ≈ S Norway

◆ Country ● Country Capital ◇ Dependent Territory ○ Dependent Territory Capital ⬖ Administrative Regions ✈ International Airport ▲ Mountain ▲▲ Mountain Range Volcano ≈ River ◎ Lake ⊠ Reservoir

112 *F13* **Glamoč** ◈ Federacija Bosna I Hercegovina, NE Boznia and Herzegovina
97 *J22* **Glamorgan** *cultural region* S Wales, UK
95 *G24* **Glamsbjerg** Fyn, C Denmark
171 *Q8* **Glan** Mindanao, S Philippines
109 *T9* **Glan** ≈ SE Austria
101 *F19* **Glan** ≈ W Germany
95 *M17* **Glan** ◎ S Sweden
Glaris *see* Glarus
108 *H9* **Glarner Alpen** *Eng.* Glarus Alps. ▲▲ E Switzerland
108 *H8* **Glarus** Glarus, E Switzerland
108 *H9* **Glarus** *Fr.* Glaris. ◈ *canton* C Switzerland
Glarus Alps *see* Glarner Alpen
27 *N3* **Glasco** Kansas, C USA
96 *I12* **Glasgow** S Scotland, UK
20 *K7* **Glasgow** Kentucky, S USA
27 *T4* **Glasgow** Missouri, C USA
33 *W7* **Glasgow** Montana, NW USA
21 *T6* **Glasgow** Virginia, NE USA
96 *I12* **Glasgow** ✈ W Scotland, UK
9 *S14* **Glaslyn** Saskatchewan, S Canada
18 *I16* **Glassboro** New Jersey, NE USA
24 *L10* **Glass Mountains** ▲▲ Texas, SW USA
97 *K23* **Glastonbury** SW England, UK
Glatz *see* Kłodzko
101 *N16* **Glauchau** Sachsen, E Germany
Glavn'a Morava *see* Velika Morava
113 *N16* **Glavnik** Kosovo, S Serbia
127 *T1* **Glazov** Udmurtskaya Respublika, NW Russian Federation
Głda *see* Gwda
109 *U8* **Gleinalpe** ▲▲ SE Austria
109 *W8* **Gleisdorf** Steiermark, SE Austria
Gleiwitz *see* Gliwice
39 *S11* **Glenallen** Alaska, USA
102 *F7* **Glénan, Îles** *island group* NW France
185 *G21* **Glenavy** Canterbury, South Island, New Zealand
10 *H5* **Glenboyle** Yukon Territory, NW Canada
21 *X3* **Glen Burnie** Maryland, NE USA
36 *L8* **Glen Canyon** *canyon* Utah, W USA
36 *L8* **Glen Canyon Dam** *dam* Arizona, SW USA
30 *K15* **Glen Carbon** Illinois, N USA
14 *E17* **Glencoe** Ontario, S Canada
83 *K22* **Glencoe** KwaZulu/Natal, E South Africa
29 *U9* **Glencoe** Minnesota, N USA
96 *H10* **Glen Coe** *valley* N Scotland, UK
36 *K13* **Glendale** Arizona, SW USA
35 *S15* **Glendale** California, W USA
182 *G5* **Glendambo** South Australia
33 *Y8* **Glendive** Montana, NW USA
33 *Y15* **Glendo** Wyoming, C USA
55 *S10* **Glendor Mountians** ▲▲ C Guyana
182 *K12* **Glenelg River** ≈ South Australia/Victoria, SE Australia
29 *P4* **Glenfield** North Dakota, N USA
25 *V12* **Glen Flora** Texas, SW USA
181 *P7* **Glen Helen** Northern Territory, N Australia
183 *U5* **Glen Innes** New South Wales, SE Australia
31 *P6* **Glen Lake** ◎ Michigan, N USA
10 *I7* **Glenlyon Peak** ▲ Yukon Territory, W Canada
37 *N16* **Glenn, Mount** ▲ Arizona, SW USA
33 *N15* **Glenns Ferry** Idaho, NW USA
23 *W6* **Glennville** Georgia, SE USA
10 *J10* **Glenora** British Columbia, W Canada
182 *M11* **Glenorchy** Victoria, SE Australia
183 *V5* **Glenreagh** New South Wales, SE Australia
33 *X15* **Glenrock** Wyoming, C USA
96 *K11* **Glenrothes** E Scotland, UK
18 *L9* **Glens Falls** New York, NE USA
97 *D14* **Glenties** *Ir.* Na Gleannta. Donegal, NW Ireland
28 *L5* **Glen Ullin** North Dakota, N USA
21 *R4* **Glenville** West Virginia, NE USA
27 *T12* **Glenwood** Arkansas, C USA
29 *S15* **Glenwood** Iowa, C USA
29 *T7* **Glenwood** Minnesota, N USA
36 *L5* **Glenwood** Utah, W USA
30 *I5* **Glenwood City** Wisconsin, N USA
37 *Q4* **Glenwood Springs** Colorado, C USA
108 *F10* **Gletsch** Valais, S Switzerland
Glevum *see* Gloucester
29 *U14* **Glidden** Iowa, C USA
112 *E9* **Glina** Sisak-Moslavina, NE Croatia
94 *F11* **Glittertind** ▲ S Norway
111 *J16* **Gliwice** *Ger.* Gleiwitz. Śląskie, S Poland
36 *M14* **Globe** Arizona, SW USA
Globino *see* Hlobyne
108 *L9* **Glockturm** ▲ SW Austria
116 *L9* **Glodeni** *Rus.* Glodyany. N Moldova
109 *S9* **Glödnitz** Kärnten, S Austria
Glodyany *see* Glodeni
Glogau *see* Głogów
109 *W6* **Gloggnitz** Niederösterreich, E Austria
110 *F13* **Głogów** *Ger.* Glogau, Glogow. Dolnośląskie, SW Poland
Glogow *see* Głogów
111 *I16* **Głogówek** *Ger.* Oberglogau. Opolskie, S Poland
92 *G12* **Glomfjord** Nordland, C Norway
Glomma *see* Glåma
Glommen *see* Glåma
93 *I14* **Glommersträsk** Norrbotten, N Sweden
172 *I1* **Glorieuses, Nosy** *island* N Madagascar
65 *C25* **Glorious Hill** *hill* East Falkland, Falkland Islands
38 *J12* **Glory of Russia Cape** *headland* Saint Matthew Island, Alaska, USA
22 *J7* **Gloster** Mississippi, S USA
183 *U7* **Gloucester** New South Wales, SE Australia
186 *F7* **Gloucester** New Britain, E Papua New Guinea
97 *L21* **Gloucester** *hist.* Caer Glou, *Lat.* Glevum. C England, UK
19 *P10* **Gloucester** Massachusetts, NE USA
21 *X6* **Gloucester** Virginia, NE USA
97 *K21* **Gloucestershire** *cultural region* C England, UK
31 *T14* **Glouster** Ohio, N USA
42 *H3* **Glovers Reef** *reef* E Belize
18 *K10* **Gloversville** New York, NE USA
110 *K12* **Głowno** Łódź, C Poland
111 *H16* **Głubczyce** *Ger.* Leobschütz. Opolskie, S Poland
126 *L11* **Glubokiy** Rostovskaya Oblast', SW Russian Federation
145 *W9* **Glubokoye** Vostochnyy Kazakhstan, E Kazakhstan
Glubokoye *see* Hlybokaye
111 *H16* **Głuchołazy** *Ger.* Ziegenhais. Opolskie, S Poland
100 *I9* **Glückstadt** Schleswig-Holstein, N Germany
Glukhov *see* Hlukhiv
Glushkevichi *see* Hlushkavichy
Glusk/Glussk *see* Hlusk
Glybokaya *see* Hlyboka
95 *F21* **Glyngøre** Viborg, NW Denmark
127 *Q9* **Gmelinka** Volgogradskaya Oblast', SW Russian Federation
109 *R8* **Gmünd** Kärnten, S Austria
109 *U2* **Gmünd** Niederösterreich, N Austria
Gmünd *see* Schwäbisch Gmünd
109 *S5* **Gmunden** Oberösterreich, N Austria
Gmundner See *see* Traunsee
94 *N10* **Gnarp** Gävleborg, C Sweden
109 *W8* **Gnas** Steiermark, SE Austria
Gnaviyani Atoll *see* Fuammulah
Gnesen *see* Gniezno
95 *O16* **Gnesta** Södermanland, C Sweden
110 *H11* **Gniezno** *Ger.* Gnesen. Weilkopolskie, C Poland
113 *O17* **Gnjilane** *var.* Gilani, *Alb.* Gjilan. Kosovo, S Serbia
95 *K20* **Gnosjö** Jönköping, S Sweden
155 *E17* **Goa** *prev.* Old Goa, Vela Goa, Velha Goa. Goa, W India
155 *E17* **Goa** *var.* Old Goa. ◈ *state* W India
Goabddális *see* Kåbdalis
42 *H7* **Goascorán, Río** ≈ El Salvador/Honduras
77 *O16* **Goaso** *var.* Gawso. W Ghana
81 *K14* **Goba** *It.* Oromo. Oromo, C Ethiopia
83 *C20* **Gobabed** Erongo, W Namibia
83 *E19* **Gobabis** Omaheke, E Namibia
Gobannium *see* Abergavenny
64 *M7* **Goban Spur** *undersea feature* NW Atlantic Ocean
63 *H21* **Gobernador Gregores** Santa Cruz, S Argentina
61 *F14* **Gobernador Ingeniero Virasoro** Corrientes, NE Argentina
162 *L12* **Gobi** *desert* China/Mongolia
164 *I14* **Gobō** Wakayama, Honshū, SW Japan
Gobolka Awdal *see* Awdal
Gobolka Sahil *see* Sahil
Gobolka Sool *see* Sool
101 *D14* **Goch** Nordrhein-Westfalen, W Germany
83 *E20* **Gochas** Hardap, S Namibia
155 *I14* **Godāvari** *var.* Godavari. ≈ C India
Godavari *see* Godāvari
155 *L16* **Godāvari, Mouths of the** *delta* E India
15 *V5* **Godbout** Québec, SE Canada
15 *U5* **Godbout** ≈ Québec, SE Canada
15 *U5* **Godbout Est** ≈ Québec, SE Canada
27 *N6* **Goddard** Kansas, C USA
14 *E15* **Goderich** Ontario, S Canada
Godhavn *see* Qeqertarsuaq
154 *E10* **Godhra** Gujarāt, W India
Göding *see* Hodonín
111 *K22* **Gödöllő** Pest, N Hungary
62 *H11* **Godoy Cruz** Mendoza, W Argentina
9 *Y11* **Gods** ≈ Manitoba, C Canada
9 *Y13* **Gods Lake** Manitoba, C Canada
9 *X13* **Gods Lake** ◎ Manitoba, C Canada
Godthaab/Godthåb *see* Nuuk
Godwin Austen, Mount *see* K2
Goede Hoop, Kaap de *see* Good Hope, Cape of
Goedgegun *see* Nhlangano
Goeie Hoop, Kaap die *see* Good Hope, Cape of
13 *O7* **Goélands, Lac aux** ◎ Québec, SE Canada
98 *E13* **Goeree** *island* SW Netherlands
99 *F15* **Goes** Zeeland, SW Netherlands
Goettingen *see* Göttingen
19 *O10* **Goffstown** New Hampshire, NE USA
14 *E8* **Gogama** Ontario, S Canada
30 *L3* **Gogebic, Lake** ◎ Michigan, N USA
30 *K3* **Gogebic Range** *hill range* Michigan/Wisconsin, N USA
Gogi Lerr *see* Gogi, Mount
137 *V13* **Gogi, Mount** *Arm.* Gogi Lerr, *Az.* Küküdağ. ▲ Armenia/Azerbaijan
124 *F12* **Gogland, Ostrov** *island* NW Russian Federation
111 *I15* **Gogolin** Opolskie, S Poland
Gogonou *see* Gogounou
77 *S14* **Gogounou** *var.* Gogonou. N Benin
152 *I10* **Gohāna** Haryāna, N India
59 *K18* **Goianésia** Goiás, C Brazil
59 *K18* **Goiânia** *prev.* Goyania. *state capital* Goiás, C Brazil
59 *K18* **Goiás** Goiás, C Brazil
59 *J18* **Goiás** *off.* Estado de Goiás; *prev.* Goiaz, Goyaz. ◈ *state* C Brazil
Goiás, Estado de *see* Goiás
Goiaz *see* Goiás
159 *R14* **Goinsargoin** Xizang Zizhiqu, W China
60 *H10* **Goio-Erê** Paraná, SW Brazil
99 *I15* **Goirle** Noord-Brabant, S Netherlands
104 *H8* **Góis** Coimbra, N Portugal
165 *Q8* **Gojōme** Akita, Honshū, NW Japan
149 *U9* **Gojra** Punjab, E Pakistan
136 *A11* **Gökçeada** *var.* Imroz Adasī, *Gk.* Imbros. *island* NW Turkey
Gökçeada *see* İmroz
146 *F13* **Gökdepe** *Rus.* Gëkdepe, Geok-Tepe. Ahal Welaýaty, C Turkmenistan
136 *I10* **Gökīrmak** ≈ N Turkey
Goklenkuy, Solonchak *see* Geklengkui, Solonchak
136 *C16* **Gökova Körfezi** *gulf* SW Turkey
136 *K15* **Göksu** ≈ S Turkey
136 *L15* **Göksun** Kahramanmaraş, C Turkey
136 *I17* **Göksu Nehri** ≈ S Turkey
83 *J16* **Gokwe** Midlands, NW Zimbabwe
94 *F13* **Gol** Buskerud, S Norway
153 *X12* **Golāghāt** Assam, NE India
110 *H10* **Gołańcz** Wielkopolskie, C Poland
138 *G8* **Golan Heights** *Ar.* Al Jawlān, *Heb.* HaGolan. ▲▲ SW Syria
Golārā *see* Ārān
Golaya Pristan *see* Hola Prystan'
143 *T11* **Golbāf** Kermān, C Iran
136 *M15* **Gölbaşı** Adıyaman, S Turkey
109 *P9* **Gölbner** ▲ SW Austria
30 *M17* **Golconda** Illinois, N USA
35 *T3* **Golconda** Nevada, W USA
136 *E11* **Gölcük** Kocaeli, NW Turkey
108 *I7* **Goldach** Sankt Gallen, NE Switzerland
110 *N7* **Gołdap** *Ger.* Goldap. Warmińsko-Mazurskie, NE Poland
32 *E15* **Gold Beach** Oregon, NW USA
Goldberg *see* Złotoryja
183 *V3* **Gold Coast** *cultural region* Queensland, E Australia
68 *D12* **Gold Coast** *coastal region* S Ghana
39 *R10* **Gold Creek** Alaska, USA
9 *O16* **Golden** British Columbia, SW Canada
37 *T4* **Golden** Colorado, C USA
184 *I13* **Golden Bay** *bay* South Island, New Zealand
27 *R7* **Golden City** Missouri, C USA
32 *I11* **Goldendale** Washington, NW USA
Goldener Tisch *see* Zlatý Stôl
44 *L13* **Golden Grove** E Jamaica
14 *J12* **Golden Lake** ◎ Ontario, SE Canada
22 *K10* **Golden Meadow** Louisiana, S USA
45 *V10* **Golden Rock** ✈ (Basseterre) Saint Kitts, Saint Kitts and Nevis
Golden State, The *see* California
83 *K16* **Golden Valley** Mashonaland West, N Zimbabwe
35 *U9* **Goldfield** Nevada, W USA
Goldingen *see* Kuldīga
Goldmarkt *see* Zlatna
10 *K17* **Gold River** Vancouver Island, British Columbia, SW Canada
21 *V10* **Goldsboro** North Carolina, SE USA
24 *M8* **Goldsmith** Texas, SW USA
25 *R8* **Goldthwaite** Texas, SW USA
137 *R11* **Göle** Ardahan, NE Turkey
Golema Ada *see* Ostrovo
114 *H9* **Golema Planina** ▲▲ W Bulgaria
114 *F9* **Golemi Vrŭkh** ▲ W Bulgaria
110 *D8* **Goleniów** *Ger.* Gollnow. Zachodnio-pomorskie, NW Poland
143 *R3* **Golestān** ◈ *province* N Iran
35 *Q14* **Goleta** California, W USA
43 *O16* **Golfito** Puntarenas, SE Costa Rica
25 *T13* **Goliad** Texas, SW USA
113 *L14* **Golija** ▲▲ SW Serbia
Golinka *see* Gongbo'gyamda
113 *O16* **Goljak** ▲▲ SE Serbia
136 *M12* **Gölköy** Ordu, N Turkey
Gollel *see* Lavumisa
109 *X3* **Göllersbach** ≈ NE Austria
Gollnow *see* Goleniów
Golmo *see* Golmud
159 *P10* **Golmud** *var.* Ge'e'mu, Golmo, *Chin.* Ko-erh-mu. Qinghai, C China
103 *Y14* **Golo** ≈ Corse, France, C Mediterranean Sea
Golovanevsk *see* Holovanivs'k
Golovchin *see* Halowchyn
39 *N9* **Golovin** Alaska, USA
142 *M7* **Golpāyegān** *var.* Gulpaigan. Eşfahān, W Iran
Golshan *see* Ţabas
Gol'shany *see* Hal'shany
96 *J7* **Golspie** N Scotland, UK
112 *O11* **Golubac** Serbia, NE Serbia
110 *J9* **Golub-Dobrzyń** Kujawski-pomorskie, C Poland
145 *S7* **Golubovka** Pavlodar, N Kazakhstan
82 *B11* **Golungo Alto** Cuanza Norte, NW Angola
114 *M8* **Golyama Kamchiya** ≈ E Bulgaria
114 *L8* **Golyama Reka** ≈ N Bulgaria
114 *H11* **Golyama Syutkya** ▲ SW Bulgaria
114 *I12* **Golyam Perelik** ▲ S Bulgaria
114 *I11* **Golyam Persenk** ▲ S Bulgaria
79 *P19* **Goma** Nord Kivu, NE Dem. Rep. Congo
Gomati *see* Gumti
77 *X14* **Gombe** Gombe, E Nigeria
67 *U10* **Gombe** *var.* Igombe. ≈ E Tanzania
77 *Y14* **Gombi** Adamawa, E Nigeria
Gombroon *see* Bandar-e 'Abbās
Gomel' *see* Homyel'
Gomel'skaya Oblast' *see* Homyel'skaya Voblasts'
64 *N11* **Gomera** *island* Islas Canarias, Spain, NE Atlantic Ocean
40 *I5* **Gómez Farias** Chihuahua, N Mexico
40 *L8* **Gómez Palacio** Durango, C Mexico
158 *J13* **Gomo** Xizang Zizhiqu, W China
143 *T6* **Gonābād** *var.* Gunabad. Khorāsān, NE Iran
44 *L8* **Gonaïves** *var.* Les Gonaïves. N Haiti
123 *Q12* **Gonam** ≈ NE Russian Federation
44 *L9* **Gonâve, Canal de la** *var.* Canal de Sud. *channel* N Caribbean Sea
44 *K9* **Gonâve, Golfe de la** *gulf* N Caribbean Sea
Gonāveh *see* Bandar-e Gonāveh
44 *K9* **Gonâve, Île de la** *island* C Haiti
Gonbadān *see* Dow Gonbadān
143 *Q3* **Gonbad-e Kāvūs** *var.* Gunbad-i-Qawus. Golestán, N Iran
152 *M12* **Gonda** Uttar Pradesh, N India
Gondar *see* Gonder
80 *I11* **Gonder** *var.* Gondar. NW Ethiopia
78 *J13* **Gondey** Moyen-Chari, S Chad
154 *J12* **Gondia** Mahārāshtra, C India
104 *G6* **Gondomar** Porto, NW Portugal
136 *C12* **Gönen** Balıkesir, W Turkey
136 *C12* **Gönen Çayī** ≈ NW Turkey
159 *O15* **Gongbo'gyamda** *var.* Golinka. Xizang Zizhiqu, W China
159 *N16* **Gonggar** *var.* Gyixong. Xizang Zizhiqu, W China
160 *G9* **Gongga Shan** ▲ C China
159 *T10* **Gonghe** *var.* Qabqa. Qinghai, C China
158 *I5* **Gongliu** *var.* Tokkuztara. Xinjiang Uygur Zizhiqu, NW China
77 *W14* **Gongola** ≈ E Nigeria
Gongoleh State *see* Jonglei
183 *P5* **Gongolgon** New South Wales, SE Australia
159 *Q6* **Gongpoquan** Gansu, N China
Gongquan *see* Gongxian
Gongtang *see* Damxung
160 *I10* **Gongxian** *var.* Gongquan, Gong Xian. Sichuan, C China
Gong Xian *see* Gongxian
157 *V10* **Gongzhuling** *prev.* Huaide. Jilin, NE China
159 *S14* **Gonjo** Xizang Zizhiqu, W China
107 *B20* **Gonnesa** Sardegna, Italy, C Mediterranean Sea
Gonni/Gónnos *see* Gónnoi
115 *F15* **Gónnoi** *var.* Gonni, Gónnos; *prev.* Derelí. Thessalía, C Greece
164 *C13* **Gōnoura** Nagasaki, Iki, SW Japan
35 *O11* **Gonzales** California, W USA
22 *J9* **Gonzales** Louisiana, S USA
25 *T12* **Gonzales** Texas, SW USA
41 *P11* **González** Tamaulipas, C Mexico
21 *V6* **Goochland** Virginia, NE USA
195 *X14* **Goodenough, Cape** *headland* Antarctica
186 *F9* **Goodenough Island** *var.* Morata. *island* SE Papua New Guinea
Good Hope *see* Fort Good Hope
39 *N8* **Goodhope Bay** *bay* Alaska, USA
83 *D26* **Good Hope, Cape of** *Afr.* Kaap de Goede Hoop, Kaap die Goeie Hoop. *cape* SW South Africa
10 *K10* **Good Hope Lake** British Columbia, W Canada
83 *E23* **Goodhouse** Northern Cape, W South Africa
33 *O15* **Gooding** Idaho, NW USA
26 *H3* **Goodland** Kansas, C USA
173 *Y15* **Goodlands** NW Mauritius
20 *J8* **Goodlettsville** Tennessee, S USA
39 *N13* **Goodnews** Alaska, USA
25 *O3* **Goodnight** Texas, SW USA
183 *Q4* **Goodooga** New South Wales, SE Australia
29 *N4* **Goodrich** North Dakota, N USA
25 *W10* **Goodrich** Texas, SW USA
29 *X10* **Goodview** Minnesota, N USA
26 *H8* **Goodwell** Oklahoma, C USA
97 *N17* **Goole** E England, UK
183 *O8* **Goolgowi** New South Wales, SE Australia
182 *I10* **Goolwa** South Australia
181 *Y11* **Goondiwindi** Queensland, E Australia
98 *O11* **Goor** Overijssel, E Netherlands
Goose Bay *see* Happy Valley-Goose Bay
33 *V13* **Gooseberry Creek** ≈ Wyoming, C USA
21 *S14* **Goose Creek** South Carolina, SE USA
63 *M23* **Goose Green** *var* Prado del Ganso. East Falkland, Falkland Islands
16 *D8* **Goose Lake** *var.* Lago dos Gansos. ◎ California/Oregon, W USA
29 *Q4* **Goose River** ≈ North Dakota, N USA
153 *T16* **Gopalganj** Dhaka, S Bangladesh
153 *O12* **Gopālganj** Bihār, N India
Gopher State *see* Minnesota
101 *I22* **Göppingen** Baden-Württemberg, SW Germany
110 *G13* **Góra** *Ger.* Guhrau. Dolnośląskie, SW Poland
110 *M12* **Góra Kalwaria** Mazowieckie, C Poland
153 *O12* **Gorakhpur** Uttar Pradesh, N India
Gora Kyuren *see* Kurendag
Gorany *see* Harany
113 *J14* **Goražde** Fedaracija Bosna I Hercegovina, SE Bosnia and Herzegovina
Gorbovichi *see* Harbavichy
Gorče Petrov *see* Đorče Petrov
0 *E9* **Gorda Ridges** *undersea feature* NE Pacific Ocean
Gordiaz *see* Gardīz
78 *K12* **Gordil** Vakaga, N Central African Republic
23 *U5* **Gordon** Georgia, SE USA
28 *K12* **Gordon** Nebraska, C USA
25 *R7* **Gordon** Texas, SW USA
28 *L13* **Gordon Creek** ≈ Nebraska, C USA
63 *I25* **Gordon, Isla** *island* S Chile
183 *O17* **Gordon, Lake** ◎ Tasmania, SE Australia
183 *O17* **Gordon River** ≈ Tasmania, SE Australia
21 *V5* **Gordonsville** Virginia, NE USA
78 *H13* **Goré** Logone-Oriental, S Chad
80 *H13* **Gorē** Oromo, C Ethiopia
185 *D24* **Gore** Southland, South Island, New Zealand
14 *D11* **Gore Bay** Manitoulin Island, Ontario, S Canada
25 *Q5* **Goree** Texas, SW USA
137 *O11* **Görele** Giresun, NE Turkey
19 *N6* **Gore Mountain** ▲ Vermont, NE USA
39 *R13* **Gore Point** *headland* Alaska, USA
37 *R4* **Gore Range** ▲▲ Colorado, C USA
97 *F19* **Gorey** *Ir.* Guaire. Wexford, SE Ireland
143 *R12* **Gorgāb** Kermān, S Iran
143 *Q4* **Gorgān** *var.* Astarabad, Astrabad, Gurgan, *prev.* Asterābād; *anc.* Hyrcania. Golestán, N Iran
143 *Q4* **Gorgān, Rūd-e** ≈ N Iran
76 *I10* **Gorgol** ◈ *region* S Mauritania
106 *D12* **Gorgona, Isola di** *island* Archipelago Toscano, C Italy
19 *P8* **Gorham** Maine, NE USA
137 *T10* **Gori** C Georgia
98 *I13* **Gorinchem** *var.* Gorkum. Zuid-Holland, C Netherlands
137 *V13* **Goris** SE Armenia
124 *K16* **Goritsy** Tverskaya Oblast', W Russian Federation
106 *J7* **Gorizia** *Ger.* Görz. Friuli-Venezia Giulia, NE Italy
116 *G13* **Gorj** ◈ *county* SW Romania
109 *W12* **Gorjanci** *var.* Uskočke Planine, Žumberak, Žumberačko Gorje, *Ger.* Uskokengebirge; *prev.* Sichelburger Gerbirge. ▲ Croatia/Slovenia Europe *see also* Žumberačko Gorje
Görkau *see* Jirkov
Gorki *see* Horki
Gor'kiy *see* Nizhniy Novgorod
Gorkum *see* Gorinchem
95 *I23* **Gørlev** Vestsjælland, E Denmark
111 *M17* **Gorlice** Małopolskie, S Poland
101 *Q15* **Görlitz** Sachsen, E Germany
Görlitz *see* Zgorzelec
Gorlovka *see* Horlivka
25 *R7* **Gorman** Texas, SW USA
21 *T3* **Gormania** West Virginia, NE USA
Gorna Dzhumaya *see* Blagoevgrad
114 *K8* **Gorna Oryakhovitsa** Veliko Tŭrnovo, N Bulgaria
114 *J8* **Gorna Studena** Veliko Tŭrnovo, N Bulgaria
Gornja Mužlja *see* Mužlja
109 *X9* **Gornja Radgona** *Ger.* Oberradkersburg. NE Slovenia
112 *M13* **Gornji Milanovac** Serbia, C Serbia
112 *G13* **Gornji Vakuf** *var* Uskoplje. Federacija Bosna I Hercegovina, SW Bosnia and Herzegovina
122 *J13* **Gorno-Altaysk** Respublika Altay, S Russian Federation
Gorno-Altayskaya Respublika *see* Altay, Respublika
123 *N12* **Gorno-Chuyskiy** Irkutskaya Oblast', C Russian Federation
125 *V14* **Gornozavodsk** Permskaya Oblast', NW Russian Federation
125 *V14* **Gornozavodsk** Ostrov Sakhalin, Sakhalinskaya Oblast', SE Russian Federation
122 *I13* **Gornyak** Altayskiy Kray, S Russian Federation
127 *R8* **Gornyy** Chitunskaya Oblast', S Russian Federation
Gornyy Altay *see* Altay, Respublika
127 *O10* **Gornyy Balykley** Volgogradskaya Oblast', SW Russian Federation
80 *I13* **Goroch'an** ▲ W Ethiopia
Gorodenka *see* Horodenka
127 *O3* **Gorodets** Nizhegorodskaya Oblast', W Russian Federation
Gorodets *see* Haradzyets
Gorodeya *see* Haradzyeya
127 *P6* **Gorodishche** Penzenskaya Oblast', W Russian Federation
Gorodishche *see* Horodyshche
Gorodnya *see* Horodnya
Gorodok *see* Haradok
Gorodok/Gorodok Yagellonski *see* Horodok
126 *M13* **Gorodovikovsk** Respublika Kalmykiya, SW Russian Federation
186 *D7* **Goroka** Eastern Highlands, C Papua New Guinea
Gorokhov *see* Horokhiv
127 *N3* **Gorokhovets** Vladimirskaya Oblast', W Russian Federation
77 *Q11* **Gorom-Gorom** NE Burkina
171 *U13* **Gorong, Kepulauan** *island group* E Indonesia
83 *M17* **Gorongosa** Sofala, C Mozambique
171 *P11* **Gorontalo** Sulawesi, C Indonesia
Gorontalo, Teluk *see* Tomini, Gulf of
110 *L7* **Górowo Iławeckie** *Ger.* Landsberg. Warmińsko-Mazurskie, NE Poland
98 *M7* **Gorredijk** *Fris.* De Gordyk. Friesland, N Netherlands
84 *C14* **Gorringe Ridge** *undersea feature* E Atlantic Ocean
98 *M11* **Gorssel** Gelderland, E Netherlands
109 *T8* **Görtschitz** ≈ S Austria
Goryn *see* Horyn'
Görz *see* Gorizia
110 *E10* **Gorzów Wielkopolski** *Ger.* Landsberg, Landsberg an der Warthe. Lubuskie, W Poland
146 *B10* **Goşabo** *var.* Goshoba, *Rus.* Koshoba. Balkan Welaýaty, NW Turkmenistan
108 *G9* **Göschenen** Uri, C Switzerland
165 *O11* **Gosen** Niigata, Honshū, C Japan
183 *T8* **Gosford** New South Wales, SE Australia
31 *P11* **Goshen** Indiana, N USA
18 *K13* **Goshen** New York, NE USA
Goshoba *see* Goşabo
Goshoba *see* Goşoba
165 *Q7* **Goshogawara** *var.* Gosyogawara. Aomori, Honshū, C Japan
Goshquduq Qum *see* Tosquduq Qumlari
101 *J14* **Goslar** Niedersachsen, C Germany
27 *Y9* **Gosnell** Arkansas, C USA
146 *B10* **Goşoba** *var.* Goshoba, *Rus.* Koshoba. Balkanskiy Velayat, NW Turkmenistan
112 *C11* **Gospić** Lika-Senj, C Croatia
97 *N23* **Gosport** S England, UK
94 *D9* **Gossa** *island* S Norway
108 *H7* **Gossau** Sankt Gallen, NE Switzerland
99 *G20* **Gosselies** *var.* Goss'lies. Hainaut, S Belgium
77 *P10* **Gossi** Tombouctou, C Mali
Goss'lies *see* Gosselies
113 *N18* **Gostivar** W FYR Macedonia
Gostomel' *see* Hostomel'
110 *G12* **Gostyń** *var.* Gostyn. Wielkopolskie, C Poland
Gostyn *see* Gostyń
110 *K11* **Gostynin** Mazowiesckie, C Poland
Gosyogawara *see* Goshogawara
95 *J18* **Göta Älv** ≈ S Sweden
95 *N17* **Göta kanal** *canal* S Sweden
95 *K18* **Götaland** *cultural region* S Sweden
95 *H17* **Göteborg** *Eng.* Gothenburg. Västra Götaland, S Sweden
77 *X16* **Gotel Mountains** ▲▲ E Nigeria
95 *K17* **Götene** Västra Götaland, S Sweden
Gotera *see* San Francisco
101 *K16* **Gotha** Thüringen, C Germany
29 *N15* **Gothenburg** Nebraska, C USA
Gothenburg *see* Göteborg
77 *R12* **Gothèye** Tillabéri, SW Niger
Gothland *see* Gotland
95 *P19* **Gotland** *var.* Gothland, Gottland. ◈ *county* SE Sweden
95 *O18* **Gotland** *island* SE Sweden
164 *B13* **Gotō-rettō** *island group* SW Japan
114 *H12* **Gotse Delchev** *prev.* Nevrokop. Blagoevgrad, SW Bulgaria
95 *P17* **Gotska Sandön** *island* SE Sweden
101 *I15* **Göttingen** *var.* Goettingen. Niedersachsen, C Germany
Gottland *see* Gotland
93 *I16* **Gottne** Västernorrland, C Sweden
Gottschee *see* Kočevje
Gottwaldov *see* Zlín
146 *B11* **Goturdepe** *Rus.* Koturdepe. Balkan Welaýaty, W Turkmenistan
108 *I7* **Götzis** Vorarlberg, NW Austria
98 *H12* **Gouda** Zuid-Holland, C Netherlands
76 *I11* **Goudiri** *var.* Goudiry. E Senegal
Goudiry *see* Goudiri
77 *X12* **Goudoumaria** Diffa, S Niger
15 *R9* **Gouffre, Rivière du** ≈ Québec, SE Canada
65 *M19* **Gough Fracture Zone** *tectonic feature* S Atlantic Ocean
65 *M19* **Gough Island** *island* Tristan da Cunha, S Atlantic Ocean
15 *N8* **Gouin, Réservoir** ⊠ Québec, SE Canada
14 *B10* **Goulais River** Ontario, S Canada
183 *R9* **Goulburn** New South Wales, SE Australia
183 *O11* **Goulburn River** ≈ Victoria, SE Australia
195 *O10* **Gould Coast** *physical region* Antarctica
Goulimime *see* Guelmime
114 *F13* **Gouménissa** Kentrikí Makedonía, N Greece
77 *O10* **Goundam** Tombouctou, NW Mali
78 *H12* **Goundi** Moyen-Chari, S Chad
78 *G12* **Gounou-Gaya** Mayo-Kébbi, SW Chad
77 *O12* **Gourci** *var.* Gourcy. NW Burkina
Gourcy *see* Gourci
102 *M13* **Gourdon** Lot, S France
77 *W11* **Gouré** Zinder, SE Niger
102 *G6* **Gourin** Morbihan, NW France
77 *P10* **Gourma-Rharous** Tombouctou, C Mali
103 *N4* **Gournay-en-Bray** Seine-Maritime, N France
78 *J6* **Gouro** Borkou-Ennedi-Tibesti, N Chad
104 *H8* **Gouveia** Guarda, N Portugal
18 *I7* **Gouverneur** New York, NE USA
99 *L21* **Gouvy** Luxembourg, E Belgium
45 *R14* **Gouyave** *var.* Charlotte Town. NW Grenada
Goverla, Gora *see* Hoverla, Hora
59 *N20* **Governador Valadares** Minas Gerais, SE Brazil
171 *R8* **Governor Generoso** Mindanao, S Philippines
44 *I2* **Governor's Harbour** Eleuthera Island, C Bahamas
162 *F9* **Govĭ-Altay** ◈ *province* SW Mongolia
162 *I10* **Govĭ Altayn Nuruu** ▲▲ S Mongolia
154 *L9* **Govind Ballabh Pant Sāgar** ⊠ C India
152 *I7* **Govind Sāgar** ⊠ NE India

◆ Country
● Country Capital
◇ Dependent Territory
○ Dependent Territory Capital
◈ Administrative Regions
✈ International Airport
▲ Mountain
▲▲ Mountain Range
Volcano
≈ River
◎ Lake
⊠ Reservoir

162 *M8* **Govĭ-Sumber** ◈ *province* C Mongolia
Govurdak *see* Govurdak
18 *D11* **Gowanda** New York, NE USA
148 *J10* **Gowd-e Zereh, Dasht-e** *var.* Guad-i-Zirreh. *marsh* SW Afghanistan
14 *F8* **Gowganda** Ontario, S Canada
14 *G8* **Gowganda Lake** ◎ Ontario, S Canada
29 *U13* **Gowrie** Iowa, C USA
147 *N14* **Govurdak** *Rus.* Govurdak; *prev.* Guardak. Lebap Welaýaty, E Turkmenistan
61 *C15* **Goya** Corrientes, NE Argentina
Goyania *see* Goiânia
Goyaz *see* Goiás
137 *X11* **Göyçay** *Rus.* Geokchay. C Azerbaijan
146 *D10* **Goymat** *Rus.* Koymat. Balkan Welaýaty, NW Turkmenistan
146 *D10* **Goymatdag, Gory** *Rus.* Gory Koymatdag. *hill range* Balkan Welaýaty, NW Turkmenistan
136 *F12* **Göynük** Bolu, NW Turkey
165 *R9* **Goyō-san** ▲ Honshū, C Japan
78 *K11* **Goz Beïda** Ouaddaï, SE Chad
146 *M10* **G'ozg'on** *Rus.* Gazgan. Navoy Viloyati, C Uzbekistan
146 *M10* **G'ozg'on** *Rus.* Gazgan. Nawoiy Viloyati, C Uzbekistan
158 *H11* **Gozha Co** ◎ W China
121 *O15* **Gozo** *var.* Ghawdex. *island* N Malta
80 *H9* **Gōz Regeb** Kassala, NE Sudan
83 *H25* **Graaff-Reinet** Eastern Cape, S South Africa
Graasten *see* Gråsten
76 *L17* **Grabo** SW Ivory Coast
112 *P11* **Grabovica** Serbia, E Serbia
110 *I13* **Grabów nad Prosną** Wielkopolskie, C Poland
108 *I8* **Grabs** Sankt Gallen, NE Switzerland
112 *D12* **Gračac** Zadar, SW Croatia
112 *I11* **Gračanica** Federacija Bosna I Hercegovina, NE Bosnia and Herzegovina
14 *L11* **Gracefield** Québec, SE Canada
99 *K19* **Grâce-Hollogne** Liège, E Belgium
23 *R8* **Graceville** Florida, SE USA
29 *R8* **Graceville** Minnesota, N USA
42 *G6* **Gracias** Lempira, W Honduras
Gracias *see* Lempira
42 *L5* **Gracias a Dios** ◈ *department* E Honduras
43 *O6* **Gracias a Dios, Cabo de** *headland* Honduras/Nicaragua
64 *O2* **Graciosa** *var.* Ilha Graciosa. *island* Azores, Portugal, NE Atlantic Ocean
64 *Q11* **Graciosa** *island* Islas Canarias, Spain, NE Atlantic Ocean
Graciosa, Ilha *see* Graciosa
112 *I11* **Gradačac** Federacija Bosna I Hercegovina, N Bosnia and Herzegovina
59 *J15* **Gradaús, Serra dos** ▲▲ C Brazil
104 *L3* **Gradefes** Castilla-León, N Spain
Gradiška *see* Bosanska Gradiška
Gradizhsk *see* Hradyz'k
106 *J7* **Grado** Friuli-Venezia Giulia, NE Italy
104 *K2* **Grado** Asturias, N Spain
113 *P19* **Gradsko** C FYR Macedonia
37 *V11* **Grady** New Mexico, SW USA
Grad Zagreb *see* Zagreb
29 *T12* **Graettinger** Iowa, C USA
101 *M23* **Grafing** Bayern, SE Germany
25 *S6* **Graford** Texas, SW USA
183 *V5* **Grafton** New South Wales, SE Australia
29 *Q3* **Grafton** North Dakota, N USA
21 *S3* **Grafton** West Virginia, NE USA
21 *T9* **Graham** North Carolina, SE USA
25 *R6* **Graham** Texas, SW USA
Graham Bell Island *see* Greem-Bell, Ostrov
10 *I13* **Graham Island** *island* Queen Charlotte Islands, British Columbia, SW Canada
19 *S6* **Graham Lake** ◎ Maine, NE USA
194 *H4* **Graham Land** *physical region* Antarctica
37 *N15* **Graham, Mount** ▲ Arizona, SW USA
Grahamstad *see* Grahamstown
83 *I25* **Grahamstown** *Afr.* Grahamstad. Eastern Cape, S South Africa
Grahovo *see* Bosansko Grahovo
68 *C12* **Grain Coast** *coastal region* S Liberia
169 *S17* **Grajagan, Teluk** *bay* Jawa, S Indonesia
59 *L14* **Grajaú** Maranhão, E Brazil
58 *M13* **Grajaú, Rio** ≈ NE Brazil
110 *O8* **Grajewo** Podlaskie, NE Poland
95 *F24* **Gram** Sønderjylland, SW Denmark
103 *N13* **Gramat** Lot, S France
22 *H5* **Grambling** Louisiana, S USA
115 *C14* **Grámmos** ▲▲ Albania/Greece
96 *I9* **Grampian Mountains** ▲▲ C Scotland, UK
182 *L12* **Grampians, The** ▲▲ Victoria, SE Australia
98 *O9* **Gramsbergen** Overijssel, E Netherlands
113 *L21* **Gramsh** *var.* Gramshi. Elbasan, C Albania
Gramshi *see* Gramsh
Gran *see* Esztergom
Gran *see* Hron
54 *F11* **Granada** Meta, C Colombia
42 *J10* **Granada** Granada, SW Nicaragua
105 *N14* **Granada** Andalucía, S Spain
37 *W6* **Granada** Colorado, C USA
42 *J11* **Granada** ◈ *department* SW Nicaragua
105 *N14* **Granada** ◈ *province* Andalucía, S Spain
63 *I21* **Gran Antiplanicie Central** *plain* S Argentina
97 *E17* **Granard** Longford, C Ireland
63 *J20* **Gran Bajo** *basin* S Argentina
63 *J15* **Gran Bajo del Gualicho** *basin* E Argentina
63 *I21* **Gran Bajo de San Julián** *basin* SE Argentina
25 *S7* **Granbury** Texas, SW USA
15 *P12* **Granby** Québec, SE Canada
27 *S8* **Granby** Missouri, C USA
37 *S3* **Granby, Lake** ▣ Colorado, C USA
64 *O12* **Gran Canaria** *var.* Grand Canary. *island* Islas Canarias, Spain, NE Atlantic Ocean
47 *T11* **Gran Chaco** *var.* Chaco. *lowland plain* South America
45 *R14* **Grand Anse** SW Grenada
Grand-Anse *see* Portsmouth
44 *G1* **Grand Bahama Island** *island* N Bahamas
Grand Balé *see* Tui
103 *U7* **Grand Ballon** *Ger.* Ballon de Guebwiller. ▲ NE France
13 *T13* **Grand Bank** Newfoundland, Newfoundland and Labrador, SE Canada
64 *I7* **Grand Banks of Newfoundland** *undersea feature* NW Atlantic Ocean
Grand Bassa *see* Buchanan
77 *N17* **Grand-Bassam** *var.* Bassam. SE Ivory Coast
14 *E16* **Grand Bend** Ontario, S Canada
76 *L17* **Grand-Bérébi** *var.* Grand-Béréby. SW Ivory Coast
Grand-Béréby *see* Grand-Bérébi
45 *X11* **Grand-Bourg** Marie-Galante, SE Guadeloupe
44 *M6* **Grand Caicos** *var.* Middle Caicos. *island* C Turks and Caicos Islands
14 *K12* **Grand Calumet, Île du** *island* Québec, SE Canada
97 *E18* **Grand Canal** *Ir.* An Chanáil Mhór. *canal* C Ireland
Grand Canal *see* Da Yunhe
Grand Canary *see* Gran Canaria
36 *K10* **Grand Canyon** Arizona, SW USA
36 *J9* **Grand Canyon** *canyon* Arizona, SW USA
Grand Canyon State *see* Arizona
44 *D8* **Grand Cayman** *island* SW Cayman Islands
9 *R14* **Grand Centre** Alberta, SW Canada
76 *L17* **Grand Cess** SE Liberia
108 *D12* **Grand Combin** ▲ S Switzerland
32 *K8* **Grand Coulee** Washington, NW USA
32 *J8* **Grand Coulee** *valley* Washington, NW USA
45 *X5* **Grand Cul-de-Sac Marin** *bay* N Guadeloupe
Grand Duchy of Luxembourg *see* Luxembourg
63 *I22* **Grande, Bahía** *bay* S Argentina
9 *N14* **Grande Cache** Alberta, W Canada
103 *U12* **Grande Casse** ▲ E France
172 *G12* **Grande Comore** *var.* Njazidja, Great Comoro. *island* NW Comoros
61 *G18* **Grande, Cuchilla** *hill range* E Uruguay
45 *S5* **Grande de Añasco, Río** ≈ W Puerto Rico
Grande de Chiloé, Isla *see* Chiloé, Isla de
58 *J12* **Grande de Gurupá, Ilha** *river island* NE Brazil
57 *K21* **Grande de Lipez, Río** ≈ SW Bolivia
45 *U6* **Grande de Loíza, Río** ≈ E Puerto Rico
45 *T5* **Grande de Manatí, Río** ≈ C Puerto Rico
42 *L9* **Grande de Matagalpa, Río** ≈ C Nicaragua
40 *K12* **Grande de Santiago, Río** *var.* Santiago. ≈ C Mexico
43 *O15* **Grande de Térraba, Río** *var.* Río Térraba. ≈ SE Costa Rica
12 *J9* **Grande Deux, Réservoir la** ▣ Québec, E Canada
60 *O10* **Grande, Ilha** *island* SE Brazil
9 *O13* **Grande Prairie** Alberta, W Canada
74 *I8* **Grand Erg Occidental** *desert* W Algeria
74 *L9* **Grand Erg Oriental** *desert* Algeria/Tunisia
57 *M18* **Grande, Río** ≈ C Bolivia
59 *J20* **Grande, Rio** ≈ S Brazil
2 *F15* **Grande, Rio** *var.* Río Bravo, *Sp.* Río Bravo del Norte, Bravo del Norte. ≈ Mexico/USA
15 *Y7* **Grande-Rivière** Québec, SE Canada
15 *Y6* **Grande Rivière** ≈ Québec, SE Canada
44 *M8* **Grande-Rivière-du-Nord** N Haiti
62 *K9* **Grande, Salina** *var.* Gran Salitral. *salt lake* C Argentina
15 *S7* **Grandes-Bergeronnes** Québec, SE Canada
47 *W6* **Grande, Serra** ▲▲ W Brazil
40 *K4* **Grande, Sierra** ▲▲ N Mexico
103 *S12* **Grandes Rousses** ▲▲ E France
63 *K17* **Grandes, Salinas** *salt lake* E Argentina
45 *Y5* **Grande Terre** *island* E West Indies
15 *X5* **Grande-Vallée** Québec, SE Canada
45 *Y5* **Grande Vigie, Pointe de la** *headland* Grande Terre, N Guadeloupe
13 *N14* **Grand Falls** New Brunswick, SE Canada
13 *T11* **Grand Falls** Newfoundland, Newfoundland and Labrador, SE Canada
24 *L9* **Grandfalls** Texas, SW USA
21 *P9* **Grandfather Mountain** ▲ North Carolina, SE USA
26 *L13* **Grandfield** Oklahoma, C USA
9 *N17* **Grand Forks** British Columbia, SW Canada
29 *R4* **Grand Forks** North Dakota, N USA
31 *O9* **Grand Haven** Michigan, N USA
Grandichi *see* Hrandzichy
29 *P15* **Grand Island** Nebraska, C USA
31 *O3* **Grand Island** *island* Michigan, N USA
22 *K10* **Grand Isle** Louisiana, S USA
65 *A23* **Grand Jason** *island* Jason Islands, NW Falkland Islands
37 *P5* **Grand Junction** Colorado, C USA
20 *F10* **Grand Junction** Tennessee, S USA
14 *J9* **Grand-Lac-Victoria** Québec, SE Canada
14 *J9* **Grand lac Victoria** ◎ Québec, SE Canada
77 *N17* **Grand-Lahou** *var.* Grand Lahu. S Ivory Coast
Grand Lahu *see* Grand-Lahou
37 *S3* **Grand Lake** Colorado, C USA
13 *S11* **Grand Lake** ◎ Newfoundland, Newfoundland and Labrador, E Canada
22 *G9* **Grand Lake** ◎ Louisiana, S USA
31 *R5* **Grand Lake** ◎ Michigan, N USA
31 *Q13* **Grand Lake** ▣ Ohio, N USA
27 *R9* **Grand Lake O' The Cherokees** *var.* Lake O' The Cherokees. ▣ Oklahoma, C USA
31 *Q9* **Grand Ledge** Michigan, N USA
102 *I8* **Grand-Lieu, Lac de** ◎ NW France
19 *U6* **Grand Manan Channel** *channel* Canada/USA
13 *O15* **Grand Manan Island** *island* New Brunswick, SE Canada
29 *Y4* **Grand Marais** Minnesota, N USA
15 *P10* **Grand-Mère** Québec, SE Canada
37 *P5* **Grand Mesa** ▲▲ Colorado, C USA
108 *C10* **Grand Muveran** ▲ W Switzerland
104 *G12* **Grândola** Setúbal, S Portugal
Grand Paradis *see* Gran Paradiso
187 *O15* **Grand Passage** *passage* N New Caledonia
77 *R16* **Grand-Popo** S Benin
29 *Z3* **Grand Portage** Minnesota, N USA
25 *T6* **Grand Prairie** Texas, SW USA
9 *W14* **Grand Rapids** Manitoba, C Canada
31 *P9* **Grand Rapids** Michigan, N USA
29 *V5* **Grand Rapids** Minnesota, N USA
14 *L10* **Grand-Remous** Québec, SE Canada
14 *F15* **Grand River** ≈ Ontario, S Canada
31 *P9* **Grand River** ≈ Michigan, N USA
27 *T3* **Grand River** ≈ Missouri, C USA
28 *M7* **Grand River** ≈ South Dakota, N USA
45 *Q11* **Grand' Rivière** N Martinique
32 *F11* **Grand Ronde** Oregon, NW USA
32 *L11* **Grand Ronde River** ≈ Oregon/Washington, NW USA
Grand-Saint-Bernard, Col du *see* Great Saint Bernard Pass
25 *V6* **Grand Saline** Texas, SW USA
55 *X10* **Grand-Santi** W French Guiana
Grandsee *see* Grandson
172 *J16* **Grand Sœur** *island* Les Sœurs, NE Seychelles
108 *B9* **Grandson** *prev.* Grandsee. Vaud, W Switzerland
33 *S14* **Grand Teton** ▲ Wyoming, C USA
31 *P5* **Grand Traverse Bay** *lake bay* Michigan, N USA
45 *N6* **Grand Turk** ○ (Turks and Caicos Islands) Grand Turk Island, S Turks and Caicos Islands
45 *N6* **Grand Turk Island** *island* SE Turks and Caicos Islands
103 *S13* **Grand Veymont** ▲ E France
9 *W15* **Grandview** Manitoba, S Canada
27 *R4* **Grandview** Missouri, C USA
36 *I10* **Grand Wash Cliffs** *cliff* Arizona, SW USA
14 *J8* **Granet, Lac** ◎ Québec, SE Canada
95 *L14* **Grangärde** Dalarna, C Sweden
44 *H12* **Grange Hill** W Jamaica
96 *J12* **Grangemouth** C Scotland, UK
25 *T10* **Granger** Texas, SW USA
32 *J10* **Granger** Washington, NW USA
33 *T17* **Granger** Wyoming, C USA
Granges *see* Grenchen
95 *L14* **Grängesberg** Kopparberg, C Sweden
33 *N11* **Grangeville** Idaho, NW USA
10 *K13* **Granisle** British Columbia, SW Canada
30 *K15* **Granite City** Illinois, N USA
29 *S9* **Granite Falls** Minnesota, N USA
21 *Q9* **Granite Falls** North Carolina, SE USA
36 *K12* **Granite Mountain** ▲ Arizona, SW USA
33 *T12* **Granite Peak** ▲ Montana, NW USA
35 *T2* **Granite Peak** ▲ Nevada, W USA
36 *J3* **Granite Peak** ▲ Utah, W USA
Granite State *see* New Hampshire
107 *H24* **Granitola, Capo** *headland* Sicilia, Italy, C Mediterranean Sea
185 *H15* **Granity** West Coast, South Island, New Zealand
Gran Lago *see* Nicaragua, Lago de
63 *J18* **Gran Laguna Salada** ◎ S Argentina
Gran Malvina *see* West Falkland
95 *L18* **Gränna** Jönköping, S Sweden
105 *W5* **Granollers** *var.* Granollérs. Cataluña, NE Spain
Granollérs *see* Granollers
106 *A7* **Gran Paradiso** *Fr.* Grand Paradis. ▲ NW Italy
Gran Pilastro *see* Hochfeiler
Gran Salitral *see* Grande, Salina
Gran San Bernardo, Passo di *see* Great Saint Bernard Pass
Gran Santiago *see* Santiago
107 *J14* **Gran Sasso d'Italia** ▲▲ C Italy
100 *N11* **Gransee** Brandenburg, NE Germany
28 *L15* **Grant** Nebraska, C USA
27 *R1* **Grant City** Missouri, C USA
97 *N19* **Grantham** E England, UK
65 *D24* **Grantham Sound** *sound* East Falkland, Falkland Islands
194 *K13* **Grant Island** *island* Antarctica
45 *Z14* **Grantley Adams** ✈ (Bridgetown) SE Barbados
35 *S7* **Grant, Mount** ▲ Nevada, W USA
96 *J9* **Grantown-on-Spey** N Scotland, UK
35 *W8* **Grant Range** ▲▲ Nevada, W USA
37 *Q11* **Grants** New Mexico, SW USA
30 *I4* **Grantsburg** Wisconsin, N USA
32 *F15* **Grants Pass** Oregon, NW USA
36 *K3* **Grantsville** Utah, W USA
21 *R4* **Grantsville** West Virginia, NE USA
102 *I5* **Granville** Manche, N France
9 *V12* **Granville Lake** ◎ Manitoba, C Canada
25 *V8* **Grapeland** Texas, SW USA
25 *T6* **Grapevine** Texas, SW USA
83 *K20* **Graskop** Mpumalanga, NE South Africa
95 *P14* **Gräsö** Uppsala, C Sweden
93 *I19* **Gräsö** *island* C Sweden
103 *U15* **Grasse** Alpes-Maritimes, SE France
18 *E14* **Grassflat** Pennsylvania, NE USA
33 *U9* **Grassrange** Montana, NW USA
18 *J6* **Grass River** ≈ New York, NE USA
35 *P6* **Grass Valley** California, W USA
183 *N14* **Grassy** Tasmania, SE Australia
28 *K4* **Grassy Butte** North Dakota, N USA
21 *R5* **Grassy Knob** ▲ West Virginia, NE USA
95 *G24* **Gråsten** *var.* Graasten. Sønderjylland, SW Denmark
95 *J18* **Grästorp** Västra Götaland, S Sweden
Gratianopolis *see* Grenoble
109 *V8* **Gratwein** Steiermark, SE Austria
Gratz *see* Graz
108 *I9* **Graubünden** *Fr.* Grisons, *It.* Grigioni. ◈ *canton* SE Switzerland
Graudenz *see* Grudziądz
103 *N15* **Graulhet** Tarn, S France
105 *T4* **Graus** Aragón, NE Spain
61 *I16* **Gravataí** Rio Grande do Sul, S Brazil
98 *L13* **Grave** Noord-Brabant, SE Netherlands
9 *T17* **Gravelbourg** Saskatchewan, S Canada
103 *N1* **Gravelines** Nord, N France
Graven *see* Grez-Doiceau
14 *H13* **Gravenhurst** Ontario, S Canada
33 *O10* **Grave Peak** ▲ Idaho, NW USA
102 *I11* **Grave, Pointe de** *headland* W France
183 *S4* **Gravesend** New South Wales, SE Australia
97 *P22* **Gravesend** SE England, UK
107 *N17* **Gravina di Puglia** Puglia, SE Italy
103 *S8* **Gray** Haute-Saône, E France
23 *T4* **Gray** Georgia, SE USA
195 *V16* **Gray, Cape** *headland* Antarctica
32 *F9* **Grayland** Washington, NW USA
39 *N10* **Grayling** Alaska, USA
31 *Q6* **Grayling** Michigan, N USA
32 *F9* **Grays Harbor** *inlet* Washington, NW USA
21 *O5* **Grayson** Kentucky, S USA
37 *S4* **Grays Peak** ▲ Colorado, C USA
30 *M16* **Grayville** Illinois, N USA
109 *V8* **Graz** *prev.* Gratz. Steiermark, SE Austria
104 *L15* **Grazalema** Andalucía, S Spain
113 *P15* **Grdelica** Serbia, SE Serbia
44 *H1* **Great Abaco** *var.* Abaco Island. *island* N Bahamas
Great Admiralty Island *see* Manus Island
Great Alfold *see* Great Hungarian Plain
Great Ararat *see* Büyükağrı Dağı
181 *U8* **Great Artesian Basin** *lowlands* Queensland, C Australia
181 *O12* **Great Australian Bight** *bight* S Australia
64 *E11* **Great Bahama Bank** *undersea feature* E Gulf of Mexico
184 *M4* **Great Barrier Island** *island* N New Zealand
181 *X4* **Great Barrier Reef** *reef* Queensland, NE Australia
18 *L11* **Great Barrington** Massachusetts, NE USA
0 *F10* **Great Basin** *basin* W USA
8 *I8* **Great Bear Lake** *Fr.* Grand Lac de l'Ours. ◎ Northwest Territories, NW Canada
Great Belt *see* Storebælt
26 *L5* **Great Bend** Kansas, C USA
Great Bermuda *see* Bermuda
97 *A20* **Great Blasket Island** *Ir.* An Blascaod Mór. *island* SW Ireland
Great Britain *see* Britain
151 *Q23* **Great Channel** *channel* Andaman Sea/Indian Ocean
166 *J10* **Great Coco Island** *island* SW Myanmar (Burma)
Great Comoro *see* Grande Comore
Great Crosby *see* Crosby
21 *X7* **Great Dismal Swamp** *wetland* North Carolina/Virginia, SE USA
33 *V16* **Great Divide Basin** *basin* Wyoming, C USA
181 *W7* **Great Dividing Range** ▲▲ NE Australia
14 *D12* **Great Duck Island** *island* Ontario, S Canada
Great Elder Reservoir *see* Waconda Lake
195 *V8* **Greater Antarctica** *var.* East Antarctica. *physical region* Antarctica
44 *G8* **Greater Antilles** *island group* West Indies
129 *V16* **Greater Sunda Islands** *var.* Sunda Islands. *island group* Indonesia
184 *I1* **Great Exhibition Bay** *inlet* North Island, New Zealand
44 *H4* **Great Exuma Island** *island* C Bahamas
33 *R8* **Great Falls** Montana, NW USA
21 *R11* **Great Falls** South Carolina, SE USA
84 *F9* **Great Fisher Bank** *undersea feature* C North Sea
Great Glen *see* Mor, Glen
Great Grimsby *see* Grimsby
44 *I4* **Great Guana Cay** *island* C Bahamas
64 *I5* **Great Hellefiske Bank** *undersea feature* N Atlantic Ocean
111 *L24* **Great Hungarian Plain** *var.* Great Alfold, Plain of Hungary, *Hung.* Alföld. *plain* SE Europe
44 *L7* **Great Inagua** *var.* Inagua Islands. *island* S Bahamas
Great Indian Desert *see* Thar Desert
83 *G25* **Great Karoo** *var.* Great Karroo, High Veld, *Afr.* Groot Karoo, Hoë Karoo. *plateau region* S South Africa
Great Karroo *see* Great Karoo
Great Kei *see* Groot-Kei
Great Khingan Range *see* Da Hinggan Ling
14 *E11* **Great La Cloche Island** *island* Ontario, S Canada
183 *P16* **Great Lake** ◎ Tasmania, SE Australia
Great Lake *see* Tônlé Sap
9 *R15* **Great Lakes** *lakes* Ontario, Canada/USA
Great Lakes State *see* Michigan
97 *L20* **Great Malvern** W England, UK
184 *M5* **Great Mercury Island** *island* N New Zealand
Great Meteor Seamount *see* Great Meteor Tablemount
64 *K10* **Great Meteor Tablemount** *var.* Great Meteor Seamount. *undersea feature* E Atlantic Ocean
31 *Q14* **Great Miami River** ≈ Ohio, N USA
151 *Q24* **Great Nicobar** *island* Nicobar Islands, India, NE Indian Ocean
67 *T4* **Great Oasis, The** *var.* Khārga Oasis. *oasis* S Egypt
97 *O19* **Great Ouse** *var.* Ouse. ≈ E England, UK
183 *Q17* **Great Oyster Bay** *bay* Tasmania, SE Australia
44 *I13* **Great Pedro Bluff** *headland* W Jamaica
21 *T12* **Great Pee Dee River** ≈ North Carolina/South Carolina, SE USA
129 *W9* **Great Plain of China** *plain* E China
0 *F12* **Great Plains** *var.* High Plains. *plains* Canada/USA
37 *W6* **Great Plains Reservoirs** ▣ Colorado, C USA
19 *Q13* **Great Point** *headland* Nantucket Island, Massachusetts, NE USA
68 *I13* **Great Rift Valley** *var.* Rift Valley. *depression* Asia/Africa
81 *I23* **Great Ruaha** ≈ S Tanzania
18 *K10* **Great Sacandaga Lake** ▣ New York, NE USA
108 *C12* **Great Saint Bernard Pass** *Fr.* Col du Grand-Saint-Bernard, *It.* Passo del Gran San Bernardo. *pass* Italy/Switzerland
44 *F1* **Great Sale Cay** *island* N Bahamas
Great Salt Desert *see* Kavīr, Dasht-e
36 *K1* **Great Salt Lake** *salt lake* Utah, W USA
36 *J3* **Great Salt Lake Desert** *plain* Utah, W USA
26 *M8* **Great Salt Plains Lake** ▣ Oklahoma, C USA
75 *T9* **Great Sand Sea** *desert* Egypt/Libya
180 *L6* **Great Sandy Desert** *desert* Western Australia
Great Sandy Desert *see* Ar Rub 'al Khālī
Great Sandy Island *see* Fraser Island
187 *Y13* **Great Sea Reef** *reef* Vanua Levu, N Fiji
38 *H17* **Great Sitkin Island** *island* Aleutian Islands, Alaska, USA
8 *J10* **Great Slave Lake** *Fr.* Grand Lac des Esclaves. ◎ Northwest Territories, NW Canada
21 *O10* **Great Smoky Mountains** ▲▲ North Carolina/Tennessee, SE USA
10 *L11* **Great Snow Mountain** ▲ British Columbia, W Canada
64 *A12* **Great Sound** *sound* Bermuda, NW Atlantic Ocean
180 *M10* **Great Victoria Desert** *desert* South Australia/Western Australia
194 *H2* **Great Wall** *Chinese research station* South Shetland Islands, Antarctica
19 *T7* **Great Wass Island** *island* Maine, NE USA
97 *Q19* **Great Yarmouth** *var.* Yarmouth. E England, UK
139 *S1* **Great Zab** *Ar.* Az Zāb al Kabīr, *Kurd.* Zē-i Bādīnān, *Turk.* Büyükzap Suyu. ≈ Iraq/Turkey
95 *I17* **Grebbestad** Västra Götaland, S Sweden
Grebenka *see* Hrebinka
42 *M13* **Grecia** Alajuela, C Costa Rica
61 *E18* **Greco** Río Negro, W Uruguay
Greco, Cape *see* Gkréko, Akrotíri
104 *L8* **Gredos, Sierra de** ▲▲ W Spain
18 *F9* **Greece** New York, NE USA
115 *E17* **Greece** *off.* Hellenic Republic, *Gk.* Ellás; *anc.* Hellas. ◆ *republic* SE Europe
Greece Central *see* Stereá Ellás
Greece West *see* Dytikí Ellás
37 *T3* **Greeley** Colorado, C USA
29 *P14* **Greeley** Nebraska, C USA
122 *K3* **Greem-Bell, Ostrov** *Eng.* Graham Bell Island. *island* Zemlya Frantsa-Iosifa, N Russian Federation
30 *M6* **Green Bay** Wisconsin, N USA
31 *N6* **Green Bay** *lake bay* Michigan/Wisconsin, N USA
21 *S5* **Greenbrier River** ≈ West Virginia, NE USA
29 *S2* **Greenbush** Minnesota, N USA
183 *R12* **Green Cape** *headland* New South Wales, SE Australia
31 *O14* **Greencastle** Indiana, N USA
18 *F16* **Greencastle** Pennsylvania, NE USA
27 *T2* **Green City** Missouri, C USA
21 *O9* **Greeneville** Tennessee, S USA
35 *O11* **Greenfield** California, W USA
31 *P14* **Greenfield** Indiana, N USA
29 *U15* **Greenfield** Iowa, C USA
18 *M11* **Greenfield** Massachusetts, NE USA
27 *S7* **Greenfield** Missouri, C USA
31 *S14* **Greenfield** Ohio, N USA
20 *G8* **Greenfield** Tennessee, S USA
30 *M9* **Greenfield** Wisconsin, N USA
27 *T9* **Green Forest** Arkansas, C USA
37 *T7* **Greenhorn Mountain** ▲ Colorado, C USA
Green Island *see* Lü Tao
186 *I6* **Green Islands** *var.* Nissan Islands. *island group* NE Papua New Guinea
9 *S14* **Green Lake** Saskatchewan, C Canada
30 *L8* **Green Lake** ◎ Wisconsin, N USA
197 *O14* **Greenland** *Dan.* Grønland, *Inuit* Kalaallit Nunaat. ◇ *Danish external territory* NE North America
84 *D4* **Greenland** *island* NE North America
197 *R13* **Greenland Plain** *undersea feature* N Greenland Sea
197 *R14* **Greenland Sea** *sea* Arctic Ocean
37 *R4* **Green Mountain Reservoir** ▣ Colorado, C USA
18 *M8* **Green Mountains** ▲▲ Vermont, NE USA
Green Mountain State *see* Vermont
96 *H12* **Greenock** W Scotland, UK
39 *T5* **Greenough, Mount** ▲ Alaska, USA
186 *A6* **Green River** Sandaun, NW Papua New Guinea
37 *N5* **Green River** Utah, W USA
33 *U17* **Green River** Wyoming, C USA
16 *H9* **Green River** ≈ W USA
30 *K11* **Green River** ≈ Illinois, N USA
20 *J7* **Green River** ≈ Kentucky, C USA
28 *K5* **Green River** ≈ North Dakota, N USA
37 *N6* **Green River** ≈ Utah, W USA
33 *T16* **Green River** ≈ Wyoming, C USA
20 *L7* **Green River Lake** ▣ Kentucky, S USA
23 *O5* **Greensboro** Alabama, S USA
23 *U3* **Greensboro** Georgia, SE USA
21 *T9* **Greensboro** North Carolina, SE USA
31 *P14* **Greensburg** Indiana, N USA
26 *K6* **Greensburg** Kansas, C USA
20 *L7* **Greensburg** Kentucky, S USA
18 *C15* **Greensburg** Pennsylvania, NE USA
37 *O13* **Greens Peak** ▲ Arizona, SW USA
21 *V12* **Green Swamp** *wetland* North Carolina, SE USA
21 *O4* **Greenup** Kentucky, S USA
36 *M16* **Green Valley** Arizona, SW USA
76 *K17* **Greenville** *var.* Sino, Sinoe. SE Liberia
23 *P6* **Greenville** Alabama, S USA
23 *T8* **Greenville** Florida, SE USA
23 *S4* **Greenville** Georgia, SE USA
30 *L15* **Greenville** Illinois, N USA
20 *I7* **Greenville** Kentucky, S USA
19 *Q5* **Greenville** Maine, NE USA
31 *P9* **Greenville** Michigan, N USA
22 *J4* **Greenville** Mississippi, S USA
21 *W9* **Greenville** North Carolina, SE USA
31 *Q13* **Greenville** Ohio, N USA
19 *O12* **Greenville** Rhode Island, NE USA
21 *P11* **Greenville** South Carolina, SE USA
25 *U6* **Greenville** Texas, SW USA
31 *T12* **Greenwich** Ohio, N USA
27 *S11* **Greenwood** Arkansas, C USA
31 *O14* **Greenwood** Indiana, N USA
22 *K4* **Greenwood** Mississippi, S USA
21 *P12* **Greenwood** South Carolina, SE USA
21 *Q12* **Greenwood, Lake** ▣ South Carolina, SE USA
21 *P11* **Greer** South Carolina, SE USA
27 *V10* **Greers Ferry Lake** ▣ Arkansas, C USA
27 *S13* **Greeson, Lake** ▣ Arkansas, C USA
29 *O12* **Gregory** South Dakota, N USA
182 *J3* **Gregory, Lake** *salt lake* South Australia
180 *J9* **Gregory Lake** ◎ Western Australia

◆ Country
● Country Capital
◇ Dependent Territory
○ Dependent Territory Capital
◈ Administrative Regions
✈ International Airport
▲ Mountain
▲▲ Mountain Range
Volcano
≈ River
◎ Lake
▣ Reservoir

181 V5 Gregory Range ⛰ Queensland, E Australia
Greifenberg/Greifenberg in Pommern see Gryfice
Greifenhagen see Gryfino
100 O8 Greifswald Mecklenburg-Vorpommern, NE Germany
100 O8 Greifswalder Bodden bay NE Germany
109 U4 Grein Oberösterreich, N Austria
101 M17 Greiz Thüringen, C Germany
Gremicha/Gremiha see Gremikha
124 M4 Gremikha var. Gremicha, Gremiha. Murmanskaya Oblast', NW Russian Federation
125 V14 Gremyachinsk Permskaya Oblast', NW Russian Federation
Grenå see Grenaa
95 H21 Grenaa var. Grenå. Århus, C Denmark
22 L3 Grenada Mississippi, S USA
45 W15 Grenada ◆ commonwealth republic SE West Indies
47 S4 Grenada island Grenada
47 R4 Grenada Basin undersea feature W Atlantic Ocean
22 L3 Grenada Lake ⊞ Mississippi, S USA
45 Y14 Grenadines, The island group Grenada/St Vincent and the Grenadines
108 D7 Grenchen Fr. Granges. Solothurn, NW Switzerland
183 Q9 Grenfell New South Wales, SE Australia
9 V16 Grenfell Saskatchewan, S Canada
92 J1 Grenivík Nordhurland Eystra, N Iceland
103 S12 Grenoble anc. Cularo, Gratianopolis. Isère, E France
28 J2 Grenora North Dakota, N USA
92 N8 Grense-Jakobselv Finnmark, N Norway
45 S14 Grenville E Grenada
32 G11 Gresham Oregon, NW USA
Gresk see Hresk
106 B7 Gressoney-St-Jean Valle d'Aosta, NW Italy
22 K9 Gretna Louisiana, S USA
21 T7 Gretna Virginia, NE USA
98 F13 Grevelingen inlet S North Sea
100 F13 Greven Nordrhein-Westfalen, NW Germany
115 D15 Grevená Dytikí Makedonía, N Greece
101 D16 Grevenbroich Nordrhein-Westfalen, W Germany
99 N24 Grevenmacher Grevenmacher, E Luxembourg
99 M24 Grevenmacher ◈ district E Luxembourg
100 K9 Grevesmühlen Mecklenburg-Vorpommern, N Germany
185 H16 Grey ≈ South Island, New Zealand
33 V12 Greybull Wyoming, C USA
33 U13 Greybull River ≈ Wyoming, C USA
65 A24 Grey Channel sound Falkland Islands
Greyerzer See see Gruyère, Lac de la
13 T10 Grey Islands island group Newfoundland and Labrador, E Canada
18 L10 Greylock, Mount ▲ Massachusetts, NE USA
185 G17 Greymouth West Coast, South Island, New Zealand
181 U10 Grey Range ⛰ New South Wales/Queensland, E Australia
97 G18 Greystones Ir. Na Clocha Liatha. E Ireland
185 M14 Greytown Wellington, North Island, New Zealand
83 K23 Greytown KwaZulu/Natal, E South Africa
Greytown see San Juan del Norte
99 H19 Grez-Doiceau Dut. Graven. Walloon Brabant, C Belgium
115 J19 Griá, Ákrotírio headland Ándros, Kykládes, Greece, Aegean Sea
127 N8 Gribanovskiy Voronezhskaya Oblast', W Russian Federation
78 I13 Gribingui ≈ N Central African Republic
35 O6 Gridley California, W USA
83 G23 Griekwastad Northern Cape, C South Africa
23 S4 Griffin Georgia, SE USA
183 O9 Griffith New South Wales, SE Australia
14 F13 Griffith Island island Ontario, S Canada
21 W10 Grifton North Carolina, SE USA
Grigioni see Graubünden
119 H14 Grigiškes Vilnius, SE Lithuania
117 N10 Grigoriopol C Moldova
147 X7 Grigor'yevka Issyk-Kul'skaya Oblast', E Kyrgyzstan
193 U8 Grijalva Ridge undersea feature E Pacific Ocean
41 U15 Grijalva, Río var. Tabasco. ≈ Guatemala/Mexico
98 N5 Grijpskerk Groningen, NE Netherlands
83 C22 Grillenthal Karas, SW Namibia
79 J15 Grimari Ouaka, C Central African Republic
Grimaylov see Hrymayliv
99 G18 Grimbergen Vlaams Brabant, C Belgium
183 N15 Grim, Cape headland Tasmania, SE Australia
100 N8 Grimmen Mecklenburg-Vorpommern, NE Germany
14 G16 Grimsby Ontario, S Canada
97 O17 Grimsby prev. Great Grimsby. E England, UK
92 J1 Grímsey var. Grimsey. island N Iceland
Grimsey see Grímsey
9 O12 Grimshaw Alberta, W Canada
95 F18 Grimstad Aust-Agder, S Norway
92 H4 Grindavík Reykjanes, W Iceland
108 F9 Grindelwald Bern, S Switzerland
95 F23 Grindsted Ribe, W Denmark
29 W14 Grinnell Iowa, C USA
109 U10 Grintovec ▲ N Slovenia
182 H1 Griselda, Lake salt lake South Australia
Grisons see Graubünden
95 P14 Grisslehamn Stockholm, C Sweden
29 T15 Griswold Iowa, C USA
102 M1 Griz Nez, Cap headland N France
112 P13 Grljan Serbia, E Serbia
112 E11 Grmeč ⛰ NW Bosnia and Herzegovina
99 H16 Grobbendonk Antwerpen, N Belgium
Grobin see Grobiņa
118 C10 Grobiņa Ger. Grobin. Liepāja, W Latvia
83 K20 Groblersdal Mpumalanga, NE South Africa
83 G23 Groblershoop Northern Cape, W South Africa
Gródek Jagielloński see Horodok
109 Q6 Grödig Salzburg, W Austria
111 H15 Grodków Opolskie, S Poland
Grodnenskaya Oblast' see Hrodzyenskaya Voblasts'
Grodno see Hrodna
110 L12 Grodzisk Mazowiecki Mazowieckie, C Poland
110 F12 Grodzisk Wielkopolski Wielkopolskie, C Poland
Grodzyanka see Hrodzyanka
98 O12 Groenlo Gelderland, E Netherlands
83 E22 Groenrivier Karas, SE Namibia
25 U8 Groesbeck Texas, SW USA
98 L13 Groesbeek Gelderland, SE Netherlands
102 G7 Groix, Îles de island group NW France
110 M12 Grójec Mazowieckie, C Poland
65 K15 Gröll Seamount undersea feature C Atlantic Ocean
100 E13 Gronau var. Gronau in Westfalen. Nordrhein-Westfalen, NW Germany
Gronau in Westfalen see Gronau
93 F15 Grong Nord-Trøndelag, C Norway
95 N22 Grönhögen Kalmar, S Sweden
98 N5 Groningen Groningen, NE Netherlands
55 W9 Groningen Saramacca, N Suriname
98 N5 Groningen ◈ province NE Netherlands
Grønland see Greenland
108 H11 Grono Graubünden, S Switzerland
95 M20 Grönskåra Kalmar, S Sweden
25 O2 Groom Texas, SW USA
35 W9 Groom Lake ◎ Nevada, W USA
83 H25 Groot ≈ S South Africa
181 S2 Groote Eylandt island Northern Territory, N Australia
98 M6 Grootegast Groningen, NE Netherlands
83 D17 Grootfontein Otjozondjupa, N Namibia
83 E22 Groot Karasberge ⛰ S Namibia
Groot Karoo see Great Karoo
83 J25 Groot-Kei Eng. Great Kei. ≈ S South Africa
45 T10 Gros Islet N Saint Lucia
44 L8 Gros-Morne NW Haiti
13 S11 Gros Morne ▲ Newfoundland, Newfoundland and Labrador, E Canada
103 R9 Grosne ≈ C France
45 S12 Gros Piton ▲ SW Saint Lucia
Grossa, Isola see Dugi Otok
Grossbetschkerek see Zrenjanin
Grosse Isper see Grosse Ysper
Grosse Kokel see Târnava Mare
101 M21 Grosser Laaber var. Grosse Laber. ≈ SE Germany
Grosse Laber see Grosser Laaber
Grosse Morava see Velika Morava
101 O15 Grossenhain Sachsen, E Germany
109 Y4 Grossenzersdorf Niederösterreich, NE Austria
101 O21 Grosser Arber ▲ SE Germany
101 K17 Grosser Beerberg ▲ C Germany
101 G18 Grosser Feldberg ▲ W Germany
109 O8 Grosser Löffler It. Monte Lovello. ▲ Austria/Italy
109 N8 Grosser Möseler var. Mesule. ▲ Austria/Italy
100 J8 Grosser Plöner See ◎ N Germany
101 O21 Grosser Rachel ▲ SE Germany
Grosser Sund see Suur Väin
15 V6 Grosses-Roches Québec, SE Canada
109 P8 Grosses Weiesbachhorn var. Wiesbachhorn. ▲ W Austria
106 F13 Grosseto Toscana, C Italy
101 M22 Grosse Vils ≈ SE Germany
109 U4 Grosse Ysper var. Grosse Isper. ≈ N Austria
101 G19 Gross-Gerau Hessen, W Germany
109 U3 Gross Gerungs Niederösterreich, N Austria
109 P8 Grossglockner ▲ W Austria
Grosskanizsa see Nagykanizsa
Gross-Karol see Carei
Grosskikinda see Kikinda
109 W9 Grossklein Steiermark, SE Austria
Grosskoppe see Velká Deštná
Grossmeseritsch see Velké Meziříčí
Grossmichel see Michalovce
101 H19 Grossostheim Bayern, C Germany
109 X7 Grosspetersdorf Burgenland, SE Austria
109 T5 Grossraming Oberösterreich, C Austria
101 P14 Grossräschen Brandenburg, E Germany
Grossrauschenbach see Revúca
Gross-Sankt-Johannis see Suure-Jaani
Gross-Schlatten see Abrud
109 V2 Gross-Siegharts Niederösterreich, N Austria
Gross-Skaisgirren see Bol'shakovo
Gross-Steffelsdorf see Rimavská Sobota
Gross Strehlitz see Strzelce Opolskie
109 O8 Grossvenediger ▲ W Austria
Grosswardein see Oradea
Gross Wartenberg see Syców
109 U11 Grosuplje C Slovenia
99 H17 Grote Nete ≈ N Belgium
94 E10 Grotli Oppland, S Norway
19 N13 Groton Connecticut, NE USA
29 P8 Groton South Dakota, N USA
107 P18 Grottaglie Puglia, SE Italy
107 L17 Grottaminarda Campania, S Italy
106 K13 Grottammare Marche, C Italy
21 U5 Grottoes Virginia, NE USA
Grou see Grouw
13 N10 Groulx, Monts ⛰ Québec, E Canada
14 E7 Groundhog ≈ Ontario, S Canada
36 J1 Grouse Creek Utah, W USA
36 J1 Grouse Creek Mountains ⛰ Utah, W USA
98 L6 Grouw Fris. Grou. Friesland, N Netherlands
27 R8 Grove Oklahoma, C USA
31 S13 Grove City Ohio, N USA
18 B13 Grove City Pennsylvania, NE USA
23 O6 Grove Hill Alabama, S USA
33 S15 Grover Wyoming, C USA
35 P13 Grover City California, W USA
25 Y11 Groves Texas, SW USA
19 O7 Groveton New Hampshire, NE USA
25 W9 Groveton Texas, SW USA
36 J15 Growler Mountains ⛰ Arizona, SW USA
Grozdovo see Bratya Daskalovi
127 P16 Groznyy Chechenskaya Respublika, SW Russian Federation
Grubeshov see Hrubieszów
112 G9 Grubišno Polje Bjelovar-Bilogora, NE Croatia
Grudovo see Sredets
110 J9 Grudziądz Ger. Graudenz. Kujawsko-pomorskie, C Poland
25 R17 Grulla var. La Grulla. Texas, SW USA
40 K14 Grullo Jalisco, SW Mexico
67 V10 Grumeti ≈ N Tanzania
95 K16 Grums Värmland, C Sweden
109 S5 Grünau im Almtal Oberösterreich, N Austria
101 H17 Grünberg Hessen, W Germany
Grünberg/Grünberg in Schlesien see Zielona Góra
92 H3 Grundarfjördhur Vestfirdhir, W Iceland
21 P7 Grundy Virginia, NE USA
29 W13 Grundy Center Iowa, C USA
Grüneberg see Zielona Góra
25 N1 Gruver Texas, SW USA
108 C9 Gruyère, Lac de la Ger. Greyerzer See. ◎ SW Switzerland
108 C9 Gruyères Fribourg, W Switzerland
118 E11 Gruzdžiai Šiauliai, N Lithuania
Gruzinskaya SSR/Gruziya see Georgia
Gryada Akkyr see Akgyr Erezi
126 L7 Gryazi Lipetskaya Oblast', W Russian Federation
124 M14 Gryazovets Vologodskaya Oblast', NW Russian Federation
111 M17 Grybów Małopolskie, SE Poland
94 M13 Grycksbo Dalarna, C Sweden
110 E8 Gryfice Ger. Greifenberg, Greifenberg in Pommern. Zachodnio-pomorskie, NW Poland
110 D9 Gryfino Ger. Greifenhagen. Zachodnio-pomorskie, NW Poland
92 H9 Gryllefjord Troms, N Norway
95 L15 Grythyttan Örebro, C Sweden
108 D10 Gstaad Bern, W Switzerland
43 P14 Guabito Bocas del Toro, NW Panama
44 G7 Guacanayabo, Golfo de gulf S Cuba
40 I7 Guachochi Chihuahua, N Mexico
104 J11 Guadajira ≈ SW Spain
104 M13 Guadajoz ≈ S Spain
40 L13 Guadalajara Jalisco, C Mexico
105 O8 Guadalajara Ar. Wad Al-Hajarah; anc. Arriaca. Castilla-La Mancha, C Spain
105 O7 Guadalajara ◈ province Castilla-La Mancha, C Spain
104 K12 Guadalcanal Andalucía, S Spain
186 L10 Guadalcanal off. Guadalcanal Province. ◈ province C Solomon Islands
186 M9 Guadalcanal island C Solomon Islands
Guadalcanal Province see Guadalcanal
105 O12 Guadalén ≈ S Spain
105 R13 Guadalentín ≈ SE Spain
104 K15 Guadalete ≈ SW Spain
105 O13 Guadalimar ≈ S Spain
105 P12 Guadalmena ≈ S Spain
104 L11 Guadalmez ≈ W Spain
105 S7 Guadalope ≈ E Spain
104 K13 Guadalquivir ≈ W Spain
104 J14 Guadalquivir, Marismas del var. Las Marismas. wetland SW Spain
40 M11 Guadalupe Zacatecas, C Mexico
57 E16 Guadalupe Ica, W Peru
104 L10 Guadalupe Extremadura, W Spain
36 L14 Guadalupe Arizona, SW USA
35 P13 Guadalupe California, W USA
Guadalupe see Canelones
40 J3 Guadalupe Bravos Chihuahua, N Mexico
40 A4 Guadalupe, Isla island NW Mexico
37 U15 Guadalupe Mountains ⛰ New Mexico/Texas, SW USA
24 J8 Guadalupe Peak ▲ Texas, SW USA
25 R11 Guadalupe River ≈ SW USA
104 K10 Guadalupe, Sierra de ⛰ W Spain
40 K9 Guadalupe Victoria Durango, C Mexico
40 I8 Guadalupe y Calvo Chihuahua, N Mexico
105 N7 Guadarrama Madrid, C Spain
105 N7 Guadarrama ≈ C Spain
104 M7 Guadarrama, Puerto de pass C Spain
105 N9 Guadarrama, Sierra de ⛰ C Spain
105 Q9 Guadazaón ≈ C Spain
45 X10 Guadeloupe ◇ French overseas department E West Indies
47 S3 Guadeloupe island group E West Indies
45 W10 Guadeloupe Passage passage E Caribbean Sea
104 H13 Guadiana ≈ Portugal/Spain
105 O13 Guadiana Menor ≈ S Spain
105 Q8 Guadiela ≈ C Spain
105 O14 Guadix Andalucía, S Spain
Guad-i-Zirreh see Gowd-e Zereh, Dasht-e
193 T12 Guafo Fracture Zone tectonic feature SE Pacific Ocean
63 F18 Guafo, Isla island S Chile
42 I6 Guaimaca Francisco Morazán, C Honduras
54 J12 Guainía off. Comisaría del Guainía. ◈ province E Colombia
Guainía, Comisaría del see Guainía
54 K12 Guainía, Río ≈ Colombia/Venezuela
55 O9 Guaiquinima, Cerro elevation SE Venezuela
60 G10 Guaíra Paraná, S Brazil
60 L7 Guaíra São Paulo, S Brazil
62 O7 Guairá off. Departamento del Guairá. ◈ department S Paraguay
Guairá, Departamento del see Guairá
Guaire see Gorey
63 F19 Guaiteca, Isla island S Chile
44 G6 Guajaba, Cayo headland C Cuba
59 D16 Guajará-Mirim Rondônia, W Brazil
Guajira see La Guajira
Guajira, Departamento de La see La Guajira
54 H3 Guajira, Península de la peninsula N Colombia
42 J6 Gualaco Olancho, C Honduras
34 L7 Gualala California, W USA
42 E5 Gualán Zacapa, C Guatemala
61 C19 Gualeguay Entre Ríos, E Argentina
61 D18 Gualeguaychú Entre Ríos, E Argentina
61 C18 Gualeguay, Río ≈ E Argentina
63 K16 Gualicho, Salina del salt lake E Argentina
188 B15 Guam ◇ US unincorporated territory W Pacific Ocean
63 F19 Guamblin, Isla island Archipiélago de los Chonos, S Chile
61 A22 Guaminí Buenos Aires, E Argentina
40 H8 Guamúchil Sinaloa, C Mexico
54 H4 Guana var. Misión de Guana. Zulia, NW Venezuela
44 C4 Guanabacoa La Habana, W Cuba
42 K13 Guanacaste off. Provincia de Guanacaste. ◈ province NW Costa Rica
42 K12 Guanacaste, Cordillera de ⛰ NW Costa Rica
Guanacaste, Provincia de see Guanacaste
40 J8 Guanaceví Durango, C Mexico
44 A5 Guanahacabibes, Golfo de gulf W Cuba
42 K4 Guanaja, Isla de island Islas de la Bahía, N Honduras
44 C4 Guanajay La Habana, W Cuba
41 N12 Guanajuato Guanajuato, C Mexico
40 M12 Guanajuato ◈ state C Mexico
54 J6 Guanare Portuguesa, N Venezuela
54 K7 Guanare, Río ≈ W Venezuela
54 J6 Guanarito Portuguesa, NW Venezuela
160 M3 Guancen Shan ⛰ C China
62 I9 Guandacol La Rioja, W Argentina
44 A5 Guane Pinar del Río, W Cuba
161 N14 Guangdong var. Guangdong Sheng, Kuang-tung, Kwangtung, Yue. ◈ province S China
Guangdong Sheng see Guangdong
Guanghua see Laohekou
Guangju see Kwangju
160 I13 Guangnan var. Liancheng. Yunnan, SW China
161 N8 Guangshui prev. Yingshan. Hubei, C China
Guangxi see Guangxi Zhuangzu Zizhiqu
160 K14 Guangxi Zhuangzu Zizhiqu var. Guangxi, Gui, Kuang-hsi, Kwangsi, Eng. Kwangsi Chuang Autonomous Region. ◈ autonomous region S China
160 J8 Guangyuan var. Kuang-yuan, Kwangyuan. Sichuan, C China
161 N14 Guangzhou var. Kwangchow, Eng. Canton. province capital Guangdong, S China
59 N19 Guanhães Minas Gerais, SE Brazil
160 I12 Guanling var. Guanling Buyeizu Miaozu Zizhixian. Guizhou, S China
Guanling Buyeizu Miaozu Zizhixian see Guanling
55 N5 Guanta Anzoátegui, NE Venezuela
44 J8 Guantánamo Guantánamo, SE Cuba
44 J8 Guantánamo, Bahia de Eng. Guantanamo Bay. US military base SE Cuba
Guantanamo Bay see Guantánamo, Bahia de
Guanxian/Guan Xian see Dujiangyan
161 Q6 Guanyun var Yishan. Jiangsu, E China
54 C12 Guapí Cauca, SW Colombia
43 N13 Guápiles Limón, NE Costa Rica
61 I15 Guaporé Rio Grande do Sul, S Brazil
47 S8 Guaporé, Rio var. Río Iténez. ≈ Bolivia/Brazil see also Río Iténez
Guaporé, Rio see Iténez, Río
56 B7 Guaranda Bolívar, C Ecuador
60 H11 Guaraniaçu Paraná, S Brazil
59 O20 Guarapari Espírito Santo, SE Brazil
60 I12 Guarapuava Paraná, S Brazil
60 J8 Guararapes São Paulo, S Brazil
105 S4 Guara, Sierra de ⛰ NE Spain
60 N10 Guaratinguetá São Paulo, S Brazil
104 I7 Guarda Guarda, N Portugal
104 I7 Guarda ◈ district N Portugal
Guardak see Govurdak
104 M3 Guardo Castilla-León, N Spain
104 K11 Guareña Extremadura, W Spain
60 J11 Guaricana, Pico ▲ S Brazil
54 L6 Guárico off. Estado Guárico. ◈ state N Venezuela
Guárico, Estado see Guárico
44 J7 Guarico, Punta headland E Cuba
54 L7 Guárico, Río ≈ C Venezuela
60 M10 Guarujá São Paulo, SE Brazil
61 L22 Guarulhos ✕ (São Paulo) São Paulo, S Brazil
43 R17 Guarumal Veraguas, S Panama
Guasapa see Guasopa
40 H8 Guasave Sinaloa, C Mexico
54 I8 Guasdualito Apure, C Venezuela
55 Q7 Guasipati Bolívar, E Venezuela
186 I9 Guasopa var. Guasapa. Woodlark Island, SE Papua New Guinea
106 F9 Guastalla Emilia-Romagna, C Italy
42 D6 Guastatoya var. El Progreso. El Progreso, C Guatemala
42 D5 Guatemala off. Republic of Guatemala. ◆ republic Central America
42 A2 Guatemala off. Departamento de Guatemala. ◈ department S Guatemala
193 S7 Guatemala Basin undersea feature E Pacific Ocean
Guatemala City see Ciudad de Guatemala
Guatemala, Departamento de see Guatemala
Guatemala, Republic of see Guatemala
45 V14 Guatuaro Point headland Trinidad, Trinidad and Tobago
186 B8 Guavi ≈ SW Papua New Guinea
54 G13 Guaviare off. Comisaría Guaviare. ◈ province S Colombia
Guaviare, Comisaría see Guaviare
54 J11 Guaviare, Río ≈ E Colombia
61 E15 Guaviravi Corrientes, NE Argentina
54 G12 Guayabero, Río ≈ SW Colombia
45 U6 Guayama E Puerto Rico
42 J7 Guayambre, Río ≈ S Honduras
Guayanas, Macizo de las see Guiana Highlands
45 V6 Guayanés, Punta headland E Puerto Rico
42 J6 Guayape, Río ≈ C Honduras
56 B7 Guayaquil var. Santiago de Guayaquil. Guayas, SW Ecuador
Guayaquil see Simon Bolivar
56 A8 Guayaquil, Golfo de var. Gulf of Guayaquil. gulf SW Ecuador
Guayaquil, Gulf of see Guayaquil, Golfo de
56 A7 Guayas ◈ province W Ecuador
62 N7 Guaycurú, Río ≈ NE Argentina
40 F6 Guaymas Sonora, NW Mexico
45 U5 Guaynabo E Puerto Rico
80 H12 Guba Benishangul, W Ethiopia
146 H8 Gubadag Turkm. Tel'man; prev. Tel'mansk. Daşoguz Welaýaty, N Turkmenistan
125 T1 Guba Dolgaya Nenetskiy Avtonomnyy Okrug, NW Russian Federation
125 V13 Gubakha Permskaya Oblast', NW Russian Federation
106 I12 Gubbio Umbria, C Italy
100 Q13 Guben var. Wilhelm-Pieck-Stadt. Brandenburg, E Germany
Guben see Gubin
110 D12 Gubin Ger. Guben. Lubuskie, W Poland
126 K8 Gubkin Belgorodskaya Oblast', W Russian Federation
162 J9 Guchin-Us var. Arguut. Övörhangay, C Mongolia
Gudara see Ghŭdara
105 S8 Gúdar, Sierra de ⛰ E Spain
137 P8 Gudaut'a NW Georgia
94 G12 Gudbrandsdalen valley S Norway
95 G21 Gudenå var. Gudenaa. ≈ C Denmark
Gudenaa see Gudenå
127 P16 Gudermes Chechenskaya Respublika, SW Russian Federation
155 J18 Gūdūr Andhra Pradesh, E India
146 F13 Gudurolum Balkan Welaýaty, W Turkmenistan
94 D13 Gudvangen Sogn Og Fjordane, S Norway
103 U7 Guebwiller Haut-Rhin, NE France
Guéckédou see Guékédou
14 K8 Guéguen, Lac ◎ Québec, SE Canada
76 J15 Guékédou var. Guéckédou. Guinée-Forestière, S Guinea
41 R16 Guelatao Oaxaca, SE Mexico
Guelders see Gelderland
78 G11 Guélengdeng Mayo-Kébbi, W Chad
74 L5 Guelma var. Gâlma. NE Algeria
74 D8 Guelmime var. Goulimime. SW Morocco
14 G15 Guelph Ontario, S Canada
102 I7 Guémené-Penfao Loire-Atlantique, NW France
102 I7 Guer Morbihan, NW France
78 I11 Guéra off. Préfecture du Guéra. ◈ prefecture S Chad
102 H8 Guérande Loire-Atlantique, NW France
Guéra, Préfecture du see Guéra
78 K9 Guéréda Biltine, E Chad
103 N10 Guéret Creuse, C France
Guernica/Guernica y Lumo see Gernika-Lumo
33 Z15 Guernsey Wyoming, C USA
97 K25 Guernsey island Channel Islands, NW Europe
76 J10 Guérou Assaba, S Mauritania
25 R16 Guerra Texas, SW USA
41 O15 Guerrero ◈ state S Mexico
40 D6 Guerrero Negro Baja California Sur, NW Mexico
103 P9 Gueugnon Saône-et-Loire, C France
76 M17 Guéyo S Ivory Coast
107 L15 Guglionesi Molise, C Italy
188 K5 Guguan island C Northern Mariana Islands
Guhrau see Góra
Gui see Guangxi Zhuangzu Zizhiqu
Guiana see French Guiana
47 V4 Guiana Basin undersea feature W Atlantic Ocean
48 G6 Guiana Highlands var. Macizo de las Guayanas. ⛰ N South America
Guiba see Juba
102 I7 Guichen Ille-et-Vilaine, NW France
Guichi see Chizhou
61 E18 Guichón Paysandú, W Uruguay
77 U12 Guidan-Roumji Maradi, S Niger
Guidder see Guider
159 T10 Guide var. Heyin. Qinghai, C China
78 F12 Guider var. Guidder. Nord, N Cameroon
76 I11 Guidimaka ◈ region S Mauritania
77 W12 Guidimouni Zinder, S Niger
76 G10 Guier, Lac de var. Lac de Guiers. ◎ N Senegal
Guiers, Lac de see Guier, Lac de
160 L14 Guigang var. Guixian, Gui Xian. Guangxi Zhuangzu Zizhiqu, S China
76 L16 Guiglo W Ivory Coast
54 L5 Güigüe Carabobo, N Venezuela
83 M20 Guijá Gaza, S Mozambique
42 E7 Güija, Lago de ◎ El Salvador/Guatemala
160 L14 Gui Jiang var. Gui Shui. ≈ S China
104 K8 Guijuelo Castilla-León, N Spain
Guilan see Gīlān
97 N22 Guildford SE England, UK
19 R5 Guildford Maine, NE USA
19 O7 Guildhall Vermont, NE USA
103 R13 Guilherand Ardèche, E France
160 L13 Guilin var. Kuei-lin, Kweilin. Guangxi Zhuangzu Zizhiqu, S China
12 J6 Guillaume-Delisle, Lac ◎ Québec, NE Canada
103 U13 Guillestre Hautes-Alpes, SE France
104 H6 Guimarães var. Guimaráes. Braga, N Portugal
Guimarães see Guimarães
58 D11 Guimarães Rosas, Pico ▲ NW Brazil
23 N3 Guin Alabama, S USA
Güina see Wina
76 I14 Guinea off. Republic of Guinea, var. Guinée; prev. French Guinea, People's Revolutionary Republic of Guinea. ◆ republic W Africa
64 N13 Guinea Basin undersea feature E Atlantic Ocean
76 E12 Guinea-Bissau off. Republic of Guinea-Bissau, Fr. Guinée-Bissau, Port. Guiné-Bissau; prev. Portuguese Guinea. ◆ republic W Africa
Guinea-Bissau, Republic of see Guinea-Bissau
66 K7 Guinea Fracture Zone tectonic feature E Atlantic Ocean
64 O13 Guinea, Gulf of Fr. Golfe de Guinée. gulf E Atlantic Ocean
Guinea, People's Revolutionary Republic of see Guinea
Guinea, Republic of see Guinea
Guiné-Bissau see Guinea-Bissau
Guinée see Guinea
Guinée-Bissau see Guinea-Bissau
Guinée, Golfe de see Guinea, Gulf of
44 C4 Güines La Habana, W Cuba
102 G5 Guingamp Côtes d'Armor, NW France

◆ Country
● Country Capital
◇ Dependent Territory
○ Dependent Territory Capital
◈ Administrative Regions
✕ International Airport
▲ Mountain
⛰ Mountain Range
Volcano
≈ River
◎ Lake
⊞ Reservoir

105 P3 **Guipúzcoa** *Basq.* Gipuzkoa. ⬖ *province* País Vasco, N Spain
44 C5 **Güira de Melena** La Habana, W Cuba
74 G8 **Guir, Hamada du** *desert* Algeria/Morocco
55 P5 **Güiria** Sucre, NE Venezuela
Gui Shui *see* Gui Jiang
104 H2 **Guitiriz** Galicia, NW Spain
77 N17 **Guitri** S Ivory Coast
171 Q5 **Guiuan** Samar, C Philippines
Gui Xian/Guixian *see* Guigang
160 J12 **Guiyang** *var.* Kuei-Yang, Kuei-yang, Kueyang, Kweiyang; *prev.* Kweichu. *province capital* Guizhou, S China
160 J12 **Guizhou** *var.* Guizhou Sheng, Kuei-chou, Kweichow, Qian. ⬖ *province* S China
Guizhou Sheng *see* Guizhou
102 J13 **Gujan-Mestras** Gironde, SW France
154 B10 **Gujarāt** *var.* Gujerat. ⬖ *state* W India
149 V6 **Gūjar Khān** Punjab, E Pakistan
Gujerat *see* Gujarāt
149 V7 **Gujrānwāla** Punjab, NE Pakistan
149 V7 **Gujrāt** Punjab, E Pakistan
146 B8 **Gulandag** *Rus.* Gory Kulandag. ▲▲ Balkan Welaýaty, W Turkmenistan
159 U9 **Gulang** Gansu, C China
183 R6 **Gulargambone** New South Wales, SE Australia
155 G15 **Gulbarga** Karnātaka, C India
118 J8 **Gulbene** *Ger.* Alt-Schwanenburg. Gulbene, NE Latvia
147 U10 **Gul'cha** *Kir.* Gülchö. Oshskaya Oblast', SW Kyrgyzstan
Gülchö *see* Gul'cha
173 T10 **Gulden Draak Seamount** *undersea feature* E Indian Ocean
136 J16 **Gülek Boğazı** *var.* Cilician Gates. *pass* S Turkey
186 D8 **Gulf** ⬖ *province* S Papua New Guinea
23 O9 **Gulf Breeze** Florida, SE USA
Gulf of Liaotung *see* Liaodong Wan
23 V13 **Gulfport** Florida, SE USA
22 M9 **Gulfport** Mississippi, S USA
23 O9 **Gulf Shores** Alabama, S USA
141 T5 **Gulf, The** *var.* Persian Gulf, *Ar.* Khalīj al 'Arabī, *Per.* Khalīj-e Fars. *Gulf* SW Asia *see also* Persian Gulf
183 R7 **Gulgong** New South Wales, SE Australia
160 I11 **Gulin** Sichuan, C China
171 U14 **Gulir** Pulau Kasiui, E Indonesia
Gulistan *see* Guliston
147 P10 **Guliston** *Rus.* Gulistan. Sirdaryo Viloyati, E Uzbekistan
163 T6 **Guliya Shan** ▲ NE China
Gulja *see* Yining
39 S11 **Gulkana** Alaska, USA
9 S17 **Gull Lake** Saskatchewan, S Canada
31 P10 **Gull Lake** ◎ Michigan, N USA
29 T6 **Gull Lake** ◎ Minnesota, N USA
95 L16 **Gullspång** Västra Götaland, S Sweden
136 B15 **Güllük Körfezi** *prev* Akbük Limanı. *bay* W Turkey
152 H5 **Gulmarg** Jammu and Kashmir, NW India
Gulpaigan *see* Golpāyegān
99 L18 **Gulpen** Limburg, SE Netherlands
Gul'shad *see* Gul'shad
145 S13 **Gul'shad** *var.* Gul'shad. Karaganda, E Kazakhstan
81 F17 **Gulu** N Uganda
114 K10 **Gŭlŭbovo** Stara Zagora, C Bulgaria
114 I7 **Gulyantsi** Pleven, N Bulgaria
Gulyaypole *see* Hulyaypole
Guma *see* Pishan
Gümai *see* Darlag
79 K16 **Gumba** Equateur, NW Dem. Rep. Congo
Gumbinnen *see* Gusev
81 H24 **Gumbiro** Ruvuma, S Tanzania
146 B11 **Gumdag** *prev.* Kum-Dag. Balkan Welaýaty, W Turkmenistan
77 W12 **Gumel** Jigawa, N Nigeria
105 N5 **Gumiel de Hizán** Castilla-León, N Spain
153 P16 **Gumla** Jhārkhand, N India
Gumma *see* Gunma
101 F16 **Gummersbach** Nordrhein-Westfalen, W Germany
77 T13 **Gummi** Zamfara, NW Nigeria
Gumpolds *see* Humpolec
153 N13 **Gumti** *var.* Gomati. ≈ N India
Gümülcine/Gümüljina *see* Komotiní
Gümüşane *see* Gümüşhane
137 O12 **Gümüşhane** *var.* Gümüşane, Gumushkhane. Gümüşhane, NE Turkey
137 O12 **Gümüşhane** *var.* Gümüşane, Gumushkhane. ⬖ *province* NE Turkey
Gumushkhane *see* Gümüşhane
171 V14 **Gumzai** Pulau Kola, E Indonesia
154 H9 **Guna** Madhya Pradesh, C India
Gunabad *see* Gonābād
Gunan *see* Qijiang
Gunbad-i-Qawus *see* Gonbad-e Kāvūs
183 O9 **Gunbar** New South Wales, SE Australia
183 O9 **Gun Creek** *seasonal river* New South Wales, SE Australia
183 Q10 **Gundagai** New South Wales, SE Australia
79 K17 **Gundji** Equateur, N Dem. Rep. Congo
155 G20 **Gundlupet** Karnātaka, W India
136 G16 **Gündoğmuş** Antalya, S Turkey
137 O14 **Güney Doğu Toroslar** ▲▲ SE Turkey
79 J21 **Gungu** Bandundu, SW Dem. Rep. Congo
127 P17 **Gunib** Respublika Dagestan, SW Russian Federation
112 J11 **Gunja** Vukovar-Srijem, E Croatia
31 P9 **Gun Lake** ◎ Michigan, N USA
165 N12 **Gunma** *off.* Gunma-ken, *var.* Gumma. ⬖ *prefecture* Honshū, S Japan
Gunma-ken *see* Gunma
197 P15 **Gunnbjørn Fjeld** *var.* Gunnbjörns Bjerge. ▲ C Greenland
Gunnbjörns Bjerge *see* Gunnbjørn Fjeld
183 S6 **Gunnedah** New South Wales, SE Australia
173 Y15 **Gunner's Quoin** *island* N Mauritius
37 R6 **Gunnison** Colorado, C USA
36 L5 **Gunnison** Utah, W USA
37 P5 **Gunnison River** ≈ Colorado, C USA
21 X2 **Gunpowder River** ≈ Maryland, NE USA
Güns *see* Kőszeg
Gunsan *see* Kunsan
109 S4 **Gunskirchen** Oberösterreich, N Austria
Gunt *see* Ghund
155 H17 **Guntakal** Andhra Pradesh, C India
23 Q2 **Guntersville** Alabama, S USA
23 Q2 **Guntersville Lake** ⊠ Alabama, S USA
109 X4 **Guntramsdorf** Niederösterreich, E Austria
155 J16 **Guntūr** *var.* Guntur. Andhra Pradesh, SE India
168 H10 **Gunungsitoli** Pulau Nias, W Indonesia
155 M14 **Gunupur** Orissa, E India
101 J23 **Günz** ≈ S Germany
Gunzan *see* Kunsan
101 J22 **Günzburg** Bayern, S Germany
101 K21 **Gunzenhausen** Bayern, S Germany
Guolüezhen *see* Lingbao
Guovdageaidnu *see* Kautokeino
161 P7 **Guoyang** Anhui, E China
116 G11 **Gurahonţ** *Hung.* Honctő. Arad, W Romania
Gurahumora *see* Gura Humorului
116 K9 **Gura Humorului** *Ger.* Gurahumora. Suceava, NE Romania
146 H8 **Gurbansoltan Eje** *Prev.* Ýylanly, *Rus.* Il'yaly. Daşoguz Welaýaty, N Turkmenistan
146 H8 **Gurbansoltan Eje** *prev.* Ýylanly, *Rus.* Il'yaly. Daşoguz Welaýaty, N Turkmenistan
158 K4 **Gurbantünggüt Shamo** *desert* W China
152 H7 **Gurdāspur** Punjab, N India
27 T13 **Gurdon** Arkansas, C USA
Gurdzhaani *see* Gurjaani
Gurgan *see* Gorgān
152 I10 **Gurgaon** Haryāna, N India
59 M15 **Gurguéia, Rio** ≈ NE Brazil
55 Q7 **Guri, Embalse de** ⊠ E Venezuela
137 V10 **Gurjaani** *Rus.* Gurdzhaani. E Georgia
109 T8 **Gurk** Kärnten, S Austria
109 T9 **Gurk** *Slvn.* Krka. ≈ S Austria
Gurkfeld *see* Krško
114 K9 **Gurkovo** *prev.* Kolupchii. Stara Zagora, C Bulgaria
109 S9 **Gurktaler Alpen** ▲▲ S Austria
146 H8 **Gurlan** *Rus.* Gurlen. Xorazm Viloyati, W Uzbekistan
Gurlen *see* Gurlan
83 M16 **Guro** Manica, C Mozambique
136 M14 **Gürün** Sivas, C Turkey
59 K16 **Gurupi** Tocantins, C Brazil
58 L12 **Gurupi, Rio** ≈ NE Brazil
152 E14 **Guru Sikhar** ▲ NW India
162 H8 **Gurvanbulag** *var.* Höviyn Am. Bayanhongor, C Mongolia
162 K7 **Gurvanbulag** *var.* Avdzaga. Bulgan, C Mongolia
162 K7 **Gurvanbulag** *var.* Avdzaga. Bulgan, C Monogolia
162 I11 **Gurvantes** *var.* Urt. Ömnögovĭ, S Mongolia
Gur'yev/Gur'yevskaya Oblast' *see* Atyrau
77 U13 **Gusau** Zamfara, NW Nigeria
126 C3 **Gusev** *Ger.* Gumbinnen. Kaliningradskaya Oblast', W Russian Federation
146 J17 **Gushgy** *Rus.* Kushka. ≈ Mary Welaýaty, S Turkmenistan
Gushgy *see* Serhetabat
Gushiago *see* Gushiegu
77 Q14 **Gushiegu** *var.* Gushiago. NE Ghana
165 S17 **Gushikawa** Okinawa, Okinawa, SW Japan
113 L16 **Gusinje** E Montenegro
126 M4 **Gus'-Khrustal'nyy** Vladimirskaya Oblast', W Russian Federation
107 B19 **Guspini** Sardegna, Italy, C Mediterranean Sea
109 X8 **Güssing** Burgenland, SE Austria
109 V6 **Gusswerk** Steiermark, E Austria
92 O2 **Gustav Adolf Land** *physical region* NE Svalbard
195 X5 **Gustav Bull Mountains** ▲▲ Antarctica
39 W13 **Gustavus** Alaska, USA
92 O1 **Gustav V Land** *physical region* NE Svalbard
35 P9 **Gustine** California, W USA
25 R8 **Gustine** Texas, SW USA
100 M9 **Güstrow** Mecklenburg-Vorpommern, NE Germany
95 N18 **Gusum** Östergötland, S Sweden
Guta/Gúta *see* Kolárovo
Gutenstein *see* Ravne na Koroškem
101 G14 **Gütersloh** Nordrhein-Westfalen, W Germany
27 N10 **Guthrie** Oklahoma, C USA
25 P5 **Guthrie** Texas, SW USA
29 U14 **Guthrie Center** Iowa, C USA
41 Q13 **Gutiérrez Zamora** Veracruz-Llave, E Mexico
Gutta *see* Kolárovo
29 Y12 **Guttenberg** Iowa, C USA
Guttentag *see* Dobrodzień
Guttstadt *see* Dobre Miasto
162 G8 **Guulin** Govĭ-Altay, C Mongolia
153 V12 **Guwāhāti** *prev.* Gauhāti. Assam, NE India
139 R3 **Guwēr** *var.* Al Kuwayr, Al Quwayr, Quwair. N Iraq
146 A10 **Guwlumaýak** *Rus.* Kuuli-Mayak. Balkan Welaýaty, NW Turkmenistan
55 R9 **Guyana** *off.* Cooperative Republic of Guyana; *prev.* British Guiana. ◆ *republic* N South America
Guyana, Cooperative Republic of *see* Guyana
21 P5 **Guyandotte River** ≈ West Virginia, NE USA
Guyane *see* French Guiana
Guyi *see* Sanjiang
26 H8 **Guymon** Oklahoma, C USA
146 K12 **Guynuk** Lebap Welaýaty, NE Turkmenistan
Guyong *see* Jiangle
21 O9 **Guyot, Mount** ▲ North Carolina/Tennessee, SE USA
183 U5 **Guyra** New South Wales, SE Australia
159 W10 **Guyuan** Ningxia, N China
Guzar *see* G'uzor
Guzar *see* G'uzor
121 P2 **Güzelyurt** *Gk.* Mórfou, Morphou. W Cyprus
121 N2 **Güzelyurt Körfezi** *var.* Morfou Bay, Morphou Bay, *Gk.* Kólpos Mórfou. *bay* W Cyprus
Guzhou *see* Rongjiang
40 I3 **Guzmán** Chihuahua, N Mexico
147 N13 **G'uzor** *Rus.* Guzar. Qashqadaryo Viloyati, S Uzbekistan
147 N13 **G'uzor** *Rus.* Guzar. Qashqadaryo Viloyati, S Uzbekistan
119 B14 **Gvardeysk** *Ger.* Tapaiu. Kaliningradskaya Oblast', W Russian Federation
Gvardeyskoye *see* Hvardiys'ke
183 R5 **Gwabegar** New South Wales, SE Australia
148 J16 **Gwādar** *var.* Gwadur. Baluchistān, SW Pakistan
148 J16 **Gwādar East Bay** *bay* SW Pakistan
148 J16 **Gwādar West Bay** *bay* SW Pakistan
Gwadur *see* Gwādar
83 J17 **Gwai** Matabeleland North, W Zimbabwe
154 I7 **Gwalior** Madhya Pradesh, C India
83 J18 **Gwanda** Matabeleland South, SW Zimbabwe
79 N15 **Gwane** Orientale, N Dem. Rep. Congo
83 I17 **Gwayi** ≈ W Zimbabwe
110 G8 **Gwda** *var.* Glda, *Ger.* Küddow. ≈ NW Poland
97 C14 **Gweebarra Bay** *Ir.* Béal an Bheara. *inlet* W Ireland
97 D14 **Gweedore** *Ir.* Gaoth Dobhair. Donegal, NW Ireland
Gwelo *see* Gweru
97 K21 **Gwent** *cultural region* S Wales, UK
83 K17 **Gweru** *prev.* Gwelo. Midlands, C Zimbabwe
29 Q7 **Gwinner** North Dakota, N USA
77 Y13 **Gwoza** Borno, NE Nigeria
Gwy *see* Wye
183 R4 **Gwydir River** ≈ New South Wales, SE Australia
97 I19 **Gwynedd** *var.* Gwyneth. *cultural region* NW Wales, UK
Gwyneth *see* Gwynedd
159 O16 **Gyaca** *var.* Ngarrab. Xizang Zizhiqu, W China
Gya'gya *see* Saga
Gyaijêpozhanggê *see* Zhidoi
Gyaisi *see* Jiulong
115 M22 **Gyalí** *var.* Yialí. *island* Dodekánisa, Greece, Aegean Sea
Gyamotang *see* Dêngqên
Gyandzha *see* Gäncä
Gyangkar *see* Dinggyê
158 M16 **Gyangzê** Xizang Zizhiqu, W China
158 L14 **Gyaring Co** ◎ W China
159 Q12 **Gyaring Hu** ◎ C China
115 I20 **Gyáros** *var.* Yioúra. *island* Kykládes, Greece, Aegean Sea
122 J7 **Gyda** Yamalo-Nenetskiy Avtonomnyy Okrug, N Russian Federation
122 J7 **Gydanskiy Poluostrov** *Eng.* Gyda Peninsula. *peninsula* N Russian Federation
Gyda Peninsula *see* Gydanskiy Poluostrov
Gyêgu *see* Yushu
Gyéres *see* Câmpia Turzii
Gyergyószentmiklós *see* Gheorgheni
Gyergyótölgyes *see* Tulgheş
Gyertyámos *see* Cărpiniş
Gyeva *see* Detva
Gyigang *see* Zayü
Gyixong *see* Gonggar
95 I23 **Gyldenløveshøy** *hill range* C Denmark
181 Z10 **Gympie** Queensland, E Australia
166 L7 **Gyobingauk** Pegu, SW Myanmar (Burma)
111 M23 **Gyomaendrőd** Békés, SE Hungary
Gyömbér *see* Ďumbier
111 L22 **Gyöngyös** Heves, NE Hungary
111 H22 **Győr** *Ger.* Raab, *Lat.* Arrabona. Győr-Moson-Sopron, NW Hungary
111 G22 **Győr-Moson-Sopron** *off.* Győr-Moson-Sopron Megye. ⬖ *county* NW Hungary
Győr-Moson-Sopron Megye *see* Győr-Moson-Sopron
9 X15 **Gypsumville** Manitoba, S Canada
12 M4 **Gyrfalcon Islands** *island group* Northwest Territories, NE Canada
95 N14 **Gysinge** Gävleborg, C Sweden
115 F22 **Gýtheio** *var.* Githio; *prev.* Yíthion. Pelopónnisos, S Greece
146 L13 **Gyuichbirleshik** Lebap Welaýaty, E Turkmenistan
111 N24 **Gyula** *Rom.* Jula. Békés, SE Hungary
Gyulafehérvár *see* Alba Iulia
Gyulovo *see* Roza
137 T11 **Gyumri** *var.* Giumri, *Rus.* Kumayri; *prev.* Aleksandropol', Leninakan. W Armenia
146 D13 **Gyunuzyndag, Gora** ▲ Balkan Welaýaty, W Turkmenistan
146 J15 **Gyzylbaydak** *Rus.* Krasnoye Znamya. Mary Welaýaty, S Turkmenistan
Gyzyletrek *see* Etrek
146 D10 **Gyzylgaýa** *Rus.* Kizyl-Kaya. Balkan Welaýaty, NW Turkmenistan
146 A10 **Gyzylsuw** *Rus.* Kizyl-Su. Balkan Welaýaty, W Turkmenistan
Gyzyrlabat *see* Serdar
126 J3 **Gzhatsk** Smolenskaya Oblast', W Russian Federation

H

153 T12 **Ha** W Bhutan
Haabai *see* Ha'apai Group
99 H17 **Haacht** Vlaams Brabant, C Belgium
109 T4 **Haag** Niederösterreich, NE Austria
194 L8 **Haag Nunataks** ▲▲ Antarctica
92 N2 **Haakon VII Land** *physical region* NW Svalbard
98 O11 **Haaksbergen** Overijssel, E Netherlands
99 E14 **Haamstede** Zeeland, SW Netherlands
193 Y15 **Ha'ano** *island* Ha'apai Group, C Tonga
193 Y15 **Ha'apai Group** *var.* Haabai. *island group* C Tonga
93 L15 **Haapajärvi** Oulu, C Finland
93 L17 **Haapamäki** Länsi-Soumi, C Finland
93 L15 **Haapavesi** Oulu, C Finland
191 N7 **Haapiti** Moorea, W French Polynesia
118 F4 **Haapsalu** *Ger.* Hapsal. Läänemaa, W Estonia
Ha'Arava *see* 'Arabah, Wādī al
95 G24 **Haarby** *var.* Hårby. Fyn, C Denmark
98 H10 **Haarlem** *prev.* Harlem. Noord-Holland, W Netherlands
185 D19 **Haast** West Coast, South Island, New Zealand
185 C20 **Haast** ≈ South Island, New Zealand
185 D20 **Haast Pass** *pass* South Island, New Zealand
193 W16 **Ha'atua** 'Eau, E Tonga
149 P15 **Hab** ≈ SW Pakistan
141 W7 **Haba** *var.* Al Haba. Dubayy, NE United Arab Emirates
158 K2 **Habahe** *var.* Kaba. Xinjiang Uygur Zizhiqu, NW China
141 U13 **Ḩabarūt** *var.* Habrut. SW Oman
81 J18 **Habaswein** North Eastern, NE Kenya
99 L24 **Habay-la-Neuve** Luxembourg, SE Belgium
139 S8 **Ḩabbānīyah, Buḩayrat** ◎ C Iraq
Habelschwerdt *see* Bystrzyca Kłodzka
153 V14 **Habiganj** Sylhet, NE Bangladesh
163 Q12 **Habirag** Nei Mongol Zizhiqu, N China
95 L19 **Habo** Västra Götaland, S Sweden
123 V14 **Habomai Islands** *island group* Kuril'skiye Ostrova, SE Russian Federation
165 S2 **Haboro** Hokkaidō, NE Japan
153 S16 **Habra** West Bengal, NE India
Habrut *see* Ḩabarūt
143 P17 **Ḩabshān** Abū Ẓaby, C United Arab Emirates
54 E14 **Hacha** Putumayo, S Colombia
165 X13 **Hachijō** Tōkyō, Hachijō-jima, SE Japan
165 X13 **Hachijō-jima** *island* Izu-shotō, SE Japan
164 L12 **Hachiman** Gifu, Honshū, SW Japan
165 P7 **Hachimori** Akita, Honshū, C Japan
165 R7 **Hachinohe** Aomori, Honshū, C Japan
93 G17 **Hackås** Jämtland, C Sweden
18 K14 **Hackensack** New Jersey, NE USA
Hadama *see* Nazrēt
141 W13 **Ḩadbaram** S Oman
139 U13 **Ḩaddānīyah** *well* S Iraq
96 K12 **Haddington** SE Scotland, UK
141 Z8 **Ḩadd, Ra's al** *headland* NE Oman
Haded *see* Xadeed
77 W12 **Hadejia** Jigawa, N Nigeria
77 W12 **Hadejia** ≈ N Nigeria
138 F9 **Ḩadera** *var.* Khadera. Haifa, C Israel
Hadersleben *see* Haderslev
95 G24 **Haderslev** *Ger.* Hadersleben. Sønderjylland, SW Denmark
151 J21 **Hadhdhunmathi Atoll** *atoll* S Maldives
Hadhramaut *see* Ḩaḑramawt
141 W17 **Hadīboh** Suquṭrā, SE Yemen
158 K9 **Hadilik** Xinjiang Uygur Zizhiqu, W China
136 H16 **Hadım** Konya, S Turkey
140 K7 **Hadīyah** Al Madīnah, W Saudi Arabia
8 L5 **Hadley Bay** *bay* Victoria Island, Nunavut, N Canada
167 S6 **Ha Đông** *var.* Hadong. Ha Tây, N Vietnam
Hadong *see* Ha Đông
141 R15 **Ḩaḑramawt** *Eng.* Hadhramaut. ▲▲ S Yemen
Hadria *see* Adria
Hadrianopolis *see* Edirne
Hadria Picena *see* Apricena
95 G22 **Hadsten** Århus, C Denmark
95 G21 **Hadsund** Nordjylland, N Denmark
117 S4 **Hadyach** *Rus.* Gadyach. Poltavs'ka Oblast', NE Ukraine
112 I13 **Hadžići** Federacija Bosna I Hercegovina, SE Bosnia and Herzegovina
163 W14 **Haeju** S North Korea
Haerbin/Haerhpin/Ha-erh-pin *see* Harbin
141 P5 **Ḩafar al Bāṭin** Ash Sharqīyah, N Saudi Arabia
9 T15 **Hafford** Saskatchewan, S Canada
136 M13 **Hafik** Sivas, N Turkey
149 V8 **Hāfizābād** Punjab, E Pakistan
92 H4 **Hafnarfjördhur** Reykjanes, W Iceland
Hafnia *see* Denmark
Hafnia *see* København
Hafren *see* Severn
Hafun *see* Xaafuun
Hafun, Ras *see* Xaafuun, Raas
80 G10 **Hag 'Abdullah** Sinnar, E Sudan
81 K18 **Hagadera** North Eastern, E Kenya
138 G8 **HaGalil** *Eng.* Galilee. ▲▲ N Israel
14 G10 **Hagar** Ontario, S Canada
155 G18 **Hagari** *var.* Vedāvati. ≈ W India
188 B16 **Hagåtña** *var.* Agana, *var.* Agaña. ○ (Guam) NW Guam
100 M13 **Hagelberg** *hill* NE Germany
39 N14 **Hagemeister Island** *island* Alaska, USA
101 F15 **Hagen** Nordrhein-Westfalen, W Germany
100 K10 **Hagenow** Mecklenburg-Vorpommern, N Germany
10 K15 **Hagensborg** British Columbia, SW Canada
80 I13 **Hāgere Hiywet** *var.* Agere Hiywet, Ambo. Oromo, C Ethiopia
33 O15 **Hagerman** Idaho, NW USA
37 U14 **Hagerman** New Mexico, SW USA
21 V2 **Hagerstown** Maryland, NE USA
14 G16 **Hagersville** Ontario, S Canada
102 J15 **Hagetmau** Landes, SW France
95 K14 **Hagfors** Värmland, C Sweden
93 G16 **Häggenås** Jämtland, C Sweden
164 E12 **Hagi** Yamaguchi, Honshū, SW Japan
167 S5 **Ha Giang** Ha Giang, N Vietnam
Hagios Evstrátios *see* Ágios Efstrátios
HaGolan *see* Golan Heights
103 T4 **Hagondange** Moselle, NE France
97 B18 **Hag's Head** *Ir.* Ceann Caillí. *headland* W Ireland
102 I3 **Hague, Cap de la** *headland* N France
103 V5 **Haguenau** Bas-Rhin, NE France
165 X16 **Hahajima-rettō** *island group* SE Japan
15 R8 **Há Há, Lac** ◎ Québec, SE Canada
172 H13 **Hahaya** ✈ (Moroni) Grande Comore, NW Comoros
22 K9 **Hahnville** Louisiana, S USA
83 E22 **Haib** Karas, S Namibia
Haibak *see* Āybak
149 N15 **Haibo** ≈ SW Pakistan
Haibowan *see* Wuhai
163 U12 **Haicheng** Liaoning, NE China
Haicheng *see* Haiyuan
167 T6 **Hai Dương** Hai Hưng, N Vietnam
Haida *see* Nový Bor
Haidarabad *see* Hyderābād
Haidenschaft *see* Ajdovščina
138 F9 **Haifa** ⬖ *district* NW Israel
Haifa *see* Ḩefa
Haifa, Bay of *see* Ḩefa, Mifraẓ
161 P14 **Haifeng** Guangdong, S China
Haifong *see* Hai Phong
161 P3 **Hai He** ≈ E China
Haikang *see* Leizhou
160 L17 **Haikou** *var.* Hai-k'ou, Hoihow, *Fr.* Hoï-Hao. *province capital* Hainan, S China
Hai-k'ou *see* Haikou
140 M6 **Ḩā'il** Ḩā'il, NW Saudi Arabia
141 N5 **Ḩā'il** *off.* Minṭaqah Ḩā'il. ⬖ *province* N Saudi Arabia
Hai-la-erh *see* Hailar
163 S6 **Hailar** *var.* Hai-la-erh; *prev.* Hulun. Nei Mongol Zizhiqu, N China
163 S6 **Hailar He** ≈ NE China
33 P14 **Hailey** Idaho, NW USA
14 H9 **Haileybury** Ontario, S Canada
163 X9 **Hailin** Heilongjiang, NE China
Ḩā'il, Minṭaqah *see* Ḩā'il
Hailong *see* Meihekou
93 K14 **Hailuoto** *Swe.* Karlö. *island* W Finland
Haima *see* Haymā'
Haimen *see* Taizhou
160 M17 **Hainan** *var.* Hainan Sheng, Qiong. ⬖ *province* S China
160 K17 **Hainan Dao** *island* S China
Hainan Sheng *see* Hainan
Hainan Strait *see* Qiongzhou Haixia
Hainasch *see* Ainaži
Hainau *see* Chojnów
99 E20 **Hainaut** ⬖ *province* SW Belgium
Hainburg *see* Hainburg an der Donau
109 Z4 **Hainburg an der Donau** *var.* Hainburg. Niederösterreich, NE Austria
39 W12 **Haines** Alaska, USA
32 L12 **Haines** Oregon, NW USA
23 W12 **Haines City** Florida, SE USA
10 H8 **Haines Junction** Yukon Territory, W Canada
109 W4 **Hainfeld** Niederösterreich, NE Austria
101 N16 **Hainichen** Sachsen, E Germany
Hai Ninh *see* Mong Cai
167 T6 **Hai Phong** *var.* Haifong, Haiphong. N Vietnam
Haiphong *see* Hai Phong
161 S12 **Haitan Dao** *island* SE China
44 K8 **Haiti** *off.* Republic of Haiti. ◆ *republic* C West Indies
Haiti, Republic of *see* Haiti
35 T11 **Haiwee Reservoir** ⊠ California, W USA
80 I7 **Haiya** Red Sea, NE Sudan
159 T10 **Haiyan** *var.* Sanjiaocheng. Qinghai, W China
160 M13 **Haiyang Shan** ▲▲ S China
159 V10 **Haiyuan** Ningxia, N China
Hajda *see* Nový Bor
111 M22 **Hajdú-Bihar** *off.* Hajdú-Bihar Megye. ⬖ *county* E Hungary
Hajdú-Bihar Megye *see* Hajdú-Bihar
111 N22 **Hajdúböszörmény** Hajdú-Bihar, E Hungary
111 N22 **Hajdúhadház** Hajdú-Bihar, E Hungary
111 N21 **Hajdúnánás** Hajdú-Bihar, E Hungary
111 N22 **Hajdúszoboszló** Hajdú-Bihar, E Hungary
142 J3 **Ḩājī Ebrāhīm, Kūh-e** ▲ Iran/Iraq
165 O9 **Hajiki-zaki** *headland* Sado, C Japan
Hajine *see* Abū Ḩardān
153 P13 **Hājīpur** Bihār, N India
141 N14 **Ḩajjah** W Yemen
139 U11 **Ḩajjama** S Iraq
143 R12 **Ḩājjīābād** Hormozgān, C Iran
139 U14 **Ḩājj, Thaqb al** *well* S Iraq
113 L16 **Hajla** ▲ E Montenegro
110 P10 **Hajnówka** *Ger.* Hermhausen. Podlaskie, NE Poland
166 K4 **Haka** Chin State, W Myanmar (Burma)
Hakapehi *see* Punaauia
Hakâri *see* Hakkâri
137 T16 **Hakkâri** *var.* Çölemerik, Hakâri. Hakkâri, SE Turkey
137 T16 **Hakkâri** *var.* Hakkari. ⬖ *province* SE Turkey
Hakkari *see* Hakkâri
92 J12 **Hakkas** Norrbotten, N Sweden
164 J14 **Hakken-zan** ▲ Honshū, SW Japan
165 R7 **Hakkōda-san** ▲ Honshū, C Japan
165 T2 **Hako-dake** ▲ Hokkaidō, NE Japan
165 R5 **Hakodate** Hokkaidō, NE Japan
164 L11 **Hakui** Ishikawa, Honshū, SW Japan
190 B16 **Hakupu** SE Niue
164 L12 **Haku-san** ▲ Honshū, SW Japan
Hal *see* Halle
149 Q15 **Hāla** Sind, SE Pakistan
138 J3 **Ḩalab** *Eng.* Aleppo, *Fr.* Alep; *anc.* Beroea. Ḩalab, NW Syria
138 J3 **Ḩalab** *off.* Muḩāfaẓat Ḩalab, *var.* Aleppo, Halab. ⬖ *governorate* NW Syria
138 J3 **Ḩalab** ✈ Ḩalab, NW Syria
Halab *see* Ḩalab
141 O8 **Ḩalabān** *var.* Halībān. Ar Riyāḑ, C Saudi Arabia
139 V4 **Ḩalabja** NE Iraq
Ḩalab, Muḩāfaẓat *see* Ḩalab
146 L13 **Halaç** *Rus.* Khalach. Lebap Welaýaty, E Turkmenistan
190 A16 **Halagigie Point** *headland* W Niue
75 Z11 **Halaib** SE Egypt
190 G12 **Halalo** Île Uvea, N Wallis and Futuna
Halandri *see* Chalándri
141 X13 **Ḩalāniyāt, Juzur al** *var.* Jazā'ir Bin Ghalfān, *Eng.* Kuria Muria Islands. *island group* S Oman
141 W13 **Ḩalāniyāt, Khalīj al** *Eng.* Kuria Muria Bay. *bay* S Oman
Halas *see* Kiskunhalas
38 G11 **Hālawa** *var.* Halawa. Hawai'i, USA, C Pacific Ocean
Halawa *see* Hālawa
38 F9 **Halawa, Cape** *var.* Cape Halawa. *headland* Moloka'i, Hawai'i, USA
Cape Halawa *see* Hālawa, Cape
Halban *see* Tsetserleg
101 K14 **Halberstadt** Sachsen-Anhalt, C Germany
184 M12 **Halcombe** Manawatu-Wanganui, North Island, New Zealand
95 I16 **Halden** *prev.* Fredrikshald. Østfold, S Norway
100 L13 **Haldensleben** Sachsen-Anhalt, C Germany
Háldi *see* Halti
153 S17 **Haldia** West Bengal, NE India
152 K10 **Haldwāni** Uttaranchal, N India
163 P9 **Haldzan** *var.* Hatavch. Sühbaatar
38 F10 **Haleakalā** *crater* Maui, Hawai'i, USA
25 N4 **Hale Center** Texas, SW USA
99 J18 **Halen** Limburg, NE Belgium
23 O2 **Haleyville** Alabama, S USA
77 O17 **Half Assini** SW Ghana
35 R8 **Half Dome** ▲ California, W USA
185 C25 **Halfmoon Bay** *var.* Oban. Stewart Island, Southland, New Zealand
182 E5 **Half Moon Lake** *salt lake* South Australia
163 S8 **Halhgol** *var.* Tsagaannuur. Dornod, E Mongolia
163 R7 **Halhgol** Dornod, E Mongolia
Haliacmon *see* Aliákmonas
Halibān *see* Ḩalabān
14 I13 **Haliburton** Ontario, SE Canada
14 I12 **Haliburton Highlands** *var.* Madawaska Highlands. *hill range* Ontario, SE Canada
13 Q15 **Halifax** *province capital* Nova Scotia, SE Canada
97 L17 **Halifax** N England, UK
21 W8 **Halifax** North Carolina, SE USA
21 U7 **Halifax** Virginia, NE USA
13 Q15 **Halifax** ✈ Nova Scotia, SE Canada
143 T13 **Halīl Rūd** *seasonal river* SE Iran

◆ Country ● Country Capital ◇ Dependent Territory ○ Dependent Territory Capital ⬖ Administrative Regions ✈ International Airport ▲ Mountain ▲▲ Mountain Range ⛰ Volcano ◎ Lake ≈ River ⊠ Reservoir

138 I6 Ḩalīmah ▲ Lebanon/Syria
162 G8 Haliun Govĭ-Altay, W Mongolia
118 I3 Haljala Ger. Halljal. Lääne-Virumaa, N Estonia
39 Q4 Halkett, Cape headland Alaska, USA
Halkida see Chalkída
96 J6 Halkirk N Scotland, UK
15 X7 Hall 〜 Québec, SE Canada
Hall see Schwäbisch Hall
93 H15 Hälla Västerbotten, N Sweden
96 J6 Halladale 〜 N Scotland, UK
95 J21 Halland ◆ county S Sweden
23 Z15 Hallandale Florida, SE USA
95 K22 Hallandsås physical region S Sweden
9 P6 Hall Beach Nunavut, N Canada
99 G19 Halle Fr. Hal. Vlaams Brabant, C Belgium
101 M15 Halle var. Halle an der Saale. Sachsen-Anhalt, C Germany
Halle an der Saale see Halle
35 W3 Halleck Nevada, W USA
95 L15 Hällefors Örebro, C Sweden
95 N16 Hälleforsnäs Södermanland, C Sweden
109 Q6 Hallein Salzburg, N Austria
101 L15 Halle-Neustadt Sachsen-Anhalt, C Germany
25 U12 Hallettsville Texas, SW USA
195 N4 Halley UK research station Antarctica
28 L4 Halliday North Dakota, N USA
37 S2 Halligan Reservoir ⊞ Colorado, C USA
100 G7 Halligen island group N Germany
94 G13 Hallingdal valley S Norway
38 J12 Hall Island island Alaska, USA
Hall Island see Maiana
189 P15 Hall Islands island group C Micronesia
118 H6 Halliste 〜 S Estonia
Halljal see Haljala
93 I15 Hällnäs Västerbotten, N Sweden
29 R2 Hallock Minnesota, N USA
9 S6 Hall Peninsula peninsula Baffin Island, Nunavut, NE Canada
20 F9 Halls Tennessee, S USA
95 M16 Hallsberg Örebro, C Sweden
181 N5 Halls Creek Western Australia
182 L12 Halls Gap Victoria, SE Australia
95 N15 Hallstahammar Västmanland, C Sweden
109 R6 Hallstatt Salzburg, W Austria
109 R6 Hallstatter See ◎ C Austria
95 P14 Hallstavik Stockholm, C Sweden
25 X7 Hallsville Texas, SW USA
103 P1 Halluin Nord, N France
Halmahera, Laut see Halmahera Sea
171 R11 Halmahera, Pulau prev. Djailolo, Gilolo, Jailolo. island E Indonesia
171 S12 Halmahera Sea Ind. Laut Halmahera. sea E Indonesia
95 J21 Halmstad Halland, S Sweden
119 N15 Halowchyn Rus. Golovchin. Mahilyowskaya Voblasts', E Belarus
95 H20 Hals Nordjylland, N Denmark
94 F8 Halsa Møre og Romsdal, S Norway
119 I15 Hal'shany Rus. Gol'shany. Hrodzyenskaya Voblasts', W Belarus
Hälsingborg see Helsingborg
29 R5 Halstad Minnesota, N USA
27 N6 Halstead Kansas, C USA
99 G15 Halsteren Noord-Brabant, S Netherlands
93 L16 Halsua Länsi-Soumi, W Finland
101 E14 Haltern Nordrhein-Westfalen, W Germany
92 J9 Halti var. Haltiatunturi, Lapp. Háldi. ▲ Finland/Norway
Haltiatunturi see Halti
116 J6 Halych Ivano-Frankivs'ka Oblast', W Ukraine
Halycus see Platani
103 P3 Ham Somme, N France
Hama see Ḩamāh
164 F12 Hamada Shimane, Honshū, SW Japan
142 L6 Hamadān anc. Ecbatana. Hamadān, W Iran
142 L6 Hamadān off. Ostān-e Hamadān. ◆ province W Iran
Hamadān, Ostān-e see Hamadān
138 I5 Ḩamāh var. Hama; anc. Epiphania, Bibl. Hamath. Ḩamāh, W Syria
138 I5 Ḩamāh off. Muḩāfaz̧at Ḩamāh, var. Hama. ◆ governorate C Syria
Ḩamāh, Muḩāfaz̧at see Ḩamāh
165 S3 Hamamasu Hokkaidō, NE Japan
164 L14 Hamamatsu var. Hamamatu. Shizuoka, Honshū, S Japan
Hamamatu see Hamamatsu
165 W14 Hamanaka Hokkaidō, NE Japan
164 L14 Hamana-ko ◎ Honshū, S Japan
94 I13 Hamar prev. Storhammer. Hedmark, S Norway
141 U10 Ḩamārīr al Kidan, Qalamat well E Saudi Arabia
164 I12 Hamasaka Hyōgo, Honshū, SW Japan
Hamath see Ḩamāh
165 T1 Hamatonbetsu Hokkaidō, NE Japan
155 K26 Hambantota Southern Province, SE Sri Lanka
Hambourg see Hamburg
100 J9 Hamburg Hamburg, N Germany
27 V14 Hamburg Arkansas, C USA
29 S16 Hamburg Iowa, C USA
18 D10 Hamburg New York, NE USA
100 I10 Hamburg Fr. Hambourg. ◆ state N Germany
148 K5 Hamdam Āb, Dasht-e Pash. Dasht-i Hamdamab. ▲▲ W Afghanistan
Hamdamab, Dasht-i see Hamdam Āb, Dasht-e
18 M13 Hamden Connecticut, NE USA
140 K6 Ḩamḑ, Wādī al dry watercourse W Saudi Arabia
93 K18 Hämeenkyrö Länsi-Suomi, W Finland
93 L19 Hämeenlinna Swe. Tavastehus. Etelä-Suomi, S Finland
HaMelaḥ, Yam see Dead Sea
Hamelin see Hameln
100 I13 Hameln Eng. Hamelin. Niedersachsen, N Germany
180 I8 Hamersley Range ▲▲ Western Australia
163 Y12 Hamgyŏng-sanmaek ▲▲ N North Korea
163 X13 Hamhŭng C North Korea
159 O6 Hami var. Ha-mi, Uigh. Kumul, Qomul. Xinjiang Uygur Zizhiqu, NW China
Ha-mi see Hami
139 X10 Ḩāmid Amīn E Iraq
141 W11 Hamīdān, Khawr oasis SE Saudi Arabia
138 H5 Ḩamīdīyah var. Hamīdīyé. Ţarţūs, W Syria
114 L12 Hamidiye Edirne, NW Turkey
Hamīdīyé see Ḩamīdīyah
182 L12 Hamilton Victoria, SE Australia
64 B12 Hamilton ○ (Bermuda) C Bermuda
14 G16 Hamilton Ontario, S Canada
184 M7 Hamilton Waikato, North Island, New Zealand
96 I12 Hamilton S Scotland, UK
23 N3 Hamilton Alabama, S USA
38 M10 Hamilton Alaska, USA
30 J13 Hamilton Illinois, N USA
27 S3 Hamilton Missouri, C USA
33 P10 Hamilton Montana, NW USA
25 S8 Hamilton Texas, SW USA
14 G16 Hamilton ✈ Ontario, SE Canada
64 I6 Hamilton Bank undersea feature SE Labrador Sea
182 E1 Hamilton Creek seasonal river South Australia
13 R8 Hamilton Inlet inlet Newfoundland and Labrador, E Canada
27 T12 Hamilton, Lake ⊞ Arkansas, C USA
35 W6 Hamilton, Mount ▲ Nevada, W USA
75 S8 Ḩamīm, Wādī al 〜 NE Libya
93 N19 Hamina Swe. Fredrikshamn. Kymi, S Finland
9 W16 Hamiota Manitoba, S Canada
152 L13 Hamīrpur Uttar Pradesh, N India
Hamïs Musait see Khamīs Mushayt
21 T11 Hamlet North Carolina, SE USA
25 P6 Hamlin Texas, SW USA
21 P5 Hamlin West Virginia, NE USA
31 O7 Hamlin Lake ◎ Michigan, N USA
101 F14 Hamm var. Hamm in Westfalen. Nordrhein-Westfalen, W Germany
Ḩammāmāt, Khalīj al see Hammamet, Golfe de
75 N5 Hammamet, Golfe de Ar. Khalīj al Ḩammāmāt. gulf NE Tunisia
139 R3 Ḩammān al 'Alīl N Iraq
139 X12 Ḩammār, Hawr al ◎ SE Iraq
93 J20 Hammarland Åland, SW Finland
93 H16 Hammarstrand Jämtland, C Sweden
93 O17 Hammaslahti Pohjois-Karjala, SE Finland
99 F17 Hamme Oost-Vlaanderen, NW Belgium
100 H10 Hamme 〜 NW Germany
95 G22 Hammel Århus, C Denmark
101 I18 Hammelburg Bayern, C Germany
99 H18 Hamme-Mille Walloon Brabant, C Belgium
100 H10 Hamme-Oste-Kanal canal NW Germany
93 G16 Hammerdal Jämtland, C Sweden
92 K8 Hammerfest Finnmark, N Norway
101 D14 Hamminkeln Nordrhein-Westfalen, W Germany
Hamm in Westfalen see Hamm
26 K10 Hammon Oklahoma, C USA
31 N11 Hammond Indiana, N USA
22 K8 Hammond Louisiana, S USA
99 K20 Hamoir Liège, E Belgium
99 J21 Hamois Namur, SE Belgium
99 K16 Hamont Limburg, NE Belgium
185 F22 Hampden Otago, South Island, New Zealand
19 R6 Hampden Maine, NE USA
97 M23 Hampshire cultural region S England, UK
13 O15 Hampton New Brunswick, SE Canada
27 U14 Hampton Arkansas, C USA
29 V12 Hampton Iowa, C USA
19 P10 Hampton New Hampshire, NE USA
21 R14 Hampton South Carolina, SE USA
21 P8 Hampton Tennessee, S USA
21 X7 Hampton Virginia, NE USA
94 L11 Hamra Gävleborg, C Sweden
80 D10 Hamrat esh Sheikh Northern Kordofan, C Sudan
139 S5 Ḩamrīn, Jabal ▲▲ N Iraq
121 P16 Hamrun C Malta
167 U14 Ham Thuân Nam Binh Thuân, S Vietnam
Hāmūn, Daryācheh-ye see Şāberī, Hāmūn-e/Sīstān, Daryācheh-ye
Hamwih see Southampton
38 G10 Hāna var. Hana. Maui, Hawai'i, USA
Hana see Hāna
21 S14 Hanahan South Carolina, SE USA
38 B8 Hanalei Kaua'i, Hawai'i, USA
167 U10 Ha Nam Quang Nam-Đa Năng, C Vietnam
165 Q9 Hanamaki Iwate, Honshū, C Japan
38 F10 Hanamanioa, Cape headland Maui, Hawai'i, USA
190 B16 Hanan ✈ (Alofi) SW Niue
101 H18 Hanau Hessen, W Germany
162 M11 Hanbogd var. Ih Bulag. Ömnögovĭ, S Mongolia
8 L9 Hanbury 〜 Northwest Territories, NW Canada
Hâncești see Hîncești
10 M15 Hanceville British Columbia, SW Canada
23 P3 Hanceville Alabama, S USA
Hancewicze see Hantsavichy
160 L6 Hancheng Shaanxi, C China
21 V2 Hancock Maryland, NE USA
30 M3 Hancock Michigan, N USA
29 S8 Hancock Minnesota, N USA
18 I12 Hancock New York, NE USA
80 Q12 Handa Bari, NE Somalia
161 O5 Handan var. Han-tan. Hebei, E China
95 P16 Handen Stockholm, C Sweden
81 J22 Handeni Tanga, E Tanzania
37 Q7 Handies Peak ▲ Colorado, C USA
111 J19 Handlová Ger. Krickerhäu, Hung. Nyitrabánya; prev. Kriegerhaj. Trenčiansky Kraj, C Slovakia
165 O13 Haneda ✈ (Tōkyō) Tōkyō, Honshū, S Japan
138 F13 HaNegev Eng. Negev. desert S Israel
Hanfeng see Kaixian
35 Q11 Hanford California, W USA
191 V16 Hanga Roa Easter Island, Chile, E Pacific Ocean
162 I7 Hangay var. Hunt. Arhangay, C Mongolia
162 H7 Hangayn Nuruu ▲▲ C Mongolia
Hang-chou/Hangchow see Hangzhou
95 K20 Hånger Jönköping, S Sweden
Hangö see Hanko
161 R9 Hangzhou var. Hang-chou, Hangchow. province capital Zhejiang, SE China
162 J4 Hanh var. Turt. Hövsgöl, N Mongolia
162 F5 Hanhöhiy Uul ▲▲ NW Mongolia
162 K10 Hanhongor var. Ögöömör. Ömnögovĭ, S Mongolia
146 I14 Hanhowuz Rus. Khauz-Khan. Ahal Welaýaty, S Turkmenistan
146 I14 Hanhowuz Suw Howdany Rus. Khauzkhanskoye Vodokhranilishche. ◎ S Turkmenistan
146 I14 Hanhowuz Suw Howdany Rus. Khauzkhanskoye Vodoranilishche. ⊞ S Turkmenistan
137 P15 Hani Diyarbakır, SE Turkey
Hania see Chaniá
141 R11 Ḩanīsh al Kabīr, Jazīrat al island SW Yemen
Hanka, Lake see Khanka, Lake
93 M17 Hankasalmi Länsi-Suomi, C Finland
29 R7 Hankinson North Dakota, N USA
93 K20 Hanko Swe. Hangö. Etelä-Suomi, SW Finland
Han-kou/Han-k'ou/Hankow see Wuhan
36 M6 Hanksville Utah, W USA
152 K6 Hanle Jammu and Kashmir, NW India
185 I17 Hanmer Springs Canterbury, South Island, New Zealand
9 R16 Hanna Alberta, SW Canada
27 V3 Hannibal Missouri, C USA
180 M3 Hann, Mount ▲ Western Australia
100 I12 Hannover Eng. Hanover. Niedersachsen, NW Germany
99 J19 Hannut Liège, C Belgium
95 L22 Hanöbukten bay S Sweden
167 T6 Ha Nôi Eng. Hanoi, Fr. Hanoï. ● (Vietnam) N Vietnam
14 F14 Hanover Ontario, S Canada
31 P15 Hanover Indiana, N USA
18 G16 Hanover Pennsylvania, NE USA
21 W6 Hanover Virginia, NE USA
Hanover see Hannover
63 G23 Hanover, Isla island S Chile
Hanselbeck see Érd
195 X5 Hansen Mountains ▲▲ Antarctica
160 M8 Han Shui 〜 C China
152 H10 Hānsi Haryāna, NW India
95 F20 Hanstholm Viborg, NW Denmark
Han-tan see Handan
158 H6 Hantengri Feng var. Pik Khan-Tengri. ▲ China/Kazakhstan see also Khan-Tengri, Pik
119 I18 Hantsavichy Pol. Hancewicze, Rus. Gantsevichi. Brestskaya Voblasts', SW Belarus
9 Q6 Hantzsch 〜 Baffin Island, Nunavut, NE Canada
152 G9 Hanumāngarh Rājasthān, NW India
183 O9 Hanwood New South Wales, SE Australia
Hanyang see Wuhan
Hanyang see Caidian
160 H10 Hanyuan var. Fulin. Sichuan, C China
Hanyuan see Xihe
160 J7 Hanzhong Shaanxi, C China
191 W11 Hao atoll Îles Tuamotu, C French Polynesia
153 S16 Hāora prev. Howrah. West Bengal, NE India
78 K8 Haouach, Ouadi dry watercourse E Chad
92 K13 Haparanda Norrbotten, N Sweden
25 N3 Happy Texas, SW USA
34 M1 Happy Camp California, W USA
13 Q9 Happy Valley-Goose Bay prev. Goose Bay. Newfoundland and Labrador, E Canada
Hapsal see Haapsalu
152 J10 Hāpur Uttar Pradesh, N India
138 F12 HaQatan, HaMakhtesh ▲▲ S Israel
140 I4 Ḩaql Tabūk, NW Saudi Arabia
171 U14 Har Pulau Kai Besar, E Indonesia
Haraat see Tsagaandelger
141 R8 Ḩaraḑ var. Haradh. Ash Sharqīyah, E Saudi Arabia
Haradh see Ḩaraḑ
118 N12 Haradok Rus. Gorodok. Vitsyebskaya Voblasts', N Belarus
92 J13 Harads Norrbotten, N Sweden
119 G19 Haradzyets Rus. Gorodets. Brestskaya Voblasts', SW Belarus
119 J17 Haradzyeya Rus. Gorodeya. Minskaya Voblasts', C Belarus
191 V10 Haraiki atoll Îles Tuamotu, C French Polynesia
165 Q11 Haramachi Fukushima, Honshū, E Japan
118 M12 Harany Rus. Gorany. Vitsyebskaya Voblasts', N Belarus
83 L16 Harare prev. Salisbury. ● (Zimbabwe) Mashonaland East, NE Zimbabwe
83 L16 Harare ✈ Mashonaland East, NE Zimbabwe
78 J10 Haraz-Djombo Batha, C Chad
119 O16 Harbavichy Rus. Gorbovichi. Mahilyowskaya Voblasts', E Belarus
76 J16 Harbel W Liberia
163 W8 Harbin var. Haerbin, Ha-erh-pin, Kharbin; prev. Haerhpin, Pingkiang, Pinkiang. province capital Heilongjiang, NE China
31 S7 Harbor Beach Michigan, N USA
13 T13 Harbour Breton Newfoundland, Newfoundland and Labrador, E Canada
65 D25 Harbours, Bay of bay East Falkland, Falkland Islands
Hårby see Haarby
36 I13 Harcuvar Mountains ▲▲ Arizona, SW USA
108 I7 Hard Vorarlberg, NW Austria
154 H11 Harda Khas Madhya Pradesh, C India
95 D14 Hardanger physical region S Norway
95 D14 Hardangerfjorden fjord S Norway
94 E13 Hardangerjøkulen glacier S Norway
95 E14 Hardangervidda plateau S Norway
83 D20 Hardap ◆ district S Namibia
21 R15 Hardeeville South Carolina, SE USA
98 L5 Hardegarijp Fris. Hurdegaryp. Friesland, N Netherlands
98 O9 Hardenberg Overijssel, E Netherlands
183 Q9 Harden-Murrumburrah New South Wales, SE Australia
98 K10 Harderwijk Gelderland, C Netherlands
30 J14 Hardin Illinois, N USA
33 V11 Hardin Montana, NW USA
23 R5 Harding, Lake ⊞ Alabama/Georgia, SE USA
20 J6 Hardinsburg Kentucky, S USA
98 I13 Hardinxveld-Giessendam Zuid-Holland, C Netherlands
9 R15 Hardisty Alberta, SW Canada
152 L12 Hardoi Uttar Pradesh, N India
Hardwar see Haridwār
23 U4 Hardwick Georgia, SE USA
27 W9 Hardy Arkansas, C USA
94 D10 Hareid Møre og Romsdal, S Norway
8 H7 Hare Indian 〜 Northwest Territories, NW Canada
99 D18 Harelbeke var. Harlebeke. West-Vlaanderen, W Belgium
Harem see Ḩārim
100 E11 Haren Niedersachsen, NW Germany
98 N6 Haren Groningen, NE Netherlands
80 L13 Hārer E Ethiopia
95 P14 Harg Uppsala, C Sweden
Hargeisa see Hargeysa
80 M13 Hargeysa var. Hargeisa. Woqooyi Galbeed, NW Somalia
116 J10 Harghita ◆ county NE Romania
25 S17 Hargill Texas, SW USA
162 J8 Harhorin Övörhangay, C Mongolia
159 Q9 Har Hu ◎ C China
Hariana see Haryāna
141 P15 Ḩarīb W Yemen
168 M12 Hari, Batang prev. Djambi. 〜 Sumatera, W Indonesia
152 J9 Haridwār prev. Hardwar. Uttaranchal, N India
155 F18 Harihar Karnātaka, W India
185 F18 Harihari West Coast, South Island, New Zealand
138 I3 Ḩārim var. Harem. Idlib, W Syria
98 F13 Haringvliet channel SW Netherlands
98 F13 Haringvlietdam dam SW Netherlands
149 U5 Haripur North-West Frontier Province, NW Pakistan
148 J4 Harīrūd var. Tedzhen, Turkm. Tejen. 〜 Afghanistan/Iran see also Tejen
Harīrūd see Tejen
94 J11 Härjåhågnen Swe. Härjahågnen, var Härjehågna. ▲ Norway/Sweden
Härjahågnen see Østrehogna
Härjahågnen see Härjåhågnen
93 K18 Harjavalta Länsi-Suomi, W Finland
Härjehågna see Østrehogna
Härjehågna see Härjåhågnen
118 G4 Harjumaa var. Harju Maakond. ◆ province NW Estonia
Harju Maakond see Harjumaa
21 X11 Harkers Island North Carolina, SE USA
139 S1 Harki N Iraq
29 T14 Harlan Iowa, C USA
21 O7 Harlan Kentucky, S USA
29 N17 Harlan County Lake ⊞ Nebraska, C USA
116 L9 Hârlău var. Hîrlău. Iași, NE Romania
Harlebeke see Harelbeke
33 U7 Harlem Montana, NW USA
Harlem see Haarlem
95 G22 Harlev Århus, C Denmark
98 K6 Harlingen Fris. Harns. Friesland, N Netherlands
25 T17 Harlingen Texas, SW USA
97 O21 Harlow E England, UK
33 T10 Harlowton Montana, NW USA
94 N11 Harmånger Gävleborg, C Sweden
98 I11 Harmelen Utrecht, C Netherlands
29 X11 Harmony Minnesota, N USA
32 J14 Harney Basin basin Oregon, NW USA
0 F9 Harney Basin ▲▲ Oregon, NW USA
32 J14 Harney Lake ◎ Oregon, NW USA
28 J10 Harney Peak ▲ South Dakota, N USA
93 H17 Härnösand var. Hernösand. Västernorrland, C Sweden
Harns see Harlingen
162 F6 Har Nuur ◎ NW Mongolia
105 P4 Haro La Rioja, N Spain
40 F6 Haro, Cabo headland NW Mexico
94 D9 Harøy island S Norway
97 N21 Harpenden E England, UK
76 L18 Harper var. Cape Palmas. NE Liberia
26 M7 Harper Kansas, C USA
32 L13 Harper Oregon, NW USA
25 Q10 Harper Texas, SW USA
35 U13 Harper Lake salt flat California, W USA
39 T9 Harper, Mount ▲ Alaska, USA
95 J21 Harplinge Halland, S Sweden
36 J13 Harquahala Mountains ▲▲ Arizona, SW USA
141 T15 Ḩarrah SE Yemen
12 H11 Harricana 〜 Québec, SE Canada
20 M9 Harriman Tennessee, S USA
13 R11 Harrington Harbour Québec, E Canada
64 B12 Harrington Sound bay Bermuda, NW Atlantic Ocean
96 F8 Harris physical region NW Scotland, UK
27 X10 Harrisburg Arkansas, C USA
30 M17 Harrisburg Illinois, N USA
28 I14 Harrisburg Nebraska, C USA
32 F12 Harrisburg Oregon, NW USA
18 G15 Harrisburg state capital Pennsylvania, NE USA
182 F6 Harris, Lake ◎ South Australia
23 W11 Harris, Lake ◎ Florida, SE USA
83 J22 Harrismith Free State, E South Africa
27 T9 Harrison Arkansas, C USA
31 Q7 Harrison Michigan, N USA
28 I12 Harrison Nebraska, C USA
39 Q5 Harrison Bay inlet Alaska, USA
22 I6 Harrisonburg Louisiana, S USA
21 U4 Harrisonburg Virginia, NE USA
13 R7 Harrison, Cape cape Newfoundland and Labrador, E Canada
27 R5 Harrisonville Missouri, C USA
Harris Ridge see Lomonosov Ridge
192 M3 Harris Seamount undersea feature N Pacific Ocean
96 F8 Harris, Sound of strait NW Scotland, UK
31 R6 Harrisville Michigan, N USA
21 R3 Harrisville West Virginia, NE USA
20 M6 Harrodsburg Kentucky, S USA
97 M16 Harrogate N England, UK
25 Q4 Harrold Texas, SW USA
27 S5 Harry S. Truman Reservoir ⊞ Missouri, C USA
100 G13 Harsewinkel Nordrhein-Westfalen, W Germany
116 M14 Hârşova prev. Hîrşova. Constanța, SE Romania
92 H10 Harstad Troms, N Norway
31 O8 Hart Michigan, N USA
24 M4 Hart Texas, SW USA
10 I5 Hart 〜 Yukon Territory, NW Canada
83 F23 Hartbees 〜 C South Africa
109 X7 Hartberg Steiermark, SE Austria
182 I10 Hart, Cape headland South Australia
95 E14 Hårteigen ▲ S Norway
23 Q7 Hartford Alabama, S USA
27 R11 Hartford Arkansas, C USA
18 M12 Hartford state capital Connecticut, NE USA
20 J6 Hartford Kentucky, S USA
31 P10 Hartford Michigan, N USA
29 R11 Hartford South Dakota, N USA
30 M8 Hartford Wisconsin, N USA
31 P13 Hartford City Indiana, N USA
29 Q13 Hartington Nebraska, C USA
13 N14 Hartland New Brunswick, SE Canada
97 H23 Hartland Point headland SW England, UK
97 M15 Hartlepool N England, UK
29 T12 Hartley Iowa, C USA
24 M1 Hartley Texas, SW USA
32 J15 Hart Mountain ▲ Oregon, NW USA
173 U10 Hartog Ridge undersea feature W Indian Ocean
93 M18 Hartola Etelä-Suomi, S Finland
67 U14 Harts var. Hartz. 〜 N South Africa
23 P2 Hartselle Alabama, S USA
23 S3 Hartsfield Atlanta ✈ Georgia, SE USA
27 Q11 Hartshorne Oklahoma, C USA
21 S12 Hartsville South Carolina, SE USA
20 K8 Hartsville Tennessee, S USA
27 U7 Hartville Missouri, C USA
23 U2 Hartwell Georgia, SE USA
21 O11 Hartwell Lake ⊞ Georgia/South Carolina, SE USA
Hartz see Harts
Har-Us see Eslāmābād
Har-Us see Erdenebüren
162 E6 Harus Nuur ◎ NW Mongolia
30 M10 Harvard Illinois, N USA
29 P16 Harvard Nebraska, C USA
37 R5 Harvard, Mount ▲ Colorado, C USA
31 N11 Harvey Illinois, N USA
29 N4 Harvey North Dakota, N USA
97 Q21 Harwich E England, UK
152 H10 Haryāna var. Hariana. ◆ state N India
141 Y9 Ḩaryān, Ţawī al spring/well NE Oman
101 J14 Harz ▲ C Germany
Ḩasakah, Muḩāfaz̧at al see Al Ḩasakah
165 Q9 Hasama Miyagi, Honshū, C Japan
136 J15 Hasan Dağı ▲ C Turkey
139 T9 Ḩasan Ibn Ḩassūn C Iraq
149 R6 Ḩasan Khēl var. Ahmad Khel. Paktiā, SE Afghanistan
100 F12 Hase 〜 NW Germany
Haselberg see Krasnoznamensk
100 F12 Haselünne Niedersachsen, NW Germany
Hashaat see Delgerhangay
Hashemite Kingdom of Jordan see Jordan
139 V8 Hāshimah E Iraq
142 K3 Hashtrūd var Azaran. Āżarbāyjān-e Khāvarī, N Iran
141 W13 Ḩāsik S Oman
149 U10 Hāsilpur Punjab, E Pakistan
27 Q10 Haskell Oklahoma, C USA
25 Q6 Haskell Texas, SW USA
114 M11 Hasköy Edirne, NW Turkey
95 L24 Hasle Bornholm, E Denmark
97 N23 Haslemere SE England, UK
102 I16 Hasparren Pyrénées-Atlantiques, SW France
Hassakeh see Al Ḩasakah
155 G19 Hassan Karnātaka, W India
36 J13 Hassayampa River 〜 Arizona, SW USA
101 J18 Hassberge hill range C Germany
94 N10 Hassela Gävleborg, C Sweden
99 J18 Hasselt Limburg, NE Belgium
98 M9 Hasselt Overijssel, E Netherlands
Hassetché see Al Ḩasakah
101 J18 Hassfurt Bayern, C Germany
74 L9 Hassi Bel Guebbour E Algeria
74 L8 Hassi Messaoud E Algeria
95 K22 Hässleholm Skåne, S Sweden
Hasta Colonia/Hasta Pompeia see Asti
183 O13 Hastings Victoria, SE Australia
184 O11 Hastings Hawke's Bay, North Island, New Zealand
97 P23 Hastings SE England, UK
31 P9 Hastings Michigan, N USA
29 W9 Hastings Minnesota, N USA
29 P16 Hastings Nebraska, C USA
95 K22 Hästveda Skåne, S Sweden
92 J8 Hasvik Finnmark, N Norway
37 V6 Haswell Colorado, C USA
163 N11 Hatanbulag var. Ergel. Dornogovĭ, SE Mongolia
Hatansuudal see Bayanlig
163 P9 Hatavch var. Hatavch. Sühbaatar, E Mongolia
Hatavch see Hatavch
Hatavch see Haldzan
136 K17 Hatay ◆ province S Turkey
37 R15 Hatch New Mexico, SW USA
36 K7 Hatch Utah, W USA
20 F9 Hatchie River 〜 Tennessee, S USA
116 G12 Haţeg Ger. Wallenthal, Hung. Hátszeg; prev. Hatzeg, Hötzing. Hunedoara, SW Romania
165 O17 Hateruma-jima island Yaeyama-shotō, SW Japan
183 N8 Hatfield New South Wales, SE Australia
162 I5 Hatgal Hövsgöl, N Mongolia
153 V16 Hathazari Chittagong, SE Bangladesh
141 T13 Hathūt, Hişā' oasis NE Yemen
167 R14 Ha Tiên Kiên Giang, S Vietnam
167 T8 Ha Tinh Ha Tinh, N Vietnam
138 F12 Hatira, Haré hill range S Israel
167 R6 Hat Lot var Mai Son. Son La, N Vietnam
45 P16 Hato Airport ✈ (Willemstad) Curaçao, SW Netherlands Antilles
54 H9 Hato Corozal Casanare, C Colombia
Hato del Volcán see Volcán
45 P9 Hato Mayor E Dominican Republic
Hatra see Al Ḩaḑr
Hatria see Adria
Hátszeg see Haţeg
143 R16 Ḩattá Dubayy, NE United Arab Emirates
182 L9 Hattah Victoria, SE Australia
98 M9 Hattem Gelderland, E Netherlands
21 Z10 Hatteras Hatteras Island, North Carolina, SE USA
21 Rr10 Hatteras, Cape headland North Carolina, SE USA
21 Z9 Hatteras Island island North Carolina, SE USA
64 F10 Hatteras Plain undersea feature W Atlantic Ocean
93 G14 Hattfjelldal Troms, N Norway
22 M7 Hattiesburg Mississippi, S USA
29 Q4 Hatton North Dakota, N USA
Hatton Bank see Hatton Ridge
64 L6 Hatton Ridge var. Hatton Bank. undersea feature N Atlantic Ocean
191 W6 Hatutu island Îles Marquises, NE French Polynesia
111 K22 Hatvan Heves, NE Hungary
167 O16 Hat Yai var. Ban Hat Yai. Songkhla, SW Thailand
Hatzeg see Haţeg
Hatzfeld see Jimbolia

◆ Country ◇ Dependent Territory ◆ Administrative Regions ▲ Mountain ▲ Volcano ◎ Lake
● Country Capital ○ Dependent Territory Capital ✈ International Airport ▲▲ Mountain Range 〜 River ⊞ Reservoir

80 *N13* **Haud** *plateau* Ethiopia/Somalia
95 *D18* **Hauge** Rogaland, S Norway
95 *C15* **Haugesund** Rogaland, S Norway
109 *X2* **Haugsdorf** Niederösterreich, NE Austria
184 *M9* **Hauhungaroa Range** ▲ North Island, New Zealand
95 *E15* **Haukeligrend** Telemark, S Norway
93 *L14* **Haukipudas** Oulu, C Finland
93 *M17* **Haukivesi** ◎ SE Finland
93 *M17* **Haukivuori** Isä-Suomi, E Finland
Hauptkanal *see* Havelländ Grosse
187 *N10* **Hauraha** San Cristobal, SE Solomon Islands
184 *L5* **Hauraki Gulf** *gulf* North Island, N New Zealand
185 *B24* **Hauroko, Lake** ◎ South Island, New Zealand
167 *S14* **Hâu, Sông** ⁓ S Vietnam
92 *N12* **Hautajärvi** Lappi, NE Finland
74 *F7* **Haut Atlas** *Eng.* High Atlas. ▲ C Morocco
79 *M17* **Haut-Congo** *off.* Région du Haut-Congo, *prev* Haut-Zaïre. ◆ *region* NE Dem. Rep. Congo
103 *Y14* **Haute-Corse** ◆ *department* Corse, France, C Mediterranean Sea
102 *L16* **Haute-Garonne** ◆ *department* S France
79 *K14* **Haute-Kotto** ◆ *prefecture* E Central African Republic
103 *P12* **Haute-Loire** ◆ *department* C France
103 *R6* **Haute-Marne** ◆ *department* N France
102 *M3* **Haute-Normandie** ◆ *region* N France
15 *U6* **Hauterive** Québec, SE Canada
103 *T13* **Hautes-Alpes** ◆ *department* SE France
103 *S7* **Haute-Saône** ◆ *department* E France
103 *T10* **Haute-Savoie** ◆ *department* E France
99 *M20* **Hautes Fagnes** *Ger.* Hohes Venn. ▲ E Belgium
102 *K16* **Hautes-Pyrénées** ◆ *department* S France
99 *L23* **Haute Sûre, Lac de la** ⊠ NW Luxembourg
102 *M11* **Haute-Vienne** ◆ *department* C France
19 *S8* **Haut, Isle au** *island* Maine, NE USA
79 *M14* **Haut-Mbomou** ◆ *prefecture* SE Central African Republic
103 *Q2* **Hautmont** Nord, N France
79 *F19* **Haut-Ogooué** *off.* Province du Haut-Ogooué, *var.* Le Haut-Ogooué. ◆ *province* SE Gabon
Haut-Ogooué, Le *see* Haut-Ogooué
Haut-Ogooué, Province du *see* Haut-Ogooué
103 *U7* **Haut-Rhin** ◆ *department* NE France
74 *I6* **Hauts Plateaux** *plateau* Algeria/Morocco
Haut-Zaïre *see* Haut-Congo
38 *D9* **Hau'ula** *var.* Hauula. O'ahu, Hawai'i, USA
Hauula *see* Hau'ula
101 *O22* **Hauzenberg** Bayern, SE Germany
30 *K13* **Havana** Illinois, N USA
Havana *see* La Habana
97 *N23* **Havant** S England, UK
35 *Y14* **Havasu, Lake** ⊠ Arizona/ California, W USA
95 *J23* **Havdrup** Roskilde, E Denmark
100 *N10* **Havel** ⁓ NE Germany
99 *J21* **Havelange** Namur, SE Belgium
100 *M11* **Havelberg** Sachsen-Anhalt, NE Germany
149 *U5* **Havelian** North-West Frontier Province, NW Pakistan
100 *N12* **Havelländ Grosse** *var.* Hauptkanal. *canal* NE Germany
14 *J14* **Havelock** Ontario, SE Canada
185 *J14* **Havelock** Marlborough, South Island, New Zealand
21 *X11* **Havelock** North Carolina, SE USA
184 *O11* **Havelock North** Hawke's Bay, North Island, New Zealand
98 *M8* **Havelte** Drenthe, NE Netherlands
27 *N6* **Haven** Kansas, C USA
97 *H21* **Haverfordwest** SW Wales, UK
97 *P20* **Haverhill** E England, UK
19 *O10* **Haverhill** Massachusetts, NE USA
93 *G17* **Haverö** Västernorrland, C Sweden
111 *I17* **Havířov** Moravskoslezský Kraj, E Czech Republic
111 *E17* **Havlíčkův Brod** *Ger.* Deutsch-Brod; *prev.* Německý Brod. Vysočina, C Czech Republic
92 *K7* **Havøysund** Finnmark, N Norway
99 *F20* **Havré** Hainaut, S Belgium
33 *T7* **Havre** Montana, NW USA
Havre *see* le Havre
13 *P11* **Havre-St-Pierre** Québec, E Canada
136 *B10* **Havsa** Edirne, NW Turkey
38 *G11* **Hawi** *var.* Hāwī. Hawaii, USA
38 *D8* **Hawai'i** *off.* State of Hawai'i, *also known as* Aloha State, Paradise of the Pacific, *var.* Hawaii. ◆ *state* USA, C Pacific Ocean
38 *G12* **Hawai'i** *var.* Hawaii. *island* Hawaiian Islands, USA, C Pacific Ocean
192 *M5* **Hawaiian Islands** *prev.* Sandwich Islands. *island group* Hawaii, USA
192 *L5* **Hawaiian Ridge** *undersea feature* N Pacific Ocean
193 *N6* **Hawaiian Trough** *undersea feature* N Pacific Ocean
29 *R12* **Hawarden** Iowa, C USA
Hawash *see* Āwash
139 *P6* **Hawbayn al Gharbīyah** C Iraq
185 *D21* **Hawea, Lake** ◎ South Island, New Zealand
184 *K11* **Hawera** Taranaki, North Island, New Zealand
20 *J5* **Hawesville** Kentucky, S USA
38 *G11* **Hāwī** *var.* Hawi. Hawai'i, USA, C Pacific Ocean
Hawi *see* Hāwī
Hawi *see* Hawi
96 *K13* **Hawick** SE Scotland, UK
139 *S4* **Ḩawījah** C Iraq
139 *Y10* **Ḩawīzah, Hawr al** ◎ S Iraq
185 *E21* **Hawkdun Range** ▲ South Island, New Zealand
184 *P10* **Hawke Bay** *bay* North Island, New Zealand
182 *I6* **Hawker** South Australia
184 *N11* **Hawke's Bay** *off.* Hawkes Bay Region. ◆ *region* North Island, New Zealand
149 *O16* **Hawkes Bay** *bay* SE Pakistan
Hawkes Bay Region *see* Hawke's Bay
15 *N12* **Hawkesbury** Ontario, SE Canada
Hawkeye State *see* Iowa
23 *T5* **Hawkinsville** Georgia, SE USA
14 *B7* **Hawk Junction** Ontario, S Canada
21 *N10* **Haw Knob** ▲ North Carolina/ Tennessee, SE USA
21 *Q9* **Hawksbill Mountain** ▲ North Carolina, SE USA
33 *Z16* **Hawk Springs** Wyoming, C USA
Hawlêr *see* Arbīl
29 *S5* **Hawley** Minnesota, N USA
25 *P7* **Hawley** Texas, SW USA
141 *R14* **Ḩawrā'** C Yemen
139 *P7* **Ḩawrān, Wadi** *dry watercourse* W Iraq
21 *T9* **Haw River** ⁓ North Carolina, SE USA
139 *U5* **Hawshqūrah** E Iraq
35 *S7* **Hawthorne** Nevada, W USA
37 *W3* **Haxtun** Colorado, C USA
183 *N9* **Hay** New South Wales, SE Australia
9 *O10* **Hay** ⁓ W Canada
171 *S13* **Haya** Pulau Seram, E Indonesia
165 *R9* **Hayachine-san** ▲ Honshū, C Japan
103 *S4* **Hayange** Moselle, NE France
HaYarden *see* Jordan
Hayastani Hanrapetut'yun *see* Armenia
Hayasui-seto *see* Hōyo-kaikyō
39 *N9* **Haycock** Alaska, USA
36 *M14* **Hayden** Arizona, SW USA
37 *Q3* **Hayden** Colorado, C USA
28 *M10* **Hayes** South Dakota, N USA
9 *X13* **Hayes** ⁓ Manitoba, C Canada
9 *P12* **Hayes** ⁓ Nunavut, NE Canada
28 *M16* **Hayes Center** Nebraska, C USA
39 *S10* **Hayes, Mount** ▲ Alaska, USA
21 *N11* **Hayesville** North Carolina, SE USA
35 *X10* **Hayford Peak** ▲ Nevada, W USA
34 *M3* **Hayfork** California, W USA
Hayir, Qasr al *see* Ḩayr al Gharbī, Qaşr al
Haylaastay *see* Sühbaatar
14 *I12* **Hay Lake** ◎ Ontario, SE Canada
141 *X11* **Haymā'** *var.* Haima. C Oman
136 *H13* **Haymana** Ankara, C Turkey
138 *J7* **Ḩaymūr, Jabal** ▲ W Syria
Haynau *see* Chojnów
22 *G4* **Haynesville** Louisiana, S USA
23 *P6* **Hayneville** Alabama, S USA
114 *M12* **Hayrabolu** Tekirdağ, NW Turkey
136 *C10* **Hayrabolu Deresi** ⁓ NW Turkey
138 *J6* **Ḩayr al Gharbī, Qaşr al** *var.* Qasr al Hayir, Qasr al Hir al Gharbi. *ruins* Ḩimş, C Syria
138 *L5* **Ḩayr ash Sharqī, Qaşr al** *var.* Qasr al Hir Ash Sharqī. *ruins* Ḩimş, C Syria
162 *J7* **Hayrhan** *var.* Uubulan. Arhangay, C Mongolia
162 *J9* **Hayrhandulaan** *var.* Mardzad. Övörhangay, C Mongolia
8 *J10* **Hay River** Northwest Territories, W Canada
26 *K4* **Hays** Kansas, C USA
28 *K12* **Hay Springs** Nebraska, C USA
65 *H25* **Haystack, The** ▲ NE Saint Helena
27 *N7* **Haysville** Kansas, C USA
117 *O7* **Haysyn** *Rus.* Gaysin. Vinnyts'ka Oblast', C Ukraine
27 *Y9* **Hayti** Missouri, C USA
29 *Q9* **Hayti** South Dakota, N USA
117 *O8* **Hayvoron** *Rus.* Gayvorno. Kirovohrads'ka Oblast', C Ukraine
35 *N9* **Hayward** California, W USA
30 *J4* **Hayward** Wisconsin, N USA
97 *O23* **Haywards Heath** SE England, UK
146 *A11* **Hazar** *prev. Rus.* Cheleken. Balkan Welaýaty, W Turkmenistan
143 *S11* **Hazārān, Kūh-e** *var.* Kūh-e ā Hazr. ▲ SE Iran
Hazarat Imam *see* Emām Şāḩeb
21 *O7* **Hazard** Kentucky, S USA
137 *O15* **Hazar Gölü** ◎ C Turkey
153 *P15* **Hazārībāg** *var.* Hazāribāgh. Jhārkhand, N India
Hazārībāgh *see* Hazārībāg
103 *O1* **Hazebrouck** Nord, N France
30 *K9* **Hazel Green** Wisconsin, N USA
192 *K9* **Hazel Holme Bank** *undersea feature* S Pacific Ocean
10 *K13* **Hazelton** British Columbia, SW Canada
29 *N6* **Hazelton** North Dakota, N USA
35 *R5* **Hazen** Nevada, W USA
28 *L5* **Hazen** North Dakota, N USA
38 *L12* **Hazen Bay** *bay* E Bering Sea
139 *S5* **Hazīm, Bi'r** *well* C Iraq
23 *V6* **Hazlehurst** Georgia, SE USA
22 *K6* **Hazlehurst** Mississippi, S USA
18 *K15* **Hazlet** New Jersey, NE USA
146 *I9* **Hazorasp** *Rus.* Khazarosp. Xorazm Viloyati, W Uzbekistan
147 *R13* **Hazratishoh, Qatorkŭhi** *var.* Khrebet Khazretishi, *Rus.* Khrebet Khozretishi. ▲ S Tajikistan
Hazr, Kūh-e ā *see* Hazārān, Kūh-e
149 *U6* **Hazro** Punjab, E Pakistan
23 *R7* **Headland** Alabama, S USA
182 *C6* **Head of Bight** *headland* South Australia
33 *N10* **Headquarters** Idaho, NW USA
34 *M7* **Healdsburg** California, W USA
27 *N13* **Healdton** Oklahoma, C USA
183 *O12* **Healesville** Victoria, SE Australia
39 *R10* **Healy** Alaska, USA
173 *R13* **Heard and McDonald Islands** ◇ *Australian external territory* S Indian Ocean
173 *R13* **Heard Island** *island* Heard and McDonald Islands, S Indian Ocean
25 *U9* **Hearne** Texas, SW USA
12 *F12* **Hearst** Ontario, S Canada
194 *J5* **Hearst Island** *island* Antarctica
Heart of Dixie *see* Alabama
28 *L5* **Heart River** ⁓ North Dakota, N USA
31 *T13* **Heath** Ohio, N USA
183 *N11* **Heathcote** Victoria, SE Australia
97 *N22* **Heathrow** ✈ (London) SE England, UK
21 *X5* **Heathsville** Virginia, NE USA
27 *R11* **Heavener** Oklahoma, C USA
25 *R15* **Hebbronville** Texas, SW USA
163 *Q13* **Hebei** *var.* Hebei Sheng, Hopeh, Hopei, Ji; *prev.* Chihli. ◆ *province* E China
Hebei Sheng *see* Hebei
36 *M3* **Heber City** Utah, W USA
27 *V10* **Heber Springs** Arkansas, C USA
161 *N5* **Hebi** Henan, C China
32 *F11* **Hebo** Oregon, NW USA
96 *F9* **Hebrides, Sea of the** *sea* NW Scotland, UK
13 *P5* **Hebron** Newfoundland and Labrador, E Canada
31 *N11* **Hebron** Indiana, N USA
29 *Q17* **Hebron** Nebraska, C USA
28 *L5* **Hebron** North Dakota, N USA
138 *F11* **Hebron** *var.* Al Khalīl, El Khalil, *Heb.* Hevron; *anc.* Kiriath-Arba. S West Bank
Hebrus *see* Évros/Maritsa/Meriç
95 *N14* **Heby** Västmanland, C Sweden
10 *I14* **Hecate Strait** *strait* British Columbia, W Canada
41 *W12* **Hecelchakán** Campeche, SE Mexico
160 *K13* **Hechi** *var.* Jinchengjiang. Guangxi Zhuangzu Zizhiqu, S China
101 *H23* **Hechingen** Baden-Württemberg, S Germany
99 *K17* **Hechtel** Limburg, NE Belgium
160 *J9* **Hechuan** *var.* Heyang. Chongqing Shi, C China
29 *P7* **Hecla** South Dakota, N USA
29 *T9* **Hector** Minnesota, N USA
95 *F17* **Hede** Jämtland, C Sweden
Hede *see* Sheyang
95 *M14* **Hedemora** Dalarna, C Sweden
92 *K13* **Hedenäset** Norrbotten, N Sweden
95 *G23* **Hedensted** Vejle, C Denmark
95 *N14* **Hedesunda** Gävleborg, C Sweden
95 *N14* **Hedesundafjord** ◎ C Sweden
25 *O3* **Hedley** Texas, SW USA
94 *I12* **Hedmark** ◆ *county* S Norway
165 *T16* **Hedo-misaki** *headland* Okinawa, SW Japan
29 *X15* **Hedrick** Iowa, C USA
99 *L16* **Heel** Limburg, SE Netherlands
189 *Y12* **Heel Point** *point* Wake Island
98 *H9* **Heemskerk** Noord-Holland, W Netherlands
98 *M10* **Heerde** Gelderland, E Netherlands
98 *L7* **Heerenveen** *Fris.* It Hearrenfean. Friesland, N Netherlands
98 *I8* **Heerhugowaard** Noord-Holland, NW Netherlands
92 *O3* **Heer Land** *physical region* C Svalbard
99 *M18* **Heerlen** Limburg, SE Netherlands
99 *J19* **Heers** Limburg, NE Belgium
Heerwegen *see* Polkowice
98 *K13* **Heesch** Noord-Brabant, S Netherlands
99 *K15* **Heeze** Noord-Brabant, SE Netherlands
138 *F8* **Ḩefa** *var.* Haifa, *hist.* Caiffa, Caiphas; *anc.* Sycaminum. Haifa, N Israel
138 *F8* **Ḩefa, Mifraẕ** *Eng.* Bay of Haifa. *bay* N Israel
161 *Q8* **Hefei** *var.* Hofei, *hist.* Luchow. *province capital* Anhui, E China
23 *R3* **Heflin** Alabama, S USA
163 *X7* **Hegang** Heilongjiang, NE China
164 *L10* **Hegura-jima** *island* SW Japan
Heguri-jima *see* Heigun-tō
Hei *see* Heilongjiang
100 *H8* **Heide** Schleswig-Holstein, N Germany
101 *G20* **Heidelberg** Baden-Württemberg, SW Germany
83 *J21* **Heidelberg** Gauteng, NE South Africa
22 *M6* **Heidelberg** Mississippi, S USA
Heidenheim *see* Heidenheim an der Brenz
101 *J22* **Heidenheim an der Brenz** *var.* Heidenheim. Baden-Württemberg, S Germany
109 *U2* **Heidenreichstein** Niederösterreich, N Austria
164 *F14* **Heigun-tō** *var.* Heguri-jima. *island* SW Japan
163 *W5* **Heihe** *prev.* Ai-hun. Heilongjiang, NE China
162 *S8* **Hei He** ⁓ C China
Hei-ho *see* Nagqu
83 *J22* **Heilbron** Free State, N South Africa
101 *H21* **Heilbronn** Baden-Württemberg, SW Germany
Heiligenbeil *see* Mamonovo
109 *Q8* **Heiligenblut** Tirol, W Austria
100 *K7* **Heiligenhafen** Schleswig-Holstein, N Germany
Heiligenkreuz *see* Žiar nad Hronom
101 *J15* **Heiligenstadt** Thüringen, C Germany
163 *W8* **Heilongjiang** *var.* Hei, Heilongjiang Sheng, Hei-lung-chiang, Heilungkiang. ◆ *province* NE China
Heilong Jiang *see* Amur
Heilongjiang Sheng *see* Heilongjiang
98 *H9* **Heiloo** Noord-Holland, NW Netherlands
Heilsberg *see* Lidzbark Warmiński
Hei-lung-chiang/ Heilungkiang *see* Heilongjiang
Heimaæy *see* Heimaey
92 *I4* **Heimaey** *var.* Heimaæy. *island* S Iceland
94 *H8* **Heimdal** Sør-Trøndelag, S Norway
Heinaste *see* Ainaži
93 *N17* **Heinävesi** Isä-Suomi, E Finland
99 *M22* **Heinerscheid** Diekirch, N Luxembourg
98 *M10* **Heino** Overijssel, E Netherlands
93 *M18* **Heinola** Etelä-Suomi, S Finland
101 *C16* **Heinsberg** Nordrhein-Westfalen, W Germany
163 *U12* **Heishan** Liaoning, NE China
160 *H8* **Heishui** *var.* Luhua. Sichuan, C China
99 *H17* **Heist-op-den-Berg** Antwerpen, C Belgium
Heitō *see* P'ingtung
171 *X15* **Heitske** Papua, E Indonesia
Hejanah *see* Al Hījānah
Hejaz *see* Al Ḩijāz
160 *M14* **He Jiang** ⁓ S China
Hejiayan *see* Lüeyang
158 *K6* **Hejing** Xinjiang Uygur Zizhiqu, NW China
Héjjasfalva *see* Vânători
Heka *see* Hoika
137 *N14* **Hekimhan** Malatya, C Turkey
92 *J4* **Hekla** ▲ S Iceland
Hekou *see* Yanshan, Jiangxi, China
Hekou *see* Yajiang, Sichuan, China
110 *J6* **Hel** *Ger.* Hela. Pomorskie, N Poland
Hela *see* Hel
93 *F17* **Helagsfjället** ▲ C Sweden
159 *W8* **Helan** *var.* Xigang. Ningxia, N China
162 *K14* **Helan Shan** ▲ N China
99 *M16* **Helden** Limburg, SE Netherlands
27 *X12* **Helena** Arkansas, C USA
33 *R10* **Helena** *state capital* Montana, NW USA
96 *H12* **Helensburgh** W Scotland, UK
184 *K5* **Helensville** Auckland, North Island, New Zealand
95 *L20* **Helgasjön** ◎ S Sweden
100 *G8* **Helgoland** *Eng.* Heligoland. *island* NW Germany
Helgoland Bay *see* Helgoländer Bucht
100 *G8* **Helgoländer Bucht** *var.* Helgoland Bay, Heligoland Bight. *bay* NW Germany
Heligoland *see* Helgoland
Heligoland Bight *see* Helgoländer Bucht
Heliopolis *see* Baalbek
92 *I4* **Hella** Sudhurland, SW Iceland
Hellas *see* Greece
143 *N11* **Ḩelleh, Rūd-e** ⁓ S Iran
98 *N10* **Hellendoorn** Overijssel, E Netherlands
Hellenic Republic *see* Greece
121 *Q10* **Hellenic Trough** *undersea feature* Aegean Sea, C Mediterranean Sea
94 *E10* **Hellesylt** Møre og Romsdal, S Norway
98 *F13* **Hellevoetsluis** Zuid-Holland, SW Netherlands
105 *Q12* **Hellín** Castilla-La Mancha, C Spain
115 *H19* **Hellinikon** ✈ (Athína) Attikí, C Greece
32 *M12* **Hells Canyon** *valley* Idaho/ Oregon, NW USA
148 *L9* **Helmand** ◆ *province* S Afghanistan
148 *K10* **Helmand, Daryā-ye** *var.* Rūd-e Hīrmand. ⁓ Afghanistan/Iran *see also* Hīrmand, Rūd-e
Helmand, Daryā-ye *see* Hīrmand, Rūd-e
Helmantica *see* Salamanca
101 *K15* **Helme** ⁓ C Germany
99 *L15* **Helmond** Noord-Brabant, S Netherlands
96 *J7* **Helmsdale** N Scotland, UK
100 *K13* **Helmstedt** Niedersachsen, N Germany
163 *Y10* **Helong** Jilin, NE China
36 *M4* **Helper** Utah, W USA
100 *O10* **Helpter Berge** *hill* NE Germany
95 *J22* **Helsingborg** *prev.* Hälsingborg. Skåne, S Sweden
Helsingfors *see* Helsinki
95 *J22* **Helsingør** *Eng.* Elsinore. Frederiksborg, E Denmark
93 *M20* **Helsinki** *Swe.* Helsingfors. ● (Finland) Etelä-Suomi, S Finland
97 *H25* **Helston** SW England, UK
Heltau *see* Cisnădie
61 *C17* **Helvecia** Santa Fe, C Argentina
97 *K15* **Helvellyn** ▲ NW England, UK
Helvetia *see* Switzerland
75 *W8* **Helwân** *var.* Hilwân, Hulwan, Hulwân. N Egypt
97 *N21* **Hemel Hempstead** E England, UK
35 *U16* **Hemet** California, W USA
28 *J13* **Hemingford** Nebraska, C USA
21 *T13* **Hemingway** South Carolina, SE USA
92 *G13* **Hemnesberget** Nordland, C Norway
25 *Y8* **Hemphill** Texas, SW USA
25 *V11* **Hempstead** Texas, SW USA
95 *P20* **Hemse** Gotland, SE Sweden
94 *F13* **Hemsedal** *valley* S Norway
159 *T11* **Henan** *var.* Henan Mongolzu Zizhixian, Yêgainnyin. Qinghai, C China
161 *N6* **Henan** *var.* Henan Sheng, Honan, Yu. ◆ *province* C China
184 *L4* **Hen and Chickens** *island group* N New Zealand
105 *O7* **Henares** ⁓ C Spain
165 *P7* **Henashi-zaki** *headland* Honshū, C Japan
102 *I16* **Hendaye** Pyrénées-Atlantiques, SW France
136 *F11* **Hendek** Sakarya, NW Turkey
61 *B21* **Henderson** Buenos Aires, E Argentina
20 *I5* **Henderson** Kentucky, S USA
35 *X11* **Henderson** Nevada, W USA
21 *V8* **Henderson** North Carolina, SE USA
20 *G10* **Henderson** Tennessee, S USA
25 *W7* **Henderson** Texas, SW USA
30 *J12* **Henderson Creek** ⁓ Illinois, N USA
186 *M9* **Henderson Field** ✈ (Honiara) Guadalcanal, C Solomon Islands
191 *O17* **Henderson Island** *atoll* N Pitcairn Islands
21 *O10* **Hendersonville** North Carolina, SE USA
20 *J8* **Hendersonville** Tennessee, S USA
143 *O14* **Hendorābī, Jazīreh-ye** *island* S Iran
55 *V10* **Hendrik Top** *var.* Hendriktop. *elevation* C Surinam
Hendriktop *see* Hendrik Top
Hendū Kosh *see* Hindu Kush
14 *L12* **Heney, Lac** ◎ Québec, SE Canada
Hengchow *see* Hengyang
161 *S15* **Hengchun** S Taiwan
159 *R16* **Hengduan Shan** ▲ SW China
98 *N12* **Hengelo** Gelderland, E Netherlands
98 *O10* **Hengelo** Overijssel, E Netherlands
Hengnan *see* Hengyang
161 *N11* **Hengshan** Hunan, S China
160 *L4* **Hengshan** Shaanxi, C China
161 *O4* **Hengshui** Hebei, E China
161 *N12* **Hengyang** *var.* Hengnan, Heng-yang; *prev.* Hengchow. Hunan, S China
Heng-yang *see* Hengyang
117 *U11* **Heniches'k** *Rus.* Genichesk. Khersons'ka Oblast', S Ukraine
21 *Z4* **Henlopen, Cape** *headland* Delaware, NE USA
Henna *see* Enna
94 *M10* **Hennan** Gävleborg, C Sweden
102 *G7* **Hennebont** Morbihan, NW France
30 *L11* **Hennepin** Illinois, N USA
26 *M9* **Hennessey** Oklahoma, C USA
100 *N12* **Hennigsdorf** *var.* Hennigsdorf bei Berlin. Brandenburg, NE Germany
Hennigsdorf bei Berlin *see* Hennigsdorf
19 *N9* **Henniker** New Hampshire, NE USA
25 *S5* **Henrietta** Texas, SW USA
Henrique de Carvalho *see* Saurimo
30 *L12* **Henry** Illinois, N USA
21 *Y7* **Henry, Cape** *headland* Virginia, NE USA
27 *P10* **Henryetta** Oklahoma, C USA
194 *M7* **Henry Ice Rise** *ice cap* Antarctica
33 *R13* **Henrys Fork** ⁓ Idaho, NW USA
14 *E15* **Hensall** Ontario, S Canada
100 *J9* **Henstedt-Ulzburg** Schleswig-Holstein, N Germany
Hentiy *see* Batshireet
162 *M7* **Hentiyn Nuruu** ▲ N Mongolia
183 *P10* **Henty** New South Wales, SE Australia
166 *L8* **Henzada** Irrawaddy, SW Myanmar (Burma)
Heping *see* Huishui
101 *G19* **Heppenheim** Hessen, W Germany
32 *J11* **Heppner** Oregon, NW USA
160 *L15* **Hepu** *var.* Lianzhou. Guangxi Zhuangzu Zizhiqu, S China
Heracleum *see* Irákleio
92 *J2* **Heradhsvötn** ⁓ C Iceland
Herakleion *see* Irákleio
148 *K5* **Herāt** *var.* Herat; *anc.* Aria. Herāt, W Afghanistan
148 *J5* **Herāt** ◆ *province* W Afghanistan
103 *P14* **Hérault** ◆ *department* S France
103 *P15* **Hérault** ⁓ S France
9 *T16* **Herbert** Saskatchewan, S Canada
185 *F22* **Herbert** Otago, South Island, New Zealand
38 *J17* **Herbert Island** *island* Aleutian Islands, Alaska, USA
Herbertshöhe *see* Kokopo
15 *Q7* **Hébertville** Québec, SE Canada
101 *G17* **Herborn** Hessen, W Germany
113 *I17* **Herceg-Novi** *It.* Castelnuovo; *prev.* Ercegnovi. SW Montenegro
9 *X10* **Herchmer** Manitoba, C Canada
186 *E8* **Hercules Bay** *bay* E Papua New Guinea
92 *K2* **Herdhubreidh** ▲ C Iceland
42 *M13* **Heredia** Heredia, C Costa Rica
42 *M12* **Heredia** *off.* Provincia de Heredia. ◆ *province* N Costa Rica
Heredia, Provincia de *see* Heredia
97 *K21* **Hereford** W England, UK
24 *M3* **Hereford** Texas, SW USA
15 *Q13* **Hereford, Mont** ▲ Québec, SE Canada
97 *K21* **Herefordshire** *cultural region* W England, UK
191 *U11* **Hereheretue** *atoll* Îles Tuamotu, C French Polynesia
105 *N10* **Herencia** Castilla-La Mancha, C Spain
99 *H18* **Herent** Vlaams Brabant, C Belgium
99 *I16* **Herentals** *var.* Herenthals. Antwerpen, N Belgium
Herenthals *see* Herentals
99 *H17* **Herenthout** Antwerpen, N Belgium
95 *J23* **Herfølge** Roskilde, E Denmark
100 *G13* **Herford** Nordrhein-Westfalen, NW Germany
27 *O5* **Herington** Kansas, C USA
108 *H7* **Herisau** *Fr.* Hérisau. Appenzell Ausser Rhoden, NE Switzerland
Hérisau *see* Herisau
Héristal *see* Herstal
99 *J18* **Herk-de-Stad** Limburg, NE Belgium
Herkulesbad/Herkulesfürdő *see* Băile Herculane
162 *M8* **Herlenbayan-Ulaan** *var.* Dulaan. Hentiy, C Mongolia
Herlen Gol/Herlen He *see* Kerulen
35 *Q4* **Herlong** California, W USA
97 *L26* **Herm** *island* Channel Islands
109 *R9* **Hermagor** *Slvn.* Šmohor. Kärnten, S Austria
29 *S7* **Herman** Minnesota, N USA
96 *L1* **Herma Ness** *headland* NE Scotland, UK
27 *V4* **Hermann** Missouri, C USA
181 *Q8* **Hermannsburg** Northern Territory, N Australia
Hermannstadt *see* Sibiu
94 *E12* **Hermansverk** Sogn Og Fjordane, S Norway
138 *H6* **Hermel** *var.* Hirmil. NE Lebanon
Hermhausen *see* Hajnówka
183 *P6* **Hermidale** New South Wales, SE Australia
55 *X9* **Herminadorp** Sipaliwini, NE Suriname
32 *K11* **Hermiston** Oregon, NW USA
27 *T6* **Hermitage** Missouri, C USA
186 *D4* **Hermit Islands** *island group* N Papua New Guinea
25 *O7* **Hermleigh** Texas, SW USA
138 *G7* **Hermon, Mount** *Ar.* Jabal ash Shaykh. ▲ S Syria
Hermopolis Parva *see* Damanhûr
28 *J10* **Hermosa** South Dakota, N USA
40 *F5* **Hermosillo** Sonora, NW Mexico
Hermoupolis *see* Ermoúpoli
111 *N20* **Hernád** *var.* Hornád, *Ger.* Kundert. ⁓ Hungary/Slovakia
61 *C18* **Hernández** Entre Ríos, E Argentina
23 *V11* **Hernando** Florida, SE USA
22 *L1* **Hernando** Mississippi, S USA
105 *Q2* **Hernani** País Vasco, N Spain
99 *F19* **Herne** Vlaams Brabant, C Belgium
101 *E14* **Herne** Nordrhein-Westfalen, W Germany
95 *F22* **Herning** Ringkøbing, W Denmark
Hernösand *see* Härnösand
121 *U11* **Herodotus Basin** *undersea feature* E Mediterranean Sea
121 *Q12* **Herodotus Trough** *undersea feature* C Mediterranean Sea
29 *T11* **Heron Lake** Minnesota, N USA
Herowābād *see* Khalkhāl
95 *G16* **Herre** Telemark, S Norway
29 *N7* **Herreid** South Dakota, N USA
101 *H22* **Herrenberg** Baden-Württemberg, S Germany
104 *L14* **Herrera** Andalucía, S Spain
43 *R17* **Herrera** *off.* Provincia de Herrera. ◆ *province* S Panama
104 *L10* **Herrera del Duque** Extremadura, W Spain
104 *M4* **Herrera de Pisuerga** Castilla-León, N Spain
Herrera, Provincia de *see* Herrera
41 *Z13* **Herrero, Punta** *headland* SE Mexico
183 *P16* **Herrick** Tasmania, SE Australia
30 *L17* **Herrin** Illinois, N USA
20 *M6* **Herrington Lake** ⊠ Kentucky, S USA
95 *K18* **Herrljunga** Västra Götaland, S Sweden
103 *N16* **Hers** ⁓ S France
10 *I1* **Herschel Island** *island* Yukon Territory, NW Canada
99 *I17* **Herselt** Antwerpen, C Belgium
18 *G15* **Hershey** Pennsylvania, NE USA
99 *K19* **Herstal** *Fr.* Héristal. Liège, E Belgium
97 *O21* **Hertford** E England, UK
21 *X8* **Hertford** North Carolina, SE USA
97 *O21* **Hertfordshire** *cultural region* E England, UK
181 *Z9* **Hervey Bay** Queensland, E Australia
101 *O14* **Herzberg** Brandenburg, E Germany
99 *E18* **Herzele** Oost-Vlaanderen, NW Belgium
101 *K20* **Herzogenaurach** Bayern, SE Germany
109 *W4* **Herzogenburg** Niederösterreich, NE Austria
Herzogenbusch *see* 's-Hertogenbosch
103 *N2* **Hesdin** Pas-de-Calais, N France
160 *K14* **Heshan** Guangxi Zhuangzu Zizhiqu, S China
159 *X10* **Heshui** *var.* Xihuachi. Gansu, C China
99 *M25* **Hespérange** Luxembourg, SE Luxembourg
35 *U14* **Hesperia** California, W USA
37 *P7* **Hesperus Mountain** ▲ Colorado, C USA
10 *J6* **Hess** ⁓ Yukon Territory, NW Canada
Hesse *see* Hessen
101 *J21* **Hesselberg** ▲ S Germany
95 *I22* **Hesselo** *island* E Denmark
101 *H17* **Hessen** *Eng./Fr.* Hesse. ◆ *state* C Germany
192 *L6* **Hess Tablemount** *undersea feature* C Pacific Ocean
27 *N6* **Hesston** Kansas, C USA

◆ Country
● Country Capital
◇ Dependent Territory
○ Dependent Territory Capital
◆ Administrative Regions
✈ International Airport
▲ Mountain
▲ Mountain Range
▲ Volcano
⁓ River
◎ Lake
⊠ Reservoir

93 G15 **Hestkjøltoppen** ▲ C Norway
97 K18 **Heswall** NW England, UK
153 P12 **Hetauḍā** Central, C Nepal
Hétfalu see Săcele
28 K7 **Hettinger** North Dakota, N USA
101 L14 **Hettstedt** Sachsen-Anhalt, C Germany
92 P3 **Heuglin, Kapp** headland SE Svalbard
187 N10 **Heuru** San Cristobal, SE Solomon Islands
99 J17 **Heusden** Limburg, NE Belgium
98 J13 **Heusden** Noord-Brabant, S Netherlands
102 K3 **Hève, Cap de la** headland N France
99 H18 **Heverlee** Vlaams Brabant, C Belgium
111 L22 **Heves** Heves, NE Hungary
111 L22 **Heves** off. Heves Megye. ◆ county NE Hungary
Heves Megye see Heves
Hevron see Hebron
45 Y13 **Hewanorra** ✈ (Saint Lucia) S Saint Lucia
Hexian see Hezhou
160 L6 **Heyang** Shaanxi, C China
Heyang see Hechuan
Heydebrech see Kędzierzyn-Kozle
Heydekrug see Šilutė
Heyin see Guide
97 K16 **Heysham** NW England, UK
161 O14 **Heyuan** Guangdong, S China
182 L12 **Heywood** Victoria, SE Australia
180 K3 **Heywood Islands** island group Western Australia
161 O6 **Heze** var. Caozhou. Shandong, E China
159 U11 **Hezheng** Gansu, C China
160 M13 **Hezhou** var. Babu; prev. Hexian. Guangxi Zhuangzu Zizhiqu, S China
159 U11 **Hezuo** Gansu, C China
23 Z16 **Hialeah** Florida, SE USA
27 Q3 **Hiawatha** Kansas, C USA
36 M4 **Hiawatha** Utah, W USA
29 V4 **Hibbing** Minnesota, N USA
183 N17 **Hibbs, Point** headland Tasmania, SE Australia
Hibernia see Ireland
20 F8 **Hickman** Kentucky, S USA
21 Q9 **Hickory** North Carolina, SE USA
21 Q9 **Hickory, Lake** ◎ North Carolina, SE USA
184 Q7 **Hicks Bay** Gisborne, North Island, New Zealand
25 S8 **Hico** Texas, SW USA
165 T4 **Hidaka** Hokkaidō, NE Japan
164 I12 **Hidaka** Hyōgo, Honshū, SW Japan
165 T5 **Hidaka-sanmyaku** ▲▲ Hokkaidō, NE Japan
41 O6 **Hidalgo** var. Villa Hidalgo. Coahuila de Zaragoza, NE Mexico
41 N8 **Hidalgo** Nuevo León, NE Mexico
41 O10 **Hidalgo** Tamaulipas, C Mexico
41 O13 **Hidalgo** ◆ state C Mexico
40 J7 **Hidalgo del Parral** var. Parral. Chihuahua, N Mexico
100 N7 **Hiddensee** island NE Germany
80 G6 **Hidiglib, Wadi** ~ NE Sudan
109 U6 **Hieflau** Salzburg, E Austria
187 P16 **Hienghène** Province Nord, C New Caledonia
Hierosolyma see Jerusalem
64 N12 **Hierro** var. Ferro. island Islas Canarias, Spain, NE Atlantic Ocean
164 G13 **Higashi-Hiroshima** var. Higashihirosima. Hiroshima, Honshū, SW Japan
164 C12 **Higashi-suidō** strait SW Japan
Higashihirosima see Higashi-Hiroshima
25 P1 **Higgins** Texas, SW USA
31 P7 **Higgins Lake** ◎ Michigan, N USA
27 S4 **Higginsville** Missouri, C USA
High Atlas see Haut Atlas
30 M5 **High Falls Reservoir** ▣ Wisconsin, N USA
44 K12 **Highgate** C Jamaica
25 X11 **High Island** Texas, SW USA
31 O5 **High Island** island Michigan, N USA
30 K15 **Highland** Illinois, N USA
31 N10 **Highland Park** Illinois, N USA
21 O10 **Highlands** North Carolina, SE USA
9 O11 **High Level** Alberta, W Canada
29 O9 **Highmore** South Dakota, N USA
171 N3 **High Peak** ▲ Luzon, N Philippines
High Plains see Great Plains
21 S9 **High Point** North Carolina, SE USA
18 J13 **High Point** hill New Jersey, NE USA
9 P13 **High Prairie** Alberta, W Canada
9 Q16 **High River** Alberta, SW Canada
21 S9 **High Rock Lake** ▣ North Carolina, SE USA
23 V9 **High Springs** Florida, SE USA
High Veld see Great Karoo
97 J24 **High Willhays** ▲ SW England, UK
97 N22 **High Wycombe** prev. Chepping Wycombe, Chipping Wycombe. SE England, UK
41 P12 **Higos** var. El Higo. Veracruz-Llave, E Mexico
102 I16 **Higuer, Cap** headland NE Spain
45 R5 **Higüero, Punta** headland W Puerto Rico
45 P9 **Higüey** var. Salvaleón de Higüey. E Dominican Republic
190 G11 **Hihifo** ✈ (Mata'utu) Île Uvea, N Wallis and Futuna
81 N16 **Hiiraan** off. Gobolka Hiiraan. ◆ region C Somalia
Hiiraan, Gobolka see Hiiraan
118 E4 **Hiiumaa** var. Hiiumaa Maakond. ◆ province W Estonia
118 D4 **Hiiumaa** Ger. Dagden, Swe. Dagö. island W Estonia
Hiiumaa Maakond see Hiiumaa
Hijanah see Al Hījānah
105 S6 **Híjar** Aragón, NE Spain
191 V10 **Hikueru** atoll Îles Tuamotu, C French Polynesia
184 K3 **Hikurangi** Northland, North Island, New Zealand
184 Q8 **Hikurangi** ▲ North Island, New Zealand
192 L11 **Hikurangi Trench** var. Hikurangi Trough. undersea feature SW Pacific Ocean
Hikurangi Trough see Hikurangi Trench
190 B15 **Hikutavake** NW Niue
121 Q12 **Hilāl, Ra's al** headland N Libya
61 A24 **Hilario Ascasubi** Buenos Aires, E Argentina
101 K17 **Hildburghausen** Thüringen, C Germany
101 E15 **Hilden** Nordrhein-Westfalen, W Germany
100 I13 **Hildesheim** Niedersachsen, N Germany
33 T9 **Hilger** Montana, NW USA
Hili see Hilli
Hilla see Al Ḥillah
45 O14 **Hillaby, Mount** ▲ N Barbados
95 K19 **Hillared** Älvsborg, S Sweden
195 R12 **Hillary Coast** physical region Antarctica
42 G2 **Hill Bank** Orange Walk, N Belize
33 O14 **Hill City** Idaho, NW USA
26 K3 **Hill City** Kansas, C USA
29 V5 **Hill City** Minnesota, N USA
28 J10 **Hill City** South Dakota, N USA
65 C24 **Hill Cove Settlement** West Falkland, Falkland Islands
98 H10 **Hillegom** Zuid-Holland, W Netherlands
95 J22 **Hillerød** Frederiksborg, E Denmark
36 M7 **Hillers, Mount** ▲ Utah, W USA
153 S13 **Hilli** var. Hili. Rajshahi, NW Bangladesh
29 R11 **Hills** Minnesota, N USA
30 L14 **Hillsboro** Illinois, N USA
27 N5 **Hillsboro** Kansas, C USA
27 X5 **Hillsboro** Missouri, C USA
19 N10 **Hillsboro** New Hampshire, NE USA
37 Q14 **Hillsboro** New Mexico, SW USA
29 R4 **Hillsboro** North Dakota, N USA
31 R14 **Hillsboro** Ohio, N USA
32 G11 **Hillsboro** Oregon, NW USA
25 T8 **Hillsboro** Texas, SW USA
30 K8 **Hillsboro** Wisconsin, N USA
23 Y14 **Hillsboro Canal** canal Florida, SE USA
45 Y15 **Hillsborough** Carriacou, N Grenada
97 G15 **Hillsborough** E Northern Ireland, UK
21 U9 **Hillsborough** North Carolina, SE USA
31 Q10 **Hillsdale** Michigan, N USA
183 O8 **Hillston** New South Wales, SE Australia
21 R7 **Hillsville** Virginia, NE USA
96 L2 **Hillswick** NE Scotland, UK
Hill Tippera see Tripura
38 H11 **Hilo** Hawai'i, USA, C Pacific Ocean
18 F9 **Hilton** New York, NE USA
14 C10 **Hilton Beach** Ontario, S Canada
21 R16 **Hilton Head Island** South Carolina, SE USA
21 R16 **Hilton Head Island** island South Carolina, SE USA
99 J15 **Hilvarenbeek** Noord-Brabant, S Netherlands
98 J11 **Hilversum** Noord-Holland, C Netherlands
Hilwān see Helwān
152 J7 **Himāchal Pradesh** ◆ state NW India
Himalaya/Himalaya Shan see Himalayas
152 M9 **Himalayas** var. Himalaya, Chin. Himalaya Shan. ▲▲ S Asia
171 P6 **Himamaylan** Negros, C Philippines
93 K15 **Himanka** Länsi-Soumi, W Finland
Himara see Himarë
113 L23 **Himarë** var. Himara. Vlorë, S Albania
138 M2 **Ḥimār, Wādī al** dry watercourse N Syria
154 D9 **Himatnagar** Gujarāt, W India
109 Y4 **Himberg** Niederösterreich, E Austria
164 I13 **Himeji** var. Himezi. Hyōgo, Honshū, SW Japan
164 E14 **Hime-jima** island SW Japan
Himezi see Himeji
164 L13 **Himi** Toyama, Honshū, SW Japan
109 S9 **Himmelberg** Kärnten, S Austria
138 I5 **Ḥimş** var. Homs; anc. Emesa. Ḥimş, C Syria
138 K6 **Ḥimş** off. Muḥāfaẓat Hims, var. Homs. ◆ governorate C Syria
138 I5 **Ḥimş, Buḥayrat** var. Buḥayrat Qattinah. ◎ W Syria
171 R7 **Hinatuan** Mindanao, S Philippines
117 N10 **Hînceşti** var. Hânceşti; prev. Kotovsk. C Moldova
44 M9 **Hinche** C Haiti
181 X5 **Hinchinbrook Island** island Queensland, NE Australia
39 S12 **Hinchinbrook Island** island Alaska, USA
97 M19 **Hinckley** C England, UK
29 V7 **Hinckley** Minnesota, N USA
36 K5 **Hinckley** Utah, W USA
18 J9 **Hinckley Reservoir** ▣ New York, NE USA
152 I12 **Hindaun** Rājasthān, N India
Hindenburg/Hindenburg in Oberschlesien see Zabrze
Hindiya see Al Hindīyah
21 O6 **Hindman** Kentucky, S USA
182 L10 **Hindmarsh, Lake** ◎ Victoria, SE Australia
185 G19 **Hinds** Canterbury, South Island, New Zealand
185 G19 **Hinds** ~ South Island, New Zealand
95 H23 **Hindsholm** island C Denmark
149 S4 **Hindu Kush** Per. Hendū Kosh. ▲▲ Afghanistan/Pakistan
155 H19 **Hindupur** Andhra Pradesh, E India
9 O12 **Hines Creek** Alberta, W Canada
23 W6 **Hinesville** Georgia, SE USA
154 I12 **Hinganghāt** Mahārāshtra, C India
149 N15 **Hingol** ~ SW Pakistan
154 H13 **Hingoli** Mahārāshtra, C India
137 R13 **Hınıs** Erzurum, E Turkey
92 O2 **Hinlopenstretet** strait N Svalbard
92 G10 **Hinnøya** Lapp. Iinnasuolu. island C Norway
108 H10 **Hinterrhein** ~ SW Switzerland
9 O14 **Hinton** Alberta, SW Canada
26 M10 **Hinton** Oklahoma, C USA
21 R6 **Hinton** West Virginia, NE USA
Hios see Chíos
41 N8 **Hipolito** Coahuila de Zaragoza, NE Mexico
Hipponium see Vibo Valentia
164 B13 **Hirado** Nagasaki, Hirado-shima, SW Japan
164 B13 **Hirado-shima** island SW Japan
165 P16 **Hirakubo-saki** headland Ishigaki-jima, SW Japan
154 M11 **Hīrākud Reservoir** ▣ E India
Hir al Gharbi, Qasr al see Ḥayr al Gharbī, Qaşr al
165 Q16 **Hirara** Okinawa, Miyako-jima, SW Japan
164 G12 **Hirata** Shimane, Honshū, SW Japan
136 I13 **Hirfanlı Barajı** ▣ C Turkey
155 G18 **Hiriyūr** Karnātaka, W India
Hîrlău see Hârlău
148 K10 **Hirmand, Rūd-e** var. Daryā-ye Helmand. ~ Afghanistan/Iran see also Helmand, Daryā-ye
Hirmand, Rūd-e see Helmand, Daryā-ye
Hirmil see Hermel
165 T5 **Hiroo** Hokkaidō, NE Japan
165 Q7 **Hirosaki** Aomori, Honshū, C Japan
164 G13 **Hiroshima** var. Hirosima. Hiroshima, Honshū, SW Japan
164 F13 **Hiroshima** off. Hiroshima-ken, var. Hirosima. ◆ prefecture Honshū, SW Japan
Hiroshima-ken see Hiroshima
Hirosima see Hiroshima
Hirschberg/Hirschberg im Riesengebirge/Hirschberg in Schlesien see Jelenia Góra
103 Q3 **Hirson** Aisne, N France
Hîrşova see Hârşova
95 G19 **Hirtshals** Nordjylland, N Denmark
152 H10 **Hisār** Haryāna, NW India
162 K7 **Hishig Öndör** var. Maanīt. Bulgan, C Mongolia
186 E9 **Hisiu** Central, SW Papua New Guinea
147 P13 **Hisor** Rus. Gissar. W Tajikistan
Hispalis see Sevilla
Hispana/Hispania see Spain
44 M7 **Hispaniola** island Dominion Republic/Haiti
64 F11 **Hispaniola Basin** var. Hispaniola Trough. undersea feature SW Atlantic Ocean
Hispaniola Trough see Hispaniola Basin
Histonium see Vasto
139 R7 **Hīt** SW Iraq
165 P14 **Hita** Ōita, Kyūshū, SW Japan
165 P12 **Hitachi** var. Hitati. Ibaraki, Honshū, S Japan
165 P12 **Hitachi-Ōta** var. Hitatiôta. Ibaraki, Honshū, S Japan
Hitati see Hitachi
Hitatiōta see Hitachi-Ōta
97 O21 **Hitchin** E England, UK
191 Q7 **Hitiaa** Tahiti, W French Polynesia
164 D15 **Hitoyoshi** var. Hitoyosi. Kumamoto, Kyūshū, SW Japan
Hitoyosi see Hitoyoshi
94 F7 **Hitra** prev. Hitteren. island S Norway
Hitteren see Hitra
187 Q11 **Hiu** island Torres Islands, N Vanuatu
165 O11 **Hiuchiga-take** ▲ Honshū, C Japan
191 X7 **Hiva Oa** island Îles Marquises, N French Polynesia
20 M10 **Hiwassee Lake** ▣ North Carolina, SE USA
20 M10 **Hiwassee River** ~ SE USA
95 H20 **Hjallerup** Nordjylland, N Denmark
95 M16 **Hjälmaren** Eng. Lake Hjalmar. ◎ C Sweden
Hjalmar, Lake see Hjälmaren
95 C14 **Hjellestad** Hordaland, S Norway
95 D16 **Hjelmeland** Rogaland, S Norway
94 G10 **Hjerkinn** Oppland, S Norway
95 L18 **Hjo** Västra Götaland, S Sweden
95 G19 **Hjørring** Nordjylland, N Denmark
167 O1 **Hkakabo Razi** ▲ Myanmar (Burma)/China
167 N1 **Hkring Bum** ▲ N Myanmar (Burma)
83 L21 **Hlathikulu** var. Hlatikulu. S Swaziland
Hlatikulu see Hlathikulu
Hliboka see Hlyboka
111 F17 **Hlinsko** var. Hlinsko v Čechách. Pardubický Kraj, C Czech Republic
Hlinsko v Čechách see Hlinsko
117 S6 **Hlobyne** Rus. Globino. Poltavs'ka Oblast', NE Ukraine
111 H20 **Hlohovec** Ger. Freistadtl, Hung. Galgóc; prev. Frakštát. Trnavský Kraj, W Slovakia
83 J23 **Hlotse** var. Leribe. NW Lesotho
111 I17 **Hlučín** Ger. Hultschin, Pol. Hulczyn. Moravskoslezský Kraj, E Czech Republic
117 S2 **Hlukhiv** Rus. Glukhov. Sums'ka Oblast', NE Ukraine
119 K21 **Hlushkavichy** Rus. Glushkevichi. Homyel'skaya Voblasts', SE Belarus
119 L18 **Hlusk** Rus. Glusk, Glussk. Mahilyowskaya Voblasts', E Belarus
116 K8 **Hlyboka** Ger. Hliboka, Rus. Glybokaya. Chernivets'ka Oblast', W Ukraine
118 K13 **Hlybokaye** Rus. Glubokoye. Vitsyebskaya Voblasts', N Belarus
77 Q16 **Ho** SE Ghana
167 S6 **Hoa Binh** Hoa Binh, N Vietnam
83 E20 **Hoachanas** Hardap, C Namibia
Hoai Nhơn see Bông Sơn
167 T8 **Hoa Lac** Quang Binh, C Vietnam
167 S5 **Hoang Liên Sơn** ▲▲ N Vietnam
83 B17 **Hoanib** ~ NW Namibia
33 S15 **Hoback Peak** ▲ Wyoming, C USA
183 P17 **Hobart** prev. Hobarton, Hobart Town. state capital Tasmania, SE Australia
26 L11 **Hobart** Oklahoma, C USA
183 P17 **Hobart** ✈ Tasmania, SE Australia
Hobarton/Hobart Town see Hobart
37 W14 **Hobbs** New Mexico, SW USA
194 L12 **Hobbs Coast** physical region Antarctica
23 Z14 **Hobe Sound** Florida, SE USA
Hobicaurikány see Uricani
54 E12 **Hobo** Huila, S Colombia
99 G16 **Hoboken** Antwerpen, N Belgium
158 K3 **Hoboksar** var. Hoboksar Mongol Zizhixian. Xinjiang Uygur Zizhiqu, NW China
Hoboksar Mongol Zizhixian see Hoboksar
95 G21 **Hobro** Nordjylland, N Denmark
21 X10 **Hobucken** North Carolina, SE USA
95 O20 **Hoburgen** headland SE Sweden
81 P15 **Hobyo** It. Obbia. Mudug, E Somalia
109 R8 **Hochalmspitze** ▲ SW Austria
109 Q4 **Hochburg** Oberösterreich, N Austria
108 F8 **Hochdorf** Luzern, N Switzerland
109 N8 **Hochfeiler** It. Gran Pilastro. ▲ Austria/Italy
167 T14 **Hô Chi Minh** var. Ho Chi Minh City; prev. Saigon. S Vietnam
Ho Chi Minh City see Hô Chi Minh
108 I7 **Höchst** Vorarlberg, NW Austria
Höchstadt see Höchstadt an der Aisch
101 K19 **Höchstadt an der Aisch** var. Höchstadt. Bayern, C Germany
108 L9 **Hochwilde** It. L'Altissima. ▲ Austria/Italy
109 S7 **Hochwildstelle** ▲ C Austria
31 T14 **Hocking River** ~ Ohio, N USA
Hoctúm see Hoctún
41 X12 **Hoctún** var. Hoctúm. Yucatán, E Mexico
Hodeida see Al Ḥudaydah
20 K6 **Hodgenville** Kentucky, S USA
9 T17 **Hodgeville** Saskatchewan, S Canada
76 L9 **Hodh ech Chargui** ◆ region E Mauritania
Hodh el Garbi see Hodh el Gharbi
76 J10 **Hodh el Gharbi** var. Hodh el Garbi. ◆ region S Mauritania
111 L25 **Hódmezővásárhely** Csongrád, SE Hungary
74 J6 **Hodna, Chott El** var. Chott el-Hodna, Ar. Shatt al-Hodna. salt lake N Algeria
Hodna, Chott el-/Hodna, Shatt al- see Hodna, Chott El
111 G19 **Hodonín** Ger. Göding. Jihomoravský Kraj, SE Czech Republic
Hödrögö see Nömrög
Hodság/Hodschag see Odžaci
39 R7 **Hodzana River** ~ Alaska, USA
Hoei see Huy
99 H19 **Hoeilaart** Vlaams Brabant, C Belgium
Hoë Karoo see Great Karoo
98 F12 **Hoek van Holland** Eng. Hook of Holland. Zuid-Holland, W Netherlands
98 L11 **Hoenderloo** Gelderland, E Netherlands
99 L18 **Hoensbroek** Limburg, SE Netherlands
163 Y11 **Hoeryŏng** NE North Korea
99 K18 **Hoeselt** Limburg, NE Belgium
98 K11 **Hoevelaken** Gelderland, C Netherlands
Hoey see Huy
101 M18 **Hof** Bayern, SE Germany
Höfdhakaupstadhur see Skagaströnd
Hofei see Hefei
101 G18 **Hofheim am Taunus** Hessen, W Germany
Hofmarkt see Odorheiu Secuiesc
92 L3 **Höfn** Austurland, SE Iceland
94 N13 **Hofors** Gävleborg, C Sweden
92 J6 **Hofsjökull** glacier C Iceland
92 J1 **Hofsós** Nordhurland Vestra, N Iceland
164 E13 **Hōfu** Yamaguchi, Honshū, SW Japan
Hofuf see Al Hufūf
95 J22 **Höganäs** Skåne, S Sweden
183 P14 **Hogan Group** island group Tasmania, SE Australia
23 R4 **Hogansville** Georgia, SE USA
39 P8 **Hogatza River** ~ Alaska, USA
28 I14 **Hogback Mountain** ▲ Nebraska, C USA
95 G14 **Høgevarde** ▲ S Norway
Högfors see Karkkila
31 P5 **Hog Island** island Michigan, N USA
21 Y6 **Hog Island** island Virginia, NE USA
Hogoley Islands see Chuuk Islands
95 N20 **Högsby** Kalmar, S Sweden
36 K1 **Hogup Mountains** ▲▲ Utah, W USA
101 E17 **Hohe Acht** ▲ W Germany
Hohenelbe see Vrchlabí
108 I7 **Hohenems** Vorarlberg, W Austria
Hohenmauth see Vysoké Mýto
Hohensalza see Inowrocław
Hohenstadt see Zábřeh
Hohenstein in Ostpreussen see Olsztynek
20 I9 **Hohenwald** Tennessee, S USA
101 L17 **Hohenwarte-stausee** ▣ C Germany
Hohes Venn see Hautes Fagnes
109 Q8 **Hohe Tauern** ▲▲ W Austria
163 O13 **Hohhot** var. Huhehot, Huhohaote, Mong. Kukukhoto; prev. Kweisui, Kwesui. Nei Mongol Zizhiqu, N China
162 F7 **Hohmorīt** var. Sayn-Ust. Govī-Altay, W Mongolia
103 U5 **Hohneck** ▲ NE France
77 Q16 **Hohoe** E Ghana
164 E12 **Hōhoku** Yamaguchi, Honshū, SW Japan
159 O11 **Hoh Sai Hu** ◎ C China
159 N11 **Hoh Xil Hu** ◎ C China
158 L11 **Hoh Xil Shan** ▲ W China
167 U10 **Hôi An** prev. Faifo. Quang Nam-Đa Nẵng, C Vietnam
Hoï-Hao/Hoihow see Haikou
159 S11 **Hoika** prev. Heka. Qinghai, W China
81 F17 **Hoima** W Uganda
26 L5 **Hoisington** Kansas, C USA
146 D12 **Hojagala** Rus. Khodzhakala. Balkan Welaýaty, W Turkmenistan
146 M13 **Hojambaz** Rus. Khodzhambas. Labap Welaýaty, E Turkmenistan
95 H23 **Højby** Fyn, C Denmark
95 F24 **Højer** Sønderjylland, SW Denmark
164 E14 **Hōjō** var. Hôzyô. Ehime, Shikoku, SW Japan
184 J3 **Hokianga Harbour** inlet SE Tasman Sea
185 F17 **Hokitika** West Coast, South Island, New Zealand
165 U4 **Hokkai-dō** ◆ territory Hokkaidō, NE Japan
165 T3 **Hokkaidō** prev. Ezo, Yeso, Yezo. island NE Japan
95 G15 **Hokksund** Buskerud, S Norway
143 S4 **Hokmābād** KhorāsānRazavī, N Iran
Hokō see P'ohang
Hoko-guntō/Hoko-shotō see P'enghu Liehtao
Hoktemberyan see Armavir
94 F13 **Hol** Buskerud, S Norway
117 R11 **Hola Prystan'** Rus. Golaya Pristan. Khersons'ka Oblast', S Ukraine
95 I23 **Holbæk** Vestsjælland, E Denmark
Holboo see Santmargats
183 P10 **Holbrook** New South Wales, SE Australia
37 N11 **Holbrook** Arizona, SW USA
27 S5 **Holden** Missouri, C USA
36 K5 **Holden** Utah, W USA
27 O11 **Holdenville** Oklahoma, C USA
29 O16 **Holdrege** Nebraska, C USA
35 X3 **Hole in the Mountain Peak** ▲ Nevada, W USA
155 G20 **Hole Narsipur** Karnātaka, W India
111 H18 **Holešov** Ger. Holleschau. Zlínský Kraj, E Czech Republic
45 N14 **Holetown** prev. Jamestown. W Barbados
31 Q12 **Holgate** Ohio, N USA
44 I7 **Holguín** Holguín, SE Cuba
23 V12 **Holiday** Florida, SE USA
39 O12 **Holitna River** ~ Alaska, USA
94 J13 **Höljes** Värmland, C Sweden
109 X3 **Hollabrunn** Niederösterreich, NE Austria
36 L3 **Holladay** Utah, W USA
9 X16 **Holland** Manitoba, S Canada
31 O9 **Holland** Michigan, N USA
25 T9 **Holland** Texas, SW USA
Holland see Netherlands
22 K4 **Hollandale** Mississippi, S USA
Hollandia see Jayapura
Hollandsch Diep see Hollands Diep
99 H14 **Hollands Diep** var. Hollandsch Diep. channel SW Netherlands
Holleschau see Holešov
25 R5 **Holliday** Texas, SW USA
18 E15 **Hollidaysburg** Pennsylvania, NE USA
21 S6 **Hollins** Virginia, NE USA
26 J12 **Hollis** Oklahoma, C USA
35 O10 **Hollister** California, W USA
27 T8 **Hollister** Missouri, C USA
93 M19 **Hollola** Etelä-Suomi, S Finland
98 K4 **Hollum** Friesland, N Netherlands
95 J23 **Höllviksnäs** Skåne, S Sweden
37 W6 **Holly** Colorado, C USA
31 R9 **Holly** Michigan, N USA
21 S14 **Holly Hill** South Carolina, SE USA
21 W11 **Holly Ridge** North Carolina, SE USA
22 L1 **Holly Springs** Mississippi, S USA
23 Z15 **Hollywood** Florida, SE USA
8 J6 **Holman** Victoria Island, Northwest Territories, N Canada
92 I2 **Hólmavík** Vestfirdhir, NW Iceland
30 J7 **Holmen** Wisconsin, N USA
23 R8 **Holmes Creek** ~ Alabama/Florida, SE USA
95 H16 **Holmestrand** Vestfold, S Norway
93 J16 **Holmön** island N Sweden
95 E22 **Holmsland Klit** beach W Denmark
93 J16 **Holmsund** Västerbotten, N Sweden
95 Q18 **Holmudden** headland SE Sweden
138 F10 **Ḥolon** var Kholon. Tel Aviv, C Israel
163 P7 **Hölönbuyr** var. Bayan. Dornod, E Mongolia
163 P7 **Hölönbuyr** var. Bayan. Dornod, E Mongolia
117 P8 **Holovanivs'k** Rus. Golovanevsk. Kirovohrads'ka Oblast', C Ukraine
95 F21 **Holstebro** Ringkøbing, W Denmark
95 F23 **Holsted** Ribe, W Denmark
29 T13 **Holstein** Iowa, C USA
Holsteinborg/Holsteinsborg/Holstenborg/Holstensborg see Sisimiut
21 O8 **Holston River** ~ Tennessee, S USA
31 Q9 **Holt** Michigan, N USA
98 N10 **Holten** Overijssel, E Netherlands
27 P3 **Holton** Kansas, C USA
27 U5 **Holts Summit** Missouri, C USA
35 X17 **Holtville** California, W USA
98 L5 **Holwerd** Fris. Holwert. Friesland, N Netherlands
Holwert see Holwerd
39 O11 **Holy Cross** Alaska, USA
37 R4 **Holy Cross, Mount Of The** ▲ Colorado, C USA
97 I18 **Holyhead** Wel. Caer Gybi. NW Wales, UK
97 H18 **Holy Island** island NW Wales, UK
96 L12 **Holy Island** island NE England, UK
37 W3 **Holyoke** Colorado, C USA
18 M11 **Holyoke** Massachusetts, NE USA
101 I14 **Holzminden** Niedersachsen, C Germany
81 G19 **Homa Bay** Nyanza, W Kenya
Homāyūnshahr see Khomeynīshahr
77 P11 **Hombori** Mopti, S Mali
101 E20 **Homburg** Saarland, SW Germany
9 R5 **Home Bay** bay Baffin Bay, Nunavut, NE Canada
Homenau see Humenné
39 Q13 **Homer** Alaska, USA
22 H4 **Homer** Louisiana, S USA
18 H10 **Homer** New York, NE USA
23 V7 **Homerville** Georgia, SE USA
23 Y16 **Homestead** Florida, SE USA
27 O9 **Hominy** Oklahoma, C USA
94 H8 **Hommelvik** Sør-Trøndelag, S Norway
95 C16 **Hommersåk** Rogaland, S Norway
155 H15 **Homnābād** Karnātaka, C India
22 J7 **Homochitto River** ~ Mississippi, S USA
83 N20 **Homoine** Inhambane, SE Mozambique
112 O12 **Homoljske Planine** ▲▲ E Serbia
Homonna see Humenné
Homs see Al Khums, Libya
Homs see Ḥimş
119 P19 **Homyel'** Rus. Gomel'. Homyel'skaya Voblasts', SE Belarus
118 L12 **Homyel'** Vitsyebskaya Voblasts', N Belarus
119 L19 **Homyel'skaya Voblasts'** prev. Rus. Gomel'skaya Oblast'. ◆ province SE Belarus
Honan see Luoyang, China
Honan see Henan, China
164 U4 **Honbetsu** Hokkaidō, NE Japan
Honctō see Gurahonţ
54 E9 **Honda** Tolima, C Colombia
83 D24 **Hondeklip** Afr. Hondeklipbaai. Northern Cape, W South Africa
Hondeklipbaai see Hondeklip
9 Q13 **Hondo** Alberta, W Canada
164 C15 **Hondo** Kumamoto, Shimo-jima, SW Japan
25 Q12 **Hondo** Texas, SW USA
42 G1 **Hondo** ~ Central America
Hondo see Honshū
42 G6 **Honduras** off. Republic of Honduras. ◆ republic Central America
Honduras, Golfo de see Honduras, Gulf of
42 H4 **Honduras, Gulf of** Sp. Golfo de Honduras. gulf W Caribbean Sea
Honduras, Republic of see Honduras
9 V12 **Hone** Manitoba, C Canada
21 P12 **Honea Path** South Carolina, SE USA
95 H14 **Hønefoss** Buskerud, S Norway
31 S12 **Honey Creek** ~ Ohio, N USA
25 V5 **Honey Grove** Texas, SW USA
35 Q4 **Honey Lake** ◎ California, W USA
102 L4 **Honfleur** Calvados, N France
Hon Gai see Hông Gai
161 O8 **Hong'an** prev. Huang'an. Hubei, C China
Hongay see Hông Gai
167 T6 **Hông Gai** var. Hon Gai, Hongay. Quang Ninh, N Vietnam
161 O15 **Honghai Wan** bay N South China Sea
Hông Hà, Sông see Red River

◆ Country ● Country Capital ◇ Dependent Territory ○ Dependent Territory Capital ◆ Administrative Regions ✈ International Airport ▲ Mountain ▲▲ Mountain Range Volcano ~ River ◎ Lake ▣ Reservoir

161 O7 **Hong He** C China
161 N9 **Hong Hu** ◎ C China
160 L11 **Hongjiang** Hunan, S China
Hongjiang see Wangcang
161 O15 **Hong Kong** Chin. Xianggang. Hong Kong, S China
160 L4 **Hongliu He** C China
159 P8 **Hongliuwan** var. Aksay, Aksay Kazakzu Zizhixian. Gansu, N China
159 P7 **Hongliuyuan** Gansu, N China
Hongor see Delgereh
161 S8 **Hongqiao** ✕ (Shanghai) Shanghai Shi, E China
160 K14 **Hongshui He** S China
160 M5 **Hongtong** Shanxi, C China
164 J15 **Hongū** Wakayama, Honshū, SW Japan
Honguedo, Détroit d' see Honguedo Passage
15 Y5 **Honguedo Passage** var. Honguedo Strait, Fr. Détroit d'Honguedo. strait Québec, E Canada
Honguedo Strait see Honguedo Passage
Hongwan see Hongwansi
159 S8 **Hongwansi** var. Sunan, Sunan Yugurzu Zizhixian; prev. Hongwan. Gansu, N China
163 X13 **Hongwŏn** E North Korea
160 H7 **Hongyuan** var. Qiongxi; prev. Hurama. Sichuan, C China
161 Q7 **Hongze Hu** var. Hung-tse Hu. ◎ E China
186 L9 **Honiara** ● (Solomon Islands) Guadalcanal, C Solomon Islands
165 P8 **Honjō** var. Honzyô. Akita, Honshū, C Japan
93 K18 **Honkajoki** Länsi-Soumi, SW Finland
92 K7 **Honningsvåg** Finnmark, N Norway
95 I19 **Hönö** Västra Götaland, S Sweden
38 G11 **Honoka'a** var. Honokaa. Hawai'i, USA, C Pacific Ocean
38 G11 **Honoka'a** Hawaii, USA
Honokaa see Honoka'a
38 D9 **Honolulu** state capital O'ahu, Hawai'i, USA
38 H11 **Honomú** var. Honomu. Hawai'i, USA, C Pacific Ocean
105 P10 **Honrubia** Castilla-La Mancha, C Spain
164 M12 **Honshū** var. Hondo, Honsyû. island SW Japan
Honsyû see Honshū
Honte see Westerschelde
Honzyô see Honjō
8 K8 **Hood** Nunavut, NW Canada
Hood Island see Española, Isla
32 H11 **Hood, Mount** ▲ Oregon, NW USA
32 H11 **Hood River** Oregon, NW USA
98 H10 **Hoofddorp** Noord-Holland, W Netherlands
99 G15 **Hoogerheide** Noord-Brabant, S Netherlands
98 N8 **Hoogeveen** Drenthe, NE Netherlands
98 O6 **Hoogezand-Sappemeer** Groningen, NE Netherlands
98 J8 **Hoogkarspel** Noord-Holland, NW Netherlands
98 N5 **Hoogkerk** Groningen, NE Netherlands
98 G13 **Hoogvliet** Zuid-Holland, SW Netherlands
26 J8 **Hooker** Oklahoma, C USA
97 E21 **Hook Head** Ir. Rinn Duáin. headland SE Ireland
Hook of Holland see Hoek van Holland
Hoolt see Tögrög
39 W13 **Hoonah** Chichagof Island, Alaska, USA
38 L11 **Hooper Bay** Alaska, USA
31 N13 **Hoopeston** Illinois, N USA
95 K22 **Höör** Skåne, S Sweden
98 I9 **Hoorn** Noord-Holland, NW Netherlands
18 L10 **Hoosic River** New York, NE USA
Hoosier State see Indiana
35 Y11 **Hoover Dam** dam Arizona/Nevada, W USA
Höövör see Baruunbayan-Ulaan
137 Q11 **Hopa** Artvin, NE Turkey
18 J14 **Hopatcong** New Jersey, NE USA
10 M17 **Hope** British Columbia, SW Canada
39 R12 **Hope** Alaska, USA
27 T14 **Hope** Arkansas, C USA
31 P14 **Hope** Indiana, N USA
29 Q5 **Hope** North Dakota, N USA
13 Q7 **Hopedale** Newfoundland and Labrador, NE Canada
Hopeh/Hopei see Hebei
180 K13 **Hope, Lake** salt lake Western Australia
41 X13 **Hopelchén** Campeche, SE Mexico
21 U11 **Hope Mills** North Carolina, SE USA
183 O7 **Hope, Mount** New South Wales, SE Australia
92 P4 **Hopen** island SE Svalbard
197 Q4 **Hope, Point** headland Alaska, USA
12 M3 **Hopes Advance, Cap** cape Québec, NE Canada
182 L10 **Hopetoun** Victoria, SE Australia
83 H23 **Hopetown** Northern Cape, W South Africa
21 W6 **Hopewell** Virginia, NE USA
109 O7 **Hopfgarten im Brixental** Tirol, W Austria
181 N8 **Hopkins Lake** salt lake Western Australia
182 M12 **Hopkins River** Victoria, SE Australia
20 I7 **Hopkinsville** Kentucky, S USA
34 M6 **Hopland** California, W USA
95 G24 **Hoptrup** Sønderjylland, SW Denmark
Hoqin Zuoyi Zhongji see Baokang
32 F9 **Hoquiam** Washington, NW USA
29 R6 **Horace** North Dakota, N USA
137 R12 **Horasan** Erzurum, NE Turkey
101 G22 **Horb am Neckar** Baden-Württemberg, S Germany
95 K23 **Hörby** Skåne, S Sweden
43 P16 **Horconcitos** Chiriquí, W Panama
95 C14 **Hordaland** ◐ county S Norway
116 H13 **Horezu** Vâlcea, SW Romania
108 G7 **Horgen** Zürich, N Switzerland
Horgo see Tariat
Hörin see Fenglin
163 O13 **Horinger** Nei Mongol Zizhiqu, N China
Horiult see Bogd
9 U17 **Horizon** Saskatchewan, S Canada
192 K9 **Horizon Bank** undersea feature S Pacific Ocean
192 L10 **Horizon Deep** undersea feature W Pacific Ocean
95 L14 **Hörken** Örebro, S Sweden
119 O15 **Horki** Rus. Gorki. Mahilyowskaya Voblasts', E Belarus
195 O10 **Horlick Mountains** ▲▲ Antarctica
117 X7 **Horlivka** Rom. Adâncata, Rus. Gorlovka. Donets'ka Oblast', E Ukraine
143 V11 **Ḩormak** Sīstān va Balūchestān, SE Iran
143 R13 **Hormozgān** off. Ostān-e Hormozgān. ◐ province S Iran
Hormozgān, Ostān-e see Hormozgān
Hormoz, Tangeh-ye see Hormuz, Strait of
141 W6 **Hormuz, Strait of** var. Strait of Ormuz, Per. Tangeh-ye Hormoz. strait Iran/Oman
109 W2 **Horn** Niederösterreich, NE Austria
95 M18 **Horn** Östergötland, S Sweden
8 J9 **Horn** Northwest Territories, NW Canada
Hornád see Hernád
8 I6 **Hornaday** Northwest Territories, NW Canada
92 H13 **Hornavan** ◎ N Sweden
65 C24 **Hornby Mountains** hill range West Falkland, Falkland Islands
Horn, Cape see Hornos, Cabo de
97 O18 **Horncastle** E England, UK
95 N14 **Horndal** Dalarna, C Sweden
93 I16 **Hörnefors** Västerbotten, N Sweden
18 F11 **Hornell** New York, NE USA
Horné Nové Mesto see Kysucké Nové Mesto
12 F12 **Hornepayne** Ontario, S Canada
94 D10 **Hornindalsvatnet** ◎ S Norway
101 G22 **Hornisgrinde** ▲ SW Germany
22 M9 **Horn Island** island Mississippi, S USA
Hornja Łužica see Oberlausitz
63 J26 **Hornos, Cabo de** Eng. Cape Horn. cape S Chile
117 S10 **Hornostayivka** Khersons'ka Oblast', S Ukraine
183 T9 **Hornsby** New South Wales, SE Australia
97 O16 **Hornsea** E England, UK
94 O11 **Hornslandet** peninsula C Sweden
95 H22 **Hornslet** Århus, C Denmark
92 O4 **Hornsundtind** ▲ S Svalbard
Horochów see Horokhiv
116 J7 **Horodenka** Rus. Gorodenka. Ivano-Frankivs'ka Oblast', W Ukraine
117 Q2 **Horodnya** Rus. Gorodnya. Chernihivs'ka Oblast', NE Ukraine
116 K6 **Horodok** Khmel'nyts'ka Oblast', W Ukraine
116 H5 **Horodok** Pol. Gródek Jagielloński, Rus. Gorodok, Gorodok Yagellonski. L'vivs'ka Oblast', NW Ukraine
117 Q6 **Horodyshche** Rus. Gorodishche. Cherkas'ka Oblast', C Ukraine
165 T3 **Horokanai** Hokkaidō, NE Japan
116 J4 **Horokhiv** Pol. Horochów, Rus. Gorokhov. Volyns'ka Oblast', NW Ukraine
165 T4 **Horoshiri-dake** var. Horosiri Dake. ▲ Hokkaidō, N Japan
Horosiri Dake see Horoshiri-dake
111 C17 **Hořovice** Ger. Horowitz. Střední Čechy, W Czech Republic
Horowitz see Hořovice
Horqin Zuoyi Houqi see Ganjig
Horqin Zuoyi Zhongqi see Bayan Huxu
62 O5 **Horqueta** Concepción, C Paraguay
55 O12 **Horqueta Minas** Amazonas, S Venezuela
95 J20 **Horred** Älvsborg, S Sweden
151 J19 **Horsburgh Atoll** atoll N Maldives
20 K7 **Horse Cave** Kentucky, S USA
37 V6 **Horse Creek** Colorado, C USA
27 S6 **Horse Creek** Missouri, C USA
18 G11 **Horseheads** New York, NE USA
37 P13 **Horse Mount** ▲ New Mexico, SW USA
95 G22 **Horsens** Vejle, C Denmark
65 F25 **Horse Pasture Point** headland W Saint Helena
33 N13 **Horseshoe Bend** Idaho, NW USA
36 L13 **Horseshoe Reservoir** ▣ Arizona, SW USA
64 M9 **Horseshoe Seamounts** undersea feature E Atlantic Ocean
182 L11 **Horsham** Victoria, SE Australia
97 O23 **Horsham** SE England, UK
99 M15 **Horst** Limburg, SE Netherlands
64 N2 **Horta** Faial, Azores, Portugal, NE Atlantic Ocean
95 H16 **Horten** Vestfold, S Norway
111 M23 **Hortobágy-Berettyó** E Hungary
27 Q3 **Horton** Kansas, C USA
8 I7 **Horton** Northwest Territories, NW Canada
95 I23 **Hørve** Vestsjælland, E Denmark
95 L22 **Hörvik** Blekinge, S Sweden
138 E11 **Horvot Haluza** var Khorvot Khalutsa. ruins Southern, S Israel
14 E7 **Horwood Lake** ◎ Ontario, S Canada
116 K4 **Horyn'** Rus. Goryn. NW Ukraine
81 I14 **Hosa'ina** var. Hosseina, It. Hosanna. Southern, S Ethiopia
Hosanna see Hosa'ina
101 H18 **Hösbach** Bayern, C Germany
Hose Mountains see Hose, Pegunungan
169 T9 **Hose, Pegunungan** var. Hose Mountains. ▲▲ East Malaysia
148 L15 **Hoshāb** Baluchistān, SW Pakistan
154 H10 **Hoshangābād** Madhya Pradesh, C India
116 L4 **Hoshcha** Rivnens'ka Oblast', NW Ukraine
152 I7 **Hoshiārpur** Punjab, NW India
Hōshööt see Öldziyt
99 M23 **Hosingen** Diekirch, NE Luxembourg
186 G7 **Hoskins** New Britain, E Papua New Guinea
155 G17 **Hospet** Karnātaka, C India
104 K4 **Hospital de Orbigo** Castilla-León, N Spain
Hospitalet see L'Hospitalet de Llobregat
92 N13 **Hossa** Oulu, E Finland
Hosseina see Hosa'ina
Hosszúmezjő see Câmpulung Moldovenesc
63 I25 **Hoste, Isla** island S Chile
117 O4 **Hostomel'** Rus. Gostomel'. Kyyivs'ka Oblast', N Ukraine
155 H20 **Hosūr** Tamil Nādu, SE India
167 N8 **Hot** Chiang Mai, NW Thailand
158 G10 **Hotan** var. Khotan, Chin. Ho-t'ien. Xinjiang Uygur Zizhiqu, NW China
158 H9 **Hotan He** NW China
83 G22 **Hotazel** Northern Cape, N South Africa
37 Q5 **Hotchkiss** Colorado, C USA
35 V7 **Hot Creek Range** ▲▲ Nevada, W USA
Hote see Hoti
171 T13 **Hoti** var. Hote. Pulau Seram, E Indonesia
Ho-t'ien see Hotan
Hotin see Khotyn
93 H15 **Hoting** Jämtland, C Sweden
162 L14 **Hotong Qagan Nur** ◎ N China
162 J8 **Hotont** Arhangay, C Mongolia
27 T12 **Hot Springs** Arkansas, C USA
28 J11 **Hot Springs** South Dakota, N USA
21 S5 **Hot Springs** Virginia, NE USA
35 Q4 **Hot Springs Peak** ▲ California, W USA
27 T12 **Hot Springs Village** Arkansas, C USA
Hotspur Bank see Hotspur Seamount
65 J16 **Hotspur Seamount** var. Hotspur Bank. undersea feature C Atlantic Ocean
8 J8 **Hottah Lake** ◎ Northwest Territories, NW Canada
44 K9 **Hotte, Massif de la** ▲▲ SW Haiti
99 K21 **Hotton** Luxembourg, SE Belgium
Hötzing see Haţeg
187 P17 **Houaïlou** Province Nord, C New Caledonia
74 K5 **Houari Boumediène** ✕ (Alger) N Algeria
167 P6 **Houayxay** var. Ban Houayxay. Bokèo, N Laos
103 N5 **Houdan** Yvelines, N France
99 F20 **Houdeng-Goegnies** var. Houdeng-Gœgnies. Hainaut, S Belgium
102 K14 **Houeillès** Lot-et-Garonne, SW France
99 L22 **Houffalize** Luxembourg, SE Belgium
30 M3 **Houghton** Michigan, N USA
31 Q7 **Houghton Lake** Michigan, N USA
31 Q7 **Houghton Lake** ◎ Michigan, N USA
19 T3 **Houlton** Maine, NE USA
160 M5 **Houma** Shanxi, C China
193 U15 **Houma** 'Eua, C Tonga
193 U16 **Houma** Tongatapu, S Tonga
22 J10 **Houma** Louisiana, S USA
196 V16 **Houma Taloa** headland Tongatapu, S Tonga
77 O13 **Houndé** SW Burkina
102 J13 **Hourtin-Carcans, Lac d'** ◎ SW France
36 J5 **House Range** ▲▲ Utah, W USA
10 K13 **Houston** British Columbia, SW Canada
39 R11 **Houston** Alaska, USA
29 X10 **Houston** Minnesota, N USA
22 M3 **Houston** Mississippi, S USA
27 V7 **Houston** Missouri, C USA
25 W11 **Houston** Texas, SW USA
25 W11 **Houston** ✕ Texas, SW USA
98 J12 **Houten** Utrecht, C Netherlands
99 K17 **Houthalen** Limburg, NE Belgium
99 I22 **Houyet** Namur, SE Belgium
95 H22 **Hov** Århus, C Denmark
95 L17 **Hova** Västra Götaland, S Sweden
162 E6 **Hovd** var. Khovd, Kobdo; prev. Jirgalanta. Hovd, W Mongolia
162 E6 **Hovd** var. Dund-Us. Hovd, W Mongolia
162 E7 **Hovd** ◐ province W Mongolia
Hovd see Bogd
162 C5 **Hovd Gol** NW Mongolia
97 O23 **Hove** SE England, UK
29 N8 **Hoven** South Dakota, N USA
116 I8 **Hoverla, Hora** Rus. Gora Goverla. ▲ W Ukraine
Höviyn Am see Gurvanbulag
95 M21 **Hovmantorp** Kronoberg, S Sweden
163 N11 **Hövsgöl** Dornogovĭ, SE Mongolia
162 I5 **Hövsgöl** ◐ province N Mongolia
Hovsgol, Lake see Hövsgöl Nuur
162 J5 **Hövsgöl Nuur** var. Lake Hovsgol. ◎ N Mongolia
78 L9 **Howa, Ouadi** var. Wādi Howar. Chad/Sudan see also Howar, Wādi
Howa, Ouadi see Howar, Wādi
27 P7 **Howard** Kansas, C USA
29 Q10 **Howard** South Dakota, N USA
25 N10 **Howard Draw** valley Texas, SW USA
29 U8 **Howard Lake** Minnesota, N USA
80 B8 **Howar, Wādi** var. Ouadi Howa. Chad/Sudan see also Howa, Ouadi
Howar, Wādi see Howa, Ouadi
25 U5 **Howe** Texas, SW USA
183 R12 **Howe, Cape** cape New South Wales/Victoria, SE Australia
31 R9 **Howell** Michigan, N USA
28 L9 **Howes** South Dakota, N USA
83 K23 **Howick** KwaZulu/Natal, E South Africa
Howrah see Hāora
27 W9 **Hoxie** Arkansas, C USA
26 J3 **Hoxie** Kansas, C USA
101 I14 **Höxter** Nordrhein-Westfalen, W Germany
158 K6 **Hoxud** Xinjiang Uygur Zizhiqu, NW China
96 J5 **Hoy** island N Scotland, UK
43 S17 **Hoya, Cerro** ▲ S Panama
94 D12 **Høyanger** Sogn Og Fjordane, S Norway
101 P15 **Hoyerswerda** Lus. Wojerecy. Sachsen, E Germany
164 R14 **Hōyo-kaikyō** var. Hayasui-seto. strait SW Japan
104 J8 **Hoyos** Extremadura, W Spain
29 W4 **Hoyt Lakes** Minnesota, N USA
87 V2 **Hoyvík** Streymoy, N Faeroe Islands
137 O14 **Hozat** Tunceli, E Turkey
Hôzyô see Hōjō
111 F16 **Hradec Králové** Ger. Königgrätz. Královéhradecký Kraj, N Czech Republic
Hradecký Kraj see Královéhradecký Kraj
111 B16 **Hradiště** Ger. Burgstadlberg. ▲ NW Czech Republic
117 R6 **Hradyz'k** Rus. Gradizhsk. Poltavs'ka Oblast', NE Ukraine
119 M16 **Hradzyanka** Rus. Grodzyanka. Mahilyowskaya Voblasts', E Belarus
119 F16 **Hrandzichy** Rus. Grandichi. Hrodzyenskaya Voblasts', W Belarus
111 H18 **Hranice** Ger. Mährisch-Weisskirchen. Olomoucký Kraj, E Czech Republic
112 I13 **Hrasnica** Federacija Bosna I Hercegovina, SE Bosnia and Herzegovina
109 V11 **Hrastnik** C Slovenia
137 U12 **Hrazdan** Rus. Razdan. C Armenia
137 T12 **Hrazdan** var. Zanga, Rus. Razdan. C Armenia
117 R5 **Hrebinka** Rus. Grebenka. Poltavs'ka Oblast', NE Ukraine
119 K17 **Hresk** Rus. Gresk. Minskaya Voblasts', C Belarus
Hrisoupoli see Chrysoúpoli
119 F16 **Hrodna** Pol. Grodno. Hrodzyenskaya Voblasts', W Belarus
119 F16 **Hrodzyenskaya Voblasts'** prev. Rus. Grodnenskaya Oblast'. ◐ province W Belarus
111 J21 **Hron** Ger. Gran, Hung. Garam. C Slovakia
111 Q14 **Hrubieszów** Rus. Grubeshov. Lubelskie, E Poland
112 F13 **Hrvace** Split-Dalmacija, SE Croatia
Hrvatska see Croatia
112 F10 **Hrvatska Kostajnica** var. Kostajnica. Sisak-Moslavina, C Croatia
Hrvatsko Grahovi see Bosansko Grahovo
116 K6 **Hrymayliv** Pol. Gizymałów, Rus. Grimaylov. Ternopil's'ka Oblast', W Ukraine
167 N4 **Hsenwi** Shan State, E Myanmar (Burma)
Hsia-men see Xiamen
Hsiang-t'an see Xiangtan
Hsi Chiang see Xi Jiang
167 N6 **Hsihseng** Shan State, C Myanmar (Burma)
161 S13 **Hsinchu** N Taiwan
Hsing-K'ai Hu see Khanka, Lake
Hsi-ning/Hsining see Xining
Hsinking see Changchun
Hsin-yang see Xinyang
161 S14 **Hsinying** var. Sinying, Jap. Shinei. C Taiwan
167 N4 **Hsipaw** Shan State, C Myanmar (Burma)
Hsu-chou see Xuzhou
161 S13 **Hsüeh Shan** ▲ N Taiwan
Hu see Shanghai Shi
161 Q7 **Huaiyin** Jiangsu, E China
83 B18 **Huab** W Namibia
57 M21 **Huacaya** Chuquisaca, S Bolivia
57 J19 **Huachacalla** Oruro, SW Bolivia
159 X9 **Huachi** var. Rouyuanchengzi. Gansu, C China
57 N16 **Huachi, Laguna** ◎ N Bolivia
57 D14 **Huacho** Lima, W Peru
163 Y7 **Huachuan** Heilongjiang, NE China
163 P12 **Huade** Nei Mongol Zizhiqu, N China
163 W10 **Huadian** Jilin, NE China
56 E13 **Huagaruncho, Cordillera** ▲▲ C Peru
Hua Hin see Ban Hua Hin
191 S10 **Huahine** island Îles Sous le Vent, W French Polynesia
Huahua, Río see Wawa, Río
167 R8 **Huai** E Thailand
161 Q7 **Huai'an** var. Qingjiang; prev. Huaiyin. Jiangsu, E China
161 P6 **Huaibei** Anhui, E China
Huaide see Gongzhuling
157 T10 **Huai He** C China
160 L11 **Huaihua** Hunan, S China
161 N14 **Huaiji** Guangdong, S China
161 O2 **Huailai** var. Shacheng. Hebei, E China
161 P7 **Huainan** var. Huai-nan, Hwainan. Anhui, E China
Huai-nan see Huainan
161 N2 **Huairen** Shanxi, C China
161 O7 **Huaiyang** Henan, C China
Huaiyin see Huai'an
167 N16 **Huai Yot** Trang, SW Thailand
41 Q15 **Huajuapan** var. Huajuapan de León. Oaxaca, SE Mexico
Huajuapan de León see Huajuapan
41 O9 **Hualahuises** Nuevo León, NE Mexico
36 I11 **Hualapai Mountains** ▲▲ Arizona, SW USA
36 I11 **Hualapai Peak** ▲ Arizona, SW USA
62 J7 **Hualfín** Catamarca, N Argentina
161 T13 **Hualien** var. Hwalien, Jap. Karen. C Taiwan
56 E10 **Huallaga, Río** N Peru
56 C11 **Huamachuco** La Libertad, C Peru
41 Q14 **Huamantla** Tlaxcala, S Mexico
82 C13 **Huambo** Port. Nova Lisboa. Huambo, C Angola
82 B13 **Huambo** ◐ province C Angola
41 P15 **Huamuxtitlán** Guerrero, S Mexico
163 Y8 **Huanan** Heilongjiang, NE China
63 H17 **Huancache, Sierra** ▲▲ SW Argentina
57 I17 **Huancané** Puno, SE Peru
57 F16 **Huancapi** Ayacucho, C Peru
57 E15 **Huancavelica** Huancavelica, SW Peru
57 E15 **Huancavelica** off. Departamento de Huancavelica. ◐ department W Peru
Huancavelica, Departamento de see Huancavelica
57 E14 **Huancayo** Junín, C Peru
57 K20 **Huanchaca, Cerro** ▲ S Bolivia
56 C12 **Huandoy, Nevado** ▲ W Peru
Huang'an see Hong'an
161 O8 **Huangchuan** Henan, C China
161 O9 **Huanggang** Hubei, C China
Huang Hai see Yellow Sea
157 Q8 **Huang He** var. Yellow River. C China
161 Q4 **Huanghe Kou** delta E China
160 L5 **Huangling** Shaanxi, C China
161 O9 **Huangpi** Hubei, C China
163 P13 **Huangqi Hai** ◎ N China
161 Q9 **Huangshan** var. Tunxi. Anhui, E China
161 Q9 **Huang Shan** tourist site Anhui, E China
161 O9 **Huangshi** var. Huang-shih, Hwangshih. Hubei, C China
Huang-shih see Huangshi
160 L5 **Huangtu Gaoyuan** plateau C China
61 B22 **Huanguelén** Buenos Aires, E Argentina
161 S10 **Huangyan** Zhejiang, SE China
159 T10 **Huangyuan** Qinghai, C China
159 T10 **Huangzhong** var. Lushar. Qinghai, C China
163 W12 **Huanren** var. Huanren Manzu Zizhixian. Liaoning, NE China
Huanren Manzu Zizhixian see Huanren
57 F15 **Huanta** Ayacucho, C Peru
56 E13 **Huánuco** Huánuco, C Peru
56 D13 **Huánuco** off. Departamento de Huánuco. ◐ department C Peru
Huánuco, Departamento de see Huánuco
57 K19 **Huanuni** Oruro, W Bolivia
159 X9 **Huanxian** Gansu, C China
161 S12 **Huap'ing Yu** island N Taiwan
62 H3 **Huara** Tarapacá, N Chile
57 D14 **Huaral** Lima, W Peru
Huarás see Huaraz
56 D13 **Huaraz** var. Huarás. Ancash, W Peru
57 I16 **Huari Huari, Río** S Peru
56 C13 **Huarmey** Ancash, W Peru
40 H4 **Huásabas** Sonora, NW Mexico
56 D8 **Huasaga, Río** Ecuador/Peru
167 O15 **Hua Sai** Nakhon Si Thammarat, SW Thailand
56 D12 **Huascarán, Nevado** ▲ W Peru
62 G8 **Huasco** Atacama, N Chile
62 G8 **Huasco, Río** C Chile
159 S11 **Huashikia** Qinghai, W China
40 G7 **Huatabampo** Sonora, NW Mexico
159 W10 **Huating** Gansu, C China
167 S7 **Huatt, Phou** ▲ N Vietnam
41 Q14 **Huatusco** var. Huatusco de Chicuellar. Veracruz-Llave, C Mexico
Huatusco de Chicuellar see Huatusco
41 P13 **Huauchinango** Puebla, S Mexico
Huaunta see Wounta
41 R15 **Huautla** var. Huautla de Jiménez. Oaxaca, SE Mexico
Huautla de Jiménez see Huautla
161 O5 **Huaxian** var. Daokou, Hua Xian. Henan, C China
Hua Xian see Huaxian
Huazangsi see Tianzhu
29 V13 **Hubbard** Iowa, C USA
25 U8 **Hubbard** Texas, SW USA
25 Q6 **Hubbard Creek Lake** ◎ Texas, SW USA
31 R6 **Hubbard Lake** ◎ Michigan, N USA
160 M9 **Hubei** var. E, Hubei Sheng, Hupeh, Hupei. ◐ province C China
Hubei Sheng see Hubei
109 P8 **Huben** Tirol, W Austria
31 R13 **Huber Heights** Ohio, N USA
155 F17 **Hubli** Karnātaka, SW India
163 X12 **Huch'ang** N North Korea
97 M18 **Hucknall** C England, UK
97 L17 **Huddersfield** N England, UK
95 O16 **Huddinge** Stockholm, C Sweden
94 N11 **Hudiksvall** Gävleborg, C Sweden
29 W13 **Hudson** Iowa, C USA
19 O11 **Hudson** Massachusetts, NE USA
31 Q11 **Hudson** Michigan, N USA
30 H6 **Hudson** Wisconsin, N USA
9 V14 **Hudson Bay** Saskatchewan, S Canada
12 G6 **Hudson Bay** bay NE Canada
195 T16 **Hudson, Cape** headland Antarctica
Hudson, Détroit d' see Hudson Strait
27 Q9 **Hudson, Lake** ▣ Oklahoma, C USA
18 K9 **Hudson River** New Jersey/New York, NE USA
10 M12 **Hudson's Hope** British Columbia, W Canada
12 L2 **Hudson Strait** Fr. Détroit d'Hudson. strait Northwest Territories/Québec, NE Canada
Ḩudūd ash Shamālīyah, Minṭaqat al see Al Ḩudūd ash Shamālīyah
Hudur see Xuddur
167 U9 **Huê** Th,a Thiên-Huê, C Vietnam
104 J7 **Huebra** W Spain
24 H8 **Hueco Mountains** ▲▲ Texas, SW USA
116 G10 **Huedin** Hung. Bánffyhunyad. Cluj, NW Romania
40 J10 **Huehuento, Cerro** ▲ C Mexico
42 B5 **Huehuetenango** Huehuetenango, W Guatemala
42 B4 **Huehuetenango** off. Departamento de Huehuetenango. ◐ department W Guatemala
Huehuetenango, Departamento de see Huehuetenango
40 L11 **Huejuquilla** Jalisco, SW Mexico
41 P12 **Huejutla** var. Huejutla de Reyes. Hidalgo, C Mexico
Huejutla de Reyes see Huejutla
102 G6 **Huelgoat** Finistère, NW France
105 O13 **Huelma** Andalucía, S Spain
104 I14 **Huelva** anc. Onuba. Andalucía, SW Spain
104 I13 **Huelva** ◐ province Andalucía, SW Spain
104 J13 **Huelva** SW Spain
105 Q14 **Huercal-Overa** Andalucía, S Spain
37 Q9 **Huerfano Mountain** ▲ New Mexico, SW USA
37 T7 **Huerfano River** Colorado, C USA
105 S12 **Huertas, Cabo** cape SE Spain
105 R6 **Huerva** N Spain
105 S4 **Huesca** anc. Osca. Aragón, NE Spain
105 T4 **Huesca** ◐ province Aragón, NE Spain
105 P13 **Huéscar** Andalucía, S Spain
41 N15 **Huetamo** var. Huetamo de Núñez. Michoacán de Ocampo, SW Mexico
Huetamo de Núñez see Huetamo
105 P8 **Huete** Castilla-La Mancha, C Spain
23 P4 **Hueytown** Alabama, S USA
28 L16 **Hugh Butler Lake** ▣ Nebraska, C USA
181 V6 **Hughenden** Queensland, NE Australia
182 A6 **Hughes** South Australia
39 P8 **Hughes** Alaska, USA
27 X11 **Hughes** Arkansas, C USA
25 W6 **Hughes Springs** Texas, SW USA
37 V5 **Hugo** Colorado, C USA
27 Q13 **Hugo** Oklahoma, C USA
27 Q13 **Hugo Lake** ▣ Oklahoma, C USA
26 H7 **Hugoton** Kansas, C USA
Huhehot/Huhohaote see Hohhot
Huhttán see Kvikkjokk
161 R13 **Hui'an** var. Luocheng. Fujian, SE China
184 O9 **Huiarau Range** ▲▲ North Island, New Zealand
83 D22 **Huib-Hoch Plateau** plateau S Namibia
41 O13 **Huichapán** Hidalgo, C Mexico
Huicheng see Shexian
163 W13 **Hŭich'ŏn** C North Korea
83 B15 **Huíla** ◐ province SW Angola
54 E12 **Huila** off. Departamento del Huila. ◐ province S Colombia
Huila, Departamento del see Huila
54 D11 **Huila, Nevado del** elevation C Colombia
83 B15 **Huíla Plateau** plateau S Angola
160 G12 **Huili** Sichuan, C China
161 P4 **Huimin** Shandong, E China
163 W11 **Huinan** var. Chaoyang. Jilin, NE China
62 K12 **Huinca Renancó** Córdoba, C Argentina
159 V10 **Huining** var. Huishi. Gansu, C China
Huishi see Huining
160 J12 **Huishui** var. Heping. Guizhou, S China
102 L6 **Huisne** NW France
98 L12 **Huissen** Gelderland, SE Netherlands
159 N11 **Huiten Nur** ◎ C China
93 K19 **Huittinen** Länsi-Soumi, SW Finland
41 O15 **Huitzuco** var. Huitzuco de los Figueroa. Guerrero, S Mexico
Huitzuco de los Figueroa see Huitzuco
159 W11 **Huixian** var. Hui Xian. Gansu, C China
Hui Xian see Huixian
41 V17 **Huixtla** Chiapas, SE Mexico

◆ Country
● Country Capital
◇ Dependent Territory
○ Dependent Territory Capital
◐ Administrative Regions
✕ International Airport
▲ Mountain
▲▲ Mountain Range
Volcano
River
◎ Lake
▣ Reservoir

160 *H12* **Huize** *var.* Zhongping. Yunnan, SW China
98 *J10* **Huizen** Noord-Holland, C Netherlands
161 *O14* **Huizhou** Guangdong, S China
162 *J6* **Hujirt** Arhangay, C Mongolia
Hujirt *see* Tsetserleg
Hujirt *see* Delgerhaan
Hukagawa *see* Fukagawa
Hŭksan-chedo *see* Hŭksan-gundo
163 *W17* **Hŭksan-gundo** *var.* Hŭksan-chedo. *island group* SW South Korea
Hukue *see* Fukue
Hukui *see* Fukui
83 *G20* **Hukuntsi** Kgalagadi, SW Botswana
Hukuoka *see* Fukuoka
Hukusima *see* Fukushima
Hukutiyama *see* Fukuchiyama
Hukuyama *see* Fukuyama
163 *W8* **Hulan** Heilongjiang, NE China
163 *W8* **Hulan He** NE China
31 *Q4* **Hulbert Lake** Michigan, N USA
Hulczyn *see* Hlučín
Huliao *see* Dabu
163 *Z8* **Hulin** Heilongjiang, NE China
163 *S9* **Hulingol** *prev.* Huolin Gol. Nei Mongol Zizhiqu, N China
14 *L12* **Hull** Québec, SE Canada
29 *S12* **Hull** Iowa, C USA
Hull *see* Kingston upon Hull
Hull Island *see* Orona
99 *F16* **Hulst** Zeeland, SW Netherlands
Hulstay Dornod *see* Choybalsan
Hultschin *see* Hlučín
95 *M19* **Hultsfred** Kalmar, S Sweden
163 *T13* **Huludao** *prev.* Jinxi, Lianshan. Liaoning, NE China
Hulun *see* Hailar
Hu-lun Ch'ih *see* Hulun Nur
163 *Q6* **Hulun Nur** *var.* Hu-lun Ch'ih; *prev.* Dalai Nor. NE China
Hulwan/Hulwân *see* Helwân
117 *V8* **Hulyaypole** *Rus.* Gulyaypole. Zaporiz'ka Oblast', SE Ukraine
163 *V4* **Huma** Heilongjiang, NE China
45 *V6* **Humacao** E Puerto Rico
163 *U4* **Huma He** NE China
62 *J5* **Humahuaca** Jujuy, N Argentina
59 *E14* **Humaitá** Amazonas, N Brazil
62 *N7* **Humaitá** Ñeembucú, S Paraguay
83 *H26* **Humansdorp** Eastern Cape, S South Africa
27 *S6* **Humansville** Missouri, C USA
40 *I8* **Humaya, Río** C Mexico
83 *C16* **Humbe** Cunene, SW Angola
97 *N17* **Humber** *estuary* E England, UK
97 *N17* **Humberside** *cultural region* E England, UK
Humberto *see* Umberto
25 *W11* **Humble** Texas, SW USA
9 *U15* **Humboldt** Saskatchewan, S Canada
29 *U12* **Humboldt** Iowa, C USA
27 *Q6* **Humboldt** Kansas, C USA
29 *S17* **Humboldt** Nebraska, C USA
35 *S3* **Humboldt** Nevada, W USA
20 *G9* **Humboldt** Tennessee, S USA
34 *K3* **Humboldt Bay** *bay* California, W USA
35 *S4* **Humboldt Lake** Nevada, W USA
35 *S4* **Humboldt River** Nevada, W USA
35 *T5* **Humboldt Salt Marsh** *wetland* Nevada, W USA
183 *P11* **Hume, Lake** New South Wales/Victoria, SE Australia
111 *N19* **Humenné** *Ger.* Homenau, *Hung.* Homonna. Prešovský Kraj, E Slovakia
29 *V15* **Humeston** Iowa, C USA
54 *J5* **Humocaro Bajo** Lara, N Venezuela
29 *Q14* **Humphrey** Nebraska, C USA
35 *S9* **Humphreys, Mount** California, W USA
36 *L11* **Humphreys Peak** Arizona, SW USA
111 *E17* **Humpolec** *Ger.* Gumpolds, Humpoletz. Vysočina, C Czech Republic
Humpoletz *see* Humpolec
93 *K19* **Humppila** Etelä-Suomi, S Finland
32 *F8* **Humptulips** Washington, NW USA
42 *H7* **Humuya, Río** W Honduras
75 *P9* **Hūn** N Libya
92 *I1* **Húnaflói** *bay* NW Iceland
160 *M11* **Hunan** *var.* Hunan Sheng, Xiang. *province* S China
Hunan Sheng *see* Hunan
163 *Y10* **Hunchun** Jilin, NE China
95 *I22* **Hundested** Frederiksborg, E Denmark
Hundred Mile House *see* 100 Mile House
116 *G12* **Hunedoara** *Ger.* Eisenmarkt, *Hung.* Vajdahunyad. Hunedoara, SW Romania
116 *G12* **Hunedoara** *county* W Romania
101 *I17* **Hünfeld** Hessen, C Germany
Hungarian People's Republic *see* Hungary
111 *H23* **Hungary** *off.* Republic of Hungary, *Ger.* Ungarn, *Hung.* Magyarország, *Rom.* Ungaria, *SCr.* Madarska, *Ukr.* Uhorshchyna; *prev.* Hungarian People's Republic. *republic* C Europe
Hungary, Plain of *see* Great Hungarian Plain
Hungary, Republic of *see* Hungary
Hungiy *see* Urgamal
163 *X13* **Hŭngnam** E North Korea
33 *P8* **Hungry Horse Reservoir** Montana, NW USA
Hungt'ou *see* Lan Yü
Hung-tse Hu *see* Hongze Hu
167 *T6* **Hưng Yên** Hai H,ng, N Vietnam
Hunjiang *see* Baishan
95 *I18* **Hunnebostrand** Västra Götaland, S Sweden
101 *E19* **Hunsrück** W Germany
97 *P18* **Hunstanton** E England, UK
155 *G20* **Hunsūr** Karnātaka, E India
Hunt *see* Hangay
100 *G12* **Hunte** NW Germany
29 *Q5* **Hunter** North Dakota, N USA
25 *S11* **Hunter** Texas, SW USA
185 *D20* **Hunter** South Island, New Zealand
183 *N15* **Hunter Island** *island* Tasmania, SE Australia
18 *K11* **Hunter Mountain** New York, NE USA
185 *B23* **Hunter Mountains** South Island, New Zealand
183 *S7* **Hunter River** New South Wales, SE Australia
32 *L7* **Hunters** Washington, NW USA
185 *F20* **Hunters Hills, The** *hill range* South Island, New Zealand
184 *M12* **Hunterville** Manawatu-Wanganui, North Island, New Zealand
31 *N16* **Huntingburg** Indiana, N USA
97 *O20* **Huntingdon** E England, UK
18 *E15* **Huntingdon** Pennsylvania, NE USA
20 *G9* **Huntingdon** Tennessee, S USA
97 *O20* **Huntingdonshire** *cultural region* C England, UK
31 *P12* **Huntington** Indiana, N USA
32 *L13* **Huntington** Oregon, NW USA
25 *X9* **Huntington** Texas, SW USA
36 *M5* **Huntington** Utah, W USA
21 *P5* **Huntington** West Virginia, NE USA
35 *T16* **Huntington Beach** California, W USA
35 *W4* **Huntington Creek** Nevada, W USA
184 *L7* **Huntly** Waikato, North Island, New Zealand
96 *K8* **Huntly** NE Scotland, UK
10 *K8* **Hunt, Mount** Yukon Territory, NW Canada
14 *H12* **Huntsville** Ontario, S Canada
23 *P2* **Huntsville** Alabama, S USA
27 *S9* **Huntsville** Arkansas, C USA
27 *U3* **Huntsville** Missouri, C USA
20 *M8* **Huntsville** Tennessee, S USA
25 *V10* **Huntsville** Texas, SW USA
36 *L2* **Huntsville** Utah, W USA
41 *W12* **Hunucmá** Yucatán, SE Mexico
149 *W3* **Hunza** *var.* Karīmābād. Jammu and Kashmir, NE Pakistan
149 *W3* **Hunza** NE Pakistan
Hunze *see* Oostermoers Vaart
158 *H4* **Huocheng** *var.* Shuiding. Xinjiang Uygur Zizhiqu, NW China
161 *N6* **Huojia** Henan, C China
Huolin Gol *see* Hulingol
186 *N14* **Huon** *reef* N New Caledonia
186 *E7* **Huon Peninsula** *headland* C Papua New Guinea
Huoshao Dao *see* Lü Tao
Huoshao Tao *see* Lan Yü
Hupeh/Hupei *see* Hubei
Hurama *see* Hongyuan
95 *H14* **Hurdalssjøen** S Norway
14 *E13* **Hurd, Cape** *headland* Ontario, S Canada
Hurdegaryp *see* Hardegarijp
29 *N4* **Hurdsfield** North Dakota, N USA
Hüremt *see* Sayhan
Hüremt *see* Taragt
75 *X9* **Hurghada** *var.* Al Ghurdaqah, Ghurdaqah. E Egypt
67 *V9* **Huri Hills** NW Kenya
37 *P15* **Hurley** New Mexico, SW USA
30 *K4* **Hurley** Wisconsin, N USA
21 *Y4* **Hurlock** Maryland, NE USA
162 *K11* **Hürmen** *var.* Tsoohor. Ömnögovĭ, S Mongolia
29 *P10* **Huron** South Dakota, N USA
31 *S6* **Huron, Lake** Canada/USA
31 *N3* **Huron Mountains** *hill range* Michigan, N USA
36 *J8* **Hurricane** Utah, W USA
21 *P5* **Hurricane** West Virginia, NE USA
36 *J8* **Hurricane Cliffs** *cliff* Arizona, SW USA
23 *V6* **Hurricane Creek** Georgia, SE USA
94 *E12* **Hurrungane** S Norway
101 *E16* **Hürth** Nordrhein-Westfalen, W Germany
Hurukawa *see* Furukawa
185 *I17* **Hurunui** South Island, New Zealand
95 *F21* **Hurup** Viborg, NW Denmark
117 *T14* **Hurzuf** Respublika Krym, S Ukraine
Huș *see* Huși
95 *B19* **Húsavík** *Dan.* Husevig. Sandoy, C Faeroe Islands
92 *K1* **Húsavík** Nordhurland Eystra, NE Iceland
Husevig *see* Húsavík
116 *M10* **Huși** *var.* Huș. Vaslui, E Romania
95 *L19* **Huskvarna** Jönköping, S Sweden
39 *P8* **Huslia** Alaska, USA
Husn *see* Al Ḩuṣn
95 *C15* **Husnes** Hordaland, S Norway
94 *D8* **Hustadvika** *sea area* S Norway
Husté *see* Khust
100 *H7* **Husum** Schleswig-Holstein, N Germany
93 *I16* **Husum** Västernorrland, C Sweden
116 *K6* **Husyatyn** Ternopil's'ka Oblast', W Ukraine
Huszt *see* Khust
Hutag *see* Hutag-Öndör
162 *K6* **Hutag-Öndör** *var.* Hutag. Bulgan, N Mongolia
26 *M6* **Hutchinson** Kansas, C USA
29 *U9* **Hutchinson** Minnesota, N USA
23 *Y13* **Hutchinson Island** *island* Florida, SE USA
36 *L11* **Hutch Mountain** Arizona, SW USA
141 *O14* **Ḩūth** NW Yemen
186 *I7* **Hutjena** Buka Island, NE Papua New Guinea
109 *T8* **Hüttenberg** Kärnten, S Austria
25 *T10* **Hutto** Texas, SW USA
Huttu *see* Futtsu
108 *E8* **Huttwil** Bern, W Switzerland
158 *K5* **Hutubi** Xinjiang Uygur Zizhiqu, NW China
161 *N4* **Hutuo He** C China
Hutyû *see* Fuchū
185 *E20* **Huxley, Mount** South Island, New Zealand
99 *J20* **Huy** *Dut.* Hoei, Hoey. Liège, E Belgium
161 *R8* **Huzhou** *var.* Wuxing. Zhejiang, SE China
Huzi *see* Fuji
Huzieda *see* Fujieda
Huzinomiya *see* Fujinomiya
Huzisawa *see* Fujisawa
92 *I2* **Hvammstangi** Nordhurland Vestra, N Iceland
92 *K4* **Hvannadalshnúkur** S Iceland
113 *E15* **Hvar** *It.* Lesina. Split-Dalmacija, S Croatia
113 *F15* **Hvar** *It.* Lesina; *anc.* Pharus. *island* S Croatia
117 *T13* **Hvardiys'ke** *Rus.* Gvardeyskoye. Respublika Krym, S Ukraine
92 *I4* **Hveragerdhi** Sudhurland, SW Iceland
95 *E22* **Hvide Sande** Ringkøbing, W Denmark
92 *I3* **Hvítá** C Iceland
95 *G15* **Hvittingfoss** Buskerud, S Norway
92 *I4* **Hvolsvöllur** Sudhurland, SW Iceland
Hwach'ŏn-chŏsuji *see* P'aro-ho
Hwainan *see* Huainan
Hwalien *see* Hualien
83 *I16* **Hwange** *prev.* Wankie. Matabeleland North, W Zimbabwe
Hwang-Hae *see* Yellow Sea
Hwangshih *see* Huangshi
83 *L17* **Hwedza** Mashonaland East, E Zimbabwe
63 *G20* **Hyades, Cerro** S Chile
162 *K6* **Hyalganat** *var.* Selenge. Bulgan, N Mongolia
19 *Q12* **Hyannis** Massachusetts, NE USA
28 *L13* **Hyannis** Nebraska, C USA
162 *F6* **Hyargas Nuur** NW Mongolia
Hybla/Hybla Major *see* Paternò
39 *Y14* **Hydaburg** Prince of Wales Island, Alaska, USA
185 *F22* **Hyde** Otago, South Island, New Zealand
21 *O7* **Hyden** Kentucky, S USA
18 *K12* **Hyde Park** New York, NE USA
39 *Z14* **Hyder** Alaska, USA
155 *I15* **Hyderābād** *var.* Haidarabad. *state capital* Andhra Pradesh, C India
149 *Q16* **Hyderābād** *var.* Haidarabad. Sind, SE Pakistan
103 *T16* **Hyères** Var, SE France
103 *T16* **Hyères, Îles d'** *island group* S France
118 *K12* **Hyermanavichy** *Rus.* Germanovichi. Vitsyebskaya Voblasts', N Belarus
163 *X12* **Hyesan** NE North Korea
10 *K8* **Hyland** Yukon Territory, NW Canada
95 *K20* **Hyltebruk** Halland, S Sweden
18 *D16* **Hyndman** Pennsylvania, NE USA
33 *P14* **Hyndman Peak** Idaho, NW USA
164 *I13* **Hyōgo** *off.* Hyōgo-ken. *prefecture* Honshū, SW Japan
Hyōgo-ken *see* Hyōgo
Hypsas *see* Belice
Hyrcania *see* Gorgān
36 *L1* **Hyrum** Utah, W USA
93 *N14* **Hyrynsalmi** Oulu, C Finland
33 *V10* **Hysham** Montana, NW USA
9 *N13* **Hythe** Alberta, W Canada
97 *Q23* **Hythe** SE England, UK
Hyvinge *see* Hyvinkää
93 *L19* **Hyvinkää** *Swe.* Hyvinge. Uusimaa, S Finland

I

116 *J9* **Iacobeni** *Ger.* Jakobeny. Suceava, NE Romania
Iader *see* Zadar
172 *I7* **Iakora** Fianarantsoa, SE Madagascar
116 *K14* **Ialomița** *var.* Jalomitsa. *county* SE Romania
116 *K14* **Ialomița** SE Romania
117 *N10* **Ialoveni** *Rus.* Yaloveny. C Moldova
117 *N11* **Ialpug** *var.* Ialpugul Mare, *Rus.* Yalpug. Moldova/Ukraine
Ialpugul Mare *see* Ialpug
23 *T8* **Iamonia, Lake** Florida, SE USA
116 *L13* **Ianca** Brăila, SE Romania
116 *M10* **Iași** *Ger.* Jassy. Iași, NE Romania
116 *L9* **Iași** *Ger.* Jassy, Yassy. *county* NE Romania
114 *J13* **Íasmos** Anatolikí Makedonía kai Thráki, NE Greece
22 *H6* **Iatt, Lake** Louisiana, S USA
58 *B11* **Iauretê** Amazonas, NW Brazil
171 *N3* **Iba** Luzon, N Philippines
77 *S16* **Ibadan** Oyo, SW Nigeria
54 *E10* **Ibagué** Tolima, C Colombia
60 *J10* **Ibaiti** Paraná, S Brazil
36 *J4* **Ibapah Peak** Utah, W USA
113 *M15* **Ibar** *Alb.* Ibër. C Serbia
165 *P13* **Ibaraki** *off.* Ibaraki-ken. *prefecture* Honshū, S Japan
Ibaraki-ken *see* Ibaraki
56 *C5* **Ibarra** *var.* San Miguel de Ibarra. Imbabura, N Ecuador
Ibaşfalău *see* Dumbrăveni
141 *O16* **Ibb** W Yemen
100 *F13* **Ibbenbüren** Nordrhein-Westfalen, NW Germany
79 *H16* **Ibenga** N Congo
Ibër *see* Ibar
57 *I14* **Iberia** Madre de Dios, E Peru
Iberia *see* Spain
66 *M1* **Iberian Basin** *undersea feature* E Atlantic Ocean
Iberian Mountains *see* Ibérico, Sistema
84 *D12* **Iberian Peninsula** *physical region* Portugal/Spain
64 *M8* **Iberian Plain** *undersea feature* E Atlantic Ocean
Ibérica, Cordillera *see* Ibérico, Sistema
105 *P6* **Ibérico, Sistema** *var.* Cordillera Ibérica, *Eng.* Iberian Mountains. NE Spain
12 *K7* **Iberville Lac d'** Québec, NE Canada
77 *T14* **Ibeto** Niger, W Nigeria
77 *W15* **Ibi** Taraba, C Nigeria
105 *S11* **Ibi** País Valenciano, E Spain
59 *L20* **Ibiá** Minas Gerais, SE Brazil
61 *F15* **Ibicuí, Rio** S Brazil
61 *C19* **Ibicuy** Entre Ríos, E Argentina
61 *F16* **Ibirapuitã** S Brazil
105 *V10* **Ibiza** *var.* Iviza, *Cast.* Eivissa; *anc.* Ebusus. *island* Islas Baleares, Spain, W Mediterranean Sea
Ibiza *see* Eivissa
138 *J4* **Ibn Wardān, Qaşr** *ruins* Ḩamāh, C Syria
Ibo *see* Sassandra
188 *E9* **Ibobang** Babeldaob, N Palau
171 *V13* **Ibonma** Papua, E Indonesia
59 *N17* **Ibotirama** Bahia, E Brazil
141 *Y8* **Ibrā** NE Oman
127 *Q4* **Ibresi** Chuvashskaya Respublika, W Russian Federation
141 *X8* **'Ibrī** NW Oman
164 *C16* **Ibusuki** Kagoshima, Kyūshū, SW Japan
57 *E16* **Ica** Ica, SW Peru
57 *E16* **Ica** *off.* Departamento de Ica. *department* SW Peru
Ica, Departamento de *see* Ica
58 *C11* **Içana** Amazonas, NW Brazil
Icaria *see* Ikaría
58 *B13* **Içá, Rio** *var.* Río Putumayo. NW South America *see also* Putumayo, Río
Içá, Rio *see* Putumayo, Río
İçel *see* Mersin
92 *I3* **Iceland** *off.* Republic of Iceland, *Dan.* Island, *Icel.* Ísland. *republic* N Atlantic Ocean
86 *B6* **Iceland** *island* N Atlantic Ocean
64 *L5* **Iceland Basin** *undersea feature* N Atlantic Ocean
Icelandic Plateau *see* Iceland Plateau
197 *Q15* **Iceland Plateau** *var.* Icelandic Plateau. *undersea feature* S Greenland Sea
Iceland, Republic of *see* Iceland
155 *E16* **Ichalkaranji** Mahārāshtra, W India
164 *D15* **Ichifusa-yama** Kyūshū, SW Japan
Ichili *see* Mersin
164 *K13* **Ichinomiya** *var.* Itinomiya. Aichi, Honshū, SW Japan
165 *Q9* **Ichinoseki** *var.* Itinoseki. Iwate, Honshū, C Japan
117 *R3* **Ichnya** Chernihivs'ka Oblast', NE Ukraine
57 *L17* **Ichoa, Río** C Bolivia
I-ch'un *see* Yichun
Iconium *see* Konya
Iculisma *see* Angoulême
39 *U12* **Icy Bay** *inlet* Alaska, USA
39 *N5* **Icy Cape** *headland* Alaska, USA
39 *W13* **Icy Strait** *strait* Alaska, USA
27 *R13* **Idabel** Oklahoma, C USA
29 *T13* **Ida Grove** Iowa, C USA
77 *U16* **Idah** Kogi, S Nigeria
33 *N13* **Idaho** *off.* State of Idaho, *also known as* Gem of the Mountains, Gem State. *state* NW USA
33 *N14* **Idaho City** Idaho, NW USA
33 *R14* **Idaho Falls** Idaho, NW USA
121 *P2* **Idálion** *var.* Dali, Dhali. C Cyprus
25 *N5* **Idalou** Texas, SW USA
104 *I9* **Idanha-a-Nova** Castelo Branco, C Portugal
101 *E19* **Idar-Oberstein** Rheinland-Pfalz, SW Germany
118 *J3* **Ida-Virumaa** *var.* Ida-Viru Maakond. *province* NE Estonia
Ida-Viru Maakond *see* Ida-Virumaa
124 *J8* **Idel'** Respublika Kareliya, NW Russian Federation
79 *C15* **Idenao** Sud-Ouest, SW Cameroon
Idensalmi *see* Iisalmi
162 *I6* **Ider** *var.* Dzuunmod. Hövsgöl, C Mongolia
Ider *see* Galt
75 *X10* **Idfu** *var.* Edfu. SE Egypt
Ídhi Óros *see* Ídi
Ídhra *see* Ýdra
168 *H7* **Idi** Sumatera, W Indonesia
115 *I25* **Ídi** *var.* Ídhi Óros. Kríti, Greece, E Mediterranean Sea
Idi Amin, Lac *see* Edward, Lake
106 *G10* **Idice** N Italy
76 *G9* **Idini** Trarza, W Mauritania
79 *J21* **Idiofa** Bandundu, SW Dem. Rep. Congo
39 *O10* **Iditarod River** Alaska, USA
95 *M14* **Idkerberget** Dalarna, C Sweden
138 *I3* **Idlib** Idlib, NW Syria
138 *I4* **Idlib** *off.* Muḩāfaẓat Idlib. *governorate* NW Syria
Idlib, Muḩāfaẓat *see* Idlib
Idra *see* Ýdra
94 *J11* **Idre** Dalarna, C Sweden
Idria *see* Idrija
109 *S11* **Idrija** *It.* Idria. W Slovenia
101 *G18* **Idstein** Hessen, W Germany
83 *J25* **Idutywa** Eastern Cape, SE South Africa
Idzhevan *see* Ijevan
118 *G9* **Iecava** Bauska, S Latvia
165 *T16* **Ie-jima** *island* Nansei-shotō, SW Japan
99 *B18* **Ieper** *Fr.* Ypres. West-Vlaanderen, W Belgium
115 *K25* **Ierápetra** Kríti, Greece, E Mediterranean Sea
115 *G22* **Iérax, Ákrotirio** *cape* S Greece
Ierisós *see* Ierissós
115 *H14* **Ierissós** *var.* Ierisós. Kentrikí Makedonía, N Greece
116 *I11* **Iernut** *Hung.* Radnót. Mureș, C Romania
106 *J12* **Iesi** *var.* Jesi. Marche, C Italy
92 *K9* **Iešjávri** N Norway
Iesolo *see* Jesolo
188 *K16* **Ifalik Atoll** *atoll* Caroline Islands, C Micronesia
172 *I6* **Ifanadiana** Fianarantsoa, SE Madagascar
77 *T16* **Ife** Osun, SW Nigeria
77 *V8* **Iferouâne** Agadez, N Niger
Iferten *see* Yverdon
92 *L8* **Ifjord** Finnmark, N Norway
77 *R8* **Ifôghas, Adrar des** *var.* Adrar des Iforas. NE Mali
Iforas, Adrar des *see* Ifôghas, Adrar des
182 *D6* **Ifould lake** *salt lake* South Australia
74 *G6* **Ifrane** C Morocco
171 *S11* **Iga** Pulau Halmahera, E Indonesia
81 *G18* **Iganga** SE Uganda
60 *L7* **Igarapava** São Paulo, S Brazil
122 *K9* **Igarka** Krasnoyarskiy Kray, N Russian Federation
Igaunija *see* Estonia
137 *T12* **Iğdır** *province* E Turkey
I.G.Duca *see* General Toshevo
Igel *see* Jihlava
94 *N11* **Iggesund** Gävleborg, C Sweden
39 *P7* **Igikpak, Mount** Alaska, USA
39 *P13* **Igiugig** Alaska, USA
Iglau/Iglawa/Igława *see* Jihlava
107 *B20* **Iglesias** Sardegna, Italy, C Mediterranean Sea
127 *V4* **Iglino** Respublika Bashkortostan, W Russian Federation
Igló *see* Spišská Nová Ves
9 *O6* **Igloolik** Nunavut, N Canada
12 *B11* **Ignace** Ontario, S Canada
118 *I12* **Ignalina** Utena, E Lithuania
127 *Q5* **Ignatovka** Ul'yanovskaya Oblast', W Russian Federation
124 *K12* **Ignatovo** Vologodskaya Oblast', NW Russian Federation
114 *N11* **İğneada** Kırklareli, NW Turkey
121 *S7* **İğneada Burnu** *headland* NW Turkey
Igombe *see* Gombe
115 *B16* **Igoumenítsa** Ípeiros, W Greece
127 *T2* **Igra** Udmurtskaya Respublika, NW Russian Federation
122 *H9* **Igrim** Khanty-Mansiyskiy Avtonomnyy Okrug, N Russian Federation
60 *G12* **Iguaçu, Rio** *Sp.* Río Iguazú. Argentina/Brazil *see also* Iguazú, Río
59 *I22* **Iguaçu, Salto do** *Sp.* Cataratas del Iguazú; *prev.* Victoria Falls. *waterfall* Argentina/Brazil *see also* Iguazú, Cataratas del
Iguaçu, Salto do *see* Iguazú, Cataratas del
41 *O15* **Iguala** *var.* Iguala de la Independencia. Guerrero, S Mexico
105 *V5* **Igualada** Cataluña, NE Spain
Iguala de la Independencia *see* Iguala
60 *G12* **Iguazú, Cataratas del** *Port.* Salto do Iguaçu; *prev.* Victoria Falls. *waterfall* Argentina/Brazil *see also* Iguaçu, Salto do
Iguazú, Cataratas del *see* Iguaçu, Salto do
62 *Q6* **Iguazú, Río** Argentina/Brazil
Iguazú, Río *see* Iguaçu, Rio
79 *D19* **Iguéla** Ogooué-Maritime, SW Gabon
Iguid, Erg *see* Iguîdi, 'Erg
67 *M5* **Iguîdi, 'Erg** *var.* Erg Iguid. *desert* Algeria/Mauritania
172 *K2* **Iharaña** *prev.* Vohémar. Antsiranana, NE Madagascar
151 *K18* **Ihavandippolhu Atoll** *atoll* N Maldives
Ih Bulag *see* Hanbogd
165 *T16* **Iheya-jima** *island* Nansei-shotō, SW Japan
Ihhayrhan *see* Bayan-Önjüül
163 *N9* **Ihhet** *var.* Bayan. Dornogovĭ, SE Mongolia
163 *N9* **Ihhet** *var* Bayan. Dornogovĭ, SE Mongolia
172 *I6* **Ihosy** Fianarantsoa, S Madagascar
Ihsüüj *see* Bayanchandmanĭ
162 *I7* **Ihtamir** *var.* Dzaanhushuu. Arhangay, C Mongolia
162 *H6* **Ih-Uul** *var.* Bayan-Uhaa. Dzavhan, C Mongolia
162 *J6* **Ih-Uul** *var.* Selenge. Hövsgöl, N Mongolia
93 *L14* **Ii** Oulu, C Finland
164 *M13* **Iida** Nagano, Honshū, S Japan
93 *M14* **Iijoki** C Finland
Iinnasuolu *see* Hinnøya
118 *J4* **Iisaku** *Ger.* Isaak. Ida-Virumaa, NE Estonia
93 *M16* **Iisalmi** *var.* Idensalmi. Isä-Suomi, C Finland
165 *N11* **Iiyama** Nagano, Honshū, S Japan
77 *S16* **Ijebu-Ode** Ogun, SW Nigeria
137 *U11* **Ijevan** *Rus.* Idzhevan. N Armenia
98 *H9* **IJmuiden** Noord-Holland, W Netherlands
98 *M12* **IJssel** *var.* Yssel. Netherlands
98 *J8* **IJsselmeer** *prev.* Zuider Zee. N Netherlands
98 *L9* **IJsselmuiden** Overijssel, E Netherlands
98 *I12* **IJsselstein** Utrecht, C Netherlands
61 *G14* **Ijuí** Rio Grande do Sul, S Brazil
61 *G14* **Ijuí, Rio** S Brazil
189 *R8* **Ijuw** NE Nauru
99 *E16* **IJzendijke** Zeeland, SW Netherlands
99 *A18* **Ijzer** W Belgium
93 *K18* **Ikaalinen** Länsi-Suomi, W Finland
172 *I6* **Ikalamavony** Fianarantsoa, SE Madagascar
185 *G16* **Ikamatua** West Coast, South Island, New Zealand
77 *U16* **Ikare** Ondo, SW Nigeria
115 *L20* **Ikaría** *var.* Kariot, Nicaria, Nikaria; *anc.* Icaria. *island* Dodekánisa, Greece, Aegean Sea
95 *F22* **Ikast** Ringkøbing, W Denmark
184 *O9* **Ikawhenua Range** North Island, New Zealand
165 *U4* **Ikeda** Hokkaidō, NE Japan
164 *H14* **Ikeda** Tokushima, Shikoku, SW Japan
77 *S16* **Ikeja** Lagos, SW Nigeria
79 *L19* **Ikela** Equateur, C Dem. Rep. Congo
114 *H10* **Ikhtiman** Sofiya, W Bulgaria
164 *C13* **Iki** *island* SW Japan
127 *O13* **Iki Burul** Respublika Kalmykiya, SW Russian Federation
137 *P11* **İkizdere** Rize, NE Turkey
39 *P14* **Ikolik, Cape** *headland* Kodiak Island, Alaska, USA
77 *V17* **Ikom** Cross River, SE Nigeria
172 *I6* **Ikongo** *prev.* Fort-Carnot. Fianarantsoa, SE Madagascar
39 *P5* **Ikpikpuk River** Alaska, USA
190 *H1* **Iku** *atoll* Tungaru, W Kiribati
164 *I12* **Ikuno** Hyōgo, Honshū, SW Japan
190 *H16* **Ikurangi** Rarotonga, S Cook Islands
171 *X14* **Ilaga** Papua, E Indonesia
171 *O2* **Ilagan** Luzon, N Philippines
142 *J7* **Īlām** *var.* Elam. Īlām, W Iran
153 *R12* **Ilam** Eastern, E Nepal
142 *J8* **Īlām** *off.* Ostān-e Īlām. *province* W Iran
Īlām, Ostān-e *see* Īlām
161 *T13* **Ilan** *Jap.* Giran. N Taiwan
146 *G9* **Ilanly Obvodnitel'nyy Kanal** *canal* N Turkmenistan
122 *L12* **Ilanskiy** Krasnoyarskiy Kray, S Russian Federation
108 *H9* **Ilanz** Graubünden, S Switzerland
77 *S16* **Ilaro** Ogun, SW Nigeria
57 *I17* **Ilave** Puno, S Peru
110 *K8* **Iława** *Ger.* Deutsch-Eylau. Warmińsko-Mazurskie, NE Poland
123 *P10* **Il'benge** Respublika Sakha (Yakutiya), NE Russian Federation
129 *R7* **Ile** *var.* Ili, *Chin.* Ili He, *Rus.* Reka Ili. China/Kazakhstan *see also* Ili He
Ile *see* Ili He
9 *S13* **Île-à-la-Crosse** Saskatchewan, C Canada
79 *J21* **Ilebo** *prev.* Port-Francqui. Kasai Occidental, W Dem. Rep. Congo
103 *N5* **Île-de-France** *region* N France
144 *I9* **Ilek** *Kaz.* Elek. Kazakhstan/Russian Federation
Ilerda *see* Lleida
77 *T16* **Ilesha** Osun, SW Nigeria
187 *Q16* **Îles Loyauté, Province des** *province* E New Caledonia
9 *X12* **Ilford** Manitoba, C Canada
116 *K14* **Ilfov** *county* S Romania
97 *I23* **Ilfracombe** SW England, UK
136 *I11* **Ilgaz Dağları** N Turkey
136 *G15* **Ilgın** Konya, W Turkey
60 *I7* **Ilha Solteira** São Paulo, S Brazil
104 *G7* **Ílhavo** Aveiro, N Portugal
59 *O18* **Ilhéus** Bahia, E Brazil
116 *G11* **Ilia** *Hung.* Marosillye. Hunedoara, SW Romania
39 *P13* **Iliamna** Alaska, USA
39 *P13* **Iliamna Lake** Alaska, USA
137 *N13* **İliç** Erzincan, C Turkey
Il'ichevsk *see* Şărur
Il'ichevsk *see* Illichivs'k
Ilici *see* Elche
37 *V2* **Iliff** Colorado, C USA
171 *Q7* **Iligan** *off.* Iligan City. Mindanao, S Philippines
171 *Q7* **Iligan Bay** *bay* S Philippines
Iligan City *see* Iligan
158 *I5* **Ili He** *var.* Ili, *Kaz.* Ile, *Rus.* Reka Ili. China/Kazakhstan *see also* Ile
Ili He *see* Ile
56 *C6* **Iliniza** N Ecuador
Ilinski *see* Il'inskiy
125 *U14* **Il'inskiy** *var.* Ilinski. Permskaya Oblast', NW Russian Federation
125 *U14* **Il'inskiy** Ostrov Sakhalin, Sakhalinskaya Oblast', SE Russian Federation
18 *I10* **Ilion** New York, NE USA
38 *E9* **'Ilio Point** *var.* Ilio Point. *headland* Moloka'i, Hawai'i, USA
Ilio Point *see* 'Ilio Point
109 *T13* **Ilirska Bistrica** *prev.* Bistrica, *Ger.* Feistritz, Illyrisch-Feistritz, *It.* Villa del Nevoso. SW Slovenia
137 *Q16* **Ilisu Barajı** SE Turkey
155 *G17* **Ilkal** Karnātaka, C India
97 *M19* **Ilkeston** C England, UK
121 *O16* **Il-Kullana** *headland* SW Malta
108 *J8* **Ill** W Austria
103 *U6* **Ill** NE France
62 *G10* **Illapel** Coquimbo, C Chile
Illaue Fartak Trench *see* Alula-Fartak Trench
182 *C2* **Illbillee, Mount** South Australia
102 *I6* **Ille-et-Vilaine** *department* NW France
77 *T11* **Illéla** Tahoua, SW Niger
101 *J24* **Iller** S Germany
101 *J23* **Illertissen** Bayern, S Germany
105 *X9* **Illes Baleares** *autonomous community* E Spain
105 *N8* **Illescas** Castilla-La Mancha, C Spain
Ille-sur-la-Têt *see* Ille-sur-Têt

◆ Country
● Country Capital
◇ Dependent Territory
○ Dependent Territory Capital
Administrative Regions
International Airport
Mountain
Mountain Range
Volcano
River
Lake
Reservoir

103 *O17* **Ille-sur-Têt** *var.* Ille-sur-la-Têt. Pyrénées-Orientales, S France
Illi *see* Ile/Ili He
Illiberis *see* Elne
117 *P11* **Illichivs'k** *Rus.* Il'ichevsk. Odes'ka Oblast', SW Ukraine
Illicis *see* Elche
102 *M6* **Illiers-Combray** Eure-et-Loir, C France
30 *K12* **Illinois** *off.* State of Illinois, *also known as* Prairie State, Sucker State. ◈ *state* C USA
30 *J13* **Illinois River** ≈ Illinois, N USA
117 *N6* **Illintsi** Vinnyts'ka Oblast', C Ukraine
Illiturgis *see* Andújar
74 *M10* **Illizi** SE Algeria
27 *Y7* **Illmo** Missouri, C USA
Illurco *see* Lorca
Illuro *see* Mataró
Illyrisch-Feistritz *see* Ilirska Bistrica
101 *K16* **Ilm** ≈ C Germany
101 *K17* **Ilmenau** Thüringen, C Germany
124 *H14* **Il'men', Ozero** ◎ NW Russian Federation
57 *H18* **Ilo** Moquegua, SW Peru
171 *O6* **Iloilo** *off.* Iloilo City. Panay Island, C Philippines
Iloilo City *see* Iloilo
112 *K10* **Ilok** *Hung.* Újlak. Vojvodina, NW Serbia
93 *O16* **Ilomantsi** Pohjois-Karjala, SE Finland
42 *F8* **Ilopango, Lago de** *volcanic lake* C El Salvador
77 *T15* **Ilorin** Kwara, W Nigeria
117 *X8* **Ilovays'k** *Rus.* Ilovaysk. Donets'ka Oblast', SE Ukraine
Ilovaysk *see* Ilovays'k
127 *O10* **Ilovlya** Volgogradskaya Oblast', SW Russian Federation
127 *O10* **Ilovlya** ≈ SW Russian Federation
126 *K14* **Il'skiy** Krasnodarskiy Kray, SW Russian Federation
182 *B2* **Iltur** South Australia
171 *Y13* **Ilugwa** Papua, E Indonesia
Iluh *see* Batman
118 *I11* **Ilūkste** Daugvapils, SE Latvia
171 *Y13* **Ilur** Pulau Gorong, E Indonesia
32 *F10* **Ilwaco** Washington, NW USA
Il'yaly *see* Gurbansoltan Eje
Il'yaly *see* Gurbansoltan Eje
Ilyasbaba Burnu *see* Tekke Burnu
125 *U9* **Ilych** ≈ NW Russian Federation
101 *O21* **Ilz** ≈ SE Germany
111 *M14* **Iłża** Radom, SE Poland
164 *G13* **Imabari** *var.* Imaharu. Ehime, Shikoku, SW Japan
Imaharu *see* Imabari
165 *O12* **Imaichi** *var.* Imaiti. Tochigi, Honshū, S Japan
Imaiti *see* Imaichi
164 *K12* **Imajō** Fukui, Honshū, SW Japan
139 *R9* **Imām Ibn Hāshim** C Iraq
139 *T11* **Imān 'Abd Allāh** S Iraq
124 *J4* **Imandra, Ozero** ◎ NW Russian Federation
164 *F15* **Imano-yama** ▲ Shikoku, SW Japan
164 *C13* **Imari** Saga, Kyūshū, SW Japan
Imarssuak Mid-Ocean Seachannel *see* Imarssuak Seachannel
64 *J6* **Imarssuak Seachannel** *var.* Imarssuak Mid-Ocean Seachannel. *channel* N Atlantic Ocean
93 *N18* **Imatra** Kymi, SE Finland
164 *K13* **Imazu** Shiga, Honshū, SW Japan
56 *C6* **Imbabura** ◈ *province* N Ecuador
55 *R9* **Imbaimadai** W Guyana
61 *K14* **Imbituba** Santa Catarina, S Brazil
27 *W9* **Imboden** Arkansas, C USA
Imbros *see* Gökçeada
Imeni 26 Bakinskikh Komissarov *see* 26 Bakı Komissarı
Imeni 26 Bakinskikh Komissarov *see* Uzboý
125 *N13* **Imeni Babushkina** Vologodskaya Oblast', NW Russian Federation
126 *J7* **Imeni Karla Libknekhta** Kurskaya Oblast', W Russian Federation
Imeni Mollanepesa *see* Mollanepes Adyndaky
Imeni S. A. Niyazova *see* S. A.Nyýazow Adyndaky
Imeni Sverdlova Rudnik *see* Sverdlovs'k
188 *E9* **Imeong** Babeldaob, N Palau
81 *L14* **Īmī** Somali, E Ethiopia
115 *M21* **Imia** *Turk.* Kardak. *island* Dodekánisa, Greece, Aegean Sea
Imishli *see* İmişli
137 *X12* **İmişli** *Rus.* Imishli. C Azerbaijan
163 *X14* **Imjin-gang** ≈ North Korea/South Korea
35 *S3* **Imlay** Nevada, W USA
31 *S9* **Imlay City** Michigan, N USA
23 *X15* **Immokalee** Florida, SE USA
77 *U17* **Imo** ◈ *state* SE Nigeria
106 *G10* **Imola** Emilia-Romagna, N Italy
186 *A5* **Imonda** Sandaun, NW Papua New Guinea
Imoschi *see* Imotski
113 *G14* **Imotski** *It.* Imoschi. Split-Dalmacija, SE Croatia
59 *L14* **Imperatriz** Maranhão, NE Brazil
106 *B10* **Imperia** Liguria, NW Italy
57 *E15* **Imperial** Lima, W Peru
35 *X17* **Imperial** California, W USA
28 *L16* **Imperial** Nebraska, C USA
24 *M9* **Imperial** Texas, SW USA
35 *Y17* **Imperial Dam** *dam* California, W USA
79 *I17* **Impfondo** La Likouala, NE Congo
153 *X14* **Imphāl** *state capital* Manipur, NE India
103 *P9* **Imphy** Nièvre, C France
106 *G11* **Impruneta** Toscana, C Italy
115 *K15* **İmroz** *var.* Gökçeada. Çanakkale, NW Turkey
Imroz Adasī *see* Gökçeada
108 *L7* **Imst** Tirol, W Austria
40 *F3* **Imuris** Sonora, NW Mexico
164 *M13* **Ina** Nagano, Honshū, S Japan
65 *M18* **Inaccessible Island** *island* W Tristan da Cunha
115 *F20* **Ínachos** ≈ S Greece
188 *H6* **I Naftan, Puntan** *headland* Saipan, S Northern Mariana Islands
Inagua Islands *see* Little Inagua
Inagua Islands *see* Great Inagua
185 *H15* **Inangahua** West Coast, South Island, New Zealand
57 *I14* **Iñapari** Madre de Dios, E Peru
188 *B17* **Inarajan** SE Guam
92 *L10* **Inari** *Lapp.* Anár, Aanaar. Lappi, N Finland
92 *L10* **Inarijärvi** *Lapp.* Aanaarjävri, *Swe.* Enareträsk. ◎ N Finland
92 *L9* **Inarijoki** *Lapp.* Anárjohka. ≈ Finland/Norway
Inău *see* Ineu
165 *P11* **Inawashiro-ko** *var.* Inawasiro Ko. ◎ Honshū, C Japan
Inawasiro Ko *see* Inawashiro-ko
105 *X9* **Inca** Mallorca, Spain, W Mediterranean Sea
62 *H7* **Inca de Oro** Atacama, N Chile
115 *J15* **İnce Burnu** *cape* NW Turkey
136 *K9* **İnce Burnu** *headland* N Turkey
136 *I17* **İncekum Burnu** *headland* S Turkey
76 *G7* **Inchiri** ◈ *region* NW Mauritania
163 *X15* **Inch'ŏn** *off.* Inch'ŏn-gwangyŏksi, *Jap.* Jinsen; *prev.* Chemulpo. NW South Korea
161 *X15* **Inch'on** ✈ (Sŏul) NW South Korea
Inch'ŏn-gwangyŏksi *see* Inch'ŏn
83 *M17* **Inchope** Manica, C Mozambique
Incoronata *see* Kornat
103 *Y15* **Incudine, Monte** ▲ Corse, France, C Mediterranean Sea
60 *M10* **Indaiatuba** São Paulo, S Brazil
93 *H17* **Indal** Västernorrland, C Sweden
93 *H17* **Indalsälven** ≈ C Sweden
40 *K8* **Inde** Durango, C Mexico
Indefatigable Island *see* Santa Cruz, Isla
35 *S10* **Independence** California, W USA
29 *X13* **Independence** Iowa, C USA
27 *P7* **Independence** Kansas, C USA
20 *M4* **Independence** Kentucky, S USA
27 *R4* **Independence** Missouri, C USA
21 *R8* **Independence** Virginia, NE USA
30 *J7* **Independence** Wisconsin, N USA
197 *R12* **Independence Fjord** *fjord* N Greenland
Independence Island *see* Malden Island
35 *W2* **Independence Mountains** ▲▲ Nevada, W USA
57 *K18* **Independencia** Cochabamba, C Bolivia
57 *E16* **Independencia, Bahía de la** *bay* W Peru
Independencia, Monte *see* Adam, Mount
116 *M12* **Independenţa** Galaţi, SE Romania
Inderagiri *see* Indragiri, Sungai
Inderbor *see* Inderborskiy
144 *F11* **Inderborskiy** *Kaz.* Inderbor. Atyrau, W Kazakhstan
151 *I14* **India** *off.* Republic of India, *var.* Indian Union, Union of India, *Hind.* Bhārat. ◆ *republic* S Asia
India *see* Inđija
18 *D14* **Indiana** Pennsylvania, NE USA
31 *N13* **Indiana** *off.* State of Indiana, *also known as* Hoosier State. ◈ *state* N USA
31 *O14* **Indianapolis** *state capital* Indiana, N USA
9 *O10* **Indian Cabins** Alberta, W Canada
42 *G1* **Indian Church** Orange Walk, N Belize
Indian Desert *see* Thar Desert
9 *U16* **Indian Head** Saskatchewan, S Canada
31 *O4* **Indian Lake** ◎ Michigan, N USA
18 *K9* **Indian Lake** ◎ New York, NE USA
31 *R13* **Indian Lake** ⊞ Ohio, N USA
172-173 **Indian Ocean** *ocean*
29 *V15* **Indianola** Iowa, C USA
22 *K4* **Indianola** Mississippi, S USA
36 *J6* **Indian Peak** ▲ Utah, W USA
23 *Y13* **Indian River** *lagoon* Florida, SE USA
35 *W10* **Indian Springs** Nevada, W USA
23 *Y14* **Indiantown** Florida, SE USA
Indian Union *see* India
59 *K19* **Indiara** Goiás, S Brazil
India, Republic of *see* India
India, Union of *see* India
125 *Q4* **Indiga** Nenetskiy Avtonomnyy Okrug, NW Russian Federation
123 *R9* **Indigirka** ≈ NE Russian Federation
112 *L10* **Inđija** *Hung.* India; *prev.* Indjija. Vojvodina, N Serbia
35 *V16* **Indio** California, W USA
42 *M12* **Indio, Río** ≈ SE Nicaragua
152 *I10* **Indira Gandhi International** ✈ (Delhi) Delhi, N India
151 *Q23* **Indira Point** *headland* Andaman and Nicobar Island, India, NE Indian Ocean
Indjija *see* Inđija
129 *Q13* **Indo-Australian Plate** *tectonic feature*
173 *N11* **Indomed Fracture Zone** *tectonic feature* SW Indian Ocean
170 *L12* **Indonesia** *off.* Republic of Indonesia, *Ind.* Republik Indonesia; *prev.* Dutch East Indies, Netherlands East Indies, United States of Indonesia. ◆ *republic* SE Asia
Indonesian Borneo *see* Kalimantan
Indonesia, Republic of *see* Indonesia
Indonesia, Republik *see* Indonesia
Indonesia, United States of *see* Indonesia
154 *G10* **Indore** Madhya Pradesh, C India
168 *L11* **Indragiri, Sungai** *var.* Batang Kuantan, Inderagiri. ≈ Sumatera, W Indonesia
Indramajoe/Indramaju *see* Indramayu
169 *P15* **Indramayu** *prev.* Indramajoe, Indramaju. Jawa, C Indonesia
155 *K14* **Indrāvati** ≈ S India
103 *N9* **Indre** ◈ *department* C France
102 *M8* **Indre** ≈ C France
94 *D13* **Indre Ålvik** Hordaland, S Norway
102 *L8* **Indre-et-Loire** ◈ *department* C France
Indreville *see* Châteauroux
152 *G3* **Indus** *Chin.* Yindu He; *prev.* Yin-tu Ho. ≈ S Asia
Indus Cone *see* Indus Fan
173 *P3* **Indus Fan** *var.* Indus Cone. *undersea feature* N Arabian Sea
149 *P17* **Indus, Mouths of the** *delta* S Pakistan
83 *I24* **Indwe** Eastern Cape, SE South Africa
136 *I10* **İnebolu** Kastamonu, N Turkey
77 *P8* **I-n-Échaï** *oasis* C Mali
114 *M13* **İnecik** Tekirdağ, NW Turkey
136 *E12* **İnegöl** Bursa, NW Turkey
Inessa *see* Biancavilla
116 *F10* **Ineu** *Hung.* Borosjenő; *prev.* Inău. Arad, W Romania
Ineul/Ineu, Vîrful *see* Ineu, Vârful
116 *J9* **Ineu, Vârful** *var.* Ineul; *prev.* Vîrful Ineu. ▲ N Romania
21 *P6* **Inez** Kentucky, S USA
74 *E8* **Inezgane** ✈ (Agadir) W Morocco
41 *T17* **Inferior, Laguna** *lagoon* S Mexico
40 *M15* **Infiernillo, Presa del** ⊞ S Mexico
104 *L2* **Infiesto** Asturias, N Spain
93 *L20* **Ingå** *Fin.* Inkoo. Etelä-Suomi, S Finland
77 *U10* **Ingal** *var.* I-n-Gall. Agadez, C Niger
I-n-Gall *see* Ingal
99 *C18* **Ingelmunster** West-Vlaanderen, W Belgium
79 *I18* **Ingende** Equateur, W Dem. Rep. Congo
62 *L5* **Ingeniero Guillermo Nueva Juárez** Formosa, N Argentina
63 *H16* **Ingeniero Jacobacci** Río Negro, C Argentina
14 *F16* **Ingersoll** Ontario, S Canada
Ingettolgoy *see* Selenge
181 *W5* **Ingham** Queensland, NE Australia
146 *M11* **Ingichka** Samarqand Viloyati, C Uzbekistan
97 *L16* **Ingleborough** ▲ N England, UK
25 *T14* **Ingleside** Texas, SW USA
184 *K10* **Inglewood** Taranaki, North Island, New Zealand
35 *S15* **Inglewood** California, W USA
101 *L21* **Ingolstadt** Bayern, S Germany
33 *V9* **Ingomar** Montana, NW USA
13 *R14* **Ingonish Beach** Cape Breton Island, Nova Scotia, SE Canada
153 *S14* **Ingrāj Bāzār** *prev.* English Bazar. West Bengal, NE India
25 *Q11* **Ingram** Texas, SW USA
195 *X7* **Ingrid Christensen Coast** *physical region* Antarctica
74 *K14* **I-n-Guezzam** S Algeria
Ingulets *see* Inhulets'
Inguri *see* Enguri
Ingushetia/Ingushetiya, Respublika *see* Ingushskaya Respublika
127 *O15* **Ingushskaya Respublika** *var.* Respublika Ingushetiya, *Eng.* Ingushetia. ◈ *autonomous republic* SW Russian Federation
83 *N20* **Inhambane** Inhambane, SE Mozambique
83 *M20* **Inhambane** *off.* Província de Inhambane. ◈ *province* S Mozambique
Inhambane, Província de *see* Inhambane
83 *N17* **Inhaminga** Sofala, C Mozambique
83 *N20* **Inharrime** Inhambane, SE Mozambique
83 *M18* **Inhassoro** Inhambane, E Mozambique
117 *S9* **Inhulets'** *Rus.* Ingulets. Dnipropetrovs'ka Oblast', E Ukraine
117 *R10* **Inhulets'** *Rus.* Ingulets. ≈ S Ukraine
105 *Q10* **Iniesta** Castilla-La Mancha, C Spain
I-ning *see* Yining
54 *K11* **Inírida, Río** ≈ E Colombia
Inis *see* Ennis
Inis Ceithleann *see* Enniskillen
Inis Córthaidh *see* Enniscorthy
Inis Díomáin *see* Ennistimon
97 *A17* **Inishbofin** *Ir.* Inis Bó Finne. *island* W Ireland
97 *B18* **Inisheer** *var.* Inishere, *Ir.* Inis Oírr. *island* W Ireland
Inishere *see* Inisheer
97 *B18* **Inishmaan** *Ir.* Inis Meáin. *island* W Ireland
97 *A18* **Inishmore** *Ir.* Árainn. *island* W Ireland
96 *E13* **Inishtrahull** *Ir.* Inis Trá Tholl. *island* NW Ireland
97 *A17* **Inishturk** *Ir.* Inis Toirc. *island* W Ireland
Inkoo *see* Ingå
185 *J16* **Inland Kaikoura Range** ▲▲ South Island, New Zealand
Inland Sea *see* Seto-naikai
21 *P11* **Inman** South Carolina, SE USA
108 *L7* **Inn** ≈ C Europe
197 *O11* **Innaanganeq** *var.* Kap York. *headland* NW Greenland
182 *K2* **Innamincka** South Australia
92 *G12* **Inndyr** Nordland, C Norway
42 *G3* **Inner Channel** *inlet* SE Belize
96 *F11* **Inner Hebrides** *island group* W Scotland, UK
172 *H15* **Inner Islands** *var.* Central Group. *island group* NE Seychelles
Inner Mongolia/Inner Mongolian Autonomous Region *see* Nei Mongol Zizhiqu
96 *G8* **Inner Sound** *strait* NW Scotland, UK
100 *J13* **Innerste** ≈ C Germany
181 *W5* **Innisfail** Queensland, NE Australia
9 *Q15* **Innisfail** Alberta, SW Canada
Inniskilling *see* Enniskillen
39 *O11* **Innoko River** ≈ Alaska, USA
Innsbruch *see* Innsbruck
108 *M7* **Innsbruck** *var.* Innsbruch. Tirol, W Austria
79 *I19* **Inongo** Bandundu, W Dem. Rep. Congo
Inoucdjouac *see* Inukjuak
Inowrazlaw *see* Inowrocław
110 *I10* **Inowrocław** *Ger.* Hohensalza; *prev.* Inowrazlaw. Kujawski-pomorskie, C Poland
57 *K18* **Inquisivi** La Paz, W Bolivia
Inrin *see* Yüanlin
74 *J10* **I-n-Salah** *var.* In Salah. C Algeria
127 *O5* **Insar** Respublika Mordoviya, W Russian Federation
189 *X15* **Insiaf** Kosrae, E Micronesia
94 *L13* **Insjön** Dalarna, C Sweden
Insterburg *see* Chernyakhovsk
Insula *see* Lille
116 *L13* **Însurăţei** Brăila, SE Romania
125 *V6* **Inta** Respublika Komi, NW Russian Federation
77 *R9* **I-n-Tebezas** Kidal, E Mali
Interamna *see* Teramo
Interamna Nahars *see* Terni
28 *L11* **Interior** South Dakota, N USA
108 *E9* **Interlaken** Bern, SW Switzerland
29 *V2* **International Falls** Minnesota, N USA
167 *O7* **Inthanon, Doi** ▲ NW Thailand
42 *G7* **Intibucá** ◈ *department* SW Honduras
42 *G8* **Intipucá** La Unión, SE El Salvador
61 *B15* **Intiyaco** Santa Fe, C Argentina
116 *K12* **Întorsura Buzăului** *Ger.* Bozau, *Hung.* Bodzafordulő. Covasna, E Romania
22 *H9* **Intracoastal Waterway** *inland waterway system* Louisiana, S USA
25 *V13* **Intracoastal Waterway** *inland waterway system* Texas, SW USA
108 *G11* **Intragna** Ticino, S Switzerland
165 *P14* **Inubō-zaki** *headland* Honshū, S Japan
164 *E14* **Inukai** Ōita, Kyūshū, SW Japan
12 *I5* **Inukjuak** *var.* Inoucdjouac; *prev.* Port Harrison. Québec, NE Canada
63 *I24* **Inútil, Bahía** *bay* S Chile
Inuuvik *see* Inuvik
9 *R8* **Inuvik** *var.* Inuuvik. Northwest Territories, NW Canada
164 *L13* **Inuyama** Aichi, Honshū, SW Japan
56 *G13* **Inuya, Río** ≈ E Peru
125 *U13* **In'va** ≈ NW Russian Federation
96 *H11* **Inveraray** W Scotland, UK
185 *C24* **Invercargill** Southland, South Island, New Zealand
183 *T5* **Inverell** New South Wales, SE Australia
96 *I8* **Invergordon** N Scotland, UK
9 *P16* **Invermere** British Columbia, SW Canada
13 *R14* **Inverness** Cape Breton Island, Nova Scotia, SE Canada
96 *I8* **Inverness** N Scotland, UK
23 *V11* **Inverness** Florida, SE USA
96 *I9* **Inverness** *cultural region* NW Scotland, UK
96 *K9* **Inverurie** NE Scotland, UK
182 *F8* **Investigator Group** *island group* South Australia
173 *T7* **Investigator Ridge** *undersea feature* E Indian Ocean
182 *H10* **Investigator Strait** *strait* South Australia
29 *R11* **Inwood** Iowa, C USA
123 *S10* **Inya** ≈ E Russian Federation
Inyanga *see* Nyanga
83 *M16* **Inyangani** ▲ NE Zimbabwe
83 *J17* **Inyathi** Matabeleland North, SW Zimbabwe
35 *T12* **Inyokern** California, W USA
35 *T10* **Inyo Mountains** ▲▲ California, W USA
127 *P6* **Inza** Ul'yanovskaya Oblast', W Russian Federation
127 *W5* **Inzer** Respublika Bashkortostan, W Russian Federation
127 *N7* **Inzhavino** Tambovskaya Oblast', W Russian Federation
115 *C16* **Ioánnina** *var.* Janina, Yannina. Ípeiros, W Greece
164 *B17* **Iō-jima** *var.* Iwojima. *island* Nansei-shotō, SW Japan
124 *L4* **Iokan'ga** ≈ NW Russian Federation
27 *Q6* **Iola** Kansas, C USA
Iolcus *see* Iolkós
115 *G16* **Iolkós** *anc.* Iolcus. *site of ancient city* Thessalía, C Greece
Iolotan' *see* Ýolöten
83 *A16* **Iona** Namibe, SW Angola
96 *F11* **Iona** *island* W Scotland, UK
116 *M15* **Ion Corvin** Constanţa, SE Romania
35 *P7* **Ione** California, W USA
116 *I13* **Ioneşti** Vâlcea, SW Romania
31 *Q9* **Ionia** Michigan, N USA
Ionia Basin *see* Ionian Basin
121 *O10* **Ionian Basin** *var.* Ionia Basin. *undersea feature* Ionian Sea, C Mediterranean Sea
115 *B17* **Iónia Nisiá** *var.* Iónioi Nísoi, *Eng.* Ionian Islands. *island group* W Greece
Ionian Islands *see* Iónia Nísiá/Iónioi Nísoi
121 *O10* **Ionian Sea** *Gk.* Iónio Pélagos, *It.* Mar Ionio. *sea* C Mediterranean Sea
115 *B17* **Iónioi Nísoi** *Eng.* Ionian Islands. ◈ *region* W Greece
Iónioi Nísoi *see* Iónia Nisiá
Ionio, Mar/Iónio Pélagos *see* Ionian Sea
Iordan *see* Yordan
137 *U10* **Iori** *var.* Qabırrı. ≈ Azerbaijan/Georgia
Iorrais, Ceann *see* Erris Head
115 *J22* **Íos** *var.* Nio. *island* Kykládes, Greece, Aegean Sea
Íos *see* Chóra
22 *G9* **Iowa** Louisiana, S USA
29 *V13* **Iowa** *off.* State of Iowa, *also known as* Hawkeye State. ◈ *state* C USA
29 *Y14* **Iowa City** Iowa, C USA
29 *V13* **Iowa Falls** Iowa, C USA
25 *R4* **Iowa Park** Texas, SW USA
29 *Y14* **Iowa River** ≈ Iowa, C USA
119 *M19* **Ipa** ≈ SE Belaeus
59 *N20* **Ipatinga** Minas Gerais, SE Brazil
127 *N13* **Ipatovo** Stavropol'skiy Kray, SW Russian Federation
115 *C16* **Ípeiros** *Eng.* Epirus. ◈ *region* W Greece
Ipek *see* Peć
111 *J21* **Ipel'** *var.* Ipoly, *Ger.* Eipel. ≈ Hungary/Slovakia
54 *C13* **Ipiales** Nariño, SW Colombia
189 *V14* **Ipis** *atoll* Chuuk Islands, C Micronesia
59 *A14* **Ipixuna** Amazonas, W Brazil
168 *J8* **Ipoh** Perak, Peninsular Malaysia
Ipoly *see* Ipel'
187 *S15* **Ipota** Erromango, S Vanuatu
79 *K14* **Ippy** Ouaka, C Central African Republic
114 *L13* **İpsala** Edirne, NW Turkey
Ipsario *see* Ypsário
183 *V3* **Ipswich** Queensland, E Australia
97 *Q20* **Ipswich** *hist.* Gipeswic. E England, UK
29 *O8* **Ipswich** South Dakota, N USA
119 *P18* **Iputs'** ≈ Belarus/Russian Federation
9 *R7* **Iqaluit** *prev.* Frobisher Bay. *province capital* Baffin Island, Nunavut, NE Canada
159 *P9* **Iqe** Qinghai, W China
159 *P9* **Iqe He** ≈ C China
Iqlid *see* Eqlīd
62 *G3* **Iquique** Tarapacá, N Chile
56 *G8* **Iquitos** Loreto, N Peru
25 *N9* **Iraan** Texas, SW USA
79 *K14* **Ira Banda** Haute-Kotto, E Central African Republic
165 *P16* **Irabu-jima** *island* Miyako-shotō, SW Japan
55 *Y9* **Iracoubo** N French Guiana
60 *H13* **Iraí** Rio Grande do Sul, S Brazil
114 *G12* **Irákleia** Kentrikí Makedonía, N Greece
115 *J21* **Irákleia** *island* Kykládes, Greece, Aegean Sea
115 *J25* **Irákleio** *var.* Herakleion, *Eng.* Candia; *prev.* Iráklion. Kríti, Greece, E Mediterranean Sea
115 *F15* **Irákleio** *anc.* Heracleum. *castle* Kentrikí Makedonía, N Greece
115 *J25* **Irákleio** ✈ Kríti, Greece, E Mediterranean Sea
Iráklion *see* Irákleio
143 *O7* **Iran** *off.* Islamic Republic of Iran; *prev.* Persia. ◆ *republic* SW Asia
58 *F13* **Iranduba** Amazonas, NW Brazil
85 *P13* **Iranian Plate** *tectonic feature*
143 *Q9* **Iranian Plateau** *var.* Plateau of Iran. *plateau* N Iran
Iran, Islamic Republic of *see* Iran
169 *U9* **Iran, Pegunungan** ▲▲ Indonesia/Malaysia
Iran, Plateau of *see* Iranian Plateau
143 *W13* **Īrānshahr** Sīstān va Balūchestān, SE Iran
55 *P5* **Irapa** Sucre, NE Venezuela
41 *N13* **Irapuato** Guanajuato, C Mexico
139 *R7* **Iraq** *off.* Republic of Iraq, *Ar.* 'Irāq. ◆ *republic* SW Asia
'Irāq *see* Iraq
Iraq, Republic of *see* Iraq
60 *J12* **Irati** Paraná, S Brazil
105 *R3* **Irati** ≈ N Spain
125 *T8* **Irayël'** Respublika Komi, NW Russian Federation
43 *N13* **Irazú, Volcán** ⛰ C Costa Rica
Irbenskiy Zaliv/Irbes Šaurums *see* Irbe Strait
118 *D7* **Irbe Strait** *Est.* Kura Kurk, *Latv.* Irbes Šaurums, Irbenskiy Zaliv; *prev. Est.* Irbe Väin. *strait* Estonia/Latvia
Irbe Väin *see* Irbe Strait
138 *G9* **Irbid** Irbid, N Jordan
138 *G9* **Irbid** *off.* Muḩāfaẓat Irbid. ◈ *governorate* N Jordan
Irbid, Muḩāfaẓat *see* Irbid
Irbīl *see* Arbīl
109 *S6* **Irdning** Steiermark, SE Austria
79 *I18* **Irebu** Equateur, W Dem. Rep. Congo
97 *D17* **Ireland** *off.* Republic of Ireland, *Ir.* Éire. ◆ *republic* NW Europe
84 *C9* **Ireland** *Lat.* Hibernia. *island* Ireland/UK
64 *A12* **Ireland Island North** *island* W Bermuda
64 *A12* **Ireland Island South** *island* W Bermuda
Ireland, Republic of *see* Ireland
125 *V15* **Iren'** ≈ NW Russian Federation
185 *A22* **Irene, Mount** ▲ South Island, New Zealand
Irgalem *see* Yirga 'Alem
144 *L11* **Irgiz** Aktyubinsk, C Kazakhstan
Irian *see* New Guinea
Irian Barat *see* Papua
Irian Jaya *see* Papua
Cendrawasih, Teluk *see* Cenderawasih, Teluk
78 *K9* **Iriba** Biltine, NE Chad
127 *X7* **Iriklinskoye Vodokhranilishche** ⊞ W Russian Federation
81 *H23* **Iringa** Iringa, C Tanzania
81 *H23* **Iringa** ◈ *region* S Tanzania
165 *O16* **Iriomote-jima** *island* Sakishima-shotō, SW Japan
42 *L4* **Iriona** Colón, NE Honduras
47 *U7* **Iriri** ≈ N Brazil
58 *I13* **Iriri, Rio** ≈ C Brazil
Iris *see* Yeşilırmak
35 *W9* **Irish, Mount** ▲ Nevada, W USA
97 *H17* **Irish Sea** *Ir.* Muir Éireann. *sea* C British Isles
139 *U12* **Irjal ash Shaykhīyah** S Iraq
147 *U11* **Irkeshtam** Oshskaya Oblast', SW Kyrgyzstan
122 *M13* **Irkutsk** Irkutskaya Oblast', S Russian Federation
122 *M12* **Irkutskaya Oblast'** ◈ *province* S Russian Federation
Irlir, Gora *see* Irlir Tog'I
146 *K8* **Irlir Tog'I** *var.* Gora Irlir. ▲ N Uzbekistan
Irminger Basin *see* Reykjanes Basin
21 *R12* **Irmo** South Carolina, SE USA
102 *E6* **Iroise** *sea* NW France
189 *X2* **Iroj** *var.* Eroj. *island* Ratak Chain, SE Marshall Islands
182 *H7* **Iron Baron** South Australia
14 *C10* **Iron Bridge** Ontario, S Canada
20 *H10* **Iron City** Tennessee, S USA
14 *I13* **Irondale** ≈ Ontario, SE Canada
182 *H7* **Iron Knob** South Australia
30 *M5* **Iron Mountain** Michigan, N USA
30 *M4* **Iron River** Michigan, N USA
30 *J3* **Iron River** Wisconsin, N USA
27 *X6* **Ironton** Missouri, C USA
31 *S15* **Ironton** Ohio, N USA
30 *K4* **Ironwood** Michigan, N USA
12 *H12* **Iroquois Falls** Ontario, S Canada
31 *N12* **Iroquois River** ≈ Illinois/Indiana, N USA
164 *M15* **Irō-zaki** *headland* Honshū, S Japan
Irpen' *see* Irpin'
117 *O4* **Irpin'** *Rus.* Irpen'. Kyyivs'ka Oblast', N Ukraine
117 *O4* **Irpin'** *Rus.* Irpen'. ≈ N Ukraine
141 *Q16* **'Irqah** SW Yemen
166 *K8* **Irrawaddy** *var.* Ayeyarwady. ◈ *division* SW Myanmar (Burma)
166 *L6* **Irrawaddy** *var.* Ayeyarwady. ≈ W Myanmar (Burma)
166 *K8* **Irrawaddy, Mouths of the** *delta* SW Myanmar (Burma)
117 *N4* **Irsha** ≈ N Ukraine
116 *H7* **Irshava** Zakarpats'ka Oblast', W Ukraine
107 *N18* **Irsina** Basilicata, S Italy
Irtish *see* Irtysh
129 *R5* **Irtysh** *var.* Irtish, *Kaz.* Ertis. ≈ C Asia
145 *S7* **Irtyshsk** *Kaz.* Ertis. Pavlodar, NE Kazakhstan
79 *P17* **Irumu** Orientale, E Dem. Rep. Congo
105 *Q2* **Irún** País Vasco, N Spain
Iruña *see* Pamplona
105 *Q3* **Irurzun** Navarra, N Spain
96 *I13* **Irvine** W Scotland, UK
21 *N6* **Irvine** Kentucky, S USA
25 *T6* **Irving** Texas, SW USA
20 *K5* **Irvington** Kentucky, S USA
Isaak *see* Iisaku
28 *L8* **Isabel** South Dakota, N USA
186 *L8* **Isabel** *off.* Isabel Province. ◈ *province* N Solomon Islands
171 *O8* **Isabela** Basilan Island, SW Philippines
45 *S5* **Isabela** W Puerto Rico
45 *N8* **Isabela, Cabo** *headland* NW Dominican Republic
57 *A18* **Isabela, Isla** *var.* Albemarle Island. *island* Galapagos Islands, Ecuador, E Pacific Ocean
40 *I12* **Isabela, Isla** *island* C Mexico
42 *K9* **Isabella, Cordillera** ▲▲ NW Nicaragua
35 *S12* **Isabella Lake** ⊞ California, W USA
31 *N2* **Isabelle, Point** *headland* Michigan, N USA
Isabel Province *see* Isabel
Isabel Segunda *see* Vieques
116 *M13* **Isaccea** Tulcea, E Romania
92 *H1* **Ísafjarđardjúp** *inlet* NW Iceland
92 *H1* **Ísafjördhur** Vestfirdhir, NW Iceland
164 *C14* **Isahaya** Nagasaki, Kyūshū, SW Japan
149 *S7* **Īsa Khel** Punjab, E Pakistan
172 *H7* **Isalo** *var.* Massif de L'Isalo. ▲▲ SW Madagascar
79 *K20* **Isandja** Kasai Occidental, C Dem. Rep. Congo
187 *R15* **Isangel** Tanna, S Vanuatu
79 *M18* **Isangi** Orientale, C Dem. Rep. Congo
101 *L24* **Isar** ≈ Austria/Germany
101 *M23* **Isar-Kanal** *canal* SE Germany
Isbarta *see* Isparta
Isca Damnoniorum *see* Exeter
107 *K18* **Ischia** *var.* Isola d'Ischea; *anc.* Aenaria. Campania, S Italy
107 *J18* **Ischia, Isola d'** *island* S Italy
54 *B12* **Iscuandé** *var.* Santa Bárbara. Nariño, SW Colombia
164 *K14* **Ise** Mie, Honshū, SW Japan
100 *J12* **Ise** ≈ N Germany
95 *I23* **Isefjord** *fjord* E Denmark
Iseghem *see* Izegem
192 *M14* **Iselin Seamount** *undersea feature* S Pacific Ocean
Isenhof *see* Püssi
106 *E7* **Iseo** Lombardia, N Italy
103 *U12* **Iseran, Col de l'** *pass* E France

◆ Country
● Country Capital
◇ Dependent Territory
○ Dependent Territory Capital
◈ Administrative Regions
✈ International Airport
▲ Mountain
▲▲ Mountain Range
⛰ Volcano
≈ River
◎ Lake
⊞ Reservoir

103 S11 **Isère** ◐ *department* E France
103 S12 **Isère** ≈ E France
101 F15 **Iserlohn** Nordrhein-Westfalen, W Germany
107 K16 **Isernia** var. Æsernia. Molise, C Italy
165 N12 **Isesaki** Gunma, Honshū, S Japan
129 Q5 **Iset'** ≈ C Russian Federation
77 S15 **Iseyin** Oyo, W Nigeria
Isfahan *see* Eşfahān
147 Q11 **Isfana** Batkenskaya Oblast', SW Kyrgyzstan
147 R11 **Isfara** N Tajikistan
149 O4 **Isfi Maidān** Ghowr, N Afghanistan
92 O3 **Isfjorden** *fjord* W Svalbard
Isgender *see* Kul'mach
Isha Baydhabo *see* Baydhabo
125 V11 **Isherim, Gora** ▲ NW Russian Federation
127 Q5 **Isheyevka** Ul'yanovskaya Oblast', W Russian Federation
165 P16 **Ishigaki** Okinawa, Ishigaki-jima, SW Japan
165 P16 **Ishigaki-jima** *island* Sakishima-shotō, SW Japan
165 R3 **Ishikari-wan** *bay* Hokkaidō, NE Japan
165 S16 **Ishikawa** var. Isikawa. Okinawa, Okinawa, SW Japan
164 K11 **Ishikawa** off. Ishikawa-ken, var. Isikawa. ◐ *prefecture* Honshū, SW Japan
Ishikawa-ken *see* Ishikawa
122 H11 **Ishim** Tyumenskaya Oblast', C Russian Federation
129 R6 **Ishim** Kaz. Esil. ≈ Kazakhstan/Russian Federation
127 V6 **Ishimbay** Respublika Bashkortostan, W Russian Federation
145 O9 **Ishimskoye** Akmola, C Kazakhstan
165 Q10 **Ishinomaki** var. Isinomaki. Miyagi, Honshū, C Japan
165 P13 **Ishioka** var. Isioka. Ibaraki, Honshū, S Japan
Ishkashim *see* Ishkoshim
Ishkashimskiy Khrebet *see* Ishkoshim, Qatorkŭhi
147 S15 **Ishkoshim** Rus. Ishkashim. S Tajikistan
147 S15 **Ishkoshim, Qatorkŭhi** Rus. Ishkashimskiy Khrebet. ▲▲ SE Tajikistan
31 N4 **Ishpeming** Michigan, N USA
147 N11 **Ishtikhon** Rus. Ishtykhan. Samarqand Viloyati, C Uzbekistan
Ishtykhan *see* Ishtikhon
153 T15 **Ishurdi** var Iswardi. Rajshahi, W Bangladesh
61 G17 **Isidoro Noblia** Cerro Largo, NE Uruguay
102 J4 **Isigny-sur-Mer** Calvados, N France
Isikawa *see* Ishikawa
136 C11 **Işıklar Dağı** ▲▲ NW Turkey
107 C19 **Isili** Sardegna, Italy, C Mediterranean Sea
122 H12 **Isil'kul'** Omskaya Oblast', C Russian Federation
Isinomaki *see* Ishinomaki
Isioka *see* Ishioka
81 I18 **Isiolo** Eastern, C Kenya
79 O16 **Isiro** Orientale, NE Dem. Rep. Congo
92 P2 **Isispynten** *headland* NE Svalbard
123 P11 **Isit** Respublika Sakha (Yakutiya), NE Russian Federation
149 O2 **Iskabad Canal** *canal* N Afghanistan
147 Q9 **Iskandar** Rus. Iskander. Toshkent Viloyati, E Uzbekistan
Iskander *see* Iskandar
Iskăr *see* Iskŭr
121 Q2 **İskele** var. Trikomo, Gk. Tríkomon. E Cyprus
136 K17 **İskenderun** Eng. Alexandretta. Hatay, S Turkey
138 H2 **İskenderun Körfezi** Eng. Gulf of Alexandretta. *gulf* S Turkey
136 J11 **İskilip** Çorum, N Turkey
Iski-Nauket *see* Eski-Nookat
114 J11 **Iskra** prev. Popovo. Khaskovska Oblast, S Bulgaria
114 G10 **Iskŭr** var. Iskăr. ≈ NW Bulgaria
114 H10 **Iskŭr, Yazovir** prev. Yazovir Stalin. ⊠ W Bulgaria
41 S15 **Isla** Veracruz-Llave, SE Mexico
119 J15 **Islach** Rus. Isloch'. ≈ C Belarus
104 H14 **Isla Cristina** Andalucía, S Spain
Isla de León *see* San Fernando
149 U6 **Islāmābād** ● (Pakistan) Federal Capital Territory Islāmābād, NE Pakistan
149 U6 **Islāmābād** ✕ Federal Capital Territory Islāmābād, NE Pakistan
Islamabad *see* Anantnāg
149 R17 **Islamkot** Sind, SE Pakistan
23 Y17 **Islamorada** Florida Keys, Florida, SE USA
153 P14 **Islāmpur** Bihār, N India
Islam Qala *see* Eslām Qal'eh
18 K16 **Island Beach** *spit* New Jersey, NE USA
19 S4 **Island Falls** Maine, NE USA
Island/Ísland *see* Iceland
182 H6 **Island Lagoon** ◎ South Australia
9 Y13 **Island Lake** ◎ Manitoba, C Canada
29 W5 **Island Lake Reservoir** ⊠ Minnesota, N USA
77 O8 **I-n-Sâkâne, 'Erg** *desert* N Mali
33 R13 **Island Park** Idaho, NW USA
19 N6 **Island Pond** Vermont, NE USA
184 K2 **Islands, Bay of** *inlet* North Island, New Zealand
103 R7 **Is-sur-Tille** Côte d'Or, C France
42 J3 **Islas de la Bahía** ◐ *department* N Honduras
65 L20 **Islas Orcadas Rise** *undersea feature* S Atlantic Ocean
96 F12 **Islay** *island* SW Scotland, UK
116 I15 **Islaz** Teleorman, S Romania
29 V7 **Isle** Minnesota, N USA
102 M12 **Isle** ≈ W France
97 I16 **Isle of Man** ◇ *UK crown dependency* NW Europe
21 X7 **Isle of Wight** Virginia, NE USA
97 M24 **Isle of Wight** *cultural region* S England, UK
191 Y3 **Isles Lagoon** ◎ Kiritimati, E Kiribati
37 R11 **Isleta Pueblo** New Mexico, SW USA
Isloch' *see* Islach
61 E19 **Ismael Cortinas** Flores, S Uruguay
Ismailia *see* Ismâ'ilîya
75 W7 **Ismâ'ilîya** var. Ismailia. N Egypt
Ismailly *see* İsmayıllı
137 X11 **İsmayıllı** Rus. Ismailly. N Azerbaijan
Ismid *see* İzmit
75 X10 **Isna** var. Esna. SE Egypt
93 K18 **Isojoki** Länsi-Soumi, W Finland
82 M12 **Isoka** Northern, NE Zambia
Isola d'Ischea *see* Ischia
Isola d'Istria *see* Izola
Isonzo *see* Soča
15 U4 **Isoukustouc** ≈ Québec, SE Canada
136 F15 **Isparta** var. Isbarta. Isparta, SW Turkey
136 F15 **Isparta** var. Isbarta. ◐ *province* SW Turkey
114 M7 **Isperikh** prev. Kemanlar. Razgrad, N Bulgaria
107 L26 **Ispica** Sicilia, Italy, C Mediterranean Sea
148 J14 **Ispikān** Baluchistān, SW Pakistan
137 Q12 **İspir** Erzurum, NE Turkey
138 E12 **Israel** off. State of Israel, var. Medinat Israel, Heb. Yisrael, Yisra'el. ◆ *republic* SW Asia
Israel, State of *see* Israel
Issa *see* Vis
55 S9 **Issano** C Guyana
76 M16 **Issia** SW Ivory Coast
Issiq Kŭl *see* Issyk-Kul', Ozero
103 P11 **Issoire** Puy-de-Dôme, C France
103 N9 **Issoudun** anc. Uxellodunum. Indre, C France
81 H22 **Issuna** Singida, C Tanzania
Issyk *see* Yesik
Issyk-Kul' *see* Balykchy
147 X7 **Issyk-Kul', Ozero** var. Issiq Köl, Kir. Ysyk-Köl. ◎ E Kyrgyzstan
147 X7 **Issyk-Kul'skaya Oblast'** Kir. Ysyk-Köl Oblasty. ◐ *province* E Kyrgyzstan
149 Q7 **Istādeh-ye Moqor, Āb-e-** var. Āb-i-Istāda. ◎ SE Afghanistan
136 D11 **İstanbul** Bul. Tsarigrad, Eng. Istanbul, prev. Constantinople; anc. Byzantium. Istanbul, NW Turkey
114 P12 **İstanbul** ◐ *province* NW Turkey
114 P12 **İstanbul Boğazı** var. Bosporus Thracius, Eng. Bosphorus, Bosporus, Turk. Karadeniz Boğazi. *strait* NW Turkey
Istarska Županija *see* Istra
115 G19 **Isthmía** Pelopónnisos, S Greece
115 G17 **Istiaía** Évvoia, C Greece
54 D9 **Istmina** Chocó, W Colombia
23 W13 **Istokpoga, Lake** ◎ Florida, SE USA
112 A9 **Istra** off. Istarska Županija. ◐ *province* NW Croatia
112 I10 **Istra** Eng. Istria, Ger. Istrien. *cultural region* NW Croatia
103 R15 **Istres** Bouches-du-Rhône, SE France
Istria/Istrien *see* Istra
Iswardi *see* Ishurdi
127 V7 **Isyangulovo** Respublika Bashkortostan, W Russian Federation
62 O6 **Itá** Central, S Paraguay
59 O17 **Itaberaba** Bahia, E Brazil
59 M20 **Itabira** prev. Presidente Vargas. Minas Gerais, SE Brazil
59 O18 **Itabuna** Bahia, E Brazil
59 J18 **Itacaiu** Mato Grosso, S Brazil
58 G12 **Itacoatiara** Amazonas, N Brazil
54 D9 **Itagüí** Antioquia, W Colombia
60 D13 **Itá Ibaté** Corrientes, NE Argentina
60 G11 **Itaipú, Represa de** ⊠ Brazil/Paraguay
58 H13 **Itaituba** Pará, NE Brazil
60 K13 **Itajaí** Santa Catarina, S Brazil
Italia/Italiana, Republica/Italian Republic, The *see* Italy
Italian Somaliland *see* Somalia
25 T7 **Italy** Texas, SW USA
106 G12 **Italy** off. The Italian Republic, It. Italia, Repubblica Italiana. ◆ *republic* S Europe
59 O19 **Itamaraju** Bahia, E Brazil
59 C14 **Itamarati** Amazonas, W Brazil
59 M19 **Itambé, Pico de** ▲ SE Brazil
164 J13 **Itami** ✕ (Ōsaka) Ōsaka, Honshū, SW Japan
115 H15 **Itámos** ▲ N Greece
153 W11 **Itānagar** *state capital* Arunāchal Pradesh, NE India
Itany *see* Litani
59 N19 **Itaobim** Minas Gerais, SE Brazil
59 P15 **Itaparica, Represa de** ⊠ E Brazil
58 M13 **Itapecuru-Mirim** Maranhão, E Brazil
60 Q8 **Itaperuna** Rio de Janeiro, SE Brazil
59 O18 **Itapetinga** Bahia, E Brazil
60 L10 **Itapetininga** São Paulo, S Brazil
60 K10 **Itapeva** São Paulo, S Brazil
47 W6 **Itapicuru, Rio** ≈ NE Brazil
58 O13 **Itapipoca** Ceará, E Brazil
60 M9 **Itapira** São Paulo, S Brazil
60 K8 **Itápolis** São Paulo, S Brazil
60 K10 **Itaporanga** São Paulo, S Brazil
62 P7 **Itapúa** off. Departamento de Itapúa. ◐ *department* SE Paraguay
Itapúa, Departamento de *see* Itapúa
59 E15 **Itapuã do Oeste** Rondônia, W Brazil
61 E15 **Itaqui** Rio Grande do Sul, S Brazil
60 K10 **Itararé** São Paulo, S Brazil
60 K10 **Itararé, Rio** ≈ S Brazil
154 H11 **Itārsi** Madhya Pradesh, C India
25 T7 **Itasca** Texas, SW USA
Itassi *see* Vieille Case
60 D13 **Itatí** Corrientes, NE Argentina
60 K10 **Itatinga** São Paulo, S Brazil
115 F18 **Itéas, Kólpos** *gulf* C Greece
57 N15 **Iténez, Río** var. Rio Guaporé. ≈ Bolivia/Brazil *see also* Rio Guaporé
Iténez, Río *see* Guaporé, Rio
54 H11 **Iteviate, Río** ≈ C Colombia
100 I13 **Ith** *hill range* C Germany
31 Q8 **Ithaca** Michigan, N USA
18 H11 **Ithaca** New York, NE USA
115 C18 **Itháki** *island* Iónia Nísiá, Greece, C Mediterranean Sea
Itháki *see* Vathy
It Hearrenfean *see* Heerenveen
79 L17 **Itimbiri** ≈ N Dem. Rep. Congo
Itinomiya *see* Ichinomiya
Itinoseki *see* Ichinoseki
39 Q5 **Itkilik River** ≈ Alaska, USA
164 M11 **Itoigawa** Niigata, Honshū, C Japan
15 R6 **Itomamo, Lac** ◎ Québec, SE Canada
165 S17 **Itoman** Okinawa, SW Japan
102 M5 **Iton** ≈ N France
57 M16 **Itonamas Río** ≈ NE Bolivia
Itoupé, Mont *see* Sommet Tabulaire
Itseqqortoormiit *see* Ittoqqortoormiit
22 K4 **Itta Bena** Mississippi, S USA
107 B17 **Ittiri** Sardegna, Italy, C Mediterranean Sea
197 Q14 **Ittoqqortoormiit** var. Itseqqortoormiit, Dan. Scoresbysund, Eng. Scoresby Sound. Tunu, C Greenland
60 M10 **Itu** São Paulo, S Brazil
54 D8 **Ituango** Antioquia, NW Colombia
59 A14 **Ituí, Rio** ≈ NW Brazil
79 O20 **Itula** Sud Kivu, E Dem. Rep. Congo
59 K19 **Itumbiara** Goiás, C Brazil
55 T9 **Ituni** E Guyana
41 X13 **Iturbide** Campeche, SE Mexico
Ituri *see* Aruwimi
123 V13 **Iturup, Ostrov** *island* Kuril'skiye Ostrova, SE Russian Federation
60 L7 **Ituverava** São Paulo, S Brazil
59 C15 **Ituxi, Rio** ≈ W Brazil
61 E14 **Ituzaingó** Corrientes, NE Argentina
101 K18 **Itz** ≈ C Germany
100 I9 **Itzehoe** Schleswig-Holstein, N Germany
23 N2 **Iuka** Mississippi, S USA
60 I11 **Ivaiporã** Paraná, S Brazil
60 I11 **Ivaí, Rio** ≈ S Brazil
92 L10 **Ivalo** Lapp. Avveel, Avvil. Lappi, N Finland
92 L10 **Ivalojoki** Lapp. Avveel. ≈ N Finland
119 H20 **Ivanava** Pol. Janów, Janów Poleski, Rus. Ivanovo. Brestskaya Voblasts', SW Belarus
Ivangorod *see* Dęblin
Ivangrad *see* Berane
183 N7 **Ivanhoe** New South Wales, SE Australia
29 S9 **Ivanhoe** Minnesota, N USA
14 D8 **Ivanhoe** ≈ Ontario, S Canada
112 E8 **Ivanić-Grad** Sisak-Moslavina, N Croatia
117 T10 **Ivanivka** Khersons'ka Oblast', S Ukraine
117 P10 **Ivanivka** Odes'ka Oblast', SW Ukraine
113 L14 **Ivanjica** Serbia, C Serbia
112 G11 **Ivanjska** var Potkozarje. Republika Srpska, NW Bosnia and Herzegovina
111 H21 **Ivanka** ✕ (Bratislava) Bratislavský Kraj, W Slovakia
117 O3 **Ivankiv** Rus. Ivankov. Kyyivs'ka Oblast', N Ukraine
Ivankov *see* Ivankiv
39 O15 **Ivanof Bay** Alaska, USA
116 J7 **Ivano-Frankivs'k** Ger. Stanislau, Pol. Stanisławów, Rus. Ivano-Frankovsk; prev. Stanislav. Ivano-Frankivs'ka Oblast', W Ukraine
Ivano-Frankivs'k *see* Ivano-Frankivs'ka Oblast'
116 I7 **Ivano-Frankivs'ka Oblast'** var. Ivano-Frankivs'k, Rus. Ivano-Frankovskaya Oblast'; prev. Stanislavskaya Oblast'. ◐ *province* W Ukraine
Ivano-Frankovsk *see* Ivano-Frankivs'k
Ivano-Frankovskaya Oblast' *see* Ivano-Frankivs'ka Oblast'
124 M16 **Ivanovo** Ivanovskaya Oblast', W Russian Federation
Ivanovo *see* Ivanava
124 M16 **Ivanovskaya Oblast'** ◐ *province* W Russian Federation
35 X12 **Ivanpah Lake** ◎ California, W USA
112 E7 **Ivanšćica** ▲▲ NE Croatia
114 M8 **Ivanski** Shumen, NE Bulgaria
127 R7 **Ivanteyevka** Saratovskaya Oblast', W Russian Federation
Ivantsevichi/Ivatsevichi *see* Ivatsevichy
116 I4 **Ivanychi** Volyns'ka Oblast', NW Ukraine
119 H18 **Ivatsevichy** Pol. Iwacewicze, Rus. Ivantsevichi, Ivatsevichi. Brestskaya Voblasts', SW Belarus
114 L12 **Ivaylovgrad** Khaskovska Oblast, S Bulgaria
114 K11 **Ivaylovgrad, Yazovir** ⊠ S Bulgaria
122 G9 **Ivdel'** Sverdlovskaya Oblast', C Russian Federation
Ivenets *see* Ivyanyets
116 L12 **Iveşti** Galaţi, E Romania
Ivgovuotna *see* Lyngen
Ivigtut *see* Ivittuut
79 F18 **Ivindo** ≈ Congo/Gabon
59 I21 **Ivinheima** Mato Grosso do Sul, SW Brazil
196 M15 **Ivittuut** var. Ivigtut. Kitaa, S Greenland
Iviza *see* Ibiza
Iviza *see* Eivissa
172 I6 **Ivohibe** Fianarantsoa, SE Madagascar
Ivoire, Côte d' *see* Ivory Coast
76 L15 **Ivory Coast** off. Republic of the Ivory Coast, Fr. Côte d'Ivoire, République de la Côte d'Ivoire. ◆ *republic* W Africa
68 C12 **Ivory Coast** Fr. Côte d'Ivoire. *coastal region* S Ivory Coast
Ivory Coast, Republic of the *see* Ivory Coast
95 L22 **Ivösjön** ◎ S Sweden
106 B7 **Ivrea** anc. Eporedia. Piemonte, NW Italy
12 J2 **Ivujivik** Québec, NE Canada
119 J16 **Ivyanyets** Rus. Ivenets. Minskaya Voblasts', C Belarus
Iv'ye *see* Iwye
Iwacewicze *see* Ivatsevichy
165 R8 **Iwaizumi** Iwate, Honshū, NE Japan
165 P12 **Iwaki** Fukushima, Honshū, N Japan
164 F13 **Iwakuni** Yamaguchi, Honshū, SW Japan
165 S4 **Iwamizawa** Hokkaidō, NE Japan
165 R4 **Iwanai** Hokkaidō, NE Japan
165 Q10 **Iwanuma** Miyagi, Honshū, C Japan
164 L14 **Iwata** Shizuoka, Honshū, S Japan
165 R8 **Iwate** Iwate, Honshū, N Japan
165 R8 **Iwate** off. Iwate-ken. ◐ *prefecture* Honshū, C Japan
Iwate-ken *see* Iwate
77 S16 **Iwo** Oyo, SW Nigeria
Iwojima *see* Iō-jima
119 I16 **Iwye** Pol. Iwje, Rus. Iv'ye. Hrodzyenskaya Voblasts', W Belarus
42 C4 **Ixcán, Río** ≈ Guatemala/Mexico
99 G18 **Ixelles** Dut. Elsene. Brussels, C Belgium
57 J16 **Ixiamas** La Paz, NW Bolivia
41 O13 **Ixmiquilpan** var. Ixmiquilpán. Hidalgo, C Mexico
Ixmiquilpán *see* Ixmiquilpan
83 K23 **Ixopo** KwaZulu/Natal, E South Africa
Ixtaccíhuatal, Volcán *see* Iztaccíhuatl, Volcán
40 M16 **Ixtapa** Guerrero, S Mexico
41 S16 **Ixtepec** Oaxaca, SE Mexico
40 K12 **Ixtlán** var. Ixtlán del Río. Nayarit, C Mexico
Ixtlán del Río *see* Ixtlán
122 H11 **Iyevlevo** Tyumenskaya Oblast', C Russian Federation
164 F14 **Iyo** Ehime, Shikoku, SW Japan
164 E14 **Iyo-nada** *sea* S Japan
42 E4 **Izabal** off. Departamento de Izabal. ◐ *department* E Guatemala
Izabal, Departamento de *see* Izabal
42 F5 **Izabal, Lago de** prev. Golfo Dulce. ◎ E Guatemala
143 O9 **Izad Khvāst** Fārs, C Iran
41 X12 **Izamal** Yucatán, SE Mexico
127 Q16 **Izberbash** Respublika Dagestan, SW Russian Federation
99 C18 **Izegem** prev. Iseghem. West-Vlaanderen, W Belgium
142 M9 **Īzeh** Khūzestān, SW Iran
165 T16 **Izena-jima** *island* Nansei-shotō, SW Japan
114 N10 **Izgrev** Burgas, E Bulgaria
127 T2 **Izhevsk** prev. Ustinov. Udmurtskaya Respublika, NW Russian Federation
125 S7 **Izhma** Respublika Komi, NW Russian Federation
125 S7 **Izhma** ≈ NW Russian Federation
141 X8 **Izkī** NE Oman
Izmail *see* Izmayil
117 N13 **Izmayil** Rus. Izmail. Odes'ka Oblast', SW Ukraine
136 B14 **İzmir** prev. Smyrna. İzmır, W Turkey
136 C14 **İzmir** prev. Smyrna. ◐ *province* W Turkey
136 E11 **İzmit** var. Ismid; anc. Astacus. Kocaeli, NW Turkey
104 M14 **Iznájar** Andalucía, S Spain
104 M14 **Iznajar, Embalse de** ⊠ S Spain
105 N14 **Iznalloz** Andalucía, S Spain
136 E11 **İznik** Bursa, NW Turkey
136 E12 **İznik Gölü** ◎ NW Turkey
126 M14 **Izobil'nyy** Stavropol'skiy Kray, SW Russian Federation
109 S13 **Izola** It. Isola d'Istria. SW Slovenia
138 H9 **Izra'** var. Ezra, Ezraa. Dar'ā, S Syria
41 P14 **Iztaccíhuati, Volcán** var. Volcán Ixtaccíhuatal. ⧗ S Mexico
42 C7 **Iztapa** Escuintla, SE Guatemala
Izúcar de Matamoros *see* Matamoros
165 N14 **Izu-hantō** *peninsula* Honshū, S Japan
164 C12 **Izuhara** Nagasaki, Tsushima, SW Japan
164 J14 **Izumiōtsu** Ōsaka, Honshū, SW Japan
164 I14 **Izumi-Sano** Ōsaka, Honshū, SW Japan
164 G12 **Izumo** Shimane, Honshū, SW Japan
192 H5 **Izu Trench** *undersea feature* NW Pacific Ocean
122 K6 **Izvestiy TsIK, Ostrova** *island* N Russian Federation
116 G10 **Izvor** Pernik, W Bulgaria
116 L5 **Izyaslav** Khmel'nyts'ka Oblast', W Ukraine
117 W6 **Izyum** Kharkivs'ka Oblast', E Ukraine

J

93 M18 **Jaala** Kymi, S Finland
140 J5 **Jabal ash Shifā** *desert* NW Saudi Arabia
141 U8 **Jabal az Ẓannah** var. Jebel Dhanna. Abū Ẓaby, W United Arab Emirates
138 E11 **Jabalīya** var. Jabāliyah. NE Gaza Strip
Jabāliyah *see* Jabalīya
105 N11 **Jabalón** ≈ C Spain
154 J10 **Jabalpur** prev. Jubbulpore. Madhya Pradesh, C India
141 N15 **Jabal Zuuqar, Jazīrat** var. Az Zuqur. *island* SW Yemen
Jabat *see* Jabwot
138 J3 **Jabbūl, Sabkhat al** *sabkha* NW Syria
181 P1 **Jabiru** Northern Territory, N Australia
138 H4 **Jablah** var. Jeble, Fr. Djéblé. Al Lādhiqīyah, W Syria
112 C11 **Jablanac** Lika-Senj, W Croatia
113 H14 **Jablanica** Federacija Bosna I Hercegovina, SW Bosnia and Herzegovina
113 M20 **Jablanica** Alb. Mali i Jabllanicës, var. Malet e Jabllanicës. ▲ Albania/FYR Macedonia *see also* Jabllanicës, Mali i
Jabllanicës, Malet e *see* Jablanica/Jabllanicës, Mali i
113 M20 **Jabllanicës, Mali i**, Mac. Jablanica. ▲ Albania/FYR Macedonia *see also* Jablanica
111 E15 **Jablonec nad Nisou** Ger. Gablonz an der Neisse. Liberecký Kraj, N Czech Republic
Jablonków/Jablunkau *see* Jablunkov
110 J9 **Jabłonowo Pomorskie** Kujawski-pomorskie, C Poland
111 J17 **Jablunkov** Ger. Jablunkau, Pol. Jabłonków. Moravskoslezský Kraj, E Czech Republic
59 Q15 **Jaboatão** Pernambuco, E Brazil
60 L8 **Jaboticabal** São Paulo, S Brazil
189 U7 **Jabwot** var. Jabat, Jebat, Jōwat. *island* Ralik Chain, S Marshall Islands
105 S4 **Jaca** Aragón, NE Spain
42 B4 **Jacaltenango** Huehuetenango, W Guatemala
59 G14 **Jacaré-a-Canga** Pará, NE Brazil
60 N10 **Jacareí** São Paulo, S Brazil
59 I18 **Jaciara** Mato Grosso, W Brazil
59 E15 **Jaciparaná** Rondônia, W Brazil
19 P5 **Jackman** Maine, NE USA
35 X1 **Jackpot** Nevada, W USA
20 M8 **Jacksboro** Tennessee, S USA
25 S6 **Jacksboro** Texas, SW USA
23 N7 **Jackson** Alabama, S USA
35 P7 **Jackson** California, W USA
23 T4 **Jackson** Georgia, SE USA
21 O6 **Jackson** Kentucky, S USA
22 J8 **Jackson** Louisiana, S USA
31 Q10 **Jackson** Michigan, N USA
29 T11 **Jackson** Minnesota, N USA
22 K5 **Jackson** *state capital* Mississippi, S USA
27 Y7 **Jackson** Missouri, C USA
21 W8 **Jackson** North Carolina, SE USA
31 T15 **Jackson** Ohio, NE USA
20 G9 **Jackson** Tennessee, S USA
33 S14 **Jackson** Wyoming, C USA
185 C19 **Jackson Bay** *bay* South Island, New Zealand
186 E9 **Jackson Field** ✕ (Port Moresby) Central/National Capital District, S Papua New Guinea
185 C20 **Jackson Head** *headland* South Island, New Zealand
23 S8 **Jackson, Lake** ◎ Florida, SE USA
33 S13 **Jackson Lake** ◎ Wyoming, C USA
194 J6 **Jackson, Mount** ▲ Antarctica
37 U3 **Jackson Reservoir** ◎ Colorado, C USA
23 Q3 **Jacksonville** Alabama, S USA
27 V11 **Jacksonville** Arkansas, C USA
23 W8 **Jacksonville** Florida, SE USA
30 K14 **Jacksonville** Illinois, N USA
21 W11 **Jacksonville** North Carolina, SE USA
25 W7 **Jacksonville** Texas, SW USA
23 X9 **Jacksonville Beach** Florida, SE USA
44 L9 **Jacmel** var. Jaquemel. S Haiti
Jacob *see* Nkayi
149 Q12 **Jacobābād** Sind, SE Pakistan
55 T11 **Jacobs Ladder Falls** *waterfall* S Guyana
45 O11 **Jaco, Pointe** *headland* N Dominica
15 Q9 **Jacques-Cartier** ≈ Québec, SE Canada
13 P11 **Jacques-Cartier, Détroit de** var. Jacques-Cartier Passage. *strait* Gulf of St. Lawrence/St. Lawrence River
15 W6 **Jacques-Cartier, Mont** ▲ Québec, SE Canada
Jacques-Cartier Passage *see* Jacques-Cartier, Détroit de
61 H16 **Jacuí, Rio** ≈ S Brazil
60 L11 **Jacupiranga** São Paulo, S Brazil
100 G10 **Jade** ≈ NW Germany
100 G10 **Jadebusen** *bay* NW Germany
Jadotville *see* Likasi
Jadransko More/Jadransko Morje *see* Adriatic Sea
105 O7 **Jadraque** Castilla-La Mancha, C Spain
95 I22 **Jægerspris** Frederiksborg, E Denmark
56 C10 **Jaén** Cajamarca, N Peru
105 N13 **Jaén** Andalucía, SW Spain
105 N13 **Jaén** ◐ *province* Andalucía, S Spain
95 C17 **Jæren** *physical region* S Norway
155 J23 **Jaffna** Northern Province, N Sri Lanka
155 K23 **Jaffna Lagoon** *lagoon* N Sri Lanka
19 N10 **Jaffrey** New Hampshire, NE USA
138 H13 **Jafr, Qā' al** var. El Jafr. *salt pan* S Jordan
152 J9 **Jagādhri** Haryāna, N India
118 H4 **Jägala** var. Jägala Jõgi, Ger. Jaggowal. ≈ NW Estonia
Jägala Jõgi *see* Jägala
Jagannath *see* Puri
155 L14 **Jagdalpur** Chhattīsgarh, C India
163 U5 **Jagdaqi** Nei Mongol Zizhiqu, N China
Jägerndorf *see* Krnov
Jaggowal *see* Jägala
139 O2 **Jaghjaghah, Nahr** ≈ N Syria
112 N13 **Jagodina** prev. Svetozarevo. Serbia, C Serbia
112 K12 **Jagodnja** ▲▲ W Serbia
101 I20 **Jagst** ≈ SW Germany
155 I14 **Jagtiāl** Andhra Pradesh, C India
61 H18 **Jaguarão** Rio Grande do Sul, S Brazil
61 H18 **Jaguarão, Rio** var. Río Yaguarón. ≈ Brazil/Uruguay
60 K11 **Jaguariaíva** Paraná, S Brazil
44 D5 **Jagüey Grande** Matanzas, W Cuba
153 P14 **Jahānābād** Bihār, N India
Jahra *see* Al Jahrā'
143 P12 **Jahrom** var. Jahrum. Fārs, S Iran
Jahrum *see* Jahrom
Jailolo *see* Halmahera, Pulau
Jainat *see* Chai Nat
Jainti *see* Jayanti
152 H12 **Jaipur** prev. Jeypore. *state capital* Rājasthān, N India
153 T14 **Jaipur Hat** Rajshahi, NW Bangladesh
152 D11 **Jaisalmer** Rājasthān, NW India
154 O12 **Jājapur** Orissa, E India
143 R4 **Jājarm** Khorāsān-e Shemālī, NE Iran
112 G12 **Jajce** Federacija Bosna I Hercegovina, W Bosnia and Herzegovina
Jajī *see* 'Alī Kheyl
83 D17 **Jakalsberg** Otjozondjupa, N Namibia
169 O15 **Jakarta** prev. Djakarta, Dut. Batavia. ● (Indonesia) Jawa, C Indonesia
10 I8 **Jakes Corner** Yukon Territory, W Canada
152 H9 **Jākhal** Haryāna, NW India
Jakobeny *see* Iacobeni
93 K16 **Jakobstad** Fin. Pietarsaari. Länsi-Suomi, W Finland
Jakobstadt *see* Jēkabpils
113 O18 **Jakupica** ▲▲ C FYR Macedonia
37 W15 **Jal** New Mexico, SW USA
141 P7 **Jalājil** var. Ğalāğil. Ar Riyāḍ, C Saudi Arabia
149 S5 **Jalālābād** var. Jalalabad, Jelalabad. Nangarhār, E Afghanistan
Jalal-Abad *see* Dzhalal-Abad
Jalal-Abad Oblasty *see* Dzhalal-Abadskaya Oblast'
149 V7 **Jalālpur** Punjab, E Pakistan
149 T11 **Jalālpur Pīrwāla** Punjab, E Pakistan
152 H8 **Jalandhar** prev. Jullundur. Punjab, N India
42 J7 **Jalán, Río** ≈ S Honduras
42 E6 **Jalapa** Jalapa, C Guatemala
42 J7 **Jalapa** Nueva Segovia, NW Nicaragua
42 A3 **Jalapa** off. Departamento de Jalapa. ◐ *department* SE Guatemala
Jalapa, Departamento de *see* Jalapa
42 E6 **Jalapa, Río** ≈ SE Guatemala
143 X13 **Jālaq** Sīstān va Balūchestān, SE Iran
93 K17 **Jalasjärvi** Länsi-Soumi, W Finland
149 O8 **Jaldak** Zābol, SE Afghanistan
60 J7 **Jales** São Paulo, S Brazil
154 P11 **Jaleshwar** var. Jaleswar. Orissa, NE India
Jaleswar *see* Jaleshwar
154 F12 **Jalgaon** Mahārāshtra, C India
139 W12 **Jalībah** S Iraq
139 W13 **Jalīb Shahāb** S Iraq
77 X15 **Jalingo** Taraba, E Nigeria
40 K13 **Jalisco** ◐ *state* SW Mexico
154 G13 **Jālna** Mahārāshtra, W India
Jalomitsa *see* Ialomiţa
105 R5 **Jalón** ≈ N Spain
152 E13 **Jālor** Rājasthān, N India
112 K11 **Jalovik** Serbia, W Serbia
40 L12 **Jalpa** Zacatecas, C Mexico
153 S12 **Jalpāiguri** West Bengal, NE India
41 O12 **Jalpán** var. Jalpan. Querétaro de Arteaga, C Mexico
Jalpan *see* Jalpán
67 P2 **Jalta** *island* N Tunisia
75 S9 **Jālū** var. Jūlā. NE Libya
189 U8 **Jaluit Atoll** var. Jālwōj. *atoll* Ralik Chain, S Marshall Islands
Jālwōj *see* Jaluit Atoll
81 L18 **Jamaame** It. Giamame; prev. Margherita. Jubbada Hoose, S Somalia
77 W13 **Jamaare** ≈ NE Nigeria
44 G9 **Jamaica** ◆ *island state* W West Indies
47 P3 **Jamaica** *island* W West Indies
44 I9 **Jamaica Channel** *channel* Haiti/Jamaica
153 T14 **Jamalpur** Dhaka, N Bangladesh
153 Q14 **Jamālpur** Bihār, NE India
168 L9 **Jamaluang** var. Jemaluang. Johor, Peninsular Malaysia
59 I14 **Jamanxim, Rio** ≈ C Brazil
56 B8 **Jambeli, Canal de** *channel* S Ecuador
99 I20 **Jambes** Namur, SE Belgium
168 L12 **Jambi** var. Telanaipura; prev. Djambi. Sumatera, W Indonesia
168 K12 **Jambi** off. Propinsi Jambi, var. Djambi. ◐ *province* W Indonesia
Jambi, Propinsi *see* Jambi
Jamdena *see* Yamdena, Pulau
12 H8 **James Bay** *bay* Ontario/Québec, E Canada

◆ Country ● Country Capital ◇ Dependent Territory ○ Dependent Territory Capital ◐ Administrative Regions ✕ International Airport ▲ Mountain ▲▲ Mountain Range ⧗ Volcano ≈ River ◎ Lake ⊠ Reservoir

63 F19 **James, Isla** *island* Archipiélago de los Chonos, S Chile
181 Q8 **James Ranges** ▲▲ Northern Territory, C Australia
29 P8 **James River** ≈ North Dakota/South Dakota, N USA
21 X7 **James River** ≈ Virginia, NE USA
194 H4 **James Ross Island** *island* Antarctica
182 I8 **Jamestown** South Australia
65 G25 **Jamestown** ○ (Saint Helena) NW Saint Helena
35 P8 **Jamestown** California, W USA
20 L7 **Jamestown** Kentucky, S USA
18 D11 **Jamestown** New York, NE USA
29 P5 **Jamestown** North Dakota, N USA
20 L8 **Jamestown** Tennessee, S USA
Jamestown *see* Holetown
15 N10 **Jamet** ≈ Québec, SE Canada
41 Q17 **Jamiltepec** *var.* Santiago Jamiltepec. Oaxaca, SE Mexico
95 F20 **Jammerbugten** *bay* Skagerrak, E North Sea
152 H6 **Jammu** *prev.* Jummoo. *state capital* Jammu and Kashmir, NW India
152 I5 **Jammu and Kashmir** *var.* Jammu-Kashmir, Kashmir. ◈ *state* NW India
149 V4 **Jammu and Kashmīr** *disputed region* India/Pakistan
Jammu-Kashmir *see* Jammu and Kashmir
154 B10 **Jāmnagar** *prev.* Navanagar. Gujarāt, W India
149 S11 **Jāmpur** Punjab, E Pakistan
93 L18 **Jämsä** Länsi-Soumi, C Finland
93 L18 **Jämsänkoski** Länsi-Soumi, C Finland
153 Q16 **Jamshedpur** Jhārkhand, NE India
94 K9 **Jämtland** ◈ *county* C Sweden
153 Q14 **Jamūi** Bihār, NE India
153 T14 **Jamuna** ≈ N Bangladesh
Jamuna *see* Brahmaputra
Jamundá *see* Nhamundá, Rio
54 D11 **Jamundí** Valle del Cauca, SW Colombia
153 Q12 **Janakpur** Central, C Nepal
59 N18 **Janaúba** Minas Gerais, SE Brazil
58 K11 **Janaucu, Ilha** *island* NE Brazil
143 Q7 **Jandaq** Eşfahān, C Iran
64 Q11 **Jandia, Punta de** *headland* Fuerteventura, Islas Canarias, Spain, NE Atlantic Ocean
59 B14 **Jandiatuba, Rio** ≈ NW Brazil
105 N12 **Jándula** ≈ S Spain
29 V10 **Janesville** Minnesota, N USA
30 L9 **Janesville** Wisconsin, N USA
149 N13 **Jangal** Baluchistān, SW Pakistan
83 N20 **Jangamo** Inhambane, SE Mozambique
155 J14 **Jangaon** Andhra Pradesh, C India
153 S14 **Jangīpur** West Bengal, NE India
Janina *see* Ioánnina
Janischken *see* Joniškis
112 J11 **Janja** NE Bosnia and Herzegovina
Jankovac *see* Jánoshalma
197 Q15 **Jan Mayen** ◇ *Norwegian dependency* N Atlantic Ocean
84 D5 **Jan Mayen** *island* N Atlantic Ocean
197 R15 **Jan Mayen Fracture Zone** *tectonic feature* Greenland Sea/Norwegian Sea
197 R15 **Jan Mayen Ridge** *undersea feature* Greenland Sea/ Norwegian Sea
40 H3 **Janos** Chihuahua, N Mexico
111 K25 **Jánoshalma** *SCr.* Jankovac. Bács-Kiskun, S Hungary
Janów *see* Ivanava, Belarus
110 H10 **Janowiec Wielkopolski** *Ger.* Janowitz. Kujawski-pomorskie, C Poland
Janowitz *see* Janowiec Wielkopolski
Janow/Janów *see* Jonava, Lithuania
111 O15 **Janów Lubelski** Lubelski, E Poland
Janów Poleski *see* Ivanava
83 H25 **Jansenville** Eastern Cape, S South Africa
59 M18 **Januária** Minas Gerais, SE Brazil
Janūbīyah, Al Bādiyah al *see* Ash Shāmīyah
102 I7 **Janzé** Ille-et-Vilaine, NW France
154 F10 **Jaora** Madhya Pradesh, C India
171 Y9 **Japan** *var.* Nippon, *Jap.* Nihon. ◆ *monarchy* E Asia
129 Y9 **Japan** *island group* E Asia
192 H4 **Japan Basin** *undersea feature* N Sea of Japan
129 Y8 **Japan, Sea of** *var.* East Sea, *Rus.* Yapanskoye More. *sea* NW Pacific Ocean *see also* East Sea
192 H4 **Japan Trench** *undersea feature* NW Pacific Ocean
Japen *see* Yapen, Pulau
59 A15 **Japiim** *var.* Máncio Lima. Acre, W Brazil
58 D12 **Japurá** Amazonas, N Brazil
58 C12 **Japurá, Rio** *var.* Río Caquetá, Yapurá. ≈ Brazil/Colombia *see also* Caquetá, Río
Japurá, Rio *see* Caquetá, Río
43 W17 **Jaqué** Darién, SE Panama
Jaquemel *see* Jacmel
Jarablos *see* Jarābulus
138 K2 **Jarābulus** *var.* Jarablos, Jerablus, *Fr.* Djérablous. Ḩalab, N Syria
60 K13 **Jaraguá do Sul** Santa Catarina, S Brazil
104 K9 **Jaraicejo** Extremadura, W Spain
104 K9 **Jaraíz de la Vera** Extremadura, W Spain
105 O7 **Jarama** ≈ C Spain
63 J20 **Jaramillo** Santa Cruz, SE Argentina
Jarandilla de la Vega *see* Jarandilla de la Vera
104 K8 **Jarandilla de la Vera** *var.* Jarandilla de la Vega. Extremadura, W Spain
149 V9 **Jarānwāla** Punjab, E Pakistan
138 G9 **Jarash** *var.* Jerash; *anc.* Gerasa. Irbid, NW Jordan
Jarbah, Jazīrat *see* Jerba, Île de
94 N13 **Järbo** Gävleborg, C Sweden
Jardan *see* Yordan
44 F7 **Jardines de la Reina, Archipiélago de los** *island group* C Cuba
162 I8 **Jargalant** Bayanhongor, C Mongolia
162 K6 **Jargalant** Bulgan, N Mongolia
162 G7 **Jargalant** *var.* Buyanbat. Govĭ-Altay, W Mongolia
162 I6 **Jargalant** *var.* Orgil. Hövsgöl, C Mongolia
Jargalant *see* Battsengel
Jargalant *see* Bulgan
Jargalant *see* Biger
Jarīd, Shaṭṭ al *see* Jerid, Chott el
58 I11 **Jari, Rio** *var.* Jary. ≈ N Brazil
141 N7 **Jarīr, Wādī al** *dry watercourse* C Saudi Arabia
Jarja *see* Yur'ya
94 L13 **Järna** *var.* Dala-Jarna. Dalarna, C Sweden
95 O16 **Järna** Stockholm, C Sweden
102 K11 **Jarnac** Charente, W France
110 H12 **Jarocin** Wielkopolskie, C Poland
111 F16 **Jaroměř** *Ger.* Jermer. Královéhradecký Kraj, N Czech Republic
Jaroslau *see* Jarosław
111 O16 **Jarosław** *Ger.* Jaroslau, *Rus.* Yaroslav. Podkarpackie, SE Poland
93 F16 **Järpen** Jämtland, C Sweden
147 O14 **Jarqo'rg'on** *Rus.* Dzharkurgan. Surkhondaryo Viloyati, S Uzbekistan
139 P2 **Jarrāh, Wadi** *dry watercourse* NE Syria
Jars, Plain of *see* Xiangkhoang, Plateau de
162 K14 **Jartai Yanchi** ◎ N China
59 E16 **Jaru** Rondônia, W Brazil
Jarud Qi *see* Lubei
118 I4 **Järva-Jaani** *Ger.* Sankt-Johannis. Järvamaa, N Estonia
118 G5 **Järvakandi** *Ger.* Jerwakant. Raplamaa, NW Estonia
118 H4 **Järvamaa** *var.* Järva Maakond. ◈ *province* N Estonia
Järva Maakond *see* Järvamaa
93 L19 **Järvenpää** Uusimaa, S Finland
14 G17 **Jarvis** Ontario, S Canada
177 R8 **Jarvis Island** ◇ *US unincorporated territory* C Pacific Ocean
94 M11 **Järvsö** Gävleborg, C Sweden
Jary *see* Jari, Rio
112 M9 **Jaša Tomić** Vojvodina, NE Serbia
112 D12 **Jasenice** Zadar, SW Croatia
138 I11 **Jashshat al 'Adlah, Wādī al** *dry watercourse* C Jordan
77 Q16 **Jasikan** E Ghana
Jāsk *see* Bandar-e Jāsk
146 F6 **Jasliq** *Rus.* Zhaslyk. Qoraqalpoghiston Respublikasi, NW Uzbekistan
111 N17 **Jasło** Podkarpackie, SE Poland
9 U16 **Jasmin** Saskatchewan, S Canada
65 A23 **Jason Islands** *island group* NW Falkland Islands
194 I4 **Jason Peninsula** *peninsula* Antarctica
31 N15 **Jasonville** Indiana, N USA
9 O15 **Jasper** Alberta, SW Canada
14 L13 **Jasper** Ontario, SE Canada
23 O3 **Jasper** Alabama, S USA
27 T9 **Jasper** Arkansas, C USA
23 U8 **Jasper** Florida, SE USA
31 N16 **Jasper** Indiana, N USA
29 R11 **Jasper** Minnesota, N USA
27 S7 **Jasper** Missouri, C USA
20 K10 **Jasper** Tennessee, S USA
25 Y9 **Jasper** Texas, SW USA
9 O15 **Jasper National Park** *national park* Alberta/British Columbia, SW Canada
Jassy *see* Iaşi
113 N14 **Jastrebac** ▲▲ SE Serbia
112 D9 **Jastrebarsko** Grad Zagreb, N Croatia
Jastrow *see* Jastrowie
110 G9 **Jastrowie** *Ger.* Jastrow. Wielkopolskie, C Poland
111 J17 **Jastrzębie-Zdrój** Śląskie, S Poland
111 L22 **Jászapáti** Jász-Nagykun-Szolnok, E Hungary
111 L22 **Jászberény** Jász-Nagykun-Szolnok, E Hungary
111 L23 **Jász-Nagykun-Szolnok** *off.* Jász-Nagykun-Szolnok Megye. ◈ *county* E Hungary
Jász-Nagykun-Szolnok Megye *see* Jász-Nagykun-Szolnok
59 J19 **Jataí** Goiás, C Brazil
58 G12 **Jatapu, Serra do** ▲▲ N Brazil
41 W16 **Jatate, Río** ≈ SE Mexico
149 P17 **Jāti** Sind, SE Pakistan
44 F6 **Jatibonico** Sancti Spíritus, C Cuba
169 O16 **Jatiluhur, Danau** ◎ Jawa, S Indonesia
Jativa *see* Xátiva
149 S11 **Jattoi** Punjab, E Pakistan
60 L9 **Jaú** São Paulo, S Brazil
58 F11 **Jauaperi, Rio** ≈ N Brazil
99 I19 **Jauche** Walloon Brabant, C Belgium
Jauer *see* Jawor
Jauf *see* Al Jawf
149 U7 **Jauharābād** Punjab, E Pakistan
57 E14 **Jauja** Junín, C Peru
41 O10 **Jaumave** Tamaulipas, C Mexico
118 H10 **Jaunjelgava** *Ger.* Friedrichstadt. Aizkraukle, S Latvia
Jaunlatgale *see* Pytalovo
118 I8 **Jaunpiebalga** Gulbene, NE Latvia
118 E9 **Jaunpils** Tukums, C Latvia
153 N13 **Jaunpur** Uttar Pradesh, N India
29 N8 **Java** South Dakota, N USA
Java *see* Jawa
105 R9 **Javalambre** ▲ E Spain
173 V7 **Java Ridge** *undersea feature* E Indian Ocean
59 A14 **Javari, Rio** *var.* Yavarí. ≈ Brazil/Peru
Javarthushuu *see* Bayan-Uul
169 Q15 **Java Sea** *Ind.* Laut Jawa. *sea* W Indonesia
173 U7 **Java Trench** *var.* Sunda Trench. *undersea feature* E Indian Ocean
143 Q10 **Javazm** *var* Jowzam. Kermān, C Iran
105 T11 **Jávea** *Cat.* Xàbia. País Valenciano, E Spain
Javhlant *see* Bayan-Ovoo
63 G20 **Javier, Isla** *island* S Chile
113 L14 **Javor** ▲▲ Bosnia and Herzegovina/Serbia
111 K20 **Javorie** *Hung.* Jávoros. ▲ S Slovakia
Jávoros *see* Javorie
93 J14 **Jävre** Norrbotten, N Sweden
192 E8 **Jawa** *Eng.* Java; *prev.* Djawa. *island* C Indonesia
169 O16 **Jawa Barat** *off.* Propinsi Jawa Barat, *Eng.* West Java. ◈ *province* S Indonesia
Jawa Barat, Propinsi *see* Jawa Barat
Jawa, Laut *see* Java Sea
139 R3 **Jawān** NW Iraq
169 P16 **Jawa Tengah** *off.* Propinsi Jawa Tengah, *Eng.* Central Java. ◈ *province* S Indonesia
Jawa Tengah, Propinsi *see* Jawa Tengah
169 R16 **Jawa Timur** *off.* Propinsi Jawa Timur, *Eng.* East Java. ◈ *province* S Indonesia
Jawa Timur, Propinsi *see* Jawa Timur
81 N17 **Jawhar** *var.* Jowhar, *It.* Giohar. Shabeellaha Dhexe, S Somalia
111 F14 **Jawor** *Ger.* Jauer. Dolnośląskie, SW Poland
Jaworów *see* Yavoriv
111 J16 **Jaworzno** Śląskie, S Poland
Jaxartes *see* Syr Darya
27 R9 **Jay** Oklahoma, C USA
Jayabum *see* Chaiyaphum
Jayanath *see* Chai Nat
153 T12 **Jayanti** *prev.* Jainti. West Bengal, NE India
171 X14 **Jaya, Puncak** *prev.* Puntjak Carstensz, Puntjak Sukarno. ▲ Papua, E Indonesia
171 Z13 **Jayapura** *var.* Djajapura, *Dut.* Hollandia; *prev.* Kotabaru, Sukarnapura. Papua, E Indonesia
Jayhawker State *see* Kansas
147 S12 **Jayilgan** *Rus.* Dzhailgan, Dzhayilgan. C Tajikistan
155 L14 **Jaypur** *var.* Jeypore, Jeypur. Orissa, E India
25 O6 **Jayton** Texas, SW USA
143 U13 **Jaz Mūrīān, Hāmūn-e** ◎ SE Iran
138 M4 **Jazrah** Ar Raqqah, C Syria
138 G6 **Jbaïl** *var.* Jebeil, Jubayl, Jubeil; *anc.* Biblical Gebal, Bybles. W Lebanon
25 O7 **J. B. Thomas, Lake** ⊠ Texas, SW USA
Jdaïdé *see* Judaydah
35 X12 **Jean** Nevada, W USA
22 I9 **Jeanerette** Louisiana, S USA
44 L8 **Jean-Rabel** NW Haiti
143 T12 **Jebāl Bārez, Kūh-e** ▲▲ SE Iran
Jebat *see* Jabwot
77 T15 **Jebba** Kwara, W Nigeria
Jebeil *see* Jbaïl
116 E12 **Jebel** *Hung.* Széphely; *prev. Hung.* Zsebely. Timiş, W Romania
146 B11 **Jebel** *Rus.* Dzhebel. Balkan Welaýaty, W Turkmenistan
Jebel, Bahr el *see* White Nile
Jebel Dhanna *see* Jabal az Ẓannah
Jeble *see* Jablah
96 K13 **Jedburgh** SE Scotland, UK
Jedda *see* Jiddah
111 L15 **Jędrzejów** *Ger.* Endersdorf. Świętokrzyskie, C Poland
100 K12 **Jeetze** *var.* Jeetzel. ≈ C Germany
Jeetzel *see* Jeetze
29 U14 **Jefferson** Iowa, C USA
21 Q8 **Jefferson** North Carolina, SE USA
25 X6 **Jefferson** Texas, SW USA
30 M9 **Jefferson** Wisconsin, N USA
27 U5 **Jefferson City** *state capital* Missouri, C USA
33 R10 **Jefferson City** Montana, NW USA
21 N9 **Jefferson City** Tennessee, S USA
35 U7 **Jefferson, Mount** ▲ Nevada, W USA
32 H12 **Jefferson, Mount** ▲ Oregon, NW USA
20 L5 **Jeffersontown** Kentucky, S USA
31 P16 **Jeffersonville** Indiana, N USA
33 V15 **Jeffrey City** Wyoming, C USA
77 T13 **Jega** Kebbi, NW Nigeria
Jehol *see* Chengde
62 P5 **Jejui-Guazú, Río** ≈ E Paraguay
118 I10 **Jēkabpils** *Ger.* Jakobstadt. Jēkabpils, S Latvia
23 W7 **Jekyll Island** *island* Georgia, SE USA
169 R13 **Jelai, Sungai** ≈ Borneo, N Indonesia
Jelalabad *see* Jalālābād
111 H14 **Jelcz-Laskowice** Dolnośląskie, SW Poland
111 E14 **Jelenia Góra** *Ger.* Hirschberg, Hirschberg im Riesengebirge, Hirschberg im Riesengebirge, Hirschberg in Schlesien. Dolnośląskie, SW Poland
153 S11 **Jelep La** *pass* N India
118 F9 **Jelgava** *Ger.* Mitau. Jelgava, C Latvia
113 L14 **Jelica** ▲ C Serbia
20 M8 **Jellico** Tennessee, S USA
95 G23 **Jelling** Vejle, C Denmark
169 N9 **Jemaja, Pulau** *island* W Indonesia
Jemaluang *see* Jamaluang
99 E20 **Jemappes** Hainaut, S Belgium
169 S17 **Jember** *prev.* Djember. Jawa, C Indonesia
99 I20 **Jemeppe-sur-Sambre** Namur, S Belgium
37 R10 **Jemez Pueblo** New Mexico, SW USA
158 K2 **Jeminay** Xinjiang Uygur Zizhiqu, NW China
189 U5 **Jemo Island** *atoll* Ratak Chain, C Marshall Islands
169 U11 **Jempang, Danau** ◎ Borneo, N Indonesia
101 L16 **Jena** Thüringen, C Germany
22 I6 **Jena** Louisiana, S USA
108 I8 **Jenaz** Graubünden, SE Switzerland
109 N7 **Jenbach** Tirol, W Austria
171 N15 **Jeneponto** *prev.* Djeneponto. Sulawesi, C Indonesia
138 F9 **Jenin** N West Bank
21 P7 **Jenkins** Kentucky, S USA
27 P9 **Jenks** Oklahoma, C USA
Jenné *see* Djenné
109 X8 **Jennersdorf** Burgenland, SE Austria
22 H9 **Jennings** Louisiana, S USA
9 N7 **Jenny Lind Island** *island* Nunavut, N Canada
23 Y13 **Jensen Beach** Florida, SE USA
9 P6 **Jens Munk Island** *island* Nunavut, NE Canada
59 O17 **Jequié** Bahia, E Brazil
59 O18 **Jequitinhonha, Rio** ≈ E Brazil
Jerablus *see* Jarābulus
74 H6 **Jerada** NE Morocco
Jerash *see* Jarash
75 N7 **Jerba, Île de** *var.* Djerba, Jazīrat Jarbah. *island* E Tunisia
44 K9 **Jérémie** SW Haiti
Jeréz *see* Jeréz de García Salinas, Mexico
Jerez *see* Jeréz de la Frontera, Spain
40 L11 **Jerez de García Salinas** *var.* Jeréz. Zacatecas, C Mexico
104 J15 **Jeréz de la Frontera** *var.* Jerez; *prev.* Xeres. Andalucía, SW Spain
104 I12 **Jeréz de los Caballeros** Extremadura, W Spain
Jergucati *see* Jorgucat
138 G10 **Jericho** *Ar.* Arīḩā, *Heb.* Yeriḥo. E West Bank
74 M7 **Jerid, Chott el** *var.* Shaṭṭ al Jarīd. *salt lake* SW Tunisia
183 O10 **Jerilderie** New South Wales, SE Australia
Jerischmarkt *see* Câmpia Turzii
92 K11 **Jerisjärvi** ◎ NW Finland
Jermak *see* Aksu
Jermentau *see* Yermentau
Jermer *see* Jaroměř
36 K11 **Jerome** Arizona, SW USA
33 O15 **Jerome** Idaho, NW USA
97 L26 **Jersey** *island* NW Europe
18 K14 **Jersey City** New Jersey, NE USA
18 F13 **Jersey Shore** Pennsylvania, NE USA
30 K14 **Jerseyville** Illinois, N USA
104 K8 **Jerte** ≈ W Spain
138 F10 **Jerusalem** *Ar.* Al Quds, Al Quds ash Sharīf, *Heb.* Yerushalayim; *anc.* Hierosolyma. ● (Israel) Jerusalem, NE Israel
138 G10 **Jerusalem** ◈ *district* E Israel
183 S10 **Jervis Bay** New South Wales, SE Australia
183 S10 **Jervis Bay Territory** ◈ *territory* SE Australia
Jerwakant *see* Järvakandi
109 S10 **Jesenice** *Ger.* Assling. NW Slovenia
111 H16 **Jeseník** *Ger.* Freiwaldau. Olomoucký Kraj, E Czech Republic
Jesi *see* Iesi
106 I8 **Jesolo** *var.* Iesolo. Veneto, NE Italy
Jesselton *see* Kota Kinabalu
95 I14 **Jessheim** Akershus, S Norway
153 T15 **Jessore** Khulna, W Bangladesh
23 W6 **Jesup** Georgia, SE USA
41 S15 **Jesús Carranza** Veracruz-Llave, SE Mexico
62 K10 **Jesús María** Córdoba, C Argentina
26 K6 **Jetmore** Kansas, C USA
103 Q2 **Jeumont** Nord, N France
95 H14 **Jevnaker** Oppland, S Norway
Jewe *see* Jõhvi
25 V9 **Jewett** Texas, SW USA
19 N12 **Jewett City** Connecticut, NE USA
Jeypore *see* Jaipur, Rājasthān, India
Jeypore/Jeypur *see* Jaypur, Orissa, India
113 L17 **Jezercës, Maja e** ▲ N Albania
111 B18 **Jezerní Hora** ▲ SW Czech Republic
154 F10 **Jhābua** Madhya Pradesh, C India
152 H14 **Jhālāwār** Rājasthān, N India
Jhang/Jhang Sadar *see* Jhang Sadr
149 U9 **Jhang Sadr** *var.* Jhang, Jhang Sadar. Punjab, NE Pakistan
152 J13 **Jhānsi** Uttar Pradesh, N India
153 O16 **Jhārkhand** ◈ *state* NE India
154 M11 **Jhārsuguda** Orissa, E India
149 V7 **Jhelum** Punjab, NE Pakistan
129 P9 **Jhelum** ≈ E Pakistan
Jhenaidaha *see* Jhenida
153 T15 **Jhenida** *var.* Jhenaidaha. Dhaka, W Bangladesh
149 P16 **Jhimpīr** Sind, SE Pakistan
Jhind *see* Jīnd
149 R16 **Jhudo** Sind, SE Pakistan
Jhumra *see* Chak Jhumra
152 H11 **Jhunjhunūn** Rājasthān, N India
Ji *see* Hebei, China
Ji *see* Jilin, China
Jiading *see* Xinfeng
153 S14 **Jiāganj** West Bengal, NE India
Jiaji *see* Qionghai
160 J7 **Jialing Jiang** ≈ C China
163 Y7 **Jiamusi** *var.* Chia-mu-ssu, Kiamusze. Heilongjiang, NE China
161 O11 **Ji'an** Jiangxi, S China
163 W12 **Ji'an** Jilin, NE China
163 T13 **Jianchang** Liaoning, NE China
Jianchang *see* Nancheng
Jiancheng *see* Jianyang
160 F11 **Jianchuan** *var.* Jinhuan. Yunnan, SW China
158 M4 **Jiangjunmiao** Xinjiang Uygur Zizhiqu, W China
160 K11 **Jiangkou** *var.* Shuangjiang. Guizhou, S China
Jiangkou *see* Fengkai
161 Q12 **Jiangle** *var.* Guyong. Fujian, SE China
161 N15 **Jiangmen** Guangdong, S China
Jiangna *see* Yanshan
161 Q10 **Jiangshan** Zhejiang, SE China
161 Q7 **Jiangsu** *var.* Chiang-su, Jiangsu Sheng, Kiangsu, Su. ◈ *province* E China
Jiangsu *see* Nanjing
Jiangsu Sheng *see* Jiangsu
161 O11 **Jiangxi** *var.* Chiang-hsi, Gan, Jiangxi Sheng, Kiangsi. ◈ *province* S China
Jiangxi Sheng *see* Jiangxi
160 I8 **Jiangyou** *prev.* Zhongba. Sichuan, C China
161 N9 **Jianli** *var.* Rongcheng. Hubei, C China
161 Q11 **Jian'ou** Fujian, SE China
163 S12 **Jianping** *var.* Yebaishou. Liaoning, NE China
Jianshe *see* Baiyü
160 L9 **Jianshi** *var.* Yezhou. Hubei, C China
129 V11 **Jian Xi** ≈ SE China
161 Q11 **Jianyang** Fujian, SE China
160 I9 **Jianyang** *var.* Jiancheng. Sichuan, C China
163 X10 **Jiaohe** Jilin, NE China
Jiaojiang *see* Taizhou
Jiaoxian *see* Jiaozhou
161 R5 **Jiaozhou** *prev.* Jiaoxian. Shandong, E China
161 N6 **Jiaozuo** Henan, C China
Jiashan *see* Mingguang
158 F8 **Jiashi** *var.* Payzawat. Xinjiang Uygur Zizhiqu, NW China
154 L9 **Jiāwān** Madhya Pradesh, C India
161 S9 **Jiaxing** Zhejiang, SE China
Jiayi *see* Chiai
163 X6 **Jiayin** *var.* Chaoyang. Heilongjiang, NE China
159 R8 **Jiayuguan** Gansu, N China
Jibhalanta *see* Uliastay
138 M4 **Jibli** Ar Raqqah, C Syria
116 H9 **Jibou** *Hung.* Zsibó. Sălaj, NW Romania
141 Z9 **Jibsh, Ra's al** *headland* E Oman
Jibuti *see* Djibouti
111 E15 **Jičín** *Ger.* Jitschin. Královéhradecký Kraj, N Czech Republic
140 K10 **Jiddah** *Eng.* Jedda. ● (Saudi Arabia) Makkah, W Saudi Arabia
141 W11 **Jiddat al Ḩarāsīs** *desert* C Oman
Jiesjavrre *see* Iešjávri
160 M4 **Jiexiu** Shanxi, C China
161 P14 **Jieyang** Guangdong, S China
119 F14 **Jieznas** Kaunas, S Lithuania
Jifa', Bi'r *see* Jif'īyah, Bi'r
141 P15 **Jif'īyah, Bi'r** *var.* Bi'r Jifa'. *well* C Yemen
77 W13 **Jigawa** ◈ *state* N Nigeria
146 J10 **Jigerbent** *Rus.* Dzhigirbent. Lebap Welaýaty, NE Turkmenistan
44 I7 **Jiguaní** Granma, E Cuba
159 T12 **Jigzhi** *var.* Chugqênsumdo. Qinghai, C China
Jih-k'a-tse *see* Xigazê
111 E18 **Jihlava** *Ger.* Iglau, *Pol.* Igława. Vysocina, S Czech Republic
111 E18 **Jihlava** *var.* Igel, *Ger.* Iglawa. ≈ Vysočina, C Czech Republic
Jihlavský Kraj *see* Vysočina
111 C18 **Jihočeský Kraj** *prev.* Budějovický Kraj. ◈ *region* Czech Republic
111 G19 **Jihomoravský Kraj** *prev.* Brněnský Kraj. ◈ *region* SE Czech Republic
74 L5 **Jijel** *var.* Djidjel; *prev.* Djidjelli. NE Algeria
116 L9 **Jijia** ≈ N Romania
80 L13 **Jijiga** *It.* Giggiga. Somali, E Ethiopia
105 S12 **Jijona** *var.* Xixona. País Valenciano, E Spain
Jilf al Kabīr, Haḑabat al *see* Gilf Kebir Plateau
81 L18 **Jilib** *It.* Gelib. Jubbada Dhexe, S Somalia
163 W10 **Jilin** *var.* Chi-lin, Girin, Kirin; *prev.* Yungki, Yunki. Jilin, NE China
163 W10 **Jilin** *var.* Chi-lin, Girin, Ji, Jilin Sheng, Kirin. ◈ *province* NE China
163 W11 **Jilin Hada Ling** ▲▲ NE China
Jilin Sheng *see* Jilin
163 S4 **Jiliu He** ≈ NE China
105 Q6 **Jiloca** ≈ N Spain
81 I14 **Jīma** *var.* Jimma, *It.* Gimma. Oromo, C Ethiopia
44 M9 **Jimaní** W Dominican Republic
116 E11 **Jimbolia** *Ger.* Hatzfeld, *Hung.* Zsombolya. Timiş, W Romania
104 K16 **Jimena de la Frontera** Andalucía, S Spain
40 K7 **Jiménez** Chihuahua, N Mexico
41 N5 **Jiménez** Coahuila de Zaragoza, NE Mexico
41 P9 **Jiménez** *var.* Santander Jiménez. Tamaulipas, C Mexico
40 L10 **Jiménez del Teul** Zacatecas, C Mexico
77 Y14 **Jimeta** Adamawa, E Nigeria
Jimma *see* Jīma
158 M5 **Jimsar** Xinjiang Uygur Zizhiqu, NW China
18 I14 **Jim Thorpe** Pennsylvania, NE USA
Jin *see* Shanxi
Jin *see* Tianjin Shi
161 P5 **Jinan** *var.* Chinan, Chi-nan, Tsinan. *province capital* Shandong, E China
Jin'an *see* Songpan
Jinbi *see* Dayao
159 T8 **Jinchang** Gansu, N China
161 N5 **Jincheng** Shanxi, C China
Jincheng *see* Wuding
Jinchengjiang *see* Hechi
152 I9 **Jīnd** *prev.* Jhind. Haryāna, NW India
183 Q11 **Jindabyne** New South Wales, SE Australia
111 O18 **Jindřichův Hradec** *Ger.* Neuhaus. Jihočeský Kraj, S Czech Republic
Jing *see* Beijing Shi
Jing *see* Jinghe, China
159 X10 **Jingchuan** Gansu, C China
161 Q10 **Jingdezhen** Jiangxi, S China
161 O12 **Jinggangshan** Jiangxi, S China
161 P3 **Jinghai** Tianjin Shi, E China
158 I4 **Jinghe** *var.* Jing. Xinjiang Uygur Zizhiqu, NW China
160 K6 **Jing He** ≈ C China
160 F15 **Jinghong** *var.* Yunjinghong. Yunnan, SW China
160 M9 **Jingmen** Hubei, C China
163 X10 **Jingpo Hu** ◎ NE China
160 M8 **Jing Shan** ▲▲ C China
159 V9 **Jingtai** *var.* Yitiaoshan. Gansu, C China
160 J14 **Jingxi** *var.* Xinjing. Guangxi Zhuangzu Zizhiqu, S China
Jing Xian *see* Jingzhou
163 W11 **Jingyu** Jilin, NE China
159 V10 **Jingyuan** Gansu, C China
160 M9 **Jingzhou** *prev.* Shashi, Shashih, Shasi. Hubei, C China
160 L12 **Jingzhou** *var.* Jing Xian, Jingzhou Miaouzu Dongzu Zizhixian, Quyang. Hunan, S China
Jingzhou Miaouzu Dongzu Zizhixian *see* Jingzhou
Jinhe *see* Jinping
161 R10 **Jinhua** Zhejiang, SE China
Jinhuan *see* Jianchuan
163 P13 **Jining** Nei Mongol Zizhiqu, N China
161 P5 **Jining** Shandong, E China
81 G18 **Jinja** S Uganda
161 R13 **Jinjiang** *var.* Qingyang. Fujian, SE China
161 O11 **Jin Jiang** ≈ S China
Jinjiang *see* Chengmei
171 V15 **Jin, Kepulauan** *island group* E Indonesia
Jinmen Dao *see* Chinmen Tao
42 J9 **Jinotega** Jinotega, NW Nicaragua
42 K7 **Jinotega** ◈ *department* N Nicaragua
42 J11 **Jinotepe** Carazo, SW Nicaragua
160 L13 **Jinping** *var.* Sanjiang. Guizhou, S China
160 H14 **Jinping** *var* Jinhe. Yunnan, SW China
Jinsen *see* Inch'ŏn
160 J11 **Jinsha** Guizhou, S China
157 N12 **Jinsha Jiang** *Eng* Yangtze. ≈ SW China
160 M10 **Jinshi** Hunan, S China
Jinshi *see* Xinning
162 I9 **Jinst** *var.* Bodĭ. Bayanhongor, C Mongolia
159 R7 **Jinta** Gansu, N China
161 Q12 **Jin Xi** ≈ SE China
Jinxi *see* Huludao
163 U14 **Jinxian** Liaoning, NE China
161 P6 **Jinxiang** Shandong, E China
161 P8 **Jinzhai** *var.* Meishan. Anhui, E China
161 N4 **Jinzhong** *var.* Yuci. Shanxi, C China
163 T12 **Jinzhou** *var.* Chin-chou, Chinchow; *prev.* Chinhsien. Liaoning, NE China
Jinzhou *see* Daocheng
138 H12 **Jinz, Qā' al** ◎ C Jordan
47 S8 **Jiparaná, Rio** ≈ W Brazil
56 A7 **Jipijapa** Manabí, W Ecuador
42 F8 **Jiquilisco** Usulután, S El Salvador
Jirgalanta *see* Hovd
147 S12 **Jirgatol** *Rus.* Dzhirgatal'. C Tajikistan
Jirjā *see* Girga
111 B15 **Jirkov** *Ger.* Görkau. Ústecký Kraj, NW Czech Republic
Jiroft *see* Sabzvārān
160 L11 **Jishou** Hunan, S China
Jisr ash Shadadi *see* Ash Shadādah
116 I14 **Jitaru** Olt, S Romania
Jitschin *see* Jičín
116 H14 **Jiu** *Ger.* Schil, Schyl, *Hung.* Zsil, Zsily. ≈ S Romania
161 R11 **Jiufeng Shan** ▲▲ SE China
161 P9 **Jiujiang** Jiangxi, S China
161 O10 **Jiuling Shan** ▲▲ S China
160 G10 **Jiulong** *var.* Garba, *Tib.* Gyaisi. Sichuan, C China
161 Q13 **Jiulong Jiang** ≈ SE China
161 Q12 **Jiulong Xi** ≈ SE China
159 R8 **Jiuquan** *var.* Suzhou. Gansu, N China
160 K17 **Jiusuo** Hainan, S China
163 W10 **Jiutai** Jilin, NE China
160 K13 **Jiuwan Dashan** ▲▲ S China
160 I7 **Jiuzhaigou** *prev.* Nanping. Sichuan, C China
148 I16 **Jīwani** Baluchistān, SW Pakistan
163 Y8 **Jixi** Heilongjiang, NE China
163 Y7 **Jixian** Heilongjiang, NE China
160 M5 **Jixian** *var.* Ji Xian. Shanxi, C China
Ji Xian *see* Jixian
Jiza *see* Al Jīzah
141 N13 **Jīzān** *var.* Qīzān. Jīzān, SW Saudi Arabia
141 N13 **Jīzān** *var.* Minţaqat Jīzān. ◈ *province* SW Saudi Arabia
Jīzān, Minţaqat *see* Jīzān
140 K6 **Jīzl, Wādī al** *dry watercourse* W Saudi Arabia
164 H12 **Jizō-zaki** *headland* Honshū, SW Japan
141 U14 **Jiz', Wādī al** *dry watercourse* E Yemen
147 O11 **Jizzax** *Rus.* Dzhizak. Jizzax Viloyati, C Uzbekistan
147 N10 **Jizzax Viloyati** *Rus.* Dzhizakskaya Oblast'. ◈ *province* C Uzbekistan
60 I13 **Joaçaba** Santa Catarina, S Brazil
Joal *see* Joal-Fadiout
76 F11 **Joal-Fadiout** *prev.* Joal. W Senegal
76 E10 **João Barrosa** Boa Vista, E Cape Verde
João Belo *see* Xai-Xai
João de Almeida *see* Chibia
59 Q15 **João Pessoa** *prev.* Paraíba. *state capital* Paraíba, E Brazil
25 X7 **Joaquin** Texas, SW USA

◆ Country
● Country Capital
◇ Dependent Territory
○ Dependent Territory Capital
◈ Administrative Regions
✈ International Airport
▲ Mountain
▲▲ Mountain Range
Volcano
≈ River
◎ Lake
⊠ Reservoir

62 K6 **Joaquín V. González** Salta, N Argentina
Joazeiro see Juazeiro
Job'urg see Johannesburg
109 O7 **Jochberger Ache** ≈ W Austria
Jo-ch'iang see Ruoqiang
92 K12 **Jock** Norrbotten, N Sweden
42 I5 **Jocón** Yoro, N Honduras
105 O13 **Jódar** Andalucía, S Spain
152 F12 **Jodhpur** Rājasthān, NW India
99 I19 **Jodoigne** Walloon Brabant, C Belgium
93 O16 **Joensuu** Itä-Suomi, SE Finland
37 W4 **Joes** Colorado, C USA
191 Z3 **Joe's Hill** *hill* Kiritimati, NE Kiribati
165 N11 **Jōetsu** *var.* Zyôetu. Niigata, Honshū, C Japan
83 M18 **Jofane** Inhambane, S Mozambique
153 R12 **Jogbani** Bihār, NE India
118 I5 **Jõgeva** *Ger.* Laisholm. Jõgevamaa, E Estonia
118 I4 **Jõgevamaa** *off.* Jõgeva Maakond. ◈ *province* E Estonia
Jõgeva Maakond see Jõgevamaa
155 E18 **Jog Falls** *Waterfall* Karnātaka, W India
143 S4 **Joghatāy** Khorāsān, NE Iran
153 U12 **Jogighopa** Assam, NE India
152 I7 **Jogindarnagar** Himāchal Pradesh, N India
Jogjakarta see Yogyakarta
164 L11 **Jōhana** Toyama, Honshū, SW Japan
Johanna Island see Anjouan
83 J21 **Johannesburg** *var.* Egoli, Erautini, Gauteng, *abbrev.* Job'urg. Gauteng, NE South Africa
35 T13 **Johannesburg** California, W USA
83 I21 **Johannesburg** ✈ Gauteng, NE South Africa
Johannisburg see Pisz
149 P14 **Johi** Sind, SE Pakistan
55 T13 **Johi Village** S Guyana
32 K13 **John Day** Oregon, NW USA
32 I11 **John Day River** ≈ Oregon, NW USA
18 L14 **John F Kennedy** ✈ (New York) Long Island, New York, NE USA
21 V8 **John H. Kerr Reservoir** *var.* Buggs Island Lake, Kerr Lake. ⊠ North Carolina/ Virginia, SE USA
37 V6 **John Martin Reservoir** ⊠ Colorado, C USA
96 K6 **John o'Groats** N Scotland, UK
27 P5 **John Redmond Reservoir** ⊠ Kansas, C USA
39 Q7 **John River** ≈ Alaska, USA
26 H6 **Johnson** Kansas, C USA
18 M7 **Johnson** Vermont, NE USA
18 D13 **Johnsonburg** Pennsylvania, NE USA
18 H11 **Johnson City** New York, NE USA
21 P8 **Johnson City** Tennessee, S USA
25 R10 **Johnson City** Texas, SW USA
35 S12 **Johnsondale** California, W USA
10 I8 **Johnsons Crossing** Yukon Territory, W Canada
21 T13 **Johnsonville** South Carolina, SE USA
21 Q13 **Johnston** South Carolina, SE USA
192 M6 **Johnston Atoll** ◇ *US unincorporated territory* C Pacific Ocean
175 Q3 **Johnston Atoll** *atoll* C Pacific Ocean
30 L17 **Johnston City** Illinois, N USA
180 K12 **Johnston, Lake** *salt lake* Western Australia
31 S13 **Johnstown** Ohio, N USA
18 D15 **Johnstown** Pennsylvania, NE USA
168 L10 **Johor** *var.* Johore. ◈ *state* Peninsular Malaysia
Johor Baharu see Johor Bahru
168 K10 **Johor Bahru** *var.* Johor Baharu, Johore Bahru. Johor, Peninsular Malaysia
Johore see Johor
Johore Bahru see Johor Bahru
118 K3 **Jõhvi** *Ger.* Jewe. Ida-Virumaa, NE Estonia
103 P7 **Joigny** Yonne, C France
Joinvile see Joinville
60 K12 **Joinville** *var.* Joinvile. Santa Catarina, S Brazil
103 R6 **Joinville** Haute-Marne, N France
194 H3 **Joinville Island** *island* Antarctica
41 O15 **Jojutla** *var.* Jojutla de Juárez. Morelos, S Mexico
Jojutla de Juárez see Jojutla
92 I12 **Jokkmokk** *Lapp.* Dálvvadis. Norrbotten, N Sweden
92 L2 **Jökulsá á Dal** ≈ E Iceland
92 K2 **Jökulsá á Fjöllum** ≈ NE Iceland
Jokyakarta see Yogyakarta
30 M11 **Joliet** Illinois, N USA
15 O11 **Joliette** Québec, SE Canada
171 O8 **Jolo** Jolo Island, SW Philippines
94 D11 **Jølstervatnet** ◎ S Norway
169 S16 **Jombang** *prev.* Djombang. Jawa, S Indonesia
159 R14 **Jomda** Xizang Zizhiqu, W China
56 A6 **Jome, Punta de** *headland* W Ecuador
118 G13 **Jonava** *Ger.* Janow, *Pol.* Janów. Kaunas, C Lithuania
146 L11 **Jondor** *Rus.* Zhondor. Buxoro Viloyati, C Uzbekistan
159 V11 **Jonê** Gansu, C China
27 X9 **Jonesboro** Arkansas, C USA
23 S4 **Jonesboro** Georgia, SE USA
30 L17 **Jonesboro** Illinois, N USA
22 H5 **Jonesboro** Louisiana, S USA
21 P8 **Jonesboro** Tennessee, S USA
19 T6 **Jonesport** Maine, NE USA
0 J4 **Jones Sound** *channel* Nunavut, N Canada
22 I6 **Jonesville** Louisiana, S USA
31 Q10 **Jonesville** Michigan, N USA
21 Q11 **Jonesville** South Carolina, SE USA
146 K10 **Jongeldi** *Rus.* Dzhankel'dy. Buxoro Viloyati, C Uzbekistan
81 F14 **Jonglei** Jonglei, SE Sudan
81 F14 **Jonglei** *var.* Gongoleh State. ◈ *state* SE Sudan
81 F14 **Jonglei Canal** *canal* S Sudan
118 F11 **Joniškėlis** Panevėžys, N Lithuania
118 F10 **Joniškis** *Ger.* Janischken. Šiauliai, N Lithuania
95 L19 **Jönköping** Jönköping, S Sweden
95 K20 **Jönköping** ◈ *county* S Sweden
15 Q7 **Jonquière** Québec, SE Canada
41 V15 **Jonuta** Tabasco, SE Mexico
102 K12 **Jonzac** Charente-Maritime, W France
27 R7 **Joplin** Missouri, C USA
33 W8 **Jordan** Montana, NW USA
138 H12 **Jordan** *off.* Hashemite Kingdom of Jordan, *Ar.* Al Mamlaka al Urduniya al Hashemiyah, Al Urdunn; *prev.* Transjordan. ◆ *monarchy* SW Asia
138 G9 **Jordan** *Ar.* Urdunn, *Heb.* HaYarden. ≈ SW Asia
Jordan Lake see B. Everett Jordan Reservoir
111 K17 **Jordanów** Małopolskie, S Poland
32 M15 **Jordan Valley** Oregon, NW USA
138 G9 **Jordan Valley** *valley* N Israel
57 D15 **Jorge Chávez International** *var.* Lima. ✈ (Lima) Lima, W Peru
113 L23 **Jorgucat** *var.* Jergucati, Jorgucati. Gjirokastër, S Albania
Jorgucati see Jorgucat
153 X12 **Jorhāt** Assam, NE India
93 J14 **Jörn** Västerbotten, N Sweden
37 R14 **Jornada Del Muerto** *valley* New Mexico, SW USA
93 N17 **Joroinen** Isä-Suomi, E Finland
95 C16 **Jørpeland** Rogaland, S Norway
77 W14 **Jos** Plateau, C Nigeria
171 Q8 **Jose Abad Santos** *var.* Trinidad. Mindanao, S Philippines
61 F19 **José Batlle y Ordóñez** *var.* Batlle y Ordóñez. Florida, C Uruguay
63 H18 **José de San Martín** Chubut, S Argentina
61 E19 **José Enrique Rodó** *var.* Rodó, José E.Rodo; *prev.* Drabble, Drable. Soriano, SW Uruguay
José E.Rodo see José Enrique Rodó
Josefsdorf see Žabalj
44 C4 **José Martí** ✈ (La Habana) Cuidad de La Habana, N Cuba
61 F19 **José Pedro Varela** *var.* José P.Varela. Lavalleja, S Uruguay
181 N2 **Joseph Bonaparte Gulf** *gulf* N Australia
37 N11 **Joseph City** Arizona, SW USA
13 O9 **Joseph, Lake** ◎ Newfoundland and Labrador, E Canada
14 G13 **Joseph, Lake** ◎ Ontario, S Canada
186 C6 **Josephstaal** Madang, N Papua New Guinea
José P.Varela see José Pedro Varela
59 J14 **José Rodrigues** Pará, N Brazil
152 K9 **Joshimath** Uttaranchal, N India
25 T7 **Joshua** Texas, SW USA
35 V15 **Joshua Tree** California, W USA
77 V14 **Jos Plateau** *plateau* C Nigeria
102 H6 **Josselin** Morbihan, NW France
Jos Sudarso see Yos Sudarso, Pulau
94 E11 **Jostedalsbreen** *glacier* S Norway
94 F12 **Jotunheimen** ▲▲ S Norway
138 G7 **Joûnié** *var.* Juniyah. W Lebanon
25 R13 **Jourdanton** Texas, SW USA
98 L7 **Joure** *Fris.* De Jouwer. Friesland, N Netherlands
93 M18 **Joutsa** Länsi-Suomi, C Finland
93 N18 **Joutseno** Etelä-Suomi, SE Finland
92 M12 **Joutsijärvi** Lappi, NE Finland
108 A9 **Joux, Lac de** ◎ W Switzerland
44 D5 **Jovellanos** Matanzas, W Cuba
153 V13 **Jowai** Meghālaya, NE India
Jöwat see Jabwot
Jowhar see Jawhar
143 O12 **Jowkān** Fārs, S Iran
Jowzam see Javazm
149 N2 **Jowzjān** ◈ *province* N Afghanistan
Józseffalva see Žabalj
J.Storm Thurmond Reservoir see Clark Hill Lake
45 T6 **Juana Díaz** C Puerto Rico
40 L9 **Juan Aldama** Zacatecas, C Mexico
0 E9 **Juan de Fuca Plate** *tectonic feature*
32 F7 **Juan de Fuca, Strait of** *strait* Canada/USA
Juan Fernandez Islands see Juan Fernández, Islas
193 S11 **Juan Fernández, Islas** *Eng.* Juan Fernandez Islands. *island group* W Chile
55 O4 **Juangriego** Nueva Esparta, NE Venezuela
56 D11 **Juanjuí** *var.* Juanjuy. San Martín, N Peru
Juanjuy see Juanjuí
93 N16 **Juankoski** Kuopio, C Finland
Juan Lacaze see Juan L. Lacaze
61 E20 **Juan L. Lacaze** *var.* Juan Lacaze, Puerto Sauce; *prev.* Sauce. Colonia, SW Uruguay
62 L5 **Juan Solá** Salta, N Argentina
63 F21 **Juan Stuven, Isla** *island* S Chile
59 H16 **Juará** Mato Grosso, W Brazil
41 N7 **Juárez** *var.* Villa Juárez. Coahuila de Zaragoza, NE Mexico
40 C2 **Juárez, Sierra de** ▲▲ NW Mexico
59 O15 **Juazeiro** *prev.* Joazeiro. Bahia, E Brazil
59 P14 **Juazeiro do Norte** Ceará, E Brazil
81 F15 **Juba** *var.* Jūbā. Bahr el Gabel, S Sudan
81 L17 **Juba** *Amh.* Genalē Wenz, *It.* Guiba, *Som.* Ganaane, Webi Jubba. ≈ Ethiopia/Somalia
194 H2 **Jubany** *Argentinian research station* Antarctica
Jubayl see Jbaïl
81 L18 **Jubbada Dhexe** *off.* Gobolka Jubbada Dhexe. ◈ *region* SW Somalia
Jubbada Dhexe, Gobolka see Jubbada Dhexe
81 K18 **Jubbada Hoose** ◈ *region* SW Somalia
Jubba, Webi see Juba
Jubbulpore see Jabalpur
Jubeil see Jbaïl
74 B9 **Juby, Cap** *headland* SW Morocco
105 R10 **Júcar** *var.* Jucar. ≈ C Spain
40 L12 **Juchipila** Zacatecas, C Mexico
41 S16 **Juchitán** *var.* Juchitán de Zaragosa. Oaxaca, SE Mexico
Juchitán de Zaragosa see Juchitán
138 G11 **Judaea** *cultural region* Israel/ West Bank
138 F11 **Judaean Hills** *Heb.* Haré Yehuda. *hill range* E Israel
138 H8 **Judaydah** *Fr.* Jdaidé. Dimashq, W Syria
139 P11 **Judayyidat Hāmir** S Iraq
109 U8 **Judenburg** Steiermark, C Austria
33 T8 **Judith River** ≈ Montana, NW USA
27 V11 **Judsonia** Arkansas, C USA
141 P14 **Jufrah, Wādī al** *dry watercourse* NW Yemen
Jugar see Sêrxü
Jugoslavija see Serbia
42 K10 **Juigalpa** Chontales, S Nicaragua
161 T13 **Juishui** C Taiwan
100 E9 **Juist** *island* NW Germany
59 M21 **Juiz de Fora** Minas Gerais, SE Brazil
62 J5 **Jujuy** *off.* Provincia de Jujuy. ◈ *province* N Argentina
Jujuy see San Salvador de Jujuy
Jujuy, Provincia de see Jujuy
92 J11 **Jukkasjärvi** *Lapp.* Čohkkiras. Norrbotten, N Sweden
Jula see Gyula, Hungary
Jūlā see Jālū, Libya
37 W2 **Julesburg** Colorado, C USA
Julia Beterrae see Béziers
57 I17 **Juliaca** Puno, SE Peru
181 U6 **Julia Creek** Queensland, C Australia
35 V17 **Julian** California, W USA
98 H7 **Julianadorp** Noord-Holland, NW Netherlands
109 S11 **Julian Alps** *Ger.* Julische Alpen, *It.* Alpi Giulie, *Slvn.* Julijske Alpe. ▲▲ Italy/Slovenia
55 V11 **Juliana Top** ▲ C Suriname
Julianehåb see Qaqortoq
Julijske Alpe see Julian Alps
40 J6 **Julimes** Chihuahua, N Mexico
Julio Briga see Bragança
Juliobriga see Logroño
61 G15 **Júlio de Castilhos** Rio Grande do Sul, S Brazil
Juliomagus see Angers
Julische Alpen see Julian Alps
Jullundur see Jalandhar
147 N11 **Juma** *Rus.* Dzhuma. Samarqand Viloyati, C Uzbekistan
161 O3 **Juma He** ≈ E China
81 L18 **Jumboo** Jubbada Hoose, S Somalia
35 Y11 **Jumbo Peak** ▲ Nevada, W USA
105 R12 **Jumilla** Murcia, SE Spain
153 N10 **Jumla** Mid Western, NW Nepal
Jummoo see Jammu
Jumna see Yamuna
Jumporn see Chumphon
30 K5 **Jump River** ≈ Wisconsin, N USA
154 B11 **Jūnāgadh** *var.* Junagarh. Gujarāt, W India
Junagarh see Jūnāgadh
161 Q6 **Junan** *var.* Shizilu. Shandong, E China
62 G11 **Juncal, Cerro** ▲ C Chile
25 Q10 **Junction** Texas, SW USA
36 K6 **Junction** Utah, W USA
27 O4 **Junction City** Kansas, C USA
32 F13 **Junction City** Oregon, NW USA
60 M10 **Jundiaí** São Paulo, S Brazil
39 X12 **Juneau** *state capital* Alaska, USA
30 M8 **Juneau** Wisconsin, N USA
105 U6 **Juneda** Cataluña, NE Spain
183 Q9 **Junee** New South Wales, SE Australia
35 R8 **June Lake** California, W USA
Jungbunzlau see Mladá Boleslav
158 L4 **Junggar Pendi** *Eng.* Dzungarian Basin. *basin* NW China
99 N24 **Junglinster** Grevenmacher, C Luxembourg
18 F14 **Juniata River** ≈ Pennsylvania, NE USA
61 B20 **Junín** Buenos Aires, E Argentina
57 E14 **Junín** Junín, C Peru
57 F14 **Junín** *off.* Departamento de Junín. ◈ *department* C Peru
63 H15 **Junín de los Andes** Neuquén, W Argentina
Junín, Departamento de see Junín
57 D14 **Junín, Lago de** ◎ C Peru
Juniyah see Joûnié
Junkseylon see Phuket
160 I11 **Junlian** Sichuan, C China
25 O11 **Juno** Texas, SW USA
92 J11 **Junosuando** *Lapp.* Čunusavvon. Norrbotten, N Sweden
93 H16 **Junsele** Västernorrland, C Sweden
Junten see Sunch'ŏn
32 L14 **Juntura** Oregon, NW USA
93 N14 **Juntusranta** Oulu, E Finland
118 H11 **Juodupė** Panevėžys, NE Lithuania
119 H14 **Juozapinės Kalnas** ▲ SE Lithuania
99 K19 **Juprelle** Liège, E Belgium
80 D13 **Jur** ≈ C Sudan
103 S9 **Jura** ◈ *department* E France
108 C7 **Jura** ◈ *canton* NW Switzerland
108 B8 **Jura** *var.* Jura Mountains. ▲▲ France/Switzerland
96 G12 **Jura** *island* SW Scotland, UK
Juraciszki see Yuratsishki
54 C8 **Juradó** Chocó, NW Colombia
Jura Mountains see Jura
96 G12 **Jura, Sound of** *strait* W Scotland, UK
139 V15 **Juraybīyāt, Bi'r** *well* S Iraq
118 E13 **Jurbarkas** *Ger.* Georgenburg, Jurburg. Tauragė, W Lithuania
99 F20 **Jurbise** Hainaut, SW Belgium
Jurburg see Jurbarkas
118 F9 **Jūrmala** Rīga, C Latvia
58 D13 **Juruá** Amazonas, NW Brazil
48 F7 **Juruá, Rio** *var.* Río Yuruá. ≈ Brazil/Peru
59 G16 **Juruena** Mato Grosso, W Brazil
59 G16 **Juruena, Rio** ≈ W Brazil
165 Q6 **Jūsan-ko** ◎ Honshū, C Japan
25 O6 **Justiceburg** Texas, SW USA
Justinianopolis see Kirşehir
62 K11 **Justo Daract** San Luis, C Argentina
59 C14 **Jutaí** Amazonas, W Brazil
58 C13 **Jutaí, Rio** ≈ NW Brazil
100 N13 **Jüterbog** Brandenburg, E Germany
42 E6 **Jutiapa** Jutiapa, S Guatemala
42 A3 **Jutiapa** *off.* Departamento de Jutiapa. ◈ *department* SE Guatemala
Jutiapa, Departamento de see Jutiapa
42 J6 **Juticalpa** Olancho, C Honduras
82 I13 **Jutila** North Western, NW Zambia
Jutland see Jylland
84 F8 **Jutland Bank** *undersea feature* SE North Sea
93 N16 **Juuka** Pohjois-Karjala, E Finland
93 N17 **Juva** Isä-Suomi, E Finland
Juvavum see Salzburg
44 A6 **Juventud, Isla de la** *var.* Isla de Pinos, *Eng.* Isle of Youth; *prev.* The Isle of the Pines. *island* W Cuba
161 Q5 **Juxian** *var.* Chengyang, Ju Xian. Shandong, E China
Ju Xian see Juxian
161 P6 **Juye** Shandong, E China
113 O15 **Južna Morava** *Ger.* Südliche Morava. ≈ SE Serbia
83 H20 **Jwaneng** Southern, S Botswana Africa
95 I23 **Jyderup** Vestsjælland, E Denmark
95 F22 **Jylland** *Eng.* Jutland. *peninsula* W Denmark
Jyrgalan see Dzhergalan
93 M17 **Jyväskylä** Länsi-Soumi, C Finland

K

38 D9 **Ka'a'awa** *var.* Kaaawa. Hawai'i, O'ahu, USA, C Pacific Ocean
Kaaawa see Ka'a'awa
81 G16 **Kaabong** NE Uganda
Kaaden see Kadaň
Kaafu Atoll see Male' Atoll
55 V9 **Kaaimanston** Sipaliwini, N Suriname
Kaakhka see Kaka
Kaala see Caála
187 O16 **Kaala-Gomen** Province Nord, W New Caledonia
92 L9 **Kaamanen** *Lapp.* Gámas. Lappi, N Finland
Kaapstad see Cape Town
Kaarasjoki see Karasjok
Kaaresuanto see Karesuando
92 J10 **Kaaresuvanto** *Lapp.* Gárassavon. Lappi, N Finland
93 K19 **Kaarina** Länsi-Soumi, SW Finland
99 I14 **Kaatsheuvel** Noord-Brabant, S Netherlands
93 N16 **Kaavi** Itä-Suomi, C Finland
Kaba see Habahe
171 O14 **Kabaena, Pulau** *island* C Indonesia
Kabakly see Gabakly
76 J14 **Kabala** N Sierra Leone
81 E19 **Kabale** SW Uganda
55 U10 **Kabalebo Rivier** ≈ W Suriname
79 N22 **Kabalo** Katanga, SE Dem. Rep. Congo
79 O21 **Kabambare** Maniema, E Dem. Rep. Congo
145 W13 **Kabanbay** *Kaz.* Qabanbay; *prev.* Andreyevka, *Kaz.* Andreevka. Almaty, SE Kazakhstan
187 Y15 **Kabara** *prev.* Kambara. *island* Lau Group, E Fiji
Kabardino-Balkaria see Kabardino-Balkarskaya Respublika
126 M15 **Kabardino-Balkarskaya Respublika** *Eng.* Kabardino-Balkaria. ◈ *autonomous republic* SW Russian Federation
79 O19 **Kabare** Sud Kivu, E Dem. Rep. Congo
171 T11 **Kabarei** Papua, E Indonesia
171 P7 **Kabasalan** Mindanao, S Philippines
77 U15 **Kabba** Kogi, S Nigeria
92 I13 **Kåbdalis** *Lapp.* Goabddális. Norrbotten, N Sweden
138 M6 **Kabd aş Şārim** *hill range* E Syria
14 B7 **Kabenung Lake** ◎ Ontario, S Canada
29 W3 **Kabetogama Lake** ◎ Minnesota, N USA
Kabia, Pulau see Kabin, Pulau
79 M22 **Kabinda** Kasai Oriental, SE Dem. Rep. Congo
Kabinda see Cabinda
171 O15 **Kabin, Pulau** *var.* Pulau Kabia. *island* W Indonesia
171 P16 **Kabir** Pulau Pantar, S Indonesia
149 T10 **Kabīrwāla** Punjab, E Pakistan
78 I13 **Kabo** Ouham, NW Central African Republic
149 Q5 **Kābol** *var.* Kabul, *Pash.* Kābul. ● (Afghanistan) Kābul, E Afghanistan
149 Q5 **Kābol** *Eng.* Kabul, *Pash.* Kābul. ◈ *province* E Afghanistan
149 Q5 **Kābol** ✈ Kābul, E Afghanistan
83 H14 **Kabompo** North Western, W Zambia
83 H14 **Kabompo** ≈ W Zambia
79 M22 **Kabongo** Katanga, SE Dem. Rep. Congo
120 K11 **Kaboudia, Rass** *headland* E Tunisia
143 U4 **Kabūd Gonbad** Khorāsān, NE Iran
142 L5 **Kabūd Rāhang** Hamadān, W Iran
82 L12 **Kabuko** Northern, NE Zambia
149 R5 **Kabul** *var.* Daryā-ye Kābul. ≈ Afghanistan/Pakistan *see also* Kābul, Daryā-ye
Kābul see Kābol
Kabul see Kābul, Daryā-ye
149 S5 **Kābul, Daryā-ye** *var.* Kabul. ≈ Afghanistan/Pakistan *see also* Kabul
Kābul, Daryā-ye see Kabul
79 O25 **Kabunda** Katanga, SE Dem. Rep. Congo
171 R9 **Kaburuang, Pulau** *island* Kepulauan Talaud, N Indonesia
80 G8 **Kabushiya** River Nile, NE Sudan
83 J14 **Kabwe** Central, C Zambia
186 E7 **Kabwum** Morobe, C Papua New Guinea
113 N17 **Kačanik** Kosovo, S Serbia
118 F13 **Kačerginė** Kaunas, C Lithuania
117 S13 **Kacha** Respublika Krym, S Ukraine
154 A10 **Kachchh, Gulf of** *var.* Gulf of Cutch, Gulf of Kutch. *gulf* W India
154 I11 **Kachchhīdhāna** Madhya Pradesh, C India
149 Q11 **Kachchh, Rann of** *var.* Rann of Kachh, Rann of Kutch. *salt marsh* India/Pakistan
39 Q13 **Kachemak Bay** *bay* Alaska, USA
Kachh, Rann of see Kachchh, Rann of
77 V14 **Kachia** Kaduna, C Nigeria
167 N2 **Kachin State** ◈ *state* N Myanmar (Burma)
145 T7 **Kachiry** Pavlodar, NE Kazakhstan
137 Q11 **Kaçkar Dağları** ▲▲ NE Turkey
155 C21 **Kadamatt Island** *island* Lakshadweep, India, N Indian Ocean
111 B15 **Kadaň** *Ger.* Kaaden. Ústecký Kraj, NW Czech Republic
1667 N11 **Kadan Kyun** *prev.* King Island. *island* Mergui Archipelago, S Myanmar (Burma)
187 X15 **Kadavu** *prev.* Kandavu. *island* S Fiji
187 X15 **Kadavu Passage** *channel* S Fiji
79 G16 **Kadéï** ≈ Cameroon/Central African Republic
Kadhimain see Al Kāẓimīyah
Kadijica see Kadiytsa
114 M13 **Kadıköy Barajı** ⊠ NW Turkey
182 I8 **Kadina** South Australia
136 H15 **Kadınhanı** Konya, C Turkey
76 M14 **Kadiolo** Sikasso, S Mali
136 L16 **Kadirli** Osmaniye, S Turkey
114 G11 **Kadiytsa** *Mac.* Kadijica. ▲ Bulgaria/FYR Macedonia
28 L10 **Kadoka** South Dakota, N USA
127 N5 **Kadom** Ryazanskaya Oblast', W Russian Federation
83 K16 **Kadoma** *prev.* Gatooma. Mashonaland West, C Zimbabwe
80 E12 **Kadugli** Southern Kordofan, S Sudan
77 V14 **Kaduna** Kaduna, C Nigeria
77 V14 **Kaduna** ◈ *state* C Nigeria
77 V15 **Kaduna** ≈ N Nigeria
124 K14 **Kaduy** Vologodskaya Oblast', NW Russian Federation
154 E13 **Kadwa** ≈ W India
123 S9 **Kadykchan** Magadanskaya Oblast', E Russian Federation
Kadzharan see K'ajaran
125 T7 **Kadzherom** Respublika Komi, NW Russian Federation
147 X8 **Kadzhi-Say** *Kir.* Kajisay. Issyk-Kul'skaya Oblast', NE Kyrgyzstan
76 I10 **Kaédi** Gorgol, S Mauritania
78 G12 **Kaélé** Extrême-Nord, N Cameroon
38 C9 **Ka'ena Point** *var.* Kaena Point. *headland* O'ahu, Hawai'i, USA
184 J2 **Kaeo** Northland, North Island, New Zealand
163 X14 **Kaesŏng** *var.* Kaesŏng-si. S North Korea
Kaesŏng-si see Kaesŏng
Kaewieng see Kavieng
79 L24 **Kafakumba** Shaba, S Dem. Rep. Congo
Kafan see Kapan
77 V14 **Kafanchan** Kaduna, C Nigeria
Kaffa see Feodosiya
76 G11 **Kaffrine** C Senegal
115 I19 **Kafiréos, Stenó** *strait* Évvoia/ Kykládes, Greece, Aegean Sea
Kafirnigan see Kofarnihon
Kafo see Kafu
Kafr ash Shaykh/Kafrel Sheik see Kafr el Sheikh
75 W7 **Kafr el Sheikh** *var.* Kafr ash Shaykh, Kafrel Sheik. N Egypt
81 F17 **Kafu** *var.* Kafo. ≈ W Uganda
83 J15 **Kafue** Lusaka, SE Zambia
83 I14 **Kafue** ≈ C Zambia
67 T13 **Kafue Flats** *plain* C Zambia
164 K12 **Kaga** Ishikawa, Honshū, SW Japan
79 J14 **Kaga Bandoro** *prev.* Fort-Crampel. Nana-Grébizi, C Central African Republic
81 E18 **Kagadi** W Uganda
38 H17 **Kagalaska Island** *island* Aleutian Islands, Alaska, USA
Kagan see Kogon
Kaganovichabad see Kolkhozobod
Kagarlyk see Kaharlyk
164 H14 **Kagawa** *off.* Kagawa-ken. ◈ *prefecture* Shikoku, SW Japan
Kagawa-ken see Kagawa
154 J13 **Kagaznagar** Andhra Pradesh, C India
93 J14 **Kåge** Västerbotten, N Sweden
81 E19 **Kagera** *var.* Ziwa Magharibi, *Eng.* West Lake. ◈ *region* NW Tanzania
81 E19 **Kagera** *var.* Akagera. ≈ Rwanda/Tanzania *see also* Akagera
76 L5 **Kâgheț** *var.* Karet. *physical region* N Mauritania
Kagi see Chiai
137 S12 **Kağızman** Kars, NE Turkey
188 I6 **Kagman Point** *headland* Saipan, S Northern Mariana Islands
164 C16 **Kagoshima** *var.* Kagosima. Kagoshima, Kyūshū, SW Japan
164 C16 **Kagoshima** *off.* Kagoshima-ken, *var.* Kagosima. ◈ *prefecture* Kyūshū, SW Japan
Kagoshima-ken see Kagoshima
Kagosima see Kagoshima
Kagul see Cahul
Kagul, Ozero see Kahul, Ozero
38 B8 **Kahala Point** *headland* Kaua'i, Hawai'i, USA
81 F21 **Kahama** Shinyanga, NW Tanzania
117 P5 **Kaharlyk** *Rus.* Kagarlyk. Kyyivs'ka Oblast', N Ukraine
169 T13 **Kahayan, Sungai** ≈ Borneo, C Indonesia
79 I22 **Kahemba** Bandundu, SW Dem. Rep. Congo
185 A23 **Kaherekoau Mountains** ▲▲ South Island, New Zealand
143 W14 **Kahīrī** *var.* Kūhīrī. Sīstān va Balūchestān, SE Iran
101 L16 **Kahla** Thüringen, C Germany
101 G15 **Kahler Asten** ▲ W Germany
149 Q4 **Kahmard, Daryā-ye** *prev.* Darya-i-surkhab. ≈ NE Afghanistan
143 T13 **Kahnūj** Kermān, SE Iran
27 V1 **Kahoka** Missouri, C USA
38 E10 **Kaho'olawe** *var.* Kahoolawe. *island* Hawaiian Islands, Hawai'i, USA
Kahoolawe see Kaho'olawe
136 M16 **Kahramanmaraş** *var.* Kahraman Maraş, Maraş, Marash. Kahramanmaraş, S Turkey
136 L15 **Kahramanmaraş** *var.* Kahraman Maraş, Maraş, Marash. ◈ *province* C Turkey
Kahraman Maraş see Kahramanmaraş
Kahror/Kahror Pakka see Karor Pacca
137 N15 **Kâhta** Adıyaman, S Turkey
38 D8 **Kahuku** O'ahu, Hawai'i, USA
38 D8 **Kahuku Point** *headland* O'ahu, Hawai'i, USA
116 M12 **Kahul, Ozero** *var.* Lacul Cahul, *Rus.* Ozero Kagul. ◎ Moldova/Ukraine
143 V11 **Kahūrak** Sīstān va Balūchestān, SE Iran
184 G13 **Kahurangi Point** *headland* South Island, New Zealand
149 V6 **Kahūta** Punjab, E Pakistan
77 S14 **Kaiama** Kwara, W Nigeria
186 D7 **Kaiapit** Morobe, C Papua New Guinea
185 I18 **Kaiapoi** Canterbury, South Island, New Zealand
36 K9 **Kaibab Plateau** *plain* Arizona, SW USA
171 U14 **Kai Besar, Pulau** *island* Kepulauan Kai, E Indonesia
36 L9 **Kaibito Plateau** *plain* Arizona, SW USA
158 K6 **Kaidu He** *var.* Karaxahar. ≈ NW China
55 S10 **Kaieteur Falls** *waterfall* C Guyana
161 O6 **Kaifeng** Henan, C China
184 J3 **Kaihu** Northland, North Island, New Zealand
Kaihua see Wenshan
171 U14 **Kai Kecil, Pulau** *island* Kepulauan Kai, E Indonesia
169 U16 **Kai, Kepulauan** *prev.* Kei Islands. *island group* Maluku, SE Indonesia
184 J3 **Kaikohe** Northland, North Island, New Zealand
185 J16 **Kaikoura** Canterbury, South Island, New Zealand
185 J16 **Kaikoura Peninsula** *peninsula* South Island, New Zealand
Kailas Range see Gangdisê Shan
160 K12 **Kaili** Guizhou, S China
38 F10 **Kailua** Maui, Hawaii, USA
38 F10 **Kailua** Maui, Hawaii, USA, C Pacific Ocean
Kailua see Kalaoa
38 G11 **Kailua-Kona** *var.* Kona. Hawai'i, USA, C Pacific Ocean
186 B7 **Kaim** ≈ W Papua New Guinea
171 X14 **Kaima** Papua, E Indonesia
184 M7 **Kaimai Range** ▲▲ North Island, New Zealand
114 E13 **Kaïmaktsalán** ▲ Greece/FYR Macedonia
185 C20 **Kaimanawa Mountains** ▲▲ North Island, New Zealand
118 E4 **Käina** *Ger.* Keinis; *prev.* Keina. Hiiumaa, W Estonia
109 V7 **Kainach** ≈ SE Austria
164 I14 **Kainan** Tokushima, Shikoku, SW Japan
164 H15 **Kainan** Wakayama, Honshū, SW Japan
147 U7 **Kaindy** *Kir.* Kayyngdy. Chuyskaya Oblast', N Kyrgyzstan
77 T14 **Kainji Dam** *dam* W Nigeria
Kainji Lake see Kainji Reservoir

◆ Country
● Country Capital
◇ Dependent Territory
○ Dependent Territory Capital
◈ Administrative Regions
✈ International Airport
▲ Mountain
▲▲ Mountain Range
Volcano
≈ River
◎ Lake
⊠ Reservoir

77 T14 **Kainji Reservoir** *var.* Kainji Lake. ⊠ W Nigeria
186 D8 **Kaintiba** *var.* Kamina. Gulf, S Papua New Guinea
92 K12 **Kainulaisjärvi** Norrbotten, N Sweden
184 K5 **Kaipara Harbour** *harbor* North Island, New Zealand
152 I10 **Kairāna** Uttar Pradesh, N India
74 M6 **Kairouan** *var.* Al Qayrawān. E Tunisia
Kaisaria *see* Kayseri
101 F20 **Kaiserslautern** Rheinland-Pfalz, SW Germany
118 G13 **Kaišiadorys** Kaunas, S Lithuania
184 I2 **Kaitaia** Northland, North Island, New Zealand
185 E24 **Kaitangata** Otago, South Island, New Zealand
152 I9 **Kaithal** Haryāna, NW India
Kaitong *see* Tongyu
169 N13 **Kait, Tanjung** *cape* Sumatera, W Indonesia
38 E9 **Kaiwi Channel** *channel* Hawai'i, USA, C Pacific Ocean
160 K9 **Kaixian** *var.* Hanfeng. Sichuan, C China
163 V11 **Kaiyuan** *var.* K'ai-yüan. Liaoning, NE China
160 H14 **Kaiyuan** Yunnan, SW China
K'ai-yüan *see* Kaiyuan
39 O9 **Kaiyuh Mountains** ▲▲ Alaska, USA
93 M15 **Kajaani** *Swe.* Kajana. Oulu, C Finland
149 N7 **Kajaki, Band-e** ◎ C Afghanistan
Kajan *see* Kayan, Sungai
Kajana *see* Kajaani
137 V13 **K'ajaran** *Rus.* Kadzharan. SE Armenia
Kajisay *see* Kadzhi-Say
113 O20 **Kajmakčalan** ▲ S FYR Macedonia
Kajnar *see* Kaynar
149 N6 **Kajrān** Dāikondī, C Afghanistan
149 N5 **Kaj Rūd** ≈ C Afghanistan
146 G14 **Kaka** *Rus.* Kaakhka. Ahal Welaýaty, S Turkmenistan
12 C12 **Kakabeka Falls** Ontario, S Canada
83 F23 **Kakamas** Northern Cape, W South Africa
81 H18 **Kakamega** Western, W Kenya
112 H13 **Kakanj** Federacija Bosna I Hercegovina, C Bosnia and Herzegovina
185 F22 **Kakanui Mountains** ▲▲ South Island, New Zealand
184 K11 **Kakaramea** Taranaki, North Island, New Zealand
76 J16 **Kakata** C Liberia
184 M11 **Kakatahi** Manawatu-Wanganui, North Island, New Zealand
113 M23 **Kakavi** Gjirokastër, S Albania
147 O14 **Kakaydi** Surkhondaryo Viloyati, S Uzbekistan
164 F13 **Kake** Hiroshima, Honshū, SW Japan
39 X13 **Kake** Kupreanof Island, Alaska, USA
171 P14 **Kakea** Pulau Wowoni, C Indonesia
164 M14 **Kakegawa** Shizuoka, Honshū, S Japan
165 V16 **Kakeromajima** Kagoshima, SW Japan
143 T6 **Kākhak** Khorāsān, E Iran
118 L11 **Kakhanavichy** *Rus.* Kokhanovichi. Vitsyebskaya Voblasts', N Belarus
39 P13 **Kakhonak** Alaska, USA
117 S10 **Kakhovka** Khersons'ka Oblast', S Ukraine
117 U9 **Kakhovs'ke Vodoskhovyshche** *Rus.* Kakhovskoye Vodokhranilishche. ⊠ SE Ukraine
Kakhovskoye Vodokhranilishche *see* Kakhovs'ke Vodoskhovyshche
117 T11 **Kakhovs'kyy Kanal** *canal* S Ukraine
Kakia *see* Khakhea
155 L16 **Kākināda** *prev.* Cocanada. Andhra Pradesh, E India
Kākisalmi *see* Priozersk
164 I13 **Kakogawa** Hyōgo, Honshū, SW Japan
81 F18 **Kakoge** C Uganda
145 O7 **Kak, Ozero** ◎ N Kazakhstan
Ka-Krem *see* Malyy Yenisey
Kakshaal-Too, Khrebet *see* Kokshaal-Tau
39 S5 **Kaktovik** Alaska, USA
165 Q11 **Kakuda** Miyagi, Honshū, C Japan
165 Q8 **Kakunodate** Akita, Honshū, C Japan
Kalaallit Nunaat *see* Greenland
149 T7 **Kālābāgh** Punjab, E Pakistan
171 Q16 **Kalabahi** Pulau Alor, S Indonesia
188 I5 **Kalabera** Saipan, S Northern Mariana Islands
83 G14 **Kalabo** Western, W Zambia
126 M9 **Kalach** Voronezhskaya Oblast', W Russian Federation
127 N10 **Kalach-na-Donu** Volgogradskaya Oblast', SW Russian Federation
166 K5 **Kaladan** ≈ W Myanmar (Burma)
14 K14 **Kaladar** Ontario, SE Canada
38 G13 **Ka Lae** *var.* South Cape, South Point. *headland* Hawai'i, USA, C Pacific Ocean
83 G19 **Kalahari Desert** *desert* Southern Africa
38 B8 **Kalāheo** *var.* Kalaheo. Kaua'i, Hawai'i, USA
Kalaheo *see* Kalāheo
Kalaikhum *see* Qal'aikhum
Kala-i-Mor *see* Galaýmor
93 K15 **Kalajoki** Oulu, W Finland
Kalak *see* Eski Kaļak
Kal al Sraghna *see* El Kelâa Srarhna
32 G10 **Kalama** Washington, NW USA
Kalámai *see* Kalámata
115 G14 **Kalamariá** Kentrikí Makedonía, N Greece
115 C15 **Kalamás** *var.* Thiamis, *prev* Thýamis. ≈ W Greece
115 E21 **Kalámata** *prev.* Kalámai. Pelopónnisos, S Greece
31 P10 **Kalamazoo** Michigan, N USA
31 P9 **Kalamazoo River** ≈ Michigan, N USA
Kalambaka *see* Kalampáka
117 S13 **Kalamits'ka Zatoka** *Rus.* Kalamitskiy Zaliv. *gulf* S Ukraine
Kalamitskiy Zaliv *see* Kalamits'ka Zatoka
115 H18 **Kálamos** Attikí, C Greece
115 C18 **Kálamos** *island* Iónioi Nísia, Greece, C Mediterranean Sea
115 D15 **Kalampáka** *var.* Kalambaka. Thessalía, C Greece
Kalan *see* Călan, Romania
Kalan *see* Tunceli, Turkey
117 S11 **Kalanchak** Khersons'ka Oblast', S Ukraine
38 G11 **Kalaoa** *var.* Kailua. Hawai'i, USA, C Pacific Ocean
171 O15 **Kalaotoa, Pulau** *island* W Indonesia
155 J24 **Kala Oya** ≈ NW Sri Lanka
Kalarash *see* Călărași
93 H17 **Kälarne** Jämtland, C Sweden
143 V15 **Kalar Rūd** ≈ SE Iran
169 R9 **Kalasin** *var.* Muang Kalasin. Kalasin, E Thailand
149 O11 **Kalāt** *var.* Kelat, Khelat. Baluchistān, SW Pakistan
Kalāt *see* Qalāt
115 J14 **Kalathriá, Ákrotirio** *headland* Samothráki, NE Greece
193 W17 **Kalau** *island* Tongatapu Group, SE Tonga
38 E9 **Kalaupapa** Moloka'i, Hawai'i, USA
127 N13 **Kalaus** ≈ SW Russian Federation
Kalávrita *see* Kalávryta
115 E19 **Kalávryta** *var.* Kalávrita. Dytikí Ellás, S Greece
141 Y10 **Kalbān** W Oman
180 H11 **Kalbarri** Western Australia
145 X10 **Kalbinskiy Khrebet** *Kaz.* Qalba Zhotasy. ▲▲ E Kazakhstan
144 G10 **Kaldygayty** ≈ W Kazakhstan
136 I12 **Kalecik** Ankara, N Turkey
79 O19 **Kalehe** Sud Kivu, E Dem. Rep. Congo
79 P22 **Kalemie** *prev.* Albertville. Katanga, SE Dem. Rep. Congo
166 L4 **Kalemyo** Sagaing, W Myanmar (Burma)
82 H12 **Kalene Hill** North Western, NW Zambia
Kale Sultanie *see* Çanakkale
124 I7 **Kalevala** Respublika Kareliya, NW Russian Federation
166 L4 **Kalewa** Sagaing, C Myanmar (Burma)
Kalgan *see* Zhangjiakou
39 Q12 **Kalgin Island** *island* Alaska, USA
180 L12 **Kalgoorlie** Western Australia
Kali *see* Sārda
115 E17 **Kaliakoúda** ▲ C Greece
114 O8 **Kaliakra, Nos** *cape* NE Bulgaria
115 F19 **Kaliánoi** Pelopónnisos, S Greece
115 N24 **Kalí Límni** ▲ Kárpathos, SE Greece
79 N20 **Kalima** Maniema, E Dem. Rep. Congo
169 S11 **Kalimantan** *Eng.* Indonesian Borneo. *geopolitical region* Borneo, C Indonesia
169 Q11 **Kalimantan Barat** *off.* Propinsi Kalimantan Berat, *Eng.* West Borneo, West Kalimantan. ◐ *province* N Indonesia
Kalimantan Barat, Propinsi *see* Kalimantan Barat
169 T13 **Kalimantan Selatan** *off.* Propinsi Kalimantan Selatan, *Eng.* South Borneo, South Kalimantan. ◐ *province* N Indonesia
Kalimantan Selatan, Propinsi *see* Kalimantan Selatan
169 R12 **Kalimantan Tengah** *off.* Propinsi Kalimantan Tengah, *Eng.* Central Borneo, Central Kalimantan. ◐ *province* N Indonesia
Kalimantan Tengah, Propinsi *see* Kalimantan Tengah
169 U10 **Kalimantan Timur** *off.* Propinsi Kalimantan Timur, *Eng.* East Borneo, East Kalimantan. ◐ *province* N Indonesia
Kalimantan Timur, Propinsi *see* Kalimantan Timur
Kálimnos *see* Kálymnos
153 S12 **Kālimpang** West Bengal, NE India
Kalinin *see* Tver'
Kalinin *see* Boldumsaz
Kalininabad *see* Kalininobod
126 B3 **Kaliningrad** Kaliningradskaya Oblast', W Russian Federation
Kaliningrad *see* Kaliningradskaya Oblast'
126 A3 **Kaliningradskaya Oblast'** *var.* Kaliningrad. ◐ *province and enclave* W Russian Federation
Kalinino *see* Tashir
147 P14 **Kalininobod** *Rus.* Kalininabad. SW Tajikistan
127 O8 **Kalininsk** Saratovskaya Oblast', W Russian Federation
Kalininsk *see* Boldumsaz
Kalinisk *see* Cupcina
119 M19 **Kalinkavichy** *Rus.* Kalinkovichi. Homyel'skaya Voblasts', SE Belarus
Kalinkovichi *see* Kalinkavichy
81 G18 **Kaliro** SE Uganda
Kalisch/Kalish *see* Kalisz
33 O7 **Kalispell** Montana, NW USA
110 I13 **Kalisz** *Ger.* Kalisch, *Rus.* Kalish; *anc.* Calisia. Wielkopolskie, C Poland
110 F9 **Kalisz Pomorski** *Ger.* Kallies. Zachodnio-pomorskie, NW Poland
126 M10 **Kalitva** ≈ SW Russian Federation
81 F21 **Kaliua** Tabora, C Tanzania
92 K13 **Kalix** Norrbotten, N Sweden
92 K12 **Kalixälven** ≈ N Sweden
92 J11 **Kalixfors** Norrbotten, N Sweden
145 T8 **Kalkaman** Pavlodar, NE Kazakhstan
Kalkandelen *see* Tetovo
181 O4 **Kalkarindji** Northern Territory, N Australia
31 P6 **Kalkaska** Michigan, N USA
93 F16 **Kall** Jämtland, C Sweden
189 X2 **Kallalen** *var.* Calalen. *island* Ratak Chain, SE Marshall Islands
118 J5 **Kallaste** *Ger.* Krasnogor. Tartumaa, SE Estonia
93 N16 **Kallavesi** ◎ SE Finland
115 F17 **Kallídromo** ▲▲ C Greece
Kallies *see* Kalisz Pomorski
95 M22 **Kallinge** Blekinge, S Sweden
115 L16 **Kalloní** Lésvos, E Greece
93 F16 **Kallsjön** ◎ C Sweden
95 N21 **Kalmar** *var.* Calmar. Kalmar, S Sweden
95 M19 **Kalmar** *var.* Calmar. ◐ *county* S Sweden
95 N20 **Kalmarsund** *strait* S Sweden
148 L16 **Kalmat, Khor** *Eng.* Kalmat Lagoon. *lagoon* SW Pakistan
Kalmat Lagoon *see* Kalmat, Khor
117 X9 **Kal'mius** ≈ E Ukraine
99 H15 **Kalmthout** Antwerpen, N Belgium
Kalmykia/Kalmykiya-Khal'mg Tangch, Respublika *see* Kalmykiya, Respublika
127 O12 **Kalmykiya, Respublika** *var.* Respublika Kalmykiya-Khal'mg Tangch, *Eng.* Kalmykia; *prev.* Kalmytskaya ASSR. ◐ *autonomous republic* SW Russian Federation
Kalmytskaya ASSR *see* Kalmykiya, Respublika
118 F9 **Kalnciems** Jelgava, C Latvia
114 L10 **Kalnitsa** ≈ SE Bulgaria
111 J24 **Kalocsa** Bács-Kiskun, S Hungary
114 J9 **Kalofer** Plovdiv, C Bulgaria
38 E10 **Kalohi Channel** *channel* C Pacific Ocean
83 I16 **Kalomo** Southern, S Zambia
29 X14 **Kalona** Iowa, C USA
115 K22 **Kalotási, Ákrotirio** *cape* Amorgós, Kykládes, Greece, Aegean Sea
152 J8 **Kalpa** Himāchal Pradesh, N India
115 C15 **Kalpáki** Ípeiros, W Greece
155 C22 **Kalpeni Island** *island* Lakshadweep, India, N Indian Ocean
152 K13 **Kālpi** Uttar Pradesh, N India
158 G7 **Kalpin** Xinjiang Uygur Zizhiqu, NW China
149 P16 **Kalri Lake** ◎ SE Pakistan
143 R5 **Kāl Shūr** ≈ N Iran
39 N11 **Kalskag** Alaska, USA
Kalsø *see* Kalsoy
95 B18 **Kalsoy** *Dan.* Kalsø. *island* N Faeroe Islands
39 O9 **Kaltag** Alaska, USA
108 H7 **Kaltbrunn** Sankt Gallen, NE Switzerland
Kaltdorf *see* Pruszków
77 X14 **Kaltungo** Gombe, E Nigeria
126 K4 **Kaluga** Kaluzhskaya Oblast', W Russian Federation
155 J26 **Kalu Ganga** ≈ S Sri Lanka
82 J13 **Kalulushi** Copperbelt, C Zambia
180 M2 **Kalumburu** Western Australia
95 H23 **Kalundborg** Vestsjælland, E Denmark
82 K11 **Kalungwishi** ≈ N Zambia
149 T8 **Kalūr Kot** Punjab, E Pakistan
116 I6 **Kalush** *Pol.* Kałusz. Ivano-Frankivs'ka Oblast', W Ukraine
Kałusz *see* Kalush
110 N11 **Kałuszyn** Mazowieckie, C Poland
155 J26 **Kalutara** Western Province, SW Sri Lanka
Kaluwawa *see* Fergusson Island
126 I5 **Kaluzhskaya Oblast'** ◐ *province* W Russian Federation
119 E14 **Kalvarija** *Pol.* Kalwaria. Marijampol'e, S Lithuania
93 K15 **Kälviä** Länsi-Soumi, W Finland
109 U6 **Kalwang** Steiermark, E Austria
Kalwaria *see* Kalvarija
154 D13 **Kalyān** Mahārāshtra, W India
124 K16 **Kalyazin** Tverskaya Oblast', W Russian Federation
115 D18 **Kalydón** *anc.* Calydon. *site of ancient city* Dytikí Ellás, C Greece
115 M21 **Kálymnos** *var.* Kálimnos. Kálymnos, Dodekánisa, Greece, Aegean Sea
115 M21 **Kálymnos** *var.* Kálimnos. *island* Dodekánisa, Greece, Aegean Sea
117 O5 **Kalynivka** Kyyivs'ka Oblast', N Ukraine
117 N6 **Kalynivka** Vinnyts'ka Oblast', C Ukraine
42 M10 **Kama** *var.* Cama. Región Autónoma Atlántico Sur, SE Nicaragua
165 R9 **Kamaishi** *var.* Kamaisi. Iwate, Honshū, C Japan
Kamaisi *see* Kamaishi
118 H11 **Kamajai** Panevėžys, NE Lithuania
118 H13 **Kamajai** Utena, E Lithuania
149 U9 **Kamālia** Punjab, NE Pakistan
83 I14 **Kamalondo** North Western, NW Zambia
136 I13 **Kaman** Kırşehir, C Turkey
79 O20 **Kamanyola** Sud Kivu, E Dem. Rep. Congo
141 N14 **Kamarān** *island* W Yemen
55 R9 **Kamarang** W Guyana
Kāmāreddi/Kamareddy *see* Rāmāreddi
Kama Reservoir *see* Kamskoye Vodokhranilishche
148 K13 **Kamarod** Baluchistān, SW Pakistan
171 P14 **Kamaru** Pulau Buton, C Indonesia
147 N12 **Kamashi** Qashqadaryo Viloyati, S Uzbekistan
77 S13 **Kamba** Kebbi, NW Nigeria
Kambaeng Petch *see* Kamphaeng Phet
180 L12 **Kambalda** Western Australia
149 P13 **Kambar** *var.* Qambar. Sind, SE Pakistan
Kambara *see* Kabara
76 I14 **Kambia** W Sierra Leone
Kambos *see* Kámpos
79 N25 **Kambove** Katanga, SE Dem. Rep. Congo
Kambryk *see* Cambrai
123 V10 **Kamchatka** ≈ E Russian Federation
Kamchatka *see* Kamchatka, Poluostrov
Kamchatka Basin *see* Komandorskaya Basin
123 U10 **Kamchatka, Poluostrov** *Eng.* Kamchatka. *peninsula* E Russian Federation
123 V10 **Kamchatskaya Oblast'** ◐ *province* E Russian Federation
123 V10 **Kamchatskiy Zaliv** *gulf* E Russian Federation
114 N9 **Kamchiya** ≈ E Bulgaria
114 L9 **Kamchiya, Yazovir** ◎ E Bulgaria
Kamdesh *see* Kāmdeysh
149 T4 **Kāmdeysh** *var.* Kamdesh. Nūrestān, E Afghanistan
118 M13 **Kamen'** *Rus.* Kamen'. Vitsyebskaya Voblasts', N Belarus
Kamenets *see* Kamyanyets
Kamenets-Podol'skaya Oblast' *see* Khmel'nyts'ka Oblast'
Kamenets-Podol'skiy *see* Kam"yanets'-Podil's'kyy
113 Q18 **Kamenica** NE Macedonia
112 A11 **Kamenjak, Rt** *headland* NW Croatia
144 F8 **Kamenka** Zapadnyy Kazakhstan, NW Kazakhstan
125 O6 **Kamenka** Arkhangel'skaya Oblast', NW Russian Federation
126 6 **Kamenka** Penzenskaya Oblast', W Russian Federation
127 L8 **Kamenka** Voronezhskaya Oblast', W Russian Federation
Kamenka *see* Camenca
Kamenka *see* Kam"yanka
Kamenka-Bugskaya *see* Kam"yanka-Buz'ka
Kamenka Dneprovskaya *see* Kam"yanka-Dniprovs'ka
Kamen Kashirskiy *see* Kamin'-Kashyrs'kyy
126 L15 **Kamennomostskiy** Respublika Adygeya, SW Russian Federation
126 L11 **Kamenolomni** Rostovskaya Oblast', SW Russian Federation
127 P8 **Kamenskiy** Saratovskaya Oblast', W Russian Federation
Kamenskoye *see* Dniprodzerzhyns'k
126 L11 **Kamensk-Shakhtinskiy** Rostovskaya Oblast', SW Russian Federation
101 P15 **Kamenz** Sachsen, E Germany
164 J13 **Kameoka** Kyōto, Honshū, SW Japan
126 M3 **Kameshkovo** Vladimirskaya Oblast', W Russian Federation
164 C11 **Kami-Agata** Nagasaki, Tsushima, SW Japan
33 N10 **Kamiah** Idaho, NW USA
Kamień Koszyrski *see* Kamin'-Kashyrs'kyy
110 H9 **Kamień Krajeński** *Ger.* Kamin in Westpreussen. Kujawski-pomorskie, C Poland
111 F15 **Kamienna Góra** *Ger.* Landeshut, Landeshut in Schlesien. Dolnośląskie, SW Poland
110 D8 **Kamień Pomorski** *Ger.* Cummin in Pommern. Zachodnio-pomorskie, NW Poland
165 R5 **Kamiiso** Hokkaidō, NE Japan
79 L22 **Kamiji** Kasai Oriental, S Dem. Rep. Congo
165 T3 **Kamikawa** Hokkaidō, NE Japan
164 B15 **Kami-Koshiki-jima** *island* SW Japan
79 M23 **Kamina** Shaba, S Dem. Rep. Congo
Kamina *see* Kaintiba
42 C6 **Kaminaljuyú** *ruins* Guatemala, C Guatemala
Kamin in Westpreussen *see* Kamień Krajeński
116 J2 **Kamin'-Kashyrs'kyy** *Pol.* Kamień Koszyrski, *Rus.* Kamen Kashirskiy. Volyns'ka Oblast', NW Ukraine
165 Q5 **Kaminokuni** Hokkaidō, NE Japan
165 P10 **Kaminoyama** Yamagata, Honshū, C Japan
39 Q13 **Kamishak Bay** *bay* Alaska, USA
165 U4 **Kami-Shihoro** Hokkaidō, NE Japan
Kamishli *see* Al Qāmishlī
Kamissar *see* Kamsar
164 C11 **Kami-Tsushima** Nagasaki, Tsushima, SW Japan
79 O20 **Kamituga** Sud Kivu, E Dem. Rep. Congo
164 B17 **Kamiyaku** Kagoshima, Yaku-shima, SW Japan
9 N16 **Kamloops** British Columbia, SW Canada
107 G25 **Kamma** Sicilia, Italy, C Mediterranean Sea
192 K4 **Kammu Seamount** *undersea feature* N Pacific Ocean
109 U11 **Kamnik** *Ger.* Stein. C Slovenia
Kamniške Alpe *see* Kamniško-Savinjske Alpe
109 T10 **Kamniško-Savinjske Alpe** *var.* Kamniške Alpe, Sanntaler Alpen, *Ger* Steiner Alpen. ▲▲ N Slovenia
Kamo *see* Gavarr
165 O14 **Kamogawa** Chiba, Honshū, S Japan
149 W8 **Kāmoke** Punjab, E Pakistan
82 L13 **Kamoto** Eastern, E Zambia
109 V3 **Kamp** ≈ N Austria
81 F18 **Kampala** ● (Uganda) S Uganda
168 K11 **Kampar, Sungai** ≈ Sumatera, W Indonesia
98 L9 **Kampen** Overijssel, E Netherlands
79 N20 **Kampene** Maniema, E Dem. Rep. Congo
29 Q9 **Kampeska, Lake** ◎ South Dakota, N USA
167 O9 **Kamphaeng Phet** *var.* Kambaeng Petch. Kamphaeng Phet, W Thailand
Kampo *see* Campo, Cameroon
Kampo *see* Ntem, Cameroon/Equatorial Guinea
167 S12 **Kâmpóng Cham** *prev.* Kompong Cham. Kâmpóng Cham, C Cambodia
167 R12 **Kâmpóng Chhnăng** *prev.* Kompong. Kâmpóng Chhnăng, C Cambodia
167 R12 **Kâmpóng Khleăng** *prev.* Kompong Kleang. Siĕmréab, NW Cambodia
167 Q14 **Kâmpóng Saôm** *prev.* Kompong Som, Sihanoukville. Kâmpóng Saôm, SW Cambodia
167 R13 **Kâmpóng Spoe** *prev.* Kompong Speu. Kâmpóng Spœ, S Cambodia
121 O2 **Kámpos** *var.* Kambos. NW Cyprus
167 R14 **Kâmpôt** Kâmpôt, SW Cambodia
Kamptee *see* Kāmthi
77 O14 **Kampti** SW Burkina
Kampuchea *see* Cambodia
Kampuchea, Democratic *see* Cambodia
Kampuchea, People's Democratic Republic of *see* Cambodia
169 Q9 **Kampung Sirik** Sarawak, East Malaysia
9 V15 **Kamsack** Saskatchewan, S Canada
76 H13 **Kamsar** *var.* Kamissar. Guinée-Maritime, W Guinea
127 R4 **Kamskoye Ust'ye** Respublika Tatarstan, W Russian Federation
125 U14 **Kamskoye Vodokhranilishche** *var.* Kama Reservoir. ⊠ NW Russian Federation
154 I12 **Kāmthi** *prev.* Kamptee. Mahārāshtra, C India
Kamuela *see* Waimea
165 R3 **Kamuenai** Hokkaidō, NE Japan
165 T5 **Kamui-dake** △ Hokkaidō, NE Japan
165 R3 **Kamui-misaki** *headland* Hokkaidō, NE Japan
43 O15 **Kámuk, Cerro** ▲ SE Costa Rica
116 K7 **Kam"yanets'-Podil's'kyy** *Rus.* Kamenets-Podol'skiy. Khmel'nyts'ka Oblast', W Ukraine
117 Q6 **Kam"yanka** *Rus.* Kamenka. Cherkas'ka Oblast', C Ukraine
116 I5 **Kam"yanka-Buz'ka** *Rus.* Kamenka-Bugskaya. L'vivs'ka Oblast', NW Ukraine
117 T9 **Kam"yanka-Dniprovs'ka** *Rus.* Kamenka Dneprovskaya. Zaporiz'ka Oblast', SE Ukraine
119 F19 **Kamyanyets** *Rus.* Kamenets. Brestskaya Voblasts', SW Belarus
127 P9 **Kamyshin** Volgogradskaya Oblast', SW Russian Federation
127 Q13 **Kamyzyak** Astrakhanskaya Oblast', SW Russian Federation
12 K8 **Kanaaupscow** ≈ Québec, C Canada
36 K8 **Kanab** Utah, W USA
36 K9 **Kanab Creek** ≈ Arizona/Utah, SW USA
187 Y14 **Kanacea** *prev.* Kanathea. Taveuni, N Fiji
38 G17 **Kanaga Island** *island* Aleutian Islands, Alaska, USA
38 G17 **Kanaga Volcano** ▲ Kanaga Island, Alaska, USA
164 N14 **Kanagawa** *off.* Kanagawa-ken. ◐ *prefecture* Honshū, S Japan
Kanagawa-ken *see* Kanagawa
13 Q8 **Kanairiktok** ≈ Newfoundland and Labrador, E Canada
Kanaky *see* New Caledonia
79 K22 **Kananga** *prev.* Luluabourg. Kasai Occidental, S Dem. Rep. Congo
Kananur *see* Cannanore
Kanara *see* Karnātaka
36 J7 **Kanarraville** Utah, W USA
127 Q4 **Kanash** Chuvashskaya Respublika, W Russian Federation
Kanathea *see* Kanacea
21 Q4 **Kanawha River** ≈ West Virginia, NE USA
164 L13 **Kanayama** Gifu, Honshū, SW Japan
164 L11 **Kanazawa** Ishikawa, Honshū, SW Japan
166 M4 **Kanbalu** Sagaing, C Myanmar (Burma)
166 L8 **Kanbe** Yangon, SW Myanmar (Burma)
167 O11 **Kanchanaburi** Kanchanaburi, W Thailand
Kanchanjańghā *see* Kangchenjunga
Kānchenjunga *see* Kangchenjunga
145 V11 **Kanchingiz, Khrebet** ▲▲ E Kazakhstan
155 J19 **Kānchīpuram** *prev.* Conjeeveram. Tamil Nādu, SE India
149 N8 **Kandahār** *Per.* Qandahār. Kandahār, S Afghanistan
149 N9 **Kandahār** *Per.* Qandahār. ◐ *province* SE Afghanistan
Kandalakša *see* Kandalaksha
124 I5 **Kandalaksha** *var.* Kandalakša, *Fin.* Kantalahti. Murmanskaya Oblast', NW Russian Federation
Kandalaksha Gulf/Kandalakshskaya Guba *see* Kandalakshskiy Zaliv
124 K6 **Kandalakshskiy Zaliv** *var.* Kandalakshskaya Guba, *Eng.* Kandalaksha Gulf. *bay* NW Russian Federation
Kandalangodi *see* Kandalengoti
83 G17 **Kandalengoti** *var.* Kandalangodi. Ngamiland, NW Botswana
169 U13 **Kandangan** Borneo, C Indonesia
Kandau *see* Kandava
118 E8 **Kandava** *Ger.* Kandau. Tukums, W Latvia
Kandavu *see* Kadavu
77 R14 **Kandé** *var.* Kanté. NE Togo
101 F23 **Kandel** ▲ SW Germany
186 C7 **Kandep** Enga, W Papua New Guinea
149 R12 **Kandh kot** Sind, SE Pakistan
77 S13 **Kandi** N Benin
149 P14 **Kandiāro** Sind, SE Pakistan
136 F11 **Kandıra** Kocaeli, NW Turkey
183 S8 **Kandos** New South Wales, SE Australia
148 M16 **Kandrāch** *var.* Kanrach. Baluchistān, SW Pakistan
172 I4 **Kandreho** Mahajanga, C Madagascar
186 F7 **Kandrian** New Britain, E Papua New Guinea
Kandukur *see* Kondukūr
155 K25 **Kandy** Central Province, C Sri Lanka
144 I10 **Kandyagash** *Kaz.* Qandyaghash; *prev.* Oktyab'rsk. Aktyubinsk, W Kazakhstan
18 D12 **Kane** Pennsylvania, NE USA
64 I11 **Kane Fracture Zone** *tectonic feature* NW Atlantic Ocean
Kanëka *see* Kanëvka
78 G9 **Kanem** *off.* Préfecture du Kanem. ◐ *prefecture* W Chad
Kanem, Préfecture du *see* Kanem
38 D9 **Kāne'ohe** *var.* Kaneohe. O'ahu, Hawai'i, USA
Kanestron, Akra *see* Palioúri, Ákrotírio
Kanëv *see* Kaniv
124 M5 **Kanëvka** *var.* Kanëka. Murmanskaya Oblast', NW Russian Federation
126 K13 **Kanevskaya** Krasnodarskiy Kray, SW Russian Federation
Kanevskoye Vodokhranilishche *see* Kanivs'ke Vodoskhovyshche
165 P9 **Kaneyama** Yamagata, Honshū, C Japan
83 G20 **Kang** Kgalagadi, C Botswana
76 L13 **Kangaba** Koulikoro, SW Mali
136 M13 **Kangal** Sivas, C Turkey
143 O13 **Kangan** Būshehr, S Iran
Kangān *see* Bandar-e Kangān
168 J6 **Kangar** Perlis, Peninsular Malaysia
76 L13 **Kangaré** Sikasso, S Mali
182 F10 **Kangaroo Island** *island* South Australia
93 M17 **Kangasniemi** Isä-Suomi, E Finland
142 K6 **Kangāvar** *var.* Kangāwar. Kermānshāhān, W Iran
Kangāwar *see* Kangāvar
153 S11 **Kangchenjunga** *var.* Kānchenjunga, *Nep.* Kanchanjańghā. ▲ NE India
160 G9 **Kangding** *var.* Lucheng, *Tib.* Dardo. Sichuan, C China
169 U16 **Kangean, Kepulauan** *island group* S Indonesia
169 T16 **Kangean, Pulau** *island* Kepulauan Kangean, S Indonesia
67 U8 **Kangen** *var.* Kengen. ≈ SE Sudan
197 N14 **Kangerlussuaq** *Dan.* Sondre Strømfjord. ✈ Kitaa, W Greenland
197 Q15 **Kangertittivaq** *Dan.* Scoresby Sund. *fjord* E Greenland
167 O2 **Kangfang** Kachin State, N Myanmar (Burma)
163 X12 **Kanggye** N North Korea
197 P15 **Kangikajik** *var.* Kap Brewster. *headland* E Greenland
13 N5 **Kangiqsualujjuaq** *prev.* George River, Port-Nouveau-Québec. Québec, E Canada
12 L2 **Kangiqsujuaq** *prev.* Maricourt, Wakeham Bay. Québec, NE Canada
12 M4 **Kangirsuk** *prev.* Bellin, Payne. Québec, E Canada
Kangle *see* Wanzai
158 M16 **Kangmar** Xizang Zizhiqu, W China
158 J15 **Kangmar** Xizang Zizhiqu, W China
163 Y14 **Kangnŭng** *Jap.* Kōryō. NE South Korea
79 D18 **Kango** Estuaire, NW Gabon
152 I7 **Kāngra** Himāchal Pradesh, NW India
153 Q16 **Kangsabati Reservoir** ⊠ N India
159 O17 **Kangto** ▲ China/India
159 W12 **Kangxian** *var.* Kang Xian, Zuitai, Zuitaizi. Gansu, C China
Kang Xian *see* Kangxian
76 M15 **Kani** NW Ivory Coast
166 L4 **Kani** Sagaing, C Myanmar (Burma)
79 M23 **Kaniama** Katanga, S Dem. Rep. Congo
Kanibadam *see* Konibodom
169 V6 **Kanibongan** Sabah, East Malaysia
185 F17 **Kaniere** West Coast, South Island, New Zealand
185 G17 **Kaniere, Lake** ◎ South Island, New Zealand
188 E17 **Kanifaay** Yap, W Micronesia
125 O4 **Kanin Kamen'** ▲▲ NW Russian Federation

◆ Country ● Country Capital ◇ Dependent Territory ○ Dependent Territory Capital ◐ Administrative Regions ✈ International Airport ▲ Mountain ▲▲ Mountain Range △ Volcano ≈ River ◎ Lake ⊠ Reservoir

125 N3 **Kanin Nos** Nenetskiy Avtonomnyy Okrug, NW Russian Federation
125 N3 **Kanin Nos, Mys** cape NW Russian Federation
125 O5 **Kanin, Poluostrov** peninsula NW Russian Federation
139 V8 **Kānī Sakht** E Iraq
139 T3 **Kānī Sulaymān** N Iraq
165 Q6 **Kanita** Aomori, Honshū, C Japan
117 Q5 **Kaniv** Rus. Kanëv. Cherkas'ka Oblast', C Ukraine
182 K11 **Kaniva** Victoria, SE Australia
117 Q5 **Kanivs'ke Vodoskhovyshche** Rus. Kanevskoye Vodokhranilishche. ◎ C Ukraine
112 L8 **Kanjiža** Ger. Altkanischa, Hung. Magyarkanizsa, Ókanizsa; prev. Stara Kanjiža. Vojvodina, N Serbia
93 K18 **Kankaanpää** Länsi-Soumi, SW Finland
30 M12 **Kankakee** Illinois, N USA
31 O11 **Kankakee River** ~ Illinois/Indiana, N USA
76 K14 **Kankan** Haute-Guinée, E Guinea
154 K13 **Kānker** Chhattīsgarh, C India
76 J10 **Kankossa** Assaba, S Mauritania
169 N12 **Kanmaw Kyun** var. Kisseraing, Kithareng. island Mergui Archipelago, S Myanmar (Burma)
164 F12 **Kanmuri-yama** ▲ Kyūshū, SW Japan
21 R10 **Kannapolis** North Carolina, SE USA
93 L16 **Kannonkoski** Länsi-Soumi, C Finland
Kannur see Cannanore
93 K15 **Kannus** Länsi-Soumi, W Finland
77 V13 **Kano** Kano, N Nigeria
77 V13 **Kano** ◐ state N Nigeria
77 V13 **Kano** ✈ Kano, N Nigeria
164 G14 **Kan'onji** var. Kanonzi. Kagawa, Shikoku, SW Japan
Kanonzi see Kan'onji
26 M5 **Kanopolis Lake** ◎ Kansas, C USA
36 K5 **Kanosh** Utah, W USA
169 R9 **Kanowit** Sarawak, East Malaysia
164 C16 **Kanoya** Kagoshima, Kyūshū, SW Japan
152 L13 **Kānpur** Eng. Cawnpore. Uttar Pradesh, N India
Kanrach see Kandrāch
164 I14 **Kansai** ✈ (Ōsaka) Ōsaka, Honshū, SW Japan
27 R9 **Kansas** Oklahoma, C USA
26 L5 **Kansas** off. State of Kansas, also known as Jayhawker State, Sunflower State. ◐ state C USA
27 R4 **Kansas City** Kansas, C USA
27 R4 **Kansas City** Missouri, C USA
27 R3 **Kansas City** ✈ Missouri, C USA
27 P4 **Kansas River** ~ Kansas, C USA
122 L14 **Kansk** Krasnoyarskiy Kray, S Russian Federation
Kansu see Gansu
147 V7 **Kant** Chuyskaya Oblast', N Kyrgyzstan
Kantalahti see Kandalaksha
167 N16 **Kantang** var. Ban Kantang. Trang, SW Thailand
115 H25 **Kántanos** Kríti, Greece, E Mediterranean Sea
77 R12 **Kantchari** E Burkina
Kanté see Kandé
Kantemir see Cantemir
126 L9 **Kantemirovka** Voronezhskaya Oblast', W Russian Federation
167 R11 **Kantharalak** Si Sa Ket, E Thailand
Kantipur see Kathmandu
39 Q9 **Kantishna River** ~ Alaska, USA
191 S3 **Kanton** var. Abariringa, Canton Island; prev. Mary Island. atoll Phoenix Islands, C Kiribati
97 C20 **Kanturk** Ir. Ceann Toirc. Cork, SW Ireland
55 T11 **Kanuku Mountains** ▲▲ S Guyana
165 O12 **Kanuma** Tochigi, Honshū, S Japan
83 H20 **Kanye** Southern, SE Botswana
83 H17 **Kanyu** Ngamiland, C Botswana
166 M7 **Kanyutkwin** Pegu, C Myanmar (Burma)
79 M24 **Kanzenze** Shaba, SE Dem. Rep. Congo
193 Y15 **Kao** island Kotu Group, W Tonga
161 S14 **Kaohsiung** var. Gaoxiong, Jap. Takao, Takow. S Taiwan
161 S14 **Kaohsiung** ✈ S Taiwan
Kaokaona see Kirakira
83 B17 **Kaoko Veld** ▲▲ N Namibia
76 G11 **Kaolack** var. Kaolak. W Senegal
Kaolak see Kaolack
Kaolan see Lanzhou
186 M8 **Kaolo** San Jorge, N Solomon Islands
83 H14 **Kaoma** Western, W Zambia
38 B8 **Kapa'a** var. Kapaa. Kaua'i, Hawai'i, USA, C pacific Ocean
Kapaa see Kapa'a
113 J16 **Kapa Moračka** ▲ C Montenegro
137 V13 **Kapan** Rus. Kafan; prev. Ghap'an. SE Armenia
82 L13 **Kapandashila** Northern, NE Zambia
79 L23 **Kapanga** Katanga, S Dem. Rep. Congo
145 U15 **Kapchagay** Kaz. Kapshaghay. Almaty, SE Kazakhstan
145 V15 **Kapchagayskoye Vodokhranilishche** Kaz. Qapshagay Böyeni. ◎ SE Kazakhstan
99 F15 **Kapelle** Zeeland, SW Netherlands
99 G16 **Kapellen** Antwerpen, N Belgium
95 P15 **Kapellskär** Stockholm, C Sweden
81 H18 **Kapenguria** Rift Valley, W Kenya
109 V6 **Kapfenberg** Steiermark, C Austria
83 J14 **Kapiri Mposhi** Central, C Zambia
149 R4 **Kāpīsā** ◐ province E Afghanistan
12 G10 **Kapiskau** ~ Ontario, C Canada
184 K13 **Kapiti Island** island C New Zealand
78 K9 **Kapka, Massif du** ▲▲ E Chad
Kaplamada see Kaubalatmada, Gunung
22 H9 **Kaplan** Louisiana, S USA
Kaplangky, Plato see Gaplaňgyr Platosy
111 D19 **Kaplice** Ger. Kaplitz. Jihočeský Kraj, S Czech Republic
Kaplitz see Kaplice
Kapoche see Capoche
171 T12 **Kapocol** Papua, E Indonesia
167 N14 **Kapoe** Ranong, SW Thailand
Kapoeas see Kapuas, Sungai
81 G15 **Kapoeta** Eastern Equatoria, SE Sudan
111 I25 **Kapos** ~ S Hungary
111 H25 **Kaposvár** Somogy, SW Hungary
94 H13 **Kapp** Oppland, S Norway
100 I7 **Kappeln** Schleswig-Holstein, N Germany
Kaproncza see Koprivnica
109 P7 **Kaprun** Salzburg, C Austria
Kapshaghay see Kapchagay
Kapstad see Cape Town
Kapsukas see Marijampolė
171 Y13 **Kaptiau** Papua, E Indonesia
119 L19 **Kaptsevichy** Rus. Koptsevichi. Homyel'skaya Voblasts', SE Belarus
Kapuas Hulu, Banjaran/Kapuas Hulu, Pegunungan see Kapuas Mountains
169 S10 **Kapuas Mountains** Ind. Banjaran Kapuas Hulu, Pegunungan Kapuas Hulu. ▲▲ Indonesia/Malaysia
169 P11 **Kapuas, Sungai** ~ Borneo, N Indonesia
169 T13 **Kapuas, Sungai** prev. Kapoeas. ~ Borneo, C Indonesia
182 J9 **Kapunda** South Australia
152 H8 **Kapūrthala** Punjab, N India
12 G12 **Kapuskasing** Ontario, S Canada
14 D6 **Kapuskasing** ~ Ontario, S Canada
127 P11 **Kapustin Yar** Astrakhanskaya Oblast', SW Russian Federation
82 K11 **Kaputa** Northern, NE Zambia
111 G22 **Kapuvár** Győr-Moson-Sopron, NW Hungary
Kapydzhik, Gora see Qazangödağ
119 J17 **Kapyl'** Rus. Kopyl'. Minskaya Voblasts', C Belarus
43 N9 **Kara** var. Cara. Región Autónoma Atlántico Sur, E Nicaragua
77 R14 **Kara** var. Lama-Kara. NE Togo
77 Q14 **Kara** ~ N Togo
147 U7 **Kara-Balta** Chuyskaya Oblast', N Kyrgyzstan
144 L7 **Karabalyk** Kaz. Komsomol, var. Komsomolets. Kostanay, N Kazakhstan
144 G11 **Karabau** Atyrau, W Kazakhstan
146 E7 **Karabaur', Uval** Kaz. Korabavur Pastligi, Uzb. Qorabowur Kirlari. physical region Kazakhstan/Uzbekistan
Karabekaul see Garabekewül
Karabil', Vozvyshennost' see Garabil Belentligi
Kara-Bogaz-Gol see Garabogazköl
Kara-Bogaz-Gol, Zaliv see Garabogaz Aylagy
Kara-Bogazkol see Garabogazköl
145 R15 **Karaboget** Kaz. Qaraböget. Zhambyl, S Kazakhstan
136 H11 **Karabük** Karabük, NW Turkey
136 H11 **Karabük** ◐ province NW Turkey
122 L12 **Karabula** Krasnoyarskiy Kray, C Russian Federation
145 V14 **Karabulak** Kaz. Qarabulaq. Taldykorgan, SE Kazakhstan
145 Y11 **Karabulak** Kaz. Qarabulaq. Vostochnyy Kazakhstan, E Kazakhstan
145 Q17 **Karabulak** Kaz. Qarabulaq. Yuzhnyy Kazakhstan, S Kazakhstan
136 C17 **Kara Burnu** headland SW Turkey
144 K10 **Karabutak** Kaz. Qarabutaq. Aktyubinsk, W Kazakhstan
136 D12 **Karacabey** Bursa, NW Turkey
114 O12 **Karacaköy** İstanbul, NW Turkey
114 M12 **Karacaoğlan** Kırklareli, NW Turkey
Karachay-Cherkessia see Karachayevo-Cherkesskaya Respublika
126 L15 **Karachayevo-Cherkesskaya Respublika** Eng. Karachay-Cherkessia. ◐ autonomous republic SW Russian Federation
126 M15 **Karachayevsk** Karachayevo-Cherkesskaya Respublika, SW Russian Federation
126 J6 **Karachev** Bryanskaya Oblast', W Russian Federation
149 O16 **Karāchi** Sind, SE Pakistan
149 O16 **Karāchi** ✈ Sind, S Pakistan
Karácsonkő see Piatra-Neamţ
155 E15 **Karād** Mahārāshtra, W India
136 H16 **Karadağ** ▲ S Turkey
147 T10 **Karadar'ya** Uzb. Qoradaryo. ~ Kyrgyzstan/Uzbekistan
Karadeniz see Black Sea
Karadeniz Boğazi see İstanbul Boğazi
146 B13 **Karadepe** Balkan Welaýaty, W Turkmenistan
Karadzhar see Qorajar
Karaferiye see Véroia
Karagan see Garagan
145 R10 **Karaganda** Kaz. Qaraghandy. Karaganda, C Kazakhstan
145 R10 **Karaganda** off. Karagandinskaya Oblast', Kaz. Qaraghandy Oblysy. ◐ province C Kazakhstan
Karagandinskaya Oblast' see Karaganda
145 T10 **Karagayly** Kaz. Qaraghayly. Karaganda, C Kazakhstan
Karagel' see Garagöl'
123 U9 **Karaginskiy, Ostrov** island E Russian Federation
197 T1 **Karaginskiy Zaliv** bay E Russian Federation
137 P13 **Karagöl Dağları** ▲▲ NE Turkey
Karagumskiy Kanal see Garagum Kanaly
114 L13 **Karahisar** Edirne, NW Turkey
127 V3 **Karaidel'** Respublika Bashkortostan, W Russian Federation
127 V3 **Karaidel'skiy** Respublika Bashkortostan, W Russian Federation
114 L13 **Karaidemir Barajı** ◎ NW Turkey
155 J21 **Kāraikāl** Pondicherry, SE India
155 I22 **Kāraikkudi** Tamil Nādu, SE India
145 Y11 **Kara Irtysh** Rus. Chërnyy Irtysh. ~ NE Kazakhstan
143 N5 **Karaj** Tehrān, N Iran
168 K8 **Karak** Pahang, Peninsular Malaysia
Karak see Al Karak
147 T11 **Kara-Kabak** Oshskaya Oblast', SW Kyrgyzstan
Kara-Kala see Magtymguly
Karakala see Oqqal'a
Karakalpakstan, Respublika see Qoraqalpog'iston Respublikasi
Karakalpakya see Qoraqalpog'iston
Karakax see Moyu
158 G10 **Karakax He** ~ NW China
121 X8 **Karakaya Barajı** ◎ C Turkey
171 Q9 **Karakelang, Pulau** island N Indonesia
Karakılısse see Ağrı
Karak, Muḥāfaẓat al see Al Karak
147 Y7 **Karakol** prev. Przheval'sk. Issyk-Kul'skaya Oblast', NE Kyrgyzstan
147 X8 **Karakol** var. Karakolka. Issyk-Kul'skaya Oblast', NE Kyrgyzstan
Kara-Köl see Kara-Kul'
Karakolka see Karakol
149 W2 **Karakoram Highway** road China/Pakistan
149 Z3 **Karakoram Pass** Chin. Karakoram Shankou. pass C Asia
152 I3 **Karakoram Range** ▲▲ C Asia
Karakoram Shankou see Karakoram Pass
Karaköse see Ağrı
145 P14 **Karakoyyn, Ozero** Kaz. Qaraqoyyn. ◎ C Kazakhstan
83 F19 **Karakubis** Ghanzi, W Botswana
147 T9 **Kara-Kul'** Kir. Kara-Köl. Dzhalal-Abadskaya Oblast', W Kyrgyzstan
Karakul' see Qarokŭl
Karakul' see Qorako'l
147 U10 **Kara-Kul'dzha** Oshskaya Oblast', SW Kyrgyzstan
127 T3 **Karakulino** Udmurtskaya Respublika, NW Russian Federation
Karakul', Ozero see Qarokŭl
Kara Kum see Garagum
Kara Kum Canal/Karakumskiy Kanal see Garagum Kanaly
Karakumy, Peski see Garagum
83 E17 **Karakuwisa** Okavango, NE Namibia
122 M13 **Karam** Irkutskaya Oblast', S Russian Federation
Karamai see Karamay
169 T14 **Karamain, Pulau** island N Indonesia
136 I16 **Karaman** Karaman, S Turkey
136 H16 **Karaman** ◐ province S Turkey
114 M8 **Karamandere** ~ NE Bulgaria
158 J4 **Karamay** var. Karamai, Kelamayi; prev. Chin. K'o-la-ma-i. Xinjiang Uygur Zizhiqu, NW China
169 U14 **Karambu** Borneo, N Indonesia
185 H14 **Karamea** West Coast, South Island, New Zealand
185 H14 **Karamea** ~ South Island, New Zealand
185 G15 **Karamea Bight** gulf South Island, New Zealand
Karamet-Niyaz see Garamätnyýaz
158 K10 **Karamiran He** ~ NW China
147 S11 **Karamyk** Oshskaya Oblast', SW Kyrgyzstan
169 U17 **Karangasem** Bali, S Indonesia
154 H12 **Kāranja** Mahārāshtra, C India
Karanpur see Karanpura
152 F9 **Karanpura** var. Karanpur. Rājasthān, NW India
Karánsebes/Karansebesch see Caransebeş
145 T14 **Karaoy** Kaz. Qaraoy. Almaty, SE Kazakhstan
114 N7 **Karapelit** Rom. Stejarul. Dobrich, NE Bulgaria
136 I15 **Karapınar** Konya, C Turkey
83 D22 **Karas** ◐ district S Namibia
147 Y8 **Kara-Say** Issyk-Kul'skaya Oblast', NE Kyrgyzstan
83 E22 **Karasburg** Karas, S Namibia
Kara Sea see Karskoye More
92 K9 **Kárášjohka** var Karašjokka. ~ N Norway
Kárášjohka see Karasjok
92 L9 **Karasjok** Fin. Kaarasjoki, Lapp. Kárášjohka. Finnmark, N Norway
Karašjokka see Kárášjohka
Kara Strait see Karskiye Vorota, Proliv
145 N8 **Karasu** Kaz. Qarasū. Kostanay, N Kazakhstan
136 F11 **Karasu** Sakarya, NW Turkey
Kara Su see Mesta/Néstos
Karasubazar see Bilohirs'k
122 I12 **Karasuk** Novosibirskaya Oblast', C Russian Federation
145 U13 **Karatal** Kaz. Qaratal. ~ SE Kazakhstan
136 K17 **Karataş** Adana, S Turkey
145 Q16 **Karatau** Kaz. Qarataū. Zhambyl, S Kazakhstan
Karatau see Karatau, Khrebet
145 P16 **Karatau, Khrebet** var. Karatau, Kaz. Qarataū. ▲▲ S Kazakhstan
144 G13 **Karaton** Kaz. Qaraton. Atyrau, W Kazakhstan
164 C13 **Karatsu** var. Karatu. Saga, Kyūshū, SW Japan
Karatu see Karatsu
122 K8 **Karaul** Taymyrskiy (Dolgano-Nenetskiy) Avtonomnyy Okrug, N Russian Federation
Karaulbazar see Qorowulbozor
Karauzyak see Qorao'zak
115 D16 **Karáva** ▲ C Greece
Karavanke see Karawanken
115 F22 **Karavás** Kýthira, S Greece
113 J20 **Karavastasë, Laguna e** var. Kënet' e Karavastas, Kravasta Lagoon. lagoon W Albania
Karavastas, Kënet' e see Karavastasë, Laguna e
118 I5 **Karavere** Tartumaa, E Estonia
115 L23 **Karavonísia** island Kykládes, Greece, Aegean Sea
169 O15 **Karawang** prev. Krawang. Jawa, C Indonesia
109 T10 **Karawanken** Slvn. Karavanke. ▲▲ Austria/Serbia
Karaxahar see Kaidu He
137 R13 **Karayazı** Erzurum, NE Turkey
145 Q12 **Karazhal** Karaganda, C Kazakhstan
139 S9 **Karbalā'** var. Kerbala, Kerbela. S Iraq
94 L11 **Kårböle** Gävleborg, C Sweden
111 M23 **Karcag** Jász-Nagykun-Szolnok, E Hungary
Kardak see Imia
114 N7 **Kardam** Dobrich, NE Bulgaria
115 M22 **Kardámaina** Kos, Dodekánisa, Greece, Aegean Sea
Kardamila see Kardámyla
115 L18 **Kardámyla** var. Kardamila, Kardhámila. Chíos, E Greece
Kardeljevo see Ploče
Kardh see Qardho
Kardhámila see Kardámyla
Kardhítsa see Kardítsa
115 E16 **Kardítsa** var. Kardhítsa. Thessalía, C Greece
118 E4 **Kärdla** Ger. Kertel. Hiiumaa, W Estonia
Kărdžali see Kŭrdzhali
Karelia see Kareliya, Respublika
119 I16 **Karelichy** Pol. Korelicze, Rus. Korelichi. Hrodzyenskaya Voblasts', W Belarus
124 I10 **Kareliya, Respublika** prev. Karel'skaya ASSR, Eng. Karelia. ◐ autonomous republic NW Russian Federation
Karel'skaya ASSR see Kareliya, Respublika
81 E22 **Karema** Rukwa, W Tanzania
Karen see Hualien
83 I14 **Karenda** Central, C Zambia
167 N8 **Karen State** var. Kawthule State, Kayin State. ◐ state S Myanmar (Burma)
92 J10 **Karesuando** Fin. Kaaresuanto, Lapp. Gárasavvon. Norrbotten, N Sweden
Karet see Kâghet
Kareyz-e-Elyās/Kārez Iliās see Kārīz-e Elyās
122 J11 **Kargasok** Tomskaya Oblast', C Russian Federation
122 I12 **Kargat** Novosibirskaya Oblast', C Russian Federation
136 J11 **Kargı** Çorum, N Turkey
152 I5 **Kargil** Jammu and Kashmir, NW India
Kargilik see Yecheng
124 L11 **Kargopol'** Arkhangel'skaya Oblast', NW Russian Federation
110 F12 **Kargowa** Ger. Unruhstadt. Lubuskie, W Poland
77 X13 **Kari** Bauchi, E Nigeria
83 J15 **Kariba** Mashonaland West, N Zimbabwe
83 J16 **Kariba, Lake** ◎ Zambia/Zimbabwe
165 Q4 **Kariba-yama** ▲ Hokkaidō, NE Japan
83 C19 **Karibib** Erongo, C Namibia
Karies see Karyés
92 L9 **Karigasniemi** Lapp. Garegegasnjárga. Lappi, N Finland
184 J2 **Karikari, Cape** headland North Island, New Zealand
Karīmābād see Hunza
169 P12 **Karimata, Kepulauan** island group N Indonesia
169 P12 **Karimata, Pulau** island Kepulauan Karimata, N Indonesia
169 O11 **Karimata, Selat** strait W Indonesia
155 I14 **Karīmnagar** Andhra Pradesh, C India
186 C7 **Karimui** Chimbu, C Papua New Guinea
169 Q15 **Karimunjawa, Pulau** island S Indonesia
80 N12 **Karin** Woqooyi Galbeed, N Somalia
Kariot see Ikaría
93 L20 **Karis** Fin. Karjaa. Etelä-Suomi, SW Finland
Káristos see Kárystos
148 J4 **Kārīz-e Elyās** var. Kareyz-e-Elyās, Kārez Iliās. Herāt, NW Afghanistan
Karjaa see Karis
145 T10 **Karkaralinsk** Kaz. Qarqaraly. Karaganda, E Kazakhstan
186 D6 **Karkar Island** island N Papua New Guinea
143 N7 **Karkas, Kūh-e** ▲ C Iran
142 K8 **Karkheh, Rūd-e** ~ SW Iran
115 L20 **Karkinági** var Karkinagrio. Ikaría, Dodekánisa, Greece, Aegean Sea
Karkinagrio see Karkinági
117 R12 **Karkinits'ka Zatoka** Rus. Karkinitskiy Zaliv. gulf S Ukraine
Karkinitskiy Zaliv see Karkinits'ka Zatoka
93 L19 **Karkkila** Swe. Högfors. Uusimaa, S Finland
93 M19 **Kärkölä** Etelä-Suomi, S Finland
182 G9 **Karkoo** South Australia
Karkūk see Kirkūk
118 D5 **Kärla** Ger. Kergel. Saaremaa, W Estonia
Karleby see Kokkola
110 F7 **Karlino** Ger. Körlin an der Persante. Zachodnio-pomorskie, NW Poland
137 Q13 **Karlıova** Bingöl, E Turkey
117 U6 **Karlivka** Poltavs'ka Oblast', C Ukraine
Karl-Marx-Stadt see Chemnitz
Karlö see Hailuoto
112 C11 **Karlobag** It. Carlopago. Lika-Senj, W Croatia
112 D9 **Karlovac** Ger. Karlstadt, Hung. Károlyváros. Karlovac, C Croatia
112 C10 **Karlovac** off. Karlovačka Županija. ◐ province C Croatia
Karlovačka Županija see Karlovac
111 A16 **Karlovarsky Kraj** ◐ W Czech Republic
115 M19 **Karlovási** var. Neon Karlovási, Neon Karlovásion. Sámo, Greece, Aegean Sea
115 M19 **Karlovási** var. Néon Karlovásion, Néon Karlovasi. Sámos, Dodekánisa, Greece, Aegean Sea
114 J9 **Karlovo** prev. Levskigrad. Plovdiv, C Bulgaria
111 A16 **Karlovy Vary** Ger. Karlsbad; prev. Eng. Carlsbad. Karlovarský Kraj, W Czech Republic
Karlsbad see Karlovy Vary
95 L17 **Karlsborg** Västra Götaland, S Sweden
Karlsburg see Alba Iulia
95 L22 **Karlshamn** Blekinge, S Sweden
95 L16 **Karlskoga** Örebro, C Sweden
95 M22 **Karlskrona** Blekinge, S Sweden
101 G21 **Karlsruhe** var. Carlsruhe. Baden-Württemberg, SW Germany
95 K16 **Karlstad** Värmland, C Sweden
29 R3 **Karlstad** Minnesota, N USA
101 I18 **Karlstadt** Bayern, C Germany
Karlstadt see Karlovac
39 Q14 **Karluk** Kodiak Island, Alaska, USA
Karluk see Qarluq
119 O17 **Karma** Rus. Korma. Homyel'skaya Voblasts', SE Belarus
155 F14 **Karmāla** Mahārāshtra, W India
146 M11 **Karmana** Navoiy Viloyati, C Uzbekistan
138 G8 **Karmi'él** var. Carmiel. Northern, N Israel
95 B16 **Karmøy** island S Norway
152 I9 **Karnāl** Haryāna, N India
153 W15 **Karnaphuli Reservoir** ◎ NE India
155 F17 **Karnātaka** var. Kanara; prev. Maisur, Mysore. ◐ state W India
25 S13 **Karnes City** Texas, SW USA
109 P9 **Karnische Alpen** It. Alpi Carniche. ▲▲ Austria/Italy
114 M9 **Karnobat** Burgas, E Bulgaria
109 Q9 **Kärnten** off. Land Kärten, Eng. Carinthi, Slvn. Koroška. ◐ state S Austria
Karnul see Kurnool
83 K16 **Karoi** Mashonaland West, N Zimbabwe
Karol see Carei
Károly-Fehérvár see Alba Iulia
Károlyváros see Karlovac
82 M12 **Karonga** Northern, N Malawi
147 W10 **Karool-Tëbë** Narynskaya Oblast', C Kyrgyzstan
182 J9 **Karoonda** South Australia
149 S9 **Karor Lāl Esan** Punjab, E Pakistan
149 T11 **Karor Pacca** var. Kahror, var. Kahror Pakka. Punjab, E Pakistan
171 N12 **Karosa** var. Karosa. Sulawesi, C Indonesia
Karosa see Karosa
Karpaten see Carpathian Mountains
115 L22 **Karpáthio Pélagos** sea Dodekánisa, Greece, Aegean Sea
115 N24 **Kárpathos** Kárpathos, SE Greece
115 N24 **Kárpathos** It. Scarpanto; anc. Carpathos, Carpathus. island SE Greece
Karpathos Strait see Karpathou, Stenó
115 N24 **Karpathou, Stenó** var. Karpathos Strait, Scarpanto Strait. strait Dodekánisa, Greece, Aegean Sea
Karpaty see Carpathian Mountains
115 E17 **Karpenísi** prev. Karpenísion. Stereá Ellás, C Greece
Karpenision see Karpenísi
Karpilovka see Aktsyabrski
125 O8 **Karpogory** Arkhangel'skaya Oblast', NW Russian Federation
180 I7 **Karratha** Western Australia
137 S12 **Kars** var. Qars. Kars, NE Turkey
137 S12 **Kars** var. Qars. ◐ province NE Turkey
145 O12 **Karsakpay** Kaz. Qarsaqbay. Karaganda, C Kazakhstan
93 L15 **Kärsämäki** Oulu, C Finland
Karsau see Kārsava
118 K9 **Kārsava** Ger. Karsau; prev. Rus. Korsovka. Ludza, E Latvia
Karshi see Garşy
Karshi see Qarshi, Uzbekistan
Karshinskaya Step see Qarshi Cho'li
Karshinskiy Kanal see Qarshi Kanali
84 I5 **Karskiye Vorota, Proliv** Eng. Kara Strait. strait N Russian Federation
122 J6 **Karskoye More** Eng. Kara Sea. sea Arctic Ocean
93 L17 **Karstula** Länsi-Soumi, C Finland
127 Q5 **Karsun** Ul'yanovskaya Oblast', W Russian Federation
122 F11 **Kartaly** Chelyabinskaya Oblast', C Russian Federation
18 E13 **Karthaus** Pennsylvania, NE USA
110 I7 **Kartuzy** Pomorskie, NW Poland
165 R8 **Karumai** Iwate, Honshū, C Japan
181 U4 **Karumba** Queensland, NE Australia
142 L10 **Kārūn** var. Rūd-e Kārūn. ~ SW Iran
92 K13 **Karungi** Norrbotten, N Sweden
92 K13 **Karunki** Lappi, N Finland
Kārūn, Rūd-e see Kārūn
155 H21 **Karūr** Tamil Nādu, SE India
93 K17 **Karvia** Länsi-Soumi, SW Finland
111 J17 **Karviná** Ger. Karwin, Pol. Karwina; prev. Nová Karvinná. Moravskoslezský Krajj, E Czech Republic
155 E17 **Kārwār** Karnātaka, W India
108 M7 **Karwendelgebirge** ▲▲ Austria/Germany
Karwin/Karwina see Karviná
115 I14 **Karyés** var. Karies. Ágion Óros, N Greece
115 I19 **Kárystos** var. Káristos. Évvoia, C Greece
136 E17 **Kaş** Antalya, SW Turkey
39 Y14 **Kasaan** Prince of Wales Island, Alaska, USA
164 I13 **Kasai** Hyōgo, Honshū, SW Japan
79 K21 **Kasai** var. Cassai, Kassai. ~ Angola/Dem. Rep. Congo
79 K22 **Kasai Occidental** off. Région Kasai Occidental. ◐ region S Dem. Rep. Congo
Kasai Occidental, Région see Kasai Occidental
79 L21 **Kasai Oriental** off. Région Kasai Oriental. ◐ region C Dem. Rep. Congo
Kasai Oriental, Région see Kasai Oriental
79 L24 **Kasaji** Katanga, S Dem. Rep. Congo
82 L12 **Kasama** Northern, N Zambia
Kasan see Koson
83 H16 **Kasane** North-West, NE Botswana
81 E23 **Kasanga** Rukwa, W Tanzania
79 G21 **Kasangulu** Bas-Congo, W Dem. Rep. Congo
Kasansay see Kosonsoy
Kasargen see Kasari
155 E20 **Kāsaragod** Kerala, SW India
118 P13 **Kasari** var. Kasari Jõgi, Ger. Kasargen. ~ W Estonia
Kasari Jõgi see Kasari
8 L11 **Kasba Lake** ◎ Northwest Territories, Nunavut N Canada
Kaschau see Košice
164 B16 **Kaseda** Kagoshima, Kyūshū, SW Japan
83 I14 **Kasempa** North Western, NW Zambia
79 O24 **Kasenga** Katanga, SE Dem. Rep. Congo
79 P17 **Kasenye** var. Kasenyi. Orientale, NE Dem. Rep. Congo
Kasenyi see Kasenye
79 O19 **Kasese** Maniema, E Dem. Rep. Congo
81 E18 **Kasese** SW Uganda
152 J11 **Kāsganj** Uttar Pradesh, N India
143 U4 **Kashaf Rūd** ~ NE Iran
143 N7 **Kāshān** Eşfahān, C Iran
126 M10 **Kashary** Rostovskaya Oblast', SW Russian Federation
39 O12 **Kashegelok** Alaska, USA
Kashgar see Kashi
158 E7 **Kashi** Chin. Kaxgar, K'o-shih, Uigh. Kashgar. Xinjiang Uygur Zizhiqu, NW China
164 J14 **Kashihara** var. Kasihara. Nara, Honshū, SW Japan
165 P13 **Kashima-nada** gulf S Japan
124 K15 **Kashin** Tverskaya Oblast', W Russian Federation
152 K10 **Kāshīpur** Uttarānchal, N India
126 L4 **Kashira** Moskovskaya Oblast', W Russian Federation
165 N11 **Kashiwazaki** var. Kasiwazaki. Niigata, Honshū, C Japan
Kashkadar'inskaya Oblast' see Qashqadaryo Viloyati
143 T5 **Kāshmar** var. Turshiz; prev. Solṭānābād, Torshiz. Khorāsān, NE Iran
Kashmir see Jammu and Kashmir
149 R12 **Kashmor** Sind, SE Pakistan
149 S5 **Kashmūnd Ghar** Eng. Kashmund Range. ▲▲ E Afghanistan
Kashmund Range see Kashmūnd Ghar
Kasi see Vārānasi
153 O12 **Kasia** Uttar Pradesh, N India
39 N12 **Kasigluk** Alaska, USA
Kasihara see Kashihara
39 R12 **Kasilof** Alaska, USA
Kasimköj see General Toshevo
126 M4 **Kasimov** Ryazanskaya Oblast', W Russian Federation
79 P18 **Kasindi** Nord Kivu, E Dem. Rep. Congo
82 M12 **Kasitu** ~ N Malawi
Kasiwazaki see Kashiwazaki
30 L14 **Kaskaskia River** ~ Illinois, N USA
93 J17 **Kaskinen** Swe. Kaskö. Länsi-Soumi, W Finland
Kaskö see Kaskinen
Kas Kong see Kŏng, Kaôh
9 O17 **Kaslo** British Columbia, SW Canada
Kåsmark see Kežmarok
169 T12 **Kasongan** Borneo, C Indonesia
79 N21 **Kasongo** Maniema, E Dem. Rep. Congo

◆ Country ● Country Capital ◇ Dependent Territory ○ Dependent Territory Capital ◐ Administrative Regions ✈ International Airport ▲ Mountain ▲▲ Mountain Range Volcano ~ River ◎ Lake ◎ Reservoir

79 H22 **Kasongo-Lunda** Bandundu, SW Dem. Rep. Congo
115 M24 **Kásos** island S Greece
Kasos Strait see Kasou, Stenó
115 M25 **Kasou, Stenó** var. Kasos Strait. strait Dodekánisa/Kríti, Greece, Aegean Sea
137 T10 **Kaspi** C Georgia
114 M8 **Kaspichan** Shumen, NE Bulgaria
Kaspīy Mangy Oypaty see Caspian Depression
127 Q16 **Kaspiysk** Respublika Dagestan, SW Russian Federation
Kaspiyskiy see Lagan'
Kaspiyskoye More/Kaspiy Tengizi see Caspian Sea
Kassa see Košice
Kassai see Kasai
80 I9 **Kassala** Kassala, E Sudan
80 H9 **Kassala** ⬖ state NE Sudan
115 G15 **Kassándra** prev. Pallíni; anc. Pallene. peninsula NE Greece
115 G15 **Kassándras, Akrotírio** cape N Greece
115 H15 **Kassándras, Kólpos** var. Kólpos Toronaíos. gulf N Greece
139 Y11 **Kassārah** E Iraq
101 I15 **Kassel** prev. Cassel. Hessen, C Germany
74 M6 **Kasserine** var. Al Qaşrayn. W Tunisia
14 J14 **Kasshabog Lake** ◎ Ontario, SE Canada
139 O5 **Kassīr, Sabkhat al** ◎ E Syria
29 W10 **Kasson** Minnesota, N USA
115 C17 **Kassópeia** Var. Kassópi. site of ancient city Ípeiros, W Greece
Kassópi see Kassópeia
115 N24 **Kastállou, Akrotírio** headland Kárpathos, SE Greece
136 I11 **Kastamonu** var. Castamoni, Kastamuni. Kastamonu, N Turkey
136 I10 **Kastamonu** var. Kastamuni. ⬖ province N Turkey
Kastamuni see Kastamonu
115 E14 **Kastaneá** Kentrikí Makedonía, N Greece
Kastélli see Kíssamos
Kastellórizon see Megísti
95 N21 **Kastlösa** Kalmar, S Sweden
115 D14 **Kastoría** Dytikí Makedonía, N Greece
126 K7 **Kastornoye** Kurskaya Oblast', W Russian Federation
115 I21 **Kástro** Sífnos, Kykládes, Greece, Aegean Sea
95 J23 **Kastrup** ✈ (København) København, E Denmark
119 Q17 **Kastsyukovichy** Rus. Kostyukovichi. Mahilyowskaya Voblasts', E Belarus
119 O18 **Kastsyukowka** Rus. Kostyukovka. Homyel'skaya Voblasts', SE Belarus
164 D13 **Kasuga** Fukuoka, Kyūshū, SW Japan
164 L13 **Kasugai** Aichi, Honshū, SW Japan
81 E21 **Kasulu** Kigoma, W Tanzania
164 I12 **Kasumi** Hyōgo, Honshū, SW Japan
127 R17 **Kasumkent** Respublika Dagestan, SW Russian Federation
82 M13 **Kasungu** Central, C Malawi
149 W9 **Kasūr** Punjab, E Pakistan
83 G15 **Kataba** Western, W Zambia
19 R4 **Katahdin, Mount** ▲ Maine, NE USA
79 M20 **Katako-Kombe** Kasai Oriental, C Dem. Rep. Congo
39 T12 **Katalla** Alaska, USA
Katana see Qaṭanā
79 L24 **Katanga** off. Région du Katanga, prev Shaba. ⬖ region SE Dem. Rep. Congo
122 M11 **Katanga** ~ C Russian Federation
Katanga, Région du see Katanga
154 J11 **Katāngi** Madhya Pradesh, C India
180 J13 **Katanning** Western Australia
181 P8 **Kata Tjuta** var. Mount Olga. ▲ Northern Territory, C Australia
Katawaz see Zarghūn Shahr
151 Q22 **Katchall Island** island Nicobar Islands, India, NE Indian Ocean
115 F14 **Kateríni** Kentrikí Makedonía, N Greece
117 P7 **Katerynopil'** Cherkas'ka Oblast', C Ukraine
166 M3 **Katha** Sagaing, N Myanmar (Burma)
181 P2 **Katherine** Northern Territory, N Australia
154 B11 **Kāthiāwār Peninsula** peninsula W India
153 P11 **Kathmandu** prev. Kantipur. ● (Nepal) Central, C Nepal
152 H7 **Kathua** Jammu and Kashmir, NW India
76 L12 **Kati** Koulikoro, SW Mali
153 R13 **Katihār** Bihār, NE India
184 N7 **Katikati** Bay of Plenty, North Island, New Zealand
83 H16 **Katima Mulilo** Caprivi, NE Namibia
77 N15 **Katiola** C Ivory Coast
191 V10 **Katiu** atoll Îles Tuamotu, C French Polynesia
117 N12 **Katlabukh, Ozero** ◎ SW Ukraine
39 P14 **Katmai, Mount** ▲ Alaska, USA
154 J9 **Katni** Madhya Pradesh, C India
115 D19 **Káto Achaïa** var. Kato Ahaia, Káto Akhaía. Dytikí Ellás, S Greece
Kato Ahaia/Káto Akhaía see Káto Achaïa
121 P2 **Kato Lakatámeia** var. Kato Lakatamia. C Cyprus
Kato Lakatamia see Kato Lakatámeia
79 N22 **Katompi** Katanga, SE Dem. Rep. Congo
83 K14 **Katondwe** Lusaka, C Zambia
114 H12 **Káto Nevrokópi** prev. Káto Nevrokópion. Anatolikí Makedonía kai Thráki, NE Greece
Káto Nevrokópion see Káto Nevrokópi
81 E18 **Katonga** ~ S Uganda
115 F15 **Káto Ólympos** ▲▲ C Greece
115 D17 **Katoúna** Dytikí Ellás, C Greece
115 E19 **Káto Vlasiá** Dytikí Makedonía, S Greece
111 J16 **Katowice** Ger. Kattowitz. Śląskie, S Poland
153 S15 **Kātoya** West Bengal, NE India
136 E16 **Katrançik Dağı** ▲▲ SW Turkey
95 N16 **Katrineholm** Södermanland, C Sweden
96 I11 **Katrine, Loch** ◎ C Scotland, UK
77 V12 **Katsina** Katsina, N Nigeria
77 U12 **Katsina** ⬖ state N Nigeria
67 P8 **Katsina Ala** ~ S Nigeria
164 C13 **Katsumoto** Nagasaki, Iki, SW Japan
165 P13 **Katsuta** var. Katuta. Ibaraki, Honshū, S Japan
165 O14 **Katsuura** var. Katuura. Chiba, Honshū, S Japan
164 K12 **Katsuyama** var. Katuyama. Fukui, Honshū, SW Japan
164 H12 **Katsuyama** Okayama, Honshū, SW Japan
Kattakurgan see Kattaqo'rg'on
147 N11 **Kattaqo'rg'on** Rus. Kattakurgan. Samarqand Viloyati, C Uzbekistan
115 O23 **Kattavía** Ródos, Dodekánisa, Greece, Aegean Sea
95 I21 **Kattegat** Dan. Kattegatt. strait N Europe
Kattegatt see Kattegat
95 P19 **Katthammarsvik** Gotland, SE Sweden
Kattowitz see Katowice
122 J13 **Katun'** ~ S Russian Federation
Katuta see Katsuta
Katuura see Katsuura
Katuyama see Katsuyama
Katwijk see Katwijk aan Zee
98 G11 **Katwijk aan Zee** var. Katwijk. Zuid-Holland, W Netherlands
38 B8 **Kaua'i** var. Kauai. island Hawaiian Islands, Hawai'i, USA, C PacificOcean
Kauai see Kaua'i
38 C8 **Kaua'i Channel** var. Kauai Channel. channel Hawai'i, USA, C Pacific Ocean
Kauai Channel see Kaua'i Channel
171 R13 **Kaubalatmada, Gunung** ▲ Pulau Buru, E Indonesia
191 U10 **Kauehi** atoll Îles Tuamotu, C French Polynesia
Kauen see Kaunas
101 K24 **Kaufbeuren** Bayern, S Germany
25 U7 **Kaufman** Texas, SW USA
101 I15 **Kaufungen** Hessen, C Germany
93 K17 **Kauhajoki** Länsi-Soumi, W Finland
93 K16 **Kauhava** Länsi-Soumi, W Finland
30 M7 **Kaukauna** Wisconsin, N USA
92 L11 **Kaukonen** Lappi, N Finland
38 A8 **Kaulakahi Channel** channel Hawai'i, USA, C Pacific Ocean
38 E9 **Kaunakakai** Moloka'i, Hawai'i, USA, C Pacific Ocean
38 F12 **Kaunā Point** var. Kauna Point. headland Hawai'i, USA, C Pacific Ocean
Kauna Point see Kaunā Point
118 F13 **Kaunas** Ger. Kauen, Pol. Kowno; prev. Rus. Kovno. Kaunas, C Lithuania
118 F13 **Kaunas** ⬖ province C Lithuania
186 C6 **Kaup** East Sepik, NW Papua New Guinea
77 U12 **Kaura Namoda** Zamfara, NW Nigeria
Kaushany see Căuşeni
93 K16 **Kaustinen** Länsi-Soumi, W Finland
99 M23 **Kautenbach** Diekirch, NE Luxembourg
92 K10 **Kautokeino** Lapp. Guovdageaidnu. Finnmark, N Norway
Kavadar see Kavadarci
113 P19 **Kavadarci** Turk. Kavadar. C Macedonia
Kavaja see Kavajë
113 K20 **Kavajë** It. Cavaia, Kavaja. Tiranë, W Albania
114 M13 **Kavak Çayı** ~ NW Turkey
Kavakli see Topolovgrad
114 I13 **Kavála** prev. Kaválla. Anatolikí Makedonía kai Thráki, NE Greece
114 I13 **Kaválas, Kólpos** gulf Aegean Sea, NE Mediterranean Sea
155 J17 **Kāvali** Andhra Pradesh, E India
Kaválla see Kavála
Kavango see Cubango/Okavango
155 C21 **Kavaratti** Lakshadweep, SW India
114 O8 **Kavarna** Dobrich, NE Bulgaria
118 G12 **Kavarskas** Utena, E Lithuania
76 I13 **Kavendou** ▲ C Guinea
Kavengo see Cubango/Okavango
155 F20 **Kāveri** var. Cauvery. ~ S India
186 G5 **Kavieng** var. Kaewieng. New Ireland, NE Papua New Guinea
83 H16 **Kavimba** North-West, NE Botswana
83 I15 **Kavingu** Southern, S Zambia
143 Q6 **Kavīr, Dasht-e** var. Great Salt Desert. salt pan N Iran
Kavirondo Gulf see Winam Gulf
Kavkaz see Caucasus
95 K23 **Kävlinge** Skåne, S Sweden
82 G12 **Kavungo** Moxico, E Angola
165 Q8 **Kawabe** Akita, Honshū, C Japan
165 R9 **Kawai** Iwate, Honshū, C Japan
38 A8 **Kawaihoa Point** headland Ni'ihau, Hawai'i, USA, C Pacific Ocean
184 K3 **Kawakawa** Northland, North Island, New Zealand
82 I13 **Kawama** North Western, NW Zambia
82 K11 **Kawambwa** Luapula, N Zambia
154 K11 **Kawardha** Chhattīsgarh, C India
14 I14 **Kawartha Lakes** ◎ Ontario, SE Canada
165 O13 **Kawasaki** Kanagawa, Honshū, S Japan
171 R12 **Kawassi** Pulau Obi, E Indonesia
165 R6 **Kawauchi** Aomori, Honshū, C Japan
184 L5 **Kawau Island** island N New Zealand
184 N10 **Kaweka Range** ▲▲ North Island, New Zealand
Kawelecht see Puhja
184 O8 **Kawerau** Bay of Plenty, North Island, New Zealand
184 L8 **Kawhia** Waikato, North Island, New Zealand
184 K8 **Kawhia Harbour** inlet North Island, New Zealand
35 V8 **Kawich Peak** ▲ Nevada, W USA
35 V9 **Kawich Range** ▲▲ Nevada, W USA
14 G12 **Kawigamog Lake** ◎ Ontario, S Canada
171 P9 **Kawio, Kepulauan** island group N Indonesia
167 N9 **Kawkareik** Karen State, S Myanmar (Burma)
27 O8 **Kaw Lake** ⊠ Oklahoma, C USA
166 M3 **Kawlin** Sagaing, N Myanmar (Burma)
Kawm Umbū see Kôm Ombo
Kawthule State see Karen State
Kaxgar see Kashi
158 D7 **Kaxgar He** ~ NW China
158 J5 **Kax He** ~ NW China
77 P12 **Kaya** C Burkina
167 N6 **Kayah State** ⬖ state C Myanmar (Burma)
39 T12 **Kayak Island** island Alaska, USA
114 M11 **Kayalıköy Barajı** ⊠ NW Turkey
155 G23 **Kāyankulam** Kerala, SW India
166 M8 **Kayan** Yangon, SW Myanmar (Burma)
Kayangel Islands see Ngcheangel
169 V9 **Kayan, Sungai** prev. Kajan. ~ Borneo, C Indonesia
144 F14 **Kaydak, Sor** salt flat SW Kazakhstan
Kaydanovo see Dzyarzhynsk Belarus
37 N9 **Kayenta** Arizona, SW USA
76 J11 **Kayes** Kayes, W Mali
76 J11 **Kayes** ⬖ region SW Mali
Kayin State see Karen State
145 U10 **Kaynar** var. Kajnar. Vostochnyy Kazakhstan, E Kazakhstan
Kaynary see Căinari
83 H15 **Kayoya** Western, W Zambia
Kayrakkum see Qayroqqum
Kayrakkumskoye Vodokhranilishche see Qayroqqum, Obanbori
136 K14 **Kayseri** var. Kaisaria; anc. Caesarea Mazaca, Mazaca. Kayseri, C Turkey
136 K14 **Kayseri** var. Kaisaria. ⬖ province C Turkey
36 L2 **Kaysville** Utah, W USA
Kayyngdy see Kaindy
14 L11 **Kazabazua** Québec, SE Canada
14 L12 **Kazabazua** ~ Québec, SE Canada
123 Q7 **Kazach'ye** Respublika Sakha (Yakutiya), NE Russian Federation
Kazakdar'ya see Qozoqdaryo
146 E9 **Kazakhlyshor, Solonchak** var. Solonchak Shorkazakhly. salt marsh NW Turkmenistan
Kazakhskaya SSR/Kazakh Soviet Socialist Republic see Kazakhstan
145 R9 **Kazakhskiy Melkosopochnik** Eng. Kazakh Uplands, Kirghiz Steppe, Kaz. Saryarqa. uplands C Kazakhstan
144 L12 **Kazakhstan** off. Republic of Kazakhstan, var. Kazakstan, Kaz. Qazaqstan, Qazaqstan Respublikasy; prev. Kazakh Soviet Socialist Republic, Rus. Kazakhskaya SSR. ◆ republic C Asia
Kazakhstan, Republic of see Kazakhstan
Kazakh Uplands see Kazakhskiy Melkosopochnik
Kazakstan see Kazakhstan
144 L14 **Kazalinsk** Kzyl-Orda, S Kazakhstan
127 R4 **Kazan'** Respublika Tatarstan, W Russian Federation
8 M10 **Kazan** ~ Nunavut, NW Canada
127 R4 **Kazan'** ✈ Respublika Tatarstan, W Russian Federation
Kazandzhik see Bereket
117 R8 **Kazanka** Mykolayivs'ka Oblast', S Ukraine
Kazanketken see Qozonketkan
Kazanlik see Kazanlŭk
114 J9 **Kazanlŭk** prev. Kazanlik. Stara Zagorat, C Bulgaria
165 Y16 **Kazan-rettō** Eng. Volcano Islands. island group SE Japan
117 V12 **Kazantip, Mys** headland S Ukraine
147 U9 **Kazarman** Narynskaya Oblast', C Kyrgyzstan
Kazatin see Kozyatyn
Kazbegi see Qazbegi
Kazbegi see Kazbek
137 T9 **Kazbek** var. Kazbegi, Geor. Mqinvartsveri. ▲ N Georgia
82 M13 **Kazembe** Eastern, NE Zambia
143 N11 **Kāzerūn** Fārs, S Iran
125 R12 **Kazhym** Respublika Komi, NW Russian Federation
Kazi Ahmad see Qāzi Ahmad
Kazi Magomed see Qazimämmäd
136 H16 **Kazımkarabekir** Karaman, S Turkey
111 M20 **Kazincbarcika** Borsod-Abaúj-Zemplén, NE Hungary
119 H17 **Kazlowshchyna** Pol. Kozlowszczyzna, Rus. Kozlovshchina. Hrodzyenskaya Voblasts', W Belarus
119 E14 **Kazlų Rūda** Marijampolė, S Lithuania
144 E9 **Kaztalovka** Zapadnyy Kazakhstan, W Kazakhstan
79 K22 **Kazumba** Kasai Occidental, S Dem. Rep. Congo
165 Q8 **Kazuno** Akita, Honshū, C Japan
Kazvin see Qazvīn
118 J12 **Kaz'yany** Rus. Koz'yany. Vitsyebskaya Voblasts', NW Belarus
122 H9 **Kazym** ~ N Russian Federation
110 H10 **Kcynia** Ger. Exin. Kujawsko-pomorskie, C Poland
Kéa see Tziá
38 H11 **Kea'au** var. Keaau. Hawai'i, USA, C Pacific Ocean
Keaau see Kea'au
38 F11 **Keāhole Point** var. Keahole Point. headland Hawai'i, USA, C Pacific Ocean
38 G12 **Kealakekua** Hawai'i, USA, C Pacific Ocean
38 H11 **Kea, Mauna** ▲ Hawaii, USA
37 N10 **Keams** Arizona, SW USA
Kéamu see Aneityum
29 O16 **Kearney** Nebraska, C USA
36 L3 **Kearns** Utah, W USA
115 H20 **Kéas, Stenó** strait SE Greece
137 O14 **Keban Barajı** dam C Turkey
137 O14 **Keban Barajı** ⊠ C Turkey
77 S13 **Kebbi** ⬖ state NW Nigeria
76 G10 **Kébémèr** NW Senegal
74 M7 **Kebili** var. Qibilī. C Tunisia
138 H4 **Kebir, Nahr el** ~ NW Syria
80 A10 **Kebkabiya** Northern Darfur, W Sudan
92 I11 **Kebnekaise** ▲ N Sweden
81 M14 **K'ebrī Dehar** Somali, E Ethiopia
148 K15 **Kech** ~ SW Pakistan
10 K10 **Kechika** ~ British Columbia, W Canada
111 K23 **Kecskemét** Bács-Kiskun, C Hungary
168 J6 **Kedah** ⬖ state Peninsular Malaysia
118 F12 **Kėdainiai** Kaunas, C Lithuania
Kedder see Kehra
13 N13 **Kedgwick** New Brunswick, SE Canada
169 R16 **Kediri** Jawa, C Indonesia
171 Y13 **Kedir Sarmi** Papua, E Indonesia
163 V7 **Kedong** Heilongjiang, NE China
76 I12 **Kédougou** SE Senegal
122 I11 **Kedrovyy** Tomskaya Oblast', C Russian Federation
111 H16 **Kędzierzyn-Kozle** Ger. Heydebrech. Opolskie, S Poland
8 H8 **Keele** ~ Northwest Territories, NW Canada
10 K6 **Keele Peak** ▲ Yukon Territory, NW Canada
Keelung see Chilung
19 N10 **Keene** New Hampshire, NE USA
99 H17 **Keerbergen** Vlaams Brabant, C Belgium
83 E21 **Keetmanshoop** Karas, S Namibia
12 A11 **Keewatin** Ontario, S Canada
29 V4 **Keewatin** Minnesota, N USA
Kefallinía see Kefallonía
115 B18 **Kefallonía** var. Kefallinía. island Iónioi Nísoi, Greece, C Mediterranean Sea
115 M22 **Kéfalos** Kos, Dodekánisa, Greece, Aegean Sea
171 Q17 **Kefamenanu** Timor, C Indonesia
138 F10 **Kefar Sava** var. Kfar Saba. Central, C Israel
Kefe see Feodosiya
77 V15 **Keffi** Nassarawa, C Nigeria
92 H4 **Keflavík** Reykjanes, W Iceland
92 H4 **Keflavík** ✈ (Reykjavík) Reykjanes, W Iceland
Kegalee see Kegalla
155 J25 **Kegalla** var. Kegalee, Kegalle. Sabaragamuwa Province, C Sri Lanka
Kegalle see Kegalla
Kegayli see Kegeyli
Kegel see Keila
145 W16 **Kegen** Almaty, SE Kazakhstan
146 H7 **Kegeyli** Rus. Kegayli. Qoraqalpoghiston Respublikasi, W Uzbekistan
101 F22 **Kehl** Baden-Württemberg, SW Germany
118 H3 **Kehra** Ger. Kedder. Harjumaa, NW Estonia
117 U6 **Kehychivka** Kharkivs'ka Oblast', E Ukraine
97 L17 **Keighley** N England, UK
Kei Islands see Kai, Kepulauan
Keijō see Sŏul
118 G3 **Keila** Ger. Kegel. Harjumaa, NW Estonia
Keilberg see Klínovec
83 F23 **Keimoes** Northern Cape, W South Africa
Keina/Keinis see Käina
Keishū see Kyŏngju
77 T11 **Keïta** Tahoua, C Niger
78 J12 **Kéita, Bahr** var. Doka. ~ S Chad
93 M16 **Keitele** ◎ C Finland
182 K10 **Keith** South Australia
96 K8 **Keith** NE Scotland, UK
26 K3 **Keith Sebelius Lake** ⊠ Kansas, C USA
32 G11 **Keizer** Oregon, NW USA
38 A8 **Kekaha** Kaua'i, Hawai'i, USA
147 U10 **Kek-Art** prev. Alaykel', Alay-Kuu. Oshskaya Oblast', SW Kyrgyzstan
147 W10 **Këk-Aygyr** var. Keyaygyr. Narynskaya Oblast', C Kyrgyzstan
147 V9 **Këk-Dzhar** Narynskaya Oblast', C Kyrgyzstan
14 L8 **Kekek** ~ Québec, SE Canada
185 K15 **Kekerengu** Canterbury, South Island, New Zealand
111 L21 **Kékes** ▲ N Hungary
171 P17 **Kekneno, Gunung** ▲ Timor, S Indonesia
147 S9 **Këk-Tash** Kir. Kök-Tash. Dzhalal-Abadskaya Oblast', W Kyrgyzstan
81 M15 **K'elafo** Somali, E Ethiopia
169 U10 **Kelai, Sungai** ~ Borneo, N Indonesia
Kelamayi see Karamay
Kelang see Klang
168 K7 **Kelantan** ⬖ state Peninsular Malaysia
Kelantan see Kelantan, Sungai
168 K7 **Kelantan, Sungai** var. Kelantan. ~ Peninsular Malaysia
Kelat see Kalāt
Këlcyra see Këlcyrë
113 L22 **Këlcyrë** var. Këlcyra. Gjirokastër, S Albania
Kelifskiy Uzboy see Kelifskiy Uzboýy
146 L14 **Kelifskiy Uzboýy** Rus. Kelifskiy Uzboy. salt marsh Lebap Welaýaty, E Turkmenistan
137 O12 **Kelkit** Gümüşhane, NE Turkey
136 M12 **Kelkit Çayı** ~ N Turkey
79 G18 **Kéllé** Cuvette-Quest, W Congo
77 W11 **Kellé** Zinder, S Niger
145 P7 **Kellerovka** Severnyy Kazakhstan, N Kazakhstan
8 I5 **Kellett, Cape** headland Banks Island, Northwest Territories, NW Canada
31 S11 **Kelleys Island** island Ohio, N USA
33 N8 **Kellogg** Idaho, NW USA
92 M12 **Kelloselkä** Lappi, N Finland
97 F17 **Kells** Ir. Ceanannas. Meath, E Ireland
118 E12 **Kelmė** Šiauliai, C Lithuania
99 M19 **Kelmis** var. La Calamine. Liège, E Belgium
78 H12 **Kélo** Tandjilé, SW Chad
83 I14 **Kelongwa** North Western, NW Zambia
9 N17 **Kelowna** British Columbia, SW Canada
9 X12 **Kelsey** Manitoba, C Canada
34 M6 **Kelseyville** California, W USA
96 K13 **Kelso** SE Scotland, UK
32 G10 **Kelso** Washington, NW USA
195 W15 **Keltie, Cape** headland Antarctica
Keltsy see Kielce
168 L9 **Keluang** var. Kluang. Johor, Peninsular Malaysia
168 M11 **Kelume** Pulau Lingga, W Indonesia
9 U15 **Kelvington** Saskatchewan, S Canada
124 J7 **Kem'** Respublika Kareliya, NW Russian Federation
124 I7 **Kem'** ~ NW Russian Federation
137 O13 **Kemah** Erzincan, E Turkey
137 N13 **Kemaliye** Erzincan, C Turkey
Kemaman see Cukai
Kemanlar see Isperikh
10 K14 **Kemano** British Columbia, SW Canada
Kemarat see Khemmarat
171 P12 **Kembani** Pulau Peleng, N Indonesia
136 F17 **Kemer** Antalya, SW Turkey
122 J12 **Kemerovo** prev. Shcheglovsk. Kemerovskaya Oblast', C Russian Federation
122 K12 **Kemerovskaya Oblast'** ⬖ province S Russian Federation
92 L13 **Kemi** Lappi, NW Finland
92 M12 **Kemijärvi** Swe. Kemiträsk. Lappi, N Finland
92 M12 **Kemijärvi** ◎ N Finland
92 L13 **Kemijoki** ~ NW Finland
147 V7 **Kemin** prev. Bystrovka. Chuyskaya Oblast', N Kyrgyzstan
92 L13 **Keminmaa** Lappi, NW Finland
Kemins Island see Nikumaroro
Kemiö see Kimito
Kemiträsk see Kemijärvi
127 P5 **Kemlya** Respublika Mordoviya, W Russian Federation
99 B18 **Kemmel** West-Vlaanderen, W Belgium
33 S16 **Kemmerer** Wyoming, C USA
Kemmuna see Comino
79 I14 **Kémo** ⬖ prefecture S Central African Republic
25 U7 **Kemp** Texas, SW USA
93 L14 **Kempele** Oulu, C Finland
101 D15 **Kempen** Nordrhein-Westfalen, W Germany
25 Q5 **Kemp, Lake** ◎ Texas, SW USA
195 W5 **Kemp Land** physical region Antarctica
25 S9 **Kempner** Texas, SW USA
44 H3 **Kemp's Bay** Andros Island, W Bahamas
183 U6 **Kempsey** New South Wales, SE Australia
101 J24 **Kempten** Bayern, S Germany
15 N9 **Kempt, Lac** ◎ Québec, SE Canada
183 P17 **Kempton** Tasmania, SE Australia
154 J9 **Ken** ~ C India
39 R12 **Kenai** Alaska, USA
0 D5 **Kenai Mountains** ▲▲ Alaska, USA
39 R12 **Kenai Peninsula** peninsula Alaska, USA
21 V11 **Kenansville** North Carolina, SE USA
146 A10 **Kenar** prev. Rus. Ufra. Balkan Welaýaty, NW Turkmenistan
121 U13 **Kenâyis, Râs el-** headland N Egypt
97 K16 **Kendal** NW England, UK
23 Y16 **Kendall** Florida, SE USA
9 O8 **Kendall, Cape** headland Nunavut, E Canada
18 J15 **Kendall Park** New Jersey, NE USA
31 Q11 **Kendallville** Indiana, N USA
171 P14 **Kendari** Sulawesi, C Indonesia
169 Q13 **Kendawangan** Borneo, C Indonesia
154 O12 **Kendrāpāra** var. Kendrāparha. Orissa, E India
Kendrāparha see Kendrāpāra
154 O11 **Kendujhargarh** prev. Keonjihargarh. Orissa, E India
25 S13 **Kenedy** Texas, SW USA
Kënekesir see Kënekesir
76 J15 **Kenema** SE Sierra Leone
29 P16 **Kenesaw** Nebraska, C USA
Këneurgench see Këneurgench
79 H21 **Kenge** Bandundu, SW Dem. Rep. Congo
Kengen see Kangen
167 O5 **Keng Tung** var. Kentung. Shan State, E Myanmar (Burma)
83 F23 **Kenhardt** Northern Cape, W South Africa
76 J12 **Kéniéba** Kayes, W Mali
Kenimekh see Konimex
169 U7 **Keningau** Sabah, East Malaysia
74 F6 **Kénitra** prev. Port-Lyautey. NW Morocco
21 V9 **Kenly** North Carolina, SE USA
97 B21 **Kenmare** Ir. Neidín. Kerry, S Ireland
28 L2 **Kenmare** North Dakota, N USA
97 A21 **Kenmare River** Ir. An Ribhéar. inlet NE Atlantic Ocean
18 D10 **Kenmore** New York, NE USA
25 W8 **Kennard** Texas, SW USA
29 N10 **Kennebec** South Dakota, N USA
19 Q7 **Kennebec River** ~ Maine, NE USA
19 P9 **Kennebunk** Maine, NE USA
39 R13 **Kennedy Entrance** strait Alaska, USA
166 L3 **Kennedy Peak** ▲ W Myanmar (Burma)
22 K9 **Kenner** Louisiana, S USA
180 I8 **Kenneth Range** ▲▲ Western Australia
27 Y9 **Kennett** Missouri, C USA
18 I16 **Kennett Square** Pennsylvania, NE USA
32 K10 **Kennewick** Washington, NW USA
12 E11 **Kenogami** ~ Ontario, S Canada
15 Q7 **Kénogami, Lac** ◎ Québec, SE Canada
14 G8 **Kenogami Lake** Ontario, S Canada
14 F7 **Kenogamissi Lake** ◎ Ontario, S Canada
10 I6 **Keno Hill** Yukon Territory, NW Canada
12 A11 **Kenora** Ontario, S Canada
31 N9 **Kenosha** Wisconsin, N USA
13 P14 **Kensington** Prince Edward Island, SE Canada
26 L3 **Kensington** Kansas, C USA
32 I11 **Kent** Oregon, NW USA
24 J9 **Kent** Texas, SW USA
32 H8 **Kent** Washington, NW USA
97 P22 **Kent** cultural region SE England, UK
145 P16 **Kentau** Yuzhnyy Kazakhstan, S Kazakhstan
183 P14 **Kent Group** island group Tasmania, SE Australia
31 N12 **Kentland** Indiana, N USA
31 R12 **Kenton** Ohio, N USA
8 K7 **Kent Peninsula** peninsula Nunavut, N Canada
115 F14 **Kentrikí Makedonía** Eng. Macedonia Central. ⬖ region N Greece
20 J6 **Kentucky** off. Commonwealth of Kentucky, also known as Bluegrass State. ⬖ state C USA
20 H8 **Kentucky Lake** ⊠ Kentucky/Tennessee, S USA
Kentung see Keng Tung
13 P15 **Kentville** Nova Scotia, SE Canada
22 K8 **Kentwood** Louisiana, S USA
31 P9 **Kentwood** Michigan, N USA
81 H17 **Kenya** off. Republic of Kenya. ◆ republic E Africa
Kenya, Mount see Kirinyaga
Kenya, Republic of see Kenya
168 L7 **Kenyir, Tasik** var. Tasek Kenyir. ◎ Peninsular Malaysia
29 W10 **Kenyon** Minnesota, N USA
29 Y16 **Keokuk** Iowa, C USA
Keonjihargarh see Kendujhargarh
Kéos see Tziá
29 X16 **Keosauqua** Iowa, C USA
29 X15 **Keota** Iowa, C USA
21 O11 **Keowee, Lake** ⊠ South Carolina, SE USA
124 I7 **Kepa** var. Kepe. Respublika Kareliya, NW Russian Federation
Kepe see Kepa
189 O13 **Kepirohi Falls** waterfall Pohnpei, E Micronesia
185 B22 **Kepler Mountains** ▲▲ South Island, New Zealand
111 I14 **Kepno** Wielkopolskie, C Poland
65 C24 **Keppel Island** island N Falkland Islands
Keppel Island see Niuatoputapu
65 C23 **Keppel Sound** sound N Falkland Islands
136 D12 **Kepsut** Balıkesir, NW Turkey
168 M11 **Kepulauan Riau** off. Propinsi Kepulauan Riau. ⬖ province NW Indonesia
171 V13 **Kerai** Papua, E Indonesia
Kerak see Al Karak
155 F22 **Kerala** ⬖ state S India
165 R16 **Kerama-rettō** island group SW Japan
183 N10 **Kerang** Victoria, SE Australia
Kerasunt see Giresun
115 H19 **Keratéa** var. Keratea. Attikí, C Greece
Keratea see Keratéa
93 M19 **Kerava** Swe. Kervo. Etelä-Suomi, S Finland
Kerbala/Kerbela see Karbalā'
32 F15 **Kerby** Oregon, NW USA

◆ Country
● Country Capital
◇ Dependent Territory
○ Dependent Territory Capital
⬖ Administrative Regions
✈ International Airport
▲ Mountain
▲▲ Mountain Range
Volcano
~ River
◎ Lake
⊠ Reservoir

117 W12 **Kerch** Rus. Kerch'. Respublika Krym, SE Ukraine
Kerch' see Kerch
Kerchens'ka Protska/Kerchenskiy Proliv see Kerch Strait
117 V13 **Kerchens'kyy Pivostriv** peninsula S Ukraine
121 V4 **Kerch Strait** var. Bosporus Cimmerius, Enikale Strait, Rus. Kerchenskiy Proliv, Ukr. Kerchens'ka Protska. strait Black Sea/Sea of Azov
152 K8 **Kerdārnāth** Uttaranchal, N India
Kerdilio see Kerdýlio
114 H13 **Kerdýlio** var. Kerdilio. ▲ N Greece
186 D8 **Kerema** Gulf, S Papua New Guinea
Keremitlik see Lyulyakovo
136 J9 **Kerempe Burnu** headland N Turkey
80 J9 **Keren** var. Cheren. C Eritrea
25 U7 **Kerens** Texas, SW USA
184 M6 **Kerepehi** Waikato, North Island, New Zealand
145 P10 **Kerey, Ozero** ◎ C Kazakhstan
Kergel see Kärla
173 Q12 **Kerguelen** island C French Southern and Antarctic Territories
173 Q13 **Kerguelen Plateau** undersea feature S Indian Ocean
115 C20 **Kerí** Zákynthos, Iónioi Nísoi, Greece, C Mediterranean Sea
81 H19 **Kericho** Rift Valley, W Kenya
184 K2 **Kerikeri** Northland, North Island, New Zealand
93 O17 **Kerimäki** Isä-Suomi, E Finland
168 K12 **Kerinci, Gunung** ▲ Sumatera, W Indonesia
Keriya see Yutian
158 H9 **Keriya He** ∽ NW China
98 J9 **Kerkbuurt** Noord-Holland, C Netherlands
98 J13 **Kerkdriel** Gelderland, C Netherlands
75 N6 **Kerkenah, Îles de** var. Kerkenna Islands, Ar. Juzur Qarqannah. island group E Tunisia
Kerkenna Islands see Kerkenah, Îles de
115 M20 **Kerketévs** ▲ Sámos, Dodekánisa, Greece, Aegean Sea
29 T8 **Kerkhoven** Minnesota, N USA
Kerki see Atamyrat
Kerkichi see Kerkiçi
146 M14 **Kerkiçi** Rus. Kerkichi. Lebap Welaýaty, E Turkmenistan
115 F16 **Kerkíneo** prehistoric site Thessalía, C Greece
114 G12 **Kerkíni, Límni** var. Kerkinitis Límni. ◎ N Greece
Kérkira see Kérkyra
99 M18 **Kerkrade** Limburg, SE Netherlands
Kerkuk see Kirkūk
115 B16 **Kérkyra** var. Kérkira, Eng. Corfu. Kérkyra, Iónioi Nísoi, Greece, C Mediterranean Sea
115 B16 **Kerkyra** ✈ Kérkyra, Iónioi Nísoi, Greece, C Mediterranean Sea
115 A16 **Kérkyra** var. Kérkira, Eng. Corfu. island Iónioi Nísoi, Greece, C Mediterranean Sea
192 K10 **Kermadec Islands** island group New Zealand, SW Pacific Ocean
175 R10 **Kermadec Ridge** undersea feature SW Pacific Ocean
175 R11 **Kermadec Trench** undersea feature SW Pacific Ocean
143 S10 **Kermān** var. Kirman; anc. Carmana. Kermān, C Iran
143 R11 **Kermān** off. Ostān-e Kermān, var. Kirman; anc. Carmania. ◈ province SE Iran
143 U12 **Kermān, Biābān-e** desert SE Iran
Kermān, Ostān-e see Kermān
142 K6 **Kermānshāh** var. Qahremānshahr; prev. Bākhtarān. Kermānshāhān, W Iran
143 Q9 **Kermānshāh** Yazd, C Iran
142 J6 **Kermānshāh** off. Ostān-e Kermānshāhān; prev. Bākhtarān. ◈ province W Iran
Kermānshāhān, Ostān-e see Kermānshāh
114 L10 **Kermen** Sliven, C Bulgaria
24 L8 **Kermit** Texas, SW USA
21 P6 **Kermit** West Virginia, NE USA
21 S9 **Kernersville** North Carolina, SE USA
35 S12 **Kern River** ∽ California, W USA
35 S12 **Kernville** California, W USA
115 K21 **Kéros** island Kykládes, Greece, Aegean Sea
76 K14 **Kérouané** Haute-Guinée, SE Guinea
101 D16 **Kerpen** Nordrhein-Westfalen, W Germany
146 I11 **Kerpichli** Lebap Welaýaty, NE Turkmenistan
24 M1 **Kerrick** Texas, SW USA
Kerr Lake see John H. Kerr Reservoir
9 S15 **Kerrobert** Saskatchewan, S Canada
25 Q11 **Kerrville** Texas, SW USA
97 B20 **Kerry** Ir. Ciarraí. ◈ county SW Ireland
21 S11 **Kershaw** South Carolina, SE USA
Kertel see Kärdla
95 H23 **Kerteminde** Fyn, C Denmark
163 Q7 **Kerulen** Chin. Herlen He, Mong. Herlen Gol. ∽ China/Mongolia
Kervo see Kerava
Kerýneia see Girne
12 H11 **Kesagami Lake** ◎ Ontario, SE Canada
93 O17 **Kesälahti** Pohjois-Karjala, SE Finland
136 B11 **Keşan** Edirne, NW Turkey
165 R9 **Kesennuma** Miyagi, Honshū, C Japan
163 V7 **Keshan** Heilongjiang, NE China
30 M6 **Keshena** Wisconsin, N USA
136 I13 **Keskin** Kırıkkale, C Turkey
Késmárk see Kežmarok
124 I6 **Kesten'ga** var. Kest Enga. Respublika Kareliya, NW Russian Federation
Kest Enga see Kesten'ga
98 K12 **Kesteren** Gelderland, C Netherlands
14 H14 **Keswick** Ontario, S Canada
97 K15 **Keswick** NW England, UK
111 H24 **Keszthely** Zala, SW Hungary
122 K11 **Ket'** ∽ C Russian Federation
77 R17 **Keta** SE Ghana
169 Q12 **Ketapang** Borneo, C Indonesia
127 O12 **Ketchenery** prev. Sovetskoye. Respublika Kalmykiya, SW Russian Federation
39 Y14 **Ketchikan** Revillagigedo Island, Alaska, USA
33 O14 **Ketchum** Idaho, NW USA
Kete/Kete Krakye see Kete-Krachi
77 Q15 **Kete-Krachi** var. Kete, Kete Krakye. E Ghana
98 L9 **Ketelmeer** channel E Netherlands
149 P17 **Keti Bandar** Sind, SE Pakistan
145 W16 **Ketmen', Khrebet** ▲▲ SE Kazakhstan
77 S16 **Kétou** SE Benin
110 M7 **Kętrzyn** Ger. Rastenburg. Warmińsko-Mazurskie, NE Poland
97 N20 **Kettering** C England, UK
31 R14 **Kettering** Ohio, N USA
18 F13 **Kettle Creek** ∽ Pennsylvania, NE USA
32 L7 **Kettle Falls** Washington, NW USA
14 D16 **Kettle Point** headland Ontario, S Canada
29 V6 **Kettle River** ∽ Minnesota, N USA
186 B7 **Ketu** ∽ W Papua New Guinea
18 G10 **Keuka Lake** ◎ New York, NE USA
Keupriya see Primorsko
93 L17 **Keuruu** Länsi-Suomi, C Finland
Kevevára see Kovin
92 L9 **Kevo** Lapp. Geavvú. Lappi, N Finland
44 M6 **Kew** North Caicos, N Turks and Caicos Islands
30 K11 **Kewanee** Illinois, N USA
31 N7 **Kewaunee** Wisconsin, N USA
30 M3 **Keweenaw Bay** ◎ Michigan, N USA
31 N2 **Keweenaw Peninsula** peninsula Michigan, N USA
31 N2 **Keweenaw Point** peninsula Michigan, N USA
29 N12 **Keya Paha River** ∽ Nebraska/South Dakota, N USA
Keyaygyr see Këk-Aygyr
23 Z16 **Key Biscayne** Florida, SE USA
26 G8 **Keyes** Oklahoma, C USA
23 Y17 **Key Largo** Key Largo, Florida, SE USA
21 U3 **Keyser** West Virginia, NE USA
27 O9 **Keystone Lake** ▣ Oklahoma, C USA
36 L16 **Keystone Peak** ▲ Arizona, SW USA
Keystone State see Pennsylvania
21 U7 **Keysville** Virginia, NE USA
27 T3 **Keytesville** Missouri, C USA
23 W17 **Key West** Florida Keys, Florida, SE USA
127 T1 **Kez** Udmurtskaya Respublika, NW Russian Federation
Kezdivásárhely see Târgu Secuiesc
122 M12 **Kezhma** Krasnoyarskiy Kray, C Russian Federation
111 L18 **Kežmarok** Ger. Käsmark, Hung. Késmárk. Prešovský Kraj, E Slovakia
Kfar Saba see Kefar Sava
83 F20 **Kgalagadi** ◈ district SW Botswana
83 I20 **Kgatleng** ◈ district SE Botswana
188 F8 **Kgkeklau** Babeldaob, N Palau
125 R6 **Khabarikha** var. Chabaricha. Respublika Komi, NW Russian Federation
123 S14 **Khabarovsk** Khabarovskiy Kray, SE Russian Federation
123 R11 **Khabarovskiy Kray** ◈ territory E Russian Federation
141 W7 **Khabb** Abū Ẓaby, E United Arab Emirates
Khabour, Nahr al see Khābūr, Nahr al
Khabura see Al Khābūrah
139 N2 **Khābūr, Nahr al** var. Nahr al Khabour. ∽ Syria/Turkey
Khachmas see Xaçmaz
80 B12 **Khadari** ∽ W Sudan
Khadera see Hadera
141 X12 **Khādhil** var. Khudal. SE Oman
155 E14 **Khadki** prev. Kirkee. Mahārāshtra, W India
126 L14 **Khadyzhensk** Krasnodarskiy Kray, SW Russian Federation
114 N9 **Khadzhiyska Reka** ∽ E Bulgaria
117 P10 **Khadzhybeys'kyy Lyman** ◎ SW Ukraine
138 K3 **Khafsah** Ḥalab, N Syria
152 M13 **Khāga** Uttar Pradesh, N India
153 Q13 **Khagaria** Bihār, NE India
149 Q13 **Khairpur** Sind, SE Pakistan
122 K13 **Khakasiya, Respublika** prev. Khakasskaya Avtonomnaya Oblast', Eng. Khakassia. ◈ autonomous republic C Russian Federation
Khakassia/Khakasskaya Avtonomnaya Oblast' see Khakasiya, Respublika
167 N9 **Kha Khaeng, Khao** ▲ W Thailand
83 G20 **Khakhea** var. Kakia. Southern, S Botswana
Khalach see Halaç
Khalándrion see Chalándri
Khalīj-e Fars see Gulf, The
127 W7 **Khalilovo** Orenburgskaya Oblast', W Russian Federation
Khalkabad see Xalqobod
142 L3 **Khalkhāl** prev. Herowābād. Ardabīl, NW Iran
Khalkidhikí see Chalkidikí
Khalkís see Chalkída
125 W3 **Khal'mer-Yu** Respublika Komi, NW Russian Federation
119 M14 **Khalopyenichy** Rus. Kholopenichi. Minskaya Voblasts', NE Belarus
Khalturin see Orlov
141 Y10 **Khalūf** var. Al Khaluf. E Oman
154 K10 **Khamaria** Madhya Pradesh, C India
154 D11 **Khambhāt** Gujarāt, W India
154 C12 **Khambhāt, Gulf of** Eng. Gulf of Cambay. gulf W India
167 U10 **Khâm Đưc** Quang Nam-Đa Năng, C Vietnam
154 G12 **Khāmgaon** Mahārāshtra, C India
141 O14 **Khamir** var. Khamr. W Yemen
141 N12 **Khamīs Mushayt** var. Hamīs Musait. 'Asīr, SW Saudi Arabia
123 P10 **Khampa** Respublika Sakha (Yakutiya), NE Russian Federation
Khamr see Khamir
83 C19 **Khan** ∽ W Namibia
149 Q2 **Khānābād** Kunduz, NE Afghanistan
Khân Abou Châmâte/Khan Abou Ech Cham see Khān Abū Shāmāt
138 I7 **Khān Abū Shāmāt** var. Khân Abou Châmâte, Khan Abou Ech Cham. Dimashq, W Syria
Khān al Baghdādī see Al Baghdādī
Khān al Maḥāwīl see Al Maḥāwīl
139 T7 **Khān al Mashāhidah** C Iraq
139 T10 **Khān al Muşallá** S Iraq
139 U6 **Khānaqīn** E Iraq
139 T11 **Khān ar Ruḥbah** S Iraq
139 P2 **Khān as Sūr** N Iraq
139 T8 **Khān Āzād** C Iraq
154 N13 **Khandaparha** prev. Khandpara. Orissa, E India
Khandpara see Khandaparha
149 T2 **Khandūd** var. Khandud, Wakhan. Badakhshān, NE Afghanistan
Khandud see Khandūd
154 G11 **Khandwa** Madhya Pradesh, C India
123 R10 **Khandyga** Respublika Sakha (Yakutiya), NE Russian Federation
149 T10 **Khānewāl** Punjab, NE Pakistan
149 S10 **Khāngarh** Punjab, E Pakistan
Khanh Hung see Soc Trăng
Khaniá see Chaniá
Khanka see Xonqa
163 Z8 **Khanka, Lake** var. Hsing-K'ai Hu, Lake Hanka, Chin. Xingkai Hu, Rus. Ozero Khanka. ◎ China/Russian Federation
Khanka, Ozero see Khanka, Lake
Khankendi see Xankändi
Khanlar see Xanlar
123 O9 **Khannya** ∽ NE Russian Federation
149 S12 **Khānpur** Punjab, SE Pakistan
149 S12 **Khānpur** Punjab, E Pakistan
138 I4 **Khān Shaykhūn** var. Khan Sheikhun. Idlib, NW Syria
Khan Sheikhun see Khān Shaykhūn
145 S15 **Khantau** Zhambyl, S Kazakhstan
145 W16 **Khan Tengri, Pik** ▲ SE Kazakhstan
Khan-Tengri, Pik see Hantengri Feng
167 S9 **Khanthabouli** var. Savannakhét. S Laos
127 V8 **Khanty-Mansiysk** prev. Ostyako-Voguls'k. Khanty-Mansiyskiy Avtonomnyy Okrug, C Russian Federation
125 V8 **Khanty-Mansiyskiy Avtonomnyy Okrug** ◈ autonomous district C Russian Federation
139 R4 **Khānūqah** C Iraq
138 E11 **Khān Yūnis** var. Khān Yūnus. S Gaza Strip
Khān Yūnus see Khān Yūnis
Khanzi see Ghanzi
139 U5 **Khān Zūr** E Iraq
167 N10 **Khao Laem Reservoir** ▣ W Thailand
123 O14 **Khapcheranga** Chitinskaya Oblast', S Russian Federation
127 Q12 **Kharabali** Astrakhanskaya Oblast', SW Russian Federation
153 R16 **Kharagpur** West Bengal, NE India
139 V11 **Kharā'ib 'Abd al Karīm** S Iraq
143 Q8 **Kharānaq** Yazd, C Iran
Kharbin see Harbin
146 H13 **Khardzhagaz** Ahal Welaýaty, C Turkmenistan
Khārga Oasis see Great Oasis, The
154 F11 **Khargon** Madhya Pradesh, C India
149 V7 **Khāriān** Punjab, NE Pakistan
117 X8 **Kharisyz'k** Donets'ka Oblast', E Ukraine
117 V5 **Kharkiv** Rus. Khar'kov. Kharkivs'ka Oblast', NE Ukraine
117 V5 **Kharkiv** ✈ Kharkivs'ka Oblast', E Ukraine
Kharkiv see Kharkivs'ka Oblast'
117 U5 **Kharkivs'ka Oblast'** var. Kharkiv, Rus. Khar'kovskaya Oblast'. ◈ province E Ukraine
Khar'kov see Kharkiv
Khar'kovskaya Oblast' see Kharkivs'ka Oblast'
124 L3 **Kharlovka** Murmanskaya Oblast', NW Russian Federation
114 K11 **Kharmanli** Khaskovo, S Bulgaria
114 K11 **Kharmanliyska Reka** ∽ S Bulgaria
124 M13 **Kharovsk** Vologodskaya Oblast', NW Russian Federation
80 F9 **Khartoum** var. El Khartûm, Khartum. ● (Sudan) Khartoum, C Sudan
80 F9 **Khartoum** ◈ state NE Sudan
80 F9 **Khartoum** ✈ Khartoum, C Sudan
80 F9 **Khartoum North** Khartoum, C Sudan
117 X8 **Khartsyz'k** Rus. Khartsyzsk. Donets'ka Oblast', SE Ukraine
Khartsyzsk see Khartsyz'k
Khartum see Khartoum
Khasab see Al Khaşab
123 S15 **Khasan** Primorskiy Kray, SE Russian Federation
127 P16 **Khasavyurt** Respublika Dagestan, SW Russian Federation
143 W12 **Khāsh** prev. Vāsht. Sīstān va Balūchestān, SE Iran
148 K8 **Khāsh, Dasht-e** Eng. Khash Desert. desert SW Afghanistan
Khash Desert see Khāsh, Dasht-e
Khashim Al Qirba/Khashm al Qirbah see Khashm el Girba
80 H9 **Khashm el Girba** var. Khashim Al Qirba, Khashm al Qirbah. Kassala, E Sudan
138 G14 **Khashsh, Jabal al** ▲▲ S Jordan
137 S10 **Khashuri** C Georgia
153 V13 **Khāsi Hills** hill range NE India
114 K11 **Khaskovo** Khaskovo, S Bulgaria
114 K11 **Khaskovo** ◈ province S Bulgaria
122 M7 **Khatanga** ∽ N Russian Federation
Khatanga, Gulf of see Khatangskiy Zaliv
123 N7 **Khatangskiy Zaliv** var. Gulf of Khatanga. bay N Russian Federation
141 W7 **Khatmat al Malāḥah** N Oman
143 S16 **Khaṭmat al Malāḥah** Ash Shāriqah, E United Arab Emirates
123 V7 **Khatyrka** Chukotskiy Avtonomnyy Okrug, NE Russian Federation
Khauz-Khan see Hanhowuz
Khauzkhanskoye Vodokhranilishche see Hanhowuz Suw Howdany
Khauzkhanskoye Vodoranilishche see Hanhowuz Suw Howdany
Khavaling see Khovaling
Khavast see Xovos
139 W10 **Khawrah, Nahr al** ∽ S Iraq
Khawr Barakah see Baraka
141 W7 **Khawr Fakkān** var. Khor Fakkan. Ash Shāriqah, NE United Arab Emirates
140 L6 **Khaybar** Al Madīnah, NW Saudi Arabia
Khaybar, Kowtal-e see Khyber Pass
147 S11 **Khaydarkan** var. Khaydarken. Batkenskaya Oblast', SW Kyrgyzstan
Khaydarken see Khaydarkan
125 U2 **Khaypudyrskaya Guba** bay NW Russian Federation
139 S1 **Khayrūzuk** E Iraq
Khazar, Baḥr-e/Khazar, Daryā-ye see Caspian Sea
Khazarosp see Hazorasp
Khazretishi, Khrebet see Hazratishoh, Qatorkŭhi
Khelat see Kalāt
74 F6 **Khemisset** NW Morocco
167 R10 **Khemmarat** var. Kemarat. Ubon Ratchathani, E Thailand
74 L6 **Khenchela** var. Khenchla. NE Algeria
Khenchla see Khenchela
74 G7 **Khénifra** C Morocco
Khersān, Rūd-e see Garm, Āb-e
117 R10 **Kherson** Khersons'ka Oblast', S Ukraine
Kherson see Khersons'ka Oblast'
117 S14 **Khersones, Mys** Rus. Mys Khersonesskiy. headland S Ukraine
Khersonesskiy, Mys see Khersones, Mys
117 R10 **Khersons'ka Oblast'** var. Kherson, Rus. Khersonskaya Oblast'. ◈ province S Ukraine
Khersonskaya Oblast' see Khersons'ka Oblast'
122 L8 **Kheta** ∽ N Russian Federation
167 S8 **Khe Ve** Quang Binh, C Vietnam
149 U7 **Khewra** Punjab, E Pakistan
Khiam see El Khiyam
124 J4 **Khibiny** ▲▲ NW Russian Federation
126 K3 **Khimki** Moskovskaya Oblast', W Russian Federation
147 S12 **Khingov** Rus. Obi-Khingou. ∽ C Tajikistan
Khíos see Chíos
149 R15 **Khipro** Sind, SE Pakistan
139 S10 **Khirr, Wādī al** dry watercourse S Iraq
114 I10 **Khisarya** Plovdiv, C Bulgaria
Khiva/Khiwa see Xiva
167 N9 **Khlong Khlung** Kamphaeng Phet, W Thailand
167 N15 **Khlong Thom** Krabi, SW Thailand
167 P12 **Khlung** Chantaburi, S Thailand
Khmel'nik see Khmil'nyk
Khmel'nitskaya Oblast' see Khmel'nyts'ka Oblast'
Khmel'nitskiy see Khmel 'nyts'kyy
116 K5 **Khmel'nyts'ka Oblast'** var. Khmel'nyts'kyy, Rus. Khmel'nitskaya Oblast'; prev. Kamenets-Podol'skaya Oblast'. ◈ province NW Ukraine
116 L6 **Khmel 'nyts'kyy** Rus. Khmel'nitskiy; prev. Proskurov. Khmel'nyts'ka Oblast', W Ukraine
Khmel'nyts'kyy see Khmel'nyts'ka Oblast'
116 M6 **Khmil'nyk** Rus. Khmel'nik. Vinnyts'ka Oblast', C Ukraine
144 I10 **Khobda** prev. Novoalekseyevka. Aktyubinsk, W Kazakhstan
137 R9 **Khobi** W Georgia
119 P15 **Khodasy** Rus. Khodosy. Mahilyowskaya Voblasts', E Belarus
116 I6 **Khodoriv** Pol. Chodorów, Rus. Khodorov. L'vivs'ka Oblast', NW Ukraine
Khodorov see Khodoriv
Khodosy see Khodasy
Khodzhakala see Hojagala
146 M13 **Khodzhambas** Rus. Khodzhambas. Lebap Welaýaty, E Turkmenistan
Khodzhambas see Hojambaz
Khodzhambas see Khodzhambas
Khodzhent see Khŭjand
Khodzheyli see Xo'jayli
Khoi see Khvoy
Khojend see Khŭjand
Khokand see Qo'qon
126 L8 **Khokhol'skiy** Voronezhskaya Oblast', W Russian Federation
167 P10 **Khok Samrong** Lop Buri, C Thailand
149 P2 **Kholm** var. Tashqurghan, Pash. Khulm. Balkh, N Afghanistan
124 H15 **Kholm** Novgorodskaya Oblast', W Russian Federation
Kholm see Chełm
Kholmech' see Kholmyech
123 T13 **Kholmsk** Ostrov Sakhalin, Sakhalinskaya Oblast', SE Russian Federation
119 O19 **Kholmyech** Rus. Kholmech'. Homyel'skaya Voblasts', SE Belarus
Kholon see Holon
Kholopenichi see Khalopyenichy
83 D19 **Khomas** ◈ district C Namibia
83 D19 **Khomas Hochland** var. Khomasplato. plateau C Namibia
Khomasplato see Khomas Hochland
Khomein see Khomeyn
142 M7 **Khomeyn** var. Khomein, Khumain. Markazī, W Iran
143 N8 **Khomeynishahr** prev. Homāyūnshahr. Eşfahān, C Iran
Khoms see Al Khums
Khong Sedone see Muang Khôngxédôn
167 Q9 **Khon Kaen** var. Muang Khon Kaen. Khon Kaen, E Thailand
Khonqa see Xonqa
167 Q9 **Khon San** Khon Kaen, E Thailand
123 R8 **Khonuu** Respublika Sakha (Yakutiya), NE Russian Federation
127 N8 **Khopër** var. Khoper. ∽ SW Russian Federation
Khoper see Khopër
123 S14 **Khor** Khabarovskiy Kray, SE Russian Federation
143 U9 **Khorāsān-e Janūbī** off. Ostan-e Khorāsān-e Janūbi. ◈ province E Iran
143 S3 **Khorāsān-e Shemālī** off. Ostan-e Khorāsān-e Shemālī. ◈ province NE Iran
143 U5 **Khorāsān-Razavī** off. Ostan-e Khorāsān-Razavi. ◈ province NE Iran
Khorat see Nakhon Ratchasima
154 O13 **Khordha** prev. Khurda. Orissa, E India
125 U4 **Khorey-Ver** Nenetskiy Avtonomnyy Okrug, NW Russian Federation
Khorezmskaya Oblast' see Xorazm Viloyati
Khor Fakkan see Khawr Fakkān
145 W15 **Khorgos** Almaty, SE Kazakhstan
123 N13 **Khorinsk** Respublika Buryatiya, S Russian Federation
83 C18 **Khorixas** Kunene, NW Namibia
141 O17 **Khormaksar** var. Aden. ✈ ('Aden) SW Yemen
Khormal see Khurmāl
Khormuj see Khvormūj
Khorog see Khorugh
117 S5 **Khorol** Poltavs'ka Oblast', NE Ukraine
142 L7 **Khorramābād** var. Khurramabad. Lorestān, W Iran
142 K10 **Khorramshahr** var. Khurramshahr, Muhammerah; prev. Mohammerah. Khūzestān, SW Iran
147 S14 **Khorugh** Rus. Khorog. S Tajikistan
Khorvot Khalutsa see Horvot Haluza
127 Q12 **Khosheutovo** Astrakhanskaya Oblast', SW Russian Federation
Khotan see Hotan
Khotimsk see Khotsimsk
Khotin see Khotyn
119 R16 **Khotsimsk** Rus. Khotimsk. Mahilyowskaya Voblasts', E Belarus
116 K7 **Khotyn** Rom. Hotin, Rus. Khotin. Chernivets'ka Oblast', W Ukraine
74 F7 **Khouribga** C Morocco
147 Q13 **Khovaling** Rus. Khavaling. SW Tajikistan
Khovd see Hovd
149 R6 **Khowst** Khowst, E Afghanistan
149 S6 **Khowst** ◈ province E Afghanistan
Khoy see Khvoy
119 N20 **Khoyniki** Rus. Khoyniki. Homyel'skaya Voblasts', SE Belarus
Khozretishi, Khrebet see Hazratishoh, Qatorkŭhi
Khrebet Babatag see Bototgot', Tizmasi
Khrisoúpolis see Chrysoúpoli
144 J10 **Khromtau** Kaz. Khromtaū. Aktyubinsk, W Kazakhstan
Khromtaū see Khromtau
Khrysokhou Bay see Chrysochoú, Kólpos
117 O7 **Khrystynivka** Cherkas'ka Oblast', C Ukraine
167 R10 **Khuang Nai** Ubon Ratchathani, E Thailand
Khudal see Khādhil
Khudat see Xudat
149 W9 **Khudiān** Punjab, E Pakistan
Khudzhand see Khŭjand
147 O13 **Khufar** Surkhondaryo Viloyati, S Uzbekistan
83 G21 **Khuis** Kgalagadi, SW Botswana
147 Q11 **Khŭjand** var. Khodzhent, Khojend, Rus. Khudzhand; prev. Leninabad, Taj. Leninobod. N Tajikistan
167 R11 **Khukhan** Si Sa Ket, E Thailand
Khulm see Kholm
153 T16 **Khulna** Khulna, SW Bangladesh
153 T16 **Khulna** ◈ division SW Bangladesh
Khumain see Khomeyn
Khums see Al Khums
149 W2 **Khunjerāb Pass** pass China/Pakistan
Khūnjerāb Pass see Kunjirap Daban
153 P16 **Khunti** Jhārkhand, N India
167 N7 **Khun Yuam** Mae Hong Son, NW Thailand
Khurais see Khurayş
141 R7 **Khurayş** var. Khurais. Ash Sharqīyah, C Saudi Arabia
Khurda see Khordha
152 J11 **Khurja** Uttar Pradesh, N India
139 V4 **Khurmāl** var. Khormal. NE Iraq
Khurramabad see Khorramābād
Khurramshahr see Khorramshahr
149 U7 **Khushāb** Punjab, NE Pakistan
116 H8 **Khust** Cz. Chust, var. Husté, Hung. Huszt. Zakarpats'ka Oblast', W Ukraine
80 D11 **Khuwei** Western Kordofan, C Sudan
149 O13 **Khuzdār** Baluchistān, SW Pakistan
142 L9 **Khūzestān** off. Ostān-e Khūzestān, var. Khuzistan, prev. Arabistan; anc. Susiana. ◈ province SW Iran
Khūzestān, Ostān-e see Khūzestān
Khuzistan see Khūzestān
149 R2 **Khvājeh Ghār** var. Khwajaghar, Khwaja-i-Ghar. Takhār, NE Afghanistan
127 Q7 **Khvalynsk** Saratovskaya Oblast', W Russian Federation
143 N12 **Khvormūj** var. Khormuj. Būshehr, S Iran
142 I2 **Khvoy** var. Khoi, Khoy. Āžarbāyjān-e Bākhtarī, NW Iran
Khwajaghar/Khwaja-i-Ghar see Khvājeh Ghār
149 S5 **Khyber Pass** var. Kowtal-e Khaybar. pass Afghanistan/Pakistan
186 L8 **Kia** Santa Isabel, N Solomon Islands
183 S10 **Kiama** New South Wales, SE Australia
79 O22 **Kiambi** Katanga, SE Dem. Rep. Congo
27 Q12 **Kiamichi Mountains** ▲▲ Oklahoma, C USA
27 Q12 **Kiamichi River** ∽ Oklahoma, C USA
14 M10 **Kiamika, Réservoir** ▣ Québec, SE Canada
Kiamusze see Jiamusi
39 N7 **Kiana** Alaska, USA
Kiangmai see Chiang Mai
Kiang-ning see Nanjing
Kiangsi see Jiangxi
Kiangsu see Jiangsu
93 M14 **Kiantajärvi** ◎ E Finland
115 F19 **Kiáto** prev. Kiáton. Pelopónnisos, S Greece
Kiáton see Kiáto
Kiayi see Chiai
95 F22 **Kibæk** Ringkøbing, W Denmark
67 T9 **Kibali** var. Uele (upper course). ∽ NE Dem. Rep. Congo
79 E20 **Kibangou** Le Niari, SW Congo
Kibarty see Kybartai
92 M8 **Kiberg** Finnmark, N Norway
79 N20 **Kibombo** Maniema, E Dem. Rep. Congo
81 E20 **Kibondo** Kigoma, NW Tanzania
81 J15 **Kibre Mengist** var. Adola. Oromo, C Ethiopia
Kıbrıs see Cyprus
Kıbrıs/Kıbrıs Cumhuriyeti see Cyprus
81 E20 **Kibungo** var. Kibungu. SE Rwanda
Kibungu see Kibungo
113 N19 **Kičevo** SW FYR Macedonia
125 P13 **Kichmengskiy Gorodok** Vologodskaya Oblast', NW Russian Federation
30 J8 **Kickapoo River** ∽ Wisconsin, N USA
9 P16 **Kicking Horse Pass** pass Alberta/British Columbia, SW Canada
77 R9 **Kidal** Kidal, C Mali
77 Q8 **Kidal** ◈ region NE Mali
171 Q7 **Kidapawan** Mindanao, S Philippines
97 L20 **Kidderminster** C England, UK
76 I11 **Kidira** E Senegal
184 O11 **Kidnappers, Cape** headland North Island, New Zealand
100 J8 **Kiel** Schleswig-Holstein, N Germany
111 L15 **Kielce** Rus. Keltsy. Świętokrzyskie, C Poland
100 K7 **Kieler Bucht** bay N Germany
100 J7 **Kieler Förde** inlet N Germany
167 U13 **Kiên Đưc** var. Đak Lap. Đắc Lắc, S Vietnam
79 N24 **Kienge** Katanga, SE Dem. Rep. Congo

◆ Country
● Country Capital
◇ Dependent Territory
○ Dependent Territory Capital
◈ Administrative Regions
✈ International Airport
▲ Mountain
▲▲ Mountain Range
Volcano
∽ River
◎ Lake
▣ Reservoir

100 Q12 **Kietz** Brandenburg, NE Germany
Kiev *see* Kyyiv
Kiev Reservoir *see* Kyyivs'ke Vodoskhovyshche
76 J10 **Kiffa** Assaba, S Mauritania
115 H19 **Kifisiá** Attikí, C Greece
115 F18 **Kifisós** ≈ C Greece
139 U5 **Kifrī** N Iraq
81 D20 **Kigali** ● (Rwanda) C Rwanda
81 E20 **Kigali** ✈ C Rwanda
137 P13 **Kiğı** Bingöl, E Turkey
81 E21 **Kigoma** Kigoma, W Tanzania
81 E21 **Kigoma** ◈ *region* W Tanzania
38 F10 **Kihei** *var.* Kihei. Maui, Hawaii, USA
38 F10 **Kihei** *var.* Kihei. Maui, Hawai'i, USA, C Pacific Ocean
Kihei *see* Kihei
Kihei *see* Kihei
93 K17 **Kihniö** Länsi-Suomi, W Finland
118 F6 **Kihnu** *var.* Kihnu Saar, *Ger.* Kühnö. *island* SW Estonia
Kihnu Saar *see* Kihnu
38 A8 **Kii Landing** Ni'ihau, Hawai'i, USA
93 L14 **Kiiminki** Oulu, C Finland
164 J14 **Kii-Nagashima** *var.* Nagashima. Mie, Honshū, SW Japan
164 J14 **Kii-sanchi** ▲▲ Honshū, SW Japan
92 L11 **Kiistala** Lappi, N Finland
164 I15 **Kii-suidō** *strait* S Japan
165 V16 **Kikai-shima** *island* Nansei-shotō, SW Japan
112 M8 **Kikinda** *Ger.* Grosskikinda, *Hung.* Nagykikinda; *prev.* Velika Kikinda. Vojvodina, N Serbia
Kikládhes *see* Kykládes
165 Q5 **Kikonai** Hokkaidō, NE Japan
186 C8 **Kikori** Gulf, S Papua New Guinea
186 C8 **Kikori** ≈ W Papua New Guinea
165 O14 **Kikuchi** *var.* Kikuti. Kumamoto, Kyūshū, SW Japan
Kikuti *see* Kikuchi
127 N8 **Kikvidze** Volgogradskaya Oblast', SW Russian Federation
14 I10 **Kikwissi, Lac** ◎ Québec, SE Canada
79 I21 **Kikwit** Bandundu, W Dem. Rep. Congo
95 K15 **Kil** Värmland, C Sweden
94 N12 **Kilafors** Gävleborg, C Sweden
38 B8 **Kilauea** Kauai, Hawaii, USA, C Pacific Ocean
38 B8 **Kilauea** *var.* Kilauea. Kaua'i, Hawai'i, USA, C Pacific Ocean
38 H12 **Kilauea Caldera** *var.* Kilauea Caldera. *crater* Hawai'i, USA, C Pacific Ocean
Kilauea Caldera *see* Kilauea Caldera
109 V4 **Kilb** Niederösterreich, C Austria
39 O12 **Kilbuck Mountains** ▲▲ Alaska, USA
163 Y12 **Kilchu** NE North Korea
97 F18 **Kilcock** *Ir.* Cill Choca. Kildare, E Ireland
183 V2 **Kilcoy** Queensland, E Australia
97 F18 **Kildare** *Ir.* Cill Dara. Kildare, E Ireland
97 F18 **Kildare** *Ir.* Cill Dara. ◈ *county* E Ireland
124 K2 **Kil'din, Ostrov** *island* NW Russian Federation
25 W7 **Kilgore** Texas, SW USA
Kilien Mountains *see* Qilian Shan
114 K9 **Kilifarevo** Veliko Tŭrnovo, N Bulgaria
81 K20 **Kilifi** Coast, SE Kenya
189 U9 **Kili Island** *var.* Kōle. *island* Ralik Chain, S Marshall Islands
149 V2 **Kilik Pass** *pass* Afghanistan/China
Kilimane *see* Quelimane
81 I21 **Kilimanjaro** ◈ *region* E Tanzania
81 I20 **Kilimanjaro** *var.* Uhuru Peak. ⛰ NE Tanzania
Kilimbangara *see* Kolombangara
Kilinailau Islands *see* Tulun Islands
81 K23 **Kilindoni** Pwani, E Tanzania
118 H6 **Kilingi-Nõmme** *Ger.* Kurkund. Pärnumaa, SW Estonia
136 M17 **Kilis** Kilis, S Turkey
136 M16 **Kilis** ◈ *province* S Turkey
117 N12 **Kiliya** *Rom.* Chilia-Nouă. Odes'ka Oblast', SW Ukraine
97 B19 **Kilkee** *Ir.* Cill Chaoi. Clare, W Ireland
97 E19 **Kilkenny** *Ir.* Cill Chainnigh. Kilkenny, S Ireland
97 E19 **Kilkenny** *Ir.* Cill Chainnigh. ◈ *county* S Ireland
97 B18 **Kilkieran Bay** *Ir.* Cuan Chill Chiaráin. *bay* W Ireland
114 G13 **Kilkís** Kentrikí Makedonía, N Greece
97 C15 **Killala Bay** *Ir.* Cuan Chill Ala. *inlet* NW Ireland
9 R15 **Killam** Alberta, SW Canada
183 U3 **Killarney** Queensland, E Australia
9 W17 **Killarney** Manitoba, S Canada
14 E11 **Killarney** Ontario, S Canada
97 B20 **Killarney** *Ir.* Cill Airne. Kerry, SW Ireland
28 K4 **Killdeer** North Dakota, N USA
28 J4 **Killdeer Mountains** ▲▲ North Dakota, N USA
45 V15 **Killdeer River** ≈ Trinidad, Trinidad and Tobago
25 S9 **Killeen** Texas, SW USA
39 P6 **Killik River** ≈ Alaska, USA
9 T7 **Killinek Island** *island* Nunavut, NE Canada
Killini *see* Kyllíni
115 C19 **Killínis, Ákrotírio** *cape* S Greece
97 D15 **Killybegs** *Ir.* Na Cealla Beaga. NW Ireland
Kilmain *see* Quelimane
96 I13 **Kilmarnock** W Scotland, UK
21 X6 **Kilmarnock** Virginia, NE USA
125 S16 **Kil'mez'** Kirovskaya Oblast', NW Russian Federation
127 S2 **Kil'mez'** Udmurtskaya Respublika, NW Russian Federation
125 R16 **Kil'mez'** ≈ NW Russian Federation
67 V11 **Kilombero** ≈ S Tanzania
92 J10 **Kilpisjarvi** Lappi, N Finland
97 B19 **Kilrush** *Ir.* Cill Rois. Clare, W Ireland
79 O24 **Kilwa** Katanga, SE Dem. Rep. Congo
Kilwa *see* Kilwa Kivinje
81 J24 **Kilwa Kivinje** *var.* Kilwa. Lindi, SE Tanzania
81 J24 **Kilwa Masoko** Lindi, SE Tanzania
171 T13 **Kilwo** Pulau Seram, E Indonesia
114 P12 **Kilyos** İstanbul, NW Turkey
37 V8 **Kim** Colorado, C USA
169 U7 **Kimanis, Teluk** *bay* Sabah, East Malaysia
182 H8 **Kimba** South Australia
28 I15 **Kimball** Nebraska, C USA
29 O11 **Kimball** South Dakota, N USA
79 I21 **Kimbao** Bandundu, SW Dem. Rep. Congo
186 F7 **Kimbe** New Britain, E Papua New Guinea
186 G7 **Kimbe Bay** *inlet* New Britain, E Papua New Guinea
9 P17 **Kimberley** British Columbia, SW Canada
83 H23 **Kimberley** Northern Cape, C South Africa
180 M4 **Kimberley Plateau** *plateau* Western Australia
33 P15 **Kimberly** Idaho, NW USA
163 Y12 **Kimch'aek** *prev.* Sŏngjin. E North Korea
163 Y15 **Kimch'ŏn** C South Korea
163 Z16 **Kim Hae** *var.* Pusan. ✈ (Pusan) SE South Korea
93 K20 **Kimito** *Swe.* Kemiö. Länsi-Soumi, SW Finland
165 R4 **Kimobetsu** Hokkaidō, NE Japan
115 I21 **Kímolos** *island* Kykládes, Greece, Aegean Sea
115 I21 **Kímolou Sífnou, Stenó** *strait* Kykládes, Greece, Aegean Sea
126 L5 **Kimovsk** Tul'skaya Oblast', W Russian Federation
163 X15 **Kimpo** ✈ NW South Korea
Kimpolung *see* Câmpulung Moldovenesc
124 K16 **Kimry** Tverskaya Oblast', W Russian Federation
79 H21 **Kimvula** Bas-Congo, SW Dem. Rep. Congo
169 U6 **Kinabalu, Gunung** ▲ East Malaysia
Kinabatangan *see* Kinabatangan, Sungai
169 V7 **Kinabatangan, Sungai** *var.* Kinabatangan. ≈ East Malaysia
115 L21 **Kínaros** *island* Kykládes, Greece, Aegean Sea
9 O15 **Kinbasket Lake** ⊠ British Columbia, SW Canada
96 I7 **Kinbrace** N Scotland, UK
14 E14 **Kincardine** Ontario, S Canada
96 K10 **Kincardine** *cultural region* E Scotland, UK
79 K21 **Kinda** Kasai Occidental, SE Dem. Rep. Congo
79 M24 **Kinda** Katanga, SE Dem. Rep. Congo
166 L3 **Kindat** Sagaing, N Myanmar (Burma)
109 V6 **Kindberg** Steiermark, C Austria
22 H8 **Kinder** Louisiana, S USA
98 H13 **Kinderdijk** Zuid-Holland, SW Netherlands
97 M17 **Kinder Scout** ▲ C England, UK
9 S16 **Kindersley** Saskatchewan, S Canada
76 I14 **Kindia** Guinée-Maritime, SW Guinea
64 B11 **Kindley Field** *air base* E Bermuda
29 R6 **Kindred** North Dakota, N USA
79 N20 **Kindu** *prev.* Kindu-Port-Empain. Maniema, C Dem. Rep. Congo
Kindu-Port-Empain *see* Kindu
127 S6 **Kinel'** Samarskaya Oblast', W Russian Federation
125 N15 **Kineshma** Ivanovskaya Oblast', W Russian Federation
King *see* King William's Town
140 K10 **King Abdul Aziz** ✈ (Makkah) Makkah, W Saudi Arabia
21 X6 **King and Queen Court House** Virginia, NE USA
King Charles Islands *see* Kong Karls Land
King Christian IX Land *see* Kong Christian IX Land
King Christian X Land *see* Kong Christian X Land
35 O11 **King City** California, W USA
27 R2 **King City** Missouri, C USA
38 M16 **King Cove** Alaska, USA
26 M10 **Kingfisher** Oklahoma, C USA
King Frederik VI Coast *see* Kong Frederik VI Kyst
King Frederik VIII Land *see* Kong Frederik VIII Land
65 B24 **King George Bay** *bay* West Falkland, Falkland Islands
194 G3 **King George Island** *var.* King George Land. *island* South Shetland Islands, Antarctica
12 I6 **King George Islands** *island group* Northwest Territories, C Canada
King George Land *see* King George Island
124 G13 **Kingisepp** Leningradskaya Oblast', NW Russian Federation
183 N14 **King Island** *island* Tasmania, SE Australia
10 J15 **King Island** *island* British Columbia, SW Canada
King Island *see* Kadan Kyun
Kingissepp *see* Kuressaare
141 Q7 **King Khalid** ✈ (Ar Riyāḍ) Ar Riyāḍ, C Saudi Arabia
35 S2 **King Lear Peak** ▲ Nevada, W USA
195 Y8 **King Leopold and Queen Astrid Land** *physical region* Antarctica
180 M4 **King Leopold Ranges** ▲▲ Western Australia
36 I11 **Kingman** Arizona, SW USA
26 M6 **Kingman** Kansas, C USA
192 L7 **Kingman Reef** ◇ *US territory* C Pacific Ocean
79 N20 **Kingombe** Maniema, E Dem. Rep. Congo
182 F5 **Kingoonya** South Australia
194 J10 **King Peninsula** *peninsula* Antarctica
39 P13 **King Salmon** Alaska, USA
35 Q6 **Kings Beach** California, W USA
35 R11 **Kingsburg** California, W USA
182 I10 **Kingscote** South Australia
King's County *see* Offaly
194 H2 **King Sejong** *South Korean research station* Antarctica
183 T9 **Kingsford Smith** ✈ (Sydney) New South Wales, SE Australia
9 P17 **Kingsgate** British Columbia, SW Canada
23 W8 **Kingsland** Georgia, SE USA
29 S13 **Kingsley** Iowa, C USA
97 O19 **King's Lynn** *var.* Bishop's Lynn, Kings Lynn, Lynn, Lynn Regis. E England, UK
Kings Lynn *see* King's Lynn
21 Q10 **Kings Mountain** North Carolina, SE USA
180 K4 **King Sound** *sound* Western Australia
37 N2 **Kings Peak** ▲ Utah, W USA
21 O8 **Kingsport** Tennessee, S USA
35 R11 **Kings River** ≈ California, W USA
183 P17 **Kingston** Tasmania, SE Australia
14 K14 **Kingston** Ontario, SE Canada
44 K13 **Kingston** ● (Jamaica) E Jamaica
185 C22 **Kingston** Otago, South Island, New Zealand
19 P12 **Kingston** Massachusetts, NE USA
27 S3 **Kingston** Missouri, C USA
18 K12 **Kingston** New York, NE USA
31 S14 **Kingston** Ohio, N USA
19 O13 **Kingston** Rhode Island, NE USA
20 M9 **Kingston** Tennessee, S USA
35 W12 **Kingston Peak** ▲ California, W USA
182 J11 **Kingston Southeast** South Australia
97 N17 **Kingston upon Hull** *var.* Hull. E England, UK
97 N22 **Kingston upon Thames** SE England, UK
45 P14 **Kingstown** ● (Saint Vincent and the Grenadines) Saint Vincent, Saint Vincent and the Grenadines
Kingstown *see* Dún Laoghaire
21 T13 **Kingstree** South Carolina, SE USA
64 L8 **Kings Trough** *undersea feature* E Atlantic Ocean
14 C18 **Kingsville** Ontario, S Canada
25 S15 **Kingsville** Texas, SW USA
21 W6 **King William** Virginia, NE USA
8 M7 **King William Island** *island* Nunavut, N Canada Arctic Ocean
83 I25 **King William's Town** *var.* King, Kingwilliamstown. Eastern Cape, S South Africa
Kingwilliamstown *see* King William's Town
21 T3 **Kingwood** West Virginia, NE USA
136 C13 **Kınık** İzmir, W Turkey
79 G21 **Kinkala** Le Pool, S Congo
165 R10 **Kinka-san** *headland* Honshū, C Japan
184 M8 **Kinleith** Waikato, North Island, New Zealand
95 J19 **Kinna** Älvsborg, S Sweden
96 L8 **Kinnaird Head** *var.* Kinnairds Head. *headland* NE Scotland, UK
Kinnairds Head *see* Kinnaird Head
95 K20 **Kinnared** Halland, S Sweden
Kinneret, Yam *see* Tiberias, Lake
155 K24 **Kinniyai** Eastern Province, NE Sri Lanka
93 L16 **Kinnula** Länsi-Soumi, C Finland
14 I8 **Kinojévis** ≈ Québec, SE Canada
164 I14 **Kino-kawa** ≈ Honshū, SW Japan
9 U11 **Kinoosao** Saskatchewan, C Canada
99 L17 **Kinrooi** Limburg, NE Belgium
96 J11 **Kinross** C Scotland, UK
96 J11 **Kinross** *cultural region* C Scotland, UK
97 C21 **Kinsale** *Ir.* Cionn tSáile. Cork, SW Ireland
95 D14 **Kinsarvik** Hordaland, S Norway
79 G21 **Kinshasa** *prev.* Léopoldville. ● Kinshasa, W Dem. Rep. Congo
79 G21 **Kinshasa** *off.* Ville de Kinshasa, *var.* Kinshasa City. ◈ *region* (Dem. Rep. Congo) SW Dem. Rep. Congo
79 G21 **Kinshasa** ✈ Kinshasa, SW Dem. Rep. Congo
Kinshasa City *see* Kinshasa
117 U9 **Kins'ka** ≈ SE Ukraine
26 K6 **Kinsley** Kansas, C USA
21 W10 **Kinston** North Carolina, SE USA
77 P15 **Kintampo** W Ghana
182 B1 **Kintore, Mount** ▲ South Australia
96 G13 **Kintyre** *peninsula* W Scotland, UK
96 G13 **Kintyre, Mull of** *headland* W Scotland, UK
166 M4 **Kin-u** Sagaing, C Myanmar (Burma)
12 G8 **Kinushseo** ≈ Ontario, C Canada
9 P13 **Kinuso** Alberta, W Canada
154 I13 **Kinwat** Mahārāshtra, C India
81 F16 **Kinyeti** ▲ S Sudan
101 I17 **Kinzig** ≈ SW Germany
Kioga, Lake *see* Kyoga, Lake
26 M8 **Kiowa** Kansas, C USA
27 P12 **Kiowa** Oklahoma, C USA
Kiparissia *see* Kyparissia
14 H10 **Kipawa, Lac** ◎ Québec, SE Canada
81 G24 **Kipengere Range** ▲▲ SW Tanzania
81 E23 **Kipili** Rukwa, W Tanzania
81 K20 **Kipini** Coast, SE Kenya
9 V16 **Kipling** Saskatchewan, S Canada
38 M13 **Kipnuk** Alaska, USA
97 F18 **Kippure** *Ir.* Cipiúr. ▲ E Ireland
79 N25 **Kipushi** Katanga, SE Dem. Rep. Congo
187 N10 **Kirakira** *var.* Kaokaona. San Cristobal, SE Solomon Islands
155 K14 **Kirandul** *var.* Bailādila. Chhattīsgarh, C India
155 I21 **Kīranūr** Tamil Nādu, SE India
119 N21 **Kiraw** *Rus.* Kirovo. Homyel'skaya Voblasts', SE Belarus
119 M17 **Kirawsk** *Rus.* Kirovsk; *prev.* Startsy. Mahilyowskaya Voblasts', E Belarus
118 F5 **Kirbla** Läänemaa, W Estonia
25 Y9 **Kirbyville** Texas, SW USA
114 M12 **Kırcasalih** Edirne, NW Turkey
109 W8 **Kirchbach** *var.* Kirchbach in Steiermark. Steiermark, SE Austria
Kirchbach in Steiermark *see* Kirchbach
108 H7 **Kirchberg** Sankt Gallen, NE Switzerland
109 S5 **Kirchdorf an der Krems** Oberösterreich, N Austria
Kirchheim *see* Kirchheim unter Teck
101 I22 **Kirchheim unter Teck** *var.* Kirchheim. Baden-Württemberg, SW Germany
Kirdzhali *see* Kŭrdzhali
123 N13 **Kirenga** ≈ S Russian Federation
123 N12 **Kirensk** Irkutskaya Oblast', C Russian Federation
Kirghizia *see* Kyrgyzstan
145 S16 **Kirghiz Range** *Rus.* Kirgizskiy Khrebet; *prev.* Alexander Range. ▲▲ Kazakhstan/Kyrgyzstan
Kirghiz SSR *see* Kyrgyzstan
Kirghiz Steppe *see* Kazakhskiy Melkosopochnik
Kirgizskaya SSR *see* Kyrgyzstan
Kirgizskiy Khrebet *see* Kirghiz Range
79 I19 **Kiri** Bandundu, W Dem. Rep. Congo
Kiriath-Arba *see* Hebron
191 R3 **Kiribati** *off.* Republic of Kiribati. ◆ *republic* C Pacific Ocean
Kiribati, Republic of *see* Kiribati
136 L17 **Kırıkhan** Hatay, S Turkey
136 I13 **Kırıkkale** Kırıkkale, C Turkey
136 C10 **Kırıkkale** ◈ *province* C Turkey
124 L13 **Kirillov** Vologodskaya Oblast', NW Russian Federation
Kirin *see* Jilin
81 I18 **Kirinyaga** *prev.* Mount Kenya. ▲ C Kenya
124 H13 **Kirishi** *var.* Kirisi. Leningradskaya Oblast', NW Russian Federation
164 C16 **Kirishima-yama** ▲ Kyūshū, SW Japan
Kirisi *see* Kirishi
191 Y2 **Kiritimati** ✈ Kiritimati, E Kiribati
191 Y2 **Kiritimati** *prev.* Christmas Island. *atoll* Line Islands, E Kiribati
186 G9 **Kiriwina Island** *Eng.* Trobriand Island. *island* SE Papua New Guinea
186 G9 **Kiriwina Islands** *var.* Trobriand Islands. *island group* S Papua New Guinea
96 K12 **Kirkcaldy** E Scotland, UK
97 I14 **Kirkcudbright** S Scotland, U
97 I14 **Kirkcudbright** *cultural region* S Scotland, UK
Kirkee *see* Khadki
95 I14 **Kirkenær** Hedmark, S Norway
92 M8 **Kirkenes** *Fin.* Kirkkoniemi. Finnmark, N Norway
92 J4 **Kirkjubæjarklaustur** Sudhurland, S Iceland
Kirk-Kilissa *see* Kırklareli
Kirkkoniemi *see* Kirkenes
93 L20 **Kirkkonummi** *Swe.* Kyrkslätt. Uusimaa, S Finland
14 G7 **Kirkland Lake** Ontario, S Canada
136 C9 **Kırklareli** *prev.* Kirk-Kilissa. Kırklareli, NW Turkey
136 I13 **Kırklareli** ◈ *province* NW Turkey
185 F20 **Kirkliston Range** ▲▲ South Island, New Zealand
14 D10 **Kirkpatrick Lake** ◎ Ontario, S Canada
195 Q11 **Kirkpatrick, Mount** ▲ Antarctica
27 U2 **Kirksville** Missouri, C USA
139 T4 **Kirkūk** *var.* Karkūk, Kerkuk. N Iraq
139 U7 **Kir Kush** E Iraq
96 K5 **Kirkwall** NE Scotland, UK
83 H25 **Kirkwood** Eastern Cape, S South Africa
27 X5 **Kirkwood** Missouri, C USA
Kirman *see* Kermān
Kir Moab *see* Al Karak
Kir of Moab *see* Al Karak
126 I5 **Kirov** Kaluzhskaya Oblast', W Russian Federation
125 R14 **Kirov** *prev.* Vyatka. Kirovskaya Oblast', NW Russian Federation
Kirov *see* Balpyk Bi
Kirovabad *see* Gäncä
Kirovakan *see* Vanadzor
Kirov/Kirova *see* Kopbirlik
Kirovo *see* Kiraw
Kirovo *see* Beshariq
125 R14 **Kirovo-Chepetsk** Kirovskaya Oblast', NW Russian Federation
117 R7 **Kirovohrad** *Rus.* Kirovograd; *prev.* Kirovo, Yelizavetgrad, Zinov'yevsk. Kirovohrads'ka Oblast', C Ukraine
Kirovohrad *see* Kirovohrads'ka Oblast'
117 P7 **Kirovohrads'ka Oblast'** *var.* Kirovohrad, *Rus.* Kirovogradskaya Oblast'. ◈ *province* C Ukraine
Kirovo/Kirovograd *see* Kirovohrad
124 J4 **Kirovsk** Murmanskaya Oblast', NW Russian Federation
117 X7 **Kirovs'k** Luhans'ka Oblast', E Ukraine
Kirovsk *see* Kirawsk, Belarus
Kirovsk *see* Babadaýhan, Turkmenistan
122 E9 **Kirovskaya Oblast'** ◈ *province* NW Russian Federation
117 X8 **Kirov'ske** Donets'ka Oblast', E Ukraine
117 U13 **Kirovs'ke** *Rus.* Kirovskoye. Respublika Krym, S Ukraine
Kirovskiy *see* Balpyk Bi
Kirovskiy *see* Ust'yevoye
Kirovskoye *see* Kyzyl-Adyr
Kirovskoye *see* Kirovs'ke
146 E11 **Kirpili** Ahal Welaýaty, C Turkmenistan
96 K10 **Kirriemuir** E Scotland, UK
125 S13 **Kirs** Kirovskaya Oblast', NW Russian Federation
127 N7 **Kirsanov** Tambovskaya Oblast', W Russian Federation
136 J14 **Kırşehir** *anc.* Justinianopolis. Kırşehir, C Turkey
136 I13 **Kırşehir** ◈ *province* C Turkey
149 P4 **Kirthar Range** ▲▲ S Pakistan
37 P9 **Kirtland** New Mexico, SW USA
92 J11 **Kiruna** *Lapp.* Giron. Norrbotten, N Sweden
79 M18 **Kirundu** Orientale, NE Dem. Rep. Congo
Kirun/Kirun' *see* Chilung
26 L3 **Kirwin Reservoir** ⊠ Kansas, C USA
127 Q4 **Kirya** Chavash Respubliki, W Russian Federation
95 M18 **Kisa** Östergötland, S Sweden
165 P9 **Kisakata** Akita, Honshū, C Japan
Kisalföld *see* Little Alföld
79 L18 **Kisangani** *prev.* Stanleyville. Orientale, NE Dem. Rep. Congo
39 N12 **Kisaralik River** ≈ Alaska, USA
165 O14 **Kisarazu** Chiba, Honshū, S Japan
111 I22 **Kisbér** Komárom-Esztergom, NW Hungary
9 V17 **Kisbey** Saskatchewan, S Canada
122 J13 **Kiselevsk** Kemerovskaya Oblast', S Russian Federation
153 R13 **Kishanganj** Bihār, NE India
152 G12 **Kishangarh** Rājasthān, N India
Kishegyes *see* Mali Idoš
77 S15 **Kishi** Oyo, W Nigeria
Kishinev *see* Chişinău
Kishiözen *see* Malyy Uzen'
164 I14 **Kishiwada** *var.* Kisiwada. Ōsaka, Honshū, SW Japan
143 P14 **Kish, Jazīreh-ye** *island* S Iran
145 R7 **Kishkenekol'** *prev.* Kzyltu, *Kaz.* Qyzyltū. Kokshetau, N Kazakhstan
152 I6 **Kishtwār** Jammu and Kashmir, NW India
81 H19 **Kisii** Nyanza, SW Kenya
81 J23 **Kisiju** Pwani, E Tanzania
Kisiwada *see* Kishiwada
Kisjenő *see* Chişineu-Criş
38 E17 **Kiska Island** *island* Aleutian Islands, Alaska, USA
Kiskapus *see* Copşa Mică
111 M22 **Kiskőrei-víztároló** ⊠ E Hungary
Kis-Küküllo *see* Târnava Mică
111 L24 **Kiskunfélegyháza** *var.* Félegyháza. Bács-Kiskun, C Hungary
111 K25 **Kiskunhalas** *var.* Halas. Bács-Kiskun, S Hungary
111 K24 **Kiskunmajsa** Bács-Kiskun, S Hungary
127 N15 **Kislovodsk** Stavropol'skiy Kray, SW Russian Federation
81 L18 **Kismaayo** *var.* Chisimayu, Kismayu, *It.* Chisimaio. Jubbada Hoose, S Somalia
Kismayu *see* Kismaayo
164 M13 **Kiso-sanmyaku** ▲▲ Honshū, S Japan
115 H24 **Kíssamos** *prev* Kastélli. Kríti, Greece, E Mediterranean Sea
Kisseraing *see* Kanmaw Kyun
76 K14 **Kissidougou** Guinée-Forestière, S Guinea
23 X12 **Kissimmee** Florida, SE USA
23 X12 **Kissimmee, Lake** ◎ Florida, SE USA
23 X13 **Kissimmee River** ≈ Florida, SE USA
9 V13 **Kississing Lake** ◎ Manitoba, C Canada
111 L24 **Kistelek** Csongrád, SE Hungary
Kistna *see* Krishna
111 M23 **Kisújszállás** Jász-Nagykun-Szolnok, E Hungary
164 G12 **Kisuki** Shimane, Honshū, SW Japan
81 H18 **Kisumu** *prev.* Port Florence. Nyanza, W Kenya
Kisutzaneustadtl *see* Kysucké Nové Mesto
111 O20 **Kisvárda** *Ger.* Kleinwardein. Szabolcs-Szatmár-Bereg, E Hungary
81 J24 **Kiswere** Lindi, SE Tanzania
Kiszucaújhely *see* Kysucké Nové Mesto
76 K12 **Kita** Kayes, W Mali
197 N14 **Kitaa** ◈ *province* W Greenland
Kitab *see* Kitob
165 Q4 **Kitahiyama** Hokkaidō, NE Japan
165 P12 **Kita-Ibaraki** Ibaraki, Honshū, S Japan
165 X16 **Kita-Iō-jima** *island* SE Japan
165 Q9 **Kitakami** Iwate, Honshū, C Japan
165 P11 **Kitakata** Fukushima, Honshū, C Japan
164 D13 **Kitakyūshū** *var.* Kitakyûsyû. Fukuoka, Kyūshū, SW Japan
Kitakyûsyû *see* Kitakyūshū
81 H18 **Kitale** Rift Valley, W Kenya
165 U3 **Kitami** Hokkaidō, NE Japan
165 T2 **Kitami-sanchi** ▲▲ Hokkaidō, NE Japan
37 W5 **Kit Carson** Colorado, C USA
180 M12 **Kitchener** Western Australia
14 F16 **Kitchener** Ontario, S Canada
93 O17 **Kitee** Itä-Suomi, SE Finland
81 G16 **Kitgum** N Uganda
Kithareng *see* Kanmaw Kyun
Kíthira *see* Kýthira
Kíthnos *see* Kýthnos
10 J13 **Kitimat** British Columbia, SW Canada
92 L11 **Kitinen** ≈ N Finland
147 N12 **Kitob** *Rus.* Kitab. Qashqadaryo Viloyati, S Uzbekistan
116 K7 **Kitsman'** *Ger.* Kotzman, *Rom.* Cozmeni, *Rus.* Kitsman. Chernivets'ka Oblast', W Ukraine
164 E14 **Kitsuki** *var.* Kituki. Ōita, Kyūshū, SW Japan
18 C14 **Kittanning** Pennsylvania, NE USA
19 P10 **Kittery** Maine, NE USA
92 L11 **Kittilä** Lappi, N Finland
109 Z4 **Kittsee** Burgenland, E Austria
81 J19 **Kitui** Eastern, S Kenya
Kituki *see* Kitsuki
81 G22 **Kitunda** Tabora, C Tanzania
10 K13 **Kitwanga** British Columbia, SW Canada
82 J13 **Kitwe** *var.* Kitwe-Nkana. Copperbelt, C Zambia
Kitwe-Nkana *see* Kitwe
109 O7 **Kitzbühel** Tirol, W Austria
109 O7 **Kitzbüheler Alpen** ▲▲ W Austria
101 J19 **Kitzingen** Bayern, SE Germany
153 Q14 **Kiul** Bihār, NE India
186 A7 **Kiunga** Western, SW Papua New Guinea
93 M16 **Kiuruvesi** Kuopio, C Finland
38 M7 **Kivalina** Alaska, USA
92 L13 **Kivalo** *ridge* C Finland
116 J3 **Kivertsi** *Pol.* Kiwerce, *Rus.* Kivertsy. Volyns'ka Oblast', NW Ukraine
Kivertsy *see* Kivertsi
93 L16 **Kivijärvi** Länsi-Soumi, C Finland
95 L23 **Kivik** Skåne, S Sweden
118 J3 **Kiviõli** Ida-Virumaa, NE Estonia
Kivu, Lac *see* Kivu, Lake
67 U10 **Kivu, Lake** *Fr.* Lac Kivu. ◎ Rwanda/Dem. Rep. Congo
186 C9 **Kiwai Island** *island* SW Papua New Guinea
39 N8 **Kiwalik** Alaska, USA
Kiwerce *see* Kivertsi
Kiyev *see* Kyyiv
145 R10 **Kiyevka** Karaganda, C Kazakhstan
Kiyevskaya Oblast' *see* Kyyivs'ka Oblast'
Kiyevskoye Vodokhranilishche *see* Kyyivs'ke Vodoskhovyshche
136 D10 **Kıyıköy** Kırklareli, NW Turkey
145 O9 **Kiyma** Akmola, C Kazakhstan
125 V13 **Kizel** Permskaya Oblast', NW Russian Federation
125 O12 **Kizema** *var.* Kizëma. Arkhangel'skaya Oblast', NW Russian Federation
Kizëma *see* Kizema
Kizilagach *see* Elkhovo
136 H12 **Kızılcahamam** Ankara, N Turkey
136 J10 **Kızıl Irmak** ≈ C Turkey
Kizil Kum *see* Kyzyl Kum
137 P16 **Kızıltepe** Mardin, SE Turkey
Ki Zil Uzen *see* Qezel Owzan, Rūd-e
127 Q16 **Kizilyurt** Respublika Dagestan, SW Russian Federation
127 Q15 **Kizlyar** Respublika Dagestan, SW Russian Federation
127 S3 **Kizner** Udmurtskaya Respublika, NW Russian Federation
Kizyl-Arvat *see* Serdar
Kizyl-Atrek *see* Etrek
Kizyl-Kaya *see* Gyzylgaýa
Kizyl-Su *see* Gyzylsuw
95 H16 **Kjerkøy** *island* S Norway
92 L7 **Kjøllefjord** Finnmark, N Norway
92 H11 **Kjøpsvik** Nordland, C Norway
169 N12 **Klabat, Teluk** *bay* Pulau Bangka, W Indonesia
112 I12 **Kladanj** ◈ Federacija Bosna I Hercegovina, E Bosnia and Herzegovina
171 X16 **Kladar** Papua, E Indonesia
111 C16 **Kladno** Středni Čechy, NW Czech Republic
112 P11 **Kladovo** Serbia, E Serbia
167 P12 **Klaeng** Rayong, S Thailand
109 T9 **Klagenfurt** *Slvn.* Celovec. Kärnten, S Austria
118 B11 **Klaipėda** *Ger.* Memel. Klaipeda, NW Lithuania
118 C11 **Klaipėda** ◈ *province* W Lithuania
Klaksvig *see* Klaksvík
95 B18 **Klaksvík** *Dan.* Klaksvig. Bordhoy, N Faeroe Islands
34 L2 **Klamath** California, W USA
32 H16 **Klamath Falls** Oregon, NW USA
34 M1 **Klamath Mountains** ▲▲ California/Oregon, W USA
34 L2 **Klamath River** ≈ California/Oregon, W USA
168 K9 **Klang** *var.* Kelang; *prev.* Port Swettenham. Selangor, Peninsular Malaysia
94 J13 **Klarälven** ≈ Norway/Sweden
111 B15 **Klášterec nad Ohří** *Ger.* Klösterle an der Eger. Ústecky Kraj, NW Czech Republic
111 B18 **Klatovy** *Ger.* Klattau. Plzeňský Kraj, W Czech Republic
Klattau *see* Klatovy
Klausenburg *see* Cluj-Napoca
39 Y14 **Klawock** Prince of Wales Island, Alaska, USA
98 P8 **Klazienaveen** Drenthe, NE Netherlands
Kleck *see* Klyetsk

◆ Country ● Country Capital ◇ Dependent Territory ○ Dependent Territory Capital ◈ Administrative Regions ✈ International Airport ▲ Mountain ▲▲ Mountain Range ⛰ Volcano ≈ River ◎ Lake ⊠ Reservoir

110 H11 **Kłecko** Weilkopolskie, C Poland
110 I11 **Kleczew** Wielkopolskie, C Poland
10 L15 **Kleena Kleene** British Columbia, SW Canada
83 D20 **Klein Aub** Hardap, C Namibia
Kleine Donau *see* Mosoni-Duna
101 O14 **Kleine Elster** ≈ E Germany
Kleine Kokel *see* Târnava Mică
99 I16 **Kleine Nete** ≈ N Belgium
Kleines Ungarisches Tiefland *see* Little Alföld
83 E22 **Klein Karas** Karas, S Namibia
Kleinkopisch *see* Copşa Mică
Klein-Marien *see* Väike-Maarja
Kleinschlatten *see* Zlatna
83 D23 **Kleinsee** Northern Cape, W South Africa
Kleinwardein *see* Kisvárda
115 C16 **Kleisoúra** Ípeiros, W Greece
95 C17 **Klepp** Rogaland, S Norway
83 I22 **Klerksdorp** North-West, N South Africa
126 I5 **Kletnya** Bryanskaya Oblast', W Russian Federation
Kletsk *see* Klyetsk
101 D14 **Kleve** *Eng.* Cleves, *Fr.* Clèves; *prev.* Cleve. Nordrhein-Westfalen, W Germany
113 J16 **Kličevo** C Montenegro
119 M16 **Klichaw** *Rus.* Klichev. Mahilyowskaya Voblasts', E Belarus
Klichev *see* Klichaw
119 Q16 **Klimavichy** *Rus.* Klimovichi. Mahilyowskaya Voblasts', E Belarus
114 M7 **Kliment** Shumen, NE Bulgaria
Klimovichi *see* Klimavichy
93 G14 **Klimpfjäll** Västerbotten, N Sweden
126 K3 **Klin** Moskovskaya Oblast', W Russian Federation
113 M16 **Klina** Kosovo, S Serbia
111 B15 **Klínovec** *Ger.* Keilberg. ▲ NW Czech Republic
95 P19 **Klintehamn** Gotland, SE Sweden
127 R8 **Klintsovka** Saratovskaya Oblast', W Russian Federation
126 H6 **Klintsy** Bryanskaya Oblast', W Russian Federation
95 K22 **Klippan** Skåne, S Sweden
92 G13 **Klippen** Västerbotten, N Sweden
121 P2 **Klírou** W Cyprus
114 I9 **Klisura** Plovdiv, C Bulgaria
95 F20 **Klitmøller** Viborg, NW Denmark
112 F11 **Ključ** ◈ Federacija Bosna I Hercegovina, NW Bosnia and Herzegovina
111 J14 **Kłobuck** Śląskie, S Poland
110 J11 **Kłodawa** Wielkopolskie, C Poland
111 G16 **Kłodzko** *Ger.* Glatz. Dolnośląskie, SW Poland
95 I14 **Kløfta** Akershus, S Norway
112 P12 **Klokočevac** Serbia, E Serbia
118 G3 **Klooga** *Ger.* Lodensee. Harjumaa, NW Estonia
99 F15 **Kloosterzande** Zeeland, SW Netherlands
113 L19 **Klos** *var.* Klosi. Dibër, C Albania
Klosi *see* Klos
Klösterle an der Eger *see* Klášterec nad Ohří
109 X3 **Klosterneuburg** Niederösterreich, NE Austria
108 J9 **Klosters** Graubünden, SE Switzerland
108 G7 **Kloten** Zürich, N Switzerland
108 G7 **Kloten** ✈ (Zürich) Zürich, N Switzerland
100 K12 **Klötze** Sachsen-Anhalt, C Germany
12 K3 **Klotz, Lac** ◎ Québec, NE Canada
101 O15 **Klotzsche** ✈ (Dresden) Sachsen, E Germany
10 H7 **Kluane Lake** ◎ Yukon Territory, W Canada
Kluang *see* Keluang
111 I14 **Kluczbork** *Ger.* Kreuzburg, Kreuzburg in Oberschlesien. Opolskie, S Poland
39 W12 **Klukwan** Alaska, USA
Klyastitsy *see* Klyastsitsy
118 L11 **Klyastsitsy** *Rus.* Klyastitsy. Vitsyebskaya Voblasts', N Belarus
127 T5 **Klyavlino** Samarskaya Oblast', W Russian Federation
84 K9 **Klyaz'in** ≈ W Russian Federation
127 N3 **Klyaz'ma** ≈ W Russian Federation
119 J17 **Klyetsk** *Pol.* Kleck, *Rus.* Kletsk. Minskaya Voblasts', SW Belarus
147 S8 **Klyuchevka** Talasskaya Oblast', NW Kyrgyzstan
123 V10 **Klyuchevskaya Sopka, Vulkan** ✱ E Russian Federation
95 D17 **Knaben** Vest-Agder, S Norway
95 K21 **Knäred** Halland, S Sweden
97 M16 **Knaresborough** N England, UK
114 H8 **Knezha** Vratsa, NW Bulgaria
25 O9 **Knickerbocker** Texas, SW USA
28 K5 **Knife River** ≈ North Dakota, N USA
10 K16 **Knight Inlet** *inlet* British Columbia, W Canada
39 S12 **Knight Island** *island* Alaska, USA
97 K20 **Knighton** E Wales, UK
35 O7 **Knights Landing** California, W USA
112 E13 **Knin** Šibenik-Knin, S Croatia
25 Q12 **Knippal** Texas, SW USA
109 U7 **Knittelfeld** Steiermark, C Austria
95 O15 **Knivsta** Uppsala, C Sweden
113 P14 **Knjaževac** Serbia, E Serbia
27 S4 **Knob Noster** Missouri, C USA
99 D15 **Knokke-Heist** West-Vlaanderen, NW Belgium
95 H20 **Knøsen** *hill* N Denmark
Knosós *see* Knossos
115 J25 **Knossos** *Gk.* Knosós. *prehistoric site* Kríti, Greece, E Mediterranean Sea
25 N7 **Knott** Texas, SW USA
194 K5 **Knowles, Cape** *headland* Antarctica
31 O11 **Knox** Indiana, N USA
29 O3 **Knox** North Dakota, N USA
18 C13 **Knox** Pennsylvania, NE USA
189 X8 **Knox Atoll** *var.* Nadikdik, Narikrik. *atoll* Ratak Chain, SE Marshall Islands
10 H13 **Knox, Cape** *headland* Graham Island, British Columbia, SW Canada
25 P5 **Knox City** Texas, SW USA
195 Y11 **Knox Coast** *physical region* Antarctica
31 T12 **Knox Lake** ⊠ Ohio, N USA
23 T5 **Knoxville** Georgia, SE USA
30 K12 **Knoxville** Illinois, N USA
29 W15 **Knoxville** Iowa, C USA
21 N9 **Knoxville** Tennessee, S USA
197 P11 **Knud Rasmussen Land** *physical region* N Greenland
Knüll *see* Knüllgebirge
101 I16 **Knüllgebirge** *var.* Knüll. ▲▲ C Germany
Knyazhevo *see* Sredishte
Knyazhitsy *see* Knyazhytsy
119 O15 **Knyazhytsy** *Rus.* Knyazhitsy. Mahilyowskaya Voblasts', E Belarus
83 G26 **Knysna** Western Cape, SW South Africa
Koartac *see* Quaqtaq
169 N13 **Koba** Pulau Bangka, W Indonesia
164 D16 **Kobayashi** *var.* Kobayasi. Miyazaki, Kyūshū, SW Japan
Kobayasi *see* Kobayashi
Kobdo *see* Hovd
164 I13 **Kōbe** Hyōgo, Honshū, SW Japan
Kobelyaki *see* Kobelyaky
117 T6 **Kobelyaky** *Rus.* Kobelyaki. Poltavs'ka Oblast', NE Ukraine
95 J22 **København** *Eng.* Copenhagen; *anc.* Hafnia. ● (Denmark) Sjælland, København, E Denmark
95 J23 **København** *off.* Københavns Amt. ◈ *county* E Denmark
Københavns Amt *see* København
76 K10 **Kobenni** Hodh el Gharbi, S Mauritania
171 T13 **Kobi** Pulau Seram, E Indonesia
101 F17 **Koblenz** *prev.* Coblenz, *Fr.* Coblence; *anc.* Confluentes. Rheinland-Pfalz, W Germany
108 F6 **Koblenz** Aargau, N Switzerland
124 J14 **Kabozha** Novgorodskaya Oblast', W Russian Federation
Kobrin *see* Kobryn
171 V15 **Kobroor, Pulau** *island* Kepulauan Aru, E Indonesia
119 G19 **Kobryn** *Pol.* Kobryn, *Rus.* Kobrin. Brestskaya Voblasts', SW Belarus
39 O7 **Kobuk** Alaska, USA
39 O7 **Kobuk River** ≈ Alaska, USA
137 Q10 **K'obulet'i** W Georgia
123 P10 **Kobyay** Respublika Sakha (Yakutiya), NE Russian Federation
136 E11 **Kocaeli** ◈ *province* NW Turkey
113 P18 **Kočani** NE FYR Macedonia
112 K12 **Koceljevo** Serbia, W Serbia
109 U12 **Kočevje** *Ger.* Gottschee. S Slovenia
153 T12 **Koch Bihār** West Bengal, NE India
122 M9 **Kochechum** ≈ N Russian Federation
101 I20 **Kocher** ≈ SW Germany
125 T13 **Kochevo** Komi-Permyatskiy Avtonomnyy Okrug, NW Russian Federation
164 G14 **Kōchi** *var.* Kôti. Kōchi, Shikoku, SW Japan
164 G14 **Kōchi** *off.* Kōchi-ken, *var.* Kôti. ◈ *prefecture* Shikoku, SW Japan
Kochi *see* Cochin
Kōchi-ken *see* Kōchi
Kochiu *see* Gejiu
Kochkor *see* Kochkorka
147 V8 **Kochkorka** *Kir.* Kochkor. Narynskaya Oblast', C Kyrgyzstan
125 V5 **Kochmes** Respublika Komi, NW Russian Federation
127 P15 **Kochubey** Respublika Dagestan, SW Russian Federation
115 I17 **Kochýlas** ▲ Skńyros, Vóreioi Sporádes, Greece, Aegean Sea
110 O13 **Kock** Lubelskie, E Poland
81 J19 **Kodacho** *spring/well* S Kenya
155 K24 **Koddiyar Bay** *bay* NE Sri Lanka
39 Q14 **Kodiak** Kodiak Island, Alaska, USA
39 Q14 **Kodiak Island** *island* Alaska, USA
154 B12 **Kodīnār** Gujarāt, W India
124 M9 **Kodino** Arkhangel'skaya Oblast', NW Russian Federation
122 M12 **Kodinsk** Krasnoyarskiy Kray, C Russian Federation
80 F12 **Kodok** Upper Nile, SE Sudan
117 N8 **Kodyma** Odes'ka Oblast', SW Ukraine
Koedoes *see* Kudus
99 B17 **Koekelare** West-Vlaanderen, W Belgium
Koeln *see* Köln
Koepang *see* Kupang
Ko-erh-mu *see* Golmud
99 J17 **Koersel** Limburg, NE Belgium
83 E21 **Koës** Karas, SE Namibia
Koetai *see* Mahakam, Sungai
Koetaradja *see* Bandaaceh
36 I14 **Kofa Mountains** ▲▲ Arizona, SW USA
171 Y15 **Kofarau** Papua, E Indonesia
147 P13 **Kofarnihon** *Rus.* Kofarnikhon; *prev.* Ordzhonikidzeabad, *Taj* Orjonikidzeobod, Yangi-Bazar. W Tajikistan
147 P14 **Kofarnihon** *Rus.* Kafirnigan. ≈ SW Tajikistan
Kofarnikhon *see* Kofarnihon
114 M11 **Kofçaz** Kırklareli, NW Turkey
115 J25 **Kófinas** ▲ Kríti, Greece, E Mediterranean Sea
121 P3 **Kofínou** *var.* Kophinou. S Cyprus
109 V8 **Köflach** Steiermark, SE Austria
77 Q17 **Koforidua** SE Ghana
164 H12 **Kōfu** Tottori, Honshū, SW Japan
164 M13 **Kōfu** *var.* Kôhu. Yamanashi, Honshū, S Japan
81 F22 **Koga** Tabora, C Tanzania
Kogălniceanu *see* Mihail Kogălniceanu
13 P6 **Kogaluk** ≈ Newfoundland and Labrador, E Canada
12 J4 **Kogaluk** ≈ Québec, NE Canada
122 I10 **Kogalym** Khanty-Mansiyskiy Avtonomnyy Okrug, C Russian Federation
95 J23 **Køge** Roskilde, E Denmark
95 J23 **Køge Bugt** *bay* E Denmark
77 U16 **Kogi** ◈ *state* C Nigeria
146 L11 **Kogon** *Rus.* Kagan. Buxoro Viloyati, C Uzbekistan
163 Y17 **Kōgŭm-do** *island* S South Korea
Kōhalom *see* Rupea
149 T6 **Kohāt** North-West Frontier Province, NW Pakistan
142 L10 **Kohgīlūyeh va Būyer Aḥmad** *off.* Ostān-e Kohkīlūyeh va Būyer Aḥmadī, *var.* Boyer Ahmadī va Kohkīlūyeh. ◈ *province* SW Iran
118 G4 **Kohila** *Ger.* Koil. Raplamaa, NW Estonia
153 X13 **Kohīma** *state capital* Nāgāland, E India
Koh I Noh *see* Büyükağrı Dağı
Kohkīlūyeh va Būyer Aḥmadī, Ostān-e *see* Kohgīlūyeh va Būyer Aḥmad
Kohsān *see* Kūhestān
118 J3 **Kohtla-Järve** Ida-Virumaa, NE Estonia
Kōhu *see* Kōfu
117 N10 **Kohyl'nyk** *Rom.* Cogîlnic. ≈ Moldova/Ukraine
165 N11 **Koide** Niigata, Honshū, C Japan
10 G7 **Koidern** Yukon Territory, W Canada
76 J15 **Koidu** E Sierra Leone
118 I4 **Koigi** Järvamaa, C Estonia
Koil *see* Kohila
172 H13 **Koimbani** Grande Comore, NW Comoros
139 T3 **Koi Sanjaq** *var.* Koysanjaq, Küysanjaq. N Iraq
93 O16 **Koitere** ◎ E Finland
Koivisto *see* Primorsk
163 Z16 **Kōje-do** *Jap.* Kyōsai-tō. *island* S South Korea
80 J13 **K'ok'a Hāyk'** ◎ C Ethiopia
Kokand *see* Qo'qon
182 F6 **Kokatha** South Australia
146 M10 **Ko'kcha** *Rus.* Kokcha. Boxoro Viloyati, C Uzbekistan
146 M10 **Ko'kcha** *Rus.* Kokcha. Buxoro Viloyati, C Uzbekistan
Kokcha *see* Ko'kcha
Kokcha *see* Ko'kcha
Kokchetav *see* Kokshetau
93 K18 **Kokemäenjoki** ≈ SW Finland
171 W14 **Kokenau** *var.* Kokonau. Papua, E Indonesia
83 E22 **Kokerboom** Karas, SE Namibia
119 N14 **Kokhanava** *Rus.* Kokhanovo. Vitsyebskaya Voblasts', NE Belarus
Kokhanovichi *see* Kakhanavichy
Kokhanovo *see* Kokhanava
Kök-Janggak *see* Kok-Yangak
93 K16 **Kokkola** *Swe.* Karleby; *prev. Swe.* Gamlakarleby. Länsi-Soumi, W Finland
118 H9 **Koknese** Aizkraukle, C Latvia
77 T13 **Koko** Kebbi, W Nigeria
186 E9 **Kokoda** Northern, S Papua New Guinea
76 K12 **Kokofata** Kayes, W Mali
39 N6 **Kokolik River** ≈ Alaska, USA
31 O13 **Kokomo** Indiana, N USA
Kokonau *see* Kokenau
Koko Nor *see* Qinghai Hu, China
Koko Nor *see* Qinghai, China
186 H6 **Kokopo** *var.* Kopopo; *prev.* Herbertshöhe. New Britain, E Papua New Guinea
145 X10 **Kokpekti** *Kaz.* Kökpekti. Semipalatinsk, E Kazakhstan
145 X11 **Kokpekti** ≈ E Kazakhstan
Kökpekti *see* Kokpekti
39 P9 **Kokrines** Alaska, USA
39 P9 **Kokrines Hills** ▲▲ Alaska, USA
145 P17 **Koksaray** Yuzhnyy Kazakhstan, S Kazakhstan
147 X9 **Kokshaal-Tau** *Rus.* Khrebet Kakshaal-Too. ▲▲ China/Kyrgyzstan
145 P7 **Kokshetau** *Kaz.* Kökshetaū; *prev.* Kokchetav. Kokshetau, N Kazakhstan
Kökshetaū *see* Kokshetau
99 A17 **Koksijde** West-Vlaanderen, W Belgium
12 M5 **Koksoak** ≈ Québec, E Canada
83 K24 **Kokstad** KwaZulu/Natal, E South Africa
145 V14 **Koksu** *Kaz.* Rūdnīchnyy. Almaty, SE Kazakhstan
145 W15 **Koktal** *Kaz.* Köktal. Almaty, SE Kazakhstan
145 Q12 **Koktas** ≈ C Kazakhstan
Kök-Tash *see* Kĕk-Tash
Koktokay *see* Fuyun
147 T9 **Kok-Yangak** *Kir.* Kök-Janggak. Dzhalal-Abadskaya Oblast', W Kyrgyzstan
158 F9 **Kokyar** Xinjiang Uygur Zizhiqu, W China
149 O13 **Kolāchi** *var.* Kulachi. ≈ SW Pakistan
76 J15 **Kolahun** N Liberia
171 O14 **Kolaka** Sulawesi, C Indonesia
Kolam *see* Quilon
K'o-la-ma-i *see* Karamay
Kola Peninsula *see* Kol'skiy Poluostrov
155 H19 **Kolār** Karnātaka, E India
155 H19 **Kolār Gold Fields** Karnātaka, E India
92 K11 **Kolari** Lappi, NW Finland
111 I21 **Kolárovo** *Ger.* Gutta; *prev.* Guta, *Hung.* Gúta. Nitriansky Kraj, SW Slovakia
113 K16 **Kolašin** E Montenegro
152 F11 **Kolāyat** Rājasthān, NW India
95 N15 **Kolbäck** Västmanland, C Sweden
Kolbcha *see* Kowbcha
197 Q15 **Kolbeinsey Ridge** *undersea feature* Denmark Strait/ Norwegian Sea
Kolberg *see* Kołobrzeg
95 H15 **Kolbotn** Akershus, S Norway
111 N16 **Kolbuszowa** Podkarpackie, SE Poland
126 L3 **Kol'chugino** Vladimirskaya Oblast', W Russian Federation
76 H12 **Kolda** S Senegal
95 G23 **Kolding** Vejle, C Denmark
79 K20 **Kole** Kasai Oriental, SW Dem. Rep. Congo
79 M17 **Kole** Orientale, N Dem. Rep. Congo
Kōle *see* Kili Island
84 F6 **Kölen** ▲▲ Norway/Sweden
Kolepom, Pulau *see* Yos Sudarso, Pulau
118 H3 **Kolga Laht** *Ger.* Kolko-Wiek. *bay* N Estonia
125 Q3 **Kolguyev, Ostrov** *island* NW Russian Federation
155 E16 **Kolhāpur** Mahārāshtra, SW India
151 K21 **Kolhumadulu Atoll** *atoll* S Maldives
93 O16 **Koli** *var.* Kolinkylä. Pohjois-Karjala, E Finland
39 O13 **Koliganek** Alaska, USA
111 E16 **Kolín** *Ger.* Kolin. Střední Čechy, C Czech Republic
Kolinkylä *see* Koli
190 E12 **Koliu** Île Futuna, W Wallis and Futuna
118 E7 **Kolka** Talsi, NW Latvia
118 E7 **Kolkasrags** *prev. Eng.* Cape Domesnes. *cape* NW Latvia
153 S16 **Kolkata** *prev.* Calcutta. *state capital* West Bengal, NE India
Kolkhozabad *see* Kolkhozobod
147 P14 **Kolkhozobod** *Rus.* Kolkhozabad; *prev.* Kaganovichabad, Tugalan. SW Tajikistan
Kolki/Kołki *see* Kolky
Kolko-Wiek *see* Kolga Laht
116 K3 **Kolky** *Pol.* Kołki, *Rus.* Kolki. Volyns'ka Oblast', NW Ukraine
Kollam *see* Quilon
155 G20 **Kollegāl** Karnātaka, W India
98 M5 **Kollum** Friesland, N Netherlands
Kolmar *see* Colmar
101 E16 **Köln** *var.* Koeln, *Eng./Fr.* Cologne, *prev.* Cöln; *anc.* Colonia Agrippina, Oppidum Ubiorum. Nordrhein-Westfalen, W Germany
110 N9 **Kolno** Podlaskie, NE Poland
110 J12 **Koło** Wielkopolskie, C Poland
38 B8 **Kōloa** *var.* Koloa. Kaua'i, Hawai'i, USA
Koloa *see* Kōloa
110 E7 **Kołobrzeg** *Ger.* Kolberg. Zachodnio-pomorskie, NW Poland
126 H4 **Kolodnya** Smolenskaya Oblast', W Russian Federation
190 E13 **Kolofau, Mont** ✱ Île Alofi, S Wallis and Futuna
125 O14 **Kologriv** Kostromskaya Oblast', NW Russian Federation
76 L12 **Kolokani** Koulikoro, W Mali
77 N13 **Koloko** W Burkina
186 K8 **Kolombangara** *var.* Kilimbangara, Nduke. *island* New Georgia Islands, NW Solomon Islands
Kolomea *see* Kolomyya
126 L4 **Kolomna** Moskovskaya Oblast', W Russian Federation
116 J7 **Kolomyya** *Ger.* Kolomea. Ivano-Frankivs'ka Oblast', W Ukraine
76 M13 **Kolondiéba** Sikasso, SW Mali
193 V15 **Kolonga** Tongatapu, S Tonga
189 U16 **Kolonia** *var.* Colonia. Pohnpei, E Micronesia
Kolonja *see* Kolonjë
113 K21 **Kolonjë** *var.* Kolonja. Fier, C Albania
Kolonjë *see* Ersekë
Kolotambu *see* Avuavu
193 U15 **Kolovai** Tongatapu, S Tonga
Kolozsvár *see* Cluj-Napoca
112 C9 **Kolpa** *Ger.* Kulpa, *SCr.* Kupa. ≈ Croatia/Slovenia
122 J11 **Kolpashevo** Tomskaya Oblast', C Russian Federation
124 H13 **Kolpino** Leningradskaya Oblast', NW Russian Federation
100 M10 **Kölpinsee** ◎ NE Germany
146 K8 **Ko'lquduq** *Rus.* Kulkuduk. Navoiy Viloyati, N Uzbekistan
146 K8 **Ko'lquduq** *Rus.* Kulkuduk. Nawoiy Viloyati, N Uzbekistan
124 K5 **Kol'skiy Poluostrov** *Eng.* Kola Peninsula. *peninsula* NW Russian Federation
127 T6 **Koltubanovskiy** Orenburgskaya Oblast', W Russian Federation
112 L11 **Kolubara** ≈ C Serbia
Kolupchii *see* Gurkovo
110 K13 **Koluszki** Łódźskie, C Poland
125 T6 **Kolva** ≈ NW Russian Federation
93 E14 **Kolvereid** Nord-Trøndelag, W Norway
148 L15 **Kolwa** Balūchistān, SW Pakistan
79 M24 **Kolwezi** Katanga, S Dem. Rep. Congo
123 S7 **Kolyma** ≈ NE Russian Federation
Kolyma Lowland *see* Kolymskaya Nizmennost'
Kolyma Range/Kolymskiy, Khrebet *see* Kolymskoye Nagor'ye
123 S7 **Kolymskaya Nizmennost'** *Eng.* Kolyma Lowland. *lowlands* NE Russian Federation
123 S7 **Kolymskoye** Respublika Sakha (Yakutiya), NE Russian Federation
123 U8 **Kolymskoye Nagor'ye** *var.* Khrebet Kolymskiy, *Eng.* Kolyma Range. ▲▲ E Russian Federation
123 V5 **Kolyuchinskaya Guba** *bay* NE Russian Federation
145 W15 **Kol'zhat** Almaty, SE Kazakhstan
114 G8 **Kom** ▲ NW Bulgaria
80 I13 **Koma** Oromo, C Ethiopia
77 X12 **Komadugu Gana** ≈ NE Nigeria
164 M13 **Komagane** Nagano, Honshū, S Japan
79 P17 **Komanda** Orientale, NE Dem. Rep. Congo
197 U1 **Komandorskaya Basin** *var.* Kamchatka Basin. *undersea feature* SW Bering Sea
125 Pp9 **Komandorskiye Ostrova** *Eng.* Commander Islands. *island group* E Russian Federation
Komárfalva *see* Comăneşti
111 I22 **Komárno** *Ger.* Komorn, *Hung.* Komárom. Nitriansky Kraj, SW Slovakia
111 I22 **Komárom** Komárom-Esztergom, NW Hungary
Komárom *see* Komárno
111 I22 **Komárom-Esztergom** *off.* Komárom-Esztergom Megye. ◈ *county* N Hungary
Komárom-Esztergom Megye *see* Komárom-Esztergom
164 K11 **Komatsu** *var.* Komatu. Ishikawa, Honshū, SW Japan
Komatu *see* Komatsu
83 D17 **Kombat** Otjozondjupa, N Namibia
Kombissiguiri *see* Kombissiri
77 P13 **Kombissiri** *var.* Kombissiguiri. C Burkina
188 E10 **Komebail Lagoon** *lagoon* N Palau
81 F20 **Kome Island** *island* N Tanzania
Komeyo *see* Wandai
117 P10 **Kominternivs'ke** Odes'ka Oblast', SW Ukraine
125 R12 **Komi-Permyatskiy Avtonomnyy Okrug** ◈ *autonomous district* W Russian Federation
125 R8 **Komi, Respublika** ◈ *autonomous republic* NW Russian Federation
111 I25 **Komló** Baranya, SW Hungary
Kommunarsk *see* Alchevs'k
147 S12 **Kommunizm, Qullai** ▲ E Tajikistan
186 B7 **Komo** Southern Highlands, W Papua New Guinea
170 M16 **Komodo, Pulau** *island* Nusa Tenggara, S Indonesia
77 N15 **Komoé** *var.* Komoé Fleuve. ≈ E Ivory Coast
Komoé Fleuve *see* Komoé
75 X11 **Kôm Ombo** *var.* Kawm Umbū. SE Egypt
79 F20 **Komono** La Lékoumou, SW Congo
171 Y16 **Komoran** Papua, E Indonesia
171 Y16 **Komoran, Pulau** *island* E Indonesia
Komorn *see* Komárno
Komornok *see* Comorâşte
Komosolabad *see* Komsomolobod
Komotau *see* Chomutov
114 K13 **Komotiní** *var.* Gümüljina, *Turk.* Gümülcine. Anatolikí Makedonía kai Thráki, NE Greece
113 K16 **Komovi** ▲▲ E Montenegro
117 R8 **Kompaniyivka** Kirovohrads'ka Oblast', C Ukraine
Kompong *see* Kâmpóng Chhnăng
Kompong Cham *see* Kâmpóng Cham
Kompong Kleang *see* Kâmpóng Khleăng
Kompong Som *see* Kâmpóng Saôm
Kompong Speu *see* Kâmpóng Spoe
Komrat *see* Comrat
Komsomol *see* Komsomol'skiy
122 K14 **Komsomolets, Ostrov** *island* Severnaya Zemlya, N Russian Federation
144 F13 **Komsomolets, Zaliv** *lake gulf* SW Kazakhstan
Komsomol/Komsomolets *see* Karabalyk, Kostanay, Kazakhstan
147 Q12 **Komsomolobod** *Rus.* Komosolabad. C Tajikistan
124 M16 **Komsomol'sk** Ivanovskaya Oblast', W Russian Federation
117 S6 **Komsomol's'k** Poltavs'ka Oblast', C Ukraine
146 M11 **Komsomol'sk** Navoiy Viloyati, N Uzbekistan
144 G12 **Komsomol'skiy** *Kaz.* Komsomol. Atyrau, W Kazakhstan
125 W4 **Komsomol'skiy** Respublika Komi, NW Russian Federation
123 S13 **Komsomol'sk-na-Amure** Khabarovskiy Kray, SE Russian Federation
Komsomol'sk-na-Ustyurte *see* Komsomol'sk-Ustyurt
144 K10 **Komsomol'skoye** Aktyubinsk, NW Kazakhstan
127 Q8 **Komsomol'skoye** Saratovskaya Oblast', W Russian Federation
145 P10 **Kon** ≈ C Kazakhstan
Kona *see* Kailua-Kona
124 K16 **Konakovo** Tverskaya Oblast', W Russian Federation
149 S4 **Konar** *Per.* Konarhā, *Pash.* Kunar. ◈ *province* E Afghanistan
143 V15 **Konārak** Sīstān va Balūchestān, SE Iran
Konarhā *see* Konar
27 O11 **Konawa** Oklahoma, C USA
122 H10 **Konda** ≈ C Russian Federation
154 L13 **Kondagaon** Chhattīsgarh, C India
14 K10 **Kondiaronk, Lac** ◎ Québec, SE Canada
180 J13 **Kondinin** Western Australia
81 H21 **Kondoa** Dodoma, C Tanzania
127 P6 **Kondol'** Penzenskaya Oblast', W Russian Federation
114 N10 **Kondolovo** Burgas, E Bulgaria
171 Z16 **Kondomirat** Papua, E Indonesia
124 J10 **Kondopoga** Respublika Kareliya, NW Russian Federation
149 Q2 **Kondoz** *var.* Kondoz, Kundūz, Qondūz, *Per.* Kondūz. Kunduz, NE Afghanistan
149 Q2 **Kondoz** *Pash.* Kunduz. ◈ *province* NE Afghanistan
Kondoz *see* Kondoz
155 J17 **Kondukūr** *var.* Kandukur. Andhra Pradesh, E India
Kondūz *see* Kondoz
187 P16 **Koné** Province Nord, W New Caledonia
146 E13 **Kënekesir** *Rus.* Kënekesir. Balkan Welaýaty, W Turkmenistan
146 G8 **Këneurgench** *var.* Köneürgench, *Rus.* Këneurgench; *prev.* Kunya-Urgench. Daşoguz Welaýaty, N Turkmenistan
Köneürgench *see* Këneurgench
77 N15 **Kong** N Ivory Coast
39 S5 **Kongakut River** ≈ Alaska, USA
197 O14 **Kong Christian IX Land** *Eng.* King Christian IX Land. *physical region* SE Greenland
197 P13 **Kong Christian X Land** *Eng.* King Christian X Land. *physical region* E Greenland
197 N13 **Kong Frederik IX Land** *physical region* SW Greenland
197 Q12 **Kong Frederik VIII Land** *Eng.* King Frederik VIII Land. *physical region* NE Greenland
197 N15 **Kong Frederik VI Kyst** *Eng.* King Frederik VI Coast. *physical region* SE Greenland
167 P13 **Kông, Kaôh** *prev.* Kas Kong. *island* SW Cambodia
92 P2 **Kong Karls Land** *Eng.* King Charles Islands. *island group* SE Svalbard
81 G14 **Kong Kong** ≈ SE Sudan
Kongo *see* Congo (river)
83 G16 **Kongola** Caprivi, NE Namibia
79 N21 **Kongolo** Katanga, E Dem. Rep. Congo
81 F14 **Kongor** Jonglei, SE Sudan
197 Q14 **Kong Oscar Fjord** *fjord* E Greenland
77 P12 **Kongoussi** N Burkina
95 G15 **Kongsberg** Buskerud, S Norway
92 Q2 **Kongsøya** *island* Kong Karls Land, E Svalbard
95 I14 **Kongsvinger** Hedmark, S Norway
Kongtong *see* Pingliang
167 T11 **Kông, Tônle** *var.* Xê Kong. ≈ Cambodia/Laos
158 E8 **Kongur Shan** ▲ NW China
81 I22 **Kongwa** Dodoma, C Tanzania
Kong, Xê *see* Kông, Tônle
Konia *see* Konya
147 R11 **Konibodom** *Rus.* Kanibadam. N Tajikistan
111 K15 **Koniecpol** Śląskie, S Poland
Konieh *see* Konya
Königgrätz *see* Hradec Králové
Königinhof an der Elbe *see* Dvůr Králové nad Labem
101 K23 **Königsbrunn** Bayern, S Germany
Königshütte *see* Chorzów
101 O24 **Königssee** ◎ SE Germany
109 S8 **Königstuhl** ▲ S Austria
109 U3 **Königswiesen** Oberösterreich, N Austria
101 E17 **Königswinter** Nordrhein-Westfalen, W Germany
146 M11 **Konimex** *Rus.* Kenimekh. Navoiy Viloyati, N Uzbekistan
110 I12 **Konin** *Ger.* Kuhnau. Wielkopolskie, C Poland
Koninkrijk der Nederlanden *see* Netherlands
113 L24 **Konispol** *var.* Konispoli. Vlorë, S Albania
Konispoli *see* Konispol
115 C15 **Kónitsa** Ípeiros, W Greece
Konitz *see* Chojnice
108 D8 **Köniz** Bern, W Switzerland
113 H14 **Konjic** ◈ Federacija Bosna I Hercegovina, S Bosnia and Herzegovina
92 J10 **Könkämäälven** ≈ Finland/Sweden
155 D14 **Konkan** *plain* W India
83 D22 **Konkiep** ≈ S Namibia
76 I14 **Konkouré** ≈ W Guinea
77 O11 **Konna** Mopti, S Mali
186 H6 **Konogaiang, Mount** ▲ New Ireland, NE Papua New Guinea
186 H5 **Konogogo** New Ireland, NE Papua New Guinea
108 E9 **Konolfingen** Bern, W Switzerland
77 P16 **Konongo** C Ghana
186 H5 **Konos** New Ireland, NE Papua New Guinea
124 M12 **Konosha** Arkhangel'skaya Oblast', NW Russian Federation
117 R3 **Konotop** Sums'ka Oblast', NE Ukraine
158 L7 **Konqi He** ≈ NW China
111 L14 **Końskie** Śiętokrzyskie, C Poland
Konstantinovka *see* Kostyantynivka
126 M11 **Konstantinovsk** Rostovskaya Oblast', SW Russian Federation
101 H24 **Konstanz** *var.* Constanz, *Eng.* Constance, *hist.* Kostnitz; *anc.* Constantia. Baden-Württemberg, S Germany
Konstanza *see* Constanţa
77 T14 **Kontagora** Niger, W Nigeria
78 E13 **Kontcha** Nord, N Cameroon
99 G17 **Kontich** Antwerpen, N Belgium

93 O16 **Kontiolahti** Itä-Suomi, SE Finland
93 M15 **Kontiomäki** Oulu, C Finland
167 U11 **Kon Tum** *var.* Kontum. Kon Tum, C Vietnam
Kontum *see* Kon Tum
Konur *see* Sulakyurt
136 H15 **Konya** *var.* Konieh, *prev.* Konia; *anc.* Iconium. Konya, C Turkey
136 H15 **Konya** *var.* Konia, Konieh. ◐ *province* C Turkey
Konya Reservoir *see* Shivāji Sāgar
145 T13 **Konyrat** *var.* Kounradskiy, *Kaz.* Qongyrat. Karaganda, SE Kazakhstan
145 W15 **Konyrolen** Almaty, SE Kazakhstan
81 I19 **Konza** Eastern, S Kenya
98 I9 **Koog aan den Zaan** Noord-Holland, C Netherlands
182 E7 **Koonibba** South Australia
31 O11 **Koontz Lake** Indiana, N USA
171 U12 **Koor** Papua, E Indonesia
183 R9 **Koorawatha** New South Wales, SE Australia
118 J5 **Koosa** Tartumaa, E Estonia
33 N7 **Kootenai** *var.* Kootenay. ≈ Canada/USA *see also* Kootenay
9 P17 **Kootenay** ≈ Canada/USA
Kootenay *see* Kootenai
83 F24 **Kootjieskolk** Northern Cape, W South Africa
113 M15 **Kopaonik** ▲▲ S Serbia
Kopar *see* Koper
92 K1 **Kópasker** Nordhurland Eystra, N Iceland
92 H4 **Kópavogur** Reykjanes, W Iceland
145 U13 **Kopbirlik** *prev.* Kirov, Kirova. Almaty, SE Kazakhstan
109 S13 **Koper** *It.* Capodistria; *prev.* Kopar. SW Slovenia
95 C16 **Kopervik** Rogaland, S Norway
Köpetdag Gershi/Kopetdag, Khrebet *see* Koppeh Dāgh
Kophinou *see* Kofínou
182 G8 **Kopi** South Australia
153 W12 **Kopili** ≈ NE India
95 M15 **Köping** Västmanland, C Sweden
113 K17 **Koplik** *var.* Kopliku. Shkodër, NW Albania
Kopliku *see* Koplik
Kopopo *see* Kokopo
94 I11 **Koppang** Hedmark, S Norway
Kopparberg *see* Dalarna
143 S3 **Koppeh Dāgh** *Rus.* Khrebet Kopetdag, *Turkm.* Köpetdag Gershi. ▲▲ Iran/Turkmenistan
Koppename *see* Coppename Rivier
95 J15 **Koppom** Värmland, C Sweden
Kopreinitz *see* Koprivnica
114 K9 **Koprinka, Yazovir** *prev.* Yazovir Georgi Dimitrov. ⊠ C Bulgaria
112 F7 **Koprivnica** *Ger.* Kopreinitz, *Hung.* Kaproncza. Koprivnica-Križevci, N Croatia
112 F8 **Koprivnica-Križevci** *off.* Koprivničko-Križevačka Županija. ◐ *province* N Croatia
111 I17 **Kopřivnice** *Ger.* Nesselsdorf. Moravskoslezský Kraj, E Czech Republic
Koprivničko-Križevačka Županija *see* Koprivnica-Križevci
Köprülü *see* Veles
Koptsevichi *see* Kaptsevichy
Kopyl' *see* Kapyl'
119 O14 **Kopys'** *Rus.* Kopys'. Vitsyebskaya Voblasts', NE Belarus
113 M18 **Korab** ▲ Albania/FYR Macedonia
Korabavur Pastligi *see* Karabaur', Uval
81 M14 **K'orahē** Somali, E Ethiopia
115 L16 **Kórakas, Ákrotirio** *cape* Lésvos, E Greece
112 D9 **Korana** ≈ C Croatia
155 L14 **Korāput** Orissa, E India
Korat *see* Nakhon Ratchasima
167 Q9 **Korat Plateau** *plateau* E Thailand
139 T1 **Kōrāwa, Sar-i** ▲ NE Iraq
154 L11 **Korba** Chhattīsgarh, C India
101 H15 **Korbach** Hessen, C Germany
Korça *see* Korçë
113 M21 **Korçë** *var.* Korça, *Gk.* Korytsa, *It.* Corriza; *prev.* Koritsa. Korçë, SE Albania
113 M21 **Korçë** ◐ *district* SE Albania
113 G15 **Korčula** *It.* Curzola. Dubrovnik-Neretva, S Croatia
113 F15 **Korčula** *It.* Curzola; *anc.* Corcyra Nigra. *island* S Croatia
113 F15 **Korčulanski Kanal** *channel* S Croatia
145 T6 **Korday** *prev.* Georgiyevka. Zhambyl, SE Kazakhstan
142 J5 **Kordestān** *off.* Ostān-e Kordestān, *var.* Kurdestan. ◐ *province* W Iran
Kordestān, Ostān-e *see* Kordestān
143 P4 **Kord Kūy** *var.* Kurd Kui. Golestān, N Iran
163 V13 **Korea Bay** *bay* China/North Korea
Korea, Democratic People's Republic of *see* North Korea
171 T15 **Koreare** Pulau Yamdena, E Indonesia
Korea, Republic of *see* South Korea
163 Z17 **Korea Strait** *Jap.* Chōsen-kaikyō, *Kor.* Taehan-haehyŏp. *channel* Japan/South Korea
Korelichi/Korelicze *see* Karelichy
80 J11 **Korem** ◐ Tigrai, N Ethiopia
77 U11 **Korén Adoua** ≈ C Niger
126 J7 **Korenevo** Kurskaya Oblast', W Russian Federation
126 L13 **Korenovsk** Krasnodarskiy Kray, SW Russian Federation
116 L4 **Korets'** *Pol.* Korzec, *Rus.* Korets. Rivnens'ka Oblast', NW Ukraine
Korets *see* Korets'
194 L7 **Korff Ice Rise** *ice cap* Antarctica
145 Q10 **Korgalzhyn** *var.* Kurgal'dzhino, Kurgal'dzhinsky, *Kaz.* Qorgazhyn. Akmola, C Kazakhstan
92 G13 **Korgen** Troms, N Norway
147 R9 **Korgon-Dëbë** Dzhalal-Abadskaya Oblast', W Kyrgyzstan
76 M14 **Korhogo** N Ivory Coast
115 F19 **Korinthiakós Kólpos** *Eng.* Gulf of Corinth; *anc.* Corinthiacus Sinus. *gulf* C Greece
115 F19 **Kórinthos** *anc.* Corinthus *Eng.* Corinth. Pelopónnisos, S Greece
113 M18 **Koritnik** ▲ S Serbia
Koritsa *see* Korçë
165 P11 **Kōriyama** Fukushima, Honshū, C Japan
136 E16 **Korkuteli** Antalya, SW Turkey
158 K6 **Korla** *Chin.* K'u-erh-lo. Xinjiang Uygur Zizhiqu, NW China
122 J10 **Korliki** Khanty-Mansiyskiy Avtonomnyy Okrug, C Russian Federation
Körlin an der Persante *see* Karlino
Korma *see* Karma
14 D8 **Kormak** Ontario, S Canada
Kormakíti, Akrotíri/Kormakiti, Cape/Kormakítis *see* Koruçam Burnu
111 G23 **Körmend** Vas, W Hungary
139 T5 **Kōrmōr** E Iraq
112 C13 **Kornat** *It.* Incoronata. *island* W Croatia
Korneshty *see* Corneşti
109 X3 **Korneuburg** Niederösterreich, NE Austria
145 P7 **Korneyevka** Severnyy Kazakhstan, N Kazakhstan
95 I17 **Kornsjø** Østfold, S Norway
77 O11 **Koro** Mopti, S Mali
187 Y14 **Koro** *island* C Fiji
186 B7 **Koroba** Southern Highlands, W Papua New Guinea
126 K8 **Korocha** Belgorodskaya Oblast', W Russian Federation
136 H12 **Köroğlu Dağları** ▲▲ C Turkey
183 V6 **Korogoro Point** *headland* New South Wales, SE Australia
81 J21 **Korogwe** Tanga, E Tanzania
182 L13 **Koroit** Victoria, SE Australia
187 X15 **Korolevu** Viti Levu, W Fiji
190 I17 **Koromiri** *island* S Cook Islands
171 Q8 **Koronadal** Mindanao, S Philippines
114 G13 **Koróneia, Límni** *var.* Límni Korónia. ◎ N Greece
115 E22 **Koróni** Pelopónnisos, S Greece
Korónia, Límni *see* Koróneia, Límni
110 I9 **Koronowo** *Ger.* Krone an der Brahe. Kujawski-pomorskie,C Poland
117 R2 **Korop** Chernihivs'ka Oblast', N Ukraine
115 H19 **Koropí** Attikí, C Greece
188 C8 **Koror** *var.* Oreor. ● (Palau) Oreor, N Palau
Koror *see* Oreor
111 L23 **Kőrös** ≈ E Hungary
Körös *see* Križevci
Kőrösbánya *see* Baia de Criş
187 Y14 **Koro Sea** *sea* C Fiji
Koroška *see* Kärnten
117 N3 **Korosten'** Zhytomyrs'ka Oblast', NW Ukraine
Korostyshev *see* Korostyshiv
117 N4 **Korostyshiv** *Rus.* Korostyshev. Zhytomyrs'ka Oblast', N Ukraine
125 V3 **Korotaikha** ≈ NW Russian Federation
122 J9 **Korotchayevo** Yamalo-Nenetskiy Avtonomnyy Okrug, N Russian Federation
78 I8 **Koro Toro** Borkou-Ennedi-Tibesti, N Chad
39 N16 **Korovin Island** *island* Shumagin Islands, Alaska, USA
187 X14 **Korovou** Viti Levu, W Fiji
93 M17 **Korpilahti** Länsi-Soumi, C Finland
92 K12 **Korpilombolo** *Lapp.* Dállogilli. Norrbotten, N Sweden
123 T13 **Korsakov** Ostrov Sakhalin, Sakhalinskaya Oblast', SE Russian Federation
93 J16 **Korsholm** *Fin.* Mustasaari. Länsi-Soumi, W Finland
95 I23 **Korsør** Vestsjælland, E Denmark
Korsovka *see* Kārsava
117 P6 **Korsun'-Shevchenkivs'kyy** *Rus.* Korsun'-Shevchenkovskiy. Cherkas'ka Oblast', C Ukraine
Korsun'-Shevchenkovskiy *see* Korsun'-Shevchenkivs'kyy
99 C17 **Kortemark** West-Vlaanderen, W Belgium
99 H18 **Kortenberg** Vlaams Brabant, C Belgium
99 K18 **Kortessem** Limburg, NE Belgium
99 E14 **Kortgene** Zeeland, SW Netherlands
80 F8 **Korti** Northern, N Sudan
99 C18 **Kortrijk** *Fr.* Courtrai. West-Vlaanderen, W Belgium
121 O2 **Koruçam Burnu** *var.* Cape Kormakiti, Kormakítis, *Gk.* Akrotíri Kormakití. *cape* N Cyprus
183 O13 **Korumburra** Victoria, SE Australia
Koryak Range *see* Koryakskoye Nagor'ye
123 V8 **Koryakskiy Avtonomnyy Okrug** ◐ *autonomous district* E Russian Federation
Koryakskiy Khrebet *see* Koryakskoye Nagor'ye
123 V7 **Koryakskoye Nagor'ye** *var.* Koryakskiy Khrebet, *Eng.* Koryak Range. ▲▲ NE Russian Federation
125 P11 **Koryazhma** Arkhangel'skaya Oblast', NW Russian Federation
Kōryō *see* Kangnŭng
Korytsa *see* Korçë
117 Q2 **Koryukivka** Chernihivs'ka Oblast', N Ukraine
Korzec *see* Korets'
115 N21 **Kos** Kos, Dodekánisa, Greece, Aegean Sea
115 M21 **Kos** *It.* Coo; *anc.* Cos. *island* Dodekánisa, Greece, Aegean Sea
125 T12 **Kosa** Permskaya Oblast', NW Russian Federation
125 T13 **Kosa** ≈ NW Russian Federation
164 B12 **Kō-saki** *headland* Nagasaki, Tsushima, SW Japan
163 X13 **Kosan** SE North Korea
119 H18 **Kosava** *Rus.* Kosovo. Brestskaya Voblasts', SW Belarus
Kosch *see* Kose
144 G12 **Koschagyl** *Kaz.* Qosshaghyl. Atyrau, W Kazakhstan
110 G12 **Kościan** *Ger.* Kosten. Wielkopolskie, C Poland
110 I7 **Kościerzyna** Pomorskie, NW Poland
22 L4 **Kosciusko** Mississippi, S USA
Kosciusko, Mount *see* Kosciuszko, Mount
183 R11 **Kosciuszko, Mount** *prev.* Mount Kosciusko. ▲ New South Wales, SE Australia
118 H4 **Kose** *Ger.* Kosch. Harjumaa, NW Estonia
114 G6 **Koshava** Vidin, NW Bulgaria
147 U9 **Kosh-Dëbë** *var.* Koshtebë. Narynskaya Oblast', C Kyrgyzstan
K'o-shih *see* Kashi
164 B12 **Koshikijima-rettō** *var.* Kosikizima Rettô. *island group* SW Japan
145 W13 **Koshkarkol', Ozero** ◎ SE Kazakhstan
30 L9 **Koshkonong, Lake** ◎ Wisconsin, N USA
Koshoba *see* Goşabo
Koshoba *see* Goşoba
164 M12 **Kōshoku** *var.* Kôsyoku. Nagano, Honshū, S Japan
Koshtebë *see* Kosh-Dëbë
Kōshū *see* Kwangju
111 N19 **Košice** *Ger.* Kaschau, *Hung.* Kassa. Košický Kraj, E Slovakia
111 M20 **Košický Kraj** ◐ E Slovakia
Kosikizima Rettô *see* Koshikijima-rettō
153 R12 **Kosi Reservoir** ⊠ E Nepal
116 J8 **Kosiv** Ivano-Frankivs'ka Oblast', W Ukraine
145 O11 **Koskol'** Karaganda, C Kazakhstan
125 Q9 **Koslan** Respublika Komi, NW Russian Federation
Köslin *see* Koszalin
146 M12 **Koson** *Rus.* Kasan. Qashqadaryo Viloyati, S Uzbekistan
163 Y13 **Kosŏng** SE North Korea
147 S9 **Kosonsoy** *Rus.* Kasansay. Namangan Viloyati, E Uzbekistan
113 M16 **Kosovo** *prev.* Autonomous Province of Kosovo and Metohija. ◐ *province* S Serbia
Kosovo *see* Kosava
Kosovo and Metohija, Autonomous Province of *see* Kosovo
113 N16 **Kosovo Polje** Kosovo, S Serbia
113 O16 **Kosovska Kamenica** Kosovo, SE Serbia
113 M16 **Kosovska Mitrovica** *Alb.* Mitrovicë; *prev.* Mitrovica, Titova Mitrovica. Kosovo, S Serbia
189 X17 **Kosrae** ◐ *state* E Micronesia
189 Y14 **Kosrae** *prev.* Kusaie. *island* Caroline Islands, E Micronesia
25 U9 **Kosse** Texas, SW USA
109 P6 **Kössen** Tirol, W Austria
76 M16 **Kossou, Lac de** ◎ C Ivory Coast
Kossukavak *see* Krumovgrad
Kostajnica *see* Hrvatska Kostajnica
Kostamus *see* Kostomuksha
144 M7 **Kostanay** *var.* Kustanay, *Kaz.* Qostanay. Kustanay, N Kazakhstan
144 L8 **Kostanay** *var.* Kostanayskaya Oblast', *Kaz.* Qostanay Oblysy. ◐ *province* N Kazakhstan
Kostanayskaya Oblast' *see* Kostanay
Kosten *see* Kościan
114 H10 **Kostenets** *prev.* Georgi Dimitrov. Sofiya, W Bulgaria
80 F10 **Kosti** White Nile, C Sudan
Kostnitz *see* Konstanz
124 H7 **Kostomuksha** *Fin.* Kostamus. Respublika Kareliya, NW Russian Federation
116 K3 **Kostopil'** *Rus.* Kostopol'. Rivnens'ka Oblast', NW Ukraine
Kostopol' *see* Kostopil'
124 M15 **Kostroma** Kostromskaya Oblast', NW Russian Federation
125 N14 **Kostroma** ≈ NW Russian Federation
125 N14 **Kostromskaya Oblast'** ◐ *province* NW Russian Federation
110 D11 **Kostrzyn** *Ger.* Cüstrin, Küstrin. Lubuskie, W Poland
110 H11 **Kostrzyn** Weilkopolskie, C Poland
117 X7 **Kostyantynivka** *Rus.* Konstantinovka. Donets'ka Oblast', SE Ukraine
Kostyukovichi *see* Kastsyukovichy
Kostyukovka *see* Kastsyukowka
Kôsyoku *see* Kōshoku
125 U6 **Kos'yu** Respublika Komi, NW Russian Federation
125 U6 **Kos'yu** ≈ NW Russian Federation
110 F7 **Koszalin** *Ger.* Köslin. Zachodnio-pomorskie, NW Poland
111 F22 **Kőszeg** *Ger.* Güns. Vas, W Hungary
152 H13 **Kota** *prev.* Kotah. Rājasthān, N India
Kota Baharu *see* Kota Bharu
Kota Bahru *see* Kota Bharu
169 U13 **Kotabaru** Pulau Laut, C Indonesia
168 K12 **Kota Baru** Sumatera, W Indonesia
Kotabaru *see* Jayapura
168 K6 **Kota Bharu** *var.* Kota Baharu, Kota Bahru. Kelantan, Peninsular Malaysia
Kotaboemi *see* Kotabumi
168 M14 **Kotabumi** *prev.* Kotaboemi. Sumatera, W Indonesia
149 S10 **Kot Addu** Punjab, E Pakistan
Kotah *see* Kota
169 U7 **Kota Kinabalu** *prev.* Jesselton. Sabah, East Malaysia
169 U7 **Kota Kinabalu** ✈ Sabah, East Malaysia
92 M12 **Kotala** Lappi, N Finland
Kotamobagoe *see* Kotamobagu
171 Q11 **Kotamobagu** *prev.* Kotamobagoe. Sulawesi, C Indonesia
155 L14 **Kotapad** *var.* Kotapārh. Orissa, E India
Kotapārh *see* Kotapad
166 N17 **Ko Ta Ru Tao** *island* SW Thailand
169 R13 **Kotawaringin, Teluk** *bay* Borneo, C Indonesia
149 Q13 **Kot Dīji** Sind, SE Pakistan
152 K9 **Kotdwāra** Uttaranchal, N India
125 Q14 **Kotel'nich** Kirovskaya Oblast', NW Russian Federation
127 N12 **Kotel'nikovo** Volgogradskaya Oblast', SW Russian Federation
123 Q6 **Kotel'nyy, Ostrov** *island* Novosibirskiye Ostrova, N Russian Federation
117 T5 **Kotel'va** Poltavs'ka Oblast', C Ukraine
101 M14 **Köthen** *var.* Cöthen. Sachsen-Anhalt, C Germany
Kôti *see* Kōchi
81 G17 **Kotido** NE Uganda
93 N19 **Kotka** Kymi, S Finland
125 P11 **Kotlas** Arkhangel'skaya Oblast', NW Russian Federation
38 M10 **Kotlik** Alaska, USA
77 Q17 **Kotoka** ✈ (Accra) S Ghana
Kotonu *see* Cotonou
113 J17 **Kotor** *It.* Cattaro. SW Montenegro
Kotor *see* Kotoriba
112 F7 **Kotoriba** *Hung.* Kotor. Medimurje, N Croatia
113 I17 **Kotorska, Boka** *It.* Bocche di Cattaro. *bay* SW Montenegro
112 H11 **Kotorsko** ◐ Republika Srpska, N Bosnia and Herzegovina
112 G11 **Kotor Varoš** ◐ Republika Srpska, N Bosnia and Herzegovina
Koto Sho/Kotosho *see* Lan Yü
126 M7 **Kotovsk** Tambovskaya Oblast', W Russian Federation
117 O9 **Kotovs'k** *Rus.* Kotovsk. Odes'ka Oblast', SW Ukraine
Kotovsk *see* Hînceşti
119 G16 **Kotra** *Rus.* Kotra. ≈ W Belarus
149 P16 **Kotri** Sind, SE Pakistan
109 Q9 **Kötschach** Kärnten, S Austria
155 K15 **Kottagūdem** Andhra Pradesh, E India
155 F21 **Kottappadi** Kerala, SW India
155 G23 **Kottayam** Kerala, SW India
Kottbus *see* Cottbus
Kotte *see* Sri Jayawardanapura
79 K15 **Kotto** ≈ Central African Republic/Dem. Rep. Congo
193 X15 **Kotu Group** *island group* W Tonga
Koturdepe *see* Goturdepe
122 M9 **Kotuy** ≈ N Russian Federation
83 M16 **Kotwa** Mashonaland East, NE Zimbabwe
39 N7 **Kotzebue** Alaska, USA
38 M7 **Kotzebue Sound** *inlet* Alaska, USA
Kotzenan *see* Chocianów
Kotzman *see* Kitsman'
77 R14 **Kouandé** NW Benin
79 J15 **Kouango** Ouaka, S Central African Republic
77 O13 **Koudougou** C Burkina
98 K7 **Koudum** Friesland, N Netherlands
115 L25 **Koufonísi** *island* SE Greece
115 K21 **Koufonísi** *island* Kykládes, Greece, Aegean Sea
38 M8 **Kougarok Mountain** ▲ Alaska, USA
79 E20 **Kouilou** ≈ S Congo
121 O3 **Koúklia** SW Cyprus
79 E19 **Koulamoutou** Ogooué-Lolo, C Gabon
76 L12 **Koulikoro** Koulikoro, SW Mali
76 L11 **Koulikoro** ◐ *region* SW Mali
187 P16 **Koumac** Province Nord, W New Caledonia
165 N12 **Koumi** Nagano, Honshū, S Japan
78 I13 **Koumra** Moyen-Chari, S Chad
Kounadougou *see* Koundougou
76 M15 **Kounahiri** C Ivory Coast
76 I12 **Koundâra** Moyenne-Guinée, NW Guinea
77 N13 **Koundougou** *var.* Kounadougou. C Burkina
76 H11 **Koungheul** C Senegal
Kounradskiy *see* Konyrat
25 X10 **Kountze** Texas, SW USA
77 Q13 **Koupéla** C Burkina
77 N13 **Kouri** Sikasso, SW Mali
55 Y9 **Kourou** N French Guiana
114 J12 **Kouroú** ≈ NE Greece
76 K14 **Kouroussa** Haute-Guinée, C Guinea
Kousseir *see* Al Quşayr
78 G11 **Kousséri** *prev.* Fort-Foureau. Extrême-Nord, NE Cameroon
Kouteifé *see* Al Quţayfah
76 M13 **Koutiala** Sikasso, S Mali
76 M14 **Kouto** NW Ivory Coast
93 M19 **Kouvola** Kymi, S Finland
79 G18 **Kouyou** ≈ C Congo
112 M10 **Kovačica** *Hung.* Antafalva; *prev.* Kovacsicza. Vojvodina, N Serbia
Kovacsicza *see* Kovačica
Kővárhosszúfalu *see* Satulung
Kovászna *see* Covasna
124 I4 **Kovdor** Murmanskaya Oblast', NW Russian Federation
124 I5 **Kovdozero, Ozero** ◎ NW Russian Federation
116 J3 **Kovel'** *Pol.* Kowel. Volyns'ka Oblast', NW Ukraine
112 M11 **Kovin** *Hung.* Kevevára; *prev.* Temes-Kubin. Vojvodina, NE Serbia
Kovno *see* Kaunas
127 N3 **Kovrov** Vladimirskaya Oblast', W Russian Federation
127 O5 **Kovylkino** Respublika Mordoviya, W Russian Federation
110 J11 **Kowal** Kujawsko-pomorskie, C Poland
110 J9 **Kowalewo Pomorskie** *Ger.* Schönsee. Kujawsko-pomorskie, N Poland
Kowasna *see* Covasna
119 M16 **Kowbcha** *Rus.* Kolbcha. Mahilyowskaya Voblasts', E Belarus
Koweit *see* Kuwait
Kowel *see* Kovel'
185 F17 **Kowhitirangi** West Coast, South Island, New Zealand
161 O15 **Kowloon** Hong Kong, S China
Kowno *see* Kaunas
158 L3 **Kok Kuduk** *spring/well* N China
159 N7 **Kox Kuduk** *spring/well* NW China
136 D16 **Köyceğiz** Muğla, SW Turkey
125 N6 **Koyda** Arkhangel'skaya Oblast', NW Russian Federation
Koymat *see* Goymat
Koymatdag, Gory *see* Goymatdag, Gory
151 E15 **Koyna Reservoir** ⊠ W India
165 P9 **Koyoshi-gawa** ≈ Honshū, C Japan
Koysanjaq *see* Koi Sanjaq
Koytash *see* Qo'ytosh
Koytash *see* Qo'ytosh
146 M14 **Köytendag** *prev. Rus.* Charshanga, Charshangy, *Turkm.* Charshangngy. Lebap Welaýaty, E Turkmenistan
39 N9 **Koyuk** Alaska, USA
39 N9 **Koyuk River** ≈ Alaska, USA
39 O9 **Koyukuk** Alaska, USA
39 O9 **Koyukuk River** ≈ Alaska, USA
136 J13 **Kozaklı** Nevşehir, C Turkey
136 K16 **Kozan** Adana, S Turkey
115 E14 **Kozáni** Dytikí Makedonía, N Greece
112 F10 **Kozara** ▲▲ NW Bosnia and Herzegovina
Kozarska Dubica *see* Bosanska Dubica
117 P3 **Kozelets'** *Rus.* Kozelets. Chernihivs'ka Oblast', NE Ukraine
Kozelets *see* Kozelets'
117 S6 **Kozel'shchyna** Poltavs'ka Oblast', C Ukraine
126 J5 **Kozel'sk** Kaluzhskaya Oblast', W Russian Federation
Kozhikode *see* Calicut
125 U6 **Kozhim** Respublika Komi, NW Russian Federation
125 V9 **Kozhimiz, Gora** ▲ NW Russian Federation
124 L9 **Kozhozero, Ozero** ◎ NW Russian Federation
125 T7 **Kozhva** Respublika Komi, NW Russian Federation
125 T7 **Kozhva** ≈ NW Russian Federation
110 N13 **Kozienice** Mazowieckie, C Poland
109 S13 **Kozina** SW Slovenia
114 H7 **Kozloduy** Vratsa, NW Bulgaria
127 Q3 **Kozlovka** Chuvashskaya Respublika, W Russian Federation
Kozlovshchina/Kozlowszczyzna *see* Kazlowshchyna
127 P3 **Koz'modem'yansk** Respublika Mariy El, W Russian Federation
116 J6 **Kozova** Ternopil's'ka Oblast', W Ukraine
113 P20 **Kožuf** ▲ S Macedonia
165 N15 **Kōzu-shima** *island* E Japan
Koz'yany *see* Kaz'yany
117 N5 **Kozyatyn** *Rus.* Kazatin. Vinnyts'ka Oblast', C Ukraine
77 Q16 **Kpalimé** *var.* Palimé. SW Togo
77 Q16 **Kpandu** E Ghana
99 F15 **Krabbendijke** Zeeland, SW Netherlands
167 N15 **Krabi** *var.* Muang Krabi. Krabi, SW Thailand
167 N13 **Kra Buri** Ranong, SW Thailand
167 S12 **Krâchéh** *prev.* Kratie. Krâchéh, E Cambodia
Kradnovodskiy Zaliv *see* Krasnovodskiy Zaliv
95 G17 **Kragerø** Telemark, S Norway
112 M13 **Kragujevac** Serbia, C Serbia
Krainburg *see* Kranj
166 N13 **Kra, Isthmus of** *isthmus* Malaysia/Thailand
112 D12 **Krajina** *cultural region* SW Croatia
Krakatau, Pulau *see* Rakata, Pulau
Krakau *see* Kraków
111 L16 **Kraków** *Eng.* Cracow, *Ger.* Krakau; *anc.* Cracovia. Małopolskie, S Poland
100 L9 **Krakower See** ◎ NE Germany
167 Q11 **Krâlănh** Siĕmréab, NW Cambodia
45 Q16 **Kralendijk** Bonaire, E Netherlands Antilles
112 B10 **Kraljevica** *It.* Porto Re. Primorje-Gorski Kotar, NW Croatia
112 M13 **Kraljevo** *prev.* Rankovićevo. Serbia, C Serbia
185 B16 **Kralovarský Kraj** ◐ W Czech Republic
111 E16 **Královehradecký Kraj** *prev.* Hradecký Kraj. ◐ *region* N Czech Republic
Kralup an der Moldau *see* Kralupy nad Vltavou
111 C16 **Kralupy nad Vltavou** *Ger.* Kralup an der Moldau. Středni Čechy, NW Czech Republic
117 W7 **Kramators'k** *Rus.* Kramatorsk. Donets'ka Oblast', SE Ukraine
Kramatorsk *see* Kramators'k
93 H17 **Kramfors** Västernorrland, C Sweden
Kranéa *see* Kraniá
108 M7 **Kranebitten** ✈ (Innsbruck) Tirol, W Austria
115 D15 **Kraniá** *var* Kranéa. Dytikí Makedonía, N Greece
115 G20 **Kranídi** Pelopónnisos, S Greece
109 T11 **Kranj** *Ger.* Krainburg. NW Slovenia
115 F16 **Krannón** *battleground* Thessalía, C Greece
Kranz *see* Zelenogradsk
112 D7 **Krapina** Krapina-Zagorje, N Croatia
112 E8 **Krapina** ≈ N Croatia
112 D8 **Krapina-Zagorje** *off.* Krapinsko-Zagorska Županija. ◐ *province* N Croatia
114 L7 **Krapinets** ≈ NE Bulgaria
Krapinsko-Zagorska Županija *see* Krapina-Zagorje
111 I15 **Krapkowice** *Ger.* Krappitz. Opolskie, SW Poland
Krappitz *see* Krapkowice
125 O12 **Krasavino** Vologodskaya Oblast', NW Russian Federation
122 H6 **Krasino** Novaya Zemlya, Arkhangel'skaya Oblast', N Russian Federation
123 S15 **Kraskino** Primorskiy Kray, SE Russian Federation
118 J11 **Krāslava** Krāslava, SE Latvia
119 M14 **Krasnaluki** *Rus.* Krasnoluki. Vitsyebskaya Voblasts', N Belarus
119 P17 **Krasnapollye** *Rus.* Krasnopol'ye. Mahilyowskaya Voblasts', E Belarus
126 L15 **Krasnaya Polyana** Krasnodarskiy Kray, SW Russian Federation
Krasnaya Slabada/Krasnaya Sloboda *see* Chyrvonaya Slabada
Krasnaya Slabada / Krasnaya Sloboda *see* Chyrvonaya Slabada
119 J15 **Krasnaye** *Rus.* Krasnoye. Minskaya Voblasts', C Belarus
111 O14 **Kraśnik** *Ger.* Kratznick. Lubelskie, E Poland
117 O9 **Krasni Okny** Odes'ka Oblast', SW Ukraine
127 P8 **Krasnoarmeysk** Saratovskaya Oblast', W Russian Federation
Krasnoarmeysk *see* Tayynsha
Krasnoarmeysk *see* Krasnoarmiys'k/Tayynsha
123 T6 **Krasnoarmeyskiy** Chukotskiy Avtonomnyy Okrug, NE Russian Federation
117 W7 **Krasnoarmiys'k** *Rus.* Krasnoarmeysk. Donets'ka Oblast', SE Ukraine
125 P11 **Krasnoborsk** Arkhangel'skaya Oblast', NW Russian Federation
126 K14 **Krasnodar** *prev.* Ekaterinodar, Yekaterinodar. Krasnodarskiy Kray, SW Russian Federation
126 K13 **Krasnodarskiy Kray** ◐ *territory* SW Russian Federation
117 Z7 **Krasnodon** Luhans'ka Oblast', E Ukraine
Krasnogor *see* Kallaste
127 T2 **Krasnogorskoye** *Latv.* Sarkaņi. Udmurtskaya Respublika, NW Russian Federation
Krasnograd *see* Krasnohrad
Krasnogvardeysk *see* Bulungh'ur
126 M13 **Krasnogvardeyskoye** Stavropol'skiy Kray, SW Russian Federation
Krasnogvardeyskoye *see* Krasnohvardiys'ke
117 U6 **Krasnohrad** *Rus.* Krasnograd. Kharkivs'ka Oblast', E Ukraine
117 S12 **Krasnohvardiys'ke** *Rus.* Krasnogvardeyskoye. Respublika Krym, S Ukraine
123 P14 **Krasnokamensk** Chitinskaya Oblast', S Russian Federation
125 U14 **Krasnokamsk** Permskaya Oblast', W Russian Federation
127 U8 **Krasnokholm** Orenburgskaya Oblast', W Russian Federation
117 U5 **Krasnokuts'k** *Rus.* Krasnokutsk. Kharkivs'ka Oblast', E Ukraine
Krasnokutsk *see* Krasnokuts'k
126 L7 **Krasnolesnyy** Voronezhskaya Oblast', W Russian Federation
Krasnoluki *see* Krasnaluki
Krasnoosol'skoye Vodokhranilishche *see* Chervonooskil's'ke Vodoskhovyshche
117 S11 **Krasnoperekops'k** *Rus.* Krasnoperekopsk. Respublika Krym, S Ukraine
Krasnoperekopsk *see* Krasnoperekops'k
117 U4 **Krasnopillya** Sums'ka Oblast', NE Ukraine
Krasnopol'ye *see* Krasnapollye
124 L5 **Krasnoshchel'ye** Murmanskaya Oblast', NW Russian Federation
127 O5 **Krasnoslobodsk** Respublika Mordoviya, W Russian Federation
127 T2 **Krasnoslobodsk** Volgogradskaya Oblast', SW Russian Federation
Krasnostav *see* Krasnystaw
127 V5 **Krasnousol'skiy** Respublika Bashkortostan, W Russian Federation
125 U12 **Krasnovishersk** Permskaya Oblast', NW Russian Federation

◆ Country
● Country Capital
◇ Dependent Territory
○ Dependent Territory Capital
◐ Administrative Regions
✈ International Airport
▲ Mountain
▲▲ Mountain Range
Volcano
≈ River
◎ Lake
⊠ Reservoir

Krasnovodsk see Turkmenbaşy
145 A10 **Krasnovodskiy Zaliv** prev. Rus. Kradnovodskiy Zaliv, Turkm. Krasnowodsk Aylagy. lake gulf W Turkmenistan
Krasnovodskiy Zaliv see Türkmenbasy Aylagy
146 B10 **Krasnovodskoye Plato** Turkm. Krasnowodsk Platosy. plateau Krasnowodsk Platosy, NW Turkmenistan
Krasnowodsk Aylagy see Türkmenbasy Aylagy
Krasnowodsk Aylagy see Krasnovodskiy Zaliv
Krasnowodsk Platosy see Krasnovodskoye Plato
122 K12 **Krasnoyarsk** Krasnoyarskiy Kray, S Russian Federation
127 X7 **Krasnoyarskiy** Orenburgskaya Oblast', W Russian Federation
122 K11 **Krasnoyarskiy Kray** ◐ territory C Russian Federation
Krasnoye see Krasnaye
Krasnoye Znamya see Gyzylbaydak
125 R11 **Krasnozatonskiy** Respublika Komi, NW Russian Federation
118 D13 **Krasnoznamensk** prev. Lasdehnen, Ger. Haselberg. Kaliningradskaya Oblast', W Russian Federation
126 K3 **Krasnoznamensk** Moskovskaya Oblast', W Russian Federation
117 R11 **Krasnoznam"yans'kyy Kanal** canal S Ukraine
111 P14 **Krasnystaw** Rus. Krasnostav. Lubelskie, SE Poland
126 H4 **Krasnyy** Smolenskaya Oblast', W Russian Federation
127 P2 **Krasnyye Baki** Nizhegorodskaya Oblast', W Russian Federation
127 Q13 **Krasnyye Barrikady** Astrakhanskaya Oblast', SW Russian Federation
124 K15 **Krasnyy Kholm** Tverskaya Oblast', W Russian Federation
127 Q8 **Krasnyy Kut** Saratovskaya Oblast', W Russian Federation
Krasnyy Liman see Krasnyy Lyman
117 Y7 **Krasnyy Luch** prev. Krindachevka. Luhans'ka Oblast', E Ukraine
117 X6 **Krasnyy Lyman** Rus. Krasnyy Liman. Donets'ka Oblast', SE Ukraine
127 R3 **Krasnyy Steklovar** Respublika Mariy El, W Russian Federation
127 P8 **Krasnyy Tekstil'shchik** Saratovskaya Oblast', W Russian Federation
127 R13 **Krasnyy Yar** Astrakhanskaya Oblast', SW Russian Federation
Krassóvár see Caraşova
116 L5 **Krasyliv** Khmel'nyts'ka Oblast', W Ukraine
111 O21 **Kraszna** Rom. Crasna. ∽ Hungary/Romania
Kratie see Krâchéh
113 P17 **Kratovo** NE FYR Macedonia
Kratznick see Kraśnik
171 Y13 **Krau** Papua, E Indonesia
167 Q13 **Krâvanh, Chuŏr Phnum** Eng. Cardamom Mountains, Fr. Chaîne des Cardamomes. ▲▲ W Cambodia
Kravasta Lagoon see Karavastasë, Laguna e
Krawang see Karawang
127 Q15 **Kraynovka** Respublika Dagestan, SW Russian Federation
118 D12 **Kražiai** Šiaulai, C Lithuania
27 P11 **Krebs** Oklahoma, C USA
101 D15 **Krefeld** Nordrhein-Westfalen, W Germany
Kreisstadt see Krosno Odrzańskie
115 D17 **Kremastón, Technití Límni** ⊠ C Greece
Kremenchug see Kremenchuk
Kremenchugskoye Vodokhranilishche/Kremenchuk Reservoir see Kremenchuts'ke Vodoskhovyshche
117 S6 **Kremenchuk** Rus. Kremenchug. Poltavs'ka Oblast', NE Ukraine
117 R6 **Kremenchuts'ke Vodoskhovyshche** Eng. Kremenchuk Reservoir, Rus. Kremenchugskoye Vodokhranilishche. ⊠ C Ukraine
116 K5 **Kremenets'** Pol. Krzemieniec, Rus. Kremenets. Ternopil's'ka Oblast', W Ukraine
Kremennaya see Kreminna
117 X6 **Kreminna** Rus. Kremennaya. Luhans'ka Oblast', E Ukraine
37 R4 **Kremmling** Colorado, C USA
109 V3 **Krems** ∽ NE Austria
Krems see Krems an der Donau
109 W3 **Krems an der Donau** var. Krems. Niederösterreich, N Austria
Kremsier see Kroměříž
109 S4 **Kremsmünster** Oberösterreich, N Austria
38 M17 **Krenitzin Islands** island Aleutian Islands, Alaska, USA
Kresena see Kresna
114 G11 **Kresna** var. Kresena. Blagoevgrad, SW Bulgaria
112 O12 **Krespoljin** Serbia, E Serbia
25 N4 **Kress** Texas, SW USA
123 V6 **Kresta, Zaliv** bay E Russian Federation
115 D20 **Kréstena** prev. Selinoús. Dytikí Elláda, S Greece
124 H14 **Kresttsy** Novgorodskaya Oblast', W Russian Federation
Kretikon Delagos see Kritikó Pélagos
118 C11 **Kretinga** Ger. Krottingen. Klaipėda, NW Lithuania
Kreutz see Cristuru Secuiesc
Kreuz see Križevci
Kreuz see Risti
Kreuzburg/Kreuzburg in Oberschlesien see Kluczbork
Kreuzingen see Bol'shakovo
108 H6 **Kreuzlingen** Thurgau, NE Switzerland
101 K25 **Kreuzspitze** ▲ S Germany
101 F16 **Kreuztal** Nordrhein-Westfalen, W Germany
119 I15 **Kreva** Rus. Krevo. Hrodzyenskaya Voblasts', W Belarus
Krevo see Kreva
Kría Vrísi see Krýa Vrýsi
79 D16 **Kribi** Sud, SW Cameroon
Krichëv see Krychaw
Krickerhäu/Kriegerhaj see Handlová
109 W6 **Krieglach** Steiermark, E Austria
108 F8 **Kriens** Luzern, W Switzerland
Krievija see Russian Federation
Krimmitschau see Crimmitschau
98 H12 **Krimpen aan den IJssel** Zuid-Holland, SW Netherlands
Krindachevka see Krasnyy Luch
115 G25 **Kríos, Ákrotírio** headland Kríti, Greece, E Mediterranean Sea
155 J16 **Krishna** prev. Kistna. ∽ C India
155 H20 **Krishnagiri** Tamil Nādu, SE India
155 K17 **Krishna, Mouths of the** delta SE India
153 S15 **Krishnanagar** West Bengal, N India
155 G20 **Krishnarājāsāgara Reservoir** ⊠ W India
95 N19 **Kristdala** Kalmar, S Sweden
Kristiania see Oslo
95 E18 **Kristiansand** var. Christiansand. Vest-Agder, S Norway
95 L22 **Kristianstad** Skåne, S Sweden
94 F8 **Kristiansund** var. Christiansund. Møre og Romsdal, S Norway
Kristiinankaupunki see Kristinestad
93 I14 **Kristineberg** Västerbotten, N Sweden
95 L16 **Kristinehamn** Värmland, C Sweden
93 J17 **Kristinestad** Fin. Kristiinankaupunki. Länsi-Soumi, W Finland
Kristyor see Crişcior
115 J25 **Kríti** Eng. Crete. ◐ region Greece, Aegean Sea
115 J24 **Kríti** Eng. Crete. island Greece, Aegean Sea
115 J23 **Kritikó Pélagos** var. Kretikon Delagos, Eng. Sea of Crete; anc. Mare Creticum. sea Greece, Aegean Sea
Kriulyany see Criuleni
112 I12 **Krivaja** ∽ NE Bosnia and Herzegovina
Krivaja see Mali Idoš
113 P17 **Kriva Palanka** Turk. Eğri Palanka. NE Macedonia
Krivichi see Kryvychy
114 H8 **Krivodol** Vratsa, NW Bulgaria
126 M10 **Krivorozh'ye** Rostovskaya Oblast', SW Russian Federation
Krivoshin see Kryvoshyn
Krivoy Rog see Kryvyy Rih
112 F7 **Križevci** Ger. Kreuz, Hung. Kőrös. Varaždin, NE Croatia
112 B10 **Krk** It. Veglia. Primorje-Gorski Kotar, NW Croatia
112 B10 **Krk** It. Veglia; anc. Curieta. island NW Croatia
109 V12 **Krka** ∽ SE Slovenia
Krka see Gurk
109 R11 **Krn** ▲ NW Slovenia
111 H16 **Krnov** Ger. Jägerndorf. Moravskoslezský Kraj, E Czech Republic
Kroatien see Croatia
95 G14 **Krøderen** Buskerud, S Norway
95 G14 **Krøderen** ◎ S Norway
Kroi see Krui
95 N17 **Krokek** Östergötland, S Sweden
Krokodil see Crocodile
93 G16 **Krokom** Jämtland, C Sweden
117 S2 **Krolevets'** Rus. Krolevets. Sums'ka Oblast', NE Ukraine
Krolevets see Krolevets'
Królewska Huta see Chorzów
111 H18 **Kroměříž** Ger. Kremsier. Zlínský Kraj, E Czech Republic
98 I9 **Krommenie** Noord-Holland, C Netherlands
126 J6 **Kromy** Orlovskaya Oblast', W Russian Federation
101 L18 **Kronach** Bayern, E Germany
Krone an der Brahe see Koronowo
167 Q13 **Krŏng Kaôh Kŏng** Kaôh Kông, SW Cambodia
95 K21 **Kronoberg** ◐ county S Sweden
123 V10 **Kronotskiy Zaliv** bay E Russian Federation
195 O2 **Kronprinsesse Märtha Kyst** physical region Antarctica
195 V3 **Kronprins Olav Kyst** physical region Antarctica
124 G12 **Kronshtadt** Leningradskaya Oblast', NW Russian Federation
Kronstadt see Braşov
83 I22 **Kroonstad** Free State, C South Africa
123 O12 **Kropotkin** Irkutskaya Oblast', C Russian Federation
126 L14 **Kropotkin** Krasnodarskiy Kray, SW Russian Federation
110 J11 **Krośniewice** Łódzkie, C Poland
111 N17 **Krosno** Ger. Krossen. Podkarpackie, SE Poland
110 E12 **Krosno Odrzańskie** Ger. Crossen, Kreisstadt. Lubuskie, W Poland
Krossen see Krosno
Krotoschin see Krotoszyn
110 H13 **Krotoszyn** Ger. Krotoschin. Wielkopolskie, C Poland
Krottingen see Kretinga
Krousón see Krousónas
115 J25 **Krousónas** prev. Krousón, Kroussón. Kríti, Greece, E Mediterranean Sea
Kroussón see Krousónas
Krraba see Krrabë
113 L20 **Krrabë** var. Krraba. Tiranë, C Albania
113 L17 **Krrabit, Mali i** ▲▲ N Albania
109 W12 **Krško** Ger. Gurkfeld; prev. Videm-Krško. E Slovenia
83 K19 **Kruger National Park** national park Northern, N South Africa
83 J21 **Krugersdorp** Gauteng, NE South Africa
38 D16 **Krugloi Point** headland Agattu Island, Alaska, USA
Krugloye see Kruhlaye
119 N15 **Kruhlaye** Rus. Krugloye. Mahilyowskaya Voblasts', E Belarus
168 L15 **Krui** var. Kroi. Sumatera, SW Indonesia
99 G16 **Kruibeke** Oost-Vlaanderen, N Belgium
83 G25 **Kruidfontein** Western Cape, SW South Africa
99 F15 **Kruiningen** Zeeland, SW Netherlands
Kruja see Krujë
113 L19 **Krujë** var. Kruja, It. Croia. Durrës, C Albania
Krulevshchina/Krulewshchyna see Krulyewshchyna
118 K13 **Krulyewshchyna** Rus. Krulevshchina, Krulewshchyna. Vitsyebskaya Voblasts', N Belarus
25 T6 **Krum** Texas, SW USA
101 J23 **Krumbach** Bayern, S Germany
113 M17 **Krumë** Kukës, NE Albania
Krummau see Český Krumlov
114 K12 **Krumovgrad** prev. Kossukavak. Yambol, E Bulgaria
114 K12 **Krumovitsa** ∽ S Bulgaria
114 L10 **Krumovo** Yambol, E Bulgaria
167 O11 **Krung Thep** var. Krung Thep Mahanakhon, Eng. Bangkok. ● (Thailand) Bangkok, C Thailand
167 O11 **Krung Thep, Ao** var. Bight of Bangkok. bay S Thailand
Krung Thep Mahanakhon see Krung Thep
Krupa/Krupa na Uni see Bosanska Krupa
119 M15 **Krupki** Rus. Krupki. Minskaya Voblasts', C Belarus
95 G24 **Kruså** var. Krusaa. Sønderjylland, SW Denmark
Krusaa see Kruså
113 N14 **Kruševac** Serbia, C Serbia
113 N19 **Kruševo** SW FYR Macedonia
111 A15 **Krušné Hory** Eng. Ore Mountains, Ger. Erzgebirge. ▲▲ Czech Republic/Germany see also Erzgebirge
Krušné Hory see Erzgebirge
39 W13 **Kruzof Island** island Alexander Archipelago, Alaska, USA
114 F13 **Krýa Vrýsi** var. Kría Vrísi. Kentrikí Makedonía, N Greece
119 P16 **Krychaw** Rus. Krichëv. Mahilyowskaya Voblasts', E Belarus
64 K11 **Krylov Seamount** undersea feature E Atlantic Ocean
Krym see Krym, Respublika
117 S13 **Krym, Respublika** var. Krym, Eng. Crimea, Crimean Oblast; prev. Rus. Krymskaya ASSR, Krymskaya Oblast'. ◐ province SE Ukraine
126 K14 **Krymsk** Krasnodarskiy Kray, SW Russian Federation
Krymskaya ASSR/Krymskaya Oblast' see Krym, Respublika
117 T13 **Kryms'ki Hory** ▲▲ S Ukraine
117 T13 **Kryms'kyy Pivostriv** peninsula S Ukraine
111 M18 **Krynica** Ger. Tannenhof. Małopolskie, S Poland
117 P8 **Kryve Ozero** Odes'ka Oblast', SW Ukraine
119 I18 **Kryvoshyn** Rus. Krivoshin. Brestskaya Voblasts', SW Belarus
119 K14 **Kryvychy** Rus. Krivichi. Minskaya Voblasts', C Belarus
117 S8 **Kryvyy Rih** Rus. Krivoy Rog. Dnipropetrovs'ka Oblast', SE Ukraine
117 N8 **Kryzhopil'** Vinnyts'ka Oblast', C Ukraine
Krzemieniec see Kremenets'
111 J14 **Krzepice** Śląskie, S Poland
110 F10 **Krzyż Wielkopolskie** Wielkopolskie, W Poland
Ksar al Kabir see Ksar-el-Kebir
Ksar al Soule see Er-Rachidia
74 J5 **Ksar El Boukhari** N Algeria
74 G5 **Ksar-el-Kebir** var. Alcázar, Ksar al Kabir, Ksar-el-Kébir, Ar. Al-Kasr al-Kebir, Al-Qsar al-Kbir, Sp. Alcazarquivir. NW Morocco
Ksar-el-Kébir see Ksar-el-Kebir
110 H12 **Książ Wielkopolski** Ger. Xions. Weilkopolskie, W Poland
127 O3 **Kstovo** Nizhegorodskaya Oblast', W Russian Federation
169 T8 **Kuala Belait** W Brunei
Kuala Dungun see Dungun
169 S10 **Kualakerian** Borneo, C Indonesia
169 S12 **Kualakuayan** Borneo, C Indonesia
168 K8 **Kuala Lipis** Pahang, Peninsular Malaysia
168 K9 **Kuala Lumpur** ● (Malaysia) Kuala Lumpur, Peninsular Malaysia
168 K9 **Kuala Lumpur International** ✈ Selangor, Peninsular Malaysia
Kuala Pelabohan Kelang see Pelabuhan Klang
169 U7 **Kuala Penyu** Sabah, East Malaysia
38 E9 **Kualapu'u** var. Kualapuu. Moloka'i, Hawai'i, USA
Kualapuu see Kualapu'u
168 L7 **Kuala Terengganu** var. Kuala Trengganu. Terengganu, Peninsular Malaysia
168 L11 **Kualatungkal** Sumatera, W Indonesia
171 P11 **Kuandang** Sulawesi, N Indonesia
163 V12 **Kuandian** var. Kuandian Manzu Zizhixian. Liaoning, NE China
Kuandian Manzu Zizhixian see Kuandian
Kuando-Kubango see Cuando Cubango
Kuang-chou see Guangzhou
Kuang-hsi see Guangxi Zhuangzu Zizhiqu
Kuang-tung see Guangdong
Kuang-yuan see Guangyuan
Kuantan, Batang see Indragiri, Sungai
Kuanza Norte see Cuanza Norte
Kuanza Sul see Cuanza Sul
Kuanzhou see Qingjian
Kuba see Quba
Kubango see Cubango/Okavango
141 X8 **Kubārah** NW Oman
93 H16 **Kubbe** Västernorrland, C Sweden
80 A11 **Kubbum** Southern Darfur, W Sudan
124 L13 **Kubenskoye, Ozero** ◎ NW Russian Federation
146 G6 **Komsomol'sk-Ustyurt** Rus. Komsomol'sk-na-Ustyurte. Qoraqalpoghiston Respublikasi, NW Uzbekistan
164 G15 **Kubokawa** Kōchi, Shikoku, SW Japan
114 L7 **Kubrat** prev. Balbunar. Razgrad, N Bulgaria
112 O13 **Kučajske Planine** ▲▲ E Serbia
165 T1 **Kuccharo-ko** ◎ Hokkaidō, N Japan
112 O11 **Kučevo** Serbia, NE Serbia
Kuchan see Qūchān
169 Q10 **Kuching** prev. Sarawak. Sarawak, East Malaysia
169 Q10 **Kuching** ✈ Sarawak, East Malaysia
164 B17 **Kuchinoerabu-jima** island Nansei-shotō, SW Japan
164 C14 **Kuchinotsu** Nagasaki, Kyūshū, SW Japan
109 Q6 **Kuchl** Salzburg, NW Austria
148 L9 **Kūchnay Darweyshān** Helmand, S Afghanistan
Kuchurgan see Kuchurhan
117 O9 **Kuchurhan** Rus. Kuchurgan. ∽ NE Ukraine
Kuçova see Kuçovë
113 L21 **Kuçovë** var. Kuçova; prev. Qyteti Stalin. Berat, C Albania
136 D11 **Küçük Çekmece** İstanbul, NW Turkey
164 F14 **Kudamatsu** var. Kudamatu. Yamaguchi, Honshū, SW Japan
Kudamatu see Kudamatsu
Kudara see Ghŭdara
169 V6 **Kudat** Sabah, East Malaysia
Küddow see Gwda
155 G17 **Kūdligi** Karnātaka, W India
Kudowa see Kudowa-Zdrój
111 F16 **Kudowa-Zdrój** Ger. Kudowa. Wałbrzych, SW Poland
117 P9 **Kudryavtsivka** Mykolayivs'ka Oblast', S Ukraine
169 R16 **Kudus** prev. Koedoes. Jawa, C Indonesia
125 T13 **Kudymkar** Permskaya Oblast', NW Russian Federation
Kudzsir see Cugir
Kuei-chou see Guizhou
Kuei-lin see Guilin
Kuei-Yang/Kuei-yang see Guiyang
K'u-erh-lo see Korla
Kueyang see Guiyang
Kufa see Al Kūfah
136 E14 **Küfiçayı** ∽ C Turkey
109 O6 **Kufstein** Tirol, W Austria
145 V14 **Kugaly** Kaz. Qoghaly. Almaty, SE Kazakhstan
8 K8 **Kugluktuk** var. Qurlurtuuq; prev. Coppermine. Nunavut, NW Canada
143 Y13 **Kūhak** Sīstān va Balūchestān, SE Iran
143 R9 **Kūhbonān** Kermān, C Iran
148 J5 **Kūhestān** var. Kohsān. Herāt, W Afghanistan
Kūhīrī see Kahīrī
93 N15 **Kuhmo** Oulu, E Finland
93 L18 **Kuhmoinen** Länsi-Soumi, C Finland
Kuhnau see Konin
Kūhnō see Kihnu
143 O8 **Kūhpāyeh** Eşfahān, C Iran
167 O12 **Kui Buri** var. Ban Kui Nua. Prachuap Khiri Khan, SW Thailand
Kuibyshev see Kuybyshevskoye Vodokhranilishche
82 D13 **Kuito** Port. Silva Porto. Bié, C Angola
39 X14 **Kuiu Island** island Alexander Archipelago, Alaska, USA
93 L15 **Kuivaniemi** Oulu, C Finland
77 V14 **Kujama** Kaduna, C Nigeria
110 I10 **Kujawsko-pomorskie** ◐ province C Poland
165 R8 **Kuji** var. Kuzi. Iwate, Honshū, C Japan
Kujto, Ozero see Kuyto, Ozero
Kujū-renzan see Kujū-san
164 D14 **Kujū-san** var. Kujū-renzan. ▲ Kyūshū, SW Japan
43 N7 **Kukalaya, Rio** var. Rio Cuculaya, Rio Kukulaya. ∽ NE Nicaragua
113 O16 **Kukavica** var. Vlajna. ▲ SE Serbia
113 M18 **Kukës** var. Kukësi. Kukës, NE Albania
113 L18 **Kukës** ◐ district NE Albania
Kukësi see Kukës
186 D8 **Kukipi** Gulf, S Papua New Guinea
127 S3 **Kukmor** Respublika Tatarstan, W Russian Federation
Kukong see Shaoguan
39 N6 **Kukpowruk River** ∽ Alaska, USA
38 M6 **Kukpuk River** ∽ Alaska, USA
Kükúdağ see Gogi, Mount
Kukukhoto see Hohhot
Kukulaya, Rio see Kukalaya, Rio
189 W12 **Kuku Point** headland NW Wake Island
146 G11 **Kukurtli** Ahal Welaýaty, C Turkmenistan
Kül see Kül, Rūd-e
114 F7 **Kula** Vidin, NW Bulgaria
112 K9 **Kula** Vojvodina, NW Serbia
136 D14 **Kula** Manisa, W Turkey
149 S8 **Kulāchi** North-West Frontier Province, NW Pakistan
Kulachi see Kolāchi
144 F11 **Kulagino** Kaz. Külagīno. Atyrau, W Kazakhstan
Külagīno see Kulagino
168 L10 **Kulai** Johor, Peninsular Malaysia
114 M7 **Kulak** ∽ NE Bulgaria
153 T11 **Kula Kangri** var. Kulhakangri. ▲ Bhutan/China
144 E13 **Kulaly, Ostrov** island SW Kazakhstan
145 S16 **Kulan** Kaz. Qulan; prev. Lugovoy, Lugovoye. Zhambyl, S Kazakhstan
147 V9 **Kulanak** Narynskaya Oblast', C Kyrgyzstan
Gory Kulandag see Gulandag
153 V14 **Kulaura** Sylhet, NE Bangladesh
118 D9 **Kuldīga** Ger. Goldingen. Kuldiga, W Latvia
Kuldja see Yining
Kul'dzhuktau, Gory see QuljuqtovTog'lari
127 N4 **Kulebaki** Nizhegorodskaya Oblast', W Russian Federation
112 E11 **Kulen Vakuf** var. Spasovo. ◐ Federacija Bosna I Hercegovina, NW Bosnia and Herzegovina
181 Q9 **Kulgera Roadhouse** Northern Territory, N Australia
Kulhakangri see Kula Kangri
127 T1 **Kuliga** Udmurtskaya Respublika, NW Russian Federation
Kulkuduk see Ko'lquduq
Kulkuduk see Ko'lquduq
118 G4 **Kullamaa** Läänemaa, W Estonia
197 O12 **Kullorsuaq** var. Kuvdlorssuak. ◐ Kitaa, C Greenland
29 O6 **Kulm** North Dakota, N USA
Kulm see Chełmno
146 D12 **Kul'mach** prev. Turkm. Isgender. Balkan Welaýaty, W Turkmenistan
101 L18 **Kulmbach** Bayern, SE Germany
Kulmsee see Chełmża
147 Q14 **Kŭlob** Rus. Kulyab. SW Tajikistan
92 M13 **Kuloharju** Lappi, N Finland
125 N7 **Kuloy** Arkhangel'skaya Oblast', NW Russian Federation
125 N7 **Kuloy** ∽ NW Russian Federation
137 Q14 **Kulp** Dıyarbakır, SE Turkey
Kulpa see Kolpa
77 P14 **Kulpawn** ∽ N Ghana
143 R13 **Kül, Rūd-e** var. Kül. ∽ S Iran
144 G12 **Kul'sary** Kaz. Qulsary. Atyrau, W Kazakhstan
153 R15 **Kulti** West Bengal, NE India
93 G14 **Kultsjön** ◎ N Sweden
136 I14 **Kulu** Konya, W Turkey
123 S9 **Kulu** ∽ E Russian Federation
122 I13 **Kulunda** Altayskiy Kray, S Russian Federation
145 T7 **Kulunda Steppe** Kaz. Qulyndy Zhazyghy, Rus. Kulundinskaya Ravnina. grassland Kazakhstan/Russian Federation
Kulundinskaya Ravnina see Kulunda Steppe
182 M9 **Kulwin** Victoria, SE Australia
Kulyab see Kŭlob
117 Q3 **Kulykivka** Chernihivs'ka Oblast', N Ukraine
Kum see Qom
164 F14 **Kuma** Ehime, Shikoku, SW Japan
127 P14 **Kuma** ∽ SW Russian Federation
165 O12 **Kumagaya** Saitama, Honshū, S Japan
165 Q5 **Kumaishi** Hokkaidō, NE Japan
169 R13 **Kumai, Teluk** bay Borneo, C Indonesia
127 Y7 **Kumak** Orenburgskaya Oblast', W Russian Federation
164 C14 **Kumamoto** Kumamoto, Kyūshū, SW Japan
164 D15 **Kumamoto** off. Kumamoto-ken. ◐ prefecture Kyūshū, SW Japan
Kumamoto-ken see Kumamoto
164 J15 **Kumano** Mie, Honshū, SW Japan
Kumanova see Kumanovo
113 O17 **Kumanovo** Turk. Kumanova. N Macedonia
185 G17 **Kumara** West Coast, South Island, New Zealand
180 J8 **Kumarina Roadhouse** Western Australia
153 T15 **Kumarkhali** Khulna, W Bangladesh
77 P16 **Kumasi** prev. Coomassie. C Ghana
Kumayri see Gyumri
79 D15 **Kumba** Sud-Ouest, W Cameroon
114 N13 **Kumbağ** Tekirdağ, NW Turkey
155 J21 **Kumbakonam** Tamil Nādu, SE India
Kum-Dag see Gumdag
165 R16 **Kume-jima** island Nansei-shotō, SW Japan
127 V6 **Kumertau** Respublika Bashkortostan, W Russian Federation
Kumillā see Comilla
35 R4 **Kumiva Peak** ▲ Nevada, W USA
159 N7 **Kumkuduk** Xinjiang Uygur Zizhiqu, W China
159 N8 **Kum Kuduk** spring/well NW China
Kumkurgan see Qumqo'rg'on
95 M16 **Kumla** Örebro, C Sweden
136 E17 **Kumluca** Antalya, SW Turkey
100 N9 **Kummerower See** ◎ NE Germany
77 X14 **Kumo** Gombi, E Nigeria
145 O13 **Kumola** ∽ C Kazakhstan
167 N1 **Kumon Range** ▲▲ N Myanmar (Burma)
83 F22 **Kums** Karas, SE Namibia
155 E18 **Kumta** Karnātaka, W India
158 L6 **Kümük** Xinjiang Uygur Zizhiqu, W China
38 H12 **Kumukahi, Cape** headland Hawai'i, USA, C Pacific Ocean
127 Q17 **Kumukh** Respublika Dagestan, SW Russian Federation
Kumul see Hami
127 N9 **Kumylzhenskaya** Volgogradskaya Oblast', SW Russian Federation
141 W6 **Kumzār** N Oman
Kunar see Konar
Kunashiri see Kunashir, Ostrov
123 U14 **Kunashir, Ostrov** var. Kunashiri. island Kuril'skiye Ostrova, SE Russian Federation
118 I3 **Kunda** Lääne-Virumaa, NE Estonia
152 M13 **Kunda** Uttar Pradesh, N India
155 E19 **Kundāpura** var. Coondapoor. Karnātaka, W India
79 O24 **Kundelungu, Monts** ▲▲ S Dem. Rep. Congo
Kundert see Hernád
186 D7 **Kundiawa** Chimbu, W Papua New Guinea
Kundla see Sāvarkundla
168 L10 **Kundur, Pulau** island W Indonesia
Kunduz see Kondoz
Kunduz/Kundūz see Kondoz
Kuneitra see Al Qunayţirah
83 B18 **Kunene** ◐ district NE Namibia
83 A16 **Kunene** var. Cunene. ∽ Angola/Namibia see also Cunene
Kunene see Cunene
Künes see Xinyuan
158 J5 **Künes He** ∽ NW China
95 I19 **Kungälv** Västra Götaland, S Sweden
147 W7 **Kungei Ala-Tau** Rus. Khrebet Kyungëy Ala-Too, Kir. Küngöy Ala-Too. ▲▲ Kazakhstan/Kyrgyzstan
Küngöy Ala-Too see Kungei Ala-Tau
Kungrad see Qo'ng'irot
95 J19 **Kungsbacka** Halland, S Sweden
95 I18 **Kungshamn** Västra Götaland, S Sweden
95 M16 **Kungsör** Västmanland, C Sweden
79 J16 **Kungu** Equateur, NW Dem. Rep. Congo
125 V15 **Kungur** Permskaya Oblast', NW Russian Federation
166 L9 **Kungyangon** Yangon, SW Myanmar (Burma)
111 M22 **Kunhegyes** Jász-Nagykun-Szolnok, E Hungary
167 O5 **Kunhing** Shan State, E Myanmar (Burma)
158 D9 **Kunjirap Daban** var. Khūnjerāb Pass. pass China/Pakistan
Kunjirap Daban see Khunjerāb Pass
Kunlun Mountains see Kunlun Shan
158 H10 **Kunlun Shan** Eng. Kunlun Mountains. ▲▲ NW China
159 P11 **Kunlun Shankou** pass C China
160 G13 **Kunming** var. K'un-ming; prev. Yunnan. province capital Yunnan, SW China
K'un-ming see Kunming
Kunø see Kunoy
95 B18 **Kunoy** Dan. Kunø. island N Faeroe Islands
163 X16 **Kunsan** var. Gunsan, Jap. Gunzan. W South Korea
111 L24 **Kunszentmárton** Jász-Nagykun-Szolnok, E Hungary
111 J23 **Kunszentmiklós** Bács-Kiskun, C Hungary
181 N3 **Kununurra** Western Australia
Kunyang see Pingyang
Kunya-Urgench see Köneürgench
Kunyé see Pins, Île des
169 T11 **Kunyi** Borneo, C Indonesia
101 I20 **Künzelsau** Baden-Württemberg, S Germany
161 S10 **Kuocang Shan** ▲▲ SE China
124 H5 **Kuoloyarvi** var. Luolajarvi. Murmanskaya Oblast', NW Russian Federation
93 N16 **Kuopio** Kuopio, C Finland
93 N17 **Kuopio** ◐ province C Finland
93 K17 **Kuortane** Länsi-Soumi, W Finland
93 M18 **Kuortti** Isäsuomi, E Finland
Kupa see Kolpa
171 P17 **Kupang** prev. Koepang. Timor, C Indonesia
39 Q5 **Kuparuk River** ∽ Alaska, USA
Kupchino see Cupcina
186 E9 **Kupiano** Central, S Papua New Guinea
180 M4 **Kupingarri** Western Australia
122 I12 **Kupino** Novosibirskaya Oblast', C Russian Federation
118 H11 **Kupiškis** Panevėžys, NE Lithuania
114 L13 **Küplü** Edirne, NW Turkey
39 X13 **Kupreanof Island** island Alexander Archipelago, Alaska, USA
39 O16 **Kupreanof Point** headland Alaska, USA
112 G13 **Kupres** ◐ Federacija Bosna I Hercegovina, SW Bosnia and Herzegovina
117 W5 **Kup"yans'k** Rus. Kupyansk. Kharkivs'ka Oblast', E Ukraine
Kupyansk see Kup"yans'k

◆ Country ● Country Capital ◇ Dependent Territory ○ Dependent Territory Capital ◐ Administrative Regions ✈ International Airport ▲ Mountain ▲▲ Mountain Range Volcano ∽ River ◎ Lake ⊠ Reservoir

117 W5 **Kup"yans'k-Vuzlovyy** Kharkivs'ka Oblast', E Ukraine
158 I6 **Kuqa** Xinjiang Uygur Zizhiqu, NW China
Kür see Kura
137 W11 **Kura** Az. Kür, Geor. Mtkvari, Turk. Kura Nehri. ≈ SW Asia
55 R8 **Kuracki** NW Guyana
Kura Kurk see Irbe Strait
147 Q10 **Kurama Range** Rus. Kuraminskiy Khrebet. ▲▲ Tajikistan/Uzbekistan
Kuraminskiy Khrebet see Kurama Range
Kura Nehri see Kura
119 J14 **Kuranyets** Rus. Kurenets. Minskaya Voblasts', C Belarus
164 H13 **Kurashiki** var. Kurasiki. Okayama, Honshū, SW Japan
154 L10 **Kurasia** Chhattīsgarh, C India
Kurasiki see Kurashiki
164 H12 **Kurayoshi** var. Kurayosi. Tottori, Honshū, SW Japan
Kurayosi see Kurayoshi
163 X6 **Kurbin He** ≈ NE China
145 X10 **Kurchum** Kaz. Kürshim. Vostochnyy Kazakhstan, E Kazakhstan
145 Y10 **Kurchum** ≈ E Kazakhstan
137 X11 **Kürdämir** Rus. Kyurdamir. C Azerbaijan
Kurdestan see Kordestān
139 S1 **Kurdistan** cultural region SW Asia
Kurd Kui see Kord Küy
155 F15 **Kurduvādi** Mahārāshtra, W India
114 J11 **Kŭrdzhali** var. Kirdzhali, Kărdžali. Kŭrdzhali, S Bulgaria
114 K11 **Kŭrdzhali** ◈ province S Bulgaria
114 J11 **Kŭrdzhali, Yazovir** ▣ S Bulgaria
164 F13 **Kure** Hiroshima, Honshū, SW Japan
192 K5 **Kure Atoll** var. Ocean Island. atoll Hawaiian Islands, Hawaii, USA
136 J10 **Küre Dağları** ▲▲ N Turkey
146 C11 **Kurendag** rus Gora Kyuren. ▲ W Turkmenistan
Kurenets see Kuranyets
118 E6 **Kuressaare** Ger. Arensburg; prev. Kingissepp. Saaremaa, W Estonia
122 K9 **Kureyka** Krasnoyarskiy Kray, N Russian Federation
122 K9 **Kureyka** ≈ N Russian Federation
Kurgal'dzhino/Kurgal'dzhinsky see Korgalzhyn
122 G11 **Kurgan** Kurganskaya Oblast', C Russian Federation
126 L14 **Kurganinsk** Krasnodarskiy Kray, SW Russian Federation
122 G11 **Kurganskaya Oblast'** ◈ province C Russian Federation
Kurgan-Tyube see Qŭrghonteppa
191 O2 **Kuria** prev. Woodle Island. island Tungaru, W Kiribati
Kuria Muria Bay see Ḥalānīyāt, Khalīj al
Kuria Muria Islands see Ḥalānīyāt, Juzur al
153 T13 **Kurigram** Rajshahi, N Bangladesh
93 K17 **Kurikka** Länsi-Soumi, W Finland
192 I3 **Kurile Basin** undersea feature NW Pacific Ocean
Kurile Islands see Kuril'skiye Ostrova
Kurile-Kamchatka Depression see Kurile Trench
192 J3 **Kurile Trench** var. Kurile-Kamchatka Depression. undersea feature NW Pacific Ocean
127 Q9 **Kurilovka** Saratovskaya Oblast', W Russian Federation
123 U13 **Kuril'sk** Kuril'skiye Ostrova, Sakhalinskaya Oblats', SE Russian Federation
122 G11 **Kuril'skiye Ostrova** Eng. Kurile Islands. island group SE Russian Federation
42 M9 **Kurinwas, Río** ≈ E Nicaragua
Kurisches Haff see Courland Lagoon
Kurkund see Kilingi-Nõmme
126 M4 **Kurlovskiy** Vladimirskaya Oblast', W Russian Federation
80 G12 **Kurmuk** Blue Nile, SE Sudan
Kurna see Al Qurnah
155 H17 **Kurnool** var. Karnul. Andhra Pradesh, S India
164 M11 **Kurobe** Toyama, Honshū, SW Japan
165 Q7 **Kuroishi** var. Kuroisi. Aomori, Honshū, C Japan
Kuroisi see Kuroishi
165 O12 **Kuroiso** Tochigi, Honshū, S Japan
165 Q4 **Kuromatsunai** Hokkaidō, NE Japan
164 B17 **Kuro-shima** island SW Japan
185 F21 **Kurow** Canterbury, South Island, New Zealand
127 N15 **Kursavka** Stavropol'skiy Kray, SW Russian Federation
118 E11 **Kuršėnai** Šiauliai, N Lithuania
Kürshim see Kurchum
Kurshskaya Kosa/Kuršių Nerija see Courland Spit
126 J7 **Kursk** Kurskaya Oblast', W Russian Federation
126 I7 **Kurskaya Oblast'** ◈ province W Russian Federation
Kurskiy Zaliv see Courland Lagoon
113 N15 **Kuršumlija** Serbia, S Serbia
137 R15 **Kurtalan** Siirt, SE Turkey
Kurtbunar see Tervel
Kurt-Dere see Vŭlchidol
Kurtitsch/Kürtös see Curtici
Kurtty see Kurtty
145 U15 **Kurtty** var. Kurtty. ≈ SE Kazakhstan
93 L18 **Kuru** Länsi-Suomi, W Finland
80 C13 **Kuru** ≈ W Sudan
114 M13 **Kuru Dağı** ▲▲ NW Turkey
158 L7 **Kuruktag** ▲▲ NW China
83 G22 **Kuruman** Northern Cape, N South Africa
67 T14 **Kuruman** ≈ W South Africa
164 D14 **Kurume** Fukuoka, Kyūshū, SW Japan
123 N13 **Kurumkan** Respublika Buryatiya, S Russian Federation
155 J25 **Kurunegala** North Western Province, C Sri Lanka
55 T10 **Kurupukari** C Guyana
125 U10 **Kur"ya** Respublika Komi, NW Russian Federation
144 E15 **Kuryk** var. Yeraliyev. Mangistau, SW Kazakhstan
136 B15 **Kuşadası** Aydın, SW Turkey
115 M19 **Kuşadası Körfezi** gulf SW Turkey
164 A17 **Kusagaki-guntō** island SW Japan
Kusaie see Kosrae
145 T12 **Kusak** ≈ C Kazakhstan
Kusary see Qusar
167 P7 **Ku Sathan, Doi** ▲ NW Thailand
164 J13 **Kusatsu** var. Kusatu. Shiga, Honshū, SW Japan
Kusatu see Kusatsu
138 F11 **Kuseifa** Southern, C Israel
136 C12 **Kuş Gölü** ◎ NW Turkey
126 L12 **Kushchevskaya** Krasnodarskiy Kray, SW Russian Federation
164 D16 **Kushima** var. Kusima. Miyazaki, Kyūshū, SW Japan
164 I15 **Kushimoto** Wakayama, Honshū, SW Japan
165 V4 **Kushiro** var. Kusiro. Hokkaidō, NE Japan
148 K4 **Kūshk** Herāt, W Afghanistan
Kushka see Serhetabat
Kushka see Gushgy
145 N8 **Kushmurun** Kaz. Qusmuryn. Kostanay, N Kazakhstan
145 N8 **Kushmurun, Ozero** Kaz. Qusmuryn. ◎ N Kazakhstan
127 U4 **Kushnarenkovo** Respublika Bashkortostan, W Russian Federation
Kushrabat see Qo'shrabot
Kushrabat see Qo'shrabot
153 T15 **Kushtia** var. Kustia. Khulna, W Bangladesh
Kusima see Kushima
Kusiro see Kushiro
38 M13 **Kuskokwim Bay** bay Alaska, USA
39 P11 **Kuskokwim Mountains** ▲▲ Alaska, USA
39 N12 **Kuskokwim River** ≈ Alaska, USA
108 G7 **Küsnacht** Zürich, N Switzerland
165 V4 **Kussharo-ko** var. Kussyaro. ◎ Hokkaidō, NE Japan
Küssnacht see Küssnacht am Rigi
108 F8 **Küssnacht am Rigi** var. Küssnacht. Schwyz, C Switzerland
Kussyaro see Kussharo-ko
Kustanay see Kostanay
Küstence/Küstendje see Constanța
100 F11 **Küstenkanal** var. Ems-Hunte Canal. canal NW Germany
Kustia see Kushtia
Küstrin see Kostrzyn
171 R11 **Kusu** Pulau Halmahera, E Indonesia
170 L16 **Kuta** Pulau Lombok, S Indonesia
139 T4 **Kutabān** N Iraq
136 E13 **Kütahya** prev. Kutaia. Kütahya, W Turkey
136 E13 **Kütahya** var. Kutaia. ◈ province W Turkey
Kutai see Mahakam, Sungai
Kutaia see Kütahya
137 R9 **K'ut'aisi** W Georgia
Kūt al 'Amārah see Al Kūt
Kut al Hai/Kūt al Ḩayy see Al Ḩayy
Kut al Imara see Al Kūt
123 Q11 **Kutana** Respublika Sakha (Yakutiya), NE Russian Federation
Kutaradja/Kutaraja see Bandaaceh
165 R4 **Kutchan** Hokkaidō, NE Japan
Kutch, Gulf of see Kachchh, Gulf of
Kutch, Rann of see Kachchh, Rann of
112 F9 **Kutina** Sisak-Moslavina, NE Croatia
112 H9 **Kutjevo** Požega-Slavonija, NE Croatia
111 E17 **Kutná Hora** Ger. Kuttenberg. Střední Čechy, C Czech Republic
110 K12 **Kutno** Łódzkie, C Poland
Kuttenberg see Kutná Hora
79 I20 **Kutu** Bandundu, W Dem. Rep. Congo
153 V17 **Kutubdia Island** island SE Bangladesh
80 B10 **Kutum** Northern Darfur, W Sudan
147 Y7 **Kuturgu** Issyk-Kul'skaya Oblast', E Kyrgyzstan
12 M5 **Kuujjuaq** prev. Fort-Chimo. Québec, E Canada
12 I7 **Kuujjuarapik** Québec, C Canada
Kuuli-Mayak see Guwlumaýak
118 I6 **Kuulse magi** ▲ S Estonia
92 N13 **Kuusamo** Oulu, E Finland
93 M19 **Kuusankoski** Kymi, S Finland
127 W7 **Kuvandyk** Orenburgskaya Oblast', W Russian Federation
Kuvango see Cubango
Kuvasay see Quvasoy
Kuvdlorssuak see Kullorsuaq
124 I16 **Kuvshinovo** Tverskaya Oblast', W Russian Federation
141 Q4 **Kuwait** off. State of Kuwait, var. Dawlat al Kuwait, Koweit, Kuweit. ◆ monarchy SW Asia
Kuwait see Al Kuwayt
Kuwait Bay see Kuwayt, Jūn al
Kuwait City see Al Kuwayt
Kuwait, Dawlat al see Kuwait
Kuwait, State of see Kuwait
Kuwajleen see Kwajalein Atoll
164 K13 **Kuwana** Mie, Honshū, SW Japan
139 X9 **Kuwayt** E Iraq
142 K11 **Kuwayt, Jūn al** var. Kuwait Bay. bay E Kuwait
Kuweit see Kuwait
117 P10 **Kuyal'nyts'kyy Lyman** ◎ SW Ukraine
122 I12 **Kuybyshev** Novosibirskaya Oblast', C Russian Federation
Kuybyshev see Bolgar, Respublika Tatarstan, Russian Federation
Kuybyshev see Samara
117 W9 **Kuybysheve** Rus. Kuybyshevo. Zaporiz'ka Oblast', SE Ukraine
Kuybyshevo see Kuybysheve
Kuybyshev Reservoir see Kuybyshevskoye Vodokhranilishche
Kuybyshevskaya Oblast' see Samarskaya Oblast'
Kuybyshevskiy see Novoishimskiy
127 R4 **Kuybyshevskoye Vodokhranilishche** var. Kuibyshev, Eng. Kuybyshev Reservoir. ▣ W Russian Federation
123 S9 **Kuydusun** Respublika Sakha (Yakutiya), NE Russian Federation
125 U16 **Kuyeda** Permskaya Oblast', NW Russian Federation
Küysanjaq see Koi Sanjaq
124 I7 **Kuyto, Ozero** var. Ozero Kujto. ◎ NW Russian Federation
158 J4 **Kuytun** Xinjiang Uygur Zizhiqu, NW China
122 M13 **Kuytun** Irkutskaya Oblast', S Russian Federation
55 S12 **Kuyuwini Landing** S Guyana
Kuzi see Kuji
38 M9 **Kuzitrin River** ≈ Alaska, USA
127 P6 **Kuznetsk** Penzenskaya Oblast', W Russian Federation
116 K3 **Kuznetsovs'k** Rivnens'ka Oblast', NW Ukraine
124 K6 **Kuzomen'** Murmanskaya Oblast', NW Russian Federation
165 R8 **Kuzumaki** Iwate, Honshū, C Japan
95 H24 **Kværndrup** Fyn, C Denmark
92 H9 **Kvaløya** island N Norway
92 K8 **Kvalsund** Finnmark, N Norway
94 G11 **Kvam** Oppland, S Norway
127 X7 **Kvarkeno** Orenburgskaya Oblast', W Russian Federation
93 G15 **Kvarnbergsvattnet** var. Frostviken. ◎ N Sweden
112 A11 **Kvarner** var. Carnaro, It. Quarnero. gulf W Croatia
112 B11 **Kvarnerić** channel W Croatia
39 O14 **Kvichak Bay** bay Alaska, USA
92 H12 **Kvikkjokk** Lapp. Huhttán. Norrbotten, N Sweden
95 D17 **Kvina** ≈ S Norway
95 F16 **Kvitseid** Telemark, S Norway
92 Q1 **Kvitøya** island NE Svalbard
79 H20 **Kwa** ≈ W Dem. Rep. Congo
77 Q15 **Kwadwokurom** C Ghana
186 M8 **Kwailibesi** Malaita, N Solomon Islands
189 S6 **Kwajalein Atoll** var. Kuwajleen. atoll Ralik Chain, C Marshall Islands
55 W9 **Kwakoegron** Brokopondo, N Suriname
81 J21 **Kwale** Coast, S Kenya
77 U17 **Kwale** Delta, S Nigeria
79 H20 **Kwamouth** Bandundu, W Dem. Rep. Congo
Kwando see Cuando
Kwangchow see Guangzhou
Kwangchu see Kwangju
163 X16 **Kwangju** off. Kwangju-gwangyŏksi, var. Guangju, Kwangchu, Jap. Kōshū. SW South Korea
Kwangju-gwangyŏksi see Kwangju
79 H20 **Kwango** Port. Cuango. ≈ Angola/Dem. Rep. Congo
Kwango see Cuango
Kwangsi/Kwangsi Chuang Autonomous Region see Guangxi Zhuangzu Zizhiqu
Kwangtung see Guangdong
Kwangyuan see Guangyuan
81 F17 **Kwania, Lake** ◎ C Uganda
Kwanza see Cuanza
77 S15 **Kwara** ◈ state SW Nigeria
83 K22 **KwaZulu/Natal** off. KwaZulu/Natal Province; prev. Natal. ◈ province E South Africa
KwaZulu/Natal Province see KwaZulu/Natal
Kweichow see Guizhou
Kweichu see Guiyang
Kweilin see Guilin
Kweisui see Hohhot
Kweiyang see Guiyang
83 K17 **Kwekwe** prev. Que Que. Midlands, C Zimbabwe
83 G20 **Kweneng** ◈ district S Botswana
Kwesui see Hohhot
39 N12 **Kwethluk** Alaska, USA
39 N12 **Kwethluk River** ≈ Alaska, USA
110 J8 **Kwidzyń** Ger. Marienwerder. Pomorskie, N Poland
38 M13 **Kwigillingok** Alaska, USA
186 E9 **Kwikila** Central, S Papua New Guinea
79 I20 **Kwilu** ≈ W Dem. Rep. Congo
Kwito see Cuito
171 U12 **Kwoka, Gunung** ▲ Papua, E Indonesia
78 I12 **Kyabé** Moyen-Chari, S Chad
183 O11 **Kyabram** Victoria, SE Australia
166 M9 **Kyaikkami** prev. Amherst. Mon State, S Myanmar (Burma)
166 L9 **Kyaiklat** Irrawaddy, SW Myanmar (Burma)
166 M8 **Kyaikto** Mon State, S Myanmar (Burma)
123 N14 **Kyakhta** Respublika Buryatiya, S Russian Federation
182 G8 **Kyancutta** South Australia
167 T8 **Ky Anh** Ha Tinh, N Vietnam
166 L5 **Kyaukpadaung** Mandalay, C Myanmar (Burma)
166 J6 **Kyaukpyu** Arakan State, W Myanmar (Burma)
166 M5 **Kyaukse** Mandalay, C Myanmar (Burma)
166 L8 **Kyaunggon** Irrawaddy, SW Myanmar (Burma)
119 E14 **Kybartai** Pol. Kibarty. Marijampolė, S Lithuania
152 I7 **Kyelang** Himāchal Pradesh, NW India
111 G19 **Kyjov** Ger. Gaya. Jihomoravský Kraj, SE Czech Republic
115 J21 **Kykládes** var. Kikládhes, Eng. Cyclades. island group SE Greece
25 S11 **Kyle** Texas, SW USA
96 G9 **Kyle of Lochalsh** N Scotland, UK
101 D18 **Kyll** ≈ W Germany
115 F19 **Kyllíni** var. Killini. ▲ S Greece
115 H18 **Kými** Évvoia, C Greece
93 L19 **Kymi** ◈ province SE Finland
115 H18 **Kými, Ákrotírio** cape Évvoia, C Greece
93 M19 **Kymijoki** ≈ S Finland
115 H18 **Kýmis, Akrotírio** headland C Greece
125 W14 **Kyn** Permskaya Oblast', NW Russian Federation
183 N12 **Kyneton** Victoria, SE Australia
81 G17 **Kyoga, Lake** var. Lake Kioga. ◎ C Uganda
164 J12 **Kyōga-misaki** headland Honshū, SW Japan
183 V4 **Kyogle** New South Wales, SE Australia
163 W15 **Kyŏnggi-man** bay NW South Korea
163 Z16 **Kyŏngju** Jap. Keishū. SE South Korea
Kyŏngsŏng see Sŏul
Kyōsai-tō see Kŏje-do
81 F19 **Kyotera** S Uganda
164 J13 **Kyōto** Kyōto, Honshū, SW Japan
164 J13 **Kyōto** off. Kyōto-fu, var. Kyōto Hu. ◈ urban prefecture Honshū, SW Japan
Kyōto-fu/Kyōto Hu see Kyōto
115 D21 **Kyparissía** var. Kiparissía. Pelopónnisos, S Greece
115 D20 **Kyparissiakós Kólpos** gulf S Greece
Kyperounda see Kyperoúnta
121 P3 **Kyperoúnta** var. Kyperounda. C Cyprus
Kypros see Cyprus
115 H16 **Kyrá Panagía** island Vóreies Sporádes, Greece, Aegean Sea
Kyrenia see Girne
Kyrenia Mountains see Beşparmak Dağları
Kyrgyz Republic see Kyrgyzstan
147 U9 **Kyrgyzstan** off. Kyrgyz Republic, var. Kirghizia; prev. Kirgizskaya SSR, Kirghiz SSR, Republic of Kyrgyzstan. ◆ republic C Asia
Kyrgyzstan, Republic of see Kyrgyzstan
Kyriat Gat see Qiryat Gat
100 M11 **Kyritz** Brandenburg, NE Germany
94 G8 **Kyrksæterøra** Sør-Trøndelag, S Norway
Kyrkslätt see Kirkkonummi
125 U8 **Kyrta** Respublika Komi, NW Russian Federation
111 J18 **Kysucké Nové Mesto** prev. Horné Nové Mesto, Ger. Kisutzaneustadtl, Oberneustadtl, Hung. Kiszucaújhely. Žilinský Kraj, N Slovakia
117 N12 **Kytay, Ozero** ◎ SW Ukraine
115 F23 **Kýthira** var. Kíthira, It. Cerigo, Lat. Cythera. Kńythira, S Greece
115 F23 **Kýthira** var. Kíthira, It. Cerigo, Lat. Cythera. island S Greece
115 I20 **Kýthnos** Kńythnos, Kykládes, Greece, Aegean Sea
115 I20 **Kýthnos** var. Kíthnos, Thermiá, It. Termia; anc. Cythnos. island Kykládes, Greece, Aegean Sea
115 I20 **Kýthnou, Stenó** strait Kykládes, Greece, Aegean Sea
Kyungëy Ala-Too, Khrebet see Kungei Ala-Tau
Kyurdamir see Kürdämir
164 D15 **Kyūshū** var. Kyûsyû. island SW Japan
192 H6 **Kyushu-Palau Ridge** var. Kyusyu-Palau Ridge. undersea feature W Pacific Ocean
114 F10 **Kyustendil** anc. Pautalia. Kyustendil, W Bulgaria
114 G11 **Kyustendil** ◈ province W Bulgaria
Kyûsyû see Kyūshū
Kyusyu-Palau Ridge see Kyushu-Palau Ridge
123 P8 **Kyusyur** Respublika Sakha (Yakutiya), NE Russian Federation
183 P10 **Kywong** New South Wales, SE Australia
117 P4 **Kyyiv** Eng. Kiev, Rus. Kiyev. ● (Ukraine) Kyyivs'ka Oblast', N Ukraine
Kyyiv see Kyyivs'ka Oblast'
117 O4 **Kyyivs'ka Oblast'** var. Kyyiv, Rus. Kiyevskaya Oblast'. ◈ province N Ukraine
117 P3 **Kyyivs'ke Vodoskhovyshche** Eng. Kiev Reservoir, Rus. Kiyevskoye Vodokhranilishche. ▣ N Ukraine
93 L16 **Kyyjärvi** Länsi-Soumi, C Finland
122 K14 **Kyzyl** Respublika Tyva, C Russian Federation
147 S8 **Kyzyl-Adyr** var. Kirovskoye. Talasskaya Oblast', NW Kyrgyzstan
145 V14 **Kyzylagash** Almaty, SE Kazakhstan
146 C13 **Kyzylbair** Balkan Welaýaty, W Turkmenistan
Kyzyl-Dzhiik, Pereval see Uzbel Shankou
145 S7 **Kyzylkak, Ozero** ◎ NE Kazakhstan
145 X11 **Kyzylkesek** Vostochnyy Kazakhstan, E Kazakhstan
147 S10 **Kyzyl-Kiya** Kir. Kyzyl-Kyya. Batkenskaya Oblast', SW Kyrgyzstan
144 L11 **Kyzylkol', Ozero** ◎ C Kazakhstan
122 K14 **Kyzyl Kum** var. Kizil Kum, Qizil Qum, Uz. Qizilqum. desert Kazakhstan/Uzbekistan
Kyzyl-Kyya see Kyzyl-Kiya
145 N15 **Kyzylorda** var. Kzyl-Orda, Qizil Orda, Qyzylorda; prev. Perovsk. Kyzylorda, S Kazakhstan
144 L14 **Kyzylorda** off. Kyzylordinskaya Oblast', Kaz. Qyzylorda Oblysy. ◈ province S Kazakhstan
Kyzylordinskaya Oblast' see Kyzylorda
Kyzylrabat see Qizilravot
Kyzylrabot see Qizilrabot
Kyzylsu see Kyzyl-Suu
147 X7 **Kyzyl-Suu** prev. Pokrovka. Issyk-Kul'skaya Oblast', NE Kyrgyzstan
147 S12 **Kyzyl-Suu** var. Kyzylsu. ≈ Kyrgyzstan/Tajikistan
147 X8 **Kyzyl-Tuu** Issyk-Kul'skaya Oblast', E Kyrgyzstan
145 Q12 **Kyzylzhar** Kaz. Qyzylzhar. Karaganda, C Kazakhstan
145 N15 **Kzyl-Orda** Kzyl-Orda, S Kazakhstan
144 L14 **Kzylorda** ◈ province S Kazakhstan
Kzyl-Orda see Kyzylorda
Kzyltu see Kishkenekol'

L

109 X2 **Laa an der Thaya** Niederösterreich, NE Austria
63 K15 **La Adela** La Pampa, SE Argentina
Laagen see Numedalslågen
109 S5 **Laakirchen** Oberösterreich, N Austria
Laaland see Lolland
104 I11 **La Albuera** Extremadura, W Spain
105 O7 **La Alcarria** physical region C Spain
104 K14 **La Algaba** Andalucía, S Spain
105 P9 **La Almarcha** Castilla-La Mancha, C Spain
105 R6 **La Almunia de Doña Godina** Aragón, NE Spain
41 N5 **La Amistad, Presa** ▣ NW Mexico
118 F4 **Läänemaa** var. Lääne Maakond. ◈ province NW Estonia
Lääne Maakond see Läänemaa
118 I3 **Lääne-Virumaa** off Lääne-Viru Maakond. ◈ province NE Estonia
Lääne-Viru Maakond see Lääne-Virumaa
62 J9 **La Antigua, Salina** salt lake W Argentina
99 E17 **Laarne** Oost-Vlaanderen, NW Belgium
80 O13 **Laas Caanood** Sool, N Somalia
41 O9 **La Ascensión** Nuevo León, NE Mexico
80 N12 **Laas Dhaareed** Sanaag, N Somalia
55 O4 **La Asunción** Nueva Esparta, NE Venezuela
Laatokka see Ladozhskoye, Ozero
100 I13 **Laatzen** Niedersachsen, NW Germany
38 E9 **La'au Point** var. Laau Point. headland Moloka'i, Hawai'i, USA
Laau Point see La'au Point
42 D6 **La Aurora** ✈ (Ciudad de Guatemala) Guatemala, C Guatemala
74 C9 **Laâyoune** var. Aaiún. ● (Western Sahara) NW Western Sahara
126 L14 **Laba** ≈ SW Russian Federation
40 M6 **La Babia** Coahuila de Zaragoza, NE Mexico
15 R7 **La Baie** Québec, SE Canada
171 P16 **Labala** Pulau Lomblen, S Indonesia
62 K8 **La Banda** Santiago del Estero, N Argentina
La Banda Oriental see Uruguay
104 K4 **La Bañeza** Castilla-León, N Spain
40 M13 **La Barca** Jalisco, SW Mexico
40 K14 **La Barra de Navidad** Jalisco, C Mexico
187 Y13 **Labasa** prev. Lambasa. Vanua Levu, N Fiji
102 H8 **la Baule-Escoublac** Loire-Atlantique, NW France
76 I13 **Labé** NW Guinea
Labe see Elbe
15 N11 **Labelle** Québec, SE Canada
23 X14 **La Belle** Florida, SE USA
10 H7 **Laberge, Lake** ◎ Yukon Territory, W Canada
Labes see Łobez
Labiau see Polessk
112 A10 **Labin** It. Albona. Istra, NW Croatia
126 L14 **Labinsk** Krasnodarskiy Kray, SW Russian Federation
105 X5 **La Bisbal d'Empordà** Cataluña, NE Spain
119 P16 **Labkovichy** Rus. Lobkovichi. Mahilyowskaya Voblasts', E Belarus
15 S4 **La Blache, Lac de** ◎ Québec, SE Canada
171 P4 **Labo** Luzon, N Philippines
Laboehanbadjo see Labuhanbajo
Laborca see Laborec
111 N18 **Laborec** Hung. Laborca. ≈ E Slovakia
108 D11 **La Borgne** ≈ S Switzerland
45 T12 **Laborie** SW Saint Lucia
79 F21 **La Bouenza** ◈ province S Congo
102 J14 **Labouheyre** Landes, SW France
62 L12 **Laboulaye** Córdoba, C Argentina
13 Q7 **Labrador** cultural region Newfoundland and Labrador, SW Canada
64 I6 **Labrador Basin** var. Labrador Sea Basin. undersea feature Labrador Sea
13 N9 **Labrador City** Newfoundland and Labrador, E Canada
13 Q5 **Labrador Sea** sea NW Atlantic Ocean
Labrador Sea Basin see Labrador Basin
Labrang see Xiahe
54 G9 **Labranzagrande** Boyacá, C Colombia
59 D14 **Lábrea** Amazonas, N Brazil
45 U15 **La Brea** Trinidad, Trinidad and Tobago
15 S6 **Labrieville** Québec, SE Canada
102 K14 **Labrit** Landes, SW France
108 C9 **La Broye** ≈ SW Switzerland
103 N15 **Labruguière** Tarn, S France
168 M11 **Labu** Pulau Singkep, W Indonesia
169 T7 **Labuan** var. Victoria. Labuan, East Malaysia
169 T7 **Labuan** ◈ federal territory East Malaysia
Labuan see Labuan, Pulau
169 T7 **Labuan, Pulau** var. Labuan. island East Malaysia
Labudalin see Ergun
171 N16 **Labuhanbajo** prev. Laboehanbadjo. Flores, S Indonesia
168 J9 **Labuhanbilik** Sumatera, N Indonesia
168 G8 **Labuhanhaji** Sumatera, W Indonesia
Labuk see Labuk, Sungai
Labuk Bay see Labuk, Teluk
169 V7 **Labuk, Sungai** var. Labuk. ≈ East Malaysia
169 W6 **Labuk, Teluk** var. Labuk Bay, Telukan Labuk. bay S Sulu Sea
Labuk, Telukan see Labuk, Teluk
166 K9 **Labutta** Irrawaddy, SW Myanmar (Burma)
122 I8 **Labytnangi** Yamalo-Nenetskiy Avtonomnyy Okrug, N Russian Federation
113 K19 **Laç** var. Laci. Lezhë, C Albania
78 F10 **Lac** off. Préfecture du Lac. ◈ prefecture W Chad
57 K19 **Lacajahuira, Rio** ≈ W Bolivia
La Calamine see Kelmis
62 G11 **La Calera** Valparaíso, C Chile
13 P11 **Lac-Allard** Québec, E Canada
104 L13 **La Campana** Andalucía, S Spain
102 J12 **Lacanau** Gironde, SW France
42 C2 **Lacandón, Sierra del** ▲▲ Guatemala/Mexico
La Cañiza see A Cañiza
41 W16 **Lacantún, Río** ≈ SE Mexico
103 Q3 **la Capelle** Aisne, N France
112 K10 **Laćarak** Vojvodina, NW Serbia
62 L11 **La Carlota** Córdoba, C Argentina
104 L13 **La Carlota** Andalucía, S Spain
105 N12 **La Carolina** Andalucía, S Spain
103 O15 **Lacaune** Tarn, S France
15 P7 **Lac-Bouchette** Québec, SE Canada
Laccadive Islands/Laccadive Minicoy and Amindivi Islands, the see Lakshadweep
9 Y16 **Lac du Bonnet** Manitoba, S Canada
30 L4 **Lac du Flambeau** Wisconsin, N USA
15 P8 **Lac-Édouard** Québec, SE Canada
42 I4 **La Ceiba** Atlántida, N Honduras
54 E9 **La Ceja** Antioquia, W Colombia
182 J11 **Lacepede Bay** bay South Australia
32 G9 **Lacey** Washington, NW USA
103 P12 **la Chaise-Dieu** Haute-Loire, C France
114 G13 **Lachanás** Kentrikí Makedonía, N Greece
124 L11 **Lacha, Ozero** ◎ NW Russian Federation
103 O8 **la Charité-sur-Loire** Nièvre, C France
103 N9 **la Châtre** Indre, C France
108 C8 **La Chaux-de-Fonds** Neuchâtel, W Switzerland
Lach Dera see Dheere Laaq
108 G8 **Lachen** Schwyz, C Switzerland
183 Q8 **Lachlan River** ≈ New South Wales, SE Australia
43 T15 **La Chorrera** Panamá, C Panama
15 V7 **Lac-Humqui** Québec, SE Canada
15 N12 **Lachute** Québec, SE Canada
Lachyn see Laçın
Laci see Laç
137 W13 **Laçın** Rus. Lachyn. SW Azerbaijan
103 S16 **la Ciotat** anc. Citharista. Bouches-du-Rhône, SE France
18 D10 **Lackawanna** New York, NE USA
9 Q13 **Lac La Biche** Alberta, SW Canada
Lac la Martre see Wha Ti
Lac la Martre see Wha Ti
15 R12 **Lac-Mégantic** var. Mégantic. Québec, SE Canada
Lacobriga see Lagos
40 G5 **La Colorada** Sonora, NW Mexico
9 P15 **Lacombe** Alberta, SW Canada
30 L12 **Lacon** Illinois, N USA
43 P16 **La Concepción** var. Concepción. Chiriquí, W Panama
54 H5 **La Concepción** Zulia, NW Venezuela
107 C19 **Laconi** Sardegna, Italy, C Mediterranean Sea
19 O9 **Laconia** New Hampshire, NE USA
61 H19 **La Coronilla** Rocha, E Uruguay
La Coruña see A Coruña
103 O11 **la Courtine** Creuse, C France
Lac, Préfecture du see Lac
102 J16 **Lacq** Pyrénées-Atlantiques, SW France

◆ Country ● Country Capital ◇ Dependent Territory C Dependent Territory Capital ◈ Administrative Regions ✈ International Airport ▲ Mountain ▲▲ Mountain Range Volcano ≈ River ◎ Lake ▣ Reservoir

15 *P9* **La Croche** Québec, SE Canada
29 *X3* **la Croix, Lac** ◎ Canada/USA
26 *K5* **La Crosse** Kansas, C USA
21 *V7* **La Crosse** Virginia, NE USA
32 *L9* **La Crosse** Washington, NW USA
30 *J7* **La Crosse** Wisconsin, N USA
54 *C13* **La Cruz** Nariño, SW Colombia
42 *K12* **La Cruz** Guanacaste, NW Costa Rica
40 *I10* **La Cruz** Sinaloa, W Mexico
61 *F19* **La Cruz** Florida, S Uruguay
42 *M9* **La Cruz de Río Grande** Región Autónoma Atlántico Sur, E Nicaragua
54 *J4* **La Cruz de Taratara** Falcón, N Venezuela
15 *Q10* **Lac-St-Charles** Québec, SE Canada
40 *M6* **La Cuesta** Coahuila de Zaragoza, NE Mexico
57 *A17* **La Cumbra, Volcán** ⛰ Galapagos Islands, Ecuador, E Pacific Ocean
152 *J5* **Ladākh Range** ▲▲ NE India
26 *I5* **Ladder Creek** 〰 Kansas, C USA
45 *X10* **la Désirade** *atoll* E Guadeloupe
Lādhiqīyah, Muḥāfaẓat al *see* Al Lādhiqīyah
83 *F25* **Ladismith** Western Cape, SW South Africa
152 *G11* **Lādnūn** Rājasthān, NW India
Ladoga, Lake *see* Ladozhskoye, Ozero
115 *E19* **Ládon** 〰 S Greece
54 *E9* **La Dorada** Caldas, C Colombia
124 *H11* **Ladozhskoye, Ozero** ***Eng.*** Lake Ladoga, ***Fin.*** Laatokka. ◎ NW Russian Federation
37 *R12* **Ladron Peak** ▲ New Mexico, SW USA
124 *J11* **Ladva-Vetka** Respublika Kareliya, NW Russian Federation
183 *Q15* **Lady Barron** Tasmania, SE Australia
14 *G9* **Lady Evelyn Lake** ◎ Ontario, S Canada
23 *W11* **Lady Lake** Florida, SE USA
10 *L17* **Ladysmith** Vancouver Island, British Columbia, SW Canada
83 *J22* **Ladysmith** KwaZulu/Natal, E South Africa
30 *J5* **Ladysmith** Wisconsin, N USA
145 *P9* **Ladyzhenka** Akmola, C Kazakhstan
186 *E7* **Lae** Morobe, W Papua New Guinea
189 *R6* **Lae Atoll** *atoll* Ralik Chain, W Marshall Islands
40 *C3* **La Encantada, Cerro de** ▲ NW Mexico
94 *E12* **Lærdalsøyri** Sogn Og Fjordane, S Norway
55 *N11* **La Esmeralda** Amazonas, S Venezuela
95 *H20* **Læso** *Island* N Denmark
42 *G7* **La Esperanza** Intibucá, SW Honduras
30 *K8* **La Farge** Wisconsin, N USA
23 *R5* **Lafayette** Alabama, S USA
37 *T4* **Lafayette** Colorado, C USA
23 *R2* **La Fayette** Georgia, SE USA
31 *O13* **Lafayette** Indiana, N USA
22 *I9* **Lafayette** Louisiana, S USA
20 *K8* **Lafayette** Tennessee, S USA
19 *N7* **Lafayette, Mount** ▲ New Hampshire, NE USA
La Fe *see* Santa Fé
103 *P3* **la Fère** Aisne, N France
102 *L6* **la Ferté-Bernard** Sarthe, NW France
102 *K5* **la Ferté-Macé** Orne, N France
103 *N7* **la Ferté-St-Aubin** Loiret, C France
103 *P5* **la Ferté-sous-Jouarre** Seine-et-Marne, N France
77 *V15* **Lafia** Nassarawa, C Nigeria
77 *T15* **Lafiagi** Kwara, W Nigeria
9 *T17* **Lafleche** Saskatchewan, S Canada
102 *K7* **la Flèche** Sarthe, NW France
109 *X7* **Lafnitz** ***Hung.*** Lapines. 〰 Austria/Hungary
187 *P17* **La Foa** Province Sud, S New Caledonia
20 *M8* **La Follette** Tennessee, S USA
15 *N12* **Lafontaine** Québec, SE Canada
22 *K10* **Lafourche, Bayou** 〰 Louisiana, S USA
62 *K6* **La Fragua** Santiago del Estero, N Argentina
54 *H7* **La Fría** Táchira, NW Venezuela
104 *J7* **La Fuente de San Esteban** Castilla-León, N Spain
186 *C7* **Lagaip** 〰 W Papua New Guinea
61 *B15* **La Gallareta** Santa Fe, C Argentina
127 *Q14* **Lagan'** ***prev.*** Kaspiyskiy. Respublika Kalmykiya, SW Russian Federation
95 *L20* **Lagan** Kronoberg, S Sweden
95 *K21* **Lågan** 〰 S Sweden
92 *L2* **Lagarfljót** ***var.*** Lögurinn. ◎ E Iceland
37 *R7* **La Garita Mountains** ▲▲ Colorado, C USA
171 *O2* **Lagawe** Luzon, N Philippines
78 *F13* **Lagdo** Nord, N Cameroon
78 *F13* **Lagdo, Lac de** ◎ N Cameroon
100 *H13* **Lage** Nordrhein-Westfalen, W Germany
94 *H12* **Lågen** 〰 S Norway
61 *J14* **Lages** Santa Catarina, S Brazil
Lágesvuotna *see* Laksefjorden
149 *R4* **Laghmān** ◈ *province* E Afghanistan
74 *J6* **Laghouat** N Algeria
105 *Q10* **La Gineta** Castilla-La Mancha, C Spain
115 *E21* **Lagkáda** ***var.*** Langada. Pelopónnisos, S Greece
114 *G13* **Lagkadás** ***var.*** Langades, Langadhás. Kentrikí Makedonía, N Greece
115 *E20* **Lagkádia** ***var.*** Langádhia, ***cont.*** Langadia. Pelopónnisos, S Greece
54 *F6* **La Gloria** Cesar, N Colombia
41 *O7* **La Gloria** Nuevo León, NE Mexico
92 *N3* **Lågneset** *headland* W Svalbard
104 *G14* **Lagoa** Faro, S Portugal
La Goagira *see* La Guajira
Lago Agrio *see* Nueva Loja
61 *I14* **Lagoa Vermelha** Rio Grande do Sul, S Brazil
137 *V10* **Lagodekhi** SE Georgia
42 *C7* **La Gomera** Escuintla, S Guatemala
Lagone *see* Logone
107 *M19* **Lagonegro** Basilicata, S Italy
63 *G16* **Lago Ranco** Los Lagos, S Chile
77 *S16* **Lagos** Lagos, SW Nigeria
104 *F14* **Lagos** ***anc.*** Lacobriga. Faro, S Portugal
77 *S16* **Lagos** ◈ *state* SW Nigeria
40 *M12* **Lagos de Moreno** Jalisco, SW Mexico
Lagosta *see* Lastovo
74 *A12* **Lagouira** SW Western Sahara
92 *O1* **Lågøya** *island* N Svalbard
32 *L11* **La Grande** Oregon, NW USA
103 *Q14* **la Grande-Combe** Gard, S France
12 *K9* **La Grande Rivière** ***var.*** Fort George. 〰 Québec, SE Canada
23 *R4* **La Grange** Georgia, SE USA
31 *P11* **Lagrange** Indiana, N USA
20 *L5* **La Grange** Kentucky, S USA
27 *V2* **La Grange** Missouri, C USA
21 *V10* **La Grange** North Carolina, SE USA
25 *U11* **La Grange** Texas, SW USA
105 *N7* **La Granja** Castilla-León, N Spain
55 *Q9* **La Gran Sabana** *grassland* E Venezuela
54 *H7* **La Grita** Táchira, NW Venezuela
La Grulla *see* Grulla
15 *R11* **La Guadeloupe** Québec, SE Canada
64 *F12* **La Guaira** Distrito Federal, N Venezuela
54 *G4* **La Guajira** ***off.*** Departamento de La Guajira, ***var.*** Guajira, La Goagira. ◈ *province* NE Colombia
188 *I4* **Lagua Lichan, Punta** *headland* Saipan, S Northern Mariana Islands
105 *P4* **Laguardia** ***Basq*** Biasteri. País Vasco, N Spain
18 *K14* **La Guardia** ✈ (New York) Long Island, New York, NE USA
La Guardia/Laguardia *see* A Guarda
La Gudiña *see* A Gudiña
103 *O9* **la Guerche-sur-l'Aubois** Cher, C France
103 *O13* **Laguiole** Aveyron, S France
83 *F26* **L'Agulhas** ***var.*** Agulhas. Western Cape, SW South Africa
61 *K14* **Laguna** Santa Catarina, S Brazil
37 *Q11* **Laguna** New Mexico, SW USA
35 *T16* **Laguna Beach** California, W USA
35 *Y17* **Laguna Dam** *dam* Arizona/California, W USA
40 *L7* **Laguna El Rey** Coahuila de Zaragoza, N Mexico
35 *V17* **Laguna Mountains** ▲▲ California, W USA
61 *B17* **Laguna Paiva** Santa Fe, C Argentina
62 *H3* **Lagunas** Tarapacá, N Chile
56 *E9* **Lagunas** Loreto, N Peru
57 *M20* **Lagunillas** Santa Cruz, SE Bolivia
54 *H6* **Lagunillas** Mérida, NW Venezuela
44 *C4* **La Habana** ***var.*** Havana. ● (Cuba) Ciudad de La Habana, W Cuba
169 *W7* **Lahad Datu** Sabah, East Malaysia
169 *W7* **Lahad Datu, Teluk** ***var.*** Telukan Lahad Datu, Teluk Darvel, Teluk Datu; ***prev.*** Darvel Bay. *bay* Sabah, East Malaysia, C Pacific Ocean
Lahad Datu, Telukan *see* Lahad Datu, Teluk
38 *F10* **Lahaina** Maui, Hawai'i, USA
168 *L14* **Lahat** Sumatera, W Indonesia
La Haye *see* 's-Gravenhage
Lahej *see* Laḥij
62 *G9* **La Higuera** Coquimbo, N Chile
141 *S13* **Lahī, Ḥisā' al** *spring/well* NE Yemen
141 *O16* **Laḥij** ***var.*** Laḥj, ***Eng.*** Lahej. SW Yemen
142 *M3* **Lāhījān** Gīlān, NW Iran
119 *I19* **Lahishyn** ***Pol.*** Lohiszyn, ***Rus.*** Logishin. Brestskaya Voblasts', SW Belarus
Laḥj *see* Laḥij
101 *F18* **Lahn** 〰 W Germany
Lähn *see* Wleń
95 *J21* **Laholm** Halland, S Sweden
95 *J21* **Laholmsbukten** *bay* S Sweden
35 *R6* **Lahontan Reservoir** ⊞ Nevada, W USA
149 *W8* **Lahore** Punjab, NE Pakistan
149 *W8* **Lahore** ✈ Punjab, E Pakistan
55 *Q6* **La Horqueta** Delta Amacuro, NE Venezuela
119 *K15* **Lahoysk** ***Rus.*** Logoysk. Minskaya Voblasts', C Belarus
101 *F22* **Lahr** Baden-Württemberg, S Germany
93 *M19* **Lahti** ***Swe.*** Lahtis. Etelä-Suomi, S Finland
Lahtis *see* Lahti
40 *M14* **La Huacana** Michoacán de Ocampo, SW Mexico
40 *K14* **La Huerta** Jalisco, SW Mexico
78 *H12* **Laï** ***prev.*** Behagle, De Behagle. Tandjilé, S Chad
Laibach *see* Ljubljana
167 *Q5* **Lai Châu** Lai Châu, N Vietnam
Laichow Bay *see* Laizhou Wan
38 *D9* **Lā'ie** ***var.*** Laie. O'ahu, Hawai'i, USA
Laie *see* Lā'ie
102 *L5* **l'Aigle** Orne, N France
103 *Q7* **Laignes** Côte d'Or, C France
93 *K17* **Laihia** Länsi-Soumi, W Finland
Laila *see* Laylā
83 *F25* **Laingsburg** Western Cape, SW South Africa
109 *U2* **Lainsitz** ***Cz.*** Lužnice. 〰 Austria/Czech Republic
96 *I7* **Lairg** N Scotland, UK
81 *I17* **Laisamis** Eastern, N Kenya
Laisberg *see* Leisi
127 *R4* **Laishevo** Respublika Tatarstan, W Russian Federation
Laisholm *see* Jõgeva
92 *H13* **Laisvall** Norrbotten, N Sweden
93 *K19* **Laitila** Länsi-Soumi, SW Finland
161 *P5* **Laiwu** Shandong, E China
161 *R4* **Laixi** ***var.*** Shuiji. Shandong, E China
161 *R4* **Laiyang** Shandong, E China
161 *O3* **Laiyuan** Hebei, E China
161 *R4* **Laizhou** ***var.*** Ye Xian. Shandong, E China
161 *Q4* **Laizhou Wan** ***var.*** Laichow Bay. *bay* E China
37 *S8* **La Jara** Colorado, C USA
61 *I15* **Lajeado** Rio Grande do Sul, S Brazil
112 *L12* **Lajkovac** Serbia, C Serbia
111 *K23* **Lajosmizse** Bács-Kiskun, C Hungary
Lajta *see* Leitha
40 *I6* **La Junta** Chihuahua, N Mexico
37 *V7* **La Junta** Colorado, C USA
92 *J13* **Lakaträsk** Norrbotten, N Sweden
Lak Dera *see* Dheere Laaq
Lakeamu *see* Lakekamu
29 *P12* **Lake Andes** South Dakota, N USA
22 *H9* **Lake Arthur** Louisiana, S USA
187 *Z15* **Lakeba** ***prev.*** Lakemba. *island* Lau Group, E Fiji
187 *Z14* **Lakeba Passage** *channel* E Fiji
29 *S10* **Lake Benton** Minnesota, N USA
23 *V9* **Lake Butler** Florida, SE USA
183 *P8* **Lake Cargelligo** New South Wales, SE Australia
22 *G9* **Lake Charles** Louisiana, S USA
27 *X9* **Lake City** Arkansas, C USA
37 *Q7* **Lake City** Colorado, C USA
23 *V9* **Lake City** Florida, SE USA
29 *U13* **Lake City** Iowa, C USA
31 *P7* **Lake City** Michigan, N USA
29 *W9* **Lake City** Minnesota, N USA
21 *T13* **Lake City** South Carolina, SE USA
29 *Q7* **Lake City** South Dakota, N USA
20 *M8* **Lake City** Tennessee, S USA
10 *L17* **Lake Cowichan** Vancouver Island, British Columbia, SW Canada
29 *U10* **Lake Crystal** Minnesota, N USA
25 *T6* **Lake Dallas** Texas, SW USA
97 *K15* **Lake District** *physical region* NW England, UK
18 *D10* **Lake Erie Beach** New York, NE USA
29 *T11* **Lakefield** Minnesota, N USA
25 *V6* **Lake Fork Reservoir** ◎ Texas, SW USA
30 *M9* **Lake Geneva** Wisconsin, N USA
18 *L9* **Lake George** New York, NE USA
9 *R7* **Lake Harbour** Baffin Island, Nunavut, NE Canada
36 *I12* **Lake Havasu City** Arizona, SW USA
25 *W12* **Lake Jackson** Texas, SW USA
186 *D8* **Lakekamu** ***var.*** Lakeamu. 〰 S Papua New Guinea
180 *K13* **Lake King** Western Australia
23 *V12* **Lakeland** Florida, SE USA
23 *U7* **Lakeland** Georgia, SE USA
181 *W4* **Lakeland Downs** Queensland, NE Australia
9 *P16* **Lake Louise** Alberta, SW Canada
Lakemba *see* Lakeba
29 *V11* **Lake Mills** Iowa, C USA
39 *Q10* **Lake Minchumina** Alaska, USA
Lakemti *see* Nek'emtē
186 *A7* **Lake Murray** Western, SW Papua New Guinea
31 *R9* **Lake Orion** Michigan, N USA
190 *B16* **Lakepa** NE Niue
29 *T11* **Lake Park** Iowa, C USA
18 *K7* **Lake Placid** New York, NE USA
18 *K9* **Lake Pleasant** New York, NE USA
34 *M6* **Lakeport** California, W USA
29 *Q10* **Lake Preston** South Dakota, N USA
22 *J5* **Lake Providence** Louisiana, S USA
185 *E20* **Lake Pukaki** Canterbury, South Island, New Zealand
183 *Q12* **Lakes Entrance** Victoria, SE Australia
37 *N12* **Lakeside** Arizona, SW USA
35 *V17* **Lakeside** California, W USA
23 *S9* **Lakeside** Florida, SE USA
28 *K13* **Lakeside** Nebraska, C USA
32 *E13* **Lakeside** Oregon, NW USA
21 *W6* **Lakeside** Virginia, NE USA
Lakes State *see* El Buhayrat
Lake State *see* Michigan
185 *F20* **Lake Tekapo** Canterbury, South Island, New Zealand
21 *O10* **Lake Toxaway** North Carolina, SE USA
29 *T13* **Lake View** Iowa, C USA
32 *I16* **Lakeview** Oregon, NW USA
25 *O3* **Lakeview** Texas, SW USA
27 *W14* **Lake Village** Arkansas, C USA
23 *W12* **Lake Wales** Florida, SE USA
37 *T4* **Lakewood** Colorado, C USA
18 *K15* **Lakewood** New Jersey, NE USA
18 *C11* **Lakewood** New York, NE USA
31 *T11* **Lakewood** Ohio, N USA
23 *Y13* **Lakewood Park** Florida, SE USA
23 *Z14* **Lake Worth** Florida, SE USA
152 *H4* **Lake Wular** ◎ NE India
124 *H11* **Lakhdenpokh'ya** Respublika Kareliya, NW Russian Federation
152 *L11* **Lakhīmpur** Uttar Pradesh, N India
154 *J11* **Lakhnādon** Madhya Pradesh, C India
Lakhnau *see* Lucknow
154 *A9* **Lakhpat** Gujarāt, W India
119 *K19* **Lakhva** ***Rus.*** Lakhva. Brestskaya Voblasts', SW Belarus
26 *I6* **Lakin** Kansas, C USA
149 *S7* **Lakki Marwat** North-West Frontier Province, NW Pakistan
115 *F21* **Lakonía** *historical region* S Greece
115 *F22* **Lakonikós Kólpos** *gulf* S Greece
76 *M17* **Lakota** S Ivory Coast
29 *U11* **Lakota** Iowa, C USA
29 *P3* **Lakota** North Dakota, N USA
Lak Sao *see* Ban Lakxao
92 *L8* **Laksefjorden** ***Lapp.*** Lágesvuotna. *fjord* N Norway
92 *K8* **Lakselv** ***Lapp.*** Leavdnja. Finnmark, N Norway
155 *B21* **Lakshadweep** ***prev.*** the Laccadive Minicoy and Amindivi Islands. ◈ *union territory* India, N Indian Ocean
155 *C22* **Lakshadweep** ***Eng.*** Laccadive Islands. *island group* India, N Indian Ocean
153 *S17* **Lakshmikāntapur** West Bengal, NE India
112 *G11* **Laktaši** ◈ Republika Srpska, N Bosnia and Herzegovina
149 *V7* **Lāla Mūsa** Punjab, NE Pakistan
la Laon *see* Laon
114 *M11* **Lalapaşa** Edirne, NW Turkey
83 *P14* **Lalaua** Nampula, N Mozambique
105 *S9* **L'Alcora** ***var*** Alcora. País Valenciano, E Spain
105 *S10* **L'Alcúdia** ***var.*** L'Alcudia. País Valenciano, E Spain
79 *F20* **La Lékoumou** ◈ *province* SW Congo
42 *E8* **La Libertad** La Libertad, SW El Salvador
42 *E3* **La Libertad** Petén, N Guatemala
42 *H6* **La Libertad** Comayagua, SW Honduras
40 *E4* **La Libertad** ***var.*** Puerto Libertad. Sonora, NW Mexico
42 *K10* **La Libertad** Chontales, S Nicaragua
42 *A9* **La Libertad** ◈ *department* SW El Salvador
56 *B11* **La Libertad** ◈ *department* W Peru
62 *G11* **La Ligua** Valparaíso, C Chile
139 *U5* **La'lī Khān** E Iraq
79 *H16* **La Likouala** ◈ *province* NE Congo
104 *H3* **Lalín** Galicia, NW Spain
102 *L13* **Lalinde** Dordogne, SW France
104 *K16* **La Línea** ***var.*** La Línea de la Concepción. Andalucía, S Spain
La Línea de la Concepción *see* La Línea
152 *J14* **Lalitpur** Uttar Pradesh, N India
153 *P11* **Lalitpur** Central, C Nepal
152 *K10* **Lālkua** Uttarachal, N India
153 *T12* **Lalmanirhat** Rājshāhi, N Bangladesh
9 *R12* **La Loche** Saskatchewan, C Canada
102 *M6* **la Loupe** Eure-et-Loir, C France
99 *G20* **La Louvière** Hainaut, S Belgium
L'Altissima *see* Hochwilde
104 *L14* **La Luisiana** Andalucía, S Spain
37 *S14* **La Luz** New Mexico, SW USA
107 *D16* **la Maddalena** Sardegna, Italy, C Mediterranean Sea
62 *J7* **La Madrid** Tucumán, N Argentina
Lama-Kara *see* Kara
15 *S8* **La Malbaie** Québec, SE Canada
167 *T10* **Lamam** Xékong, S Laos
105 *P10* **La Mancha** *physical region* C Spain
la Manche *see* English Channel
187 *R13* **Lamap** Malekula, C Vanuatu
37 *W6* **Lamar** Colorado, C USA
27 *S7* **Lamar** Missouri, C USA
21 *S12* **Lamar** South Carolina, SE USA
107 *C19* **La Marmora, Punta** ▲ Sardegna, Italy, C Mediterranean Sea
8 *I9* **La Martre, Lac** ◎ Northwest Territories, NW Canada
56 *D10* **Lamas** San Martín, N Peru
42 *I5* **La Masica** Atlántida, NW Honduras
103 *R12* **Lamastre** Ardèche, E France
La Matepec *see* Santa Ana, Volcán de
44 *I7* **La Maya** Santiago de Cuba, E Cuba
109 *S5* **Lambach** Oberösterreich, N Austria
168 *I11* **Lambak** Pulau Pini, W Indonesia
102 *H5* **Lamballe** Côtes d'Armor, NW France
79 *D18* **Lambaréné** Moyen-Ogooué, W Gabon
Lambasa *see* Labasa
56 *B11* **Lambayeque** Lambayeque, W Peru
56 *A10* **Lambayeque** ***off.*** Departamento de Lambayeque. ◈ *department* NW Peru
Lambayeque, Departamento de *see* Lambayeque
97 *G17* **Lambay Island** ***Ir.*** Reachrainn. *island* E Ireland
186 *G6* **Lambert, Cape** *headland* New Britain, E Papua New Guinea
195 *W6* **Lambert Glacier** *glacier* Antarctica
29 *T10* **Lamberton** Minnesota, N USA
27 *X4* **Lambert-Saint Louis** ✈ Missouri, C USA
31 *R11* **Lambertville** Michigan, N USA
18 *J15* **Lambertville** New Jersey, NE USA
171 *N12* **Lambogo** Sulawesi, N Indonesia
106 *D8* **Lambro** 〰 N Italy
33 *W11* **Lame Deer** Montana, NW USA
104 *H6* **Lamego** Viseu, N Portugal
187 *Q14* **Lamen Bay** Épi, C Vanuatu
45 *X6* **Lamentin** Basse Terre, N Guadeloupe
Lamentin *see* le Lamentin
182 *K10* **Lameroo** South Australia
54 *F10* **La Mesa** Cundinamarca, C Colombia
35 *U17* **La Mesa** California, W USA
37 *R16* **La Mesa** New Mexico, SW USA
25 *N6* **Lamesa** Texas, SW USA
107 *N21* **Lamezia Terme** Calabria, SE Italy
115 *F17* **Lamía** Stereá Ellás, C Greece
171 *O8* **Lamitan** Basilan Island, SW Philippines
187 *Y14* **Lamiti** Gau, C Fiji
171 *T11* **Lamlam** Papua, E Indonesia
188 *B16* **Lamlam, Mount** ▲ SW Guam
109 *Q6* **Lammer** 〰 E Austria
185 *E23* **Lammerlaw Range** ▲▲ South Island, New Zealand
95 *L20* **Lammhult** Kronoberg, S Sweden
93 *L18* **Lammi** Etelä-Suomi, S Finland
189 *U11* **Lamoil** *island* Chuuk, C Micronesia
35 *W3* **Lamoille** Nevada, W USA
18 *M7* **Lamoille River** 〰 Vermont, NE USA
30 *J13* **La Moine River** 〰 Illinois, N USA
171 *P4* **Lamon Bay** *bay* Luzon, N Philippines
29 *V16* **Lamoni** Iowa, C USA
35 *R13* **Lamont** California, W USA
27 *N8* **Lamont** Oklahoma, C USA
54 *E13* **La Montañita** ***var.*** Montañita. Caquetá, S Colombia
43 *N8* **La Mosquitia** ***var.*** Miskito Coast, ***Eng.*** Mosquito Coast. *coastal region* E Nicaragua
102 *I9* **la Mothe-Achard** Vendée, NW France
188 *L15* **Lamotrek Atoll** *atoll* Caroline Islands, C Micronesia
29 *P6* **La Moure** North Dakota, N USA
167 *O8* **Lampang** ***var.*** Muang Lampang. Lampang, NW Thailand
167 *R9* **Lam Pao Reservoir** ⊞ E Thailand
25 *S9* **Lampasas** Texas, SW USA
25 *S9* **Lampasas River** 〰 Texas, SW USA
41 *N7* **Lampazos** ***var.*** Lampazos de Naranjo. Nuevo León, NE Mexico
Lampazos de Naranjo *see* Lampazos
115 *E19* **Lámpeia** Dytikí Ellás, S Greece
101 *G19* **Lampertheim** Hessen, W Germany
97 *I20* **Lampeter** SW Wales, UK
167 *O7* **Lamphun** ***var.*** Lampun, Muang Lamphun. Lamphun, NW Thailand
9 *X10* **Lamprey** Manitoba, C Canada
Lampun *see* Lamphun
168 *M15* **Lampung** ***off.*** Propinsi Lampung. ◈ *province* SW Indonesia
Lampung, Propinsi *see* Lampung
126 *K6* **Lamskoye** Lipetskaya Oblast', W Russian Federation
81 *K20* **Lamu** Coast, SE Kenya
43 *N14* **La Muerte, Cerro** ▲ C Costa Rica
103 *S13* **la Mure** Isère, E France
37 *S10* **Lamy** New Mexico, SW USA
119 *J18* **Lan'** ***Rus.*** Lan'. 〰 C Belarus
38 *E10* **Lāna'i** ***var.*** Lanai. *island* Hawai'i, USA, C Pacific Ocean
38 *E10* **Lāna'i City** ***var.*** Lanai City. Lanai, Hawai'i, USA, C Pacific Ocean
Lanai City *see* Lāna'i City
99 *L18* **Lanaken** Limburg, NE Belgium
171 *Q7* **Lanao, Lake** ***var.*** Lake Sultan Alonto. ◎ Mindanao, S Philippines
96 *J12* **Lanark** S Scotland, UK
96 *I13* **Lanark** *cultural region* C Scotland, UK
104 *L9* **La Nava de Ricomalillo** Castilla-La Mancha, C Spain
166 *M13* **Lanbi Kyun** ***prev.*** Sullivan Island. *island* Mergui Archipelago, S Myanmar (Burma)
Lancang Jiang *see* Mekong
97 *K17* **Lancashire** *cultural region* N England, UK
15 *N13* **Lancaster** Ontario, SE Canada
97 *K16* **Lancaster** NW England, UK
35 *T14* **Lancaster** California, W USA
20 *M6* **Lancaster** Kentucky, S USA
27 *U1* **Lancaster** Missouri, C USA
19 *O7* **Lancaster** New Hampshire, NE USA
18 *D10* **Lancaster** New York, NE USA
31 *T14* **Lancaster** Ohio, N USA
18 *H16* **Lancaster** Pennsylvania, NE USA
21 *R11* **Lancaster** South Carolina, SE USA
25 *U7* **Lancaster** Texas, SW USA
21 *X5* **Lancaster** Virginia, NE USA
30 *J9* **Lancaster** Wisconsin, N USA
197 *N10* **Lancaster Sound** *sound* Nunavut, N Canada
Lan-chou/Lan-chow/Lanchow *see* Lanzhou
107 *K14* **Lanciano** Abruzzo, C Italy
111 *O16* **Łańcut** Podkarpackie, SE Poland
169 *Q11* **Landak, Sungai** 〰 Borneo, N Indonesia
Landao *see* Lantau Island
Landau *see* Landau an der Isar
Landau *see* Landau in der Pfalz
101 *N22* **Landau an der Isar** ***var.*** Landau. Bayern, SE Germany
101 *F20* **Landau in der Pfalz** ***var.*** Landau. Rheinland-Pfalz, SW Germany
Land Burgenland *see* Burgenland
108 *K8* **Landeck** Tirol, W Austria
99 *J19* **Landen** Vlaams Brabant, C Belgium
33 *U15* **Lander** Wyoming, C USA
102 *F5* **Landerneau** Finistère, NW France
95 *K20* **Landeryd** Halland, S Sweden
102 *J15* **Landes** ◈ *department* SW France
Landeshut/Landeshut in Schlesien *see* Kamienna Góra
105 *R9* **Landete** Castilla-La Mancha, C Spain
99 *M18* **Landgraaf** Limburg, SE Netherlands
102 *F5* **Landivisiau** Finistère, NW France
Land Kärten *see* Kärnten
Land of Enchantment *see* New Mexico
The Land of Opportunity *see* Arkansas
Land of Steady Habits *see* Connecticut
Land of the Midnight Sun *see* Alaska
108 *I8* **Landquart** Graubünden, SE Switzerland
108 *J9* **Landquart** 〰 Austria/Switzerland
21 *P10* **Landrum** South Carolina, SE USA
Landsberg *see* Gorzów Wielkopolski, Lubuskie, Poland
Landsberg *see* Górowo Iławeckie, Warmińsko-Mazurskie, NE Poland
101 *K23* **Landsberg am Lech** Bayern, S Germany
Landsberg an der Warthe *see* Gorzów Wielkopolski
97 *G25* **Land's End** *headland* SW England, UK
101 *M22* **Landshut** Bayern, SE Germany
Landskron *see* Lanškroun
95 *J22* **Landskrona** Skåne, S Sweden
98 *I10* **Landsmeer** Noord-Holland, C Netherlands
95 *J19* **Landvetter** ✈ (Göteborg) Västra Götaland, S Sweden
Landwarów *see* Lentvaris
23 *R5* **Lanett** Alabama, S USA
108 *C8* **La Neuveville** ***var.*** Neuveville, ***Ger.*** Neuenstadt. Neuchâtel, W Switzerland
95 *G21* **Langå** ***var.*** Langaa. Århus, C Denmark
Langaa *see* Langå
158 *G14* **La'nga Co** ◎ W China
Langada *see* Lagkáda
Langades/Langadhás *see* Lagkadás
Langádhia/ *see* Lagkádia
147 *T14* **Langar** ***Rus.*** Lyangar. SE Tajikistan
146 *M10* **Langar** ***Rus.*** Lyangar. Navoiy Viloyati, C Uzbekistan
142 *M3* **Langarūd** Gīlān, NW Iran
9 *V16* **Langbank** Saskatchewan, S Canada
29 *P2* **Langdon** North Dakota, N USA
103 *P12* **Langeac** Haute-Loire, C France
102 *L8* **Langeais** Indre-et-Loire, C France
80 *I8* **Langeb, Wadi** 〰 NE Sudan
Långed *see* Dals Långed
95 *G25* **Langeland** *island* S Denmark
99 *B18* **Langemark** West-Vlaanderen, W Belgium
101 *G18* **Langen** Hessen, W Germany
101 *J22* **Langenau** Baden-Württemberg, S Germany
9 *V16* **Langenburg** Saskatchewan, S Canada
108 *L8* **Längenfeld** Tirol, W Austria
101 *E16* **Langenfeld** Nordrhein-Westfalen, W Germany
100 *I12* **Langenhagen** Niedersachsen, N Germany
100 *I12* **Langenhagen** ✈ (Hannover) Niedersachsen, NW Germany
109 *W3* **Langenlois** Niederösterreich, NE Austria
108 *E7* **Langenthal** Bern, NW Switzerland
109 *W6* **Langenwang** Steiermark, E Austria
109 *X3* **Langenzersdorf** Niederösterreich, E Austria
100 *F9* **Langeoog** *island* NW Germany
95 *H23* **Langeskov** Fyn, C Denmark
95 *G16* **Langesund** Telemark, S Norway
95 *G17* **Langesundsfjorden** *fjord* S Norway
94 *D10* **Langevågen** Møre og Romsdal, S Norway
161 *P3* **Langfang** Hebei, E China
94 *E9* **Langfjorden** *fjord* S Norway
29 *Q8* **Langford** South Dakota, N USA
168 *I10* **Langgapayung** Sumatera, W Indonesia
106 *E9* **Langhirano** Emilia-Romagna, C Italy
97 *K14* **Langholm** S Scotland, UK
92 *I3* **Langjökull** *glacier* C Iceland
168 *I6* **Langkawi, Pulau** *island* Peninsular Malaysia
166 *M14* **Langkha Tuk, Khao** ▲ SW Thailand
14 *L8* **Langlade** Québec, SE Canada
10 *M17* **Langley** British Columbia, SW Canada
167 *S7* **Lang Mô** Thanh Hoa, N Vietnam
Langnau *see* Langnau im Emmental
108 *E8* **Langnau im Emmental** ***var.*** Langnau. Bern, W Switzerland
103 *Q13* **Langogne** Lozère, S France
102 *K13* **Langon** Gironde, SW France
La Ngounié *see* Ngounié
92 *G10* **Langøya** *island* C Norway
158 *G14* **Langqên Zangbo** 〰 China/India
104 *K2* **Langreo** ***var.*** Sama de Langreo. Asturias, N Spain
103 *S7* **Langres** Haute-Marne, N France
103 *R8* **Langres, Plateau de** *plateau* C France
168 *H8* **Langsa** Sumatera, W Indonesia
93 *H16* **Långsele** Västernorrland, C Sweden
162 *L12* **Lang Shan** ▲▲ N China
95 *M14* **Långshyttan** Dalarna, C Sweden

◆ Country
● Country Capital
◇ Dependent Territory
○ Dependent Territory Capital
◈ Administrative Regions
✈ International Airport
▲ Mountain
▲▲ Mountain Range
⛰ Volcano
〰 River
◎ Lake
⊞ Reservoir

167 T5 **Lang Sơn** *var.* Langson. Lang Sơn, N Vietnam
Langson *see* Lang Sơn
167 N14 **Lang Suan** Chumphon, SW Thailand
93 J14 **Långträsk** Norrbotten, N Sweden
25 N11 **Langtry** Texas, SW USA
103 P16 **Languedoc** *cultural region* S France
103 P15 **Languedoc-Roussillon** ◐ *region* S France
27 X10 **L'Anguille River** ≈ Arkansas, C USA
93 I16 **Långviksmon** Västernorrland, N Sweden
101 K22 **Langweid** Bayern, S Germany
160 J8 **Langzhong** Sichuan, C China
Lan Hsü *see* Lan Yü
9 U15 **Lanigan** Saskatchewan, S Canada
116 K5 **Lanivtsi** Ternopil's'ka Oblast', W Ukraine
137 Y13 **Länkäran** *Rus.* Lenkoran'. S Azerbaijan
102 L16 **Lannemezan** Hautes-Pyrénées, S France
102 G5 **Lannion** Côtes d'Armor, NW France
14 M11 **L'Annonciation** Québec, SE Canada
105 V5 **L'Anoia** ≈ NE Spain
18 I15 **Lansdale** Pennsylvania, NE USA
14 L14 **Lansdowne** Ontario, SE Canada
152 K9 **Lansdowne** Uttaranchal, N India
30 M3 **L'Anse** Michigan, N USA
15 S7 **L'Anse-St-Jean** Québec, SE Canada
29 Y11 **Lansing** Iowa, C USA
27 R4 **Lansing** Kansas, C USA
31 Q9 **Lansing** *state capital* Michigan, N USA
93 K18 **Länsi-Suomi** ◐ *province* W Finland
92 J12 **Lansjärv** Norrbotten, N Sweden
111 G17 **Lanškroun** *Ger.* Landskron. Pardubický Kraj, E Czech Republic
167 N16 **Lanta, Ko** *island* S Thailand
161 O15 **Lantau Island** *Cant.* Tai Yue Shan, *Chin.* Landao. *island* Hong Kong, S China
Lantian *see* Lianyuan
Lan-ts'ang Chiang *see* Mekong
Lantung, Gulf of *see* Liaodong Wan
171 O11 **Lanu** Sulawesi, N Indonesia
107 D19 **Lanusei** Sardegna, Italy, C Mediterranean Sea
102 H7 **Lanvaux, Landes de** *physical region* NW France
163 W8 **Lanxi** Heilongjiang, NE China
161 R10 **Lanxi** Zhejiang, SE China
La Nyanga *see* Nyanga
161 T15 **Lan Yü** *var.* Huoshao Tao, *var.* Hungt'ou, Lan Hsü, Lanyü, *Eng.* Orchid Island; *prev.* Kotosho, Koto Sho. *island* SE Taiwan
Lanyü *see* Lan Yü
64 P11 **Lanzarote** *island* Islas Canarias, Spain, NE Atlantic Ocean
159 V10 **Lanzhou** *var.* Lan-chou, Lanchow, Lan-chow; *prev.* Kaolan. *province capital* Gansu, C China
106 B8 **Lanzo Torinese** Piemonte, NE Italy
171 O11 **Laoag** Luzon, N Philippines
171 Q5 **Laoang** Samar, C Philippines
167 R5 **Lao Cai** Lao Cai, N Vietnam
Laodicea/Laodicea ad Mare *see* Al Lādhiqīyah
Laoet *see* Laut, Pulau
163 T11 **Laoha He** ≈ NE China
160 M8 **Laohekou** *var.* Guanghua. Hubei, C China
Laoi, An *see* Lee
97 E19 **Laois** *prev.* Leix, Queen's County. ◐ *county* C Ireland
Laojunmiao *see* Yumen
163 W12 **Lao Ling** ▲▲ N China
64 Q11 **La Oliva** *var.* Oliva. Fuerteventura, Islas Canarias, Spain, NE Atlantic Ocean
Lao, Loch *see* Belfast Lough
Laolong *see* Longchuan
Lao Mangnai *see* Mangnai
103 P3 **Laon** *var.* la Laon; *anc.* Laudunum. Aisne, N France
Lao People's Democratic Republic *see* Laos
54 M3 **La Orchila, Isla** *island* N Venezuela
64 O11 **La Orotava** Tenerife, Islas Canarias, Spain, NE Atlantic Ocean
57 E14 **La Oroya** Junín, C Peru
167 Q7 **Laos** *off.* Lao People's Democratic Republic. ◆ *republic* SE Asia
161 R5 **Laoshan Wan** *bay* E China
163 Y10 **Laoye Ling** ▲▲ NE China
60 J12 **Lapa** Paraná, S Brazil
103 P10 **Lapalisse** Allier, C France
54 F9 **La Palma** Cundinamarca, C Colombia
42 F7 **La Palma** Chalatenango, N El Salvador
43 W16 **La Palma** Darién, SE Panama
64 N11 **La Palma** *island* Islas Canarias, Spain, NE Atlantic Ocean
104 J14 **La Palma del Condado** Andalucía, S Spain
61 F18 **La Paloma** Durazno, C Uruguay
61 G20 **La Paloma** Rocha, E Uruguay
61 A21 **La Pampa** *off.* Provincia de La Pampa. ◐ *province* C Argentina
La Pampa, Provincia de *see* La Pampa
55 P8 **La Paragua** Bolívar, E Venezuela
119 O16 **Lapatsichy** *Rus.* Lopatichi. Mahilyowskaya Voblasts', E Belarus
61 C16 **La Paz** Entre Ríos, E Argentina
62 I11 **La Paz** Mendoza, C Argentina
57 J18 **La Paz** *var.* La Paz de Ayacucho. ● (Bolivia-legislative and administrative capital) La Paz, W Bolivia
42 H6 **La Paz** La Paz, SW Honduras
40 F9 **La Paz** Baja California Sur, NW Mexico
61 F20 **La Paz** Canelones, S Uruguay
57 J16 **La Paz** ◐ *department* W Bolivia
42 B9 **La Paz** ◐ *department* S El Salvador
42 G7 **La Paz** ◐ *department* SW Honduras
La Paz *see* El Alto
La Paz *see* Robles
La Paz *see* La Paz Centro
40 F9 **La Paz, Bahía de** *bay* W Mexico
42 I10 **La Paz Centro** *var.* La Paz. León, W Nicaragua
La Paz de Ayacucho *see* La Paz
54 J15 **La Pedrera** Amazonas, SE Colombia
31 S9 **Lapeer** Michigan, N USA
40 K6 **La Perla** Chihuahua, N Mexico
165 T1 **La Perouse Strait** *Jap.* Sōya-kaikyō, *Rus.* Proliv Laperuza. *strait* Japan/Russian Federation
63 I14 **La Perra, Salitral de** *salt lake* C Argentina
Laperuza, Proliv *see* La Perouse Strait
41 Q10 **La Pesca** Tamaulipas, C Mexico
40 M13 **La Piedad Cabadas** Michoacán de Ocampo, C Mexico
Lapines *see* Lafnitz
93 M16 **Lapinlahti** Kuopio, C Finland
Lápithos *see* Lapta
22 K9 **Laplace** Louisiana, S USA
45 X12 **La Plaine** SE Dominica
173 P16 **La Plaine-des-Palmistes** C Réunion
92 K11 **Lapland** *Fin.* Lappi, *Swe.* Lappland. *cultural region* N Europe
28 M8 **La Plant** South Dakota, N USA
61 D20 **La Plata** Buenos Aires, E Argentina
54 D12 **La Plata** Huila, SW Colombia
21 W4 **La Plata** Maryland, NE USA
La Plata *see* Sucre
45 U6 **la Plata, Río de** ≈ C Puerto Rico
105 W4 **La Pobla de Lillet** Cataluña, NE Spain
105 U4 **La Pobla de Segur** Cataluña, NE Spain
15 S9 **La Pocatière** Québec, SE Canada
104 L3 **La Pola de Gordón** Castilla-León, N Spain
31 O11 **La Porte** Indiana, N USA
18 H13 **Laporte** Pennsylvania, NE USA
29 X13 **La Porte City** Iowa, C USA
62 J8 **La Posta** Catamarca, C Argentina
40 E8 **La Poza Grande** Baja California Sur, W Mexico
93 K16 **Lappajärvi** Länsi-Soumi, W Finland
93 L16 **Lappajärvi** ◎ W Finland
93 N18 **Lappeenranta** *Swe.* Villmanstrand. Etelä-Suomi, SE Finland
93 J17 **Lappfjärd** *Fin.* Lapväärtti. Länsi-Soumi, W Finland
92 L12 **Lappi** *Swe.* Lappland. ◐ *province* N Finland
Lappi/Lappland *see* Lapland
Lappland *see* Lappi
Lappo *see* Lapua
61 C23 **Laprida** Buenos Aires, E Argentina
25 P13 **La Pryor** Texas, SW USA
136 B11 **Lâpseki** Çanakkale, NW Turkey
121 P2 **Lapta** *Gk.* Lápithos. NW Cyprus
Laptev Sea *see* Laptevykh, More
122 N6 **Laptevykh, More** *Eng.* Laptev Sea. *sea* Arctic Ocean
93 K16 **Lapua** *Swe.* Lappo. Länsi-Soumi, W Finland
105 P3 **La Puebla de Arganzón** País Vasco, N Spain
104 L14 **La Puebla de Cazalla** Andalucía, S Spain
104 M9 **La Puebla de Montalbán** Castilla-La Mancha, C Spain
54 I6 **La Puerta** Trujillo, NW Venezuela
Lapurdum *see* Bayonne
40 E7 **La Purísima** Baja California Sur, W Mexico
Lapväärtti *see* Lappfjärd
110 O10 **Łapy** Podlaskie, NE Poland
80 D6 **Laqiya Arba'in** Northern, NW Sudan
62 J4 **La Quiaca** Jujuy, N Argentina
107 J14 **L'Aquila** *var.* Aquila, Aquila degli Abruzzi. Abruzzo, C Italy
143 Q13 **Lār** Fārs, S Iran
54 J5 **Lara** *off.* Estado Lara. ◐ *state* NW Venezuela
104 G2 **Laracha** Galicia, NW Spain
74 G5 **Larache** *var.* al Araïch, El Araïch, *prev.* El Araïche; *anc.* Lixus. NW Morocco
Lara, Estado *see* Lara
103 T14 **Laragne-Montéglin** Hautes-Alpes, SE France
104 M13 **La Rambla** Andalucía, S Spain
33 Y17 **Laramie** Wyoming, C USA
33 X15 **Laramie Mountains** ▲▲ Wyoming, C USA
33 Y16 **Laramie River** ≈ Wyoming, C USA
60 H12 **Laranjeiras do Sul** Paraná, S Brasil
Larantoeka *see* Larantuka
171 P16 **Larantuka** *prev.* Larantoeka. Flores, C Indonesia
171 U15 **Larat** Pulau Larat, E Indonesia
171 U15 **Larat, Pulau** *island* Kepulauan Tanimbar, E Indonesia
95 P19 **Lärbro** Gotland, SE Sweden
106 A9 **Larche, Col de** *pass* France/Italy
14 H8 **Larder Lake** Ontario, S Canada
105 O2 **Laredo** Cantabria, N Spain
25 Q15 **Laredo** Texas, SW USA
40 H9 **La Reforma** Sinaloa, W Mexico
98 N11 **Laren** Gelderland, E Netherlands
98 J11 **Laren** Noord-Holland, C Netherlands
102 K13 **la Réole** Gironde, SW France
La Réunion *see* Réunion
Largeau *see* Faya
105 U13 **l'Argentière-la-Bessée** Hautes-Alpes, SE France
149 O4 **Lar Gerd** *var.* Largird. Balkh, N Afghanistan
Largird *see* Lar Gerd
23 V12 **Largo** Florida, SE USA
37 Q9 **Largo, Canon** *valley* New Mexico, SW USA
44 D6 **Largo, Cayo** *island* W Cuba
23 Z17 **Largo, Key** *island* Florida Keys, Florida, SE USA
96 H12 **Largs** W Scotland, UK
102 I16 **la Rhune** *var.* Larrún. ▲ France/Spain *see also* Larrún
la Rhune *see* Larrún
la Riege *see* Ariège
29 Q4 **Larimore** North Dakota, N USA
107 L15 **Larino** Molise, C Italy
Lario *see* Como, Lago di
62 J9 **La Rioja** La Rioja, NW Argentina
62 I9 **La Rioja** *off.* Provincia de La Rioja. ◐ *province* NW Argentina
105 O4 **La Rioja** ◐ *autonomous community* N Spain
La Rioja, Provincia de *see* La Rioja
115 F16 **Lárisa** *var.* Larissa. Thessalía, C Greece
Larissa *see* Lárisa
149 Q13 **Lārkāna** *var.* Larkhana. Sind, SE Pakistan
Larkhana *see* Lārkāna
Larnaca *see* Lárnaka
121 Q3 **Lárnaka** *var.* Larnaca, Larnax. SE Cyprus
121 Q3 **Lárnaka** ✕ SE Cyprus
Larnax *see* Lárnaka
97 G14 **Larne** *Ir.* Latharna. E Northern Ireland, UK
26 L5 **Larned** Kansas, C USA
104 L3 **La Robla** Castilla-León, N Spain
104 J10 **La Roca de la Sierra** Extremadura, W Spain
99 K22 **La Roche-en-Ardenne** Luxembourg, SE Belgium
102 L11 **la Rochefoucauld** Charente, W France
102 J10 **la Rochelle** *anc.* Rupella. Charente-Maritime, W France
102 I9 **la Roche-sur-Yon** *prev.* Bourbon Vendée, Napoléon-Vendée. Vendée, NW France
105 Q10 **La Roda** Castilla-La Mancha, C Spain
104 L14 **La Roda de Andalucía** Andalucía, S Spain
45 P9 **La Romana** E Dominican Republic
9 T13 **La Ronge** Saskatchewan, C Canada
9 U13 **La Ronge, Lac** ◎ Saskatchewan, C Canada
22 K10 **Larose** Louisiana, S USA
42 M7 **La Rosita** Región Autónoma Atlántico Norte, NE Nicaragua
181 Q3 **Larrimah** Northern Territory, N Australia
62 N11 **Larroque** Entre Ríos, E Argentina
105 Q2 **Larrún** *Fr.* la Rhune. ▲ France/Spain *see also* la Rhune
Larrún *see* la Rhune
195 X6 **Lars Christensen Coast** *physical region* Antarctica
39 Q14 **Larsen Bay** Kodiak Island, Alaska, USA
194 I5 **Larsen Ice Shelf** *ice shelf* Antarctica
8 M6 **Larsen Sound** *sound* Nunavut, N Canada
La Rúa *see* A Rúa de Valdeorras
102 K16 **Laruns** Pyrénées-Atlantiques, SW France
95 G16 **Larvik** Vestfold, S Norway
La-sa *see* Lhasa
171 S13 **Lasahata** Pulau Seram, E Indonesia
Lasahau *see* Lasihao
37 O6 **La Sal** Utah, W USA
14 C17 **La Salle** Ontario, S Canada
30 L11 **La Salle** Illinois, N USA
45 O9 **Las Americas** ✕ (Santo Domingo) S Dominican Republic
79 G17 **La Sangha** ◐ *province* N Congo
37 V6 **Las Animas** Colorado, C USA
108 D10 **La Sarine** *var.* Sarine. ≈ SW Switzerland
108 B9 **La Sarraz** Vaud, W Switzerland
12 H12 **La Sarre** Québec, SE Canada
54 L3 **Las Aves, Islas** *var.* Islas de Aves. *island group* N Venezuela
55 N7 **Las Bonitas** Bolívar, C Venezuela
104 K15 **Las Cabezas de San Juan** Andalucía, S Spain
61 G19 **Lascano** Rocha, E Uruguay
62 I5 **Lascar, Volcán** ⛰ N Chile
41 T15 **Las Choapas** *var.* Choapas. Veracruz-Llave, SE Mexico
37 R15 **Las Cruces** New Mexico, SW USA
Lasdehnen *see* Krasnoznamensk
105 V4 **La See d'Urgel** *var.* La Seu d'Urgell, Seo de Urgel. Cataluña, NE Spain
La Selle *see* Selle, Pic de la
62 G9 **La Serena** Coquimbo, C Chile
104 K11 **La Serena** *physical region* W Spain
La Seu d'Urgell *see* La See d'Urgel
103 T16 **la Seyne-sur-Mer** Var, SE France
61 D21 **Las Flores** Buenos Aires, E Argentina
62 H9 **Las Flores** San Juan, W Argentina
9 S14 **Lashburn** Saskatchewan, S Canada
62 I11 **Las Heras** Mendoza, W Argentina
148 M8 **Lashkar Gāh** *var.* Lash-Kar-Gar'. Helmand, S Afghanistan
Lash-Kar-Gar' *see* Lashkar Gāh
171 P14 **Lasihao** *var.* Lasahau. Pulau Muna, C Indonesia
107 N21 **La Sila** ▲▲ SW Italy
63 H23 **La Silueta, Cerro** ▲ S Chile
42 L9 **La Sirena** Región Autónoma Atlántico Sur, E Nicaragua
110 J13 **Łask** Łódzkie, C Poland
109 V11 **Laško** *Ger.* Tüffer. C Slovenia
63 H14 **Las Lajas** Neuquén, W Argentina
63 H15 **Las Lajas, Cerro** ▲ W Argentina
62 M6 **Las Lomitas** Formosa, N Argentina
41 V16 **Las Margaritas** Chiapas, SE Mexico
Las Marismas *see* Guadalquivir, Marismas del
54 M6 **Las Mercedes** Guárico, N Venezuela
42 F6 **Las Minas, Cerro** ▲ W Honduras
105 O11 **La Solana** Castilla-La Mancha, C Spain
45 Q14 **La Soufrière** ▲ Saint Vincent, Saint Vincent and the Grenadines
102 M10 **la Souterraine** Creuse, C France
62 N7 **Las Palmas** Chaco, N Argentina
43 Q16 **Las Palmas** Veraguas, W Panama
64 P12 **Las Palmas** *var.* Las Palmas de Gran Canaria. Gran Canaria, Islas Canarias, Spain, NE Atlantic Ocean
64 P12 **Las Palmas** ◐ *province* Islas Canarias, Spain, NE Atlantic Ocean
64 Q12 **Las Palmas** ✕ Gran Canaria, Islas Canarias, Spain, NE Atlantic Ocean
Las Palmas de Gran Canaria *see* Las Palmas
40 D6 **Las Palomas** Baja California Sur, W Mexico
105 P10 **Las Pedroñeras** Castilla-La Mancha, C Spain
106 E10 **La Spezia** Liguria, NW Italy
61 F20 **Las Piedras** Canelones, S Uruguay
63 J18 **Las Plumas** Chubut, S Argentina
61 B18 **Las Rosas** Santa Fe, C Argentina
Lassa *see* Lhasa
35 O4 **Lassen Peak** ▲ California, W USA
194 K6 **Lassiter Coast** *physical region* Antarctica
109 V9 **Lassnitz** ≈ SE Austria
15 O12 **L'Assomption** Québec, SE Canada
15 N11 **L'Assomption** ≈ Québec, SE Canada
43 S17 **Las Tablas** Los Santos, S Panama
Lastarria, Volcán *see* Azufre, Volcán
37 V4 **Last Chance** Colorado, C USA
Last Frontier, The *see* Alaska
9 U16 **Last Mountain Lake** ◎ Saskatchewan, S Canada
62 H9 **Las Tórtolas, Cerro** ▲ W Argentina
61 C14 **Las Toscas** Santa Fe, C Argentina
79 F19 **Lastoursville** Ogooué-Lolo, E Gabon
113 F16 **Lastovo** *It.* Lagosta. *island* SW Croatia
113 F16 **Lastovski Kanal** *channel* SW Croatia
40 E6 **Las Tres Vírgenes, Volcán** ⛰ W Mexico
40 F4 **Las Trincheras** Sonora, NW Mexico
55 N8 **Las Trincheras** Bolívar, E Venezuela
44 H7 **Las Tunas** *var.* Victoria de las Tunas. Las Tunas, E Cuba
La Suisse *see* Switzerland
40 I5 **Las Varas** Chihuahua, N Mexico
40 J12 **Las Varas** Nayarit, C Mexico
62 L10 **Las Varillas** Córdoba, E Argentina
35 X11 **Las Vegas** Nevada, W USA
37 T10 **Las Vegas** New Mexico, SW USA
187 P10 **Lata** Nendö, Solomon Islands
13 R10 **La Tabatière** Québec, E Canada
56 C6 **Latacunga** Cotopaxi, C Ecuador
194 I7 **Latady Island** *island* Antarctica
54 E14 **La Tagua** Putumayo, S Colombia
Latakia *see* Al Lādhiqīyah
92 J10 **Lätäseno** ≈ NW Finland
14 H9 **Latchford** Ontario, S Canada
14 J13 **Latchford Bridge** Ontario, SE Canada
193 Y14 **Late** *island* Vava'u Group, N Tonga
153 P15 **Lātehār** Jhārkhand, N India
15 R7 **Laterrière** Québec, SE Canada
102 J13 **la Teste** Gironde, SW France
25 V8 **Latexo** Texas, SW USA
18 L10 **Latham** New York, NE USA
Latharna *see* Larne
108 B9 **La Thielle** *var.* Thièle. ≈ W Switzerland
27 R3 **Lathrop** Missouri, C USA
107 I16 **Latina** *prev.* Littoria. Lazio, C Italy
41 R14 **La Tinaja** Veracruz-Llave, S Mexico
106 J7 **Latisana** Friuli-Venezia Giulia, NE Italy
Latium *see* Lazio
115 K25 **Lató** *site of ancient city* Kríti, Greece, E Mediterranean Sea
187 Q17 **La Tontouta** ✕ (Noumea) Province Sud, S New Caledonia
55 N4 **La Tortuga, Isla** *var.* Isla Tortuga. *island* N Venezuela
108 C10 **La Tour-de-Peilz** *var.* La Tour de Peilz. Vaud, SW Switzerland
La Tour de Peilz *see* La Tour-de-Peilz
103 S11 **la Tour-du-Pin** Isère, E France
102 J11 **la Tremblade** Charente-Maritime, W France
102 L10 **la Trimouille** Vienne, W France
42 J9 **La Trinidad** Estelí, NW Nicaragua
41 V16 **La Trinitaria** Chiapas, SE Mexico
45 Q11 **la Trinité** E Martinique
15 U7 **La Trinité-des-Monts** Québec, SE Canada
18 C15 **Latrobe** Pennsylvania, NE USA
183 P13 **La Trobe River** ≈ Victoria, SE Australia
Lattakia/Lattaquié *see* Al Lādhiqīyah
171 S13 **Latu** Pulau Seram, E Indonesia
15 P9 **La Tuque** Québec, SE Canada
155 G14 **Lātūr** Mahārāshtra, C India
118 G8 **Latvia** *off.* Republic of Latvia, *Ger.* Lettland, *Latv.* Latvija, Latvijas Republika; *prev.* Latvian SSR, *Rus.* Latviyskaya SSR. ◆ *republic* NE Europe
Latvian SSR/Latvija/Latvijas Republika/Latviyskaya SSR *see* Latvia
Latvia, Republic of *see* Latvia
186 H7 **Lau** New Britain, E Papua New Guinea
175 R9 **Lau Basin** *undersea feature* S Pacific Ocean
101 O15 **Lauchhammer** Brandenburg, E Germany
Laudunum *see* Laon
Laudus *see* St-Lô
Lauenburg/Lauenburg in Pommern *see* Lębork
101 L20 **Lauf an der Pegnitz** Bayern, SE Germany
108 D7 **Laufen** Basel, NW Switzerland
109 P5 **Lauffen** Salzburg, NW Austria
92 I2 **Laugarbakki** Nordhurland Vestra, N Iceland
92 I4 **Laugarvatn** Sudhurland, SW Iceland
31 O3 **Laughing Fish Point** *headland* Michigan, N USA
187 Z14 **Lau Group** *island group* E Fiji
Lauis *see* Lugano
93 M17 **Laukaa** Länsi-Soumi, C Finland
118 D12 **Laukuva** Tauragė, W Lithuania
Laun *see* Louny
183 P16 **Launceston** Tasmania, SE Australia
97 I24 **Launceston** *anc.* Dunheved. SW England, UK
54 C13 **La Unión** Nariño, SW Colombia
42 H8 **La Unión** La Unión, SE El Salvador
42 I6 **La Unión** Olancho, C Honduras
40 M15 **La Unión** Guerrero, S Mexico
41 Y14 **La Unión** Quintana Roo, E Mexico
105 S13 **La Unión** Murcia, SE Spain
54 L7 **La Unión** Barinas, C Venezuela
42 B10 **La Unión** ◐ *department* E El Salvador
38 H11 **Laupāhoehoe** *var.* Laupahoehoe. Hawai'i, USA, C Pacific Ocean
Laupahoehoe *see* Laupāhoehoe
101 I23 **Laupheim** Baden-Württemberg, S Germany
181 W3 **Laura** Queensland, NE Australia
189 X2 **Laura** *atoll* Majuro Atoll, SE Marshall Islands
Laurana *see* Lovran
54 L8 **La Urbana** Bolívar, C Venezuela
21 Y4 **Laurel** Delaware, NE USA
23 V14 **Laurel** Florida, SE USA
21 W3 **Laurel** Maryland, NE USA
22 M6 **Laurel** Mississippi, S USA
33 U11 **Laurel** Montana, NW USA
29 R13 **Laurel** Nebraska, C USA
18 H15 **Laureldale** Pennsylvania, NE USA
18 C16 **Laurel Hill** *ridge* Pennsylvania, NE USA
29 T12 **Laurens** Iowa, C USA
21 P11 **Laurens** South Carolina, SE USA
Laurentian Highlands *see* Laurentian Mountains
15 P10 **Laurentian Mountains** *var.* Laurentian Highlands, *Fr.* Les Laurentides. *plateau* Newfoundland and Labrador/Québec, Canada
15 O12 **Laurentides** Québec, SE Canada
Laurentides, Les *see* Laurentian Mountains
107 M19 **Lauria** Basilicata, S Italy
194 I1 **Laurie Island** *island* Antarctica
21 T11 **Laurinburg** North Carolina, SE USA
30 M2 **Laurium** Michigan, N USA
Lauru *see* Choiseul
108 B9 **Lausanne** *It.* Losanna. Vaud, SW Switzerland
101 Q16 **Lausche** *var.* Luže. ▲ Czech Republic/Germany *see also* Luže
Lausche *see* Luže
101 Q16 **Lausitzer Bergland** *var.* Lausitzer Gebirge, *Cz.* Gory Lužyckie, Lužické Hory', *Eng.* Lusatian Mountains. ▲▲ E Germany
Lausitzer Gebirge *see* Lausitzer Bergland
Lausitzer Neisse *see* Neisse
103 T12 **Lautaret, Col du** *pass* SE France
63 G15 **Lautaro** Araucanía, C Chile
101 F21 **Lauter** ≈ W Germany
108 I7 **Lauterach** Vorarlberg, NW Austria
101 I17 **Lauterbach** Hessen, C Germany
108 E9 **Lauterbrunnen** Bern, C Switzerland
169 U14 **Laut Kecil, Kepulauan** *island group* N Indonesia
187 X14 **Lautoka** Viti Levu, W Fiji
169 O8 **Laut, Pulau** *prev.* Laoet. *island* Borneo, C Indonesia
169 V14 **Laut, Pulau** *island* Kepulauan Natuna, W Indonesia
169 U13 **Laut, Selat** *strait* Borneo, C Indonesia
168 H8 **Laut Tawar, Danau** ◎ Sumatera, NW Indonesia
189 V14 **Lauvergne Island** *island* Chuuk, C Micronesia
98 M5 **Lauwers Meer** ◎ N Netherlands
98 M4 **Lauwersoog** Groningen, NE Netherlands
102 M14 **Lauzerte** Tarn-et-Garonne, S France
25 U13 **Lavaca Bay** *bay* Texas, SW USA
25 U12 **Lavaca River** ≈ Texas, SW USA
15 O12 **Laval** Québec, SE Canada
102 J6 **Laval** Mayenne, NW France
15 T6 **Laval** ≈ Québec, SE Canada
105 S9 **La Vall d'Uixó** *var.* Vall d'Uxo. País Valenciano, E Spain
105 S9 **La Vall D'Uixó** *var.* Vall D'Uxó. País Valenciano, E Spain
61 F19 **Lavalleja** ◐ *department* S Uruguay
15 O12 **Lavaltrie** Québec, SE Canada
186 M10 **Lavanggu** Rennell, S Solomon Islands
143 O14 **Lāvān, Jazīreh-ye** *island* S Iran
109 U8 **Lavant** ≈ S Austria
118 G5 **Lavassaare** *Ger.* Lawassaar. Pärnumaa, SW Estonia
104 L3 **La Vecilla de Curueño** Castilla-León, N Spain
45 N8 **La Vega** *var.* Concepción de la Vega. C Dominican Republic
La Vela *see* La Vela de Coro
54 J4 **La Vela de Coro** *var.* La Vela. Falcón, N Venezuela
103 N17 **Lavelanet** Ariège, S France
107 M17 **Lavello** Basilicata, S Italy
36 J8 **La Verkin** Utah, W USA
26 J8 **Laverne** Oklahoma, C USA
25 S12 **La Vernia** Texas, SW USA
93 K18 **Lavia** Länsi-Soumi, SW Finland
14 I12 **Lavieille, Lake** ◎ Ontario, SE Canada
94 C12 **Lavik** Sogn Og Fjordane, S Norway
La Vila Joíosa *see* Villajoyosa
33 U10 **Lavina** Montana, NW USA
194 H5 **Lavoisier Island** *island* Antarctica
23 U2 **Lavonia** Georgia, SE USA
103 R13 **la Voulte-sur-Rhône** Ardèche, E France
123 W5 **Lavrentiya** Chukotskiy Avtonomnyy Okrug, NE Russian Federation
115 H20 **Lávrio** *prev.* Lávrion. Attikí, C Greece
Lávrion *see* Lávrio
83 L22 **Lavumisa** *prev.* Gollel. SE Swaziland
149 T4 **Lawarai Pass** *pass* N Pakistan
Lawassaar *see* Lavassaare
141 P16 **Lawdar** SW Yemen
25 Q7 **Lawn** Texas, SW USA
195 Y4 **Law Promontory** *headland* Antarctica
77 O14 **Lawra** NW Ghana
185 E23 **Lawrence** Otago, South Island, New Zealand
31 P14 **Lawrence** Indiana, N USA
27 Q4 **Lawrence** Kansas, C USA
19 O10 **Lawrence** Massachusetts, NE USA
20 L5 **Lawrenceburg** Kentucky, S USA
20 I10 **Lawrenceburg** Tennessee, S USA
23 T3 **Lawrenceville** Georgia, SE USA
31 N15 **Lawrenceville** Illinois, N USA
21 V7 **Lawrenceville** Virginia, NE USA
27 S3 **Lawson** Missouri, C USA
26 L12 **Lawton** Oklahoma, C USA
140 I4 **Lawz, Jabal al** ▲ NW Saudi Arabia
95 L16 **Laxå** Örebro, C Sweden
125 T5 **Laya** ≈ NW Russian Federation
57 I19 **La Yarada** Tacna, SW Peru
141 S15 **Layjūn** C Yemen
141 Q9 **Laylā** *var.* Laila. Ar Riyāḍ, C Saudi Arabia
23 P4 **Lay Lake** ▣ Alabama, S USA
45 P14 **Layou** Saint Vincent, Saint Vincent and the Grenadines
La Youne *see* El Ayoun
192 L5 **Laysan Island** *island* Hawaiian Islands, Hawaii, USA
36 L2 **Layton** Utah, W USA
34 L5 **Laytonville** California, N USA
172 H17 **Lazare, Pointe** *headland* Mahé, NE Seychelles
123 T12 **Lazarev** Khabarovskiy Kray, SE Russian Federation
112 L12 **Lazarevac** Serbia, C Serbia
65 N22 **Lazarev Sea** *sea* Antarctica
40 M15 **Lázaro Cárdenas** Michoacán de Ocampo, SW Mexico
119 F15 **Lazdijai** Alytus, S Lithuania
107 H15 **Lazio** *anc.* Latium. ◐ *region* C Italy
111 A16 **Lázně Kynžvart** *Ger.* Bad Königswart. Karlovarský Kraj, W Czech Republic
Lazovsk *see* Singerei
167 R12 **Leach** Poŭthĭsăt, W Cambodia
27 X9 **Leachville** Arkansas, C USA
28 I9 **Lead** South Dakota, N USA
9 S16 **Leader** Saskatchewan, S Canada
19 S6 **Lead Mountain** ▲ Maine, NE USA
37 R5 **Leadville** Colorado, C USA
9 V12 **Leaf Rapids** Manitoba, C Canada
22 M7 **Leaf River** ≈ Mississippi, S USA
25 W11 **League City** Texas, SW USA
92 K8 **Leaibevuotna** *Nor.* Olderfjord. Finnmark, N Norway
23 N7 **Leakesville** Mississippi, S USA
25 Q11 **Leakey** Texas, SW USA
Leal *see* Lihula
83 G15 **Lealui** Western, W Zambia
Leamhcán *see* Lucan

◆ Country
● Country Capital
◇ Dependent Territory
○ Dependent Territory Capital
◐ Administrative Regions
✕ International Airport
▲ Mountain
▲▲ Mountain Range
⛰ Volcano
≈ River
◎ Lake
▣ Reservoir

14 C18 **Leamington** Ontario, S Canada
Leamington/Leamington Spa see Royal Leamington Spa
Leammi see Lemmenjoki
25 S10 **Leander** Texas, SW USA
60 F13 **Leandro N. Alem** Misiones, NE Argentina
97 A20 **Leane, Lough** Ir. Loch Léin. ◎ SW Ireland
180 G8 **Learmouth** Western Australia
Leau see Zoutleeuw
L'Eau d'Heure see Plate Taille, Lac de la
190 D12 **Leava** Île Futuna, S Wallis and Futuna
Leavdnja see Lakselv
27 R3 **Leavenworth** Kansas, C USA
32 I8 **Leavenworth** Washington, NW USA
92 L8 **Leavvajohka** var. Levvajok. Finnmark, N Norway
27 R4 **Leawood** Kansas, C USA
110 H6 **Łeba** Ger. Leba. Pomorskie, N Poland
110 I6 **Łeba** Ger. Leba. ≈ N Poland
Leba see Łeba
101 D20 **Lebach** Saarland, SW Germany
Łeba, Jezioro see Łebsko, Jezioro
171 P8 **Lebak** Mindanao, S Philippines
31 O13 **Lebanon** Indiana, N USA
20 L6 **Lebanon** Kentucky, S USA
27 U6 **Lebanon** Missouri, C USA
19 N9 **Lebanon** New Hampshire, NE USA
32 G12 **Lebanon** Oregon, NW USA
18 H15 **Lebanon** Pennsylvania, NE USA
20 J8 **Lebanon** Tennessee, S USA
21 P7 **Lebanon** Virginia, NE USA
138 G6 **Lebanon** off. Republic of Lebanon, Ar. Al Lubnān, Fr. Liban. ◆ republic SW Asia
20 K6 **Lebanon Junction** Kentucky, S USA
Lebanon, Mount see Liban, Jebel
Lebanon, Republic of see Lebanon
146 J10 **Lebap** Lebapskiy Velayat, NE Turkmenistan
Lebapskiy Velayat see Lebap Welaýaty
146 J11 **Lebap Welaýaty** Rus Lebapskiy Velayat; prev. Rus. Chardzhevskaya Oblast, Turkm. Chärjew Oblasty. ◈ province E Turkmenistan
Lebasee see Łebsko, Jezioro
99 F17 **Lebbeke** Oost-Vlaanderen, NW Belgium
35 S14 **Lebec** California, W USA
Lebedin see Lebedyn
123 Q11 **Lebedinyy** Respublika Sakha (Yakutiya), NE Russian Federation
126 L6 **Lebedyan'** Lipetskaya Oblast', W Russian Federation
117 T4 **Lebedyn** Rus. Lebedin. Sums'ka Oblast', NE Ukraine
12 I12 **Lebel-sur-Quévillon** Québec, SE Canada
92 L8 **Lebesby** Finnmark, N Norway
102 M9 **le Blanc** Indre, C France
79 L15 **Lebo** Orientale, N Dem. Rep. Congo
27 P5 **Lebo** Kansas, C USA
110 H6 **Lębork** var. Lębórk, Ger. Lauenburg, Lauenburg in Pommern. Pomorskie, N Poland
103 O17 **le Boulou** Pyrénées-Orientales, S France
108 A9 **Le Brassus** Vaud, W Switzerland
104 J15 **Lebrija** Andalucía, S Spain
110 G6 **Łebsko, Jezioro** Ger. Lebasee; prev. Jezioro Łeba. ◎ N Poland
63 F14 **Lebu** Bío Bío, C Chile
Lebyazh'ye see Akku
104 F6 **Leça da Palmeira** Porto, N Portugal
103 U15 **le Cannet** Alpes-Maritimes, SE France
Le Cap see Cap-Haïtien
103 P2 **le Cateau-Cambrésis** Nord, N France
107 Q18 **Lecce** Puglia, SE Italy
106 D7 **Lecco** Lombardia, N Italy
29 V10 **Le Center** Minnesota, N USA
108 J7 **Lech** Vorarlberg, W Austria
101 K22 **Lech** ≈ Austria/Germany
115 D19 **Lechainá** var. Lehena, Lekhainá. Dytikí Ellás, S Greece
102 J11 **le Château d'Oléron** Charente-Maritime, W France
103 R3 **le Chesne** Ardennes, N France
103 R13 **le Cheylard** Ardèche, E France
108 K7 **Lechtaler Alpen** ▲▲ W Austria
100 H6 **Leck** Schleswig-Holstein, N Germany
14 L9 **Lecointre, Lac** ◎ Québec, SE Canada
22 H7 **Lecompte** Louisiana, S USA
103 Q9 **le Creusot** Saône-et-Loire, C France
Lecumberri see Lekunberri
110 P13 **Łęczna** Lublin, E Poland
110 J12 **Łęczyca** Ger. Lentschiza, Rus. Lenchitsa. Łódzkie, C Poland
100 F10 **Leda** ≈ NW Germany
109 Y9 **Ledava** ≈ NE Slovenia
99 F17 **Lede** Oost-Vlaanderen, NW Belgium
104 K6 **Ledesma** Castilla-León, N Spain
45 Q12 **le Diamant** SW Martinique
172 J16 **Le Digue** island Inner Islands, NE Seychelles
103 Q10 **le Donjon** Allier, C France
102 M10 **le Dorat** Haute-Vienne, C France
Ledo Salinarius see Lons-le-Saunier
9 Q14 **Leduc** Alberta, SW Canada
123 V7 **Ledyanaya, Gora** ▲ E Russian Federation
97 C21 **Lee** Ir. An Laoi. ≈ SW Ireland
29 U5 **Leech Lake** ◎ Minnesota, N USA
26 K10 **Leedey** Oklahoma, C USA
97 M17 **Leeds** N England, UK
23 P4 **Leeds** Alabama, S USA
29 O3 **Leeds** North Dakota, N USA
98 N6 **Leek** Groningen, NE Netherlands
99 K15 **Leende** Noord-Brabant, SE Netherlands
100 F10 **Leer** Niedersachsen, NW Germany
98 J13 **Leerdam** Zuid-Holland, C Netherlands
98 K12 **Leersum** Utrecht, C Netherlands
23 W11 **Leesburg** Florida, SE USA
21 V3 **Leesburg** Virginia, NE USA
27 R4 **Lees Summit** Missouri, C USA
22 G7 **Leesville** Louisiana, S USA
25 S12 **Leesville** Texas, SW USA
31 U13 **Leesville Lake** ▣ Ohio, N USA
Leesville Lake see Smith Mountain Lake
183 P9 **Leeton** New South Wales, SE Australia
98 L6 **Leeuwarden** Fris. Ljouwert. Friesland, N Netherlands
180 I14 **Leeuwin, Cape** headland Western Australia
35 R8 **Lee Vining** California, W USA
45 V8 **Leeward Islands** island group E West Indies
Leeward Islands see Sotavento, Ilhas de
Leeward Islands see Vent, Îles Sous le
79 G20 **Léfini** ≈ SE Congo
115 C17 **Lefkáda** prev. Levkás. Lefkáda, Iónioi Nísoi, Greece, C Mediterranean Sea
115 B17 **Lefkáda** It. Santa Maura, prev. Levkás; anc. Leucas. island Iónioi Nísoi, Greece, C Mediterranean Sea
115 H25 **Lefká Óri** ▲▲ Kríti, Greece, E Mediterranean Sea
115 B16 **Lefkímmi** var. Levkímmi. Kérkyra, Iónia Nisiá, Greece, C Mediterranean Sea
Lefkosía/Lefkoşa see Nicosia
25 O2 **Lefors** Texas, SW USA
45 R12 **le François** E Martinique
180 L12 **Lefroy, Lake** salt lake Western Australia
Legaceaster see Chester
105 N8 **Leganés** Madrid, C Spain
Leghorn see Livorno
110 M11 **Legionowo** Mazowieckie, C Poland
99 K24 **Léglise** Luxembourg, SE Belgium
106 G8 **Legnago** Lombardia, NE Italy
106 D7 **Legnano** Veneto, NE Italy
111 F14 **Legnica** Ger. Liegnitz. Dolnośląskie, SW Poland
35 Q9 **Le Grand** California, W USA
103 Q15 **le Grau-du-Roi** Gard, S France
183 U3 **Legume** New South Wales, SE Australia
102 L4 **le Havre** Eng. Havre; prev. le Havre-de-Grâce. Seine-Maritime, N France
le Havre-de-Grâce see le Havre
Lehena see Lechainá
36 L3 **Lehi** Utah, W USA
18 I14 **Lehighton** Pennsylvania, NE USA
29 O6 **Lehr** North Dakota, N USA
38 A8 **Lehua Island** island Hawaiian Islands, Hawai'i, USA
149 S9 **Leiāh** Punjab, NE Pakistan
109 W9 **Leibnitz** Steiermark, SE Austria
97 M19 **Leicester** Lat. Batae Coritanorum. C England, UK
97 M19 **Leicestershire** cultural region C England, UK
Leicheng see Leizhou
93 H11 **Leiden** prev. Leyden; anc. Lugdunum Batavorum. Zuid-Holland, W Netherlands
98 H11 **Leiderdorp** Zuid-Holland, W Netherlands
98 G11 **Leidschendam** Zuid-Holland, W Netherlands
99 D18 **Leie** Fr. Lys. ≈ Belgium/France
Leifear see Lifford
184 L4 **Leigh** Auckland, North Island, New Zealand
97 K17 **Leigh** NW England, UK
182 I5 **Leigh Creek** South Australia
23 O2 **Leighton** Alabama, S USA
97 M21 **Leighton Buzzard** E England, UK
Léim an Bhradáin see Leixlip
Léim An Mhadaidh see Limavady
Léime, Ceann see Loop Head, Ireland
Léime, Ceann see Slyne Head, Ireland
101 G20 **Leimen** Baden-Württemberg, SW Germany
100 I13 **Leine** ≈ NW Germany
101 J15 **Leinefelde** Thüringen, C Germany
Léin, Loch see Leane, Lough
97 D19 **Leinster** Ir. Cúige Laighean. cultural region E Ireland
97 F19 **Leinster, Mount** Ir. Stua Laighean. ▲ SE Ireland
119 F15 **Leipalingis** Alytus, S Lithuania
92 J12 **Leipojärvi** Norrbotten, N Sweden
31 R12 **Leipsic** Ohio, N USA
Leipsic see Leipzig
115 M20 **Leipsoí** island Dodekánisa, Greece, Aegean Sea
101 M15 **Leipzig** Pol. Lipsk, hist. Leipsic; anc. Lipsia. Sachsen, E Germany
101 M15 **Leipzig Halle** ✈ Sachsen, E Germany
104 G9 **Leiria** anc. Collipo. Leiria, C Portugal
104 F9 **Leiria** ◈ district C Portugal
95 C15 **Leirvik** Hordaland, S Norway
118 E5 **Leisi** Ger. Laisberg. Saaremaa, W Estonia
104 J3 **Leitariegos, Puerto de** pass NW Spain
20 J6 **Leitchfield** Kentucky, S USA
109 Y5 **Leitha** Hung. Lajta. ≈ Austria/Hungary
Leitir Ceanainn see Letterkenny
97 D16 **Leitrim** Ir. Liatroim. ◈ county NW Ireland
Leiváďia see Livádeia
Leix see Laois
97 F18 **Leixlip** Eng. Salmon Leap, Ir. Léim an Bhradáin. Kildare, E Ireland
64 N8 **Leixões** Porto, N Portugal
161 N12 **Leiyang** Hunan, S China
160 L16 **Leizhou** var. Haikang, Leicheng. Guangdong, S China
160 L16 **Leizhou Bandao** var. Luichow Peninsula. peninsula S China
98 H13 **Lek** ≈ SW Netherlands
114 I13 **Lekánis** ▲▲ NE Greece
172 H13 **Le Kartala** ▲ Grande Comore, NW Comoros
Le Kef see El Kef
79 G20 **Lékéti, Monts de la** ▲▲ S Congo
Lekhainá see Lechainá
114 H8 **Lekhchevo** Montana, NW Bulgaria
92 G11 **Leknes** Nordland, C Norway
79 E21 **Le Kouilou** ◈ province SW Congo
94 L13 **Leksand** Dalarna, C Sweden
124 H8 **Leksozero, Ozero** ◎ NW Russian Federation
105 Q3 **Lekunberri** var. Lecumberri. Navarra, N Spain
171 S11 **Lelai, Tanjung** headland Pulau Halmahera, N Indonesia
45 Q12 **le Lamentin** var. Lamentin. C Martinique
45 Q12 **le Lamentin** ✈ (Fort-de-France) C Martinique
31 P6 **Leland** Michigan, N USA
22 J4 **Leland** Mississippi, S USA
95 J16 **Lelång** var. Lelången. ◎ S Sweden
Lelången see Lelång
Lel'chitsy see Lyel'chytsy
le Léman see Geneva, Lake
Leli see Tianlin
25 O3 **Lelia Lake** Texas, SW USA
113 I14 **Lelija** ▲ SE Bosnia and Herzegovina
108 C8 **Le Locle** Neuchâtel, W Switzerland
189 Y14 **Lelu** Kosrae, E Micronesia
Lelu see Lelu Island
189 Y14 **Lelu Island** var. Lelu. island Kosrae, E Micronesia
55 W9 **Lelydorp** Wanica, N Suriname
98 K9 **Lelystad** Flevoland, C Netherlands
63 K25 **Le Maire, Estrecho de** strait S Argentina
168 L10 **Lemang** Pulau Rangsang, W Indonesia
186 I7 **Lemankoa** Buka Island, NE Papua New Guinea
Léman, Lac see Geneva, Lake
102 L6 **le Mans** Sarthe, NW France
29 S12 **Le Mars** Iowa, C USA
109 S3 **Lembach im Mühlkreis** Oberösterreich, N Austria
101 G23 **Lemberg** ▲ SW Germany
Lemberg see L'viv
Lemdiyya see Médéa
121 P3 **Lemesós** var. Limassol. SW Cyprus
100 H13 **Lemgo** Nordrhein-Westfalen, W Germany
33 P13 **Lemhi Range** ▲▲ Idaho, NW USA
9 S6 **Lemieux Islands** island group Nunavut, NE Canada
171 O11 **Lemito** Sulawesi, N Indonesia
92 L10 **Lemmenjoki** Lapp. Leammi. ≈ NE Finland
98 L7 **Lemmer** Fris. De Lemmer. Friesland, N Netherlands
28 L7 **Lemmon** South Dakota, N USA
36 M15 **Lemmon, Mount** ▲ Arizona, SW USA
Lemnos see Límnos
31 O14 **Lemon, Lake** ◎ Indiana, N USA
102 J5 **le Mont St-Michel** castle Manche, N France
35 Q11 **Lemoore** California, W USA
189 T13 **Lemotol Bay** bay Chuuk Islands, C Micronesia
45 Y5 **le Moule** var. Moule. Grande Terre, NE Guadeloupe
Lemovices see Limoges
Le Moyen-Ogooué see Moyen-Ogooué
12 M6 **le Moyne, Lac** ◎ Québec, E Canada
93 L18 **Lempäälä** Länsi-Suomi, W Finland
42 E7 **Lempa, Río** ≈ Central America
42 F7 **Lempira** prev. Gracias. ◈ department SW Honduras
Lemsalu see Limbaži
107 N17 **Le Murge** ▲▲ SE Italy
125 V6 **Lemva** ≈ NW Russian Federation
95 F21 **Lemvig** Ringkøbing, W Denmark
166 K8 **Lemyethna** Irrawaddy, SW Myanmar (Burma)
30 K10 **Lena** Illinois, N USA
129 V4 **Lena** ≈ NE Russian Federation
173 N13 **Lena Tablemount** undersea feature S Indian Ocean
Lenchitsa see Łęczyca
59 N17 **Lençóis** Bahia, E Brazil
60 K9 **Lençóis Paulista** São Paulo, S Brazil
109 Y9 **Lendava** Hung. Lendva, Ger. Unterlimbach; prev. Dolnja Lendava. NE Slovenia
83 F20 **Lendepas** Hardap, SE Namibia
124 H9 **Lendery** Respublika Kareliya, NW Russian Federation
Lendum see Lens
Lendva see Lendava
27 R4 **Lenexa** Kansas, C USA
109 Q5 **Lengau** Oberösterreich, N Austria
145 Q17 **Lenger** Yuzhnyy Kazakhstan, S Kazakhstan
Lenghu see Lenghuzhen
159 O9 **Lenghuzhen** var. Lenghu. Qinghai, C China
159 T9 **Lenglong Ling** ▲▲ N China
108 D7 **Lengnau** Bern, W Switzerland
Lengshuitan see Yongzhou
95 M20 **Lenhovda** Kronoberg, S Sweden
79 E20 **Le Niari** ◈ province SW Congo
Lenīn see Uzynkol'
Lenin see Akdepe
Leninabad see Khŭjand
Leninakan see Gyumri
Lenina, Pik see Lenin Peak
117 V12 **Lenine** Rus. Lenino. Respublika Krym, S Ukraine
Leningor see Leninogorsk
147 Q13 **Leningrad** Rus. Leningradskiy; prev. Mŭ'minobod, Rus. Muminabad. SW Tajikistan
Leningrad see Sankt-Peterburg
126 L13 **Leningradskaya** Krasnodarskiy Kray, SW Russian Federation
195 S16 **Leningradskaya** Russian research station Antarctica
124 H12 **Leningradskaya Oblast'** ◈ province NW Russian Federation
Leningradskiy see Leningrad
Lenino see Lyenina
Lenino see Lenine
Leninobod see Khŭjand
145 X9 **Leninogorsk** Kaz. Leningor. Vostochnyy Kazakhstan, E Kazakhstan
127 T5 **Leninogorsk** Respublika Tatarstan, W Russian Federation
147 T12 **Lenin Peak** Rus. Pik Lenina, Taj. Qullai Lenin. ▲ Kyrgyzstan/Tajikistan
147 S8 **Leninpol'** Talasskaya Oblast', NW Kyrgyzstan
Lenin, Qullai see Lenin Peak
127 P11 **Leninsk** Volgogradskaya Oblast', SW Russian Federation
Leninsk see Baykonyr
Leninsk see Akdepe
Leninsk see Asaka
145 T8 **Leninskiy** Pavlodar, E Kazakhstan
122 I13 **Leninsk-Kuznetskiy** Kemerovskaya Oblast', S Russian Federation
125 P15 **Leninskoye** Kirovskaya Oblast', NW Russian Federation
Leninskoye see Uzynkol'
Lenin-Turkmenski see Türkmenabat
Leninváros see Tiszaújváros
Lenkoran' see Länkäran
101 F15 **Lenne** ≈ W Germany
101 G16 **Lennestadt** Nordrhein-Westfalen, W Germany
29 R11 **Lennox** South Dakota, N USA
63 J25 **Lennox, Isla** Eng. Lennox Island. island S Chile
Lennox Island see Lennox, Isla
21 Q9 **Lenoir** North Carolina, SE USA
20 M9 **Lenoir City** Tennessee, S USA
108 C7 **Le Noirmont** Jura, NW Switzerland
14 L9 **Lenôtre, Lac** ◎ Québec, SE Canada
29 U15 **Lenox** Iowa, C USA
103 O2 **Lens** anc. Lendum, Lentium. Pas-de-Calais, N France
123 O11 **Lensk** Respublika Sakha (Yakutiya), NE Russian Federation
111 F24 **Lenti** Zala, SW Hungary
Lentia see Linz
93 N14 **Lentiira** Oulu, E Finland
107 L25 **Lentini** anc. Leontini. Sicilia, Italy, C Mediterranean Sea
Lentium see Lens
Lentschiza see Łęczyca
93 N15 **Lentua** ◎ E Finland
119 H14 **Lentvaris** Pol. Landwarów. Vilnius, SE Lithuania
108 F7 **Lenzburg** Aargau, N Switzerland
109 R5 **Lenzing** Oberösterreich, N Austria
77 P13 **Léo** SW Burkina
109 V7 **Leoben** Steiermark, C Austria
Leobschütz see Głubczyce
44 L9 **Léogâne** S Haiti
171 O11 **Leok** Sulawesi, N Indonesia
29 O7 **Leola** South Dakota, N USA
97 K20 **Leominster** W England, UK
19 N11 **Leominster** Massachusetts, NE USA
102 I15 **Léon** Landes, SW France
40 M12 **León** var. León de los Aldamas. Guanajuato, C Mexico
42 I10 **León** León, NW Nicaragua
104 L4 **León** Castilla-León, NW Spain
29 V16 **Leon** Iowa, C USA
42 I9 **León** ◈ department W Nicaragua
104 K4 **León** ◈ province Castilla-León, NW Spain
León see Cotopaxi
25 V9 **Leona** Texas, SW USA
180 K11 **Leonara** Western Australia
25 U5 **Leonard** Texas, SW USA
107 H15 **Leonardo da Vinci** prev. Fiumicino. ✈ (Roma) Lazio, C Italy
21 X5 **Leonardtown** Maryland, NE USA
25 Q13 **Leona River** ≈ Texas, SW USA
41 Z11 **Leona Vicario** Quintana Roo, SE Mexico
101 H21 **Leonberg** Baden-Württemberg, SW Germany
62 M3 **León, Cerro** ▲ NW Paraguay
León de los Aldamas see León
109 T4 **Leonding** Oberösterreich, N Austria
107 I14 **Leonessa** Lazio, C Italy
107 K24 **Leonforte** Sicilia, Italy, C Mediterranean Sea
183 O13 **Leongatha** Victoria, SE Australia
115 F21 **Leonídio** var. Leonídi. Pelopónnisos, S Greece
Leonídi see Leonídio
104 J4 **León, Montes de** ▲▲ NW Spain
25 S8 **Leon River** ≈ Texas, SW USA
Leontini see Lentini
Léopold II, Lac see Mai-Ndombe, Lac
99 J17 **Leopoldsburg** Limburg, NE Belgium
Léopoldville see Kinshasa
26 I5 **Leoti** Kansas, C USA
116 M11 **Leova** Rus. Leovo. SW Moldova
Leovo see Leova
102 G8 **le Palais** Morbihan, NW France
27 X10 **Lepanto** Arkansas, C USA
169 N13 **Lepar, Pulau** island W Indonesia
104 I14 **Lepe** Andalucía, S Spain
Lepel' see Lyepyel'
83 I19 **Lephepe** Kweneng, SE Botswana
161 Q10 **Leping** Jiangxi, S China
Lépontiennes, Alpes/Lepontine, Alpi see Lepontine Alps
108 G10 **Lepontine Alps** Fr. Alpes Lépontiennes, It. Alpi Lepontine. ▲▲ Italy/Switzerland
79 G20 **Le Pool** ◈ province S Congo
173 O16 **Le Port** NW Réunion
103 N1 **le Portel** Pas-de-Calais, N France
93 N17 **Leppävirta** Itä-Suomi, C Finland
45 Q11 **le Prêcheur** NW Martinique
Lepsi see Lepsy
145 V13 **Lepsy** Kaz. Lepsi. Taldykorgan, SE Kazakhstan
145 V13 **Lepsy** Kaz. Lepsi. ≈ SE Kazakhstan
Le Puglie see Puglia
103 Q12 **le Puy** prev. le Puy-en-Velay, hist. Anicium, Podium Anicensis. Haute-Loire, C France
le Puy-en-Velay see le Puy
45 X11 **le Raizet** var. Le Raizet. ✈ (Pointe-à-Pitre) Grande Terre, C Guadeloupe
107 J24 **Lercara Friddi** Sicilia, Italy, C Mediterranean Sea
78 G12 **Léré** Mayo-Kébbi, SW Chad
Leribe see Hlotse
106 E10 **Lerici** Liguria, NW Italy
54 I14 **Lérida** Vaupés, SE Colombia
Lérida see Lleida
105 N5 **Lerma** Castilla-León, N Spain
40 M13 **Lerma, Río** ≈ C Mexico
Lerna see Lérni
115 F20 **Lérni** var Lerna. prehistoric site Pelopónnisos, S Greece
45 R11 **le Robert** E Martinique
115 M21 **Léros** island Dodekánisa, Greece, Aegean Sea
30 L13 **Le Roy** Illinois, N USA
27 Q6 **Le Roy** Kansas, C USA
29 W11 **Le Roy** Minnesota, N USA
18 E10 **Le Roy** New York, NE USA
Lerrnayin Gharabakh see Nagorno-Karabakh
95 J19 **Lerum** Älvsborg, S Sweden
96 M2 **Lerwick** NE Scotland, UK
45 Y6 **les Abymes** var. Abymes. Grande Terre, C Guadeloupe
les Albères see Albères, Chaîne des
102 M4 **les Andelys** Eure, N France
45 Q12 **les Anses-d'Arlets** SW Martinique
105 U6 **Les Borges Blanques** var. Borjas Blancas. Cataluña, NE Spain
Lesbos see Lésvos
Les Cayes see Cayes
31 Q4 **Les Cheneaux Islands** island Michigan, N USA
105 T8 **Les Coves de Vinromá** Cast. Cuevas de Vinromá. País Valenciano, E Spain
103 T12 **les Écrins** ▲ E France
108 C10 **Le Sépey** Vaud, W Switzerland
15 T7 **Les Escoumins** Québec, SE Canada
Les Gonaïves see Gonaïves
160 H9 **Leshan** Sichuan, C China
108 D11 **Les Haudères** Valais, SW Switzerland
102 J9 **les Herbiers** Vendée, NW France
Lesh/Leshi see Lezhë
125 O8 **Leshukonskoye** Arkhangel'skaya Oblast', NW Russian Federation
Lesina see Hvar
107 M15 **Lesina, Lago di** ◎ SE Italy
114 K13 **Lesitse** ▲▲ NE Greece
94 G10 **Lesja** Oppland, S Norway
95 L15 **Lesjöfors** Värmland, C Sweden
111 O18 **Lesko** Podkarpackie, SE Poland
113 O15 **Leskovac** Serbia, SE Serbia
113 M22 **Leskovik** var. Leskoviku. Korçë, S Albania
Leskoviku see Leskovik
33 P14 **Leslie** Idaho, NW USA
31 Q10 **Leslie** Michigan, N USA
Leśna/Lesnaya see Lyasnaya
Lesnaya see Lyasnaya
102 F5 **Lesneven** Finistère, NW France
112 J11 **Lešnica** Serbia, W Serbia
125 S13 **Lesnoy** Kirovskaya Oblast', NW Russian Federation
122 G10 **Lesnoy** Sverdlovskaya Oblast', C Russian Federation
122 K12 **Lesosibirsk** Krasnoyarskiy Kray, C Russian Federation
83 J23 **Lesotho** off. Kingdom of Lesotho; prev. Basutoland. ◆ monarchy S Africa
Lesotho, Kingdom of see Lesotho
102 J12 **Lesparre-Médoc** Gironde, SW France
108 C8 **Les Ponts-de-Martel** Neuchâtel, W Switzerland
103 P1 **Lesquin** ✈ Nord, N France
102 I9 **les Sables-d'Olonne** Vendée, NW France
109 S7 **Lessach** var. Lessachbach. ≈ E Austria
Lessachbach see Lessach
45 W11 **les Saintes** var. Îles des Saintes. island group S Guadeloupe
74 L5 **Les Salines** ✈ (Annaba) NE Algeria
99 J22 **Lesse** ≈ SE Belgium
95 M21 **Lessebo** Kronoberg, S Sweden
194 M10 **Lesser Antarctica** var. West Antarctica. physical region Antarctica
45 P15 **Lesser Antilles** island group E West Indies
137 T10 **Lesser Caucasus** Rus. Malyy Kavkaz. ▲▲ SW Asia
Lesser Khingan Range see Xiao Hinggan Ling
9 P13 **Lesser Slave Lake** ◎ Alberta, W Canada
99 E19 **Lessines** Hainaut, SW Belgium
103 R16 **les Stes-Maries-de-la-Mer** Bouches-du-Rhône, SE France
14 G15 **Lester B. Pearson** var. Toronto. ✈ (Toronto) Ontario, S Canada
29 U9 **Lester Prairie** Minnesota, N USA
93 L16 **Lestijärvi** Länsi-Soumi, W Finland
L'Estuaire see Estuaire
29 U9 **Le Sueur** Minnesota, N USA
108 B8 **Les Verrières** Neuchâtel, W Switzerland
115 L17 **Lésvos** anc. Lesbos. island E Greece
110 G12 **Leszno** Ger. Lissa. Wielkopolskie, C Poland
83 L20 **Letaba** Northern, NE South Africa
173 P17 **Le Tampon** SW Réunion
97 O21 **Letchworth** E England, UK
111 G25 **Letenye** Zala, SW Hungary
9 Q17 **Lethbridge** Alberta, SW Canada
55 S11 **Lethem** S Guyana
83 H18 **Letiahau** ≈ W Botswana
54 J18 **Leticia** Amazonas, S Colombia
171 S16 **Leti, Kepulauan** island group E Indonesia
83 I18 **Letlhakane** Central, C Botswana
83 H20 **Letlhakeng** Kweneng, SE Botswana
114 J8 **Letnitsa** Lovech, N Bulgaria
103 N1 **le Touquet-Paris-Plage** Pas-de-Calais, N France
166 L8 **Letpadan** Pegu, SW Myanmar (Burma)
166 K6 **Letpan** Arakan State, W Myanmar (Burma)
102 M2 **le Tréport** Seine-Maritime, N France
166 M12 **Letsôk-aw Kyun** var. Letsutan Island; prev. Domel Island. island Mergui Archipelago, S Myanmar (Burma)
Letsutan Island see Letsôk-aw Kyun
97 E14 **Letterkenny** Ir. Leitir Ceanainn. Donegal, NW Ireland
Lettland see Latvia
116 M6 **Letychiv** Khmel'nyts'ka Oblast', W Ukraine
Lëtzebuerg see Luxembourg
116 H14 **Leu** Dolj, SW Romania
Leucas see Lefkáda
103 P17 **Leucate** Aude, S France
103 P17 **Leucate, Étang de** ◎ S France
108 E10 **Leuk** Valais, SW Switzerland
108 E10 **Leukerbad** Valais, SW Switzerland
Leusden see Leusden-Centrum
98 K11 **Leusden-Centrum** var. Leusden. Utrecht, C Netherlands
Leutschau see Levoča
99 H18 **Leuven** Fr. Louvain, Ger. Löwen. Vlaams Brabant, C Belgium
99 I20 **Leuze** Namur, C Belgium
Leuze see Leuze-en-Hainaut
99 E19 **Leuze-en-Hainaut** var. Leuze. Hainaut, SW Belgium
Léva see Levice
36 L4 **Levan** Utah, W USA
93 E16 **Levanger** Nord-Trøndelag, C Norway
106 D10 **Levanto** Liguria, W Italy
107 H23 **Levanzo, Isola di** island Isole Egadi, S Italy
127 Q17 **Levashi** Respublika Dagestan, SW Russian Federation
24 M5 **Levelland** Texas, SW USA
39 P13 **Levelock** Alaska, USA
101 E16 **Leverkusen** Nordrhein-Westfalen, W Germany
111 J21 **Levice** Ger. Lewentz, Hung. Léva, Lewenz. Nitriansky Kraj, SW Slovakia
106 G6 **Levico Terme** Trentino-Alto Adige, N Italy
115 E20 **Levídi** Pelopónnisos, S Greece
103 P14 **le Vigan** Gard, S France
184 L13 **Levin** Manawatu-Wanganui, North Island, New Zealand
15 R10 **Lévis** var. Levis. Québec, SE Canada
Levis see Lévis
21 P6 **Levisa Fork** ≈ Kentucky/Virginia, S USA
115 L21 **Levítha** island Kykládes, Greece, Aegean Sea
18 L14 **Levittown** Long Island, New York, NE USA
18 J15 **Levittown** Pennsylvania, NE USA
Levkás see Lefkáda
Levkímmi see Lefkímmi
111 L19 **Levoča** Ger. Leutschau, Hung. Locse. Prešovský Kraj, E Slovakia
Lévrier, Baie du see Nouâdhibou, Dakhlet
103 N9 **Levroux** Indre, C France
114 J8 **Levski** Pleven, N Bulgaria
Levskigrad see Karlovo
126 L6 **Lev Tolstoy** Lipetskaya Oblast', W Russian Federation
187 X14 **Levuka** Ovalau, C Fiji
Levvajok see Leavvajohka
166 L6 **Lewe** Mandalay, C Myanmar (Burma)
Lewentz/Lewenz see Levice
97 O23 **Lewes** SE England, UK
21 Z4 **Lewes** Delaware, NE USA
29 Q12 **Lewis And Clark Lake** ▣ Nebraska/South Dakota, N USA
18 G14 **Lewisburg** Pennsylvania, NE USA
20 J10 **Lewisburg** Tennessee, S USA
21 S6 **Lewisburg** West Virginia, NE USA
96 F6 **Lewis, Butt of** headland NW Scotland, UK
96 F7 **Lewis, Isle of** island NW Scotland, UK
35 U4 **Lewis, Mount** ▲ Nevada, W USA
185 H16 **Lewis Pass** pass South Island, New Zealand
33 P7 **Lewis Range** ▲▲ Montana, NW USA
23 O3 **Lewis Smith Lake** ▣ Alabama, S USA

◆ Country ● Country Capital ◇ Dependent Territory ○ Dependent Territory Capital ◈ Administrative Regions ✈ International Airport ▲ Mountain ▲▲ Mountain Range Volcano ◎ Lake ≈ River ▣ Reservoir

32 M10 **Lewiston** Idaho, NW USA
19 P7 **Lewiston** Maine, NE USA
29 X10 **Lewiston** Minnesota, N USA
18 D9 **Lewiston** New York, NE USA
36 L1 **Lewiston** Utah, W USA
30 K13 **Lewistown** Illinois, N USA
33 T9 **Lewistown** Montana, NW USA
27 T14 **Lewisville** Arkansas, C USA
25 T6 **Lewisville** Texas, SW USA
25 T6 **Lewisville, Lake** ▣ Texas, SW USA
Le Woleu-Ntem *see* Woleu-Ntem
23 U3 **Lexington** Georgia, SE USA
20 M5 **Lexington** Kentucky, S USA
22 L4 **Lexington** Mississippi, S USA
27 S4 **Lexington** Missouri, C USA
29 N16 **Lexington** Nebraska, C USA
20 S9 **Lexington** North Carolina, SE USA
27 N11 **Lexington** Oklahoma, C USA
21 R12 **Lexington** South Carolina, SE USA
20 G9 **Lexington** Tennessee, S USA
25 T10 **Lexington** Texas, SW USA
21 T6 **Lexington** Virginia, NE USA
21 X5 **Lexington Park** Maryland, NE USA
Leyden *see* Leiden
102 J14 **Leyre** ≈ SW France
171 Q5 **Leyte** *island* C Philippines
171 Q6 **Leyte Gulf** *gulf* E Philippines
111 O16 **Leżajsk** Podkarpackie, SE Poland
Lezha *see* Lezhë
113 K18 **Lezhë** *var.* Lezha; *prev.* Lesh, Leshi. Lezhë, NW Albania
113 K18 **Lezhë** ◈ *district* NW Albania
103 O16 **Lézignan-Corbières** Aude, S France
126 J7 **L'gov** Kurskaya Oblast', W Russian Federation
159 P15 **Lhari** Xizang Zizhiqu, W China
159 N16 **Lhasa** *var.* La-sa, Lassa. Xizang Zizhiqu, W China
159 O15 **Lhasa He** ≈ W China
Lhaviyani Atoll *see* Faadhippolhu Atoll
158 K16 **Lhazê** *var* Quxar. Xizang Zizhiqu, W China
158 K14 **Lhazhong** Xizang Zizhiqu, W China
168 H7 **Lhoksukon** Sumatera, W Indonesia
159 Q15 **Lhorong** *var.* Zito. Xizang Zizhiqu, W China
105 W6 **L'Hospitalet de Llobregat** *var.* Hospitalet. Cataluña, NE Spain
153 R11 **Lhotse** ▲ China/Nepal
159 N17 **Lhozhag** *var.* Garbo. Xizang Zizhiqu, W China
159 O16 **Lhünzê** *var.* Xingba. Xizang Zizhiqu, W China
159 N15 **Lhünzhub** *var.* Ganqu. Xizang Zizhiqu, W China
167 N8 **Li** Lamphun, NW Thailand
115 L21 **Liádi** *var* Livádi. *island* Kykládes, Greece, Aegean Sea
Liancheng *see* Lianjiang
Liancheng *see* Qinglong
Liancheng *see* Guangnan
Lianfeng *see* Liangcheng
161 P12 **Liangcheng** *var.* Lianfeng. Fujian, SE China
160 K9 **Liangping** *var.* Liangshan. Sichuan, C China
Liangshan *see* Liangping
Liangzhou *see* Wuwei
161 O9 **Liangzi Hu** ▣ C China
161 R12 **Lianjiang** Fujian, SE China
160 L15 **Lianjiang** *var* Liancheng. Guangdong, S China
Lianjiang *see* Xingguo
161 O13 **Lianping** *var.* Yuanshan. Guangdong, S China
Lianshan *see* Huludao
Lian Xian *see* Lianzhou
160 M11 **Lianyuan** *prev.* Lantian. Hunan, S China
161 Q6 **Lianyungang** *var.* Xinpu. Jiangsu, E China
161 N13 **Lianzhou** *var.* Linxian; *prev.* Lian Xian. Guangdong, S China
Lianzhou *see* Hepu
Liao *see* Liaoning
161 P5 **Liaocheng** Shandong, E China
163 U13 **Liaodong Bandao** *var.* Liaotung Peninsula. *peninsula* NE China
163 T13 **Liaodong Wan** *Eng.* Gulf of Lantung, Gulf of Liaotung. *gulf* NE China
163 U11 **Liao He** ≈ NE China
163 U12 **Liaoning** *var.* Liao, Liaoning Sheng, Shengking, *hist.* Fengtien, Shenking. ◈ *province* NE China
Liaoning Sheng *see* Liaoning
Liaotung Peninsula *see* Liaodong Bandao
163 V12 **Liaoyang** *var.* Liao-yang. Liaoning, NE China
Liao-yang *see* Liaoyang
163 V11 **Liaoyuan** *var.* Dongliao, Shuang-liao, *Jap.* Chengchiatun. Jilin, NE China
163 U12 **Liaozhong** Liaoning, NE China
Liaqatabad *see* Piplān
10 M10 **Liard** ≈ W Canada
Liard *see* Fort Liard
10 L10 **Liard River** British Columbia, W Canada
149 O15 **Liāri** Baluchistān, SW Pakistan
Liatroim *see* Leitrim
189 S6 **Lib** *var.* Ellep. *island* Ralik Chain, C Marshall Islands
Liban *see* Lebanon
138 H6 **Liban, Jebel** *Ar.* Jabal al Gharbt, Jabal Lubnān, *Eng.* Mount Lebanon. ▲▲ C Lebanon
Libau *see* Liepāja
33 N7 **Libby** Montana, NW USA
79 I16 **Libenge** Equateur, NW Dem. Rep. Congo
26 I7 **Liberal** Kansas, C USA
27 R7 **Liberal** Missouri, C USA
Liberalitas Julia *see* Évora
111 D15 **Liberec** *Ger.* Reichenberg. Liberecký Kraj, N Czech Republic
111 D15 **Liberecky Kraj** ◈ *region* N Czech Republic
42 K12 **Liberia** Guanacaste, NW Costa Rica
76 K17 **Liberia** *off.* Republic of Liberia. ◆ *republic* W Africa
Liberia, Republic of *see* Liberia
61 D16 **Libertad** Corrientes, NE Argentina
61 E20 **Libertad** San José, S Uruguay
54 I7 **Libertad** Barinas, NW Venezuela
54 K6 **Libertad** Cojedes, N Venezuela
62 G12 **Libertador** *off.* Región del Libertador General Bernardo O'Higgins. ◈ *region* C Chile
Libertador General Bernardo O'Higgins, Región del *see* Libertador
Libertador General San Martín *see* Ciudad de Libertador General San Martín
20 L6 **Liberty** Kentucky, S USA
22 J7 **Liberty** Mississippi, S USA
27 R4 **Liberty** Missouri, C USA
18 J12 **Liberty** New York, NE USA
21 T9 **Liberty** North Carolina, SE USA
Libian Desert *see* Libyan Desert
99 J23 **Libin** Luxembourg, SE Belgium
Lībīyah, Aş Şaḩrā' al *see* Libyan Desert
160 K13 **Libo** *var.* Yuping. Guizhou, S China
Libohova *see* Libohovë
113 L23 **Libohovë** *var.* Libohova. Gjirokastër, S Albania
81 K18 **Liboi** North Eastern, E Kenya
102 K13 **Libourne** Gironde, SW France
99 K23 **Libramont** Luxembourg, SE Belgium
113 M20 **Librazhd** *var.* Librazhdi. Elbasan, E Albania
Librazhdi *see* Librazhd
79 C18 **Libreville** ● (Gabon) Estuaire, NW Gabon
75 P10 **Libya** *off.* Socialist People's Libyan Arab Jamahiriya, *Ar.* Al Jamāhīrīyah al 'Arabīyah al Lībīyah ash Sha'bīyah al Ishtirākīy; *prev.* Libyan Arab Republic. ◆ *islamic state* N Africa
Libyan Arab Republic *see* Libya
75 T11 **Libyan Desert** *var.* Libian Desert, *Ar.* Aş Şaḩrā' al Lībīyah. *desert* N Africa
75 T8 **Libyan Plateau** *var.* Aḑ Diffah. *plateau* Egypt/Libya
62 G12 **Licantén** Maule, C Chile
107 J25 **Licata** *anc.* Phintias. Sicilia, Italy, C Mediterranean Sea
137 P14 **Lice** Dıyarbakır, SE Turkey
97 L19 **Lichfield** C England, UK
83 N14 **Lichinga** Niassa, N Mozambique
109 V3 **Lichtenau** Niederösterreich, N Austria
83 I21 **Lichtenburg** North-West, N South Africa
101 K18 **Lichtenfels** Bayern, SE Germany
98 O12 **Lichtenvoorde** Gelderland, E Netherlands
Lichtenwald *see* Sevnica
99 C17 **Lichtervelde** West-Vlaanderen, W Belgium
160 L9 **Lichuan** Hubei, C China
27 V7 **Licking** Missouri, C USA
20 M4 **Licking River** ≈ Kentucky, S USA
112 C11 **Lički Osik** Lika-Senj, C Croatia
Ličko-Senjska Županija *see* Lika-Senj
107 K19 **Licosa, Punta** *headland* S Italy
119 H16 **Lida** *Rus.* Lida. Hrodzyenskaya Voblasts', W Belarus
93 H17 **Liden** Västernorrland, C Sweden
29 R7 **Lidgerwood** North Dakota, N USA
Lidhorikíon *see* Lidoríki
95 K21 **Lidhult** Kronoberg, S Sweden
95 P16 **Lidingö** Stockholm, C Sweden
95 K17 **Lidköping** Västra Götaland, S Sweden
Lido di Iesolo *see* Lido di Jesolo
106 I8 **Lido di Jesolo** *var.* Lido di Iesolo. Veneto, NE Italy
107 H15 **Lido di Ostia** Lazio, C Italy
Lidokhorikion *see* Lidoríki
115 E18 **Lidoríki** *prev.* Lidhorikíon, Lidokhorikion. Stereá Ellás, C Greece
110 K9 **Lidzbark** Warmińsko-Mazurskie, NE Poland
110 L7 **Lidzbark Warmiński** *Ger.* Heilsberg. Olsztyn, N Poland
109 U3 **Liebenau** Oberösterreich, N Austria
181 P7 **Liebig, Mount** ▲ Northern Territory, C Australia
109 V8 **Lieboch** Steiermark, SE Austria
108 I8 **Liechtenstein** *off.* Principality of Liechtenstein. ◆ *principality* C Europe
Liechtenstein, Principality of *see* Liechtenstein
99 F18 **Liedekerke** Vlaams Brabant, C Belgium
99 K19 **Liège** *Dut.* Luik, *Ger.* Lüttich. Liège, E Belgium
99 K20 **Liège** *Dut.* Luik. ◈ *province* E Belgium
Liegnitz *see* Legnica
93 O16 **Lieksa** Pohjois-Karjala, E Finland
118 F10 **Lielupe** ≈ Latvia/Lithuania
118 G9 **Lielvārde** Ogre, C Latvia
167 U13 **Liên Hương** *var.* Tuy Phong. Binh Thuận, S Vietnam
Liên Nghia *see* Đưc Trong
109 P9 **Lienz** Tirol, W Austria
118 B10 **Liepāja** *Ger.* Libau. Liepāja, W Latvia
99 H17 **Lier** *Fr.* Lierre. Antwerpen, N Belgium
95 H15 **Lierbyen** Buskerud, S Norway
99 L21 **Lierneux** Liège, E Belgium
Lierre *see* Lier
101 D18 **Lieser** ≈ W Germany
109 U7 **Liesing** ≈ E Austria
108 E6 **Liestal** Basel-Land, N Switzerland
Lietuva *see* Lithuania
Lievenhof *see* Līvāni
103 O2 **Liévin** Pas-de-Calais, N France
14 M9 **Lièvre, Rivière du** ≈ Québec, SE Canada
109 T6 **Liezen** Steiermark, C Austria
97 E14 **Lifford** *Ir.* Leifear. Donegal, NW Ireland
187 Q16 **Lifou** *island* Îles Loyauté, E New Caledonia
193 Y15 **Lifuka** *island* Ha'apai Group, C Tonga
171 P4 **Ligao** Luzon, N Philippines
Liger *see* Loire
42 H2 **Lighthouse Reef** *reef* E Belize
183 Q4 **Lightning Ridge** New South Wales, SE Australia
103 N9 **Lignières** Cher, C France
103 S5 **Ligny-en-Barrois** Meuse, NE France
83 P15 **Ligonha** ≈ NE Mozambique
31 P11 **Ligonier** Indiana, N USA
81 I25 **Ligunga** Ruvuma, S Tanzania
106 D9 **Ligure, Appennino** *Eng.* Ligurian Mountains. ▲▲ NW Italy
Ligure, Mar *see* Ligurian Sea
106 C9 **Liguria** ◈ *region* NW Italy
Ligurian Mountains *see* Ligure, Appennino
120 K6 **Ligurian Sea** *Fr.* Mer Ligurienne, *It.* Mar Ligure. *sea* N Mediterranean Sea
Ligurienne, Mer *see* Ligurian Sea
186 H5 **Lihir Group** *island group* NE Papua New Guinea
38 B8 **Līhu'e** *var.* Lihue. Kaua'i, Hawai'i, USA North America
38 B8 **Lihue** *var.* Līhu'e. Kauai, Hawaii, USA
Lihue *see* Līhu'e
Līhu'e *see* Lihue
118 F5 **Lihula** *Ger.* Leal. Läänemaa, W Estonia
124 I2 **Liinakhamari** *var.* Linacmamari. Murmanskaya Oblast', NW Russian Federation
Liivi Laht *see* Riga, Gulf of
160 F11 **Lijiang** *var.* Dayan, Lijiang Naxizu Zizhixian. Yunnan, SW China
Lijiang Naxizu Zizhixian *see* Lijiang
112 C11 **Lika-Senj** *off.* Ličko-Senjska Županija. ◈ *province* W Croatia
79 N25 **Likasi** *prev.* Jadotville. Shaba, SE Dem. Rep. Congo
79 L16 **Likati** Orientale, N Dem. Rep. Congo
10 M15 **Likely** British Columbia, SW Canada
153 Y11 **Likhapāni** Assam, NE India
124 J16 **Likhoslavl'** Tverskaya Oblast', W Russian Federation
189 U5 **Likiep Atoll** *atoll* Ratak Chain, C Marshall Islands
95 D18 **Liknes** Vest-Agder, S Norway
79 H18 **Likouala** ≈ N Congo
79 H18 **Likouala aux Herbes** ≈ E Congo
190 B16 **Liku** E Niue
Likupang, Selat *see* Bangka, Selat
27 Y8 **Lilbourn** Missouri, C USA
103 X14 **l'Île-Rousse** Corse, France, C Mediterranean Sea
109 W5 **Lilienfeld** Niederösterreich, NE Austria
161 N11 **Liling** Hunan, S China
95 J18 **Lilla Edet** Älvsborg, S Sweden
103 P1 **Lille** *var.* l'Isle, *Dut.* Rijssel, *Flem.* Ryssel, *prev.* Lisle; *anc.* Insula. Nord, N France
95 G24 **Lillebælt** *var.* Lille Bælt, *Eng.* Little Belt. *strait* S Denmark
Lille Bælt *see* Lillebælt
102 L3 **Lillebonne** Seine-Maritime, N France
94 H12 **Lillehammer** Oppland, S Norway
103 O1 **Lillers** Pas-de-Calais, N France
95 F18 **Lillesand** Aust-Agder, S Norway
95 I15 **Lillestrøm** Akershus, S Norway
93 F18 **Lillhärdal** Jämtland, C Sweden
21 U10 **Lillington** North Carolina, SE USA
105 O9 **Lillo** Castilla-La Mancha, C Spain
10 M16 **Lillooet** British Columbia, SW Canada
83 M14 **Lilongwe** ● (Malawi) Central, W Malawi
83 M14 **Lilongwe** ✈ Central, W Malawi
83 M14 **Lilongwe** ≈ W Malawi
171 P7 **Liloy** Mindanao, S Philippines
Lilybaeum *see* Marsala
182 J7 **Lilydale** South Australia
183 P16 **Lilydale** Tasmania, SE Australia
113 J14 **Lim** ≈ SE Europe
57 D15 **Lima** ● (Peru) Lima, W Peru
94 K13 **Lima** Dalarna, C Sweden
31 R12 **Lima** Ohio, NE USA
57 D14 **Lima** ◈ *department* W Peru
Lima *see* Jorge Chávez International
111 L17 **Limanowa** Małopolskie, S Poland
104 G5 **Lima, Rio** *Sp.* Limia. ≈ Portugal/Spain *see also* Limia
Lima, Rio Limia
168 M11 **Limas** Pulau Sebangka, W Indonesia
Limassol *see* Lemesós
97 F14 **Limavady** *Ir.* Léim An Mhadaidh. NW Northern Ireland, UK
63 J14 **Limay Mahuida** La Pampa, C Argentina
63 H15 **Limay, Río** ≈ W Argentina
101 N16 **Limbach-Oberfrohna** Sachsen, E Germany
81 F22 **Limba Limba** ≈ C Tanzania
107 C17 **Limbara, Monte** ▲ Sardegna, Italy, C Mediterranean Sea
118 G7 **Limbaži** *Est.* Lemsalu. Limbaži, N Latvia
44 M8 **Limbé** N Haiti
99 L19 **Limbourg** Liège, E Belgium
99 K17 **Limbourg** ◈ *province* NE Belgium
99 L16 **Limburg** ◈ *province* SE Netherlands
101 F17 **Limburg an der Lahn** Hessen, W Germany
94 K13 **Limedsforsen** Dalarna, C Sweden
60 L9 **Limeira** São Paulo, S Brazil
97 C19 **Limerick** *Ir.* Luimneach. Limerick, SW Ireland
97 C20 **Limerick** *Ir.* Luimneach. ◈ *county* SW Ireland
19 S2 **Limestone** Maine, NE USA
25 U9 **Limestone, Lake** ◎ Texas, SW USA
39 P12 **Lime Village** Alaska, USA
95 F20 **Limfjorden** *fjord* N Denmark
95 J23 **Limhamn** Skåne, S Sweden
104 H5 **Limia** *Port.* Rio Lima. ≈ Portugal/Spain *see also* Lima,Rio
Limia Lima, Rio
93 L14 **Liminka** Oulu, C Finland
Limín Vathéos *see* Sámos
115 G17 **Límni** Évvoia, C Greece
Límni Distos *see* Dýstos, Límni
Límni Doïranis *see* Doïrani, Límni
Límni Kerkinitis *see* Kerkíni, Límni
115 J15 **Límnos** *anc.* Lemnos. *island* E Greece
102 M11 **Limoges** *anc.* Augustoritum Lemovicensium, Lemovices. Haute-Vienne, C France
43 O13 **Limón** *var.* Puerto Limón. Limón, E Costa Rica
42 K4 **Limón** Colón, NE Honduras
37 U5 **Limon** Colorado, C USA
43 N13 **Limón** *off.* Provincia de Limón. ◈ *province* E Costa Rica
106 A10 **Limone Piemonte** Piemonte, NE Italy
Limones *see* Valdéz
Limón, Provincia de *see* Limón
Limonum *see* Poitiers
103 N11 **Limousin** ◈ *region* C France
103 N16 **Limoux** Aude, S France
83 J20 **Limpopo** *off.* Limpopo Province; *prev.* Northern, Northern Transvaal. ◈ *province* NE South Africa
83 L19 **Limpopo** *var.* Crocodile. ≈ S Africa
Limpopo Province *see* Limpopo
160 K17 **Limu Ling** ▲▲ S China
113 M20 **Lin** *var.* Lini. Elbasan, E Albania
Linacmamari *see* Liinakhamari
62 G13 **Linares** Maule, C Chile
54 C13 **Linares** Nariño, SW Colombia
41 O9 **Linares** Nuevo León, NE Mexico
105 N12 **Linares** Andalucía, S Spain
107 G15 **Linaro, Capo** *headland* C Italy
106 D8 **Linate** ✈ (Milano) Lombardia, N Italy
167 T8 **Lin Camh** *prev.* Đưc Tho. Ha Tinh, N Vietnam
160 F13 **Lincang** Yunnan, SW China
Lincheng *see* Lingao
161 P11 **Linchuan** *prev.* Linchuan. Jiangxi, S China
Linchuan *see* Linchuan
61 B20 **Lincoln** Buenos Aires, E Argentina
185 H19 **Lincoln** Canterbury, South Island, New Zealand
97 N18 **Lincoln** *anc.* Lindum, Lindum Colonia. E England, UK
35 O6 **Lincoln** California, W USA
30 L13 **Lincoln** Illinois, N USA
26 M4 **Lincoln** Kansas, C USA
19 S5 **Lincoln** Maine, NE USA
27 T5 **Lincoln** Missouri, C USA
29 R16 **Lincoln** *state capital* Nebraska, C USA
32 F11 **Lincoln City** Oregon, NW USA
167 X10 **Lincoln Island** *island* E Paracel Islands
197 Q11 **Lincoln Sea** *sea* Arctic Ocean
97 N18 **Lincolnshire** *cultural region* E England, UK
21 R10 **Lincolnton** North Carolina, SE USA
25 V7 **Lindale** Texas, SW USA
101 I25 **Lindau** *var.* Lindau am Bodensee. Bayern, S Germany
Lindau am Bodensee *see* Lindau
123 P9 **Linde** ≈ NE Russian Federation
55 T9 **Linden** E Guyana
23 O6 **Linden** Alabama, S USA
20 H9 **Linden** Tennessee, S USA
25 X6 **Linden** Texas, SW USA
18 J16 **Lindenwold** New Jersey, NE USA
95 M15 **Lindesberg** Örebro, C Sweden
95 D18 **Lindesnes** *headland* S Norway
Líndhos *see* Líndos
81 K24 **Lindi** Lindi, SE Tanzania
81 J24 **Lindi** ◈ *region* SE Tanzania
79 N17 **Lindi** ≈ NE Dem. Rep. Congo
163 V7 **Lindian** Heilongjiang, NE China
185 E21 **Lindis Pass** *pass* South Island, New Zealand
83 J22 **Lindley** Free State, C South Africa
95 J19 **Lindome** Västra Götaland, S Sweden
163 S10 **Lindong** *var.* Bairin Zuoqi. Nei Mongol Zizhiqu, N China
115 O23 **Líndos** *var.* Líndhos. Ródos, Dodekánisa, Greece, Aegean Sea
14 I14 **Lindsay** Ontario, SE Canada
35 R11 **Lindsay** California, W USA
33 X8 **Lindsay** Montana, NW USA
27 N11 **Lindsay** Oklahoma, C USA
27 N5 **Lindsborg** Kansas, C USA
95 N21 **Lindsdal** Kalmar, S Sweden
Lindum/Lindum Colonia *see* Lincoln
191 W3 **Line Islands** *island group* E Kiribati
Linëvo *see* Linova
160 M5 **Linfen** *var.* Lin-fen. Shanxi, C China
Lin-fen *see* Linfen
155 F18 **Linganamakki Reservoir** ▣ SW India
160 L17 **Lingao** *var.* Lincheng. Hainan, S China
171 N3 **Lingayen** Luzon, N Philippines
160 M6 **Lingbao** *var.* Guolüezhen. Henan, C China
94 N12 **Lingbo** Gävleborg, C Sweden
Lingcheng *see* Beiliu
Lingeh *see* Bandar-e Langeh
100 E12 **Lingen** *var.* Lingen an der Ems. Niedersachsen, NW Germany
Lingen an der Ems *see* Lingen
168 M11 **Lingga, Kepulauan** *island group* W Indonesia
168 L11 **Lingga, Pulau** *island* Kepulauan Lingga, W Indonesia
14 J14 **Lingham Lake** ◎ Ontario, SE Canada
94 M13 **Linghed** Dalarna, C Sweden
Lingheng *see* Lingshan
33 Z15 **Lingle** Wyoming, C USA
18 G15 **Linglestown** Pennsylvania, NE USA
79 K18 **Lingomo 11** Equateur, NW Dem. Rep. Congo
160 L15 **Lingshan** *var* Lingheng. Guangxi Zhuangzu Zizhiqu, S China
160 L17 **Lingshui** *var.* Lingshui Lizu Zizhixian. Hainan, S China
Lingshui Lizu Zizhixian *see* Lingshui
155 G16 **Lingsugūr** Karnātaka, C India
107 L23 **Linguaglossa** Sicilia, Italy, C Mediterranean Sea
76 H10 **Linguère** N Senegal
159 W8 **Lingwu** Ningxia, N China
Lingxi *see* Yongshun
Lingxi *see* Cangnan
Lingxian/Ling Xian *see* Yanling
163 S12 **Lingyuan** Liaoning, NE China
163 U4 **Linhai** Heilongjiang, NE China
161 S10 **Linhai** *var.* Taizhou. Zhejiang, SE China
59 O20 **Linhares** Espírito Santo, SE Brazil
162 M13 **Linhe** Nei Mongol Zizhiqu, N China
Lini *see* Lin
139 S1 **Līnik, Chiyā-ē** ▲ N Iraq
95 M18 **Linköping** Östergötland, S Sweden
163 Y8 **Linkou** Heilongjiang, NE China
118 F11 **Linkuva** Šiaulai, N Lithuania
27 V5 **Linn** Missouri, C USA
25 S16 **Linn** Texas, SW USA
27 T2 **Linneus** Missouri, C USA
96 H10 **Linnhe, Loch** *inlet* W Scotland, UK
119 G19 **Linova** *Rus.* Linëvo. Brestskaya Voblasts', SW Belarus
161 O5 **Linqing** Shandong, E China
161 N6 **Linruzhen** Henan, C China
60 K8 **Lins** São Paulo, S Brazil
93 F17 **Linsell** Jämtland, C Sweden
160 J9 **Linshui** Sichuan, C China
44 K12 **Linstead** C Jamaica
159 U11 **Lintan** Gansu, N China
159 V11 **Lintao** Gansu, C China
15 S12 **Lintère** ≈ Québec, SE Canada
108 H8 **Linth** ≈ NW Switzerland
108 H8 **Linthal** Glarus, NE Switzerland
31 N15 **Linton** Indiana, N USA
29 N6 **Linton** North Dakota, N USA
163 R11 **Linxi** Nei Mongol Zizhiqu, N China
159 U11 **Linxia** *var.* Linxia Huizu Zizhizhou. Gansu, C China
Linxia Huizu Zizhizhou *see* Linxia
Linxian *see* Lianzhou
161 P4 **Linyi** Shandong, E China
161 Q6 **Linyi** Shandong, S China
160 M6 **Linyi** Shanxi, C China
109 T4 **Linz** *anc.* Lentia. Oberösterreich, N Austria
159 S8 **Linze** *var.* Shahepu. Gansu, N China
44 J13 **Lionel Town** C Jamaica
103 Q16 **Lion, Golfe du** *Eng.* Gulf of Lion, Gulf of Lions; *anc.* Sinus Gallicus. *gulf* S France
Lion, Gulf of/Lions, Gulf of *see* Lion, Golfe du
83 K16 **Lions Den** Mashonaland West, N Zimbabwe
14 F13 **Lion's Head** Ontario, S Canada
Lios Ceannúir, Bá *see* Liscannor Bay
Lios Mór *see* Lismore
Lios na gCearrbhach *see* Lisburn
Lios Tuathail *see* Listowel
79 G17 **Liouesso** La Sangha, N Congo
Liozno *see* Lyozna
171 O4 **Lipa** *off.* Lipa City. Luzon, N Philippines
Lipa City *see* Lipa
25 S7 **Lipan** Texas, SW USA
Lipari Islands/Lipari, Isole *see* Eolie, Isole
107 L22 **Lipari, Isola** *island* Isole Eolie, S Italy
116 L8 **Lipcani** *Rus.* Lipkany. N Moldova
93 N17 **Liperi** Pohjois-Karjala, SE Finland
126 L7 **Lipetsk** Lipetskaya Oblast', W Russian Federation
126 K6 **Lipetskaya Oblast'** ◈ *province* W Russian Federation
57 K22 **Lipez, Cordillera de** ▲▲ SW Bolivia
110 E10 **Lipiany** *Ger.* Lippehne. Zachodnio-pomorskie, W Poland
112 G9 **Lipik** Požega-Slavonija, NE Croatia
124 L12 **Lipin Bor** Vologodskaya Oblast', NW Russian Federation
160 L12 **Liping** *var.* Defeng. Guizhou, S China
Lipkany *see* Lipcani
119 H15 **Lipnishki** *Rus.* Lipnishki. Hrodzyenskaya Voblasts', W Belarus
110 J10 **Lipno** Kujawsko-pomorskie, C Poland
116 F11 **Lipova** *Hung.* Lippa. Arad, W Romania
Lipovets *see* Lypovets'
Lippa *see* Lipova
101 E14 **Lippe** ≈ W Germany
Lippehne *see* Lipiany
101 G14 **Lippstadt** Nordrhein-Westfalen, W Germany
25 P1 **Lipscomb** Texas, SW USA
Lipsia/Lipsk *see* Leipzig
Liptau-Sankt-Nikolaus/Liptószentmiklós *see* Liptovský Mikuláš
111 K19 **Liptovský Mikuláš** *Ger.* Liptau-Sankt-Nikolaus, *Hung.* Liptószentmiklós. Žilinský Kraj, N Slovakia
183 O13 **Liptrap, Cape** *headland* Victoria, SE Australia
160 L13 **Lipu** Guangxi Zhuangzu Zizhiqu, S China
141 X12 **Liqbi** S Oman
81 G17 **Lira** N Uganda
57 F15 **Lircay** Huancavelica, C Peru
107 K17 **Liri** ≈ C Italy
144 M8 **Lisakovsk** Kustanay, NW Kazakhstan
79 K17 **Lisala** Equateur, N Dem. Rep. Congo
104 F11 **Lisboa** *Eng.* Lisbon; *anc.* Felicitas Julia, Olisipo. ● (Portugal) Lisboa, W Portugal
104 F10 **Lisboa** *Eng.* Lisbon. ◈ *district* C Portugal
19 N7 **Lisbon** New Hampshire, NE USA
29 Q6 **Lisbon** North Dakota, N USA
Lisbon *see* Lisboa
19 Q8 **Lisbon Falls** Maine, NE USA
97 G15 **Lisburn** *Ir.* Lios na gCearrbhach. E Northern Ireland, UK
38 L6 **Lisburne, Cape** *headland* Alaska, USA
97 B19 **Liscannor Bay** *Ir.* Bá Lios Ceannúir. *inlet* W Ireland
113 Q18 **Lisec** ▲ E FYR Macedonia
160 F13 **Lishe Jiang** ≈ SW China
160 M4 **Lishi** Shanxi, C China
163 V10 **Lishu** Jilin, NE China
161 R10 **Lishui** Zhejiang, SE China
192 L5 **Lisianski Island** *island* Hawaiian Islands, Hawaii, USA
Lisichansk *see* Lysychans'k
102 L4 **Lisieux** *anc.* Noviomagus. Calvados, N France
126 L8 **Liski** *prev.* Georgiu-Dezh. Voronezhskaya Oblast', W Russian Federation
103 N4 **l'Isle-Adam** Val-d'Oise, N France
Lisle/l'Isle *see* Lille
103 R15 **l'Isle-sur-la-Sorgue** Vaucluse, SE France
15 S9 **L'Islet** Québec, SE Canada
182 M12 **Lismore** Victoria, SE Australia
97 D20 **Lismore** *Ir.* Lios Mór. S Ireland
Lissa *see* Vis
Lissa *see* Leszno
98 H11 **Lisse** Zuid-Holland, W Netherlands
114 K13 **Lissos** *var.* Filiouri. ≈ NE Greece
95 D18 **Lista** *peninsula* S Norway
95 D18 **Listafjorden** *fjord* S Norway
195 R13 **Lister, Mount** ▲ Antarctica
126 M8 **Listopadovka** Voronezhskaya Oblast', W Russian Federation
14 F15 **Listowel** Ontario, S Canada
97 B20 **Listowel** *Ir.* Lios Tuathail. Kerry, SW Ireland
160 L14 **Litang** Guangxi Zhuangzu Zizhiqu, S China
160 F9 **Litang** *var.* Gaocheng. Sichuan, C China
160 F10 **Litang Qu** ≈ C China
55 X12 **Litani** *var.* Itany. ≈ French Guiana/Suriname
138 G8 **Lītani, Nahr el** *var.* Nahr al Litant. ≈ C Lebanon
Lītant, Nahr al *see* Lītani, Nahr el
Litauen *see* Lithuania
30 K14 **Litchfield** Illinois, N USA
29 U8 **Litchfield** Minnesota, N USA
36 K13 **Litchfield Park** Arizona, SW USA
183 S8 **Lithgow** New South Wales, SE Australia
115 I26 **Líthino, Akrotírio** *headland* Kríti, Greece, E Mediterranean Sea
118 D12 **Lithuania** *off.* Republic of Lithuania, *Ger.* Litauen, *Lith.* Lietuva, *Pol.* Litwa, *Rus.* Litva; *prev.* Lithuanian SSR, *Rus.* Litovskaya SSR. ◆ *republic* NE Europe
Lithuanian SSR *see* Lithuania
Lithuania, Republic of *see* Lithuania
109 U11 **Litija** *Ger.* Littai. C Slovenia
18 H15 **Lititz** Pennsylvania, NE USA
115 F15 **Litóchoro** *var.* Litohoro, Litókhoron. Kentrikí Makedonía, N Greece
Litohoro/Litókhoron *see* Litóchoro
111 C15 **Litoměřice** Ústecký Kraj, NW Czech Republic
111 F17 **Litomyšl** Pardubický Kraj, C Czech Republic
111 G17 **Litovel** *Ger.* Littau. Olomoucký Kraj, E Czech Republic
123 S13 **Litovko** Khabarovskiy Kray, SE Russian Federation
Litovskaya SSR *see* Lithuania
Littai *see* Litija
Littau *see* Litovel
44 G1 **Little Abaco** *var.* Abaco Island. *island* N Bahamas
111 I21 **Little Alföld** *Ger.* Kleines Ungarisches Tiefland, *Hung.* Kisalföld, *Slvk.* Podunajská Rovina. *plain* Hungary/Slovakia
151 Q20 **Little Andaman** *island* Andaman Islands, India, NE Indian Ocean
26 M5 **Little Arkansas River** ≈ Kansas, C USA
184 L4 **Little Barrier Island** *island* N New Zealand
Little Belt *see* Lillebælt
38 M11 **Little Black River** ≈ Alaska, USA

27 O2 Little Blue River Kansas/Nebraska, C USA
44 D8 Little Cayman island E Cayman Islands
9 X11 Little Churchill Manitoba, C Canada
166 J10 Little Coco Island island SW Myanmar (Burma)
36 L10 Little Colorado River Arizona, SW USA
14 E11 Little Current Manitoulin Island, Ontario, S Canada
12 E11 Little Current Ontario, S Canada
38 L8 Little Diomede Island island Alaska, USA
44 I4 Little Exuma island C Bahamas
29 U7 Little Falls Minnesota, N USA
18 J10 Little Falls New York, NE USA
24 M5 Littlefield Texas, SW USA
29 V3 Littlefork Minnesota, N USA
29 V3 Little Fork River Minnesota, N USA
9 N16 Little Fort British Columbia, SW Canada
9 Y14 Little Grand Rapids Manitoba, C Canada
97 N23 Littlehampton SE England, UK
35 T2 Little Humboldt River Nevada, W USA
44 K6 Little Inagua var. Inagua Islands. island S Bahamas
21 Q4 Little Kanawha River West Virginia, NE USA
83 F25 Little Karoo plateau S South Africa
39 O16 Little Koniuji Island island Shumagin Islands, Alaska, USA
44 H12 Little London W Jamaica
13 R10 Little Mecatina Fr. Rivière du Petit Mécatina. Newfoundland and Labrador/Québec, E Canada
96 F8 Little Minch, The strait NW Scotland, UK
27 T13 Little Missouri River Arkansas, USA
28 J7 Little Missouri River NW USA
28 J3 Little Muddy River North Dakota, N USA
151 Q22 Little Nicobar island Nicobar Islands, India, NE Indian Ocean
27 R6 Little Osage River Missouri, C USA
97 P20 Little Ouse E England, UK
149 V2 Little Pamir Pash. Pāmīr-e Khord, Rus. Malyy Pamir. ⛰ Afghanistan/Tajikistan
21 U12 Little Pee Dee River North Carolina/South Carolina, SE USA
27 V10 Little Red River Arkansas, C USA
Little Rhody see Rhode Island
185 I19 Little River Canterbury, South Island, New Zealand
21 U12 Little River South Carolina, SE USA
27 Y9 Little River Arkansas/Missouri, C USA
27 R13 Little River Arkansas/Oklahoma, USA
23 T7 Little River Georgia, SE USA
22 H6 Little River Louisiana, S USA
25 T10 Little River Texas, SW USA
27 V12 Little Rock state capital Arkansas, C USA
31 N8 Little Sable Point headland Michigan, N USA
103 U11 Little Saint Bernard Pass Fr. Col du Petit St-Bernard, It. Colle del Piccolo San Bernardo. pass France/Italy
36 K7 Little Salt Lake Utah, W USA
180 K8 Little Sandy Desert desert Western Australia
29 S13 Little Sioux River Iowa, C USA
38 E17 Little Sitkin Island island Aleutian Islands, Alaska, USA
9 O13 Little Smoky Alberta, W Canada
9 O14 Little Smoky Alberta, W Canada
37 P3 Little Snake River Colorado, C USA
64 A12 Little Sound bay Bermuda, NW Atlantic Ocean
37 T4 Littleton Colorado, C USA
19 N7 Littleton New Hampshire, NE USA
18 D11 Little Valley New York, NE USA
30 M15 Little Wabash River Illinois, N USA
14 D10 Little White River Ontario, S Canada
28 M12 Little White River South Dakota, N USA
25 R5 Little Wichita River Texas, SW USA
142 I4 Little Zab Ar. Nahraz Zāb aş Şaghīr, Kurd. Zē-i Kōya, Per. Rūdkhāneh-ye Zāb-e Kūchek. Iran/Iraq
79 D15 Littoral ◈ province W Cameroon
Littoria see Latina
Litva/Litwa see Lithuania
111 B15 Litvínov Ústecký Kraj, NW Czech Republic
116 M6 Lityn Vinnyts'ka Oblast', C Ukraine
Liu-chou/Liuchow see Liuzhou
163 W11 Liuhe Jilin, NE China
83 Q15 Liúpo Nampula, NE Mozambique
83 G14 Liuwa Plain plain W Zambia
160 L13 Liuzhou var. Liu-chou, Liuchow. Guangxi Zhuangzu Zizhiqu, S China
116 H8 Livada Hung. Sárköz. Satu Mare, NW Romania
115 J20 Liváda, Ákrotírio headland Tínos, Kykládes, Greece, Aegean Sea
115 F18 Livádeia prev. Levádia. Stereá Ellás, C Greece
Livádi see Liádi
Livanátai see Livanátes
115 G18 Livanátes prev. Livanátai. Stereá Ellás, C Greece
118 I10 Līvāni Ger. Lievenhof. Preiļi, SE Latvia
65 E25 Lively Island island SE Falkland Islands
65 D25 Lively Sound sound SE Falkland Islands
39 R8 Livengood Alaska, USA
106 I7 Livenza NE Italy
35 O6 Live Oak California, W USA
23 U9 Live Oak Florida, SE USA
35 O9 Livermore California, W USA
20 I6 Livermore Kentucky, S USA
19 Q7 Livermore Falls Maine, NE USA
24 J10 Livermore, Mount ▲ Texas, SW USA
13 P16 Liverpool Nova Scotia, SE Canada
97 K17 Liverpool NW England, UK
183 S7 Liverpool Range ⛰ New South Wales, SE Australia
42 F4 Livingston Izabal, E Guatemala
96 J12 Livingston C Scotland, UK
23 N5 Livingston Alabama, S USA
35 P9 Livingston California, W USA
22 J8 Livingston Louisiana, S USA
33 S11 Livingston Montana, NW USA
20 L8 Livingston Tennessee, S USA
25 W9 Livingston Texas, SW USA
83 I16 Livingstone var. Maramba. Southern, S Zambia
185 B22 Livingstone Mountains ⛰ South Island, New Zealand
80 K13 Livingstone Mountains ⛰ S Tanzania
82 N12 Livingstonia Northern, N Malawi
194 G4 Livingston Island island Antarctica
25 W9 Livingston, Lake Texas, SW USA
112 F13 Livno ◈ Federicija Bosna I Hercegovina, SW Bosnia and Herzegovina
126 K7 Livny Orlovskaya Oblast', W Russian Federation
93 M14 Livojoki C Finland
31 R10 Livonia Michigan, N USA
106 E11 Livorno Eng. Leghorn. Toscana, C Italy
Livramento see Santana do Livramento
141 U8 Liwā var. Al Liwā'. oasis region S United Arab Emirates
81 I24 Liwale Lindi, SE Tanzania
159 W9 Liwangbu Ningxia, N China
83 N15 Liwonde Southern, S Malawi
159 V11 Lixian Gansu, C China
160 H8 Lixian var. Li Xian, Zagunao. Sichuan, C China
Li Xian see Lixian
Li Xian see Lixian
Lixian Jiang see Black River
115 B18 Lixoúri prev. Lixoúrion. Kefallinía, Iónia Nisiá, Greece, C Mediterranean Sea
Lixoúrion see Lixoúri
Lixus see Larache
33 U15 Lizard Head Peak ▲ Wyoming, C USA
97 H25 Lizard Point headland SW England, UK
Lizarra see Estella
112 L12 Ljig Serbia, C Serbia
Ljouwert see Leeuwarden
Ljubelj see Loibl Pass
109 U11 Ljubljana Ger. Laibach, It. Lubiana; anc. Aemona, Emona. ● (Slovenia) C Slovenia
109 T11 Ljubljana ✈ C Slovenia
113 N17 Ljuboten ▲ S Serbia
95 P19 Ljugarn Gotland, SE Sweden
84 G7 Ljungan N Sweden
93 F17 Ljungan C Sweden
95 K21 Ljungby Kronoberg, S Sweden
95 M17 Ljungsbro Östergötland, S Sweden
95 I18 Ljungskile Västra Götaland, S Sweden
94 M11 Ljusdal Gävleborg, C Sweden
94 M11 Ljusnan C Sweden
94 N12 Ljusne Gävleborg, C Sweden
95 P15 Ljusterö Stockholm, C Sweden
109 X9 Ljutomer Ger. Luttenberg. NE Slovenia
63 G15 Llaima, Volcán S Chile
105 X4 Llançà var. Llansá. Cataluña, NE Spain
97 J21 Llandovery C Wales, UK
97 J20 Llandrindod Wells E Wales, UK
97 J18 Llandudno N Wales, UK
97 I21 Llanelli prev. Llanelly. SW Wales, UK
Llanelly see Llanelli
104 M2 Llanes Asturias, N Spain
97 K19 Llangollen NE Wales, UK
25 R10 Llano Texas, SW USA
25 Q10 Llano River Texas, SW USA
54 I9 Llanos physical region Colombia/Venezuela
63 G16 Llanquihue, Lago S Chile
Llansá see Llançà
105 U5 Lleida Cast. Lérida; anc. Ilerda. Cataluña, NE Spain
105 U5 Lérida ◈ province Cataluña, NE Spain
104 K12 Llerena Extremadura, W Spain
105 S9 Lliria País Valenciano, E Spain
105 W4 Llivia Cataluña, NE Spain
105 O3 Llodio País Vasco, N Spain
105 X5 Lloret de Mar Cataluña, NE Spain
Llorri see Tossal de l'Orri
10 L11 Lloyd George, Mount ▲ British Columbia, W Canada
9 R14 Lloydminster Alberta/Saskatchewan, SW Canada
105 X9 Llucmajor Mallorca, Spain, W Mediterranean Sea
36 L6 Loa Utah, W USA
169 S8 Loagan Bunut East Malaysia
38 G12 Loa, Mauna ▲ Hawaii, USA
Loanda see Luanda
79 J22 Loange S Dem. Rep. Congo
79 E21 Loango Le Kouilou, S Congo
106 B10 Loano Liguria, NW Italy
62 H4 Loa, Río N Chile
83 I20 Lobatse var. Lobatsi. Kgatleng, SE Botswana
Lobatsi see Lobatse
101 Q15 Löbau Sachsen, E Germany
79 H16 Lobaye ◈ prefecture SW Central African Republic
79 I16 Lobaye SW Central African Republic
99 G21 Lobbes Hainaut, S Belgium
61 D23 Lobería Buenos Aires, E Argentina
110 F8 Łobez Ger. Labes. Zacodnio-pomorskie, NW Poland
82 A13 Lobito Benguela, W Angola
Lobkovichi see Labkovichy
Lob Nor see Lop Nur
171 V13 Lobo Papua, E Indonesia
104 J11 Lobón Extremadura, W Spain
61 D20 Lobos Buenos Aires, E Argentina
40 E4 Lobos, Cabo headland NW Mexico
40 F6 Lobos, Isla island NW Mexico
Lobositz see Lovosice
Lobsens see Łobżenica
Loburi see Lop Buri
110 H9 Łobżenica Ger. Lobsens. Wielkopolskie, C Poland
108 G11 Locarno Ger. Luggarus. Ticino, S Switzerland
96 E9 Lochboisdale NW Scotland, UK
98 N11 Lochem Gelderland, E Netherlands
102 M8 Loches Indre-et-Loire, C France
Loch Garman see Wexford
96 H12 Lochgilphead W Scotland, UK
96 H7 Lochinver N Scotland, UK
96 F8 Lochmaddy NW Scotland, UK
96 J10 Lochnagar ▲ C Scotland, UK
99 E17 Lochristi Oost-Vlaanderen, NW Belgium
96 H9 Lochy, Loch N Scotland, UK
182 G8 Lock South Australia
97 J14 Lockerbie S Scotland, UK
27 S13 Lockesburg Arkansas, C USA
183 P10 Lockhart New South Wales, SE Australia
25 S11 Lockhart Texas, SW USA
18 F13 Lock Haven Pennsylvania, NE USA
25 N4 Lockney Texas, SW USA
100 O12 Löcknitz NE Germany
18 E9 Lockport New York, NE USA
167 T13 Lôc Ninh Sông Be, S Vietnam
107 N23 Locri Calabria, SW Italy
Locse see Levoča
27 T2 Locust Creek Missouri, C USA
23 P3 Locust Fork Alabama, S USA
27 Q9 Locust Grove Oklahoma, C USA
94 E11 Lodalskåpa ▲ S Norway
183 N10 Loddon River Victoria, SE Australia
Lodensee see Klooga
103 P15 Lodève anc. Luteva. Hérault, S France
124 I12 Lodeynoye Pole Leningradskaya Oblast', NW Russian Federation
33 V11 Lodge Grass Montana, NW USA
28 J15 Lodgepole Creek Nebraska/Wyoming, C USA
149 T11 Lodhrān Punjab, E Pakistan
106 D8 Lodi Lombardia, NW Italy
35 O8 Lodi California, W USA
31 T12 Lodi Ohio, N USA
92 H10 Lødingen Nordland, C Norway
79 L20 Lodja Kasai Oriental, C Dem. Rep. Congo
37 O3 Lodore, Canyon of canyon Colorado, C USA
105 Q4 Lodosa Navarra, N Spain
81 H16 Lodwar Rift Valley, NW Kenya
110 K12 Łódź Rus. Lodz. Łódzkie, C Poland
110 E12 Łódzkie ◈ province C Poland
167 P8 Loei var. Loey, Muang Loei. Loei, C Thailand
98 I11 Loenen Utrecht, C Netherlands
167 R9 Loeng Nok Tha Yasothon, E Thailand
83 F24 Loeriesfontein Northern Cape, W South Africa
Loewoek see Luwuk
Loey see Loei
76 J16 Lofa N Liberia
109 P6 Lofer Salzburg, C Austria
92 F11 Lofoten var. Lofoten Islands. island group C Norway
Lofoten Islands see Lofoten
95 N18 Loftahammar Kalmar, S Sweden
127 O10 Log Volgogradskaya Oblast', SW Russian Federation
77 S12 Loga Dosso, SW Niger
29 S14 Logan Iowa, C USA
26 K3 Logan Kansas, C USA
31 T14 Logan Ohio, N USA
36 L1 Logan Utah, W USA
21 P6 Logan West Virginia, NE USA
35 Y10 Logandale Nevada, W USA
19 O11 Logan International ✈ (Boston) Massachusetts, NE USA
9 N16 Logan Lake British Columbia, SW Canada
23 Q4 Logan Martin Lake Alabama, S USA
10 G8 Logan, Mount ▲ Yukon Territory, W Canada
32 I7 Logan, Mount ▲ Washington, NW USA
33 P7 Logan Pass pass Montana, NW USA
31 O12 Logansport Indiana, N USA
22 F6 Logansport Louisiana, S USA
Logar see Lowgar
67 R11 Loge NW Angola
Logishin see Lahishyn
Log na Coille see Lugnaquillia Mountain
78 G11 Logone var. Lagone. Cameroon/Chad
78 G13 Logone-Occidental off. Préfecture du Logone-Occidental. ◈ prefecture SW Chad
78 H13 Logone Occidental SW Chad
Logone-Occidental, Préfecture du see Logone-Occidental
78 G13 Logone-Oriental off. Préfecture du Logone-Oriental. ◈ prefecture SW Chad
78 H13 Logone Oriental SW Chad
Logone Oriental see Pendé
Logone-Oriental, Préfecture du see Logone-Oriental
L'Ogooué-Ivindo see Ogooué-Ivindo
L'Ogooué-Lolo see Ogooué-Lolo
L'Ogooué-Maritime see Ogooué-Maritime
Logoysk see Lahoysk
105 P4 Logroño anc. Vareia, Lat. Juliobriga. La Rioja, N Spain
104 L10 Logrosán Extremadura, W Spain
95 G20 Løgstør Nordjylland, N Denmark
95 H22 Løgten Århus, C Denmark
95 F24 Løgumkloster Sønderjylland, SW Denmark
Lögurinn see Lagarfljót
153 P15 Lohārdaga Jhārkhand, N India
152 H10 Lohāru Haryāna, N India
101 D15 Lohausen ✈ (Düsseldorf) Nordrhein-Westfalen, W Germany
189 O14 Lohd Pohnpei, E Micronesia
92 L12 Lohiniva Lappi, N Finland
Lohiszyn see Lahishyn
93 L20 Lohja var. Lojo. Etelä-Suomi, S Finland
169 V11 Lohjanan Borneo, C Indonesia
25 Q9 Lohn Texas, SW USA
100 G12 Lohne Niedersachsen, NW Germany
Lohr see Lohr am Main
101 I18 Lohr am Main var. Lohr. Bayern, C Germany
109 T10 Loibl Pass Ger. Loiblpass, Slvn. Ljubelj. pass Austria/Slovenia
Loiblpass see Loibl Pass
167 N6 Loi-Kaw Kayah State, C Myanmar (Burma)
93 K19 Loimaa Länsi-Soumi, SW Finland
103 O6 Loing C France
167 R6 Loi, Phou ▲ N Laos
102 L7 Loir C France
103 Q11 Loire ◈ department E France
102 M7 Loire var. Liger. C France
102 I7 Loire-Atlantique ◈ department NW France
103 O7 Loiret ◈ department C France
102 M8 Loir-et-Cher ◈ department C France
101 L24 Loisach SE Germany
56 B9 Loja Loja, S Ecuador
104 M14 Loja Andalucía, S Spain
56 B9 Loja ◈ province S Ecuador
Lojo see Lohja
116 J4 Lokachi Volyns'ka Oblast', NW Ukraine
79 M20 Lokandu Maniema, C Dem. Rep. Congo
92 M11 Lokan Tekojärvi NE Finland
137 Z11 Lökbatan Rus. Lokbatan. E Azerbaijan
Lokbatan see Lökbatan
99 F17 Lokeren Oost-Vlaanderen, NW Belgium
Lokhvitsa see Lokhvytsya
117 S4 Lokhvytsya Rus. Lokhvitsa. Poltavs'ka Oblast', NE Ukraine
81 H17 Lokichar Rift Valley, NW Kenya
81 G16 Lokichokio Rift Valley, NW Kenya
81 H16 Lokitaung Rift Valley, NW Kenya
92 M11 Lokka Lappi, N Finland
94 G8 Løkken Verk Sør-Trøndelag, S Norway
124 G16 Loknya Pskovskaya Oblast', W Russian Federation
77 V15 Loko Nassarawa, C Nigeria
77 U15 Lokoja Kogi, C Nigeria
81 H17 Lokori Rift Valley, W Kenya
77 R16 Lokossa S Benin
118 I3 Loksa Ger. Loxa. Harjumaa, NW Estonia
9 T7 Loks Land island Nunavut, NE Canada
80 C13 Lol S Sudan
76 K15 Lola Guinée-Forestière, SE Guinea
35 Q5 Lola, Mount ▲ California, W USA
81 H20 Loliondo Arusha, NE Tanzania
95 H25 Lolland prev. Laaland. island S Denmark
186 G6 Lolobau Island island E Papua New Guinea
79 E16 Lolodorf Sud, SW Cameroon
114 G7 Lom prev. Lom-Palanka. Montana, NW Bulgaria
114 G7 Lom NW Bulgaria
79 M19 Lomami C Dem. Rep. Congo
57 F17 Lomas Arequipa, SW Peru
63 I23 Lomas, Bahía bay S Chile
61 D20 Lomas de Zamora Buenos Aires, E Argentina
61 D20 Loma Verde Buenos Aires, E Argentina
180 K4 Lombadina Western Australia
106 E6 Lombardia Eng. Lombardy. ◈ region N Italy
Lombardy see Lombardia
102 M15 Lombez Gers, S France
171 Q16 Lomblen, Pulau island Nusa Tenggara, S Indonesia
173 W7 Lombok Basin undersea feature E Indian Ocean
170 L16 Lombok, Pulau island Nusa Tenggara, C Indonesia
77 Q16 Lomé ● (Togo) S Togo
77 Q16 Lomé ✈ S Togo
79 L19 Lomela Kasai Oriental, C Dem. Rep. Congo
25 R9 Lometa Texas, SW USA
79 F16 Lomié Est, SE Cameroon
30 M8 Lomira Wisconsin, N USA
95 K23 Lomma Skåne, S Sweden
99 J16 Lommel Limburg, N Belgium
96 I11 Lomond, Loch C Scotland, UK
197 R9 Lomonosov Ridge var. Harris Ridge, Rus. Khrebet Homonsova. undersea feature Arctic Ocean
Lomonsova, Khrebet see Lomonosov Ridge
Lom-Palanka see Lom
Lomphat see Lumphăt
35 P14 Lompoc California, W USA
167 P9 Lom Sak var. Muang Lom Sak. Phetchabun, C Thailand
110 N9 Łomża Rus. Lomzha. Podlaskie, NE Poland
Lomzha see Łomża
Lonaula see Lonāvale
155 D14 Lonāvale prev. Lonaula. Mahārāshtra, W India
63 G15 Loncoche Araucanía, C Chile
63 H14 Loncopue Neuquén, W Argentina
99 G17 Londerzeel Vlaams Brabant, C Belgium
Londinium see London
14 E16 London Ontario, S Canada
191 Y2 London Kiritimati, E Kiribati
97 O22 London anc. Augusta, Lat. Londinium. ● (UK) SE England, UK
21 N7 London Kentucky, S USA
31 S13 London Ohio, NE USA
25 Q10 London Texas, SW USA
97 O22 London City ✈ SE England, UK
97 E14 Londonderry var. Derry, Ir. Doire. NW Northern Ireland, UK
97 F14 Londonderry cultural region NW Northern Ireland, UK
180 M2 Londonderry, Cape cape Western Australia
63 H25 Londonderry, Isla island S Chile
43 O7 Londres, Cayos reef NE Nicaragua
60 I10 Londrina Paraná, S Brazil
27 N13 Lone Grove Oklahoma, C USA
14 E12 Lonely Island island Ontario, S Canada
35 T8 Lone Mountain ▲ Nevada, W USA
25 V6 Lone Oak Texas, SW USA
35 T11 Lone Pine California, W USA
Lone Star State see Texas
83 D14 Longa Cuando Cubango, C Angola
82 B12 Longa W Angola
83 E15 Longa SE Angola
Long'an see Pingwu
197 S4 Longa, Proliv Eng. Long Strait. strait NE Russian Federation
44 J13 Long Bay bay W Jamaica
21 V13 Long Bay bay North Carolina/South Carolina, E USA
35 T16 Long Beach California, W USA
22 M9 Long Beach Mississippi, S USA
18 L14 Long Beach Long Island, New York, NE USA
32 F9 Long Beach Washington, NW USA
18 K16 Long Beach Island island New Jersey, NE USA
65 M25 Longbluff headland SW Tristan da Cunha
23 U13 Longboat Key island Florida, SE USA
18 K15 Long Branch New Jersey, NE USA
44 J5 Long Cay island SE Bahamas
Longcheng see Xiaoxian
161 P14 Longchuan var. Laolong. Guangdong, S China
Longchuan see Nanhua
Longchuan Jiang see Shweli
32 K12 Long Creek Oregon, NW USA
159 W10 Longde Ningxia, N China
183 P16 Longford Tasmania, SE Australia
97 D17 Longford Ir. An Longfort. Longford, C Ireland
97 E17 Longford Ir. An Longfort. ◈ county C Ireland
Longgang see Dazu
163 W11 Longgang Shan ⛰ NE China
161 P1 Longhua Hebei, E China
169 U11 Longiram Borneo, C Indonesia
44 J4 Long Island island C Bahamas
12 H8 Long Island island Northwest Territories, C Canada
186 D7 Long Island var. Arop Island. island N Papua New Guinea
18 L14 Long Island island New York, NE USA
Long Island see Bermuda
18 M14 Long Island Sound sound NE USA
163 U7 Longjiang Heilongjiang, NE China
160 K13 Long Jiang S China
163 Y10 Longjing var. Yanji. Jilin, NE China
161 R4 Longkou Shandong, E China
12 E11 Longlac Ontario, S Canada
19 S1 Long Lake Maine, NE USA
31 R5 Long Lake Michigan, N USA
31 O6 Long Lake Michigan, N USA
29 N6 Long Lake North Dakota, N USA
30 J4 Long Lake Wisconsin, N USA
99 K23 Longlier Luxembourg, SE Belgium
160 I13 Longlin var. Longlin Gezu Zizhixian, Xinzhou. Guangxi Zhuangzu Zizhiqu, S China
Longlin Gezu Zizhixian see Longlin
37 T3 Longmont Colorado, C USA
157 P10 Longnan var. Wudu. Gansu, C China
29 N13 Long Pine Nebraska, C USA
Longping see Luodian
14 F17 Long Point headland Ontario, S Canada
14 K15 Long Point headland Ontario, SE Canada
184 P10 Long Point headland North Island, New Zealand
30 L2 Long Point headland Michigan, N USA
14 G17 Long Point Bay lake bay Ontario, S Canada
29 T7 Long Prairie Minnesota, N USA
Longquan see Fenggang
13 S11 Long Range Mountains hill range Newfoundland, Newfoundland and Labrador, E Canada
65 H25 Long Range Point headland SE Saint Helena
181 V8 Longreach Queensland, E Australia
160 H7 Longriba Sichuan, C China
160 L10 Longshan var. Min'an. Hunan, S China
37 S3 Longs Peak ▲ Colorado, C USA
Long Strait see Longa, Proliv
102 K8 Longué Maine-et-Loire, NW France
13 P11 Longue-Pointe Québec, E Canada
103 S4 Longuyon Meurthe-et-Moselle, NE France
25 W7 Longview Texas, SW USA
32 G10 Longview Washington, NW USA
65 H25 Longwood C Saint Helena
25 P7 Longworth Texas, SW USA
103 S3 Longwy Meurthe-et-Moselle, NE France
159 V11 Longxi Gansu, C China
Longxian see Wengyuan
167 S14 Long Xuyên var. Longxuyen. An Giang, S Vietnam
Longxuyen see Long Xuyên
161 Q13 Longyan Fujian, SE China
92 O3 Longyearbyen ○ (Svalbard) Spitsbergen, W Svalbard
160 J15 Longzhou Guangxi Zhuangzu Zizhiqu, S China
Longzhouping see Changyang
100 F12 Löningen Niedersachsen, NW Germany
27 V11 Lonoke Arkansas, C USA
95 L21 Lönsboda Skåne, S Sweden
103 S9 Lons-le-Saunier anc. Ledo Salinarius. Jura, E France
31 O15 Loogootee Indiana, N USA
31 Q9 Looking Glass River Michigan, N USA
21 X11 Lookout, Cape cape North Carolina, SE USA
39 O6 Lookout Ridge ridge Alaska, USA
181 N11 Loongana Western Australia
99 I14 Loon op Zand Noord-Brabant, S Netherlands
97 A19 Loop Head Ir. Ceann Léime. promontory W Ireland
109 V4 Loosdorf Niederösterreich, NE Austria
158 G10 Lop Xinjiang Uygur Zizhiqu, NW China
112 J11 Lopare ◈ Republika Srpska, NE Bosnia and Herzegovina
Lopatichi see Lapatsichy
127 Q15 Lopatin Respublika Dagestan, SW Russian Federation
127 P7 Lopatino Penzenskaya Oblast', W Russian Federation
167 P10 Lop Buri var. Loburi. Lop Buri, C Thailand
25 R16 Lopeno Texas, SW USA
79 C18 Lopez, Cap cape W Gabon
98 I12 Lopik Utrecht, C Netherlands
Lop Nor see Lop Nur
158 M7 Lop Nur var. Lob Nor, Lop Nor, Lo-pu Po. seasonal lake NW China
Lopnur see Yuli
79 K17 Lopori NW Dem. Rep. Congo
98 O5 Loppersum Groningen, NE Netherlands
92 I8 Lopphavet sound N Norway
Lo-pu Po see Lop Nur
Lora see Lowrah
182 F3 Lora Creek seasonal river South Australia
104 K13 Lora del Río Andalucía, S Spain
148 M11 Lora, Hāmūn-i wetland SW Pakistan
31 T11 Lorain Ohio, N USA
25 O7 Loraine Texas, SW USA
31 R13 Loramie, Lake Ohio, N USA
105 Q13 Lorca Ar. Lurka; anc. Eliocroca, Lat. Illurco. Murcia, S Spain
192 I10 Lord Howe Island island E Australia
Lord Howe Island see Ontong Java Atoll
175 O10 Lord Howe Rise undersea feature SW Pacific Ocean
192 J10 Lord Howe Seamounts undersea feature W Pacific Ocean
37 P15 Lordsburg New Mexico, SW USA
186 E5 Lorengau var. Lorungau. Manus Island, N Papua New Guinea
25 N5 Lorenzo Texas, SW USA
142 K7 Lorestān off. Ostān-e Lorestān, var. Luristan. ◈ province W Iran
Lorestān, Ostān-e see Lorestān
57 M17 Loreto Beni, N Bolivia
106 J12 Loreto Marche, C Italy
40 F8 Loreto Baja California Sur, W Mexico
40 M11 Loreto Zacatecas, C Mexico
56 E9 Loreto off. Departamento de Loreto. ◈ department NE Peru
Loreto, Departamento de see Loreto
81 K18 Lorian Swamp swamp E Kenya
54 E6 Lorica Córdoba, NW Colombia
102 G7 Lorient prev. l'Orient. Morbihan, NW France
l'Orient see Lorient
111 K22 Lőrinci Heves, NE Hungary
14 G11 Loring Ontario, S Canada
33 V6 Loring Montana, NW USA
103 R13 Loriol-sur-Drôme Drôme, E France
21 U12 Loris South Carolina, SE USA
57 I18 Loriscota, Laguna S Peru
183 N13 Lorne Victoria, SE Australia
96 G11 Lorn, Firth of inlet W Scotland, UK
Loro Sae see East Timor
101 F24 Lörrach Baden-Württemberg, S Germany

◆ Country ● Country Capital ◇ Dependent Territory ○ Dependent Territory Capital ◈ Administrative Regions ✈ International Airport ▲ Mountain ⛰ Mountain Range Volcano River Lake Reservoir

103 T5 **Lorraine** ⬖ region NE France
Lorungau *see* Lorengau
94 L11 **Los** Gävleborg, C Sweden
35 P14 **Los Alamos** California, W USA
37 S10 **Los Alamos** New Mexico, SW USA
42 F5 **Los Amates** Izabal, E Guatemala
63 G14 **Los Ángeles** Bío Bío, C Chile
35 S15 **Los Angeles** California, W USA
35 S15 **Los Angeles** ✈ California, W USA
35 T13 **Los Angeles Aqueduct** aqueduct California, W USA
Losanna *see* Lausanne
63 H20 **Los Antiguos** Santa Cruz, SW Argentina
189 Q16 **Losap Atoll** atoll C Micronesia
35 P10 **Los Banos** California, W USA
104 K16 **Los Barrios** Andalucía, S Spain
62 L5 **Los Blancos** Salta, N Argentina
42 L12 **Los Chiles** Alajuela, NW Costa Rica
105 O2 **Los Corrales de Buelna** Cantabria, N Spain
25 T17 **Los Fresnos** Texas, SW USA
35 N9 **Los Gatos** California, W USA
110 O11 **Łosice** Mazowieckie, C Poland
112 B11 **Lošinj** Ger. Lussin, It. Lussino. island W Croatia
Los Jardines *see* Ngetik Atoll
63 G15 **Los Lagos** Los Lagos, C Chile
63 F17 **Los Lagos** off. Región de los Lagos. ⬖ region C Chile
los Lagos, Región de *see* Los Lagos
Loslau *see* Wodzisław Śląski
64 N11 **Los Llanos** var. Los Llanos de Aridane. La Palma, Islas Canarias, Spain, NE Atlantic Ocean
Los Llanos de Aridane *see* Los Llanos
37 R11 **Los Lunas** New Mexico, SW USA
63 I16 **Los Menucos** Río Negro, C Argentina
40 H8 **Los Mochis** Sinaloa, C Mexico
35 N4 **Los Molinos** California, W USA
104 M9 **Los Navalmorales** Castilla-La Mancha, C Spain
25 S15 **Los Olmos Creek** ≈ Texas, SW USA
Losonc/Losontz *see* Lučenec
167 S5 **Lô, Sông** var. Panlong Jiang. ≈ China/Vietnam
44 B5 **Los Palacios** Pinar del Río, W Cuba
104 K14 **Los Palacios y Villafranca** Andalucía, S Spain
37 R12 **Los Pinos Mountains** ▲▲ New Mexico, SW USA
37 R11 **Los Ranchos de Albuquerque** New Mexico, SW USA
40 M14 **Los Reyes** Michoacán de Ocampo, SW Mexico
56 B7 **Los Ríos** ⬖ province C Ecuador
64 O11 **Los Rodeos** ✈ (Santa Cruz de Tenerife) Tenerife, Islas Canarias, Spain, NE Atlantic Ocean
54 L4 **Los Roques, Islas** island group N Venezuela
43 S17 **Los Santos** Los Santos, S Panama
43 S17 **Los Santos** off. Provincia de Los Santos. ⬖ province S Panama
Los Santos *see* Los Santos de Maimona
104 J12 **Los Santos de Maimona** var. Los Santos. Extremadura, W Spain
Los Santos, Provincia de *see* Los Santos
98 P10 **Losser** Overijssel, E Netherlands
96 J8 **Lossiemouth** NE Scotland, UK
61 B14 **Los Tábanos** Santa Fe, C Argentina
54 J4 **Los Taques** Falcón, N Venezuela
14 G11 **Lost Channel** Ontario, S Canada
54 L5 **Los Teques** Miranda, N Venezuela
35 Q12 **Lost Hills** California, W USA
36 J7 **Lost Peak** ▲ Utah, W USA
33 P11 **Lost Trail Pass** pass Montana, NW USA
186 G9 **Losuia** Kiriwina Island, SE Papua New Guinea
62 G10 **Los Vilos** Coquimbo, C Chile
105 N10 **Los Yébenes** Castilla-La Mancha, C Spain
103 N13 **Lot** ⬖ department S France
103 N13 **Lot** ≈ S France
63 F14 **Lota** Bío Bío, C Chile
81 G15 **Lotagipi Swamp** wetland Kenya/Sudan
102 K14 **Lot-et-Garonne** ⬖ department SW France
83 K21 **Lothair** Mpumalanga, NE South Africa
33 R7 **Lothair** Montana, NW USA
79 L20 **Loto** Kasai Oriental, C Dem. Rep. Congo
108 E10 **Lötschbergtunnel** tunnel Valais, SW Switzerland
25 T9 **Lott** Texas, SW USA
124 H3 **Lotta** var. Lutto. ≈ Finland/Russian Federation
184 Q7 **Lottin Point** headland North Island, New Zealand
Loualaba *see* Lualaba
167 P6 **Louangnamtha** var. Luong Nam Tha. Louang Namtha, N Laos
167 Q7 **Louangphabang** var. Louangphrabang, Luang Prabang. Louangphabang, N Laos
Louangphabang *see* Louangphabang
194 H5 **Loubet Coast** physical region Antarctica
Loubomo *see* Dolisie
Louch *see* Loukhi
102 H6 **Loudéac** Côtes d'Armor, NW France
160 M11 **Loudi** Hunan, S China
79 F21 **Loudima** La Bouenza, S Congo
20 M9 **Loudon** Tennessee, S USA
31 T12 **Loudonville** Ohio, N USA
102 L8 **Loudun** Vienne, W France
102 K7 **Loué** Sarthe, NW France
76 G10 **Louga** NW Senegal
97 M19 **Loughborough** C England, UK
97 C18 **Loughrea** Ir. Baile Locha Riach. Galway, W Ireland
103 S9 **Louhans** Saône-et-Loire, C France
21 P5 **Louisa** Kentucky, S USA
21 V5 **Louisa** Virginia, NE USA
21 V9 **Louisburg** North Carolina, SE USA
25 U12 **Louise** Texas, SW USA
15 P11 **Louiseville** Québec, SE Canada
27 W3 **Louisiana** Missouri, C USA
22 G8 **Louisiana** off. State of Louisiana, also known as Creole State, Pelican State. ⬖ state S USA
83 K19 **Louis Trichardt** Northern, NE South Africa
23 V4 **Louisville** Georgia, SE USA
30 M15 **Louisville** Illinois, N USA
20 K5 **Louisville** Kentucky, S USA
22 M4 **Louisville** Mississippi, S USA
29 S15 **Louisville** Nebraska, C USA
192 L11 **Louisville Ridge** undersea feature S Pacific Ocean
124 J6 **Loukhi** var. Louch. Respublika Kareliya, NW Russian Federation
79 H19 **Loukoléla** Cuvette, E Congo
104 G14 **Loulé** Faro, S Portugal
111 C16 **Louny** Ger. Laun. Ústecký Kraj, NW Czech Republic
29 O15 **Loup City** Nebraska, C USA
29 P15 **Loup River** ≈ Nebraska, C USA
15 S9 **Loup, Rivière du** ≈ Québec, SE Canada
12 K7 **Loups Marins, Lacs des** ◎ Québec, NE Canada
102 K16 **Lourdes** Hautes-Pyrénées, S France
Lourenço Marques *see* Maputo
104 F11 **Loures** Lisboa, C Portugal
104 F10 **Lourinhã** Lisboa, C Portugal
115 C16 **Loúros** ≈ W Greece
104 G8 **Lousã** Coimbra, N Portugal
160 M10 **Lou Shui** ≈ C China
183 O5 **Louth** New South Wales, SE Australia
97 O18 **Louth** E England, UK
97 F17 **Louth** Ir. Lú. ⬖ county NE Ireland
115 H15 **Loutrá** Kentrikí Makedonía, N Greece
115 G19 **Loutráki** Pelopónnisos, S Greece
Louvain *see* Leuven
99 H19 **Louvain-la Neuve** Walloon Brabant, C Belgium
14 J8 **Louvicourt** Québec, SE Canada
102 M4 **Louviers** Eure, N France
30 K14 **Lou Yaeger, Lake** ⊠ Illinois, N USA
93 J15 **Lövånger** Västerbotten, N Sweden
124 J14 **Lovat'** ≈ NW Russian Federation
113 J17 **Lovćen** ▲ SW Montenegro
114 J8 **Lovech** Lovech, N Bulgaria
114 I9 **Lovech** ⬖ province N Bulgaria
25 V9 **Lovelady** Texas, SW USA
37 T3 **Loveland** Colorado, C USA
33 U12 **Lovell** Wyoming, C USA
Lovello, Monte *see* Grosser Löffler
35 S4 **Lovelock** Nevada, W USA
106 E7 **Lovere** Lombardia, N Italy
30 L10 **Loves Park** Illinois, N USA
26 M2 **Lovewell Reservoir** ⊠ Kansas, C USA
93 M19 **Loviisa** Swe. Lovisa. Etelä-Suomi, S Finland
37 V15 **Loving** New Mexico, SW USA
21 U6 **Lovingston** Virginia, NE USA
37 V14 **Lovington** New Mexico, SW USA
Lovisa *see* Loviisa
111 C15 **Lovosice** Ger. Lobositz. Ústecký Kraj, NW Czech Republic
124 K4 **Lovozero** Murmanskaya Oblast', NW Russian Federation
124 K4 **Lovozero, Ozero** ◎ NW Russian Federation
112 B9 **Lovran** It. Laurana. Primorje-Gorski Kotar, NW Croatia
116 E11 **Lovrin** Ger. Lowrin. Timiş, W Romania
82 E10 **Lóvua** Lunda Norte, NE Angola
82 G12 **Lóvua** Moxico, E Angola
65 D25 **Low Bay** bay East Falkland, Falkland Islands
9 P9 **Low, Cape** headland Nunavut, E Canada
33 N10 **Lowell** Idaho, NW USA
19 O10 **Lowell** Massachusetts, NE USA
Löwen *see* Leuven
Löwenberg in Schlesien *see* Lwówek Śląski
Lower Austria *see* Niederösterreich
Lower Bann *see* Bann
Lower California *see* Baja California
Lower Danube *see* Niederösterreich
185 L14 **Lower Hutt** Wellington, North Island, New Zealand
39 N11 **Lower Kalskag** Alaska, USA
35 O1 **Lower Klamath Lake** ◎ California, W USA
35 Q2 **Lower Lake** ◎ California/Nevada, W USA
97 E15 **Lower Lough Erne** ◎ SW Northern Ireland, UK
Lower Lusatia *see* Niederlausitz
Lower Normandy *see* Basse-Normandie
10 K9 **Lower Post** British Columbia, W Canada
29 T4 **Lower Red Lake** ◎ Minnesota, N USA
Lower Rhine *see* Neder Rijn
Lower Saxony *see* Niedersachsen
97 Q19 **Lowestoft** E England, UK
149 Q5 **Lowgar** var. Logar. ⬖ province E Afghanistan
182 H7 **Low Hill** South Australia
110 K12 **Łowicz** Łódzkie, C Poland
33 N13 **Lowman** Idaho, NW USA
149 P8 **Lowrah** var. Lora. ≈ SE Afghanistan
Lowrin *see* Lovrin
183 N17 **Low Rocky Point** headland Tasmania, SE Australia
18 I8 **Lowville** New York, NE USA
Loxa *see* Loksa
182 K9 **Loxton** South Australia
81 G21 **Loya** Tabora, C Tanzania
30 K6 **Loyal** Wisconsin, N USA
18 G13 **Loyalsock Creek** ≈ Pennsylvania, NE USA
35 Q5 **Loyalton** California, W USA
Lo-yang *see* Luoyang
187 Q16 **Loyauté, Îles** island group S New Caledonia
Loyev *see* Loyew
119 O20 **Loyew** Rus. Loyev. Homyel'skaya Voblasts', SE Belarus
125 S13 **Loyno** Kirovskaya Oblast', NW Russian Federation
103 P13 **Lozère** ⬖ department S France
103 Q14 **Lozère, Mont** ▲ S France
112 J11 **Loznica** Serbia, W Serbia
117 V7 **Lozova** Rus. Lozovaya. Kharkivs'ka Oblast', E Ukraine
Lozovaya *see* Lozova
105 N7 **Lozoyuela** Madrid, C Spain
Lu *see* Shandong
Lú *see* Louth
82 F12 **Luacano** Moxico, E Angola
79 N21 **Lualaba** Fr. Loualaba. ≈ SE Dem. Rep. Congo
83 H14 **Luampa** Western, NW Zambia
83 H15 **Luampa Kuta** Western, W Zambia
161 P8 **Lu'an** Anhui, E China
104 K2 **Luanco** Asturias, N Spain
82 A11 **Luanda** var. Loanda, Port. São Paulo de Loanda. ● Luanda, NW Angola
82 A11 **Luanda** ⬖ province (Angola) NW Angola
82 A11 **Luanda** ✈ Luanda, NW Angola
82 D12 **Luando** ≈ C Angola
Luang *see* Tapi, Mae Nam
83 G14 **Luanginga** var. Luanguinga. ≈ Angola/Zambia
167 N15 **Luang, Khao** ▲ SW Thailand
Luang Prabang *see* Louangphabang
167 P8 **Luang Prabang Range** Th. Thiukhaoluang Phrahang. ▲▲ Laos/Thailand
167 N16 **Luang, Thale** lagoon S Thailand
Luangua, Rio *see* Luangwa
82 E11 **Luangue** ≈ NE Angola
Luanguinga *see* Luanginga
83 K15 **Luangwa** var. Aruângua. Lusaka, C Zambia
83 K14 **Luangwa** , var. Rio Luangua. ≈ Mozambique/Zambia
161 Q2 **Luan He** ≈ E China
190 G11 **Luaniva, Île** island E Wallis and Futuna
161 P2 **Luanping** var. Anjiangying. Hebei, E China
82 J13 **Luanshya** Copperbelt, C Zambia
62 K13 **Luan Toro** La Pampa, C Argentina
161 Q2 **Luanxian** var. Luan Xian. Hebei, E China
Luan Xian *see* Luanxian
82 J12 **Luapula** ⬖ province N Zambia
79 O25 **Luapula** ≈ Dem. Rep. Congo/Zambia
104 J2 **Luarca** Asturias, N Spain
169 R10 **Luar, Danau** ◎ Borneo, N Indonesia
79 L25 **Luashi** Katanga, S Dem. Rep. Congo
82 G12 **Luau** Port. Vila Teixeira de Sousa. Moxico, NE Angola
79 C16 **Luba** prev. San Carlos. Isla de Bioco, NW Equatorial Guinea
42 F4 **Lubaantun** ruins Toledo, S Belize
111 P16 **Lubaczów** var. Lúbaczów. Podkarpackie, SE Poland
Lubale *see* Lubalo
82 E11 **Lubalo** Lunda Norte, NE Angola
82 E11 **Lubalo** var. Lubale. ≈ Angola/Dem. Rep. Congo
118 J9 **Lubāna** Madona, E Latvia
Lubānas Ezers *see* Lubāns
171 N4 **Lubang Island** island N Philippines
83 B15 **Lubango** Port. Sá da Bandeira. Huíla, SW Angola
118 J9 **Lubāns** var. Lubānas Ezers. ◎ E Latvia
79 M21 **Lubao** Kasai Oriental, C Dem. Rep. Congo
110 O13 **Lubartów** Ger. Qumälisch. Lublin, E Poland
100 G13 **Lübbecke** Nordrhein-Westfalen, NW Germany
100 O13 **Lübben** Brandenburg, E Germany
101 P14 **Lübbenau** Brandenburg, E Germany
25 N5 **Lubbock** Texas, SW USA
Lubcz *see* Lyubcha
19 U6 **Lubec** Maine, NE USA
100 K9 **Lübeck** Schleswig-Holstein, N Germany
100 K8 **Lübecker Bucht** bay N Germany
79 M21 **Lubefu** Kasai Oriental, C Dem. Rep. Congo
163 T10 **Lubei** var. Jarud Qi. Nei Mongol Zizhiqu, N China
111 O14 **Lubelska, Wyżyna** plateau SE Poland
110 O13 **Lubelskie** ⬖ province E Poland
Lubembe *see* Luembe
Lüben *see* Lubin
144 H9 **Lubenka** Zapadnyy Kazakhstan, W Kazakhstan
79 P18 **Lubero** Nord Kivu, E Dem. Rep. Congo
79 L22 **Lubi** ≈ S Dem. Rep. Congo
Lubiana *see* Ljubljana
110 J11 **Lubień Kujawski** Kujawsko-pomorskie, C Poland
67 T11 **Lubilandji** ≈ S Dem. Rep. Congo
110 F13 **Lubin** Ger. Lüben. Dolnośląskie, SW Poland
111 O14 **Lublin** Rus. Lyublin. Lubelskie, E Poland
111 J15 **Lubliniec** Śląskie, S Poland
Lubnān, Jabal *see* Liban, Jebel
117 R5 **Lubny** Poltavs'ka Oblast', NE Ukraine
Luboml *see* Lyuboml'
110 G11 **Luboń** Ger. Peterhof. Wielkolpolskie, C Poland
110 D12 **Lubsko** Ger. Sommerfeld. Lubuskie, W Poland
79 N24 **Lubudi** Katanga, SE Dem. Rep. Congo
168 L13 **Lubukilinggau** Sumatera, W Indonesia
79 N25 **Lubumbashi** prev. Élisabethville. Shaba, SE Dem. Rep. Congo
83 I14 **Lubungu** Central, C Zambia
110 E12 **Lubuskie** ⬖ province W Poland
Lubuskie *see* Dobiegniew
79 N18 **Lubutu** Maniema, E Dem. Rep. Congo
Luca *see* Lucca
82 C11 **Lucala** ≈ W Angola
14 E16 **Lucan** Ontario, S Canada
97 F18 **Lucan** Ir. Leamhcán. Dublin, E Ireland
Lucanian Mountains *see* Lucano, Appennino
107 M18 **Lucano, Appennino** Eng. Lucanian Mountains. ▲▲ S Italy
82 F11 **Lucapa** var. Lukapa. Lunda Norte, NE Angola
29 V15 **Lucas** Iowa, C USA
61 C18 **Lucas González** Entre Ríos, E Argentina
65 C25 **Lucas Point** headland West Falkland, Falkland Islands
31 S15 **Lucasville** Ohio, N USA
106 F11 **Lucca** anc. Luca. Toscana, C Italy
44 H12 **Lucea** W Jamaica
97 H15 **Luce Bay** inlet SW Scotland, UK
22 M8 **Lucedale** Mississippi, S USA
171 O4 **Lucena** off. Lucena City. Luzon, N Philippines
104 M14 **Lucena** Andalucía, S Spain
Lucena City *see* Lucena
105 S8 **Lucena del Cid** País Valenciano, E Spain
111 D15 **Lučenec** Ger. Losontz, Hung. Losonc. Banskobystrický Kraj, C Slovakia
Lucentum *see* Alicante
107 M16 **Lucera** Puglia, SE Italy
Lucerna/Lucerne *see* Luzern
Lucerne, Lake of *see* Vierwaldstätter See
40 J4 **Lucero** Chihuahua, N Mexico
123 S14 **Luchegorsk** Primorskiy Kray, SE Russian Federation
105 Q13 **Luchena** ≈ SE Spain
Lucheng *see* Kangding
82 N13 **Lucheringo** var. Luchulingo. ≈ N Mozambique
Luchesa *see* Luchosa
Luchin *see* Luchyn
118 N13 **Luchosa** Rus. Luchesa. ≈ N Belarus
100 K11 **Lüchow** Mecklenburg-Vorpommern, N Germany
Luchow *see* Hefei
Luchulingo *see* Lucheringo
119 N17 **Luchyn** Rus. Luchin. Homyel'skaya Voblasts', SE Belarus
55 U11 **Lucie Rivier** ≈ W Suriname
182 K11 **Lucindale** South Australia
83 A14 **Lucira** Namibe, SW Angola
Łuck *see* Luts'k
101 O14 **Luckau** Brandenburg, E Germany
100 N13 **Luckenwalde** Brandenburg, E Germany
14 E15 **Lucknow** Ontario, S Canada
152 L12 **Lucknow** var. Lakhnau. state capital Uttar Pradesh, N India
102 J10 **Luçon** Vendée, NW France
44 I7 **Lucrecia, Cabo** headland E Cuba
82 F13 **Lucusse** Moxico, E Angola
Luda *see* Dalian
114 M9 **Luda Kamchiya** ≈ E Bulgaria
Ludasch *see* Luduş
114 I10 **Luda Yana** ≈ C Bulgaria
112 F7 **Ludbreg** Varaždin, N Croatia
29 P7 **Ludden** North Dakota, N USA
101 F15 **Lüdenscheid** Nordrhein-Westfalen, W Germany
83 C21 **Lüderitz** prev. Angra Pequena. Karas, SW Namibia
152 H8 **Ludhiāna** Punjab, N India
31 O7 **Ludington** Michigan, N USA
97 K20 **Ludlow** W England, UK
35 W14 **Ludlow** California, W USA
28 J7 **Ludlow** South Dakota, N USA
18 M9 **Ludlow** Vermont, NE USA
114 L7 **Ludogorie** physical region NE Bulgaria
23 W6 **Ludowici** Georgia, SE USA
Ludsan *see* Ludza
116 I10 **Luduş** Ger. Ludasch, Hung. Marosludas. Mureş, C Romania
95 M14 **Ludvika** Dalarna, C Sweden
101 H21 **Ludwigsburg** Baden-Württemberg, SW Germany
100 O13 **Ludwigsfelde** Brandenburg, NE Germany
101 G20 **Ludwigshafen** var. Ludwigshafen am Rhein. Rheinland-Pfalz, W Germany
Ludwigshafen am Rhein *see* Ludwigshafen
101 L20 **Ludwigskanal** canal SE Germany
100 L10 **Ludwigslust** Mecklenburg-Vorpommern, N Germany
118 K10 **Ludza** Ger. Ludsan. Ludza, E Latvia
79 K21 **Luebo** Kasai Occidental, SW Dem. Rep. Congo
25 Q6 **Lueders** Texas, SW USA
79 N20 **Lueki** Maniema, C Dem. Rep. Congo
82 F10 **Luembe** var. Lubembe. ≈ Angola/Dem. Rep. Congo
82 E13 **Luena** var. Lwena, Port. Luso. Moxico, E Angola
79 M24 **Luena** Katanga, SE Dem. Rep. Congo
82 K12 **Luena** Northern, NE Zambia
82 F13 **Luena** ≈ E Angola
83 F16 **Luengue** ≈ SE Angola
67 V13 **Luenha** ≈ W Mozambique
83 G15 **Lueti** ≈ Angola/Zambia
160 J7 **Lüeyang** var. Hejiayan. Shaanxi, C China
161 P14 **Lufeng** Guangdong, S China
79 N24 **Lufira** ≈ SE Dem. Rep. Congo
79 N25 **Lufira, Lac de Retenue de la** var. Lac Tshangalele. ◎ SE Dem. Rep. Congo
25 W8 **Lufkin** Texas, SW USA
82 L11 **Lufubu** ≈ N Zambia
124 G14 **Luga** Leningradskaya Oblast', NW Russian Federation
124 G13 **Luga** ≈ NW Russian Federation
Luganer See *see* Lugano, Lago di
108 H11 **Lugano** Ger. Lauis. Ticino, S Switzerland
108 H12 **Lugano, Lago di** var. Ceresio, Ger. Luganer See. ◎ S Switzerland
Lugansk *see* Luhans'k
187 Q13 **Luganville** Espiritu Santo, C Vanuatu
Lugdunum *see* Lyon
Lugdunum Batavorum *see* Leiden
83 O15 **Lugela** Zambézia, NE Mozambique
83 O16 **Lugela** ≈ C Mozambique
82 P13 **Lugenda, Rio** ≈ N Mozambique
Luggarus *see* Locarno
Lugh Ganana *see* Luuq
97 G19 **Lugnaquillia Mountain** Ir. Log na Coille. ▲ E Ireland
106 H10 **Lugo** Emilia-Romagna, N Italy
104 I3 **Lugo** anc. Lugus Augusti. Galicia, NW Spain
104 I3 **Lugo** ⬖ province Galicia, NW Spain
21 R12 **Lugoff** South Carolina, SE USA
116 F12 **Lugoj** Ger. Lugosch, Hung. Lugos. Timiş, W Romania
Lugos/Lugosch *see* Lugoj
Lugovoy/Lugovoye *see* Kulan
158 I13 **Lugu** Xizang Zizhiqu, W China
Lugus Augusti *see* Lugo
Luguvallium/Luguvallum *see* Carlisle
117 Y7 **Luhans'k** Rus. Lugansk; prev. Voroshilovgrad. Luhans'ka Oblast', E Ukraine
117 Y7 **Luhans'k** ✈ Luhans'ka Oblast', E Ukraine
Luhans'k *see* Luhans'ka Oblast'
117 X6 **Luhans'ka Oblast'** var. Luhans'k; prev. Voroshilovgrad, Rus. Voroshilovgradskaya Oblast'. ⬖ province E Ukraine
161 Q7 **Luhe** Jiangsu, E China
171 S13 **Luhu** Pulau Seram, E Indonesia
Luhua *see* Heishui
160 G8 **Luhuo** var. Xindu, Tib. Zhaggo. Sichuan, C China
116 M3 **Luhyny** Zhytomyrs'ka Oblast', N Ukraine
83 G15 **Lui** ≈ W Zambia
83 G16 **Luiana** ≈ SE Angola
83 L15 **Luia, Rio** var. Ruya. ≈ Mozambique/Zimbabwe
Luichow Peninsula *see* Leizhou Bandao
Luik *see* Liège
82 C13 **Luimbale** Huambo, C Angola
Luimneach *see* Limerick
106 D6 **Luino** Lombardia, N Italy
82 E13 **Luio** ≈ E Angola
92 L11 **Luiro** ≈ NE Finland
79 N25 **Luishia** Katanga, SE Dem. Rep. Congo
59 M19 **Luislândia do Oeste** Minas Gerais, SE Brazil
40 K5 **Luis L. León, Presa** ⊠ N Mexico
Luis Muñoz Marin *see* San Juan
195 N5 **Luitpold Coast** physical region Antarctica
79 K22 **Luiza** Kasai Occidental, S Dem. Rep. Congo
61 D20 **Luján** Buenos Aires, E Argentina
79 N24 **Lukafu** Katanga, SE Dem. Rep. Congo
Lukapa *see* Lucapa
112 I11 **Lukavac** ⬖ Federacija Bosna I Hercegovina, NE Bosnia and Herzegovina
79 I20 **Lukenie** ≈ C Dem. Rep. Congo
79 H19 **Lukolela** Equateur, W Dem. Rep. Congo
119 M14 **Lukoml'skaye, Vozyera** Rus. Ozero Lukoml'skoye. ◎ N Belarus
Lukoml'skoye, Ozero *see* Lukoml'skaye, Vozyera
114 I8 **Lukovit** Lovech, N Bulgaria
110 O12 **Łuków** Ger. Bogendorf. Lubelskie, E Poland
127 O4 **Lukoyanov** Nizhegorodskaya Oblast', W Russian Federation
79 N22 **Lukuga** ≈ SE Dem. Rep. Congo
79 F21 **Lukula** Bas-Congo, SW Dem. Rep. Congo
83 G14 **Lukulu** Western, NW Zambia
189 R17 **Lukunor Atoll** atoll Mortlock Islands, C Micronesia
82 J12 **Lukwesa** Luapula, NE Zambia
93 K14 **Luleå** Norrbotten, N Sweden
92 J13 **Luleälven** ≈ N Sweden
136 C10 **Lüleburgaz** Kırklareli, NW Turkey
160 M4 **Lüliang Shan** ▲▲ C China
79 O21 **Lulimba** Maniema, E Dem. Rep. Congo
22 K9 **Luling** Louisiana, S USA
25 T11 **Luling** Texas, SW USA
79 I18 **Lulonga** ≈ NW Dem. Rep. Congo
79 K22 **Lulua** ≈ S Dem. Rep. Congo
Luluabourg *see* Kananga
192 L17 **Luma** Ta'ū, E American Samoa
169 S17 **Lumajang** Jawa, C Indonesia
158 G12 **Lumajangdong Co** ◎ W China
82 G13 **Lumbala Kaquengue** Moxico, E Angola
83 F14 **Lumbala N'Guimbo** var. Nguimbo, Gago Coutinho, Port. Vila Gago Coutinho. Moxico, E Angola
21 T11 **Lumber River** ≈ North Carolina/South Carolina, SE USA
Lumber State *see* Maine
22 L8 **Lumberton** Mississippi, S USA
21 U11 **Lumberton** North Carolina, SE USA
105 R4 **Lumbier** Navarra, N Spain
83 Q15 **Lumbo** Nampula, NE Mozambique
124 M4 **Lumbovka** Murmanskaya Oblast', NW Russian Federation
104 J7 **Lumbrales** Castilla-León, N Spain
153 W13 **Lumding** Assam, NE India
82 F12 **Lumege** var. Lumeje. Moxico, E Angola
Lumeje *see* Lumege
99 J17 **Lummen** Limburg, NE Belgium
93 J20 **Lumparland** Åland, SW Finland
167 T11 **Lumphăt** prev. Lomphat. Rôtânôkiri, NE Cambodia
9 U16 **Lumsden** Saskatchewan, S Canada
185 C23 **Lumsden** Southland, South Island, New Zealand
169 N14 **Lumut, Tanjung** cape Sumatera, W Indonesia
157 P4 **Lün** Töv, C Mongolia
116 I13 **Lunca Corbului** Argeş, S Romania
95 K23 **Lund** Skåne, S Sweden
35 X6 **Lund** Nevada, W USA
82 D11 **Lunda Norte** ⬖ province NE Angola
82 E12 **Lunda Sul** ⬖ province NE Angola
82 M13 **Lundazi** Eastern, NE Zambia
95 G16 **Lunde** Telemark, S Norway
Lundenburg *see* Břeclav
95 C17 **Lundevatnet** ◎ S Norway
Lundi *see* Runde
97 I23 **Lundy** island SW England, UK
100 J10 **Lüneburg** Niedersachsen, N Germany
100 J11 **Lüneburger Heide** heathland NW Germany
103 Q15 **Lunel** Hérault, S France
101 F14 **Lünen** Nordrhein-Westfalen, W Germany
13 P16 **Lunenburg** Nova Scotia, SE Canada
21 V7 **Lunenburg** Virginia, NE USA
103 T5 **Lunéville** Meurthe-et-Moselle, NE France
83 I14 **Lunga** ≈ C Zambia
Lunga, Isola *see* Dugi Otok
158 H12 **Lungdo** Xizang Zizhiqu, W China
158 I14 **Lunggar** Xizang Zizhiqu, W China
76 I15 **Lungi** ✈ (Freetown) W Sierra Leone
Lungkiang *see* Qiqihar
Lungleh *see* Lunglei
153 W15 **Lunglei** prev. Lungleh. Mizoram, NE India
158 L15 **Lungsang** Xizang Zizhiqu, W China
82 E13 **Lungué-Bungo** var. Lungwebungu. ≈ Angola/Zambia *see also* Lungwebungu
Lungué-Bungo *see* Lungwebungu
83 G14 **Lungwebungu** var. Lungué-Bungo. ≈ Angola/Zambia *see also* Lungué-Bungo
Lungwebungu *see* Lungué-Bungo
152 F12 **Lūni** Rājasthān, N India
152 F12 **Lūni** ≈ N India
Luninets *see* Luninyets
35 S7 **Luning** Nevada, W USA
Łuniniec *see* Luninyets
127 P6 **Lunino** Penzenskaya Oblast', W Russian Federation
119 J19 **Luninyets** Pol. Łuniniec, Rus. Luninets. Brestskaya Voblasts', SW Belarus
152 F10 **Lūnkaransar** Rājasthān, NW India
119 G17 **Lunna** Pol. Łunna, Rus. Lunna. Hrodzyenskaya Voblasts', W Belarus
76 I15 **Lunsar** W Sierra Leone
83 K14 **Lunsemfwa** ≈ C Zambia
158 J6 **Luntai** var. Bügür. Xinjiang Uygur Zizhiqu, NW China
98 K11 **Lunteren** Gelderland, C Netherlands
109 U5 **Lunz am See** Niederösterreich, C Austria
163 Y7 **Luobei** var. Fengxiang. Heilongjiang, NE China
Luocheng *see* Hui'an
Luocheng *see* Luoding
160 J13 **Luodian** var. Longping. Guizhou, S China
160 M15 **Luoding** var. Luocheng. Guangdong, S China
161 N7 **Luohe** Henan, C China
160 M6 **Luo He** ≈ C China
160 L5 **Luo He** ≈ C China
Luolajarvi *see* Kuoloyarvi
Luong Nam Tha *see* Louangnamtha
160 L13 **Luoqing Jiang** ≈ S China
161 O8 **Luoshan** Henan, C China
161 O12 **Luoxiao Shan** ▲▲ S China
161 N6 **Luoyang** var. Honan, Lo-yang. Henan, C China
161 R12 **Luoyuan** var. Fengshan. Fujian, SE China
79 F21 **Luozi** Bas-Congo, W Dem. Rep. Congo
83 J17 **Lupane** Matabeleland North, W Zimbabwe
160 I12 **Lupanshui** prev. Shuicheng. Guizhou, S China
169 R10 **Lupar, Batang** ≈ East Malaysia
Lupatia *see* Altamura
116 G12 **Lupeni** Hung. Lupény. Hunedoara, SW Romania
Lupény *see* Lupeni
82 N13 **Lupiliche** Niassa, N Mozambique
83 E14 **Lupire** Cuando Cubango, E Angola

79 L22 **Luputa** Kasai Oriental, S Dem. Rep. Congo
121 P16 **Luqa** ✈ (Valletta) S Malta
159 U11 **Luqu** var. Ma'ai. Gansu, C China
45 U5 **Luquillo, Sierra de** ▲▲ E Puerto Rico
26 L4 **Luray** Kansas, C USA
21 U4 **Luray** Virginia, NE USA
103 T7 **Lure** Haute-Saône, E France
82 D11 **Luremo** Lunda Norte, NE Angola
97 F15 **Lurgan** Ir. An Lorgain. S Northern Ireland, UK
57 K18 **Luribay** La Paz, W Bolivia
Luring see Gêrzê
83 Q14 **Lúrio** Nampula, NE Mozambique
83 P14 **Lúrio, Rio** ≈ NE Mozambique
Luristan see Lorestān
Lurka see Lorca
83 J15 **Lusaka** ● (Zambia) Lusaka, SE Zambia
83 J15 **Lusaka** ◆ province C Zambia
83 J15 **Lusaka** ✈ Lusaka, C Zambia
79 L21 **Lusambo** Kasai Oriental, C Dem. Rep. Congo
186 F8 **Lusancay Islands and Reefs** island group SE Papua New Guinea
79 I21 **Lusanga** Bandundu, SW Dem. Rep. Congo
79 N21 **Lusangi** Maniema, E Dem. Rep. Congo
Lusatian Mountains see Lausitzer Bergland
Lushar see Huangzhong
Lushnja see Lushnjë
113 K21 **Lushnjë** var. Lushnja. Fier, C Albania
81 J21 **Lushoto** Tanga, E Tanzania
102 L10 **Lusignan** Vienne, W France
33 Z15 **Lusk** Wyoming, C USA
Luso see Luena
102 L10 **Lussac-les-Châteaux** Vienne, W France
Lussin/Lussino see Lošinj
Lussinpiccolo see Mali Lošinj
108 I7 **Lustenau** Vorarlberg, W Austria
161 T14 **Lü Tao** var. Huoshao Dao, Lütao, Eng. Green Island. island SE Taiwan
Lütao see Lü Tao
Lūt, Baḩrat/Lut, Bahret see Dead Sea
22 K9 **Lutcher** Louisiana, S USA
143 T9 **Lūt, Dasht-e** var. Kavīr-e Lūt. desert E Iran
83 F14 **Lutembo** Moxico, E Angola
Lutetia/Lutetia Parisiorum see Paris
Luteva see Lodève
14 G15 **Luther Lake** ◎ Ontario, S Canada
186 K8 **Luti** Choiseul Island, NW Solomon Islands
Lūt, Kavīr-e see Lūt, Dasht-e
97 N21 **Luton** E England, UK
97 N21 **Luton** ✈ (London) SE England, UK
108 B10 **Lutry** Vaud, SW Switzerland
8 K10 **Łutselk'e** prev. Snowdrift. Northwest Territories, W Canada
29 Y4 **Lutsen** Minnesota, N USA
116 J4 **Luts'k** Pol. Łuck, Rus. Lutsk. Volyns'ka Oblast', NW Ukraine
Lutsk see Luts'k
Luttenberg see Ljutomer
Lüttich see Liège
83 G25 **Luttig** Western Cape, SW South Africa
Lutto see Lotta
82 E13 **Lutuai** Moxico, E Angola
117 Y7 **Lutuhyne** Luhans'ka Oblast', E Ukraine
171 V14 **Lutur, Pulau** island Kepulauan Aru, E Indonesia
23 V12 **Lutz** Florida, SE USA
Lutzow-Holm Bay see Lützow Holmbukta
195 V2 **Lützow Holmbukta** var. Lutzow-Holm Bay. bay Antarctica
81 L16 **Luuq** It. Lugh Ganana. Gedo, SW Somalia
92 M12 **Luusua** Lappi, NE Finland
23 Q6 **Luverne** Alabama, S USA
29 S11 **Luverne** Minnesota, N USA
79 O22 **Luvua** ≈ SE Dem. Rep. Congo
82 F13 **Luvuei** Moxico, E Angola
81 H24 **Luwego** ≈ S Tanzania
82 K12 **Luwingu** Northern, NE Zambia
171 P12 **Luwuk** prev. Loewoek. Sulawesi, C Indonesia
23 N3 **Luxapallila Creek** ≈ Alabama/Mississippi, S USA
99 M25 **Luxembourg** ● (Luxembourg) Luxembourg, S Luxembourg
99 M25 **Luxembourg** off. Grand Duchy of Luxembourg, var. Lëtzebuerg, Luxemburg. ◆ monarchy NW Europe
99 J23 **Luxembourg** ◆ province SE Belgium
99 L24 **Luxembourg** ◆ district S Luxembourg
31 N6 **Luxemburg** Wisconsin, N USA
Luxemburg see Luxembourg
103 U7 **Luxeuil-les-Bains** Haute-Saône, E France
160 E13 **Luxi** prev. Mangshi. Yunnan, SW China
82 E10 **Luxico** ≈ Angola/Dem. Rep. Congo
75 X10 **Luxor** Ar. Al Uqṣur. E Egypt
75 X10 **Luxor** ✈ C Egypt
160 M4 **Luya Shan** ▲▲ C China
102 J15 **Luy de Béarn** ≈ SW France
102 J15 **Luy de France** ≈ SW France
125 P12 **Luza** Kirovskaya Oblast', NW Russian Federation
125 Q12 **Luza** ≈ NW Russian Federation
104 I16 **Luz, Costa de la** coastal region SW Spain
111 K20 **Luže** var. Lausche. ▲ Czech Republic/Germany see also Lausche
Luže see Lausche
108 F8 **Luzern** Fr. Lucerne, It. Lucerna. Luzern, C Switzerland
108 E8 **Luzern** Fr. Lucerne. ◆ canton C Switzerland
160 L13 **Luzhai** Guangxi Zhuangzu Zizhiqu, S China
118 K12 **Luzhki** Rus. Luzhki. Vitsyebskaya Voblasts', N Belarus
160 I10 **Luzhou** Sichuan, C China
Lužická Nisa see Neisse
Lužické Hory' see Lausitzer Bergland
Lužnice see Lainsitz
171 O2 **Luzon** island N Philippines
171 N1 **Luzon Strait** strait Philippines/Taiwan
Lużyckie, Gory see Lausitzer Bergland
116 I5 **L'viv** Ger. Lemberg, Pol. Lwów, Rus. L'vov. L'vivs'ka Oblast', W Ukraine
L'viv see L'vivs'ka Oblast'
116 I4 **L'vivs'ka Oblast'** var. L'viv, Rus. L'vovskaya Oblast'. ◆ province NW Ukraine
L'vov see L'viv
L'vovskaya Oblast' see L'vivs'ka Oblast'
Lwena see Luena
Lwów see L'viv
110 F11 **Lwówek** Ger. Neustadt bei Pinne. Wielkopolskie, C Poland
111 E14 **Lwówek Śląski** Ger. Löwenberg in Schlesien. Jelenia Góra, SW Poland
119 I18 **Lyakhavichy** Rus. Lyakhovichi. Brestskaya Voblasts', SW Belarus
Lyakhovichi see Lyakhavichy
185 B22 **Lyall, Mount** ▲ South Island, New Zealand
Lyallpur see Faisalābād
Lyangar see Langar
124 H11 **Lyaskelya** Respublika Kareliya, NW Russian Federation
119 I18 **Lyasnaya** Rus. Lesnaya. Brestskaya Voblasts', SW Belarus
119 F19 **Lyasnaya** Pol. Leśna, Rus. Lesnaya. ≈ SW Belarus
124 H15 **Lychkovo** Novgorodskaya Oblast', W Russian Federation
Lyck see Ełk
93 I15 **Lycksele** Västerbotten, N Sweden
18 G13 **Lycoming Creek** ≈ Pennsylvania, NE USA
Lycopolis see Asyût
195 N3 **Lyddan Island** island Antarctica
83 K20 **Lydenburg** Mpumalanga, NE South Africa
119 L20 **Lyel'chytsy** Rus. Lel'chitsy. Homyel'skaya Voblasts', SE Belarus
119 P14 **Lyenina** Rus. Lenino. Mahilyowskaya Voblasts', E Belarus
118 L13 **Lyepyel'** Rus. Lepel'. Vitsyebskaya Voblasts', N Belarus
25 S17 **Lyford** Texas, SW USA
95 E17 **Lygna** ≈ S Norway
18 G14 **Lykens** Pennsylvania, NE USA
115 E21 **Lykódimo** ▲ S Greece
97 K24 **Lyme Bay** bay S England, UK
97 K24 **Lyme Regis** S England, UK
110 L7 **Łyna** Ger. Alle. ≈ N Poland
29 P12 **Lynch** Nebraska, C USA
20 J10 **Lynchburg** Tennessee, S USA
21 T6 **Lynchburg** Virginia, NE USA
21 T12 **Lynches River** ≈ South Carolina, SE USA
32 H6 **Lynden** Washington, NW USA
182 I5 **Lyndhurst** South Australia
27 Q5 **Lyndon** Kansas, C USA
19 N7 **Lyndonville** Vermont, NE USA
95 D18 **Lyngdal** Vest-Agder, S Norway
92 I9 **Lyngen** Lapp. Ivgovuotna. inlet Arctic Ocean
95 G17 **Lyngør** Aust-Agder, S Norway
92 I9 **Lyngseidet** Troms, N Norway
19 P11 **Lynn** Massachusetts, NE USA
Lynn see King's Lynn
23 R9 **Lynn Haven** Florida, SE USA
9 V11 **Lynn Lake** Manitoba, C Canada
Lynn Regis see King's Lynn
118 I13 **Lyntupy** Rus. Lyntupy. Vitsyebskaya Voblasts', NW Belarus
103 R11 **Lyon** Eng. Lyons; anc. Lugdunum. Rhône, E France
8 I6 **Lyon, Cape** headland Northwest Territories, NW Canada
18 K6 **Lyon Mountain** ▲ New York, NE USA
103 Q11 **Lyonnais, Monts du** ▲▲ C France
65 N25 **Lyon Point** headland SE Tristan da Cunha
182 E5 **Lyons** South Australia
37 T3 **Lyons** Colorado, C USA
23 V6 **Lyons** Georgia, SE USA
26 M5 **Lyons** Kansas, C USA
29 R14 **Lyons** Nebraska, C USA
18 G10 **Lyons** New York, NE USA
Lyons see Lyon
118 O13 **Lyozna** Rus. Liozno. Vitsyebskaya Voblasts', NE Belarus
117 S4 **Lypova Dolyna** Sums'ka Oblast', NE Ukraine
117 N6 **Lypovets'** Rus. Lipovets. Vinnyts'ka Oblast', C Ukraine
Lys see Leie
111 I18 **Lysá Hora** ▲ E Czech Republic
95 D16 **Lysefjorden** fjord S Norway
95 I18 **Lysekil** Västra Götaland, S Sweden
Lysi see Akdoğan
33 V14 **Lysite** Wyoming, C USA
127 P3 **Lyskovo** Nizhegorodskaya Oblast', W Russian Federation
108 D8 **Lyss** Bern, W Switzerland
95 H22 **Lystrup** Århus, C Denmark
125 V14 **Lys'va** Permskaya Oblast', NW Russian Federation
117 P6 **Lysyanka** Cherkas'ka Oblast', C Ukraine
117 X6 **Lysychans'k** Rus. Lisichansk. Luhans'ka Oblast', E Ukraine
97 K17 **Lytham St Anne's** NW England, UK
185 I19 **Lyttelton** Canterbury, South Island, New Zealand
10 M17 **Lytton** British Columbia, SW Canada
119 L18 **Lyuban'** Rus. Lyuban'. Minskaya Voblasts', S Belarus
119 L18 **Lyubanskaye Vodaskhovishcha** ⊞ C Belarus
116 M5 **Lyubar** Zhytomyrs'ka Oblast', N Ukraine
Lyubashëvka see Lyubashivka
117 O8 **Lyubashivka** Rus. Lyubashëvka. Odes'ka Oblast', SW Ukraine
119 I16 **Lyubcha** Pol. Lubcz, Rus. Lyubcha. Hrodzyenskaya Voblasts', W Belarus
126 L4 **Lyubertsy** Moskovskaya Oblast', W Russian Federation
116 K2 **Lyubeshiv** Volyns'ka Oblast', NW Ukraine
124 M14 **Lyubim** Yaroslavskaya Oblast', NW Russian Federation
114 K11 **Lyubimets** Khaskovo, S Bulgaria
Lyublin see Lublin
116 I3 **Lyuboml'** Pol. Luboml. Volyns'ka Oblast', NW Ukraine
Lyubotin see Lyubotyn
117 U5 **Lyubotyn** Rus. Lyubotin. Kharkivs'ka Oblast', E Ukraine
126 I5 **Lyudinovo** Kaluzhskaya Oblast', W Russian Federation
127 T2 **Lyuk** Udmurtskaya Respublika, NW Russian Federation
114 M9 **Lyulyakovo** prev. Keremitlik. Burgas, E Bulgaria
119 I18 **Lyusina** Rus. Lyusino. Brestskaya Voblasts', SW Belarus
Lyusino see Lyusina

M

138 G9 **Ma'ād** Irbid, N Jordan
Ma'ai see Luqu
Maalahti see Malax
Maale see Male'
138 G13 **Ma'ān** Ma'ān, SW Jordan
138 H13 **Ma'ān** off. Muḩāfaẓat Ma'ān, var. Ma'an, Ma'ān. ◆ governorate S Jordan
93 M16 **Maaninka** Isä-Suomi, C Finland
Maanīt see Bayan, Töv, Mongolia
Maanīt see Hishig Öndör, Bulgan, Mongolia
Ma'ān, Muḩāfaẓat see Ma'ān
93 N15 **Maanselkä** Oulu, C Finland
161 Q8 **Ma'anshan** Anhui, E China
188 F16 **Maap** island Caroline Islands, W Micronesia
118 H3 **Maardu** Ger. Maart. Harjumaa, NW Estonia
Ma'aret-en-Nu'man see Ma'arrat an Nu'mān
99 K16 **Maarheeze** Noord-Brabant, SE Netherlands
Maarianhamina see Mariehamn
138 I4 **Ma'arrat an Nu'mān** var. Ma'aret-en-Nu'man, Fr. Maarret enn Naamâne. Idlib, NW Syria
Maarret enn Naamâne see Ma'arrat an Nu'mān
98 I11 **Maarssen** Utrecht, C Netherlands
Maart see Maardu
99 L17 **Maas** Fr. Meuse. ≈ W Europe see also Meuse
Maas see Meuse
99 M15 **Maasbree** Limburg, SE Netherlands
99 L17 **Maaseik** prev. Maeseyck. Limburg, NE Belgium
171 Q6 **Maasin** Leyte, C Philippines
99 L17 **Maasmechelen** Limburg, NE Belgium
98 G12 **Maassluis** Zuid-Holland, SW Netherlands
99 L18 **Maastricht** var. Maestricht; anc. Traiectum ad Mosam, Traiectum Tungorum. Limburg, SE Netherlands
183 N18 **Maatsuyker Group** island group Tasmania, SE Australia
Maba see Qujiang
83 L20 **Mabalane** Gaza, S Mozambique
25 V7 **Mabank** Texas, SW USA
97 O18 **Mablethorpe** E England, UK
171 V12 **Maboi** Papua, E Indonesia
83 M19 **Mabote** Inhambane, S Mozambique
32 J10 **Mabton** Washington, NW USA
83 H20 **Mabutsane** Southern, S Botswana
63 G19 **Macá, Cerro** ▲ S Chile
60 Q9 **Macaé** Rio de Janeiro, SE Brazil
82 N13 **Macaloge** Niassa, N Mozambique
Macan see Bonerate, Kepulauan
161 N15 **Macao** Chin. Aomen, Port. Macau. E Asia
104 H9 **Mação** Santarém, C Portugal
58 J11 **Macapá** state capital Amapá, N Brazil
43 S17 **Macaracas** Los Santos, S Panama
55 P6 **Macare, Caño** ≈ NE Venezuela
55 Q6 **Macareo, Caño** ≈ NE Venezuela
Macarsca see Makarska
182 L12 **Macarthur** Victoria, SE Australia
MacArthur see Ormoc
56 C7 **Macas** Morona Santiago, SE Ecuador
Macassar see Makassar
59 Q14 **Macau** Rio Grande do Norte, E Brazil
Macău see Makó, Hungary
Macau see Macao
65 E24 **Macbride Head** headland East Falkland, Falkland Islands
23 V9 **Macclenny** Florida, SE USA
97 L18 **Macclesfield** C England, UK
192 F6 **Macclesfield Bank** undersea feature N South China Sea
MacCluer Gulf see Berau, Teluk
181 N7 **Macdonald, Lake** salt lake Northern Territory/Western Australia
181 Q7 **Macdonnell Ranges** ▲▲ Northern Territory, C Australia
96 K8 **Macduff** NE Scotland, UK
104 I6 **Macedo de Cavaleiros** Bragança, N Portugal
Macedonia see Macedonia, FYR
Macedonia Central see Kentrikí Makedonía
Macedonia East and Thrace see Anatolikí Makedonía kai Thráki
113 O19 **Macedonia, FYR** off. the Former Yugoslav Republic of Macedonia, var. Macedonia, Mac. Makedonija, abbrev. FYR Macedonia. ◆ republic SE Europe
Macedonia, the Former Yugoslav Republic of see Macedonia, FYR
Macedonia West see Dytikí Makedonía
59 Q16 **Maceió** state capital Alagoas, E Brazil
76 K15 **Macenta** SE Guinea
106 J12 **Macerata** Marche, C Italy
9 S11 **MacFarlane** ≈ Saskatchewan, C Canada
182 H7 **Macfarlane, Lake** var. Lake Mcfarlane. ◎ South Australia
Macgillicuddy's Reeks Mountains see Macgillycuddy's Reeks
97 B21 **Macgillycuddy's Reeks** var. Macgillicuddy's Reeks Mountains, Ir. Na Cruacha Dubha. ▲▲ SW Ireland
9 X16 **MacGregor** Manitoba, S Canada
149 O10 **Mach** Baluchistān, SW Pakistan
56 C6 **Machachi** Pichincha, C Ecuador
83 M19 **Machaila** Gaza, S Mozambique
Machaire Fíolta see Magherafelt
Machaire Rátha see Maghera
81 I19 **Machakos** Eastern, S Kenya
56 B8 **Machala** El Oro, SW Ecuador
Machali see Madoi
83 J19 **Machaneng** Central, SE Botswana
83 M18 **Machanga** Sofala, E Mozambique
80 G13 **Machar Marshes** wetland SE Sudan
102 I8 **Machecoul** Loire-Atlantique, NW France
161 O8 **Macheng** Hubei, C China
155 J16 **Mācherla** Andhra Pradesh, C India
153 O11 **Machhapuchhre** ▲ C Nepal
19 T6 **Machias** Maine, NE USA
19 R3 **Machias River** ≈ Maine, NE USA
19 T6 **Machias River** ≈ Maine, NE USA
64 P5 **Machico** Madeira, Portugal, NE Atlantic Ocean
155 K16 **Machilipatnam** var. Bandar Masulipatnam. Andhra Pradesh, E India
54 G5 **Machiques** Zulia, NW Venezuela
57 G15 **Machupicchu** Cusco, C Peru
83 M20 **Macia** var. Vila de Macia. Gaza, S Mozambique
Macías Nguema Biyogo see Bioco, Isla de
116 M13 **Măcin** Tulcea, SE Romania
183 T4 **Macintyre River** ≈ New South Wales/Queensland, SE Australia
181 Y7 **Mackay** Queensland, NE Australia
181 O7 **Mackay, Lake** salt lake Northern Territory/Western Australia
10 M13 **Mackenzie** British Columbia, W Canada
8 I9 **Mackenzie** ≈ Northwest Territories, NW Canada
195 Y6 **Mackenzie Bay** bay Antarctica
10 J1 **Mackenzie Bay** bay NW Canada
2 D9 **Mackenzie Delta** delta Northwest Territories, NW Canada
197 P8 **Mackenzie King Island** island Queen Elizabeth Islands, Northwest Territories, N Canada
8 H8 **Mackenzie Mountains** ▲▲ Northwest Territories, NW Canada
31 Q5 **Mackinac, Straits of** ◎ Michigan, N USA
194 K5 **Mackintosh, Cape** headland Antarctica
9 R15 **Macklin** Saskatchewan, S Canada
183 V6 **Macksville** New South Wales, SE Australia
183 V5 **Maclean** New South Wales, SE Australia
83 J24 **Maclear** Eastern Cape, SE South Africa
183 U6 **Macleay River** ≈ New South Wales, SE Australia
MacLeod see Fort Macleod
180 G9 **Macleod, Lake** ◎ Western Australia
10 I6 **Macmillan** ≈ Yukon Territory, NW Canada
30 J12 **Macomb** Illinois, N USA
107 B18 **Macomer** Sardegna, Italy, C Mediterranean Sea
82 Q13 **Macomia** Cabo Delgado, NE Mozambique
103 R10 **Mâcon** anc. Matisco, Matisco Ædourum. Saône-et-Loire, C France
23 T5 **Macon** Georgia, SE USA
23 N4 **Macon** Mississippi, S USA
27 U3 **Macon** Missouri, C USA
22 J6 **Macon, Bayou** ≈ Arkansas/Louisiana, S USA
82 G13 **Macondo** Moxico, E Angola
83 M16 **Macossa** Manica, C Mozambique
9 T12 **Macoun Lake** ◎ Saskatchewan, C Canada
30 K14 **Macoupin Creek** ≈ Illinois, N USA
Macouria see Tonate
83 N18 **Macovane** Inhambane, SE Mozambique
183 N17 **Macquarie Harbour** inlet Tasmania, SE Australia
192 J13 **Macquarie Island** island New Zealand, SW Pacific Ocean
183 T8 **Macquarie, Lake** lagoon New South Wales, SE Australia
183 Q6 **Macquarie Marshes** wetland New South Wales, SE Australia
175 O13 **Macquarie Ridge** undersea feature SW Pacific Ocean
183 Q6 **Macquarie River** ≈ New South Wales, SE Australia
183 P17 **Macquarie River** ≈ Tasmania, SE Australia
195 V5 **Mac. Robertson Land** physical region Antarctica
97 C21 **Macroom** Ir. Maigh Chromtha. Cork, SW Ireland
42 G5 **Macuelizo** Santa Bárbara, NW Honduras
182 G2 **Macumba River** ≈ South Australia
57 I16 **Macusani** Puno, S Peru
56 E8 **Macusari, Río** ≈ N Peru
41 U15 **Macuspana** Tabasco, SE Mexico
138 G10 **Ma'dabā** var. Mādabā, Madeba; anc. Medeba. Ma'dabā, NW Jordan
138 G11 **Ma'dabā** off. Muḩāfaẓat Ma'dabā. ◆ governorate C Jordan
Mādabā see Ma'dabā
172 G2 **Madagascar** off. Democratic Republic of Madagascar, Malg. Madagasikara; prev. Malagasy Republic. ◆ republic W Indian Ocean
172 I5 **Madagascar** island W Indian Ocean
128 L17 **Madagascar Basin** undersea feature W Indian Ocean
Madagascar, Democratic Republic of see Madagascar
128 L16 **Madagascar Plain** undersea feature W Indian Ocean
67 Y14 **Madagascar Plateau** var. Madagascar Ridge, Madagascar Rise, Rus. Madagaskarskiy Khrebet. undersea feature W Indian Ocean
Madagascar Rise/Madagascar Ridge see Madagascar Plateau
Madagasikara see Madagascar
Madagaskarskiy Khrebet see Madagascar Plateau
64 N2 **Madalena** Pico, Azores, Portugal, NE Atlantic Ocean
77 Y6 **Madama** Agadez, NE Niger
114 J12 **Madan** Smolyan, S Bulgaria
155 I19 **Madanapalle** Andhra Pradesh, E India
186 D7 **Madang** Madang, N Papua New Guinea
186 C6 **Madang** ◆ province N Papua New Guinea
146 G7 **Madaniyat** Rus. Madeniyet. Qoraqalpog'iston Respublikasi, W Uzbekistan
Madanīyīn see Médenine
77 U11 **Madaoua** Tahoua, SW Niger
Madaras see Vtáčnik
153 U15 **Madaripur** Dhaka, C Bangladesh
77 U12 **Madarounfa** Maradi, S Niger
Mađarska see Hungary
Madau see Madau
186 H9 **Madau Island** island SE Papua New Guinea
146 B13 **Madau** Rus. Madau. Balkan Welaýaty, W Turkmenistan
19 S1 **Madawaska** Maine, NE USA
14 J13 **Madawaska** ≈ Ontario, SE Canada
Madawaska Highlands see Haliburton Highlands
166 M4 **Madaya** Mandalay, C Myanmar (Burma)
107 K17 **Maddaloni** Campania, S Italy
29 O3 **Maddock** North Dakota, N USA
99 I14 **Made** Noord-Brabant, S Netherlands
Madeba see Ma'dabā
64 L9 **Madeira** var. Ilha de Madeira. island Madeira, Portugal, NE Atlantic Ocean
Madeira, Ilha de see Madeira
64 O5 **Madeira Islands** Port. Região Autoónoma da Madeira. ◆ autonomous region Madeira, Portugal, NE Atlantic Ocean
64 L9 **Madeira Plain** undersea feature E Atlantic Ocean
Madeira, Região Autoónoma da see Madeira Islands
64 L9 **Madeira Ridge** undersea feature E Atlantic Ocean
59 F14 **Madeira, Rio** var. Río Madera. ≈ Bolivia/Brazil see also Madera, Río
Madeira, Rio see Madera, Río
101 J25 **Mädelegabel** ▲ Austria/Germany
15 X6 **Madeleine** ≈ Québec, SE Canada
15 X5 **Madeleine, Cap de la** headland Québec, SE Canada
13 Q13 **Madeleine, Îles de la** Eng. Magdalen Islands. island group Québec, E Canada
29 U10 **Madelia** Minnesota, N USA
35 P3 **Madeline** California, W USA
30 K3 **Madeline Island** island Apostle Islands, Wisconsin, N USA
137 O15 **Maden** Elazığ, SE Turkey
145 V12 **Madeniyet** Vostochnyy Kazakhstan, E Kazakhstan
Madeniyet see Madaniyat
40 H5 **Madera** Chihuahua, N Mexico
35 Q10 **Madera** California, W USA
56 L13 **Madera, Río** Port. Rio Madeira. ≈ Bolivia/Brazil see also Madeira, Rio
Madera, Río see Madeira, Rio
106 D6 **Madesimo** Lombardia, N Italy
141 O14 **Madhāb, Wādī** dry watercourse NW Yemen
153 R13 **Madhepura** prev. Madhipure. Bihār, NE India
Madhipure see Madhepura
153 Q13 **Madhubani** Bihār, N India
153 Q15 **Madhupur** Jhārkhand, NE India
154 I10 **Madhya Pradesh** prev. Central Provinces and Berar. ◆ state C India
57 K15 **Madidi, Río** ≈ W Bolivia
155 F20 **Madikeri** prev. Mercara. Karnātaka, W India
27 O13 **Madill** Oklahoma, C USA
79 G21 **Madimba** Bas-Congo, SW Dem. Rep. Congo
138 M4 **Ma'dīn** Ar Raqqah, C Syria
Madīnah, Minṭaqat al see Al Madīnah
76 M14 **Madinani** NW Ivory Coast
141 O17 **Madīnat ash Sha'b** prev. Al Ittiḩād. SW Yemen
138 K3 **Madīnat ath Thawrah** var. Ath Thawrah. Ar Raqqah, N Syria Asia
173 O6 **Madingley Rise** undersea feature W Indian Ocean
79 E21 **Madingo-Kayes** Le Kouilou, S Congo
79 F21 **Madingou** La Bouenza, S Congo
Madioen see Madiun
23 U8 **Madison** Florida, SE USA
23 T3 **Madison** Georgia, SE USA
31 P15 **Madison** Indiana, N USA
27 P6 **Madison** Kansas, C USA
19 Q6 **Madison** Maine, NE USA
29 S9 **Madison** Minnesota, N USA
22 K5 **Madison** Mississippi, S USA
29 Q14 **Madison** Nebraska, C USA
29 R10 **Madison** South Dakota, N USA
21 V5 **Madison** Virginia, NE USA
21 Q5 **Madison** West Virginia, NE USA
30 L9 **Madison** state capital Wisconsin, N USA
21 T6 **Madison Heights** Virginia, NE USA
20 I6 **Madisonville** Kentucky, S USA
20 M10 **Madisonville** Tennessee, S USA
25 V9 **Madisonville** Texas, SW USA
Madisonville see Taiohae
169 R16 **Madiun** prev. Madioen. Jawa, C Indonesia
Madjene see Majene
14 J14 **Madoc** Ontario, SE Canada
Madoera see Madura, Pulau
81 J18 **Mado Gashi** North Eastern, E Kenya
159 R11 **Madoi** var. Machali. Qinghai, C China
189 O13 **Madolenihmw** Pohnpei, E Micronesia
118 I9 **Madona** Ger. Modohn. Madona, E Latvia
107 J23 **Madonie** ▲▲ Sicilia, Italy, C Mediterranean Sea
141 Y11 **Madrakah, Ra's** headland E Oman
32 I12 **Madras** Oregon, NW USA
Madras see Tamil Nādu
Madras see Chennai
57 H14 **Madre de Dios** off. Departamento de Madre de Dios. ◆ department E Peru
Madre de Dios, Departamento de see Madre de Dios
63 F22 **Madre de Dios, Isla** island S Chile
57 J14 **Madre de Dios, Río** ≈ Bolivia/Peru
41 Q9 **Madre, Laguna** lagoon NE Mexico
25 T16 **Madre, Laguna** lagoon Texas, SW USA
37 Q12 **Madre Mount** ▲ New Mexico, SW USA
105 N8 **Madrid** ● (Spain) Madrid, C Spain
29 V14 **Madrid** Iowa, C USA
105 N7 **Madrid** ◆ autonomous community C Spain
105 N10 **Madridejos** Castilla-La Mancha, C Spain
104 L7 **Madrigal de las Altas Torres** Castilla-León, N Spain
104 K10 **Madrigalejo** Extremadura, W Spain
34 L3 **Mad River** ≈ California, W USA
42 J8 **Madriz** ◆ department NW Nicaragua
104 K10 **Madroñera** Extremadura, W Spain
181 N12 **Madura** Western Australia
Madura see Madurai
155 H22 **Madurai** prev. Madura, Mathurai. Tamil Nādu, S India
169 S16 **Madura, Pulau** prev. Madoera. island C Indonesia
169 S16 **Madura, Selat** strait C Indonesia
127 Q17 **Madzhalis** Respublika Dagestan, SW Russian Federation
114 K12 **Madzharovo** Khaskovo, S Bulgaria
83 M14 **Madzimoyo** Eastern, E Zambia
165 O12 **Maebashi** var. Maebasi, Mayebashi. Gunma, Honshū, S Japan
Maebasi see Maebashi
167 O6 **Mae Chan** Chiang Rai, NW Thailand
167 N7 **Mae Hong Son** var. Maehongson, Muai To. Mae Hong Son, NW Thailand
Maehongson see Mae Hong Son
Mae Nam Khong see Mekong
167 Q7 **Mae Nam Nan** ≈ NW Thailand
167 O10 **Mae Nam Tha Chin** ≈ W Thailand
167 P7 **Mae Nam Yom** ≈ W Thailand
37 O3 **Maeser** Utah, W USA

◆ Country ● Country Capital ◇ Dependent Territory ○ Dependent Territory Capital ◆ Administrative Regions ✈ International Airport ▲ Mountain ▲▲ Mountain Range ⩚ Volcano ≈ River ◎ Lake ⊞ Reservoir

Maeseyck *see* Maaseik
167 *N9* **Mae Sot** *var.* Ban Mae Sot. Tak, W Thailand
Maestricht *see* Maastricht
167 *O7* **Mae Suai** *var.* Ban Mae Suai. Chiang Rai, NW Thailand
167 *O7* **Mae Tho, Doi** ▲ NW Thailand
172 *I4* **Maevatanana** Mahajanga, C Madagascar
187 *R13* **Maéwo** *prev.* Aurora. *island* C Vanuatu
171 *S11* **Mafa** Pulau Halmahera, E Indonesia
83 *I23* **Mafeteng** W Lesotho
99 *J21* **Maffe** Namur, SE Belgium
183 *P12* **Maffra** Victoria, SE Australia
81 *K23* **Mafia** *island* E Tanzania
81 *J23* **Mafia Channel** *sea waterway* E Tanzania
83 *I21* **Mafikeng** North-West, N South Africa
60 *J12* **Mafra** Santa Catarina, S Brazil
104 *F10* **Mafra** Lisboa, C Portugal
143 *Q17* **Mafraq** Abū Ẓaby, C United Arab Emirates
Mafraq/Muḥāfaẓat al Mafraq *see* Al Mafraq
123 *T10* **Magadan** Magadanskaya Oblast', E Russian Federation
123 *T9* **Magadanskaya Oblast'** ◈ *province* E Russian Federation
108 *G11* **Magadino** Ticino, S Switzerland
63 *G23* **Magallanes** *var.* Región de Magallanes y de la Antártica Chilena. ◈ *region* S Chile
Magallanes *see* Punta Arenas
Magallanes, Estrecho de *see* Magellan, Strait of
Magallanes y de la Antártica Chilena, Región de *see* Magallanes
14 *I10* **Maganasipi, Lac** ◎ Québec, SE Canada
54 *F6* **Magangué** Bolívar, N Colombia
Magareva *see* Mangareva
77 *V12* **Magaria** Zinder, S Niger
186 *F10* **Magarida** Central, SW Papua New Guinea
171 *O2* **Magat** ≈ Luzon, N Philippines
27 *T11* **Magazine Mountain** ▲ Arkansas, C USA
76 *I15* **Magburaka** C Sierra Leone
123 *Q13* **Magdagachi** Amurskaya Oblast', SE Russian Federation
62 *O12* **Magdalena** Buenos Aires, E Argentina
57 *M15* **Magdalena** Beni, N Bolivia
40 *F4* **Magdalena** Sonora, NW Mexico
37 *Q13* **Magdalena** New Mexico, SW USA
54 *F5* **Magdalena** *off.* Departamento del Magdalena. ◈ *province* N Colombia
40 *E9* **Magdalena, Bahía** *bay* W Mexico
Magdalena, Departamento del *see* Magdalena
63 *G19* **Magdalena, Isla** *island* Archipiélago de los Chonos, S Chile
40 *D8* **Magdalena, Isla** *island* W Mexico
47 *P6* **Magdalena, Río** ≈ C Colombia
40 *F4* **Magdalena, Río** ≈ NW Mexico
Magdalen Islands *see* Madeleine, Îles de la
100 *L13* **Magdeburg** Sachsen-Anhalt, C Germany
22 *L6* **Magee** Mississippi, S USA
169 *Q16* **Magelang** Jawa, C Indonesia
192 *K7* **Magellan Rise** *undersea feature* C Pacific Ocean
63 *H24* **Magellan, Strait of** *Sp.* Estrecho de Magallanes. *strait* Argentina/Chile
106 *D7* **Magenta** Lombardia, NW Italy
Magerøy *see* Magerøya
92 *K7* **Magerøya** *var.* Magerøy, *Lapp.* Máhkarávju. *island* N Norway
164 *C17* **Mage-shima** *island* Nansei-shotō, SW Japan
108 *G11* **Maggia** Ticino, S Switzerland
108 *G10* **Maggia** ≈ SW Switzerland
Maggiore, Lago *see* Maggiore, Lake
106 *C6* **Maggiore, Lake** *It.* Lago Maggiore. ◎ Italy/Switzerland
44 *I12* **Maggotty** W Jamaica
76 *I10* **Maghama** Gorgol, S Mauritania
97 *F14* **Maghera** *Ir.* Machaire Rátha. C Northern Ireland, UK
97 *F15* **Magherafelt** *Ir.* Machaire Fíolta. C Northern Ireland, UK
188 *H6* **Magicienne Bay** *bay* Saipan, S Northern Mariana Islands
105 *O13* **Magina** ▲ S Spain
81 *H24* **Magingo** Ruvuma, S Tanzania
112 *H11* **Maglaj** ◈ Federacija Bosna I Hercegovina, N Bosnia and Herzegovina
107 *Q19* **Maglie** Puglia, SE Italy
36 *L2* **Magna** Utah, W USA
Magnesia *see* Manisa
14 *G12* **Magnetawan** ≈ Ontario, S Canada
27 *T14* **Magnolia** Arkansas, C USA
22 *K7* **Magnolia** Mississippi, S USA
25 *V10* **Magnolia** Texas, SW USA
Magnolia State *see* Mississippi
95 *J15* **Magnor** Hedmark, S Norway
187 *Y14* **Mago** *prev.* Mango. *island* Lau Group, E Fiji
83 *L15* **Màgoé** Tete, NW Mozambique
15 *Q13* **Magog** Québec, SE Canada
83 *J15* **Magoye** Southern, S Zambia
41 *Q12* **Magozal** Veracruz-Llave, C Mexico
14 *B7* **Magpie** ≈ Ontario, S Canada
9 *Q17* **Magrath** Alberta, SW Canada
105 *R10* **Magro** ≈ E Spain
76 *I9* **Magta' Lahjar** *var.* Magta Lahjar, Magta' Lahjar, Magtá Lahjar. Brakna, SW Mauritania
146 *D12* **Magtymguly** *prev.* Garrygala, *Rus.* Kara-Kala. Balkan Welaýaty, W Turkmenistan
83 *L20* **Magude** Maputo, S Mozambique
77 *Y12* **Magumeri** Borno, NE Nigeria
189 *O14* **Magur Islands** *island group* Caroline Islands, C Micronesia
Magway *see* Magwe
166 *L6* **Magwe** *var.* Magway. Magwe, W Myanmar (Burma)
166 *L6* **Magwe** *var.* Magway. ◈ *division* C Myanmar (Burma)
Magyar-Becse *see* Bečej
Magyarkanizsa *see* Kanjiža
Magyarország *see* Hungary
Magyarzsombor *see* Zimbor
142 *J4* **Mahābād** *var.* Mehabad; *prev.* Sāūjbulāgh. Āzarbāyjān-e Gharbī, NW Iran
172 *H5* **Mahabo** Toliara, W Madagascar
Maha Chai *see* Samut Sakhon
155 *D14* **Mahād** Mahārāshtra, W India
81 *N17* **Mahadday Weyne** Shabeellaha Dhexe, C Somalia
79 *Q17* **Mahagi** Orientale, NE Dem. Rep. Congo
Mahāil *see* Muhāyil
172 *I4* **Mahajamba** *seasonal river* NW Madagascar
152 *G10* **Mahājan** Rājasthān, NW India
172 *I3* **Mahajanga** *var.* Majunga. Mahajanga, NW Madagascar
172 *I3* **Mahajanga** ◈ *province* W Madagascar
172 *I3* **Mahajanga** ✈ Mahajanga, NW Madagascar
169 *U19* **Mahakam, Sungai** *var.* Koetai, Kutai. ≈ Borneo, C Indonesia
83 *I19* **Mahalapye** *var.* Mahalatswe. Central, SE Botswana
Mahalatswe *see* Mahalapye
Mahalla el Kubra *see* El Maḥalla el Kubra
171 *O13* **Mahalona** Sulawesi, C Indonesia
Mahameru *see* Semeru, Gunung
143 *S11* **Mahān** Kermān, E Iran
154 *N12* **Mahanādi** ≈ E India
172 *J5* **Mahanoro** Toamasina, E Madagascar
153 *P13* **Mahārājganj** Bihār, N India
154 *G13* **Mahārāshtra** ◈ *state* W India
172 *I4* **Mahavavy** *seasonal river* N Madagascar
155 *K24* **Mahaweli Ganga** ≈ C Sri Lanka
Mahbés *see* El Mahbas
155 *J15* **Mahbūbābād** Andhra Pradesh, E India
155 *H16* **Mahbūbnagar** Andhra Pradesh, C India
140 *M8* **Mahd adh Dhahab** Al Madīnah, W Saudi Arabia
55 *S9* **Mahdia** C Guyana
75 *N6* **Mahdia** *var.* Al Mahdīyah, Mehdia. NE Tunisia
155 *F20* **Mahe** *Fr.* Mahé; *prev.* Mayyali. Pondicherry, SW India
172 *I16* **Mahé** ✈ Mahé, NE Seychelles
172 *H16* **Mahé** *island* Inner Islands, NE Seychelles
Mahé *see* Mahe
173 *Y17* **Mahebourg** SE Mauritius
152 *L10* **Mahendranagar** Far Western, W Nepal
81 *I23* **Mahenge** Morogoro, SE Tanzania
185 *F22* **Maheno** Otago, South Island, New Zealand
154 *D9* **Mahesāna** Gujarāt, W India
154 *F11* **Maheshwar** Madhya Pradesh, C India
151 *F14* **Mahi** ≈ N India
184 *Q10* **Mahia Peninsula** *peninsula* North Island, New Zealand
119 *O16* **Mahilyow** *Rus.* Mogilëv. Mahilyowskaya Voblasts', E Belarus
119 *M16* **Mahilyowskaya Voblasts'** *prev. Rus.* Mogilëvskaya Oblast'. ◈ *province* E Belarus
191 *P7* **Mahina** Tahiti, W French Polynesia
185 *E23* **Mahinerangi, Lake** ◎ South Island, New Zealand
Máhkarávju *see* Magerøya
83 *L22* **Mahlabatini** KwaZulu/Natal, E South Africa
166 *L5* **Mahlaing** Mandalay, C Myanmar (Burma)
109 *X8* **Mahldorf** Steiermark, SE Austria
Mahmūd-e 'Erāqī *see* Maḥmūd-e Rāqī
149 *R4* **Maḥmūd-e Rāqī** *var.* Mahmūd-e 'Erāqī. Kāpīsā, NE Afghanistan
Mahmudiya *see* Al Maḥmūdīyah
29 *S5* **Mahnomen** Minnesota, N USA
152 *K14* **Mahoba** Uttar Pradesh, N India
105 *Z9* **Mahón** *Cat.* Maó, *Eng.* Port Mahon; *anc.* Portus Magonis. Menorca, Spain, W Mediterranean Sea
18 *D14* **Mahoning Creek Lake** ⊠ Pennsylvania, NE USA
105 *Q10* **Mahora** Castilla-La Mancha, C Spain
Mähren *see* Moravia
Mährisch-Budwitz *see* Moravské Budějovice
Mährisch-Kromau *see* Moravský Krumlov
Mährisch-Neustadt *see* Uničov
Mährisch-Schönberg *see* Šumperk
Mährisch-Trübau *see* Moravská Třebová
Mährisch-Weisskirchen *see* Hranice
Māh-Shahr *see* Bandar-e Māhshahr
79 *N19* **Mahulu** Maniema, E Dem. Rep. Congo
154 *C12* **Mahuva** Gujarāt, W India
114 *N11* **Mahya Dağı** ▲ NW Turkey
105 *T6* **Maials** *var.* Mayals. Cataluña, NE Spain
191 *O2* **Maiana** *prev.* Hall Island. *atoll* Tungaru, W Kiribati
191 *S11* **Maiao** *var.* Tapuaemanu, Tubuai-Manu. *island* Îles du Vent, W French Polynesia
54 *H4* **Maicao** La Guajira, N Colombia
Mai Ceu/Mai Chio *see* Maych'ew
103 *U8* **Maîche** Doubs, E France
97 *N22* **Maidenhead** S England, UK
9 *S15* **Maidstone** Saskatchewan, S Canada
97 *P22* **Maidstone** SE England, UK
77 *Y13* **Maiduguri** Borno, NE Nigeria
108 *I8* **Maienfeld** Sankt Gallen, NE Switzerland
116 *J12* **Măieruș** *Hung.* Szászmagyarós. Brașov, C Romania
Maigh Chromtha *see* Macroom
Maigh Eo *see* Mayo
55 *N9* **Maigualida, Sierra** ▲▲ S Venezuela
154 *K9* **Maihar** Madhya Pradesh, C India
154 *K11* **Maikala Range** ▲▲ C India
67 *T10* **Maiko** ≈ W Dem. Rep. Congo
Mailand *see* Milano
152 *L11* **Mailāni** Uttar Pradesh, N India
149 *U10* **Māilsi** Punjab, E Pakistan
147 *R8* **Maimak** Talasskaya Oblast', NW Kyrgyzstan
Maimāna *see* Meymaneh
Maimansingh *see* Mymensingh
171 *V13* **Maimawa** Papua, E Indonesia
Maimuna *see* Al Maymūnah
101 *G18* **Main** ≈ C Germany
115 *F22* **Maïna** *ancient monument* Pelopónnisos, S Greece
115 *E20* **Maínalo** ▲▲ S Greece
101 *L22* **Mainburg** Bayern, SE Germany
Main Camp *see* Banana
14 *E12* **Main Channel** *lake channel* Ontario, S Canada
79 *I20* **Mai-Ndombe, Lac** *prev.* Lac Léopold II. ◎ W Dem. Rep. Congo
101 *K20* **Main-Donau-Kanal** *canal* SE Germany
19 *R6* **Maine** *off.* State of Maine, *also known as* Lumber State, Pine Tree State. ◈ *state* NE USA
102 *K6* **Maine** *cultural region* NW France
102 *J7* **Maine-et-Loire** ◈ *department* NW France
19 *Q9* **Maine, Gulf of** *gulf* NE USA
77 *X12* **Maïné-Soroa** Diffa, SE Niger
167 *N2* **Maingkwan** *var.* Mungkawn. Kachin State, N Myanmar (Burma)
Main Island *see* Bermuda
Mainistir Fhear Maí *see* Fermoy
Mainistirna Búille *see* Boyle
Mainistir na Corann *see* Midleton
Mainistir na Féile *see* Abbeyfeale
96 *J5* **Mainland** *island* N Scotland, UK
96 *L2* **Mainland** *island* NE Scotland, UK
159 *P16* **Mainling** *var.* Tungdor. Xizang Zizhiqu, W China
152 *K12* **Mainpuri** Uttar Pradesh, N India
103 *N5* **Maintenon** Eure-et-Loir, C France
172 *H4* **Maintirano** Mahajanga, W Madagascar
93 *M15* **Mainua** Oulu, C Finland
101 *G18* **Mainz** *Fr.* Mayence. Rheinland-Pfalz, SW Germany
76 *I9* **Maio** *var.* Vila do Maio. Maio, S Cape Verde
76 *E10* **Maio** *var.* Mayo. *island* Ilhas de Sotavento, SE Cape Verde
62 *G12* **Maipo, Río** ≈ C Chile
62 *H12* **Maipo, Volcán** ⛰ W Argentina
61 *E22* **Maipú** Buenos Aires, E Argentina
62 *I11* **Maipú** Mendoza, E Argentina
62 *H11* **Maipú** Santiago, C Chile
106 *A9* **Maira** ≈ NW Italy
108 *I10* **Maira** *It.* Mera. ≈ Italy/Switzerland
153 *V12* **Mairābari** Assam, NE India
44 *K7* **Maisí** Guantánamo, E Cuba
118 *H13* **Maišiagala** Vilnius, SE Lithuania
153 *V17* **Maiskhal Island** *island* SE Bangladesh
167 *N13* **Mai Sombun** Chumphon, SW Thailand
Mai Son *see* Hat Lot
Maisur *see* Karnātaka, India
Maisur *see* Mysore, India
183 *T8* **Maitland** New South Wales, SE Australia
182 *I9* **Maitland** South Australia
14 *F15* **Maitland** ≈ Ontario, S Canada
195 *R1* **Maitri** *Indian research station* Antarctica
159 *N15* **Maizhokunggar** Xizang Zizhiqu, W China
43 *O10* **Maíz, Islas del** *var.* Corn Islands. *island group* SE Nicaragua
164 *J12* **Maizuru** Kyōto, Honshū, SW Japan
54 *F6* **Majagual** Sucre, N Colombia
41 *Z13* **Majahual** Quintana Roo, E Mexico
Mājeej *see* Mejit Island
171 *N13* **Majene** *prev.* Madjene. Sulawesi, C Indonesia
43 *V15* **Majé, Serranía de** ▲▲ E Panama
112 *I11* **Majevica** ▲▲ NE Bosnia and Herzegovina
81 *H15* **Majī** Southern, S Ethiopia
141 *X7* **Majīs** NW Oman
Majorca *see* Mallorca
105 *X9* **Major, Puig** ▲ Mallorca, Spain, W Mediterranean Sea
Mājro *see* Majuro Atoll
Majunga *see* Mahajanga
189 *Y3* **Majuro** ✈ Majuro Atoll, SE Marshall Islands
189 *Y2* **Majuro Atoll** *var.* Mājro. *atoll* Ratak Chain, SE Marshall Islands
189 *X2* **Majuro Lagoon** *lagoon* Majuro Atoll, SE Marshall Islands
76 *H11* **Maka** C Senegal
79 *F20* **Makabana** Le Niari, SW Congo
38 *D9* **Mākaha** *var.* Makaha. O'ahu, Hawai'i, USA
38 *B8* **Makahū'ena Point** *var.* Makahuena Point. *headland* Kaua'i, Hawai'i, USA
38 *D9* **Makakilo City** O'ahu, Hawai'i, USA
83 *H18* **Makalamabedi** Central, C Botswana
Makale *see* Mek'elē
158 *K17* **Makalu** *Chin.* Makaru Shan. ▲ China/Nepal
81 *G23* **Makampi** Mbeya, S Tanzania
145 *X12* **Makanchi** *Kaz.* Maqanshy. Vostochnyy Kazakhstan, E Kazakhstan
42 *M8* **Makantaka** Región Autónoma Atlántico Norte, NE Nicaragua
190 *B16* **Makapu Point** *headland* W Niue
185 *C24* **Makarewa** Southland, South Island, New Zealand
117 *O4* **Makariv** Kyyivs'ka Oblast', N Ukraine
185 *D20* **Makarora** ≈ South Island, New Zealand
123 *T13* **Makarov** Ostrov Sakhalin, Sakhalinskaya Oblast', SE Russian Federation
197 *R9* **Makarov Basin** *undersea feature* Arctic Ocean
192 *I5* **Makarov Seamount** *undersea feature* W Pacific Ocean
113 *F15* **Makarska** *It.* Macarsca. Split-Dalmacija, SE Croatia
Makaru Shan *see* Makalu
125 *O15* **Makar'yev** Kostromskaya Oblast', NW Russian Federation
82 *L11* **Makasa** Northern, NE Zambia
Makasar *see* Makassar
Makasar, Selat *see* Makassar Straits
170 *M14* **Makassar** *var.* Macassar, Makasar; *prev.* Ujungpandang. Sulawesi, C Indonesia
192 *F7* **Makassar Straits** *Ind.* Makasar Selat. *strait* C Indonesia
144 *G12* **Makat** *Kaz.* Maqat. Atyrau, SW Kazakhstan
191 *T10* **Makatea** *island* Îles Tuamotu, C French Polynesia
139 *U7* **Makātū** E Iraq
172 *H6* **Makay** *var.* Massif du Makay. ▲▲ SW Madagascar
Makay, Massif du *see* Makay
114 *J12* **Makaza** *pass* Bulgaria/Greece
Makedonija *see* Macedonia, FYR
190 *B16* **Makefu** W Niue
191 *V10* **Makemo** *atoll* Îles Tuamotu, C French Polynesia
76 *I15* **Makeni** C Sierra Leone
Makenzen *see* Orlyak
Makeyevka *see* Makiyivka
127 *Q16* **Makhachkala** *prev.* Petrovsk-Port. Respublika Dagestan, SW Russian Federation
144 *F11* **Makhambet** Atyrau, W Kazakhstan
Makharadze *see* Ozurget'i
139 *W13* **Makhfar Al Buṣayyah** S Iraq
139 *R4* **Makhmūr** N Iraq
138 *I11* **Makhrūq, Wadi al** *dry watercourse* E Jordan
139 *R4* **Makḥūl, Jabal** ▲ C Iraq
141 *R13* **Makhyah, Wādī** *dry watercourse* N Yemen
171 *V13* **Maki** Papua, E Indonesia
185 *G21* **Makikihi** Canterbury, South Island, New Zealand
191 *O2* **Makin** *prev.* Pitt Island. *atoll* Tungaru, W Kiribati
81 *I20* **Makindu** Eastern, S Kenya
145 *Q8* **Makinsk** Akmola, N Kazakhstan
187 *N10* **Makira** *off.* Makira Province. ◈ *province* SE Solomon Islands
Makira *see* San Cristobal
Makira Province *see* Makira
117 *X8* **Makiyivka** *Rus.* Makeyevka; *prev.* Dmitriyevsk. Donets'ka Oblast', E Ukraine
140 *L10* **Makkah** *Eng.* Mecca. Makkah, W Saudi Arabia
140 *M10* **Makkah** *var.* Minṭaqat Makkah. ◈ *province* W Saudi Arabia
Makkah, Minṭaqat *see* Makkah
13 *R7* **Makkovik** Newfoundland and Labrador, NE Canada
98 *K6* **Makkum** Friesland, N Netherlands
111 *M25* **Makó** *Rom.* Macău. Csongrád, SE Hungary
Mako *see* Makung
14 *G9* **Makobe Lake** ◎ Ontario, S Canada
79 *F18* **Makokou** Ogooué-Ivindo, NE Gabon
81 *G23* **Makongolosi** Mbeya, S Tanzania
81 *E19* **Makota** SW Uganda
79 *G18* **Makoua** Cuvette, C Congo
110 *M10* **Maków Mazowiecki** Mazowieckie, C Poland
111 *K17* **Maków Podhalański** Małopolskie, S Poland
143 *V14* **Makran** *cultural region* Iran/Pakistan
152 *G12* **Makrāna** Rājasthān, N India
143 *U15* **Makran Coast** *coastal region* SE Iran
119 *F20* **Makrany** *Rus.* Mokrany. Brestskaya Voblasts', SW Belarus
Makrinoros *see* Makrynóros
115 *H20* **Makrónisosi** *island* Kykládes, Greece, Aegean Sea
115 *D17* **Makrynóros** *var.* Makrinoros. ▲▲ C Greece
115 *G19* **Makryplági** ▲ C Greece
Maksamaa *see* Maxmo
Maksatha *see* Maksatikha
Maksaticha *see* Maksatikha
124 *J15* **Maksatikha** *var.* Maksatha, Maksaticha. Tverskaya Oblast', W Russian Federation
154 *G10* **Maksi** Madhya Pradesh, C India
142 *I1* **Mākū** Āzarbāyjān-e Gharbī, NW Iran
153 *Y11* **Makum** Assam, NE India
Makun *see* Makung
161 *R14* **Makung** *prev.* Mako, Makun. W Taiwan
164 *B16* **Makurazaki** Kagoshima, Kyūshū, SW Japan
77 *V15* **Makurdi** Benue, C Nigeria
38 *L17* **Makushin Volcano** ⛰ Unalaska Island, Alaska, USA
83 *K16* **Makwiro** Mashonaland West, N Zimbabwe
57 *D15* **Mala** Lima, W Peru
Mala *see* Mallow, Ireland
Mala *see* Malaita, Solomon Islands
93 *I14* **Malå** Västerbotten, N Sweden
190 *G12* **Mala'atoli** Île Uvea, E Wallis and Futuna
171 *P8* **Malabang** Mindanao, S Philippines
155 *E21* **Malabār Coast** *coast* SW India
79 *C16* **Malabo** *prev.* Santa Isabel. ● (Equatorial Guinea) Isla de Bioco, NW Equatorial Guinea
79 *C16* **Malabo** ✈ Isla de Bioco, N Equatorial Guinea
Malaca *see* Málaga
Malacca *see* Melaka
168 *I7* **Malacca, Strait of** *Ind.* Selat Malaka. *strait* Indonesia/Malaysia
Malacka *see* Malacky
111 *G20* **Malacky** *Hung.* Malacka. Bratislavský Kraj, W Slovakia
33 *R16* **Malad City** Idaho, NW USA
117 *Q4* **Mala Divytsya** Chernihivs'ka Oblast', N Ukraine
119 *J15* **Maladzyechna** *Pol.* Molodeczno, *Rus.* Molodechno. Minskaya Voblasts', C Belarus
190 *D12* **Malaee** Île Futuna, N Wallis and Futuna
54 *G8* **Málaga** Santander, C Colombia
104 *M15* **Málaga** *anc.* Malaca. Andalucía, S Spain
37 *V15* **Malaga** New Mexico, SW USA
104 *L15* **Málaga** ◈ *province* Andalucía, S Spain
104 *M15* **Málaga** ✈ Andalucía, S Spain
Malagasy Republic *see* Madagascar
105 *N10* **Malagón** Castilla-La Mancha, C Spain
97 *G18* **Malahide** *Ir.* Mullach Íde. Dublin, E Ireland
187 *N9* **Malaita** *off.* Malaita Province. ◈ *province* N Solomon Islands
187 *N8* **Malaita** *var.* Mala. *island* N Solomon Islands
Malaita Province *see* Malaita
80 *F13* **Malakal** Upper Nile, S Sudan
112 *C10* **Mala Kapela** ▲▲ NW Croatia
25 *V7* **Malakoff** Texas, SW USA
Malakula *see* Malekula
149 *V7* **Malakwāl** *var.* Mālikwāla. Punjab, E Pakistan
186 *E7* **Malalamai** Madang, W Papua New Guinea
171 *O13* **Malamala** Sulawesi, C Indonesia
169 *S17* **Malang** Jawa, C Indonesia
83 *O14* **Malanga** Niassa, N Mozambique
Malange *see* Malanje
92 *I9* **Malangen** *sound* N Norway
82 *C11* **Malanje** *var.* Malange. Malanje, NW Angola
82 *C11* **Malanje** *var.* Malange. ◈ *province* N Angola
148 *M16* **Malān, Rās** *cape* SW Pakistan
77 *S13* **Malanville** NE Benin
Malapane *see* Ozimek
155 *F21* **Malappuram** Kerala, SW India
43 *T17* **Mala, Punta** *headland* S Panama
95 *N16* **Mälaren** ◎ C Sweden
62 *H13* **Malargüe** Mendoza, W Argentina
14 *J8* **Malartic** Québec, SE Canada
119 *F20* **Malaryta** *Pol.* Maloryta, *Rus.* Malorita. Brestskaya Voblasts', SW Belarus
63 *J19* **Malaspina** Chubut, SE Argentina
39 *U12* **Malaspina Glacier** *glacier* Alaska, USA
137 *N15* **Malatya** *anc.* Melitene. Malatya, SE Turkey
136 *M14* **Malatya** ◈ *province* C Turkey
Malavate *see* Pédima
117 *Q7* **Mala Vyska** *Rus.* Malaya Viska. Kirovohrads'ka Oblast', S Ukraine
83 *M14* **Malawi** *off.* Republic of Malaŵi; *prev.* Nyasaland, Nyasaland Protectorate. ◆ *republic* S Africa
Malawi, Lake *see* Nyasa, Lake
Malaŵi, Republic of *see* Malawi
93 *J17* **Malax** *Fin.* Maalahti. Länsi-Soumi, W Finland
124 *H14* **Malaya Vishera** Novgorodskaya Oblast', W Russian Federation
Malaya Viska *see* Mala Vyska
171 *Q7* **Malaybalay** Mindanao, S Philippines
142 *L6* **Malāyer** *prev.* Daulatabad. Hamadān, W Iran
168 *J7* **Malay Peninsula** *peninsula* Malaysia/Thailand
168 *L7* **Malaysia** *var.* Federation of Malaysia; *prev.* the separate territories of Federation of Malaya, Sarawak and Sabah (North Borneo) and Singapore. ◆ *monarchy* SE Asia
Malaysia, Federation of *see* Malaysia
137 *R14* **Malazgirt** Muş, E Turkey
15 *R8* **Malbaie** ≈ Québec, SE Canada
77 *T12* **Malbaza** Tahoua, S Niger
110 *J7* **Malbork** *Ger.* Marienburg, Marienburg in Westpreussen. Pomorskie, N Poland
100 *N9* **Malchin** Mecklenburg-Vorpommern, N Germany
100 *M9* **Malchiner See** ◎ NE Germany
99 *D16* **Maldegem** Oost-Vlaanderen, NW Belgium
98 *L13* **Malden** Gelderland, SE Netherlands
19 *O11* **Malden** Massachusetts, NE USA
27 *Y8* **Malden** Missouri, C USA
191 *X4* **Malden Island** *prev.* Independence Island. *atoll* E Kiribati
173 *Q6* **Maldives** *off.* Maldivian Divehi, Republic of Maldives. ◆ *republic* N Indian Ocean
Maldives, Republic of *see* Maldives
Maldivian Divehi *see* Maldives
97 *P21* **Maldon** E England, UK
61 *G20* **Maldonado** Maldonado, S Uruguay
61 *G20* **Maldonado** ◈ *department* S Uruguay
41 *P17* **Maldonado, Punta** *headland* S Mexico
106 *G6* **Malè** Trentino-Alto Adige, N Italy
151 *K19* **Male'** *Div.* Maale. ● (Maldives) Male' Atoll, C Maldives
76 *K13* **Maléa** *var.* Maléya. NE Guinea
Maléas, Ákra *see* Agriliá, Akrotírio
115 *G22* **Maléas, Akrotírio** *cape* S Greece
151 *K19* **Male' Atoll** *var.* Kaafu Atoll. *atoll* C Maldives
Malebo, Pool *see* Stanley Pool
154 *E12* **Mālegaon** Mahārāshtra, W India
81 *F15* **Malek** Jonglei, S Sudan
187 *Q13* **Malekula** *var.* Malakula; *prev.* Mallicolo. *island* W Vanuatu
189 *Y15* **Malem** Kosrae, E Micronesia
83 *O15* **Malema** Nampula, N Mozambique
79 *N23* **Malemba-Nkulu** Katanga, SE Dem. Rep. Congo
124 *K9* **Malen'ga** Respublika Kareliya, NW Russian Federation
95 *M20* **Målerås** Kalmar, S Sweden
103 *O6* **Malesherbes** Loiret, C France
115 *G18* **Malesína** Stereá Ellás, E Greece
Maléya *see* Maléa
127 *O15* **Malgobek** Chechenskaya Respublika, SW Russian Federation
105 *X5* **Malgrat de Mar** Cataluña, NE Spain
80 *C9* **Malha** Northern Darfur, W Sudan
139 *Q5* **Malḥāt** C Iraq
32 *K14* **Malheur Lake** ◎ Oregon, NW USA
32 *L14* **Malheur River** ≈ Oregon, NW USA
76 *I13* **Mali** NW Guinea
77 *O9* **Mali** *off.* Republic of Mali, *Fr.* République du Mali; *prev.* French Sudan, Sudanese Republic. ◆ *republic* W Africa
171 *Q16* **Maliana** W East Timor
167 *O2* **Mali Hka** ≈ N Myanmar (Burma)
Mali Idjoš *see* Mali Iđoš
112 *K8* **Mali Iđoš** *var.* Mali Idjoš, *Hung.* Kishegyes; *prev.* Krivaja. Vojvodina, N Serbia
112 *K9* **Mali Kanal** *canal* N Serbia
171 *P12* **Maliku** Sulawesi, N Indonesia
Malik, Wadi al *see* Milk, Wadi el
Mālikwāla *see* Malakwāl
167 *N11* **Mali Kyun** *var.* Tavoy Island. *island* Mergui Archipelago, S Myanmar (Burma)
95 *M19* **Målilla** Kalmar, S Sweden
112 *B11* **Mali Lošinj** *It.* Lussinpiccolo. Primorje-Gorski Kotar, W Croatia
Malin *see* Malyn
171 *P7* **Malindang, Mount** ▲ Mindanao, S Philippines
81 *K20* **Malindi** Coast, SE Kenya
Malines *see* Mechelen
96 *E13* **Malin Head** *Ir.* Cionn Mhálanna. *headland* NW Ireland
171 *O11* **Malino, Gunung** ▲ Sulawesi, N Indonesia
113 *M21* **Maliq** *var.* Maliqi. Korçë, SE Albania
Maliqi *see* Maliq
Mali, Republic of *see* Mali
Mali, République du *see* Mali
171 *Q8* **Malita** Mindanao, S Philippines
154 *G12* **Malkāpur** Mahārāshtra, C India
136 *B10* **Malkara** Tekirdağ, NW Turkey
119 *J19* **Mal'kavichy** *Rus.* Mal'kovichi. Brestskaya Voblasts', SW Belarus
Malkiye *see* Al Mālikīyah
114 *L11* **Malko Sharkovo, Yazovir** ⊠ SE Bulgaria
114 *N11* **Malko Tŭrnovo** Burgas, E Bulgaria
Mal'kovichi *see* Mal'kavichy
183 *R12* **Mallacoota** Victoria, SE Australia
96 *G10* **Mallaig** N Scotland, UK
182 *I9* **Mallala** South Australia
75 *W9* **Mallawi** C Egypt
105 *R5* **Mallén** Aragón, NE Spain
106 *F5* **Malles Venosta** *Ger.* Mals im Vinschgau. Trentino-Alto Adige, N Italy
Mallicolo *see* Malekula
109 *Q8* **Mallnitz** Salzburg, S Austria
105 *W9* **Mallorca** *Eng.* Majorca; *anc.* Baleares Major. *island* Islas Baleares, Spain, W Mediterranean Sea
97 *C20* **Mallow** *Ir.* Mala. SW Ireland
93 *E15* **Malm** Nord-Trøndelag, C Norway
95 *L19* **Malmbäck** Jönköping, S Sweden
92 *J12* **Malmberget** *Lapp.* Malmivaara. Norrbotten, N Sweden
99 *M20* **Malmédy** Liège, E Belgium
83 *E25* **Malmesbury** Western Cape, SW South Africa
Malmivaara *see* Malmberget
95 *N16* **Malmköping** Södermanland, C Sweden
95 *K23* **Malmö** Skåne, S Sweden
95 *K23* **Malmo** ✈ Skåne, S Sweden
45 *Q16* **Malmok** *headland* Bonaire, S Netherlands Antilles
95 *M18* **Malmslätt** Östergötland, S Sweden
125 *R16* **Malmyzh** Kirovskaya Oblast', NW Russian Federation
187 *Q13* **Malo** *island* W Vanuatu
126 *J7* **Maloarkhangel'sk** Orlovskaya Oblast', W Russian Federation
Maloelap *see* Maloelap Atoll
189 *V6* **Maloelap Atoll** *var.* Maloelap. *atoll* E Marshall Islands
Maloenda *see* Malunda

◆ Country ● Country Capital ◇ Dependent Territory ○ Dependent Territory Capital ◈ Administrative Regions ✈ International Airport ▲ Mountain ▲▲ Mountain Range ⛰ Volcano ≈ River ◎ Lake ⊠ Reservoir

108 I10 Maloja Graubünden, S Switzerland
82 L12 Malole Northern, NE Zambia
171 O3 Malolos Luzon, N Philippines
18 K6 Malone New York, NE USA
79 K25 Malonga Katanga, S Dem. Rep. Congo
111 L17 Małopolskie ◈ province SE Poland
Malorita/Maloryta see Malaryta
124 K9 Maloshuyka Arkhangel'skaya Oblast', NW Russian Federation
114 G10 Mal'ovitsa ▲ W Bulgaria
145 V15 Malovodnoye Almaty, SE Kazakhstan
94 C10 Måløy Sogn Og Fjordane, S Norway
126 K4 Maloyaroslavets Kaluzhskaya Oblast', W Russian Federation
122 G7 Malozemel'skaya Tundra physical region NW Russian Federation
104 J10 Malpartida de Cáceres Extremadura, W Spain
104 K9 Malpartida de Plasencia Extremadura, W Spain
106 C7 Malpensa ✈ (Milano) Lombardia, N Italy
76 J6 Malqteïr desert N Mauritania
Mals im Vinschgau see Malles Venosta
118 J10 Malta Rēzekne, SE Latvia
33 V7 Malta Montana, NW USA
120 M11 Malta off. Republic of Malta. ◆ republic C Mediterranean Sea
109 R8 Malta var. Maltabach. ≈ S Austria
120 M11 Malta island Malta, C Mediterranean Sea
Maltabach see Malta
Malta, Canale di see Malta Channel
120 M11 Malta Channel It. Canale di Malta. strait Italy/Malta
83 D20 Maltahöhe Hardap, SW Namibia
Malta, Republic of see Malta
97 N16 Malton N England, UK
171 R13 Maluku off. Propinsi Maluku, Dut. Molukken, Eng. Moluccas. ◈ province E Indonesia
171 R13 Maluku Dut. Molukken, Eng. Moluccas; prev. Spice Islands. island group E Indonesia
Maluku, Laut see Molucca Sea
Maluku, Propinsi see Maluku
171 R11 Maluku Utara off. Propinsi Maluku Utara. ◈ province E Indonesia
Maluku Utara, Propinsi see Maluku Utara
77 V13 Malumfashi Katsina, N Nigeria
171 N13 Malunda prev. Maloenda. Sulawesi, C Indonesia
94 K13 Malung Dalarna, C Sweden
94 K13 Malungsfors Dalarna, C Sweden
186 M8 Maluu var. Malu'u. Malaita, N Solomon Islands
Malu'u see Maluu
155 D16 Mālvan Mahārāshtra, W India
Malventum see Benevento
27 U12 Malvern Arkansas, C USA
29 S15 Malvern Iowa, C USA
44 I13 Malvern ▲ W Jamaica
Malvinas, Islas see Falkland Islands
117 N4 Malyn Rus. Malin. Zhytomyrs'ka Oblast', N Ukraine
127 O11 Malyye Derbety Respublika Kalmykiya, SW Russian Federation
Malyy Kavkaz see Lesser Caucasus
123 Q6 Malyy Lyakhovskiy, Ostrov island NE Russian Federation
Malyy Pamir see Little Pamir
122 N5 Malyy Taymyr, Ostrov island Severnaya Zemlya, N Russian Federation
144 E10 Malyy Uzen' Kaz. Kishiözen. ≈ Kazakhstan/Russian Federation
122 L14 Malyy Yenisey var. Ka-Krem. ≈ S Russian Federation
127 S3 Mamadysh Respublika Tatarstan, W Russian Federation
117 N14 Mamaia Constanța, E Romania
187 W14 Mamanuca Group island group Yasawa Group, W Fiji
146 L13 Mamash Lebap Welaýaty, E Turkmenistan
79 O17 Mambasa Orientale, NE Dem. Rep. Congo
171 X13 Mamberamo, Sungai ≈ Papua, E Indonesia
79 G15 Mambéré ≈ SW Central African Republic
79 G15 Mambéré-Kadéï ◈ prefecture SW Central African Republic
Mambij see Manbij
79 H18 Mambili ≈ W Congo
83 N18 Mambone var. Nova Mambone. Inhambane, E Mozambique
171 O4 Mamburao Mindoro, N Philippines
172 I16 Mamelles island Inner Islands, NE Seychelles
99 M25 Mamer Luxembourg, SW Luxembourg
102 L6 Mamers Sarthe, NW France
79 D15 Mamfe Sud-Ouest, W Cameroon
145 P6 Mamlyutka Severnyy Kazakhstan, N Kazakhstan
36 M15 Mammoth Arizona, SW USA
33 S12 Mammoth Hot Springs Wyoming, C USA
Mamoedjoe see Mamuju
119 A14 Mamonovo Ger. Heiligenbeil. Kaliningradskaya Oblast', W Russian Federation
57 L14 Mamoré, Rio ≈ Bolivia/Brazil
76 I14 Mamou W Guinea
22 H8 Mamou Louisiana, S USA
172 I14 Mamoudzou ○ (Mayotte) C Mayotte
172 I3 Mampikony Mahajanga, N Madagascar
77 P16 Mampong C Ghana
110 M7 Mamry, Jezioro Ger. Mauersee. ◎ NE Poland
171 N13 Mamuju prev. Mamoedjoe. Sulawesi, S Indonesia
83 F19 Mamuno Ghanzi, W Botswana
113 K19 Mamuras var. Mamurasi, Mamurras. Lezhë, C Albania
Mamurasi/Mamurras see Mamuras
76 L16 Man W Ivory Coast
55 X9 Mana NW French Guiana
56 A6 Manabí ◈ province W Ecuador
42 G4 Manabique, Punta var. Cabo Tres Puntas. headland E Guatemala
54 G11 Manacacías, Río ≈ C Colombia
58 F13 Manacapuru Amazonas, N Brazil
105 Y9 Manacor Mallorca, Spain, W Mediterranean Sea
171 Q11 Manado prev. Menado. Sulawesi, C Indonesia
188 H5 Managaha island S Northern Mariana Islands
99 G20 Manage Hainaut, S Belgium
42 J10 Managua ● (Nicaragua) Managua, W Nicaragua
42 J10 Managua ◈ department W Nicaragua
42 J10 Managua ✈ Managua, W Nicaragua
42 J10 Managua, Lago de var. Xolotlán. ◎ W Nicaragua
Manah see Bilād Manaḩ
18 K16 Manahawkin New Jersey, NE USA
184 K11 Manaia Taranaki, North Island, New Zealand
172 J6 Manakara Fianarantsoa, SE Madagascar
152 J7 Manāli Himāchal Pradesh, NW India
129 U12 Ma, Nam Vtn. Sông Mã. ≈ Laos/Vietnam
Manama see Al Manāmah
186 D6 Manam Island island N Papua New Guinea
67 Y13 Mananara ≈ SE Madagascar
182 M9 Manangatang Victoria, SE Australia
172 J6 Mananjary Fianarantsoa, SE Madagascar
76 L14 Manankoro Sikasso, SW Mali
76 J12 Manantali, Lac de ⊠ W Mali
Manáos see Manaus
185 B23 Manapouri Southland, South Island, New Zealand
185 B23 Manapouri, Lake ◎ South Island, New Zealand
58 F13 Manaquiri Amazonas, NW Brazil
Manar see Mannar
158 K5 Manas Xinjiang Uygur Zizhiqu, NW China
153 U12 Manās var. Dangme Chu. ≈ Bhutan/India
153 P10 Manāslu var. Manaslu. ▲ C Nepal
147 R8 Manas, Gora ▲ Kyrgyzstan/Uzbekistan
158 K3 Manas Hu ◎ NW China
Manaslu see Manāslu
37 S8 Manassa Colorado, C USA
21 W4 Manassas Virginia, NE USA
45 T5 Manatí C Puerto Rico
186 E8 Manau Northern, S Papua New Guinea
54 H4 Manaure La Guajira, N Colombia
58 F12 Manaus prev. Manáos. state capital Amazonas, NW Brazil
136 G17 Manavgat Antalya, SW Turkey
184 M13 Manawatu ≈ North Island, New Zealand
184 L11 Manawatu-Wanganui off. Manawatu-Wanganui Region. ◈ region North Island, New Zealand
Manawatu-Wanganui Region see Manawatu-Wanganui
171 R7 Manay Mindanao, S Philippines
138 K2 Manbij var. Mambij, Fr. Membidj. Ḩalab, N Syria
105 N13 Mancha Real Andalucía, S Spain
102 I4 Manche ◈ department N France
97 L17 Manchester Lat. Mancunium. NW England, UK
23 S5 Manchester Georgia, SE USA
29 Y13 Manchester Iowa, C USA
21 N7 Manchester Kentucky, S USA
19 O10 Manchester New Hampshire, NE USA
20 K10 Manchester Tennessee, S USA
18 M9 Manchester Vermont, NE USA
97 L18 Manchester ✈ NW England, UK
149 P15 Manchhar Lake ◎ SE Pakistan
Man-chou-li see Manzhouli
129 X7 Manchurian Plain plain NE China
Máncio Lima see Japiim
Mancunium see Manchester
148 J15 Mand Baluchistān, SW Pakistan
Mand see Mand, Rūd-e
81 H25 Manda Iringa, SW Tanzania
172 H6 Mandabe Toliara, W Madagascar
162 M10 Mandah var. Töhöm. Dornogovĭ, SE Mongolia
95 E18 Mandal Vest-Agder, S Norway
Mandal see Arbulag, Hövsgöl, Mongolia
Mandal see Batsümber, Töv, Mongolia
166 L5 Mandalay Mandalay, C Myanmar (Burma)
166 M6 Mandalay ◈ division C Myanmar (Burma)
162 L9 Mandalgovĭ Dundgovĭ, C Mongolia
139 V7 Mandalī Diyālá, E Iraq
162 K10 Mandal-Ovoo var. Sharhulsan. Ömnögovĭ, S Mongolia
95 E18 Mandalselva ≈ S Norway
163 P11 Mandalt var. Sonid Zuoqi. Nei Mongol Zizhiqu, N China
28 M5 Mandan North Dakota, N USA
Mandargiri Hill see Mandār Hill
153 R14 Mandār Hill prev. Mandargiri Hill. Bihār, NE India
170 M13 Mandar, Teluk bay Sulawesi, C Indonesia
107 C19 Mandas Sardegna, Italy, C Mediterranean Sea
Mandasor see Mandsaur
81 L16 Mandera North Eastern, NE Kenya
33 V13 Manderson Wyoming, C USA
44 J12 Mandeville C Jamaica
22 K9 Mandeville Louisiana, S USA
152 I7 Mandi Himāchal Pradesh, NW India
76 K14 Mandiana E Guinea
149 U10 Mandi Būrewāla var. Būrewāla. Punjab, E Pakistan
152 G9 Mandi Dabwāli Haryāna, NW India
Mandidzudzure see Chimanimani
83 M15 Mandié Manica, NW Mozambique
83 N14 Mandimba Niassa, N Mozambique
57 Q19 Mandioré, Laguna ◎ E Bolivia
154 J10 Mandla Madhya Pradesh, C India
83 M20 Mandlakazi var. Manjacaze. Gaza, S Mozambique
95 E24 Mandø var. Manø. island W Denmark
Mandoúdhion/Mandoudi see Mantoúdi
115 G19 Mándra Attikí, C Greece
172 I7 Mandrare ≈ S Madagascar
114 M10 Mandra, Yazovir salt lake SE Bulgaria
107 L23 Mandrazzi, Portella pass Sicilia, Italy, C Mediterranean Sea
172 J3 Mandritsara Mahajanga, N Madagascar
143 O13 Mand, Rūd-e var. Mand. ≈ S Iran
154 F9 Mandsaur prev. Mandasor. Madhya Pradesh, C India
154 F11 Māndu Madhya Pradesh, C India
169 W8 Mandul, Pulau island N Indonesia
83 G15 Mandundu Western, W Zambia
180 I13 Mandurah Western Australia
107 P18 Manduria Puglia, SE Italy
155 G20 Mandya Karnātaka, C India
77 P12 Mané C Burkina
106 E8 Manerbio Lombardia, NW Italy
Manevichi see Manevychi
116 K3 Manevychi Pol. Maniewicze, Rus. Manevichi. Volyns'ka Oblast', NW Ukraine
107 N16 Manfredonia Puglia, SE Italy
107 N16 Manfredonia, Golfo di gulf Adriatic Sea, N Mediterranean Sea
77 P13 Manga C Burkina
59 L16 Mangabeiras, Chapada das ▲ E Brazil
79 J20 Mangai Bandundu, W Dem. Rep. Congo
190 L17 Mangaia island group S Cook Islands
184 M9 Mangakino Waikato, North Island, New Zealand
116 M15 Mangalia anc. Callatis. Constanța, SE Romania
78 J11 Mangalmé Guéra, SE Chad
155 E19 Mangalore Karnātaka, W India
191 Y13 Mangareva var. Magareva. island Îles Tuamotu, SE French Polynesia
83 I23 Mangaung Free State, C South Africa
Mangaung see Bloemfontein
154 K9 Mangawān Madhya Pradesh, C India
184 M11 Mangaweka Manawatu-Wanganui, North Island, New Zealand
184 N11 Mangaweka ▲ North Island, New Zealand
79 P17 Mangbwalu Orientale, NE Dem. Rep. Congo
101 L24 Mangfall ≈ SE Germany
169 P13 Manggar Pulau Belitung, W Indonesia
166 M2 Mangin Range ▲▲ N Myanmar (Burma)
139 R1 Mangish N Iraq
144 F15 Mangistau Kaz. Mangqystaū Oblysy; prev. Mangyshlaskaya. ◈ province SW Kazakhstan
Mangit see Mang'it
146 H8 Mang'it Rus. Mangit. Qoraqalpog'iston Respublikasi, W Uzbekistan
54 A13 Manglares, Cabo headland SW Colombia
149 V6 Mangla Reservoir ⊠ NE Pakistan
159 N9 Mangnai var. Lao Mangnai. Qinghai, C China
Mango see Mago, Fiji
Mango see Sansanné-Mango, Togo
Mangoche see Mangochi
83 N14 Mangochi var. Mangoche; prev. Fort Johnston. Southern, SE Malawi
77 N14 Mangodara SW Burkina
172 H6 Mangoky ≈ W Madagascar
171 Q12 Mangole, Pulau island Kepulauan Sula, E Indonesia
184 J2 Mangonui Northland, North Island, New Zealand
Mangqystaū Oblysy see Mangistau
Mangqystaū Shyghanaghy see Mangyshlakskiy Zaliv
Mangshi see Luxi
104 H7 Mangualde Viseu, N Portugal
61 H18 Mangueira, Lagoa ◎ S Brazil
77 X6 Manguéni, Plateau du ▲ NE Niger
163 T4 Mangui Nei Mongol Zizhiqu, N China
26 K11 Mangum Oklahoma, C USA
79 O18 Manguredjipa Nord Kivu, E Dem. Rep. Congo
83 L16 Mangwendi Mashonaland East, E Zimbabwe
144 F15 Mangyshlak, Plato plateau SW Kazakhstan
144 E14 Mangyshlakskiy Zaliv Kaz. Mangqystaū Shyghanaghy. gulf SW Kazakhstan
Mangyshlaskaya see Mangistau
162 E7 Manhan var. Tögrög. Hovd, W Mongolia
Manhan see Alag-Erdene
27 O4 Manhattan Kansas, C USA
99 L21 Manhay Luxembourg, SE Belgium
83 L21 Manhiça prev. Vila de Manhiça. Maputo, S Mozambique
83 L21 Manhoca Maputo, S Mozambique
59 N20 Manhuaçu Minas Gerais, SE Brazil
54 H10 Maní Casanare, C Colombia
143 R11 Mānī Kermān, C Iran
83 M17 Manica var. Vila de Manica. Manica, W Mozambique
83 M17 Manica off. Província de Manica. ◈ province W Mozambique
83 L17 Manicaland ◈ province E Zimbabwe
Manica, Província de see Manica
15 U5 Manic Deux, Réservoir ⊠ Québec, SE Canada
Manich see Manych
59 F14 Manicoré Amazonas, N Brazil
13 N11 Manicouagan Québec, SE Canada
13 N11 Manicouagan ≈ Québec, SE Canada
15 U6 Manicouagan, Péninsule de peninsula Québec, SE Canada
13 N11 Manicouagan, Réservoir ◎ Québec, E Canada
15 T4 Manic Trois, Réservoir ⊠ Québec, SE Canada
79 M20 Maniema off. Région du Maniema. ◈ region E Dem. Rep. Congo
Maniema, Région du see Maniema
Maniewicze see Manevychi
160 F8 Maniganggo Sichuan, C China
9 Y15 Manigotagan Manitoba, S Canada
153 R13 Manihāri Bihār, N India
191 U9 Manihi island Îles Tuamotu, C French Polynesia
190 L13 Manihiki atoll N Cook Islands
175 U8 Manihiki Plateau undersea feature C Pacific Ocean
196 M14 Maniitsoq var. Manîtsoq, Dan. Sukkertoppen. ◈ Kitaa, S Greenland
153 T15 Manikganj Dhaka, C Bangladesh
152 M14 Mānikpur Uttar Pradesh, N India
171 N4 Manila off. City of Manila. ● (Philippines) Luzon, N Philippines
27 Y9 Manila Arkansas, C USA
Manila, City of see Manila
189 N16 Manila Reef reef W Micronesia
183 T5 Manilla New South Wales, SE Australia
192 P5 Maniloa island Tongatapu Group, S Tonga
123 U8 Manily Koryakskiy Avtonomnyy Okrug, E Russian Federation
171 V12 Manim, Pulau island E Indonesia
168 I11 Maninjau, Danau ◎ Sumatera, W Indonesia
153 W13 Manipur ◈ state NE India
153 X14 Manipur Hills hill range E India
136 C14 Manisa var. Manissa, prev. Saruhan; anc. Magnesia. Manisa, W Turkey
136 C13 Manisa var. Manissa. ◈ province W Turkey
Manissa see Manisa
31 O7 Manistee Michigan, N USA
31 P7 Manistee River ≈ Michigan, N USA
31 O4 Manistique Michigan, N USA
31 P4 Manistique Lake ◎ Michigan, N USA
9 W13 Manitoba ◈ province S Canada
9 X16 Manitoba, Lake ◎ Manitoba, S Canada
9 X17 Manitou Manitoba, S Canada
31 N2 Manitou Island island Michigan, N USA
14 H11 Manitou Lake ◎ Ontario, SE Canada
12 G15 Manitoulin Island island Ontario, S Canada
37 T5 Manitou Springs Colorado, C USA
14 G12 Manitouwabing Lake ◎ Ontario, S Canada
12 E12 Manitouwadge Ontario, S Canada
12 G15 Manitowaning Manitoulin Island, Ontario, S Canada
14 B7 Manitowik Lake ◎ Ontario, S Canada
31 N7 Manitowoc Wisconsin, N USA
Manîtsoq see Maniitsoq
139 O7 Mānī', Wādī al dry watercourse W Iraq
12 J14 Maniwaki Québec, SE Canada
171 W13 Maniwori Papua, E Indonesia
54 E10 Manizales Caldas, W Colombia
112 F11 Manjača ▲▲ NW Bosnia and Herzegovina
Manjacaze see Mandlakazi
180 J14 Manjimup Western Australia
109 V4 Mank Niederösterreich, C Austria
79 I17 Mankanza Equateur, NW Dem. Rep. Congo
153 N12 Mankāpur Uttar Pradesh, N India
26 M3 Mankato Kansas, C USA
29 U10 Mankato Minnesota, N USA
117 O7 Man'kivka Cherkas'ka Oblast', C Ukraine
76 M15 Mankono C Ivory Coast
9 T17 Mankota Saskatchewan, S Canada
155 K23 Mankulam Northern Province, N Sri Lanka
162 L10 Manlay var. Üydzen. Ömnögovĭ, S Mongolia
39 Q9 Manley Hot Springs Alaska, USA
18 H10 Manlius New York, NE USA
105 W5 Manlleu Cataluña, NE Spain
29 V11 Manly Iowa, C USA
154 E13 Manmād Mahārāshtra, W India
182 J7 Mannahill South Australia
155 J23 Mannar var. Manar. Northern Province, NW Sri Lanka
155 I24 Mannar, Gulf of gulf India/Sri Lanka
155 J23 Mannar Island island N Sri Lanka
Mannersdorf see Mannersdorf am Leithagebirge
109 Y5 Mannersdorf am Leithagebirge var. Mannersdorf. Niederösterreich, E Austria
109 Y6 Mannersdorf an der Rabnitz Burgenland, E Austria
101 G20 Mannheim Baden-Württemberg, SW Germany
9 O12 Manning Alberta, W Canada
29 T14 Manning Iowa, C USA
28 K5 Manning North Dakota, N USA
21 S13 Manning South Carolina, SE USA
191 Y2 Manning, Cape headland Kiritimati, NE Kiribati
21 S3 Mannington West Virginia, NE USA
182 A1 Mann Ranges ▲▲ South Australia
107 C19 Mannu ≈ Sardegna, Italy, C Mediterranean Sea
9 R14 Mannville Alberta, SW Canada
76 J15 Mano ≈ Liberia/Sierra Leone
Manø see Mandø
39 O13 Manokotak Alaska, USA
171 V12 Manokwari Papua, E Indonesia
79 N22 Manono Shabo, SE Dem. Rep. Congo
25 T10 Manor Texas, SW USA
97 D16 Manorhamilton Ir. Cluainín. Leitrim, NW Ireland
103 S15 Manosque Alpes-de-Haute-Provence, SE France
12 L11 Manouane, Lac ◎ Québec, SE Canada
163 W12 Manp'o var. Manp'ojin. NW North Korea
Manp'ojin see Manp'o
191 T4 Manra prev. Sydney Island. atoll Phoenix Islands, C Kiribati
105 V5 Manresa Cataluña, NE Spain
152 H9 Mānsa Punjab, NW India
82 J12 Mansa prev. Fort Rosebery. Luapula, N Zambia
76 G12 Mansa Konko C Gambia
15 Q11 Manseau Québec, SE Canada
149 U5 Mānsehra North-West Frontier Province, NW Pakistan
9 Q9 Mansel Island island Nunavut, NE Canada
183 O12 Mansfield Victoria, SE Australia
97 M18 Mansfield C England, UK
27 S11 Mansfield Arkansas, C USA
22 G6 Mansfield Louisiana, S USA
19 O12 Mansfield Massachusetts, NE USA
31 T12 Mansfield Ohio, N USA
18 G12 Mansfield Pennsylvania, NE USA
18 M7 Mansfield, Mount ▲ Vermont, NE USA
59 M16 Mansidão Bahia, E Brazil
102 L11 Mansle Charente, W France
76 G12 Mansôa C Guinea-Bissau
47 V8 Manso, Rio ≈ C Brazil
Manşûra see El Manşûra
Mansurabad see Mehrān, Rūd-e
56 A6 Manta Manabí, W Ecuador
56 A6 Manta, Bahía de bay W Ecuador
57 F14 Mantaro, Río ≈ C Peru
35 O8 Manteca California, W USA
54 J7 Mantecal Apure, C Venezuela
31 N11 Manteno Illinois, N USA
21 Y9 Manteo Roanoke Island, North Carolina, SE USA
Mantes-Gassicourt see Mantes-la-Jolie
103 N5 Mantes-la-Jolie prev. Mantes-Gassicourt, Mantes-sur-Seine; anc. Medunta. Yvelines, N France
Mantes-sur-Seine see Mantes-la-Jolie
36 L5 Manti Utah, W USA
Mantinea see Mantíneia
115 F20 Mantíneia anc. Mantinea. site of ancient city Pelopónnisos, S Greece
59 M21 Mantiqueira, Serra da ▲▲ S Brazil
29 W10 Mantorville Minnesota, N USA
115 G17 Mantoúdi var. Mandoudi; prev. Mandoúdhion. Évvoia, C Greece
Mantoue see Mantova
106 F8 Mantova Eng. Mantua, Fr. Mantoue. Lombardia, NW Italy
93 M19 Mäntsälä Etelä-Suomi, S Finland
93 L17 Mänttä Länsi-Suomi, W Finland
Mantua see Mantova
125 O14 Manturovo Kostromskaya Oblast', NW Russian Federation
93 M18 Mäntyharju Isä-Suomi, SE Finland
92 M13 Mäntyjärvi Lappi, N Finland
190 L16 Manuae island S Cook Islands
191 Q10 Manuae atoll Îles Sous le Vent, W French Polynesia
192 L16 Manua Islands island group E American Samoa
40 L5 Manuel Benavides Chihuahua, N Mexico
61 D21 Manuel J. Cobo Buenos Aires, E Argentina
58 M12 Manuel Luís, Recife reef E Brazil
61 F15 Manuel Viana Rio Grande do Sul, S Brazil
59 I14 Manuel Zinho Pará, N Brazil
191 V11 Manuhangi atoll Îles Tuamotu, C French Polynesia
185 E22 Manuherikia ≈ South Island, New Zealand
171 P13 Manui, Pulau island N Indonesia
Manukau see Manurewa
184 L6 Manukau Harbour harbor North Island, New Zealand
191 Z2 Manulu Lagoon ◎ Kiritimati, E Kiribati
182 J7 Manunda Creek seasonal river South Australia
57 K15 Manupari, Río ≈ N Bolivia
184 L6 Manurewa var. Manukau. Auckland, North Island, New Zealand
57 K15 Manurimi, Río ≈ NW Bolivia
186 D5 Manus ◈ province N Papua New Guinea
186 D5 Manus Island var. Great Admiralty Island. island N Papua New Guinea
171 T16 Manuwui Pulau Babar, E Indonesia
29 Q3 Manvel North Dakota, N USA
33 Z14 Manville Wyoming, C USA
22 G6 Many Louisiana, S USA
81 H21 Manyara, Lake ◎ NE Tanzania
126 L12 Manych var. Manich. ≈ SW Russian Federation
127 N13 Manych-Gudilo, Ozero salt lake SW Russian Federation
83 H14 Manyinga North Western, NW Zambia
105 O11 Manzanares Castilla-La Mancha, C Spain
44 H7 Manzanillo Granma, E Cuba
40 K14 Manzanillo Colima, SW Mexico
40 K14 Manzanillo, Bahía bay SW Mexico
37 S11 Manzano Mountains ▲▲ New Mexico, SW USA
37 R12 Manzano Peak ▲ New Mexico, SW USA
163 R6 Manzhouli var. Man-chou-li. Nei Mongol Zizhiqu, N China
Manzil Bū Ruqaybah see Menzel Bourguiba
139 X9 Manzilīyah E Iraq
83 L21 Manzini prev. Bremersdorp. C Swaziland
83 L21 Manzini ✈ (Mbabane) C Swaziland
78 G10 Mao Kanem, W Chad
45 N8 Mao NW Dominican Republic
Maó see Mahón
Maoemere see Maumere
159 W9 Maojing Gansu, N China
171 Y14 Maoke, Pegunungan Dut. Sneeuw-gebergte, Eng. Snow Mountains. ▲▲ Papua, E Indonesia
Maol Réidh, Caoc see Mweelrea
160 M15 Maoming Guangdong, S China
160 H8 Maoxian var. Mao Xian; prev. Fengyizhen. Sichuan, C China
Mao Xian see Maoxian
83 L19 Mapai Gaza, SW Mozambique
158 H15 Mapam Yumco ◎ W China
83 I15 Mapanza Southern, S Zambia
54 J4 Mapararí Falcón, N Venezuela
41 U17 Mapastepec Chiapas, SE Mexico
169 V9 Mapat, Pulau island N Indonesia
171 Y15 Mapi Papua, E Indonesia
171 V11 Mapia, Kepulauan island group E Indonesia
40 L8 Mapimí Durango, C Mexico
83 N19 Mapinhane Inhambane, SE Mozambique
55 N7 Mapire Monagas, NE Venezuela
9 S17 Maple Creek Saskatchewan, S Canada
31 Q9 Maple River ≈ Michigan, N USA
29 P7 Maple River ≈ North Dakota/South Dakota, N USA
29 S13 Mapleton Iowa, C USA
29 U10 Mapleton Minnesota, N USA
29 R5 Mapleton North Dakota, N USA
32 F13 Mapleton Oregon, NW USA
36 L3 Mapleton Utah, W USA
192 K5 Mapmaker Seamounts undersea feature N Pacific Ocean
186 B6 Maprik East Sepik, NW Papua New Guinea
83 L21 Maputo prev. Lourenço Marques. ● (Mozambique) Maputo, S Mozambique
83 L21 Maputo ◈ province S Mozambique
67 V14 Maputo ≈ S Mozambique
83 L21 Maputo ✈ Maputo, S Mozambique
Maqanshy see Makanchi
Maqat see Makat
113 K19 Maqë ≈ NW Albania
113 M19 Maqellarë Dibër, C Albania
159 S12 Maqên var. Dawu; prev. Dawu. Qinghai, C China
159 S11 Maqen Kangri ▲ C China
159 U12 Maqu var. Nyinma. Gansu, C China
104 M9 Maqueda Castilla-La Mancha, C Spain
82 B9 Maquela do Zombo Uíge, NW Angola
63 I16 Maquinchao Río Negro, C Argentina
29 Z13 Maquoketa Iowa, C USA
29 Y13 Maquoketa River ≈ Iowa, C USA
14 F13 Mar Ontario, S Canada
95 F14 Mår ◎ S Norway
81 G19 Mara ◈ region N Tanzania
58 D12 Maraã Amazonas, NW Brazil
191 P8 Maraa Tahiti, W French Polynesia
191 O8 Maraa, Pointe headland Tahiti, W French Polynesia
59 K14 Marabá Pará, NE Brazil
54 H5 Maracaibo Zulia, NW Venezuela

◆ Country
● Country Capital
◇ Dependent Territory
○ Dependent Territory Capital
◈ Administrative Regions
✈ International Airport
▲ Mountain
▲▲ Mountain Range
Volcano
≈ River
◎ Lake
⊠ Reservoir

Maracaibo, Gulf of see Venezuela, Golfo de
54 H5 **Maracaibo, Lago de** var. Lake Maracaibo. inlet NW Venezuela
Maracaibo, Lake see Maracaibo, Lago de
58 K10 **Maracá, Ilha de** island NE Brazil
59 H20 **Maracaju, Serra de** ▲▲ S Brazil
58 I11 **Maracanaquará, Planalto** ▲▲ NE Brazil
54 L5 **Maracay** Aragua, N Venezuela
Marada see Marādah
75 R9 **Marādah** var. Marada. N Libya
77 U12 **Maradi** Maradi, S Niger
77 U11 **Maradi** ⬖ department S Niger
81 E21 **Maragarazi** var. Muragarazi. ≈ Burundi/Tanzania
Maragha see Marāgheh
142 J3 **Marāgheh** var. Maragha. Āžarbāyjān-e Khāvarī, NW Iran
141 P7 **Marāh** var. Marrāt. Ar Riyāḑ, C Saudi Arabia
55 N11 **Marahuaca, Cerro** ▲ S Venezuela
27 R5 **Marais des Cygnes River** ≈ Kansas/Missouri, C USA
58 L11 **Marajó, Baía de** bay N Brazil
59 K12 **Marajó, Ilha de** island N Brazil
191 O2 **Marakei** atoll Tungaru, W Kiribati
Marakesh see Marrakech
81 I18 **Maralal** Rift Valley, C Kenya
83 G21 **Maralaleng** Kgalagadi, S Botswana
145 U8 **Maraldy, Ozero** ◎ NE Kazakhstan
182 C5 **Maralinga** South Australia
Máramarossziget see Sighetu Marmaţiei
187 N9 **Maramasike** var. Small Malaita. island N Solomon Islands
Maramba see Livingstone
194 H3 **Marambio** Argentinian research station Antarctica
116 H9 **Maramureş** ⬖ county NW Romania
36 L15 **Marana** Arizona, SW USA
105 P7 **Maranchón** Castilla-La Mancha, C Spain
142 J2 **Marand** var. Merend. Āžarbāyjān-e Sharqī, NW Iran
Marandellas see Marondera
58 L13 **Maranhão** off. Estado do Maranhão. ⬖ state E Brazil
104 H10 **Maranhão, Barragem do** ⊠ C Portugal
Maranhão, Estado do see Maranhão
149 O11 **Mārān, Koh-i** ▲ SW Pakistan
106 J7 **Marano, Laguna di** lagoon NE Italy
56 E9 **Marañón, Río** ≈ N Peru
102 J10 **Marans** Charente-Maritime, W France
83 M20 **Marão** Inhambane, S Mozambique
185 B23 **Mararoa** ≈ South Island, New Zealand
Maraş/Marash see Kahramanmaraş
107 M19 **Maratea** Basilicata, S Italy
104 G11 **Marateca** Setúbal, S Portugal
115 B20 **Marathiá, Akrotírio** headland Zákynthos, Iónia Nisiá, Greece, C Mediterranean Sea
12 E12 **Marathon** Ontario, S Canada
23 Y17 **Marathon** Florida Keys, Florida, SE USA
24 L10 **Marathon** Texas, SW USA
Marathón see Marathónas
115 H19 **Marathónas** prev. Marathón. Attikí, C Greece
169 W9 **Maratua, Pulau** island N Indonesia
59 O18 **Maraú** Bahia, SE Brazil
143 R3 **Marāveh Tappeh** Golestán, N Iran
24 L11 **Maravillas Creek** ≈ Texas, SW USA
186 D8 **Marawaka** Eastern Highlands, C Papua New Guinea
171 Q7 **Marawi** Mindanao, S Philippines
137 Y11 **Märäzä** Rus. Maraza. E Azerbaijan
Maraza see Märäzä
Marbat see Mirbāţ
104 L16 **Marbella** Andalucía, S Spain
180 J7 **Marble Bar** Western Australia
36 L9 **Marble Canyon** canyon Arizona, SW USA
25 S10 **Marble Falls** Texas, SW USA
27 Y7 **Marble Hill** Missouri, C USA
33 T15 **Marbleton** Wyoming, C USA
Marburg see Marburg an der Lahn
Marburg see Maribor
101 H16 **Marburg an der Lahn** hist. Marburg. Hessen, W Germany
111 H23 **Marcal** ≈ W Hungary
42 G7 **Marcala** La Paz, SW Honduras
111 H24 **Marcali** Somogy, SW Hungary
83 A16 **Marca, Ponta da** headland SW Angola
59 I16 **Marcelândia** Mato Grosso, W Brazil
27 T3 **Marceline** Missouri, C USA
60 I13 **Marcelino Ramos** Rio Grande do Sul, S Brazil
55 Y12 **Marcel, Mont** ▲ S French Guiana
97 O19 **March** E England, UK
109 Z3 **March** var. Morava. ≈ C Europe see also Morava
March see Morava
106 I12 **Marche** Eng. Marches. ⬖ region C Italy
103 N11 **Marche** cultural region C France
99 J21 **Marche-en-Famenne** Luxembourg, SE Belgium
104 K14 **Marchena** Andalucía, S Spain
57 B17 **Marchena, Isla** var. Bindloe Island. island Galapagos Islands, Ecuador, E Pacific Ocean
Marches see Marche
99 J20 **Marchin** Liège, E Belgium
181 S1 **Marchinbar Island** island Wessel Islands, Northern Territory, N Australia
62 L9 **Mar Chiquita, Laguna** ◎ C Argentina
103 Q10 **Marcigny** Saône-et-Loire, C France
23 W16 **Marco** Florida, SE USA
Marcodurum see Düren
59 O15 **Marcolândia** Pernambuco, E Brazil
106 I8 **Marco Polo** ✕ (Venezia) Veneto, NE Italy
Marcounda see Markounda
Marcq see Mark
116 M8 **Mărculeşti** Rus. Markuleshty. N Moldova
29 S12 **Marcus** Iowa, C USA
39 S11 **Marcus Baker, Mount** ▲ Alaska, USA
192 I5 **Marcus Island** var. Minami Tori Shima. island E Japan
18 K8 **Marcy, Mount** ▲ New York, NE USA
149 T5 **Mardān** North-West Frontier Province, N Pakistan
63 N14 **Mar del Plata** Buenos Aires, E Argentina
137 Q16 **Mardin** Mardin, SE Turkey
137 Q16 **Mardin** ⬖ province SE Turkey
137 Q16 **Mardin Dağları** ▲▲ SE Turkey
Mardzad see Hayrhandulaan
187 R17 **Maré** island Îles Loyauté, E New Caledonia
Marea Neagră see Black Sea
105 Z8 **Mare de Déu del Toro** var. El Toro. ▲ Menorca, Spain, W Mediterranean Sea
181 W4 **Mareeba** Queensland, NE Australia
96 G8 **Maree, Loch** ◎ N Scotland, UK
Mareeq see Mereeg
Marek see Dupnitsa
76 J11 **Maréna** Kayes, W Mali
190 I2 **Marenanuka** atoll Tungaru, W Kiribati
29 X14 **Marengo** Iowa, C USA
102 J11 **Marennes** Charente-Maritime, W France
107 G23 **Marettimo, Isola** island Isole Egadi, S Italy
24 K10 **Marfa** Texas, SW USA
57 P17 **Marfil, Laguna** ◎ E Bolivia
Marganets see Marhanets'
25 Q4 **Margaret** Texas, SW USA
180 I14 **Margaret River** Western Australia
186 C7 **Margarima** Southern Highlands, W Papua New Guinea
55 N4 **Margarita, Isla de** island N Venezuela
115 I25 **Margarítes** Kríti, Greece, E Mediterranean Sea
97 Q22 **Margate** prev. Mergate. SE England, UK
23 Z15 **Margate** Florida, SE USA
Margelan see Marg'ilon
103 P13 **Margeride, Montagnes de la** ▲▲ C France
Margherita see Jamaame
107 N16 **Margherita di Savoia** Puglia, SE Italy
Margherita, Lake see Ābaya Hāyk'
81 E18 **Margherita Peak** Fr. Pic Marguerite. ▲ Uganda/Dem. Rep. Congo
149 O4 **Marghī** Bāmīān, N Afghanistan
116 G9 **Marghita** Hung. Margitta. Bihor, NW Romania
Margilan see Marg'ilon
147 S10 **Marg'ilon** var. Margelan, Rus. Margilan. Farg'ona Viloyati, E Uzbekistan
116 K8 **Marginea** Suceava, NE Romania
Margitta see Marghita
148 K9 **Mārgow, Dasht-e** desert SW Afghanistan
99 L18 **Margraten** Limburg, SE Netherlands
10 M15 **Marguerite** British Columbia, SW Canada
15 V3 **Marguerite** ≈ Québec, SE Canada
194 I6 **Marguerite Bay** bay Antarctica
Marguerite, Pic see Margherita Peak
117 T9 **Marhanets'** Rus. Marganets. Dnipropetrovs'ka Oblast', E Ukraine
186 B9 **Mari** Western, SW Papua New Guinea
191 Y12 **Maria** atoll Groupe Actéon, SE French Polynesia
191 R12 **Maria** island Îles Australes, SW French Polynesia
40 I12 **María Cleofas, Isla** island C Mexico
62 H4 **María Elena** var. Oficina María Elena. Antofagasta, N Chile
95 G21 **Mariager** Århus, C Denmark
61 C22 **María Ignacia** Buenos Aires, E Argentina
183 P17 **Maria Island** island Tasmania, SE Australia
40 H12 **María Madre, Isla** island C Mexico
40 I12 **María Magdalena, Isla** island C Mexico
192 H6 **Mariana Islands** island group Guam/Northern Mariana Islands
175 N3 **Mariana Trench** var. Challenger Deep. undersea feature W Pacific Ocean
153 X12 **Mariāni** Assam, NE India
27 X11 **Marianna** Arkansas, C USA
23 R8 **Marianna** Florida, SE USA
172 J16 **Marianne** island Inner Islands, NE Seychelles
95 M19 **Mariannelund** Jönköping, S Sweden
61 D15 **Mariano I. Loza** Corrientes, NE Argentina
Mariano Machado see Ganda
111 A16 **Mariánské Lázně** Ger. Marienbad. Karlovarský Kraj, W Czech Republic
Máriaradna see Radna
33 S7 **Marias River** ≈ Montana, NW USA
Maria-Theresiopel see Subotica
Máriatölgyes see Dubnica nad Váhom
184 H1 **Maria van Diemen, Cape** headland North Island, New Zealand
109 V5 **Mariazell** Steiermark, E Austria
141 P15 **Mar'ib** W Yemen
95 I25 **Maribo** Storstrøm, S Denmark
109 W9 **Maribor** Ger. Marburg. NE Slovenia
35 R13 **Maricopa** California, W USA
Maricourt see Kangiqsujuaq
81 D15 **Maridi** Western Equatoria, SW Sudan
194 M11 **Marie Byrd Land** physical region Antarctica
193 P14 **Marie Byrd Seamount** undersea feature N Amundsen Sea
45 X11 **Marie-Galante** var. Ceyre to the Caribs. island SE Guadeloupe
45 Y6 **Marie-Galante, Canal de** channel S Guadeloupe
93 J20 **Mariehamn** Fin. Maarianhamina. Åland, SW Finland
44 C4 **Mariel** La Habana, W Cuba
99 H22 **Mariembourg** Namur, S Belgium
Marienbad see Mariánské Lázně
Marienburg see Alūksne, Latvia
Marienburg see Malbork, Poland
Marienburg see Feldioara, Romania
Marienburg in Westpreussen see Malbork
Marienhausen see Viļaka
83 D20 **Mariental** Hardap, SW Namibia
18 D13 **Marienville** Pennsylvania, NE USA
Marienwerder see Kwidzyń
58 C12 **Marié, Rio** ≈ NW Brazil
95 K17 **Mariestad** Västra Götaland, S Sweden
23 S3 **Marietta** Georgia, SE USA
31 U14 **Marietta** Ohio, N USA
27 N13 **Marietta** Oklahoma, C USA
81 H18 **Marigat** Rift Valley, W Kenya
103 S16 **Marignane** Bouches-du-Rhône, SE France
Marignano see Melegnano
45 O11 **Marigot** NE Dominica
122 K12 **Mariinsk** Kemerovskaya Oblast', S Russian Federation
127 Q3 **Mariinskiy Posad** Respublika Mariy El, W Russian Federation
119 E14 **Marijampolė** prev. Kapsukas. Marijampolė, S Lithuania
114 G12 **Marikostenovo** Blagoevgrad, SW Bulgaria
60 J9 **Marília** São Paulo, S Brazil
82 D11 **Marimba** Malanje, NW Angola
139 T1 **Marī Mīlā** E Iraq
104 G4 **Marín** Galicia, NW Spain
35 N10 **Marina** California, W USA
Mar'ina Gorka see Mar"ina Horka
119 L17 **Mar"ina Horka** Rus. Mar'ina Gorka. Minskaya Voblasts', C Belarus
171 O4 **Marinduque** island C Philippines
31 S9 **Marine City** Michigan, N USA
31 N6 **Marinette** Wisconsin, N USA
60 I10 **Maringá** Paraná, S Brazil
83 N16 **Maringuè** Sofala, C Mozambique
104 F9 **Marinha Grande** Leiria, C Portugal
107 I15 **Marino** Lazio, C Italy
59 A15 **Mário Lobão** Acre, W Brazil
23 O5 **Marion** Alabama, S USA
27 Y11 **Marion** Arkansas, C USA
30 L17 **Marion** Illinois, N USA
31 P13 **Marion** Indiana, N USA
29 X13 **Marion** Iowa, C USA
27 O5 **Marion** Kansas, C USA
20 H6 **Marion** Kentucky, S USA
21 P9 **Marion** North Carolina, SE USA
31 S12 **Marion** Ohio, N USA
21 T12 **Marion** South Carolina, SE USA
21 Q7 **Marion** Virginia, NE USA
27 O5 **Marion Lake** ⊠ Kansas, C USA
21 S13 **Marion, Lake** ⊠ South Carolina, SE USA
27 S8 **Marionville** Missouri, C USA
55 N7 **Maripa** Bolívar, E Venezuela
55 X11 **Maripasoula** W French Guiana
35 Q9 **Mariposa** California, W USA
61 G19 **Mariscala** Lavalleja, S Uruguay
62 M4 **Mariscal Estigarribia** Boquerón, NW Paraguay
56 C6 **Mariscal Sucre** var. Quito. ✕ (Quito) Pichincha, C Ecuador
30 K16 **Marissa** Illinois, N USA
103 U14 **Maritime Alps** Fr. Alpes Maritimes, It. Alpi Marittime. ▲▲ France/Italy
Maritimes, Alpes see Maritime Alps
Maritime Territory see Primorskiy Kray
114 K11 **Maritsa** var. Marica, Gk. Évros, Turk. Meriç; anc. Hebrus. ≈ SW Europe see also Évros/Meriç
Maritsa see Simeonovgrad
Maritsa see Évros
Maritsa see Meriç
Marittime, Alpi see Maritime Alps
Maritzburg see Pietermaritzburg
117 X9 **Mariupol'** prev. Zhdanov. Donets'ka Oblast', SE Ukraine
55 Q6 **Mariusa, Caño** ≈ NE Venezuela
142 J5 **Marīvān** prev. Dezh Shāhpūr. Kordestān, W Iran
127 R3 **Mariyets** Respublika Mariy El, W Russian Federation
118 G4 **Märjamaa** Ger. Merjama. Raplamaa, NW Estonia
99 I15 **Mark** Fr. Marcq. ≈ Belgium/Netherlands
81 N17 **Marka** var. Merca. Shabeellaha Hoose, S Somalia
145 Z10 **Markakol', Ozero** Kaz. Marqakōl. ◎ E Kazakhstan
76 M12 **Markala** Ségou, W Mali
159 S15 **Markam** var. Gartog. Xizang Zizhiqu, W China
95 K21 **Markaryd** Kronoberg, S Sweden
142 L7 **Markazī** off. Ostān-e Markazī. ⬖ province W Iran
Markazī, Ostān-e see Markazī
14 F14 **Markdale** Ontario, S Canada
27 X10 **Marked Tree** Arkansas, C USA
98 N11 **Markelo** Overijssel, E Netherlands
98 J9 **Markermeer** ◎ C Netherlands
97 N20 **Market Harborough** C England, UK
97 N18 **Market Rasen** E England, UK
123 O10 **Markha** ≈ NE Russian Federation
12 H16 **Markham** Ontario, S Canada
25 V12 **Markham** Texas, SW USA
186 E7 **Markham** ≈ C Papua New Guinea
195 Q11 **Markham, Mount** ▲ Antarctica
110 M11 **Marki** Mazowieckie, C Poland
158 F8 **Markit** Xinjiang Uygur Zizhiqu, NW China
117 Y5 **Markivka** Rus. Markovka. Luhans'ka Oblast', E Ukraine
35 Q7 **Markleeville** California, W USA
98 L8 **Marknesse** Flevoland, N Netherlands
79 H14 **Markounda** var. Marcounda. Ouham, NW Central African Republic
Markovka see Markivka
123 U7 **Markovo** Chukotskiy Avtonomnyy Okrug, NE Russian Federation
127 P8 **Marks** Saratovskaya Oblast', W Russian Federation
22 K2 **Marks** Mississippi, S USA
22 I7 **Marksville** Louisiana, S USA
101 I19 **Marktheidenfeld** Bayern, C Germany
101 J24 **Marktoberdorf** Bayern, S Germany
101 M18 **Marktredwitz** Bayern, E Germany
Markt-Übelbach see Übelbach
27 V3 **Mark Twain Lake** ⊠ Missouri, C USA
Markuleshty see Mărculeşti
101 E14 **Marl** Nordrhein-Westfalen, W Germany
182 F2 **Marla** South Australia
181 Y8 **Marlborough** Queensland, E Australia
97 M22 **Marlborough** S England, UK
185 I15 **Marlborough** off. Marlborough District. ⬖ unitary authority South Island, New Zealand
Marlborough District see Marlborough
103 P3 **Marle** Aisne, N France
31 S8 **Marlette** Michigan, N USA
25 T9 **Marlin** Texas, SW USA
21 S5 **Marlinton** West Virginia, NE USA
26 M12 **Marlow** Oklahoma, C USA
155 E17 **Marmagao** Goa, W India
Marmanda see Marmande
102 L13 **Marmande** anc. Marmanda. Lot-et-Garonne, SW France
136 C11 **Marmara** Balıkesir, NW Turkey
136 D11 **Marmara Denizi** Eng. Sea of Marmara. sea NW Turkey
114 N13 **Marmaraereğlisi** Tekirdağ, NW Turkey
Marmara, Sea of see Marmara Denizi
136 C16 **Marmaris** Muğla, SW Turkey
28 J6 **Marmarth** North Dakota, N USA
21 Q5 **Marmet** West Virginia, NE USA
106 H5 **Marmolada, Monte** ▲ N Italy
104 M13 **Marmolejo** Andalucía, S Spain
14 J14 **Marmora** Ontario, SE Canada
39 Q14 **Marmot Bay** bay Alaska, USA
103 Q4 **Marne** ⬖ department N France
103 Q4 **Marne** ≈ N France
137 U10 **Marneuli** prev. Borchalo, Sarvani. S Georgia
78 I13 **Maro** Moyen-Chari, S Chad
54 L12 **Maroa** Amazonas, S Venezuela
172 J3 **Maroantsetra** Toamasina, NE Madagascar
191 W11 **Marokau** atoll Îles Tuamotu, C French Polynesia
172 J5 **Marolambo** Toamasina, E Madagascar
172 J2 **Maromokotro** ▲ N Madagascar
83 L16 **Marondera** prev. Marandellas. Mashonaland East, NE Zimbabwe
55 X9 **Maroni** Dut. Marowijne. ≈ French Guiana/Suriname
183 V2 **Maroochydore-Mooloolaba** Queensland, E Australia
171 N14 **Maros** Sulawesi, C Indonesia
116 H11 **Maros** var. Mureş, Mureşul, Ger. Marosch, Mieresch. ≈ Hungary/Romania see also Mureş
Marosch see Maros/Mureş
Maroshevíz see Toplița
Marosillye see Ilia
Marosludas see Luduş
Marosújvár/Marosújvárakna see Ocna Mureş
Marosvásárhely see Târgu Mureş
191 V14 **Marotiri** var. Îlots de Bass, Morotiri. island group Îles Australes, SW French Polynesia
78 G12 **Maroua** Extrême-Nord, N Cameroon
55 X12 **Marouini Rivier** ≈ SE Suriname
172 I3 **Marovoay** Mahajanga, NW Madagascar
55 W9 **Marowijne** ⬖ district NE Suriname
Marowijne see Maroni
Marqakōl see Markakol', Ozero
193 P8 **Marquesas Fracture Zone** tectonic feature E Pacific Ocean
Marquesas Islands see Marquises, Îles
23 W17 **Marquesas Keys** island group Florida, SE USA
29 Y12 **Marquette** Iowa, C USA
31 N3 **Marquette** Michigan, N USA
103 N1 **Marquise** Pas-de-Calais, N France
191 X7 **Marquises, Îles** Eng. Marquesas Islands. island group N French Polynesia
183 Q6 **Marra Creek** ≈ New South Wales, SE Australia
80 B10 **Marra Hills** plateau W Sudan
80 B11 **Marra, Jebel** ▲ W Sudan
74 E7 **Marrakech** var. Marakesh, Eng. Marrakesh; prev. Morocco. W Morocco
Marrakesh see Marrakech
Marrāt see Marāh
183 N15 **Marrawah** Tasmania, SE Australia
182 I4 **Marree** South Australia
81 L17 **Marrehan** ▲▲ SW Somalia
83 N17 **Marromeu** Sofala, C Mozambique
104 J17 **Marroquí, Punta** headland SW Spain
183 N8 **Marrowie Creek** seasonal river New South Wales, SE Australia
83 O14 **Marrupa** Niassa, N Mozambique
182 D1 **Marryat** South Australia
75 Y10 **Marsa 'Alam** SE Egypt
75 R8 **Marsá al Burayqah** var. Al Burayqah. N Libya
81 J17 **Marsabit** Eastern, N Kenya
107 H23 **Marsala** anc. Lilybaeum. Sicilia, Italy, C Mediterranean Sea
121 P16 **Marsaxlokk Bay** bay SE Malta
65 G15 **Mars Bay** bay Ascension Island, C Atlantic Ocean
101 H15 **Marsberg** Nordrhein-Westfalen, W Germany
9 R15 **Marsden** Saskatchewan, S Canada
98 H7 **Marsdiep** strait NW Netherlands
103 R16 **Marseille** Eng. Marseilles; anc. Massilia. Bouches-du-Rhône, SE France
Marseille-Marignane see Provence
30 M11 **Marseilles** Illinois, N USA
Marseilles see Marseille
76 J16 **Marshall** W Liberia
39 N11 **Marshall** Alaska, USA
27 U9 **Marshall** Arkansas, C USA
31 N14 **Marshall** Illinois, N USA
31 Q10 **Marshall** Michigan, N USA
29 S9 **Marshall** Minnesota, N USA
27 T4 **Marshall** Missouri, C USA
21 O9 **Marshall** North Carolina, SE USA
25 X6 **Marshall** Texas, SW USA
189 S4 **Marshall Islands** off. Republic of the Marshall Islands. ◆ republic W Pacific Ocean
175 Q3 **Marshall Islands** island group W Pacific Ocean
Marshall Islands, Republic of the see Marshall Islands
192 K6 **Marshall Seamounts** undersea feature SW Pacific Ocean
29 W13 **Marshalltown** Iowa, C USA
19 P12 **Marshfield** Massachusetts, NE USA
27 T7 **Marshfield** Missouri, C USA
30 K6 **Marshfield** Wisconsin, N USA
44 H1 **Marsh Harbour** Great Abaco, W Bahamas
19 S3 **Mars Hill** Maine, NE USA
21 P9 **Mars Hill** North Carolina, SE USA
22 H10 **Marsh Island** island Louisiana, S USA
21 S11 **Marshville** North Carolina, SE USA
15 W5 **Marsoui** Québec, SE Canada
15 R8 **Mars, Rivière à** ≈ Québec, SE Canada
95 O15 **Märsta** Stockholm, C Sweden
95 H24 **Marstal** Fyn, C Denmark
95 I19 **Marstrand** Västra Götaland, S Sweden
25 U8 **Mart** Texas, SW USA
166 M9 **Martaban** var. Moktama. Mon State, S Myanmar (Burma)
166 L9 **Martaban, Gulf of** gulf S Myanmar (Burma)
107 Q19 **Martano** Puglia, SE Italy
Martapoera see Martapura
169 T13 **Martapura** prev. Martapoera. Borneo, C Indonesia
99 L23 **Martelange** Luxembourg, SE Belgium
114 L7 **Marten** Ruse, N Bulgaria
14 H10 **Marten River** Ontario, S Canada
9 T15 **Martensville** Saskatchewan, S Canada
Marteskirch see Târnăveni
Martes Tolosane see Martres-Tolosane
115 K25 **Mártha** Kríti, Greece, E Mediterranean Sea
183 Q6 **Marthaguy Creek** ≈ New South Wales, SE Australia
19 P13 **Martha's Vineyard** island Massachusetts, NE USA
108 C11 **Martigny** Valais, SW Switzerland
103 R16 **Martigues** Bouches-du-Rhône, SE France
111 J19 **Martin** Ger. Sankt Martin, Hung. Turócszentmárton; prev. Turčianský Svätý Martin. Žilinský Kraj, N Slovakia
28 L11 **Martin** South Dakota, N USA
20 G8 **Martin** Tennessee, S USA
105 S7 **Martín** ≈ E Spain
107 P18 **Martina Franca** Puglia, SE Italy
185 M14 **Martinborough** Wellington, North Island, New Zealand
25 S11 **Martindale** Texas, SW USA
35 N8 **Martinez** California, W USA
23 V3 **Martinez** Georgia, SE USA
41 Q13 **Martínez de La Torre** Veracruz-Llave, E Mexico
45 Y12 **Martinique** ◇ French overseas department E West Indies
1 O15 **Martinique** island E West Indies
Martinique Channel see Martinique Passage
45 X12 **Martinique Passage** var. Dominica Channel, Martinique Channel. channel Dominica/Martinique
23 Q5 **Martin Lake** ⊠ Alabama, S USA
115 G18 **Martíno** prev. Martínon. Stereá Ellás, C Greece
Martínon see Martíno
194 J11 **Martin Peninsula** peninsula Antarctica
39 S5 **Martin Point** headland Alaska, USA
109 V3 **Martinsberg** Niederösterreich, NE Austria
21 V3 **Martinsburg** West Virginia, NE USA
31 V13 **Martins Ferry** Ohio, N USA
Martinskirch see Târnăveni
31 O14 **Martinsville** Indiana, N USA
21 S8 **Martinsville** Virginia, NE USA
65 K16 **Martin Vaz, Ilhas** island group E Brazil
Martök see Martuk
184 M12 **Marton** Manawatu-Wanganui, North Island, New Zealand
105 N13 **Martos** Andalucía, S Spain
102 M16 **Martres-Tolosane** var. Martes Tolosane. Haute-Garonne, S France
92 M11 **Martti** Lappi, NE Finland
144 I9 **Martuk** Kaz. Martök. Aktyubinsk, NW Kazakhstan
137 U12 **Martuni** E Armenia
58 L11 **Marudá** Pará, E Brazil
169 V6 **Marudu, Teluk** bay East Malaysia
149 O8 **Ma'rūf** Kandahār, SE Afghanistan
164 H13 **Marugame** Kagawa, Shikoku, SW Japan
185 H16 **Maruia** ≈ South Island, New Zealand
98 M6 **Marum** Groningen, NE Netherlands
187 R13 **Marum, Mount** ▲ Ambrym, C Vanuatu
79 P23 **Marungu** ▲▲ SE Dem. Rep. Congo
191 Y12 **Marutea** atoll Groupe Actéon, C French Polynesia
143 O11 **Marv Dasht** var. Mervdasht. Fārs, S Iran
103 P13 **Marvejols** Lozère, S France
27 X12 **Marvell** Arkansas, C USA
36 L6 **Marvine, Mount** ▲ Utah, W USA
139 Q7 **Marwānīyah** C Iraq
152 F13 **Mārwār** var. Marwar Junction. Rājasthān, N India
Marwar Junction see Mārwār
9 R14 **Marwayne** Alberta, SW Canada
146 I14 **Mary** prev. Merv. Mary Welaýaty, S Turkmenistan
Mary see Mary Welaýaty
181 Z9 **Maryborough** Queensland, E Australia
182 M11 **Maryborough** Victoria, SE Australia
Maryborough see Port Laoise
83 G23 **Marydale** Northern Cape, W South Africa
117 W8 **Mar"yinka** Donets'ka Oblast', E Ukraine
Mary Island see Kanton
21 W4 **Maryland** off. State of Maryland, also known as America in Miniature, Cockade State, Free State, Old Line State. ⬖ state NE USA
Maryland, State of see Maryland
25 P7 **Maryneal** Texas, SW USA
97 J15 **Maryport** NW England, UK
13 U13 **Marystown** Newfoundland, Newfoundland and Labrador, SE Canada
36 K6 **Marysvale** Utah, W USA
35 O6 **Marysville** California, W USA
27 O3 **Marysville** Kansas, C USA
31 S13 **Marysville** Michigan, N USA
31 S9 **Marysville** Ohio, NE USA
32 H7 **Marysville** Washington, NW USA
27 R2 **Maryville** Missouri, C USA
21 N9 **Maryville** Tennessee, S USA
146 I15 **Mary Welaýaty** var. Mary, Rus. Maryyskiy Velayat. ⬖ province S Turkmenistan
Maryyskiy Velayat see Mary Welaýaty
Marzūq see Murzuq
42 J11 **Masachapa** var. Puerto Masachapa. Managua, W Nicaragua
81 G19 **Masai Mara National Reserve** reserve C Kenya
81 I21 **Masai Steppe** grassland NW Tanzania
81 F19 **Masaka** SW Uganda
169 T15 **Masalembo Besar, Pulau** island S Indonesia
137 Y13 **Masallı** Rus. Masally. S Azerbaijan
Masally see Masallı
171 N13 **Masamba** Sulawesi, C Indonesia
Masampo see Masan
163 Y16 **Masan** prev. Masampo. S South Korea
Masandam Peninsula see Musandam Peninsula
81 J25 **Masasi** Mtwara, SE Tanzania
Masawa see Massawa
42 J10 **Masaya** Masaya, W Nicaragua
42 J10 **Masaya** ⬖ department W Nicaragua
171 P5 **Masbate** Masbate, N Philippines
171 P5 **Masbate** island C Philippines
74 I6 **Mascara** var. Mouaskar. NW Algeria
173 O7 **Mascarene Basin** undersea feature W Indian Ocean
173 O9 **Mascarene Islands** island group W Indian Ocean
173 N9 **Mascarene Plain** undersea feature W Indian Ocean
173 O7 **Mascarene Plateau** undersea feature W Indian Ocean
194 H5 **Mascart, Cape** headland Adelaide Island, Antarctica
62 J10 **Mascasín, Salinas de** salt lake C Argentina
40 K13 **Mascota** Jalisco, C Mexico

◆ Country ● Country Capital ◇ Dependent Territory ○ Dependent Territory Capital ⬖ Administrative Regions ✕ International Airport ▲ Mountain ▲▲ Mountain Range Volcano ≈ River ◎ Lake ⊠ Reservoir

15 O12 **Mascouche** Québec, SE Canada
124 J9 **Masel'gskaya** Respublika Kareliya, NW Russian Federation
83 J23 **Maseru** ● (Lesotho) W Lesotho
83 J23 **Maseru** ✈ W Lesotho
Mashaba see Mashava
160 K14 **Mashan** var. Baishan. Guangxi Zhuangzu Zizhiqu, S China
83 K17 **Mashava** prev. Mashaba. Masvingo, SE Zimbabwe
143 U4 **Mashhad** var. Meshed. Khorāsān-Razavī, NE Iran
165 S3 **Mashike** Hokkaidō, NE Japan
Mashīz see Bardsīr
149 N14 **Mashkai** ≈ SW Pakistan
143 X13 **Māshkel** var. Rūd-i Māshkel, Rūd-e Māshkīd. ≈ Iran/Pakistan
148 K12 **Māshkel, Hāmūn-i** salt marsh SW Pakistan
Māshkel, Rūd-i/Māshkīd, Rūd-e see Māshkel
83 K15 **Mashonaland Central** ◈ province N Zimbabwe
83 K16 **Mashonaland East** ◈ province NE Zimbabwe
83 J16 **Mashonaland West** ◈ province NW Zimbabwe
Mashtagi see Maştağa
141 S14 **Masīlah, Wādī al** dry watercourse SE Yemen
79 I21 **Masi-Manimba** Bandundu, SW Dem. Rep. Congo
81 F17 **Masindi** W Uganda
81 I19 **Masinga Reservoir** ▣ S Kenya
Masīra see Maşīrah, Jazīrat
Masīra, Gulf of see Maşīrah, Khalīj
141 Y10 **Maşīrah, Jazīrat** var. Masīra. island E Oman
141 Y10 **Maşīrah, Khalīj** var. Gulf of Masira. bay E Oman
Masis see Büyükağrı Dağı
79 O19 **Masisi** Nord Kivu, E Dem. Rep. Congo
Masjed-e Soleymān see Masjed Soleymān
142 L9 **Masjed Soleymān** var. Masjed-e Soleymān, Masjid-i Sulaiman. Khūzestān, SW Iran
Masjid-i Sulaiman see Masjed Soleymān
Maskat see Masqaţ
139 Q7 **Maskhān** C Iraq
141 X8 **Maskin** var. Miskin. NW Oman
97 B17 **Mask, Lough** Ir. Loch Measca. ◎ W Ireland
114 N10 **Maslen Nos** headland E Bulgaria
172 K3 **Masoala, Tanjona** headland NE Madagascar
Masohi see Amahai
31 Q9 **Mason** Michigan, N USA
31 R14 **Mason** Ohio, N USA
25 Q10 **Mason** Texas, SW USA
21 P4 **Mason** West Virginia, NE USA
185 B25 **Mason Bay** bay Stewart Island, New Zealand
30 K13 **Mason City** Illinois, N USA
29 V12 **Mason City** Iowa, C USA
Mâ, Sông see Ma, Nam
18 B16 **Masontown** Pennsylvania, NE USA
141 Y8 **Masqaţ** var. Maskat, Eng. Muscat. ● (Oman) NE Oman
106 E10 **Massa** Toscana, C Italy
18 M11 **Massachusetts** off. Commonwealth of Massachusetts, also known as Bay State, Old Bay State, Old Colony State. ◈ state NE USA
19 P11 **Massachusetts Bay** bay Massachusetts, NE USA
35 R2 **Massacre Lake** ◎ Nevada, W USA
107 O18 **Massafra** Puglia, SE Italy
108 G11 **Massagno** Ticino, S Switzerland
78 G11 **Massaguet** Chari-Baguirmi, W Chad
Massakori see Massakory
78 G10 **Massakory** var. Massakori; prev. Dagana. Chari-Baguirmi, W Chad
78 H11 **Massalassef** Chari-Baguirmi, SW Chad
106 F13 **Massa Marittima** Toscana, C Italy
82 B11 **Massangano** Cuanza Norte, NW Angola
83 M18 **Massangena** Gaza, S Mozambique
80 J9 **Massawa** var. Masawa, Amh. Mits'iwa. E Eritrea
80 K9 **Massawa Channel** channel E Eritrea
18 J6 **Massena** New York, NE USA
78 H11 **Massenya** Chari-Baguirmi, SW Chad
10 I13 **Masset** Graham Island, British Columbia, SW Canada
102 L16 **Masseube** Gers, S France
14 E11 **Massey** Ontario, S Canada
103 P12 **Massiac** Cantal, C France
103 P12 **Massif Central** plateau C France
Massif de L'Isalo see Isalo
Massilia see Marseille
31 U12 **Massillon** Ohio, N USA
77 N12 **Massina** Ségou, W Mali
83 N19 **Massinga** Inhambane, SE Mozambique
83 L20 **Massingir** Gaza, SW Mozambique
195 Z10 **Masson Island** island Antarctica
Massoukou see Franceville
137 Z11 **Maştağa** Rus. Mashtagi, Mastaga. E Azerbaijan
Mastanli see Momchilgrad
184 M13 **Masterton** Wellington, North Island, New Zealand
18 M14 **Mastic** Long Island, New York, NE USA
149 O10 **Mastung** Baluchistān, SW Pakistan
119 J20 **Mastva** Rus. Mostva. ≈ SW Belarus
119 G17 **Masty** Rus. Mosty. Hrodzyenskaya Voblasts', W Belarus
164 F12 **Masuda** Shimane, Honshū, SW Japan
92 J11 **Masugnsbyn** Norrbotten, N Sweden
Masuku see Franceville
83 K17 **Masvingo** prev. Fort Victoria, Nyanda, Victoria. Masvingo, SE Zimbabwe
83 K18 **Masvingo** prev. Victoria. ◈ province SE Zimbabwe
138 H5 **Maşyāf** Fr. Misiaf. Ḩamāh, C Syria
110 E9 **Maszewo** Zachodniopomorskie, NW Poland
83 I17 **Matabeleland North** ◈ province W Zimbabwe
83 J18 **Matabeleland South** ◈ province S Zimbabwe
82 O13 **Mataca** Niassa, N Mozambique
14 G8 **Matachewan** Ontario, S Canada
163 Q8 **Matad** var. Dzüünbulag. Dornod, E Mongolia
79 F22 **Matadi** Bas-Congo, W Dem. Rep. Congo
25 O4 **Matador** Texas, SW USA
42 J9 **Matagalpa** Matagalpa, C Nicaragua
42 K9 **Matagalpa** ◈ department W Nicaragua
12 I12 **Matagami** Québec, S Canada
25 U13 **Matagorda** Texas, SW USA
25 U13 **Matagorda Bay** inlet Texas, SW USA
25 U14 **Matagorda Island** island Texas, SW USA
25 V13 **Matagorda Peninsula** headland Texas, SW USA
191 Q8 **Mataiea** Tahiti, W French Polynesia
191 T9 **Mataiva** atoll Îles Tuamotu, C French Polynesia
183 O7 **Matakana** New South Wales, SE Australia
184 N7 **Matakana Island** island NE New Zealand
83 C15 **Matala** Huíla, SW Angola
190 G12 **Matala'a Pointe** headland Île Uvea, N Wallis and Futuna
155 K25 **Matale** Central Province, C Sri Lanka
190 E12 **Matalesina, Pointe** headland Île Alofi, W Wallis and Futuna
76 I10 **Matam** NE Senegal
184 M8 **Matamata** Waikato, North Island, New Zealand
77 V12 **Matamey** Zinder, S Niger
40 L8 **Matamoros** Coahuila de Zaragoza, NE Mexico
41 P15 **Matamoros** var. Izúcar de Matamoros. Puebla, S Mexico
41 Q8 **Matamoros** Tamaulipas, C Mexico
75 S13 **Ma'ţan as Sārah** SE Libya
82 J12 **Matanda** Luapula, N Zambia
81 J24 **Matandu** ≈ S Tanzania
15 V6 **Matane** Québec, SE Canada
15 V6 **Matane** ≈ Québec, SE Canada
77 S12 **Matankari** Dosso, SW Niger
39 R11 **Matanuska River** ≈ Alaska, USA
54 G7 **Matanza** Santander, N Colombia
44 D4 **Matanzas** Matanzas, NW Cuba
15 V7 **Matapédia** ≈ Québec, SE Canada
15 V6 **Matapédia, Lac** ◎ Québec, SE Canada
190 B17 **Mata Point** headland SE Niue
190 D12 **Matapu, Pointe** headland Île Futuna, W Wallis and Futuna
62 G12 **Mataquito, Río** ≈ C Chile
155 K26 **Matara** Southern Province, S Sri Lanka
115 D18 **Matarágka** var. Mataránga. Dytikí Ellás, C Greece
171 K16 **Mataram** Pulau Lombok, C Indonesia
Mataránga see Matarágka
181 Q3 **Mataranka** Northern Territory, N Australia
105 W6 **Mataró** anc. Illuro. Cataluña, E Spain
184 O8 **Matata** Bay of Plenty, North Island, New Zealand
192 K16 **Matātula, Cape** headland Tutuila, W American Samoa
185 D24 **Mataura** Southland, South Island, New Zealand
185 D24 **Mataura** ≈ South Island, New Zealand
Mata Uta see Matā'utu
192 H16 **Matāutu** Upolu, C Samoa
190 G11 **Matā'utu** var. Mata Uta. ○ (Wallis and Futuna) Île Uvea, Wallis and Futuna
190 G12 **Matā'utu, Baie de** bay Île Uvea, Wallis and Futuna
191 P7 **Matavai, Baie de** bay Tahiti, W French Polynesia
190 I16 **Matavera** Rarotonga, S Cook Islands
191 V16 **Mataveri** Easter Island, Chile, E Pacific Ocean
191 V17 **Mataveri** ✈ (Easter Island) Easter Island, Chile, E Pacific Ocean
184 P9 **Matawai** Gisborne, North Island, New Zealand
15 O10 **Matawin** ≈ Québec, SE Canada
145 V13 **Matay** Almaty, SE Kazakhstan
14 K8 **Matchi-Manitou, Lac** ◎ Québec, SE Canada
41 O10 **Matehuala** San Luis Potosí, C Mexico
45 V13 **Matelot** Trinidad, Trinidad and Tobago
83 M15 **Matenge** Tete, NW Mozambique
107 O18 **Matera** Basilicata, S Italy
111 O21 **Mátészalka** Szabolcs-Szatmár-Bereg, E Hungary
93 H17 **Matfors** Västernorrland, C Sweden
102 K11 **Matha** Charente-Maritime, W France
0 F15 **Mathematicians Seamounts** undersea feature E Pacific Ocean
21 X6 **Mathews** Virginia, NE USA
25 S14 **Mathis** Texas, SW USA
152 J11 **Mathura** prev. Muttra. Uttar Pradesh, N India
Mathurai see Madurai
171 R7 **Mati** Mindanao, S Philippines
Matianus see Orūmīyeh, Daryācheh-ye
Matiara see Matiāri
149 Q15 **Matiāri** var. Matiara. Sind, SE Pakistan
41 S16 **Matías Romero** Oaxaca, SE Mexico
43 O13 **Matina** Limón, E Costa Rica
14 D10 **Matinenda Lake** ◎ Ontario, S Canada
19 R8 **Matinicus Island** island Maine, NE USA
Matisco/Matisco Ædourum see Mâcon
149 Q16 **Mātli** Sind, SE Pakistan
97 M18 **Matlock** C England, UK
59 F18 **Mato Grosso** prev. Vila Bela da Santissima Trindade. Mato Grosso, W Brazil
59 G17 **Mato Grosso** off. Estado de Mato Grosso; prev. Matto Grosso. ◈ state W Brazil
60 H8 **Mato Grosso do Sul** off. Estado de Mato Grosso do Sul. ◈ state S Brazil
Mato Grosso do Sul, Estado de see Mato Grosso do Sul
Mato Grosso, Estado de see Mato Grosso
59 I18 **Mato Grosso, Planalto de** plateau C Brazil
83 L21 **Matola** Maputo, S Mozambique
104 G6 **Matosinhos** prev. Matozinhos. Porto, NW Portugal
Matou see Pingguo
55 Z10 **Matoury** NE French Guiana
Matozinhos see Matosinhos
111 L21 **Mátra** ▲▲ N Hungary
141 Y8 **Maţraḩ** var. Mutrah. NE Oman
116 L12 **Mătrașești** Vrancea, E Romania
108 M8 **Matrei am Brenner** Tirol, W Austria
109 P8 **Matrei in Osttirol** Tirol, W Austria
76 I15 **Matru** SW Sierra Leone
75 U7 **Maţrūḩ** var. Mersa Maţrūḩ; anc. Paraetonium. NW Egypt
165 U16 **Matsubara** var. Matubara. Kagoshima, Tokuno-shima, SW Japan
164 G12 **Matsue** var. Matsuye, Matue. Shimane, Honshū, SW Japan
165 Q6 **Matsumae** Hokkaidō, NE Japan
164 M12 **Matsumoto** var. Matumoto. Nagano, Honshū, S Japan
164 K14 **Matsusaka** var. Matsuzaka, Matusaka. Mie, Honshū, SW Japan
161 S12 **Matsu Tao** Chin. Mazu Dao. island NW Taiwan
Matsutō see Mattō
164 F14 **Matsuyama** var. Matuyama. Ehime, Shikoku, SW Japan
Matsuye see Matsue
Matsuzaka see Matsusaka
164 M14 **Matsuzaki** Shizuoka, Honshū, S Japan
14 F8 **Mattagami** ≈ Ontario, S Canada
14 F8 **Mattagami Lake** ◎ Ontario, S Canada
62 K12 **Mattaldi** Córdoba, C Argentina
21 Y9 **Mattamuskeet, Lake** ◎ North Carolina, SE USA
21 W6 **Mattaponi River** ≈ Virginia, NE USA
14 I11 **Mattawa** Ontario, SE Canada
14 I11 **Mattawa** ≈ Ontario, SE Canada
19 S5 **Mattawamkeag** Maine, NE USA
19 S4 **Mattawamkeag Lake** ◎ Maine, NE USA
108 D11 **Matterhorn** It. Monte Cervino. ▲ Italy/Switzerland see also Cervino, Monte
32 L12 **Matterhorn** var. Sacajawea Peak. ▲ Oregon, NW USA
35 W1 **Matterhorn** ▲ Nevada, W USA
Matterhorn see Cervino, Monte
35 R8 **Matterhorn Peak** ▲ California, W USA
109 Y5 **Mattersburg** Burgenland, E Austria
108 E11 **Matter Vispa** ≈ S Switzerland
55 R7 **Matthews Ridge** N Guyana
44 K7 **Matthew Town** Great Inagua, S Bahamas
109 Q4 **Mattighofen** Oberösterreich, NW Austria
107 N16 **Mattinata** Puglia, SE Italy
141 T9 **Maţţī, Sabkhat** sabkha Saudi Arabia/United Arab Emirates
18 M14 **Mattituck** Long Island, New York, NE USA
164 L11 **Mattō** var. Matsutō. Ishikawa, Honshū, SW Japan
Matto Grosso see Mato Grosso
30 M14 **Mattoon** Illinois, N USA
57 L16 **Mattos, Río** ≈ C Bolivia
Mattu see Metu
169 R9 **Matu** Sarawak, East Malaysia
Matubara see Matsubara
57 E14 **Matucana** Lima, W Peru
Matue see Matsue
187 Y15 **Matuku** island S Fiji
112 B9 **Matulji** Primorje-Gorski Kotar, NW Croatia
Matumoto see Matsumoto
55 P5 **Maturín** Monagas, NE Venezuela
Matusaka see Matsusaka
Matuyama see Matsuyama
126 K11 **Matveyev Kurgan** Rostovskaya Oblast', SW Russian Federation
127 O8 **Matyshevo** Volgogradskaya Oblast', SW Russian Federation
153 O13 **Mau** var. Maunāth Bhanjan. Uttar Pradesh, N India
83 O14 **Maúa** Niassa, N Mozambique
102 M17 **Maubermé, Pic de** var. Tuc de Moubermé, Sp. Pico Mauberme; prev. Tuc de Maubermé. ▲ France/Spain see also Moubermé, Tuc de
Maubermé, Pic de see Moubermé, Tuc de
Mauberme, Pico see Maubermé, Pic de/Moubermé, Tuc de
Maubermé, Tuc de see Maubermé, Pic de/Moubermé, Tuc de
103 Q2 **Maubeuge** Nord, N France
166 L8 **Maubin** Irrawaddy, SW Myanmar (Burma)
152 L13 **Maudaha** Uttar Pradesh, N India
183 N9 **Maude** New South Wales, SE Australia
195 P3 **Maudheimvidda** physical region Antarctica
65 N22 **Maud Rise** undersea feature S Atlantic Ocean
109 Q4 **Mauerkirchen** Oberösterreich, NW Austria
Mauersee see Mamry, Jezioro
188 K2 **Maug Islands** island group N Northern Mariana Islands
103 Q15 **Mauguio** Hérault, S France
193 N5 **Maui** island Hawai'i, USA, C Pacific Ocean
190 M16 **Mauke** atoll S Cook Islands
62 G13 **Maule** var. Región del Maule. ◈ region C Chile
102 J9 **Mauléon** Deux-Sèvres, W France
102 J16 **Mauléon-Licharre** Pyrénées-Atlantiques, SW France
Maule, Región del see Maule
62 G13 **Maule, Río** ≈ C Chile
63 G17 **Maullín** Los Lagos, S Chile
Maulmain see Moulmein
31 R11 **Maumee** Ohio, N USA
31 Q12 **Maumee River** ≈ Indiana/Ohio, N USA
27 U11 **Maumelle** Arkansas, C USA
27 T11 **Maumelle, Lake** ▣ Arkansas, C USA
171 O16 **Maumere** prev. Maoemere. Flores, S Indonesia
83 G17 **Maun** North-West, C Botswana
Maunāth Bhanjan see Mau
Maunawai see Waimea
190 H16 **Maungaroa** ▲ Rarotonga, S Cook Islands
184 K3 **Maungatapere** Northland, North Island, New Zealand
184 K4 **Maungaturoto** Northland, North Island, New Zealand
191 R10 **Maupiti** var. Maurua. island Îles Sous le Vent, W French Polynesia
152 K14 **Mau Rānīpur** Uttar Pradesh, N India
22 K9 **Maurepas, Lake** ◎ Louisiana, S USA
103 T16 **Maures** ▲▲ SE France
103 O12 **Mauriac** Cantal, C France
Maurice see Mauritius
65 J20 **Maurice Ewing Bank** undersea feature SW Atlantic Ocean
182 C4 **Maurice, Lake** salt lake South Australia
18 I17 **Maurice River** ≈ New Jersey, NE USA
25 Y10 **Mauriceville** Texas, SW USA
98 K12 **Maurik** Gelderland, C Netherlands
76 H8 **Mauritania** off. Islamic Republic of Mauritania, Ar. Mūrītānīyah. ◆ republic W Africa
Mauritania, Islamic Republic of see Mauritania
173 W15 **Mauritius** off. Republic of Mauritius, Fr. Maurice. ◆ republic W Indian Ocean
128 M17 **Mauritius** island W Indian Ocean
Mauritius, Republic of see Mauritius
173 N9 **Mauritius Trench** undersea feature W Indian Ocean
102 H6 **Mauron** Morbihan, NW France
103 N13 **Maurs** Cantal, C France
Maurua see Maupiti
Maury Mid-Ocean Channel see Maury Seachannel
64 L6 **Maury Seachannel** var. Maury Mid-Ocean Channel. undersea feature N Atlantic Ocean
30 K8 **Mauston** Wisconsin, N USA
109 R8 **Mauterndorf** Salzburg, NW Austria
109 T4 **Mauthausen** Oberösterreich, N Austria
109 Q9 **Mauthen** Kärnten, S Austria
83 F15 **Mavinga** Cuando Cubango, SE Angola
83 M17 **Mavita** Manica, W Mozambique
115 K22 **Mavrópetra, Akrotírio** cape Santoríni, Kykládes, Greece, Aegean Sea
115 F16 **Mavrovoúni** ▲ C Greece
184 Q8 **Mawhai Point** headland North Island, New Zealand
166 L3 **Mawlaik** Sagaing, C Myanmar (Burma)
Mawlamyine see Moulmein
141 N14 **Mawr, Wādī** dry watercourse NW Yemen
195 X5 **Mawson** Australian research station Antarctica
195 X5 **Mawson Coast** physical region Antarctica
28 M4 **Max** North Dakota, N USA
41 W12 **Maxcanú** Yucatán, SE Mexico
Maxesibebi see Mount Ayliff
109 Q5 **Maxglan** ✈ (Salzburg) Salzburg, W Austria
93 K16 **Maxmo** Fin. Maksamaa. Länsi-Soumi, W Finland
21 T11 **Maxton** North Carolina, SE USA
25 R8 **May** Texas, SW USA
186 B6 **May** ≈ NW Papua New Guinea
123 R10 **Maya** ≈ E Russian Federation
151 Q19 **Māyābandar** Andaman and Nicobar Islands, India, E Indian Ocean
Mayadin see Al Mayādīn
44 L5 **Mayaguana** island SE Bahamas
44 L5 **Mayaguana Passage** passage SE Bahamas
45 S6 **Mayagüez** W Puerto Rico
45 R6 **Mayagüez, Bahía de** bay W Puerto Rico
Mayals see Maials
79 G20 **Mayama** Le Pool, SE Congo
37 V8 **Maya, Mesa De** ▲ Colorado, C USA
143 R4 **Mayamey** Semnān, N Iran
42 F3 **Maya Mountains** Sp. Montañas Mayas. ▲▲ Belize/Guatemala
44 I7 **Mayarí** Holguín, E Cuba
Mayas, Montañas see Maya Mountains
18 I17 **May, Cape** headland New Jersey, NE USA
80 J11 **Maych'ew** var. Mai Chio, It. Mai Ceu. Tigray, N Ethiopia
138 I2 **Maydān Ikbiz** Ḩalab, N Syria
Maydān Shahr see Meydān Shahr
80 O12 **Maydh** Sanaag, N Somalia
Maydī see Midī
Mayebashi see Maebashi
Mayence see Mainz
102 K6 **Mayenne** Mayenne, NW France
102 J6 **Mayenne** ◈ department NW France
102 J7 **Mayenne** ≈ N France
36 K12 **Mayer** Arizona, SW USA
22 J4 **Mayersville** Mississippi, S USA
9 P14 **Mayerthorpe** Alberta, SW Canada
21 S12 **Mayesville** South Carolina, SE USA
185 G19 **Mayfield** Canterbury, South Island, New Zealand
33 N14 **Mayfield** Idaho, NW USA
20 G7 **Mayfield** Kentucky, S USA
36 L5 **Mayfield** Utah, W USA
Mayhan see Sant
37 T14 **Mayhill** New Mexico, SW USA
145 T9 **Maykain** Kaz. Mayqayyng. Pavlodar, NE Kazakhstan
126 L14 **Maykop** Respublika Adygeya, SW Russian Federation
Maylibash see Maylybas
Mayli-Say see Mayluu-Suu
147 T9 **Mayluu-Suu** prev. Mayli-Say, Kir. Mayly-Say. Dzhalal-Abadskaya Oblast', W Kyrgyzstan
144 L14 **Maylybas** prev. Maylibash. Kzylorda, S Kazakhstan
Mayly-Say see Mayluu-Suu
Maymana see Meymaneh
166 M5 **Maymyo** Mandalay, C Myanmar (Burma)
123 V7 **Mayn** ≈ NE Russian Federation
127 Q5 **Mayna** Ul'yanovskaya Oblast', W Russian Federation
21 N8 **Maynardville** Tennessee, S USA
14 J13 **Maynooth** Ontario, SE Canada
10 I6 **Mayo** Yukon Territory, NW Canada
23 U9 **Mayo** Florida, SE USA
97 B16 **Mayo** Ir. Maigh Eo. ◈ county W Ireland
Mayo see Maio
78 G12 **Mayo-Kébbi** off. Préfecture du Mayo-Kébbu, var. Mayo-Kébi. ◈ prefecture SW Chad
Mayo-Kébbu, Préfecture du see Mayo-Kébbi
Mayo-Kébi see Mayo-Kébbi
79 F19 **Mayoko** Le Niari, SW Congo
171 P4 **Mayon Volcano** ⛰ Luzon, N Philippines
61 A24 **Mayor Buratovich** Buenos Aires, E Argentina
104 L4 **Mayorga** Castilla-León, N Spain
184 N6 **Mayor Island** island NE New Zealand
Mayor Pablo Lagerenza see Capitán Pablo Lagerenza
173 I14 **Mayotte** ◇ French territorial collectivity E Africa
Mayoumba see Mayumba
44 J13 **May Pen** C Jamaica
Mayqayyng see Maykain
171 O1 **Mayraira Point** headland Luzon, N Philippines
109 N8 **Mayrhofen** Tirol, W Austria
186 A6 **May River** East Sepik, NW Papua New Guinea
123 R13 **Mayskiy** Amurskaya Oblast', SE Russian Federation
127 O15 **Mayskiy** Kabardino-Balkarskaya Respublika, SW Russian Federation
145 U9 **Mayskoye** Pavlodar, NE Kazakhstan
18 J17 **Mays Landing** New Jersey, NE USA
21 N4 **Maysville** Kentucky, S USA
27 R2 **Maysville** Missouri, C USA
79 D20 **Mayumba** var. Mayoumba. Nyanga, S Gabon
31 S8 **Mayville** Michigan, N USA
18 C11 **Mayville** New York, NE USA
29 Q4 **Mayville** North Dakota, N USA
Mayyali see Mahe
Mayyit, Al Baḩr al see Dead Sea
83 J15 **Mazabuka** Southern, S Zambia
Mazaca see Kayseri
Mazagan see El-Jadida
32 J7 **Mazama** Washington, NW USA
103 O15 **Mazamet** Tarn, S France
143 O4 **Māzandarān** off. Ostān-e Māzandarān. ◈ province N Iran
Māzandarān, Ostān-e see Māzandarān
156 F7 **Mazar** Xinjiang Uygur Zizhiqu, NW China
107 H24 **Mazara del Vallo** Sicilia, Italy, C Mediterranean Sea
149 O2 **Mazār-e Sharīf** var. Mazār-i Sharif. Balkh, N Afghanistan
Mazār-i Sharif see Mazār-e Sharīf
105 R13 **Mazarrón** Murcia, SE Spain
105 R14 **Mazarrón, Golfo de** gulf SE Spain
55 S9 **Mazaruni River** ≈ N Guyana
42 B6 **Mazatenango** Suchitepéquez, SW Guatemala
40 I10 **Mazatlán** Sinaloa, C Mexico
36 L12 **Mazatzal Mountains** ▲▲ Arizona, SW USA
118 D10 **Mažeikiai** Telšiai, NW Lithuania
118 D7 **Mazirbe** Talsi, NW Latvia
40 G5 **Mazocahui** Sonora, NW Mexico
57 I18 **Mazocruz** Puno, S Peru
Mazoe, Rio see Mazowe
79 N21 **Mazomeno** Maniema, E Dem. Rep. Congo
159 Q6 **Mazong Shan** ▲ N China
83 L16 **Mazowe** var. Rio Mazoe. ≈ Mozambique/Zimbabwe
110 M11 **Mazowieckie** ◈ province C Poland
Mazra'a see Al Mazra'ah
138 G6 **Mazraat Kfar Debiâne** C Lebanon
118 H7 **Mazsalaca** Est. Väike-Salatsi, Ger. Salisburg. Valmiera, N Latvia
Mazu Dao see Matsu Tao
110 L9 **Mazury** physical region NE Poland
119 M20 **Mazyr** Rus. Mozyr'. Homyel'skaya Voblasts', SE Belarus
107 K25 **Mazzarino** Sicilia, Italy, C Mediterranean Sea
Mba see Ba
83 L21 **Mbabane** ● (Swaziland) NW Swaziland
Mbacké see Mbaké
77 N15 **Mbahiakro** E Ivory Coast
79 I16 **Mbaïki** var. M'Baiki. Lobaye, SW Central African Republic
M'Baiki see Mbaïki
79 F14 **Mbakaou, Lac de** ◎ C Cameroon
76 G11 **Mbaké** var. Mbacké. W Senegal
82 L11 **Mbala** prev. Abercorn. Northern, NE Zambia
83 J18 **Mbalabala** prev. Balla Balla. Matabeleland South, SW Zimbabwe
81 G18 **Mbale** E Uganda
79 E16 **Mbalmayo** var. M'Balmayo. Centre, S Cameroon
M'Balmayo see Mbalmayo
81 H25 **Mbamba Bay** Ruvuma, S Tanzania
79 I18 **Mbandaka** prev. Coquilhatville. Equateur, NW Dem. Rep. Congo
82 B9 **M'Banza Congo** var. Mbanza Congo; prev. São Salvador, São Salvador do Congo. Dem. Rep. Congo, NW Angola
79 G21 **Mbanza-Ngungu** Bas-Congo, W Dem. Rep. Congo
67 V11 **Mbarangandu** ≈ E Tanzania
81 E19 **Mbarara** SW Uganda
79 L15 **Mbari** ≈ SE Central African Republic
81 I24 **Mbarika Mountains** ▲▲ S Tanzania
83 J24 **Mbashe** ≈ S South Africa
78 F13 **Mbé** Nord, N Cameroon
81 J24 **Mbemkuru** var. Mbwemkuru. ≈ S Tanzania
Mbengga see Beqa
172 H13 **Mbéni** Grande Comore, NW Comoros
83 K18 **Mberengwa** Midlands, S Zimbabwe
81 G24 **Mbeya** Mbeya, SW Tanzania
81 G23 **Mbeya** ◈ region S Tanzania
79 E19 **Mbigou** Ngounié, C Gabon
Mbilua see Vella Lavella
79 F19 **Mbinda** Le Niari, SW Congo
79 D17 **Mbini** W Equatorial Guinea
Mbini see Uolo, Río
83 L18 **Mbizi** Masvingo, SE Zimbabwe
81 G23 **Mbogo** Mbeya, W Tanzania
79 N15 **Mboki** Haut-Mbomou, SE Central African Republic
79 G18 **Mbomo** Cuvette, NW Congo
79 L15 **Mbomou** ◈ prefecture SE Central African Republic
Mbomou/M'Bomu/Mbomu see Bomu
76 F11 **Mbour** W Senegal
76 I10 **Mbout** Gorgol, S Mauritania
79 J14 **Mbrès** var. Mbrés. Nana-Grébizi, C Central African Republic
Mbrés see Mbrès
79 L22 **Mbuji-Mayi** prev. Bakwanga. Kasai Oriental, S Dem. Rep. Congo
81 H21 **Mbulu** Manyara, N Tanzania
186 E5 **M'bunai** var. Bunai. Manus Island, N Papua New Guinea
62 N8 **Mburucuyá** Corrientes, NE Argentina
Mbutha see Buca
Mbwemkuru see Mbemkuru
81 G21 **Mbwikwe** Singida, C Tanzania
13 O15 **McAdam** New Brunswick, SE Canada
25 O5 **McAdoo** Texas, SW USA
35 V2 **McAfee Peak** ▲ Nevada, W USA
27 P11 **McAlester** Oklahoma, C USA
25 S17 **McAllen** Texas, SW USA
21 S11 **McBee** South Carolina, SE USA
9 N14 **McBride** British Columbia, SW Canada
24 M9 **McCamey** Texas, SW USA
33 R15 **McCammon** Idaho, NW USA
35 X11 **McCarran** ✈ (Las Vegas) Nevada, W USA
39 T11 **McCarthy** Alaska, USA
30 M5 **McCaslin Mountain** hill Wisconsin, N USA
25 O2 **McClellan Creek** ≈ Texas, SW USA
21 T14 **McClellanville** South Carolina, SE USA
8 L6 **McClintock Channel** channel Nunavut, N Canada
195 R12 **McClintock, Mount** ▲ Antarctica
35 N2 **McCloud** California, W USA
35 N3 **McCloud River** ≈ California, W USA
35 Q9 **McClure, Lake** ▣ California, W USA
197 O8 **McClure Strait** strait Northwest Territories, N Canada
29 N4 **McClusky** North Dakota, N USA
21 T11 **McColl** South Carolina, SE USA
22 K7 **McComb** Mississippi, S USA
18 E16 **McConnellsburg** Pennsylvania, NE USA

◆ Country
● Country Capital
◇ Dependent Territory
○ Dependent Territory Capital
◈ Administrative Regions
✈ International Airport
▲ Mountain
▲▲ Mountain Range
⛰ Volcano
≈ River
◎ Lake
▣ Reservoir

31 T14 **McConnelsville** Ohio, N USA
28 M17 **McCook** Nebraska, C USA
21 P13 **McCormick** South Carolina, SE USA
9 W16 **McCreary** Manitoba, S Canada
27 W11 **McCrory** Arkansas, C USA
25 T10 **McDade** Texas, SW USA
23 O8 **McDavid** Florida, SE USA
35 T1 **McDermitt** Nevada, W USA
23 S4 **McDonough** Georgia, SE USA
36 L12 **McDowell Mountains** ⛰ Arizona, SW USA
20 H8 **McEwen** Tennessee, S USA
35 R12 **McFarland** California, W USA
Mcfarlane, Lake *see* Macfarlane, Lake
27 P12 **McGee Creek Lake** ⊠ Oklahoma, C USA
27 W13 **McGehee** Arkansas, C USA
35 X5 **Mcgill** Nevada, W USA
14 K11 **McGillivray, Lac** ◎ Québec, SE Canada
39 P10 **McGrath** Alaska, USA
25 T8 **McGregor** Texas, SW USA
33 O12 **McGuire, Mount** ▲ Idaho, NW USA
83 M14 **Mchinji** *prev.* Fort Manning. Central, W Malawi
28 M7 **McIntosh** South Dakota, N USA
9 S7 **McKeand** ≈ Baffin Island, Nunavut, NE Canada
191 R4 **McKean Island** *island* Phoenix Islands, C Kiribati
30 J13 **McKee Creek** ≈ Illinois, N USA
18 C15 **Mckeesport** Pennsylvania, NE USA
21 V7 **McKenney** Virginia, NE USA
20 G8 **McKenzie** Tennessee, S USA
185 B20 **McKerrow, Lake** ◎ South Island, New Zealand
39 Q10 **McKinley, Mount** *var.* Denali. ⛰ Alaska, USA
39 R10 **McKinley Park** Alaska, USA
34 K3 **McKinleyville** California, W USA
25 U6 **McKinney** Texas, SW USA
26 I5 **McKinney, Lake** ◎ Kansas, C USA
28 M7 **McLaughlin** South Dakota, N USA
25 O2 **McLean** Texas, SW USA
30 M16 **Mcleansboro** Illinois, N USA
9 O13 **McLennan** Alberta, W Canada
14 L9 **McLennan, Lac** ◎ Québec, SE Canada
10 M13 **McLeod Lake** British Columbia, W Canada
27 N10 **McLoud** Oklahoma, C USA
32 G15 **McLoughlin, Mount** ▲ Oregon, NW USA
37 U15 **McMillan, Lake** ⊠ New Mexico, SW USA
32 G11 **McMinnville** Oregon, NW USA
20 K9 **McMinnville** Tennessee, S USA
195 R13 **McMurdo** *US research station* Antarctica
37 N13 **Mcnary** Arizona, SW USA
24 H9 **McNary** Texas, SW USA
27 N5 **McPherson** Kansas, C USA
McPherson *see* Fort McPherson
23 U6 **McRae** Georgia, SE USA
29 P4 **McVille** North Dakota, N USA
83 J25 **Mdantsane** Eastern Cape, SE South Africa
167 T6 **Me** Ninh Binh, N Vietnam
26 J7 **Meade** Kansas, C USA
39 O5 **Meade River** ≈ Alaska, USA
35 Y11 **Mead, Lake** ⊠ Arizona/Nevada, W USA
24 M5 **Meadow** Texas, SW USA
9 S14 **Meadow Lake** Saskatchewan, C Canada
35 Y10 **Meadow Valley Wash** ≈ Nevada, W USA
22 J7 **Meadville** Mississippi, S USA
18 B12 **Meadville** Pennsylvania, NE USA
14 F14 **Meaford** Ontario, S Canada
Meáin, Inis *see* Inishmaan
104 G8 **Mealhada** Aveiro, N Portugal
13 R8 **Mealy Mountains** ⛰ Newfoundland and Labrador, E Canada
9 O10 **Meander River** Alberta, W Canada
32 E11 **Meares, Cape** *headland* Oregon, NW USA
47 V6 **Mearim, Rio** ≈ NE Brazil
Measca, Loch *see* Mask, Lough
97 F17 **Meath** *Ir.* An Mhí. ⬖ *county* E Ireland
9 T14 **Meath Park** Saskatchewan, S Canada
103 O5 **Meaux** Seine-et-Marne, N France
21 T9 **Mebane** North Carolina, SE USA
171 U12 **Mebo, Gunung** ▲ Papua, E Indonesia
94 I8 **Mebonden** Sør-Trøndelag, S Norway
82 A10 **Mebridege** ≈ NW Angola
35 W16 **Mecca** California, W USA
Mecca *see* Makkah
29 Y14 **Mechanicsville** Iowa, C USA
18 L10 **Mechanicville** New York, NE USA
99 H17 **Mechelen** *Eng.* Mechlin, *Fr.* Malines. Antwerpen, C Belgium
188 C8 **Mecherchar** *var.* Eil Malk. *island* Palau Islands, Palau
101 D17 **Mechernich** Nordrhein-Westfalen, W Germany
126 L12 **Mechetinskaya** Rostovskaya Oblast', SW Russian Federation
114 J11 **Mechka** ≈ S Bulgaria
Mechlin *see* Mechelen
61 D23 **Mechongué** Buenos Aires, E Argentina
115 L14 **Mecidiye** Edirne, NW Turkey
101 I24 **Meckenbeuren** Baden-Württemberg, S Germany
100 L8 **Mecklenburger Bucht** *bay* N Germany
100 M10 **Mecklenburgische Seenplatte** *wetland* NE Germany
100 L9 **Mecklenburg-Vorpommern** ⬖ *state* NE Germany
83 Q15 **Meconta** Nampula, NE Mozambique
111 I25 **Mecsek** ⛰ SW Hungary
83 P14 **Mecubúri** ≈ N Mozambique
83 Q14 **Mecúfi** Cabo Delgado, NE Mozambique
82 O13 **Mecula** Niassa, N Mozambique
168 I8 **Medan** Sumatera, E Indonesia
51 A24 **Médanos** *var.* Medanos. Buenos Aires, E Argentina
61 C19 **Médanos** Entre Ríos, E Argentina
155 K24 **Medawachchiya** North Central Province, N Sri Lanka
106 C8 **Mede** Lombardia, N Italy
74 J5 **Médéa** *var.* El Mediyya, Lemdiyya. N Algeria
Medeba *see* Ma'dabā
54 E8 **Medellín** Antioquia, NW Colombia
100 H9 **Medem** ≈ NW Germany
98 J8 **Medemblik** Noord-Holland, NW Netherlands
75 N7 **Médenine** *var.* Madanīyīn. SE Tunisia
76 G9 **Mederdra** Trarza, SW Mauritania
Medeshamstede *see* Peterborough
42 F4 **Medesto Mendez** Izabal, NE Guatemala
19 O11 **Medford** Massachusetts, NE USA
27 N8 **Medford** Oklahoma, C USA
32 G15 **Medford** Oregon, NW USA
30 K6 **Medford** Wisconsin, N USA
39 P10 **Medfra** Alaska, USA
116 M14 **Medgidia** Constanţa, SE Romania
Medgyes *see* Mediaş
43 O5 **Media Luna, Arrecifes de la** *reef* E Honduras
60 G11 **Medianeira** Paraná, S Brazil
29 Y15 **Mediapolis** Iowa, C USA
116 I11 **Mediaş** *Ger.* Mediasch, *Hung.* Medgyes. Sibiu, C Romania
41 S15 **Medias Aguas** Veracruz-Llave, SE Mexico
Mediasch *see* Mediaş
106 G10 **Medicina** Emilia-Romagna, C Italy
33 X16 **Medicine Bow** Wyoming, C USA
37 S2 **Medicine Bow Mountains** ⛰ Colorado/Wyoming, C USA
33 X16 **Medicine Bow River** ≈ Wyoming, C USA
9 R17 **Medicine Hat** Alberta, SW Canada
26 L7 **Medicine Lodge** Kansas, C USA
26 L7 **Medicine Lodge River** ≈ Kansas/Oklahoma, C USA
112 E7 **Međimurje** *off.* Međimurska Županija. ⬖ *province* N Croatia
Međimurska Županija *see* Međimurje
54 G10 **Medina** Cundinamarca, C Colombia
18 E9 **Medina** New York, NE USA
29 O5 **Medina** North Dakota, N USA
31 T11 **Medina** Ohio, N USA
25 Q11 **Medina** Texas, SW USA
Medina *see* Al Madīnah
105 P6 **Medinaceli** Castilla-León, N Spain
104 L6 **Medina del Campo** Castilla-León, N Spain
104 L5 **Medina de Ríoseco** Castilla-León, N Spain
Médina Gonassé *see* Médina Gounas
76 H12 **Médina Gounas** *var.* Médina Gonassé. S Senegal
25 S12 **Medina River** ≈ Texas, SW USA
104 K16 **Medina Sidonia** Andalucía, S Spain
Medinat Israel *see* Israel
119 H14 **Medininkai** Vilnius, SE Lithuania
153 R16 **Medinīpur** West Bengal, NE India
Mediolanum *see* Saintes, France
Mediolanum *see* Milano, Italy
Mediomatrica *see* Metz
121 Q11 **Mediterranean Ridge** *undersea feature* C Mediterranean Sea
121 O16 **Mediterranean Sea** *Fr.* Mer Méditerranée. *sea* Africa/Asia/Europe
Méditerranée, Mer *see* Mediterranean Sea
79 N17 **Medje** Orientale, NE Dem. Rep. Congo
Medjerda, Oued *see* Mejerda
114 G7 **Medkovets** Montana, NW Bulgaria
93 J15 **Medle** Västerbotten, N Sweden
127 W7 **Mednogorsk** Orenburgskaya Oblast', W Russian Federation
123 W9 **Mednyy, Ostrov** *island* E Russian Federation
102 J12 **Médoc** *cultural region* SW France
159 Q16 **Mêdog** Xizang Zizhiqu, W China
28 J5 **Medora** North Dakota, N USA
79 E17 **Médouneu** Woleu-Ntem, N Gabon
106 I7 **Meduna** ≈ NE Italy
Medunta *see* Mantes-la-Jolie
Medvedica *see* Medveditsa
124 J16 **Medveditsa** *var.* Medvedica. ≈ W Russian Federation
127 O9 **Medveditsa** ≈ SW Russian Federation
112 E8 **Medvednica** ⛰ NE Croatia
125 R15 **Medvedok** Kirovskaya Oblast', NW Russian Federation
123 S6 **Medvezh'i, Ostrova** *island group* NE Russian Federation
124 J9 **Medvezh'yegorsk** Respublika Kareliya, NW Russian Federation
109 T11 **Medvode** *Ger.* Zwischenwässern. NW Slovenia
126 J4 **Medyn'** Kaluzhskaya Oblast', W Russian Federation
180 J10 **Meekatharra** Western Australia
37 Q4 **Meeker** Colorado, C USA
13 T12 **Meelpaeg Lake** ◎ Newfoundland, Newfoundland and Labrador, E Canada
Meemu Atoll *see* Mulaku Atoll
Meenen *see* Menen
101 M16 **Meerane** Sachsen, E Germany
101 D15 **Meerbusch** Nordrhein-Westfalen, W Germany
98 I12 **Meerkerk** Zuid-Holland, C Netherlands
99 L18 **Meerssen** *var.* Mersen. Limburg, SE Netherlands
152 J10 **Meerut** Uttar Pradesh, N India
33 U13 **Meeteetse** Wyoming, C USA
99 K17 **Meeuwen** Limburg, NE Belgium
81 J16 **Mēga** Oromo, C Ethiopia
81 J16 **Mēga Escarpment** *escarpment* S Ethiopia
Megála Kalívia *see* Megála Kalývia
115 E16 **Megála Kalývia** *var.* Megála Kalívia. Thessalía, C Greece
115 H14 **Megáli Panagiá** *var.* Megáli Panayía. Kentrikí Makedonía, N Greece
Megáli Panayía *see* Megáli Panagiá
Megáli Préspa, Límni *see* Prespa, Lake
114 K12 **Megálo Livádi** ▲ Bulgaria/Greece
115 E20 **Megalópoli** *prev.* Megalópolis. Pelopónnisos, S Greece
Megalópolis *see* Megalópoli
171 U12 **Megamo** Papua, E Indonesia
115 C18 **Meganísi** *island* Iónia Nisiá, Greece, C Mediterranean Sea
Meganom, Mys *see* Mehanom, Mys
Mégantic *see* Lac-Mégantic
15 R12 **Mégantic, Mont** ▲ Québec, SE Canada
115 G19 **Mégara** Attikí, C Greece
25 R5 **Megargel** Texas, SW USA
98 K13 **Megen** Noord-Brabant, S Netherlands
153 U13 **Meghālaya** ⬖ *state* NE India
153 U16 **Meghna** ≈ S Bangladesh
137 V14 **Meghri** *Rus.* Megri. SE Armenia
115 Q23 **Megísti** *var.* Kastellórizon. *island* SE Greece
Megri *see* Meghri
Mehabad *see* Mahābād
116 F13 **Mehadia** *Hung.* Mehádia. Caraş-Severin, SW Romania
Mehádia *see* Mehadia
92 L7 **Mehamn** Finnmark, N Norway
117 U13 **Mehanom, Mys** *Rus.* Mys Meganom. *headland* S Ukraine
149 P14 **Mehar** Sind, SE Pakistan
180 J8 **Meharry, Mount** ▲ Western Australia
Mehdia *see* Mahdia
116 G14 **Mehedinţi** ⬖ *county* SW Romania
153 S15 **Meherpur** Khulna, W Bangladesh
21 W8 **Meherrin River** ≈ North Carolina/Virginia, SE USA
Meheso *see* Mī'ēso
191 T11 **Mehetia** *island* Îles du Vent, W French Polynesia
118 K6 **Mehikoorma** Tartumaa, E Estonia
Me Hka *see* Nmai Hka
143 N5 **Mehrabad** ✕ (Tehrān) Tehrān, N Iran
142 J7 **Mehrān** Īlām, W Iran
143 Q14 **Mehrān, Rūd-e** *prev.* Mansurabad. ≈ W Iran
143 Q9 **Mehrīz** Yazd, C Iran
149 R5 **Mehtar Lām** *var.* Mehtarlām, Meterlam, Methariam, Metharlam. Laghmān, E Afghanistan
Mehtarlām *see* Mehtar Lām
103 N8 **Mehun-sur-Yèvre** Cher, C France
79 G14 **Meiganga** Adamaoua, NE Cameroon
160 H10 **Meigu** *var.* Bapu. Sichuan, C China
163 W11 **Meihekou** *var.* Hailong. Jilin, NE China
99 L15 **Meijel** Limburg, SE Netherlands
Meijiang *see* Ningdu
166 M5 **Meiktila** Mandalay, C Myanmar (Burma)
Meilbhe, Loch *see* Melvin, Lough
108 G7 **Meilen** Zürich, N Switzerland
Meilu *see* Wuchuan
161 T12 **Meinhua Yu** *island* N Taiwan
101 J17 **Meiningen** Thüringen, C Germany
108 F9 **Meiringen** Bern, S Switzerland
Meishan *see* Jinzhai
101 O15 **Meissen** *Ger.* Meißen. Sachsen, E Germany
Meißen *see* Meissen
101 I15 **Meissner** ▲ C Germany
99 K25 **Meix-devant-Virton** Luxembourg, SE Belgium
Meixian *see* Meizhou
Meixing *see* Xinjin
161 P13 **Meizhou** *var.* Meixian, Mei Xian. Guangdong, S China
67 P2 **Mejerda** *var.* Oued Medjerda, Wādī Majardah. ≈ Algeria/Tunisia *see also* Medjerda, Oued
42 F7 **Mejicanos** San Salvador, C El Salvador
Méjico *see* Mexico
62 G5 **Mejillones** Antofagasta, N Chile
189 V5 **Mejit Island** *var.* Mājeej. *island* Ratak Chain, NE Marshall Islands
79 F17 **Mékambo** Ogooué-Ivindo, NE Gabon
80 J10 **Mek'elē** *var.* Makale. Tigray, N Ethiopia
74 I10 **Mekerrhane, Sebkha** *var.* Sebkha Meqerghane, Sebkra Mekerrhane. *salt flat* C Algeria
Mekerrhane, Sebkra *see* Mekerrhane, Sebkha
76 G10 **Mékhé** NW Senegal
146 G14 **Mekhinli** Ahal Welaýaty, C Turkmenistan
15 P9 **Mékinac, Lac** ◎ Québec, SE Canada
Meklong *see* Samut Songhram
74 G6 **Meknès** N Morocco
129 U12 **Mekong** *var.* Lan-ts'ang Chiang, *Cam.* Mékôngk, *Chin.* Lancang Jiang, *Lao.* Mènam Khong, *Th.* Mae Nam Khong, *Tib.* Dza Chu, *Vtn.* Sông Tiên Giang. ≈ SE Asia
Mékôngk *see* Mekong
167 T15 **Mekong, Mouths of the** *delta* S Vietnam
38 L12 **Mekoryuk** Nunivak Island, Alaska, USA
77 R14 **Mékrou** ≈ N Benin
168 K9 **Melaka** *var.* Malacca. Melaka, Peninsular Malaysia
168 L9 **Melaka** *var.* Malacca. ⬖ *state* Peninsular Malaysia
Melaka, Selat *see* Malacca, Strait of
175 O6 **Melanesia** *island group* W Pacific Ocean
175 P5 **Melanesian Basin** *undersea feature* W Pacific Ocean
171 R9 **Melanguane** Pulau Karakelang, N Indonesia
169 R11 **Melawi, Sungai** ≈ Borneo, N Indonesia
183 N12 **Melbourne** *state capital* Victoria, SE Australia
27 V9 **Melbourne** Arkansas, C USA
23 Y12 **Melbourne** Florida, SE USA
29 W14 **Melbourne** Iowa, C USA
92 G10 **Melbu** Nordland, C Norway
Melchor de Mencos *see* Ciudad Melchor de Mencos
63 F19 **Melchor, Isla** *island* Archipiélago de los Chonos, S Chile
40 M9 **Melchor Ocampo** Zacatecas, C Mexico
14 C11 **Meldrum Bay** Manitoulin Island, Ontario, S Canada
Meleda *see* Mljet
106 D8 **Melegnano** *prev.* Marignano. Lombardia, N Italy
Melekeiok *see* Melekeok
188 F9 **Melekeok** *var.* Melekeiok. Babeldaob, N Palau
112 L9 **Melenci** *Hung.* Melencze. Vojvodina, N Serbia
Melencze *see* Melenci
127 N4 **Melenki** Vladimirskaya Oblast', W Russian Federation
127 V6 **Meleuz** Respublika Bashkortostan, W Russian Federation
12 L6 **Mélèzes, Rivière aux** ≈ Québec, C Canada
78 I11 **Melfi** Guéra, S Chad
107 M17 **Melfi** Basilicata, S Italy
9 U14 **Melfort** Saskatchewan, S Canada
104 H4 **Melgaço** Viana do Castelo, N Portugal
105 N4 **Melgar de Fernamental** Castilla-León, N Spain
74 L6 **Melghir, Chott** *var.* Chott Melrhir. *salt lake* E Algeria
94 H8 **Melhus** Sør-Trøndelag, S Norway
104 H3 **Melide** Galicia, NW Spain
Meligalá *see* Meligalás
115 E21 **Meligalás** *prev.* Meligalá. Pelopónnisos, S Greece
60 L12 **Mel, Ilha do** *island* S Brazil
120 E10 **Melilla** *anc.* Rusaddir, Russadir. Melilla, Spain, N Africa
71 N1 **Melilla** *enclave* Spain, N Africa
63 G18 **Melimoyu, Monte** ▲ S Chile
169 V11 **Melintang, Danau** ◎ Borneo, N Indonesia
117 U7 **Melioratyvne** Dnipropetrovs'ka Oblast', E Ukraine
62 G11 **Melipilla** Santiago, C Chile
115 I25 **Mélissa, Akrotírio** *cape* Kríti, Greece, E Mediterranean Sea
11 W17 **Melita** Manitoba, S Canada
Melita *see* Mljet
Melitene *see* Malatya
107 M23 **Melito di Porto Salvo** Calabria, SW Italy
117 U10 **Melitopol'** Zaporiz'ka Oblast', SE Ukraine
109 V4 **Melk** Niederösterreich, NE Austria
95 K15 **Mellan-Fryken** ◎ C Sweden
99 E17 **Melle** Oost-Vlaanderen, NW Belgium
100 G13 **Melle** Niedersachsen, NW Germany
95 J17 **Mellerud** Västra Götaland, S Sweden
102 K10 **Melle-sur-Bretonne** Deux-Sèvres, W France
29 P8 **Mellette** South Dakota, N USA
121 O15 **Mellieħa** E Malta
80 B10 **Mellit** Northern Darfur, W Sudan
75 N7 **Mellita** ✕ SE Tunisia
63 G21 **Mellizo Sur, Cerro** ▲ S Chile
100 G9 **Mellum** *island* NW Germany
83 L22 **Melmoth** KwaZulu/Natal, E South Africa
111 D16 **Mělník** *Ger.* Melnik. Středočeský Kraj, NW Czech Republic
122 J12 **Mel'nikovo** Tomskaya Oblast', C Russian Federation
61 G18 **Melo** Cerro Largo, NE Uruguay
Melodunum *see* Melun
Melrhir, Chott *see* Melghir, Chott
183 P7 **Melrose** New South Wales, SE Australia
182 I7 **Melrose** South Australia
29 T7 **Melrose** Minnesota, N USA
33 Q11 **Melrose** Montana, NW USA
37 V12 **Melrose** New Mexico, SW USA
108 I8 **Mels** Sankt Gallen, NE Switzerland
Melsetter *see* Chimanimani
33 V9 **Melstone** Montana, NW USA
101 I16 **Melsungen** Hessen, C Germany
92 L12 **Meltaus** Lappi, NW Finland
97 N19 **Melton Mowbray** C England, UK
82 Q13 **Meluco** Cabo Delgado, NE Mozambique
103 O5 **Melun** *anc.* Melodunum. Seine-et-Marne, N France
80 F12 **Melut** Upper Nile, SE Sudan
27 P5 **Melvern Lake** ⊠ Kansas, C USA
9 V16 **Melville** Saskatchewan, S Canada
Melville Bay/Melville Bugt *see* Qimusseriarsuaq
45 O11 **Melville Hall** ✕ (Dominica) NE Dominica
181 O1 **Melville Island** *island* Northern Territory, N Australia
197 O8 **Melville Island** *island* Parry Islands, Northwest Territories, NW Canada
9 W9 **Melville, Lake** ◎ Newfoundland and Labrador, E Canada
9 O7 **Melville Peninsula** *peninsula* Nunavut, NE Canada
Melville Sound *see* Viscount Melville Sound
25 Q9 **Melvin** Texas, SW USA
97 D15 **Melvin, Lough** *Ir.* Loch Meilbhe. ◎ S Northern Ireland, UK/Ireland
169 S12 **Memala** Borneo, C Indonesia
113 L22 **Memaliaj** Gjirokastër, S Albania
83 Q14 **Memba** Nampula, NE Mozambique
83 Q14 **Memba, Baia de** *inlet* NE Mozambique
Membidj *see* Manbij
Memel *see* Neman, NE Europe
Memel *see* Klaipeda, Lithuania
101 J23 **Memmingen** Bayern, S Germany
27 U1 **Memphis** Missouri, C USA
20 E10 **Memphis** Tennessee, S USA
25 P3 **Memphis** Texas, SW USA
20 E10 **Memphis** ✕ Tennessee, S USA
15 Q13 **Memphrémagog, Lac** *var.* Lake Memphremagog. ◎ Canada/USA *see also* Lake Memphremagog
19 N6 **Memphremagog, Lake** *var.* Lac Memphrémagog. ◎ Canada/USA *see also* Memphrémagog, Lac
117 Q2 **Mena** Chernihivs'ka Oblast', NE Ukraine
27 S12 **Mena** Arkansas, C USA
Menaam *see* Menaldum
Menado *see* Manado
106 D6 **Menaggio** Lombardia, N Italy
29 T6 **Menahga** Minnesota, N USA
77 R10 **Ménaka** Goa, E Mali
98 K5 **Menaldum** *Fris.* Menaam. Friesland, N Netherlands
Mènam Khong *see* Mekong
74 E7 **Menara** ✕ (Marrakech) C Morocco
25 Q9 **Menard** Texas, SW USA
193 Q12 **Menard Fracture Zone** *tectonic feature* E Pacific Ocean
30 M7 **Menasha** Wisconsin, N USA
Mencezi Garagum *see* Merkezi Garagumy
Mencezi Garagum *see* Merkezi Garagumy
193 U9 **Mendaña Fracture Zone** *tectonic feature* E Pacific Ocean
169 S13 **Mendawai, Sungai** ≈ Borneo, C Indonesia
103 P13 **Mende** *anc.* Mimatum. Lozère, S France
81 J14 **Mendebo** ⛰ C Ethiopia
80 J9 **Mendefera** *prev.* Adi Ugri. S Eritrea
197 S7 **Mendeleyev Ridge** *undersea feature* Arctic Ocean
127 T3 **Mendeleyevsk** Respublika Tatarstan, W Russian Federation
101 F15 **Menden** Nordrhein-Westfalen, W Germany
22 L6 **Mendenhall** Mississippi, S USA
38 L13 **Mendenhall, Cape** *headland* Nunivak Island, Alaska, USA
41 P9 **Méndez** *var.* Villa de Méndez. Tamaulipas, C Mexico
80 H13 **Mendī** Oromo C Ethiopia
186 C7 **Mendi** Southern Highlands, W Papua New Guinea
97 K22 **Mendip Hills** *var.* Mendips. *hill range* S England, UK
Mendips *see* Mendip Hills
34 L6 **Mendocino** California, W USA
34 J3 **Mendocino, Cape** *headland* California, W USA
0 B8 **Mendocino Fracture Zone** *tectonic feature* NE Pacific Ocean
35 P10 **Mendota** California, W USA
30 L11 **Mendota** Illinois, N USA
30 K8 **Mendota, Lake** ◎ Wisconsin, N USA
62 I11 **Mendoza** Mendoza, W Argentina
62 I12 **Mendoza** *off.* Provincia de Mendoza. ⬖ *province* W Argentina
Mendoza, Provincia de *see* Mendoza
108 H12 **Mendrisio** Ticino, S Switzerland
168 L10 **Mendung** Pulau Mendol, W Indonesia
54 I5 **Mene de Mauroa** Falcón, NW Venezuela
54 I5 **Mene Grande** Zulia, NW Venezuela
136 B14 **Menemen** İzmir, W Turkey
99 C18 **Menen** *var.* Meenen, *Fr.* Menin. West-Vlaanderen, W Belgium
163 Q8 **Menengiyn Tal** *plain* E Mongolia
189 R9 **Meneng Point** *headland* SW Nauru
92 L10 **Menesjärvi** *Lapp.* Menešjávri. Lappi, N Finland
Menešjávri *see* Menesjärvi
107 I24 **Menfi** Sicilia, Italy, C Mediterranean Sea
161 P7 **Mengcheng** Anhui, E China
160 F15 **Menghai** Yunnan, SW China
160 F15 **Mengla** Yunnan, SW China
65 F24 **Menguera Point** *headland* East Falkland, Falkland Islands
160 M13 **Mengzhu Ling** ⛰ S China
160 H14 **Mengzi** Yunnan, SW China
114 H13 **Meníkio** *var.* Menoíkio. ▲ NE Greece
Menin *see* Menen
182 L7 **Menindee** New South Wales, SE Australia
182 L7 **Menindee Lake** ◎ New South Wales, SE Australia
182 J10 **Meningie** South Australia
103 O5 **Mennecy** Essonne, N France
29 Q12 **Menno** South Dakota, N USA
114 H13 **Menoíkio** ⛰ NE Greece
Menoíkio *see* Meníkio
31 N5 **Menominee** Michigan, N USA
30 M5 **Menominee River** ≈ Michigan/Wisconsin, N USA
30 M8 **Menomonee Falls** Wisconsin, N USA
30 I6 **Menomonie** Wisconsin, N USA
83 D14 **Menongue** *var.* Vila Serpa Pinto, *Port.* Serpa Pinto. Cuando Cubango, C Angola
120 H8 **Menorca** *Eng.* Minorca; *anc.* Balearis Minor. *island* Islas Baleares, Spain, W Mediterranean Sea
105 S13 **Menor, Mar** *lagoon* SE Spain
39 S10 **Mentasta Lake** ◎ Alaska, USA
39 S10 **Mentasta Mountains** ⛰ Alaska, USA
168 I13 **Mentawai, Kepulauan** *island group* W Indonesia
168 I12 **Mentawai, Selat** *strait* W Indonesia
168 M12 **Mentok** Pulau Bangka, W Indonesia
103 V15 **Menton** *It.* Mentone. Alpes-Maritimes, SE France
24 K8 **Mentone** Texas, SW USA
Mentone *see* Menton
31 U11 **Mentor** Ohio, N USA
169 U10 **Menyapa, Gunung** ▲ Borneo, N Indonesia
159 T9 **Menyuan** *var.* Menyuan Huizu Zizhixian. Qinghai, C China
Menyuan Huizu Zizhixian *see* Menyuan
74 M5 **Menzel Bourguiba** *var.* Manzil Bū Ruqaybah; *prev.* Ferryville. N Tunisia
136 M15 **Menzelet Barajı** ⊠ C Turkey
127 T4 **Menzelinsk** Respublika Tatarstan, W Russian Federation
180 K11 **Menzies** Western Australia
195 V6 **Menzies, Mount** ▲ Antarctica
40 J6 **Meoqui** Chihuahua, N Mexico
83 N14 **Meponda** Niassa, NE Mozambique
98 M8 **Meppel** Drenthe, NE Netherlands
100 E12 **Meppen** Niedersachsen, NW Germany
Meqerghane, Sebkha *see* Mekerrhane, Sebkha
105 T6 **Mequinenza, Embalse de** ⊠ NE Spain
30 M8 **Mequon** Wisconsin, N USA
Mera *see* Maira
182 D3 **Meramangye, Lake** *salt lake* South Australia
27 W5 **Meramec River** ≈ Missouri, C USA
Meran *see* Merano
168 K13 **Merangin** ≈ Sumatera, W Indonesia
106 G5 **Merano** *Ger.* Meran. Trentino-Alto Adige, N Italy
168 K8 **Merapuh Lama** Pahang, Peninsular Malaysia
106 D7 **Merate** Lombardia, N Italy
169 U13 **Meratus, Pegunungan** ⛰ Borneo, N Indonesia
171 Y16 **Merauke, Sungai** ≈ Papua, E Indonesia
182 L9 **Merbein** Victoria, SE Australia
99 F21 **Merbes-le-Château** Hainaut, S Belgium
Merca *see* Marka
54 C13 **Mercaderes** Cauca, SW Colombia
Mercara *see* Madikeri
35 P9 **Merced** California, W USA
61 C20 **Mercedes** Buenos Aires, E Argentina
61 D15 **Mercedes** Corrientes, NE Argentina
62 J11 **Mercedes** *prev.* Villa Mercedes. San Luis, C Argentina
61 D19 **Mercedes** Soriano, SW Uruguay
25 S17 **Mercedes** Texas, SW USA
35 R9 **Merced Peak** ▲ California, W USA
35 P9 **Merced River** ≈ California, W USA
18 B13 **Mercer** Pennsylvania, NE USA
99 G18 **Merchtem** Vlaams Brabant, C Belgium
15 O13 **Mercier** Québec, SE Canada
25 Q9 **Mercury** Texas, SW USA
184 M5 **Mercury Islands** *island group* N New Zealand
19 O9 **Meredith** New Hampshire, NE USA
65 B25 **Meredith, Cape** *var.* Cabo Belgrano. *headland* West Falkland, Falkland Islands
37 V6 **Meredith, Lake** ◎ Colorado, C USA
25 N2 **Meredith, Lake** ⊠ Texas, SW USA
81 O16 **Mereeg** *var.* Mareeq, *It.* Meregh. Galguduud, E Somalia
117 V5 **Merefa** Kharkivs'ka Oblast', E Ukraine
Meregh *see* Mereeg
99 E17 **Merelbeke** Oost-Vlaanderen, NW Belgium
Merend *see* Marand
167 T12 **Mereuch** Môndól Kiri, E Cambodia
Mergate *see* Margate
144 F9 **Mergenevo** Zapadnyy Kazakhstan, NW Kazakhstan
167 N12 **Mergui** Tenasserim, S Myanmar (Burma)
166 M12 **Mergui Archipelago** *island group* S Myanmar (Burma)
114 L12 **Meriç** Edirne, NW Turkey
114 L12 **Meriç** *Bul.* Maritsa, *Gk.* Évros; *anc.* Hebrus. ≈ SE Europe *see also* Évros/Maritsa
41 X12 **Mérida** Yucatán, SW Mexico
104 J11 **Mérida** *anc.* Augusta Emerita. Extremadura, W Spain
54 I6 **Mérida** Mérida, W Venezuela
54 H7 **Mérida** *off.* Estado Mérida. ⬖ *state* W Venezuela
Mérida, Estado *see* Mérida
18 M13 **Meriden** Connecticut, NE USA

◆ Country ● Country Capital ◇ Dependent Territory ○ Dependent Territory Capital ⬖ Administrative Regions ✕ International Airport ▲ Mountain ⛰ Mountain Range ⩕ Volcano ≈ River ◎ Lake ⊠ Reservoir

22 M5 **Meridian** Mississippi, S USA
25 S8 **Meridian** Texas, SW USA
102 J13 **Mérignac** Gironde, SW France
102 J13 **Mérignac** ✕ (Bordeaux) Gironde, SW France
93 J18 **Merikarvia** Länsi-Soumi, SW Finland
183 R12 **Merimbula** New South Wales, SE Australia
182 L9 **Meringur** Victoria, SE Australia
Merín, Laguna see Mirim Lagoon
97 J19 **Merioneth** *cultural region* W Wales, UK
188 A11 **Merir** *island* Palau Islands, N Palau
188 B17 **Merizo** SW Guam
Merjama see Märjamaa
145 S16 **Merke** Zhambyl, S Kazakhstan
25 P7 **Merkel** Texas, SW USA
146 E12 **Merkezi Garagumy** var. Mencezi Garagum, Rus. Tsentral'nyye Nizmennyye Garagumy. *desert* C Turkmenistan
146 E12 **Merkezi Garagumy** var. Mencezi Garagum, Rus. Tsentral'nyye Nizmennyye Garagumy. *desert* C Turkmenistan
119 F15 **Merkinė** Alytus, S Lithuania
99 G16 **Merksem** Antwerpen, N Belgium
99 I15 **Merksplas** Antwerpen, N Belgium
Merkulovichi see Myerkulavichy
119 G15 **Merkys** ≈ S Lithuania
32 F15 **Merlin** Oregon, NW USA
61 C20 **Merlo** Buenos Aires, E Argentina
138 G8 **Meron, Haré** ▲ N Israel
74 K6 **Merouane, Chott** *salt lake* NE Algeria
80 F7 **Merowe** Northern, N Sudan
180 J12 **Merredin** Western Australia
97 I14 **Merrick** ▲ S Scotland, UK
32 H16 **Merrill** Oregon, NW USA
30 L5 **Merrill** Wisconsin, N USA
31 N11 **Merrillville** Indiana, N USA
19 O10 **Merrimack River** ≈ Massachusetts/New Hampshire, NE USA
28 L12 **Merriman** Nebraska, C USA
9 N17 **Merritt** British Columbia, SW Canada
23 Y12 **Merritt Island** Florida, SE USA
23 Y11 **Merritt Island** *island* Florida, SE USA
28 M12 **Merritt Reservoir** ▣ Nebraska, C USA
183 S7 **Merriwa** New South Wales, SE Australia
183 O8 **Merriwagga** New South Wales, SE Australia
22 G8 **Merryville** Louisiana, S USA
80 K9 **Mersa Fatma** E Eritrea
102 M7 **Mer St-Aubin** Loir-et-Cher, C France
Mersa Maṭrûḥ see Maṭrûḥ
99 M24 **Mersch** Luxembourg, C Luxembourg
101 M15 **Merseburg** Sachsen-Anhalt, C Germany
Mersen see Meerssen
97 K18 **Mersey** ≈ NW England, U K
136 J17 **Mersin** Mersin, S Turkey
136 I17 **Mersin** prev. İçel, Ichili. ◈ *province* S Turkey
168 L9 **Mersing** Johor, Peninsular Malaysia
118 E8 **Mērsrags** Talsi, NW Latvia
152 G12 **Merta** var. Merta City. Rājasthān, N India
Merta City see Merta
152 F12 **Merta Road** Rājasthān, N India
97 J21 **Merthyr Tydfil** S Wales, UK
104 H13 **Mértola** Beja, S Portugal
144 G14 **Mertvyy Kultuk, Sor** *salt flat* SW Kazakhstan
195 V16 **Mertz Glacier** *glacier* Antarctica
99 M24 **Mertzig** Diekirch, C Luxembourg
25 O9 **Mertzon** Texas, SW USA
103 N4 **Méru** Oise, N France
81 I18 **Meru** Eastern, C Kenya
81 I20 **Meru, Mount** ▲ NE Tanzania
Merv see Mary
Mervdasht see Marv Dasht
136 K11 **Merzifon** Amasya, N Turkey
101 D20 **Merzig** Saarland, SW Germany
36 L14 **Mesa** Arizona, SW USA
29 V4 **Mesabi Range** ▲▲ Minnesota, N USA
54 H6 **Mesa Bolívar** Mérida, NW Venezuela
107 Q18 **Mesagne** Puglia, SE Italy
39 P12 **Mesa Mountain** ▲ Alaska, USA
115 J25 **Mesará** *lowland* Kríti, Greece, E Mediterranean Sea
37 S14 **Mescalero** New Mexico, SW USA
101 G15 **Meschede** Nordrhein-Westfalen, W Germany
137 Q12 **Mescit Dağları** ▲▲ NE Turkey
189 V13 **Mesegon** *island* Chuuk, C Micronesia
Meseritz see Międzyrzecz
54 F11 **Mesetas** Meta, C Colombia
Meshchera Lowland see Meshcherskaya Nizina
126 M4 **Meshcherskaya Nizina** Eng. Meshchera Lowland. *basin* W Russian Federation
126 J5 **Meshchovsk** Kaluzhskaya Oblast', W Russian Federation
125 R9 **Meshchura** Respublika Komi, NW Russian Federation
Meshed see Mashhad
Meshed-i-Sar see Bābolsar
80 E13 **Meshra'er Req** Warab, S Sudan
37 R15 **Mesilla** New Mexico, SW USA
108 H10 **Mesocco** Ger. Misox. Ticino, S Switzerland
115 D18 **Mesolóngi** prev. Mesolóngion. Dytikí Elláds, W Greece
Mesolóngion see Mesolóngi
14 E8 **Mesomikenda Lake** ◎ Ontario, S Canada
61 D15 **Mesopotamia** var. Mesopotamia Argentina. *physical region* NE Argentina
Mesopotamia Argentina see Mesopotamia
35 Y10 **Mesquite** Nevada, W USA
82 Q13 **Messalo, Rio** var. Mualo. ≈ NE Mozambique
Messana/Messene see Messina
99 L25 **Messancy** Luxembourg, SE Belgium
107 M23 **Messina** var. Messana, Messene; anc. Zancle. Sicilia, Italy, C Mediterranean Sea
Messina see Musina
Messina, Strait of see Messina, Stretto di
107 M23 **Messina, Stretto di** Eng. Strait of Messina. *strait* SW Italy
115 E21 **Messíni** Pelopónnisos, S Greece
115 E21 **Messinía** *peninsula* S Greece
115 E22 **Messiniakós Kólpos** *gulf* S Greece
122 J8 **Messoyakha** ≈ N Russian Federation
114 H11 **Mesta** Gk. Néstos, Turk. Kara Su. ≈ Bulgaria/Greece see also Néstos
Mesta see Néstos
Mestghanem see Mostaganem
137 R8 **Mestia** var. Mestiya. N Georgia
Mestiya see Mestia
115 K18 **Mestón, Akrotírio** *cape* Chíos, E Greece
106 H8 **Mestre** Veneto, NE Italy
59 M16 **Mestre, Espigão** ▲▲ E Brazil
169 N14 **Mesuji** ≈ Sumatera, W Indonesia
Mesule see Grosser Möseler
10 J10 **Meszah Peak** ▲ British Columbia, W Canada
54 G11 **Meta** off. Departamento del Meta. ◈ *province* C Colombia
15 Q8 **Metabetchouane** ≈ Québec, SE Canada
Meta, Departamento del see Meta
9 S7 **Meta Incognita Peninsula** *peninsula* Baffin Island, Nunavut, NE Canada
22 K9 **Metairie** Louisiana, S USA
32 M6 **Metaline Falls** Washington, NW USA
62 K6 **Metán** Salta, N Argentina
82 N13 **Metangula** Niassa, N Mozambique
42 E7 **Metapán** Santa Ana, NW El Salvador
54 K9 **Meta, Río** ≈ Colombia/Venezuela
106 I11 **Metauro** ≈ C Italy
80 H11 **Metema** Amhara, N Ethiopia
115 D15 **Metéora** *religious building* Thessalía, C Greece
65 O20 **Meteor Rise** *undersea feature* SW Indian Ocean
186 G5 **Meteran** New Hanover, NE Papua New Guinea
Meterlam see Mehtar Lām
115 G20 **Methanon** *peninsula* S Greece
Methariam/Metharlam see Mehtar Lām
32 J6 **Methow River** ≈ Washington, NW USA
19 O10 **Methuen** Massachusetts, NE USA
185 G19 **Methven** Canterbury, South Island, New Zealand
Metis see Metz
113 G15 **Metković** Dubrovnik-Neretva, SE Croatia
39 Y14 **Metlakatla** Annette Island, Alaska, USA
109 V13 **Metlika** Ger. Möttling. SE Slovenia
109 T8 **Metnitz** Kärnten, S Austria
27 W12 **Meto, Bayou** ≈ Arkansas, C USA
168 M15 **Metro** Sumatera, W Indonesia
30 M17 **Metropolis** Illinois, N USA
Metropolitan see Santiago
35 N8 **Metropolitan Oakland** ✕ California, W USA
115 D15 **Métsovo** prev. Métsovon. Ípeiros, C Greece
Métsovon see Métsovo
23 V5 **Metter** Georgia, SE USA
99 H21 **Mettet** Namur, S Belgium
101 D20 **Mettlach** Saarland, SW Germany
Mettu see Metu
80 H13 **Metu** var. Mattu, Mettu. Oromo, C Ethiopia
169 T10 **Metulang** Borneo, N Indonesia
138 G8 **Metulla** Northern, N Israel
103 T4 **Metz** anc. Divodurum Mediomatricum, Mediomatrica, Metis. Moselle, NE France
101 H22 **Metzingen** Baden-Württemberg, S Germany
168 G8 **Meulaboh** Sumatera, W Indonesia
99 D18 **Meulebeke** West-Vlaanderen, W Belgium
103 U6 **Meurthe** ≈ NE France
103 S5 **Meurthe-et-Moselle** ◈ *department* NE France
103 S4 **Meuse** ◈ *department* NE France
84 F10 **Meuse** Dut. Maas. ≈ W Europe see also Maas
Meuse see Maas
Mexcala, Río see Balsas, Río
25 U8 **Mexia** Texas, SW USA
58 K11 **Mexiana, Ilha** *island* NE Brazil
40 C1 **Mexicali** Baja California, NW Mexico
Mexicanos, Estados Unidos see Mexico
41 O14 **México** var. Ciudad de México, Eng. Mexico City. ● (Mexico) México, C Mexico
27 V4 **Mexico** Missouri, C USA
18 H9 **Mexico** New York, NE USA
40 L7 **Mexico** off. United Mexican States, var. Méjico, México, Sp. Estados Unidos Mexicanos. ◆ *federal republic* N Central America
41 O13 **México** ◈ *state* S Mexico
México see Mexico
0 J13 **Mexico Basin** var. Sigsbee Deep. *undersea feature* C Gulf of Mexico
Mexico City see México
México, Golfo de see Mexico, Gulf of
44 B4 **Mexico, Gulf of** Sp. Golfo de México. *gulf* W Atlantic Ocean
Meyadine see Al Mayādīn
149 Q5 **Meydān Shahr** var. Maydān Shahr. Vardak, E Afghanistan
39 Y14 **Meyers Chuck** Etolin Island, Alaska, USA
148 M3 **Meymaneh** var. Maimāna, Maymana. Fāryāb, NW Afghanistan
143 N7 **Meymeh** Eşfahān, C Iran
123 V7 **Meynypil'gyno** Chukotskiy Avtonomnyy Okrug, NE Russian Federation
108 A10 **Meyrin** Genève, SW Switzerland
166 L7 **Mezaligon** Irrawaddy, SW Myanmar (Burma)
41 O15 **Mezcala** Guerrero, S Mexico
114 H8 **Mezdra** Vratsa, NW Bulgaria
103 P16 **Mèze** Hérault, S France
125 O6 **Mezen'** Arkhangel'skaya Oblast', NW Russian Federation
125 P8 **Mezen'** ≈ NW Russian Federation
Mezen, Bay of see Mezenskaya Guba
103 Q13 **Mézenc, Mont** ▲ C France
125 O8 **Mezenskaya Guba** var. Bay of Mezen. *bay* NW Russian Federation
Mezha see Myazha
122 H6 **Mezhdusharskiy, Ostrov** *island* Novaya Zemlya, N Russian Federation
Mezhëvo see Myezhava
127 W5 **Mezhgor'ye** Respublika Bashkortostan, W Russian Federation
Mezhgor'ye see Mizhhir"ya
117 V8 **Mezhova** Dnipropetrovs'ka Oblast', E Ukraine
10 J12 **Meziadin Junction** British Columbia, W Canada
111 G16 **Mezileské Sedlo** var. Przełęcz Międzyleska. *pass* Czech Republic/Poland
102 L14 **Mézin** Lot-et-Garonne, SW France
111 M24 **Mezőberény** Békés, SE Hungary
111 M25 **Mezőhegyes** Békés, SE Hungary
111 M25 **Mezőkovácsháza** Békés, SE Hungary
111 M21 **Mezőkövesd** Borsod-Abaúj-Zemplén, NE Hungary
Mezőtelegd see Tileagd
111 M23 **Mezőtúr** Jász-Nagykun-Szolnok, E Hungary
40 K10 **Mezquital** Durango, C Mexico
106 G6 **Mezzolombardo** Trentino-Alto Adige, N Italy
82 L13 **Mfuwe** Northern, N Zambia
121 O15 **Mġarr** Gozo, N Malta
126 H6 **Mglin** Bryanskaya Oblast', W Russian Federation
Mhálanna, Cionn see Malin Head
154 G10 **Mhow** Madhya Pradesh, C India
Miadzioł Nowy see Myadzyel
171 O6 **Miagao** Panay Island, C Philippines
41 R17 **Miahuatlán** var. Miahuatlán de Porfirio Díaz. Oaxaca, SE Mexico
Miahuatlán de Porfirio Díaz see Miahuatlán
104 K10 **Miajadas** Extremadura, W Spain
Miajlar see Myājlār
36 M14 **Miami** Arizona, SW USA
23 Z16 **Miami** Florida, SE USA
27 R8 **Miami** Oklahoma, C USA
25 O2 **Miami** Texas, SW USA
23 Z16 **Miami** ✕ Florida, SE USA
23 Z16 **Miami Beach** Florida, SE USA
23 Y15 **Miami Canal** *canal* Florida, SE USA
31 R14 **Miamisburg** Ohio, N USA
149 U10 **Miān Channūn** Punjab, E Pakistan
142 J4 **Miāndowāb** var. Mianduab, Miyāndoāb. Āžarbāyjān-e Gharbī, NW Iran
172 H5 **Miandrivazo** Toliara, C Madagascar
Mianduab see Miāndowāb
142 K3 **Miāneh** var. Miyāneh. Āžarbāyjān-e Sharqī, NW Iran
149 O16 **Miāni Hōr** *lagoon* S Pakistan
160 G10 **Mianning** Sichuan, C China
149 T7 **Miānwāli** Punjab, NE Pakistan
160 J7 **Mianxian** var. Mian Xian. Shaanxi, C China
Mian Xian see Mianxian
160 I8 **Mianyang** Sichuan, C China
Mianyang see Xiantao
161 R3 **Miaodao Qundao** *island group* E China
161 S13 **Miaoli** N Taiwan
122 F11 **Miass** Chelyabinskaya Oblast', C Russian Federation
110 G8 **Miastko** Ger. Rummelsburg in Pommern. Pomorskie, N Poland
Miava see Myjava
9 O15 **Mica Creek** British Columbia, SW Canada
160 J7 **Micang Shan** ▲▲ C China
Mi Chai see Nong Khai
111 O19 **Michalovce** Ger. Grossmichel, Hung. Nagymihály. Košický Kraj, E Slovakia
99 M20 **Michel, Baraque** *hill* E Belgium
39 S5 **Michelson, Mount** ▲ Alaska, USA
45 P9 **Miches** E Dominican Republic
30 M4 **Michigamme, Lake** ◎ Michigan, N USA
30 M4 **Michigamme Reservoir** ▣ Michigan, N USA
31 N4 **Michigamme River** ≈ Michigan, N USA
31 O7 **Michigan** off. State of Michigan, also known as Great Lakes State, Lake State, Wolverine State. ◈ *state* N USA
31 O11 **Michigan City** Indiana, N USA
31 O8 **Michigan, Lake** ◎ N USA
31 P2 **Michipicoten Bay** *lake bay* Ontario, N Canada
14 A8 **Michipicoten Island** *island* Ontario, S Canada
14 B7 **Michipicoten River** Ontario, S Canada
Michurin see Tsarevo
126 M6 **Michurinsk** Tambovskaya Oblast', W Russian Federation
Mico, Punta/Mico, Punto see Monkey Point
42 L10 **Mico, Río** ≈ SE Nicaragua
45 T12 **Micoud** SE Saint Lucia
189 N16 **Micronesia** off. Federated States of Micronesia. ◆ *federation* W Pacific Ocean
175 P4 **Micronesia** *island group* W Pacific Ocean
Micronesia, Federated States of see Micronesia
169 O9 **Midai, Pulau** *island* Kepulauan Natuna, W Indonesia
Mid-Atlantic Cordillera see Mid-Atlantic Ridge
65 M17 **Mid-Atlantic Ridge** var. Mid-Atlantic Cordillera, Mid-Atlantic Rise, Mid-Atlantic Swell. *undersea feature* Atlantic Ocean
Mid-Atlantic Rise/Mid-Atlantic Swell see Mid-Atlantic Ridge
99 E15 **Middelburg** Zeeland, SW Netherlands
83 H24 **Middelburg** Eastern Cape, S South Africa
83 K21 **Middelburg** Mpumalanga, NE South Africa
95 G23 **Middelfart** Fyn, C Denmark
98 G13 **Middelharnis** Zuid-Holland, SW Netherlands
99 B16 **Middelkerke** West-Vlaanderen, W Belgium
98 I9 **Middenbeemster** Noord-Holland, C Netherlands
98 I8 **Middenmeer** Noord-Holland, NW Netherlands
35 Q2 **Middle Alkali Lake** ◎ California, W USA
193 S6 **Middle America Trench** *undersea feature* E Pacific Ocean
151 P19 **Middle Andaman** *island* Andaman Islands, India, NE Indian Ocean
Middle Atlas see Moyen Atlas
21 R3 **Middlebourne** West Virginia, NE USA
23 W9 **Middleburg** Florida, SE USA
Middleburg Island see 'Eua
Middle Caicos see Grand Caicos
25 N8 **Middle Concho River** ≈ Texas, SW USA
Middle Congo see Congo (Republic of)
39 R6 **Middle Fork Chandalar River** ≈ Alaska, USA
39 Q7 **Middle Fork Koyukuk River** ≈ Alaska, USA
33 O12 **Middle Fork Salmon River** ≈ Idaho, NW USA
9 T15 **Middle Lake** Saskatchewan, S Canada
28 L13 **Middle Loup River** ≈ Nebraska, C USA
185 E22 **Middlemarch** Otago, South Island, New Zealand
31 T15 **Middleport** Ohio, N USA
29 U14 **Middle Raccoon River** ≈ Iowa, C USA
29 R3 **Middle River** ≈ Minnesota, N USA
21 N8 **Middlesboro** Kentucky, S USA
97 M15 **Middlesbrough** N England, UK
42 G3 **Middlesex** Stann Creek, C Belize
97 N22 **Middlesex** *cultural region* SE England, UK
13 P15 **Middleton** Nova Scotia, SE Canada
20 F10 **Middleton** Tennessee, S USA
30 L9 **Middleton** Wisconsin, N USA
39 S13 **Middleton Island** *island* Alaska, USA
34 M7 **Middletown** California, W USA
21 Y2 **Middletown** Delaware, NE USA
18 K15 **Middletown** New Jersey, NE USA
18 K13 **Middletown** New York, NE USA
31 R14 **Middletown** Ohio, N USA
18 G15 **Middletown** Pennsylvania, NE USA
141 N14 **Mīdī** var. Maydī. NW Yemen
103 O16 **Midi, Canal du** *canal* S France
102 K17 **Midi de Bigorre, Pic du** ▲ S France
102 K17 **Midi d'Ossau, Pic du** ▲ SW France
173 R7 **Mid-Indian Basin** *undersea feature* N Indian Ocean
173 P7 **Mid-Indian Ridge** var. Central Indian Ridge. *undersea feature* C Indian Ocean
103 N14 **Midi-Pyrénées** ◈ *region* S France
25 N8 **Midkiff** Texas, SW USA
14 G13 **Midland** Ontario, S Canada
31 R8 **Midland** Michigan, N USA
28 M10 **Midland** South Dakota, N USA
24 M8 **Midland** Texas, SW USA
83 K17 **Midlands** ◈ *province* C Zimbabwe
97 D21 **Midleton** Ir. Mainistir na Corann. SW Ireland
25 T7 **Midlothian** Texas, SW USA
96 K12 **Midlothian** *cultural region* S Scotland, UK
172 I7 **Midongy** Fianarantsoa, S Madagascar
102 K15 **Midou** ≈ SW France
192 J6 **Mid-Pacific Mountains** var. Mid-Pacific Seamounts. *undersea feature* NW Pacific Ocean
Mid-Pacific Seamounts see Mid-Pacific Mountains
171 Q7 **Midsayap** Mindanao, S Philippines
36 L3 **Midway** Utah, W USA
192 L5 **Midway Islands** ◇ *US territory* C Pacific Ocean
33 X14 **Midwest** Wyoming, C USA
27 N10 **Midwest City** Oklahoma, C USA
152 M10 **Mid Western** ◈ *zone* W Nepal
98 P5 **Midwolda** Groningen, NE Netherlands
137 Q16 **Midyat** Mardin, SE Turkey
114 F8 **Midžhur** SCr. Midžor. ▲ Bulgaria/Serbia see also Midžor
Midzhur see Midžor
113 Q14 **Midžor** Bul. Midzhur. ▲ Bulgaria/Serbia see also Midzhur
Midžor see Midzhur
164 K14 **Mie** off. Mie-ken. ◈ *prefecture* Honshū, SW Japan
111 L16 **Miechów** Małopolskie, S Poland
110 F11 **Międzychód** Ger. Mitteldorf. Wielkopolskie, C Poland
Międzyleska, Przełęcz see Mezileské Sedlo
110 O12 **Międzyrzec Podlaski** Lubelskie, E Poland
110 E11 **Międzyrzecz** Ger. Meseritz. Lubuskie, W Poland
Mie-ken see Mie
102 L16 **Miélan** Gers, S France
111 N16 **Mielec** Podkarpackie, SE Poland
95 L21 **Mien** ◎ S Sweden
41 O8 **Mier** Tamaulipas, C Mexico
116 J11 **Miercurea-Ciuc** Ger. Szeklerburg, Hung. Csíkszereda. Harghita, C Romania
Mieresch see Maros/Mureş
Mieres del Camín see Mieres del Camino
104 K2 **Mieres del Camino** var. Mieres del Camín. Asturias, NW Spain
99 K15 **Mierlo** Noord-Brabant, SE Netherlands
41 O10 **Mier y Noriega** Nuevo León, NE Mexico
Mies see Stříbro
80 K13 **Mī'ēso** var. Meheso, Miesso. Oromo, C Ethiopia
Miesso see Mī'ēso
110 D10 **Mieszkowice** Ger. Bärwalde Neumark. Zachodnio-pomorskie, W Poland
18 G14 **Mifflinburg** Pennsylvania, NE USA
18 F14 **Mifflintown** Pennsylvania, NE USA
41 R15 **Miguel Alemán, Presa** ▣ SE Mexico
40 L9 **Miguel Asua** var. Miguel Auza. Zacatecas, C Mexico
Miguel Auza see Miguel Asua
43 S15 **Miguel de la Borda** var. Donoso. Colón, C Panama
41 N13 **Miguel Hidalgo** ✕ (Guadalajara) Jalisco, SW Mexico
40 H7 **Miguel Hidalgo, Presa** ▣ W Mexico
116 J14 **Mihăileşti** Giurgiu, S Romania
116 M14 **Mihail Kogălniceanu** var. Kogălniceanu; prev. Caramurat, Ferdinand. Constanţa, SE Romania
117 N14 **Mihai Viteazu** Constanţa, SE Romania
136 G12 **Mihalıççık** Eskişehir, NW Turkey
164 G13 **Mihara** Hiroshima, Honshū, SW Japan
165 N14 **Mihara-yama** (volcano) Miyako-jima, SE Japan
105 S8 **Mijares** ≈ E Spain
98 I11 **Mijdrecht** Utrecht, C Netherlands
165 S4 **Mikasa** Hokkaidō, NE Japan
Mikashevichi see Mikashevichy
119 K19 **Mikashevichy** Pol. Mikaszewicze, Rus. Mikashevichi. Brestskaya Voblasts', SW Belarus
Mikaszewicze see Mikashevichy
126 L5 **Mikhaylov** Ryazanskaya Oblast', W Russian Federation
Mikhaylovgrad see Montana
195 Z8 **Mikhaylov Island** *island* Antarctica
145 T6 **Mikhaylovka** Pavlodar, N Kazakhstan
127 N9 **Mikhaylovka** Volgogradskaya Oblast', SW Russian Federation
Mikhaylovka see Mykhaylivka
81 K24 **Mikindani** Mtwara, SE Tanzania
93 N18 **Mikkeli** Swe. Sankt Michel. Itä-Suomi, SE Finland
110 M8 **Mikołajki** Ger. Nikolaiken. Warmińsko-Mazurskie, NE Poland
Míkonos see Mýkonos
114 I9 **Mikre** Lovech, N Bulgaria
114 C13 **Mikrí Préspa, Límni** ◎ N Greece
125 P4 **Mikulkin, Mys** *cape* NW Russian Federation
81 I23 **Mikumi** Morogoro, SE Tanzania
125 R10 **Mikun'** Respublika Komi, NW Russian Federation
164 K13 **Mikuni** Fukui, Honshū, SW Japan
165 X13 **Mikura-jima** *island* E Japan
29 V7 **Milaca** Minnesota, N USA
62 J10 **Milagro** La Rioja, C Argentina
56 B7 **Milagro** Guayas, SW Ecuador
31 P4 **Milakokia Lake** ◎ Michigan, N USA
30 J1 **Milan** Illinois, N USA
31 R10 **Milan** Michigan, N USA
27 T2 **Milan** Missouri, C USA
37 Q11 **Milan** New Mexico, SW USA
20 G9 **Milan** Tennessee, S USA
Milan see Milano
95 F15 **Miland** Telemark, S Norway
83 N15 **Milange** Zambézia, NE Mozambique
106 D8 **Milano** Eng. Milan, Ger. Mailand; anc. Mediolanum. Lombardia, N Italy
25 U10 **Milano** Texas, SW USA
136 C15 **Milas** Muğla, SW Turkey
119 K21 **Milashavichy** Rus. Milashevichi. Homyel'skaya Voblasts', SE Belarus
Milashevichi see Milashavichy
119 I18 **Milavidy** Rus. Milovidy. Brestskaya Voblasts', SW Belarus
107 L23 **Milazzo** anc. Mylae. Sicilia, Italy, C Mediterranean Sea
29 R8 **Milbank** South Dakota, N USA
19 T7 **Milbridge** Maine, NE USA
100 L11 **Milde** ≈ C Germany
14 F14 **Mildmay** Ontario, S Canada
182 L9 **Mildura** Victoria, SE Australia
137 X12 **Mil Düzü** Rus. Mil'skaya Ravnina, Mil'skaya Step'. *physical region* C Azerbaijan
160 H13 **Mile** var. Miyang. Yunnan, SW China
Mile see Mili Atoll
181 Y10 **Miles** Queensland, E Australia
25 P8 **Miles** Texas, SW USA
33 X9 **Miles City** Montana, NW USA
9 U17 **Milestone** Saskatchewan, S Canada
107 N22 **Mileto** Calabria, SW Italy
107 K16 **Miletto, Monte** ▲ C Italy
18 M13 **Milford** Connecticut, NE USA
21 Y3 **Milford** var. Milford City. Delaware, NE USA
29 T11 **Milford** Iowa, C USA
19 S6 **Milford** Maine, NE USA
29 R16 **Milford** Nebraska, C USA
19 O10 **Milford** New Hampshire, NE USA
18 J13 **Milford** Pennsylvania, NE USA
25 T7 **Milford** Texas, SW USA
36 K6 **Milford** Utah, W USA
Milford see Milford Haven
Milford City see Milford
97 H21 **Milford Haven** prev. Milford. SW Wales, UK
27 O4 **Milford Lake** ▣ Kansas, C USA
185 B21 **Milford Sound** Southland, South Island, New Zealand
185 B21 **Milford Sound** *inlet* South Island, New Zealand
Milhau see Millau
Milḥ, Baḥr al see Razāzah, Buḥayrat ar
139 T10 **Milḥ, Wādī al** *dry watercourse* S Iraq
189 W8 **Mili Atoll** var. Mile. *atoll* Ratak Chain, SE Marshall Islands
110 H13 **Milicz** Dolnośląskie, SW Poland
107 L25 **Militello in Val di Catania** Sicilia, Italy, C Mediterranean Sea
9 R17 **Milk River** Alberta, SW Canada
44 J13 **Milk River** ≈ C Jamaica
33 W7 **Milk River** ≈ Montana, NW USA
80 D9 **Milk, Wadi el** var. Wadi al Malik. ≈ C Sudan
99 L14 **Mill** Noord-Brabant, SE Netherlands
103 P14 **Millau** var. Milhau; anc. Æmilianum. Aveyron, S France
14 I14 **Millbrook** Ontario, SE Canada
23 U4 **Milledgeville** Georgia, SE USA
12 C12 **Mille Lacs, Lac des** ◎ Ontario, S Canada
29 V6 **Mille Lacs Lake** ◎ Minnesota, N USA
23 V4 **Millen** Georgia, SE USA
191 Y5 **Millennium Island** prev. Caroline Island, Thornton Island. *atoll* Line Islands, E Kiribati
29 O9 **Miller** South Dakota, N USA
30 K5 **Miller Dam Flowage** ◎ Wisconsin, N USA
39 U12 **Miller, Mount** ▲ Alaska, USA
126 L10 **Millerovo** Rostovskaya Oblast', SW Russian Federation
37 N17 **Miller Peak** ▲ Arizona, SW USA
31 T12 **Millersburg** Ohio, N USA
18 G15 **Millersburg** Pennsylvania, NE USA
185 D23 **Millers Flat** Otago, South Island, New Zealand
25 Q8 **Millersview** Texas, SW USA
106 B10 **Millesimo** Piemonte, NE Italy
12 C12 **Milles Lacs, Lac des** ◎ Ontario, SW Canada
25 Q13 **Millett** Texas, SW USA
103 N11 **Millevaches, Plateau de** *plateau* C France
182 K12 **Millicent** South Australia
98 M13 **Millingen aan den Rijn** Gelderland, SE Netherlands
20 E10 **Millington** Tennessee, S USA
19 R4 **Millinocket** Maine, NE USA
19 R4 **Millinocket Lake** ◎ Maine, NE USA
195 Z11 **Mill Island** *island* Antarctica
183 T3 **Millmerran** Queensland, E Australia
109 R9 **Millstatt** Kärnten, S Austria
97 B19 **Milltown Malbay** Ir. Sráid na Cathrach. W Ireland
18 J17 **Millville** New Jersey, NE USA
27 S13 **Millwood Lake** ▣ Arkansas, C USA
Milne Bank see Milne Seamounts
186 G10 **Milne Bay** ◈ *province* SE Papua New Guinea
64 J8 **Milne Seamounts** var. Milne Bank. *undersea feature* N Atlantic Ocean
29 Q6 **Milnor** North Dakota, N USA
19 R5 **Milo** Maine, NE USA
115 I22 **Mílos** *island* Kykládes, Greece, Aegean Sea
Mílos see Pláka
110 H11 **Miłosław** Wielkopolskie, C Poland
113 K19 **Milot** var. Miloti. Lezhë, C Albania
Miloti see Milot
117 Z5 **Milove** Luhans'ka Oblast', E Ukraine
Milovidy see Milavidy
182 L4 **Milparinka** New South Wales, SE Australia
35 N9 **Milpitas** California, W USA
Mil'skaya Ravnina/Mil'skaya Step' see Mil Düzü
14 G15 **Milton** Ontario, S Canada
185 E24 **Milton** Otago, South Island, New Zealand
21 Y4 **Milton** Delaware, NE USA
23 P8 **Milton** Florida, SE USA
18 G14 **Milton** Pennsylvania, NE USA
18 L7 **Milton** Vermont, NE USA

◆ Country ● Country Capital ◇ Dependent Territory ○ Dependent Territory Capital ◈ Administrative Regions ✕ International Airport ▲ Mountain ▲▲ Mountain Range (volcano) Volcano ≈ River ◎ Lake ▣ Reservoir

32 K11 **Milton-Freewater** Oregon, NW USA
97 N21 **Milton Keynes** SE England, UK
27 N3 **Miltonvale** Kansas, C USA
161 N10 **Miluo** Hunan, S China
30 M9 **Milwaukee** Wisconsin, N USA
Milyang see Miryang
Mimatum see Mende
37 Q15 **Mimbres Mountains** ▲▲ New Mexico, SW USA
182 D2 **Mimili** South Australia
102 J14 **Mimizan** Landes, SW France
Mimmaya see Minmaya
79 E19 **Mimongo** Ngounié, C Gabon
Min see Fujian
35 T7 **Mina** Nevada, W USA
143 S14 **Mīnāb** Hormozgān, SE Iran
Mina Baranis see Berenice
149 R9 **Mīna Bāzār** Baluchistān, SW Pakistan
165 X17 **Minami-Iō-jima** *Eng.* San Augustine. *island* SE Japan
165 R5 **Minami-Kayabe** Hokkaidō, NE Japan
164 C17 **Minamitane** Kagoshima, Tanega-shima, SW Japan
Minami Tori Shima see Marcus Island
Min'an see Longshan
62 J4 **Mina Pirquitas** Jujuy, NW Argentina
173 O3 **Mīnā' Qābūs** NE Oman
61 F19 **Minas** Lavalleja, S Uruguay
13 P15 **Minas Basin** *bay* Nova Scotia, SE Canada
61 F17 **Minas de Corrales** Rivera, NE Uruguay
44 A5 **Minas de Matahambre** Pinar del Río, W Cuba
104 J13 **Minas de Ríotinto** Andalucía, S Spain
60 K7 **Minas Gerais** *off.* Estado de Minas Gerais. ❖ *state* E Brazil
Minas Gerais, Estado de see Minas Gerais
42 E5 **Minas, Sierra de las** ▲▲ E Guatemala
41 T15 **Minatitlán** Veracruz-Llave, E Mexico
166 L6 **Minbu** Magwe, W Myanmar (Burma)
149 V10 **Minchinābād** Punjab, E Pakistan
63 G17 **Minchinmávida, Volcán** ⛰ S Chile
96 G7 **Minch, The** *var.* North Minch. *strait* NW Scotland, UK
106 F8 **Mincio** *anc.* Mincius. ≈ N Italy
Mincius see Mincio
26 M11 **Minco** Oklahoma, C USA
171 Q7 **Mindanao** *island* S Philippines
Mindanao Sea see Bohol Sea
101 J23 **Mindel** ≈ S Germany
101 J23 **Mindelheim** Bayern, S Germany
Mindello see Mindelo
76 C9 **Mindelo** *var.* Mindello; *prev.* Porto Grande. São Vicente, N Cape Verde
14 I13 **Minden** Ontario, SE Canada
100 H13 **Minden** *anc.* Minthun. Nordrhein-Westfalen, NW Germany
22 G5 **Minden** Louisiana, S USA
29 O16 **Minden** Nebraska, C USA
35 Q6 **Minden** Nevada, W USA
182 L8 **Mindona Lake** *seasonal lake* New South Wales, SE Australia
171 O4 **Mindoro** *island* N Philippines
171 N5 **Mindoro Strait** *strait* W Philippines
159 S9 **Mine** Gansu, N China
97 J23 **Minehead** SW England, UK
97 E21 **Mine Head** *Ir.* Mionn Ard. *headland* S Ireland
59 J19 **Mineiros** Goiás, C Brazil
25 V6 **Mineola** Texas, SW USA
25 S13 **Mineral** Texas, SW USA
127 N15 **Mineral'nyye Vody** Stavropol'skiy Kray, SW Russian Federation
30 K9 **Mineral Point** Wisconsin, N USA
25 S6 **Mineral Wells** Texas, SW USA
36 K6 **Minersville** Utah, W USA
31 U12 **Minerva** Ohio, N USA
107 N17 **Minervino Murge** Puglia, SE Italy
103 O16 **Minervois** *physical region* S France
158 I10 **Minfeng** *var.* Niya. Xinjiang Uygur Zizhiqu, NW China
79 O25 **Minga** Katanga, SE Dem. Rep. Congo
137 W11 **Mingäçevir** *Rus.* Mingechaur, Mingechevir. C Azerbaijan
137 W11 **Mingäçevir Su Anbarı** *Rus.* Mingechaurskoye Vodokhranilishche, Mingechevirskoye Vodokhranilishche. ⊠ NW Azerbaijan
166 L8 **Mingaladon** ✈ (Yangon) Yangon, SW Myanmar (Burma)
13 P11 **Mingan** Québec, E Canada
149 U5 **Mingãora** *var.* Mingora, Mongora. North-West Frontier Province, N Pakistan
146 K8 **Mingbuloq** *Rus.* Mynbulak. Navoiy Viloyati, N Uzbekistan
146 K9 **Mingbuloq Botig'I** *Rus.* Vpadina Mynbulak. *depression* N Uzbekistan
Mingechaur/Mingechevir see Mingäçevir
Mingechaurskoye Vodokhranilishche/ Mingechevirskoye Vodokhranilishche see Mingäçevir Su Anbarı
161 Q7 **Mingguang** *prev.* Jiashan. Anhui, SE China
166 L4 **Mingin** Sagaing, C Myanmar (Burma)
105 Q10 **Minglanilla** Castilla-La Mancha, C Spain
31 V13 **Mingo Junction** Ohio, N USA
Mingora see Mingãora
163 V7 **Mingshui** Heilongjiang, NE China
Mingtekl Daban see Mintaka Pass
83 Q14 **Minguri** Nampula, NE Mozambique
Mingzhou see Suide
159 U10 **Minhe** *var.* Shangchuankou. Qinghai, C China
166 L6 **Minhla** Magwe, W Myanmar (Burma)
167 S14 **Minh Lương** Kiên Giang, S Vietnam
104 G5 **Minho** *former province* N Portugal
104 G5 **Minho, Rio** *Sp.* Miño. ≈ Portugal/Spain *see also* Miño
Minho, Rio see Miño
155 C24 **Minicoy Island** *island* SW India
33 P15 **Minidoka** Idaho, NW USA
118 C11 **Minija** ≈ W Lithuania
180 G9 **Minilya** Western Australia
14 E8 **Minisinakwa Lake** ◎ Ontario, S Canada
45 T12 **Ministre Point** *headland* S Saint Lucia
9 V15 **Minitonas** Manitoba, S Canada
Minius see Miño
161 R12 **Min Jiang** ≈ SE China
160 H10 **Min Jiang** ≈ C China
182 H9 **Minlaton** South Australia
165 Q6 **Minmaya** *var.* Mimmaya. Aomori, Honshū, C Japan
77 U14 **Minna** Niger, C Nigeria
165 P16 **Minna-jima** *island* Sakishima-shotō, SW Japan
27 N4 **Minneapolis** Kansas, C USA
29 U9 **Minneapolis** Minnesota, N USA
29 V8 **Minneapolis-Saint Paul** ✈ Minnesota, N USA
11 W16 **Minnedosa** Manitoba, S Canada
26 J7 **Minneola** Kansas, C USA
29 S7 **Minnesota** *off.* State of Minnesota, *also known as* Gopher State, New England of the West, North Star State. ❖ *state* N USA
29 S9 **Minnesota River** ≈ Minnesota/South Dakota, N USA
29 V9 **Minnetonka** Minnesota, N USA
29 O3 **Minnewaukan** North Dakota, N USA
182 F7 **Minnipa** South Australia
104 H2 **Miño** Galicia, NW Spain
104 G5 **Miño** *var.* Miño, Minius, *Port.* Rio Minho. ≈ Portugal/Spain *see also* Minho, Rio
Miño see Minho, Rio
30 L4 **Minocqua** Wisconsin, N USA
30 L12 **Minonk** Illinois, N USA
Minorca see Menorca
28 M3 **Minot** North Dakota, N USA
159 U8 **Minqin** Gansu, N China
119 J16 **Minsk** ● (Belarus) Minskaya Voblasts', C Belarus
119 L16 **Minsk** ✈ Minskaya Voblasts', C Belarus
Minskaya Oblast' see Minskaya Voblasts'
119 K16 **Minskaya Voblasts'** *prev. Rus.* Minskaya Oblast'. ❖ *province* C Belarus
119 J16 **Minskaya Wzvyshsha** ▲▲ C Belarus
110 N12 **Mińsk Mazowiecki** *var.* Nowo-Minsk. Mazowieckie, C Poland
31 Q13 **Minster** Ohio, N USA
79 F15 **Minta** Centre, C Cameroon
149 W2 **Mintaka Pass** *Chin.* Mingtekl Daban. *pass* China/Pakistan
115 D20 **Mínthi** ▲ S Greece
Minthun see Minden
13 O14 **Minto** New Brunswick, SE Canada
10 H6 **Minto** Yukon Territory, W Canada
39 R9 **Minto** Alaska, USA
29 Q3 **Minto** North Dakota, N USA
12 K6 **Minto, Lac** ◎ Québec, C Canada
195 R16 **Minto, Mount** ▲ Antarctica
9 U17 **Minton** Saskatchewan, S Canada
189 R15 **Minto Reef** *atoll* Caroline Islands, C Micronesia
37 R4 **Minturn** Colorado, C USA
107 J16 **Minturno** Lazio, C Italy
122 K13 **Minusinsk** Krasnoyarskiy Kray, S Russian Federation
108 G11 **Minusio** Ticino, S Switzerland
79 E17 **Minvoul** Woleu-Ntem, N Gabon
141 R13 **Minwakh** N Yemen
159 V11 **Minxian** *var.* Min Xian. Gansu, C China
Min Xian see Minxian
Minya see El Minya
31 R6 **Mio** Michigan, N USA
Mionn Ard see Mine Head
158 L5 **Miquan** Xinjiang Uygur Zizhiqu, NW China
119 I17 **Mir** Hrodzyenskaya Voblasts', W Belarus
106 H8 **Mira** Veneto, NE Italy
104 G13 **Mira, Rio** ≈ S Portugal
12 K15 **Mirabel** *var.* Montreal. ✈ (Montréal) Québec, SE Canada
60 Q8 **Miracema** Rio de Janeiro, SE Brazil
54 G9 **Miraflores** Boyacá, C Colombia
40 G10 **Miraflores** Baja California Sur, W Mexico
44 L9 **Miragoâne** S Haiti
155 E16 **Miraj** Mahārāshtra, W India
61 E23 **Miramar** Buenos Aires, E Argentina
103 R15 **Miramas** Bouches-du-Rhône, SE France
102 K12 **Mirambeau** Charente-Maritime, W France
102 L13 **Miramont-de-Guyenne** Lot-et-Garonne, SW France
115 L25 **Mirampéllou Kólpos** *gulf* Kríti, Greece, E Mediterranean Sea
158 L8 **Miran** Xinjiang Uygur Zizhiqu, NW China
54 M5 **Miranda** *off.* Estado Miranda. ❖ *state* N Venezuela
Miranda de Corvo see Miranda do Corvo
105 O3 **Miranda de Ebro** La Rioja, N Spain
104 G8 **Miranda do Corvo** *var.* Miranda de Corvo. Coimbra, N Portugal
104 J6 **Miranda do Douro** Bragança, N Portugal
Miranda, Estado see Miranda
102 L15 **Mirande** Gers, S France
104 I6 **Mirandela** Bragança, N Portugal
25 R15 **Mirando City** Texas, SW USA
106 G9 **Mirandola** Emilia-Romagna, N Italy
60 I8 **Mirandópolis** São Paulo, S Brazil
60 K8 **Mirassol** São Paulo, S Brazil
44 J3 **Miravalles** ▲ NW Spain
42 L12 **Miravalles, Volcán** ⛰ NW Costa Rica
141 W13 **Mirbāṭ** *var.* Marbat. S Oman
44 M9 **Mirebalais** C Haiti
103 T6 **Mirecourt** Vosges, NE France
103 N16 **Mirepoix** Ariège, S France
Mirgorod see Myrhorod
139 W10 **Mīr Ḥājī Khalīl** E Iraq
169 T8 **Miri** Sarawak, East Malaysia
77 W12 **Miria** Zinder, S Niger
182 F5 **Mirikata** South Australia
54 K4 **Mirimire** Falcón, N Venezuela
61 H18 **Mirim Lagoon** *var.* Lake Mirim, *Sp.* Laguna Merín. *lagoon* Brazil/Uruguay
Mirim, Lake see Mirim Lagoon
Mírina see Mýrina
172 H14 **Miringoni** Mohéli, S Comoros
143 W11 **Mīrjāveh** Sīstān va Balūchestān, SE Iran
195 Z9 **Mirny** *Russian research station* Antarctica
124 M10 **Mirnyy** Arkhangel'skaya Oblast', NW Russian Federation
123 O10 **Mirnyy** Respublika Sakha (Yakutiya), NE Russian Federation
Mironovka see Myronivka
110 F9 **Mirosławiec** Zachodnio-pomorskie, NW Poland
Mirovo see Vrattsa
100 N10 **Mirow** Mecklenburg-Vorpommern, N Germany
152 G6 **Mīrpur** Jammu and Kashmir, NW India
Mīrpur see New Mīrpur
149 P17 **Mīrpur Batoro** Sind, SE Pakistan
149 Q16 **Mīrpur Khās** Sind, SE Pakistan
149 P17 **Mīrpur Sakro** Sind, SE Pakistan
143 T14 **Mīr Shahdād** Hormozgān, S Iran
Mirtoan Sea see Mirtóo Pélagos
115 G21 **Mirtóo Pélagos** *Eng.* Mirtoan Sea; *anc.* Myrtoum Mare. *sea* S Greece
163 Z16 **Miryang** *var.* Milyang, *Jap.* Mitsuō. SE South Korea
Mirzachirla see Murzechirla
164 E14 **Misaki** Ehime, Shikoku, SW Japan
41 Q13 **Misantla** Veracruz-Llave, E Mexico
165 R7 **Misawa** Aomori, Honshū, C Japan
57 G14 **Mishagua, Río** ≈ C Peru
163 Z8 **Mishan** Heilongjiang, NE China
31 O11 **Mishawaka** Indiana, N USA
39 N6 **Misheguk Mountain** ▲ Alaska, USA
165 N14 **Mishima** *var.* Misima. Shizuoka, Honshū, S Japan
164 E12 **Mi-shima** *island* SW Japan
127 V4 **Mishkino** Respublika Bashkortostan, W Russian Federation
153 Y10 **Mishmi Hills** *hill range* NE India
161 N11 **Mi Shui** ≈ S China
Misiaf see Maṣyāf
107 J23 **Misilmeri** Sicilia, Italy, C Mediterranean Sea
Misima see Mishima
Misión de Guana see Guana
60 F13 **Misiones** *off.* Provincia de Misiones. ❖ *province* NE Argentina
62 P8 **Misiones** *off.* Departamento de las Misiones. ❖ *department* S Paraguay
Misiones, Departamento de las see Misiones
Misiones, Provincia de see Misiones
Misión San Fernando see San Fernando
Miskin see Maskin
Miskito Coast see La Mosquitia
43 O7 **Miskitos, Cayos** *island group* NE Nicaragua
111 M21 **Miskolc** Borsod-Abaúj-Zemplén, NE Hungary
171 T12 **Misool, Pulau** *island* Maluku, E Indonesia
Misox see Mesocco
29 Y3 **Misquah Hills** *hill range* Minnesota, N USA
75 P7 **Miṣrātah** *var.* Misurata. NW Libya
75 P7 **Miṣrātah, Râs** *headland* N Libya
14 C7 **Missanabie** Ontario, S Canada
58 E10 **Missão Catrimani** Roraima, N Brazil
14 D6 **Missinaibi** ≈ Ontario, S Canada
14 C7 **Missinaibi Lake** ◎ Ontario, S Canada
9 T13 **Missinipe** Saskatchewan, C Canada
28 M11 **Mission** South Dakota, N USA
25 S17 **Mission** Texas, SW USA
12 F10 **Missisa Lake** ◎ Ontario, C Canada
18 M6 **Missisquoi Bay** *lake bay* Canada/USA
14 C10 **Mississagi** ≈ Ontario, S Canada
14 G15 **Mississauga** Ontario, S Canada
31 P12 **Mississinewa Lake** ⊠ Indiana, N USA
31 P12 **Mississinewa River** ≈ Indiana/Ohio, N USA
22 K4 **Mississippi** *off.* State of Mississippi, *also known as* Bayou State, Magnolia State. ❖ *state* SE USA
14 K13 **Mississippi** ≈ Ontario, SE Canada
0 J11 **Mississippi River** ≈ C USA
47 N1 **Mississippi Fan** *undersea feature* N Gulf of Mexico
14 L13 **Mississippi Lake** ◎ Ontario, SE Canada
22 M10 **Mississippi Delta** *delta* Louisiana, S USA
22 M9 **Mississippi Sound** *sound* Alabama/Mississippi, S USA
33 P9 **Missoula** Montana, NW USA
27 T5 **Missouri** *off.* State of Missouri, *also known as* Bullion State, Show Me State. ❖ *state* C USA
25 V11 **Missouri City** Texas, SW USA
0 J10 **Missouri River** ≈ C USA
15 Q6 **Mistassibi** ≈ Québec, SE Canada
15 P6 **Mistassini** Québec, SE Canada
15 P6 **Mistassini** ≈ Québec, SE Canada
12 J11 **Mistassini, Lac** ◎ Québec, SE Canada
109 Y3 **Mistelbach an der Zaya** Niederösterreich, NE Austria
107 L24 **Misterbianco** Sicilia, Italy, C Mediterranean Sea
95 N19 **Misterhult** Kalmar, S Sweden
57 H17 **Misti, Volcán** ⛰ S Peru
Mistras see Mystrás
107 K23 **Mistretta** *anc.* Amestratus. Sicilia, Italy, C Mediterranean Sea
164 F12 **Misumi** Shimane, Honshū, SW Japan
Misurata see Miṣrātah
83 O14 **Mitande** Niassa, N Mozambique
40 J13 **Mita, Punta de** *headland* C Mexico
55 W12 **Mitaraka, Massif du** ▲ NE South America
Mitau see Jelgava
181 X9 **Mitchell** Queensland, E Australia
14 E15 **Mitchell** Ontario, S Canada
28 I13 **Mitchell** Nebraska, C USA
32 J12 **Mitchell** Oregon, NW USA
29 P11 **Mitchell** South Dakota, N USA
23 P5 **Mitchell Lake** ⊠ Alabama, S USA
31 P7 **Mitchell, Lake** ◎ Michigan, N USA
21 P9 **Mitchell, Mount** ▲ North Carolina, SE USA
181 V3 **Mitchell River** ≈ Queensland, NE Australia
97 D20 **Mitchelstown** *Ir.* Baile Mhistéala. SW Ireland
14 M9 **Mitchinamécus, Lac** ◎ Québec, SE Canada
Mitèmboni see Mitemele, Río
79 D17 **Mitemele, Río** *var.* Mitèmboni, Temboni, Utamboni. ≈ S Equatorial Guinea
149 S12 **Mithānkot** Punjab, E Pakistan
149 T7 **Mitha Tiwāna** Punjab, E Pakistan
149 R17 **Mithi** Sind, SE Pakistan
Míthimna see Míthymna
Mi Tho see My Tho
115 L16 **Míthymna** *var.* Míthimna. Lésvos, E Greece
190 L16 **Mitiaro** *island* S Cook Islands
Mitilíni see Mytilíni
15 U7 **Mitis** ≈ Québec, SE Canada
41 R16 **Mitla** Oaxaca, SE Mexico
165 P13 **Mito** Ibaraki, Honshū, S Japan
92 N2 **Mitra, Kapp** *headland* W Svalbard
184 M13 **Mitre** ▲ North Island, New Zealand
185 B21 **Mitre Peak** ▲ South Island, New Zealand
39 O15 **Mitrofania Island** *island* Alaska, USA
Mitrovica/Mitrovicë see Kosovska Mitrovica, Serbia
Mitrovica/Mitrowitz see Sremska Mitrovica, Serbia
172 H12 **Mitsamiouli** Grande Comore, NW Comoros
172 I3 **Mitsinjo** Mahajanga, NW Madagascar
Mits'iwa see Massawa
172 H13 **Mitsoudjé** Grande Comore, NW Comoros
Mitspe Ramon see Mizpé Ramon
165 T5 **Mitsuishi** Hokkaidō, NE Japan
165 O11 **Mitsuke** *var.* Mituke. Niigata, Honshū, C Japan
Mitsuō see Miryang
164 C12 **Mitsushima** Nagasaki, Tsushima, SW Japan
100 G12 **Mittellandkanal** *canal* NW Germany
108 J7 **Mittelberg** Vorarlberg, NW Austria
Mitteldorf see Międzychód
Mittelstadt see Baia Sprie
Mitterburg see Pazin
109 P7 **Mittersill** Salzburg, NW Austria
101 N16 **Mittweida** Sachsen, E Germany
54 J13 **Mitú** Vaupés, SE Colombia
Mituke see Mitsuke
Mitumba, Chaîne des/Mitumba Range see Mitumba, Monts
79 O22 **Mitumba, Monts** *var.* Chaîne des Mitumba, Mitumba Range. ▲▲ E Dem. Rep. Congo
79 N23 **Mitwaba** Katanga, SE Dem. Rep. Congo
79 E18 **Mitzic** Woleu-Ntem, N Gabon
82 K11 **Miueru Wantipa, Lake** ◎ N Zambia
165 N14 **Miura** Kanagawa, Honshū, S Japan
165 Q10 **Miyagi** *off.* Miyagi-ken. ❖ *prefecture* Honshū, C Japan
Miyagi-ken see Miyagi
138 M7 **Miyāh, Wādī al** *dry watercourse* E Syria
165 X13 **Miyake** Tōkyō, Miyako-jima, SE Japan
165 R8 **Miyako** Iwate, Honshū, C Japan
165 Q16 **Miyako-jima** *island* Sakishima-shotō, SW Japan
164 D16 **Miyakonojō** *var.* Miyakonzyô. Miyazaki, Kyūshū, SW Japan
Miyakonzyô see Miyakonojō
165 Q16 **Miyako-shotō** *island group* SW Japan
144 G11 **Miyaly** Atyrau, W Kazakhstan
Miyāndoāb see Mīāndowāb
Miyāneh see Mīāneh
Miyang see Mile
164 D16 **Miyazaki** Miyazaki, Kyūshū, SW Japan
164 D16 **Miyazaki** *off.* Miyazaki-ken. ❖ *prefecture* Kyūshū, SW Japan
Miyazaki-ken see Miyazaki
164 J12 **Miyazu** Kyōto, Honshū, SW Japan
Miyory see Myory
164 G12 **Miyoshi** *var.* Miyosi. Hiroshima, Honshū, SW Japan
Miyosi see Miyoshi
Miza see Mizë
81 H14 **Mīzan Teferī** Southern, S Ethiopia
Mizda see Mizdah
75 O8 **Mizdah** *var.* Mizda. NW Libya
113 K20 **Mizë** *var.* Miza. Fier, W Albania
97 A22 **Mizen Head** *Ir.* Carn Uí Néid. *headland* SW Ireland
116 H7 **Mizhhir"ya** *Rus.* Mezhgor'ye. Zakarpats'ka Oblast', W Ukraine
160 L4 **Mizhi** Shaanxi, C China
116 K13 **Mizil** Prahova, SE Romania
114 H7 **Miziya** Vratsa, NW Bulgaria
153 W15 **Mizo Hills** *hill range* E India
153 W15 **Mizoram** ❖ *state* NE India
138 F12 **Mizpé Ramon** *var.* Mitspe Ramon. Southern, S Israel
57 L19 **Mizque** Cochabamba, C Bolivia
57 M19 **Mizque, Río** ≈ C Bolivia
165 Q9 **Mizusawa** Iwate, Honshū, C Japan
95 M18 **Mjölby** Östergötland, S Sweden
95 G15 **Mjøndalen** Buskerud, S Norway
95 J19 **Mjörn** ◎ S Sweden
94 I13 **Mjøsa** *var.* Mjøsen. ◎ S Norway
Mjøsen see Mjøsa
81 G21 **Mkalama** Singida, C Tanzania
80 K13 **Mkata** ≈ C Tanzania
83 K14 **Mkushi** Central, C Zambia
83 L22 **Mkuze** KwaZulu/Natal, E South Africa
81 J22 **Mkwaja** Tanga, E Tanzania
111 D16 **Mladá Boleslav** *Ger.* Jungbunzlau. Středočeský Kraj, N Czech Republic
112 M12 **Mladenovac** Serbia, C Serbia
114 L11 **Mladinovo** Khaskovo, S Bulgaria
113 O17 **Mlado Nagoričane** N FYR Macedonia
Mlanje see Mulanje
112 N12 **Mlava** ≈ E Serbia
110 L9 **Mława** Mazowieckie, C Poland
113 G16 **Mljet** *It.* Meleda; *anc.* Melita. *island* S Croatia
116 K4 **Mlyniv** Rivnens'ka Oblast', NW Ukraine
83 I21 **Mmabatho** North-West, N South Africa
83 I19 **Mmashoro** Central, E Botswana
44 J7 **Moa** Holguín, E Cuba
76 J15 **Moa** ≈ Guinea/Sierra Leone
37 O6 **Moab** Utah, W USA
181 V1 **Moa Island** *island* Queensland, NE Australia
187 Y15 **Moala** *island* S Fiji
83 L21 **Moamba** Maputo, SW Mozambique
79 F19 **Moanda** *var.* Mouanda. Haut-Ogooué, SE Gabon
83 M15 **Moatize** Tete, NW Mozambique
79 P22 **Moba** Katanga, E Dem. Rep. Congo
Mobay see Montego Bay
79 K15 **Mobaye** Basse-Kotto, S Central African Republic
79 K15 **Mobayi-Mbongo** Equateur, NW Dem. Rep. Congo
25 P2 **Mobeetie** Texas, SW USA
27 U3 **Moberly** Missouri, C USA
23 N8 **Mobile** Alabama, S USA
23 N9 **Mobile Bay** *bay* Alabama, S USA
23 N8 **Mobile River** ≈ Alabama, S USA
29 N8 **Mobridge** South Dakota, N USA
Mobutu Sese Seko, Lac see Albert, Lake
45 N8 **Moca** N Dominican Republic
83 Q15 **Moçambique** Nampula, NE Mozambique Africa
Moçâmedes see Namibe
167 S6 **Mộc Châu** Sơn La, N Vietnam
187 Z15 **Moce** *island* Lau Group, E Fiji
Mocha see Al Mukhā
193 T11 **Mocha Fracture Zone** *tectonic feature* SE Pacific Ocean
63 F14 **Mocha, Isla** *island* C Chile
56 C12 **Moche, Río** ≈ W Peru
167 S14 **Mộc Hóa** Long An, S Vietnam
83 I20 **Mochudi** Kgatleng, SE Botswana
82 Q13 **Mocímboa da Praia** *var.* Vila de Mocímboa da Praia. Cabo Delgado, N Mozambique
94 L13 **Mockfjärd** Dalarna, C Sweden
21 R9 **Mocksville** North Carolina, SE USA
32 F8 **Moclips** Washington, NW USA
82 C13 **Môco** *var.* Morro de Môco. ▲ W Angola
54 D13 **Mocoa** Putumayo, SW Colombia
60 M8 **Mococa** São Paulo, S Brazil
Môco, Morro de see Môco
40 H8 **Mocorito** Sinaloa, C Mexico
40 J4 **Moctezuma** Chihuahua, N Mexico
41 N11 **Moctezuma** San Luis Potosí, C Mexico
40 G4 **Moctezuma** Sonora, NW Mexico
41 P12 **Moctezuma, Río** ≈ C Mexico
Mó, Cuan see Clew Bay
83 O16 **Mocuba** Zambézia, NE Mozambique
103 U12 **Modane** Savoie, E France
106 F9 **Modena** *anc.* Mutina. Emilia-Romagna, N Italy
36 I7 **Modena** Utah, W USA
35 O9 **Modesto** California, W USA
107 L25 **Modica** *anc.* Motyca. Sicilia, Italy, C Mediterranean Sea
83 J20 **Modimolle** *prev.* Nylstroom. Limpopo, NE South Africa
79 K17 **Modjamboli** Equateur, N Dem. Rep. Congo
109 X4 **Mödling** Niederösterreich, NE Austria
Modohn see Madona
Modot see Tsenhermandal
171 V14 **Modowi** Papua, E Indonesia
112 I12 **Modračko Jezero** ⊠ NE Bosnia and Herzegovina
112 I10 **Modriča** Republika Srpska, N Bosnia and Herzegovina
183 O13 **Moe** Victoria, SE Australia
Moearatewe see Muaratewe
Moei, Mae Nam see Thaungyin
94 H13 **Moelv** Hedmark, S Norway
92 I10 **Moen** Troms, N Norway
Möen see Møn, Denmark
Moen see Weno, Micronesia
Moena see Muna, Pulau
36 M10 **Moenkopi Wash** ≈ Arizona, SW USA
185 F22 **Moeraki Point** *headland* South Island, New Zealand
99 F16 **Moerbeke** Oost-Vlaanderen, NW Belgium
99 H14 **Moerdijk** Noord-Brabant, S Netherlands
Moero, Lac see Mweru, Lake
101 D15 **Moers** *var.* Mörs. Nordrhein-Westfalen, W Germany
Moesi see Musi, Air
Moeskroen see Mouscron
96 J13 **Moffat** S Scotland, UK
185 C22 **Moffat Peak** ▲ South Island, New Zealand
79 N19 **Moga** Sud Kivu, E Dem. Rep. Congo
152 H8 **Moga** Punjab, N India
Mogadiscio/Mogadishu see Muqdisho
Mogador see Essaouira
104 J6 **Mogadouro** Bragança, N Portugal
167 N2 **Mogaung** Kachin State, N Myanmar (Burma)
110 L13 **Mogielnica** Mazowieckie, C Poland
Mogilëv see Mahilyow
Mogilev-Podol'skiy see Mohyliv-Podil's'kyy
Mogilëvskaya Oblast' see Mahilyowskaya Voblasts'
110 I11 **Mogilno** Kujawsko-pomorskie, C Poland
60 L9 **Mogi-Mirim** *var.* Moji-Mirim. São Paulo, S Brazil
83 Q15 **Mogincual** Nampula, NE Mozambique
114 E13 **Moglenítsas** ≈ N Greece
106 H8 **Mogliano Veneto** Veneto, NE Italy
113 M21 **Moglicë** Korçë, SE Albania
123 O13 **Mogocha** Chitinskaya Oblast', S Russian Federation
122 J11 **Mogochin** Tomskaya Oblast', C Russian Federation
80 F13 **Mogogh** Jonglei, SE Sudan
171 U12 **Mogoi** Papua, E Indonesia
166 M4 **Mogok** Mandalay, C Myanmar (Burma)
37 P14 **Mogollon Mountains** ▲▲ New Mexico, SW USA
36 M12 **Mogollon Rim** *cliff* Arizona, SW USA
61 E23 **Mogotes, Punta** *headland* E Argentina
42 J8 **Mogotón** ▲ NW Nicaragua
104 I14 **Moguer** Andalucía, S Spain
111 J26 **Mohács** Baranya, SW Hungary
185 C20 **Mohaka** ≈ North Island, New Zealand
28 M2 **Mohall** North Dakota, N USA
Moḩammadābād see Dargaz
74 F6 **Mohammedia** *prev.* Fédala. NW Morocco
74 F6 **Mohammed V** ✈ (Casablanca) W Morocco
Mohammerah see Khorramshahr
36 H10 **Mohave, Lake** ⊠ Arizona/Nevada, W USA
36 I12 **Mohave Mountains** ▲▲ Arizona, SW USA
36 I15 **Mohawk Mountains** ▲▲ Arizona, SW USA
18 J10 **Mohawk River** ≈ New York, NE USA
163 T3 **Mohe** *var.* Xilinji. Heilongjiang, NE China
95 L20 **Moheda** Kronoberg, S Sweden
172 H13 **Mohéli** *var.* Mwali, Mohilla, Mohila, *Fr.* Moili. *island* S Comoros
152 I11 **Mahendragarh** Haryāna, N India
38 K12 **Mohican, Cape** *headland* Nunivak Island, Alaska, USA
Mohila see Mohéli
Mohilla see Mohéli
Mohn see Muhu
101 G15 **Möhne** ≈ W Germany
101 G15 **Möhne-Stausee** ⊠ W Germany
92 P2 **Mohn, Kapp** *headland* NW Svalbard
197 S14 **Mohns Ridge** *undersea feature* Greenland Sea/Norwegian Sea
57 I17 **Moho** Puno, SE Peru
Mohokare see Caledon
95 L17 **Moholm** Västra Götaland, S Sweden
36 J11 **Mohon Peak** ▲ Arizona, SW USA
81 J23 **Mohoro** Pwani, E Tanzania
Mohra see Moravice
Mohrungen see Morąg
116 M7 **Mohyliv-Podil's'kyy** *Rus.* Mogilev-Podol'skiy. Vinnyts'ka Oblast', C Ukraine
95 D17 **Moi** Rogaland, S Norway
Moili see Mohéli
116 K11 **Moinești** *Hung.* Mojnest. Bacău, E Romania
Móinteach Mílic see Mountmellick
14 J14 **Moira** ≈ Ontario, SE Canada
92 G13 **Mo i Rana** Nordland, C Norway
153 X14 **Moirāng** Manipur, NE India
115 J25 **Moíres** Kríti, Greece, E Mediterranean Sea

◆ Country ● Country Capital ◇ Dependent Territory ○ Dependent Territory Capital ❖ Administrative Regions ✈ International Airport ▲ Mountain ▲▲ Mountain Range ⛰ Volcano ≈ River ◎ Lake ⊠ Reservoir

118 H6 **Mõisaküla** *Ger.* Moiseküll. Viljandimaa, S Estonia
Moiseküll *see* Mõisaküla
15 W4 **Moisie** Québec, E Canada
15 W3 **Moisie** ≈ Québec, SE Canada
102 M14 **Moissac** Tarn-et-Garonne, S France
78 I13 **Moïssala** Moyen-Chari, S Chad
55 O7 **Moitaco** Bolívar, E Venezuela
95 P15 **Möja** Stockholm, C Sweden
105 Q14 **Mojácar** Andalucía, S Spain
35 T13 **Mojave** California, W USA
35 V13 **Mojave Desert** *plain* California, W USA
35 V13 **Mojave River** ≈ California, W USA
Moji-Mirim *see* Mogi-Mirim
113 K15 **Mojkovac** E Montenegro
Mojnest *see* Moineşti
Mõka *see* Mooka
153 Q13 **Mokāma** *prev.* Mokameh, Mukama. Bihār, N India
79 O25 **Mokambo** Katanga, SE Dem. Rep. Congo
Mokameh *see* Mokāma
38 D9 **Mōkapu Point** *var* Mokapu Point. *headland* O'ahu, Hawai'i, USA
184 L9 **Mokau** Waikato, North Island, New Zealand
184 L9 **Mokau** ≈ North Island, New Zealand
35 P7 **Mokelumne River** ≈ California, W USA
83 J23 **Mokhotlong** NE Lesotho
Mokil Atoll *see* Mwokil Atoll
95 N14 **Möklinta** Västmanland, C Sweden
184 L4 **Mokohinau Islands** *island group* N New Zealand
153 X12 **Mokokchūng** Nāgāland, NE India
78 F12 **Mokolo** Extrême-Nord, N Cameroon
83 J20 **Mokopane** *prev.* Potgietersrus. Limpopo, NE South Africa
185 D24 **Mokoreta** ≈ South Island, New Zealand
163 X17 **Mokp'o** *Jap.* Moppo. SW South Korea
113 L16 **Mokra Gora** ▲▲ S Serbia
Mokrany *see* Makrany
127 O5 **Moksha** ≈ W Russian Federation
Moktama *see* Martaban
77 T14 **Mokwa** Niger, W Nigeria
99 J16 **Mol** *prev.* Moll. Antwerpen, N Belgium
107 O17 **Mola di Bari** Puglia, SE Italy
Molai *see* Moláoi
41 P13 **Molango** Hidalgo, C Mexico
115 F22 **Moláoi** *var.* Molai. Pelopónnisos, S Greece
41 Z12 **Molas del Norte, Punta** *var.* Punta Molas. *headland* SE Mexico
Molas, Punta *see* Molas del Norte, Punta
105 R11 **Molatón** ▲ C Spain
97 K18 **Mold** NE Wales, UK
Moldau *see* Vltava, Czech Republic
Moldau *see* Moldova
Moldavia *see* Moldova
Moldavian SSR/ Moldavskaya SSR *see* Moldova
94 E9 **Molde** Møre og Romsdal, S Norway
Moldotau, Khrebet *see* Moldo-Too, Khrebet
147 V9 **Moldo-Too, Khrebet** *prev.* Khrebet Moldotau. ▲▲ C Kyrgyzstan
116 L9 **Moldova** *off.* Republic of Moldova, *var.* Moldavia; *prev.* Moldavian SSR, *Rus.* Moldavskaya SSR. ◆ *republic* SE Europe
116 K9 **Moldova** *Eng.* Moldavia, *Ger.* Moldau. *former province* NE Romania
116 K9 **Moldova** ≈ N Romania
116 F13 **Moldova Nouă** *Ger.* Neumoldowa, *Hung.* Újmoldova. Caraş-Severin, SW Romania
Moldova, Republic of *see* Moldova
116 F13 **Moldova Veche** *Ger.* Altmoldowa, *Hung.* Ómoldova. Caraş-Severin, SW Romania
Moldoveanul *see* Vârful Moldoveanu
83 I20 **Molepolole** Kweneng, SE Botswana
44 L8 **Môle-St-Nicolas** NW Haiti
118 H13 **Molėtai** Utena, E Lithuania
107 O17 **Molfetta** Puglia, SE Italy
171 P11 **Molibagu** Sulawesi, N Indonesia
62 G12 **Molina** Maule, C Chile
105 Q7 **Molina de Aragón** Castilla-La Mancha, C Spain
105 R13 **Molina de Segura** Murcia, SE Spain
30 J11 **Moline** Illinois, N USA
27 P7 **Moline** Kansas, C USA
79 P23 **Moliro** Katanga, SE Dem. Rep. Congo
107 K16 **Molise** ◈ *region* S Italy
95 K15 **Molkom** Värmland, C Sweden
109 Q9 **Möll** ≈ S Austria
Moll *see* Mol
146 I14 **Mollanepes Adyndaky** *Rus.* Imeni Mollanepesa. Mary Welaýaty, S Turkmenistan
95 J22 **Mölle** Skåne, S Sweden
57 H18 **Mollendo** Arequipa, SW Peru
105 U5 **Mollerussa** Cataluña, NE Spain
108 H8 **Mollis** Glarus, NE Switzerland
95 J19 **Mölndal** Västra Götaland, S Sweden
95 J19 **Mölnlycke** Västra Götaland, S Sweden
117 U9 **Molochans'k** *Rus.* Molochansk. Zaporiz'ka Oblast', SE Ukraine
117 U10 **Molochna** *Rus.* Molochnaya. ≈ S Ukraine
Molochnaya *see* Molochna
117 U10 **Molochnyy Lyman** *bay* N Black Sea
Molodechno/Molodeczno *see* Maladzyechna
195 V3 **Molodezhnaya** *Russian research station* Antarctica
124 J14 **Mologa** ≈ NW Russian Federation
38 E9 **Moloka'i** *var.* Molokai. *island* Hawaiian Islands, Hawai'i, USA
175 X3 **Molokai Fracture Zone** *tectonic feature* NE Pacific Ocean
124 K15 **Molokovo** Tverskaya Oblast', W Russian Federation
125 Q14 **Moloma** ≈ NW Russian Federation
183 R8 **Molong** New South Wales, SE Australia
83 H21 **Molopo** *seasonal river* Botswana/South Africa
115 F17 **Mólos** Stereá Ellás, C Greece
171 O11 **Molosipat** Sulawesi, N Indonesia
Molotov *see* Severodvinsk, Arkhangel'skaya Oblast', Russian Federation
Molotov *see* Perm', Permskaya Oblast', Russian Federation
79 G17 **Moloundou** Est, SE Cameroon
103 U5 **Molsheim** Bas-Rhin, NE France
11 X13 **Molson Lake** ◎ Manitoba, C Canada
Moluccas *see* Maluku
171 Q12 **Molucca Sea** *Ind.* Laut Maluku. *sea* E Indonesia
Molukken *see* Maluku
83 O15 **Molumbo** Zambézia, N Mozambique
171 T15 **Molu, Pulau** *island* Maluku, E Indonesia
83 P16 **Moma** Nampula, NE Mozambique
171 X14 **Momats** ≈ Papua, E Indonesia
42 J11 **Mombacho, Volcán** ⛰ SW Nicaragua
81 K21 **Mombasa** Coast, SE Kenya
81 J21 **Mombasa** ✈ Coast, SE Kenya
Mombetsu *see* Monbetsu
114 J12 **Momchilgrad** *prev.* Mastanli. Kŭrdzhali, S Bulgaria
99 F23 **Momignies** Hainaut, S Belgium
54 E6 **Momil** Córdoba, NW Colombia
42 I10 **Momotombo, Volcán** ⛰ W Nicaragua
56 B5 **Mompiche, Ensenada de** *bay* NW Ecuador
79 K18 **Mompono** Equateur, NW Dem. Rep. Congo
54 F6 **Mompós** Bolívar, NW Colombia
95 J24 **Møn** *prev.* Möen. *island* SE Denmark
36 L4 **Mona** Utah, W USA
Mona, Canal de la *see* Mona Passage
96 E8 **Monach Islands** *island group* NW Scotland, UK
103 V14 **Monaco** *var.* Monaco-Ville; *anc.* Monoecus. ● (Monaco) S Monaco
103 V14 **Monaco** *off.* Principality of Monaco. ◆ *monarchy* W Europe
Monaco *see* München
Monaco Basin *see* Canary Basin
Monaco, Principality of *see* Monaco
Monaco-Ville *see* Monaco
96 I9 **Monadhliath Mountains** ▲▲ N Scotland, UK
55 O6 **Monagas** *off.* Estado Monagas. ◈ *state* NE Venezuela
Monagas, Estado *see* Monagas
97 F16 **Monaghan** *Ir.* Muineachán. Monaghan, N Ireland
97 E16 **Monaghan** *Ir.* Muineachán. ◈ *county* N Ireland
43 S15 **Monagrillo** Herrera, S Panama
24 L8 **Monahans** Texas, SW USA
45 Q9 **Mona, Isla** *island* W Puerto Rico
45 Q9 **Mona Passage** *Sp.* Canal de la Mona. *channel* Dominican Republic/Puerto Rico
43 O14 **Mona, Punta** *headland* E Costa Rica
155 K25 **Monaragala** Uva Province, SE Sri Lanka
33 S9 **Monarch** Montana, NW USA
10 H14 **Monarch Mountain** ▲ British Columbia, SW Canada
Monasterio *see* Monesterio
Monasterzyska *see* Monastyrys'ka
Monastir *see* Bitola
Monastyriska *see* Monastyrys'ka
117 O7 **Monastyryshche** Cherkas'ka Oblast', C Ukraine
116 J6 **Monastyrys'ka** *Pol.* Monasterzyska, *Rus.* Monastyriska. Ternopil's'ka Oblast', W Ukraine
79 E15 **Monatélé** Centre, SW Cameroon
165 U2 **Monbetsu** *var.* Mombetsu, Monbetu. Hokkaidō, NE Japan
Monbetu *see* Monbetsu
106 B8 **Moncalieri** Piemonte, NW Italy
104 G4 **Monção** Viana do Castelo, N Portugal
105 Q5 **Moncayo** ▲ N Spain
105 Q5 **Moncayo, Sierra del** ▲▲ N Spain
124 J4 **Monchegorsk** Murmanskaya Oblast', NW Russian Federation
101 D15 **Mönchengladbach** *prev.* München-Gladbach. Nordrhein-Westfalen, W Germany
104 F14 **Monchique** Faro, S Portugal
104 G14 **Monchique, Serra de** ▲▲ S Portugal
21 S14 **Moncks Corner** South Carolina, SE USA
41 N7 **Monclova** Coahuila de Zaragoza, NE Mexico
Moncorvo *see* Torre de Moncorvo
13 P14 **Moncton** New Brunswick, SE Canada
104 F8 **Mondego, Cabo** *cape* N Portugal
104 G8 **Mondego, Rio** ≈ N Portugal
104 I2 **Mondoñedo** Galicia, NW Spain
99 N25 **Mondorf-les-Bains** Grevenmacher, SE Luxembourg
102 M7 **Mondoubleau** Loir-et-Cher, C France
30 J6 **Mondovi** Wisconsin, N USA
106 B9 **Mondovì** Piemonte, NW Italy
Mondragón *see* Arrasate
107 J17 **Mondragone** Campania, S Italy
109 R5 **Mondsee** ◎ N Austria
115 G22 **Monemvasiá** *var.* Monemvasía. Pelopónnisos, S Greece
18 B15 **Monessen** Pennsylvania, NE USA
104 J12 **Monesterio** *var.* Monasterio. Extremadura, W Spain
14 L8 **Monet** Québec, SE Canada
27 S8 **Monett** Missouri, C USA
27 X9 **Monette** Arkansas, C USA
14 G11 **Monetville** Ontario, S Canada
106 J7 **Monfalcone** Friuli-Venezia Giulia, NE Italy
104 H10 **Monforte** Portalegre, C Portugal
104 I4 **Monforte de Lemos** Galicia, NW Spain
79 L16 **Monga** Orientale, N Dem. Rep. Congo
81 I24 **Monga** Lindi, SE Tanzania
81 F15 **Mongalla** Bahr el Gabel, S Sudan
153 U11 **Mongar** E Bhutan
167 U6 **Mong Cai** *var.* Hai Ninh. Quang Ninh, N Vietnam
180 I11 **Mongers Lake** *salt lake* Western Australia
186 K8 **Mongga** Kolombangara, NW Solomon Islands
167 O6 **Möng Hpayak** Shan State, E Myanmar (Burma)
Monghyr *see* Munger
106 B10 **Mongioie, Monte** ▲ NW Italy
Mongla *see* Mungla
188 C15 **Mongmong** C Guam
167 N6 **Möng Nai** Shan State, E Myanmar (Burma)
78 I11 **Mongo** Guéra, C Chad
76 I14 **Mongo** ≈ N Sierra Leone
163 I8 **Mongolia** *Mong.* Mongol Uls. ◆ *republic* E Asia
129 V8 **Mongolia, Plateau of** *plateau* E Mongolia
Mongolküre *see* Zhaosu
Mongol Uls *see* Mongolia
79 E17 **Mongomo** E Equatorial Guinea
162 M7 **Möngönmorĭt** *var.* Bulag. Töv, C Mongolia
77 Y12 **Mongonu** *var.* Monguno. Borno, NE Nigeria
Mongora *see* Mingāora
78 K11 **Mongororo** Ouaddaï, SE Chad
Mongos, Chaîne des *see* Bongo, Massif des
79 I16 **Mongoumba** Lobaye, SW Central African Republic
Mongrove, Punta *see* Cayacal, Punta
83 G15 **Mongu** Western, W Zambia
76 I10 **Mônguel** Gorgol, SW Mauritania
Monguno *see* Mongonu
167 N4 **Möng Yai** Shan State, E Myanmar (Burma)
167 O5 **Möng Yang** Shan State, E Myanmar (Burma)
167 N3 **Möng Yu** Shan State, E Myanmar (Burma)
Mönhbulag *see* Yösöndzüyl
163 O8 **Mönhhaan** *var.* Bayasgalant. Sühbaatar, E Mongolia
162 E7 **Mönhhayrhan** *var.* Tsenher. Hovd, W Mongolia
Mönh Sarĭdag *see* Munku-Sardyk, Gora
186 P9 **Moni** ≈ S Papau New Guinea
115 I15 **Moní Megístis Lávras** *monastery* Kentrikí Makedonía, N Greece
115 F18 **Moní Osíou Loúkas** *monastery* Stereá Ellás, C Greece
54 F9 **Moniquirá** Boyacá, C Colombia
103 Q12 **Monistrol-sur-Loire** Haute-Loire, C France
35 V7 **Monitor Range** ▲▲ Nevada, W USA
115 I14 **Moní Vatopedíou** *monastery* Kentrikí Makedonía, N Greece
Monkchester *see* Newcastle upon Tyne
83 N14 **Monkey Bay** Southern, SE Malawi
43 N11 **Monkey Point** *var.* Punta Mico, Punte Mono, Punto Mico. *headland* SE Nicaragua
Monkey River *see* Monkey River Town
42 G3 **Monkey River Town** *var.* Monkey River. Toledo, SE Belize
14 M13 **Monkland** Ontario, SE Canada
79 J19 **Monkoto** Equateur, NW Dem. Rep. Congo
97 K21 **Monmouth** *Wel.* Trefynwy. SE Wales, UK
30 J12 **Monmouth** Illinois, N USA
32 F12 **Monmouth** Oregon, NW USA
97 K21 **Monmouth** *cultural region* SE Wales, UK
98 I10 **Monnickendam** Noord-Holland, C Netherlands
77 R15 **Mono** ≈ C Togo
Monoecus *see* Monaco
35 R8 **Mono Lake** ◎ California, W USA
115 O23 **Monólithos** Ródos, Dodekánisa, Greece, Aegean Sea
19 Q12 **Monomoy Island** *island* Massachusetts, NE USA
31 O12 **Monon** Indiana, N USA
29 Y12 **Monona** Iowa, C USA
30 L9 **Monona** Wisconsin, N USA
18 B15 **Monongahela** Pennsylvania, NE USA
18 B16 **Monongahela River** ≈ NE USA
107 P17 **Monopoli** Puglia, SE Italy
Mono, Punte *see* Monkey Point
111 K23 **Monor** Pest, C Hungary
Monostor *see* Beli Manastir
78 K8 **Monou** Borkou-Ennedi-Tibesti, NE Chad
105 S12 **Monovar** *Cat.* Monover. País Valenciano, E Spain
Monover *see* Monovar
105 R7 **Monreal del Campo** Aragón, NE Spain
107 I23 **Monreale** Sicilia, Italy, C Mediterranean Sea
23 T3 **Monroe** Georgia, SE USA
29 W14 **Monroe** Iowa, C USA
22 I5 **Monroe** Louisiana, S USA
31 S10 **Monroe** Michigan, N USA
18 K13 **Monroe** New York, NE USA
21 S11 **Monroe** North Carolina, SE USA
36 L6 **Monroe** Utah, W USA
32 H7 **Monroe** Washington, NW USA
30 L9 **Monroe** Wisconsin, N USA
27 V3 **Monroe City** Missouri, C USA
31 O15 **Monroe Lake** ⊠ Indiana, N USA
23 O7 **Monroeville** Alabama, S USA
18 C15 **Monroeville** Pennsylvania, NE USA
76 J16 **Monrovia** ● (Liberia) W Liberia
76 J16 **Monrovia** ✈ W Liberia
105 T7 **Monroyo** Aragón, NE Spain
99 F20 **Mons** *Dut.* Bergen. Hainaut, S Belgium
104 I8 **Monsanto** Castelo Branco, C Portugal
106 H8 **Monselice** Veneto, NE Italy
166 M9 **Mon State** ◈ *state* S Myanmar (Burma)
98 G12 **Monster** Zuid-Holland, W Netherlands
95 N20 **Mönsterås** Kalmar, S Sweden
101 F17 **Montabaur** Rheinland-Pfalz, W Germany
106 G8 **Montagnana** Veneto, NE Italy
35 N1 **Montague** California, W USA
25 S5 **Montague** Texas, SW USA
183 S11 **Montague Island** *island* New South Wales, SE Australia
39 S12 **Montague Island** *island* Alaska, USA
39 S13 **Montague Strait** *strait* N Gulf of Alaska
102 J8 **Montaigu** Vendée, NW France
Montaigu *see* Scherpenheuvel
105 S7 **Montalbán** Aragón, NE Spain
106 G13 **Montalcino** Toscana, C Italy
104 H5 **Montalegre** Vila Real, N Portugal
114 G8 **Montana** *prev.* Ferdinand, Mikhaylovgrad. Montana, NW Bulgaria
108 D10 **Montana** Valais, SW Switzerland
39 R11 **Montana** Alaska, USA
114 G8 **Montana** ◈ *province* NW Bulgaria
33 T9 **Montana** *off.* State of Montana, *also known as* Mountain State, Treasure State. ◈ *state* NW USA
104 J10 **Montánchez** Extremadura, W Spain
Montañita *see* La Montañita
15 Q8 **Mont-Apica** Québec, SE Canada
104 G10 **Montargil** Portalegre, C Portugal
104 G10 **Montargil, Barragem de** ⊠ C Portugal
103 O7 **Montargis** Loiret, C France
103 O4 **Montataire** Oise, N France
102 M14 **Montauban** Tarn-et-Garonne, S France
19 N14 **Montauk** Long Island, New York, NE USA
19 N14 **Montauk Point** *headland* Long Island, New York, NE USA
103 Q7 **Montbard** Côte d'Or, C France
103 U7 **Montbéliard** Doubs, E France
25 W11 **Mont Belvieu** Texas, SW USA
105 U6 **Montblanc** *var.* Montblanch. Cataluña, NE Spain
Montblanch *see* Montblanc
103 Q11 **Montbrison** Loire, E France
Montcalm, Lake *see* Dogai Coring
103 Q9 **Montceau-les-Mines** Saône-et-Loire, C France
103 U12 **Mont Cenis, Col du** *pass* E France
102 K15 **Mont-de-Marsan** Landes, SW France
103 O3 **Montdidier** Somme, N France
187 Q17 **Mont-Dore** Province Sud, S New Caledonia
20 K10 **Monteagle** Tennessee, S USA
57 M20 **Monteagudo** Chuquisaca, S Bolivia
41 R16 **Monte Albán** *ruins* Oaxaca, S Mexico
105 R11 **Montealegre del Castillo** Castilla-La Mancha, C Spain
59 N18 **Monte Azul** Minas Gerais, SE Brazil
14 M12 **Montebello** Québec, SE Canada
106 H7 **Montebelluna** Veneto, NE Italy
60 G13 **Montecarlo** Misiones, NE Argentina
61 D16 **Monte Caseros** Corrientes, NE Argentina
60 J13 **Monte Castelo** Santa Catarina, S Brazil
106 F11 **Montecatini Terme** Toscana, C Italy
42 H7 **Montecillos, Cordillera de** ▲▲ W Honduras
62 I12 **Monte Comén** Mendoza, W Argentina
44 M8 **Monte Cristi** *var.* San Fernando de Monte Cristi. NW Dominican Republic
58 C13 **Monte Cristo** Amazonas, W Brazil
107 E14 **Montecristo, Isola di** *island* Archipelago Toscano, C Italy
Monte Croce Carnico, Passo di *see* Plöcken Pass
58 J12 **Monte Dourado** Pará, NE Brazil
40 L11 **Monte Escobedo** Zacatecas, C Mexico
106 I13 **Montefalco** Umbria, C Italy
107 H14 **Montefiascone** Lazio, C Italy
105 N14 **Montefrío** Andalucía, S Spain
44 I11 **Montego Bay** *var.* Mobay. W Jamaica
Montego Bay *see* Sangster
104 J8 **Montehermoso** Extremadura, W Spain
104 F10 **Montejunto, Serra de** ▲ C Portugal
Monteleone di Calabria *see* Vibo Valentia
54 E7 **Montelíbano** Córdoba, NW Colombia
103 R13 **Montélimar** *anc.* Acunum Acusio, Montilium Adhemari. Drôme, E France
104 K15 **Montellano** Andalucía, S Spain
35 Y2 **Montello** Nevada, W USA
30 L8 **Montello** Wisconsin, N USA
63 J18 **Montemayor, Meseta de** *plain* SE Argentina
41 O9 **Montemorelos** Nuevo León, NE Mexico
104 G11 **Montemor-o-Novo** Évora, S Portugal
104 G8 **Montemor-o-Velho** *var.* Montemor-o-Vélho. Coimbra, N Portugal
Montemor-o-Vélho *see* Montemor-o-Velho
104 H7 **Montemuro, Serra de** ▲ N Portugal
102 K12 **Montendre** Charente-Maritime, W France
61 I15 **Montenegro** Rio Grande do Sul, S Brazil
113 J16 **Montenegro** *Serb.* Crna Gora. ◆ SW Europe
62 G10 **Monte Patria** Coquimbo, N Chile
45 O9 **Monte Plata** E Dominican Republic
83 P14 **Montepuez** Cabo Delgado, N Mozambique
83 P14 **Montepuez** ≈ N Mozambique
106 G13 **Montepulciano** Toscana, C Italy
62 L6 **Monte Quemado** Santiago del Estero, N Argentina
103 O6 **Montereau-Faut-Yonne** *anc.* Condate. Seine-St-Denis, N France
35 N11 **Monterey** California, W USA
20 L9 **Monterey** Tennessee, S USA
21 T5 **Monterey** Virginia, NE USA
Monterey *see* Monterrey
35 N10 **Monterey Bay** *bay* California, W USA
54 D6 **Montería** Córdoba, NW Colombia
57 N18 **Montero** Santa Cruz, C Bolivia
62 J7 **Monteros** Tucumán, C Argentina
104 I5 **Monterrei** Galicia, NW Spain
41 O8 **Monterrey** *var.* Monterey. Nuevo León, NE Mexico
32 F9 **Montesano** Washington, NW USA
107 M19 **Montesano sulla Marcellana** Campania, S Italy
107 N16 **Monte Sant' Angelo** Puglia, SE Italy
59 O16 **Monte Santo** Bahia, E Brazil
107 D18 **Monte Santu, Capo di** *headland* Sardegna, Italy, C Mediterranean Sea
59 M19 **Montes Claros** Minas Gerais, SE Brazil
107 K14 **Montesilvano Marina** Abruzzo, C Italy
23 P4 **Montevallo** Alabama, S USA
106 G12 **Montevarchi** Toscana, C Italy
61 F20 **Montevideo** ● (Uruguay) Montevideo, S Uruguay
29 S9 **Montevideo** Minnesota, N USA
37 S7 **Monte Vista** Colorado, C USA
23 T5 **Montezuma** Georgia, SE USA
29 W14 **Montezuma** Iowa, C USA
26 J6 **Montezuma** Kansas, C USA
103 U12 **Montgenèvre, Col de** *pass* France/Italy
97 K20 **Montgomery** E Wales, UK
23 Q5 **Montgomery** *state capital* Alabama, S USA
29 V9 **Montgomery** Minnesota, N USA
18 G13 **Montgomery** Pennsylvania, NE USA
21 Q5 **Montgomery** West Virginia, NE USA
97 K19 **Montgomery** *cultural region* E Wales, UK
Montgomery *see* Sāhīwāl
27 V4 **Montgomery City** Missouri, C USA
35 S8 **Montgomery Pass** *pass* Nevada, W USA
102 K12 **Montguyon** Charente-Maritime, W France
108 C10 **Monthey** Valais, SW Switzerland
27 V13 **Monticello** Arkansas, C USA
23 T4 **Monticello** Florida, SE USA
23 T8 **Monticello** Georgia, SE USA
30 M13 **Monticello** Illinois, N USA
31 O12 **Monticello** Indiana, N USA
29 Y13 **Monticello** Iowa, C USA
20 L7 **Monticello** Kentucky, S USA
29 V8 **Monticello** Minnesota, N USA
22 K7 **Monticello** Mississippi, S USA
27 V2 **Monticello** Missouri, C USA
18 J12 **Monticello** New York, NE USA
37 O7 **Monticello** Utah, W USA
106 F8 **Montichiari** Lombardia, N Italy
102 M12 **Montignac** Dordogne, SW France
99 G21 **Montignies-le-Tilleul** *var.* Montigny-le-Tilleul. Hainaut, S Belgium
14 J8 **Montigny, Lac de** ◎ Québec, SE Canada
103 S6 **Montigny-le-Roi** Haute-Marne, N France
Montigny-le-Tilleul *see* Montignies-le-Tilleul
43 R16 **Montijo** Veraguas, S Panama
104 F11 **Montijo** Setúbal, W Portugal
104 J11 **Montijo** Extremadura, W Spain
Montilium Adhemari *see* Montélimar
104 M13 **Montilla** Andalucía, S Spain
102 L3 **Montivilliers** Seine-Maritime, N France
15 U7 **Mont-Joli** Québec, SE Canada
14 M10 **Mont-Laurier** Québec, SE Canada
15 X5 **Mont-Louis** Québec, SE Canada
103 N17 **Mont-Louis** *var.* Mont Louis. Pyrénées-Orientales, S France
103 O10 **Montluçon** Allier, C France
15 R10 **Montmagny** Québec, SE Canada
103 S3 **Montmédy** Meuse, NE France
103 P5 **Montmirail** Marne, N France
15 R9 **Montmorency** ≈ Québec, SE Canada
102 M10 **Montmorillon** Vienne, W France
107 J14 **Montorio al Vomano** Abruzzo, C Italy
104 M13 **Montoro** Andalucía, S Spain
33 S16 **Montpelier** Idaho, NW USA
29 P6 **Montpelier** North Dakota, N USA
18 M7 **Montpelier** *state capital* Vermont, NE USA
103 Q15 **Montpellier** Hérault, S France
102 L12 **Montpon-Ménestérol** Dordogne, SW France
12 K15 **Montréal** *Eng.* Montreal. Québec, SE Canada
14 C8 **Montreal** ≈ Ontario, S Canada
14 G8 **Montreal** ≈ Ontario, S Canada
Montreal *see* Mirabel
9 T14 **Montreal Lake** ◎ Saskatchewan, C Canada
14 B9 **Montreal River** Ontario, S Canada
103 N2 **Montreuil** Pas-de-Calais, N France
102 K8 **Montreuil-Bellay** Maine-et-Loire, NW France
108 C10 **Montreux** Vaud, SW Switzerland
108 B9 **Montricher** Vaud, W Switzerland
96 K10 **Montrose** E Scotland, UK
27 W14 **Montrose** Arkansas, C USA
37 Q6 **Montrose** Colorado, C USA
29 Y16 **Montrose** Iowa, C USA
18 H12 **Montrose** Pennsylvania, NE USA
21 X5 **Montross** Virginia, NE USA
15 O12 **Mont-St-Hilaire** Québec, SE Canada
103 S3 **Mont-St-Martin** Meurthe-et-Moselle, NE France
45 V10 **Montserrat** *var.* Emerald Isle. ◇ *UK dependent territory* E West Indies
105 V5 **Montserrat** ▲ NE Spain
104 M7 **Montuenga** Castilla-León, N Spain
99 M19 **Montzen** Liège, E Belgium
37 N8 **Monument Valley** *valley* Arizona/Utah, SW USA
166 L4 **Monywa** Sagaing, C Myanmar (Burma)
106 D7 **Monza** Lombardia, N Italy
83 J15 **Monze** Southern, S Zambia
105 T5 **Monzón** Aragón, NE Spain
25 T9 **Moody** Texas, SW USA
98 L13 **Mook** Limburg, SE Netherlands
165 O12 **Mooka** *var.* Mōka. Tochigi, Honshū, S Japan
182 K3 **Moomba** South Australia
14 G13 **Moon** ≈ Ontario, S Canada
Moon *see* Muhu
181 Y10 **Moonie** Queensland, E Australia
193 O5 **Moonless Mountains** *undersea feature* E Pacific Ocean
182 L13 **Moonlight Head** *headland* Victoria, SE Australia
Moon-Sund *see* Väinameri
182 H8 **Moonta** South Australia
Moor *see* Mór
180 I12 **Moora** Western Australia
98 H12 **Moordrecht** Zuid-Holland, C Netherlands
33 T9 **Moore** Montana, NW USA
27 N11 **Moore** Oklahoma, C USA
25 R12 **Moore** Texas, SW USA
191 S10 **Moorea** *island* Îles du Vent, W French Polynesia
21 U3 **Moorefield** West Virginia, NE USA
23 X14 **Moore Haven** Florida, SE USA
180 J11 **Moore, Lake** ◎ Western Australia
19 N7 **Moore Reservoir** ⊠ New Hampshire/Vermont, NE USA
44 G1 **Moores Island** *island* N Bahamas
21 R10 **Mooresville** North Carolina, SE USA
29 R5 **Moorhead** Minnesota, N USA
22 K4 **Moorhead** Mississippi, S USA
99 F18 **Moorsel** Oost-Vlaanderen, C Belgium
99 C18 **Moorslede** West-Vlaanderen, W Belgium
18 L8 **Moosalamoo, Mount** ▲ Vermont, NE USA
101 M22 **Moosburg an der Isar** Bayern, SE Germany
33 S14 **Moose** Wyoming, C USA
12 H11 **Moose** ≈ Ontario, S Canada
12 H10 **Moose Factory** Ontario, S Canada
19 Q4 **Moosehead Lake** ◎ Maine, NE USA
9 U16 **Moose Jaw** Saskatchewan, S Canada
9 V14 **Moose Lake** Manitoba, C Canada
29 W6 **Moose Lake** Minnesota, N USA
19 P6 **Mooselookmeguntic Lake** ◎ Maine, NE USA
39 R12 **Moose Pass** Alaska, USA
19 P5 **Moose River** ≈ Maine, NE USA
18 J9 **Moose River** ≈ New York, NE USA
9 V16 **Moosomin** Saskatchewan, S Canada
12 H10 **Moosonee** Ontario, SE Canada

◆ Country
● Country Capital
◇ Dependent Territory
○ Dependent Territory Capital
◈ Administrative Regions
✈ International Airport
▲ Mountain
▲▲ Mountain Range
⛰ Volcano
≈ River
◎ Lake
⊠ Reservoir

19 N12 **Moosup** Connecticut, NE USA
83 N16 **Mopeia** Zambézia, NE Mozambique
83 H18 **Mopipi** Central, C Botswana
Moppo see Mokp'o
77 N11 **Mopti** Mopti, C Mali
77 O11 **Mopti** ⬗ region S Mali
57 H18 **Moquegua** Moquegua, SE Peru
57 H18 **Moquegua** off. Departamento de Moquegua. ⬗ department S Peru
Moquegua, Departamento de see Moquegua
111 I23 **Mór** Ger. Moor. Fejér, C Hungary
78 G11 **Mora** Extrême-Nord, N Cameroon
104 G11 **Mora** Évora, S Portugal
105 N9 **Mora** Castilla-La Mancha, C Spain
94 L12 **Mora** Dalarna, C Sweden
29 V7 **Mora** Minnesota, N USA
37 T10 **Mora** New Mexico, SW USA
113 J17 **Morača** ≈ S Montenegro
152 K10 **Morādābād** Uttar Pradesh, N India
105 U6 **Móra d'Ebre** var. Mora de Ebro. Cataluña, NE Spain
Mora de Ebro see Móra d'Ebre
105 S8 **Mora de Rubielos** Aragón, NE Spain
172 H4 **Morafenobe** Mahajanga, W Madagascar
110 K8 **Morąg** Ger. Mohrungen. Warmińsko-Mazurskie, N Poland
111 L25 **Mórahalom** Csongrád, S Hungary
105 N11 **Moral de Calatrava** Castilla-La Mancha, C Spain
63 G19 **Moraleda, Canal** strait SE Pacific Ocean
54 J3 **Morales** Bolívar, N Colombia
54 D12 **Morales** Cauca, SW Colombia
42 F5 **Morales** Izabal, E Guatemala
172 J5 **Moramanga** Toamasina, E Madagascar
27 Q6 **Moran** Kansas, C USA
25 Q7 **Moran** Texas, SW USA
181 X7 **Moranbah** Queensland, NE Australia
44 L13 **Morant Bay** E Jamaica
96 G10 **Morar, Loch** ◎ N Scotland, UK
Morata see Goodenough Island
105 Q12 **Moratalla** Murcia, SE Spain
108 C8 **Morat, Lac de** Ger. Murtensee. ◎ W Switzerland
84 I11 **Morava** var. March. ≈ C Europe see also March
Morava see March
Morava see Moravia, Czech Republic
Morava see Velika Morava, Serbia
29 W15 **Moravia** Iowa, C USA
111 F18 **Moravia** Cz. Morava, Ger. Mähren. cultural region E Czech Republic
111 H17 **Moravice** Ger. Mohra. ≈ NE Czech Republic
116 E12 **Moravița** Timiș, SW Romania
111 G17 **Moravská Třebová** Ger. Mährisch-Trübau. Pardubický Kraj, C Czech Republic
111 E19 **Moravské Budějovice** Ger. Mährisch-Budwitz. Vysočina, C Czech Republic
111 H17 **Moravskoslezský Kraj** prev. Ostravský Kraj. ⬗ region E Czech Republic
111 F19 **Moravský Krumlov** Ger. Mährisch-Kromau. Jihomoravský Kraj, SE Czech Republic
96 J8 **Moray** cultural region N Scotland, UK
96 J8 **Moray Firth** inlet N Scotland, UK
42 B10 **Morazán** ⬗ department NE El Salvador
154 C10 **Morbi** Gujarāt, W India
102 G7 **Morbihan** ⬗ department NW France
Mörbisch see Mörbisch am See
109 Y5 **Mörbisch am See** var. Mörbisch. Burgenland, E Austria
95 N21 **Mörbylånga** Kalmar, S Sweden
102 J14 **Morcenx** Landes, SW France
Morcheh Khort see Mürcheh Khvort
163 T5 **Mordaga** Nei Mongol Zizhiqu, N China
11 X17 **Morden** Manitoba, S Canada
Mordovia see Mordoviya, Respublika
127 N5 **Mordoviya, Respublika** prev. Mordovskaya ASSR, Eng. Mordovia, var. Mordvinia. ⬗ autonomous republic W Russian Federation
126 M7 **Mordovo** Tambovskaya Oblast', W Russian Federation
Mordovskaya ASSR/Mordvinia see Mordoviya, Respublika
Morea see Pelopónnisos
28 K8 **Moreau River** ≈ South Dakota, N USA
97 K16 **Morecambe** NW England, UK
97 K16 **Morecambe Bay** inlet NW England, UK
183 S4 **Moree** New South Wales, SE Australia
21 N5 **Morehead** Kentucky, S USA
21 X11 **Morehead City** North Carolina, SE USA
27 Y8 **Morehouse** Missouri, C USA
108 E10 **Mörel** Valais, SW Switzerland
54 D13 **Morelia** Caquetá, S Colombia
41 N14 **Morelia** Michoacán de Ocampo, S Mexico
105 T7 **Morella** País Valenciano, E Spain
40 I7 **Morelos** Chihuahua, N Mexico
41 O15 **Morelos** ⬗ state S Mexico
154 H7 **Morena** Madhya Pradesh, C India
104 L12 **Morena, Sierra** ▲▲ S Spain
37 O14 **Morenci** Arizona, SW USA
31 R11 **Morenci** Michigan, N USA
116 J13 **Moreni** Dâmbovița, S Romania
94 D9 **Møre og Romsdal** ⬗ county S Norway
10 I14 **Moresby Island** island Queen Charlotte Islands, British Columbia, SW Canada
183 W2 **Moreton Island** island Queensland, E Australia
103 O3 **Moreuil** Somme, N France
35 V7 **Morey Peak** ▲ Nevada, W USA
125 U4 **More-Yu** ≈ NW Russian Federation
103 T9 **Morez** Jura, E France
Mórfou see Güzelyurt
Morfou Bay/Mórfou, Kólpos see Güzelyurt Körfezi
182 J8 **Morgan** South Australia
23 S7 **Morgan** Georgia, SE USA
25 S8 **Morgan** Texas, SW USA
22 J10 **Morgan City** Louisiana, S USA
20 H6 **Morganfield** Kentucky, S USA
35 O10 **Morgan Hill** California, W USA
21 Q9 **Morganton** North Carolina, SE USA
20 J7 **Morgantown** Kentucky, S USA
21 S2 **Morgantown** West Virginia, NE USA
108 B10 **Morges** Vaud, SW Switzerland
Morghāb, Daryā-ye see Murgap
148 M4 **Morghāb, Daryā-ye** Rus. Murgab, Murghab, Turk. Murgap, Deryasy Murgap. ≈ Afghanistan/Turkmenistan see also Murgap
96 I9 **Mor, Glen** var. Glen Albyn, Great Glen. valley N Scotland, UK
103 T5 **Morhange** Moselle, NE France
158 M5 **Mori** var. Mori Kazak Zizhixian. Xinjiang Uygur Zizhiqu, NW China
165 R5 **Mori** Hokkaidō, NE Japan
35 Y6 **Moriah, Mount** ▲ Nevada, W USA
37 S11 **Moriarty** New Mexico, SW USA
54 J12 **Morichal** Guaviare, E Colombia
Mori Kazak Zizhixian see Mori
Morin Dawa Daurzu Zizhiqi see Nirji
11 Q14 **Morinville** Alberta, SW Canada
165 R8 **Morioka** Iwate, Honshū, C Japan
183 T8 **Morisset** New South Wales, SE Australia
165 Q8 **Moriyoshi-yama** ▲ Honshū, C Japan
92 K13 **Morjärv** Norrbotten, N Sweden
127 R3 **Morki** Respublika Mariy El, W Russian Federation
123 N10 **Morkoka** ≈ NE Russian Federation
102 F5 **Morlaix** Finistère, NW France
95 M20 **Mörlunda** Kalmar, S Sweden
107 N19 **Mormanno** Calabria, SW Italy
36 L11 **Mormon Lake** ◎ Arizona, SW USA
35 Y10 **Mormon Peak** ▲ Nevada, W USA
Mormon State see Utah
45 Y5 **Morne-à-l'Eau** Grande Terre, N Guadeloupe
29 Y15 **Morning Sun** Iowa, C USA
193 S12 **Mornington Abyssal Plain** undersea feature SE Pacific Ocean
63 F22 **Mornington, Isla** island S Chile
181 T4 **Mornington Island** island Wellesley Islands, Queensland, N Australia
115 E18 **Mórnos** ≈ C Greece
149 P14 **Moro** Sind, SE Pakistan
32 I11 **Moro** Oregon, NW USA
186 E8 **Morobe** Morobe, C Papua New Guinea
186 E8 **Morobe** ⬗ province C Papua New Guinea
31 N12 **Morocco** Indiana, N USA
74 E8 **Morocco** off. Kingdom of Morocco, Ar. Al Mamlakah. ◆ monarchy N Africa
Morocco see Marrakech
Morocco, Kingdom of see Morocco
81 I22 **Morogoro** Morogoro, E Tanzania
81 H24 **Morogoro** ⬗ region SE Tanzania
171 Q7 **Moro Gulf** gulf S Philippines
41 N13 **Moroleón** Guanajuato, C Mexico
172 H6 **Morombe** Toliara, W Madagascar
44 G5 **Morón** Ciego de Ávila, C Cuba
163 N8 **Mörön** Hentiy, C Mongolia
162 I6 **Mörön** Hövsgöl, N Mongolia
54 K5 **Morón** Carabobo, N Venezuela
Morón see Morón de la Frontera
56 D8 **Morona, Río** ≈ N Peru
56 C8 **Morona Santiago** ⬗ province E Ecuador
172 H5 **Morondava** Toliara, W Madagascar
104 K14 **Morón de la Frontera** var. Morón. Andalucía, S Spain
172 G13 **Moroni** ● (Comoros) Grande Comore, NW Comoros
171 S10 **Morotai, Pulau** island Maluku, E Indonesia
Morotiri see Marotiri
81 H17 **Moroto** NE Uganda
Morozov see Bratan
126 M11 **Morozovsk** Rostovskaya Oblast', SW Russian Federation
97 L14 **Morpeth** N England, UK
Morphou see Güzelyurt
Morphou Bay see Güzelyurt Körfezi
28 I13 **Morrill** Nebraska, C USA
27 U11 **Morrilton** Arkansas, C USA
9 Q16 **Morrin** Alberta, SW Canada
184 M7 **Morrinsville** Waikato, North Island, New Zealand
9 X16 **Morris** Manitoba, S Canada
30 M11 **Morris** Illinois, N USA
29 S8 **Morris** Minnesota, N USA
14 M13 **Morrisburg** Ontario, SE Canada
197 R11 **Morris Jesup, Kap** headland N Greenland
182 B1 **Morris, Mount** ▲ South Australia
30 K10 **Morrison** Illinois, N USA
36 K13 **Morristown** Arizona, SW USA
18 J14 **Morristown** New Jersey, NE USA
21 O8 **Morristown** Tennessee, S USA
42 L11 **Morrito** Río San Juan, SW Nicaragua
35 P13 **Morro Bay** California, W USA
95 L22 **Mörrum** Blekinge, S Sweden
83 N16 **Morrumbala** Zambézia, NE Mozambique
83 N20 **Morrumbene** Inhambane, SE Mozambique
95 F21 **Mors** island NW Denmark
Mörs see Moers
25 N1 **Morse** Texas, SW USA
127 N6 **Morshansk** Tambovskaya Oblast', W Russian Federation
102 L5 **Mortagne-au-Perche** Orne, N France
102 J8 **Mortagne-sur-Sèvre** Vendée, NW France
104 G8 **Mortágua** Viseu, N Portugal
102 J5 **Mortain** Manche, N France
106 C8 **Mortara** Lombardia, N Italy
59 J17 **Mortes, Rio das** ≈ C Brazil
182 M12 **Mortlake** Victoria, SE Australia
Mortlock Group see Takuu Islands
189 Q17 **Mortlock Islands** prev. Nomoi Islands. island group C Micronesia
29 T9 **Morton** Minnesota, N USA
22 L5 **Morton** Mississippi, S USA
24 M5 **Morton** Texas, SW USA
32 H9 **Morton** Washington, NW USA
0 D7 **Morton Seamount** undersea feature NE Pacific Ocean
45 U15 **Moruga** Trinidad, Trinidad and Tobago
183 P9 **Morundah** New South Wales, SE Australia
Moruroa see Mururoa
183 S11 **Moruya** New South Wales, SE Australia
103 Q8 **Morvan** physical region C France
185 G21 **Morven** Canterbury, South Island, New Zealand
183 O13 **Morwell** Victoria, SE Australia
125 N6 **Morzhovets, Ostrov** island NW Russian Federation
126 J4 **Mosal'sk** Kaluzhskaya Oblast', W Russian Federation
101 H20 **Mosbach** Baden-Württemberg, SW Germany
95 E18 **Mosby** Vest-Agder, S Norway
33 V9 **Mosby** Montana, NW USA
32 M9 **Moscow** Idaho, NW USA
20 F10 **Moscow** Tennessee, S USA
Moscow see Moskva
101 D19 **Mosel** Fr. Moselle. ≈ W Europe see also Moselle
Mosel see Moselle
103 T4 **Moselle** ⬗ department NE France
103 T6 **Moselle** Ger. Mosel. ≈ W Europe see also Mosel
Moselle see Mosel
32 K9 **Moses Lake** ◎ Washington, NW USA
83 I18 **Mosetse** Central, E Botswana
92 H4 **Mosfellsbær** Sudhurland, SW Iceland
185 F23 **Mosgiel** Otago, South Island, New Zealand
124 M11 **Mosha** ≈ NW Russian Federation
81 I20 **Moshi** Kilimanjaro, NE Tanzania
110 G12 **Mosina** Wielkolpolskie, C Poland
30 L6 **Mosinee** Wisconsin, N USA
92 F13 **Mosjøen** Nordland, C Norway
123 S12 **Moskal'vo** Ostrov Sakhalin, Sakhalinskaya Oblast', SE Russian Federation
92 I13 **Moskosel** Norrbotten, N Sweden
126 K4 **Moskovskaya Oblast'** ⬗ province W Russian Federation
Moskovskiy see Moskva
126 J3 **Moskva** Eng. Moscow. ● (Russian Federation) Gorod Moskva, W Russian Federation
147 Q14 **Moskva** Rus. Moskovskiy; prev. Chubek. SW Tajikistan
126 L4 **Moskva** ≈ W Russian Federation
83 I20 **Mosomane** Kgatleng, SE Botswana
Moson and Magyaróvár see Mosonmagyaróvár
111 H21 **Mosoni-Duna** Ger. Kleine Donau. ≈ NW Hungary
111 H21 **Mosonmagyaróvár** Ger. Wieselburg-Ungarisch-Altenburg; prev. Moson and Magyaróvár, Ger. Wieselburg and Ungarisch-Altenburg. Győr-Moson-Sopron, NW Hungary
Mospino see Mospyne
117 X8 **Mospyne** Rus. Mospino. Donets'ka Oblast', E Ukraine
54 B12 **Mosquera** Nariño, SW Colombia
37 U10 **Mosquero** New Mexico, SW USA
Mosquito Coast see La Mosquitia
31 U11 **Mosquito Creek Lake** ⊠ Ohio, N USA
Mosquito Gulf see Mosquitos, Golfo de los
23 X11 **Mosquito Lagoon** wetland Florida, SE USA
43 N10 **Mosquito, Punta** headland E Nicaragua
43 W14 **Mosquito, Punta** headland NE Panama
43 Q15 **Mosquitos, Golfo de los** Eng. Mosquito Gulf. gulf N Panama
95 H16 **Moss** Østfold, S Norway
Mossâmedes see Namibe
22 G8 **Moss Bluff** Louisiana, S USA
185 C23 **Mossburn** Southland, South Island, New Zealand
83 G26 **Mosselbaai** var. Mosselbai, Eng. Mossel Bay. Western Cape, SW South Africa
Mosselbai/Mossel Bay see Mosselbaai
79 F20 **Mossendjo** Le Niari, SW Congo
183 N8 **Mossgiel** New South Wales, SE Australia
101 H22 **Mössingen** Baden-Württemberg, S Germany
181 W4 **Mossman** Queensland, NE Australia
59 P14 **Mossoró** Rio Grande do Norte, NE Brazil
23 N9 **Moss Point** Mississippi, S USA
183 S9 **Moss Vale** New South Wales, SE Australia
32 G9 **Mossyrock** Washington, NW USA
111 B15 **Most** Ger. Brüx. Ústecký Kraj, NW Czech Republic
162 E7 **Möst** var. Ulaantolgoy. Hovd, W Mongolia
121 P16 **Mosta** var. Musta. C Malta
74 I5 **Mostaganem** var. Mestghanem. NW Algeria
113 H14 **Mostar** Federacija Bosna I Hercegovina, S Bosnia and Herzegovina
61 J17 **Mostardas** Rio Grande do Sul, S Brazil
116 K14 **Mostiștea** ≈ S Romania
Mostva see Mastva
Mosty see Masty
116 H5 **Mostys'ka** L'vivs'ka Oblast', W Ukraine
Mosul see Al Mawşil
95 F15 **Møsvatnet** ◎ S Norway
80 J12 **Mot'a** Amhara, N Ethiopia
79 H16 **Motaba** ≈ N Congo
105 O10 **Mota del Cuervo** Castilla-La Mancha, C Spain
104 L5 **Mota del Marqués** Castilla-León, N Spain
42 F5 **Motagua, Río** ≈ Guatemala/Honduras
119 H19 **Motal'** Brestskaya Voblasts', SW Belarus
95 L17 **Motala** Östergötland, S Sweden
191 X7 **Motane** island Îles Marquises, NE French Polynesia
152 K13 **Moth** Uttar Pradesh, N India
Mother of Presidents/Mother of States see Virginia
96 I12 **Motherwell** C Scotland, UK
153 P12 **Motīhāri** Bihār, N India
105 Q10 **Motilla del Palancar** Castilla-La Mancha, C Spain
184 N7 **Motiti Island** island NE New Zealand
65 E25 **Motley Island** island SE Falkland Islands
83 J19 **Motloutse** ≈ E Botswana
41 V17 **Motozintla de Mendoza** Chiapas, SE Mexico
105 N15 **Motril** Andalucía, S Spain
116 G13 **Motru** Gorj, SW Romania
165 Q4 **Motsuta-misaki** headland Hokkaidō, NE Japan
28 L6 **Mott** North Dakota, N USA
Möttling see Metlika
107 O18 **Mottola** Puglia, SE Italy
184 P8 **Motu** ≈ North Island, New Zealand
185 I14 **Motueka** Tasman, South Island, New Zealand
185 I14 **Motueka** ≈ South Island, New Zealand
Motu Iti see Tupai
41 X12 **Motul** var. Motul de Felipe Carrillo Puerto. Yucatán, SE Mexico
Motul de Felipe Carrillo Puerto see Motul
191 U17 **Motu Nui** island Easter Island, Chile, E Pacific Ocean
191 Q10 **Motu One** var. Bellingshausen. atoll Îles Sous le Vent, W French Polynesia
190 I16 **Motutapu** island E Cook Islands
193 V15 **Motu Tapu** island Tongatapu Group, S Tonga
184 L5 **Motutapu Island** island N New Zealand
Motyca see Modica
Mouanda see Moanda
Mouaskar see Mascara
105 U3 **Moubermé, Tuc de** Fr. Pic de Maubermé, Sp. Pico Mauberme; prev. Tuc de Maubermé. ▲ France/Spain see also Maubermé, Pic de
Moubermé, Tuc de see Maubermé, Pic de
45 N7 **Mouchoir Passage** passage SE Turks and Caicos Islands
76 I9 **Moudjéria** Tagant, SW Mauritania
108 C9 **Moudon** Vaud, W Switzerland
Mouhoun see Black Volta
79 E19 **Mouila** Ngounié, C Gabon
79 K14 **Mouka** Haute-Kotto, C Central African Republic
Moukden see Shenyang
183 N10 **Moulamein** New South Wales, SE Australia
Moulamein Creek see Billabong Creek
74 F6 **Moulay-Bousselham** NW Morocco
Moule see le Moule
80 M11 **Moulhoulé** N Djibouti
103 P9 **Moulins** Allier, C France
166 M9 **Moulmein** var. Maulmain, Mawlamyine. Mon State, S Myanmar (Burma)
166 L8 **Moulmeingyun** Irrawaddy, SW Myanmar (Burma)
74 G6 **Moulouya** var. Mulucha, Muluya, Mulwiya. seasonal river NE Morocco
23 O2 **Moulton** Alabama, S USA
29 W16 **Moulton** Iowa, C USA
25 T11 **Moulton** Texas, SW USA
23 T7 **Moultrie** Georgia, SE USA
21 S14 **Moultrie, Lake** ⊠ South Carolina, SE USA
22 K3 **Mound Bayou** Mississippi, S USA
30 L17 **Mound City** Illinois, N USA
27 R6 **Mound City** Kansas, C USA
27 Q2 **Mound City** Missouri, C USA
29 N7 **Mound City** South Dakota, N USA
78 H13 **Moundou** Logone-Occidental, SW Chad
27 P10 **Mounds** Oklahoma, C USA
21 R2 **Moundsville** West Virginia, NE USA
167 Q12 **Moŭng Roessei** Bătdâmbâng, W Cambodia
Moun Hou see Black Volta
8 H8 **Mountain** ≈ Northwest Territories, NW Canada
37 S12 **Mountainair** New Mexico, SW USA
35 V1 **Mountain City** Nevada, W USA
21 Q8 **Mountain City** Tennessee, S USA
27 U7 **Mountain Grove** Missouri, C USA
27 U9 **Mountain Home** Arkansas, C USA
33 N15 **Mountain Home** Idaho, NW USA
25 Q11 **Mountain Home** Texas, SW USA
29 W4 **Mountain Iron** Minnesota, N USA
29 T10 **Mountain Lake** Minnesota, N USA
23 S3 **Mountain Park** Georgia, SE USA
35 W12 **Mountain Pass** pass California, W USA
27 T12 **Mountain Pine** Arkansas, C USA
39 Y14 **Mountain Point** Annette Island, Alaska, USA
Mountain State see Montana
Mountain State see West Virginia
27 V7 **Mountain View** Arkansas, C USA
38 H12 **Mountain View** Hawai'i, USA, C Pacific Ocean
27 V10 **Mountain View** Missouri, C USA
38 M11 **Mountain Village** Alaska, USA
21 R8 **Mount Airy** North Carolina, SE USA
83 K24 **Mount Ayliff** Xh. Maxesibebi. Eastern Cape, SE South Africa
29 U16 **Mount Ayr** Iowa, C USA
182 J9 **Mount Barker** South Australia
180 J14 **Mount Barker** Western Australia
183 P11 **Mount Beauty** Victoria, SE Australia
14 E16 **Mount Brydges** Ontario, S Canada
31 N16 **Mount Carmel** Illinois, N USA
30 K10 **Mount Carroll** Illinois, N USA
31 S9 **Mount Clemens** Michigan, N USA
185 E19 **Mount Cook** Canterbury, South Island, New Zealand
83 L16 **Mount Darwin** Mashonaland Central, NE Zimbabwe
19 S7 **Mount Desert Island** island Maine, NE USA
23 W11 **Mount Dora** Florida, SE USA
182 G5 **Mount Eba** South Australia
25 W8 **Mount Enterprise** Texas, SW USA
182 J4 **Mount Fitton** South Australia
83 J24 **Mount Fletcher** Eastern Cape, SE South Africa
14 F15 **Mount Forest** Ontario, S Canada
182 K12 **Mount Gambier** South Australia
181 W5 **Mount Garnet** Queensland, NE Australia
21 P6 **Mount Gay** West Virginia, NE USA
31 S12 **Mount Gilead** Ohio, N USA
186 C7 **Mount Hagen** Western Highlands, C Papua New Guinea
18 J16 **Mount Holly** New Jersey, NE USA
21 R10 **Mount Holly** North Carolina, SE USA
27 T12 **Mount Ida** Arkansas, C USA
181 T6 **Mount Isa** Queensland, C Australia
21 U4 **Mount Jackson** Virginia, NE USA
18 D12 **Mount Jewett** Pennsylvania, NE USA
18 L13 **Mount Kisco** New York, NE USA
18 B15 **Mount Lebanon** Pennsylvania, NE USA
182 J8 **Mount Lofty Ranges** ▲▲ South Australia
180 J10 **Mount Magnet** Western Australia
184 N7 **Mount Maunganui** Bay of Plenty, North Island, New Zealand
97 E18 **Mountmellick** Ir. Móinteach Mílic. Laois, C Ireland
30 L10 **Mount Morris** Illinois, N USA
31 R9 **Mount Morris** Michigan, N USA
18 F10 **Mount Morris** New York, NE USA
18 B16 **Mount Morris** Pennsylvania, NE USA
30 K15 **Mount Olive** Illinois, N USA
21 V10 **Mount Olive** North Carolina, SE USA
21 N4 **Mount Olivet** Kentucky, S USA
29 Y15 **Mount Pleasant** Iowa, C USA
31 Q8 **Mount Pleasant** Michigan, N USA
18 C15 **Mount Pleasant** Pennsylvania, NE USA
21 T14 **Mount Pleasant** South Carolina, SE USA
20 I9 **Mount Pleasant** Tennessee, S USA
25 W6 **Mount Pleasant** Texas, SW USA
36 L4 **Mount Pleasant** Utah, W USA
63 N23 **Mount Pleasant** ✈ (Stanley) East Falkland, Falkland Islands
97 G25 **Mount's Bay** inlet SW England, UK
35 N2 **Mount Shasta** California, W USA
30 J13 **Mount Sterling** Illinois, N USA
21 N5 **Mount Sterling** Kentucky, S USA
18 E15 **Mount Union** Pennsylvania, NE USA
23 V6 **Mount Vernon** Georgia, SE USA
30 L16 **Mount Vernon** Illinois, N USA
20 M6 **Mount Vernon** Kentucky, S USA
27 S7 **Mount Vernon** Missouri, C USA
31 T13 **Mount Vernon** Ohio, N USA
32 K13 **Mount Vernon** Oregon, NW USA
25 W6 **Mount Vernon** Texas, SW USA
32 H7 **Mount Vernon** Washington, NW USA
20 L5 **Mount Washington** Kentucky, S USA
182 F8 **Mount Wedge** South Australia
30 L14 **Mount Zion** Illinois, N USA
181 Y9 **Moura** Queensland, NE Australia
58 F12 **Moura** Amazonas, NW Brazil
104 H12 **Moura** Beja, S Portugal
104 I12 **Mourão** Évora, S Portugal
76 L11 **Mourdiah** Koulikoro, W Mali
78 K7 **Mourdi, Dépression du** desert lowland Chad/Sudan
102 J16 **Mourenx** Pyrénées-Atlantiques, SW France
Mourgana see Mourgkána
115 C15 **Mourgkána** var. Mourgana. ▲ Albania/Greece
97 G16 **Mourne Mountains** Ir. Beanna Boirche. ▲▲ SE Northern Ireland, UK
115 I15 **Moúrtzeflos, Ákrotírio** headland Límnos, E Greece
99 C19 **Mouscron** Dut. Moeskroen. Hainaut, W Belgium
Mouse River see Souris River
78 H10 **Moussoro** Kanem, W Chad
103 T11 **Moûtiers** Savoie, E France
172 J14 **Moutsamoudou** var. Mutsamudu. Anjouan, SE Comoros
74 K11 **Mouydir, Monts de** ▲▲ S Algeria
79 F20 **Mouyondzi** La Bouenza, S Congo
115 E16 **Mouzáki** prev. Mouzákion. Thessalía, C Greece
Mouzákion see Mouzáki
29 S13 **Moville** Iowa, C USA
82 E13 **Moxico** ⬗ province E Angola
172 I14 **Moya** Anjouan, SE Comoros
40 L12 **Moyahua** Zacatecas, C Mexico
81 J16 **Moyalē** Oromo, C Ethiopia
76 I15 **Moyamba** W Sierra Leone
74 G7 **Moyen Atlas** Eng. Middle Atlas. ▲▲ N Morocco
78 H13 **Moyen-Chari** off. Préfecture du Moyen-Chari. ⬗ prefecture S Chad
Moyen-Chari, Préfecture du see Moyen-Chari
Moyen-Congo see Congo (Republic of)
83 J24 **Moyeni** var. Quthing. SW Lesotho
79 D18 **Moyen-Ogooué** off. Province du Moyen-Ogooué, var. Le Moyen-Ogooué. ⬗ province C Gabon
Moyen-Ogooué, Province du see Moyen-Ogooué
103 S4 **Moyeuvre-Grande** Moselle, NE France
33 N7 **Moyie Springs** Idaho, NW USA
146 G6 **Mo'ynoq** Rus. Muynak. Qoraqalpog'iston Respublikasi, NW Uzbekistan
81 F16 **Moyo** NW Uganda
56 D10 **Moyobamba** San Martín, NW Peru
78 H10 **Moyto** Chari-Baguirmi, W Chad
158 G9 **Moyu** var. Karakax. Xinjiang Uygur Zizhiqu, NW China
122 M9 **Moyyero** ≈ N Russian Federation
145 S15 **Moyynkum** var. Furmanovka, Kaz. Fūrmanov. Zhambyl, S Kazakhstan
145 Q15 **Moyynkum, Peski** Kaz. Moyynqum. desert S Kazakhstan
Moyynqum see Moyynkum, Peski
145 S12 **Moyynty** Karaganda, C Kazakhstan
145 S12 **Moyynty** ≈ Karaganda, C Kazakhstan
Mozambika, Lakandranon' i see Mozambique Channel
83 M18 **Mozambique** off. Republic of Mozambique; prev. People's Republic of Mozambique, Portuguese East Africa. ◆ republic S Africa
Mozambique Basin see Natal Basin
Mozambique, Canal de see Mozambique Channel
83 P17 **Mozambique Channel** Fr. Canal de Mozambique, Mal. Lakandranon' i Mozambika. strait W Indian Ocean
172 L11 **Mozambique Escarpment** var. Mozambique Scarp. undersea feature SW Indian Ocean
Mozambique, People's Republic of see Mozambique
172 L10 **Mozambique Plateau** var. Mozambique Rise. undersea feature SW Indian Ocean
Mozambique, Republic of see Mozambique
Mozambique Rise see Mozambique Plateau
Mozambique Scarp see Mozambique Escarpment
127 O15 **Mozdok** Respublika Severnaya Osetiya, SW Russian Federation
57 K17 **Mozetenes, Serranías de** ▲▲ C Bolivia
126 J4 **Mozhaysk** Moskovskaya Oblast', W Russian Federation

◆ Country
● Country Capital
◇ Dependent Territory
○ Dependent Territory Capital
⬗ Administrative Regions
✈ International Airport
▲ Mountain
▲▲ Mountain Range
Volcano
≈ River
◎ Lake
⊠ Reservoir

127 T3 **Mozhga** Udmurtskaya Respublika, NW Russian Federation
Mozyr' see Mazyr
79 P22 **Mpala** Katanga, E Dem. Rep. Congo
79 G19 **Mpama** ≈ C Congo
81 E22 **Mpanda** Rukwa, W Tanzania
82 L11 **Mpande** Northern, NE Zambia
83 J18 **Mphoengs** Matabeleland South, SW Zimbabwe
81 F18 **Mpigi** S Uganda
82 L13 **Mpika** Northern, NE Zambia
83 J14 **Mpima** Central, C Zambia
82 J13 **Mpongwe** Copperbelt, C Zambia
82 K11 **Mporokoso** Northern, N Zambia
79 H20 **Mpouya** Plateaux, SE Congo
77 P16 **Mpraeso** C Ghana
82 L11 **Mpulungu** Northern, N Zambia
83 K21 **Mpumalanga** prev. Eastern Transvaal, Afr. Oos-Transvaal. ◈ province NE South Africa
83 D16 **Mpungu** Okavango, N Namibia
81 I22 **Mpwapwa** Dodoma, C Tanzania
Mqinvartsveri see Kazbek
110 M8 **Mragowo** Ger. Sensburg. Warmińsko-Mazurskie, NE Poland
127 V6 **Mrakovo** Respublika Bashkortostan, W Russian Federation
172 I13 **Mramani** Anjouan, E Comoros
112 F12 **Mrkonjić Grad** ◈ Republika Srpska, W Bosnia and Herzegovina
110 H9 **Mrocza** Kujawsko-pomorskie, C Poland
124 I14 **Msta** ≈ NW Russian Federation
Mstislavl' see Mstsislaw
119 P15 **Mstsislaw** Rus. Mstislavl'. Mahilyowskaya Voblasts', E Belarus
Mtkvari see Kura
Mtoko see Mutoko
126 K6 **Mtsensk** Orlovskaya Oblast', W Russian Federation
81 K24 **Mtwara** Mtwara, SE Tanzania
81 J25 **Mtwara** ◈ region SE Tanzania
104 G14 **Mu** ▲ S Portugal
193 V15 **Mu'a** Tongatapu, S Tonga
Muai To see Mae Hong Son
83 P16 **Mualama** Zambézia, NE Mozambique
Mualo see Messalo, Rio
79 E22 **Muanda** Bas-Congo, SW Dem. Rep. Congo
Muang Chiang Rai see Chiang Rai
167 R6 **Muang Ham** Houaphan, N Laos
167 S8 **Muang Hinboun** Khammouan, C Laos
Muang Kalasin see Kalasin
Muang Khammouan see Thakhèk
167 S11 **Muang Không** Champasak, S Laos
167 S10 **Muang Khôngxédôn** var. Khong Sedone. Salavan, S Laos
Muang Khon Kaen see Khon Kaen
167 Q6 **Muang Khoua** Phôngsali, N Laos
Muang Krabi see Krabi
Muang Lampang see Lampang
Muang Lamphun see Lamphun
Muang Loei see Loei
Muang Lom Sak see Lom Sak
Muang Nakhon Sawan see Nakhon Sawan
167 Q6 **Muang Namo** Oudômxai, N Laos
Muang Nan see Nan
167 Q6 **Muang Ngoy** Louangphabang, N Laos
167 Q5 **Muang Ou Tai** Phôngsali, N Laos
Muang Pak Lay see Pak Lay
Muang Pakxan see Pakxan
167 T10 **Muang Pakxong** Champasak, S Laos
167 S9 **Muang Phalan** var. Muang Phalane. Savannakhét, S Laos
Muang Phalane see Muang Phalan
Muang Phan see Phan
Muang Phayao see Phayao
Muang Phichit see Phichit
167 T9 **Muang Phin** Savannakhét, S Laos
Muang Phitsanulok see Phitsanulok
Muang Phrae see Phrae
Muang Roi Et see Roi Et
Muang Sakon Nakhon see Sakon Nakhon
Muang Samut Prakan see Samut Prakan
167 P6 **Muang Sing** Louang Namtha, N Laos
Muang Ubon see Ubon Ratchathani
Muang Uthai Thani see Uthai Thani
167 P7 **Muang Vangviang** Viangchan, C Laos
Muang Xaignabouri see Xaignabouli
Muang Xay see Xai
167 S9 **Muang Xépôn** var. Sepone. Savannakhét, S Laos
168 K10 **Muar** var. Bandar Maharani. Johor, Peninsular Malaysia
168 J9 **Muara** Sumatera, W Indonesia
168 L13 **Muarabeliti** Sumatera, W Indonesia
168 K12 **Muarabungo** Sumatera, W Indonesia
168 L13 **Muaraenim** Sumatera, W Indonesia
169 T11 **Muarajuloi** Borneo, C Indonesia
169 U12 **Muarakaman** Borneo, C Indonesia
168 H12 **Muarasigep** Pulau Siberut, W Indonesia
168 L12 **Muaratembesi** Sumatera, W Indonesia
169 T12 **Muaratewe** var. Muarateweh; prev. Moearatewe. Borneo, C Indonesia
Muarateweh see Muaratewe
169 U10 **Muarawahau** Borneo, N Indonesia
138 G13 **Mubārak, Jabal** ▲ S Jordan
153 N13 **Mubārakpur** Uttar Pradesh, N India
Mubarek see Muborak
81 F18 **Mubende** SW Uganda
77 Y14 **Mubi** Adamawa, NE Nigeria
146 M12 **Muborak** Rus. Mubarek. Qashqadaryo Viloyati, S Uzbekistan
171 U12 **Mubrani** Papua, E Indonesia
67 U12 **Muchinga Escarpment** escarpment NE Zambia
127 N7 **Muchkapskiy** Tambovskaya Oblast', W Russian Federation
96 G10 **Muck** island W Scotland, UK
82 Q13 **Mucojo** Cabo Delgado, N Mozambique
82 F12 **Muconda** Lunda Sul, NE Angola
54 I10 **Muco, Río** ≈ E Colombia
83 O16 **Mucubela** Zambézia, NE Mozambique
42 J5 **Mucupina, Monte** ▲ N Honduras
136 J14 **Mucur** Kirşehir, C Turkey
143 U8 **Mūd** Khorāsān-e Janūbī, E Iran
163 Y9 **Mudanjiang** var. Mu-tan-chiang. Heilongjiang, NE China
163 Y9 **Mudan Jiang** ≈ NE China
136 D11 **Mudanya** Bursa, NW Turkey
28 K8 **Mud Butte** South Dakota, N USA
155 G16 **Muddebihāl** Karnātaka, C India
27 P12 **Muddy Boggy Creek** ≈ Oklahoma, C USA
36 M6 **Muddy Creek** ≈ Utah, W USA
37 V7 **Muddy Creek Reservoir** ⊠ Colorado, C USA
33 W15 **Muddy Gap** Wyoming, C USA
35 Y11 **Muddy Peak** ▲ Nevada, W USA
183 R7 **Mudgee** New South Wales, SE Australia
29 S3 **Mud Lake** ◎ Minnesota, N USA
29 P7 **Mud Lake Reservoir** ⊠ South Dakota, N USA
167 N9 **Mudon** Mon State, S Myanmar (Burma)
81 O14 **Mudug** off. Gobolka Mudug. ◈ region NE Somalia
81 O14 **Mudug** var. Mudugh. plain N Somalia
Mudug, Gobolka see Mudug
Mudugh see Mudug
83 Q15 **Muecate** Nampula, NE Mozambique
82 Q13 **Mueda** Cabo Delgado, NE Mozambique
42 L10 **Muelle de los Bueyes** Región Autónoma Atlántico Sur, SE Nicaragua
Muenchen see München
83 M14 **Muende** Tete, NW Mozambique
25 T5 **Muenster** Texas, SW USA
Muenster see Münster
43 O6 **Muerto, Cayo** reef NE Nicaragua
41 T17 **Muerto, Mar** lagoon SE Mexico
64 F11 **Muertos Trough** undersea feature N Caribbean Sea
83 H14 **Mufaya Kuta** Western, NW Zambia
82 J13 **Mufulira** Copperbelt, C Zambia
161 O10 **Mufu Shan** ▲▲ C China
Mugalzhar Taūlary see Mugodzhary, Gory
137 Y12 **Muğan Düzü** Rus. Muganskaya Ravnina, Muganskaya Step'. physical region S Azerbaijan
Muganskaya Ravnina/ Muganskaya Step' see Muğan Düzü
106 K8 **Múggia** Friuli-Venezia Giulia, NE Italy
153 N14 **Mughal Sarāi** Uttar Pradesh, N India
Mughla see Muğla
141 W11 **Mughshin** var. Muqshin. S Oman
147 S12 **Mughsu** Rus. Muksu. ≈ C Tajikistan
164 H14 **Mugi** Tokushima, Shikoku, SW Japan
136 C16 **Muğla** var. Mughla. Muğla, SW Turkey
136 C16 **Muğla** var. Mughla. ◈ province SW Turkey
144 J11 **Mugodzhary, Gory** Kaz. Mugalzhar Taūlary. ▲▲ W Kazakhstan
83 O15 **Mugulama** Zambézia, NE Mozambique
Muḩāfaẓat Hims see Ḩimş
Muḩāfaẓat Ma'dabā see Ma'dabā
139 U9 **Muḩammad** E Iraq
139 R8 **Muḩammadīyah** C Iraq
80 I6 **Muhammad Qol** Red Sea, NE Sudan
75 Y9 **Muhammad, Râs** headland E Egypt
Muhammerah see Khorramshahr
Muḩāṭazat Al 'Aqabah see Al 'Aqabah
140 M12 **Muḩāyil** var. Mahāil. 'Asīr, SW Saudi Arabia
139 O7 **Muḩaywīr** W Iraq
101 H21 **Mühlacker** Baden-Württemberg, SW Germany
Mühlbach see Sebeş
Mühldorf see Mühldorf am Inn
101 N23 **Mühldorf am Inn** var. Mühldorf. Bayern, SE Germany
101 J15 **Mühlhausen** var. Mühlhausen in Thüringen. Thüringen, C Germany
Mühlhausen in Thüringen see Mühlhausen
195 Q2 **Mühlig-Hofmann Mountains** ▲▲ Antarctica
93 L14 **Muhos** Oulu, C Finland
138 K6 **Mūḩ, Sabkhat al** ◎ C Syria
118 E5 **Muhu** Ger. Mohn, Moon. island W Estonia
81 F19 **Muhutwe** Kagera, NW Tanzania
Muhu Väin see Väinameri
98 J10 **Muiden** Noord-Holland, C Netherlands
193 W15 **Mui Hopohoponga** headland Tongatapu, S Tonga
Muinchille see Cootehill
Muineachán see Monaghan
97 F19 **Muine Bheag** Eng. Bagenalstown. Carlow, SE Ireland
56 B5 **Muisne** Esmeraldas, NW Ecuador
83 P14 **Muite** Nampula, NE Mozambique
41 Z11 **Mujeres, Isla** island E Mexico
116 G7 **Mukacheve** Hung. Munkács, Rus. Mukachevo. Zakarpats'ka Oblast', W Ukraine
Mukachevo see Mukacheve
169 R9 **Mukah** Sarawak, East Malaysia
Mukalla see Al Mukallā
Mukama see Mokāma
Mukāshafa/Mukashshafah see Mukayshīfah
139 S6 **Mukayshīfah** var. Mukāshafa, Mukashshafah. N Iraq
167 R9 **Mukdahan** Mukdahan, E Thailand
Mukden see Shenyang
165 Y15 **Mukojima-rettō** Eng. Parry group. island group SE Japan
146 M14 **Mukry** Lebap Welaýaty, E Turkmenistan
Muksu see Mughsu
153 U14 **Muktagacha** var. Muktagachha. Dhaka. N Bangladesh
Muktagachha Dhaka see Muktagacha
82 K13 **Mukuku** Central, C Zambia
82 K11 **Mukupa Kaoma** Northern, NE Zambia
81 I18 **Mukutan** Rift Valley, W Kenya
83 F16 **Mukwe** Caprivi, NE Namibia
105 R13 **Mula** Murcia, SE Spain
151 K20 **Mulaku Atoll** var. Meemu Atoll. atoll C Maldives
83 J15 **Mulalika** Lusaka, C Zambia
163 X8 **Mulan** Heilongjiang, NE China
83 N15 **Mulanje** var. Mlanje. Southern, S Malawi
40 H5 **Mulatos** Sonora, NW Mexico
23 P3 **Mulberry Fork** ≈ Alabama, S USA
39 P12 **Mulchatna River** ≈ Alaska, USA
125 W4 **Mul'da** Respublika Komi, NW Russian Federation
101 M14 **Mulde** ≈ E Germany
27 R10 **Muldrow** Oklahoma, C USA
40 E7 **Mulegé** Baja California Sur, W Mexico
108 I10 **Mulegns** Graubünden, S Switzerland
79 M21 **Mulenda** Kasai Oriental, C Dem. Rep. Congo
24 M4 **Muleshoe** Texas, SW USA
83 O15 **Mulevala** Zambézia, NE Mozambique
183 P5 **Mulgoa Creek** seasonal river New South Wales, SE Australia
105 O15 **Mulhacén** var. Cerro de Mulhacén. ▲ S Spain
Mulhacén, Cerro de see Mulhacén
Mülhausen see Mulhouse
101 E24 **Mülheim** Baden-Württemberg, SW Germany
101 E15 **Mülheim** var. Mulheim an der Ruhr. Nordrhein-Westfalen, W Germany
Mulheim an der Ruhr see Mülheim
103 U7 **Mulhouse** Ger. Mülhausen. Haut-Rhin, NE France
160 G11 **Muli** var. Qiaowa, Muli Zangzu Zizhixian. Sichuan, C China
171 X15 **Muli** channel Papua, E Indonesia
163 Y9 **Muling** Heilongjiang, NE China
Muli Zangzu Zizhixian see Muli
Mullach Íde see Malahide
Mullaitivu see Mullaittivu
155 K23 **Mullaittivu** var. Mullaitivu. Northern Province, N Sri Lanka
33 N8 **Mullan** Idaho, NW USA
28 M13 **Mullen** Nebraska, C USA
183 Q6 **Mullengudgery** New South Wales, SE Australia
21 Q6 **Mullens** West Virginia, NE USA
Müller-gerbergte see Muller, Pegunungan
169 T10 **Muller, Pegunungan** Dut. Müller-gerbergte. ▲▲ Borneo, C Indonesia
31 Q5 **Mullett Lake** ◎ Michigan, N USA
18 J16 **Mullica River** ≈ New Jersey, NE USA
25 R8 **Mullin** Texas, SW USA
97 E17 **Mullingar** Ir. An Muileann gCearr. C Ireland
21 T12 **Mullins** South Carolina, SE USA
96 G11 **Mull, Isle of** island W Scotland, UK
127 R5 **Mullovka** Ul'yanovskaya Oblast', W Russian Federation
95 K19 **Mullsjö** Västra Götaland, S Sweden
183 V4 **Mullumbimby** New South Wales, SE Australia
83 H15 **Mulobezi** Western, SW Zambia
83 C15 **Mulondo** Huíla, SW Angola
83 G15 **Mulonga Plain** plain W Zambia
79 N23 **Mulongo** Katanga, SE Dem. Rep. Congo
149 T10 **Multān** Punjab, E Pakistan
93 L17 **Multia** Länsi-Soumi, C Finland
Mulucha see Moulouya
83 J14 **Mulungushi** Central, C Zambia
83 K14 **Mulungwe** Central, C Zambia
Muluya see Moulouya
27 N7 **Mulvane** Kansas, C USA
183 O10 **Mulwala** New South Wales, SE Australia
Mulwiya see Moulouya
182 K6 **Mulyungarie** South Australia
154 D13 **Mumbai** prev. Bombay. state capital Mahārāshtra, W India
154 D13 **Mumbai** ✕ Mahārāshtra, W India
83 D14 **Mumbué** Bié, C Angola
186 E8 **Mumeng** Morobe, C Papua New Guinea
171 V12 **Mumi** Papua, E Indonesia
Muminabad/Mŭ'minobod see Leningrad
127 Q13 **Mumra** Astrakhanskaya Oblast', SW Russian Federation
41 X12 **Muna** Yucatán, SE Mexico
123 O9 **Muna** ≈ NE Russian Federation
152 C12 **Munābāo** Rājasthān, NW India
Munamägi see Suur Munamägi
171 O14 **Muna, Pulau** prev. Moena. island C Indonesia
101 L18 **Münchberg** Bayern, E Germany
101 L23 **München** var. Muenchen, Eng. Munich, It. Monaco. Bayern, SE Germany
München-Gladbach see Mönchengladbach
108 E6 **Münchenstein** Basel-Land, NW Switzerland
10 L10 **Muncho Lake** British Columbia, W Canada
31 P13 **Muncie** Indiana, N USA
18 G13 **Muncy** Pennsylvania, NE USA
9 Q14 **Mundare** Alberta, SW Canada
25 Q5 **Munday** Texas, SW USA
31 N10 **Mundelein** Illinois, N USA
101 I15 **Münden** Niedersachsen, C Germany
105 Q12 **Mundo** ≈ S Spain
82 B12 **Munenga** Cuanza Sul, NW Angola
105 P11 **Munera** Castilla-La Mancha, C Spain
20 E9 **Munford** Tennessee, S USA
20 K7 **Munfordville** Kentucky, S USA
182 D5 **Mungala** South Australia
83 M16 **Mungári** Manica, C Mozambique
79 O16 **Mungbere** Orientale, NE Dem. Rep. Congo
153 Q13 **Munger** prev. Monghyr. Bihār, NE India
182 I2 **Mungeranie** South Australia
Mu Nggava see Rennell
169 O10 **Mungguresak, Tanjung** cape Borneo, N Indonesia
Mungiki see Bellona
183 R4 **Mungindi** New South Wales, SE Australia
Mungkawn see Maingkwan
153 T16 **Mungla** var. Mongla. Khulna, S Bangladesh
82 C13 **Mungo** Huambo, W Angola
188 F16 **Munguuy Bay** bay Yap, W Micronesia
82 E13 **Munhango** Bié, C Angola
Munich see München
105 S7 **Muniesa** Aragón, NE Spain
31 O4 **Munising** Michigan, N USA
Munkács see Mukacheve
95 I17 **Munkedal** Västra Götaland, S Sweden
95 K15 **Munkfors** Värmland, C Sweden
122 M14 **Munku-Sardyk, Gora** var. Mönh Sarĭdag. ▲ Mongolia/Russian Federation
99 E18 **Munkzwalm** Oost-Vlaanderen, NW Belgium
167 R10 **Mun, Mae Nam** ≈ E Thailand
153 U15 **Munshiganj** Dhaka, C Bangladesh
108 D8 **Münsingen** Bern, W Switzerland
103 U6 **Munster** Haut-Rhin, NE France
100 J11 **Munster** Niedersachsen, NW Germany
100 F13 **Münster** var. Muenster, Münster in Westfalen. Nordrhein-Westfalen, W Germany
108 F10 **Münster** Valais, S Switzerland
97 B20 **Munster** Ir. Cúige Mumhan. cultural region S Ireland
Münsterberg in Schlesien see Ziębice
Münster in Westfalen see Münster
100 E13 **Münsterland** cultural region NW Germany
100 F13 **Münster-Osnabruck** ✕ Nordrhein-Westfalen, NW Germany
31 R4 **Munuscong Lake** ◎ Michigan, N USA
83 K17 **Munyati** ≈ C Zimbabwe
109 R3 **Münzkirchen** Oberösterreich, N Austria
92 K11 **Muodoslompolo** Norrbotten, N Sweden
92 M13 **Muojärvi** ◎ NE Finland
167 S6 **Mương Khến** Hoa Binh, N Vietnam
Muong Sai see Xai
167 Q7 **Muong Xiang Ngeun** var. Xieng Ngeun. Louangphabang, N Laos
92 K11 **Muonio** Lappi, N Finland
Muonioälv/Muoniojoki see Muonionjoki
92 K11 **Muonionjoki** var. Muoniojoki, Swe. Muonioälv. ≈ Finland/Sweden
83 N17 **Mupa** ≈ C Mozambique
83 E16 **Mupini** Okavango, NE Namibia
80 F8 **Muqaddam, Wadi** ≈ N Sudan
138 K9 **Muqāṭ** Al Mafraq, E Jordan
141 X7 **Muqaz** N Oman
81 N17 **Muqdisho** Eng. Mogadishu, It. Mogadiscio. ● (Somalia) Banaadir, S Somalia
81 N17 **Muqdisho** ✕ Banaadir, E Somalia
Muqshin see Mughshin
109 T8 **Mur** SCr. Mura. ≈ C Europe
109 X9 **Mura** ≈ NE Slovenia
Mura see Mur
137 T14 **Muradiye** Van, E Turkey
Muragarazi see Maragarazi
165 O10 **Murakami** Niigata, Honshū, C Japan
63 G22 **Murallón, Cerro** ▲ S Argentina
81 E20 **Muramvya** C Burundi
81 I19 **Murang'a** prev. Fort Hall. Central, SW Kenya
81 H16 **Murangering** Rift Valley, NW Kenya
Murapara see Murupara
140 M5 **Murār, Bi'r al** well NW Saudi Arabia
125 Q13 **Murashi** Kirovskaya Oblast', NW Russian Federation
103 O12 **Murat** Cantal, C France
114 N12 **Muratlı** Tekirdağ, NW Turkey
137 R14 **Murat Nehri** var. Eastern Euphrates; anc. Arsanias. ≈ NE Turkey
107 D20 **Muravera** Sardegna, Italy, C Mediterranean Sea
165 P10 **Murayama** Yamagata, Honshū, C Japan
121 R13 **Muraysah, Ra's al** headland N Libya
104 I6 **Murça** Vila Real, N Portugal
80 Q11 **Murcanyo** Bari, NE Somalia
143 N8 **Mürcheh Khvort** var. Morcheh Khort. Eşfahān, C Iran
185 H15 **Murchison** Tasman, South Island, New Zealand
185 B22 **Murchison Mountains** ▲▲ South Island, New Zealand
180 I10 **Murchison River** ≈ Western Australia
105 R13 **Murcia** Murcia, SE Spain
105 Q13 **Murcia** ◈ autonomous community SE Spain
103 O13 **Mur-de-Barrez** Aveyron, S France
182 G8 **Murdinga** South Australia
28 M10 **Murdo** South Dakota, N USA
15 X6 **Murdochville** Québec, SE Canada
109 W9 **Mureck** Steiermark, SE Austria
114 M13 **Mürefte** Tekirdağ, NW Turkey
116 I10 **Mureş** ◈ county N Romania
84 J11 **Mureş** ≈ Hungary/Romania
Mureş see Maros
Mureşul see Maros/Mureş
102 M16 **Muret** Haute-Garonne, S France
27 T13 **Murfreesboro** Arkansas, C USA
21 W8 **Murfreesboro** North Carolina, SE USA
20 J9 **Murfreesboro** Tennessee, S USA
Murgab see Morghāb, Daryā-ye/Murgap
Murgab see Murghob
146 I14 **Murgap** Rus. Murgap. Mary Welaýaty, S Turkmenistan
146 J16 **Murgap** var. Deryasy Murgap, Murghab, Pash. Daryā-ye Morghāb, Rus. Murgab. ≈ Afghanistan/Turkmenistan see also Morghāb, Daryā-ye
Murgap see Morghāb, Daryā-ye
Murgap, Deryasy see Morghāb, Daryā-ye/Murgap
114 H9 **Murgash** ▲ W Bulgaria
Murghab see Morghāb, Daryā-ye/Murgap
147 U13 **Murghob** Rus. Murgab. SE Tajikistan
147 U13 **Murghob** Rus. Murgab. ≈ SE Tajikistan
181 Z10 **Murgon** Queensland, E Australia
190 I16 **Muri** Rarotonga, S Cook Islands
108 F7 **Muri** Aargau, W Switzerland
108 D8 **Muri** var. Muri bei Bern. Bern, W Switzerland
104 K3 **Murias de Paredes** Castilla-León, N Spain
Muri bei Bern see Muri
82 F11 **Muriege** Lunda Sul, NE Angola
189 P14 **Murilo Atoll** atoll Hall Islands, C Micronesia
Mūrītāniyah see Mauritania
100 N10 **Müritz** var. Müritzee. ◎ NE Germany
Müritzee see Müritz
100 L10 **Müritz-Elde-Kanal** canal N Germany
184 K6 **Muriwai Beach** Auckland, North Island, New Zealand
92 J13 **Murjek** Norrbotten, N Sweden
124 J3 **Murmansk** Murmanskaya Oblast', NW Russian Federation
124 I4 **Murmanskaya Oblast'** ◈ province NW Russian Federation
197 V14 **Murmansk Rise** undersea feature SW Barents Sea
124 J3 **Murmashi** Murmanskaya Oblast', NW Russian Federation
126 M5 **Murmino** Ryazanskaya Oblast', W Russian Federation
101 K24 **Murnau** Bayern, SE Germany
103 X16 **Muro, Capo di** headland Corse, France, C Mediterranean Sea
107 M18 **Muro Lucano** Basilicata, S Italy
127 N4 **Murom** Vladimirskaya Oblast', W Russian Federation
122 I11 **Muromtsevo** Omskaya Oblast', C Russian Federation
165 R5 **Muroran** Hokkaidō, NE Japan
104 G3 **Muros** Galicia, NW Spain
104 F3 **Muros e Noia, Ría de** estuary NW Spain
164 H15 **Muroto** Kōchi, Shikoku, SW Japan
164 H15 **Muroto-zaki** Shikoku, SW Japan
116 L7 **Murovani Kurylivtsi** Vinnyts'ka Oblast', C Ukraine
110 G11 **Murowana Goślina** Wielkolpolskie, W Poland
32 M14 **Murphy** Idaho, NW USA
21 N10 **Murphy** North Carolina, SE USA
35 P8 **Murphys** California, W USA
30 L17 **Murphysboro** Illinois, N USA
29 V15 **Murray** Iowa, C USA
20 H8 **Murray** Kentucky, S USA
182 J10 **Murray Bridge** SE Australia
175 X2 **Murray Fracture Zone** tectonic feature NE Pacific Ocean
192 H11 **Murray, Lake** ◎ SW Papua New Guinea
21 P12 **Murray, Lake** ⊠ South Carolina, SE USA
10 K8 **Murray, Mount** ▲ Yukon Territory, NW Canada
Murray Range see Murray Ridge
173 O3 **Murray Ridge** var. Murray Range. undersea feature N Arabian Sea
183 N10 **Murray River** ≈ SE Australia
182 K10 **Murrayville** Victoria, SE Australia
149 U5 **Murree** Punjab, E Pakistan
101 I21 **Murrhardt** Baden-Württemberg, S Germany
183 O9 **Murrumbidgee River** ≈ New South Wales, SE Australia
83 P15 **Murrupula** Nampula, NE Mozambique
183 T7 **Murrurundi** New South Wales, SE Australia
109 X9 **Murska Sobota** Ger. Olsnitz. NE Slovenia
154 G12 **Murtajāpur** prev. Murtazapur. Mahārāshtra, C India
77 S16 **Murtala Muhammed** ✕ (Lagos) Ogun, SW Nigeria
Murtazapur see Murtajāpur
108 C8 **Murten** Neuchâtel, W Switzerland
Murtensee see Morat, Lac de
182 L11 **Murtoa** Victoria, SE Australia
92 N13 **Murtovaara** Oulu, E Finland
Murua Island see Woodlark Island
155 D14 **Murud** Mahārāshtra, W India
184 O9 **Murupara** var. Murapara. Bay of Plenty, North Island, New Zealand
191 X12 **Mururoa** var. Moruroa. atoll Îles Tuamotu, SE French Polynesia
Murviedro see Sagunto
154 J9 **Murwāra** Madhya Pradesh, N India
183 V4 **Murwillumbah** New South Wales, SE Australia
146 H11 **Murzechirla** prev. Mirzachirla. Ahal Welaýaty, C Turkmenistan
Murzuk see Murzuq
75 O11 **Murzuq** var. Marzūq, Murzuk. SW Libya
Murzuq, Edeyin see Murzuq, Idhān
75 N11 **Murzuq, Ḩamādat** plateau W Libya
75 O11 **Murzuq, Idhān** var. Edeyin Murzuq. desert SW Libya
109 W6 **Mürzzuschlag** Steiermark, E Austria
137 Q14 **Muş** var. Mush. Muş, E Turkey
137 Q14 **Muş** var. Mush. ◈ province E Turkey
118 G11 **Mūša** ≈ Latvia/Lithuania
186 F9 **Musa** ≈ S Papua New Guinea
75 X8 **Mûsa, Gebel** ▲ NE Egypt
Musaiyib see Al Musayyib
Musa Khel see Mūsa Khel Bāzār
149 R9 **Mūsa Khel Bāzār** var. Musa Khel. Baluchistān, SW Pakistan
114 H10 **Musala** ▲ W Bulgaria
168 H10 **Musala, Pulau** island W Indonesia
83 I15 **Musale** Southern, S Zambia
141 Y9 **Muşalla** NE Oman
141 W6 **Musandam Peninsula** Ar. Masandam Peninsula. peninsula N Oman
Musay'id see Umm Sa'id
Muscat see Masqaṭ
Muscat and Oman see Oman
29 Y14 **Muscatine** Iowa, C USA
Muscat Slb Airport see Seeb
31 O15 **Muscatuck River** ≈ Indiana, N USA
30 K8 **Muscoda** Wisconsin, N USA
185 F19 **Musgrave, Mount** ▲ South Island, New Zealand
181 P9 **Musgrave Ranges** ▲▲ South Australia
Mush see Muş
138 H12 **Mushayyish, Qaşr al** castle Ma'ān, C Jordan
79 H20 **Mushie** Bandundu, W Dem. Rep. Congo
168 M13 **Musi, Air** prev. Moesi. ≈ Sumatera, W Indonesia
192 M4 **Musicians Seamounts** undersea feature N Pacific Ocean
83 K19 **Musina** prev. Messina. Limpopo, NE South Africa
54 D8 **Musinga, Alto** ▲ NW Colombia
29 T2 **Muskeg Bay** lake bay Minnesota, N USA
31 O8 **Muskegon** Michigan, N USA
31 O8 **Muskegon Heights** Michigan, N USA
31 P8 **Muskegon River** ≈ Michigan, N USA
31 T14 **Muskingum River** ≈ Ohio, N USA
95 P16 **Muskö** Stockholm, C Sweden
Muskogean see Tallahassee
27 Q10 **Muskogee** Oklahoma, C USA
14 H13 **Muskoka, Lake** ◎ Ontario, S Canada
80 H8 **Musmar** Red Sea, NE Sudan
83 K14 **Musofu** Central, C Zambia
81 G19 **Musoma** Mara, N Tanzania
82 L13 **Musoro** Central, C Zambia
186 F4 **Mussau Island** island NE Papua New Guinea
98 P7 **Musselkanaal** Groningen, NE Netherlands
33 V9 **Musselshell River** ≈ Montana, NW USA
82 C12 **Mussende** Cuanza Sul, NW Angola
102 L12 **Mussidan** Dordogne, SW France
99 L25 **Musson** Luxembourg, SE Belgium
152 J9 **Mussoorie** Uttaranchal, N India
Musta see Mosta
152 M13 **Mustafābād** Uttar Pradesh, N India

◆ Country ● Country Capital ◇ Dependent Territory ○ Dependent Territory Capital ◈ Administrative Regions ✕ International Airport ▲ Mountain ▲▲ Mountain Range Volcano ≈ River ◎ Lake ⊠ Reservoir

136 *D12* **Mustafakemalpaşa** Bursa, NW Turkey
Mustafa-Pasha *see* Svilengrad
81 *M15* **Mustahīl** Somali, E Ethiopia
24 *M7* **Mustang Draw** *valley* Texas, SW USA
25 *T14* **Mustang Island** *island* Texas, SW USA
Mustasaari *see* Korsholm
Mustér *see* Disentis
63 *I19* **Musters, Lago** ◎ S Argentina
45 *Y14* **Mustique** *island* C Saint Vincent and the Grenadines
118 *I6* **Mustla** Viljandimaa, S Estonia
118 *J4* **Mustvee** ***Ger.*** Tschorna. Jõgevamaa, E Estonia
42 *L9* **Musún, Cerro** ▲ NE Nicaragua
183 *T7* **Muswellbrook** New South Wales, SE Australia
111 *M18* **Muszyna** Małopolskie, SE Poland
75 *V10* **Mût** ***var.*** Mut. C Egypt
136 *I17* **Mut** Mersin, S Turkey
109 *V9* **Muta** N Slovenia
190 *B15* **Mutalau** N Niue
Mu-tan-chiang *see* Mudanjiang
82 *I13* **Mutanda** North Western, NW Zambia
59 *O17* **Mutá, Ponta do** *headland* E Brazil
83 *L17* **Mutare** ***var.*** Mutari; ***prev.*** Umtali. Manicaland, E Zimbabwe
Mutari *see* Mutare
54 *D8* **Mutatá** Antioquia, NW Colombia
Mutina *see* Modena
83 *L16* **Mutoko** ***prev.*** Mtoko. Mashonaland East, NE Zimbabwe
81 *J20* **Mutomo** Eastern, S Kenya
Mutrah *see* Maṭraḥ
Mutsamudu *see* Moutsamoudou
79 *M24* **Mutshatsha** Katanga, S Dem. Rep. Congo
165 *R6* **Mutsu** ***var.*** Mutu. Aomori, Honshū, N Japan
165 *R6* **Mutsu-wan** *bay* N Japan
108 *E6* **Muttenz** Basel-Land, NW Switzerland
185 *A26* **Muttonbird Islands** *island group* SW New Zealand
Muttra *see* Mathura
Mutu *see* Mutsu
83 *O15* **Mutuáli** Nampula, N Mozambique
82 *D13* **Mutumbo** Bié, C Angola
189 *Y14* **Mutunte, Mount** ***var.*** Mount Buache. ▲ Kosrae, E Micronesia
155 *K24* **Mutur** Eastern Province, E Sri Lanka
92 *L13* **Muurola** Lappi, NW Finland
162 *M14* **Mu Us Shadi** ***var.*** Ordos Desert; ***prev.*** Mu Us Shamo. *desert* N China
Mu Us Shamo *see* Mu Us Shadi
82 *B11* **Muxima** Bengo, NW Angola
124 *I8* **Muyezerskiy** Respublika Kareliya, NW Russian Federation
81 *E20* **Muyinga** NE Burundi
42 *K9* **Muy Muy** Matagalpa, C Nicaragua
Muynak *see* Moʻynoq
79 *N22* **Muyumba** Katanga, SE Dem. Rep. Congo
149 *V5* **Muzaffarābād** Jammu and Kashmir, NE Pakistan
149 *S10* **Muzaffargarh** Punjab, E Pakistan
152 *J9* **Muzaffarnagar** Uttar Pradesh, N India
153 *P13* **Muzaffarpur** Bihār, N India
158 *H6* **Muzat He** ≈ W China
83 *L15* **Muze** Tete, NW Mozambique
122 *H8* **Muzhi** Yamalo-Nenetskiy Avtonomnyy Okrug, N Russian Federation
102 *H7* **Muzillac** Morbihan, NW France
Muzkol, Khrebet *see* Muzqŭl, Qatorkŭhi
112 *L9* **Mužlja** ***Hung.*** Felsőmuzslya; ***prev.*** Gornja Mužlja. Vojvodina, N Serbia
54 *F9* **Muzo** Boyacá, C Colombia
83 *J15* **Muzoka** Southern, S Zambia
39 *Y15* **Muzon, Cape** *headland* Dall Island, Alaska, USA
40 *M6* **Múzquiz** Coahuila de Zaragoza, NE Mexico
147 *U13* **Muzqŭl, Qatorkŭhi** ***Rus.*** Khrebet Muzkol. ▲▲ SE Tajikistan
158 *G10* **Muztag** ▲ NW China
158 *K10* **Muztag** ▲ W China
158 *D8* **Muztagata** ▲ NW China
83 *K17* **Mvuma** ***prev.*** Umvuma. Midlands, C Zimbabwe
Mwali *see* Mohéli
82 *L13* **Mwanya** Eastern, E Zambia
79 *N23* **Mwanza** Katanga, SE Dem. Rep. Congo
81 *G20* **Mwanza** Mwanza, NW Tanzania
81 *F20* **Mwanza** ⬖ *region* N Tanzania
82 *M13* **Mwase Lundazi** Eastern, E Zambia
97 *B17* **Mweelrea** ***Ir.*** Caoc Maol Réidh. ▲ W Ireland
79 *K21* **Mweka** Kasai Occidental, C Dem. Rep. Congo
82 *K12* **Mwenda** Luapula, N Zambia
79 *L22* **Mwene-Ditu** Kasai Oriental, S Dem. Rep. Congo
83 *L18* **Mwenezi** ≈ S Zimbabwe
79 *O20* **Mwenga** Sud Kivu, E Dem. Rep. Congo
82 *K11* **Mweru, Lake** ***var.*** Lac Moero. ◎ Dem. Rep. Congo/Zambia
82 *H13* **Mwinilunga** North Western, NW Zambia
189 *V16* **Mwokil Atoll** ***prev.*** Mokil Atoll. *atoll* Caroline Islands, E Micronesia
Myadel' *see* Myadzyel
118 *J13* **Myadzyel** ***Pol.*** Miadzioł Nowy, ***Rus.*** Myadel'. Minskaya Voblasts', N Belarus
152 *C12* **Myājlār** ***var.*** Miajlar. Rājasthān, NW India
123 *T9* **Myakit** Magadanskaya Oblast', E Russian Federation
23 *W13* **Myakka River** ≈ Florida, SE USA
124 *L14* **Myaksa** Vologodskaya Oblast', NW Russian Federation
183 *U8* **Myall Lake** ◎ New South Wales, SE Australia
166 *L7* **Myanaung** Irrawaddy, SW Myanmar (Burma)
166 *M4* **Myanmar** ***off.*** Union of Myanmar. ◆ *military dictatorship* SE Asia
166 *K8* **Myaungmya** Irrawaddy, SW Myanmar (Burma)
118 *N11* **Myazha** ***Rus.*** Mezha. Vitsyebskaya Voblasts', NE Belarus
119 *O18* **Myerkulavichy** ***Rus.*** Merkulovichi. Homyel'skaya Voblasts', SE Belarus
119 *N14* **Myezhava** ***Rus.*** Mezhëvo. Vitsyebskaya Voblasts', NE Belarus
Myggenaes *see* Mykines
166 *L5* **Myingyan** Mandalay, C Myanmar (Burma)
167 *N12* **Myitkyina** Kachin State, N Myanmar (Burma)
166 *M5* **Myittha** Mandalay, C Myanmar (Burma)
111 *H19* **Myjava** ***Hung.*** Miava. Trenčiansky Kraj, W Slovakia
Myjeldino *see* Myyëldino
117 *U9* **Mykhaylivka** ***Rus.*** Mikhaylovka. Zaporiz'ka Oblast', SE Ukraine
95 *A18* **Mykines** ***Dan.*** Myggenaes. *island* W Faeroe Islands
116 *I5* **Mykolayiv** L'vivs'ka Oblast', W Ukraine
117 *Q10* **Mykolayiv** ***Rus.*** Nikolayev. Mykolayivs'ka Oblast', S Ukraine
117 *Q10* **Mykolayiv** ✕ Mykolayivs'ka Oblast', S Ukraine
Mykolayiv *see* Mykolayivs'ka Oblast'
117 *P9* **Mykolayivka** Odes'ka Oblast', SW Ukraine
117 *S13* **Mykolayivka** Respublika Krym, S Ukraine
117 *P9* **Mykolayivs'ka Oblast'** ***var.*** Mykolayiv, ***Rus.*** Nikolayevskaya Oblast'. ⬖ *province* S Ukraine
115 *J20* **Mýkonos** Mńykonos, Kykládes, Greece, Aegean Sea
115 *K20* **Mýkonos** ***var.*** Míkonos. *island* Kykládes, Greece, Aegean Sea
125 *R7* **Myla** Respublika Komi, NW Russian Federation
Mylae *see* Milazzo
93 *M19* **Myllykoski** Etelä-Suomi, S Finland
Mymensing *see* Mymensingh
153 *U14* **Mymensingh** ***var.*** Maimansingh, Mymensing; ***prev.*** Nasirābād. Dhaka, N Bangladesh
93 *K19* **Mynämäki** Länsi-Soumi, SW Finland
145 *S14* **Mynaral** ***Kaz.*** Myngaral. Zhambyl, S Kazakhstan
Mynbulak *see* Mingbuloq
Mynbulak, Vpadina *see* Mingbuloq BotigʻI
Myngaral *see* Mynaral
166 *K5* **Myohaung** Arakan State, W Myanmar (Burma)
163 *W13* **Myohyang-sanmaek** ▲▲ C North Korea
164 *M11* **Myōkō-san** ▲ Honshū, S Japan
83 *J15* **Myooye** Central, C Zambia
118 *K12* **Myory** ***prev.*** Miyory. Vitsyebskaya Voblasts', N Belarus
92 *J4* **Mýrdalsjökull** *glacier* S Iceland
92 *G10* **Myre** Nordland, C Norway
117 *S5* **Myrhorod** ***Rus.*** Mirgorod. Poltavs'ka Oblast', NE Ukraine
115 *J15* **Mýrina** ***var.*** Mírina. Límnos, SE Greece
117 *P5* **Myronivka** ***Rus.*** Mironovka. Kyyivs'ka Oblast', N Ukraine
21 *U13* **Myrtle Beach** South Carolina, SE USA
32 *F14* **Myrtle Creek** Oregon, NW USA
183 *P11* **Myrtleford** Victoria, SE Australia
32 *E14* **Myrtle Point** Oregon, NW USA
115 *K25* **Mýrtos** Kríti, Greece, E Mediterranean Sea
Myrtoum Mare *see* Mirtóo Pélagos
93 *G17* **Myrviken** Jämtland, C Sweden
95 *I15* **Mysen** Østfold, S Norway
124 *L15* **Myshkin** Yaroslavskaya Oblast', NW Russian Federation
111 *K17* **Myślenice** Malopolskie, S Poland
110 *D10* **Myślibórz** Zachodnio-pomorskie, NW Poland
155 *G20* **Mysore** ***var.*** Maisur. Karnātaka, W India
Mysore *see* Karnātaka
115 *F21* **Mystrás** ***var.*** Mistras. Pelopónnisos, S Greece
125 *T12* **Mysy** Permskaya Oblast', NW Russian Federation
111 *K15* **Myszków** Ślaskie, S Poland
167 *T14* **My Tho** ***var.*** Mi Tho. Tiên Giang, S Vietnam
Mytilene *see* Mytilíni
115 *L17* **Mytilíni** ***var.*** Mitilíni; ***anc.*** Mytilene. Lésvos, E Greece
126 *K3* **Mytishchi** Moskovskaya Oblast', W Russian Federation
37 *N3* **Myton** Utah, W USA
92 *K2* **Mývatn** ◎ C Iceland
125 *T11* **Myyëldino** ***var.*** Myjeldino. Respublika Komi, NW Russian Federation
82 *M13* **Mzimba** Northern, NW Malawi
82 *M12* **Mzuzu** Northern, N Malawi

N

101 *M19* **Naab** ≈ SE Germany
98 *G12* **Naaldwijk** Zuid-Holland, W Netherlands
38 *G12* **Nāʻālehu** ***var.*** Naalehu. Hawaiʻi, USA, C Pacific Ocean
93 *K19* **Naantali** ***Swe.*** Nådendal. Länsi-Soumi, SW Finland
98 *J10* **Naarden** Noord-Holland, C Netherlands
109 *U4* **Naarn** ≈ N Austria
97 *F18* **Naas** ***Ir.*** An Nás, Nás na Ríogh. Kildare, C Ireland
92 *M9* **Näätämöjoki** ***Lapp.*** Njávdám. ≈ NE Finland
83 *E23* **Nababeep** ***var.*** Nababiep. Northern Cape, W South Africa
Nababiep *see* Nababeep
Nabadwip *see* Navadwīp
164 *J14* **Nabari** Mie, Honshū, SW Japan
Nabatié *see* Nabatîyé
138 *G8* **Nabatîyé** ***var.*** An Nabatīyah at Taḥtā, Nabatié, Nabatiyet et Tahta. SW Lebanon
Nabatiyet et Tahta *see* Nabatîyé
187 *X14* **Nabavatu** Vanua Levu, N Fiji
190 *I2* **Nabeina** *island* Tungaru, W Kiribati
127 *T4* **Naberezhnyye Chelny** ***prev.*** Brezhnev. Respublika Tatarstan, W Russian Federation
39 *T10* **Nabesna** Alaska, USA
39 *T10* **Nabesna River** ≈ Alaska, USA
75 *N5* **Nabeul** ***var.*** Nābul. NE Tunisia
152 *I9* **Nābha** Punjab, NW India
171 *W13* **Nabire** Papua, E Indonesia
141 *O15* **Nabī Shuʻayb, Jabal an** ▲ W Yemen
138 *F10* **Nablus** ***var.*** Nābulus, ***Heb.*** Shekhem; ***anc.*** Neapolis, ***Bibl.*** Shechem. N West Bank
187 *X14* **Nabouwalu** Vanua Levu, N Fiji
Nābul *see* Nabeul
Nābulus *see* Nablus
187 *Y13* **Nabuna** Vanua Levu, N Fiji
83 *Q14* **Nacala** Nampula, NE Mozambique
42 *H8* **Nacaome** Valle, S Honduras
Na Cealla Beaga *see* Killybegs
Na-Ch'ii *see* Nagqu
164 *J15* **Nachikatsuura** ***var.*** Nachi-Katsuura. Wakayama, Honshū, SE Japan
Nachi-Katsuura *see* Nachikatsuura
81 *J24* **Nachingwea** Lindi, SE Tanzania
111 *F16* **Náchod** Královéhradecký Kraj, N Czech Republic
Na Clocha Liatha *see* Greystones
40 *G3* **Naco** Sonora, NW Mexico
25 *X8* **Nacogdoches** Texas, SW USA
40 *G4* **Nacozari de García** Sonora, NW Mexico
Nada *see* Danzhou
77 *O14* **Nadawli** NW Ghana
104 *I3* **Nadela** Galicia, NW Spain
Nådendal *see* Naantali
144 *M7* **Nadezhdinka** ***prev.*** Nadezhdinskiy. Kostanay, N Kazakhstan
Nadezhdinskiy *see* Nadezhdinka
Nadgan *see* Nadqān, Qalamat
187 *W14* **Nadi** ***prev.*** Nandi. Viti Levu, W Fiji
187 *X14* **Nadi** ***prev.*** Nandi. ✕ Viti Levu, W Fiji
154 *D10* **Nadiād** Gujarāt, W India
Ṇadikdik *see* Knox Atoll
116 *E11* **Nădlac** ***Ger.*** Nadlak, ***Hung.*** Nagylak. Arad, W Romania
Nadlak *see* Nădlac
74 *H6* **Nador** ***prev.*** Villa Nador. NE Morocco
141 *S9* **Nadqān, Qalamat** ***var.*** Nadgan. *well* E Saudi Arabia
111 *N22* **Nádudvar** Hajdú-Bihar, E Hungary
121 *O15* **Nadur** Gozo, N Malta
187 *X13* **Naduri** ***prev.*** Nanduri. Vanua Levu, N Fiji
116 *I7* **Nadvirna** ***Pol.*** Nadwórna, ***Rus.*** Nadvornaya. Ivano-Frankivs'ka Oblast', W Ukraine
124 *J8* **Nadvoitsy** Respublika Kareliya, NW Russian Federation
Nadvornaya/Nadwórna *see* Nadvirna
122 *I9* **Nadym** Yamalo-Nenetskiy Avtonomnyy Okrug, N Russian Federation
122 *I9* **Nadym** ≈ C Russian Federation
186 *E7* **Nadzab** Morobe, C Papua New Guinea
95 *C17* **Nærbø** Rogaland, S Norway
95 *I24* **Næstved** Storstrøm, SE Denmark
77 *X13* **Nafada** Gombe, E Nigeria
108 *H8* **Näfels** Glarus, NE Switzerland
115 *E18* **Náfpaktos** ***var.*** Návpaktos. Dytikí Ellás, C Greece
115 *F20* **Náfplio** ***prev.*** Návplion. Pelopónnisos, S Greece
139 *U6* **Nafṭ Khāneh** E Iraq
149 *N13* **Nāg** Baluchistān, SW Pakistan
171 *P4* **Naga** ***off.*** Naga City; ***prev.*** Nueva Caceres. Luzon, N Philippines
Nagaarzê *see* Nagarzê
Naga City *see* Naga
12 *F11* **Nagagami** ≈ Ontario, S Canada
164 *F14* **Nagahama** Ehime, Shikoku, SW Japan
153 *X12* **Nāga Hills** ▲▲ NE India
165 *P10* **Nagai** Yamagata, Honshū, C Japan
Na Gaibhlte *see* Galty Mountains
39 *N16* **Nagai Island** *island* Shumagin Islands, Alaska, USA
153 *X12* **Nāgāland** ⬖ *state* NE India
164 *M11* **Nagano** Nagano, Honshū, S Japan
164 *M12* **Nagano** ***off.*** Nagano-ken. ⬖ *prefecture* Honshū, S Japan
Nagano-ken *see* Nagano
165 *N11* **Nagaoka** Niigata, Honshū, C Japan
153 *W12* **Nagaon** ***var.*** Nowgong. Assam, NE India
155 *J21* **Nāgappattinam** ***var.*** Negapatam, Negapattinam. Tamil Nādu, SE India
Nagara Nayok *see* Nakhon Nayok
Nagara Panom *see* Nakhon Phanom
Nagara Pathom *see* Nakhon Pathom
Nagara Sridharmaraj *see* Nakhon Si Thammarat
Nagara Svarga *see* Nakhon Sawan
155 *H16* **Nāgārjuna Sāgar** ⊠ E India
42 *I10* **Nagarote** León, SW Nicaragua
158 *M16* **Nagarzê** ***var.*** Nagaarzê. Xizang Zizhiqu, W China
164 *C14* **Nagasaki** Nagasaki, Kyūshū, SW Japan
164 *C14* **Nagasaki** ***off.*** Nagasaki-ken. ⬖ *prefecture* Kyūshū, SW Japan
Nagasaki-ken *see* Nagasaki
Nagashima *see* Kii-Nagashima
164 *E12* **Nagato** Yamaguchi, Honshū, SW Japan
152 *F11* **Nāgaur** Rājasthān, NW India
154 *F10* **Nāgda** Madhya Pradesh, C India
98 *L8* **Nagele** Flevoland, N Netherlands
155 *H24* **Nāgercoil** Tamil Nādu, SE India
153 *X12* **Nāginimāra** Nāgāland, NE India
Na Gleannta *see* Glenties
165 *T16* **Nago** Okinawa, Okinawa, SW Japan
154 *K9* **Nāgod** Madhya Pradesh, C India
155 *J26* **Nagoda** Southern Province, S Sri Lanka
101 *G22* **Nagold** Baden-Württemberg, SW Germany
137 *V12* **Nagorno-Karabakh** ***var.*** Nagorno- Karabakhskaya Avtonomnaya Oblast, ***Arm.*** Lerrnayin Gharabakh, ***Az.*** Dağliq Quarabağ, ***Rus.*** Nagornyy Karabakh. *former autonomous region* SW Azerbaijan
Nagorno- Karabakhskaya Avtonomnaya Oblast *see* Nagorno-Karabakh
123 *Q12* **Nagornyy** Respublika Sakha (Yakutiya), NE Russian Federation
Nagornyy Karabakh *see* Nagorno-Karabakh
125 *R13* **Nagorsk** Kirovskaya Oblast', NW Russian Federation
164 *K13* **Nagoya** Aichi, Honshū, SW Japan
154 *I12* **Nāgpur** Mahārāshtra, C India
156 *K10* **Nagqu** ***Chin.*** Na-Ch'ii; ***prev.*** Hei-ho. Xizang Zizhiqu, W China
152 *J8* **Nāg Tibba Range** ▲▲ N India
45 *O8* **Nagua** NE Dominican Republic
111 *H25* **Nagyatád** Somogy, SW Hungary
Nagybánya *see* Baia Mare
Nagybecskerek *see* Zrenjanin
Nagydisznód *see* Cisnădie
Nagyenyed *see* Aiud
111 *N21* **Nagykálló** Szabolcs-Szatmár-Bereg, E Hungary
111 *G25* **Nagykanizsa** ***Ger.*** Grosskanizsa. Zala, SW Hungary
Nagykároly *see* Carei
111 *K22* **Nagykáta** Pest, C Hungary
Nagykikinda *see* Kikinda
111 *K23* **Nagykőrös** Pest, C Hungary
Nagy-Küküllő *see* Târnava Mare
Nagylak *see* Nădlac
Nagymihály *see* Michalovce
Nagyrőce *see* Revúca
Nagysomkút *see* Şomcuta Mare
Nagysurány *see* Šurany
Nagyszalonta *see* Salonta
Nagyszeben *see* Sibiu
Nagyszentmiklós *see* Sânnicolau Mare
Nagyszöllös *see* Vynohradiv
Nagyszombat *see* Trnava
Nagytapolcsány *see* Topoľčany
Nagyvárad *see* Oradea
165 *S17* **Naha** Okinawa, Okinawa, SW Japan
152 *J8* **Nāhan** Himāchal Pradesh, NW India
Nahang, Rūd-e *see* Nihing
Nahariya *see* Nahariyya
138 *F8* **Nahariyya** ***var.*** Nahariya. Northern, N Israel
142 *L6* **Nahāvand** ***var.*** Nehavend. Hamadān, W Iran
101 *F19* **Nahe** ≈ SW Germany
Na H-Iarmhidhe *see* Westmeath
189 *O13* **Nahnalaud** ▲ Pohnpei, E Micronesia
Nahoi, Cape *see* Cumberland, Cape
Nahtavárr *see* Nattavaara
63 *H16* **Nahuel Huapí, Lago** ◎ W Argentina
23 *W7* **Nahunta** Georgia, SE USA
40 *J6* **Naica** Chihuahua, N Mexico
9 *U15* **Naicam** Saskatchewan, S Canada
Naiman Qi *see* Daqin Tal
158 *M4* **Naimin Bulak** *spring* NW China
13 *P6* **Nain** Newfoundland and Labrador, NE Canada
143 *P8* **Nā'īn** Eşfahān, C Iran
152 *K10* **Naini Tāl** Uttaranchal, N India
154 *J11* **Nainpur** Madhya Pradesh, C India
96 *J8* **Nairn** N Scotland, UK
96 *I8* **Nairn** *cultural region* NE Scotland, UK
81 *I19* **Nairobi** ● (Kenya) Nairobi Area, S Kenya
81 *I19* **Nairobi** ✕ Nairobi Area, S Kenya
82 *P13* **Nairoto** Cabo Delgado, NE Mozambique
118 *G3* **Naissaar** *island* N Estonia
Naissus *see* Niš
187 *Z14* **Naitaba** ***var.*** Naitauba; ***prev.*** Naitamba. *island* Lau Group, E Fiji
Naitamba/Naitauba *see* Naitaba
81 *I19* **Naivasha** Rift Valley, SW Kenya
81 *H19* **Naivasha, Lake** ◎ SW Kenya
Najaf *see* An Najaf
143 *N8* **Najafābād** ***var.*** Nejafabad. Eşfahān, C Iran
141 *N7* **Najd** ***var.*** Nejd. *cultural region* C Saudi Arabia
105 *O4* **Nájera** La Rioja, N Spain
105 *P4* **Najerilla** ≈ N Spain
163 *U7* **Naji** ***var.*** Arun Qi. Nei Mongol Zizhiqu, N China
152 *J9* **Najībābād** Uttar Pradesh, N India
Najima *see* Fukuoka
163 *Y11* **Najin** NE North Korea
139 *T9* **Najm al Ḩassūn** C Iraq
141 *O13* **Najrān** ***var.*** Abā as Suʻūd. Najrān, S Saudi Arabia
141 *P12* **Najrān** ***var.*** Minṭaqat al Najrān. ⬖ *province* S Saudi Arabia
Najrān, Minṭaqat al *see* Najrān
165 *T2* **Nakagawa** Hokkaidō, NE Japan
38 *F9* **Nākālele Point** ***var.*** Nakalele Point. *headland* Maui, Hawaiʻi, USA
164 *D13* **Nakama** Fukuoka, Kyūshū, SW Japan
Nakambé *see* White Volta
Nakamti *see* Nek'emtē
164 *F15* **Nakamura** Kōchi, Shikoku, SW Japan
186 *H7* **Nakanai Mountains** ▲▲ New Britain, E Papua New Guinea
164 *H11* **Nakano-shima** *island* Oki-shotō, SW Japan
165 *Q6* **Nakasato** Aomori, Honshū, C Japan
165 *T5* **Nakasatsunai** Hokkaidō, NE Japan
165 *W4* **Nakashibetsu** Hokkaidō, NE Japan
81 *F18* **Nakasongola** C Uganda
165 *T1* **Nakatonbetsu** Hokkaidō, NE Japan
164 *L13* **Nakatsugawa** ***var.*** Nakatugawa. Gifu, Honshū, SW Japan
Nakatugawa *see* Nakatsugawa
Nakdong *see* Naktong-gang
Nakel *see* Nakło nad Notecią
80 *J8* **Nakfa** N Eritrea
Nakhichevan' *see* Naxçıvan
123 *S15* **Nakhodka** Primorskiy Kray, SE Russian Federation
122 *J8* **Nakhodka** Yamalo-Nenetskiy Avtonomnyy Okrug, N Russian Federation
Nakhon Navok *see* Nakhon Nayok
167 *P11* **Nakhon Nayok** ***var.*** Nagara Nayok, Nakhon Navok. Nakhon Nayok, C Thailand
167 *O11* **Nakhon Pathom** ***var.*** Nagara Pathom, Nakorn Pathom. Nakhon Pathom, W Thailand
167 *R8* **Nakhon Phanom** ***var.*** Nagara Panom. Nakhon Phanom, E Thailand
167 *Q10* **Nakhon Ratchasima** ***var.*** Khorat, Korat. Nakhon Ratchasima, E Thailand
167 *O9* **Nakhon Sawan** ***var.*** Muang Nakhon Sawan, Nagara Svarga. Nakhon Sawan, W Thailand
167 *N15* **Nakhon Si Thammarat** ***var.*** Nagara Sridharmaraj, Nakhon Sithamnaraj. Nakhon Si Thammarat, SW Thailand
Nakhon Sithamnaraj *see* Nakhon Si Thammarat
139 *Y11* **Nakhrash** SE Iraq
10 *I9* **Nakina** British Columbia, W Canada
110 *H9* **Nakło nad Notecią** ***Ger.*** Nakel. Kujawsko-pomorskie, C Poland
39 *P13* **Naknek** Alaska, USA
152 *H8* **Nakodar** Punjab, NW India
82 *M11* **Nakonde** Northern, NE Zambia
Nakorn Pathom *see* Nakhon Pathom
95 *H24* **Nakskov** Storstrøm, SE Denmark
163 *Y15* **Naktong-gang** ***var.*** Nakdong, ***Jap.*** Rakutō-kō. ≈ C South Korea
81 *H18* **Nakuru** Rift Valley, SW Kenya
81 *H19* **Nakuru, Lake** ◎ Rift Valley, C Kenya
9 *O17* **Nakusp** British Columbia, SW Canada
149 *N15* **Nāl** ≈ W Pakistan
162 *M7* **Nalayh** Töv, C Mongolia
153 *V12* **Nalbāri** Assam, NE India
63 *G19* **Nalcayec, Isla** *island* Archipiélago de los Chonos, S Chile
127 *N15* **Nal'chik** Kabardino-Balkarskaya Respublika, SW Russian Federation
155 *I16* **Nalgonda** Andhra Pradesh, C India
153 *S14* **Nalhāti** West Bengal, NE India
153 *U14* **Nalitabari** Dhaka, N Bangladesh
155 *I17* **Nallamala Hills** ▲▲ E India
136 *G12* **Nallıhan** Ankara, NW Turkey
104 *K2* **Nalón** ≈ NW Spain
167 *N3* **Nalong** Kachin State, N Myanmar (Burma)
75 *N8* **Nālūt** NW Libya
171 *T14* **Nama** Pulau Manawoka, E Indonesia
189 *Q16* **Nama** *island* C Micronesia
83 *O16* **Namacurra** Zambézia, NE Mozambique
188 *F9* **Namai Bay** *bay* Babeldaob, N Palau
29 *W2* **Namakan Lake** ◎ Canada/USA
143 *O6* **Namak, Daryācheh-ye** *marsh* N Iran
143 *T6* **Namak, Kavīr-e** *salt pan* NE Iran
167 *O6* **Namaklwe** Shan State, E Myanmar (Burma)
Namaksār, Kowl-e/ Namakzār, Daryācheh-ye *see* Namakzar
148 *I5* **Namakzar** ***Pash.*** Daryācheh-ye Namakzār, Kowl-e Namaksār. *marsh* Afghanistan/Iran
171 *V15* **Namalau** Pulau Jursian, E Indonesia
81 *I20* **Namanga** Rift Valley, S Kenya
147 *S10* **Namangan** Namangan Viloyati, E Uzbekistan
Namanganskaya Oblast' *see* Namangan Viloyati
147 *R10* **Namangan Viloyati** ***Rus.*** Namanganskaya Oblast'. ⬖ *province* E Uzbekistan
83 *Q14* **Namapa** Nampula, NE Mozambique
83 *C21* **Namaqualand** *physical region* S Namibia
81 *G18* **Namasagali** C Uganda
186 *H6* **Namatanai** New Ireland, NE Papua New Guinea
83 *I14* **Nambala** Central, C Zambia
81 *J23* **Nambanje** Lindi, SE Tanzania
83 *G16* **Nambiya** North West, N Botswana
183 *V2* **Nambour** Queensland, E Australia
183 *V6* **Nambucca Heads** New South Wales, SE Australia
159 *N15* **Nam Co** ◎ W China
167 *R5* **Nâm Cum** Lai Châu, N Vietnam
Namdik *see* Namorik Atoll
167 *T6* **Nam Đinh** Nam Ha, N Vietnam
99 *I20* **Namêche** Namur, SE Belgium
30 *J4* **Namekagon Lake** ◎ Wisconsin, N USA
188 *F10* **Namekakl Passage** *passage* Babeldaob, N Palau
Namen *see* Namur
83 *P15* **Nametil** Nampula, NE Mozambique
163 *X14* **Nam-gang** ≈ C North Korea
163 *Y16* **Nam-gang** ≈ S South Korea
163 *Y17* **Namhae-do** ***Jap.*** Nankai-tō. *island* S South Korea
Namhoi *see* Foshan
83 *C19* **Namib Desert** *desert* W Namibia
83 *A15* **Namibe** ***Port.*** Moçâmedes, Mossâmedes. Namibe, SW Angola
83 *A15* **Namibe** ⬖ *province* SE Angola
83 *C18* **Namibia** ***off.*** Republic of Namibia, ***var.*** South West Africa, ***Afr.*** Suidwes-Afrika, ***Ger.*** Deutsch-Südwestafrika; ***prev.*** German Southwest Africa, South-West Africa. ◆ *republic* S Africa
65 *O17* **Namibia Plain** *undersea feature* S Atlantic Ocean
Namibia, Republic of *see* Namibia
165 *Q11* **Namie** Fukushima, Honshū, C Japan
165 *Q7* **Namioka** Aomori, Honshū, C Japan
40 *I5* **Namiquipa** Chihuahua, N Mexico
159 *P15* **Namjagbarwa Feng** ▲ W China
Namka *see* Doilungdêqên
171 *R13* **Namlea** Pulau Buru, E Indonesia
158 *L16* **Namling** Xizang Zizhiqu, W China
Namnetes *see* Nantes
167 *R8* **Nam Ngum** ≈ C Laos
Namo *see* Namu Atoll
183 *R5* **Namoi River** ≈ New South Wales, SE Australia
189 *Q17* **Namoluk Atoll** *atoll* Mortlock Islands, C Micronesia
189 *O15* **Namonuito Atoll** *atoll* Caroline Islands, C Micronesia
189 *T9* **Namorik Atoll** ***var.*** Namdik. *atoll* Ralik Chain, S Marshall Islands
167 *Q6* **Nam Ou** ≈ N Laos
32 *M14* **Nampa** Idaho, NW USA
76 *M11* **Nampala** Ségou, W Mali
163 *W14* **Namp'o** SW North Korea
83 *P15* **Nampula** Nampula, NE Mozambique
83 *P15* **Nampula** ***off.*** Província de Nampula. ⬖ *province* NE Mozambique
Nampula, Província de *see* Nampula
163 *W13* **Namsan-ni** NW North Korea
Namslau *see* Namysłów
93 *E15* **Namsos** Nord-Trøndelag, C Norway
93 *F14* **Namsskogan** Nord-Trøndelag, C Norway
167 *O6* **Nam Teng** ≈ E Myanmar (Burma)
167 *P6* **Nam Tha** ≈ N Laos
123 *Q10* **Namsty** Respublika Sakha (Yakutiya), NE Russian Federation
167 *N4* **Namtu** Shan State, E Myanmar (Burma)
10 *J15* **Namu** British Columbia, SW Canada
189 *T7* **Namu Atoll** ***var.*** Namo. *atoll* Ralik Chain, C Marshall Islands
187 *Y15* **Namuka-i-lau** *island* Lau Group, E Fiji
83 *O15* **Namuli, Mont** ▲ NE Mozambique
83 *P14* **Namuno** Cabo Delgado, N Mozambique
99 *I20* **Namur** ***Dut.*** Namen. Namur, SE Belgium
99 *H21* **Namur** ***Dut.*** Namen. ⬖ *province* S Belgium
83 *D17* **Namutoni** Kunene, N Namibia
163 *Y16* **Namwŏn** ***Jap.*** Nangen. S South Korea
111 *H14* **Namysłów** ***Ger.*** Namslau. Opole, SW Poland
167 *P7* **Nan** ***var.*** Muang Nan. Nan, NW Thailand
79 *G15* **Nana** ≈ W Central African Republic
165 *R5* **Nanae** Hokkaidō, NE Japan
79 *I14* **Nana-Grébizi** ⬖ *prefecture* N Central African Republic
10 *L17* **Nanaimo** Vancouver Island, British Columbia, SW Canada
38 *C9* **Nānākuli** ***var.*** Nanakuli. Oʻahu, Hawaiʻi, USA
79 *G15* **Nana-Mambéré** ⬖ *prefecture* W Central African Republic
161 *R13* **Nan'an** Fujian, SE China

◆ Country
● Country Capital
◇ Dependent Territory
○ Dependent Territory Capital
⬖ Administrative Regions
✕ International Airport
▲ Mountain
▲▲ Mountain Range
Volcano
≈ River
◎ Lake
⊠ Reservoir

183 U2 **Nanango** Queensland, E Australia
164 L11 **Nanao** Ishikawa, Honshū, SW Japan
161 Q14 **Nan'ao Dao** island S China
164 L10 **Nanatsu-shima** island SW Japan
56 F8 **Nanay, Río** ≈ NE Peru
160 J8 **Nanbu** Sichuan, C China
163 X7 **Nancha** Heilongjiang, NE China
161 P10 **Nanchang** var. Nan-ch'ang, Nanch'ang-hsien. province capital Jiangxi, S China
Nan-ch'ang see Nanchang
Nanch'ang-hsien see Nanchang
161 P11 **Nancheng** var. Jianchang. Jiangxi, S China
Nan-ching see Nanjing
160 J9 **Nanchong** Sichuan, C China
160 J10 **Nanchuan** Chongqing Shi, C China
103 T5 **Nancy** Meurthe-et-Moselle, NE France
185 A22 **Nancy Sound** sound South Island, New Zealand
152 L9 **Nanda Devi** ▲ NW India
42 J11 **Nandaime** Granada, SW Nicaragua
160 K13 **Nandan** Guangxi Zhuangzu Zizhiqu, S China
155 H14 **Nānded** Mahārāshtra, C India
183 S5 **Nandewar Range** ▲▲ New South Wales, SE Australia
Nandi see Nadi
160 E13 **Nanding He** ≈ China/Vietnam
Nándorhgy see Oţelu Roşu
154 E11 **Nandurbār** Mahārāshtra, W India
Nanduri see Naduri
155 I17 **Nandyāl** Andhra Pradesh, E India
161 P11 **Nanfeng** var. Qincheng. Jiangxi, S China
Nang see Nangxian
79 E15 **Nanga Eboko** Centre, C Cameroon
Nangah Serawai see Nangaserawai
149 W4 **Nanga Parbat** ▲ India/Pakistan
169 R11 **Nangapinoh** Borneo, C Indonesia
149 R5 **Nangarhār** ⬖ province E Afghanistan
169 S11 **Nangaserawai** var. Nangah Serawai. Borneo, C Indonesia
169 Q12 **Nangatayap** Borneo, C Indonesia
Nangen see Namwŏn
103 P5 **Nangis** Seine-et-Marne, N France
163 X13 **Nangnim-sanmaek** ▲▲ C North Korea
161 O4 **Nangong** Hebei, E China
159 Q14 **Nangqên** var. Xangda. Qinghai, C China
167 Q10 **Nang Rong** Buri Ram, E Thailand
159 O16 **Nangxian** var. Nang. Xizang Zizhiqu, W China
Nan Hai see South China Sea
160 L8 **Nan He** ≈ C China
160 F12 **Nanhua** var. Longchuan. Yunnan, SW China
Naniwa see Ōsaka
155 G20 **Nanjangūd** Karnātaka, W India
161 Q8 **Nanjing** var. Nan-ching, Nanking; prev. Chianning, Chian-ning, Kiang-ning, Jiangsu. province capital Jiangsu, E China
Nankai-tō see Namhae-do
161 O12 **Nankang** var. Rongjiang. Jiangxi, S China
Nanking see Nanjing
161 N13 **Nan Ling** ▲▲ S China
160 L15 **Nanliu Jiang** ≈ S China
189 P13 **Nan Madol** ruins Temwen Island, E Micronesia
160 K15 **Nanning** var. Nan-ning; prev. Yung-ning. Guangxi Zhuangzu Zizhiqu, S China
Nan-ning see Nanning
196 M15 **Nanortalik** ⬖ Kitaa, S Greenland
Nanouki see Aranuka
160 H13 **Nanpan Jiang** ≈ S China
152 M11 **Nānpāra** Uttar Pradesh, N India
161 Q12 **Nanping** var. Nan-p'ing; prev. Yenping. Fujian, SE China
Nan-p'ing see Nanping
Nanping see Jiuzhaigou
Nanpu see Pucheng
161 R12 **Nanri Dao** island SE China
165 S16 **Nansei-shotō** Eng. Ryukyu Islands. island group SW Japan
Nansei Syotō Trench see Ryukyu Trench
197 T10 **Nansen Basin** undersea feature Arctic Ocean
197 T10 **Nansen Cordillera** var. Arctic Mid Oceanic Ridge, Nansen Ridge. undersea feature Arctic Ocean
Nansen Ridge see Nansen Cordillera
129 T9 **Nan Shan** ▲▲ C China
Nansha Qundao see Spratly Islands
12 K3 **Nantais, Lac** ◎ Québec, NE Canada
103 N5 **Nanterre** Hauts-de-Seine, N France
102 I8 **Nantes** Bret. Naoned; anc. Condivincum, Namnetes. Loire-Atlantique, NW France
14 G17 **Nanticoke** Ontario, S Canada
18 H13 **Nanticoke** Pennsylvania, NE USA
21 Y4 **Nanticoke River** ≈ Delaware/Maryland, NE USA
9 Q17 **Nanton** Alberta, SW Canada
161 S8 **Nantong** Jiangsu, E China
161 S13 **Nant'ou** W Taiwan
103 S10 **Nantua** Ain, E France
19 Q13 **Nantucket** Nantucket Island, Massachusetts, NE USA
19 Q13 **Nantucket Island** island Massachusetts, NE USA
19 Q13 **Nantucket Sound** sound Massachusetts, NE USA
82 P13 **Nantulo** Cabo Delgado, N Mozambique
189 O12 **Nanuh** Pohnpei, E Micronesia
190 D6 **Nanumaga** atoll NW Tuvalu
190 D5 **Nanumea Atoll** atoll NW Tuvalu
59 O19 **Nanuque** Minas Gerais, SE Brazil
171 R10 **Nanusa, Kepulauan** island group N Indonesia
163 U4 **Nanweng He** ≈ NE China
160 I10 **Nanxi** Sichuan, C China
161 N10 **Nanxian** var. Nan Xian, Nanzhou. Hunan, S China
Nan Xian see Nanxian
161 N7 **Nanyang** var. Nan-yang. Henan, C China
Nan-yang see Nanyang
161 P6 **Nanyang Hu** ◎ E China
165 P10 **Nan'yō** Yamagata, Honshū, C Japan
81 I18 **Nanyuki** Central, C Kenya
160 M8 **Nanzhang** Hubei, C China
Nanzhou see Nanxian
105 T11 **Nao, Cabo de La** cape E Spain
12 M9 **Naococane, Lac** ◎ Québec, E Canada
153 S14 **Naogaon** Rajshahi, NW Bangladesh
Naokot see Naukot
187 R13 **Naone** Maewo, C Vanuatu
Naoned see Nantes
115 E14 **Náousa** Kentrikí Makedonía, N Greece
35 N8 **Napa** California, W USA
39 O11 **Napaimiut** Alaska, USA
39 N12 **Napakiak** Alaska, USA
122 J7 **Napalkovo** Yamalo-Nenetskiy Avtonomnyy Okrug, N Russian Federation
12 I16 **Napanee** Ontario, SE Canada
39 N12 **Napaskiak** Alaska, USA
167 S5 **Na Phac** Cao Băng, N Vietnam
184 O11 **Napier** Hawke's Bay, North Island, New Zealand
195 X3 **Napier Mountains** ▲▲ Antarctica
15 O13 **Napierville** Québec, SE Canada
23 W15 **Naples** Florida, SE USA
25 W5 **Naples** Texas, SW USA
Naples see Napoli
160 I14 **Napo** Guangxi Zhuangzu Zizhiqu, S China
56 C6 **Napo** ⬖ province NE Ecuador
29 O6 **Napoleon** North Dakota, N USA
31 R11 **Napoleon** Ohio, N USA
Napoléon-Vendée see la Roche-sur-Yon
22 J9 **Napoleonville** Louisiana, S USA
107 K17 **Napoli** Eng. Naples, Ger. Neapel; anc. Neapolis. Campania, S Italy
107 J18 **Napoli, Golfo di** gulf S Italy
57 F7 **Napo, Río** ≈ Ecuador/Peru
191 W9 **Napuka** island Îles Tuamotu, C French Polynesia
142 J3 **Naqadeh** Āžarbāyjān-e Bākhtarī, NW Iran
139 U6 **Naqnah** E Iraq
Nar see Nera
164 J14 **Nara** Nara, Honshū, SW Japan
76 L11 **Nara** Koulikoro, W Mali
149 R14 **Nāra Canal** irrigation canal S Pakistan
182 K11 **Naracoorte** South Australia
183 P8 **Naradhan** New South Wales, SE Australia
Naradhivas see Narathiwat
56 B8 **Naranjal** Guayas, W Ecuador
57 Q19 **Naranjos** Santa Cruz, E Bolivia
41 Q12 **Naranjos** Veracruz-Llave, E Mexico
159 Q6 **Naran Sebstein Bulag** spring NW China
143 X12 **Narānū** Sīstān va Balūchestān, SE Iran
164 B14 **Narao** Nagasaki, Nakadōri-jima, SW Japan
155 J16 **Narasaraopet** Andhra Pradesh, E India
158 J5 **Narat** Xinjiang Uygur Zizhiqu, W China
167 P17 **Narathiwat** var. Naradhivas. Narathiwat, SW Thailand
37 V10 **Nara Visa** New Mexico, SW USA
Nārāyāni see Gandak
Narbada see Narmada
Narbo Martius see Narbonne
103 P16 **Narbonne** anc. Narbo Martius. Aude, S France
Narborough Island see Fernandina, Isla
104 J2 **Narcea** ≈ NW Spain
152 J9 **Narendranagar** Uttaranchal, N India
Nares Abyssal Plain see Nares Plain
64 G11 **Nares Plain** var. Nares Abyssal Plain. undersea feature NW Atlantic Ocean
Nares Stræde see Nares Strait
197 P10 **Nares Strait** Dan. Nares Stræde. strait Canada/Greenland
110 O9 **Narew** ≈ E Poland
155 F17 **Nargund** Karnātaka, W India
83 D20 **Narib** Hardap, S Namibia
Narikrik see Knox Atoll
Narin Gol see Dong He
54 B13 **Nariño** off. Departamento de Nariño. ⬖ province SW Colombia
165 P13 **Narita** Chiba, Honshū, S Japan
165 P13 **Narita** ✈ (Tōkyō) Chiba, Honshū, S Japan
Narīya see An Nu'ayrīyah
162 F5 **Nariyn Gol** ≈ Mongolia/Russian Federation
162 J8 **Nariynteel** var. Tsagaan-Ovoo. Övörhangay, C Mongolia
152 J8 **Nārkanda** Himāchal Pradesh, NW India
92 L13 **Narkaus** Lappi, NW Finland
154 E11 **Narmada** var. Narbada. ≈ C India
152 H11 **Narnaul** var. Nārnaul. Haryāna, N India
107 I14 **Narni** Umbria, C Italy
107 J24 **Naro** Sicilia, Italy, C Mediterranean Sea
Narodichi see Narodychi
125 V7 **Narodnaya, Gora** ▲ NW Russian Federation
117 N3 **Narodychi** Rus. Narodichi. Zhytomyrs'ka Oblast', N Ukraine
126 J4 **Naro-Fominsk** Moskovskaya Oblast', W Russian Federation
81 H19 **Narok** Rift Valley, SW Kenya
104 H2 **Narón** Galicia, NW Spain
183 S11 **Narooma** New South Wales, SE Australia
Narova see Narva
Narovlya see Narowlya
149 W8 **Nārowāl** Punjab, E Pakistan
119 N20 **Narowlya** Rus. Narovlya. Homyel'skaya Voblasts', SE Belarus
93 J17 **Närpes** Fin. Närpiö. Länsi-Soumi, W Finland
Närpiö see Närpes
183 S5 **Narrabri** New South Wales, SE Australia
183 P9 **Narrandera** New South Wales, SE Australia
183 Q4 **Narran Lake** ◎ New South Wales, SE Australia
183 Q4 **Narran River** ≈ New South Wales/Queensland, SE Australia
180 J13 **Narrogin** Western Australia
183 Q7 **Narromine** New South Wales, SE Australia
21 R6 **Narrows** Virginia, NE USA
196 M15 **Narsarsuaq** ✈ Kitaa, S Greenland
154 I10 **Narsimhapur** Madhya Pradesh, C India
Narsingdi see Narsinghdi
153 U15 **Narsinghdi** var. Narsingdi. Dhaka, C Bangladesh
154 H9 **Narsinghgarh** Madhya Pradesh, C India
163 Q11 **Nart** Nei Mongol Zizhiqu, N China
Nartës, Gjol i/Nartës, Laguna e see Nartës, Liqeni i
113 J22 **Nartës, Liqeni i** var. Gjol i Nartës, Laguna e Nartës. ◎ SW Albania
115 F17 **Narthákí** ▲ C Greece
127 O15 **Nartkala** Kabardino-Balkarskaya Respublika, SW Russian Federation
118 K3 **Narva** Ida-Virumaa, NE Estonia
118 K4 **Narva** prev. Narova. ≈ Estonia/Russian Federation
118 J3 **Narva Bay** Est. Narva Laht, Ger. Narwa-Bucht, Rus. Narvskiy Zaliv. bay Estonia/Russian Federation
Narva Laht see Narva Bay
124 F13 **Narva Reservoir** Est. Narva Veehoidla, Rus. Narvskoye Vodokhranilishche. ⊠ Estonia/Russian Federation
Narva Veehoidla see Narva Reservoir
92 H10 **Narvik** Nordland, C Norway
Narvskiy Zaliv see Narva Bay
Narvskoye Vodokhranilishche see Narva Reservoir
Narwa-Bucht see Narva Bay
152 I9 **Narwāna** Haryāna, NW India
125 R4 **Nar'yan-Mar** prev. Beloshchel'ye, Dzerzhinskiy. Nenetskiy Avtonomnyy Okrug, NW Russian Federation
122 J12 **Narym** Tomskaya Oblast', C Russian Federation
145 Y10 **Narymskiy Khrebet** Kaz. Naryn Zhotasy. ▲▲ E Kazakhstan
147 W9 **Naryn** Narynskaya Oblast', C Kyrgyzstan
147 U8 **Naryn** ≈ Kyrgyzstan/Uzbekistan
145 W16 **Narynkol** Kaz. Narynqol. Almaty, SE Kazakhstan
Naryn Oblasty see Narynskaya Oblast'
Narynqol see Narynkol
147 V9 **Narynskaya Oblast'** Kir. Naryn Oblasty. ⬖ province C Kyrgyzstan
Naryn Zhotasy see Narymskiy Khrebet
126 J6 **Naryshkino** Orlovskaya Oblast', W Russian Federation
95 L14 **Nås** Dalarna, C Sweden
92 G13 **Nasafjellet** Lapp. Násávárre. ▲ C Norway
93 H16 **Nasåker** Västernorrland, C Sweden
187 Y14 **Nasau** Koro, C Fiji
116 I9 **Năsăud** Ger. Nussdorf, Hung. Naszód. Bistrița-Năsăud, N Romania
Násávárre see Nasafjellet
103 P13 **Nasbinals** Lozère, S France
Na Sceirí see Skerries
Nase see Naze
185 E22 **Naseby** Otago, South Island, New Zealand
143 R10 **Nāşerīyeh** Kermān, C Iran
25 X5 **Nash** Texas, SW USA
154 E13 **Nāshik** prev. Nāsik. Mahārāshtra, W India
56 E7 **Nashiño, Río** ≈ Ecuador/Peru
29 W12 **Nashua** Iowa, C USA
33 W7 **Nashua** Montana, NW USA
19 O10 **Nashua** New Hampshire, NE USA
27 S13 **Nashville** Arkansas, C USA
23 U7 **Nashville** Georgia, SE USA
30 L16 **Nashville** Illinois, N USA
31 O14 **Nashville** Indiana, N USA
21 V9 **Nashville** North Carolina, SE USA
20 J8 **Nashville** state capital Tennessee, S USA
20 J9 **Nashville** ✈ Tennessee, S USA
64 H10 **Nashville Seamount** undersea feature NW Atlantic Ocean
112 H9 **Našice** Osijek-Baranja, E Croatia
110 M11 **Nasielsk** Mazowieckie, C Poland
93 K18 **Näsijärvi** ◎ SW Finland
Nāsik see Nāshik
80 G13 **Nasir** Upper Nile, SE Sudan
149 Q12 **Nasīrābād** Baluchistān, SW Pakistan
148 K15 **Nasīrābād** Baluchistān, SW Pakistan
Nasīrābād see Mymensingh
Nasir, Buhayrat/Nâşir, Buḥeiret see Nasser, Lake
Nāsiri see Ahvāz
Nasiriya see An Nāşirīyah
Nás na Ríogh see Naas
107 L23 **Naso** Sicilia, Italy, C Mediterranean Sea
Nasratabad see Zābol
10 J11 **Nass** ≈ British Columbia, SW Canada
77 V15 **Nassarawa** Nassarawa, C Nigeria
44 H2 **Nassau** ● (Bahamas) New Providence, N Bahamas
44 H2 **Nassau** ✈ New Providence, C Bahamas
190 J13 **Nassau** island N Cook Islands
23 W8 **Nassau Sound** sound Florida, SE USA
108 L7 **Nassereith** Tirol, W Austria
75 X11 **Nasser, Lake** ◎ Egypt/Sudan
80 F5 **Nasser, Lake** var. Buhayrat Nasir, Buḥayrat Nāşir, Buḥeiret Nâşir. ◎ Egypt/Sudan
95 L19 **Nässjö** Jönköping, S Sweden
99 K22 **Nassogne** Luxembourg, SE Belgium
12 J6 **Nastapoka Islands** island group Northwest Territories, C Canada
93 M19 **Nastola** Etelä-Suomi, S Finland
171 O4 **Nasugbu** Luzon, N Philippines
94 N11 **Näsviken** Gävleborg, C Sweden
Naszód see Năsăud
83 I17 **Nata** Central, NE Botswana
54 E11 **Natagaima** Tolima, C Colombia
59 Q14 **Natal** state capital Rio Grande do Norte, E Brazil
168 I11 **Natal** Sumatera, N Indonesia
Natal see KwaZulu/Natal
173 L10 **Natal Basin** var. Mozambique Basin. undersea feature W Indian Ocean
25 R12 **Natalia** Texas, SW USA
67 W15 **Natal Valley** undersea feature SW Indian Ocean
Natanya see Netanya
143 O7 **Naţanz** Eşfahān, C Iran
13 Q11 **Natashquan** Québec, E Canada
13 Q10 **Natashquan** ≈ Newfoundland and Labrador/Québec, E Canada
22 J7 **Natchez** Mississippi, S USA
22 G6 **Natchitoches** Louisiana, S USA
108 E10 **Naters** Valais, S Switzerland
Nathanya see Netanya
92 O3 **Nathorst Land** physical region W Svalbard
186 E9 **National Capital District** ⬖ province S Papua New Guinea
35 U17 **National City** California, W USA
184 M10 **National Park** Manawatu-Wanganui, North Island, New Zealand
77 R14 **Natitingou** NW Benin
40 B5 **Natividad, Isla** island W Mexico
165 Q10 **Natori** Miyagi, Honshū, C Japan
18 C14 **Natrona Heights** Pennsylvania, NE USA
81 H20 **Natron, Lake** ◎ Kenya/Tanzania
Natsrat see Nazerat
166 L7 **Nattalin** Pegu, C Myanmar (Burma)
92 J12 **Nattavaara** Lapp. Nahtavárr. Norrbotten, N Sweden
109 S3 **Natternbach** Oberösterreich, N Austria
95 M22 **Nättraby** Blekinge, S Sweden
169 P10 **Natuna Besar, Pulau** island Kepulauan Natuna, W Indonesia
Natuna Islands see Natuna, Kepulauan
169 O9 **Natuna, Kepulauan** var. Natuna Islands. island group W Indonesia
169 N9 **Natuna, Laut** sea W Indonesia
21 N6 **Natural Bridge** tourist site Kentucky, C USA
173 V11 **Naturaliste Fracture Zone** tectonic feature E Indian Ocean
174 J10 **Naturaliste Plateau** undersea feature E Indian Ocean
Nau see Nov
103 O14 **Naucelle** Aveyron, S France
83 D20 **Nauchas** Hardap, C Namibia
108 K9 **Nauders** Tirol, W Austria
Naugard see Nowogard
118 F12 **Naujamiestis** Panevėžys, C Lithuania
118 E10 **Naujoji Akmenė** Šiaulai, NW Lithuania
149 R16 **Naukot** var. Naokot. Sind, SE Pakistan
101 L16 **Naumburg** var. Naumburg an der Saale. Sachsen-Anhalt, C Germany
Naumburg am Queis see Nowogrodziec
Naumburg an der Saale see Naumburg
191 W15 **Naunau** ancient monument Easter Island, Chile, E Pacific Ocean
138 G10 **Nā'ūr** 'Ammān, W Jordan
189 Q8 **Nauru** off. Republic of Nauru; prev. Pleasant Island. ◆ republic W Pacific Ocean
175 P5 **Nauru** island W Pacific Ocean
189 Q9 **Nauru International** ✈ S Nauru
Nauru, Republic of see Nauru
Nausari see Navsāri
19 Q12 **Nauset Beach** beach Massachusetts, NE USA
Naushahra see Nowshera
149 P14 **Naushahro Fīroz** Sind, SE Pakistan
Naushara see Nowshera
187 X14 **Nausori** Viti Levu, W Fiji
56 F9 **Nauta** Loreto, N Peru
153 O12 **Nautanwa** Uttar Pradesh, N India
41 R13 **Nautla** Veracruz-Llave, E Mexico
Nauzad see Now Zād
41 N6 **Nava** Coahuila de Zaragoza, NE Mexico
Navabad see Navobod
104 L6 **Nava del Rey** Castilla-León, N Spain
153 S15 **Navadwīp** prev. Nabadwip. West Bengal, NE India
104 M9 **Navahermosa** Castilla-La Mancha, C Spain
119 I16 **Navahrudak** Pol. Nowogródek, Rus. Novogrudok. Hrodzyenskaya Voblasts', W Belarus
119 I16 **Navahrudskaye Wzvyshsha** ▲ W Belarus
36 M8 **Navajo Mount** ▲ Utah, W USA
37 Q9 **Navajo Reservoir** ⊠ New Mexico, SW USA
104 K9 **Navalmoral de la Mata** Extremadura, W Spain
104 K10 **Navalvillar de Pelea** Extremadura, W Spain
97 F17 **Navan** Ir. An Uaimh. E Ireland
Navanagar see Jāmnagar
118 L12 **Navapolatsk** Rus. Novopolotsk. Vitsyebskaya Voblasts', N Belarus
149 P6 **Nāvar, Dasht-e** Pash. Dasht-i-Nawar. desert C Afghanistan
123 W6 **Navarin, Mys** cape NE Russian Federation
63 I25 **Navarino, Isla** island S Chile
105 Q4 **Navarra** Eng./Fr. Navarre. ⬖ autonomous community N Spain
Navarre see Navarra
105 P4 **Navarrete** La Rioja, N Spain
61 C20 **Navarro** Buenos Aires, E Argentina
105 O12 **Navas de San Juan** Andalucía, S Spain
25 V10 **Navasota** Texas, SW USA
25 U9 **Navasota River** ≈ Texas, SW USA
44 I9 **Navassa Island** ◇ US unincorporated territory C West Indies
119 L19 **Navasyolki** Rus. Novosëlki. Homyel'skaya Voblasts', SE Belarus
119 H17 **Navayel'nya** Pol. Nowojelnia, Rus. Novoyel'nya. Hrodzyenskaya Voblasts', W Belarus
171 Y13 **Naver** Papua, E Indonesia
118 H5 **Navesti** ≈ C Estonia
104 J2 **Navia** Asturias, N Spain
104 J2 **Navia** ≈ NW Spain
59 I21 **Naviraí** Mato Grosso do Sul, SW Brazil
126 I6 **Navlya** Bryanskaya Oblast', W Russian Federation
187 X13 **Navoalevu** Vanua Levu, N Fiji
147 R12 **Navobod** Rus. Navabad, Novabad. C Tajikistan
147 P13 **Navobod** Rus. Navabad. W Tajikistan
Navoi see Navoiy
146 M11 **Navoiy** Rus. Navoi. Navoiy Viloyati, C Uzbekistan
Navoiyskaya Oblast' see Navoiy Viloyati
146 K8 **Navoiy Viloyati** Rus. Navoiyskaya Oblast'. ⬖ province N Uzbekistan
40 G7 **Navojoa** Sonora, NW Mexico
Navolat see Navolato
40 H9 **Navolato** var. Navolat. Sinaloa, C Mexico
187 Q13 **Navonda** Ambae, C Vanuatu
Návpaktos see Náfpaktos
Návplion see Náfplio
77 P14 **Navrongo** N Ghana
154 D12 **Navsāri** var. Nausari. Gujarāt, W India
187 X15 **Navua** Viti Levu, W Fiji
138 H8 **Nawá** Dar'ā, S Syria
Nawabashah see Nawābshāh
153 S14 **Nawabganj** Rajshahi, NW Bangladesh
153 S14 **Nawābganj** Uttar Pradesh, N India
149 Q15 **Nawābshāh** var. Nawabashah. Sind, S Pakistan
153 P14 **Nawāda** Bihār, N India
152 H11 **Nawalgarh** Rājasthān, N India
Nawāl, Sabkhat an see Noual, Sebkhet en
Nawar, Dasht-i- see Nāvar, Dasht-e
167 N4 **Nawnghkio** var. Nawngkio. Shan State, C Myanmar (Burma)
Nawngkio see Nawnghkio
137 U13 **Naxçıvan** Rus. Nakhichevan'. SW Azerbaijan
160 I10 **Naxi** Sichuan, C China
115 K21 **Náxos** var. Naxos. Náxos, Kykládes, Greece, Aegean Sea
115 K21 **Náxos** island Kykládes, Greece, Aegean Sea
40 J11 **Nayarit** ⬖ state C Mexico
187 Y14 **Nayau** island Lau Group, E Fiji
143 S8 **Nāy Band** Yazd, E Iran
165 T2 **Nayoro** Hokkaidō, NE Japan
104 F9 **Nazaré** var. Nazare. Leiria, C Portugal
Nazare see Nazaré
24 M4 **Nazareth** Texas, SW USA
Nazareth see Nazerat
173 O8 **Nazareth Bank** undersea feature W Indian Ocean
40 K9 **Nazas** Durango, C Mexico
57 F16 **Nazca** Ica, S Peru
0 L17 **Nazca Plate** tectonic feature
193 U9 **Nazca Ridge** undersea feature E Pacific Ocean
165 V15 **Naze** var. Nase. Kagoshima, Amami-ōshima, SW Japan
138 G9 **Nazerat** var. Natsrat, Ar. En Nazira, Eng. Nazareth. Northern, N Israel
137 R14 **Nazik Gölü** ◎ E Turkey
136 C15 **Nazilli** Aydın, SW Turkey
137 P14 **Nazimiye** Tunceli, E Turkey
Nazinon see Red Volta
10 L15 **Nazko** British Columbia, SW Canada
127 O16 **Nazran'** Ingushskaya Respublika, SW Russian Federation
80 J13 **Nazrēt** var. Adama, Hadama. Oromo, C Ethiopia
Nazwāh see Nizwá
82 J13 **Nchanga** Copperbelt, C Zambia
82 J11 **Nchelenge** Luapula, N Zambia
Ncheu see Ntcheu
Ndaghamcha, Sebkra de see Te-n-Dghâmcha, Sebkhet
81 G21 **Ndala** Tabora, C Tanzania
82 B11 **N'Dalatando** Port. Salazar, Vila Salazar. Cuanza Norte, NW Angola
77 S14 **Ndali** C Benin
81 E18 **Ndeke** SW Uganda
78 J13 **Ndélé** Bamingui-Bangoran, N Central African Republic
79 E19 **Ndendé** Ngounié, S Gabon
79 E20 **Ndindi** Nyanga, S Gabon
78 G11 **Ndjamena** var. N'Djamena; prev. Fort-Lamy. ● (Chad) Chari-Baguirmi, W Chad
78 G11 **Ndjamena** ✈ Chari-Baguirmi, W Chad
N'Djamena see Ndjamena
79 D18 **Ndjolé** Moyen-Ogooué, W Gabon
82 J13 **Ndola** Copperbelt, C Zambia
Ndrhamcha, Sebkha de see Te-n-Dghâmcha, Sebkhet
79 L15 **Ndu** Orientale, N Dem. Rep. Congo
81 H21 **Nduguti** Singida, C Tanzania
186 M9 **Nduindui** Guadalcanal, C Solomon Islands
Nduke see Kolombangara
115 F16 **Néa Anchiálos** var. Nea Anhialos, Néa Ankhíalos. Thessalía, C Greece
Nea Anhialos/Néa Ankhíalos see Néa Anchiálos
115 H18 **Néa Artáki** Évvoia, C Greece
97 F15 **Neagh, Lough** ◎ E Northern Ireland, UK
32 F7 **Neah Bay** Washington, NW USA
115 J22 **Nea Kaméni** island Kykládes, Greece, Aegean Sea
181 O8 **Neale, Lake** ◎ Northern Territory, C Australia
182 G2 **Neales River** seasonal river South Australia
115 G14 **Néa Moudanía** var. Néa Moudhaniá. Kentrikí Makedonía, N Greece
Néa Moudhaniá see Néa Moudanía
116 K10 **Neamţ** ⬖ county NE Romania
Neapel see Napoli
115 D14 **Neápoli** prev. Neápolis. Dytikí Makedonía, N Greece
115 K25 **Neápoli** Kríti, Greece, E Mediterranean Sea
115 G22 **Neápoli** Pelopónnisos, S Greece
Neápolis see Neápoli, Greece
Neapolis see Napoli, Italy
Neapolis see Nablus, West Bank
38 D16 **Near Islands** island group Aleutian Islands, Alaska, USA
97 J21 **Neath** S Wales, UK
114 H13 **Néa Zíchni** var. Néa Zíkhni; prev. Néa Zíkhna. Kentrikí Makedonía, NE Greece
Néa Zíkhna/Néa Zíkhni see Néa Zíchni
42 C5 **Nebaj** Quiché, W Guatemala
77 P13 **Nebbou** S Burkina
Nebitdag see Balkanabat
54 M13 **Neblina, Pico da** ▲ NW Brazil
124 I13 **Nebolchi** Novgorodskaya Oblast', W Russian Federation
36 L4 **Nebo, Mount** ▲ Utah, W USA
28 L14 **Nebraska** off. State of Nebraska, also known as Blackwater State, Cornhusker State, Tree Planters State. ⬖ state C USA
29 S16 **Nebraska City** Nebraska, C USA
107 K23 **Nebrodi, Monti** var. Monti Caronie. ▲▲ Sicilia, Italy, C Mediterranean Sea
10 L14 **Nechako** ≈ British Columbia, SW Canada
29 Q2 **Neche** North Dakota, N USA
25 V8 **Neches** Texas, SW USA
25 W8 **Neches River** ≈ Texas, SW USA
101 H20 **Neckar** ≈ SW Germany
101 H20 **Neckarsulm** Baden-Württemberg, SW Germany
192 L5 **Necker Island** island C British Virgin Islands
175 U3 **Necker Ridge** undersea feature N Pacific Ocean
61 D23 **Necochea** Buenos Aires, E Argentina
104 H2 **Neda** Galicia, NW Spain
115 E20 **Néda** var. Nédas. ≈ S Greece
Nédas see Néda
25 Y11 **Nederland** Texas, SW USA
Nederland see Netherlands
98 K12 **Neder Rijn** Eng. Lower Rhine. ≈ C Netherlands
99 L16 **Nederweert** Limburg, SE Netherlands
95 G16 **Nedre Tokke** ◎ S Norway
Nedrigaylov see Nedryhayliv
117 S3 **Nedryhayliv** Rus. Nedrigaylov. Sums'ka Oblast', NE Ukraine
98 O11 **Neede** Gelderland, E Netherlands
33 T13 **Needle Mountain** ▲ Wyoming, C USA
35 Y14 **Needles** California, W USA
97 M24 **Needles, The** rocks S England, UK
62 O7 **Ñeembucú** off. Departamento de Ñeembucú. ⬖ department SW Paraguay
Ñeembucú, Departamento de see Ñeembucú
30 M7 **Neenah** Wisconsin, N USA
9 W16 **Neepawa** Manitoba, S Canada
99 K16 **Neerpelt** Limburg, NE Belgium
74 M6 **Nefta** ✈ W Tunisia
126 L15 **Neftegorsk** Krasnodarskiy Kray, SW Russian Federation
127 U3 **Neftekamsk** Respublika Bashkortostan, W Russian Federation
127 O14 **Neftekumsk** Stavropol'skiy Kray, SW Russian Federation
Neftezavodsk see Seýdi
82 C10 **Negage** var. N'Gage. Uíge, NW Angola
Negapatam/Negapattinam see Nāgappattinam
169 T17 **Negara** Bali, Indonesia
169 T13 **Negara** Borneo, C Indonesia
Negara Brunei Darussalam see Brunei

◆ Country
● Country Capital
◇ Dependent Territory
○ Dependent Territory Capital
⬖ Administrative Regions
✈ International Airport
▲ Mountain
▲▲ Mountain Range
Volcano
≈ River
◎ Lake
⊠ Reservoir

31 N4 **Negaunee** Michigan, N USA
81 J15 **Negēlē** var. Negelli, It. Neghelli. Oromo, C Ethiopia
Negelli see Negēlē
Negeri Pahang Darul Makmur see Pahang
Negeri Selangor Darul Ehsan see Selangor
168 K9 **Negeri Sembilan** var. Negri Sembilan. ◐ state Peninsular Malaysia
92 P3 **Negerpynten** headland S Svalbard
Negev see HaNegev
Neghelli see Negēlē
116 I12 **Negoiu** var. Negoiul. ▲ S Romania
Negoiul see Negoiu
82 P13 **Negomane** var. Negomano. Cabo Delgado, N Mozambique
Negomano see Negomane
155 J25 **Negombo** Western Province, SW Sri Lanka
Negoreloye see Nyeharelaye
112 P12 **Negotin** Serbia, E Serbia
113 P19 **Negotino** C Macedonia
56 A10 **Negra, Punta** point NW Peru
104 G3 **Negreira** Galicia, NW Spain
116 L10 **Negrești** Vaslui, E Romania
Negrești see Negrești-Oaș
116 H8 **Negrești-Oaș** Hung. Avasfelsőfalu; prev. Negrești. Satu Mare, NE Romania
44 H12 **Negril** W Jamaica
Negri Sembilan see Negeri Sembilan
63 K15 **Negro, Río** ≈ E Argentina
62 N7 **Negro, Río** ≈ NE Argentina
57 N17 **Negro, Río** ≈ E Bolivia
48 F6 **Negro, Rio** ≈ N South America
61 E18 **Negro, Río** ≈ Brazil/Uruguay
62 O5 **Negro, Río** ≈ C Paraguay
Negro, Río see Chixoy, Río
Negro, Río see Sico Tinto, Río
171 P6 **Negros** island C Philippines
116 M15 **Negru Vodă** Constanța, SE Romania
13 P13 **Neguac** New Brunswick, SE Canada
14 B7 **Negwazu, Lake** ◎ Ontario, S Canada
Négyfalu see Săcele
32 F10 **Nehalem** Oregon, NW USA
32 F10 **Nehalem River** ≈ Oregon, NW USA
Nehavend see Nahāvand
143 V9 **Nehbandān** Khorāsān, E Iran
163 V6 **Nehe** Heilongjiang, NE China
193 Y14 **Neiafu** 'Uta Vava'u, N Tonga
45 N9 **Neiba** var. Neyba. SW Dominican Republic
Néid, Carn Uí see Mizen Head
92 M9 **Neiden** Finnmark, N Norway
Neidín see Kenmare
Néifinn see Nephin
103 S10 **Neige, Crêt de la** ▲ E France
173 O16 **Neiges, Piton des** ▲ C Réunion
15 R9 **Neiges, Rivière des** ≈ Québec, SE Canada
160 I10 **Neijiang** Sichuan, C China
30 K6 **Neillsville** Wisconsin, N USA
Nei Monggol Zizhiqu/Nei Mongol see Nei Mongol Zizhiqu
163 Q10 **Nei Mongol Gaoyuan** plateau NE China
163 O12 **Nei Mongol Zizhiqu** var. Nei Mongol, Eng. Inner Mongolia, Inner Mongolian Autonomous Region; prev. Nei Monggol Zizhiqu. ◐ autonomous region N China
161 O4 **Neiqiu** Hebei, E China
Neiriz see Neyriz
101 Q16 **Neisse** Pol. Nisa Cz. Lužická Nisa, Ger. Lausitzer Neisse, Nysa Łużycka. ≈ C Europe
Neisse see Nysa
54 E11 **Neiva** Huila, S Colombia
160 M7 **Neixiang** Henan, C China
Nejafabad see Najafābād
9 V9 **Nejanilini Lake** ◎ Manitoba, C Canada
Nejd see Najd
80 I13 **Nek'emtē** var. Lakemti, Nakamti. Oromo, C Ethiopia
126 M9 **Nekhayevskiy** Volgogradskaya Oblast', SW Russian Federation
30 K7 **Nekoosa** Wisconsin, N USA
Neksø Bornholm see Nexø
115 C16 **Nekyomanteío** ancient monument Ípeiros, W Greece
104 H7 **Nelas** Viseu, N Portugal
124 H16 **Nelidovo** Tverskaya Oblast', W Russian Federation
29 P13 **Neligh** Nebraska, C USA
123 R11 **Nel'kan** Khabarovskiy Kray, E Russian Federation
92 M10 **Nellim** var. Nellimö, Lapp. Njellim. Lappi, N Finland
Nellimö see Nellim
155 J18 **Nellore** Andhra Pradesh, E India
123 T14 **Nel'ma** Khabarovskiy Kray, SE Russian Federation
61 B17 **Nelson** Santa Fe, C Argentina
9 O17 **Nelson** British Columbia, SW Canada
185 I14 **Nelson** Nelson, South Island, New Zealand
97 L17 **Nelson** NW England, UK
29 P17 **Nelson** Nebraska, C USA
185 J14 **Nelson** ◐ unitary authority South Island, New Zealand
9 X12 **Nelson** ≈ Manitoba, C Canada
183 U8 **Nelson Bay** New South Wales, SE Australia
182 K13 **Nelson, Cape** headland Victoria, SE Australia
63 G23 **Nelson, Estrecho** strait SE Pacific Ocean
9 W12 **Nelson House** Manitoba, C Canada
30 J4 **Nelson Lake** ◎ Wisconsin, N USA
31 T14 **Nelsonville** Ohio, N USA
27 S2 **Nelsoon River** ≈ Iowa/Missouri, C USA
83 K21 **Nelspruit** Mpumalanga, NE South Africa
76 L10 **Néma** Hodh ech Chargui, SE Mauritania
118 D13 **Neman** Ger. Ragnit. Kaliningradskaya Oblast', W Russian Federation
84 I9 **Neman** Bel. Nyoman, Ger. Memel, Lith. Nemunas, Pol. Niemen, Rus. Neman. ≈ NE Europe
Nemausus see Nîmes
115 F19 **Neméa** Pelopónnisos, S Greece
Německý Brod see Havlíčkův Brod
14 D7 **Nemegosenda** ≈ Ontario, S Canada
14 D8 **Nemegosenda Lake** ◎ Ontario, S Canada
119 H14 **Nemenčinė** Vilnius, SE Lithuania
Nemetocenna see Arras
Nemirov see Nemyriv
103 O6 **Nemours** Seine-et-Marne, N France
Nemunas see Neman
165 W4 **Nemuro** Hokkaidō, NE Japan
165 W4 **Nemuro-hantō** peninsula Hokkaidō, NE Japan
165 W3 **Nemuro-kaikyō** strait Japan/Russian Federation
165 W4 **Nemuro-wan** bay N Japan
116 H5 **Nemyriv** Rus. Nemirov. L'vivs'ka Oblast', NW Ukraine
117 N7 **Nemyriv** Rus. Nemirov. Vinnyts'ka Oblast', C Ukraine
97 D19 **Nenagh** Ir. An tAonach. Tipperary, C Ireland
39 R9 **Nenana** Alaska, USA
39 R9 **Nenana River** ≈ Alaska, USA
187 P10 **Nendö** var. Swallow Island. island Santa Cruz Islands, E Solomon Islands
97 O19 **Nene** ≈ E England, UK
125 R4 **Nenetskiy Avtonomnyy Okrug** ◐ autonomous district NW Russian Federation
191 W11 **Nengonengo** atoll Îles Tuamotu, C French Polynesia
163 V6 **Nenjiang** Heilongjiang, NE China
163 U6 **Nen Jiang** var. Nonni. ≈ NE China
189 P16 **Neoch** atoll Caroline Islands, C Micronesia
115 D18 **Neochóri** Dytikí Ellás, C Greece
27 Q7 **Neodesha** Kansas, C USA
29 S14 **Neola** Iowa, C USA
Néon Karlovasi/Néon Karlovásion see Karlovási
115 E16 **Néo Monastíri** Thessalía, C Greece
Néon Monastiri see Néo Monastíri
27 R8 **Neosho** Missouri, C USA
27 Q7 **Neosho River** ≈ Kansas/Oklahoma, C USA
123 N12 **Nepa** ≈ C Russian Federation
153 N10 **Nepal** off. Kingdom of Nepal. ◆ monarchy S Asia
152 M11 **Nepālganj** Mid Western, SW Nepal
Nepal, Kingdom of see Nepal
14 L13 **Nepean** Ontario, SE Canada
36 L4 **Nephi** Utah, W USA
97 B16 **Nephin** Ir. Néifinn. ▲ W Ireland
67 T9 **Nepoko** ≈ NE Dem. Rep. Congo
18 K15 **Neptune** New Jersey, NE USA
182 G10 **Neptune Islands** island group South Australia
107 I14 **Nera** anc. Nar. ≈ C Italy
102 L14 **Nérac** Lot-et-Garonne, SW France
111 D16 **Neratovice** Ger. Neratowitz. Středocesky Kraj, C Czech Republic
Neratowitz see Neratovice
123 O13 **Nercha** ≈ S Russian Federation
123 O13 **Nerchinsk** Chitinskaya Oblast', S Russian Federation
123 P14 **Nerchinskiy Zavod** Chitinskaya Oblast', S Russian Federation
124 M15 **Nerekhta** Kostromskaya Oblast', NW Russian Federation
118 H10 **Nereta** Aizkraukle, S Latvia
106 K13 **Nereto** Abruzzo, C Italy
113 H15 **Neretva** ≈ Bosnia and Herzegovina/Croatia
115 C17 **Nerikós** ruins Lefkáda, Iónia Nisiá, Greece, C Mediterranean Sea
83 F15 **Neriquinha** Cuando Cubango, SE Angola
118 I13 **Neris** Bel. Viliya, Pol. Wilia; prev. Pol. Wilja. ≈ Belarus/Lithuania
Neris see Viliya
105 N15 **Nerja** Andalucía, S Spain
124 L16 **Nerl'** ≈ W Russian Federation
105 P12 **Nerpio** Castilla-La Mancha, C Spain
104 J13 **Nerva** Andalucía, S Spain
98 L4 **Nes** Friesland, N Netherlands
94 G13 **Nesbyen** Buskerud, S Norway
92 L2 **Neskaupstadhur** Austurland, E Iceland
92 F13 **Nesna** Nordland, C Norway
26 K5 **Ness City** Kansas, C USA
Nesselsdorf see Kopřivnice
108 H7 **Nesslau** Sankt Gallen, NE Switzerland
96 I9 **Ness, Loch** ◎ N Scotland, UK
Nesterov see Zhovkva
114 I12 **Néstos** Bul. Mesta, Turk. Kara Su. ≈ Bulgaria/Greece see also Mesta
Néstos see Mesta
95 C14 **Nesttun** Hordaland, S Norway
Nesvizh see Nyasvizh
138 F9 **Netanya** var. Natanya, Nathanya. Central, C Israel
98 I9 **Netherlands** off. Kingdom of the Netherlands, var. Holland, Dut. Koninkrijk der Nederlanden, Nederland. ◆ monarchy NW Europe
45 S9 **Netherlands Antilles** prev. Dutch West Indies. ◇ Dutch autonomous region S Caribbean Sea
Netherlands East Indies see Indonesia
Netherlands Guiana see Surinam
Netherlands, Kingdom of the see Netherlands
Netherlands New Guinea see Papua
116 L4 **Netishyn** Khmel'nyts'ka Oblast', W Ukraine
138 E11 **Netivot** Southern, S Israel
107 O21 **Neto** ≈ S Italy
9 Q6 **Nettilling Lake** ◎ Baffin Island, Nunavut, N Canada
29 V3 **Nett Lake** ◎ Minnesota, N USA
107 I16 **Nettuno** Lazio, C Italy
Netum see Noto
41 U16 **Netzahualcóyotl, Presa** ⊠ SE Mexico
Netze see Noteć
Neu Amerika see Puławy
Neubetsche see Novi Bečej
Neubidschow see Nový Bydžov
Neubistritz see Nová Bystřice
100 N9 **Neubrandenburg** Mecklenburg-Vorpommern, NE Germany
101 K22 **Neuburg an der Donau** Bayern, S Germany
108 C8 **Neuchâtel** Ger. Neuenburg. Neuchâtel, W Switzerland
108 C8 **Neuchâtel** Ger. Neuenburg. ◐ canton W Switzerland
108 C8 **Neuchâtel, Lac de** Ger. Neuenburger See. ◎ W Switzerland
Neudorf see Spišská Nová Ves
100 L10 **Neue Elde** canal N Germany
Neuenburg see Neuchâtel
Neuenburg an der Elbe see Nymburk
Neuenburger See see Neuchâtel, Lac de
108 F7 **Neuenhof** Aargau, N Switzerland
100 H11 **Neuenland** ✈ (Bremen) Bremen, NW Germany
Neuenstadt see La Neuveville
101 C18 **Neuerburg** Rheinland-Pfalz, W Germany
99 K24 **Neufchâteau** Luxembourg, SE Belgium
103 S6 **Neufchâteau** Vosges, NE France
102 M3 **Neufchâtel-en-Bray** Seine-Maritime, N France
109 S3 **Neufelden** Oberösterreich, N Austria
Neugradisk see Nova Gradiška
Neuhaus see Jindřichův Hradec
Neuhäusel see Nové Zámky
108 G6 **Neuhausen** var. Neuhausen am Rheinfall. Schaffhausen, N Switzerland
Neuhausen am Rheinfall see Neuhausen
101 I17 **Neuhof** Hessen, C Germany
Neuhof see Zgierz
Neukuhren see Pionerskiy
Neu-Langenburg see Tukuyu
109 W4 **Neulengbach** Niederösterreich, NE Austria
113 G15 **Neum** ◐ Federacija Bosna I Hercegovina, S Bosnia and Herzegovina
Neumark see Nowy Targ
Neumark see Nowe Miasto Lubawskie, Warmińsko-Mazurskie, Poland
Neumarkt see Neumarkt im Hausruckkreis, Oberösterreich, Austria
Neumarkt see Neumarkt am Wallersee, Salzburg, Austria
Neumarkt see Środa Śląska, Dolnośląskie, Poland
Neumarkt see Târgu Secuiesc, Covasna, Romania
Neumarkt see Târgu Mureș
109 Q5 **Neumarkt am Wallersee** var. Neumarkt. Salzburg, NW Austria
109 R4 **Neumarkt im Hausruckkreis** var. Neumarkt. Oberösterreich, N Austria
101 L20 **Neumarkt in der Oberpfalz** Bayern, SE Germany
Neumarktl see Tržič
Neumoldowa see Moldova Nouă
100 J8 **Neumünster** Schleswig-Holstein, N Germany
109 X5 **Neunkirchen** var. Neunkirchen am Steinfeld. Niederösterreich, E Austria
101 E20 **Neunkirchen** Saarland, SW Germany
Neunkirchen am Steinfeld see Neunkirchen
Neuoderberg see Bohumín
63 I15 **Neuquén** Neuquén, SE Argentina
63 H14 **Neuquén** off. Provincia de Neuquén. ◐ province W Argentina
Neuquén, Provincia de see Neuquén
63 H14 **Neuquén, Río** ≈ W Argentina
Neurode see Nowa Ruda
100 N11 **Neuruppin** Brandenburg, NE Germany
Neusalz an der Oder see Nowa Sól
Neu Sandec see Nowy Sącz
101 K22 **Neusäss** Bayern, S Germany
Neusatz see Novi Sad
Neuschliss see Gherla
21 N8 **Neuse River** ≈ North Carolina, SE USA
109 Z5 **Neusiedl am See** Burgenland, E Austria
111 G22 **Neusiedler See** Hung. Fertő. ◎ Austria/Hungary
Neusohl see Banská Bystrica
101 D15 **Neuss** anc. Novaesium, Novesium. Nordrhein-Westfalen, W Germany
Neuss see Nyon
Neustadt see Neustadt bei Coburg, Bayern, Germany
Neustadt see Neustadt an der Aisch, Bayern, Germany
Neustadt see Prudnik, Opole, Poland
Neustadt see Baia Mare, Maramureș, Romania
100 I12 **Neustadt am Rübenberge** Niedersachsen, N Germany
101 J19 **Neustadt an der Aisch** var. Neustadt. Bayern, C Germany
Neustadt an der Haardt see Neustadt an der Weinstrasse
101 F20 **Neustadt an der Weinstrasse** prev. Neustadt an der Haardt, hist. Niewenstat; anc. Nova Civitas. Rheinland-Pfalz, SW Germany
101 K18 **Neustadt bei Coburg** var. Neustadt. Bayern, C Germany
Neustadt bei Pinne see Lwówek
Neustadt in Oberschlesien see Prudnik
Neustadtl see Novo mesto
Neustadtl in Mähren see Nové Město na Moravě
Neustettin see Szczecinek
108 M8 **Neustift im Stubaital** var. Stubaital. Tirol, W Austria
100 N10 **Neustrelitz** Mecklenburg-Vorpommern, NE Germany
Neutitschein see Nový Jičín
Neutra see Nitra
101 J22 **Neu-Ulm** Bayern, S Germany
Neuveville see La Neuveville
103 N12 **Neuvic** Corrèze, C France
Neuwarp see Nowe Warpno
100 G9 **Neuwerk** island NW Germany
101 E17 **Neuwied** Rheinland-Pfalz, W Germany
Neuzen see Terneuzen
124 H12 **Neva** ≈ NW Russian Federation
29 V14 **Nevada** Iowa, C USA
27 R6 **Nevada** Missouri, C USA
35 R5 **Nevada** off. State of Nevada, also known as Battle Born State, Sagebrush State, Silver State. ◐ state W USA
35 P6 **Nevada City** California, W USA
124 G16 **Nevel'** Pskovskaya Oblast', W Russian Federation
123 T14 **Nevel'sk** Ostrov Sakhalin, Sakhalinskaya Oblast', SE Russian Federation
123 Q13 **Never** Amurskaya Oblast', SE Russian Federation
127 Q6 **Neverkino** Penzenskaya Oblast', W Russian Federation
103 P9 **Nevers** anc. Noviodunum. Nièvre, C France
18 J12 **Neversink River** ≈ New York, NE USA
183 Q6 **Nevertire** New South Wales, SE Australia
113 H15 **Nevesinje** ◐ Republika Srpska, S Bosnia and Herzegovina
118 G12 **Nevežis** ≈ C Lithuania
126 M14 **Nevinnomyssk** Stavropol'skiy Kray, SW Russian Federation
45 W10 **Nevis** island Saint Kitts and Nevis
Nevoso, Monte see Veliki Snežnik
Nevrokop see Gotse Delchev
136 J14 **Nevşehir** var. Nevshehr. Nevşehir, C Turkey
136 J14 **Nevşehir** var. Nevshehr. ◐ province C Turkey
Nevshehr see Nevşehir
122 G10 **Nev'yansk** Sverdlovskaya Oblast', C Russian Federation
81 J25 **Newala** Mtwara, SE Tanzania
31 P16 **New Albany** Indiana, N USA
22 M2 **New Albany** Mississippi, S USA
29 Y11 **New Albin** Iowa, C USA
55 U8 **New Amsterdam** E Guyana
183 Q4 **New Angledool** New South Wales, SE Australia
21 Y2 **Newark** Delaware, NE USA
18 K14 **Newark** New Jersey, NE USA
18 G10 **Newark** New York, NE USA
31 T13 **Newark** Ohio, N USA
Newark see Newark-on-Trent
35 W5 **Newark Lake** ◎ Nevada, W USA
97 N18 **Newark-on-Trent** var. Newark. C England, UK
22 M7 **New Augusta** Mississippi, S USA
19 P12 **New Bedford** Massachusetts, NE USA
32 G11 **Newberg** Oregon, NW USA
21 X10 **New Bern** North Carolina, SE USA
20 F8 **Newbern** Tennessee, S USA
31 P4 **Newberry** Michigan, N USA
21 Q12 **Newberry** South Carolina, SE USA
18 F15 **New Bloomfield** Pennsylvania, NE USA
25 X5 **New Boston** Texas, SW USA
25 S11 **New Braunfels** Texas, SW USA
31 Q13 **New Bremen** Ohio, N USA
97 F18 **Newbridge** Ir. An Droichead Nua. Kildare, C Ireland
18 B14 **New Brighton** Pennsylvania, NE USA
18 M12 **New Britain** Connecticut, NE USA
186 G7 **New Britain** island E Papua New Guinea
192 I8 **New Britain Trench** undersea feature W Pacific Ocean
18 J15 **New Brunswick** New Jersey, NE USA
15 V8 **New Brunswick** Fr. Nouveau-Brunswick. ◐ province SE Canada
18 K13 **Newburgh** New York, NE USA
97 M22 **Newbury** S England, UK
19 P10 **Newburyport** Massachusetts, NE USA
77 T14 **New Bussa** Niger, W Nigeria
187 O17 **New Caledonia** var. Kanaky, Fr. Nouvelle-Calédonie. ◇ French overseas territory SW Pacific Ocean
187 O15 **New Caledonia** island SW Pacific Ocean
175 O10 **New Caledonia Basin** undersea feature W Pacific Ocean
183 T8 **Newcastle** New South Wales, SE Australia
13 O14 **Newcastle** New Brunswick, SE Canada
14 I15 **Newcastle** Ontario, SE Canada
83 K22 **Newcastle** KwaZulu/Natal, E South Africa
97 G16 **Newcastle** Ir. An Caisleán Nua. SE Northern Ireland, UK
31 P13 **New Castle** Indiana, N USA
20 L5 **New Castle** Kentucky, S USA
27 N11 **Newcastle** Oklahoma, C USA
18 B13 **New Castle** Pennsylvania, NE USA
25 R6 **Newcastle** Texas, SW USA
36 J7 **Newcastle** Utah, W USA
21 S6 **New Castle** Virginia, NE USA
33 Z13 **Newcastle** Wyoming, C USA
45 W10 **Newcastle** ✈ Nevis, Saint Kitts and Nevis
97 L14 **Newcastle** ✈ NE England, UK
Newcastle see Newcastle upon Tyne
97 L18 **Newcastle-under-Lyme** C England, UK
97 M14 **Newcastle upon Tyne** var. Newcastle, hist. Monkchester, Lat. Pons Aelii. NE England, UK
181 Q4 **Newcastle Waters** Northern Territory, N Australia
Newchwang see Yingkou
18 K13 **New City** New York, NE USA
31 U13 **Newcomerstown** Ohio, N USA
18 G15 **New Cumberland** Pennsylvania, NE USA
21 R1 **New Cumberland** West Virginia, NE USA
152 I10 **New Delhi** ● (India) Delhi, N India
9 O17 **New Denver** British Columbia, SW Canada
28 J9 **Newell** South Dakota, N USA
21 Q13 **New Ellenton** South Carolina, SE USA
22 J6 **Newellton** Louisiana, S USA
28 K6 **New England** North Dakota, N USA
19 P8 **New England** cultural region NE USA
New England of the West see Minnesota
183 U5 **New England Range** ▲▲ New South Wales, SE Australia
64 G9 **New England Seamounts** var. Bermuda-New England Seamount Arc. undersea feature W Atlantic Ocean
38 M14 **Newenham, Cape** headland Alaska, USA
138 F11 **Newé Zohar** Southern, E Israel
18 D9 **Newfane** New York, NE USA
97 M23 **New Forest** physical region S England, UK
13 T12 **Newfoundland** Fr. Terre-Neuve. island Newfoundland and Labrador, SE Canada
13 R9 **Newfoundland and Labrador** Fr. Terre Neuve. ◐ province E Canada
65 J8 **Newfoundland Basin** undersea feature NW Atlantic Ocean
64 I8 **Newfoundland Ridge** undersea feature NW Atlantic Ocean
64 J8 **Newfoundland Seamounts** undersea feature N Sargasso Sea
18 G16 **New Freedom** Pennsylvania, NE USA
186 K9 **New Georgia** island New Georgia Islands, NW Solomon Islands
186 K8 **New Georgia Islands** island group NW Solomon Islands
186 L8 **New Georgia Sound** var. The Slot. sound E Solomon Sea
30 L9 **New Glarus** Wisconsin, N USA
13 Q15 **New Glasgow** Nova Scotia, SE Canada
New Goa see Panaji
186 A6 **New Guinea** Dut. Nieuw Guinea, Ind. Irian. island Indonesia/Papua New Guinea
192 H8 **New Guinea Trench** undersea feature SW Pacific Ocean
32 I6 **Newhalem** Washington, NW USA
39 P13 **Newhalen** Alaska, USA
29 X13 **Newhall** Iowa, C USA
14 F16 **New Hamburg** Ontario, S Canada
19 N9 **New Hampshire** off. State of New Hampshire, also known as Granite State. ◐ state NE USA
29 W12 **New Hampton** Iowa, C USA
186 G5 **New Hanover** island NE Papua New Guinea
97 P23 **Newhaven** SE England, UK
18 M13 **New Haven** Connecticut, NE USA
31 Q12 **New Haven** Indiana, N USA
27 W5 **New Haven** Missouri, C USA
10 K13 **New Hazelton** British Columbia, SW Canada
New Hebrides see Vanuatu
175 P9 **New Hebrides Trench** undersea feature N Coral Sea
18 H15 **New Holland** Pennsylvania, NE USA
22 I9 **New Iberia** Louisiana, S USA
186 G5 **New Ireland** ◐ province NE Papua New Guinea
186 G5 **New Ireland** island NE Papua New Guinea
65 A24 **New Island** island W Falkland Islands
18 J15 **New Jersey** off. State of New Jersey, also known as The Garden State. ◐ state NE USA
18 C14 **New Kensington** Pennsylvania, NE USA
21 W6 **New Kent** Virginia, NE USA
27 O8 **Newkirk** Oklahoma, C USA
21 Q9 **Newland** North Carolina, SE USA
28 L6 **New Leipzig** North Dakota, N USA
14 H9 **New Liskeard** Ontario, S Canada
22 G7 **Newllano** Louisiana, S USA
19 N13 **New London** Connecticut, NE USA
29 Y15 **New London** Iowa, C USA
29 T8 **New London** Minnesota, N USA
27 V3 **New London** Missouri, C USA
30 M7 **New London** Wisconsin, N USA
27 Y8 **New Madrid** Missouri, C USA
180 J8 **Newman** Western Australia
194 M13 **Newman Island** island Antarctica
14 H15 **Newmarket** Ontario, S Canada
97 P20 **Newmarket** E England, UK
19 P10 **Newmarket** New Hampshire, NE USA
21 U4 **New Market** Virginia, NE USA
21 R2 **New Martinsville** West Virginia, NE USA
31 U14 **New Matamoras** Ohio, N USA
32 M12 **New Meadows** Idaho, NW USA
26 R12 **New Mexico** off. State of New Mexico, also known as Land of Enchantment, Sunshine State. ◐ state SW USA
149 V6 **New Mīrpur** var. Mīrpur. Sind, SE Pakistan
151 N15 **New Moore Island** Island E India
23 S4 **Newnan** Georgia, SE USA
183 P17 **New Norfolk** Tasmania, SE Australia
22 K9 **New Orleans** Louisiana, S USA
22 K9 **New Orleans** ✈ Louisiana, S USA
18 K12 **New Paltz** New York, NE USA
31 U12 **New Philadelphia** Ohio, N USA
184 K10 **New Plymouth** Taranaki, North Island, New Zealand
97 M24 **Newport** S England, UK
97 K22 **Newport** SE Wales, UK
27 W10 **Newport** Arkansas, C USA
31 N13 **Newport** Indiana, N USA
20 M3 **Newport** Kentucky, S USA
29 W9 **Newport** Minnesota, N USA
32 F12 **Newport** Oregon, NW USA
19 O13 **Newport** Rhode Island, NE USA
21 O9 **Newport** Tennessee, S USA
19 N6 **Newport** Vermont, NE USA
32 M7 **Newport** Washington, NW USA
21 X7 **Newport News** Virginia, NE USA
97 N20 **Newport Pagnell** SE England, UK
23 U12 **New Port Richey** Florida, SE USA
29 V9 **New Prague** Minnesota, N USA
44 H3 **New Providence** island N Bahamas
97 I20 **New Quay** SW Wales, UK
97 H24 **Newquay** SW England, UK
29 V10 **New Richland** Minnesota, N USA
15 X7 **New-Richmond** Québec, SE Canada
31 R15 **New Richmond** Ohio, N USA
30 I5 **New Richmond** Wisconsin, N USA
42 G1 **New River** ≈ N Belize
55 T12 **New River** ≈ SE Guyana
21 R6 **New River** ≈ West Virginia, NE USA
42 G1 **New River Lagoon** ◎ N Belize
22 J8 **New Roads** Louisiana, S USA
18 L14 **New Rochelle** New York, NE USA
29 O4 **New Rockford** North Dakota, N USA
97 P23 **New Romney** SE England, UK
97 F20 **New Ross** Ir. Ros Mhic Thriúin. Wexford, SE Ireland
97 F16 **Newry** Ir. An tIúr. SE Northern Ireland, UK
28 M5 **New Salem** North Dakota, N USA
New Sarum see Salisbury
29 W14 **New Sharon** Iowa, C USA
New Siberian Islands see Novosibirskiye Ostrova
23 X11 **New Smyrna Beach** Florida, SE USA
183 O7 **New South Wales** ◐ state SE Australia
39 O13 **New Stuyahok** Alaska, USA
21 N8 **New Tazewell** Tennessee, S USA
38 M12 **Newtok** Alaska, USA
23 S7 **Newton** Georgia, SE USA
29 W14 **Newton** Iowa, C USA
27 N6 **Newton** Kansas, C USA
19 O11 **Newton** Massachusetts, NE USA
22 M5 **Newton** Mississippi, S USA
18 J14 **Newton** New Jersey, NE USA
21 R9 **Newton** North Carolina, SE USA
25 Y9 **Newton** Texas, SW USA
97 J24 **Newton Abbot** SW England, UK
96 K13 **Newton St Boswells** SE Scotland, UK
97 I14 **Newton Stewart** S Scotland, UK
92 O2 **Newtontoppen** ▲ C Svalbard
97 J20 **Newtown** E Wales, UK
28 K3 **New Town** North Dakota, N USA
97 G15 **Newtownabbey** Ir. Baile na Mainistreach. E Northern Ireland, UK
97 G15 **Newtownards** Ir. Baile Nua na hArda. SE Northern Ireland, UK
29 U10 **New Ulm** Minnesota, N USA
28 K10 **New Underwood** South Dakota, N USA
25 V10 **New Waverly** Texas, SW USA
18 K14 **New York** New York, NE USA
18 G10 **New York** ◐ state NE USA
35 X13 **New York Mountains** ▲▲ California, W USA
184 K12 **New Zealand** ◆ commonwealth republic SW Pacific Ocean
95 M24 **Nexø** var. Neksø Bornholm. E Denmark
125 O15 **Neya** Kostromskaya Oblast', NW Russian Federation
Neyba see Neiba
143 Q12 **Neyrīz** var. Neiriz, Niriz. Fārs, S Iran
143 T4 **Neyshābūr** var. Nishapur. Khorāsān-Razavī, NE Iran
155 J21 **Neyveli** Tamil Nādu, SE India
Nezhin see Nizhyn
33 N10 **Nezperce** Idaho, NW USA
22 H8 **Nezpique, Bayou** ≈ Louisiana, S USA
77 Y13 **Ngadda** ≈ NE Nigeria
N'Gage see Negage
185 G16 **Ngahere** West Coast, South Island, New Zealand
77 Z12 **Ngala** Borno, NE Nigeria

◆ Country
● Country Capital
◇ Dependent Territory
○ Dependent Territory Capital
◐ Administrative Regions
✈ International Airport
▲ Mountain
▲▲ Mountain Range
Volcano
≈ River
◎ Lake
⊠ Reservoir

158 K16 **Ngamring** Xizang Zizhiqu, W China
81 K19 **Ngangerabeli Plain** *plain* SE Kenya
158 I14 **Ngangla Ringco** ◎ W China
158 G13 **Nganglong Kangri** ▲ W China
158 K15 **Ngangzê Co** ◎ W China
79 F14 **Ngaoundéré** *var.* N'Gaoundéré. Adamaoua, N Cameroon
N'Gaoundéré *see* Ngaoundéré
81 E20 **Ngara** Kagera, NW Tanzania
188 F8 **Ngardmau Bay** *bay* Babeldaob, N Palau
188 F7 **Ngaregur** *island* Palau Islands, N Palau
Ngarrab *see* Gyaca
184 L7 **Ngaruawahia** Waikato, North Island, New Zealand
184 N11 **Ngaruroro** ≈ North Island, New Zealand
190 I16 **Ngatangiia** Rarotonga, S Cook Islands
184 M6 **Ngatea** Waikato, North Island, New Zealand
166 L8 **Ngathainggyaung** Irrawaddy, SW Myanmar (Burma)
Ngatik *see* Ngetik Atoll
Ngau *see* Gau
Ngawa *see* Aba
188 C7 **Ngcheangel** *var.* Kayangel Islands. *island* Palau Islands, N Palau
188 E10 **Ngchemiangel** Babeldaob, N Palau
188 C8 **Ngeaur** *var.* Angaur. *island* Palau Islands, S Palau
188 E10 **Ngerkeai** Babeldaob, N Palau
188 F9 **Ngermechau** Babeldaob, N Palau
188 C8 **Ngeruktabel** *prev.* Urukthapel. *island* Palau Islands, S Palau
188 F8 **Ngetbong** Babeldaob, N Palau
189 T17 **Ngetik Atoll** *var.* Ngatik; *prev.* Los Jardines. *atoll* Caroline Islands, E Micronesia
188 E10 **Ngetkip** Babeldaob, N Palau
Nghia Dan *see* Thai Hoa
83 C16 **N'Giva** *var.* Ondjiva, *Port.* Vila Pereira de Eça. Cunene, S Angola
79 G20 **Ngo** Plateaux, SE Congo
167 S7 **Ngoc Lac** Thanh Hoa, N Vietnam
79 G17 **Ngoko** ≈ Cameroon/Congo
81 H19 **Ngorengore** Rift Valley, SW Kenya
159 Q11 **Ngoring Hu** ◎ C China
Ngorolaka *see* Banifing
81 H20 **Ngorongoro Crater** *crater* N Tanzania
79 D19 **Ngounié** *off.* Province de la Ngounié, *var.* La Ngounié. ◈ *province* S Gabon
79 D19 **Ngounié** ≈ Congo/Gabon
Ngounié, Province de la *see* Ngounié
78 H10 **Ngoura** *var.* NGoura. Chari-Baguirmi, W Chad
NGoura *see* Ngoura
78 G10 **Ngouri** *var.* NGouri; *prev.* Fort-Millot. Lac, W Chad
NGouri *see* Ngouri
77 Y10 **Ngourti** Diffa, E Niger
77 Y11 **Nguigmi** *var.* N'Guigmi. Diffa, SE Niger
N'Guigmi *see* Nguigmi
Nguimbo *see* Lumbala N'Guimbo
188 F15 **Ngulu Atoll** *atoll* Caroline Islands, W Micronesia
187 R14 **Nguna** *island* C Vanuatu
N'Gunza *see* Sumbe
169 U17 **Ngurah Rai** ✈ (Bali) Bali, S Indonesia
77 W12 **Nguru** Yobe, NE Nigeria
Ngwaketze *see* Southern
83 I16 **Ngweze** ≈ S Zambia
83 M17 **Nhamatanda** Sofala, C Mozambique
58 G12 **Nhamundá, Rio** *var.* Jamundá, Yamundá. ≈ N Brazil
60 J7 **Nhandeara** São Paulo, S Brazil
82 D12 **Nharêa** *var.* N'Harea, Nhareia. Bié, W Angola
N'Harea *see* Nharêa
Nhareia *see* Nharêa
167 V12 **Nha Trang** Khanh Hoa, S Vietnam
182 L11 **Nhill** Victoria, SE Australia
83 L22 **Nhlangano** *prev.* Goedgegun. SW Swaziland
181 S1 **Nhulunbuy** Northern Territory, N Australia
77 N10 **Niafounké** Tombouctou, W Mali
31 N5 **Niagara** Wisconsin, N USA
14 H16 **Niagara** ≈ Ontario, S Canada
14 G15 **Niagara Escarpment** *hill range* Ontario, S Canada
14 H16 **Niagara Falls** Ontario, S Canada
18 D9 **Niagara Falls** New York, NE USA
14 H16 **Niagara Falls** *waterfall* Canada/USA
76 K12 **Niagassola** *var.* Nyagassola. Haute-Guinée, NE Guinea
77 R12 **Niamey** ● (Niger) Niamey, SW Niger
77 R12 **Niamey** ✈ Niamey, SW Niger
77 R14 **Niamtougou** N Togo
79 O16 **Niangara** Orientale, NE Dem. Rep. Congo
77 O10 **Niangay, Lac** ◎ E Mali
77 N14 **Niangoloko** SW Burkina
27 U6 **Niangua River** ≈ Missouri, C USA
79 O17 **Nia-Nia** Orientale, NE Dem. Rep. Congo
19 N13 **Niantic** Connecticut, NE USA
163 U7 **Nianzishan** Heilongjiang, NE China
168 H10 **Nias, Pulau** *island* W Indonesia
82 O13 **Niassa** *off.* Província do Niassa. ◈ *province* N Mozambique
Niassa, Província do *see* Niassa
191 U10 **Niau** *island* Îles Tuamotu, C French Polynesia
95 G20 **Nibe** Nordjylland, N Denmark
189 Q8 **Nibok** N Nauru
118 C10 **Nīca** Liepāja, W Latvia
Nicaea *see* Nice
42 J9 **Nicaragua** *off.* Republic of Nicaragua. ◆ *republic* Central America
42 K11 **Nicaragua, Lago de** *var.* Cocibolca, Gran Lago, *Eng.* Lake Nicaragua. ◎ S Nicaragua
Nicaragua, Lake *see* Nicaragua, Lago de
64 D11 **Nicaraguan Rise** *undersea feature* NW Caribbean Sea
Nicaragua, Republic of *see* Nicaragua
Nicaria *see* Ikaría
107 N21 **Nicastro** Calabria, SW Italy
103 V15 **Nice** *It.* Nizza; *anc.* Nicaea. Alpes-Maritimes, SE France
Nice *see* Côte d'Azur
Nicephorium *see* Ar Raqqah
12 M9 **Nichicun, Lac** ◎ Québec, E Canada
164 D16 **Nichinan** *var.* Nitinan. Miyazaki, Kyūshū, SW Japan
44 E4 **Nicholas Channel** *channel* N Cuba
Nicholas II Land *see* Severnaya Zemlya
149 U2 **Nicholas Range** *Pash.* Selselehye Kuhe Vākhān, *Taj.* Qatorkŭhi Vakhon. ▲▲ Afghanistan/Tajikistan
20 M6 **Nicholasville** Kentucky, S USA
44 G2 **Nicholls Town** Andros Island, NW Bahamas
21 U12 **Nichols** South Carolina, SE USA
55 U9 **Nickerie** ◈ *district* NW Surinam
55 V9 **Nickerie Rivier** ≈ NW Surinam
151 P22 **Nicobar Islands** *island group* India, E Indian Ocean
116 L9 **Nicolae Bălcescu** Botoşani, NE Romania
15 P11 **Nicolet** Québec, SE Canada
15 Q12 **Nicolet** ≈ Québec, SE Canada
31 Q4 **Nicolet, Lake** ◎ Michigan, N USA
29 U10 **Nicollet** Minnesota, N USA
61 F19 **Nico Pérez** Florida, S Uruguay
Nicopolis *see* Nikopol, Bulgaria
Nicopolis *see* Nikópoli, Greece
121 P2 **Nicosia** *Gk.* Lefkosía, *Turk.* Lefkoşa. ● (Cyprus) C Cyprus
107 K24 **Nicosia** Sicilia, Italy, C Mediterranean Sea
107 N22 **Nicotera** Calabria, SW Italy
42 K13 **Nicoya** Guanacaste, W Costa Rica
42 L14 **Nicoya, Golfo de** *gulf* W Costa Rica
42 L14 **Nicoya, Península de** *peninsula* NW Costa Rica
Nictheroy *see* Niterói
118 B12 **Nida** *Ger.* Nidden. Klaipėda, SW Lithuania
111 L15 **Nida** ≈ S Poland
Nidaros *see* Trondheim
108 D8 **Nidau** Bern, W Switzerland
101 H17 **Nidda** ≈ W Germany
Nidden *see* Nida
95 F17 **Nidelva** ≈ S Norway
110 L9 **Nidzica** *Ger.* Niedenburg. Warmińsko Mazurskie, NE Poland
100 H6 **Niebüll** Schleswig-Holstein, N Germany
Niedenburg *see* Nidzica
99 N25 **Niederanven** Luxembourg, C Luxembourg
103 V4 **Niederbronn-les-Bains** Bas-Rhin, NE France
Niederdonau *see* Niederösterreich
109 S7 **Niedere Tauern** ▲▲ C Austria
101 P14 **Niederlausitz** *Eng.* Lower Lusatia, *Lus.* Donja Łužica. *physical region* E Germany
109 U5 **Niederösterreich** *off.* Land Niederösterreich, *Eng.* Lower Austria, *Ger.* Niederdonau; *prev.* Lower Danube. ◈ *state* NE Austria
Niederösterreich, Land *see* Niederösterreich
100 G12 **Niedersachsen** *Eng.* Lower Saxony, *Fr.* Basse-Saxe. ◈ *state* NW Germany
79 D17 **Niefang** *var.* Sevilla de Niefang. NW Equatorial Guinea
83 G23 **Niekerkshoop** Northern Cape, W South Africa
99 G17 **Niel** Antwerpen, N Belgium
Niélé *see* Niellé
76 M14 **Niellé** *var.* Niélé. N Ivory Coast
79 O22 **Niemba** Katanga, E Dem. Rep. Congo
111 G15 **Niemcza** *Ger.* Nimptsch. Dolnośląskie, SW Poland
Niemen *see* Neman
92 J13 **Niemisel** Norrbotten, N Sweden
111 H15 **Niemodlin** *Ger.* Falkenberg. Opolskie, SW Poland
76 M13 **Niéna** Sikasso, SW Mali
100 H12 **Nienburg** Niedersachsen, N Germany
100 N13 **Nieplitz** ≈ NE Germany
111 L16 **Niepołomice** Malopolskie, S Poland
101 D14 **Niers** ≈ Germany/Netherlands
101 Q15 **Niesky** *Lus.* Niska. Sachsen, E Germany
Nieśwież *see* Nyasvizh
Nieuport *see* Nieuwpoort
98 O8 **Nieuw-Amsterdam** Drenthe, NE Netherlands
55 W9 **Nieuw Amsterdam** Commewijne, NE Surinam
99 M14 **Nieuw-Bergen** Limburg, SE Netherlands
98 O7 **Nieuw-Buinen** Drenthe, NE Netherlands
98 J12 **Nieuwegein** Utrecht, C Netherlands
98 P6 **Nieuwe Pekela** Groningen, NE Netherlands
98 P5 **Nieuweschans** Groningen, NE Netherlands
Nieuw Guinea *see* New Guinea
98 I11 **Nieuwkoop** Zuid-Holland, C Netherlands
98 M9 **Nieuwleusen** Overijssel, S Netherlands
98 J11 **Nieuw-Loosdrecht** Noord-Holland, C Netherlands
55 U9 **Nieuw Nickerie** Nickerie, NW Surinam
98 P5 **Nieuwolda** Groningen, NE Netherlands
99 B17 **Nieuwpoort** *var.* Nieuport. West-Vlaanderen, W Belgium
99 G14 **Nieuw-Vossemeer** Noord-Brabant, S Netherlands
98 P7 **Nieuw-Weerdinge** Drenthe, NE Netherlands
40 L10 **Nieves** Zacatecas, C Mexico
64 O11 **Nieves, Pico de las** ▲ Gran Canaria, Islas Canarias, Spain, NE Atlantic Ocean
103 P8 **Nièvre** ◈ *department* C France
Niewenstat *see* Neustadt an der Weinstrasse
136 J15 **Niğde** Niğde, C Turkey
136 J15 **Niğde** ◈ *province* C Turkey
83 J21 **Nigel** Gauteng, NE South Africa
77 V10 **Niger** *off.* Republic of Niger. ◆ *republic* W Africa
77 T14 **Niger** ◈ *state* C Nigeria
67 P8 **Niger** ≈ W Africa
Niger Cone *see* Niger Fan
67 P9 **Niger Delta** *delta* S Nigeria
67 P9 **Niger Fan** *var.* Niger Cone. *undersea feature* E Atlantic Ocean
77 T13 **Nigeria** *off.* Federal Republic of Nigeria. ◆ *federal republic* W Africa
Nigeria, Federal Republic of *see* Nigeria
77 T17 **Niger, Mouths of the** *delta* S Nigeria
Niger, Republic of *see* Niger
185 C24 **Nightcaps** Southland, South Island, New Zealand
14 F7 **Night Hawk Lake** ◎ Ontario, S Canada
65 M19 **Nightingale Island** *island* S Tristan da Cunha, S Atlantic Ocean
38 M12 **Nightmute** Alaska, USA
114 G13 **Nigríta** Kentrikí Makedonía, NE Greece
148 J15 **Nihing** *Per.* Rūd-e Nahang. ≈ Iran/Pakistan
191 V10 **Nihiru** *atoll* Îles Tuamotu, C French Polynesia
Nihommatsu *see* Nihonmatsu
Nihon *see* Japan
165 P11 **Nihonmatsu** *var.* Nihommatsu, Nihonmatu. Fukushima, Honshū, C Japan
Nihonmatu *see* Nihonmatsu
62 I12 **Nihuil, Embalse del** ◎ W Argentina
165 O10 **Niigata** Niigata, Honshū, C Japan
165 O11 **Niigata** *off.* Niigata-ken. ◈ *prefecture* Honshū, C Japan
Niigata-ken *see* Niigata
165 G14 **Niihama** Ehime, Shikoku, SW Japan
38 A8 **Ni'ihau** *var.* Niihau. *island* Hawai'i, USA, C Pacific Ocean
165 X12 **Nii-jima** *island* E Japan
165 H12 **Niimi** Okayama, Honshū, SW Japan
165 O10 **Niitsu** *var.* Niitu. Niigata, Honshū, C Japan
Niitu *see* Niitsu
105 P15 **Nijar** Andalucía, S Spain
98 K11 **Nijkerk** Gelderland, C Netherlands
99 H16 **Nijlen** Antwerpen, N Belgium
98 L13 **Nijmegen** *Ger.* Nimwegen; *anc.* Noviomagus. Gelderland, SE Netherlands
98 N10 **Nijverdal** Overijssel, E Netherlands
190 G16 **Nikao** Rarotonga, S Cook Islands
Nikaria *see* Ikaría
124 I2 **Nikel'** Murmanskaya Oblast', NW Russian Federation
171 Q17 **Nikiniki** Timor, S Indonesia
129 Q15 **Nikitin Seamount** *undersea feature* E Indian Ocean
77 S14 **Nikki** E Benin
Niklasmarkt *see* Gheorgheni
39 P10 **Nikolai** Alaska, USA
Nikolaiken *see* Mikołajki
Nikolainkaupunki *see* Vaasa
Nikolayev *see* Mykolayiv
145 O6 **Nikolayevka** Severnyy Kazakhstan, N Kazakhstan
Nikolayevka *see* Zhetigen
127 P9 **Nikolayevsk** Volgogradskaya Oblast', SW Russian Federation
Nikolayevskaya Oblast' *see* Mykolayivs'ka Oblast'
123 S12 **Nikolayevsk-na-Amure** Khabarovskiy Kray, SE Russian Federation
127 P6 **Nikol'sk** Penzenskaya Oblast', W Russian Federation
125 O13 **Nikol'sk** Vologodskaya Oblast', NW Russian Federation
Nikol'sk *see* Ussuriysk
38 K17 **Nikolski** Umnak Island, Alaska, USA
Nikol'skiy *see* Satpayev
127 V7 **Nikol'skoye** Orenburgskaya Oblast', W Russian Federation
Nikol'sk-Ussuriyskiy *see* Ussuriysk
114 J7 **Nikopol** *anc.* Nicopolis. Pleven, N Bulgaria
117 S9 **Nikopol'** Dnipropetrovs'ka Oblast', SE Ukraine
115 C17 **Nikópoli** *anc.* Nicopolis. *site of ancient city* Ípeiros, W Greece
136 M12 **Niksar** Tokat, N Turkey
143 V14 **Nīkshahr** Sīstān va Balūchestān, SE Iran
113 J16 **Nikšić** C Montenegro
191 R4 **Nikumaroro**; *prev.* Gardner Island. *atoll* Phoenix Islands, C Kiribati
191 P3 **Nikunau** *var.* Nukunau; *prev.* Byron Island. *atoll* Tungaru, W Kiribati
155 G21 **Nilambūr** Kerala, SW India
35 X16 **Niland** California, W USA
80 G8 **Nile** *former province* NW Uganda
67 T3 **Nile** *Ar.* Nahr an Nīl. ≈ N Africa
75 W7 **Nile Delta** *delta* N Egypt
67 T3 **Nile Fan** *undersea feature* E Mediterranean Sea
31 O11 **Niles** Michigan, N USA
31 V11 **Niles** Ohio, N USA
155 F20 **Nileswaram** Kerala, SW India
14 K10 **Nilgaut, Lac** ◎ Québec, SE Canada
149 O6 **Nīlī** Dāikondī, C Afghanistan
158 I5 **Nilka** Xinjiang Uygur Zizhiqu, NW China
Nīl, Nahr an *see* Nile
93 N16 **Nilsiä** Itä-Suomi, C Finland
154 F9 **Nimach** Madhya Pradesh, C India
152 G14 **Nimbāhera** Rājasthān, N India
76 L15 **Nimba, Monts** *var.* Nimba Mountains. ▲▲ W Africa
Nimba Mountains *see* Nimba, Monts
Nimburg *see* Nymburk
103 Q15 **Nîmes** *anc.* Nemausus, Nismes. Gard, S France
152 H11 **Nīm ka Thāna** Rājasthān, N India
183 R11 **Nimmitabel** New South Wales, SE Australia
Nimptsch *see* Niemcza
195 R11 **Nimrod Glacier** *glacier* Antarctica
Nimroze *see* Nīmrūz
148 K8 **Nīmrūz** *var.* Nimroze; *prev.* Chakhānsūr. ◈ *province* SW Afghanistan
81 F16 **Nimule** Eastern Equatoria, S Sudan
Nimwegen *see* Nijmegen
155 C23 **Nine Degree Channel** *channel* India/Maldives
18 G9 **Ninemile Point** *headland* New York, NE USA
173 S8 **Ninetyeast Ridge** *undersea feature* E Indian Ocean
183 P13 **Ninety Mile Beach** *beach* Victoria, SE Australia
184 I2 **Ninety Mile Beach** *beach* North Island, New Zealand
21 P12 **Ninety Six** South Carolina, SE USA
163 Y9 **Ning'an** Heilongjiang, NE China
161 S9 **Ningbo** *var.* Ning-po, Yin-hsien; *prev.* Ninghsien. Zhejiang, SE China
161 U12 **Ningde** Fujian, SE China
161 P12 **Ningdu** *var.* Meijiang. Jiangxi, S China
Ning'er *see* Pu'er
186 A7 **Ningerum** Western, SW Papua New Guinea
161 R9 **Ningguo** Anhui, E China
161 S9 **Ninghai** Zhejiang, SE China
Ning-hsia *see* Ningxia
Ninghsien *see* Ningbo
160 J15 **Ningming** *var.* Chengzhong. Guangxi Zhuangzu Zizhiqu, S China
160 H11 **Ningnan** *var.* Pisha. Sichuan, C China
Ning-po *see* Ningbo
Ningsia/Ningsia Hui/Ningsia Hui Autonomous Region *see* Ningxia
160 J5 **Ningxia** *off.* Ningxia Huizu Zizhiqu, *var.* Ning-hsia, Ningsia, *Eng.* Ningsia Hui, Ningsia Hui Autonomous Region. ◈ *autonomous region* N China
Ningxia Huizu Zizhiqu *see* Ningxia
159 X10 **Ningxian** Gansu, N China
167 T7 **Ninh Binh** Ninh Binh, N Vietnam
167 V12 **Ninh Hoa** Khanh Hoa, S Vietnam
186 C4 **Ninigo Group** *island group* N Papua New Guinea
39 Q12 **Ninilchik** Alaska, USA
27 N7 **Ninnescah River** ≈ Kansas, C USA
195 U16 **Ninnis Glacier** *glacier* Antarctica
165 R8 **Ninohe** Iwate, Honshū, C Japan
99 F18 **Ninove** Oost-Vlaanderen, C Belgium
171 O4 **Ninoy Aquino** ✈ (Manila) Luzon, N Philippines
Nio *see* Íos
29 P12 **Niobrara** Nebraska, C USA
28 M12 **Niobrara River** ≈ Nebraska/Wyoming, C USA
79 I20 **Nioki** Bandundu, W Dem. Rep. Congo
76 M11 **Niono** Ségou, C Mali
76 K11 **Nioro** *var.* Nioro du Sahel. Kayes, W Mali
76 G11 **Nioro du Rip** SW Senegal
Nioro du Sahel *see* Nioro
102 K10 **Niort** Deux-Sèvres, W France
172 H14 **Nioumachoua** Mohéli, S Comoros
186 C7 **Nipa** Southern Highlands, W Papua New Guinea
9 U14 **Nipawin** Saskatchewan, S Canada
12 D12 **Nipigon** Ontario, S Canada
12 D11 **Nipigon, Lake** ◎ Ontario, S Canada
9 S13 **Nipin** ≈ Saskatchewan, C Canada
14 G11 **Nipissing, Lake** ◎ Ontario, S Canada
35 P13 **Nipomo** California, W USA
Nippon *see* Japan
138 K6 **Niqniqīyah, Jabal an** ▲ C Syria
62 I9 **Niquivil** San Juan, W Argentina
171 Y13 **Nirabotong** Papua, E Indonesia
Niriz *see* Neyrīz
163 U7 **Nirji** *var.* Morin Dawa Daurzu Zizhiqi. Nei Mongol Zizhiqu, N China
155 I14 **Nirmal** Andhra Pradesh, C India
153 Q13 **Nirmāli** Bihār, NE India
113 O14 **Niš** *Eng.* Nish, *Ger.* Nisch; *anc.* Naissus. Serbia, SE Serbia
104 H9 **Nisa** Portalegre, C Portugal
Nisa *see* Neisse
141 P4 **Nişab** Al Ḩudūd ash Shamālīyah, N Saudi Arabia
141 Q15 **Nişāb** *var.* Anşāb. SW Yemen
113 P14 **Nišava** *Bul.* Nishava. ≈ Bulgaria/Serbia *see also* Nishava
Nišava *see* Nishava
107 K25 **Niscemi** Sicilia, Italy, C Mediterranean Sea
Nisch/Nish *see* Niš
165 R4 **Niseko** Hokkaidō, NE Japan
Nishapur *see* Neyshābūr
114 G9 **Nishava** *var.* Nišava. ≈ Bulgaria/Serbia *see also* Nišava
Nishava *see* Nišava
118 L11 **Nishcha** ≈ N Belarus
165 C17 **Nishinoomote** Kagoshima, Tanega-shima, SW Japan
165 X15 **Nishino-shima** *Eng.* Rosario. *island* Ogasawara-shotō, SE Japan
165 I13 **Nishiwaki** *var.* Nisiwaki. Hyōgo, Honshū, SW Japan
141 U14 **Nishtūn** SE Yemen
Nisibin *see* Nusaybin
Nisiros *see* Nísyros
Nisiwaki *see* Nishiwaki
Niska *see* Niesky
113 O14 **Niška Banja** Serbia, SE Serbia
12 D6 **Niskibi** ≈ Ontario, C Canada
111 O15 **Nisko** Podkrapackie, SE Poland
10 H7 **Nisling** ≈ Yukon Territory, W Canada
99 H22 **Nismes** Namur, S Belgium
Nismes *see* Nîmes
116 M10 **Nisporeni** *Rus.* Nisporeny. W Moldova
Nisporeny *see* Nisporeni
95 K20 **Nissan** ≈ S Sweden
Nissan Islands *see* Green Islands
95 F16 **Nisser** ◎ S Norway
95 E21 **Nissum Bredning** *inlet* NW Denmark
29 U6 **Nisswa** Minnesota, N USA
Nistru *see* Dniester
115 M22 **Nísyros** *var.* Nisiros. *island* Dodekánisa, Greece, Aegean Sea
118 H8 **Nītaure** Cēsis, C Latvia
60 P10 **Niterói** *prev.* Nictheroy. Rio de Janeiro, SE Brazil
14 F16 **Nith** ≈ Ontario, S Canada
96 J13 **Nith** ≈ S Scotland, UK
Nitinan *see* Nichinan
111 I21 **Nitra** *Ger.* Neutra, *Hung.* Nyitra. Nitriansky Kraj, SW Slovakia
111 I20 **Nitra** *Ger.* Neutra, *Hung.* Nyitra. ≈ W Slovakia
111 I21 **Nitriansky Kraj** ◈ *region* SW Slovakia
21 Q5 **Nitro** West Virginia, NE USA
95 H14 **Nittedal** Akershus, S Norway
Niuatobutabu *see* Niuatoputapu
193 X13 **Niuatoputapu** *var.* Niuatobutabu; *prev.* Keppel Island. *island* N Tonga
193 U15 **Niu'Aunofa** *headland* Tongatapu, S Tonga
Niuchwang *see* Yingkou
190 B16 **Niue** ◇ *self-governing territory in free association with New Zealand* S Pacific Ocean
190 F10 **Niulakita** *var.* Nurakita. *atoll* S Tuvalu
190 E6 **Niutao** *atoll* NW Tuvalu
93 L15 **Nivala** Oulu, C Finland
102 I15 **Nive** ≈ SW France
99 G19 **Nivelles** Walloon Brabant, C Belgium
103 P8 **Nivernais** *cultural region* C France
15 N8 **Niverville, Lac** ◎ Québec, SE Canada
27 T7 **Nixa** Missouri, C USA
35 R5 **Nixon** Nevada, W USA
25 S12 **Nixon** Texas, SW USA
Niya *see* Minfeng
155 H14 **Nizāmābād** Andhra Pradesh, C India
155 H15 **Nizām Sāgar** ◎ C India
125 N16 **Nizhegorodskaya Oblast'** ◈ *province* W Russian Federation
Nizhnegorskiy *see* Nyzhn'ohirs'kyy
127 S4 **Nizhnekamsk** Respublika Tatarstan, W Russian Federation
127 U3 **Nizhnekamskoye Vodokhranilishche** ▣ W Russian Federation
123 S14 **Nizhneleninskoye** Yevreyskaya Avtonomnaya Oblast', SE Russian Federation
122 L13 **Nizhneudinsk** Irkutskaya Oblast', S Russian Federation
122 I10 **Nizhnevartovsk** Khanty-Mansiyskiy Avtonomnyy Okrug, C Russian Federation
123 Q7 **Nizhneyansk** Respublika Sakha (Yakutiya), NE Russian Federation
127 Q11 **Nizhniy Baskunchak** Astrakhanskaya Oblast', SW Russian Federation
127 O6 **Nizhniy Lomov** Penzenskaya Oblast', W Russian Federation
127 P3 **Nizhniy Novgorod** *prev.* Gor'kiy. Nizhegorodskaya Oblast', W Russian Federation
125 T8 **Nizhniy Odes** Respublika Komi, NW Russian Federation
Nizhniy Pyandzh *see* Panji Poyon
122 G10 **Nizhniy Tagil** Sverdlovskaya Oblast', C Russian Federation
125 T9 **Nizhnyaya-Omra** Respublika Komi, NW Russian Federation
125 P5 **Nizhnyaya Pesha** Nenetskiy Avtonomnyy Okrug, NW Russian Federation
117 Q3 **Nizhyn** *Rus.* Nezhin. Chernihivs'ka Oblast', NE Ukraine
136 M17 **Nizip** Gaziantep, S Turkey
141 X8 **Nizwá** *var.* Nazwāh. NE Oman
Nizza *see* Nice
106 C9 **Nizza Monferrato** Piemonte, NE Italy
Njávdám *see* Näätämöjoki
Njazidja *see* Grande Comore
Njellim *see* Nellim
81 H24 **Njombe** Iringa, S Tanzania
81 G23 **Njombe** ≈ C Tanzania
Njuk, Ozero *see* Nyuk, Ozero
Njuksenica *see* Nyuksenitsa
92 I10 **Njunis** ▲ N Norway
93 H17 **Njurunda** Västernorrland, C Sweden
94 N11 **Njutånger** Gävleborg, C Sweden
79 D14 **Nkambe** Nord-Ouest, NW Cameroon
Nkata Bay *see* Nkhata Bay
79 F21 **Nkayi** *prev.* Jacob. La Bouenza, S Congo
83 J17 **Nkayi** Matabeleland North, W Zimbabwe
82 N13 **Nkhata Bay** *var.* Nkata Bay. Northern, N Malawi
81 E22 **Nkonde** Kigoma, N Tanzania
79 D15 **Nkongsamba** *var.* N'Kongsamba. Littoral, W Cameroon
N'Kongsamba *see* Nkongsamba
83 E16 **Nkurenkuru** Okavango, N Namibia
77 Q15 **Nkwanta** E Ghana
167 O2 **Nmai Hka** *var.* Me Hka. ≈ N Myanmar (Burma)
Noardwâlde *see* Noordwolde
39 N7 **Noatak** Alaska, USA
39 N7 **Noatak River** ≈ Alaska, USA
164 E15 **Nobeoka** Miyazaki, Kyūshū, SW Japan
27 N11 **Noble** Oklahoma, C USA
31 P13 **Noblesville** Indiana, N USA
165 R5 **Noboribetsu** *var.* Noboribetu. Hokkaidō, NE Japan
Noboribetu *see* Noboribetsu
59 H18 **Nobres** Mato Grosso, W Brazil
107 N21 **Nocera Terinese** Calabria, S Italy
41 Q16 **Nochixtlán** *var.* Asunción Nochixtlán. Oaxaca, SE Mexico
25 S5 **Nocona** Texas, SW USA
63 K21 **Nodales, Bahía de los** *bay* S Argentina
27 Q2 **Nodaway River** ≈ Iowa/Missouri, C USA
27 R8 **Noel** Missouri, C USA
40 H3 **Nogales** Chihuahua, NW Mexico
40 F3 **Nogales** Sonora, NW Mexico
36 M17 **Nogales** Arizona, SW USA
Nogal Valley *see* Dooxo Nugaaleed
102 K15 **Nogaro** Gers, S France
110 J7 **Nogat** ≈ N Poland
164 D12 **Nōgata** Fukuoka, Kyūshū, SW Japan
127 P15 **Nogayskaya Step'** *steppe* SW Russian Federation
102 M6 **Nogent-le-Rotrou** Eure-et-Loir, C France
103 O4 **Nogent-sur-Oise** Oise, N France
103 P6 **Nogent-sur-Seine** Aube, N France
122 L10 **Noginsk** Evenkiyskiy Avtonomnyy Okrug, N Russian Federation
126 L3 **Noginsk** Moskovskaya Oblast', W Russian Federation
123 T12 **Nogliki** Ostrov Sakhalin, Sakhalinskaya Oblast', SE Russian Federation
164 K12 **Nōgōhaku-san** ▲ Honshū, SW Japan
162 D5 **Nogoonnuur** Bayan-Ölgiy, NW Mongolia
61 C18 **Nogoyá** Entre Ríos, E Argentina
111 K21 **Nógrád** *off.* Nógrád Megye. ◈ *county* N Hungary
Nógrád Megye *see* Nógrád
105 U5 **Noguera Pallaresa** ≈ NE Spain
105 U4 **Noguera Ribagorçana** ≈ NE Spain
101 E19 **Nohfelden** Saarland, SW Germany
38 A8 **Nohili Point** *headland* Kaua'i, Hawai'i, USA
104 G3 **Noia** Galicia, NW Spain
103 N16 **Noire, Montagne** ▲▲ S France
15 P12 **Noire, Rivière** ≈ Québec, SE Canada
14 J10 **Noire, Rivière** ≈ Québec, SE Canada
Noire, Rivi`ere *see* Black River
102 G6 **Noires, Montagnes** ▲▲ NW France
102 H8 **Noirmoutier-en-l'Île** Vendée, NW France
102 H8 **Noirmoutier, Île de** *island* NW France
187 Q10 **Noka** Nendö, E Solomon Islands
83 G17 **Nokaneng** North West, NW Botswana
93 L18 **Nokia** Länsi-Suomi, W Finland
148 K11 **Nok Kundi** Baluchistān, SW Pakistan
30 L14 **Nokomis** Illinois, N USA
30 K5 **Nokomis, Lake** ▣ Wisconsin, N USA
78 G9 **Nokou** Kanem, W Chad
187 Q12 **Nokuku** Espiritu Santo, W Vanuatu
95 J18 **Nol** Västra Götaland, S Sweden
79 H16 **Nola** Sangha-Mbaéré, SW Central African Republic
25 P7 **Nolan** Texas, SW USA
125 R16 **Nolinsk** Kirovskaya Oblast', NW Russian Federation
Nolsø *see* Nólsoy
95 B19 **Nólsoy** *Dan.* Nolsø. *island* E Faeroe Islands
186 B7 **Nomad** Western, SW Papua New Guinea
164 B16 **Noma-zaki** Kyūshū, SW Japan
40 K10 **Nombre de Dios** Durango, C Mexico
42 I5 **Nombre de Dios, Cordillera** ▲▲ N Honduras
38 M9 **Nome** Alaska, USA
29 Q6 **Nome** North Dakota, N USA
38 M9 **Nome, Cape** *headland* Alaska, USA
162 K11 **Nomgon** *var.* Sangiyn Dalay. Ömnögovĭ, S Mongolia
14 M11 **Nominingue, Lac** ◎ Québec, SE Canada
Nomoi Islands *see* Mortlock Islands
164 B16 **Nomo-zaki** *headland* Kyūshū, SW Japan
162 G6 **Nömrög** *var.* Hödrögö. Dzavhan, N Mongolia
193 X15 **Nomuka** *island* Nomuka Group, C Tonga
193 X15 **Nomuka Group** *island group* W Tonga

◆ Country ● Country Capital ◇ Dependent Territory ○ Dependent Territory Capital ◈ Administrative Regions ✈ International Airport ▲ Mountain ▲▲ Mountain Range Volcano ≈ River ◎ Lake ▣ Reservoir

189 Q15 **Nomwin Atoll** atoll Hall Islands, C Micronesia
8 L10 **Nonacho Lake** ⊚ Northwest Territories, NW Canada
Nondaburi see Nonthaburi
39 P12 **Nondalton** Alaska, USA
163 V10 **Nong'an** Jilin, NE China
169 P10 **Nong Bua Khok** Nakhon Ratchasima, C Thailand
167 Q9 **Nong Bua Lamphu** Udon Thani, E Thailand
167 R7 **Nông Hèt** Xiangkhoang, N Laos
Nongkaya see Nong Khai
167 Q8 **Nong Khai** var. Mi Chai, Nongkaya. Nong Khai, E Thailand
167 N14 **Nong Met** Surat Thani, SW Thailand
83 L22 **Nongoma** KwaZulu/Natal, E South Africa
167 P9 **Nong Phai** Phetchabun, C Thailand
153 U13 **Nongstoin** Meghālaya, NE India
83 C19 **Nonidas** Erongo, N Namibia
Nonni see Nen Jiang
40 I7 **Nonoava** Chihuahua, N Mexico
191 O3 **Nonouti** prev. Sydenham Island. atoll Tungaru, W Kiribati
167 O11 **Nonthaburi** var. Nondaburi, Nontha Buri. Nonthaburi, C Thailand
Nontha Buri see Nonthaburi
102 L11 **Nontron** Dordogne, SW France
181 P1 **Noonamah** Northern Territory, N Australia
28 K2 **Noonan** North Dakota, N USA
99 E14 **Noord-Beveland** var. North Beveland. island SW Netherlands
99 J14 **Noord-Brabant** Eng. North Brabant. ◐ province S Netherlands
98 H7 **Noorder Haaks** spit NW Netherlands
98 H9 **Noord-Holland** Eng. North Holland. ◐ province NW Netherlands
Noordhollandsch Kanaal see Noordhollands Kanaal
98 H8 **Noordhollands Kanaal** var. Noordhollandsch Kanaal. canal NW Netherlands
Noord-Kaap see Northern Cape
98 L8 **Noordoostpolder** island N Netherlands
45 P16 **Noordpunt** headland Curaçao, C Netherlands Antilles
98 I8 **Noord-Scharwoude** Noord-Holland, NW Netherlands
Noordwes see North-West
98 G11 **Noordwijk aan Zee** Zuid-Holland, W Netherlands
98 H11 **Noordwijkerhout** Zuid-Holland, W Netherlands
98 M7 **Noordwolde** Fris. Noardwâlde. Friesland, N Netherlands
Noordzee see North Sea
98 H10 **Noordzee-Kanaal** canal NW Netherlands
93 K18 **Noormarkku** Swe. Norrmark. Länsi-Soumi, SW Finland
39 N8 **Noorvik** Alaska, USA
10 J17 **Nootka Sound** inlet British Columbia, W Canada
82 A9 **Nóqui** Dem. Rep. Congo, NW Angola
95 L15 **Nora** Örebro, C Sweden
147 Q13 **Norak** Rus. Nurek. W Tajikistan
13 I13 **Noranda** Québec, SE Canada
29 W12 **Nora Springs** Iowa, C USA
95 M14 **Norberg** Västmanland, C Sweden
14 K13 **Norcan Lake** ⊚ Ontario, SE Canada
197 R12 **Nord** Avannaarsua, N Greenland
78 F13 **Nord** Eng. North. ◐ province N Cameroon
103 P2 **Nord** ◐ department N France
92 P1 **Nordaustlandet** island NE Svalbard
95 G24 **Nordborg** Ger. Nordburg. Sønderjylland, SW Denmark
Nordburg see Nordborg
95 F23 **Nordby** Ribe, W Denmark
9 P15 **Nordegg** Alberta, SW Canada
100 E9 **Norden** Niedersachsen, NW Germany
100 G10 **Nordenham** Niedersachsen, NW Germany
122 M6 **Nordenshel'da, Arkhipelag** island group N Russian Federation
92 O3 **Nordenskiold Land** physical region W Svalbard
100 E9 **Norderney** island NW Germany
100 J9 **Norderstedt** Schleswig-Holstein, N Germany
94 D11 **Nordfjord** fjord S Norway
94 C11 **Nordfjord** physical region S Norway
94 D11 **Nordfjordeid** Sogn Og Fjordane, S Norway
92 G11 **Nordfold** Nordland, C Norway
Nordfriesische Inseln see North Frisian Islands
100 H7 **Nordfriesland** cultural region N Germany
101 K15 **Nordhausen** Thüringen, C Germany
25 T13 **Nordheim** Texas, SW USA
94 C13 **Nordhordland** physical region S Norway
100 E12 **Nordhorn** Niedersachsen, NW Germany
92 I1 **Nordhurfjördhur** Vestfirdhir, NW Iceland
92 J1 **Nordhurland Eystra** ◐ region N Iceland
92 I2 **Nordhurland Vestra** ◐ region N Iceland
172 H16 **Nord, Île du** island Inner Islands, NE Seychelles
95 F20 **Nordjylland** var. Nordjyllands Amt. ◐ county N Denmark
Nordjyllands Amt see Nordjylland
92 K7 **Nordkapp** Eng. North Cape. headland N Norway
92 O1 **Nordkapp** headland N Svalbard
92 L7 **Nordkinn** headland N Norway
79 N19 **Nord Kivu** off. Région du Nord Kivu. ◐ region E Dem. Rep. Congo
Nord Kivu, Région du see Nord Kivu
92 G12 **Nordland** ◐ county C Norway
101 J21 **Nördlingen** Bayern, S Germany
93 I16 **Nordmaling** Västerbotten, N Sweden
95 K15 **Nordmark** Värmland, C Sweden
Nord, Mer du see North Sea
94 F8 **Nordmøre** physical region S Norway
100 I8 **Nord-Ostsee-Kanal** canal N Germany
0 J3 **Nordostrundingen** cape NE Greenland
79 D14 **Nord-Ouest** Eng. North-West. ◐ province NW Cameroon
Nord-Ouest, Territoires du see Northwest Territories
103 N2 **Nord-Pas-de-Calais** ◐ region N France
101 F19 **Nordpfälzer Bergland** ⛰ W Germany
Nord, Pointe see Fatua, Pointe
187 P16 **Nord, Province** ◐ province C New Caledonia
101 D14 **Nordrhein-Westfalen** Eng. North Rhine-Westphalia, Fr. Rhénanie du Nord-Westphalie. ◐ state W Germany
Nordsee/Nordsjøen/Nordsøen see North Sea
100 H7 **Nordstrand** island N Germany
93 E15 **Nord-Trøndelag** ◐ county C Norway
97 E19 **Nore** Ir. An Fheoir. ≈ S Ireland
29 Q14 **Norfolk** Nebraska, C USA
21 X7 **Norfolk** Virginia, NE USA
97 P19 **Norfolk** cultural region E England, UK
192 K10 **Norfolk Island** ◇ Australian external territory SW Pacific Ocean
175 P9 **Norfolk Ridge** undersea feature W Pacific Ocean
27 U8 **Norfork Lake** ⊠ Arkansas/Missouri, C USA
98 N6 **Norg** Drenthe, NE Netherlands
Norge see Norway
95 D14 **Norheimsund** Hordaland, S Norway
25 S16 **Norias** Texas, SW USA
164 L12 **Norikura-dake** ▲ Honshū, S Japan
122 K8 **Noril'sk** Taymyrskiy (Dolgano-Nenetskiy) Avtonomnyy Okrug, N Russian Federation
14 I13 **Norland** Ontario, SE Canada
21 V8 **Norlina** North Carolina, SE USA
30 L13 **Normal** Illinois, N USA
27 N11 **Norman** Oklahoma, C USA
Norman see Tulita
186 G9 **Normanby Island** island SE Papua New Guinea
Normandes, Îles see Channel Islands
58 G9 **Normandia** Roraima, N Brazil
102 L5 **Normandie** Eng. Normandy. cultural region N France
102 J5 **Normandie, Collines de** hill range NW France
Normandy see Normandie
25 V9 **Normangee** Texas, SW USA
21 Q10 **Norman, Lake** ⊠ North Carolina, SE USA
44 K13 **Norman Manley** ✈ (Kingston) E Jamaica
181 U5 **Norman River** ≈ Queensland, NE Australia
181 U4 **Normanton** Queensland, NE Australia
8 I8 **Norman Wells** Northwest Territories, NW Canada
12 H12 **Normétal** Québec, S Canada
163 O7 **Norovlin** var. Uldz. Hentiy, NE Mongolia
9 V15 **Norquay** Saskatchewan, S Canada
94 N11 **Norra Dellen** ⊚ C Sweden
93 G15 **Norråker** Jämtland, C Sweden
94 N12 **Norrala** Gävleborg, C Sweden
Norra Ny see Stöllet
92 G13 **Norra Storjfjället** ▲ N Sweden
92 I13 **Norrbotten** ◐ county N Sweden
95 G23 **Nørre Aaby** var. Nørre Åby. Fyn, C Denmark
Nørre Åby see Nørre Aaby
95 I24 **Nørre Alslev** Storstrøm, SE Denmark
95 E23 **Nørre Nebel** Ribe, W Denmark
95 G20 **Nørresundby** Nordjylland, N Denmark
21 N8 **Norris Lake** ⊠ Tennessee, S USA
18 I15 **Norristown** Pennsylvania, NE USA
95 N17 **Norrköping** Östergötland, S Sweden
Norrmark see Noormarkku
94 N13 **Norrsundet** Gävleborg, C Sweden
95 P15 **Norrtälje** Stockholm, C Sweden
180 L12 **Norseman** Western Australia
93 I14 **Norsjö** Västerbotten, N Sweden
95 G16 **Norsjø** ⊚ S Norway
123 R13 **Norsk** Amurskaya Oblast', SE Russian Federation
Norske Havet see Norwegian Sea
187 Q13 **Norsup** Malekula, C Vanuatu
191 V15 **Norte, Cabo** cape Easter Island, Chile, E Pacific Ocean
54 F7 **Norte de Santander** off. Departamento de Norte de Santander. ◐ province N Colombia
Norte de Santander, Departamento de see Norte de Santander
61 E21 **Norte, Punta** headland E Argentina
21 R13 **North** South Carolina, SE USA
North see Nord
18 L10 **North Adams** Massachusetts, NE USA
113 L17 **North Albanian Alps** Alb. Bjeshkët e Namuna, SCr. Prokletije. ⛰ SE Europe
97 M15 **Northallerton** N England, UK
180 J12 **Northam** Western Australia
83 J20 **Northam** Northern, N South Africa
1 **North America** continent
1 N12 **North American Basin** undersea feature W Sargasso Sea
0 C5 **North American Plate** tectonic feature
18 M11 **North Amherst** Massachusetts, NE USA
97 N20 **Northampton** C England, UK
97 M20 **Northamptonshire** cultural region C England, UK
151 P18 **North Andaman** island Andaman Islands, India, NE Indian Ocean
65 D25 **North Arm** East Falkland, Falkland Islands
21 Q13 **North Augusta** South Carolina, SE USA
173 W8 **North Australian Basin** Fr. Bassin Nord de l' Australie. undersea feature E Indian Ocean
31 R11 **North Baltimore** Ohio, N USA
9 T15 **North Battleford** Saskatchewan, S Canada
14 H11 **North Bay** Ontario, S Canada
12 H6 **North Belcher Islands** island group Belcher Islands, Nunavut, C Canada
29 R15 **North Bend** Nebraska, C USA
32 E14 **North Bend** Oregon, NW USA
96 K12 **North Berwick** SE Scotland, UK
North Beveland see Noord-Beveland
North Borneo see Sabah
183 P5 **North Bourke** New South Wales, SE Australia
North Brabant see Noord-Brabant
182 F2 **North Branch Neales** seasonal river South Australia
44 M6 **North Caicos** island NW Turks and Caicos Islands
26 L10 **North Canadian River** ≈ Oklahoma, C USA
31 U12 **North Canton** Ohio, N USA
13 R13 **North, Cape** headland Cape Breton Island, Nova Scotia, SE Canada
184 I1 **North Cape** headland North Island, New Zealand
186 G5 **North Cape** headland New Ireland, NE Papua New Guinea
North Cape see Nordkapp
18 J17 **North Cape May** New Jersey, NE USA
12 C9 **North Caribou Lake** ⊚ Ontario, C Canada
21 U10 **North Carolina** off. State of North Carolina, also known as Old North State, Tar Heel State, Turpentine State. ◐ state SE USA
North Celebes see Sulawesi Utara
155 J24 **North Central Province** ◐ province N Sri Lanka
31 S4 **North Channel** lake channel Canada/USA
97 G14 **North Channel** strait Northern Ireland/Scotland, UK
21 S14 **North Charleston** South Carolina, SE USA
31 N10 **North Chicago** Illinois, N USA
195 Y10 **Northcliffe Glacier** glacier Antarctica
31 Q14 **North College Hill** Ohio, N USA
25 O8 **North Concho River** ≈ Texas, SW USA
19 O8 **North Conway** New Hampshire, NE USA
27 V14 **North Crossett** Arkansas, C USA
28 L4 **North Dakota** off. State of North Dakota, also known as Flickertail State, Peace Garden State, Sioux State. ◐ state N USA
North Devon Island see Devon Island
97 O22 **North Downs** hill range SE England, UK
18 C11 **North East** Pennsylvania, NE USA
83 I18 **North East** ◐ district NE Botswana
65 G15 **North East Bay** bay Ascension Island, C Atlantic Ocean
38 L10 **Northeast Cape** headland Saint Lawrence Island, Alaska, USA
81 J17 **North Eastern** ◐ province Kenya
North East Frontier Agency/North East Frontier Agency of Assam see Arunāchal Pradesh
65 E25 **North East Island** island E Falkland Islands
189 V11 **Northeast Island** island Chuuk, C Micronesia
44 L6 **Northeast Point** headland Great Inagua, S Bahamas
44 K5 **Northeast Point** headland Acklins Island, SE Bahamas
44 L12 **North East Point** headland E Jamaica
191 Z2 **Northeast Point** headland Kiritimati, E Kiribati
44 H2 **Northeast Providence Channel** channel N Bahamas
101 J14 **Northeim** Niedersachsen, C Germany
29 X14 **North English** Iowa, C USA
138 G8 **Northern** ◐ district N Israel
82 M12 **Northern** ◐ region N Malawi
186 F8 **Northern** ◐ province S Papua New Guinea
80 D7 **Northern** ◐ state N Sudan
82 K12 **Northern** ◐ province NE Zambia
Northern see Limpopo
80 B13 **Northern Bahr el Ghazal** ◐ state SW Sudan
Northern Border Region see Al Ḩudūd ash Shamālīyah
83 F24 **Northern Cape** off. Northern Cape Province, Afr. Noord-Kaap. ◐ province W South Africa
Northern Cape Province see Northern Cape
190 K14 **Northern Cook Islands** island group N Cook Islands
80 B8 **Northern Darfur** ◐ state NW Sudan
Northern Dvina see Severnaya Dvina
97 F14 **Northern Ireland** var. The Six Counties. cultural region Northern Ireland, UK
80 D9 **Northern Kordofan** ◐ state C Sudan
187 Z14 **Northern Lau Group** island group Lau Group, NE Fiji
188 K3 **Northern Mariana Islands** ◇ US commonwealth territory W Pacific Ocean
155 J23 **Northern Province** ◐ province N Sri Lanka
Northern Rhodesia see Zambia
Northern Sporades see Vóreies Sporádes
182 D1 **Northern Territory** ◐ territory N Australia
Northern Transvaal see Limpopo
Northern Ural Hills see Severnyye Uvaly
84 I9 **North European Plain** plain N Europe
27 V2 **North Fabius River** ≈ Missouri, C USA
65 D24 **North Falkland Sound** sound N Falkland Islands
29 V9 **Northfield** Minnesota, N USA
19 O9 **Northfield** New Hampshire, NE USA
175 Q8 **North Fiji Basin** undersea feature N Coral Sea
97 Q22 **North Foreland** headland SE England, UK
35 P6 **North Fork American River** ≈ California, W USA
39 R7 **North Fork Chandalar River** ≈ Alaska, USA
28 K7 **North Fork Grand River** ≈ North Dakota/South Dakota, N USA
21 O6 **North Fork Kentucky River** ≈ Kentucky, S USA
39 Q7 **North Fork Koyukuk River** ≈ Alaska, USA
39 Q10 **North Fork Kuskokwim River** ≈ Alaska, USA
26 K11 **North Fork Red River** ≈ Oklahoma/Texas, SW USA
26 K3 **North Fork Solomon River** ≈ Kansas, C USA
23 W14 **North Fort Myers** Florida, SE USA
31 P5 **North Fox Island** island Michigan, N USA
100 G6 **North Frisian Islands** var. Nordfriesische Inseln. island group N Germany
197 N9 **North Geomagnetic Pole** pole Arctic Ocean
18 M13 **North Haven** Connecticut, NE USA
184 J5 **North Head** headland North Island, New Zealand
18 L6 **North Hero** Vermont, NE USA
35 O7 **North Highlands** California, W USA
North Holland see Noord-Holland
81 I16 **North Horr** Eastern, N Kenya
151 K21 **North Huvadhu Atoll** var. Gaafu Alifu Atoll. atoll S Maldives
65 A24 **North Island** island W Falkland Islands
184 N9 **North Island** island N New Zealand
21 U14 **North Island** island South Carolina, SE USA
31 O11 **North Judson** Indiana, N USA
North Kazakhstan see Severnyy Kazakhstan
31 V10 **North Kingsville** Ohio, N USA
163 Y13 **North Korea** off. Democratic People's Republic of Korea, Kor. Chosŏn-minjujuŭi-inmin-kanghwaguk. ◆ republic E Asia
153 X11 **North Lakhimpur** Assam, NE India
184 J3 **Northland** off. Northland Region. ◐ region North Island, New Zealand
192 K11 **Northland Plateau** undersea feature S Pacific Ocean
Northland Region see Northland
35 X11 **North Las Vegas** Nevada, W USA
31 O11 **North Liberty** Indiana, N USA
29 X14 **North Liberty** Iowa, C USA
27 V12 **North Little Rock** Arkansas, C USA
28 M13 **North Loup River** ≈ Nebraska, C USA
151 K18 **North Maalhosmadulu Atoll** var. North Malosmadulu Atoll, Raa Atoll. atoll N Maldives
31 U10 **North Madison** Ohio, N USA
North Malosmadulu Atoll see North Maalhosmadulu Atoll
31 P12 **North Manchester** Indiana, N USA
31 P6 **North Manitou Island** island Michigan, N USA
29 U10 **North Mankato** Minnesota, N USA
23 Z15 **North Miami** Florida, SE USA
151 K18 **North Miladhunmadulu Atoll** atoll N Maldives
North Minch see Minch, The
23 W15 **North Naples** Florida, SE USA
175 P8 **North New Hebrides Trench** undersea feature N Coral Sea
23 Y15 **North New River Canal** ≈ Florida, SE USA
151 K20 **North Nilandhe Atoll** atoll C Maldives
36 L2 **North Ogden** Utah, W USA
North Ossetia see Severnaya Osetiya-Alaniya, Respublika
35 S10 **North Palisade** ▲ California, W USA
189 U11 **North Pass** passage Chuuk Islands, C Micronesia
28 M15 **North Platte** Nebraska, C USA
33 X17 **North Platte River** ≈ C USA
65 G14 **North Point** headland Ascension Island, C Atlantic Ocean
172 I16 **North Point** headland Mahé, NE Seychelles
31 R5 **North Point** headland Michigan, N USA
31 S6 **North Point** headland Michigan, N USA
39 S9 **North Pole** Alaska, USA
197 R9 **North Pole** pole Arctic Ocean
23 O4 **Northport** Alabama, S USA
23 W14 **North Port** Florida, SE USA
32 L6 **Northport** Washington, NW USA
32 L12 **North Powder** Oregon, NW USA
29 U13 **North Raccoon River** ≈ Iowa, C USA
North Rhine-Westphalia see Nordrhein-Westfalen
97 M16 **North Riding** cultural region N England, UK
96 G5 **North Rona** island NW Scotland, UK
96 K4 **North Ronaldsay** island NE Scotland, UK
36 L2 **North Salt Lake** Utah, W USA
9 P15 **North Saskatchewan** ≈ Alberta/Saskatchewan, S Canada
35 X5 **North Schell Peak** ▲ Nevada, W USA
North Scotia Ridge see South Georgia Ridge
86 D10 **North Sea** Dan. Nordsøen, Dut. Noordzee, Fr. Mer du Nord, Ger. Nordsee, Nor. Nordsjøen; prev. German Ocean, Lat. Mare Germanicum. sea NW Europe
35 T6 **North Shoshone Peak** ▲ Nevada, W USA
North Siberian Lowland/North Siberian Plain see Severo-Sibirskaya Nizmennost'
29 R13 **North Sioux City** South Dakota, N USA
96 K4 **North Sound, The** sound N Scotland, UK
183 T4 **North Star** New South Wales, SE Australia
North Star State see Minnesota
183 V3 **North Stradbroke Island** island Queensland, E Australia
North Sulawesi see Sulawesi Utara
North Sumatra see Sumatera Utara
14 D17 **North Sydenham** ≈ Ontario, S Canada
18 H9 **North Syracuse** New York, NE USA
184 K9 **North Taranaki Bight** gulf North Island, New Zealand
12 H9 **North Twin Island** island Nunavut, C Canada
96 E8 **North Uist** island NW Scotland, UK
97 L14 **Northumberland** cultural region N England, UK
181 Y7 **Northumberland Isles** island group Queensland, NE Australia
13 Q14 **Northumberland Strait** strait SE Canada
32 G14 **North Umpqua River** ≈ Oregon, NW USA
45 Q13 **North Union** Saint Vincent, Saint Vincent and the Grenadines
10 L17 **North Vancouver** British Columbia, SW Canada
18 K9 **Northville** New York, NE USA
97 Q19 **North Walsham** E England, UK
39 T10 **Northway** Alaska, USA
83 G17 **North-West** ◐ district NW Botswana
83 G21 **North-West** off. North-West Province, Afr. Noordwes. ◐ province N South Africa
North-West see Nord-Ouest
64 I6 **Northwest Atlantic Mid-Ocean Canyon** undersea feature N Atlantic Ocean
180 G8 **North West Cape** cape Western Australia
38 J9 **Northwest Cape** headland Saint Lawrence Island, Alaska, USA
82 H13 **North Western** ◐ province W Zambia
155 J24 **North Western Province** ◐ province W Sri Lanka
149 U4 **North-West Frontier Province** ◐ province NW Pakistan
96 H8 **North West Highlands** ⛰ N Scotland, UK
192 J4 **Northwest Pacific Basin** undersea feature NW Pacific Ocean
191 Y2 **Northwest Point** headland Kiritimati, E Kiribati
44 G1 **Northwest Providence Channel** channel N Bahamas
North-West Province see North-West
13 Q8 **North West River** Newfoundland and Labrador, E Canada
8 J9 **Northwest Territories** Fr. Territoires du Nord-Ouest. ◐ territory NW Canada
97 K18 **Northwich** C England, UK
25 Q5 **North Wichita River** ≈ Texas, SW USA
18 J17 **North Wildwood** New Jersey, NE USA
21 R9 **North Wilkesboro** North Carolina, SE USA
19 P8 **North Windham** Maine, NE USA
197 Q6 **Northwind Plain** undersea feature Arctic Ocean
29 V11 **Northwood** Iowa, C USA
29 Q4 **Northwood** North Dakota, N USA
97 M15 **North York Moors** moorland N England, UK
25 V9 **North Zulch** Texas, SW USA
26 K2 **Norton** Kansas, C USA
31 S13 **Norton** Ohio, N USA
21 P7 **Norton** Virginia, NE USA
39 N9 **Norton Bay** bay Alaska, USA
Norton de Matos see Balombo
31 O9 **Norton Shores** Michigan, N USA
38 M10 **Norton Sound** inlet Alaska, USA
27 Q3 **Nortonville** Kansas, C USA
102 I8 **Nort-sur-Erdre** Loire-Atlantique, NW France
195 N2 **Norvegia, Cape** headland Antarctica
18 L13 **Norwalk** Connecticut, NE USA
29 V14 **Norwalk** Iowa, C USA
31 S11 **Norwalk** Ohio, N USA
19 P7 **Norway** Maine, NE USA
31 N5 **Norway** Michigan, N USA
93 E17 **Norway** off. Kingdom of Norway, Nor. Norge. ◆ monarchy N Europe
9 X13 **Norway House** Manitoba, C Canada
Norway, Kingdom of see Norway
197 R16 **Norwegian Basin** undersea feature NW Norwegian Sea
84 D6 **Norwegian Sea** var. Norske Havet. sea NE Atlantic Ocean
197 S17 **Norwegian Trench** undersea feature NE North Sea
14 F16 **Norwich** Ontario, S Canada
97 Q19 **Norwich** E England, UK
19 N13 **Norwich** Connecticut, NE USA
18 I11 **Norwich** New York, NE USA
29 U9 **Norwood** Minnesota, N USA
31 Q15 **Norwood** Ohio, N USA
14 H11 **Nosbonsing, Lake** ⊚ Ontario, S Canada
Nösen see Bistrița
165 T1 **Noshappu-misaki** headland Hokkaidō, NE Japan
165 P7 **Noshiro** var. Nosiro; prev. Noshirominato. Akita, Honshū, C Japan
Noshirominato/Nosiro see Noshiro
117 Q3 **Nosivka** Rus. Nosovka. Chernihivs'ka Oblast', NE Ukraine
67 T14 **Nosop** var. Nossob, Nossop. ≈ Botswana/Namibia
125 S4 **Nosovaya** Nenetskiy Avtonomnyy Okrug, NW Russian Federation
Nosovka see Nosivka
143 V11 **Noṣratābād** Sīstān va Balūchestān, E Iran
95 J18 **Nossebro** Västra Götaland, S Sweden
96 K6 **Noss Head** headland N Scotland, UK
Nossi-Bé see Be, Nosy
83 E20 **Nossob** ≈ E Namibia
Nossob/Nossop see Nosop
172 J2 **Nosy Be** ✈ Antsirãnana, N Madagascar
172 J6 **Nosy Varika** Fianarantsoa, SE Madagascar
14 L10 **Notawassi** ≈ Québec, SE Canada
14 M9 **Notawassi, Lac** ⊚ Québec, SE Canada
36 J5 **Notch Peak** ▲ Utah, W USA
110 G10 **Noteć** Ger. Netze. ≈ NW Poland
Nótiès Sporádes see Dodekánisa
115 J22 **Nótion Aigaíon** Eng. Aegean South. ◐ region E Greece
115 H18 **Nótios Evvoïkós Kólpos** gulf E Greece
115 B16 **Nótio Stenó Kérkyras** strait W Greece
107 L25 **Noto** anc. Netum. Sicilia, Italy, C Mediterranean Sea
164 M10 **Noto** Ishikawa, Honshū, SW Japan
95 G15 **Notodden** Telemark, S Norway
107 L25 **Noto, Golfo di** gulf Sicilia, Italy, C Mediterranean Sea
164 L10 **Noto-hantō** peninsula Honshū, SW Japan
164 L11 **Noto-jima** island SW Japan
13 T11 **Notre Dame Bay** bay Newfoundland, Newfoundland and Labrador, E Canada
15 P6 **Notre-Dame-de-Lorette** Québec, SE Canada
14 L11 **Notre-Dame-de-Pontmain** Québec, SE Canada
15 T8 **Notre-Dame-du-Lac** Québec, SE Canada
15 Q6 **Notre-Dame-du-Rosaire** Québec, SE Canada
15 U8 **Notre-Dame, Monts** ⛰ Québec, S Canada
77 R16 **Notsé** S Togo
14 G14 **Nottawasaga** ≈ Ontario, S Canada
14 G14 **Nottawasaga Bay** lake bay Ontario, S Canada
12 I11 **Nottaway** ≈ Québec, SE Canada
23 S1 **Nottely Lake** ⊠ Georgia, SE USA
95 H16 **Nøtterøy** island S Norway
97 M19 **Nottingham** C England, UK
9 E14 **Nottingham Island** island Nunavut, NE Canada
97 N18 **Nottinghamshire** cultural region C England, UK
21 V7 **Nottoway** Virginia, NE USA
21 V7 **Nottoway River** ≈ Virginia, NE USA
76 G7 **Nouâdhibou** prev. Port-Étienne. Dakhlet Nouâdhibou, W Mauritania
76 G7 **Nouâdhibou** ✈ Dakhlet Nouâdhibou, W Mauritania
76 F7 **Nouâdhibou, Dakhlet** prev. Baie du Lévrier. bay W Mauritania
76 F7 **Nouâdhibou, Râs** prev. Cap Blanc. headland NW Mauritania
76 G9 **Nouakchott** ● (Mauritania) Nouakchott District, SW Mauritania
76 G9 **Nouakchott** ✈ Trarza, SW Mauritania
120 J11 **Noual, Sebkhet en** var. Sabkhat an Nawāl. salt flat C Tunisia

76 G8 **Nouâmghâr** *var.* Nouamrhar. Dakhlet Nouâdhibou, W Mauritania
Nouamrhar *see* Nouâmghâr
Nouă Sulița *see* Novoselytsya
187 Q17 **Nouméa** ○ (New Caledonia) Province Sud, S New Caledonia
79 E15 **Noun** ≈ C Cameroon
77 N12 **Nouna** W Burkina
83 H24 **Noupoort** Northern Cape, C South Africa
Nouveau-Brunswick *see* New Brunswick
Nouveau-Comptoir *see* Wemindji
15 T4 **Nouvel, Lacs** ◎ Québec, SE Canada
15 W7 **Nouvelle** Québec, SE Canada
15 W7 **Nouvelle** ≈ Québec, SE Canada
Nouvelle-Calédonie *see* New Caledonia
Nouvelle Écosse *see* Nova Scotia
103 R3 **Nouzonville** Ardennes, N France
147 Q11 **Nov** *Rus.* Nau. NW Tajikistan
59 I21 **Nova Alvorada** Mato Grosso do Sul, SW Brazil
Novabad *see* Navobod
111 D19 **Nová Bystřice** *Ger.* Neubistritz. Jihočeský Kraj, S Czech Republic
116 H13 **Novaci** Gorj, SW Romania
Nova Civitas *see* Neustadt an der Weinstrasse
Novaesium *see* Neuss
60 H10 **Nova Esperança** Paraná, S Brazil
106 H11 **Novafeltria** Marche, C Italy
60 Q9 **Nova Friburgo** Rio de Janeiro, SE Brazil
82 D12 **Nova Gaia** *var.* Cambundi-Catembo. Malanje, NE Angola
109 S12 **Nova Gorica** W Slovenia
112 G10 **Nova Gradiška** *Ger.* Neugradisk, *Hung.* Újgradiska. Brod-Posavina, NE Croatia
60 K7 **Nova Granada** São Paulo, S Brazil
60 O10 **Nova Iguaçu** Rio de Janeiro, SE Brazil
117 S10 **Nova Kakhovka** *Rus.* Novaya Kakhovka. Khersons'ka Oblast', SE Ukraine
Nová Karvinná *see* Karviná
Nova Lamego *see* Gabú
Nova Lisboa *see* Huambo
112 C11 **Novalja** Lika-Senj, W Croatia
119 M14 **Novalukoml'** *Rus.* Novolukoml'. Vitsyebskaya Voblasts', N Belarus
Nova Mambone *see* Mambone
83 P16 **Nova Nabúri** Zambézia, NE Mozambique
117 Q9 **Nova Odesa** *var.* Novaya Odessa. Mykolayivs'ka Oblast', S Ukraine
60 H10 **Nova Olímpia** Paraná, S Brazil
61 I15 **Nova Prata** Rio Grande do Sul, S Brazil
14 H12 **Novar** Ontario, S Canada
106 C7 **Novara** *anc.* Novaria. Piemonte, NW Italy
Novaria *see* Novara
117 P7 **Novarkanels'k** Kirovohrads'ka Oblast', C Ukraine
13 P15 **Nova Scotia** *Fr.* Nouvelle Écosse. ⬖ *province* SE Canada
0 M9 **Nova Scotia** *physical region* SE Canada
34 M8 **Novato** California, W USA
192 M7 **Nova Trough** *undersea feature* W Pacific Ocean
116 L7 **Nova Ushtsya** Khmel'nyts'ka Oblast', W Ukraine
83 M17 **Nova Vanduzi** Manica, C Mozambique
117 U5 **Nova Vodolaha** *Rus.* Novaya Vodolaga. Kharkivs'ka Oblast', E Ukraine
123 O12 **Novaya Chara** Chitinskaya Oblast', S Russian Federation
122 M12 **Novaya Igirma** Irkutskaya Oblast', C Russian Federation
Novaya Kakhovka *see* Nova Kakhovka
144 E10 **Novaya Kazanka** Zapadnyy Kazakhstan, W Kazakhstan
124 I12 **Novaya Ladoga** Leningradskaya Oblast', NW Russian Federation
127 R5 **Novaya Malykla** Ul'yanovskaya Oblast', W Russian Federation
Novaya Odessa *see* Nova Odesa
123 Q5 **Novaya Sibir', Ostrov** *island* Novosibirskiye Ostrova, NE Russian Federation
Novaya Vodolaga *see* Nova Vodolaha
119 P17 **Novaya Yel'nya** *Rus.* Novaya Yel'nya. Mahilyowskaya Voblasts', E Belarus
122 I6 **Novaya Zemlya** *island group* N Russian Federation
Novaya Zemlya Trough *see* East Novaya Zemlya Trough
114 K10 **Nova Zagora** Sliven, C Bulgaria
105 S12 **Novelda** País Valenciano, E Spain
111 H19 **Nové Mesto nad Váhom** *Ger.* Waagneustadtl, *Hung.* Vágújhely. Trenčiansky Kraj, W Slovakia
111 F17 **Nové Město na Moravě** *Ger.* Neustadtl in Mähren. Vysočina, C Czech Republic
Novesium *see* Neuss
111 I21 **Nové Zámky** *Ger.* Neuhäusel, *Hung.* Érsekújvár. Nitriansky Kraj, SW Slovakia
Novgorod *see* Velikiy Novgorod
Novgorod-Severskiy *see* Novhorod-Sivers'kyy
122 C7 **Novgorodskaya Oblast'** ⬖ *province* W Russian Federation
117 R8 **Novhorodka** Kirovohrads'ka Oblast', C Ukraine
117 R2 **Novhorod-Sivers'kyy** *Rus.* Novgorod-Severskiy. Chernihivs'ka Oblast', NE Ukraine
31 R10 **Novi** Michigan, N USA
Novi *see* Novi Vinodolski
112 L9 **Novi Bečej** *prev.* Új-Becse, Vološinovo, *Ger.* Neubetsche, *Hung.* Törökbecse. Vojvodina, N Serbia
25 Q8 **Novice** Texas, SW USA
112 A9 **Novigrad** Istra, NW Croatia
Novi Grad *see* Bosanski Novi
114 G9 **Novi Iskŭr** Sofiya-Grad, W Bulgaria
106 C9 **Novi Ligure** Piemonte, NW Italy
99 L22 **Noville** Luxembourg, SE Belgium
194 I10 **Noville Peninsula** *peninsula* Thurston Island, Antarctica
Noviodunum *see* Soissons, Aisne, France
Noviodunum *see* Nevers, Nièvre, France
Noviodunum *see* Nyon, Vaud, Switzerland
Noviomagus *see* Lisieux, Calvados, France
Noviomagus *see* Nijmegen, Netherlands
114 M8 **Novi Pazar** Shumen, NE Bulgaria
113 M15 **Novi Pazar** *Turk.* Yenipazar. Serbia, S Serbia
112 K10 **Novi Sad** *Ger.* Neusatz, *Hung.* Újvidék. Vojvodina, N Serbia
117 T6 **Novi Sanzhary** Poltavs'ka Oblast', C Ukraine
112 H12 **Novi Travnik** *prev.* Pučarevo. ⬖ Federacija Bosna I Hercegovina, C Bosnia and Herzegovina
112 B10 **Novi Vinodolski** *var.* Novi. Primorje-Gorski Kotar, NW Croatia
58 F12 **Novo Airão** Amazonas, N Brazil
127 N14 **Novoaleksandrovsk** Stavropol'skiy Kray, SW Russian Federation
Novoalekseyevka *see* Khobda
127 N9 **Novoanninskiy** Volgogradskaya Oblast', SW Russian Federation
58 F13 **Novo Aripuanã** Amazonas, N Brazil
117 Y6 **Novoaydar** Luhans'ka Oblast', E Ukraine
117 X9 **Novoazovs'k** *Rus.* Novoazovsk. Donets'ka Oblast', E Ukraine
123 R14 **Novobureyskiy** Amurskaya Oblast', SE Russian Federation
127 Q3 **Novocheboksarsk** Chavash Respubliki, W Russian Federation
127 R5 **Novocheremshansk** Ul'yanovskaya Oblast', W Russian Federation
126 L12 **Novocherkassk** Rostovskaya Oblast', SW Russian Federation
127 R6 **Novodevich'ye** Samarskaya Oblast', W Russian Federation
124 M8 **Novodvinsk** Arkhangel'skaya Oblast', NW Russian Federation
Novograd-Volynskiy *see* Novohrad-Volyns'kyy
Novogrudok *see* Navahrudak
61 I15 **Novo Hamburgo** Rio Grande do Sul, S Brazil
59 H16 **Novo Horizonte** Mato Grosso, W Brazil
60 K8 **Novo Horizonte** São Paulo, S Brazil
116 M4 **Novohrad-Volyns'kyy** *Rus.* Novograd-Volynskiy. Zhytomyrs'ka Oblast', N Ukraine
145 O7 **Novoishimskiy** *prev.* Kuybyshevskiy. Severnyy Kazakhstan, N Kazakhstan
Novokazalinsk *see* Ayteke Bi
126 M8 **Novokhopersk** Voronezhskaya Oblast', W Russian Federation
127 R6 **Novokuybyshevsk** Samarskaya Oblast', W Russian Federation
122 J13 **Novokuznetsk** *prev.* Stalinsk. Kemerovskaya Oblast', S Russian Federation
195 R1 **Novolazarevskaya** *Russian research station* Antarctica
Novolukoml' *see* Novalukoml'
109 V12 **Novo mesto** *Ger.* Rudolfswert; *prev. Ger.* Neustadtl. SE Slovenia
126 K15 **Novomikhaylovskiy** Krasnodarskiy Kray, SW Russian Federation
112 L8 **Novo Miloševo** Vojvodina, N Serbia
Novomirgorod *see* Novomyrhorod
126 L5 **Novomoskovsk** Tul'skaya Oblast', W Russian Federation
117 U7 **Novomoskovs'k** *Rus.* Novomoskovsk. Dnipropetrovs'ka Oblast', E Ukraine
117 V8 **Novomykolayivka** Zaporiz'ka Oblast', SE Ukraine
117 Q7 **Novomyrhorod** *Rus.* Novomirgorod. Kirovohrads'ka Oblast', S Ukraine
127 N8 **Novonikolayevskiy** Volgogradskaya Oblast', SW Russian Federation
127 P10 **Novonikol'skoye** Volgogradskaya Oblast', SW Russian Federation
127 X7 **Novoorsk** Orenburgskaya Oblast', W Russian Federation
126 M13 **Novopokrovskaya** Krasnodarskiy Kray, SW Russian Federation
Novopolotsk *see* Navapolatsk
117 Y5 **Novopskov** Luhans'ka Oblast', E Ukraine
Novoradomsk *see* Radomsko
Novo Redondo *see* Sumbe
127 R8 **Novorepnoye** Saratovskaya Oblast', W Russian Federation
126 K14 **Novorossiysk** Krasnodarskiy Kray, SW Russian Federation
Novorossiyskiy/Novorossiyskoye *see* Akzhar
124 F15 **Novorzhev** Pskovskaya Oblast', W Russian Federation
Novoselitsa *see* Novoselytsya
117 S12 **Novoselivs'ke** Respublika Krym, S Ukraine
Novosëlki *see* Navasyolki
114 G6 **Novo Selo** Vidin, NW Bulgaria
113 M14 **Novo Selo** Serbia, C Serbia
116 K8 **Novoselytsya** *Rom.* Nouă Sulița, *Rus.* Novoselitsa. Chernivets'ka Oblast', W Ukraine
127 U7 **Novosergiyevka** Orenburgskaya Oblast', W Russian Federation
126 L11 **Novoshakhtinsk** Rostovskaya Oblast', SW Russian Federation
122 J12 **Novosibirsk** Novosibirskaya Oblast', C Russian Federation
122 J12 **Novosibirskaya Oblast'** ⬖ *province* C Russian Federation
122 M4 **Novosibirskiye Ostrova** *Eng.* New Siberian Islands. *island group* N Russian Federation
126 K6 **Novosil'** Orlovskaya Oblast', W Russian Federation
124 G16 **Novosokol'niki** Pskovskaya Oblast', W Russian Federation
127 Q6 **Novospasskoye** Ul'yanovskaya Oblast', W Russian Federation
Novotroickoje *see* Brlik
127 X8 **Novotroitsk** Orenburgskaya Oblast', W Russian Federation
Novotroitskoye *see* Brlik, Kazakhstan
Novotroitskoye *see* Novotroyits'ke, Ukraine
117 T11 **Novotroyits'ke** *Rus.* Novotroitskoye. Khersons'ka Oblast', S Ukraine
Novoukrainka *see* Novoukrayinka
117 Q8 **Novoukrayinka** *Rus.* Novoukrainka. Kirovohrads'ka Oblast', C Ukraine
127 Q5 **Novoul'yanovsk** Ul'yanovskaya Oblast', W Russian Federation
127 W8 **Novouralets** Orenburgskaya Oblast', W Russian Federation
Novo-Urgench *see* Urganch
116 I4 **Novovolyns'k** *Rus.* Novovolynsk. Volyns'ka Oblast', NW Ukraine
117 S9 **Novovorontsovka** Khersons'ka Oblast', S Ukraine
147 Y7 **Novovoznesenovka** Issyk-Kul'skaya Oblast', E Kyrgyzstan
125 R14 **Novovyatsk** Kirovskaya Oblast', NW Russian Federation
Novoyel'nya *see* Navayel'nya
124 I7 **Novoye Yushkozero** Respublika Kareliya, NW Russian Federation
117 O6 **Novozhyvotiv** Vinnyts'ka Oblast', C Ukraine
126 H6 **Novozybkov** Bryanskaya Oblast', W Russian Federation
112 F9 **Novska** Sisak-Moslavina, NE Croatia
Nový Bohumín *see* Bohumín
111 D15 **Nový Bor** *Ger.* Haida; *prev.* Bor u České Lípy, Hajda. Liberecký Kraj, N Czech Republic
111 E16 **Nový Bydžov** *Ger.* Neubidschow. Královéhradecký Kraj, N Czech Republic
119 G18 **Novy Dvor** *Rus.* Novyy Dvor. Hrodzyenskaya Voblasts', W Belarus
111 I17 **Nový Jičín** *Ger.* Neutitschein. Moravskoslezský Kraj, E Czech Republic
118 K12 **Novy Pahost** *Rus.* Novyy Pogost. Vitsyebskaya Voblasts', NW Belarus
Novyy Bug *see* Novyy Buh
117 R9 **Novyy Buh** *Rus.* Novyy Bug. Mykolayivs'ka Oblast', S Ukraine
117 Q4 **Novyy Bykiv** Chernihivs'ka Oblast', N Ukraine
Novyy Dvor *see* Novy Dvor
Novyye Aneny *see* Anenii Noi
127 P7 **Novyye Burasy** Saratovskaya Oblast', W Russian Federation
Novyy Margilan *see* Farg'ona
126 K8 **Novyy Oskol** Belgorodskaya Oblast', W Russian Federation
Novyy Pogost *see* Novy Pahost
127 R2 **Novyy Tor"yal** Respublika Mariy El, W Russian Federation
123 N12 **Novyy Uoyan** Respublika Buryatiya, S Russian Federation
122 J9 **Novyy Urengoy** Yamalo-Nenetskiy Avtonomnyy Okrug, N Russian Federation
Novyy Uzen' *see* Zhanaozen
111 N16 **Nowa Dęba** Podkarpackie, SE Poland
111 G15 **Nowa Ruda** *Ger.* Neurode. Dolnośląskie, SW Poland
110 F12 **Nowa Sól** *var.* Nowasól, *Ger.* Neusalz an der Oder. Lubuskie, W Poland
Nowasól *see* Nowa Sól
27 Q8 **Nowata** Oklahoma, C USA
142 M6 **Nowbarān** Markazi, W Iran
110 H8 **Nowe** Kujawski-pomorskie, N Poland
110 K9 **Nowe Miasto Lubawskie** *Ger.* Neumark. Warmińsko-Mazurskie, NE Poland
110 L13 **Nowe Miasto nad Pilicą** Mazowieckie, C Poland
110 D8 **Nowe Warpno** *Ger.* Neuwarp. Zachodnio-pomorskie, NW Poland
Nowgong *see* Nagaon
110 E8 **Nowogard** *var.* Nowógard, *Ger.* Naugard. Zachodnio-pomorskie, NW Poland
110 N9 **Nowogród** Podlaskie, NE Poland
Nowogródek *see* Navahrudak
111 E14 **Nowogrodziec** *Ger.* Naumburg am Queis. Dolnośląskie, SW Poland
Nowojelnia *see* Navayel'nya
Nowo-Minsk *see* Mińsk Mazowiecki
33 V13 **Nowood River** ≈ Wyoming, C USA
Nowo-Święciany *see* Švenčionėliai
183 S10 **Nowra-Bomaderry** New South Wales, SE Australia
149 T5 **Nowshera** *var.* Naushahra, Naushara. North-West Frontier Province, NE Pakistan
110 J7 **Nowy Dwór Gdański** *Ger.* Tiegenhof. Pomorskie, N Poland
110 L11 **Nowy Dwór Mazowiecki** Mazowieckie, C Poland
111 M17 **Nowy Sącz** *Ger.* Neu Sandec. Małopolskie, S Poland
111 L18 **Nowy Targ** *Ger.* Neumark. Małopolskie, S Poland
110 F11 **Nowy Tomyśl** *var.* Nowy Tomysl. Wielkopolskie, C Poland
Nowy Tomysl *see* Nowy Tomyśl
148 M7 **Now Zād** *var.* Nauzad. Helmand, S Afghanistan
23 N4 **Noxubee River** ≈ Alabama/Mississippi, S USA
122 I10 **Noyabr'sk** Yamalo-Nenetskiy Avtonomnyy Okrug, N Russian Federation
102 L8 **Noyant** Maine-et-Loire, NW France
39 X14 **Noyes Island** *island* Alexander Archipelago, Alaska, USA
103 O3 **Noyon** Oise, N France
102 I7 **Nozay** Loire-Atlantique, NW France
82 L12 **Nsando** Northern, NE Zambia
83 N16 **Nsanje** Southern, S Malawi
77 Q17 **Nsawam** SE Ghana
79 E16 **Nsimalen** ✈ Centre, C Cameroon
82 K12 **Nsombo** Northern, NE Zambia
82 H13 **Ntambu** North Western, NW Zambia
83 N14 **Ntcheu** *var.* Ncheu. Central, S Malawi
79 D17 **Ntem** *prev.* Campo, *var.* Kampo. ≈ Cameroon/Equatorial Guinea
83 I14 **Ntemwa** North Western, NW Zambia
Ntlenyana, Mount *see* Thabana Ntlenyana
79 I19 **Ntomba, Lac** *var.* Lac Tumba. ◎ NW Dem. Rep. Congo
115 I19 **Ntóro, Kávo** *prev.* Ákrotirio Kafiréas. *cape* Évvoia, C Greece
81 E19 **Ntungamo** SW Uganda
81 E18 **Ntusi** SW Uganda
83 H18 **Ntwetwe Pan** *salt lake* NE Botswana
93 M15 **Nuasjärvi** ◎ C Finland
80 F11 **Nuba Mountains** ▲▲ C Sudan
68 J9 **Nubian Desert** *desert* NE Sudan
116 G10 **Nucet** *Hung.* Diófás. Bihor, W Romania
Nu Chiang *see* Salween
145 U9 **Nuclear Testing Ground** *nuclear site* Pavlodar, E Kazakhstan
56 E9 **Nucuray, Río** ≈ N Peru
25 R14 **Nueces River** ≈ Texas, SW USA
9 V9 **Nueltin Lake** ◎ Manitoba/Northwest Territories, C Canada
99 K15 **Nuenen** Noord-Brabant, S Netherlands
62 G6 **Nuestra Señora, Bahía** *bay* N Chile
61 D14 **Nuestra Señora Rosario de Caa Catí** Corrientes, NE Argentina
54 J9 **Nueva Antioquia** Vichada, E Colombia
Nueva Caceres *see* Naga
41 O7 **Nueva Ciudad Guerrera** Tamaulipas, C Mexico
55 N4 **Nueva Esparta** *off.* Estado Nueva Esparta. ⬖ *state* NE Venezuela
Nueva Esparta, Estado *see* Nueva Esparta
44 C5 **Nueva Gerona** Isla de la Juventud, S Cuba
42 H8 **Nueva Guadalupe** San Miguel, E El Salvador
42 M11 **Nueva Guinea** Región Autónoma Atlántico Sur, SE Nicaragua
61 D19 **Nueva Helvecia** Colonia, SW Uruguay
63 J25 **Nueva, Isla** *island* S Chile
40 M14 **Nueva Italia** Michoacán de Ocampo, SW Mexico
56 D6 **Nueva Loja** *var.* Lago Agrio. Sucumbíos, NE Ecuador
42 F6 **Nueva Ocotepeque** *prev.* Ocotepeque. Ocotepeque, W Honduras
61 D19 **Nueva Palmira** Colonia, SW Uruguay
41 N6 **Nueva Rosita** Coahuila de Zaragoza, NE Mexico
42 E7 **Nueva San Salvador** *prev.* Santa Tecla. La Libertad, SW El Salvador
42 J8 **Nueva Segovia** ⬖ *department* NW Nicaragua
Nueva Tabarca *see* Plana, Isla
Nueva Villa de Padilla *see* Nuevo Padilla
61 B21 **Nueve de Julio** Buenos Aires, E Argentina
44 H6 **Nuevitas** Camagüey, E Cuba
61 D18 **Nuevo Berlín** Río Negro, W Uruguay
40 I4 **Nuevo Casas Grandes** Chihuahua, N Mexico
43 T14 **Nuevo Chagres** Colón, C Panama
41 W15 **Nuevo Coahuila** Campeche, E Mexico
63 K17 **Nuevo, Golfo** *gulf* S Argentina
41 O7 **Nuevo Laredo** Tamaulipas, NE Mexico
41 N8 **Nuevo León** ⬖ *state* NE Mexico
41 P10 **Nuevo Padilla** *var.* Nueva Villa de Padilla. Tamaulipas, C Mexico
56 E6 **Nuevo Rocafuerte** Orellana, E Ecuador
Nuga *see* Dzavhanmandal
80 O13 **Nugaal** *off.* Gobolka Nugaal. ⬖ *region* N Somalia
Nugaal, Gobolka *see* Nugaal
185 E24 **Nugget Point** *headland* South Island, New Zealand
186 J5 **Nuguria Islands** *island group* E Papua New Guinea
184 P10 **Nuhaka** Hawke's Bay, North Island, New Zealand
138 M10 **Nuhaydayn, Wādī an** *dry watercourse* W Iraq
190 E7 **Nui Atoll** *atoll* W Tuvalu
Nu Jiang *see* Salween
Nûk *see* Nuuk
182 G7 **Nukey Bluff** *hill* South Australia
Nukha *see* Şäki
123 T9 **Nukh Yablonevyy, Gora** ▲ E Russian Federation
186 K7 **Nukiki** Choiseul Island, NW Solomon Islands
186 B6 **Nuku** Sandaun, NW Papua New Guinea
193 W15 **Nuku** *island* Tongatapu Group, NE Tonga
193 U15 **Nuku'alofa** Tongatapu, S Tonga
193 Y16 **Nuku'alofa** ● (Tonga) Tongatapu, S Tonga
190 G12 **Nukuatea** *island* N Wallis and Futuna
190 F7 **Nukufetau Atoll** *atoll* C Tuvalu
190 G12 **Nukuhifala** *island* E Wallis and Futuna
191 W7 **Nuku Hiva** *island* Îles Marquises, NE French Polynesia
191 W7 **Nuku Hiva Island** *island* Îles Marquises, N French Polynesia
190 F9 **Nukulaelae Atoll** *var.* Nukulailai. *atoll* E Tuvalu
Nukulailai *see* Nukulaelae Atoll
190 G11 **Nukuloa** *island* N Wallis and Futuna
186 L6 **Nukumanu Islands** *prev.* Tasman Group. *island group* NE Papua New Guinea
Nukunau *see* Nikunau
190 J9 **Nukunonu Atoll** *island* C Tokelau
190 J9 **Nukunonu Village** Nukunonu Atoll, C Tokelau
189 S18 **Nukuoro Atoll** *atoll* Caroline Islands, S Micronesia
146 H8 **Nukus** Qoraqalpog'iston Respublikasi, W Uzbekistan
190 G11 **Nukutapu** *island* N Wallis and Futuna
39 O9 **Nulato** Alaska, USA
39 O10 **Nulato Hills** ▲▲ Alaska, USA
105 T9 **Nules** País Valenciano, E Spain
Nuling *see* Sultan Kudarat
182 C6 **Nullarbor** South Australia
180 M11 **Nullarbor Plain** *plateau* South Australia/Western Australia
163 S12 **Nulu'erhu Shan** ▲▲ N China
77 X14 **Numan** Adamawa, E Nigeria
165 S3 **Numata** Hokkaidō, NE Japan
81 C15 **Numatinna** ≈ W Sudan
95 F14 **Numedalen** *valley* S Norway
95 G14 **Numedalslågen** *var.* Laagen. ≈ S Norway
93 L19 **Nummela** Etelä-Suomi, S Finland
183 O11 **Numurkah** Victoria, SE Australia
196 L16 **Nunap Isua** *var.* Uummannarsuaq, *Dan.* Kap Farvel, *Eng.* Cape Farewell. *cape* S Greenland
9 N8 **Nunavut** ⬖ *territory* N Canada
54 H9 **Nunchia** Casanare, C Colombia
97 M20 **Nuneaton** C England, UK
153 W14 **Nungba** Manipur, NE India
38 L12 **Nunivak Island** *island* Alaska, USA
152 I5 **Nun Kun** ▲ NW India
98 L10 **Nunspeet** Gelderland, E Netherlands
107 C18 **Nuoro** Sardegna, Italy, C Mediterranean Sea
75 R12 **Nuqayy, Jabal** *hill range* S Libya
54 C9 **Nuquí** Chocó, W Colombia
143 O4 **Nūr** Māzandarān, N Iran
145 Q9 **Nura** ≈ N Kazakhstan
143 N11 **Nūrābād** Fārs, C Iran
Nurakita *see* Niulakita
Nurata *see* Nurota
Nuratau, Khrebet *see* Nurota Tizmasi
136 L17 **Nur Dağları** ▲▲ S Turkey
Nurek *see* Norak
Nuremberg *see* Nürnberg
149 S4 **Nūrestān** ⬖ *province* C Afghanistan
136 M15 **Nurhak** Kahramanmaraş, S Turkey
182 J9 **Nuriootpa** South Australia
127 S5 **Nurlat** Respublika Tatarstan, W Russian Federation
93 N15 **Nurmes** Itä-Suomi, E Finland
101 K20 **Nürnberg** *Eng.* Nuremberg. Bayern, S Germany
101 K20 **Nürnberg** ✈ Bayern, SE Germany
146 M10 **Nurota** *Rus.* Nurata. Navoiy Viloyati, C Uzbekistan
147 N10 **Nurota Tizmasi** *Rus.* Khrebet Nuratau. ▲▲ C Uzbekistan
149 T8 **Nūrpur** Punjab, E Pakistan
183 P6 **Nurri, Mount** *hill* New South Wales, SE Australia
25 T13 **Nursery** Texas, SW USA
169 V17 **Nusa Tenggara Barat** *off.* Propinsi Nusa Tenggara Barat, *Eng.* West Nusa Tenggara. ⬖ *province* S Indonesia
Nusa Tenggara Barat, Propinsi *see* Nusa Tenggara Barat
171 O16 **Nusa Tenggara Timur** *off.* Propinsi Nusa Tenggara Timur, *Eng.* East Nusa Tenggara. ⬖ *province* S Indonesia
Nusa Tenggara Timur, Propinsi *see* Nusa Tenggara Timur
171 U14 **Nusawulan** Papua, E Indonesia
137 Q16 **Nusaybin** *var.* Nisibin. Manisa, SE Turkey
39 O14 **Nushagak Bay** *bay* Alaska, USA
39 O13 **Nushagak Peninsula** *headland* Alaska, USA
39 O13 **Nushagak River** ≈ Alaska, USA
160 E11 **Nu Shan** ▲▲ SW China
149 N11 **Nushki** Baluchistān, SW Pakistan
Nussdorf *see* Năsăud
112 J9 **Nuštar** Vukovar-Srijem, E Croatia
99 L18 **Nuth** Limburg, SE Netherlands
100 N13 **Nuthe** ≈ NE Germany
Nutmeg State *see* Connecticut
39 T10 **Nutzotin Mountains** ▲▲ Alaska, USA
64 I5 **Nuuk** *var.* Nûk, *Dan.* Godthaab, Godthåb. ○ (Greenland) Kitaa, SW Greenland
92 L13 **Nuupas** Lappi, NW Finland
191 O7 **Nuupere, Pointe** *headland* Moorea, W French Polynesia
191 O7 **Nuuroa, Pointe** *headland* Tahiti, W French Polynesia
Nüürst *see* Baganuur
Nuwara *see* Nuwara Eliya
155 K25 **Nuwara Eliya** *var.* Nuwara. Central Province, S Sri Lanka
182 E7 **Nuyts Archipelago** *island group* South Australia
83 F17 **Nxaunxau** North West, NW Botswana
39 N12 **Nyac** Alaska, USA
122 H9 **Nyagan'** Khanty-Mansiyskiy Avtonomnyy Okrug, N Russian Federation
Nyagassola *see* Niagassola
Nyagquka *see* Yajiang
81 I18 **Nyahururu** Central, W Kenya
182 M10 **Nyah West** Victoria, SE Australia
158 M15 **Nyainqêntanglha Feng** ▲ W China
159 N15 **Nyainqêntanglha Shan** ▲▲ W China
80 B11 **Nyala** Southern Darfur, W Sudan
83 M16 **Nyamapanda** Mashonaland East, NE Zimbabwe
81 H25 **Nyamtumbo** Ruvuma, S Tanzania
Nyanda *see* Masvingo
124 M11 **Nyandoma** Arkhangel'skaya Oblast', NW Russian Federation
83 M16 **Nyanga** *prev.* Inyanga. Manicaland, E Zimbabwe
79 D20 **Nyanga** *off.* Province de la Nyanga, *var.* La Nyanga. ⬖ *province* SW Gabon
79 E20 **Nyanga** ≈ Congo/Gabon
Nyanga, Province de la *see* Nyanga
81 F20 **Nyantakara** Kagera, NW Tanzania
81 G19 **Nyanza** ⬖ *province* W Kenya
81 E21 **Nyanza-Lac** S Burundi
68 J14 **Nyasa, Lake** *var.* Lake Malawi; *prev.* Lago Nyassa. ◎ E Africa
Nyasaland/Nyasaland Protectorate *see* Malawi
Nyassa, Lago *see* Nyasa, Lake
119 J17 **Nyasvizh** *Pol.* Nieśwież, *Rus.* Nesvizh. Minskaya Voblasts', C Belarus
166 M8 **Nyaunglebin** Pegu, SW Myanmar (Burma)
166 M5 **Nyaung-u** Magwe, C Myanmar (Burma)
95 H24 **Nyborg** Fyn, C Denmark
95 N21 **Nybro** Kalmar, S Sweden
119 J16 **Nyeharelaye** *Rus.* Negoreloye. Minskaya Voblasts', C Belarus
195 W3 **Nye Mountains** ▲▲ Antarctica
81 I19 **Nyeri** Central, C Kenya
118 M11 **Nyeshcharda, Vozyera** ◎ N Belarus
92 O2 **Ny-Friesland** *physical region* N Svalbard
95 L14 **Nyhammar** Dalarna, C Sweden
160 F7 **Nyikog Qu** ≈ C China
158 L14 **Nyima** Xizang Zizhiqu, W China
83 L14 **Nyimba** Eastern, E Zambia
159 P16 **Nyingchi** *var.* Pula. Xizang Zizhiqu, W China
Nyinma *see* Maqu
111 O21 **Nyírbátor** Szabolcs-Szatmár-Bereg, E Hungary
111 N21 **Nyíregyháza** Szabolcs-Szatmár-Bereg, NE Hungary
Nyiro *see* Ewaso Ng'iro
Nyitra *see* Nitra
Nyitrabánya *see* Handlová
93 K16 **Nykarleby** *Fin.* Uusikaarlepyy. Länsi-Soumi, W Finland
95 I25 **Nykøbing** Storstrøm, SE Denmark
95 I22 **Nykøbing** Vestsjælland, C Denmark
95 F21 **Nykøbing** Viborg, NW Denmark
95 N17 **Nyköping** Södermanland, S Sweden
95 L15 **Nykroppa** Värmland, C Sweden
Nylstroom *see* Modimolle
183 P7 **Nymagee** New South Wales, SE Australia
183 V5 **Nymboida** New South Wales, SE Australia
183 U5 **Nymboida River** ≈ New South Wales, SE Australia
111 D16 **Nymburk** *var.* Neuenburg an der Elbe, *Ger.* Nimburg. Středočeský Kraj, C Czech Republic
95 O16 **Nynäshamn** Stockholm, C Sweden
183 Q6 **Nyngan** New South Wales, SE Australia
Nyoman *see* Neman
108 A10 **Nyon** *Ger.* Neuss; *anc.* Noviodunum. Vaud, SW Switzerland
79 D16 **Nyong** ≈ SW Cameroon
103 S14 **Nyons** Drôme, E France
79 D14 **Nyos, Lac** *Eng.* Lake Nyos. ◎ NW Cameroon
Nyos, Lake *see* Nyos, Lac

125 *U11* **Nyrob** *var.* Nyrov. Permskaya Oblast', NW Russian Federation
Nyrov *see* Nyrob
111 *H15* **Nysa** *Ger.* Neisse. Opolskie, S Poland
Nysa Łużycka *see* Neisse
Nyslott *see* Savonlinna
32 *M13* **Nyssa** Oregon, NW USA
Nystad *see* Uusikaupunki
95 *I25* **Nysted** Storstrøm, SE Denmark
125 *U14* **Nytva** Permskaya Oblast', NW Russian Federation
165 *P8* **Nyūdō-zaki** *headland* Honshū, C Japan
125 *P9* **Nyukhcha** Arkhangel'skaya Oblast', NW Russian Federation
124 *H8* **Nyuk, Ozero** *var.* Ozero Njuk. ⊚ NW Russian Federation
125 *O12* **Nyuksenitsa** *var.* Njuksenica. Vologodskaya Oblast', NW Russian Federation
79 *O22* **Nyunzu** Katanga, SE Dem. Rep. Congo
123 *O10* **Nyurba** Respublika Sakha (Yakutiya), NE Russian Federation
123 *O11* **Nyuya** Respublika Sakha (Yakutiya), NE Russian Federation
146 *K12* **Niyazow** *Rus.* Nyyazov. Lebap Welaýaty, NE Turkmenistan
Nyyazov *see* Niyazow
117 *T10* **Nyzhni Sirohozy** Khersons'ka Oblast', S Ukraine
117 *U12* **Nyzhn'ohirs'kyy** *Rus.* Nizhnegorskiy. Respublika Krym, S Ukraine
NZ *see* New Zealand
81 *G21* **Nzega** Tabora, C Tanzania
76 *K15* **Nzérékoré** SE Guinea
82 *A10* **N'Zeto** *prev.* Ambrizete. Zaire, NW Angola
79 *M24* **Nzilo, Lac** *prev.* Lac Delcommune. ⊚ SE Dem. Rep. Congo
Nzwani *see* Anjouan

O

29 *O11* **Oacoma** South Dakota, N USA
29 *N9* **Oahe Dam** *dam* South Dakota, N USA
28 *M9* **Oahe, Lake** ⊠ North Dakota/South Dakota, N USA
38 *C9* **Oa'hu** *var.* Oahu. *island* Hawaiian Islands, Hawai'i, USA
165 *V4* **O-Akan-dake** ▲ Hokkaidō, NE Japan
182 *K8* **Oakbank** South Australia
19 *P13* **Oak Bluffs** Martha's Vineyard, New York, NE USA
36 *K4* **Oak City** Utah, W USA
37 *R3* **Oak Creek** Colorado, C USA
35 *P8* **Oakdale** California, W USA
22 *H8* **Oakdale** Louisiana, S USA
29 *P7* **Oakes** North Dakota, N USA
22 *J4* **Oak Grove** Louisiana, S USA
97 *N19* **Oakham** C England, UK
32 *H7* **Oak Harbor** Washington, NW USA
21 *R5* **Oak Hill** West Virginia, NE USA
35 *N8* **Oakland** California, W USA
29 *T15* **Oakland** Iowa, C USA
19 *Q7* **Oakland** Maine, NE USA
21 *T3* **Oakland** Maryland, NE USA
29 *R14* **Oakland** Nebraska, C USA
31 *N11* **Oak Lawn** Illinois, N USA
33 *P16* **Oakley** Idaho, NW USA
26 *I4* **Oakley** Kansas, C USA
31 *N10* **Oak Park** Illinois, N USA
9 *X16* **Oak Point** Manitoba, S Canada
32 *G13* **Oakridge** Oregon, NW USA
20 *M9* **Oak Ridge** Tennessee, S USA
184 *K10* **Oakura** Taranaki, North Island, New Zealand
22 *L7* **Oak Vale** Mississippi, S USA
14 *G16* **Oakville** Ontario, S Canada
25 *V8* **Oakwood** Texas, SW USA
185 *F22* **Oamaru** Otago, South Island, New Zealand
96 *F13* **Oa, Mull of** *headland* W Scotland, UK
171 *O11* **Oan** Sulawesi, N Indonesia
185 *J17* **Oaro** Canterbury, South Island, New Zealand
35 *X2* **Oasis** Nevada, W USA
195 *S15* **Oates Land** *physical region* Antarctica
183 *P17* **Oatlands** Tasmania, SE Australia
36 *I11* **Oatman** Arizona, SW USA
41 *R16* **Oaxaca** *var.* Oaxaca de Juárez; *prev.* Antequera. Oaxaca, SE Mexico
41 *Q16* **Oaxaca** ◈ *state* SE Mexico
Oaxaca de Juárez *see* Oaxaca
122 *I19* **Ob'** ≈ C Russian Federation
14 *G9* **Obabika Lake** ⊚ Ontario, S Canada
Obagan *see* Ubagan
118 *M12* **Obal'** *Rus.* Obol'. Vitsyebskaya Voblasts', N Belarus
79 *E16* **Obala** Centre, SW Cameroon
14 *C6* **Oba Lake** ⊚ Ontario, S Canada
164 *J12* **Obama** Fukui, Honshū, SW Japan
96 *H11* **Oban** W Scotland, UK
Oban *see* Halfmoon Bay
Obando *see* Puerto Inírida
104 *I4* **O Barco** *var.* El Barco, El Barco de Valdeorras, O Barco de Valdeorras. Galicia, NW Spain
O Barco de Valdeorras *see* O Barco
Obbia *see* Hobyo
93 *J16* **Obbola** Västerbotten, N Sweden
Obbrovazzo *see* Obrovac
Obchuga *see* Abchuha
Obdorsk *see* Salekhard
Óbecse *see* Bečej
118 *I11* **Obeliai** Panevėžys, NE Lithuania
60 *F13* **Oberá** Misiones, NE Argentina
108 *E8* **Oberburg** Bern, W Switzerland
109 *Q9* **Oberdrauburg** Salzburg, S Austria
Oberglogau *see* Głogówek
109 *W4* **Ober Grafendorf** Niederösterreich, NE Austria
101 *E15* **Oberhausen** Nordrhein-Westfalen, W Germany
Oberhollabrunn *see* Tulln
Oberlaibach *see* Vrhnika
101 *Q15* **Oberlausitz** *var.* Hornja Łužica. *physical region* E Germany
26 *J2* **Oberlin** Kansas, C USA
22 *H8* **Oberlin** Louisiana, S USA
31 *T11* **Oberlin** Ohio, N USA
103 *U5* **Obernai** Bas-Rhin, NE France
109 *R4* **Obernberg am Inn** Oberösterreich, N Austria
Oberndorf *see* Oberndorf am Neckar
101 *G23* **Oberndorf am Neckar** *var.* Oberndorf. Baden-Württemberg, SW Germany
109 *Q5* **Oberndorf bei Salzburg** Salzburg, W Austria
Oberneustadtl *see* Kysucké Nové Mesto
183 *S8* **Oberon** New South Wales, SE Australia
109 *Q4* **Oberösterreich** *off.* Land Oberösterreich, *Eng.* Upper Austria. ◈ *state* NW Austria
Oberösterreich, Land *see* Oberösterreich
Oberpahlen *see* Põltsamaa
101 *M19* **Oberpfälzer Wald** ▲▲ SE Germany
109 *Y6* **Oberpullendorf** Burgenland, E Austria
Oberradkersburg *see* Gornja Radgona
101 *G18* **Oberursel** Hessen, W Germany
109 *Q8* **Obervellach** Salzburg, S Austria
109 *X7* **Oberwart** Burgenland, SE Austria
Oberwischau *see* Vişeu de Sus
109 *T7* **Oberwölz** *var.* Oberwölz-Stadt. Steiermark, SE Austria
Oberwölz-Stadt *see* Oberwölz
31 *S13* **Obetz** Ohio, N USA
Ob', Gulf of *see* Obskaya Guba
54 *G8* **Obia** Santander, C Colombia
58 *H12* **Óbidos** Pará, NE Brazil
104 *F10* **Óbidos** Leiria, C Portugal
Obidovichi *see* Abidavichy
147 *Q13* **Obigarm** W Tajikistan
165 *T2* **Obihiro** Hokkaidō, NE Japan
Obi-Khingou *see* Khingov
147 *P13* **Obikiik** SW Tajikistan
113 *N16* **Obilić** Kosovo, S Serbia
127 *O12* **Obil'noye** Respublika Kalmykiya, SW Russian Federation
20 *F8* **Obion** Tennessee, S USA
20 *F8* **Obion River** ≈ Tennessee, S USA
171 *S12* **Obi, Pulau** *island* Maluku, E Indonesia
165 *S2* **Obira** Hokkaidō, NE Japan
127 *N11* **Oblivskaya** Rostovskaya Oblast', SW Russian Federation
123 *R14* **Obluch'ye** Yevreyskaya Avtonomnaya Oblast', SE Russian Federation
126 *K4* **Obninsk** Kaluzhskaya Oblast', W Russian Federation
114 *J8* **Obnova** Pleven, N Bulgaria
79 *N15* **Obo** Haut-Mbomou, E Central African Republic
159 *T9* **Obo** Qinghai, C China
80 *M11* **Obock** E Djibouti
Obol' *see* Obal'
Obolyanka *see* Abalyanka
171 *V13* **Obome** Papua, E Indonesia
110 *G11* **Oborniki** Wielkolpolskie, W Poland
79 *G19* **Obouya** Cuvette, C Congo
126 *J8* **Oboyan'** Kurskaya Oblast', W Russian Federation
124 *M9* **Obozerskiy** Arkhangel'skaya Oblast', NW Russian Federation
112 *L11* **Obrenovac** Serbia, N Serbia
112 *D12* **Obrovac** *It.* Obbrovazzo. Zadar, SW Croatia
Obrovo *see* Abrova
35 *Q3* **Observation Peak** ▲ California, W USA
122 *J8* **Obskaya Guba** *Eng.* Gulf of Ob. *gulf* N Russian Federation
173 *N13* **Ob' Tablemount** *undersea feature* S Indian Ocean
173 *T10* **Ob' Trench** *undersea feature* E Indian Ocean
77 *P16* **Obuasi** S Ghana
117 *P5* **Obukhiv** *Rus.* Obukhov. Kyyivs'ka Oblast', N Ukraine
Obukhov *see* Obukhiv
125 *U14* **Obva** ≈ NW Russian Federation
117 *V10* **Obytichna Kosa** *spit* SE Ukraine
117 *V10* **Obytichna Zatoka** *gulf* SE Ukraine
105 *O3* **Oca** ≈ N Spain
23 *W10* **Ocala** Florida, SE USA
40 *M7* **Ocampo** Coahuila de Zaragoza, NE Mexico
54 *G7* **Ocaña** Norte de Santander, N Colombia
105 *N9* **Ocaña** Castilla-La Mancha, C Spain
104 *H4* **O Carballiño** *Cast.* Carballiño. Galicia, NW Spain
37 *T9* **Ocate** New Mexico, SW USA
Ocavango *see* Okavango
57 *D14* **Occidental, Cordillera** ▲▲ W Colombia
54 *I4* **Occidental, Cordillera** ▲▲ W Colombia
21 *Q6* **Oceana** West Virginia, NE USA
21 *Z4* **Ocean City** Maryland, NE USA
18 *J17* **Ocean City** New Jersey, NE USA
10 *K15* **Ocean Falls** British Columbia, SW Canada
Ocean Island *see* Banaba
Ocean Island *see* Kure Atoll
64 *J9* **Oceanographer Fracture Zone** *tectonic feature* NW Atlantic Ocean
35 *U17* **Oceanside** California, W USA
22 *M9* **Ocean Springs** Mississippi, S USA
Ocean State *see* Rhode Island
25 *O9* **O C Fisher Lake** ⊠ Texas, SW USA
117 *Q10* **Ochakiv** *Rus.* Ochakov. Mykolayivs'ka Oblast', S Ukraine
Ochakov *see* Ochakiv
Ochamchira *see* Och'amch'ire
137 *Q9* **Och'amch'ire** *Rus.* Ochamchira. W Georgia
Ochansk *see* Okhansk
125 *T15* **Ocher** Permskaya Oblast', NW Russian Federation
115 *I19* **Óchi** ▲ Évvoia, C Greece
165 *W4* **Ochiishi-misaki** *headland* Hokkaidō, NE Japan
23 *S9* **Ochlockonee River** ≈ Florida/Georgia, SE USA
44 *K12* **Ocho Rios** C Jamaica
Ochrida *see* Ohrid
Ochrida, Lake *see* Ohrid, Lake
101 *J19* **Ochsenfurt** Bayern, C Germany
23 *U7* **Ocilla** Georgia, SE USA
94 *N13* **Ockelbo** Gävleborg, C Sweden
Ocker *see* Oker
95 *I19* **Öckerö** Västra Götaland, S Sweden
23 *U6* **Ocmulgee River** ≈ Georgia, SE USA
116 *H11* **Ocna Mureş** *Hung.* Marosújvár; *prev.* Ocna Mureşului, *prev. Hung.* Marosújvárakna. Alba, C Romania
Ocna Mureşului *see* Ocna Mureş
116 *H11* **Ocna Sibiului** *Ger.* Salzburg, *Hung.* Vizakna. Sibiu, C Romania
116 *H13* **Ocnele Mari** *prev.* Vioara. Vâlcea, S Romania
116 *L7* **Ocniţa** *Rus.* Oknitsa. N Moldova
23 *U4* **Oconee, Lake** ⊠ Georgia, SE USA
23 *U5* **Oconee River** ≈ Georgia, SE USA
30 *M9* **Oconomowoc** Wisconsin, N USA
30 *M6* **Oconto** Wisconsin, N USA
30 *M6* **Oconto Falls** Wisconsin, N USA
30 *M6* **Oconto River** ≈ Wisconsin, N USA
104 *I3* **O Corgo** Galicia, NW Spain
41 *V16* **Ocosingo** Chiapas, SE Mexico
42 *J8* **Ocotal** Nueva Segovia, NW Nicaragua
42 *F6* **Ocotepeque** ◈ *department* W Honduras
Ocotepeque *see* Nueva Ocotepeque
40 *L13* **Ocotlán** Jalisco, SW Mexico
41 *R16* **Ocotlán** *var.* Ocotlán de Morelos. Oaxaca, SE Mexico
Ocotlán de Morelos *see* Ocotlán
41 *U16* **Ocozocuautla** Chiapas, SE Mexico
21 *Y10* **Ocracoke Island** *island* North Carolina, SE USA
102 *I3* **Octeville** Manche, N France
October Revolution Island *see* Oktyabr'skoy Revolyutsii, Ostrov
43 *R17* **Ocú** Herrera, S Panama
83 *Q14* **Ocua** Cabo Delgado, NE Mozambique
Ocumare *see* Ocumare del Tuy
54 *M5* **Ocumare del Tuy** *var.* Ocumare. Miranda, N Venezuela
77 *P17* **Oda** SE Ghana
165 *G12* **Ōda** *var.* Oda. Shimane, Honshū, SW Japan
92 *K3* **Ódadhahraun** *lava flow* C Iceland
165 *Q7* **Ōdate** Akita, Honshū, C Japan
165 *N14* **Odawara** Kanagawa, Honshū, S Japan
95 *D14* **Odda** Hordaland, S Norway
95 *G22* **Odder** Århus, C Denmark
Oddur *see* Xuddur
29 *T13* **Odebolt** Iowa, C USA
104 *H14* **Odeleite** Faro, S Portugal
25 *Q4* **Odell** Texas, SW USA
25 *T14* **Odem** Texas, SW USA
104 *F13* **Odemira** Beja, S Portugal
136 *C14* **Ödemiş** İzmir, SW Turkey
Ödenburg *see* Sopron
83 *I22* **Odendaalsrus** Free State, C South Africa
Odenpäh *see* Otepää
95 *H23* **Odense** Fyn, C Denmark
101 *H19* **Odenwald** ▲▲ W Germany
84 *H10* **Oder** *Cz./Pol.* Odra. ≈ C Europe
Oderberg *see* Bohumín
100 *P11* **Oderbruch** *wetland* Germany/Poland
Oderhaff *see* Szczeciński, Zalew
100 *O11* **Oder-Havel-Kanal** *canal* NE Germany
Oderhellen *see* Odorheiu Secuiesc
100 *P13* **Oder-Spree-Kanal** *canal* NE Germany
Odertal *see* Zdzieszowice
106 *I7* **Oderzo** Veneto, NE Italy
117 *P10* **Odesa** *Rus.* Odessa. Odes'ka Oblast', SW Ukraine
Odesa *see* Odes'ka Oblast'
95 *L18* **Ödeshög** Östergötland, S Sweden
117 *O9* **Odes'ka Oblast'** *var.* Odesa, *Rus.* Odesskaya Oblast'. ◈ *province* SW Ukraine
24 *M8* **Odessa** Texas, SW USA
32 *K8* **Odessa** Washington, NW USA
Odessa *see* Odesa
Odesskaya Oblast' *see* Odes'ka Oblast'
122 *H12* **Odesskoye** Omskaya Oblast', C Russian Federation
Odessus *see* Varna
102 *F6* **Odet** ≈ NW France
104 *I14* **Odiel** ≈ SW Spain
76 *L14* **Odienné** NW Ivory Coast
171 *O4* **Odiongan** Tablas Island, C Philippines
116 *L12* **Odobeşti** Vrancea, E Romania
110 *H13* **Odolanów** *Ger.* Adelnau. Wielkopolskie, C Poland
167 *R13* **Ŏdôngk** Kâmpóng Spoe, S Cambodia
25 *N6* **O'donnell** Texas, SW USA
98 *O7* **Odoorn** Drenthe, NE Netherlands
Odorhei *see* Odorheiu Secuiesc
116 *J11* **Odorheiu Secuiesc** *Ger.* Oderhellen, *Hung.* Vámosudvarhely; *prev.* Odorhei, *Ger.* Hofmarkt. Harghita, C Romania
Odra *see* Oder
112 *J9* **Odžaci** *Ger.* Hodschag, *Hung.* Hodság. Vojvodina, NW Serbia
59 *N14* **Oeiras** Piauí, E Brazil
104 *F11* **Oeiras** Lisboa, C Portugal
101 *G14* **Oelde** Nordrhein-Westfalen, W Germany
28 *J11* **Oelrichs** South Dakota, N USA
101 *M17* **Oelsnitz** Sachsen, E Germany
Oels/Oels in Schlesien *see* Oleśnica
29 *X12* **Oelwein** Iowa, C USA
Oeniadae *see* Oiniádes
191 *N17* **Oeno Island** *atoll* Pitcairn Islands, C Pacific Ocean
Oesel *see* Saaremaa
108 *L7* **Oetz** *var.* Ötz. Tirol, W Austria
137 *P11* **Of** Trabzon, NE Turkey
30 *K15* **O'Fallon** Illinois, N USA
27 *W4* **O'Fallon** Missouri, C USA
107 *N16* **Ofanto** ≈ S Italy
97 *D18* **Offaly** *Ir.* Ua Uíbh Fhailí; *prev.* King's County. ◈ *county* C Ireland
101 *H18* **Offenbach** *var.* Offenbach am Main. Hessen, W Germany
Offenbach am Main *see* Offenbach
101 *F22* **Offenburg** Baden-Württemberg, SW Germany
182 *C2* **Officer Creek** *seasonal river* South Australia
Oficina María Elena *see* María Elena
Oficina Pedro de Valdivia *see* Pedro de Valdivia
115 *K22* **Ofidoússa** *island* Kykládes, Greece, Aegean Sea
Ofiral *see* Sharm el Sheikh
92 *H10* **Ofotfjorden** *fjord* N Norway
192 *L16* **Ofu** *island* Manua Islands, E American Samoa
165 *R9* **Ōfunato** Iwate, Honshū, C Japan
165 *P8* **Oga** Akita, Honshū, C Japan
Ogaadeen *see* Ogaden
165 *Q9* **Ogachi** Akita, Honshū, C Japan
165 *P9* **Ogachi-tōge** *pass* Honshū, C Japan
81 *N14* **Ogaden** *Som.* Ogaadeen. *plateau* Ethiopia/Somalia
165 *P8* **Oga-hantō** *peninsula* Honshū, C Japan
165 *K13* **Ōgaki** Gifu, Honshū, SW Japan
28 *L15* **Ogallala** Nebraska, C USA
168 *M14* **Ogan, Air** ≈ Sumatera, W Indonesia
165 *Y15* **Ogasawara-shotō** *Eng.* Bonin Islands. *island group* SE Japan
14 *I9* **Ogascanane, Lac** ⊚ Québec, SE Canada
165 *R7* **Ogawara-ko** ⊚ Honshū, C Japan
77 *T15* **Ogbomosho** *var.* Ogmoboso. Oyo, W Nigeria
29 *U13* **Ogden** Iowa, C USA
36 *L2* **Ogden** Utah, W USA
18 *I6* **Ogdensburg** New York, NE USA
23 *W5* **Ogeechee River** ≈ Georgia, SE USA
Oger *see* Ogre
165 *N10* **Ogi** Niigata, Sado, C Japan
10 *H5* **Ogilvie** Yukon Territory, NW Canada
10 *H4* **Ogilvie** ≈ Yukon Territory, NW Canada
10 *H5* **Ogilvie Mountains** ▲▲ Yukon Territory, NW Canada
Oginskiy Kanal *see* Ahinski Kanal
162 *J7* **Ögiynuur** *var.* Dzegstey. Arhangay, C Mongolia
146 *F6* **Og'iyon Sho'rxogi** *wetland* NW Uzbekistan
146 *F6* **Og'iyon Sho'rxogi** *wetland* NW Uzbekistan
146 *B10* **Oglanly** Balkan Welaýaty, W Turkmenistan
23 *T5* **Oglethorpe** Georgia, SE USA
23 *T2* **Oglethorpe, Mount** ▲ Georgia, SE USA
106 *F7* **Oglio** *anc.* Ollius. ≈ N Italy
Ogmoboso *see* Ogbomosho
103 *T8* **Ognon** ≈ E France
123 *R13* **Ogodzha** Amurskaya Oblast', S Russian Federation
77 *W16* **Ogoja** Cross River, S Nigeria
12 *C10* **Ogoki** ≈ Ontario, S Canada
12 *D11* **Ogoki Lake** ⊚ Ontario, C Canada
Ögöömör *see* Hanhongor
79 *F19* **Ogooué** ≈ Congo/Gabon
79 *E18* **Ogooué-Ivindo** *off.* Province de l'Ogooué-Ivindo, *var.* L'Ogooué-Ivindo. ◈ *province* N Gabon
Ogooué-Ivindo, Province de l' *see* Ogooué-Ivindo
79 *E19* **Ogooué-Lolo** *off.* Province de l'Ogooué-Lolo, *var.* L'Ogooué-Lolo. ◈ *province* C Gabon
Ogooué-Lolo, Province de l' *see* Ogooué-Lolo
79 *C19* **Ogooué-Maritime** *off.* Province de l'Ogooué-Maritime, *var.* L'Ogooué-Maritime. ◈ *province* W Gabon
Ogooué-Maritime, Province de l' *see* Ogooué-Maritime
165 *D14* **Ogōri** Fukuoka, Kyūshū, SW Japan
114 *H7* **Ogosta** ≈ NW Bulgaria
112 *Q9* **Ogražden** *Bul.* Ograzhden. ▲ Bulgaria/FYR Macedonia *see also* Ograzhden
114 *G12* **Ograzhden** *Mac.* Orgražden. ▲ Bulgaria/FYR Macedonia *see also* Orgražden
Ograzhden *see* Ogražden
118 *G9* **Ogre** *Ger.* Oger. Ogre, C Latvia
118 *H9* **Ogre** ≈ C Latvia
112 *C10* **Ogulin** Karlovac, NW Croatia
77 *S16* **Ogun** ◈ *state* SW Nigeria
Ogurdzhaly, Ostrov *see* OgurjalyAdasy
146 *A12* **OgurjalyAdasy** *Rus.* Ogurdzhaly, Ostrov. *island* W Turkmenistan
77 *U16* **Ogwashi-Uku** Delta, S Nigeria
185 *B23* **Ohai** Southland, South Island, New Zealand
147 *Q10* **Ohangaron** *Rus.* Akhangaran. Toshkent Viloyati, E Uzbekistan
147 *Q10* **Ohangaron** *Rus.* Akhangaran. ≈ E Uzbekistan
83 *C16* **Ohangwena** ◈ *district* N Namibia
30 *M10* **O'Hare** ✕ (Chicago) Illinois, N USA
165 *R6* **Ōhata** Aomori, Honshū, C Japan
184 *L13* **Ohau** Manawatu-Wanganui, North Island, New Zealand
185 *E20* **Ohau, Lake** ⊚ South Island, New Zealand
Ohcejohka *see* Utsjoki
99 *J20* **Ohey** Namur, SE Belgium
191 *X15* **O'Higgins, Cabo** *cape* Easter Island, Chile, E Pacific Ocean
O'Higgins, Lago *see* San Martín, Lago
31 *S12* **Ohio** *off.* State of Ohio, *also known as* Buckeye State. ◈ *state* N USA
0 *L10* **Ohio River** ≈ N USA
Ohlau *see* Oława
101 *H16* **Ohm** ≈ C Germany
193 *W16* **Ohonua** 'Eua, E Tonga
23 *V5* **Ohoopee River** ≈ Georgia, SE USA
100 *L12* **Ohre** *Ger.* Eger. ≈ Czech Republic/Germany
Ohri *see* Ohrid
113 *M20* **Ohrid** *Turk.* Ochrida, Ohri. SW FYR Macedonia
113 *M20* **Ohrid, Lake** *var.* Lake Ochrida, *Alb.* Liqeni i Ohrit, *Mac.* Ohridsko Ezero. ⊚ Albania/FYR Macedonia
Ohridsko Ezero/Ohrit, Liqeni i *see* Ohrid, Lake
184 *L9* **Ohura** Manawatu-Wanganui, North Island, New Zealand
58 *J9* **Oiapoque** Amapá, E Brazil
58 *J10* **Oiapoque, Rio** *var.* Fleuve l'Oyapok, Oyapock. ≈ Brazil/French Guiana *see also* Oyapok, Fleuve l'
Oiapoque, Rio *see* Oyapok, Fleuve l'
15 *O9* **Oies, Île aux** *island* Québec, SE Canada
92 *L13* **Oijärvi** Oulu, C Finland
92 *L12* **Oikarainen** Lappi, N Finland
188 *F10* **Oikuul** Babeldaob, N Palau
18 *C13* **Oil City** Pennsylvania, NE USA
18 *C12* **Oil Creek** ≈ Pennsylvania, NE USA
35 *R13* **Oildale** California, W USA
Oileán Ciarral *see* Castleisland
Oil Islands *see* Chagos Archipelago
115 *D18* **Oiniádes** *anc.* Oeniadae. *site of ancient city* Dytikí Ellás, W Greece
115 *L18* **Oinoússes** *island* E Greece
Oírr, Inis *see* Inisheer
99 *J15* **Oirschot** Noord-Brabant, S Netherlands
103 *N4* **Oise** ◈ *department* N France
103 *P3* **Oise** ≈ N France
99 *J14* **Oisterwijk** Noord-Brabant, S Netherlands
45 *O14* **Oistins** S Barbados
165 *E4* **Ōita** Ōita, Kyūshū, SW Japan
165 *D14* **Ōita** *off.* Ōita-ken. ◈ *prefecture* Kyūshū, SW Japan
Ōita-ken *see* Ōita
115 *E17* **Oíti** ▲ C Greece
165 *S4* **Oiwake** Hokkaidō, NE Japan
35 *R14* **Ojai** California, W USA
94 *K13* **Öje** Dalarna, C Sweden
93 *J14* **Öjebyn** Norrbotten, N Sweden
165 *B13* **Ojika-jima** *island* SW Japan
40 *K5* **Ojinaga** Chihuahua, N Mexico
40 *M11* **Ojo Caliente** *var.* Ojocaliente. Zacatecas, C Mexico
Ojocaliente *see* Ojo Caliente
40 *D6* **Ojo de Liebre, Laguna** *var.* Laguna Scammon, Scammon Lagoon. *lagoon* W Mexico
62 *I7* **Ojos del Salado, Cerro** ▲ W Argentina
105 *R7* **Ojos Negros** Aragón, NE Spain
40 *M12* **Ojuelos de Jalisco** Aguascalientes, C Mexico
127 *N4* **Oka** ≈ W Russian Federation
83 *D19* **Okahandja** Otjozondjupa, C Namibia
184 *L9* **Okahukura** Manawatu-Wanganui, North Island, New Zealand
184 *J3* **Okaihau** Northland, North Island, New Zealand
83 *D18* **Okakarara** Otjozondjupa, N Namibia
13 *P5* **Okak Islands** *island group* Newfoundland and Labrador, E Canada
10 *M17* **Okanagan** ≈ British Columbia, SW Canada
9 *N17* **Okanagan Lake** ⊚ British Columbia, SW Canada
Ókanizsa *see* Kanjiža
83 *C16* **Okankolo** Otjikoto, N Namibia
32 *K6* **Okanogan River** ≈ Washington, NW USA
83 *D18* **Okaputa** Otjozondjupa, N Namibia
149 *V9* **Okāra** Punjab, E Pakistan
26 *M10* **Okarche** Oklahoma, C USA
Okarem *see* Ekerem
189 *X14* **Okat Harbor** *harbor* Kosrae, E Micronesia
22 *M5* **Okatibbee Creek** ≈ Mississippi, S USA
83 *C17* **Okaukuejo** Kunene, N Namibia
Okavanggo *see* Cubango/Okavango
83 *E17* **Okavango** ◈ *district* NW Namibia
83 *G17* **Okavango** *var.* Cubango, Kavango, Kavengo, Kubango, Okavanggo, *Port.* Ocavango. ≈ S Africa *see also* Cubango
Okavango *see* Cubango
83 *G17* **Okavango Delta** *wetland* N Botswana
164 *M12* **Okaya** Nagano, Honshū, S Japan
164 *H13* **Okayama** Okayama, Honshū, SW Japan
164 *H13* **Okayama** *off.* Okayama-ken. ◈ *prefecture* Honshū, SW Japan
Okayama-ken *see* Okayama
164 *L14* **Okazaki** Aichi, Honshū, C Japan
110 *M12* **Okęcie** ✕ (Warszawa) Mazowieckie, C Poland
23 *Y13* **Okeechobee** Florida, SE USA
23 *Y14* **Okeechobee, Lake** ⊚ Florida, SE USA
26 *M9* **Okeene** Oklahoma, C USA
23 *V8* **Okefenokee Swamp** *wetland* Georgia, SE USA
97 *J24* **Okehampton** SW England, UK
27 *P10* **Okemah** Oklahoma, C USA
77 *U16* **Okene** Kogi, S Nigeria
100 *K13* **Oker** *var.* Ocker. ≈ NW Germany
101 *J14* **Oker-Stausee** ⊚ C Germany
123 *T12* **Okha** Ostrov Sakhalin, Sakhalinskaya Oblast', SE Russian Federation
125 *U15* **Okhansk** *var.* Ochansk. Permskaya Oblast', NW Russian Federation
123 *S10* **Okhotsk** Khabarovskiy Kray, E Russian Federation
192 *J2* **Okhotsk, Sea of** *sea* NW Pacific Ocean
117 *T4* **Okhtyrka** *Rus.* Akhtyrka. Sums'ka Oblast', NE Ukraine
83 *E23* **Okiep** Northern Cape, W South Africa
Oki-guntō *see* Oki-shotō
164 *H11* **Oki-kaikyō** *strait* SW Japan
165 *P16* **Okinawa** Okinawa, SW Japan
165 *S16* **Okinawa** *off.* Okinawa-ken. ◈ *prefecture* Okinawa, SW Japan
165 *S16* **Okinawa** *island* SW Japan
Okinawa-ken *see* Okinawa
165 *U16* **Okinoerabu-jima** *island* Nansei-shotō, SW Japan
164 *F15* **Okino-shima** *island* SW Japan
164 *H11* **Oki-shotō** *var.* Oki-guntō. *island group* SW Japan
77 *T16* **Okitipupa** Ondo, SW Nigeria
166 *L8* **Okkan** Pegu, SW Myanmar (Burma)
27 *N10* **Oklahoma** *off.* State of Oklahoma, *also known as* The Sooner State. ◈ *state* C USA
27 *N11* **Oklahoma City** *state capital* Oklahoma, C USA
25 *Q4* **Oklaunion** Texas, SW USA
23 *W10* **Oklawaha River** ≈ Florida, SE USA
27 *P10* **Okmulgee** Oklahoma, C USA
Oknitsa *see* Ocniţa
22 *M3* **Okolona** Mississippi, S USA
165 *U2* **Okoppe** Hokkaidō, NE Japan
9 *Q16* **Okotoks** Alberta, SW Canada
80 *H6* **Oko, Wadi** ≈ NE Sudan
79 *G19* **Okoyo** Cuvette, W Congo
77 *S15* **Okpara** ≈ Benin/Nigeria
92 *I8* **Øksfjord** Finnmark, N Norway
125 *R4* **Oksino** Nenetskiy Avtonomnyy Okrug, NW Russian Federation
92 *G13* **Oksskolten** ▲ C Norway
Oksu *see* Oqsu
144 *M8* **Oktyabr'sk** Kostanay, N Kazakhstan
186 *B7* **Ok Tedi** Western, W Papua New Guinea
Oktemberyan *see* Armavir
166 *M7* **Oktwin** Pegu, C Myanmar (Burma)
127 *R6* **Oktyabr'sk** Samarskaya Oblast', W Russian Federation
Oktyab'rsk *see* Kandyagash
125 *N12* **Oktyabr'skiy** Arkhangel'skaya Oblast', NW Russian Federation
122 *E10* **Oktyabr'skiy** Kamchatskaya Oblast', E Russian Federation
127 *T5* **Oktyabr'skiy** Respublika Bashkortostan, W Russian Federation
127 *O11* **Oktyabr'skiy** Volgogradskaya Oblast', SW Russian Federation
Oktyabr'skiy *see* Aktsyabrski
127 *V7* **Oktyabr'skoye** Orenburgskaya Oblast', W Russian Federation
122 *M5* **Oktyabr'skoy Revolyutsii, Ostrov** *Eng.* October Revolution Island. *island* Severnaya Zemlya, N Russian Federation
164 *C15* **Ōkuchi** *var.* Ōkuti. Kagoshima, Kyūshū, SW Japan
Okulovka *see* Uglovka
165 *Q4* **Okushiri-tō** *var.* Okusiri Tô. *island* NE Japan
Okusiri Tô *see* Okushiri-tō
77 *S15* **Okuta** Kwara, W Nigeria
Ōkuti *see* Ōkuchi
83 *F19* **Okwa** *var.* Chapman's. ≈ Botswana/Namibia
123 *T10* **Ola** Magadanskaya Oblast', E Russian Federation
27 *T11* **Ola** Arkansas, C USA
Ola *see* Ala
35 *T11* **Olacha Peak** ▲ California, W USA
92 *J1* **Ólafsfjördhur** Nordhurland Eystra, N Iceland
92 *H3* **Ólafsvík** Vesturland, W Iceland
Oláhbrettye *see* Bretea-Română
Oláhszentgyörgy *see* Sângeorz-Băi
Oláh-Toplicza *see* Toplița
35 *T11* **Olancha** California, W USA
42 *J5* **Olanchito** Yoro, C Honduras
42 *J6* **Olancho** ◈ *department* E Honduras
95 *O20* **Öland** *island* S Sweden
95 *O19* **Ölands norra udde** *headland* S Sweden
95 *N22* **Ölands södra udde** *headland* S Sweden
182 *K7* **Olary** South Australia
27 *R4* **Olathe** Kansas, C USA
61 *C22* **Olavarría** Buenos Aires, E Argentina

◆ Country
● Country Capital
◇ Dependent Territory
○ Dependent Territory Capital
◈ Administrative Regions
✕ International Airport
▲ Mountain
▲▲ Mountain Range
Volcano
≈ River
⊚ Lake
⊠ Reservoir

92 O2 **Olav V Land** *physical region* C Svalbard
111 H14 **Oława** *Ger.* Ohlau. Dolnośląskie, SW Poland
107 D17 **Olbia** *prev.* Terranova Pausania. Sardegna, Italy, C Mediterranean Sea
44 G5 **Old Bahama Channel** *channel* Bahamas/Cuba
Old Bay State/Old Colony State *see* Massachusetts
10 H2 **Old Crow** Yukon Territory, NW Canada
Old Dominion *see* Virginia
Oldeberkeap *see* Oldeberkoop
98 M7 **Oldeberkoop** *Fris.* Oldeberkeap. Friesland, N Netherlands
98 L10 **Oldebroek** Gelderland, E Netherlands
98 L8 **Oldemarkt** Overijssel, N Netherlands
94 E11 **Olden** Sogn Og Fjordane, C Norway
100 G10 **Oldenburg** Niedersachsen, NW Germany
100 K8 **Oldenburg** *var.* Oldenburg in Holstein. Schleswig-Holstein, N Germany
Oldenburg in Holstein *see* Oldenburg
98 P10 **Oldenzaal** Overijssel, E Netherlands
Olderfjord *see* Leaibevuotna
18 J8 **Old Forge** New York, NE USA
Old Goa *see* Goa
97 L17 **Oldham** NW England, UK
39 Q14 **Old Harbor** Kodiak Island, Alaska, USA
44 J13 **Old Harbour** C Jamaica
97 C22 **Old Head of Kinsale** *Ir.* An Seancheann. *headland* SW Ireland
20 J8 **Old Hickory Lake** ⊠ Tennessee, S USA
Old Line State *see* Maryland
Old North State *see* North Carolina
81 I17 **Ol Doinyo Lengeyo** ▲▲ C Kenya
9 Q16 **Olds** Alberta, SW Canada
19 O7 **Old Speck Mountain** ▲ Maine, NE USA
19 S6 **Old Town** Maine, NE USA
9 T17 **Old Wives Lake** ◎ Saskatchewan, S Canada
162 J7 **Öldziyt** *var.* Höshööt. Arhangay, C Mongolia
162 I8 **Öldziyt** *var.* Ulaan-Uul. Bayanhongor, C Mongolia
162 L10 **Öldziyt** *var.* Rashaant. Dundgovĭ, C Mongolia
162 K8 **Öldziyt** *var.* Sangiyn Dalay. Övörhangay, C Mongolia
Öldziyt *see* Erdenemandal, Arhangay, Mongolia
Öldziyt *see* Sayhandulaan, Dornogovĭ, Mongolia
188 H6 **Oleai** *var.* San Jose. Saipan, S Northern Mariana Islands
18 E11 **Olean** New York, NE USA
110 O7 **Olecko** *Ger.* Treuburg. Warmińsko-Mazurskie, NE Poland
106 C7 **Oleggio** Piemonte, NE Italy
123 P11 **Olëkma** Amurskaya Oblast', SE Russian Federation
123 P12 **Olëkma** ≈ C Russian Federation
123 P11 **Olëkminsk** Respublika Sakha (Yakutiya), NE Russian Federation
117 W7 **Oleksandrivka** Donets'ka Oblast', E Ukraine
117 R7 **Oleksandrivka** *Rus.* Aleksandrovka. Kirovohrads'ka Oblast', C Ukraine
117 Q9 **Oleksandrivka** Mykolayivs'ka Oblast', S Ukraine
117 S7 **Oleksandriya** *Rus.* Aleksandriya. Kirovohrads'ka Oblast', C Ukraine
93 B20 **Ølen** Hordaland, S Norway
124 J4 **Olenegorsk** Murmanskaya Oblast', NW Russian Federation
123 N9 **Olenëk** Respublika Sakha (Yakutiya), NE Russian Federation
123 N9 **Olenëk** ≈ NE Russian Federation
123 O7 **Olenëkskiy Zaliv** *bay* N Russian Federation
124 K6 **Olenitsa** Murmanskaya Oblast', NW Russian Federation
102 I11 **Oléron, Île d'** *island* W France
111 H14 **Oleśnica** *Ger.* Oels, Oels in Schlesien. Dolnośląskie, SW Poland
111 I15 **Olesno** *Ger.* Rosenberg. Opolskie, S Poland
116 M3 **Olevs'k** *Rus.* Olevsk. Zhytomyrs'ka Oblast', N Ukraine
Olevsk *see* Olevs'k
123 S15 **Ol'ga** Primorskiy Kray, SE Russian Federation
Olga, Mount *see* Kata Tjuta
92 P2 **Olgastretet** *strait* E Svalbard
162 D5 **Ölgiy** Bayan-Ölgiy, W Mongolia
95 F23 **Ølgod** Ribe, W Denmark
104 H14 **Olhão** Faro, S Portugal
93 L14 **Olhava** Oulu, C Finland
112 B12 **Olib** *It.* Ulbo. *island* W Croatia
83 B16 **Olifa** Kunene, NW Namibia
83 E20 **Olifants** *var.* Elephant River. ≈ E Namibia
83 E25 **Olifants** *var.* Elefantes. ≈ SW South Africa
83 G22 **Olifantshoek** Northern Cape, N South Africa
188 L15 **Olimarao Atoll** *atoll* Caroline Islands, C Micronesia
Ólimbos *see* Ólympos
Olimpo *see* Fuerte Olimpo
59 Q15 **Olinda** Pernambuco, E Brazil
Olinthos *see* Ólynthos
83 I20 **Oliphants Drift** Kgatleng, SE Botswana
Olisipo *see* Lisboa
Olita *see* Alytus
105 Q4 **Olite** Navarra, N Spain
62 K10 **Oliva** Córdoba, C Argentina
105 T11 **Oliva** País Valenciano, E Spain
Oliva *see* La Oliva
104 I12 **Oliva de la Frontera** Extremadura, W Spain
Olivares *see* Olivares de Júcar
62 H9 **Olivares, Cerro de** ▲ N Chile
105 P9 **Olivares de Júcar** *var.* Olivares. Castilla-La Mancha, C Spain
22 L1 **Olive Branch** Mississippi, S USA
21 O5 **Olive Hill** Kentucky, S USA
35 O6 **Olivehurst** California, W USA
104 G7 **Oliveira de Azeméis** Aveiro, N Portugal
104 I11 **Olivenza** Extremadura, W Spain
9 N17 **Oliver** British Columbia, SW Canada
103 N7 **Olivet** Loiret, C France
29 Q12 **Olivet** South Dakota, N USA
29 T9 **Olivia** Minnesota, N USA
185 C20 **Olivine Range** ▲▲ South Island, New Zealand
108 H10 **Olivone** Ticino, S Switzerland
Ölkeyek *see* Ul'kayak
127 O9 **Ol'khovka** Volgogradskaya Oblast', SW Russian Federation
111 K16 **Olkusz** Małopolskie, S Poland
22 I6 **Olla** Louisiana, S USA
62 I4 **Ollagüe, Volcán** *var.* Oyahue, Volcán Oyahue. ⛰ N Chile
189 U13 **Ollan** *island* Chuuk, C Micronesia
188 F7 **Ollei** Babeldaob, N Palau
Ollius *see* Oglio
108 C10 **Ollon** Vaud, W Switzerland
147 Q10 **Olmaliq** *Rus.* Almalyk. Toshkent Viloyati, E Uzbekistan
104 M6 **Olmedo** Castilla-León, N Spain
55 B10 **Olmos** Lambayeque, W Peru
Olmütz *see* Olomouc
30 M15 **Olney** Illinois, N USA
25 R5 **Olney** Texas, SW USA
95 L22 **Olofström** Blekinge, S Sweden
187 N9 **Olomburi** Malaita, N Solomon Islands
111 H17 **Olomouc** *Ger.* Olmütz, *Pol.* Ołomuniec. Olomoucký Kraj, E Czech Republic
111 H18 **Olomoucký Kraj** ◈ *region* E Czech Republic
Ołomuniec *see* Olomouc
122 D7 **Olonets** Respublika Kareliya, NW Russian Federation
171 N3 **Olongapo** *off.* Olongapo City. Luzon, N Philippines
Olongapo City *see* Olongapo
102 J16 **Oloron-Ste-Marie** Pyrénées-Atlantiques, SW France
192 L16 **Olosega** *island* Manua Islands, E American Samoa
105 W4 **Olot** Cataluña, NE Spain
146 K12 **Olot** *Rus.* Alat. Buxoro Viloyati, C Uzbekistan
112 I12 **Olovo** ◈ Federacija Bosna I Hercegovina, E Bosnia and Herzegovina
123 O14 **Olovyannaya** Chitinskaya Oblast', S Russian Federation
123 T7 **Oloy** ≈ NE Russian Federation
101 F16 **Olpe** Nordrhein-Westfalen, W Germany
109 N8 **Olperer** ▲ SW Austria
Olshanka *see* Vil'shanka
Ol'shany *see* Al'shany
Olsnitz *see* Murska Sobota
98 M10 **Olst** Overijssel, E Netherlands
110 L8 **Olsztyn** *Ger.* Allenstein. Warmińsko-Mazurskie, N Poland
110 L8 **Olsztynek** *Ger.* Hohenstein in Ostpreussen. Warmińsko-Mazurskie, N Poland
116 I14 **Olt** ◈ *county* SW Romania
116 I14 **Olt** *var.* Oltul, *Ger.* Alt. ≈ S Romania
108 E7 **Olten** Solothurn, NW Switzerland
116 K14 **Oltenița** *prev. Eng.* Oltenitsa; *anc.* Constantiola. Călărași, SE Romania
Oltenitsa *see* Oltenița
116 H14 **Olteț** ≈ S Romania
24 M4 **Olton** Texas, SW USA
137 R12 **Oltu** Erzurum, NE Turkey
Oltul *see* Olt
146 G7 **Oltynko'l** Qoraqalpog'iston Respublikasi, NW Uzbekistan
161 S15 **Oluan Pi** *Eng.* Cape Olwanpi. *cape* S Taiwan
Ólubló *see* Stará L'ubovňa
137 R11 **Olur** Erzurum, NE Turkey
104 L15 **Olvera** Andalucía, S Spain
Ol'viopol' *see* Pervomays'k
Olwanpi, Cape *see* Oluan Pi
115 D20 **Olympía** Dytikí Ellás, S Greece
32 G9 **Olympia** *state capital* Washington, NW USA
182 H5 **Olympic Dam** South Australia
32 F7 **Olympic Mountains** ▲▲ Washington, NW USA
121 O3 **Ólympos** *var.* Troodos, *Eng.* Mount Olympus. ▲ C Cyprus
115 F15 **Ólympos** *var.* Ólimbos, *Eng.* Mount Olympus. ▲ N Greece
115 L17 **Ólympos** ▲ Lésvos, E Greece
16 C5 **Olympus, Mount** ▲ Washington, NW USA
Olympus, Mount *see* Ólympos
115 G14 **Ólynthos** *var.* Olinthos; *anc.* Olynthus. *site of ancient city* Kentrikí Makedonía, N Greece
Olynthus *see* Ólynthos
117 Q3 **Olyshivka** Chernihivs'ka Oblast', N Ukraine
123 W8 **Olyutorskiy, Mys** *headland* E Russian Federation
123 V8 **Olyutorskiy Zaliv** *bay* E Russian Federation
186 M10 **Om** ≈ W Papua New Guinea
129 S6 **Om'** ≈ N Russian Federation
158 I13 **Oma** Xizang Zizhiqu, W China
165 R6 **Ōma** Aomori, Honshū, C Japan
125 P6 **Oma** ≈ NW Russian Federation
164 M12 **Ōmachi** *var.* Ōmati. Nagano, Honshū, S Japan
165 Q8 **Ōmagari** Akita, Honshū, C Japan
97 E15 **Omagh** *Ir.* An Ómaigh. W Northern Ireland, UK
29 S15 **Omaha** Nebraska, C USA
83 E19 **Omaheke** ◈ *district* W Namibia
141 W10 **Oman** *off.* Sultanate of Oman, *Ar.* Salṭanat 'Umān; *prev.* Muscat and Oman. ◆ *monarchy* SW Asia
129 O10 **Oman Basin** *var.* Bassin d'Oman. *undersea feature* N Indian Ocean
Oman, Bassin d' *see* Oman Basin
129 N10 **Oman, Gulf of** *Ar.* Khalīj 'Umān. *gulf* N Arabian Sea
Oman, Sultanate of *see* Oman
184 J3 **Omapere** Northland, North Island, New Zealand
185 E20 **Omarama** Canterbury, South Island, New Zealand
112 F11 **Omarska** ◈ Republika Srpska, NW Bosnia and Herzegovina
83 C18 **Omaruru** Erongo, NW Namibia
83 C19 **Omaruru** ≈ W Namibia
83 E17 **Omatako** ≈ NE Namibia
Ōmati *see* Ōmachi
83 E18 **Omawewozonyanda** Omaheke, E Namibia
165 R6 **Ōma-zaki** *headland* Honshū, C Japan
Omba *see* Ambae
Ombai *see* Alor, Pulau
83 C16 **Ombalantu** Omusati, N Namibia
79 H15 **Ombella-Mpoko** ◈ *prefecture* S Central African Republic
Ombetsu *see* Onbetsu
83 B17 **Ombombo** Kunene, NW Namibia
79 D19 **Omboué** Ogooué-Maritime, W Gabon
106 G13 **Ombrone** ≈ C Italy
80 F9 **Omdurman** *var.* Umm Durmān. Khartoum, C Sudan
165 N13 **Ōme** Tōkyō, Honshū, S Japan
106 C6 **Omegna** Piemonte, NE Italy
183 P12 **Omeo** Victoria, SE Australia
138 F11 **'Omer** Southern, C Israel
41 P16 **Ometepec** Guerrero, S Mexico
42 K11 **Ometepe, Isla de** *island* S Nicaragua
Om Hager *see* Om Hajer
80 I10 **Om Hajer** *var.* Om Hager. SW Eritrea
165 J13 **Ōmi-Hachiman** *var.* Ōmihachiman. Shiga, Honshū, SW Japan
Ōmihachiman *see* Ōmi-Hachiman
10 L12 **Omineca Mountains** ▲▲ British Columbia, W Canada
113 F14 **Omiš** *It.* Almissa. Split-Dalmacija, S Croatia
112 B10 **Omišalj** Primorje-Gorski Kotar, NW Croatia
83 D19 **Omitara** Khomas, C Namibia
41 O16 **Omitlán, Río** ≈ S Mexico
39 X14 **Ommaney, Cape** *headland* Baranof Island, Alaska, USA
98 N9 **Ommen** Overijssel, E Netherlands
163 N7 **Ömnödelgar** *var.* Bayanbulag. Hentiy, C Mongolia
163 N7 **Ömnödelger** *var.* Bayanbulag. Hentiy, C Mongolia
162 K11 **Ömnögovĭ** ◈ *province* S Mongolia
191 X7 **Omoa** Fatu Hira, NE French Polynesia
Omo Botego *see* Omo Wenz
Ömoldova *see* Moldova Veche
123 T7 **Omolon** Chukotskiy Avtonomnyy Okrug, NE Russian Federation
123 T7 **Omolon** ≈ NE Russian Federation
123 Q8 **Omoloy** ≈ NE Russian Federation
165 P8 **Omono-gawa** ≈ Honshū, C Japan
81 I14 **Omo Wenz** *var.* Omo Botego. ≈ Ethiopia/Kenya
122 H12 **Omsk** Omskaya Oblast', C Russian Federation
122 H11 **Omskaya Oblast'** ◈ *province* C Russian Federation
165 U2 **Ōmu** Hokkaidō, NE Japan
110 M9 **Omulew** ≈ NE Poland
116 J12 **Omul, Vârful** *prev.* Vîrful Omu. ▲ C Romania
83 D16 **Omundaungilo** Ohangwena, N Namibia
164 C14 **Ōmura** Nagasaki, Kyūshū, SW Japan
83 B17 **Omusati** ◈ *district* N Namibia
164 C14 **Ōmuta** Fukuoka, Kyūshū, SW Japan
125 S14 **Omutninsk** Kirovskaya Oblast', NW Russian Federation
Omu, Vîrful *see* Omul, Vârful
29 V7 **Onamia** Minnesota, N USA
21 Y5 **Onancock** Virginia, NE USA
14 E10 **Onaping Lake** ◎ Ontario, S Canada
30 M12 **Onarga** Illinois, N USA
15 R6 **Onatchiway, Lac** ◎ Québec, SE Canada
29 S14 **Onawa** Iowa, C USA
165 U5 **Onbetsu** *var.* Ombetsu. Hokkaidō, NE Japan
83 B16 **Oncócua** Cunene, SW Angola
105 S9 **Onda** País Valenciano, E Spain
111 N18 **Ondava** ≈ NE Slovakia
Ondjiva *see* N'Giva
77 T16 **Ondo** Ondo, SW Nigeria
77 T16 **Ondo** ◈ *state* SW Nigeria
163 N8 **Öndörhaan** *var.* Undur Khan; *prev.* Tsetsen Khan. Hentiy, E Mongolia
162 M9 **Öndörshil** *var.* Böhöt. Dundgovĭ, C Mongolia
162 L8 **Öndörshireet** *var.* Bayshint. Töv, C Mongolia
162 I7 **Öndör-Ulaan** *var.* Teel. Arhangay, C Mongolia
83 D18 **Ondundazongonda** Otjozondjupa, N Namibia
151 K21 **One and Half Degree Channel** *channel* S Maldives
187 Z15 **Oneata** *island* Lau Group, E Fiji
124 L9 **Onega** Arkhangel'skaya Oblast', NW Russian Federation
124 L9 **Onega** ≈ NW Russian Federation
Onega Bay *see* Onezhskaya Guba
Onega, Lake *see* Onezhskoye Ozero
18 I10 **Oneida** New York, NE USA
20 M8 **Oneida** Tennessee, S USA
18 H9 **Oneida Lake** ◎ New York, NE USA
29 P13 **O'Neill** Nebraska, C USA
123 V12 **Onekotan, Ostrov** *island* Kuril'skiye Ostrova, SE Russian Federation
23 P3 **Oneonta** Alabama, S USA
18 J11 **Oneonta** New York, NE USA
190 I16 **Oneroa** *island* S Cook Islands
116 K11 **Onești** *Hung.* Onyest; *prev.* Gheorghe Gheorghiu-Dej. Bacău, E Romania
193 V15 **Onevai** *island* Tongatapu Group, S Tonga
108 A11 **Onex** Genève, SW Switzerland
124 K8 **Onezhskaya Guba** *Eng.* Onega Bay. *bay* NW Russian Federation
122 D7 **Onezhskoye Ozero** *Eng.* Lake Onega. ◎ NW Russian Federation
83 C16 **Ongandjera** Omusati, N Namibia
184 N12 **Ongaonga** Hawke's Bay, North Island, New Zealand
Ongi *see* Sayhan-Ovoo, Dundgovĭ, Mongolia
Ongi *see* Uyanga
163 W14 **Ongjin** SW North Korea
155 J17 **Ongole** Andhra Pradesh, E India
Ongon *see* Bürd
Ongtüstik Qazaqstan Oblysy *see* Yuzhnyy Kazakhstan
99 I21 **Onhaye** Namur, S Belgium
166 M8 **Onhne** Pegu, SW Myanmar (Burma)
137 S9 **Oni** N Georgia
29 N9 **Onida** South Dakota, N USA
164 F15 **Onigajō-yama** ▲ Shikoku, SW Japan
172 H7 **Onilahy** ≈ S Madagascar
77 U16 **Onitsha** Anambra, S Nigeria
164 K12 **Ōno** Fukui, Honshū, SW Japan
164 I13 **Ōno** Hyōgo, Honshū, SW Japan
187 K15 **Ono** *island* SW Fiji
164 E13 **Onoda** Yamaguchi, Honshū, SW Japan
187 Z16 **Ono-i-lau** *island* SE Fiji
164 D13 **Ōnojō** *var.* Ōnozyô. Fukuoka, Kyūshū, SW Japan
163 O7 **Onon Gol** ≈ N Mongolia
Ononte *see* Orontes
55 N6 **Onoto** Anzoátegui, NE Venezuela
191 O3 **Onotoa** *prev.* Clerk Island. *atoll* Tungaru, W Kiribati
Ōnozyô *see* Ōnojō
95 I19 **Onsala** Halland, S Sweden
83 E23 **Onseepkans** Northern Cape, W South Africa
104 F4 **Ons, Illa de** *island* NW Spain
180 H7 **Onslow** Western Australia
21 W11 **Onslow Bay** *bay* North Carolina, E USA
98 P6 **Onstwedde** Groningen, NE Netherlands
164 C16 **On-take** ▲ Kyūshū, SW Japan
35 T15 **Ontario** California, W USA
32 M13 **Ontario** Oregon, NW USA
12 D10 **Ontario** ◈ *province* S Canada
9 P14 **Ontario, Lake** ◎ Canada/USA
0 L9 **Ontario Peninsula** *peninsula* Canada/USA
Onteniente *see* Ontinyent
105 S11 **Ontinyent** *var.* Onteniente. País Valenciano, E Spain
93 N15 **Ontojärvi** ◎ E Finland
30 L3 **Ontonagon** Michigan, N USA
30 L3 **Ontonagon River** ≈ Michigan, N USA
186 M7 **Ontong Java Atoll** *prev.* Lord Howe Island. *atoll* N Solomon Islands
175 N5 **Ontong Java Rise** *undersea feature* W Pacific Ocean
Onuba *see* Huelva
55 W9 **Onverwacht** Para, N Surinam
Onyest *see* Onești
Oodeypore *see* Udaipur
182 J7 **Oodla Wirra** South Australia
182 F2 **Oodnadatta** South Australia
182 C5 **Ooldea** South Australia
27 Q8 **Oologah Lake** ⊠ Oklahoma, C USA
Oos-Kaap *see* Eastern Cape
Oos-Londen *see* East London
99 E17 **Oostakker** Oost-Vlaanderen, NW Belgium
99 D15 **Oostburg** Zeeland, SW Netherlands
98 K9 **Oostelijk-Flevoland** *polder* C Netherlands
99 B16 **Oostende** *Eng.* Ostend, *Fr.* Ostende. West-Vlaanderen, NW Belgium
99 B16 **Oostende** ✈ West-Vlaanderen, NW Belgium
98 L12 **Oosterbeek** Gelderland, SE Netherlands
99 I14 **Oosterhout** Noord-Brabant, S Netherlands
98 O6 **Oostermoers Vaart** *var.* Hunze. ≈ NE Netherlands
99 F14 **Oosterschelde** *Eng.* Eastern Scheldt. *inlet* SW Netherlands
99 E14 **Oosterscheldedam** *dam* SW Netherlands
98 M7 **Oosterwolde** *Fris.* Easterwâlde. Friesland, N Netherlands
98 I9 **Oosthuizen** Noord-Holland, NW Netherlands
99 H16 **Oostmalle** Antwerpen, N Belgium
Oos-Transvaal *see* Mpumalanga
99 E15 **Oost-Souburg** Zeeland, SW Netherlands
99 E17 **Oost-Vlaanderen** *Eng.* East Flanders. ◈ *province* NW Belgium
98 J5 **Oost-Vlieland** Friesland, N Netherlands
98 F12 **Oostvoorne** Zuid-Holland, SW Netherlands
Ootacamund *see* Udagamandalam
98 O10 **Ootmarsum** Overijssel, E Netherlands
10 K14 **Ootsa Lake** ⊠ British Columbia, SW Canada
114 L8 **Opaka** Türgovishte, N Bulgaria
79 M18 **Opala** Orientale, C Dem. Rep. Congo
125 Q13 **Oparino** Kirovskaya Oblast', NW Russian Federation
14 H8 **Opasatica, Lac** ◎ Québec, SE Canada
112 B9 **Opatija** *It.* Abbazia. Primorje-Gorski Kotar, NW Croatia
111 N15 **Opatów** Świętokrzyskie, C Poland
111 I17 **Opava** *Ger.* Troppau. Moravskoslezský Kraj, E Czech Republic
111 H16 **Opava** *Ger.* Oppa. ≈ NE Czech Republic
Opazova *see* Stara Pazova
Opécska *see* Pecica
14 E8 **Opeepeesway Lake** ◎ Ontario, S Canada
23 R5 **Opelika** Alabama, S USA
22 I8 **Opelousas** Louisiana, S USA
186 G6 **Open Bay** *bay* New Britain, E Papua New Guinea
14 I12 **Opeongo Lake** ◎ Ontario, SE Canada
99 K17 **Opglabbeek** Limburg, NE Belgium
33 W6 **Opheim** Montana, NW USA
39 P10 **Ophir** Alaska, USA
Ophiusa *see* Formentera
79 N18 **Opienge** Orientale, E Dem. Rep. Congo
185 G20 **Opihi** ≈ South Island, New Zealand
12 J9 **Opinaca** ≈ Québec, C Canada
12 J10 **Opinaca, Réservoir** ⊠ Québec, E Canada
117 T5 **Opishnya** *Rus.* Oposhnya. Poltavs'ka Oblast', NE Ukraine
98 I8 **Opmeer** Noord-Holland, NW Netherlands
77 V17 **Opobo** Akwa Ibom, S Nigeria
124 F16 **Opochka** Pskovskaya Oblast', W Russian Federation
110 L13 **Opoczno** Łodzkie, C Poland
111 I15 **Opole** *Ger.* Oppeln. Opolskie, S Poland
111 H15 **Opolskie** ◈ *province* S Poland
Opornyy *see* Borankul
104 G4 **O Porriño** *var.* Porriño. Galicia, NW Spain
Oporto *see* Porto
Oposhnya *see* Opishnya
184 P8 **Opotiki** Bay of Plenty, North Island, New Zealand
23 Q7 **Opp** Alabama, S USA
Oppa *see* Opava
94 G9 **Oppdal** Sør-Trøndelag, S Norway
Oppeln *see* Opole
107 N23 **Oppido Mamertina** Calabria, SW Italy
Oppidum Ubiorum *see* Köln
94 F12 **Oppland** ◈ *county* S Norway
118 J12 **Opsa** *Rus.* Opsa. Vitsyebskaya Voblasts', NW Belarus
26 I8 **Optima Lake** ⊠ Oklahoma, C USA
184 J11 **Opunake** Taranaki, North Island, New Zealand
191 N6 **Opunohu, Baie d'** *bay* Moorea, W French Polynesia
83 B17 **Opuwo** Kunene, NW Namibia
146 H6 **Oqqal'a** *var.* Akkala, *Rus.* Karakala. Qoraqalpog'iston Respublikasi, NW Uzbekistan
147 V13 **Oqsu** *Rus.* Oksu. ≈ SE Tajikistan
147 P14 **Oqtogh, Qatorkŭhi** *Rus.* Khrebet Aktau. ▲▲ SW Tajikistan
146 M11 **Oqtosh** *Rus.* Aktash. Samarqand Viloyati, C Uzbekistan
147 N11 **Oqtow Tizmasi** *var.* Khrebet Aktau. ▲▲ C Uzbekistan
30 J12 **Oquawka** Illinois, N USA
144 J10 **Or'** *Kaz.* Or. ≈ Kazakhstan/Russian Federation
36 M15 **Oracle** Arizona, SW USA
147 N15 **O'radaryo** *Rus.* Uradar'ya. ≈ S Uzbekistan
147 N13 **O'radaryo** *Rus.* Uradar'ya. ≈ S Uzbekistan
116 F9 **Oradea** *prev.* Oradea Mare, *Ger.* Grosswardein, *Hung.* Nagyvárad. Bihor, NW Romania
Oradea Mare *see* Oradea
113 M17 **Orahovac** *Alb.* Rahovec. Kosovo, S Serbia
112 H9 **Orahovica** Virovitica-Podravina, NE Croatia
152 K13 **Orai** Uttar Pradesh, N India
92 K12 **Orajärvi** Lappi, NW Finland
Or Akiva *see* Or 'Aqiva
Oral *see* Ural'sk
74 I5 **Oran** *var.* Ouahran, Wahran. NW Algeria
183 R8 **Orange** New South Wales, SE Australia
103 R14 **Orange** *anc.* Arausio. Vaucluse, SE France
25 Y10 **Orange** Texas, SW USA
21 V5 **Orange** Virginia, NE USA
21 R13 **Orangeburg** South Carolina, SE USA
58 J9 **Orange, Cabo** *headland* NE Brazil
29 S12 **Orange City** Iowa, C USA
Orange Cone *see* Orange Fan
172 J10 **Orange Fan** *var.* Orange Cone. *undersea feature* SW Indian Ocean
Orange Free State *see* Free State
25 S14 **Orange Grove** Texas, SW USA
18 K13 **Orange Lake** New York, NE USA
23 V10 **Orange Lake** ◎ Florida, SE USA
Orange Mouth/Orangemund *see* Oranjemund
23 W9 **Orange Park** Florida, SE USA
83 E23 **Orange River** *Afr.* Oranjerivier. ≈ S Africa
14 G15 **Orangeville** Ontario, S Canada
36 M5 **Orangeville** Utah, W USA
42 G1 **Orange Walk** Orange Walk, N Belize
42 F1 **Orange Walk** ◈ *district* NW Belize
100 N11 **Oranienburg** Brandenburg, NE Germany
98 O7 **Oranjekanaal** *canal* NE Netherlands
83 D23 **Oranjemund** *var.* Orangemund; *prev.* Orange Mouth. Karas, SW Namibia
Oranjerivier *see* Orange River
45 N16 **Oranjestad** ○ (Aruba) W Aruba
Oranje Vrystaat *see* Free State
Orany *see* Varėna
83 H18 **Orapa** Central, C Botswana
138 F9 **Or 'Aqiva** *var* Or Akiva. Haifa, W Israel
112 I10 **Orašje** ◈ Federacija Bosna I Herecegovina, N Bosnia and Herzegovina
116 G11 **Orăștie** *Ger.* Broos, *Hung.* Szászváros. Hunedoara, W Romania
Orașul Stalin *see* Brașov
111 K18 **Orava** *Hung.* Árva, *Pol.* Orawa. ≈ N Slovakia
Oravainen *see* Oravais
93 K16 **Oravais** *Fin.* Oravainen. Länsi-Soumi, W Finland
Oravicabánya *see* Oravița
116 F13 **Oravița** *Ger.* Orawitza, *Hung.* Oravicabánya. Caraș-Severin, SW Romania
Orawa *see* Orava
185 B24 **Orawia** Southland, South Island, New Zealand
Orawitza *see* Oravița
103 P16 **Orb** ≈ S France
106 C9 **Orba** ≈ NW Italy
158 H12 **Orba Co** ◎ W China
108 B9 **Orbe** Vaud, W Switzerland
107 G14 **Orbetello** Toscana, C Italy
104 K3 **Orbigo** ≈ NW Spain
183 Q12 **Orbost** Victoria, SE Australia
95 O14 **Örbyhus** Uppsala, C Sweden
194 I1 **Orcadas** *Argentinian research station* South Orkney Islands, Antarctica
105 P12 **Orcera** Andalucía, S Spain
33 P9 **Orchard Homes** Montana, NW USA
37 P5 **Orchard Mesa** Colorado, C USA
18 D10 **Orchard Park** New York, NE USA
Orchid Island *see* Lan Yü
115 G18 **Orchómenos** *var.* Orhomenos, Orkhómenos, *prev.* Skripón; *anc.* Orchomenus. Stereá Ellás, C Greece
Orchomenus *see* Orchómenos
106 B7 **Orco** ≈ NW Italy
103 R8 **Or, Côte d'** *physical region* C France
29 O14 **Ord** Nebraska, C USA
119 O15 **Ordats'** *Rus.* Ordat'. Mahilyowskaya Voblasts', E Belarus
36 K8 **Orderville** Utah, W USA
104 H2 **Ordes** Galicia, NW Spain
35 V14 **Ord Mountain** ▲ California, W USA
163 N14 **Ordos** *prev.* Dongsheng. Nei Mongol Zizhiqu, N China
Ordos Desert *see* Mu Us Shadi
188 B16 **Ordot** C Guam
137 N11 **Ordu** *anc.* Cotyora. Ordu, N Turkey
136 M11 **Ordu** ◈ *province* N Turkey
137 V14 **Ordubad** SW Azerbaijan
Orduña *see* Urduña
37 U6 **Ordway** Colorado, C USA
117 T9 **Ordzhonikidze** Dnipropetrovs'ka Oblast', E Ukraine
Ordzhonikidze *see* Denisovka, Kazakhstan
Ordzhonikidze *see* Vladikavkaz, Russian Federation
Ordzhonikidze *see* Yenakiyeve, Ukraine
Ordzhonikidzeabad *see* Kofarnihon
55 U9 **Orealla** E Guyana
113 G15 **Orebić** *It.* Sabbioncello. Dubrovnik-Neretva, S Croatia
95 M16 **Örebro** Örebro, C Sweden
95 L16 **Örebro** ◈ *county* C Sweden
25 W6 **Ore City** Texas, SW USA
30 L10 **Oregon** Illinois, N USA
27 Q2 **Oregon** Missouri, C USA
31 R11 **Oregon** Ohio, N USA
32 H13 **Oregon** *off.* State of Oregon, *also known as* Beaver State, Sunset State, Valentine State, Webfoot State. ◈ *state* NW USA
32 G11 **Oregon City** Oregon, NW USA
Oregon, State of *see* Oregon
95 P14 **Öregrund** Uppsala, C Sweden
Orekhov *see* Orikhiv
126 L3 **Orekhovo-Zuyevo** Moskovskaya Oblast', W Russian Federation
Orekhovsk *see* Arekhawsk
126 J6 **Orël** Orlovskaya Oblast', W Russian Federation
Orel *see* Oril'
56 E11 **Orellana** Loreto, N Peru
56 E6 **Orellana** ◈ *province* NE Ecuador
104 L11 **Orellana, Embalse de** ⊠ W Spain
36 L3 **Orem** Utah, W USA
Ore Mountains *see* Erzgebirge/Krušné Hory
127 V7 **Orenburg** *prev.* Chkalov. Orenburgskaya Oblast', W Russian Federation
127 V7 **Orenburg** ✈ Orenburgskaya Oblast', W Russian Federation
127 T7 **Orenburgskaya Oblast'** ◈ *province* W Russian Federation
Orense *see* Ourense
188 C8 **Oreor** *var.* Koror. *island* N Palau

◆ Country ● Country Capital ◇ Dependent Territory ○ Dependent Territory Capital ◈ Administrative Regions ✈ International Airport ▲ Mountain ▲▲ Mountain Range ⛰ Volcano ≈ River ◎ Lake ⊠ Reservoir

Oreor see Koror
185 B24 **Orepuki** Southland, South Island, New Zealand
114 L12 **Orestiáda** prev. Orestiás. Anatolikí Makedonía kai Thráki, NE Greece
Orestiás see Orestiáda
Øresund/Öresund see Sound, The
185 C23 **Oreti** ≈ South Island, New Zealand
184 L5 **Orewa** Auckland, North Island, New Zealand
65 A25 **Orford, Cape** headland West Falkland, Falkland Islands
44 B5 **Órganos, Sierra de los** ▲▲ W Cuba
37 R15 **Organ Peak** ▲ New Mexico, SW USA
105 N9 **Orgaz** Castilla-La Mancha, C Spain
Orgeyev see Orhei
Orgil see Jargalant
105 O15 **Orgiva** var. Orjiva. Andalucía, S Spain
163 O10 **Örgön** var. Senj. Dornogovĭ, SE Mongolia
Örgön see Bayangovĭ
Orgražden see Ograzhden
117 N9 **Orhei** var. Orheiu, Rus. Orgeyev. N Moldova
Orheiu see Orhei
105 R3 **Orhi** var. Orhy, Pico de Orhy, Pic d'Orhy. ▲ France/Spain see also Orhy
Orhi see Orhy
Orhomenos see Orchómenos
162 K6 **Orhon** ◈ province N Mongolia
162 L6 **Orhon Gol** ≈ N Mongolia
102 J16 **Orhy** var. Orhi, Pico de Orhy, Pic d'Orhy. ▲ France/Spain see also Orhi
Orhy see Orhi
Orhy, Pic d'/Orhy, Pico de see Orhi/Orhy
34 L2 **Orick** California, W USA
32 L6 **Orient** Washington, NW USA
48 D6 **Oriental, Cordillera** ▲▲ Bolivia/Peru
48 D6 **Oriental, Cordillera** ▲▲ C Colombia
57 H16 **Oriental, Cordillera** ▲▲ C Peru
63 M15 **Oriente** Buenos Aires, E Argentina
105 R12 **Orihuela** País Valenciano, E Spain
117 V9 **Orikhiv** Rus. Orekhov. Zaporiz'ka Oblast', SE Ukraine
113 K22 **Orikum** var. Orikumi. Vlorë, SW Albania
Orikumi see Orikum
117 V6 **Oril'** Rus. Orel. ≈ E Ukraine
14 H14 **Orillia** Ontario, S Canada
93 M19 **Orimattila** Etelä-Suomi, S Finland
33 Y15 **Orin** Wyoming, C USA
47 R4 **Orinoco, Río** ≈ Colombia/Venezuela
186 C9 **Oriomo** Western, SW Papua New Guinea
30 K11 **Orion** Illinois, N USA
29 Q5 **Oriska** North Dakota, N USA
153 P17 **Orissa** ◈ state NE India
Orissaar see Orissaare
118 E5 **Orissaare** Ger. Orissaar. Saaremaa, W Estonia
107 B19 **Oristano** Sardegna, Italy, C Mediterranean Sea
107 A19 **Oristano, Golfo di** gulf Sardegna, Italy, C Mediterranean Sea
54 D13 **Orito** Putumayo, SW Colombia
93 L18 **Orivesi** Häme, W Finland
93 N17 **Orivesi** ◎ Länsi-Suomi, SE Finland
58 H12 **Oriximiná** Pará, NE Brazil
41 Q14 **Orizaba** Veracruz-Llave, E Mexico
41 Q14 **Orizaba, Volcán Pico de** var. Citlaltépetl. ▲ S Mexico
95 I16 **Ørje** Østfold, S Norway
113 I16 **Orjen** ▲▲ Bosnia and Herzegovina/Montenegro
Orjiva see Orgiva
Orjonikidzeobod see Kofarnihon
94 G8 **Orkanger** Sør-Trøndelag, S Norway
94 G8 **Orkdalen** valley S Norway
95 K22 **Örkelljunga** Skåne, S Sweden
Orkhaniye see Botevgrad
Orkhómenos see Orchómenos
94 H9 **Orkla** ≈ S Norway
Orkney see Orkney Islands
65 J22 **Orkney Deep** undersea feature Scotia Sea/Weddell Sea
96 J4 **Orkney Islands** var. Orkney, Orkneys. island group N Scotland, UK
Orkneys see Orkney Islands
24 K8 **Orla** Texas, SW USA
35 N5 **Orland** California, W USA
23 X11 **Orlando** Florida, SE USA
23 X12 **Orlando** ✕ Florida, SE USA
107 K23 **Orlando, Capo d'** headland Sicilia, Italy, C Mediterranean Sea
Orlau see Orlová
103 N6 **Orléanais** cultural region C France
103 N7 **Orléans** anc. Aurelianum. Loiret, C France
34 L2 **Orleans** California, W USA
19 Q12 **Orleans** Massachusetts, NE USA
15 R10 **Orléans, Île d'** island Québec, SE Canada
Orléansville see Chlef
111 F16 **Orlice** Ger. Adler. ≈ NE Czech Republic
122 L13 **Orlik** Respublika Buryatiya, S Russian Federation
125 Q14 **Orlov** prev. Khalturin. Kirovskaya Oblast', NW Russian Federation
111 I17 **Orlová** Ger. Orlau, Pol. Orłowa. Moravskoslezský Kraj, E Czech Republic
Orlov, Mys see Orlovskiy, Mys
126 I6 **Orlovskaya Oblast'** ◈ province W Russian Federation
124 M5 **Orlovskiy, Mys** var. Mys Orlov. headland NW Russian Federation
Orłowa see Orlová
103 O5 **Orly** ✕ (Paris) Essonne, N France
119 G16 **Orlya** Rus. Orlya. Hrodzyenskaya Voblasts', W Belarus
114 M7 **Orlyak** prev. Makenzen, Trubchular, Rom. Trupcilar. Dobrich, NE Bulgaria
148 L16 **Ormāra** Baluchistān, SW Pakistan
171 P5 **Ormoc** off. Ormoc City, var. MacArthur. Leyte, C Philippines
Ormoc City see Ormoc
23 X10 **Ormond Beach** Florida, SE USA
109 X10 **Ormož** Ger. Friedau. NE Slovenia
14 J13 **Ormsby** Ontario, SE Canada
97 K17 **Ormskirk** NW England, UK
Ormsö see Vormsi
15 N13 **Ormstown** Québec, SE Canada
Ormuz, Strait of see Hormuz, Strait of
103 T8 **Ornans** Doubs, E France
102 K5 **Orne** ◈ department N France
102 K5 **Orne** ≈ N France
92 G12 **Ørnes** Nordland, C Norway
110 L7 **Orneta** Warmińsko-Mazurskie, NE Poland
95 P16 **Ornö** Stockholm, C Sweden
37 Q3 **Orno Peak** ▲ Colorado, C USA
93 I16 **Örnsköldsvik** Västernorrland, C Sweden
163 X13 **Oro** E North Korea
45 T6 **Orocovis** C Puerto Rico
54 H10 **Orocué** Casanare, E Colombia
77 N13 **Orodara** SW Burkina
105 S4 **Oroel, Peña de** ▲ N Spain
33 N10 **Orofino** Idaho, NW USA
162 I9 **Orog Nuur** ◎ S Mongolia
35 U14 **Oro Grande** California, W USA
37 S15 **Orogrande** New Mexico, SW USA
191 Q7 **Orohena, Mont** ⛰ Tahiti, W French Polynesia
Orolaunum see Arlon
Orol Dengizi see Aral Sea
189 S15 **Oroluk Atoll** atoll Caroline Islands, C Micronesia
80 J13 **Oromo** ◈ region C Ethiopia
Oromo see Goba
13 O15 **Oromocto** New Brunswick, SE Canada
191 S4 **Orona** prev. Hull Island. atoll Phoenix Islands, C Kiribati
191 V17 **Orongo** ancient monument Easter Island, Chile, E Pacific Ocean
138 I3 **Orontes** var. Ononte, Nahr el Aassi, Ar. Nahr al 'Aşī. ≈ SW Asia
104 L9 **Oropesa** Castilla-La Mancha, C Spain
105 T8 **Oropesa** País Valenciano, E Spain
Oropeza see Cochabamba
Oroqen Zizhiqi see Alihe
171 P7 **Oroquieta** var. Oroquieta City. Mindanao, S Philippines
Oroquieta City see Oroquieta
40 J8 **Oro, Río del** ≈ C Mexico
59 O14 **Orós, Açude** ⊞ E Brazil
107 D18 **Orosei, Golfo di** gulf Tyrrhenian Sea, C Mediterranean Sea
111 M24 **Orosháza** Békés, SE Hungary
Orosirá Rodhópis see Rhodope Mountains
111 I22 **Oroszlány** Komárom-Esztergom, W Hungary
188 B16 **Orote Peninsula** peninsula W Guam
123 T9 **Orotukan** Magadanskaya Oblast', E Russian Federation
35 O5 **Oroville** California, W USA
32 K6 **Oroville** Washington, NW USA
35 O5 **Oroville, Lake** ⊞ California, W USA
0 G15 **Orozco Fracture Zone** tectonic feature E Pacific Ocean
64 I7 **Orphan Knoll** undersea feature NW Atlantic Ocean
29 V3 **Orr** Minnesota, N USA
95 M21 **Orrefors** Kalmar, S Sweden
182 I7 **Orroroo** South Australia
31 T12 **Orrville** Ohio, N USA
94 L12 **Orsa** Dalarna, C Sweden
Orschowa see Orşova
Orschütz see Orzyc
119 O14 **Orsha** Rus. Orsha. Vitsyebskaya Voblasts', NE Belarus
127 Q2 **Orshanka** Respublika Mariy El, W Russian Federation
108 C11 **Orsières** Valais, SW Switzerland
127 X8 **Orsk** Orenburgskaya Oblast', W Russian Federation
116 F13 **Orşova** Ger. Orschowa, Hung. Orsova. Mehedinţi, SW Romania
94 D10 **Ørsta** Møre og Romsdal, S Norway
95 O15 **Örsundsbro** Uppsala, C Sweden
136 D16 **Ortaca** Muğla, SW Turkey
107 M16 **Orta Nova** Puglia, SE Italy
136 I17 **Orta Toroslar** ▲▲ S Turkey
54 E11 **Ortega** Tolima, W Colombia
104 H1 **Ortegal, Cabo** cape NW Spain
Ortelsburg see Szczytno
102 J15 **Orthez** Pyrénées-Atlantiques, SW France
57 K14 **Orthon, Río** ≈ N Bolivia
60 J10 **Ortigueira** Paraná, S Brazil
104 H1 **Ortigueira** Galicia, NW Spain
106 H5 **Ortisei** Ger. Sankt-Ulrich. Trentino-Alto Adige, N Italy
40 F6 **Ortiz** Sonora, NW Mexico
54 L5 **Ortiz** Guárico, N Venezuela
Ortler see Ortles
106 F5 **Ortles** Ger. Ortler. ▲ N Italy
107 K14 **Ortona** Abruzzo, C Italy
29 R8 **Ortonville** Minnesota, N USA
147 W8 **Orto-Tokoy** Issyk-Kul'skaya Oblast', NE Kyrgyzstan
93 I15 **Orträsk** Västerbotten, N Sweden
100 J12 **Örtze** ≈ NW Germany
Oruba see Aruba
142 I3 **Orūmīyeh** var. Rizaiyeh, Urmia, Urmiyeh; prev. Rezā'īyeh. Āzarbāyjān-e Gharbī, NW Iran
142 J3 **Orūmīyeh, Daryācheh-ye** var. Matianus, Sha Hi, Urumi Yeh, Eng. Lake Urmia; prev. Daryācheh-ye Rezā'īyeh. ◎ NW Iran
57 K19 **Oruro** Oruro, W Bolivia
57 J19 **Oruro** ◈ department W Bolivia
95 I18 **Orust** island S Sweden
149 O7 **Orūzgān** var. Oruzgān. Pash. Urūzgān. Urūzgān, C Afghanistan
149 N6 **Orūzgān** Pash. Orūzgān. ◈ province C Afghanistan
Orūzgān see Orūzgān
Oruzgān see Orūzgān
106 H13 **Orvieto** anc. Velsuna. Umbria, C Italy
194 K7 **Orville Coast** physical region Antarctica
114 H7 **Oryakhovo** Vratsa, NW Bulgaria
Oryokko see Yalu
117 R5 **Orzhytsya** Poltavs'ka Oblast', C Ukraine
110 M9 **Orzyc** Ger. Orschütz. ≈ NE Poland
110 N8 **Orzysz** Ger. Arys. Warmińsko-Mazurskie, NE Poland
94 I10 **Os** Hedmark, S Norway
125 U15 **Osa** Permskaya Oblast', NW Russian Federation
29 W11 **Osage** Iowa, C USA
27 U5 **Osage Beach** Missouri, C USA
27 P5 **Osage City** Kansas, C USA
27 U7 **Osage Fork River** ≈ Missouri, C USA
27 U5 **Osage River** ≈ Missouri, C USA
164 J13 **Ōsaka** hist. Naniwa. Ōsaka, Honshū, SW Japan
164 I13 **Ōsaka** off. Ōsaka-fu, var. Ōsaka Hu. ◈ urban prefecture Honshū, SW Japan
Ōsaka-fu/Ōsaka Hu see Ōsaka
145 R10 **Osakarovka** Karaganda, C Kazakhstan
29 T7 **Osakis** Minnesota, N USA
43 N16 **Osa, Península de** peninsula S Costa Rica
60 M10 **Osasco** São Paulo, S Brazil
27 R5 **Osawatomie** Kansas, C USA
26 L3 **Osborne** Kansas, C USA
173 S8 **Osborn Plateau** undersea feature E Indian Ocean
95 L21 **Osby** Skåne, S Sweden
Osca see Huesca
92 N2 **Oscar II Land** physical region W Svalbard
27 Y10 **Osceola** Arkansas, C USA
29 V15 **Osceola** Iowa, C USA
27 S6 **Osceola** Missouri, C USA
29 Q15 **Osceola** Nebraska, C USA
101 N15 **Oschatz** Sachsen, E Germany
100 K13 **Oschersleben** Sachsen-Anhalt, C Germany
31 R7 **Oscoda** Michigan, N USA
Ösel see Saaremaa
94 H6 **Osen** Sør-Trøndelag, S Norway
94 I12 **Osensjøen** ◎ S Norway
164 A14 **Ōse-zaki** Fukue-jima, SW Japan
147 T10 **Osh** Oshskaya Oblast', SW Kyrgyzstan
83 C16 **Oshakati** Oshana, N Namibia
83 C16 **Oshana** ◈ district N Namibia
14 H15 **Oshawa** Ontario, SE Canada
165 R10 **Oshika-hantō** peninsula Honshū, C Japan
83 C16 **Oshikango** Ohangwena, N Namibia
Oshikoto see Otjikoto
165 P5 **Ō-shima** island NE Japan
165 N14 **Ō-shima** island S Japan
165 Q5 **Oshima-hantō** ▲▲ Hokkaidō, NE Japan
83 D17 **Oshivelo** Otjikoto, N Namibia
28 K14 **Oshkosh** Nebraska, C USA
30 M7 **Oshkosh** Wisconsin, N USA
Oshmyany see Ashmyany
Osh Oblasty see Oshskaya Oblast'
77 T16 **Oshogbo** var. Osogbo. Osun, W Nigeria
147 S11 **Oshskaya Oblast'** Kir. Osh Oblasty. ◈ province SW Kyrgyzstan
Oshun see Osun
79 J20 **Oshwe** Bandundu, C Dem. Rep. Congo
Osiek see Osijek
112 I9 **Osijek** prev. Osiek, Osjek, Ger. Esseg, Hung. Eszék. Osijek-Baranja, E Croatia
112 I9 **Osijek-Baranja** off. Osječko-Baranjska Županija. ◈ province E Croatia
106 J12 **Osimo** Marche, C Italy
122 M12 **Osinovka** Irkutskaya Oblast', C Russian Federation
Osintorf see Asintorf
112 N11 **Osipaonica** Serbia, NE Serbia
Osipenko see Berdyans'k
Osipovichi see Asipovichy
Osječko-Baranjska Županija see Osijek-Baranja
Osjek see Osijek
29 W15 **Oskaloosa** Iowa, C USA
27 Q4 **Oskaloosa** Kansas, C USA
95 N20 **Oskarshamn** Kalmar, S Sweden
95 J21 **Oskarström** Halland, S Sweden
14 M8 **Oskélanéo** Québec, SE Canada
Öskemen see Ust'-Kamenogorsk
Oskil see Oskol
117 W5 **Oskol** Ukr. Oskil. ≈ Russian Federation/Ukraine
93 D20 **Oslo** prev. Christiania, Kristiania. ● (Norway) Oslo, S Norway
93 D20 **Oslo** ◈ county S Norway
93 D21 **Oslofjorden** fjord S Norway
155 G15 **Osmānābād** Mahārāshtra, C India
136 J11 **Osmancık** Çorum, N Turkey
136 L16 **Osmaniye** Osmaniye, S Turkey
136 L16 **Osmaniye** ◈ province S Turkey
95 O16 **Ösmo** Stockholm, C Sweden
118 E3 **Osmussaar** island W Estonia
100 G13 **Osnabrück** Niedersachsen, NW Germany
110 D11 **Ośno Lubuskie** Ger. Drossen. Lubuskie, W Poland
Osogbo see Oshogbo
113 P19 **Osogov Mountains** var. Osogovske Planine, Osogovski Planina, Mac. Osogovski Planini. ▲▲ Bulgaria/FYR Macedonia
Osogovske Planine/ Osogovski Planina/ Osogovski Planini see Osogov Mountains
165 R6 **Osore-yama** ▲ Honshū, C Japan
Oşorhei see Târgu Mureş
61 J16 **Osório** Rio Grande do Sul, S Brazil
63 G16 **Osorno** Los Lagos, C Chile
104 M4 **Osorno** Castilla-León, N Spain
9 N17 **Osoyoos** British Columbia, SW Canada
95 C14 **Osøyro** Hordaland, S Norway
54 J6 **Ospino** Portuguesa, N Venezuela
98 K13 **Oss** Noord-Brabant, S Netherlands
115 F15 **Óssa** ▲▲ C Greece
104 H11 **Ossa** ▲ S Portugal
23 X6 **Ossabaw Island** island Georgia, SE USA
23 X6 **Ossabaw Sound** sound Georgia, SE USA
183 O16 **Ossa, Mount** ▲ Tasmania, SE Australia
104 H11 **Ossa, Serra d'** ▲▲ SE Portugal
77 U16 **Osse** ≈ S Nigeria
30 J6 **Osseo** Wisconsin, N USA
109 S9 **Ossiacher See** ◎ S Austria
18 K13 **Ossining** New York, NE USA
123 V9 **Ossora** Koryakskiy Avtonomnyy Okrug, E Russian Federation
Ostān-e Āzarbāyjān-e Sharqī see Āžarbāyjān-e Sharqī
Ostān-e Khorāsān-e Janūbī see Khorāsān-e Janūbī
Ostān-e Khorāsān-Razavī see Khorāsān-Razavī
124 I15 **Ostashkov** Tverskaya Oblast', W Russian Federation
100 H9 **Oste** ≈ NW Germany
Ostee see Baltic Sea
Ostend/Ostende see Oostende
117 P3 **Oster** Chernihivs'ka Oblast', N Ukraine
95 O14 **Österbybruk** Uppsala, C Sweden
95 M19 **Österbymo** Östergötland, S Sweden
94 K12 **Österdalälven** ≈ C Sweden
94 I12 **Østerdalen** valley S Norway
95 L18 **Östergötland** ◈ county S Sweden
100 H10 **Osterholz-Scharmbeck** Niedersachsen, NW Germany
Östermark see Teuva
Östermyra see Seinäjoki
Østerø see Eysturoy
101 J14 **Osterode am Harz** Niedersachsen, C Germany
Osterode/Osterode in Ostpreussen see Ostróda
94 C13 **Osterøy** island S Norway
Österreich see Austria
93 G16 **Östersund** Jämtland, C Sweden
95 N14 **Östervåla** Västmanland, C Sweden
101 H22 **Ostfildern** Baden-Württemberg, SW Germany
95 H16 **Østfold** ◈ county S Norway
100 E9 **Ostfriesische Inseln** Eng. East Frisian Islands. island group NW Germany
100 F10 **Ostfriesland** historical region NW Germany
95 P14 **Östhammar** Uppsala, C Sweden
Ostia Aterni see Pescara
106 G8 **Ostiglia** Lombardia, N Italy
95 J14 **Östmark** Värmland, C Sweden
95 K22 **Östra Ringsjön** ◎ S Sweden
111 I17 **Ostrava** Moravskoslezský Kraj, E Czech Republic
Ostravský Kraj see Moravskoslezský Kraj
94 J11 **Østrehogna** Swe. Härjahågnen, Härjehågna. ▲ Norway/Sweden
110 K8 **Ostróda** Ger. Osterode, Osterode in Ostpreussen. Warmińsko-Mazurskie, NE Poland
Ostrog/Ostróg see Ostroh
126 L8 **Ostrogozhsk** Voronezhskaya Oblast', W Russian Federation
116 L4 **Ostroh** Pol. Ostróg, Rus. Ostrog. Rivnens'ka Oblast', NW Ukraine
110 N9 **Ostrołęka** Ger. Wiesenhof, Rus. Ostrolenka. Mazowieckie, C Poland
Ostrolenka see Ostrołęka
111 A16 **Ostrov** Ger. Schlackenwerth. Karlovarský Kraj, W Czech Republic
124 F15 **Ostrov** Latv. Austrava. Pskovskaya Oblast', W Russian Federation
Ostrovets see Ostrowiec Świętokrzyski
113 M21 **Ostrovicës, Mali i** ▲ SE Albania
165 Z2 **Ostrov Iturup** island NE Russian Federation
124 M4 **Ostrovnoy** Murmanskaya Oblast', NW Russian Federation
114 L7 **Ostrovo** prev. Golema Ada. Razgrad, N Bulgaria
125 N15 **Ostrovskoye** Kostromskaya Oblast', NW Russian Federation
Ostrów see Ostrów Wielkopolski
Ostrowiec see Ostrowiec Świętokrzyski
111 M14 **Ostrowiec Świętokrzyski** var. Ostrowiec, Rus. Ostrovets. Świętokrzyskie, C Poland
110 P13 **Ostrów Lubelski** Lubelskie, E Poland
110 N10 **Ostrów Mazowiecka** var. Ostrów Mazowiecki. Mazowieckie, NE Poland
Ostrów Mazowiecki see Ostrów Mazowiecka
Ostrowo see Ostrów Wielkopolski
110 H13 **Ostrów Wielkopolski** var. Ostrów, Ger. Ostrowo. Wielkopolskie, C Poland
Ostryna see Astryna
110 I13 **Ostrzeszów** Wielkopolskie, C Poland
107 P18 **Ostuni** Puglia, SE Italy
Ostyako-Voguls'k see Khanty-Mansiysk
114 I9 **Osŭm** ≈ N Bulgaria
Osum see Osumit, Lumi i
164 C17 **Ōsumi-hantō** ▲▲ Kyūshū, SW Japan
164 C17 **Ōsumi-kaikyō** strait SW Japan
113 L22 **Osumit, Lumi i** var. Osum. ≈ SE Albania
77 T16 **Osun** var. Oshun. ◈ state SW Nigeria
104 L14 **Osuna** Andalucía, S Spain
60 J8 **Osvaldo Cruz** São Paulo, S Brazil
Osveya see Asvyeya
18 J7 **Oswegatchie River** ≈ New York, NE USA
27 Q7 **Oswego** Kansas, C USA
18 H9 **Oswego** New York, NE USA
97 K19 **Oswestry** W England, UK
111 J16 **Oświęcim** Ger. Auschwitz. Małopolskie, S Poland
185 E22 **Otago** off. Otago Region. ◈ region South Island, New Zealand
185 F23 **Otago Peninsula** peninsula South Island, New Zealand
Otago Region see Otago
165 F13 **Ōtake** Hiroshima, Honshū, SW Japan
184 L13 **Otaki** Wellington, North Island, New Zealand
93 M15 **Otanmäki** Oulu, C Finland
145 T15 **Otar** Zhambyl, SE Kazakhstan
165 R4 **Otaru** Hokkaidō, NE Japan
185 C24 **Otatara** Southland, South Island, New Zealand
185 C24 **Otautau** Southland, South Island, New Zealand
93 M18 **Otava** Isä-Suomi, E Finland
111 B18 **Otava** Ger. Wottawa. ≈ SW Czech Republic
56 C6 **Otavalo** Imbabura, N Ecuador
83 D17 **Otavi** Otjozondjupa, N Namibia
165 P12 **Ōtawara** Tochigi, Honshū, S Japan
83 B16 **Otchinjau** Cunene, SW Angola
116 F12 **Oţelu Roşu** Ger. Ferdinandsberg, Hung. Nándorhgy. Caras-Severin, SW Romania
185 E21 **Otematata** Canterbury, South Island, New Zealand
118 I6 **Otepää** Ger. Odenpäh. Valgamaa, SE Estonia
162 H7 **Otgon** var. Buyant. Dzavhan, C Mongolia
32 K9 **Othello** Washington, NW USA
115 A15 **Othonoí** island Iónia Nisiá, Greece, C Mediterranean Sea
Othris see Óthrys
115 F17 **Óthrys** var. Othris. ▲▲ C Greece
77 Q14 **Oti** ≈ N Togo
40 K10 **Otinapa** Durango, C Mexico
185 G17 **Otira** West Coast, South Island, New Zealand
37 V3 **Otis** Colorado, C USA
12 L10 **Otish, Monts** ▲▲ Québec, E Canada
83 C17 **Otjikondo** Kunene, N Namibia
83 C17 **Otjikoto** var. Oshikoto. ◈ district N Namibia
83 E18 **Otjinene** Omaheke, NE Namibia
83 D18 **Otjiwarongo** Otjozondjupa, N Namibia
83 D18 **Otjosondu** var. Otjosundu. Otjozondjupa, C Namibia
Otjosundu see Otjosondu
83 D18 **Otjozondjupa** ◈ district C Namibia
112 C11 **Otočac** Lika-Senj, W Croatia
Otog Qi see Ulan
112 J10 **Otok** Vukovar-Srijem, E Croatia
116 K14 **Otopeni** ✕ (Bucureşti) Ilfov, S Romania
184 L8 **Otorohanga** Waikato, North Island, New Zealand
12 D9 **Otoskwin** ≈ Ontario, C Canada
165 G14 **Ōtoyo** Kōchi, Shikoku, SW Japan
95 E16 **Otra** ≈ S Norway
107 R19 **Otranto** Puglia, SE Italy
Otranto, Canale d' see Otranto, Strait of
107 Q18 **Otranto, Strait of** It. Canale d'Otranto. strait Albania/Italy
111 H18 **Otrokovice** Ger. Otrokowitz. Zlínský Kraj, E Czech Republic
Otrokowitz see Otrokovice
31 P10 **Otsego** Michigan, N USA
31 Q6 **Otsego Lake** ◎ Michigan, N USA
18 I11 **Otselic River** ≈ New York, NE USA
164 J14 **Ōtsu** var. Ōtu. Shiga, Honshū, SW Japan
94 G11 **Otta** Oppland, S Norway
189 U13 **Otta** island Chuuk, C Micronesia
94 F11 **Otta** ≈ S Norway
189 U13 **Otta Pass** passage Chuuk Islands, C Micronesia
95 J22 **Ottarp** Skåne, S Sweden
14 L12 **Ottawa** ● (Canada) Ontario, SE Canada
30 L11 **Ottawa** Illinois, N USA
27 Q5 **Ottawa** Kansas, C USA
31 R12 **Ottawa** Ohio, N USA
14 L12 **Ottawa** var. Uplands. ✕ Ontario, SE Canada
14 M12 **Ottawa** Fr. Outaouais. ≈ Ontario/Québec, SE Canada
12 I4 **Ottawa Islands** island group Nunavut, C Canada
18 L8 **Otter Creek** ≈ Vermont, NE USA
36 L6 **Otter Creek Reservoir** ⊞ Utah, W USA
98 L11 **Otterlo** Gelderland, E Netherlands
94 D9 **Otterøya** island S Norway
29 S6 **Otter Tail Lake** ◎ Minnesota, N USA
29 R7 **Otter Tail River** ≈ Minnesota, C USA
95 H23 **Otterup** Fyn, C Denmark
99 H19 **Ottignies** Wallon Brabant, C Belgium
101 L23 **Ottobrunn** Bayern, SE Germany
29 X15 **Ottumwa** Iowa, C USA
Ōtu see Ōtsu
83 B16 **Otuazuma** Kunene, NW Namibia
77 V16 **Oturkpo** Benue, S Nigeria
193 Y15 **Otu Tolu Group** island group SE Tonga
182 M13 **Otway, Cape** headland Victoria, SE Australia
63 H24 **Otway, Seno** inlet S Chile
Ötz see Oetz
108 L8 **Ötztaler Ache** ≈ W Austria
108 L9 **Ötztaler Alpen** It. Alpi Venoste. ▲▲ SW Austria
27 T12 **Ouachita, Lake** ⊞ Arkansas, C USA
27 R11 **Ouachita Mountains** ▲▲ Arkansas/Oklahoma, C USA
27 U13 **Ouachita River** ≈ Arkansas/Louisiana, C USA
Ouadaï see Ouaddaï
76 J7 **Ouadâne** var. Ouadane. Adrar, C Mauritania
78 K13 **Ouadda** Haute-Kotto, N Central African Republic
78 J10 **Ouaddaï** off. Préfecture du Ouaddaï, var. Ouadaï, Wadai. ◈ prefecture SE Chad
Ouaddaï, Préfecture du see Ouaddaï
77 P13 **Ouagadougou** var. Wagadugu. ● (Burkina) C Burkina
77 P13 **Ouagadougou** ✕ C Burkina
77 O12 **Ouahigouya** NW Burkina
Ouahran see Oran
79 J14 **Ouaka** ◈ prefecture C Central African Republic
79 J15 **Ouaka** ≈ S Central African Republic
Oualam see Ouallam
76 M9 **Oualâta** var. Oualata. Hodh ech Chargui, SE Mauritania
77 R11 **Ouallam** var. Oualam. Tillabéri, W Niger
172 H14 **Ouanani** Mohéli, S Comoros
55 Z10 **Ouanary** E French Guiana
78 L13 **Ouanda Djallé** Vakaga, NE Central African Republic
79 N14 **Ouando** Haut-Mbomou, SE Central African Republic
79 L15 **Ouango** Mbomou, S Central African Republic
77 N14 **Ouangolodougou** var. Wangolodougou. N Ivory Coast
172 I13 **Ouani** Anjouan, SE Comoros
79 M15 **Ouara** ≈ E Central African Republic
76 K7 **Ouarâne** desert C Mauritania
15 O11 **Ouareau** ≈ Québec, SE Canada
74 K7 **Ouargla** var. Wargla. NE Algeria
74 F8 **Ouarzazate** S Morocco
77 Q11 **Ouatagouna** Gao, E Mali
74 G6 **Ouazzane** var. Ouezzane, Ar. Wazan, Wazzan. N Morocco
Oubangui see Ubangi
Oubangui-Chari see Central African Republic
Oubangui-Chari, Territoire de l' see Central African Republic
Oubari, Edeyen d' see Awbāri, Idhān
98 G13 **Oud-Beijerland** Zuid-Holland, SW Netherlands
98 F13 **Ouddorp** Zuid-Holland, SW Netherlands
77 P9 **Oudeïka** oasis C Mali
98 G13 **Oude Maas** ≈ SW Netherlands
99 E18 **Oudenaarde** Fr. Audenarde. Oost-Vlaanderen, SW Belgium
99 H14 **Oudenbosch** Noord-Brabant, S Netherlands
98 P6 **Oude Pekela** Groningen, NE Netherlands
Ouderkerk see Ouderkerk aan den Amstel
98 I10 **Ouderkerk aan den Amstel** var. Ouderkerk. Noord-Holland, C Netherlands
98 I6 **Oudeschild** Noord-Holland, NW Netherlands
99 G14 **Oude-Tonge** Zuid-Holland, SW Netherlands
98 I12 **Oudewater** Utrecht, C Netherlands
Oudjda see Oujda
98 L5 **Oudkerk** Friesland, N Netherlands
102 J7 **Oudon** ≈ NW France
98 I9 **Oudorp** Noord-Holland, NW Netherlands
83 G25 **Oudtshoorn** Western Cape, SW South Africa
99 I16 **Oud-Turnhout** Antwerpen, N Belgium
74 F7 **Oued-Zem** C Morocco
187 P16 **Ouégoa** Province Nord, C New Caledonia
76 L13 **Ouéléssébougou** var. Oulossébougou. Koulikoro, SW Mali
77 N16 **Ouellé** E Ivory Coast
77 R16 **Ouémé** ≈ C Benin
77 O13 **Ouessa** S Burkina
102 D5 **Ouessant, Île d'** Eng. Ushant. island NW France
79 H17 **Ouésso** La Sangha, NW Congo
79 D15 **Ouest** Eng. West. ◈ province W Cameroon
190 G11 **Ouest, Baie del'** bay Îles Wallis, E Wallis and Futuna
15 Y7 **Ouest, Pointe de l'** headland Québec, SE Canada
Ouezzane see Ouazzane
99 K20 **Ouffet** Liège, E Belgium
79 H14 **Ouham** ◈ prefecture NW Central African Republic
78 I13 **Ouham** ≈ Central African Republic/Chad
79 G14 **Ouham-Pendé** ◈ prefecture W Central African Republic
77 R16 **Ouidah** Eng. Whydah, var. Wida. S Benin

◆ Country ● Country Capital ◇ Dependent Territory ○ Dependent Territory Capital ◈ Administrative Regions ✕ International Airport ▲ Mountain ▲▲ Mountain Range ⛰ Volcano ≈ River ◎ Lake ⊞ Reservoir

74 H6 Oujda *Ar.* Oudjda, Ujda. NE Morocco
76 I7 Oujeft Adrar, C Mauritania
93 L15 Oulainen Oulu, C Finland
Ould Yanja *see* Ould Yenjé
76 J10 Ould Yenjé *var.* Ould Yanja. Guidimaka, S Mauritania
93 L14 Oulu *Swe.* Uleåborg. Oulu, C Finland
93 M14 Oulu *Swe.* Uleåborg. ◈ *province* N Finland
93 L15 Oulujärvi *Swe.* Uleträsk. ◎ C Finland
93 M14 Oulujoki *Swe.* Uleälv. ≈ C Finland
93 L14 Oulunsalo Oulu, C Finland
106 A8 Oulx Piemonte, NE Italy
78 J9 Oum-Chalouba Borkou-Ennedi-Tibesti, NE Chad
76 M16 Oumé C Ivory Coast
74 F7 Oum er Rbia ≈ C Morocco
78 J10 Oum-Hadjer Batha, E Chad
92 K10 Ounasjoki ≈ N Finland
78 J7 Ounianga Kébir Borkou-Ennedi-Tibesti, N Chad
Ouolossébougou *see* Ouéléssébougou
Oup *see* Auob
99 K19 Oupeye Liège, E Belgium
99 N21 Our ≈ NW Europe
37 Q7 Ouray Colorado, C USA
103 R7 Ource ≈ C France
104 G9 Ourém Santarém, C Portugal
104 H4 Ourense *Cast.* Orense, *Lat.* Aurium. Galicia, NW Spain
104 I4 Ourense *Cast.* Orense. ◈ *province* Galicia, NW Spain
59 O15 Ouricuri Pernambuco, E Brazil
60 J9 Ourinhos São Paulo, S Brazil
104 G13 Ourique Beja, S Portugal
59 M20 Ouro Preto Minas Gerais, NE Brazil
Ours, Grand Lac de l' *see* Great Bear Lake
99 K20 Ourthe ≈ E Belgium
165 Q9 Ōu-sanmyaku ▲▲ Honshū, C Japan
97 M17 Ouse ≈ N England, UK
Ouse *see* Great Ouse
102 H7 Oust ≈ NW France
Outaouais *see* Ottawa
15 T4 Outardes Quatre, Réservoir ⊠ Québec, SE Canada
15 T5 Outardes, Rivière aux ≈ Québec, SE Canada
96 E8 Outer Hebrides *var.* Western Isles. *island group* NW Scotland, UK
30 K3 Outer Island *island* Apostle Islands, Wisconsin, N USA
35 S16 Outer Santa Barbara Passage *passage* California, SW USA
104 G3 Outes Galicia, NW Spain
83 C18 Outjo Kunene, N Namibia
9 T16 Outlook Saskatchewan, S Canada
93 N16 Outokumpu Itä-Suomi, E Finland
96 M2 Out Skerries *island group* NE Scotland, UK
187 Q16 Ouvéa *island* Îles Loyauté, NE New Caledonia
103 S14 Ouvèze ≈ SE France
182 L9 Ouyen Victoria, SE Australia
39 Q14 Ouzinkie Kodiak Island, Alaska, USA
137 O13 Ovacık Tunceli, E Turkey
106 C9 Ovada Piemonte, NE Italy
187 X14 Ovalau *island* C Fiji
62 G9 Ovalle Coquimbo, N Chile
83 C17 Ovamboland *physical region* N Namibia
54 L10 Ovana, Cerro ▲ S Venezuela
104 G7 Ovar Aveiro, N Portugal
114 L10 Ovcharitsa, Yazovir ⊠ SE Bulgaria
54 E6 Ovejas Sucre, NW Colombia
101 E16 Overath Nordrhein-Westfalen, W Germany
98 F13 Overflakkee *island* SW Netherlands
99 H19 Overijse Vlaams Brabant, C Belgium
98 N10 Overijssel ◈ *province* E Netherlands
98 M9 Overijssels Kanaal *canal* E Netherlands
92 K13 Överkalix Norrbotten, N Sweden
27 R4 Overland Park Kansas, C USA
99 L14 Overloon Noord-Brabant, SE Netherlands
99 K16 Overpelt Limburg, NE Belgium
35 Y10 Overton Nevada, W USA
25 W7 Overton Texas, SW USA
92 K13 Övertorneå Norrbotten, N Sweden
95 N18 Överum Kalmar, S Sweden
92 G13 Överuman ◎ N Sweden
117 P11 Ovidiopol' Odes'ka Oblast', SW Ukraine
116 M14 Ovidiu Constanţa, SE Romania
45 N10 Oviedo SW Dominican Republic
104 K2 Oviedo *anc.* Asturias. Asturias, NW Spain
104 K2 Oviedo ✕ Asturias, N Spain
Ovilava *see* Wels
118 D7 Oviši Ventspils, W Latvia
146 K10 Ovminzatovo Tog'lari ▲▲ N Uzbekistan
146 K10 Ovminzatovo Tog'lari *Rus.* Gory Auminzatau. ▲▲ N Uzbekistan
Övögdiy *see* Telmen
Ovoot *see* Dariganga
157 O4 Övörhangay ◈ *province* C Mongolia
94 E12 Øvre Årdal Sogn Og Fjordane, S Norway
95 J14 Övre Fryken ◎ C Sweden
92 J11 Övre Soppero *Lapp.* Badje-Sohppar. Norrbotten, N Sweden
117 N3 Ovruch Zhytomyrs'ka Oblast', N Ukraine
Övt *see* Bat-Öldziy
185 E24 Owaka Otago, South Island, New Zealand
79 H18 Owando *prev.* Fort Rousset. Cuvette, C Congo
164 J14 Owase Mie, Honshū, SW Japan
27 P9 Owasso Oklahoma, C USA
29 V10 Owatonna Minnesota, N USA
173 O4 Owen Fracture Zone *tectonic feature* W Arabian Sea
185 H15 Owen, Mount ▲ South Island, New Zealand
185 H15 Owen River Tasman, South Island, New Zealand
44 D8 Owen Roberts ✕ Grand Cayman, Cayman Islands
20 I6 Owensboro Kentucky, S USA
35 T11 Owens Lake *salt flat* California, W USA
14 F14 Owen Sound Ontario, S Canada
14 F13 Owen Sound ◎ Ontario, S Canada
35 T10 Owens River ≈ California, W USA
186 F9 Owen Stanley Range ▲▲ S Papua New Guinea
27 V5 Owensville Missouri, C USA
20 M4 Owenton Kentucky, S USA
77 U17 Owerri Imo, S Nigeria
184 M10 Owhango Manawatu-Wanganui, North Island, New Zealand
21 N5 Owingsville Kentucky, S USA
77 T16 Owo Ondo, SW Nigeria
31 R9 Owosso Michigan, N USA
35 V1 Owyhee Nevada, W USA
32 L14 Owyhee, Lake ◎ Oregon, NW USA
32 L15 Owyhee River ≈ Idaho/Oregon, NW USA
92 K1 Öxarfjörðhur *var.* Axarfjördhur. *fjord* N Iceland
94 K12 Oxberg Dalarna, C Sweden
9 V17 Oxbow Saskatchewan, S Canada
95 O17 Oxelösund Södermanland, S Sweden
185 H18 Oxford Canterbury, South Island, New Zealand
97 M21 Oxford *Lat.* Oxonia. S England, UK
23 Q3 Oxford Alabama, S USA
22 L2 Oxford Mississippi, S USA
29 N16 Oxford Nebraska, C USA
18 I11 Oxford New York, NE USA
21 U8 Oxford North Carolina, SE USA
31 Q14 Oxford Ohio, N USA
18 H16 Oxford Pennsylvania, NE USA
9 X12 Oxford House Manitoba, C Canada
29 Y13 Oxford Junction Iowa, C USA
9 X12 Oxford Lake ◎ Manitoba, C Canada
97 M21 Oxfordshire *cultural region* S England, UK
Oxia *see* Oxyá
41 X12 Oxkutzcab Yucatán, SE Mexico
35 R15 Oxnard California, W USA
Oxonia *see* Oxford
14 I12 Oxtongue ≈ Ontario, SE Canada
Oxus *see* Amu Darya
115 E15 Oxyá *var.* Oxia. ▲ C Greece
164 L11 Oyabe Toyama, Honshū, SW Japan
Oyahue/Oyahue, Volcán *see* Ollagüe, Volcán
165 O12 Oyama Tochigi, Honshū, S Japan
47 U5 Oyapock ≈ E French Guiana
Oyapock *see* Oiapoque, Rio/Oyapok, Fleuve l'
55 Z10 Oyapok, Baie de L' *bay* Brazil/French Guiana South America W Atlantic Ocean
55 Z11 Oyapok, Fleuve l' *var.* Rio Oiapoque, Oyapock. ≈ Brazil/French Guiana *see also* Oiapoque, Rio
Oyapok, Fleuve l' *see* Oiapoque, Rio
79 E17 Oyem Woleu-Ntem, N Gabon
9 R16 Oyen Alberta, SW Canada
95 I15 Øyeren ◎ S Norway
Oygon *see* Tüdevtey
96 I7 Oykel ≈ N Scotland, UK
123 R9 Oymyakon Respublika Sakha (Yakutiya), NE Russian Federation
79 H19 Oyo Cuvette, C Congo
77 S15 Oyo Oyo, W Nigeria
77 S15 Oyo ◈ *state* SW Nigeria
56 D13 Oyón Lima, C Peru
103 S10 Oyonnax Ain, E France
146 L10 Oyoqog'itma *Rus.* Ayakagytma. Buxoro Viloyati, C Uzbekistan
146 M9 Oyoqquduq *Rus.* Ayakkuduk. Navoiy Viloyati, N Uzbekistan
32 F9 Oysterville Washington, NW USA
95 D14 Øystese Hordaland, S Norway
145 S16 Oytal Zhambyl, S Kazakhstan
147 U10 Oy-Tal Oshskaya Oblast', SW Kyrgyzstan
147 T10 Oy-Tal ≈ SW Kyrgyzstan
Oyyl *see* Uil
Ozarichi *see* Azarychy
23 R7 Ozark Alabama, S USA
27 S10 Ozark Arkansas, C USA
27 T8 Ozark Missouri, C USA
27 T8 Ozark Plateau *plain* Arkansas/Missouri, C USA
27 T6 Ozarks, Lake of the ⊠ Missouri, C USA
192 L10 Ozbourn Seamount *undersea feature* W Pacific Ocean
111 L20 Ózd Borsod-Abaúj-Zemplén, NE Hungary
112 D11 Ozeblin ▲ C Croatia
123 V11 Ozernovskiy Kamchatskaya Oblast', E Russian Federation
144 M7 Ozërnoye *var.* Ozërnyy. Kostanay, N Kazakhstan
124 J15 Ozërnyy Tverskaya Oblast', W Russian Federation
Ozërnyy *see* Ozërnoye
115 D18 Ozerós, Límni ◎ W Greece
122 F11 Ozërsk Chelyabinskaya Oblast', C Russian Federation
119 D14 Ozersk *prev.* Darkehnen, *Ger.* Angerapp. Kaliningradskaya Oblast', W Russian Federation
126 L4 Ozery Moskovskaya Oblast', W Russian Federation
Özgön *see* Uzgen
107 C17 Ozieri Sardegna, Italy, C Mediterranean Sea
111 I15 Ozimek *Ger.* Malapane. Opolskie, SW Poland
127 R8 Ozinki Saratovskaya Oblast', W Russian Federation
25 O10 Ozona Texas, SW USA
Ozorkov *see* Ozorków
110 J12 Ozorków *Rus.* Ozorkov. Łódź, C Poland
164 F14 Ōzu Ehime, Shikoku, SW Japan
137 R10 Ozurget'i *prev.* Makharadze. W Georgia

P

99 J17 Paal Limburg, NE Belgium
196 M14 Paamiut *var.* Pâmiut, *Dan.* Frederikshåb. S Greenland
167 N8 Pa-an Karen State, S Myanmar (Burma)
101 L22 Paar ≈ SE Germany
83 E26 Paarl Western Cape, SW South Africa
93 L15 Paavola Oulu, C Finland
96 E8 Pabbay *island* NW Scotland, UK
153 T15 Pabna Rajshahi, W Bangladesh
109 U4 Pabneukirchen Oberösterreich, N Austria
118 H13 Pabradė *Pol.* Podbrodzie. Vilnius, SE Lithuania
56 L13 Pacahuaras, Río ≈ N Bolivia
Pacaraima, Sierra/Pacaraim, Serra *see* Pakaraima Mountains
56 B11 Pacasmayo La Libertad, W Peru
42 D6 Pacaya, Volcán de ▲ S Guatemala
115 K23 Pacheía *var.* Pachía. *island* Kykládes, Greece, Aegean Sea
Pachía *see* Pacheía
107 L26 Pachino Sicilia, Italy, C Mediterranean Sea
56 F12 Pachitea, Río ≈ C Peru
154 I11 Pachmarhi Madhya Pradesh, C India
121 P3 Páchna *var.* Pakhna. SW Cyprus
115 H25 Páchnes ▲ Kríti, Greece, E Mediterranean Sea
54 F9 Pacho Cundinamarca, C Colombia
154 F12 Pāchora Mahārāshtra, C India
41 P13 Pachuca *var.* Pachuca de Soto. Hidalgo, C Mexico
Pachuca de Soto *see* Pachuca
27 W5 Pacific Missouri, C USA
192 L14 Pacific-Antarctic Ridge *undersea feature* S Pacific Ocean
32 F8 Pacific Beach Washington, NW USA
35 N10 Pacific Grove California, W USA
29 S15 Pacific Junction Iowa, C USA
192-193 Pacific Ocean *ocean*
129 Z10 Pacific Plate *tectonic feature*
113 J15 Pačir ▲ N Montenegro
182 L5 Packsaddle New South Wales, SE Australia
32 H9 Packwood Washington, NW USA
Padalung *see* Phatthalung
168 J12 Padang Sumatera, W Indonesia
168 L9 Padang Endau Pahang, Peninsular Malaysia
Padangpandjang *see* Padangpanjang
168 I11 Padangpanjang *prev.* Padangpandjang. Sumatera, W Indonesia
168 I10 Padangsidempuan *prev.* Padangsidimpoean. Sumatera, W Indonesia
Padangsidimpoean *see* Padangsidempuan
124 I9 Padany Respublika Kareliya, NW Russian Federation
93 M18 Padasjoki Etelä-Suomi, S Finland
57 M22 Padcaya Tarija, S Bolivia
101 H14 Paderborn Nordrhein-Westfalen, NW Germany
Padeşul/Padeş, Vîrful *see* Padeş, Vârful
116 F12 Padeş, Vârful *var.* Padeşul; *prev.* Vîrful Padeş. ▲ W Romania
112 L10 Padinska Skela Serbia, N Serbia
153 S14 Padma *var.* Ganges. ≈ Bangladesh/India *see also* Ganges
Padma *see* Brahmaputra
Padma *see* Ganges
106 H8 Padova *Eng.* Padua; *anc.* Patavium. Veneto, NE Italy
82 A10 Padrão, Ponta do *headland* NW Angola
25 T16 Padre Island *island* Texas, SW USA
104 G3 Padrón Galicia, NW Spain
118 K13 Padsvillye *Rus.* Podsvil'ye. Vitsyebskaya Voblasts', N Belarus
182 K11 Padthaway South Australia
Padua *see* Padova
20 G7 Paducah Kentucky, S USA
25 P4 Paducah Texas, SW USA
105 N15 Padul Andalucía, S Spain
191 P8 Paea Tahiti, W French Polynesia
185 L14 Paekakariki Wellington, North Island, New Zealand
163 X11 Paektu-san *var.* Baitou Shan. ▲ China/North Korea
163 V15 Paengnyŏng-do *island* NW South Korea
184 M7 Paeroa Waikato, North Island, New Zealand
54 D12 Páez Cauca, SW Colombia
121 O3 Páfos *var.* Paphos. W Cyprus
121 O3 Páfos ✕ SW Cyprus
83 L19 Pafúri Gaza, SW Mozambique
112 C12 Pag *It.* Pago. Lika-Senj, SW Croatia
112 B11 Pag *It.* Pago. *island* Zadar, C Croatia
171 P7 Pagadian Mindanao, S Philippines
168 J13 Pagai Selatan, Pulau *island* Kepulauan Mentawai, W Indonesia
168 J13 Pagai Utara, Pulau *island* Kepulauan Mentawai, W Indonesia
188 K4 Pagan *island* C Northern Mariana Islands
115 G16 Pagasitikós Kólpos *gulf* E Greece
36 L8 Page Arizona, SW USA
29 Q5 Page North Dakota, N USA
118 D13 Pagėgiai *Ger.* Pogegen. Tauragė, SW Lithuania
21 S11 Pageland South Carolina, SE USA
81 G16 Pager ≈ NE Uganda
149 Q5 Paghmān Kābol, E Afghanistan
Pago *see* Pag
188 C16 Pago Bay *bay* E Guam, W Pacific Ocean
115 M20 Pagóndas *var.* Pagóndhas. Sámos, Dodekánisa, Greece, Aegean Sea
Pagóndhas *see* Pagóndas
192 J16 Pago Pago ○ (American Samoa) Tutuila, W American Samoa
37 R8 Pagosa Springs Colorado, C USA
38 H12 Pāhala *var.* Pahala. Hawai'i, USA, C Pacific Ocean
168 K8 Pahang *var.* Negeri Pahang Darul Makmur. ◈ *state* Peninsular Malaysia
Pahang *see* Pahang, Sungai
168 L8 Pahang, Sungai *var.* Pahang, Sungei Pahang. ≈ Peninsular Malaysia
149 S8 Pahārpur North-West Frontier Province, NW Pakistan
185 B24 Pahia Point *headland* South Island, New Zealand
184 M13 Pahiatua Manawatu-Wanganui, North Island, New Zealand
38 H12 Pāhoa *var.* Pahoa. Hawai'i, USA, C Pacific Ocean
23 Y14 Pahokee Florida, SE USA
35 X9 Pahranagat Range ▲▲ Nevada, W USA
35 W11 Pahrump Nevada, W USA
Pahsien *see* Chongqing
35 V9 Pahute Mesa ▲▲ Nevada, W USA
167 N7 Pai Mae Hong Son, NW Thailand
38 F10 Pa'ia *var.* Paia. Maui, Hawai'i, USA, C Pacific Ocean
Paia *see* Pa'ia
Pai-ch'eng *see* Baicheng
118 H4 Paide *Ger.* Weissenstein. Järvamaa, N Estonia
97 J24 Paignton SW England, UK
184 K3 Paihia Northland, North Island, New Zealand
93 M18 Päijänne ◎ S Finland
114 F13 Páïko ▲ N Greece
57 M17 Paila, Río ≈ C Bolivia
167 Q12 Pailin Bătdâmbâng, W Cambodia
Pailing *see* Chun'an
54 F6 Pailitas Cesar, N Colombia
38 F9 Pailolo Channel *channel* Hawai'i, USA, C Pacific Ocean
93 K19 Paimio *Swe.* Pemar. Länsi-Soumi, SW Finland
165 O16 Paimi-saki *var.* Yaeme-saki. *headland* Iriomote-jima, SW Japan
102 G5 Paimpol Côtes d'Armor, NW France
168 J12 Painan Sumatera, W Indonesia
63 G23 Paine, Cerro ▲ S Chile
31 U11 Painesville Ohio, N USA
31 S14 Paint Creek ≈ Ohio, N USA
36 L10 Painted Desert *desert* Arizona, SW USA
Paint Hills *see* Wemindji
30 M4 Paint River ≈ Michigan, N USA
25 P8 Paint Rock Texas, SW USA
21 O6 Paintsville Kentucky, S USA
Paisance *see* Piacenza
96 I12 Paisley W Scotland, UK
32 I15 Paisley Oregon, NW USA
105 R10 País Valenciano *var.* Valencia, *Cat.* València; *anc.* Valentia. ◈ *autonomous community* NE Spain
105 O3 País Vasco *Basq.* Euskadi, *Eng.* The Basque Country, *Sp.* Provincias Vascongadas. ◈ *autonomous community* N Spain
56 A9 Paita Piura, NW Peru
169 V6 Paitan, Teluk *bay* Sabah, East Malaysia
104 H7 Paiva, Rio ≈ N Portugal
92 K12 Pajala Norrbotten, N Sweden
104 K3 Pajares, Puerto de *pass* NW Spain
54 G9 Pajarito Boyacá, C Colombia
54 G4 Pajaro La Guajira, S Colombia
Pakanbaru *see* Pekanbaru
55 Q10 Pakaraima Mountains *var.* Serra Pacaraim, Sierra Pacaraima. ▲▲ N South America
167 P10 Pak Chong Nakhon Ratchasima, C Thailand
123 V8 Pakhachi Koryakskiy Avtonomnyy Okrug, E Russian Federation
Pakhna *see* Páchna
189 U16 Pakin Atoll *atoll* Caroline Islands, E Micronesia
149 Q12 Pakistan *off.* Islamic Republic of Pakistan, *var.* Islami Jamhuriya e Pakistan. ◆ *republic* S Asia
Pakistan, Islamic Republic of *see* Pakistan
Pakistan, Islami Jamhuriya e *see* Pakistan
167 P8 Pak Lay *var.* Muang Pak Lay. Xaignabouli, C Laos
Paknam *see* Samut Prakan
166 L5 Pakokku Magwe, C Myanmar (Burma)
110 I10 Pakość *Ger.* Pakosch. Kujawski-pomorskie, C Poland
Pakosch *see* Pakość
149 V10 Pākpattan Punjab, E Pakistan
167 O15 Pak Phanang *var.* Ban Pak Phanang. Nakhon Si Thammarat, SW Thailand
112 G9 Pakrac *Hung.* Pakrácz. Požega-Slavonija, NE Croatia
Pakrácz *see* Pakrac
118 F11 Pakruojis Šiaulai, N Lithuania
111 J24 Paks Tolna, S Hungary
Pak Sane *see* Pakxan
Paksé *see* Pakxé
167 Q10 Pak Thong Chai Nakhon Ratchasima, C Thailand
149 R6 Paktīā ◈ *province* SE Afghanistan
149 Q7 Paktīkā ◈ *province* SE Afghanistan
171 N12 Pakuli Sulawesi, C Indonesia
81 F17 Pakwach NW Uganda
167 R8 Pakxan *var.* Muang Pakxan, Pak Sane. Bolikhamxai, C Laos
167 S10 Pakxé *var.* Paksé. Champasak, S Laos
78 G12 Pala Mayo-Kébbi, SW Chad
61 A17 Palacios Santa Fe, C Argentina
25 V13 Palacios Texas, SW USA
105 X5 Palafrugell Cataluña, NE Spain
107 L24 Palagonia Sicilia, Italy, C Mediterranean Sea
113 E17 Palagruža *It.* Pelagosa. *island* SW Croatia
115 G20 Palaiá Epídavros Pelopónnisos, S Greece
121 P3 Palaichóri *var.* Palekhori. C Cyprus
115 H25 Palaiochóra Kríti, Greece, E Mediterranean Sea
115 A15 Palaiolastrítsa *religious building* Kérkyra, Iónia Nisiá, Greece, C Mediterranean Sea
115 J19 Palaiópoli Ándros, Kykládes, Greece, Aegean Sea
103 N5 Palaiseau Essonne, N France
Palakkad *see* Pālghāt
154 N11 Pāla Laharha Orissa, E India
83 G19 Palamakoloi Ghanzi, C Botswana
115 E16 Palamás Thessalía, C Greece
105 X5 Palamós Cataluña, NE Spain
118 J5 Palamuse *Ger.* Sankt-Bartholomäi. Jõgevamaa, E Estonia
183 Q14 Palana Tasmania, SE Australia
123 U9 Palana Koryakskiy Avtonomnyy Okrug, E Russian Federation
118 C11 Palanga *Ger.* Polangen. Klaipėda, NW Lithuania
143 V10 Palangān, Kūh-e ▲ E Iran
Palangkaraja *see* Palangkaraya
169 T12 Palangkaraya *prev.* Palangkaraja. Borneo, C Indonesia
155 H22 Palani Tamil Nādu, SE India
Palanka *see* Bačka Palanka
154 D9 Pālanpur Gujarāt, W India
Palantia *see* Palencia
83 I19 Palapye Central, SE Botswana
155 J19 Palār ≈ SE India
104 H3 Palas de Rei Galicia, NW Spain
123 T9 Palatka Magadanskaya Oblast', E Russian Federation
23 W10 Palatka Florida, SE USA
188 B9 Palau *var.* Belau. ◆ *republic* W Pacific Ocean
129 Y14 Palau Islands *island group* N Palau
192 G16 Palauli Bay *bay* Savai'i, C Samoa, C Pacific Ocean
167 N11 Palaw Tenasserim, S Myanmar (Burma)
170 M6 Palawan *island* W Philippines
171 N6 Palawan Passage *passage* W Philippines
192 E7 Palawan Trough *undersea feature* S South China Sea
155 H23 Pālayankottai Tamil Nādu, SE India
107 L25 Palazzolo Acreide *anc.* Acrae. Sicilia, Italy, C Mediterranean Sea
118 G3 Paldiski *prev.* Baltiski, *Eng* Baltic Port, *Ger.* Baltischport. Harjumaa, NW Estonia
112 I13 Pale ◈ Republika Srpska, SE Bosnia and Herzegovina
Palekhori *see* Palaichóri
168 L13 Palembang Sumatera, W Indonesia
63 G18 Palena Los Lagos, S Chile
63 G18 Palena, Río ≈ S Chile
104 M5 Palencia *anc.* Palantia, Pallantia. Castilla-León, NW Spain
104 M3 Palencia ◈ *province* Castilla-León, N Spain
35 X15 Palen Dry Lake ◎ California, W USA
41 V15 Palenque Chiapas, SE Mexico
41 V15 Palenque *var.* Ruinas de Palenque. *ruins* Chiapas, SE Mexico
45 O9 Palenque, Punta *headland* S Dominican Republic
Palenque, Ruinas de *see* Palenque
Palerme *see* Palermo
107 I23 Palermo *Fr.* Palerme; *anc.* Panhormus, Panormus. Sicilia, Italy, C Mediterranean Sea
25 V8 Palestine Texas, SW USA
25 V7 Palestine, Lake ⊠ Texas, SW USA
107 I15 Palestrina Lazio, C Italy
166 K5 Paletwa Chin State, W Myanmar (Burma)
155 G21 Pālghāt *var.* Palakkad; *prev.* Pulicat. Kerala, SW India
152 F13 Pāli Rājasthān, N India
167 N16 Palian Trang, SW Thailand
189 O12 Palikir ● (Micronesia) Pohnpei, E Micronesia
Palimé *see* Kpalimé
107 L19 Palinuro, Capo *headland* S Italy
115 H15 Palioúri, Ákrotírio *var.* Akra Kanestron. *headland* N Greece
33 R14 Palisades Reservoir ⊠ Idaho, NW USA
99 J23 Paliseul Luxembourg, SE Belgium
154 C11 Pālitāna Gujarāt, W India
118 F4 Palivere Läänemaa, W Estonia
41 V14 Palizada Campeche, SE Mexico
93 L18 Pälkäne Länsi-Suomi, W Finland
155 J22 Palk Strait *strait* India/Sri Lanka
155 J23 Pallai Northern Province, NW Sri Lanka
Pallantia *see* Palencia
106 C6 Pallanza Piemonte, NE Italy
127 Q9 Pallasovka Volgogradskaya Oblast', SW Russian Federation
Pallene/Pallíni *see* Kassándra
185 L15 Palliser Bay *bay* North Island, New Zealand
185 L15 Palliser, Cape *headland* North Island, New Zealand
191 U9 Palliser, Îles *island group* Îles Tuamotu, C French Polynesia
82 Q12 Palma Cabo Delgado, N Mozambique
105 X9 Palma *var.* Palma de Mallorca. Mallorca, Spain, W Mediterranean Sea
105 X9 Palma ✕ Mallorca, Spain, W Mediterranean Sea
105 X10 Palma, Badia de *bay* Mallorca, Spain, W Mediterranean Sea
104 L13 Palma del Río Andalucía, S Spain
Palma de Mallorca *see* Palma
107 J25 Palma di Montechiaro Sicilia, Italy, C Mediterranean Sea
106 J7 Palmanova Friuli-Venezia Giulia, NE Italy
54 J7 Palmarito Apure, C Venezuela
43 N15 Palmar Sur Puntarenas, SE Costa Rica
60 I12 Palmas Paraná, S Brazil
59 K16 Palmas *var* Palmas do Tocantins. Tocantins, C Brazil
76 L18 Palmas, Cape *Fr.* Palmès, Cap des. *headland* SW Ivory Coast
Palmas do Tocantins *see* Palmas
54 D11 Palmaseca ✕ (Cali) Valle del Cauca, SW Colombia
107 B21 Palmas, Golfo di *gulf* Sardegna, Italy, C Mediterranean Sea
44 I7 Palma Soriano Santiago de Cuba, E Cuba
23 Y12 Palm Bay Florida, SE USA
35 T14 Palmdale California, W USA
61 H14 Palmeira das Missões Rio Grande do Sul, S Brazil
82 A11 Palmeirinhas, Ponta das *headland* NW Angola
39 R11 Palmer Alaska, USA
19 N11 Palmer Massachusetts, NE USA
25 U7 Palmer Texas, SW USA
194 H4 Palmer *US research station* Antarctica
15 R11 Palmer ≈ Québec, SE Canada
37 T5 Palmer Lake Colorado, C USA
194 J6 Palmer Land *physical region* Antarctica
14 F15 Palmerston Ontario, SE Canada
185 F22 Palmerston Otago, South Island, New Zealand
190 K15 Palmerston *island* S Cook Islands
Palmerston *see* Darwin
184 M12 Palmerston North Manawatu-Wanganui, North Island, New Zealand
Palmès, Cap des *see* Palmas, Cape
23 V13 Palmetto Florida, SE USA
The Palmetto State *see* South Carolina
107 M22 Palmi Calabria, SW Italy
54 D11 Palmira Valle del Cauca, W Colombia
56 F8 Palmira, Río ≈ N Peru
61 D19 Palmitas Soriano, SW Uruguay
Palmnicken *see* Yantarnyy
35 V15 Palm Springs California, W USA
27 V2 Palmyra Missouri, C USA
18 G10 Palmyra New York, NE USA
18 G15 Palmyra Pennsylvania, NE USA
21 V5 Palmyra Virginia, NE USA
Palmyra *see* Tudmur
192 L7 Palmyra Atoll ◇ *US privately owned unincorporated territory* C Pacific Ocean
154 P12 Palmyras Point *headland* E India
35 N9 Palo Alto California, W USA
25 O1 Palo Duro Creek ≈ Texas, SW USA
Paloe *see* Denpasar, Bali, C Indonesia
Paloe *see* Palu
168 L9 Paloh Johor, Peninsular Malaysia
80 F12 Paloich Upper Nile, SE Sudan
40 I3 Palomas Chihuahua, N Mexico
107 I15 Palombara Sabina Lazio, C Italy
105 S13 Palos, Cabo de *cape* SE Spain
104 I14 Palos de la Frontera Andalucía, S Spain
60 G11 Palotina Paraná, S Brazil
32 M9 Palouse Washington, NW USA
32 L9 Palouse River ≈ Washington, NW USA
35 Y16 Palo Verde California, W USA
57 E16 Palpa Ica, W Peru
95 M16 Pålsboda Örebro, C Sweden
93 M15 Paltamo Oulu, C Finland
171 N12 Palu *prev.* Paloe. Sulawesi, C Indonesia
137 P14 Palu Elazığ, E Turkey
152 I11 Palwal Haryāna, N India
123 U6 Palyavaam ≈ NE Russian Federation
77 Q13 Pama SE Burkina
172 J14 Pamandzi ✕ (Mamoudzou) Petite-Terre, E Mayotte
Pamangkat *see* Pemangkat
143 R11 Pā Mazār Kermān, C Iran
83 N19 Pambarra Inhambane, SE Mozambique
171 X12 Pamdai Papua, E Indonesia
103 N16 Pamiers Ariège, S France
147 T14 Pamir *var.* Daryā-ye Pāmīr, *Taj.* Dar"yoi Pomir. ≈ Afghanistan/Tajikistan *see also* Pāmīr, Daryā-ye

◆ Country ● Country Capital ◇ Dependent Territory ○ Dependent Territory Capital ◈ Administrative Regions ✕ International Airport ▲ Mountain ▲▲ Mountain Range ▲ Volcano ≈ River ◎ Lake ⊠ Reservoir

Pamir see Pāmīr, Daryā-ye
149 U1 **Pāmīr, Daryā-ye** var. Pamir, Taj. Dar"yoi Pomir. ⇝ Afghanistan/Tajikistan see also Pamir
Pāmīr, Daryā-ye see Pamir
Pāmīr-e Khord see Little Pamir
Pamir/Pāmīr, Daryā-ye see Pamirs
129 Q8 **Pamirs** Pash. Daryā-ye Pāmīr, Rus. Pamir. ▲▲ C Asia
Pâmiut see Paamiut
21 X10 **Pamlico River** ⇝ North Carolina, SE USA
21 Y10 **Pamlico Sound** sound North Carolina, SE USA
25 O2 **Pampa** Texas, SW USA
Pampa Aullagas, Lago see Poopó, Lago
61 B21 **Pampa Húmeda** grassland E Argentina
56 A10 **Pampa las Salinas** salt lake NW Peru
57 F15 **Pampas** Huancavelica, C Peru
62 K13 **Pampas** plain C Argentina
55 O4 **Pampatar** Nueva Esparta, NE Venezuela
Pampeluna see Pamplona
104 H8 **Pampilhosa da Serra** var. Pampilhosa de Serra. Coimbra, N Portugal
173 Y15 **Pamplemousses** N Mauritius
54 G7 **Pamplona** Norte de Santander, N Colombia
105 Q3 **Pamplona** Basq. Iruña, prev. Pampeluna; anc. Pompaelo. Navarra, N Spain
114 I11 **Pamporovo** prev. Vasil Kolarov. Smolyan, S Bulgaria
136 D15 **Pamukkale** Denizli, W Turkey
21 W5 **Pamunkey River** ⇝ Virginia, NE USA
152 K5 **Pamzal** Jammu and Kashmir, NW India
30 L14 **Pana** Illinois, N USA
41 Y11 **Panabá** Yucatán, SE Mexico
35 Y8 **Panaca** Nevada, W USA
115 E19 **Panachaikó** ▲▲ S Greece
14 F11 **Panache Lake** ◎ Ontario, S Canada
114 I10 **Panagyurishte** Pazardzhik, C Bulgaria
168 M16 **Panaitan, Pulau** island S Indonesia
115 D18 **Panaitolikó** ▲▲ C Greece
155 E17 **Panaji** var. Pangim, Panjim, New Goa. state capital Goa, W India
43 T15 **Panamá** var. Ciudad de Panama, Eng. Panama City. ● (Panama) Panamá, C Panama
43 T14 **Panama** off. Republic of Panama. ◆ republic Central America
43 U14 **Panamá** off. Provincia de Panamá. ◈ province E Panama
43 U15 **Panamá, Bahía de** bay N Gulf of Panama
193 T7 **Panama Basin** undersea feature E Pacific Ocean
43 T15 **Panama Canal** shipping canal E Panama
23 R9 **Panama City** Florida, SE USA
43 T14 **Panama City** ✕ Panamá, C Panama
Panama City see Panamá
23 Q9 **Panama City Beach** Florida, SE USA
43 T17 **Panamá, Golfo de** var. Gulf of Panama. gulf S Panama
Panama, Gulf of see Panamá, Golfo de
Panama, Isthmus of see Panama, Istmo de
43 T15 **Panama, Istmo de** Eng. Isthmus of Panama; prev. Isthmus of Darien. isthmus E Panama
Panamá, Provincia de see Panamá
Panama, Republic of see Panama
35 U11 **Panamint Range** ▲▲ California, W USA
107 L22 **Panarea, Isola** island Isole Eolie, S Italy
106 G9 **Panaro** ⇝ N Italy
171 P5 **Panay Island** island C Philippines
35 W7 **Pancake Range** ▲▲ Nevada, W USA
112 M11 **Pančevo** Ger. Pantschowa, Hung. Pancsova. Vojvodina, N Serbia
113 M15 **Pančićev Vrh** ▲ SW Serbia
116 L12 **Panciu** Vrancea, E Romania
116 F10 **Pâncota** Hung. Pankota; prev. Pîncota. Arad, W Romania
Pancsova see Pančevo
83 N20 **Panda** Inhambane, SE Mozambique
171 X12 **Pandaidori, Kepulauan** island group E Indonesia
25 N11 **Pandale** Texas, SW USA
169 P12 **Pandang Tikar, Pulau** island N Indonesia
61 F20 **Pan de Azúcar** Maldonado, S Uruguay
118 H11 **Pandėlys** Panevėžys, NE Lithuania
155 F15 **Pandharpur** Mahārāshtra, W India
182 J1 **Pandie Pandie** South Australia
171 O12 **Pandiri** Sulawesi, C Indonesia
61 F20 **Pando** Canelones, S Uruguay
57 J14 **Pando** ◈ department N Bolivia
192 K9 **Pandora Bank** undersea feature W Pacific Ocean
95 G20 **Pandrup** Nordjylland, N Denmark
79 J15 **Pandu** Equateur, NW Dem. Rep. Congo
153 V12 **Pandu** Assam, NE India
Paneas see Bāniyās
59 F15 **Panelas** Mato Grosso, W Brazil
118 G12 **Panevėžys** Panevėžys, C Lithuania
118 G11 **Panevėžys** ◈ province NW Lithuania
Panfilov see Zharkent
127 N9 **Panfilovo** Volgogradskaya Oblast', SW Russian Federation
79 N17 **Panga** Orientale, N Dem. Rep. Congo
193 Y15 **Pangai** Lifuka, C Tonga
114 H13 **Pangaío** ▲▲ N Greece
79 G20 **Pangala** Le Pool, S Congo
81 J22 **Pangani** Tanga, E Tanzania
81 I21 **Pangani** ⇝ NE Tanzania
186 K8 **Panggoe** Choiseul Island, NW Solomon Islands
79 N20 **Pangi** Maniema, E Dem. Rep. Congo
Pangim see Panaji
168 H8 **Pangkalanbrandan** Sumatera, W Indonesia
Pangkalanbun see Pangkalanbuun
169 R13 **Pangkalanbuun** var. Pangkalanbun. Borneo, C Indonesia
169 N12 **Pangkalpinang** Pulau Bangka, W Indonesia
9 U17 **Pangman** Saskatchewan, S Canada
Pang-Nga see Phang-Nga
9 S6 **Pangnirtung** Baffin Island, Nunavut, NE Canada
152 K6 **Pangong Tso** var. Bangong Co. ◎ China/India see also Bangong Co
Pangong Tso see Bangong Co
36 K7 **Panguitch** Utah, W USA
186 J7 **Panguna** Bougainville Island, NE Papua New Guinea
171 N8 **Pangutaran Group** island group Sulu Archipelago, SW Philippines
25 N2 **Panhandle** Texas, SW USA
Panhormus see Palermo
171 W14 **Paniai, Danau** ◎ Papua, E Indonesia
79 L21 **Pania-Mutombo** Kasai Oriental, C Dem. Rep. Congo
Panicherevo see Dolno Panicherevo
187 P16 **Panié, Mont** ▲ C New Caledonia
152 I10 **Pānīpat** Haryāna, N India
147 Q14 **Panj** Rus. Pyandzh; prev. Kirovabad. SW Tajikistan
147 P15 **Panj** Rus. Pyandzh. ⇝ Afghanistan/Tajikistan
149 O5 **Panjāb** Bāmīān, C Afghanistan
147 O12 **Panjakent** Rus. Pendzhikent. W Tajikistan
148 L14 **Panjgūr** Baluchistān, SW Pakistan
Panjim see Panaji
163 U12 **Panjin** Liaoning, NE China
147 P14 **Panji Poyon** Rus. Nizhniy Pyandzh. SW Tajikistan
149 S4 **Panjshīr** ◈ province NE Afghanistan
149 Q4 **Panjshīr** ⇝ E Afghanistan
Pankota see Pâncota
77 W14 **Pankshin** Plateau, C Nigeria
163 Y10 **Pan Ling** ▲▲ N China
Panlong Jiang see Lô, Sông
154 J9 **Panna** Madhya Pradesh, C India
99 M16 **Panningen** Limburg, SE Netherlands
149 R13 **Pāno Āqil** Sind, SE Pakistan
121 P3 **Páno Léfkara** S Cyprus
121 O3 **Páno Panagiá** var. Pano Panayia. W Cyprus
Pano Panayia see Páno Panagiá
Panopolis see Akhmīm
29 U14 **Panora** Iowa, C USA
60 I8 **Panorama** São Paulo, S Brazil
115 I24 **Pánormos** Kríti, Greece, E Mediterranean Sea
Panormus see Palermo
163 W11 **Panshi** Jilin, NE China
59 H19 **Pantanal** var. Pantanalmato-Grossense. swamp SW Brazil
Pantanalmato-Grossense see Pantanal
61 H16 **Pântano Grande** Rio Grande do Sul, S Brazil
171 Q16 **Pantar, Pulau** island Kepulauan Alor, S Indonesia
21 X9 **Pantego** North Carolina, SE USA
107 G25 **Pantelleria** anc. Cossyra, Cosyra. Sicilia, Italy, C Mediterranean Sea
107 G25 **Pantelleria, Isola di** island SW Italy
Pante Macassar/Pante Makassar see Pante Makasar
171 Q16 **Pante Makasar** var. Pante Macassar, Pante Makassar. W East Timor
152 K10 **Pantnagar** Uttaranchal, N India
115 A15 **Pantokrátoras** ▲ Kérkyra, Iónia Nisiá, Greece, C Mediterranean Sea
Pantschowa see Pančevo
41 P11 **Pánuco** Veracruz-Llave, E Mexico
41 P11 **Pánuco, Río** ⇝ C Mexico
160 I12 **Panxian** Guizhou, S China
168 I10 **Panyabungan** Sumatera, N Indonesia
77 W14 **Panyam** Plateau, C Nigeria
157 N13 **Panzhihua** prev. Dukou, Tu-k'ou. Sichuan, C China
79 I22 **Panzi** Bandundu, SW Dem. Rep. Congo
42 E5 **Panzós** Alta Verapaz, E Guatemala
Pao-chi/Paoki see Baoji
Pao-king see Shaoyang
107 N20 **Paola** Calabria, SW Italy
121 P16 **Paola** E Malta
27 R5 **Paola** Kansas, C USA
31 O15 **Paoli** Indiana, N USA
187 R14 **Paonangisu** Éfaté, C Vanuatu
171 S13 **Paoni** var. Pauni. Pulau Seram, E Indonesia
37 Q5 **Paonia** Colorado, C USA
191 O7 **Paopao** Moorea, W French Polynesia
Pao-shan see Baoshan
Pao-ting see Baoding
Pao-t'ou/Paotow see Baotou
79 H14 **Paoua** Ouham-Pendé, W Central African Republic
Pap see Pop
111 H23 **Pápa** Veszprém, W Hungary
42 J12 **Papagayo, Golfo de** gulf NW Costa Rica
38 H11 **Pāpa'ikou** var. Papaikou. Hawai'i, USA, C Pacific Ocean
41 R15 **Papaloapan, Río** ⇝ S Mexico
184 L6 **Papakura** Auckland, North Island, New Zealand
41 Q13 **Papantla** var. Papantla de Olarte. Veracruz-Llave, E Mexico
Papantla de Olarte see Papantla
191 P8 **Papara** Tahiti, W French Polynesia
184 K4 **Paparoa** Northland, North Island, New Zealand
185 G16 **Paparoa Range** ▲▲ South Island, New Zealand
115 K20 **Pápas, Akrotírio** cape Ikaría, Dodekánisa, Greece, Aegean Sea
96 L2 **Papa Stour** island NE Scotland, UK
184 L6 **Papatoetoe** Auckland, North Island, New Zealand
185 E25 **Papatowai** Otago, South Island, New Zealand
96 K4 **Papa Westray** island NE Scotland, UK
191 T10 **Papeete** ○ (French Polynesia) Tahiti, W French Polynesia
100 F11 **Papenburg** Niedersachsen, NW Germany
98 H13 **Papendrecht** Zuid-Holland, SW Netherlands
191 Q7 **Papenoo** Tahiti, W French Polynesia
191 Q7 **Papenoo Rivière** ⇝ Tahiti, W French Polynesia
191 N7 **Papetoai** Moorea, W French Polynesia
92 L3 **Papey** island E Iceland
Paphos see Páfos
40 H5 **Papigochic, Río** ⇝ NW Mexico
118 E10 **Papilė** Šiaulai, NW Lithuania
29 S15 **Papillion** Nebraska, C USA
15 T5 **Papinachois** ⇝ Québec, SE Canada
171 X13 **Papua** var. Irian Barat, West Irian, West New Guinea, West Papua; prev. Dutch New Guinea, Irian Jaya, Netherlands New Guinea. ◈ province E Indonesia
Papua and New Guinea, Territory of see Papua New Guinea
186 C9 **Papua, Gulf of** gulf S Papua New Guinea
186 C8 **Papua New Guinea** off. Independent State of Papua New Guinea; prev. Territory of Papua and New Guinea. ◆ commonwealth republic NW Melanesia
Papua New Guinea, Independent State of see Papua New Guinea
192 H8 **Papua Plateau** undersea feature N Coral Sea
112 G9 **Papuk** ▲▲ NE Croatia
167 N8 **Papun** Karen State, S Myanmar (Burma)
42 L14 **Paquera** Puntarenas, W Costa Rica
58 I13 **Pará** off. Estado do Pará. ◈ state NE Brazil
55 V9 **Para** ◈ district N Surinam
Pará see Belém
180 I8 **Paraburdoo** Western Australia
57 E16 **Paracas, Península de** peninsula W Peru
59 L19 **Paracatu** Minas Gerais, NE Brazil
192 E6 **Paracel Islands** ◇ disputed territory SE Asia
182 I6 **Parachilna** South Australia
149 R6 **Pārachinār** North-West Frontier Province, NW Pakistan
112 N13 **Paraćin** Serbia, C Serbia
14 K8 **Paradis** Québec, SE Canada
39 N11 **Paradise** var. Paradise Hill. Alaska, USA
35 O5 **Paradise** California, W USA
35 X11 **Paradise** Nevada, W USA
Paradise Hill see Paradise
37 R11 **Paradise Hills** New Mexico, SW USA
Paradise of the Pacific see Hawai'i
36 L13 **Paradise Valley** Arizona, SW USA
35 T2 **Paradise Valley** Nevada, W USA
115 O22 **Paradisi** ✕ (Ródos) Ródos, Dodekánisa, Greece, Aegean Sea
154 P12 **Pārādwīp** Orissa, E India
Pará, Estado do see Pará
Paraetonium see Maṭrūḥ
117 R4 **Parafiyivka** Chernihivs'ka Oblast', N Ukraine
36 K2 **Paragonah** Utah, W USA
27 X9 **Paragould** Arkansas, C USA
47 X8 **Paraguaçu** var. Paraguassú. ⇝ E Brazil
60 J9 **Paraguaçu Paulista** São Paulo, S Brazil
54 H4 **Paraguaipoa** Zulia, NW Venezuela
62 O6 **Paraguarí** Paraguarí, S Paraguay
62 O7 **Paraguarí** off. Departamento de Paraguarí. ◈ department S Paraguay
Paraguarí, Departamento de see Paraguarí
57 O16 **Paraguá, Río** ⇝ NE Bolivia
55 O8 **Paragua, Río** ⇝ SE Venezuela
Paraguassú see Paraguaçu
62 N5 **Paraguay** ◆ republic C South America
47 U10 **Paraguay** var. Río Paraguay. ⇝ C South America
Paraguay, Río see Paraguay
Parahiba/Parahyba see Paraíba
59 P15 **Paraíba** off. Estado da Paraíba; prev. Parahiba, Parahyba. ◈ state E Brazil
Paraíba see João Pessoa
60 P9 **Paraíba do Sul, Rio** ⇝ SE Brazil
Paraíba, Estado da see Paraíba
Parainen see Pargas
43 N14 **Paraíso** Cartago, C Costa Rica
41 U14 **Paraíso** Tabasco, SE Mexico
57 O17 **Paraíso, Río** ⇝ E Bolivia
Parajd see Praid
77 S14 **Parakou** C Benin
115 F20 **Paralía Tyrou** Pelopónnisos, S Greece
121 Q2 **Paralímni** E Cyprus
115 G18 **Paralímni, Límni** ◎ C Greece
55 W8 **Paramaribo** ● (Surinam) Paramaribo, N Surinam
55 W9 **Paramaribo** ◈ district N Surinam
55 W9 **Paramaribo** ✕ Paramaribo, N Surinam
Paramithiá see Paramythiá
56 C13 **Paramonga** Lima, W Peru
123 V12 **Paramushir, Ostrov** island SE Russian Federation
115 C16 **Paramythiá** var. Paramithiá. Ípeiros, W Greece
62 M10 **Paraná** Entre Ríos, E Argentina
60 H11 **Paraná** off. Estado do Paraná. ◈ state S Brazil
47 U11 **Paraná** var. Alto Paraná. ⇝ C South America
Paraná, Estado do see Paraná
60 K12 **Paranaguá** Paraná, S Brazil
59 J20 **Paranaíba, Rio** ⇝ E Brazil
61 C19 **Paraná Ibicuy, Río** ⇝ E Argentina
59 H15 **Paranaíta** Mato Grosso, W Brazil
60 H9 **Paranapanema, Rio** ⇝ S Brazil
60 K11 **Paranapiacaba, Serra do** ▲▲ S Brazil
60 H9 **Paranavaí** Paraná, S Brazil
143 N5 **Parandak** Markazī, W Iran
114 I12 **Paranésti** var Paranestio. Anatolikí Makedonía kai Thráki, NE Greece
Paranestio see Paranésti
191 W11 **Paraoa** atoll Îles Tuamotu, C French Polynesia
184 L13 **Paraparaumu** Wellington, North Island, New Zealand
57 N20 **Parapetí, Río** ⇝ SE Bolivia
54 L10 **Paraque, Cerro** ▲ W Venezuela
154 I11 **Parāsiya** Madhya Pradesh, C India
115 M23 **Paraspóri, Ákrotírio** cape Kárpathos, SE Greece
60 O10 **Parati** Rio de Janeiro, SE Brazil
59 K14 **Parauapebas** Pará, N Brazil
103 Q10 **Paray-le-Monial** Saône-et-Loire, C France
Parbatsar see Parvatsar
154 G13 **Parbhani** Mahārāshtra, C India
100 L10 **Parchim** Mecklenburg-Vorpommern, N Germany
Parchwitz see Prochowice
110 P13 **Parczew** Lubelskie, E Poland
60 L8 **Pardo, Rio** ⇝ S Brazil
111 E16 **Pardubice** Ger. Pardubitz. Pardubický Kraj, C Czech Republic
111 E17 **Pardubický Kraj** ◈ region N Czech Republic
Pardubitz see Pardubice
119 F16 **Parechcha** Pol. Porzecze, Rus. Porech'ye. Hrodzyenskaya Voblasts', W Belarus
59 F17 **Parecis, Chapada dos** var. Serra dos Parecis. ▲▲ W Brazil
Parecis, Serra dos see Parecis, Chapada dos
104 M4 **Paredes de Nava** Castilla-León, N Spain
189 U12 **Parem** island Chuuk, C Micronesia
189 O12 **Parem Island** island E Micronesia
184 I1 **Parengarenga Harbour** inlet North Island, New Zealand
15 N8 **Parent** Québec, SE Canada
102 J14 **Parentis-en-Born** Landes, SW France
Parenzo see Poreč
185 G20 **Pareora** Canterbury, South Island, New Zealand
171 N14 **Parepare** Sulawesi, C Indonesia
115 B16 **Párga** Ípeiros, W Greece
93 K20 **Pargas** Swe. Parainen. Länsi-Soumi, SW Finland
64 O5 **Pargo, Ponta do** headland Madeira, Portugal, NE Atlantic Ocean
Paria, Golfo de see Paria, Gulf of
55 N6 **Pariaguán** Anzoátegui, NE Venezuela
45 X17 **Paria, Gulf of** var. Golfo de Paria. gulf Trinidad and Tobago/Venezuela
57 I15 **Pariamanu, Río** ⇝ E Peru
36 L8 **Paria River** ⇝ Utah, W USA
Parichi see Parychy
40 M14 **Paricutín, Volcán** ⛰ C Mexico
43 P16 **Parida, Isla** island SW Panama
55 T8 **Parika** NE Guyana
93 O18 **Parikkala** Etelä-Suomi, SE Finland
58 E10 **Parima, Serra** var. Sierra Parima. ▲▲ Brazil/Venezuela see also Parima, Sierra
55 N11 **Parima, Sierra** var. Serra Parima. ▲▲ Brazil/Venezuela see also Parima, Serra
57 F17 **Parinacochas, Laguna** ◎ SW Peru
56 A9 **Pariñas, Punta** headland NW Peru
58 H12 **Parintins** Amazonas, N Brazil
103 O5 **Paris** anc. Lutetia, Lutetia Parisiorum, Parisii. ● (France) Paris, N France
191 Y2 **Paris** Kiritimati, E Kiribati
27 S11 **Paris** Arkansas, C USA
33 S16 **Paris** Idaho, NW USA
31 N14 **Paris** Illinois, N USA
20 M5 **Paris** Kentucky, S USA
27 V3 **Paris** Missouri, C USA
20 H8 **Paris** Tennessee, S USA
25 V5 **Paris** Texas, SW USA
Parisii see Paris
43 S16 **Parita** Herrera, S Panama
43 S16 **Parita, Bahía de** bay S Panama
93 K18 **Parkano** Länsi-Suomi, W Finland
Parkan/Párkány see Štúrovo
27 N6 **Park City** Kansas, C USA
36 L3 **Park City** Utah, W USA
36 I12 **Parker** Arizona, SW USA
23 R9 **Parker** Florida, SE USA
29 R11 **Parker** South Dakota, N USA
35 Z14 **Parker Dam** California, W USA
29 W13 **Parkersburg** Iowa, C USA
21 Q3 **Parkersburg** West Virginia, NE USA
29 T7 **Parkers Prairie** Minnesota, N USA
171 P8 **Parker Volcano** ⛰ Mindanao, S Philippines
181 W13 **Parkes** New South Wales, SE Australia
30 K4 **Park Falls** Wisconsin, N USA
Parkhar see Farkhor
14 E16 **Parkhill** Ontario, S Canada
29 T5 **Park Rapids** Minnesota, N USA
29 Q3 **Park River** North Dakota, N USA
29 Q11 **Parkston** South Dakota, N USA
10 L17 **Parksville** Vancouver Island, British Columbia, SW Canada
37 S3 **Parkview Mountain** ▲ Colorado, C USA
105 N8 **Parla** Madrid, C Spain
29 S8 **Parle, Lac qui** ▣ Minnesota, N USA
155 G14 **Parli Vaijnāth** Mahārāshtra, C India
106 F9 **Parma** Emilia-Romagna, N Italy
31 T11 **Parma** Ohio, N USA
Parnahyba see Parnaíba
58 N13 **Parnaíba** var. Parnahyba. Piauí, E Brazil
65 J14 **Parnaíba Ridge** undersea feature C Atlantic Ocean
58 N13 **Parnaíba, Rio** ⇝ NE Brazil
115 F18 **Parnassós** ▲▲ C Greece
185 J17 **Parnassus** Canterbury, South Island, New Zealand
182 H10 **Parndana** South Australia
115 H19 **Párnitha** ▲▲ C Greece
Parnon see Párnonas
115 F21 **Párnonas** var. Parnon. ▲▲ S Greece
118 G5 **Pärnu** Ger. Pernau, Latv. Pērnava; prev. Rus. Pernov. Pärnumaa, SW Estonia
118 G6 **Pärnu** var. Parnu Jõgi, Ger. Pernau. ⇝ SW Estonia
118 G5 **Pärnu-Jaagupi** Ger. Sankt-Jakobi. Pärnumaa, SW Estonia
Parnu Jõgi see Pärnu
118 G5 **Pärnu Laht** Ger. Pernauer Bucht. bay SW Estonia
118 F5 **Pärnumaa** var. Pärnu Maakond. ◈ province SW Estonia
Pärnu Maakond see Pärnumaa
153 T11 **Paro** W Bhutan
153 T11 **Paro** ✕ (Thimphu) W Bhutan
185 G17 **Paroa** West Coast, South Island, New Zealand
163 X14 **P'aro-ho** var. Hwach'ŏn-chŏsuji. ▣ N South Korea
115 J21 **Pároikiá** prev. Páros. Páros, Kykládes, Greece, Aegean Sea
183 N6 **Paroo River** seasonal river New South Wales/Queensland, SE Australia
Paropamisus Range see Sefīd Kūh, Selseleh-ye
Paropamisus Range see Safīdkūh, Selseleh-ye
115 J21 **Páros** island Kykládes, Greece, Aegean Sea
Páros see Pároikiá
36 K7 **Parowan** Utah, W USA
103 U13 **Parpaillon** ▲▲ SE France
108 I9 **Parpan** Graubünden, S Switzerland
62 G13 **Parral** Maule, C Chile
Parral see Hidalgo del Parral
183 T9 **Parramatta** New South Wales, SE Australia
21 Y6 **Parramore Island** island Virginia, NE USA
40 M8 **Parras** var. Parras de la Fuente. Coahuila de Zaragoza, NE Mexico
Parras de la Fuente see Parras
42 M14 **Parrita** Puntarenas, S Costa Rica
Parry group see Mukojima-rettō
14 G13 **Parry Island** island Ontario, S Canada
197 O9 **Parry Islands** island group Nunavut, NW Canada
14 G12 **Parry Sound** Ontario, S Canada
110 F7 **Parsęta** Ger. Persante. ⇝ NW Poland
28 L3 **Parshall** North Dakota, N USA
27 Q7 **Parsons** Kansas, C USA
20 H9 **Parsons** Tennessee, S USA
21 T3 **Parsons** West Virginia, NE USA
Parsonstown see Birr
100 P11 **Parsteiner See** ◎ NE Germany
107 I24 **Partanna** Sicilia, Italy, C Mediterranean Sea
108 J8 **Partenen** Graubünden, E Switzerland
102 K9 **Parthenay** Deux-Sèvres, W France
95 J19 **Partille** Västra Götaland, S Sweden
107 I23 **Partinico** Sicilia, Italy, C Mediterranean Sea
111 I20 **Partizánske** prev. Šimonovany, Hung. Simony. Trenčiansky Kraj, W Slovakia
58 H11 **Paru de Oeste, Rio** ⇝ N Brazil
182 K9 **Paruna** South Australia
58 I11 **Paru, Rio** ⇝ N Brazil
149 Q5 **Parvān** Pash. Parwān. ◈ province E Afghanistan
155 M14 **Pārvatipuram** Andhra Pradesh, E India
152 G12 **Parvatsar** prev. Parbatsar. Rājasthān, N India
Parwān see Parvān
158 I15 **Paryang** Xizang Zizhiqu, W China
119 M18 **Parychy** Rus. Parichi. Homyel'skaya Voblasts', SE Belarus
83 J21 **Parys** Free State, C South Africa
35 T15 **Pasadena** California, W USA
25 W11 **Pasadena** Texas, SW USA
56 B8 **Pasaje** El Oro, SW Ecuador
137 T9 **P'asanauri** N Georgia
168 I13 **Pasapuat** Pulau Pagai Utara, W Indonesia
167 N7 **Pasawng** Kayah State, C Myanmar (Burma)
114 L13 **Paşayiğit** Edirne, NW Turkey
23 N9 **Pascagoula** Mississippi, S USA
22 M8 **Pascagoula River** ⇝ Mississippi, S USA
116 F12 **Paşcani** Hung. Páskán. Iaşi, NE Romania
109 T4 **Pasching** Oberösterreich, N Austria
32 K10 **Pasco** Washington, NW USA
56 E13 **Pasco** off. Departamento de Pasco. ◈ department C Peru
Pasco, Departamento de see Pasco
191 N11 **Pascua, Isla de** var. Rapa Nui, Easter Island. island E Pacific Ocean
63 G21 **Pascua, Río** ⇝ S Chile
103 N1 **Pas-de-Calais** ◈ department N France
100 P10 **Pasewalk** Mecklenburg-Vorpommern, NE Germany
9 T10 **Pasfield Lake** ◎ Saskatchewan, C Canada
Pa-shih Hai-hsia see Bashi Channel
Pashkeni see Bolyarovo
Pashmakli see Smolyan
153 X10 **Pāsighāt** Arunāchel Pradesh, NE India
137 Q12 **Pasinler** Erzurum, NE Turkey
Pasi Oloy, Qatorkŭhi see Zaalayskiy Khrebet
42 E3 **Pasión, Río de la** ⇝ N Guatemala
168 J12 **Pasirganting** Sumatera, W Indonesia
Pasirpangarayan see Bagansiapiapi
168 K6 **Pasir Puteh** var. Pasir Putih. Kelantan, Peninsular Malaysia
Pasir Putih see Pasir Puteh
169 R9 **Pasir, Tanjung** cape East Malaysia
95 N20 **Påskallavik** Kalmar, S Sweden
Páskán see Paşcani
Paskevicha, Zaliv see Tushybas, Zaliv
110 K7 **Pasłęk** Ger. Preußisch Holland. Warmińsko-Mazurskie, NE Poland
110 K7 **Pasłęka** Ger. Passarge. ⇝ N Poland
148 K16 **Pasni** Baluchistān, SW Pakistan
63 I18 **Paso de Indios** Chubut, S Argentina
54 L7 **Paso del Caballo** Guárico, N Venezuela
61 E15 **Paso de los Libres** Corrientes, NE Argentina
61 E18 **Paso de los Toros** Tacuarembó, C Uruguay
Pasoeroean see Pasuruan
35 P12 **Paso Robles** California, W USA
15 Y7 **Paspébiac** Québec, SE Canada
9 U14 **Pasquia Hills** ▲▲ Saskatchewan, S Canada
149 W7 **Pasrūr** Punjab, E Pakistan
30 M1 **Passage Island** island Michigan, N USA
65 B24 **Passage Islands** island group W Falkland Islands
8 K5 **Passage Point** headland Banks Island, Northwest Territories, NW Canada
Passarge see Pasłęka
115 C15 **Passarón** ancient monument Ípeiros, W Greece
Passarowitz see Požarevac
101 O22 **Passau** Bayern, SE Germany
22 M9 **Pass Christian** Mississippi, S USA
107 L26 **Passero, Capo** headland Sicilia, Italy, C Mediterranean Sea
171 P5 **Passi** Panay Island, C Philippines
61 H14 **Passo Fundo** Rio Grande do Sul, S Brazil
60 H13 **Passo Fundo, Barragem de** ▣ S Brazil
61 H15 **Passo Real, Barragem de** ▣ S Brazil
59 L20 **Passos** Minas Gerais, NE Brazil
167 X10 **Passu Keah** island S Paracel Islands
118 J13 **Pastavy** Pol. Postawy, Rus. Postavy. Vitsyebskaya Voblasts', NW Belarus
56 D7 **Pastaza** ◈ province E Ecuador
56 D9 **Pastaza, Río** ⇝ Ecuador/Peru
61 A21 **Pasteur** Buenos Aires, E Argentina
15 V3 **Pasteur** ⇝ Québec, SE Canada
147 Q12 **Pastigav** Rus. Pastigov. W Tajikistan
Pastigov see Pastigav
54 C13 **Pasto** Nariño, SW Colombia
38 M10 **Pastol Bay** bay Alaska, USA
37 O8 **Pastora Peak** ▲ Arizona, SW USA
105 O8 **Pastrana** Castilla-La Mancha, C Spain
169 S16 **Pasuruan** prev. Pasoeroean. Jawa, C Indonesia
118 F11 **Pasvalys** Panevėžys, N Lithuania
111 K21 **Pásztó** Nógrád, N Hungary
189 U12 **Pata** var. Patta. atoll Chuuk Islands, C Micronesia
36 M16 **Patagonia** Arizona, SW USA
63 H20 **Patagonia** semi arid region Argentina/Chile
Patalung see Phatthalung
154 D9 **Pātan** Gujarāt, W India
154 J10 **Pātan** Madhya Pradesh, C India
171 S11 **Patani** Pulau Halmahera, E Indonesia
Patani see Pattani
15 V7 **Patapédia Est** ⇝ Québec, SE Canada
116 K13 **Pătâriagele** prev. Pătîriagele. Buzău, SE Romania
Patavium see Padova
182 I5 **Patawarta Hill** ▲ South Australia
182 L10 **Patchewollock** Victoria, SE Australia

184 K11 **Patea** Taranaki, North Island, New Zealand
184 K11 **Patea** ≈ North Island, New Zealand
77 U15 **Pategi** Kwara, C Nigeria
81 K20 **Pate Island** *var.* Patta Island. *island* SE Kenya
105 S10 **Paterna** País Valenciano, E Spain
109 R9 **Paternion** *Slvn.* Špatrjan. Kärnten, S Austria
107 L24 **Paternò** *anc.* Hybla, Hybla Major. Sicilia, Italy, C Mediterranean Sea
32 J7 **Pateros** Washington, NW USA
18 J14 **Paterson** New Jersey, NE USA
32 J10 **Paterson** Washington, NW USA
185 C25 **Paterson Inlet** *inlet* Stewart Island, New Zealand
98 N6 **Paterswolde** Drenthe, NE Netherlands
152 H7 **Pathānkot** Himāchal Pradesh, N India
Pathein *see* Bassein
33 W15 **Pathfinder Reservoir** ⊠ Wyoming, C USA
167 O11 **Pathum Thani** *var.* Patumdhani, Prathum Thani. Pathum Thani, C Thailand
54 C12 **Patía** *var.* El Bordo. Cauca, SW Colombia
152 I9 **Patiāla** *var.* Puttiala. Punjab, NW India
54 B12 **Patía, Río** ≈ SW Colombia
188 D15 **Pati Point** *headland* NE Guam
Pātiriagele *see* Pătâriagele
56 C13 **Pativilca** Lima, W Peru
166 M1 **Pātkai Bum** *var.* Patkai Range. ▲▲ Myanmar (Burma)/India
Patkai Range *see* Pātkai Bum
115 L20 **Pátmos** Pátmos, Dodekánisa, Greece, Aegean Sea
115 L20 **Pátmos** *island* Dodekánisa, Greece, Aegean Sea
153 P13 **Patna** *var.* Azimabad. *state capital* Bihār, N India
154 M12 **Patnāgarh** Orissa, E India
171 O5 **Patnongon** Panay Island, C Philippines
137 S13 **Patnos** Ağrı, E Turkey
60 H12 **Pato Branco** Paraná, S Brazil
31 O16 **Patoka Lake** ◎ Indiana, N USA
92 L9 **Patoniva** *Lapp.* Buoddobohki. Lappi, N Finland
113 K21 **Patos** *var.* Patosi. Fier, SW Albania
Patos *see* Patos de Minas
59 K19 **Patos de Minas** *var.* Patos. Minas Gerais, NE Brazil
Patosi *see* Patos
61 I17 **Patos, Lagoa dos** *lagoon* S Brazil
62 J9 **Patquía** La Rioja, C Argentina
115 E19 **Pátra** *Eng.* Patras; *prev.* Pátrai. Dytikí Ellás, S Greece
115 D18 **Patraïkós Kólpos** *gulf* S Greece
Pátrai/Patras *see* Pátra
92 G2 **Patreksfjördhur** Vestfirdhir, W Iceland
24 M7 **Patricia** Texas, SW USA
63 F21 **Patricio Lynch, Isla** *island* S Chile
Patta *see* Pata
Patta Island *see* Pate Island
167 O16 **Pattani** *var.* Patani. Pattani, SW Thailand
167 P12 **Pattaya** Chon Buri, S Thailand
19 S4 **Patten** Maine, NE USA
35 O9 **Patterson** California, W USA
22 J10 **Patterson** Louisiana, S USA
35 R7 **Patterson, Mount** ▲ California, W USA
31 P4 **Patterson, Point** *headland* Michigan, N USA
107 L23 **Patti** Sicilia, Italy, C Mediterranean Sea
107 L23 **Patti, Golfo di** *gulf* Sicilia, Italy
93 L14 **Pattijoki** Oulu, W Finland
193 Q4 **Patton Escarpment** *undersea feature* E Pacific Ocean
27 S2 **Pattonsburg** Missouri, C USA
0 D6 **Patton Seamount** *undersea feature* NE Pacific Ocean
10 J12 **Pattullo, Mount** ▲ British Columbia, W Canada
42 M5 **Patuca, Río** ≈ E Honduras
153 U16 **Patuakhali** *var.* Patukhali. Barisal, S Bangladesh
Patukhali *see* Patuakhali
Patumdhani *see* Pathum Thani
40 M14 **Pátzcuaro** Michoacán de Ocampo, SW Mexico
42 C6 **Patzicía** Chimaltenango, S Guatemala
102 K16 **Pau** Pyrénées-Atlantiques, SW France
102 J12 **Pauillac** Gironde, SW France
166 L5 **Pauk** Magwe, W Myanmar (Burma)
8 I6 **Paulatuk** Northwest Territories, NW Canada
42 K5 **Paulayá, Río** ≈ NE Honduras
22 M6 **Paulding** Mississippi, S USA
31 Q12 **Paulding** Ohio, N USA
29 S12 **Paullina** Iowa, C USA
59 P15 **Paulo Afonso** Bahia, E Brazil
38 M16 **Pauloff Harbor** *var.* Pavlor Harbour. Sanak Island, Alaska, USA
27 N12 **Pauls Valley** Oklahoma, C USA
166 L7 **Paungde** Pegu, C Myanmar (Burma)
Pauni *see* Paoni
152 K9 **Pauri** Uttaranchal, N India
Pautalia *see* Kyustendil
142 J5 **Pāveh** Kermānshāhān, NW Iran
126 L5 **Pavelets** Ryazanskaya Oblast', W Russian Federation
106 D8 **Pavia** *anc.* Ticinum. Lombardia, N Italy
118 C9 **Pāvilosta** Liepāja, W Latvia
125 P14 **Pavino** Kostromskaya Oblast', NW Russian Federation
114 J8 **Pavlikeni** Veliko Tŭrnovo, N Bulgaria
145 T8 **Pavlodar** Pavlodar, NE Kazakhstan
145 S9 **Pavlodar** *off.* Pavlodarskaya Oblast', *Kaz.* Pavlodar Oblysy. ◈ *province* NE Kazakhstan
Pavlodar Oblysy/Pavlodarskaya Oblast' *see* Pavlodar
Pavlograd *see* Pavlohrad
117 U7 **Pavlohrad** *Rus.* Pavlograd. Dnipropetrovs'ka Oblast', E Ukraine
Pavlor Harbour *see* Pauloff Harbor
145 R9 **Pavlovka** Akmola, C Kazakhstan
127 V4 **Pavlovka** Respublika Bashkortostan, W Russian Federation
127 Q7 **Pavlovka** Ul'yanovskaya Oblast', W Russian Federation
127 N3 **Pavlovo** Nizhegorodskaya Oblast', W Russian Federation
126 L9 **Pavlovsk** Voronezhskaya Oblast', W Russian Federation
126 L13 **Pavlovskaya** Krasnodarskiy Kray, SW Russian Federation
117 S7 **Pavlysh** Kirovohrads'ka Oblast', C Ukraine
106 F10 **Pavullo nel Frignano** Emilia-Romagna, C Italy
27 P8 **Pawhuska** Oklahoma, C USA
21 U13 **Pawleys Island** South Carolina, SE USA
167 N6 **Pawn** ≈ C Myanmar (Burma)
30 K14 **Pawnee** Illinois, N USA
27 O9 **Pawnee** Oklahoma, C USA
37 U2 **Pawnee Buttes** ▲ Colorado, C USA
29 S17 **Pawnee City** Nebraska, C USA
26 K5 **Pawnee River** ≈ Kansas, C USA
31 O10 **Paw Paw** Michigan, N USA
31 O10 **Paw Paw Lake** Michigan, N USA
19 O12 **Pawtucket** Rhode Island, NE USA
Pax Augusta *see* Badajoz
115 I25 **Paximádia** *island* SE Greece
Pax Julia *see* Beja
115 B16 **Paxoí** *island* Iónia Nisiá, Greece, C Mediterranean Sea
39 S10 **Paxson** Alaska, USA
147 O11 **Paxtakor** Jizzax Viloyati, C Uzbekistan
30 M13 **Paxton** Illinois, N USA
124 J11 **Pay** Respublika Kareliya, NW Russian Federation
166 M8 **Payagyi** Pegu, SW Myanmar (Burma)
108 C9 **Payerne** *Ger.* Peterlingen. Vaud, W Switzerland
32 M13 **Payette** Idaho, NW USA
32 M13 **Payette River** ≈ Idaho, NW USA
125 V2 **Pay-Khoy, Khrebet** ▲▲ NW Russian Federation
Payne *see* Kangirsuk
12 K4 **Payne, Lac** ◎ Québec, NE Canada
29 T8 **Paynesville** Minnesota, N USA
169 S8 **Payong, Tanjung** *cape* East Malaysia
Payo Obispo *see* Chetumal
61 D18 **Paysandú** Paysandú, W Uruguay
61 D17 **Paysandú** ◈ *department* W Uruguay
102 I7 **Pays de la Loire** ◈ *region* NW France
36 L12 **Payson** Arizona, SW USA
36 L4 **Payson** Utah, W USA
125 W4 **Payyer, Gora** ▲ NW Russian Federation
Payzawat *see* Jiashi
137 Q11 **Pazar** Rize, NE Turkey
136 F10 **Pazarbaşı Burnu** *headland* NW Turkey
136 M16 **Pazarcık** Kahramanmaraş, S Turkey
114 I10 **Pazardzhik** *prev.* Tatar Pazardzhik. Pazardzhik, SW Bulgaria
64 H11 **Pazardzhik** ◈ *province* C Bulgaria
54 H9 **Paz de Ariporo** Casanare, E Colombia
111 B17 **Pazeňský-Kraj** ◈ *region* W Czech Republic
112 A10 **Pazin** *Ger.* Mitterburg, *It.* Pisino. Istra, NW Croatia
42 D7 **Paz, Río** ≈ El Salvador/Guatemala
113 O18 **Pčinja** ≈ N Macedonia
193 V15 **Pea** Tongatapu, S Tonga
27 O6 **Peabody** Kansas, C USA
9 O12 **Peace** ≈ Alberta/British Columbia, W Canada
Peace Garden State *see* North Dakota
9 Q10 **Peace Point** Alberta, C Canada
9 O12 **Peace River** Alberta, W Canada
23 W13 **Peace River** ≈ Florida, SE USA
9 N17 **Peachland** British Columbia, SW Canada
36 J10 **Peach Springs** Arizona, SW USA
Peach State *see* Georgia
23 S4 **Peachtree City** Georgia, SE USA
189 Y13 **Peacock Point** *point* SE Wake Island
97 M18 **Peak District** *physical region* C England, UK
183 Q7 **Peak Hill** New South Wales, SE Australia
65 G15 **Peak, The** ▲ C Ascension Island
105 O13 **Peal de Becerro** Andalucía, S Spain
189 X11 **Peale Island** *island* N Wake Island
37 O6 **Peale, Mount** ▲ Utah, W USA
39 O4 **Peard Bay** *bay* Alaska, USA
23 Q7 **Pea River** ≈ Alabama/Florida, S USA
25 W11 **Pearland** Texas, SW USA
38 D9 **Pearl City** O'ahu, Hawai'i, USA
38 D9 **Pearl Harbor** *inlet* O'ahu, Hawai'i, USA, C Pacific Ocean
Pearl Islands *see* Perlas, Archipiélago de las
Pearl Lagoon *see* Perlas, Laguna de
22 M5 **Pearl River** ≈ Louisiana/Mississippi, S USA
25 Q13 **Pearsall** Texas, SW USA
23 U7 **Pearson** Georgia, SE USA
25 P4 **Pease River** ≈ Texas, SW USA
12 F7 **Peawanuk** Ontario, C Canada
83 P16 **Pebane** Zambézia, NE Mozambique
65 C23 **Pebble Island** *island* N Falkland Islands
65 C23 **Pebble Island Settlement** Pebble Island, N Falkland Islands
113 L16 **Peć** *Alb.* Pejë, *Turk.* Ipek. Kosovo, S Serbia
25 R8 **Pecan Bayou** ≈ Texas, SW USA
22 H10 **Pecan Island** Louisiana, S USA
60 L12 **Peças, Ilha das** *island* S Brazil
30 L10 **Pecatonica River** ≈ Illinois/Wisconsin, N USA
108 G10 **Peccia** Ticino, S Switzerland
Pechenegi *see* Pechenihy
Pechenezhskoye Vodokhranilishche *see* Pecheniz'ke Vodoskhovyshche
124 I2 **Pechenga** *Fin.* Petsamo. Murmanskaya Oblast', NW Russian Federation
117 V5 **Pechenihy** *Rus.* Pechenegi. Kharkivs'ka Oblast', E Ukraine
117 V5 **Pecheniz'ke Vodoskhovyshche** *Rus.* Pechenezhskoye Vodokhranilishche. ⊠ E Ukraine
125 U7 **Pechora** Respublika Komi, NW Russian Federation
125 R6 **Pechora** ≈ NW Russian Federation
Pechora Bay *see* Pechorskaya Guba
Pechora Sea *see* Pechorskoye More
125 S3 **Pechorskaya Guba** *Eng.* Pechora Bay. *bay* NW Russian Federation
122 H7 **Pechorskoye More** *Eng.* Pechora Sea. *sea* NW Russian Federation
116 E11 **Pecica** *Ger.* Petschka, *Hung.* Ópécska. Arad, W Romania
24 K8 **Pecos** Texas, SW USA
25 N11 **Pecos River** ≈ New Mexico/Texas, SW USA
111 I25 **Pécs** *Ger.* Fünfkirchen, *Lat.* Sopianae. Baranya, SW Hungary
43 T17 **Pedasí** Los Santos, S Panama
Pedde *see* Pedja
183 O17 **Pedder, Lake** ◎ Tasmania, SE Australia
44 M10 **Pedernales** SW Dominican Republic
55 Q5 **Pedernales** Delta Amacuro, NE Venezuela
25 R10 **Pedernales River** ≈ Texas, SW USA
62 H6 **Pedernales, Salar de** *salt lake* N Chile
Pedhoulas *see* Pedoulás
55 X11 **Pédima** *var.* Malavate. SW French Guiana
182 F1 **Pedirka** South Australia
171 S11 **Pediwang** Pulau Halmahera, E Indonesia
118 I5 **Pedja** *var.* Pedja Jõgi, *Ger.* Pedde. ≈ E Estonia
Pedja Jõgi *see* Pedja
121 O3 **Pedoulás** *var.* Pedhoulas. W Cyprus
59 N18 **Pedra Azul** Minas Gerais, NE Brazil
104 I3 **Pedrafita, Porto de** *var.* Puerto de Piedrafita. *pass* NW Spain
76 E9 **Pedra Lume** Sal, NE Cape Verde
43 P16 **Pedregal** Chiriquí, W Panama
54 J4 **Pedregal** Falcón, N Venezuela
40 L9 **Pedriceña** Durango, C Mexico
60 L11 **Pedro Barros** São Paulo, S Brazil
39 Q13 **Pedro Bay** Alaska, USA
62 H4 **Pedro de Valdivia** *var.* Oficina Pedro de Valdivia. Antofagasta, N Chile
62 P4 **Pedro Juan Caballero** Amambay, E Paraguay
63 L15 **Pedro Luro** Buenos Aires, E Argentina
105 O10 **Pedro Muñoz** Castilla-La Mancha, C Spain
155 J22 **Pedro, Point** *headland* NW Sri Lanka
182 K9 **Peebinga** South Australia
96 J13 **Peebles** SE Scotland, UK
31 S15 **Peebles** Ohio, N USA
96 J12 **Peebles** *cultural region* SE Scotland, UK
18 K13 **Peekskill** New York, NE USA
97 I16 **Peel** W Isle of Man
8 G7 **Peel** ≈ Northwest Territories/Yukon Territory, NW Canada
8 K5 **Peel Point** *headland* Victoria Island, Northwest Territories, NW Canada
8 M5 **Peel Sound** *passage* Nunavut, N Canada
100 N9 **Peene** ≈ NE Germany
99 K17 **Peer** Limburg, NE Belgium
14 H14 **Pefferlaw** Ontario, S Canada
185 I18 **Pegasus Bay** *bay* South Island, New Zealand
121 O3 **Pégeia** *var.* Peyia. SW Cyprus
109 V7 **Peggau** Steiermark, SE Austria
101 L19 **Pegnitz** Bayern, SE Germany
101 L19 **Pegnitz** ≈ SE Germany
105 T11 **Pego** País Valenciano, E Spain
166 L8 **Pegu** *var.* Bago. Pegu, SW Myanmar (Burma)
166 L7 **Pegu** ◈ *division* S Myanmar (Burma)
189 N13 **Pehleng** Pohnpei, E Micronesia
114 M12 **Pehlivanköy** Kırklareli, NW Turkey
77 R14 **Péhonko** C Benin
61 B21 **Pehuajó** Buenos Aires, E Argentina
Pei-ching *see* Beijing/Beijing Shi
100 J13 **Peine** Niedersachsen, C Germany
Pei-p'ing *see* Beijing/Beijing Shi
Peipsi Järv/Peipus-See *see* Peipus, Lake
118 J5 **Peipus, Lake** *Est.* Peipsi Järv, *Ger.* Peipus-See, *Rus.* Chudskoye Ozero. ◎ Estonia/Russian Federation
115 H19 **Peiraías** *prev.* Piraiévs, *Eng.* Piraeus. Attikí, C Greece
Peisern *see* Pyzdry
60 I8 **Peixe, Rio do** ≈ S Brazil
59 I16 **Peixoto de Azevedo** Mato Grosso, W Brazil
168 O11 **Pejantan, Pulau** *island* W Indonesia
Pejë *see* Peć
167 R7 **Pèk** *var.* Xieng Khouang; *prev.* Xiangkhoang. Xiangkhoang, N Laos
112 N11 **Pek** ≈ E Serbia
169 Q16 **Pekalongan** Jawa, C Indonesia
168 K11 **Pekanbaru** *var.* Pakanbaru. Sumatera, W Indonesia
30 L12 **Pekin** Illinois, N USA
Peking *see* Beijing/Beijing Shi
Pelabohan Kelang/Pelabuhan Kelang *see* Pelabuhan Klang
168 J9 **Pelabuhan Klang** *var.* Kuala Pelabohan Kelang, Pelabohan Kelang, Pelabuhan Kelang, Port Klang, Port Swettenham. Selangor, Peninsular Malaysia
120 L11 **Pelagie, Isole** *island group* SW Italy
Pelagosa *see* Palagruža
22 L5 **Pelahatchie** Mississippi, S USA
169 T14 **Pelaihari** *var.* Pleihari. Borneo, C Indonesia
103 U14 **Pelat, Mont** ▲ SE France
116 F12 **Peleaga, Vârful** *prev.* Vîrful Peleaga. ▲ W Romania
Peleaga, Vîrful *see* Peleaga, Vârful
123 O11 **Peleduy** Respublika Sakha (Yakutiya), NE Russian Federation
14 C18 **Pelee Island** *island* Ontario, S Canada
45 Q11 **Pelée, Montagne** ▲ N Martinique
14 D18 **Pelee, Point** *headland* Ontario, S Canada
171 P12 **Pelei** Pulau Peleng, N Indonesia
Peleliu *see* Beliliou
171 P12 **Peleng, Pulau** *island* Kepulauan Banggai, N Indonesia
23 T7 **Pelham** Georgia, SE USA
111 E18 **Pelhřimov** *Ger.* Pilgram. Vysočina, C Czech Republic
39 W13 **Pelican** Chichagof Island, Alaska, USA
191 Z3 **Pelican Lagoon** ◎ Kiritimati, E Kiribati
29 V3 **Pelican Lake** ◎ Minnesota, N USA
29 U6 **Pelican Lake** ◎ Minnesota, N USA
30 L5 **Pelican Lake** ◎ Wisconsin, N USA
44 G1 **Pelican Point** Grand Bahama Island, N Bahamas
83 B19 **Pelican Point** *headland* W Namibia
29 S6 **Pelican Rapids** Minnesota, N USA
Pelican State *see* Louisiana
9 U13 **Pelikan Narrows** Saskatchewan, C Canada
115 L18 **Pelinaío** ▲ Chíos, E Greece
Pelinnaeum *see* Pelinnaío
115 E16 **Pelinnaío** *anc.* Pelinnaeum. *ruins* Thessalía, C Greece
113 N20 **Pelister** ▲ SW FYR Macedonia
113 G15 **Pelješac** *peninsula* S Croatia
92 M12 **Pelkosenniemi** Lappi, NE Finland
29 W15 **Pella** Iowa, C USA
114 F13 **Pélla** *site of ancient city* Kentrikí Makedonía, N Greece
23 Q3 **Pell City** Alabama, S USA
61 A22 **Pellegrini** Buenos Aires, E Argentina
92 K12 **Pello** Lappi, NW Finland
100 G7 **Pellworm** *island* N Germany
10 H6 **Pelly** ≈ Yukon Territory, NW Canada
9 N7 **Pelly Bay** Nunavut, N Canada
10 I8 **Pelly Mountains** ▲▲ Yukon Territory, W Canada
Pélmonostor *see* Beli Manastir
37 P13 **Pelona Mountain** ▲ New Mexico, SW USA
Peloponnese/Peloponnesus *see* Pelopónnisos
115 E20 **Pelopónnisos** *Eng.* Peloponnese. ◈ *region* S Greece
115 E20 **Pelopónnisos** *var.* Morea, *Eng.* Peloponnese; *anc.* Peloponnesus. *peninsula* S Greece
107 L23 **Peloritani, Monti** *anc.* Pelorus and Neptunius. ▲▲ Sicilia, Italy, C Mediterranean Sea
107 M22 **Peloro, Capo** *var.* Punta del Faro. *headland* S Italy
Pelorus and Neptunius *see* Peloritani, Monti
61 H17 **Pelotas** Rio Grande do Sul, S Brazil
61 I14 **Pelotas, Rio** ≈ S Brazil
92 K10 **Peltovuoma** *Lapp.* Bealdovuopmi. Lappi, N Finland
19 R4 **Pemadumcook Lake** ◎ Maine, NE USA
169 Q16 **Pemalang** Jawa, C Indonesia
169 P10 **Pemangkat** *var.* Pamangkat. Borneo, C Indonesia
Pemar *see* Paimio
168 I9 **Pematangsiantar** Sumatera, W Indonesia
83 Q14 **Pemba** *prev.* Port Amelia, Porto Amélia. Cabo Delgado, NE Mozambique
81 J22 **Pemba** ◈ *region* E Tanzania
81 K21 **Pemba** *island* E Tanzania
83 Q14 **Pemba, Baia de** *inlet* NE Mozambique
81 J21 **Pemba Channel** *channel* E Tanzania
180 J14 **Pemberton** Western Australia
10 M16 **Pemberton** British Columbia, SW Canada
29 Q2 **Pembina** North Dakota, N USA
9 P15 **Pembina** ≈ Alberta, SW Canada
29 Q2 **Pembina** ≈ Canada/USA
171 X16 **Pembre** Papua, E Indonesia
14 K12 **Pembroke** Ontario, SE Canada
97 H21 **Pembroke** SW Wales, UK
23 W6 **Pembroke** Georgia, SE USA
21 U11 **Pembroke** North Carolina, SE USA
21 R7 **Pembroke** Virginia, NE USA
97 H21 **Pembroke** *cultural region* SW Wales, UK
Pembuang, Sungai *see* Seruyan, Sungai
43 S15 **Peña Blanca, Cerro** ▲ C Panama
104 K8 **Peña de Francia, Sierra de la** ▲▲ W Spain
104 G6 **Penafiel** *var.* Peñafiel. Porto, N Portugal
105 N6 **Peñafiel** Castilla-León, N Spain
Peñafiel *see* Penafiel
105 S8 **Peñagolosa** ▲ E Spain
105 N7 **Peñalara, Pico de** ▲ C Spain
171 X16 **Penambo, Banjaran** *var.* Banjaran Tama Abu, Penambo Range. ▲▲ Indonesia/Malaysia
Penambo Range *see* Penambo, Banjaran
41 O10 **Peña Nevada, Cerro** ▲ C Mexico
Penang *see* Pinang, Pulau, Peninsular Malaysia
Penang *see* Pinang
Penang *see* George Town
60 J8 **Penápolis** São Paulo, S Brazil
104 L7 **Peñaranda de Bracamonte** Castilla-León, N Spain
105 S8 **Peñarroya** ▲ E Spain
104 L12 **Peñarroya-Pueblonuevo** Andalucía, S Spain
97 K22 **Penarth** S Wales, UK
104 K1 **Peñas, Cabo de** *cape* N Spain
63 F20 **Penas, Golfo de** *gulf* S Chile
Pen-ch'i *see* Benxi
79 H14 **Pendé** *var.* Logone Oriental. ≈ Central African Republic/Chad
76 I14 **Pendembu** E Sierra Leone
29 R13 **Pender** Nebraska, C USA
Penderma *see* Bandırma
32 K11 **Pendleton** Oregon, NW USA
32 M7 **Pend Oreille, Lake** ◎ Idaho, NW USA
32 M7 **Pend Oreille River** ≈ Idaho/Washington, NW USA
Pendzhikent *see* Panjakent
Peneius *see* Pineiós
104 G8 **Penela** Coimbra, N Portugal
14 G13 **Penetanguishene** Ontario, S Canada
151 H15 **Penganga** ≈ C India
161 T12 **P'engchia Yu** *island* N Taiwan
79 M21 **Penge** Kasai Oriental, C Dem. Rep. Congo
Penghu Archipelago/P'enghu Ch'üntao/Penghu Islands *see* P'enghu Liehtao
161 R14 **P'enghu Liehtao** *var.* P'enghu Ch'üntao, Penghu Islands, *Eng.* Penghu Archipelago, Pescadores, *Jap.* Hoko-guntō, Hoko-shotō. *island group* W Taiwan
Penghu Shuidao/P'enghu Shuitao *see* Pescadores Channel
161 R4 **Penglai** *var.* Dengzhou. Shandong, E China
Peng-pu *see* Bengbu
Penhsihu *see* Benxi
Penibético, Sistema *see* Béticos, Sistemas
104 F10 **Peniche** Leiria, W Portugal
169 U17 **Penida, Nusa** *island* S Indonesia
Peninsular State *see* Florida
105 T8 **Peñíscola** País Valenciano, E Spain
40 M13 **Pénjamo** Guanajuato, C Mexico
Penki *see* Benxi
102 F7 **Penmarch, Pointe de** *headland* NW France
107 L15 **Penna, Punta della** *headland* C Italy
107 K14 **Penne** Abruzzo, C Italy
Penner *see* Penneru
155 J18 **Penneru** *var.* Penner. ≈ C India
182 I10 **Penneshaw** South Australia
18 C14 **Penn Hills** Pennsylvania, NE USA
Penninae, Alpes/Pennine, Alpi *see* Pennine Alps
108 D11 **Pennine Alps** *Fr.* Alpes Pennines, *It.* Alpi Pennine, *Lat.* Alpes Penninae. ▲▲ Italy/Switzerland
Pennine Chain *see* Pennines
97 L15 **Pennines** *var.* Pennine Chain. ▲▲ N England, UK
Pennines, Alpes *see* Pennine Alps
21 O8 **Pennington Gap** Virginia, NE USA
18 I16 **Penns Grove** New Jersey, NE USA
18 I16 **Pennsville** New Jersey, NE USA
18 E14 **Pennsylvania** *off.* Commonwealth of Pennsylvania, *also known as* Keystone State. ◈ *state* NE USA
18 G10 **Penn Yan** New York, NE USA
124 H16 **Peno** Tverskaya Oblast', W Russian Federation
19 R7 **Penobscot Bay** *bay* Maine, NE USA
19 S5 **Penobscot River** ≈ Maine, NE USA
182 K12 **Penola** South Australia
40 K9 **Peñón Blanco** Durango, C Mexico
182 E7 **Penong** South Australia
43 S16 **Penonomé** Coclé, C Panama
190 L13 **Penrhyn** *atoll* N Cook Islands
192 M9 **Penrhyn Basin** *undersea feature* C Pacific Ocean
183 S9 **Penrith** New South Wales, SE Australia
97 K15 **Penrith** NW England, UK
23 O9 **Pensacola** Florida, SE USA
23 O9 **Pensacola Bay** *bay* Florida, SE USA
195 N7 **Pensacola Mountains** ▲▲ Antarctica
182 L12 **Penshurst** Victoria, SE Australia
187 R13 **Pentecost** *Fr.* Pentecôte. *island* C Vanuatu
15 V4 **Pentecôte** ≈ Québec, SE Canada
Pentecôte *see* Pentecost
15 V4 **Pentecôte, Lac** ◎ Québec, SE Canada
8 H15 **Penticton** British Columbia, SW Canada
96 J6 **Pentland Firth** *strait* N Scotland, UK
96 J12 **Pentland Hills** *hill range* S Scotland, UK
171 Q12 **Penu** Pulau Taliabu, E Indonesia
155 H18 **Penukonda** Andhra Pradesh, E India
166 L7 **Penwegon** Pegu, C Myanmar (Burma)
24 M8 **Penwell** Texas, SW USA
97 J21 **Pen y Fan** ▲ SE Wales, UK
97 L16 **Pen-y-ghent** ▲ N England, UK
127 O6 **Penza** Penzenskaya Oblast', W Russian Federation
97 G25 **Penzance** SW England, UK
127 N6 **Penzenskaya Oblast'** ◈ *province* W Russian Federation
123 U7 **Penzhina** ≈ E Russian Federation
123 U9 **Penzhinskaya Guba** *bay* E Russian Federation
Penzig *see* Pieńsk
36 K13 **Peoria** Arizona, SW USA
30 L12 **Peoria** Illinois, N USA
30 L12 **Peoria Heights** Illinois, N USA
31 N11 **Peotone** Illinois, N USA
18 J11 **Pepacton Reservoir** ⊠ New York, NE USA
76 I15 **Pepel** W Sierra Leone
30 I6 **Pepin, Lake** ⊠ Minnesota/Wisconsin, N USA
99 L20 **Pepinster** Liège, E Belgium
113 L20 **Peqin** *var.* Peqini. Elbasan, C Albania
Peqini *see* Peqin
40 D7 **Pequeña, Punta** *headland* W Mexico
168 J8 **Perak** ◈ *state* Peninsular Malaysia
105 R7 **Perales del Alfambra** Aragón, NE Spain
115 C15 **Pérama** *var.* Perama. Ípeiros, W Greece
Perama *see* Pérama
92 M13 **Perä-Posio** Lappi, NE Finland
15 Z6 **Percé** Québec, SE Canada
15 Z6 **Percé, Rocher** *island* Québec, S Canada
102 L5 **Perche, Collines de** ▲▲ N France
109 X4 **Perchtoldsdorf** Niederösterreich, NE Austria
180 L6 **Percival Lakes** *lakes* Western Australia
105 T3 **Perdido, Monte** ▲ NE Spain
23 O8 **Perdido River** ≈ Alabama/Florida, S USA
Perece Vela Basin *see* West Mariana Basin
116 G7 **Perechyn** Zakarpats'ka Oblast', W Ukraine
54 E10 **Pereira** Risaralda, W Colombia
60 I7 **Pereira Barreto** São Paulo, S Brazil
59 G15 **Pereirinha** Pará, N Brazil
127 N10 **Perelazovskiy** Volgogradskaya Oblast', SW Russian Federation
127 S7 **Perelyub** Saratovskaya Oblast', W Russian Federation
31 P7 **Pere Marquette River** ≈ Michigan, N USA
Peremyshl *see* Przemyśl
116 I5 **Peremyshlyany** L'vivs'ka Oblast', W Ukraine
Pereshchepino *see* Pereshchepyne
116 L9 **Pereshchepyne** *Rus.* Pereshchepino. Dnipropetrovs'ka Oblast', E Ukraine
124 L16 **Pereslavl'-Zalesskiy** Yaroslavskaya Oblast', W Russian Federation
117 Y7 **Pereval's'k** Luhans'ka Oblast', E Ukraine
127 U7 **Perevolotskiy** Orenburgskaya Oblast', W Russian Federation
Pereyaslav-Khmel'nitskiy *see* Pereyaslav-Khmel'nyts'kyy
117 Q5 **Pereyaslav-Khmel'nyts'kyy** *Rus.* Pereyaslav-Khmel'nitskiy. Kyyivs'ka Oblast', N Ukraine
109 U4 **Perg** Oberösterreich, N Austria
61 B19 **Pergamino** Buenos Aires, E Argentina
106 G6 **Pergine Valsugana** *Ger.* Persen. Trentino-Alto Adige, N Italy
29 S6 **Perham** Minnesota, N USA
93 L16 **Perho** Länsi-Soumi, W Finland
116 E11 **Periam** *Ger.* Perjamosch, *Hung.* Perjámos. Timiş, W Romania
15 Q6 **Péribonca** ≈ Québec, SE Canada
12 L11 **Péribonca, Lac** ◎ Québec, SE Canada
15 Q6 **Péribonca, Petite Rivière** ≈ Québec, SE Canada
15 Q7 **Péribonka** Québec, SE Canada
40 I9 **Pericos** Sinaloa, C Mexico
169 Q10 **Perigi** Borneo, C Indonesia
102 L12 **Périgueux** *anc.* Vesuna. Dordogne, SW France
54 G5 **Perijá, Serranía de** ▲▲ Columbia/Venezuela
115 H17 **Peristéra** *island* Vóreioi Sporádes, Greece, Aegean Sea
63 H20 **Perito Moreno** Santa Cruz, S Argentina
155 G22 **Periyāl** *var.* Periyār. ≈ SW India
Periyār *see* Periyāl
155 G23 **Periyār Lake** ◎ S India
Perjámos/Perjamosch *see* Periam
27 O9 **Perkins** Oklahoma, C USA
116 L7 **Perkivtsi** Chernivets'ka Oblast', W Ukraine

◆ Country ● Country Capital ◇ Dependent Territory ○ Dependent Territory Capital ◈ Administrative Regions ✈ International Airport ▲ Mountain ▲▲ Mountain Range ᐱ Volcano ≈ River ◎ Lake ⊠ Reservoir

43 U15 **Perlas, Archipiélago de las** *Eng.* Pearl Islands. *island group* SE Panama
43 O10 **Perlas, Cayos de** *reef* SE Nicaragua
43 N9 **Perlas, Laguna de** *Eng.* Pearl Lagoon. *lagoon* E Nicaragua
43 N10 **Perlas, Punta de** *headland* E Nicaragua
100 L11 **Perleberg** Brandenburg, N Germany
Perlepe *see* Prilep
168 I6 **Perlis** ◐ *state* Peninsular Malaysia
125 U14 **Perm'** *prev.* Molotov. Permskaya Oblast', NW Russian Federation
113 M22 **Përmet** *var.* Përmeti, Prëmet. Gjirokastër, S Albania
Përmeti *see* Përmet
125 U15 **Permskaya Oblast'** ◐ *province* NW Russian Federation
59 P15 **Pernambuco** *off.* Estado de Pernambuco. ◐ *state* E Brazil
Pernambuco *see* Recife
Pernambuco Abyssal Plain *see* Pernambuco Plain
Pernambuco, Estado de *see* Pernambuco
47 Y6 **Pernambuco Plain** *var.* Pernambuco Abyssal Plain. *undersea feature* E Atlantic Ocean
65 K15 **Pernambuco Seamounts** *undersea feature* C Atlantic Ocean
182 H6 **Pernatty Lagoon** *salt lake* South Australia
Pernau *see* Pärnu
Pernauer Bucht *see* Pärnu Laht
Pērnava *see* Pärnu
114 G9 **Pernik** *prev.* Dimitrovo. Pernik, W Bulgaria
114 G10 **Pernik** ◐ *province* W Bulgaria
93 K20 **Perniö** *Swe.* Bjärnå. Länsi-Soumi, SW Finland
109 X5 **Pernitz** Niederösterreich, E Austria
Pernov *see* Pärnu
103 O3 **Péronne** Somme, N France
14 L8 **Péronne, Lac** ◎ Québec, SE Canada
106 A8 **Perosa Argentina** Piemonte, NE Italy
41 Q14 **Perote** Veracruz-Llave, E Mexico
Pérouse *see* Perugia
191 W15 **Pérouse, Bahía de la** *bay* Easter Island, Chile, E Pacific Ocean
Perovsk *see* Kyzylorda
103 O17 **Perpignan** Pyrénées-Orientales, S France
113 M20 **Përrenjas** *var.* Përrenjasi, Prenjas, Prenjasi. Elbasan, E Albania
Përrenjasi *see* Përrenjas
92 O2 **Perriertoppen** ▲ C Svalbard
25 S6 **Perrin** Texas, SW USA
23 Y16 **Perrine** Florida, SE USA
37 S12 **Perro, Laguna del** ◎ New Mexico, SW USA
102 G5 **Perros-Guirec** Côtes d'Armor, NW France
23 T9 **Perry** Florida, SE USA
23 T5 **Perry** Georgia, SE USA
29 U14 **Perry** Iowa, C USA
18 E10 **Perry** New York, NE USA
27 N9 **Perry** Oklahoma, C USA
27 Q3 **Perry Lake** ▣ Kansas, C USA
31 R11 **Perrysburg** Ohio, N USA
25 O1 **Perryton** Texas, SW USA
39 O15 **Perryville** Alaska, USA
27 U11 **Perryville** Arkansas, C USA
27 Y6 **Perryville** Missouri, C USA
Persante *see* Parsęta
Persen *see* Pergine Valsugana
Pershay *see* Pyarshai
117 V7 **Pershotravens'k** Dnipropetrovs'ka Oblast', E Ukraine
117 W9 **Pershotravneve** Donets'ka Oblast', E Ukraine
Persia *see* Iran
141 T5 **Persian Gulf** *var.* The Gulf, *Ar.* Khalīj al 'Arabī, *Per.* Khalīj-e Fars. *Gulf* SW Asia *see also* Gulf, The
Persis *see* Fārs
95 K22 **Perstorp** Skåne, S Sweden
137 O14 **Pertek** Tunceli, C Turkey
183 P16 **Perth** Tasmania, SE Australia
180 I13 **Perth** *state capital* Western Australia
14 L13 **Perth** Ontario, SE Canada
96 J11 **Perth** C Scotland, UK
96 J10 **Perth** *cultural region* C Scotland, UK
180 I12 **Perth** ✈ Western Australia
173 V10 **Perth Basin** *undersea feature* SE Indian Ocean
103 S15 **Pertuis** Vaucluse, SE France
103 Y16 **Pertusato, Capo** *headland* Corse, France, C Mediterranean Sea
30 L11 **Peru** Illinois, N USA
31 P12 **Peru** Indiana, N USA
57 E13 **Peru** *off.* Republic of Peru. ◆ *republic* W South America
Peru *see* Beru
193 T9 **Peru Basin** *undersea feature* E Pacific Ocean
193 U8 **Peru-Chile Trench** *undersea feature* E Pacific Ocean
112 F13 **Perućko Jezero** ◎ S Croatia
106 H13 **Perugia** *Fr.* Pérouse; *anc.* Perusia. Umbria, C Italy
Perugia, Lake of *see* Trasimeno, Lago
61 D15 **Perugorría** Corrientes, NE Argentina
60 M11 **Peruíbe** São Paulo, S Brazil
155 B21 **Perumalpār** *reef* India, N Indian Ocean
Peru, Republic of *see* Peru
Perusia *see* Perugia
99 D20 **Péruwelz** Hainaut, SW Belgium
137 R15 **Pervari** Siirt, SE Turkey
127 O4 **Pervomaysk** Nizhegorodskaya Oblast', W Russian Federation
117 X7 **Pervomays'k** Luhans'ka Oblast', E Ukraine
117 P8 **Pervomays'k** *prev.* Ol'viopol'. Mykolayivs'ka Oblast', S Ukraine
117 S12 **Pervomays'ke** Respublika Krym, S Ukraine
125 R14 **Pervomayskiy** Kirovskaya Oblast', NW Russian Federation
127 V7 **Pervomayskiy** Orenburgskaya Oblast', W Russian Federation
126 M6 **Pervomayskiy** Tambovskaya Oblast', W Russian Federation
117 V6 **Pervomays'kyy** Kharkivs'ka Oblast', E Ukraine
122 F10 **Pervoural'sk** Sverdlovskaya Oblast', C Russian Federation
123 V11 **Pervyy Kuril'skiy Proliv** *strait* E Russian Federation
99 I19 **Perwez** Walloon Brabant, C Belgium
106 I11 **Pesaro** *anc.* Pisaurum. Marche, C Italy
35 N9 **Pescadero** California, W USA
Pescadores *see* P'enghu Liehtao
161 S14 **Pescadores Channel** *var.* Penghu Shuidao, P'enghu Shuitao. *channel* W Taiwan
107 K14 **Pescara** *anc.* Aternum, Ostia Aterni. Abruzzo, C Italy
107 K15 **Pescara** ≈ C Italy
106 F11 **Pescia** Toscana, C Italy
108 C8 **Peseux** Neuchâtel, W Switzerland
125 P6 **Pesha** ≈ NW Russian Federation
149 T5 **Peshāwar** North-West Frontier Province, N Pakistan
149 T6 **Peshāwar** ✈ North-West Frontier Province, N Pakistan
113 M19 **Peshkopi** *var.* Peshkopia, Peshkopija. Dibër, NE Albania
Peshkopia/Peshkopija *see* Peshkopi
114 I11 **Peshtera** Pazardzhik, C Bulgaria
31 N6 **Peshtigo** Wisconsin, N USA
31 N6 **Peshtigo River** ≈ Wisconsin, N USA
Peski *see* Pyeski
125 S13 **Peskovka** Kirovskaya Oblast', NW Russian Federation
103 S8 **Pesmes** Haute-Saône, E France
104 H6 **Peso da Régua** *var.* Pêso da Regua. Vila Real, N Portugal
40 F5 **Pesqueira** Sonora, NW Mexico
102 J13 **Pessac** Gironde, SW France
111 J23 **Pest** *off.* Pest Megye. ◐ *county* C Hungary
Pest Megye *see* Pest
124 J14 **Pestovo** Novgorodskaya Oblast', W Russian Federation
40 M15 **Petacalco, Bahía** *bay* W Mexico
Petach-Tikva *see* Petah Tiqwa
138 F10 **Petah Tiqwa** *var.* Petach-Tikva, Petah Tiqva, Petakh Tikva. Tel Aviv, C Israel
93 L17 **Petäjävesi** Länsi-Soumi, C Finland
Petakh Tikva/Petah Tiqva *see* Petah Tiqwa
22 M7 **Petal** Mississippi, S USA
115 I19 **Petalioí** *island* C Greece
115 H19 **Petalión, Kólpos** *gulf* E Greece
115 J19 **Pétalo** ▲ Ándros, Kykládes, Greece, Aegean Sea
34 M8 **Petaluma** California, W USA
99 L25 **Pétange** Luxembourg, SW Luxembourg
54 M5 **Petare** Miranda, N Venezuela
41 N16 **Petatlán** Guerrero, S Mexico
83 L14 **Petauke** Eastern, E Zambia
14 J12 **Petawawa** Ontario, SE Canada
14 J11 **Petawawa** ≈ Ontario, SE Canada
Petchaburi *see* Phetchaburi
42 D2 **Petén** *off.* Departamento del Petén. ◐ *department* N Guatemala
Petén, Departamento del *see* Petén
42 D2 **Petén Itzá, Lago** *var.* Lago de Flores. ◎ N Guatemala
30 K7 **Petenwell Lake** ▣ Wisconsin, N USA
14 D6 **Peterbell** Ontario, S Canada
182 I7 **Peterborough** South Australia
14 I14 **Peterborough** Ontario, SE Canada
97 N20 **Peterborough** *prev.* Medeshamstede. E England, UK
19 N10 **Peterborough** New Hampshire, NE USA
96 L8 **Peterhead** NE Scotland, UK
Peterhof *see* Luboń
193 Q14 **Peter I Island** ◇ *Norwegian dependency* Antarctica
194 H9 **Peter I Island** *var.* Peter I øy. *island* Antarctica
Peter I øy *see* Peter I Island
97 M14 **Peterlee** N England, UK
Peterlingen *see* Payerne
197 P14 **Petermann Bjerg** ▲ C Greenland
9 S12 **Peter Pond Lake** ◎ Saskatchewan, C Canada
39 X13 **Petersburg** Mytkof Island, Alaska, USA
30 K13 **Petersburg** Illinois, N USA
31 N16 **Petersburg** Indiana, N USA
29 Q3 **Petersburg** North Dakota, N USA
25 N5 **Petersburg** Texas, SW USA
21 V7 **Petersburg** Virginia, NE USA
21 T4 **Petersburg** West Virginia, NE USA
100 H12 **Petershagen** Nordrhein-Westfalen, NW Germany
55 S9 **Peters Mine** *var.* Peter's Mine. N Guyana
107 O21 **Petilia Policastro** Calabria, SW Italy
44 M9 **Pétionville** S Haiti
45 X6 **Petit-Bourg** Basse Terre, C Guadeloupe
15 Y5 **Petit-Cap** Québec, SE Canada
45 Y6 **Petit Cul-de-Sac Marin** *bay* C Guadeloupe
44 M9 **Petite-Rivière-de-l'Artibonite** C Haiti
173 X16 **Petite Rivière Noire, Piton de la** ▲ C Mauritius
15 R9 **Petite-Rivière-St-François** Québec, SE Canada
44 L9 **Petit-Goâve** S Haiti
Petitjean *see* Sidi-Kacem
13 N10 **Petit Lac Manicouagan** ◎ Québec, E Canada
19 T7 **Petit Manan Point** *headland* Maine, NE USA
Petit Mécatina, Rivière du *see* Little Mecatina
9 N10 **Petitot** ≈ Alberta/British Columbia, W Canada
45 S12 **Petit Piton** ▲ SW Saint Lucia
Petit-Popo *see* Aného
Petit St-Bernard, Col du *see* Little Saint Bernard Pass
13 O8 **Petitsikapau Lake** ◎ Newfoundland and Labrador, E Canada
92 L11 **Petkula** Lappi, N Finland
41 X12 **Peto** Yucatán, SE Mexico
62 G10 **Petorca** Valparaíso, C Chile
31 Q5 **Petoskey** Michigan, N USA
138 G14 **Petra** *archaeological site* Ma'ān, W Jordan
Petra *see* Wādī Mūsā
115 F14 **Pétras, Sténa** *pass* N Greece
123 S16 **Petra Velikogo, Zaliv** *bay* SE Russian Federation
Petrel *see* Petrer
14 K15 **Petre, Point** *headland* Ontario, SE Canada
105 S12 **Petrer** *var.* Petrel. País Valenciano, E Spain
125 U11 **Petretsovo** Permskaya Oblast', NW Russian Federation
114 G12 **Petrich** Blagoevegrad, SW Bulgaria
187 P15 **Petrie, Récif** *reef* N New Caledonia
37 N11 **Petrified Forest** *prehistoric site* Arizona, SW USA
Petrikau *see* Piotrków Trybunalski
Petrikov *see* Pyetrykaw
116 H12 **Petrila** *Hung.* Petrilla. Hunedoara, W Romania
Petrilla *see* Petrila
112 E9 **Petrinja** Sisak-Moslavina, C Croatia
Petroaleksandrovsk *see* To'rtkok'l
Petrőcz *see* Bački Petrovac
124 G12 **Petrodvorets** *Fin.* Pietarhovi. Leningradskaya Oblast', NW Russian Federation
Petrograd *see* Sankt-Peterburg
Petrokov *see* Piotrków Trybunalski
54 G6 **Petrólea** Norte de Santander, NE Colombia
14 D16 **Petrolia** Ontario, S Canada
25 S4 **Petrolia** Texas, SW USA
59 O15 **Petrolina** Pernambuco, E Brazil
45 T6 **Petrona, Punta** *headland* C Puerto Rico
Petropavl *see* Petropavlovsk
117 V7 **Petropavlivka** Dnipropetrovs'ka Oblast', E Ukraine
145 P6 **Petropavlovsk** *Kaz.* Petropavl. Severnyy Kazakhstan, N Kazakhstan
123 V11 **Petropavlovsk-Kamchatskiy** Kamchatskaya Oblast', E Russian Federation
60 P9 **Petrópolis** Rio de Janeiro, SE Brazil
116 H12 **Petroșani** *var.* Petroșeni, *Ger.* Petroschen, *Hung.* Petrozsény. Hunedoara, W Romania
Petroschen/Petroșeni *see* Petroșani
Petroskoi *see* Petrozavodsk
112 N12 **Petrovac** Serbia, E Serbia
Petrovac *see* Bosanski Petrovac
113 J17 **Petrovac na Moru** S Montenegro
Petrovac/Petrovácz *see* Bački Petrovac
117 S8 **Petrove** Kirovohrads'ka Oblast', C Ukraine
113 O18 **Petrovec** C FYR Macedonia
Petrovgrad *see* Zrenjanin
127 P7 **Petrovsk** Saratovskaya Oblast', W Russian Federation
124 J9 **Petrovskiy Yam** Respublika Kareliya, NW Russian Federation
Petrovsk-Port *see* Makhachkala
127 P9 **Petrov Val** Volgogradskaya Oblast', SW Russian Federation
124 J11 **Petrozavodsk** *Fin.* Petroskoi. Respublika Kareliya, NW Russian Federation
Petrozsény *see* Petroșani
83 D20 **Petrusdal** Hardap, C Namibia
117 T7 **Petrykivka** Dnipropetrovs'ka Oblast', E Ukraine
Petsamo *see* Pechenga
Petschka *see* Pecica
Pettau *see* Ptuj
109 S5 **Pettenbach** Oberösterreich, C Austria
25 S13 **Pettus** Texas, SW USA
122 G12 **Petukhovo** Kurganskaya Oblast', C Russian Federation
Petuna *see* Songyuan
109 R4 **Peuerbach** Oberösterreich, N Austria
62 G12 **Peumo** Libertador, C Chile
123 T6 **Pevek** Chukotskiy Avtonomnyy Okrug, NE Russian Federation
27 X5 **Pevely** Missouri, C USA
Peyia *see* Pégeia
102 J15 **Peyrehorade** Landes, SW France
124 J14 **Peza** ≈ NW Russian Federation
103 P16 **Pézenas** Hérault, S France
111 H20 **Pezinok** *Ger.* Bösing, *Hung.* Bazin. Bratislavský Kraj, W Slovakia
101 L22 **Pfaffenhofen an der Ilm** Bayern, SE Germany
108 G7 **Pfäffikon** Schwyz, C Switzerland
101 F20 **Pfälzer Wald** *hill range* W Germany
101 N22 **Pfarrkirchen** Bayern, SE Germany
101 G21 **Pforzheim** Baden-Württemberg, SW Germany
101 H24 **Pfullendorf** Baden-Württemberg, S Germany
108 K8 **Pfunds** Tirol, W Austria
101 G19 **Pfungstadt** Hessen, W Germany
83 L20 **Phalaborwa** Limpopo, NE South Africa
152 E11 **Phalodi** Rājasthān, NW India
152 E12 **Phalsund** Rājasthān, NW India
155 E15 **Phaltan** Mahārāshtra, W India
167 O7 **Phan** *var.* Muang Phan. Chiang Rai, NW Thailand
167 O14 **Phangan, Ko** *island* SW Thailand
166 M15 **Phang-Nga** *var.* Pang-Nga, Phangnga. Phangnga, SW Thailand
Phangnga *see* Phang-Nga
Phan Rang/Phanrang *see* Phan Rang-Thap Cham
167 V13 **Phan Rang-Thap Cham** *var.* Phanrang, Phan Rang, Phan Rang Thap Cham. Ninh Thuân, S Vietnam
167 U13 **Phan Ri** Binh Thuân, S Vietnam
167 U13 **Phan Thiêt** Binh Thuân, S Vietnam
Pharnacia *see* Giresun
25 S17 **Pharr** Texas, SW USA
Pharus *see* Hvar
167 N16 **Phatthalung** *var.* Padalung, Patalung. Phatthalung, SW Thailand
167 O7 **Phayao** *var.* Muang Phayao. Phayao, NW Thailand
9 U10 **Phelps Lake** ◎ Saskatchewan, C Canada
21 X9 **Phelps Lake** ◎ North Carolina, SE USA
23 R5 **Phenix City** Alabama, S USA
167 T8 **Pheo** Quang Binh, C Vietnam
Phet Buri *see* Phetchaburi
167 O11 **Phetchaburi** *var.* Bejraburi, Petchaburi, Phet Buri. Phetchaburi, SW Thailand
167 O9 **Phichit** *var.* Bichitra, Muang Phichit, Pichit. Phichit, C Thailand
22 M5 **Philadelphia** Mississippi, S USA
18 I7 **Philadelphia** New York, NE USA
18 I16 **Philadelphia** Pennsylvania, NE USA
18 I16 **Philadelphia** ✈ Pennsylvania, NE USA
Philadelphia *see* 'Ammān
28 L10 **Philip** South Dakota, N USA
99 H22 **Philippeville** Namur, S Belgium
Philippeville *see* Skikda
21 S3 **Philippi** West Virginia, NE USA
Philippi *see* Fílippoi
195 Y9 **Philippi Glacier** *glacier* Antarctica
192 G6 **Philippine Basin** *undersea feature* W Pacific Ocean
129 X12 **Philippine Plate** *tectonic feature*
171 O5 **Philippines** *off.* Republic of the Philippines. ◆ *republic* SE Asia
129 X13 **Philippines** *island group* W Pacific Ocean
171 P3 **Philippine Sea** *sea* W Pacific Ocean
Philippines, Republic of the *see* Philippines
192 F6 **Philippine Trench** *undersea feature* W Philippine Sea
83 H23 **Philippolis** Free State, C South Africa
Philippopolis *see* Plovdiv
Philippopolis *see* Shahbā', Syria
45 V9 **Philipsburg** Sint Maarten, N Netherlands Antilles
33 P10 **Philipsburg** Montana, NW USA
39 R6 **Philip Smith Mountains** ▲▲ Alaska, USA
152 H8 **Phillaur** Punjab, N India
183 N13 **Phillip Island** *island* Victoria, SE Australia
25 N2 **Phillips** Texas, SW USA
30 K5 **Phillips** Wisconsin, N USA
26 K3 **Phillipsburg** Kansas, C USA
18 I14 **Phillipsburg** New Jersey, NE USA
21 S7 **Philpott Lake** ▣ Virginia, NE USA
Phintias *see* Licata
167 P9 **Phitsanulok** *var.* Bisnulok, Muang Phitsanulok, Pitsanulok. Phitsanulok, C Thailand
Phlórina *see* Flórina
Phnom Penh *see* Phnum Penh
167 S13 **Phnum Penh** *var.* Phnom Penh. ● (Cambodia) Phnum Penh, S Cambodia
167 S11 **Phnum Tbêng Meanchey** Preăh Vihéar, N Cambodia
36 K13 **Phoenix** *state capital* Arizona, SW USA
Phoenix Island *see* Rawaki
191 R3 **Phoenix Islands** *island group* C Kiribati
18 I15 **Phoenixville** Pennsylvania, NE USA
83 K22 **Phofung** *var.* Mont-aux-Sources. ▲ N Lesotho
167 Q10 **Phon** Khon Kaen, E Thailand
167 Q5 **Phôngsali** *var.* Phong Saly. Phôngsali, N Laos
Phong Saly *see* Phôngsali
167 Q8 **Phônhông** C Laos
167 R5 **Phô Rang** *var* Bao Yèn. Lao Cai, N Vietnam
Phort Láirge, Cuan *see* Waterford Harbour
167 N10 **Phra Chedi Sam Ong** Kanchanaburi, W Thailand
167 O8 **Phrae** *var.* Muang Phrae, Prae. Phrae, NW Thailand
Phra Nakhon Si Ayutthaya *see* Ayutthaya
167 M14 **Phra Thong, Ko** *island* SW Thailand
Phu Cŭong *see* Thu Dâu Môt
166 M15 **Phuket** *var.* Bhuket, Puket, *Mal.* Ujung Salang; *prev.* Junkseylon, Salang. Phuket, SW Thailand
166 M15 **Phuket** ✈ Phuket, SW Thailand
166 M15 **Phuket, Ko** *island* SW Thailand
154 N12 **Phulabāni** *prev.* Phulbani. Orissa, E India
Phulbani *see* Phulabāni
167 U9 **Phu Lôc** Th,a Thiên-Huê, C Vietnam
167 S13 **Phumĭ Banam** Prey Vêng, S Cambodia
167 R13 **Phumĭ Chŏâm** Kâmpóng Spœ, SW Cambodia
167 T11 **Phumĭ Kalêng** Stœng Trêng, NE Cambodia
167 S12 **Phumĭ Kâmpóng Trâbêk** *prev.* Phum Kompong Trabek. Kâmpóng Thum, C Cambodia
167 Q11 **Phumĭ Koŭk Kduŏch** Bătdâmbâng, NW Cambodia
167 T11 **Phumĭ Labăng** Rôtânôkiri, NE Cambodia
167 S11 **Phumĭ Mlu Prey** Preăh Vihéar, N Cambodia
167 R11 **Phumĭ Moŭng** Siĕmréab, NW Cambodia
167 Q12 **Phumĭ Prâmaôy** Poŭthĭsăt, W Cambodia
167 Q13 **Phumĭ Samĭt** Kaôh Kông, SW Cambodia
167 R11 **Phumĭ Sâmraông** *prev.* Phum Samrong. Siĕmréab, NW Cambodia
167 S12 **Phumĭ Siĕmbok** Stœng Trêng, N Cambodia
167 S11 **Phumĭ Thalabârĭvăt** Stœng Trêng, N Cambodia
167 R13 **Phumĭ Veal Renh** Kâmpôt, SW Cambodia
167 P13 **Phumĭ Yeay Sên** Kaôh Kông, SW Cambodia
Phum Kompong Trabek *see* Phumĭ Kâmpóng Trâbêk
Phum Samrong *see* Phumĭ Sâmraông
167 V11 **Phu My** Binh Đinh, C Vietnam
167 S14 **Phung Hiêp** Cân Thơ, S Vietnam
153 T12 **Phuntsholing** SW Bhutan
167 R15 **Phươc Long** Minh Hai, S Vietnam
167 R14 **Phu Quôc, Đao** *var.* Phu Quoc Island. *island* S Vietnam
Phu Quoc Island *see* Phu Quôc, Đao
167 S6 **Phu Tho** Vinh Phu, N Vietnam
Phu Vinh *see* Tra Vinh
189 T13 **Piaanu Pass** *passage* Chuuk Islands, C Micronesia
106 E8 **Piacenza** *Fr.* Paisance; *anc.* Placentia. Emilia-Romagna, N Italy
107 K14 **Pianella** Abruzzo, C Italy
107 M15 **Pianosa, Isola** *island* Archipelago Toscano, C Italy
171 U13 **Piar** Papua, E Indonesia
45 U14 **Piarco** *var.* Port of Spain. ✈ (Port-of-Spain) Trinidad, Trinidad and Tobago
110 M12 **Piaseczno** Mazowieckie, C Poland
116 I15 **Piatra** Teleorman, S Romania
116 L10 **Piatra-Neamț** *Hung.* Karácsonkő. Neamț, NE Romania
Piauhy *see* Piauí
59 N15 **Piauí** *off.* Estado do Piauí; *prev.* Piauhy. ◐ *state* E Brazil
Piauí, Estado do *see* Piauí
106 I7 **Piave** ≈ NE Italy
107 K24 **Piazza Armerina** *var.* Chiazza. Sicilia, Italy, C Mediterranean Sea
81 G14 **Pibor** *Amh.* Pībor Wenz. ≈ Ethiopia/Sudan
81 G14 **Pibor Post** Jonglei, SE Sudan
Pībor Wenz *see* Pibor
Pibrans *see* Příbram
36 K11 **Picacho Butte** ▲ Arizona, SW USA
40 D4 **Picachos, Cerro** ▲ NW Mexico
103 O4 **Picardie** *Eng.* Picardy. ◐ *region* N France
Picardy *see* Picardie
22 L8 **Picayune** Mississippi, S USA
Piccolo San Bernardo, Colle di *see* Little Saint Bernard Pass
PicdeBälaitous *see* Balaïtous
62 K5 **Pichanal** Salta, N Argentina
147 P12 **Pichandar** W Tajikistan
27 R8 **Picher** Oklahoma, C USA
62 G12 **Pichilemu** Libertador, C Chile
40 F9 **Pichilingue** Baja California Sur, W Mexico
56 B6 **Pichincha** ◐ *province* N Ecuador
56 C6 **Pichincha** ▲ N Ecuador
Pichit *see* Phichit
41 U15 **Pichucalco** Chiapas, SE Mexico
22 L5 **Pickens** Mississippi, S USA
21 O11 **Pickens** South Carolina, SE USA
14 G11 **Pickerel** ≈ Ontario, S Canada
14 H15 **Pickering** Ontario, S Canada
97 N16 **Pickering** N England, UK
31 S13 **Pickerington** Ohio, N USA
12 C10 **Pickle Lake** Ontario, C Canada
29 P12 **Pickstown** South Dakota, N USA
25 V6 **Pickton** Texas, SW USA
23 N1 **Pickwick Lake** ▣ S USA
64 N2 **Pico** *var.* Ilha do Pico. *island* Azores, Portugal, NE Atlantic Ocean
63 J19 **Pico de Salamanca** Chubut, SE Argentina
1 P9 **Pico Fracture Zone** *tectonic feature* NW Atlantic Ocean
Pico, Ilha do *see* Pico
59 O14 **Picos** Piauí, E Brazil
63 I20 **Pico Truncado** Santa Cruz, SE Argentina
183 S9 **Picton** New South Wales, SE Australia
14 K15 **Picton** Ontario, SE Canada
185 K14 **Picton** Marlborough, South Island, New Zealand
63 H15 **Pićun Leufú, Arroyo** ≈ SW Argentina
Pidálion *see* Gkréko, Akrotíri
155 K25 **Pidurutalagala** ▲ S Sri Lanka
116 K6 **Pidvolochys'k** Ternopil's'ka Oblast', W Ukraine
107 K16 **Piedimonte Matese** Campania, S Italy
27 X7 **Piedmont** Missouri, C USA
21 P11 **Piedmont** South Carolina, SE USA
17 S12 **Piedmont** *escarpment* E USA
Piedmont *see* Piemonte
31 U13 **Piedmont Lake** ▣ Ohio, N USA
104 M11 **Piedrabuena** Castilla-La Mancha, C Spain
Piedrafita, Puerto de *see* Pedrafita, Porto de
104 L8 **Piedrahita** Castilla-León, N Spain
41 N6 **Piedras Negras** *var.* Ciudad Porfirio Díaz. Coahuila de Zaragoza, NE Mexico
61 E21 **Piedras, Punta** *headland* E Argentina
57 I14 **Piedras, Río de las** ≈ E Peru
111 J16 **Piekary Śląskie** Śląskie, S Poland
93 M17 **Pieksämäki** Isä-Suomi, E Finland
109 V5 **Pielach** ≈ NE Austria
93 M16 **Pielavesi** Itä-Suomi, C Finland
93 N16 **Pielinen** *var.* Pielisjärvi. ◎ E Finland
Pielisjärvi *see* Pielinen
106 A8 **Piemonte** *Eng.* Piedmont. ◐ *region* NW Italy
111 L18 **Pieniny** ▲▲ S Poland
111 E14 **Pieńsk** *Ger.* Penzig. Dolnośląskie, SW Poland
29 Q13 **Pierce** Nebraska, C USA
9 R14 **Pierceland** Saskatchewan, C Canada
115 E14 **Piéria** ▲▲ N Greece
29 N10 **Pierre** *state capital* South Dakota, N USA
102 K16 **Pierrefitte-Nestalas** Hautes-Pyrénées, S France
103 R14 **Pierrelatte** Drôme, E France
15 P11 **Pierreville** Québec, SE Canada
15 O7 **Pierriche** ≈ Québec, SE Canada
111 H20 **Piešt'any** *Ger.* Pistyan, *Hung.* Pöstyén. Tranavský Kraj, W Slovakia
109 X5 **Piesting** ≈ E Austria
Pietarhovi *see* Petrodvorets
Pietari *see* Sankt-Peterburg
Pietarsaari *see* Jakobstad
83 K23 **Pietermaritzburg** *var.* Maritzburg. KwaZulu/Natal, E South Africa
Pietersburg *see* Polokwane
107 K24 **Pietraperzia** Sicilia, Italy, C Mediterranean Sea
107 N22 **Pietra Spada, Passo della** *pass* SW Italy
83 K22 **Piet Retief** Mpumalanga, E South Africa
116 J10 **Pietrosul, Vârful** *prev.* Vîrful Pietrosu. ▲ N Romania
116 I9 **Pietrosul, Vârful** *prev.* Vîrful Pietrosu. ▲ N Romania
Pietrosu, Vîrful *see* Pietrosul, Vârful
106 I6 **Pieve di Cadore** Veneto, NE Italy
14 C18 **Pigeon Bay** *lake bay* Ontario, S Canada
27 X8 **Piggott** Arkansas, C USA
83 L21 **Piggs Peak** NW Swaziland
Pigs, Bay of *see* Cochinos, Bahía de
61 A23 **Pigüé** Buenos Aires, E Argentina
41 O12 **Piguícas** ▲ C Mexico
193 W15 **Piha Passage** *passage* S Tonga
Pihkva Järv *see* Pskov, Lake
93 N18 **Pihlajavesi** ◎ SE Finland
93 J18 **Pihlava** Länsi-Soumi, SW Finland
93 L16 **Pihtipudas** Länsi-Soumi, C Finland
40 L14 **Pihuamo** Jalisco, SW Mexico
189 U11 **Piis Moen** *var.* Pis. *atoll* Chuuk Islands, C Micronesia
41 U17 **Pijijiapán** Chiapas, SE Mexico
98 G12 **Pijnacker** Zuid-Holland, W Netherlands
42 H5 **Pijol, Pico** ▲ NW Honduras
Pikaar *see* Bikar Atoll
124 I13 **Pikalevo** Leningradskaya Oblast', NW Russian Federation
188 M15 **Pikelot** *island* Caroline Islands, C Micronesia
30 M5 **Pike River** ≈ Wisconsin, N USA
37 T5 **Pikes Peak** ▲ Colorado, C USA
21 P6 **Pikeville** Kentucky, S USA
20 L9 **Pikeville** Tennessee, S USA
Pikinni *see* Bikini Atoll
79 H18 **Pikounda** La Sangha, C Congo
110 G9 **Piła** *Ger.* Schneidemühl. Wielkopolskie, C Poland
62 N6 **Pilagá, Riacho** ≈ NE Argentina
61 D20 **Pilar** Buenos Aires, E Argentina
62 N7 **Pilar** *var.* Villa del Pilar. Ñeembucú, S Paraguay
62 N6 **Pilcomayo, Rio** ≈ C South America
147 R12 **Pildon** *Rus.* Pil'don. C Tajikistan
Piles *see* Pylés
Pilgram *see* Pelhřimov
152 L10 **Pīlībhīt** Uttar Pradesh, N India
110 M13 **Pilica** ≈ C Poland
115 G16 **Pílio** ▲▲ C Greece
111 J22 **Pilisvörösvár** Pest, N Hungary
65 G15 **Pillar Bay** *bay* Ascension Island, C Atlantic Ocean
183 P17 **Pillar, Cape** *headland* Tasmania, SE Australia
Pillau *see* Baltiysk
183 R5 **Pilliga** New South Wales, SE Australia
44 H8 **Pilón** Granma, E Cuba
Pilos *see* Pýlos
9 W17 **Pilot Mound** Manitoba, S Canada
21 S8 **Pilot Mountain** North Carolina, SE USA
39 O14 **Pilot Point** Alaska, USA
25 T5 **Pilot Point** Texas, SW USA
32 K11 **Pilot Rock** Oregon, NW USA
38 M11 **Pilot Station** Alaska, USA
Pilsen *see* Plzeň
111 K18 **Pilsko** ▲ N Slovakia
Pilten *see* Piltene
118 D8 **Piltene** *Ger.* Pilten. Ventspils, W Latvia
111 M16 **Pilzno** Podkarpackie, SE Poland
Pilzno *see* Plzeň
37 N14 **Pima** Arizona, SW USA
58 H13 **Pimenta** Pará, N Brazil

◆ Country
● Country Capital
◇ Dependent Territory
○ Dependent Territory Capital
◐ Administrative Regions
✈ International Airport
▲ Mountain
▲▲ Mountain Range
Volcano
≈ River
◎ Lake
▣ Reservoir

59 F16 **Pimenta Bueno** Rondônia, W Brazil
56 B11 **Pimentel** Lambayeque, W Peru
105 S6 **Pina** Aragón, NE Spain
119 I20 **Pina** ≈ SW Belarus
40 E2 **Pinacate, Sierra del** ▲ NW Mexico
63 H22 **Pináculo, Cerro** ▲ S Argentina
191 X11 **Pinaki** *atoll* Îles Tuamotu, E French Polynesia
37 N15 **Pinaleno Mountains** ⛰ Arizona, SW USA
171 P4 **Pinamalayan** Mindoro, N Philippines
169 Q10 **Pinang** Borneo, C Indonesia
168 J7 **Pinang** *var.* Penang. ⬖ *state* Peninsular Malaysia
Pinang *see* George Town
Pinang *see* Pinang, Pulau, Peninsular Malaysia
168 J7 **Pinang, Pulau** *var.* Penang, Pinang; *prev.* Prince of Wales Island. *island* Peninsular Malaysia
44 B5 **Pinar del Río** Pinar del Río, W Cuba
114 N11 **Pınarhisar** Kırklareli, NW Turkey
171 O3 **Pinatubo, Mount** 🌋 Luzon, N Philippines
9 Y16 **Pinawa** Manitoba, S Canada
9 Q17 **Pincher Creek** Alberta, SW Canada
30 L16 **Pinckneyville** Illinois, N USA
Pincota *see* Pâncota
111 L15 **Pińczów** Świętokrzyskie, C Poland
149 U7 **Pind Dādan Khān** Punjab, E Pakistan
Píndhos/Píndhos Óros *see* Píndos
149 V8 **Pindi Bhattiān** Punjab, E Pakistan
149 U6 **Pindi Gheb** Punjab, E Pakistan
115 D15 **Píndos** *var.* Píndhos Óros, *Eng.* Pindus Mountains; *prev.* Píndhos. ⛰ C Greece
Pindus Mountains *see* Píndos
18 J16 **Pine Barrens** *physical region* New Jersey, NE USA
27 V12 **Pine Bluff** Arkansas, C USA
23 X11 **Pine Castle** Florida, SE USA
29 V7 **Pine City** Minnesota, N USA
181 P2 **Pine Creek** Northern Territory, N Australia
35 V4 **Pine Creek** ≈ Nevada, W USA
18 F13 **Pine Creek** ≈ Pennsylvania, NE USA
27 Q13 **Pine Creek Lake** ⊠ Oklahoma, C USA
33 T15 **Pinedale** Wyoming, C USA
9 X15 **Pine Dock** Manitoba, S Canada
9 Y16 **Pine Falls** Manitoba, S Canada
35 R10 **Pine Flat Lake** ⊠ California, W USA
125 N8 **Pinega** Arkhangel'skaya Oblast', NW Russian Federation
125 N8 **Pinega** ≈ NW Russian Federation
15 N12 **Pine Hill** Québec, SE Canada
9 T12 **Pinehouse Lake** ◎ Saskatchewan, C Canada
21 T10 **Pinehurst** North Carolina, SE USA
115 D19 **Pineiós** ≈ S Greece
115 E16 **Pineiós** *var.* Piniós; *anc.* Peneius. ≈ C Greece
29 W10 **Pine Island** Minnesota, N USA
23 V15 **Pine Island** *island* Florida, SE USA
194 K10 **Pine Island Glacier** *glacier* Antarctica
25 X9 **Pineland** Texas, SW USA
23 V13 **Pinellas Park** Florida, SE USA
10 M13 **Pine Pass** *pass* British Columbia, W Canada
8 J10 **Pine Point** Northwest Territories, W Canada
28 K12 **Pine Ridge** South Dakota, N USA
29 U6 **Pine River** Minnesota, N USA
31 Q8 **Pine River** ≈ Michigan, N USA
30 M4 **Pine River** ≈ Wisconsin, N USA
106 A8 **Pinerolo** Piemonte, NE Italy
115 I15 **Pínes, Akrotírio** *var.* Akrotírio Pínnes. *headland* N Greece
25 W6 **Pines, Lake O' the** ⊠ Texas, SW USA
Pines, The Isle of the *see* Juventud, Isla de la
Pine Tree State *see* Maine
21 N7 **Pineville** Kentucky, S USA
22 H7 **Pineville** Louisiana, S USA
27 R8 **Pineville** Missouri, C USA
21 R10 **Pineville** North Carolina, SE USA
21 Q6 **Pineville** West Virginia, NE USA
33 V8 **Piney Buttes** *physical region* Montana, NW USA
160 H14 **Pingbian** *var.* Pingbian Miaozu Zizhixian, Yuping. Yunnan, SW China
Pingbian Miaozu Zizhixian *see* Pingbian
157 S9 **Pingdingshan** Henan, C China
161 R4 **Pingdu** Shandong, E China
189 W16 **Pingelap Atoll** *atoll* Caroline Islands, E Micronesia
160 K14 **Pingguo** *var.* Matou. Guangxi Zhuangzu Zizhiqu, S China
161 Q13 **Pinghe** *var.* Xiaoxi. Fujian, SE China
P'ing-hsiang *see* Pingxiang
161 N10 **Pingjiang** Hunan, S China
Pingkiang *see* Harbin
160 L8 **Pingli** Shaanxi, C China
159 W10 **Pingliang** *var.* Kongtong, P'ing-liang. Gansu, C China
P'ing-liang *see* Pingliang
159 W8 **Pingluo** Ningxia, N China
Pingma *see* Tiandong
167 O7 **Ping, Mae Nam** ≈ W Thailand
161 Q1 **Pingquan** Hebei, E China
29 P5 **Pingree** North Dakota, N USA
163 W9 **Pingshan** Jilin, NE China
Pingsiang *see* Pingxiang
161 S14 **P'ingtung** *Jap.* Heitō. S Taiwan
160 I8 **Pingwu** *var.* Long'an. Sichuan, C China
160 J15 **Pingxiang** Guangxi Zhuangzu Zizhiqu, S China
161 O11 **Pingxiang** *var.* P'ing-hsiang; *prev.* Pingsiang. Jiangxi, S China
161 S11 **Pingyang** *var.* Kunyang. Zhejiang, SE China
161 P5 **Pingyi** Shandong, E China
161 P5 **Pingyin** Shandong, E China
60 H13 **Pinhalzinho** Santa Catarina, S Brazil
60 I12 **Pinhão** Paraná, S Brazil
61 H17 **Pinheiro Machado** Rio Grande do Sul, S Brazil
104 I7 **Pinhel** Guarda, N Portugal
Piniós *see* Pineiós
168 I11 **Pini, Pulau** *island* Kepulauan Batu, W Indonesia
109 Y7 **Pinka** ≈ SE Austria
109 X7 **Pinkafeld** Burgenland, SE Austria
Pinkiang *see* Harbin
10 M12 **Pink Mountain** British Columbia, W Canada
166 M3 **Pinlebu** Sagaing, N Myanmar (Burma)
38 J12 **Pinnacle Island** *island* Alaska, USA
180 I12 **Pinnacles, The** *tourist site* Western Australia
182 K10 **Pinnaroo** South Australia
Pinne *see* Pniewy
100 I9 **Pinneberg** Schleswig-Holstein, N Germany
115 I15 **Pínnes, Akrotírio** *cape* N Greece
Pínnes, Akrotírio *see* Pínes, Akrotírio
Pinos, Isla de *see* Juventud, Isla de la
35 R14 **Pinos, Mount** ▲ California, W USA
105 R12 **Pinoso** País Valenciano, E Spain
105 N14 **Pinos-Puente** Andalucía, S Spain
41 Q17 **Pinotepa Nacional** *var.* Santiago Pinotepa Nacional. Oaxaca, SE Mexico
114 F13 **Pínovo** ▲ N Greece
187 R17 **Pins, Île des** *var.* Kunyé. *island* E New Caledonia
119 I20 **Pinsk** *Pol.* Pińsk. Brestskaya Voblasts', SW Belarus
14 D18 **Pins, Pointe aux** *headland* Ontario, S Canada
57 B16 **Pinta, Isla** *var.* Abingdon. *island* Galapagos Islands, Ecuador, E Pacific Ocean
125 Q12 **Pinyug** Kirovskaya Oblast', NW Russian Federation
57 B17 **Pinzón, Isla** *var.* Duncan Island. *island* Galapagos Islands, Ecuador, E Pacific Ocean
35 Y8 **Pioche** Nevada, W USA
106 F13 **Piombino** Toscana, C Italy
0 C9 **Pioneer Fracture Zone** *tectonic feature* NE Pacific Ocean
122 L5 **Pioner, Ostrov** *island* Severnaya Zemlya, N Russian Federation
118 A13 **Pionerskiy** *Ger.* Neukuhren. Kaliningradskaya Oblast', W Russian Federation
110 N13 **Pionki** Mazowieckie, C Poland
184 L9 **Piopio** Waikato, North Island, New Zealand
110 K13 **Piotrków Trybunalski** *Ger.* Petrikau, *Rus.* Petrokov. Lodzkie, C Poland
152 F12 **Pīpār Road** Rājasthān, N India
115 I16 **Pipéri** *island* Vóreioi Sporádes, Greece, Aegean Sea
29 S10 **Pipestone** Minnesota, N USA
12 C9 **Pipestone** ≈ Ontario, C Canada
61 E21 **Pipinas** Buenos Aires, E Argentina
149 T7 **Piplān** *prev.* Liaqatabad. Punjab, E Pakistan
15 R5 **Pipmuacan, Réservoir** ⊠ Québec, SE Canada
Piqan *see* Shanshan
31 R13 **Piqua** Ohio, N USA
105 P5 **Piqueras, Puerto de** *pass* N Spain
60 H11 **Piquiri, Rio** ≈ S Brazil
60 L9 **Piracicaba** São Paulo, S Brazil
Piraeus/Piraiévs *see* Peiraías
60 K10 **Piraju** São Paulo, S Brazil
60 K9 **Pirajuí** São Paulo, S Brazil
63 G21 **Pirámide, Cerro** ▲ S Chile
Piramiva *see* Pyramíva
109 R13 **Piran** *It.* Pirano. SW Slovenia
62 N6 **Piranė** Formosa, N Argentina
59 J18 **Piranhas** Goiás, S Brazil
Pirano *see* Piran
142 I4 **Pīrānshahr** Āžarbāyjān-e Gharbī, NW Iran
59 M19 **Pirapora** Minas Gerais, NE Brazil
60 I9 **Pirapòzinho** São Paulo, S Brazil
61 G19 **Piraraja** Lavalleja, S Uruguay
60 L9 **Pirassununga** São Paulo, S Brazil
45 V6 **Pirata, Monte** ▲ E Puerto Rico
60 I13 **Piratuba** Santa Catarina, S Brazil
114 I9 **Pirdop** *prev.* Strednogorie. Sofiya, W Bulgaria
191 P7 **Pirea** Tahiti, W French Polynesia
59 K18 **Pirenópolis** Goiás, S Brazil
153 S13 **Pirganj** Rajshahi, NW Bangladesh
Pirgi *see* Pyrgí
Pírgos *see* Pýrgos
61 F20 **Piriápolis** Maldonado, S Uruguay
114 G11 **Pirin** ⛰ SW Bulgaria
Pirineos *see* Pyrenees
58 N13 **Piripiri** Piauí, E Brazil
118 H4 **Pirita** *var.* Pirita Jõgi. ≈ NW Estonia
Pirita Jõgi *see* Pirita
54 J6 **Píritu** Portuguesa, N Venezuela
93 L18 **Pirkkala** Länsi-Suomi, W Finland
101 F20 **Pirmasens** Rheinland-Pfalz, SW Germany
101 P16 **Pirna** Sachsen, E Germany
Piroe *see* Piru
113 Q15 **Pirot** Serbia, SE Serbia
152 H6 **Pīr Panjāl Range** ⛰ NE India
43 W16 **Pirre, Cerro** ▲ SE Panama
137 Y11 **Pirsaat** *Rus.* Pirsagat. ≈ E Azerbaijan
Pirsagat *see* Pirsaat
143 V11 **Pīr Shūrān, Selseleh-ye** ⛰ SE Iran
92 M12 **Pirttikoski** Lappi, N Finland
Pirttikylä *see* Pörtom
171 R13 **Piru** *prev.* Piroe. Pulau Seram, E Indonesia
Piryatin *see* Pyryatyn
Pis *see* Piis Moen
106 F11 **Pisa** *var.* Pisae. Toscana, C Italy
Pisae *see* Pisa
189 V12 **Pisar** *atoll* Chuuk Islands, C Micronesia
Pisaurum *see* Pesaro
14 M10 **Piscatosine, Lac** ◎ Québec, SE Canada
109 W7 **Pischeldorf** Steiermark, SE Austria
Pischk *see* Simeria
107 L19 **Pisciotta** Campania, S Italy
57 E16 **Pisco** Ica, SW Peru
116 G9 **Pişcolt** *Hung.* Piskolt. Satu Mare, NW Romania
57 E16 **Pisco, Río** ≈ E Peru
111 C18 **Písek** Budějovický Kraj, S Czech Republic
31 R14 **Pisgah** Ohio, N USA
Pisha *see* Ningnan
158 F9 **Pishan** *var.* Guma. Xinjiang Uygur Zizhiqu, NW China
117 N8 **Pishchanka** Vinnyts'ka Oblast', C Ukraine
113 K21 **Pishë** Fier, SW Albania
143 X14 **Pīshīn** Sīstān va Balūchestān, SE Iran
149 O9 **Pishīn** North-West Frontier Province, NW Pakistan
149 N11 **Pishin Lora** *var.* Psein Lora, *Pash.* Pseyn Bowr. ≈ SW Pakistan
Pishma *see* Pizhma
Pishpek *see* Bishkek
171 O14 **Pising** Pulau Kabaena, C Indonesia
Pisino *see* Pazin
Piski *see* Simeria
Piskolt *see* Pişcolt
147 Q9 **Piskom** *Rus.* Pskem. ≈ E Uzbekistan
Piskom Tizmasi *see* Pskemskiy Khrebet
35 P13 **Pismo Beach** California, W USA
77 P12 **Pissila** C Burkina
62 H8 **Pissis, Monte** ▲ N Argentina
41 X12 **Piste** Yucatán, E Mexico
107 O18 **Pisticci** Basilicata, S Italy
106 F11 **Pistoia** *anc.* Pistoria, Pistoriæ. Toscana, C Italy
32 E15 **Pistol River** Oregon, NW USA
Pistoria/Pistoriæ *see* Pistoia
15 U5 **Pistuacanis** ≈ Québec, SE Canada
Pistyan *see* Piešt'any
104 M5 **Pisuerga** ≈ N Spain
110 N8 **Pisz** *Ger.* Johannisburg. Warmińsko-Mazurskie, NE Poland
76 I13 **Pita** NW Guinea
54 D12 **Pitalito** Huila, S Colombia
60 I11 **Pitanga** Paraná, S Brazil
182 M9 **Pitarpunga Lake** *salt lake* New South Wales, SE Australia
193 P10 **Pitcairn Island** *island* S Pitcairn Islands
193 P10 **Pitcairn Islands** ◇ *UK dependent territory* C Pacific Ocean
93 J14 **Piteå** Norrbotten, N Sweden
92 I13 **Piteälven** ≈ N Sweden
116 I13 **Piteşti** Argeş, S Romania
Pithagorio *see* Pythagóreio
180 I12 **Pithara** Western Australia
103 N6 **Pithiviers** Loiret, C France
152 L9 **Pithorāgarh** Uttaranchal, N India
188 B16 **Piti** W Guam
106 G13 **Pitigliano** Toscana, C Italy
40 F3 **Pitiquito** Sonora, NW Mexico
Pitkäranta *see* Pitkyaranta
38 M11 **Pitkas Point** Alaska, USA
124 H11 **Pitkyaranta** *Fin.* Pitkäranta. Respublika Kareliya, NW Russian Federation
96 J10 **Pitlochry** C Scotland, UK
18 I16 **Pitman** New Jersey, NE USA
146 I9 **Pitnak** *var.* Drujba, *Rus.* Druzhba. Xorazm Viloyati, W Uzbekistan
112 G8 **Pitomača** Virovitica-Podravina, NE Croatia
35 O2 **Pit River** ≈ California, W USA
63 G15 **Pitrufquén** Araucanía, S Chile
Pitsanulok *see* Phitsanulok
Pitschen *see* Byczyna
Pitsunda *see* Bichvint'a
109 X6 **Pitten** ≈ E Austria
10 J14 **Pitt Island** *island* British Columbia, W Canada
Pitt Island *see* Makin
22 M3 **Pittsboro** Mississippi, S USA
21 T9 **Pittsboro** North Carolina, SE USA
27 R7 **Pittsburg** Kansas, C USA
25 W6 **Pittsburg** Texas, SW USA
18 B14 **Pittsburgh** Pennsylvania, NE USA
30 J14 **Pittsfield** Illinois, N USA
19 R6 **Pittsfield** Maine, NE USA
18 L11 **Pittsfield** Massachusetts, NE USA
183 U3 **Pittsworth** Queensland, E Australia
62 I8 **Pituil** La Rioja, NW Argentina
56 A10 **Piura** Piura, NW Peru
56 A9 **Piura** *off.* Departamento de Piura. ⬖ *department* NW Peru
Piura, Departamento de *see* Piura
35 S13 **Piute Peak** ▲ California, W USA
113 J15 **Piva** ≈ NW Montenegro
117 V5 **Pivdenne** Kharkivs'ka Oblast', E Ukraine
117 P8 **Pivdennyy Buh** *Rus.* Yuzhnyy Bug. ≈ S Ukraine
54 F5 **Pivijay** Magdalena, N Colombia
109 T13 **Pivka** *prev.* Šent Peter, *Ger.* Sankt Peter, *It.* San Pietro del Carso. SW Slovenia
117 U13 **Pivnichno-Kryms'kyy Kanal** *canal* S Ukraine
113 J15 **Pivsko Jezero** ◎ NW Montenegro
111 M18 **Piwniczna** Małopolskie, S Poland
35 R12 **Pixley** California, W USA
125 Q15 **Pizhma** *var.* Pishma. ≈ NW Russian Federation
13 U13 **Placentia** Newfoundland, Newfoundland and Labrador, SE Canada
Placentia *see* Piacenza
13 U13 **Placentia Bay** *inlet* Newfoundland, Newfoundland and Labrador, SE Canada
171 P5 **Placer** Masbate, N Philippines
35 P7 **Placerville** California, W USA
44 F5 **Placetas** Villa Clara, C Cuba
113 Q18 **Plačkovica** ⛰ E Macedonia
36 L2 **Plain City** Utah, W USA
22 G4 **Plain Dealing** Louisiana, S USA
31 O14 **Plainfield** Indiana, N USA
18 K14 **Plainfield** New Jersey, NE USA
33 O8 **Plains** Montana, NW USA
24 L6 **Plains** Texas, SW USA
29 X10 **Plainview** Minnesota, N USA
29 Q13 **Plainview** Nebraska, C USA
25 N4 **Plainview** Texas, SW USA
26 K4 **Plainville** Kansas, C USA
115 I22 **Pláka** *var.* Mílos. Mílos, Kykládes, Greece, Aegean Sea
115 J15 **Pláka, Ákrotírio** *headland* Kríti, Greece, E Mediterranean Sea
115 J15 **Pláka, Akrotírio** *headland* Límnos, E Greece
113 N19 **Plakenska Planina** ⛰ SW Macedonia
44 K5 **Plana Cays** *islets* SE Bahamas
105 S12 **Plana, Isla** *var.* Nueva Tabarca. *island* E Spain
59 L18 **Planaltina** Goiás, S Brazil
83 O14 **Planalto Moçambicano** *plateau* N Mozambique
112 N10 **Plandište** Vojvodina, NE Serbia
100 N13 **Plane** ≈ NE Germany
54 E6 **Planeta Rica** Córdoba, NW Colombia
29 P11 **Plankinton** South Dakota, N USA
30 M11 **Plano** Illinois, N USA
25 U6 **Plano** Texas, SW USA
23 W12 **Plant City** Florida, SE USA
22 J9 **Plaquemine** Louisiana, S USA
104 K9 **Plasencia** Extremadura, W Spain
110 P7 **Plaska** Podlaskie, NE Poland
112 C10 **Plaški** Karlovac, C Croatia
113 N19 **Plasnica** SW FYR Macedonia
13 N14 **Plaster Rock** New Brunswick, SE Canada
107 J24 **Platani** *anc.* Halycus. ≈ Sicilia, Italy, C Mediterranean Sea
115 G17 **Plataniá** Thessalía, C Greece
115 G24 **Plátanos** Kríti, Greece, E Mediterranean Sea
65 H18 **Plata, Río de la** *var.* River Plate. *estuary* Argentina/Uruguay
77 V15 **Plateau** ⬖ *state* C Nigeria
79 G19 **Plateaux** *var.* Région des Plateaux. ⬖ *province* C Congo
Plateaux, Région des *see* Plateaux
92 P1 **Platen, Kapp** *headland* NE Svalbard
Plate, River *see* Plata, Río de la
99 G22 **Plate Taille, Lac de la** *var.* L'Eau d'Heure. ◎ SE Belgium
Plathe *see* Płoty
39 N13 **Platinum** Alaska, USA
54 F5 **Plato** Magdalena, N Colombia
29 O11 **Platte** South Dakota, N USA
27 R3 **Platte City** Missouri, C USA
Plattensee *see* Balaton
27 R3 **Platte River** ≈ Iowa/Missouri, USA
29 Q15 **Platte River** ≈ Nebraska, C USA
37 T3 **Platteville** Colorado, C USA
30 K9 **Platteville** Wisconsin, N USA
101 N21 **Plattling** Bayern, SE Germany
27 R3 **Plattsburg** Missouri, C USA
18 L6 **Plattsburgh** New York, NE USA
29 S15 **Plattsmouth** Nebraska, C USA
101 M17 **Plauen** *var.* Plauen im Vogtland. Sachsen, E Germany
Plauen im Vogtland *see* Plauen
100 M10 **Plauer See** ◎ NE Germany
113 L16 **Plav** E Montenegro
118 I10 **Pļaviņas** *Ger.* Stockmannshof. Aizkraukle, S Latvia
126 K5 **Plavsk** Tul'skaya Oblast', W Russian Federation
41 Z12 **Playa del Carmen** Quintana Roo, E Mexico
40 J12 **Playa Los Corchos** Nayarit, SW Mexico
37 P16 **Playas Lake** ◎ New Mexico, SW USA
41 S15 **Playa Vicenté** Veracruz-Llave, SE Mexico
167 U11 **Plây Cu** *var.* Pleiku. Gia Lai, C Vietnam
28 L3 **Plaza** North Dakota, N USA
63 I15 **Plaza Huincul** Neuquén, C Argentina
36 L3 **Pleasant Grove** Utah, W USA
29 V14 **Pleasant Hill** Iowa, C USA
27 R4 **Pleasant Hill** Missouri, C USA
Pleasant Island *see* Nauru
36 K13 **Pleasant, Lake** ⊠ Arizona, SW USA
19 P8 **Pleasant Mountain** ▲ Maine, NE USA
27 R5 **Pleasanton** Kansas, C USA
25 R12 **Pleasanton** Texas, SW USA
185 G20 **Pleasant Point** Canterbury, South Island, New Zealand
19 R5 **Pleasant River** ≈ Maine, NE USA
18 J17 **Pleasantville** New Jersey, NE USA
103 N12 **Pléaux** Cantal, C France
111 B19 **Plechý** *var.* Plöckenstein. ▲ Austria/Czech Republic
Pleebo *see* Plibo
Pleihari *see* Pelaihari
Pleiku *see* Plây Cu
101 M16 **Pleisse** ≈ E Germany
Plencia *see* Plentzia
184 O7 **Plenty, Bay of** *bay* North Island, New Zealand
33 Y6 **Plentywood** Montana, NW USA
105 O2 **Plentzia** *var.* Plencia. País Vasco, N Spain
102 H5 **Plérin** Côtes d'Armor, NW France
124 M10 **Plesetsk** Arkhangel'skaya Oblast', NW Russian Federation
Pleshchenitsy *see* Plyeshchanitsy
Pleskau *see* Pskov
Pleskauer See *see* Pskov, Lake
Pleskava *see* Pskov
112 E8 **Pleso International** ✈ (Zagreb) Zagreb, NW Croatia
Pless *see* Pszczyna
15 Q11 **Plessisville** Québec, SE Canada
110 H12 **Pleszew** Wielkopolskie, C Poland
12 L10 **Plétipi, Lac** ◎ Québec, SE Canada
101 F15 **Plettenberg** Nordrhein-Westfalen, W Germany
114 I8 **Pleven** *prev.* Plevna. Pleven, N Bulgaria
114 I8 **Pleven** ⬖ *province* N Bulgaria
Plevlja/Plevlje *see* Pljevlja
Plevna *see* Pleven
Plezzo *see* Bovec
Pliberk *see* Bleiburg
76 L17 **Plibo** *var.* Pleebo. SE Liberia
121 R11 **Pliny Trench** *undersea feature* C Mediterranean Sea
118 K13 **Plisa** *Rus.* Plissa. Vitsyebskaya Voblasts', N Belarus
Plissa *see* Plisa
112 D11 **Plitvica Selo** Lika-Senj, W Croatia
112 D11 **Plješevica** ⛰ C Croatia
113 K14 **Pljevlja** *prev.* Plevlja, Plevlje. N Montenegro
Ploça *see* Ploçë
Plocce *see* Ploče
113 K22 **Ploçë** *var.* Ploça. Vlorë, SW Albania
113 G15 **Ploče** *It.* Plocce; *prev.* Kardeljevo. Dubrovnik-Neretva, SE Croatia
110 K11 **Płock** *Ger.* Plozk. Mazowieckie, C Poland
109 Q10 **Plöcken Pass** *Ger.* Plöckenpass, *It.* Passo di Monte Croce Carnico. *pass* SW Austria
Plöckenpass *see* Plöcken Pass
Plöckenstein *see* Plechý
99 B19 **Ploegsteert** Hainaut, W Belgium
102 H6 **Ploërmel** Morbihan, NW France
Ploeşti *see* Ploieşti
116 K13 **Ploieşti** *prev.* Ploeşti. Prahova, SE Romania
115 L17 **Plomári** *prev.* Plomárion. Lésvos, E Greece
Plomárion *see* Plomári
103 O12 **Plomb du Cantal** ▲ C France
183 V6 **Plomer, Point** *headland* New South Wales, SE Australia
100 J8 **Plön** Schleswig-Holstein, N Germany
110 L11 **Płońsk** Mazowieckie, C Poland
119 J20 **Plotnitsa** *Rus.* Plotnitsa. Brestskaya Voblasts', SW Belarus
110 E8 **Płoty** *Ger.* Plathe. Zachodnio-pomorskie, NW Poland
102 G7 **Plouay** Morbihan, NW France
111 D15 **Ploučnice** *Ger.* Polzen. ≈ NE Czech Republic
114 I10 **Plovdiv** *prev.* Eumolpias; *anc.* Evmolpia, Philippopolis, *Lat.* Trimontium. Plovdiv, C Bulgaria
114 I11 **Plovdiv** ⬖ *province* C Bulgaria
30 L6 **Plover** Wisconsin, N USA
Plozk *see* Płock
27 U11 **Plumerville** Arkansas, C USA
19 P10 **Plum Island** *island* Massachusetts, NE USA
32 M9 **Plummer** Idaho, NW USA
83 J18 **Plumtree** Matabeleland South, SW Zimbabwe
118 D11 **Plungė** Telšiai, W Lithuania
113 J15 **Plužine** NW Montenegro
119 K14 **Plyeshchanitsy** *Rus.* Pleshchenitsy. Minskaya Voblasts', N Belarus
45 V10 **Plymouth** ○ (Montserrat) SW Montserrat
97 I24 **Plymouth** SW England, UK
31 O11 **Plymouth** Indiana, N USA
19 P12 **Plymouth** Massachusetts, NE USA
19 N8 **Plymouth** New Hampshire, NE USA
21 X9 **Plymouth** North Carolina, SE USA
30 M8 **Plymouth** Wisconsin, N USA
97 J20 **Plynlimon** ▲ C Wales, UK
124 G14 **Plyussa** Pskovskaya Oblast', W Russian Federation
111 B17 **Plzeň** *Ger.* Pilsen, *Pol.* Pilzno. Plzeňský Kraj, W Czech Republic
111 B17 **Plzeňský Kraj** ⬖ *region* W Czech Republic
110 F11 **Pniewy** *Ger.* Pinne. Wielkolpolskie, W Poland
77 P13 **Pô** S Burkina
106 D8 **Po** ≈ N Italy
42 M13 **Poás, Volcán** 🌋 NW Costa Rica
77 S16 **Pobè** S Benin
123 S8 **Pobeda, Gora** ▲ NE Russian Federation
Pobeda Peak *see* Pobedy, Pik/Tomur Feng
147 Z7 **Pobedy, Pik** *Chin.* Tomür Feng. ▲ China/Kyrgyzstan *see also* Tomür Feng
Pobedy, Pik *see* Tomur Feng
110 H11 **Pobiedziska** *Ger.* Pudewitz. Wielkolpolskie, C Poland
Po, Bocche del *see* Po, Foci del
27 W9 **Pocahontas** Arkansas, C USA
29 U12 **Pocahontas** Iowa, C USA
33 Q15 **Pocatello** Idaho, NW USA
167 S13 **Pochentong** ✈ (Phnum Penh) Phnum Penh, S Cambodia
126 I6 **Pochep** Bryanskaya Oblast', W Russian Federation
126 H4 **Pochinok** Smolenskaya Oblast', W Russian Federation
41 R17 **Pochutla** *var.* San Pedro Pochutla. Oaxaca, SE Mexico
62 I6 **Pocitos, Salar** *var.* Salar Quiróm. *salt lake* NW Argentina
101 O22 **Pocking** Bayern, SE Germany
186 I10 **Pocklington Reef** *reef* SE Papua New Guinea
59 P15 **Poço da Cruz, Açude** ⊠ E Brazil
27 R11 **Pocola** Oklahoma, C USA
21 Y5 **Pocomoke City** Maryland, NE USA
59 L21 **Poços de Caldas** Minas Gerais, NE Brazil
124 H14 **Podberez'ye** Novgorodskaya Oblast', NW Russian Federation
Podbrodzie *see* Pabradė
125 U8 **Podcher'ye** Respublika Komi, NW Russian Federation
111 E16 **Poděbrady** *Ger.* Podiebrad. Středočeský Kraj, C Czech Republic
126 L9 **Podgorenskiy** Voronezhskaya Oblast', W Russian Federation
113 J17 **Podgorica** *prev.* Titograd. ● S Montenegro
113 K17 **Podgorica** ✈ S Montenegro
109 T13 **Podgrad** SW Slovenia
Podiebrad *see* Poděbrady
116 M5 **Podil's'ka Vysochina** *plateau* W Ukraine
Podium Anicensis *see* le Puy
122 L11 **Podkamennaya Tunguska** *Eng.* Stony Tunguska. ≈ C Russian Federation
111 N17 **Podkarpackie** ⬖ *province* SW Poland
Pod Klošter *see* Arnoldstein
110 P9 **Podlaskie** ⬖ *province* Mazowieckie, C Poland
127 Q8 **Podlesnoye** Saratovskaya Oblast', W Russian Federation
126 K4 **Podol'sk** Moskovskaya Oblast', W Russian Federation
76 H10 **Podor** N Senegal
125 P12 **Podosinovets** Kirovskaya Oblast', NW Russian Federation
124 I12 **Podporozh'ye** Leningradskaya Oblast', NW Russian Federation
Podravska Slatina *see* Slatina
112 J13 **Podromanlja** ⬖ Republika Srpska, SE Bosnia and Herzegovina
Podsvil'ye *see* Padsvillye
116 L9 **Podu Iloaiei** *prev.* Podul Iloaiei. Iaşi, NE Romania
113 N15 **Podujevo** Kosovo, S Serbia
Podul Iloaiei *see* Podu Iloaiei
Podunajská Rovina *see* Little Alföld
124 M12 **Podyuga** Arkhangel'skaya Oblast', NW Russian Federation
56 A9 **Poechos, Embalse** ◎ NW Peru
55 W10 **Poeketi** Sipaliwini, E Surinam
100 L8 **Poel** *island* N Germany
83 M20 **Poelela, Lagoa** ◎ S Mozambique
Poerwodadi *see* Purwodadi
Poerwokerto *see* Purwokerto
Poerworedjo *see* Purworejo
Poetovio *see* Ptuj
83 E23 **Pofadder** Northern Cape, W South Africa
106 I9 **Po, Foci del** *var.* Bocche del Po. ≈ NE Italy
116 E12 **Pogăniş** ≈ W Romania
Pogegen *see* Pagėgiai
106 G12 **Poggibonsi** Toscana, C Italy
107 I14 **Poggio Mirteto** Lazio, C Italy
109 V4 **Pöggstall** Niederösterreich, N Austria
116 L13 **Pogoanele** Buzău, SE Romania
Pogónion *see* Delvináki
113 M21 **Pogradec** *var.* Pogradeci. Korçë, SE Albania
Pogradeci *see* Pogradec
123 S15 **Pogranichnyy** Primorskiy Kray, SE Russian Federation
38 M16 **Pogromni Volcano** ▲ Unimak Island, Alaska, USA
163 Z15 **P'ohang** *Jap.* Hokō. E South Korea
15 T9 **Pohénégamook, Lac** ◎ Québec, SE Canada
93 L20 **Pohja** *Swe.* Pojo. Etelä-Suomi, SW Finland
Pohjanlahti *see* Bothnia, Gulf of
189 U16 **Pohnpei** ⬖ *state* E Micronesia
189 O12 **Pohnpei** ✈ Pohnpei, E Micronesia
189 O12 **Pohnpei** *prev.* Ponape Ascension Island. *island* E Micronesia
111 F19 **Pohořelice** *Ger.* Pohrlitz. Jihomoravský Kraj, SE Czech Republic
109 V10 **Pohorje** *Ger.* Bacher. ⛰ N Slovenia
117 N6 **Pohrebyshche** Vinnyts'ka Oblast', C Ukraine
Pohrlitz *see* Pohořelice
161 P9 **Po Hu** ⊠ E China
116 G15 **Poiana Mare** Dolj, S Romania
Poictiers *see* Poitiers
127 N6 **Poim** Penzenskaya Oblast', W Russian Federation
159 N15 **Poindo** Xigzang Zizhiqu, W China
195 Y13 **Poinsett, Cape** *cape* Antarctica
29 R9 **Poinsett, Lake** ◎ South Dakota, N USA
22 I10 **Point Au Fer Island** *island* Louisiana, S USA
39 X14 **Point Baker** Prince of Wales Island, Alaska, USA
25 U13 **Point Comfort** Texas, SW USA
Point de Galle *see* Galle
44 K10 **Pointe à Gravois** *headland* SW Haiti
22 L10 **Pointe a la Hache** Louisiana, S USA
45 Y6 **Pointe-à-Pitre** Grande Terre, C Guadeloupe

◆ Country
● Country Capital
◇ Dependent Territory
○ Dependent Territory Capital
⬖ Administrative Regions
✈ International Airport
▲ Mountain
⛰ Mountain Range
🌋 Volcano
≈ River
◎ Lake
⊠ Reservoir

15 *U7* **Pointe-au-Père** Québec, SE Canada
15 *V5* **Pointe-aux-Anglais** Québec, SE Canada
45 *T10* **Pointe Du Cap** *headland* N Saint Lucia
79 *E21* **Pointe-Noire** Le Kouilou, S Congo
45 *X6* **Pointe Noire** Basse Terre, W Guadeloupe
79 *E21* **Pointe-Noire** ✈ Le Kouilou, S Congo
45 *U15* **Point Fortin** Trinidad, Trinidad and Tobago
38 *M6* **Point Hope** Alaska, USA
39 *N5* **Point Lay** Alaska, USA
18 *B16* **Point Marion** Pennsylvania, NE USA
18 *K16* **Point Pleasant** New Jersey, NE USA
21 *P4* **Point Pleasant** West Virginia, NE USA
45 *R14* **Point Salines** ✈ (St. George's) SW Grenada
102 *L9* **Poitiers** ***prev.*** Poictiers; ***anc.*** Limonum. Vienne, W France
102 *K9* **Poitou** *cultural region* W France
102 *K10* **Poitou-Charentes** ⬖ *region* W France
103 *N3* **Poix-de-Picardie** Somme, N France
Pojo *see* Pohja
37 *S10* **Pojoaque** New Mexico, SW USA
152 *E11* **Pokaran** Rājasthān, NW India
183 *R4* **Pokataroo** New South Wales, SE Australia
119 *P18* **Pokats'** ***Rus.*** Pokot'. 〜 SE Belarus
29 *V5* **Pokegama Lake** ◎ Minnesota, N USA
184 *L6* **Pokeno** Waikato, North Island, New Zealand
153 *O11* **Pokharā** Western, C Nepal
127 *T6* **Pokhvistnevo** Samarskaya Oblast', W Russian Federation
55 *W10* **Pokigron** Sipaliwini, C Suriname
92 *L10* **Pokka** ***Lapp.*** Bohkká. Lappi, N Finland
79 *N16* **Poko** Orientale, NE Dem. Rep. Congo
Pokot' *see* Pokats'
Po-ko-to Shan *see* Bogda Shan
147 *S7* **Pokrovka** Talasskaya Oblast', NW Kyrgyzstan
Pokrovka *see* Kyzyl-Suu
117 *V8* **Pokrovs'ke** ***Rus.*** Pokrovskoye. Dnipropetrovs'ka Oblast', E Ukraine
Pokrovskoye *see* Pokrovs'ke
Pola *see* Pula
37 *N10* **Polacca** Arizona, SW USA
104 *L2* **Pola de Laviana** Asturias, N Spain
104 *K2* **Pola de Lena** Asturias, N Spain
104 *L2* **Pola de Siero** Asturias, N Spain
191 *Y3* **Poland** Kiritimati, E Kiribati
110 *H12* **Poland** ***off.*** Republic of Poland, ***var.*** Polish Republic, ***Pol.*** Polska, Rzeczpospolita Polska; ***prev. Pol.*** Polska Rzeczpospolita Ludowa, The Polish People's Republic. ◆ *republic* C Europe
Poland, Republic of *see* Poland
Polangen *see* Palanga
110 *G7* **Polanów** ***Ger.*** Pollnow. Zachodnio-pomorskie, NW Poland
136 *H13* **Polatlı** Ankara, C Turkey
118 *L12* **Polatsk** ***Rus.*** Polotsk. Vitsyebskaya Voblasts', N Belarus
110 *F8* **Połczyn-Zdrój** ***Ger.*** Bad Polzin. Zachodnio-pomorskie, NW Poland
149 *R5* **Pol-e-'Alam** Lowgar, E Afghanistan
Polekhatum *see* Pulhatyn
149 *Q3* **Pol-e Khomrī** ***var.*** Pul-i-Khumri. Baghlān, NE Afghanistan
197 *S10* **Pole Plain** *undersea feature* Arctic Ocean
143 *P5* **Pol-e Safīd** ***var.*** Pol-e-Sefid, Pul-i-Sefid. Māzandarān, N Iran
Pol-e-Sefid *see* Pol-e Safīd
118 *B13* **Polessk** ***Ger.*** Labiau. Kaliningradskaya Oblast', W Russian Federation
Polesskoye *see* Polis'ke
171 *N13* **Polewali** Sulawesi, C Indonesia
114 *G11* **Polezhan** ▲ SW Bulgaria
78 *F13* **Poli** Nord, N Cameroon
Poli *see* Pólis
107 *M19* **Policastro, Golfo di** *gulf* S Italy
110 *D8* **Police** ***Ger.*** Politz. Zachodnio-pomorskie, NW Poland
172 *I17* **Police, Pointe** *headland* Mahé, NE Seychelles
115 *L17* **Polichnítos** ***var.*** Polihnitos, Políkhnitos. Lésvos, E Greece
Poligiros *see* Polýgyros
107 *P17* **Polignano a Mare** Puglia, SE Italy
103 *S9* **Poligny** Jura, E France
Polihnitos *see* Polichnítos
Polikastro/Políkastron *see* Polýkastro
Políkhnitos *see* Polichnítos
114 *K8* **Polikrayshte** Veliko Tŭrnovo, N Bulgaria
171 *O3* **Polillo Islands** *island group* N Philippines
109 *Q9* **Polinik** ▲ SW Austria
115 *J15* **Políochni** ***var.*** Polýochni. *site of ancient city* Límnos, E Greece
121 *O2* **Pólis** ***var.*** Poli. W Cyprus
Polish People's Republic, The *see* Poland
Polish Republic *see* Poland
117 *O3* **Polis'ke** ***Rus.*** Polesskoye. Kyyivs'ka Oblast', N Ukraine
107 *N22* **Polistena** Calabria, SW Italy
Politz *see* Police
Políyiros *see* Polýgyros
29 *V14* **Polk City** Iowa, C USA
110 *F13* **Polkowice** ***Ger.*** Heerwegen. Dolnośląskie, W Poland
155 *G22* **Pollāchi** Tamil Nādu, SE India
109 *W7* **Pöllau** Steiermark, SE Austria
189 *T13* **Polle** *atoll* Chuuk Islands, C Micronesia
105 *X9* **Pollença** Mallorca, Spain, W Mediterranean Sea
Pollnow *see* Polanów
29 *N7* **Pollock** South Dakota, N USA
92 *L8* **Polmak** Finnmark, N Norway
30 *L10* **Polo** Illinois, N USA
193 *V15* **Poloa** *island* Tongatapu Group, N Tonga
42 *E5* **Polochic, Río** 〜 C Guatemala
Pologi *see* Polohy
117 *V9* **Polohy** ***Rus.*** Pologi. Zaporiz'ka Oblast', SE Ukraine
83 *K20* **Polokwane** ***prev.*** Pietersburg. Limpopo, NE South Africa
14 *M10* **Polonais, Lac des** ◎ Québec, SE Canada
61 *G20* **Polonio, Cabo** *headland* E Uruguay
155 *K24* **Polonnaruwa** North Central Province, C Sri Lanka
116 *L5* **Polonne** ***Rus.*** Polonnoye. Khmel'nyts'ka Oblast', NW Ukraine
Polonnoye *see* Polonne
Polotsk *see* Polatsk
109 *T7* **Pöls** ***var.*** Pölsbach. 〜 E Austria
Pölsbach *see* Pöls
Polska/Polska, Rzeczpospolita/Polska Rzeczpospolita Ludowa *see* Poland
114 *L10* **Polski Gradets** Stara Zagora, C Bulgaria
114 *K8* **Polsko Kosovo** Ruse, N Bulgaria
33 *P8* **Polson** Montana, NW USA
117 *T6* **Poltava** Poltavs'ka Oblast', NE Ukraine
Poltava *see* Poltavs'ka Oblast'
117 *R5* **Poltavs'ka Oblast'** ***var.*** Poltava, ***Rus.*** Poltavskaya Oblast'. ⬖ *province* NE Ukraine
Poltavskaya Oblast' *see* Poltavs'ka Oblast'
Poltoratsk *see* Aşgabat
118 *I5* **Põltsamaa** ***Ger.*** Oberpahlen. Jõgevamaa, E Estonia
118 *I4* **Põltsamaa** ***var.*** Põltsamaa Jõgi. 〜 C Estonia
Põltsamaa Jõgi *see* Põltsamaa
122 *I8* **Poluy** 〜 N Russian Federation
118 *J6* **Põlva** ***Ger.*** Pölwe. Põlvamaa, SE Estonia
93 *N16* **Polvijärvi** Itä-Suomi, SE Finland
Pölwe *see* Põlva
115 *I22* **Polýaigos** *island* Kykládes, Greece, Aegean Sea
115 *I22* **Polyaígou Folégandrou, Stenó** *strait* Kykládes, Greece, Aegean Sea
124 *J3* **Polyarnyy** Murmanskaya Oblast', NW Russian Federation
125 *W5* **Polyarnyy Ural** ▲▲ NW Russian Federation
115 *G14* **Polýgyros** ***var.*** Poligiros, Políyiros. Kentrikí Makedonía, N Greece
114 *F13* **Polýkastro** ***var.*** Polikastro; ***prev.*** Políkastron. Kentrikí Makedonía, N Greece
193 *O9* **Polynesia** *island group* C Pacific Ocean
Polýochni *see* Políochni
41 *Y13* **Polyuc** Quintana Roo, E Mexico
109 *V10* **Polzela** C Slovenia
Polzen *see* Ploučnice
56 *D12* **Pomabamba** Ancash, C Peru
185 *D23* **Pomahaka** 〜 South Island, New Zealand
106 *F12* **Pomarance** Toscana, C Italy
104 *G9* **Pombal** Leiria, C Portugal
76 *D9* **Pombas** Santo Antão, NW Cape Verde
83 *N19* **Pomene** Inhambane, SE Mozambique
110 *G8* **Pomerania** *cultural region* Germany/Poland
110 *D7* **Pomeranian Bay** ***Ger.*** Pommersche Bucht, ***Pol.*** Zatoka Pomorska. *bay* Germany/Poland
31 *T15* **Pomeroy** Ohio, N USA
32 *L10* **Pomeroy** Washington, NW USA
117 *Q8* **Pomichna** Kirovohrads'ka Oblast', C Ukraine
186 *H7* **Pomio** New Britain, E Papua New Guinea
Pomir, Dar"yoi *see* Pamir/Pāmīr, Daryā-ye
27 *T6* **Pomme de Terre Lake** ⊠ Missouri, C USA
29 *S8* **Pomme de Terre River** 〜 Minnesota, N USA
Pommersche Bucht *see* Pomeranian Bay
35 *T15* **Pomona** California, W USA
114 *N9* **Pomorie** Burgas, E Bulgaria
Pomorska, Zatoka *see* Pomeranian Bay
110 *H8* **Pomorskie** ⬖ *province* N Poland
125 *Q4* **Pomorskiy Proliv** *strait* NW Russian Federation
125 *T10* **Pomozdino** Respublika Komi, NW Russian Federation
Pompaelo *see* Pamplona
23 *Z15* **Pompano Beach** Florida, SE USA
107 *K18* **Pompei** Campania, S Italy
33 *V10* **Pompeys Pillar** Montana, NW USA
Ponape Ascension Island *see* Pohnpei
29 *R13* **Ponca** Nebraska, C USA
27 *O8* **Ponca City** Oklahoma, C USA
45 *T6* **Ponce** C Puerto Rico
23 *X10* **Ponce de Leon Inlet** *inlet* Florida, SE USA
22 *K8* **Ponchatoula** Louisiana, S USA
26 *M8* **Pond Creek** Oklahoma, C USA
155 *J20* **Pondicherry** ***var.*** Puduchcheri, ***Fr.*** Pondichéry. Pondicherry, SE India
151 *I20* **Pondicherry** ***var.*** Puduchcheri, ***Fr.*** Pondichéry. ⬖ *union territory* India
Pondichéry *see* Pondicherry
197 *N11* **Pond Inlet** Baffin Island, Nunavut, NE Canada
187 *P16* **Ponérihouen** Province Nord, C New Caledonia
104 *J4* **Ponferrada** Castilla-León, NW Spain
184 *N13* **Pongaroa** Manawatu-Wanganui, North Island, New Zealand
167 *Q12* **Pong Nam Ron** Chantaburi, S Thailand
81 *C14* **Pongo** 〜 S Sudan
152 *I7* **Pong Reservoir** ⊠ N India
111 *N14* **Poniatowa** Lubelskie, E Poland
167 *R12* **Pônley** Kâmpóng Chhnăng, C Cambodia
155 *I20* **Ponnaiyār** 〜 SE India
9 *Q15* **Ponoka** Alberta, SW Canada
127 *U6* **Ponomarevka** Orenburgskaya Oblast', W Russian Federation
169 *Q17* **Ponorogo** Jawa, C Indonesia
124 *M5* **Ponoy** Murmanskaya Oblast', NW Russian Federation
122 *F6* **Ponoy** 〜 NW Russian Federation
102 *K11* **Pons** Charente-Maritime, W France
Pons *see* Ponts
Pons Aelii *see* Newcastle upon Tyne
Pons Vetus *see* Pontevedra
99 *G20* **Pont-à-Celles** Hainaut, S Belgium
102 *K16* **Pontacq** Pyrénées-Atlantiques, SW France
64 *P3* **Ponta Delgada** São Miguel, Azores, Portugal, NE Atlantic Ocean
64 *P3* **Ponta Delgado** ✈ São Miguel, Azores, Portugal, NE Atlantic Ocean
64 *N2* **Ponta do Pico** ▲ Pico, Azores, Portugal, NE Atlantic Ocean
60 *J11* **Ponta Grossa** Paraná, S Brazil
103 *S5* **Pont-à-Mousson** Meurthe-et-Moselle, NE France
103 *T9* **Pontarlier** Doubs, E France
106 *G11* **Pontassieve** Toscana, C Italy
102 *L4* **Pont-Audemer** Eure, N France
22 *K9* **Pontchartrain, Lake** ◎ Louisiana, S USA
102 *I8* **Pontchâteau** Loire-Atlantique, NW France
103 *R10* **Pont-de-Vaux** Ain, E France
104 *G4* **Ponteareas** Galicia, NW Spain
106 *J6* **Pontebba** Friuli-Venezia Giulia, NE Italy
104 *G4* **Ponte Caldelas** Galicia, NW Spain
107 *J16* **Pontecorvo** Lazio, C Italy
104 *G5* **Ponte da Barca** Viana do Castelo, N Portugal
104 *G5* **Ponte de Lima** Viana do Castelo, N Portugal
106 *F11* **Pontedera** Toscana, C Italy
104 *H10* **Ponte de Sor** Portalegre, C Portugal
104 *H2* **Pontedeume** Galicia, NW Spain
106 *F6* **Ponte di Legno** Lombardia, N Italy
9 *T17* **Ponteix** Saskatchewan, S Canada
59 *N20* **Ponte Nova** Minas Gerais, NE Brazil
59 *G18* **Pontes e Lacerda** Mato Grosso, W Brazil
104 *G4* **Pontevedra** ***anc.*** Pons Vetus. Galicia, NW Spain
104 *G3* **Pontevedra** ⬖ *province* Galicia, NW Spain
104 *G4* **Pontevedra, Ría de** *estuary* NW Spain
30 *M12* **Pontiac** Illinois, N USA
31 *R9* **Pontiac** Michigan, N USA
169 *P11* **Pontianak** Borneo, C Indonesia
107 *I16* **Pontino, Agro** *plain* C Italy
Pontisarae *see* Pontoise
102 *H6* **Pontivy** Morbihan, NW France
102 *F6* **Pont-l'Abbé** Finistère, NW France
103 *N4* **Pontoise** ***anc.*** Briva Isarae, Cergy-Pontoise, Pontisarae. Val-d'Oise, N France
9 *W13* **Ponton** Manitoba, C Canada
102 *J5* **Pontorson** Manche, N France
22 *M2* **Pontotoc** Mississippi, S USA
25 *R9* **Pontotoc** Texas, SW USA
106 *E10* **Pontremoli** Toscana, C Italy
108 *J10* **Pontresina** Graubünden, S Switzerland
105 *U5* **Ponts** ***var.*** Pons. Cataluña, NE Spain
103 *R14* **Pont-St-Esprit** Gard, S France
97 *K21* **Pontypool** ***Wel.*** Pontypŵl. SE Wales, UK
97 *J22* **Pontypridd** S Wales, UK
Pontypŵl *see* Pontypool
43 *R17* **Ponuga** Veraguas, SE Panama
184 *L6* **Ponui Island** *island* N New Zealand
119 *K14* **Ponya** 〜 N Belarus
107 *I17* **Ponza, Isola di** *Island* Isole Ponziane, S Italy
107 *I17* **Ponziane, Isole** *island* C Italy
182 *F7* **Poochera** South Australia
97 *L24* **Poole** S England, UK
25 *S6* **Poolville** Texas, SW USA
Poona *see* Pune
182 *M8* **Pooncarie** New South Wales, SE Australia
183 *N6* **Poopelloe Lake** *seasonal lake* New South Wales, SE Australia
57 *K19* **Poopó** Oruro, C Bolivia
57 *K19* **Poopó, Lago** ***var.*** Lago Pampa Aullagas. ◎ W Bolivia
184 *L3* **Poor Knights Islands** *island* N New Zealand
39 *P10* **Poorman** Alaska, USA
182 *E3* **Pootnoura** South Australia
147 *R10* **Pop** ***Rus.*** Pap. Namangan Viloyati, E Uzbekistan
117 *X7* **Popasna** ***Rus.*** Popasnaya. Luhans'ka Oblast', E Ukraine
Popasnaya *see* Popasna
54 *D12* **Popayán** Cauca, SW Colombia
99 *B18* **Poperinge** West-Vlaanderen, W Belgium
123 *N7* **Popigay** Taymyrskiy (Dolgano-Nenetskiy) Avtonomnyy Okrug, N Russian Federation
123 *N7* **Popigay** 〜 N Russian Federation
117 *O5* **Popil'nya** Zhytomyrs'ka Oblast', N Ukraine
182 *K8* **Popiltah Lake** *seasonal lake* New South Wales, SE Australia
33 *X7* **Poplar** Montana, NW USA
9 *Y14* **Poplar** 〜 Manitoba, C Canada
27 *X8* **Poplar Bluff** Missouri, C USA
33 *X6* **Poplar River** 〜 Montana, NW USA
41 *P14* **Popocatépetl** ⛰ S Mexico
79 *H21* **Popokabaka** Bandundu, SW Dem. Rep. Congo
107 *J15* **Popoli** Abruzzo, C Italy
186 *F9* **Popondetta** Northern, S Papua New Guinea
112 *F9* **Popovača** Sisak-Moslavina, NE Croatia
114 *J10* **Popovitsa** Loveshka Oblast, C Bulgaria
114 *L8* **Popovo** Tŭrgovishte, N Bulgaria
Popovo *see* Iskra
Popper *see* Poprad
30 *M5* **Popple River** 〜 Wisconsin, N USA
111 *L19* **Poprad** ***Ger.*** Deutschendorf, ***Hung.*** Poprád. Prešovský Kraj, E Slovakia
111 *L18* **Poprad** ***Ger.*** Popper, ***Hung.*** Poprád. 〜 Poland/Slovakia
111 *L19* **Poprad-Tatry** ✈ (Poprad) Prešovský Kraj, E Slovakia
21 *X7* **Poquoson** Virginia, NE USA
149 *O15* **Porāli** 〜 SW Pakistan
184 *N12* **Porangahau** Hawke's Bay, North Island, New Zealand
59 *K17* **Porangatu** Goiás, C Brazil
119 *G18* **Porazava** ***Pol.*** Porozow, ***Rus.*** Porozovo. Hrodzyenskaya Voblasts', W Belarus
154 *A11* **Porbandar** Gujarāt, W India
10 *I13* **Porcher Island** *island* British Columbia, SW Canada
104 *M13* **Porcuna** Andalucía, S Spain
14 *F7* **Porcupine** Ontario, S Canada
64 *M6* **Porcupine Bank** *undersea feature* N Atlantic Ocean
9 *V15* **Porcupine Hills** ▲▲ Manitoba/Saskatchewan, S Canada
30 *L3* **Porcupine Mountains** *hill range* Michigan, N USA
64 *M7* **Porcupine Plain** *undersea feature* E Atlantic Ocean
8 *G7* **Porcupine River** 〜 Canada/USA
106 *I7* **Pordenone** ***anc.*** Portenau. Friuli-Venezia Giulia, NE Italy
54 *H9* **Pore** Casanare, E Colombia
112 *A9* **Poreč** ***It.*** Parenzo. Istra, NW Croatia
60 *I9* **Porecatu** Paraná, S Brazil
Porech'ye *see* Parechcha
127 *P4* **Poretskoye** Chuvashskaya Respublika, W Russian Federation
77 *Q13* **Porga** N Benin
186 *B7* **Porgera** Enga, W Papua New Guinea
93 *K18* **Pori** ***Swe.*** Björneborg. Länsi-Soumi, SW Finland
185 *L14* **Porirua** Wellington, North Island, New Zealand
92 *I12* **Porjus** ***Lapp.*** Bårjås. Norrbotten, N Sweden
124 *G14* **Porkhov** Pskovskaya Oblast', W Russian Federation
55 *O4* **Porlamar** Nueva Esparta, NE Venezuela
102 *I8* **Pornic** Loire-Atlantique, NW France
186 *B7* **Poroma** Southern Highlands, W Papua New Guinea
123 *T13* **Poronaysk** Ostrov Sakhalin, Sakhalinskaya Oblast', SE Russian Federation
115 *G20* **Póros** Póros, S Greece
115 *C19* **Póros** Kefallinía, Iónia Nisiá, Greece, C Mediterranean Sea
115 *G20* **Póros** *island* S Greece
81 *G24* **Poroto Mountains** ▲▲ SW Tanzania
112 *B10* **Porozina** Primorje-Gorski Kotar, NW Croatia
Porozovo/Porozow *see* Porazava
195 *X15* **Porpoise Bay** *bay* Antarctica
65 *G15* **Porpoise Point** *headland* NE Ascension Island
65 *C25* **Porpoise Point** *headland* East Falkland, Falkland Islands
108 *C6* **Porrentruy** Jura, NW Switzerland
106 *F10* **Porretta Terme** Emilia-Romagna, C Italy
Porriño *see* O Porriño
Pors *see* Porsangenfijorden
92 *L7* **Porsangenfijorden** ***Lapp.*** Pors. *fjord* N Norway
92 *K8* **Porsangerhalvøya** *peninsula* N Norway
95 *G16* **Porsgrunn** Telemark, S Norway
136 *E13* **Porsuk Çayı** 〜 C Turkey
Porsy *see* Boldumsaz
57 *N18* **Portachuelo** Santa Cruz, C Bolivia
182 *I9* **Port Adelaide** South Australia
97 *F15* **Portadown** ***Ir.*** Port An Dúnáin. S Northern Ireland, UK
31 *P10* **Portage** Michigan, N USA
18 *D15* **Portage** Pennsylvania, NE USA
30 *K8* **Portage** Wisconsin, N USA
30 *M3* **Portage Lake** ◎ Michigan, N USA
9 *X16* **Portage la Prairie** Manitoba, S Canada
31 *R11* **Portage River** 〜 Ohio, N USA
27 *Y8* **Portageville** Missouri, C USA
28 *L2* **Portal** North Dakota, N USA
10 *L17* **Port Alberni** Vancouver Island, British Columbia, SW Canada
14 *E15* **Port Albert** Ontario, S Canada
104 *I10* **Portalegre** ***anc.*** Ammaia, Amoea. Portalegre, E Portugal
104 *H10* **Portalegre** ⬖ *district* C Portugal
37 *V12* **Portales** New Mexico, SW USA
39 *X14* **Port Alexander** Baranof Island, Alaska, USA
83 *I25* **Port Alfred** Eastern Cape, S South Africa
10 *J16* **Port Alice** Vancouver Island, British Columbia, SW Canada
22 *J8* **Port Allen** Louisiana, S USA
Port Amelia *see* Pemba
Port An Dúnáin *see* Portadown
32 *G7* **Port Angeles** Washington, NW USA
44 *L12* **Port Antonio** NE Jamaica
115 *D16* **Pórta Panagiá** *religious building* Thessalía, C Greece
25 *T14* **Port Aransas** Texas, SW USA
97 *E18* **Portarlington** ***Ir.*** Cúil an tSúdaire. Laois/Offaly, C Ireland
183 *P17* **Port Arthur** Tasmania, SE Australia
25 *Y11* **Port Arthur** Texas, SW USA
96 *G12* **Port Askaig** W Scotland, UK
182 *I7* **Port Augusta** South Australia
44 *M9* **Port-au-Prince** ● (Haiti) C Haiti
44 *M9* **Port-au-Prince** ✈ E Haiti
22 *I8* **Port Barre** Louisiana, S USA
151 *Q19* **Port Blair** Andaman and Nicobar Islands, SE India
25 *X12* **Port Bolivar** Texas, SW USA
105 *X4* **Portbou** Cataluña, NE Spain
77 *N17* **Port Bouet** ✈ (Abidjan) SE Ivory Coast
182 *I8* **Port Broughton** South Australia
14 *F17* **Port Burwell** Ontario, S Canada
12 *G17* **Port Burwell** Québec, NE Canada
182 *M13* **Port Campbell** Victoria, SE Australia
15 *V4* **Port-Cartier** Québec, SE Canada
185 *F23* **Port Chalmers** Otago, South Island, New Zealand
23 *W14* **Port Charlotte** Florida, SE USA
38 *L9* **Port Clarence** Alaska, USA
10 *I13* **Port Clements** Graham Island, British Columbia, SW Canada
31 *S11* **Port Clinton** Ohio, N USA
14 *H17* **Port Colborne** Ontario, S Canada
15 *Y7* **Port-Daniel** Québec, SE Canada
Port Darwin *see* Darwin
183 *O17* **Port Davey** *headland* Tasmania, SE Australia
44 *K8* **Port-de-Paix** NW Haiti
181 *W4* **Port Douglas** Queensland, NE Australia
10 *J13* **Port Edward** British Columbia, SW Canada
83 *K24* **Port Edward** KwaZulu/Natal, SE South Africa
58 *J12* **Portel** Pará, NE Brazil
104 *H12* **Portel** Évora, S Portugal
14 *E14* **Port Elgin** Ontario, S Canada
45 *Y14* **Port Elizabeth** Bequia, Saint Vincent and the Grenadines
83 *I26* **Port Elizabeth** Eastern Cape, S South Africa
96 *G13* **Port Ellen** W Scotland, UK
Portenau *see* Pordenone
97 *H16* **Port Erin** SW Isle of Man
45 *Q13* **Porter Point** *headland* Saint Vincent, Saint Vincent and the Grenadines
185 *G18* **Porters Pass** *pass* South Island, New Zealand
83 *E25* **Porterville** Western Cape, SW South Africa
35 *R12* **Porterville** California, W USA
Port-Étienne *see* Nouâdhibou
182 *L13* **Port Fairy** Victoria, SE Australia
184 *M4* **Port Fitzroy** Great Barrier Island, Auckland, NE New Zealand
Port Florence *see* Kisumu
Port-Francqui *see* Ilebo
79 *C18* **Port-Gentil** Ogooué-Maritime, W Gabon
182 *I7* **Port Germein** South Australia
22 *J6* **Port Gibson** Mississippi, S USA
39 *Q13* **Port Graham** Alaska, USA
77 *U17* **Port Harcourt** Rivers, S Nigeria
10 *J16* **Port Hardy** Vancouver Island, British Columbia, SW Canada
Port Harrison *see* Inukjuak
13 *R14* **Port Hawkesbury** Cape Breton Island, Nova Scotia, SE Canada
180 *I6* **Port Hedland** Western Australia
39 *O15* **Port Heiden** Alaska, USA
97 *I19* **Porthmadog** ***var.*** Portmadoc. NW Wales, UK
14 *I15* **Port Hope** Ontario, SE Canada
13 *S9* **Port Hope Simpson** Newfoundland and Labrador, E Canada
65 *C24* **Port Howard Settlement** West Falkland, Falkland Islands
31 *T9* **Port Huron** Michigan, N USA
107 *K17* **Portici** Campania, S Italy
137 *Y13* **Port-İliç** ***Rus.*** Port Il'ich. SE Azerbaijan
Port Il'ich *see* Port-İliç
104 *G14* **Portimão** ***var.*** Vila Nova de Portimão. Faro, S Portugal
25 *T17* **Port Isabel** Texas, SW USA
18 *J13* **Port Jervis** New York, NE USA
55 *S7* **Port Kaituma** NW Guyana
126 *K12* **Port Katon** Rostovskaya Oblast', SW Russian Federation
183 *S9* **Port Kembla** New South Wales, SE Australia
182 *F8* **Port Kenny** South Australia
Port Klang *see* Pelabuhan Klang
Port Láirge *see* Waterford
183 *S8* **Portland** New South Wales, SE Australia
182 *L13* **Portland** Victoria, SE Australia
184 *K4* **Portland** Northland, North Island, New Zealand
31 *Q13* **Portland** Indiana, N USA
19 *P8* **Portland** Maine, NE USA
31 *Q9* **Portland** Michigan, N USA
29 *Q4* **Portland** North Dakota, N USA
32 *G11* **Portland** Oregon, NW USA
20 *J8* **Portland** Tennessee, S USA
25 *T14* **Portland** Texas, SW USA
32 *G11* **Portland** ✈ Oregon, NW USA
182 *L13* **Portland Bay** *bay* Victoria, SE Australia
44 *K13* **Portland Bight** *bay* S Jamaica
97 *L24* **Portland Bill** ***var.*** Bill of Portland. *headland* S England, UK
Portland, Bill of *see* Portland Bill
183 *P15* **Portland, Cape** *headland* Tasmania, SE Australia
10 *J12* **Portland Inlet** *inlet* British Columbia, W Canada
184 *P11* **Portland Island** *island* E New Zealand
65 *F15* **Portland Point** *headland* SW Ascension Island
44 *J13* **Portland Point** *headland* C Jamaica
103 *P16* **Port-la-Nouvelle** Aude, S France
Portlaoighise *see* Port Laoise
97 *E18* **Port Laoise** ***var.*** Portlaoise, ***Ir.*** Portlaoighise; ***prev.*** Maryborough. C Ireland
Portlaoise *see* Port Laoise
25 *U13* **Port Lavaca** Texas, SW USA
182 *G9* **Port Lincoln** South Australia
39 *Q14* **Port Lions** Kodiak Island, Alaska, USA
76 *I15* **Port Loko** W Sierra Leone
65 *E24* **Port Louis** East Falkland, Falkland Islands
45 *Y5* **Port-Louis** Grande Terre, N Guadeloupe
173 *X16* **Port Louis** ● (Mauritius) NW Mauritius
Port Louis *see* Scarborough
Port-Lyautey *see* Kénitra
182 *K12* **Port MacDonnell** South Australia
183 *U7* **Port Macquarie** New South Wales, SE Australia
Portmadoc *see* Porthmadog
Port Mahon *see* Mahón
44 *K12* **Port Maria** C Jamaica
10 *K16* **Port McNeill** Vancouver Island, British Columbia, SW Canada
13 *P11* **Port-Menier** Île d'Anticosti, Québec, E Canada
39 *N15* **Port Moller** Alaska, USA
44 *L13* **Port Morant** E Jamaica
44 *K13* **Portmore** C Jamaica
186 *D9* **Port Moresby** ● (Papua New Guinea) Central/National Capital District, SW Papua New Guinea
Port Natal *see* Durban
25 *Y11* **Port Neches** Texas, SW USA
182 *G9* **Port Neill** South Australia
15 *S6* **Portneuf** 〜 Québec, SE Canada
15 *R6* **Portneuf, Lac** ◎ Québec, SE Canada
83 *D23* **Port Nolloth** Northern Cape, W South Africa
18 *J17* **Port Norris** New Jersey, NE USA
Port-Nouveau-Québec *see* Kangiqsualujjuaq
104 *G6* **Porto** ***Eng.*** Oporto; ***anc.*** Portus Cale. Porto, NW Portugal
104 *G6* **Porto** ***var.*** Pôrto. ⬖ *district* N Portugal
104 *G6* **Porto** ✈ Porto, W Portugal
Pôrto *see* Porto
61 *I16* **Porto Alegre** ***var.*** Pôrto Alegre. *state capital* Rio Grande do Sul, S Brazil
Porto Alexandre *see* Tombua
82 *B12* **Porto Amboim** Cuanza Sul, NW Angola
Porto Amélia *see* Pemba
Porto Bello *see* Portobelo
43 *T14* **Portobelo** ***var.*** Porto Bello, Puerto Bello. Colón, N Panama
60 *G10* **Pôrto Camargo** Paraná, S Brazil
25 *U13* **Port O'Connor** Texas, SW USA
Pôrto de Mós *see* Porto de Moz
58 *J12* **Porto de Moz** ***var.*** Pôrto de Mós. Pará, NE Brazil
64 *O5* **Porto do Moniz** Madeira, Portugal, NE Atlantic Ocean
59 *H16* **Porto dos Gaúchos** Mato Grosso, W Brazil
Porto Edda *see* Sarandë
107 *J24* **Porto Empedocle** Sicilia, Italy, C Mediterranean Sea
59 *H20* **Porto Esperança** Mato Grosso do Sul, SW Brazil
106 *E13* **Portoferraio** Toscana, C Italy
96 *G6* **Port of Ness** NW Scotland, UK
45 *U14* **Port-of-Spain** ● (Trinidad and Tobago) Trinidad, Trinidad and Tobago
Port of Spain *see* Piarco
103 *X15* **Porto, Golfe de** *gulf* Corse, France, C Mediterranean Sea
Porto Grande *see* Mindelo
106 *I7* **Portogruaro** Veneto, NE Italy
35 *P5* **Portola** California, W USA
187 *Q13* **Port-Olry** Espiritu Santo, C Vanuatu
93 *J17* **Pörtom** ***Fin.*** Pirttikylä. Länsi-Soumi, W Finland
Port Omna *see* Portumna
59 *G21* **Porto Murtinho** Mato Grosso do Sul, SW Brazil
59 *K16* **Porto Nacional** Tocantins, C Brazil
77 *S16* **Porto-Novo** ● (Benin) S Benin
23 *X10* **Port Orange** Florida, SE USA
32 *G8* **Port Orchard** Washington, NW USA
Porto Re *see* Kraljevica
32 *E15* **Port Orford** Oregon, NW USA
Porto Rico *see* Puerto Rico
106 *J13* **Porto San Giorgio** Marche, C Italy
64 *P5* **Porto Santo** ***var.*** Vila Baleira. Porto Santo, Madeira, Portugal, NE Atlantic Ocean
64 *Q5* **Porto Santo** ✈ Porto Santo, Madeira, Portugal, NE Atlantic Ocean

◆ Country
● Country Capital
◇ Dependent Territory
○ Dependent Territory Capital
⬖ Administrative Regions
✈ International Airport
▲ Mountain
▲▲ Mountain Range
⛰ Volcano
〜 River
◎ Lake
⊠ Reservoir

64 P5 **Porto Santo** *var.* Ilha do Porto Santo. *island* Madeira, Portugal, NE Atlantic Ocean
Porto Santo, Ilha do *see* Porto Santo
107 F14 **Porto Santo Stefano** Toscana, C Italy
60 H9 **Porto São José** Paraná, S Brazil
59 O19 **Porto Seguro** Bahia, E Brazil
107 B17 **Porto Torres** Sardegna, Italy, C Mediterranean Sea
59 J23 **Porto União** Santa Catarina, S Brazil
103 Y16 **Porto-Vecchio** Corse, France, C Mediterranean Sea
59 E15 **Porto Velho** *var.* Velho. *state capital* Rondônia, W Brazil
56 A6 **Portoviejo** *var.* Puertoviejo. Manabí, W Ecuador
185 B26 **Port Pegasus** *bay* Stewart Island, New Zealand
14 H15 **Port Perry** Ontario, SE Canada
183 N12 **Port Phillip Bay** *harbor* Victoria, SE Australia
182 I8 **Port Pirie** South Australia
96 G9 **Portree** N Scotland, UK
Port Rex *see* East London
Port Rois *see* Portrush
44 K13 **Port Royal** E Jamaica
21 R15 **Port Royal** South Carolina, SE USA
21 R15 **Port Royal Sound** *inlet* South Carolina, SE USA
97 F14 **Portrush** *Ir.* Port Rois. N Northern Ireland, UK
75 W7 **Port Said** *Ar.* Būr Sa'īd. N Egypt
23 R9 **Port Saint Joe** Florida, SE USA
23 Y11 **Port Saint John** Florida, SE USA
83 K24 **Port St. Johns** Eastern Cape, SE South Africa
103 R16 **Port-St-Louis-du-Rhône** Bouches-du-Rhône, SE France
44 K10 **Port Salut** SW Haiti
65 E24 **Port Salvador** *inlet* East Falkland, Falkland Islands
65 D24 **Port San Carlos** East Falkland, Falkland Islands
13 S10 **Port Saunders** Newfoundland, Newfoundland and Labrador, SE Canada
83 K24 **Port Shepstone** KwaZulu/Natal, E South Africa
45 O11 **Portsmouth** *var.* Grand-Anse. NW Dominica
97 N24 **Portsmouth** S England, UK
19 P10 **Portsmouth** New Hampshire, NE USA
31 S15 **Portsmouth** Ohio, N USA
21 X7 **Portsmouth** Virginia, NE USA
14 E17 **Port Stanley** Ontario, S Canada
Port Stanley *see* Stanley
65 B25 **Port Stephens** *inlet* West Falkland, Falkland Islands
65 B25 **Port Stephens Settlement** West Falkland, Falkland Islands
97 F14 **Portstewart** *Ir.* Port Stíobhaird. N Northern Ireland, UK
Port Stíobhaird *see* Portstewart
80 I7 **Port Sudan** Red Sea, NE Sudan
22 L10 **Port Sulphur** Louisiana, S USA
Port Swettenham *see* Klang/Pelabuhan Klang
97 J22 **Port Talbot** S Wales, UK
92 L11 **Porttipahdan Tekojärvi** ◎ N Finland
32 G7 **Port Townsend** Washington, NW USA
104 H9 **Portugal** *off.* Republic of Portugal. ◆ *republic* SW Europe
105 O2 **Portugalete** País Vasco, N Spain
Portugal, Republic of *see* Portugal
54 J6 **Portuguesa** *off.* Estado Portuguesa. ◈ *state* N Venezuela
Portuguesa, Estado *see* Portuguesa
Portuguese East Africa *see* Mozambique
Portuguese Guinea *see* Guinea-Bissau
Portuguese Timor *see* East Timor
Portuguese West Africa *see* Angola
97 D18 **Portumna** *Ir.* Port Omna. Galway, W Ireland
Portus Cale *see* Porto
Portus Magnus *see* Almería
Portus Magonis *see* Mahón
103 P17 **Port-Vendres** *var.* Port Vendres. Pyrénées-Orientales, S France
182 H9 **Port Victoria** South Australia
187 Q14 **Port-Vila** *var.* Vila. ● (Vanuatu) Éfaté, C Vanuatu
Port Vila *see* Bauer Field
182 I9 **Port Wakefield** South Australia
31 N8 **Port Washington** Wisconsin, N USA
57 J14 **Porvenir** Pando, NW Bolivia
63 I24 **Porvenir** Magallanes, S Chile
61 D18 **Porvenir** Paysandú, W Uruguay
93 M19 **Porvoo** *Swe.* Borgå. Etelä-Suomi, S Finland
Porzecze *see* Parechcha
104 M10 **Porzuna** Castilla-La Mancha, C Spain
61 E14 **Posadas** Misiones, NE Argentina
104 L13 **Posadas** Andalucía, S Spain
Poschega *see* Požega
108 J11 **Poschiavino** ~ Italy/Switzerland
108 J10 **Poschiavo** *Ger.* Puschlav. Graubünden, S Switzerland
112 D12 **Posedarje** Zadar, SW Croatia
Posen *see* Poznań
124 L14 **Poshekhon'ye** Yaroslavskaya Oblast', W Russian Federation
92 M13 **Posio** Lappi, NE Finland
Poskam *see* Zepu
Posnania *see* Poznań
171 O12 **Poso** Sulawesi, C Indonesia
171 O12 **Poso, Danau** ◎ Sulawesi, C Indonesia
137 R10 **Posof** Ardahan, NE Turkey
25 R6 **Possum Kingdom Lake** ⊞ Texas, SW USA
25 N6 **Post** Texas, SW USA
Postavy/Postawy *see* Pastavy
12 I7 **Poste-de-la-Baleine** Québec, NE Canada
99 M17 **Posterholt** Limburg, SE Netherlands
83 G22 **Postmasburg** Northern Cape, N South Africa
Pôsto Diuarum *see* Campo de Diauarum
59 I16 **Pôsto Jacaré** Mato Grosso, W Brazil
109 T12 **Postojna** *Ger.* Adelsberg, *It.* Postumia. SW Slovenia
Postumia *see* Postojna
29 X12 **Postville** Iowa, C USA
Pöstyén *see* Piešťany
113 G14 **Posušje** ◈ Federacija Bosna I Hercegovina, SW Bosnia and Herzegovina
171 O16 **Pota** Flores, C Indonesia
115 G23 **Potamós** Antikýthira, S Greece
55 S9 **Potaru River** ~ C Guyana
83 I21 **Potchefstroom** North-West, N South Africa
27 R11 **Poteau** Oklahoma, C USA
25 R12 **Poteet** Texas, SW USA
115 G14 **Poteídaia** *site of ancient city* Kentrikí Makedonía, N Greece
Potentia *see* Potenza
107 M18 **Potenza** *anc.* Potentia. Basilicata, S Italy
185 A24 **Poteriteri, Lake** ◎ South Island, New Zealand
104 M2 **Potes** Cantabria, N Spain
Potgietersrus *see* Mokopane
25 S12 **Poth** Texas, SW USA
32 J9 **Potholes Reservoir** ⊞ Washington, NW USA
137 Q9 **P'ot'i** W Georgia
77 X13 **Potiskum** Yobe, NE Nigeria
Potkozarje *see* Ivanjska
32 M9 **Potlatch** Idaho, NW USA
33 N9 **Pot Mountain** ▲ Idaho, NW USA
113 H14 **Potoci** ◈ Federacija Bosna I Hercegovina, S Bosnia and Herzegovina
21 V3 **Potomac River** ~ NE USA
57 L20 **Potosí** Potosí, S Bolivia
42 H9 **Potosí** Chinandega, NW Nicaragua
27 W6 **Potosi** Missouri, C USA
57 K21 **Potosí** ◈ *department* SW Bolivia
62 H7 **Potrerillos** Atacama, N Chile
42 H5 **Potrerillos** Cortés, NW Honduras
62 H8 **Potro, Cerro del** ▲ N Chile
100 N12 **Potsdam** Brandenburg, NE Germany
18 J7 **Potsdam** New York, NE USA
109 X5 **Pottendorf** Niederösterreich, E Austria
109 X5 **Pottenstein** Niederösterreich, E Austria
18 I15 **Pottstown** Pennsylvania, NE USA
18 H14 **Pottsville** Pennsylvania, NE USA
155 L25 **Pottuvil** Eastern Province, SE Sri Lanka
149 U6 **Potwar Plateau** *plateau* NE Pakistan
102 J7 **Pouancé** Maine-et-Loire, W France
15 R6 **Poulin de Courval, Lac** ◎ Québec, SE Canada
18 L9 **Poultney** Vermont, NE USA
187 O16 **Poum** Province Nord, W New Caledonia
59 L21 **Pouso Alegre** Minas Gerais, NE Brazil
192 I16 **Poutasi** Upolu, SE Samoa
167 R12 **Poŭthĭsăt** *prev.* Pursat. Poŭthĭsăt, W Cambodia
167 R12 **Poŭthĭsăt, Stœ̆ng** *prev.* Pursat. ~ W Cambodia
102 J9 **Pouzauges** Vendée, NW France
Po, Valle del *see* Po Valley
106 F8 **Po Valley** *It.* Valle del Po. *valley* N Italy
111 I19 **Považská Bystrica** *Ger.* Waagbistritz, *Hung.* Vágbeszterce. Trenčiansky Kraj, W Slovakia
124 J10 **Povenets** Respublika Kareliya, NW Russian Federation
184 Q9 **Poverty Bay** *inlet* North Island, New Zealand
112 K12 **Povlen** ▲▲ W Serbia
104 G6 **Póvoa de Varzim** Porto, NW Portugal
127 N8 **Povorino** Voronezhskaya Oblast', W Russian Federation
Povungnituk *see* Puvirnituq
12 J3 **Povungnituk, Rivière de** ~ Québec, NE Canada
14 H11 **Powassan** Ontario, S Canada
35 U17 **Poway** California, W USA
33 W14 **Powder River** Wyoming, C USA
33 Y10 **Powder River** ~ Montana/Wyoming, NW USA
32 L12 **Powder River** ~ Oregon, NW USA
33 W13 **Powder River Pass** *pass* Wyoming, C USA
33 U12 **Powell** Wyoming, C USA
65 I22 **Powell Basin** *undersea feature* NW Weddell Sea
36 M8 **Powell, Lake** ◎ Utah, W USA
37 R4 **Powell, Mount** ▲ Colorado, C USA
10 L17 **Powell River** British Columbia, SW Canada
31 N5 **Powers** Michigan, N USA
28 K2 **Powers Lake** North Dakota, N USA
21 V6 **Powhatan** Virginia, NE USA
31 V13 **Powhatan Point** Ohio, N USA
97 J20 **Powys** *cultural region* E Wales, UK
187 P17 **Poya** Province Nord, C New Caledonia
161 P10 **Poyang Hu** ◎ S China
30 L7 **Poygan, Lake** ◎ Wisconsin, N USA
109 Y2 **Poysdorf** Niederösterreich, NE Austria
112 N11 **Požarevac** *Ger.* Passarowitz. Serbia, NE Serbia
41 Q13 **Poza Rica** *var.* Poza Rica de Hidalgo. Veracruz-Llave, E Mexico
Poza Rica de Hidalgo *see* Poza Rica
112 L13 **Požega** *prev.* Slavonska Požega, *Ger.* Poschega, *Hung.* Pozsega. Požega-Slavonija, NE Croatia
112 H9 **Požega-Slavonija** *off.* Požeško-Slavonska Županija. ◈ *province* NE Croatia
Požeško-Slavonska Županija *see* Požega-Slavonija
125 U13 **Pozhva** Permskaya Oblast', NW Russian Federation
110 G11 **Poznań** *Ger.* Posen, Posnania. Wielkolpolskie, C Poland
105 O13 **Pozo Alcón** Andalucía, S Spain
62 H3 **Pozo Almonte** Tarapacá, N Chile
104 L12 **Pozoblanco** Andalucía, S Spain
105 Q11 **Pozo Cañada** Castilla-La Mancha, C Spain
62 N5 **Pozo Colorado** Presidente Hayes, C Paraguay
63 J20 **Pozos, Punta** *headland* S Argentina
Pozsega *see* Požega
Pozsony *see* Bratislava
55 N5 **Pozuelos** Anzoátegui, NE Venezuela
107 L26 **Pozzallo** Sicilia, Italy, C Mediterranean Sea
107 K17 **Pozzuoli** *anc.* Puteoli. Campania, S Italy
77 P17 **Pra** ~ S Ghana
111 C19 **Prachatice** *Ger.* Prachatitz. Jihočeský Kraj, S Czech Republic
Prachatitz *see* Prachatice
167 P11 **Prachin Buri** *var.* Prachinburi. Prachin Buri, C Thailand
Prachinburi *see* Prachin Buri
Prachuab Girikhand *see* Prachuap Khiri Khan
167 O12 **Prachuap Khiri Khan** *var.* Prachuab Girikhand. Prachuap Khiri Khan, SW Thailand
111 H16 **Praděd** *Ger.* Altvater. ▲ NE Czech Republic
54 D11 **Pradera** Valle del Cauca, SW Colombia
103 O17 **Prades** Pyrénées-Orientales, S France
59 O19 **Prado** Bahia, SE Brazil
54 E11 **Prado** Tolima, C Colombia
Prado del Ganso *see* Goose Green
Prae *see* Phrae
95 I24 **Præstø** Storstrøm, SE Denmark
Prag/Praga/Prague *see* Praha
27 O10 **Prague** Oklahoma, C USA
111 D16 **Praha** *Eng.* Prague, *Ger.* Prag, *Pol.* Praga. ● (Czech Republic) Středočeský Kraj, NW Czech Republic
116 J13 **Prahova** ◈ *county* SE Romania
116 J13 **Prahova** ~ S Romania
76 E10 **Praia** ● (Cape Verde) Santiago, S Cape Verde
83 M21 **Praia do Bilene** Gaza, S Mozambique
83 M20 **Praia do Xai-Xai** Gaza, S Mozambique
116 J10 **Praid** *Hung.* Parajd. Harghita, C Romania
26 J3 **Prairie Dog Creek** ~ Kansas/Nebraska, C USA
30 J9 **Prairie du Chien** Wisconsin, N USA
27 S9 **Prairie Grove** Arkansas, C USA
31 P10 **Prairie River** ~ Michigan, N USA
Prairie State *see* Illinois
25 V11 **Prairie View** Texas, SW USA
167 Q10 **Prakhon Chai** Buri Ram, E Thailand
109 R4 **Pram** ~ N Austria
109 S4 **Prambachkirchen** Oberösterreich, N Austria
118 H2 **Prangli** *island* N Estonia
154 J13 **Prānhita** ~ C India
172 I15 **Praslin** *island* Inner Islands, NE Seychelles
115 O23 **Prasonísi, Ákrotírio** *cape* Ródos, Dodekánisa, Greece, Aegean Sea
111 I14 **Praszka** Opolskie, S Poland
Pratas Island *see* Tungsha Tao
119 M18 **Pratasy** *Rus.* Protasy. Homyel'skaya Voblasts', SE Belarus
167 Q10 **Prathai** Nakhon Ratchasima, E Thailand
Prathet Thai *see* Thailand
Prathum Thani *see* Pathum Thani
63 F21 **Prat, Isla** *island* S Chile
106 G11 **Prato** Toscana, C Italy
103 O17 **Prats-de-Mollo-la-Preste** Pyrénées-Orientales, S France
26 L6 **Pratt** Kansas, C USA
108 E6 **Pratteln** Basel-Land, NW Switzerland
193 O2 **Pratt Seamount** *undersea feature* N Pacific Ocean
23 P5 **Prattville** Alabama, S USA
Praust *see* Pruszcz Gdański
114 M7 **Pravda** *prev.* Dogrular. Silistra, NE Bulgaria
119 B14 **Pravdinsk** *Ger.* Friedland. Kaliningradskaya Oblast', W Russian Federation
104 K2 **Pravia** Asturias, N Spain
118 L12 **Prazaroki** *Rus.* Prozoroki. Vitsyebskaya Voblasts', N Belarus
Prázsmár *see* Prejmer
167 S11 **Preăh Vihéar** Preăh Vihéar, N Cambodia
116 J12 **Predeal** *Hung.* Predeál. Brașov, C Romania
109 S8 **Predlitz** Steiermark, SE Austria
9 V15 **Preeceville** Saskatchewan, S Canada
Preenkuln *see* Priekule
102 K6 **Pré-en-Pail** Mayenne, NW France
109 T4 **Pregarten** Oberösterreich, N Austria
54 H7 **Pregonero** Táchira, NW Venezuela
118 J10 **Preiļi** *Ger.* Preli. Preiļi, SE Latvia
116 J12 **Prejmer** *Ger.* Tartlau, *Hung.* Prázsmár. Brașov, S Romania
113 J16 **Prekornica** ▲▲ C Montenegro
Preli *see* Preiļi
Prëmet *see* Përmet
100 M12 **Premnitz** Brandenburg, NE Germany
25 S15 **Premont** Texas, SW USA
113 H14 **Prenj** ▲▲ S Bosnia and Herzegovina
Prenjas/Prenjasi *see* Përrenjas
22 L7 **Prentiss** Mississippi, S USA
Preny *see* Prienai
100 O10 **Prenzlau** Brandenburg, NE Germany
123 N11 **Preobrazhenka** Irkutskaya Oblast', C Russian Federation
166 J9 **Preparis Island** *island* SW Myanmar (Burma)
Prerau *see* Přerov
111 H18 **Přerov** *Ger.* Prerau. Olomoucký Kraj, E Czech Republic
Preschau *see* Prešov
14 M14 **Prescott** Ontario, SE Canada
36 K12 **Prescott** Arizona, SW USA
27 T13 **Prescott** Arkansas, C USA
32 L10 **Prescott** Washington, NW USA
30 H6 **Prescott** Wisconsin, N USA
185 A24 **Preservation Inlet** *inlet* South Island, New Zealand
112 O7 **Preševo** Serbia, SE Serbia
29 N10 **Presho** South Dakota, N USA
58 M13 **Presidente Dutra** Maranhão, E Brazil
60 I8 **Presidente Epitácio** São Paulo, S Brazil
62 N5 **Presidente Hayes** *off.* Departamento de Presidente Hayes. ◈ *department* C Paraguay
Presidente Hayes, Departamento de *see* Presidente Hayes
60 I9 **Presidente Prudente** São Paulo, S Brazil
Presidente Stroessner *see* Ciudad del Este
Presidente Vargas *see* Itabira
60 I8 **Presidente Venceslau** São Paulo, S Brazil
193 O10 **President Thiers Seamount** *undersea feature* C Pacific Ocean
24 J11 **Presidio** Texas, SW USA
Preslav *see* Veliki Preslav
111 M19 **Prešov** *var.* Preschau, *Ger.* Eperies, *Hung.* Eperjes. Prešovský Kraj, E Slovakia
111 M19 **Prešovský Kraj** ◈ *region* E Slovakia
113 N20 **Prespa, Lake** *Alb.* Liqen i Prespës, *Gk.* Límni Megáli Préspa, Limni Prespa, *Mac.* Prespansko Ezero, *Serb.* Prespansko Jezero. ◎ SE Europe
Prespa, Limni/Prespansko Ezero/Prespansko Jezero/Prespës, Liqen i *see* Prespa, Lake
19 S2 **Presque Isle** Maine, NE USA
18 B11 **Presque Isle** *headland* Pennsylvania, NE USA
Pressburg *see* Bratislava
77 P17 **Prestea** SW Ghana
111 B17 **Přeštice** *Ger.* Pschestitz. Plzeňský Kraj, W Czech Republic
97 K17 **Preston** NW England, UK
23 S6 **Preston** Georgia, SE USA
33 R16 **Preston** Idaho, NW USA
29 Z13 **Preston** Iowa, C USA
29 X11 **Preston** Minnesota, N USA
21 O6 **Prestonsburg** Kentucky, S USA
96 I13 **Prestwick** W Scotland, UK
Pretoria *see* Tshwane
Pretoria-Witwatersrand-Vereeniging *see* Gauteng
Pretusha *see* Pretushë
113 M21 **Pretushë** *var.* Pretusha. Korçë, SE Albania
Preussisch Eylau *see* Bagrationovsk
Preußisch Holland *see* Pasłęk
Preussisch-Stargard *see* Starogard Gdański
115 C17 **Préveza** Ípeiros, W Greece
37 V3 **Prewitt Reservoir** ⊞ Colorado, C USA
167 S13 **Prey Vêng** Prey Vêng, S Cambodia
144 M12 **Priaral'skiye Karakumy, Peski** *desert* SW Kazakhstan
123 P14 **Priargunsk** Chitinskaya Oblast', S Russian Federation
38 K14 **Pribilof Islands** *island group* Alaska, USA
113 K14 **Priboj** Serbia, W Serbia
111 C17 **Příbram** *Ger.* Pibrans. Středočeský Kraj, W Czech Republic
36 M4 **Price** Utah, W USA
37 N5 **Price River** ~ Utah, W USA
23 N8 **Prichard** Alabama, S USA
25 R8 **Priddy** Texas, SW USA
105 P8 **Priego** Castilla-La Mancha, C Spain
104 M14 **Priego de Córdoba** Andalucía, S Spain
118 C10 **Priekule** *Ger.* Preenkuln. Liepāja, SW Latvia
118 C12 **Priekulė** *Ger.* Prökuls. Klaipėda, W Lithuania
119 F14 **Prienai** *Pol.* Preny. Kaunas, S Lithuania
83 G23 **Prieska** Northern Cape, C South Africa
32 M7 **Priest Lake** ◎ Idaho, NW USA
32 M7 **Priest River** Idaho, NW USA
104 M3 **Prieta, Peña** ▲ N Spain
40 J10 **Prieto, Cerro** ▲ C Mexico
111 J19 **Prievidza** *var.* Priewitz, *Ger.* Priwitz, *Hung.* Privigye. Trenčiansky Kraj, W Slovakia
Priewitz *see* Prievidza
112 F10 **Prijedor** ◈ Republika Srpska, NW Bosnia and Herzegovina
113 K14 **Prijepolje** Serbia, W Serbia
Prikaspiyskaya Nizmennost' *see* Caspian Depression
113 O19 **Prilep** *Turk.* Perlepe. S FYR Macedonia
108 B9 **Prilly** Vaud, SW Switzerland
Priluki *see* Pryluky
62 L10 **Primero, Río** ~ C Argentina
29 S12 **Primghar** Iowa, C USA
112 B9 **Primorje-Gorski Kotar** *off.* Primorsko-Goranska Županija. ◈ *province* NW Croatia
118 A13 **Primorsk** *Ger.* Fischhausen. Kaliningradskaya Oblast', W Russian Federation
124 G12 **Primorsk** *Fin.* Koivisto. Leningradskaya Oblast', NW Russian Federation
123 S14 **Primorskiy Kray** *prev. Eng.* Maritime Territory. ◈ *territory* SE Russian Federation
114 N10 **Primorsko** *prev.* Keupriya. Burgas, E Bulgaria
126 K13 **Primorsko-Akhtarsk** Krasnodarskiy Kray, SW Russian Federation
Primorsko-Goranska Županija *see* Primorje-Gorski Kotar
Primorsk/Primorskoye *see* Prymors'k
117 U13 **Primors'kyy** Respublika Krym, S Ukraine
113 D14 **Primošten** Šibenik-Knin, S Croatia
9 R13 **Primrose Lake** ◎ Saskatchewan, C Canada
9 T14 **Prince Albert** Saskatchewan, S Canada
83 G25 **Prince Albert** Western Cape, SW South Africa
8 J5 **Prince Albert Peninsula** *peninsula* Victoria Island, Northwest Territories, NW Canada
8 J6 **Prince Albert Sound** *inlet* Northwest Territories, N Canada
9 P6 **Prince Charles Island** *island* Nunavut, NE Canada
195 W6 **Prince Charles Mountains** ▲▲ Antarctica
Prince-Édouard, Île-du *see* Prince Edward Island
172 M13 **Prince Edward Fracture Zone** *tectonic feature* SW Indian Ocean
13 P14 **Prince Edward Island** *Fr.* Île-du Prince-Édouard. ◈ *province* SE Canada
13 Q14 **Prince Edward Island** *Fr.* Île-du Prince-Édouard. *island* SE Canada
173 M12 **Prince Edward Islands** *island group* S South Africa
21 X4 **Prince Frederick** Maryland, NE USA
10 M14 **Prince George** British Columbia, SW Canada
21 W6 **Prince George** Virginia, NE USA
197 O8 **Prince Gustaf Adolf Sea** *sea* Nunavut, N Canada
197 Q3 **Prince of Wales, Cape** *headland* Alaska, USA
181 V1 **Prince of Wales Island** *island* Queensland, E Australia
8 L5 **Prince of Wales Island** *island* Queen Elizabeth Islands, Nunavut, NW Canada
39 Y14 **Prince of Wales Island** *island* Alexander Archipelago, Alaska, USA
Prince of Wales Island *see* Pinang, Pulau
8 J5 **Prince of Wales Strait** *strait* Northwest Territories, N Canada
197 O8 **Prince Patrick Island** *island* Parry Islands, Northwest Territories, NW Canada
9 N5 **Prince Regent Inlet** *channel* Nunavut, N Canada
10 J13 **Prince Rupert** British Columbia, SW Canada
Prince's Island *see* Príncipe
21 Y5 **Princess Anne** Maryland, NE USA
195 R1 **Princess Astrid Kyst** *physical region* Antarctica
181 W2 **Princess Charlotte Bay** *bay* Queensland, NE Australia
195 W7 **Princess Elizabeth Land** *physical region* Antarctica
10 J14 **Princess Royal Island** *island* British Columbia, SW Canada
45 U15 **Princes Town** Trinidad, Trinidad and Tobago
9 N17 **Princeton** British Columbia, SW Canada
30 L11 **Princeton** Illinois, N USA
31 N16 **Princeton** Indiana, N USA
29 Z14 **Princeton** Iowa, C USA
20 H7 **Princeton** Kentucky, S USA
29 V8 **Princeton** Minnesota, N USA
27 S1 **Princeton** Missouri, C USA
18 J15 **Princeton** New Jersey, NE USA
21 R6 **Princeton** West Virginia, NE USA
39 S12 **Prince William Sound** *inlet* Alaska, USA
67 P9 **Príncipe** *var.* Príncipe Island, *Eng.* Prince's Island. *island* N Sao Tome and Principe
Príncipe Island *see* Príncipe
32 I13 **Prineville** Oregon, NW USA
28 J11 **Pringle** South Dakota, N USA
25 N1 **Pringle** Texas, SW USA
99 H14 **Prinsenbeek** Noord-Brabant, S Netherlands
98 L6 **Prinses Margriet Kanaal** *canal* N Netherlands
195 T2 **Prinsesse Ragnhild Kyst** *physical region* Antarctica
195 U2 **Prins Harald Kyst** *physical region* Antarctica
92 N2 **Prins Karls Forland** *island* W Svalbard
43 N8 **Prinzapolka** Región Autónoma Atlántico Norte, NE Nicaragua
42 L8 **Prinzapolka, Río** ~ NE Nicaragua
122 H9 **Priob'ye** Khanty-Mansiyskiy Avtonomnyy Okrug, N Russian Federation
104 H1 **Prior, Cabo** *cape* NW Spain
29 V9 **Prior Lake** Minnesota, N USA
124 H11 **Priozersk** *Fin.* Käkisalmi. Leningradskaya Oblast', NW Russian Federation
119 J20 **Pripet** *Bel.* Prypyats', *Ukr.* Pryp"yat'. ~ Belarus/Ukraine
119 J20 **Pripet Marshes** *forested and swampy region* Belarus/Ukraine
Prishtinë *see* Priština
126 J8 **Pristen'** Kurskaya Oblast', W Russian Federation
113 N16 **Priština** *Alb.* Prishtinë. Kosovo, S Serbia
100 M10 **Pritzwalk** Brandenburg, NE Germany
103 R13 **Privas** Ardèche, E France
107 I16 **Priverno** Lazio, C Italy
Privigye *see* Prievidza
112 C12 **Privlaka** Zadar, SW Croatia
124 M15 **Privolzhsk** Ivanovskaya Oblast', NW Russian Federation
127 P7 **Privolzhskaya Vozvyshennost'** *var.* Volga Uplands. ▲▲ W Russian Federation
127 P8 **Privolzhskoye** Saratovskaya Oblast', W Russian Federation
Priwitz *see* Prievidza
127 N13 **Priyutnoye** Respublika Kalmykiya, SW Russian Federation
113 M17 **Prizren** *Alb.* Prizreni. Kosovo, S Serbia
Prizreni *see* Prizren
107 I24 **Prizzi** Sicilia, Italy, C Mediterranean Sea
113 P18 **Probištip** NE FYR Macedonia
169 S16 **Probolinggo** Jawa, C Indonesia
Probstberg *see* Wyszków
111 F14 **Prochowice** *Ger.* Parchwitz. Dolnośląskie, SW Poland
29 W5 **Proctor** Minnesota, N USA
25 R8 **Proctor** Texas, SW USA
25 R8 **Proctor Lake** ⊞ Texas, SW USA
155 I18 **Proddatūr** Andhra Pradesh, E India
104 H9 **Proença-a-Nova** *var.* Proença a Nova. Castelo Branco, C Portugal
Proença a Nova *see* Proença-a-Nova
99 I21 **Profondeville** Namur, SE Belgium
41 W11 **Progreso** Yucatán, SE Mexico
123 R14 **Progress** Amurskaya Oblast', SE Russian Federation
127 O15 **Prokhladnyy** Kabardino-Balkarskaya Respublika, SW Russian Federation
Prokletije *see* North Albanian Alps
Prökuls *see* Priekulė
113 O15 **Prokuplje** Serbia, SE Serbia
124 H14 **Proletariy** Novgorodskaya Oblast', W Russian Federation
126 M12 **Proletarsk** Rostovskaya Oblast', SW Russian Federation
126 J8 **Proletarskiy** Belgorodskaya Oblast', W Russian Federation
166 L7 **Prome** *var.* Pyè. Pegu, C Myanmar (Burma)
60 J8 **Promissão** São Paulo, S Brazil
60 J8 **Promissão, Represa de** ⊞ S Brazil
125 V4 **Promyshlennyy** Respublika Komi, NW Russian Federation
119 O16 **Pronya** ~ E Belarus
10 M11 **Prophet River** British Columbia, W Canada
30 K11 **Prophetstown** Illinois, N USA
Propinsi Kepulauan Riau *see* Kepulauan Riau
59 P16 **Propriá** Sergipe, E Brazil
103 X16 **Propriano** Corse, France, C Mediterranean Sea
Prościejów *see* Prostějov
Proskurov *see* Khmel'nyts'kyy
114 H12 **Prosotsáni** Anatolikí Makedonía kai Thráki, NE Greece
171 Q7 **Prosperidad** Mindanao, S Philippines
32 J10 **Prosser** Washington, NW USA
Prossnitz *see* Prostějov
111 G18 **Prostějov** *Ger.* Prossnitz, *Pol.* Prościejów. Olomoucký Kraj, E Czech Republic
117 V8 **Prosyana** Dnipropetrovs'ka Oblast', E Ukraine
111 L16 **Proszowice** Małopolskie, S Poland
Protasy *see* Pratasy
172 J11 **Protea Seamount** *undersea feature* SW Indian Ocean
115 D21 **Próti** *island* S Greece
114 N8 **Provadiya** Varna, E Bulgaria
103 T14 **Provence** *cultural region* SE France
103 S15 **Provence** *prev.* Marseille-Marignane. ✈ (Marseille) Bouches-du-Rhône, SE France
103 T14 **Provence-Alpes-Côte d'Azur** ◈ *region* SE France
20 H6 **Providence** Kentucky, S USA
19 N12 **Providence** *state capital* Rhode Island, NE USA
36 L1 **Providence** Utah, W USA
Providence *see* Fort Providence
Providence *see* Providence Atoll
67 X10 **Providence Atoll** *var.* Providence. *atoll* S Seychelles
14 D12 **Providence Bay** Manitoulin Island, Ontario, S Canada
23 R6 **Providence Canyon** *valley* Alabama/Georgia, S USA
22 I5 **Providence, Lake** ◎ Louisiana, S USA
35 X13 **Providence Mountains** ▲▲ California, W USA
44 L6 **Providenciales** *island* W Turks and Caicos Islands
19 Q12 **Provincetown** Massachusetts, NE USA
103 P5 **Provins** Seine-et-Marne, N France

◆ Country ● Country Capital ◇ Dependent Territory ○ Dependent Territory Capital ◈ Administrative Regions ✈ International Airport ▲ Mountain ▲▲ Mountain Range Volcano ~ River ◎ Lake ⊞ Reservoir

36 L3 **Provo** Utah, W USA
9 R15 **Provost** Alberta, SW Canada
112 G13 **Prozor** ◐ Federacija Bosna I Hercegovina, SW Bosnia and Herzegovina
Prozoroki *see* Prazaroki
60 I11 **Prudentópolis** Paraná, S Brazil
39 R5 **Prudhoe Bay** Alaska, USA
39 R4 **Prudhoe Bay** *bay* Alaska, USA
111 H16 **Prudnik** *Ger.* Neustadt, Neustadt in Oberschlesien. Opole, SW Poland
119 J16 **Prudy** *Rus.* Prudy. Minskaya Voblasts', C Belarus
101 D18 **Prüm** Rheinland-Pfalz, W Germany
101 D18 **Prüm** ≈ W Germany
Prusa *see* Bursa
110 J7 **Pruszcz Gdański** *Ger.* Praust. Pomorskie, N Poland
110 M12 **Pruszków** *Ger.* Kaltdorf. Mazowieckie, C Poland
116 K8 **Prut** *Ger.* Pruth. ≈ E Europe
Pruth *see* Prut
108 L8 **Prutz** Tirol, W Austria
Pružana *see* Pruzhany
119 G19 **Pruzhany** *Pol.* Prużana. Brestskaya Voblasts', SW Belarus
124 I11 **Pryazha** Respublika Kareliya, NW Russian Federation
117 U10 **Pryazovs'ke** Zaporiz'ka Oblast', SE Ukraine
Prychornomor'ska Nyzovyna *see* Black Sea Lowland
Prydniprovs'ka Nyzovyna/ Prydnyaprowskaya Nizina *see* Dnieper Lowland
195 Y7 **Prydz Bay** *bay* Antarctica
117 R4 **Pryluky** *Rus.* Priluki. Chernihivs'ka Oblast', NE Ukraine
117 V10 **Prymors'k** *Rus.* Primorsk; *prev.* Primorskoye. Zaporiz'ka Oblast', SE Ukraine
27 Q9 **Pryor** Oklahoma, C USA
33 U11 **Pryor Creek** ≈ Montana, NW USA
Pryp"yat'/Prypyats' *see* Pripet
110 M10 **Przasnysz** Mazowieckie, C Poland
111 K14 **Przedbórz** Lodzkie, S Poland
111 P17 **Przemyśl** *Rus.* Peremyshl. Podkarpackie, C Poland
111 O16 **Przeworsk** Podkarpackie, SE Poland
Przheval'sk *see* Karakol
110 L13 **Przysucha** Mazowieckie, SE Poland
115 H18 **Psachná** *var.* Psahna, Psakhná. Évvoia, C Greece
Psahna/Psakhná *see* Psachná
115 K18 **Psará** *island* E Greece
115 I16 **Psathoúra** *island* Vóreioi Sporádes, Greece, Aegean Sea
Pschestitz *see* Přeštice
Psein Lora *see* Pishin Lora
117 S5 **Psël** ≈ Russian Federation/Ukraine
115 M21 **Psérimos** *island* Dodekánisa, Greece, Aegean Sea
Pseyn Bowr *see* Pishin Lora
Pskem *see* Piskom
147 R8 **Pskemskiy Khrebet** *Uzb.* Piskom Tizmasi. ▲▲ Kyrgyzstan/Uzbekistan
124 F14 **Pskov** *Ger.* Pleskau, *Latv.* Pleskava. Pskovskaya Oblast', W Russian Federation
118 K6 **Pskov, Lake** *Est.* Pihkva Järv, *Ger.* Pleskauer See, *Rus.* Pskovskoye Ozero. ◎ Estonia/Russian Federation
124 F15 **Pskovskaya Oblast'** ◐ *province* W Russian Federation
Pskovskoye Ozero *see* Pskov, Lake
112 G9 **Psunj** ▲▲ NE Croatia
111 J17 **Pszczyna** *Ger.* Pless. Śląskie, S Poland
Ptačnik/Ptacsnik *see* Vtáčnik
115 D17 **Ptéri** ▲ C Greece
Ptich' *see* Ptsich
115 E14 **Ptolemaïda** *prev.* Ptolemaïs. Dytikí Makedonía, N Greece
Ptolemaïs *see* Ptolemaïda, Greece
Ptolemaïs *see* 'Akko, Israel
119 M19 **Ptsich** *Rus.* Ptich'. Homyel'skaya Voblasts', SE Belarus
119 M18 **Ptsich** *Rus.* Ptich'. ≈ SE Belarus
109 X10 **Ptuj** *Ger.* Pettau; *anc.* Poetovio. NE Slovenia
61 A23 **Puán** Buenos Aires, E Argentina
192 H15 **Pu'apu'a** Savai'i, C Samoa
192 G15 **Puava, Cape** *cape* Savai'i, NW Samoa
56 F12 **Pucallpa** Ucayali, C Peru
57 J17 **Pucarani** La Paz, NW Bolivia
Pučarevo *see* Novi Travnik
157 U12 **Pucheng** Shaanxi, SE China
160 L6 **Pucheng** *var.* Nanpu. Fujian, C China
125 N16 **Puchezh** Ivanovskaya Oblast', W Russian Federation
111 I19 **Púchov** *Hung.* Puhó. Trenčiansky Kraj, W Slovakia
116 J13 **Pucioasa** Dâmbovița, S Romania
110 I6 **Puck** Pomorskie, N Poland
30 L8 **Puckaway Lake** ◎ Wisconsin, N USA
63 G15 **Pucón** Araucanía, S Chile
93 M14 **Pudasjärvi** Oulu, C Finland
148 L8 **Pūdeh Tal, Shelleh-ye** ≈ SW Afghanistan
127 S1 **Pudem** Udmurtskaya Respublika, NW Russian Federation
Pudewitz *see* Pobiedziska
124 K11 **Pudozh** Respublika Kareliya, NW Russian Federation
97 M17 **Pudsey** N England, UK
Puduchcheri *see* Pondicherry
151 H21 **Pudukkottai** Tamil Nādu, SE India
171 Z13 **Pue** Papua, E Indonesia
41 P14 **Puebla** *var.* Puebla de Zaragoza. Puebla, S Mexico
41 P15 **Puebla** ◐ *state* S Mexico
104 L11 **Puebla de Alcocer** Extremadura, W Spain
Puebla de Don Fabrique *see* Puebla de Don Fadrique
105 P13 **Puebla de Don Fadrique** *var.* Puebla de Don Fabrique. Andalucía, S Spain
104 J11 **Puebla de la Calzada** Extremadura, W Spain
104 J5 **Puebla de Sanabria** Castilla-León, N Spain
Puebla de Trives *see* A Pobla de Trives
Puebla de Zaragoza *see* Puebla
37 T6 **Pueblo** Colorado, C USA
37 N10 **Pueblo Colorado Wash** *valley* Arizona, SW USA
61 C16 **Pueblo Libertador** Corrientes, NE Argentina
40 J10 **Pueblo Nuevo** Durango, C Mexico
42 J8 **Pueblo Nuevo** Estelí, NW Nicaragua
54 J3 **Pueblo Nuevo** Falcón, N Venezuela
42 B6 **Pueblo Nuevo Tiquisate** *var.* Tiquisate. Escuintla, SW Guatemala
41 Q11 **Pueblo Viejo, Laguna de** *lagoon* E Mexico
63 J14 **Puelches** La Pampa, C Argentina
104 L14 **Puente-Genil** Andalucía, S Spain
105 Q3 **Puente la Reina** *Bas.* Gares. Navarra, N Spain
104 L12 **Puente Nuevo, Embalse de** ⊠ S Spain
57 D14 **Puente Piedra** Lima, W Peru
160 F14 **Pu'er** *var.* Ning'er. Yunnan, SW China
45 V6 **Puerca, Punta** *headland* E Puerto Rico
37 R12 **Puerco, Rio** ≈ New Mexico, SW USA
57 J17 **Puerto Acosta** La Paz, W Bolivia
63 G19 **Puerto Aisén** Aisén, S Chile
41 R17 **Puerto Ángel** Oaxaca, SE Mexico
Puerto Argentino *see* Stanley
41 T17 **Puerto Arista** Chiapas, SE Mexico
43 O16 **Puerto Armuelles** Chiriquí, SW Panama
Puerto Arrecife *see* Arrecife
54 D14 **Puerto Asís** Putumayo, SW Colombia
54 L9 **Puerto Ayacucho** Amazonas, SW Venezuela
57 C18 **Puerto Ayora** Galapagos Islands, Ecuador, E Pacific Ocean
57 C18 **Puerto Baquerizo Moreno** *var.* Baquerizo Moreno. Galapagos Islands, Ecuador, E Pacific Ocean
42 G4 **Puerto Barrios** Izabal, E Guatemala
Puerto Bello *see* Portobelo
54 F8 **Puerto Berrío** Antioquia, C Colombia
54 F9 **Puerto Boyaca** Boyacá, C Colombia
54 K4 **Puerto Cabello** Carabobo, N Venezuela
43 N7 **Puerto Cabezas** *var.* Bilwi. Región Autónoma Atlántico Norte, NE Nicaragua
54 L9 **Puerto Carreño** Vichada, E Colombia
54 E4 **Puerto Colombia** Atlántico, N Colombia
42 H4 **Puerto Cortés** Cortés, NW Honduras
54 J4 **Puerto Cumarebo** Falcón, N Venezuela
Puerto de Cabras *see* Puerto del Rosario
55 Q5 **Puerto de Hierro** Sucre, NE Venezuela
64 O11 **Puerto de la Cruz** Tenerife, Islas Canarias, Spain, NE Atlantic Ocean
64 Q11 **Puerto del Rosario** *var.* Puerto de Cabras. Fuerteventura, Islas Canarias, Spain, NE Atlantic Ocean
63 J20 **Puerto Deseado** Santa Cruz, SE Argentina
40 F8 **Puerto Escondido** Baja California Sur, W Mexico
41 R17 **Puerto Escondido** Oaxaca, SE Mexico
60 G12 **Puerto Esperanza** Misiones, NE Argentina
56 D6 **Puerto Francisco de Orellana** *var.* Coca. Orellana, N Ecuador
54 H10 **Puerto Gaitán** Meta, C Colombia
Puerto Gallegos *see* Río Gallegos
60 G12 **Puerto Iguazú** Misiones, NE Argentina
56 F12 **Puerto Inca** Huánuco, N Peru
54 L11 **Puerto Inírida** *var.* Obando. Guainía, E Colombia
42 K13 **Puerto Jesús** Guanacaste, NW Costa Rica
41 Z11 **Puerto Juárez** Quintana Roo, SE Mexico
55 N5 **Puerto La Cruz** Anzoátegui, NE Venezuela
54 E14 **Puerto Leguízamo** Putumayo, S Colombia
43 N5 **Puerto Lempira** Gracias a Dios, E Honduras
Puerto Libertad *see* La Libertad
54 I11 **Puerto Limón** Meta, E Colombia
54 D13 **Puerto Limón** Putumayo, SW Colombia
Puerto Limón *see* Limón
105 N11 **Puertollano** Castilla-La Mancha, C Spain
63 K17 **Puerto Lobos** Chubut, SE Argentina
54 I3 **Puerto López** La Guajira, N Colombia
105 Q14 **Puerto Lumbreras** Murcia, SE Spain
41 V17 **Puerto Madero** Chiapas, SE Mexico
63 K17 **Puerto Madryn** Chubut, S Argentina
Puerto Magdalena *see* Bahía Magdalena
57 J15 **Puerto Maldonado** Madre de Dios, E Peru
Puerto Masachapa *see* Masachapa
Puerto México *see* Coatzacoalcos
63 G17 **Puerto Montt** Los Lagos, C Chile
41 Z12 **Puerto Morelos** Quintana Roo, SE Mexico
54 L10 **Puerto Nariño** Vichada, E Colombia
63 H23 **Puerto Natales** Magallanes, S Chile
43 X15 **Puerto Obaldía** San Blas, NE Panama
44 H6 **Puerto Padre** Las Tunas, E Cuba
54 L9 **Puerto Páez** Apure, C Venezuela
40 E3 **Puerto Peñasco** Sonora, NW Mexico
55 N5 **Puerto Píritu** Anzoátegui, NE Venezuela
45 N8 **Puerto Plata** *var.* San Felipe de Puerto Plata. N Dominican Republic
45 N8 **Puerto Plata** ✈ N Dominican Republic
Puerto Presidente Stroessner *see* Ciudad del Este
171 N6 **Puerto Princesa** *off.* Puerto Princesa City. Palawan, W Philippines
Puerto Princesa City *see* Puerto Princesa
Puerto Príncipe *see* Camagüey
Puerto Quellón *see* Quellón
60 F13 **Puerto Rico** Misiones, NE Argentina
57 K14 **Puerto Rico** Pando, N Bolivia
54 E12 **Puerto Rico** Caquetá, S Colombia
45 U5 **Puerto Rico** *off.* Commonwealth of Puerto Rico; *prev.* Porto Rico. ◇ *US commonwealth territory* C West Indies
64 F11 **Puerto Rico** *island* C West Indies
Puerto Rico, Commonwealth of *see* Puerto Rico
64 G11 **Puerto Rico Trench** *undersea feature* NE Caribbean Sea
54 I8 **Puerto Rondón** Arauca, E Colombia
Puerto San José *see* San José
63 J21 **Puerto San Julián** *var.* San Julián. Santa Cruz, SE Argentina
63 I22 **Puerto Santa Cruz** *var.* Santa Cruz. Santa Cruz, SE Argentina
Puerto Sauce *see* Juan L. Lacaze
57 Q20 **Puerto Suárez** Santa Cruz, E Bolivia
54 D13 **Puerto Umbría** Putumayo, SW Colombia
40 J13 **Puerto Vallarta** Jalisco, SW Mexico
63 G16 **Puerto Varas** Los Lagos, C Chile
42 M13 **Puerto Viejo** Heredia, NE Costa Rica
Puertoviejo *see* Portoviejo
57 B18 **Puerto Villamil** *var.* Villamil. Galapagos Islands, Ecuador, E Pacific Ocean
54 F8 **Puerto Wilches** Santander, N Colombia
63 H20 **Pueyrredón, Lago** *var.* Lago Cochrane. ◎ S Argentina
127 R7 **Pugachëv** Saratovskaya Oblast', W Russian Federation
127 T3 **Pugachëvo** Udmurtskaya Respublika, NW Russian Federation
32 H8 **Puget Sound** *sound* Washington, NW USA
107 O17 **Puglia** *var.* Le Puglie, *Eng.* Apulia. ◐ *region* SE Italy
107 N17 **Puglia, Canosa di** *anc.* Canusium. Puglia, SE Italy
118 I6 **Puhja** *Ger.* Kawelecht. Tartumaa, SE Estonia
Puhó *see* Púchov
105 V4 **Puigcerdà** Cataluña, NE Spain
Puigmal *see* Puigmal d'Err
103 N17 **Puigmal d'Err** *var.* Puigmal. ▲ S France
76 I16 **Pujehun** S Sierra Leone
Puka *see* Pukë
185 E20 **Pukaki, Lake** ◎ South Island, New Zealand
38 F10 **Pukalani** Maui, Hawai'i, USA
190 J13 **Pukapuka** *atoll* N Cook Islands
191 X9 **Pukapuka** *atoll* Îles Tuamotu, E French Polynesia
Pukari Neem *see* Purekkari Neem
191 X11 **Pukarua** *var.* Pukaruha. *atoll* Îles Tuamotu, E French Polynesia
Pukaruha *see* Pukarua
14 A7 **Pukaskwa** ≈ Ontario, S Canada
9 V12 **Pukatawagan** Manitoba, C Canada
191 X16 **Pukatikei, Maunga** ⩯ Easter Island, Chile, E Pacific Ocean
182 C1 **Pukatja** *var.* Ernabella. South Australia
163 Y12 **Pukch'ŏng** E North Korea
113 L18 **Pukë** *var.* Puka. Shkodër, N Albania
184 L6 **Pukekohe** Auckland, North Island, New Zealand
184 L7 **Pukemiro** Waikato, North Island, New Zealand
190 D12 **Puke, Mont** ▲ Île Futuna, W Wallis and Futuna
Puket *see* Phuket
185 C20 **Puketeraki Range** ▲▲ South Island, New Zealand
184 N13 **Puketoi Range** ▲▲ North Island, New Zealand
185 F21 **Pukeuri Junction** Otago, South Island, New Zealand
119 L16 **Pukhavichy** *Rus.* Pukhovichi. Minskaya Voblasts', C Belarus
Pukhovichi *see* Pukhavichy
124 M10 **Puksoozero** Arkhangel'skaya Oblast', NW Russian Federation
112 A10 **Pula** *It.* Pola; *prev.* Pulj. Istra, NW Croatia
Pula *see* Nyingchi
163 U14 **Pulandian** *var.* Xinjin. Liaoning, NE China
163 T14 **Pulandian Wan** *bay* NE China
189 O15 **Pulap Atoll** *atoll* Caroline Islands, C Micronesia
18 H9 **Pulaski** New York, NE USA
20 I10 **Pulaski** Tennessee, S USA
21 R7 **Pulaski** Virginia, NE USA
171 Y14 **Pulau, Sungai** ≈ Papua, E Indonesia
110 N13 **Puławy** *Ger.* Neu Amerika. Lubelskie, E Poland
146 I16 **Pulhatyn** *Rus.* Polekhatum; *prev.* Pul'-I-Khatum. Ahal Welaýaty, S Turkmenistan
101 E16 **Pulheim** Nordrhein-Westfalen, W Germany
Pulicat *see* Pālghāt
155 J19 **Pulicat Lake** *lagoon* SE India
Pul'-I-Khatum *see* Pulhatyn
Pul-i-Khumri *see* Pol-e Khomrī
Pul-i-Sefid *see* Pol-e Safīd
Pulj *see* Pula
109 W2 **Pulkau** ≈ NE Austria
93 L15 **Pulkkila** Oulu, C Finland
122 C7 **Pul'kovo** ✈ (Sankt-Peterburg) Leningradskaya Oblast', NW Russian Federation
32 M9 **Pullman** Washington, NW USA
108 B10 **Pully** Vaud, SW Switzerland
40 F7 **Púlpita, Punta** *headland* W Mexico
110 M10 **Pułtusk** Mazowieckie, C Poland
158 H10 **Pulu** Xinjiang Uygur Zizhiqu, W China
137 P13 **Pülümür** Tunceli, E Turkey
189 N16 **Pulusuk** *island* Caroline Islands, C Micronesia
189 N16 **Puluwat Atoll** *atoll* Caroline Islands, C Micronesia
25 N11 **Pumpville** Texas, SW USA
191 P7 **Punaauia** *var.* Hakapehi. Tahiti, W French Polynesia
56 B8 **Puná, Isla** *island* SW Ecuador
185 G16 **Punakaiki** West Coast, South Island, New Zealand
153 T11 **Punakha** C Bhutan
57 L18 **Punata** Cochabamba, C Bolivia
155 E14 **Pune** *prev.* Poona. Mahārāshtra, W India
83 M17 **Pungoè, Rio** *var.* Púnguè, Pungwe. ≈ C Mozambique
21 X10 **Pungo River** ≈ North Carolina, SE USA
Púnguè/Pungwe *see* Pungoè, Rio
79 N19 **Punia** Maniema, E Dem. Rep. Congo
62 H8 **Punilla, Sierra de la** ▲▲ W Argentina
161 P14 **Puning** Guangdong, S China
62 G10 **Punitaqui** Coquimbo, C Chile
152 H8 **Punjab** ◐ *state* NW India
149 T9 **Punjab** *prev.* West Punjab, Western Punjab. ◐ *province* E Pakistan
129 Q9 **Punjab Plains** *plain* N India
93 O17 **Punkaharju** *var.* Punkasalmi. Isä-Suomi, E Finland
Punkasalmi *see* Punkaharju
57 I17 **Puno** Puno, SE Peru
57 H17 **Puno** *off.* Departamento de Puno. ◐ *department* S Peru
Puno, Departamento de *see* Puno
61 B24 **Punta Alta** Buenos Aires, E Argentina
63 H24 **Punta Arenas** *prev.* Magallanes. Magallanes, S Chile
45 T6 **Punta, Cerro de** ▲ C Puerto Rico
43 T15 **Punta Chame** Panamá, C Panama
57 G17 **Punta Colorada** Arequipa, SW Peru
40 F9 **Punta Coyote** Baja California Sur, W Mexico
62 G8 **Punta de Díaz** Atacama, N Chile
61 G20 **Punta del Este** Maldonado, S Uruguay
63 K17 **Punta Delgada** Chubut, SE Argentina
55 O5 **Punta de Mata** Monagas, NE Venezuela
55 O4 **Punta de Piedras** Nueva Esparta, NE Venezuela
42 F4 **Punta Gorda** Toledo, SE Belize
43 N11 **Punta Gorda** Región Autónoma Atlántico Sur, SE Nicaragua
23 W14 **Punta Gorda** Florida, SE USA
42 M11 **Punta Gorda, Río** ≈ SE Nicaragua
62 H6 **Punta Negra, Salar de** *salt lake* N Chile
40 D5 **Punta Prieta** Baja California, NW Mexico
42 L13 **Puntarenas** Puntarenas, W Costa Rica
42 L13 **Puntarenas** *off.* Provincia de Puntarenas. ◐ *province* W Costa Rica
Puntarenas, Provincia de *see* Puntarenas
80 P13 **Puntland** *cultural region* NE Somalia
54 J4 **Punto Fijo** Falcón, N Venezuela
105 S4 **Puntón de Guara** ▲ N Spain
18 D14 **Punxsutawney** Pennsylvania, NE USA
93 M14 **Puolanka** Oulu, C Finland
57 J17 **Pupuya, Nevado** ▲ W Bolivia
Puqi *see* Chibi
57 F16 **Puquio** Ayacucho, S Peru
122 I9 **Pur** ≈ N Russian Federation
186 D7 **Purari** ≈ S Papua New Guinea
27 N11 **Purcell** Oklahoma, C USA
9 O16 **Purcell Mountains** ▲▲ British Columbia, SW Canada
105 P14 **Purchena** Andalucía, S Spain
27 S8 **Purdy** Missouri, C USA
118 I2 **Purekkari Neem** *prev.* Pukari Neem. *headland* N Estonia
37 U7 **Purgatoire River** ≈ Colorado, C USA
Purgstall *see* Purgstall an der Erlauf
109 V5 **Purgstall an der Erlauf** *var.* Purgstall. Niederösterreich, NE Austria
154 O13 **Puri** *var.* Jagannath. Orissa, E India
Puriramya *see* Buriram
109 X4 **Purkersdorf** Niederösterreich, NE Austria
98 I9 **Purmerend** Noord-Holland, C Netherlands
151 G16 **Pūrna** ≈ C India
Purnea *see* Pūrnia
153 R13 **Pūrnia** *prev.* Purnea. Bihār, NE India
Pursat *see* Poŭthĭsăt, Poŭthĭsăt, W Cambodia
Pursat *see* Poŭthĭsăt, Stœng, W, Cambodia
Purulia *see* Puruliya
150 L13 **Puruliya** *prev.* Purulia. West Bengal, NE India
47 G7 **Purus, Rio** *var.* Río Purús. ≈ Brazil/Peru
186 C9 **Purutu Island** *island* SW Papua New Guinea
93 N17 **Puruvesi** ◎ SE Finland
22 L7 **Purvis** Mississippi, S USA
114 J11 **Pŭrvomay** *prev.* Borisovgrad. Plovdiv, C Bulgaria
169 R16 **Purwodadi** *prev.* Poerwodadi. Jawa, C Indonesia
169 P16 **Purwokerto** *prev.* Poerwokerto. Jawa, C Indonesia
169 P16 **Purworejo** *prev.* Poerworedjo. Jawa, C Indonesia
20 H8 **Puryear** Tennessee, S USA
154 H13 **Pusad** Mahārāshtra, C India
163 Z16 **Pusan** *off.* Pusan-gwangyŏksi, *var.* Busan, *Jap.* Fusan. SE South Korea
Pusan *see* Kim Hae
Pusan-gwangyŏksi *see* Pusan
168 H7 **Pusatgajo, Pegunungan** ▲▲ Sumatera, NW Indonesia
Puschlav *see* Poschiavo
Pushkin *see* Tsarskoye Selo
127 Q8 **Pushkino** Saratovskaya Oblast', W Russian Federation
Pushkino *see* Biläsuvar
111 M22 **Püspökladány** Hajdú-Bihar, E Hungary
118 J3 **Püssi** *Ger.* Isenhof. Ida-Virumaa, NE Estonia
116 I5 **Pustomyty** L'vivs'ka Oblast', W Ukraine
124 F16 **Pustoshka** Pskovskaya Oblast', W Russian Federation
Pusztakalán *see* Călan
167 N1 **Putao** *prev.* Fort Hertz. Kachin State, N Myanmar (Burma)
184 M8 **Putaruru** Waikato, North Island, New Zealand
Puteoli *see* Pozzuoli
161 R12 **Putian** Fujian, SE China
107 O17 **Putignano** Puglia, SE Italy
Puting *see* De'an
Putivl' *see* Putyvl'
41 Q16 **Putla** *var.* Putla de Guerrero. Oaxaca, SE Mexico
Putla de Guerrero *see* Putla
19 N12 **Putnam** Connecticut, NE USA
25 Q7 **Putnam** Texas, SW USA
18 M10 **Putney** Vermont, NE USA
111 L20 **Putnok** Borsod-Abaúj-Zemplén, NE Hungary
Putorana, Gory/Putorana Mountains *see* Putorana, Plato
122 L8 **Putorana, Plato** *var.* Gory Putorana, *Eng.* Putorana Mountains. ▲▲ N Russian Federation
168 K9 **Putrajaya** ● (Malaysia) Kuala Lumpur, Peninsular Malaysia
62 H2 **Putre** Tarapacá, N Chile
155 J24 **Puttalam** North Western Province, W Sri Lanka
155 J24 **Puttalam Lagoon** *lagoon* W Sri Lanka
99 H17 **Putte** Antwerpen, C Belgium
94 E10 **Puttegga** ▲ S Norway
98 K11 **Putten** Gelderland, C Netherlands
100 K7 **Puttgarden** Schleswig-Holstein, N Germany
Puttiala *see* Patiāla
101 D20 **Püttlingen** Saarland, SW Germany
54 D14 **Putumayo** *off.* Intendencia del Putumayo. ◐ *province* S Colombia
Putumayo, Intendencia del *see* Putumayo
48 E7 **Putumayo, Río** *var.* Içá, Rio. ≈ NW South America *see also* Içá, Rio
Putumayo, Río *see* Içá, Rio
169 P11 **Putus, Tanjung** *cape* Borneo, N Indonesia
116 J8 **Putyla** Chernivets'ka Oblast', W Ukraine
117 S3 **Putyvl'** *Rus.* Putivl'. Sums'ka Oblast', NE Ukraine
93 M18 **Puula** ◎ SE Finland
93 N18 **Puumala** Isä-Suomi, E Finland
118 I5 **Puurmani** *Ger.* Talkhof. Jõgevamaa, E Estonia
99 G17 **Puurs** Antwerpen, N Belgium
38 F10 **Pu'u 'Ula'ula** *var.* Red Hill. ▲ Maui, Hawai'i, USA
38 A8 **Pu'uwai** *var* Puuwai. Ni'ihau, Hawai'i, USA
12 J4 **Puvirnituq** *prev.* Povungnituk. Québec, NE Canada
32 H8 **Puyallup** Washington, NW USA
161 O5 **Puyang** Henan, C China
161 R9 **Puyang Jiang** *var.* Tsien Tang. ≈ SE China
103 O11 **Puy-de-Dôme** ◐ *department* C France
103 N15 **Puylaurens** Tarn, S France
102 M13 **Puy-l'Evêque** Lot, S France
103 N17 **Puymorens, Col de** *pass* S France
56 C7 **Puyo** Pastaza, C Ecuador
185 A24 **Puysegur Point** *headland* South Island, New Zealand
148 J8 **Pūzak, Hāmūn-e** *Pash.* Hāmūn-i-Puzak. ◎ SW Afghanistan
Puzak, Hāmūn-i- *see* Pūzak, Hāmūn-e
81 J23 **Pwani** *Eng.* Coast. ◐ *region* E Tanzania
79 O23 **Pweto** Katanga, SE Dem. Rep. Congo
97 I19 **Pwllheli** NW Wales, UK
189 O14 **Pwok** Pohnpei, E Micronesia
122 I9 **Pyakupur** ≈ N Russian Federation
124 M6 **Pyalitsa** Murmanskaya Oblast', NW Russian Federation
124 K10 **Pyal'ma** Respublika Kareliya, NW Russian Federation
Pyandzh *see* Panj
124 I6 **Pyaozero, Ozero** ◎ NW Russian Federation
166 L9 **Pyapon** Irrawaddy, SW Myanmar (Burma)
119 J15 **Pyarshai** *Rus.* Pershay. Minskaya Voblasts', C Belarus
122 K8 **Pyasina** ≈ N Russian Federation
114 I10 **Pyasŭchnik, Yazovir** ⊠ C Bulgaria
Pyatikhatki *see* P"yatykhatky
117 S7 **P"yatykhatky** *Rus.* Pyatikhatki. Dnipropetrovs'ka Oblast', E Ukraine
166 M6 **Pyawbwe** Mandalay, C Myanmar (Burma)
127 T3 **Pychas** Udmurtskaya Respublika, NW Russian Federation
Pyè *see* Prome
166 K6 **Pyechin** Chin State, W Myanmar (Burma)
119 G17 **Pyeski** *Rus.* Peski. Hrodzyenskaya Voblasts', W Belarus
119 L19 **Pyetrykaw** *Rus.* Petrikov. Homyel'skaya Voblasts', SE Belarus
93 O17 **Pyhäjärvi** ◎ SE Finland
93 M16 **Pyhäjärvi** ◎ C Finland
93 L15 **Pyhäjoki** Oulu, W Finland
93 L15 **Pyhäjoki** ≈ W Finland
93 M15 **Pyhäntä** Oulu, C Finland
93 M16 **Pyhäsalmi** Oulu, C Finland
93 O17 **Pyhäselkä** ◎ SE Finland
93 M19 **Pyhtää** *Swe.* Pyttis. Etelä-Suomi, S Finland
166 M6 **Pyinmana** (Myanmar (Burma)) Mandalay, C Myanmar (Burma)
115 N24 **Pylés** *var.* Piles. Kárpathos, SE Greece
115 D21 **Pýlos** *var.* Pilos. Pelopónnisos, S Greece
18 B12 **Pymatuning Reservoir** ⊠ Ohio/Pennsylvania, NE USA
163 X15 **P'yŏngt'aek** NW South Korea
163 V14 **P'yŏngyang** *var.* P'yŏngyang-si, *Eng.* Pyongyang. ● (North Korea) SW North Korea
P'yŏngyang-si *see* P'yŏngyang
35 Q4 **Pyramid Lake** ◎ Nevada, W USA
37 P15 **Pyramid Mountains** ▲▲ New Mexico, SW USA
37 R5 **Pyramid Peak** ▲ Colorado, C USA
115 D17 **Pyramíva** *var.* Piramiva. ▲ C Greece
Pyrenaei Montes *see* Pyrenees
86 B12 **Pyrenees** *Fr.* Pyrénées, *Sp.* Pirineos; *anc.* Pyrenaei Montes. ▲▲ SW Europe
102 J16 **Pyrénées-Atlantiques** ◐ *department* SW France
103 N17 **Pyrénées-Orientales** ◐ *department* S France
115 L19 **Pyrgí** *var.* Pirgi. Chíos, E Greece
115 D20 **Pýrgos** *var.* Pírgos. Dytikí Ellás, S Greece
Pyritz *see* Pyrzyce
115 E19 **Pýrros** ≈ S Greece
117 R4 **Pyryatyn** *Rus.* Piryatin. Poltavs'ka Oblast', NE Ukraine
110 D9 **Pyrzyce** *Ger.* Pyritz. Zachodnio-pomorskie, NW Poland
124 F15 **Pytalovo** *Latv.* Abrene; *prev.* Jaunlatgale. Pskovskaya Oblast', W Russian Federation
115 M20 **Pythagóreio** *var.* Pithagorio. Sámos, Dodekánisa, Greece, Aegean Sea
14 L11 **Pythonga, Lac** ◎ Québec, SE Canada
Pyttis *see* Pyhtää
166 M7 **Pyu** Pegu, C Myanmar (Burma)
166 M8 **Pyuntaza** Pegu, SW Myanmar (Burma)
153 N11 **Pyuthan** Mid Western, W Nepal
110 H12 **Pyzdry** *Ger.* Peisern. Wielkopolskie, C Poland

Q

138 H13 **Qā' al Jafr** ◎ S Jordan
197 O11 **Qaanaaq** *var.* Qânâq, *Dan.* Thule. ◐ Avannaarsua, N Greenland
Qabanbay *see* Kabanbay
138 G7 **Qabb Eliâs** E Lebanon
Qabil *see* Al Qābil
Qabırrı *see* Iori
Qābis *see* Gabès
Qābis, Khalīj *see* Gabès, Golfe de
Qabqa *see* Gonghe
141 S14 **Qabr Hūd** C Yemen
Qacentina *see* Constantine
148 L4 **Qādes** Bādghīs, NW Afghanistan
139 T11 **Qādisīyah** S Iraq
143 O4 **Qa'emshahr** *prev.* 'Aliābad, Shāhī. Māzandarān, N Iran
143 U7 **Qā'en** *var.* Qain, Qāyen. Khorāsān-Razavī, E Iran
141 U13 **Qafa** *spring/well* SW Oman
Qafşah *see* Gafsa
163 Q12 **Qagan Nur** *var.* Xulun Hobot Qagan, Zhengxiangbai Qi. Nei Mongol Zizhiqu, N China
163 V9 **Qagan Nur** ◎ NE China
163 Q11 **Qagan Nur** ◎ N China
Qagan Us *see* Dulan
158 H13 **Qagcaka** Xizang Zizhiqu, W China
Qagchêng *see* Xiangcheng
Qahremānshahr *see* Kermānshāh
159 Q10 **Qaidam He** ≈ C China
156 L8 **Qaidam Pendi** *basin* C China
Qain *see* Qā'en
Qala Āhangarān *see* Chaghcharān

139 U3 **Qaļā Diza** *var.* Qal 'at Dīzah. NE Iraq
Qal'ah Sālih *see* Qal'at Şāliḩ
147 R13 **Qal'aikhum** *Rus.* Kalaikhum. S Tajikistan
Qala Nau *see* Qal'eh-ye Now
141 V17 **Qalansīyah** Suquṭrā, W Yemen
Qala Panja *see* Qal'eh-ye Panjeh
Qala Shāhar *see* Qal'eh Shahr
149 O8 **Qalāt** *Per.* Kalāt. Zābol, S Afghanistan
139 W9 **Qal'at Aḩmad** E Iraq
141 N11 **Qal'at Bīshah** 'Asīr, SW Saudi Arabia
138 H4 **Qal'at Burzay** Ḩamāh, W Syria
Qal 'at Dīzah *see* Qaļā Diza
139 W9 **Qal'at Ḩusayh** E Iraq
139 V10 **Qal'at Majnūnah** S Iraq
139 X11 **Qal'at Şāliḩ** *var.* Qal'ah Sālih. E Iraq
139 V10 **Qal'at Sukkar** SE Iraq
Qalba Zhotasy *see* Kalbinskiy Khrebet
143 Q12 **Qal'eh Biābān** Fārs, S Iran
149 N4 **Qal'eh Shahr** *Pash.* Qala Shāhar. Sar-e Pol, N Afghanistan
148 L4 **Qal'eh-ye Now** *var.* Qala Nau. Bādghīs, NW Afghanistan
149 T2 **Qal'eh-ye Panjeh** *var.* Qala Panja. Badakhshān, NE Afghanistan
Qamar Bay *see* Qamar, Ghubbat al
141 U14 **Qamar, Ghubbat al** *Eng.* Qamar Bay. *bay* Oman/Yemen
141 V13 **Qamar, Jabal al** ▲▲ SW Oman
147 N12 **Qamashi** Qashqadaryo Viloyati, S Uzbekistan
Qambar *see* Kambar
159 R14 **Qamdo** Xizang Zizhiqu, W China
75 R7 **Qamīnis** NE Libya
Qamishly *see* Al Qāmishlī
Qânâq *see* Qaanaaq
Qandahār *see* Kandahār
80 Q11 **Qandala** Bari, NE Somalia
Qandyaghash *see* Kandyagash
138 L2 **Qanţārī** Ar Raqqah, N Syria
Qapiciğ Daği *see* Qazangödağ
158 H5 **Qapqal** *var.* Qapqal Xibe Zizhixian. Xinjiang Uygur Zizhiqu, NW China
Qapqal Xibe Zizhixian *see* Qapqal
Qapshagay Böyeni *see* Kapchagayskoye Vodokhranilishche
Qapugtang *see* Zadoi
196 M15 **Qaqortoq** *Dan.* Julianehåb. ◆ Kitaa, S Greenland
75 U8 **Qâra** *var.* Qārah. NW Egypt
139 T4 **Qara Anjīr** N Iraq
Qarabāgh *see* Qarah Bāgh
Qaraböget *see* Karaboget
Qarabulaq *see* Karabulak
Qarabutaq *see* Karabutak
Qaraghandy/Qaraghandy Oblysy *see* Karaganda
Qaraghayly *see* Karagayly
139 U4 **Qara Gol** NE Iraq
Qārah *see* Qâra
148 J4 **Qarah Bāgh** *var.* Qarabāgh. Herāt, NW Afghanistan
138 G7 **Qaraoun, Lac de** *var.* Buḩayrat al Qir'awn. ◎ S Lebanon
Qaraoy *see* Karaoy
Qaraqoyyn *see* Karakoyyn, Ozero
Qara Qum *see* Garagum
Qarasū *see* Karasu
Qaratal *see* Karatal
Qarataū *see* Karatau, Khrebet, Kazakhstan
Qarataū *see* Karatau, Zhambyl, Kazakhstan
Qaraton *see* Karaton
80 P13 **Qardho** *var.* Kardh, *It.* Gardo. Bari, N Somalia
142 M6 **Qareh Chāy** ⚡ N Iran
142 K2 **Qareh Sū** ⚡ NW Iran
Qariateïne *see* Al Qaryatayn
Qarkilik *see* Ruoqiang
147 O13 **Qarluq** *Rus.* Karluk. Surkhondaryo Viloyati, S Uzbekistan
147 U12 **Qarokŭl** *Rus.* Karakul'. E Tajikistan
147 T12 **Qarokŭl** *Rus.* Ozero Karakul'. ◎ E Tajikistan
Qarqan *see* Qiemo
158 K9 **Qarqan He** ⚡ NW China
Qarqannah, Juzur *see* Kerkenah, Îles de
Qarqaraly *see* Karkaralinsk
149 O1 **Qarqīn** Jowzjān, N Afghanistan
Qars *see* Kars
Qarsaqbay *see* Karsakpay
146 M12 **Qarshi** *Rus.* Karshi; *prev.* Bek-Budi. Qashqadaryo Viloyati, S Uzbekistan
146 L12 **Qarshi Cho'li** *Rus.* Karshinskaya Step. *grassland* S Uzbekistan
146 M13 **Qarshi Kanali** *Rus.* Karshinskiy Kanal. *canal* Turkmenistan/Uzbekistan
Qaryatayn *see* Al Qaryatayn
Qāsh, Nahr al *see* Gash
146 M12 **Qashqadaryo Viloyati** *Rus.* Kashkadar'inskaya Oblast'. ◆ *province* S Uzbekistan
Qasigianguit *see* Qasigiannguit
197 N13 **Qasigiannguit** *var.* Qasigianguit, *Dan.* Christianshåb. ◆ Kitaa, C Greenland
Qaşim, Minţaqat *see* Al Qaşīm
Qasr al Hir Ash Sharqī *see* Ḩayr ash Sharqī, Qaşr al
139 P8 **Qaşr 'Amīj** C Iraq
139 R9 **Qaşr Darwīshāh** C Iraq
142 J6 **Qaşr-e Shīrīn** Kermānshāhān, W Iran
75 V10 **Qasr Farâfra** W Egypt
Qassim *see* Al Qaşīm
141 O16 **Qa'ţabah** SW Yemen
138 H7 **Qaţanā** *var.* Katana. Dimashq, S Syria
143 N15 **Qatar** *off.* State of Qatar, *Ar.* Dawlat Qaţar. ◆ *monarchy* SW Asia
Qatar, State of *see* Qatar
Qatrana *see* Al Qaţrānah
143 Q12 **Qaţrūyeh** Fārs, S Iran
Qattara Depression/ Qaţţārah, Munkhafaḑ al *see* Qaţţâra, Monkhafad el
75 U8 **Qaţţâra, Monkhafad el** *var.* Munkhafaḑ al Qaţţārah, *Eng.* Qattara Depression. *desert* NW Egypt
Qattinah, Buhayrat *see* Ḩimş, Buḩayrat
Qaydār *see* Qeydār
Qāyen *see* Qā'en
147 Q11 **Qayroqqum** *Rus.* Kayrakkum. NW Tajikistan
147 Q10 **Qayroqqum, Obanbori** *Rus.* Kayrakkumskoye Vodokhranilishche. ▣ NW Tajikistan
137 V13 **Qazangödağ** *Rus.* Gora Kapydzhik, *Turk.* Qapiciğ Daği. ▲ SW Azerbaijan
139 U7 **Qazānīyah** *var.* Dhū Shaykh. E Iraq
Qazaqstan/Qazaqstan Respublikasy *see* Kazakhstan
137 T9 **Qazbegi** *Rus.* Kazbegi. NE Georgia
149 P15 **Qāzi Ahmad** *var.* Kazi Ahmad. Sind, SE Pakistan
137 Y12 **Qazimämmäd** *Rus.* Kazi Magomed. SE Azerbaijan
Qazris *see* Cáceres
142 M4 **Qazvīn** *var.* Kazvin. Qazvīn, N Iran
142 M5 **Qazvīn** ◆ *province* N Iran
187 Z13 **Qelelevu Lagoon** *lagoon* NE Fiji
75 X10 **Qena** *var.* Qinā; *anc.* Caene, Caenepolis. E Egypt
113 L23 **Qeparo** Vlorë, S Albania
Qeqertarssuaq *see* Qeqertarsuaq
197 N13 **Qeqertarsuaq** *var.* Qeqertarssuaq, *Dan.* Godhavn. ◆ Kitaa, S Greenland
196 M13 **Qeqertarsuaq** *island* W Greenland
197 N13 **Qeqertarsuup Tunua** *Dan.* Disko Bugt. *inlet* W Greenland
Qerveh *see* Qorveh
143 S14 **Qeshm** Hormozgān, S Iran
143 R14 **Qeshm** *var.* Jazīreh-ye Qeshm, Qeshm Island. *island* S Iran
Qeshm Island/Qeshm, Jazīreh-ye *see* Qeshm
142 L4 **Qeydār** *var.* Qaydār. Zanjān, NW Iran
142 K5 **Qezel Owzan, Rūd-e** *var.* Ki Zil Uzen, Qi Zil Uzun. ⚡ NW Iran
Qian *see* Guizhou
161 Q2 **Qian'an** Hebei, E China
Qiandao Hu *see* Xin'anjiang Shuiku
Qiandaohu *see* Chun'an
Qian Gorlo/Qian Gorlos/ Qian Gorlos Mongolzu Zizhixian/Quianguozhen *see* Qianguo
163 V9 **Qianguo** *var.* Qian Gorlo, Qian Gorlos, Qian Gorlos Mongolzu Zizhixian, Quianguozhen. Jilin, NE China
161 N9 **Qianjiang** Hubei, C China
160 K10 **Qianjiang** Sichuan, C China
160 L14 **Qian Jiang** ⚡ S China
160 G9 **Qianning** *var.* Gartar. Sichuan, C China
163 U13 **Qian Shan** ▲▲ NE China
160 H10 **Qianwei** *var.* Yujin. Sichuan, C China
160 J11 **Qianxi** Guizhou, S China
Qiaotou *see* Datong
Qiaowa *see* Muli
159 Q7 **Qiaowan** Gansu, N China
Qibilī *see* Kebili
158 K9 **Qiemo** *var.* Qarqan. Xinjiang Uygur Zizhiqu, NW China
160 J10 **Qijiang** *var.* Gunan. Chongqing Shi, C China
159 N5 **Qijiaojing** Xinjiang Uygur Zizhiqu, NW China
Qike *see* Xunke
149 P9 **Qila Saifullāh** Baluchistān, SW Pakistan
159 S9 **Qilian** *var.* Babao. Qinghai, C China
159 N8 **Qilian Shan** *var.* Kilien Mountains. ▲▲ N China
197 O11 **Qimusseriarsuaq** *Dan.* Melville Bugt, *Eng.* Melville Bay. *bay* NW Greenland
Qinā *see* Qena
159 W11 **Qin'an** Gansu, C China
Qincheng *see* Nanfeng
Qing *see* Qinghai
163 W7 **Qing'an** Heilongjiang, NE China
161 R5 **Qingdao** *var.* Ching-Tao, Ch'ing-tao, Tsingtao, Tsintao, *Ger.* Tsingtau. Shandong, E China
163 V8 **Qinggang** Heilongjiang, NE China
Qinggil *see* Qinghe
159 P11 **Qinghai** *var.* Chinghai, Koko Nor, Qing, Qinghai Sheng, Tsinghai. ◆ *province* C China
159 S10 **Qinghai Hu** *var.* Ch'ing Hai, Tsing Hai, *Mong.* Koko Nor. ◎ C China
Qinghai Sheng *see* Qinghai
158 M3 **Qinghe** *var.* Qinggil. Xinjiang Uygur Zizhiqu, NW China
160 L4 **Qingjian** *var* Kuanzhou, *prev* Xiuyan. Shaanxi, C China
160 L9 **Qing Jiang** ⚡ C China
Qingjiang *see* Huai'an
Qingkou *see* Ganyu
160 I12 **Qinglong** *var.* Liancheng. Guizhou, S China
161 Q2 **Qinglong** Hebei, E China
Qingshan *see* Wudalianchi
159 R12 **Qingshuihe** Qinghai, C China
159 X10 **Qingyang** *var.* Xifeng. Gansu, C China
Qingyang *see* Jinjiang
161 N14 **Qingyuan** Guangdong, S China
163 V11 **Qingyuan** *var.* Qingyuan Manzu Zizhixian. Liaoning, NE China
Qingyuan Manzu Zizhixian *see* Qingyuan
158 L13 **Qingzang Gaoyuan** *var.* Xizang Gaoyuan, *Eng.* Plateau of Tibet. *plateau* W China
161 Q4 **Qingzhou** *prev.* Yidu. Shandong, E China
157 R9 **Qin He** ⚡ C China
161 Q2 **Qinhuangdao** Hebei, E China
160 K7 **Qin Ling** ▲▲ C China
161 N5 **Qinxian** *var.* Qin Xian. Shanxi, C China
Qin Xian *see* Qinxian
161 N6 **Qinyang** Henan, C China
160 K15 **Qinzhou** Guangxi Zhuangzu Zizhiqu, S China
Qiong *see* Hainan
160 L17 **Qionghai** *prev.* Jiaji. Hainan, S China
160 H9 **Qionglai** Sichuan, C China
160 H8 **Qionglai Shan** ▲▲ C China
Qiongxi *see* Hongyuan
160 L17 **Qiongzhou Haixia** *var.* Hainan Strait. *strait* S China
163 U7 **Qiqihar** *var.* Ch'i-ch'i-ha-erh, Tsitsihar; *prev.* Lungkiang. Heilongjiang, NE China
Qir *see* Qīr-va-Kārzīn
158 H10 **Qira** Xinjiang Uygur Zizhiqu, NW China
Qir'awn, Buḩayrat al *see* Qaraoun, Lac de
143 P12 **Qīr-va-Kārzīn** *var* Qir. Fārs, S Iran
138 F11 **Qiryat Gat** *var.* Kyriat Gat. Southern, C Israel
138 G8 **Qiryat Shemona** Northern, N Israel
Qishlaq *see* Garmsār
141 U14 **Qishn** SE Yemen
138 G9 **Qishon, Naḩal** ⚡ N Israel
Qita Ghazzah *see* Gaza Strip
156 K5 **Qitai** Xinjiang Uygur Zizhiqu, NW China
163 Y8 **Qitaihe** Heilongjiang, NE China
141 W12 **Qitbīt, Wādī** *dry watercourse* S Oman
161 O5 **Qixian** *var.* Qi Xian, Zhaoge. Henan, C China
Qi Xian *see* Qixian
Qīzān *see* Jīzān
Qizil Orda *see* Kyzylorda
Qizil Qum/Qizilqum *see* Kyzyl Kum
147 V14 **Qizilrabot** *Rus.* Kyzylrabot. SE Tajikistan
146 J10 **Qizilravot** *Rus.* Kyzylrabat. Buxoro Viloyati, C Uzbekistan
Qi Zil Uzun *see* Qezel Owzan, Rūd-e
139 S4 **Qizil Yār** N Iraq
Qoghaly *see* Kugaly
Qogir Feng *see* K2
143 N6 **Qom** *var.* Kum, Qum. Qom, N Iran
143 N6 **Qom** ◆ *province* N Iran
Qomisheh *see* Shahreẕā
Qomolangma Feng *see* Everest, Mount
142 M7 **Qom, Rūd-e** ⚡ C Iran
Qomsheh *see* Shahreẕā
Qomul *see* Hami
Qondūz *see* Kondoz
146 G7 **Qo'ng'irot** *Rus.* Kungrad. Qoraqalpog'iston Respublikasi, NW Uzbekistan
Qongyrat *see* Konyrat
Qoqek *see* Tacheng
147 R10 **Qo'qon** *var.* Khokand, *Rus.* Kokand. Farg'ona Voliyati, E Uzbekistan
Qorabowur Kirlari *see* Karabaur', Uval
Qoradaryo *see* Karadar'ya
146 G6 **Qorajar** *Rus.* Karadzhar. Qoraqalpoghiston Respublikasi, NW Uzbekistan
146 K12 **Qorako'l** *Rus.* Karakul'. Buxoro Viloyati, C Uzbekistan
146 H7 **Qorao'zak** *Rus.* Karauzyak. Qoraqalpoghiston Respublikasi, NW Uzbekistan
146 E5 **Qoraqalpog'iston** *Rus.* Karakalpakya. Qoraqalpog'iston Respublikasi, NW Uzbekistan
146 G7 **Qoraqalpog'iston Respublikasi** *Rus.* Respublika Karakalpakstan. ◆ *autonomous republic* NW Uzbekistan
Qorgazhyn *see* Korgalzhyn
138 H6 **Qornet es Saouda** ▲ NE Lebanon
146 L12 **Qorowulbozor** *Rus.* Karaulbazar. Buxoro Viloyati, C Uzbekistan
142 K5 **Qorveh** *var.* Qerveh, Qurveh. Kordestān, W Iran
147 N11 **Qo'shrabot** *Rus.* Kushrabat. Samarqand Viloyati, C Uzbekistan
147 N11 **Qo'shrabot** *Rus.* Kushrabat. Samarqand Viloyati, C Uzbekistan
Qosshaghyl *see* Koschagyl
Qostanay/Qostanay Oblysy *see* Kostanay
143 P12 **Qoţbābād** Fārs, S Iran
143 R13 **Qoţbābād** Hormozgān, S Iran
138 H6 **Qoubaïyât** *var.* Al Qubayyāt. N Lebanon
Qoussantina *see* Constantine
Qowowuyag *see* Cho Oyu
147 O11 **Qo'ytosh** *Rus.* Koytash. Jizzakh Viloyati, C Uzbekistan
147 O11 **Qo'ytosh** *Rus.* Koytash. Jizzax Viloyati, C Uzbekistan
146 G7 **Qozonketkan** *Rus.* Kazanketken. Qoraqalpogh'iston Respublikasi, NW Uzbekistan
146 H6 **Qozoqdaryo** *Rus.* Kazakdar'ya. Qoraqalpoghiston Respublikasi, NW Uzbekistan
19 N11 **Quabbin Reservoir** ▣ Massachusetts, NE USA
100 F12 **Quakenbrück** Niedersachsen, NW Germany
18 I15 **Quakertown** Pennsylvania, NE USA
182 M10 **Quambatook** Victoria, SE Australia
25 Q4 **Quanah** Texas, SW USA
167 V10 **Quang Ngai** *var.* Quangngai, Quang Nghia. Quang Ngai, C Vietnam
Quangngai *see* Quang Ngai
Quang Nghia *see* Quang Ngai
167 T9 **Quang Tri** *var.* Trièu Hai. Quang Tri, C Vietnam
Quanjiang *see* Suichuan
Quan Long *see* Ca Mau
152 L4 **Quanshuigou** China/India
161 R13 **Quanzhou** *var.* Ch'uan-chou, Tsinkiang; *prev.* Chin-chiang. Fujian, SE China
160 M12 **Quanzhou** Guangxi Zhuangzu Zizhiqu, S China
9 V16 **Qu'Appelle** ⚡ Saskatchewan, S Canada
12 M3 **Quaqtaq** *prev.* Koartac. Québec, NE Canada
61 E16 **Quaraí** Rio Grande do Sul, S Brazil
59 H24 **Quaraí, Rio** *Sp.* Río Cuareim. ⚡ Brazil/Uruguay *see also* Cuareim, Río
Quaraí, Rio *see* Cuareim, Río
171 N13 **Quarles, Pegunungan** ▲▲ Sulawesi, C Indonesia
Quarnero *see* Kvarner
107 C20 **Quartu Sant' Elena** Sardegna, Italy, C Mediterranean Sea
29 X13 **Quasqueton** Iowa, C USA
173 X16 **Quatre Bornes** W Mauritius
172 I17 **Quatre Bornes** Mahé, NE Seychelles
137 X10 **Quba** *Rus.* Kuba. N Azerbaijan
Qubba *see* Ba'qūbah
143 T3 **Qūchān** *var.* Kuchan. Khorāsān-Razavī, NE Iran
183 R10 **Queanbeyan** New South Wales, SE Australia
15 Q10 **Québec** *var.* Quebec. *province capital* Québec, SE Canada
14 K10 **Québec** *var.* Quebec. ◆ *province* SE Canada
61 D17 **Quebracho** Paysandú, W Uruguay
101 K14 **Quedlinburg** Sachsen-Anhalt, C Germany
138 H10 **Queen Alia** ✈ ('Ammān) 'Ammān, C Jordan
10 L16 **Queen Bess, Mount** ▲ British Columbia, SW Canada
10 I14 **Queen Charlotte** British Columbia, SW Canada
65 B24 **Queen Charlotte Bay** *bay* West Falkland, W Falkland Islands
10 H14 **Queen Charlotte Islands** *Fr.* Îles de la Reine-Charlotte. *island group* British Columbia, SW Canada
10 I15 **Queen Charlotte Sound** *sea area* British Columbia, W Canada
10 J16 **Queen Charlotte Strait** *strait* British Columbia, W Canada
27 U1 **Queen City** Missouri, C USA
25 X5 **Queen City** Texas, SW USA
197 O9 **Queen Elizabeth Islands** *Fr.* Îles de la Reine-Élisabeth. *island group* Nunavut, N Canada
195 Y10 **Queen Mary Coast** *physical region* Antarctica
65 N24 **Queen Mary's Peak** ▲ C Tristan da Cunha
196 M8 **Queen Maud Gulf** *gulf* Arctic Ocean
195 P11 **Queen Maud Mountains** ▲▲ Antarctica
Queen's County *see* Laois
181 U7 **Queensland** ◆ *state* N Australia
192 I9 **Queensland Plateau** *undersea feature* N Coral Sea
183 O16 **Queenstown** Tasmania, SE Australia
185 C22 **Queenstown** Otago, South Island, New Zealand
83 I24 **Queenstown** Eastern Cape, S South Africa
Queenstown *see* Cobh
32 F8 **Queets** Washington, NW USA
61 D18 **Queguay Grande, Río** ⚡ W Uruguay
59 O16 **Queimadas** Bahia, E Brazil
82 D11 **Quela** Malanje, NW Angola
83 O16 **Quelimane** *var.* Kilimane, Kilmain, Quilimane. Zambézia, NE Mozambique
63 G18 **Quellón** *var.* Puerto Quellón. Los Lagos, S Chile
Quelpart *see* Cheju-do
37 P12 **Quemado** New Mexico, SW USA
25 O12 **Quemado** Texas, SW USA
44 K7 **Quemado, Punta de** *headland* E Cuba
Quemoy *see* Chinmen Tao
62 K13 **Quemú Quemú** La Pampa, E Argentina
155 E17 **Quepem** Goa, W India
42 M14 **Quepos** Puntarenas, S Costa Rica
Que Que *see* Kwekwe
61 D23 **Quequén** Buenos Aires, E Argentina
61 D23 **Quequén Grande, Río** ⚡ E Argentina
61 C23 **Quequén Salado, Río** ⚡ E Argentina
Quera *see* Chur
41 N13 **Querétaro** Querétaro de Arteaga, C Mexico
40 F4 **Querobabi** Sonora, NW Mexico
42 M13 **Quesada** *var.* Ciudad Quesada, San Carlos. Alajuela, N Costa Rica
105 O13 **Quesada** Andalucía, S Spain
161 O7 **Queshan** Henan, C China
10 M15 **Quesnel** British Columbia, SW Canada
37 S9 **Questa** New Mexico, SW USA
102 H7 **Questembert** Morbihan, NW France
57 K22 **Quetena, Río** ⚡ SW Bolivia
149 O10 **Quetta** Baluchistān, SW Pakistan
Quetzalcoalco *see* Coatzacoalcos
Quetzaltenango *see* Quezaltenango
56 B6 **Quevedo** Los Ríos, C Ecuador
42 B6 **Quezaltenango** *var.* Quetzaltenango. Quezaltenango, W Guatemala
42 A2 **Quezaltenango** *off.* Departamento de Quezaltenango, *var.* Quetzaltenango. ◆ *department* SW Guatemala
Quezaltenango, Departamento de *see* Quezaltenango
42 E6 **Quezaltepeque** Chiquimula, SE Guatemala
170 M6 **Quezon** Palawan, W Philippines
161 P5 **Qufu** Shandong, E China
82 B12 **Quibala** Cuanza Sul, NW Angola
82 B11 **Quibaxe** *var.* Quibaxi. Cuanza Norte, NW Angola
Quibaxi *see* Quibaxe
54 D9 **Quibdó** Chocó, W Colombia
102 G7 **Quiberon** Morbihan, NW France
102 G7 **Quiberon, Baie de** *bay* NW France
54 J5 **Quíbor** Lara, N Venezuela
42 C4 **Quiché** *off.* Departamento del Quiché. ◆ *department* W Guatemala
Quiché, Departamento del *see* Quiché
99 E21 **Quiévrain** Hainaut, S Belgium
40 I9 **Quila** Sinaloa, C Mexico
83 B14 **Quilengues** Huíla, SW Angola
Quilimane *see* Quelimane
57 G15 **Quillabamba** Cusco, C Peru
57 L18 **Quillacollo** Cochabamba, C Bolivia
62 H4 **Quillagua** Antofagasta, N Chile
103 N17 **Quillan** Aude, S France
9 U15 **Quill Lakes** ◎ Saskatchewan, S Canada
62 G11 **Quillota** Valparaíso, C Chile
155 G23 **Quilon** *var.* Kolam, Kollam. Kerala, SW India
181 V9 **Quilpie** Queensland, C Australia
149 O4 **Quil-Qala** Bāmīān, N Afghanistan
62 L7 **Quimilí** Santiago del Estero, C Argentina
57 O19 **Quimome** Santa Cruz, E Bolivia
102 F6 **Quimper** *anc.* Quimper Corentin. Finistère, NW France
Quimper Corentin *see* Quimper
102 G7 **Quimperlé** Finistère, NW France
32 F8 **Quinault** Washington, NW USA
32 F8 **Quinault River** ⚡ Washington, NW USA
35 P5 **Quincy** California, W USA
23 S8 **Quincy** Florida, SE USA
30 I13 **Quincy** Illinois, N USA
19 O11 **Quincy** Massachusetts, NE USA
32 J9 **Quincy** Washington, NW USA
54 E10 **Quindío** *off.* Departamento del Quindío. ◆ *province* C Colombia
54 E10 **Quindío, Nevado del** ▲ C Colombia
62 J10 **Quines** San Luis, C Argentina
39 N13 **Quinhagak** Alaska, USA
76 G13 **Quinhámel** W Guinea-Bissau
Qui Nhon/Quinhon *see* Quy Nhơn
Quinindé *see* Rosa Zárate
25 U6 **Quinlan** Texas, SW USA
61 H17 **Quinta** Rio Grande do Sul, S Brazil
105 O10 **Quintanar de la Orden** Castilla-La Mancha, C Spain
41 X13 **Quintana Roo** ◆ *state* SE Mexico
105 S6 **Quinto** Aragón, NE Spain
108 G10 **Quinto** Ticino, S Switzerland
27 Q11 **Quinton** Oklahoma, C USA
62 K12 **Quinto, Río** ⚡ C Argentina
82 A10 **Quinzau** Dem. Rep. Congo, NW Angola
14 H8 **Quinze, Lac des** ◎ Québec, SE Canada
83 B15 **Quipungo** Huíla, C Angola
62 G13 **Quirihue** Bío Bío, C Chile
82 D12 **Quirima** Malanje, NW Angola
183 T6 **Quirindi** New South Wales, SE Australia
55 P5 **Quiriquire** Monagas, NE Venezuela
14 D10 **Quirke Lake** ◎ Ontario, S Canada
61 B21 **Quiroga** Buenos Aires, E Argentina
104 I4 **Quiroga** Galicia, NW Spain
Quiróm, Salar *see* Pocitos, Salar
56 B9 **Quiroz, Río** ⚡ NW Peru
82 Q13 **Quissanga** Cabo Delgado, NE Mozambique
83 M20 **Quissico** Inhambane, S Mozambique
25 O4 **Quitaque** Texas, SW USA
82 Q13 **Quiterajo** Cabo Delgado, NE Mozambique
23 T6 **Quitman** Georgia, SE USA
22 M6 **Quitman** Mississippi, S USA
25 V6 **Quitman** Texas, SW USA
56 C6 **Quito** ● (Ecuador) Pichincha, N Ecuador
Quito *see* Mariscal Sucre
58 P13 **Quixadá** Ceará, E Brazil
83 Q15 **Quixaxe** Nampula, NE Mozambique
161 N13 **Qujiang** *var.* Maba. Guangdong, S China
160 J9 **Qu Jiang** ⚡ C China
161 R10 **Qu Jiang** ⚡ SE China
160 H12 **Qujing** Yunnan, SW China
Qulan *see* Kulan
163 T8 **Qulin Gol** *prev.* Chaor He. ⚡ NE China
146 L10 **QuljuqtovTog'lari** *Rus.* Gory Kul'dzhuktau. ▲▲ C Uzbekistan
Qulsary *see* Kul'sary
Qulyndy Zhazyghy *see* Kulunda Steppe
Qum *see* Qom
Qumälisch *see* Lubartów
159 P11 **Qumar He** ⚡ C China
159 Q12 **Qumarlêb** *var.* Yuegaitan. Qinghai, C China
Qumisheh *see* Shahreẕā
147 O14 **Qumqo'rg'on** *Rus.* Kumkurgan. Surkhondaryo Viloyati, S Uzbekistan
Qunaytirah/Qunayţirah, Muḩāfaẓat al *see* Al Qunayţirah
189 V12 **Quoi** *island* Chuuk, C Micronesia
9 N8 **Quoich** ⚡ Nunavut, NE Canada
83 E26 **Quoin Point** *headland* SW South Africa
182 I7 **Quorn** South Australia
Qurein *see* Al Kuwayt
147 P14 **Qŭrghonteppa** *Rus.* Kurgan-Tyube. SW Tajikistan
Qurlurtuuq *see* Kugluktuk
Qurveh *see* Qorveh
Qusair *see* Quseir
137 X10 **Qusar** *Rus.* Kusary. NE Azerbaijan
Quşayr *see* Al Quşayr
75 Y10 **Quseir** *var.* Al Quşayr, Qusair. E Egypt
142 I2 **Qūshchī** Āżarbāyjān-e Gharbī, N Iran
Qusmuryn *see* Kushmurun, Ozero
Qusmuryn *see* Kushmurun, Kostanay, Kazakhstan
Quţayfah/Qutayfe/Quteife *see* Al Quţayfah
Quthing *see* Moyeni
147 S10 **Quvasoy** *Rus.* Kuvasay. Farg'ona Viloyati, E Uzbekistan
Quwair *see* Guwêr
Quxar *see* Lhazê
Qu Xian *see* Quzhou
159 N16 **Qŭxŭ** *var.* Xoi. Xizang Zizhiqu, W China
Quyang *see* Jingzhou
167 V13 **Quy Chanh** Ninh Thuận, S Vietnam
167 V11 **Quy Nhơn** *var.* Quinhon, Qui Nhon. Binh Định, C Vietnam
161 R10 **Quzhou** *var.* Qu Xian. Zhejiang, SE China
Qyteti Stalin *see* Kuçovë
Qyzylorda/Qyzylorda Oblysy *see* Kyzylorda
Qyzyltū *see* Kishkenekol'
Qyzylzhar *see* Kyzylzhar

R

Raa Atoll *see* North Maalhosmadulu Atoll
109 R4 **Raab** Oberösterreich, N Austria
109 X8 **Raab** *Hung.* Rába. ⚡ Austria/Hungary
Raab *see* Rába
Raab *see* Győr
109 V2 **Raabs an der Thaya** Niederösterreich, E Austria
93 L14 **Raahe** *Swe.* Brahestad. Oulu, W Finland
98 M10 **Raalte** Overijssel, E Netherlands
99 I14 **Raamsdonksveer** Noord-Brabant, S Netherlands
92 L12 **Raanujärvi** Lappi, NW Finland
96 G9 **Raasay** *island* NW Scotland, UK
118 H3 **Raasiku** *Ger.* Rasik. Harjumaa, NW Estonia
112 B11 **Rab** *It.* Arbe. Primorje-Gorski Kotar, NW Croatia
112 B11 **Rab** *It.* Arbe. *island* NW Croatia
171 N16 **Raba** Sumbawa, S Indonesia
111 G22 **Rába** *Ger.* Raab. ⚡ Austria/Hungary *see also* Raab
112 A10 **Rabac** Istra, NW Croatia
104 I2 **Rábade** Galicia, NW Spain
80 F10 **Rabak** White Nile, C Sudan
186 G9 **Rabaraba** Milne Bay, SE Papua New Guinea
102 K16 **Rabastens-de-Bigorre** Hautes-Pyrénées, S France
121 O16 **Rabat** W Malta
74 F6 **Rabat** *var.* al Dar al Baida. ● (Morocco) NW Morocco
Rabat *see* Victoria
186 H6 **Rabaul** New Britain, E Papua New Guinea
Rabbah Ammon/Rabbath Ammon *see* 'Ammān
28 K8 **Rabbit Creek** ⚡ South Dakota, N USA
14 H10 **Rabbit Lake** ◎ Ontario, S Canada
187 Y14 **Rabi** *prev.* Rambi. *island* N Fiji
140 K9 **Rābigh** Makkah, W Saudi Arabia
42 D5 **Rabinal** Baja Verapaz, C Guatemala
168 G9 **Rabi, Pulau** *island* NW Indonesia, East Indies
111 L17 **Rabka** Małopolskie, S Poland
155 F16 **Rabkavi** Karnātaka, W India
Râbnița *see* Rîbnița
109 Y6 **Rabnitz** ⚡ E Austria
124 J7 **Rabocheostrovsk** Respublika Kareliya, NW Russian Federation
23 U1 **Rabun Bald** ▲ Georgia, SE USA
75 S11 **Rabyānah** SE Libya
75 S11 **Rabyānah, Ramlat** *var.* Rebiana Sand Sea, Şaḩrā' Rabyānah. *desert* SE Libya
Rabyānah, Şaḩrā' *see* Rabyānah, Ramlat
116 L11 **Răcăciuni** Bacău, E Romania
Racaka *see* Riwoqê
107 J24 **Racalmuto** Sicilia, Italy, C Mediterranean Sea
116 J14 **Răcari** Dâmbovița, SE Romania
Răcari *see* Durankulak
116 F13 **Răcășdia** *Hung.* Rakasd. Caraș-Severin, SW Romania
106 B9 **Racconigi** Piemonte, NE Italy
31 T15 **Raccoon Creek** ⚡ Ohio, N USA
13 V13 **Race, Cape** *cape* Newfoundland, Newfoundland and Labrador, E Canada
22 K10 **Raceland** Louisiana, S USA
19 Q12 **Race Point** *headland* Massachusetts, NE USA
167 S14 **Rach Gia** Kiên Giang, S Vietnam
167 S14 **Rach Gia, Vinh** *bay* S Vietnam
76 J8 **Rachid** Tagant, C Mauritania
110 L10 **Raciąż** Mazowieckie, C Poland
111 I16 **Racibórz** *Ger.* Ratibor. Śląskie, S Poland

31 *N9* **Racine** Wisconsin, N USA
14 *D7* **Racine Lake** ◎ Ontario, S Canada
111 *J23* **Ráckeve** Pest, C Hungary
Rácz-Becse *see* Bečej
141 *O15* **Radā'** *var.* Ridā'. W Yemen
113 *O15* **Radan** ▲ SE Serbia
63 *J19* **Rada Tilly** Chubut, SE Argentina
116 *K8* **Rădăuţi** *Ger.* Radautz, *Hung.* Rádóc. Suceava, N Romania
116 *L8* **Rădăuţi-Prut** Botoşani, NE Romania
Radautz *see* Rădăuţi
Radbusa *see* Radbuza
111 *A17* **Radbuza** *Ger.* Radbusa. ⚞ SE Czech Republic
20 *K6* **Radcliff** Kentucky, S USA
139 *O2* **Radd, Wādī ar** *dry watercourse* N Syria
95 *H16* **Råde** Østfold, S Norway
109 *V11* **Radeče** *Ger.* Ratschach. C Slovenia
Radein *see* Radenci
116 *J4* **Radekhiv** *Pol.* Radziechów, *Rus.* Radekhov. L'vivs'ka Oblast', W Ukraine
Radekhov *see* Radekhiv
109 *X9* **Radenci** *Ger.* Radein; *prev.* Radinci. NE Slovenia
109 *S9* **Radenthein** Kärnten, S Austria
21 *R7* **Radford** Virginia, NE USA
154 *C9* **Rādhanpur** Gujarāt, W India
Radinci *see* Radenci
127 *Q6* **Radishchevo** Ul'yanovskaya Oblast', W Russian Federation
12 *I9* **Radisson** Québec, E Canada
9 *P16* **Radium Hot Springs** British Columbia, SW Canada
116 *F11* **Radna** *Hung.* Máriaradna. Arad, W Romania
114 *K10* **Radnevo** Stara Zagora, C Bulgaria
97 *J20* **Radnor** *cultural region* E Wales, UK
Radnót *see* Iernut
Rádóc *see* Rădăuţi
101 *H24* **Radolfzell am Bodensee** Baden-Württemberg, S Germany
110 *M13* **Radom** Mazowieckie, C Poland
116 *I14* **Radomireşti** Olt, S Romania
111 *K14* **Radomsko** *Rus.* Novoradomsk. Łódzkie, C Poland
117 *N4* **Radomyshl'** Zhytomyrs'ka Oblast', N Ukraine
113 *P19* **Radoviš** *prev.* Radovište. E Macedonia
Radovište *see* Radoviš
94 *B13* **Radøy** *island* S Norway
109 *R7* **Radstadt** Salzburg, NW Austria
182 *E8* **Radstock, Cape** *headland* South Australia
109 *U10* **Raduha** ▲ N Slovenia
119 *G15* **Radun'** *Rus.* Radun'. Hrodzyenskaya Voblasts', W Belarus
126 *M3* **Raduzhnyy** Vladimirskaya Oblast', W Russian Federation
118 *F11* **Radviliškis** Šiaulai, N Lithuania
9 *U17* **Radville** Saskatchewan, S Canada
140 *K7* **Raḍwá, Jabal** ▲ W Saudi Arabia
111 *P16* **Radymno** Podkarpackie, SE Poland
116 *J5* **Radyvyliv** Rivnens'ka Oblast', NW Ukraine
Radziechów *see* Radekhiv
110 *I11* **Radziejów** Kujawsko-pomorskie, C Poland
110 *O12* **Radzyń Podlaski** Lubelskie, E Poland
8 *J7* **Rae** ⚞ Nunavut, NW Canada
152 *M13* **Rāe Bareli** Uttar Pradesh, N India
Rae-Edzo *see* Edzo
21 *T11* **Raeford** North Carolina, SE USA
99 *M19* **Raeren** Liège, E Belgium
9 *N7* **Rae Strait** *strait* Nunavut, N Canada
184 *L11* **Raetihi** Manawatu-Wanganui, North Island, New Zealand
191 *U13* **Raevavae** *var* Raivavae. *island* Îles Australes, SW French Polynesia
Rafa *see* Rafah
62 *M10* **Rafaela** Santa Fe, E Argentina
138 *E11* **Rafah** *var.* Rafa, Rafaḥ, *Heb.* Rafiaḥ, *var.* Raphiah. SW Gaza Strip
79 *L15* **Rafaï** Mbomou, SE Central African Republic
141 *O4* **Rafḥah** Al Ḥudūd ash Shamālīyah, N Saudi Arabia
Rafiaḥ *see* Rafah
143 *R10* **Rafsanjān** Kermān, C Iran
80 *B13* **Raga** Western Bahr el Ghazal, SW Sudan
19 *S8* **Ragged Island** *island* Maine, NE USA
44 *I5* **Ragged Island Range** *island group* S Bahamas
184 *L7* **Raglan** Waikato, North Island, New Zealand
22 *G8* **Ragley** Louisiana, S USA
Ragnit *see* Neman
107 *K25* **Ragusa** Sicilia, Italy, C Mediterranean Sea
Ragusa *see* Dubrovnik
Ragusavecchia *see* Cavtat
171 *P14* **Raha** Pulau Muna, C Indonesia
119 *N17* **Rahachow** *Rus.* Rogachëv. Homyel'skaya Voblasts', SE Belarus
67 *U6* **Rahad** *var.* Nahr ar Rahad. ⚞ W Sudan
Rahad, Nahr ar *see* Rahad
Rahaeng *see* Tak
138 *F11* **Rahat** Southern, C Israel
140 *L8* **Rahaṭ, Ḥarrat** *lava flow* W Saudi Arabia
149 *S12* **Rahimyār Khān** Punjab, SE Pakistan
95 *I14* **Råholt** Akershus, S Norway
Rahovec *see* Orahovac
191 *S10* **Raiatea** *island* Îles Sous le Vent, W French Polynesia
155 *H16* **Rāichūr** Karnātaka, C India
Raidestos *see* Tekirdağ
153 *S13* **Rāiganj** West Bengal, NE India
154 *M11* **Raigarh** Chhattīsgarh, C India
183 *O16* **Railton** Tasmania, SE Australia
36 *L8* **Rainbow Bridge** *natural arch* Utah, W USA
23 *Q3* **Rainbow City** Alabama, S USA
9 *N11* **Rainbow Lake** Alberta, W Canada
21 *R5* **Rainelle** West Virginia, NE USA
32 *G10* **Rainier** Oregon, NW USA
32 *H9* **Rainier, Mount** ⛰ Washington, NW USA
23 *Q2* **Rainsville** Alabama, S USA
12 *B11* **Rainy Lake** ◎ Canada/USA
12 *A11* **Rainy River** Ontario, C Canada
Raippaluoto *see* Replot
154 *K12* **Raipur** Chhattīsgarh, C India
154 *H10* **Raisen** Madhya Pradesh, C India
15 *N13* **Raisin** ⚞ Ontario, SE Canada
31 *R11* **Raisin, River** ⚞ Michigan, N USA
Raivavae *see* Raevavae
149 *W9* **Rāiwind** Punjab, E Pakistan
171 *T12* **Raja Ampat, Kepulauan** *island group* E Indonesia
155 *L16* **Rājahmundry** Andhra Pradesh, E India
155 *I18* **Rājampet** Andhra Pradesh, E India
Rajang *see* Rajang, Batang
169 *S9* **Rajang, Batang** *var.* Rajang. ⚞ East Malaysia
149 *S11* **Rājanpur** Punjab, E Pakistan
155 *H23* **Rājapālaiyam** Tamil Nādu, SE India
152 *E12* **Rājasthān** ◆ *state* NW India
153 *T15* **Rajbari** Dhaka, C Bangladesh
153 *R12* **Rajbiraj** Eastern, E Nepal
154 *G9* **Rājgarh** Madhya Pradesh, C India
152 *H10* **Rājgarh** Rājasthān, NW India
153 *P14* **Rājgīr** Bihār, N India
110 *O8* **Rajgród** Podlaskie, NE Poland
154 *L12* **Rājim** Chhattīsgarh, C India
112 *C11* **Rajinac, Mali** ▲ W Croatia
154 *B10* **Rājkot** Gujarāt, W India
153 *R14* **Rājmahal** Jhārkhand, NE India
153 *Q14* **Rājmahāl Hills** *hill range* N India
154 *K12* **Rāj Nāndgaon** Chhattīsgarh, C India
152 *I8* **Rājpura** Punjab, NW India
153 *S14* **Rajshahi** *prev.* Rampur Boalia. Rajshahi, W Bangladesh
153 *S13* **Rajshahi** ◆ *division* NW Bangladesh
190 *K13* **Rakahanga** *atoll* N Cook Islands
185 *H19* **Rakaia** Canterbury, South Island, New Zealand
185 *G19* **Rakaia** ⚞ South Island, New Zealand
152 *H3* **Rakaposhi** ▲ N India
Rakasd *see* Răcăşdia
169 *N15* **Rakata, Pulau** *var.* Pulau Krakatau. *island* S Indonesia
141 *U10* **Rakbah, Qalamat ar** *well* SE Saudi Arabia
Rakhine State *see* Arakan State
116 *I8* **Rakhiv** Zakarpats'ka Oblast', W Ukraine
141 *V13* **Rakhyūt** SW Oman
192 *K9* **Rakiraki** Viti Levu, W Fiji
Rakka *see* Ar Raqqah
118 *I4* **Rakke** Lääne-Virumaa, NE Estonia
95 *I16* **Rakkestad** Østfold, S Norway
110 *F12* **Rakoniewice** *Ger.* Rakwitz. Wielkopolskie, C Poland
Rakonitz *see* Rakovník
83 *H18* **Rakops** Central, C Botswana
111 *C16* **Rakovník** *Ger.* Rakonitz. Středočeský Kraj, W Czech Republic
114 *J10* **Rakovski** Plovdiv, C Bulgaria
Rakutō-kō *see* Naktong-gang
118 *I3* **Rakvere** *Ger.* Wesenberg. Lääne-Virumaa, N Estonia
Rakwitz *see* Rakoniewice
22 *L6* **Raleigh** Mississippi, S USA
21 *U9* **Raleigh** *state capital* North Carolina, SE USA
21 *Y11* **Raleigh Bay** *bay* North Carolina, SE USA
21 *U9* **Raleigh-Durham** ✈ North Carolina, SE USA
189 *S6* **Ralik Chain** *island group* Ralik Chain, W Marshall Islands
25 *N5* **Ralls** Texas, SW USA
18 *G13* **Ralston** Pennsylvania, NE USA
141 *O16* **Ramādah** W Yemen
Ramadi *see* Ar Ramādī
105 *N2* **Ramales de la Victoria** Cantabria, N Spain
138 *F10* **Ramallah** C West Bank
61 *C19* **Ramallo** Buenos Aires, E Argentina
155 *H20* **Rāmanagaram** Karnātaka, E India
155 *I23* **Rāmanāthapuram** Tamil Nādu, SE India
154 *N12* **Rāmapur** Orissa, E India
155 *I14* **Rāmāreddi** *var.* Kāmāreddi, Kamareddy. Andhra Pradesh, C India
138 *F10* **Ramat Gan** Tel Aviv, W Israel
103 *T6* **Rambervillers** Vosges, NE France
Rambi *see* Rabi
103 *N5* **Rambouillet** Yvelines, N France
186 *E5* **Rambutyo Island** *island* N Papua New Guinea
153 *Q12* **Ramechhāp** Central, C Nepal
183 *R12* **Rame Head** *headland* Victoria, SE Australia
126 *L4* **Ramenskoye** Moskovskaya Oblast', W Russian Federation
124 *J15* **Rameshki** Tverskaya Oblast', W Russian Federation
153 *P14* **Rāmgarh** Jhārkhand, N India
152 *D11* **Rāmgarh** Rājasthān, NW India
142 *M9* **Rāmhormoz** *var.* Ram Hormuz, Ramuz. Khūzestān, SW Iran
Ram Hormuz *see* Rāmhormoz
Ram, Jebel *see* Ramm, Jabal
138 *F10* **Ramla** *var.* Ramle, Ramleh, *Ar.* Er Ramle. Central, C Israel
Ramle/Ramleh *see* Ramla
138 *F14* **Ramm, Jabal** *var.* Jebel Ram. ▲ SW Jordan
152 *K10* **Rāmnagar** Uttaranchal, N India
95 *N15* **Ramnäs** Västmanland, C Sweden
Râmnicul-Sărat *see* Râmnicu Sărat
116 *L12* **Râmnicu Sărat** *prev.* Râmnicul-Sărat, Rîmnicu-Sărat. Buzău, E Romania
116 *I13* **Râmnicu Vâlcea** *prev.* Rîmnicu Vîlcea. Vâlcea, C Romania
Ramokgwebana *see* Ramokgwebane
83 *J18* **Ramokgwebane** *var.* Ramokgwebana. Central, NE Botswana
126 *L7* **Ramon'** Voronezhskaya Oblast', W Russian Federation
35 *V17* **Ramona** California, W USA
56 *A10* **Ramón, Laguna** ◎ NW Peru
14 *G7* **Ramore** Ontario, S Canada
40 *M11* **Ramos** San Luis Potosí, C Mexico
41 *N8* **Ramos Arizpe** Coahuila de Zaragoza, NE Mexico
40 *J9* **Ramos, Río de** ⚞ C Mexico
83 *J21* **Ramotswa** South East, S Botswana
39 *R8* **Rampart** Alaska, USA
8 *H8* **Ramparts** ⚞ Northwest Territories, NW Canada
152 *K10* **Rāmpur** Uttar Pradesh, N India
154 *F9* **Rāmpura** Madhya Pradesh, C India
Rampur Boalia *see* Rajshahi
166 *K6* **Ramree Island** *island* W Myanmar (Burma)
141 *W6* **Rams** *var.* Ar Rams. Ra's al Khaymah, NE United Arab Emirates
143 *N4* **Rāmsar** *prev.* Sakhtsar. Māzandarān, N Iran
93 *H16* **Ramsele** Västernorrland, N Sweden
21 *T9* **Ramseur** North Carolina, SE USA
97 *I16* **Ramsey** NE Isle of Man
97 *I16* **Ramsey Bay** *bay* NE Isle of Man
14 *E9* **Ramsey Lake** ◎ Ontario, S Canada
97 *Q22* **Ramsgate** SE England, UK
94 *M10* **Ramsjö** Gävleborg, C Sweden
154 *I12* **Rāmtek** Mahārāshtra, C India
Ramtha *see* Ar Ramthā
Ramuz *see* Rāmhormoz
118 *G12* **Ramygala** Panevėžys, C Lithuania
152 *H14* **Rāna Pratāp Sāgar** ◎ N India
169 *V7* **Ranau** Sabah, East Malaysia
168 *L14* **Ranau, Danau** ◎ Sumatera, W Indonesia
62 *H12* **Rancagua** Libertador, C Chile
99 *G22* **Rance** Hainaut, S Belgium
102 *H6* **Rance** ⚞ NW France
60 *J9* **Rancharia** São Paulo, S Brazil
153 *P15* **Rānchi** Jhārkhand, N India
61 *D21* **Ranchos** Buenos Aires, E Argentina
37 *S9* **Ranchos De Taos** New Mexico, SW USA
63 *G16* **Ranco, Lago** ◎ C Chile
95 *C16* **Randaberg** Rogaland, S Norway
29 *U7* **Randall** Minnesota, N USA
107 *L23* **Randazzo** Sicilia, Italy, C Mediterranean Sea
95 *G21* **Randers** Århus, C Denmark
92 *I12* **Randijaure** ◎ N Sweden
21 *T9* **Randleman** North Carolina, SE USA
19 *O11* **Randolph** Massachusetts, NE USA
29 *Q13* **Randolph** Nebraska, C USA
36 *M1* **Randolph** Utah, W USA
100 *P9* **Randow** ⚞ NE Germany
95 *H14* **Randsfjorden** ◎ S Norway
92 *K13* **Råneå** Norrbotten, N Sweden
92 *G12* **Ranelva** ⚞ C Norway
93 *F15* **Ranemsletta** Nord-Trøndelag, C Norway
76 *H10* **Ranérou** C Senegal
Råneś *see* Ringvassøya
185 *E22* **Ranfurly** Otago, South Island, New Zealand
167 *P17* **Rangae** Narathiwat, SW Thailand
153 *V16* **Rangamati** Chittagong, SE Bangladesh
184 *I2* **Rangaunu Bay** *bay* North Island, New Zealand
19 *P6* **Rangeley** Maine, NE USA
37 *O4* **Rangely** Colorado, C USA
25 *R7* **Ranger** Texas, SW USA
14 *C9* **Ranger Lake** Ontario, S Canada
14 *C9* **Ranger Lake** ◎ Ontario, S Canada
153 *V12* **Rangia** Assam, NE India
185 *I18* **Rangiora** Canterbury, South Island, New Zealand
191 *T9* **Rangiroa** *atoll* Îles Tuamotu, W French Polynesia
184 *N9* **Rangitaiki** ⚞ North Island, New Zealand
185 *F19* **Rangitata** ⚞ South Island, New Zealand
184 *M12* **Rangitikei** ⚞ North Island, New Zealand
184 *L6* **Rangitoto Island** *island* N New Zealand
Rangkasbitoeng *see* Rangkasbitung
169 *N16* **Rangkasbitung** *prev.* Rangkasbitoeng. Jawa, SW Indonesia
167 *P9* **Rang, Khao** ▲ C Thailand
147 *V13* **Rangkŭl** *Rus.* Rangkul'. SE Tajikistan
Rangkul' *see* Rangkŭl
Rangoon *see* Yangon
153 *T13* **Rangpur** Rajshahi, N Bangladesh
155 *F18* **Rānibennur** Karnātaka, W India
153 *R15* **Rāniganj** West Bengal, NE India
149 *Q13* **Rānīpur** Sind, SE Pakistan
Rāniyah *see* Ŗānya
25 *N9* **Rankin** Texas, SW USA
9 *O9* **Rankin Inlet** Nunavut, C Canada
183 *P8* **Rankins Springs** New South Wales, SE Australia
Rankovićevo *see* Kraljevo
108 *I7* **Rankweil** Vorarlberg, W Austria
Rann *see* Brežice
127 *T8* **Ranneye** Orenburgskaya Oblast', W Russian Federation
96 *I10* **Rannoch, Loch** ◎ C Scotland, UK
191 *U17* **Rano Kau** *var.* Rano Kao. *crater* Easter Island, Chile, E Pacific Ocean
167 *N14* **Ranong** Ranong, SW Thailand
186 *J8* **Ranongga** *var.* Ghanongga. *island* NW Solomon Islands
191 *W16* **Rano Raraku** *ancient monument* Easter Island, Chile, E Pacific Ocean
171 *V12* **Ransiki** Papua, E Indonesia
92 *K12* **Rantajärvi** Norrbotten, N Sweden
93 *N17* **Rantasalmi** Itä-Suomi, SE Finland
169 *U13* **Rantau** Borneo, C Indonesia
168 *L10* **Rantau, Pulau** *var.* Pulau Tebingtinggi. *island* W Indonesia
171 *N13* **Rantepao** Sulawesi, C Indonesia
30 *M13* **Rantoul** Illinois, N USA
93 *L15* **Rantsila** Oulu, C Finland
92 *L13* **Ranua** Lappi, NW Finland
139 *T3* **Ŗānya** *var.* Rāniyah. NE Iraq
157 *X3* **Raohe** Heilongjiang, NE China
74 *H9* **Raoui, Erg er** *desert* W Algeria
193 *O10* **Rapa** *island* Îles Australes, S French Polynesia
191 *V14* **Rapa Iti** *island* Îles Australes, SW French Polynesia
106 *D10* **Rapallo** Liguria, NW Italy
Rapa Nui *see* Pascua, Isla de
Raphiah *see* Rafah
21 *V5* **Rapidan River** ⚞ Virginia, NE USA
28 *J10* **Rapid City** South Dakota, N USA
15 *P8* **Rapide-Blanc** Québec, SE Canada
14 *I8* **Rapide-Deux** Québec, SE Canada
118 *K6* **Räpina** *Ger.* Rappin. Põlvamaa, SE Estonia
118 *G4* **Rapla** *Ger.* Rappel. Raplamaa, NW Estonia
118 *G4* **Raplamaa** *var.* Rapla Maakond. ◆ *province* NW Estonia
Rapla Maakond *see* Raplamaa
21 *X6* **Rappahannock River** ⚞ Virginia, NE USA
Rappel *see* Rapla
108 *G7* **Rapperswil** Sankt Gallen, NE Switzerland
Rappin *see* Räpina
153 *N12* **Rāpti** ⚞ N India
57 *K16* **Rapulo, Río** ⚞ E Bolivia
Raqqah/Raqqah, Muḥāfaẓat al *see* Ar Raqqah
18 *J8* **Raquette Lake** ◎ New York, NE USA
18 *J6* **Raquette River** ⚞ New York, NE USA
191 *V10* **Raraka** *atoll* Îles Tuamotu, C French Polynesia
191 *V10* **Raroia** *atoll* Îles Tuamotu, C French Polynesia
190 *H15* **Rarotonga** ✈ Rarotonga, S Cook Islands, C Pacific Ocean
190 *H16* **Rarotonga** *island* S Cook Islands, C Pacific Ocean
147 *P12* **Rarz** W Tajikistan
Ras al 'Ain *see* Ra's al 'Ayn
139 *N2* **Ra's al 'Ayn** *var.* Ras al'Ain. Al Ḥasakah, N Syria
138 *H3* **Ra's al Basīṭ** Al Lādhiqīyah, W Syria
Ra's al-Hafǧī *see* Ra's al Khafjī
141 *R5* **Ra's al Khafjī** *var.* Ra's al-Hafǧī. Ash Sharqīyah, NE Saudi Arabia
Ras al-Khaimah/Ras al Khaimah *see* Ra's al Khaymah
143 *R15* **Ra's al Khaymah** *var.* Ras al Khaimah. Ra's al Khaymah, NE United Arab Emirates
143 *R15* **Ra's al Khaymah** *var.* Ras al-Khaimah. ✈ Ra's al Khaymah, NE United Arab Emirates
138 *G13* **Ra's an Naqb** Ma'ān, S Jordan
61 *B26* **Rasa, Punta** *headland* E Argentina
171 *V12* **Rasawi** Papua, E Indonesia
Râşcani *see* Rîşcani
80 *J10* **Ras Dashen Terara** ▲ N Ethiopia
151 *K19* **Rasdu Atoll** *atoll* C Maldives
118 *E12* **Raseiniai** Kaunas, C Lithuania
75 *X8* **Ras Ghārib** E Egypt
162 *J6* **Rashaant** Hövsgöl, N Mongolia
Rashaant *see* Delüün, Bayan-Ölgiy, Mongolia
Rashaant *see* Öldziyt, Dundgovĭ, Mongolia
75 *V7* **Rashîd** *Eng.* Rosetta. N Egypt
139 *Y11* **Rashīd** E Iraq
142 *M3* **Rasht** *var.* Resht. Gīlān, NW Iran
139 *S2* **Rashwān** N Iraq
Rasik *see* Raasiku
113 *M15* **Raška** Serbia, C Serbia
119 *P15* **Rasna** *Rus.* Ryasna. Mahilyowskaya Voblasts', E Belarus
116 *J12* **Râşnov** *prev.* Rişno, Rozsnyó, *Hung.* Barcarozsnyó. Braşov, C Romania
118 *L11* **Rasony** *Rus.* Rossony. Vitsyebskaya Voblasts', N Belarus
Ra's Shamrah *see* Ugarit
127 *N7* **Rasskazovo** Tambovskaya Oblast', W Russian Federation
119 *O16* **Rasta** ⚞ E Belarus
Rastadt *see* Rastatt
Rastâne *see* Ar Rastān
141 *S6* **Ra's Tannūrah** *Eng.* Ras Tanura. Ash Sharqīyah, NE Saudi Arabia
Ras Tanura *see* Ra's Tannūrah
101 *G21* **Rastatt** *var.* Rastadt. Baden-Württemberg, SW Germany
Rastenburg *see* Kętrzyn
149 *V7* **Rasūlnagar** Punjab, E Pakistan
189 *U6* **Ratak Chain** *island group* Ratak Chain, E Marshall Islands
119 *K15* **Ratamka** *Rus.* Ratomka. Minskaya Voblasts', C Belarus
93 *G17* **Ratan** Jämtland, C Sweden
152 *G11* **Ratangarh** Rājasthān, NW India
Rat Buri *see* Ratchaburi
167 *O11* **Ratchaburi** *var.* Rat Buri. Ratchaburi, W Thailand
29 *W15* **Rathbun Lake** ⊠ Iowa, C USA
Ráth Caola *see* Rathkeale
166 *K5* **Rathedaung** Arakan State, W Myanmar (Burma)
100 *M12* **Rathenow** Brandenburg, NE Germany
97 *C19* **Rathkeale** *Ir.* Ráth Caola. Limerick, SW Ireland
96 *F13* **Rathlin Island** *Ir.* Reachlainn. *island* N Northern Ireland, UK
97 *C20* **Ráthluirc** *Ir.* An Ráth. Cork, SW Ireland
Ratibor *see* Racibórz
Ratisbon/Ratisbona/Ratisbonne *see* Regensburg
Rätische Alpen *see* Rhaetian Alps
38 *E17* **Rat Island** *island* Aleutian Islands, Alaska, USA
38 *E17* **Rat Islands** *island group* Aleutian Islands, Alaska, USA
154 *F10* **Ratlām** *prev.* Rutlam. Madhya Pradesh, C India
155 *D15* **Ratnāgiri** Mahārāshtra, W India
155 *K26* **Ratnapura** Sabaragamuwa Province, S Sri Lanka
116 *J2* **Ratne** *Rus.* Ratno. Volyns'ka Oblast', NW Ukraine
Ratno *see* Ratne
Ratomka *see* Ratamka
37 *U8* **Raton** New Mexico, SW USA
139 *O7* **Ratqah, Wādī ar** *dry watercourse* W Iraq
Ratschach *see* Radeče
167 *O16* **Rattaphum** Songkhla, SW Thailand
26 *L6* **Rattlesnake Creek** ⚞ Kansas, C USA
94 *L13* **Rättvik** Dalarna, C Sweden
100 *K9* **Ratzeburg** Mecklenburg-Vorpommern, N Germany
100 *K9* **Ratzeburger See** ◎ N Germany
10 *J10* **Ratz, Mount** ▲ British Columbia, SW Canada
61 *D22* **Rauch** Buenos Aires, E Argentina
41 *U16* **Raudales** Chiapas, SE Mexico
Raudhatain *see* Ar Rawḍatayn
Raudnitz an der Elbe *see* Roudnice nad Labem
92 *K1* **Raufarhöfn** Nordhurland Eystra, NE Iceland
94 *H13* **Raufoss** Oppland, S Norway
Raukawa *see* Cook Strait
184 *Q8* **Raukumara** ▲ North Island, New Zealand
192 *K11* **Raukumara Plain** *undersea feature* N Coral Sea
184 *P8* **Raukumara Range** ⛰ North Island, New Zealand
154 *N11* **Raurkela** *var.* Raurkela; *prev.* Rourkela. Orissa, E India
95 *F15* **Rauland** Telemark, S Norway
93 *J19* **Rauma** *Swe.* Raumo. Länsi-Soumi, SW Finland
94 *F10* **Rauma** ⚞ S Norway
Raumo *see* Rauma
118 *H8* **Rauna** Cēsis, C Latvia
169 *T17* **Raung, Gunung** ▲ Jawa, S Indonesia
Raurkela *see* Rāurkela
95 *J22* **Raus** Skåne, S Sweden
165 *W3* **Rausu** Hokkaidō, NE Japan
165 *W3* **Rausu-dake** ▲ Hokkaidō, NE Japan
93 *M17* **Rautalampi** Itä-Suomi, C Finland
93 *N16* **Rautavaara** Itä-Suomi, C Finland
116 *M9* **Răutel** ⚞ C Moldova
93 *O18* **Rautjärvi** Etelä-Suomi, SE Finland
Rautu *see* Sosnovo
191 *V11* **Ravahere** *atoll* Îles Tuamotu, C French Polynesia
107 *J25* **Ravanusa** Sicilia, Italy, C Mediterranean Sea
143 *S9* **Rāvar** Kermān, C Iran
147 *Q11* **Ravat** Batkenskaya Oblast', SW Kyrgyzstan
18 *K11* **Ravena** New York, NE USA
106 *H10* **Ravenna** Emilia-Romagna, N Italy
29 *O15* **Ravenna** Nebraska, C USA
31 *U11* **Ravenna** Ohio, N USA
101 *I24* **Ravensburg** Baden-Württemberg, S Germany
181 *W4* **Ravenshoe** Queensland, NE Australia
180 *K13* **Ravensthorpe** Western Australia
21 *Q4* **Ravenswood** West Virginia, NE USA
149 *U9* **Rāvi** ⚞ India/Pakistan
112 *C9* **Ravna Gora** Primorje-Gorski Kotar, NW Croatia
109 *U10* **Ravne na Koroškem** *Ger.* Gutenstein. N Slovenia
139 *P6* **Rāwah** W Iraq
191 *T4* **Rawaki** *prev.* Phoenix Island. *atoll* Phoenix Islands, C Kiribati
149 *U6* **Rāwalpindi** Punjab, NE Pakistan
110 *L13* **Rawa Mazowiecka** Łódzkie, C Poland
139 *T2* **Ŗawāndiz** *var.* Rawandoz, Rawāndūz. N Iraq
Rawandoz/Rawāndūz *see* Ŗawāndiz
171 *U12* **Rawas** Papua, E Indonesia
139 *O4* **Rawḍah** ◎ E Syria
110 *G13* **Rawicz** *Ger.* Rawitsch. Wielkopolskie, C Poland
Rawitsch *see* Rawicz
180 *M11* **Rawlinna** Western Australia
33 *W16* **Rawlins** Wyoming, C USA
63 *K17* **Rawson** Chubut, SE Argentina
159 *R16* **Rawu** Xizang Zizhiqu, W China
153 *P12* **Raxaul** Bihār, N India
28 *K3* **Ray** North Dakota, N USA
169 *S11* **Raya, Bukit** ▲ Borneo, C Indonesia
155 *I18* **Rāyachoti** Andhra Pradesh, E India
Rāyadrug *see* Rāyagarha
155 *M14* **Rāyagarha** *prev.* Rāyadrug. Orissa, E India
138 *H7* **Rayak** *var.* Rayaq, Riyāq. E Lebanon
Rayaq *see* Rayak
139 *T2* **Rāyat** E Iraq
169 *N12* **Raya, Tanjung** *cape* Pulau Bangka, W Indonesia
13 *R13* **Ray, Cape** *cape* Newfoundland, Newfoundland and Labrador, E Canada
123 *Q13* **Raychikhinsk** Amurskaya Oblast', SE Russian Federation
127 *U5* **Rayevskiy** Respublika Bashkortostan, W Russian Federation
9 *Q17* **Raymond** Alberta, SW Canada
22 *K6* **Raymond** Mississippi, S USA
32 *F9* **Raymond** Washington, NW USA
183 *T8* **Raymond Terrace** New South Wales, SE Australia
25 *T17* **Raymondville** Texas, SW USA
9 *U16* **Raymore** Saskatchewan, S Canada
39 *Q8* **Ray Mountains** ⛰ Alaska, USA
22 *H9* **Rayne** Louisiana, S USA
41 *O12* **Rayón** San Luis Potosí, C Mexico
40 *G4* **Rayón** Sonora, NW Mexico
167 *P12* **Rayong** Rayong, S Thailand
25 *T5* **Ray Roberts, Lake** ◎ Texas, SW USA
18 *E15* **Raystown Lake** ⊠ Pennsylvania, NE USA
141 *V13* **Raysūt** SW Oman
27 *R4* **Raytown** Missouri, C USA
22 *I5* **Rayville** Louisiana, S USA
142 *L5* **Razan** Hamadān, W Iran
139 *S9* **Razāzah, Buḥayrat ar** *var.* Baḥr al Milḥ. ◎ C Iraq
114 *L9* **Razboyna** ▲ E Bulgaria
Razdan *see* Hrazdan
Razdolnoye *see* Rozdol'ne
Razelm, Lacul *see* Razim, Lacul
139 *U2* **Razga** E Iraq
114 *L8* **Razgrad** Razgrad, N Bulgaria
114 *L8* **Razgrad** ◆ *province* NE Bulgaria
117 *N13* **Razim, Lacul** *prev.* Lacul Razelm. *lagoon* NW Black Sea
114 *G11* **Razlog** Blagoevgrad, SW Bulgaria
118 *K10* **Rāznas Ezers** ◎ SE Latvia
102 *E6* **Raz, Pointe du** *headland* NW France
Reachlainn *see* Rathlin Island
Reachrainn *see* Lambay Island
97 *N22* **Reading** S England, UK
18 *H15* **Reading** Pennsylvania, NE USA
48 *C7* **Real, Cordillera** ⛰ C Ecuador
62 *K12* **Realicó** La Pampa, C Argentina
25 *R15* **Realitos** Texas, SW USA
108 *G9* **Realp** Uri, C Switzerland
167 *Q12* **Reăng Kesei** Bătdâmbâng, W Cambodia
191 *Y11* **Reao** *atoll* Îles Tuamotu, E French Polynesia
Reate *see* Rieti
180 *L11* **Rebecca, Lake** ◎ Western Australia
Rebiana Sand Sea *see* Rabyānah, Ramlat
124 *H8* **Reboly** Respublika Kareliya, NW Russian Federation
165 *S1* **Rebun** Rebun-tō, NE Japan
165 *S1* **Rebun-tō** *island* NE Japan
106 *J12* **Recanati** Marche, C Italy
Rechitsa *see* Rechytsa
109 *Y7* **Rechnitz** Burgenland, SE Austria
119 *J20* **Rechytsa** *Rus.* Rechitsa. Brestskaya Voblasts', SW Belarus
119 *O19* **Rechytsa** *Rus.* Rechitsa. Homyel'skaya Voblasts', SE Belarus
59 *Q15* **Recife** *prev.* Pernambuco. *state capital* Pernambuco, E Brazil
83 *I26* **Recife, Cape** *Afr.* Kaap Recife. *headland* S South Africa
Recife, Kaap *see* Recife, Cape
172 *I16* **Récifs, Îles aux** *island* Inner Islands, NE Seychelles
101 *E14* **Recklinghausen** Nordrhein-Westfalen, W Germany
100 *M8* **Recknitz** ⚞ NE Germany
99 *K23* **Recogne** Luxembourg, SE Belgium
61 *C15* **Reconquista** Santa Fe, C Argentina
195 *O6* **Recovery Glacier** *glacier* Antarctica
59 *G15* **Recreio** Mato Grosso, W Brazil
27 *X9* **Rector** Arkansas, C USA
110 *E9* **Recz** *Ger.* Reetz Neumark. Zachodnio-pomorskie, NW Poland
99 *L24* **Redange** *var.* Redange-sur-Attert. Diekirch, W Luxembourg
Redange-sur-Attert *see* Redange
18 *C13* **Redbank Creek** ⚞ Pennsylvania, NE USA
13 *S9* **Red Bay** Québec, E Canada
23 *N2* **Red Bay** Alabama, S USA
35 *N4* **Red Bluff** California, W USA
24 *J8* **Red Bluff Reservoir** ⊠ New Mexico/Texas, SW USA
30 *K16* **Red Bud** Illinois, N USA
30 *J5* **Red Cedar River** ⚞ Wisconsin, N USA
9 *R17* **Redcliff** Alberta, SW Canada
83 *K17* **Redcliff** Midlands, C Zimbabwe
182 *L9* **Red Cliffs** Victoria, SE Australia
29 *P17* **Red Cloud** Nebraska, C USA
22 *L8* **Red Creek** ⚞ Mississippi, S USA
9 *P15* **Red Deer** Alberta, SW Canada
9 *Q16* **Red Deer** ⚞ Alberta, SW Canada
39 *O11* **Red Devil** Alaska, USA
35 *N3* **Redding** California, W USA
97 *L20* **Redditch** W England, UK
29 *P9* **Redfield** South Dakota, N USA
24 *J12* **Redford** Texas, SW USA
45 *V13* **Redhead** Trinidad, Trinidad and Tobago
182 *I8* **Red Hill** South Australia
Red Hill *see* Pu'u 'Ula'ula

◆ Country
● Country Capital
◇ Dependent Territory
○ Dependent Territory Capital
◆ Administrative Regions
✈ International Airport
▲ Mountain
⛰ Mountain Range
⛰ Volcano
⚞ River
◎ Lake
⊠ Reservoir

26 K7 Red Hills hill range Kansas, C USA
13 T12 Red Indian Lake ◎ Newfoundland, Newfoundland and Labrador, E Canada
124 J16 Redkino Tverskaya Oblast', W Russian Federation
12 A10 Red Lake Ontario, C Canada
36 I10 Red Lake salt flat Arizona, SW USA
29 S4 Red Lake Falls Minnesota, N USA
29 R4 Red Lake River ≈ Minnesota, N USA
35 U15 Redlands California, W USA
18 G16 Red Lion Pennsylvania, NE USA
33 U11 Red Lodge Montana, NW USA
32 H13 Redmond Oregon, NW USA
36 L5 Redmond Utah, W USA
32 H8 Redmond Washington, NW USA
Rednitz see Regnitz
29 T15 Red Oak Iowa, C USA
18 K12 Red Oaks Mill New York, NE USA
102 I7 Redon Ille-et-Vilaine, NW France
45 W10 Redonda island SW Antigua and Barbuda
104 G4 Redondela Galicia, NW Spain
104 H11 Redondo Évora, S Portugal
39 Q12 Redoubt Volcano ▲ Alaska, USA
9 Y16 Red River ≈ Canada/USA
129 U12 Red River var. Yuan, Chin. Yuan Jiang, Vtn. Sông Hông Hà. ≈ China/Vietnam
25 W4 Red River ≈ S USA
22 H7 Red River ≈ Louisiana, S USA
30 M6 Red River ≈ Wisconsin, N USA
Red Rock, Lake see Red Rock Reservoir
29 W14 Red Rock Reservoir var. Lake Red Rock. ⊠ Iowa, C USA
80 H7 Red Sea ◐ state NE Sudan
75 Y9 Red Sea var. Sinus Arabicus. sea Africa/Asia
21 T11 Red Springs North Carolina, SE USA
8 I9 Redstone ≈ Northwest Territories, NW Canada
9 V17 Redvers Saskatchewan, S Canada
77 P13 Red Volta var. Nazinon, Fr. Volta Rouge. ≈ Burkina/Ghana
9 Q14 Redwater Alberta, SW Canada
28 M16 Red Willow Creek ≈ Nebraska, C USA
29 W9 Red Wing Minnesota, N USA
35 N9 Redwood City California, W USA
29 T9 Redwood Falls Minnesota, N USA
31 P7 Reed City Michigan, N USA
28 K6 Reeder North Dakota, N USA
35 R11 Reedley California, W USA
33 T11 Reedpoint Montana, NW USA
30 K8 Reedsburg Wisconsin, N USA
32 E13 Reedsport Oregon, NW USA
187 Q9 Reef Islands island group Santa Cruz Islands, E Solomon Islands
185 H16 Reefton West Coast, South Island, New Zealand
20 F8 Reelfoot Lake ◎ Tennessee, S USA
97 D17 Ree, Lough Ir. Loch Rí. ◎ C Ireland
Reengus see Rīngas
35 U4 Reese River ≈ Nevada, W USA
98 M8 Reest ≈ E Netherlands
Reetz Neumark see Recz
Reevhtse see Røsvatnet
137 N13 Refahiye Erzincan, C Turkey
23 N4 Reform Alabama, S USA
95 K20 Refteles Jönköping, S Sweden
25 T14 Refugio Texas, SW USA
110 E8 Rega ≈ NW Poland
Regar see Tursunzoda
101 O21 Regen Bayern, SE Germany
101 M20 Regen ≈ SE Germany
101 M21 Regensburg Eng. Ratisbon, Fr. Ratisbonne, hist. Ratisbona; anc. Castra Regina, Reginum. Bayern, SE Germany
101 M21 Regenstauf Bayern, SE Germany
74 I10 Reggane C Algeria
98 N9 Regge ≈ E Netherlands
Reggio see Reggio nell'Emilia
Reggio Calabria see Reggio di Calabria
107 M23 Reggio di Calabria var. Reggio Calabria, Gk. Rhegion; anc. Regium, Rhegium. Calabria, SW Italy
Reggio Emilia see Reggio nell'Emilia
106 F9 Reggio nell'Emilia var. Reggio Emilia, abbrev. Reggio; anc. Regium Lepidum. Emilia-Romagna, N Italy
116 I10 Reghin Ger. Sächsisch-Reen, Hung. Szászrégen; prev. Reghinul Săsesc, Ger. Sächsisch-Regen. Mureş, C Romania
Reghinul Săsesc see Reghin
9 U16 Regina province capital Saskatchewan, S Canada
55 Z10 Régina E French Guiana
9 U16 Regina ✈ Saskatchewan, S Canada
9 U16 Regina Beach Saskatchewan, S Canada
Reginum see Regensburg
Région du Haut-Congo see Haut-Congo
Registan see Rīgestān
60 L11 Registro São Paulo, S Brazil
Regium see Reggio di Calabria
Regium Lepidum see Reggio nell'Emilia
101 K19 Regnitz var. Rednitz. ≈ SE Germany
40 K10 Regocijo Durango, W Mexico
104 H12 Reguengos de Monsaraz Évora, S Portugal
101 M18 Rehau Bayern, E Germany
83 D19 Rehoboth Hardap, C Namibia
21 Z4 Rehoboth Beach Delaware, NE USA
Rehoboth/Rehovot see Rehovot
138 F10 Rehovot var. Rehoboth, Rekhovoth, Rehovoth. Central, C Israel
81 J20 Rei spring/well S Kenya
Reichenau see Rychnov nad Kněžnou
Reichenau see Bogatynia, Poland
101 M17 Reichenbach var. Reichenbach im Vogtland. Sachsen, E Germany
Reichenbach see Dzierżoniów
Reichenbach im Vogtland see Reichenbach
Reichenberg see Liberec
181 O11 Reid Western Australia
23 V6 Reidsville Georgia, SE USA
21 T8 Reidsville North Carolina, SE USA
Reifnitz see Ribnica
97 O22 Reigate SE England, UK
Reikjavik see Reykjavík
102 I10 Ré, Île de island W France
37 N15 Reiley Peak ▲ Arizona, SW USA
103 Q4 Reims Eng. Rheims; anc. Durocortorum, Remi. Marne, N France
63 G23 Reina Adelaida, Archipiélago island group S Chile
45 O16 Reina Beatrix ✈ (Oranjestad) C Aruba
108 F7 Reinach Aargau, W Switzerland
108 E6 Reinach Basel-Land, NW Switzerland
64 O11 Reina Sofía ✈ (Tenerife) Tenerife, Islas Canarias, Spain, NE Atlantic Ocean
29 W13 Reinbeck Iowa, C USA
100 J10 Reinbek Schleswig-Holstein, N Germany
9 U12 Reindeer ≈ Saskatchewan, C Canada
9 U11 Reindeer Lake ◎ Manitoba/Saskatchewan, C Canada
Reine-Charlotte, Îles de la see Queen Charlotte Islands
Reine-Élisabeth, Îles de la see Queen Elizabeth Islands
94 F13 Reineskarvet ▲ S Norway
184 H1 Reinga, Cape headland North Island, New Zealand
105 N3 Reinosa Cantabria, N Spain
109 R8 Reisseck ▲ S Austria
21 W3 Reisterstown Maryland, NE USA
Reisui see Yŏsu
98 N5 Reitdiep ≈ NE Netherlands
191 V10 Reitoru atoll Îles Tuamotu, C French Polynesia
95 M17 Rejmyre Östergötland, S Sweden
Reka see Rijeka
Reka Ili see Ile/Ili He
95 N16 Rekarne Västmanland, C Sweden
Rekhovoth see Rehovot
8 K9 Reliance Northwest Territories, C Canada
33 U16 Reliance Wyoming, C USA
74 I5 Relizane var. Ghelîzâne, Ghilizane. NW Algeria
182 I7 Remarkable, Mount ▲ South Australia
54 E8 Remedios Antioquia, N Colombia
43 Q16 Remedios Veraguas, W Panama
42 D8 Remedios, Punta headland SW El Salvador
Remi see Reims
99 N25 Remich Grevenmacher, SE Luxembourg
99 J19 Remicourt Liège, E Belgium
14 H8 Rémigny, Lac ◎ Québec, SE Canada
55 Z10 Rémire NE French Guiana
127 N13 Remontnoye Rostovskaya Oblast', SW Russian Federation
171 U14 Remoon Pulau Kur, E Indonesia
99 L20 Remouchamps Liège, E Belgium
103 R15 Remoulins Gard, S France
173 X16 Rempart, Mont du hill W Mauritius
101 E15 Remscheid Nordrhein-Westfalen, W Germany
29 S12 Remsen Iowa, C USA
94 I12 Rena Hedmark, S Norway
94 I11 Renåa ≈ S Norway
Renaix see Ronse
118 H7 Rencēni Valmiera, N Latvia
118 D9 Renda Kuldīga, W Latvia
107 N20 Rende Calabria, SW Italy
99 K21 Rendeux Luxembourg, SE Belgium
Rendina see Rentína
30 L16 Rend Lake ⊠ Illinois, N USA
186 K9 Rendova island New Georgia Islands, NW Solomon Islands
100 I8 Rendsburg Schleswig-Holstein, N Germany
108 B9 Renens Vaud, SW Switzerland
14 K12 Renfrew Ontario, SE Canada
96 I12 Renfrew cultural region SW Scotland, UK
168 L11 Rengat Sumatera, W Indonesia
153 W12 Rengma Hills ▲▲ NE India
62 H12 Rengo Libertador, C Chile
116 M12 Reni Odes'ka Oblast', SW Ukraine
80 F11 Renk Upper Nile, E Sudan
93 L19 Renko Etelä-Suomi, S Finland
98 L12 Renkum Gelderland, SE Netherlands
182 K9 Renmark South Australia
186 L10 Rennell var. Mu Nggava. island S Solomon Islands
181 Q4 Renner Springs Roadhouse Northern Territory, N Australia
102 I6 Rennes Bret. Roazon; anc. Condate. Ille-et-Vilaine, NW France
195 S16 Rennick Glacier glacier Antarctica
9 Y16 Rennie Manitoba, S Canada
35 Q5 Reno Nevada, W USA
106 H10 Reno ≈ N Italy
35 Q5 Reno-Cannon ✈ Nevada, W USA
83 F24 Renoster ≈ SW South Africa
15 T5 Renouard, Lac ◎ Québec, SE Canada
18 F13 Renovo Pennsylvania, NE USA
161 O3 Renqiu Hebei, E China
160 I9 Renshou Sichuan, C China
31 N12 Rensselaer Indiana, N USA
18 L11 Rensselaer New York, NE USA
Rentería see Errenteria
115 E17 Rentína var. Rendina. Thessalía, C Greece
29 T9 Renville Minnesota, N USA
77 O13 Réo W Burkina
15 O12 Repentigny Québec, SE Canada
146 K13 Repetek Lebap Welaýaty, E Turkmenistan
93 J16 Replot Fin. Raippaluoto. island W Finland
Reppen see Rzepin
Reps see Rupea
27 T7 Republic Missouri, C USA
32 K7 Republic Washington, NW USA
27 N3 Republican River ≈ Kansas/Nebraska, C USA
Republika Srpska see Foča
9 O7 Repulse Bay Northwest Territories, N Canada
56 F9 Requena Loreto, NE Peru
105 R10 Requena País Valenciano, E Spain
103 O14 Réquista Aveyron, S France
136 M12 Reşadiye Tokat, N Turkey
Reschenpass see Resia, Passo di
Reschitza see Reşiţa
113 N20 Resen Turk. Resne. SW FYR Macedonia
60 J11 Reserva Paraná, S Brazil
9 V15 Reserve Saskatchewan, S Canada
37 P13 Reserve New Mexico, SW USA
Reshetilovka see Reshetylivka
117 S6 Reshetylivka Rus. Reshetilovka. Poltavs'ka Oblast', NE Ukraine
Resht see Rasht
106 F5 Resia, Passo di Ger. Reschenpass. pass Austria/Italy
Resicabánya see Reşiţa
62 N7 Resistencia Chaco, NE Argentina
116 F12 Reşiţa Ger. Reschitza, Hung. Resicabánya. Caraş-Severin, W Romania
Resne see Resen
197 N9 Resolute Cornwallis Island, Nunavut, N Canada
Resolution see Fort Resolution
9 T7 Resolution Island island Nunavut, NE Canada
185 A23 Resolution Island island SW New Zealand
15 W7 Restigouche Québec, SE Canada
9 W17 Reston Manitoba, S Canada
14 H11 Restoule Lake ◎ Ontario, S Canada
54 F10 Restrepo Meta, C Colombia
42 B6 Retalhuleu Retalhuleu, SW Guatemala
42 A1 Retalhuleu off. Departamento de Retalhuleu. ◐ department SW Guatemala
Retalhuleu, Departamento de see Retalhuleu
97 N18 Retford C England, UK
103 Q3 Rethel Ardennes, N France
Rethimno/Réthimnon see Réthymno
115 I25 Réthymno prev. Rethimno, Réthimnon. Kríti, Greece, E Mediterranean Sea
Retiche, Alpi see Rhaetian Alps
99 J16 Retie Antwerpen, N Belgium
111 J21 Rétság Nógrád, N Hungary
109 W2 Retz Niederösterreich, NE Austria
173 N15 Réunion off. La Réunion. ◇ French overseas department W Indian Ocean
128 L17 Réunion island W Indian Ocean
105 U6 Reus Cataluña, E Spain
99 J15 Reusel Noord-Brabant, S Netherlands
108 F7 Reuss ≈ NW Switzerland
Reuţel see Ciuhuru
101 H22 Reutlingen Baden-Württemberg, S Germany
108 L7 Reutte Tirol, W Austria
99 M16 Reuver Limburg, SE Netherlands
28 K7 Reva South Dakota, N USA
Reval/Revel see Tallinn
124 J4 Revda Murmanskaya Oblast', NW Russian Federation
122 F6 Revda Sverdlovskaya Oblast', C Russian Federation
103 N16 Revel Haute-Garonne, S France
9 O16 Revelstoke British Columbia, SW Canada
43 N13 Reventazón, Río ≈ E Costa Rica
106 G9 Revere Lombardia, N Italy
39 Y14 Revillagigedo Island island Alexander Archipelago, Alaska, USA
103 R3 Revin Ardennes, N France
92 O3 Revnosa headland C Svalbard
Revolyutsii, Pik see Revolyutsiya, Qullai
147 T13 Revolyutsiya, Qullai Rus. Pik Revolyutsii. ▲ SE Tajikistan
111 L19 Revúca Ger. Grossrauschenbach, Hung. Nagyrőce. Banskobystrický Kraj, C Slovakia
154 K9 Rewa Madhya Pradesh, C India
152 I11 Rewāri Haryāna, N India
33 R14 Rexburg Idaho, NW USA
78 G13 Rey Bouba Nord, NE Cameroon
92 L3 Reydharfjördhur Austurland, E Iceland
57 K16 Reyes Beni, NW Bolivia
34 L8 Reyes, Point headland California, W USA
54 B12 Reyes, Punta headland SW Colombia
136 L17 Reyhanlı Hatay, S Turkey
43 U16 Rey, Isla del island Archipiélago de las Perlas, SE Panama
92 H2 Reykhólar Vestfirdhir, W Iceland
92 K2 Reykjahlídh Nordhurland Eystra, NE Iceland
92 I4 Reykjanes ◐ region SW Iceland
197 O16 Reykjanes Basin var. Irminger Basin. undersea feature N Atlantic Ocean
197 N17 Reykjanes Ridge undersea feature N Atlantic Ocean
92 H4 Reykjavík var. Reikjavik. ● (Iceland) Höfudhborgarsvaedhi, W Iceland
18 D13 Reynoldsville Pennsylvania, NE USA
41 P8 Reynosa Tamaulipas, C Mexico
Reẕā'īyeh see Orūmīyeh
Reẕā'īyeh, Daryācheh-ye see Orūmīyeh, Daryācheh-ye
102 I8 Rezé Loire-Atlantique, NW France
118 K10 Rēzekne Ger. Rositten; prev. Rus. Rezhitsa. Rēzekne, SE Latvia
Rezhitsa see Rēzekne
117 N9 Rezina NE Moldova
114 N11 Rezovo Turk. Rezve. Burgas, E Bulgaria
114 N11 Rezovska Reka Turk. Rezve Deresi. ≈ Bulgaria/Turkey see also Rezve Deresi
Rezovska Reka see Rezve Deresi
Rezve see Rezovo
114 N11 Rezve Deresi Bul. Rezovska Reka. ≈ Bulgaria/Turkey see also Rezovska Reka
Rezve Deresi see Rezovska Reka
Rhadames see Ghadāmis
Rhaedestus see Tekirdağ
108 J10 Rhaetian Alps Fr. Alpes Rhétiques, Ger. Rätische Alpen, It. Alpi Retiche. ▲▲ C Europe
108 I8 Rhätikon ▲▲ C Europe
101 G14 Rheda-Wiedenbrück Nordrhein-Westfalen, W Germany
98 M12 Rheden Gelderland, E Netherlands
Rhegion/Rhegium see Reggio di Calabria
Rheims see Reims
Rhein see Rhine
101 E17 Rheinbach Nordrhein-Westfalen, W Germany
100 F13 Rheine var. Rheine in Westfalen. Nordrhein-Westfalen, NW Germany
Rheine in Westfalen see Rheine
Rheinfeld see Rheinfelden
101 F24 Rheinfelden Baden-Württemberg, S Germany
108 E6 Rheinfelden var. Rheinfeld. Aargau, N Switzerland
101 E17 Rheinisches Schiefergebirge var. Rhine State Uplands, Eng. Rhenish Slate Mountains. ▲▲ W Germany
101 D18 Rheinland-Pfalz Eng. Rhineland-Palatinate, Fr. Rhénanie-Palatinat. ◐ state W Germany
101 G18 Rhein/Main ✈ (Frankfurt am Main) Hessen, W Germany
Rhénanie du Nord-Westphalie see Nordrhein-Westfalen
Rhénanie-Palatinat see Rheinland-Pfalz
98 K12 Rhenen Utrecht, C Netherlands
Rhenish Slate Mountains see Rheinisches Schiefergebirge
Rhétiques, Alpes see Rhaetian Alps
100 N10 Rhin ≈ NE Germany
Rhin see Rhine
84 F10 Rhine Dut. Rijn, Fr. Rhin, Ger. Rhein. ≈ W Europe
30 L5 Rhinelander Wisconsin, N USA
Rhineland-Palatinate see Rheinland-Pfalz
Rhine State Uplands see Rheinisches Schiefergebirge
100 N11 Rhinkanal canal NE Germany
81 F17 Rhino Camp NW Uganda
74 D7 Rhir, Cap headland W Morocco
106 D7 Rho Lombardia, N Italy
19 N12 Rhode Island off. State of Rhode Island and Providence Plantations, also known as Little Rhody, Ocean State. ◐ state NE USA
19 O13 Rhode Island island Rhode Island, NE USA
19 O13 Rhode Island Sound sound Maine/Rhode Island, NE USA
Rhodes see Ródos
Rhode-Saint-Genèse see Sint-Genesius-Rode
84 L14 Rhodes Basin undersea feature E Mediterranean Sea
Rhodesia see Zimbabwe
114 I12 Rhodope Mountains var. Rodhópi Óri, Bul. Rhodope Planina, Rodopi, Gk. Orosirá Rodhópis, Turk. Dospad Dagh. ▲▲ Bulgaria/Greece
Rhodope Planina see Rhodope Mountains
101 I18 Rhön ▲▲ C Germany
103 Q10 Rhône ◐ department E France
86 C12 Rhône ≈ France/Switzerland
103 R12 Rhône-Alpes ◐ region E France
98 G13 Rhoon Zuid-Holland, SW Netherlands
96 G9 Rhum var. Rum. island W Scotland, UK
Rhuthun see Ruthin
97 J18 Rhyl NE Wales, UK
59 K18 Rialma Goiás, S Brazil
104 L3 Riaño Castilla-León, N Spain
105 O9 Riansáres ≈ C Spain
152 H6 Riāsi Jammu and Kashmir, NW India
168 K10 Riau off. Propinsi Riau. ◐ province W Indonesia
Riau Archipelago see Riau, Kepulauan
168 M11 Riau, Kepulauan var. Riau Archipelago, Dut. Riouw-Archipel. island group W Indonesia
Riau, Propinsi see Riau
105 O6 Riaza Castilla-León, N Spain
105 N6 Riaza ≈ N Spain
81 K17 Riba spring/well NE Kenya
104 H4 Ribadavia Galicia, NW Spain
104 J2 Ribadeo Galicia, NW Spain
104 L2 Ribadesella Asturias, N Spain
104 G10 Ribatejo former province C Portugal
83 P15 Ribáuè Nampula, N Mozambique
97 K17 Ribble ≈ NW England, UK
95 F23 Ribe Ribe, W Denmark
95 F23 Ribe off. Ribe Amt, var. Ripen. ◐ county W Denmark
Ribe Amt see Ribe
104 G3 Ribeira Galicia, NW Spain
64 O5 Ribeira Brava Madeira, Portugal, NE Atlantic Ocean
64 P3 Ribeira Grande São Miguel, Azores, Portugal, NE Atlantic Ocean
60 L8 Ribeirão Preto São Paulo, S Brazil
60 L11 Ribeira, Rio ≈ S Brazil
107 I24 Ribera Sicilia, Italy, C Mediterranean Sea
57 L14 Riberalta Beni, N Bolivia
105 W4 Ribes de Freser Cataluña, NE Spain
30 L6 Rib Mountain ▲ Wisconsin, N USA
109 U12 Ribnica Ger. Reifnitz. S Slovenia
117 N9 Rîbniţa var. Râbniţa, Rus. Rybnitsa. NE Moldova
100 M8 Ribnitz-Damgarten Mecklenburg-Vorpommern, NE Germany
111 D16 Říčany Ger. Ritschan. Středočesky Kraj, W Czech Republic
29 U7 Rice Minnesota, N USA
30 J5 Rice Lake Wisconsin, N USA
14 E8 Rice Lake ◎ Ontario, S Canada
14 I15 Rice Lake ◎ Ontario, SE Canada
23 V3 Richard B. Russell Lake ⊠ Georgia, SE USA
25 U6 Richardson Texas, SW USA
9 R11 Richardson ≈ Alberta, C Canada
10 I3 Richardson Mountains ▲▲ Yukon Territory, NW Canada
185 C21 Richardson Mountains ▲▲ South Island, New Zealand
42 F3 Richardson Peak ▲ SE Belize
76 G10 Richard Toll N Senegal
28 L5 Richardton North Dakota, N USA
14 F13 Rich, Cape headland Ontario, S Canada
102 L8 Richelieu Indre-et-Loire, C France
33 P15 Richfield Idaho, NW USA
36 K5 Richfield Utah, W USA
18 J10 Richfield Springs New York, NE USA
18 M6 Richford Vermont, NE USA
27 R6 Rich Hill Missouri, C USA
13 P14 Richibucto New Brunswick, SE Canada
108 G8 Richisau Glarus, NE Switzerland
23 S6 Richland Georgia, SE USA
27 U6 Richland Missouri, C USA
25 U8 Richland Texas, SW USA
32 K10 Richland Washington, NW USA
30 K8 Richland Center Wisconsin, N USA
21 W11 Richlands North Carolina, SE USA
21 Q7 Richlands Virginia, NE USA
25 R9 Richland Springs Texas, SW USA
183 S8 Richmond New South Wales, SE Australia
10 L17 Richmond British Columbia, SW Canada
14 L13 Richmond Ontario, SE Canada
15 Q12 Richmond Québec, SE Canada
185 I14 Richmond Tasman, South Island, New Zealand
35 N8 Richmond California, W USA
31 Q14 Richmond Indiana, N USA
20 M6 Richmond Kentucky, S USA
27 S4 Richmond Missouri, C USA
25 V11 Richmond Texas, SW USA
36 L1 Richmond Utah, W USA
21 W6 Richmond state capital Virginia, NE USA
14 H15 Richmond Hill Ontario, S Canada
185 J15 Richmond Range ▲▲ South Island, New Zealand
27 S12 Rich Mountain ▲ Arkansas, C USA
31 S13 Richwood Ohio, N USA
21 R5 Richwood West Virginia, NE USA
104 K5 Ricobayo, Embalse de ⊠ NW Spain
Ricomagus see Riom
Ridā' see Radā'
98 H13 Ridderkerk Zuid-Holland, SW Netherlands
33 N16 Riddle Idaho, NW USA
32 F14 Riddle Oregon, NW USA
14 L13 Rideau ≈ Ontario, SE Canada
35 T12 Ridgecrest California, W USA
18 L13 Ridgefield Connecticut, NE USA
22 K5 Ridgeland Mississippi, S USA
21 R15 Ridgeland South Carolina, SE USA
20 F8 Ridgely Tennessee, S USA
14 D17 Ridgetown Ontario, S Canada
21 R12 Ridgeway South Carolina, SE USA
Ridgeway see Ridgway
18 D13 Ridgway var. Ridgeway. Pennsylvania, NE USA
9 W16 Riding Mountain ▲▲ Manitoba, S Canada
Ried see Ried im Innkreis
109 R4 Ried im Innkreis var. Ried. Oberösterreich, NW Austria
109 X8 Riegersburg Steiermark, SE Austria
108 E6 Riehen Basel-Stadt, NW Switzerland
92 J9 Riehppegáisá var. Rieppe. ▲ N Norway
99 K18 Riemst Limburg, NE Belgium
Rieppe see Riehppegáisá
101 O15 Riesa Sachsen, E Germany
63 H24 Riesco, Isla island S Chile
107 K25 Riesi Sicilia, Italy, C Mediterranean Sea
83 F25 Riet ≈ SW South Africa
83 I23 Riet ≈ SW South Africa
118 D11 Rietavas Telšiai, W Lithuania
83 F19 Rietfontein Omaheke, E Namibia
107 I14 Rieti anc. Reate. Lazio, C Italy
84 D14 Rif var. Riff, Er Rif, Er Riff. ▲▲ N Morocco
Riff see Rif
37 Q4 Rifle Colorado, C USA
31 R7 Rifle River ≈ Michigan, N USA
81 H18 Rift Valley ◐ province Kenya
Rift Valley see Great Rift Valley
118 F9 Rīga Eng. Riga. ● (Latvia) Rīga, C Latvia
Rigaer Bucht see Riga, Gulf of
118 F6 Riga, Gulf of Est. Liivi Laht, Ger. Rigaer Bucht, Latv. Rīgas Jūras Līcis, Rus. Rizhskiy Zaliv; prev. Est. Riia Laht. gulf Estonia/Latvia
143 U12 Rīgān Kermān, SE Iran
Rīgas Jūras Līcis see Riga, Gulf of
15 N12 Rigaud ≈ Ontario/Québec, SE Canada
33 R14 Rigby Idaho, NW USA
148 M10 Rīgestān var. Registan. desert region S Afghanistan
32 M11 Riggins Idaho, NW USA
13 R8 Rigolet Newfoundland and Labrador, NE Canada
78 G9 Rig-Rig Kanem, W Chad
118 F4 Riguldi Läänemaa, W Estonia
Riia Laht see Riga, Gulf of
93 L19 Riihimäki Etelä-Suomi, S Finland
195 O2 Riiser-Larsen Ice Shelf ice shelf Antarctica
195 U2 Riiser-Larsen Peninsula peninsula Antarctica
65 P22 Riiser-Larsen Sea sea Antarctica
40 D2 Riíto Sonora, NW Mexico
112 B9 Rijeka Ger. Sankt Veit am Flaum, It. Fiume, Slvn. Reka; anc. Tarsatica. Primorje-Gorski Kotar, NW Croatia
99 I14 Rijen Noord-Brabant, S Netherlands
99 H15 Rijkevorsel Antwerpen, N Belgium
Rijn see Rhine
98 G11 Rijnsburg Zuid-Holland, W Netherlands
Rijssel see Lille
98 N10 Rijssen Overijssel, E Netherlands
98 G12 Rijswijk Eng. Ryswick. Zuid-Holland, W Netherlands
92 I10 Riksgränsen Norrbotten, N Sweden
165 U4 Rikubetsu Hokkaidō, NE Japan
165 R9 Rikuzen-Takata Iwate, Honshū, C Japan
27 O4 Riley Kansas, C USA
99 I17 Rillaar Vlaams Brabant, C Belgium
Rí, Loch see Ree, Lough
114 G11 Rilska Reka ≈ W Bulgaria
77 T12 Rima ≈ N Nigeria
141 N7 Rimah, Wādī ar var. Wādī ar Rummah. dry watercourse C Saudi Arabia
Rimaszombat see Rimavská Sobota
191 R12 Rimatara island Îles Australes, SW French Polynesia
111 L20 Rimavská Sobota Ger. Gross-Steffelsdorf, Hung. Rimaszombat. Bankobystrický Kraj, C Slovakia
9 Q15 Rimbey Alberta, SW Canada
95 P15 Rimbo Stockholm, C Sweden
95 M18 Rimforsa Östergötland, S Sweden
106 I11 Rimini anc. Ariminum. Emilia-Romagna, N Italy
Rîmnicu-Sărat see Râmnicu Sărat
Rîmnicu Vîlcea see Râmnicu Vâlcea
149 Y3 Rimo Muztāgh ▲▲ India/Pakistan
15 U7 Rimouski Québec, SE Canada
158 M16 Rinbung Xizang Zizhiqu, W China
Rinchinlhumbe see Dzöölön
62 I5 Rincón, Cerro ▲ N Chile
104 M15 Rincón de la Victoria Andalucía, S Spain
Rincón del Bonete, Lago Artificial de see Río Negro, Embalse del
105 Q4 Rincón de Soto La Rioja, N Spain
94 G8 Rindal Møre og Romsdal, S Norway
115 J20 Ríneia island Kykládes, Greece, Aegean Sea
152 H11 Rīngas prev. Reengus, Ringus. Rājasthān, N India
95 H24 Ringe Fyn, C Denmark
94 H11 Ringebu Oppland, S Norway
Ringen see Rõngu
186 K8 Ringgi Kolombangara, NW Solomon Islands
23 R1 Ringgold Georgia, SE USA
22 G5 Ringgold Louisiana, S USA
25 S5 Ringgold Texas, SW USA
95 E22 Ringkøbing Ringkøbing, W Denmark
95 E21 Ringkøbing var. Ringkøbing Amt. ◐ county W Denmark
Ringkøbing Amt see Ringkøbing

◆ Country
● Country Capital
◇ Dependent Territory
○ Dependent Territory Capital
◐ Administrative Regions
✈ International Airport
▲ Mountain
▲▲ Mountain Range
Volcano
≈ River
◎ Lake
⊠ Reservoir

95 E22 **Ringkøbing Fjord** *fjord* W Denmark
33 S10 **Ringling** Montana, NW USA
27 N13 **Ringling** Oklahoma, C USA
94 H13 **Ringsaker** Hedmark, S Norway
95 I23 **Ringsted** Vestsjælland, E Denmark
Ringus *see* Rīngas
92 I9 **Ringvassøya** *Lapp.* Ráneš. *island* N Norway
18 K13 **Ringwood** New Jersey, NE USA
Rinn Duáin *see* Hook Head
100 H13 **Rinteln** Niedersachsen, NW Germany
115 E18 **Río** Dytikí Ellás, S Greece
Rio *see* Rio de Janeiro
56 C7 **Riobamba** Chimborazo, C Ecuador
60 P9 **Rio Bonito** Rio de Janeiro, SE Brazil
59 C16 **Rio Branco** *state capital* Acre, W Brazil
61 H18 **Río Branco** Cerro Largo, NE Uruguay
Rio Branco, Território de *see* Roraima
41 P8 **Río Bravo** Tamaulipas, C Mexico
63 G16 **Río Bueno** Los Lagos, C Chile
55 P5 **Río Caribe** Sucre, NE Venezuela
54 M5 **Río Chico** Miranda, N Venezuela
63 H18 **Río Cisnes** Aisén, S Chile
60 L9 **Rio Claro** São Paulo, S Brazil
45 V14 **Rio Claro** Trinidad, Trinidad and Tobago
54 J5 **Río Claro** Lara, N Venezuela
63 K15 **Río Colorado** Río Negro, E Argentina
62 K11 **Río Cuarto** Córdoba, C Argentina
60 P10 **Rio de Janeiro** *var.* Rio. *state capital* Rio de Janeiro, SE Brazil
60 P9 **Rio de Janeiro** *off.* Estado do Rio de Janeiro. ⬖ *state* SE Brazil
Rio de Janeiro, Estado do *see* Rio de Janeiro
43 R17 **Río de Jesús** Veraguas, S Panama
34 K3 **Rio Dell** California, W USA
60 K13 **Rio do Sul** Santa Catarina, S Brazil
63 I23 **Río Gallegos** *var.* Gallegos, Puerto Gallegos. Santa Cruz, S Argentina
63 J24 **Río Grande** Tierra del Fuego, S Argentina
61 I18 **Rio Grande** *var.* São Pedro do Rio Grande do Sul. Rio Grande do Sul, S Brazil
40 L10 **Río Grande** Zacatecas, C Mexico
42 J9 **Río Grande** León, NW Nicaragua
45 V5 **Río Grande** E Puerto Rico
24 I9 **Rio Grande** 〰 Texas, SW USA
25 R17 **Rio Grande City** Texas, SW USA
59 P14 **Rio Grande do Norte** *off.* Estado do Rio Grande do Norte. ⬖ *state* E Brazil
Rio Grande do Norte, Estado do *see* Rio Grande do Norte
61 G15 **Rio Grande do Sul** *off.* Estado do Rio Grande do Sul. ⬖ *state* S Brazil
Rio Grande do Sul, Estado do *see* Rio Grande do Sul
65 M17 **Rio Grande Fracture Zone** *tectonic feature* C Atlantic Ocean
65 J18 **Rio Grande Gap** *undersea feature* S Atlantic Ocean
Rio Grande Plateau *see* Rio Grande Rise
65 J18 **Rio Grande Rise** *var.* Rio Grande Plateau. *undersea feature* SW Atlantic Ocean
54 G4 **Ríohacha** La Guajira, N Colombia
43 S16 **Río Hato** Coclé, C Panama
25 T17 **Rio Hondo** Texas, SW USA
56 D10 **Rioja** San Martín, N Peru
41 Y11 **Río Lagartos** Yucatán, SE Mexico
103 P11 **Riom** *anc.* Ricomagus. Puy-de-Dôme, C France
104 F10 **Rio Maior** Santarém, C Portugal
103 O12 **Riom-ès-Montagnes** Cantal, C France
60 J12 **Rio Negro** Paraná, S Brazil
63 I15 **Río Negro** *off.* Provincia de Río Negro. ⬖ *province* C Argentina
61 D18 **Río Negro** ⬖ *department* W Uruguay
47 V12 **Río Negro, Embalse del** *var.* Lago Artificial de Rincón del Bonete. ⊠ C Uruguay
Río Negro, Provincia de *see* Río Negro
107 M17 **Rionero in Vulture** Basilicata, S Italy
137 S9 **Rioni** 〰 W Georgia
105 P11 **Riópar** Castilla-La Mancha, C Spain
61 H16 **Rio Pardo** Rio Grande do Sul, S Brazil
37 R11 **Rio Rancho Estates** New Mexico, SW USA
42 L11 **Río San Juan** ⬖ *department* S Nicaragua
54 E9 **Riosucio** Caldas, W Colombia
54 C7 **Ríosucio** Chocó, NW Colombia
62 K10 **Río Tercero** Córdoba, C Argentina
54 J5 **Río Tocuyo** Lara, N Venezuela
Riouw-Archipel *see* Riau, Kepulauan
59 J19 **Rio Verde** Goiás, C Brazil
41 O12 **Río Verde** *var.* Rioverde. San Luis Potosí, C Mexico
Rioverde *see* Río Verde
35 O8 **Rio Vista** California, W USA
112 M11 **Ripanj** Serbia, N Serbia
106 J13 **Ripatransone** Marche, C Italy
Ripen *see* Ribe
22 M2 **Ripley** Mississippi, S USA
31 R15 **Ripley** Ohio, N USA
20 F9 **Ripley** Tennessee, S USA
21 Q4 **Ripley** West Virginia, NE USA
105 W4 **Ripoll** Cataluña, NE Spain
97 M16 **Ripon** N England, UK
30 M7 **Ripon** Wisconsin, N USA
107 L24 **Riposto** Sicilia, Italy, C Mediterranean Sea
99 L14 **Rips** Noord-Brabant, SE Netherlands
54 D9 **Risaralda** *off.* Departamento de Risaralda. ⬖ *province* C Colombia
Risaralda, Departamento de *see* Risaralda
116 L8 **Rîşcani** *var.* Râşcani, *Rus.* Ryshkany. NW Moldova
152 J9 **Rishikesh** Uttaranchal, N India
165 S1 **Rishiri-tō** *var.* Risiri Tô. *island* NE Japan
165 S1 **Rishiri-yama** 🌋 Rishiri-tō, NE Japan
25 R7 **Rising Star** Texas, SW USA
31 Q15 **Rising Sun** Indiana, N USA
Risiri Tô *see* Rishiri-tō
102 L4 **Risle** 〰 N France
Rîşno *see* Râşnov
27 V13 **Rison** Arkansas, C USA
95 G17 **Risør** Aust-Agder, S Norway
92 H10 **Risøyhamn** Nordland, C Norway
101 I23 **Riss** 〰 S Germany
118 G4 **Risti** *Ger.* Kreuz. Läänemaa, W Estonia
15 V8 **Ristigouche** 〰 Québec, SE Canada
93 N18 **Ristiina** Isä-Suomi, E Finland
93 N14 **Ristijärvi** Oulu, C Finland
188 C14 **Ritidian Point** *headland* N Guam
Ritschan *see* Říčany
35 R9 **Ritter, Mount** ▲ California, W USA
31 T12 **Rittman** Ohio, N USA
32 L9 **Ritzville** Washington, NW USA
Riva *see* Riva del Garda
61 A21 **Rivadavia** Buenos Aires, E Argentina
106 F7 **Riva del Garda** *var.* Riva. Trentino-Alto Adige, N Italy
106 B8 **Rivarolo Canavese** Piemonte, W Italy
42 K11 **Rivas** Rivas, SW Nicaragua
42 J11 **Rivas** ⬖ *department* SW Nicaragua
103 R11 **Rive-de-Gier** Loire, E France
61 A22 **Rivera** Buenos Aires, E Argentina
61 F16 **Rivera** Rivera, NE Uruguay
61 F17 **Rivera** ⬖ *department* NE Uruguay
35 P9 **Riverbank** California, W USA
76 K17 **River Cess** SW Liberia
28 M4 **Riverdale** North Dakota, N USA
30 I6 **River Falls** Wisconsin, N USA
9 T16 **Riverhurst** Saskatchewan, S Canada
183 O10 **Riverina** *physical region* New South Wales, SE Australia
80 G8 **River Nile** ⬖ *state* NE Sudan
63 F19 **Rivero, Isla** *island* Archipiélago de los Chonos, S Chile
9 W16 **Rivers** Manitoba, S Canada
77 U17 **Rivers** ⬖ *state* S Nigeria
185 D23 **Riversdale** Southland, South Island, New Zealand
83 F26 **Riversdale** Western Cape, SW South Africa
35 U15 **Riverside** California, W USA
25 W9 **Riverside** Texas, SW USA
37 U3 **Riverside Reservoir** ⊠ Colorado, C USA
10 K15 **Rivers Inlet** British Columbia, SW Canada
10 K15 **Rivers Inlet** *inlet* British Columbia, SW Canada
11 X15 **Riverton** Manitoba, S Canada
185 C24 **Riverton** Southland, South Island, New Zealand
30 L13 **Riverton** Illinois, N USA
36 L3 **Riverton** Utah, W USA
33 V15 **Riverton** Wyoming, C USA
14 G10 **River Valley** Ontario, S Canada
13 P14 **Riverview** New Brunswick, SE Canada
103 O17 **Rivesaltes** Pyrénées-Orientales, S France
36 H11 **Riviera** Arizona, SW USA
25 S15 **Riviera** Texas, SW USA
23 Z14 **Riviera Beach** Florida, SE USA
15 Q10 **Rivière-à-Pierre** Québec, SE Canada
15 T9 **Rivière-Bleue** Québec, SE Canada
15 T8 **Rivière-du-Loup** Québec, SE Canada
173 Y15 **Rivière du Rempart** NE Mauritius
45 R12 **Rivière-Pilote** S Martinique
173 O17 **Rivière St-Etienne, Point de la** *headland* SW Réunion
13 S10 **Rivière-St-Paul** Québec, E Canada
Rivière Sèche *see* Bel Air
116 K4 **Rivne** *Pol.* Równe, *Rus.* Rovno. Rivnens'ka Oblast', NW Ukraine
Rivne *see* Rivnens'ka Oblast'
116 K3 **Rivnens'ka Oblast'** *var.* Rivne, *Rus.* Rovenskaya Oblast'. ⬖ *province* NW Ukraine
106 B8 **Rivoli** Piemonte, NW Italy
159 Q14 **Riwoqê** *var.* Racaka. Xizang Zizhiqu, W China
99 H19 **Rixensart** Walloon Brabant, C Belgium
Riyadh/Riyāḑ, Minţaqat ar *see* Ar Riyāḑ
Riyāq *see* Rayak
Rizaiyeh *see* Orūmīyeh
137 P11 **Rize** Rize, NE Turkey
137 P11 **Rize** *prev.* Çoruh. ⬖ *province* NE Turkey
161 R5 **Rizhao** Shandong, E China
Rizhskiy Zaliv *see* Riga, Gulf of
Rizokarpaso/Rizokárpason *see* Dipkarpaz
107 O21 **Rizzuto, Capo** *headland* S Italy
95 F15 **Rjukan** Telemark, S Norway
95 D16 **Rjuven** ▲▲ S Norway
76 H9 **Rkîz** Trarza, W Mauritania
115 Q23 **Ro** *prev.* Ágios Geórgios. *island* SE Greece
95 H14 **Roa** Oppland, S Norway
105 N5 **Roa** Castilla-León, N Spain
45 T9 **Road Town** ○ (British Virgin Islands) Tortola, C British Virgin Islands
96 F6 **Roag, Loch** *inlet* NW Scotland, UK
37 O5 **Roan Cliffs** *cliff* Colorado/Utah, W USA
21 P9 **Roan High Knob** *var.* Roan Mountain. ▲ North Carolina/Tennessee, SE USA
Roan Mountain *see* Roan High Knob
103 Q10 **Roanne** *anc.* Rodunma. Loire, E France
23 R4 **Roanoke** Alabama, S USA
21 S7 **Roanoke** Virginia, NE USA
21 Z9 **Roanoke Island** *island* North Carolina, SE USA
21 W8 **Roanoke Rapids** North Carolina, SE USA
21 X9 **Roanoke River** 〰 North Carolina/Virginia, SE USA
37 O4 **Roan Plateau** *plain* Utah, W USA
37 R5 **Roaring Fork River** 〰 Colorado, C USA
25 O5 **Roaring Springs** Texas, SW USA
42 J4 **Roatán** *var.* Coxen Hole, Coxin Hole. Islas de la Bahía, N Honduras
42 I4 **Roatán, Isla de** *island* Islas de la Bahía, N Honduras
Roat Kampuchea *see* Cambodia
Roazon *see* Rennes
143 T7 **Robāţ-e Chāh Gonbad** Yazd, E Iran
143 R7 **Robāţ-e Khān** Yazd, C Iran
143 T7 **Robāţ-e Khvosh Āb** Yazd, E Iran
143 R8 **Robāţ-e Posht-e Bādām** Yazd, NE Iran
143 Q8 **Robāţ-e Rīzāb** Yazd, C Iran
175 S8 **Robbie Ridge** *undersea feature* W Pacific Ocean
21 T10 **Robbins** North Carolina, SE USA
183 N15 **Robbins Island** *island* Tasmania, SE Australia
21 N10 **Robbinsville** North Carolina, SE USA
182 J12 **Robe** South Australia
21 W9 **Robersonville** North Carolina, SE USA
25 P8 **Robert Lee** Texas, SW USA
35 V5 **Roberts Creek Mountain** ▲ Nevada, W USA
93 J15 **Robertsfors** Västerbotten, N Sweden
27 R11 **Robert S. Kerr Reservoir** ⊠ Oklahoma, C USA
38 L12 **Roberts Mountain** ▲ Nunivak Island, Alaska, USA
83 F26 **Robertson** Western Cape, SW South Africa
194 H4 **Robertson Island** *island* Antarctica
76 J16 **Robertsport** W Liberia
182 J8 **Robertstown** South Australia
Robert Williams *see* Caála
15 P7 **Roberval** Québec, SE Canada
31 N15 **Robinson** Illinois, N USA
193 U11 **Róbinson Crusoe, Isla** *island* Islas Juan Fernández, Chile, E Pacific Ocean
180 J9 **Robinson Range** ▲▲ Western Australia
182 M9 **Robinvale** Victoria, SE Australia
105 P11 **Robledo** Castilla-La Mancha, C Spain
54 G5 **Robles** *var.* La Paz, Robles La Paz. Cesar, N Colombia
Robles La Paz *see* Robles
9 V15 **Roblin** Manitoba, S Canada
9 S17 **Robsart** Saskatchewan, S Canada
9 N15 **Robson, Mount** ▲ British Columbia, SW Canada
25 T14 **Robstown** Texas, SW USA
25 P6 **Roby** Texas, SW USA
104 E11 **Roca, Cabo da** *cape* C Portugal
Rocadas *see* Xangongo
41 S14 **Roca Partida, Punta** *headland* C Mexico
47 X6 **Rocas, Atol das** *island* E Brazil
107 L18 **Roccadaspide** *var.* Rocca d'Aspide. Campania, S Italy
Rocca d'Aspide *see* Roccadaspide
107 K15 **Roccaraso** Abruzzo, C Italy
106 H10 **Rocca San Casciano** Emilia-Romagna, C Italy
106 G13 **Roccastrada** Toscana, C Italy
61 G20 **Rocha** Rocha, E Uruguay
61 G19 **Rocha** ⬖ *department* E Uruguay
97 L17 **Rochdale** NW England, UK
102 L11 **Rochechouart** Haute-Vienne, C France
99 J22 **Rochefort** Namur, SE Belgium
102 J11 **Rochefort** *var.* Rochefort sur Mer. Charente-Maritime, W France
Rochefort sur Mer *see* Rochefort
125 N10 **Rochegda** Arkhangel'skaya Oblast', NW Russian Federation
30 L10 **Rochelle** Illinois, N USA
25 Q9 **Rochelle** Texas, SW USA
15 V3 **Rochers Ouest, Rivière aux** 〰 Québec, SE Canada
97 O22 **Rochester** *anc.* Durobrivae. SE England, UK
31 O12 **Rochester** Indiana, N USA
29 W10 **Rochester** Minnesota, N USA
19 O9 **Rochester** New Hampshire, NE USA
18 F9 **Rochester** New York, NE USA
25 P5 **Rochester** Texas, SW USA
31 S9 **Rochester Hills** Michigan, N USA
Rocheuses, Montagnes/Rockies *see* Rocky Mountains
64 M6 **Rockall** *island* N Atlantic Ocean, UK
64 L6 **Rockall Bank** *undersea feature* N Atlantic Ocean
84 B8 **Rockall Rise** *undersea feature* N Atlantic Ocean
84 C9 **Rockall Trough** *undersea feature* N Atlantic Ocean
35 U2 **Rock Creek** 〰 Nevada, W USA
25 T10 **Rockdale** Texas, SW USA
195 N12 **Rockefeller Plateau** *plateau* Antarctica
30 K11 **Rock Falls** Illinois, N USA
23 Q5 **Rockford** Alabama, S USA
30 L10 **Rockford** Illinois, N USA
15 Q12 **Rock Forest** Québec, SE Canada
9 T17 **Rockglen** Saskatchewan, S Canada
181 Y8 **Rockhampton** Queensland, E Australia
21 R11 **Rock Hill** South Carolina, SE USA
180 I13 **Rockingham** Western Australia
21 T11 **Rockingham** North Carolina, SE USA
30 J11 **Rock Island** Illinois, N USA
25 U12 **Rock Island** Texas, SW USA
14 C10 **Rock Lake** Ontario, S Canada
29 O2 **Rock Lake** North Dakota, N USA
14 I12 **Rock Lake** ◎ Ontario, SE Canada
14 M12 **Rockland** Ontario, SE Canada
19 R7 **Rockland** Maine, NE USA
182 L11 **Rocklands Reservoir** ⊠ Victoria, SE Australia
35 O7 **Rocklin** California, W USA
23 R3 **Rockmart** Georgia, SE USA
31 N16 **Rockport** Indiana, N USA
27 Q1 **Rock Port** Missouri, C USA
25 T14 **Rockport** Texas, SW USA
32 I7 **Rockport** Washington, NW USA
29 S11 **Rock Rapids** Iowa, C USA
30 K11 **Rock River** 〰 Illinois/Wisconsin, N USA
44 I3 **Rock Sound** Eleuthera Island, C Bahamas
25 P11 **Rocksprings** Texas, SW USA
33 U17 **Rock Springs** Wyoming, C USA
55 T9 **Rockstone** C Guyana
29 S12 **Rock Valley** Iowa, C USA
31 N14 **Rockville** Indiana, N USA
21 W3 **Rockville** Maryland, NE USA
25 U6 **Rockwall** Texas, SW USA
29 U13 **Rockwell City** Iowa, C USA
31 S10 **Rockwood** Michigan, N USA
20 M9 **Rockwood** Tennessee, S USA
25 Q8 **Rockwood** Texas, SW USA
37 U6 **Rocky Ford** Colorado, C USA
14 D9 **Rocky Island Lake** ◎ Ontario, S Canada
21 V9 **Rocky Mount** North Carolina, SE USA
21 S7 **Rocky Mount** Virginia, NE USA
33 Q8 **Rocky Mountain** ▲ Montana, NW USA
9 P15 **Rocky Mountain House** Alberta, SW Canada
37 T3 **Rocky Mountain National Park** *national park* Colorado, C USA
2 E12 **Rocky Mountains** *var.* Rockies, *Fr.* Montagnes Rocheuses. ▲▲ Canada/USA
42 H1 **Rocky Point** *headland* NE Belize
83 A17 **Rocky Point** *headland* NW Namibia
95 F14 **Rødberg** Buskerud, S Norway
95 I25 **Rødby** Storstrøm, SE Denmark
95 I25 **Rødbyhavn** Storstrøm, SE Denmark
13 T10 **Roddickton** Newfoundland, Newfoundland and Labrador, SE Canada
95 F23 **Rødding** Sønderjylland, SW Denmark
95 M22 **Rödeby** Blekinge, S Sweden
98 N6 **Roden** Drenthe, NE Netherlands
62 H9 **Rodeo** San Juan, W Argentina
103 O14 **Rodez** *anc.* Segodunum. Aveyron, S France
Rodholívos *see* Rodolívos
Rodhópi Óri *see* Rhodope Mountains
Ródhos *see* Ródos
Ródhos/Rodi *see* Ródos
Rodi *see* Ródos
107 N15 **Rodi Garganico** Puglia, SE Italy
101 N20 **Roding** Bayern, SE Germany
113 J19 **Rodinit, Kepi i** *headland* W Albania
116 I9 **Rodnei, Munţii** ▲▲ N Romania
184 L4 **Rodney, Cape** *headland* North Island, New Zealand
38 L9 **Rodney, Cape** *headland* Alaska, USA
124 M16 **Rodniki** Ivanovskaya Oblast', W Russian Federation
119 Q16 **Rodnya** *Rus.* Rodnya. Mahilyowskaya Voblasts', E Belarus
Rodó *see* José Enrique Rodó
114 H13 **Rodolívos** *var.* Rodholívos. Kentrikí Makedonía, NE Greece
Rodopi *see* Rhodope Mountains
115 O22 **Ródos** *var.* Ródhos, *Eng.* Rhodes, *It.* Rodi. Ródos, Dodekánisa, Greece, Aegean Sea
115 O22 **Ródos** *var.* Ródhos, *Eng.* Rhodes, *It.* Rodi; *anc.* Rhodos. *island* Dodekánisa, Greece, Aegean Sea
Rodosto *see* Tekirdağ
59 A14 **Rodrigues** Amazonas, W Brazil
173 P8 **Rodrigues** *var.* Rodriquez. *island* E Mauritius
Rodriquez *see* Rodrigues
Rodunma *see* Roanne
180 I7 **Roebourne** Western Australia
83 J20 **Roedtan** Limpopo, NE South Africa
98 H11 **Roelofarendsveen** Zuid-Holland, W Netherlands
Roepat *see* Rupat, Pulau
Roer *see* Rur
99 M16 **Roermond** Limburg, SE Netherlands
99 C18 **Roeselare** *Fr.* Roulers; *prev.* Rousselaere. West-Vlaanderen, W Belgium
9 P8 **Roes Welcome Sound** *strait* Nunavut, N Canada
Roeteng *see* Ruteng
Rofreit *see* Rovereto
Rogachëv *see* Rahachow
57 L15 **Rogagua, Laguna** ◎ NW Bolivia
95 C16 **Rogaland** ⬖ *county* S Norway
25 Y9 **Roganville** Texas, SW USA
109 W11 **Rogaška Slatina** *Ger.* Rohitsch-Sauerbrunn; *prev.* Rogatec-Slatina. E Slovenia
Rogatec-Slatina *see* Rogaška Slatina
112 J13 **Rogatica** ⬖ Republika Srpska, SE Bosnia and Herzegovina
Rogatin *see* Rohatyn
93 F17 **Rogen** ◎ C Sweden
27 S9 **Rogers** Arkansas, C USA
29 P5 **Rogers** North Dakota, N USA
25 T9 **Rogers** Texas, SW USA
31 R5 **Rogers City** Michigan, N USA
Roger Simpson Island *see* Abemama
35 T14 **Rogers Lake** *salt flat* California, W USA
21 Q8 **Rogers, Mount** ▲ Virginia, NE USA
33 O16 **Rogerson** Idaho, NW USA
9 O16 **Rogers Pass** *pass* British Columbia, SW Canada
21 O8 **Rogersville** Tennessee, S USA
99 L16 **Roggel** Limburg, SE Netherlands
Roggeveen *see* Roggewein, Cabo
193 R10 **Roggeveen Basin** *undersea feature* E Pacific Ocean
191 X16 **Roggewein, Cabo** *var.* Roggeveen. *cape* Easter Island, Chile, E Pacific Ocean
103 Y13 **Rogliano** Corse, France, C Mediterranean Sea
107 N21 **Rogliano** Calabria, SW Italy
92 G12 **Rognan** Nordland, C Norway
100 K10 **Rögnitz** 〰 N Germany
Rogozhina/Rogozhinë *see* Rrogozhinë
110 G10 **Rogoźno** Wielkopolskie, C Poland
32 E15 **Rogue River** 〰 Oregon, NW USA
116 I6 **Rohatyn** *Rus.* Rogatin. Ivano-Frankivs'ka Oblast', W Ukraine
189 O14 **Rohi** Pohnpei, E Micronesia
Rohitsch-Sauerbrunn *see* Rogaška Slatina
149 Q13 **Rohri** Sind, SE Pakistan
152 I10 **Rohtak** Haryāna, N India
Roi Ed *see* Roi Et
167 R9 **Roi Et** *var.* Muang Roi Et, Roi Ed. Roi Et, E Thailand
191 U9 **Roi Georges, Îles du** *island group* Îles Tuamotu, C French Polynesia
153 Y10 **Roing** Arunāchal Pradesh, NE India
118 E7 **Roja** Talsi, NW Latvia
61 B20 **Rojas** Buenos Aires, E Argentina
149 R12 **Rojhān** Punjab, E Pakistan
41 Q12 **Rojo, Cabo** *headland* C Mexico
45 Q10 **Rojo, Cabo** *cape* W Puerto Rico
168 K10 **Rokan Kiri, Sungai** 〰 Sumatera, W Indonesia
118 I11 **Rokiškis** Panevėžys, NE Lithuania
165 R7 **Rokkasho** Aomori, Honshū, C Japan
111 B17 **Rokycany** *Ger.* Rokytzan. Plzeňský Kraj, W Czech Republic
117 P6 **Rokytne** Kyyivs'ka Oblast', N Ukraine
116 L3 **Rokytne** Rivnens'ka Oblast', NW Ukraine
Rokytzan *see* Rokycany
158 L11 **Rola Co** ◎ W China
29 V13 **Roland** Iowa, C USA
95 D15 **Røldal** Hordaland, S Norway
98 O7 **Rolde** Drenthe, NE Netherlands
29 O2 **Rolette** North Dakota, N USA
27 V6 **Rolla** Missouri, C USA
29 O2 **Rolla** North Dakota, N USA
108 A10 **Rolle** Vaud, W Switzerland
181 X8 **Rolleston** Queensland, E Australia
185 H19 **Rolleston** Canterbury, South Island, New Zealand
185 G18 **Rolleston Range** ▲▲ South Island, New Zealand
14 H8 **Rollet** Québec, SE Canada
22 J4 **Rolling Fork** Mississippi, S USA
20 L6 **Rolling Fork** 〰 Kentucky, S USA
14 J11 **Rolphton** Ontario, SE Canada
Röm *see* Rømø
181 X10 **Roma** Queensland, E Australia
107 I15 **Roma** *Eng.* Rome. ● (Italy) Lazio, C Italy
95 P19 **Roma** Gotland, SE Sweden
21 T14 **Romain, Cape** *headland* South Carolina, SE USA
13 P11 **Romaine** 〰 Newfoundland and Labrador/Québec, E Canada
25 R17 **Roma Los Saenz** Texas, SW USA
114 H8 **Roman** Vratsa, NW Bulgaria
116 L10 **Roman** *Hung.* Románvásár. Neamţ, NE Romania
64 M13 **Romanche Fracture Zone** *tectonic feature* E Atlantic Ocean
61 C15 **Romang** Santa Fe, C Argentina
171 R15 **Romang, Pulau** *var.* Pulau Roma. *island* Kepulauan Damar, E Indonesia
171 R15 **Romang, Selat** *strait* Nusa Tenggara, S Indonesia
116 J11 **Romania** *Bul.* Rumŭniya, *Ger.* Rumänien, *Hung.* Románia, *Rom.* România, *SCr.* Rumunjska, *Ukr.* Rumuniya, *prev.* Republica Socialistă România, Roumania, Rumania, Socialist Republic of Romania, *prev.Rom.* Romînia. ◆ *republic* SE Europe
România, Republica Socialistă *see* Romania
Romania, Socialist Republic of *see* Romania
117 T14 **Roman-Kash** ▲ S Ukraine
23 W16 **Romano, Cape** *headland* Florida, SE USA
44 G5 **Romano, Cayo** *island* C Cuba
123 O13 **Romanovka** Respublika Buryatiya, S Russian Federation
127 N8 **Romanovka** Saratovskaya Oblast', W Russian Federation
108 I6 **Romanshorn** Thurgau, NE Switzerland
103 R12 **Romans-sur-Isère** Drôme, E France
189 U12 **Romanum** *island* Chuuk, C Micronesia
Románvásár *see* Roman
39 S5 **Romanzof Mountains** ▲▲ Alaska, USA
Roma, Pulau *see* Romang, Pulau
103 S4 **Rombas** Moselle, NE France
23 R2 **Rome** Georgia, SE USA
18 I9 **Rome** New York, NE USA
Rome *see* Roma
31 S9 **Romeo** Michigan, N USA
Römerstadt *see* Rýmařov
Rometan *see* Romiton
103 P5 **Romilly-sur-Seine** Aube, N France
Romînia *see* Romania
146 L11 **Romiton** *Rus.* Rometan. Buxoro Viloyati, C Uzbekistan
21 U3 **Romney** West Virginia, NE USA
117 S4 **Romny** Sums'ka Oblast', NE Ukraine
95 E24 **Rømø** *Ger.* Röm. *island* SW Denmark
117 S5 **Romodan** Poltavs'ka Oblast', NE Ukraine
127 P5 **Romodanovo** Respublika Mordoviya, W Russian Federation
Romorantin *see* Romorantin-Lanthenay
103 N8 **Romorantin-Lanthenay** *var.* Romorantin. Loir-et-Cher, C France
94 F9 **Romsdal** *physical region* S Norway
94 F10 **Romsdalen** *valley* S Norway
94 E9 **Romsdalsfjorden** *fjord* S Norway
33 P8 **Ronan** Montana, NW USA
59 M14 **Roncador** Maranhão, E Brazil
186 M7 **Roncador Reef** *reef* N Solomon Islands
59 J17 **Roncador, Serra do** ▲▲ C Brazil
21 S6 **Ronceverte** West Virginia, NE USA
107 H14 **Ronciglione** Lazio, C Italy
104 L15 **Ronda** Andalucía, S Spain
94 G11 **Rondane** ▲▲ S Norway
104 L15 **Ronda, Serranía de** ▲▲ S Spain
95 H22 **Rønde** Århus, C Denmark
Ronde, Île *see* Round Island
Rōndik *see* Rongrik Atoll
59 E16 **Rondônia** *off.* Estado de Rondônia; *prev.* Território de Rondônia. ⬖ *state* W Brazil
Rondônia, Estado de *see* Rondônia
Rondônia, Território de *see* Rondônia
59 I18 **Rondonópolis** Mato Grosso, W Brazil
94 G11 **Rondslottet** ▲ S Norway
95 P20 **Ronehamn** Gotland, SE Sweden
160 L13 **Rong'an** *var.* Chang'an, Rongan. Guangxi Zhuangzu Zizhiqu, S China
Rongan *see* Rong'an
Rongcheng *see* Jianli, Hubei, China
189 R4 **Rongelap Atoll** *var.* Rōnlap. *atoll* Ralik Chain, NW Marshall Islands
Rongerik *see* Rongrik Atoll
160 K12 **Rongjiang** *var.* Guzhou. Guizhou, S China
160 L13 **Rong Jiang** 〰 S China
Rongjiang *see* Nankang
Rong, Kas *see* Rŭng, Kaôh
167 P8 **Rong Kwang** Phrae, NW Thailand
189 T4 **Rongrik Atoll** *var.* Rōndik, Rongerik. *atoll* Ralik Chain, N Marshall Islands
189 X2 **Rongrong** *island* SE Marshall Islands
160 L13 **Rongshui** *var.* Rongshui Miaozu Zizhixian. Guangxi Zhuangzu Zizhiqu, S China
Rongshui Miaozu Zizhixian *see* Rongshui
118 I6 **Rōngu** *Ger.* Ringen. Tartumaa, SE Estonia
160 L15 **Rongxian** *var.* Rongcheng. Guangxi Zhuangzu Zizhiqu, S China
Rong Xian *see* Rongxian, Guangxi, China
Rongzhag *see* Danba
Roniu *see* Ronui, Mont
189 N13 **Ronkiti** Pohnpei, E Micronesia
Rōnlap *see* Rongelap Atoll
95 L24 **Rønne** Bornholm, E Denmark
95 M22 **Ronneby** Blekinge, S Sweden
194 J7 **Ronne Entrance** *inlet* Antarctica
194 L6 **Ronne Ice Shelf** *ice shelf* Antarctica
99 E19 **Ronse** *Fr.* Renaix. Oost-Vlaanderen, SW Belgium
191 R8 **Ronui, Mont** *var.* Roniu. 🌋 Tahiti, W French Polynesia
30 K14 **Roodhouse** Illinois, N USA
83 C19 **Rooibank** Erongo, W Namibia
Rooke Island *see* Umboi Island
65 N24 **Rookery Point** *headland* NE Tristan da Cunha
171 V13 **Roon, Pulau** *island* E Indonesia
173 V7 **Roo Rise** *undersea feature* E Indian Ocean
152 J9 **Roorkee** Uttaranchal, N India
99 H15 **Roosendaal** Noord-Brabant, S Netherlands
25 P10 **Roosevelt** Texas, SW USA
37 N3 **Roosevelt** Utah, W USA
47 T8 **Roosevelt** 〰 W Brazil
195 O13 **Roosevelt Island** *island* Antarctica
10 L10 **Roosevelt, Mount** ▲ British Columbia, W Canada

◆ Country ● Country Capital ◇ Dependent Territory ○ Dependent Territory Capital ⬖ Administrative Regions ✈ International Airport ▲ Mountain ▲▲ Mountain Range 🌋 Volcano 〰 River ◎ Lake ⊠ Reservoir

9 P17 **Roosville** British Columbia, SW Canada
29 X10 **Root River** ≈ Minnesota, N USA
111 N16 **Ropczyce** Podkarpackie, SE Poland
181 Q3 **Roper Bar** Northern Territory, N Australia
24 M5 **Ropesville** Texas, SW USA
102 K14 **Roquefort** Landes, SW France
61 C21 **Roque Pérez** Buenos Aires, E Argentina
58 E10 **Roraima** *off.* Estado de Roraima; *prev.* Território de Rio Branco, Território de Roraima. ⬖ *state* N Brazil
Roraima, Estado de *see* Roraima
58 F9 **Roraima, Mount** ▲ N South America
Roraima, Território de *see* Roraima
94 I9 **Røros** Sør-Trøndelag, S Norway
108 I7 **Rorschach** Sankt Gallen, NE Switzerland
93 E14 **Rørvik** Nord-Trøndelag, C Norway
119 G17 **Ros'** *Rus.* Ross'. Hrodzyenskaya Voblasts', W Belarus
119 G17 **Ros'** *Rus.* Ross'. ≈ W Belarus
117 O6 **Ros'** ≈ N Ukraine
44 K7 **Rosa, Lake** ◎ Great Inagua, S Bahamas
32 M9 **Rosalia** Washington, NW USA
191 W15 **Rosalia, Punta** *headland* Easter Island, Chile, E Pacific Ocean
45 P12 **Rosalie** E Dominica
35 T14 **Rosamond** California, W USA
35 S14 **Rosamond Lake** *salt flat* California, W USA
61 B18 **Rosario** Santa Fe, C Argentina
40 J11 **Rosario** Sinaloa, C Mexico
40 G6 **Rosario** Sonora, NW Mexico
62 O6 **Rosario** San Pedro, C Paraguay
61 E20 **Rosario** Colonia, SW Uruguay
54 H5 **Rosario** Zulia, NW Venezuela
Rosario *see* Nishino-shima
Rosario *see* Rosarito
40 B4 **Rosario, Bahía del** *bay* NW Mexico
62 K6 **Rosario de la Frontera** Salta, N Argentina
61 C18 **Rosario del Tala** Entre Ríos, E Argentina
61 F16 **Rosário do Sul** Rio Grande do Sul, S Brazil
59 H18 **Rosário Oeste** Mato Grosso, W Brazil
40 B1 **Rosarito** *var.* Rosario. Baja California, NW Mexico
40 E7 **Rosarito** Baja California, NW Mexico
40 E7 **Rosarito** Baja California Sur, W Mexico
104 L9 **Rosarito, Embalse del** ⊠ W Spain
107 N22 **Rosarno** Calabria, SW Italy
56 B5 **Rosa Zárate** *var.* Quinindé. Esmeraldas, SW Ecuador
Roscianum *see* Rossano
29 O8 **Roscoe** South Dakota, N USA
25 P7 **Roscoe** Texas, SW USA
102 F5 **Roscoff** Finistère, NW France
Ros Comáin *see* Roscommon
97 C17 **Roscommon** *Ir.* Ros Comáin. C Ireland
31 Q7 **Roscommon** Michigan, N USA
97 C17 **Roscommon** *Ir.* Ros Comáin. ⬖ *county* C Ireland
Ros. Cré *see* Roscrea
97 D19 **Roscrea** *Ir.* Ros. Cré. C Ireland
45 X12 **Roseau** *prev.* Charlotte Town. ● (Dominica) SW Dominica
29 S2 **Roseau** Minnesota, N USA
173 Y16 **Rose Belle** SE Mauritius
183 O16 **Rosebery** Tasmania, SE Australia
21 U11 **Roseboro** North Carolina, SE USA
25 T9 **Rosebud** Texas, SW USA
33 W10 **Rosebud Creek** ≈ Montana, NW USA
32 F14 **Roseburg** Oregon, NW USA
22 J3 **Rosedale** Mississippi, S USA
99 H21 **Rosée** Namur, S Belgium
55 U8 **Rose Hall** E Guyana
173 X16 **Rose Hill** W Mauritius
80 H12 **Roseires, Reservoir** *var.* Lake Rusayris. ⊠ E Sudan
Rosenau *see* Rožnov pod Radhoštěm
Rosenau *see* Rožňava
25 V11 **Rosenberg** Texas, SW USA
Rosenberg *see* Olesno
Rosenberg *see* Ružomberok
100 I10 **Rosengarten** Niedersachsen, N Germany
101 M24 **Rosenheim** Bayern, S Germany
Rosenhof *see* Zilupe
105 X4 **Roses** Cataluña, NE Spain
105 X4 **Roses, Golf de** *gulf* NE Spain
107 K14 **Roseto degli Abruzzi** Abruzzo, C Italy
9 S16 **Rosetown** Saskatchewan, S Canada
Rosetta *see* Rashîd
35 O7 **Roseville** California, W USA
30 J12 **Roseville** Illinois, N USA
29 V8 **Roseville** Minnesota, N USA
29 R7 **Rosholt** South Dakota, N USA
106 F12 **Rosignano Marittimo** Toscana, C Italy
116 I14 **Roşiori de Vede** Teleorman, S Romania
114 K8 **Rositsa** ≈ N Bulgaria
Rositten *see* Rēzekne
95 J23 **Roskilde** Roskilde, E Denmark
95 I23 **Roskilde** *off.* Roskilde Amt. ⬖ *county* E Denmark
Roskilde Amt *see* Roskilde
Ros Láir *see* Rosslare
126 H5 **Roslavl'** Smolenskaya Oblast', W Russian Federation
32 I8 **Roslyn** Washington, NW USA
99 K14 **Rosmalen** Noord-Brabant, S Netherlands
Ros Mhic Thriúin *see* New Ross
113 P19 **Rosoman** C FYR Macedonia
102 F6 **Rosporden** Finistère, NW France
185 F17 **Ross** West Coast, South Island, New Zealand
10 J7 **Ross** ≈ Yukon Territory, W Canada
Ross' *see* Ros'
96 H8 **Ross and Cromarty** *cultural region* N Scotland, UK
107 O20 **Rossano** *anc.* Roscianum. Calabria, SW Italy
22 L5 **Ross Barnett Reservoir** ⊠ Mississippi, S USA
9 W16 **Rossburn** Manitoba, S Canada
14 H13 **Rosseau** Ontario, S Canada
14 H13 **Rosseau, Lake** ◎ Ontario, S Canada
186 I10. **Rossel Island** *prev.* Yela Island. *island* SE Papua New Guinea
195 P12 **Ross Ice Shelf** *ice shelf* Antarctica
13 P16 **Rossignol, Lake** ◎ Nova Scotia, SE Canada
83 C19 **Rössing** Erongo, W Namibia
195 Q14 **Ross Island** *island* Antarctica
Rossitten *see* Rybachiy
Rossiyskaya Federatsiya *see* Russian Federation
9 N17 **Rossland** British Columbia, SW Canada
97 F20 **Rosslare** *Ir.* Ros Láir. Wexford, SE Ireland
97 F20 **Rosslare Harbour** Wexford, SE Ireland
101 M14 **Rosslau** Sachsen-Anhalt, E Germany
76 G10 **Rosso** Trarza, SW Mauritania
103 X14 **Rosso, Cap** *headland* Corse, France, C Mediterranean Sea
93 H16 **Rossön** Jämtland, C Sweden
97 K21 **Ross-on-Wye** W England, UK
Rossony *see* Rasony
126 L9 **Rossosh'** Voronezhskaya Oblast', W Russian Federation
181 Q7 **Ross River** Northern Territory, N Australia
10 J7 **Ross River** Yukon Territory, W Canada
195 O15 **Ross Sea** *sea* Antarctica
92 G13 **Røssvatnet** *Lapp* Reevhtse. ◎ C Norway
23 R1 **Rossville** Georgia, SE USA
143 P14 **Rostāq** Hormozgān, S Iran
117 N5 **Rostavytsya** ≈ N Ukraine
9 T15 **Rosthern** Saskatchewan, S Canada
100 M8 **Rostock** Mecklenburg-Vorpommern, NE Germany
124 L16 **Rostov** Yaroslavskaya Oblast', W Russian Federation
Rostov *see* Rostov-na-Donu
126 L12 **Rostov-na-Donu** *var.* Rostov, *Eng.* Rostov-on-Don. Rostovskaya Oblast', SW Russian Federation
Rostov-on-Don *see* Rostov-na-Donu
126 L10 **Rostovskaya Oblast'** ⬖ *province* SW Russian Federation
93 J14 **Rosvik** Norrbotten, N Sweden
23 S3 **Roswell** Georgia, SE USA
37 U14 **Roswell** New Mexico, SW USA
94 K12 **Rot** Dalarna, C Sweden
101 I23 **Rot** ≈ S Germany
104 J15 **Rota** Andalucía, S Spain
188 K9 **Rota** *island* S Northern Mariana Islands
25 P6 **Rotan** Texas, SW USA
Rotcher Island *see* Tamana
100 I11 **Rotenburg** Niedersachsen, NW Germany
Rotenburg *see* Rotenburg an der Fulda
101 I16 **Rotenburg an der Fulda** *var.* Rotenburg. Thüringen, C Germany
101 L18 **Roter Main** ≈ E Germany
101 K20 **Roth** Bayern, SE Germany
101 G16 **Rothaargebirge** ▲▲ W Germany
Rothenburg *see* Rothenburg ob der Tauber
101 J20 **Rothenburg ob der Tauber** *var.* Rothenburg. Bayern, S Germany
194 H6 **Rothera** *UK research station* Antarctica
185 I17 **Rotherham** Canterbury, South Island, New Zealand
97 M17 **Rotherham** N England, UK
108 E7 **Rothrist** Aargau, N Switzerland
96 H12 **Rothesay** W Scotland, UK
194 H6 **Rothschild Island** *island* Antarctica
171 P17 **Roti, Pulau** *island* S Indonesia
183 O8 **Roto** New South Wales, SE Australia
184 N8 **Rotoiti, Lake** ◎ North Island, New Zealand
Rotomagus *see* Rouen
107 N19 **Rotondella** Basilicata, S Italy
103 X15 **Rotondo, Monte** ▲ Corse, France, C Mediterranean Sea
185 I15 **Rotoroa, Lake** ◎ South Island, New Zealand
184 N8 **Rotorua** Bay of Plenty, North Island, New Zealand
184 N8 **Rotorua, Lake** ◎ North Island, New Zealand
101 N22 **Rott** ≈ SE Germany
108 F10 **Rotten** ≈ S Switzerland
109 T6 **Rottenmann** Steiermark, E Austria
98 H12 **Rotterdam** Zuid-Holland, SW Netherlands
18 K10 **Rotterdam** New York, NE USA
95 M21 **Rottnen** ◎ S Sweden
98 N4 **Rottumeroog** *island* Waddeneilanden, NE Netherlands
98 N4 **Rottumerplaat** *island* Waddeneilanden, NE Netherlands
101 G23 **Rottweil** Baden-Württemberg, S Germany
191 O7 **Rotui, Mont** ☼ Moorea, W French Polynesia
103 P1 **Roubaix** Nord, N France
111 C15 **Roudnice nad Labem** *Ger.* Raudnitz an der Elbe. Ústecký Kraj, NW Czech Republic
102 M4 **Rouen** *anc.* Rotomagus. Seine-Maritime, N France
171 X13 **Rouffaer Reserves** *reserve* Papua, E Indonesia
15 N10 **Rouge, Rivière** ≈ Québec, SE Canada
20 J6 **Rough River** ≈ Kentucky, S USA
20 J6 **Rough River Lake** ⊠ Kentucky, S USA
Rouhaïbé *see* Ar Ruḩaybah
102 K11 **Rouillac** Charente, W France
Roulers *see* Roeselare
Roumania *see* Romania
173 Y15 **Round Island** *var.* Île Ronde. *island* NE Mauritius
14 J12 **Round Lake** ◎ Ontario, SE Canada
35 U7 **Round Mountain** Nevada, W USA
25 R10 **Round Mountain** Texas, SW USA
183 U5 **Round Mountain** ▲ New South Wales, SE Australia
25 S10 **Round Rock** Texas, SW USA
33 U10 **Roundup** Montana, NW USA
55 Y10 **Roura** NE French Guiana
Rourkela *see* Rāurkela
96 J4 **Rousay** *island* N Scotland, UK
Rousselaere *see* Roeselare
103 O17 **Roussillon** *cultural region* S France
15 V7 **Routhierville** Québec, SE Canada
99 K25 **Rouvroy** Luxembourg, SE Belgium
14 I7 **Rouyn-Noranda** Québec, SE Canada
Rouyuanchengzi *see* Huachi
92 L12 **Rovaniemi** Lappi, N Finland
106 E7 **Rovato** Lombardia, N Italy
125 N11 **Rovdino** Arkhangel'skaya Oblast', NW Russian Federation
Roven'ki *see* Roven'ky
117 Y8 **Roven'ky** *var.* Roven'ki. Luhans'ka Oblast', E Ukraine
Rovenskaya Oblast' *see* Rivnens'ka Oblast'
Rovenskaya Sloboda *see* Rovyenskaya Slabada
106 G7 **Rovereto** *Ger.* Rofreit. Trentino-Alto Adige, N Italy
167 S12 **Rôviěng Tbong** Preăh Vihéar, N Cambodia
Rovigno *see* Rovinj
106 H8 **Rovigo** Veneto, NE Italy
112 A10 **Rovinj** *It.* Rovigno. Istra, NW Croatia
54 E10 **Rovira** Tolima, C Colombia
Rovno *see* Rivne
127 P9 **Rovnoye** Saratovskaya Oblast', W Russian Federation
82 Q12 **Rovuma, Rio** *var.* Ruvuma. ≈ Mozambique/Tanzania
see also Ruvuma
Rovuma, Rio *see* Ruvuma
119 O19 **Rovyenskaya Slabada** *Rus.* Rovenskaya Sloboda. Homyel'skaya Voblasts', SE Belarus
183 R5 **Rowena** New South Wales, SE Australia
21 T11 **Rowland** North Carolina, SE USA
9 P5 **Rowley** ≈ Baffin Island, Nunavut, NE Canada
9 P6 **Rowley Island** *island* Nunavut, NE Canada
173 W8 **Rowley Shoals** *reef* NW Australia
Równe *see* Rivne
171 O4 **Roxas** Mindoro, N Philippines
171 P5 **Roxas City** Panay Island, C Philippines
21 U8 **Roxboro** North Carolina, SE USA
185 D23 **Roxburgh** Otago, South Island, New Zealand
96 K13 **Roxburgh** *cultural region* SE Scotland, UK
182 H5 **Roxby Downs** South Australia
95 M17 **Roxen** ◎ S Sweden
25 V5 **Roxton** Texas, SW USA
15 P12 **Roxton-Sud** Québec, SE Canada
33 U8 **Roy** Montana, NW USA
37 U10 **Roy** New Mexico, SW USA
97 E17 **Royal Canal** *Ir.* An Chanáil Ríoga. *canal* C Ireland
30 L1 **Royale, Isle** *island* Michigan, N USA
37 S6 **Royal Gorge** *valley* Colorado, C USA
97 M20 **Royal Leamington Spa** *var.* Leamington, Leamington Spa. C England, UK
97 O23 **Royal Tunbridge Wells** *var.* Tunbridge Wells. SE England, UK
24 L9 **Royalty** Texas, SW USA
102 J11 **Royan** Charente-Maritime, W France
65 B24 **Roy Cove Settlement** West Falkland, Falkland Islands
103 O3 **Roye** Somme, N France
95 H15 **Røyken** Buskerud, S Norway
93 F14 **Røyrvik** Nord-Trøndelag, C Norway
25 U6 **Royse City** Texas, SW USA
97 O21 **Royston** E England, UK
23 U2 **Royston** Georgia, SE USA
114 L10 **Roza** *prev.* Gyulovo. Yambol, E Bulgaria
113 L16 **Rožaje** E Montenegro
110 M10 **Różan** Mazowieckie, C Poland
117 O10 **Rozdil'na** Odes'ka Oblast', SW Ukraine
117 S12 **Rozdol'ne** *Rus.* Razdolnoye. Respublika Krym, S Ukraine
145 Q9 **Rozhdestvenka** Akmola, C Kazakhstan
116 I6 **Rozhnyativ** Ivano-Frankivs'ka Oblast', W Ukraine
116 J3 **Rozhyshche** Volyns'ka Oblast', NW Ukraine
Roznau am Radhost *see* Rožnov pod Radhoštěm
111 L19 **Rožňava** *Ger.* Rosenau, *Hung.* Rozsnyó. Košický Kraj, E Slovakia
116 K10 **Roznov** Neamţ, NE Romania
111 I18 **Rožnov pod Radhoštěm** *Ger.* Rosenau, Roznau am Radhost. Zlínský Kraj, E Czech Republic
Rózsahegy *see* Ružomberok
Rozsnyó *see* Râşnov
Rozsnyó *see* Rožňava
113 K18 **Rranxë** Shkodër, NW Albania
113 L18 **Rrëshen** *var.* Rresheni, Rrshen. Lezhë, C Albania
Rresheni *see* Rrëshen
Rrogozhina *see* Rrogozhinë
113 K20 **Rrogozhinë** *var.* Rogozhina, Rogozhinë, Rrogozhina. Tiranë, W Albania
Rrshen *see* Rrëshen
112 O13 **Rtanj** ▲ E Serbia
127 O7 **Rtishchevo** Saratovskaya Oblast', W Russian Federation
184 N12 **Ruahine Range** *var.* Ruarine. ▲▲ North Island, New Zealand
185 L14 **Ruamahanga** ≈ North Island, New Zealand
Ruanda *see* Rwanda
184 M10 **Ruapehu, Mount** ☼ North Island, New Zealand
185 C25 **Ruapuke Island** *island* SW New Zealand
Ruarine *see* Ruahine Range
184 O9 **Ruatahuna** Bay of Plenty, North Island, New Zealand
184 Q8 **Ruatoria** Gisborne, North Island, New Zealand
184 K4 **Ruawai** Northland, North Island, New Zealand
15 N8 **Ruban** ≈ Québec, SE Canada
81 I22 **Rubeho Mountains** ▲▲ C Tanzania
165 U3 **Rubeshibe** Hokkaidō, NE Japan
Rubezhnoye *see* Rubizhne
113 L18 **Rubik** Lezhë, C Albania
54 H7 **Rubio** Táchira, W Venezuela
117 X6 **Rubizhne** *Rus.* Rubezhnoye. Luhans'ka Oblast', E Ukraine
81 F20 **Rubondo Island** *island* N Tanzania
122 I13 **Rubtsovsk** Altayskiy Kray, S Russian Federation
39 P9 **Ruby** Alaska, USA
35 W3 **Ruby Dome** ▲ Nevada, W USA
35 W4 **Ruby Lake** ◎ Nevada, W USA
35 W4 **Ruby Mountains** ▲▲ Nevada, W USA
33 Q12 **Ruby Range** ▲▲ Montana, NW USA
118 C10 **Rucava** Liepāja, SW Latvia
143 S13 **Rūdān** *var.* Dehbārez. Hormozgān, S Iran
Rudelstadt *see* Ciechanowiec
Rudensk *see* Rudzyensk
119 G14 **Rūdiškės** Vilnius, S Lithuania
95 H24 **Rudkøbing** Fyn, C Denmark
125 S13 **Rudnichnyy** Kirovskaya Oblast', NW Russian Federation
Rūdnīchnyy *see* Koksu
114 N9 **Rudnik** Varna, E Bulgaria
Rudny *see* Rudnyy
126 H4 **Rudnya** Smolenskaya Oblast', W Russian Federation
127 O8 **Rudnya** Volgogradskaya Oblast', SW Russian Federation
144 M7 **Rudnyy** *var.* Rudny. Kostanay, N Kazakhstan
122 K3 **Rudol'fa, Ostrov** *island* Zemlya Frantsa-Iosifa, NW Russian Federation
Rudolf, Lake *see* Turkana, Lake
Rudolfswert *see* Novo mesto
101 L17 **Rudolstadt** Thüringen, C Germany
31 Q4 **Rudyard** Michigan, N USA
33 S7 **Rudyard** Montana, NW USA
119 K16 **Rudzyensk** *Rus.* Rudensk. Minskaya Voblasts', C Belarus
104 L6 **Rueda** Castilla-León, N Spain
114 F10 **Ruen** ▲ Bulgaria/FYR Macedonia
80 G10 **Rufa'a** Gezira, C Sudan
102 L10 **Ruffec** Charente, W France
21 R14 **Ruffin** South Carolina, SE USA
81 J23 **Rufiji** ≈ E Tanzania
61 A20 **Rufino** Santa Fe, C Argentina
76 F11 **Rufisque** W Senegal
83 K14 **Rufunsa** Lusaka, C Zambia
118 J9 **Rugāji** Balvi, E Latvia
161 R7 **Rugao** Jiangsu, E China
97 M20 **Rugby** C England, UK
29 N3 **Rugby** North Dakota, N USA
100 N7 **Rügen** *cape* NE Germany
Ruhaybeh *see* Ar Ruḩaybah
81 E19 **Ruhengeri** NW Rwanda
Ruhja *see* Rūjiena
100 M10 **Ruhner Berg** *hill* N Germany
118 F7 **Ruhnu** *var.* Ruhnu Saar, *Swe.* Runö. *island* SW Estonia
Ruhnu Saar *see* Ruhnu
101 G15 **Ruhr** ≈ W Germany
91 W6 **Ruhr Valley** *industrial region* W Germany
161 S11 **Rui'an** *var.* Rui an. Zhejiang, SE China
Rui an *see* Rui'an
161 P10 **Ruichang** Jiangxi, S China
24 J11 **Ruidosa** Texas, SW USA
37 S14 **Ruidoso** New Mexico, SW USA
161 P12 **Ruijin** Jiangxi, S China
160 D13 **Ruili** Yunnan, SW China
98 N8 **Ruinen** Drenthe, NE Netherlands
99 D17 **Ruiselede** West-Vlaanderen, W Belgium
64 P5 **Ruivo de Santana, Pico** ▲ Madeira, Portugal, NE Atlantic Ocean
40 J12 **Ruiz** Nayarit, SW Mexico
54 E10 **Ruiz, Nevado del** ☼ W Colombia
138 J9 **Rujaylah, Ḩarrat ar** *salt lake* N Jordan
Rujen *see* Rūjiena
118 H7 **Rūjiena** *Est.* Ruhja, *Ger.* Rujen. Valmiera, N Latvia
79 I18 **Ruki** ≈ W Dem. Rep. Congo
81 E22 **Rukwa** ⬖ *region* SW Tanzania
81 F23 **Rukwa, Lake** ◎ SE Tanzania
25 P6 **Rule** Texas, SW USA
22 K3 **Ruleville** Mississippi, S USA
Rum *see* Rhum
112 K10 **Ruma** Vojvodina, N Serbia
Rumadiya *see* Ar Ramādī
141 Q7 **Rumāḩ** Ar Riyāḑ, C Saudi Arabia
Rumaitha *see* Ar Rumaythah
Rumania/Rumänien *see* Romania
Rumänisch-Sankt-Georgen *see* Sângeorz-Băi
139 Y13 **Rumaylah** SE Iraq
139 P2 **Rumaylah, Wādī** *dry watercourse* NE Syria
171 U13 **Rumbati** Papua, E Indonesia
81 E14 **Rumbek** El Buhayrat, S Sudan
Rumburg *see* Rumburk
111 D14 **Rumburk** *Ger.* Rumburg. Ústecký Kraj, NW Czech Republic
44 J4 **Rum Cay** *island* C Bahamas
99 M26 **Rumelange** Luxembourg, S Luxembourg
99 D20 **Rumes** Hainaut, SW Belgium
19 P7 **Rumford** Maine, NE USA
110 I6 **Rumia** Pomorskie, N Poland
113 J17 **Rumija** ▲▲ S Montenegro
103 T11 **Rumilly** Haute-Savoie, E France
139 O6 **Rūmiyah** W Iraq
Rummah, Wādī ar *see* Rimah, Wādī ar
Rummelsburg in Pommern *see* Miastko
165 S3 **Rumoi** Hokkaidō, NE Japan
82 M12 **Rumphi** *var.* Rumpi. Northern, N Malawi
Rumpi *see* Rumphi
29 V7 **Rum River** ≈ Minnesota, N USA
188 F16 **Rumung** *island* Caroline Islands, W Micronesia
Rumuniya/Rumŭniya/Rumunjska *see* Romania
185 G16 **Runanga** West Coast, South Island, New Zealand
184 P7 **Runaway, Cape** *headland* North Island, New Zealand
97 K18 **Runcorn** C England, UK
118 K10 **Rundāni** Ludza, E Latvia
83 L18 **Runde** *var.* Lundi. ≈ SE Zimbabwe
83 E16 **Rundu** *var.* Runtu. Okavango, NE Namibia
93 I16 **Rundvik** Västerbotten, N Sweden
81 G20 **Runere** Mwanza, N Tanzania
25 S13 **Runge** Texas, SW USA
167 Q13 **Rŭng, Kaôh** *prev.* Kas Rong. *island* SW Cambodia
79 O16 **Rungu** Orientale, NE Dem. Rep. Congo
81 F23 **Rungwa** Rukwa, W Tanzania
81 G22 **Rungwa** Singida, C Tanzania
94 M13 **Runn** ◎ C Sweden
24 M4 **Running Water Draw** *valley* New Mexico/Texas, SW USA
Runö *see* Ruhnu
Runtu *see* Rundu
189 V12 **Ruo** *island* Caroline Islands, C Micronesia
158 L9 **Ruoqiang** *var.* Jo-ch'iang, *Uigh.* Charkhlik, Charkhliq, Qarkilik. Xinjiang Uygur Zizhiqu, NW China
159 S7 **Ruo Shui** ≈ N China
92 L8 **Ruostekfielbmá** *var.* Rustefjelbma Finnmark. Finnmark, N Norway
93 L18 **Ruovesi** Länsi-Suomi, W Finland
112 B9 **Rupa** Primorje-Gorski Kotar, NW Croatia
182 M11 **Rupanyup** Victoria, SE Australia
168 K9 **Rupat, Pulau** *prev.* Roepat. *island* W Indonesia
168 K10 **Rupat, Selat** *strait* Sumatera, W Indonesia
116 J11 **Rupea** *Ger.* Reps, *Hung.* Kőhalom; *prev.* Cohalm. Braşov, C Romania
99 G17 **Rupel** ≈ N Belgium
Rupella *see* la Rochelle
33 P15 **Rupert** Idaho, NW USA
21 R5 **Rupert** West Virginia, NE USA
Rupert House *see* Fort Rupert
12 J10 **Rupert, Rivière de** ≈ Québec, C Canada
194 M13 **Ruppert Coast** *physical region* Antarctica
100 N11 **Ruppiner Kanal** *canal* NE Germany
55 S11 **Rupununi River** ≈ S Guyana
101 D16 **Rur** *Dut.* Roer. ≈ Germany/Netherlands
58 H13 **Rurópolis Presidente Medici** Pará, N Brazil
191 S12 **Rurutu** *island* Îles Australes, SW French Polynesia
Rusaddir *see* Melilla
83 L17 **Rusape** Manicaland, E Zimbabwe
Rusayris, Lake *see* Roseires, Reservoir
Ruschuk/Rusçuk *see* Ruse
114 K7 **Ruse** *var.* Ruschuk, Rustchuk, *Turk.* Rusçuk. Ruse, N Bulgaria
109 W10 **Ruše** NE Slovenia
114 L7 **Ruse** ⬖ *province* N Bulgaria
114 K7 **Rusenski Lom** ≈ N Bulgaria
97 G17 **Rush** *Ir.* An Ros. Dublin, E Ireland
161 S4 **Rushan** *var.* Xiacun. Shandong, E China
Rushan *see* Rŭshon
Rushanskiy Khrebet *see* Rushon, Qatorkŭhi
29 V7 **Rush City** Minnesota, N USA
37 V5 **Rush Creek** ≈ Colorado, C USA
29 X10 **Rushford** Minnesota, N USA
154 N13 **Rushikulya** ≈ E India
14 D8 **Rush Lake** ◎ Ontario, S Canada
30 M7 **Rush Lake** ◎ Wisconsin, N USA
28 J10 **Rushmore, Mount** ▲ South Dakota, N USA
147 S13 **Rŭshon** *Rus.* Rushan. S Tajikistan
147 S14 **Rushon, Qatorkŭhi** *Rus.* Rushanskiy Khrebet. ▲▲ SE Tajikistan
26 M12 **Rush Springs** Oklahoma, C USA
45 V15 **Rushville** Trinidad, Trinidad and Tobago
30 J13 **Rushville** Illinois, N USA
28 K12 **Rushville** Nebraska, C USA
183 O11 **Rushworth** Victoria, SE Australia
25 W8 **Rusk** Texas, SW USA
93 I14 **Rusksele** Västerbotten, N Sweden
118 C12 **Rusnė** Klaipėda, W Lithuania
114 M10 **Rusokastrenska Reka** ≈ E Bulgaria
Russadir *see* Melilla
109 X3 **Russbach** ≈ NE Austria
9 V16 **Russell** Manitoba, S Canada
184 K2 **Russell** Northland, North Island, New Zealand
26 L4 **Russell** Kansas, C USA
21 O4 **Russell** Kentucky, S USA
20 L7 **Russell Springs** Kentucky, S USA
23 O2 **Russellville** Alabama, S USA
27 T11 **Russellville** Arkansas, C USA
20 J7 **Russellville** Kentucky, S USA
101 G18 **Rüsselsheim** Hessen, W Germany
Russia *see* Russian Federation
Russian America *see* Alaska
122 J11 **Russian Federation** *off.* Russian Federation, *var.* Russia, *Latv.* Krievija, *Rus.* Rossiyskaya Federatsiya. ◆ *republic* Asia/Europe
Russian Federation *see* Russian Federation
39 N11 **Russian Mission** Alaska, USA
34 M7 **Russian River** ≈ California, W USA
194 L13 **Russkaya** *Russian research station* Antarctica
122 J5 **Russkaya Gavan'** Novaya Zemlya, Arkhangel'skaya Oblast', N Russian Federation
122 J5 **Russkiy, Ostrov** *island* N Russian Federation
109 Y5 **Rust** Burgenland, E Austria
Rustaq *see* Ar Rustāq
137 U10 **Rust'avi** SE Georgia
21 T7 **Rustburg** Virginia, NE USA
Rustchuk *see* Ruse
Rustefjelbma Finnmark *see* Ruostekfielbmá
83 I21 **Rustenburg** North-West, N South Africa
22 H5 **Ruston** Louisiana, S USA
81 E21 **Rutana** SE Burundi
62 I4 **Rutana, Volcán** ☼ N Chile
Rutanzige, Lake *see* Edward, Lake
Rutba *see* Ar Ruṭbah
104 M14 **Rute** Andalucía, S Spain
171 N16 **Ruteng** *prev.* Roeteng. Flores, C Indonesia
194 L8 **Rutford Ice Stream** *ice feature* Antarctica
35 X6 **Ruth** Nevada, W USA
101 G15 **Rüthen** Nordrhein-Westfalen, W Germany
14 D17 **Rutherford** Ontario, S Canada
21 Q10 **Rutherfordton** North Carolina, SE USA
97 J18 **Ruthin** *Wel.* Rhuthun. NE Wales, UK
108 G7 **Rüti** Zürich, N Switzerland
Rutlam *see* Ratlām
18 M9 **Rutland** Vermont, NE USA
97 N19 **Rutland** *cultural region* C England, UK
21 N8 **Rutledge** Tennessee, S USA
158 G12 **Rutög** *var.* Rutog, Rutok. Xizang Zizhiqu, W China
Rutok *see* Rutög
79 P19 **Rutshuru** Nord Kivu, E Dem. Rep. Congo
98 L8 **Rutten** Flevoland, N Netherlands
127 Q17 **Rutul** Respublika Dagestan, SW Russian Federation
93 L14 **Ruukki** Oulu, C Finland
98 N11 **Ruurlo** Gelderland, E Netherlands
143 S15 **Ru'ūs al Jibāl** *cape* Oman/United Arab Emirates
138 I7 **Ru'ūs aṭ Ṭiwāl, Jabal** ▲▲ W Syria
81 H23 **Ruvuma** ⬖ *region* SE Tanzania
81 I25 **Ruvuma** *var.* Rio Rovuma. ≈ Mozambique/Tanzania
see also Rovuma, Rio
Ruvuma *see* Rovuma, Rio
Ruwais *see* Ar Ruways
138 L9 **Ruwayshid, Wadi ar** *dry watercourse* NE Jordan
141 Z10 **Ruways, Ra's ar** *headland* E Oman
79 P18 **Ruwenzori** ▲▲ Uganda/Dem. Rep. Congo
141 Y8 **Ruwī** NE Oman
114 F9 **Ruy** ▲ Bulgaria/Serbia and Montenegro
Ruya *see* Luia, Rio
81 E20 **Ruyigi** E Burundi
127 P5 **Ruzayevka** Respublika Mordoviya, W Russian Federation
119 G18 **Ruzhany** *Rus.* Ruzhany. Brestskaya Voblasts', SW Belarus
114 I10 **Rŭzhevo Konare** *var.* Rŭzhevo Konare. Plovdiv, C Bulgaria
Ruzhin *see* Ruzhyn
114 G7 **Ruzhintsi** Vidin, NW Bulgaria
161 N6 **Ruzhou** Henan, C China
117 N5 **Ruzhyn** *Rus.* Ruzhin. Zhytomyrs'ka Oblast', N Ukraine
111 K19 **Ružomberok** *Ger.* Rosenberg, *Hung.* Rózsahegy. Žilinský Kraj, N Slovakia
111 C16 **Ruzyně** ✈ (Praha) Praha, C Czech Republic
81 D19 **Rwanda** *off.* Rwandese Republic; *prev.* Ruanda. ◆ *republic* C Africa
Rwandese Republic *see* Rwanda
95 G22 **Ry** Århus, C Denmark
Ryasna *see* Rasna
126 L5 **Ryazan'** Ryazanskaya Oblast', W Russian Federation
126 L5 **Ryazanskaya Oblast'** ⬖ *province* W Russian Federation
126 M6 **Ryazhsk** Ryazanskaya Oblast', W Russian Federation
118 B13 **Rybachiy** *Ger.* Rossitten. Kaliningradskaya Oblast', W Russian Federation
124 J2 **Rybachiy, Poluostrov** *peninsula* NW Russian Federation
Rybach'ye *see* Balykchy
124 L15 **Rybinsk** *prev.* Andropov. Yaroslavskaya Oblast', W Russian Federation
124 K14 **Rybinskoye Vodokhranilishche** *Eng.* Rybinsk Reservoir, Rybinsk Sea. ⊠ W Russian Federation

◆ Country ● Country Capital ◇ Dependent Territory ○ Dependent Territory Capital ⬖ Administrative Regions ✈ International Airport ▲ Mountain ▲▲ Mountain Range ☼ Volcano ≈ River ◎ Lake ⊠ Reservoir

Rybinsk Reservoir/ Rybinsk Sea see Rybinskoye Vodokhranilishche
111 I16 **Rybnik** Śląskie, S Poland
Rybnitsa see Rîbniţa
111 F16 **Rychnov nad Kněžnou** Ger. Reichenau. Královéhradecký Kraj, N Czech Republic
110 I12 **Rychwał** Wielkopolskie, C Poland
9 O13 **Rycroft** Alberta, W Canada
95 L21 **Ryd** Kronoberg, S Sweden
95 L20 **Rydaholm** Jönköping, S Sweden
194 I8 **Rydberg Peninsula** *peninsula* Antarctica
97 P23 **Rye** SE England, UK
33 T10 **Ryegate** Montana, NW USA
35 S3 **Rye Patch Reservoir** Nevada, W USA
95 D15 **Ryfylke** *physical region* S Norway
95 H16 **Rygge** Østfold, S Norway
110 N13 **Ryki** Lubelskie, E Poland
Rykovo see Yenakiyeve
126 I7 **Ryl'sk** Kurskaya Oblast', W Russian Federation
183 S8 **Rylstone** New South Wales, SE Australia
111 H17 **Rýmařov** Ger. Römerstadt. Moravskoslezský Kraj, E Czech Republic
144 E11 **Ryn-Peski** *desert* W Kazakhstan
165 N10 **Ryōtsu** var. Ryôtu. Niigata, Sado, C Japan
Ryôtu see Ryōtsu
110 K10 **Rypin** Kujawsko-pomorskie, C Poland
Ryshkany see Rîşcani
Ryssel see Lille
Ryswick see Rijswijk
95 M24 **Rytterknægten** *hill* E Denmark
Ryukyu Islands see Nansei-shotō
192 G5 **Ryukyu Trench** var. Nansei Syotō Trench. *undersea feature* S East China Sea
110 D11 **Rzepin** Ger. Reppen. Lubuskie, W Poland
111 N16 **Rzeszów** Podkarpackie, SE Poland
124 I16 **Rzhev** Tverskaya Oblast', W Russian Federation
Rzhishchev see Rzhyshchiv
117 P5 **Rzhyshchiv** Rus. Rzhishchev. Kyyivs'ka Oblast', N Ukraine

S

138 E11 **Sa'ad** Southern, W Israel
109 P7 **Saalach** W Austria
101 L14 **Saale** C Germany
101 L17 **Saalfeld** var. Saalfeld an der Saale. Thüringen, C Germany
Saalfeld see Zalewo
Saalfeld an der Saale see Saalfeld
108 C8 **Saane** W Switzerland
101 D19 **Saar** Fr. Sarre. France/Germany
101 E20 **Saarbrücken** Fr. Sarrebruck. Saarland, SW Germany
Saarburg see Sarrebourg
118 D6 **Sääre** var. Sjar. Saaremaa, W Estonia
Saare see Saaremaa
118 D5 **Saaremaa** off. Saare Maakond. ◐ *province* W Estonia
118 E6 **Saaremaa** Ger. Oesel, Ösel; prev. Saare. *island* W Estonia
Saare Maakond see Saaremaa
92 L12 **Saarenkylä** Lappi, N Finland
Saargemund see Sarreguemines
93 L17 **Saarijärvi** Länsi-Soumi, C Finland
Saar in Mähren see Žd'ár nad Sázavou
92 M10 **Saariselkä** Lapp. Suoločielgi. Lappi, N Finland
92 L10 **Saariselkä** *hill range* NE Finland
101 D20 **Saarland** Fr. Sarre. ◐ *state* SW Germany
Saarlautern see Saarlouis
101 D20 **Saarlouis** prev. Saarlautern. Saarland, SW Germany
108 E11 **Saaser Vispa** S Switzerland
137 X12 **Saatlı** Rus. Saatly. C Azerbaijan
Saatly see Saatlı
Saaz see Žatec
45 V9 **Saba** *island* N Netherlands Antilles
138 J7 **Sab' Ābār** var. Sab'a Biyar, Sa'b Bi'ār. Ḥimṣ, C Syria
Sab'a Biyar see Sab' Ābār
112 K11 **Šabac** Serbia, W Serbia
105 W5 **Sabadell** Cataluña, E Spain
164 K12 **Sabae** Fukui, Honshū, SW Japan
169 V7 **Sabah** prev. British North Borneo, North Borneo. ◐ *state* East Malaysia
168 J8 **Sabak** var. Sabak Bernam. Selangor, Peninsular Malaysia
Sabak Bernam see Sabak
38 D16 **Sabak, Cape** *headland* Agattu Island, Alaska, USA
81 J20 **Sabaki** S Kenya
142 L2 **Sabalān, Kuhhā-ye** ▲ NW Iran
154 H7 **Sabalgarh** Madhya Pradesh, C India
44 E4 **Sabana, Archipiélago de** *island group* C Cuba
42 H7 **Sabanagrande** var. Sabana Grande. Francisco Morazán, S Honduras
Sabana Grande see Sabanagrande
54 E5 **Sabanalarga** Atlántico, N Colombia
41 W14 **Sabancuy** Campeche, SE Mexico
45 N8 **Sabaneta** NW Dominican Republic
54 J4 **Sabaneta** Falcón, N Venezuela
188 H4 **Sabaneta, Puntan** prev. Ushi Point. *headland* Saipan, S Northern Mariana Islands
171 X14 **Sabang** Papua, E Indonesia
116 L10 **Săbăoani** Neamţ, NE Romania
155 J26 **Sabaragamuwa Province** ◐ *province* C Sri Lanka
Sabaria see Szombathely
154 D10 **Sābarmati** NW India
171 S10 **Sabatai** Pulau Morotai, E Indonesia
141 Q15 **Sab'atayn, Ramlat as** *desert* C Yemen
107 I16 **Sabaudia** Lazio, C Italy
57 J19 **Sabaya** Oruro, S Bolivia
Sa'b Bi'ār see Sab' Ābār
Sabbioncello see Orebić
148 I8 **Şāberī, Hāmūn-e** var. Daryācheh-ye Hāmun, Daryācheh-ye Sīstān. Afghanistan/Iran *see also* Sīstān, Daryācheh-ye
Şāberī, Hāmūn-e see Sīstān, Daryācheh-ye
27 P2 **Sabetha** Kansas, C USA
75 P10 **Sabhā** C Libya
67 V13 **Sabi** var. Rio Save. Mozambique/Zimbabwe *see also* Save, Rio
Sabi see Save
118 E8 **Sabile** Ger. Zabeln. Talsi, NW Latvia
31 R14 **Sabina** Ohio, N USA
40 I3 **Sabinal** Chihuahua, N Mexico
25 Q12 **Sabinal** Texas, SW USA
25 Q11 **Sabinal River** Texas, SW USA
105 S4 **Sabiñánigo** Aragón, NE Spain
41 N6 **Sabinas** Coahuila de Zaragoza, NE Mexico
41 O8 **Sabinas Hidalgo** Nuevo León, NE Mexico
41 N6 **Sabinas, Río** NE Mexico
22 F9 **Sabine Lake** Louisiana/Texas, S USA
92 O3 **Sabine Land** *physical region* C Svalbard
25 W7 **Sabine River** Louisiana/Texas, SW USA
137 X12 **Sabirabad** C Azerbaijan
Sabkha see As Sabkhah
171 O4 **Sablayan** Mindoro, N Philippines
13 P16 **Sable, Cape** *cape* Newfoundland and Labrador, SE Canada
23 X17 **Sable, Cape** *headland* Florida, SE USA
13 R16 **Sable Island** *island* Nova Scotia, SE Canada
14 L11 **Sables, Lac des** Québec, SE Canada
14 E10 **Sables, Rivière aux** Ontario, S Canada
102 K7 **Sable-sur-Sarthe** Sarthe, NW France
125 U7 **Sablya, Gora** ▲ NW Russian Federation
77 U14 **Sabon Birnin Gwari** Kaduna, C Nigeria
77 V11 **Sabon Kafi** Zinder, C Niger
104 H6 **Sabor, Rio** N Portugal
14 J8 **Sabourin, Lac** Québec, SE Canada
102 J14 **Sabres** Landes, SW France
195 X13 **Sabrina Coast** *physical region* Antarctica
140 M11 **Sabt al Ulayā** 'Asīr, SW Saudi Arabia
104 I8 **Sabugal** Guarda, N Portugal
29 Z13 **Sabula** Iowa, C USA
141 N13 **Şabyā** Jīzān, SW Saudi Arabia
Sabzawar see Sabzevār
Sabzawaran see Sabzvārān
143 S4 **Sabzevār** var. Sabzawar. Khorāsān-Razavī, NE Iran
143 T12 **Sabzvārān** var. Sabzawaran; prev. Jiroft. Kermān, SE Iran
Sacajawea Peak see Matterhorn
82 C9 **Sacandica** Uíge, NW Angola
42 A2 **Sacatepéquez** off. Departamento de Sacatepéquez. ◐ *department* S Guatemala
Sacatepéquez, Departamento de see Sacatepéquez
104 F11 **Sacavém** Lisboa, W Portugal
29 T13 **Sac City** Iowa, C USA
105 P8 **Sacedón** Castilla-La Mancha, C Spain
116 J12 **Săcele** Ger. Vierdörfer, Hung. Négyfalu; prev. Ger. Sieben Dörfer, Hung. Hétfalu. Braşov, C Romania
12 C8 **Sachigo** Ontario, C Canada
12 C7 **Sachigo** Ontario, C Canada
12 C8 **Sachigo Lake** Ontario, C Canada
163 Y16 **Sach'ŏn** Jap. Sansenhō; prev. Samch'ŏnpŏ. S South Korea
101 O15 **Sachsen** Eng. Saxony, Fr. Saxe. ◐ *state* E Germany
101 K14 **Sachsen-Anhalt** Eng. Saxony-Anhalt. ◐ *state* C Germany
109 R9 **Sachsenburg** Salzburg, S Austria
Sachsenfeld see Žalec
8 I5 **Sachs Harbour** Banks Island, Northwest Territories, N Canada
Sächsisch-Reen/Sächsisch-Regen see Reghin
18 H8 **Sackets Harbor** New York, NE USA
13 P14 **Sackville** New Brunswick, SE Canada
19 P9 **Saco** Maine, NE USA
19 P8 **Saco River** Maine/New Hampshire, NE USA
35 O7 **Sacramento** *state capital* California, W USA
37 T14 **Sacramento Mountains** ▲▲ New Mexico, SW USA
35 N6 **Sacramento River** California, W USA
35 N5 **Sacramento Valley** *valley* California, W USA
36 I10 **Sacramento Wash** *valley* Arizona, SW USA
105 N15 **Sacratif, Cabo** *cape* S Spain
116 F9 **Săcueni** prev. Săcuieni, Hung. Székelyhíd. Bihor, W Romania
Săcuieni see Săcueni
105 R4 **Sádaba** Aragón, NE Spain
Sá da Bandeira see Lubango
138 I6 **Şadad** Ḥimş, W Syria
141 O13 **Şa'dah** NW Yemen
167 O16 **Sadao** Songkhla, SW Thailand
142 L8 **Sadd-e Dez, Daryācheh-ye** W Iran
19 S3 **Saddleback Mountain** *hill* Maine, NE USA
19 P6 **Saddleback Mountain** ▲ Maine, NE USA
141 W13 **Sadḩ** S Oman
76 J11 **Sadiola** Kayes, W Mali
149 R12 **Sādiqābād** Punjab, E Pakistan
153 Y10 **Sadiya** Assam, NE India
139 W9 **Sa'dīyah, Hawr as** E Iraq
165 N9 **Sado** var. Sadoga-shima. *island* C Japan
Sadoga-shima see Sado
104 F12 **Sado, Rio** S Portugal
114 I8 **Sadovets** Pleven, N Bulgaria
127 O11 **Sadovoye** Respublika Kalmykiya, SW Russian Federation
105 W9 **Sa Dragonera** var. Isla Dragonera. *island* Islas Baleares, Spain, W Mediterranean Sea
95 H20 **Sæby** Nordjylland, N Denmark
105 P9 **Saelices** Castilla-La Mancha, C Spain
Saena Julia see Siena
Saetabicula see Alzira
114 O12 **Safaalan** Tekirdağ, NW Turkey
Safad see Ẕefat
Şafāqis see Sfax
192 I16 **Safata Bay** *bay* Upolo, Samoa, C Pacific Ocean
Safed see Ẕefat
139 X11 **Şaffāf, Ḩawr aş** *marshy lake* S Iraq
95 J16 **Säffle** Värmland, C Sweden
37 N15 **Safford** Arizona, SW USA
74 E7 **Safi** W Morocco
143 V9 **Şafīdābeh** Khorāsān-e Janūbī, E Iran
148 K5 **Safīdkūh, Selseleh-ye** Eng. Paropamisus Range. ▲▲ W Afghanistan
142 M4 **Safīd, Rūd-e** NW Iran
126 I4 **Safonovo** Smolenskaya Oblast', W Russian Federation
136 H11 **Safranbolu** Karabük, NW Turkey
139 Y13 **Safwān** SE Iraq
158 J16 **Saga** var. Gya'gya. Xizang Zizhiqu, W China
164 C14 **Saga** Saga, Kyūshū, SW Japan
164 C13 **Saga** off. Saga-ken. ◐ *prefecture* Kyūshū, SW Japan
165 P10 **Sagae** Yamagata, Honshū, C Japan
166 L3 **Sagaing** Sagaing, C Myanmar (Burma)
166 L5 **Sagaing** ◐ *division* N Myanmar (Burma)
Saga-ken see Saga
165 N13 **Sagamihara** Kanagawa, Honshū, S Japan
165 N14 **Sagami-nada** *inlet* SW Japan
Sagan see Żagań
29 Y3 **Saganaga Lake** Minnesota, N USA
155 F18 **Sāgar** Karnātaka, W India
154 I9 **Sāgar** prev. Saugor. Madhya Pradesh, C India
15 S8 **Sagard** Québec, SE Canada
Sagarmāthā see Everest, Mount
Sagebrush State see Nevada
143 V11 **Sāghand** Yazd, C Iran
19 N14 **Sag Harbor** Long Island, New York, NE USA
Saghez see Saqqez
31 R8 **Saginaw** Michigan, N USA
31 R8 **Saginaw Bay** *lake bay* Michigan, N USA
144 H11 **Sagiz** Atyrau, W Kazakhstan
64 H6 **Saglek Bank** *undersea feature* W Labrador Sea
13 P5 **Saglek Bay** *bay* SW Labrador Sea
Saglouc/Sagluk see Salluit
103 X15 **Sagonne, Golfe de** *gulf* Corse, France, C Mediterranean Sea
105 P13 **Sagra** ▲ S Spain
104 F14 **Sagres** Faro, S Portugal
37 S7 **Saguache** Colorado, C USA
44 J7 **Sagua de Tánamo** Holguín, E Cuba
44 E5 **Sagua la Grande** Villa Clara, C Cuba
15 R7 **Saguenay** Québec, SE Canada
74 C9 **Saguia al Hamra** var. As Saqia al Hamra. N Western Sahara
105 S9 **Sagunto** Cat. Sagunt, Ar. Murviedro; anc. Saguntum. País Valenciano, E Spain
Sagunt/Saguntum see Sagunto
138 H10 **Saḩāb** 'Ammān, NW Jordan
54 E6 **Sahagún** Córdoba, NW Colombia
104 L4 **Sahagún** Castilla-León, N Spain
141 X8 **Saḩam** N Oman
68 F9 **Sahara** *desert* Libya/Algeria
75 U9 **Sahara el Gharbîya** var. Aş Şaḩrā' al Gharbīyah, Eng. Western Desert. *desert* C Egypt
75 X9 **Sahara el Sharqîya** var. Aş Şaḩrā' ash Sharqīyah, Eng. Arabian Desert, Eastern Desert. *desert* E Egypt
Saharan Atlas see Atlas Saharien
152 J9 **Sahāranpur** Uttar Pradesh, N India
64 L10 **Saharan Seamounts** var. Saharian Seamounts. *undersea feature* E Atlantic Ocean
Saharian Seamounts see Saharan Seamounts
153 Q13 **Saharsa** Bihār, NE India
67 O7 **Sahel** *physical region* C Africa
153 R14 **Sāhibganj** Jhārkhand, NE India
80 N12 **Sahil** off. Gobolka Sahil. ◐ *region* N Somalia
139 Q7 **Sāhilīyah** C Iraq
138 H4 **Sāḩilīyah, Jibāl as** ▲▲ NW Syria
114 M13 **Şahin** Tekirdağ, NW Turkey
149 U9 **Sāhīwāl** prev. Montgomery. Punjab, E Pakistan
149 U8 **Sāhīwāl** Punjab, E Pakistan
141 W11 **Saḩmah, Ramlat as** *desert* C Oman
139 T13 **Şaḩrā' al Ḩijārah** *desert* S Iraq
40 H5 **Sahuaripa** Sonora, NW Mexico
36 M16 **Sahuarita** Arizona, SW USA
40 L13 **Sahuayo** var. Sahuayo de José Mariá Morelos; prev. Sahuayo de Díaz, Sahuayo de Porfirio Díaz. Michoacán de Ocampo, SW Mexico
Sahuayo de Díaz/Sahuayo de José Mariá Morelos/ Sahuayo de Porfirio Díaz see Sahuayo
173 W8 **Sahul Shelf** *undersea feature* N Timor Sea
167 P17 **Sai Buri** Pattani, SW Thailand
74 I6 **Saïda** NW Algeria
138 G7 **Saïda** var. Şaydā, Sayida; anc. Sidon. W Lebanon
Sa'īdābād see Sīrjān
80 B13 **Sa'id Bundas** Western Bahr el Ghazal, SW Sudan
186 E7 **Saidor** Madang, N Papua New Guinea
153 S13 **Saidpur** var. Syedpur. Rajshahi, NW Bangladesh
108 C7 **Saignelégier** Jura, NW Switzerland
164 H11 **Saigō** Shimane, Dōgo, SW Japan
Saigon see Hô Chi Minh
163 P11 **SaihanTal** var. Sonid Youqi. Nei Mongol Zizhiqu, N China
162 I12 **Saihan Toroi** Nei Mongol Zizhiqu, N China
Sai Hun see Syr Darya
92 M11 **Saija** Lappi, NE Finland
164 G14 **Saijō** Ehime, Shikoku, SW Japan
164 E15 **Saiki** Ōita, Kyūshū, SW Japan
93 N18 **Saimaa** SE Finland
93 N18 **Saimaa Canal** Fin. Saimaan Kanava, Rus. Saymenskiy Kanal. *canal* Finland/Russian Federation
Saimaan Kanava see Saimaa Canal
40 L10 **Saín Alto** Zacatecas, C Mexico
96 L12 **St Abb's Head** *headland* SE Scotland, UK
9 Y16 **St. Adolphe** Manitoba, S Canada
103 O15 **St-Affrique** Aveyron, S France
15 Q10 **St-Agapit** Québec, SE Canada
97 O21 **St Albans** anc. Verulamium. E England, UK
18 L6 **Saint Albans** Vermont, NE USA
21 Q5 **Saint Albans** West Virginia, NE USA
St. Alban's Head see St Aldhelm's Head
9 Q14 **St. Albert** Alberta, SW Canada
97 M24 **St Aldhelm's Head** var. St. Alban's Head. *headland* S England, UK
15 S8 **St-Alexandre** Québec, SE Canada
15 O11 **St-Alexis-des-Monts** Québec, SE Canada
103 P2 **St-Amand-les-Eaux** Nord, N France
103 O9 **St-Amand-Montrond** var. St-Amand-Mont-Rond. Cher, C France
15 Q7 **St-Ambroise** Québec, SE Canada
173 P16 **St-André** NE Réunion
14 M12 **St-André-Avellin** Québec, SE Canada
102 K12 **St-André-de-Cubzac** Gironde, SW France
96 K11 **St Andrews** E Scotland, UK
23 Q9 **Saint Andrews Bay** *bay* Florida, SE USA
23 W7 **Saint Andrew Sound** *sound* Georgia, SE USA
Saint Anna Trough see Svyataya Anna Trough
44 J11 **St. Ann's Bay** C Jamaica
13 T10 **St. Anthony** Newfoundland, Newfoundland and Labrador, SE Canada
33 R13 **Saint Anthony** Idaho, NW USA
182 M11 **Saint Arnaud** Victoria, SE Australia
185 I15 **St. Arnaud Range** ▲▲ South Island, New Zealand
15 T8 **St-Arsène** Québec, SE Canada
13 R10 **St-Augustin** Québec, E Canada
23 X9 **Saint Augustine** Florida, SE USA
97 H24 **St Austell** SW England, UK
103 T4 **St-Avold** Moselle, NE France
103 N17 **St-Barthélemy** ▲ S France
102 L17 **St-Béat** Haute-Garonne, S France
97 I15 **St Bees Head** *headland* NW England, UK
173 P16 **St-Benoit** E Réunion
103 T13 **St-Bonnet** Hautes-Alpes, SE France
St.Botolph's Town see Boston
97 G21 **St Brides Bay** *inlet* SW Wales, UK
102 H5 **St-Brieuc** Côtes d'Armor, NW France
102 H5 **St-Brieuc, Baie de** *bay* NW France
102 L7 **St-Calais** Sarthe, NW France
15 Q10 **St-Casimir** Québec, SE Canada
14 H16 **St. Catharines** Ontario, S Canada
45 S14 **St. Catherine, Mount** ▲ N Grenada
64 C11 **St Catherine Point** *headland* E Bermuda
23 X6 **Saint Catherines Island** *island* Georgia, SE USA
97 M24 **St Catherine's Point** *headland* S England, UK
103 N13 **St-Céré** Lot, S France
108 A10 **St. Cergue** Vaud, W Switzerland
103 R11 **St-Chamond** Loire, E France
33 S16 **Saint Charles** Idaho, NW USA
27 X4 **Saint Charles** Missouri, C USA
103 P13 **St-Chély-d'Apcher** Lozère, S France
Saint Christopher and Nevis, Federation of see Saint Kitts and Nevis
Saint Christopher-Nevis see Saint Kitts and Nevis
31 S9 **Saint Clair** Michigan, N USA
14 D17 **St. Clair** Canada/USA
183 O17 **St. Clair, Lake** Tasmania, SE Australia
14 C17 **St. Clair, Lake** var. Lac à L'Eau Claire. Canada/USA
31 S10 **Saint Clair Shores** Michigan, N USA
103 S10 **St-Claude** anc. Condate. Jura, E France
45 X6 **St-Claude** Basse Terre, SW Guadeloupe
23 X12 **Saint Cloud** Florida, SE USA
29 U8 **Saint Cloud** Minnesota, N USA
45 T9 **Saint Croix** *island* S Virgin Islands (US)
30 J4 **Saint Croix Flowage** Wisconsin, N USA
19 T5 **Saint Croix River** Canada/USA
29 W7 **Saint Croix River** Minnesota/Wisconsin, N USA
45 S14 **St. David's** SE Grenada
97 H21 **St David's** SW Wales, UK
97 G21 **St David's Head** *headland* SW Wales, UK
64 C12 **St David's Island** *island* E Bermuda
173 O16 **St-Denis** ○ (Réunion) NW Réunion
103 U6 **St-Dié** Vosges, NE France
103 R5 **St-Dizier** anc. Desiderii Fanum. Haute-Marne, N France
15 N11 **St-Donat** Québec, SE Canada
15 N11 **Ste-Adèle** Québec, SE Canada
15 N11 **Ste-Agathe-des-Monts** Québec, SE Canada
9 Y16 **Ste. Anne** Manitoba, S Canada
45 R12 **Ste-Anne** Grande Terre, E Guadeloupe
45 Y6 **Ste-Anne** SE Martinique
15 Q10 **Ste-Anne** Québec, SE Canada
172 I16 **Sainte Anne** *island* Inner Islands, NE Seychelles
15 W6 **Ste-Anne-des-Monts** Québec, SE Canada
14 M10 **Ste-Anne-du-Lac** Québec, SE Canada
15 U4 **Ste-Anne, Lac** Québec, SE Canada
15 S10 **Ste-Apolline** Québec, SE Canada
15 U7 **Ste-Blandine** Québec, SE Canada
15 R10 **Ste-Claire** Québec, SE Canada
15 Q10 **Ste-Croix** Québec, SE Canada
108 B8 **Ste. Croix** Vaud, SW Switzerland
103 P14 **Ste-Énimie** Lozère, S France
27 Y6 **Sainte Genevieve** Missouri, C USA
103 S12 **St-Egrève** Isère, E France
39 T12 **Saint Elias, Cape** *headland* Kayak Island, Alaska, USA
39 U11 **Saint Elias, Mount** ▲ Alaska, USA
10 G8 **Saint Elias Mountains** ▲▲ Canada/USA
55 Y10 **St-Élie** N French Guiana
103 O10 **St-Eloy-les-Mines** Puy-de-Dôme, C France
15 S7 **Ste-Maguerite Nord-Est** Québec, SE Canada
15 V4 **Ste-Marguerite, Pointe** *headland* Québec, SE Canada
15 R10 **Ste-Marie** Québec, SE Canada
45 Q11 **Ste-Marie** NE Martinique
173 P16 **Ste-Marie** NE Réunion
103 U6 **Ste-Marie-aux-Mines** Haut-Rhin, NE France
Sainte Marie, Cap see Vohimena, Tanjona
12 J14 **Ste-Marie, Lac** Québec, S Canada
172 K4 **Sainte Marie, Nosy** *island* E Madagascar
102 L8 **Ste-Maure-de-Touraine** Indre-et-Loire, C France
103 R4 **Ste-Menehould** Marne, NE France
Ste-Perpétue see Ste-Perpétue-de-l'Islet
15 S9 **Ste-Perpétue-de-l'Islet** var. Ste-Perpétue. Québec, SE Canada
45 X11 **Ste-Rose** Basse Terre, N Guadeloupe
173 P16 **Ste-Rose** E Réunion
9 W15 **Ste. Rose du Lac** Manitoba, S Canada
102 J11 **Saintes** anc. Mediolanum. Charente-Maritime, W France
45 X7 **Saintes, Canal des** *channel* SW Guadeloupe
Saintes, Îles des see les Saintes
173 P16 **Ste-Suzanne** N Réunion
15 P10 **Ste-Thècle** Québec, SE Canada
103 Q12 **St-Étienne** Loire, E France
102 M4 **St-Étienne-du-Rouvray** Seine-Maritime, N France
Saint Eustatius see Sint Eustatius
14 M11 **Ste-Véronique** Québec, SE Canada
15 T7 **St-Fabien** Québec, SE Canada
15 P7 **St-Félicien** Québec, SE Canada
15 O11 **St-Félix-de-Valois** Québec, SE Canada
103 Y14 **St-Florent** Corse, France, C Mediterranean Sea
103 Y14 **St-Florent, Golfe de** *gulf* Corse, France, C Mediterranean Sea
103 P6 **St-Florentin** Yonne, C France
103 N9 **St-Florent-sur-Cher** Cher, C France
103 P12 **St-Flour** Cantal, C France
26 H2 **Saint Francis** Kansas, C USA
83 H26 **St. Francis, Cape** *headland* S South Africa
27 X10 **Saint Francis River** Arkansas/Missouri, C USA
22 J8 **Saint Francisville** Louisiana, S USA
45 Y6 **St-François** Grande Terre, E Guadeloupe
15 Q12 **St-François** Québec, SE Canada
15 R11 **St-François, Lac** Québec, SE Canada
27 X7 **Saint Francois Mountains** ▲▲ Missouri, C USA
St-Gall see St-Gall/Saint Gall/St.Gallen
St-Gall/Saint Gall/St. Gallen see Sankt Gallen
102 L16 **St-Gaudens** Haute-Garonne, S France
15 R12 **St-Gédéon** Québec, SE Canada
181 X10 **St George** Queensland, E Australia
64 B12 **St George** N Bermuda
38 K15 **Saint George** Saint George Island, Alaska, USA
21 S14 **Saint George** South Carolina, SE USA
36 J8 **Saint George** Utah, W USA
13 R12 **St. George, Cape** *cape* Newfoundland, Newfoundland and Labrador, E Canada
186 I6 **St. George, Cape** *headland* New Ireland, NE Papua New Guinea
38 J15 **Saint George Island** *island* Pribilof Islands, Alaska, USA
23 S10 **Saint George Island** *island* Florida, SE USA
99 J19 **Saint-Georges** Liège, E Belgium
15 R11 **St-Georges** Québec, SE Canada
55 Z11 **St-Georges** E French Guiana
45 R14 **St. George's** ● (Grenada) SW Grenada
13 R12 **St. George's Bay** *inlet* Newfoundland, Newfoundland and Labrador, E Canada
97 G21 **Saint George's Channel** *channel* Ireland/Wales, UK
186 H6 **St. George's Channel** *channel* NE Papua New Guinea
64 B11 **St George's Island** *island* E Bermuda
99 I21 **Saint-Gérard** Namur, S Belgium
St-Germain see St-Germain-en-Laye
15 P12 **St-Germain-de-Grantham** Québec, SE Canada
103 N5 **St-Germain-en-Laye** var. St-Germain. Yvelines, N France
102 H8 **St-Gildas, Pointe du** *headland* NW France
103 R15 **St-Gilles** Gard, S France
102 I9 **St-Gilles-Croix-de-Vie** Vendée, NW France
173 O16 **St-Gilles-les-Bains** W Réunion
102 M16 **St-Girons** Ariège, S France
Saint Gotthard see Szentgotthárd
108 G9 **St. Gotthard Tunnel** *tunnel* Ticino, S Switzerland
97 H22 **St Govan's Head** *headland* SW Wales, UK
34 M7 **Saint Helena** California, W USA
65 F24 **Saint Helena** ◇ *UK dependent territory* C Atlantic Ocean
67 O12 **Saint Helena** *island* C Atlantic Ocean
83 E25 **St. Helena Bay** *bay* SW South Africa
65 M16 **Saint Helena Fracture Zone** *tectonic feature* C Atlantic Ocean
34 M7 **Saint Helena, Mount** ▲ California, W USA
21 S15 **Saint Helena Sound** *inlet* South Carolina, SE USA
31 Q7 **Saint Helen, Lake** Michigan, N USA
183 Q16 **Saint Helens** Tasmania, SE Australia
97 K18 **St Helens** NW England, UK
32 G10 **Saint Helens** Oregon, NW USA
32 H10 **Saint Helens, Mount** Washington, NW USA
97 L26 **St Helier** ○ (Jersey) S Jersey, Channel Islands
15 S9 **St-Hilarion** Québec, SE Canada
99 K22 **Saint-Hubert** Luxembourg, SE Belgium
15 T8 **St-Hubert** Québec, SE Canada
15 P12 **St-Hyacinthe** Québec, SE Canada
St.Iago de la Vega see Spanish Town
31 Q4 **Saint Ignace** Michigan, N USA
15 O10 **St-Ignace-du-Lac** Québec, SE Canada
12 D12 **St. Ignace Island** *island* Ontario, S Canada
108 C7 **St. Imier** Bern, W Switzerland
97 G25 **St Ives** SW England, UK
29 U10 **Saint James** Minnesota, N USA
10 I15 **St. James, Cape** *headland* Graham Island, British Columbia, SW Canada
15 O13 **St-Jean** var. St-Jean-sur-Richelieu. Québec, SE Canada
55 X9 **St-Jean** NW French Guiana
15 R8 **St-Jean** Québec, SE Canada
Saint-Jean-d'Acre see 'Akko
102 K11 **St-Jean-d'Angély** Charente-Maritime, W France
103 N7 **St-Jean-de-Braye** Loiret, C France
102 I16 **St-Jean-de-Luz** Pyrénées-Atlantiques, SW France
103 T12 **St-Jean-de-Maurienne** Savoie, E France
102 I9 **St-Jean-de-Monts** Vendée, NW France
103 Q14 **St-Jean-du-Gard** Gard, S France
15 Q7 **St-Jean, Lac** Québec, SE Canada
102 I16 **St-Jean-Pied-de-Port** Pyrénées-Atlantiques, SW France
15 S9 **St-Jean-Port-Joli** Québec, SE Canada
St-Jean-sur-Richelieu see St-Jean
15 N12 **St-Jérôme** Québec, SE Canada
25 T5 **Saint Jo** Texas, SW USA
13 O15 **St. John** New Brunswick, SE Canada
26 L6 **Saint John** Kansas, C USA
19 Q2 **Saint John** Fr. Saint-John. Canada/USA
76 K16 **Saint John** C Liberia
45 T9 **Saint John** *island* C Virgin Islands (US)
Saint-John see Saint John

◆ Country ● Country Capital ◇ Dependent Territory ○ Dependent Territory Capital ◐ Administrative Regions ✈ International Airport ▲ Mountain ▲▲ Mountain Range Volcano River Lake Reservoir

22 *I6* **Saint John, Lake** ◎ Louisiana, S USA
45 *W10* **St John's** ● (Antigua and Barbuda) Antigua, Antigua and Barbuda
13 *V12* **St. John's** *province capital* Newfoundland, Newfoundland and Labrador, E Canada
37 *O12* **Saint Johns** Arizona, SW USA
31 *Q9* **Saint Johns** Michigan, N USA
13 *V12* **St. John's** ✈ Newfoundland, Newfoundland and Labrador, E Canada
23 *X11* **Saint Johns River** ≈ Florida, SE USA
45 *N12* **St. Joseph** W Dominica
173 *P17* **St-Joseph** S Réunion
22 *J6* **Saint Joseph** Louisiana, S USA
31 *O10* **Saint Joseph** Michigan, N USA
27 *R3* **Saint Joseph** Missouri, C USA
20 *I10* **Saint Joseph** Tennessee, S USA
22 *R9* **Saint Joseph Bay** *bay* Florida, SE USA
15 *R11* **St-Joseph-de-Beauce** Québec, SE Canada
12 *C10* **St. Joseph, Lake** ◎ Ontario, C Canada
31 *Q11* **Saint Joseph River** ≈ N USA
14 *C11* **Saint Joseph's Island** *island* Ontario, S Canada
15 *N11* **St-Jovite** Québec, SE Canada
121 *P16* **St Julian's** N Malta
St-Julien *see* St-Julien-en-Genevois
103 *T10* **St-Julien-en-Genevois** *var.* St-Julien. Haute-Savoie, E France
102 *M11* **St-Junien** Haute-Vienne, C France
103 *Q11* **St-Just-St-Rambert** Loire, E France
96 *D8* **St Kilda** *island* NW Scotland, UK
45 *V10* **Saint Kitts** *island* Saint Kitts and Nevis
45 *U10* **Saint Kitts and Nevis** *off.* Federation of Saint Christopher and Nevis, *var.* Saint Christopher-Nevis. ◆ *commonwealth republic* E West Indies
9 *X16* **St. Laurent** Manitoba, S Canada
St-Laurent *see* St-Laurent-du-Maroni
55 *X9* **St-Laurent-du-Maroni** *var.* St-Laurent. NW French Guiana
St-Laurent, Fleuve *see* St. Lawrence
102 *J12* **St-Laurent-Médoc** Gironde, SW France
13 *N12* **St. Lawrence** *Fr.* Fleuve St-Laurent. ≈ Canada/USA
13 *Q12* **St. Lawrence, Gulf of** *gulf* NW Atlantic Ocean
38 *K10* **Saint Lawrence Island** *island* Alaska, USA
14 *M14* **Saint Lawrence River** ≈ Canada/USA
99 *L25* **Saint-Léger** Luxembourg, SE Belgium
13 *N14* **St. Léonard** New Brunswick, SE Canada
15 *P11* **St-Léonard** Québec, SE Canada
173 *O17* **St-Leu** W Réunion
102 *J4* **St-Lô** *anc.* Briovera, Laudus. Manche, N France
9 *T15* **St. Louis** Saskatchewan, S Canada
103 *V7* **St-Louis** Haut-Rhin, NE France
173 *O17* **St-Louis** S Réunion
76 *G10* **Saint Louis** NW Senegal
27 *X4* **Saint Louis** Missouri, C USA
29 *W5* **Saint Louis River** ≈ Minnesota, N USA
103 *T7* **St-Loup-sur-Semouse** Haute-Saône, E France
15 *O12* **St-Luc** Québec, SE Canada
83 *L22* **St. Lucia** KwaZulu/Natal, E South Africa
45 *X13* **Saint Lucia** ◆ *independent island state* SE West Indies
47 *S3* **Saint Lucia** *island* SE West Indies
83 *L22* **St. Lucia, Cape** *headland* E South Africa
45 *Y13* **Saint Lucia Channel** *channel* Martinique/Saint Lucia
23 *Y14* **Saint Lucie Canal** *canal* Florida, SE USA
23 *Z13* **Saint Lucie Inlet** *inlet* Florida, SE USA
96 *L2* **St Magnus Bay** *bay* N Scotland, UK
102 *K10* **St-Maixent-l'École** Deux-Sèvres, W France
9 *Y16* **St. Malo** Manitoba, S Canada
102 *I5* **St-Malo** Ille-et-Vilaine, NW France
102 *H4* **St-Malo, Golfe de** *gulf* NW France
44 *L9* **St-Marc** C Haiti
44 *L9* **St-Marc, Canal de** *channel* W Haiti
103 *S12* **St-Marcellin-le-Mollard** Isère, E France
55 *Y12* **Saint-Marcel, Mont** ▲ S French Guiana
96 *K5* **St Margaret's Hope** NE Scotland, UK
32 *M9* **Saint Maries** Idaho, NW USA
23 *T9* **Saint Marks** Florida, SE USA
108 *D11* **St. Martin** Valais, SW Switzerland
Saint Martin *see* Sint Maarten
31 *O5* **Saint Martin Island** *island* Michigan, N USA
22 *I9* **Saint Martinville** Louisiana, S USA
185 *E20* **St. Mary, Mount** ▲ South Island, New Zealand
186 *E8* **St. Mary, Mount** ▲ S Papua New Guinea
182 *I6* **Saint Mary Peak** ▲ South Australia
183 *Q16* **Saint Marys** Tasmania, SE Australia
14 *E16* **St. Marys** Ontario, S Canada
38 *M11* **Saint Marys** Alaska, USA
23 *W8* **Saint Marys** Georgia, SE USA
27 *P4* **Saint Marys** Kansas, C USA
31 *Q4* **Saint Marys** Ohio, N USA
21 *R3* **Saint Marys** West Virginia, NE USA
23 *W8* **Saint Marys River** ≈ Florida/Georgia, SE USA
31 *Q4* **Saint Marys River** ≈ Michigan, N USA
102 *D6* **St-Mathieu, Pointe** *headland* NW France
38 *J12* **Saint Matthew Island** *island* Alaska, USA
21 *R13* **Saint Matthews** South Carolina, SE USA
St.Matthew's Island *see* Zadetkyi Kyun
186 *G4* **St. Matthias Group** *island group* NE Papua New Guinea
108 *C11* **St. Maurice** Valais, SW Switzerland
15 *P9* **St-Maurice** ≈ Québec, SE Canada
102 *J13* **St-Médard-en-Jalles** Gironde, SW France
39 *N10* **Saint Michael** Alaska, USA
15 *N10* **St-Michel-des-Saints** Québec, SE Canada
103 *S5* **St-Mihiel** Meuse, NE France
108 *J10* **St. Moritz** *Ger.* Sankt Moritz, *Rmsch.* San Murezzan. Graubünden, SE Switzerland
102 *H8* **St-Nazaire** Loire-Atlantique, NW France
Saint Nicholas *see* São Nicolau
Saint-Nicolas *see* Sint-Niklaas
103 *N1* **St-Omer** Pas-de-Calais, N France
102 *J11* **Saintonge** *cultural region* W France
15 *S9* **St-Pacôme** Québec, SE Canada
15 *S10* **St-Pamphile** Québec, SE Canada
15 *S9* **St-Pascal** Québec, SE Canada
14 *J11* **St-Patrice, Lac** ◎ Québec, SE Canada
9 *R14* **St. Paul** Alberta, SW Canada
173 *O16* **St-Paul** NW Réunion
38 *K14* **Saint Paul** Saint Paul Island, Alaska, USA
29 *V8* **Saint Paul** *state capital* Minnesota, N USA
29 *P15* **Saint Paul** Nebraska, C USA
21 *P7* **Saint Paul** Virginia, NE USA
77 *Q17* **Saint Paul, Cape** *headland* S Ghana
103 *O17* **St-Paul-de-Fenouillet** Pyrénées-Orientales, S France
65 *K14* **Saint Paul Fracture Zone** *tectonic feature* E Atlantic Ocean
38 *J14* **Saint Paul Island** *island* Pribilof Islands, Alaska, USA
102 *J15* **St-Paul-les-Dax** Landes, SW France
21 *U11* **Saint Pauls** North Carolina, SE USA
Saint Paul's Bay *see* San Pawl il-Bahar
191 *R16* **St Paul's Point** *headland* Pitcairn Island, Pitcairn Islands
29 *U10* **Saint Peter** Minnesota, N USA
97 *L26* **St Peter Port** ○ (Guernsey) C Guernsey, Channel Islands
23 *V13* **Saint Petersburg** Florida, SE USA
Saint Petersburg *see* Sankt-Peterburg
23 *V13* **Saint Petersburg Beach** Florida, SE USA
173 *P17* **St-Philippe** SE Réunion
45 *Q11* **St-Pierre** NW Martinique
173 *O17* **St-Pierre** SW Réunion
13 *S13* **St-Pierre and Miquelon** *Fr.* Îles St-Pierre et Miquelon. ◇ *French territorial collectivity* NE North America
15 *P11* **St-Pierre, Lac** ◎ Québec, SE Canada
102 *F5* **St-Pol-de-Léon** Finistère, NW France
103 *O2* **St-Pol-sur-Ternoise** Pas-de-Calais, N France
St. Pons *see* St-Pons-de-Thomières
103 *O16* **St-Pons-de-Thomières** *var.* St. Pons. Hérault, S France
103 *P10* **St-Pourçain-sur-Sioule** Allier, C France
15 *S11* **St-Prosper** Québec, SE Canada
103 *P3* **St-Quentin** Aisne, N France
15 *R10* **St-Raphaël** Québec, SE Canada
103 *U15* **St-Raphaël** Var, SE France
15 *Q10* **St-Raymond** Québec, SE Canada
33 *O9* **Saint Regis** Montana, NW USA
18 *J7* **Saint Regis River** ≈ New York, NE USA
103 *R15* **St-Rémy-de-Provence** Bouches-du-Rhône, SE France
15 *V6* **St-René-de-Matane** Québec, SE Canada
102 *M9* **St-Savin** Vienne, W France
15 *S8* **St-Siméon** Québec, SE Canada
23 *X7* **Saint Simons Island** *island* Georgia, SE USA
191 *Y2* **Saint Stanislas Bay** *bay* Kiritimati, E Kiribati
13 *O15* **St. Stephen** New Brunswick, SE Canada
39 *X12* **Saint Terese** Alaska, USA
14 *E17* **St. Thomas** Ontario, S Canada
29 *Q2* **Saint Thomas** North Dakota, N USA
45 *T9* **Saint Thomas** *island* W Virgin Islands (US)
Saint Thomas *see* São Tomé, Sao Tome and Principe
Saint Thomas *see* Charlotte Amalie, Virgin Islands (US)
15 *P10* **St-Tite** Québec, SE Canada
Saint-Trond *see* Sint-Truiden
103 *U16* **St-Tropez** Var, SE France
Saint Ubes *see* Setúbal
102 *L3* **St-Valéry-en-Caux** Seine-Maritime, N France
103 *Q9* **St-Vallier** Saône-et-Loire, C France
106 *B7* **St-Vincent** Valle d'Aosta, NW Italy
45 *Q14* **Saint Vincent** *island* N Saint Vincent and the Grenadines
Saint Vincent *see* São Vicente
45 *W14* **Saint Vincent and the Grenadines** ◆ *commonwealth republic* SE West Indies
Saint Vincent, Cape *see* São Vicente, Cabo de
102 *I15* **St-Vincent-de-Tyrosse** Landes, SW France
182 *I9* **Saint Vincent, Gulf** *gulf* South Australia
23 *R10* **Saint Vincent Island** *island* Florida, SE USA
45 *T12* **Saint Vincent Passage** *passage* Saint Lucia/Saint Vincent and the Grenadines
183 *N18* **Saint Vincent, Point** *headland* Tasmania, SE Australia
Saint-Vith *see* Sankt-Vith
9 *S14* **St. Walburg** Saskatchewan, S Canada
St Wolfgangsee *see* Wolfgangsee
102 *M11* **St-Yrieix-la-Perche** Haute-Vienne, C France
Saint Yves *see* Setúbal
15 *Y5* **St-Yvon** Québec, SE Canada
188 *H5* **Saipan** *island* ● (Northern Mariana Islands) S Northern Mariana Islands
188 *H6* **Saipan Channel** *channel* S Northern Mariana Islands
188 *H6* **Saipan International Airport** ✈ Saipan, S Northern Mariana Islands
74 *G6* **Sais** ✈ (Fès) C Morocco
Saishū *see* Cheju-do
Saishū *see* Cheju
102 *J16* **Saison** ≈ SW France
169 *R10* **Sai, Sungai** ≈ Borneo, N Indonesia
165 *N13* **Saitama** *off.* Saitama-ken. ◈ *prefecture* Honshū, S Japan
Saitama-ken *see* Saitama
Saiyid Abid *see* Sayyid 'Abid
57 *J19* **Sajama, Nevado** ▲ W Bolivia
141 *V13* **Sājir, Ras** *headland* S Oman
111 *M20* **Sajószentpéter** Borsod-Abaúj-Zemplén, NE Hungary
83 *F24* **Sak** ≈ SW South Africa
81 *J18* **Saka** Coast, E Kenya
167 *P11* **Sa Kaeo** Prachin Buri, C Thailand
164 *J14* **Sakai** Ōsaka, Honshū, SW Japan
164 *H14* **Sakaide** Kagawa, Shikoku, SW Japan
164 *H12* **Sakaiminato** Tottori, Honshū, SW Japan
140 *M3* **Sakākah** Al Jawf, NW Saudi Arabia
28 *L4* **Sakakawea, Lake** ⊠ North Dakota, N USA
12 *J9* **Sakami, Lac** ◎ Québec, C Canada
79 *O26* **Sakania** Katanga, SE Dem. Rep. Congo
146 *K12* **Sakar** Lebap Welaýaty, E Turkmenistan
172 *H7* **Sakaraha** Toliara, SW Madagascar
146 *I14* **Sakarçäge** *var.* Sakarchäge, *Rus.* Sakar-Chaga. Mary Welaýaty, C Turkmenistan
Sakar-Chaga/Sakarchäge *see* Sakarçäge
Sak'art'velo *see* Georgia
136 *F11* **Sakarya** ◈ *province* NW Turkey
136 *F12* **Sakarya Nehri** ≈ NW Turkey
144 *K13* **Sakasaul'skiy** *var.* Saksaul'skoye, *Kaz.* Sekseūil. Kzylorda, S Kazakhstan
165 *P9* **Sakata** Yamagata, Honshū, C Japan
123 *P9* **Sakha (Yakutiya), Respublika** *var.* Respublika Yakutiya, *Eng.* Yakutia. ◈ *autonomous republic* NE Russian Federation
Sakhalin *see* Sakhalin, Ostrov
192 *I3* **Sakhalin, Ostrov** *var.* Sakhalin. *island* SE Russian Federation
123 *U12* **Sakhalinskaya Oblast'** ◈ *province* SE Russian Federation
123 *T12* **Sakhalinskiy Zaliv** *gulf* E Russian Federation
Sakhnovshchina *see* Sakhnovshchyna
117 *U6* **Sakhnovshchyna** *Rus.* Sakhnovshchina. Kharkivs'ka Oblast', E Ukraine
Sakhon Nakhon *see* Sakon Nakhon
Sakhtsar *see* Rāmsar
137 *W10* **Şäki** *Rus.* Sheki; *prev.* Nukha. NW Azerbaijan
Saki *see* Saky
118 *E13* **Šakiai** *Ger.* Schaken. Marijampolė, S Lithuania
165 *O16* **Sakishima-shotō** *var.* Sakisima Syotô. *island group* SW Japan
Sakisima Syotô *see* Sakishima-shotō
Sakiz *see* Saqqez
Sakiz-Adasi *see* Chíos
155 *F19* **Sakleshpur** Karnātaka, E India
167 *S9* **Sakon Nakhon** *var.* Muang Sakon Nakhon, Sakhon Nakhon. E Thailand
149 *P15* **Sakrand** Sind, SE Pakistan
83 *F24* **Sak River** *Afr.* Sakrivier. Northern Cape, W South Africa
Sakrivier *see* Sak River
Saksaul'skoye *see* Sakasaul'skiy
95 *I25* **Sakskøbing** Storstrøm, SE Denmark
165 *N12* **Saku** Nagano, Honshū, S Japan
117 *S13* **Saky** *Rus.* Saki. Respublika Krym, S Ukraine
76 *E9* **Sal** *island* Ilhas de Barlavento, NE Cape Verde
127 *N12* **Sal** ≈ SW Russian Federation
111 *I21* **Sal'a** *Hung.* Sellye, Vágsellye. Nitriansky Kraj, SW Slovakia
95 *N15* **Sala** Västmanland, C Sweden
15 *N13* **Salaberry-de-Valleyfield** *var* Valleyfield. Québec, SE Canada
118 *G7* **Salacgrīva** *Est.* Salatsi. Limbaži, N Latvia
107 *M18* **Sala Consilina** Campania, S Italy
40 *C2* **Salada, Laguna** ◎ NW Mexico
61 *D14* **Saladas** Corrientes, NE Argentina
61 *C21* **Saladillo** Buenos Aires, E Argentina
61 *B16* **Saladillo, Río** ≈ C Argentina
25 *T9* **Salado** Texas, SW USA
63 *J16* **Salado, Arroyo** ≈ SE Argentina
61 *D21* **Salado, Río** ≈ E Argentina
62 *J12* **Salado, Río** ≈ C Argentina
41 *N7* **Salado, Río** ≈ NE Mexico
37 *Q12* **Salado, Río** ≈ New Mexico, SW USA
143 *N6* **Salafchegān** *var.* Sarafjagān. Quom, N Iran
77 *Q15* **Salaga** C Ghana
192 *G5* **Sala'ilua** Savai'i, W Samoa
116 *G9* **Sălaj** ◈ *county* NW Romania
83 *H20* **Salajwe** Kweneng, SE Botswana
78 *H9* **Salal** Kanem, W Chad
80 *I6* **Salala** Red Sea, NE Sudan
141 *V13* **Şalālah** SW Oman
42 *D5* **Salamá** Baja Verapaz, C Guatemala
42 *J6* **Salamá** Olancho, C Honduras
62 *G10* **Salamanca** Coquimbo, C Chile
41 *N13* **Salamanca** Guanajuato, C Mexico
104 *K7* **Salamanca** *anc.* Helmantica, Salmantica. Castilla-León, NW Spain
18 *D11* **Salamanca** New York, NE USA
104 *J7* **Salamanca** ◈ *province* Castilla-León, W Spain
63 *J19* **Salamanca, Pampa de** *plain* S Argentina
78 *J12* **Salamat** *off.* Préfecture du Salamat. ◈ *prefecture* SE Chad
78 *I12* **Salamat, Bahr** ≈ S Chad
Salamat, Préfecture du *see* Salamat
54 *F5* **Salamina** Magdalena, N Colombia
115 *G19* **Salamína** *var.* Salamís. Salamína, C Greece
115 *G19* **Salamína** *island* C Greece
Salamís *see* Salamína
138 *I5* **Salamīyah** *var.* As Salamīyah. Ḥamāh, W Syria
31 *P12* **Salamonie Lake** ⊠ Indiana, N USA
31 *P12* **Salamonie River** ≈ Indiana, N USA
Salang *see* Phuket
192 *I16* **Salani** Upolu, SE Samoa
118 *C11* **Salantai** Klaipėda, NW Lithuania
104 *K2* **Salas** Asturias, N Spain
105 *O5* **Salas de los Infantes** Castilla-León, N Spain
102 *M16* **Salat** ≈ S France
189 *V13* **Salat** *island* Chuuk, C Micronesia
169 *Q16* **Salatiga** Jawa, C Indonesia
189 *V13* **Salat Pass** *passage* W Pacific Ocean
Salatsi *see* Salacgrīva
167 *T10* **Salavan** *var.* Saravan, Saravane. Salavan, S Laos
127 *V6* **Salavat** Respublika Bashkortostan, W Russian Federation
56 *C12* **Salaverry** La Libertad, N Peru
171 *T12* **Salawati, Pulau** *island* E Indonesia
193 *R10* **Sala y Gomez** *island* Chile, E Pacific Ocean
Sala y Gomez Fracture Zone *see* Sala y Gomez Ridge
193 *S10* **Sala y Gomez Ridge** *var.* Sala y Gomez Fracture Zone. *tectonic feature* SE Pacific Ocean
61 *A22* **Salazar** Buenos Aires, E Argentina
54 *G7* **Salazar** Norte de Santander, N Colombia
Salazar *see* N'Dalatando
173 *P16* **Salazie** C Réunion
103 *N8* **Salbris** Loir-et-Cher, C France
57 *G15* **Salcantay, Nevado** ▲ C Peru
45 *O8* **Salcedo** N Dominican Republic
39 *S9* **Salcha River** ≈ Alaska, USA
119 *H15* **Šalčininkai** Vilnius, SE Lithuania
Saldae *see* Béjaïa
54 *E11* **Saldaña** Tolima, C Colombia
104 *M4* **Saldaña** Castilla-León, N Spain
83 *E25* **Saldanha** Western Cape, SW South Africa
Salduba *see* Zaragoza
61 *B23* **Saldungaray** Buenos Aires, E Argentina
118 *D9* **Saldus** *Ger.* Frauenburg. Saldus, W Latvia
183 *P13* **Sale** Victoria, SE Australia
74 *F6* **Salé** NW Morocco
74 *F6* **Salé** ✈ (Rabat) W Morocco
Salehābād *see* Andīmeshk
170 *M16* **Saleh, Teluk** *bay* Nusa Tenggara, S Indonesia
122 *H8* **Salekhard** *prev.* Obdorsk. Yamalo-Nenetskiy Avtonomnyy Okrug, N Russian Federation
192 *H16* **Sālelologa** Savai'i, C Samoa
155 *H21* **Salem** Tamil Nādu, SE India
27 *V9* **Salem** Arkansas, C USA
30 *L15* **Salem** Illinois, N USA
31 *P15* **Salem** Indiana, N USA
19 *P11* **Salem** Massachusetts, NE USA
27 *V6* **Salem** Missouri, C USA
18 *I16* **Salem** New Jersey, NE USA
31 *U12* **Salem** Ohio, N USA
32 *G12* **Salem** *state capital* Oregon, NW USA
29 *Q11* **Salem** South Dakota, N USA
36 *L4* **Salem** Utah, W USA
21 *S7* **Salem** Virginia, NE USA
21 *R3* **Salem** West Virginia, NE USA
107 *H23* **Salemi** Sicilia, Italy, C Mediterranean Sea
Salemy *see* As Sālimī
94 *K12* **Sälen** Dalarna, C Sweden
107 *Q18* **Salentina, Campi** Puglia, SE Italy
107 *Q18* **Salentina, Penisola** *peninsula* SE Italy
107 *L18* **Salerno** *anc.* Salernum. Campania, S Italy
107 *L18* **Salerno, Golfo di** *Eng.* Gulf of Salerno. *gulf* S Italy
Salerno, Gulf of *see* Salerno, Golfo di
Salernum *see* Salerno
97 *K17* **Salford** NW England, UK
Salgir *see* Salhyr
111 *K21* **Salgótarján** Nógrád, N Hungary
59 *O15* **Salgueiro** Pernambuco, E Brazil
94 *C13* **Salhus** Hordaland, S Norway
117 *T12* **Salhyr** *Rus.* Salgir. ≈ S Ukraine
171 *Q9* **Salibabu, Pulau** *island* N Indonesia
37 *S6* **Salida** Colorado, C USA
102 *J15* **Salies-de-Béarn** Pyrénées-Atlantiques, SW France
136 *C14* **Salihli** Manisa, W Turkey
119 *K18* **Salihorsk** *Rus.* Soligorsk. Minskaya Voblasts', S Belarus
119 *K18* **Salihorskaye Vodaskhovishcha** ⊠ C Belarus
83 *N14* **Salima** Central, C Malawi
166 *L5* **Salin** Magwe, W Myanmar (Burma)
27 *N4* **Salina** Kansas, C USA
36 *L5* **Salina** Utah, W USA
41 *S17* **Salina Cruz** Oaxaca, SE Mexico
107 *L22* **Salina, Isola** *island* Isole Eolie, S Italy
44 *J5* **Salina Point** *headland* Acklins Island, SE Bahamas
56 *A7* **Salinas** Guayas, W Ecuador
40 *M11* **Salinas** *var.* Salinas de Hidalgo. San Luis Potosí, C Mexico
45 *T6* **Salinas** C Puerto Rico
35 *O10* **Salinas** California, W USA
Salinas, Cabo de *see* Salines, Cap de ses
Salinas de Hidalgo *see* Salinas
82 *A13* **Salinas, Ponta das** *headland* W Angola
45 *O10* **Salinas, Punta** *headland* S Dominican Republic
Salinas, Río *see* Chixoy, Río
35 *O11* **Salinas River** ≈ California, W USA
22 *H6* **Saline Lake** ◎ Louisiana, S USA
25 *R17* **Salineno** Texas, SW USA
27 *V14* **Saline River** ≈ Arkansas, C USA
30 *M17* **Saline River** ≈ Illinois, N USA
105 *X10* **Salines, Cap de ses** *var.* Cabo de Salinas. *cape* Mallorca, Spain, W Mediterranean Sea
Salisburg *see* Mazsalaca
45 *O12* **Salisbury** *var.* Baroui. W Dominica
97 *M23* **Salisbury** *var.* New Sarum. S England, UK
21 *Y4* **Salisbury** Maryland, NE USA
27 *T3* **Salisbury** Missouri, C USA
21 *S9* **Salisbury** North Carolina, SE USA
Salisbury *see* Harare
9 *Q7* **Salisbury Island** *island* Nunavut, NE Canada
Salisbury, Lake *see* Bisina, Lake
97 *L23* **Salisbury Plain** *plain* S England, UK
21 *R14* **Salkehatchie River** ≈ South Carolina, SE USA
138 *I9* **Şalkhad** As Suwaydā', SW Syria
92 *M12* **Salla** Lappi, NE Finland
Sállan *see* Sørøya
103 *U11* **Sallanches** Haute-Savoie, E France
105 *V5* **Sallent** Cataluña, NE Spain
61 *A22* **Salliqueló** Buenos Aires, E Argentina
27 *R10* **Sallisaw** Oklahoma, C USA
80 *I7* **Sallom** Red Sea, NE Sudan
12 *J2* **Salluit** *prev.* Saglouc, Sagluk. Québec, NE Canada
Sallūm, Khalīj as *see* Salûm, Gulf of
Sallyana *see* Şalyan
13 *S11* **Sally's Cove** Newfoundland and Labrador, E Canada
139 *W9* **Salmān Bin 'Arāzah** E Iraq
Salmantica *see* Salamanca
142 *I2* **Salmās** *prev.* Dilman, Shāpūr. Āžarbāyjān-e Gharbī, NW Iran
124 *I11* **Salmi** Respublika Kareliya, NW Russian Federation
33 *P12* **Salmon** Idaho, NW USA
9 *N16* **Salmon Arm** British Columbia, SW Canada
192 *L5* **Salmon Bank** *undersea feature* N Pacific Ocean
Salmon Leap *see* Leixlip
34 *L2* **Salmon Mountains** ▲▲ California, W USA
14 *J15* **Salmon Point** *headland* Ontario, SE Canada
33 *N11* **Salmon River** ≈ Idaho, NW USA
18 *K6* **Salmon River** ≈ New York, NE USA
33 *N12* **Salmon River Mountains** ▲▲ Idaho, NW USA
18 *I9* **Salmon River Reservoir** ⊠ New York, NE USA
93 *K19* **Salo** Länsi-Soumi, SW Finland
106 *F7* **Salò** Lombardia, N Italy
Salona/Salonae *see* Solin
103 *S15* **Salon-de-Provence** Bouches-du-Rhône, SE France
Salonica/Salonika *see* Thessaloníki
115 *I14* **Salonikiós, Akrotírio** *var.* Akrotírio Salonikós. *cape* Thásos, E Greece
116 *F10* **Salonta** *Hung.* Nagyszalonta. Bihor, W Romania
104 *I9* **Salor** ≈ W Spain
105 *U6* **Salou** Cataluña, NE Spain
76 *H11* **Saloum** ≈ C Senegal
42 *H4* **Sal, Punta** *headland* NW Honduras
92 *N3* **Salpynten** *headland* W Svalbard
138 *I3* **Salqīn** Idlib, W Syria
93 *F14* **Salsbruket** Nord-Trøndelag, C Norway
126 *M13* **Sal'sk** Rostovskaya Oblast', SW Russian Federation
107 *K25* **Salso** ≈ Sicilia, Italy, C Mediterranean Sea
107 *J25* **Salso** ≈ Sicilia, Italy, C Mediterranean Sea
106 *E9* **Salsomaggiore Terme** Emilia-Romagna, N Italy
Salt *see* As Salt
62 *J6* **Salta** Salta, NW Argentina
62 *K6* **Salta** *off.* Provincia de Salta. ◈ *province* N Argentina
Salta, Provincia de *see* Salta
97 *I24* **Saltash** SW England, UK
24 *I8* **Salt Basin** *basin* Texas, SW USA
9 *V16* **Saltcoats** Saskatchewan, S Canada
30 *L13* **Salt Creek** ≈ Illinois, N USA
24 *J9* **Salt Draw** ≈ Texas, SW USA
97 *F21* **Saltee Islands** *island group* SE Ireland
92 *G12* **Saltfjorden** *inlet* C Norway
24 *I8* **Salt Flat** Texas, SW USA
27 *N8* **Salt Fork Arkansas River** ≈ Oklahoma, C USA
31 *T13* **Salt Fork Lake** ⊠ Ohio, N USA
26 *J11* **Salt Fork Red River** ≈ Oklahoma/Texas, C USA
26 *J11* **Salt Fork Red River** ≈ Oklahoma/Texas, C USA
95 *J23* **Saltholm** *island* E Denmark
41 *N8* **Saltillo** Coahuila de Zaragoza, NE Mexico
182 *L5* **Salt Lake** *salt lake* New South Wales, SE Australia
37 *V15* **Salt Lake** ◎ New Mexico, SW USA
36 *K2* **Salt Lake City** *state capital* Utah, W USA
61 *C20* **Salto** Buenos Aires, E Argentina
61 *D17* **Salto** Salto, N Uruguay
61 *E17* **Salto** ◈ *department* N Uruguay
107 *J14* **Salto** ≈ C Italy
62 *Q6* **Salto del Guairá** Canindeyú, E Paraguay
61 *D17* **Salto Grande, Embalse de** *var.* Lago de Salto Grande. ⊠ Argentina/Uruguay
Salto Grande, Lago de *see* Salto Grande, Embalse de
35 *W16* **Salton Sea** ◎ California, W USA
60 *I12* **Salto Santiago, Represa de** ⊠ S Brazil
149 *U7* **Salt Range** ▲▲ E Pakistan
36 *M13* **Salt River** ≈ Arizona, SW USA
20 *L5* **Salt River** ≈ Kentucky, S USA
27 *V3* **Salt River** ≈ Missouri, C USA
95 *F17* **Saltrød** Aust-Agder, S Norway
95 *P16* **Saltsjöbaden** Stockholm, C Sweden
92 *G12* **Saltstraumen** Nordland, C Norway
21 *Q7* **Saltville** Virginia, NE USA
Saluces/Saluciae *see* Saluzzo
21 *Q12* **Saluda** South Carolina, SE USA
21 *X6* **Saluda** Virginia, NE USA
21 *Q12* **Saluda River** ≈ South Carolina, SE USA
75 *T7* **Salûm** *var.* As Sallūm. NW Egypt
152 *F14* **Salūmbar** Rājasthān, N India
75 *T7* **Salûm, Gulf of** *Ar.* Khalīj as Sallūm. *gulf* Egypt/Libya
171 *O11* **Salumpaga** Sulawesi, N Indonesia
155 *M14* **Salūr** Andhra Pradesh, E India
55 *Y9* **Salut, Îles du** *island group* N French Guiana
106 *A9* **Saluzzo** *Fr.* Saluces; *anc.* Saluciae. Piemonte, NW Italy
63 *F23* **Salvación, Bahía** *bay* S Chile
59 *P17* **Salvador** *prev.* São Salvador. *state capital* Bahia, E Brazil
65 *E24* **Salvador** East Falkland, Falkland Islands
22 *K10* **Salvador, Lake** ◎ Louisiana, S USA
Salvaleón de Higüey *see* Higüey
104 *F10* **Salvaterra de Magos** Santarém, C Portugal
41 *N13* **Salvatierra** Guanajuato, C Mexico
105 *P3* **Salvatierra** *Basq.* Agurain. País Vasco, N Spain
Salwa/Salwah *see* As Salwā
166 *M7* **Salween** *Bur.* Thanlwin, *Chin.* Nu Chiang, Nu Jiang. ≈ SE Asia
137 *Y12* **Salyan** *Rus.* Sal'yany. SE Azerbaijan
153 *N11* **Şalyan** *var.* Sallyana. Mid Western, W Nepal
Sal'yany *see* Salyan
21 *O6* **Salyersville** Kentucky, S USA
109 *V6* **Salza** ≈ E Austria
109 *Q7* **Salzach** ≈ Austria/Germany
109 *Q6* **Salzburg** *anc.* Juvavum. Salzburg, N Austria
109 *O8* **Salzburg** *off.* Land Salzburg. ◈ *state* C Austria
Salzburg *see* Ocna Sibiului
Salzburg Alps *see* Salzburger Kalkalpen
109 *Q7* **Salzburger Kalkalpen** *Eng.* Salzburg Alps. ▲▲ C Austria
Salzburg, Land *see* Salzburg
100 *J13* **Salzgitter** *prev.* Watenstedt-Salzgitter. Niedersachsen, C Germany
101 *G14* **Salzkotten** Nordrhein-Westfalen, W Germany
100 *K11* **Salzwedel** Sachsen-Anhalt, N Germany
152 *D11* **Sām** Rājasthān, NW India
104 *K2* **Sama** *var.* Sama de Langreo. Asturias, N Spain
Šamac *see* Bosanski Šamac
54 *G9* **Samacá** Boyacá, C Colombia
40 *I7* **Samachique** Chihuahua, N Mexico
141 *Y8* **Şamad** NE Oman
Sama de Langreo *see* Langreo
Sama de Langreo *see* Sama
Samaden *see* Samedan
57 *M19* **Samaipata** Santa Cruz, C Bolivia
167 *T10* **Samakhixai** *var.* Attapu, Attopeu. Attapu, S Laos
Samakov *see* Samokov
42 *B6* **Samalá, Río** ≈ SW Guatemala
40 *J3* **Samalayuca** Chihuahua, N Mexico
155 *L16* **Sāmalkot** Andhra Pradesh, E India
45 *P8* **Samaná** *var.* Santa Bárbara de Samaná. E Dominican Republic

◆ Country ● Country Capital ◇ Dependent Territory ○ Dependent Territory Capital ◈ Administrative Regions ✈ International Airport ▲ Mountain ▲▲ Mountain Range Volcano ◎ Lake ≈ River ⊠ Reservoir

45 P8 **Samaná, Bahía de** *bay* E Dominican Republic
44 K4 **Samana Cay** *island* SE Bahamas
136 K17 **Samandağı** Hatay, S Turkey
149 P3 **Samangān** ◈ *province* N Afghanistan
Samangān *see* Āybak
165 T5 **Samani** Hokkaidō, NE Japan
54 C13 **Samaniego** Nariño, SW Colombia
171 Q5 **Samar** *island* C Philippines
127 S6 **Samara** *prev.* Kuybyshev. Samarskaya Oblast', W Russian Federation
127 T7 **Samara** ~ W Russian Federation
127 S6 **Samara** ✈ Samarskaya Oblast', W Russian Federation
117 V7 **Samara** ~ E Ukraine
186 G10 **Samarai** Milne Bay, SE Papua New Guinea
Samarang *see* Semarang
138 G9 **Samarian Hills** *hill range* N Israel
54 L9 **Samariapo** Amazonas, C Venezuela
169 V11 **Samarinda** Borneo, C Indonesia
Samarkand *see* Samarqand
Samarkandskaya Oblast' *see* Samarqand Viloyati
Samarkandski/Samarkandskoye *see* Temirtau
Samarobriva *see* Amiens
147 N11 **Samarqand** *Rus.* Samarkand. Samarqand Viloyati, C Uzbekistan
146 M11 **Samarqand Viloyati** *Rus.* Samarkandskaya Oblast'. ◈ *province* C Uzbekistan
139 S6 **Sāmarrā'** C Iraq
127 R7 **Samarskaya Oblast'** *prev.* Kuybyshevskaya Oblast'. ◈ *province* W Russian Federation
153 Q13 **Samastīpur** Bihār, N India
76 L14 **Samatiguila** NW Ivory Coast
119 Q17 **Samatsevichy** *Rus.* Samotevichi. Mahilyowskaya Voblasts', E Belarus
Samawa *see* As Samāwah
137 Y11 **Şamaxı** *Rus.* Shemakha. E Azerbaijan
79 K18 **Samba** Equateur, NW Dem. Rep. Congo
79 N21 **Samba** Maniema, E Dem. Rep. Congo
152 H6 **Samba** Jammu and Kashmir, NW India
169 W10 **Sambaliung, Pegunungan** ▲▲ Borneo, N Indonesia
154 M11 **Sambalpur** Orissa, E India
67 X12 **Sambao** ~ W Madagascar
169 Q10 **Sambas, Sungai** ~ Borneo, N Indonesia
172 K2 **Sambava** Antsiranana, NE Madagascar
152 J10 **Sambhal** Uttar Pradesh, N India
152 H12 **Sāmbhar Salt Lake** ◎ N India
107 N21 **Sambiase** Calabria, SW Italy
116 H5 **Sambir** *Rus.* Sambor. L'vivs'ka Oblast', NW Ukraine
82 C13 **Sambo** Huambo, C Angola
Sambor *see* Sambir
61 E21 **Samborombón, Bahía** *bay* NE Argentina
99 H20 **Sambre** ~ Belgium/France
43 V16 **Sambú, Río** ~ SE Panama
163 Z14 **Samch'ŏk** *Jap.* Sanchoku. NE South Korea
Samch'ŏnpŏ *see* Sach'ŏn
81 I21 **Same** Kilimanjaro, NE Tanzania
108 J10 **Samedan** *Ger.* Samaden. Graubünden, S Switzerland
82 K12 **Samfya** Luapula, N Zambia
141 W13 **Samḥān, Jabal** ▲▲ SW Oman
115 C18 **Sámi** Kefallonía, Iónia Nisiá, Greece, C Mediterranean Sea
56 F10 **Samiria, Río** ~ N Peru
Samirum *see* Semīrom
137 V11 **Şämkir** *Rus.* Shamkhor. NW Azerbaijan
167 S7 **Sam, Nam** *Vtn.* Sông Chu. ~ Laos/Vietnam
Samnān *see* Semnān
Sam Neua *see* Xam Nua
75 P10 **Samnū** C Libya
192 H15 **Samoa** *off.* Independent State of Western Samoa, *var.* Sāmoa, *prev* Western Samoa. ◆ *monarchy* W Polynesia
192 L9 **Sāmoa** *island group* American Samoa
Sāmoa *see* Samoa
175 T9 **Samoa Basin** *undersea feature* W Pacific Ocean
112 D8 **Samobor** Zagreb, N Croatia
114 H10 **Samokov** *var.* Samakov. Sofiya, W Bulgaria
111 H21 **Šamorín** *Ger.* Sommerein, *Hung.* Somorja. Trnavský Kraj, W Slovakia
115 M19 **Sámos** *prev.* Limín Vathéos. Sámos, Dodekánisa, Greece, Aegean Sea
115 M20 **Sámos** *island* Dodekánisa, Greece, Aegean Sea
Samosch *see* Szamos
168 I9 **Samosir, Pulau** *island* W Indonesia
Samotevichi *see* Samatsevichy
Samothrace *see* Samothráki
115 K14 **Samothráki** Samothráki, NE Greece
115 J14 **Samothráki** *anc.* Samothrace. *island* NE Greece
115 A15 **Samothráki** *island* Iónia Nisiá, Greece, C Mediterranean Sea
Samotschin *see* Szamocin
Sampê *see* Xiangcheng
169 S13 **Sampit** Borneo, C Indonesia
169 S12 **Sampit, Sungai** ~ Borneo, N Indonesia
Sampoku *see* Sanpoku
186 H7 **Sampun** New Britain, E Papua New Guinea
79 N24 **Sampwe** Katanga, SE Dem. Rep. Congo
25 X8 **Sam Rayburn Reservoir** ▣ Texas, SW USA
167 Q6 **Sam Sao, Phou** ▲▲ Laos/Thailand
95 H22 **Samsø** *island* E Denmark
95 H23 **Samsø Bælt** *channel* E Denmark
167 T7 **Sâm Sơn** Thanh Hoa, N Vietnam
136 L11 **Samsun** *anc.* Amisus. Samsun, N Turkey
136 K11 **Samsun** ◈ *province* N Turkey
137 R9 **Samtredia** W Georgia
59 E15 **Samuel, Represa de** ▣ W Brazil
167 O14 **Samui, Ko** *island* SW Thailand
Samundari *see* Samundri
149 U9 **Samundri** *var.* Samundari. Punjab, E Pakistan
137 X10 **Samur** ~ Azerbaijan/Russian Federation
137 Y11 **Samur-Abşeron Kanalı** *Rus.* Sam ur-Apsheronskiy Kanal. *canal* E Azerbaijan
Sam ur-Apsheronskiy Kanal *see* Samur-Abşeron Kanalı
167 O11 **Samut Prakan** *var.* Muang Samut Prakan, Paknam. Samut Prakan, C Thailand
167 O11 **Samut Sakhon** *var.* Maha Chai, Samut Sakorn, Tha Chin. Samut Sakhon, C Thailand
Samut Sakorn *see* Samut Sakhon
167 O11 **Samut Songhram** *prev.* Meklong. Samut Songkhram, SW Thailand
77 N12 **San** Ségou, C Mali
111 O15 **San** ~ SE Poland
141 O15 **Şan'ā'** *Eng.* Sana. ● (Yemen) W Yemen
112 F11 **Sana** ~ NW Bosnia and Herzegovina
80 O12 **Sanaag** *off.* Gobolka Sanaag. ◈ *region* N Somalia
Sanaag, Gobolka *see* Sanaag
114 J8 **Sanadinovo** Pleven, N Bulgaria
195 P1 **Sanae** *South African research station* Antarctica
139 Y10 **Sanāf, Hawr as** ◎ S Iraq
79 E15 **Sanaga** ~ C Cameroon
54 D12 **San Agustín** Huila, SW Colombia
171 R8 **San Agustin, Cape** *headland* Mindanao, S Philippines
37 Q13 **San Agustin, Plains of** *plain* New Mexico, SW USA
38 M16 **Sanak Island** *island* Aleutian Islands, Alaska, USA
193 U10 **San Ambrosio, Isla** *Eng.* San Ambrosio Island. *island* W Chile
San Ambrosio Island *see* San Ambrosio, Isla
171 Q12 **Sanana** Pulau Sanana, E Indonesia
171 Q12 **Sanana, Pulau** *island* Maluku, E Indonesia
142 K5 **Sanandaj** *prev.* Sinneh. Kordestān, W Iran
35 P8 **San Andreas** California, W USA
2 C13 **San Andreas Fault** *fault* W USA
54 G8 **San Andrés** Santander, C Colombia
61 C20 **San Andrés de Giles** Buenos Aires, E Argentina
37 R14 **San Andres Mountains** ▲▲ New Mexico, SW USA
41 S15 **San Andrés Tuxtla** *var.* Tuxtla. Veracruz-Llave, E Mexico
25 P8 **San Angelo** Texas, SW USA
107 A20 **San Antioco, Isola di** *island* W Italy
42 F4 **San Antonio** Toledo, S Belize
62 G11 **San Antonio** Valparaíso, C Chile
188 H6 **San Antonio** Saipan, S Northern Mariana Islands
37 R13 **San Antonio** New Mexico, SW USA
25 R12 **San Antonio** Texas, SW USA
54 M11 **San Antonio** Amazonas, S Venezuela
54 I7 **San Antonio** Barinas, C Venezuela
55 O5 **San Antonio** Monagas, NE Venezuela
25 S12 **San Antonio** ✈ Texas, SW USA
San Antonio *see* San Antonio del Táchira
San Antonio Abad *see* Sant Antonio de Portmany
San Antonio Abad *see* Sant Antoni de Portmany
25 U13 **San Antonio Bay** *inlet* Texas, SW USA
61 E22 **San Antonio, Cabo** *headland* E Argentina
44 A5 **San Antonio, Cabo de** *cape* W Cuba
105 T11 **San Antonio, Cabo de** *cape* E Spain
54 H7 **San Antonio de Caparo** Táchira, W Venezuela
62 J5 **San Antonio de los Cobres** Salta, NE Argentina
54 H7 **San Antonio del Táchira** *var.* San Antonio. Táchira, W Venezuela
35 T15 **San Antonio, Mount** ▲ California, W USA
63 K16 **San Antonio Oeste** Río Negro, E Argentina
25 T13 **San Antonio River** ~ Texas, SW USA
54 J5 **Sanare** Lara, N Venezuela
103 T16 **Sanary-sur-Mer** Var, SE France
25 X8 **San Augustine** Texas, SW USA
San Augustine *see* Minami-Iō-jima
141 T13 **Sanāw** *var.* Sanaw. NE Yemen
41 O11 **San Bartolo** San Luis Potosí, C Mexico
107 L16 **San Bartolomeo in Galdo** Campania, S Italy
106 K13 **San Benedetto del Tronto** Marche, C Italy
42 E3 **San Benito** Petén, N Guatemala
25 T17 **San Benito** Texas, SW USA
54 E6 **San Benito Abad** Sucre, N Colombia
35 P11 **San Benito Mountain** ▲ California, W USA
35 O10 **San Benito River** ~ California, W USA
108 H10 **San Bernardino** Graubünden, S Switzerland
35 U15 **San Bernardino** California, W USA
35 U15 **San Bernardino Mountains** ▲▲ California, W USA
62 H11 **San Bernardo** Santiago, C Chile
40 J8 **San Bernardo** Durango, C Mexico
164 G12 **Sanbe-san** ▲ Kyūshū, SW Japan
San Bizenti-Barakaldo *see* San Vicente de Barakaldo
40 J12 **San Blas** Nayarit, C Mexico
40 H8 **San Blas** Sinaloa, C Mexico
43 V14 **San Blas** *off.* Comarca de San Blas. ◈ *special territory* NE Panama
43 U14 **San Blas, Archipiélago de** *island group* NE Panama
23 Q10 **San Blas, Cape** *headland* Florida, SE USA
San Blas, Comarca de *see* San Blas
43 V14 **San Blas, Cordillera de** ▲▲ NE Panama
62 J8 **San Blas de los Sauces** Catamarca, NW Argentina
106 G8 **San Bonifacio** Veneto, NE Italy
29 S12 **Sanborn** Iowa, C USA
40 M7 **San Buenaventura** Coahuila de Zaragoza, NE Mexico
105 S5 **San Caprasio** ▲ N Spain
60 L19 **San Carlos** São Paulo, SE Brazil
62 G13 **San Carlos** Bío Bío, C Chile
40 E9 **San Carlos** Baja California Sur, W Mexico
41 N5 **San Carlos** Coahuila de Zaragoza, NE Mexico
41 P9 **San Carlos** Tamaulipas, C Mexico
42 L12 **San Carlos** Río San Juan, S Nicaragua
43 T16 **San Carlos** Panamá, C Panama
171 N3 **San Carlos** *off.* San Carlos City. Luzon, N Philippines
61 G20 **San Carlos** Maldonado, S Uruguay
36 M14 **San Carlos** Arizona, SW USA
54 K5 **San Carlos** Cojedes, N Venezuela
San Carlos *see* Quesada, Costa Rica
San Carlos *see* Luba, Equatorial Guinea
61 B17 **San Carlos Centro** Santa Fe, C Argentina
171 P6 **San Carlos City** Negros, C Philippines
San Carlos City *see* San Carlos
San Carlos de Ancud *see* Ancud
63 H16 **San Carlos de Bariloche** Río Negro, SW Argentina
61 B21 **San Carlos de Bolívar** Buenos Aires, E Argentina
54 H6 **San Carlos del Zulia** Zulia, W Venezuela
54 L12 **San Carlos de Río Negro** Amazonas, S Venezuela
San Carlos, Estrecho de *see* Falkland Sound
36 M14 **San Carlos Reservoir** ▣ Arizona, SW USA
42 M12 **San Carlos, Río** ~ N Costa Rica
65 D24 **San Carlos Settlement** East Falkland, Falkland Islands
61 C23 **San Cayetano** Buenos Aires, E Argentina
103 O8 **Sancerre** Cher, C France
158 G7 **Sanchakou** Xinjiang Uygur Zizhiqu, NW China
Sanchoku *see* Samch'ŏk
41 O12 **San Ciro** San Luis Potosí, C Mexico
105 P10 **San Clemente** Castilla-La Mancha, C Spain
35 T16 **San Clemente** California, W USA
61 E21 **San Clemente del Tuyú** Buenos Aires, E Argentina
35 S17 **San Clemente Island** *island* Channel Islands, California, W USA
103 O9 **Sancoins** Cher, C France
61 B16 **San Cristóbal** Santa Fe, C Argentina
44 B4 **San Cristóbal** Pinar del Río, W Cuba
45 O9 **San Cristóbal** *var.* Benemérita de San Cristóbal. S Dominican Republic
54 H7 **San Cristóbal** Táchira, W Venezuela
187 N10 **San Cristobal** *var.* Makira. *island* SE Solomon Islands
San Cristóbal *see* San Cristóbal de Las Casas
41 U16 **San Cristóbal de Las Casas** *var.* San Cristóbal. Chiapas, SE Mexico
187 N10 **San Cristóbal, Isla** *var.* Chatham Island. *island* Galapagos Islands, Ecuador, E Pacific Ocean
42 D5 **San Cristóbal Verapaz** Alta Verapaz, C Guatemala
44 F6 **Sancti Spíritus** Sancti Spíritus, C Cuba
103 O11 **Sancy, Puy de** ▲ C France
95 D15 **Sand** Rogaland, S Norway
169 W7 **Sandakan** Sabah, East Malaysia
182 K9 **Sandalwood** South Australia
Sandalwood Island *see* Sumba, Pulau
94 D11 **Sandane** Sogn Og Fjordane, S Norway
114 G12 **Sandanski** *prev.* Sveti Vrach. Blagoevgrad, SW Bulgaria
76 J11 **Sandaré** Kayes, W Mali
95 J19 **Sandared** Västra Götaland, S Sweden
94 N12 **Sandarne** Gävleborg, C Sweden
186 B5 **Sandaun** *prev.* West Sepik. ◈ *province* NW Papua New Guinea
96 K4 **Sanday** *island* NE Scotland, UK
31 P15 **Sand Creek** ~ Indiana, N USA
95 H15 **Sande** Vestfold, S Norway
95 H16 **Sandefjord** Vestfold, S Norway
77 O15 **Sandégué** E Ivory Coast
77 P14 **Sandema** N Ghana
37 O11 **Sanders** Arizona, SW USA
24 M11 **Sanderson** Texas, SW USA
23 U4 **Sandersville** Georgia, SE USA
92 H4 **Sandgerdhi** Sudhurland, SW Iceland
28 K14 **Sand Hills** ▲▲ Nebraska, C USA
25 S14 **Sandia** Texas, SW USA
35 T17 **San Diego** California, W USA
25 S14 **San Diego** Texas, SW USA
136 F14 **Sandıklı** Afyon, W Turkey
152 L12 **Sandila** Uttar Pradesh, N India
San Dimitri Point *see* San Dimitri, Ras
121 N15 **San Dimitri, Ras** *var.* San Dimitri Point. *headland* Gozo, NW Malta
168 J13 **Sanding, Selat** *strait* W Indonesia
30 J3 **Sand Island** *island* Apostle Islands, Wisconsin, N USA
95 C16 **Sandnes** Rogaland, S Norway
92 F13 **Sandnessjøen** Nordland, C Norway
Sandø *see* Sandoy
79 L24 **Sandoa** Katanga, S Dem. Rep. Congo
111 N15 **Sandomierz** *Rus.* Sandomir. Świętokrzyskie, C Poland
Sandomir *see* Sandomierz
54 C13 **Sandoná** Nariño, SW Colombia
106 I7 **San Donà di Piave** Veneto, NE Italy
124 K14 **Sandovo** Tverskaya Oblast', W Russian Federation
166 K7 **Sandoway** Arakan State, W Myanmar (Burma)
97 M24 **Sandown** S England, UK
95 B19 **Sandoy** *Dan.* Sandø. *island* C Faeroe Islands
39 N16 **Sand Point** Popof Island, Alaska, USA
32 M7 **Sandpoint** Idaho, NW USA
65 N24 **Sand Point** *headland* E Tristan da Cunha
31 R7 **Sand Point** *headland* Michigan, N USA
93 H14 **Sandsele** Västerbotten, N Sweden
10 I14 **Sandspit** Moresby Island, British Columbia, SW Canada
27 P9 **Sand Springs** Oklahoma, C USA
29 W7 **Sandstone** Minnesota, N USA
36 K15 **Sand Tank Mountains** ▲▲ Arizona, SW USA
31 S8 **Sandusky** Michigan, N USA
31 S11 **Sandusky** Ohio, N USA
31 S12 **Sandusky River** ~ Ohio, N USA
83 D22 **Sandverhaar** Karas, S Namibia
95 L24 **Sandvig** Bornholm, E Denmark
95 H15 **Sandvika** Akershus, S Norway
94 N13 **Sandviken** Gävleborg, C Sweden
30 M11 **Sandwich** Illinois, N USA
Sandwich Island *see* Éfaté
Sandwich Islands *see* Hawaiian Islands
153 V16 **Sandwip Island** *island* S Bangladesh
9 U12 **Sandy Bay** Saskatchewan, C Canada
183 N16 **Sandy Cape** *headland* Tasmania, SE Australia
36 L3 **Sandy City** Utah, W USA
31 U12 **Sandy Creek** ~ Ohio, N USA
146 J15 **Sandykachi** *var.* Sandykgachy, *Rus* Sandykachi. Maryyskiy Velayat, S Turkmenistan
21 O5 **Sandy Hook** Kentucky, S USA
18 K15 **Sandy Hook** *headland* New Jersey, NE USA
Sandykachi *see* Sandykachi
Sandykachi/Sandykgachy *see* Sandykgaçy
Sandykgachy *see* Sandykachi
146 J15 **Sandykgaçy** *var.* Sandykgachy, *Rus.* Sandykachi. Mary Welaýaty, S Turkmenistan
146 L13 **Sandykly Gumy** *Rus.* Peski Sandykly. *desert* E Turkmenistan
Sandykly, Peski *see* Sandykly Gumy
9 Q13 **Sandy Lake** Alberta, W Canada
12 B8 **Sandy Lake** Ontario, C Canada
12 B8 **Sandy Lake** ◎ Ontario, C Canada
23 S3 **Sandy Springs** Georgia, SE USA
24 H8 **San Elizario** Texas, SW USA
99 L25 **Sanem** Luxembourg, SW Luxembourg
42 K5 **San Esteban** Olancho, C Honduras
105 O6 **San Esteban de Gormaz** Castilla-León, N Spain
40 E5 **San Esteban, Isla** *island* NW Mexico
San Eugenio/San Eugenio del Cuareim *see* Artigas
62 H11 **San Felipe** *var.* San Felipe de Aconcagua. Valparaíso, C Chile
40 D3 **San Felipe** Baja California, NW Mexico
40 N12 **San Felipe** Guanajuato, C Mexico
54 K5 **San Felipe** Yaracuy, NW Venezuela
44 B5 **San Felipe, Cayos de** *island group* W Cuba
San Felipe de Aconcagua *see* San Felipe
San Felipe de Puerto Plata *see* Puerto Plata
37 R11 **San Felipe Pueblo** New Mexico, SW USA
San Feliú de Guixols *see* Sant Feliu de Guíxols
193 T10 **San Félix, Isla** *Eng.* San Felix Island. *island* W Chile
San Felix Island *see* San Félix, Isla
54 L11 **San Fernanado de Atabapo** Amazonas, S Venezuela
40 C4 **San Fernando** *var.* Misión San Fernando. Baja California, NW Mexico
41 P9 **San Fernando** Tamaulipas, C Mexico
171 N2 **San Fernando** Luzon, N Philippines
171 O3 **San Fernando** Luzon, N Philippines
104 J16 **San Fernando** *prev.* Isla de León. Andalucía, S Spain
45 U14 **San Fernando** Trinidad, Trinidad and Tobago
35 S15 **San Fernando** California, W USA
54 L7 **San Fernando** *var.* San Fernando de Apure. Apure, C Venezuela
San Fernando de Apure *see* San Fernando
62 L8 **San Fernando del Valle de Catamarca** *var.* Catamarca. Catamarca, NW Argentina
San Fernando de Monte Cristi *see* Monte Cristi
41 P9 **San Fernando, Río** ~ C Mexico
23 X11 **Sanford** Florida, SE USA
19 P9 **Sanford** Maine, NE USA
21 T10 **Sanford** North Carolina, SE USA
25 N2 **Sanford** Texas, SW USA
39 T10 **Sanford, Mount** ▲ Alaska, USA
42 G8 **San Francisco** *var.* Gotera, San Francisco Gotera. Morazán, E El Salvador
43 R16 **San Francisco** Veraguas, C Panama
171 N2 **San Francisco** *var.* Aurora. Luzon, N Philippines
35 L8 **San Francisco** California, W USA
54 H5 **San Francisco** Zulia, NW Venezuela
34 M8 **San Francisco** ✈ California, W USA
35 N9 **San Francisco Bay** *bay* California, W USA
61 C24 **San Francisco de Bellocq** Buenos Aires, E Argentina
40 I6 **San Francisco de Borja** Chihuahua, N Mexico
42 J6 **San Francisco de la Paz** Olancho, C Honduras
40 J7 **San Francisco del Oro** Chihuahua, N Mexico
40 M12 **San Francisco del Rincón** Jalisco, SW Mexico
45 O8 **San Francisco de Macorís** C Dominican Republic
San Francisco de Satipo *see* Satipo
San Francisco Gotera *see* San Francisco
San Francisco Telixtlahuaca *see* Telixtlahuaca
107 K23 **San Fratello** Sicilia, Italy, C Mediterranean Sea
San Fructuoso *see* Tacuarembó
82 C12 **Sanga** Cuanza Sul, NW Angola
56 C5 **San Gabriel** Carchi, N Ecuador
159 S15 **Sa'ngain** Xizang Zizhiqu, W China
154 E13 **Sangamner** Mahārāshtra, W India
152 H12 **Sāngāner** Rājasthān, N India
Sangan, Koh-i- *see* Sangān, Kūh-e
149 N6 **Sangān, Kūh-e** *Pash.* Koh-i-Sangan. ▲ C Afghanistan
123 P10 **Sangar** Respublika Sakha (Yakutiya), NE Russian Federation
169 V11 **Sangasanga** Borneo, C Indonesia
103 N1 **Sangatte** Pas-de-Calais, N France
107 B19 **San Gavino Monreale** Sardegna, Italy, C Mediterranean Sea
57 D16 **Sangayan, Isla** *island* W Peru
30 L14 **Sangchris Lake** ▣ Illinois, N USA
171 N16 **Sangeang, Pulau** *island* S Indonesia
116 I10 **Sângeorgiu de Pădure** *prev.* Erdăt-Sângeorz, Sîngeorgiu de Pădure, *Hung.* Erdőszentgyörgy. Mureş, C Romania
116 I9 **Sângeorz-Băi** *var.* Singeroz Băi, *Ger.* Rumänisch-Sankt-Georgen, *Hung.* Oláhszentgyőrgy; *prev.* Sîngeorz-Băi. Bistriţa-Năsăud, N Romania
35 R10 **Sanger** California, W USA
25 T5 **Sanger** Texas, SW USA
Sângerei *see* Sîngerei
101 L15 **Sangerhausen** Sachsen-Anhalt, C Germany
45 S6 **San Germán** W Puerto Rico
San Germano *see* Cassino
161 N2 **Sanggan He** ~ E China
169 Q11 **Sanggau** Borneo, C Indonesia
79 H16 **Sangha** ~ Central African Republic/Congo
79 G16 **Sangha-Mbaéré** ◈ *prefecture* SW Central African Republic
149 Q15 **Sānghar** Sind, SE Pakistan
115 F22 **Sangiás** ▲ S Greece
Sangihe, Kepulauan *see* Sangir, Kepulauan
171 Q9 **Sangihe, Pulau** *var.* Sangir. *island* N Indonesia
54 G8 **San Gil** Santander, C Colombia
106 F12 **San Gimignano** Toscana, C Italy
148 M8 **Sangīn** *var.* Sangin. Helmand, S Afghanistan
Sangin *see* Sangīn
107 O21 **San Giovanni in Fiore** Calabria, SW Italy
107 M16 **San Giovanni Rotondo** Puglia, SE Italy
106 G12 **San Giovanni Valdarno** Toscana, C Italy
Sangir *see* Sangihe, Pulau
171 Q10 **Sangir, Kepulauan** *var* Kepulauan Sangihe. *island group* N Indonesia
Sangiyn Dalay *see* Erdenedalay, Dundgovĭ, Mongolia
Sangiyn Dalay *see* Erdene, Govĭ-Altay, Mongolia
Sangiyn Dalay *see* Nomgon, Ömnögovĭ, Mongolia
Sangiyn Dalay *see* Öldziyt, Övörhangay, Mongolia
163 Y15 **Sangju** *Jap.* Shōshū. C South Korea
167 R11 **Sangkha** Surin, E Thailand
169 W10 **Sangkulirang** Borneo, N Indonesia
169 W10 **Sangkulirang, Teluk** *bay* Borneo, N Indonesia
155 E16 **Sāngli** Mahārāshtra, W India
79 E16 **Sangmélima** Sud, S Cameroon
35 V15 **San Gorgonio Mountain** ▲ California, W USA
37 T8 **Sangre de Cristo Mountains** ▲▲ Colorado/New Mexico, C USA
61 A20 **San Gregorio** Santa Fe, C Argentina
61 F18 **San Gregorio de Polanco** Tacuarembó, C Uruguay
45 V14 **Sangre Grande** Trinidad, Trinidad and Tobago
159 N16 **Sangri** Xizang Zizhiqu, W China
152 H9 **Sangrūr** Punjab, NW India
44 I11 **Sangster** *off.* Sir Donald Sangster International Airport, *var.* Montego Bay. ✈ (Montego Bay) W Jamaica
59 G17 **Sangue, Rio do** ~ W Brazil
105 R4 **Sangüesa** Navarra, N Spain
61 C16 **San Gustavo** Entre Ríos, E Argentina
Sangyuan *see* Wuqiao
40 C6 **San Hipólito, Punta** *headland* W Mexico
23 W15 **Sanibel** Sanibel Island, Florida, SE USA
23 V15 **Sanibel Island** *island* Florida, SE USA
60 F13 **San Ignacio** Misiones, NE Argentina
42 F2 **San Ignacio** *prev.* Cayo, El Cayo. Cayo, W Belize
57 L16 **San Ignacio** Beni, N Bolivia
57 O18 **San Ignacio** Santa Cruz, E Bolivia
42 M14 **San Ignacio** *var.* San Ignacio de Acosta. San José, W Costa Rica
40 E6 **San Ignacio** Baja California Sur, W Mexico
40 J10 **San Ignacio** Sinaloa, W Mexico
56 B9 **San Ignacio** Cajamarca, N Peru
San Ignacio de Acosta *see* San Ignacio
40 D7 **San Ignacio, Laguna** *lagoon* W Mexico
12 I6 **Sanikiluaq** Belcher Islands, Nunavut, C Canada
171 O3 **San Ildefonso Peninsula** *peninsula* Luzon, N Philippines
Saniquillie *see* Sanniquellie
61 D20 **San Isidro** Buenos Aires, E Argentina
43 N14 **San Isidro** *var.* San Isidro de El General. San José, SE Costa Rica
San Isidro de El General *see* San Isidro
54 E5 **San Jacinto** Bolívar, N Colombia
35 U16 **San Jacinto** California, W USA
35 V15 **San Jacinto Peak** ▲ California, W USA
61 F14 **San Javier** Misiones, NE Argentina
61 C16 **San Javier** Santa Fe, C Argentina
105 S13 **San Javier** Murcia, SE Spain
61 D18 **San Javier** Río Negro, W Uruguay
61 C16 **San Javier, Río** ~ C Argentina
160 L12 **Sanjiang** *var.* Guyi, Sanjiang Dongzu Zizhixian. Guangxi Zhuangzu Zizhiqu, S China
Sanjiang *see* Jinping, Guizhou
Sanjiang Dongzu Zizhixian *see* Sanjiang
Sanjiaocheng *see* Haiyan
165 N11 **Sanjō** *var.* Sanzyô. Niigata, Honshū, C Japan
57 M15 **San Joaquín** Beni, N Bolivia
55 O6 **San Joaquín** Anzoátegui, NE Venezuela
35 O9 **San Joaquin River** ~ California, W USA
35 P10 **San Joaquin Valley** *valley* California, W USA
61 A18 **San Jorge** Santa Fe, C Argentina
40 D3 **San Jorge, Bahía de** *bay* NW Mexico
63 J19 **San Jorge, Golfo** *var.* Gulf of San Jorge. *gulf* S Argentina
San Jorge, Gulf of *see* San Jorge, Golfo
61 F14 **San José** Misiones, NE Argentina
57 P19 **San José** *var.* San José de Chiquitos. Santa Cruz, E Bolivia
42 M14 **San José** ● (Costa Rica) San José, C Costa Rica
42 C7 **San José** *var.* Puerto San José. Escuintla, S Guatemala
40 G6 **San José** Sonora, NW Mexico
188 K8 **San Jose** Tinian, S Northern Mariana Islands
105 U11 **San José** Eivissa, Spain, W Mediterranean Sea
35 N9 **San Jose** California, W USA
54 H5 **San José** Zulia, NW Venezuela
42 M14 **San José** *off.* Provincia de San José. ◈ *province* W Costa Rica
61 E19 **San José** ◈ *department* S Uruguay
42 M13 **San José** ✈ Alajuela, C Costa Rica
San José *see* San José del Guaviare, Colombia
San Jose *see* Oleai
San Jose *see* Sant Josep de sa Talaia, Ibiza, Spain
San José *see* San José de Mayo, Uruguay
171 O3 **San Jose City** Luzon, N Philippines
San José de Chiquitos *see* San José
San José de Cúcuta *see* Cúcuta

◆ Country
● Country Capital
◇ Dependent Territory
○ Dependent Territory Capital
◈ Administrative Regions
✈ International Airport
▲ Mountain
▲▲ Mountain Range
☗ Volcano
~ River
◎ Lake
▣ Reservoir

61 D16 **San José de Feliciano** Entre Ríos, E Argentina
55 O6 **San José de Guanipa** var. El Tigrito. Anzoátegui, NE Venezuela
62 I9 **San José de Jáchal** San Juan, W Argentina
40 G10 **San José del Cabo** Baja California Sur, W Mexico
54 G12 **San José del Guaviare** var. San José. Guaviare, S Colombia
61 E20 **San José de Mayo** var. San José. San José, S Uruguay
54 I10 **San José de Ocuné** Vichada, E Colombia
41 O9 **San José de Raíces** Nuevo León, NE Mexico
63 K17 **San José, Golfo** gulf E Argentina
40 F9 **San José, Isla** island W Mexico
43 U16 **San José, Isla** island SE Panama
San Jose, Isla see Weddell Island
25 U14 **San Jose Island** island Texas, SW USA
San José, Provincia de see San José
62 I10 **San Juan** San Juan, W Argentina
45 N9 **San Juan** var. San Juan de la Maguana. C Dominican Republic
57 E17 **San Juan** Ica, S Peru
45 U5 **San Juan** ○ (Puerto Rico) NE Puerto Rico
62 H10 **San Juan** off. Provincia de San Juan. ◈ province W Argentina
45 U5 **San Juan** var. Luis Muñoz Marín. ✕ NE Puerto Rico
San Juan see San Juan de los Morros
62 O7 **San Juan Bautista** Misiones, S Paraguay
35 O10 **San Juan Bautista** California, W USA
San Juan Bautista see Villahermosa
San Juan Bautista Cuicatlán see Cuicatlán
San Juan Bautista Tuxtepec see Tuxtepec
79 C17 **San Juan, Cabo** cape S Equatorial Guinea
105 S12 **San Juan de Alicante** País Valenciano, E Spain
54 H7 **San Juan de Colón** Táchira, NW Venezuela
40 L9 **San Juan de Guadalupe** Durango, C Mexico
San Juan de la Maguana see San Juan
54 G4 **San Juan del Cesar** La Guajira, N Colombia
40 L15 **San Juan de Lima, Punta** headland SW Mexico
42 I8 **San Juan de Limay** Estelí, NW Nicaragua
43 N12 **San Juan del Norte** var. Greytown. Río San Juan, SE Nicaragua
54 K4 **San Juan de los Cayos** Falcón, N Venezuela
40 M12 **San Juan de los Lagos** Jalisco, C Mexico
54 L5 **San Juan de los Morros** var. San Juan. Guárico, N Venezuela
40 K9 **San Juan del Río** Durango, C Mexico
41 O13 **San Juan del Río** Querétaro de Arteaga, C Mexico
42 J11 **San Juan del Sur** Rivas, SW Nicaragua
54 M9 **San Juan de Manapiare** Amazonas, S Venezuela
40 E7 **San Juanico** Baja California Sur, W Mexico
40 D7 **San Juanico, Punta** headland W Mexico
32 G6 **San Juan Islands** island group Washington, NW USA
40 I6 **San Juanito** Chihuahua, N Mexico
40 I12 **San Juanito, Isla** island C Mexico
37 R8 **San Juan Mountains** ▲▲ Colorado, C USA
54 E5 **San Juan Nepomuceno** Bolívar, NW Colombia
44 E5 **San Juan, Pico** ▲ C Cuba
San Juan, Provincia de see San Juan
191 W15 **San Juan, Punta** headland Easter Island, Chile, E Pacific Ocean
42 M12 **San Juan, Río** ≈ Costa Rica/Nicaragua
41 S15 **San Juan, Río** ≈ SE Mexico
37 O8 **San Juan River** ≈ Colorado/Utah, W USA
San Julián see Puerto San Julián
61 B17 **San Justo** Santa Fe, C Argentina
109 W5 **Sankt Aegyd am Neuwalde** Niederösterreich, E Austria
109 U9 **Sankt Andrä** Slvn. Šent Andraž. Kärnten, S Austria
Sankt Andrä see Szentendre
Sankt Anna see Sântana
108 K8 **Sankt Anton am Arlberg** Vorarlberg, W Austria
101 E16 **Sankt Augustin** Nordrhein-Westfalen, W Germany
Sankt-Bartholomäi see Palamuse
101 F24 **Sankt Blasien** Baden-Württemberg, SW Germany
109 R3 **Sankt Florian am Inn** Oberösterreich, N Austria
108 I7 **Sankt Gallen** var. St. Gallen, Eng. Saint Gall, Fr. St-Gall. Sankt Gallen, NE Switzerland
108 H8 **Sankt Gallen** var. St.Gallen, Eng. Saint Gall, Fr. St-Gall. ◈ canton NE Switzerland
108 J8 **Sankt Gallenkirch** Vorarlberg, W Austria
109 Q5 **Sankt Georgen** Salzburg, N Austria
Sankt Georgen see Đurđevac
Sankt-Georgen see Sfântu Gheorghe
109 R6 **Sankt Gilgen** Salzburg, NW Austria
Sankt Gotthard see Szentgotthárd
101 E20 **Sankt Ingbert** Saarland, SW Germany
Sankt-Jakobi see Viru-Jaagupi, Lääne-Virumaa, Estonia
Sankt-Jakobi see Pärnu-Jaagupi, Pärnumaa, Estonia
Sankt Johann see Sankt Johann in Tirol
109 T7 **Sankt Johann am Tauern** Steiermark, E Austria
109 Q7 **Sankt Johann im Pongau** Salzburg, NW Austria
109 P6 **Sankt Johann in Tirol** var. Sankt Johann. Tirol, W Austria
Sankt-Johannis see Järva-Jaani
108 L8 **Sankt Leonhard** Tirol, W Austria
Sankt Margarethen see Sankt Margarethen im Burgenland
109 Y5 **Sankt Margarethen im Burgenland** var. Sankt Margarethen. Burgenland, E Austria
Sankt Martin see Martin
109 X8 **Sankt Martin an der Raab** Burgenland, SE Austria
109 U7 **Sankt Michael in Obersteiermark** Steiermark, SE Austria
Sankt Michel see Mikkeli
Sankt Moritz see St. Moritz
108 E11 **Sankt Niklaus** Valais, S Switzerland
109 S7 **Sankt Nikolai** var. Sankt Nikolai im Sölktal. Steiermark, SE Austria
Sankt Nikolai im Sölktal see Sankt Nikolai
109 U9 **Sankt Paul** var. Sankt Paul im Lavanttal. Kärnten, S Austria
Sankt Paul im Lavanttal see Sankt Paul
Sankt Peter see Pivka
109 W9 **Sankt Peter am Ottersbach** Steiermark, SE Austria
124 J13 **Sankt-Peterburg** prev. Leningrad, Petrograd, Eng. Saint Petersburg, Fin. Pietari. Leningradskaya Oblast', NW Russian Federation
100 H8 **Sankt Peter-Ording** Schleswig-Holstein, N Germany
109 V4 **Sankt Pölten** Niederösterreich, N Austria
109 W7 **Sankt Ruprecht** var. Sankt Ruprecht an der Raab. Steiermark, SE Austria
Sankt Ruprecht an der Raab see Sankt Ruprecht
Sankt-Ulrich see Ortisei
109 T4 **Sankt Valentin** Niederösterreich, C Austria
Sankt Veit am Flaum see Rijeka
109 T9 **Sankt Veit an der Glan** Slvn. Št. Vid. Kärnten, S Austria
99 M21 **Sankt-Vith** var. Saint-Vith. Liège, E Belgium
101 E20 **Sankt Wendel** Saarland, SW Germany
109 R6 **Sankt Wolfgang** Salzburg, NW Austria
79 K21 **Sankuru** ≈ C Dem. Rep. Congo
40 D8 **San Lázaro, Cabo** headland W Mexico
137 O16 **Şanlıurfa** prev. Sanli Urfa, Urfa; anc. Edessa. şanlıurfa, S Turkey
137 O16 **Şanlıurfa** prev. Urfa. ◈ province SE Turkey
Sanli Urfa see Şanlıurfa
137 O16 **Şanlıurfa Yaylası** plateau SE Turkey
61 B18 **San Lorenzo** Santa Fe, C Argentina
57 M21 **San Lorenzo** Tarija, S Bolivia
56 C5 **San Lorenzo** Esmeraldas, N Ecuador
42 H8 **San Lorenzo** Valle, S Honduras
56 A6 **San Lorenzo, Cabo** headland W Ecuador
105 N8 **San Lorenzo de El Escorial** var. El Escorial. Madrid, C Spain
40 E5 **San Lorenzo, Isla** island NW Mexico
57 C14 **San Lorenzo, Isla** island W Peru
63 G20 **San Lorenzo, Monte** ▲ S Argentina
40 I9 **San Lorenzo, Río** ≈ C Mexico
104 J15 **Sanlúcar de Barrameda** Andalucía, S Spain
104 J14 **Sanlúcar la Mayor** Andalucía, S Spain
40 E6 **San Lucas** var. Cabo San Lucas. Baja California Sur, W Mexico
40 F11 **San Lucas** Baja California Sur, NW Mexico
40 G11 **San Lucas, Cabo** var. San Lucas Cape. headland W Mexico
San Lucas Cape see San Lucas, Cabo
62 J11 **San Luis** San Luis, C Argentina
42 E4 **San Luis** Petén, NE Guatemala
40 D2 **San Luis** var. San Luis Río Colorado. Sonora, NW Mexico
42 M7 **San Luis** Región Autónoma Atlántico Norte, NE Nicaragua
36 H15 **San Luis** Arizona, SW USA
37 T8 **San Luis** Colorado, C USA
54 J4 **San Luis** Falcón, N Venezuela
62 J11 **San Luis** off. Provincia de San Luis. ◈ province C Argentina
41 N12 **San Luis de la Paz** Guanajuato, C Mexico
40 K8 **San Luis del Cordero** Durango, C Mexico
40 D4 **San Luis, Isla** island NW Mexico
42 E6 **San Luis Jilotepeque** Jalapa, SE Guatemala
57 M16 **San Luis, Laguna de** ◎ NW Bolivia
35 P13 **San Luis Obispo** California, W USA
37 R7 **San Luis Peak** ▲ Colorado, C USA
41 N11 **San Luis Potosí** San Luis Potosí, C Mexico
41 N11 **San Luis Potosí** ◈ state C Mexico
San Luis, Provincia de see San Luis
35 O10 **San Luis Reservoir** ▦ California, W USA
San Luis Río Colorado see San Luis
37 S8 **San Luis Valley** basin Colorado, C USA
107 C19 **Sanluri** Sardegna, Italy, C Mediterranean Sea
61 D23 **San Manuel** Buenos Aires, E Argentina
36 M15 **San Manuel** Arizona, SW USA
106 F11 **San Marcello Pistoiese** Toscana, C Italy
107 N20 **San Marco Argentano** Calabria, SW Italy
54 E6 **San Marcos** Sucre, N Colombia
42 M14 **San Marcos** San José, C Costa Rica
42 B5 **San Marcos** San Marcos, W Guatemala
42 F6 **San Marcos** Ocotepeque, SW Honduras
41 O16 **San Marcos** Guerrero, S Mexico
25 S11 **San Marcos** Texas, SW USA
42 A5 **San Marcos** off. Departamento de San Marcos. ◈ department W Guatemala
San Marcos de Arica see Arica
San Marcos, Departamento de see San Marcos
40 E6 **San Marcos, Isla** island W Mexico
106 H11 **San Marino** ● (San Marino) C San Marino
106 I11 **San Marino** off. Republic of San Marino. ◆ republic S Europe
San Marino, Republic of see San Marino
62 I11 **San Martín** Mendoza, C Argentina
54 F11 **San Martín** Meta, C Colombia
56 D11 **San Martín** off. Departamento de San Martín. ◈ department C Peru
194 I5 **San Martín** Argentinian research station Antarctica
63 H16 **San Martín de los Andes** Neuquén, W Argentina
San Martín, Departamento de see San Martín
104 M8 **San Martín de Valdeiglesias** Madrid, C Spain
63 G21 **San Martín, Lago** var. Lago O'Higgins. ◎ S Argentina
106 H6 **San Martino di Castrozza** Trentino-Alto Adige, N Italy
57 N16 **San Martín, Río** ≈ N Bolivia
San Martín Texmelucan see Texmelucan
35 N9 **San Mateo** California, W USA
55 O6 **San Mateo** Anzoátegui, NE Venezuela
42 B4 **San Mateo Ixtatán** Huehuetenango, W Guatemala
57 Q18 **San Matías** Santa Cruz, E Bolivia
63 K16 **San Matías, Golfo** var. Gulf of San Matías. gulf E Argentina
San Matías, Gulf of see San Matías, Golfo
15 O8 **Sanmaur** Québec, SE Canada
161 T10 **Sanmen Wan** bay E China
160 M6 **Sanmenxia** var. Shan Xian. Henan, C China
Sânmiclăuş Mare see Sânnicolau Mare
61 D14 **San Miguel** Corrientes, NE Argentina
57 L16 **San Miguel** Beni, N Bolivia
42 G8 **San Miguel** San Miguel, SE El Salvador
40 L6 **San Miguel** Coahuila de Zaragoza, N Mexico
40 J9 **San Miguel** var. San Miguel de Cruces. Durango, C Mexico
43 U16 **San Miguel** Panamá, SE Panama
35 P12 **San Miguel** California, W USA
42 B9 **San Miguel** ◈ department E El Salvador
41 N13 **San Miguel de Allende** Guanajuato, C Mexico
San Miguel de Cruces see San Miguel
San Miguel de Ibarra see Ibarra
61 D21 **San Miguel del Monte** Buenos Aires, E Argentina
62 J7 **San Miguel de Tucumán** var. Tucumán. Tucumán, N Argentina
43 V16 **San Miguel, Golfo de** gulf S Panama
35 P15 **San Miguel Island** island California, W USA
42 L11 **San Miguelito** Río San Juan, S Nicaragua
43 T15 **San Miguelito** Panamá, C Panama
57 N18 **San Miguel, Río** ≈ E Bolivia
56 D6 **San Miguel, Río** ≈ Colombia/Ecuador
40 I7 **San Miguel, Río** ≈ N Mexico
42 F7 **San Miguel, Volcán de** Ѫ SE El Salvador
161 Q12 **Sanming** Fujian, SE China
106 F11 **San Miniato** Toscana, C Italy
San Murezzan see St. Moritz
Sannär see Sennar
107 M15 **Sannicandro Garganico** Puglia, SE Italy
40 H6 **San Nicolás** Sonora, NW Mexico
61 C19 **San Nicolás de los Arroyos** Buenos Aires, E Argentina
35 R16 **San Nicolas Island** island Channel Islands, California, W USA
Sânnicolaul-Mare see Sânnicolau Mare
116 E11 **Sânnicolau Mare** var. Sânnicolaul-Mare, Hung. Nagyszentmiklós; prev. Sânmiclăuş Mare, Sînnicolau Mare. Timiş, W Romania
123 Q6 **Sannikova, Proliv** strait NE Russian Federation
76 K16 **Sanniquellie** var. Saniquillie. NE Liberia
165 R7 **Sannohe** Aomori, Honshū, C Japan
Sanntaler Alpen see Kamniško-Savinjske Alpe
111 O17 **Sanok** Podkarpackie, SE Poland
54 E5 **San Onofre** Sucre, NW Colombia
57 K21 **San Pablo** Potosí, S Bolivia
171 O4 **San Pablo** off. San Pablo City. Luzon, N Philippines
San Pablo Balleza see Balleza
35 N8 **San Pablo Bay** bay California, W USA
San Pablo City see San Pablo
40 C6 **San Pablo, Punta** headland W Mexico
43 R16 **San Pablo, Río** ≈ C Panama
171 P4 **San Pascual** Burias Island, C Philippines
121 Q16 **San Pawl il-Bahar** Eng. Saint Paul's Bay. E Malta
61 C19 **San Pedro** Buenos Aires, E Argentina
62 K5 **San Pedro** Jujuy, N Argentina
60 G13 **San Pedro** Misiones, NE Argentina
42 H1 **San Pedro** Corozal, NE Belize
76 M17 **San-Pédro** S Ivory Coast
40 L8 **San Pedro** var. San Pedro de las Colonias. Coahuila de Zaragoza, NE Mexico
62 O5 **San Pedro** San Pedro, SE Paraguay
62 O6 **San Pedro** off. Departamento de San Pedro. ◈ department C Paraguay
44 G6 **San Pedro** ≈ C Cuba
77 N16 **San Pedro** ✕ (Yamoussoukro) C Ivory Coast
San Pedro see San Pedro del Pinatar
42 D5 **San Pedro Carchá** Alta Verapaz, C Guatemala
35 S16 **San Pedro Channel** channel California, W USA
62 I5 **San Pedro de Atacama** Antofagasta, N Chile
San Pedro de Durazno see Durazno
40 G5 **San Pedro de la Cueva** Sonora, NW Mexico
San Pedro de las Colonias see San Pedro
56 B11 **San Pedro de Lloc** La Libertad, NW Peru
105 S13 **San Pedro del Pinatar** var. San Pedro. Murcia, SE Spain
45 P9 **San Pedro de Macorís** SE Dominican Republic
San Pedro, Departamento de see San Pedro
40 C3 **San Pedro Mártir, Sierra** ▲▲ NW Mexico
San Pedro Pochutla see Pochutla
42 D2 **San Pedro, Río** ≈ Guatemala/Mexico
40 K10 **San Pedro, Río** ≈ C Mexico
104 J10 **San Pedro, Sierra de** ▲▲ W Spain
42 G5 **San Pedro Sula** Cortés, NW Honduras
San Pedro Tapanatepec see Tapanatepec
62 I4 **San Pedro, Volcán** Ѫ N Chile
106 E7 **San Pellegrino Terme** Lombardia, N Italy
25 T16 **San Perlita** Texas, SW USA
San Pietro see Supetar
San Pietro del Carso see Pivka
107 A20 **San Pietro, Isola di** island W Italy
32 K7 **Sanpoil River** ≈ Washington, NW USA
165 O9 **Sanpoku** var. Sampoku. Niigata, Honshū, C Japan
40 C3 **San Quintín** Baja California, NW Mexico
40 B3 **San Quintín, Bahía de** bay NW Mexico
40 B3 **San Quintín, Cabo** headland NW Mexico
62 I12 **San Rafael** Mendoza, W Argentina
41 N9 **San Rafael** Nuevo León, NE Mexico
34 M8 **San Rafael** California, W USA
37 Q11 **San Rafael** New Mexico, SW USA
54 H4 **San Rafael** var. El Moján. Zulia, NW Venezuela
42 J8 **San Rafael del Norte** Jinotega, NW Nicaragua
42 J10 **San Rafael del Sur** Managua, SW Nicaragua
36 M5 **San Rafael Knob** ▲ Utah, W USA
35 Q14 **San Rafael Mountains** ▲▲ California, W USA
42 M13 **San Ramón** Alajuela, C Costa Rica
57 E14 **San Ramón** Junín, C Peru
61 F19 **San Ramón** Canelones, S Uruguay
62 K5 **San Ramón de la Nueva Orán** Salta, N Argentina
57 O16 **San Ramón, Río** ≈ E Bolivia
106 B11 **San Remo** Liguria, NW Italy
54 J3 **San Román, Cabo** headland NW Venezuela
61 C15 **San Roque** Corrientes, NE Argentina
188 I4 **San Roque** Saipan, S Northern Mariana Islands
104 K16 **San Roque** Andalucía, S Spain
25 R9 **San Saba** Texas, SW USA
25 Q9 **San Saba River** ≈ Texas, SW USA
61 D17 **San Salvador** Entre Ríos, E Argentina
42 F7 **San Salvador** ● (El Salvador) San Salvador, SW El Salvador
42 A10 **San Salvador** ◈ department C El Salvador
44 K4 **San Salvador** prev. Watlings Island. island E Bahamas
42 F8 **San Salvador** ✕ La Paz, S El Salvador
62 J5 **San Salvador de Jujuy** var. Jujuy. Jujuy, N Argentina
42 F7 **San Salvador, Volcán de** Ѫ C El Salvador
77 Q14 **Sansanné-Mango** var. Mango. N Togo
45 S5 **San Sebastián** W Puerto Rico
63 J24 **San Sebastián, Bahía** bay S Argentina
Sansenhō see Sach'ŏn
106 H12 **Sansepolcro** Toscana, C Italy
107 M16 **San Severo** Puglia, SE Italy
112 F11 **Sanski Most** ◈ Federacija Bosna I Hercegovina, NW Bosnia and Herzegovina
171 W12 **Sansundi** Papua, E Indonesia
162 K9 **Sant** var. Mayhan. Övörhangay, C Mongolia
104 K11 **Santa Amalia** Extremadura, W Spain
60 F13 **Santa Ana** Misiones, NE Argentina
57 L16 **Santa Ana** Beni, N Bolivia
42 E7 **Santa Ana** Santa Ana, NW El Salvador
40 F4 **Santa Ana** Sonora, NW Mexico
35 T16 **Santa Ana** California, W USA
55 N6 **Santa Ana** Nueva Esparta, NE Venezuela
42 A9 **Santa Ana** ◈ department NW El Salvador
Santa Ana de Coro see Coro
35 U16 **Santa Ana Mountains** ▲▲ California, W USA
42 E7 **Santa Ana, Volcán de** var. La Matepec. Ѫ W El Salvador
42 G6 **Santa Bárbara** Santa Bárbara, W Honduras
40 J7 **Santa Barbara** Chihuahua, N Mexico
35 Q14 **Santa Barbara** California, W USA
54 L11 **Santa Bárbara** Amazonas, S Venezuela
54 I7 **Santa Bárbara** Barinas, W Venezuela
42 F5 **Santa Bárbara** ◈ department NW Honduras
Santa Bárbara see Iscuandé
35 Q15 **Santa Barbara Channel** channel California, W USA
Santa Bárbara de Samaná see Samaná
35 R16 **Santa Barbara Island** island Channel Islands, California, W USA
54 E5 **Santa Catalina** Bolívar, N Colombia
43 R15 **Santa Catalina** Bocas del Toro, W Panama
35 T17 **Santa Catalina, Gulf of** gulf California, W USA
40 F8 **Santa Catalina, Isla** island W Mexico
35 S16 **Santa Catalina Island** island Channel Islands, California, W USA
41 N8 **Santa Catarina** Nuevo León, NE Mexico
60 H13 **Santa Catarina** off. Estado de Santa Catarina. ◈ state S Brazil
Santa Catarina de Tepehuanes see Tepehuanes
Santa Catarina, Estado de see Santa Catarina
60 L13 **Santa Catarina, Ilha de** island S Brazil
45 Q16 **Santa Catherina** Curaçao, C Netherlands Antilles
44 E5 **Santa Clara** Villa Clara, C Cuba
35 N9 **Santa Clara** California, W USA
36 J8 **Santa Clara** Utah, W USA
Santa Clara see Santa Clara de Olimar
61 F18 **Santa Clara de Olimar** var. Santa Clara. Cerro Largo, NE Uruguay
61 A17 **Santa Clara de Saguier** Santa Fe, C Argentina
Santa Coloma see Santa Coloma de Gramanet
105 X5 **Santa Coloma de Farners** var. Santa Coloma de Farnés. Cataluña, NE Spain
Santa Coloma de Farnés see Santa Coloma de Farners
105 W6 **Santa Coloma de Gramanet** var. Santa Coloma. Cataluña, NE Spain
104 G2 **Santa Comba** Galicia, NW Spain
Santa Comba see Uaco Cungo
104 H8 **Santa Comba Dão** Viseu, N Portugal
82 C10 **Santa Cruz** Uíge, NW Angola
57 N19 **Santa Cruz** var. Santa Cruz de la Sierra. Santa Cruz, C Bolivia
62 G12 **Santa Cruz** Libertador, C Chile
42 K13 **Santa Cruz** Guanacaste, W Costa Rica
44 I12 **Santa Cruz** W Jamaica
64 P6 **Santa Cruz** Madeira, Portugal, NE Atlantic Ocean
35 N10 **Santa Cruz** California, W USA
63 H20 **Santa Cruz** off. Provincia de Santa Cruz. ◈ province S Argentina
57 O18 **Santa Cruz** ◈ department E Bolivia
Santa Cruz see Puerto Santa Cruz
Santa Cruz see Viru-Viru
Santa Cruz Barillas see Barillas
59 O18 **Santa Cruz Cabrália** Bahia, E Brazil
Santa Cruz de El Seibo see El Seibo
64 N11 **Santa Cruz de la Palma** La Palma, Islas Canarias, Spain, NE Atlantic Ocean
Santa Cruz de la Sierra see Santa Cruz
105 O9 **Santa Cruz de la Zarza** Castilla-La Mancha, C Spain
42 C5 **Santa Cruz del Quiché** Quiché, W Guatemala
105 N8 **Santa Cruz del Retamar** Castilla-La Mancha, C Spain
Santa Cruz del Seibo see El Seibo
44 G7 **Santa Cruz del Sur** Camagüey, C Cuba
105 O11 **Santa Cruz de Mudela** Castilla-La Mancha, C Spain
64 Q11 **Santa Cruz de Tenerife** Tenerife, Islas Canarias, Spain, NE Atlantic Ocean
64 P11 **Santa Cruz de Tenerife** ◈ province Islas Canarias, Spain, NE Atlantic Ocean
60 K9 **Santa Cruz do Rio Pardo** São Paulo, S Brazil
61 H15 **Santa Cruz do Sul** Rio Grande do Sul, S Brazil
57 C17 **Santa Cruz, Isla** var. Indefatigable Island, Isla Chávez. island Galapagos Islands, Ecuador, E Pacific Ocean
40 F8 **Santa Cruz, Isla** island W Mexico
35 Q15 **Santa Cruz Island** island California, W USA
187 Q10 **Santa Cruz Islands** island group E Solomon Islands
Santa Cruz, Provincia de see Santa Cruz
63 I22 **Santa Cruz, Río** ≈ S Argentina
36 L15 **Santa Cruz River** ≈ Arizona, SW USA
61 C17 **Santa Elena** Entre Ríos, E Argentina
42 F2 **Santa Elena** Cayo, W Belize
25 R16 **Santa Elena** Texas, SW USA
56 A7 **Santa Elena, Bahía de** bay W Ecuador
55 R10 **Santa Elena de Uairén** Bolívar, E Venezuela
42 K12 **Santa Elena, Península** peninsula NW Costa Rica
56 A7 **Santa Elena, Punta** headland W Ecuador
104 L11 **Santa Eufemia** Andalucía, S Spain
107 N21 **Santa Eufemia, Golfo di** gulf S Italy
105 S4 **Santa Eulalia de Gállego** Aragón, NE Spain
105 V11 **Santa Eulalia del Río** Ibiza, Spain, W Mediterranean Sea
61 B17 **Santa Fe** Santa Fe, C Argentina
44 C6 **Santa Fé** var. La Fe. Isla de la Juventud, W Cuba
43 R16 **Santa Fé** Veraguas, C Panama
105 N14 **Santa Fe** Andalucía, S Spain
37 S10 **Santa Fe** state capital New Mexico, SW USA
61 B15 **Santa Fe** off. Provincia de Santa Fe. ◈ province C Argentina
Santa Fe see Bogotá
Santa Fe de Bogotá see Bogotá
60 J7 **Santa Fé do Sul** São Paulo, S Brazil
57 B18 **Santa Fe, Isla** var. Barrington Island. island Galapagos Islands, Ecuador, E Pacific Ocean
Santa Fe, Provincia de see Santa Fe
23 V9 **Santa Fe River** ≈ Florida, SE USA
59 M15 **Santa Filomena** Piauí, E Brazil
40 G10 **Santa Genoveva** ▲ W Mexico
153 S14 **Santahar** Rajshahi, NW Bangladesh
60 G11 **Santa Helena** Paraná, S Brazil
54 J5 **Santa Inés** Lara, N Venezuela
63 G24 **Santa Inés, Isla** island S Chile
62 J13 **Santa Isabel** La Pampa, C Argentina
43 U14 **Santa Isabel** Colón, N Panama
186 L8 **Santa Isabel** var. Bughotu. island N Solomon Islands
Santa Isabel see Malabo
58 D11 **Santa Isabel do Rio Negro** Amazonas, NW Brazil
61 C15 **Santa Lucia** Corrientes, NE Argentina
57 I17 **Santa Lucía** Puno, S Peru
61 F20 **Santa Lucía** var. Santa Lucia. Canelones, S Uruguay
42 B6 **Santa Lucía Cotzumalguapa** Escuintla, SW Guatemala
107 L23 **Santa Lucia del Mela** Sicilia, Italy, C Mediterranean Sea
35 O11 **Santa Lucia Range** ▲▲ California, W USA
40 D9 **Santa Margarita, Isla** island W Mexico
62 J7 **Santa María** Catamarca, N Argentina
61 G15 **Santa Maria** Rio Grande do Sul, S Brazil
35 P13 **Santa Maria** California, W USA
64 Q4 **Santa Maria** ✕ Santa Maria, Azores, Portugal, NE Atlantic Ocean
64 P3 **Santa Maria** island Azores, Portugal, NE Atlantic Ocean
Santa Maria see Gaua
Santa María Asunción Tlaxiaco see Tlaxiaco
40 G9 **Santa María, Bahía** bay W Mexico
83 L21 **Santa Maria, Cabo de** headland S Mozambique
104 G15 **Santa Maria, Cabo de** cape S Portugal
44 J4 **Santa Maria, Cape** headland Long Island, C Bahamas
107 J17 **Santa Maria Capua Vetere** Campania, S Italy
104 G7 **Santa Maria da Feira** Aveiro, N Portugal
59 M17 **Santa Maria da Vitória** Bahia, E Brazil
55 N9 **Santa Maria de Erebato** Bolívar, SE Venezuela
55 N6 **Santa María de Ipire** Guárico, C Venezuela
Santa Maria del Buen Aire see Buenos Aires
40 J8 **Santa María del Oro** Durango, C Mexico
41 N12 **Santa María del Río** San Luis Potosí, C Mexico
Santa Maria di Castellabate see Castellabate
107 Q20 **Santa Maria di Leuca, Capo** headland SE Italy
108 K10 **Santa Maria-im-Münstertal** Graubünden, SE Switzerland
57 B18 **Santa María, Isla** var. Isla Floreana, Charles Island. island Galapagos Islands, Ecuador, E Pacific Ocean
40 J3 **Santa María, Laguna de** ◎ N Mexico

◆ Country ◇ Dependent Territory ◈ Administrative Regions ▲ Mountain Ѫ Volcano ◎ Lake
● Country Capital ○ Dependent Territory Capital ✕ International Airport ▲▲ Mountain Range ≈ River ▦ Reservoir

61 *G16* **Santa Maria, Rio** ≈ S Brazil
43 *R16* **Santa María, Río** ≈ C Panama
36 *J12* **Santa Maria River** ≈ Arizona, SW USA
107 *G15* **Santa Marinella** Lazio, C Italy
54 *F4* **Santa Marta** Magdalena, N Colombia
104 *J11* **Santa Marta** Extremadura, W Spain
Santa Maura *see* Lefkáda
35 *S15* **Santa Monica** California, W USA
116 *F10* **Sântana** *Ger.* Sankt Anna, *Hung.* Újszentanna; *prev.* Sintana. Arad, W Romania
61 *F16* **Santana, Coxilha de** *hill range* S Brazil
61 *H16* **Santana da Boa Vista** Rio Grande do Sul, S Brazil
61 *F16* **Santana do Livramento** *prev.* Livramento. Rio Grande do Sul, S Brazil
105 *N2* **Santander** Cantabria, N Spain
54 *F8* **Santander** *off.* Departamento de Santander. ◈ *province* C Colombia
Santander, Departamento de *see* Santander
Santander Jiménez *see* Jiménez
Sant'Andrea *see* Svetac
107 *B20* **Sant'Antioco** Sardegna, Italy, C Mediterranean Sea
105 *V11* **Sant Antonio de Portmany** *Cas.* San Antonio Abad. Ibiza, Spain, W Mediterranean Sea
105 *Y10* **Sant Antoni de Portmany** *Cas.* San Antonio Abad. Ibiza, Spain, W Mediterranean
105 *Y10* **Santanyí** Mallorca, Spain, W Mediterranean Sea
104 *J13* **Santa Olalla del Cala** Andalucía, S Spain
35 *R15* **Santa Paula** California, W USA
36 *L4* **Santaquin** Utah, W USA
58 *I12* **Santarém** Pará, N Brazil
104 *G10* **Santarém** *anc.* Scalabis. Santarém, W Portugal
104 *G10* **Santarém** ◈ *district* C Portugal
44 *F4* **Santaren Channel** *channel* W Bahamas
54 *K10* **Santa Rita** Vichada, E Colombia
188 *B16* **Santa Rita** SW Guam
42 *H5* **Santa Rita** Cortés, NW Honduras
40 *E9* **Santa Rita** Baja California Sur, W Mexico
54 *H5* **Santa Rita** Zulia, NW Venezuela
59 *I19* **Santa Rita de Araguaia** Goiás, S Brazil
Santa Rita de Cassia *see* Cássia
61 *D14* **Santa Rosa** Corrientes, NE Argentina
62 *K13* **Santa Rosa** La Pampa, C Argentina
61 *G14* **Santa Rosa** Rio Grande do Sul, S Brazil
58 *E10* **Santa Rosa** Roraima, N Brazil
56 *B8* **Santa Rosa** El Oro, SW Ecuador
57 *I16* **Santa Rosa** Puno, S Peru
34 *M7* **Santa Rosa** California, W USA
37 *U11* **Santa Rosa** New Mexico, SW USA
55 *O6* **Santa Rosa** Anzoátegui, NE Venezuela
42 *A3* **Santa Rosa** *off.* Departamento de Santa Rosa. ◈ *department* SE Guatemala
Santa Rosa *see* Santa Rosa de Copán
63 *J15* **Santa Rosa, Bajo de** *basin* E Argentina
42 *F6* **Santa Rosa de Copán** *var.* Santa Rosa. Copán, W Honduras
54 *E8* **Santa Rosa de Osos** Antioquia, C Colombia
Santa Rosa, Departamento de *see* Santa Rosa
35 *Q15* **Santa Rosa Island** *island* California, W USA
23 *O9* **Santa Rosa Island** *island* Florida, SE USA
40 *E6* **Santa Rosalía** Baja California Sur, W Mexico
54 *K6* **Santa Rosalía** Portuguesa, NW Venezuela
188 *C15* **Santa Rosa, Mount** ▲ NE Guam
35 *V16* **Santa Rosa Mountains** ▲▲ California, W USA
35 *T2* **Santa Rosa Range** ▲▲ Nevada, W USA
62 *M8* **Santa Sylvina** Chaco, N Argentina
Santa Tecla *see* Nueva San Salvador
61 *B19* **Santa Teresa** Santa Fe, C Argentina
59 *O20* **Santa Teresa** Espírito Santo, SE Brazil
107 *M23* **San Teresa di Riva** Sicilia, Italy, C Mediterranean Sea
61 *E21* **Santa Teresita** Buenos Aires, E Argentina
61 *H19* **Santa Vitória do Palmar** Rio Grande do Sul, S Brazil
35 *Q14* **Santa Ynez River** ≈ California, W USA
Sant Carles de la Rápida *see* Sant Carles de la Ràpita
105 *U7* **Sant Carles de la Ràpita** *var.* Sant Carles de la Rápida. Cataluña, NE Spain
105 *W5* **Sant Celoni** Cataluña, NE Spain
35 *U17* **Santee** California, W USA
21 *T13* **Santee River** ≈ South Carolina, SE USA
40 *K15* **San Telmo, Punta** *headland* SW Mexico
107 *O17* **Santeramo in Colle** Puglia, SE Italy
105 *X5* **Sant Feliu de Guíxols** *var.* San Feliú de Guixols. Cataluña, NE Spain
105 *W6* **Sant Feliu de Llobregat** Cataluña, NE Spain
106 *C7* **Santhià** Piemonte, NE Italy
61 *F15* **Santiago** Rio Grande do Sul, S Brazil
62 *H11* **Santiago** *var.* Gran Santiago. ● (Chile) Santiago, C Chile
45 *N8* **Santiago** *var.* Santiago de los Caballeros. N Dominican Republic
40 *G10* **Santiago** Baja California Sur, W Mexico
41 *O8* **Santiago** Nuevo León, NE Mexico
43 *R16* **Santiago** Veraguas, S Panama
57 *E16* **Santiago** Ica, SW Peru
104 *G3* **Santiago** *var.* Santiago de Compostela, *Eng.* Compostella; *anc.* Campus Stellae. Galicia, NW Spain
62 *H11* **Santiago** *off.* Región Metropolitana de Santiago, *var.* Metropolitan. ◈ *region* C Chile
76 *D10* **Santiago** *var.* São Tiago. *island* Ilhas de Sotavento, S Cape Verde
62 *H11* **Santiago** ✕ Santiago, C Chile
104 *G3* **Santiago** ✕ Galicia, NW Spain
Santiago *see* Santiago de Cuba, Cuba
Santiago *see* Grande de Santiago, Río, Mexico
42 *B6* **Santiago Atitlán** Sololá, SW Guatemala
43 *Q16* **Santiago, Cerro** ▲ W Panama
Santiago de Compostela *see* Santiago
44 *I8* **Santiago de Cuba** *var.* Santiago. Santiago de Cuba, E Cuba
Santiago de Guayaquil *see* Guayaquil
62 *K8* **Santiago del Estero** Santiago del Estero, C Argentina
61 *A15* **Santiago del Estero** *off.* Provincia de Santiago del Estero. ◈ *province* N Argentina
Santiago del Estero, Provincia de *see* Santiago del Estero
40 *I8* **Santiago de los Caballeros** Sinaloa, W Mexico
Santiago de los Caballeros *see* Santiago, Dominican Republic
Santiago de los Caballeros *see* Ciudad de Guatemala, Guatemala
42 *F8* **Santiago de María** Usulután, SE El Salvador
104 *F12* **Santiago do Cacém** Setúbal, S Portugal
40 *J12* **Santiago Ixcuintla** Nayarit, C Mexico
Santiago Jamiltepec *see* Jamiltepec
24 *L11* **Santiago Mountains** ▲▲ Texas, SW USA
40 *J9* **Santiago Papasquiaro** Durango, C Mexico
Santiago Pinotepa Nacional *see* Pinotepa Nacional
Santiago, Región Metropolitana de *see* Santiago
56 *C8* **Santiago, Río** ≈ N Peru
40 *M10* **San Tiburcio** Zacatecas, C Mexico
105 *N2* **Santillana** Cantabria, N Spain
54 *I5* **San Timoteo** Zulia, NW Venezuela
Santi Quaranta *see* Sarandë
Santissima Trinidad *see* Chilung
105 *O12* **Santisteban del Puerto** Andalucía, S Spain
105 *U7* **Sant Jordi, Golf de** *gulf* NE Spain
105 *U11* **Sant Josep de sa Talaia** *var.* San Jose. Ibiza, Spain, W Mediterranean Sea
162 *G6* **Santmargats** *var.* Holboo. Dzavhan, W Mongolia
105 *T8* **Sant Mateu** País Valenciano, E Spain
25 *S7* **Santo** Texas, SW USA
Santo *see* Espiritu Santo
60 *M10* **Santo Amaro, Ilha de** *island* SE Brazil
61 *G14* **Santo Ângelo** Rio Grande do Sul, S Brazil
76 *C9* **Santo Antão** *island* Ilhas de Barlavento, N Cape Verde
60 *J10* **Santo Antônio da Platina** Paraná, S Brazil
58 *C13* **Santo Antônio do Içá** Amazonas, N Brazil
57 *Q18* **Santo Corazón, Río** ≈ E Bolivia
44 *E5* **Santo Domingo** Villa Clara, C Cuba
45 *O9* **Santo Domingo** *prev.* Ciudad Trujillo. ● (Dominican Republic) SE Dominican Republic
40 *E8* **Santo Domingo** Baja California Sur, W Mexico
40 *M10* **Santo Domingo** San Luis Potosí, C Mexico
42 *L10* **Santo Domingo** Chontales, S Nicaragua
105 *P4* **Santo Domingo de la Calzada** La Rioja, N Spain
56 *B6* **Santo Domingo de los Colorados** Pichincha, NW Ecuador
Santo Domingo Tehuantepec *see* Tehuantepec
55 *O6* **San Tomé** Anzoátegui, NE Venezuela
San Tomé de Guayana *see* Ciudad Guayana
105 *R13* **Santomera** Murcia, SE Spain
105 *O2* **Santoña** Cantabria, N Spain
Santorin *see* Santoríni
115 *K22* **Santoríni** *var.* Santorin, *prev.* Thíra; *anc.* Thera. *island* Kykládes, Greece, Aegean Sea
60 *M10* **Santos** São Paulo, S Brazil
65 *J17* **Santos Plateau** *undersea feature* SW Atlantic Ocean
104 *G6* **Santo Tirso** Porto, N Portugal
40 *B2* **Santo Tomás** Baja California, NW Mexico
42 *L10* **Santo Tomás** Chontales, S Nicaragua
42 *G5* **Santo Tomás de Castilla** Izabal, E Guatemala
40 *B2* **Santo Tomás, Punta** *headland* NW Mexico
57 *H16* **Santo Tomás, Río** ≈ C Peru
57 *B18* **Santo Tomás, Volcán** ⩚ Galapagos Islands, Ecuador, E Pacific Ocean
61 *F14* **Santo Tomé** Corrientes, NE Argentina
Santo Tomé de Guayana *see* Ciudad Guayana
98 *H10* **Santpoort** Noord-Holland, W Netherlands
Santurce *see* Santurtzi
105 *O2* **Santurtzi** *var.* Santurce, Santurzi. País Vasco, N Spain
Santurzi *see* Santurtzi
63 *G20* **San Valentín, Cerro** ▲ S Chile
42 *F8* **San Vicente** San Vicente, C El Salvador
40 *C2* **San Vicente** Baja California, NW Mexico
188 *H6* **San Vicente** Saipan, S Northern Mariana Islands
42 *B9* **San Vicente** ◈ *department* E El Salvador
104 *I10* **San Vicente de Alcántara** Extremadura, W Spain
105 *N2* **San Vicente de Barakaldo** *var.* Baracaldo, *Basq.* San Bizenti-Barakaldo. País Vasco, N Spain
57 *E15* **San Vicente de Cañete** *var.* Cañete. Lima, W Peru
104 *M2* **San Vicente de la Barquera** Cantabria, N Spain
54 *E12* **San Vicente del Caguán** Caquetá, S Colombia
42 *F8* **San Vicente, Volcán de** ⩚ C El Salvador
43 *O15* **San Vito** Puntarenas, SE Costa Rica
106 *I7* **San Vito al Tagliamento** Friuli-Venezia Giulia, NE Italy
107 *H23* **San Vito, Capo** *headland* Sicilia, Italy, C Mediterranean Sea
107 *P18* **San Vito dei Normanni** Puglia, SE Italy
160 *L17* **Sanya** *var.* Ya Xian. Hainan, S China
83 *J16* **Sanyati** ≈ N Zimbabwe
25 *Q16* **San Ygnacio** Texas, SW USA
160 *L6* **Sanyuan** Shaanxi, C China
123 *P11* **Sanyyakhtakh** Respublika Sakha (Yakutiya), NE Russian Federation
146 *J15* **S. A.Nyýazow Adyndaky** *Rus.* Imeni S. A. Niyazova. Maryyskiy Velayat, S Turkmenistan
82 *C10* **Sanza Pombo** Uíge, NW Angola
Sanzyô *see* Sanjō
104 *G14* **São Bartolomeu de Messines** Faro, S Portugal
60 *M10* **São Bernardo do Campo** São Paulo, S Brazil
61 *F15* **São Borja** Rio Grande do Sul, S Brazil
104 *H14* **São Brás de Alportel** Faro, S Portugal
60 *M10* **São Caetano do Sul** São Paulo, S Brazil
60 *L9* **São Carlos** São Paulo, S Brazil
59 *P16* **São Cristóvão** Sergipe, E Brazil
61 *F15* **São Francisco de Assis** Rio Grande do Sul, S Brazil
58 *K13* **São Félix** Pará, NE Brazil
São Félix *see* São Félix do Araguaia
59 *J16* **São Félix do Araguaia** *var.* São Félix. Mato Grosso, W Brazil
59 *J14* **São Félix do Xingu** Pará, NE Brazil
60 *Q9* **São Fidélis** Rio de Janeiro, SE Brazil
76 *D10* **São Filipe** Fogo, S Cape Verde
60 *K12* **São Francisco do Sul** Santa Catarina, S Brazil
60 *K12* **São Francisco, Ilha de** *island* S Brazil
59 *P16* **São Francisco, Rio** ≈ E Brazil
61 *G16* **São Gabriel** Rio Grande do Sul, S Brazil
60 *P10* **São Gonçalo** Rio de Janeiro, SE Brazil
81 *H23* **Sao Hill** Iringa, S Tanzania
58 *M12* **São João de Cortes** Maranhão
60 *R9* **São João da Barra** Rio de Janeiro, SE Brazil
104 *G7* **São João da Madeira** Aveiro, N Portugal
58 *M12* **São João de Cortês** Maranhão, E Brazil
59 *M21* **São João del Rei** Minas Gerais, NE Brazil
59 *N15* **São João do Piauí** Piauí, E Brazil
59 *N14* **São João dos Patos** Maranhão, E Brazil
58 *C11* **São Joaquim** Amazonas, NW Brazil
61 *J14* **São Joaquim** Santa Catarina, S Brazil
60 *L7* **São Joaquim da Barra** São Paulo, S Brazil
64 *N2* **São Jorge** *island* Azores, Portugal, NE Atlantic Ocean
61 *K14* **São José** Santa Catarina, S Brazil
60 *M8* **São José do Rio Pardo** São Paulo, S Brazil
60 *K8* **São José do Rio Preto** São Paulo, S Brazil
60 *N10* **São Jose dos Campos** São Paulo, S Brazil
61 *I17* **São Lourenço do Sul** Rio Grande do Sul, S Brazil
58 *M12* **São Luís** *state capital* Maranhão, NE Brazil
58 *F11* **São Luís** Roraima, N Brazil
58 *M12* **São Luís, Ilha de** *island* NE Brazil
61 *F14* **São Luiz Gonzaga** Rio Grande do Sul, S Brazil
104 *I10* **São Mamede** ▲ C Portugal
São Mandol *see* São Manuel, Rio
47 *U8* **São Manuel** ≈ C Brazil
59 *H15* **São Manuel, Rio** *var.* São Mandol, Teles Pirés. ≈ C Brazil
58 *C11* **São Marcelino** Amazonas, NW Brazil
58 *N12* **São Marcos, Baía de** *bay* N Brazil
59 *O20* **São Mateus** Espírito Santo, SE Brazil
60 *J12* **São Mateus do Sul** Paraná, S Brazil
64 *P3* **São Miguel** *island* Azores, Portugal, NE Atlantic Ocean
60 *G13* **São Miguel d'Oeste** Santa Catarina, S Brazil
45 *P9* **Saona, Isla** *island* SE Dominican Republic
172 *H12* **Saondzou** ▲ Grande Comore, NW Comoros
103 *R10* **Saône** ≈ E France
103 *Q9* **Saône-et-Loire** ◈ *department* C France
76 *D9* **São Nicolau** *Eng.* Saint Nicholas. *island* Ilhas de Barlavento, N Cape Verde
60 *M10* **São Paulo** *state capital* São Paulo, S Brazil
60 *K9* **São Paulo** *off.* Estado de São Paulo. ◈ *state* S Brazil
São Paulo de Loanda *see* Luanda
São Paulo, Estado de *see* São Paulo
São Pedro do Rio Grande do Sul *see* Rio Grande
104 *H7* **São Pedro do Sul** Viseu, N Portugal
64 *K13* **São Pedro e São Paulo** *undersea feature* C Atlantic Ocean
59 *M14* **São Raimundo das Mangabeiras** Maranhão, E Brazil
59 *Q14* **São Roque, Cabo de** *headland* E Brazil
São Salvador *see* Salvador, Brazil
São Salvador/São Salvador do Congo *see* M'Banza Congo, Angola
60 *N10* **São Sebastião, Ilha de** *island* S Brazil
83 *N19* **São Sebastião, Ponta** *headland* C Mozambique
104 *F13* **São Teotónio** Beja, S Portugal
São Tiago *see* Santiago
79 *B18* **São Tomé** ● (Sao Tome and Principe) São Tomé, S Sao Tome and Principe
79 *B18* **São Tomé** ✕ São Tomé, S Sao Tome and Principe
79 *B18* **São Tomé** *Eng.* Saint Thomas. *island* S Sao Tome and Principe
79 *B17* **Sao Tome and Principe** *off.* Democratic Republic of Sao Tome and Principe. ◆ *republic* E Atlantic Ocean
Sao Tome and Principe, Democratic Republic of *see* Sao Tome and Principe
74 *H9* **Saoura, Oued** ≈ NW Algeria
60 *M10* **São Vicente** *Eng.* Saint Vincent. São Paulo, S Brazil
64 *O5* **São Vicente** Madeira, Portugal, NE Atlantic Ocean
76 *C9* **São Vicente** *Eng.* Saint Vincent. *island* Ilhas de Barlavento, N Cape Verde
104 *F14* **São Vicente, Cabo de** *Eng.* Cape Saint Vincent, *Port.* Cabode São Vicente. *cape* S Portugal
São Vicente, Cabo de *see* São Vicente, Cabo de
Sápai *see* Sápes
Sapaleri, Cerro *see* Zapaleri, Cerro
Saparoea *see* Saparua
171 *S13* **Saparua** *prev.* Saparoea. Pulau Saparau, C Indonesia
168 *L11* **Sapat** Sumatera, W Indonesia
77 *U17* **Sapele** Delta, S Nigeria
23 *X7* **Sapelo Island** *island* Georgia, SE USA
23 *X7* **Sapelo Sound** *sound* Georgia, SE USA
114 *K13* **Sápes** *var.* Sápai. Anatolikí Makedonía kai Thráki, NE Greece
Sapiéntza *see* Sapiénza
115 *D22* **Sapiénza** *var* Sapiéntza. *island* S Greece
Sapir *see* Sappir
61 *I15* **Sapiranga** Rio Grande do Sul, S Brazil
114 *K13* **Sápka** ▲▲ NE Greece
105 *X9* **Sa Pobla** Mallorca, Spain, W Mediterranean Sea
56 *D11* **Saposoa** San Martín, N Peru
119 *F16* **Sapotskin** *Pol.* Sopockinie, *Rus.* Sapotskino, Sopotskin. Hrodzyenskaya Voblasts', W Belarus
77 *P13* **Sapoui** *var.* Sapouy. S Burkina
Sapouy *see* Sapoui
138 *F12* **Sappir** *var* Sapir. Southern, S Israel
165 *S4* **Sapporo** Hokkaidō, NE Japan
107 *M19* **Sapri** Campania, S Italy
169 *T16* **Sapudi, Pulau** *island* S Indonesia
27 *P9* **Sapulpa** Oklahoma, C USA
142 *J4* **Saqqez** *var.* Saghez, Sakiz, Saqqiz. Kordestān, NW Iran
Saqqiz *see* Saqqez
139 *U8* **Sarābādī** E Iraq
167 *P10* **Sara Buri** *var.* Saraburi. Saraburi, C Thailand
Saraburi *see* Sara Buri
Sarafjagān *see* Salafchegān
24 *K9* **Saragosa** Texas, SW USA
Saragossa *see* Zaragoza
Saragt *see* Sarahs
56 *B8* **Saraguro** Loja, S Ecuador
146 *I15* **Sarahs** *var.* Saragt, *Rus.* Serakhs. Ahal Welaýaty, S Turkmenistan
126 *M6* **Sarai** Ryazanskaya Oblast', W Russian Federation
Sarāi *see* Sarāy
154 *M12* **Saraipāli** Chhattīsgarh, C India
149 *T9* **Sarāi Sidhu** Punjab, E Pakistan
93 *M15* **Säräisniemi** Oulu, C Finland
113 *I14* **Sarajevo** ● (Bosnia and Herzegovina) Federacija Bosna I Hercegovina, SE Bosnia and Herzegovina
112 *I13* **Sarajevo** ✕ Federacija Bosna I Hercegovina, C Bosnia and Herzegovina
143 *V4* **Sarakhs** Khorāsān-Razavī, NE Iran
115 *H17* **Sarakíniko, Ákrotírio** *headland* Évvoia, C Greece
115 *I18* **Sarakinó** *island* Vóreioi Sporádes, Greece, Aegean Sea
127 *V7* **Saraktash** Orenburgskaya Oblast', W Russian Federation
30 *L15* **Sara, Lake** ▣ Illinois, N USA
23 *N8* **Saraland** Alabama, S USA
55 *V9* **Saramacca** ◈ *district* N Surinam
55 *V10* **Saramacca Rivier** ≈ C Surinam
166 *M2* **Saramati** ▲ N Myanmar (Burma)
145 *R10* **Saran'** *Kaz.* Saran. Karaganda, C Kazakhstan
18 *K7* **Saranac Lake** New York, NE USA
18 *K7* **Saranac River** ≈ New York, NE USA
Saranda *see* Sarandë
113 *L23* **Sarandë** *var.* Saranda, *It.* Porto Edda; *prev.* Santi Quaranta. Vlorë, S Albania
61 *H14* **Sarandi** Rio Grande do Sul, S Brazil
61 *F19* **Sarandí del Yí** Durazno, C Uruguay
61 *F19* **Sarandí Grande** Florida, S Uruguay
171 *Q8* **Sarangani Islands** *island group* S Philippines
127 *P5* **Saransk** Respublika Mordoviya, W Russian Federation
115 *C14* **Sarantáporos** ≈ N Greece
114 *H9* **Sarantsi** Sofiya, W Bulgaria
127 *T3* **Sarapul** Udmurtskaya Respublika, NW Russian Federation
Sarâqeb *see* Sarāqib
138 *I3* **Sarāqib** *Fr.* Sarâqeb. Idlib, N Syria
54 *J5* **Sarare** Lara, N Venezuela
55 *O10* **Sarariña** Amazonas, S Venezuela
143 *S10* **Sar Ashk** Kermān, C Iran
23 *V13* **Sarasota** Florida, SE USA
117 *O11* **Sarata** Odes'ka Oblast', SW Ukraine
116 *I10* **Sărăţel** *Hung.* Szeretfalva. Bistriţa-Năsăud, N Romania
25 *X10* **Saratoga** Texas, SW USA
18 *K10* **Saratoga Springs** New York, NE USA
127 *P8* **Saratov** Saratovskaya Oblast', W Russian Federation
127 *P8* **Saratovskaya Oblast'** ◈ *province* W Russian Federation
127 *Q7* **Saratovskoye Vodokhranilishche** ▣ W Russian Federation
Saravan/Saravane *see* Salavan
169 *S9* **Sarawak** ◈ *state* East Malaysia
Sarawak *see* Kuching
139 *U6* **Sarāy** *var.* Sarāi. E Iraq
136 *D10* **Saray** Tekirdağ, NW Turkey
76 *J12* **Saraya** SE Senegal
143 *W14* **Sarbāz** Sīstān va Balūchestān, SE Iran
143 *U8* **Sarbīsheh** Khorāsān, E Iran
111 *J24* **Sárbogárd** Fejér, C Hungary
Şarcad *see* Sarkad
27 *S7* **Sarcoxie** Missouri, C USA
152 *L11* **Sārda** *Nep.* Kali. ≈ India/Nepal
152 *G10* **Sardārshahr** Rājasthān, NW India
107 *C18* **Sardegna** *Eng.* Sardinia. ◈ *region* Italy, C Mediterranean Sea
107 *A18* **Sardegna** *Eng.* Sardinia. *island* Italy, C Mediterranean Sea
42 *K13* **Sardinal** Guanacaste, NW Costa Rica
54 *G7* **Sardinata** Norte de Santander, N Colombia
Sardinia *see* Sardegna
120 *K8* **Sardinia-Corsica Trough** *undersea feature* Tyrrhenian Sea, C Mediterranean Sea
22 *L2* **Sardis** Mississippi, S USA
22 *L2* **Sardis Lake** ▣ Mississippi, S USA
27 *P12* **Sardis Lake** ▣ Oklahoma, C USA
92 *H12* **Sarek** ▲▲ N Sweden
92 *H11* **Sarektjåhkkå** ▲ N Sweeden
149 *N3* **Sar-e Pol** *var.* Sar-i-Pul. Sar-e Pol, N Afghanistan
149 *O3* **Sar-e Pol** ◈ *province* N Afghanistan
Sar-e Pol *see* Sar-e Pol-e Žahāb
142 *J6* **Sar-e Pol-e Žahāb** *var.* Sar-e Pol, Sar-i Pul. Kermānshāhān, W Iran
Teluk Sarera *see* Cenderawasih, Teluk
92 *H11* **Stortoppen** ▲ N Sweden
147 *T13* **Sarez, Kŭli** *Rus.* Sarezskoye Ozero. ◎ SE Tajikistan
Sarezskoye Ozero *see* Sarez, Kŭli
64 *G10* **Sargasso Sea** *sea* W Atlantic Ocean
149 *U8* **Sargodha** Punjab, NE Pakistan
78 *I13* **Sarh** *prev.* Fort-Archambault. Moyen-Chari, S Chad
143 *P4* **Sārī** *var.* Sari, Sāri. Māzandarān, N Iran
115 *N23* **Saría** *island* SE Greece
Sariasiya *see* Sariosiyo
40 *F3* **Saric** Sonora, NW Mexico
188 *K6* **Sarigan** *island* C Northern Mariana Islands
136 *D14* **Sarıgöl** Manisa, SW Turkey
139 *T6* **Sārihah** E Iraq
137 *R12* **Sarıkamış** Kars, NE Turkey
169 *R9* **Sarikei** Sarawak, East Malaysia
147 *U12* **Sarikol Range** *Rus.* Sarykol'skiy Khrebet. ▲▲ China/Tajikistan
181 *Y7* **Sarina** Queensland, NE Australia
Sarine *see* La Sarine
105 *S5* **Sariñena** Aragón, NE Spain
147 *O13* **Sariosiyo** *Rus.* Sariasiya. Surkhondaryo Viloyati, S Uzbekistan
Sar-i-Pul *see* Sar-e Pol
Sar-i Pul *see* Sar-e Pol-e Žahāb
Sariqamish Kŭli *see* Sarygamyş Köli
149 *V1* **Sarī Qūl** *Rus.* Ozero Zurkul', *Taj.* Zŭrkŭl. ◎ Afghanistan/ Tajikistan *see also* Zŭrkŭl
Sarī Qūl *see* Zŭrkŭl
75 *Q12* **Sarīr Tibistī** *var.* Serir Tibesti. *desert* S Libya
25 *S15* **Sarita** Texas, SW USA
163 *W14* **Sariwŏn** SW North Korea
114 *P12* **Sarıyer** İstanbul, NW Turkey
97 *L26* **Sark** *Fr.* Sercq. *island* Channel Islands
111 *N24* **Sarkad** *Rom.* Şărcad. Békés, SE Hungary
145 *W14* **Sarkand** Almaty, SW Kazakhstan
Sarkaņi *see* Krasnogorskoye
152 *D11* **Sarkāri Tala** Rājasthān, NW India
136 *G15* **Şarkikaraağaç** *var.* Şarki Karaağaç. Isparta, SW Turkey
Şarki Karaağaç *see* Şarkikaraağaç
136 *L13* **Şarkışla** Sivas, C Turkey
136 *C11* **Şarköy** Tekirdağ, NW Turkey
Sárköz *see* Livada
Sarlat *see* Sarlat-la-Canéda
102 *M13* **Sarlat-la-Canéda** *var.* Sarlat. Dordogne, SW France
109 *S3* **Sarleinsbach** Oberösterreich, N Austria
Šarma *see* Ash Sharmah
171 *Y12* **Sarmi** Papua, E Indonesia
63 *I19* **Sarmiento** Chubut, S Argentina
63 *H25* **Sarmiento, Monte** ▲ S Chile
94 *J11* **Särna** Dalarna, C Sweden
108 *F8* **Sarnen** Obwalden, C Switzerland
108 *F9* **Sarner See** ◎ C Switzerland
14 *D16* **Sarnia** Ontario, S Canada
116 *L3* **Sarny** Rivnens'ka Oblast', NW Ukraine
171 *O13* **Saroako** Sulawesi, C Indonesia
118 *L13* **Sarochyna** *Rus.* Sorochino. Vitsyebskaya Voblasts', N Belarus
168 *L12* **Sarolangun** Sumatera, W Indonesia
165 *U3* **Saroma** Hokkaidō, NE Japan
165 *V3* **Saroma-ko** ◎ Hokkaidō, NE Japan
Saronic Gulf *see* Saronikós Kólpos
115 *H20* **Saronikós Kólpos** *Eng.* Saronic Gulf. *gulf* S Greece
106 *D7* **Saronno** Lombardia, N Italy
136 *B11* **Saros Körfezi** *gulf* NW Turkey
111 *N20* **Sárospatak** Borsod-Abaúj-Zemplén, NE Hungary
127 *O4* **Sarov** *prev.* Sarova. Respublika Mordoviya, SW Russian Federation
Sarova *see* Sarov
127 *P12* **Sarpa** Respublika Kalmykiya, SW Russian Federation
127 *P12* **Sarpa, Ozero** ◎ SW Russian Federation
113 *M18* **Šar Planina** ▲▲ FYR Macedonia/Serbia
95 *I16* **Sarpsborg** Østfold, S Norway
139 *U5* **Sarqalā** N Iraq
103 *U4* **Sarralbe** Moselle, NE France
Sarre *see* Saar
Sarre *see* Saarland
103 *U5* **Sarrebourg** *Ger.* Saarburg. Moselle, NE France
Sarrebruck *see* Saarbrücken
103 *U4* **Sarreguemines** *prev.* Saargemund. Moselle, NE France
104 *I3* **Sarria** Galicia, NW Spain
105 *S8* **Sarrión** Aragón, NE Spain
42 *F4* **Sarstoon** *Sp.* Río Sarstún. ≈ Belize/Guatemala
Sarstún, Río *see* Sarstoon
123 *Q9* **Sartang** ≈ NE Russian Federation
103 *X16* **Sartène** Corse, France, C Mediterranean Sea
102 *K7* **Sarthe** ◈ *department* NW France
102 *K7* **Sarthe** ≈ N France
115 *H15* **Sárti** Kentrikí Makedonía, N Greece
Sartu *see* Daqing
165 *T1* **Sarufutsu** Hokkaidō, NE Japan
Saruhan *see* Manisa
152 *G9* **Sarūpsar** Rājasthān, NW India
137 *U13* **Şärur** *prev.* Il'ichevsk. SW Azerbaijan
Sarvani *see* Marneuli
111 *G23* **Sárvár** Vas, W Hungary
143 *P11* **Sarvestān** Fārs, S Iran
171 *W12* **Sarwon** Papua, E Indonesia
Saryagach *see* Saryagash
145 *P17* **Saryagash** *var.* Saryagach, *Kaz.* Saryaghash. Yuzhnyy Kazakhstan, S Kazakhstan
Saryaghash *see* Saryagash
Saryarqa *see* Kazakhskiy Melkosopochnik
147 *W8* **Sary-Bulak** Narynskaya Oblast', C Kyrgyzstan
147 *U10* **Sary-Bulak** Oshskaya Oblast', SW Kyrgyzstan
117 *S14* **Sarych, Mys** *headland* S Ukraine
147 *Z7* **Sary-Dzhaz** *var.* Aksu He. ≈ China/Kyrgyzstan *see also* Aksu He
Sary-Dzhaz *see* Aksu He
146 *F8* **Sarygamyş Köli** *Rus.* Sarykamyshkoye Ozero, *Uzb.* Sariqamish Kŭli. *salt lake* Kazakhstan/Uzbekistan
144 *G13* **Sarykamys** *Kaz.* Saryqamys. Mangistau, SW Kazakhstan
Sarykamyshkoye Ozero *see* Sarygamyş Köli
145 *N7* **Sarykol'** *prev.* Uritskiy. Kustanay, N Kazakhstan
Sarykol'skiy Khrebet *see* Sarikol Range
144 *M10* **Sarykopa, Ozero** ◎ C Kazakhstan
145 *V15* **Saryozek** *Kaz.* Saryözek. Almaty, SE Kazakhstan
Saryqamys *see* Sarykamys
145 *S13* **Saryshagan** *Kaz.* Saryshahan. Karaganda, SE Kazakhstan
Saryshahan *see* Saryshagan
145 *O13* **Sarysu** ≈ S Kazakhstan
147 *T11* **Sary-Tash** Oshskaya Oblast', SW Kyrgyzstan
145 *T12* **Saryterek** Karaganda, C Kazakhstan
146 *J15* **Saryýazy Suw Howdany** *Rus.* Saryyazynskoye Vodokhranilishche. ▣ S Turkmenistan
Saryyazynskoye Vodokhranilishche *see* Saryýazy Suw Howdany

◆ Country
● Country Capital
◇ Dependent Territory
○ Dependent Territory Capital
◈ Administrative Regions
✕ International Airport
▲ Mountain
▲▲ Mountain Range
⩚ Volcano
≈ River
◎ Lake
▣ Reservoir

145 T14 **Saryesik-Atyrau, Peski** *desert* E Kazakhstan
106 E10 **Sarzana** Liguria, NW Italy
188 B17 **Sasalaguan, Mount** ▲ S Guam
153 O14 **Sasarām** Bihār, N India
186 M8 **Sasari, Mount** ▲ Santa Isabel, N Solomon Islands
164 C13 **Sasebo** Nagasaki, Kyūshū, SW Japan
14 I9 **Saseginaga, Lac** ◎ Québec, SE Canada
Saseno *see* Sazan
9 R13 **Saskatchewan** ◈ *province* SW Canada
9 U14 **Saskatchewan** ≈ Manitoba/ Saskatchewan, C Canada
9 T15 **Saskatoon** Saskatchewan, S Canada
9 T15 **Saskatoon** ✈ Saskatchewan, S Canada
123 N7 **Saskylakh** Respublika Sakha (Yakutiya), NE Russian Federation
42 L7 **Saslaya, Cerro** ▲ N Nicaragua
38 G17 **Sasmik, Cape** *headland* Tanaga Island, Alaska, USA
119 N19 **Sasnovy Bor** *Rus.* Sosnovyy Bor. Homyel'skaya Voblasts', SE Belarus
127 N5 **Sasovo** Ryazanskaya Oblast', W Russian Federation
25 S12 **Saspamco** Texas, SW USA
109 W9 **Sass** *var.* Sassbach. ≈ SE Austria
76 M17 **Sassandra** S Ivory Coast
76 M17 **Sassandra** *var.* Ibo, Sassandra Fleuve. ≈ S Ivory Coast
Sassandra Fleuve *see* Sassandra
107 B17 **Sassari** Sardegna, Italy, C Mediterranean Sea
Sassbach *see* Sass
98 H11 **Sassenheim** Zuid-Holland, W Netherlands
Sassmacken *see* Valdemārpils
100 O7 **Sassnitz** Mecklenburg-Vorpommern, NE Germany
99 E16 **Sas van Gent** Zeeland, SW Netherlands
145 W12 **Sasykkol', Ozero** ◎ E Kazakhstan
117 O12 **Sasyk Kunduk, Ozero** ◎ SW Ukraine
76 J12 **Satadougou** Kayes, SW Mali
164 C17 **Sata-misaki** Kyūshū, SW Japan
26 I7 **Satanta** Kansas, C USA
155 E15 **Sātāra** Mahārāshtra, W India
192 G15 **Sātaua** Savai'i, NW Samoa
188 M16 **Satawal** *island* Caroline Islands, C Micronesia
189 R17 **Satawan Atoll** *atoll* Mortlock Islands, C Micronesia
23 Y12 **Satellite Beach** Florida, SE USA
95 M14 **Säter** Dalarna, C Sweden
Sathmar *see* Satu Mare
23 V7 **Satilla River** ≈ Georgia, SE USA
57 F14 **Satipo** *var.* San Francisco de Satipo. Junín, C Peru
122 F11 **Satka** Chelyabinskaya Oblast', C Russian Federation
153 T16 **Satkhira** Khulna, SW Bangladesh
146 J13 **Şatlyk** *Rus.* Shatlyk. Mary Welaýaty, C Turkmenistan
154 K9 **Satna** *prev.* Sutna. Madhya Pradesh, C India
103 R11 **Satolas** ✈ (Lyon) Rhône, E France
111 N20 **Sátoraljaújhely** Borsod-Abaúj-Zemplén, NE Hungary
145 O12 **Satpayev** *prev.* Nikol'skiy. Karaganda, C Kazakhstan
154 G11 **Sātpura Range** ▲▲ C India
167 P12 **Sattahip** *var.* Ban Sattahip, Ban Sattahipp. Chon Buri, S Thailand
92 L11 **Sattanen** Lappi, NE Finland
Satul *see* Satun
116 H9 **Satulung** *Hung.* Kővárhosszúfalu. Maramureş, N Romania
Satul-Vechi *see* Staro Selo
116 G8 **Satu Mare** *Ger.* Sathmar, *Hung.* Szatmárrnémeti. Satu Mare, NW Romania
116 G8 **Satu Mare** ◈ *county* NW Romania
167 N16 **Satun** *var.* Satul, Setul. Satun, SW Thailand
192 G16 **Satupaiteau** Savai'i, W Samoa
Sau *see* Sava
14 F14 **Sauble** ≈ Ontario, S Canada
14 F13 **Sauble Beach** Ontario, S Canada
61 C16 **Sauce** Corrientes, NE Argentina
Sauce *see* Juan L. Lacaze
36 K15 **Sauceda Mountains** ▲▲ Arizona, SW USA
61 C17 **Sauce de Luna** Entre Ríos, E Argentina
63 L15 **Sauce Grande, Río** ≈ E Argentina
40 K6 **Saucillo** Chihuahua, N Mexico
95 D15 **Sauda** Rogaland, S Norway
145 Q16 **Saudakent** *Kaz.* Saūdakent; *prev.* Baykadam, *Kaz.* Bayqadam. Zhambyl, S Kazakhstan
92 J2 **Saudhárkrókur** Nordhurland Vestra, N Iceland
141 P9 **Saudi Arabia** *off.* Kingdom of Saudi Arabia, Al 'Arabīyah as Su'ūdīyah, *Ar.* Al Mamlakah al 'Arabīyah as Su'ūdīyah. ◆ *monarchy* SW Asia
Saudi Arabia, Kingdom of *see* Saudi Arabia
101 D19 **Sauer** *var.* Sûre. ≈ NW Europe *see also* Sûre
Sauer *see* Sûre
101 F15 **Sauerland** *forest* W Germany
14 F14 **Saugeen** ≈ Ontario, S Canada
18 K12 **Saugerties** New York, NE USA
Saugor *see* Sāgar
10 K15 **Saugstad, Mount** ▲ British Columbia, SW Canada
Sāūjbulāgh *see* Mahābād
102 J11 **Saujon** Charente-Maritime, W France
29 T7 **Sauk Centre** Minnesota, N USA
30 L8 **Sauk City** Wisconsin, N USA
29 U7 **Sauk Rapids** Minnesota, N USA
55 Y11 **Saül** C French Guiana
103 O7 **Sauldre** ≈ C France
101 I23 **Saulgau** Baden-Württemberg, SW Germany
103 Q8 **Saulieu** Côte d'Or, C France
118 G8 **Saulkrasti** Riga, C Latvia
15 S6 **Sault-aux-Cochons, Rivière du** ≈ Québec, SE Canada
31 Q4 **Sault Sainte Marie** Michigan, N USA
12 F14 **Sault Ste. Marie** Ontario, S Canada
145 P7 **Saumalkol'** *prev.* Volodarskoye. Severnyy Kazakhstan, N Kazakhstan
190 E13 **Sauma, Pointe** *headland* Île Alofi, W Wallis and Futuna
171 T16 **Saumlaki** *var.* Saumlakki. Pulau Yamdena, E Indonesia
Saumlakki *see* Saumlaki
15 R12 **Saumon, Rivière au** ≈ Québec, SE Canada
102 K8 **Saumur** Maine-et-Loire, NW France
185 F23 **Saunders, Cape** *headland* South Island, New Zealand
195 N13 **Saunders Coast** *physical region* Antarctica
65 B23 **Saunders Island** *island* NW Falkland Islands
65 C24 **Saunders Island Settlement** Saunders Island, NW Falkland Islands
82 F11 **Saurimo** *Port.* Henrique de Carvalho, Vila Henrique de Carvalho. Lunda Sul, NE Angola
55 S11 **Sauriwaunawa** S Guyana
82 D12 **Sautar** Malanje, NW Angola
45 S13 **Sauteurs** N Grenada
102 K13 **Sauveterre-de-Guyenne** Gironde, SW France
119 O14 **Sava** *Rus.* Sava. Mahilyowskaya Voblasts', E Belarus
42 J5 **Savá** Colón, N Honduras
84 H11 **Sava** *Eng.* Save, *Ger.* Sau, *Hung.* Száva. ≈ SE Europe
33 Y8 **Savage** Montana, NW USA
183 N16 **Savage River** Tasmania, SE Australia
77 R15 **Savalou** S Benin
30 K10 **Savanna** Illinois, N USA
23 X6 **Savannah** Georgia, SE USA
27 R2 **Savannah** Missouri, C USA
20 H10 **Savannah** Tennessee, S USA
21 O12 **Savannah River** ≈ Georgia/ South Carolina, SE USA
Savannakhét *see* Khanthabouli
44 H12 **Savanna-La-Mar** W Jamaica
12 B10 **Savant Lake** ◎ Ontario, S Canada
155 F17 **Savanūr** Karnātaka, W India
93 J16 **Sävar** Västerbotten, N Sweden
Savaria *see* Szombathely
154 C11 **Sāvarkundla** *var.* Kundla. Gujarāt, W India
116 F11 **Săvârşin** *Hung.* Soborsin; *prev.* Săvirşin. Arad, W Romania
136 C13 **Savaştepe** Balıkesir, W Turkey
Savat *see* Savot
Sāvdijāri *see* Skaulo
77 R15 **Savè** SE Benin
83 N18 **Save** Inhambane, E Mozambique
102 L16 **Save** ≈ S France
83 L17 **Save** *var.* Sabi. ≈ Mozambique/Zimbabwe *see also* Sabi
Save *see* Sava
142 M6 **Sāveh** Markazī, W Iran
116 L8 **Săveni** Botoşani, NE Romania
103 N16 **Saverdun** Ariège, S France
Save, Rio *see* Sabi
103 U5 **Saverne** *var.* Zabern; *anc.* Tres Tabernae. Bas-Rhin, NE France
106 B9 **Savigliano** Piemonte, NW Italy
Savigsivik *see* Savissivik
Savinichi *see* Savinichy
119 Q16 **Savinichy** *Rus.* Savinichi. Mahilyowskaya Voblasts', E Belarus
109 U10 **Savinja** ≈ N Slovenia
106 H11 **Savio** ≈ C Italy
Săvirşin *see* Săvârşin
197 O11 **Savissivik** *var.* Savigsivik. ◈ Avannaarsua, N Greenland
93 N18 **Savitaipale** Etelä-Suomi, SE Finland
113 J15 **Šavnik** C Montenegro
108 I9 **Savognin** Graubünden, S Switzerland
103 T12 **Savoie** ◈ *department* E France
106 C10 **Savona** Liguria, NW Italy
93 N17 **Savonlinna** *Swe.* Nyslott. Isä-Suomi, E Finland
93 N17 **Savonranta** Isä-Suomi, E Finland
38 K10 **Savoonga** Saint Lawrence Island, Alaska, USA
147 P11 **Savot** *Rus.* Savat. Sirdaryo Viloyati, E Uzbekistan
147 P11 **Savot** *Rus.* Savat. Sirdaryo Viloyati, E Uzbekistan
30 M13 **Savoy** Illinois, N USA
117 O8 **Savran'** Odes'ka Oblast', SW Ukraine
137 R11 **Şavşat** Artvin, NE Turkey
95 L19 **Sävsjö** Jönköping, S Sweden
Savu, Kepulauan *see* Sawu, Kepulauan
92 M11 **Savukoski** Lappi, NE Finland
Savu, Pulau *see* Sawu, Pulau
187 Y14 **Savusavu** Vanua Levu, N Fiji
171 O17 **Savu Sea** *Ind.* Laut Sawu. *sea* S Indonesia
83 H17 **Savute** North-West, N Botswana
139 N7 **Şawāb Uqlat'** *well* W Iraq
138 M7 **Sawāb, Wādī as** *dry watercourse* W Iraq
152 H13 **Sawāi Mādhopur** Rājasthān, N India
Sawakin *see* Suakin
167 R8 **Sawang Daen Din** Sakon Nakhon, E Thailand
167 O8 **Sawankhalok** *var.* Swankalok. Sukhothai, NW Thailand
165 P13 **Sawara** Chiba, Honshū, S Japan
37 R5 **Sawatch Range** ▲▲ Colorado, C USA
141 N12 **Sawdā', Jabal** ▲▲ SW Saudi Arabia
75 P9 **Sawdā', Jabal as** ▲▲ C Libya
Sawdirī *see* Sodiri
97 F14 **Sawel Mountain** ▲ C Northern Ireland, UK
Sawhāj *see* Sohâg
77 O15 **Sawla** N Ghana
141 X12 **Şawqirah** *var.* Suqrah. S Oman
141 X12 **Şawqirah, Dawḥat** *var.* Ghubbat Sawqirah, Sukra Bay, Suqrah Bay. *bay* S Oman
Sawqirah, Ghubbat *see* Şawqirah, Dawḥat
183 V5 **Sawtell** New South Wales, SE Australia
138 K7 **Şawt, Wādī aş** *dry watercourse* S Syria
171 O17 **Sawu, Kepulauan** *var.* Kepulauan Savu. *island group* S Indonesia
Sawu, Laut *see* Savu Sea
171 O17 **Sawu, Pulau** *var.* Pulau Sawu. *island* Kepulauan Sawu, S Indonesia
105 S12 **Sax** País Valenciano, E Spain
Saxe *see* Sachsen
108 C11 **Saxon** Valais, SW Switzerland
Saxony *see* Sachsen
Saxony-Anhalt *see* Sachsen-Anhalt
77 R12 **Say** Niamey, SW Niger
15 V7 **Sayabec** Québec, SE Canada
Sayaboury *see* Xaignabouli
145 U12 **Sayak** *Kaz.* Sayaq. Karaganda, E Kazakhstan
57 D14 **Sayán** Lima, W Peru
129 T6 **Sayanskiy Khrebet** ▲▲ S Russian Federation
Sayaq *see* Sayak
146 K13 **Saýat** *Rus.* Sayat. Lebap Welaýaty, E Turkmenistan
42 D3 **Sayaxché** Petén, N Guatemala
Şaydā/Sayida *see* Saïda
162 J7 **Sayhan** *var.* Hüremt. Bulgan, C Mongolia
163 N10 **Sayhandulaan** *var.* Öldziyt. Dornogovĭ, SE Mongolia
162 K9 **Sayhan-Ovoo** *var.* Ongi. Dundgovĭ, C Mongolia
141 T15 **Sayḥūt** E Yemen
29 U14 **Saylorville Lake** ⊠ Iowa, C USA
Saymenskiy Kanal *see* Saimaa Canal
163 N10 **Saynshand** Dornogovĭ, SE Mongolia
Saynshand *see* Sevrey
Sayn-Ust *see* Hohmorit
Say-Ötesh *see* Say-Utës
138 J7 **Şayqal, Baḥr** ◎ S Syria
Sayrab *see* Sayrob
158 H4 **Sayram Hu** ◎ NW China
26 K11 **Sayre** Oklahoma, C USA
18 H12 **Sayre** Pennsylvania, NE USA
18 K15 **Sayreville** New Jersey, NE USA
147 N13 **Sayrob** *Rus.* Sayrab. Surkhondaryo Viloyati, S Uzbekistan
40 L13 **Sayula** Jalisco, SW Mexico
141 R14 **Say'ūn** *var.* Saywūn. C Yemen
144 G14 **Say-Utës** *Kaz.* Say-Ötesh. Mangistau, SW Kazakhstan
10 K16 **Sayward** Vancouver Island, British Columbia, SW Canada
Saywūn *see* Say'ūn
Sayyāl *see* As Sayyāl
139 U8 **Sayyid 'Abīd** *var.* Saiyid Abid. E Iraq
113 J22 **Sazan** *var.* Ishulli i Sazanit, *It.* Saseno. *island* SW Albania
Sazanit, Ishulli i *see* Sazan
Sazau/Sazawa *see* Sázava
111 E17 **Sázava** *var.* Sazau, *Ger.* Sazawa. ≈ C Czech Republic
124 J14 **Sazonovo** Vologodskaya Oblast', NW Russian Federation
102 G6 **Scaër** Finistère, NW France
97 J15 **Scafell Pike** ▲ NW England, UK
Scalabis *see* Santarém
96 M2 **Scalloway** N Scotland, UK
38 M11 **Scammon Bay** Alaska, USA
Scammon Lagoon/ Scammon, Laguna *see* Ojo de Liebre, Laguna
84 F7 **Scandinavia** *geophysical region* NW Europe
96 K5 **Scapa Flow** *sea basin* N Scotland, UK
107 K26 **Scaramia, Capo** *headland* Sicilia, Italy, C Mediterranean Sea
14 H15 **Scarborough** Ontario, SE Canada
45 Z16 **Scarborough** *prev.* Port Louis. Tobago, Trinidad and Tobago
97 N16 **Scarborough** N England, UK
185 I17 **Scargill** Canterbury, South Island, New Zealand
96 E7 **Scarp** *island* NW Scotland, UK
Scarpanto *see* Kárpathos
Scarpanto Strait *see* Karpathou, Stenó
107 G25 **Scauri** Sicilia, Italy, C Mediterranean Sea
Scealg, Bá na *see* Ballinskelligs Bay
Scebeli *see* Shebeli
100 K10 **Schaale** ≈ N Germany
100 K9 **Schaalsee** ◎ N Germany
99 G18 **Schaerbeek** Brussels, C Belgium
108 G6 **Schaffhausen** *Fr.* Schaffhouse. Schaffhausen, N Switzerland
108 G6 **Schaffhausen** *Fr.* Schaffhouse. ◈ *canton* N Switzerland
Schaffhouse *see* Schaffhausen
98 I8 **Schagen** Noord-Holland, NW Netherlands
Schaken *see* Šakiai
98 M10 **Schalkhaar** Overijssel, E Netherlands
109 R3 **Schärding** Oberösterreich, N Austria
100 G9 **Scharhörn** *island* NW Germany
Schässburg *see* Sighişoara
Schaulen *see* Šiauliai
30 M10 **Schaumburg** Illinois, N USA
Schebschi Mountains *see* Shebshi Mountains
98 P6 **Scheemda** Groningen, NE Netherlands
100 I10 **Scheessel** Niedersachsen, NW Germany
13 N8 **Schefferville** Québec, E Canada
Schelde *see* Scheldt
99 D18 **Scheldt** *Dut.* Schelde, *Fr.* Escaut. ≈ W Europe
35 X5 **Schell Creek Range** ▲▲ Nevada, W USA
18 K10 **Schenectady** New York, NE USA
99 I17 **Scherpenheuvel** *Fr.* Montaigu. Vlaams Brabant, C Belgium
98 K11 **Scherpenzeel** Gelderland, C Netherlands
25 S12 **Schertz** Texas, SW USA
98 G11 **Scheveningen** Zuid-Holland, W Netherlands
98 G12 **Schiedam** Zuid-Holland, SW Netherlands
99 M24 **Schieren** Diekirch, NE Luxembourg
98 M4 **Schiermonnikoog** *Fris.* Skiermûntseach. Friesland, N Netherlands
98 M4 **Schiermonnikoog** *Fris.* Skiermûntseach. *island* Waddeneilanden, N Netherlands
99 K14 **Schijndel** Noord-Brabant, S Netherlands
Schil *see* Jiu
99 H16 **Schilde** Antwerpen, N Belgium
Schillen *see* Zhilino
103 V5 **Schiltigheim** Bas-Rhin, NE France
106 G7 **Schio** Veneto, NE Italy
98 H10 **Schiphol** ✈ (Amsterdam) Noord-Holland, C Netherlands
Schippenbeil *see* Sępopol
Schiria *see* Şiria
Schivelbein *see* Świdwin
115 D22 **Schíza** *island* S Greece
175 U3 **Schjetman Reef** *reef* Antarctica
Schlackenwerth *see* Ostrov
109 R7 **Schladming** Steiermark, SE Austria
Schlan *see* Slaný
Schlanders *see* Silandro
100 I7 **Schlei** *inlet* N Germany
101 D17 **Schleiden** Nordrhein-Westfalen, W Germany
Schlelau *see* Szydłowiec
100 I7 **Schleswig** Schleswig-Holstein, N Germany
29 T13 **Schleswig** Iowa, C USA
100 H8 **Schleswig-Holstein** ◈ *state* N Germany
Schlettstadt *see* Sélestat
108 F7 **Schlieren** Zürich, N Switzerland
Schlochau *see* Człuchów
Schloppe *see* Człopa
101 I18 **Schlüchtern** Hessen, C Germany
101 J17 **Schmalkalden** Thüringen, C Germany
109 W2 **Schmida** ≈ NE Austria
65 P19 **Schmidt-Ott Seamount** *var.* Schmitt-Ott Seamount, Schmitt-Ott Tablemount. *undersea feature* SW Indian Ocean
Schmiegel *see* Śmigiel
Schmitt-Ott Seamount/ Schmitt-Ott Tablemount *see* Schmidt-Ott Seamount
15 V3 **Schmon** ≈ Québec, SE Canada
101 M18 **Schneeberg** ▲ W Germany
Schneeberg *see* Veliki Snežnik
Schnee-Eifel *see* Schneifel
Schneekoppe *see* Sněžka
Schneidemühl *see* Piła
101 D18 **Schneifel** *var.* Schnee-Eifel. *plateau* W Germany
Schnelle Körös/Schnelle Kreisch *see* Crişul Repede
100 I11 **Schneverdingen** *var.* Schneverdingen (Wümme). Niedersachsen, NW Germany
Schneverdingen (Wümme) *see* Schneverdingen
Schoden *see* Skuodas
45 Q12 **Schœlcher** W Martinique
18 K10 **Schoharie** New York, NE USA
18 K11 **Schoharie Creek** ≈ New York, NE USA
115 J21 **Schoinoússa** *island* Kykládes, Greece, Aegean Sea
100 L13 **Schönebeck** Sachsen-Anhalt, C Germany
Schöneck *see* Skarszewy
100 O12 **Schönefeld** ✈ (Berlin) Berlin, NE Germany
101 K24 **Schongau** Bayern, S Germany
100 K13 **Schöningen** Niedersachsen, C Germany
Schönlanke *see* Trzcianka
Schönsee *see* Kowalewo Pomorskie
31 P10 **Schoolcraft** Michigan, N USA
98 O8 **Schoonebeek** Drenthe, NE Netherlands
98 I12 **Schoonhoven** Zuid-Holland, C Netherlands
98 H8 **Schoorl** Noord-Holland, NW Netherlands
Schooten *see* Schoten
101 F24 **Schopfheim** Baden-Württemberg, SW Germany
101 I21 **Schorndorf** Baden-Württemberg, S Germany
100 F10 **Schortens** Niedersachsen, NW Germany
99 H16 **Schoten** *var.* Schooten. Antwerpen, N Belgium
183 Q17 **Schouten Island** *island* Tasmania, SE Australia
186 C5 **Schouten Islands** *island group* NW Papua New Guinea
98 E13 **Schouwen** *island* SW Netherlands
Schreiberhau *see* Szklarska Poręba
109 U2 **Schrems** Niederösterreich, E Austria
101 L22 **Schrobenhausen** Bayern, SE Germany
18 L8 **Schroon Lake** ◎ New York, NE USA
108 J8 **Schruns** Vorarlberg, W Austria
Schubin *see* Szubin
25 U11 **Schulenburg** Texas, SW USA
Schuls *see* Scuol
108 E8 **Schüpfheim** Luzern, C Switzerland
35 S6 **Schurz** Nevada, W USA
101 I24 **Schussen** ≈ S Germany
Schüttenhofen *see* Sušice
29 R15 **Schuyler** Nebraska, C USA
18 L10 **Schuylerville** New York, NE USA
101 K20 **Schwabach** Bayern, SE Germany
Schwabenalb *see* Schwäbische Alb
101 I23 **Schwäbische Alb** *var.* Schwabenalb, *Eng.* Swabian Jura. ▲▲ S Germany
101 I22 **Schwäbisch Gmünd** *var.* Gmünd. Baden-Württemberg, SW Germany
101 I21 **Schwäbisch Hall** *var.* Hall. Baden-Württemberg, SW Germany
101 H16 **Schwalm** ≈ C Germany
109 V9 **Schwanberg** Steiermark, SE Austria
108 H8 **Schwanden** Glarus, E Switzerland
101 M20 **Schwandorf** Bayern, SE Germany
109 S5 **Schwanenstadt** Oberösterreich, NW Austria
169 S11 **Schwaner, Pegunungan** ▲▲ Borneo, N Indonesia
109 W5 **Schwarza** ≈ E Austria
109 P9 **Schwarzach** ≈ S Austria
101 M20 **Schwarzach** *Cz.* Černice. ≈ Czech Republic/Germany
Schwarzach *see* Schwarzach im Pongau
109 Q7 **Schwarzach im Pongau** *var.* Schwarzach. Salzburg, NW Austria
Schwarzawa *see* Svratka
101 N14 **Schwarze Elster** ≈ E Germany
Schwarze Körös *see* Crişul Negru
108 D9 **Schwarzenburg** Bern, W Switzerland
83 D21 **Schwarzrand** ▲▲ S Namibia
101 G23 **Schwarzwald** *Eng.* Black Forest. ▲▲ SW Germany
Schwarzwasser *see* Wda
39 P7 **Schwatka Mountains** ▲▲ Alaska, USA
109 N7 **Schwaz** Tirol, W Austria
109 Y4 **Schwechat** Niederösterreich, NE Austria
109 Y4 **Schwechat** ✈ (Wien) Wien, E Austria
100 P11 **Schwedt** Brandenburg, NE Germany
101 D19 **Schweich** Rheinland-Pfalz, SW Germany
Schweidnitz *see* Świdnica
101 J18 **Schweinfurt** Bayern, SE Germany
Schweiz *see* Switzerland
100 L9 **Schwerin** Mecklenburg-Vorpommern, N Germany
Schwerin *see* Skwierzyna
100 L9 **Schweriner See** ◎ N Germany
Schwertberg *see* Świecie
101 F15 **Schwerte** Nordrhein-Westfalen, W Germany
Schwiebus *see* Świebodzin
100 P13 **Schwielochsee** ◎ NE Germany
Schwihau *see* Švihov
Schwiz *see* Schwyz
108 G8 **Schwyz** *var.* Schwiz. Schwyz, C Switzerland
108 G8 **Schwyz** *var.* Schwiz. ◈ *canton* C Switzerland
14 J11 **Schyan** ≈ Québec, SE Canada
Schyl *see* Jiu
107 I24 **Sciacca** Sicilia, Italy, C Mediterranean Sea
Sciasciamana *see* Shashemenē
107 L26 **Scicli** Sicilia, Italy, C Mediterranean Sea
97 F25 **Scilly, Isles of** *island group* SW England, UK
111 H17 **Ščinawa** *Ger.* Steinau an der Elbe. Dolnośląskie, SW Poland
Scio *see* Chíos
31 S14 **Scioto River** ≈ Ohio, N USA
36 L5 **Scipio** Utah, W USA
33 X6 **Scobey** Montana, NW USA
183 T7 **Scone** New South Wales, SE Australia
Scoresby Sound/ Scoresbysund *see* Ittoqqortoormiit
Scoresby Sund *see* Kangertittivaq
Scorno, Punta dello *see* Caprara, Punta
34 K3 **Scotia** California, W USA
47 Y14 **Scotia Plate** *tectonic feature*
47 V15 **Scotia Ridge** *undersea feature* S Atlantic Ocean
194 H2 **Scotia Sea** *sea* SW Atlantic Ocean
29 Q12 **Scotland** South Dakota, N USA
25 R5 **Scotland** Texas, SW USA
96 H11 **Scotland** *cultural region* Scotland, U K
21 W8 **Scotland Neck** North Carolina, SE USA
195 R13 **Scott Base** *NZ research station* Antarctica
10 J16 **Scott, Cape** *headland* Vancouver Island, British Columbia, SW Canada
26 I5 **Scott City** Kansas, C USA
27 Y7 **Scott City** Missouri, C USA
195 R14 **Scott Coast** *physical region* Antarctica
18 C15 **Scottdale** Pennsylvania, NE USA
195 Y11 **Scott Glacier** *glacier* Antarctica
195 Q17 **Scott Island** *island* Antarctica
26 L11 **Scott, Mount** ▲ Oklahoma, USA
32 G15 **Scott, Mount** ▲ Oregon, NW USA
34 M1 **Scott River** ≈ California, W USA
28 I13 **Scottsbluff** Nebraska, C USA
23 Q2 **Scottsboro** Alabama, S USA
31 P15 **Scottsburg** Indiana, N USA
183 P16 **Scottsdale** Tasmania, SE Australia
36 L13 **Scottsdale** Arizona, SW USA
45 O12 **Scotts Head Village** *var.* Cachacrou. S Dominica
192 L14 **Scott Shoal** *undersea feature* S Pacific Ocean
20 K7 **Scottsville** Kentucky, S USA
29 U14 **Scranton** Iowa, C USA
18 I13 **Scranton** Pennsylvania, NE USA
186 B6 **Screw** ≈ NW Papua New Guinea
29 R14 **Scribner** Nebraska, C USA
Scrobesbyrig' *see* Shrewsbury
14 I14 **Scugog** ≈ Ontario, SE Canada
14 I14 **Scugog, Lake** ◎ Ontario, SE Canada
97 N17 **Scunthorpe** E England, UK
108 K9 **Scuol** *Ger.* Schuls. Graubünden, E Switzerland
Scupi *see* Skopje
Scutari *see* Shkodër
113 K17 **Scutari, Lake** *Alb.* Liqeni i Shkodrës, *SCr.* Skadarsko Jezero. ◎ Albania/Montenegro
Scyros *see* Skýros
Scythopolis *see* Bet She'an
25 U13 **Seadrift** Texas, SW USA
21 Y4 **Seaford** *var.* Seaford City. Delaware, NE USA
Seaford City *see* Seaford
14 E15 **Seaforth** Ontario, S Canada
24 M6 **Seagraves** Texas, SW USA
9 X9 **Seal** ≈ Manitoba, C Canada
182 M10 **Sea Lake** Victoria, SE Australia
83 G26 **Seal, Cape** *headland* S South Africa
65 D26 **Sea Lion Islands** *island group* SE Falkland Islands
19 S8 **Seal Island** *island* Maine, NE USA
25 V11 **Sealy** Texas, SW USA
35 X12 **Searchlight** Nevada, W USA
27 V11 **Searcy** Arkansas, C USA
19 R7 **Searsport** Maine, NE USA
35 N10 **Seaside** California, W USA
32 F10 **Seaside** Oregon, NW USA
18 K16 **Seaside Heights** New Jersey, NE USA
32 H8 **Seattle** Washington, NW USA
32 H9 **Seattle-Tacoma** ✈ Washington, NW USA
185 J16 **Seaward Kaikoura Range** ▲▲ South Island, New Zealand
42 J9 **Sébaco** Matagalpa, W Nicaragua
19 P8 **Sebago Lake** ◎ Maine, NE USA
169 S13 **Sebangan, Teluk** *bay* Borneo, C Indonesia
169 S13 **Sebanganu, Teluk** *bay* Borneo, C Indonesia
Sebaste/Sebastia *see* Sivas
23 Y12 **Sebastian** Florida, SE USA
40 C5 **Sebastían Vizcaíno, Bahía** *bay* NW Mexico
19 R6 **Sebasticook Lake** ◎ Maine, NE USA
34 M7 **Sebastopol** California, W USA
Sebastopol *see* Sevastopol'
169 W8 **Sebatik, Pulau** *island* N Indonesia
19 R5 **Sebec Lake** ◎ Maine, NE USA
76 K12 **Sébékoro** Kayes, W Mali
Sebenico *see* Šibenik
40 G6 **Seberi, Cerro** ▲ NW Mexico
116 H11 **Sebeş** *Ger.* Mühlbach, *Hung.* Szászsebes; *prev.* Sebeşu Săsesc. Alba, W Romania
Sebes-Körös *see* Crişul Repede
Sebeşu Săsesc *see* Sebeş
31 R8 **Sebewaing** Michigan, N USA
124 F16 **Sebezh** Pskovskaya Oblast', W Russian Federation
137 N12 **Şebinkarahisar** Giresun, N Turkey
116 F11 **Sebiş** *Hung.* Borossebes. Arad, W Romania
Sebkra Azz el Matti *see* Azzel Matti, Sebkha
19 Q4 **Seboomook Lake** ◎ Maine, NE USA
74 G6 **Sebou** *var.* Sebu. ≈ N Morocco
20 I6 **Sebree** Kentucky, S USA
23 X13 **Sebring** Florida, SE USA
Sebta *see* Ceuta
Sebu *see* Sebou
169 U13 **Sebuku, Pulau** *island* N Indonesia
169 W8 **Sebuku, Teluk** *bay* Borneo, N Indonesia
106 F10 **Secchia** ≈ N Italy
10 L17 **Sechelt** British Columbia, SW Canada
56 C12 **Sechín, Río** ≈ W Peru
56 A10 **Sechura, Bahía de** *bay* NW Peru
185 A22 **Secretary Island** *island* SW New Zealand
155 I15 **Secunderābād** *var.* Sikandarabad. Andhra Pradesh, C India
57 L17 **Sécure, Río** ≈ C Bolivia
118 D10 **Seda** Telšiai, NW Lithuania
27 T5 **Sedalia** Missouri, C USA
103 R3 **Sedan** Ardennes, N France
27 P7 **Sedan** Kansas, C USA
105 N3 **Sedano** Castilla-León, N Spain
104 H10 **Seda, Ribeira de** *stream* C Portugal
185 K15 **Seddon** Marlborough, South Island, New Zealand
185 H15 **Seddonville** West Coast, South Island, New Zealand
143 U7 **Sedeh** Khorāsān-e Janūbī, E Iran
138 E11 **Sederot** Southern, S Israel
65 B23 **Sedge Island** *island* NW Falkland Islands
76 G12 **Sédhiou** SW Senegal
9 U16 **Sedley** Saskatchewan, S Canada
Sedlez *see* Siedlce
117 Q2 **Sedniv** Chernihivs'ka Oblast', N Ukraine
36 L11 **Sedona** Arizona, SW USA
Sedunum *see* Sion
118 F12 **Šeduva** Šiauliai, N Lithuania
141 Y8 **Seeb** *var.* Muscat Sīb Airport. ✈ (Masqaṭ) NE Oman
Seeb *see* As Sīb
108 M7 **Seefeld in Tirol** Tirol, W Austria
83 E22 **Seeheim Noord** Karas, S Namibia
Seeland *see* Sjælland
195 N9 **Seelig, Mount** ▲ Antarctica

◆ Country ● Country Capital ◇ Dependent Territory ○ Dependent Territory Capital ◈ Administrative Regions ✈ International Airport ▲ Mountain ▲▲ Mountain Range Volcano ≈ River ◎ Lake ⊠ Reservoir

Seeonee see Seoni
Seer see Dörgön
102 L5 **Sées** Orne, N France
101 J14 **Seesen** Niedersachsen, C Germany
Seesker Höhe see Szeska Góra
100 J10 **Seevetal** Niedersachsen, N Germany
109 V6 **Seewiesen** Steiermark, E Austria
136 J13 **Şefaatli** var. Kızılkoca. Yozgat, C Turkey
149 N3 **Sefid, Darya-ye** Pash. Āb-i-safed. ≈ N Afghanistan
148 K5 **Sefid Kūh, Selseleh-ye** Eng. Paropamisus Range. ▲ W Afghanistan
74 G6 **Sefrou** N Morocco
185 E19 **Sefton, Mount** ▲ South Island, New Zealand
171 S13 **Segaf, Kepulauan** island group E Indonesia
169 W7 **Segama, Sungai** ≈ East Malaysia
168 L9 **Segamat** Johor, Peninsular Malaysia
77 S13 **Ségbana** NE Benin
Segestica see Sisak
Segesvár see Sighişoara
171 T12 **Seget** Papua, E Indonesia
Segewold see Sigulda
124 J9 **Segezha** Respublika Kareliya, NW Russian Federation
Seghedin see Szeged
Segna see Senj
107 I16 **Segni** Lazio, C Italy
Segodunum see Rodez
105 S9 **Segorbe** País Valenciano, E Spain
76 M12 **Ségou** var. Segu. Ségou, C Mali
76 M12 **Ségou** ◈ region SW Mali
54 E8 **Segovia** Antioquia, N Colombia
105 N7 **Segovia** Castilla-León, C Spain
104 M6 **Segovia** ◈ province Castilla-León, N Spain
Segoviao Wangkí see Coco, Río
124 J9 **Segozero, Ozero** ◎ NW Russian Federation
102 J7 **Segré** Maine-et-Loire, NW France
105 U5 **Segre** ≈ NE Spain
Segu see Ségou
38 I17 **Seguam Island** island Aleutian Islands, Alaska, USA
38 I17 **Seguam Pass** strait Aleutian Islands, Alaska, USA
77 Y7 **Séguédine** Agadez, NE Niger
76 M15 **Séguéla** W Ivory Coast
25 S11 **Seguin** Texas, SW USA
38 E17 **Segula Island** island Aleutian Islands, Alaska, USA
62 K10 **Segundo, Río** ≈ C Argentina
105 Q12 **Segura** ≈ S Spain
105 P13 **Segura, Sierra de** ▲▲ S Spain
83 G18 **Sehithwa** North-West, N Botswana
154 H10 **Sehore** Madhya Pradesh, C India
186 G9 **Sehulea** Normanby Island, S Papua New Guinea
149 P15 **Sehwān** Sind, SE Pakistan
109 V8 **Seiersberg** Steiermark, SE Austria
26 L9 **Seiling** Oklahoma, C USA
103 S9 **Seille** ≈ E France
99 J20 **Seilles** Namur, SE Belgium
93 K17 **Seinäjoki** Swe. Östermyra. Länsi-Soumi, W Finland
12 B12 **Seine** ≈ Ontario, S Canada
102 M4 **Seine** ≈ N France
102 K4 **Seine, Baie de la** bay N France
Seine, Banc de la see Seine Seamount
103 O5 **Seine-et-Marne** ◈ department N France
102 L3 **Seine-Maritime** ◈ department N France
84 B14 **Seine Plain** undersea feature E Atlantic Ocean
84 B15 **Seine Seamount** var. Banc de la Seine. undersea feature E Atlantic Ocean
102 E6 **Sein, Île de** island NW France
171 Y14 **Seinma** Papua, E Indonesia
Seisbierrum see Sexbierum
109 U5 **Seitenstetten Markt** Niederösterreich, C Austria
Seiyu see Chŏnju
95 H22 **Sejerø** island E Denmark
110 P7 **Sejny** Podlaskie, NE Poland
81 G20 **Seke** Shinyanga, N Tanzania
164 L13 **Seki** Gifu, Honshū, SW Japan
161 U12 **Sekibi-sho** island China/Japan/Taiwan
165 U3 **Sekihoku-tōge** pass Hokkaidō, NE Japan
Sekondi see Sekondi-Takoradi
77 P17 **Sekondi-Takoradi** var. Sekondi. S Ghana
80 J11 **Sek'ot'a** Amhara, N Ethiopia
Sekseüil see Sakasaul'skiy
32 I9 **Selah** Washington, NW USA
168 J8 **Selangor** var. Negeri Selangor Darul Ehsan. ◈ state Peninsular Malaysia
Selānik see Thessaloníki
168 K10 **Selapanjang** Pulau Rantau, W Indonesia
167 R10 **Selaphum** Roi Et, E Thailand
171 T16 **Selaru, Pulau** island Kepulauan Tanimbar, E Indonesia
171 U13 **Selassi** Papua, E Indonesia
168 J7 **Selatan, Selat** strait Peninsular Malaysia
39 N8 **Selawik** Alaska, USA
39 N8 **Selawik Lake** ◎ Alaska, USA
171 N14 **Selayar, Selat** strait Sulawesi, C Indonesia
95 C14 **Selbjørnsfjorden** fjord S Norway
94 H8 **Selbusjøen** ◎ S Norway
97 M17 **Selby** N England, UK
29 N8 **Selby** South Dakota, N USA
21 Z4 **Selbyville** Delaware, NE USA
136 B15 **Selçuk** var. Akıncılar. İzmir, SW Turkey
39 Q13 **Seldovia** Alaska, USA
107 M18 **Sele** anc. Silarius. ≈ S Italy
83 J19 **Selebi-Phikwe** Central, E Botswana
42 B5 **Selegua, Río** ≈ W Guatemala
129 X7 **Selemdzha** ≈ SE Russian Federation
129 U7 **Selenga** Mong. Selenge Mörön. ≈ Mongolia/Russian Federation
79 I19 **Selenge** Bandundu, W Dem. Rep. Congo
162 K6 **Selenge** var. Ingettolgoy. Bulgan, N Mongolia
162 L6 **Selenge** ◈ province N Mongolia
Selenge see Hyalganat, Bulgan, Mongolia
Selenge see Ih-Uul, Hövsgöl, Mongolia
Selenge Mörön see Selenga
123 N14 **Selenginsk** Respublika Buryatiya, S Russian Federation
Selenica see Selenicë
113 K22 **Selenicë** var. Selenica. Vlorë, SW Albania
123 Q8 **Selennyakh** ≈ NE Russian Federation
100 J8 **Selenter See** ◎ N Germany
Sele Sound see Soela Väin
103 U6 **Sélestat** Ger. Schlettstadt. Bas-Rhin, NE France
Selety see Sileti
Seleucia see Silifke
92 I4 **Selfoss** Sudhurland, SW Iceland
28 M7 **Selfridge** North Dakota, N USA
76 I15 **Seli** ≈ N Sierra Leone
76 I11 **Sélibabi** var. Sélibaby. Guidimaka, S Mauritania
Sélibaby see Sélibabi
Selidovka/Selidovo see Selydove
124 I15 **Seliger, Ozero** ◎ W Russian Federation
36 J11 **Seligman** Arizona, SW USA
27 S8 **Seligman** Missouri, C USA
80 E6 **Selima Oasis** oasis N Sudan
76 L13 **Sélingué, Lac de** ⊠ S Mali
Selinoús see Kréstena
18 G14 **Selinsgrove** Pennsylvania, NE USA
Selishche see Syelishcha
124 I16 **Selizharovo** Tverskaya Oblast', W Russian Federation
94 C10 **Selje** Sogn Og Fjordane, S Norway
9 X16 **Selkirk** Manitoba, S Canada
96 K13 **Selkirk** SE Scotland, UK
96 K13 **Selkirk** cultural region SE Scotland, UK
9 O16 **Selkirk Mountains** ▲▲ British Columbia, SW Canada
193 T11 **Selkirk Rise** undersea feature SE Pacific Ocean
115 F21 **Sellasía** Pelopónnisos, S Greece
44 M9 **Selle, Pic de la** var. La Selle. ▲ SE Haiti
102 M8 **Selles-sur-Cher** Loir-et-Cher, C France
36 K16 **Sells** Arizona, SW USA
Sellye see Sal'a
23 P5 **Selma** Alabama, S USA
35 Q11 **Selma** California, W USA
20 G10 **Selmer** Tennessee, S USA
173 N17 **Sel, Pointe au** headland W Réunion
Selselehye Kuhe Vākhān see Nicholas Range
127 S2 **Selty** Udmurtskaya Respublika, NW Russian Federation
Selukwe see Shurugwi
62 L9 **Selva** Santiago del Estero, N Argentina
9 T9 **Selwyn Lake** ◎ Northwest Territories/Saskatchewan, C Canada
10 K6 **Selwyn Mountains** ▲▲ Yukon Territory, NW Canada
181 T6 **Selwyn Range** ▲▲ Queensland, C Australia
117 W8 **Selydove** var. Selidovka, Rus. Selidovo. Donets'ka Oblast', SE Ukraine
Selzaete see Zelzate
Seman see Semanit, Lumi i
168 M15 **Semangka, Teluk** bay Sumatera, SW Indonesia
113 D22 **Semanit, Lumi i** var. Seman. ≈ W Albania
169 Q16 **Semarang** var. Samarang. Jawa, C Indonesia
169 Q10 **Sematan** Sarawak, East Malaysia
171 P17 **Semau, Pulau** island S Indonesia
169 V8 **Sembakung, Sungai** ≈ Borneo, N Indonesia
79 G17 **Sembé** La Sangha, NW Congo
169 S13 **Sembulu, Danau** ◎ Borneo, N Indonesia
Semendria see Smederevo
117 R1 **Semenivka** Chernihivs'ka Oblast', N Ukraine
117 S6 **Semenivka** Rus. Semenovka. Poltavs'ka Oblast', NE Ukraine
127 O3 **Semenov** Nizhegorodskaya Oblast', W Russian Federation
Semenovka see Semenivka
169 S17 **Semeru, Gunung** var. Mahameru. ▲ Jawa, S Indonesia
Semey see Semipalatinsk
Semezhevo see Syemyezhava
126 L7 **Semiluki** Voronezhskaya Oblast', W Russian Federation
33 W16 **Seminoe Reservoir** ⊠ Wyoming, C USA
27 O11 **Seminole** Oklahoma, C USA
24 M6 **Seminole** Texas, SW USA
23 S8 **Seminole, Lake** ⊠ Florida/Georgia, SE USA
Semiozernoye see Auliyekol'
145 V9 **Semipalatinsk** Kaz. Semey. Vostochnyy Kazakhstan, E Kazakhstan
143 O9 **Semīrom** var. Samirum. Eşfahān, C Iran
38 F17 **Semisopochnoi Island** island Aleutian Islands, Alaska, USA
169 R11 **Semitau** Borneo, C Indonesia
81 E18 **Semliki** ≈ Uganda/Dem. Rep. Congo
143 P5 **Semnān** var. Samnān. Semnān, N Iran
143 Q5 **Semnān** off. Ostān-e Semnān. ◈ province N Iran
Semnān, Ostān-e see Semnān
99 K24 **Semois** ≈ SE Belgium
108 E8 **Sempacher See** ◎ C Switzerland
Sena see Vila de Sena
30 L12 **Senachwine Lake** ◎ Illinois, N USA
59 O14 **Senador Pompeu** Ceará, E Brazil
Sena Gallica see Senigallia
59 C15 **Sena Madureira** Acre, W Brazil
155 L25 **Senanayake Samudra** ◎ E Sri Lanka
83 G15 **Senanga** Western, SW Zambia
27 Y9 **Senath** Missouri, C USA
22 L2 **Senatobia** Mississippi, S USA
164 C16 **Sendai** Kagoshima, Kyūshū, SW Japan
165 Q10 **Sendai** Miyagi, Honshū, C Japan
165 Q11 **Sendai-wan** bay E Japan
101 J23 **Senden** Bayern, S Germany
154 F11 **Sendhwa** Madhya Pradesh, C India
111 H21 **Senec** Ger. Wartberg, Hung. Szenc; prev. Szempcz. Bratislavský Kraj, W Slovakia
27 P3 **Seneca** Kansas, C USA
27 R8 **Seneca** Missouri, C USA
32 K13 **Seneca** Oregon, NW USA
21 O11 **Seneca** South Carolina, SE USA
18 G11 **Seneca Lake** ◎ New York, NE USA
31 U13 **Senecaville Lake** ⊠ Ohio, N USA
76 G11 **Senegal** off. Republic of Senegal, Fr. Sénégal. ◆ republic W Africa
76 H9 **Senegal** Fr. Sénégal. ≈ W Africa
Senegal, Republic of see Senegal
31 O4 **Seney Marsh** wetland Michigan, N USA
101 P14 **Senftenberg** Brandenburg, E Germany
82 L11 **Senga Hill** Northern, NE Zambia
158 G13 **Sênggê Zangbo** ≈ W China
171 Z13 **Senggi** Papua, E Indonesia
127 R5 **Sengiley** Ul'yanovskaya Oblast', W Russian Federation
63 I19 **Senguerr, Río** ≈ S Argentina
83 J16 **Sengwa** ≈ C Zimbabwe
Senia see Senj
111 H19 **Senica** Ger. Senitz, Hung. Szenice. Trnavský Kraj, W Slovakia
Seniça see Sjenica
106 J11 **Senigallia** anc. Sena Gallica. Marche, C Italy
136 F15 **Senirkent** Isparta, SW Turkey
Senitz see Senica
112 C10 **Senj** Ger. Zengg, It. Segna; anc. Senia. Lika-Senj, NW Croatia
Senj see Örgön
92 H9 **Senja** prev. Senjen. island N Norway
Senjen see Senja
161 U12 **Senkaku-shotō** island group SW Japan
137 R12 **Şenkaya** Erzurum, NE Turkey
83 I16 **Senkobo** Southern, S Zambia
103 O4 **Senlis** Oise, N France
167 T12 **Senmonorom** Môndól Kiri, E Cambodia
80 G10 **Sennar** var. Sannār. Sinnar, C Sudan
Senno see Syanno
Senones see Sens
109 W11 **Senovo** E Slovenia
103 P6 **Sens** anc. Agendicum, Senones. Yonne, C France
Sensburg see Mrągowo
167 S11 **Sên, Stœng** ≈ C Cambodia
42 F7 **Sensuntepeque** Cabañas, NE El Salvador
112 L8 **Senta** Hung. Zenta. Vojvodina, N Serbia
Šent Andraž see Sankt Andrä
171 Y13 **Sentani, Danau** ◎ Papua, E Indonesia
28 J5 **Sentinel Butte** ▲ North Dakota, N USA
10 M13 **Sentinel Peak** ▲ British Columbia, W Canada
59 N16 **Sento Sé** Bahia, E Brazil
Šent Peter see Pivka
Št. Vid see Sankt Veit an der Glan
Seo de Urgel see La Seu d'Urgel
154 I7 **Seondha** Madhya Pradesh, C India
154 J11 **Seoni** prev. Seeonee. Madhya Pradesh, C India
Seoul see Sŏul
184 I13 **Separation Point** headland South Island, New Zealand
169 V10 **Sepasu** Borneo, N Indonesia
186 B6 **Sepik** ≈ Indonesia/Papua New Guinea
Sepone see Muang Xépôn
110 M7 **Sępopol** Ger. Schippenbeil. Warmińsko-Mazurskie, N Poland
116 F10 **Şepreuş** Hung. Seprős. Arad, W Romania
Seprős see Şepreuş
Şepşi-Sângeorz/Sepsiszentgyőrgy see Sfântu Gheorghe
15 W4 **Sept-Îles** Québec, SE Canada
105 N6 **Sepúlveda** Castilla-León, N Spain
104 K8 **Sequeros** Castilla-León, N Spain
104 L5 **Sequillo** ≈ NW Spain
32 G7 **Sequim** Washington, NW USA
35 S11 **Sequoia National Park** national park California, W USA
137 Q14 **Şerafettin Dağları** ▲▲ E Turkey
127 N10 **Serafimovich** Volgogradskaya Oblast', SW Russian Federation
171 Q10 **Serai** Sulawesi, N Indonesia
99 K19 **Seraing** Liège, E Belgium
Sêraitang see Baima
Serajgonj see Shirajganj Ghat
Serakhs see Sarahs
171 W13 **Serami** Papua, E Indonesia
Seram, Laut see Ceram Sea
Serampore/Serampur see Shrīrāmpur
171 S13 **Seram, Pulau** var. Serang, Eng. Ceram. island Maluku, E Indonesia
169 N15 **Serang** Jawa, C Indonesia
Serang see Seram, Pulau
169 P9 **Serasan, Pulau** island Kepulauan Natuna, W Indonesia
169 P9 **Serasan, Selat** strait Indonesia/Malaysia
112 M13 **Serbia** off. Federal Republic of Serbia; prev. Yugoslavia, SCr. Jugoslavija. ◆ federal republic SE Europe
112 M12 **Serbia** Ger. Serbien, Serb. Srbija. ◈ republic Serbia
Serbia, Federal Republic of see Serbia
Serbien see Serbia
Sercq see Sark
146 D12 **Serdar** prev. Rus. Gyzyrlabat, Kizyl-Arvat. Balkan Welaýaty, W Turkmenistan
Serdica see Sofiya
127 O7 **Serdobsk** Penzenskaya Oblast', W Russian Federation
145 X9 **Serebryansk** Vostochnyy Kazakhstan, E Kazakhstan
123 Q12 **Serebryanyy Bor** Respublika Sakha (Yakutiya), NE Russian Federation
111 H20 **Sered'** Hung. Szered. Trnavský Kraj, W Slovakia
117 S1 **Seredyna-Buda** Sums'ka Oblast', NE Ukraine
118 E13 **Seredžius** Tauragė, C Lithuania
136 H14 **Şereflikoçhisar** Ankara, C Turkey
106 D7 **Seregno** Lombardia, N Italy
103 P7 **Serein** ≈ C France
168 K9 **Seremban** Negeri Sembilan, Peninsular Malaysia
81 H20 **Serengeti Plain** plain N Tanzania
82 K13 **Serenje** Central, E Zambia
Seres see Sérres
116 J5 **Seret** ≈ W Ukraine
Seret/Sereth see Siret
115 I21 **Serfopoúla** island Kykládes, Greece, Aegean Sea
127 P4 **Sergach** Nizhegorodskaya Oblast', W Russian Federation
29 S13 **Sergeant Bluff** Iowa, C USA
163 P7 **Sergelen** Dornod, NE Mongolia
Sergelen see Tuvshinshiree
168 H8 **Sergeulangit, Pegunungan** ▲▲ Sumatera, NW Indonesia
122 L5 **Sergeya Kirova, Ostrova** island N Russian Federation
Sergeyevichi see Syarhyeyevichy
145 O7 **Sergeyevka** Severnyy Kazakhstan, N Kazakhstan
Sergiopol see Ayagoz
59 P16 **Sergipe** off. Estado de Sergipe. ◈ state E Brazil
Sergipe, Estado de see Sergipe
126 L3 **Sergiyev Posad** Moskovskaya Oblast', W Russian Federation
124 K5 **Sergozero, Ozero** ◎ NW Russian Federation
146 J17 **Serhetabat** prev. Rus. Gushgy, Kushka. Mary Welaýaty, S Turkmenistan
169 Q10 **Serian** Sarawak, East Malaysia
115 I21 **Sérifos** anc. Seriphos. island Kykládes, Greece, Aegean Sea
115 I21 **Sérifou, Stenó** strait SE Greece
136 F16 **Serik** Antalya, SW Turkey
106 E7 **Serio** ≈ N Italy
Seriphos see Sérifos
Serir Tibesti see Sarīr Tībistī
Sêrkog see Sêrtar
127 S5 **Sernovodsk** Samarskaya Oblast', W Russian Federation
127 R2 **Sernur** Respublika Mariy El, W Russian Federation
110 M11 **Serock** Mazowieckie, C Poland
61 B18 **Serodino** Santa Fe, C Argentina
Seroei see Serui
105 P14 **Serón** Andalucía, S Spain
99 E14 **Serooskerke** Zeeland, SW Netherlands
105 T6 **Serós** Cataluña, NE Spain
122 G10 **Serov** Sverdlovskaya Oblast', C Russian Federation
83 I19 **Serowe** Central, SE Botswana
104 H13 **Serpa** Beja, S Portugal
Serpa Pinto see Menongue
182 A4 **Serpentine Lakes** salt lake South Australia
45 T15 **Serpent's Mouth, The** Sp. Boca de la Serpiente. strait Trinidad and Tobago/Venezuela
Serpiente, Boca de la see Serpent's Mouth, The
126 K4 **Serpukhov** Moskovskaya Oblast', W Russian Federation
60 K13 **Serra do Mar** ▲▲
Sérrai see Sérres
107 N22 **Serra San Bruno** Calabria, SW Italy
103 S14 **Serres** Hautes-Alpes, SE France
114 H13 **Sérres** var. Seres; prev. Sérrai. Kentrikí Makedonía, NE Greece
62 J9 **Serrezuela** Córdoba, C Argentina
59 O16 **Serrinha** Bahia, E Brazil
59 M19 **Serro** var. Sêrro. Minas Gerais, NE Brazil
Sêrro see Serro
Sert see Siirt
104 H9 **Sertã** var. Sertá. Castelo Branco, C Portugal
Sertá see Sertã
60 L8 **Sertãozinho** São Paulo, S Brazil
160 F7 **Sêrtar** var. Sêrkog. Sichuan, C China
171 W13 **Serui** prev. Seroei. Papua, E Indonesia
83 J19 **Serule** Central, E Botswana
169 S12 **Seruyan, Sungai** var. Sungai Pembuang. ≈ Borneo, N Indonesia
115 E14 **Sérvia** Dytikí Makedonía, N Greece
160 E7 **Sêrxü** var. Jugar. Sichuan, C China
123 R13 **Seryshevo** Amurskaya Oblast', SE Russian Federation
Sesana see Sežana
169 V8 **Sesayap, Sungai** ≈ Borneo, N Indonesia
Sesdlets see Siedlce
79 N17 **Sese** Orientale, N Dem. Rep. Congo
81 F18 **Sese Islands** island group S Uganda
83 H16 **Sesheke** var. Sesheko. Western, SE Zambia
Sesheko see Sesheke
106 C8 **Sesia** anc. Sessites. ≈ NW Italy
104 F11 **Sesimbra** Setúbal, S Portugal
115 N22 **Seskliό** island Dodekánisa, Greece, Aegean Sea
30 L16 **Sesser** Illinois, N USA
Sessites see Sesia
106 G11 **Sesto Fiorentino** Toscana, C Italy
106 E7 **Sesto San Giovanni** Lombardia, N Italy
106 A8 **Sestriere** Piemonte, NE Italy
106 D10 **Sestri Levante** Liguria, NW Italy
107 C20 **Sestu** Sardegna, Italy, C Mediterranean Sea
112 E8 **Sesvete** Zagreb, N Croatia
118 G12 **Šeta** Kaunas, C Lithuania
Setabis see Xátiva
165 Q4 **Setana** Hokkaidō, NE Japan
103 Q16 **Sète** prev. Cette. Hérault, S France
58 J11 **Sete Ilhas** Amapá, NE Brazil
59 L20 **Sete Lagoas** Minas Gerais, NE Brazil
60 G10 **Sete Quedas, Ilha das** island S Brazil
92 I10 **Setermoen** Troms, N Norway
95 E17 **Setesdal** valley S Norway
43 W16 **Setetule, Cerro** ▲ SE Panama
21 Q5 **Seth** West Virginia, NE USA
Setia see Sezze
74 K5 **Sétif** var. Stif. N Algeria
164 L5 **Seto** Aichi, Honshū, SW Japan
164 G13 **Seto-naikai** Eng. Inland Sea. sea S Japan
165 V16 **Setouchi** var. Setoushi. Kagoshima, Amami-Ō-shima, SW Japan
Setoushi see Setouchi
74 F6 **Settat** W Morocco
79 D20 **Setté Cama** Ogooué-Maritime, SW Gabon
9 W13 **Setting Lake** ◎ Manitoba, C Canada
97 L16 **Settle** N England, UK
189 Y12 **Settlement** E Wake Island
104 F11 **Setúbal** Eng. Saint Ubes, Saint Yves. Setúbal, W Portugal
104 F11 **Setúbal** ◈ district S Portugal
104 F12 **Setúbal, Baía de** bay W Portugal
Setul see Satun
12 B10 **Seul, Lac** ◎ Ontario, S Canada
103 R8 **Seurre** Côte d'Or, C France
137 U11 **Sevan** C Armenia
137 V12 **Sevana Lich** Eng. Lake Sevan, Rus. Ozero Sevan. ◎ E Armenia
Sevan, Lake/Sevan, Ozero see Sevana Lich
77 N11 **Sévaré** Mopti, C Mali
117 S14 **Sevastopol'** Eng. Sebastopol. Respublika Krym, S Ukraine
25 R14 **Seven Sisters** Texas, SW USA
10 K13 **Seven Sisters Peaks** ▲ British Columbia, SW Canada
99 M15 **Sevenum** Limburg, SE Netherlands
103 P14 **Séverac-le-Château** Aveyron, S France
14 H13 **Severn** ≈ Ontario, S Canada
97 L21 **Severn** Wel. Hafren. ≈ England/Wales, UK
125 O11 **Severnaya Dvina** var. Northern Dvina. ≈ NW Russian Federation
127 N16 **Severnaya Osetiya-Alaniya, Respublika** Eng. North Ossetia; prev. Respublika Severnaya Osetiya, Severo-Osetinskaya SSR. ◈ autonomous republic SW Russian Federation
Severnaya Osetiya, Respublika see Severnaya Osetiya-Alaniya, Respublika
122 M5 **Severnaya Zemlya** var. Nicholas II Land. island group N Russian Federation
127 T5 **Severnoye** Orenburgskaya Oblast', W Russian Federation
35 S3 **Severn Troughs Range** ▲▲ Nevada, W USA
125 W3 **Severnyy** Respublika Komi, NW Russian Federation
144 I13 **Severnyy Chink Ustyurta** ▲ W Kazakhstan
125 Q13 **Severnyye Uvaly** var. Northern Ural Hills. hill range NW Russian Federation
145 O6 **Severnyy Kazakhstan** off. Severo-Kazakhstanskaya Oblast', var. North Kazakhstan, Kaz. Soltūstik Qazaqstan Oblysy. ◈ province N Kazakhstan
125 V9 **Severnyy Ural** ▲▲ NW Russian Federation
Severo-Alichurskiy Khrebet see Alichuri Shimolí, Qatorkŭhi
123 N12 **Severobaykal'sk** Respublika Buryatiya, S Russian Federation
Severodonetsk see Syeverodonets'k
124 M8 **Severodvinsk** prev. Molotov, Sudostroy. Arkhangel'skaya Oblast', NW Russian Federation
Severo-Kazakhstanskaya Oblast' see Severnyy Kazakhstan
123 U11 **Severo-Kuril'sk** Sakhalinskaya Oblast', SE Russian Federation
124 J3 **Severomorsk** Murmanskaya Oblast', NW Russian Federation
Severo-Osetinskaya SSR see Severnaya Osetiya-Alaniya, Respublika
122 M7 **Severo-Sibirskaya Nizmennost'** var. North Siberian Plain, Eng. North Siberian Lowland. lowlands N Russian Federation
122 G10 **Severoural'sk** Sverdlovskaya Oblast', C Russian Federation
122 L11 **Severo-Yeniseyskiy** Krasnoyarskiy Kray, C Russian Federation
122 J12 **Seversk** Tomskaya Oblast', C Russian Federation
126 M11 **Severskiy Donets** Ukr. Sivers'kyy Donets'. ≈ Russian Federation/Ukraine see also Sivers'kyy Donets'
Severskiy Donets see Sivers'kyy Donets'
92 M9 **Sevettijärvi** Lappi, N Finland
36 M5 **Sevier Bridge Reservoir** ⊠ Utah, W USA
36 J4 **Sevier Desert** plain Utah, W USA
36 J5 **Sevier Lake** ◎ Utah, W USA
21 N9 **Sevierville** Tennessee, S USA
104 J14 **Sevilla** Eng. Seville; anc. Hispalis. Andalucía, SW Spain
104 J13 **Sevilla** ◈ province Andalucía, SW Spain
Sevilla de Niefang see Niefang
43 O16 **Sevilla, Isla** island SW Panama
Seville see Sevilla
114 J9 **Sevlievo** Gabrovo, N Bulgaria
Sevluš/Sevlyush see Vynohradiv
109 V11 **Sevnica** Ger. Lichtenwald. E Slovenia
162 J11 **Sevrey** var. Saynshand. Ömnögovĭ, S Mongolia
126 I7 **Sevsk** Bryanskaya Oblast', W Russian Federation
76 J15 **Sewa** ≈ E Sierra Leone
39 R12 **Seward** Alaska, USA
29 R15 **Seward** Nebraska, C USA
10 G8 **Seward Glacier** glacier Yukon Territory, W Canada
197 Q3 **Seward Peninsula** peninsula Alaska, USA
Seward's Folly see Alaska
62 H12 **Sewell** Libertador, C Chile
98 K5 **Sexbierum** Fris. Seisbierrum. Friesland, N Netherlands
9 O13 **Sexsmith** Alberta, W Canada
41 W13 **Seybaplaya** Campeche, SE Mexico
173 N6 **Seychelles** off. Republic of Seychelles. ◆ republic W Indian Ocean
67 Z9 **Seychelles** island group NE Seychelles
173 N6 **Seychelles Bank** var. Le Banc des Seychelles. undersea feature W Indian Ocean
Seychelles, Le Banc des see Seychelles Bank
Seychelles, Republic of see Seychelles
172 H17 **Seychellois, Morne** ▲ Mahé, NE Seychelles
92 L2 **Seydhisfjördhur** Austurland, E Iceland
146 J12 **Seýdi** Rus. Seydi; prev. Neftezavodsk. Lebap Welaýaty, E Turkmenistan
136 G16 **Seydişehir** Konya, SW Turkey
136 J13 **Seyfe Gölü** ◎ C Turkey
Seyhan see Adana
136 K16 **Seyhan Barajı** ⊠ S Turkey
136 K17 **Seyhan Nehri** ≈ S Turkey
136 F13 **Seyitgazi** Eskişehir, W Turkey
126 J7 **Seym** ≈ W Russian Federation
117 S3 **Seym** ≈ N Ukraine
123 T9 **Seymchan** Magadanskaya Oblast', E Russian Federation
114 N12 **Seymen** Tekirdağ, NW Turkey
183 O11 **Seymour** Victoria, SE Australia
83 I25 **Seymour** Eastern Cape, S South Africa
29 W16 **Seymour** Iowa, C USA
27 U7 **Seymour** Missouri, C USA
25 Q5 **Seymour** Texas, SW USA
114 M12 **Şeytan Deresi** ≈ NW Turkey
109 S12 **Sežana** It. Sesana. SW Slovenia
103 P5 **Sézanne** Marne, N France
107 I16 **Sezze** anc. Setia. Lazio, C Italy
Sfákia see Chóra Sfakíon
115 D21 **Sfaktiría** island S Greece
116 J11 **Sfântu Gheorghe** Ger. Sankt-Georgen, Hung. Sepsiszentgyőrgy; prev. Şepşi-Sângeorz, Sfintu Gheorghe. Covasna, C Romania
117 N13 **Sfântu Gheorghe, Braţul** var. Gheorghe Braţul. ≈ E Romania
75 N6 **Sfax** Ar. Şafāqis. E Tunisia
75 N6 **Sfax** ✈ E Tunisia
Sfintu Gheorghe see Sfântu Gheorghe
98 H13 **'s-Gravendeel** Zuid-Holland, SW Netherlands
98 F11 **'s-Gravenhage** var. Den Haag, Eng. The Hague, Fr. La Haye. ● (Netherlands-seat of government) Zuid-Holland, W Netherlands
98 G12 **'s-Gravenzande** Zuid-Holland, W Netherlands
Shaan/Shaanxi Sheng see Shaanxi
159 X11 **Shaanxi** var. Shaan, Shaanxi Sheng, Shan-hsi, Shenshi, Shensi. ◈ province C China
Shaartuz see Shahrtuz
Shaba see Katanga
Shabani see Zvishavane
81 N17 **Shabeellaha Dhexe** off. Gobolka Shabeellaha Dhexe. ◈ region E Somalia
Shabeellaha Dhexe, Gobolka see Shabeellaha Dhexe
81 L17 **Shabeellaha Hoose** off. Gobolka Shabeellaha Hoose. ◈ region S Somalia
Shabeellaha Hoose, Gobolka see Shabeellaha Hoose
Shabeelle, Webi see Shebeli
114 O7 **Shabla** Dobrich, NE Bulgaria
114 O7 **Shabla, Nos** headland NE Bulgaria
13 N9 **Shabogama Lake** ◎ Newfoundland and Labrador, E Canada
79 N20 **Shabunda** Sud Kivu, E Dem. Rep. Congo
141 Q15 **Shabwah** C Yemen
158 F8 **Shache** var. Yarkant. Xinjiang Uygur Zizhiqu, NW China
Shacheng see Huailai
195 R12 **Shackleton Coast** physical region Antarctica
195 Z10 **Shackleton Ice Shelf** ice shelf Antarctica

◆ Country
● Country Capital
◇ Dependent Territory
○ Dependent Territory Capital
◈ Administrative Regions
✈ International Airport
▲ Mountain
▲▲ Mountain Range
Volcano
≈ River
◎ Lake
⊠ Reservoir

Shaddādī see Ash Shadādah
28 K7 **Shadehill Reservoir** ▣ South Dakota, N USA
122 G11 **Shadrinsk** Kurganskaya Oblast', C Russian Federation
31 O12 **Shafer, Lake** ▣ Indiana, N USA
35 R13 **Shafter** California, W USA
24 J11 **Shafter** Texas, SW USA
97 L23 **Shaftesbury** S England, UK
185 F22 **Shag** ⌇ South Island, New Zealand
145 V9 **Shagan** ⌇ E Kazakhstan
39 O11 **Shageluk** Alaska, USA
122 K14 **Shagonar** Respublika Tyva, S Russian Federation
185 F22 **Shag Point** *headland* South Island, New Zealand
144 J12 **Shagyray, Plato** *plain* SW Kazakhstan
Shāhābād see Eslāmābād
168 K9 **Shah Alam** Selangor, Peninsular Malaysia
117 O12 **Shahany, Ozero** ◎ SW Ukraine
138 H9 **Shahbā'** *anc.* Philippopolis. As Suwaydā', S Syria
Shahbān see Ad Dayr
149 P17 **Shāhbandar** Sind, SE Pakistan
149 P13 **Shāhdād Kot** Sind, SW Pakistan
143 T10 **Shahdād, Namakzār-e** *salt pan* E Iran
149 Q15 **Shāhdādpur** Sind, SE Pakistan
154 K10 **Shahdol** Madhya Pradesh, C India
161 N7 **Sha He** ⌇ C China
Shahepu see Linze
153 N13 **Shāhganj** Uttar Pradesh, N India
152 C11 **Shāhgarh** Rājasthān, NW India
Sha Hi see Orūmīyeh, Daryācheh-ye
Shāhī see Qā'emshahr
139 Q6 **Shāhīmah** *var.* Shahma. C Iraq
Shāhjahanabad see Delhi
152 L11 **Shāhjahānpur** Uttar Pradesh, N India
Shahma see Shāhīmah
149 U7 **Shāhpur** Punjab, E Pakistan
Shāhpur see Shāhpur Chākar
152 G13 **Shāhpura** Rājasthān, N India
149 Q15 **Shāhpur Chākar** *var.* Shāhpur. Sind, SE Pakistan
148 M5 **Shahrak** Ghowr, C Afghanistan
143 Q11 **Shahr-e Bābak** Kermān, C Iran
143 N8 **Shahr-e Kord** *var.* Shahr Kord. Chahār MaḨall va Bakhtiārī, C Iran
143 O9 **Shahreẓā** *var.* Qomisheh, Qumisheh, Shahriza; *prev.* Qomsheh. Eṣfahān, C Iran
147 S10 **Shahrikhon** *Rus.* Shakhrikhan. Andijon Viloyati, E Uzbekistan
147 P11 **Shahriston** *Rus.* Shakhristan. NW Tajikistan
Shahriza see Shahreẓā
Shahr-i-Zabul see Zābol
Shahr Kord see Shahr-e Kord
147 P14 **Shahrtuz** *Rus.* Shaartuz. SW Tajikistan
143 Q4 **Shāhrūd** *prev.* Emāmrūd, Emāmshahr. Semnān, N Iran
Shahsavār/Shahsawar see Tonekābon
Shaidara see Step' Nardara
Shaikh Ābid see Shaykh 'Ābid
Shaikh Fāris see Shaykh Fāris
Shaikh Najm see Shaykh Najm
138 K5 **Shā'īr, Jabal** ▲ C Syria
154 G10 **Shājāpur** Madhya Pradesh, C India
80 J8 **Shakal, Ras** *headland* NE Sudan
83 G17 **Shakawe** North West, NW Botswana
Shakhdarinskiy Khrebet see Shokhdara, Qatorkŭhi
Shakhrikhan see Shahrikhon
Shakhrisabz see Sharixon
Shakhristan see Shahriston
117 X8 **Shakhtars'k** *Rus.* Shakhtërsk. Donets'ka Oblast', SE Ukraine
Shakhtërsk see Shakhtars'k
145 R10 **Shakhtinsk** Karaganda, C Kazakhstan
126 L11 **Shakhty** Rostovskaya Oblast', SW Russian Federation
127 P2 **Shakhun'ya** Nizhegorodskaya Oblast', W Russian Federation
77 S15 **Shaki** Oyo, W Nigeria
81 J15 **Shakiso** Oromo, C Ethiopia
117 X8 **Shakmars'k** Donets'ka Oblast', E Ukraine
29 V9 **Shakopee** Minnesota, N USA
165 R3 **Shakotan-misaki** *headland* Hokkaidō, NE Japan
39 N9 **Shaktoolik** Alaska, USA
81 J14 **Shala Hāyk'** ◎ C Ethiopia
124 M10 **Shalakusha** Arkhangel'skaya Oblast', NW Russian Federation
145 U8 **Shalday** Pavlodar, NE Kazakhstan
127 P16 **Shali** Chechenskaya Respublika, SW Russian Federation
141 W12 **Shalīm** *var.* Shelim. S Oman
Shaliuhe see Gangca
144 K12 **Shalkar** *var.* Chelkar. Aktyubinsk, W Kazakhstan
144 F9 **Shalkar, Ozero** *prev* Chelkar Ozero. ◎ W Kazakhstan
21 V12 **Shallotte** North Carolina, SE USA
25 N5 **Shallowater** Texas, SW USA
124 K11 **Shal'skiy** Respublika Kareliya, NW Russian Federation
160 F9 **Shaluli Shan** ▲▲ C China
81 F22 **Shama** ⌇ C Tanzania
9 Z11 **Shamattawa** Manitoba, C Canada
12 F8 **Shamattawa** ⌇ Ontario, C Canada
Shām, Bādiyat ash see Syrian Desert
Shamiya see Ash Shāmīyah
141 X8 **Shām, Jabal ash** *var.* Jebel Sham. ▲ NW Oman
Sham, Jebel see Shām, Jabal ash
Shamkhor see Şämkir
18 G14 **Shamokin** Pennsylvania, NE USA
25 P2 **Shamrock** Texas, SW USA
Sha'nabī, Jabal ash see Chambi, Jebel
139 Y12 **Shanāwah** E Iraq
Shancheng see Taining
159 T8 **Shandan** Gansu, N China
Shandī see Shendi
161 Q5 **Shandong** *var.* Lu, Shandong Sheng, Shantung. ◆ *province* E China
161 R4 **Shandong Bandao** *var.* Shantung Peninsula. *peninsula* E China
Shandong Sheng see Shandong
139 U8 **Shandrūkh** E Iraq
83 J17 **Shangani** ⌇ W Zimbabwe
161 O15 **Shangchuan Dao** *island* S China
Shangchuankou see Minhe
163 P12 **Shangdu** Nei Mongol Zizhiqu, N China
161 O11 **Shanggao** *var.* Aoyang. Jiangxi, S China
161 S8 **Shanghai** *var.* Shang-hai. Shanghai Shi, E China
161 S8 **Shanghai Shi** *var.* Hu, Shanghai. ◆ *municipality* E China
161 P13 **Shanghang** Fujian, SE China
160 K14 **Shanglin** *var.* Dafeng. Guangxi Zhuangzu Zizhiqu, S China
160 L7 **Shangluo** *var.* Shangxian. Shaanxi, C China
160 L7 **Shangluo** *var.* Shangxian, Shangzhou. Shaanxi, C China
83 G15 **Shangombo** Western, W Zambia
Shangpai/Shangpaihe see Feixi
161 O6 **Shangqiu** *var.* Zhuji. Henan, C China
161 Q10 **Shangrao** Jiangxi, S China
Shangxian see Shangluo
Shangxian see Shangluo
161 S9 **Shangyu** *var.* Baiguan. Zhejiang, SE China
163 X9 **Shangzhi** Heilongjiang, NE China
Shangzhou see Shangluo
Shanhe see Zhengning
163 W9 **Shanhetun** Heilongjiang, NE China
Shan-hsi see Shaanxi, China
Shan-hsi see Shanxi, China
159 O6 **Shankou** Xinjiang Uygur Zizhiqu, W China
184 M13 **Shannon** Manawatu-Wanganui, North Island, New Zealand
97 C17 **Shannon** *Ir.* An tSionainn. ⌇ W Ireland
97 B19 **Shannon** ✈ W Ireland
167 N6 **Shan Plateau** *plateau* E Myanmar (Burma)
Shanshan see Piqan
158 M6 **Shanshan** *var.* Piqan. Xinjiang Uygur Zizhiqu, NW China
Shansi see Shanxi
167 N5 **Shan State** ◆ *state* E Myanmar (Burma)
Shantar Islands see Shantarskiye Ostrova
123 S12 **Shantarskiye Ostrova** *Eng.* Shantar Islands. *island group* E Russian Federation
161 Q14 **Shantou** *var.* Shan-t'ou, Swatow. Guangdong, S China
Shan-t'ou see Shantou
Shantung see Shandong
Shantung Peninsula see Shandong Bandao
163 O14 **Shanxi** *var.* Jin, Shan-hsi, Shansi, Shanxi Sheng. ◆ *province* C China
161 P6 **Shanxian** *var.* Shan Xian. Shandong, E China
Shan Xian see Sanmenxia
Shan Xian see Shanxian
Shanxi Sheng see Shanxi
160 L7 **Shanyang** Shaanxi, C China
151 N13 **Shanyin** *var.* Daiyue. Shanxi, C China E Asia
161 O13 **Shaoguan** *var.* Shao-kuan, *Cant.* Kukong; *prev.* Ch'u-chiang. Guangdong, S China
Shao-kuan see Shaoguan
161 Q11 **Shaowu** Fujian, SE China
161 S9 **Shaoxing** Zhejiang, SE China
160 M12 **Shaoyang** *var.* Tangdukou. Hunan, S China
160 M11 **Shaoyang** *var.* Baoqing, Shao-yang; *prev.* Pao-king. Hunan, S China
Shao-yang see Shaoyang
96 K5 **Shapinsay** *island* NE Scotland, UK
125 S4 **Shapkina** ⌇ NW Russian Federation
Shāpūr see Salmās
158 M4 **Shaqiuhe** Xinjiang Uygur Zizhiqu, W China
139 T2 **Shaqlāwa** *var.* Shaqlāwah. E Iraq
Shaqlāwah see Shaqlāwa
138 I8 **Shaqqā** As Suwaydā', S Syria
141 P7 **Shaqrā'** Ar Riyāḍ, C Saudi Arabia
Shaqrā see Shuqrah
145 W10 **Shar** *var.* Charsk. Vostochnyy Kazakhstan, E Kazakhstan
149 O6 **Sharan** Dāikondī, SE Afghanistan
149 Q7 **Sharan** *var.* Zareh Sharan. Paktīkā, E Afghanistan
Sharaqpur see Sharqpur
Sharbaqty see Shcherbakty
141 X12 **Sharbatāt** S Oman
Sharbatāt, Ra's see Sharbithāt, Ras
141 X12 **Sharbithāt, Ras** *var.* Ra's Sharbatāt. *headland* S Oman
14 K14 **Sharbot Lake** Ontario, SE Canada
145 P17 **Shardara** *var.* Chardara. Yuzhnyy Kazakhstan, S Kazakhstan
Shardara Dalasy see Step' Nardara
162 F8 **Sharga** Govĭ-Altay, W Mongolia
Sharga see Tsagaan-Uul
116 M7 **Sharhorod** Vinnyts'ka Oblast', C Ukraine
Sharhulsan see Mandal-Ovoo
165 V3 **Shari** Hokkaidō, NE Japan
Shari see Chari
139 T6 **Shārī, Buḩayrat** ◎ C Iraq
147 N12 **Sharixon** *Rus.* Shakhrisabz. Qashqadaryo Viloyati, S Uzbekistan
Sharjah see Ash Shāriqah
118 K12 **Sharkawshchyna** *var.* Sharkowshchyna, *Pol.* Szarkowszczyzna, *Rus.* Sharkovshchina. Vitsyebskaya Voblasts', NW Belarus
180 G9 **Shark Bay** *bay* Western Australia
141 Y9 **Sharkh** E Oman
Sharkovshchina/ Sharkowshchyna see Sharkawshchyna
127 U6 **Sharlyk** Orenburgskaya Oblast', W Russian Federation
Sharm ash Shaykh see Sharm el Sheikh
75 Y9 **Sharm el Sheikh** *var.* Ofiral, Sharm ash Shaykh. E Egypt
18 B13 **Sharon** Pennsylvania, NE USA
26 H4 **Sharon Springs** Kansas, C USA
31 Q14 **Sharonville** Ohio, N USA
Sharourah see Sharūrah
29 O10 **Sharpe, Lake** ▣ South Dakota, N USA
Sharqī, Al Jabal ash/Sharqi, Jebel esh see Anti-Lebanon
Sharqīyah, Al Minṭaqah ash see Ash Sharqīyah
138 I6 **Sharqīyat an Nabk, Jabal** ▲▲ W Syria
149 W8 **Sharqpur** *var.* Sharaqpur. Punjab, E Pakistan
141 Q13 **Sharūrah** *var.* Sharourah. Najrān, S Saudi Arabia
125 O14 **Shar'ya** Kostromskaya Oblast', NW Russian Federation
145 V15 **Sharyn** *var.* Charyn. ⌇ SE Kazakhstan
Sharyn see Charyn
83 J18 **Shashe** Central, NE Botswana
83 J18 **Shashe** *var.* Shashi. ⌇ Botswana/Zimbabwe
81 J14 **Shashemenē** *var.* Shashemenne, Shashhamana, *It.* Sciasciamana. Oromo, C Ethiopia
Shashemenne/Shashhamana see Shashemenē
Shashi see Shashe
Shashi/Sha-shih/Shasi see Jingzhou, Hubei
35 N3 **Shasta Lake** ▣ California, W USA
35 N2 **Shasta, Mount** ▲ California, W USA
127 O4 **Shatki** Nizhegorodskaya Oblast', W Russian Federation
Shatlyk see Şatlyk
Shatra see Ash Shaṭrah
119 K17 **Shatsk** *Rus.* Shatsk. Minskaya Voblasts', C Belarus
127 N5 **Shatsk** Ryazanskaya Oblast', W Russian Federation
26 J9 **Shattuck** Oklahoma, C USA
145 P16 **Shaul'der** Yuzhnyy Kazakhstan, S Kazakhstan
9 S17 **Shaunavon** Saskatchewan, S Canada
Shavat see Shovot
158 K4 **Shawan** Xinjiang Uygur Zizhiqu, NW China
14 G12 **Shawanaga** Ontario, S Canada
30 M6 **Shawano** Wisconsin, N USA
30 M6 **Shawano Lake** ◎ Wisconsin, N USA
15 P10 **Shawinigan** *prev.* Shawinigan Falls. Québec, SE Canada
Shawinigan Falls see Shawinigan
15 P10 **Shawinigan-Sud** Québec, SE Canada
138 J5 **Shawmarīyah, Jabal ash** ▲▲ C Syria
27 O11 **Shawnee** Oklahoma, C USA
14 K12 **Shawville** Québec, SE Canada
145 Q16 **Shayan** *var.* Chayan. Yuzhnyy Kazakhstan, S Kazakhstan
Shaykh see Ash Shakk
139 W9 **Shaykh 'Ābid** *var.* Shaikh Ābid. E Iraq
139 Y10 **Shaykh Fāris** *var.* Shaikh Fāris. E Iraq
139 T7 **Shaykh Ḩātim** E Iraq
Shaykh, Jabal ash see Hermon, Mount
139 X10 **Shaykh Najm** *var.* Shaikh Najm. E Iraq
139 W9 **Shaykh Sa'd** E Iraq
147 T14 **Shazud** SE Tajikistan
119 N18 **Shchadryn** *Rus.* Shchedrin. Homyel'skaya Voblasts', SE Belarus
119 H18 **Shchara** ⌇ SW Belarus
Shchedrin see Shchadryn
Shcheglovsk see Kemerovo
126 K5 **Shchëkino** Tul'skaya Oblast', W Russian Federation
125 S7 **Shchel'yayur** Respublika Komi, NW Russian Federation
145 U8 **Shcherbakty** *Kaz.* Sharbaqty. Pavlodar, E Kazakhstan
126 K7 **Shchigry** Kurskaya Oblast', W Russian Federation
Shchitkovichi see Shchytkavichy
117 Q2 **Shchors** Chernihivs'ka Oblast', N Ukraine
117 T8 **Shchors'k** Dnipropetrovs'ka Oblast', E Ukraine
Shchuchin see Shchuchyn
145 Q7 **Shchuchinsk** *prev.* Shchuchye. Akmola, N Kazakhstan
Shchuchye see Shchuchinsk
119 G16 **Shchuchyn** *Pol.* Szczuczyn Nowogródzki, *Rus.* Shchuchin. Hrodzyenskaya Voblasts', W Belarus
119 K17 **Shchytkavichy** *Rus.* Shchitkovichi. Minskaya Voblasts', C Belarus
122 J13 **Shebalino** Respublika Altay, S Russian Federation
126 J9 **Shebekino** Belgorodskaya Oblast', W Russian Federation
Shebelē Wenz, Wabē see Shebeli
81 L14 **Shebeli** *Amh.* Wabē Shebelē Wenz, *It.* Scebeli, *Som.* Webi Shabeelle. ⌇ Ethiopia/Somalia
113 M20 **Shebenikut, Maja e** ▲ E Albania
149 N2 **Sheberghān** *var.* Shibarghān, Shiberghan, Shiberghān. Jowzjān, N Afghanistan
144 F14 **Shebir** Mangistau, SW Kazakhstan
31 N8 **Sheboygan** Wisconsin, N USA
77 X15 **Shebshi Mountains** *var.* Schebschi Mountains. ▲▲ E Nigeria
Shechem see Nablus
Shedadi see Ash Shadādah
13 P14 **Shediac** New Brunswick, SE Canada
126 L15 **Shedok** Krasnodarskiy Kray, SW Russian Federation
80 N13 **Sheekh** Togdheer, N Somalia
38 M11 **Sheenjek River** ⌇ Alaska, USA
96 D13 **Sheep Haven** *Ir.* Cuan na gCaorach. *inlet* N Ireland
35 X10 **Sheep Range** ▲▲ Nevada, W USA
98 M13 **'s-Heerenberg** Gelderland, E Netherlands
97 P22 **Sheerness** SE England, UK
13 Q15 **Sheet Harbour** Nova Scotia, SE Canada
185 H18 **Sheffield** Canterbury, South Island, New Zealand
97 M18 **Sheffield** N England, UK
23 O2 **Sheffield** Alabama, S USA
29 V12 **Sheffield** Iowa, C USA
25 N10 **Sheffield** Texas, SW USA
63 H22 **Shehuen, Río** ⌇ S Argentina
Shekhem see Nablus
149 V8 **Shekhūpura** Punjab, NE Pakistan
Sheki see Şäki
124 L14 **Sheksna** Vologodskaya Oblast', NW Russian Federation
123 T5 **Shelagskiy, Mys** *cape* NE Russian Federation
27 V3 **Shelbina** Missouri, C USA
13 P16 **Shelburne** Nova Scotia, SE Canada
14 G14 **Shelburne** Ontario, S Canada
33 R7 **Shelby** Montana, NW USA
21 Q10 **Shelby** North Carolina, SE USA
31 S12 **Shelby** Ohio, N USA
30 L14 **Shelbyville** Illinois, N USA
31 P14 **Shelbyville** Indiana, N USA
20 L5 **Shelbyville** Kentucky, S USA
27 V2 **Shelbyville** Missouri, C USA
20 J10 **Shelbyville** Tennessee, S USA
25 X8 **Shelbyville** Texas, SW USA
30 L14 **Shelbyville, Lake** ▣ Illinois, N USA
29 S12 **Sheldon** Iowa, C USA
38 M11 **Sheldons Point** Alaska, USA
Shelekhov Gulf see Shelikhova, Zaliv
123 U9 **Shelikhova, Zaliv** *Eng.* Shelekhov Gulf. *gulf* E Russian Federation
39 P14 **Shelikof Strait** *strait* Alaska, USA
Shelim see Shalīm
9 T14 **Shellbrook** Saskatchewan, S Canada
28 L3 **Shell Creek** ⌇ North Dakota, N USA
Shellif see Chelif, Oued
22 I10 **Shell Keys** *island group* Louisiana, S USA
30 I4 **Shell Lake** Wisconsin, N USA
29 W12 **Shell Rock** Iowa, C USA
185 C26 **Shelter Point** *headland* Stewart Island, New Zealand
18 L13 **Shelton** Connecticut, NE USA
32 G8 **Shelton** Washington, NW USA
Shemakha see Şamaxı
145 W9 **Shemonaikha** Vostochnyy Kazakhstan, E Kazakhstan
127 Q4 **Shemursha** Chavash Respubliki, W Russian Federation
38 D16 **Shemya Island** *island* Aleutian Islands, Alaska, USA
29 T16 **Shenandoah** Iowa, C USA
21 U4 **Shenandoah** Virginia, NE USA
21 U4 **Shenandoah Mountains** *ridge* West Virginia, NE USA
21 V3 **Shenandoah River** ⌇ West Virginia, NE USA
77 W15 **Shendam** Plateau, C Nigeria
80 G8 **Shendi** *var.* Shandī. River Nile, NE Sudan
76 I15 **Shenge** SW Sierra Leone
146 L10 **Shengeldi** *Rus.* Chingildi. Navoiy Viloyati, N Uzbekistan
146 L10 **Shengeldi** *Rus.* Chingildi. Navoiy Viloyati, N Uzbekistan
145 U15 **Shengel'dy** Almaty, SE Kazakhstan
113 K18 **Shëngjin** *var.* Shëngjini. Lezhë, NW Albania
Shëngjini see Shëngjin
Shengking see Liaoning
Sheng Xian/Shengxian see Shengzhou
161 S9 **Shengzhou** *var.* Shengxian, Sheng Xian. Zhejiang, SE China
Shenking see Liaoning
125 N11 **Shenkursk** Arkhangel'skaya Oblast', NW Russian Federation
160 L3 **Shenmu** Shaanxi, C China
113 L19 **Shën Noj i Madh** ▲ C Albania
160 L8 **Shennong Ding** *var.* Dashennongjia. ▲ C China
Shenshi/Shensi see Shaanxi
163 V12 **Shenyang** *Chin.* Shen-yang, *Eng.* Moukden, Mukden; *prev.* Fengtien. *province capital* Liaoning, NE China
Shen-yang see Shenyang
161 O15 **Shenzhen** Guangdong, S China
154 G8 **Sheopur** Madhya Pradesh, C India
116 L5 **Shepetivka** *Rus.* Shepetovka. Khmel'nyts'ka Oblast', NW Ukraine
Shepetovka see Shepetivka
25 W10 **Shepherd** Texas, SW USA
187 R14 **Shepherd Islands** *island group* C Vanuatu
20 K5 **Shepherdsville** Kentucky, S USA
183 O11 **Shepparton** Victoria, SE Australia
97 P22 **Sheppey, Isle of** *island* SE England, UK
Sherabad see Sherobod
97 L23 **Sherborne** S England, UK
76 H16 **Sherbro Island** *island* SW Sierra Leone
15 Q12 **Sherbrooke** Québec, SE Canada
29 T11 **Sherburn** Minnesota, N USA
78 H6 **Sherda** Borkou-Ennedi-Tibesti, N Chad
80 G7 **Shereik** River Nile, N Sudan
126 K3 **Sheremet'yevo** ✈ (Moskva) Moskovskaya Oblast', W Russian Federation
153 P14 **Shergāti** Bihār, N India
27 U12 **Sheridan** Arkansas, C USA
33 W12 **Sheridan** Wyoming, C USA
182 G8 **Sheringa** South Australia
25 U5 **Sherman** Texas, SW USA
194 J10 **Sherman Island** *island* Antarctica
19 S4 **Sherman Mills** Maine, NE USA
29 O15 **Sherman Reservoir** ▣ Nebraska, C USA
147 N14 **Sherobod** *Rus.* Sherabad. Surkhondaryo Viloyati, S Uzbekistan
147 O13 **Sherobod** *Rus.* Sherabad. ⌇ S Uzbekistan
153 T14 **Sherpur** Dhaka, N Bangladesh
37 T4 **Sherrelwood** Colorado, C USA
99 J14 **'s-Hertogenbosch** *Fr.* Bois-le-Duc, *Ger.* Herzogenbusch. Noord-Brabant, S Netherlands
28 M2 **Sherwood** North Dakota, N USA
9 Q14 **Sherwood Park** Alberta, SW Canada
56 F13 **Sheshea, Río** ⌇ E Peru
143 T5 **Sheshtamad** Khorāsān-Razavī, NE Iran
29 S10 **Shetek, Lake** ◎ Minnesota, N USA
96 M2 **Shetland Islands** *island group* NE Scotland, UK
144 F14 **Shetpe** Mangistau, SW Kazakhstan
154 C11 **Shetrunji** ⌇ W India
Shevchenko see Aktau
117 W5 **Shevchenkove** Kharkivs'ka Oblast', E Ukraine
81 H14 **Shewa Gīmīra** Southern, S Ethiopia
161 Q9 **Shexian** *var.* Huicheng, She Xian. Anhui, E China
She Xian see Shexian
161 R6 **Sheyang** *prev.* Hede. Jiangsu, E China
29 O4 **Sheyenne** North Dakota, N USA
29 P4 **Sheyenne River** ⌇ North Dakota, N USA
96 G7 **Shiant Islands** *island group* NW Scotland, UK
123 U12 **Shiashkotan, Ostrov** *island* Kuril'skiye Ostrova, SE Russian Federation
31 R9 **Shiawassee River** ⌇ Michigan, N USA
141 R14 **Shibām** C Yemen
Shibarghān see Sheberghān
165 O10 **Shibata** *var.* Sibata. Niigata, Honshū, C Japan
Shiberghan/Shiberghān see Sheberghān
Shibh Jazīrat Sīnā see Sinai
Shibīn al Kawm see Shibīn el Kôm
75 W8 **Shibīn el Kôm** *var.* Shibīn al Kawm. N Egypt
143 O13 **Shīb, Kūh-e** ▲ S Iran
12 D8 **Shibogama Lake** ◎ Ontario, C Canada
Shibotsu-jima see Zelënyy, Ostrov
164 B16 **Shibushi** Kagoshima, Kyūshū, SW Japan
189 U13 **Shichiyo Islands** *island group* Chuuk, C Micronesia
Shickshock Mountains see Chic-Chocs, Monts
145 S8 **Shiderti** *var.* Shiderty. Pavlodar, NE Kazakhstan
145 S9 **Shiderti** ⌇ N Kazakhstan
Shiderty see Shiderti
96 G10 **Shiel, Loch** ◎ N Scotland, UK
164 J13 **Shiga** *off.* Shiga-ken, *var.* Siga. ◆ *prefecture* Honshū, SW Japan
Shiga-ken see Shiga
Shigatse see Xigazê
141 U13 **Shiḩan** *oasis* NE Yemen
Shih-chia-chuang/Shihmen see Shijiazhuang
158 K4 **Shihezi** Xinjiang Uygur Zizhiqu, NW China
Shiichi see Shyichy
113 K19 **Shijak** *var.* Shijaku. Durrës, W Albania
Shijaku see Shijak
161 O4 **Shijiazhuang** *var.* Shih-chia-chuang; *prev.* Shihmen. *province capital* Hebei, E China
165 R5 **Shikabe** Hokkaidō, NE Japan
149 Q13 **Shikārpur** Sind, S Pakistan
127 Q7 **Shikhany** Saratovskaya Oblast', W Russian Federation
189 V12 **Shiki Islands** *island group* Chuuk, C Micronesia
164 G14 **Shikoku** *var.* Sikoku. *island* SW Japan
192 H5 **Shikoku Basin** *var.* Sikoku Basin. *undersea feature* N Philippine Sea
164 G14 **Shikoku-sanchi** ▲▲ Shikoku, SW Japan
165 X4 **Shikotan, Ostrov** *Jap.* Shikotan-tō. *island* NE Russian Federation
Shikotan-tō see Shikotan, Ostrov
165 R4 **Shikotsu-ko** *var.* Sikotu Ko. ◎ Hokkaidō, NE Japan
81 N15 **Shilabo** Somali, E Ethiopia
127 X7 **Shil'da** Orenburgskaya Oblast', W Russian Federation
139 V3 **Shilēr, Āw-e** ⌇ E Iraq
153 S12 **Shiliguri** *prev.* Siliguri. West Bengal, NE India
Shiliu see Changjiang
129 V7 **Shilka** ⌇ S Russian Federation
18 H15 **Shillington** Pennsylvania, NE USA
153 V13 **Shillong** *state capital* Meghālaya, NE India
126 M5 **Shilovo** Ryazanskaya Oblast', W Russian Federation
164 C14 **Shimabara** *var.* Simabara. Nagasaki, Kyūshū, SW Japan
164 C14 **Shimabara-wan** *bay* SW Japan
164 F12 **Shimane** *off.* Shimane-ken, *var.* Simane. ◆ *prefecture* Honshū, SW Japan
164 G11 **Shimane-hantō** *peninsula* Honshū, SW Japan
Shimane-ken see Shimane
123 Q13 **Shimanovsk** Amurskaya Oblast', SE Russian Federation
Shimbir Berris see Shimbiris
80 O12 **Shimbiris** *var.* Shimbir Berris. ▲ N Somalia
165 T4 **Shimizu** Hokkaidō, NE Japan
164 M14 **Shimizu** *var.* Simizu. Shizuoka, Honshū, S Japan
152 I8 **Shimla** *prev.* Simla. *state capital* Himāchal Pradesh, N India
165 N14 **Shimoda** *var.* Simoda. Shizuoka, Honshū, S Japan
165 O13 **Shimodate** *var.* Simodate. Ibaraki, Honshū, S Japan
155 F18 **Shimoga** Karnātaka, W India
164 C15 **Shimo-jima** *island* SW Japan
164 B15 **Shimo-Koshiki-jima** *island* SW Japan
81 J21 **Shimoni** Coast, S Kenya
164 D13 **Shimonoseki** *var.* Simonoseki, *hist.* Akamagaseki, Bakan. Yamaguchi, Honshū, SW Japan
124 G14 **Shimsk** Novgorodskaya Oblast', NW Russian Federation
141 W7 **Shināş** N Oman
148 J6 **Shīndand** Herāt, W Afghanistan
Shinei see Hsinying
162 H10 **Shinejinst** *var.* Dzalaa. Bayanhongor, C Mongolia
25 T12 **Shiner** Texas, SW USA
167 N1 **Shingbwiyang** Kachin State, N Myanmar (Burma)
145 W11 **Shingozha** Vostochnyy Kazakhstan, E Kazakhstan
164 J15 **Shingū** *var.* Singû. Wakayama, Honshū, SW Japan
14 F8 **Shining Tree** Ontario, S Canada
165 P9 **Shinjō** *var.* Sinzyô. Yamagata, Honshū, C Japan
96 I7 **Shin, Loch** ◎ N Scotland, UK
21 S3 **Shinnston** West Virginia, NE USA
138 I6 **Shinshār** *Fr.* Chinnchâr. Ḩimş, W Syria
Shinshū see Chinju
165 T4 **Shintoku** Hokkaidō, NE Japan
81 G20 **Shinyanga** Shinyanga, NW Tanzania
81 G20 **Shinyanga** ◆ *region* N Tanzania
165 Q10 **Shiogama** *var.* Siogama. Miyagi, Honshū, C Japan
164 M12 **Shiojiri** *var.* Sioziri. Nagano, Honshū, S Japan
164 I15 **Shiono-misaki** *headland* Honshū, SW Japan
165 Q12 **Shioya-zaki** *headland* Honshū, C Japan
114 J9 **Shipchenski Prokhod** *pass* C Bulgaria
160 G14 **Shiping** Yunnan, SW China
13 P13 **Shippagan** *var.* Shippegan. New Brunswick, SE Canada
Shippegan see Shippagan
18 F15 **Shippensburg** Pennsylvania, NE USA
37 P9 **Shiprock** New Mexico, SW USA
37 O9 **Ship Rock** ▲ New Mexico, SW USA
15 R6 **Shipshaw** ⌇ Québec, SE Canada
123 V10 **Shipunskiy, Mys** *cape* E Russian Federation
160 K7 **Shiquan** Shaanxi, C China
122 K13 **Shira** Respublika Khakasiya, S Russian Federation
153 T14 **Shirajganj Ghat** *var.* Serajgonj, Sirajganj. Rajshahi, C Bangladesh
165 P12 **Shirakawa** *var.* Sirakawa. Fukushima, Honshū, C Japan
164 M13 **Shirane-san** ▲ Honshū, S Japan
165 U14 **Shiranuka** Hokkaidō, NE Japan
195 N12 **Shirase Coast** *physical region* Antarctica
165 U3 **Shirataki** Hokkaidō, NE Japan
143 O11 **Shīrāz** *var.* Shīrāz. Fārs, S Iran
83 N15 **Shire** *var.* Chire. ⌇ Malawi/Mozambique
Shiree see Tsagaanhayrhan
Shireet see Bayandelger
165 W3 **Shiretoko-hantō** *headland* Hokkaidō, NE Japan
165 W3 **Shiretoko-misaki** *headland* Hokkaidō, NE Japan
127 N5 **Shiringushi** Respublika Mordoviya, W Russian Federation
148 M3 **Shīrīn Tagāb** Fāryāb, N Afghanistan
149 N2 **Shīrīn Tagāb** ⌇ N Afghanistan
165 R6 **Shiriya-zaki** *headland* Honshū, C Japan
144 I12 **Shirkala, Gryada** *plain* W Kazakhstan
165 P10 **Shiroishi** *var.* Siroisi. Miyagi, Honshū, C Japan
Shirokoye see Shyroke
165 O10 **Shirone** *var.* Sirone. Niigata, Honshū, C Japan
164 L12 **Shirotori** Gifu, Honshū, SW Japan
197 T1 **Shirshov Ridge** *undersea feature* W Bering Sea
Shirshütür/Shirshyutyur, Peski see Şirşütür Gumy
143 T3 **Shīrvān** *var.* Shirwān. Khorāsān, NE Iran
Shirwa, Lake see Chilwa, Lake
Shirwān see Shīrvān
159 N5 **Shisanjianfang** Xinjiang Uygur Zizhiqu, W China

◆ Country ● Country Capital ◇ Dependent Territory ○ Dependent Territory Capital ◆ Administrative Regions ✈ International Airport ▲ Mountain ▲▲ Mountain Range Volcano ⌇ River ◎ Lake ▣ Reservoir

38 *M16* **Shishaldin Volcano** ▲ Unimak Island, Alaska, USA
Shishchitsy *see* Shyshchytsy
38 *M8* **Shishmaref** Alaska, USA
Shisur *see* Ash Shişar
164 *L13* **Shitara** Aichi, Honshū, SW Japan
152 *D12* **Shiv** Rājasthān, NW India
151 *E15* **Shivāji Sāgar** *prev.* Konya Reservoir. ⊠ W India
154 *H8* **Shivpuri** Madhya Pradesh, C India
36 *J9* **Shivwits Plateau** *plain* Arizona, SW USA
Shiwalik Range *see* Siwalik Range
160 *M8* **Shiyan** Hubei, C China
Shizilu *see* Junan
160 *H13* **Shizong** *var.* Danfeng. Yunnan, SW China
165 *R10* **Shizugawa** Miyagi, Honshū, NE Japan
159 *W8* **Shizuishan** *var.* Dawukou. Ningxia, N China
165 *T5* **Shizunai** Hokkaidō, NE Japan
165 *M14* **Shizuoka** *var.* Sizuoka. Shizuoka, Honshū, S Japan
164 *M13* **Shizuoka** *off.* Shizuoka-ken, *var.* Sizuoka. ⬖ *prefecture* Honshū, S Japan
Shizuoka-ken *see* Shizuoka
Shklov *see* Shklow
119 *N15* **Shklow** *Rus.* Shklov. Mahilyowskaya Voblasts', E Belarus
113 *K18* **Shkodër** *var.* Shkodra, *It.* Scutari, *SCr.* Skadar. Shkodër, NW Albania
113 *K17* **Shkodër** ⬖ *district* NW Albania
Shkodra *see* Shkodër
Shkodrës, Liqeni i *see* Scutari, Lake
113 *L20* **Shkumbinit, Lumi i** *var.* Shkumbî, Shkumbin. ≈ C Albania
Shkumbî/Shkumbin *see* Shkumbinit, Lumi i
Shligigh, Cuan *see* Sligo Bay
122 *L4* **Shmidta, Ostrov** *island* Severnaya Zemlya, N Russian Federation
183 *S10* **Shoalhaven River** ≈ New South Wales, SE Australia
9 *W16* **Shoal Lake** Manitoba, S Canada
31 *O15* **Shoals** Indiana, N USA
164 *I13* **Shōdo-shima** *island* SW Japan
Shōka *see* Changhua
122 *M5* **Shokal'skogo, Proliv** *strait* N Russian Federation
147 *T14* **Shokhdara, Qatorkŭhi** *Rus.* Shakhdarinskiy Khrebet. ▲▲ SE Tajikistan
145 *P15* **Sholakkorgan** *var.* Chulakkurgan. Yuzhnyy Kazakhstan, S Kazakhstan
145 *N9* **Sholaksay** Kostanay, N Kazakhstan
Sholāpur *see* Solāpur
Sholdaneshty *see* Şoldăneşti
Shoqpar *see* Chokpar
155 *G21* **Shoranūr** Kerala, SW India
155 *G16* **Shorāpur** Karnātaka, C India
147 *O14* **Sho'rchi** *Rus.* Shurchi. Surkhondaryo Viloyati, S Uzbekistan
30 *M11* **Shorewood** Illinois, N USA
Shorkazakhly, Solonchak *see* Kazakhlyshor, Solonchak
145 *Q9* **Shortandy** Akmola, C Kazakhstan
Shortepa/Shor Tepe *see* Shūr Tappeh
186 *J7* **Shortland Island** *var.* Alu. *island* Shortland Islands, NW Solomon Islands
Shosambetsu *see* Shosanbetsu
165 *S2* **Shosanbetsu** *var.* Shosambetsu. Hokkaidō, NE Japan
33 *O15* **Shoshone** Idaho, NW USA
35 *T6* **Shoshone Mountains** ▲▲ Nevada, W USA
33 *U12* **Shoshone River** ≈ Wyoming, C USA
83 *I19* **Shoshong** Central, SE Botswana
33 *V14* **Shoshoni** Wyoming, C USA
Shōshū *see* Sangju
117 *S2* **Shostka** Sums'ka Oblast', NE Ukraine
185 *C21* **Shotover** ≈ South Island, New Zealand
146 *H9* **Shovot** *Rus.* Shavat. Xorazm Viloyati, W Uzbekistan
37 *N12* **Show Low** Arizona, SW USA
Show Me State *see* Missouri
125 *O4* **Shoyna** Nenetskiy Avtonomnyy Okrug, NW Russian Federation
124 *M11* **Shozhma** Arkhangel'skaya Oblast', NW Russian Federation
117 *Q7* **Shpola** Cherkas'ka Oblast', N Ukraine
Shqipëria/Shqipërisë, Republika e *see* Albania
22 *G5* **Shreveport** Louisiana, S USA
97 *K19* **Shrewsbury** *hist.* Scrobesbyrig'. W England, UK
152 *D11* **Shri Mohangarh** *prev.* Sri Mohangorh. Rājasthān, NW India
153 *S16* **Shrīrāmpur** *prev.* Serampore, Serampur. West Bengal, NE India
97 *K19* **Shropshire** *cultural region* W England, UK
145 *S16* **Shu** *Kaz.* Shū. Zhambyl, SE Kazakhstan
Shū *see* Shu
Shū *see* Chu
160 *G13* **Shuangbai** *var.* Tuodian. Yunnan, SW China
163 *W9* **Shuangcheng** Heilongjiang, NE China
Shuangcheng *see* Zherong
160 *E14* **Shuangjiang** *var.* Weiyuan. Yunnan, SW China
Shuangjiang *see* Jiangkou
Shuangjiang *see* Tongdao
163 *U10* **Shuangliao** *var.* Zhengjiatun. Jilin, NE China
Shuang-liao *see* Liaoyuan
Shuangshipu *see* Fengxian
163 *Y7* **Shuangyashan** *var.* Shuang-ya-shan. Heilongjiang, NE China
Shuang-ya-shan *see* Shuangyashan
Shu'aymiah *see* Shu'aymīyah
141 *W12* **Shu'aymīyah** *var.* Shu'aymiah. S Oman
144 *I10* **Shubarkuduk** *Kaz.* Shubarqudyq. Aktyubinsk, W Kazakhstan
Shubarqudyq *see* Shubarkuduk
145 *N12* **Shubar-Tengiz, Ozero** ◎ C Kazakhstan
39 *S5* **Shublik Mountains** ▲▲ Alaska, USA
Shubrā al Khaymah *see* Shubrâ el Kheima
121 *U13* **Shubrâ el Kheima** *var.* Shubrā al Khaymah. N Egypt
158 *E8* **Shufu** Xinjiang Uygur Zizhiqu, NW China
147 *S14* **Shughnon, Qatorkŭhi** *Rus.* Shugnanskiy Khrebet. ▲▲ SE Tajikistan
Shugnanskiy Khrebet *see* Shughnon, Qatorkŭhi
161 *Q6* **Shu He** ≈ E China
Shuicheng *see* Lupanshui
Shuiding *see* Huocheng
Shuidong *see* Dianbai
Shuiji *see* Laixi
Shū-Ile Taūlary *see* Chu-Iliyskiye Gory
Shuilocheng *see* Zhuanglang
149 *T10* **Shujāābād** Punjab, E Pakistan
163 *W9* **Shulan** Jilin, NE China
158 *E8* **Shule** Xinjiang Uygur Zizhiqu, NW China
Shuleh *see* Shule He
159 *Q8* **Shule He** *var.* Shuleh, Sulo. ≈ C China
30 *K9* **Shullsburg** Wisconsin, N USA
Shulu *see* Xinji
39 *N16* **Shumagin Islands** *island group* Alaska, USA
146 *G7* **Shumanay** Qoraqalpoghiston Respublikasi, W Uzbekistan
114 *M8* **Shumen** Shumen, NE Bulgaria
114 *M8* **Shumen** ⬖ *province* NE Bulgaria
127 *P4* **Shumerlya** ChuvashRespubliki, W Russian Federation
122 *G11* **Shumikha** Kurganskaya Oblast', C Russian Federation
118 *M12* **Shumilina** *Rus.* Shumilino. Vitsyebskaya Voblasts', NE Belarus
Shumilino *see* Shumilina
123 *V11* **Shumshu, Ostrov** *island* SE Russian Federation
116 *K5* **Shums'k** Ternopil's'ka Oblast', W Ukraine
39 *O7* **Shungnak** Alaska, USA
Shunsen *see* Ch'unch'ŏn
Shuoxian *see* Shuozhou
161 *N3* **Shuozhou** *var.* Shuoxian. Shanxi, C China
141 *P16* **Shuqrah** *var.* Shaqrā. SW Yemen
Shurab *see* Shŭrob
Shurchi *see* Sho'rchi
147 *R11* **Shŭrob** *Rus.* Shurab. NW Tajikistan
143 *T10* **Shūr, Rūd-e** ≈ E Iran
149 *O2* **Shūr Tappeh** *var.* Shortepa, Shor Tepe. Balkh, N Afghanistan
83 *K17* **Shurugwi** *prev.* Selukwe. Midlands, C Zimbabwe
142 *L8* **Shūsh** *anc.* Susa, *Bibl.* Shushan. Khūzestān, SW Iran
Shushan *see* Shūsh
142 *L9* **Shūshtar** *var.* Shustar, Shushter. Khūzestān, SW Iran
Shushter/Shustar *see* Shūshtar
141 *T9* **Shuṭfah, Qalamat** *well* E Saudi Arabia
139 *V9* **Shuwayjah, Hawr ash** *var.* Hawr as Suwayqiyah. ◎ E Iraq
124 *M16* **Shuya** Ivanovskaya Oblast', W Russian Federation
39 *Q14* **Shuyak Island** *island* Alaska, USA
166 *M4* **Shwebo** Sagaing, C Myanmar (Burma)
166 *L7* **Shwedaung** Pegu, W Myanmar (Burma)
166 *M7* **Shwegyin** Pegu, SW Myanmar (Burma)
167 *N4* **Shweli** *Chin.* Longchuan Jiang. ≈ Myanmar (Burma)/China
166 *M6* **Shwemyo** Mandalay, C Myanmar (Burma)
145 *T12* **Vostochno-Kounradskiy** *Kaz.* Shyghys Qongyrat. Zhezkazgan, C Kazakhstan
Shyghys Qazagastan Oblysy *see* Vostochnyy Kazakhstan
Shyghys Qongyrat *see* Vostochno-Kounradskiy
119 *M19* **Shyichy** *Rus.* Shiichi. Homyel'skaya Voblasts', SE Belarus
145 *Q17* **Shymkent** *prev.* Chimkent. Yuzhnyy Kazakhstan, S Kazakhstan
Shyngghyrlaū *see* Chingirlau
152 *J5* **Shyok** Jammu and Kashmir, NW India
117 *S9* **Shyroke** *Rus.* Shirokoye. Dnipropetrovs'ka Oblast', E Ukraine
117 *O9* **Shyryayeve** Odes'ka Oblast', SW Ukraine
117 *S5* **Shyshaky** Poltavs'ka Oblast', C Ukraine
119 *K17* **Shyshchytsy** *Rus.* Shishchitsy. Minskaya Voblasts', C Belarus
149 *Y3* **Siachen Muztāgh** ▲▲ NE Pakistan
Siadehan *see* Tākestān
148 *M13* **Siāhān Range** ▲▲ W Pakistan
142 *I1* **Sīāh Chashmeh** *var* Chālderān. Āzarbāyjān-e Gharbī, N Iran
149 *W7* **Siālkot** Punjab, NE Pakistan
186 *E7* **Sialum** Morobe, C Papua New Guinea
Siam *see* Thailand
Siam, Gulf of *see* Thailand, Gulf of
Sian *see* Xi'an
Siang *see* Brahmaputra
Siangtan *see* Xiangtan
169 *N8* **Siantan, Pulau** *island* Kepulauan Anambas, W Indonesia
54 *H11* **Siare, Río** ≈ C Colombia
171 *R6* **Siargao Island** *island* S Philippines
186 *F72* **Siassi** Umboi Island, C Papua New Guinea
115 *D14* **Siátista** Dytikí Makedonía, N Greece
166 *K4* **Siatlai** Chin State, W Myanmar (Burma)
171 *P6* **Siaton** Negros, C Philippines
171 *P6* **Siaton Point** *headland* Negros, C Philippines
118 *F11* **Šiauliai** *Ger.* Schaulen. Šiauliai, N Lithuania
118 *E11* **Šiauliai** ⬖ *province* N Lithuania
171 *Q10* **Siau, Pulau** *island* N Indonesia
83 *J15* **Siavonga** Southern, SE Zambia
Siazan' *see* Siyäzän
Sibah *see* As Sībah
107 *N20* **Sibari** Calabria, S Italy
Sibata *see* Shibata
127 *X6* **Sibay** Respublika Bashkortostan, W Russian Federation
93 *M19* **Sibbo** *Fin.* Sipoo. Etelä-Suomi, S Finland
112 *D13* **Šibenik** *It.* Sebenico. Šibenik-Knin, S Croatia
Sibenik *see* Šibenik-Knin
112 *E13* **Šibenik-Knin** *off.* Šibenska Županija, *var.* Sibenik. ⬖ *province* S Croatia
Šibenik-Knin *see* Drniš
Šibenska Županija *see* Šibenik-Knin
Siberia *see* Sibir'
Siberoet *see* Siberut, Pulau
168 *H12* **Siberut, Pulau** *prev.* Siberoet. *island* Kepulauan Mentawai, W Indonesia
168 *I12* **Siberut, Selat** *strait* W Indonesia
149 *P11* **Sibi** Baluchistān, SW Pakistan
186 *B9* **Sibidiri** Western, SW Papua New Guinea
123 *N10* **Sibir'** *var.* Siberia. *physical region* NE Russian Federation
79 *F20* **Sibiti** La Lékoumou, S Congo
81 *G21* **Sibiti** ≈ C Tanzania
116 *I12* **Sibiu** *Ger.* Hermannstadt, *Hung.* Nagyszeben. Sibiu, C Romania
116 *I11* **Sibiu** ⬖ *county* C Romania
29 *S11* **Sibley** Iowa, C USA
169 *R9* **Sibu** Sarawak, East Malaysia
42 *G2* **Sibun** ≈ E Belize
79 *I15* **Sibut** *prev.* Fort-Sibut. Kémo, S Central African Republic
171 *P4* **Sibuyan Island** *island* C Philippines
189 *U1* **Sibylla Island** *island* N Marshall Islands
9 *N16* **Sicamous** British Columbia, SW Canada
Sichelburger Gerbirge *see* Gorjanci
167 *N14* **Sichon** *var.* Ban Sichon, Si Chon. Nakhon Si Thammarat, SW Thailand
Si Chon *see* Sichon
160 *H9* **Sichuan** *var.* Chuan, Sichuan Sheng, Ssu-ch'uan, Szechuan, Szechwan. ⬖ *province* C China
160 *I9* **Sichuan Pendi** *basin* C China
Sichuan Sheng *see* Sichuan
103 *S16* **Sicie, Cap** *headland* SE France
107 *J24* **Sicilia** *Eng.* Sicily; *anc.* Trinacria. ⬖ *region* Italy, C Mediterranean Sea
107 *M24* **Sicilia** *Eng.* Sicily; *anc.* Trinacria. *island* Italy, C Mediterranean Sea
Sicilian Channel *see* Sicily, Strait of
107 *H24* **Sicily, Strait of** *var.* Sicilian Channel. *strait* C Mediterranean Sea
42 *K5* **Sico Tinto, Río** *var.* Río Negro. ≈ NE Honduras
57 *H16* **Sicuani** Cusco, S Peru
112 *J10* **Šid** Vojvodina, NW Serbia
115 *A15* **Sidári** Kérkyra, Iónia Nisiá, Greece, C Mediterranean Sea
169 *Q11* **Sidas** Borneo, C Indonesia
98 *O5* **Siddeburen** Groningen, NE Netherlands
154 *D9* **Siddhapur** *prev.* Siddhpur, Sidhpur. Gujarāt, W India
Siddhpur *see* Siddhapur
155 *I15* **Siddipet** Andhra Pradesh, C India
77 *N14* **Sidéradougou** SW Burkina
107 *N23* **Siderno** Calabria, SW Italy
Siders *see* Sierre
154 *L9* **Sidhi** Madhya Pradesh, C India
Sidhirókastron *see* Sidirókastro
Sidhpur *see* Siddhapur
75 *U7* **Sîdi Barrâni** NW Egypt
74 *I6* **Sidi Bel Abbès** *var.* Sidi bel Abbès, Sidi-Bel-Abbès. NW Algeria
74 *E7* **Sidi-Bennour** W Morocco
74 *M6* **Sidi Bouzid** *var.* Gammouda, Sīdī Bu Zayd. C Tunisia
Sīdī Bu Zayd *see* Sidi Bouzid
74 *D8* **Sidi-Ifni** SW Morocco
74 *G6* **Sidi-Kacem** *prev.* Petitjean. N Morocco
114 *G12* **Sidirókastro** *prev.* Sidhirókastron. Kentrikí Makedonía, NE Greece
194 *L12* **Sidley, Mount** ▲ Antarctica
29 *S16* **Sidney** Iowa, C USA
33 *Y7* **Sidney** Montana, NW USA
28 *J15* **Sidney** Nebraska, C USA
18 *I11* **Sidney** New York, NE USA
31 *R13* **Sidney** Ohio, N USA
23 *T2* **Sidney Lanier, Lake** ⊠ Georgia, SE USA
Sidon *see* Saïda
122 *J9* **Sidorovsk** Yamalo-Nenetskiy Avtonomnyy Okrug, N Russian Federation
Sidra *see* Surt
Sidra/Sidra, Gulf of *see* Surt, Khalīj, N Libya
Siebenbürgen *see* Transylvania
Sieben Dörfer *see* Săcele
110 *O12* **Siedlce** *Ger.* Sedlez, *Rus.* Sesdlets. Mazowieckie, C Poland
101 *E16* **Sieg** ≈ W Germany
101 *F16* **Siegen** Nordrhein-Westfalen, W Germany
109 *X4* **Sieghartskirchen** Niederösterreich, E Austria
110 *O11* **Siemiatycze** Podlaskie, NE Poland
167 *T11* **Siĕmpang** Stœng Trêng, NE Cambodia
167 *R11* **Siĕmréab** *prev.* Siemreap. Siĕmréab, NW Cambodia
Siemreap *see* Siĕmréab
106 *G12* **Siena** *Fr.* Sienne; *anc.* Saena Julia. Toscana, C Italy
Sienne *see* Siena
92 *K12* **Sieppijärvi** Lappi, NW Finland
110 *J13* **Sieradz** Sieradz, C Poland
110 *K10* **Sierpc** Mazowieckie, C Poland
24 *I9* **Sierra Blanca** Texas, SW USA
37 *S14* **Sierra Blanca Peak** ▲ New Mexico, SW USA
35 *P5* **Sierra City** California, W USA
63 *I16* **Sierra Colorada** Río Negro, S Argentina
62 *I13* **Sierra del Nevado** ▲ W Argentina
62 *I13* **Sierra del Nevado** ▲▲ W Argentina
63 *J16* **Sierra Grande** Río Negro, E Argentina
76 *G15* **Sierra Leone** *off.* Republic of Sierra Leone. ◆ *republic* W Africa
64 *M13* **Sierra Leone Basin** *undersea feature* E Atlantic Ocean
66 *K8* **Sierra Leone Fracture Zone** *tectonic feature* E Atlantic Ocean
Sierra Leone, Republic of *see* Sierra Leone
Sierra Leone Ridge *see* Sierra Leone Rise
64 *L13* **Sierra Leone Rise** *var.* Sierra Leone Ridge, Sierra Leone Schwelle. *undersea feature* E Atlantic Ocean
Sierra Leone Schwelle *see* Sierra Leone Rise
41 *U17* **Sierra Madre** *var.* Sierra de Soconusco. ▲▲ Guatemala/Mexico
37 *R2* **Sierra Madre** ▲▲ Colorado/Wyoming, C USA
0 *H15* **Sierra Madre del Sur** ▲▲ S Mexico
0 *H13* **Sierra Madre Occidental** *var.* Western Sierra Madre. ▲▲ C Mexico
0 *H13* **Sierra Madre Oriental** *var.* Eastern Sierra Madre. ▲▲ C Mexico
44 *H8* **Sierra Maestra** ▲▲ E Cuba
40 *L7* **Sierra Mojada** Coahuila de Zaragoza, NE Mexico
105 *O14* **Sierra Nevada** ▲▲ S Spain
35 *P6* **Sierra Nevada** ▲▲ W USA
54 *F4* **Sierra Nevada de Santa Marta** ▲▲ NE Colombia
54 *F4* **Sierra Nevada de Santa Marta** ▲▲ NE Colombia
42 *K5* **Sierra Río Tinto** ▲▲ NE Honduras
24 *J10* **Sierra Vieja** ▲▲ Texas, SW USA
37 *N16* **Sierra Vista** Arizona, SW USA
108 *D10* **Sierre** *Ger.* Siders. Valais, SW Switzerland
36 *L16* **Sierrita Mountains** ▲▲ Arizona, SW USA
Siete Moai *see* Ahu Akivi
76 *M15* **Sifié** W Ivory Coast
115 *I21* **Sífnos** *anc.* Siphnos. *island* Kykládes, Greece, Aegean Sea
115 *I21* **Sífnou, Stenó** *strait* SE Greece
Siga *see* Shiga
103 *P16* **Sigean** Aude, S France
Sighet *see* Sighetu Marmaţiei
Sighetul Marmaţiei *see* Sighetu Marmaţiei
116 *I8* **Sighetu Marmaţiei** *var.* Sighet, Sighetul Marmaţiei, *Hung.* Máramarossziget. Maramureş, N Romania
116 *I11* **Sighişoara** *Ger.* Schässburg, *Hung.* Segesvár. Mureş, C Romania
168 *G7* **Sigli** Sumatera, W Indonesia
92 *J1* **Siglufjördhur** Nordhurland Vestra, N Iceland
101 *H23* **Sigmaringen** Baden-Württemberg, S Germany
101 *N20* **Signalberg** ▲ SE Germany
36 *I13* **Signal Peak** ▲ Arizona, SW USA
Signan *see* Xi'an
194 *H1* **Signy** *UK research station* South Orkney Islands, Antarctica
29 *X15* **Sigourney** Iowa, C USA
115 *K17* **Sígri, Ákrotírio** *headland* Lésvos, E Greece
Sigsbee Deep *see* Mexico Basin
47 *N2* **Sigsbee Escarpment** *undersea feature* N Gulf of Mexico
56 *C8* **Sigsig** Azuay, S Ecuador
95 *O15* **Sigtuna** Stockholm, C Sweden
42 *H6* **Siguatepeque** Comayagua, W Honduras
105 *P7* **Sigüenza** Castilla-La Mancha, C Spain
105 *R4* **Sigües** Aragón, NE Spain
76 *K13* **Siguiri** NE Guinea
118 *G8* **Sigulda** *Ger.* Segewold. Rīga, C Latvia
Sihanoukville *see* Kâmpóng Saôm
108 *G8* **Sihlsee** ◎ NW Switzerland
93 *K18* **Siikainen** Länsi-Soumi, SW Finland
93 *M16* **Siilinjärvi** Itä-Suomi, C Finland
137 *R15* **Siirt** *var.* Sert; *anc.* Tigranocerta. Siirt, SE Turkey
137 *R15* **Siirt** *var.* Sert. ⬖ *province* SE Turkey
187 *N8* **Sikaiana** *var.* Stewart Islands. *island group* W Solomon Islands
Sikandarabad *see* Secunderābād
152 *J11* **Sikandra Rao** Uttar Pradesh, N India
10 *M11* **Sikanni Chief** British Columbia, W Canada
10 *M11* **Sikanni Chief** ≈ British Columbia, W Canada
152 *H11* **Sīkar** Rājasthān, N India
76 *M13* **Sikasso** Sikasso, S Mali
76 *L13* **Sikasso** ⬖ *region* SW Mali
167 *N3* **Sikaw** Kachin State, C Myanmar (Burma)
83 *H14* **Sikelenge** Western, W Zambia
27 *Y7* **Sikeston** Missouri, C USA
93 *J14* **Sikfors** Norrbotten, N Sweden
123 *T14* **Sikhote-Alin', Khrebet** ▲▲ SE Russian Federation
Siking *see* Xi'an
115 *J22* **Síkinos** *island* Kykládes, Greece, Aegean Sea
153 *S11* **Sikkim** *Tib.* Denjong. ⬖ *state* N India
111 *I26* **Siklós** Baranya, SW Hungary
Sikoku *see* Shikoku
Sikoku Basin *see* Shikoku Basin
83 *G14* **Sikongo** Western, W Zambia
Sikotu Ko *see* Shikotsu-ko
Sikouri/Sikoúrion *see* Sykoúrio
123 *P8* **Siktyakh** Respublika Sakha (Yakutiya), NE Russian Federation
118 *D12* **Šilalė** Tauragė, W Lithuania
106 *G5* **Silandro** *Ger.* Schlanders. Trentino-Alto Adige, N Italy
41 *N12* **Silao** Guanajuato, C Mexico
Silarius *see* Sele
153 *W14* **Silchar** Assam, NE India
108 *G9* **Silenen** Uri, C Switzerland
21 *T9* **Siler City** North Carolina, SE USA
33 *U11* **Silesia** Montana, NW USA
110 *F13* **Silesia** *physical region* SW Poland
74 *K12* **Silet** S Algeria
145 *R8* **Sileti** *var.* Selety. ≈ N Kazakhstan
Siletitengiz *see* Siletiteniz, Ozero
145 *R7* **Siletiteniz, Ozero** *Kaz.* Siletitengiz. ◎ N Kazakhstan
172 *H16* **Silhouette** *island* Inner Islands, SE Seychelles
136 *I17* **Silifke** *anc.* Seleucia. Mersin, S Turkey
Siliguri *see* Shiliguri
156 *J10* **Siling Co** ◎ W China
Silinhot *see* Xilinhot
192 *G14* **Silisili** ▲ Savai'i, C Samoa
114 *M6* **Silistra** *var.* Silistria; *anc.* Durostorum. Silistra, NE Bulgaria
114 *M7* **Silistra** ⬖ *province* NE Bulgaria
Silistria *see* Silistra
136 *D10* **Silivri** İstanbul, NW Turkey
94 *L13* **Siljan** ◎ C Sweden
95 *G22* **Silkeborg** Århus, C Denmark
108 *M8* **Sill** ≈ W Austria
105 *S10* **Silla** País Valenciano, E Spain
62 *H3* **Sillajguay, Cordillera** ▲ N Chile
118 *K3* **Sillamäe** *Ger.* Sillamäggi. Ida-Virumaa, NE Estonia
Sillamäggi *see* Sillamäe
Sillein *see* Žilina
109 *P9* **Sillian** Tirol, W Austria
112 *B10* **Šilo** Primorje-Gorski Kotar, NW Croatia
27 *R9* **Siloam Springs** Arkansas, C USA
25 *X10* **Silsbee** Texas, SW USA
143 *W15* **Sīlūp, Rūd-e** ≈ SE Iran
118 *C12* **Šilutė** *Ger.* Heydekrug. Klaipėda, W Lithuania
137 *Q15* **Sılvan** Dıyarbakır, SE Turkey
108 *J10* **Silvaplana** Graubünden, S Switzerland
Silva Porto *see* Kuito
58 *M12* **Silva, Recife do** *reef* E Brazil
154 *D12* **Silvassa** Dādra and Nagar Haveli, W India
29 *X4* **Silver Bay** Minnesota, N USA
37 *P15* **Silver City** New Mexico, SW USA
18 *D10* **Silver Creek** New York, NE USA
37 *N12* **Silver Creek** ≈ Arizona, SW USA
27 *P4* **Silver Lake** Kansas, C USA
32 *I14* **Silver Lake** Oregon, NW USA
35 *T9* **Silver Peak Range** ▲▲ Nevada, W USA
21 *W3* **Silver Spring** Maryland, NE USA
Silver State *see* Colorado
Silver State *see* Nevada
37 *Q7* **Silverton** Colorado, C USA
18 *K16* **Silverton** New Jersey, NE USA
32 *G11* **Silverton** Oregon, NW USA
25 *N4* **Silverton** Texas, SW USA
104 *G14* **Silves** Faro, S Portugal
54 *D12* **Silvia** Cauca, SW Colombia
108 *J9* **Silvrettagruppe** ▲▲ Austria/Switzerland
Sily-Vajdej *see* Vulcan
108 *L7* **Silz** Tirol, W Austria
172 *I13* **Sima** Anjouan, SE Comoros
Simabara *see* Shimabara
83 *H15* **Simakando** Western, W Zambia
Simane *see* Shimane
119 *L20* **Simanichy** *Rus.* Simonichi. Homyel'skaya Voblasts', SE Belarus
160 *F14* **Simao** Yunnan, SW China
153 *P12* **Simarā** Central, C Nepal
14 *I8* **Simard, Lac** ◎ Québec, SE Canada
136 *D13* **Simav** Kütahya, W Turkey
136 *D13* **Simav Çayı** ≈ NW Turkey
79 *L18* **Simba** Orientale, N Dem. Rep. Congo
186 *C7* **Simbai** Madang, N Papua New Guinea
Simbirsk *see* Ul'yanovsk
14 *F17* **Simcoe** Ontario, S Canada
14 *H14* **Simcoe, Lake** ◎ Ontario, S Canada
80 *J11* **Sīmēn** ▲▲ N Ethiopia
114 *K11* **Simeonovgrad** *prev.* Maritsa. Khaskovo, S Bulgaria
116 *G11* **Simeria** *Ger.* Pischk, *Hung.* Piski. Hunedoara, W Romania
107 *L24* **Simeto** ≈ Sicilia, Italy, C Mediterranean Sea
168 *G9* **Simeulue, Pulau** *island* NW Indonesia
117 *T13* **Simferopol'** Respublika Krym, S Ukraine
117 *T13* **Simferopol'** ✈ Respublika Krym, S Ukraine
Simi *see* Sými
152 *M9* **Simikot** Far Western, NW Nepal
54 *F7* **Simití** Bolívar, N Colombia
114 *G11* **Simitla** Blagoevgrad, SW Bulgaria
35 *S15* **Simi Valley** California, W USA
Simizu *see* Shimizu
Simla *see* Shimla
Şimlăul Silvaniei/Şimleul Silvaniei *see* Şimleu Silvaniei
116 *G9* **Şimleu Silvaniei** *Hung.* Szilágysomlyó; *prev.* Şimlăul Silvaniei, Şimleul Silvaniei. Sălaj, NW Romania
Simmer *see* Simmerbach
101 *E19* **Simmerbach** *var.* Simmer. ≈ W Germany
101 *F18* **Simmern** Rheinland-Pfalz, W Germany
22 *I7* **Simmesport** Louisiana, S USA
119 *F14* **Simnas** Alytus, S Lithuania
92 *L13* **Simo** Lappi, NW Finland
Simoda *see* Shimoda
Simodate *see* Shimodate
92 *M13* **Simojärvi** ◎ N Finland
92 *L13* **Simojoki** ≈ NW Finland
41 *U15* **Simojovel** *var.* Simojovel de Allende. Chiapas, SE Mexico
Simojovel de Allende *see* Simojovel
56 *B7* **Simon Bolivar** *var.* Guayaquil. ✈ (Quayaquil) Guayas, W Ecuador
54 *L5* **Simon Bolívar** ✈ (Caracas) Vargas, N Venezuela
Simonichi *see* Simanichy
14 *M12* **Simon, Lac** ◎ Québec, SE Canada
Simonoseki *see* Shimonoseki
Šimonovany *see* Partizánske
Simonstad *see* Simon's Town
83 *E26* **Simon's Town** *var.* Simonstad. Western Cape, SW South Africa
Simony *see* Partizánske
Simpeln *see* Simplon
99 *M18* **Simpelveld** Limburg, SE Netherlands
108 *E11* **Simplon** *var.* Simpeln. Valais, SW Switzerland
108 *E11* **Simplon Pass** *pass* S Switzerland
106 *C6* **Simplon Tunnel** *tunnel* Italy/Switzerland
Simpson *see* Fort Simpson
182 *G1* **Simpson Desert** *desert* Northern Territory/South Australia
10 *J9* **Simpson Peak** ▲ British Columbia, W Canada
9 *N7* **Simpson Peninsula** *peninsula* Nunavut, NE Canada
21 *P11* **Simpsonville** South Carolina, SE USA
95 *L23* **Simrishamn** Skåne, S Sweden
123 *U13* **Simushir, Ostrov** *island* Kuril'skiye Ostrova, SE Russian Federation
168 *G9* **Sinabang** Sumatera, W Indonesia
81 *N15* **Sina Dhaqa** Galguduud, C Somalia
75 *X8* **Sinai** *var.* Sinai Peninsula, *Ar.* Shibh Jazirat Sīna, Sīnā'. *physical region* NE Egypt
116 *J12* **Sinaia** Prahova, SE Romania
188 *B16* **Sinajana** C Guam
40 *H8* **Sinaloa** ⬖ *state* C Mexico
54 *H4* **Sinamaica** Zulia, NW Venezuela
163 *X14* **Sinan-ni** SE North Korea
Sīnā'/Sinai Peninsula *see* Sinai
Sīnāwan *see* Sīnāwin
75 *N8* **Sīnāwin** *var.* Sīnāwan. NW Libya
83 *J16* **Sinazongwe** Southern, S Zambia
166 *L6* **Sinbaungwe** Magwe, W Myanmar (Burma)
166 *L5* **Sinbyugyun** Magwe, W Myanmar (Burma)
54 *E6* **Since** Sucre, NW Colombia
54 *E6* **Sincelejo** Sucre, NW Colombia
166 *J5* **Sinchaingbyin** *var.* Zullapara. Arakan State, W Myanmar (Burma)
23 *U4* **Sinclair, Lake** ⊠ Georgia, SE USA
10 *M14* **Sinclair Mills** British Columbia, SW Canada
149 *Q14* **Sind** *var.* Sindh. ⬖ *province* SE Pakistan
154 *I8* **Sind** ≈ N India
95 *H19* **Sindal** Nordjylland, N Denmark
171 *P7* **Sindañgan** Mindanao, S Philippines
79 *D19* **Sindara** Ngounié, W Gabon
152 *E13* **Sindari** *prev.* Sindri. Rājasthān, N India
114 *N8* **Sindel** Varna, E Bulgaria
101 *H22* **Sindelfingen** Baden-Württemberg, SW Germany
155 *G16* **Sindgi** Karnātaka, C India
Sindh *see* Sind
118 *G5* **Sindi** *Ger.* Zintenhof. Pärnumaa, SW Estonia
136 *C13* **Sındırgı** Balıkesir, W Turkey
77 *N14* **Sindou** SW Burkina
Sindri *see* Sindari
149 *T9* **Sind Sāgar Doāb** *desert* E Pakistan
126 *M11* **Sinegorskiy** Rostovskaya Oblast', SW Russian Federation
123 *S9* **Sinegor'ye** Magadanskaya Oblast', E Russian Federation
114 *O12* **Sinekli** İstanbul, NW Turkey
104 *F12* **Sines** Setúbal, S Portugal
104 *F12* **Sines, Cabo de** *cape* S Portugal
92 *L12* **Sinettä** Lappi, NW Finland
186 *H6* **Sinewit, Mount** ▲ New Britain, C Papua New Guinea
80 *G11* **Singa** *var.* Sinja, Sinjah. Sinnar, E Sudan
78 *J12* **Singako** Moyen-Chari, S Chad
Singan *see* Xi'an
168 *K10* **Singapore** ● (Singapore) S Singapore
168 *L10* **Singapore** *off.* Republic of Singapore. ◆ *republic* SE Asia
Singapore, Republic of *see* Singapore
169 *U17* **Singaraja** Bali, C Indonesia
167 *O10* **Sing Buri** *var.* Singhaburi. Sing Buri, C Thailand
101 *H24* **Singen** Baden-Württemberg, S Germany

◆ Country
● Country Capital
◇ Dependent Territory
○ Dependent Territory Capital
⬖ Administrative Regions
✈ International Airport
▲ Mountain
▲▲ Mountain Range
Volcano
≈ River
◎ Lake
⊠ Reservoir

Singeorgiu de Pădure *see* Sângeorgiu de Pădure
Singeorz-Băi/Singeroz Băi *see* Sângeorz-Băi
116 M9 **Singerei** *var.* Sângerei; *prev.* Lazovsk. N Moldova
Singhaburi *see* Sing Buri
81 H21 **Singida** Singida, C Tanzania
81 G22 **Singida** ◈ *region* C Tanzania
Singidunum *see* Beograd
166 M2 **Singkaling Hkamti** Sagaing, N Myanmar (Burma)
171 N14 **Singkang** Sulawesi, C Indonesia
168 J11 **Singkarak, Danau** ◎ Sumatera, W Indonesia
169 N10 **Singkawang** Borneo, C Indonesia
168 M11 **Singkep, Pulau** *island* Kepulauan Lingga, W Indonesia
168 H9 **Singkilbaru** Sumatera, W Indonesia
183 T7 **Singleton** New South Wales, SE Australia
Singora *see* Songkhla
Singû *see* Shingū
Sining *see* Xining
107 D17 **Siniscola** Sardegna, Italy, C Mediterranean Sea
113 F14 **Sinj** Split-Dalmacija, SE Croatia
Sinjajevina *see* Sinjavina
139 P3 **Sinjār** NW Iraq
139 P2 **Sinjār, Jabal** ▲▲ N Iraq
Sinja/Sinjah *see* Singa
113 K15 **Sinjavina** *var.* Sinjajevina. ▲▲ C Montenegro
80 I7 **Sinkat** Red Sea, NE Sudan
Sinkiang/Sinkiang Uighur Autonomous Region *see* Xinjiang Uygur Zizhiqu
Sinmartin *see* Târnăveni
163 V13 **Sinmi-do** *island* NW North Korea
101 I18 **Sinn** 〰 C Germany
Sinnamarie *see* Sinnamary
55 Y9 **Sinnamary** *var.* Sinnamarie. N French Guiana
80 G11 **Sinnar** ◈ *state* E Sudan
Sinneh *see* Sanandaj
18 E13 **Sinnemahoning Creek** 〰 Pennsylvania, NE USA
Sînnicolau Mare *see* Sânnicolau Mare
Sinoe, Lacul *see* Sinoie, Lacul
Sinoia *see* Chinhoyi
117 N14 **Sinoie, Lacul** *prev.* Lacul Sinoe. *lagoon* SE Romania
59 H16 **Sinop** Mato Grosso, W Brazil
136 K10 **Sinop** *anc.* Sinope. Sinop, N Turkey
136 J10 **Sinop** ◈ *province* N Turkey
136 K10 **Sinop Burnu** *headland* N Turkey
Sinope *see* Sinop
Sino/Sinoe *see* Greenville
163 Y12 **Sinp'o** E North Korea
101 H20 **Sinsheim** Baden-Württemberg, SW Germany
Sîntana *see* Sântana
169 R11 **Sintang** Borneo, C Indonesia
99 F14 **Sint Annaland** Zeeland, SW Netherlands
98 L5 **Sint Annaparochie** Friesland, N Netherlands
45 V9 **Sint Eustatius** *Eng.* Saint Eustatius. *island* N Netherlands Antilles
99 G19 **Sint-Genesius-Rode** *Fr.* Rhode-Saint-Genèse. Vlaams Brabant, C Belgium
99 F16 **Sint-Gillis-Waas** Oost-Vlaanderen, N Belgium
99 H17 **Sint-Katelijne-Waver** Antwerpen, C Belgium
99 E18 **Sint-Lievens-Houtem** Oost-Vlaanderen, NW Belgium
45 V9 **Sint Maarten** *Eng.* Saint Martin. *island* N Netherlands Antilles
99 F14 **Sint Maartensdijk** Zeeland, SW Netherlands
99 L19 **Sint-Martens-Voeren** *Fr.* Fouron-Saint-Martin. Limburg, NE Belgium
99 J14 **Sint-Michielsgestel** Noord-Brabant, S Netherlands
Sîn-Miclăuş *see* Gheorgheni
45 O16 **Sint Nicholaas** S Aruba
99 F16 **Sint-Niklaas** *Fr.* Saint-Nicolas. Oost-Vlaanderen, N Belgium
99 K14 **Sint-Oedenrode** Noord-Brabant, S Netherlands
25 T14 **Sinton** Texas, SW USA
99 G14 **Sint Philipsland** Zeeland, SW Netherlands
99 G19 **Sint-Pieters-Leeuw** Vlaams Brabant, C Belgium
104 E11 **Sintra** *prev.* Cintra. Lisboa, W Portugal
99 J18 **Sint-Truiden** *Fr.* Saint-Trond. Limburg, NE Belgium
99 H14 **Sint Willebrord** Noord-Brabant, S Netherlands
163 V13 **Sinŭiju** W North Korea
80 P13 **Sinujiif** Nugaal, NE Somalia
Sinus Aelaniticus *see* Aqaba, Gulf of
Sinus Gallicus *see* Lion, Golfe du
Sinyang *see* Xinyang
Sinyavka *see* Sinyawka
119 I18 **Sinyawka** *Rus.* Sinyavka. Minskaya Voblasts', SW Belarus
Sinying *see* Hsinying
Sinyukha *see* Synyukha
Sinzyô *see* Shinjō
111 I24 **Sió** 〰 W Hungary
171 Q7 **Siocon** Mindanao, S Philippines
111 I24 **Siófok** Somogy, Hungary
Siogama *see* Shiogama
83 G15 **Sioma** Western, SW Zambia
108 D11 **Sion** *Ger.* Sitten; *anc.* Sedunum. Valais, SW Switzerland
103 O11 **Sioule** 〰 C France
29 S12 **Sioux Center** Iowa, C USA
29 R13 **Sioux City** Iowa, C USA
29 R11 **Sioux Falls** South Dakota, N USA
12 B11 **Sioux Lookout** Ontario, S Canada
29 T12 **Sioux Rapids** Iowa, C USA
Sioux State *see* North Dakota
Sioziri *see* Shiojiri
171 P6 **Sipalay** Negros, C Philippines
55 V11 **Sipaliwini** ◈ *district* S Suriname
45 U15 **Siparia** Trinidad, Trinidad and Tobago
Siphnos *see* Sífnos
163 V11 **Siping** *var.* Ssu-p'ing, Szeping; *prev.* Ssu-p'ing-chieh. Jilin, NE China
9 X12 **Sipiwesk** Manitoba, C Canada
9 W13 **Sipiwesk Lake** ◎ Manitoba, C Canada
195 O11 **Siple Coast** *physical region* Antarctica
194 K12 **Siple Island** *island* Antarctica
194 K13 **Siple, Mount** ▲ Siple Island, Antarctica
Sipoo *see* Sibbo
112 G12 **Šipovo** ◈ Republika Srpska, W Bosnia and Herzegovina
23 O4 **Sipsey River** 〰 Alabama, S USA
168 I13 **Sipura, Pulau** *island* W Indonesia
0 G16 **Siqueiros Fracture Zone** *tectonic feature* E Pacific Ocean
42 L10 **Siquia, Río** 〰 SE Nicaragua
43 N13 **Siquirres** Limón, E Costa Rica
54 J5 **Siquisique** Lara, N Venezuela
155 G19 **Sīra** Karnātaka, W India
95 D16 **Sira** 〰 S Norway
167 P12 **Siracha** *var.* Ban Si Racha, Si Racha. Chon Buri, S Thailand
Si Racha *see* Siracha
107 L25 **Siracusa** *Eng.* Syracuse. Sicilia, Italy, C Mediterranean Sea
Sirajganj *see* Shirajganj Ghat
Sirakawa *see* Shirakawa
9 N14 **Sir Alexander, Mount** ▲ British Columbia, W Canada
137 O12 **Şiran** Gümüşhane, NE Turkey
77 Q12 **Sirba** 〰 E Burkina
143 O17 **Şīr Banī Yās** *island* W United Arab Emirates
95 D17 **Sirdalsvatnet** ◎ S Norway
Sir Darya/Sirdaryo *see* Syr Darya
147 P10 **Sirdaryo** Sirdaryo Viloyati, E Uzbekistan
147 O11 **Sirdaryo Viloyati** *Rus.* Syrdar'inskaya Oblast'. ◈ *province* E Uzbekistan
Sir Donald Sangster International Airport *see* Sangster
181 S3 **Sir Edward Pellew Group** *island group* Northern Territory, NE Australia
116 K8 **Siret** *Ger.* Sereth, *Hung.* Szeret. Suceava, N Romania
116 K8 **Siret** *var.* Siretul, *Ger.* Sereth, *Rus.* Seret, *Ukr.* Siret. 〰 Romania/Ukraine
Siretul *see* Siret
140 K3 **Sirḩān, Wādī as** *dry watercourse* Jordan/Saudi Arabia
152 I8 **Sirhind** Punjab, N India
116 F11 **Şiria** *Ger.* Schiria. Arad, W Romania
Siria *see* Syria
143 S14 **Sīrīk** Hormozgān, SE Iran
167 P8 **Sirikit Reservoir** ◎ N Thailand
58 K12 **Sirituba, Ilha** *island* NE Brazil
143 R11 **Sīrjān** *prev.* Sa'īdābād. Kermān, S Iran
182 H9 **Sir Joseph Banks Group** *island group* South Australia
92 K11 **Sirkka** Lappi, N Finland
Sirna *see* Sýrna
137 R16 **Şırnak** Şırnak, SE Turkey
137 S16 **Şırnak** ◈ *province* SE Turkey
Siroisi *see* Shiroishi
155 J14 **Sironcha** Mahārāshtra, C India
Sirone *see* Shirone
Síros *see* Sýros
Sirotino *see* Sirotsina
118 M12 **Sirotsina** *Rus.* Sirotino. Vitsyebskaya Voblasts', N Belarus
152 H9 **Sirsa** Haryāna, NW India
173 Y17 **Sir Seewoosagur Ramgoolam** ✈ (port Louis) SE Mauritius
155 E18 **Sirsi** Karnātaka, W India
146 K12 **Şirşütür Gumy** *var.* Shirshütür, *Rus.* Peski Shirshyutyur. *desert* E Turkmenistan
Sirte *see* Surt
182 A2 **Sir Thomas, Mount** ▲ South Australia
Sirti, Gulf of *see* Surt, Khalīj
142 J5 **Sīrvān, Rūdkhāneh-ye** *var.* Nahr Diyālá, Sirwan. 〰 Iran/Iraq *see also* Diyālá, Nahr
Sīrvān, Rudkhaneh-ye *see* Diyālá, Nahr
118 H13 **Širvintos** Vilnius, SE Lithuania
Sirwan *see* Diyālá, Nahr/Sīrvān, Rudkhaneh-ye
9 N15 **Sir Wilfrid Laurier, Mount** ▲ British Columbia, SW Canada
14 M10 **Sir-Wilfrid, Mont** ▲ Québec, SE Canada
Sisačko-Moslavačka Županija *see* Sisak-Moslavina
112 E9 **Sisak** *var.* Siscia, *Ger.* Sissek, *Hung.* Sziszek; *anc.* Segestica. Sisak-Moslavina, C Croatia
167 R10 **Si Sa Ket** *var.* Sisaket, Sri Saket. Si Sa Ket, E Thailand
Sisaket *see* Si Sa Ket
112 E9 **Sisak-Moslavina** *off.* Sisačko-Moslavačka Županija. ◈ *province* C Croatia
167 O8 **Si Satchanala** Sukhothai, NW Thailand
Siscia *see* Sisak
83 G22 **Sishen** Northern Cape, NW South Africa
137 V13 **Sisian** SE Armenia
197 N13 **Sisimiut** *var.* Holsteinborg, Holsteinsborg, Holstenborg, Holstensborg. ◈ Kitaa, S Greenland
30 M1 **Siskiwit Bay** *lake bay* Michigan, N USA
34 L1 **Siskiyou Mountains** ▲▲ California/Oregon, W USA
167 Q11 **Sisŏphŏn** Bătdâmbâng, NW Cambodia
108 E7 **Sissach** Basel-Land, NW Switzerland
186 B5 **Sissano** Sandaun, NW Papua New Guinea
Sissek *see* Sisak
29 R7 **Sisseton** South Dakota, N USA
143 W9 **Sīstān, Daryācheh-ye** *var.* Daryācheh-ye Hāmūn, Hāmūn-e Şāberī. ◎ Afghanistan/Iran *see also* Şāberī, Hāmūn-e
Sīstān, Daryācheh-ye *see* Şāberī, Hāmūn-e
143 V12 **Sīstān va Balūchestān** *off.* Ostān-e Sīstān va Balūchestān, *var.* Balūchestān va Sīstān. ◈ *province* SE Iran
Sīstān va Balūchestān, Ostān-e *see* Sīstān va Balūchestān
103 T14 **Sisteron** Alpes-de-Haute-Provence, SE France
32 H13 **Sisters** Oregon, NW USA
65 G15 **Sisters Peak** ▲ N Ascension Island
21 R3 **Sistersville** West Virginia, NE USA
Sistova *see* Svishtov
Sitakund *see* Sitakunda
153 V16 **Sitakunda** *var.* Sitakund. Chittagong, SE Bangladesh
153 P12 **Sītāmarhi** Bihār, N India
152 L11 **Sītāpur** Uttar Pradesh, N India
Sitaş Cristuru *see* Cristuru Secuiesc
115 L25 **Siteía** *var.* Sitía. Kríti, Greece, E Mediterranean Sea
105 V6 **Sitges** Cataluña, NE Spain
115 H15 **Sithonía** *peninsula* NE Greece
Sitía *see* Siteía
54 F4 **Sitionuevo** Magdalena, N Colombia
39 X13 **Sitka** Baranof Island, Alaska, USA
39 Q15 **Sitkinak Island** *island* Trinity Islands, Alaska, USA
166 M7 **Sittang** *var.* Sittoung. 〰 S Myanmar (Burma)
99 L17 **Sittard** Limburg, SE Netherlands
Sitten *see* Sion
108 H7 **Sitter** 〰 NW Switzerland
109 U10 **Sittersdorf** Kärnten, S Austria
Sittoung *see* Sittang
166 K6 **Sittwe** *var.* Akyab. Arakan State, W Myanmar (Burma)
42 L8 **Siuna** Región Autónoma Atlántico Norte, NE Nicaragua
153 R15 **Siuri** West Bengal, NE India
Siut *see* Asyūt
123 Q13 **Sivaki** Amurskaya Oblast', SE Russian Federation
136 M13 **Sivas** *anc.* Sebastia, Sebaste. Sivas, C Turkey
136 M13 **Sivas** ◈ *province* C Turkey
137 O15 **Siverek** Şanlıurfa, S Turkey
117 X6 **Sivers'k** Donets'ka Oblast', E Ukraine
124 G13 **Siverskiy** Leningradskaya Oblast', NW Russian Federation
117 X6 **Sivers'kyy Donets'** *Rus.* Severskiy Donets. 〰 Russian Federation/Ukraine *see also* Severskiy Donets
Sivers'kyy Donets' *see* Severskiy Donets
125 W5 **Sivomaskinskiy** Respublika Komi, NW Russian Federation
136 G13 **Sivrihisar** Eskişehir, W Turkey
99 F22 **Sivry** Hainaut, S Belgium
123 V9 **Sivuchiy, Mys** *cape* E Russian Federation
75 U9 **Siwa** *var.* Sīwah. NW Egypt
Sīwah *see* Siwa
152 J9 **Siwalik Range** *var.* Shiwalik Range. ▲▲ India/Nepal
153 O13 **Siwān** Bihār, N India
43 O14 **Sixaola, Río** 〰 Costa Rica/Panama
Six Counties, The *see* Northern Ireland
103 T16 **Six-Fours-les-Plages** Var, SE France
161 Q7 **Sixian** *var.* Si Xian. Anhui, E China
Si Xian *see* Sixian
22 J9 **Six Mile Lake** ◎ Louisiana, S USA
139 V3 **Siyāh Gūz** E Iraq
155 L25 **Siyambalanduwa** Uva Province, SE Sri Lanka
137 Y10 **Siyäzän** *Rus.* Siazan'. NE Azerbaijan
Sizebolu *see* Sozopol
Sizuoka *see* Shizuoka
95 I24 **Sjælland** *Eng.* Zealand, *Ger.* Seeland. *island* E Denmark
Sjar *see* Sääre
113 L15 **Sjenica** *Turk.* Seniça. Serbia, SW Serbia
94 G11 **Sjoa** 〰 S Norway
95 K23 **Sjöbo** Skåne, S Sweden
94 E9 **Sjøholt** Møre og Romsdal, S Norway
92 O1 **Sjuøyane** *island group* N Svalbard
Skadar *see* Shkodër
Skadarsko Jezero *see* Scutari, Lake
117 R11 **Skadovs'k** Khersons'ka Oblast', S Ukraine
95 I24 **Skælskør** Vestsjælland, E Denmark
92 I2 **Skagaströnd** *prev.* Höfdhakaupstadhur. Nordhurland Vestra, N Iceland
95 H19 **Skagen** Nordjylland, N Denmark
Skagerak *see* Skagerrak
95 L16 **Skagern** ◎ C Sweden
197 T17 **Skagerrak** *var.* Skagerak. *channel* N Europe
94 G12 **Skaget** ▲ S Norway
32 H7 **Skagit River** 〰 Washington, NW USA
39 W12 **Skagway** Alaska, USA
92 K8 **Skaidi** Finnmark, N Norway
115 F21 **Skála** Pelopónnisos, S Greece
116 K6 **Skalat** *Pol.* Skałat. Ternopil's'ka Oblast', W Ukraine
95 J22 **Skälderviken** *inlet* Denmark/Sweden
124 J3 **Skalistyy** Murmanskaya Oblast', NW Russian Federation
92 I12 **Skalka** ◎ N Sweden
114 I12 **Skaloti** Anatolikí Makedonía kai Thráki, NE Greece
95 G22 **Skanderborg** Århus, C Denmark
95 K22 **Skåne** ◈ *county* S Sweden
75 N6 **Skanès** ✈ (Sousse) E Tunisia
95 C15 **Skånevik** Hordaland, S Norway
95 M18 **Skänninge** Östergötland, S Sweden
95 J23 **Skanör med Falsterbo** Skåne, S Sweden
115 H17 **Skantzoúra** *island* Vóreioi Sporádes, Greece, Aegean Sea
95 K18 **Skara** Västra Götaland, S Sweden
95 M17 **Skärblacka** Östergötland, S Sweden
95 I18 **Skärhamn** Västra Götaland, S Sweden
95 I14 **Skarnes** Hedmark, S Norway
119 M21 **Skarodnaye** *Rus.* Skorodnoye. Homyel'skaya Voblasts', SE Belarus
110 I8 **Skarszewy** *Ger.* Schöneck. Pomorskie, NW Poland
111 M14 **Skarżysko-Kamienna** Świętokrzyskie, C Poland
95 K16 **Skattkärr** Värmland, C Sweden
118 D12 **Skaudvilė** Tauragė, SW Lithuania
92 J12 **Skaulo** *Lapp.* Sávdijári. Norrbotten, N Sweden
111 K17 **Skawina** Małopolskie, S Poland
10 K12 **Skeena** 〰 British Columbia, SW Canada
10 J11 **Skeena Mountains** ▲▲ British Columbia, W Canada
97 O18 **Skegness** E England, UK
92 J4 **Skeidharársandur** *coast* S Iceland
93 J15 **Skellefteå** Västerbotten, N Sweden
93 I14 **Skellefteälven** 〰 N Sweden
93 J15 **Skelleftehamn** Västerbotten, N Sweden
25 O2 **Skellytown** Texas, SW USA
95 J19 **Skene** Västra Götaland, S Sweden
97 G17 **Skerries** *Ir.* Na Sceirí. Dublin, E Ireland
95 H15 **Ski** Akershus, S Norway
115 G17 **Skíathos** Skíathos, Vóreies Sporádes, Greece, Aegean Sea
115 G17 **Skíathos** *island* Vóreies Sporádes, Greece, Aegean Sea
27 P9 **Skiatook** Oklahoma, C USA
27 P9 **Skiatook Lake** ⊠ Oklahoma, C USA
97 B22 **Skibbereen** *Ir.* An Sciobairín. Cork, SW Ireland
92 I9 **Skibotn** Troms, N Norway
119 F16 **Skidal'** *Rus.* Skidel'. Hrodzyenskaya Voblasts', W Belarus
97 K15 **Skiddaw** ▲ NW England, UK
Skidel' *see* Skidal'
25 T14 **Skidmore** Texas, SW USA
95 G16 **Skien** Telemark, S Norway
Skiermûntseach *see* Schiermonnikoog
110 L12 **Skierniewice** Łódzkie, C Poland
74 L5 **Skikda** *prev.* Philippeville. NE Algeria
30 M16 **Skillet Fork** 〰 Illinois, N USA
95 L19 **Skillingaryd** Jönköping, S Sweden
115 B19 **Skinári, Akrotírio** *cape* Zákynthos, Iónia Nisiá, Greece, C Mediterranean Sea
95 M15 **Skinnskatteberg** Västmanland, C Sweden
182 M12 **Skipton** Victoria, SE Australia
97 L16 **Skipton** N England, UK
Skiropoula *see* Skyropoúla
Skiros *see* Skýros
95 F21 **Skive** Viborg, NW Denmark
94 F11 **Skjåk** Oppland, S Norway
92 K2 **Skjálfandafljót** 〰 C Iceland
95 F22 **Skjern** Ringkøbing, W Denmark
95 F22 **Skjern Å** *var.* Skjern Aa. 〰 W Denmark
Skjern Aa *see* Skjern Å
92 G12 **Skjerstad** Nordland, C Norway
92 J8 **Skjervøy** Troms, N Norway
92 I10 **Skjold** Troms, N Norway
111 I17 **Skoczów** Śląskie, S Poland
109 T11 **Škofja Loka** *Ger.* Bischoflack. NW Slovenia
94 N12 **Skog** Gävleborg, C Sweden
95 K16 **Skoghall** Värmland, C Sweden
31 N10 **Skokie** Illinois, N USA
116 H6 **Skole** L'vivs'ka Oblast', W Ukraine
115 D19 **Skóllis** ▲ S Greece
167 S13 **Skon** Kâmpóng Cham, C Cambodia
115 H17 **Skópelos** Skópelos, Vóreies Sporádes, Greece, Aegean Sea
115 H17 **Skópelos** *island* Vóreies Sporádes, Greece, Aegean Sea
126 L5 **Skopin** Ryazanskaya Oblast', W Russian Federation
113 N18 **Skopje** *var.* Üsküb, *Turk.* Üsküp, *prev.* Skoplje; *anc.* Scupi. ● (FYR Macedonia) N FYR Macedonia
113 O18 **Skopje** ✈ N FYR Macedonia
Skoplje *see* Skopje
110 I8 **Skórcz** *Ger.* Skurz. Pomorskie, N Poland
Skorodnoye *see* Skarodnaye
93 H16 **Skorped** Västernorrland, C Sweden
95 G21 **Skørping** Nordjylland, N Denmark
95 K18 **Skövde** Västra Götaland, S Sweden
123 Q13 **Skovorodino** Amurskaya Oblast', SE Russian Federation
19 Q6 **Skowhegan** Maine, NE USA
9 W15 **Skownan** Manitoba, S Canada
94 H13 **Skreia** Oppland, S Norway
Skripón *see* Orchómenos
118 H9 **Skriveri** Aizkraukle, S Latvia
118 J11 **Skrudaliena** Daugavpils, SE Latvia
118 D9 **Skrunda** Kuldīga, W Latvia
95 C16 **Skudeneshavn** Rogaland, S Norway
83 L20 **Skukuza** Mpumalanga, NE South Africa
97 B22 **Skull** *Ir.* An Scoil. SW Ireland
22 L3 **Skuna River** 〰 Mississippi, S USA
29 X15 **Skunk River** 〰 Iowa, C USA
Skuo *see* Skúvoy
118 C10 **Skuodas** *Ger.* Schoden, *Pol.* Szkudy. Klaipėda, NW Lithuania
95 K23 **Skurup** Skåne, S Sweden
Skurz *see* Skórcz
114 H8 **Skŭt** 〰 NW Bulgaria
94 O13 **Skutskär** Uppsala, C Sweden
95 B19 **Skúvoy** *Dan.* Skuø. *island* C Faeroe Islands
Skvira *see* Skvyra
117 O5 **Skvyra** *Rus.* Skvira. Kyyivs'ka Oblast', N Ukraine
39 Q11 **Skwentna** Alaska, USA
110 E11 **Skwierzyna** *Ger.* Schwerin. Lubuskie, W Poland
96 G9 **Skye, Isle of** *island* NW Scotland, UK
36 K13 **Sky Harbour** ✈ (Phoenix) Arizona, SW USA
32 I8 **Skykomish** Washington, NW USA
Skylge *see* Terschelling
63 F19 **Skyring, Peninsula** *peninsula* S Chile
63 H24 **Skyring, Seno** *inlet* S Chile
115 H17 **Skyropoúla** *var.* Skiropoula. *island* Vóreies Sporádes, Greece, Aegean Sea
115 I17 **Skýros** *var.* Skíros. Skýros, Vóreies Sporádes, Greece, Aegean Sea
115 I17 **Skýros** *var.* Skíros; *anc.* Scyros. *island* Vóreies Sporádes, Greece, Aegean Sea
118 J12 **Slabodka** *Rus.* Slobodka. Vitsyebskaya Voblasts', NW Belarus
95 I23 **Slagelse** Vestsjælland, E Denmark
93 I14 **Slagnäs** Norrbotten, N Sweden
39 T10 **Slana** Alaska, USA
97 F20 **Slaney** *Ir.* An tSláine. 〰 SE Ireland
116 J13 **Slănic** Prahova, SE Romania
116 K11 **Slănic Moldova** Bacău, E Romania
113 H16 **Slano** Dubrovnik-Neretva, SE Croatia
124 F13 **Slantsy** Leningradskaya Oblast', NW Russian Federation
111 C16 **Slaný** *Ger.* Schlan. Střední Čechy, NW Czech Republic
111 K16 **Sląskie** ◈ *province* S Poland
12 C10 **Slate Falls** Ontario, S Canada
27 T4 **Slater** Missouri, C USA
112 H9 **Slatina** *Hung.* Szlatina; *prev.* Podravska Slatina. Virovitica-Podravina, NE Croatia
116 I14 **Slatina** Olt, S Romania
25 N5 **Slaton** Texas, SW USA
95 H14 **Slattum** Akershus, S Norway
9 R10 **Slave** 〰 Alberta/Northwest Territories, C Canada
68 E12 **Slave Coast** *coastal region* W Africa
9 P13 **Slave Lake** Alberta, SW Canada
122 I13 **Slavgorod** Altayskiy Kray, S Russian Federation
Slavgorod *see* Slawharad
Slavonia *see* Slavonija
112 G9 **Slavonija** *Eng.* Slavonia, *Ger.* Slawonien, *Hung.* Szlavonia, Szlavonország. *cultural region* NE Croatia
Slavonska Požega *see* Požega
112 H10 **Slavonski Brod** *Ger.* Brod, *Hung.* Bród; *prev.* Brod, Brod na Savi. Brod-Posavina, NE Croatia
116 L4 **Slavuta** Khmel'nyts'ka Oblast', NW Ukraine
117 P2 **Slavutych** Chernihivs'ka Oblast', N Ukraine
123 R15 **Slavyanka** Primorskiy Kray, SE Russian Federation
114 J8 **Slavyanovo** Pleven, N Bulgaria
Slavyansk *see* Slov"yans'k
126 K14 **Slavyansk-na-Kubani** Krasnodarskiy Kray, SW Russian Federation
119 N20 **Slawyechna** *Rus.* Slovechna. 〰 Belarus/Ukraine
119 O16 **Slawharad** *Rus.* Slavgorod. Mahilyowskaya Voblasts', E Belarus
110 G7 **Sławno** Zachodnio-pomorskie, NW Poland
Slawonien *see* Slavonija
29 S10 **Slayton** Minnesota, N USA
97 N18 **Sleaford** E England, UK
97 A20 **Slea Head** *Ir.* Ceann Sléibhe. *headland* SW Ireland
96 G9 **Sleat, Sound of** *strait* NW Scotland, UK
Sledyuki *see* Slyedzyuki
12 I5 **Sleeper Islands** *island group* Nunavut, C Canada
31 O6 **Sleeping Bear Point** *headland* Michigan, N USA
29 T10 **Sleepy Eye** Minnesota, N USA
39 O11 **Sleetmute** Alaska, USA
Sléibhe, Ceann *see* Slea Head
Slēmānī *see* As Sulaymānīyah
195 O5 **Slessor Glacier** *glacier* Antarctica
22 L9 **Slidell** Louisiana, S USA
18 K12 **Slide Mountain** ▲ New York, NE USA
98 I13 **Sliedrecht** Zuid-Holland, C Netherlands
121 P16 **Sliema** N Malta
97 G16 **Slieve Donard** ▲ SE Northern Ireland, UK
Sligeach *see* Sligo
97 D16 **Sligo** *Ir.* Sligeach. Sligo, NW Ireland
97 C16 **Sligo** *Ir.* Sligeach. ◈ *county* NW Ireland
97 C15 **Sligo Bay** *Ir.* Cuan Shligigh. *inlet* NW Ireland
18 B13 **Slippery Rock** Pennsylvania, NE USA
95 P19 **Slite** Gotland, SE Sweden
114 L9 **Sliven** *var.* Slivno. Sliven, C Bulgaria
114 L10 **Sliven** ◈ *province* C Bulgaria
114 G9 **Slivnitsa** Sofiya, W Bulgaria
Slivno *see* Sliven
114 L7 **Slivo Pole** Ruse, N Bulgaria
29 S13 **Sloan** Iowa, C USA
35 X12 **Sloan** Nevada, W USA
Slobodka *see* Slabodka
125 R14 **Slobodskoy** Kirovskaya Oblast', NW Russian Federation
Slobodzeya *see* Slobozia
117 O10 **Slobozia** *Rus.* Slobodzeya. E Moldova
116 L14 **Slobozia** Ialomiţa, SE Romania
98 O5 **Slochteren** Groningen, NE Netherlands
119 H17 **Slonim** *Pol.* Słonim, *Rus.* Slonim. Hrodzyenskaya Voblasts', W Belarus
Słonim *see* Slonim
98 K7 **Sloter Meer** ◎ N Netherlands
Slot, The *see* New Georgia Sound
97 N22 **Slough** S England, UK
111 J20 **Slovakia** *off.* Slovenská Republika, *Ger.* Slowakei, *Hung.* Szlovákia, *Slvk.* Slovensko. ◆ *republic* C Europe
Slovak Ore Mountains *see* Slovenské rudohorie
Slovechna *see* Slawyechna
109 S12 **Slovenia** *off.* Republic of Slovenia, *Ger.* Slowenien, *Slvn.* Slovenija. ◆ *republic* SE Europe
Slovenia, Republic of *see* Slovenia
Slovenija *see* Slovenia
109 V10 **Slovenj Gradec** *Ger.* Windischgraz. N Slovenia
109 W10 **Slovenska Bistrica** *Ger.* Windischfeistritz. NE Slovenia
Slovenská Republika *see* Slovakia
109 W10 **Slovenske Konjice** E Slovenia
111 K20 **Slovenské rudohorie** *Eng.* Slovak Ore Mountains, *Ger.* Slowakisches Erzgebirge, Ungarisches Erzgebirge. ▲▲ C Slovakia
Slovensko *see* Slovakia
117 Y7 **Slov"yanoserbs'k** Luhans'ka Oblast', E Ukraine
117 W6 **Slov"yans'k** *Rus.* Slavyansk. Donets'ka Oblast', E Ukraine
Slowakei *see* Slovakia
Slowakisches Erzgebirge *see* Slovenské rudohorie
Slowenien *see* Slovenia
110 D11 **Słubice** *Ger.* Frankfurt. Lubuskie, W Poland
119 K19 **Sluch** *Rus.* Sluch'. 〰 C Belarus
116 L4 **Sluch** 〰 NW Ukraine
99 D16 **Sluis** Zeeland, SW Netherlands
112 D10 **Slunj** *Hung.* Szluin. Karlovac, C Croatia
110 I11 **Słupca** Wielkopolskie, C Poland
110 G6 **Słupia** *Ger.* Stolpe. 〰 NW Poland
110 G6 **Słupsk** *Ger.* Stolp. Pomorskie, N Poland
119 K18 **Slutsk** *Rus.* Slutsk. Minskaya Voblasts', S Belarus
119 O16 **Slyedzyuki** *Rus.* Sledyuki. Mahilyowskaya Voblasts', E Belarus
97 A17 **Slyne Head** *Ir.* Ceann Léime. *headland* W Ireland
27 U14 **Smackover** Arkansas, C USA
95 L20 **Småland** *cultural region* S Sweden
95 K20 **Smålandsstenar** Jönköping, S Sweden
Small Malaita *see* Maramasike
13 O8 **Smallwood Reservoir** ⊠ Newfoundland and Labrador, S Canada
119 N14 **Smalyany** *Rus.* Smolyany. Vitsyebskaya Voblasts', NE Belarus
119 L15 **Smalyavichy** *Rus.* Smolevichi. Minskaya Voblasts', C Belarus
74 C9 **Smara** *var.* Es Semara. N Western Sahara
119 I14 **Smarhon'** *Pol.* Smorgonie, *Rus.* Smorgon'. Hrodzyenskaya Voblasts', W Belarus
112 M11 **Smederevo** *Ger.* Semendria. Serbia, N Serbia
112 M12 **Smederevska Palanka** Serbia, C Serbia
95 M14 **Smedjebacken** Dalarna, C Sweden
116 L13 **Smeeni** Buzău, SE Romania
Smela *see* Smila
107 D16 **Smeralda, Costa** *cultural region* Sardegna, Italy, C Mediterranean Sea
111 J22 **Śmigiel** *Ger.* Schmiegel. Wielkopolskie, C Poland
117 Q6 **Smila** *Rus.* Smela. Cherkas'ka Oblast', C Ukraine
98 N7 **Smilde** Drenthe, NE Netherlands
9 S16 **Smiley** Saskatchewan, S Canada
25 T12 **Smiley** Texas, SW USA
Smilten *see* Smiltene
118 I8 **Smiltene** *Ger.* Smilten. Valka, N Latvia
123 T13 **Smirnykh** Ostrov Sakhalin, Sakhalinskaya Oblast', SE Russian Federation
9 Q13 **Smith** Alberta, W Canada
39 P4 **Smith Bay** *bay* Alaska, NW USA
12 I3 **Smith, Cape** *cape* Québec, NE Canada
26 L3 **Smith Center** Kansas, C USA
10 K13 **Smithers** British Columbia, SW Canada
21 V10 **Smithfield** North Carolina, SE USA
36 L1 **Smithfield** Utah, W USA
21 X7 **Smithfield** Virginia, NE USA
12 I3 **Smith Island** *island* Nunavut, C Canada
Smith Island *see* Sumisu-jima
20 H7 **Smithland** Kentucky, S USA
21 T7 **Smith Mountain Lake** *var.* Leesville Lake. ⊠ Virginia, NE USA
34 L1 **Smith River** California, W USA
33 R9 **Smith River** 〰 Montana, NW USA
14 L13 **Smiths Falls** Ontario, SE Canada
33 N13 **Smiths Ferry** Idaho, NW USA
20 K7 **Smiths Grove** Kentucky, S USA
183 N15 **Smithton** Tasmania, SE Australia

◆ Country ● Country Capital ◇ Dependent Territory ○ Dependent Territory Capital ◈ Administrative Regions ✈ International Airport ▲ Mountain ▲▲ Mountain Range ⛰ Volcano 〰 River ◎ Lake ⊠ Reservoir

18 *L14* **Smithtown** Long Island, New York, NE USA
20 *K9* **Smithville** Tennessee, S USA
25 *T11* **Smithville** Texas, SW USA
Šmohor *see* Hermagor
35 *Q4* **Smoke Creek Desert** *desert* Nevada, W USA
9 *O14* **Smoky** ≈ Alberta, W Canada
182 *E7* **Smoky Bay** South Australia
183 *V6* **Smoky Cape** *headland* New South Wales, SE Australia
26 *L4* **Smoky Hill River** ≈ Kansas, C USA
26 *L4* **Smoky Hills** *hill range* Kansas, C USA
9 *Q14* **Smoky Lake** Alberta, SW Canada
94 *E8* **Smøla** *island* W Norway
126 *H4* **Smolensk** Smolenskaya Oblast', W Russian Federation
126 *H4* **Smolenskaya Oblast'** ◈ *province* W Russian Federation
Smolensk-Moscow Upland *see* Smolensko-Moskovskaya Vozvyshennost'
126 *J3* **Smolensko-Moskovskaya Vozvyshennost'** *var.* Smolensk-Moscow Upland. ▲▲ W Russian Federation
Smolevichi *see* Smalyavichy
115 *C15* **Smólikas** *var.* Smolikás. ▲ W Greece
114 *I12* **Smolyan** *prev.* Pashmakli. Smolyan, S Bulgaria
114 *I12* **Smolyan** ◈ *province* S Bulgaria
Smolyany *see* Smalyany
33 *S15* **Smoot** Wyoming, C USA
12 *G12* **Smooth Rock Falls** Ontario, S Canada
Smorgon'/Smorgonie *see* Smarhon'
95 *K23* **Smygehamn** Skåne, S Sweden
194 *I7* **Smyley Island** *island* Antarctica
21 *Y3* **Smyrna** Delaware, NE USA
23 *S3* **Smyrna** Georgia, SE USA
20 *J9* **Smyrna** Tennessee, S USA
Smyrna *see* İzmir
97 *I16* **Snaefell** ▲ C Isle of Man
92 *H3* **Snaefellsjökull** ▲ W Iceland
92 *J3* **Snækollur** ▲ C Iceland
10 *J4* **Snake** ≈ Yukon Territory, NW Canada
29 *O8* **Snake Creek** ≈ South Dakota, N USA
183 *P13* **Snake Island** *island* Victoria, SE Australia
35 *Y6* **Snake Range** ▲▲ Nevada, W USA
32 *K10* **Snake River** ≈ NW USA
29 *V6* **Snake River** ≈ Minnesota, N USA
28 *L12* **Snake River** ≈ Nebraska, C USA
33 *Q14* **Snake River Plain** *plain* Idaho, NW USA
93 *F15* **Snåsa** Nord-Trøndelag, C Norway
21 *O8* **Sneedville** Tennessee, S USA
98 *K6* **Sneek** Friesland, N Netherlands
Sneeuw-gebergte *see* Maoke, Pegunungan
95 *F22* **Snejbjerg** Ringkøbing, C Denmark
124 *J3* **Snezhnogorsk** Murmanskaya Oblast', NW Russian Federation
122 *K9* **Snezhnogorsk** Taymyrskiy (Dolgano-Nenetskiy) Avtonomnyy Okrug, N Russian Federation
Snezhnoye *see* Snizhne
111 *G15* **Sněžka** *Ger.* Schneekoppe, *Pol.* Śnieżka. ▲ N Czech Republic/Poland
110 *N8* **Śniardwy, Jezioro** *Ger.* Spirdingsee. ◎ NE Poland
Sniečkus *see* Visaginas
Śnieżka *see* Sněžka
117 *R10* **Snihurivka** Mykolayivs'ka Oblast', S Ukraine
116 *I5* **Snilov** ✈ (L'viv) L'vivs'ka Oblast', W Ukraine
111 *O19* **Snina** *Hung.* Szinna. Prešovský Kraj, E Slovakia
117 *Y8* **Snizhne** *Rus.* Snezhnoye. Donets'ka Oblast', SE Ukraine
94 *G10* **Snøhetta** *var.* Snohetta. ▲ S Norway
92 *G12* **Snøtinden** ▲ C Norway
97 *I18* **Snowdon** ▲ NW Wales, UK
97 *I18* **Snowdonia** ▲▲ NW Wales, UK
8 *K10* **Snowdrift** ≈ Northwest Territories, NW Canada
Snowdrift *see* Łutselk'e
37 *N12* **Snowflake** Arizona, SW USA
21 *Y5* **Snow Hill** Maryland, NE USA
21 *W10* **Snow Hill** North Carolina, SE USA
194 *H3* **Snowhill Island** *island* Antarctica
9 *V13* **Snow Lake** Manitoba, C Canada
37 *R5* **Snowmass Mountain** ▲ Colorado, C USA
18 *M10* **Snow, Mount** ▲ Vermont, NE USA
34 *M5* **Snow Mountain** ▲ California, W USA
Snow Mountains *see* Maoke, Pegunungan
33 *N7* **Snowshoe Peak** ▲ Montana, NW USA
182 *I8* **Snowtown** South Australia
36 *K1* **Snowville** Utah, W USA
35 *X3* **Snow Water Lake** ◎ Nevada, W USA
183 *Q11* **Snowy Mountains** ▲▲ New South Wales/Victoria, SE Australia
183 *Q12* **Snowy River** ≈ New South Wales/Victoria, SE Australia
44 *K5* **Snug Corner** Acklins Island, SE Bahamas
167 *T13* **Snuŏl** Krâchéh, E Cambodia
116 *J7* **Snyatyn** *Rus.* Snyatyn. Ivano-Frankivs'ka Oblast', W Ukraine
26 *L12* **Snyder** Oklahoma, C USA
25 *O6* **Snyder** Texas, SW USA
172 *H3* **Soalala** Mahajanga, W Madagascar
172 *J4* **Soanierana-Ivongo** Toamasina, E Madagascar
171 *R11* **Soasiu** *var.* Tidore. Pulau Tidore, E Indonesia
54 *G8* **Soatá** Boyacá, C Colombia
172 *I5* **Soavinandriana** Antananarivo, C Madagascar
77 *V13* **Soba** Kaduna, C Nigeria
163 *Y16* **Sobaek-sanmaek** ▲▲ S South Korea
80 *F13* **Sobat** ≈ E Sudan
171 *Z14* **Sobger, Sungai** ≈ Papua, E Indonesia
171 *V13* **Sobiei** Papua, E Indonesia
126 *M3* **Sobinka** Vladimirskaya Oblast', W Russian Federation
127 *S7* **Sobolevo** Orenburgskaya Oblast', W Russian Federation
Soborsin *see* Săvârşin
164 *D15* **Sobo-san** ▲ Kyūshū, SW Japan
111 *G14* **Sobótka** Dolnośląskie, SW Poland
59 *O15* **Sobradinho** Bahia, E Brazil
Sobradinho, Barragem de *see* Sobradinho, Represa de
59 *O16* **Sobradinho, Represa de** *var.* Barragem de Sobradinho. ⊞ E Brazil
58 *O13* **Sobral** Ceará, E Brazil
105 *T4* **Sobrarbe** *physical region* NE Spain
109 *R10* **Soča** *It.* Isonzo. ≈ Italy/Slovenia
110 *L11* **Sochaczew** Mazowieckie, C Poland
126 *L15* **Sochi** Krasnodarskiy Kray, SW Russian Federation
114 *G13* **Sochós** *var.* Sohos, Sokhós. Kentrikí Makedonía, N Greece
Socialist People's Libyan Arab Jamahiriya *see* Libya
191 *R11* **Société, Archipel de la** *var.* Archipel de Tahiti, Îles de la Société, *Eng.* Society Islands. *island group* W French Polynesia
Société, Îles de la/Society Islands *see* Société, Archipel de la
21 *T11* **Society Hill** South Carolina, SE USA
Society Islands *see* Société, Archipel de la
175 *W9* **Society Ridge** *undersea feature* C Pacific Ocean
62 *I5* **Socompa, Volcán** ⛰ N Chile
Soconusco, Sierra de *see* Sierra Madre
54 *G8* **Socorro** Santander, C Colombia
37 *R13* **Socorro** New Mexico, SW USA
Socotra *see* Suquṭrā
167 *S14* **Soc Trăng** *var.* Khanh Hung. Soc Trăng, S Vietnam
105 *P10* **Socuéllamos** Castilla-La Mancha, C Spain
35 *W13* **Soda Lake** *salt flat* California, W USA
92 *L11* **Sodankylä** Lappi, N Finland
Sodari *see* Sodiri
33 *R15* **Soda Springs** Idaho, NW USA
Soddo/Soddu *see* Sodo
20 *L10* **Soddy Daisy** Tennessee, S USA
95 *N14* **Söderfors** Uppsala, C Sweden
94 *N12* **Söderhamn** Gävleborg, C Sweden
95 *N17* **Söderköping** Östergötland, S Sweden
95 *N17* **Södermanland** ◈ *county* C Sweden
95 *O16* **Södertälje** Stockholm, C Sweden
80 *D10* **Sodiri** *var.* Sawdirī, Sodari. Northern Kordofan, C Sudan
81 *I14* **Sodo** *var.* Soddo, Soddu. Southern, S Ethiopia
94 *N11* **Södra Dellen** ◎ C Sweden
95 *M19* **Södra Vi** Kalmar, S Sweden
18 *G9* **Sodus Point** *headland* New York, NE USA
171 *Q17* **Soe** *prev.* Soë. Timor, C Indonesia
Soebang *see* Subang
Soekaboemi *see* Sukabumi
169 *N15* **Soekarno-Hatta** ✈ (Jakarta) Jawa, S Indonesia
Soëla-Sund *see* Soela Väin
118 *E5* **Soela Väin** *prev. Eng.* Sele Sound, *Ger.* Dagden-Sund, Soëla-Sund. *strait* W Estonia
Soemba *see* Sumba, Pulau
Soembawa *see* Sumbawa
Soemenep *see* Sumenep
Soengaipenoeh *see* Sungaipenuh
Soerabaja *see* Surabaya
Soerakarta *see* Surakarta
101 *G14* **Soest** Nordrhein-Westfalen, W Germany
98 *J11* **Soest** Utrecht, C Netherlands
100 *F11* **Soeste** ≈ NW Germany
98 *J11* **Soesterberg** Utrecht, C Netherlands
115 *E16* **Sofádes** *var.* Sofádhes. Thessalía, C Greece
Sofádhes *see* Sofádes
83 *N18* **Sofala** Sofala, C Mozambique
83 *N17* **Sofala** ◈ *province* C Mozambique
83 *N18* **Sofala, Baia de** *bay* C Mozambique
172 *J3* **Sofia** *seasonal river* NW Madagascar
Sofia *see* Sofiya
115 *G19* **Sofikó** Pelopónnisos, S Greece
Sofi-Kurgan *see* Sopu-Korgon
114 *G10* **Sofiya** *var.* Sophia, *Eng.* Sofia, *Lat.* Serdica. ● (Bulgaria) Sofiya-Grad, W Bulgaria
114 *H9* **Sofiya** ◈ *province* W Bulgaria
114 *G9* **Sofiya** ✈ Sofiya-Grad, W Bulgaria
114 *G9* **Sofiya, Grad** ◈ *municipality* W Bulgaria
Sofiyevka *see* Sofiyivka
117 *S8* **Sofiyivka** *Rus.* Sofiyevka. Dnipropetrovs'ka Oblast', E Ukraine
123 *R13* **Sofiysk** Khabarovskiy Kray, SE Russian Federation
123 *R12* **Sofiysk** Khabarovskiy Kray, SE Russian Federation
124 *I6* **Sofporog** Respublika Kareliya, NW Russian Federation
115 *L23* **Sofraná** *prev* Záfora. *island* Kykládes, Greece, Aegean Sea
165 *Y14* **Sōfu-gan** *island* Izu-shotō, SE Japan
156 *K10* **Sog** Xizang Zizhiqu, W China
54 *G9* **Sogamoso** Boyacá, C Colombia
136 *I11* **Soğanlı Çayı** ≈ N Turkey
94 *E12* **Sogn** *physical region* S Norway
Sogndal *see* Sogndalsfjøra
94 *E12* **Sogndalsfjøra** *var.* Sogndal. Sogn Og Fjordane, S Norway
95 *E18* **Søgne** Vest-Agder, S Norway
94 *D12* **Sognefjorden** *fjord* NE North Sea
94 *C12* **Sogn Og Fjordane** ◈ *county* S Norway
162 *I11* **Sogo Nur** ◎ N China
159 *T12* **Sogruma** Qinghai, W China
163 *X17* **Sŏgwip'o** S South Korea
75 *X10* **Sohâg** *var.* Sawhāj, Suliag. C Egypt
Sohar *see* Şuḥār
64 *H9* **Sohm Plain** *undersea feature* NW Atlantic Ocean
100 *H7* **Soholmer Au** ≈ N Germany
Sohos *see* Sochós
Sohrau *see* Żory
99 *F20* **Soignies** Hainaut, SW Belgium
159 *R15* **Soila** Xizang Zizhiqu, W China
103 *P4* **Soissons** *anc.* Augusta Suessionum, Noviodunum. Aisne, N France
164 *H13* **Sōja** Okayama, Honshū, SW Japan
152 *F13* **Sojat** Rājasthān, N India
163 *W13* **Sŏjosŏn-man** *inlet* W North Korea
116 *I4* **Sokal'** *Rus.* Sokal. L'vivs'ka Oblast', NW Ukraine
163 *Y14* **Sokch'o** N South Korea
136 *B15* **Söke** Aydın, SW Turkey
189 *N12* **Sokehs Island** *island* E Micronesia
79 *M24* **Sokele** Katanga, SE Dem. Rep. Congo
147 *R11* **Sokh** *Uzb.* Sŭkh. ≈ Kyrgyzstan/Uzbekistan
Sokh *see* So'x
Sokhós *see* Sochós
137 *Q8* **Sokhumi** *Rus.* Sukhumi. NW Georgia
113 *O14* **Sokobanja** Serbia, E Serbia
77 *R15* **Sokodé** C Togo
123 *T10* **Sokol** Magadanskaya Oblast', E Russian Federation
124 *M13* **Sokol** Vologodskaya Oblast', NW Russian Federation
110 *P9* **Sokółka** Podlaskie, NE Poland
76 *M11* **Sokolo** Ségou, W Mali
111 *A16* **Sokolov** *Ger.* Falkenau an der Eger; *prev.* Falknov nad Ohří. Karlovarský Kraj, W Czech Republic
111 *O16* **Sokołów Małopolski** Podkarpackie, SE Poland
110 *O11* **Sokołów Podlaski** Mazowieckie, C Poland
76 *G11* **Sokone** W Senegal
77 *T12* **Sokoto** Sokoto, NW Nigeria
77 *T12* **Sokoto** ◈ *state* NW Nigeria
77 *S12* **Sokoto** ≈ NW Nigeria
Sokotra *see* Suquṭrā
147 *U7* **Sokuluk** Chuyskaya Oblast', N Kyrgyzstan
116 *L7* **Sokyryany** Chernivets'ka Oblast', W Ukraine
95 *C16* **Sola** Rogaland, S Norway
187 *R12* **Sola** Vanua Lava, N Vanuatu
95 *C17* **Sola** ✈ (Stavanger) Rogaland, S Norway
81 *H18* **Solai** Rift Valley, W Kenya
152 *I8* **Solan** Himāchal Pradesh, N India
185 *A25* **Solander Island** *island* SW New Zealand
Solano *see* Bahía Solano
155 *F15* **Solāpur** *var.* Sholāpur. Mahārāshtra, W India
93 *H16* **Solberg** Västernorrland, C Sweden
116 *K9* **Solca** *Ger.* Solka. Suceava, N Romania
105 *O16* **Sol, Costa del** *coastal region* S Spain
106 *F5* **Solda** *Ger.* Sulden. Trentino-Alto Adige, N Italy
117 *N9* **Şoldăneşti** *Rus.* Sholdaneshty. N Moldova
Soldau *see* Wkra
108 *L8* **Sölden** Tirol, W Austria
27 *P3* **Soldier Creek** ≈ Kansas, C USA
39 *R12* **Soldotna** Alaska, USA
110 *I10* **Solec Kujawski** Kujawsko-pomorskie, C Poland
61 *B16* **Soledad** Santa Fe, C Argentina
55 *E4* **Soledad** Atlántico, N Colombia
35 *O11* **Soledad** California, W USA
55 *O7* **Soledad** Anzoátegui, NE Venezuela
61 *H15* **Soledade** Rio Grande do Sul, S Brazil
Isla Soledad *see* East Falkland
103 *Y15* **Solenzara** Corse, France, C Mediterranean Sea
Soleure *see* Solothurn
94 *C12* **Solheim** Hordaland, S Norway
125 *N14* **Soligalich** Kostromskaya Oblast', NW Russian Federation
Soligorsk *see* Salihorsk
97 *L20* **Solihull** C England, UK
125 *U13* **Solikamsk** Permskaya Oblast', NW Russian Federation
127 *V8* **Sol'-Iletsk** Orenburgskaya Oblast', W Russian Federation
57 *G17* **Solimana, Nevado** ▲ S Peru
58 *E13* **Solimões, Rio** ≈ C Brazil
113 *E14* **Solin** *It.* Salona; *anc.* Salonae. Split-Dalmacija, S Croatia
101 *E15* **Solingen** Nordrhein-Westfalen, W Germany
Solka *see* Solca
93 *H16* **Sollefteå** Västernorrland, C Sweden
95 *O15* **Sollentuna** Stockholm, C Sweden
105 *x9* **Sóller** Mallorca, Spain, W Mediterranean Sea
94 *L13* **Sollerön** Dalarna, C Sweden
101 *I14* **Solling** *hill range* C Germany
95 *O16* **Solna** Stockholm, C Sweden
126 *K3* **Solnechnogorsk** Moskovskaya Oblast', W Russian Federation
123 *R10* **Solnechnyy** Khabarovskiy Kray, SE Russian Federation
122 *K13* **Solnechnyy** Krasnoyarskiy Kray, C Russian Federation
123 *S13* **Solnechnyy** Respublika Sakha (Yakutiya), NE Russian Federation
Solo *see* Surakarta
107 *L17* **Solofra** Campania, S Italy
168 *J11* **Solok** Sumatera, W Indonesia
42 *C6* **Sololá** Sololá, W Guatemala
42 *A2* **Sololá** *off.* Departamento de Sololá. ◈ *department* SW Guatemala
Sololá, Departamento de *see* Sololá
81 *J16* **Sololo** Eastern, N Kenya
42 *C4* **Soloma** Huehuetenango, W Guatemala
38 *M9* **Solomon** Alaska, USA
27 *N4* **Solomon** Kansas, C USA
187 *N9* **Solomon Islands** *prev.* British Solomon Islands Protectorate. ◆ *commonwealth republic* W Solomon Islands N Melanesia W Pacific Ocean
186 *L7* **Solomon Islands** *island group* Papua New Guinea/Solomon Islands
26 *M3* **Solomon River** ≈ Kansas, C USA
186 *H8* **Solomon Sea** *sea* W Pacific Ocean
31 *U11* **Solon** Ohio, N USA
117 *T8* **Solone** Dnipropetrovs'ka Oblast', E Ukraine
171 *P16* **Solor, Kepulauan** *island group* S Indonesia
126 *M4* **Solotcha** Ryazanskaya Oblast', W Russian Federation
108 *D7* **Solothurn** *Fr.* Soleure. Solothurn, NW Switzerland
108 *D7* **Solothurn** *Fr.* Soleure. ◈ *canton* NW Switzerland
124 *J7* **Solovetskiye Ostrova** *island group* NW Russian Federation
105 *V5* **Solsona** Cataluña, NE Spain
113 *E14* **Šolta** *It.* Solta. *island* S Croatia
Solṭānābād *see* Kāshmar
142 *L4* **Solṭānīyeh** Zanjān, NW Iran
100 *I11* **Soltau** Niedersachsen, NW Germany
124 *G14* **Sol'tsy** Novgorodskaya Oblast', W Russian Federation
Soltüstik Qazaqstan Oblysy *see* Severnyy Kazakhstan
Solun *see* Thessaloníki
113 *O19* **Solunska Glava** ▲ C FYR Macedonia
95 *L22* **Sölvesborg** Blekinge, S Sweden
97 *J15* **Solway Firth** *inlet* England/ Scotland, UK
82 *I13* **Solwezi** North Western, NW Zambia
165 *Q11* **Sōma** Fukushima, Honshū, C Japan
136 *C13* **Soma** Manisa, W Turkey
81 *M14* **Somali** ◈ *province* E Ethiopia
81 *O15* **Somalia** *off.* Somali Democratic Republic, *Som.* Jamuuriyada Demuqraadiga Soomaaliyeed, Soomaaliya; *prev.* Italian Somaliland, Somaliland Protectorate. ◆ *republic* E Africa
173 *N6* **Somali Basin** *undersea feature* W Indian Ocean
Somali Democratic Republic *see* Somalia
80 *N12* **Somaliland** ◈ *disputed territory* N Somalia
Somaliland Protectorate *see* Somalia
67 *Y8* **Somali Plain** *undersea feature* W Indian Ocean
112 *J8* **Sombor** *Hung.* Zombor. Vojvodina, NW Serbia
99 *H20* **Sombreffe** Namur, S Belgium
40 *L10* **Sombrerete** Zacatecas, C Mexico
45 *V8* **Sombrero** *island* N Anguilla
151 *Q21* **Sombrero Channel** *channel* Nicobar Islands, India
116 *H9* **Şomcuta Mare** *Hung.* Nagysomkút; *prev.* Somcuţa Mare. Maramureş, N Romania
Somcuţa Mare *see* Şomcuta Mare
167 *R9* **Somdet** Kalasin, E Thailand
99 *L15* **Someren** Noord-Brabant, SE Netherlands
93 *L19* **Somero** Länsi-Soumi, SW Finland
33 *P7* **Somers** Montana, NW USA
64 *A12* **Somerset** *var.* Somerset Village. W Bermuda
37 *Q5* **Somerset** Colorado, C USA
20 *M7* **Somerset** Kentucky, S USA
19 *O12* **Somerset** Massachusetts, NE USA
97 *K23* **Somerset** *cultural region* SW England, UK
Somerset East *see* Somerset-Oos
64 *A12* **Somerset Island** *island* W Bermuda
197 *N9* **Somerset Island** *island* Queen Elizabeth Islands, Nunavut, NW Canada
Somerset Nile *see* Victoria Nile
83 *I25* **Somerset-Oos** *var.* Somerset East. Eastern Cape, S South Africa
Somerset Village *see* Somerset
83 *E26* **Somerset-Wes** *var.* Somerset West. Western Cape, SW South Africa
Somerset West *see* Somerset-Wes
Somers Islands *see* Bermuda
18 *J17* **Somers Point** New Jersey, NE USA
19 *P9* **Somersworth** New Hampshire, NE USA
36 *H15* **Somerton** Arizona, SW USA
18 *J14* **Somerville** New Jersey, NE USA
20 *F10* **Somerville** Tennessee, S USA
25 *U10* **Somerville** Texas, SW USA
25 *T10* **Somerville Lake** ⊞ Texas, SW USA
Someş/Somesch/Someşul *see* Szamos
103 *N2* **Somme** ◈ *department* N France
103 *N2* **Somme** ≈ N France
95 *L18* **Sommen** Jönköping, S Sweden
95 *M18* **Sommen** ◎ S Sweden
101 *K16* **Sömmerda** Thüringen, C Germany
Sommerein *see* Šamorín
Sommerfeld *see* Lubsko
55 *Y11* **Sommet Tabulaire** *var.* Mont Itoupé. ▲▲ S French Guiana
111 *H25* **Somogy** *off.* Somogy Megye. ◈ *county* SW Hungary
Somogy Megye *see* Somogy
Somorja *see* Šamorín
105 *N7* **Somosierra, Puerto de** *pass* N Spain
187 *Y14* **Somosomo** Taveuni, N Fiji
42 *I9* **Somotillo** Chinandega, NW Nicaragua
42 *I8* **Somoto** Madriz, NW Nicaragua
110 *I11* **Sompolno** Wielkopolskie, C Poland
105 *S3* **Somport** *var.* Puerto de Somport, *Fr.* Col du Somport; *anc.* Summus Portus. *pass* France/Spain
Somport *see* Somport, Col du
102 *J17* **Somport, Col du** *var.* Puerto de Somport, *Sp.* Somport; *anc.* Summus Portus. *pass* France/Spain
Somport, Col du *see* Somport
Somport, Puerto de *see* Somport/Somport, Col du
99 *K15* **Son** Noord-Brabant, S Netherlands
95 *H15* **Son** ◈ Akershus, S Norway
154 *L9* **Son** *var.* Sone. ≈ C India
43 *R16* **Soná** Veraguas, W Panama
Sonag *see* Zêkog
154 *M12* **Sonapur** *prev.* Sonepur. Orissa, E India
95 *G24* **Sønderborg** *Ger.* Sonderburg. Sønderjylland, SW Denmark
Sonderburg *see* Sønderborg
95 *F24* **Sønderjylland** *var.* Sønderjyllands Amt. ◈ *county* SW Denmark
Sønderjyllands Amt *see* Sønderjylland
101 *K15* **Sondershausen** Thüringen, C Germany
Sondre Strømfjord *see* Kangerlussuaq
106 *E6* **Sondrio** Lombardia, N Italy
Sone *see* Son
Sonepur *see* Sonapur
57 *K22* **Sonequera** ▲ S Bolivia
167 *V12* **Sông Câu** Phu Yên, C Vietnam
167 *R15* **Sông Đôc** Minh Hai, S Vietnam
81 *H25* **Songea** Ruvuma, S Tanzania
163 *X10* **Songhua Hu** ◎ NE China
163 *Y7* **Songhua Jiang** *var.* Sungari. ≈ NE China
161 *S8* **Songjiang** Shanghai Shi, E China
Sŏngjin *see* Kimch'aek
167 *O16* **Songkhla** *var.* Songkla, *Mal.* Singora. Songkhla, SW Thailand
Songkla *see* Songkhla
163 *T13* **Song Ling** ▲▲ NE China
163 *W14* **Songnim** SW North Korea
82 *B10* **Songo** Uíge, NW Angola
83 *M15* **Songo** Tete, NW Mozambique
79 *F21* **Songololo** Bas-Congo, SW Dem. Rep. Congo
160 *H7* **Songpan** *var.* Jin'an, *Tib.* Sungpu. Sichuan, C China
163 *Y17* **Sŏngsan** S South Korea
161 *R11* **Songxi** Fujian, SE China
160 *M6* **Songxian** *var.* Song Xian. Henan, C China
Song Xian *see* Songxian
161 *R10* **Songyang** *var.* Xiping; *prev.* Songyin. Zhejiang, SE China
Songyin *see* Songyang
163 *V9* **Songyuan** *var.* Fu-yü, Petuna; *prev.* Fuyu. Jilin, NE China
Sonid Youqi *see* SaihanTal
Sonid Zuoqi *see* Mandalt
152 *I10* **Sonīpat** Haryāna, N India
93 *M15* **Sonkajärvi** Itä-Suomi, C Finland
167 *R6* **Sơn La** Sơn La, N Vietnam
149 *O16* **Sonmiāni** Baluchistān, S Pakistan
149 *O16* **Sonmiāni Bay** *bay* S Pakistan
101 *K18* **Sonneberg** Thüringen, C Germany
101 *N24* **Sonntagshorn** ▲ Austria/Germany
Sonoita *see* Sonoyta
40 *E3* **Sonoita, Rio** *var.* Río Sonoyta. ≈ Mexico/USA
35 *N7* **Sonoma** California, W USA
35 *T3* **Sonoma Peak** ▲ Nevada, W USA
35 *P8* **Sonora** California, W USA
25 *O10* **Sonora** Texas, SW USA
40 *F5* **Sonora** ◈ *state* NW Mexico
35 *X17* **Sonoran Desert** *var.* Desierto de Altar. *desert* Mexico/USA *see also* Altar, Desierto de
Sonoran Desert *see* Altar, Desierto de
40 *G5* **Sonora, Río** ≈ NW Mexico
40 *E2* **Sonoyta** *var.* Sonoita. Sonora, NW Mexico
Sonoyta, Río *see* Sonoita, Rio
142 *K6* **Sonqor** *var.* Sunqur. Kermānshāhān, W Iran
105 *N9* **Sonseca** *var.* Sonseca con Casalgordo. Castilla-La Mancha, C Spain
Sonseca con Casalgordo *see* Sonseca
54 *E9* **Sonsón** Antioquia, W Colombia
42 *E7* **Sonsonate** Sonsonate, W El Salvador
42 *A9* **Sonsonate** ◈ *department* SW El Salvador
188 *A10* **Sonsorol Islands** *island group* S Palau
112 *J9* **Sonta** *Hung.* Szond; *prev.* Szonta. Vojvodina, NW Serbia
167 *S6* **Sơn Tây** *var.* Sontay. Ha Tây, N Vietnam
Sontay *see* Sơn Tây
101 *J25* **Sonthofen** Bayern, S Germany
Soochow *see* Suzhou
80 *O13* **Sool** *off.* Gobolka Sool. ◈ *region* N Somali
Soomaaliya/Soomaaliyeed, Jamuuriyada Demuqraadiga *see* Somalia
Soome Laht *see* Finland, Gulf of
23 *V5* **Soperton** Georgia, SE USA
167 *S6* **Sop Hao** Houaphan, N Laos
Sophia *see* Sofiya
171 *S10* **Sopi** Pulau Morotai, E Indonesia
Sopianae *see* Pécs
171 *U13* **Sopinusa** Papua, E Indonesia
81 *B14* **Sopo** ≈ W Sudan
Sopockinie/Sopotskin/ Sopotskino *see* Sapotskin
114 *I9* **Sopot** Plovdiv, C Bulgaria
110 *I7* **Sopot** *Ger.* Zoppot. Pomorskie, N Poland
167 *O8* **Sop Prap** *var.* Ban Sop Prap. Lampang, NW Thailand
111 *G22* **Sopron** *Ger.* Ödenburg. Győr-Moson-Sopron, NW Hungary
147 *U11* **Sopu-Korgon** *var.* Sofi-Kurgan. Oshskaya Oblast', SW Kyrgyzstan
152 *H5* **Sopur** Jammu and Kashmir, NW India
107 *J15* **Sora** Lazio, C Italy
154 *N13* **Sorada** Orissa, E India
93 *H17* **Söråker** Västernorrland, C Sweden
57 *J17* **Sorata** La Paz, W Bolivia
Sorau/Sorau in der Niederlausitz *see* Żary
105 *Q14* **Sorbas** Andalucía, S Spain
Sord/Sórd Choluim Chille *see* Swords
15 *O11* **Sorel** Québec, SE Canada
183 *P17* **Sorell** Tasmania, SE Australia
183 *O17* **Sorell, Lake** ◎ Tasmania, SE Australia
106 *E8* **Soresina** Lombardia, N Italy
95 *D14* **Sørfjorden** *fjord* S Norway
94 *N11* **Sörforsa** Gävleborg, C Sweden
103 *R14* **Sorgues** Vaucluse, SE France
136 *K13* **Sorgun** Yozgat, C Turkey
105 *P5* **Soria** Castilla-León, N Spain
105 *P6* **Soria** ◈ *province* Castilla-León, N Spain
61 *D19* **Soriano** Soriano, SW Uruguay
61 *D19* **Soriano** ◈ *department* SW Uruguay
92 *O4* **Sørkapp** *headland* SW Svalbard
143 *T5* **Sorkh, Kūh-e** ▲▲ NE Iran
95 *I23* **Sorø** Vestsjælland, E Denmark
Soro *see* Ghazal, Bahr el
116 *M8* **Soroca** *Rus.* Soroki. N Moldova
60 *L10* **Sorocaba** São Paulo, S Brazil
Sorochino *see* Sarochyna
127 *T7* **Sorochinsk** Orenburgskaya Oblast', W Russian Federation
Soroki *see* Soroca
188 *H15* **Sorol** *atoll* Caroline Islands, W Micronesia
171 *T12* **Sorong** Papua, E Indonesia
81 *G17* **Soroti** C Uganda
Sørøy *see* Sørøya
92 *J8* **Sørøya** *var.* Sørøy, *Lapp.* Sállan. *island* N Norway
104 *G11* **Sorraia, Rio** ≈ C Portugal
92 *I10* **Sørreisa** Troms, N Norway
107 *K18* **Sorrento** *anc.* Surrentum. Campania, S Italy
104 *H10* **Sor, Ribeira de** *stream* C Portugal
195 *T3* **Sør Rondane Mountains** ▲▲ Antarctica
93 *H14* **Sorsele** Västerbotten, N Sweden
107 *B17* **Sorso** Sardegna, Italy, C Mediterranean Sea
171 *P4* **Sorsogon** Luzon, N Philippines
105 *U4* **Sort** Cataluña, NE Spain
124 *H11* **Sortavala** Respublika Kareliya, NW Russian Federation
107 *L25* **Sortino** Sicilia, Italy, C Mediterranean Sea
92 *G10* **Sortland** Nordland, C Norway
94 *G9* **Sør-Trøndelag** ◈ *county* S Norway
95 *I15* **Sørumsand** Akershus, S Norway
118 *D6* **Sõrve Säär** *headland* SW Estonia
95 *K22* **Sösdala** Skåne, S Sweden
105 *R4* **Sos del Rey Católico** Aragón, NE Spain
93 *F15* **Sösjöfjällen** ▲ C Sweden
126 *K7* **Sosna** ≈ W Russian Federation
62 *H12* **Sosneado, Cerro** ▲ W Argentina
125 *S9* **Sosnogorsk** Respublika Komi, NW Russian Federation
124 *J8* **Sosnovets** Respublika Kareliya, NW Russian Federation
Sosnovets *see* Sosnowiec
127 *Q3* **Sosnovka** Chavash Respubliki, W Russian Federation
125 *S16* **Sosnovka** Kirovskaya Oblast', NW Russian Federation
124 *M6* **Sosnovka** Murmanskaya Oblast', NW Russian Federation
126 *M6* **Sosnovka** Tambovskaya Oblast', W Russian Federation
124 *H12* **Sosnovo** *Fin.* Rautu. Leningradskaya Oblast', NW Russian Federation
Sosnovyy Bor *see* Sasnovy Bor
111 *J16* **Sosnowiec** *Ger.* Sosnowitz, *Rus.* Sosnovets. Śląskie, S Poland
Sosnowitz *see* Sosnowiec
117 *R2* **Sosnytsya** Chernihivs'ka Oblast', N Ukraine
109 *V10* **Šoštanj** N Slovenia
122 *G10* **Sos'va** Sverdlovskaya Oblast', C Russian Federation
54 *D12* **Sotará, Volcán** ⛰ S Colombia
76 *D10* **Sotavento, Ilhas de** *var.* Leeward Islands. *island group* S Cape Verde
93 *N15* **Sotkamo** Oulu, C Finland
109 *W11* **Sotla** ≈ E Slovenia
41 *P10* **Soto la Marina** Tamaulipas, C Mexico
41 *P10* **Soto la Marina, Río** ≈ C Mexico
95 *B14* **Sotra** *island* S Norway
41 *X12* **Sotuta** Yucatán, SE Mexico
79 *F17* **Souanké** La Sangha, NW Congo
76 *M17* **Soubré** S Ivory Coast
115 *H24* **Soúda** *var.* Soúdha, *Eng.* Suda. Kríti, Greece, E Mediterranean Sea
Soúdha *see* Soúda
Soueida *see* As Suwaydā'
114 *L12* **Souflí** *prev.* Souflíon. Anatolikí Makedonía kai Thráki, NE Greece
Souflíon *see* Souflí

◆ Country
● Country Capital
◇ Dependent Territory
○ Dependent Territory Capital
◈ Administrative Regions
✈ International Airport
▲ Mountain
▲▲ Mountain Range
⛰ Volcano
≈ River
◎ Lake
⊞ Reservoir

45 S11 **Soufrière** W Saint Lucia
45 X6 **Soufrière** ▲ Basse Terre, S Guadeloupe
102 M13 **Souillac** Lot, S France
173 Y17 **Souillac** S Mauritius
74 M5 **Souk Ahras** NE Algeria
Souk el Arba du Rharb/ Souk-el-Arba-du-Rharb/ Souk-el-Arba-el-Rhab see Souk-el-Arba-Rharb
74 E6 **Souk-el-Arba-Rharb** var. Souk el Arba du Rharb, Souk-el-Arba-du-Rharb, Souk-el-Arba-el-Rhab. NW Morocco
Soukhné see As Sukhnah
163 X14 **Sŏul** off. Sŏul-t'ŭkpyŏlsi, Eng. Seoul, Jap. Keijō; prev. Kyŏngsŏng. ● (South Korea) NW South Korea
102 J11 **Soulac-sur-Mer** Gironde, SW France
Sŏul-t'ŭkpyŏlsi see Sŏul
99 L19 **Soumagne** Liège, E Belgium
18 M14 **Sound Beach** Long Island, New York, NE USA
95 J22 **Sound, The** Dan. Øresund, Swe. Öresund. strait Denmark/Sweden
115 H20 **Soúnio, Akrotírio** cape C Greece
138 F8 **Soûr** var. Şūr; anc. Tyre. SW Lebanon
Sources, Mont-aux- see Phofung
104 G8 **Soure** Coimbra, N Portugal
9 W17 **Souris** Manitoba, S Canada
13 Q14 **Souris** Prince Edward Island, SE Canada
28 L2 **Souris River** var. Mouse River. ≈ Canada/USA
25 X10 **Sour Lake** Texas, SW USA
115 F17 **Soúrpi** Thessalía, C Greece
104 H11 **Sousel** Portalegre, C Portugal
75 N6 **Sousse** var. Sūsah. NE Tunisia
14 H11 **South** ≈ Ontario, S Canada
South see Sud
83 G23 **South Africa** off. Republic of South Africa, Afr. Suid-Afrika. ◆ republic S Africa
South Africa, Republic of see South Africa
46-47 **South America** continent
2 J17 **South American Plate** tectonic feature
97 M23 **Southampton** hist. Hamwih, Lat. Clausentum. S England, UK
19 N14 **Southampton** Long Island, New York, NE USA
9 P8 **Southampton Island** island Nunavut, NE Canada
151 P20 **South Andaman** island Andaman Islands, India, NE Indian Ocean
13 Q6 **South Aulatsivik Island** island Newfoundland and Labrador, E Canada
182 E4 **South Australia** ◐ state S Australia
South Australian Abyssal Plain see South Australian Plain
192 G11 **South Australian Basin** undersea feature SW Indian Ocean
173 X12 **South Australian Plain** var. South Australian Abyssal Plain. undersea feature SE Indian Ocean
37 R13 **South Baldy** ▲ New Mexico, SW USA
23 Y14 **South Bay** Florida, SE USA
14 E12 **South Baymouth** Manitoulin Island, Ontario, S Canada
30 L10 **South Beloit** Illinois, N USA
31 O11 **South Bend** Indiana, N USA
25 R6 **South Bend** Texas, SW USA
32 F9 **South Bend** Washington, NW USA
South Beveland see Zuid-Beveland
South Borneo see Kalimantan Selatan
21 U7 **South Boston** Virginia, NE USA
182 F2 **South Branch Neales** seasonal river South Australia
21 U3 **South Branch Potomac River** ≈ West Virginia, NE USA
185 H19 **Southbridge** Canterbury, South Island, New Zealand
19 N12 **Southbridge** Massachusetts, NE USA
183 P17 **South Bruny Island** island Tasmania, SE Australia
18 L7 **South Burlington** Vermont, NE USA
44 M6 **South Caicos** island S Turks and Caicos Islands
South Cape see Ka Lae
23 V3 **South Carolina** off. State of South Carolina, also known as The Palmetto State. ◐ state SE USA
South Carpathians see Carpații Meridionali
South Celebes see Sulawesi Selatan
21 Q5 **South Charleston** West Virginia, NE USA
192 D7 **South China Basin** undersea feature SE South China Sea
169 R8 **South China Sea** Chin. Nan Hai, Ind. Laut Cina Selatan, Vtn. Biên Đông. sea SE Asia
33 Z10 **South Dakota** off. State of South Dakota, also known as The Coyote State, Sunshine State. ◐ state N USA
23 X10 **South Daytona** Florida, SE USA
37 R10 **South Domingo Pueblo** New Mexico, SW USA
97 N23 **South Downs** hill range SE England, UK
83 I21 **South East** ◐ district SE Botswana
65 H15 **South East Bay** bay Ascension Island, C Atlantic Ocean
183 O17 **South East Cape** headland Tasmania, SE Australia
38 K10 **Southeast Cape** headland Saint Lawrence Island, Alaska, USA
South-East Celebes see Sulawesi Tenggara
192 G12 **Southeast Indian Ridge** undersea feature Indian Ocean/Pacific Ocean
Southeast Island see Tagula Island
193 P13 **Southeast Pacific Basin** var. Belling Hausen Mulde. undersea feature SE Pacific Ocean
65 H15 **South East Point** headland SE Ascension Island
183 O14 **South East Point** headland Victoria, S Australia
44 L5 **Southeast Point** headland Mayaguana, SE Bahamas
191 Z3 **South East Point** headland Kiritimati, NE Kiribati
South-East Sulawesi see Sulawesi Tenggara
9 U12 **Southend** Saskatchewan, C Canada
97 P22 **Southend-on-Sea** E England, UK
83 H20 **Southern** var. Bangwaketse, Ngwaketze. ◐ district SE Botswana
81 I15 **Southern** ◐ region S Ethiopia
138 E13 **Southern** ◐ district S Israel
83 N15 **Southern** ◐ region S Malawi
83 I15 **Southern** ◐ province S Zambia
185 E19 **Southern Alps** ▲▲ South Island, New Zealand
190 K15 **Southern Cook Islands** island group S Cook Islands
180 K12 **Southern Cross** Western Australia
80 A12 **Southern Darfur** ◐ state W Sudan
186 B7 **Southern Highlands** ◐ province W Papua New Guinea
9 V11 **Southern Indian Lake** ◎ Manitoba, C Canada
80 E11 **Southern Kordofan** ◐ state C Sudan
187 Z15 **Southern Lau Group** island group Lau Group, SE Fiji
173 S13 **Southern Ocean** ocean
21 T10 **Southern Pines** North Carolina, SE USA
155 J26 **Southern Province** ◐ province S Sri Lanka
96 I13 **Southern Uplands** ▲▲ S Scotland, UK
Southern Urals see Yuzhnyy Ural
183 P16 **South Esk River** ≈ Tasmania, SE Australia
9 U16 **Southey** Saskatchewan, S Canada
27 V2 **South Fabius River** ≈ Missouri, C USA
31 S10 **Southfield** Michigan, N USA
192 K10 **South Fiji Basin** undersea feature S Pacific Ocean
97 Q22 **South Foreland** headland SE England, UK
35 P7 **South Fork American River** ≈ California, W USA
28 K7 **South Fork Grand River** ≈ South Dakota, N USA
35 T12 **South Fork Kern River** ≈ California, W USA
39 Q7 **South Fork Koyukuk River** ≈ Alaska, USA
39 Q11 **South Fork Kuskokwim River** ≈ Alaska, USA
26 H2 **South Fork Republican River** ≈ C USA
26 L3 **South Fork Solomon River** ≈ Kansas, C USA
31 P5 **South Fox Island** island Michigan, N USA
20 G8 **South Fulton** Tennessee, S USA
195 U10 **South Geomagnetic Pole** pole Antarctica
65 J20 **South Georgia** island South Georgia and the South Sandwich Islands, SW Atlantic Ocean
65 K21 **South Georgia and the South Sandwich Islands** ◇ UK Dependent Territory SW Atlantic Ocean
47 Y14 **South Georgia Ridge** var. North Scotia Ridge. undersea feature SW Atlantic Ocean
181 Q1 **South Goulburn Island** island Northern Territory, N Australia
153 U16 **South Hatia Island** island SE Bangladesh
31 O10 **South Haven** Michigan, N USA
21 V7 **South Hill** Virginia, NE USA
South Holland see Zuid-Holland
21 P8 **South Holston Lake** ⊠ Tennessee/Virginia, S USA
175 N1 **South Honshu Ridge** undersea feature W Pacific Ocean
26 M6 **South Hutchinson** Kansas, C USA
151 K21 **South Huvadhu Atoll** atoll S Maldives
173 U14 **South Indian Basin** undersea feature Indian Ocean/Pacific Ocean
9 W11 **South Indian Lake** Manitoba, C Canada
81 I17 **South Island** island NW Kenya
185 C20 **South Island** island S New Zealand
65 B23 **South Jason** island Jason Islands, NW Falkland Islands
South Kalimantan see Kalimantan Selatan
South Kazakhstan see Yuzhnyy Kazakhstan
163 X15 **South Korea** off. Republic of Korea, Kor. Taehan Min'guk. ◆ republic E Asia
35 Q6 **South Lake Tahoe** California, W USA
25 N6 **Southland** Texas, SW USA
185 B23 **Southland** off. Southland Region. ◐ region South Island, New Zealand
Southland Region see Southland
29 N15 **South Loup River** ≈ Nebraska, C USA
151 K19 **South Maalhosmadulu Atoll** atoll N Maldives
14 E15 **South Maitland** ≈ Ontario, S Canada
192 E8 **South Makassar Basin** undersea feature E Java Sea
31 O6 **South Manitou Island** island Michigan, N USA
151 K18 **South Miladummadulu Atoll** atoll N Maldives
21 X8 **South Mills** North Carolina, SE USA
8 H9 **South Nahanni** ≈ Northwest Territories, NW Canada
39 P13 **South Naknek** Alaska, USA
14 M13 **South Nation** ≈ Ontario, SE Canada
44 F9 **South Negril Point** headland W Jamaica
151 K20 **South Nilandhe Atoll** var. Dhaalu Atoll. atoll C Maldives
36 L2 **South Ogden** Utah, W USA
18 M14 **Southold** Long Island, New York, NE USA
194 H1 **South Orkney Islands** island group Antarctica
137 S9 **South Ossetia** former autonomous region SW Georgia
South Pacific Basin see Southwest Pacific Basin
19 P7 **South Paris** Maine, NE USA
189 U13 **South Pass** passage Chuuk Islands, C Micronesia
33 U15 **South Pass** pass Wyoming, C USA
20 K10 **South Pittsburg** Tennessee, S USA
28 K15 **South Platte River** ≈ Colorado/Nebraska, C USA
31 T16 **South Point** Ohio, N USA
65 G15 **South Point** headland S Ascension Island
31 R6 **South Point** headland Michigan, N USA
South Point see Ka Lae
195 Q9 **South Pole** pole Antarctica
183 P17 **Southport** Tasmania, SE Australia
97 K17 **Southport** NW England, UK
21 V12 **Southport** North Carolina, SE USA
19 P8 **South Portland** Maine, NE USA
14 H12 **South River** Ontario, S Canada
21 U11 **South River** ≈ North Carolina, SE USA
96 K5 **South Ronaldsay** island NE Scotland, UK
36 L2 **South Salt Lake** Utah, W USA
65 L21 **South Sandwich Islands** island group SE South Georgia and South Sandwich Islands
65 K21 **South Sandwich Trench** undersea feature SW Atlantic Ocean
9 S16 **South Saskatchewan** ≈ Alberta/Saskatchewan, S Canada
65 I21 **South Scotia Ridge** undersea feature S Scotia Sea
9 V10 **South Seal** ≈ Manitoba, C Canada
194 G4 **South Shetland Islands** island group Antarctica
65 H22 **South Shetland Trough** undersea feature Atlantic Ocean/Pacific Ocean
97 M14 **South Shields** NE England, UK
29 R13 **South Sioux City** Nebraska, C USA
192 J9 **South Solomon Trench** undersea feature W Pacific Ocean
183 V3 **South Stradbroke Island** island Queensland, E Australia
South Sulawesi see Sulawesi Selatan
South Sumatra see Sumatera Selatan
184 K11 **South Taranaki Bight** bight SE Tasman Sea
South Tasmania Plateau see Tasman Plateau
36 M15 **South Tucson** Arizona, SW USA
12 H9 **South Twin Island** island Nunavut, C Canada
96 E9 **South Uist** island NW Scotland, UK
South-West see Sud-Ouest
South-West Africa/South West Africa see Namibia
65 F15 **South West Bay** bay Ascension Island, C Atlantic Ocean
183 N18 **South West Cape** headland Tasmania, SE Australia
185 B26 **South West Cape** headland Stewart Island, New Zealand
38 J10 **Southwest Cape** headland Saint Lawrence Island, Alaska, USA
Southwest Indian Ocean Ridge see Southwest Indian Ridge
173 N11 **Southwest Indian Ridge** var. Southwest Indian Ocean Ridge. undersea feature SW Indian Ocean
192 L10 **Southwest Pacific Basin** var. South Pacific Basin. undersea feature SE Pacific Ocean
44 H2 **Southwest Point** headland Great Abaco, N Bahamas
191 X3 **South West Point** headland Kiritimati, NE Kiribati
65 G25 **South West Point** headland SW Saint Helena
25 P5 **South Wichita River** ≈ Texas, SW USA
97 Q20 **Southwold** E England, UK
19 Q12 **South Yarmouth** Massachusetts, NE USA
116 J10 **Sovata** Hung. Szováta. Mureș, C Romania
107 N22 **Soverato** Calabria, SW Italy
121 O4 **Sovereign Base Area** uk military installation S Cyprus
Sovetabad see Ghafurov
126 C2 **Sovetsk** Ger. Tilsit. Kaliningradskaya Oblast', W Russian Federation
125 Q15 **Sovetsk** Kirovskaya Oblast', NW Russian Federation
127 N10 **Sovetskaya** Rostovskaya Oblast', SW Russian Federation
Sovetskoye see Ketchenery
146 I15 **Sovet"yab** prev. Sovet"yap. Ahal Welaýaty, S Turkmenistan
Sovet"yap see Sovet"yab
117 U12 **Sovyets'kyy** Respublika Krym, S Ukraine
83 I18 **Sowa** var. Sua. Central, NE Botswana
Sowa Pan see Sua Pan
83 J21 **Soweto** Gauteng, NE South Africa
147 R11 **So'x** Rus. Sokh. Farg'ona Viloyati, E Uzbekistan
Sōya-kaikyō see La Perouse Strait
165 T1 **Sōya-misaki** headland Hokkaidō, NE Japan
125 N7 **Soyana** ≈ NW Russian Federation
146 A8 **Soye, Mys** var. Mys Suz. headland NW Turkmenistan
82 A10 **Soyo** Dem. Rep. Congo, NW Angola
80 J10 **Soyra** ▲ C Eritrea
Sozaq see Suzak
119 P16 **Sozh** Rus. Sozh. ≈ NE Europe
114 N10 **Sozopol** prev. Sizebolu; anc. Apollonia. Burgas, E Bulgaria
99 L20 **Spa** Liège, E Belgium
194 I7 **Spaatz Island** island Antarctica
144 M14 **Space Launching Centre** space station Kzyl-Orda, S Kazakhstan
105 O7 **Spain** off. Kingdom of Spain, Sp. España; anc. Hispania, Iberia, Lat. Hispana. ◆ monarchy SW Europe
Spain, Kingdom of see Spain
Spalato see Split
97 O19 **Spalding** E England, UK
14 D11 **Spanish** Ontario, S Canada
36 L3 **Spanish Fork** Utah, W USA
64 B12 **Spanish Point** headland C Bermuda
14 E9 **Spanish River** ≈ Ontario, S Canada
44 K13 **Spanish Town** hist. St.Iago de la Vega. C Jamaica
35 Q5 **Sparks** Nevada, W USA
Sparnacum see Épernay
95 N16 **Sparreholm** Södermanland, C Sweden
23 U4 **Sparta** Georgia, SE USA
30 K16 **Sparta** Illinois, N USA
31 P9 **Sparta** Michigan, N USA
21 R8 **Sparta** North Carolina, SE USA
20 L9 **Sparta** Tennessee, S USA
30 I7 **Sparta** Wisconsin, N USA
Sparta see Spárti
21 Q11 **Spartanburg** South Carolina, SE USA
115 F21 **Spárti** Eng. Sparta. Pelopónnisos, S Greece
107 B21 **Spartivento, Capo** headland Sardegna, Italy, C Mediterranean Sea
9 P17 **Sparwood** British Columbia, SW Canada
126 I4 **Spas-Demensk** Kaluzhskaya Oblast', W Russian Federation
126 M4 **Spas-Klepiki** Ryazanskaya Oblast', W Russian Federation
Spasovo see Kulen Vakuf
123 R15 **Spassk-Dal'niy** Primorskiy Kray, SE Russian Federation
126 M5 **Spassk-Ryazanskiy** Ryazanskaya Oblast', W Russian Federation
115 H19 **Spáta** Attikí, C Greece
121 Q11 **Spátha, Akrotírio** var. Akrotírio Spánta. headland Kríti, Greece, E Mediterranean Sea
Špatrjan see Paternion
28 I9 **Spearfish** South Dakota, N USA
25 O1 **Spearman** Texas, SW USA
65 C25 **Speedwell Island** island S Falkland Islands
65 C25 **Speedwell Island Settlement** S Falkland Islands
65 G25 **Speery Island** island S Saint Helena
45 N14 **Speightstown** NW Barbados
106 I13 **Spello** Umbria, C Italy
39 R12 **Spenard** Alaska, USA
Spence Bay see Taloyoak
31 O14 **Spencer** Indiana, N USA
29 T12 **Spencer** Iowa, C USA
29 P12 **Spencer** Nebraska, C USA
21 S9 **Spencer** North Carolina, SE USA
20 L9 **Spencer** Tennessee, S USA
21 Q4 **Spencer** West Virginia, NE USA
30 K6 **Spencer** Wisconsin, N USA
182 G10 **Spencer, Cape** headland South Australia
39 V13 **Spencer, Cape** headland Alaska, USA
182 H9 **Spencer Gulf** gulf South Australia
18 F9 **Spencerport** New York, NE USA
31 Q12 **Spencerville** Ohio, N USA
115 E17 **Spercheiáda** var. Sperhiada, Sperkhiás. Stereá Ellás, C Greece
115 E17 **Spercheiós** ≈ C Greece
Sperhiada see Spercheiáda
95 G14 **Sperillen** ◎ S Norway
Sperkhiás see Spercheiáda
101 I18 **Spessart** hill range C Germany
Spétsai see Spétses
115 G21 **Spétses** prev. Spétsai. Spétses, S Greece
115 G21 **Spétses** island S Greece
96 J8 **Spey** ≈ NE Scotland, UK
101 G20 **Speyer** Eng. Spires; anc. Civitas Nemetum, Spira. Rheinland-Pfalz, SW Germany
101 G20 **Speyerbach** ≈ W Germany
107 N20 **Spezzano Albanese** Calabria, SW Italy
Spice Islands see Maluku
100 F9 **Spiekeroog** island NW Germany
109 W9 **Spielfeld** Steiermark, SE Austria
65 N21 **Spiess Seamount** undersea feature S Atlantic Ocean
108 E9 **Spiez** Bern, W Switzerland
98 G13 **Spijkenisse** Zuid-Holland, SW Netherlands
39 T6 **Spike Mountain** ▲ Alaska, USA
115 I25 **Spíli** Kríti, Greece, E Mediterranean Sea
108 D10 **Spillgerten** ▲ W Switzerland
118 F9 **Spilva** ✕ (Rīga) Rīga, C Latvia
107 N17 **Spinazzola** Puglia, SE Italy
149 O9 **Spīn Būldak** Kandahār, S Afghanistan
Spira see Speyer
Spirdingsee see Śniardwy, Jezioro
Spires see Speyer
29 T11 **Spirit Lake** Iowa, C USA
29 T11 **Spirit Lake** ◎ Iowa, C USA
9 N13 **Spirit River** Alberta, W Canada
9 S14 **Spiritwood** Saskatchewan, S Canada
27 R11 **Spiro** Oklahoma, C USA
111 L19 **Spišská Nová Ves** Ger. Neudorf, Zipser Neudorf, Hung. Igló. Košický Kraj, E Slovakia
137 T11 **Spitak** NW Armenia
92 O2 **Spitsbergen** island NW Svalbard
Spittal see Spittal an der Drau
109 R9 **Spittal an der Drau** var. Spittal. Kärnten, S Austria
109 V3 **Spitz** Niederösterreich, NE Austria
94 D9 **Spjelkavik** Møre og Romsdal, S Norway
25 W10 **Splendora** Texas, SW USA
113 E14 **Split** It. Spalato. Split-Dalmacija, S Croatia
113 E14 **Split** ✕ Split-Dalmacija, S Croatia
113 E14 **Split-Dalmacija** off. Splitsko-Dalmatinska Županija. ◐ province S Croatia
9 X12 **Split Lake** ◎ Manitoba, C Canada
Splitsko-Dalmatinska Županija see Split-Dalmacija
108 H10 **Splügen** Graubünden, S Switzerland
Spodnji Dravograd see Dravograd
25 P12 **Spofford** Texas, SW USA
118 J11 **Špoģi** Daugvapils, SE Latvia
32 L8 **Spokane** Washington, NW USA
32 L8 **Spokane River** ≈ Washington, NW USA
106 I13 **Spoleto** Umbria, C Italy
30 I4 **Spooner** Wisconsin, N USA
30 K12 **Spoon River** ≈ Illinois, N USA
21 W5 **Spotsylvania** Virginia, NE USA
32 L8 **Sprague** Washington, NW USA
170 J5 **Spratly Island** island SW Spratly Islands
192 E6 **Spratly Islands** Chin. Nansha Qundao. ◇ disputed territory SE Asia
32 J12 **Spray** Oregon, NW USA
112 I11 **Spreča** ≈ N Bosnia and Herzegovina
100 P13 **Spree** ≈ E Germany
100 P13 **Spreewald** marshy woodland district NE Germany
101 P14 **Spremberg** Brandenburg, E Germany
25 W11 **Spring** Texas, SW USA
31 Q10 **Spring Arbor** Michigan, N USA
83 E23 **Springbok** Northern Cape, W South Africa
18 I15 **Spring City** Pennsylvania, NE USA
20 L9 **Spring City** Tennessee, S USA
36 L4 **Spring City** Utah, W USA
35 W3 **Spring Creek** Nevada, W USA
27 S9 **Springdale** Arkansas, C USA
31 Q14 **Springdale** Ohio, N USA
100 I13 **Springe** Niedersachsen, N Germany
37 U9 **Springer** New Mexico, SW USA
37 W7 **Springfield** Colorado, C USA
23 W5 **Springfield** Georgia, SE USA
30 K14 **Springfield** state capital Illinois, N USA
20 L6 **Springfield** Kentucky, S USA
18 M12 **Springfield** Massachusetts, NE USA
29 T10 **Springfield** Minnesota, N USA
27 T7 **Springfield** Missouri, C USA
31 R13 **Springfield** Ohio, N USA
32 G13 **Springfield** Oregon, NW USA
29 Q12 **Springfield** South Dakota, N USA
20 J8 **Springfield** Tennessee, S USA
18 M9 **Springfield** Vermont, NE USA
30 K14 **Springfield, Lake** ⊠ Illinois, N USA
55 T8 **Spring Garden** NE Guyana
30 K8 **Spring Green** Wisconsin, N USA
29 X11 **Spring Grove** Minnesota, N USA
13 P15 **Springhill** Nova Scotia, SE Canada
23 V12 **Spring Hill** Florida, SE USA
27 R4 **Spring Hill** Kansas, C USA
22 G4 **Springhill** Louisiana, S USA
20 I9 **Spring Hill** Tennessee, S USA
21 U10 **Spring Lake** North Carolina, SE USA
24 M4 **Springlake** Texas, SW USA
35 W11 **Spring Mountains** ▲▲ Nevada, W USA
65 B24 **Spring Point** West Falkland, Falkland Islands
27 W9 **Spring River** ≈ Arkansas/Missouri, C USA
27 S7 **Spring River** ≈ Missouri/Oklahoma, C USA
83 J21 **Springs** Gauteng, NE South Africa
185 H16 **Springs Junction** West Coast, South Island, New Zealand
181 X8 **Springsure** Queensland, E Australia
29 W11 **Spring Valley** Minnesota, N USA
18 K13 **Spring Valley** New York, NE USA
29 N12 **Springview** Nebraska, C USA
18 D11 **Springville** New York, NE USA
36 L3 **Springville** Utah, W USA
Sprottau see Szprotawa
15 V4 **Sproule, Pointe** headland Québec, SE Canada
9 Q14 **Spruce Grove** Alberta, SW Canada
21 T4 **Spruce Knob** ▲ West Virginia, NE USA
35 X3 **Spruce Mountain** ▲ Nevada, W USA
21 P9 **Spruce Pine** North Carolina, SE USA
98 G13 **Spui** ≈ SW Netherlands
107 O19 **Spulico, Capo** headland S Italy
25 O5 **Spur** Texas, SW USA
97 O17 **Spurn Head** headland E England, UK
99 H20 **Spy** Namur, S Belgium
95 I15 **Spydeberg** Østfold, S Norway
185 J17 **Spy Glass Point** headland South Island, New Zealand
10 L17 **Squamish** British Columbia, SW Canada
19 O8 **Squam Lake** ◎ New Hampshire, NE USA
19 S2 **Squa Pan Mountain** ▲ Maine, NE USA
39 N16 **Squaw Harbor** Unga Island, Alaska, USA
14 E11 **Squaw Island** island Ontario, S Canada
107 O22 **Squillace, Golfo di** gulf S Italy
107 Q18 **Squinzano** Puglia, SE Italy
Sráid na Cathrach see Milltown Malbay
167 S11 **Srâlau** Stœng Trêng, N Cambodia
Srath an Urláir see Stranorlar
112 G10 **Srbac** ◐ Republika Srpska, N Bosnia and Herzegovina
Srbija see Serbia
Srbinje see Foča
112 K9 **Srbobran** var. Bácsszenttamás, Hung. Szenttamás. Vojvodina, N Serbia
Srbobran see Donji Vakuf
167 R13 **Srê Âmběl** Kaôh Kông, SW Cambodia
112 K13 **Srebrenica** ◐ Republika Srpska, E Bosnia and Herzegovina
112 I11 **Srebrenik** ◐ Federacija Bosna I Hercegovina, NE Bosnia and Herzegovina
114 K10 **Sredets** prev. Syulemeshlii. Stara Zagora, C Bulgaria
114 M10 **Sredets** prev. Grudovo. ◐ Burgas, E Bulgaria
114 M10 **Sredetska Reka** ≈ SE Bulgaria
123 U9 **Sredinnyy Khrebet** ▲▲ E Russian Federation
114 N7 **Sredishte** Rom. Beibunar; prev. Knyazhevo. Dobrich, NE Bulgaria
114 I10 **Sredna Gora** ▲▲ C Bulgaria
123 R7 **Srednekolymsk** Respublika Sakha (Yakutiya), NE Russian Federation
126 K7 **Srednerusskaya Vozvyshennost'** Eng. Central Russian Upland. ▲▲ W Russian Federation
122 L9 **Srednesibirskoye Ploskogor'ye** var. Central Siberian Uplands, Eng. Central Siberian Plateau. ▲▲ N Russian Federation
125 V13 **Sredniy Ural** ▲▲ NW Russian Federation
167 T12 **Srê Khtŭm** Môndól Kiri, E Cambodia
110 G12 **Śrem** Wielkopolskie, C Poland
112 K10 **Sremska Mitrovica** prev. Mitrovica, Ger. Mitrowitz. Vojvodina, NW Serbia
167 R11 **Srêng, Stœng** ≈ NW Cambodia
167 R11 **Srê Noy** Siĕmréab, NW Cambodia
Srepok, Sông see Srêpôk, Tônle
167 T12 **Srêpôk, Tônle** var. Sông Srepok. ≈ Cambodia/Vietnam
123 P13 **Sretensk** Chitinskaya Oblast', S Russian Federation
169 R10 **Sri Aman** Sarawak, East Malaysia
117 R4 **Sribne** Chernihivs'ka Oblast', N Ukraine
155 I25 **Sri Jayawardanapura** var. Sri Jayawardenepura; prev. Kotte. Western Province, W Sri Lanka
Sri Jayawardenepura see Sri Jayawardanapura
155 M14 **Srīkākulam** Andhra Pradesh, E India
155 J25 **Sri Lanka** off. Democratic Socialist Republic of Sri Lanka; prev. Ceylon. ◆ republic S Asia
130 F14 **Sri Lanka** island S Asia
Sri Lanka, Democratic Socialist Republic of see Sri Lanka
153 V14 **Srimangal** Sylhet, E Bangladesh
Sri Mohangorh see Shri Mohangarh
152 H5 **Srīnagar** state capital Jammu and Kashmir, N India
167 N10 **Srinagarind Reservoir** ◎ W Thailand
155 F19 **Sringeri** Karnātaka, W India
155 K25 **Sri Pada** Eng. Adam's Peak. ▲ S Sri Lanka
Sri Saket see Si Sa Ket
111 G14 **Środa Śląska** Ger. Neumarkt. Dolnośląskie, SW Poland
110 H12 **Środa Wielkopolska** Wielkopolskie, C Poland
Srpska Kostajnica see Bosanska Kostajnica
113 G14 **Srpska, Respublika** ◐ republic Bosnia and Herzegovina
Srpski Brod see Bosanski Brod
Ssu-ch'uan see Sichuan
Ssu-p'ing/Ssu-p'ing-chieh see Siping
Stablo see Stavelot
99 G15 **Stabroek** Antwerpen, N Belgium
Stackeln see Strenči
96 I5 **Stack Skerry** island N Scotland, UK
100 I9 **Stade** Niedersachsen, NW Germany

◆ Country
● Country Capital
◇ Dependent Territory
○ Dependent Territory Capital
◐ Administrative Regions
✕ International Airport
▲ Mountain
▲▲ Mountain Range
Volcano
≈ River
◎ Lake
⊠ Reservoir

94 C10 **Stadlandet** *peninsula* S Norway
109 R5 **Stadl-Paura** Oberösterreich, NW Austria
119 L20 **Stadolichy** *Rus.* Stodolichi. Homyel'skaya Voblasts', SE Belarus
98 P7 **Stadskanaal** Groningen, NE Netherlands
101 H16 **Stadtallendorf** Hessen, C Germany
101 K23 **Stadtbergen** Bayern, S Germany
108 G7 **Stäfa** Zürich, NE Switzerland
95 K23 **Staffanstorp** Skåne, S Sweden
101 K18 **Staffelstein** Bayern, C Germany
97 L19 **Stafford** C England, UK
26 L6 **Stafford** Kansas, C USA
21 W4 **Stafford** Virginia, NE USA
97 L19 **Staffordshire** *cultural region* C England, UK
19 N12 **Stafford Springs** Connecticut, NE USA
115 H14 **Stágira** Kentrikí Makedonía, N Greece
118 G7 **Staicele** Limbaži, N Latvia
Štaierdorf-Anina *see* Anina
109 V8 **Stainz** Steiermark, SE Austria
Stájerlakanina *see* Anina
117 Y7 **Stakhanov** Luhans'ka Oblast', E Ukraine
108 E11 **Stalden** Valais, SW Switzerland
Stalin *see* Varna
Stalinabad *see* Dushanbe
Stalingrad *see* Volgograd
Staliniri *see* Ts'khinvali
Stalino *see* Donets'k
Stalinobod *see* Dushanbe
Stalinov Štít *see* Gerlachovský štít
Stalinsk *see* Novokuznetsk
Stalins'kaya Oblast' *see* Donets'ka Oblast'
Stalinski Zaliv *see* Varnenski Zaliv
Stalin, Yazovir *see* Iskŭr, Yazovir
111 N15 **Stalowa Wola** Podkarpackie, SE Poland
114 I11 **Stamboliyski** Plovdiv, C Bulgaria
114 J8 **Stamboliyski, Yazovir** ⊠ N Bulgaria
97 N19 **Stamford** E England, UK
18 L14 **Stamford** Connecticut, NE USA
25 P6 **Stamford** Texas, SW USA
25 Q6 **Stamford, Lake** ⊠ Texas, SW USA
108 I10 **Stampa** Graubünden, SE Switzerland
Stampalia *see* Astypálaia
27 T14 **Stamps** Arkansas, C USA
92 G11 **Stamsund** Nordland, C Norway
27 R2 **Stanberry** Missouri, C USA
195 O3 **Stancomb-Wills Glacier** *glacier* Antarctica
83 K21 **Standerton** Mpumalanga, E South Africa
31 R7 **Standish** Michigan, N USA
20 M6 **Stanford** Kentucky, S USA
33 S9 **Stanford** Montana, NW USA
95 P19 **Stånga** Gotland, SE Sweden
94 I13 **Stange** Hedmark, S Norway
83 L23 **Stanger** KwaZulu/Natal, E South Africa
Stanimaka *see* Asenovgrad
Stanislau *see* Ivano-Frankivs'k
35 P8 **Stanislaus River** ≈ California, W USA
Stanislav *see* Ivano-Frankivs'k
Stanislavskaya Oblast' *see* Ivano-Frankivs'ka Oblast'
Stanisławów *see* Ivano-Frankivs'k
Stanke Dimitrov *see* Dupnitsa
183 O15 **Stanley** Tasmania, SE Australia
65 E24 **Stanley** *var.* Port Stanley, Puerto Argentino. ○ (Falkland Islands) East Falkland, Falkland Islands
33 O13 **Stanley** Idaho, NW USA
28 L3 **Stanley** North Dakota, N USA
21 U4 **Stanley** Virginia, NE USA
30 J6 **Stanley** Wisconsin, N USA
79 G21 **Stanley Pool** *var.* Pool Malebo. *lake section of river* Congo/Dem. Rep. Congo
155 H20 **Stanley Reservoir** ⊠ S India
Stanleyville *see* Kisangani
42 G3 **Stann Creek** ◈ *district* SE Belize
Stann Creek *see* Dangriga
123 Q12 **Stanovoy Khrebet** ▲▲ SE Russian Federation
108 F8 **Stans** Unterwalden, C Switzerland
97 O21 **Stansted** ✈ (London) Essex, E England, UK
183 U4 **Stanthorpe** Queensland, E Australia
21 N6 **Stanton** Kentucky, S USA
31 Q8 **Stanton** Michigan, N USA
29 Q14 **Stanton** Nebraska, C USA
28 L5 **Stanton** North Dakota, N USA
25 N7 **Stanton** Texas, SW USA
32 H7 **Stanwood** Washington, NW USA
117 Y7 **Stanychno-Luhans'ke** Luhans'ka Oblast', E Ukraine
108 K7 **Stanzach** Tirol, W Austria
98 M9 **Staphorst** Overijssel, E Netherlands
14 D18 **Staples** Ontario, S Canada
29 T6 **Staples** Minnesota, N USA
28 M14 **Stapleton** Nebraska, C USA
25 S8 **Star** Texas, SW USA
111 M14 **Starachowice** Świętokrzyskie, C Poland
Stara Kanjiža *see* Kanjiža
111 M18 **Stará L'ubovňa** *Ger.* Altlublau, *Hung.* Ólubló. Prešovský Kraj, E Slovakia
112 L10 **Stara Pazova** *Ger.* Altpasua, *Hung.* Ópazova. Vojvodina, N Serbia
Stara Planina *see* Balkan Mountains
114 L9 **Stara Reka** ≈ C Bulgaria
116 M5 **Stara Synyava** Khmel'nyts'ka Oblast', W Ukraine
116 I2 **Stara Vyzhivka** Volyns'ka Oblast', NW Ukraine
Staraya Belitsa *see* Staraya Byelitsa
119 M14 **Staraya Byelitsa** *Rus.* Staraya Belitsa. Vitsyebskaya Voblasts', NE Belarus
127 R5 **Staraya Mayna** Ul'yanovskaya Oblast', W Russian Federation
119 O18 **Staraya Rudnya** *Rus.* Staraya Rudnya. Homyel'skaya Voblasts', SE Belarus
124 H14 **Staraya Russa** Novgorodskaya Oblast', W Russian Federation
114 K10 **Stara Zagora** *Lat.* Augusta Trajana. Stara Zagora, C Bulgaria
114 K10 **Stara Zagora** ◈ *province* C Bulgaria
29 S8 **Starbuck** Minnesota, N USA
191 W4 **Starbuck Island** *prev.* Volunteer Island. *island* E Kiribati
27 V13 **Star City** Arkansas, C USA
112 F13 **Staretina** ▲▲ W Bosnia and Herzegovina
Stargard in Pommern *see* Stargard Szczeciński
110 E9 **Stargard Szczeciński** *Ger.* Stargard in Pommern. Zachodnio-pomorskie, NW Poland
187 N10 **Star Harbour** *harbor* San Cristobal, SE Solomon Islands
Stari Bečej *see* Bečej
113 F15 **Stari Grad** *It.* Cittavecchia. Split-Dalmacija, S Croatia
124 J16 **Staritsa** Tverskaya Oblast', W Russian Federation
23 V9 **Starke** Florida, SE USA
22 M4 **Starkville** Mississippi, S USA
186 B7 **Star Mountains** *Ind.* Pegunungan Sterren. ▲▲ Indonesia/Papua New Guinea
101 L23 **Starnberg** Bayern, SE Germany
101 L24 **Starnberger See** ◎ SE Germany
Starobel'sk *see* Starobil's'k
117 X8 **Starobesheve** Donets'ka Oblast', E Ukraine
117 Y6 **Starobil's'k** *Rus.* Starobel'sk. Luhans'ka Oblast', E Ukraine
119 K18 **Starobin** *var.* Starobyn. Minskaya Voblasts', S Belarus
Starobyn *see* Starobin
126 H6 **Starodub** Bryanskaya Oblast', W Russian Federation
110 I8 **Starogard Gdański** *Ger.* Preussisch-Stargard. Pomorskie, N Poland
145 P16 **Staroikan** Yuzhnyy Kazakhstan, S Kazakhstan
Starokonstantinov *see* Starokostyantyniv
116 L5 **Starokostyantyniv** *Rus.* Starokonstantinov. Khmel'nyts'ka Oblast', NW Ukraine
126 K12 **Starominskaya** Krasnodarskiy Kray, SW Russian Federation
114 L7 **Staro Selo** *Rom.* Satul-Vechi; *prev.* Star-Smil. Silistra, NE Bulgaria
126 K12 **Staroshcherbinovskaya** Krasnodarskiy Kray, SW Russian Federation
127 V6 **Starosubkhangulovo** Respublika Bashkortostan, W Russian Federation
35 S4 **Star Peak** ▲ Nevada, W USA
Star-Smil *see* Staro Selo
97 J25 **Start Point** *headland* SW England, UK
Startsy *see* Kirawsk
Starum *see* Stavoren
119 L18 **Staryya Darohi** *Rus.* Staryye Dorogi. Minskaya Voblasts', S Belarus
Staryye Dorogi *see* Staryya Darohi
127 T2 **Staryye Zyattsy** Udmurtskaya Respublika, NW Russian Federation
117 U13 **Staryy Krym** Respublika Krym, S Ukraine
126 K8 **Staryy Oskol** Belgorodskaya Oblast', W Russian Federation
116 H6 **Staryy Sambir** L'vivs'ka Oblast', W Ukraine
101 L14 **Stassfurt** *var.* Staßfurt. Sachsen-Anhalt, C Germany
Staßfurt *see* Stassfurt
111 M15 **Staszów** Świętokrzyskie, C Poland
29 W13 **State Center** Iowa, C USA
18 E14 **State College** Pennsylvania, NE USA
18 K15 **Staten Island** *island* New York, NE USA
Staten Island *see* Estados, Isla de los
23 U8 **Statenville** Georgia, SE USA
23 W5 **Statesboro** Georgia, SE USA
States, The *see* United States of America
21 R9 **Statesville** North Carolina, SE USA
95 G16 **Stathelle** Telemark, S Norway
30 K15 **Staunton** Illinois, N USA
21 T5 **Staunton** Virginia, NE USA
95 C16 **Stavanger** Rogaland, S Norway
99 L21 **Stavelot** *Dut.* Stablo. Liège, E Belgium
95 G16 **Stavern** Vestfold, S Norway
Stavers Island *see* Vostok Island
98 J7 **Stavoren** *Fris.* Starum. Friesland, N Netherlands
115 K21 **Stavrí, Akrotírio** *var.* Akrotírio Stavrós. *headland* Naxos, Kykládes, Greece, Aegean Sea
126 M14 **Stavropol'** *prev.* Voroshilovsk. Stavropol'skiy Kray, SW Russian Federation
Stavropol' *see* Tol'yatti
126 M14 **Stavropol'skaya Vozvyshennost'** ▲▲ SW Russian Federation
126 M14 **Stavropol'skiy Kray** ◈ *territory* SW Russian Federation
115 H14 **Stavrós** Kentrikí Makedonía, N Greece
115 J24 **Stavrós, Akrotírio** *cape* Kríti, Greece, E Mediterranean Sea
Stavrós, Akrotírio *see* Stavrí, Akrotírio
114 I12 **Stavroúpoli** *prev.* Stavroúpolis. Anatolikí Makedonía kai Thráki, NE Greece
Stavroúpolis *see* Stavroúpoli
117 O6 **Stavyshche** Kyyivs'ka Oblast', N Ukraine
182 M11 **Stawell** Victoria, SE Australia
110 N9 **Stawiski** Podlaskie, NE Poland
14 G14 **Stayner** Ontario, S Canada
37 R3 **Steamboat Springs** Colorado, C USA
20 M8 **Stearns** Kentucky, S USA
39 N10 **Stebbins** Alaska, USA
108 K7 **Steeg** Tirol, W Austria
27 Y9 **Steele** Missouri, C USA
29 N5 **Steele** North Dakota, N USA
194 J5 **Steele Island** *island* Antarctica
30 K16 **Steeleville** Illinois, N USA
27 W6 **Steelville** Missouri, C USA
99 G14 **Steenbergen** Noord-Brabant, S Netherlands
Steenkool *see* Bintuni
9 O10 **Steen River** Alberta, W Canada
98 M8 **Steenwijk** Overijssel, N Netherlands
65 A23 **Steeple Jason** *island* Jason Islands, NW Falkland Islands
174 J8 **Steep Point** *headland* Western Australia
116 L9 **Ştefăneşti** Botoşani, NE Romania
Stefanie, Lake *see* Ch'ew Bahir
8 L5 **Stefansson Island** *island* Nunavut, N Canada
117 O10 **Ştefan Vodă** *Rus.* Suvorovo. SE Moldova
63 H18 **Steffen, Cerro** ▲ S Chile
108 D9 **Steffisburg** Bern, C Switzerland
95 J24 **Stege** Storstrøm, SE Denmark
116 G10 **Ştei** *Hung.* Vaskohsziklás. Bihor, W Romania
Steier *see* Steyr
Steierdorf/Steierdorf-Anina *see* Anina
109 T7 **Steiermark** *off.* Land Steiermark, *Eng.* Styria. ◈ *state* C Austria
Steiermark, Land *see* Steiermark
101 J19 **Steigerwald** *hill range* C Germany
99 L17 **Stein** Limburg, SE Netherlands
Stein *see* Stein an der Donau
Stein *see* Kamnik, Slovenia
108 M8 **Steinach** Tirol, W Austria
Steinamanger *see* Szombathely
109 W3 **Stein an der Donau** *var.* Stein. Niederösterreich, NE Austria
Steinau an der Elbe *see* Ścinawa
9 Y16 **Steinbach** Manitoba, S Canada
Steiner Alpen *see* Kamniško-Savinjske Alpe
99 L24 **Steinfort** Luxembourg, W Luxembourg
100 H12 **Steinhuder Meer** ◎ NW Germany
93 E15 **Steinkjer** Nord-Trøndelag, C Norway
Stejarul *see* Karapelit
99 F16 **Stekene** Oost-Vlaanderen, NW Belgium
83 E26 **Stellenbosch** Western Cape, SW South Africa
98 F13 **Stellendam** Zuid-Holland, SW Netherlands
39 T12 **Steller, Mount** ▲ Alaska, USA
103 Y14 **Stello, Monte** ▲ Corse, France, C Mediterranean Sea
106 F5 **Stelvio, Passo dello** *pass* Italy/Switzerland
103 R3 **Stenay** Meuse, NE France
100 L12 **Stendal** Sachsen-Anhalt, C Germany
118 E8 **Stende** Talsi, NW Latvia
182 H10 **Stenhouse Bay** South Australia
95 J23 **Stenløse** Frederiksborg, E Denmark
95 L19 **Stensjön** Jönköping, S Sweden
95 K18 **Stenstorp** Västra Götaland, S Sweden
95 I18 **Stenungsund** Västra Götaland, S Sweden
Stepanakert *see* Xankändi
137 T11 **Step'anavan** N Armenia
100 K9 **Stepenitz** ≈ N Germany
29 O10 **Stephan** South Dakota, N USA
29 R3 **Stephen** Minnesota, N USA
27 T14 **Stephens** Arkansas, C USA
184 J13 **Stephens, Cape** *headland* D'Urville Island, Marlborough, SW New Zealand
21 V3 **Stephens City** Virginia, NE USA
182 L6 **Stephens Creek** New South Wales, SE Australia
184 K13 **Stephens Island** *island* C New Zealand
31 N5 **Stephenson** Michigan, N USA
13 S12 **Stephenville** Newfoundland, Newfoundland and Labrador, SE Canada
25 S7 **Stephenville** Texas, SW USA
145 P17 **Step' Nardara** *Kaz.* Shardara Dalasy; *prev.* Shaidara. *grassland* S Kazakhstan
145 R8 **Stepnogorsk** Akmola, C Kazakhstan
127 O15 **Stepnoye** Stavropol'skiy Kray, SW Russian Federation
145 Q8 **Stepnyak** Akmola, N Kazakhstan
192 J17 **Steps Point** *headland* Tutuila, W American Samoa
115 F17 **Stereá Ellás** *Eng.* Greece Central. ◈ *region* C Greece
83 J24 **Sterkspruit** Eastern Cape, SE South Africa
127 U6 **Sterlibashevo** Respublika Bashkortostan, W Russian Federation
39 R12 **Sterling** Alaska, USA
37 V3 **Sterling** Colorado, C USA
30 K11 **Sterling** Illinois, N USA
26 M5 **Sterling** Kansas, C USA
25 O8 **Sterling City** Texas, SW USA
31 S9 **Sterling Heights** Michigan, N USA
21 W3 **Sterling Park** Virginia, NE USA
37 V2 **Sterling Reservoir** ⊠ Colorado, C USA
22 I5 **Sterlington** Louisiana, S USA
127 U6 **Sterlitamak** Respublika Bashkortostan, W Russian Federation
Sternberg *see* Šternberk
111 H17 **Šternberk** *Ger.* Sternberg. Olomoucký Kraj, E Czech Republic
141 V17 **Stěroh** Suquţrā, S Yemen
Sterren, Pegunungan *see* Star Mountains
110 G11 **Stęszew** Wielkopolskie, C Poland
Stettin *see* Szczecin
Stettiner Haff *see* Szczeciński, Zalew
9 Q15 **Stettler** Alberta, SW Canada
31 V13 **Steubenville** Ohio, N USA
97 O21 **Stevenage** E England, UK
23 Q1 **Stevenson** Alabama, S USA
32 H11 **Stevenson** Washington, NW USA
182 E1 **Stevenson Creek** *seasonal river* South Australia
39 Q13 **Stevenson Entrance** *strait* Alaska, USA
30 L6 **Stevens Point** Wisconsin, N USA
39 R8 **Stevens Village** Alaska, USA
33 P10 **Stevensville** Montana, NW USA
93 E25 **Stevns Klint** *headland* E Denmark
10 J12 **Stewart** British Columbia, W Canada
10 I6 **Stewart** ≈ Yukon Territory, NW Canada
10 I6 **Stewart Crossing** Yukon Territory, NW Canada
63 H25 **Stewart, Isla** *island* S Chile
185 B25 **Stewart Island** *island* S New Zealand
Stewart Islands *see* Sikaiana
181 W6 **Stewart, Mount** ▲ Queensland, E Australia
10 H6 **Stewart River** Yukon Territory, NW Canada
27 R3 **Stewartsville** Missouri, C USA
9 S16 **Stewart Valley** Saskatchewan, S Canada
29 W10 **Stewartville** Minnesota, N USA
Steyerlak-Anina *see* Anina
109 T5 **Steyr** *var.* Steier. Oberösterreich, N Austria
109 T5 **Steyr** ≈ NW Austria
29 P11 **Stickney** South Dakota, N USA
98 L5 **Stiens** Friesland, N Netherlands
Stif *see* Sétif
27 Q11 **Stigler** Oklahoma, C USA
107 N18 **Stigliano** Basilicata, S Italy
95 N17 **Stigtomta** Södermanland, C Sweden
10 I11 **Stikine** ≈ British Columbia, W Canada
Stilida/Stilís *see* Stylída
95 G22 **Stilling** Århus, C Denmark
29 W8 **Stillwater** Minnesota, N USA
27 O9 **Stillwater** Oklahoma, C USA
35 S5 **Stillwater Range** ▲▲ Nevada, W USA
18 I8 **Stillwater Reservoir** ⊠ New York, NE USA
107 O22 **Stilo, Punta** *headland* S Italy
27 R10 **Stilwell** Oklahoma, C USA
113 N17 **Štimlje** Kosovo, S Serbia
25 N1 **Stinnett** Texas, SW USA
113 P18 **Štip** E FYR Macedonia
Stira *see* Stýra
96 J12 **Stirling** C Scotland, UK
96 I12 **Stirling** *cultural region* C Scotland, UK
180 J14 **Stirling Range** ▲▲ Western Australia
93 E16 **Stjørdalshalsen** Nord-Trøndelag, C Norway
Stochód *see* Stokhid
101 H24 **Stockach** Baden-Württemberg, S Germany
25 S12 **Stockdale** Texas, SW USA
109 X3 **Stockerau** Niederösterreich, NE Austria
93 H20 **Stockholm** ● (Sweden) Stockholm, C Sweden
95 O15 **Stockholm** ◈ *county* C Sweden
Stockmannshof *see* Pļaviņas
97 L18 **Stockport** NW England, UK
65 K15 **Stocks Seamount** *undersea feature* C Atlantic Ocean
35 O8 **Stockton** California, W USA
26 L3 **Stockton** Kansas, C USA
27 S6 **Stockton** Missouri, C USA
30 K3 **Stockton Island** *island* Apostle Islands, Wisconsin, N USA
27 S7 **Stockton Lake** ⊠ Missouri, C USA
97 M15 **Stockton-on-Tees** *var.* Stockton on Tees. N England, UK
Stockton on Tees *see* Stockton-on-Tees
24 M10 **Stockton Plateau** *plain* Texas, SW USA
28 M16 **Stockville** Nebraska, C USA
93 H17 **Stöde** Västernorrland, C Sweden
Stodolichi *see* Stadolichy
113 M19 **Stogovo Karaorman** ▲▲ W FYR Macedonia
Stoke *see* Stoke-on-Trent
97 L19 **Stoke-on-Trent** *var.* Stoke. C England, UK
182 M15 **Stokes Point** *headland* Tasmania, SE Australia
116 J2 **Stokhid** *Pol.* Stochód, *Rus.* Stokhod. ≈ NW Ukraine
Stokhod *see* Stokhid
92 I4 **Stokkseyri** Sudhurland, SW Iceland
92 G10 **Stokmarknes** Nordland, C Norway
Stol *see* Veliki Krš
113 H15 **Stolac** ◈ Federacija Bosna I Hercegovina, S Bosnia and Herzegovina
Stolbce *see* Stowbtsy
101 D16 **Stolberg** *var.* Stolberg im Rheinland. Nordrhein-Westfalen, W Germany
Stolberg im Rheinland *see* Stolberg
123 P6 **Stolbovoy, Ostrov** *island* NE Russian Federation
Stolbtsy *see* Stowbtsy
119 J20 **Stolin** *Rus.* Stolin. Brestskaya Voblasts', SW Belarus
95 K14 **Stöllet** *var.* Norra Ny. Värmland, C Sweden
Stolp *see* Słupsk
Stolpe *see* Słupia
Stolpmünde *see* Ustka
115 F15 **Stómio** Thessalía, C Greece
14 J11 **Stonecliffe** Ontario, SE Canada
96 L10 **Stonehaven** NE Scotland, UK
97 M23 **Stonehenge** *ancient monument* Wiltshire, S England, UK
23 T3 **Stone Mountain** ▲ Georgia, SE USA
9 X16 **Stonewall** Manitoba, S Canada
21 S3 **Stonewood** West Virginia, NE USA
14 D17 **Stoney Point** Ontario, S Canada
92 H10 **Stonglandseidet** Troms, N Norway
65 N25 **Stonybeach Bay** *bay* Tristan da Cunha, SE Atlantic Ocean
35 N5 **Stony Creek** ≈ California, W USA
65 N25 **Stonyhill Point** *headland* S Tristan da Cunha
14 I14 **Stony Lake** ◎ Ontario, SE Canada
9 Q14 **Stony Plain** Alberta, SW Canada
21 R9 **Stony Point** North Carolina, SE USA
18 G8 **Stony Point** *headland* New York, NE USA
9 T10 **Stony Rapids** Saskatchewan, C Canada
39 P11 **Stony River** Alaska, USA
Stony Tunguska *see* Podkamennaya Tunguska
12 G10 **Stooping** ≈ Ontario, C Canada
100 I9 **Stör** ≈ N Germany
95 M15 **Storå** Örebro, S Sweden
95 J16 **Stora Gla** ◎ C Sweden
95 I16 **Stora Le** *Nor.* Store Le. ◎ Norway/Sweden
92 I12 **Stora Lulevatten** ◎ N Sweden
92 H13 **Storavan** ◎ N Sweden
93 I20 **Storby** Åland, SW Finland
94 E10 **Stordalen** Møre og Romsdal, S Norway
95 H23 **Storebælt** *var.* Store Bælt, *Eng.* Great Belt, Storebelt. *channel* Baltic Sea/Kattegat
Store Bælt *see* Storebælt
Storebelt *see* Storebælt
95 M19 **Storebro** Kalmar, S Sweden
95 J24 **Store Heddinge** Storstrøm, SE Denmark
Store Le *see* Stora Le
93 E16 **Støren** Sør-Trøndelag, S Norway
92 O4 **Storfjorden** *fjord* S Norway
95 L15 **Storfors** Värmland, C Sweden
92 G13 **Storforshei** Nordland, C Norway
Storhammer *see* Hamar
100 L10 **Störkanal** *canal* N Germany
93 F16 **Storlien** Jämtland, C Sweden
183 P17 **Storm Bay** *inlet* Tasmania, SE Australia
29 T12 **Storm Lake** Iowa, C USA
29 S13 **Storm Lake** ◎ Iowa, C USA
96 G7 **Stornoway** NW Scotland, UK
Storojineţ *see* Storozhynets'
92 P1 **Storøya** *island* NE Svalbard
125 S10 **Storozhevsk** Respublika Komi, NW Russian Federation
Storozhinets *see* Storozhynets'
116 K8 **Storozhynets'** *Ger.* Storozynetz, *Rom.* Storojineţ, *Rus.* Storozhinets. Chernivets'ka Oblast', W Ukraine
Storozynetz *see* Storozhynets'
92 H11 **Storriten** ▲ C Norway
19 N12 **Storrs** Connecticut, NE USA
94 I11 **Storsjøen** ◎ S Norway
93 N13 **Storsjön** ◎ C Sweden
93 F16 **Storsjön** ◎ C Sweden
92 J9 **Storslett** Troms, N Norway
94 H11 **Storsølnkletten** ▲ S Norway
92 I9 **Storsteinnes** Troms, N Norway
95 I24 **Storstrøm** *var.* Storstrøms Amt. ◈ *county* SE Denmark
Storstrøms Amt *see* Storstrøm
93 J14 **Storsund** Norrbotten, N Sweden
94 J9 **Storsylen** *Swe.* Sylarna. ▲ Norway/Sweden
92 H11 **Stortoppen** ▲ N Sweden
93 H14 **Storuman** Västerbotten, N Sweden
93 H14 **Storuman** ◎ N Sweden
94 N13 **Storvik** Gävleborg, C Sweden
95 O14 **Storvreta** Uppsala, C Sweden
29 V13 **Story City** Iowa, C USA
9 V17 **Stoughton** Saskatchewan, S Canada
19 O11 **Stoughton** Massachusetts, NE USA
30 L9 **Stoughton** Wisconsin, N USA
97 L23 **Stour** ≈ E England, UK
97 P21 **Stour** ≈ S England, UK
27 T5 **Stover** Missouri, C USA
95 G21 **Støvring** Nordjylland, N Denmark
119 J17 **Stowbtsy** *Pol.* Stolbce, *Rus.* Stolbtsy. Minskaya Voblasts', C Belarus
25 X11 **Stowell** Texas, SW USA
97 P20 **Stowmarket** E England, UK
114 N8 **Stozher** Dobrich, NE Bulgaria
97 E14 **Strabane** *Ir.* An Srath Bán. W Northern Ireland, UK
121 S11 **Strabo Trench** *undersea feature* C Mediterranean Sea
27 T7 **Strafford** Missouri, C USA
183 N17 **Strahan** Tasmania, SE Australia
111 C18 **Strakonice** *Ger.* Strakonitz. Jihočeský Kraj, S Czech Republic
Strakonitz *see* Strakonice
100 N8 **Stralsund** Mecklenburg-Vorpommern, NE Germany
99 L16 **Stramproy** Limburg, SE Netherlands
83 E26 **Strand** Western Cape, SW South Africa
94 E10 **Stranda** Møre og Romsdal, S Norway
97 G15 **Strangford Lough** *Ir.* Loch Cuan. *inlet* E Northern Ireland, UK
95 N16 **Strängnäs** Södermanland, C Sweden
97 E14 **Stranorlar** *Ir.* Srath an Urláir. Donegal, NW Ireland
97 H14 **Stranraer** S Scotland, UK
9 U16 **Strasbourg** Saskatchewan, S Canada
103 V5 **Strasbourg** *Ger.* Strassburg; *anc.* Argentoratum. Bas-Rhin, NE France
37 U4 **Strasburg** Colorado, C USA
29 N7 **Strasburg** North Dakota, N USA
31 U12 **Strasburg** Ohio, N USA
21 U3 **Strasburg** Virginia, NE USA
117 N10 **Strășeni** *var.* Strasheny. C Moldova
Strasheny *see* Strășeni
109 T8 **Strassburg** Kärnten, S Austria
Strassburg *see* Strasbourg, France
Strassburg *see* Aiud, Romania
99 M25 **Strassen** Luxembourg, S Luxembourg
109 R5 **Strasswalchen** Salzburg, C Austria
14 F16 **Stratford** Ontario, S Canada
184 K10 **Stratford** Taranaki, North Island, New Zealand
35 Q11 **Stratford** California, W USA
29 V13 **Stratford** Iowa, C USA
27 O12 **Stratford** Oklahoma, C USA
25 N1 **Stratford** Texas, SW USA
30 K6 **Stratford** Wisconsin, N USA
Stratford *see* Stratford-upon-Avon
97 M20 **Stratford-upon-Avon** *var.* Stratford. C England, UK
183 O17 **Strathgordon** Tasmania, SE Australia
9 Q16 **Strathmore** Alberta, SW Canada
35 R11 **Strathmore** California, W USA
14 E16 **Strathroy** Ontario, S Canada
96 I6 **Strathy Point** *headland* N Scotland, UK
37 W4 **Stratton** Colorado, C USA
19 P6 **Stratton** Maine, NE USA
18 M10 **Stratton Mountain** ▲ Vermont, NE USA
101 N21 **Straubing** Bayern, SE Germany
100 O12 **Strausberg** Brandenburg, E Germany
32 K13 **Strawberry Mountain** ▲ Oregon, NW USA
29 X12 **Strawberry Point** Iowa, C USA
36 M3 **Strawberry Reservoir** ⊠ Utah, W USA
36 M4 **Strawberry River** ≈ Utah, W USA
25 R7 **Strawn** Texas, SW USA
113 P17 **Straža** ▲ Bulgaria/FYR Macedonia
111 I19 **Strážov** *Hung.* Sztrazsó. ▲ NW Slovakia
182 F7 **Streaky Bay** South Australia
182 E7 **Streaky Bay** *bay* South Australia
30 L12 **Streator** Illinois, N USA
Streckenbach *see* Świdnik
Strednogorie *see* Pirdop
111 C17 **Středočeský Kraj** ◈ *region* C Czech Republic
29 O6 **Streeter** North Dakota, N USA
25 U8 **Streetman** Texas, SW USA
116 G13 **Strehaia** Mehedinţi, SW Romania
Strehlen *see* Strzelin
114 I10 **Strelcha** Pazardzhik, C Bulgaria
122 L12 **Strelka** Krasnoyarskiy Kray, C Russian Federation
124 L6 **Strel'na** ≈ NW Russian Federation
118 H7 **Strenči** *Ger.* Stackeln. Valka, N Latvia
108 K8 **Strengen** Tirol, W Austria
106 C6 **Stresa** Piemonte, NE Italy
Streshin *see* Streshyn
119 N18 **Streshyn** *Rus.* Streshin. Homyel'skaya Voblasts', SE Belarus
95 B18 **Streymoy** *Dan.* Strømø. *island* N Faeroe Islands
95 G23 **Strib** Fyn, C Denmark
111 A17 **Stříbro** *Ger.* Mies. Plzeňský Kraj, W Czech Republic
186 B7 **Strickland** ≈ SW Papua New Guinea
Striegau *see* Strzegom
Strigonium *see* Esztergom
98 H13 **Strijen** Zuid-Holland, SW Netherlands
63 H21 **Strobel, Lago** ◎ S Argentina
61 B25 **Stroeder** Buenos Aires, E Argentina
115 C20 **Strofádes** *island* Iónioi Nísoi, Greece, C Mediterranean Sea
Strofilia *see* Strofyliá
115 G17 **Strofyliá** *var.* Strofilia. Évvoia, C Greece
100 O10 **Strom** ≈ NE Germany
107 L22 **Stromboli** ⛰ Isola Stromboli, SW Italy
107 L22 **Stromboli, Isola** *island* Isole Eolie, S Italy
96 H9 **Stromeferry** N Scotland, UK
96 J5 **Stromness** N Scotland, UK
Strømø *see* Streymoy
94 N11 **Strömsbruk** Gävleborg, C Sweden
29 Q15 **Stromsburg** Nebraska, C USA
95 K21 **Strömsnäsbruk** Kronoberg, S Sweden
95 I17 **Strömstad** Västra Götaland, S Sweden
93 G16 **Strömsund** Jämtland, C Sweden
93 G15 **Ströms Vattudal** *valley* N Sweden
27 V14 **Strong** Arkansas, C USA
Strongilí *see* Strongylí
107 O21 **Strongoli** Calabria, SW Italy
31 T11 **Strongsville** Ohio, N USA
115 Q23 **Strongylí** *var.* Strongilí. *island* SE Greece
96 K5 **Stronsay** *island* NE Scotland, UK
97 L21 **Stroud** C England, UK
27 O10 **Stroud** Oklahoma, C USA
18 I14 **Stroudsburg** Pennsylvania, NE USA

◆ Country
● Country Capital
◇ Dependent Territory
○ Dependent Territory Capital
◈ Administrative Regions
✈ International Airport
▲ Mountain
▲▲ Mountain Range
⛰ Volcano
≈ River
◎ Lake
⊠ Reservoir

95 F21 **Struer** Ringkøbing, W Denmark
113 M20 **Struga** SW FYR Macedonia
Strugi-Kranyse *see* Strugi-Krasnyye
124 G14 **Strugi-Krasnyye** *var.* Strugi-Kranyse. Pskovskaya Oblast', W Russian Federation
114 G11 **Struma** *Gk.* Strymónas. ≈ Bulgaria/Greece *see also* Strymónas
Struma *see* Strymónas
97 G21 **Strumble Head** *headland* SW Wales, UK
113 Q19 **Strumeshnitsa** *Mac.* Strumica. ≈ Bulgaria/FYR Macedonia
113 Q19 **Strumica** E FYR Macedonia
Strumica *see* Strumeshnitsa
114 G11 **Strumyani** Blagoevgrad, SW Bulgaria
31 V12 **Struthers** Ohio, N USA
114 I10 **Stryama** ≈ C Bulgaria
114 G13 **Strymónas** *Bul.* Struma. ≈ Bulgaria/Greece *see also* Struma
Strymónas *see* Struma
115 H14 **Strymonikós Kólpos** *gulf* N Greece
116 I6 **Stryy** L'vivs'ka Oblast', NW Ukraine
116 H6 **Stryy** ≈ W Ukraine
111 F14 **Strzegom** *Ger.* Striegau. Wałbrzych, SW Poland
110 E10 **Strzelce Krajeńskie** *Ger.* Friedeberg Neumark. Lubuskie, W Poland
111 I15 **Strzelce Opolskie** *Ger.* Gross Strehlitz. Opolskie, SW Poland
182 K3 **Strzelecki Creek** *seasonal river* South Australia
182 J3 **Strzelecki Desert** *desert* South Australia
111 G15 **Strzelin** *Ger.* Strehlen. Dolnośląskie, SW Poland
110 I11 **Strzelno** Kujawsko-pomorskie, C Poland
111 N17 **Strzyżów** Podkarpackie, SE Poland
Stua Laighean *see* Leinster, Mount
23 Y13 **Stuart** Florida, SE USA
29 U14 **Stuart** Iowa, C USA
29 O13 **Stuart** Nebraska, C USA
21 S8 **Stuart** Virginia, NE USA
10 L13 **Stuart** ≈ British Columbia, SW Canada
39 N10 **Stuart Island** *island* Alaska, USA
10 L13 **Stuart Lake** ◎ British Columbia, SW Canada
185 B22 **Stuart Mountains** ⛰ South Island, New Zealand
182 F3 **Stuart Range** *hill range* South Australia
Stubaital *see* Neustift im Stubaital
95 I24 **Stubbekøbing** Storstrøm, SE Denmark
45 P14 **Stubbs** Saint Vincent, Saint Vincent and the Grenadines
109 V6 **Stübming** ≈ E Austria
114 J11 **Studen Kladenets, Yazovir** ⊠ S Bulgaria
185 G21 **Studholme** Canterbury, South Island, New Zealand
Stuhlweissenberg *see* Székesfehérvár
Stuhm *see* Sztum
12 C7 **Stull Lake** ◎ Ontario, C Canada
126 L4 **Stupino** Moskovskaya Oblast', W Russian Federation
27 U4 **Sturgeon** Missouri, C USA
14 G10 **Sturgeon** ≈ Ontario, S Canada
31 N6 **Sturgeon Bay** Wisconsin, N USA
14 G11 **Sturgeon Falls** Ontario, S Canada
12 C11 **Sturgeon Lake** ◎ Ontario, S Canada
30 M3 **Sturgeon River** ≈ Michigan, N USA
20 H6 **Sturgis** Kentucky, S USA
31 P11 **Sturgis** Michigan, N USA
28 J9 **Sturgis** South Dakota, N USA
112 D10 **Šturlić** ⬗ Federacija Bosna I Hercegovina, NW Bosnia and Herzegovina
111 J22 **Štúrovo** *Hung.* Párkány; *prev.* Parkan. Nitriansky Kraj, SW Slovakia
182 L4 **Sturt, Mount** *hill* New South Wales, SE Australia
181 P4 **Sturt Plain** *plain* Northern Territory, N Australia
181 T9 **Sturt Stony Desert** *desert* South Australia
83 J25 **Stutterheim** Eastern Cape, S South Africa
101 H21 **Stuttgart** Baden-Württemberg, SW Germany
27 W12 **Stuttgart** Arkansas, C USA
92 H2 **Stykkishólmur** Vesturland, W Iceland
115 F17 **Stylída** *var.* Stilida, Stilís. Stereá Ellás, C Greece
116 K2 **Styr** *Rus.* Styr'. ≈ Belarus/Ukraine
115 I19 **Stýra** *var.* Stira. Évvoia, C Greece
Styria *see* Steiermark
Su *see* Jiangsu
Sua *see* Sowa
171 Q17 **Suai** W EastTimor
54 G9 **Suaita** Santander, C Colombia
80 I7 **Suakin** *var.* Sawakin. Red Sea, NE Sudan
161 T13 **Suao** *Jap.* Suō. N Taiwan
Suao *see* Suau
83 I18 **Sua Pan** *var.* Sowa Pan. *salt lake* NE Botswana
40 G6 **Suaqui Grande** Sonora, NW Mexico
61 A16 **Suardi** Santa Fe, C Argentina
54 D11 **Suárez** Cauca, SW Colombia
186 G10 **Suau** *var.* Suao. Suaul Island, SE Papua New Guinea
118 G12 **Subačius** Panevėžys, NE Lithuania
168 K9 **Subang** *prev.* Soebang. Jawa, C Indonesia
169 O16 **Subang** ✈ (Kuala Lumpur) Pahang, Peninsular Malaysia
129 S10 **Subansiri** ≈ NE India
118 I11 **Subate** Daugvapils, SE Latvia
139 N5 **Subaykhān** Dayr az Zawr, E Syria
Subei/Subei Mongolzu Zizhixian *see* Dangchengwan
169 P9 **Subi Besar, Pulau** *island* Kepulauan Natuna, W Indonesia
Subiyah *see* Aş Şubayḩiyah
26 I7 **Sublette** Kansas, C USA
112 K8 **Subotica** *Ger.* Maria-Theresiopel, *Hung.* Szabadka. Vojvodina, N Serbia
116 K9 **Suceava** *Ger.* Suczawa, *Hung.* Szucsava. Suceava, NE Romania
116 J9 **Suceava** ⬗ *county* NE Romania
116 K9 **Suceava** *Ger.* Suczawa. ≈ N Romania
112 E12 **Sučević** Zadar, SW Croatia
111 K17 **Sucha Beskidzka** Małopolskie, S Poland
111 M14 **Suchedniów** Świętokrzyskie, C Poland
42 A2 **Suchitepéquez** *off.* Departamento de Suchitepéquez. ⬗ *department* SW Guatemala
Suchitepéquez, Departamento de *see* Suchitepéquez
Su-chou *see* Suzhou
Suchow *see* Suzhou, Jiangsu, China
Suchow *see* Xuzhou, Jiangsu, China
97 D17 **Suck** ≈ C Ireland
Sucker State *see* Illinois
186 F9 **Suckling, Mount** ▲ S Papua New Guinea
57 L19 **Sucre** *hist.* Chuquisaca, La Plata. ● (Bolivia-legal capital) Chuquisaca, S Bolivia
54 E6 **Sucre** Santander, N Colombia
56 A7 **Sucre** Manabí, W Ecuador
54 E6 **Sucre** *off.* Departamento de Sucre. ⬗ *province* N Colombia
55 O5 **Sucre** *off.* Estado Sucre. ⬗ *state* NE Venezuela
Sucre, Departamento de *see* Sucre
Sucre, Estado *see* Sucre
56 D6 **Sucumbíos** ⬗ *province* NE Ecuador
113 G15 **Sućuraj** Split-Dalmacija, S Croatia
58 K10 **Sucuriju** Amapá, NE Brazil
Suczawa *see* Suceava
79 E16 **Sud** *Eng.* South. ⬗ *province* S Cameroon
124 K13 **Suda** ≈ NW Russian Federation
Suda *see* Soúda
117 U13 **Sudak** Respublika Krym, S Ukraine
24 M4 **Sudan** Texas, SW USA
80 C10 **Sudan** *off.* Republic of Sudan, *Ar.* Jumhuriyat as-Sudan; *prev.* Anglo-Egyptian Sudan. ◆ *republic* N Africa
Sudanese Republic *see* Mali
Sudan, Jumhuriyat as- *see* Sudan
Sudan, Republic of *see* Sudan
14 F10 **Sudbury** Ontario, S Canada
97 P20 **Sudbury** E England, UK
Sud, Canal de *see* Gonâve, Canal de la
80 E13 **Sudd** *swamp region* S Sudan
100 K10 **Sude** ≈ N Germany
Suderø *see* Sudhuroy
Sudest Island *see* Tagula Island
111 E15 **Sudeten** *var.* Sudetes, Sudetic Mountains, *Cz./Pol.* Sudety. ⛰ Czech Republic/Poland
Sudetes/Sudetic Mountains/ Sudety *see* Sudeten
92 G1 **Sudhureyri** Vestfirdhir, NW Iceland
92 J4 **Sudhurland** ⬗ *region* S Iceland
95 B19 **Sudhuroy** *Dan.* Suderø. *island* S Faeroe Islands
124 M15 **Sudislavl'** Kostromskaya Oblast', NW Russian Federation
Südkarpaten *see* Carpații Meridionali
79 N20 **Sud Kivu** *off.* Région Sud Kivu. ⬗ *region* E Dem. Rep. Congo
Sud Kivu, Région *see* Sud Kivu
Südliche Morava *see* Južna Morava
100 E12 **Süd-Nord-Kanal** *canal* NW Germany
126 M3 **Sudogda** Vladimirskaya Oblast', W Russian Federation
Sudostroy *see* Severodvinsk
79 C15 **Sud-Ouest** *Eng.* South-West. ⬗ *province* W Cameroon
173 X17 **Sud Ouest, Pointe** *headland* SW Mauritius
187 P17 **Sud, Province** ⬗ *province* S New Calednia
126 J8 **Sudzha** Kurskaya Oblast', W Russian Federation
81 D15 **Sue** ≈ S Sudan
105 S10 **Sueca** País Valenciano, E Spain
114 I10 **Sŭedinenie** Plovdiv, C Bulgaria
Suero *see* Alzira
75 X8 **Suez** *Ar.* As Suways, El Suweis. NE Egypt
75 W7 **Suez Canal** *Ar.* Qanāt as Suways. *canal* NE Egypt
75 X8 **Suez, Gulf of** *Ar.* Khalīj as Suways. *gulf* NE Egypt
9 R17 **Suffield** Alberta, SW Canada
21 X7 **Suffolk** Virginia, NE USA
97 P20 **Suffolk** *cultural region* E England, UK
142 J2 **Şūfiān** Āzarbāyjān-e Khāvarī, N Iran
31 N12 **Sugar Creek** ≈ Illinois, N USA
30 L13 **Sugar Creek** ≈ Illinois, N USA
31 R3 **Sugar Island** *island* Michigan, N USA
25 V11 **Sugar Land** Texas, SW USA
19 P6 **Sugarloaf Mountain** ▲ Maine, NE USA
65 G24 **Sugar Loaf Point** *headland* N Saint Helena
136 G16 **Suğla Gölü** ◎ SW Turkey
123 T8 **Sugoy** ≈ E Russian Federation
158 F7 **Sugun** Xinjiang Uygur Zizhiqu, W China
147 U11 **Sugut, Gora** ▲ SW Kyrgyzstan
169 V6 **Sugut, Sungai** ≈ East Malaysia
159 O9 **Suhai Hu** ◎ C China
162 K14 **Suhait** Nei Mongol Zizhiqu, N China
141 X7 **Şuḩār** *var.* Sohar. N Oman
162 L6 **Sühbaatar** Selenge, N Mongolia
163 P8 **Sühbaatar** *var.* Haylaastay. Sühbaatar, E Mongolia
163 P9 **Sühbaatar** ⬗ *province* E Mongolia
101 K17 **Suhl** Thüringen, C Germany
108 F7 **Suhr** Aargau, N Switzerland
Sui'an *see* Zhangpu
Suicheng *see* Suixi
161 O12 **Suichuan** *var.* Quanjiang. Jiangxi, S China
Suid-Afrika *see* South Africa
160 L4 **Suide** *var.* Mingzhou. Shaanxi, C China
Suidwes-Afrika *see* Namibia
163 Y9 **Suifenhe** Heilongjiang, NE China
Suigen *see* Suwŏn
163 W8 **Suihua** Heilongjiang, NE China
Súilí, Loch *see* Swilly, Lough
161 Q6 **Suining** Jiangsu, E China
160 I9 **Suining** Sichuan, C China
103 Q4 **Suippes** Marne, N France
97 E20 **Suir** *Ir.* An tSiúir. ≈ S Ireland
165 J13 **Suita** Ōsaka, Honshū, SW Japan
160 L16 **Suixi** *var.* Suicheng. Guangdong, S China
Sui Xian *see* Suizhou
163 T13 **Suizhong** Liaoning, NE China
161 N8 **Suizhou** *prev.* Sui Xian. Hubei, C China
149 P17 **Sujāwal** Sind, SE Pakistan
169 O16 **Sukabumi** *prev.* Soekaboemi. Jawa, C Indonesia
169 Q12 **Sukadana, Teluk** *bay* Borneo, W Indonesia
165 P11 **Sukagawa** Fukushima, Honshū, C Japan
Sukarnapura *see* Jayapura
Sukarno, Puntjak *see* Jaya, Puncak
Sükh *see* Sokh
114 N8 **Sukha Reka** ≈ NE Bulgaria
126 J5 **Sukhinichi** Kaluzhskaya Oblast', W Russian Federation
Sukhne *see* As Sukhnah
129 Q4 **Sukhona** *var.* Tot'ma. ≈ NW Russian Federation
167 O8 **Sukhothai** *var.* Sukotai. Sukhothai, W Thailand
Sukhumi *see* Sokhumi
Sukkertoppen *see* Maniitsoq
149 Q13 **Sukkur** Sind, SE Pakistan
Sukotai *see* Sukhothai
Sukra Bay *see* Şawqirah, Dawḩat
125 V15 **Suksun** Permskaya Oblast', NW Russian Federation
165 F15 **Sukumo** Kōchi, Shikoku, SW Japan
94 B12 **Sula** *island* S Norway
125 Q5 **Sula** ≈ NW Russian Federation
117 R5 **Sula** ≈ N Ukraine
42 H6 **Sulaco, Río** ≈ NW Honduras
Sulaimaniya *see* As Sulaymānīyah
149 S10 **Sulaimān Range** ⛰ C Pakistan
127 Q16 **Sulak** Respublika Dagestan, SW Russian Federation
127 Q16 **Sulak** ≈ SW Russian Federation
171 Q13 **Sula, Kepulauan** *island group* C Indonesia
136 I12 **Sulakyurt** *var.* Konur. Kırıkkale, N Turkey
171 P17 **Sulamu** Timor, S Indonesia
96 F5 **Sula Sgeir** *island* NW Scotland, UK
171 N13 **Sulawesi** *Eng.* Celebes. *island* C Indonesia
Sulawesi, Laut *see* Celebes Sea
171 N14 **Sulawesi Selatan** *off.* Propinsi Sulawesi Selatan, *Eng.* South Celebes, South Sulawesi. ⬗ *province* C Indonesia
Sulawesi Selatan, Propinsi *see* Sulawesi Selatan
171 P12 **Sulawesi Tengah** *off.* Propinsi Sulawesi Tengah, *Eng.* Central Celebes, Central Sulawesi. ⬗ *province* N Indonesia
Sulawesi Tengah, Propinsi *see* Sulawesi Tengah
171 O14 **Sulawesi Tenggara** *off.* Propinsi Sulawesi Tenggara, *Eng.* South-East Celebes, South-East Sulawesi. ⬗ *province* C Indonesia
Sulawesi Tenggara, Propinsi *see* Sulawesi Tenggara
171 P11 **Sulawesi Utara** *off.* Propinsi Sulawesi Utara, *Eng.* North Celebes, North Sulawesi. ⬗ *province* N Indonesia
Sulawesi Utara, Propinsi *see* Sulawesi Utara
139 T5 **Sulaymān Beg** N Iraq
95 D15 **Suldalsvatnet** ◎ S Norway
Sulden *see* Solda
110 E12 **Sulechów** *Ger.* Züllichau. Lubuskie, W Poland
110 E11 **Sulęcin** Lubuskie, W Poland
77 U14 **Suleja** Niger, C Nigeria
111 K14 **Sulejów** Lodzkie, S Poland
96 I5 **Sule Skerry** *island* N Scotland, UK
Suliag *see* Sohâg
76 J16 **Sulima** S Sierra Leone
117 O13 **Sulina** Tulcea, SE Romania
117 N13 **Sulina Braţul** ≈ SE Romania
100 H12 **Sulingen** Niedersachsen, NW Germany
Sulisjielmmá *see* Sulitjelma
92 H12 **Suliskongen** ▲ C Norway
92 H12 **Sulitjelma** *Lapp.* Sulisjielmmá. Nordland, C Norway
56 A9 **Sullana** Piura, NW Peru
23 N3 **Sulligent** Alabama, S USA
30 M14 **Sullivan** Illinois, N USA
31 N15 **Sullivan** Indiana, N USA
27 W5 **Sullivan** Missouri, C USA
Sullivan Island *see* Lanbi Kyun
96 M1 **Sullom Voe** NE Scotland, UK
103 O7 **Sully-sur-Loire** Loiret, C France
Sulmo *see* Sulmona
107 K15 **Sulmona** *anc.* Sulmo. Abruzzo, C Italy
Sulo *see* Shule He
114 M11 **Süloğlu** Edirne, NW Turkey
22 G9 **Sulphur** Louisiana, S USA
27 O12 **Sulphur** Oklahoma, C USA
28 K9 **Sulphur Creek** ≈ South Dakota, N USA
24 M5 **Sulphur Draw** ≈ Texas, SW USA
25 W5 **Sulphur River** ≈ Arkansas/ Texas, SW USA
25 V6 **Sulphur Springs** Texas, SW USA
24 M6 **Sulphur Springs Draw** ≈ Texas, SW USA
14 D8 **Sultan** Ontario, S Canada
Sultānābād *see* Arāk
Sultan Alonto, Lake *see* Lanao, Lake
136 G15 **Sultan Dağları** ⛰ C Turkey
114 N13 **Sultanköy** Tekirdağ, NW Turkey
171 Q7 **Sultan Kudarat** *var.* Nuling. Mindanao, S Philippines
152 M13 **Sultānpur** Uttar Pradesh, N India
171 O9 **Sulu Archipelago** *island group* SW Philippines
192 F7 **Sulu Basin** *undersea feature* SE South China Sea
Sülüktü *see* Sulyukta
Sulu, Laut *see* Sulu Sea
169 X6 **Sulu Sea** *var.* Laut Sulu. *sea* SW Philippines
145 O15 **Sulutobe** *Kaz.* Sulūtöbe. Kzylorda, S Kazakhstan
Sulūtöbe *see* Sulutobe
147 Q11 **Sulyukta** *Kir.* Sülüktü. Batkenskaya Oblast', SW Kyrgyzstan
Sulz *see* Sulz am Neckar
101 G22 **Sulz am Neckar** *var.* Sulz. Baden-Württemberg, SW Germany
101 L20 **Sulzbach-Rosenberg** Bayern, SE Germany
195 N13 **Sulzberger Bay** *bay* Antarctica
Sumail *see* Summēl
113 F15 **Sumartin** Split-Dalmacija, S Croatia
32 H6 **Sumas** Washington, NW USA
168 J10 **Sumatera** *Eng.* Sumatra. *island* W Indonesia
168 J12 **Sumatera Barat** *off.* Propinsi Sumatera Barat, *Eng.* West Sumatra. ⬗ *province* W Indonesia
Sumatera Barat, Propinsi *see* Sumatera Barat
168 L13 **Sumatera Selatan** *off.* Propinsi Sumatera Selatan, *Eng.* South Sumatra. ⬗ *province* W Indonesia
Sumatera Selatan, Propinsi *see* Sumatera Selatan
168 H10 **Sumatera Utara** *off.* Propinsi Sumatera Utara, *Eng.* North Sumatra. ⬗ *province* W Indonesia
Sumatera Utara, Propinsi *see* Sumatera Utara
Sumatra *see* Sumatera
Šumava *see* Bohemian Forest
Sumayl *see* Summēl
139 U7 **Sumayr al Muḩammad** E Iraq
171 N17 **Sumba, Pulau** *Eng.* Sandalwood Island; *prev.* Soemba. *island* Nusa Tenggara, C Indonesia
146 D12 **Sumbar** ≈ W Turkmenistan
192 E9 **Sumbawa** *prev.* Soembawa. *island* Nusa Tenggara, C Indonesia
170 L16 **Sumbawabesar** Sumbawa, S Indonesia
81 F23 **Sumbawanga** Rukwa, W Tanzania
82 B12 **Sumbe** *var.* N'Gunza, *Port.* Novo Redondo. Cuanza Sul, W Angola
96 M3 **Sumburgh Head** *headland* NE Scotland, UK
111 H23 **Sümeg** Veszprém, W Hungary
80 C12 **Sumeih** Southern Darfur, S Sudan
169 T16 **Sumenep** *prev.* Soemenep. Pulau Madura, C Indonesia
Sumgait *see* Sumqayıtçay, Azerbaijan
Sumgait *see* Sumqayıt, Azerbaijan
165 Y14 **Sumisu-jima** *Eng.* Smith Island. *island* SE Japan
139 Q2 **Summēl** *var.* Sumail, Sumayl. N Iraq
31 O5 **Summer Island** *island* Michigan, N USA
32 H15 **Summer Lake** ◎ Oregon, NW USA
9 N17 **Summerland** British Columbia, SW Canada
13 P14 **Summerside** Prince Edward Island, SE Canada
21 R5 **Summersville** West Virginia, NE USA
21 R5 **Summersville Lake** ⊠ West Virginia, NE USA
21 S13 **Summerton** South Carolina, SE USA
23 R2 **Summerville** Georgia, SE USA
21 S14 **Summerville** South Carolina, SE USA
39 R10 **Summit** Alaska, USA
35 V6 **Summit Mountain** ▲ Nevada, W USA
37 R8 **Summit Peak** ▲ Colorado, C USA
Summus Portus *see* Somport, Col du
Summus Portus *see* Somport/ Somport, Col du
29 X12 **Sumner** Iowa, C USA
22 K3 **Sumner** Mississippi, S USA
185 H17 **Sumner, Lake** ◎ South Island, New Zealand
37 U12 **Sumner, Lake** ⊠ New Mexico, SW USA
111 G17 **Šumperk** *Ger.* Mährisch-Schönberg. Olomoucký Kraj, E Czech Republic
42 F7 **Sumpul, Río** ≈ El Salvador/Honduras
137 Z11 **Sumqayıt** *Rus.* Sumgait. E Azerbaijan
137 Y11 **Sumqayıtçay** *Rus.* Sumgait. ≈ E Azerbaijan
147 R9 **Sumsar** Dzhalal-Abadskaya Oblast', W Kyrgyzstan
117 S3 **Sums'ka Oblast'** *var.* Sumy, *Rus.* Sumskaya Oblast'. ⬗ *province* NE Ukraine
Sumskaya Oblast' *see* Sums'ka Oblast'
124 J8 **Sumskiy Posad** Respublika Kareliya, NW Russian Federation
21 S12 **Sumter** South Carolina, SE USA
117 T3 **Sumy** Sums'ka Oblast', NE Ukraine
Sumy *see* Sums'ka Oblast'
159 Q15 **Sumzom** Xizang Zizhiqu, W China
125 R15 **Suna** Kirovskaya Oblast', NW Russian Federation
124 I10 **Suna** ≈ NW Russian Federation
165 S3 **Sunagawa** Hokkaidō, NE Japan
153 V13 **Sunamganj** Sylhet, NE Bangladesh
163 W14 **Sunan** ✈ (P'yŏngyang) SW North Korea
Sunan/Sunan Yugurzu Zizhixian *see* Hongwansi
19 N9 **Sunapee Lake** ◎ New Hampshire, NE USA
139 P4 **Sunaysilah** *salt marsh* N Iraq
20 M8 **Sunbright** Tennessee, S USA
33 R6 **Sunburst** Montana, NW USA
183 N12 **Sunbury** Victoria, SE Australia
21 X8 **Sunbury** North Carolina, SE USA
18 G14 **Sunbury** Pennsylvania, NE USA
61 A17 **Sunchales** Santa Fe, C Argentina
163 W13 **Sunch'ŏn** SW North Korea
163 Y16 **Sunch'ŏn** *Jap.* Junten. S South Korea
36 K13 **Sun City** Arizona, SW USA
19 O9 **Suncook** New Hampshire, NE USA
161 P5 **Suncun** *prev.* Xinwen. Shandong, E China
Sunda Islands *see* Greater Sunda Islands
33 Z12 **Sundance** Wyoming, C USA
153 T17 **Sundarbans** *wetland* Bangladesh/India
154 M11 **Sundargarh** Orissa, E India
129 U15 **Sunda Shelf** *undersea feature* S South China Sea
Sunda Trench *see* Java Trench
129 U17 **Sunda Trough** *undersea feature* E Indian Ocean
95 O16 **Sundbyberg** Stockholm, C Sweden
97 M14 **Sunderland** *var.* Wearmouth. NE England, UK
101 F15 **Sundern** Nordrhein-Westfalen, W Germany
136 F12 **Sündiken Dağları** ⛰ C Turkey
24 M5 **Sundown** Texas, SW USA
9 P16 **Sundre** Alberta, SW Canada
14 H12 **Sundridge** Ontario, S Canada
93 H17 **Sundsvall** Västernorrland, C Sweden
26 H4 **Sunflower, Mount** ▲ Kansas, C USA
Sunflower State *see* Kansas
169 N14 **Sungaibuntu** Sumatera, SW Indonesia
168 K12 **Sungaidareh** Sumatera, W Indonesia
167 P17 **Sungai Kolok** *var.* Sungai Ko-Lok. Narathiwat, SW Thailand
Sungai Ko-Lok *see* Sungai Kolok
168 K12 **Sungaipenuh** *prev.* Soengaipenoeh. Sumatera, W Indonesia
169 P11 **Sungaipinyuh** Borneo, C Indonesia
Sungari *see* Songhua Jiang
Sungaria *see* Dzungaria
Sungei Pahang *see* Pahang, Sungai
167 O8 **Sung Men** Phrae, NW Thailand
83 M15 **Sungo** Tete, NW Mozambique
Sungpu *see* Songpan
168 M13 **Sungsang** Sumatera, W Indonesia
114 M9 **Sungurlare** Burgas, E Bulgaria
136 J12 **Sungurlu** Çorum, N Turkey
112 F9 **Sunja** Sisak-Moslavina, C Croatia
153 Q12 **Sun Koshi** ≈ E Nepal
94 F9 **Sunndalen** *valley* S Norway
94 F9 **Sunndalsøra** Møre og Romsdal, S Norway
95 K15 **Sunne** Värmland, C Sweden
95 O15 **Sunnersta** Uppsala, C Sweden
94 C11 **Sunnfjord** *physical region* S Norway
95 C15 **Sunnhordland** *physical region* S Norway
94 D10 **Sunnmøre** *physical region* S Norway
37 N4 **Sunnyside** Utah, W USA
32 J10 **Sunnyside** Washington, NW USA
35 N9 **Sunnyvale** California, W USA
30 L8 **Sun Prairie** Wisconsin, N USA
Sunqur *see* Sonqor
25 N1 **Sunray** Texas, SW USA
22 I8 **Sunset** Louisiana, S USA
25 S5 **Sunset** Texas, SW USA
Sunset State *see* Oregon
181 Z10 **Sunshine Coast** *cultural region* Queensland, E Australia
Sunshine State *see* Florida
Sunshine State *see* New Mexico
Sunshine State *see* South Dakota
123 O10 **Suntar** Respublika Sakha (Yakutiya), NE Russian Federation
39 R10 **Suntrana** Alaska, USA
148 J15 **Suntsar** Baluchistān, SW Pakistan
163 W15 **Sunwi-do** *island* SW North Korea
163 W6 **Sunwu** Heilongjiang, NE China
77 O16 **Sunyani** W Ghana
Suō *see* Suao
93 M17 **Suolahti** Länsi-Soumi, C Finland
Suoločielgi *see* Saariselkä
Suomenlahti *see* Finland, Gulf of
Suomen Tasavalta/Suomi *see* Finland
93 N14 **Suomussalmi** Oulu, E Finland
165 E13 **Suō-nada** *sea* SW Japan
93 M17 **Suonenjoki** Itä-Suomi, C Finland
167 S13 **Suŏng** Kâmpóng Cham, C Cambodia
124 I10 **Suoyarvi** Respublika Kareliya, NW Russian Federation
Supanburi *see* Suphan Buri
57 D14 **Supe** Lima, W Peru
15 V7 **Supérieur, Lac** ◎ Québec, SE Canada
Supérieur, Lac *see* Superior, Lake
36 M14 **Superior** Arizona, SW USA
33 O9 **Superior** Montana, NW USA
29 P17 **Superior** Nebraska, C USA
30 I3 **Superior** Wisconsin, N USA
41 S17 **Superior, Laguna** *lagoon* S Mexico
31 N2 **Superior, Lake** *Fr.* Lac Supérieur. ◎ Canada/USA
36 L13 **Superstition Mountains** ⛰ Arizona, SW USA
113 F14 **Supetar** *It.* San Pietro. Split-Dalmacija, S Croatia
167 O10 **Suphan Buri** *var.* Supanburi. Suphan Buri, W Thailand
171 V12 **Supiori, Pulau** *island* E Indonesia
188 K2 **Supply Reef** *reef* N Northern Mariana Islands
195 O7 **Support Force Glacier** *glacier* Antarctica
137 R10 **Sup'sa** *var.* Supsa. ≈ W Georgia
Supsa *see* Sup'sa
Sūq 'Abs *see* 'Abs
139 W12 **Sūq ash Shuyūkh** SE Iraq
138 H4 **Şuqaylibīyah** Ḩamāh, W Syria
161 Q6 **Suqian** Jiangsu, E China
Suqrah *see* Şawqirah
Suqrah Bay *see* Şawqirah, Dawḩat
141 V16 **Suquṭrā** *var.* Sokotra, *Eng.* Socotra. *island* SE Yemen
141 Z8 **Şūr** NE Oman
Şūr *see* Soûr
127 P5 **Sura** Penzenskaya Oblast', W Russian Federation
127 P4 **Sura** ≈ W Russian Federation
149 N12 **Sūrāb** Baluchistān, SW Pakistan
Surabaja *see* Surabaya
192 E8 **Surabaya** *prev.* Surabaja, Soerabaja. Jawa, C Indonesia
95 N15 **Surahammar** Västmanland, C Sweden
169 Q16 **Surakarta** *Eng.* Solo; *prev.* Soerakarta. Jawa, S Indonesia
Surakhany *see* Suraxanı
137 S10 **Surami** C Georgia
143 X13 **Sūrān** Sīstān va Balūchestān, SE Iran
111 I21 **Šurany** *Hung.* Nagysurány. Nitriansky Kraj, SW Slovakia
154 D12 **Sūrat** Gujarāt, W India
Suratdhani *see* Surat Thani
152 G9 **Sūratgarh** Rājasthān, NW India
167 N14 **Surat Thani** *var.* Suratdhani. Surat Thani, SW Thailand
119 Q16 **Suraw** *Rus.* Surov. ≈ E Belarus
137 Z11 **Suraxanı** *Rus.* Surakhany. E Azerbaijan
141 Y11 **Surayr** E Oman
138 K2 **Suraysāt** Ḩalab, N Syria
118 O12 **Surażh** *Rus.* Surazh. Vitsyebskaya Voblasts', NE Belarus
126 H6 **Surazh** Bryanskaya Oblast', W Russian Federation
191 V17 **Sur, Cabo** *cape* Easter Island, Chile, E Pacific Ocean
112 L11 **Surčin** Serbia, N Serbia
116 H9 **Surduc** *Hung.* Szurduk. Sălaj, NW Romania
113 P16 **Surdulica** Serbia, SE Serbia
99 L24 **Sûre** *var.* Sauer. ≈ W Europe *see also* Sauer
Sûre *see* Sauer
154 C10 **Surendranagar** Gujarāt, W India
18 K16 **Surf City** New Jersey, NE USA
183 V3 **Surfers Paradise** Queensland, E Australia
21 U13 **Surfside Beach** South Carolina, SE USA
102 J10 **Surgères** Charente-Maritime, W France
122 H10 **Surgut** Khanty-Mansiyskiy Avtonomnyy Okrug, C Russian Federation
122 K10 **Surgutikha** Krasnoyarskiy Kray, N Russian Federation
98 M6 **Surhuisterveen** Friesland, N Netherlands
105 V5 **Súria** Cataluña, NE Spain
143 P10 **Sūriān** Fārs, S Iran
155 J15 **Suriāpet** Andhra Pradesh, C India
171 Q6 **Surigao** Mindanao, S Philippines
167 R10 **Surin** Surin, E Thailand
55 U11 **Suriname** *off.* Republic of Suriname; *prev.* Dutch Guiana, Netherlands Guiana. ◆ *republic* N South America
Suriname, Republic of *see* Suriname
Sūrīya/Sūrīyah, Al-Jumhūrīyah al-'Arabīyah as- *see* Syria
Surkhab, Darya-i- *see* Kahmard, Daryā-ye
Surkhandar'inskaya Oblast' *see* Surkhondaryo Viloyati
Surkhandar'ya *see* Surxondaryo
Surkhet *see* Birendranagar
147 R12 **Surkhob** ≈ C Tajikistan
147 N13 **Surkhondaryo Viloyati** *Rus.* Surkhandar'inskaya Oblast'. ⬗ *province* S Uzbekistan
137 P11 **Sürmene** Trabzon, NE Turkey
Surov *see* Suraw
127 N11 **Surovikino** Volgogradskaya Oblast', SW Russian Federation

◆ Country
● Country Capital
◇ Dependent Territory
○ Dependent Territory Capital
⬗ Administrative Regions
✈ International Airport
▲ Mountain
⛰ Mountain Range
Volcano
≈ River
◎ Lake
⊠ Reservoir

35 N11 **Sur, Point** *headland* California, W USA
187 N15 **Surprise, Île** *island* N New Caledonia
61 E22 **Sur, Punta** *headland* E Argentina
Surrentum *see* Sorrento
28 M3 **Surrey** North Dakota, N USA
97 O22 **Surrey** *cultural region* SE England, UK
21 X7 **Surry** Virginia, NE USA
108 F8 **Sursee** Luzern, W Switzerland
127 P6 **Sursk** Penzenskaya Oblast', W Russian Federation
127 P5 **Surskoye** Ul'yanovskaya Oblast', W Russian Federation
75 P8 **Surt** *var.* Sidra, Sirte. N Libya
95 I19 **Surte** Västra Götaland, S Sweden
75 Q8 **Surt, Khalīj** *Eng.* Gulf of Sidra, Gulf of Sirti, Sidra. *gulf* N Libya
92 I5 **Surtsey** *island* S Iceland
137 N17 **Suruç** Şanlıurfa, S Turkey
168 L13 **Surulangun** Sumatera, W Indonesia
147 P13 **Surxondaryo** *Rus.* Surkhandar'ya. Tajikistan/Uzbekistan
Süs *see* Susch
106 A8 **Susa** Piemonte, NE Italy
165 E12 **Susa** Yamaguchi, Honshū, SW Japan
Susa *see* Shūsh
113 E16 **Sušac** *It.* Cazza. *island* SW Croatia
Sūsah *see* Sousse
164 G14 **Susaki** Kōchi, Shikoku, SW Japan
165 I15 **Susami** Wakayama, Honshū, SW Japan
142 K9 **Sūsangerd** *var.* Susangird. Khūzestān, SW Iran
Susangird *see* Sūsangerd
35 P4 **Susanville** California, W USA
108 J9 **Susch** *var.* Süs. Graubünden, SE Switzerland
137 N12 **Suşehri** Sivas, N Turkey
Susiana *see* Khūzestān
111 B18 **Sušice** *Ger.* Schüttenhofen. Plzeňský Kraj, W Czech Republic
39 R11 **Susitna** Alaska, USA
39 R11 **Susitna River** Alaska, USA
127 Q3 **Suslonger** Respublika Mariy El, W Russian Federation
105 N14 **Suspiro del Moro, Puerto del** *pass* S Spain
18 H16 **Susquehanna River** New York/Pennsylvania, NE USA
13 O15 **Sussex** New Brunswick, SE Canada
18 J13 **Sussex** New Jersey, NE USA
21 W7 **Sussex** Virginia, NE USA
97 O23 **Sussex** *cultural region* S England, UK
183 S10 **Sussex Inlet** New South Wales, SE Australia
99 L17 **Susteren** Limburg, SE Netherlands
10 K12 **Sustut Peak** ▲ British Columbia, W Canada
123 S9 **Susuman** Magadanskaya Oblast', E Russian Federation
188 H6 **Susupe** Saipan, S Northern Mariana Islands
136 D12 **Susurluk** Balıkesir, NW Turkey
114 M13 **Susuzmüsellim** Tekirdağ, NW Turkey
136 F15 **Sütçüler** Isparta, SW Turkey
116 L13 **Şuţeşti** Brăila, SE Romania
83 F25 **Sutherland** Western Cape, SW South Africa
28 L15 **Sutherland** Nebraska, C USA
96 I7 **Sutherland** *cultural region* N Scotland, UK
185 B21 **Sutherland Falls** *waterfall* South Island, New Zealand
32 F14 **Sutherlin** Oregon, NW USA
149 V10 **Sutlej** India/Pakistan
Sutna *see* Satna
35 P7 **Sutter Creek** California, W USA
39 R11 **Sutton** Alaska, USA
29 Q16 **Sutton** Nebraska, C USA
21 R4 **Sutton** West Virginia, NE USA
12 F8 **Sutton** Ontario, C Canada
97 M19 **Sutton Coldfield** C England, UK
21 R4 **Sutton Lake** West Virginia, NE USA
15 P13 **Sutton, Monts** *hill range* Québec, SE Canada
12 F8 **Sutton Ridges** ▲▲ Ontario, C Canada
165 Q4 **Suttsu** Hokkaidō, NE Japan
39 P15 **Sutwik Island** *island* Alaska, USA
Süüj *see* Dashinchilen
118 H5 **Suure-Jaani** *Ger.* Gross-Sankt-Johannis. Viljandimaa, S Estonia
118 J7 **Suur Munamägi** *var.* Munamägi, *Ger.* Eier-Berg. ▲ SE Estonia
118 F5 **Suur Väin** *Ger.* Grosser Sund. *strait* W Estonia
147 U8 **Suusamyr** Chuyskaya Oblast', C Kyrgyzstan
187 X14 **Suva** ● (Fiji) Viti Levu, W Fiji
187 X15 **Suva** ✕ Viti Levu, C Fiji
113 N18 **Suva Gora** ▲▲ WFYR Macedonia
118 H11 **Suvainiškis** Panevėžys, NE Lithuania
Suvalkai/Suvalki *see* Suwałki
113 P15 **Suva Planina** ▲▲ SE Serbia
113 M17 **Suva Reka** Kosovo, S Serbia
126 K5 **Suvorov** Tul'skaya Oblast', W Russian Federation
117 N12 **Suvorove** Odes'ka Oblast', SW Ukraine
Suvorovo *see* Ştefan Vodă
Suwaik *see* As Suwayq
Suwaira *see* Aş Şuwayrah
110 O7 **Suwałki** *Lith.* Suvalkai, *Rus.* Suvalki. Podlaskie, NE Poland
167 R10 **Suwannaphum** Roi Et, E Thailand
23 V8 **Suwannee River** Florida/Georgia, SE USA
Şuwār *see* Aş Şuwār
190 K14 **Suwarrow** *atoll* N Cook Islands
143 R16 **Suwaydān** *var.* Sweiham. Abū Ẓaby, E United Arab Emirates
Suwaydá/Suwaydā', Muḩāfaẓat as *see* As Suwaydā'
Suwayqiyah, Hawr as *see* Shuwayjah, Hawr ash
Suways, Khalīj as *see* Suez, Gulf of
Suways, Qanāt as *see* Suez Canal
Suweida *see* As Suwaydā'
Suweon *see* Suwŏn
163 X15 **Suwŏn** *var.* Suweon, *Jap.* Suigen. NW South Korea
Su Xian *see* Suzhou
143 R14 **Sūzā** Hormozgān, S Iran
145 P15 **Suzak** *Kaz.* Sozaq. Yuzhnyy Kazakhstan, S Kazakhstan
Suzaka *see* Suzuka
126 M3 **Suzdal'** Vladimirskaya Oblast', W Russian Federation
161 P7 **Suzhou** *var.* Su Xian. Anhui, E China
161 R8 **Suzhou** *var.* Soochow, Su-chou, Suchow; *prev.* Wuhsien. Jiangsu, E China
Suzhou *see* Jiuquan
Suz, Mys *see* Soye, Mys
165 M10 **Suzu** Ishikawa, Honshū, SW Japan
165 K14 **Suzuka** Mie, Honshū, SW Japan
165 N12 **Suzuka** *var.* Suzaka. Nagano, Honshū, S Japan
165 M10 **Suzu-misaki** *headland* Honshū, SW Japan
Svågälv *see* Svågan
94 M10 **Svågan** *var.* Svågälv. C Sweden
Svalava/Svaljava *see* Svalyava
92 O2 **Svalbard** ◇ *Norwegian dependency* Arctic Ocean
92 J2 **Svalbardhseyri** Nordhurland Eystra, N Iceland
95 K22 **Svalöv** Skåne, S Sweden
116 H7 **Svalyava** *Cz.* Svalava, Svaljava, *Hung.* Szolyva. Zakarpats'ka Oblast', W Ukraine
92 O2 **Svanbergfjellet** ▲ C Svalbard
95 M24 **Svaneke** Bornholm, E Denmark
95 L22 **Svängsta** Blekinge, S Sweden
95 J16 **Svanskog** Värmland, C Sweden
95 L16 **Svartå** Örebro, C Sweden
95 L15 **Svartälven** C Sweden
92 G12 **Svartisen** *glacier* C Norway
117 X6 **Svatove** *Rus.* Svatovo. Luhans'ka Oblast', E Ukraine
Svatovo *see* Svatove
Sväty Kríž nad Hronom *see* Žiar nad Hronom
167 Q11 **Svay Chék, Stœng** Cambodia/Thailand
167 S13 **Svay Riĕng** Svay Riĕng, S Cambodia
92 O3 **Sveagruva** Spitsbergen, W Svalbard
95 K23 **Svedala** Skåne, S Sweden
118 H12 **Svėdesai** Utena, NE Lithuania
93 G18 **Sveg** Jämtland, C Sweden
118 C12 **Švėkšna** Klaipėda, W Lithuania
94 C11 **Svelgen** Sogn Og Fjordane, S Norway
95 H15 **Svelvik** Vestfold, S Norway
118 I13 **Švenčionėliai** *Pol.* Nowo-Święciany. Vilnius, SE Lithuania
118 I13 **Švenčionys** *Pol.* Swięciany. Vilnius, SE Lithuania
95 H24 **Svendborg** Fyn, C Denmark
95 K19 **Svenljunga** Västra Götaland, S Sweden
92 P2 **Svenskøya** *island* E Svalbard
93 G17 **Svenstavik** Jämtland, C Sweden
95 G20 **Svenstrup** Nordjylland, N Denmark
118 H12 **Šventoji** C Lithuania
117 Z8 **Sverdlovs'k** *Rus.* Sverdlovsk; *prev.* Imeni Sverdlova Rudnik. Luhans'ka Oblast', E Ukraine
Sverdlovsk *see* Yekaterinburg
127 W2 **Sverdlovskaya Oblast'** ⬖ *province* C Russian Federation
122 K6 **Sverdrup, Ostrov** *island* N Russian Federation
Sverige *see* Sweden
113 D15 **Svetac** *prev.* Sveti Andrea, *It.* Sant'Andrea. *island* SW Croatia
Sveti Andrea *see* Svetac
Sveti Nikola *see* Sveti Nikole
113 O18 **Sveti Nikole** *prev.* Sveti Nikola. C FYR Macedonia
Sveti Vrach *see* Sandanski
123 T14 **Svetlaya** Primorskiy Kray, SE Russian Federation
126 B2 **Svetlogorsk** Kaliningradskaya Oblast', W Russian Federation
122 K9 **Svetlogorsk** Krasnoyarskiy Kray, N Russian Federation
Svetlogorsk *see* Svyetlahorsk
127 N14 **Svetlograd** Stavropol'skiy Kray, SW Russian Federation
Svetlovodsk *see* Svitlovods'k
119 A14 **Svetlyy** *Ger.* Zimmerbude. Kaliningradskaya Oblast', W Russian Federation
127 Y8 **Svetlyy** Orenburgskaya Oblast', W Russian Federation
127 P7 **Svetlyy** Saratovskaya Oblast', W Russian Federation
124 G11 **Svetogorsk** *Fin.* Enso. Leningradskaya Oblast', NW Russian Federation
Svetozarevo *see* Jagodina
111 B18 **Švihov** *Ger.* Schwihau. Plzeňský Kraj, W Czech Republic
112 E13 **Svilaja** ▲▲ SE Croatia
112 N12 **Svilajnac** Serbia, C Serbia
114 L11 **Svilengrad** *prev.* Mustafa-Pasha. Khaskovo, S Bulgaria
Svinecea Mare, Munte *see* Svinecea Mare, Vârful
116 F13 **Svinecea Mare, Vârful** *var.* Munte Svinecea Mare. ▲ SW Romania
Svinø *see* Svínoy
95 B18 **Svínoy** *Dan.* Svinø. *island* NE Faeroe Islands
147 N14 **Svintsovyy Rudnik** *Turkm.* Swintsowyy Rudnik. Lebap Welaýaty, E Turkmenistan
118 I13 **Svir** *Rus.* Svir'. Minskaya Voblasts', NW Belarus
124 I12 **Svir'** *canal* NW Russian Federation
Svir', Ozero *see* Svir, Vozyera
119 I14 **Svir, Vozyera** *Rus.* Ozero Svir'. C Belarus
114 J7 **Svishtov** *prev.* Sistova. Veliko Tŭrnovo, N Bulgaria
119 F18 **Svislach** *Pol.* Świsłocz, *Rus.* Svisloch'. Hrodzyenskaya Voblasts', W Belarus
119 M17 **Svislach** *Rus.* Svisloch'. Mahilyowskaya Voblasts', E Belarus
119 L17 **Svislach** *Rus.* Svisloch'. E Belarus
Svisloch' *see* Svislach
111 F17 **Svitavy** *Ger.* Zwittau. Pardubický Kraj, C Czech Republic
117 S6 **Svitlovods'k** *Rus.* Svetlovodsk. Kirovohrads'ka Oblast', C Ukraine
Svizzera *see* Switzerland
123 Q13 **Svobodnyy** Amurskaya Oblast', SE Russian Federation
114 G9 **Svoge** Sofiya, W Bulgaria
92 G11 **Svolvær** Nordland, C Norway
111 F18 **Svratka** *Ger.* Schwarzawa. SE Czech Republic
113 P14 **Svrljig** Serbia, E Serbia
197 U10 **Svyataya Anna Trough** *var.* Saint Anna Trough. *undersea feature* N Kara Sea
124 M4 **Svyatoy Nos, Mys** *headland* NW Russian Federation
119 N18 **Svyetlahorsk** *Rus.* Svetlogorsk. Homyel'skaya Voblasts', SE Belarus
Swabian Jura *see* Schwäbische Alb
97 P19 **Swaffham** E England, UK
23 V5 **Swainsboro** Georgia, SE USA
83 C19 **Swakop** W Namibia
83 C19 **Swakopmund** Erongo, W Namibia
97 M15 **Swale** N England, UK
Swallow Island *see* Nendö
99 M16 **Swalmen** Limburg, SE Netherlands
12 G8 **Swan** Ontario, C Canada
97 L24 **Swanage** S England, UK
182 M10 **Swan Hill** Victoria, SE Australia
9 P13 **Swan Hills** Alberta, W Canada
65 D24 **Swan Island** *island* C Falkland Islands
Swankalok *see* Sawankhalok
29 U10 **Swan Lake** Minnesota, N USA
21 Y10 **Swanquarter** North Carolina, SE USA
182 J9 **Swan Reach** South Australia
9 V15 **Swan River** Manitoba, S Canada
183 P17 **Swansea** Tasmania, SE Australia
97 J22 **Swansea** *Wel.* Abertawe. S Wales, UK
21 R13 **Swansea** South Carolina, SE USA
19 S7 **Swans Island** *island* Maine, NE USA
28 L17 **Swanson Lake** Nebraska, C USA
31 R11 **Swanton** Ohio, N USA
110 G11 **Swarzędz** Poznań, W Poland
Swatow *see* Shantou
83 L22 **Swaziland** *off.* Kingdom of Swaziland. ◆ *monarchy* S Africa
Swaziland, Kingdom of *see* Swaziland
93 G18 **Sweden** *off.* Kingdom of Sweden, *Swe.* Sverige. ◆ *monarchy* N Europe
Sweden, Kingdom of *see* Sweden
Swedru *see* Agona Swedru
25 V12 **Sweeny** Texas, SW USA
33 R6 **Sweetgrass** Montana, NW USA
32 G12 **Sweet Home** Oregon, NW USA
25 T12 **Sweet Home** Texas, SW USA
27 T4 **Sweet Springs** Missouri, C USA
20 M10 **Sweetwater** Tennessee, S USA
25 P7 **Sweetwater** Texas, SW USA
33 V15 **Sweetwater River** Wyoming, C USA
Sweiham *see* Suwaydān
83 F26 **Swellendam** Western Cape, SW South Africa
111 G15 **Świdnica** *Ger.* Schweidnitz. Wałbrzych, SW Poland
111 O14 **Świdnik** *Ger.* Streckenbach. Lubelskie, E Poland
110 F8 **Świdwin** *Ger.* Schivelbein. Zachodnio-pomorskie, NW Poland
111 F15 **Świebodzice** *Ger.* Freiburg in Schlesien, Swiebodzice. Walbrzych, SW Poland
110 E11 **Świebodzin** *Ger.* Schwiebus. Lubuskie, W Poland
Święciany *see* Švenčionys
110 I9 **Świecie** *Ger.* Schwertberg. Kujawsko-pomorskie, C Poland
111 L15 **Świętokrzyskie** ⬖ *province* S Poland
9 T16 **Swift Current** Saskatchewan, S Canada
98 K9 **Swifterbant** Flevoland, C Netherlands
183 Q12 **Swifts Creek** Victoria, SE Australia
96 E13 **Swilly, Lough** *Ir.* Loch Súílí. *inlet* N Ireland
97 M22 **Swindon** S England, UK
Swinemünde *see* Świnoujście
110 D8 **Świnoujście** *Ger.* Swinemünde. Zachodnio-pomorskie, NW Poland
Swintsowyy Rudnik *see* Svintsovyy Rudnik
Świsłocz *see* Svislach
Swiss Confederation *see* Switzerland
108 E9 **Switzerland** *off.* Swiss Confederation, *Fr.* La Suisse, *Ger.* Schweiz, *It.* Svizzera; *anc.* Helvetia. ◆ *federal republic* C Europe
97 F17 **Swords** *Ir.* Sord, Sórd Choluim Chille. Dublin, E Ireland
18 H13 **Swoyersville** Pennsylvania, NE USA
124 I10 **Syamozera, Ozero** NW Russian Federation
124 M13 **Syamzha** Vologodskaya Oblast', NW Russian Federation
118 N13 **Syanno** *Rus.* Senno. Vitsyebskaya Voblasts', NE Belarus
119 K16 **Syarhyeyevichy** *Rus.* Sergeyevichi. Minskaya Voblasts', C Belarus
124 I12 **Syas'stroy** Leningradskaya Oblast', NW Russian Federation
Sycaminum *see* Hefa
30 M10 **Sycamore** Illinois, N USA
126 J3 **Sychëvka** Smolenskaya Oblast', W Russian Federation
111 H14 **Syców** *Ger.* Gross Wartenberg. Dolnosląskie, SW Poland
14 E17 **Sydenham** Ontario, S Canada
Sydenham Island *see* Nonouti
183 T9 **Sydney** *state capital* New South Wales, SE Australia
13 R14 **Sydney** Cape Breton Island, Nova Scotia, SE Canada
Sydney Island *see* Manra
13 R14 **Sydney Mines** Cape Breton Island, Nova Scotia, SE Canada
Syedpur *see* Saidpur
119 K18 **Syelishcha** *Rus.* Selishche. Minskaya Voblasts', C Belarus
119 J18 **Syemyezhava** *Rus.* Semezhevo. Minskaya Voblasts', C Belarus
Syene *see* Aswân
117 X6 **Syeverodonets'k** *Rus.* Severodonetsk. Luhans'ka Oblast', E Ukraine
100 H11 **Syke** Niedersachsen, NW Germany
94 D10 **Sykkylven** Møre og Romsdal, S Norway
Sykoúri *see* Sykoúrio
115 F15 **Sykoúrio** *var.* Sikouri, Sykoúri; *prev.* Sikoúrion. Thessalía, C Greece
125 R11 **Syktyvkar** *prev.* Ust'-Sysol'sk. Respublika Komi, NW Russian Federation
23 Q4 **Sylacauga** Alabama, S USA
Sylarna *see* Storsylen
153 V14 **Sylhet** Sylhet, NE Bangladesh
153 V13 **Sylhet** ⬖ *division* NE Bangladesh
100 G6 **Sylt** *island* NW Germany
21 O10 **Sylva** North Carolina, SE USA
125 V15 **Sylva** NW Russian Federation
23 W5 **Sylvania** Georgia, SE USA
31 R11 **Sylvania** Ohio, N USA
9 Q15 **Sylvan Lake** Alberta, SW Canada
33 T13 **Sylvan Pass** *pass* Wyoming, C USA
23 T7 **Sylvester** Georgia, SE USA
25 P6 **Sylvester** Texas, SW USA
10 L11 **Sylvia, Mount** ▲ British Columbia, W Canada
122 K11 **Sym** C Russian Federation
115 N22 **Sými** *var.* Simi. *island* Dodekánisa, Greece, Aegean Sea
117 U8 **Synel'nykove** Dnipropetrovs'ka Oblast', E Ukraine
125 U6 **Synya** Respublika Komi, NW Russian Federation
117 P7 **Synyukha** *Rus.* Sinyukha. S Ukraine
195 V2 **Syowa** *Japanese research station* Antarctica
26 H6 **Syracuse** Kansas, C USA
29 S16 **Syracuse** Nebraska, C USA
18 H10 **Syracuse** New York, NE USA
Syracuse *see* Siracusa
Syrdar'inskaya Oblast' *see* Sirdaryo Viloyati
Syrdariya *see* Syr Darya
144 L14 **Syr Darya** *var.* Sai Hun, Sir Darya, Syrdarya, *Kaz.* Syrdariya, *Rus.* Syrdar'ya, *Uzb.* Sirdaryo; *anc.* Jaxartes. C Asia
Syrdarya *see* Syr Darya
138 J6 **Syria** *off.* Syrian Arab Republic, *var.* Siria, Syrie, *Ar.* Al-Jumhūrīyah al-'Arabīyah as-Sūrīyah, Sūrīya. ◆ *republic* SW Asia
Syrian Arab Republic *see* Syria
138 L9 **Syrian Desert** *Ar.* Al Hamad, Bādiyat ash Shām. *desert* SW Asia
Syrie *see* Syria
115 L22 **Sýrna** *var.* Sirna. *island* Kykládes, Greece, Aegean Sea
115 I20 **Sýros** *var.* Síros. *island* Kykládes, Greece, Aegean Sea
93 M18 **Sysmä** Etelä-Suomi, S Finland
125 R12 **Sysola** NW Russian Federation
Syulemeshlii *see* Sredets
127 S2 **Syumsi** Udmurtskaya Respublika, NW Russian Federation
114 K10 **Syuyutliyka** C Bulgaria
Syvash, Zaliv *see* Syvash, Zatoka
117 U12 **Syvash, Zatoka** *Rus.* Zaliv Syvash. *inlet* S Ukraine
127 Q6 **Syzran'** Samarskaya Oblast', W Russian Federation
Szabadka *see* Subotica
111 N21 **Szabolcs-Szatmár-Bereg** *off.* Szabolcs-Szatmár-Bereg Megye. ⬖ *county* E Hungary
Szabolcs-Szatmár-Bereg Megye *see* Szabolcs-Szatmár-Bereg
110 G10 **Szamocin** *Ger.* Samotschin. Wielkopolskie, C Poland
116 H8 **Szamos** *var.* Someş, Someşul, *Ger.* Samosch, Somesch. Hungary/Romania
Szamosújvár *see* Gherla
110 G11 **Szamotuły** Poznań, W Poland
Szarkowszczyzna *see* Sharkawshchyna
111 M24 **Szarvas** Békés, SE Hungary
Szászmagyarós *see* Măieruş
Szászrégen *see* Reghin
Szászsebes *see* Sebeş
Szászváros *see* Orăştie
Szatmárrnémeti *see* Satu Mare
Száva *see* Sava
111 P15 **Szczebrzeszyn** Lubelskie, E Poland
110 D9 **Szczecin** *Eng./Ger.* Stettin. Zachodnio-pomorskie, NW Poland
110 G8 **Szczecinek** *Ger.* Neustettin. Zachodnio-pomorskie, NW Poland
110 D8 **Szczeciński, Zalew** *var.* Stettiner Haff, *Ger.* Oderhaff. *bay* Germany/Poland
111 K15 **Szczekociny** Śląskie, S Poland
110 N8 **Szczuczyn** Podlaskie, NE Poland
Szczuczyn Nowogródzki *see* Shchuchyn
110 M8 **Szczytno** *Ger.* Ortelsburg. Warmińsko-Mazurskie, NE Poland
Szechuan/Szechwan *see* Sichuan
111 K21 **Szécsény** Nógrád, N Hungary
111 L25 **Szeged** *Ger.* Szegedin, *Rom.* Seghedin. Csongrád, SE Hungary
Szegedin *see* Szeged
111 N23 **Szeghalom** Békés, SE Hungary
Székelyhid *see* Săcueni
Székelykeresztúr *see* Cristuru Secuiesc
111 I23 **Székesfehérvár** *Ger.* Stuhlweissenberg; *anc.* Alba Regia. Fejér, W Hungary
Szeklerburg *see* Miercurea-Ciuc
Szekler Neumarkt *see* Târgu Secuiesc
111 J25 **Szekszárd** Tolna, S Hungary
Szempcz/Szenc *see* Senec
Szenice *see* Senica
Szentágota *see* Agnita
111 J22 **Szentendre** *Ger.* Sankt Andrä. Pest, N Hungary
111 L24 **Szentes** Csongrád, SE Hungary
111 F23 **Szentgotthárd** *Eng.* Saint Gotthard, *Ger.* Sankt Gotthard. Vas, W Hungary
Szentgyörgy *see* Đurđevac
Szenttamás *see* Srbobran
Széphely *see* Jebel
Szeping *see* Siping
Szered *see* Sered'
111 N21 **Szerencs** Borsod-Abaúj-Zemplén, NE Hungary
Szeret *see* Siret
Szeretfalva *see* Sărăţel
110 N7 **Szeska Góra** *var.* Szeskie Wygórza, *Ger.* Seesker Höhe. *hill* NE Poland
Szeskie Wygórza *see* Szeska Góra
111 H25 **Szigetvár** Baranya, SW Hungary
Szilágysomlyó *see* Şimleu Silvaniei
Szinna *see* Snina
Sziszek *see* Sisak
Szitás-Keresztúr *see* Cristuru Secuiesc
111 E15 **Szklarska Poręba** *Ger.* Schreiberhau. Dolnośląskie, SW Poland
Szkudy *see* Skuodas
Szlatina *see* Slatina
Szlavonia/Szlavonország *see* Slavonija
Szlovákia *see* Slovakia
Szluin *see* Slunj
111 L23 **Szolnok** Jász-Nagykun-Szolnok, C Hungary
Szolyva *see* Svalyava
111 G23 **Szombathely** *Ger.* Steinamanger; *anc.* Sabaria, Savaria. Vas, W Hungary
Szond/Szonta *see* Sonta
Szováta *see* Sovata
110 F13 **Szprotawa** *Ger.* Sprottau. Lubuskie, W Poland
Sztálinváros *see* Dunaújváros
Sztrazsó *see* Strážov
110 J8 **Sztum** *Ger.* Stuhm. Pomorskie, N Poland
110 H10 **Szubin** *Ger.* Schubin. Kujawsko-pomorskie, C Poland
Szucsava *see* Suceava
Szurduk *see* Surduc
111 M14 **Szydłowiec** *Ger.* Schlelau. Mazowieckie, C Poland

T

Taalintehdas *see* Dalsbruk
171 O4 **Taal, Lake** Luzon, NW Philippines
95 J23 **Taastrup** *var.* Tåstrup. København, E Denmark
111 I24 **Tab** Somogy, W Hungary
171 P4 **Tabaco** Luzon, N Philippines
186 G4 **Tabalo** Mussau Island, NE PNG
104 K5 **Tábara** Castilla-León, N Spain
186 H5 **Tabar Islands** *island group* NE Papua New Guinea
Tabariya, Bahrat *see* Tiberias, Lake
143 S7 **Ţabas** *var.* Golshan. Yazd, C Iran
43 P15 **Tabasará, Serranía de** ▲▲ W Panama
41 U15 **Tabasco** ⬖ *state* SE Mexico
Tabasco *see* Grijalva, Río
127 Q2 **Tabashino** Respublika Mariy El, W Russian Federation
58 B13 **Tabatinga** Amazonas, N Brazil
74 G9 **Tabelbala** W Algeria
9 Q17 **Taber** Alberta, SW Canada
171 V15 **Taberfane** Pulau Trangan, E Indonesia
95 L19 **Taberg** Jönköping, S Sweden
191 O3 **Tabiteuea** *prev.* Drummond Island. *atoll* Tungaru, W Kiribati
171 O5 **Tablas Island** *island* C Philippines
184 Q10 **Table Cape** *headland* North Island, New Zealand
13 S13 **Table Mountain** ▲ Newfoundland, Newfoundland and Labrador, E Canada
173 P17 **Table, Pointe de la** *headland* SE Réunion
27 S8 **Table Rock Lake** Arkansas/Missouri, C USA
36 K14 **Table Top** ▲ Arizona, SW USA
186 D8 **Tabletop, Mount** ▲ C Papua New Guinea
111 D18 **Tábor** Jihočeský Kraj, S Czech Republic
123 R7 **Tabor** Respublika Sakha (Yakutiya), NE Russian Federation
29 S15 **Tabor** Iowa, C USA
81 F21 **Tabora** Tabora, W Tanzania
81 F21 **Tabora** ⬖ *region* C Tanzania
21 U12 **Tabor City** North Carolina, SE USA
147 Q10 **Taboshar** NW Tajikistan
76 L18 **Tabou** *var.* Tabu. S Ivory Coast
142 J2 **Tabrīz** *var.* Tebriz; *anc.* Tauris. Āzarbāyjān-e Sharqi, NW Iran
Tabu *see* Tabou
191 W1 **Tabuaeran** *prev.* Fanning Island. *atoll* Line Islands, E Kiribati
171 O2 **Tabuk** Luzon, N Philippines
140 J4 **Tabūk** Tabūk, NW Saudi Arabia
140 J5 **Tabūk** *off.* Minţaqat Tabūk. ⬖ *province* NW Saudi Arabia
Tabūk, Minţaqat *see* Tabūk
187 Q13 **Tabwemasana, Mount** ▲ Espiritu Santo, W Vanuatu
95 O15 **Täby** Stockholm, C Sweden
41 N14 **Tacámbaro** Michoacán de Ocampo, SW Mexico
42 A5 **Tacaná, Volcán** Guatemala/Mexico
43 X16 **Tacarcuna, Cerro** ▲ SE Panama
Tachau *see* Tachov
158 J3 **Tacheng** *var.* Qoqek. Xinjiang Uygur Zizhiqu, NW China
54 H7 **Táchira** *off.* Estado Táchira. ⬖ *state* W Venezuela
Táchira, Estado *see* Táchira
161 T13 **Tachoshui** N Taiwan
111 A17 **Tachov** *Ger.* Tachau. Plveňský Kraj, W Czech Republic
171 Q5 **Tacloban** *off.* Tacloban City. Leyte, C Philippines
Tacloban City *see* Tacloban
57 I19 **Tacna** Tacna, SE Peru
57 H18 **Tacna** *off.* Departamento de Tacna. ⬖ *department* S Peru
Tacna, Departamento de *see* Tacna
32 H8 **Tacoma** Washington, NW USA
18 L11 **Taconic Range** ▲▲ NE USA
62 L6 **Taco Pozo** Formosa, N Argentina
57 M20 **Tacsara, Cordillera de** ▲▲ S Bolivia
61 F17 **Tacuarembó** *prev.* San Fructuoso. Tacuarembó, C Uruguay
61 E18 **Tacuarembó** ⬖ *department* C Uruguay
61 F17 **Tacuarembó, Río** C Uruguay
83 I14 **Taculi** North Western, NW Zambia
171 Q8 **Tacurong** Mindanao, S Philippines
77 V8 **Tadek** NW Niger
74 J9 **Tademaït, Plateau du** *plateau* C Algeria
187 R17 **Tadine** Province des Îles Loyauté, E New Caledonia
80 M11 **Tadjoura, Golfe de** *Eng.* Gulf of Tajura. *inlet* E Djibouti
80 L11 **Tadjourah** E Djibouti
Tadmor/Tadmur *see* Tudmur
9 W10 **Tadoule Lake** Manitoba, C Canada
15 S8 **Tadoussac** Québec, SE Canada
155 H18 **Tādpatri** Andhra Pradesh, E India
Tadzhikabad *see* Tojikobod
Tadzhikistan *see* Tajikistan
163 Y14 **T'aebaek-sanmaek** ▲▲ E South Korea
163 V15 **Taechŏng-do** *island* NW South Korea
163 X13 **Taedong-gang** C North Korea
163 Y16 **Taegu** *off.* Taegu-gwangyŏksi, *var.* Daegu, *Jap.* Taikyū. SE South Korea
Taegu-gwangyŏksi *see* Taegu
Taehan-haehyŏp *see* Korea Strait
Taehan Min'guk *see* South Korea
163 Y15 **Taejŏn** *off.* Taejŏn-gwangyŏksi, *Jap.* Taiden. C South Korea
Taejŏn-gwangyŏksi *see* Taejŏn
193 Z13 **Tafahi** *island* N Tonga
105 Q4 **Tafalla** Navarra, N Spain
75 M12 **Tafassâsset, Oued** SE Algeria
77 W7 **Tafassâsset, Ténéré du** *desert* N Niger
55 U11 **Tafelberg** ▲ S Suriname
97 J21 **Taff** SE Wales, UK
Tafila/Ţafīlah, Muḩāfaẓat aţ *see* Aţ Ţafīlah
77 N15 **Tafiré** N Ivory Coast
142 M6 **Tafresh** Markazī, W Iran
143 Q9 **Taft** Yazd, C Iran
35 R13 **Taft** California, W USA
25 T14 **Taft** Texas, SW USA
143 W12 **Taftān, Kūh-e** ▲ SE Iran
35 R13 **Taft Heights** California, W USA
189 Y14 **Tafunsak** Kosrae, E Micronesia
192 G16 **Tāga** Savai'i, SW Samoa
149 O6 **Tagāb** Dāikondī, E Afghanistan
39 O8 **Tagagawik River** Alaska, USA
165 Q10 **Tagajō** *var.* Tagazyô. Miyagi, Honshū, C Japan
126 K12 **Taganrog** Rostovskaya Oblast', SW Russian Federation
126 K12 **Taganrog, Gulf of** *Rus.* Taganrogskiy Zaliv, *Ukr.* Tahanroz'ka Zatoka. *gulf* Russian Federation/Ukraine
Taganrogskiy Zaliv *see* Taganrog, Gulf of
76 J8 **Tagant** ⬖ *region* C Mauritania

◆ Country
● Country Capital
◇ Dependent Territory
○ Dependent Territory Capital
⬖ Administrative Regions
✕ International Airport
▲ Mountain
▲▲ Mountain Range
Volcano
River
Lake
Reservoir

148 M14 Tagas Baluchistān, SW Pakistan
171 O4 Tagaytay Luzon, N Philippines
Tagazyō see Tagajō
171 P6 Tagbilaran var. Tagbilaran City. Bohol, C Philippines
Tagbilaran City see Tagbilaran
106 B10 Taggia Liguria, NW Italy
77 V9 Taghouaji, Massif de ▲ C Niger
107 J15 Tagliacozzo Lazio, C Italy
106 I7 Tagliamento ⇝ NE Italy
149 N3 Tagow Bāy var. Bai. Sar-e Pol, N Afghanistan
146 H9 Tagta var. Tahta, Rus. Takhta. Daşoguz Welaýaty, N Turkmenistan
146 J16 Tagtabazar var. Takhtabazar. Mary Welaýaty, S Turkmenistan
59 L17 Taguatinga Tocantins, C Brazil
186 I10 Tagula Tagula Island, SE Papua New Guinea
186 I11 Tagula Island prev. Southeast Island, Sudest Island. island SE Papua New Guinea
171 Q7 Tagum Mindanao, S Philippines
54 C7 Tagún, Cerro elevation Colombia/Panama
105 P7 Tagus Port. Rio Tejo, Sp. Río Tajo. ⇝ Portugal/Spain
64 M9 Tagus Plain undersea feature E Atlantic Ocean
191 S10 Tahaa island Îles Sous le Vent, W French Polynesia
191 U10 Tahanea atoll Îles Tuamotu, C French Polynesia
Tahanroz'ka Zatoka see Taganrog, Gulf of
74 K12 Tahat ▲ SE Algeria
163 U4 Tahe Heilongjiang, NE China
163 V12 Ta He ⇝ NE China
Tahilt see Tsogt
191 T10 Tahiti island Îles du Vent, W French Polynesia
Tahiti, Archipel de see Société, Archipel de la
118 E4 Tahkuna nina headland W Estonia
148 K12 Tāhlāb ⇝ W Pakistan
148 K12 Tāhlāb, Dasht-i desert SW Pakistan
27 R10 Tahlequah Oklahoma, C USA
35 Q6 Tahoe City California, W USA
35 P6 Tahoe, Lake ◎ California/Nevada, W USA
25 N6 Tahoka Texas, SW USA
32 F8 Taholah Washington, NW USA
77 T11 Tahoua Tahoua, W Niger
77 T11 Tahoua ◈ department W Niger
31 P3 Tahquamenon Falls waterfall Michigan, N USA
31 P4 Tahquamenon River ⇝ Michigan, N USA
139 V10 Taḩrīr S Iraq
10 K17 Tahsis Vancouver Island, British Columbia, SW Canada
75 W9 Ṭahṭa C Egypt
Tahta see Tagta
136 L15 Tahtalı Dağları ▲▲ C Turkey
57 I14 Tahuamanu, Río ⇝ Bolivia/Peru
56 F13 Tahuanía, Río ⇝ E Peru
191 X7 Tahuata island Îles Marquises, NE French Polynesia
76 L17 Taï SW Ivory Coast
161 P5 Tai'an Shandong, E China
191 R8 Taiarapu, Presqu'île de peninsula Tahiti, W French Polynesia
Taibad see Tāybād
160 K7 Taibai Shan ▲ C China
105 Q12 Taibilla, Sierra de ▲▲ S Spain
Taibus Qi see Baochang
Taichū see T'aichung
161 S13 T'aichung Jap. Taichū; prev. Taiwan. C Taiwan
Taiden see Taejŏn
185 E23 Taieri ⇝ South Island, New Zealand
115 E21 Taïgetos ▲▲ S Greece
161 N4 Taihang Shan ▲▲ C China
184 M11 Taihape Manawatu-Wanganui, North Island, New Zealand
161 O7 Taihe Anhui, E China
161 O12 Taihe var. Chengjiang. Jiangxi, S China
Taihoku see T'aipei
161 P9 Taihu Anhui, E China
161 R8 Tai Hu ◎ E China
159 O9 Taikang var. Dorbod, Dorbod Mongolzu Zizhixian. Heilongjiang, NE China
161 O6 Taikang Henan, C China
165 T5 Taiki Hokkaidō, NE Japan
166 L8 Taikkyi Yangon, SW Myanmar (Burma)
Taikyū see Taegu
163 U8 Tailai Heilongjiang, NE China
168 I12 Taileleo Pulau Siberut, W Indonesia
182 J10 Tailem Bend South Australia
96 I8 Tain N Scotland, UK
161 S14 T'ainan Jap. Tainan; prev. Dainan. S Taiwan
115 E22 Taínaro, Ákrotírio cape S Greece
161 Q11 Taining var. Shancheng. Fujian, SE China
191 W7 Taiohae prev. Madisonville. Nuku Hiva, NE French Polynesia
161 T13 T'aipei Jap. Taihoku; prev. Daihoku. ● (Taiwan) N Taiwan
168 J7 Taiping Perak, Peninsular Malaysia
163 S8 Taiping Ling ▲ NE China
165 Q4 Taisei Hokkaidō, NE Japan
165 G12 Taisha Shimane, Honshū, SW Japan
109 R4 Taiskirchen Oberösterreich, NW Austria
63 F20 Taitao, Peninsula de peninsula S Chile
Taitō see T'aitung
161 T14 T'aitung Jap. Taitō. S Taiwan
92 M13 Taivalkoski Oulu, E Finland
93 K19 Taivassalo Länsi-Soumi, SW Finland
161 T14 Taiwan off. Republic of China, var. Formosa, Formo'sa. ◆ republic E Asia
192 F5 Taiwan var. Formosa. island E Asia
Taiwan see T'aichung
T'aiwan Haihsia/Taiwan Haixia see Taiwan Strait
Taiwan Shan see Chungyang Shanmo
161 R13 Taiwan Strait var. Formosa Strait, Chin. T'aiwan Haihsia, Taiwan Haixia. strait China/Taiwan
161 N4 Taiyuan var. T'ai-yuan, T'ai-yüan; prev. Yangku. province capital Shanxi, C China
T'ai-yuan/T'ai-yüan see Taiyuan
161 R7 Taizhou Jiangsu, E China
161 S10 Taizhou var. Jiaojiang; prev. Haimen. Zhejiang, SE China
Taizhou see Linhai
141 O16 Ta'izz SW Yemen
141 O16 Ta'izz ✕ SW Yemen
75 P12 Tajarhī SW Libya
147 P13 Tajikistan off. Republic of Tajikistan, Rus. Tadzhikistan, Taj. Jumhurii Tojikiston; prev. Tajik S.S.R. ◆ republic C Asia
Tajikistan, Republic of see Tajikistan
Tajik S.S.R see Tajikistan
165 O11 Tajima Fukushima, Honshū, C Japan
Tajoe see Tayu
Tajo, Río see Tagus
42 B5 Tajumulco, Volcán ▲ W Guatemala
105 P7 Tajuña ⇝ C Spain
Tajura, Gulf of see Tadjoura, Golfe de
167 O9 Tak var. Rahaeng. Tak, W Thailand
189 U4 Taka Atoll var. Tōke. atoll Ratak Chain, N Marshall Islands
165 P12 Takahagi Ibaraki, Honshū, S Japan
165 H13 Takahashi var. Takahasi. Okayama, Honshū, SW Japan
Takahasi see Takahashi
189 P12 Takaieu Island island E Micronesia
184 I13 Takaka Tasman, South Island, New Zealand
170 M14 Takalar Sulawesi, C Indonesia
165 H13 Takamatsu var. Takamatu. Kagawa, Shikoku, SW Japan
Takamatu see Takamatsu
165 D14 Takamori Kumamoto, Kyūshū, SW Japan
165 D16 Takanabe Miyazaki, Kyūshū, SW Japan
170 M16 Takan, Gunung ▲ Pulau Sumba, S Indonesia
165 Q7 Takanosu Akita, Honshū, C Japan
Takao see Kaohsiung
165 L11 Takaoka Toyama, Honshū, SW Japan
184 N12 Takapau Hawke's Bay, North Island, New Zealand
191 U9 Takapoto atoll Îles Tuamotu, C French Polynesia
184 L5 Takapuna Auckland, North Island, New Zealand
165 J3 Takarazuka Hyōgo, Honshū, SW Japan
191 U9 Takaroa atoll Îles Tuamotu, C French Polynesia
165 N12 Takasaki Gunma, Honshū, S Japan
164 L12 Takayama Gifu, Honshū, SW Japan
164 K12 Takefu var. Takehu. Fukui, Honshū, SW Japan
Takehu see Takefu
164 C14 Takeo Saga, Kyūshū, SW Japan
Takeo see Takêv
164 C17 Take-shima island Nansei-shotō, SW Japan
142 M5 Tākestān var. Takistan; prev. Siadehan. Qazvin, N Iran
164 D14 Taketa Ōita, Kyūshū, SW Japan
167 R13 Takêv prev. Takeo. Takêv, S Cambodia
167 O10 Tak Fah Nakhon Sawan, C Thailand
139 T13 Takhādīd well S Iraq
149 R3 Takhār ◈ province NE Afghanistan
Takhiatash see Takhiatosh
167 S13 Ta Khmau Kândal, S Cambodia
Takhta see Tagta
Takhtabazar see Tagtabazar
145 O8 Takhtabrod Severnyy Kazakhstan, N Kazakhstan
Takhtakupyr see Taxtako'pir
142 M8 Takht-e Shāh, Kūh-e ▲▲ C Iran
77 V12 Takiéta Zinder, S Niger
8 J8 Takijuq Lake ◎ Nunavut, NW Canada
165 S3 Takikawa Hokkaidō, NE Japan
165 U3 Takinoue Hokkaidō, NE Japan
Takistan see Tākestān
185 B23 Takitimu Mountains ▲▲ South Island, New Zealand
Takkaze see Tekezē
165 R7 Takko Aomori, Honshū, C Japan
10 L13 Takla Lake ◎ British Columbia, SW Canada
Takla Makan Desert see Taklimakan Shamo
158 H9 Taklimakan Shamo Eng. Takla Makan Desert. desert NW China
167 T12 Takôk Môndól Kiri, E Cambodia
39 P10 Takotna Alaska, USA
Takow see Kaohsiung
123 O12 Taksimo Respublika Buryatiya, S Russian Federation
164 C13 Taku Saga, Kyūshū, SW Japan
10 I10 Taku ⇝ British Columbia, W Canada
166 M15 Takua Pa var. Ban Takua Pa. Phangnga, SW Thailand
77 W16 Takum Taraba, E Nigeria
191 V10 Takume atoll Îles Tuamotu, C French Polynesia
190 L16 Takutea island S Cook Islands
186 K6 Takuu Islands prev. Mortlock Group. island group NE Papua New Guinea
119 L18 Tal' Rus. Tal'. Minskaya Voblasts', S Belarus
40 L13 Tala Jalisco, C Mexico
61 F19 Tala Canelones, S Uruguay
Talabriga see Aveiro
Talabriga see Talavera de la Reina
119 N14 Talachyn Rus. Tolochin. Vitsyebskaya Voblasts', NE Belarus
149 U7 Talagang Punjab, E Pakistan
105 V11 Talaiassa ▲ Ibiza, Spain, W Mediterranean Sea
155 J23 Talaimannar Northern Province, NW Sri Lanka
117 R3 Talalayivka Chernihivs'ka Oblast', N Ukraine
43 O15 Talamanca, Cordillera de ▲▲ S Costa Rica
56 A9 Talara Piura, NW Peru
104 L11 Talarrubias Extremadura, W Spain
147 S8 Talas Talasskaya Oblast', NW Kyrgyzstan
147 S8 Talas ⇝ NW Kyrgyzstan
186 G7 Talasea New Britain, E Papua New Guinea
Talas Oblasty see Talasskaya Oblast'
147 S8 Talasskaya Oblast' Kir. Talas Oblasty. ◈ province NW Kyrgyzstan
147 S8 Talasskiy Alatau, Khrebet ▲▲ Kazakhstan/Kyrgyzstan
77 U12 Talata Mafara Zamfara, NW Nigeria
171 R9 Talaud, Kepulauan island group E Indonesia
104 M9 Talavera de la Reina anc. Caesarobriga, Talabriga. Castilla-La Mancha, C Spain
104 J11 Talavera la Real Extremadura, W Spain
186 F7 Talawe, Mount ▲ New Britain, C Papua New Guinea
23 S5 Talbotton Georgia, SE USA
183 R7 Talbragar River ⇝ New South Wales, SE Australia
62 G13 Talca Maule, C Chile
62 F13 Talcahuano Bío Bío, C Chile
154 N12 Tālcher Orissa, E India
25 W5 Talco Texas, SW USA
145 V14 Taldykorgan Kaz. Taldyqorghan; prev. Taldy-Kurgan. Taldykorgan, SE Kazakhstan
Taldy-Kurgan/Taldyqorghan see Taldykorgan
147 Y7 Taldy-Suu Issyk-Kul'skaya Oblast', E Kyrgyzstan
147 U10 Taldy-Suu Oshskaya Oblast', SW Kyrgyzstan
Tal-e Khosravī see Yāsūj
193 Y15 Taleki Tonga island Otu Tolu Group, C Tonga
193 Y15 Taleki Vavu'u island Otu Tolu Group, C Tonga
102 J13 Talence Gironde, SW France
145 U16 Talgar Kaz. Talghar. Almaty, SE Kazakhstan
Talghar see Talgar
171 Q12 Taliabu, Pulau island Kepulauan Sula, C Indonesia
115 L22 Taliarós, Ákrotírio cape Astypálaia, Kykládes, Greece, Aegean Sea
Ta-lien see Dalian
27 Q12 Talihina Oklahoma, C USA
Talimardzhan see Tollimarjon
137 T12 T'alin Rus. Talin; prev. Verin T'alin. W Armenia
Talin see T'alin
81 E15 Tali Post Bahr el Gabel, S Sudan
Taliq-an see Tāloqān
Taliş Dağları see Talish Mountains
142 L2 Talish Mountains Az. Taliş Dağları, Per. Kūhhā-ye Ţavālesh, Rus. Talyshskiye Gory. ▲▲ Azerbaijan/Iran
170 M16 Taliwang Sumbawa, C Indonesia
119 L17 Tal'ka Rus. Tal'ka. Minskaya Voblasts', C Belarus
39 R11 Talkeetna Alaska, USA
39 R11 Talkeetna Mountains ▲▲ Alaska, USA
Talkhof see Puurmani
92 H2 Tálknafjördhur Vestfirdhir, W Iceland
139 Q3 Tall 'Abṭah N Iraq
138 M2 Tall Abyaḑ var. Tell Abiad. Ar Raqqah, N Syria
23 Q4 Talladega Alabama, S USA
139 Q2 Tall 'Afar N Iraq
23 S8 Tallahassee prev. Muskogean. state capital Florida, SE USA
22 L2 Tallahatchie River ⇝ Mississippi, S USA
Tall al Abyaḑ see At Tall al Abyaḑ
139 W12 Tall al Laḩm S Iraq
183 P11 Tallangatta Victoria, SE Australia
23 R4 Tallapoosa River ⇝ Alabama/Georgia, S USA
103 T13 Tallard Hautes-Alpes, SE France
139 Q3 Tall ash Sha'īr N Iraq
23 Q5 Tallassee Alabama, S USA
139 R4 Tall 'Azbah NW Iraq
138 I5 Tall Bīsah Ḩimş, W Syria
139 Q3 Tall Ḩassūnah N Iraq
139 Q2 Tall Ḩuqnah var. Tell Huqnah. N Iraq
Tallin see Tallinn
118 G3 Tallinn Ger. Reval, Rus. Tallin; prev. Revel. ● (Estonia) Harjumaa, NW Estonia
118 H3 Tallinn ✕ Harjumaa, NW Estonia
138 H5 Tall Kalakh var. Tell Kalakh. Ḩimş, C Syria
139 R2 Tall Kayf NW Iraq
Tall Kūchak see Tall Kūshik
139 P2 Tall Kūshik var. Tall Kūchak. Al Ḩasakah, E Syria
31 U12 Tallmadge Ohio, N USA
22 J5 Tallulah Louisiana, S USA
139 Q2 Tall 'Uwaynāt NW Iraq
139 Q2 Tall Zāhir N Iraq
122 J13 Tal'menka Altayskiy Kray, S Russian Federation
122 K8 Talnakh Taymyrskiy (Dolgano-Nenetskiy) Avtonomnyy Okrug, N Russian Federation
117 P7 Tal'ne Rus. Tal'noye. Cherkas'ka Oblast', C Ukraine
Tal'noye see Tal'ne
80 E12 Talodi Southern Kordofan, C Sudan
188 B16 Talofofo SE Guam
188 B16 Talofofo Bay bay SE Guam
26 L9 Taloga Oklahoma, C USA
123 T10 Talon Magadanskaya Oblast', E Russian Federation
14 H11 Talon, Lake ◎ Ontario, S Canada
149 R2 Tāloqān var. Taliq-an. Takhār, NE Afghanistan
126 M8 Talovaya Voronezhskaya Oblast', W Russian Federation
9 N6 Taloyoak prev. Spence Bay. Nunavut, N Canada
25 Q8 Talpa Texas, SW USA
40 K13 Talpa de Allende Jalisco, C Mexico
23 S9 Talquin, Lake ⊠ Florida, SE USA
Talsen see Talsi
Talshand see Chandmanī
118 E8 Talsi Ger. Talsen. Talsi, NW Latvia
143 V11 Tal Sīāh Sīstān va Balūchestān, SE Iran
62 G6 Taltal Antofagasta, N Chile
8 K10 Taltson ⇝ Northwest Territories, NW Canada
168 K11 Taluk Sumatera, W Indonesia
92 J8 Talvik Finnmark, N Norway
182 M7 Talyawalka Creek ⇝ New South Wales, SE Australia
Talyshskiye Gory see Talish Mountains
29 W14 Tama Iowa, C USA
Tama Abu, Banjaran see Penambo, Banjaran
169 U9 Tamabo, Banjaran ▲▲ East Malaysia
190 B16 Tamakautoga SW Niue
127 N7 Tamala Penzenskaya Oblast', W Russian Federation
77 P15 Tamale C Ghana
191 P3 Tamana prev. Rotcher Island. atoll Tungaru, W Kiribati
74 K12 Tamanrasset var. Tamenghest. S Algeria
74 J13 Tamanrasset wadi Algeria/Mali
166 M2 Tamanthi Sagaing, N Myanmar (Burma)
97 I24 Tamar ⇝ SW England, UK
Tamar see Tudmur
54 H9 Támara Casanare, C Colombia
54 F7 Tamar, Alto de ▲ C Colombia
173 X16 Tamarin E Mauritius
105 T5 Tamarite de Litera var. Tararite de Llitera. Aragón, NE Spain
111 I24 Tamási Tolna, S Hungary
Tamatave see Toamasina
41 O9 Tamaulipas ◈ state C Mexico
41 P10 Tamaulipas, Sierra de ▲▲ C Mexico
56 F12 Tamaya, Río ⇝ E Peru
40 J9 Tamazula Durango, C Mexico
40 L14 Tamazula Jalisco, C Mexico
Tamazulápam see Tamazulapán
41 Q15 Tamazulapán var. Tamazulápam. Oaxaca, SE Mexico
41 P12 Tamazunchale San Luis Potosí, C Mexico
76 H11 Tambacounda SE Senegal
83 M16 Tambara Manica, C Mozambique
77 T13 Tambawel Sokoto, NW Nigeria
186 M9 Tambea Guadalcanal, C Solomon Islands
169 N10 Tambelan, Kepulauan island group W Indonesia
57 E15 Tambo de Mora Ica, W Peru
170 L16 Tambora, Gunung ▲▲ Sumbawa, S Indonesia
61 E17 Tambores Paysandú, W Uruguay
57 F14 Tambo, Río ⇝ C Peru
56 F7 Tamboryacu, Río ⇝ N Peru
126 M7 Tambov Tambovskaya Oblast', W Russian Federation
126 L6 Tambovskaya Oblast' ◈ province W Russian Federation
104 H3 Tambre ⇝ NW Spain
169 V7 Tambunan Sabah, East Malaysia
81 C15 Tambura Western Equatoria, SW Sudan
Tamchaket see Tâmchekket
76 J9 Tâmchekket var. Tamchaket. Hodh el Gharbi, S Mauritania
167 T7 Tam Điệp Ninh Bình, N Vietnam
Tamdybulak see Tomdibuloq
54 H8 Tame Arauca, C Colombia
104 H6 Tâmega, Rio Sp. Río Támega. ⇝ Portugal/Spain
Támega, Río see Tâmega, Rio
115 H20 Taméos, Ákrotírio headland Tziá, Kykládes, Greece, Aegean Sea
Tamenghest see Tamanrasset
77 V8 Tamgak, Adrar ▲ C Niger
76 I13 Tamgue ▲ NW Guinea
41 Q12 Tamiahua Veracruz-Llave, E Mexico
41 Q12 Tamiahua, Laguna de lagoon E Mexico
23 Y16 Tamiami Canal canal Florida, SE USA
188 F17 Tamil Harbor harbor Yap, W Micronesia
155 H21 Tamil Nādu prev. Madras. ◈ state SE India
99 H20 Tamines Namur, S Belgium
116 E12 Tamiš Ger. Temesch, Hung. Temes, SCr. Tamiš. ⇝ Romania/Serbia
167 U10 Tam Ky Quang Nam-fa Năng, C Vietnam
Tammerfors see Tampere
Tammisaari see Ekenäs
95 N14 Tämnaren ◎ C Sweden
191 Q7 Tamotoe, Passe passage Tahiti, W French Polynesia
23 V12 Tampa Florida, SE USA
23 V12 Tampa ✕ Florida, SE USA
23 V13 Tampa Bay bay Florida, SE USA
93 L18 Tampere Swe. Tammerfors. Länsi-Suomi, W Finland
41 Q11 Tampico Tamaulipas, C Mexico
171 P14 Tampo Pulau Muna, C Indonesia
167 V11 Tam Quan Bình Định, C Vietnam
162 J13 Tamsag Muchang Nei Mongol Zizhiqu, N China
Tamsal see Tamsalu
118 I4 Tamsalu Ger. Tamsal. Lääne-Virumaa, NE Estonia
109 S8 Tamsweg Salzburg, SW Austria
41 P12 Tamuín San Luis Potosí, C Mexico
188 C15 Tamuning NW Guam
183 T6 Tamworth New South Wales, SE Australia
97 M19 Tamworth C England, UK
81 K19 Tana ⇝ SE Kenya
Tana see Deatnu/Tana
Tana see Deatnu
164 I15 Tanabe Wakayama, Honshū, SW Japan
92 L8 Tana Bru Finnmark, N Norway
39 T10 Tanacross Alaska, USA
92 L7 Tanafjorden Lapp. Deanuvuotna. fjord N Norway
38 G17 Tanaga Island island Aleutian Islands, Alaska, USA
38 G17 Tanaga Volcano ▲ Tanaga Island, Alaska, USA
107 M18 Tanagro ⇝ S Italy
80 H11 T'ana Hāyk' var. Lake Tana. ◎ NW Ethiopia
168 H11 Tanahbela, Pulau island Kepulauan Batu, W Indonesia
171 H15 Tanahjampea, Pulau island W Indonesia
168 H11 Tanahmasa, Pulau island Kepulauan Batu, W Indonesia
Tanais see Don
152 L10 Tanakpur Uttaranchal, N India
Tana, Lake see T'ana Hāyk'
181 P5 Tanami Desert desert Northern Territory, N Australia
167 T14 Tân An Long An, S Vietnam
39 Q9 Tanana Alaska, USA
Tananarive see Antananarivo
39 Q9 Tanana River ⇝ Alaska, USA
95 C16 Tananger Rogaland, S Norway
188 H5 Tanapag Saipan, S Northern Mariana Islands
188 H5 Tanapag, Puetton bay Saipan, S Northern Mariana Islands
106 C9 Tanaro ⇝ N Italy
163 Y12 Tanch'ŏn E North Korea
40 M14 Tancítaro, Cerro ♜ C Mexico
153 N12 Tānda Uttar Pradesh, N India
77 O15 Tanda E Ivory Coast
116 L14 Ţăndărei Ialomiţa, SE Romania
63 N14 Tandil Buenos Aires, E Argentina
78 H12 Tandjilé off. Préfecture du Tandjilé. ◈ prefecture SW Chad
Tandjilé, Préfecture du see Tandjilé
Tandjoeng see Tanjung
Tandjoengkarang see Bandar Lampung
Tandjoengpandan see Tanjungpandan
Tandjoengpinang see Tanjungpinang
Tandjoengredeb see Tanjungredeb
149 Q16 Tando Allāhyār Sind, SE Pakistan
149 Q17 Tando Bāgo Sind, SE Pakistan
149 Q16 Tando Muhammad Khān Sind, SE Pakistan
182 L7 Tandou Lake seasonal lake New South Wales, SE Australia
94 L11 Tandsjöborg Gävleborg, C Sweden
155 H15 Tāndūr Andhra Pradesh, C India
164 C17 Tanega-shima island Nansei-shotō, SW Japan
165 R7 Taneichi Iwate, Honshū, C Japan
Tanen Taunggyi see Tane Range
167 N8 Tane Range Bur. Tanen Taunggyi. ▲▲ W Thailand
111 P15 Tanew ⇝ SE Poland
21 W2 Taneytown Maryland, NE USA
74 H12 Tanezrouft desert Algeria/Mali
138 L7 Ţanf, Jabal aţ ▲ SE Syria
81 J21 Tanga Tanga, E Tanzania
81 I22 Tanga ◈ region E Tanzania
153 T14 Tangail Dhaka, C Bangladesh
186 I5 Tanga Islands island group NE Papua New Guinea
155 K26 Tangalla Southern Province, S Sri Lanka
Tanganyika and Zanzibar see Tanzania
68 J13 Tanganyika, Lake ◎ E Africa
56 E7 Tangarana, Río ⇝ N Peru
191 V16 Tangaroa, Maunga ♜ Easter Island, Chile, E Pacific Ocean
Tangdukou see Shaoyang
74 G5 Tanger var. Tangiers, Tangier, Fr./Ger. Tangerk, Sp. Tánger; anc. Tingis. NW Morocco
169 N15 Tangerang Jawa, C Indonesia
Tangerk see Tanger
100 M12 Tangermünde Sachsen-Anhalt, C Germany
159 O12 Tanggulashan var. Togton Heyan, var. Tuotuoheyan. Qinghai, C China
156 K10 Tanggula Shan var. Dangla, Tangla Range. ▲▲ W China
159 N13 Tanggula Shan ▲ W China
156 K10 Tanggula Shankou Tib. Dang La. pass W China
161 N7 Tanghe Henan, C China
149 T5 Tāngi North-West Frontier Province, NW Pakistan
Tangier see Tanger
21 Y5 Tangier Island island Virginia, NE USA
Tangiers see Tanger
22 K8 Tangipahoa River ⇝ Louisiana, S USA
Tangla Range see Tanggula Shan
164 J12 Tango-hantō peninsula Honshū, SW Japan
156 I10 Tangra Yumco var. Tangro Tso. ◎ W China
Tangro Tso see Tangra Yumco
157 T7 Tangshan var. T'ang-shan. Hebei, E China
T'ang-shan see Tangshan
77 R14 Tanguiéta NW Benin
163 X7 Tangwang He ⇝ NE China
163 X7 Tangyuan Heilongjiang, NE China
92 M11 Tanhua Lappi, N Finland
171 U16 Tanimbar, Kepulauan island group Maluku, E Indonesia
Tanintharyi see Tenasserim
139 U4 Tānjarō ⇝ E Iraq
129 T15 Tanjong Piai headland Peninsular Malaysia
Tanjore see Thanjāvūr
169 U12 Tanjung prev. Tandjoeng. Borneo, C Indonesia
169 W9 Tanjungbatu Borneo, N Indonesia
Tanjungkarang/Tanjungkarang-Telukbetung see Bandar Lampung
169 N13 Tanjungpandan prev. Tandjoengpandan. Pulau Belitung, W Indonesia
168 M10 Tanjungpinang prev. Tandjoengpinang. Pulau Bintan, W Indonesia
169 V9 Tanjungredeb var. Tanjungredep; prev. Tandjoengredeb. Borneo, C Indonesia
Tanjungredep see Tanjungredeb
149 S8 Tānk North-West Frontier Province, NW Pakistan
187 S15 Tanna island S Vanuatu
93 F17 Tännäs Jämtland, C Sweden
Tannenhof see Krynica
108 K7 Tannheim Tirol, W Austria
Tannu-Tuva see Tyva, Respublika
171 Q12 Tano Pulau Taliabu, E Indonesia
77 O17 Tano ⇝ S Ghana
152 D10 Tanot Rājasthān, NW India
77 V11 Tanout Zinder, C Niger
Tân Phu see Đinh Quan
41 P12 Tanquián San Luis Potosí, C Mexico
77 R13 Tansarga E Burkina
167 T13 Tan Son Nhat ✕ (Hô Chi Minh) Tây Ninh, S Vietnam
75 V8 Tanta var. Tantā, Tanta. N Egypt
74 D9 Tan-Tan SW Morocco
41 P12 Tantoyuca Veracruz-Llave, E Mexico
152 J12 Tāntpur Uttar Pradesh, N India
Tan-tung see Dandong
38 M12 Tanunak Alaska, USA
166 L5 Ta-nyaung Magwe, W Myanmar (Burma)
167 S5 Tân Yên Tuyên Quang, N Vietnam
81 F22 Tanzania off. United Republic of Tanzania, Swa. Jamhuri ya Muungano wa Tanzania; prev. German East Africa, Tanganyika and Zanzibar. ◆ republic E Africa
Tanzania, Jamhuri ya Muungano wa see Tanzania
Tanzania, United Republic of see Tanzania
Taoan/Tao'an see Taoan
163 T8 Tao'er He ⇝ NE China
159 U11 Tao He ⇝ C China
163 U9 Taoan var. Taoan, Tao'an. Jilin, NE China
T'aon-an see Baicheng
Taongi see Bokaak Atoll
107 M23 Taormina anc. Tauromenium. Sicilia, Italy, C Mediterranean Sea
37 S9 Taos New Mexico, SW USA
Taoudenit see Taoudenni
77 O6 Taoudenni var. Taoudenit. Tombouctou, N Mali
74 G6 Taounate N Morocco
161 S13 T'aoyüan Jap. Tōen. N Taiwan
118 I3 Tapa Ger. Taps. Lääne-Virumaa, NE Estonia
41 V17 Tapachula Chiapas, SE Mexico
Tapaiu see Gvardeysk
59 H14 Tapajós, Rio var. Tapajóz. ⇝ NW Brazil
Tapajóz see Tapajós, Rio
61 C21 Tapalqué var. Tapalquén. Buenos Aires, E Argentina
Tapalquén see Tapalqué
Tapanahoni see Tapanahony Rivier
55 W11 Tapanahony Rivier var. Tapanahoni. ⇝ E Surinam
41 T16 Tapanatepec var. San Pedro Tapanatepec. Oaxaca, SE Mexico
185 D23 Tapanui Otago, South Island, New Zealand
59 E14 Tapauá Amazonas, N Brazil
47 R7 Tapauá, Rio ⇝ W Brazil
185 I14 Tapawera Tasman, South Island, New Zealand
61 I16 Tapes Rio Grande do Sul, S Brazil
76 K16 Tapeta C Liberia
154 H11 Tāpi prev. Tāpti. ⇝ W India
104 J2 Tapia de Casariego Asturias, N Spain
56 F10 Tapiche, Río ⇝ N Peru
167 N15 Tapi, Mae Nam var. Luang. ⇝ SW Thailand
186 E8 Tapini Central, S Papua New Guinea
Tapirapecó, Serra see Tapirapecó, Sierra
55 N13 Tapirapecó, Sierra Port. Serra Tapirapecó. ▲▲ Brazil/Venezuela
77 R13 Tapoa ⇝ Benin/Niger
188 H5 Tapochau, Mount ▲ Saipan, S Northern Mariana Islands
111 H24 Tapolca Veszprém, W Hungary
21 X5 Tappahannock Virginia, NE USA
31 U13 Tappan Lake ⊠ Ohio, N USA

◆ Country ● Country Capital ◇ Dependent Territory ○ Dependent Territory Capital ◈ Administrative Regions ✕ International Airport ▲ Mountain ▲▲ Mountain Range ♜ Volcano ⇝ River ◎ Lake ⊠ Reservoir

165 Q6 **Tappi-zaki** *headland* Honshū, C Japan
Taps *see* Tapa
Tāpti *see* Tāpi
Tapuaemanu *see* Maiao
185 J16 **Tapuaenuku** ▲ South Island, New Zealand
171 N8 **Tapul Group** *island group* Sulu Archipelago, SW Philippines
58 E11 **Tapurmcuará** *var.* Tapuruquara. Amazonas, NW Brazil
Tapuruquara *see* Tapurmcuará
192 J17 **Taputapu, Cape** *headland* Tutuila, W American Samoa
141 W13 **Ţāqah** S Oman
139 T3 **Taqtaq** N Iraq
61 J15 **Taquara** Rio Grande do Sul, S Brazil
59 H19 **Taquari, Rio** ≈ C Brazil
60 L8 **Taquaritinga** São Paulo, S Brazil
122 I11 **Tara** Omskaya Oblast', C Russian Federation
83 I16 **Tara** Southern, S Zambia
113 J15 **Tara** ≈ Montenegro
112 K13 **Tara** ▲▲ W Serbia
77 W15 **Taraba** ❖ *state* E Nigeria
77 X15 **Taraba** ≈ E Nigeria
75 O7 **Ţarābulus** *var.* Ţarābulus al Gharb, *Eng.* Tripoli. ● (Libya) NW Libya
75 O7 **Ţarābulus** ✈ NW Libya
Ţarābulus al Gharb *see* Ţarābulus
Tarābulus/Ţarābulus ash Shām *see* Tripoli
105 O7 **Taracena** Castilla-La Mancha, C Spain
117 N12 **Taraclia** *Rus.* Tarakilya. S Moldova
139 V10 **Tarād al Kahf** SE Iraq
183 R10 **Tarago** New South Wales, SE Australia
162 J8 **Taragt** *var.* Hüremt. Övörhangay, C Mongolia
169 V8 **Tarakan** Borneo, C Indonesia
169 V9 **Tarakan, Pulau** *island* N Indonesia
Tarakilya *see* Taraclia
165 P16 **Tarama-jima** *island* Sakishima-shotō, SW Japan
184 K10 **Taranaki** *off.* Taranaki Region. ❖ *region* North Island, New Zealand
184 K10 **Taranaki, Mount** *var.* Egmont. ⛰ North Island, New Zealand
Taranaki Region *see* Taranaki
105 O9 **Tarancón** Castilla-La Mancha, C Spain
188 M15 **Tarang Reef** *reef* C Micronesia
96 E7 **Taransay** *island* NW Scotland, UK
107 P18 **Taranto** *var.* Tarentum. Puglia, SE Italy
107 O19 **Taranto, Golfo di** *Eng.* Gulf of Taranto. *gulf* S Italy
Taranto, Gulf of *see* Taranto, Golfo di
62 G3 **Tarapacá** *off.* Región de Tarapacá. ❖ *region* N Chile
Tarapacá, Región de *see* Tarapacá
187 N9 **Tarapaina** Maramasike Island, N Solomon Islands
56 D10 **Tarapoto** San Martín, N Peru
138 M6 **Taraq an Na'jah** *hill range* E Syria
138 M6 **Taraq Sidāwī** *hill range* E Syria
103 Q11 **Tarare** Rhône, E France
Tararite de Llitera *see* Tamarite de Litera
184 M13 **Tararua Range** ▲▲ North Island, New Zealand
151 Q22 **Tarāsa Dwīp** *island* Nicobar Islands, India, NE Indian Ocean
103 Q15 **Tarascon** Bouches-du-Rhône, SE France
102 M17 **Tarascon-sur-Ariège** Ariège, S France
117 P6 **Tarashcha** Kyyivs'ka Oblast', N Ukraine
57 L18 **Tarata** Cochabamba, C Bolivia
57 I18 **Tarata** Tacna, SW Peru
190 H2 **Taratai** *atoll* Tungaru, W Kiribati
59 B15 **Tarauacá** Acre, W Brazil
59 B15 **Tarauacá, Rio** ≈ NW Brazil
191 Q8 **Taravao** Tahiti, W French Polynesia
191 R8 **Taravao, Baie de** *bay* Tahiti, W French Polynesia
191 Q8 **Taravao, Isthme de** *isthmus* Tahiti, W French Polynesia
103 X16 **Taravo** ≈ Corse, France, C Mediterranean Sea
190 J3 **Tarawa** ✈ Tarawa, W Kiribati
190 H2 **Tarawa** *atoll* Tungaru, W Kiribati
184 N10 **Tarawera** Hawke's Bay, North Island, New Zealand
184 N8 **Tarawera, Lake** ◎ North Island, New Zealand
184 N8 **Tarawera, Mount** ▲ North Island, New Zealand
105 S8 **Tarayuela** ▲ N Spain
145 R16 **Taraz** *prev.* Aulie Ata, Auliye-Ata, Dzhambul, Zhambyl. Zhambyl, S Kazakhstan
105 Q5 **Tarazona** Aragón, NE Spain
105 Q10 **Tarazona de la Mancha** Castilla-La Mancha, C Spain
145 X12 **Tarbagatay, Khrebet** ▲▲ China/Kazakhstan
96 J8 **Tarbat Ness** *headland* N Scotland, UK
149 U5 **Tarbela Reservoir** ⊠ N Pakistan
96 H12 **Tarbert** W Scotland, UK
96 F7 **Tarbert** NW Scotland, UK
102 K16 **Tarbes** *anc.* Bigorra. Hautes-Pyrénées, S France
21 W9 **Tarboro** North Carolina, SE USA
Tarca *see* Torysa
106 J6 **Tarcento** Friuli-Venezia Giulia, NE Italy
182 F5 **Tarcoola** South Australia
105 S5 **Tardienta** Aragón, NE Spain
102 L11 **Tardoire** ≈ W France
183 U7 **Taree** New South Wales, SE Australia
92 K12 **Tärendö** *Lapp.* Deargget. Norrbotten, N Sweden
Tarentum *see* Taranto
74 C9 **Tarfaya** SW Morocco
116 J13 **Târgovişte** *prev.* Tîrgovişte. Dâmboviţa, S Romania
Târgovište *see* Türgovishte
116 M12 **Târgu Bujor** *prev.* Tîrgu Bujor. Galaţi, E Romania
116 H13 **Târgu Cărbuneşti** *prev.* Tîrgu. Gorj, SW Romania
116 L9 **Târgu Frumos** *prev.* Tîrgu Frumos. Iaşi, NE Romania
116 H13 **Târgu Jiu** *prev.* Tîrgu Jiu. Gorj, W Romania
116 H9 **Târgu Lăpuş** *prev.* Tîrgu Lăpuş. Maramureş, N Romania
Târgul-Neamţ *see* Târgu-Neamţ
Târgul-Săcuiesc *see* Târgu Secuiesc
116 I10 **Târgu Mureş** *prev.* Oşorhei, Tîrgu Mures, *Ger.* Neumarkt, *Hung.* Marosvásárhely. Mureş, C Romania
116 K9 **Târgu-Neamţ** *var.* Târgul-Neamţ; *prev.* Tîrgu-Neamţ. Neamţ, NE Romania
116 K11 **Târgu Ocna** *Hung.* Aknavásár; *prev.* Tîrgu Ocna. Bacău, E Romania
116 K11 **Târgu Secuiesc** *Ger.* Neumarkt, Szekler Neumarkt, *Hung.* Kezdivásárhely; *prev.* Chezdi-Oşorheiu, Târgul-Săcuiesc, Tîrgu Secuiesc. Covasna, E Romania
145 X10 **Targyn** Vostochnyy Kazakhstan, E Kazakhstan
Tar Heel State *see* North Carolina
186 C7 **Tari** Southern Highlands, W Papua New Guinea
162 J6 **Tarialan** *var.* Badrah. Hövsgöl, N Mongolia
162 I7 **Tariat** *var.* Horgo. Arhangay, C Mongolia
143 P17 **Ţarīf** Abū Ẓaby, C United Arab Emirates
104 K16 **Tarifa** Andalucía, S Spain
84 C14 **Tarifa, Punta de** *cape* SW Spain
57 M21 **Tarija** Tarija, S Bolivia
57 M21 **Tarija** ❖ *department* S Bolivia
141 R14 **Tarīm** C Yemen
Tarim Basin *see* Tarim Pendi
81 G19 **Tarime** Mara, N Tanzania
129 S8 **Tarim He** ≈ NW China
159 H8 **Tarim Pendi** *Eng.* Tarim Basin. *basin* NW China
149 N7 **Tarīn Kowt** *var.* Terinkot. Orūzgān, C Afghanistan
171 O12 **Taripa** Sulawesi, C Indonesia
117 Q12 **Tarkhankut, Mys** *headland* S Ukraine
27 Q1 **Tarkio** Missouri, C USA
122 J9 **Tarko-Sale** Yamalo-Nenetskiy Avtonomnyy Okrug, N Russian Federation
77 P17 **Tarkwa** S Ghana
171 O3 **Tarlac** Luzon, N Philippines
95 F22 **Tarm** Ringkøbing, W Denmark
57 E14 **Tarma** Junín, C Peru
103 N15 **Tarn** ❖ *department* S France
102 M15 **Tarn** ≈ S France
111 L22 **Tarna** ≈ C Hungary
92 G13 **Tärnaby** Västerbotten, N Sweden
149 P8 **Tarnak Rūd** ≈ SE Afghanistan
116 J11 **Târnava Mare** *Ger.* Grosse Kokel, *Hung.* Nagy-Küküllő; *prev.* Tirnava Mare. ≈ S Romania
116 I11 **Târnava Mică** *Ger.* Kleine Kokel, *Hung.* Kis-Küküllo; *prev.* Tirnava Mică. ≈ C Romania
116 I11 **Târnăveni** *Ger.* Marteskirch, Martinskirch, *Hung.* Dicsőszentmárton; *prev.* Sînmartin, Tirnăveni. Mureş, C Romania
102 L14 **Tarn-et-Garonne** ❖ *department* S France
111 P18 **Tarnica** ▲ SE Poland
111 N15 **Tarnobrzeg** Podkarpackie, SE Poland
125 N12 **Tarnogskiy Gorodok** Vologodskaya Oblast', NW Russian Federation
Tarnopol *see* Ternopil'
111 M16 **Tarnów** Małopolskie, S Poland
Tarnowice/Tarnowitz *see* Tarnowskie Góry
111 J16 **Tarnowskie Góry** *var.* Tarnowice, Tarnowskie Gory, *Ger.* Tarnowitz. Śląskie, S Poland
95 N14 **Tärnsjö** Västmanland, C Sweden
106 E9 **Taro** ≈ NW Italy
186 I6 **Taron** New Ireland, NE Papua New Guinea
74 E8 **Taroudannt** *var.* Taroudant. SW Morocco
Taroudant *see* Taroudannt
23 V12 **Tarpon, Lake** ◎ Florida, SE USA
23 V12 **Tarpon Springs** Florida, SE USA
107 G14 **Tarquinia** *anc.* Tarquinii, *hist.* Corneto. Lazio, C Italy
Tarquinii *see* Tarquinia
Tarraco *see* Tarragona
76 D10 **Tarrafal** Santiago, S Cape Verde
105 V6 **Tarragona** *anc.* Tarraco. Cataluña, E Spain
105 T7 **Tarragona** ❖ *province* Cataluña, NE Spain
183 O17 **Tarraleah** Tasmania, SE Australia
23 P3 **Tarrant City** Alabama, S USA
185 D21 **Tarras** Otago, South Island, New Zealand
Tarrasa *see* Terrassa
105 U5 **Tàrrega** *var.* Tarrega. Cataluña, NE Spain
21 W9 **Tar River** ≈ North Carolina, SE USA
Tarsatica *see* Rijeka
136 J17 **Tarsus** Mersin, S Turkey
62 K4 **Tartagal** Salta, N Argentina
137 V12 **Tärtär** *Rus.* Terter. ≈ SW Azerbaijan
102 J15 **Tartas** Landes, SW France
139 Q6 **Tārtasah** C Iraq
Tartlau *see* Prejmer
Tartous/Tartouss *see* Ţarţūs
118 J5 **Tartu** *Ger.* Dorpat; *prev. Rus* Yurev, Yury'ev. Tartumaa, SE Estonia
118 I5 **Tartumaa** *off.* Tartu Maakond. ❖ *province* E Estonia
Tartu Maakond *see* Tartumaa
138 H5 **Ţarţūs** *Fr.* Tartouss; *anc.* Tortosa. Tarţūs, W Syria
138 H5 **Ţarţūs** *off.* Muḩāfaẓat Ţarţūs, *var.* Tartous, Tartus. ❖ *governorate* W Syria
Ţarţūs, Muḩāfaẓat *see* Ţarţūs
164 C16 **Tarumizu** Kagoshima, Kyūshū, SW Japan
126 K4 **Tarusa** Kaluzhskaya Oblast', W Russian Federation
117 N11 **Tarutyne** Odes'ka Oblast', SW Ukraine
162 I7 **Tarvagatyn Nuruu** ▲▲ N Mongolia
106 J6 **Tarvisio** Friuli-Venezia Giulia, NE Italy
Tarvisium *see* Treviso
57 O16 **Tarvo, Río** ≈ E Bolivia
14 G8 **Tarzwell** Ontario, S Canada
40 K5 **Tasajera, Sierra de la** ▲▲ N Mexico
145 S13 **Tasaral** Karaganda, C Kazakhstan
Tasböget *see* Tasbuget
145 N15 **Tasbuget** *Kaz.* Tasböget. Kzylorda, S Kazakhstan
108 E11 **Täsch** Valais, SW Switzerland
Tasek Kenyir *see* Kenyir, Tasik
122 J14 **Tashanta** Respublika Altay, S Russian Federation
Tashauz *see* Daşoguz
Tashi Chho Dzong *see* Thimphu
153 U11 **Tashigang** E Bhutan
137 T11 **Tashir** *prev.* Kalinino. N Armenia
143 Q11 **Ţashk, Daryācheh-ye** ◎ C Iran
Tashkent *see* Toshkent
Tashkentskaya Oblast' *see* Toshkent Viloyati
Tashkepri *see* Daşköpri
Tash-Kömür *see* Tash-Kumyr
147 S9 **Tash-Kumyr** *Kir.* Tash-Kömür. Dzhalal-Abadskaya Oblast', W Kyrgyzstan
127 T7 **Tashla** Orenburgskaya Oblast', W Russian Federation
Tashqurghan *see* Kholm
122 J13 **Tashtagol** Kemerovskaya Oblast', S Russian Federation
95 H24 **Tåsinge** *island* C Denmark
12 M5 **Tasiujaq** Québec, E Canada
77 W11 **Tasker** Zinder, C Niger
145 W12 **Taskesken** Vostochnyy Kazakhstan, E Kazakhstan
136 J10 **Taşköprü** Kastamonu, N Turkey
Taskuduk, Peski *see* Tosquduq Qumlari
186 G5 **Taskul** New Ireland, NE Papua New Guinea
137 S13 **Taşlıçay** Ağrı, E Turkey
185 H14 **Tasman** *off.* Tasman District. ❖ *unitary authority* South Island, New Zealand
192 J12 **Tasman Basin** *var.* East Australian Basin. *undersea feature* S Tasman Sea
185 I14 **Tasman Bay** *inlet* South Island, New Zealand
Tasman District *see* Tasman
192 I13 **Tasman Fracture Zone** *tectonic feature* S Indian Ocean
185 E19 **Tasman Glacier** *glacier* South Island, New Zealand
Tasman Group *see* Nukumanu Islands
183 N15 **Tasmania** *prev.* Van Diemen's Land. ❖ *state* SE Australia
183 Q16 **Tasmania** *island* SE Australia
185 H14 **Tasman Mountains** ▲▲ South Island, New Zealand
183 P17 **Tasman Peninsula** *peninsula* Tasmania, SE Australia
192 I11 **Tasman Plain** *undersea feature* W Tasman Sea
192 I12 **Tasman Plateau** *var.* South Tasmania Plateau. *undersea feature* SW Tasman Sea
192 I11 **Tasman Sea** *sea* SW Pacific Ocean
116 G9 **Tăşnad** *Ger.* Trestenberg, Trestendorf, *Hung.* Tasnád. Satu Mare, NW Romania
136 L11 **Taşova** Amasya, N Turkey
77 T10 **Tassara** Tahoua, W Niger
12 K4 **Tassialouc, Lac** ◎ Québec, C Canada
Tassili du Hoggar *see* Tassili ta-n-Ahaggar
74 L11 **Tassili-n-Ajjer** *plateau* E Algeria
74 K14 **Tassili ta-n-Ahaggar** *var.* Tassili du Hoggar. *plateau* S Algeria
59 M15 **Tasso Fragoso** Maranhão, E Brazil
Tåstrup *see* Taastrup
145 O9 **Tasty-Taldy** Akmola, C Kazakhstan
143 W10 **Tāsūkī** Sīstān va Balūchestān, SE Iran
111 I22 **Tata** *Ger.* Totis. Komárom-Esztergom, NW Hungary
74 E8 **Tata** SW Morocco
Tataaihoa, Pointe *see* Vénus, Pointe
111 I22 **Tatabánya** Komárom-Esztergom, NW Hungary
191 X10 **Tatakoto** *atoll* Îles Tuamotu, E French Polynesia
75 N7 **Tataouine** *var.* Taţāwīn. SE Tunisia
55 O5 **Tataracual, Cerro** ▲ NE Venezuela
117 O12 **Tatarbunary** Odes'ka Oblast', SW Ukraine
119 M17 **Tatarka** *Rus.* Tatarka. Mahilyowskaya Voblasts', E Belarus
Tatar Pazardzhik *see* Pazardzhik
122 I12 **Tatarsk** Novosibirskaya Oblast', C Russian Federation
Tatarskaya ASSR *see* Tatarstan, Respublika
123 T13 **Tatarskiy Proliv** *Eng.* Tatar Strait. *strait* SE Russian Federation
127 R4 **Tatarstan, Respublika** *prev.* Tatarskaya ASSR. ❖ *autonomous republic* W Russian Federation
Tatar Strait *see* Tatarskiy Proliv
Taţāwīn *see* Tataouine
171 N12 **Tate** Sulawesi, N Indonesia
141 N11 **Tathlīth** 'Asīr, S Saudi Arabia
141 O11 **Tathlīth, Wādī** *dry watercourse* S Saudi Arabia
183 R11 **Tathra** New South Wales, SE Australia
127 P8 **Tatishchevo** Saratovskaya Oblast', W Russian Federation
39 S12 **Tatitlek** Alaska, USA
10 L15 **Tatla Lake** British Columbia, SW Canada
121 Q2 **Tatlısu** *Gk.* Akanthoú. N Cyprus
9 Z10 **Tatnam, Cape** *headland* Manitoba, C Canada
111 K18 **Tatra Mountains** *Ger.* Tatra, *Hung.* Tátra, *Pol./Slvk.* Tatry. ▲▲ Poland/Slovakia
Tatra/Tátra *see* Tatra Mountains
Tatry *see* Tatra Mountains
164 I13 **Tatsuno** *var.* Tatuno. Hyōgo, Honshū, SW Japan
145 S16 **Tatti** *var.* Tatty. Zhambyl, S Kazakhstan
Tatty *see* Tatti
60 L10 **Tatuí** São Paulo, S Brazil
37 V14 **Tatum** New Mexico, SW USA
25 X7 **Tatum** Texas, SW USA
Ta-t'ung/Tatung *see* Datong
Tatuno *see* Tatsuno
137 R14 **Tatvan** Bitlis, SE Turkey
95 C16 **Tau** Rogaland, S Norway
192 L17 **Ta'ū** *island* Manua Islands, E American Samoa
193 W15 **Tau** *island* Tongatapu Group, N Tonga
59 O14 **Tauá** Ceará, E Brazil
60 N10 **Taubaté** São Paulo, S Brazil
101 I19 **Tauber** ≈ SW Germany
101 I19 **Tauberbiscofsheim** Baden-Württemberg, C Germany
144 E14 **Tauchik** *Kaz.* Taŭshyq. Mangistau, SW Kazakhstan
191 W10 **Tauere** *atoll* Îles Tuamotu, C French Polynesia
101 H17 **Taufstein** ▲ C Germany
190 I17 **Taukoka** *island* SE Cook Islands
145 T15 **Taukum, Peski** *desert* SE Kazakhstan
184 L10 **Taumarunui** Manawatu-Wanganui, North Island, New Zealand
59 A15 **Taumaturgo** Acre, W Brazil
27 X6 **Taum Sauk Mountain** ▲ Missouri, C USA
83 H22 **Taung** North-West, N South Africa
166 L6 **Taungdwingyi** Magwe, C Myanmar (Burma)
166 M6 **Taunggyi** Shan State, C Myanmar (Burma)
166 L5 **Taungtha** Mandalay, C Myanmar (Burma)
166 K7 **Taungup** Arakan State, W Myanmar (Burma)
149 S9 **Taunsa** Punjab, E Pakistan
97 K23 **Taunton** SW England, UK
19 O12 **Taunton** Massachusetts, NE USA
101 F18 **Taunus** ▲▲ W Germany
101 G18 **Taunusstein** Hessen, W Germany
184 N9 **Taupo** Waikato, North Island, New Zealand
184 M9 **Taupo, Lake** ◎ North Island, New Zealand
109 R8 **Taurach** *var.* Taurachbach. ≈ E Austria
Taurachbach *see* Taurach
118 D12 **Tauragė** *Ger.* Tauroggen. Tauragė, SW Lithuania
118 D13 **Tauragė** ❖ *province* Lithuania
54 G10 **Tauramena** Casanare, C Colombia
184 N7 **Tauranga** Bay of Plenty, North Island, New Zealand
15 O10 **Taureau, Réservoir** ⊠ Québec, SE Canada
107 N22 **Taurianova** Calabria, SW Italy
Tauris *see* Tabrīz
184 I2 **Tauroa Point** *headland* North Island, New Zealand
Tauroggen *see* Tauragė
Tauromenium *see* Taormina
Taurus Mountains *see* Toros Dağları
Taus *see* Domažlice
Taŭshyq *see* Tauchik
105 R5 **Tauste** Aragón, NE Spain
191 V16 **Tautara, Motu** *island* Easter Island, Chile, E Pacific Ocean
191 R8 **Tautira** Tahiti, W French Polynesia
Tauz *see* Tovuz
Ţavālesh, Kūhhā-ye *see* Talish Mountains
136 D15 **Tavas** Denizli, SW Turkey
Tavastehus *see* Hämeenlinna
Tavau *see* Davos
122 G10 **Tavda** Sverdlovskaya Oblast', C Russian Federation
122 G10 **Tavda** ≈ C Russian Federation
105 T11 **Tavernes de la Valldigna** País Valenciano, E Spain
81 I20 **Taveta** Coast, S Kenya
187 Y14 **Taveuni** *island* N Fiji
147 R13 **Tavildara** *Rus.* Tavil'dara, Tovil'-Dora. C Tajikistan
Tavin *see* Adaatsag
104 H14 **Tavira** Faro, S Portugal
97 I24 **Tavistock** SW England, UK
167 N10 **Tavoy** *var.* Dawei. Tenasserim, S Myanmar (Burma)
Tavoy Island *see* Mali Kyun
115 E16 **Tavropoú, Techníti Límni** ⊠ C Greece
136 E13 **Tavşanlı** Kütahya, NW Turkey
187 X14 **Tavua** Viti Levu, W Fiji
97 J23 **Taw** ≈ SW England, UK
185 L14 **Tawa** Wellington, North Island, New Zealand
25 V6 **Tawakoni, Lake** ⊠ Texas, SW USA
153 V11 **Tawang** Arunāchal Pradesh, NE India
169 R17 **Tawang, Teluk** *bay* Jawa, S Indonesia
31 R7 **Tawas Bay** ◎ Michigan, N USA
31 R7 **Tawas City** Michigan, N USA
169 V8 **Tawau** Sabah, East Malaysia
141 U10 **Ţawīl, Qalamat aţ** *well* SE Saudi Arabia
171 N9 **Tawitawi** *island* Tawitawi Group, SW Philippines
Ţawkar *see* Tokar
Tāwūq *see* Dāqūq
Tawzar *see* Tozeur
41 O15 **Taxco** *var.* Taxco de Alarcón. Guerrero, S Mexico
Taxco de Alarcón *see* Taxco
146 H8 **Takhiatosh** *Rus.* Takhiatash. Qoraqalpoghiston Respublikasi, W Uzbekistan
158 D9 **Taxkorgan** *var.* Taxkorgan Tajik Zizhixian. Xinjiang Uygur Zizhiqu, NW China
Taxkorgan Tajik Zizhixian *see* Taxkorgan
146 H7 **Taxtako'pir** *Rus.* Takhtakupyr. Qoraqalpog'iston Respublikasi, NW Uzbekistan
96 J10 **Tay** ≈ C Scotland, UK
143 V6 **Tāybād** *var.* Taibad, Tāyybād, Tayyebāt. Khorāsān-Razavī, NE Iran
Taybert at Turkz *see* Ţayyibat at Turkī
124 J3 **Taybola** Murmanskaya Oblast', NW Russian Federation
81 M16 **Tayeeglow** Bakool, C Somalia
96 K11 **Tay, Firth of** *inlet* E Scotland, UK
122 J12 **Tayga** Kemerovskaya Oblast', S Russian Federation
Taygan *see* Delger
123 T9 **Taygonos, Mys** *cape* E Russian Federation
96 I11 **Tay, Loch** ◎ C Scotland, UK
9 N12 **Taylor** British Columbia, W Canada
29 O14 **Taylor** Nebraska, C USA
18 I13 **Taylor** Pennsylvania, NE USA
25 T10 **Taylor** Texas, SW USA
37 Q11 **Taylor, Mount** ▲ New Mexico, SW USA
37 R5 **Taylor Park Reservoir** ⊠ Colorado, C USA
37 R6 **Taylor River** ≈ Colorado, C USA
21 P11 **Taylors** South Carolina, SE USA
20 L5 **Taylorsville** Kentucky, S USA
21 R6 **Taylorsville** North Carolina, SE USA
30 L14 **Taylorville** Illinois, N USA
140 K5 **Taymā'** Tabūk, NW Saudi Arabia
122 M10 **Taymura** ≈ C Russian Federation
123 O7 **Taymylyr** Respublika Sakha (Yakutiya), NE Russian Federation
122 L7 **Taymyr, Ozero** ◎ N Russian Federation
122 M6 **Taymyr, Poluostrov** *peninsula* N Russian Federation
122 L8 **Taymyrskiy (Dolgano-Nenetskiy) Avtonomnyy Okrug** *var.* Taymyrskiy Avtonomyy Okrug. ❖ *autonomous district* N Russian Federation
Taymyrskiy Avtonomnyy Okrug *see* Taymyrskiy (Dolgano-Nenetskiy) Avtonomnyy Okrug
167 S13 **Tây Ninh** Tây Ninh, S Vietnam
122 L12 **Tayshet** Irkutskaya Oblast', S Russian Federation
162 G8 **Tayshir** *var.* Tsagaan-Olom. Govĭ-Altay, C Mongolia
171 N5 **Taytay** Palawan, W Philippines
169 Q16 **Tayu** *prev.* Tajoe. Jawa, C Indonesia
Tāyybād/Tayyebāt *see* Tāybād
138 L5 **Ţayyibah** *var.* At Taybé. Ḩimş, C Syria
138 I4 **Ţayyibat at Turkī** *var.* Taybert at Turkz. Ḩamāh, W Syria
145 P7 **Tayynsha** *prev.* Krasnoarmeysk. Severnyy Kazakhstan, N Kazakhstan
122 J10 **Taz** ≈ N Russian Federation
74 G6 **Taza** NE Morocco
139 T4 **Tāza Khurmātū** E Iraq
165 Q8 **Tazawa-ko** ◎ Honshū, C Japan
21 N8 **Tazewell** Tennessee, S USA
21 Q7 **Tazewell** Virginia, NE USA
75 S11 **Tāzirbū** SE Libya
39 S11 **Tazlina Lake** ◎ Alaska, USA
122 J8 **Tazovskiy** Yamalo-Nenetskiy Avtonomnyy Okrug, N Russian Federation
137 U10 **T'bilisi** *Eng.* Tiflis. ● (Georgia) SE Georgia
137 T10 **T'bilisi** ✈ S Georgia
79 E14 **Tchabal Mbabo** ▲ NW Cameroon
Tchad *see* Chad
Tchad, Lac *see* Chad, Lake
77 S15 **Tchaourou** E Benin
79 E20 **Tchibanga** Nyanga, S Gabon
Tchien *see* Zwedru
77 Z6 **Tchigaï, Plateau du** ▲ NE Niger
77 V9 **Tchighozérine** Agadez, C Niger
77 T10 **Tchin-Tabaradene** Tahoua, W Niger
78 G13 **Tcholliré** Nord, NE Cameroon
Tchongking *see* Chongqing
22 K4 **Tchula** Mississippi, S USA
110 I7 **Tczew** *Ger.* Dirschau. Pomorskie, N Poland
116 I10 **Teaca** *Ger.* Tekendorf, *Hung.* Teke; *prev. Ger.* Teckendorf. Bistriţa-Năsăud, N Romania
40 J11 **Teacapán** Sinaloa, C Mexico
190 A10 **Teafuafou** *island* Funafuti Atoll, C Tuvalu
25 U8 **Teague** Texas, SW USA
191 R9 **Teahupoo** Tahiti, W French Polynesia
190 H15 **Te Aiti Point** *headland* Rarotonga, S Cook Islands
65 D24 **Teal Inlet** East Falkland, Falkland Islands
185 B22 **Te Anau** Southland, South Island, New Zealand
185 B22 **Te Anau, Lake** ◎ South Island, New Zealand
41 U15 **Teapa** Tabasco, SE Mexico
184 Q7 **Te Araroa** Gisborne, North Island, New Zealand
184 M7 **Te Aroha** Waikato, North Island, New Zealand
Teate *see* Chieti
190 A9 **Te Ava Fuagea** *channel* Funafuti Atoll, SE Tuvalu
190 B8 **Te Ava I Te Lape** *channel* Funafuti Atoll, SE Tuvalu
190 B9 **Te Ava Pua Pua** *channel* Funafuti Atoll, SE Tuvalu
184 M8 **Te Awamutu** Waikato, North Island, New Zealand
171 X12 **Teba** Papua, E Indonesia
104 L15 **Teba** Andalucía, S Spain
126 M15 **Teberda** Karachayevo-Cherkesskaya Respublika, SW Russian Federation
74 M6 **Tébessa** NE Algeria
62 O7 **Tebicuary, Río** ≈ S Paraguay
168 L13 **Tebingtinggi** Sumatera, W Indonesia
168 I8 **Tebingtinggi** Sumatera, N Indonesia
Tebingtinggi, Pulau *see* Rantau, Pulau
Tebriz *see* Tabrīz
137 U9 **Tebulos Mt'a** *Rus.* Gora Tebulosmta. ▲ Georgia/Russian Federation
Tebulosmta, Gora *see* Tebulos Mt'a
41 Q14 **Tecamachalco** Puebla, S Mexico
40 B1 **Tecate** Baja California, NW Mexico
136 M13 **Tecer Dağları** ▲▲ C Turkey
103 O17 **Tech** ≈ S France
77 P16 **Techiman** W Ghana
117 N15 **Techirghiol** Constanţa, SE Romania
74 A12 **Techla** *var.* Techlé. SW Western Sahara
Techlé *see* Techla
63 H18 **Tecka, Sierra de** ▲▲ SW Argentina
Teckendorf *see* Teaca
40 L13 **Tecolotlán** Jalisco, SW Mexico
40 K14 **Tecomán** Colima, SW Mexico
35 V12 **Tecopa** California, W USA
40 G5 **Tecoripa** Sonora, NW Mexico
41 N16 **Tecpan** *var.* Tecpan de Galeana. Guerrero, S Mexico
Tecpan de Galeana *see* Tecpan
40 J11 **Tecuala** Nayarit, C Mexico
116 L12 **Tecuci** Galaţi, E Romania
31 R10 **Tecumseh** Michigan, N USA
29 S16 **Tecumseh** Nebraska, C USA
27 O11 **Tecumseh** Oklahoma, C USA
Tedzhen *see* Harīrūd/Tejen
Tedzhen *see* Tejen
146 H15 **Tedzhenstroy** *Turkm.* Tejenstroy. Ahal Welaýaty, S Turkmenistan
Teel *see* Öndör-Ulaan
97 L15 **Tees** ≈ N England, UK
14 E15 **Teeswater** Ontario, S Canada
190 A10 **Tefala** *island* Funafuti Atoll, C Tuvalu
58 D13 **Tefé** Amazonas, N Brazil
74 K11 **Tefedest** ▲▲ S Algeria
136 E16 **Tefenni** Burdur, SW Turkey
58 D13 **Tefé, Rio** ≈ NW Brazil
169 P16 **Tegal** Jawa, C Indonesia
100 O12 **Tegel** ✈ (Berlin) Berlin, NE Germany
99 M15 **Tegelen** Limburg, SE Netherlands
101 L24 **Tegernsee** ◎ SE Germany
107 M18 **Teggiano** Campania, S Italy
77 U14 **Tegina** Niger, C Nigeria
42 I7 **Tegucigalpa** ● (Honduras) Francisco Morazán, SW Honduras
42 H7 **Tegucigalpa** ✈ Central District, C Honduras
Tegucigalpa *see* Central District
Tegucigalpa *see* Francisco Morazán
77 U9 **Teguidda-n-Tessoumt** Agadez, C Niger
64 Q11 **Teguise** Lanzarote, Islas Canarias, Spain, NE Atlantic Ocean
122 K12 **Tegul'det** Tomskaya Oblast', C Russian Federation
35 S13 **Tehachapi** California, W USA
35 S13 **Tehachapi Mountains** ▲▲ California, W USA
Tehama *see* Tihāmah
Teheran *see* Tehrān
77 O14 **Téhini** NE Ivory Coast
143 N5 **Tehrān** *var.* Teheran. ● (Iran) Tehrān, N Iran
143 N6 **Tehrān** *off.* Ostān-e Tehrān, *var.* Tehran. ❖ *province* N Iran
Tehrān, Ostān-e *see* Tehrān
152 K9 **Tehri** Uttaranchal, N India
Tehri *see* Tikamgarh
41 Q15 **Tehuacán** Puebla, S Mexico
41 S17 **Tehuantepec** *var.* Santo Domingo Tehuantepec. Oaxaca, SE Mexico
41 S17 **Tehuantepec, Golfo de** *var.* Gulf of Tehuantepec. *gulf* S Mexico
Tehuantepec, Gulf of *see* Tehuantepec, Golfo de
Tehuantepec, Isthmus of *see* Tehuantepec, Istmo de
41 T16 **Tehuantepec, Istmo de** *var.* Isthmus of Tehuantepec. *isthmus* SE Mexico
0 I16 **Tehuantepec Ridge** *undersea feature* E Pacific Ocean
41 S16 **Tehuantepec, Río** ≈ SE Mexico
191 W10 **Tehuata** *atoll* Îles Tuamotu, C French Polynesia
64 O11 **Teide, Pico de** ▲ Gran Canaria, Islas Canarias, Spain, NE Atlantic Ocean
97 I21 **Teifi** ≈ SW Wales, UK
80 B9 **Teiga Plateau** *plateau* W Sudan
97 J24 **Teignmouth** SW England, UK
Teisen *see* Chech'ŏn
116 H11 **Teiuş** *Ger.* Dreikirchen, *Hung.* Tövis. Alba, C Romania
169 U17 **Tejakula** Bali, C Indonesia
146 H14 **Tejen** *Rus.* Tedzhen. Ahal Welaýaty, S Turkmenistan
146 I15 **Tejen** *Per.* Harīrūd, *Rus.* Tedzhen. ≈ Afghanistan/Iran *see also* Harīrūd

Tejen *see* Harīrūd
Tejenstroy *see* Tedzhenstroy
35 *S14* **Tejon Pass** *pass* California, W USA
Tejo, Rio *see* Tagus
41 *O14* **Tejupilco** *var.* Tejupilco de Hidalgo. México, S Mexico
Tejupilco de Hidalgo *see* Tejupilco
184 *P7* **Te Kaha** Bay of Plenty, North Island, New Zealand
29 *S14* **Tekamah** Nebraska, C USA
184 *I1* **Te Kao** Northland, North Island, New Zealand
185 *F20* **Tekapo** ≈ South Island, New Zealand
185 *F19* **Tekapo, Lake** ◎ South Island, New Zealand
184 *P9* **Te Karaka** Gisborne, North Island, New Zealand
184 *L7* **Te Kauwhata** Waikato, North Island, New Zealand
41 *X12* **Tekax** *var.* Tekax de Álvaro Obregón. Yucatán, SE Mexico
Tekax de Álvaro Obregón *see* Tekax
136 *A14* **Teke Burnu** *headland* W Turkey
114 *M12* **Teke Deresi** ≈ NW Turkey
146 *D10* **Tekedzhik, Gory** *hill range* NW Turkmenistan
145 *V14* **Tekeli** Almaty, SE Kazakhstan
145 *R7* **Teke, Ozero** ◎ N Kazakhstan
158 *I5* **Tekes** Xinjiang Uygur Zizhiqu, NW China
145 *W16* **Tekes** Almaty, SE Kazakhstan
Tekes *see* Tekes He
158 *H5* **Tekes He** *Rus.* Tekes. ≈ China/Kazakhstan
Teke/Tekendorf *see* Teaca
80 *I10* **Tekezē** *var.* Takkaze. ≈ Eritrea/Ethiopia
Tekhtin *see* Tsyakhtsin
136 *C10* **Tekirdağ** *It.* Rodosto; *anc.* Bisanthe, Raidestos, Rhaedestus. Tekirdağ, NW Turkey
136 *C10* **Tekirdağ** ◈ *province* NW Turkey
155 *N14* **Tekkali** Andhra Pradesh, E India
115 *K15* **Tekke Burnu** *Turk.* İlyasbaba Burnu. *headland* NW Turkey
137 *Q13* **Tekman** Erzurum, NE Turkey
32 *M9* **Tekoa** Washington, NW USA
190 *H16* **Te Kou** ▲ Rarotonga, S Cook Islands
Tekrit *see* Tikrīt
171 *P12* **Teku** Sulawesi, N Indonesia
184 *L9* **Te Kuiti** Waikato, North Island, New Zealand
42 *H4* **Tela** Atlántida, NW Honduras
138 *F12* **Telalim** Southern, S Israel
Telanaipura *see* Jambi
137 *U10* **T'elavi** E Georgia
138 *F10* **Tel Aviv** ◈ *district* W Israel
Tel Aviv-Jaffa *see* Tel Aviv-Yafo
138 *F10* **Tel Aviv-Yafo** *var.* Tel Aviv-Jaffa. Tel Aviv, C Israel
138 *F10* **Tel Aviv-Yafo** ✈ Tel Aviv, C Israel
111 *E18* **Telč** *Ger.* Teltsch. Vysočina, C Czech Republic
186 *B6* **Telefomin** Sandaun, NW Papua New Guinea
10 *J10* **Telegraph Creek** British Columbia, W Canada
190 *B10* **Telele** *island* Funafuti Atoll, C Tuvalu
60 *J11* **Telêmaco Borba** Paraná, S Brazil
95 *E15* **Telemark** ◈ *county* S Norway
62 *J13* **Telén** La Pampa, C Argentina
Teleneshty *see* Telenești
116 *M9* **Telenești** *Rus.* Teleneshty. C Moldova
104 *J4* **Teleno, El** ▲ NW Spain
116 *I15* **Teleorman** ◈ *county* S Romania
116 *I14* **Teleorman** ≈ S Romania
25 *V5* **Telephone** Texas, SW USA
35 *U11* **Telescope Peak** ▲ California, W USA
Teles Pirés *see* São Manuel, Rio
97 *L19* **Telford** W England, UK
108 *L7* **Telfs** Tirol, W Austria
42 *I9* **Telica** León, NW Nicaragua
42 *J6* **Telica, Río** ≈ C Honduras
76 *I13* **Télimélé** W Guinea
43 *O14* **Telire, Río** ≈ Costa Rica/Panama
114 *I8* **Telish** *prev.* Azizie. Pleven, N Bulgaria
41 *R16* **Telixtlahuaca** *var.* San Francisco Telixtlahuaca. Oaxaca, SE Mexico
10 *K13* **Telkwa** British Columbia, SW Canada
25 *P4* **Tell** Texas, SW USA
Tell Abiad *see* Tall Abyaḍ
Tell Abiad/Tell Abyad *see* At Tall al Abyaḍ
31 *O16* **Tell City** Indiana, N USA
38 *M9* **Teller** Alaska, USA
Tell Huqnah *see* Tall Ḥuqnah
155 *F20* **Tellicherry** *var.* Thalassery. Kerala, SW India
20 *M10* **Tellico Plains** Tennessee, S USA
Tell Kalakh *see* Tall Kalakh
Tell Mardīkh *see* Ebla
54 *E11* **Tello** Huila, C Colombia
Tell Shedadi *see* Ash Shadādah
37 *Q7* **Telluride** Colorado, C USA
117 *X9* **Tel'manove** Donets'ka Oblast', E Ukraine
Tel'man/Tel'mansk *see* Gubadag
162 *H6* **Telmen** *var.* Övögdiy. Dzavhan, C Mongolia
162 *H6* **Telmen Nuur** ◎ NW Mongolia
Teloekbetoeng *see* Bandar Lampung
41 *O15* **Teloloapán** Guerrero, S Mexico
Telo Martius *see* Toulon
125 *V8* **Telposiz, Gora** ▲ NW Russian Federation
Telschen *see* Telšiai
63 *J17* **Telsen** Chubut, S Argentina
118 *D11* **Telšiai** *Ger.* Telschen. Telšiai, NW Lithuania
118 *D11* **Telšiai** ◈ *province* NW Lithuania
Teltsch *see* Telč
Telukbetung *see* Bandar Lampung
168 *H10* **Telukdalam** Pulau Nias, W Indonesia
14 *H9* **Temagami** Ontario, S Canada
14 *G9* **Temagami, Lake** ◎ Ontario, S Canada
190 *H16* **Te Manga** ▲ Rarotonga, S Cook Islands
191 *W12* **Tematangi** *atoll* Îles Tuamotu, S French Polynesia
41 *X11* **Temax** Yucatán, SE Mexico
171 *E14* **Tembagapura** Papua, E Indonesia
129 *U5* **Tembenchi** ≈ N Russian Federation
55 *P6* **Temblador** Monagas, NE Venezuela
105 *N9* **Tembleque** Castilla-La Mancha, C Spain
Temboni *see* Mitemele, Río
35 *U16* **Temecula** California, W USA
168 *K7* **Temengor, Tasik** ◎ Peninsular Malaysia
112 *L9* **Temerin** Vojvodina, N Serbia
Temeschburg/Temeschwar *see* Timișoara
Temes-Kubin *see* Kovin
Temes/Temesch *see* Tamiš
Temesvár/Temeswar *see* Timișoara
Teminaboean *see* Teminabuan
171 *U12* **Teminabuan** *prev.* Teminaboean. Papua, E Indonesia
145 *P17* **Temirlanovka** Yuzhnyy Kazakhstan, S Kazakhstan
145 *R10* **Temirtau** *prev.* Samarkandski, Samarkandskoye. Karaganda, C Kazakhstan
14 *H10* **Témiscaming** Québec, SE Canada
Témiscamingue, Lac *see* Timiskaming, Lake
15 *T8* **Témiscouata, Lac** ◎ Québec, SE Canada
127 *N5* **Temnikov** Respublika Mordoviya, W Russian Federation
191 *Y13* **Temoe** *island* Îles Gambier, E French Polynesia
183 *Q9* **Temora** New South Wales, SE Australia
40 *H7* **Témoris** Chihuahua, W Mexico
40 *I5* **Temósachic** Chihuahua, N Mexico
187 *Q10* **Temotu** *var.* Temotu Province. ◈ *province* E Solomon Islands
Temotu Province *see* Temotu
36 *L14* **Tempe** Arizona, SW USA
Tempelburg *see* Czaplinek
107 *C17* **Tempio Pausania** Sardegna, Italy, C Mediterranean Sea
42 *K12* **Tempisque, Río** ≈ NW Costa Rica
25 *T9* **Temple** Texas, SW USA
100 *O12* **Templehof** ✈ (Berlin) Berlin, NE Germany
97 *D19* **Templemore** *Ir.* An Teampall Mór. Tipperary, C Ireland
100 *O11* **Templin** Brandenburg, NE Germany
41 *P12* **Tempoal** *var.* Tempoal de Sánchez. Veracruz-Llave, E Mexico
Tempoal de Sánchez *see* Tempoal
41 *P13* **Tempoal, Río** ≈ C Mexico
83 *E14* **Tempué** Moxico, C Angola
126 *J14* **Temryuk** Krasnodarskiy Kray, SW Russian Federation
99 *G17* **Temse** Oost-Vlaanderen, N Belgium
63 *F15* **Temuco** Araucanía, C Chile
185 *G20* **Temuka** Canterbury, South Island, New Zealand
189 *P13* **Temwen Island** *island* E Micronesia
56 *C6* **Tena** Napo, C Ecuador
41 *W13* **Tenabo** Campeche, E Mexico
Tenaghau *see* Aola
25 *X7* **Tenaha** Texas, SW USA
39 *X13* **Tenake** Chichagof Island, Alaska, USA
155 *K16* **Tenāli** Andhra Pradesh, E India
Tenan *see* Ch'ŏnan
41 *O14* **Tenancingo** *var.* Tenencingo de Degollado. México, S Mexico
191 *X12* **Tenararo** *island* Groupe Actéon, SE French Polynesia
167 *N12* **Tenasserim** Tenasserim, S Myanmar (Burma)
167 *N11* **Tenasserim** *var.* Tanintharyi. ◈ *division* S Myanmar (Burma)
98 *O5* **Ten Boer** Groningen, NE Netherlands
97 *I21* **Tenby** SW Wales, UK
80 *K11* **Tendaho** Afar, NE Ethiopia
103 *V14* **Tende** Alpes Maritimes, SE France
151 *Q20* **Ten Degree Channel** *strait* Andaman and Nicobar Islands, India, E Indian Ocean
80 *F11* **Tendelti** White Nile, E Sudan
76 *G8* **Te-n-Dghâmcha, Sebkhet** *var.* Sebkha de Ndrhamcha, Sebkra de Ndaghamcha. *salt lake* W Mauritania
165 *P10* **Tendō** Yamagata, Honshū, C Japan
74 *H7* **Tendrara** NE Morocco
117 *Q11* **Tendrivs'ka Kosa** *spit* S Ukraine
117 *Q11* **Tendrivs'ka Zatoka** *gulf* S Ukraine
Tenencingo de Degollado *see* Tenancingo
77 *N11* **Ténenkou** Mopti, C Mali
77 *W9* **Ténéré** *physical region* C Niger
77 *W9* **Ténére, Erg du** *desert* C Niger
64 *O11* **Tenerife** *island* Islas Canarias, Spain, NE Atlantic Ocean
74 *J5* **Ténès** NW Algeria
170 *M15* **Tengah, Kepulauan** *island group* C Indonesia
Tengcheng *see* Tengxian
169 *V11* **Tenggarong** Borneo, C Indonesia
162 *J15* **Tengger Shamo** *desert* N China
168 *L8* **Tenggul, Pulau** *island* Peninsular Malaysia
Tengiz Köl *see* Tengiz, Ozero
145 *P9* **Tengiz, Ozero** *Kaz.* Tengiz Köl. *salt lake* C Kazakhstan
76 *M14* **Tengréla** *var.* Tingréla. N Ivory Coast
160 *M14* **Tengxian** *var.* Tengcheng, Teng Xian. Guangxi Zhuangzu Zizhiqu, S China
Teng Xian *see* Tengxian
194 *H2* **Teniente Rodolfo Marsh** *Chilean research station* South Shetland Islands, Antarctica
32 *G9* **Tenino** Washington, NW USA
112 *I9* **Tenja** Osijek-Baranja, E Croatia
188 *B16* **Tenjo, Mount** ▲ W Guam
155 *H23* **Tenkāsi** Tamil Nādu, SE India
79 *N24* **Tenke** Katanga, SE Dem. Rep. Congo
Tenke *see* Tinca
123 *Q7* **Tenkeli** Respublika Sakha (Yakutiya), NE Russian Federation
27 *R10* **Tenkiller Ferry Lake** ⊠ Oklahoma, C USA
77 *Q13* **Tenkodogo** S Burkina
181 *Q5* **Tennant Creek** Northern Territory, C Australia
20 *G9* **Tennessee** *off.* State of Tennessee, *also known as* The Volunteer State. ◈ *state* SE USA
37 *R5* **Tennessee Pass** *pass* Colorado, C USA
20 *H10* **Tennessee River** ≈ S USA
23 *N2* **Tennessee Tombigbee Waterway** *canal* Alabama/Mississippi, S USA
99 *K22* **Tenneville** Luxembourg, SE Belgium
92 *M11* **Tenniöjoki** ≈ NE Finland
92 *L9* **Tenojoki** *Lapp.* Deatnu, *Nor.* Tana. ≈ Finland/Norway *see also* Deatnu
Tenojoki *see* Deatnu
169 *U7* **Tenom** Sabah, East Malaysia
Tenos *see* Tínos
41 *V15* **Tenosique** *var.* Tenosique de Pino Suárez. Tabasco, SE Mexico
Tenosique de Pino Suárez *see* Tenosique
22 *I6* **Tensas River** ≈ Louisiana, S USA
23 *O8* **Tensaw River** ≈ Alabama, S USA
74 *E7* **Tensift** *seasonal river* W Morocco
171 *O12* **Tentena** *var.* Tenteno. Sulawesi, C Indonesia
Tenteno *see* Tentena
183 *U4* **Tenterfield** New South Wales, SE Australia
23 *X16* **Ten Thousand Islands** *island group* Florida, SE USA
60 *H9* **Teodoro Sampaio** São Paulo, S Brazil
59 *N19* **Teófilo Otoni** *var.* Theophilo Ottoni. Minas Gerais, NE Brazil
116 *K5* **Teofipol'** Khmel'nyts'ka Oblast', W Ukraine
191 *Q8* **Teohatu** Tahiti, W French Polynesia
41 *P14* **Teotihuacán** *ruins* México, S Mexico
Teotilán *see* Teotitlán del Camino
41 *Q15* **Teotitlán del Camino** *var.* Teotilán. Oaxaca, S Mexico
190 *G12* **Tepa** Île Uvea, E Wallis and Futuna
191 *P8* **Tepaee, Récif** *reef* Tahiti, W French Polynesia
40 *L14* **Tepalcatepec** Michoacán de Ocampo, SW Mexico
190 *A16* **Tepa Point** *headland* SW Niue
40 *L13* **Tepatitlán** *var.* Tepatitlán de Morelos. Jalisco, SW Mexico
Tepatitlán de Morelos *see* Tepatitlán
40 *J9* **Tepehuanes** *var.* Santa Catarina de Tepehuanes. Durango, C Mexico
Tepelena *see* Tepelenë
113 *L22* **Tepelenë** *var.* Tepelena, *It.* Tepeleni. Gjirokastër, S Albania
Tepeleni *see* Tepelenë
40 *K12* **Tepic** Nayarit, C Mexico
111 *C15* **Teplice** *Ger.* Teplitz; *prev.* Teplice-Šanov, Teplitz-Schönau. Ústecký Kraj, NW Czech Republic
Teplice-Šanov/Teplitz/Teplitz-Schönau *see* Teplice
117 *O7* **Teplyk** Vinnyts'ka Oblast', C Ukraine
123 *R10* **Teplyy Klyuch** Respublika Sakha (Yakutiya), NE Russian Federation
40 *E5* **Tepoca, Cabo** *headland* NW Mexico
191 *W9* **Tepoto** *island* Îles du Désappointement, C French Polynesia
92 *L11* **Tepsa** Lappi, N Finland
190 *B8* **Tepuka** *atoll* Funafuti Atoll, C Tuvalu
184 *N7* **Te Puke** Bay of Plenty, North Island, New Zealand
40 *L13* **Tequila** Jalisco, SW Mexico
41 *O13* **Tequisquiapan** Querétaro de Arteaga, C Mexico
77 *Q12* **Téra** Tillabéri, W Niger
104 *J5* **Tera** ≈ NW Spain
191 *V1* **Teraina** *prev.* Washington Island. *atoll* Line Islands, E Kiribati
81 *F15* **Terakeka** Bahr el Gabel, S Sudan
107 *J14* **Teramo** *anc.* Interamna. Abruzzi, C Italy
98 *P7* **Ter Apel** Groningen, NE Netherlands
104 *H11* **Tera, Ribeira de** ≈ S Portugal
185 *K14* **Terawhiti, Cape** *headland* North Island, New Zealand
98 *N12* **Terborg** Gelderland, E Netherlands
137 *P13* **Tercan** Erzincan, NE Turkey
64 *O2* **Terceira** ✈ Terceira, Azores, Portugal, NE Atlantic Ocean
64 *O2* **Terceira** *var.* Ilha Terceira. *island* Azores, Portugal, NE Atlantic Ocean
Terceira, Ilha *see* Terceira
116 *K6* **Terebovlya** Ternopil's'ka Oblast', W Ukraine
127 *O15* **Terek** ≈ SW Russian Federation
Terekhovka *see* Tsyerakhowka
147 *R9* **Terek-Say** Dzhalal-Abadskaya Oblast', W Kyrgyzstan
145 *Z10* **Terekty** *Kaz.* Alekseevka. Vostochnyy Kazakhstan, E Kazakhstan
145 *Z10* **Terekty** *prev.* Alekseevka, Alekseyevka. Vostochnyy Kazakhstan, E Kazakhstan
168 *L7* **Terengganu** *var.* Trengganu. ◈ *state* Peninsular Malaysia
127 *X7* **Terensay** Orenburgskaya Oblast', W Russian Federation
58 *N13* **Teresina** *var.* Therezina. *state capital* Piauí, NE Brazil
60 *P9* **Teresópolis** Rio de Janeiro, SE Brazil
110 *P12* **Terespol** Lubelskie, E Poland
191 *V16* **Terevaka, Maunga** ⛰ Easter Island, Chile, E Pacific Ocean
103 *P3* **Tergnier** Aisne, N France
43 *O14* **Teribe, Río** ≈ NW Panama
124 *K3* **Teriberka** Murmanskaya Oblast', NW Russian Federation
Terijoki *see* Zelenogorsk
Terinkot *see* Tarīn Kowt
145 *O10* **Tersakkan** *Kaz.* Terisaqqan. ≈ C Kazakhstan
Terisaqqan *see* Tersakkan
24 *K12* **Terlingua** Texas, SW USA
24 *K11* **Terlingua Creek** ≈ Texas, SW USA
62 *K7* **Termas de Río Hondo** Santiago del Estero, N Argentina
136 *M11* **Terme** Samsun, N Turkey
Termez *see* Termiz
Termia *see* Kýthnos
107 *J23* **Termini Imerese** *anc.* Thermae Himerenses. Sicilia, Italy, C Mediterranean Sea
41 *V14* **Términos, Laguna de** *lagoon* SE Mexico
77 *X10* **Termit-Kaoboul** Zinder, C Niger
147 *O14* **Termiz** *Rus.* Termez. Surkhondaryo Viloyati, S Uzbekistan
107 *L15* **Termoli** Molise, C Italy
Termonde *see* Dendermonde
98 *P5* **Termunten** Groningen, NE Netherlands
171 *R11* **Ternate** Pulau Ternate, E Indonesia
109 *T5* **Ternberg** Oberösterreich, N Austria
99 *E15* **Terneuzen** *var.* Neuzen. Zeeland, SW Netherlands
123 *T14* **Terney** Primorskiy Kray, SE Russian Federation
107 *I14* **Terni** *anc.* Interamna Nahars. Umbria, C Italy
109 *X6* **Ternitz** Niederösterreich, E Austria
117 *V7* **Ternivka** Dnipropetrovs'ka Oblast', E Ukraine
116 *K6* **Ternopil'** *Pol.* Tarnopol, *Rus.* Ternopol'. Ternopil's'ka Oblast', W Ukraine
Ternopil' *see* Ternopil's'ka Oblast'
116 *I6* **Ternopil's'ka Oblast'** *var.* Ternopil', *Rus.* Ternopol'skaya Oblast'. ◈ *province* NW Ukraine
Ternopol' *see* Ternopil'
Ternopol'skaya Oblast' *see* Ternopil's'ka Oblast'
123 *U13* **Terpeniya, Mys** *cape* Ostrov Sakhalin, SE Russian Federation
Térraba, Río *see* Grande de Térraba, Río
10 *J13* **Terrace** British Columbia, W Canada
12 *D12* **Terrace Bay** Ontario, S Canada
107 *I16* **Terracina** Lazio, C Italy
93 *F14* **Terråk** Troms, N Norway
26 *M13* **Terral** Oklahoma, C USA
107 *B19* **Terralba** Sardegna, Italy, C Mediterranean Sea
Terranova di Sicilia *see* Gela
Terranova Pausania *see* Olbia
105 *W5* **Terrassa** *Cast.* Tarrasa. Cataluña, E Spain
15 *O12* **Terrebonne** Québec, SE Canada
22 *J11* **Terrebonne Bay** *bay* Louisiana, SE USA
31 *N14* **Terre Haute** Indiana, N USA
25 *U6* **Terrell** Texas, SW USA
Terre Neuve *see* Newfoundland and Labrador
33 *Q14* **Terreton** Idaho, NW USA
103 *T7* **Territoire-de-Belfort** ◈ *department* E France
33 *X9* **Terry** Montana, NW USA
28 *I9* **Terry Peak** ▲ South Dakota, N USA
136 *H14* **Tersakan Gölü** ◎ C Turkey
98 *J4* **Terschelling** *Fris.* Skylge. *island* Waddeneilanden, N Netherlands
78 *H10* **Tersef** Chari-Baguirmi, C Chad
147 *X8* **Terskey Ala-Too, Khrebet** ▲▲ Kazakhstan/Kyrgyzstan
Terter *see* Tärtär
105 *R8* **Teruel** *anc.* Turba. Aragón, E Spain
105 *R7* **Teruel** ◈ *province* Aragón, E Spain
114 *M7* **Tervel** *prev.* Kurtbunar, *Rom.* Curtbunar. Dobrich, NE Bulgaria
93 *M16* **Tervo** Itä-Suomi, C Finland
92 *L13* **Tervola** Lappi, NW Finland
Tervueren *see* Tervuren
99 *H18* **Tervuren** *var.* Tervueren. Vlaams Brabant, C Belgium
162 *G5* **Tes** *var.* Dzür. Dzavhan, W Mongolia
112 *H11* **Tešanj** ◈ Federacija Bosna I Hercegovina, N Bosnia and Herzegovina
Teschen *see* Cieszyn
83 *M19* **Tesenane** Inhambane, S Mozambique
80 *I9* **Teseney** *var.* Tessenei. W Eritrea
39 *P5* **Teshekpuk Lake** ◎ Alaska, USA
162 *K6* **Teshig** Bulgan, N Mongolia
165 *T2* **Teshio** Hokkaidō, NE Japan
165 *T2* **Teshio-sanchi** ▲▲ Hokkaidō, NE Japan
Těšín *see* Cieszyn
Tesiyn Gol *see* Tes-Khem
129 *T7* **Tes-Khem** *var.* Tesiyn Gol. ≈ Mongolia/Russian Federation
112 *H11* **Teslić** ◈ Republika Srpska, N Bosnia and Herzegovina
10 *I9* **Teslin** Yukon Territory, W Canada
10 *I8* **Teslin** ≈ British Columbia/Yukon Territory, W Canada
77 *Q8* **Tessalit** Kidal, NE Mali
77 *V12* **Tessaoua** Maradi, S Niger
99 *J17* **Tessenderlo** Limburg, NE Belgium
Tessenei *see* Teseney
14 *L7* **Tessier, Lac** ◎ Québec, SE Canada
Tessin *see* Ticino
97 *M23* **Test** ≈ S England, UK
Testama *see* Tõstamaa
55 *P4* **Testigos, Islas los** *island group* N Venezuela
37 *S10* **Tesuque** New Mexico, SW USA
103 *O17* **Têt** *var.* Tet. ≈ S France
Tet *see* Têt
54 *G5* **Tetas, Cerro de las** ▲ NW Venezuela
83 *M15* **Tete** Tete, NW Mozambique
83 *M15* **Tete** *off.* Província de Tete. ◈ *province* NW Mozambique
9 *N15* **Tête Jaune Cache** British Columbia, SW Canada
184 *O8* **Te Teko** Bay of Plenty, North Island, New Zealand
186 *K9* **Tetepare** *island* New Georgia Islands, NW Solomon Islands
Tete, Província de *see* Tete
Teterev *see* Teteriv
116 *M5* **Teteriv** *Rus.* Teterev. ≈ N Ukraine
100 *M9* **Teterow** Mecklenburg-Vorpommern, NE Germany
114 *I9* **Teteven** Lovech, N Bulgaria
191 *T10* **Tetiaroa** *atoll* Îles du Vent, W French Polynesia
105 *P14* **Tetica de Bacares** ▲ S Spain
Tetiyev *see* Tetiyiv
117 *O6* **Tetiyiv** *Rus.* Tetiyev. Kyyivs'ka Oblast', N Ukraine
39 *T10* **Tetlin** Alaska, USA
33 *R8* **Teton River** ≈ Montana, NW USA
74 *G5* **Tétouan** *var.* Tetouan, Tetuán. N Morocco
Tetova/Tetovë *see* Tetovo
114 *L7* **Tetovo** Razgrad, N Bulgaria
113 *N18* **Tetovo** *Alb.* Tetova, Tetovë, *Turk.* Kalkandelen. NW FYR Macedonia
115 *E20* **Tetrázio** ▲▲ S Greece
Tetschen *see* Děčín
Tetuán *see* Tétouan
191 *Q8* **Tetufera, Mont** ▲ Tahiti, W French Polynesia
127 *R4* **Tetyushi** Respublika Tatarstan, W Russian Federation
108 *I7* **Teufen** Sankt Gallen, NE Switzerland
40 *L12* **Teul** *var.* Teul de Gonzáles Ortega. Zacatecas, C Mexico
107 *B21* **Teulada** Sardegna, Italy, C Mediterranean Sea
Teul de Gonzáles Ortega *see* Teul
9 *X16* **Teulon** Manitoba, S Canada
42 *I7* **Teupasenti** El Paraíso, S Honduras
165 *S2* **Teuri-tō** *island* NE Japan
100 *G13* **Teutoburger Wald** *Eng.* Teutoburg Forest. *hill range* NW Germany
Teutoburg Forest *see* Teutoburger Wald
93 *K17* **Teuva** *Swe.* Östermark. Länsi-Soumi, W Finland
107 *H15* **Tevere** *Eng.* Tiber. ≈ C Italy
138 *G9* **Teverya** *var.* Tiberias, Tverya. Northern, N Israel
96 *K13* **Teviot** ≈ SE Scotland, UK
Tevli *see* Tewli
122 *H11* **Tevriz** Omskaya Oblast', C Russian Federation
185 *B24* **Te Waewae Bay** *bay* South Island, New Zealand
97 *L21* **Tewkesbury** C England, UK
119 *F19* **Tewli** *Rus.* Tevli. Brestskaya Voblasts', SW Belarus
159 *U12* **Têwo** *var.* Dêngkagoin. Gansu, C China
25 *U12* **Texana, Lake** ◎ Texas, SW USA
27 *S14* **Texarkana** Arkansas, C USA
25 *X5* **Texarkana** Texas, SW USA
25 *N9* **Texas** *off.* State of Texas, *also known as* Lone Star State. ◈ *state* S USA
25 *W12* **Texas City** Texas, SW USA
41 *P14* **Texcoco** México, C Mexico
98 *I6* **Texel** *island* Waddeneilanden, NW Netherlands
26 *H8* **Texhoma** Oklahoma, C USA
25 *N1* **Texhoma** Texas, SW USA
37 *W12* **Texico** New Mexico, SW USA
24 *L1* **Texline** Texas, SW USA
41 *P14* **Texmelucan** *var.* San Martín Texmelucan. Puebla, S Mexico
27 *O13* **Texoma, Lake** ⊠ Oklahoma/Texas, C USA
25 *N9* **Texon** Texas, SW USA
83 *J23* **Teyateyaneng** NW Lesotho
124 *M16* **Teykovo** Ivanovskaya Oblast', W Russian Federation
124 *M16* **Teza** ≈ W Russian Federation
41 *Q13* **Teziutlán** Puebla, S Mexico
153 *W12* **Tezpur** Assam, NE India
9 *N10* **Tha-Anne** ≈ Nunavut, NE Canada
83 *K23* **Thabana Ntlenyana** *var.* Thabantshonyana, Mount Ntlenyana. ▲ E Lesotho
Thabantshonyana *see* Thabana Ntlenyana
83 *J23* **Thaba Putsoa** ▲ C Lesotho
167 *Q8* **Tha Bo** Nong Khai, E Thailand
103 *T12* **Thabor, Pic du** ▲ E France
Tha Chin *see* Samut Sakhon
166 *M7* **Thagaya** Pegu, C Myanmar (Burma)
Thai, Ao *see* Thailand, Gulf of
167 *T6* **Thai Binh** Thai Binh, N Vietnam
167 *S7* **Thai Hoa** *var.* Nghia Dan. Nghê An, N Vietnam
167 *P9* **Thailand** *off.* Kingdom of Thailand, *Th.* Prathet Thai; *prev.* Siam. ◆ *monarchy* SE Asia
167 *P13* **Thailand, Gulf of** *var.* Gulf of Siam, *Th.* Ao Thai, *Vtn.* Vinh Thai Lan. *gulf* SE Asia
Thailand, Kingdom of *see* Thailand
Thai Lan, Vinh *see* Thailand, Gulf of
167 *T6* **Thai Nguyên** Bắc Thai, N Vietnam
167 *S8* **Thakhèk** *var.* Muang Khammouan. Khammouan, C Laos
153 *S13* **Thakurgaon** Rajshahi, NW Bangladesh
149 *S6* **Thal** North-West Frontier Province, NW Pakistan
166 *M15* **Thalang** Phuket, SW Thailand
Thalassery *see* Tellicherry
167 *Q10* **Thalat Khae** Nakhon Ratchasima, C Thailand
109 *Q5* **Thalgau** Salzburg, NW Austria
108 *G7* **Thalwil** Zürich, NW Switzerland
83 *I20* **Thamaga** Kweneng, SE Botswana
Thamarīd *see* Thamarīt
141 *V13* **Thamarīt** *var.* Thamarīd, Thumrayt. SW Oman
141 *P16* **Thamar, Jabal** ▲ SW Yemen
184 *M6* **Thames** Waikato, North Island, New Zealand
14 *D17* **Thames** ≈ Ontario, S Canada
97 *O22* **Thames** ≈ S England, UK
184 *M6* **Thames, Firth of** *gulf* North Island, New Zealand
14 *D17* **Thamesville** Ontario, S Canada
141 *S13* **Thamūd** N Yemen
167 *N9* **Thanbyuzayat** Mon State, S Myanmar (Burma)
152 *I9* **Thānesar** Haryāna, NW India
167 *T7* **Thanh Hoa** Thanh Hoa, N Vietnam
Thanintari Taungdan *see* Bilauktaung Range
155 *I21* **Thanjāvūr** *prev.* Tanjore. Tamil Nādu, SE India
Thanlwin *see* Salween
103 *U7* **Thann** Haut-Rhin, NE France
167 *O16* **Tha Nong Phrom** Phatthalung, SW Thailand
167 *N13* **Thap Sakae** *var.* Thap Sakau. Prachuap Khiri Khan, SW Thailand
Thap Sakau *see* Thap Sakae
98 *L10* **'t Harde** Gelderland, E Netherlands
152 *D11* **Thar Desert** *var.* Great Indian Desert, Indian Desert. *desert* India/Pakistan
181 *V10* **Thargomindah** Queensland, C Australia
150 *D11* **Thar Pārkar** *desert* SE Pakistan
139 *S7* **Tharthār al Furāt, Qanāt ath** *canal* C Iraq
139 *R7* **Tharthār, Buḩayrat ath** ◎ C Iraq
139 *R5* **Tharthār, Wādī ath** *dry watercourse* N Iraq
167 *N13* **Tha Sae** Chumphon, SW Thailand
167 *N15* **Tha Sala** Nakhon Si Thammarat, SW Thailand
114 *I13* **Thásos** Thásos, E Greece
115 *I14* **Thásos** *island* E Greece
37 *N14* **Thatcher** Arizona, SW USA
167 *T5* **Thât Khê** *var.* Trâng Dinh. Lang Sơn, N Vietnam
166 *M8* **Thaton** Mon State, S Myanmar (Burma)
167 *S9* **That Phanom** Nakhon Phanom, E Thailand
167 *R10* **Tha Tum** Surin, E Thailand
103 *P16* **Thau, Bassin de** *var.* Étang de Thau. ◎ S France
Thau, Étang de *see* Thau, Bassin de
166 *L3* **Thaungdut** Sagaing, N Myanmar (Burma)
167 *O8* **Thaungyin** *Th.* Mae Nam Moei. ≈ Myanmar (Burma)/Thailand
167 *R8* **Tha Uthen** Nakhon Phanom, E Thailand
109 *W2* **Thaya** *var.* Dyje. ≈ Austria/Czech Republic *see also* Dyje
Thaya *see* Dyje
27 *V8* **Thayer** Missouri, C USA
166 *L6* **Thayetmyo** Magwe, C Myanmar (Burma)
33 *S15* **Thayne** Wyoming, C USA
166 *M5* **Thazi** Mandalay, C Myanmar (Burma)
Thebes *see* Thíva
44 *L5* **The Carlton** *var.* Abraham Bay. Mayaguana, SE Bahamas
45 *O14* **The Crane** *var.* Crane. S Barbados
32 *I11* **The Dalles** Oregon, NW USA
28 *M14* **Thedford** Nebraska, C USA
The Flatts Village *see* Flatts Village
The Hague *see* 's-Gravenhage
Theiss *see* Tisa/Tisza
8 *M9* **Thelon** ≈ Northwest Territories, N Canada
9 *V15* **Theodore** Saskatchewan, S Canada
23 *N8* **Theodore** Alabama, S USA
36 *L13* **Theodore Roosevelt Lake** ⊠ Arizona, SW USA
Theodosia *see* Feodosiya
Theophilo Ottoni *see* Teófilo Otoni
11 *V13* **The Pas** Manitoba, C Canada
31 *T14* **The Plains** Ohio, N USA
Thera *see* Santoríni
172 *H17* **Thérèse, Île** *island* Inner Islands, NE Seychelles
Therezina *see* Teresina
115 *L20* **Thérma** Ikaría, Dodekánisa, Greece, Aegean Sea
Thermae Himerenses *see* Termini Imerese
Thermae Pannonicae *see* Baden
Thermaic Gulf/Thermaicus Sinus *see* Thermaïkós Kólpos
121 *Q8* **Thermaïkós Kólpos** *Eng.* Thermaic Gulf; *anc.* Thermaicus Sinus. *gulf* N Greece
Thermiá *see* Kýthnos
115 *L17* **Thermís** Lésvos, E Greece

◆ Country ● Country Capital ◇ Dependent Territory ○ Dependent Territory Capital ◈ Administrative Regions ✈ International Airport ▲ Mountain ▲▲ Mountain Range ⛰ Volcano ≈ River ◎ Lake ⊠ Reservoir

115 E18 **Thérmo** Dytikí Ellás, C Greece
33 V14 **Thermopolis** Wyoming, C USA
183 P10 **The Rock** New South Wales, SE Australia
195 O5 **Theron Mountains** ▲▲ Antarctica
The Sooner State see Oklahoma
115 G18 **Thespiés** Stereá Ellás, C Greece
115 E16 **Thessalía** Eng. Thessaly. ◈ region C Greece
14 C10 **Thessalon** Ontario, S Canada
115 G14 **Thessaloníki** Eng. Salonica, Salonika, SCr. Solun, Turk. Selânik. Kentrikí Makedonía, N Greece
115 G14 **Thessaloníki** ✈ Kentrikí Makedonía, N Greece
Thessaly see Thessalía
84 B12 **Theta Gap** undersea feature E Atlantic Ocean
97 P20 **Thetford** E England, UK
15 R11 **Thetford-Mines** Québec, SE Canada
113 K17 **Theth** var. Thethi. Shkodër, N Albania
Thethi see Theth
99 L20 **Theux** Liège, E Belgium
45 V9 **The Valley** ○ (Anguilla) E Anguilla
27 N10 **The Village** Oklahoma, C USA
The Volunteer State see Tennessee
25 W10 **The Woodlands** Texas, SW USA
Thiamis see Kalamás
Thian Shan see Tien Shan
Thibet see Xizang Zizhiqu
22 J9 **Thibodaux** Louisiana, S USA
29 S3 **Thief Lake** ◎ Minnesota, N USA
29 S3 **Thief River** ≈ Minnesota, C USA
29 S3 **Thief River Falls** Minnesota, N USA
Thièle see La Thielle
32 G14 **Thielsen, Mount** ▲ Oregon, NW USA
Thielt see Tielt
106 G7 **Thiene** Veneto, NE Italy
Thienen see Tienen
103 P11 **Thiers** Puy-de-Dôme, C France
76 F11 **Thiès** W Senegal
81 I19 **Thika** Central, S Kenya
Thikombia see Cikobia
151 K18 **Thiladhunmathi Atoll** var. Tiladummati Atoll. atoll N Maldives
Thimbu see Thimphu
153 T11 **Thimphu** var. Thimbu; prev. Tashi Chho Dzong. ● (Bhutan) W Bhutan
92 H2 **Thingeyri** Vestfirdhir, NW Iceland
92 I3 **Thingvellir** Sudhurland, SW Iceland
187 Q17 **Thio** Province Sud, C New Caledonia
103 T4 **Thionville** Ger. Diedenhofen. Moselle, NE France
115 K22 **Thíra** Santorini, Kykládes, Greece, Aegean Sea
Thíra see Santoríni
115 J22 **Thirasía** island Kykládes, Greece, Aegean Sea
97 M16 **Thirsk** N England, UK
14 F12 **Thirty Thousand Islands** island group Ontario, S Canada
Thiruvanathapuram see Trivandrum
95 F20 **Thisted** Viborg, NW Denmark
Thistil Fjord see Thistilfjördhur
92 L1 **Thistilfjördhur** var. Thistil Fjord. fjord NE Iceland
182 G9 **Thistle Island** island South Australia
Thithia see Cicia
Thiukhaoluang Phrahang see Luang Prabang Range
115 G18 **Thíva** Eng. Thebes; prev. Thívai. Stereá Ellás, C Greece
Thívai see Thíva
102 M12 **Thiviers** Dordogne, SW France
92 J4 **Thjórsá** ≈ C Iceland
9 N10 **Thlewiaza** ≈ Nunavut, NE Canada
8 L10 **Thoa** ≈ Northwest Territories, NW Canada
99 G14 **Tholen** Zeeland, SW Netherlands
99 F14 **Tholen** island SW Netherlands
26 L10 **Thomas** Oklahoma, C USA
21 T3 **Thomas** West Virginia, NE USA
27 U3 **Thomas Hill Reservoir** ▣ Missouri, C USA
23 S5 **Thomaston** Georgia, SE USA
19 R7 **Thomaston** Maine, NE USA
25 T12 **Thomaston** Texas, SW USA
23 O6 **Thomasville** Alabama, S USA
23 T8 **Thomasville** Georgia, SE USA
21 S9 **Thomasville** North Carolina, SE USA
35 N5 **Thomes Creek** ≈ California, W USA
9 W12 **Thompson** Manitoba, C Canada
29 R4 **Thompson** North Dakota, N USA
0 F8 **Thompson** ≈ Alberta/British Columbia, SW Canada
33 O8 **Thompson Falls** Montana, NW USA
29 Q10 **Thompson, Lake** ◎ South Dakota, N USA
34 M3 **Thompson Peak** ▲ California, W USA
27 S2 **Thompson River** ≈ Missouri, C USA
185 A22 **Thompson Sound** sound South Island, New Zealand
8 J5 **Thomsen** ≈ Banks Island, Northwest Territories, NW Canada
23 V4 **Thomson** Georgia, SE USA
103 T10 **Thonon-les-Bains** Haute-Savoie, E France
103 O15 **Thoré** var. Thore. ≈ S France
Thore see Thoré
37 P11 **Thoreau** New Mexico, SW USA
Thorenburg see Turda
92 J3 **Thórisvatn** ◎ C Iceland
92 P4 **Thor, Kapp** headland S Svalbard
92 I4 **Thorlákshöfn** Sudhurland, SW Iceland
Thorn see Toruń
25 T10 **Thorndale** Texas, SW USA
14 H10 **Thorne** Ontario, S Canada
97 J14 **Thornhill** S Scotland, UK
25 U8 **Thornton** Texas, SW USA
Thornton Island see Millennium Island
14 H16 **Thorold** Ontario, S Canada
32 I9 **Thorp** Washington, NW USA
Thorshavn see Tórshavn
195 S3 **Thorshavnheiane** physical region Antarctica
92 L1 **Thórshöfn** Nordhurland Eystra, NE Iceland
Thospitis see Van Gölü
167 S14 **Thôt Nôt** Cân Thơ, S Vietnam
102 K8 **Thouars** Deux-Sèvres, W France
153 X14 **Thoubal** Manipur, NE India
102 K9 **Thouet** ≈ W France
Thoune see Thun
18 H7 **Thousand Islands** island Canada/USA
35 S15 **Thousand Oaks** California, W USA
114 L12 **Thrace** cultural region SE Europe
114 J13 **Thracian Sea** Gk. Thrakikó Pélagos; anc. Thracium Mare. sea Greece/Turkey
Thracium Mare/Thrakikó Pélagos see Thracian Sea
Thrá Lí, Bá see Tralee Bay
33 R11 **Three Forks** Montana, NW USA
162 M8 **Three Gorges Dam** dam Hubei, C China
160 L9 **Three Gorges Reservoir** ▣ C China
9 Q16 **Three Hills** Alberta, SW Canada
183 N15 **Three Hummock Island** island Tasmania, SE Australia
184 H1 **Three Kings Islands** island group N New Zealand
175 P10 **Three Kings Rise** undersea feature W Pacific Ocean
77 O18 **Three Points, Cape** headland S Ghana
31 P10 **Three Rivers** Michigan, N USA
25 S13 **Three Rivers** Texas, SW USA
83 G24 **Three Sisters** Northern Cape, SW South Africa
32 H13 **Three Sisters** ▲ Oregon, NW USA
187 N10 **Three Sisters Islands** island group SE Solomon Islands
Thrissur see Trichūr
25 Q6 **Throckmorton** Texas, SW USA
180 M10 **Throssell, Lake** salt lake Western Australia
115 K25 **Thryptís** var. Thrýptis. ▲ Kríti, Greece, E Mediterranean Sea
167 T13 **Thu Dâu Môt** var. Phu Cường. Sông Be, S Vietnam
167 S6 **Thu Do** ✈ (Ha Nôi) Ha Nôi, N Vietnam
99 G21 **Thuin** Hainaut, S Belgium
149 Q12 **Thul** Sind, SE Pakistan
Thule see Qaanaaq
83 J18 **Thuli** var. Tuli. ≈ S Zimbabwe
Thumrayt see Thamarīt
108 D9 **Thun** Fr. Thoune. Bern, W Switzerland
12 C12 **Thunder Bay** Ontario, S Canada
30 M1 **Thunder Bay** lake bay S Canada
31 R6 **Thunder Bay** lake bay Michigan, N USA
31 R6 **Thunder Bay River** ≈ Michigan, N USA
27 N11 **Thunderbird, Lake** ◎ Oklahoma, C USA
28 L8 **Thunder Butte Creek** ≈ South Dakota, N USA
108 E9 **Thuner See** ◎ C Switzerland
167 N15 **Thung Song** var. Cha Mai. Nakhon Si Thammarat, SW Thailand
108 H7 **Thur** ≈ N Switzerland
108 G6 **Thurgau** Fr. Thurgovie. ◈ canton NE Switzerland
Thurgovie see Thurgau
Thuringe see Thüringen
108 J7 **Thüringen** Vorarlberg, W Austria
101 J17 **Thüringen** Eng. Thuringia, Fr. Thuringe. ◈ state C Germany
101 J17 **Thüringer Wald** Eng. Thuringian Forest. ▲▲ C Germany
Thuringia see Thüringen
Thuringian Forest see Thüringer Wald
97 D19 **Thurles** Ir. Durlas. S Ireland
21 W2 **Thurmont** Maryland, NE USA
Thurø see Thurø By
95 H24 **Thurø By** var. Thurø. Fyn, C Denmark
14 M12 **Thurso** Québec, SE Canada
96 J6 **Thurso** N Scotland, UK
194 I10 **Thurston Island** island Antarctica
108 I9 **Thusis** Graubünden, S Switzerland
Thýamis see Kalamás
95 E21 **Thyborøn** var. Tyborøn. Ringkøbing, W Denmark
195 U3 **Thyer Glacier** glacier Antarctica
115 L20 **Thýmaina** island Dodekánisa, Greece, Aegean Sea
83 N15 **Thyolo** var. Cholo. Southern, S Malawi
183 U6 **Tia** New South Wales, SE Australia
54 H5 **Tía Juana** Zulia, NW Venezuela
Tiancheng see Chongyang
160 J14 **Tiandong** var. Pingma. Guangxi Zhuangzu Zizhiqu, S China
161 O3 **Tianjin** var. Tientsin. Tianjin Shi, E China
Tianjin see Tianjin Shi
161 P3 **Tianjin Shi** var. Jin, Tianjin, T'ien-ching, Tientsin. ◈ municipality E China
159 S10 **Tianjun** var. Xinyuan. Qinghai, C China
160 J13 **Tianlin** var. Leli. Guangxi Zhuangzu Zizhiqu, S China
Tian Shan see Tien Shan
159 W11 **Tianshui** Gansu, C China
150 I7 **Tianshuihai** Xinjiang Uygur Zizhiqu, W China
161 S10 **Tiantai** Zhejiang, SE China
160 J14 **Tianyang** var. Tianzhou. Guangxi Zhuangzu Zizhiqu, S China
Tianzhou see Tianyang
159 U9 **Tianzhu** var. Huazangsi, Tianzhu Zangzu Zizhixian. Gansu, C China
Tianzhu Zangzu Zizhixian see Tianzhu
191 Q7 **Tiarei** Tahiti, W French Polynesia
74 J6 **Tiaret** var. Tihert. NW Algeria
77 N17 **Tiassalé** S Ivory Coast
192 I16 **Ti'avea** Upolu, SE Samoa
Tiba see Chiba
60 J11 **Tibagi** var. Tibaji. Paraná, S Brazil
60 J10 **Tibagi, Rio** var. Rio Tibají. ≈ S Brazil
Tibaji see Tibagi
Tibají, Rio see Tibagi, Rio
139 Q9 **Tibal, Wādī** dry watercourse S Iraq
54 G9 **Tibaná** Boyacá, C Colombia
79 F14 **Tibati** Adamaoua, N Cameroon
76 K15 **Tibé, Pic de** ▲ SE Guinea
Tiber see Tevere, Italy
Tiber see Tivoli, Italy
Tiberias see Teverya
138 G8 **Tiberias, Lake** var. Chinnereth, Sea of Bahr Tabariya, Sea of Galilee, Ar. Bahrat Tabariya, Heb. Yam Kinneret. ◎ N Israel
67 Q5 **Tibesti** var. Tibesti Massif, Ar. Tibistī. ▲▲ N Africa
Tibesti Massif see Tibesti
Tibet see Xizang Zizhiqu
Tibetan Autonomous Region see Xizang Zizhiqu
Tibet, Plateau of see Qingzang Gaoyuan
Tibistī see Tibesti
14 K7 **Tiblemont, Lac** ◎ Québec, SE Canada
139 X9 **Ţīb, Nahr aţ** ≈ S Iraq
Tibnī see At Tibnī
182 L4 **Tibooburra** New South Wales, SE Australia
95 L18 **Tibro** Västra Götaland, S Sweden
40 E5 **Tiburón, Isla** var. Isla del Tiburón. island NW Mexico
Tiburón, Isla del see Tiburón, Isla
23 W14 **Tice** Florida, SE USA
Tichau see Tychy
114 L8 **Ticha, Yazovir** ◎ NE Bulgaria
76 K9 **Tichit** var. Tichitt. Tagant, C Mauritania
Tichitt see Tichit
108 G11 **Ticino** Fr./Ger. Tessin. ◈ canton S Switzerland
106 D8 **Ticino** ≈ Italy/Switzerland
108 H11 **Ticino** Ger. Tessin. ≈ SW Switzerland
Ticinum see Pavia
41 X12 **Ticul** Yucatán, SE Mexico
95 K18 **Tidaholm** Västra Götaland, S Sweden
Tidjikdja see Tidjikja
76 J8 **Tidjikja** var. Tidjikdja; prev. Fort-Cappolani. Tagant, C Mauritania
Tidore see Soasiu
171 R11 **Tidore, Pulau** island E Indonesia
Tidra, Ile see Et Tîdra
77 N16 **Tiébissou** var. Tiebissou. C Ivory Coast
Tiebissou see Tiébissou
Tiefa see Diaobingshan
108 I9 **Tiefencastel** Graubünden, S Switzerland
Tiegenhof see Nowy Dwór Gdański
T'ieh-ling see Tieling
98 K13 **Tiel** Gelderland, C Netherlands
163 W7 **Tieli** Heilongjiang, NE China
163 V11 **Tieling** var. T'ieh-ling. Liaoning, NE China
152 L4 **Tielongtan** China/India
99 D17 **Tielt** var. Thielt. West-Vlaanderen, W Belgium
T'ien-ching see Tianjin Shi
99 I18 **Tienen** var. Thienen, Fr. Tirlemont. Vlaams Brabant, C Belgium
Tiên Giang, Sông see Mekong
147 X9 **Tien Shan** Chin. Thian Shan, Tian Shan, T'ien Shan, Rus. Tyan'-Shan'. ▲▲ C Asia
Tientsin see Tianjin
167 U6 **Tiên Yên** Quang Ninh, N Vietnam
95 O14 **Tierp** Uppsala, C Sweden
62 H7 **Tierra Amarilla** Atacama, N Chile
37 R9 **Tierra Amarilla** New Mexico, SW USA
41 R15 **Tierra Blanca** Veracruz-Llave, E Mexico
41 O16 **Tierra Colorada** Guerrero, S Mexico
63 J17 **Tierra Colorada, Bajo de la** basin SE Argentina
63 I25 **Tierra del Fuego** off. Provincia de la Tierra del Fuego. ◈ province S Argentina
63 J24 **Tierra del Fuego** island Argentina/Chile
Tierra del Fuego, Provincia de la see Tierra del Fuego
54 D7 **Tierralta** Córdoba, NW Colombia
104 K9 **Tiétar** ≈ W Spain
60 L10 **Tietê** São Paulo, S Brazil
60 J8 **Tietê, Rio** ≈ S Brazil
32 I9 **Tieton** Washington, NW USA
32 J6 **Tiffany Mountain** ▲ Washington, NW USA
31 S12 **Tiffin** Ohio, N USA
31 Q11 **Tiffin River** ≈ Ohio, N USA
Tiflis see T'bilisi
23 U7 **Tifton** Georgia, SE USA
171 R13 **Tifu** Pulau Buru, E Indonesia
38 L17 **Tigalda Island** island Aleutian Islands, Alaska, USA
115 I15 **Tigáni, Ákrotírio** headland Límnos, E Greece
169 V6 **Tiga Tarok** Sabah, East Malaysia
117 O10 **Tighina** Rus. Bendery; prev. Bender. E Moldova
145 X9 **Tigiretskiy Khrebet** ▲▲ E Kazakhstan
79 F14 **Tignère** Adamaoua, N Cameroon
13 P14 **Tignish** Prince Edward Island, SE Canada
Tigranocerta see Siirt
80 I11 **Tigray** ◈ province N Ethiopia
41 O11 **Tigre, Cerro del** ▲ C Mexico
56 F8 **Tigre, Río** ≈ N Peru
139 X10 **Tigris** Ar. Dijlah, Turk. Dicle. ≈ Iraq/Turkey
76 G9 **Tiguent** Trarza, SW Mauritania
74 M10 **Tiguentourine** E Algeria
77 V10 **Tiguidit, Falaise de** ridge C Niger
141 N13 **Tihāmah** var. Tehama. plain Saudi Arabia/Yemen
Tihert see Tiaret
Ti-hua/Tihwa see Ürümqi
41 Q13 **Tihuatlán** Veracruz-Llave, E Mexico
40 B1 **Tijuana** Baja California, NW Mexico
42 E2 **Tikal** Petén, N Guatemala
154 I9 **Tīkamgarh** prev. Tehri. Madhya Pradesh, C India
158 L7 **Tikanlik** Xinjiang Uygur Zizhiqu, NW China
77 P12 **Tikaré** N Burkina
39 O12 **Tikchik Lakes** lakes Alaska, USA
191 T9 **Tikehau** atoll Îles Tuamotu, C French Polynesia
191 V9 **Tikei** island Îles Tuamotu, C French Polynesia
126 L13 **Tikhoretsk** Krasnodarskiy Kray, SW Russian Federation
124 I13 **Tikhvin** Leningradskaya Oblast', NW Russian Federation
193 P9 **Tiki Basin** undersea feature S Pacific Ocean
76 K13 **Tikinsso** ≈ NE Guinea
184 Q8 **Tikitiki** Gisborne, North Island, New Zealand
79 D16 **Tiko** Sud-Ouest, SW Cameroon
139 S6 **Tikrīt** var. Tekrit. N Iraq
124 I8 **Tiksha** Respublika Kareliya, NW Russian Federation
124 I6 **Tikshozero, Ozero** ◎ NW Russian Federation
123 P7 **Tiksi** Respublika Sakha (Yakutiya), NE Russian Federation
Tiladummati Atoll see Thiladhunmathi Atoll
42 A6 **Tilapa** San Marcos, SW Guatemala
42 L13 **Tilarán** Guanacaste, NW Costa Rica
99 J14 **Tilburg** Noord-Brabant, S Netherlands
14 D17 **Tilbury** Ontario, S Canada
182 K4 **Tilcha** South Australia
Tilcha Creek see Callabonna Creek
29 Q14 **Tilden** Nebraska, C USA
25 R13 **Tilden** Texas, SW USA
14 H10 **Tilden Lake** Ontario, S Canada
116 G9 **Tileagd** Hung. Mezőtelegd. Bihor, W Romania
77 Q8 **Tilemsi, Vallée de** ≈ C Mali
123 V8 **Tilichiki** Koryakskiy Avtonomnyy Okrug, E Russian Federation
Tiligul see Tilihul
Tiligul'skiy Liman see Tilihul's'kyy Lyman
117 P9 **Tilihul** Rus. Tiligul. ≈ SW Ukraine
117 P10 **Tilihul's'kyy Lyman** Rus. Tiligul'skiy Liman. ◎ S Ukraine
Tilimsen see Tlemcen
Tilio Martius see Toulon
77 R11 **Tillabéri** var. Tillabéry. Tillabéri, W Niger
77 R11 **Tillabéri** ◈ department SW Niger
Tillabéry see Tillabéri
32 F11 **Tillamook** Oregon, NW USA
32 E11 **Tillamook Bay** inlet Oregon, NW USA
151 Q22 **Tillanchāng Dwīp** island Nicobar Islands, India, NE Indian Ocean
95 N15 **Tillberga** Västmanland, C Sweden
Tillenberg see Dyleń
21 S10 **Tillery, Lake** ▣ North Carolina, SE USA
77 T10 **Tillia** Tahoua, W Niger
23 N8 **Tillmans Corner** Alabama, S USA
14 F17 **Tillsonburg** Ontario, S Canada
115 N22 **Tílos** island Dodekánisa, Greece, Aegean Sea
183 N5 **Tilpa** New South Wales, SE Australia
Tilsit see Sovetsk
31 N13 **Tilton** Illinois, N USA
126 K7 **Tim** Kurskaya Oblast', W Russian Federation
54 D12 **Timaná** Huila, S Colombia
Timan Ridge see Timanskiy Kryazh
125 Q6 **Timanskiy Kryazh** Eng. Timan Ridge. ridge NW Russian Federation
185 G20 **Timaru** Canterbury, South Island, New Zealand
127 S6 **Timashevo** Samarskaya Oblast', W Russian Federation
126 K13 **Timashevsk** Krasnodarskiy Kray, SW Russian Federation
Timbaki/Timbákion see Tympáki
22 K10 **Timbalier Bay** bay Louisiana, S USA
22 K11 **Timbalier Island** island Louisiana, S USA
76 L10 **Timbedgha** var. Timbédra. Hodh ech Chargui, SE Mauritania
Timbédra see Timbedgha
32 G10 **Timber** Oregon, NW USA
181 O3 **Timber Creek** Northern Territory, N Australia
28 M8 **Timber Lake** South Dakota, N USA
54 D12 **Timbío** Cauca, SW Colombia
54 C12 **Timbiquí** Cauca, SW Colombia
83 O17 **Timbue, Ponta** headland C Mozambique
Timbuktu see Tombouctou
169 W8 **Timbun Mata, Pulau** island E Malaysia
77 P8 **Timétrine** var. Ti-n-Kâr. oasis C Mali
Timfi see Týmfi
Timfristos see Tymfristós
77 V9 **Timia** Agadez, C Niger
171 X14 **Timika** Papua, E Indonesia
74 I9 **Timimoun** C Algeria
Timiris, Cap see Timirist, Râs
76 F8 **Timirist, Râs** var. Cap Timiris. headland NW Mauritania
145 O7 **Timiryazevo** Severnyy Kazakhstan, N Kazakhstan
116 E11 **Timiş** ◈ county SW Romania
14 H9 **Timiskaming, Lake** Fr. Lac Témiscamingue. ◎ Ontario/Québec, SE Canada
116 E11 **Timişoara** Ger. Temeschwar, Temeswar, Hung. Temesvár; prev. Temeschburg. Timiş, W Romania
116 E11 **Timisoara** ✈ Timiş, SW Romania
Timkovichi see Tsimkavichy
77 U8 **Ti-m-Meghsoï** ≈ NW Niger
100 K8 **Timmerdorfer Strand** Schleswig-Holstein, N Germany
14 F7 **Timmins** Ontario, S Canada
21 S12 **Timmonsville** South Carolina, SE USA
30 K5 **Timms Hill** ▲ Wisconsin, N USA
112 P12 **Timok** ≈ E Serbia
58 N13 **Timon** Maranhão, E Brazil
171 Q17 **Timor Sea** sea E Indian Ocean
Timor Timur see East Timor
Timor Trench see Timor Trough
192 G8 **Timor Trough** var. Timor Trench. undersea feature NE Timor Sea
61 A21 **Timote** Buenos Aires, E Argentina
54 I6 **Timotes** Mérida, NW Venezuela
25 X8 **Timpson** Texas, SW USA
123 Q11 **Timpton** ≈ NE Russian Federation
93 H17 **Timrå** Västernorrland, C Sweden
20 J10 **Tims Ford Lake** ▣ Tennessee, S USA
168 L7 **Timur, Banjaran** ▲▲ Peninsular Malaysia
171 Q8 **Tinaca Point** headland Mindanao, S Philippines
54 K5 **Tinaco** Cojedes, N Venezuela
64 Q11 **Tinajo** Lanzarote, Islas Canarias, Spain, NE Atlantic Ocean
187 P10 **Tinakula** island Santa Cruz Islands, E Solomon Islands
54 K5 **Tinaquillo** Cojedes, N Venezuela
116 F10 **Tinca** Hung. Tenke. Bihor, W Romania
155 J20 **Tindivanam** Tamil Nādu, SE India
74 E9 **Tindouf** W Algeria
74 E9 **Tindouf, Sebkha de** salt lake W Algeria
104 J2 **Tineo** Asturias, N Spain
77 R9 **Ti-n-Essako** Kidal, E Mali
183 T5 **Tingha** New South Wales, SE Australia
Tingis see Tanger
Tinglett see Tinglev
95 F24 **Tinglev** Ger. Tinglett. Sønderjylland, SW Denmark
56 E12 **Tingo María** Huánuco, C Peru
Tingréla see Tengréla
158 K16 **Tingri** var. Xégar. Xizang Zizhiqu, W China
95 M21 **Tingsryd** Kronoberg, S Sweden
95 P19 **Tingstäde** Gotland, SE Sweden
62 H12 **Tinguiririca, Volcán** ⛰ C Chile
94 F9 **Tingvoll** Møre og Romsdal, S Norway
188 K8 **Tinian** island S Northern Mariana Islands
Ti-n-Kâr see Timétrine
Tinnevelly see Tirunelveli
95 G15 **Tinnoset** Telemark, S Norway
95 F15 **Tinnsjø** ◎ S Norway
Tino see Chino
115 J20 **Tínos** Tínos, Kykládes, Greece, Aegean Sea
115 J20 **Tínos** anc. Tenos. island Kykládes, Greece, Aegean Sea
153 R14 **Tinpahar** Jhārkhand, NE India
153 X11 **Tinsukia** Assam, NE India
76 K10 **Tîntâne** Hodh el Gharbi, S Mauritania
62 L7 **Tintina** Santiago del Estero, N Argentina
182 K10 **Tintinara** South Australia
104 I14 **Tinto** ≈ SW Spain
77 S8 **Ti-n-Zaouâtene** Kidal, NE Mali
Tiobraid Árann see Tipperary
28 K3 **Tioga** North Dakota, N USA
18 G12 **Tioga** Pennsylvania, NE USA
25 T5 **Tioga** Texas, SW USA
35 Q8 **Tioga Pass** pass California, W USA
18 G12 **Tioga River** ≈ New York/Pennsylvania, NE USA
Tioman Island see Tioman, Pulau
168 M9 **Tioman, Pulau** var. Tioman Island. island Peninsular Malaysia
18 C12 **Tionesta** Pennsylvania, NE USA
18 D12 **Tionesta Creek** ≈ Pennsylvania, NE USA
168 J13 **Tiop** Pulau Pagai Selatan, W Indonesia
77 O12 **Tiou** NW Burkina
18 H11 **Tioughnioga River** ≈ New York, NE USA
74 J5 **Tipasa** var. Tipaza. N Algeria
Tipaza see Tipasa
42 J10 **Tipitapa** Managua, W Nicaragua
31 R13 **Tipp City** Ohio, N USA
31 O12 **Tippecanoe River** ≈ Indiana, N USA
97 D20 **Tipperary** Ir. Tiobraid Árann. S Ireland
97 D19 **Tipperary** Ir. Tiobraid Árann. ◈ county S Ireland
35 R12 **Tipton** California, W USA
31 P13 **Tipton** Indiana, N USA
29 Y14 **Tipton** Iowa, C USA
27 U5 **Tipton** Missouri, C USA
36 I10 **Tipton, Mount** ▲ Arizona, SW USA
20 F8 **Tiptonville** Tennessee, S USA
12 E12 **Tip Top Mountain** ▲ Ontario, S Canada
155 G19 **Tiptūr** Karnātaka, W India
Tiquisate see Pueblo Nuevo Tiquisate
58 L13 **Tiracambu, Serra do** ▲▲ E Brazil
Tirana see Tiranë
113 K19 **Tirana Rinas** ✈ Durrës, W Albania
113 L20 **Tiranë** var. Tirana. ● (Albania) Tiranë, C Albania
113 K20 **Tiranë** ◈ district W Albania
140 I5 **Tirān, Jazīrat** island Egypt/Saudi Arabia
106 F6 **Tirano** Lombardia, N Italy
182 I2 **Tirari Desert** desert South Australia
117 O10 **Tiraspol** Rus. Tiraspol'. E Moldova
Tiraspol' see Tiraspol
184 M8 **Tirau** Waikato, North Island, New Zealand
136 C14 **Tire** İzmir, SW Turkey
137 O11 **Tirebolu** Giresun, N Turkey
96 F11 **Tiree** island W Scotland, UK
Tîrgovişte see Târgovişte
Tîrgu see Târgu Cărbuneşti
Tîrgu Bujor see Târgu Bujor
Tîrgu Frumos see Târgu Frumos
Tîrgu Jiu see Târgu Jiu
Tîrgu Lăpuş see Târgu Lăpuş
Tîrgu Mures see Târgu Mureş
Tîrgu-Neamţ see Târgu-Neamţ
Tîrgu Ocna see Târgu Ocna
Tîrgu Secuiesc see Târgu Secuiesc
149 T3 **Tirich Mīr** ▲ NW Pakistan
76 J5 **Tiris Zemmour** ◈ region N Mauritania
Tirlemont see Tienen
127 W5 **Tirlyanskiy** Respublika Bashkortostan, W Russian Federation
Tîrnava Mare see Târnava Mare
Tîrnava Mică see Târnava Mică
Tîrnăveni see Târnăveni
Tírnavos see Týrnavos
Tirnovo see Veliko Tŭrnovo
154 J11 **Tirodi** Madhya Pradesh, C India
108 K8 **Tirol** off. Land Tirol, var. Tyrol, It. Tirolo. ◈ state W Austria
Tirol, Land see Tirol
Tirolo see Tirol
Tirreno, Mare see Tyrrhenian Sea
107 B19 **Tirso** ≈ Sardegna, Italy, C Mediterranean Sea
95 H22 **Tirstrup** ✈ (Århus) Århus, C Denmark
155 I21 **Tiruchchirāppalli** prev. Trichinopoly. Tamil Nādu, SE India
155 H23 **Tirunelveli** var. Tinnevelly. Tamil Nādu, SE India
155 J19 **Tirupati** Andhra Pradesh, E India
155 I20 **Tiruppattūr** Tamil Nādu, SE India
155 H21 **Tiruppur** Tamil Nādu, SW India
155 I20 **Tiruvannāmalai** Tamil Nādu, SE India
112 L10 **Tisa** Ger. Theiss, Hung. Tisza, Rus. Tissa, Ukr. Tysa. ≈ SE Europe see also Tisza
Tisa see Tisza
Tischnowitz see Tišnov
9 U14 **Tisdale** Saskatchewan, S Canada
27 O13 **Tishomingo** Oklahoma, C USA
95 M17 **Tisnaren** ◎ S Sweden
111 F18 **Tišnov** Ger. Tischnowitz. Jihomoravský Kraj, SE Czech Republic
Tissa see Tisa/Tisza
74 J6 **Tissemsilt** N Algeria
153 S12 **Tista** ≈ NE India
112 L8 **Tisza** Ger. Theiss, Rom./Slvn./SCr. Tisa, Rus. Tissa, Ukr. Tysa. ≈ SE Europe see also Tisa
Tisza see Tisa
111 L23 **Tiszaföldvár** Jász-Nagykun-Szolnok, E Hungary
111 M22 **Tiszafüred** Jász-Nagykun-Szolnok, E Hungary
111 L23 **Tiszakécske** Bács-Kiskun, C Hungary
111 M21 **Tiszaújváros** prev. Leninváros. Borsod-Abaúj-Zemplén, NE Hungary
111 N21 **Tiszavasvári** Szabolcs-Szatmár-Bereg, NE Hungary
57 J17 **Titicaca, Lake** ◎ Bolivia/Peru
190 H17 **Titikaveka** Rarotonga, S Cook Islands
154 M13 **Titilāgarh** Orissa, E India
168 K8 **Titiwangsa, Banjaran** ▲▲ Peninsular Malaysia
Titograd see Podgorica
Titose see Chitose
Titova Mitrovica see Kosovska Mitrovica
Titovo Užice see Užice
113 M18 **Titov Vrv** ▲ NW FYR Macedonia
94 F7 **Titran** Sør-Trøndelag, S Norway
31 Q8 **Tittabawassee River** ≈ Michigan, N USA
116 J13 **Titu** Dâmboviţa, S Romania
79 M16 **Titule** Orientale, N Dem. Rep. Congo
23 X11 **Titusville** Florida, SE USA
18 C12 **Titusville** Pennsylvania, NE USA
76 G11 **Tivaouane** W Senegal

◆ Country
● Country Capital
◇ Dependent Territory
○ Dependent Territory Capital
◈ Administrative Regions
✈ International Airport
▲ Mountain
▲▲ Mountain Range
⛰ Volcano
≈ River
◎ Lake
▣ Reservoir

113 I17 **Tivat** SW Montenegro
14 E14 **Tiverton** Ontario, S Canada
97 J23 **Tiverton** SW England, UK
19 O12 **Tiverton** Rhode Island, NE USA
107 I15 **Tivoli** *anc.* Tiber. Lazio, C Italy
25 U13 **Tivoli** Texas, SW USA
141 Z8 **Ṭīwī** NE Oman
41 Y11 **Tizimín** Yucatán, SE Mexico
74 K5 **Tizi Ouzou** *var.* Tizi-Ouzou. N Algeria
Tizi-Ouzou *see* Tizi Ouzou
74 D8 **Tiznit** SW Morocco
95 F23 **Tjæreborg** Ribe, W Denmark
113 I14 **Tjentište** ◈ Republika Srpska, SE Bosnia and Herzegovina
98 L7 **Tjeukemeer** ◎ N Netherlands
Tjiamis *see* Ciamis
Tjiandjoer *see* Cianjur
Tjilatjap *see* Cilacap
Tjirebon *see* Cirebon
95 I18 **Tjörn** *island* S Sweden
92 O3 **Tjuvfjorden** *fjord* S Svalbard
Tkvarcheli *see* Tqvarch'eli
40 L8 **Tlahualilo** Durango, N Mexico
41 P14 **Tlalnepantla** México, C Mexico
41 Q13 **Tlapacoyán** Veracruz-Llave, E Mexico
41 P16 **Tlapa de Comonfort** Guerrero, S Mexico
40 L13 **Tlaquepaque** Jalisco, C Mexico
Tlascala *see* Tlaxcala
41 P14 **Tlaxcala** *var.* Tlascala, Tlaxcala de Xicohténcatl. Tlaxcala, C Mexico
41 P14 **Tlaxcala** ◈ *state* S Mexico
Tlaxcala de Xicohténcatl *see* Tlaxcala
41 P14 **Tlaxco** *var.* Tlaxco de Morelos. Tlaxcala, S Mexico
Tlaxco de Morelos *see* Tlaxco
41 Q16 **Tlaxiaco** *var.* Santa María Asunción Tlaxiaco. Oaxaca, S Mexico
74 I6 **Tlemcen** *var.* Tilimsen, Tlemsen. NW Algeria
Tlemsen *see* Tlemcen
138 L4 **Tlété Ouâte Rharbi, Jebel** ▲ N Syria
116 J7 **Tlumach** Ivano-Frankivs'ka Oblast', W Ukraine
127 P17 **Tlyarata** Respublika Dagestan, SW Russian Federation
116 K10 **Toaca, Vârful** *prev.* Vîrful Toaca. ▲ NE Romania
Toaca, Vîrful *see* Toaca, Vârful
187 R13 **Toak** Ambrym, C Vanuatu
172 J4 **Toamasina** *var.* Tamatave. Toamasina, E Madagascar
172 J4 **Toamasina** ◈ *province* E Madagascar
172 J4 **Toamasina** ✈ Toamasina, E Madagascar
21 X6 **Toano** Virginia, NE USA
191 U10 **Toau** *atoll* Îles Tuamotu, C French Polynesia
45 T6 **Toa Vaca, Embalse** ▣ C Puerto Rico
62 K13 **Toay** La Pampa, C Argentina
159 R14 **Toba** Xizang Zizhiqu, W China
164 K14 **Toba** Mie, Honshū, SW Japan
168 I9 **Toba, Danau** ◎ Sumatera, W Indonesia
45 Y16 **Tobago** *island* NE Trinidad and Tobago
149 Q9 **Toba Kākar Range** ▲▲ NW Pakistan
105 Q12 **Tobarra** Castilla-La Mancha, C Spain
149 U9 **Toba Tek Singh** Punjab, E Pakistan
171 R11 **Tobelo** Pulau Halmahera, E Indonesia
14 E12 **Tobermory** Ontario, S Canada
96 G10 **Tobermory** W Scotland, UK
165 S4 **Tōbetsu** Hokkaidō, NE Japan
180 M6 **Tobin Lake** ◎ Western Australia
9 U14 **Tobin Lake** ◎ Saskatchewan, C Canada
35 T4 **Tobin, Mount** ▲ Nevada, W USA
165 O9 **Tobi-shima** *island* C Japan
169 N13 **Toboali** Pulau Bangka, W Indonesia
144 M8 **Tobol** *Kaz.* Tobyl. Kustanay, N Kazakhstan
144 L8 **Tobol** *Kaz.* Tobyl. ≈ Kazakhstan/Russian Federation
122 H11 **Tobol'sk** Tyumenskaya Oblast', C Russian Federation
Tobruch/Tobruk *see* Ṭubruq
125 R3 **Tobseda** Nenetskiy Avtonomnyy Okrug, NW Russian Federation
Tobyl *see* Tobol
125 Q6 **Tobysh** ≈ NW Russian Federation
54 F10 **Tocaima** Cundinamarca, C Colombia
59 K16 **Tocantins** *off.* Estado do Tocantins. ◈ *state* C Brazil
Tocantins, Estado do *see* Tocantins
59 K15 **Tocantins, Rio** ≈ N Brazil
23 T2 **Toccoa** Georgia, SE USA
165 O12 **Tochigi** *off.* Tochigi-ken, *var.* Totigi. ◈ *prefecture* Honshū, S Japan
Tochigi-ken *see* Tochigi
165 O11 **Tochio** *var.* Totio. Niigata, Honshū, C Japan
95 I15 **Töcksfors** Värmland, C Sweden
42 J5 **Tocoa** Colón, N Honduras
62 H4 **Tocopilla** Antofagasta, N Chile
62 I4 **Tocorpuri, Cerro de** ▲ Bolivia/Chile
183 O10 **Tocumwal** New South Wales, SE Australia
54 K4 **Tocuyo de La Costa** Falcón, NW Venezuela
152 H13 **Toda Rāisingh** Rājasthān, N India
106 H13 **Todi** Umbria, C Italy
108 G9 **Tödi** ▲ NE Switzerland
171 T12 **Todlo** Papua, E Indonesia
165 S9 **Todoga-saki** *headland* Honshū, C Japan
59 P17 **Todos os Santos, Baía de** *bay* E Brazil
40 F10 **Todos Santos** Baja California Sur, W Mexico
40 B2 **Todos Santos, Bahía de** *bay* NW Mexico
Toeban *see* Tuban
Toekang Besi Eilanden *see* Tukangbesi, Kepulauan
Toeloengagoeng *see* Tulungagung
Tōen *see* T'aoyüan
185 D25 **Toetoes Bay** *bay* South Island, New Zealand
9 Q14 **Tofield** Alberta, SW Canada
10 K17 **Tofino** Vancouver Island, British Columbia, SW Canada
189 X17 **Tofol** Kosrae, E Micronesia
95 J20 **Tofta** Halland, S Sweden
95 H15 **Tofte** Buskerud, S Norway
95 F24 **Toftlund** Sønderjylland, SW Denmark
193 X15 **Tofua** *island* Ha'apai Group, C Tonga
187 Q12 **Toga** *island* Torres Islands, N Vanuatu
80 N13 **Togdheer** *off.* Gobolka Togdheer. ◈ *region* NW Somalia
Togdheer, Gobolka *see* Togdheer
Toghyzaq *see* Toguzak
164 L11 **Togi** Ishikawa, Honshū, SW Japan
39 N13 **Togiak** Alaska, USA
171 O11 **Togian, Kepulauan** *island group* C Indonesia
77 Q15 **Togo** *off.* Togolese Republic; *prev.* French Togoland. ◆ *republic* W Africa
Togolese Republic *see* Togo
162 F8 **Tögrög** Govĭ-Altay, SW Mongolia
162 F8 **Tögrög** *var.* Hoolt. Övörhangay, C Mongolia
Tögrög *see* Manhan
159 N12 **Togton He** *var.* Tuotuo He. ≈ C China
Togton Heyan *see* Tanggulashan
144 L7 **Toguzak** *Kaz.* Toghyzaq. ≈ Kazakhstan/Russian Federation
37 P10 **Tohatchi** New Mexico, SW USA
191 O7 **Tohiea, Mont** ⛰ Moorea, W French Polynesia
137 N14 **Tohma Çayı** ≈ C Turkey
93 O17 **Tohmajärvi** Itä-Suomi, SE Finland
93 L16 **Toholampi** Länsi-Soumi, W Finland
Tōhōm *see* Mandah
23 X12 **Tohopekaliga, Lake** ◎ Florida, SE USA
164 M14 **Toi** Shizuoka, Honshū, S Japan
190 B15 **Toi** N Niue
93 L19 **Toijala** Länsi-Suomi, SW Finland
171 P12 **Toima** Sulawesi, N Indonesia
164 D17 **Toi-misaki** Kyūshū, SW Japan
171 Q17 **Toineke** Timor, S Indonesia
Toirc, Inis *see* Inishturk
35 U6 **Toiyabe Range** ▲▲ Nevada, W USA
Tojikiston, Jumhurii *see* Tajikistan
147 R12 **Tojikobod** *Rus.* Tadzhikabad. C Tajikistan
164 G12 **Tōjō** Hiroshima, Honshū, SW Japan
39 T10 **Tok** Alaska, USA
164 K13 **Tōkai** Aichi, Honshū, SW Japan
111 N21 **Tokaj** Borsod-Abaúj-Zemplén, NE Hungary
165 N11 **Tōkamachi** Niigata, Honshū, C Japan
185 D25 **Tokanui** Southland, South Island, New Zealand
80 I7 **Tokar** *var.* Ṭawkar. Red Sea, NE Sudan
136 L12 **Tokat** Tokat, N Turkey
136 L12 **Tokat** ◈ *province* N Turkey
163 X15 **Tŏkchŏk-gundo** *island group* NW South Korea
Tōke *see* Taka Atoll
190 J9 **Tokelau** ◇ *NZ overseas territory* W Polynesia
Tökéterebes *see* Trebišov
Tokhtamyshbek *see* Tŭkhtamish
24 M6 **Tokio** Texas, SW USA
Tokio *see* Tōkyō
189 W11 **Toki Point** *point* NW Wake Island
Tokkuztara *see* Gongliu
147 V7 **Tokmak** *Kir.* Tokmok. Chuyskaya Oblast', N Kyrgyzstan
117 V9 **Tokmak** *var.* Velykyy Tokmak. Zaporiz'ka Oblast', SE Ukraine
Tokmok *see* Tokmak
184 Q8 **Tokomaru Bay** Gisborne, North Island, New Zealand
165 V3 **Tokoro** Hokkaidō, NE Japan
184 M8 **Tokoroa** Waikato, North Island, New Zealand
76 K14 **Tokounou** C Guinea
38 M12 **Toksook Bay** Alaska, USA
Toksu *see* Xinhe
Toksum *see* Toksun
158 L6 **Toksun** *var.* Toksum. Xinjiang Uygur Zizhiqu, NW China
147 T8 **Toktogul** Talasskaya Oblast', NW Kyrgyzstan
147 T9 **Toktogul'skoye Vodokhranilishche** ▣ W Kyrgyzstan
Toktomush *see* Tŭkhtamish
193 Y14 **Toku** *island* Vava'u Group, N Tonga
165 U16 **Tokunoshima** Kagoshima, Tokuno-shima, SW Japan
165 U16 **Tokuno-shima** *island* Nansei-shotō, SW Japan
164 I14 **Tokushima** *var.* Tokusima. Tokushima, Shikoku, SW Japan
164 H14 **Tokushima** *off.* Tokushima-ken, *var.* Tokusima. ◈ *prefecture* Shikoku, SW Japan
Tokushima-ken *see* Tokushima
Tokusima *see* Tokushima
164 E13 **Tokuyama** Yamaguchi, Honshū, SW Japan
165 N13 **Tōkyō** *var.* Tokio. ● (Japan) Tōkyō, Honshū, S Japan
165 O13 **Tōkyō** *off.* Tōkyō-to. ◈ *capital district* Honshū, S Japan
Tōkyō-to *see* Tōkyō
145 T12 **Tokyrau** ≈ C Kazakhstan
149 O3 **Tokzār** *Pash.* Tukzār. Sar-e Pol, N Afghanistan
145 W13 **Tokzhaylau** *prev.* Dzerzhinskoye. Almaty, SE Kazakhstan
189 U12 **Tol** *atoll* Chuuk Islands, C Micronesia
184 Q9 **Tolaga Bay** Gisborne, North Island, New Zealand
172 I7 **Tôlañaro** *prev.* Faradofay, Fort-Dauphin. Toliara, SE Madagascar
162 D6 **Tolbo** Bayan-Ölgiy, W Mongolia
Tolbukhin *see* Dobrich
60 G11 **Toledo** Paraná, S Brazil
54 G8 **Toledo** Norte de Santander, N Colombia
105 N9 **Toledo** *anc.* Toletum. Castilla-La Mancha, C Spain
30 M14 **Toledo** Illinois, N USA
29 W13 **Toledo** Iowa, C USA
31 R11 **Toledo** Ohio, N USA
32 F12 **Toledo** Oregon, NW USA
32 G9 **Toledo** Washington, NW USA
42 F3 **Toledo** ◈ *district* S Belize
105 M9 **Toledo** ◈ *province* Castilla-La Mancha, C Spain
25 Y7 **Toledo Bend Reservoir** ▣ Louisiana/Texas, SW USA
104 M10 **Toledo, Montes de** ▲▲ C Spain
106 J12 **Tolentino** Marche, C Italy
Toletum *see* Toledo
94 H10 **Tolga** Hedmark, S Norway
158 J3 **Toli** Xinjiang Uygur Zizhiqu, NW China
172 H7 **Toliara** *var.* Toliary; *prev.* Tuléar. Toliara, SW Madagascar
172 H7 **Toliara** ◈ *province* SW Madagascar
Toliary *see* Toliara
54 D11 **Tolima** *off.* Departmento del Tolima. ◈ *province* C Colombia
Tolima, Departamento del *see* Tolima
171 N11 **Tolitoli** Sulawesi, C Indonesia
95 K22 **Tollarp** Skåne, S Sweden
100 N9 **Tollense** ≈ NE Germany
100 N10 **Tollensesee** ◎ NE Germany
36 K13 **Tolleson** Arizona, SW USA
146 M13 **Tollimarjon** *Rus.* Talimardzhan. Qashqadaryo Viloyati, S Uzbekistan
Tolmein *see* Tolmin
106 J6 **Tolmezzo** Friuli-Venezia Giulia, NE Italy
109 S11 **Tolmin** *Ger.* Tolmein, *It.* Tolmino. W Slovenia
Tolmino *see* Tolmin
111 J25 **Tolna** *Ger.* Tolnau. Tolna, S Hungary
111 I24 **Tolna** *off.* Tolna Megye. ◈ *county* SW Hungary
Tolna Megye *see* Tolna
Tolnau *see* Tolna
79 I20 **Tolo** Bandundu, W Dem. Rep. Congo
Tolochin *see* Talachyn
190 D12 **Toloke** Île Futuna, W Wallis and Futuna
30 M13 **Tolono** Illinois, N USA
105 Q3 **Tolosa** País Vasco, N Spain
Tolosa *see* Toulouse
171 O13 **Tolo, Teluk** *bay* Sulawesi, C Indonesia
39 R9 **Tolovana River** ≈ Alaska, USA
123 U10 **Tolstoy, Mys** *cape* E Russian Federation
63 G15 **Toltén** Araucanía, C Chile
63 G15 **Toltén, Río** ≈ S Chile
54 E6 **Tolú** Sucre, NW Colombia
41 O14 **Toluca** *var.* Toluca de Lerdo. México, S Mexico
Toluca de Lerdo *see* Toluca
41 O14 **Toluca, Nevado de** ⛰ C Mexico
127 R6 **Tol'yatti** *prev.* Stavropol'. Samarskaya Oblast', W Russian Federation
77 O12 **Toma** NW Burkina
30 K7 **Tomah** Wisconsin, N USA
30 L5 **Tomahawk** Wisconsin, N USA
117 T8 **Tomakivka** Dnipropetrovs'ka Oblast', E Ukraine
165 S4 **Tomakomai** Hokkaidō, NE Japan
165 S2 **Tomamae** Hokkaidō, NE Japan
104 G9 **Tomar** Santarém, W Portugal
123 T13 **Tomari** Ostrov Sakhalin, Sakhalinskaya Oblast', SE Russian Federation
115 C16 **Tómaros** ▲ W Greece
Tomaschow *see* Tomaszów Mazowiecki
Tomaschow *see* Tomaszów Lubelski
61 E16 **Tomás Gomensoro** Artigas, N Uruguay
117 N7 **Tomashpil'** Vinnyts'ka Oblast', C Ukraine
Tomaszów *see* Tomaszów Mazowiecki
111 P15 **Tomaszów Lubelski** *Ger.* Tomaschow. Lubelskie, E Poland
Tomaszów Mazowiecka *see* Tomaszów Mazowiecki
110 L13 **Tomaszów Mazowiecki** *var.* Tomaszów Mazowiecka; *prev.* Tomaszów, *Ger.* Tomaschow. Łódzkie, C Poland
40 J13 **Tomatlán** Jalisco, C Mexico
81 F15 **Tombe** Jonglei, S Sudan
23 N4 **Tombigbee River** ≈ Alabama/Mississippi, S USA
82 A10 **Tomboco** Dem. Rep. Congo, NW Angola
77 O10 **Tombouctou** *Eng.* Timbuktu. Tombouctou, N Mali
77 N9 **Tombouctou** ◈ *region* W Mali
37 N16 **Tombstone** Arizona, SW USA
83 A15 **Tombua** *Port.* Porto Alexandre. Namibe, SW Angola
83 J19 **Tom Burke** Limpopo, NE South Africa
146 L9 **Tomdibuloq** *Rus.* Tamdybulak. Navoiy Viloyati, N Uzbekistan
146 L9 **Tomditov-Togʻlari** ▲▲ N Uzbekistan
62 G13 **Tomé** Bío Bío, C Chile
58 L12 **Tomé-Açu** Pará, NE Brazil
95 L23 **Tomelilla** Skåne, S Sweden
105 O10 **Tomelloso** Castilla-La Mancha, C Spain
14 H10 **Tomiko Lake** ◎ Ontario, S Canada
77 N12 **Tominian** Ségou, C Mali
171 N12 **Tomini, Gulf of** *var.* Teluk Tomini; *prev.* Teluk Gorontalo. *bay* Sulawesi, C Indonesia
Tomini, Teluk *see* Tomini, Gulf of
165 Q11 **Tomioka** Fukushima, Honshū, C Japan
113 G14 **Tomislavgrad** ◈ Federacija Bosna I Hercegovina, SW Bosnia and Herzegovina
181 O9 **Tomkinson Ranges** ▲▲ South Australia/Western Australia
123 Q11 **Tommot** Respublika Sakha (Yakutiya), NE Russian Federation
171 Q11 **Tomohon** Sulawesi, N Indonesia
54 K9 **Tomo, Río** ≈ E Colombia
113 L21 **Tomorrit, Mali i** ▲ S Albania
9 S17 **Tompkins** Saskatchewan, S Canada
20 K8 **Tompkinsville** Kentucky, S USA
171 N11 **Tompo** Sulawesi, N Indonesia
180 I8 **Tom Price** Western Australia
122 J12 **Tomsk** Tomskaya Oblast', C Russian Federation
122 I11 **Tomskaya Oblast'** ◈ *province* C Russian Federation
18 K16 **Toms River** New Jersey, NE USA
Tom Steed Lake *see* Tom Steed Reservoir
26 L12 **Tom Steed Reservoir** *var.* Tom Steed Lake. ▣ Oklahoma, C USA
171 U13 **Tomu** Papua, E Indonesia
158 H6 **Tomur Feng** *var.* Pobeda Peak, *Rus.* Pik Pobedy. ▲ China/Kyrgyzstan *see also* Pobedy, Pik
Tomür Feng *see* Pobedy, Pik
189 N13 **Tomworoahlang** Pohnpei, E Micronesia
41 U17 **Tonalá** Chiapas, SE Mexico
106 F6 **Tonale, Passo del** *pass* N Italy
164 I11 **Tonami** Toyama, Honshū, SW Japan
58 C12 **Tonantins** Amazonas, W Brazil
32 K6 **Tonasket** Washington, NW USA
55 Y9 **Tonate** *var.* Macouria. N French Guiana
18 D10 **Tonawanda** New York, NE USA
171 Q11 **Tondano** Sulawesi, C Indonesia
104 H7 **Tondela** Viseu, N Portugal
95 F24 **Tønder** *Ger.* Tondern. Sønderjylland, SW Denmark
Tondern *see* Tønder
143 N4 **Tonekābon** *var.* Shahsawar, Tonkābon; *prev.* Shahsavār. Māzandarān, N Iran
Tonezh *see* Tonyezh
193 Y14 **Tonga** *off.* Kingdom of Tonga, *var.* Friendly Islands. ◆ *monarchy* SW Pacific Ocean
175 R9 **Tonga** *island group* SW Pacific Ocean
83 K23 **Tongaat** KwaZulu/Natal, E South Africa
Tonga, Kingdom of *see* Tonga
161 Q13 **Tong'an** *var.* Datong, Tong an. Fujian, SE China
Tong an *see* Tong'an
27 Q4 **Tonganoxie** Kansas, C USA
39 Y13 **Tongass National Forest** *reserve* Alaska, USA
193 Y16 **Tongatapu** ✈ Tongatapu, S Tonga
193 Y16 **Tongatapu** *island* Tongatapu Group, S Tonga
193 Y16 **Tongatapu Group** *island group* S Tonga
175 S9 **Tonga Trench** *undersea feature* S Pacific Ocean
161 N8 **Tongbai Shan** ▲▲ C China
161 P8 **Tongcheng** Anhui, E China
160 L6 **Tongchuan** Shaanxi, C China
160 L12 **Tongdao** *var.* Tongdao Dongzu Zizhixian; *prev.* Shuangjiang. Hunan, S China
Tongdao Dongzu Zizhixian *see* Tongdao
159 T11 **Tongde** *var.* Gabasumdo. Qinghai, C China
99 K19 **Tongeren** *Fr.* Tongres. Limburg, NE Belgium
163 Y14 **Tonghae** NE South Korea
160 G13 **Tonghai** *var.* Xiushan. Yunnan, SW China
163 X8 **Tonghe** Heilongjiang, NE China
163 W11 **Tonghua** Jilin, NE China
163 Z6 **Tongjiang** Heilongjiang, NE China
163 Y13 **Tongjosŏn-man** *prev.* Broughton Bay. *bay* E North Korea
163 V7 **Tongken He** ≈ NE China
167 T7 **Tongking, Gulf of** *Chin.* Beibu Wan, *Vtn.* Vinh Bắc Bộ. *gulf* China/Vietnam
163 U10 **Tongliao** Nei Mongol Zizhiqu, N China
161 Q9 **Tongling** Anhui, E China
161 R9 **Tonglu** Zhejiang, SE China
187 R14 **Tongoa** *island* Shepherd Islands, S Vanuatu
62 G9 **Tongoy** Coquimbo, C Chile
160 L11 **Tongren** Guizhou, S China
159 T11 **Tongren** *var.* Rongwo. Qinghai, C China
Tongres *see* Tongeren
153 U11 **Tongsa** *var.* Tongsa Dzong. C Bhutan
Tongsa Dzong *see* Tongsa
Tongshan Fuding, Fujian, China
Tongshan *see* Xuzhou, Jiangsu, China
Tongshi *see* Wuzhishan
159 P12 **Tongtian He** ≈ C China
96 I6 **Tongue** N Scotland, UK
44 H3 **Tongue of the Ocean** *strait* C Bahamas
33 X10 **Tongue River** ≈ Montana, NW USA
33 W11 **Tongue River Reservoir** ▣ Montana, NW USA
159 V11 **Tongwei** Gansu, C China
159 W9 **Tongxin** Ningxia, N China
163 U9 **Tongyu** *var.* Kaitong. Jilin, NE China
160 J11 **Tongzi** Guizhou, S China
162 F8 **Tonhil** *var.* Dzüyl. Govĭ-Altay, SW Mongolia
40 G5 **Tónichi** Sonora, NW Mexico
81 D14 **Tonj** Warab, SW Sudan
152 H13 **Tonk** Rājasthān, N India
Tonkābon *see* Tonekābon
27 N8 **Tonkawa** Oklahoma, C USA
167 Q12 **Tônlé Sap** *Eng.* Great Lake. ◎ W Cambodia
102 L14 **Tonneins** Lot-et-Garonne, SW France
103 Q7 **Tonnerre** Yonne, C France
Tonoas *see* Dublon
35 U8 **Tonopah** Nevada, W USA
164 H13 **Tonoshō** Okayama, Shōdo-shima, SW Japan
43 S17 **Tonosí** Los Santos, S Panama
95 H16 **Tønsberg** Vestfold, S Norway
39 T11 **Tonsina** Alaska, USA
95 D17 **Tonstad** Vest-Agder, S Norway
193 X15 **Tonumea** *island* Nomuka Group, W Tonga
137 O11 **Tonya** Trabzon, NE Turkey
119 K20 **Tonyezh** *Rus.* Tonezh. Homyel'skaya Voblasts', SE Belarus
36 L3 **Tooele** Utah, W USA
122 L13 **Toora-Khem** Respublika Tyva, S Russian Federation
183 O5 **Toorale East** New South Wales, SE Australia
83 H25 **Toorberg** ▲ S South Africa
118 G5 **Tootsi** Pärnumaa, SW Estonia
183 U3 **Toowoomba** Queensland, E Australia
27 Q4 **Topeka** *state capital* Kansas, C USA
111 M18 **Topľa** *Hung.* Toplya. ≈ NE Slovakia
122 J12 **Topki** Kemerovskaya Oblast', S Russian Federation
Toplicza *see* Toplița
116 J10 **Toplița** *Ger.* Töplitz, *Hung.* Maroshevíz; *prev.* Toplița Română, *Hung.* Oláh-Toplicza, Toplicza. Harghita, C Romania
Toplița Română/Töplitz *see* Toplița
Toplya *see* Topľa
111 I20 **Topoľčany** *Hung.* Nagytapolcsány. Nitriansky Kraj, W Slovakia
40 G8 **Topolobampo** Sinaloa, C Mexico
116 I13 **Topoloveni** Argeș, S Romania
114 L11 **Topolovgrad** *prev.* Kavakli. Khaskovo, S Bulgaria
Topolya *see* Bačka Topola
124 I6 **Topozero, Ozero** ◎ NW Russian Federation
32 J10 **Toppenish** Washington, NW USA
181 P4 **Top Springs Roadhouse** Northern Territory, N Australia
189 U11 **Tora** *island* Chuuk, C Micronesia
Toraigh *see* Tory Island
189 U11 **Tora Island Pass** *passage* Chuuk Islands, C Micronesia
143 U5 **Torbat-e Ḩeydarīyeh** *var.* Turbat-i-Haidari. Khorāsān-Razavī, NE Iran
143 V5 **Torbat-e Jām** *var.* Turbat-i-Jam. Khorāsān-Razavī, NE Iran
39 Q11 **Torbert, Mount** ▲ Alaska, USA
31 P6 **Torch Lake** ◎ Michigan, N USA
Törcsvár *see* Bran
Torda *see* Turda
104 L6 **Tordesillas** Castilla-León, N Spain
92 K13 **Töre** Norrbotten, N Sweden
95 L17 **Töreboda** Västra Götaland, S Sweden
95 J21 **Torekov** Skåne, S Sweden
92 O3 **Torell Land** *physical region* SW Svalbard
117 Y8 **Torez** Donets'ka Oblast', SE Ukraine
101 N14 **Torgau** Sachsen, E Germany
Torgay *see* Turgay
Torgay Üstirti *see* Turgayskaya Stolovaya Strana
Torghay *see* Turgay
95 N22 **Torhamn** Blekinge, S Sweden
99 C17 **Torhout** West-Vlaanderen, W Belgium
106 B8 **Torino** *Eng.* Turin. Piemonte, NW Italy
165 U15 **Tori-shima** *island* Izu-shotō, SE Japan
81 F16 **Torit** Eastern Equatoria, S Sudan
186 H6 **Toriu** New Britain, E Papua New Guinea
148 M4 **Torkestān, Selseleh-ye Band-e** *var.* Bandi-i Turkistan. ▲▲ NW Afghanistan
104 L7 **Tormes** ≈ W Spain
Tornacum *see* Tournai
Torneå *see* Tornio
92 K12 **Torneälven** *var.* Tornionjoki, *Fin.* Tornionjoki. ≈ Finland/Sweden
92 I11 **Torneträsk** ◎ N Sweden
13 O4 **Torngat Mountains** ▲▲ Newfoundland and Labrador, NE Canada
24 H8 **Tornillo** Texas, SW USA
92 K13 **Tornio** *Swe.* Torneå. Lappi, NW Finland
Torniojoki/Tornionjoki *see* Torneälven
61 B23 **Tornquist** Buenos Aires, E Argentina
104 L6 **Toro** Castilla-León, N Spain
62 H9 **Toro, Cerro del** ▲ N Chile
77 R12 **Torodi** Tillabéri, SW Niger
Törökbecse *see* Novi Bečej
186 J7 **Torokina** Bougainville Island, NE Papua New Guinea
111 L23 **Törökszentmiklós** Jász-Nagykun-Szolnok, E Hungary
42 G7 **Torola, Río** ≈ El Salvador/Honduras
Toronaíos, Kólpos *see* Kassándras, Kólpos
14 H15 **Toronto** *province capital* Ontario, S Canada
31 V12 **Toronto** Ohio, N USA
Toronto *see* Lester B. Pearson
27 P6 **Toronto Lake** ▣ Kansas, C USA
35 V16 **Toro Peak** ▲ California, W USA
124 H16 **Toropets** Tverskaya Oblast', W Russian Federation
81 G18 **Tororo** E Uganda
136 H16 **Toros Dağları** *Eng.* Taurus Mountains. ▲▲ S Turkey
183 N13 **Torquay** Victoria, SE Australia
97 J24 **Torquay** SW England, UK
104 M5 **Torquemada** Castilla-León, N Spain
35 S16 **Torrance** California, W USA
104 G12 **Torrão** Setúbal, S Portugal
104 H8 **Torre, Alto da** ▲ C Portugal
107 K18 **Torre Annunziata** Campania, S Italy
105 T8 **Torreblanca** País Valenciano, E Spain
104 L15 **Torrecilla** ▲ S Spain
105 P4 **Torrecilla en Cameros** La Rioja, N Spain
105 N13 **Torredelcampo** Andalucía, S Spain
107 K17 **Torre del Greco** Campania, S Italy
104 I6 **Torre de Moncorvo** *var.* Moncorvo, Tôrre de Moncorvo. Bragança, N Portugal
104 J9 **Torrejoncillo** Extremadura, W Spain
105 O8 **Torrejón de Ardoz** Madrid, C Spain
105 N7 **Torrelaguna** Madrid, C Spain
105 N2 **Torrelavega** Cantabria, N Spain
107 M16 **Torremaggiore** Puglia, SE Italy
104 M15 **Torremolinos** Andalucía, S Spain
182 I6 **Torrens, Lake** *salt lake* South Australia
105 S10 **Torrent** *Cas.* Torrente, *var.* Torrent de l'Horta. País Valenciano, E Spain
Torrent de l'Horta/Torrente *see* Torrent
40 L8 **Torreón** Coahuila de Zaragoza, NE Mexico
105 R13 **Torre Pacheco** Murcia, SE Spain
106 A8 **Torre Pellice** Piemonte, NE Italy
105 O13 **Torreperogil** Andalucía, S Spain
61 J15 **Torres** Rio Grande do Sul, S Brazil
Torrès, Îles *see* Torres Islands
187 Q11 **Torres Islands** *Fr.* Îles Torrès. *island group* N Vanuatu
104 G9 **Torres Novas** Santarém, C Portugal
181 V1 **Torres Strait** *strait* Australia/Papua New Guinea
104 F10 **Torres Vedras** Lisboa, C Portugal
105 S13 **Torrevieja** País Valenciano, E Spain
186 B6 **Torricelli Mountains** ▲▲ NW Papua New Guinea
96 G8 **Torridon, Loch** *inlet* NW Scotland, UK
106 D9 **Torriglia** Liguria, NW Italy
104 M9 **Torrijos** Castilla-La Mancha, C Spain
18 L12 **Torrington** Connecticut, NE USA
33 Z15 **Torrington** Wyoming, C USA
Torröjen *see* Torrön
94 F16 **Torrön** *prev.* Torröjen. ◎ C Sweden
105 N15 **Torrox** Andalucía, S Spain
94 N13 **Torsåker** Gävleborg, C Sweden
95 N21 **Torsås** Kalmar, S Sweden
95 J14 **Torsby** Värmland, C Sweden
95 N16 **Torshälla** Södermanland, C Sweden
95 B19 **Tórshavn** *Dan.* Thorshavn. ○ Streymoy, N Faeroe Islands Europe
Torshiz *see* Kāshmar
146 I9 **To'rtkokʻl** *var* Türtkül, *Rus.* Turtkul'; *prev.* Petroaleksandrovsk. Qoraqalpogʻiston Respublikasi, W Uzbekistan
Tortoise Islands *see* Colón, Archipiélago de
45 T9 **Tortola** *island* C British Virgin Islands
106 D9 **Tortona** *anc.* Dertona. Piemonte, NW Italy
107 L23 **Tortorici** Sicilia, Italy, C Mediterranean Sea
105 U7 **Tortosa** *anc.* Dertosa. Cataluña, E Spain
Tortosa *see* Ṭarṭūs
105 U7 **Tortosa, Cap** *cape* E Spain
44 L8 **Tortue, Île de la** *var.* Tortuga Island. *island* N Haiti
55 Y10 **Tortue, Montagne** ▲ C French Guiana
Tortuga, Isla *see* La Tortuga, Isla
Tortuga Island *see* Tortue, Île de la
54 C11 **Tortugas, Golfo** *gulf* W Colombia
45 T5 **Tortuguero, Laguna** *lagoon* N Puerto Rico
137 Q12 **Tortum** Erzurum, NE Turkey
Torugart, Pereval *see* Turugart Shankou
137 O12 **Torul** Gümüşhane, NE Turkey
110 J10 **Toruń** *Ger.* Thorn. Toruń, Kujawsko-pomorskie, C Poland
95 K20 **Torup** Halland, S Sweden
118 I6 **Tõrva** *Ger.* Törwa. Valgamaa, S Estonia
Törwa *see* Tõrva
96 D13 **Tory Island** *Ir.* Toraigh. *island* NW Ireland

◆ Country ● Country Capital ◇ Dependent Territory ○ Dependent Territory Capital ◈ Administrative Regions ✈ International Airport ▲ Mountain ▲▲ Mountain Range ⛰ Volcano ≈ River ◎ Lake ▣ Reservoir

111 N19 **Torysa** Hung. Tarca. ≈ NE Slovakia
Törzburg see Bran
124 J16 **Torzhok** Tverskaya Oblast', W Russian Federation
164 F15 **Tosa-Shimizu** var. Tosasimizu. Kôchi, Shikoku, SW Japan
Tosasimizu see Tosa-Shimizu
164 G15 **Tosa-wan** bay SW Japan
83 H21 **Tosca** North-West, N South Africa
106 F12 **Toscana** Eng. Tuscany. ⬖ region C Italy
107 E14 **Toscano, Arcipelago** Eng. Tuscan Archipelago. island group C Italy
106 G10 **Tosco-Emiliano, Appennino** Eng. Tuscan-Emilian Mountains. ▲▲ C Italy
Tōsei see Tungshih
165 N15 **To-shima** island Izu-shotō, SE Japan
147 Q9 **Toshkent** Eng./Rus. Tashkent. ● Toshkent Viloyati, E Uzbekistan
147 Q9 **Toshkent** ✕ Toshkent Viloyati, E Uzbekistan
147 P9 **Toshkent Viloyati** Rus. Tashkentskaya Oblast'. ⬖ province E Uzbekistan
124 H13 **Tosno** Leningradskaya Oblast', NW Russian Federation
159 Q10 **Toson Hu** ◎ C China
162 H6 **Tosontsengel** Dzavhan, NW Mongolia
162 J6 **Tosontsengel** var. Tsengel. Hövsgöl, N Mongolia
146 I8 **Tosquduq Qumlari** var. Goshquduq Qum, Taskuduk, Peski. desert W Uzbekistan
105 U4 **Tossal de l'Orri** var. Llorri. ▲ NE Spain
61 A15 **Tostado** Santa Fe, C Argentina
118 F6 **Tõstamaa** Ger. Testama. Pärnumaa, SW Estonia
100 I10 **Tostedt** Niedersachsen, NW Germany
136 J11 **Tosya** Kastamonu, N Turkey
95 F15 **Totak** ◎ S Norway
105 R13 **Totana** Murcia, SE Spain
94 H13 **Toten** physical region S Norway
83 G18 **Toteng** North-West, C Botswana
102 M3 **Tôtes** Seine-Maritime, N France
Totigi see Tochigi
Totio see Tochio
Totis see Tata
189 U13 **Totiw** island Chuuk, C Micronesia
125 N13 **Tot'ma** var. Totma. Vologodskaya Oblast', NW Russian Federation
Tot'ma see Sukhona
55 V9 **Totness** Coronie, N Suriname
42 C5 **Totonicapán** Totonicapán, W Guatemala
42 A2 **Totonicapán** off. Departamento de Totonicapán. ⬖ department W Guatemala
Totonicapán, Departamento de see Totonicapán
61 B18 **Totoras** Santa Fe, C Argentina
187 Y15 **Totoya** island S Fiji
183 Q7 **Tottenham** New South Wales, SE Australia
164 I12 **Tottori** Tottori, Honshū, SW Japan
164 H12 **Tottori** off. Tottori-ken. ⬖ prefecture Honshū, SW Japan
Tottori-ken see Tottori
76 I6 **Touâjîl** Tiris Zemmour, N Mauritania
76 L15 **Touba** W Ivory Coast
76 G11 **Touba** W Senegal
74 E7 **Toubkal, Jbel** ▲ W Morocco
32 K10 **Touchet** Washington, NW USA
103 P7 **Toucy** Yonne, C France
77 O12 **Tougan** W Burkina
74 L7 **Touggourt** NE Algeria
77 Q12 **Tougouri** N Burkina
76 J13 **Tougué** NW Guinea
76 K12 **Toukoto** Kayes, W Mali
103 S5 **Toul** Meurthe-et-Moselle, NE France
76 L16 **Touléplou** var. Toulobli. W Ivory Coast
161 S14 **Touliu** C Taiwan
15 U3 **Toulnustouc** ≈ Québec, SE Canada
Toulobli see Touléplou
103 T16 **Toulon** anc. Telo Martius, Tilio Martius. Var, SE France
30 K12 **Toulon** Illinois, N USA
102 M15 **Toulouse** anc. Tolosa. Haute-Garonne, S France
102 M15 **Toulouse** ✕ Haute-Garonne, S France
77 N16 **Toumodi** C Ivory Coast
74 G9 **Tounassine, Hamada** hill range W Algeria
166 M7 **Toungoo** Pegu, C Myanmar (Burma)
102 L8 **Touraine** cultural region C France
Tourane see Đà Nẵng
103 P1 **Tourcoing** Nord, N France
104 F2 **Touriñán, Cabo** cape NW Spain
76 J6 **Tourine** Tiris Zemmour, N Mauritania
102 J3 **Tourlaville** Manche, N France
99 D19 **Tournai** var. Tournay, Dut. Doornik; anc. Tornacum. Hainaut, SW Belgium
102 L16 **Tournay** Hautes-Pyrénées, S France
Tournay see Tournai
103 R12 **Tournon** Ardèche, E France
103 R9 **Tournus** Saône-et-Loire, C France
59 Q14 **Touros** Rio Grande do Norte, E Brazil
102 L8 **Tours** anc. Caesarodunum, Turoni. Indre-et-Loire, C France
183 Q17 **Tourville, Cape** headland Tasmania, SE Australia
162 L8 **Töv** ⬖ province C Mongolia
54 H7 **Tovar** Mérida, NW Venezuela
126 L5 **Tovarkovskiy** Tul'skaya Oblast', W Russian Federation
Tovil'-Dora see Tavildara
Tövis see Teiuş
137 V11 **Tovuz** Rus. Tauz. W Azerbaijan
165 R7 **Towada** Aomori, Honshū, C Japan
184 K3 **Towai** Northland, North Island, New Zealand
18 H12 **Towanda** Pennsylvania, NE USA
29 W4 **Tower** Minnesota, N USA
171 N12 **Towera** Sulawesi, N Indonesia
Tower Island see Genovesa, Isla
180 M13 **Tower Peak** ▲ Western Australia
35 U11 **Towne Pass** pass California, W USA
29 N3 **Towner** North Dakota, N USA
33 R10 **Townsend** Montana, NW USA
181 X6 **Townsville** Queensland, NE Australia
Towoeti Meer see Towuti, Danau
148 K4 **Towraghoudī** Herāt, NW Afghanistan
21 X3 **Towson** Maryland, NE USA
171 O13 **Towuti, Danau** Dut. Towoeti Meer. ◎ Sulawesi, C Indonesia
Toxkan He see Ak-say
24 K9 **Toyah** Texas, SW USA
165 R4 **Tōya-ko** ◎ Hokkaidō, NE Japan
164 L11 **Toyama** Toyama, Honshū, SW Japan
164 L11 **Toyama** off. Toyama-ken. ⬖ prefecture Honshū, SW Japan
Toyama-ken see Toyama
164 L11 **Toyama-wan** bay W Japan
164 H15 **Tōyo** Kōchi, Shikoku, SW Japan
Toyohara see Yuzhno-Sakhalinsk
164 L14 **Toyohashi** var. Toyohasi. Aichi, Honshū, SW Japan
Toyohasi see Toyohashi
164 L14 **Toyokawa** Aichi, Honshū, SW Japan
164 I14 **Toyooka** Hyōgo, Honshū, SW Japan
164 L13 **Toyota** Aichi, Honshū, SW Japan
165 T1 **Toyotomi** Hokkaidō, NE Japan
147 Q10 **To'ytepa** Toshkent Viloyati, E Uzbekistan
147 Q10 **To'ytepa** Rus. Toytepa. Toshkent Viloyati, E Uzbekistan
Toytepa see To'ytepa
74 M6 **Tozeur** var. Tawzar. W Tunisia
39 Q8 **Tozi, Mount** ▲ Alaska, USA
137 Q9 **Tqvarch'eli** Rus. Tkvarcheli. NW Georgia
Trâblous see Tripoli
137 O11 **Trabzon** Eng. Trebizond; anc. Trapezus. Trabzon, NE Turkey
137 O11 **Trabzon** Eng. Trebizond. ⬖ province NE Turkey
13 P13 **Tracadie** New Brunswick, SE Canada
Trachenberg see Żmigród
15 O11 **Tracy** Québec, SE Canada
35 O8 **Tracy** California, W USA
29 S10 **Tracy** Minnesota, N USA
20 K10 **Tracy City** Tennessee, S USA
106 D7 **Tradate** Lombardia, N Italy
84 F6 **Traena Bank** undersea feature E Norwegian Sea
29 W13 **Traer** Iowa, C USA
104 J16 **Trafalgar, Cabo de** cape SW Spain
Traiectum ad Mosam/Traiectum Tungorum see Maastricht
Tráigh Mhór see Tramore
9 O17 **Trail** British Columbia, SW Canada
58 B11 **Traíra, Serra do** ▲▲ NW Brazil
109 V5 **Traisen** Niederösterreich, NE Austria
109 W4 **Traisen** ≈ NE Austria
109 X4 **Traiskirchen** Niederösterreich, NE Austria
Trajani Portus see Civitavecchia
Trajectum ad Rhenum see Utrecht
119 H14 **Trakai** Ger. Traken, Pol. Troki. Vilnius, SE Lithuania
Traken see Trakai
97 B20 **Tralee** Ir. Trá Lí. SW Ireland
97 A20 **Tralee Bay** Ir. Bá Thrá Lí. bay SW Ireland
Trá Lí see Tralee
Trälleborg see Trelleborg
Tralles Aydin see Aydın
61 J16 **Tramandaí** Rio Grande do Sul, S Brazil
108 C7 **Tramelan** Bern, W Switzerland
Trá Mhór see Tramore
97 E20 **Tramore** Ir. Tráigh Mhór, Trá Mhór. Waterford, S Ireland
95 L18 **Tranås** Jönköping, S Sweden
62 J7 **Trancas** Tucumán, N Argentina
104 I7 **Trancoso** Guarda, N Portugal
95 H22 **Tranebjerg** Århus, C Denmark
95 K19 **Tranemo** Västra Götaland, S Sweden
167 N16 **Trang** Trang, S Thailand
171 V15 **Trangan, Pulau** island Kepulauan Aru, E Indonesia
Trâng Dinh see Thất Khê
183 Q7 **Trangie** New South Wales, SE Australia
94 K12 **Trängslet** Dalarna, C Sweden
107 N16 **Trani** Puglia, SE Italy
61 F17 **Tranqueras** Rivera, NE Uruguay
63 G17 **Tranqui, Isla** island S Chile
39 V6 **Trans-Alaska pipeline** oil pipeline Alaska, USA
195 Q10 **Transantarctic Mountains** ▲▲ Antarctica
Transcarpathian Oblast see Zakarpats'ka Oblast'
Transilvania see Transylvania
Transilvaniei, Alpi see Carpaţii Meridionali
Transjordan see Jordan
172 L11 **Transkei Basin** undersea feature SW Indian Ocean
117 O10 **Transnistria** cultural region E Moldavia
122 E9 **Trans-Siberian Railway** railroad Russian Federation
Transsylvanische Alpen/Transylvanian Alps see Carpaţii Meridionali
94 K12 **Transtrand** Dalarna, C Sweden
116 G10 **Transylvania** Eng. Ardeal, Transilvania, Ger. Siebenbürgen, Hung. Erdély. cultural region NW Romania
167 S14 **Tra Ôn** Vinh Long, S Vietnam
107 H23 **Trapani** anc. Drepanum. Sicilia, Italy, C Mediterranean Sea
167 S12 **Trâpeăng Vêng** Kâmpóng Thum, C Cambodia
Trapezus see Trabzon
114 L9 **Trapoklovo** Sliven, C Bulgaria
183 P13 **Traralgon** Victoria, SE Australia
76 H9 **Trarza** ⬖ region SW Mauritania
Trasimenischersee see Trasimeno, Lago
106 H12 **Trasimeno, Lago** Eng. Lake of Perugia, Ger. Trasimenischersee. ◎ C Italy
95 J20 **Träslövsläge** Halland, S Sweden
Trás-os-Montes see Cucumbi
104 I6 **Trás-os-Montes e Alto Douro** former province N Portugal
167 Q12 **Trat** var. Bang Phra. Trat, S Thailand
Trá Tholl, Inis see Inishtrahull
Traù see Trogir
109 T4 **Traun** Oberösterreich, N Austria
109 S5 **Traun** ≈ N Austria
Traun, Lake see Traunsee
101 N23 **Traunreut** Bayern, SE Germany
109 S5 **Traunsee** var. Gmundner See, Eng. Lake Traun. ◎ N Austria
Trautenau see Trutnov
21 P11 **Travelers Rest** South Carolina, SE USA
182 L8 **Travellers Lake** seasonal lake New South Wales, SE Australia
31 P6 **Traverse City** Michigan, N USA
29 R7 **Traverse, Lake** ◎ Minnesota/South Dakota, N USA
185 I16 **Travers, Mount** ▲ South Island, New Zealand
9 P17 **Travers Reservoir** ⊠ Alberta, SW Canada
167 T14 **Tra Vinh** var. Phu Vinh. Tra Vinh, S Vietnam
25 S10 **Travis, Lake** ⊠ Texas, SW USA
112 H12 **Travnik** ⬖ Federacija Bosna I Hercegovina, C Bosnia and Herzegovina
109 V11 **Trbovlje** Ger. Trifail. C Slovenia
23 V13 **Treasure Island** Florida, SE USA
Treasure State see Montana
186 I8 **Treasury Islands** island group NW Solomon Islands
106 D9 **Trebbia** anc. Trebia. ≈ NW Italy
100 N8 **Trebel** ≈ NE Germany
103 O16 **Trèbes** Aude, S France
Trebia see Trebbia
111 F18 **Třebíč** Ger. Trebitsch. Vysočina, C Czech Republic
113 I16 **Trebinje** ⬖ Republika Srpska, S Bosnia and Herzegovina
Trebišnica see Trebišnjica
113 H16 **Trebišnjica** var. Trebišnica. ≈ S Bosnia and Herzegovina
111 N20 **Trebišov** Hung. Tőketerebes. Košický Kraj, E Slovakia
Trebitsch see Třebíč
Trebizond see Trabzon
Trebnitz see Trzebnica
109 V12 **Trebnje** SE Slovenia
111 D19 **Třeboň** Ger. Wittingau. Jihočeský Kraj, S Czech Republic
104 J15 **Trebujena** Andalucía, S Spain
100 I7 **Treene** ≈ N Germany
Tree Planters State see Nebraska
109 S9 **Treffen** Kärnten, S Austria
Trefynwy see Monmouth
102 G5 **Tréguier** Côtes d'Armor, NW France
61 G18 **Treinta y Tres** Treinta y Tres, E Uruguay
61 F18 **Treinta y Tres** ⬖ department E Uruguay
122 F11 **Trëkhgornyy** Chelyabinskaya Oblast', C Russian Federation
114 F9 **Treklyanska Reka** ≈ W Bulgaria
102 K8 **Trélazé** Maine-et-Loire, NW France
63 K17 **Trelew** Chubut, SE Argentina
95 K23 **Trelleborg** var. Trälleborg. Skåne, S Sweden
113 P15 **Trem** ▲ SE Serbia
15 N11 **Tremblant, Mont** ▲ Québec, SE Canada
99 H17 **Tremelo** Vlaams Brabant, C Belgium
107 M15 **Tremiti, Isole** island group SE Italy
30 K12 **Tremont** Illinois, N USA
36 L1 **Tremonton** Utah, W USA
105 U4 **Tremp** Cataluña, NE Spain
30 J7 **Trempealeau** Wisconsin, N USA
15 P8 **Trenche** ≈ Québec, SE Canada
15 O7 **Trenche, Lac** ◎ Québec, SE Canada
111 I20 **Trenčiansky Kraj** ⬖ region W Slovakia
111 I19 **Trenčín** Ger. Trentschin, Hung. Trencsén. Trenčiansky Kraj, W Slovakia
Trencsén see Trenčín
Trengganu see Terengganu
Trengganu, Kuala see Kuala Terengganu
61 A21 **Trenque Lauquen** Buenos Aires, E Argentina
14 J14 **Trent** ≈ Ontario, SE Canada
97 N18 **Trent** ≈ C England, UK
Trent see Trento
106 F5 **Trentino-Alto Adige** prev. Venezia Tridentina. ⬖ region N Italy
106 G6 **Trento** Eng. Trent, Ger. Trient; anc. Tridentum. Trentino-Alto Adige, N Italy
14 J15 **Trenton** Ontario, SE Canada
23 V10 **Trenton** Florida, SE USA
23 R1 **Trenton** Georgia, SE USA
31 S10 **Trenton** Michigan, N USA
27 S2 **Trenton** Missouri, C USA
28 M17 **Trenton** Nebraska, C USA
18 J15 **Trenton** state capital New Jersey, NE USA
21 W10 **Trenton** North Carolina, SE USA
20 G9 **Trenton** Tennessee, S USA
36 L1 **Trenton** Utah, W USA
Trentschin see Trenčín
Treptow an der Rega see Trzebiatów
61 C23 **Tres Arroyos** Buenos Aires, E Argentina
61 J15 **Três Cachoeiras** Rio Grande do Sul, S Brazil
106 E7 **Trescore Balneario** Lombardia, N Italy
41 V17 **Tres Cruces, Cerro** ▲ SE Mexico
57 K18 **Tres Cruces, Cordillera** ▲▲ W Bolivia
113 N18 **Treska** ≈ NW FYR Macedonia
113 I14 **Treskavica** ▲▲ SE Bosnia and Herzegovina
59 J20 **Três Lagoas** Mato Grosso do Sul, SW Brazil
40 H12 **Tres Marías, Islas** island group C Mexico
59 M19 **Três Marias, Represa** ⊠ SE Brazil
63 F20 **Tres Montes, Península** headland S Chile
105 O3 **Trespaderne** Castilla-León, N Spain
60 G13 **Três Passos** Rio Grande do Sul, S Brazil
61 A23 **Tres Picos, Cerro** ▲ E Argentina
63 G17 **Tres Picos, Cerro** ▲ SW Argentina
60 I12 **Três Pinheiros** Paraná, S Brazil
59 M21 **Três Pontas** Minas Gerais, SE Brazil
Tres Puntas, Cabo see Manabique, Punta
60 P9 **Três Rios** Rio de Janeiro, SE Brazil
Tres Tabernae see Saverne
Trestenberg/Trestendorf see Tăşnad
41 R15 **Tres Valles** Veracruz-Llave, SE Mexico
94 H12 **Tretten** Oppland, S Norway
Treuburg see Olecko
101 K21 **Treuchtlingen** Bayern, S Germany
100 N13 **Treuenbrietzen** Brandenburg, E Germany
95 F16 **Treungen** Telemark, S Norway
63 H17 **Trevelin** Chubut, SW Argentina
Treves/Trèves see Trier
106 I13 **Trevi** Umbria, C Italy
106 E7 **Treviglio** Lombardia, N Italy
104 J4 **Trevinca, Peña** ▲ NW Spain
105 P3 **Treviño** Castilla-León, N Spain
106 I7 **Treviso** anc. Tarvisium. Veneto, NE Italy
97 G24 **Trevose Head** headland SW England, UK
Trg see Feldkirchen in Kärnten
183 P17 **Triabunna** Tasmania, SE Australia
21 W4 **Triangle** Virginia, NE USA
83 L18 **Triangle** Masvingo, SE Zimbabwe
115 L23 **Tría Nisía** island Kykládes, Greece, Aegean Sea
Triberg see Triberg im Schwarzwald
101 G23 **Triberg im Schwarzwald** var. Triberg. Baden-Württemberg, SW Germany
153 P11 **Tribhuvan** ✕ (Kathmandu) Central, C Nepal
54 C9 **Tribugá, Golfo de** gulf W Colombia
181 W4 **Tribulation, Cape** cape Queensland, NE Australia
108 M8 **Tribulaun** ▲ SW Austria
9 U17 **Tribune** Saskatchewan, S Canada
26 H5 **Tribune** Kansas, C USA
107 N18 **Tricarico** Basilicata, S Italy
107 Q19 **Tricase** Puglia, SE Italy
Trichinopoly see Tiruchchirāppalli
115 D18 **Trichonída, Límni** ◎ C Greece
155 G22 **Trichūr** var. Thrissur. Kerala, SW India
Tricorno see Triglav
183 O8 **Trida** New South Wales, SE Australia
35 S1 **Trident Peak** ▲ Nevada, W USA
Tridentum/Trient see Trento
109 T6 **Trieben** Steiermark, SE Austria
101 D19 **Trier** Eng. Treves, Fr. Trèves; anc. Augusta Treverorum. Rheinland-Pfalz, SW Germany
106 K7 **Trieste** Slvn. Trst. Friuli-Venezia Giulia, NE Italy
Trieste, Golfo di/Triest, Golf von see Trieste, Gulf of
106 J8 **Trieste, Gulf of** Cro. Tršćanski Zaljev, Ger. Golf von Triest, It. Golfo di Trieste, Slvn. Tržaški Zaliv. gulf S Europe
109 W4 **Triesting** ≈ W Austria
Triêu Hai see Quang Tri
Trifail see Trbovlje
116 L9 **Trifeşti** Iaşi, NE Romania
109 S10 **Triglav** It. Tricorno. ▲ NW Slovenia
104 I14 **Trigueros** Andalucía, S Spain
115 E16 **Tríkala** prev. Trikkala. Thessalía, C Greece
115 E17 **Trikeriótis** ≈ C Greece
Trikkala see Tríkala
Trikomo/Tríkomon see Iskele
97 F17 **Trim** Ir. Baile Átha Troim. Meath, E Ireland
108 E7 **Trimbach** Solothurn, NW Switzerland
109 Q5 **Trimmelkam** Oberösterreich, N Austria
29 U11 **Trimont** Minnesota, N USA
Trimontium see Plovdiv
Trinacria see Sicilia
155 K24 **Trincomalee** var. Trinkomali. Eastern Province, NE Sri Lanka
65 K16 **Trindade, Ilha da** island Brazil, W Atlantic Ocean
47 Y9 **Trindade Spur** undersea feature SW Atlantic Ocean
111 J17 **Třinec** Ger. Trzynietz. Moravskoslezský Kraj, E Czech Republic
57 M16 **Trinidad** Beni, N Bolivia
54 H9 **Trinidad** Casanare, E Colombia
44 E6 **Trinidad** Sancti Spíritus, C Cuba
61 E19 **Trinidad** Flores, S Uruguay
37 U8 **Trinidad** Colorado, C USA
45 Y17 **Trinidad** island C Trinidad and Tobago
Trinidad see Jose Abad Santos
45 Y16 **Trinidad and Tobago** off. Republic of Trinidad and Tobago. ◆ republic SE West Indies
Trinidad and Tobago, Republic of see Trinidad and Tobago
63 F22 **Trinidad, Golfo** gulf S Chile
61 B24 **Trinidad, Isla** island E Argentina
107 N16 **Trinitapoli** Puglia, SE Italy
55 X10 **Trinité, Montagnes de la** ▲▲ C French Guiana
25 W9 **Trinity** Texas, SW USA
13 U12 **Trinity Bay** inlet Newfoundland, Newfoundland and Labrador, E Canada
39 P15 **Trinity Islands** island group Alaska, USA
35 N2 **Trinity Mountains** ▲▲ California, W USA
35 S4 **Trinity Peak** ▲ Nevada, W USA
35 S5 **Trinity Range** ▲▲ Nevada, W USA
35 N2 **Trinity River** ≈ California, W USA
25 V8 **Trinity River** ≈ Texas, SW USA
Trinkomali see Trincomalee
173 Y15 **Triolet** NW Mauritius
107 O20 **Trionto, Capo** headland S Italy
Tripiti, Ákra see Trypití, Akrotírio
115 F20 **Trípoli** prev. Trípolis. Pelopónnisos, S Greece
138 G6 **Tripoli** var. Tarābulus, Ţarābulus ash Shām, Trâblous; anc. Tripolis. N Lebanon
29 X12 **Tripoli** Iowa, C USA
Tripoli see Ţarābulus
Trípolis see Trípoli, Greece
Tripolis see Tripoli, Lebanon
29 Q12 **Tripp** South Dakota, N USA
153 V15 **Tripura** var. Hill Tippera. ⬖ state NE India
108 K8 **Trisanna** ≈ W Austria
100 H8 **Trischen** island NW Germany
65 M24 **Tristan da Cunha** ◇ dependency of Saint Helena SE Atlantic Ocean
67 P15 **Tristan da Cunha** island SE Atlantic Ocean
65 L18 **Tristan da Cunha Fracture Zone** tectonic feature S Atlantic Ocean
167 S14 **Tri Tôn** An Giang, S Vietnam
167 W10 **Triton Island** island S Paracel Islands
155 G24 **Trivandrum** var. Thiruvanathapuram. state capital Kerala, SW India
111 H20 **Trnava** Ger. Tyrnau, Hung. Nagyszombat. Trnavský Kraj, W Slovakia
111 H20 **Trnavský Kraj** ⬖ region W Slovakia
Trnovo see Veliko Tŭrnovo
Trobriand Island see Kiriwina Island
Trobriand Islands see Kiriwina Islands
9 Q16 **Trochu** Alberta, SW Canada
109 U7 **Trofaiach** Steiermark, SE Austria
93 F14 **Trofors** Troms, N Norway
113 E14 **Trogir** It. Traù. Split-Dalmacija, S Croatia
112 F13 **Troglav** ▲ Bosnia and Herzegovina/Croatia
107 M16 **Troia** Puglia, SE Italy
107 K24 **Troina** Sicilia, Italy, C Mediterranean Sea
173 O16 **Trois-Bassins** W Réunion
101 E17 **Troisdorf** Nordrhein-Westfalen, W Germany
74 H5 **Trois Fourches, Cap des** cape NE Morocco
15 T8 **Trois-Pistoles** Québec, SE Canada
99 L21 **Trois-Ponts** Liège, E Belgium
15 P11 **Trois-Rivières** Québec, SE Canada
55 Y12 **Trois Sauts** S French Guiana
99 M22 **Troisvierges** Diekirch, N Luxembourg
122 F11 **Troitsk** Chelyabinskaya Oblast', S Russian Federation
125 T9 **Troitsko-Pechorsk** Respublika Komi, NW Russian Federation
127 V7 **Troitskoye** Orenburgskaya Oblast', W Russian Federation
Troki see Trakai
94 F9 **Trolla** ▲ S Norway
95 J18 **Trollhättan** Västra Götaland, S Sweden
94 G9 **Trollheimen** ▲▲ S Norway
94 E9 **Trolltindane** ▲ S Norway
58 H11 **Trombetas, Rio** ≈ NE Brazil
128 L16 **Tromelin, Île** island N Réunion
92 I9 **Troms** ⬖ county N Norway
92 I9 **Tromsø** Fin. Tromssa. Troms, N Norway
84 F5 **Tromsøflaket** undersea feature W Barents Sea
Tromssa see Tromsø
94 H10 **Trona** ▲ S Norway
35 U12 **Trona** California, W USA
63 G16 **Tronador, Cerro** ▲ S Chile
94 H8 **Trondheim** Ger. Drontheim; prev. Nidaros, Trondhjem. Sør-Trøndelag, S Norway
94 H7 **Trondheimsfjorden** fjord S Norway
Trondhjem see Trondheim
107 J14 **Tronto** ≈ C Italy
121 P3 **Troódos** var. Troodos Mountains. ▲▲ C Cyprus
Troodos see Ólympos
Troodos Mountains see Troódos
96 I13 **Troon** W Scotland, UK
107 M22 **Tropea** Calabria, SW Italy
36 L7 **Tropic** Utah, W USA
64 L10 **Tropic Seamount** var. Banc du Tropique. undersea feature E Atlantic Ocean
Tropique, Banc du see Tropic Seamount
Tropoja see Tropojë
113 L17 **Tropojë** var. Tropoja. Kukës, N Albania
Troppau see Opava
95 O16 **Trosa** Södermanland, C Sweden
118 H12 **Troškūnai** Utena, E Lithuania
101 G23 **Trossingen** Baden-Württemberg, SW Germany
117 T4 **Trostyanets'** Rus. Trostyanets. Sums'ka Oblast', NE Ukraine
117 N7 **Trostyanets'** Rus. Trostyanets. Vinnyts'ka Oblast', C Ukraine
Trostyanets see Trostyanets'
116 L11 **Trotuş** ≈ E Romania
44 M8 **Trou-du-Nord** N Haiti
25 W7 **Troup** Texas, SW USA
8 I10 **Trout** ≈ Northwest Territories, NW Canada
33 N8 **Trout Creek** Montana, NW USA
32 H10 **Trout Lake** Washington, NW USA
12 B9 **Trout Lake** ◎ Ontario, S Canada
33 T12 **Trout Peak** ▲ Wyoming, C USA
102 L4 **Trouville** Calvados, N France
97 L22 **Trowbridge** S England, UK
23 Q6 **Troy** Alabama, S USA
27 Q3 **Troy** Kansas, C USA
27 W4 **Troy** Missouri, C USA
18 L10 **Troy** New York, NE USA
21 S10 **Troy** North Carolina, SE USA
31 R13 **Troy** Ohio, N USA
25 T9 **Troy** Texas, SW USA
114 I9 **Troyan** Lovech, N Bulgaria
114 I9 **Troyanski Prokhod** pass N Bulgaria
145 N6 **Troyebratskiy** Severnyy Kazakhstan, N Kazakhstan
103 Q6 **Troyes** anc. Augustobona Tricassium. Aube, N France
117 X5 **Troyits'ke** Luhans'ka Oblast', E Ukraine
35 W7 **Troy Peak** ▲ Nevada, W USA
113 G15 **Trpanj** Dubrovnik-Neretva, S Croatia
Tršćanski Zaljev see Trieste, Gulf of
Trst see Trieste
113 N14 **Trstenik** Serbia, C Serbia
126 I6 **Trubchevsk** Bryanskaya Oblast', W Russian Federation
Trubchular see Orlyak
37 S10 **Truchas Peak** ▲ New Mexico, SW USA
143 P16 **Trucial Coast** physical region C United Arab Emirates
Trucial States see United Arab Emirates
35 Q6 **Truckee** California, W USA
35 R5 **Truckee River** ≈ Nevada, W USA
127 Q13 **Trudfront** Astrakhanskaya Oblast', SW Russian Federation
14 I9 **Truite, Lac à la** ◎ Québec, SE Canada
42 K4 **Trujillo** Colón, NE Honduras
56 C12 **Trujillo** La Libertad, NW Peru
104 K10 **Trujillo** Extremadura, W Spain
54 I6 **Trujillo** Trujillo, NW Venezuela
54 I6 **Trujillo** off. Estado Trujillo. ⬖ state W Venezuela
Trujillo, Estado see Trujillo
Truk see Chuuk
Truk Islands see Chuuk Islands
29 U10 **Truman** Minnesota, N USA
27 X10 **Trumann** Arkansas, C USA
36 J9 **Trumbull, Mount** ▲ Arizona, SW USA
114 F9 **Trŭn** Pernik, W Bulgaria
183 Q8 **Trundle** New South Wales, SE Australia
129 U13 **Trung Phân** physical region S Vietnam
Trupcilar see Orlyak
13 Q15 **Truro** Nova Scotia, SE Canada
97 H25 **Truro** SW England, UK
25 P5 **Truscott** Texas, SW USA
116 K9 **Truşeşti** Botoşani, NE Romania
116 H6 **Truskavets'** L'vivs'ka Oblast', W Ukraine
95 H22 **Trustrup** Århus, C Denmark
10 M11 **Trutch** British Columbia, W Canada
37 Q14 **Truth Or Consequences** New Mexico, SW USA
111 F15 **Trutnov** Ger. Trautenau. Královéhradecký Kraj, N Czech Republic
103 P13 **Truyère** ≈ C France
114 K9 **Tryavna** Lovech, N Bulgaria
28 M14 **Tryon** Nebraska, C USA
115 J16 **Trypití, Akrotírio** var. Ákra Tripití. headland Ágios Efstrátios, E Greece
94 J12 **Trysil** Hedmark, S Norway
94 I11 **Trysilelva** ≈ S Norway
112 D10 **Tržac** ⬖ Federacija Bosna I Hercegovina, NW Bosnia and Herzegovina
Tržaški Zaliv see Trieste, Gulf of
110 G10 **Trzcianka** Ger. Schönlanke. Pila, Wielkopolskie, C Poland
110 E7 **Trzebiatów** Ger. Treptow an der Rega. Zachodnio-pomorskie, NW Poland
111 G14 **Trzebnica** Ger. Trebnitz. Dolnośląskie, SW Poland
109 T10 **Tržič** Ger. Neumarktl. NW Slovenia
Trzynietz see Třinec
Tsabong see Tshabong
162 G7 **Tsagaanchuluut** Dzavhan, C Mongolia
162 M8 **Tsagaandelger** var. Haraat. Dundgovĭ, C Mongolia
Tsagaanders see Bayantümen
162 G7 **Tsagaanhayrhan** var. Shiree. Dzavhan, W Mongolia
Tsagaannuur see Halhgol

◆ Country
● Country Capital
◇ Dependent Territory
○ Dependent Territory Capital
⬖ Administrative Regions
✕ International Airport
▲ Mountain
▲▲ Mountain Range
☒ Volcano
≈ River
◎ Lake
⊠ Reservoir

Tsagaan-Olom *see* Tayshir
Tsagaan-Ovoo *see* Nariynteel
Tsagaantüngi *see* Altantsögts
162 *H6* **Tsagaan-Uul** *var.* Sharga. Hövsgöl, N Mongolia
162 *J5* **Tsagaan-Üür** *var.* Bulgan. Hövsgöl, N Mongolia
127 *P12* **Tsagan Aman** Respublika Kalmykiya, SW Russian Federation
23 *V11* **Tsala Apopka Lake** ◎ Florida, SE USA
Tsamkong *see* Zhanjiang
Tsangpo *see* Brahmaputra
Tsant *see* Deren
83 *G17* **Tsao** North-West, NW Botswana
172 *I4* **Tsaratanana** Mahajanga, C Madagascar
114 *N10* **Tsarevo** *prev.* Michurin. Burgas, E Bulgaria
Tsarigrad *see* İstanbul
Tsaritsyn *see* Volgograd
124 *G13* **Tsarskoye Selo** *prev.* Pushkin. Leningradskaya Oblast', NW Russian Federation
117 *T7* **Tsarychanka** Dnipropetrovs'ka Oblast', E Ukraine
83 *H21* **Tsatsu** Southern, S Botswana
81 *J20* **Tsavo** Coast, S Kenya
83 *E21* **Tsawisis** Karas, S Namibia
Tschakathurn *see* Čakovec
Tschaslau *see* Čáslav
Tschenstochau *see* Częstochowa
Tschernembl *see* Črnomelj
28 *K6* **Tschida, Lake** ⊠ North Dakota, N USA
Tschorna *see* Mustvee
83 *I17* **Tsebanana** Central, NE Botswana
162 *G8* **Tseel** Govĭ-Altay, SW Mongolia
Tsefat *see* Ẕefat
126 *M13* **Tselina** Rostovskaya Oblast', SW Russian Federation
Tselinograd *see* Astana
Tselinogradskaya Oblast *see* Akmola
Tsengel *see* Tosontsengel
162 *J8* **Tsenher** *var.* Altan-Ovoo. Arhangay, C Mongolia
Tsenher *see* Mönhhayrhan
163 *N8* **Tsenhermandal** *var.* Modot. Hentiy, C Mongolia
Tsentral'nyye Nizmennyye Garagumy *see* Merkezi Garagumy
Tsentral'nyye Nizmennyye Garagumy *see* Merkezi Garagumy
83 *E21* **Tses** Karas, S Namibia
Tseshevlya *see* Tsyeshawlya
162 *E7* **Tsetseg** *var.* Tsetsegnuur. Hovd, W Mongolia
Tsetsegnuur *see* Tsetseg
Tsetsen Khan *see* Öndörhaan
162 *J6* **Tsetserleg** *var.* Hujirt. Arhangay, C Mongolia
162 *J8* **Tsetserleg** Arhangay, C Mongolia
162 *H6* **Tsetserleg** *var.* Halban. Hövsgöl, N Mongolia
77 *R16* **Tsévié** S Togo
83 *G21* **Tshabong** *var.* Tsabong. Kgalagadi, SW Botswana
83 *G20* **Tshane** Kgalagadi, SW Botswana
Tshangalele, Lac *see* Lufira, Lac de Retenue de la
83 *H17* **Tshauxaba** Central, C Botswana
79 *F21* **Tshela** Bas-Congo, W Dem. Rep. Congo
79 *K22* **Tshibala** Kasai Occidental, S Dem. Rep. Congo
79 *J22* **Tshikapa** Kasai Occidental, SW Dem. Rep. Congo
79 *L22* **Tshilenge** Kasai Oriental, S Dem. Rep. Congo
79 *L24* **Tshimbalanga** Katanga, S Dem. Rep. Congo
79 *L22* **Tshimbulu** Kasai Occidental, S Dem. Rep. Congo
Tshiumbe *see* Chiumbe
79 *M21* **Tshofa** Kasai Oriental, C Dem. Rep. Congo
79 *K18* **Tshuapa** ≈ C Dem. Rep. Congo
83 *J21* **Tshwane** *var.* Epitoli; *prev.* Pretoria. ● Gauteng, NE South Africa
114 *G7* **Tsibritsa** ≈ NW Bulgaria
Tsien Tang *see* Puyang Jiang
114 *I12* **Tsigansko Gradishte** ▲ Bulgaria/Greece
Tsihombe *see* Tsiombe
8 *H7* **Tsiigehtchic** *prev.* Arctic Red River. Northwest Territories, NW Canada
125 *Q7* **Tsil'ma** ≈ NW Russian Federation
119 *J17* **Tsimkavichy** *Rus.* Timkovichi. Minskaya Voblasts', C Belarus
126 *M11* **Tsimlyansk** Rostovskaya Oblast', SW Russian Federation
127 *N11* **Tsimlyanskoye Vodokhranilishche** *var.* Tsimlyansk Vodoskhovshche, *Eng.* Tsimlyansk Reservoir. ⊠ SW Russian Federation
Tsimlyansk Reservoir *see* Tsimlyanskoye Vodokhranilishche
Tsimlyansk Vodoskhovshche *see* Tsimlyanskoye Vodokhranilishche
Tsinan *see* Jinan
Tsing Hai *see* Qinghai Hu, China
Tsinghai *see* Qinghai, China
Tsingtao/Tsingtau *see* Qingdao
Tsingyuan *see* Baoding
Tsinkiang *see* Quanzhou
Tsintao *see* Qingdao
83 *D17* **Tsintsabis** Otjikoto, N Namibia
172 *H8* **Tsiombe** *var.* Tsihombe. Toliara, S Madagascar
123 *O13* **Tsipa** ≈ S Russian Federation
172 *H5* **Tsiribihina** ≈ W Madagascar
172 *I5* **Tsiroanomandidy** Antananarivo, C Madagascar
189 *U13* **Tsis** *island* Chuuk, C Micronesia
Tsitsihar *see* Qiqihar
127 *Q3* **Tsivil'sk** Chuvashskaya Respublika, W Russian Federation
137 *T9* **Ts'khinvali** *prev.* Staliniri. C Georgia
119 *J19* **Tsna** ≈ Sw Belarus
124 *I15* **Tsna** *var.* Zna. ≈ W Russian Federation
162 *G9* **Tsogt** *var.* Tahilt. Govĭ-Altay, W Mongolia
162 *K10* **Tsogt-Ovoo** *var.* Doloon. Ömnögovĭ, S Mongolia
162 *L10* **Tsogttsetsiy** Ömnögovĭ, S Mongolia
162 *L10* **Tsogttsetsiy** *var.* Baruunsuu. Ömnögovĭ, S Mongolia
Tsoohor *see* Hürmen
164 *K14* **Tsu** *var.* Tu. Mie, Honshū, SW Japan
165 *O10* **Tsubame** *var.* Tubame. Niigata, Honshū, C Japan
165 *V3* **Tsubetsu** Hokkaidō, NE Japan
165 *O13* **Tsuchiura** *var.* Tutiura. Ibaraki, Honshū, S Japan
165 *Q6* **Tsugaru-kaikyō** *strait* N Japan
164 *E14* **Tsukumi** *var.* Tukumi. Ōita, Kyūshū, SW Japan
Tsul-Ulaan *see* Bayannuur
Tsul-Ulaan *see* Bayannuur
83 *D17* **Tsumeb** Otjikoto, N Namibia
83 *F17* **Tsumkwe** Otjozondjupa, NE Namibia
164 *D15* **Tsuno** Miyazaki, Kyūshū, SW Japan
164 *D12* **Tsuno-shima** *island* SW Japan
164 *K12* **Tsuruga** *var.* Turuga. Fukui, Honshū, SW Japan
164 *H12* **Tsurugi-san** ▲ Shikoku, SW Japan
165 *P9* **Tsuruoka** *var.* Turuoka. Yamagata, Honshū, C Japan
164 *C12* **Tsushima** *var.* Tsushima-tō, Tusima. *island group* SW Japan
Tsushima-tō *see* Tsushima
164 *H12* **Tsuyama** *var.* Tuyama. Okayama, Honshū, SW Japan
83 *G19* **Tswaane** Ghanzi, W Botswana
119 *N16* **Tsyakhtsin** *Rus.* Tekhtin. Mahilyowskaya Voblasts', E Belarus
119 *P19* **Tsyerakhowka** *Rus.* Terekhovka. Homyel'skaya Voblasts', SE Belarus
119 *I17* **Tsyeshawlya** *Rus.* Cheshevlya, Tseshevlya. Brestskaya Voblasts', SW Belarus
Tsyurupinsk *see* Tsyurupyns'k
117 *R10* **Tsyurupyns'k** *Rus.* Tsyurupinsk. Khersons'ka Oblast', S Ukraine
Tu *see* Tsu
186 *C7* **Tua** ≈ C Papua New Guinea
Tuaim *see* Tuam
184 *L6* **Tuakau** Waikato, North Island, New Zealand
97 *C17* **Tuam** *Ir.* Tuaim. Galway, W Ireland
185 *K14* **Tuamarina** Marlborough, South Island, New Zealand
Tuamotu, Archipel des *see* Tuamotu, Îles
193 *Q9* **Tuamotu Fracture Zone** *tectonic feature* E Pacific Ocean
191 *W9* **Tuamotu, Îles** *var.* Archipel des Tuamotu, Dangerous Archipelago, Tuamotu Islands. *island group* N French Polynesia
Tuamotu Islands *see* Tuamotu, Îles
175 *X10* **Tuamotu Ridge** *undersea feature* C Pacific Ocean
167 *R5* **Tuân Giao** Lai Châu, N Vietnam
171 *O2* **Tuao** Luzon, N Philippines
190 *B15* **Tuapa** NW Niue
43 *N7* **Tuapi** Región Autónoma Atlántico Norte, NE Nicaragua
126 *K15* **Tuapse** Krasnodarskiy Kray, SW Russian Federation
169 *U6* **Tuaran** Sabah, East Malaysia
104 *I6* **Tua, Rio** ≈ N Portugal
192 *H15* **Tuasivi** Savai'i, C Samoa
185 *B24* **Tuatapere** Southland, South Island, New Zealand
36 *M9* **Tuba City** Arizona, SW USA
138 *H11* **Ṭūbah, Qaṣr aṭ** *castle* 'Ammān, C Jordan
Tubame *see* Tsubame
169 *R16* **Tuban** *prev.* Toeban. Jawa, C Indonesia
141 *O16* **Tuban, Wādī** *dry watercourse* SW Yemen
61 *K14* **Tubarão** Santa Catarina, S Brazil
98 *O10* **Tubbergen** Overijssel, E Netherlands
Tubeke *see* Tubize
101 *H22* **Tübingen** *var.* Tuebingen. Baden-Württemberg, SW Germany
127 *W6* **Tubinskiy** Respublika Bashkortostan, W Russian Federation
99 *G19* **Tubize** *Dut.* Tubeke. Walloon Brabant, C Belgium
76 *J16* **Tubmanburg** NW Liberia
75 *T7* **Ṭubruq** *Eng.* Tobruk, *It.* Tobruch. NE Libya
191 *T13* **Tubuai** *island* Îles Australes, SW French Polynesia
Tubuai, Îles/Tubuai Islands *see* Australes, Îles
Tubuai-Manu *see* Maiao
40 *F3* **Tubutama** Sonora, NW Mexico
54 *K4* **Tucacas** Falcón, N Venezuela
59 *P16* **Tucano** Bahia, E Brazil
57 *P19* **Tucavaca, Río** ≈ E Bolivia
110 *H8* **Tuchola** Kujawsko-pomorskie, C Poland
111 *M17* **Tuchów** Małopolskie, S Poland
23 *S3* **Tucker** Georgia, SE USA
27 *W10* **Tuckerman** Arkansas, C USA
64 *B12* **Tucker's Town** E Bermuda
Tuckum *see* Tukums
36 *M15* **Tucson** Arizona, SW USA
62 *J7* **Tucumán** *off.* Provincia de Tucumán. ◈ *province* N Argentina
Tucumán *see* San Miguel de Tucumán
Tucumán, Provincia de *see* Tucumán
37 *V11* **Tucumcari** New Mexico, SW USA
58 *H13* **Tucunaré** Pará, N Brazil
55 *Q6* **Tucupita** Delta Amacuro, NE Venezuela
58 *K13* **Tucuruí, Represa de** ⊠ NE Brazil
110 *F9* **Tuczno** Zachodnio-pomorskie, NW Poland
Tuddo *see* Tudu
105 *Q5* **Tudela** *Basq.* Tutera; *anc.* Tutela. Navarra, N Spain
104 *M6* **Tudela de Duero** Castilla-León, N Spain
162 *G6* **Tüdevtey** *var.* Oygon. Dzavhan, N Mongolia
138 *K6* **Tudmur** *var.* Tadmur, Tamar, *Gk.* Palmyra, *Bibl.* Tadmor. Ḥimṣ, C Syria
118 *J4* **Tudu** *Ger.* Tuddo. Lääne-Virumaa, NE Estonia
Tuebingen *see* Tübingen
122 *J14* **Tuekta** Respublika Altay, S Russian Federation
104 *I5* **Tuela, Rio** ≈ N Portugal
153 *X12* **Tuensang** Nāgāland, NE India
136 *L15* **Tufanbeyli** Adana, C Turkey
Tüffer *see* Laško
186 *F9* **Tufi** Northern, S Papua New Guinea
193 *O3* **Tufts Plain** *undersea feature* N Pacific Ocean
Tugalan *see* Kolkhozobod
67 *V14* **Tugela** ≈ SE South Africa
21 *P6* **Tug Fork** ≈ S USA
39 *P15* **Tugidak Island** *island* Trinity Islands, Alaska, USA
171 *O2* **Tuguegarao** Luzon, N Philippines
123 *S12* **Tugur** Khabarovskiy Kray, SE Russian Federation
161 *P4* **Tuhai He** ≈ E China
104 *G4* **Tui** Galicia, NW Spain
77 *O13* **Tui** *var.* Grand Balé. ≈ W Burkina
57 *J16* **Tuichi, Río** ≈ W Bolivia
64 *Q11* **Tuineje** Fuerteventura, Islas Canarias, Spain, NE Atlantic Ocean
43 *X16* **Tuira, Río** ≈ SE Panama
Tuisarkan *see* Tūysarkān
Tujiabu *see* Yongxiu
127 *W5* **Tukan** Respublika Bashkortostan, W Russian Federation
171 *P14* **Tukangbesi, Kepulauan** *Dut.* Toekang Besi Eilanden. *island group* C Indonesia
147 *V13* **Tŭkhtamish** *Rus.* Toktomush; *prev.* Tokhtamyshbek. SE Tajikistan
184 *O12* **Tukituki** ≈ North Island, New Zealand
Tu-k'ou *see* Panzhihua
121 *P12* **Tūkrah** NE Libya
8 *H6* **Tuktoyaktuk** Northwest Territories, NW Canada
168 *I9* **Tuktuk** Pulau Samosir, W Indonesia
Tukumi *see* Tsukumi
118 *E9* **Tukums** *Ger.* Tuckum. W Latvia
81 *G24* **Tukuyu** *prev.* Neu-Langenburg. Mbeya, S Tanzania
Tukzār *see* Tokzār
41 *O13* **Tula** *var.* Tula de Allende. Hidalgo, C Mexico
41 *O11* **Tula** Tamaulipas, C Mexico
126 *K5* **Tula** Tul'skaya Oblast', W Russian Federation
Tulach Mhór *see* Tullamore
Tula de Allende *see* Tula
159 *N10* **Tulage Ar Gol** ≈ W China
186 *M9* **Tulaghi** *var.* Tulagi. Florida Islands, C Solomon Islands
Tulagi *see* Tulaghi
41 *P13* **Tulancingo** Hidalgo, C Mexico
35 *R11* **Tulare** California, W USA
29 *P9* **Tulare** South Dakota, N USA
35 *Q12* **Tulare Lake Bed** *salt flat* California, W USA
37 *S14* **Tularosa** New Mexico, SW USA
37 *P13* **Tularosa Mountains** ▲▲ New Mexico, SW USA
37 *S15* **Tularosa Valley** *basin* New Mexico, SW USA
83 *E25* **Tulbagh** Western Cape, SW South Africa
56 *C5* **Tulcán** Carchi, N Ecuador
117 *N13* **Tulcea** Tulcea, E Romania
117 *N13* **Tulcea** ◈ *county* SE Romania
Tul'chin *see* Tul'chyn
117 *N7* **Tul'chyn** *Rus.* Tul'chin. Vinnyts'ka Oblast', C Ukraine
Tuléar *see* Toliara
35 *O1* **Tulelake** California, W USA
116 *J10* **Tulgheş** *Hung.* Gyergyótölgyes. Harghita, C Romania
Tuli *see* Thuli
25 *N4* **Tulia** Texas, SW USA
8 *I9* **Tulita** *prev.* Fort Norman, Norman. Northwest Territories, NW Canada
20 *J10* **Tullahoma** Tennessee, S USA
183 *N12* **Tullamarine** ✈ (Melbourne) Victoria, SE Australia
183 *Q7* **Tullamore** New South Wales, SE Australia
97 *E18* **Tullamore** *Ir.* Tulach Mhór. Offaly, C Ireland
103 *N12* **Tulle** *anc.* Tutela. Corrèze, C France
109 *X3* **Tulln** *var.* Oberhollabrunn. Niederösterreich, NE Austria
109 *W4* **Tulln** ≈ NE Austria
22 *H6* **Tullos** Louisiana, S USA
97 *F19* **Tullow** *Ir.* An Tullach. Carlow, SE Ireland
181 *W5* **Tully** Queensland, NE Australia
124 *J3* **Tuloma** ≈ NW Russian Federation
114 *K10* **Tulovo** Stara Zagora, C Bulgaria
27 *P9* **Tulsa** Oklahoma, C USA
153 *N11* **Tulsipur** Mid Western, W Nepal
126 *K6* **Tul'skaya Oblast'** ◈ *province* W Russian Federation
126 *L14* **Tul'skiy** Respublika Adygeya, SW Russian Federation
186 *E5* **Tulu** Manus Island, N Papua New Guinea
54 *D10* **Tuluá** Valle del Cauca, W Colombia
116 *M12* **Tulucești** Galați, E Romania
39 *N12* **Tuluksak** Alaska, USA
41 *Z12* **Tulum, Ruinas de** *ruins* Quintana Roo, SE Mexico
169 *R17* **Tulungagung** *prev.* Toeloengagoeng. Jawa, C Indonesia
186 *J6* **Tulun Islands** *var.* Kilinailau Islands; *prev.* Carteret Islands. *island group* NE Papua New Guinea
126 *M4* **Tuma** Ryazanskaya Oblast', W Russian Federation
54 *B12* **Tumaco** Nariño, SW Colombia
54 *B12* **Tumaco, Bahía de** *bay* SW Colombia
Tuman-gang *see* Tumen
42 *L8* **Tuma, Río** ≈ N Nicaragua
95 *O16* **Tumba** Stockholm, C Sweden
Tumba, Lac *see* Ntomba, Lac
169 *S12* **Tumbangsenamang** Borneo, C Indonesia
183 *Q10* **Tumbarumba** New South Wales, SE Australia
56 *A8* **Tumbes** Tumbes, NW Peru
56 *A9* **Tumbes** *off.* Departamento de Tumbes. ◈ *department* NW Peru
Tumbes, Departamento de *see* Tumbes
19 *P5* **Tumbledown Mountain** ▲ Maine, NE USA
9 *N13* **Tumbler Ridge** British Columbia, W Canada
167 *Q12* **Tumbŏt, Phnum** ▲ W Cambodia
182 *G9* **Tumby Bay** South Australia
163 *Y10* **Tumen** Jilin, NE China
163 *Y11* **Tumen** *Chin.* Tumen Jiang, *Kor.* Tuman-gang, *Rus.* Tumyn'tszyan. ≈ E Asia
Tumen Jiang *see* Tumen
55 *Q8* **Tumeremo** Bolívar, E Venezuela
155 *G19* **Tumkūr** Karnātaka, W India
96 *I10* **Tummel** ≈ C Scotland, UK
188 *B15* **Tumon Bay** *bay* W Guam
77 *P14* **Tumu** NW Ghana
58 *I10* **Tumuc Humac Mountains** *var.* Serra Tumucumaque. ▲▲ N South America
Tumucumaque, Serra *see* Tumuc Humac Mountains
183 *Q10* **Tumut** New South Wales, SE Australia
Tumyn'tszyan *see* Tumen
Tün *see* Ferdows
45 *U14* **Tunapuna** Trinidad, Trinidad and Tobago
60 *K11* **Tunas** Paraná, S Brazil
Tunbridge Wells *see* Royal Tunbridge Wells
114 *L11* **Tunca Nehri** *Bul.* Tundzha. ≈ Bulgaria/Turkey *see also* Tundzha
Tunca Nehri *see* Tundzha
137 *O14* **Tunceli** *var.* Kalan. Tunceli, E Turkey
137 *O14* **Tunceli** ◈ *province* C Turkey
152 *J12* **Tūndla** Uttar Pradesh, N India
81 *I25* **Tunduru** Ruvuma, S Tanzania
114 *L10* **Tundzha** *Turk.* Tunca Nehri. ≈ Bulgaria/Turkey *see also* Tunca Nehri
Tundzha *see* Tunca Nehri
162 *I6* **Tünel** *var.* Bulag. Hövsgöl, N Mongolia
155 *H17* **Tungabhadra** ≈ S India
155 *F17* **Tungabhadra Reservoir** ◎ S India
191 *P2* **Tungaru** *prev.* Gilbert Islands. *island group* W Kiribati
171 *P7* **Tungawan** Mindanao, S Philippines
Tungdor *see* Mainling
T'ung-shan *see* Xuzhou
161 *Q16* **Tungsha Tao** *Chin.* Dongsha Qundao, *Eng.* Pratas Island. *island* S Taiwan
161 *S13* **Tungshih** *Jap.* Tōsei. N Taiwan
8 *H9* **Tungsten** Northwest Territories, W Canada
Tung-t'ing Hu *see* Dongting Hu
56 *A13* **Tungurahua** ◈ *province* C Ecuador
94 *H7* **Tunhovdfjorden** ◎ S Norway
22 *K2* **Tunica** Mississippi, S USA
75 *N5* **Tunis** *var.* Tūnis. ● (Tunisia) NE Tunisia
75 *N5* **Tunis, Golfe de** *Ar.* Khalīj Tūnis. *gulf* NE Tunisia
75 *N6* **Tunisia** *off.* Republic of Tunisia, *Ar.* Al Jumhūrīyah at Tūnisīyah, *Fr.* République Tunisienne. ◆ *republic* N Africa
Tunisia, Republic of *see* Tunisia
Tunisienne, République *see* Tunisia
Tūnisīyah, Al Jumhūrīyah at *see* Tunisia
Tūnis, Khalīj *see* Tunis, Golfe de
54 *G9* **Tunja** Boyacá, C Colombia
93 *F14* **Tunnsjøen** *Lapp.* Dåtnejaevrie. ◎ C Norway
39 *N12* **Tuntutuliak** Alaska, USA
197 *P12* **Tunu** ◈ *province* E Greenland
147 *U8* **Tunuk** Chuyskaya Oblast', C Kyrgyzstan
13 *Q6* **Tunungayualok Island** *island* Newfoundland and Labrador, E Canada
62 *H11* **Tunuyán** Mendoza, W Argentina
62 *I11* **Tunuyán, Río** ≈ W Argentina
Tunxi *see* Huangshan
Tuodian *see* Shuangbai
Tuoji *see* Zhongba
35 *P9* **Tuolumne River** ≈ California, W USA
Tuong Buong *see* Tương Đương
167 *R7* **Tương Đương** *var.* Tuong Buong. Nghê An, N Vietnam
160 *I13* **Tuoniang Jiang** ≈ S China
Tuotuo He *see* Togton He
Tuotuoheyan *see* Tanggulashan
Tüp *see* Tyup
60 *J9* **Tupã** São Paulo, S Brazil
191 *S10* **Tupai** *var.* Motu Iti. *atoll* Îles Sous le Vent, W French Polynesia
61 *G15* **Tupanciretã** Rio Grande do Sul, S Brazil
22 *M2* **Tupelo** Mississippi, S USA
59 *K18* **Tupiraçaba** Goiás, S Brazil
57 *L21* **Tupiza** Potosí, S Bolivia
9 *N13* **Tupper** British Columbia, W Canada
18 *J8* **Tupper Lake** ◎ New York, NE USA
146 *J10* **Tuproqqal'a** Khorazm Viloyati, W Uzbekistan
146 *J10* **Tuproqqal'a** *Rus.* Turpakkla. Xorazm Viloyati, W Uzbekistan
62 *H11* **Tupungato, Volcán** Ѫ W Argentina
163 *T9* **Tuquan** Nei Mongol Zizhiqu, N China
54 *C13* **Túquerres** Nariño, SW Colombia
153 *U13* **Tura** Meghālaya, NE India
122 *M10* **Tura** Evenkiyskiy Avtonomnyy Okrug, N Russian Federation
122 *G10* **Tura** ≈ C Russian Federation
140 *M10* **Turabah** Makkah, W Saudi Arabia
55 *O8* **Turagua, Cerro** ▲ C Venezuela
184 *L12* **Turakina** Manawatu-Wanganui, North Island, New Zealand
185 *K15* **Turakirae Head** *headland* North Island, New Zealand
186 *B8* **Turama** ≈ S Papua New Guinea
122 *K13* **Turan** Respublika Tyva, S Russian Federation
184 *M10* **Turangi** Waikato, North Island, New Zealand
146 *F11* **Turan Lowland** *var.* Turan Plain, *Kaz.* Turan Oypaty, *Rus.* Turanskaya Nizmennost', *Turk.* Turan Pesligi, *Uzb.* Turan Pasttekisligi. *plain* C Asia
Turan Oypaty/Turan Pesligi/Turan Plain/Turanskaya Nizmennost' *see* Turan Lowland
Turan Pasttekisligi *see* Turan Lowland
138 *K7* **Ṭurāq al 'Ilab** *hill range* S Syria
119 *K20* **Turaw** *Rus.* Turov. Homyel'skaya Voblasts', SE Belarus
140 *L2* **Ṭurayf** Al Ḥudūd ash Shamālīyah, NW Saudi Arabia
Turba *see* Teruel
54 *E5* **Turbaco** Bolívar, N Colombia
148 *K15* **Turbat** Baluchistān, SW Pakistan
Turbat-i-Haidari *see* Torbat-e Ḩeydarīyeh
Turbat-i-Jam *see* Torbat-e Jām
54 *D7* **Turbo** Antioquia, NW Colombia
Turčianský Svätý Martin *see* Martin
116 *H10* **Turda** *Ger.* Thorenburg, *Hung.* Torda. Cluj, NW Romania
142 *M7* **Ṭūreh** Markazī, W Iran
191 *X12* **Tureia** *atoll* Îles Tuamotu, SE French Polynesia
110 *I12* **Turek** Wielkopolskie, C Poland
93 *L19* **Turenki** Etelä-Suomi, SW Finland
Turfan *see* Turpan
145 *R8* **Turgay** *Kaz.* Torghay. Akmola, W Kazakhstan
145 *N10* **Turgay** *Kaz.* Torgay. ≈ C Kazakhstan
144 *M8* **Turgayskaya Stolovaya Strana** *Kaz.* Torgay Üstirti. *plateau* Kazakhstan/Russian Federation
Turgel *see* Türi
114 *L8* **Türgovishte** *prev.* Eski Dzhumaya, Tărgovište. Türgovishte, N Bulgaria
114 *L8* **Türgovishte** ◈ *province* N Bulgaria
136 *C14* **Turgutlu** Manisa, W Turkey
136 *L12* **Turhal** Tokat, N Turkey
118 *H4* **Türi** *Ger.* Turgel. Järvamaa, N Estonia
105 *S9* **Turia** ≈ E Spain
58 *M12* **Turiaçu** Maranhão, E Brazil
Turin *see* Torino
116 *I3* **Turiys'k** Volyns'ka Oblast', NW Ukraine
Turja *see* Tur"ya
116 *H6* **Turka** L'vivs'ka Oblast', W Ukraine
81 *H16* **Turkana, Lake** *var.* Lake Rudolf. ◎ N Kenya
145 *P16* **Turkestan** *Kaz.* Türkistan. Yuzhnyy Kazakhstan, S Kazakhstan
147 *Q12* **Turkestan Range** *Rus.* Turkestanskiy Khrebet. ▲▲ C Asia
Turkestanskiy Khrebet *see* Turkestan Range
111 *M23* **Túrkeve** Jász-Nagykun-Szolnok, E Hungary
25 *O4* **Turkey** Texas, SW USA
136 *H14* **Turkey** *off.* Republic of Turkey, *Turk.* Türkiye Cumhuriyeti. ◆ *republic* SW Asia
181 *N4* **Turkey Creek** Western Australia
26 *M9* **Turkey Creek** ≈ Oklahoma, C USA
37 *T9* **Turkey Mountains** ▲▲ New Mexico, SW USA
Turkey, Republic of *see* Turkey
29 *X11* **Turkey River** ≈ Iowa, C USA
127 *N7* **Turki** Saratovskaya Oblast', W Russian Federation
121 *O1* **Turkish Republic of Northern Cyprus** ◇ *disputed territory* Cyprus
Türkistan *see* Turkestan
Turkistan, Bandi-i *see* Torkestān, Selseleh-ye Band-e
Türkiye Cumhuriyeti *see* Turkey
146 *K12* **Türkmenabat** *prev. Rus.* Chardzhev, Chardzhou, Chardzhui, Lenin-Turkmenski, *Turkm.* Chärjew. Lebap Welaýaty, E Turkmenistan
146 *A11* **Turkmen Aylagy** *Rus.* Turkmenskiy Zaliv. *lake gulf* W Turkmenistan
Turkmenbashi *see* Turkmenbaşy
146 *A10* **Turkmenbaşy** *Rus.* Turkmenbashi; *prev.* Krasnovodsk. Balkan Welaýaty, W Turkmenistan
146 *A10* **Türkmenbasy Aylagy** *prev. Rus.* Krasnovodskiy Zaliv, *Turkm.* Krasnowodsk Aylagy. *lake Gulf* W Turkmenistan
146 *J14* **Turkmengala** *Rus.* Turkmen-kala; *prev.* Turkmen-Kala. Mary Welaýaty, S Turkmenistan
146 *G13* **Turkmenistan**; *prev.* Turkmenskaya Soviet Socialist Republic. ◆ *republic* C Asia
Turkmen-kala/Turkmen-Kala *see* Turkmengala
Turkmenskaya Soviet Socialist Republic *see* Turkmenistan
Turkmenskiy Zaliv *see* Turkmen Aylagy
136 *L16* **Türkoğlu** Kahramanmaraş, S Turkey
44 *L6* **Turks and Caicos Islands** ◇ *UK dependent territory* N West Indies
64 *G10* **Turks and Caicos Islands** *UK dependant territory* N West Indies
45 *N6* **Turks Islands** *island group* SE Turks and Caicos Islands
93 *K19* **Turku** *Swe.* Åbo. Länsi-Soumi, SW Finland
81 *H17* **Turkwel** *seasonal river* NW Kenya
27 *P9* **Turley** Oklahoma, C USA
35 *P9* **Turlock** California, W USA
118 *I12* **Turmantas** Utena, NE Lithuania
Turmberg *see* Wieżyca
54 *L5* **Turmero** Aragua, N Venezuela South America
184 *N13* **Turnagain, Cape** *headland* North Island, New Zealand
Turnau *see* Turnov
42 *H2* **Turneffe Islands** *island group* E Belize
18 *M11* **Turners Falls** Massachusetts, NE USA
9 *P16* **Turner Valley** Alberta, SW Canada
99 *I16* **Turnhout** Antwerpen, N Belgium
109 *V5* **Türnitz** Niederösterreich, E Austria
9 *S12* **Turnor Lake** ◎ Saskatchewan, C Canada
111 *E15* **Turnov** *Ger.* Turnau. Liberecký Kraj, N Czech Republic
Türnovo *see* Veliko Türnovo
116 *I15* **Turnu Măgurele** *var.* Turnu-Măgurele. Teleorman, S Romania
Turnu Severin *see* Drobeta-Turnu Severin
Turócszentmárton *see* Martin
Turoni *see* Tours
Turov *see* Turaw
Turpakkla *see* Tuproqqal'a
158 *M6* **Turpan** *var.* Turfan. Xinjiang Uygur Zizhiqu, NW China
Turpan Depression *see* Turpan Pendi
158 *M6* **Turpan Pendi** *Eng.* Turpan Depression. *depression* NW China
158 *M5* **Turpan Zhan** Xinjiang Uygur Zizhiqu, W China
Turpentine State *see* North Carolina
44 *H8* **Turquino, Pico** ▲ E Cuba
27 *Y10* **Turrell** Arkansas, C USA
43 *N14* **Turrialba** Cartago, E Costa Rica
96 *K8* **Turriff** NE Scotland, UK
139 *V7* **Tursāq** E Iraq
Turshiz *see* Kāshmar
Tursunzade *see* Tursunzoda
147 *P13* **Tursunzoda** *Rus.* Tursunzade; *prev.* Regar. W Tajikistan
Turt *see* Hanh
Türtkül/Turtkul' *see* To'rtko'l
29 *O9* **Turtle Creek** ≈ South Dakota, N USA
30 *K4* **Turtle Flambeau Flowage** ⊠ Wisconsin, N USA
9 *S14* **Turtleford** Saskatchewan, S Canada
28 *M4* **Turtle Lake** North Dakota, N USA
92 *K12* **Turtola** Lappi, NW Finland
122 *M10* **Turu** ≈ N Russian Federation
Turuga *see* Tsuruga
147 *V10* **Turugart Pass** *pass* China/Kyrgyzstan
158 *E7* **Turugart Shankou** *var.* Pereval Torugart. *pass* China/Kyrgyzstan
122 *K9* **Turukhan** ≈ N Russian Federation
122 *K9* **Turukhansk** Krasnoyarskiy Kray, N Russian Federation
139 *N3* **Ṭurumbah** *well* NE Syria
Turuoka *see* Tsuruoka
144 *H14* **Turush** Mangistau, SW Kazakhstan
60 *K7* **Turvo, Rio** ≈ S Brazil
116 *J2* **Tur"ya** *Pol.* Turja, *Rus.* Tur'ya. ≈ NW Ukraine
23 *O4* **Tuscaloosa** Alabama, S USA
23 *O4* **Tuscaloosa, Lake** ◎ Alabama, S USA
Tuscan Archipelago *see* Toscano, Arcipelago
Tuscan-Emilian Mountains *see* Tosco-Emiliano, Appennino
Tuscany *see* Toscana
35 *V2* **Tuscarora** Nevada, W USA
18 *F15* **Tuscarora Mountain** *ridge* Pennsylvania, NE USA
30 *M14* **Tuscola** Illinois, N USA
25 *P7* **Tuscola** Texas, SW USA
23 *O2* **Tuscumbia** Alabama, S USA

◆ Country
● Country Capital
◇ Dependent Territory
○ Dependent Territory Capital
◈ Administrative Regions
✈ International Airport
▲ Mountain
▲▲ Mountain Range
Ѫ Volcano
≈ River
◎ Lake
⊠ Reservoir

92 *O4* **Tusenøyane** *island group* S Svalbard
144 *K13* **Tushybas, Zaliv** *prev.* Zaliv Paskevicha. *lake gulf* SW Kazakhstan
Tusima *see* Tsushima
171 *Y15* **Tusirah** Papua, E Indonesia
23 *Q5* **Tuskegee** Alabama, S USA
94 *E8* **Tustna** *island* S Norway
39 *R12* **Tustumena Lake** ◎ Alaska, USA
110 *K13* **Tuszyn** Łódzkie, C Poland
137 *S13* **Tutak** Ağrı, E Turkey
185 *C20* **Tutamoe Range** ▲▲ North Island, New Zealand
Tutasev *see* Tutayev
124 *L15* **Tutayev** *var.* Tutasev. Yaroslavskaya Oblast', W Russian Federation
Tutela *see* Tulle, France
Tutela *see* Tudela, Spain
Tutera *see* Tudela
155 *H23* **Tuticorin** Tamil Nādu, SE India
113 *L15* **Tutin** Serbia, S Serbia
184 *O10* **Tutira** Hawke's Bay, North Island, New Zealand
Tutiura *see* Tsuchiura
122 *K10* **Tutonchny** Evenkiyskiy Avtonomnyy Okrug, N Russian Federation
114 *L6* **Tutrakan** Silistra, NE Bulgaria
29 *N5* **Tuttle** North Dakota, N USA
26 *M11* **Tuttle** Oklahoma, C USA
27 *O3* **Tuttle Creek Lake** ⊠ Kansas, C USA
101 *H23* **Tuttlingen** Baden-Württemberg, S Germany
171 *R16* **Tutuala** East Timor
192 *K17* **Tutuila** *island* W American Samoa
83 *I18* **Tutume** Central, E Botswana
39 *N7* **Tututalak Mountain** ▲ Alaska, USA
22 *K3* **Tutwiler** Mississippi, S USA
162 *L8* **Tuul Gol** ≈ N Mongolia
93 *O16* **Tuupovaara** Itä-Suomi, E Finland
Tuva *see* Tyva, Respublika
190 *E7* **Tuvalu** *prev.* Ellice Islands. ◆ *commonwealth republic* SW Pacific Ocean
Tuvinskaya ASSR *see* Tyva, Respublika
163 *O9* **Tuvshinshiree** *var.* Sergelen. Sühbaatar, E Mongolia
141 *P9* **Ṭuwayq, Jabal** ▲▲ C Saudi Arabia
138 *H13* **Ṭuwayyil ash Shihāq** *desert* S Jordan
9 *U16* **Tuxford** Saskatchewan, S Canada
167 *U12* **Tu Xoay** Đắc Lắc, S Vietnam
40 *L14* **Tuxpan** Jalisco, C Mexico
40 *J12* **Tuxpan** Nayarit, C Mexico
41 *Q12* **Tuxpán** *var.* Tuxpán de Rodríguez Cano. Veracruz-Llave, E Mexico
Tuxpán de Rodríguez Cano *see* Tuxpán
41 *R15* **Tuxtepec** *var.* San Juan Bautista Tuxtepec. Oaxaca, S Mexico
41 *U16* **Tuxtla** *var.* Tuxtla Gutiérrez. Chiapas, SE Mexico
Tuxtla *see* San Andrés Tuxtla
Tuxtla Gutiérrez *see* Tuxtla
Tuyama *see* Tsuyama
167 *T5* **Tuyên Quang** Tuyên Quang, N Vietnam
167 *U13* **Tuy Hoa** Binh Thuân, S Vietnam
167 *V12* **Tuy Hoa** Phu Yên, S Vietnam
127 *U5* **Tuymazy** Respublika Bashkortostan, W Russian Federation
Tuy Phong *see* Liên Hương
142 *L6* **Tūysarkān** *var.* Tuisarkan, Tuyserkān. Hamadān, W Iran
Tuyserkān *see* Tūysarkān
145 *W16* **Tuyuk** *Kaz.* Tuyyq. Taldykorgan, SE Kazakhstan
Tuyyq *see* Tuyuk
136 *I14* **Tuz Gölü** ◎ C Turkey
125 *Q15* **Tuzha** Kirovskaya Oblast', NW Russian Federation
113 *K17* **Tuzi** S Montenegro
139 *T5* **Tūz Khurmātū** N Iraq
117 *N15* **Tuzla** Constanţa, SE Romania
112 *I11* **Tuzla** ◈ Federacija Bosna I Hercegovina, NE Bosnia and Herzegovina
137 *T12* **Tuzluca** İgdır, E Turkey
95 *J20* **Tvååker** Halland, S Sweden
95 *F17* **Tvedestrand** Aust-Agder, S Norway
124 *J16* **Tver'** *prev.* Kalinin. Tverskaya Oblast', W Russian Federation
126 *I15* **Tverskaya Oblast'** ◈ *province* W Russian Federation
124 *I15* **Tvertsa** ≈ W Russian Federation
Tverya *see* Teverya
110 *H13* **Twardogóra** *Ger.* Festenberg. Dolnośląskie, SW Poland
14 *J14* **Tweed** Ontario, SE Canada
96 *K13* **Tweed** ≈ England/Scotland, UK
98 *O7* **Tweede-Exloërmond** Drenthe, NE Netherlands
183 *V3* **Tweed Heads** New South Wales, SE Australia
98 *M11* **Twello** Gelderland, E Netherlands
35 *W15* **Twentynine Palms** California, W USA
25 *P9* **Twin Buttes Reservoir** ⊠ Texas, SW USA
33 *O15* **Twin Falls** Idaho, NW USA
39 *N13* **Twin Hills** Alaska, USA
9 *O11* **Twin Lakes** Alberta, W Canada
33 *O12* **Twin Peaks** ▲ Idaho, NW USA
185 *I14* **Twins, The** ▲ South Island, New Zealand
29 *S5* **Twin Valley** Minnesota, N USA
100 *G11* **Twistringen** Niedersachsen, NW Germany
185 *E20* **Twizel** Canterbury, South Island, New Zealand
29 *X5* **Two Harbors** Minnesota, N USA
9 *R14* **Two Hills** Alberta, SW Canada
31 *N7* **Two Rivers** Wisconsin, N USA
116 *H8* **Tyachiv** Zakarpats'ka Oblast', W Ukraine
Tyan'-Shan' *see* Tien Shan
166 *L3* **Tyao** ≈ Myanmar (Burma)/India
117 *R6* **Tyas'myn** ≈ N Ukraine
23 *X6* **Tybee Island** Georgia, SE USA
Tyborøn *see* Thyborøn
111 *J16* **Tychy** *Ger.* Tichau. Śląskie, S Poland
111 *O16* **Tyczyn** Podkarpackie, SE Poland
94 *I8* **Tydal** Sør-Trøndelag, S Norway
115 *H24* **Tyflós** ≈ Kríti, Greece, E Mediterranean Sea
21 *S3* **Tygart Lake** ⊠ West Virginia, NE USA
123 *Q13* **Tygda** Amurskaya Oblast', SE Russian Federation
21 *Q11* **Tyger River** ≈ South Carolina, SE USA
32 *I11* **Tygh Valley** Oregon, NW USA
94 *F12* **Tyin** ◎ S Norway
29 *S10* **Tyler** Minnesota, N USA
25 *W7* **Tyler** Texas, SW USA
25 *W7* **Tyler, Lake** ⊠ Texas, SW USA
22 *K7* **Tylertown** Mississippi, S USA
117 *P10* **Tylihuls'kyy Lyman** ◎ SW Ukraine
Tylos *see* Bahrain
115 *C15* **Týmfi** *var.* Timfi. ▲ W Greece
115 *E17* **Tymfristós** *var.* Timfristos. ▲ C Greece
115 *J25* **Tympáki** *var.* Timbaki; *prev.* Timbákion. Kríti, Greece, E Mediterranean Sea
123 *Q12* **Tynda** Amurskaya Oblast', SE Russian Federation
29 *Q12* **Tyndall** South Dakota, N USA
97 *L14* **Tyne** ≈ N England, UK
97 *M14* **Tynemouth** NE England, UK
97 *L14* **Tyneside** *cultural region* NE England, UK
94 *H10* **Tynset** Hedmark, S Norway
39 *Q12* **Tyonek** Alaska, USA
Tyôsi *see* Chōshi
Tyras *see* Dniester
Tyras *see* Bilhorod-Dnistrovs'kyy
Tyre *see* Soûr
95 *G14* **Tyrifjorden** ◎ S Norway
95 *K22* **Tyringe** Skåne, S Sweden
123 *R13* **Tyrma** Khabarovskiy Kray, SE Russian Federation
Tyrnau *see* Trnava
115 *F15* **Týrnavos** *var.* Tírnavos. Thessalía, C Greece
127 *N16* **Tyrnyauz** Kabardino-Balkarskaya Respublika, SW Russian Federation
Tyrol *see* Tirol
18 *E14* **Tyrone** Pennsylvania, NE USA
97 *E15* **Tyrone** *cultural region* W Northern Ireland, UK
Tyros *see* Bahrain
182 *M10* **Tyrrell, Lake** *salt lake* Victoria, SE Australia
84 *H14* **Tyrrhenian Basin** *undersea feature* Tyrrhenian Sea, C Mediterranean Sea
120 *L8* **Tyrrhenian Sea** *It.* Mare Tirreno. *sea* N Mediterranean Sea
94 *J12* **Tyrsil** ≈ Hedmark, S Norway
Tysa *see* Tisa/Tisza
116 *J7* **Tysmenytsya** Ivano-Frankivs'ka Oblast', W Ukraine
95 *C14* **Tysnesøya** *island* S Norway
95 *C14* **Tysse** Hordaland, S Norway
95 *D14* **Tyssedal** Hordaland, S Norway
95 *O17* **Tystberga** Södermanland, C Sweden
118 *E12* **Tytuvėnai** Šiaulai, C Lithuania
144 *D14* **Tyub-Karagan, Mys** *cape* SW Kazakhstan
147 *V8* **Tyugel'-Say** Narynskaya Oblast', C Kyrgyzstan
122 *H11* **Tyukalinsk** Omskaya Oblast', C Russian Federation
127 *V7* **Tyul'gan** Orenburgskaya Oblast', W Russian Federation
122 *G11* **Tyumen'** Tyumenskaya Oblast', C Russian Federation
122 *H11* **Tyumenskaya Oblast'** ◈ *province* C Russian Federation
147 *Y7* **Tyup** *Kir.* Tüp. Issyk-Kul'skaya Oblast', NE Kyrgyzstan
122 *L14* **Tyva, Respublika** *prev.* Tannu-Tuva, Tuva, Tuvinskaya ASSR. ◈ *autonomous republic* C Russian Federation
117 *N7* **Tyvriv** Vinnyts'ka Oblast', C Ukraine
97 *J21* **Tywi** ≈ S Wales, UK
97 *I19* **Tywyn** W Wales, UK
83 *K20* **Tzaneen** Limpopo, NE South Africa
Tzekung *see* Zigong
115 *I20* **Tziá** *prev.* Kéa, Kéos; *anc.* Ceos. *island* Kykládes, Greece, Aegean Sea
41 *X12* **Tzucacab** Yucatán, SE Mexico

U

82 *B12* **Uaco Cungo** *var.* Waku Kungo, *Port.* Santa Comba. Cuanza Sul, C Angola
UAE *see* United Arab Emirates
191 *X7* **Ua Huka** *island* Îles Marquises, NE French Polynesia
58 *E10* **Uaiacás** Roraima, N Brazil
Uamba *see* Wamba
Uanle Uen *see* Wanlaweyn
191 *W7* **Ua Pu** *island* Îles Marquises, NE French Polynesia
81 *L17* **Uar Garas** *spring/well* SW Somalia
58 *G12* **Uatumã, Rio** ≈ C Brazil
Ua Uíbh Fhailí *see* Offaly
58 *C11* **Uaupés, Rio** *var.* Río Vaupés. ≈ Brazil/Colombia *see also* Vaupés, Río
Uaupés, Rio *see* Vaupés, Río
145 *X9* **Uba** ≈ E Kazakhstan
145 *N6* **Ubagan** *Kaz.* Obagan. ≈ Kazakhstan/Russian Federation
186 *G7* **Ubai** New Britain, E Papua New Guinea
79 *J15* **Ubangi** *Fr.* Oubangui. ≈ C Africa
Ubangi-Shari *see* Central African Republic
116 *M3* **Ubarts'** *Ukr.* Ubort'. ≈ Belarus/Ukraine *see also* Ubort'
Ubarts' *see* Ubort'
54 *F9* **Ubaté** Cundinamarca, C Colombia
60 *N10* **Ubatuba** São Paulo, S Brazil
149 *R12* **Ubauro** Sind, SE Pakistan
171 *Q6* **Ubay** Bohol, C Philippines
103 *U14* **Ubaye** ≈ SE France
Ubayid, Wadi al *see* Ubayyiḍ, Wādī al
139 *N8* **Ubaylah** W Iraq
139 *O10* **Ubayyiḍ, Wādī al** *var.* Wadi al Ubayid. *dry watercourse* SW Iraq
98 *L13* **Ubbergen** Gelderland, E Netherlands
164 *E13* **Ube** Yamaguchi, Honshū, SW Japan
105 *O13* **Ubeda** Andalucía, S Spain
109 *V7* **Übelbach** *var.* Markt-Übelbach. Steiermark, SE Austria
59 *L20* **Uberaba** Minas Gerais, SE Brazil
57 *Q19* **Uberaba, Laguna** ◎ E Bolivia
59 *K19* **Uberlândia** Minas Gerais, SE Brazil
101 *H24* **Überlingen** Baden-Württemberg, S Germany
77 *U16* **Ubiaja** Edo, S Nigeria
104 *K3* **Ubiña, Peña** ▲ NW Spain
57 *H17* **Ubinas, Volcán** 🌋 S Peru
Ubol Rajadhani/Ubol Ratchathani *see* Ubon Ratchathani
167 *P9* **Ubolratna Reservoir** ⊠ C Thailand
167 *S10* **Ubon Ratchathani** *var.* Muang Ubon, Ubol Rajadhani, Ubol Ratchathani, Udon Ratchathani. Ubon Ratchathani, E Thailand
119 *L20* **Ubort'** *Bel.* Ubarts'. ≈ Belarus/Ukraine *see also* Ubarts'
Ubort' *see* Ubarts'
104 *K15* **Ubrique** Andalucía, S Spain
Ubsu-Nur, Ozero *see* Uvs Nuur
79 *M18* **Ubundu** Orientale, C Dem. Rep. Congo
146 *J13* **Uçajy** *var.* Üchajy, *Rus.* Uch-Adzhi. Mary Welaýaty, C Turkmenistan
137 *X11* **Ucar** *Rus.* Udzhary. C Azerbaijan
56 *G13* **Ucayali** *off.* Departamento de Ucayali. ◈ *department* E Peru
Ucayali, Departamento de *see* Ucayali
56 *F10* **Ucayali, Río** ≈ C Peru
Uccle *see* Ukkel
Uch-Adzhi/Üchajy *see* Uçajy
127 *X4* **Uchaly** Respublika Bashkortostan, W Russian Federation
145 *W13* **Ucharal** *Kaz.* Üsharal. Almaty, E Kazakhstan
164 *C17* **Uchinoura** Kagoshima, Kyūshū, SW Japan
165 *R5* **Uchiura-wan** *bay* NW Pacific Ocean
Uchkuduk *see* Uchquduq
Uchkurghan *see* Uchqŭrgon
147 *S9* **Uchqo'rg'on** *Rus.* Uchkurghan. Namangan Viloyati
146 *K8* **Uchquduq** *Rus.* Uchkuduk. Navoiy Viloyati, N Uzbekistan
147 *S9* **Uchqŭrgon** *Rus.* Uchkurghan. Namangan Viloyati, E Uzbekistan
Uchsay *see* Uchsoy
146 *G6* **Uchsoy** *Rus.* Uchsay. Qoraqalpog'iston Respublikasi, NW Uzbekistan
Uchtagan Gumy/Uchtagan, Peski *see* Uçtagan Gumy
123 *R11* **Uchur** ≈ E Russian Federation
100 *O10* **Uckermark** *cultural region* E Germany
10 *K17* **Ucluelet** Vancouver Island, British Columbia, SW Canada
146 *D10* **Uçtagan Gumy** *var.* Uchtagan Gumy, *Rus.* Peski Uchtagan. *desert* NW Turkmenistan
122 *M13* **Uda** ≈ S Russian Federation
123 *R12* **Uda** ≈ E Russian Federation
123 *N6* **Udachnyy** Respublika Sakha (Yakutiya), NE Russian Federation
155 *G21* **Udagamandalam** *var.* Udhagamandalam; *prev.* Ootacamund. Tamil Nādu, SW India
152 *F14* **Udaipur** *prev.* Oodeypore. Rājasthān, N India
Udayadhani *see* Uthai Thani
143 *N16* **'Udayd, Khawr al** *var.* Khor al Udeid. *inlet* Qatar/Saudi Arabia
112 *D11* **Udbina** Lika-Senj, W Croatia
95 *I18* **Uddevalla** Västra Götaland, S Sweden
Uddjaur *see* Uddjaure
92 *H13* **Uddjaure** *var.* Uddjaur. ◎ N Sweden
Udeid, Khor al *see* 'Udayd, Khawr al
99 *K14* **Uden** Noord-Brabant, SE Netherlands
Uden *see* Udenhout
99 *J14* **Udenhout** *var.* Uden. Noord-Brabant, S Netherlands
155 *H14* **Udgīr** Mahārāshtra, C India
Udhagamandalam *see* Udagamandalam
152 *H6* **Udhampur** Jammu and Kashmir, NW India
139 *X14* **'Udhaybah, 'Uqlat al** *well* S Iraq
106 *J7* **Udine** *anc.* Utina. Friuli-Venezia Giulia, NE Italy
175 *T14* **Udintsev Fracture Zone** *tectonic feature* S Pacific Ocean
Udipi *see* Udupi
Udmurtia *see* Udmurtskaya Respublika
127 *S2* **Udmurtskaya Respublika** *Eng.* Udmurtia. ◈ *autonomous republic* NW Russian Federation
124 *J15* **Udomlya** Tverskaya Oblast', W Russian Federation
Udon Ratchathani *see* Ubon Ratchathani
167 *Q8* **Udon Thani** *var.* Ban Mak Khaeng, Udorndhani. Udon Thani, N Thailand
Udorndhani *see* Udon Thani
189 *U12* **Udot** *atoll* Chuuk Islands, C Micronesia
123 *S12* **Udskaya Guba** *bay* E Russian Federation
155 *E19* **Udupi** *var.* Udipi. Karnātaka, SW India
Udzhary *see* Ucar
100 *O9* **Uecker** ≈ NE Germany
100 *P9* **Ueckermünde** Mecklenburg-Vorpommern, NE Germany
164 *M12* **Ueda** *var.* Uyeda. Nagano, Honshū, S Japan
79 *L16* **Uele** *var.* Welle. ≈ NE Dem. Rep. Congo
123 *W5* **Uelen** Chukotskiy Avtonomnyy Okrug, NE Russian Federation
Uele (upper course) *see* Kibali, Dem. Rep. Congo
Uele (upper course) *see* Uolo, Río, Equatorial Guinea/Gabon
100 *J11* **Uelzen** Niedersachsen, N Germany
164 *J14* **Ueno** Mie, Honshū, SW Japan
127 *V4* **Ufa** Respublika Bashkortostan, W Russian Federation
127 *V4* **Ufa** ≈ W Russian Federation
Ufra *see* Kenar
83 *C18* **Ugab** ≈ C Namibia
118 *D8* **Ugāle** Ventspils, NW Latvia
81 *F17* **Uganda** *off.* Republic of Uganda. ◆ *republic* E Africa
Uganda, Republic of *see* Uganda
138 *G4* **Ugarit** *Ar.* Ra's Shamrah. *site of ancient city* Al Lādhiqīyah, NW Syria
39 *O14* **Ugashik** Alaska, USA
107 *Q19* **Ugento** Puglia, SE Italy
105 *O15* **Ugíjar** Andalucía, S Spain
103 *T11* **Ugine** Savoie, E France
123 *R13* **Uglegorsk** Amurskaya Oblast', S Russian Federation
125 *V13* **Ugleural'sk** Permskaya Oblast', NW Russian Federation
124 *L15* **Uglich** Yaroslavskaya Oblast', W Russian Federation
124 *I14* **Uglovka** *var.* Okulovka. Novgorodskaya Oblast', W Russian Federation
126 *I4* **Ugra** ≈ W Russian Federation
147 *V9* **Ugyut** Narynskaya Oblast', C Kyrgyzstan
111 *H19* **Uherské Hradiště** *Ger.* Ungarisch-Hradisch. Zlínský Kraj, E Czech Republic
111 *H19* **Uherský Brod** *Ger.* Ungarisch-Brod. Zlínský Kraj, E Czech Republic
111 *B17* **Úhlava** *Ger.* Angel. ≈ W Czech Republic
Uhorshchyna *see* Hungary
31 *T13* **Uhrichsville** Ohio, N USA
Uhuru Peak *see* Kilimanjaro
96 *G8* **Uig** N Scotland, UK
82 *B10* **Uíge** *Port.* Carmona, Vila Marechal Carmona. Uíge, NW Angola
82 *B10* **Uíge** ◈ *province* N Angola
193 *Y15* **Uiha** *island* Ha'apai Group, C Tonga
189 *U13* **Uijec** *island* Chuuk, C Micronesia
163 *X14* **Ŭijŏngbu** *Jap.* Giseifu. NW South Korea
144 *H10* **Uil** *Kaz.* Oyyl. Aktyubinsk, W Kazakhstan
144 *H10* **Uil** *Kaz.* Oyyl. ≈ W Kazakhstan
36 *M3* **Uinta Mountains** ▲▲ Utah, W USA
83 *C18* **Uis** Erongo, NW Namibia
83 *I25* **Uitenhage** Eastern Cape, S South Africa
98 *H9* **Uitgeest** Noord-Holland, W Netherlands
98 *I11* **Uithoorn** Noord-Holland, C Netherlands
98 *O4* **Uithuizen** Groningen, NE Netherlands
98 *O4* **Uithuizermeeden** Groningen, NE Netherlands
189 *R6* **Ujae Atoll** *var.* Wūjae. *atoll* Ralik Chain, W Marshall Islands
Ujain *see* Ujjain
111 *I16* **Ujazd** Opolskie, S Poland
Új-Becse *see* Novi Bečej
Ujda *see* Oujda
189 *N5* **Ujelang Atoll** *var.* Wujlān. *atoll* Ralik Chain, W Marshall Islands
111 *N21* **Újfehértó** Szabolcs-Szatmár-Bereg, E Hungary
Újgradiska *see* Nova Gradiška
164 *J13* **Uji** *var.* Uzi. Kyōto, Honshū, SW Japan
81 *E21* **Ujiji** Kigoma, W Tanzania
154 *G10* **Ujjain** *prev.* Ujain. Madhya Pradesh, C India
Újlak *see* Ilok
'Ujmān *see* 'Ajmān
Újmoldova *see* Moldova Nouă
Újszentanna *see* Sântana
Ujungpandang *see* Makassar
Ujung Salang *see* Phuket
Újvidék *see* Novi Sad
UK *see* United Kingdom
154 *E11* **Ukāi Reservoir** ⊠ W India
81 *G19* **Ukara Island** *island* N Tanzania
'Ukash, Wādī *see* 'Akāsh, Wādī
81 *F19* **Ukerewe Island** *island* N Tanzania
139 *S9* **Ukhayḍhīr** C Iraq
153 *X13* **Ukhrul** Manipur, NE India
125 *S9* **Ukhta** Respublika Komi, NW Russian Federation
34 *L6* **Ukiah** California, W USA
32 *K12* **Ukiah** Oregon, NW USA
99 *G18* **Ukkel** *Fr.* Uccle. Brussels, C Belgium
118 *G13* **Ukmergė** *Pol.* Wiłkomierz. Vilnius, C Lithuania
Ukraina *see* Ukraine
116 *L6* **Ukraine** *off.* Ukraine, *Rus.* Ukraina, *Ukr.* Ukrayina; *prev.* Ukrainian Soviet Socialist Republic, Ukrainskay S.S.R. ◆ *republic* SE Europe
Ukraine *see* Ukraine
Ukrainian Soviet Socialist Republic *see* Ukraine
Ukrainskay S.S.R/Ukrayina *see* Ukraine
82 *B13* **Uku** Cuanza Sul, NW Angola
164 *B13* **Uku-jima** *island* Gotō-rettō, SW Japan
83 *F20* **Ukwi** Kgalagadi, SW Botswana
118 *M13* **Ula** *Rus.* Ulla. Vitsyebskaya Voblasts', N Belarus
136 *C16* **Ula** Muğla, SW Turkey
118 *M13* **Ula** *Rus.* Ulla. ≈ N Belarus
162 *L7* **Ulaanbaatar** *Eng.* Ulan Bator; *prev.* Urga. ● (Mongolia) Töv, C Mongolia
Ulaan-Ereg *see* Bayanmönh
162 *E5* **Ulaangom** Uvs, NW Mongolia
162 *D5* **Ulaanhus** *var.* Bilüü. Bayan-Ölgiy, W Mongolia
Ulaantolgoy *see* Möst
Ulaan-Uul *see* Öldziyt, Bayanhongor, Mongolia
Ulaan-Uul *see* Erdene, Dornogovĭ, Mongolia
162 *M14* **Ulan** *var.* Otog Qi. Nei Mongol Zizhiqu, N China
159 *R10* **Ulan** *var.* Xireg; *prev.* Xiligou. Qinghai, C China
Ulan Bator *see* Ulaanbaatar
162 *L13* **Ulan Buh Shamo** *desert* N China
Ulanhad *see* Chifeng
163 *T8* **Ulanhot** Nei Mongol Zizhiqu, N China
127 *Q14* **Ulan Khol** Respublika Kalmykiya, SW Russian Federation
162 *M13* **Ulansuhai Nur** ◎ N China
123 *N14* **Ulan-Ude** *prev.* Verkhneudinsk. Respublika Buryatiya, S Russian Federation
159 *N12* **Ulan Ul Hu** ◎ C China
187 *N9* **Ulawa Island** *island* SE Solomon Islands
138 *J7* **'Ulayyānīyah, Bi'r al** *var.* Al Hilbeh. *well* S Syria
123 *S12* **Ul'banskiy Zaliv** *strait* E Russian Federation
Ulbo *see* Olib
113 *J18* **Ulcinj** S Montenegro
Uldz *see* Norovlin
Uleåborg *see* Oulu
Uleälv *see* Oulujoki
95 *G16* **Ulefoss** Telemark, S Norway
Uleträsk *see* Oulujärvi
113 *L19* **Ulëz** *var.* Ulëza. Dibër, C Albania
Ulëza *see* Ulëz
95 *F22* **Ulfborg** Ringkøbing, W Denmark
98 *N13* **Ulft** Gelderland, E Netherlands
162 *G7* **Uliastay** *prev.* Jibhalanta. Dzavhan, W Mongolia
188 *F8* **Ulimang** Babeldaob, N Palau
67 *T10* **Ulindi** ≈ W Dem. Rep. Congo
188 *H14* **Ulithi Atoll** *atoll* Caroline Islands, W Micronesia
112 *N10* **Uljma** Vojvodina, NE Serbia
144 *L11* **Ul'kayak** *Kaz.* Ölkeyek. ≈ C Kazakhstan
145 *Q7* **Ul'ken-Karoy, Ozero** ◎ N Kazakhstan
Ülkenözen *see* Bol'shoy Uzen'
Ülkenqobda *see* Bol'shaya Khobda
104 *G3* **Ulla** ≈ NW Spain
Ulla *see* Ula
183 *S10* **Ulladulla** New South Wales, SE Australia
153 *T14* **Ullapara** Rajshahi, W Bangladesh
96 *H7* **Ullapool** N Scotland, UK
95 *J20* **Ullared** Halland, S Sweden
105 *T7* **Ulldecona** Cataluña, NE Spain
92 *I9* **Ullsfjorden** *fjord* N Norway
97 *K15* **Ullswater** ◎ NW England, UK
101 *I22* **Ulm** Baden-Württemberg, S Germany
33 *R8* **Ulm** Montana, NW USA
183 *V5* **Ulmarra** New South Wales, SE Australia
116 *K13* **Ulmeni** Buzău, C Romania
116 *K14* **Ulmeni** Călăraşi, S Romania
42 *L7* **Ulmukhuás** Región Autónoma Atlántico Norte, NE Nicaragua
188 *C8* **Ulong** *var.* Aulong. *island* Palau Islands, N Palau
83 *N14* **Ulonguè** *var.* Ulongwé. Tete, NW Mozambique
Ulongwé *see* Ulonguè
95 *K19* **Ulricehamn** Västra Götaland, S Sweden
98 *N5* **Ulrum** Groningen, NE Netherlands
163 *Z16* **Ulsan** *Jap.* Urusan. SE South Korea
94 *D10* **Ulsteinvik** Møre og Romsdal, S Norway
97 *D15* **Ulster** ◈ *province* Northern Ireland, UK/Ireland
171 *Q10* **Ulu** Pulau Siau, N Indonesia
123 *Q11* **Ulu** Respublika Sakha (Yakutiya), NE Russian Federation
42 *H5* **Ulúa, Río** ≈ NW Honduras
136 *D12* **Ulubat Gölü** ◎ NW Turkey
136 *E12* **Uludağ** ▲ NW Turkey
158 *D7* **Ulugqat** Xinjiang Uygur Zizhiqu, W China
136 *J16* **Ulukışla** Niğde, S Turkey
189 *O15* **Ulul** *island* Caroline Islands, C Micronesia
83 *L22* **Ulundi** KwaZulu/Natal, E South Africa
158 *M3* **Ulungur He** ≈ NW China
158 *K2* **Ulungur Hu** ◎ NW China
181 *P8* **Uluru** *var.* Ayers Rock. *rocky outcrop* Northern Territory, C Australia
97 *K16* **Ulverston** NW England, UK
183 *O16* **Ulverstone** Tasmania, SE Australia
94 *D13* **Ulvik** Hordaland, S Norway
93 *J18* **Ulvila** Länsi-Soumi, W Finland
117 *O8* **Ulyanivka** *Rus.* Ul'yanovka. Kirovohrads'ka Oblast', C Ukraine
Ul'yanovka *see* Ulyanivka
127 *Q5* **Ul'yanovsk** *prev.* Simbirsk. Ul'yanovskaya Oblast', W Russian Federation
127 *Q5* **Ul'yanovskaya Oblast'** ◈ *province* W Russian Federation
145 *S10* **Ul'yanovskiy** Karaganda, C Kazakhstan
Ul'yanovskiy Kanal *see* Ul'yanow Kanali
146 *M13* **Ul'yanow Kanali** *Rus.* Ul'yanovskiy Kanal. *canal* Turkmenistan/Uzbekistan
Ulyshylanshyq *see* Uly-Zhylanshyk
26 *H6* **Ulysses** Kansas, C USA
145 *O12* **Ulytau, Gory** ▲▲ C Kazakhstan
145 *N11* **Uly-Zhylanshyk** *Kaz.* Ulyshylanshyq. ≈ C Kazakhstan
112 *A9* **Umag** *It.* Umago. Istra, NW Croatia
Umago *see* Umag
41 *W12* **Umán** Yucatán, SE Mexico
117 *O7* **Uman'** *Rus.* Uman. Cherkas'ka Oblast', C Ukraine
189 *V13* **Uman** *atoll* Chuuk Islands, C Micronesia
Uman *see* Uman'
Umanak/Umanaq *see* Uummannaq
'Umān, Khalīj *see* Oman, Gulf of
'Umān, Salṭanat *see* Oman
154 *K10* **Umaria** Madhya Pradesh, C India
149 *R16* **Umar kot** Sind, SE Pakistan
188 *B17* **Umatac** SW Guam
188 *A17* **Umatac Bay** *bay* SW Guam
139 *S6* **Umayqah** C Iraq
124 *J5* **Umba** Murmanskaya Oblast', NW Russian Federation
138 *I8* **Umbāshī, Khirbat al** *ruins* As Suwaydā', S Syria
80 *A12* **Umbelasha** ≈ W Sudan
106 *H12* **Umbertide** Umbria, C Italy
61 *B17* **Umberto** *var.* Humberto. Santa Fe, C Argentina
186 *E7* **Umboi Island** *var.* Rooke Island. *island* C Papua New Guinea
124 *J4* **Umbozero, Ozero** ◎ NW Russian Federation
106 *H13* **Umbria** ◈ *region* C Italy
Umbrian-Machigian Mountains *see* Umbro-Marchigiano, Appennino
106 *I12* **Umbro-Marchigiano, Appennino** *Eng.* Umbrian-Machigian Mountains. ▲▲ C Italy
93 *J16* **Umeå** Västerbotten, N Sweden
93 *H14* **Umeälven** ≈ N Sweden
39 *Q5* **Umiat** Alaska, USA
83 *K23* **Umlazi** KwaZulu/Natal, E South Africa
139 *X10* **Umm al Baqar, Hawr** *var.* Birkat ad Dawaymah. *spring* S Iraq
141 *U12* **Umm al Ḥayt, Wādī** *var.* Wādī Amilḥayt. *seasonal river* SW Oman
Umm al Qaiwain *see* Umm al Qaywayn
143 *R15* **Umm al Qaywayn** *var.* Umm al Qaiwain. Umm al Qaywayn, NE United Arab Emirates
139 *Q5* **Umm al Tūz** C Iraq
138 *J3* **Umm 'Āmūd** Ḥalab, N Syria
141 *Y10* **Umm ar Ruṣāṣ** *var.* Umm Ruṣayṣ. W Oman
141 *X9* **Ummas Samīn** *sabkha* C Oman
141 *V9* **Umm az Zumūl** *oasis* E Saudi Arabia
80 *A9* **Umm Buru** Western Darfur, W Sudan
80 *A12* **Umm Dafag** Southern Darfur, W Sudan
Umm Durmān *see* Omdurman
138 *F9* **Umm el Fahm** Haifa, N Israel
80 *F9* **Umm Inderab** Northern Kordofan, C Sudan
80 *C10* **Umm Keddada** Northern Darfur, W Sudan
140 *J7* **Umm Lajj** Tabūk, W Saudi Arabia
138 *L10* **Umm Maḥfur** ≈ N Jordan
139 *Y13* **Umm Qaṣr** SE Iraq
Umm Ruṣayṣ *see* Umm ar Ruṣāṣ
80 *F11* **Umm Ruwaba** *var.* Umm Ruwābah, Um Ruwāba. Northern Kordofan, C Sudan
Umm Ruwābah *see* Umm Ruwaba
143 *N16* **Umm Sa'īd** *var.* Musay'īd. S Qatar
138 *K10* **Umm Ṭuways, Wādī** *dry watercourse* N Jordan
38 *J17* **Umnak Island** *island* Aleutian Islands, Alaska, USA
32 *F13* **Umpqua River** ≈ Oregon, NW USA
82 *D13* **Umpulo** Bié, C Angola
154 *I12* **Umred** Mahārāshtra, C India
139 *Y10* **Umr Sawān, Hawr** ◎ S Iraq
Um Ruwāba *see* Umm Ruwaba
Umtali *see* Mutare
83 *J24* **Umtata** Eastern Cape, SE South Africa
77 *V17* **Umuahia** Abia, SW Nigeria
60 *H10* **Umuarama** Paraná, S Brazil
Umvuma *see* Mvuma
83 *K18* **Umzingwani** ≈ S Zimbabwe
112 *D11* **Una** ≈ Bosnia and Herzegovina/Croatia
112 *E12* **Unac** ≈ W Bosnia and Herzegovina
23 *T6* **Unadilla** Georgia, SE USA
18 *I10* **Unadilla River** ≈ New York, NE USA
59 *L18* **Unaí** Minas Gerais, SE Brazil
39 *N10* **Unalakleet** Alaska, USA
38 *K17* **Unalaska Island** *island* Aleutian Islands, Alaska, USA
185 *I16* **Una, Mount** ▲ South Island, New Zealand
82 *N13* **Unango** Niassa, N Mozambique
Unao *see* Unnão
92 *L12* **Unari** Lappi, N Finland
141 *O6* **'Unayzah** *var.* Anaiza. Al Qaṣīm, C Saudi Arabia
138 *L10* **'Unayzah, Jabal** ▲ Jordan/Saudi Arabia
Unci *see* Almería
57 *K19* **Uncía** Potosí, C Bolivia
37 *Q7* **Uncompahgre Peak** ▲ Colorado, C USA
37 *P6* **Uncompahgre Plateau** *plain* Colorado, C USA
95 *L17* **Unden** ◎ S Sweden
28 *M4* **Underwood** North Dakota, N USA
171 *T13* **Undur** Pulau Seram, E Indonesia

◆ Country
● Country Capital
◇ Dependent Territory
○ Dependent Territory Capital
◈ Administrative Regions
✈ International Airport
▲ Mountain
▲▲ Mountain Range
🌋 Volcano
≈ River
◎ Lake
⊠ Reservoir

Undur Khan see Öndörhaan
126 H6 **Unecha** Bryanskaya Oblast', W Russian Federation
39 N16 **Unga** Unga Island, Alaska, USA
Ungaria see Hungary
183 P8 **Ungarie** New South Wales, SE Australia
Ungarisch-Brod see Uherský Brod
Ungarisches Erzgebirge see Slovenské rudohorie
Ungarisch-Hradisch see Uherské Hradiště
Ungarn see Hungary
12 M4 **Ungava Bay** *bay* Québec, E Canada
12 J2 **Ungava, Péninsule d'** *peninsula* Québec, SE Canada
Ungeny see Ungheni
116 M9 **Ungheni** *Rus.* Ungeny. W Moldova
Unguja see Zanzibar
146 G10 **Üngüz Angyrsyndaky Garagum** *Rus.* Zaunguzskiye Garagumy. *desert* N Turkmenistan
146 H11 **Unguz, Solonchakovyye Vpadiny** *salt marsh* C Turkmenistan
Ungvár see Uzhhorod
60 I12 **União da Vitória** Paraná, S Brazil
111 G17 **Uničov** *Ger.* Mährisch-Neustadt. Olomoucký Kraj, E Czech Republic
110 J12 **Uniejów** Łódzkie, C Poland
112 A11 **Unije** *island* W Croatia
38 L16 **Unimak Island** *island* Aleutian Islands, Alaska, USA
38 L16 **Unimak Pass** *strait* Aleutian Islands, Alaska, USA
62 J12 **Unión** San Luis, C Argentina
27 W5 **Union** Missouri, C USA
32 L12 **Union** Oregon, NW USA
21 Q11 **Union** South Carolina, SE USA
21 R6 **Union** West Virginia, NE USA
61 B25 **Unión, Bahía** *bay* E Argentina
31 Q13 **Union City** Indiana, N USA
31 Q10 **Union City** Michigan, N USA
18 C12 **Union City** Pennsylvania, NE USA
20 G8 **Union City** Tennessee, S USA
32 G14 **Union Creek** Oregon, NW USA
83 G25 **Uniondale** Western Cape, SW South Africa
40 K13 **Unión de Tula** Jalisco, SW Mexico
30 M9 **Union Grove** Wisconsin, N USA
45 Y15 **Union Island** *island* S Saint Vincent and the Grenadines
Union of Myanmar see Burma
46 K5 **Union Reefs** *reef* SW Mexico
0 D7 **Union Seamount** *undersea feature* NE Pacific Ocean
23 Q6 **Union Springs** Alabama, S USA
20 H6 **Uniontown** Kentucky, S USA
18 C16 **Uniontown** Pennsylvania, NE USA
27 T1 **Unionville** Missouri, C USA
141 V8 **United Arab Emirates** *Ar.* Al Imārāt al 'Arabīyah al Muttaḥidah, *abbrev.* UAE; *prev.* Trucial States. ◆ *federation* SW Asia
United Arab Republic see Egypt
97 H14 **United Kingdom** *off.* United Kingdom of Great Britain and Northern Ireland, *abbrev.* UK. ◆ *monarchy* NW Europe
United Kingdom of Great Britain and Northern Ireland see United Kingdom
United Mexican States see Mexico
United Provinces see Uttar Pradesh
16 L10 **United States of America** *off.* United States of America, *var.* America, The States, *abbrev.* U.S., USA. ◆ *federal republic*
United States of America see United States of America
124 J10 **Unitsa** Respublika Kareliya, NW Russian Federation
9 S15 **Unity** Saskatchewan, S Canada
Unity State see Wahda
105 Q8 **Universales, Montes** ▲▲ C Spain
27 X4 **University City** Missouri, C USA
187 Q13 **Unmet** Malekula, C Vanuatu
101 F15 **Unna** Nordrhein-Westfalen, W Germany
152 L12 **Unnāo** *prev.* Unao. Uttar Pradesh, N India
187 R15 **Unpongkor** Erromango, S Vanuatu
Unruhstadt see Kargowa
96 M1 **Unst** *island* NE Scotland, UK
101 K16 **Unstrut** ≈ C Germany
Unterdrauburg see Dravograd
Unterlimbach see Lendava
101 L23 **Unterschleissheim** Bayern, SE Germany
101 H24 **Untersee** ◎ Germany/Switzerland
100 O10 **Unterueckersee** ◎ NE Germany
108 F9 **Unterwalden** ◈ *canton* C Switzerland
55 N12 **Unturán, Sierra de** ▲▲ Brazil/Venezuela
159 N11 **Unuli Horog** Qinghai, W China
136 M11 **Ünye** Ordu, W Turkey
Unza see Unzha
125 O14 **Unzha** *var.* Unza. ≈ NW Russian Federation
79 E17 **Uolo, Río** *var.* Eyo (lower course), Mbini, Uele (upper course), Woleu; *prev.* Benito. ≈ Equatorial Guinea/Gabon
55 Q10 **Uonán** Bolívar, SE Venezuela
161 T12 **Uotsuri-shima** *island* China/Japan/Taiwan
165 M11 **Uozu** Toyama, Honshū, SW Japan
42 L12 **Upala** Alajuela, NW Costa Rica
55 P7 **Upata** Bolívar, E Venezuela
79 M23 **Upemba, Lac** ◎ SE Dem. Rep. Congo
197 O12 **Upernavik** *var.* Upernivik. ◈ Kitaa, C Greenland
Upernivik see Upernavik
83 F22 **Upington** Northern Cape, W South Africa
Uplands see Ottawa
192 I16 **Upolu** *island* SE Samoa
38 G11 **'Upolu Point** *var.* Upolu Point. *headland* Hawai'i, USA, C Pacific Ocean
Upper Austria see Oberösterreich
Upper Bann see Bann
14 M13 **Upper Canada Village** *tourist site* Ontario, SE Canada
18 I16 **Upper Darby** Pennsylvania, NE USA
28 L2 **Upper Des Lacs Lake** ⊠ North Dakota, N USA
185 L14 **Upper Hutt** Wellington, North Island, New Zealand
29 X11 **Upper Iowa River** ≈ Iowa, C USA
32 H15 **Upper Klamath Lake** ◎ Oregon, NW USA
34 M6 **Upper Lake** California, W USA
35 Q1 **Upper Lake** ◎ California, W USA
10 K9 **Upper Liard** Yukon Territory, W Canada
97 E16 **Upper Lough Erne** ◎ SW Northern Ireland, UK
80 F12 **Upper Nile** ◈ *state* E Sudan
29 T3 **Upper Red Lake** ◎ Minnesota, N USA
31 S12 **Upper Sandusky** Ohio, N USA
Upper Volta see Burkina
95 O15 **Upplandsväsby** *var.* Upplands Väsby. Stockholm, C Sweden
Upplands Väsby see Upplandsväsby
95 O15 **Uppsala** Uppsala, C Sweden
95 O14 **Uppsala** ◈ *county* C Sweden
38 J12 **Upright Cape** *headland* Saint Matthew Island, Alaska, USA
20 K6 **Upton** Kentucky, S USA
33 Y13 **Upton** Wyoming, C USA
141 N7 **'Uqlat aṣ Ṣuqūr** Al Qaṣīm, W Saudi Arabia
Uqturpan see Wushi
54 C7 **Urabá, Golfo de** *gulf* NW Colombia
Uracas see Farallon de Pajaros
Uradarya see O'radaryo
Uradar'ya see O'radaryo
Urad Qianqi see Xishanzui
165 U5 **Urahoro** Hokkaidō, NE Japan
165 T5 **Urakawa** Hokkaidō, NE Japan
127 X6 **Ural** *Kaz.* Zayyq. ≈ Kazakhstan/Russian Federation
183 T6 **Uralla** New South Wales, SE Australia
Ural Mountains see Ural'skiye Gory
144 F8 **Ural'sk** *Kaz.* Oral. Zapadnyy Kazakhstan, NW Kazakhstan
Ural'skaya Oblast' see Zapadnyy Kazakhstan
127 W5 **Ural'skiye Gory** *var.* Ural'skiy Khrebet, *Eng.* Ural Mountains. ▲▲ Kazakhstan/Russian Federation
Ural'skiy Khrebet see Ural'skiye Gory
138 I3 **Urām aṣ Ṣughrá** Ḥalab, N Syria
183 P10 **Urana** New South Wales, SE Australia
9 S10 **Uranium City** Saskatchewan, C Canada
58 F10 **Uraricoera** Roraima, N Brazil
47 S5 **Uraricoera, Rio** ≈ N Brazil
Ura-Tyube see Üroteppa
165 O13 **Urawa** Saitama, Honshū, S Japan
122 H10 **Uray** Khanty-Mansiyskiy Avtonomnyy Okrug, C Russian Federation
141 R7 **'Uray'irah** Ash Sharqīyah, E Saudi Arabia
30 M13 **Urbana** Illinois, N USA
31 R13 **Urbana** Ohio, N USA
29 V14 **Urbandale** Iowa, C USA
106 I11 **Urbania** Marche, C Italy
106 I11 **Urbino** Marche, C Italy
57 H16 **Urcos** Cusco, S Peru
144 D10 **Urda** Zapadnyy Kazakhstan, W Kazakhstan
105 N10 **Urda** Castilla-La Mancha, C Spain
Urdgol see Chandmanī
105 O3 **Urduña** *var.* Orduña. País Vasco, N Spain
Urdunn see Jordan
145 X12 **Urdzhar** *Kaz.* Ürzhar. Vostochnyy Kazakhstan, E Kazakhstan
97 L16 **Ure** ≈ N England, UK
119 K18 **Urechcha** *Rus.* Urech'ye. Minskaya Voblasts', S Belarus
Urech'ye see Urechcha
127 P2 **Uren'** Nizhegorodskaya Oblast', W Russian Federation
122 J9 **Urengoy** Yamalo-Nenetskiy Avtonomnyy Okrug, N Russian Federation
184 K10 **Urenui** Taranaki, North Island, New Zealand
187 Q12 **Ureparapara** *island* Banks Islands, N Vanuatu
40 G5 **Ures** Sonora, NW Mexico
Urfa see Şanlıurfa
Urga see Ulaanbaatar
162 F6 **Urgamal** *var.* Hungiy. Dzavhan, W Mongolia
146 H9 **Urganch** *Rus.* Urgench; *prev.* Novo-Urgench. Xorazm Viloyati, W Uzbekistan
Urgench see Urganch
136 J14 **Ürgüp** Nevşehir, C Turkey
147 O12 **Urgut** Samarqand Viloyati, C Uzbekistan
158 K3 **Urho** Xinjiang Uygur Zizhiqu, W China
152 G5 **Uri** Jammu and Kashmir, NW India
108 G9 **Uri** ◈ *canton* C Switzerland
54 F11 **Uribe** Meta, C Colombia
54 H4 **Uribia** La Guajira, N Colombia
116 G12 **Uricani** *Hung.* Hobicaurikány. Hunedoara, SW Romania
57 M21 **Uriondo** Tarija, S Bolivia
40 I7 **Urique** Chihuahua, N Mexico
40 I7 **Urique, Río** ≈ N Mexico
56 E9 **Urituyacu, Río** ≈ N Peru
Uritskiy see Sarykol'
98 K8 **Urk** Flevoland, N Netherlands
136 B14 **Urla** İzmir, W Turkey
116 K13 **Urlați** Prahova, SE Romania
127 V4 **Urman** Respublika Bashkortostan, W Russian Federation
147 P12 **Urmetan** W Tajikistan
Urmia see Orūmīyeh
Urmia, Lake see Orūmīyeh, Daryācheh-ye
Urmiyeh see Orūmīyeh
113 N17 **Uroševac** *Alb.* Ferizaj. Kosovo, S Serbia
147 P11 **Üroteppa** *Rus.* Ura-Tyube. NW Tajikistan
54 D8 **Urrao** Antioquia, W Colombia
Ursat'yevskaya see Xovos
Urt see Gurvantes
127 X7 **Urtazym** Orenburgskaya Oblast', W Russian Federation
59 K18 **Uruaçu** Goiás, C Brazil
40 M14 **Uruapan** *var.* Uruapan del Progreso. Michoacán de Ocampo, SW Mexico
Uruapan del Progreso see Uruapan
57 G15 **Urubamba, Cordillera** ▲▲ C Peru
57 G14 **Urubamba, Río** ≈ C Peru
58 G12 **Urucará** Amazonas, N Brazil
61 E16 **Uruguaiana** Rio Grande do Sul, S Brazil
Uruguai, Rio see Uruguay
61 E18 **Uruguay** *off.* Oriental Republic of Uruguay; *prev.* La Banda Oriental. ◆ *republic* E South America
61 E15 **Uruguay** *var.* Rio Uruguai, Río Uruguay. ≈ E South America
Uruguay, Oriental Republic of see Uruguay
Uruguay, Río see Uruguay
Urukthapel see Ngeruktabel
Urumchi see Ürümqi
Urumi Yeh see Orūmīyeh, Daryācheh-ye
158 L5 **Ürümqi** *var.* Tihwa, Urumchi, Urumqi, Urumtsi, Wu-lu-k'o-mu-shi, Wu-lu-mu-ch'i; *prev.* Ti-hua. Xinjiang Uygur Zizhiqu, NW China
Urumtsi see Ürümqi
Urundi see Burundi
183 V6 **Urunga** New South Wales, SE Australia
183 V6 **Urunga** New South Wales, SE Australia
188 C15 **Uruno Point** *headland* NW Guam
123 U13 **Urup, Ostrov** *island* Kuril'skiye Ostrova, SE Russian Federation
141 P11 **'Uruq al Mawārid** *desert* S Saudi Arabia
Urusan see Ulsan
127 T5 **Urussu** Respublika Tatarstan, W Russian Federation
184 K10 **Uruti** Taranaki, North Island, New Zealand
57 K19 **Uru Uru, Lago** ◎ W Bolivia
55 P9 **Uruyén** Bolívar, SE Venezuela
Urūzgān see Orūzgān
165 T3 **Uryū-gawa** ≈ Hokkaidō, NE Japan
165 T2 **Uryū-ko** ◎ Hokkaidō, NE Japan
127 N8 **Uryupinsk** Volgogradskaya Oblast', SW Russian Federation
Ürzhar see Urdzhar
125 R16 **Urzhum** Kirovskaya Oblast', NW Russian Federation
116 K13 **Urziceni** Ialomița, SE Romania
164 E14 **Usa** Ōita, Kyūshū, SW Japan
119 L16 **Usa** *Rus.* Usa. ≈ C Belarus
125 U6 **Usa** ≈ NW Russian Federation
136 E14 **Uşak** *prev.* Ushak. Uşak, W Turkey
136 D14 **Uşak** *var.* Ushak. ◈ *province* W Turkey
83 C19 **Usakos** Erongo, W Namibia
81 J21 **Usambara Mountains** ▲▲ NE Tanzania
81 G23 **Usangu Flats** *wetland* SW Tanzania
65 D24 **Usborne, Mount** ▲ East Falkland, Falkland Islands
100 O8 **Usedom** *island* NE Germany
99 M24 **Useldange** Diekirch, C Luxembourg
Ushachi see Ushachy
118 L13 **Ushachy** *Rus.* Ushachi. Vitsyebskaya Voblasts', N Belarus
Ushak see Uşak
122 L4 **Ushakova, Ostrov** *island* Severnaya Zemlya, N Russian Federation
Ushant see Ouessant, Île d'
Ūsharal see Ucharal
164 B15 **Ushibuka** *var.* Usibuka. Kumamoto, Shimo-jima, SW Japan
Ushi Point see Sabaneta, Puntan
145 V14 **Ushtobe** *Kaz.* Üshtöbe. Almaty, SE Kazakhstan
Üshtöbe see Ushtobe
63 I25 **Ushuaia** Tierra del Fuego, S Argentina
39 R10 **Usibelli** Alaska, USA
Usibuka see Ushibuka
186 D7 **Usino** Madang, N Papua New Guinea
125 U6 **Usinsk** Respublika Komi, NW Russian Federation
97 K22 **Usk** *Wel.* Wysg. ≈ SE Wales, UK
Uskočke Planine/ Uskokengebirge see Gorjanci
Uskoplje see Gornji Vakuf
Üsküb/Üsküp see Skopje
114 M11 **Üsküpdere** Kırklareli, NW Turkey
126 L7 **Usman'** Lipetskaya Oblast', W Russian Federation
118 D8 **Usmas Ezers** ◎ NW Latvia
125 U13 **Usol'ye** Permskaya Oblast', NW Russian Federation
41 T16 **Uspanapa, Río** ≈ SE Mexico
145 R11 **Uspenskiy** Karaganda, C Kazakhstan
103 O11 **Ussel** Corrèze, C France
163 Z6 **Ussuri** *var.* Usuri, Wusuri, *Chin.* Wusuli Jiang. ≈ China/Russian Federation
123 S15 **Ussuriysk** *prev.* Nikol'sk, Nikol'sk-Ussuriyskiy, Voroshilov. Primorskiy Kray, SE Russian Federation
136 J10 **Usta Burnu** *headland* N Turkey
149 P13 **Usta Muhammad** Baluchistān, SW Pakistan
123 V11 **Ust'-Bol'sheretsk** Kamchatskaya Oblast', E Russian Federation
127 N9 **Ust'-Buzulukskaya** Volgogradskaya Oblast', SW Russian Federation
111 C16 **Ustecký Kraj** ◈ *region* NW Czech Republic
108 G7 **Uster** Zürich, NE Switzerland
107 I22 **Ustica, Isola d'** *island* S Italy
122 M11 **Ust'-Ilimsk** Irkutskaya Oblast', C Russian Federation
111 C15 **Ústí nad Labem** *Ger.* Aussig. Ústecký Kraj, NW Czech Republic
111 F17 **Ústí nad Orlicí** *Ger.* Wildenschwert. Pardubický Kraj, C Czech Republic
Ustinov see Izhevsk
113 J14 **Ustiprača** ◈ Republika Srpska, SE Bosnia and Herzegovina
122 H11 **Ust'-Ishim** Omskaya Oblast', C Russian Federation
110 G6 **Ustka** *Ger.* Stolpmünde. Pomorskie, N Poland
123 V9 **Ust'-Kamchatsk** Kamchatskaya Oblast', E Russian Federation
145 X9 **Ust'-Kamenogorsk** *Kaz.* Öskemen. Vostochnyy Kazakhstan, E Kazakhstan
123 T10 **Ust'-Khayryuzovo** Koryakskiy Avtonomnyy Okrug, E Russian Federation
122 I14 **Ust'-Koksa** Respublika Altay, S Russian Federation
125 S11 **Ust'-Kulom** Respublika Komi, NW Russian Federation
123 Q8 **Ust'-Kuyga** Respublika Sakha (Yakutiya), NE Russian Federation
126 L14 **Ust'-Labinsk** Krasnodarskiy Kray, SW Russian Federation
123 R10 **Ust'-Maya** Respublika Sakha (Yakutiya), NE Russian Federation
123 R9 **Ust'-Nera** Respublika Sakha (Yakutiya), NE Russian Federation
123 P12 **Ust'-Nyukzha** Amurskaya Oblast', S Russian Federation
123 O7 **Ust'-Olenëk** Respublika Sakha (Yakutiya), NE Russian Federation
123 T9 **Ust'-Omchug** Magadanskaya Oblast', E Russian Federation
122 M13 **Ust'-Ordynskiy** Ust'-Ordynskiy Buryatskiy Avtonomnyy Okrug, S Russian Federation
122 M13 **Ust'-Ordynskiy Buryatskiy Avtonomnyy Okrug** ◈ *autonomous district* S Russian Federation
125 N8 **Ust'-Pinega** Arkhangel'skaya Oblast', NW Russian Federation
122 K8 **Ust'-Port** Taymyrskiy (Dolgano-Nenetskiy) Avtonomnyy Okrug, N Russian Federation
114 L11 **Ustrem** *prev.* Vakav. Yambol, E Bulgaria
111 O18 **Ustrzyki Dolne** Podkarpackie, SE Poland
Ust'-Sysol'sk see Syktyvkar
125 R7 **Ust'-Tsil'ma** Respublika Komi, NW Russian Federation
Ust Urt see Ustyurt Plateau
125 O11 **Ust'ya** ≈ NW Russian Federation
123 V10 **Ust'yevoye** *prev.* Kirovskiy. Kamchatskaya Oblast', E Russian Federation
117 R8 **Ustynivka** Kirovohrads'ka Oblast', C Ukraine
144 H15 **Ustyurt Plateau** *var.* Ust Urt, *Uzb.* Ustyurt Platosi. *plateau* Kazakhstan/Uzbekistan
Ustyurt Platosi see Ustyurt Plateau
124 K14 **Ustyuzhna** Vologodskaya Oblast', NW Russian Federation
158 J4 **Usu** Xinjiang Uygur Zizhiqu, NW China
171 O13 **Usu** Sulawesi, C Indonesia
164 E14 **Usuki** Ōita, Kyūshū, SW Japan
42 G8 **Usulután** Usulután, SE El Salvador
42 B9 **Usulután** ◈ *department* SE El Salvador
41 W16 **Usumacinta, Río** ≈ Guatemala/Mexico
Usumbura see Bujumbura
Usuri see Ussuri
U.S./USA see United States of America
171 W14 **Uta** Papua, E Indonesia
36 K5 **Utah** *off.* State of Utah, *also known as* Beehive State, Mormon State. ◈ *state* W USA
36 L3 **Utah Lake** ◎ Utah, W USA
Utaidhani see Uthai Thani
93 M14 **Utajärvi** Oulu, C Finland
Utamboni see Mitemele, Río
Utaradit see Uttaradit
165 T3 **Utashinai** *var.* Utasinai. Hokkaidō, NE Japan
Utasinai see Utashinai
193 Y14 **'Uta Vava'u** *island* Vava'u Group, N Tonga
37 V9 **Ute Creek** ≈ New Mexico, SW USA
118 H12 **Utena** Utena, E Lithuania
118 H12 **Utena** ◈ *province* Lithuania
37 V10 **Ute Reservoir** ⊠ New Mexico, SW USA
167 O10 **Uthai Thani** *var.* Muang Uthai Thani, Udayadhani, Utaidhani. Uthai Thani, W Thailand
149 O15 **Uthal** Baluchistān, SW Pakistan
18 I10 **Utica** New York, NE USA
105 R10 **Utiel** País Valenciano, E Spain
9 O13 **Utikuma Lake** ◎ Alberta, W Canada
42 I4 **Utila, Isla de** *island* Islas de la Bahía, N Honduras
Utina see Udine
59 O17 **Utinga** Bahia, E Brazil
Utirik see Utrik Atoll
95 M22 **Utlängan** *island* S Sweden
117 U11 **Utlyuts'kyy Lyman** *bay* S Ukraine
95 P16 **Utö** Stockholm, C Sweden
25 Q12 **Utopia** Texas, SW USA
98 J11 **Utrecht** *Lat.* Trajectum ad Rhenum. Utrecht, C Netherlands
83 K22 **Utrecht** KwaZulu/Natal, E South Africa
98 I11 **Utrecht** ◈ *province* C Netherlands
104 K14 **Utrera** Andalucía, S Spain
189 V4 **Utrik Atoll** *var.* Utirik, Utrōk, Utrōnk. *atoll* Ratak Chain, N Marshall Islands
Utrōk/Utrōnk see Utrik Atoll
95 B16 **Utsira** *island* SW Norway
92 L8 **Utsjoki** *var.* Ohcejohka. Lappi, N Finland
165 O12 **Utsunomiya** *var.* Utunomiya. Tochigi, Honshū, S Japan
127 P13 **Utta** Respublika Kalmykiya, SW Russian Federation
167 O8 **Uttaradit** *var.* Utaradit. Uttaradit, N Thailand
152 J9 **Uttaranchal** ◈ *state* N India
152 J8 **Uttarkāshi** Uttaranchal, N India
152 K11 **Uttar Pradesh** *prev.* United Provinces, United Provinces of Agra and Oudh. ◈ *state* N India
45 T5 **Utuado** C Puerto Rico
158 K3 **Utubulak** Xinjiang Uygur Zizhiqu, W China
39 N5 **Utukok River** ≈ Alaska, USA
Utunomiya see Utsunomiya
187 P10 **Utupua** *island* Santa Cruz Islands, E Soloman Islands
144 G9 **Utva** ≈ NW Kazakhstan
189 Y15 **Utwe** Kosrae, E Micronesia
189 X15 **Utwe Harbor** *harbor* Kosrae, E Micronesia
Uubulan see Hayrhan
163 O8 **Uulbayan** *var.* Dzüünbulag. Sühbaatar, E Mongolia
118 G6 **Uulu** Pärnumaa, SW Estonia
197 N13 **Uummannaq** *var.* Umanak, Umanaq. ◈ Kitaa, C Greenland
Uummannarsuaq see Nunap Isua
162 E4 **Üüreg Nuur** ◎ NW Mongolia
Uusikaarlepyy see Nykarleby
93 J19 **Uusikaupunki** *Swe.* Nystad. Länsi-Soumi, SW Finland
127 S2 **Uva** Udmurtskaya Respublika, NW Russian Federation
113 L14 **Uvac** ≈ W Serbia
25 Q12 **Uvalde** Texas, SW USA
155 K25 **Uva Province** ◈ *province* SE Sri Lanka
119 O18 **Uvaravichy** *Rus.* Uvarovichi. Homyel'skaya Voblasts', SE Belarus
54 J11 **Uvá, Río** ≈ E Colombia
Uvarovichi see Uvaravichy
127 N7 **Uvarovo** Tambovskaya Oblast', W Russian Federation
122 H10 **Uvat** Tyumenskaya Oblast', C Russian Federation
190 G12 **Uvea, Île** *island* N Wallis and Futuna
81 E21 **Uvinza** Kigoma, W Tanzania
79 O20 **Uvira** Sud Kivu, E Dem. Rep. Congo
162 E5 **Uvs** ◈ *province* NW Mongolia
162 F5 **Uvs Nuur** *var.* Ozero Ubsu-Nur. ◎ Mongolia/Russian Federation
164 F14 **Uwa** Ehime, Shikoku, SW Japan
164 F14 **Uwajima** *var.* Uwazima. Ehime, Shikoku, SW Japan
80 B5 **'Uwaynāt, Jabal al** *var.* Jebel Uweinat. ▲ Libya/Sudan
Uwazima see Uwajima
Uweinat, Jebel see 'Uwaynāt, Jabal al
14 H14 **Uxbridge** Ontario, S Canada
Uxellodunum see Issoudun
Uxin Qi see Dabqig
41 X12 **Uxmal, Ruinas** *ruins* Yucatán, SE Mexico
129 Q5 **Uy** ≈ Kazakhstan/Russian Federation
144 K15 **Uyaly** Kzylorda, S Kazakhstan
123 R8 **Uyandina** ≈ NE Russian Federation
162 J8 **Uyanga** *var.* Ongi. Övörhangay, C Mongolia
Üydzen see Manlay
Uyeda see Ueda
122 K5 **Uyedineniya, Ostrov** *island* N Russian Federation
77 V17 **Uyo** Akwa Ibom, S Nigeria
162 D8 **Üyönch** Hovd, W Mongolia
145 Q15 **Uyuk** Zhambyl, S Kazakhstan
141 V13 **'Uyūn** SW Oman
57 K20 **Uyuni** Potosí, W Bolivia
57 J20 **Uyuni, Salar de** *wetland* SW Bolivia
146 I9 **Uzbekistan** *off.* Republic of Uzbekistan. ◆ *republic* C Asia
Uzbekistan, Republic of see Uzbekistan
158 D8 **Uzbel Shankou** *Rus.* Pereval Kyzyl-Dzhiik. *pass* China/Tajikistan
146 B11 **Uzboý** *prev. Rus* Imeni 26 Bakinskikh Komissarov, *Turkm.* 26 Baku Komissarlary Adyndaky. Balkan Welaýaty, W Turkmenistan
119 J17 **Uzda** *Rus.* Uzda. Minskaya Voblasts', C Belarus
103 N12 **Uzerche** Corrèze, C France
103 R14 **Uzès** Gard, S France
147 T10 **Uzgen** *Kir.* Özgön. Oshskaya Oblast', SW Kyrgyzstan
117 O3 **Uzh** ≈ N Ukraine
Uzhgorod see Uzhhorod
116 G7 **Uzhhorod** *Rus.* Uzhgorod; *prev.* Ungvár. Zakarpats'ka Oblast', W Ukraine
Uzi see Uji
112 K13 **Užice** *prev.* Titovo Užice. Serbia, W Serbia
Uzin see Uzyn
126 L5 **Uzlovaya** Tul'skaya Oblast', W Russian Federation
108 H7 **Uznach** Sankt Gallen, NE Switzerland
145 U16 **Uzunagach** Almaty, SE Kazakhstan
136 B10 **Uzunköprü** Edirne, NW Turkey
118 D11 **Užventis** Šiauliai, C Lithuania
117 P5 **Uzyn** *Rus.* Uzin. Kyyivs'ka Oblast', N Ukraine
145 N7 **Uzynkol'** *prev.* Lenin, Leninskoye. Kustanay, N Kazakhstan

V

Vääksy see Asikkala
83 H23 **Vaal** ≈ C South Africa
93 M14 **Vaala** Oulu, C Finland
93 N19 **Vaalimaa** Etelä-Suomi, SE Finland
99 M19 **Vaals** Limburg, SE Netherlands
93 J16 **Vaasa** *Swe.* Vasa; *prev.* Nikolainkaupunki. Länsi-Soumi, W Finland
98 L10 **Vaassen** Gelderland, E Netherlands
118 G11 **Vabalninkas** Panevėžys, NE Lithuania
Vabkent see Vobkent
111 J22 **Vác** *Ger.* Waitzen. Pest, N Hungary
61 I14 **Vacaria** Rio Grande do Sul, S Brazil
35 N7 **Vacaville** California, W USA
103 R15 **Vaccarès, Étang de** ◎ SE France
44 L10 **Vache, Île à** *island* SW Haiti
173 Y16 **Vacoas** W Mauritius
32 G10 **Vader** Washington, NW USA
94 D12 **Vadheim** Sogn Og Fjordane, S Norway
154 D11 **Vadodara** *prev.* Baroda. Gujarāt, W India
92 M8 **Vadsø** *Fin.* Vesisaari. Finnmark, N Norway
95 L17 **Vadstena** Östergötland, S Sweden
108 I8 **Vaduz** ● (Liechtenstein) W Liechtenstein
Vág see Váh
125 N12 **Vaga** ≈ NW Russian Federation
94 G11 **Vågåmo** Oppland, S Norway
112 D12 **Vaganski Vrh** ▲ W Croatia
95 A19 **Vágar** *Dan.* Vågø. *island* W Faeroe Islands
Vágbeszterce see Považská Bystrica
95 L19 **Vaggeryd** Jönköping, S Sweden
137 T12 **Vagharshapat** *var.* Ejmiadzin, Ejmiatsin, Etchmiadzin, *Rus.* Echmiadzin. W Armenia
95 O16 **Vagnhärad** Södermanland, C Sweden
Vågø see Vágar
104 G7 **Vagos** Aveiro, N Portugal
Vágsellye see Sal'a
92 H10 **Vågsfjorden** *fjord* N Norway
94 C10 **Vågsøy** *island* S Norway
Vágújhely see Nové Mesto nad Váhom
111 I21 **Váh** *Ger.* Waag, *Hung.* Vág. ≈ W Slovakia
93 K16 **Vähäkyrö** Länsi-Soumi, W Finland
191 X11 **Vahitahi** *atoll* Îles Tuamotu, E French Polynesia
Váhtjer see Gällivare
Vaidei see Vulcan
22 L4 **Vaiden** Mississippi, S USA
155 I23 **Vaigai** ≈ SE India
191 V16 **Vaihu** Easter Island, Chile, E Pacific Ocean
118 I6 **Väike Emajõgi** ≈ S Estonia
118 I4 **Väike-Maarja** *Ger.* Klein-Marien. Lääne-Virumaa, NE Estonia
Väike-Salatsi see Mazsalaca
37 R4 **Vail** Colorado, C USA
193 V15 **Vaina** Tongatapu, S Tonga
118 E5 **Väinameri** *prev.* Muhu Väin, *Ger.* Moon-Sund. *sea* E Baltic Sea
93 N18 **Vainikkala** Etelä-Suomi, SE Finland
118 D10 **Vaiņode** Liepāja, SW Latvia
155 H23 **Vaippār** ≈ SE India
191 W11 **Vairaatea** *atoll* Îles Tuamotu, C French Polynesia
191 R8 **Vairao** Tahiti, W French Polynesia
103 R14 **Vaison-la-Romaine** Vaucluse, SE France
190 G11 **Vaitupu** Île Uvea, E Wallis and Futuna
190 F7 **Vaitupu** *atoll* C Tuvalu
Vajdahunyad see Hunedoara
Vajdej see Vulcan
78 K12 **Vakaga** ◈ *prefecture* NE Central African Republic
114 H10 **Vakarel** Sofiya, W Bulgaria
Vakav see Ustrem
137 O11 **Vakfıkebir** Trabzon, NE Turkey
122 J10 **Vakh** ≈ C Russian Federation
Vakhon, Qatorkŭhi see Nicholas Range
147 P14 **Vakhsh** SW Tajikistan
147 Q12 **Vakhsh** ≈ SW Tajikistan
127 P1 **Vakhtan** Nizhegorodskaya Oblast', W Russian Federation
94 C13 **Vaksdal** Hordaland, S Norway
125 O8 **Vaksha** ≈ NW Russian Federation
Valachia see Wallachia
108 D11 **Valais** *Ger.* Wallis. ◈ *canton* SW Switzerland
113 M21 **Valamarës, Mali i** ▲ SE Albania
127 S2 **Valamaz** Udmurtskaya Respublika, NW Russian Federation
113 Q19 **Valandovo** SE FYR Macedonia
111 I18 **Valašské Meziříčí** *Ger.* Wallachisch-Meseritsch, *Pol.* Wałeckie Międzyrzecze. Zlínský Kraj, E Czech Republic
115 I17 **Valáxa** *island* Vóreies Sporádes, Greece, Aegean Sea
95 K16 **Vålberg** Värmland, C Sweden
116 H12 **Vâlcea** *prev.* Vilcea. ◈ *county* SW Romania
63 J16 **Valcheta** Río Negro, E Argentina
15 P12 **Valcourt** Québec, SE Canada
Valdai Hills see Valdayskaya Vozvyshennost'
104 M3 **Valdavia** ≈ N Spain

◆ Country ● Country Capital ◇ Dependent Territory ○ Dependent Territory Capital ◈ Administrative Regions ✕ International Airport ▲ Mountain ▲▲ Mountain Range Volcano ≈ River ◎ Lake ⊠ Reservoir

124 I15 **Valday** Novgorodskaya Oblast', W Russian Federation
124 I15 **Valdayskaya Vozvyshennost'** *var.* Valdai Hills. *hill range* W Russian Federation
104 L9 **Valdecañas, Embalse de** ⊠ W Spain
118 E8 **Valdemārpils** *Ger.* Sassmacken. Talsi, NW Latvia
95 N18 **Valdemarsvik** Östergötland, S Sweden
105 N8 **Valdemoro** Madrid, C Spain
105 O11 **Valdepeñas** Castilla-La Mancha, C Spain
104 L5 **Valderaduey** ≈ NE Spain
104 L5 **Valderas** Castilla-León, N Spain
105 T7 **Valderrobres** *var.* Vall-de-roures. Aragón, NE Spain
63 K17 **Valdés, Península** *peninsula* SE Argentina
56 C5 **Valdéz** *var.* Limones. Esmeraldas, NW Ecuador
39 S11 **Valdez** Alaska, USA
Valdia *see* Weldiya
103 U11 **Val d'Isère** Savoie, E France
63 G15 **Valdivia** Los Lagos, C Chile
Valdivia Bank *see* Valdivia Seamount
65 P17 **Valdivia Seamount** *var.* Valdivia Bank. *undersea feature* E Atlantic Ocean
103 N4 **Val-d'Oise** ◆ *department* N France
14 J8 **Val-d'Or** Québec, SE Canada
23 U8 **Valdosta** Georgia, SE USA
94 G13 **Valdres** *physical region* S Norway
32 L13 **Vale** Oregon, NW USA
116 F9 **Valea lui Mihai** *Hung.* Érmihályfalva. Bihor, NW Romania
9 N15 **Valemount** British Columbia, SW Canada
59 O17 **Valença** Bahia, E Brazil
104 F4 **Valença do Minho** Viana do Castelo, N Portugal
59 N14 **Valença do Piauí** Piauí, E Brazil
103 N8 **Valençay** Indre, C France
103 R13 **Valence** *anc.* Valentia, Valentia Julia, Ventia. Drôme, E France
105 S10 **Valencia** País Valenciano, E Spain
54 K5 **Valencia** Carabobo, N Venezuela
105 R10 **Valencia** *Cat.* València. ◆ *province* País Valenciano, E Spain
105 S10 **Valencia** ✈ Valencia, E Spain
104 I10 **Valencia de Alcántara** Extremadura, W Spain
104 L4 **Valencia de Don Juan** Castilla-León, N Spain
105 U9 **Valencia, Golfo de** *var.* Gulf of Valencia. *gulf* E Spain
Valencia, Gulf of *see* Valencia, Golfo de
97 A21 **Valencia Island** *Ir.* Dairbhre. *island* SW Ireland
Valencia/València *see* País Valenciano
103 P2 **Valenciennes** Nord, N France
116 K13 **Vălenii de Munte** Prahova, SE Romania
Valentia *see* Valence, France
Valentia *see* País Valenciano
Valentia Julia *see* Valence
103 T8 **Valentigney** Doubs, E France
28 M12 **Valentine** Nebraska, C USA
24 J10 **Valentine** Texas, SW USA
Valentine State *see* Oregon
106 C8 **Valenza** Piemonte, NW Italy
94 I13 **Våler** Hedmark, S Norway
54 I6 **Valera** Trujillo, NW Venezuela
192 M11 **Valerie Guyot** *Undersea Feature* S Pacific Ocean
Valetta *see* Valletta
118 I7 **Valga** *Ger.* Walk, *Latv.* Valka. Valgamaa, S Estonia
118 I7 **Valgamaa** *var.* Valga Maakond. ◆ *province* S Estonia
Valga Maakond *see* Valgamaa
43 Q15 **Valiente, Península** *peninsula* NW Panama
103 X16 **Valinco, Golfe de** *gulf* Corse, France, C Mediterranean Sea
112 L12 **Valjevo** Serbia, W Serbia
Valjok *see* Válljohka
118 I7 **Valka** *Ger.* Walk. Valka, N Latvia
Valka *see* Valga
93 L18 **Valkeakoski** Länsi-Suomi, W Finland
93 M19 **Valkeala** Etelä-Suomi, S Finland
99 L18 **Valkenburg** Limburg, SE Netherlands
99 K15 **Valkenswaard** Noord-Brabant, S Netherlands
119 G15 **Valkininkai** Alytus, S Lithuania
117 U5 **Valky** Kharkivs'ka Oblast', E Ukraine
41 Y12 **Valladolid** Yucatán, SE Mexico
104 M5 **Valladolid** Castilla-León, NW Spain
104 L5 **Valladolid** ◆ *province* Castilla-León, N Spain
103 U15 **Vallauris** Alpes-Maritimes, SE France
Vall-de-roures *see* Valderrobres
Vall d'Uxo *see* La Vall d'Uixó
Vall D'Uxó *see* La Vall D'Uixó
95 E16 **Valle** Aust-Agder, S Norway
105 N2 **Valle** Cantabria, N Spain
42 H8 **Valle** ◆ *department* S Honduras
105 N8 **Vallecas** Madrid, C Spain
37 Q8 **Vallecito Reservoir** ⊠ Colorado, C USA
106 A7 **Valle d'Aosta** ◆ *region* NW Italy
41 O14 **Valle de Bravo** México, S Mexico
55 N5 **Valle de Guanape** Anzoátegui, N Venezuela
54 M6 **Valle de La Pascua** Guárico, N Venezuela
54 B11 **Valle del Cauca** *off.* Departamento del Valle del Cauca. ◆ *province* W Colombia
Valle del Cauca, Departamento del *see* Valle del Cauca
41 N13 **Valle de Santiago** Guanajuato, C Mexico
40 J7 **Valle de Zaragoza** Chihuahua, N Mexico
54 G5 **Valledupar** Cesar, N Colombia
76 G10 **Vallée de Ferlo** ≈ NW Senegal
57 M19 **Vallegrande** Santa Cruz, C Bolivia
41 P8 **Valle Hermoso** Tamaulipas, C Mexico
35 N8 **Vallejo** California, W USA
62 G8 **Vallenar** Atacama, N Chile
95 O15 **Vallentuna** Stockholm, C Sweden
121 P16 **Valletta** *prev.* Valetta. ● (Malta) E Malta
27 N6 **Valley Center** Kansas, C USA
29 Q5 **Valley City** North Dakota, N USA
32 I15 **Valley Falls** Oregon, NW USA
Valleyfield *see* Salaberry-de-Valleyfield
21 S4 **Valley Head** West Virginia, NE USA
25 T8 **Valley Mills** Texas, SW USA
75 W10 **Valley of the Kings** *ancient monument* E Egypt
29 R11 **Valley Springs** South Dakota, N USA
20 K5 **Valley Station** Kentucky, S USA
9 O13 **Valleyview** Alberta, W Canada
25 T5 **Valley View** Texas, SW USA
61 C21 **Vallimanca, Arroyo** ≈ E Argentina
92 L9 **Válljohka** *var.* Valjok. Finnmark, N Norway
107 M19 **Vallo della Lucania** Campania, S Italy
108 B9 **Vallorbe** Vaud, W Switzerland
105 V6 **Valls** Cataluña, NE Spain
94 N11 **Vallsta** Gävleborg, C Sweden
94 N12 **Vallvik** Gävleborg, C Sweden
9 T17 **Val Marie** Saskatchewan, S Canada
118 H7 **Valmiera** *Est.* Volmari, *Ger.* Wolmar. Valmiera, N Latvia
105 N3 **Valnera** ▲ N Spain
102 J3 **Valognes** Manche, N France
Valona *see* Vlorë
Valona Bay *see* Vlorës, Gjiri i
104 G6 **Valongo** *var.* Valongo de Gaia. Porto, N Portugal
Valongo de Gaia *see* Valongo
104 M5 **Valoria la Buena** Castilla-León, N Spain
119 J15 **Valozhyn** *Pol.* Wołożyn, *Rus.* Volozhin. Minskaya Voblasts', C Belarus
104 I5 **Valpaços** Vila Real, N Portugal
62 G11 **Valparaíso** Valparaíso, C Chile
40 L11 **Valparaíso** Zacatecas, C Mexico
23 P8 **Valparaiso** Florida, SE USA
31 N11 **Valparaiso** Indiana, N USA
62 G11 **Valparaíso** *off.* Región de Valparaíso. ◆ *region* C Chile
Valparaíso, Región de *see* Valparaíso
Valpo *see* Valpovo
112 I9 **Valpovo** *Hung.* Valpó. Osijek-Baranja, E Croatia
103 R14 **Valréas** Vaucluse, SE France
Vals *see* Vals-Platz
154 D12 **Valsād** *prev.* Bulsar. Gujarāt, W India
Valsbaai *see* False Bay
171 T12 **Valse Pisang, Kepulauan** *island group* E Indonesia
108 H9 **Vals-Platz** *var.* Vals. Graubünden, S Switzerland
171 X16 **Vals, Tanjung** *headland* Papua, SE Indonesia
93 N15 **Valtimo** Itä-Suomi, E Finland
115 D17 **Váltou** ▲▲ C Greece
127 O12 **Valuyevka** Rostovskaya Oblast', SW Russian Federation
126 K9 **Valuyki** Belgorodskaya Oblast', W Russian Federation
36 L2 **Val Verda** Utah, W USA
64 N12 **Valverde** Hierro, Islas Canarias, Spain, NE Atlantic Ocean
104 I13 **Valverde del Camino** Andalucía, S Spain
95 G23 **Vamdrup** Vejle, C Denmark
94 L12 **Våmhus** Dalarna, C Sweden
93 K18 **Vammala** Länsi-Soumi, SW Finland
Vámosudvarhely *see* Odorheiu Secuiesc
137 S14 **Van** Van, E Turkey
25 V7 **Van** Texas, SW USA
137 T14 **Van** ◆ *province* E Turkey
137 T11 **Vanadzor** *prev.* Kirovakan. N Armenia
25 U5 **Van Alstyne** Texas, SW USA
33 W10 **Vananda** Montana, NW USA
116 I11 **Vânători** *Hung.* Héjjasfalva; *prev.* Vînători. Mureş, C Romania
191 W12 **Vanavana** *atoll* Îles Tuamotu, SE French Polynesia
Vana-Vändra *see* Vändra
122 M11 **Vanavara** Evenkiyskiy Avtonomnyy Okrug, C Russian Federation
15 Q8 **Van Bruyssel** Québec, SE Canada
27 R10 **Van Buren** Arkansas, C USA
19 S1 **Van Buren** Maine, NE USA
27 W7 **Van Buren** Missouri, C USA
19 T5 **Vanceboro** Maine, NE USA
21 W10 **Vanceboro** North Carolina, SE USA
21 O4 **Vanceburg** Kentucky, S USA
Vanch *see* Vanj
10 L17 **Vancouver** British Columbia, SW Canada
32 G11 **Vancouver** Washington, NW USA
10 L17 **Vancouver** ✈ British Columbia, SW Canada
10 K16 **Vancouver Island** *island* British Columbia, SW Canada
Vanda *see* Vantaa
171 X13 **Van Daalen** ≈ Papua, E Indonesia
30 L15 **Vandalia** Illinois, N USA
27 V3 **Vandalia** Missouri, C USA
31 R13 **Vandalia** Ohio, N USA
25 U13 **Vanderbilt** Texas, SW USA
31 Q10 **Vandercook Lake** Michigan, N USA
10 L14 **Vanderhoof** British Columbia, SW Canada
18 K8 **Vanderwhacker Mountain** ▲ New York, NE USA
181 P1 **Van Diemen Gulf** *gulf* Northern Territory, N Australia
Van Diemen's Land *see* Tasmania
118 H5 **Vändra** *Ger.* Fennern; *prev.* Vana-Vändra. Pärnumaa, SW Estonia
Vandsburg *see* Więcbork
34 L4 **Van Duzen River** ≈ California, W USA
118 F13 **Vandžiogala** Kaunas, C Lithuania
41 N10 **Vanegas** San Luis Potosí, C Mexico
Vaner, Lake *see* Vänern
95 K17 **Vänern** *Eng.* Lake Vaner; *prev.* Lake Vener. ◎ S Sweden
95 J18 **Vänersborg** Västra Götaland, S Sweden
95 F12 **Vang** Oppland, S Norway
172 I7 **Vangaindrano** Fianarantsoa, SE Madagascar
137 S14 **Van Gölü** *Eng.* Lake Van; *anc.* Thospitis. *salt lake* E Turkey
186 L9 **Vangunu** *island* New Georgia Islands, NW Solomon Islands
24 J9 **Van Horn** Texas, SW USA
187 Q11 **Vanikolo** *var.* Vanikoro. *island* Santa Cruz Islands, E Solomon Islands
Vanikoro *see* Vanikolo
186 A5 **Vanimo** Sandaun, NW Papua New Guinea
123 T13 **Vanino** Khabarovskiy Kray, SE Russian Federation
155 G19 **Vāniyilāsa Sāgara** ◎ SW India
147 S13 **Vanj** *Rus.* Vanch. S Tajikistan
116 G14 **Vânju Mare** *prev.* Vinju Mare. Mehedinţi, SW Romania
15 N12 **Vankleek Hill** Ontario, SE Canada
Van, Lake *see* Van Gölü
93 I16 **Vännäs** Västerbotten, N Sweden
93 I15 **Vännäsby** Västerbotten, N Sweden
102 H7 **Vannes** *anc.* Dariorigum. Morbihan, NW France
92 I8 **Vanna** *island* N Norway
103 T12 **Vanoise, Massif de la** ▲▲ E France
83 E24 **Vanrhynsdorp** Western Cape, SW South Africa
21 P7 **Vansant** Virginia, NE USA
94 L13 **Vansbro** Dalarna, C Sweden
95 D18 **Vanse** Vest-Agder, S Norway
9 P7 **Vansittart Island** *island* Nunavut, NE Canada
93 M20 **Vantaa** *Swe.* Vanda. Etelä-Suomi, S Finland
93 L19 **Vantaa** ✈ (Helsinki) Etelä-Suomi, S Finland
32 J9 **Vantage** Washington, NW USA
187 Z14 **Vanua Balavu** *prev.* Vanua Mbalavu. *island* Lau Group, E Fiji
187 R12 **Vanua Lava** *island* Banks Islands, N Vanuatu
187 Y13 **Vanua Levu** *island* N Fiji
Vanua Mbalavu *see* Vanua Balavu
187 R12 **Vanuatu** *off.* Republic of Vanuatu; *prev.* New Hebrides. ◆ *republic* SW Pacific Ocean
175 P8 **Vanuatu** *island group* SW Pacific Ocean
Vanuatu, Republic of *see* Vanuatu
31 Q12 **Van Wert** Ohio, N USA
187 Q17 **Vao** Province Sud, S New Caledonia
Vapincum *see* Gap
117 N7 **Vapnyarka** Vinnyts'ka Oblast', C Ukraine
103 T15 **Var** ◆ *department* SE France
103 U14 **Var** ≈ SE France
95 J18 **Vara** Västra Götaland, S Sweden
Varadinska Županija *see* Varaždin
118 J10 **Varakļani** Madona, C Latvia
106 C7 **Varallo** Piemonte, NE Italy
143 O5 **Varāmīn** *var.* Veramin. Tehrān, N Iran
153 N14 **Vārānasi** *prev.* Banaras, Benares, *hist.* Kasi. Uttar Pradesh, N India
125 T3 **Varandey** Nenetskiy Avtonomnyy Okrug, NW Russian Federation
92 M8 **Varangerbotn** Finnmark, N Norway
92 M8 **Varangerfjorden** *Lapp.* Várjjatvuotna. *fjord* N Norway
92 M8 **Varangerhalvøya** *Lapp.* Várnjárga. *peninsula* N Norway
Varannó *see* Vranov nad Topl'ou
107 M15 **Varano, Lago di** ◎ SE Italy
118 J13 **Varapayeva** *Rus.* Voropayevo. Vitsyebskaya Voblasts', NW Belarus
Varasd *see* Varaždin
112 E7 **Varaždin** *Ger.* Warasdin, *Hung.* Varasd. Varaždin, N Croatia
112 E7 **Varaždin** *off.* Varadinska Županija. ◆ *province* N Croatia
106 C10 **Varazze** Liguria, NW Italy
95 J20 **Varberg** Halland, S Sweden
149 P5 **Vardak** *var.* Wardak, *Pash.* Wardag. ◆ *province* E Afghanistan
113 Q19 **Vardar** *Gk.* Axiós. ≈ FYR Macedonia/Greece *see also* Axiós
Vardar *see* Axiós
95 F23 **Varde** Ribe, W Denmark
137 V12 **Vardenis** E Armenia
92 N8 **Vardø** *Fin.* Vuoreija. Finnmark, N Norway
115 E18 **Vardoúsia** ▲▲ C Greece
Vareia *see* Logroño
100 G10 **Varel** Niedersachsen, NW Germany
119 G15 **Varėna** *Pol.* Orany. Alytus, S Lithuania
15 O12 **Varennes** Québec, SE Canada
103 P10 **Varennes-sur-Allier** Allier, C France
112 I12 **Vareš** ◆ Federacija Bosna I Hercegovina, E Bosnia and Herzegovina
106 D7 **Varese** Lombardia, N Italy
116 J12 **Vârful Moldoveanu** *var.* Moldoveanul; *prev.* Vîrful Moldoveanu. ▲ C Romania
Varganzi *see* Warganza
95 J18 **Vårgårda** Västra Götaland, S Sweden
54 L4 **Vargas** *off.* Estado Vargas. ◆ *state* N Venezuela
95 J18 **Vargön** Västra Götaland, S Sweden
95 C17 **Varhaug** Rogaland, S Norway
Várjjatvuotna *see* Varangerfjorden
93 N17 **Varkaus** Itä-Suomi, C Finland
92 J2 **Varmahlídh** Nordhurland Vestra, N Iceland
95 J15 **Värmland** ◆ *county* C Sweden
95 K16 **Värmlandsnäs** *peninsula* S Sweden
114 N8 **Varna** *prev.* Stalin; *anc.* Odessus. Varna, E Bulgaria
114 N8 **Varna** ◆ *province* E Bulgaria
114 N8 **Varna** ✈ Varna, E Bulgaria
95 L20 **Värnamo** Jönköping, S Sweden
114 N8 **Varnenski Zaliv** *prev.* Stalinski Zaliv. *bay* E Bulgaria
114 N8 **Varnensko Ezero** *estuary* E Bulgaria
118 D11 **Varniai** Telšiai, W Lithuania
Várnjárga *see* Varangerhalvøya
Varnoús *see* Baba
111 D14 **Varnsdorf** *Ger.* Warnsdorf. Ústecký Kraj, NW Czech Republic
111 I23 **Várpalota** Veszprém, W Hungary
Varshava *see* Warszawa
118 K6 **Värska** Põlvamaa, SE Estonia
98 N12 **Varsseveld** Gelderland, E Netherlands
115 D19 **Vartholomió** *prev.* Vartholomión. Dytikí Ellás, S Greece
Vartholomión *see* Vartholomió
137 Q14 **Varto** Muş, E Turkey
95 K18 **Vartofta** Västra Götaland, S Sweden
93 O17 **Värtsilä** Itä-Suomi, E Finland
Värtsilä *see* Vyartsilya
117 R4 **Varva** Chernihivs'ka Oblast', NE Ukraine
59 H18 **Várzea Grande** Mato Grosso, SW Brazil
106 D9 **Varzi** Lombardia, N Italy
Varzimanor Ayni *see* Ayní
124 K5 **Varzuga** ≈ NW Russian Federation
103 P8 **Varzy** Nièvre, C France
111 G23 **Vas** *off.* Vas Megye. ◆ *county* W Hungary
Vasa *see* Vaasa
190 A9 **Vasafua** *island* Funafuti Atoll, C Tuvalu
111 O21 **Vásárosnamény** Szabolcs-Szatmár-Bereg, E Hungary
104 H13 **Vascão, Ribeira de** ≈ S Portugal
116 G10 **Vaşcău** *Hung.* Vaskoh. Bihor, NE Romania
Vascongadas, Provincias *see* País Vasco
Vashess Bay *see* Vaskess Bay
Vāsht *see* Khāsh
Vasilevichi *see* Vasilyevichy
115 G14 **Vasiliká** Kentrikí Makedonía, NE Greece
115 C18 **Vasilikí** Lefkáda, Iónioi Nísoi, Greece, C Mediterranean Sea
115 K25 **Vasilikí** Kríti, Greece, E Mediterranean Sea
119 G16 **Vasilishki** *Pol.* Wasiliszki, *Rus.* Vasilishki. Hrodzyenskaya Voblasts', W Belarus
Vasil Kolarov *see* Pamporovo
Vasil'kov *see* Vasyl'kiv
119 N19 **Vasilyevichy** *Rus.* Vasilevichi. Homyel'skaya Voblasts', SE Belarus
191 Y3 **Vaskess Bay** *var.* Vashess Bay. *bay* Kiritimati, E Kiribati
Vaskoh *see* Vaşcău
Vaskohsziklás *see* Ştei
116 M10 **Vaslui** Vaslui, C Romania
116 L11 **Vaslui** ◆ *county* NE Romania
Vas Megye *see* Vas
31 R8 **Vassar** Michigan, N USA
95 E15 **Vassdalsegga** ▲ S Norway
60 P9 **Vassouras** Rio de Janeiro, SE Brazil
95 N15 **Västerås** Västmanland, C Sweden
93 G15 **Västerbotten** ◆ *county* N Sweden
94 K12 **Västerdalälven** ≈ C Sweden
95 O16 **Västerhaninge** Stockholm, C Sweden
94 M10 **Västernorrland** ◆ *county* C Sweden
95 N19 **Västervik** Kalmar, S Sweden
95 M15 **Västmanland** ◆ *county* C Sweden
107 L15 **Vasto** *anc.* Histonium. Abruzzo, C Italy
95 J19 **Västra Götaland** ◆ *county* S Sweden
95 J16 **Västra Silen** ◎ S Sweden
111 G23 **Vasvár** *Ger.* Eisenburg. Vas, W Hungary
117 U9 **Vasylivka** Zaporiz'ka Oblast', SE Ukraine
117 O5 **Vasyl'kiv** *var.* Vasil'kov. Kyyivs'ka Oblast', N Ukraine
122 I11 **Vasyugan** ≈ C Russian Federation
103 N8 **Vatan** Indre, C France
Vaté *see* Efate
115 C18 **Vathy** *prev.* Itháki. Itháki, Iónia Nisiá, Greece, C Mediterranean Sea
107 G15 **Vatican City** *off.* Vatican City State. ◆ *papal state* S Europe
Vatican City State *see* Vatican City
107 M22 **Vaticano, Capo** *headland* S Italy
92 K3 **Vatnajökull** *glacier* SE Iceland
95 P15 **Vätö** Stockholm, C Sweden
187 Z16 **Vatoa** *island* Lau Group, SE Fiji
172 J5 **Vatomandry** Toamasina, E Madagascar
116 J9 **Vatra Dornei** *Ger.* Dorna Watra. Suceava, NE Romania
116 J9 **Vatra Moldoviţei** Suceava, NE Romania
Vatter, Lake *see* Vättern
95 L18 **Vättern** *Eng.* Lake Vatter; *prev.* Lake Vetter. ◎ S Sweden
187 X5 **Vatulele** *island* SW Fiji
117 P7 **Vatutine** Cherkas'ka Oblast', C Ukraine
187 W15 **Vatu Vara** *island* Lau Group, E Fiji
103 R14 **Vaucluse** ◆ *department* SE France
103 S5 **Vaucouleurs** Meuse, NE France
108 B9 **Vaud** *Ger.* Waadt. ◆ *canton* SW Switzerland
15 N12 **Vaudreuil** Québec, SE Canada
37 T12 **Vaughn** New Mexico, SW USA
54 I14 **Vaupés** *off.* Comisaría del Vaupés. ◆ *province* SE Colombia
Vaupés, Comisaría del *see* Vaupés
54 J13 **Vaupés, Río** *var.* Rio Uaupés. ≈ Brazil/Colombia *see also* Uaupés, Rio
Vaupés, Río *see* Uaupés, Rio
103 Q15 **Vauvert** Gard, S France
9 R17 **Vauxhall** Alberta, SW Canada
99 K23 **Vaux-sur-Sûre** Luxembourg, SE Belgium
172 J4 **Vavatenina** Toamasina, E Madagascar
193 Y14 **Vava'u Group** *island group* N Tonga
76 M16 **Vavoua** W Ivory Coast
127 S2 **Vavozh** Udmurtskaya Respublika, NW Russian Federation
155 K23 **Vavuniya** Northern Province, N Sri Lanka
119 G17 **Vawkavysk** *Pol.* Wołkowysk, *Rus.* Volkovysk. Hrodzyenskaya Voblasts', W Belarus
119 F17 **Vawkavyskaye Wzvyshsha** *Rus.* Volkovyskiye Vysoty. *hill range* W Belarus
95 P15 **Vaxholm** Stockholm, C Sweden
95 L21 **Växjö** *var.* Vexiö. Kronoberg, S Sweden
125 T1 **Vaygach, Ostrov** *island* NW Russian Federation
137 V13 **Vayk'** *prev.* Azizbekov. SE Armenia
Vazáš *see* Vittangi
125 P8 **Vazhgort** *prev.* Chasovo. Respublika Komi, NW Russian Federation
45 V10 **V. C. Bird** ✈ (St. John's) Antigua, Antigua and Barbuda
95 C16 **Veavågen** Rogaland, S Norway
29 Q7 **Veblen** South Dakota, N USA
98 N9 **Vecht** *Ger.* Vechte. ≈ Germany/Netherlands *see also* Vechte
Vecht *see* Vechte
100 G12 **Vechta** Niedersachsen, NW Germany
100 E12 **Vechte** *Dut.* Vecht. ≈ Germany/Netherlands *see also* Vecht
Vechte *see* Vecht
118 I8 **Vecpiebalga** Cēsis, C Latvia
118 G9 **Vecumnieki** Bauska, C Latvia
Vedāvati *see* Hagari
95 J20 **Veddige** Halland, S Sweden
116 J15 **Vedea** ≈ S Romania
127 P16 **Vedeno** Chechenskaya Respublika, SW Russian Federation
95 C16 **Vedvågen** Rogaland, S Norway
98 O6 **Veendam** Groningen, NE Netherlands
98 K12 **Veenendaal** Utrecht, C Netherlands
99 E14 **Veere** Zeeland, SW Netherlands
24 M2 **Vega** Texas, SW USA
92 E13 **Vega** *island* C Norway
45 T5 **Vega Baja** C Puerto Rico
38 D17 **Vega Point** *headland* Kiska Island, Alaska, USA
95 F17 **Vegår** ◎ S Norway
99 K14 **Veghel** Noord-Brabant, S Netherlands
Veglia *see* Krk
114 E13 **Vegorítida, Límni** *var.* Límni Vegorítis. ◎ N Greece
Vegorítis, Límni *see* Vegorítida, Límni
9 Q14 **Vegreville** Alberta, SW Canada
95 K21 **Veinge** Halland, S Sweden
61 B21 **Veinticinco de Mayo** *var.* 25 de Mayo. Buenos Aires, E Argentina
63 I14 **Veinticinco de Mayo** La Pampa, C Argentina
119 F15 **Veisiejai** Alytus, S Lithuania
95 F23 **Vejen** Ribe, W Denmark
104 K16 **Vejer de la Frontera** Andalucía, S Spain
95 G23 **Vejle** Vejle, C Denmark
95 F23 **Vejle** *off.* Vejle Amt. ◆ *county* C Denmark
Vejle Amt *see* Vejle
114 M7 **Vekilski** Shumen, NE Bulgaria
54 G3 **Vela, Cabo de la** *headland* NE Colombia
Vela Goa *see* Goa
113 F15 **Vela Luka** Dubrovnik-Neretva, S Croatia
61 G19 **Velázquez** Rocha, E Uruguay
101 E15 **Velbert** Nordrhein-Westfalen, W Germany
109 S9 **Velden** Kärnten, S Austria
Veldes *see* Bled
99 K15 **Veldhoven** Noord-Brabant, S Netherlands
112 C11 **Velebit** ▲▲ C Croatia
114 N11 **Veleka** ≈ SE Bulgaria
109 V10 **Velenje** *Ger.* Wöllan. N Slovenia
190 E12 **Vele, Pointe** *headland* Île Futuna, S Wallis and Futuna
113 O18 **Veles** *Turk.* Köprülü. C FYR Macedonia
113 M20 **Velešta** SW FYR Macedonia
115 F16 **Velestíno** *prev.* Velestínon. Thessalía, C Greece
Velestínon *see* Velestíno
Velevshchina *see* Vyelyewshchyna
54 F9 **Vélez** Santander, C Colombia
105 Q13 **Vélez Blanco** Andalucía, S Spain
104 M17 **Vélez de la Gomera, Peñon de** *island group* S Spain
105 N15 **Vélez-Málaga** Andalucía, S Spain
105 Q13 **Vélez Rubio** Andalucía, S Spain
Velha Goa *see* Goa
Velho *see* Porto Velho
112 E8 **Velika Gorica** Zagreb, N Croatia
112 C9 **Velika Kapela** ▲▲ NW Croatia
Velika Kikinda *see* Kikinda
112 D10 **Velika Kladuša** ◆ Federacija Bosna I Hercegovina, NW Bosnia and Herzegovina
112 N11 **Velika Morava** *var.* Glavn'a Morava, Morava, *Ger.* Grosse Morava. ≈ C Serbia
112 N12 **Velika Plana** Serbia, C Serbia
109 U10 **Velika Raduha** ▲ N Slovenia
123 V7 **Velikaya** ≈ NE Russian Federation
124 F15 **Velikaya** ≈ W Russian Federation
Velikaya Berestovitsa *see* Vyalikaya Byerastavitsa
Velikaya Lepetikha *see* Velyka Lepetykha
Veliki Bečkerek *see* Zrenjanin
112 P12 **Veliki Krš** *var.* Stol. ▲ E Serbia
114 L8 **Veliki Preslav** *prev.* Preslav. Shumen, NE Bulgaria
112 B9 **Veliki Risnjak** ▲ NW Croatia
109 T13 **Veliki Snežnik** *Ger.* Schneeberg, *It.* Monte Nevoso. ▲ SW Slovenia
112 J13 **Veliki Stolac** ▲ E Bosnia and Herzegovina
Velikiy Bor *see* Vyaliki Bor
124 G16 **Velikiye Luki** Pskovskaya Oblast', W Russian Federation
124 H14 **Velikiy Novgorod** *prev.* Novgorod. Novgorodskaya Oblast', W Russian Federation
125 P12 **Velikiy Ustyug** Vologodskaya Oblast', NW Russian Federation
112 N11 **Veliko Gradište** Serbia, NE Serbia
155 I18 **Velikonda Range** ▲▲ SE India
Veliko Tărnovo *see* Veliko Tŭrnovo
114 K9 **Veliko Tŭrnovo** *prev.* Tirnovo, Trnovo, Tŭrnovo, Veliko Tărnovo. Veliko Tŭrnovo, N Bulgaria
114 K8 **Veliko Tŭrnovo** ◆ *province* N Bulgaria
Velikovec *see* Völkermarkt
125 R5 **Velikovisochnoye** Nenetskiy Avtonomnyy Okrug, NW Russian Federation
76 H12 **Vélingara** C Senegal
76 H11 **Vélingara** S Senegal
114 H11 **Velingrad** Pazardzhik, C Bulgaria
126 H3 **Velizh** Smolenskaya Oblast', W Russian Federation
111 F16 **Velká Deštná** *var.* Deštná, Grosskoppe, *Ger.* Deschnaer Koppe. ▲ NE Czech Republic
111 F18 **Velké Meziříčí** *Ger.* Grossmeseritsch. Vysočina, C Czech Republic
92 N1 **Velkomstpynten** *headland* NW Svalbard
111 K21 **Veľký Krtíš** Banskobystrický Kraj, C Slovakia
186 J8 **Vella Lavella** *var.* Mbilua. *island* New Georgia Islands, NW Solomon Islands
107 I15 **Velletri** Lazio, C Italy
95 K23 **Vellinge** Skåne, S Sweden
155 I19 **Vellore** Tamil Nādu, SE India
Velobriga *see* Viana do Castelo
115 G21 **Velopoúla** *island* S Greece
98 M12 **Velp** Gelderland, SE Netherlands
Velsen *see* Velsen-Noord
98 H9 **Velsen-Noord** *var.* Velsen. Noord-Holland, W Netherlands
125 N12 **Vel'sk** *var.* Velsk. Arkhangel'skaya Oblast', NW Russian Federation
Velsuna *see* Orvieto
98 K10 **Veluwemeer** *lake channel* C Netherlands
28 M3 **Velva** North Dakota, N USA
Velvendos/Velvendós *see* Velventós
115 E14 **Velventós** *var.* Velvendos, Velvendós. Dytikí Makedonía, N Greece
117 S5 **Velyka Bahachka** Poltavs'ka Oblast', C Ukraine
117 S9 **Velyka Lepetykha** *Rus.* Velikaya Lepetikha. Khersons'ka Oblast', S Ukraine
117 O10 **Velyka Mykhaylivka** Odes'ka Oblast', SW Ukraine
117 W8 **Velyka Novosilka** Donets'ka Oblast', E Ukraine
117 S9 **Velyka Oleksandrivka** Khersons'ka Oblast', S Ukraine
117 T4 **Velyka Pysanivka** Sums'ka Oblast', NE Ukraine
116 G6 **Velykyy Bereznyy** Zakarpats'ka Oblast', W Ukraine
117 W4 **Velykyy Burluk** Kharkivs'ka Oblast', E Ukraine
Velykyy Tokmak *see* Tokmak
173 P7 **Vema Fracture Zone** *tectonic feature* W Indian Ocean
65 P18 **Vema Seamount** *undersea feature* SW Indian Ocean
93 F17 **Vemdalen** Jämtland, C Sweden
95 N19 **Vena** Kalmar, S Sweden
41 N11 **Venado** San Luis Potosí, C Mexico
62 L11 **Venado Tuerto** Entre Ríos, E Argentina
61 A19 **Venado Tuerto** Santa Fe, C Argentina
107 K16 **Venafro** Molise, C Italy
55 Q9 **Venamo, Cerro** ▲ E Venezuela
106 B8 **Venaria** Piemonte, NW Italy
103 U15 **Vence** Alpes-Maritimes, SE France
104 H5 **Venda Nova** Vila Real, N Portugal

◆ Country ● Country Capital ◇ Dependent Territory ○ Dependent Territory Capital ◆ Administrative Regions ✈ International Airport ▲ Mountain ▲▲ Mountain Range Volcano ≈ River ◎ Lake ⊠ Reservoir

104 G11 **Vendas Novas** Évora, S Portugal
102 J9 **Vendée** ⬖ *department* NW France
103 Q6 **Vendeuvre-sur-Barse** Aube, NE France
102 M7 **Vendôme** Loir-et-Cher, C France
Venedig *see* Venezia
Vener, Lake *see* Vänern
106 I8 **Veneta, Laguna** *lagoon* NE Italy
Venetia *see* Venezia
39 S7 **Venetie** Alaska, USA
106 H8 **Veneto** *var.* Venezia Euganea. ⬖ *region* NE Italy
114 M7 **Venets** Shumen, NE Bulgaria
126 L5 **Venev** Tul'skaya Oblast', W Russian Federation
106 I8 **Venezia** *Eng.* Venice, *Fr.* Venise, *Ger.* Venedig; *anc.* Venetia. Veneto, NE Italy
Venezia Euganea *see* Veneto
Venezia, Golfo di *see* Venice, Gulf of
Venezia Tridentina *see* Trentino-Alto Adige
54 K8 **Venezuela** *off.* Republic of Venezuela; *prev.* Estados Unidos de Venezuela, United States of Venezuela. ◆ *republic* N South America
Venezuela, Cordillera de *see* Costa, Cordillera de la
Venezuela, Estados Unidos de *see* Venezuela
54 I4 **Venezuela, Golfo de** *Eng.* Gulf of Maracaibo, Gulf of Venezuela. *gulf* NW Venezuela
Venezuela, Gulf of *see* Venezuela, Golfo de
64 F11 **Venezuelan Basin** *undersea feature* E Caribbean Sea
Venezuela, Republic of *see* Venezuela
Venezuela, United States of *see* Venezuela
155 D16 **Vengurla** Mahārāshtra, W India
39 O15 **Veniaminof, Mount** ▲ Alaska, USA
23 V14 **Venice** Florida, SE USA
22 L10 **Venice** Louisiana, S USA
Venice *see* Venezia
106 J8 **Venice, Gulf of** *It.* Golfo di Venezia, *Slvn.* Beneški Zaliv. *gulf* N Adriatic Sea
Venise *see* Venezia
94 K13 **Venjan** Dalarna, C Sweden
94 K13 **Venjansjön** ◎ C Sweden
155 J18 **Venkatagiri** Andhra Pradesh, E India
99 M15 **Venlo** *prev.* Venloo. Limburg, SE Netherlands
Venloo *see* Venlo
95 E18 **Vennesla** Vest-Agder, S Norway
107 M17 **Venosa** *anc.* Venusia. Basilicata, S Italy
Venoste, Alpi *see* Ötztaler Alpen
Venraij *see* Venray
99 M14 **Venray** *var.* Venraij. Limburg, SE Netherlands
118 C8 **Venta** *Ger.* Windau. ≈ Latvia/Lithuania
Venta Belgarum *see* Winchester
40 G9 **Ventana, Punta Arena de la** *var.* Punta de la Ventana. *headland* W Mexico
Ventana, Punta de la *see* Ventana, Punta Arena de la
61 B23 **Ventana, Sierra de la** *hill range* E Argentina
Ventia *see* Valence
191 S11 **Vent, Îles du** *var.* Windward Islands. *island group* Archipel de la Société, W French Polynesia
191 R10 **Vent, Îles Sous le** *var.* Leeward Islands. *island group* Archipel de la Société, W French Polynesia
106 B11 **Ventimiglia** Liguria, NW Italy
97 M24 **Ventnor** S England, UK
18 J17 **Ventnor City** New Jersey, NE USA
103 S14 **Ventoux, Mont** ▲ SE France
118 C8 **Ventspils** *Ger.* Windau. Ventspils, NW Latvia
54 M10 **Ventuari, Río** ≈ S Venezuela
35 R15 **Ventura** California, W USA
182 F8 **Venus Bay** South Australia
Venusia *see* Venosa
191 P7 **Vénus, Pointe** *var.* Pointe Tataaihoa. *headland* Tahiti, W French Polynesia
41 V16 **Venustiano Carranza** Chiapas, SE Mexico
41 N7 **Venustiano Carranza, Presa** ⊠ NE Mexico
61 B15 **Vera** Santa Fe, C Argentina
105 Q14 **Vera** Andalucía, S Spain
63 K18 **Vera, Bahía** *bay* E Argentina
41 R14 **Veracruz** *var.* Veracruz Llave. Veracruz-Llave, E Mexico
Veracruz *see* Veracruz-Llave
41 Q13 **Veracruz-Llave** *var.* Veracruz. ⬖ *state* E Mexico
Veracruz Llave *see* Veracruz
43 Q16 **Veraguas** *off.* Provincia de Veraguas. ⬖ *province* W Panama
Veraguas, Provincia de *see* Veraguas
Veramin *see* Varāmīn
154 B12 **Verāval** Gujarāt, W India
106 C6 **Verbania** Piemonte, NW Italy
107 N20 **Verbicaro** Calabria, SW Italy
108 D11 **Verbier** Valais, SW Switzerland
Vercellae *see* Vercelli
106 C8 **Vercelli** *anc.* Vercellae. Piemonte, NW Italy
103 S13 **Vercors** *physical region* E France
Verdal *see* Verdalsøra
93 E16 **Verdalsøra** *var.* Verdal. Nord-Trøndelag, C Norway
Verde, Cabo *see* Cape Verde
44 J5 **Verde, Cape** *headland* Long Island, C Bahamas
104 M2 **Verde, Costa** *coastal region* N Spain
Verde Grande, Río/Verde Grande y de Belem, Río *see* Verde, Río
100 H11 **Verden** Niedersachsen, NW Germany
57 P16 **Verde, Río** ≈ Bolivia/Brazil
59 J19 **Verde, Rio** ≈ SE Brazil
40 M12 **Verde, Río** *var.* Río Verde Grande, Río Verde Grande y de Belem. ≈ C Mexico
41 Q16 **Verde, Río** ≈ SE Mexico
36 L13 **Verde River** ≈ Arizona, SW USA
Verdhikoúsa/Verdhikoússa *see* Verdikoússa
27 Q8 **Verdigris River** ≈ Kansas/Oklahoma, C USA
115 E15 **Verdikoússa** *var.* Verdhikoúsa, Verdhikoússa. Thessalía, C Greece
103 S15 **Verdon** ≈ SE France
15 O12 **Verdun** Québec, SE Canada
103 S4 **Verdun** *var.* Verdun-sur-Meuse; *anc.* Verodunum. Meuse, NE France
Verdun-sur-Meuse *see* Verdun
83 J21 **Vereeniging** Gauteng, NE South Africa
Veremeyki *see* Vyeramyeyki
125 T14 **Vereshchagino** Permskaya Oblast', NW Russian Federation
76 G14 **Verga, Cap** *headland* W Guinea
61 G18 **Vergara** Treinta y Tres, E Uruguay
108 G11 **Vergeletto** Ticino, S Switzerland
18 L8 **Vergennes** Vermont, NE USA
Veria *see* Véroia
104 I5 **Verín** Galicia, NW Spain
Verin T'alin *see* T'alin
118 K6 **Veriora** Põlvamaa, SE Estonia
117 T7 **Verkhivtseve** Dnipropetrovs'ka Oblast', E Ukraine
Verkhnedvinsk *see* Vyerkhnyadzvinsk
122 K10 **Verkhneimbatsk** Krasnoyarskiy Kray, N Russian Federation
124 I3 **Verkhnetulomskiy** Murmanskaya Oblast', NW Russian Federation
124 I3 **Verkhnetulomskoye Vodokhranilishche** ⊠ NW Russian Federation
Verkhneudinsk *see* Ulan-Ude
123 P10 **Verkhnevilyuysk** Respublika Sakha (Yakutiya), NE Russian Federation
127 W5 **Verkhniy Avzyan** Respublika Bashkortostan, W Russian Federation
127 Q11 **Verkhniy Baskunchak** Astrakhanskaya Oblast', SW Russian Federation
127 W3 **Verkhniye Kigi** Respublika Bashkortostan, W Russian Federation
117 T9 **Verkhniy Rohachyk** Khersons'ka Oblast', S Ukraine
123 Q11 **Verkhnyaya Amga** Respublika Sakha (Yakutiya), NE Russian Federation
125 V6 **Verkhnyaya Inta** Respublika Komi, NW Russian Federation
125 O10 **Verkhnyaya Toyma** Arkhangel'skaya Oblast', NW Russian Federation
126 K6 **Verkhov'ye** Orlovskaya Oblast', W Russian Federation
116 I8 **Verkhovyna** Ivano-Frankivs'ka Oblast', W Ukraine
123 P8 **Verkhoyanskiy Khrebet** ▲▲ NE Russian Federation
117 T7 **Verkn'odniprovs'k** Dnipropetrovs'ka Oblast', E Ukraine
101 G14 **Verl** Nordrhein-Westfalen, NW Germany
92 N1 **Verlegenhuken** *headland* N Svalbard
82 A9 **Vermelha, Ponta** *headland* NW Angola
103 P7 **Vermenton** Yonne, C France
9 R14 **Vermilion** Alberta, SW Canada
31 T11 **Vermilion** Ohio, N USA
22 I10 **Vermilion Bay** *bay* Louisiana, S USA
29 V4 **Vermilion Lake** ◎ Minnesota, N USA
14 F9 **Vermilion River** ≈ Ontario, S Canada
30 L12 **Vermilion River** ≈ Illinois, N USA
29 R12 **Vermillion** South Dakota, N USA
29 R12 **Vermillion River** ≈ South Dakota, N USA
15 O9 **Vermillon, Rivière** ≈ Québec, SE Canada
115 E14 **Vérmio** ▲▲ N Greece
18 L8 **Vermont** *off.* State of Vermont, *also known as* Green Mountain State. ⬖ *state* NE USA
113 K16 **Vermosh** *var.* Vermoshi. Shkodër, N Albania
Vermoshi *see* Vermosh
37 O3 **Vernal** Utah, W USA
14 G11 **Verner** Ontario, S Canada
102 M5 **Verneuil-sur-Avre** Eure, N France
114 D13 **Vérno** ▲▲ N Greece
9 N17 **Vernon** British Columbia, SW Canada
102 M4 **Vernon** Eure, N France
23 N3 **Vernon** Alabama, S USA
31 P15 **Vernon** Indiana, N USA
25 Q4 **Vernon** Texas, SW USA
32 G10 **Vernonia** Oregon, NW USA
14 G12 **Vernon, Lake** ◎ Ontario, S Canada
22 G7 **Vernon Lake** ⊠ Louisiana, S USA
23 Y13 **Vero Beach** Florida, SE USA
Verőcze *see* Virovitica
Verodunum *see* Verdun
115 E14 **Véroia** *var.* Veria, Vérroia, *Turk.* Karaferiye. Kentrikí Makedonía, N Greece
106 E8 **Verolanuova** Lombardia, N Italy
14 K14 **Verona** Ontario, SE Canada
106 G8 **Verona** Veneto, NE Italy
29 P6 **Verona** North Dakota, N USA
30 L9 **Verona** Wisconsin, N USA
61 E20 **Verónica** Buenos Aires, E Argentina
22 J9 **Verret, Lake** ◎ Louisiana, S USA
Vérroia *see* Véroia
103 N5 **Versailles** Yvelines, N France
31 P15 **Versailles** Indiana, N USA
20 M5 **Versailles** Kentucky, S USA
27 U5 **Versailles** Missouri, C USA
31 Q13 **Versailles** Ohio, N USA
Versecz *see* Vršac
108 A10 **Versoix** Genève, SW Switzerland
15 Z6 **Verte, Pointe** *headland* Québec, SE Canada
111 I22 **Vértes** ▲▲ NW Hungary
44 G6 **Vertientes** Camagüey, C Cuba
114 G13 **Vertískos** ▲▲ N Greece
102 I8 **Vertou** Loire-Atlantique, NW France
Verulamium *see* St Albans
99 L19 **Verviers** Liège, E Belgium
103 Y14 **Vescovato** Corse, France, C Mediterranean Sea
99 L20 **Vesdre** ≈ E Belgium
117 U10 **Vesele** *Rus.* Veseloye. Zaporiz'ka Oblast', S Ukraine
111 D18 **Veselí nad Lužnicí** *var.* Weseli an der Lainsitz, *Ger.* Frohenbruck. Jihočeský Kraj, S Czech Republic
114 M9 **Veselinovo** Shumen, NE Bulgaria
126 L12 **Veselovskoye Vodokhranilishche** ⊠ SW Russian Federation
Veseloye *see* Vesele
117 Q9 **Veselynove** Mykolayivs'ka Oblast', S Ukraine
Veseya *see* Vyasyeya
126 M10 **Veshenskaya** Rostovskaya Oblast', SW Russian Federation
127 Q5 **Veshkayma** Ul'yanovskaya Oblast', W Russian Federation
Vesisaari *see* Vadsø
Vesontio *see* Besançon
103 T7 **Vesoul** *anc.* Vesulium, Vesulum. Haute-Saône, E France
95 J20 **Vessigebro** Halland, S Sweden
95 D17 **Vest-Agder** ⬖ *county* S Norway
23 P4 **Vestavia Hills** Alabama, S USA
84 F6 **Vesterålen** *island* NW Norway
92 G10 **Vesterålen** *island group* N Norway
87 V3 **Vestervig** Viborg, NW Denmark
92 H2 **Vestfirdhir** ⬖ *region* NW Iceland
92 G11 **Vestfjorden** *fjord* C Norway
95 G16 **Vestfold** ⬖ *county* S Norway
Vestmanhavn *see* Vestmanna
95 B18 **Vestmanna** *Dan.* Vestmanhavn. Streymoy, N Faeroe Islands
92 I4 **Vestmannaeyjar** Sudhurland, S Iceland
94 E9 **Vestnes** Møre og Romsdal, S Norway
95 I23 **Vestsjælland** *off.* Vestsjællands Amt. ⬖ *county* E Denmark
Vestsjællands Amt *see* Vestsjælland
92 H3 **Vesturland** ⬖ *region* W Iceland
92 G11 **Vestvågøya** *island* C Norway
Vesulium/Vesulum *see* Vesoul
Vesuna *see* Périgueux
107 K17 **Vesuvio** *Eng.* Vesuvius. 🌋 S Italy
Vesuvius *see* Vesuvio
124 K14 **Ves'yegonsk** Tverskaya Oblast', W Russian Federation
111 I23 **Veszprém** *Ger.* Veszprim. Veszprém, W Hungary
111 H23 **Veszprém** *off.* Veszprém Megye. ⬖ *county* W Hungary
Veszprém Megye *see* Veszprém
Veszprim *see* Veszprém
Vetka *see* Vyetka
95 M19 **Vetlanda** Jönköping, S Sweden
127 P1 **Vetluga** Nizhegorodskaya Oblast', W Russian Federation
125 P14 **Vetluga** ≈ NW Russian Federation
125 O14 **Vetluzhskiy** Kostromskaya Oblast', NW Russian Federation
127 P2 **Vetluzhskiy** Nizhegorodskaya Oblast', W Russian Federation
107 H14 **Vetralla** Lazio, C Italy
114 M9 **Vetren** *prev.* Zhitarovo. Burgas, E Bulgaria
114 M8 **Vetrino** Varna, E Bulgaria
Vetrino *see* Vyetryna
122 L7 **Vetrovaya, Gora** ▲ N Russian Federation
Vetter, Lake *see* Vättern
106 J13 **Vettore, Monte** ▲ C Italy
99 A17 **Veurne** *var.* Furnes. West-Vlaanderen, W Belgium
31 Q15 **Vevay** Indiana, N USA
108 C10 **Vevey** *Ger.* Vivis; *anc.* Vibiscum. Vaud, SW Switzerland
Vexiö *see* Växjö
103 S13 **Veynes** Hautes-Alpes, SE France
103 N11 **Vézère** ≈ W France
114 I9 **Vezhen** ▲ C Bulgaria
136 K11 **Vezirköprü** Samsun, N Turkey
57 J18 **Viacha** La Paz, W Bolivia
27 R10 **Vian** Oklahoma, C USA
Viana de Castelo *see* Viana do Castelo
104 H12 **Viana do Alentejo** Évora, S Portugal
104 I4 **Viana do Bolo** Galicia, NW Spain
104 G5 **Viana do Castelo** *var.* Viana de Castelo; *anc.* Velobriga. Viana do Castelo, NW Portugal
104 G5 **Viana do Castelo** *var.* Viana de Castelo. ⬖ *district* N Portugal
98 J12 **Vianen** Utrecht, C Netherlands
167 Q8 **Viangchan** *Eng./Fr.* Vientiane. ● (Laos) C Laos
167 P6 **Viangphoukha** *var.* Vieng Pou Kha. Louang Namtha, N Laos
104 K13 **Viar** ≈ SW Spain
106 E11 **Viareggio** Toscana, C Italy
103 O14 **Viaur** ≈ S France
Vibiscum *see* Vevey
95 G21 **Viborg** Viborg, NW Denmark
29 R12 **Viborg** South Dakota, N USA
95 F21 **Viborg** *off.* Viborg Amt. ⬖ *county* NW Denmark
Viborg Amt *see* Viborg
107 N22 **Vibo Valentia** *prev.* Monteleone di Calabria; *anc.* Hipponium. Calabria, SW Italy
105 W5 **Vic** *var.* Vich; *anc.* Ausa, Vicus Ausonensis. Cataluña, NE Spain
102 K16 **Vic-en-Bigorre** Hautes-Pyrénées, S France
40 K10 **Vicente Guerrero** Durango, C Mexico
41 P10 **Vicente Guerrero, Presa** *var.* Presa de las Adjuntas. ⊠ NE Mexico
Vicentia *see* Vicenza
106 G8 **Vicenza** *anc.* Vicentia. Veneto, NE Italy
Vich *see* Vic
54 J10 **Vichada** *off.* Comisaría del Vichada. ⬖ *province* E Colombia
Vichada, Comisaría del *see* Vichada
54 K10 **Vichada, Río** ≈ E Colombia
61 G17 **Vichadero** Rivera, NE Uruguay
Vichegda *see* Vychegda
124 M16 **Vichuga** Ivanovskaya Oblast', W Russian Federation
103 P10 **Vichy** Allier, C France
26 K9 **Vici** Oklahoma, C USA
31 P10 **Vicksburg** Michigan, N USA
22 J5 **Vicksburg** Mississippi, S USA
103 O12 **Vic-sur-Cère** Cantal, C France
59 I21 **Víctor** Mato Grosso do Sul, SW Brazil
29 X14 **Victor** Iowa, C USA
182 I10 **Victor Harbor** South Australia
61 C18 **Victoria** Entre Ríos, E Argentina
10 L17 **Victoria** *province capital* Vancouver Island, British Columbia, SW Canada
45 R14 **Victoria** NW Grenada
42 H6 **Victoria** Yoro, NW Honduras
121 O15 **Victoria** *var.* Rabat. Gozo, NW Malta
116 I12 **Victoria** *Ger.* Viktoriastadt. Brașov, C Romania
172 H17 **Victoria** ● (Seychelles) Mahé, SW Seychelles
25 U13 **Victoria** Texas, SW USA
183 N12 **Victoria** ⬖ *state* SE Australia
174 K7 **Victoria** ≈ Western Australia
Victoria *see* Labuan, East Malaysia
Victoria *see* Masvingo, Zimbabwe
Victoria Bank *see* Vitória Seamount
9 Y15 **Victoria Beach** Manitoba, S Canada
Victoria de Durango *see* Durango
Victoria de las Tunas *see* Las Tunas
83 I16 **Victoria Falls** Matabeleland North, W Zimbabwe
83 I16 **Victoria Falls** *waterfall* Zambia/Zimbabwe
83 I16 **Victoria Falls** ✈ Matabeleland North, W Zimbabwe
Victoria Falls *see* Iguaçu, Salto do
63 F19 **Victoria, Isla** *island* Archipiélago de los Chonos, S Chile
8 K6 **Victoria Island** *island* Northwest Territories, NW Canada
182 L8 **Victoria, Lake** ◎ New South Wales, SE Australia
68 I12 **Victoria, Lake** *var.* Victoria Nyanza. ◎ E Africa
195 S13 **Victoria Land** *physical region* Antarctica
187 X14 **Victoria, Mount** ▲ Viti Levu, W Fiji
166 L5 **Victoria, Mount** ▲ W Myanmar (Burma)
186 E9 **Victoria, Mount** ▲ S Papua New Guinea
81 F17 **Victoria Nile** *var.* Somerset Nile. ≈ C Uganda
Victoria Nyanza *see* Victoria, Lake
42 G3 **Victoria Peak** ▲ SE Belize
185 H16 **Victoria Range** ▲▲ South Island, New Zealand
181 O3 **Victoria River** ≈ Northern Territory, N Australia
181 P3 **Victoria River Roadhouse** Northern Territory, N Australia
15 Q11 **Victoriaville** Québec, SE Canada
Victoria-Wes *see* Victoria West
83 G24 **Victoria West** *Afr.* Victoria-Wes. Northern Cape, W South Africa
62 J13 **Victorica** La Pampa, C Argentina
195 T3 **Victor, Mount** ▲ Antarctica
35 U14 **Victorville** California, W USA
62 G9 **Vicuña** Coquimbo, N Chile
62 K11 **Vicuña Mackenna** Córdoba, C Argentina
Vicus Ausonensis *see* Vic
Vicus Elbii *see* Viterbo
33 X7 **Vida** Montana, NW USA
23 V6 **Vidalia** Georgia, SE USA
22 J7 **Vidalia** Louisiana, S USA
95 F22 **Videbæk** Ringkøbing, C Denmark
60 I13 **Videira** Santa Catarina, S Brazil
116 J14 **Videle** Teleorman, S Romania
Videm-Krško *see* Krško
Víden *see* Wien
104 H12 **Vidigueira** Beja, S Portugal
114 J9 **Vidima** ≈ N Bulgaria
114 G7 **Vidin** *anc.* Bononia. Vidin, NW Bulgaria
114 F8 **Vidin** ⬖ *province* NW Bulgaria
154 H10 **Vidisha** Madhya Pradesh, C India
25 Y10 **Vidor** Texas, SW USA
95 L20 **Vidöstern** ◎ S Sweden
92 J13 **Vidsel** Norrbotten, N Sweden
118 H9 **Vidzemes Augstiene** ▲▲ C Latvia
118 J12 **Vidzy** *Rus.* Vidzy. Vitsyebskaya Voblasts', NW Belarus
63 L16 **Viedma** Río Negro, E Argentina
63 H22 **Viedma, Lago** ◎ S Argentina
45 O11 **Vieille Case** *var.* Itassi. N Dominica
104 M2 **Vieja, Peña** ▲ N Spain
40 E4 **Viejo, Cerro** ▲ NW Mexico
56 B9 **Viejo, Cerro** ▲ N Peru
118 E10 **Viekšniai** Telšiai, NW Lithuania
105 U3 **Vielha** *var.* Viella. Cataluña, NE Spain
Viella *see* Vielha
99 L21 **Vielsalm** Luxembourg, E Belgium
Vieng Pou Kha *see* Viangphoukha
23 T6 **Vienna** Georgia, SE USA
30 L17 **Vienna** Illinois, N USA
27 V5 **Vienna** Missouri, C USA
21 Q3 **Vienna** West Virginia, NE USA
Vienna *see* Wien, Austria
Vienna *see* Vienne, France
103 R11 **Vienne** *anc.* Vienna. Isère, E France
102 L10 **Vienne** ⬖ *department* W France
102 L9 **Vienne** ≈ W France
Vientiane *see* Viangchan
Vientos, Paso de los *see* Windward Passage
45 V6 **Vieques** *var.* Isabel Segunda. E Puerto Rico
45 V6 **Vieques, Isla de** *island* E Puerto Rico
45 V6 **Vieques, Pasaje de** *passage* E Puerto Rico
45 V5 **Vieques, Sonda de** *sound* E Puerto Rico
Vierdörfer *see* Săcele
93 M15 **Vieremä** Itä-Suomi, C Finland
99 M14 **Vierlingsbeek** Noord-Brabant, SE Netherlands
101 G20 **Viernheim** Hessen, W Germany
101 D15 **Viersen** Nordrhein-Westfalen, W Germany
108 G8 **Vierwaldstätter See** *Eng.* Lake of Lucerne. ◎ C Switzerland
103 N8 **Vierzon** Cher, C France
40 L8 **Viesca** Coahuila de Zaragoza, NE Mexico
118 H10 **Viesīte** *Ger.* Eckengraf. Jēkabpils, S Latvia
107 N15 **Vieste** Puglia, SE Italy
167 T8 **Vietnam** *off.* Socialist Republic of Vietnam, *Vtn.* Công Hoa Xa Hôi Chu Nghia Viêt Nam. ◆ *republic* SE Asia
Vietnam, Socialist Republic of *see* Vietnam
167 S5 **Viêt Quang** Ha Giang, N Vietnam
Vietri *see* Viêt Tri
167 S6 **Viêt Tri** *var.* Vietri. Vinh Phu, N Vietnam
30 L4 **Vieux Desert, Lac** ◎ Michigan/Wisconsin, N USA
45 Y13 **Vieux Fort** S Saint Lucia
45 X6 **Vieux-Habitants** Basse Terre, SW Guadeloupe
119 G14 **Vievis** Vilnius, S Lithuania
171 N2 **Vigan** Luzon, N Philippines
106 D8 **Vigevano** Lombardia, N Italy
107 N18 **Viggiano** Basilicata, S Italy
58 L12 **Vigia** Pará, NE Brazil
41 Y12 **Vigía Chico** Quintana Roo, SE Mexico
Vigie *see* George F L Charles
102 K17 **Vignemale** *var.* Pic de Vignemale. ▲ France/Spain
Vignemale, Pic de *see* Vignemale
106 G10 **Vignola** Emilia-Romagna, C Italy
104 G4 **Vigo** Galicia, NW Spain
104 G4 **Vigo, Ría de** *estuary* NW Spain
94 D9 **Vigra** *island* S Norway
95 C17 **Vigrestad** Rogaland, S Norway
93 L15 **Vihanti** Oulu, C Finland
149 U10 **Vihāri** Punjab, E Pakistan
102 K8 **Vihiers** Maine-et-Loire, NW France
111 O19 **Vihorlat** ▲ E Slovakia
93 L19 **Vihti** Etelä-Suomi, S Finland
Viipuri *see* Vyborg
93 M16 **Viitasaari** Länsi-Soumi, C Finland
118 K3 **Viivikonna** Ida-Virumaa, NE Estonia
155 K16 **Vijayawāda** *prev.* Bezwada. Andhra Pradesh, SE India
Vijosa/Vijosë *see* Aóos, Albania/Greece
Vijosa/Vijosë *see* Vjosës, Lumi i, Albania/Greece
92 J4 **Vík** Sudhurland, S Iceland
Vik *see* Vikøyri
94 L13 **Vika** Dalarna, C Sweden
92 L12 **Vikajärvi** Lappi, N Finland
94 L13 **Vikarbyn** Dalarna, C Sweden
95 J22 **Viken** Skåne, S Sweden
95 L17 **Viken** ◎ C Sweden
95 G15 **Vikersund** Buskerud, S Norway
114 G11 **Vikhren** ▲ SW Bulgaria
9 R15 **Viking** Alberta, SW Canada
84 E7 **Viking Bank** *undersea feature* N North Sea
95 M14 **Vikmanshyttan** Dalarna, C Sweden
94 D12 **Vikøyri** *var.* Vik. Sogn Og Fjordane, S Norway
93 H17 **Viksjö** Västernorrland, C Sweden
Viktoriastadt *see* Victoria
Vila *see* Port-Vila
Vila Arriaga *see* Bibala
Vila Artur de Paiva *see* Cubango
Vila Baleira *see* Porto Santo
Vila Bela da Santissima Trindade *see* Mato Grosso
58 B12 **Vila Bittencourt** Amazonas, NW Brazil
Vila da Ponte *see* Cubango
64 O2 **Vila da Praia da Vitória** Terceira, Azores, Portugal, NE Atlantic Ocean
Vila de Aljustrel *see* Cangamba
Vila de Almoster *see* Chiange
Vila de João Belo *see* Xai-Xai
Vila de Macia *see* Macia
Vila de Manhiça *see* Manhiça
Vila de Manica *see* Manica
Vila de Mocímboa da Praia *see* Mocímboa da Praia
83 N16 **Vila de Sena** *var.* Sena. Sofala, C Mozambique
104 F14 **Vila do Bispo** Faro, S Portugal
104 G6 **Vila do Conde** Porto, NW Portugal
Vila do Maio *see* Maio
64 P3 **Vila do Porto** Santa Maria, Azores, Portugal, NE Atlantic Ocean
83 K15 **Vila do Zumbo** *prev.* Vila do Zumbu, Zumbo. Tete, NW Mozambique
Vila do Zumbu *see* Vila do Zumbo
104 I6 **Vila Flor** *var.* Vila Flôr. Bragança, N Portugal
105 V6 **Vilafranca del Penedès** *var.* Villafranca del Panadés. Cataluña, NE Spain
104 F10 **Vila Franca de Xira** *var.* Vilafranca de Xira. Lisboa, C Portugal
Vila Gago Coutinho *see* Lumbala N'Guimbo
104 G3 **Vilagarcía de Arousa** *var.* Villagarcía de Arosa. Galicia, NW Spain
Vila General Machado *see* Camacupa
Vila Henrique de Carvalho *see* Saurimo
102 I7 **Vilaine** ≈ NW France
Vila João de Almeida *see* Chibia
118 K8 **Viļaka** *Ger.* Marienhausen. Balvi, NE Latvia
104 I2 **Vilalba** Galicia, NW Spain
Vila Marechal Carmona *see* Uíge
Vila Mariano Machado *see* Ganda
172 G3 **Vilanandro, Tanjona** *headland* W Madagascar
Vilanculos *see* Vilankulo
118 J10 **Viļāni** Rēzekne, E Latvia
83 N19 **Vilankulo** *var.* Vilanculos. Inhambane, E Mozambique
Vila Norton de Matos *see* Balombo
104 G6 **Vila Nova de Famalicão** *var.* Vila Nova de Famalicao. Braga, N Portugal
104 I6 **Vila Nova de Foz Côa** *var.* Vila Nova de Fozcôa. Guarda, N Portugal
Vila Nova de Fozcôa *see* Vila Nova de Foz Côa
104 F6 **Vila Nova de Gaia** Porto, NW Portugal
Vila Nova de Portimão *see* Portimão
105 V6 **Vilanova i La Geltrú** Cataluña, NE Spain
Vila Pereira de Eça *see* N'Giva
104 H6 **Vila Pouca de Aguiar** Vila Real, N Portugal
104 H6 **Vila Real** *var.* Vila Rial. Vila Real, N Portugal
104 H6 **Vila Real** ⬖ *district* N Portugal
Vila-real de los Infantes *see* Villarreal
104 H14 **Vila Real de Santo António** Faro, S Portugal
104 J7 **Vilar Formoso** Guarda, N Portugal
Vila Rial *see* Vila Real
59 J15 **Vila Rica** Mato Grosso, W Brazil
Vila Robert Williams *see* Caála
Vila Salazar *see* N'Dalatando
Vila Serpa Pinto *see* Menongue
Vila Teixeira da Silva *see* Bailundo
Vila Teixeira de Sousa *see* Luau
104 H9 **Vila Velha de Ródão** Castelo Branco, C Portugal
104 G5 **Vila Verde** Braga, N Portugal
104 H11 **Vila Viçosa** Évora, S Portugal
57 G15 **Vilcabamba, Cordillera de** ▲▲ C Peru
Vîlcea *see* Vâlcea
122 J4 **Vil'cheka, Zemlya** *Eng.* Wilczek Land. *island* Zemlya Frantsa-Iosifa, NW Russian Federation
95 F22 **Vildbjerg** Ringkøbing, C Denmark
Vileyka *see* Vilyeyka
93 H15 **Vilhelmina** Västerbotten, N Sweden
59 F17 **Vilhena** Rondônia, W Brazil
115 G19 **Vília** Attikí, C Greece
119 I14 **Viliya** *Lith.* Neris, *Rus.* Viliya. ≈ W Belarus
Viliya *see* Neris
118 H5 **Viljandi** *Ger.* Fellin. Viljandimaa, S Estonia
118 H5 **Viljandimaa** *var.* Viljandi Maakond. ⬖ *province* SW Estonia
Viljandi Maakond *see* Viljandimaa
119 E14 **Vilkaviškis** *Pol.* Wyłkowyszki. Marijampolė, SW Lithuania
118 F13 **Vilkija** Kaunas, C Lithuania
197 V9 **Vil'kitskogo, Proliv** *strait* N Russian Federation
Vilkovo *see* Vylkove
57 L21 **Villa Abecia** Chuquisaca, S Bolivia
41 N5 **Villa Acuña** *var.* Ciudad Acuña. Coahuila de Zaragoza, NE Mexico
40 J4 **Villa Ahumada** Chihuahua, N Mexico
45 O9 **Villa Altagracia** C Dominican Republic
56 L13 **Villa Bella** Beni, N Bolivia
104 J3 **Villablino** Castilla-León, N Spain
54 K6 **Villa Bruzual** Portuguesa, N Venezuela
105 O9 **Villacañas** Castilla-La Mancha, C Spain
105 O12 **Villacarrillo** Andalucía, S Spain
104 M7 **Villacastín** Castilla-León, N Spain
Villa Cecilia *see* Ciudad Madero

◆ Country
● Country Capital
◇ Dependent Territory
○ Dependent Territory Capital
⬖ Administrative Regions
✈ International Airport
▲ Mountain
▲▲ Mountain Range
🌋 Volcano
≈ River
◎ Lake
⊠ Reservoir

109 S9 **Villach** *Slvn.* Beljak. Kärnten, S Austria
107 B20 **Villacidro** Sardegna, Italy, C Mediterranean Sea
Villa Concepción *see* Concepción
104 L4 **Villada** Castilla-León, N Spain
40 M10 **Villa de Cos** Zacatecas, C Mexico
54 L5 **Villa de Cura** *var.* Cura. Aragua, N Venezuela
Villa del Nevoso *see* Ilirska Bistrica
Villa del Pilar *see* Pilar
104 M13 **Villa del Río** Andalucía, S Spain
Villa de Méndez *see* Méndez
42 H6 **Villa de San Antonio** Comayagua, W Honduras
105 N4 **Villadiego** Castilla-León, N Spain
105 T8 **Villafamés** País Valenciano, E Spain
41 U16 **Villa Flores** Chiapas, SE Mexico
104 J3 **Villafranca del Bierzo** Castilla-León, N Spain
105 S8 **Villafranca del Cid** País Valenciano, E Spain
104 J11 **Villafranca de los Barros** Extremadura, W Spain
105 N10 **Villafranca de los Caballeros** Castilla-La Mancha, C Spain
Villafranca del Panadés *see* Vilafranca del Penedès
106 F8 **Villafranca di Verona** Veneto, NE Italy
107 J23 **Villafrati** Sicilia, Italy, C Mediterranean Sea
Villagarcía de Arosa *see* Vilagarcía de Arousa
41 O9 **Villagrán** Tamaulipas, C Mexico
61 C17 **Villaguay** Entre Ríos, E Argentina
62 O6 **Villa Hayes** Presidente Hayes, S Paraguay
41 U15 **Villahermosa** *prev.* San Juan Bautista. Tabasco, SE Mexico
105 O11 **Villahermosa** Castilla-La Mancha, C Spain
64 O11 **Villahermoso** Gomera, Islas Canarias, Spain, NE Atlantic Ocean
Villa Hidalgo *see* Hidalgo
105 T12 **Villajoyosa** *Cat.* La Vila Joiosa. País Valenciano, E Spain
Villa Juárez *see* Juárez
Villalba *see* Collado Villalba
41 N8 **Villaldama** Nuevo León, NE Mexico
104 L5 **Villalón de Campos** Castilla-León, N Spain
61 A25 **Villalonga** Buenos Aires, E Argentina
104 L5 **Villalpando** Castilla-León, N Spain
40 K9 **Villa Madero** *var.* Francisco I. Madero. Durango, C Mexico
41 O9 **Villa Mainero** Tamaulipas, C Mexico
Villamaña *see* Villamañán
104 L4 **Villamañán** *var.* Villamaña. Castilla-León, N Spain
62 L10 **Villa María** Córdoba, C Argentina
61 C17 **Villa María Grande** Entre Ríos, E Argentina
57 K21 **Villa Martín** Potosí, SW Bolivia
104 K15 **Villamartín** Andalucía, S Spain
62 J8 **Villa Mazán** La Rioja, NW Argentina
Villa Mercedes *see* Mercedes
Villamil *see* Puerto Villamil
Villa Nador *see* Nador
54 G5 **Villanueva** La Guajira, N Colombia
42 H5 **Villanueva** Cortés, NW Honduras
40 L11 **Villanueva** Zacatecas, C Mexico
42 I9 **Villa Nueva** Chinandega, NW Nicaragua
37 T11 **Villanueva** New Mexico, SW USA
104 M12 **Villanueva de Córdoba** Andalucía, S Spain
105 O12 **Villanueva del Arzobispo** Andalucía, S Spain
104 K11 **Villanueva de la Serena** Extremadura, W Spain
104 L5 **Villanueva del Campo** Castilla-León, N Spain
105 O11 **Villanueva de los Infantes** Castilla-La Mancha, C Spain
61 C14 **Villa Ocampo** Santa Fe, C Argentina
40 J8 **Villa Ocampo** Durango, C Mexico
40 J7 **Villa Orestes Pereyra** Durango, C Mexico
105 N3 **Villarcayo** Castilla-León, N Spain
104 L5 **Villardefrades** Castilla-León, N Spain
105 S9 **Villar del Arzobispo** País Valenciano, E Spain
105 Q6 **Villaroya de la Sierra** Aragón, NE Spain
105 T9 **Villarreal** *var.* Vila-real de los Infantes. País Valenciano, E Spain
62 P6 **Villarrica** Guairá, SE Paraguay
63 G15 **Villarrica, Volcán** ⛰ S Chile
105 P10 **Villarrobledo** Castilla-La Mancha, C Spain
105 N10 **Villarrubia de los Ojos** Castilla-La Mancha, C Spain
18 J17 **Villas** New Jersey, NE USA
105 O3 **Villasana de Mena** Castilla-León, N Spain
107 M23 **Villa San Giovanni** Calabria, S Italy
61 D18 **Villa San José** Entre Ríos, E Argentina
Villa Sanjurjo *see* Al-Hoceïma
105 P6 **Villasayas** Castilla-León, N Spain
107 C20 **Villasimius** Sardegna, Italy, C Mediterranean Sea
41 N6 **Villa Unión** Coahuila de Zaragoza, NE Mexico
40 K10 **Villa Unión** Durango, C Mexico
40 J10 **Villa Unión** Sinaloa, C Mexico
62 K12 **Villa Valeria** Córdoba, C Argentina
105 N8 **Villaverde** Madrid, C Spain
54 F10 **Villavicencio** Meta, C Colombia
104 L2 **Villaviciosa** Asturias, N Spain
104 L12 **Villaviciosa de Córdoba** Andalucía, S Spain
57 L22 **Villazón** Potosí, S Bolivia
14 J8 **Villebon, Lac** ⊚ Québec, SE Canada
Ville de Kinshasa *see* Kinshasa
102 J5 **Villedieu-les-Poêles** Manche, N France
Villefranche *see* Villefranche-sur-Saône
103 N16 **Villefranche-de-Lauragais** Haute-Garonne, S France
103 N14 **Villefranche-de-Rouergue** Aveyron, S France
103 R10 **Villefranche-sur-Saône** *var.* Villefranche. Rhône, E France
14 H9 **Ville-Marie** Québec, SE Canada
102 M15 **Villemur-sur-Tarn** Haute-Garonne, S France
105 S11 **Villena** País Valenciano, E Spain
Villeneuve-d'Agen *see* Villeneuve-sur-Lot
102 L13 **Villeneuve-sur-Lot** *var.* Villeneuve-d'Agen, *hist.* Gajac. Lot-et-Garonne, SW France
103 P6 **Villeneuve-sur-Yonne** Yonne, C France
22 H8 **Ville Platte** Louisiana, S USA
103 R11 **Villeurbanne** Rhône, E France
101 G23 **Villingen-Schwenningen** Baden-Württemberg, S Germany
29 T15 **Villisca** Iowa, C USA
Villmanstrand *see* Lappeenranta
Vilna *see* Vilnius
119 H14 **Vilnius** *Pol.* Wilno, *Ger.* Wilna; *prev. Rus.* Vilna. ● (Lithuania) Vilnius, SE Lithuania
119 H14 **Vilnius** ✈ Vilnius, SE Lithuania
117 S7 **Vil'nohirs'k** Dnipropetrovs'ka Oblast', E Ukraine
117 U8 **Vil'nyans'k** Zaporiz'ka Oblast', SE Ukraine
93 L17 **Vilppula** Länsi-Suomi, W Finland
101 M20 **Vils** ~ SE Germany
118 C5 **Vilsandi Saar** *island* W Estonia
117 P8 **Vil'shanka** *Rus.* Olshanka. Kirovohrads'ka Oblast', C Ukraine
101 O22 **Vilshofen** Bayern, SE Germany
155 J20 **Viluppuram** Tamil Nādu, SE India
113 J16 **Vilusi** W Montenegro
99 G18 **Vilvoorde** *Fr.* Vilvorde. Vlaams Brabant, C Belgium
Vilvorde *see* Vilvoorde
119 J14 **Vilyeyka** *Pol.* Wilejka, *Rus.* Vileyka. Minskaya Voblasts', NW Belarus
122 V11 **Vilyuchinsk** Kamchatskaya Oblast', E Russian Federation
123 P10 **Vilyuy** ~ NE Russian Federation
123 P10 **Vilyuysk** Respublika Sakha (Yakutiya), NE Russian Federation
123 N10 **Vilyuyskoye Vodokhranilishche** ⊠ NE Russian Federation
104 G2 **Vimianzo** Galicia, NW Spain
95 M19 **Vimmerby** Kalmar, S Sweden
102 L5 **Vimoutiers** Orne, N France
93 L16 **Vimpeli** Länsi-Suomi, W Finland
79 G14 **Vina** ~ Cameroon/Chad
62 G11 **Viña del Mar** Valparaíso, C Chile
19 R8 **Vinalhaven Island** *island* Maine, NE USA
105 T8 **Vinaròs** País Valenciano, E Spain
Vînători *see* Vânători
31 N15 **Vincennes** Indiana, N USA
195 Y12 **Vincennes Bay** *bay* Antarctica
25 O7 **Vincent** Texas, SW USA
95 H24 **Vindeby** Fyn, C Denmark
93 I15 **Vindeln** Västerbotten, N Sweden
95 F21 **Vinderup** Ringkøbing, C Denmark
Vindhya Mountains *see* Vindhya Range
153 N14 **Vindhya Range** *var.* Vindhya Mountains. ▲▲ N India
Vindobona *see* Wien
20 K6 **Vine Grove** Kentucky, S USA
18 J17 **Vineland** New Jersey, NE USA
116 E11 **Vinga** Arad, W Romania
95 M16 **Vingåker** Södermanland, C Sweden
167 S8 **Vinh** Nghê An, N Vietnam
104 I5 **Vinhais** Bragança, N Portugal
167 T9 **Vinh Linh** Quang Tri, C Vietnam
Vinh Loi *see* Bac Liêu
167 S14 **Vinh Long** *var.* Vinhlong. Vinh Long, S Vietnam
Vinhlong *see* Vinh Long
113 Q18 **Vinica** NE FYR Macedonia
109 V13 **Vinica** SE Slovenia
114 G8 **Vinishte** Montana, NW Bulgaria
27 Q8 **Vinita** Oklahoma, C USA
Vinju Mare *see* Vânju Mare
98 I11 **Vinkeveen** Utrecht, C Netherlands
116 L6 **Vin'kivtsi** Khmel'nyts'ka Oblast', W Ukraine
112 I10 **Vinkovci** *Ger.* Winkowitz, *Hung.* Vinkovcze. Vukovar-Srijem, E Croatia
Vinkovcze *see* Vinkovci
Vinnitsa *see* Vinnytsya
Vinnitskaya Oblast'/Vinnytsya *see* Vinnyts'ka Oblast'
116 M7 **Vinnyts'ka Oblast'** *var.* Vinnytsya, *Rus.* Vinnitskaya Oblast'. ⬖ *province* C Ukraine
117 N6 **Vinnytsya** *Rus.* Vinnitsa. Vinnyts'ka Oblast', C Ukraine
117 N6 **Vinnytsya** ✈ Vinnyts'ka Oblast', N Ukraine
Vinogradov *see* Vynohradiv
194 L8 **Vinson Massif** ▲ Antarctica
94 G11 **Vinstra** Oppland, S Norway
116 K12 **Vintilă Vodă** Buzău, SE Romania
29 X13 **Vinton** Iowa, C USA
22 F9 **Vinton** Louisiana, S USA
155 J17 **Vinukonda** Andhra Pradesh, E India
Vioara *see* Ocnele Mari
83 E23 **Vioolsdrif** Northern Cape, SW South Africa
82 M13 **Viphya Mountains** ▲▲ C Malawi
171 Q4 **Virac** Catanduanes Island, N Philippines
124 K8 **Virandozero** Respublika Kareliya, NW Russian Federation
137 P16 **Viranşehir** Şanlıurfa, SE Turkey
154 D13 **Virār** Mahārāshtra, W India
9 W16 **Virden** Manitoba, S Canada
30 K14 **Virden** Illinois, N USA
Virdois *see* Virrat
102 J5 **Vire** Calvados, N France
102 J4 **Vire** ~ N France
83 A15 **Virei** Namibe, SW Angola
Virful Moldoveanu *see* Vârful Moldoveanu
35 R5 **Virgina Peak** ▲ Nevada, W USA
45 U9 **Virgin Gorda** *island* C British Virgin Islands
83 I22 **Virginia** Free State, C South Africa
30 K13 **Virginia** Illinois, N USA
29 W4 **Virginia** Minnesota, N USA
21 T6 **Virginia** *off.* Commonwealth of Virginia, *also known as* Mother of Presidents, Mother of States, Old Dominion. ⬖ *state* NE USA
21 Y7 **Virginia Beach** Virginia, NE USA
33 R11 **Virginia City** Montana, NW USA
35 Q6 **Virginia City** Nevada, W USA
14 H8 **Virginiatown** Ontario, S Canada
Virgin Islands *see* British Virgin Islands
45 T9 **Virgin Islands (US)** *var.* Virgin Islands of the United States; *prev.* Danish West Indies. ◇ *US unincorporated territory* E West Indies
Virgin Islands of the United States *see* Virgin Islands (US)
45 T9 **Virgin Passage** *passage* Puerto Rico/Virgin Islands (US)
35 Y10 **Virgin River** ~ Nevada/Utah, W USA
Virihaur *see* Virihaure
92 H12 **Virihaure** *var.* Virihaur. ⊚ N Sweden
167 T11 **Virôchey** Rôtânôkiri, NE Cambodia
93 N19 **Virolahti** Etelä-Suomi, S Finland
30 J8 **Viroqua** Wisconsin, N USA
112 G8 **Virovitica** *Ger.* Virovititz, *Hung.* Verőcze; *prev. Ger.* Werowitz. Virovitica-Podravina, NE Croatia
112 G8 **Virovitica-Podravina** *off.* Virovitičko-Podravska Županija. ⬖ *province* NE Croatia
Virovitičko-Podravska Županija *see* Virovitica-Podravina
Virovititz *see* Virovitica
113 J17 **Virpazar** S Montenegro
93 L17 **Virrat** *Swe.* Virdois. Länsi-Suomi, W Finland
95 M20 **Virserum** Kalmar, S Sweden
99 K25 **Virton** Luxembourg, SE Belgium
118 F5 **Virtsu** *Ger.* Werder. Läänemaa, W Estonia
56 C12 **Virú** La Libertad, C Peru
Virudhunagar *see* Virudunagar
155 H23 **Virudunagar** *var.* Virudhunagar. Tamil Nādu, SE India
118 I3 **Viru-Jaagupi** *Ger.* Sankt-Jakobi. Lääne-Virumaa, NE Estonia
57 N19 **Viru-Viru** *var.* Santa Cruz. ✈ (Santa Cruz) Santa Cruz, C Bolivia
113 E15 **Vis** *It.* Lissa; *anc.* Issa. *island* S Croatia
Vis *see* Fish
118 I12 **Visaginas** *prev.* Sniečkus. Utena, E Lithuania
155 M15 **Visākhapatnam** Andhra Pradesh, SE India
35 R11 **Visalia** California, W USA
Višău *see* Vişeu
95 P19 **Visby** *Ger.* Wisby. Gotland, SE Sweden
197 N9 **Viscount Melville Sound** *prev.* Melville Sound. *sound* Northwest Territories, N Canada
99 L19 **Visé** Liège, E Belgium
112 K13 **Višegrad** ⬖ Republika Srpska, SE Bosnia and Herzegovina
58 L12 **Viseu** Pará, NE Brazil
104 H7 **Viseu** *prev.* Vizeu. Viseu, N Portugal
104 H7 **Viseu** *var.* Vizeu. ⬖ *district* N Portugal
116 I8 **Vişeu** *Hung.* Visó; *prev.* Vişău. ~ NW Romania
116 I8 **Vişeu de Sus** *var.* Vişeul de Sus, *Ger.* Oberwischau, *Hung.* Felsővisó. Maramureş, N Romania
Vişeul de Sus *see* Vişeu de Sus
125 R10 **Vishera** ~ NW Russian Federation
95 J19 **Viskafors** Västra Götaland, S Sweden
95 J20 **Viskan** ~ S Sweden
95 L21 **Vislanda** Kronoberg, S Sweden
Vislinskiy Zaliv *see* Vistula Lagoon
Visó *see* Vişeu
112 H13 **Visoko** ⬖ Federacija Bosna I Hercegovina, C Bosnia and Herzegovina
106 A9 **Viso, Monte** ▲ NW Italy
108 E10 **Visp** Valais, SW Switzerland
108 E10 **Vispa** ~ S Switzerland
95 M21 **Vissefjärda** Kalmar, S Sweden
100 I11 **Visselhövede** Niedersachsen, NW Germany
95 G23 **Vissenbjerg** Fyn, C Denmark
35 U17 **Vista** California, W USA
58 C11 **Vista Alegre** Amazonas, NW Brazil
114 J13 **Vistonida, Límni** ⊚ NE Greece
Vistula *see* Wisła
119 A14 **Vistula Lagoon** *Ger.* Frisches Haff, *Pol.* Zalew Wiślany, *Rus.* Vislinskiy Zaliv. *lagoon* Poland/Russian Federation
114 I8 **Vit** ~ NW Bulgaria
Vitebsk *see* Vitsyebsk
Vitebskaya Oblast' *see* Vitsyebskaya Voblasts'
107 H14 **Viterbo** *anc.* Vicus Elbii. Lazio, C Italy
112 H12 **Vitez** ⬖ Federacija Bosna I Hercegovina, C Bosnia and Herzegovina
167 S14 **Vi Thanh** Cân Thơ, S Vietnam
Viti *see* Fiji
186 E7 **Vitiaz Strait** *strait* NE Papua New Guinea
104 J7 **Vitigudino** Castilla-León, N Spain
187 W15 **Viti Levu** *island* W Fiji
123 O11 **Vitim** ~ C Russian Federation
123 O12 **Vitimskiy** Irkutskaya Oblast', C Russian Federation
109 V2 **Vitis** Niederösterreich, N Austria
59 O20 **Vitória** *state capital* Espírito Santo, SE Brazil
Vitoria *see* Vitoria-Gasteiz
Vitoria Bank *see* Vitória Seamount
59 N18 **Vitória da Conquista** Bahia, E Brazil
105 P3 **Vitoria-Gasteiz** *var.* Vitoria, *Eng.* Vittoria. País Vasco, N Spain
65 J16 **Vitória Seamount** *var.* Victoria Bank, Vitoria Bank. *undersea feature* C Atlantic Ocean
112 F13 **Vitorog** ▲ SW Bosnia and Herzegovina
102 J6 **Vitré** Ille-et-Vilaine, NW France
103 R5 **Vitry-le-François** Marne, N France
114 D13 **Vítsi** *var.* Vítsoi. ▲ N Greece
Vítsoi *see* Vítsi
118 N13 **Vitsyebsk** *Rus.* Vitebsk. Vitsyebskaya Voblasts', NE Belarus
118 K13 **Vitsyebskaya Voblasts'** *prev. Rus.* Vitebskaya Oblast'. ⬖ *province* N Belarus
92 J11 **Vittangi** *Lapp.* Vazáš. Norrbotten, N Sweden
103 R8 **Vitteaux** Côte d'Or, C France
103 S6 **Vittel** Vosges, NE France
95 N15 **Vittinge** Västmanland, C Sweden
107 K25 **Vittoria** Sicilia, Italy, C Mediterranean Sea
Vittoria *see* Vitoria-Gasteiz
106 I7 **Vittorio Veneto** Veneto, NE Italy
175 Q9 **Vitu Levu** *island* W Fiji
175 Q7 **Vityaz Trench** *undersea feature* W Pacific Ocean
108 G8 **Vitznau** Luzern, W Switzerland
104 I1 **Viveiro** Galicia, NW Spain
105 S9 **Viver** País Valenciano, E Spain
103 Q13 **Viverais, Monts du** ▲▲ C France
122 L9 **Vivi** ~ N Russian Federation
22 F4 **Vivian** Louisiana, S USA
29 N10 **Vivian** South Dakota, N USA
103 R13 **Viviers** Ardèche, E France
Vivis *see* Vevey
83 K19 **Vivo** Limpopo, NE South Africa
102 L10 **Vivonne** Vienne, W France
Vizakna *see* Ocna Sibiului
105 O2 **Vizcaya** *Basq.* Bizkaia. ⬖ *province* País Vasco, N Spain
Vizcaya, Golfo de *see* Biscay, Bay of
136 C10 **Vize** Kırklareli, NW Turkey
122 K4 **Vize, Ostrov** *island* Severnaya Zemlya, N Russian Federation
Vizeu *see* Viseu
155 M15 **Vizianagaram** *var.* Vizianagram. Andhra Pradesh, E India
Vizianagram *see* Vizianagaram
103 S12 **Vizille** Isère, E France
125 R11 **Vizinga** Respublika Komi, NW Russian Federation
116 M13 **Viziru** Brăila, SE Romania
113 K21 **Vjosës, Lumi i** *var.* Vijosa, Vijosë, *Gk.* Aóos. ~ Albania/Greece *see also* Aóos
Vjosës, Lumi i *see* Aóos
99 H18 **Vlaams Brabant** ⬖ *province* C Belgium
Vlaanderen *see* Flanders
98 G12 **Vlaardingen** Zuid-Holland, SW Netherlands
116 F10 **Vlădeasa, Vârful** *prev.* Vîrful Vlădeasa. ▲ NW Romania
Vlădeasa, Vîrful *see* Vlădeasa, Vârful
113 P16 **Vladičin Han** Serbia, SE Serbia
127 O16 **Vladikavkaz** *prev.* Dzaudzhikau, Ordzhonikidze. Respublika Severnaya Osetiya, SW Russian Federation
126 M3 **Vladimir** Vladimirskaya Oblast', W Russian Federation
144 M7 **Vladimirovka** Kostanay, N Kazakhstan
Vladimirovka *see* Yuzhno-Sakhalinsk
126 L3 **Vladimirskaya Oblast'** ⬖ *province* W Russian Federation
126 I3 **Vladimirskiy Tupik** Smolenskaya Oblast', W Russian Federation
Vladimir-Volynskiy *see* Volodymyr-Volyns'kyy
123 Q7 **Vladivostok** Primorskiy Kray, SE Russian Federation
117 U13 **Vladyslavivka** Respublika Krym, S Ukraine
98 P6 **Vlagtwedde** Groningen, NE Netherlands
Vlajna *see* Kukavica
112 J12 **Vlasenica** ⬖ Republika Srpska, E Bosnia and Herzegovina
112 G12 **Vlašić** ▲ C Bosnia and Herzegovina
111 D17 **Vlašim** *Ger.* Wlaschim. Středočeský Kraj, C Czech Republic
113 P15 **Vlasotince** Serbia, SE Serbia
123 Q7 **Vlasovo** Respublika Sakha (Yakutiya), NE Russian Federation
98 I11 **Vleuten** Utrecht, C Netherlands
98 I5 **Vlieland** *Fris.* Flylân. *island* Waddeneilanden, N Netherlands
98 I5 **Vliestroom** *strait* NW Netherlands
99 J14 **Vlijmen** Noord-Brabant, S Netherlands
99 E15 **Vlissingen** *Eng.* Flushing, *Fr.* Flessingue. Zeeland, SW Netherlands
Vlodava *see* Włodawa
Vlonë/Vlora *see* Vlorë
113 K22 **Vlorë** *prev.* Vlonë, *It.* Valona, Vlora. Vlorë, SW Albania
113 K22 **Vlorë** ⬖ *district* SW Albania
113 K22 **Vlorës, Gjiri i** *var.* Valona Bay. *bay* SW Albania
Vlotslavsk *see* Włocławek
111 C16 **Vltava** *Ger.* Moldau. ~ W Czech Republic
126 K3 **Vnukovo** ✈ (Moskva) Gorod Moskva, W Russian Federation
146 L11 **Vobkent** Buxoro Viloyati, C Uzbekistan
146 L11 **Vobkent** *var.* Vabkent. Buxoro Viloyati, C Uzbekistan
25 Q9 **Voca** Texas, SW USA
109 R5 **Vöcklabruck** Oberösterreich, NW Austria
112 D13 **Vodice** Šibenik-Knin, S Croatia
124 K10 **Vodlozero, Ozero** ⊚ NW Russian Federation
112 A10 **Vodnjan** *It.* Dignano d'Istria. Istra, NW Croatia
125 S9 **Vodnyy** Respublika Komi, NW Russian Federation
95 G20 **Vodskov** Nordjylland, N Denmark
92 H4 **Vogar** Sudhurland, SW Iceland
Vogelkop *see* Doberai, Jazirah
77 X15 **Vogel Peak** *prev.* Dimlang. ▲ E Nigeria
101 H17 **Vogelsberg** ▲▲ C Germany
106 D8 **Voghera** Lombardia, N Italy
112 I13 **Vogošća** ⬖ Federacija Bosna I Hercegovina, SE Bosnia and Herzegovina
101 M17 **Vogtland** *historical region* E Germany
125 V12 **Vogul'skiy Kamen', Gora** ▲ NW Russian Federation
187 P16 **Voh** Province Nord, C New Caledonia
Vohémar *see* Iharaña
172 H8 **Vohimena, Tanjona** *Fr.* Cap Sainte Marie. *headland* S Madagascar
172 J6 **Vohipeno** Fianarantsoa, SE Madagascar
118 H5 **Võhma** *Ger.* Wöchma. Viljandimaa, S Estonia
81 J20 **Voi** Coast, S Kenya
76 K15 **Voinjama** N Liberia
103 S12 **Voiron** Isère, E France
109 V8 **Voitsberg** Steiermark, SE Austria
95 F24 **Vojens** *Ger.* Woyens. Sønderjylland, SW Denmark
112 K9 **Vojvodina** *Ger.* Wojwodina. Vojvodina, N Serbia
15 S6 **Volant** ~ Québec, SE Canada
Volaterrae *see* Volterra
43 P15 **Volcán** *var.* Hato del Volcán. Chiriquí, W Panama
Volcano Islands *see* Kazan-rettō
Volchansk *see* Vovchans'k
Volchya *see* Vovcha
94 D10 **Volda** Møre og Romsdal, S Norway
98 J9 **Volendam** Noord-Holland, C Netherlands
124 L15 **Volga** Yaroslavskaya Oblast', W Russian Federation
29 R10 **Volga** South Dakota, N USA
122 C11 **Volga** ~ NW Russian Federation
Volga-Baltic Waterway *see* Volgo-Baltiyskiy Kanal
Volga Uplands *see* Privolzhskaya Vozvyshennost'
124 L13 **Volgo-Baltiyskiy Kanal** *var.* Volga-Baltic Waterway. *canal* NW Russian Federation
126 M12 **Volgodonsk** Rostovskaya Oblast', SW Russian Federation
127 O10 **Volgograd** *prev.* Stalingrad, Tsaritsyn. Volgogradskaya Oblast', SW Russian Federation
127 N9 **Volgogradskaya Oblast'** ⬖ *province* SW Russian Federation
127 P10 **Volgogradskoye Vodokhranilishche** ⊠ SW Russian Federation
101 J19 **Volkach** Bayern, C Germany
109 U9 **Völkermarkt** *Slvn.* Velikovec. Kärnten, S Austria
124 I12 **Volkhov** Leningradskaya Oblast', NW Russian Federation
101 D20 **Völklingen** Saarland, SW Germany
Volkovysk *see* Vawkavysk
Volkovyskiye Vysoty *see* Vawkavyskaye Wzvyshsha
83 K22 **Volksrust** Mpumalanga, E South Africa
98 L8 **Vollenhove** Overijssel, N Netherlands
119 L16 **Volma** ~ C Belarus
Volmari *see* Valmiera
117 W9 **Volnovakha** Donets'ka Oblast', SE Ukraine
116 K6 **Volochys'k** Khmel'nyts'ka Oblast', W Ukraine
117 O6 **Volodarka** Kyyivs'ka Oblast', N Ukraine
117 W9 **Volodars'ke** Donets'ka Oblast', E Ukraine
127 R13 **Volodarskiy** Astrakhanskaya Oblast', SW Russian Federation
Volodarskoye *see* Saumalkol'
117 N8 **Volodars'k-Volyns'kyy** Zhytomyrs'ka Oblast', N Ukraine
116 K3 **Volodymerets'** Rivnens'ka Oblast', NW Ukraine
116 I3 **Volodymyr-Volyns'kyy** *Pol.* Włodzimierz, *Rus.* Vladimir-Volynskiy. Volyns'ka Oblast', NW Ukraine
124 L14 **Vologda** Vologodskaya Oblast', W Russian Federation
124 L12 **Vologodskaya Oblast'** ⬖ *province* NW Russian Federation
126 K3 **Volokolamsk** Moskovskaya Oblast', W Russian Federation
126 K9 **Volokonovka** Belgorodskaya Oblast', W Russian Federation
115 G16 **Vólos** Thessalía, C Greece
124 M11 **Voloshka** Arkhangel'skaya Oblast', NW Russian Federation
Vološinovo *see* Novi Bečej
116 H7 **Volovets'** Zakarpats'ka Oblast', W Ukraine
114 K7 **Volovo** Ruse, N Bulgaria
Volozhin *see* Valozhyn
127 Q7 **Vol'sk** Saratovskaya Oblast', W Russian Federation
77 Q17 **Volta** ~ SE Ghana
Volta Blanche *see* White Volta
77 P16 **Volta, Lake** ⊠ SE Ghana
Volta Noire *see* Black Volta
60 O9 **Volta Redonda** Rio de Janeiro, SE Brazil
Volta Rouge *see* Red Volta
106 F12 **Volterra** *anc.* Volaterrae. Toscana, C Italy
107 K17 **Volturno** ~ S Italy
113 I15 **Volujak** ▲▲ NW Montenegro
Volunteer Island *see* Starbuck Island
65 F24 **Volunteer Point** *headland* East Falkland, Falkland Islands
114 H13 **Vólvi, Límni** ⊚ N Greece
Volyn *see* Volyns'ka Oblast'
116 I3 **Volyns'ka Oblast'** *var.* Volyn, *Rus.* Volynskaya Oblast'. ⬖ *province* NW Ukraine
Volynskaya Oblast' *see* Volyns'ka Oblast'
127 Q3 **Volzhsk** Respublika Mariy El, W Russian Federation
127 O10 **Volzhskiy** Volgogradskaya Oblast', SW Russian Federation
172 I7 **Vondrozo** Fianarantsoa, SE Madagascar
114 K9 **Voneshta Voda** Veliko Tŭrnovo, N Bulgaria
39 P10 **Von Frank Mountain** ▲ Alaska, USA
115 C17 **Vónitsa** Dytikí Ellás, W Greece
118 J6 **Võnnu** *Ger.* Wendau. Tartumaa, SE Estonia
98 G12 **Voorburg** Zuid-Holland, W Netherlands
98 H11 **Voorschoten** Zuid-Holland, W Netherlands
98 M11 **Voorst** Gelderland, E Netherlands
98 K11 **Voorthuizen** Gelderland, C Netherlands
92 L2 **Vopnafjördhur** Austurland, E Iceland
92 L2 **Vopnafjördhur** *bay* E Iceland
Vora *see* Vorë
119 H15 **Voranava** *Pol.* Werenów, *Rus.* Voronovo. Hrodzyenskaya Voblasts', W Belarus
108 I8 **Vorarlberg** *off.* Land Vorarlberg. ⬖ *state* W Austria
Vorarlberg, Land *see* Vorarlberg
109 X7 **Vorau** Steiermark, E Austria
98 N11 **Vorden** Gelderland, E Netherlands
108 H9 **Vorderrhein** ~ SE Switzerland
92 J2 **Vordhufell** ▲ N Iceland
95 I24 **Vordingborg** Storstrøm, SE Denmark
113 K19 **Vorë** *var.* Vora. Tiranë, W Albania
115 H17 **Vóreies Sporádes** *var.* Vórioi Sporádhes, *Eng.* Northern Sporades. *island group* E Greece
Vóreioi Sporádes *see* Vóreies Sporádes
115 J17 **Vóreion Aigaíon** *Eng.* Aegean North. ⬖ *region* SE Greece
115 G18 **Vóreios Evvoïkós Kólpos** *var.* Voreiós Evvoïkós Kólpos. *gulf* E Greece
197 S16 **Voring Plateau** *undersea feature* N Norwegian Sea
Vórioi Sporádhes *see* Vóreies Sporádes
125 W4 **Vorkuta** Respublika Komi, NW Russian Federation
95 I14 **Vorma** ~ S Norway
118 E4 **Vormsi** *var.* Vormsi Saar, *Ger.* Worms, *Swed.* Ormsö. *island* W Estonia
Vormsi Saar *see* Vormsi
127 N7 **Vorona** ~ W Russian Federation
126 L7 **Voronezh** Voronezhskaya Oblast', W Russian Federation
126 L7 **Voronezh** ~ W Russian Federation
126 K8 **Voronezhskaya Oblast'** ⬖ *province* W Russian Federation
Voronovitsya *see* Voronovytsya
Voronovo *see* Voranava
117 N6 **Voronovytsya** *Rus.* Voronovitsya. Vinnyts'ka Oblast', C Ukraine
122 K7 **Vorontsovo** Taymyrskiy (Dolgano-Nenetskiy) Avtonomnyy Okrug, N Russian Federation
124 K3 **Voron'ya** ~ NW Russian Federation
Voropayevo *see* Varapayeva
Voroshilov *see* Ussuriysk
Voroshilovgrad *see* Luhans'k, Ukraine
Voroshilovgrad *see* Luhans'ka Oblast', Ukraine

◆ Country
● Country Capital
◇ Dependent Territory
○ Dependent Territory Capital
⬖ Administrative Regions
✈ International Airport
▲ Mountain
▲▲ Mountain Range
⛰ Volcano
~ River
⊚ Lake
⊠ Reservoir

Voroshilovgradskaya Oblast' *see* Luhans'ka Oblast'
Voroshilovsk *see* Stavropol', Russian Federation
Voroshilovsk *see* Alchevs'k
137 *V13* **Vorotan** *Az.* Bärgušad. ≈ Armenia/Azerbaijan
127 *P3* **Vorotynets** Nizhegorodskaya Oblast', W Russian Federation
117 *S3* **Vorozhba** Sums'ka Oblast', NE Ukraine
117 *T5* **Vorskla** ≈ Russian Federation/Ukraine
99 *I17* **Vorst** Antwerpen, N Belgium
83 *G21* **Vorstershoop** North-West, N South Africa
118 *H6* **Võrtsjärv** *Ger.* Wirz-See. ◎ SE Estonia
118 *J7* **Võru** *Ger.* Werro. Võrumaa, SE Estonia
147 *R11* **Vorukh** N Tajikistan
118 *I7* **Võrumaa** *off.* Võru Maakond. ⬖ *province* SE Estonia
Võru Maakond *see* Võrumaa
83 *G24* **Vosburg** Northern Cape, W South Africa
147 *Q14* **Vose'** *Rus.* Vose; *prev.* Aral. SW Tajikistan
103 *S6* **Vosges** ⬖ *department* NE France
103 *U6* **Vosges** ▲▲ NE France
126 *L4* **Voskresensk** Moskovskaya Oblast', W Russian Federation
127 *P2* **Voskresenskoye** Nizhegorodskaya Oblast', W Russian Federation
127 *V6* **Voskresenskoye** Respublika Bashkortostan, W Russian Federation
124 *K13* **Voskresenkoye** Vologodskaya Oblast', NW Russian Federation
94 *D13* **Voss** Hordaland, S Norway
94 *D13* **Voss** *physical region* S Norway
99 *I16* **Vosselaar** Antwerpen, N Belgium
94 *D13* **Vosso** ≈ S Norway
Vostochno-Kazakhstanskaya Oblast' *see* Vostochnyy Kazakhstan
123 *S5* **Vostochno-Sibirskoye More** *Eng.* East Siberian Sea. *sea* Arctic Ocean
145 *X10* **Vostochnyy Kazakhstan** *off.* Vostochno-Kazakhstanskaya Oblast', *var.* East Kazakhstan, *Kaz.* Shyghys Qazagastan Oblysy. ⬖ *province* E Kazakhstan
Vostochnyy Sayan *see* Eastern Sayans
Vostock Island *see* Vostok Island
195 *U10* **Vostok** *Russian research station* Antarctica
191 *X5* **Vostok Island** *var.* Vostock Island; *prev.* Stavers Island. *island* Line Islands, SE Kiribati
127 *T2* **Votkinsk** Udmurtskaya Respublika, NW Russian Federation
125 *U15* **Votkinskoye Vodokhranilishche** *var.* Votkinsk Reservoir. ⊠ NW Russian Federation
Votkinsk Reservoir *see* Votkinskoye Vodokhranilishche
60 *J7* **Votuporanga** São Paulo, S Brazil
104 *H7* **Vouga, Rio** ≈ N Portugal
115 *E14* **Voúrinos** ▲ N Greece
115 *G24* **Voúxa, Ákrotírio** *cape* Kríti, Greece, E Mediterranean Sea
103 *R4* **Vouziers** Ardennes, N France
117 *V7* **Vovcha** *Rus.* Volchya. ≈ E Ukraine
117 *V4* **Vovchans'k** *Rus.* Volchansk. Kharkivs'ka Oblast', E Ukraine
103 *N6* **Voves** Eure-et-Loir, C France
79 *M14* **Vovodo** ≈ S Central Africa Republic
94 *M12* **Voxna** Gävleborg, C Sweden
94 *L11* **Voxnan** ≈ C Sweden
114 *F7* **Voynishka Reka** ≈ NW Bulgaria
125 *T9* **Voyvozh** Respublika Komi, NW Russian Federation
124 *M12* **Vozhega** Vologodskaya Oblast', NW Russian Federation
124 *L12* **Vozhe, Ozero** ◎ NW Russian Federation
117 *Q9* **Voznesens'k** *Rus.* Voznesensk. Mykolayivs'ka Oblast', S Ukraine
124 *J12* **Voznesen'ye** Leningradskaya Oblast', NW Russian Federation
144 *J14* **Vozrozhdeniya, Ostrov** *Uzb.* Wozrojdeniye Oroli. *island* Kazakhstan/Uzbekistan
95 *G20* **Vrå** *var.* Vraa. Nordjylland, N Denmark
Vraa *see* Vrå
114 *H9* **Vrachesh** Sofiya, W Bulgaria
115 *C19* **Vrachíonas** ▲ Zákynthos, Iónia Nisiá, Greece, C Mediterranean Sea
117 *P8* **Vradiyivka** Mykolayivs'ka Oblast', S Ukraine
113 *G14* **Vran** ▲ SW Bosnia and Herzegovina
116 *K12* **Vrancea** ⬖ *county* E Romania
147 *T14* **Vrang** SE Tajikistan
123 *T4* **Vrangelya, Ostrov** *Eng.* Wrangel Island. *island* NE Russian Federation
112 *H13* **Vranica** ▲ C Bosnia and Herzegovina
113 *O16* **Vranje** Serbia, SE Serbia
Vranov *see* Vranov nad Topl'ou
111 *N19* **Vranov nad Topl'ou** *var.* Vranov, *Hung.* Varannó. Prešovský Kraj, E Slovakia
114 *H8* **Vratsa** Vratsa, NW Bulgaria
114 *H8* **Vratsa** ⬖ *province* NW Bulgaria
114 *F10* **Vrattsa** *prev.* Mirovo. Kyustendil, W Bulgaria
112 *G11* **Vrbanja** ≈ NW Bosnia and Herzegovina
112 *K9* **Vrbas** Vojvodina, NW Serbia
112 *G13* **Vrbas** ≈ N Bosnia and Herzegovina
112 *E8* **Vrbovec** Zagreb, N Croatia
112 *C9* **Vrbovsko** Primorje-Gorski Kotar, NW Croatia
111 *E15* **Vrchlabí** *Ger.* Hohenelbe. Královéhradecký Kraj, N Czech Republic
83 *J22* **Vrede** Free State, E South Africa
100 *E13* **Vreden** Nordrhein-Westfalen, NW Germany
83 *E25* **Vredenburg** Western Cape, SW South Africa
99 *I23* **Vresse-sur-Semois** Namur, SE Belgium
95 *L16* **Vretstorp** Örebro, C Sweden
113 *G15* **Vrgorac** *prev.* Vrhgorac. Split-Dalmacija, SE Croatia
Vrhgorac *see* Vrgorac
109 *T12* **Vrhnika** *Ger.* Oberlaibach. W Slovenia
155 *I21* **Vriddhāchalam** Tamil Nādu, SE India
98 *N6* **Vries** Drenthe, NE Netherlands
98 *O10* **Vriezenveen** Overijssel, E Netherlands
95 *L20* **Vrigstad** Jönköping, S Sweden
108 *H9* **Vrin** Graubünden, S Switzerland
112 *E13* **Vrlika** Split-Dalmacija, S Croatia
113 *M14* **Vrnjačka Banja** Serbia, C Serbia
Vrondádhes/Vrondados *see* Vrontádos
115 *L18* **Vrontádos** *var.* Vrondados; *prev.* Vrondádhes. Chíos, E Greece
98 *N9* **Vroomshoop** Overijssel, E Netherlands
112 *N10* **Vršac** *Ger.* Werschetz, *Hung.* Versecz. Vojvodina, NE Serbia
112 *M10* **Vršački Kanal** *canal* N Serbia
83 *H21* **Vryburg** North-West, N South Africa
83 *K22* **Vryheid** KwaZulu/Natal, E South Africa
111 *I18* **Vsetín** *Ger.* Wsetin. Zlínský Kraj, E Czech Republic
111 *J20* **Vtáčnik** *Hung.* Madaras, Ptacsnik; *prev.* Ptačnik. ▲ W Slovakia
Vuadil' *see* Wodil
114 *I11* **Vŭcha** ≈ SW Bulgaria
113 *N16* **Vučitrn** Kosovo, S Serbia
99 *J14* **Vught** Noord-Brabant, S Netherlands
117 *W8* **Vuhledar** Donets'ka Oblast', E Ukraine
112 *I9* **Vuka** ≈ E Croatia
113 *K17* **Vukël** *var.* Vukli. Shkodër, N Albania
Vukli *see* Vukël
112 *J9* **Vukovar** *Hung.* Vukovár. Vukovar-Srijem, E Croatia
Vukovarsko-Srijemska Županija *see* Vukovar-Srijem
112 *I10* **Vukovar-Srijem** *off.* Vukovarsko-Srijemska Županija. ⬖ *province* E Croatia
125 *U8* **Vuktyl** Respublika Komi, NW Russian Federation
9 *Q17* **Vulcan** Alberta, SW Canada
116 *G12* **Vulcan** *Ger.* Wulkan, *Hung.* Zsilyvajdevulkán; *prev.* Crivadia Vulcanului, Vaidei, *Hung.* Sily-Vajdej, Vajdej. Hunedoara, W Romania
116 *M12* **Vulcănești** *Rus.* Vulkaneshty. S Moldova
107 *L22* **Vulcano, Isola** *island* Isole Eolie, S Italy
114 *G7* **Vŭlchedrŭm** Montana, NW Bulgaria
114 *N8* **Vŭlchidol** *prev.* Kurt-Dere. Varna, E Bulgaria
Vulkaneshty *see* Vulcănești
123 *V11* **Vulkannyy** Kamchatskaya Oblast', R Russian Federation
36 *J13* **Vulture Mountains** ▲▲ Arizona, SW USA
167 *T14* **Vung Tau** *prev. Fr.* Cape Saint Jacques, Cap Saint-Jacques. Ba Ria-Vung Tau, S Vietnam
187 *X15* **Vunisea** Kadavu, SE Fiji
Vuohčču *see* Vuotso
93 *N15* **Vuokatti** Oulu, C Finland
93 *M15* **Vuolijoki** Oulu, C Finland
Vuolleriebme *see* Vuollerim
92 *J13* **Vuollerim** *Lapp.* Vuolleriebme. Norrbotten, N Sweden
Vuoreija *see* Vardø
92 *L10* **Vuotso** *Lapp.* Vuohčču. Lappi, N Finland
114 *J11* **Vŭrbitsa** *prev.* Filevo. Khaskovo, S Bulgaria
114 *J12* **Vŭrbitsa** ≈ S Bulgaria
127 *Q4* **Vurnary** Chavash Respubliki, W Russian Federation
114 *G8* **Vŭrshets** Montana, NW Bulgaria
119 *F17* **Vyalikaya Byerastavitsa** *Pol.* Brzostowica Wielka, *Rus.* Bol'shaya Berëstovitsa; *prev.* Velikaya Berestovitsa. Hrodzyenskaya Voblasts', SW Belarus
119 *N20* **Vyaliki Bor** *Rus.* Velikiy Bor. Homyel'skaya Voblasts', SE Belarus
119 *J18* **Vyaliki Rozhan** *Rus.* Bol'shoy Rozhan. Minskaya Voblasts', S Belarus
124 *H10* **Vyartsilya** *Fin.* Värtsilä. Respublika Kareliya, NW Russian Federation
119 *K17* **Vyasyeya** *Rus.* Veseya. Minskaya Voblasts', C Belarus
125 *R15* **Vyatka** ≈ NW Russian Federation
Vyatka *see* Kirov
125 *S16* **Vyatskiye Polyany** Kirovskaya Oblast', NW Russian Federation
123 *S14* **Vyazemskiy** Khabarovskiy Kray, SE Russian Federation
126 *I4* **Vyaz'ma** Smolenskaya Oblast', W Russian Federation
127 *N3* **Vyazniki** Vladimirskaya Oblast', W Russian Federation
127 *O8* **Vyazovka** Volgogradskaya Oblast', SW Russian Federation
119 *J14* **Vyazyn'** *Rus.* Vyazyn'. Minskaya Voblasts', NW Belarus
124 *G11* **Vyborg** *Fin.* Viipuri. Leningradskaya Oblast', NW Russian Federation
125 *P11* **Vychegda** *var.* Vichegda. ≈ NW Russian Federation
119 *L14* **Vyelyewshchyna** *Rus.* Velevshchina. Vitsyebskaya Voblasts', N Belarus
119 *P16* **Vyeramyeyki** *Rus.* Veremeyki. Mahilyowskaya Voblasts', E Belarus
118 *K11* **Vyerkhnyadzvinsk** *Rus.* Verkhnedvinsk. Vitsyebskaya Voblasts', N Belarus
119 *P18* **Vyetka** *Rus.* Vetka. Homyel'skaya Voblasts', SE Belarus
118 *L12* **Vyetryna** *Rus.* Vetrino. Vitsyebskaya Voblasts', N Belarus
Vygonovskoye, Ozero *see* Vyhanawskaye, Vozyera
124 *J9* **Vygozero, Ozero** ◎ NW Russian Federation
Vyhanashchanskaye Vozyera *see* Vyhanawskaye, Vozyera
119 *I18* **Vyhanawskaye, Vozyera** *var.* Vyhanashchanskaye Vozyera, *Rus.* Ozero Vygonovskoye. ◎ SW Belarus
127 *N4* **Vyksa** Nizhegorodskaya Oblast', W Russian Federation
117 *O12* **Vylkove** *Rus.* Vilkovo. Odes'ka Oblast', SW Ukraine
125 *R9* **Vym'** ≈ NW Russian Federation
116 *H8* **Vynohradiv** *Cz.* Sevluš, *Hung.* Nagyszöllös, *Rus.* Vinogradov; *prev.* Sevlyush. Zakarpats'ka Oblast', W Ukraine
124 *G13* **Vyritsa** Leningradskaya Oblast', NW Russian Federation
97 *J19* **Vyrnwy** *Wel.* Afon Efyrnwy. ≈ E Wales, UK
145 *X9* **Vyshe Ivanovskiy Belak, Gora** ▲ E Kazakhstan
117 *P4* **Vyshhorod** Kyyivs'ka Oblast', N Ukraine
124 *I15* **Vyshniy Volochek** Tverskaya Oblast', W Russian Federation
111 *G18* **Vyškov** *Ger.* Wischau. Jihomoravský Kraj, SE Czech Republic
111 *E18* **Vysočina** *prev.* Jihlavský Kraj. ⬖ *region* N Czech Republic
119 *E19* **Vysokaye** *Rus.* Vysokoye. Brestskaya Voblasts', SW Belarus
111 *F17* **Vysoké Mýto** *Ger.* Hohenmauth. Pardubický Kraj, C Czech Republic
117 *S9* **Vysokopillya** Khersons'ka Oblast', S Ukraine
126 *K3* **Vysokovsk** Moskovskaya Oblast', W Russian Federation
Vysokoye *see* Vysokaye
124 *K12* **Vytegra** Vologodskaya Oblast', NW Russian Federation
116 *J8* **Vyzhnytsya** Chernivets'ka Oblast', W Ukraine

W

77 *O14* **Wa** NW Ghana
Waadt *see* Vaud
Waag *see* Váh
Waagbistritz *see* Považská Bystrica
Waagneustadtl *see* Nové Mesto nad Váhom
81 *M16* **Waajid** Gedo, SW Somalia
98 *L13* **Waal** ≈ S Netherlands
187 *O16* **Waala** Province Nord, W New Caledonia
99 *I14* **Waalwijk** Noord-Brabant, S Netherlands
99 *E16* **Waarschoot** Oost-Vlaanderen, NW Belgium
186 *C7* **Wabag** Enga, W Papua New Guinea
15 *N7* **Wabano** ≈ Québec, SE Canada
9 *P11* **Wabasca** ≈ Alberta, SW Canada
31 *P12* **Wabash** Indiana, N USA
29 *X9* **Wabasha** Minnesota, N USA
31 *N13* **Wabash River** ≈ N USA
14 *C7* **Wabatongushi Lake** ◎ Ontario, S Canada
81 *L15* **Wabē Gestro Wenz** ≈ SE Ethiopia
14 *B9* **Wabos** Ontario, S Canada
9 *W13* **Wabowden** Manitoba, C Canada
110 *J9* **Wąbrzeźno** Kujawsko-pomorskie, C Poland
21 *U12* **Waccamaw River** ≈ South Carolina, SE USA
23 *U11* **Waccasassa Bay** *bay* Florida, SE USA
99 *F16* **Wachtebeke** Oost-Vlaanderen, NW Belgium
25 *T8* **Waco** Texas, SW USA
26 *M3* **Waconda Lake** *var.* Great Elder Reservoir. ⊠ Kansas, C USA
Wadai *see* Ouaddaï
Wad Al-Hajarah *see* Guadalajara
164 *I12* **Wadayama** Hyōgo, Honshū, SW Japan
80 *D10* **Wad Banda** Western Kordofan, C Sudan
75 *P9* **Waddān** NW Libya
98 *J4* **Waddeneilanden** *Eng.* West Frisian Islands. *island group* N Netherlands
98 *J6* **Waddenzee** *var.* Wadden Zee. *sea* SE North Sea
Wadden Zee *see* Waddenzee
10 *L16* **Waddington, Mount** ▲ British Columbia, SW Canada
98 *H12* **Waddinxveen** Zuid-Holland, C Netherlands
9 *U15* **Wadena** Saskatchewan, S Canada
29 *T6* **Wadena** Minnesota, N USA
108 *G7* **Wädenswil** Zürich, N Switzerland
21 *S11* **Wadesboro** North Carolina, SE USA
155 *G16* **Wādi** Karnātaka, C India
138 *G10* **Wādi as Sīr** *var.* Wadi es Sir. 'Ammān, NW Jordan
Wadi es Sir *see* Wādī as Sīr
80 *F5* **Wadi Halfa** *var.* Wādī Ḥalfā'. Northern, N Sudan
138 *G13* **Wādī Mūsā** *var.* Petra. Ma'ān, S Jordan
23 *V4* **Wadley** Georgia, SE USA
Wad Madanī *see* Wad Medani
80 *G10* **Wad Medani** *var.* Wad Madanī. Gezira, C Sudan
80 *F10* **Wad Nimr** White Nile, C Sudan
165 *U16* **Wadomari** Kagoshima, Okinoerabu-jima, SW Japan
111 *K17* **Wadowice** Małopolskie, S Poland
35 *R5* **Wadsworth** Nevada, W USA
31 *T12* **Wadsworth** Ohio, N USA
25 *T11* **Waelder** Texas, SW USA
Waereghem *see* Waregem
163 *U13* **Wafangdian** *var.* Fuxian, Fu Xian. Liaoning, NE China
171 *R13* **Waflia** Pulau Buru, E Indonesia
Wagadugu *see* Ouagadougou
98 *K12* **Wageningen** Gelderland, SE Netherlands
55 *V9* **Wageningen** Nickerie, NW Suriname
9 *O8* **Wager Bay** *inlet* Nunavut, N Canada
183 *P10* **Wagga Wagga** New South Wales, SE Australia
180 *J13* **Wagin** Western Australia
108 *H8* **Wägitaler See** ◎ SW Switzerland
29 *P12* **Wagner** South Dakota, N USA
27 *Q9* **Wagoner** Oklahoma, C USA
37 *U10* **Wagon Mound** New Mexico, SW USA
32 *J14* **Wagontire** Oregon, NW USA
110 *H10* **Wągrowiec** Wielkopolskie, C Poland
149 *U6* **Wāh** Punjab, NE Pakistan
171 *S13* **Wahai** Pulau Seram, E Indonesia
169 *V10* **Wahau, Sungai** ≈ Borneo, C Indonesia
Wahaybah, Ramlat Al *see* Wahībah, Ramlat Āl
80 *D13* **Wahda** *var.* Unity State. ⬖ *state* S Sudan
38 *D9* **Wahiawā** *var.* Wahiawa. O'ahu, Hawai'i, USA
Wahībah, Ramlat Ahl *see* Wahībah, Ramlat Āl
141 *Y9* **Wahībah, Ramlat Āl** *var.* Ramlat Ahl Wahībah, Ramlat Al Wahaybah, *Eng.* Wahībah Sands. *desert* N Oman
Wahībah Sands *see* Wahībah, Ramlat Āl
101 *E16* **Wahn** ✕ (Köln) Nordrhein-Westfalen, W Germany
29 *R15* **Wahoo** Nebraska, C USA
29 *R6* **Wahpeton** North Dakota, N USA
Wahran *see* Oran
36 *J6* **Wah Wah Mountains** ▲▲ Utah, W USA
38 *D9* **Waialua** O'ahu, Hawai'i, USA
38 *D9* **Wai'anae** *var.* Waianae. O'ahu, Hawai'i, USA
184 *Q8* **Waiapu** ≈ North Island, New Zealand
185 *I17* **Waiau** Canterbury, South Island, New Zealand
185 *I17* **Waiau** ≈ South Island, New Zealand
185 *B23* **Waiau** ≈ South Island, New Zealand
101 *H21* **Waiblingen** Baden-Württemberg, S Germany
Waidhofen *see* Waidhofen an der Thaya, Niederösterreich, Austria
Waidhofen *see* Waidhofen an der Ybbs, Niederösterreich, Austria
109 *V2* **Waidhofen an der Thaya** *var.* Waidhofen. Niederösterreich, NE Austria
109 *U5* **Waidhofen an der Ybbs** *var.* Waidhofen. Niederösterreich, E Austria
171 *T11* **Waigeo, Pulau** *island* Maluku, E Indonesia
184 *L5* **Waiheke Island** *island* N New Zealand
184 *M7* **Waihi** Waikato, North Island, New Zealand
185 *C20* **Waihou** ≈ North Island, New Zealand
Waikaboebak *see* Waikabubak
171 *M17* **Waikabubak** *prev.* Waikaboebak. Pulau Sumba, C Indonesia
185 *D23* **Waikaia** ≈ South Island, New Zealand
185 *D23* **Waikaka** Southland, South Island, New Zealand
184 *L13* **Waikanae** Wellington, North Island, New Zealand
184 *M7* **Waikare, Lake** ◎ North Island, New Zealand
184 *O9* **Waikaremoana, Lake** ◎ North Island, New Zealand
185 *I17* **Waikari** Canterbury, South Island, New Zealand
184 *L8* **Waikato** *off.* Waikato Region. ⬖ *region* North Island, New Zealand
184 *M8* **Waikato** ≈ North Island, New Zealand
Waikato Region *see* Waikato
182 *J9* **Waikerie** South Australia
185 *F23* **Waikouaiti** Otago, South Island, New Zealand
38 *H11* **Wailea** Hawai'i, USA, C Pacific Ocean
38 *F10* **Wailuku** Maui, Hawai'i, USA
185 *H18* **Waimakariri** ≈ South Island, New Zealand
38 *D9* **Waimānalo Beach** *var.* Waimanalo Beach. O'ahu, Hawai'i, USA
185 *G15* **Waimangaroa** West Coast, South Island, New Zealand
185 *G21* **Waimate** Canterbury, South Island, New Zealand
38 *B8* **Waimea** Kaua'i, Hawai'i, USA
38 *D9* **Waimea** *var.* Maunawai. O'ahu, Hawai'i, USA
38 *G11* **Waimea** *var.* Kamuela. Hawai'i, USA, C Pacific Ocean
99 *M20* **Waimes** Liège, E Belgium
154 *J11* **Wainganga** *var.* Wain River. ≈ C India
Waingapoe *see* Waingapu
171 *N17* **Waingapu** *prev.* Waingapoe. Pulau Sumba, C Indonesia
55 *S7* **Waini** ≈ N Guyana
55 *S7* **Waini Point** *headland* NW Guyana
Wain River *see* Wainganga
9 *R15* **Wainwright** Alberta, SW Canada
39 *O5* **Wainwright** Alaska, USA
184 *K4* **Waiotira** Northland, North Island, New Zealand
184 *M11* **Waiouru** Manawatu-Wanganui, North Island, New Zealand
171 *W14* **Waipa** Papua, E Indonesia
184 *L8* **Waipa** ≈ North Island, New Zealand
184 *P9* **Waipaoa** ≈ North Island, New Zealand
185 *D25* **Waipapa Point** *headland* South Island, New Zealand
185 *I18* **Waipara** Canterbury, South Island, New Zealand
184 *N12* **Waipawa** Hawke's Bay, North Island, New Zealand
184 *K4* **Waipu** Northland, North Island, New Zealand
184 *N12* **Waipukurau** Hawke's Bay, North Island, New Zealand
171 *U14* **Wair** Pulau Kai Besar, E Indonesia
Wairakai *see* Wairakei
184 *N9* **Wairakei** *var.* Wairakai. Waikato, North Island, New Zealand
185 *M14* **Wairarapa, Lake** ◎ North Island, New Zealand
185 *J15* **Wairau** ≈ South Island, New Zealand
184 *P10* **Wairoa** Hawke's Bay, North Island, New Zealand
184 *P10* **Wairoa** ≈ North Island, New Zealand
184 *J4* **Wairoa** ≈ North Island, New Zealand
184 *N9* **Waitahanui** Waikato, North Island, New Zealand
184 *M6* **Waitakaruru** Waikato, North Island, New Zealand
185 *F21* **Waitaki** ≈ South Island, New Zealand
184 *K10* **Waitara** Taranaki, North Island, New Zealand
184 *M7* **Waitoa** Waikato, North Island, New Zealand
184 *L8* **Waitomo Caves** Waikato, North Island, New Zealand
184 *L11* **Waitotara** Taranaki, North Island, New Zealand
184 *L11* **Waitotara** ≈ North Island, New Zealand
32 *L10* **Waitsburg** Washington, NW USA
Waitzen *see* Vác
184 *L6* **Waiuku** Auckland, North Island, New Zealand
164 *L10* **Wajima** *var.* Wazima. Ishikawa, Honshū, SW Japan
81 *K17* **Wajir** North Eastern, NE Kenya
79 *J17* **Waka** Equateur, NW Dem. Rep. Congo
81 *I14* **Waka** Southern, S Ethiopia
14 *D9* **Wakami Lake** ◎ Ontario, S Canada
164 *I12* **Wakasa** Tottori, Honshū, SW Japan
164 *J12* **Wakasa-wan** *bay* C Japan
185 *C22* **Wakatipu, Lake** ◎ South Island, New Zealand
9 *T15* **Wakaw** Saskatchewan, S Canada
164 *I14* **Wakayama** Wakayama, Honshū, SW Japan
164 *I15* **Wakayama** *off.* Wakayama-ken. ⬖ *prefecture* Honshū, SW Japan
Wakayama-ken *see* Wakayama
26 *K4* **Wa Keeney** Kansas, C USA
185 *I14* **Wakefield** Tasman, South Island, New Zealand
97 *M17* **Wakefield** N England, UK
27 *O4* **Wakefield** Kansas, C USA
30 *L4* **Wakefield** Michigan, N USA
21 *U9* **Wake Forest** North Carolina, SE USA
Wakeham Bay *see* Kangiqsujuaq
189 *Y11* **Wake Island** ◇ *US unincorporated territory* NW Pacific Ocean
189 *Y12* **Wake Island** ✕ NW Pacific Ocean
189 *Y12* **Wake Island** *atoll* NW Pacific Ocean
189 *X12* **Wake Lagoon** *lagoon* Wake Island, NW Pacific Ocean
166 *L8* **Wakema** Irrawaddy, SW Myanmar (Burma)
Wakhan *see* Khandūd
164 *H14* **Waki** Tokushima, Shikoku, SW Japan
165 *T1* **Wakkanai** Hokkaidō, NE Japan
83 *K22* **Wakkerstroom** Mpumalanga, E South Africa
14 *C10* **Wakomata Lake** ◎ Ontario, S Canada
183 *N10* **Wakool** New South Wales, SE Australia
Wakra *see* Al Wakrah
Waku Kungo *see* Uaco Cungo
186 *J7* **Wakunai** Bougainville Island, NE Papua New Guinea
Walachei/Walachia *see* Wallachia
155 *K26* **Walawe Ganga** ≈ S Sri Lanka
111 *F15* **Wałbrzych** *Ger.* Waldenburg, Waldenburg in Schlesien. Dolnośląskie, SW Poland
183 *T6* **Walcha** New South Wales, SE Australia
101 *K24* **Walchensee** ◎ SE Germany
99 *D14* **Walcheren** *island* SW Netherlands
29 *Z14* **Walcott** Iowa, C USA
33 *W16* **Walcott** Wyoming, C USA
99 *G21* **Walcourt** Namur, S Belgium
110 *G9* **Wałcz** *Ger.* Deutsch Krone. Zachodnio-pomorskie, NW Poland
108 *H7* **Wald** Zürich, N Switzerland
109 *U3* **Waldaist** ≈ N Austria
180 *I9* **Waldburg Range** ▲▲ Western Australia
37 *R3* **Walden** Colorado, C USA
18 *K13* **Walden** New York, NE USA
Waldenburg/Waldenburg in Schlesien *see* Wałbrzych
9 *T15* **Waldheim** Saskatchewan, S Canada
Waldia *see* Weldiya
101 *M23* **Waldkraiburg** Bayern, SE Germany
27 *T14* **Waldo** Arkansas, C USA
23 *V9* **Waldo** Florida, SE USA
19 *R7* **Waldoboro** Maine, NE USA
21 *W4* **Waldorf** Maryland, NE USA
32 *F12* **Waldport** Oregon, NW USA
27 *S11* **Waldron** Arkansas, C USA
195 *Y13* **Waldron, Cape** *headland* Antarctica
101 *F24* **Waldshut-Tiengen** Baden-Württemberg, S Germany
171 *P12* **Walea, Selat** *strait* Sulawesi, C Indonesia
Wałeckie Międzyrzecze *see* Valašské Meziříčí
108 *H8* **Walensee** ◎ NW Switzerland
38 *L8* **Wales** Alaska, USA
97 *J20* **Wales** *Wel.* Cymru. *cultural region* Wales, UK
9 *O7* **Wales Island** *island* Nunavut, NE Canada
77 *P14* **Walewale** N Ghana
99 *M24* **Walferdange** Luxembourg, C Luxembourg
183 *Q5* **Walgett** New South Wales, SE Australia
194 *K10* **Walgreen Coast** *physical region* Antarctica
29 *Q2* **Walhalla** North Dakota, N USA
21 *O11* **Walhalla** South Carolina, SE USA
79 *O19* **Walikale** Nord Kivu, E Dem. Rep. Congo
Walk *see* Valga, Estonia
Walk *see* Valka, Latvia
29 *U5* **Walker** Minnesota, N USA
15 *V4* **Walker, Lac** ◎ Québec, SE Canada
35 *S7* **Walker Lake** ◎ Nevada, W USA
35 *R6* **Walker River** ≈ Nevada, W USA
28 *K10* **Wall** South Dakota, N USA
173 *U9* **Wallaby Plateau** *undersea feature* E Indian Ocean
33 *N8* **Wallace** Idaho, NW USA
21 *V11* **Wallace** North Carolina, SE USA
14 *D17* **Wallaceburg** Ontario, S Canada
22 *F5* **Wallace Lake** ⊠ Louisiana, S USA
9 *P13* **Wallace Mountain** ▲ Alberta, W Canada
116 *J14* **Wallachia** *var.* Walachia, *Ger.* Walachei, *Rom.* Valachia. *cultural region* S Romania
Wallachisch-Meseritsch *see* Valašské Meziříčí
183 *U4* **Wallangarra** New South Wales, SE Australia
182 *I8* **Wallaroo** South Australia
32 *L10* **Walla Walla** Washington, NW USA
45 *V9* **Wallblake** ✕ (The Valley) C Anguilla
101 *H19* **Walldürn** Baden-Württemberg, SW Germany
100 *F12* **Wallenhorst** Niedersachsen, NW Germany
Wallenthal *see* Hațeg
109 *S4* **Wallern** Oberösterreich, N Austria
Wallern *see* Wallern im Burgenland
109 *Z5* **Wallern im Burgenland** *var.* Wallern. Burgenland, E Austria
18 *M9* **Wallingford** Vermont, NE USA
25 *V11* **Wallis** Texas, SW USA
Wallis *see* Valais
192 *K9* **Wallis and Futuna** *Fr.* Territoire de Wallis et Futuna. ◇ *French overseas territory* C Pacific Ocean
108 *G7* **Wallisellen** Zürich, N Switzerland
Wallis et Futuna, Territoire de *see* Wallis and Futuna
190 *H11* **Wallis, Îles** *island group* N Wallis and Futuna
99 *H19* **Wallon Brabant** ⬖ *province* C Belgium
31 *Q5* **Walloon Lake** ◎ Michigan, N USA
32 *K10* **Wallula** Washington, NW USA
32 *K10* **Wallula, Lake** ◎ Washington, NW USA
21 *S8* **Walnut Cove** North Carolina, SE USA
35 *N8* **Walnut Creek** California, W USA
26 *K5* **Walnut Creek** ≈ Kansas, C USA
27 *W9* **Walnut Ridge** Arkansas, C USA
25 *S7* **Walnut Springs** Texas, SW USA
182 *L10* **Walpeup** Victoria, SE Australia
187 *R17* **Walpole, Île** *island* SE New Caledonia
39 *N13* **Walrus Islands** *island group* Alaska, USA
97 *L19* **Walsall** C England, UK
37 *T7* **Walsenburg** Colorado, C USA
9 *S17* **Walsh** Alberta, SW Canada
37 *W7* **Walsh** Colorado, C USA
100 *I11* **Walsrode** Niedersachsen, NW Germany
Waltenberg *see* Zalău
21 *R14* **Walterboro** South Carolina, SE USA
Walter F.George Lake *see* Walter F. George Reservoir
23 *R6* **Walter F. George Reservoir** *var.* Walter F.George Lake. ⊠ Alabama/Georgia, SE USA
26 *M12* **Walters** Oklahoma, C USA
101 *J16* **Waltershausen** Thüringen, C Germany
173 *N10* **Walters Shoal** *var.* Walters Shoals. *reef* S Madagascar
Walters Shoals *see* Walters Shoal
22 *M3* **Walthall** Mississippi, S USA
20 *M4* **Walton** Kentucky, S USA
18 *J11* **Walton** New York, NE USA
79 *O20* **Walungu** Sud Kivu, E Dem. Rep. Congo
Walvisbaai *see* Walvis Bay

◆ Country ● Country Capital ◇ Dependent Territory ○ Dependent Territory Capital ⬖ Administrative Regions ✕ International Airport ▲ Mountain ▲▲ Mountain Range Volcano ◎ Lake ≈ River ⊠ Reservoir

83 C19 **Walvis Bay** *Afr.* Walvisbaai. Erongo, NW Namibia
83 B19 **Walvis Bay** *bay* NW Namibia
Walvish Ridge *see* Walvis Ridge
65 O17 **Walvis Ridge** *var.* Walvish Ridge. *undersea feature* E Atlantic Ocean
171 X16 **Wamal** Papua, E Indonesia
171 U15 **Wamar, Pulau** *island* Kepulauan Aru, E Indonesia
79 O17 **Wamba** Orientale, NE Dem. Rep. Congo
77 V15 **Wamba** Nassarawa, C Nigeria
79 H22 **Wamba** *var.* Uamba. ≈ Angola/Dem. Rep. Congo
27 P4 **Wamego** Kansas, C USA
18 I10 **Wampsville** New York, NE USA
42 K6 **Wampú, Río** ≈ E Honduras
171 X16 **Wan** Papua, E Indonesia
Wan *see* Anhui
183 N4 **Wanaaring** New South Wales, SE Australia
185 D21 **Wanaka** Otago, South Island, New Zealand
185 D20 **Wanaka, Lake** ◎ South Island, New Zealand
171 W14 **Wanapiri** Papua, E Indonesia
14 F9 **Wanapitei** ≈ Ontario, S Canada
14 F10 **Wanapitei Lake** ◎ Ontario, S Canada
18 K14 **Wanaque** New Jersey, NE USA
171 U12 **Wanau** Papua, E Indonesia
185 F22 **Wanbrow, Cape** *headland* South Island, New Zealand
Wancheng *see* Wanning
Wanchuan *see* Zhangjiakou
171 W13 **Wandai** *var.* Komeyo. Papua, E Indonesia
163 Z8 **Wanda Shan** ▲▲ NE China
197 R11 **Wandel Sea** *sea* Arctic Ocean
160 D13 **Wanding** *var.* Wandingzhen. Yunnan, SW China
Wandingzhen *see* Wanding
99 H20 **Wanfercée-Baulet** Hainaut, S Belgium
184 L12 **Wanganui** Manawatu-Wanganui, North Island, New Zealand
184 L11 **Wanganui** ≈ North Island, New Zealand
183 P11 **Wangaratta** Victoria, SE Australia
160 J8 **Wangcang** *var.* Donghe; *prev.* Fengjiaba, Hongjiang. Sichuan, C China
Wangda *see* Zogang
101 I24 **Wangen im Allgäu** Baden-Württemberg, S Germany
Wangerin *see* Węgorzyno
100 F9 **Wangerooge** *island* NW Germany
171 W13 **Wanggar** Papua, E Indonesia
160 J13 **Wangmo** *var.* Fuxing. Guizhou, S China
Wangolodougou *see* Ouangolodougou
161 S9 **Wangpan Yang** *sea* E China
163 Y10 **Wangqing** Jilin, NE China
167 P8 **Wang Saphung** Loei, C Thailand
167 O6 **Wan Hsa-la** Shan State, E Myanmar (Burma)
55 W9 **Wanica** ◈ *district* N Suriname
79 M18 **Wanie-Rukula** Orientale, C Dem. Rep. Congo
Wankie *see* Hwange
Wanki, Río *see* Coco, Río
81 N17 **Wanlaweyn** *var.* Wanle Weyn, *It.* Uanle Uen. Shabeellaha Hoose, SW Somalia
Wanle Weyn *see* Wanlaweyn
180 I12 **Wanneroo** Western Australia
160 L17 **Wanning** *var.* Wancheng. Hainan, S China
167 Q8 **Wanon Niwat** Sakon Nakhon, E Thailand
155 H16 **Wanparti** Andhra Pradesh, C India
Wansen *see* Wiązów
160 L11 **Wanshan** Guizhou, S China
99 M14 **Wanssum** Limburg, SE Netherlands
184 N12 **Wanstead** Hawke's Bay, North Island, New Zealand
Wanxian *see* Wanzhou
188 F16 **Wanyaan** Yap, Micronesia
160 K8 **Wanyuan** Sichuan, C China
161 O11 **Wanzai** *var.* Kangle. Jiangxi, S China
99 J20 **Wanze** Liège, E Belgium
160 K9 **Wanzhou** *var.* Wanxian. Chongqing Shi, C China
31 R12 **Wapakoneta** Ohio, N USA
12 D7 **Wapaseese** ≈ Ontario, C Canada
32 I10 **Wapato** Washington, NW USA
29 Y15 **Wapello** Iowa, C USA
9 N13 **Wapiti** ≈ Alberta/British Columbia, SW Canada
27 X7 **Wappapello Lake** ⊠ Missouri, C USA
18 K13 **Wappingers Falls** New York, NE USA
29 X13 **Wapsipinicon River** ≈ Iowa, C USA
14 L9 **Wapus** ≈ Québec, SE Canada
160 H7 **Waqên** Sichuan, C China
21 Q7 **War** West Virginia, NE USA
80 D13 **Warab** Warab, SW Sudan
81 D14 **Warab** ◈ *state* SW Sudan
155 J15 **Warangal** Andhra Pradesh, C India
Warasdin *see* Varaždin
183 O16 **Waratah** Tasmania, SE Australia
183 O14 **Waratah Bay** *bay* Victoria, SE Australia
101 H15 **Warburg** Nordrhein-Westfalen, W Germany
182 I1 **Warburton Creek** *seasonal river* South Australia
180 M9 **Warbuton** Western Australia
99 M20 **Warche** ≈ E Belgium
Wardag/Wardak *see* Vardak
32 K9 **Warden** Washington, NW USA
154 I12 **Wardha** Mahārāshtra, W India
Wardija Point *see* Wardija, Ras il-
121 N15 **Wardija, Ras il-** *var.* Wardija Point. *headland* Gozo, NW Malta
139 P3 **Wardīyah** N Iraq
185 E19 **Ward, Mount** ▲ South Island, New Zealand
10 L11 **Ware** British Columbia, W Canada
99 D18 **Waregem** *var.* Waereghem. West-Vlaanderen, W Belgium
99 J19 **Waremme** Liège, E Belgium
100 N10 **Waren** Mecklenburg-Vorpommern, NE Germany
171 W13 **Waren** Papua, E Indonesia
101 F14 **Warendorf** Nordrhein-Westfalen, W Germany
21 P12 **Ware Shoals** South Carolina, SE USA
98 N4 **Warffum** Groningen, NE Netherlands
81 O15 **Wargalo** Mudug, E Somalia
146 M12 **Warganza** *Rus.* Varganzi. Qashqadaryo Viloyati, S Uzbekistan
Wargla *see* Ouargla
183 T4 **Warialda** New South Wales, SE Australia
154 F13 **Wāri Godri** Mahārāshtra, C India
167 R10 **Warin Chamrap** Ubon Ratchathani, E Thailand
25 R11 **Waring** Texas, SW USA
39 O8 **Waring Mountains** ▲▲ Alaska, USA
110 M12 **Warka** Mazowieckie, E Poland
184 L5 **Warkworth** Auckland, North Island, New Zealand
171 U12 **Warmandi** Papua, E Indonesia
83 E22 **Warmbad** Karas, S Namibia
98 H8 **Warmenhuizen** Noord-Holland, NW Netherlands
110 M8 **Warmińsko-Mazurskie** ◈ *province* C Poland
97 L22 **Warminster** S England, UK
18 I15 **Warminster** Pennsylvania, NE USA
35 V8 **Warm Springs** Nevada, W USA
32 H12 **Warm Springs** Oregon, NW USA
21 S5 **Warm Springs** Virginia, NE USA
100 M8 **Warnemünde** Mecklenburg-Vorpommern, NE Germany
27 Q10 **Warner** Oklahoma, C USA
35 Q2 **Warner Mountains** ▲▲ California, W USA
23 T5 **Warner Robins** Georgia, SE USA
57 N18 **Warnes** Santa Cruz, C Bolivia
100 M9 **Warnow** ≈ NE Germany
Warnsdorf *see* Varnsdorf
98 M11 **Warnsveld** Gelderland, E Netherlands
154 I13 **Warora** Mahārāshtra, C India
182 L11 **Warracknabeal** Victoria, SE Australia
183 O13 **Warragul** Victoria, SE Australia
183 O4 **Warrego River** *seasonal river* New South Wales/Queensland, E Australia
183 Q6 **Warren** New South Wales, SE Australia
9 X16 **Warren** Manitoba, S Canada
27 V14 **Warren** Arkansas, C USA
31 S10 **Warren** Michigan, N USA
29 R3 **Warren** Minnesota, N USA
31 U11 **Warren** Ohio, N USA
18 D12 **Warren** Pennsylvania, NE USA
25 X10 **Warren** Texas, SW USA
97 G16 **Warrenpoint** *Ir.* An Pointe. SE Northern Ireland, UK
27 S4 **Warrensburg** Missouri, C USA
83 H22 **Warrenton** Northern Cape, N South Africa
23 U4 **Warrenton** Georgia, SE USA
27 W4 **Warrenton** Missouri, C USA
21 V8 **Warrenton** North Carolina, SE USA
21 V4 **Warrenton** Virginia, NE USA
77 U17 **Warri** Delta, S Nigeria
97 L18 **Warrington** C England, UK
23 O9 **Warrington** Florida, SE USA
23 P3 **Warrior** Alabama, S USA
182 L13 **Warrnambool** Victoria, SE Australia
29 T2 **Warroad** Minnesota, N USA
183 S6 **Warrumbungle Range** ▲▲ New South Wales, SE Australia
154 J12 **Wārsa** Mahārāshtra, C India
31 P11 **Warsaw** Indiana, N USA
20 L4 **Warsaw** Kentucky, S USA
27 T5 **Warsaw** Missouri, C USA
18 E10 **Warsaw** New York, NE USA
21 V10 **Warsaw** North Carolina, SE USA
21 X5 **Warsaw** Virginia, NE USA
Warsaw/Warschau *see* Warszawa
81 N17 **Warshiikh** Shabeellaha Dhexe, C Somalia
101 G15 **Warstein** Nordrhein-Westfalen, W Germany
110 M11 **Warszawa** *Eng.* Warsaw, *Ger.* Warschau, *Rus.* Varshava. ● (Poland) Mazowieckie, C Poland
110 J13 **Warta** Sieradz, C Poland
110 D11 **Warta** *Ger.* Warthe. ≈ W Poland
Wartberg *see* Senec
20 M9 **Wartburg** Tennessee, S USA
108 J7 **Warth** Vorarlberg, NW Austria
Warthe *see* Warta
169 U12 **Waru** Borneo, C Indonesia
171 T13 **Waru** Pulau Seram, E Indonesia
139 N6 **Wa'r, Wādī al** *dry watercourse* E Syria
183 U3 **Warwick** Queensland, E Australia
15 Q11 **Warwick** Québec, SE Canada
97 M20 **Warwick** C England, UK
18 K13 **Warwick** New York, NE USA
29 P4 **Warwick** North Dakota, N USA
19 O12 **Warwick** Rhode Island, NE USA
97 L20 **Warwickshire** *cultural region* C England, UK
14 G14 **Wasaga Beach** Ontario, S Canada
77 U13 **Wasagu** Kebbi, NW Nigeria
36 M2 **Wasatch Range** ▲▲ W USA
35 R12 **Wasco** California, W USA
29 V10 **Waseca** Minnesota, N USA
14 H13 **Washago** Ontario, S Canada
19 S2 **Washburn** Maine, NE USA
28 M5 **Washburn** North Dakota, N USA
30 K3 **Washburn** Wisconsin, N USA
31 S14 **Washburn Hill** *hill* Ohio, N USA
154 H13 **Wāshīm** Mahārāshtra, C India
97 M14 **Washington** NE England, UK
23 U3 **Washington** Georgia, SE USA
30 L12 **Washington** Illinois, N USA
31 N15 **Washington** Indiana, N USA
29 X15 **Washington** Iowa, C USA
27 O3 **Washington** Kansas, C USA
27 W5 **Washington** Missouri, C USA
21 X9 **Washington** North Carolina, SE USA
18 B15 **Washington** Pennsylvania, NE USA
25 V10 **Washington** Texas, SW USA
36 J8 **Washington** Utah, W USA
21 V4 **Washington** Virginia, NE USA
32 I9 **Washington** *off.* State of Washington, *also known as* Chinook State, Evergreen State. ◈ *state* NW USA
Washington *see* Washington Court House
31 S14 **Washington Court House** *var.* Washington. Ohio, NE USA
21 W4 **Washington DC** ● (USA) District of Columbia, NE USA
31 O5 **Washington Island** *island* Wisconsin, N USA
Washington Island *see* Teraina
19 O7 **Washington, Mount** ▲ New Hampshire, NE USA
26 M11 **Washita River** ≈ Oklahoma/Texas, C USA
97 O18 **Wash, The** *inlet* E England, UK
32 L9 **Washtucna** Washington, NW USA
Wasiliszki *see* Vasilishki
110 P9 **Wasilków** Podlaskie, NE Poland
39 R11 **Wasilla** Alaska, USA
55 U9 **Wasjabo** Sipaliwini, NW Suriname
9 X11 **Waskaiowaka Lake** ◎ Manitoba, C Canada
9 T14 **Waskesiu Lake** Saskatchewan, C Canada
25 X7 **Waskom** Texas, SW USA
110 G13 **Wąsosz** Dolnośląskie, SW Poland
42 M6 **Waspam** *var.* Waspán. Región Autónoma Atlántico Norte, NE Nicaragua
Waspán *see* Waspam
165 T3 **Wassamu** Hokkaidō, NE Japan
108 G9 **Wassen** Uri, C Switzerland
98 G11 **Wassenaar** Zuid-Holland, W Netherlands
99 N24 **Wasserbillig** Grevenmacher, E Luxembourg
Wasserburg *see* Wasserburg am Inn
101 M23 **Wasserburg am Inn** *var.* Wasserburg. Bayern, SE Germany
101 I17 **Wasserkuppe** ▲ C Germany
103 R5 **Wassy** Haute-Marne, N France
171 N14 **Watampone** *var.* Bone. Sulawesi, C Indonesia
171 R13 **Watawa** Pulau Buru, E Indonesia
Watenstedt-Salzgitter *see* Salzgitter
18 M13 **Waterbury** Connecticut, NE USA
21 R11 **Wateree Lake** ⊠ South Carolina, SE USA
21 R12 **Wateree River** ≈ South Carolina, SE USA
97 E20 **Waterford** *Ir.* Port Láirge. Waterford, S Ireland
31 S9 **Waterford** Michigan, N USA
97 E20 **Waterford** *Ir.* Port Láirge. ◈ *county* S Ireland
97 E21 **Waterford Harbour** *Ir.* Cuan Phort Láirge. *inlet* S Ireland
98 G12 **Wateringen** Zuid-Holland, W Netherlands
99 G19 **Waterloo** Walloon Brabant, C Belgium
14 F16 **Waterloo** Ontario, S Canada
15 P12 **Waterloo** Québec, SE Canada
30 K16 **Waterloo** Illinois, N USA
29 X13 **Waterloo** Iowa, C USA
18 G10 **Waterloo** New York, NE USA
30 L4 **Watersmeet** Michigan, N USA
23 V9 **Watertown** Florida, SE USA
18 I8 **Watertown** New York, NE USA
29 R9 **Watertown** South Dakota, N USA
30 M8 **Watertown** Wisconsin, N USA
22 L3 **Water Valley** Mississippi, S USA
27 O3 **Waterville** Kansas, C USA
17 V6 **Waterville** Maine, NE USA
29 V10 **Waterville** Minnesota, N USA
18 I10 **Waterville** New York, NE USA
14 E16 **Watford** Ontario, S Canada
97 N21 **Watford** E England, UK
28 K4 **Watford City** North Dakota, N USA
141 X12 **Wāṭif** S Oman
18 G11 **Watkins Glen** New York, NE USA
Watlings Island *see* San Salvador
171 U15 **Watnil** Pulau Kai Kecil, E Indonesia
26 M10 **Watonga** Oklahoma, C USA
9 T16 **Watrous** Saskatchewan, S Canada
37 T10 **Watrous** New Mexico, SW USA
79 P16 **Watsa** Orientale, NE Dem. Rep. Congo
31 N12 **Watseka** Illinois, N USA
79 J19 **Watsikengo** Equateur, C Dem. Rep. Congo
182 C5 **Watson** South Australia
9 U15 **Watson** Saskatchewan, S Canada
195 O10 **Watson Escarpment** ▲▲ Antarctica
10 K9 **Watson Lake** Yukon Territory, W Canada
35 N10 **Watsonville** California, W USA
167 Q8 **Wattay** ✈ (Viangchan) Viangchan, C Laos
109 N7 **Wattens** Tirol, W Austria
20 M9 **Watts Bar Lake** ⊠ Tennessee, S USA
108 H7 **Wattwil** Sankt Gallen, NE Switzerland
171 T14 **Watubela, Kepulauan** *island group* E Indonesia
101 N24 **Watzmann** ▲ SE Germany
186 E8 **Wau** Morobe, C Papua New Guinea
81 D14 **Wau** *var.* Wāw. Western Bahr el Ghazal, S Sudan
29 Q8 **Waubay** South Dakota, N USA
29 Q8 **Waubay Lake** ◎ South Dakota, N USA
183 U7 **Wauchope** New South Wales, SE Australia
23 W13 **Wauchula** Florida, SE USA
30 M10 **Wauconda** Illinois, N USA
182 F7 **Waukaringa** South Australia
31 N10 **Waukegan** Illinois, N USA
30 M9 **Waukesha** Wisconsin, N USA
29 X11 **Waukon** Iowa, C USA
30 L8 **Waunakee** Wisconsin, N USA
30 L7 **Waupaca** Wisconsin, N USA
30 M8 **Waupun** Wisconsin, N USA
26 M13 **Waurika** Oklahoma, C USA
26 M12 **Waurika Lake** ⊠ Oklahoma, C USA
30 L6 **Wausau** Wisconsin, N USA
31 R11 **Wauseon** Ohio, N USA
30 L7 **Wautoma** Wisconsin, N USA
30 M9 **Wauwatosa** Wisconsin, N USA
22 L9 **Waveland** Mississippi, S USA
97 Q20 **Waveney** ≈ E England, UK
184 L11 **Waverley** Taranaki, North Island, New Zealand
29 W12 **Waverly** Iowa, C USA
27 T4 **Waverly** Missouri, C USA
29 R15 **Waverly** Nebraska, C USA
18 G12 **Waverly** New York, NE USA
20 H8 **Waverly** Tennessee, S USA
21 W7 **Waverly** Virginia, NE USA
99 H19 **Wavre** Walloon Brabant, C Belgium
166 M8 **Waw** Pegu, SW Myanmar (Burma)
Wāw *see* Wau
14 B7 **Wawa** Ontario, S Canada
77 T14 **Wawa** Niger, W Nigeria
75 Q11 **Wāw al Kabīr** S Libya
43 N7 **Wawa, Río** *var.* Rio Huahua. ≈ NE Nicaragua
186 B8 **Wawoi** ≈ SW Papua New Guinea
25 T7 **Waxahachie** Texas, SW USA
158 L9 **Waxxari** Xinjiang Uygur Zizhiqu, NW China
Wayabou *see* Zichang
23 V7 **Waycross** Georgia, SE USA
180 K10 **Way, Lake** ◎ Western Australia
31 P9 **Wayland** Michigan, N USA
29 R13 **Wayne** Nebraska, C USA
18 K14 **Wayne** New Jersey, NE USA
21 P5 **Wayne** West Virginia, NE USA
23 V4 **Waynesboro** Georgia, SE USA
22 M7 **Waynesboro** Mississippi, S USA
20 H10 **Waynesboro** Tennessee, S USA
21 U5 **Waynesboro** Virginia, NE USA
18 B16 **Waynesburg** Pennsylvania, NE USA
27 U6 **Waynesville** Missouri, C USA
21 O10 **Waynesville** North Carolina, SE USA
26 L8 **Waynoka** Oklahoma, C USA
Wazan *see* Ouazzane
Wazima *see* Wajima
149 V7 **Wazīrābād** Punjab, NE Pakistan
Wazzan *see* Ouazzane
110 I8 **Wda** *var.* Czarna Woda, *Ger.* Schwarzwasser. ≈ N Poland
187 Q16 **Wé** Province des Îles Loyauté, E New Caledonia
97 O23 **Weald, The** *lowlands* SE England, UK
186 A9 **Weam** Western, SW Papua New Guinea
97 L15 **Wear** ≈ N England, UK
Wearmouth *see* Sunderland
26 L10 **Weatherford** Oklahoma, C USA
25 S6 **Weatherford** Texas, SW USA
34 M3 **Weaverville** California, W USA
27 R7 **Webb City** Missouri, C USA
192 G8 **Weber Basin** *undersea feature* S Ceram Sea
Webfoot State *see* Oregon
18 F9 **Webster** New York, NE USA
29 Q8 **Webster** South Dakota, N USA
29 V13 **Webster City** Iowa, C USA
27 X5 **Webster Groves** Missouri, C USA
21 S4 **Webster Springs** *var.* Addison. West Virginia, NE USA
171 S11 **Weda, Teluk** *bay* Pulau Halmahera, E Indonesia
65 B25 **Weddell Island** *var.* Isla San José. *island* W Falkland Islands
65 K22 **Weddell Plain** *undersea feature* SW Atlantic Ocean
65 K23 **Weddell Sea** *sea* SW Atlantic Ocean
65 B25 **Weddell Settlement** Weddell Island, W Falkland Islands
182 M11 **Wedderburn** Victoria, SE Australia
100 I9 **Wedel** Schleswig-Holstein, N Germany
92 N3 **Wedel Jarlsberg Land** *physical region* SW Svalbard
100 I12 **Wedemark** Niedersachsen, NW Germany
10 M17 **Wedge Mountain** ▲ British Columbia, SW Canada
23 R4 **Wedowee** Alabama, S USA
171 U15 **Weduar** Pulau Kai Besar, E Indonesia
35 N2 **Weed** California, W USA
15 Q12 **Weedon Centre** Québec, SE Canada
18 E13 **Weedville** Pennsylvania, NE USA
100 F10 **Weener** Niedersachsen, NW Germany
29 S16 **Weeping Water** Nebraska, C USA
99 L16 **Weert** Limburg, SE Netherlands
98 I10 **Weesp** Noord-Holland, C Netherlands
183 S5 **Wee Waa** New South Wales, SE Australia
110 N7 **Węgorzewo** *Ger.* Angerburg. Warmińsko-Mazurskie, NE Poland
110 E9 **Węgorzyno** *Ger.* Wangerin. Zachodnio-pomorskie, NW Poland
110 N11 **Węgrów** *Ger.* Bingerau. Mazowieckie, C Poland
98 N5 **Wehe-Den Hoorn** Groningen, NE Netherlands
98 M12 **Wehl** Gelderland, E Netherlands
Wehlau *see* Znamensk
168 F7 **Weh, Pulau** *island* NW Indonesia
Wei *see* Weifang
161 P1 **Weichang** *prev.* Zhuizishan. Hebei, E China
Weichang *see* Weishan
Weichsel *see* Wisła
101 M16 **Weida** Thüringen, C Germany
Weiden *see* Weiden in der Oberpfalz
101 M19 **Weiden in der Oberpfalz** *var.* Weiden. Bayern, SE Germany
161 Q4 **Weifang** *var.* Wei, Wei-fang; *prev.* Weihsien. Shandong, E China
161 S4 **Weihai** Shandong, E China
160 K6 **Wei He** ≈ C China
Weihsien *see* Weifang
101 G17 **Weilburg** Hessen, W Germany
101 K24 **Weilheim in Oberbayern** Bayern, SE Germany
183 P4 **Weilmoringle** New South Wales, SE Australia
101 L16 **Weimar** Thüringen, C Germany
25 U11 **Weimar** Texas, SW USA
160 L6 **Weinan** Shaanxi, C China
108 H6 **Weinfelden** Thurgau, NE Switzerland
101 I24 **Weingarten** Baden-Württemberg, S Germany
101 G20 **Weinheim** Baden-Württemberg, SW Germany
160 H11 **Weining** *var.* Weining Yizu Huizu Miaozu Zizhixian. Guizhou, S China
Weining Yizu Huizu Miaozu Zizhixian *see* Weining
181 V2 **Weipa** Queensland, NE Australia
9 Y11 **Weir River** Manitoba, C Canada
21 R1 **Weirton** West Virginia, NE USA
32 M13 **Weiser** Idaho, NW USA
160 F12 **Weishan** *var.* Weichang. Yunnan, SW China
161 P6 **Weishan Hu** ◎ E China
101 M15 **Weisse Elster** *Eng.* White Elster. ≈ Czech Republic/Germany
Weisse Körös/Weisse Kreisch *see* Crişul Alb
108 L7 **Weissenbach am Lech** Tirol, W Austria
Weissenburg *see* Wissembourg
Weissenburg *see* Alba Iulia
101 K21 **Weissenburg in Bayern** Bayern, SE Germany
101 M15 **Weissenfels** *var.* Weißenfels. Sachsen-Anhalt, C Germany
109 R9 **Weissensee** ◎ S Austria
Weissenstein *see* Paide
108 E11 **Weisshorn** *var.* Flüela Wisshorn. ▲ SW Switzerland
Weisskirchen *see* Bela Crkva
23 R3 **Weiss Lake** ⊠ Alabama, S USA
101 Q14 **Weisswasser** *Lus.* Běla Woda. Sachsen, E Germany
99 M22 **Weiswampach** Diekirch, N Luxembourg
109 U2 **Weitra** Niederösterreich, N Austria
161 O4 **Weixian** *var.* Wei Xian. Hebei, E China
Wei Xian *see* Weixian
159 V11 **Weiyuan** Gansu, C China
Weiyuan *see* Shuangjiang
160 F14 **Weiyuan Jiang** ≈ SW China
109 W7 **Weiz** Steiermark, SE Austria
Weizhou *see* Wenchuan
160 K16 **Weizhou Dao** *island* S China
110 I6 **Wejherowo** Pomorskie, NW Poland
27 Q8 **Welch** Oklahoma, C USA
24 M6 **Welch** Texas, SW USA
21 Q6 **Welch** West Virginia, NE USA
45 O14 **Welchman Hall** C Barbados
80 J11 **Weldiya** *var.* Waldia, *It.* Valdia. Amhara, N Ethiopia
21 W8 **Weldon** North Carolina, SE USA
25 V9 **Weldon** Texas, SW USA
99 M19 **Welkenraedt** Liège, E Belgium
193 O2 **Welker Seamount** *undersea feature* N Pacific Ocean
83 I22 **Welkom** Free State, C South Africa
14 H16 **Welland** Ontario, S Canada
14 G16 **Welland** ≈ Ontario, S Canada
97 O19 **Welland** ≈ C England, UK
14 H17 **Welland Canal** *canal* Ontario, S Canada
155 K25 **Wellawaya** Uva Province, SE Sri Lanka
Welle *see* Uele
181 T4 **Wellesley Islands** *island group* Queensland, N Australia
99 J22 **Wellin** Luxembourg, SE Belgium
97 N20 **Wellingborough** C England, UK
183 R7 **Wellington** New South Wales, SE Australia
14 J15 **Wellington** Ontario, SE Canada
185 L14 **Wellington** ● Wellington, North Island, New Zealand
83 E26 **Wellington** Western Cape, SW South Africa
37 T2 **Wellington** Colorado, C USA
27 N7 **Wellington** Kansas, C USA
35 R7 **Wellington** Nevada, W USA
31 T11 **Wellington** Ohio, N USA
25 P3 **Wellington** Texas, SW USA
36 M4 **Wellington** Utah, W USA
185 M14 **Wellington** *off.* Wellington Region. ◈ *region* (New Zealand) North Island, New Zealand
185 L14 **Wellington** ✈ Wellington, North Island, New Zealand
Wellington *see* Wellington, Isla
63 F22 **Wellington, Isla** *var.* Wellington. *island* S Chile
183 P12 **Wellington, Lake** ◎ Victoria, SE Australia
Wellington Region *see* Wellington
29 X14 **Wellman** Iowa, C USA
24 M6 **Wellman** Texas, SW USA
97 K22 **Wells** SW England, UK
29 V11 **Wells** Minnesota, N USA
35 X2 **Wells** Nevada, W USA
25 W8 **Wells** Texas, SW USA
18 F12 **Wellsboro** Pennsylvania, NE USA
21 R1 **Wellsburg** West Virginia, NE USA
184 K4 **Wellsford** Auckland, North Island, New Zealand
180 L9 **Wells, Lake** ◎ Western Australia
181 N4 **Wells, Mount** ▲ Western Australia
97 P18 **Wells-next-the-Sea** E England, UK
31 T15 **Wellston** Ohio, N USA
27 O10 **Wellston** Oklahoma, C USA
18 E11 **Wellsville** New York, NE USA
31 V12 **Wellsville** Ohio, N USA
36 L1 **Wellsville** Utah, W USA
36 I14 **Wellton** Arizona, SW USA
109 S4 **Wels** *anc.* Ovilava. Oberösterreich, N Austria
99 K15 **Welschap** ✈ (Eindhoven) Noord-Brabant, S Netherlands
100 P10 **Welse** ≈ NE Germany
22 H9 **Welsh** Louisiana, S USA
97 K19 **Welshpool** *Wel.* Y Trallwng. E Wales, UK
97 O21 **Welwyn Garden City** E England, UK
79 K18 **Wema** Equateur, NW Dem. Rep. Congo
81 G21 **Wembere** ≈ C Tanzania
9 N13 **Wembley** Alberta, W Canada
12 I9 **Wemindji** *prev.* Nouveau-Comptoir, Paint Hills. Québec, C Canada
99 G18 **Wemmel** Vlaams Brabant, C Belgium
32 J8 **Wenatchee** Washington, NW USA
160 M17 **Wenchang** Hainan, S China
161 R11 **Wencheng** *var.* Daxue. Zhejiang, SE China
77 P16 **Wenchi** W Ghana
Wen-chou/Wenchow *see* Wenzhou
160 H8 **Wenchuan** *var.* Weizhou. Sichuan, C China
Wendau *see* Võnnu
Wenden *see* Cēsis
161 S4 **Wendeng** Shandong, E China
81 J14 **Wendo** Southern, S Ethiopia
36 J2 **Wendover** Utah, W USA
14 D9 **Wenebegon** ≈ Ontario, S Canada
14 D8 **Wenebegon Lake** ◎ Ontario, S Canada
108 E9 **Wengen** Bern, W Switzerland
161 O13 **Wengyuan** *var.* Longxian. Guangdong, S China
189 P15 **Weno** *prev.* Moen. Chuuk, C Micronesia
189 V12 **Weno** *prev.* Moen. *atoll* Chuuk Islands, C Micronesia
158 N13 **Wenquan** Qinghai, C China
159 H4 **Wenquan** *var.* Arixang. Xinjiang Uygur Zizhiqu, NW China
Wenquan *see* Yingshan
160 H14 **Wenshan** *var.* Kaihua. Yunnan, SW China
158 H6 **Wensu** Xinjiang Uygur Zizhiqu, W China
182 L8 **Wentworth** New South Wales, SE Australia
27 W4 **Wentzville** Missouri, C USA
159 V12 **Wenxian** *var.* Wen Xian. Gansu, C China
Wen Xian *see* Wenxian
161 S10 **Wenzhou** *var.* Wen-chou, Wenchow. Zhejiang, SE China
34 L4 **Weott** California, W USA
99 I20 **Wépion** Namur, SE Belgium
100 O11 **Werbellinsee** ◎ NE Germany
99 L21 **Werbomont** Liège, E Belgium
83 G20 **Werda** Kgalagadi, S Botswana
81 N14 **Werdēr** Somali, E Ethiopia
Werder *see* Virtsu
Werenów *see* Voranava
171 U13 **Weri** Papua, E Indonesia
98 I13 **Werkendam** Noord-Brabant, S Netherlands
101 M20 **Wernberg-Köblitz** Bayern, SE Germany
101 J18 **Werneck** Bayern, C Germany
101 K14 **Wernigerode** Sachsen-Anhalt, C Germany
Werowitz *see* Virovitica
101 J16 **Werra** ≈ C Germany
183 N12 **Werribee** Victoria, SE Australia
183 T6 **Werris Creek** New South Wales, SE Australia
Werro *see* Võru
Werschetz *see* Vršac
101 K23 **Wertach** ≈ S Germany
101 I19 **Wertheim** Baden-Württemberg, SW Germany
98 J8 **Wervershoof** Noord-Holland, NW Netherlands
Wervicq *see* Wervik
99 C18 **Wervik** *var.* Wervicq, Werwick. West-Vlaanderen, W Belgium
Werwick *see* Wervik
101 D14 **Wesel** Nordrhein-Westfalen, W Germany
Weseli an der Lainsitz *see* Veselí nad Lužnicí
Wesenberg *see* Rakvere
100 H12 **Weser** ≈ NW Germany
Wes-Kaap *see* Western Cape
25 S17 **Weslaco** Texas, SW USA
14 J13 **Weslemkoon Lake** ◎ Ontario, SE Canada
181 R1 **Wessel Islands** *island group* Northern Territory, N Australia
29 P9 **Wessington** South Dakota, N USA
29 P10 **Wessington Springs** South Dakota, N USA
25 T8 **West** Texas, SW USA
West *see* Ouest
30 M9 **West Allis** Wisconsin, N USA

◆ Country
● Country Capital
◇ Dependent Territory
○ Dependent Territory Capital
◈ Administrative Regions
✈ International Airport
▲ Mountain
▲▲ Mountain Range
Volcano
≈ River
◎ Lake
⊠ Reservoir

182 E8 **Westall, Point** headland South Australia
West Antarctica see Lesser Antarctica
14 G11 **West Arm** Ontario, S Canada
West Australian Basin see Wharton Basin
West Azerbaijan see Āzarbāyjān-e Gharbī
9 N17 **Westbank** British Columbia, SW Canada
138 F10 **West Bank** disputed region SW Asia
14 E11 **West Bay** Manitoulin Island, Ontario, S Canada
22 L11 **West Bay** bay Louisiana, S USA
30 M8 **West Bend** Wisconsin, N USA
153 R16 **West Bengal** ◈ state NE India
West Borneo see Kalimantan Barat
29 Y14 **West Branch** Iowa, C USA
31 R7 **West Branch** Michigan, N USA
18 F13 **West Branch Susquehanna River** ~ Pennsylvania, NE USA
97 L20 **West Bromwich** C England, UK
19 P8 **Westbrook** Maine, NE USA
29 T10 **Westbrook** Minnesota, N USA
29 Y15 **West Burlington** Iowa, C USA
96 L2 **West Burra** island NE Scotland, UK
30 J8 **Westby** Wisconsin, N USA
44 L6 **West Caicos** island W Turks and Caicos Islands
185 A24 **West Cape** headland South Island, New Zealand
174 L4 **West Caroline Basin** undersea feature SW Pacific Ocean
18 I16 **West Chester** Pennsylvania, NE USA
185 E18 **West Coast** off. West Coast Region. ◈ region South Island, New Zealand
West Coast Region see West Coast
25 V12 **West Columbia** Texas, SW USA
29 W10 **West Concord** Minnesota, N USA
29 V14 **West Des Moines** Iowa, C USA
37 Q6 **West Elk Peak** ▲ Colorado, C USA
44 F1 **West End** Grand Bahama Island, N Bahamas
44 F1 **West End Point** headland Grand Bahama Island, N Bahamas
98 O7 **Westerbork** Drenthe, NE Netherlands
98 N3 **Westereems** strait Germany/Netherlands
98 O9 **Westerhaar-Vriezenveensewijk** Overijssel, E Netherlands
100 G6 **Westerland** Schleswig-Holstein, N Germany
99 I17 **Westerlo** Antwerpen, N Belgium
19 N13 **Westerly** Rhode Island, NE USA
81 G18 **Western** ◈ province W Kenya
153 N11 **Western** ◈ zone C Nepal
186 A8 **Western** ◈ province SW Papua New Guinea
186 J8 **Western** off. Western Province. ◈ province NW Solomon Islands
83 G15 **Western** ◈ province SW Zambia
180 K8 **Western Australia** ◈ state W Australia
80 A13 **Western Bahr el Ghazal** ◈ state SW Sudan
Western Bug see Bug
83 F25 **Western Cape** off. Western Cape Province, Afr. Wes-Kaap. ◈ province SW South Africa
Western Cape Province see Western Cape
80 A11 **Western Darfur** ◈ state W Sudan
Western Desert see Sahara el Gharbîya
118 G9 **Western Dvina** Bel. Dzvina, Ger. Düna, Latv. Daugava, Rus. Zapadnaya Dvina. ~ W Europe
81 D15 **Western Equatoria** ◈ state SW Sudan
155 E16 **Western Ghats** ▲▲ SW India
186 C7 **Western Highlands** ◈ province C Papua New Guinea
Western Isles see Outer Hebrides
80 C12 **Western Kordofan** ◈ state C Sudan
21 T3 **Westernport** Maryland, NE USA
155 J26 **Western Province** ◈ province SW Sri Lanka
Western Province see Western
Western Punjab see Punjab
74 B10 **Western Sahara** ◇ disputed territory N Africa
Western Samoa see Samoa
Western Samoa, Independent State of see Samoa
Western Sayans see Zapadnyy Sayan
Western Scheldt see Westerschelde
0 G13 **Western Sierra Madre** var. Western Sierra Madre. ▲▲ C Mexico
Western Sierra Madre see Western Sierra Madre
Western Sierra Madre see Sierra Madre Occidental
99 E15 **Westerschelde** Eng. Western Scheldt; prev. Honte. inlet S North Sea
31 S13 **Westerville** Ohio, N USA
101 F17 **Westerwald** ▲▲ W Germany
65 C25 **West Falkland** var. Gran Malvina. island W Falkland Islands
29 R5 **West Fargo** North Dakota, N USA
188 M15 **West Fayu Atoll** atoll Caroline Islands, C Micronesia
18 C11 **Westfield** New York, NE USA
30 L7 **Westfield** Wisconsin, N USA
West Flanders see West-Vlaanderen
27 S10 **West Fork** Arkansas, C USA
29 P16 **West Fork Big Blue River** ~ Nebraska, C USA
29 U12 **West Fork Des Moines River** ~ Iowa/Minnesota, C USA
25 S5 **West Fork Trinity River** ~ Texas, SW USA
30 L16 **West Frankfort** Illinois, N USA
98 I8 **West-Friesland** physical region NW Netherlands
West Frisian Islands see Waddeneilanden
19 T5 **West Grand Lake** ◎ Maine, NE USA
18 M12 **West Hartford** Connecticut, NE USA
18 M13 **West Haven** Connecticut, NE USA
27 X12 **West Helena** Arkansas, C USA
28 M2 **Westhope** North Dakota, N USA
195 Y8 **West Ice Shelf** ice shelf Antarctica
47 R2 **West Indies** island group SE North America
West Irian see Papua
West Java see Jawa Barat
36 L3 **West Jordan** Utah, W USA
West Kalimantan see Kalimantan Barat
99 D14 **Westkapelle** Zeeland, SW Netherlands
West Kazakhstan see Zapadnyy Kazakhstan
31 O13 **West Lafayette** Indiana, N USA
31 T13 **West Lafayette** Ohio, N USA
West Lake see Kagera
29 Y14 **West Liberty** Iowa, C USA
21 O5 **West Liberty** Kentucky, S USA
Westliche Morava see Zapadna Morava
10 J13 **Westlock** Alberta, SW Canada
14 E17 **West Lorne** Ontario, S Canada
96 J12 **West Lothian** cultural region S Scotland, UK
99 H16 **Westmalle** Antwerpen, N Belgium
192 G6 **West Mariana Basin** var. Perece Vela Basin. undersea feature W Pacific Ocean
97 E17 **Westmeath** Ir. An Iarmhí, Na H-Iarmhidhe. ◈ county C Ireland
27 Y11 **West Memphis** Arkansas, C USA
21 W2 **Westminster** Maryland, NE USA
21 O11 **Westminster** South Carolina, SE USA
22 I5 **West Monroe** Louisiana, S USA
18 D15 **Westmont** Pennsylvania, NE USA
27 O3 **Westmoreland** Kansas, C USA
35 W17 **Westmorland** California, W USA
186 E6 **West New Britain** ◈ province E Papua New Guinea
West New Guinea see Papua
83 K18 **West Nicholson** Matabeleland South, S Zimbabwe
29 T14 **West Nishnabotna River** ~ Iowa, C USA
175 P11 **West Norfolk Ridge** undersea feature W Pacific Ocean
25 P12 **West Nueces River** ~ Texas, SW USA
West Nusa Tenggara see Nusa Tenggara Barat
29 T11 **West Okoboji Lake** ◎ Iowa, C USA
33 R16 **Weston** Idaho, NW USA
21 R4 **Weston** West Virginia, NE USA
97 J22 **Weston-super-Mare** SW England, UK
23 Z14 **West Palm Beach** Florida, SE USA
West Papua see Papua
188 E9 **West Passage** passage Babeldaob, N Palau
23 O9 **West Pensacola** Florida, SE USA
27 V8 **West Plains** Missouri, C USA
35 P7 **West Point** California, W USA
23 R5 **West Point** Georgia, SE USA
22 M3 **West Point** Mississippi, S USA
29 R14 **West Point** Nebraska, C USA
21 X6 **West Point** Virginia, NE USA
182 G10 **West Point** headland South Australia
65 B24 **Westpoint Island Settlement** Westpoint Island, NW Falkland Islands
23 R4 **West Point Lake** ⊠ Alabama/Georgia, SE USA
97 B16 **Westport** Ir. Cathair na Mart. Mayo, W Ireland
185 G15 **Westport** West Coast, South Island, New Zealand
32 F10 **Westport** Oregon, NW USA
32 F9 **Westport** Washington, NW USA
31 S15 **West Portsmouth** Ohio, N USA
West Punjab see Punjab
9 V14 **Westray** Manitoba, C Canada
96 J4 **Westray** island NE Scotland, UK
14 F9 **Westree** Ontario, S Canada
97 L16 **West Riding** cultural region N England, UK
West River see Xi Jiang
30 J7 **West Salem** Wisconsin, N USA
65 H21 **West Scotia Ridge** undersea feature W Scotia Sea
West Sepik see Sandaun
173 N4 **West Sheba Ridge** undersea feature W Indian Ocean
West Siberian Plain see Zapadno-Sibirskaya Ravnina
31 S11 **West Sister Island** island Ohio, N USA
West-Skylge see West-Terschelling
West Sumatra see Sumatera Barat
98 J5 **West-Terschelling** Fris. West-Skylge. Friesland, N Netherlands
64 J7 **West Thulean Rise** undersea feature N Atlantic Ocean
29 X12 **West Union** Iowa, C USA
31 R15 **West Union** Ohio, N USA
21 R3 **West Union** West Virginia, NE USA
31 N13 **Westville** Illinois, N USA
21 R3 **West Virginia** off. State of West Virginia, also known as Mountain State. ◈ state NE USA
99 A17 **West-Vlaanderen** Eng. West Flanders. ◈ province W Belgium
35 R7 **West Walker River** ~ California/Nevada, W USA
35 P4 **Westwood** California, W USA
183 P9 **West Wyalong** New South Wales, SE Australia
171 Q16 **Wetar, Pulau** island Kepulauan Damar, E Indonesia
171 R16 **Wetar, Selat** var. Wetar Strait. strait Nusa Tenggara, S Indonesia
Wetar Strait see Wetar, Selat
9 Q15 **Wetaskiwin** Alberta, SW Canada
81 K21 **Wete** Pemba, E Tanzania
166 M4 **Wetlet** Sagaing, C Myanmar (Burma)
37 T6 **Wet Mountains** ▲▲ Colorado, C USA
101 E15 **Wetter** Nordrhein-Westfalen, W Germany
101 H17 **Wetter** ~ W Germany
99 F17 **Wetteren** Oost-Vlaanderen, NW Belgium
108 F7 **Wettingen** Aargau, N Switzerland
27 P11 **Wetumka** Oklahoma, C USA
23 Q5 **Wetumpka** Alabama, S USA
108 G7 **Wetzikon** Zürich, N Switzerland
101 G17 **Wetzlar** Hessen, W Germany
99 C18 **Wevelgem** West-Vlaanderen, W Belgium
38 M6 **Wevok** var. Wewuk. Alaska, USA
23 R9 **Wewahitchka** Florida, SE USA
186 C6 **Wewak** East Sepik, NW Papua New Guinea
27 O11 **Wewoka** Oklahoma, C USA
Wewuk see Wevok
97 F20 **Wexford** Ir. Loch Garman. SE Ireland
97 F20 **Wexford** Ir. Loch Garman. ◈ cultural region SE Ireland
30 L7 **Weyauwega** Wisconsin, N USA
9 U17 **Weyburn** Saskatchewan, S Canada
Weyer see Weyer Markt
109 U5 **Weyer Markt** var. Weyer. Oberösterreich, N Austria
100 H11 **Weyhe** Niedersachsen, NW Germany
97 L24 **Weymouth** S England, UK
19 P11 **Weymouth** Massachusetts, NE USA
99 H18 **Wezembeek-Oppem** Vlaams Brabant, C Belgium
98 M9 **Wezep** Gelderland, E Netherlands
184 M9 **Whakamaru** Waikato, North Island, New Zealand
184 O8 **Whakatane** Bay of Plenty, North Island, New Zealand
184 O8 **Whakatane** ~ North Island, New Zealand
9 O9 **Whale Cove** Nunavut, C Canada
96 M2 **Whalsay** island NE Scotland, UK
184 L11 **Whangaehu** ~ North Island, New Zealand
184 M6 **Whangamata** Waikato, North Island, New Zealand
184 Q9 **Whangara** Gisborne, North Island, New Zealand
184 K3 **Whangarei** Northland, North Island, New Zealand
184 K3 **Whangaruru Harbour** inlet North Island, New Zealand
25 V12 **Wharton** Texas, SW USA
173 U8 **Wharton Basin** var. West Australian Basin. undersea feature E Indian Ocean
185 E18 **Whataroa** West Coast, South Island, New Zealand
8 K10 **Wha Ti** var. Lac la Martre. Northwest Territories, W Canada
8 K10 **Wha Ti** prev Lac la Martre. Northwest Territories
184 K6 **Whatipu** Auckland, North Island, New Zealand
33 Y16 **Wheatland** Wyoming, C USA
14 D18 **Wheatley** Ontario, S Canada
30 M10 **Wheaton** Illinois, N USA
29 R7 **Wheaton** Minnesota, N USA
37 T4 **Wheat Ridge** Colorado, C USA
25 P2 **Wheeler** Texas, SW USA
23 O2 **Wheeler Lake** ⊠ Alabama, S USA
35 Y6 **Wheeler Peak** ▲ Nevada, W USA
37 T9 **Wheeler Peak** ▲ New Mexico, SW USA
31 S15 **Wheelersburg** Ohio, N USA
21 R2 **Wheeling** West Virginia, NE USA
97 L16 **Whernside** ▲ N England, UK
182 F9 **Whidbey, Point** headland South Australia
180 I7 **Whim Creek** Western Australia
10 L17 **Whistler** British Columbia, SW Canada
21 W8 **Whitakers** North Carolina, SE USA
14 H15 **Whitby** Ontario, S Canada
97 N15 **Whitby** N England, UK
10 G6 **White** ~ Yukon Territory, W Canada
13 T11 **White Bay** bay Newfoundland, Newfoundland and Labrador, E Canada
20 I8 **White Bluff** Tennessee, S USA
28 J6 **White Butte** ▲ North Dakota, N USA
19 R5 **White Cap Mountain** ▲ Maine, NE USA
22 J9 **White Castle** Louisiana, S USA
182 M5 **White Cliffs** New South Wales, SE Australia
31 P8 **White Cloud** Michigan, N USA
9 P14 **Whitecourt** Alberta, SW Canada
25 O2 **White Deer** Texas, SW USA
White Elster see Weisse Elster
24 M5 **Whiteface** Texas, SW USA
18 K7 **Whiteface Mountain** ▲ New York, NE USA
29 W5 **Whiteface Reservoir** ⊠ Minnesota, N USA
33 O7 **Whitefish** Montana, NW USA
31 N9 **Whitefish Bay** Wisconsin, N USA
31 Q3 **Whitefish Bay** lake bay Canada/USA
14 E11 **Whitefish Falls** Ontario, S Canada
14 B7 **Whitefish Lake** ◎ Ontario, S Canada
29 U6 **Whitefish Lake** ◎ Minnesota, C USA
31 Q3 **Whitefish Point** headland Michigan, N USA
31 O4 **Whitefish River** ~ Michigan, N USA
25 O4 **Whiteflat** Texas, SW USA
27 V12 **White Hall** Arkansas, C USA
30 K14 **White Hall** Illinois, N USA
31 O8 **Whitehall** Michigan, N USA
18 L9 **Whitehall** New York, NE USA
31 S13 **Whitehall** Ohio, N USA
30 J7 **Whitehall** Wisconsin, N USA
97 J15 **Whitehaven** NW England, UK
10 I8 **Whitehorse** territory capital Yukon Territory, W Canada
184 O7 **White Island** island NE New Zealand
14 K13 **White Lake** ◎ Ontario, SE Canada
22 H10 **White Lake** ◎ Louisiana, S USA
186 G7 **Whiteman Range** ▲▲ New Britain, E Papua New Guinea
183 Q15 **Whitemark** Tasmania, SE Australia
35 S9 **White Mountains** ▲▲ California/Nevada, W USA
19 N7 **White Mountains** ▲▲ Maine/New Hampshire, NE USA
80 F11 **White Nile** ◈ state C Sudan
67 U7 **White Nile** var. Bahr el Jebel. ~ S Sudan
81 E14 **White Nile** Ar. Al Baḩr al Abyaḑ, An Nīl al Abyaḑ, Bahr el Jebel. ~ SE Sudan
25 W5 **White Oak Creek** ~ Texas, SW USA
10 H9 **White Pass** pass Canada/USA
32 I9 **White Pass** pass Washington, NW USA
21 O9 **White Pine** Tennessee, S USA
18 K14 **White Plains** New York, NE USA
37 N13 **Whiteriver** Arizona, SW USA
28 M11 **White River** South Dakota, N USA
27 W12 **White River** ~ Arkansas, SE USA
37 P3 **White River** ~ Colorado/Utah, C USA
31 N15 **White River** ~ Indiana, N USA
31 O8 **White River** ~ Michigan, N USA
28 K11 **White River** ~ South Dakota, N USA
25 O5 **White River** ~ Texas, SW USA
18 M8 **White River** ~ Vermont, NE USA
25 O5 **White River Lake** ⊠ Texas, SW USA
32 H11 **White Salmon** Washington, NW USA
18 I10 **Whitesboro** New York, NE USA
25 T5 **Whitesboro** Texas, SW USA
21 O7 **Whitesburg** Kentucky, S USA
White Sea see Beloye More
White Sea-Baltic Canal/White Sea Canal see Belomorsko-Baltiyskiy Kanal
63 I25 **Whiteside, Canal** channel S Chile
33 S10 **White Sulphur Springs** Montana, NW USA
21 R6 **White Sulphur Springs** West Virginia, NE USA
20 J6 **Whitesville** Kentucky, S USA
32 I10 **White Swan** Washington, NW USA
21 U12 **Whiteville** North Carolina, SE USA
20 F10 **Whiteville** Tennessee, S USA
77 Q13 **White Volta** var. Nakambé, Fr. Volta Blanche. ~ Burkina/Ghana
30 M9 **Whitewater** Wisconsin, N USA
37 P14 **Whitewater Baldy** ▲ New Mexico, SW USA
23 X17 **Whitewater Bay** bay Florida, SE USA
31 Q14 **Whitewater River** ~ Indiana/Ohio, N USA
9 V16 **Whitewood** Saskatchewan, S Canada
28 J9 **Whitewood** South Dakota, N USA
25 U5 **Whitewright** Texas, SW USA
97 I15 **Whithorn** S Scotland, UK
184 M6 **Whitianga** Waikato, North Island, New Zealand
19 N11 **Whitinsville** Massachusetts, NE USA
20 M8 **Whitley City** Kentucky, S USA
21 Q11 **Whitmire** South Carolina, SE USA
31 R10 **Whitmore Lake** Michigan, N USA
195 N9 **Whitmore Mountains** ▲▲ Antarctica
14 I12 **Whitney** Ontario, SE Canada
25 T8 **Whitney** Texas, SW USA
25 S8 **Whitney, Lake** ⊠ Texas, SW USA
35 S11 **Whitney, Mount** ▲ California, W USA
181 Y6 **Whitsunday Group** island group Queensland, E Australia
25 S6 **Whitt** Texas, SW USA
29 U12 **Whittemore** Iowa, C USA
39 R12 **Whittier** Alaska, USA
35 T15 **Whittier** California, W USA
83 I25 **Whittlesea** Eastern Cape, S South Africa
20 K10 **Whitwell** Tennessee, S USA
8 L10 **Wholdaia Lake** ◎ Northwest Territories, NW Canada
182 H7 **Whyalla** South Australia
Whydah see Ouidah
14 F13 **Wiarton** Ontario, S Canada
171 O13 **Wiau** Sulawesi, C Indonesia
111 H15 **Wiązów** Ger. Wansen. Dolnośląskie, SW Poland
33 Y8 **Wibaux** Montana, NW USA
27 N6 **Wichita** Kansas, C USA
25 R5 **Wichita Falls** Texas, SW USA
26 L11 **Wichita Mountains** ▲▲ Oklahoma, C USA
25 R5 **Wichita River** ~ Texas, SW USA
96 K6 **Wick** N Scotland, UK
36 K13 **Wickenburg** Arizona, SW USA
24 L8 **Wickett** Texas, SW USA
180 I7 **Wickham** Western Australia
182 M14 **Wickham, Cape** headland Tasmania, SE Australia
20 G7 **Wickliffe** Kentucky, S USA
97 G19 **Wicklow** Ir. Cill Mhantáin. E Ireland
97 F19 **Wicklow** Ir. Cill Mhantáin. ◈ county E Ireland
97 G19 **Wicklow Head** Ir. Ceann Chill Mhantáin. headland E Ireland
97 F18 **Wicklow Mountains** Ir. Sléibhte Chill Mhantáin. ▲▲ E Ireland
14 H10 **Wicksteed Lake** ◎ Ontario, S Canada
Wida see Ouidah
65 G15 **Wideawake Airfield** ✕ (Georgetown) SW Ascension Island
97 K18 **Widnes** NW England, UK
110 H9 **Więcbork** Ger. Vandsburg. Kujawsko-pomorskie, C Poland
101 E17 **Wied** ~ W Germany
101 F16 **Wiehl** Nordrhein-Westfalen, W Germany
111 L17 **Wieliczka** Małopolskie, S Poland
110 H12 **Wielkopolskie** ◈ province SW Poland
111 J14 **Wieluń** Sieradz, C Poland
109 X4 **Wien** Eng. Vienna, Hung. Bécs, Slvk. Vídeň, Slvn. Dunaj; anc. Vindobona. ● (Austria) Wien, NE Austria
109 X4 **Wien** off. Land Wien, Eng. Vienna. ◈ state NE Austria
109 X5 **Wiener Neustadt** Niederösterreich, E Austria
Wien, Land see Wien
110 G7 **Wieprza** Ger. Wipper. ~ NW Poland
98 O10 **Wierden** Overijssel, E Netherlands
98 I7 **Wieringerwerf** Noord-Holland, NW Netherlands
Wieruschow see Wieruszów
111 I14 **Wieruszów** Ger. Wieruschow. Łódzkie, C Poland
109 V9 **Wies** Steiermark, SE Austria
Wiesbachhorn see Grosses Wiesbachhorn
101 G18 **Wiesbaden** Hessen, W Germany
Wieselburg and Ungarisch-Altenburg/Wieselburg-Ungarisch-Altenburg see Mosonmagyaróvár
Wiesenhof see Ostrołęka
101 G20 **Wiesloch** Baden-Württemberg, SW Germany
100 F10 **Wiesmoor** Niedersachsen, NW Germany
110 I7 **Wieżyca** Ger. Turmberg. hill Pomorskie, N Poland
97 L17 **Wigan** NW England, UK
37 U3 **Wiggins** Colorado, C USA
22 M8 **Wiggins** Mississippi, S USA
Wigorna Ceaster see Worcester
97 I14 **Wigtown** S Scotland, UK
97 H14 **Wigtown** cultural region SW Scotland, UK
97 I15 **Wigtown Bay** bay SW Scotland, UK
98 L13 **Wijchen** Gelderland, SE Netherlands
92 N1 **Wijdefjorden** fjord NW Svalbard
98 M10 **Wijhe** Overijssel, E Netherlands
98 J12 **Wijk bij Duurstede** Utrecht, C Netherlands
98 J13 **Wijk en Aalburg** Noord-Brabant, S Netherlands
99 H16 **Wijnegem** Antwerpen, N Belgium
14 E11 **Wikwemikong** Manitoulin Island, Ontario, S Canada
108 H7 **Wil** Sankt Gallen, NE Switzerland
29 R16 **Wilber** Nebraska, C USA
32 K8 **Wilbur** Washington, NW USA
27 Q11 **Wilburton** Oklahoma, C USA
182 M6 **Wilcannia** New South Wales, SE Australia
18 D12 **Wilcox** Pennsylvania, NE USA
Wilczek Land see Vil'cheka, Zemlya
109 U6 **Wildalpen** Steiermark, E Austria
31 O13 **Wildcat Creek** ~ Indiana, N USA
108 L9 **Wilde Kreuzspitze** It. Picco di Croce. ▲ Austria/Italy
Wildenschwert see Ústí nad Orlicí
98 O6 **Wildervank** Groningen, NE Netherlands
100 G11 **Wildeshausen** Niedersachsen, NW Germany
108 D10 **Wildhorn** ▲ SW Switzerland
9 R17 **Wild Horse** Alberta, SW Canada
27 N12 **Wildhorse Creek** ~ Oklahoma, C USA
28 L14 **Wild Horse Hill** ▲ Nebraska, C USA
109 W8 **Wildon** Steiermark, SE Austria
24 M2 **Wildorado** Texas, SW USA
29 R6 **Wild Rice River** ~ Minnesota/North Dakota, N USA
Wilejka see Vilyeyka
195 Y9 **Wilhelm II Coast** physical region Antarctica
195 X9 **Wilhelm II Land** physical region Antarctica
55 U11 **Wilhelmina Gebergte** ▲▲ C Suriname
18 B13 **Wilhelm, Lake** ⊠ Pennsylvania, NE USA
92 O2 **Wilhelmøya** island C Svalbard
Wilhelm-Pieck-Stadt see Guben
109 W4 **Wilhelmsburg** Niederösterreich, E Austria
100 G10 **Wilhelmshaven** Niedersachsen, NW Germany
Wilia/Wilja see Neris
18 H13 **Wilkes Barre** Pennsylvania, NE USA
21 R9 **Wilkesboro** North Carolina, SE USA
195 W15 **Wilkes Coast** physical region Antarctica
189 W12 **Wilkes Island** island N Wake Island
195 X12 **Wilkes Land** physical region Antarctica
9 S15 **Wilkie** Saskatchewan, S Canada
194 I6 **Wilkins Ice Shelf** ice shelf Antarctica
182 D4 **Wilkinsons Lakes** salt lake South Australia
Wiłkomierz see Ukmergė
182 K11 **Willalooka** South Australia
32 G11 **Willamette River** ~ Oregon, NW USA
183 O8 **Willandra Billabong Creek** seasonal river New South Wales, SE Australia
32 F9 **Willapa Bay** inlet Washington, NW USA
27 T7 **Willard** Missouri, C USA
37 S12 **Willard** New Mexico, SW USA
31 S12 **Willard** Ohio, N USA
36 L1 **Willard** Utah, W USA
186 G6 **Willaumez Peninsula** headland New Britain, E Papua New Guinea
37 N15 **Willcox** Arizona, SW USA
37 N16 **Willcox Playa** salt flat Arizona, SW USA
99 G17 **Willebroek** Antwerpen, C Belgium
99 G14 **Willemstad** Noord-Brabant, S Netherlands
45 P16 **Willemstad** ○ (Netherlands Antilles) Curaçao, Netherlands Antilles
9 S11 **William** ~ Saskatchewan, C Canada
23 O6 **William "Bill" Dannelly Reservoir** ⊠ Alabama, S USA
182 G3 **William Creek** South Australia
181 T15 **William, Mount** ▲ South Australia
36 K11 **Williams** Arizona, SW USA
29 X14 **Williamsburg** Iowa, C USA
20 M8 **Williamsburg** Kentucky, S USA
31 R15 **Williamsburg** Ohio, N USA
21 X6 **Williamsburg** Virginia, NE USA
10 M15 **Williams Lake** British Columbia, SW Canada
21 P6 **Williamson** West Virginia, NE USA
31 N13 **Williamsport** Indiana, N USA
18 G13 **Williamsport** Pennsylvania, NE USA
21 W9 **Williamston** North Carolina, SE USA
21 P11 **Williamston** South Carolina, SE USA
20 M4 **Williamstown** Kentucky, S USA
18 L10 **Williamstown** Massachusetts, NE USA
18 J16 **Willingboro** New Jersey, NE USA
9 Q14 **Willingdon** Alberta, SW Canada
25 W10 **Willis** Texas, SW USA
108 F8 **Willisau** Luzern, W Switzerland
83 F24 **Williston** Northern Cape, W South Africa
23 V10 **Williston** Florida, SE USA
28 J3 **Williston** North Dakota, N USA
21 Q13 **Williston** South Carolina, SE USA
10 L12 **Williston Lake** ⊠ British Columbia, W Canada
34 L5 **Willits** California, W USA
29 T8 **Willmar** Minnesota, N USA
10 K11 **Will, Mount** ▲ British Columbia, W Canada
31 T11 **Willoughby** Ohio, N USA
9 U17 **Willow Bunch** Saskatchewan, S Canada
32 J11 **Willow Creek** ~ Oregon, NW USA
39 R11 **Willow Lake** Alaska, USA
8 I9 **Willowlake** ~ Northwest Territories, NW Canada
83 H25 **Willowmore** Eastern Cape, S South Africa
30 L5 **Willow Reservoir** ⊠ Wisconsin, N USA
35 N5 **Willows** California, W USA
27 V7 **Willow Springs** Missouri, C USA
182 I7 **Wilmington** South Australia
21 Y2 **Wilmington** Delaware, NE USA
21 V12 **Wilmington** North Carolina, SE USA
31 R14 **Wilmington** Ohio, N USA
20 M6 **Wilmore** Kentucky, S USA
29 R8 **Wilmot** South Dakota, N USA
Wilna/Wilno see Vilnius
101 G16 **Wilnsdorf** Nordrhein-Westfalen, W Germany
99 G16 **Wilrijk** Antwerpen, N Belgium
100 I10 **Wilseder Berg** hill NW Germany
67 Z12 **Wilshaw Ridge** undersea feature W Indian Ocean
21 V9 **Wilson** North Carolina, SE USA
25 N5 **Wilson** Texas, SW USA
182 A7 **Wilson Bluff** headland South Australia/Western Australia
35 Y7 **Wilson Creek Range** ▲▲ Nevada, W USA
23 O1 **Wilson Lake** ⊠ Alabama, S USA
26 M4 **Wilson Lake** ⊠ Kansas, SE USA
37 P7 **Wilson, Mount** ▲ Colorado, C USA
183 P13 **Wilsons Promontory** peninsula Victoria, SE Australia

◆ Country ● Country Capital ◇ Dependent Territory ○ Dependent Territory Capital ◈ Administrative Regions ✕ International Airport ▲ Mountain ▲▲ Mountain Range Volcano ~ River ◎ Lake ⊠ Reservoir

29 *Y14* **Wilton** Iowa, C USA
19 *P7* **Wilton** Maine, NE USA
28 *M5* **Wilton** North Dakota, N USA
97 *L22* **Wiltshire** *cultural region* S England, UK
99 *M23* **Wiltz** Diekirch, NW Luxembourg
180 *K9* **Wiluna** Western Australia
99 *M23* **Wilwerwiltz** Diekirch, NE Luxembourg
29 *P5* **Wimbledon** North Dakota, N USA
42 *K7* **Wina** ***var.*** Güina. Jinotega, N Nicaragua
31 *O12* **Winamac** Indiana, N USA
81 *G19* **Winam Gulf** ***var.*** Kavirondo Gulf. *gulf* SW Kenya
83 *I22* **Winburg** Free State, C South Africa
19 *N10* **Winchendon** Massachusetts, NE USA
14 *M13* **Winchester** Ontario, SE Canada
97 *M23* **Winchester** ***hist.*** Wintanceaster, ***Lat.*** Venta Belgarum. S England, UK
32 *M10* **Winchester** Idaho, NW USA
30 *J14* **Winchester** Illinois, N USA
31 *Q13* **Winchester** Indiana, N USA
20 *M5* **Winchester** Kentucky, S USA
18 *M10* **Winchester** New Hampshire, NE USA
20 *K10* **Winchester** Tennessee, S USA
21 *V3* **Winchester** Virginia, NE USA
99 *L22* **Wincrange** Diekirch, NW Luxembourg
10 *I5* **Wind** Yukon Territory, NW Canada
183 *S8* **Windamere, Lake** ◎ New South Wales, SE Australia
Windau *see* Ventspils
Windau *see* Venta
18 *D15* **Windber** Pennsylvania, NE USA
23 *T3* **Winder** Georgia, SE USA
97 *K15* **Windermere** NW England, UK
14 *C7* **Windermere Lake** ◎ Ontario, S Canada
31 *U11* **Windham** Ohio, N USA
83 *D19* **Windhoek** ***Ger.*** Windhuk. ● (Namibia) Khomas, C Namibia
83 *D20* **Windhoek** ✈ Khomas, C Namibia
Windhuk *see* Windhoek
15 *O8* **Windigo** Québec, SE Canada
15 *O8* **Windigo** Québec, SE Canada
Windischfeistritz *see* Slovenska Bistrica
109 *T6* **Windischgarsten** Oberösterreich, W Austria
Windischgraz *see* Slovenj Gradec
37 *T16* **Wind Mountain** ▲ New Mexico, SW USA
29 *T10* **Windom** Minnesota, N USA
37 *Q7* **Windom Peak** ▲ Colorado, C USA
181 *U9* **Windorah** Queensland, C Australia
37 *O10* **Window Rock** Arizona, SW USA
31 *N9* **Wind Point** *headland* Wisconsin, N USA
33 *U14* **Wind River** Wyoming, C USA
13 *P15* **Windsor** Nova Scotia, SE Canada
14 *C17* **Windsor** Ontario, S Canada
15 *Q12* **Windsor** Québec, SE Canada
97 *N22* **Windsor** S England, UK
37 *T3* **Windsor** Colorado, C USA
18 *M12* **Windsor** Connecticut, NE USA
27 *T5* **Windsor** Missouri, C USA
21 *X9* **Windsor** North Carolina, SE USA
18 *M12* **Windsor Locks** Connecticut, NE USA
25 *R5* **Windthorst** Texas, SW USA
45 *Z14* **Windward Islands** *island group* E West Indies
Windward Islands *see* Barlavento, Ilhas de, Cape Verde
Windward Islands *see* Vent, Îles du, Archipel de la Société, French Polynesia
44 *K8* **Windward Passage** ***Sp.*** Paso de los Vientos. *channel* Cuba/Haiti
55 *T9* **Wineperu** C Guyana
23 *O3* **Winfield** Alabama, S USA
29 *Y15* **Winfield** Iowa, C USA
27 *O7* **Winfield** Kansas, C USA
25 *W6* **Winfield** Texas, SW USA
21 *Q4* **Winfield** West Virginia, NE USA
29 *N5* **Wing** North Dakota, N USA
183 *U7* **Wingham** New South Wales, SE Australia
12 *G16* **Wingham** Ontario, S Canada
33 *T8* **Winifred** Montana, NW USA
12 *E8* **Winisk** Ontario, S Canada
12 *E9* **Winisk Lake** ◎ Ontario, C Canada
24 *L8* **Wink** Texas, SW USA
36 *M14* **Winkelman** Arizona, SW USA
9 *X17* **Winkler** Manitoba, S Canada
109 *Q9* **Winklern** Tirol, W Austria
Winkowitz *see* Vinkovci
32 *G9* **Winlock** Washington, NW USA
77 *P17* **Winneba** SE Ghana
29 *U11* **Winnebago** Minnesota, N USA
29 *R13* **Winnebago** Nebraska, C USA
30 *M7* **Winnebago, Lake** ◎ Wisconsin, N USA
30 *M7* **Winneconne** Wisconsin, N USA
35 *T3* **Winnemucca** Nevada, W USA
35 *R4* **Winnemucca Lake** ◎ Nevada, W USA
101 *H21* **Winnenden** Baden-Württemberg, SW Germany
29 *N11* **Winner** South Dakota, N USA
33 *U9* **Winnett** Montana, NW USA
14 *I9* **Winneway** Québec, SE Canada
22 *H6* **Winnfield** Louisiana, S USA
29 *U4* **Winnibigoshish, Lake** ◎ Minnesota, N USA
25 *X11* **Winnie** Texas, SW USA
9 *Y16* **Winnipeg** *province capital* Manitoba, S Canada
9 *X16* **Winnipeg** ✈ Manitoba, S Canada
0 *J8* **Winnipeg** Manitoba, S Canada
9 *X16* **Winnipeg Beach** Manitoba, S Canada
9 *W14* **Winnipeg, Lake** ◎ Manitoba, C Canada
9 *W15* **Winnipegosis** Manitoba, S Canada
9 *W15* **Winnipegosis, Lake** ◎ Manitoba, C Canada
19 *O8* **Winnipesaukee, Lake** ◎ New Hampshire, NE USA
22 *I6* **Winnsboro** Louisiana, S USA
21 *R12* **Winnsboro** South Carolina, SE USA
25 *W6* **Winnsboro** Texas, SW USA
29 *X10* **Winona** Minnesota, N USA
22 *L4* **Winona** Mississippi, S USA
27 *W7* **Winona** Missouri, C USA
25 *W7* **Winona** Texas, SW USA
18 *M7* **Winooski River** Vermont, NE USA
98 *P6* **Winschoten** Groningen, NE Netherlands
100 *J10* **Winsen** Niedersachsen, N Germany
36 *M11* **Winslow** Arizona, SW USA
19 *Q7* **Winslow** Maine, NE USA
18 *M12* **Winsted** Connecticut, NE USA
32 *F14* **Winston** Oregon, NW USA
21 *S9* **Winston Salem** North Carolina, SE USA
98 *N5* **Winsum** Groningen, NE Netherlands
Wintanceaster *see* Winchester
23 *W11* **Winter Garden** Florida, SE USA
10 *J16* **Winter Harbour** Vancouver Island, British Columbia, SW Canada
23 *W12* **Winter Haven** Florida, SE USA
23 *X11* **Winter Park** Florida, SE USA
25 *P8* **Winters** Texas, SW USA
29 *U15* **Winterset** Iowa, C USA
98 *O12* **Winterswijk** Gelderland, E Netherlands
108 *G6* **Winterthur** Zürich, NE Switzerland
29 *U9* **Winthrop** Minnesota, N USA
32 *J7* **Winthrop** Washington, NW USA
181 *V7* **Winton** Queensland, E Australia
185 *C24* **Winton** Southland, South Island, New Zealand
21 *X8* **Winton** North Carolina, SE USA
101 *K15* **Wipper** C Germany
101 *K14* **Wipper** C Germany
Wipper *see* Wieprza
182 *G6* **Wirraminna** South Australia
182 *F4* **Wirrida** South Australia
182 *F7* **Wirrulla** South Australia
Wirsitz *see* Wyrzysk
Wirz-See *see* Võrtsjärv
97 *O19* **Wisbech** E England, UK
Wisby *see* Visby
19 *Q8* **Wiscasset** Maine, NE USA
Wischau *see* Vyškov
30 *J5* **Wisconsin** ***off.*** State of Wisconsin, ***also known as*** Badger State. ◆ *state* N USA
30 *L8* **Wisconsin Dells** Wisconsin, N USA
30 *L8* **Wisconsin, Lake** ⊠ Wisconsin, N USA
30 *L7* **Wisconsin Rapids** Wisconsin, N USA
30 *L7* **Wisconsin River** Wisconsin, N USA
33 *P11* **Wisdom** Montana, NW USA
21 *P7* **Wise** Virginia, NE USA
39 *Q7* **Wiseman** Alaska, USA
96 *J12* **Wishaw** W Scotland, UK
29 *O6* **Wishek** North Dakota, N USA
32 *I11* **Wishram** Washington, NW USA
111 *J17* **Wisła** Śląskie, S Poland
110 *K11* **Wisła** ***Eng.*** Vistula, ***Ger.*** Weichsel. C Poland
Wiślany, Zalew *see* Vistula Lagoon
111 *M16* **Wisłoka** SE Poland
100 *L9* **Wismar** Mecklenburg-Vorpommern, N Germany
29 *R14* **Wisner** Nebraska, C USA
103 *V4* **Wissembourg** ***var.*** Weissenburg. Bas-Rhin, NE France
30 *J6* **Wissota, Lake** ⊠ Wisconsin, N USA
97 *O18* **Witham** E England, UK
97 *O17* **Withernsea** E England, UK
37 *Q13* **Withington, Mount** ▲ New Mexico, SW USA
23 *U8* **Withlacoochee River** Florida/Georgia, SE USA
110 *H11* **Witkowo** Wielkopolskie, C Poland
97 *M21* **Witney** S England, UK
101 *E15* **Witten** Nordrhein-Westfalen, W Germany
101 *N14* **Wittenberg** Sachsen-Anhalt, E Germany
30 *L6* **Wittenberg** Wisconsin, N USA
100 *L11* **Wittenberge** Brandenburg, N Germany
103 *U7* **Wittenheim** Haut-Rhin, NE France
180 *I7* **Wittenoom** Western Australia
Wittingau *see* Třeboň
100 *K12* **Wittingen** Niedersachsen, C Germany
101 *E18* **Wittlich** Rheinland-Pfalz, SW Germany
100 *F9* **Wittmund** Niedersachsen, NW Germany
100 *M10* **Wittstock** Brandenburg, NE Germany
186 *F6* **Witu Islands** *island group* E Papua New Guinea
110 *O7* **Wiżajny** Podlaskie, NE Poland
55 *W10* **W. J. van Blommesteinmeer** ⊠ E Suriname
110 *L11* **Wkra** ***Ger.*** Soldau. C Poland
110 *I6* **Władysławowo** Pomorskie, N Poland
Wlaschim *see* Vlašim
111 *E14* **Wleń** ***Ger.*** Lähn. Dolnośląskie, SW Poland
110 *J11* **Włocławek** ***Ger./Rus.*** Vlotslavsk. Kujawsko-pomorskie, C Poland
110 *P13* **Włodawa** ***Rus.*** Vlodava. Lubelskie, SE Poland
Włodzimierz *see* Volodymyr-Volyns'kyy
111 *K15* **Włoszczowa** Świętokrzyskie, C Poland
83 *C19* **Wlotzkasbaken** Erongo, W Namibia
15 *R12* **Woburn** Québec, SE Canada
19 *O11* **Woburn** Massachusetts, NE USA
Wocheiner Feistritz *see* Bohinjska Bistrica
Wöchma *see* Võhma
147 *S11* **Wodil** ***var.*** Vuadil'. Farg'ona Viloyati, E Uzbekistan
181 *V14* **Wodonga** Victoria, SE Australia
111 *I17* **Wodzisław Śląski** ***Ger.*** Loslau. Śląskie, S Poland
98 *I11* **Woerden** Zuid-Holland, C Netherlands
98 *I8* **Wognum** Noord-Holland, NW Netherlands
Wohlau *see* Wołów
108 *F7* **Wohlen** Aargau, NW Switzerland
195 *R2* **Wohlthat Mountains** ▲▲ Antarctica
Wojerecy *see* Hoyerswerda
Wōjjā *see* Wotje Atoll
Wojwodina *see* Vojvodina
171 *V15* **Wokam, Pulau** *island* Kepulauan Aru, E Indonesia
97 *N22* **Woking** SE England, UK
Woldenberg Neumark *see* Dobiegniew
188 *K15* **Woleai Atoll** *atoll* Caroline Islands, W Micronesia
Woleu *see* Uolo, Río
79 *E17* **Woleu-Ntem** ***off.*** Province du Woleu-Ntem, ***var.*** Le Woleu-Ntem. ◆ *province* W Gabon
Woleu-Ntem, Province du *see* Woleu-Ntem
32 *F15* **Wolf Creek** Oregon, NW USA
26 *K9* **Wolf Creek** Oklahoma/Texas, SW USA
37 *R7* **Wolf Creek Pass** *pass* Colorado, C USA
19 *O9* **Wolfeboro** New Hampshire, NE USA
25 *U5* **Wolfe City** Texas, SW USA
14 *L15* **Wolfe Island** *island* Ontario, SE Canada
101 *M14* **Wolfen** Sachsen-Anhalt, E Germany
100 *J13* **Wolfenbüttel** Niedersachsen, C Germany
109 *T4* **Wolfern** Oberösterreich, N Austria
109 *Q6* **Wolfgangsee** ***var.*** Abersee, St Wolfgangsee. ◎ N Austria
39 *P9* **Wolf Mountain** ▲ Alaska, USA
33 *X7* **Wolf Point** Montana, NW USA
22 *L8* **Wolf River** Mississippi, S USA
30 *M7* **Wolf River** Wisconsin, N USA
109 *U9* **Wolfsberg** Kärnten, SE Austria
100 *K12* **Wolfsburg** Niedersachsen, N Germany
57 *B17* **Wolf, Volcán** Galapagos Islands, Ecuador, E Pacific Ocean
100 *O8* **Wolgast** Mecklenburg-Vorpommern, NE Germany
108 *F8* **Wolhusen** Luzern, W Switzerland
110 *D8* **Wolin** ***Ger.*** Wollin. Zachodnio-pomorskie, NW Poland
109 *Y3* **Wolkersdorf** Niederösterreich, NE Austria
Wołkowysk *see* Vawkavysk
Wöllan *see* Velenje
8 *J6* **Wollaston, Cape** *headland* Victoria Island, Northwest Territories, NW Canada
63 *J25* **Wollaston, Isla** *island* S Chile
9 *U11* **Wollaston Lake** Saskatchewan, C Canada
9 *T10* **Wollaston Lake** ◎ Saskatchewan, C Canada
8 *J6* **Wollaston Peninsula** *peninsula* Victoria Island, Northwest Territories/Nunavut NW Canada
Wollin *see* Wolin
183 *S9* **Wollongong** New South Wales, SE Australia
Wolmar *see* Valmiera
100 *L13* **Wolmirstedt** Sachsen-Anhalt, C Germany
110 *M11* **Wołomin** Mazowieckie, C Poland
110 *G13* **Wołów** ***Ger.*** Wohlau. Dolnośląskie, SW Poland
Wołożyn *see* Valozhyn
14 *G11* **Wolseley Bay** Ontario, S Canada
29 *P10* **Wolsey** South Dakota, N USA
110 *F12* **Wolsztyn** Wielkopolskie, C Poland
98 *M7* **Wolvega** ***Fris.*** Wolvegea. Friesland, N Netherlands
Wolvegea *see* Wolvega
97 *K19* **Wolverhampton** C England, UK
Wolverine State *see* Michigan
99 *G18* **Wolvertem** Vlaams Brabant, C Belgium
99 *H16* **Wommelgem** Antwerpen, N Belgium
186 *D7* **Wonenara** ***var.*** Wonerara. Eastern Highlands, C Papua New Guinea
Wonerara *see* Wonenara
Wongalara Lake *see* Wongalarroo Lake
183 *N6* **Wongalarroo Lake** ***var.*** Wongalara Lake. *seasonal lake* New South Wales, SE Australia
163 *Y15* **Wŏnju** ***Jap.*** Genshū. N South Korea
10 *M12* **Wonowon** British Columbia, W Canada
163 *X13* **Wŏnsan** SE North Korea
183 *O13* **Wonthaggi** Victoria, SE Australia
23 *N2* **Woodall Mountain** ▲ Mississippi, S USA
23 *W7* **Woodbine** Georgia, SE USA
29 *S14* **Woodbine** Iowa, C USA
18 *J17* **Woodbine** New Jersey, NE USA
21 *W4* **Woodbridge** Virginia, NE USA
183 *V4* **Woodburn** New South Wales, SE Australia
32 *G11* **Woodburn** Oregon, NW USA
20 *K9* **Woodbury** Tennessee, S USA
183 *V5* **Wooded Bluff** *headland* New South Wales, SE Australia
183 *V3* **Woodenbong** New South Wales, SE Australia
35 *R11* **Woodlake** California, W USA
35 *N7* **Woodland** California, W USA
19 *T5* **Woodland** Maine, NE USA
32 *G10* **Woodland** Washington, NW USA
37 *T5* **Woodland Park** Colorado, C USA
186 *I9* **Woodlark Island** ***var.*** Murua Island. *island* SE Papua New Guinea
Woodle Island *see* Kuria
9 *T17* **Wood Mountain** ▲▲ Saskatchewan, S Canada
30 *K15* **Wood River** Illinois, N USA
29 *P16* **Wood River** Nebraska, C USA
39 *R9* **Wood River** Alaska, USA
39 *O13* **Wood River Lakes** ◎ Alaska, USA
182 *C1* **Woodroffe, Mount** ▲ South Australia
21 *P11* **Woodruff** South Carolina, SE USA
30 *K4* **Woodruff** Wisconsin, N USA
25 *T14* **Woodsboro** Texas, SW USA
31 *U13* **Woodsfield** Ohio, N USA
181 *P4* **Woods, Lake** ◎ Northern Territory, N Australia
9 *Z16* **Woods, Lake of the** ***Fr.*** Lac des Bois. ◎ Canada/USA
25 *Q6* **Woodson** Texas, SW USA
13 *N14* **Woodstock** New Brunswick, SE Canada
14 *F16* **Woodstock** Ontario, S Canada
30 *M10* **Woodstock** Illinois, N USA
18 *M9* **Woodstock** Vermont, NE USA
21 *U4* **Woodstock** Virginia, NE USA
19 *N8* **Woodsville** New Hampshire, NE USA
184 *M12* **Woodville** Manawatu-Wanganui, North Island, New Zealand
22 *J7* **Woodville** Mississippi, S USA
25 *X9* **Woodville** Texas, SW USA
26 *K9* **Woodward** Oklahoma, C USA
29 *O5* **Woodworth** North Dakota, N USA
171 *W12* **Wool** Papua, E Indonesia
183 *V5* **Woolgoolga** New South Wales, E Australia
182 *H6* **Woomera** South Australia
19 *O12* **Woonsocket** Rhode Island, NE USA
29 *P10* **Woonsocket** South Dakota, N USA
31 *T12* **Wooster** Ohio, N USA
80 *L12* **Woqooyi Galbeed** ***off.*** Gobolka Woqooyi Galbeed. ◆ *region* NW Somalia
Woqooyi Galbeed, Gobolka *see* Woqooyi Galbeed
108 *E8* **Worb** Bern, C Switzerland
83 *F26* **Worcester** Western Cape, SW South Africa
97 *L20* **Worcester** ***hist.*** Wigorna Ceaster. W England, UK
19 *N11* **Worcester** Massachusetts, NE USA
97 *L20* **Worcestershire** *cultural region* C England, UK
32 *H16* **Worden** Oregon, NW USA
109 *O6* **Wörgl** Tirol, W Austria
171 *V15* **Workai, Pulau** *island* Kepulauan Aru, E Indonesia
97 *J15* **Workington** NW England, UK
98 *K7* **Workum** Friesland, N Netherlands
33 *V13* **Worland** Wyoming, C USA
Wormatia *see* Worms
99 *N25* **Wormeldange** Grevenmacher, E Luxembourg
98 *I9* **Wormer** Noord-Holland, C Netherlands
101 *G19* **Worms** ***anc.*** Augusta Vangionum, Borbetomagus, Wormatia. Rheinland-Pfalz, SW Germany
Worms *see* Vormsi
101 *K21* **Wörnitz** S Germany
25 *U8* **Wortham** Texas, SW USA
101 *G21* **Wörth am Rhein** Rheinland-Pfalz, SW Germany
109 *S9* **Wörther See** ◎ S Austria
97 *O23* **Worthing** SE England, UK
29 *S11* **Worthington** Minnesota, N USA
31 *S13* **Worthington** Ohio, N USA
35 *W8* **Worthington Peak** ▲ Nevada, W USA
171 *Y13* **Wosi** Papua, E Indonesia
171 *V13* **Wosimi** Papua, E Indonesia
189 *R5* **Wotho Atoll** ***var.*** Wōtto. *atoll* Ralik Chain, W Marshall Islands
189 *V5* **Wotje Atoll** ***var.*** Wōjjā. *atoll* Ratak Chain, E Marshall Islands
Wotoe *see* Wotu
Wottawa *see* Otava
Wōtto *see* Wotho Atoll
171 *O13* **Wotu** ***prev.*** Wotoe. Sulawesi, C Indonesia
98 *K11* **Woudenberg** Utrecht, C Netherlands
98 *I13* **Woudrichem** Noord-Brabant, S Netherlands
43 *N8* **Wounta** ***var.*** Huaunta. Región Autónoma Atlántico Norte, NE Nicaragua
171 *P14* **Wowoni, Pulau** *island* C Indonesia
81 *J17* **Woyamdero Plain** *plain* E Kenya
Woyens *see* Vojens
Wozrojdeniye Oroli *see* Vozrozhdeniya, Ostrov
Wrangel Island *see* Vrangelya, Ostrov
39 *Y13* **Wrangell** Wrangell Island, Alaska, USA
38 *C15* **Wrangell, Cape** *headland* Attu Island, Alaska, USA
39 *S11* **Wrangell, Mount** ▲ Alaska, USA
39 *T11* **Wrangell Mountains** ▲▲ Alaska, USA
197 *S7* **Wrangel Plain** *undersea feature* Arctic Ocean
96 *H6* **Wrath, Cape** *headland* N Scotland, UK
37 *W3* **Wray** Colorado, C USA
44 *K13* **Wreck Point** *headland* C Jamaica
83 *C23* **Wreck Point** *headland* W South Africa
23 *V4* **Wrens** Georgia, SE USA
97 *K18* **Wrexham** NE Wales, UK
27 *R13* **Wright City** Oklahoma, C USA
194 *J12* **Wright Island** *island* Antarctica
13 *N9* **Wright, Mont** ▲ Québec, E Canada
25 *X5* **Wright Patman Lake** ⊠ Texas, SW USA
36 *M16* **Wrightson, Mount** ▲ Arizona, SW USA
23 *U5* **Wrightsville** Georgia, SE USA
21 *W12* **Wrightsville Beach** North Carolina, SE USA
35 *T15* **Wrightwood** California, W USA
8 *H9* **Wrigley** Northwest Territories, W Canada
111 *G14* **Wrocław** ***Eng./Ger.*** Breslau. Dolnośląskie, SW Poland
110 *F10* **Wronki** ***Ger.*** Fronicken. Wielkopolskie, C Poland
110 *H11* **Września** Wielkopolskie, C Poland
110 *F12* **Wschowa** Lubuskie, W Poland
Wsetin *see* Vsetín
161 *O5* **Wu'an** Hebei, E China
180 *I12* **Wubin** Western Australia
163 *W9* **Wuchang** Heilongjiang, NE China
Wuchang *see* Wuhan
Wu-chou/Wuchow *see* Wuzhou
160 *M16* **Wuchuan** ***var.*** Meilu. Guangdong, S China
160 *K10* **Wuchuan** ***var.*** Duru, Gelaozu Miaozu Zhizhixian. Guizhou, S China
163 *O13* **Wuchuan** Nei Mongol Zizhiqu, N China
163 *V6* **Wudalianchi** ***var.*** Qingshan; ***prev.*** Dedu. Heilongjiang, NE China
159 *O11* **Wudaoliang** Qinghai, C China
141 *Q13* **Wuday'ah** *spring/well* S Saudi Arabia
77 *V13* **Wudil** Kano, N Nigeria
160 *G12* **Wuding** ***var.*** Jincheng. Yunnan, SW China
160 *L4* **Wuding He** C China
182 *G8* **Wudinna** South Australia
157 *P10* **Wudu** Gansu, C China
Wudu *see* Longnan
160 *L9* **Wufeng** Hubei, C China
161 *O11* **Wugong Shan** ▲▲ S China
157 *P7* **Wuhai** ***var.*** Haibowan. Nei Mongol Zizhiqu, N China
161 *O9* **Wuhan** ***var.*** Han-kou, Han-k'ou, Hanyang, Wuchang, Wu-han; ***prev.*** Hankow. *province capital* Hubei, C China
Wu-han *see* Wuhan
161 *Q7* **Wuhe** Anhui, E China
Wuhsien *see* Suzhou
Wuhsi/Wu-his *see* Wuxi
161 *Q8* **Wuhu** ***var.*** Wu-na-mu. Anhui, E China
Wūjae *see* Ujae Atoll
160 *K11* **Wu Jiang** C China
Wujlān *see* Ujelang Atoll
77 *W15* **Wukari** Taraba, E Nigeria
160 *H11* **Wulian Feng** ▲▲ SW China
160 *F13* **Wuliang Shan** ▲▲ SW China
160 *K11* **Wuling Shan** ▲▲ S China
109 *Y5* **Wulka** E Austria
Wulkan *see* Vulcan
109 *T3* **Wullowitz** Oberösterreich, N Austria
Wu-lu-k'o-mu-shi/Wu-lu-mu-ch'i *see* Ürümqi
79 *D14* **Wum** Nord-Ouest, NE Cameroon
160 *H12* **Wumeng Shan** ▲▲ SW China
160 *K14* **Wuming** Guangxi Zhuangzu Zizhiqu, S China
100 *I10* **Wümme** NW Germany
Wu-na-mu *see* Wuhu
171 *X13* **Wunen** Papua, E Indonesia
12 *D9* **Wunnummin Lake** ◎ Ontario, C Canada
80 *D13* **Wun Rog** Warab, S Sudan
101 *M18* **Wunsiedel** Bayern, E Germany
100 *I12* **Wunstorf** Niedersachsen, NW Germany
166 *M3* **Wuntho** Sagaing, N Myanmar (Burma)
101 *F15* **Wupper** W Germany
101 *E15* **Wuppertal** ***prev.*** Barmen-Elberfeld. Nordrhein-Westfalen, W Germany
160 *K5* **Wuqi** Shaanxi, C China
161 *P4* **Wuqiao** ***var.*** Sangyuan. Hebei, E China
101 *L23* **Würm** SE Germany
77 *T12* **Wurno** Sokoto, NW Nigeria
101 *I19* **Würzburg** Bayern, SW Germany
101 *N15* **Wurzen** Sachsen, E Germany
160 *L9* **Wu Shan** ▲▲ C China
158 *G7* **Wushi** ***var.*** Uqturpan. Xinjiang Uygur Zizhiqu, NW China
Wusih *see* Wuxi
65 *N18* **Wüst Seamount** *undersea feature* S Atlantic Ocean
Wusuli Jiang/Wusuri *see* Ussuri
161 *N3* **Wutai Shan** ***var.*** Beitai Ding. ▲ C China
160 *H10* **Wutongqiao** Sichuan, C China
159 *P6* **Wutongwozi Quan** *spring* NW China
99 *H15* **Wuustwezel** Antwerpen, N Belgium
186 *B4* **Wuvulu Island** *island* NW Papua New Guinea
159 *U9* **Wuwei** ***var.*** Liangzhou. Gansu, C China
161 *R8* **Wuxi** ***var.*** Wuhsi, Wu-hsi, Wusih. Jiangsu, E China
Wuxing *see* Huzhou
160 *L14* **Wuxuan** Guangxi Zhuangzu Zizhiqu, S China
Wuyang *see* Zhenyuan
160 *K11* **Wuyang He** S China
163 *X6* **Wuyiling** Heilongjiang, NE China
161 *Q11* **Wuyishan** ***prev.*** Chong'an. Fujian, SE China
157 *T12* **Wuyi Shan** ▲▲ SE China
162 *M13* **Wuyuan** Nei Mongol Zizhiqu, N China
160 *L17* **Wuzhishan** ***prev.*** Tongshi. Hainan, S China
160 *L17* **Wuzhi Shan** ▲ S China
159 *W8* **Wuzhong** Ningxia, N China
160 *M14* **Wuzhou** ***var.*** Wu-chou, Wuchow. Guangxi Zhuangzu Zizhiqu, S China
18 *H12* **Wyalusing** Pennsylvania, NE USA
182 *M10* **Wycheproof** Victoria, SE Australia
97 *K21* **Wye** ***Wel.*** Gwy. England/Wales, UK
Wyłkowyszki *see* Vilkaviškis
97 *P19* **Wymondham** E England, UK
29 *R17* **Wymore** Nebraska, C USA
182 *E5* **Wynbring** South Australia
181 *N3* **Wyndham** Western Australia
29 *R6* **Wyndmere** North Dakota, N USA
27 *X11* **Wynne** Arkansas, C USA
27 *N12* **Wynnewood** Oklahoma, C USA
183 *O15* **Wynyard** Tasmania, SE Australia
9 *U15* **Wynyard** Saskatchewan, S Canada
33 *V11* **Wyola** Montana, NW USA
182 *A4* **Wyola Lake** *salt lake* South Australia
31 *P9* **Wyoming** Michigan, N USA
33 *V14* **Wyoming** ***off.*** State of Wyoming, ***also known as*** Equality State. ◆ *state* C USA
33 *S15* **Wyoming Range** ▲▲ Wyoming, C USA
183 *T8* **Wyong** New South Wales, SE Australia
110 *G9* **Wyrzysk** ***Ger.*** Wirsitz. Wielkopolskie, C Poland
Wysg *see* Usk
110 *O10* **Wysokie Mazowieckie** Łomża, E Poland
110 *M11* **Wyszków** ***Ger.*** Probstberg. Mazowieckie, NE Poland
110 *L11* **Wyszogród** Mazowieckie, C Poland
21 *R7* **Wytheville** Virginia, NE USA
111 *L15* **Wyżyna Małopolska** *plateau*

X

80 *Q12* **Xaafuun** ***It.*** Hafun. Bari, NE Somalia
80 *Q12* **Xaafuun, Raas** ***var.*** Ras Hafun. *cape* NE Somalia
Xàbia *see* Jávea
42 *C4* **Xaclbal, Río** ***var.*** Xalbal. Guatemala/Mexico
137 *Y10* **Xaçmaz** ***Rus.*** Khachmas. N Azerbaijan
80 *O12* **Xadeed** ***var.*** Haded. *physical region* N Somalia
159 *O14* **Xagquka** Xizang Zizhiqu, W China
167 *Q6* **Xai** ***var.*** Muang Xay, Muong Sai. Oudômxai, N Laos
158 *F10* **Xaidulla** Xinjiang Uygur Zizhiqu, W China
167 *Q7* **Xaignabouli** ***prev*** Muang Xaignabouri, ***Fr.*** Sayaboury. Xaignabouli, N Laos
167 *R7* **Xai Lai Leng, Phou** ▲ Laos/Vietnam
158 *L15* **Xainza** Xizang Zizhiqu, W China
158 *L16* **Xaitongmoin** Xizang Zizhiqu, W China
83 *M20* **Xai-Xai** ***prev.*** João Belo, Vila de João Belo. Gaza, S Mozambique
Xalbal *see* Xaclbal, Río
80 *P13* **Xalin** Sool, N Somalia
146 *H7* **Xalqobod** ***Rus.*** Khalkabad. Qoraqalpog'iston Respublikasi, W Uzbekistan
167 *R6* **Xam Nua** ***var.*** Sam Neua. Houaphan, N Laos
82 *D11* **Xá-Muteba** ***Port.*** Cinco de Outubro. Lunda Norte, NE Angola
Xangda *see* Nangqên
83 *C16* **Xangongo** ***Port.*** Rocadas. Cunene, SW Angola
137 *W12* **Xankändi** ***Rus.*** Khankendi; ***prev.*** Stepanakert. SW Azerbaijan
137 *V11* **Xanlar** ***Rus.*** Khanlar. NW Azerbaijan
114 *J13* **Xánthi** Anatolikí Makedonía kai Thráki, NE Greece
60 *H13* **Xanxerê** Santa Catarina, S Brazil
81 *O15* **Xarardheere** Mudug, E Somalia
137 *Z11* **Xärä Zirä Adası** ***Rus.*** Ostrov Bulla. *Island* E Azerbaijan
162 *K13* **Xar Burd** ***prev.*** Bayan Nuru. Nei Mongol Zizhiqu, N China
163 *T11* **Xar Moron** NE China
Xarra *see* Xarrë
113 *L23* **Xarrë** ***var.*** Xarra. Vlorë, S Albania
82 *D12* **Xassengue** Lunda Sul, NW Angola
105 *S11* **Xátiva** ***var.*** Jativa; ***anc.*** Setabis. País Valenciano, E Spain
Xauen *see* Chefchaouen
60 *K10* **Xavantes, Represa de** ***var.*** Represa de Chavantes. ⊠ S Brazil
158 *I7* **Xayar** Xinjiang Uygur Zizhiqu, W China
Xäzär Dänizi *see* Caspian Sea
167 *S8* **Xé Bangfai** C Laos
167 *T9* **Xé Banghiang** ***var.*** Bang Hieng. S Laos
Xêgar *see* Tingri
31 *R14* **Xenia** Ohio, N USA
Xeres *see* Jeréz de la Frontera
115 *E15* **Xeriás** C Greece
115 *G17* **Xeró** ▲ Évvoia, C Greece
83 *H18* **Xhumo** Central, C Botswana
161 *N15* **Xiachuan Dao** *island* S China
Xiacun *see* Rushan
Xiaguan *see* Dali
159 *U11* **Xiahe** ***var.*** Labrang. Gansu, C China
161 *Q13* **Xiamen** ***var.*** Hsia-men; ***prev.*** Amoy. Fujian, SE China

◆ Country
● Country Capital
◇ Dependent Territory
○ Dependent Territory Capital
◆ Administrative Regions
✈ International Airport
▲ Mountain
▲▲ Mountain Range
Volcano
River
◎ Lake
⊠ Reservoir

160 L6 **Xi'an** var. Changan, Sian, Signan, Siking, Singan, Xian. province capital Shaanxi, C China
160 L10 **Xianfeng** var. Gaoleshan. Hubei, C China
Xiang see Hunan
161 N7 **Xiangcheng** Henan, C China
160 F10 **Xiangcheng** var. Sampê, Tib. Qagchêng. Sichuan, C China
160 M8 **Xiangfan** var. Xiangyang. Hubei, C China
Xianggang see Hong Kong
161 N10 **Xiang Jiang** ≈ S China
Xiangkhoang see Pèk
167 Q7 **Xiangkhoang, Plateau de** var. Plain of Jars. plateau N Laos
161 N11 **Xiangtan** var. Hsiang-t'an, Siangtan. Hunan, S China
161 N11 **Xiangxiang** Hunan, S China
Xiangyang see Xiangfan
161 S10 **Xianju** Zhejiang, SE China
Xianshui see Dawu
160 F8 **Xianshui He** ≈ C China
161 N9 **Xiantao** var. Mianyang. Hubei, C China
161 R10 **Xianxia Ling** ▲▲ SE China
160 K6 **Xianyang** Shaanxi, C China
158 L5 **Xiaocaohu** Xinjiang Uygur Zizhiqu, W China
161 O9 **Xiaogan** Hubei, C China
Xiaogang see Dongxiang
163 W6 **Xiao Hinggan Ling** Eng. Lesser Khingan Range. ▲▲ NE China
160 M6 **Xiao Shan** ▲▲ C China
160 M12 **Xiao Shui** ≈ S China
Xiaoxi see Pinghe
161 P6 **Xiaoxian** var. Longcheng, Xiao Xian. Anhui, E China
Xiao Xian see Xiaoxian
160 G11 **Xichang** Sichuan, C China
41 P11 **Xicoténcatl** Tamaulipas, C Mexico
Xieng Khouang see Pèk
Xieng Ngeun see Muong Xiang Ngeun
160 J11 **Xifeng** var. Yongjing. Guizhou, S China
Xifeng see Qingyang
Xigang see Helan
158 L16 **Xigazê** var. Jih-k'a-tse, Shigatse, Xigaze. Xizang Zizhiqu, W China
159 W11 **Xihe** var. Hanyuan. Gansu, C China
160 I8 **Xi He** ≈ C China
Xihuachi see Heshui
159 W10 **Xiji** Ningxia, N China
160 M14 **Xi Jiang** var. Hsi Chiang, Eng. West River. ≈ S China
159 Q7 **Xijian Quan** spring NW China
160 K15 **Xijin Shuiku** ▣ S China
Xilaganí see Xylaganí
Xiligou see Ulan
160 I13 **Xilin** var. Bada. Guangxi Zhuangzu Zizhiqu, S China
163 Q10 **Xilinhot** var. Silinhot. Nei Mongol Zizhiqu, N China
Xilinji see Mohe
Xilokastro see Xylókastro
Xin see Xinjiang Uygur Zizhiqu
161 R10 **Xin'anjiang Shuiku** var. Qiandao Hu. ▣ SE China
Xin'anzhen see Xinyi
Xin Barag Youqi see Altan Emel
Xin Barag Zuoqi see Amgalang
163 W12 **Xinbin** var. Xinbin Manzu Zizhixian. Liaoning, NE China
Xinbin Manzu Zizhixian see Xinbin
161 O7 **Xincai** Henan, C China
Xincheng see Zhaojue
Xindu see Luhuo
161 O13 **Xinfeng** var. Jiading. Jiangxi, S China
161 O14 **Xinfengjiang Shuiku** ▣ S China
Xing'an see Ankang
Xingba see Lhünzê
163 T13 **Xingcheng** Liaoning, NE China
Xingcheng see Xingning
82 E11 **Xinge** Lunda Norte, NE Angola
161 P12 **Xingguo** var. Lianjiang. Jiangxi, S China
159 S11 **Xinghai** var. Ziketan. Qinghai, C China
161 R7 **Xinghua** Jiangsu, E China
Xingkai Hu see Khanka, Lake
161 P13 **Xingning** var. Xingcheng. Guangdong, S China
160 I13 **Xingren** Guizhou, S China
161 O4 **Xingtai** Hebei, E China
59 J14 **Xingu, Rio** ≈ C Brazil
159 P6 **Xingxingxia** Xinjiang Uygur Zizhiqu, NW China
160 I13 **Xingyi** Guizhou, S China
158 I6 **Xinhe** var. Toksu. Xinjiang Uygur Zizhiqu, NW China
163 Q10 **Xin Hot** var. Abag Qi. Nei Mongol Zizhiqu, N China
Xinhua see Funing
163 T12 **Xinhui** var. Aohan Qi. Nei Mongol Zizhiqu, N China
159 T10 **Xining** var. Hsining, Hsi-ning, Sining. province capital Qinghai, C China
161 O4 **Xinji** prev. Shulu. Hebei, E China
161 P10 **Xinjian** Jiangxi, S China
Xinjiang see Xinjiang Uygur Zizhiqu
162 D8 **Xinjiang Uygur Zizhiqu** var. Sinkiang, Sinkiang Uighur Autonomous Region, Xin, Xinjiang. ◈ autonomous region NW China
160 H9 **Xinjin** var. Meixing, Tib. Zainlha. Sichuan, C China
Xinjin see Pulandian
Xinjing see Jingxi
163 U12 **Xinmin** Liaoning, NE China
160 M12 **Xinning** var. Jinshi. Hunan, S China
Xinpu see Lianyungang
Xinshan see Anyuan
161 P5 **Xintai** Shandong, E China
Xinwen see Suncun
Xin Xian see Xinzhou
161 N6 **Xinxiang** Henan, C China
161 O8 **Xinyang** var. Hsin-yang, Sinyang. Henan, C China
161 Q6 **Xinyi** var. Xin'anzhen. Jiangsu, E China
161 Q6 **Xinyi He** ≈ E China
161 O11 **Xinyu** Jiangxi, S China
158 I5 **Xinyuan** var. Künes. Xinjiang Uygur Zizhiqu, NW China
Xinyuan see Tianjun
162 M13 **Xinzhao Shan** ▲ N China
161 N3 **Xinzhou** var. Xin Xian. Shanxi, C China
Xinzhou see Longlin
104 H4 **Xinzo de Limia** Galicia, NW Spain
Xions see Książ Wielkopolski
161 O7 **Xiping** Henan, C China
Xiping see Songyang
159 T11 **Xiqing Shan** ▲▲ C China
59 N16 **Xique-Xique** Bahia, E Brazil
Xireg see Ulan
115 E14 **Xirovoúni** ▲ N Greece
162 M13 **Xishanzui** var. Urad Qianqi. Nei Mongol Zizhiqu, N China
160 J11 **Xishui** Guizhou, S China
Xi Ujimqin Qi see Bayan Ul
160 K11 **Xiushan** var. Zhonghe. Chongqing Shi, C China
Xiushan see Tonghai
161 O10 **Xiu Shui** ≈ S China
Xiuyan see Qingjian
146 H9 **Xiva** Rus. Khiva, Khiwa. Xorazm Viloyati, W Uzbekistan
158 J16 **Xixabangma Feng** ▲ W China
160 M7 **Xixia** Henan, C China
Xixón see Gijón
Xixona see Jijona
Xizang see Xizang Zizhiqu
Xizang Gaoyuan see Qingzang Gaoyuan
160 E9 **Xizang Zizhiqu** var. Thibet, Tibetan Autonomous Region, Xizang, Eng. Tibet. ◈ autonomous region W China
163 U14 **Xizhong Dao** island N China
Xoi see Qüxü
146 H8 **Xo'jayli** Rus. Khodzheyli. Qoraqalpog'iston Respublikasi, W Uzbekistan
Xolotlán see Managua, Lago de
147 I9 **Xonqa** var. Khonqa, Rus. Khanka. Xorazm Viloyati, W Uzbekistan
146 H9 **Xorazm Viloyati** Rus. Khorezmskaya Oblast'. ◈ province W Uzbekistan
159 N9 **Xorkol** Xinjiang Uygur Zizhiqu, NW China
147 P11 **Xovos** var. Ursat'yevskaya, Rus. Khavast. Sirdaryo Viloyati, E Uzbekistan
41 X14 **Xpujil** Quintana Roo, E Mexico
161 Q8 **Xuancheng** var. Xuanzhou. Anhui, E China
167 T9 **Xuân Đuc** Quang Binh, C Vietnam
160 L9 **Xuan'en** var. Zhushan. Hubei, C China
160 K8 **Xuanhan** Sichuan, C China
161 O2 **Xuanhua** Hebei, E China
161 P4 **Xuanhui He** ≈ E China
Xuanzhou see Xuancheng
161 N7 **Xuchang** Henan, C China
137 X10 **Xudat** Rus. Khudat. NE Azerbaijan
81 M16 **Xuddur** var. Hudur, It. Oddur. Bakool, SW Somalia
80 O13 **Xudun** Sool, N Somalia
160 L11 **Xuefeng Shan** ▲▲ S China
Xulun Hobot Qagan see Qagan Nur
42 F2 **Xunantunich** ruins Cayo, W Belize
163 W6 **Xun He** ≈ NE China
160 L7 **Xun He** ≈ C China
160 L14 **Xun Jiang** ≈ S China
163 W5 **Xunke** var. Bianjiang; prev. Qike. Heilongjiang, NE China
161 P13 **Xunwu** var. Changning. Jiangxi, S China
161 O3 **Xushui** Hebei, E China
160 L16 **Xuwen** Guangdong, S China
160 I11 **Xuyong** var. Yongning. Sichuan, C China
161 P6 **Xuzhou** var. Hsu-chou, Suchow, Tongshan; prev. T'ung-shan. Jiangsu, E China
114 K13 **Xylaganí** var. Xilaganí. Anatolikí Makedonía kai Thráki, NE Greece
115 F19 **Xylókastro** var. Xilokastro. Pelopónnisos, S Greece

Y

160 H9 **Ya'an** var. Yaan. Sichuan, C China
182 L10 **Yaapeet** Victoria, SE Australia
79 D15 **Yabassi** Littoral, W Cameroon
81 J15 **Yabēlo** Oromo, C Ethiopia
114 H9 **Yablanitsa** Lovech Oblast, N Bulgaria
43 N7 **Yablis** Región Autónoma Atlántico Norte, NE Nicaragua
123 O14 **Yablonovyy Khrebet** ▲▲ S Russian Federation
162 J14 **Yabrai Shan** ▲▲ NE China
45 U6 **Yabucoa** E Puerto Rico
160 J11 **Yachi He** ≈ S China
32 H10 **Yacolt** Washington, NW USA
54 M10 **Yacuaray** Amazonas, S Venezuela
57 M22 **Yacuiba** Tarija, S Bolivia
57 K16 **Yacuma, Río** ≈ C Bolivia
155 H16 **Yādgīr** Karnātaka, C India
21 R8 **Yadkin River** ≈ North Carolina, SE USA
21 R9 **Yadkinville** North Carolina, SE USA
127 P3 **Yadrin** Chavash Respubliki, W Russian Federation
Yaegama-shotō see Yaeyama-shotō
Yaeme-saki see Paimi-saki
165 O16 **Yaeyama-shotō** var. Yaegama-shotō. island group SW Japan
75 O8 **Yafran** NW Libya
165 S2 **Yagashiri-tō** island NE Japan
65 H21 **Yaghan Basin** undersea feature SE Pacific Ocean
123 S9 **Yagodnoye** Magadanskaya Oblast', E Russian Federation
Yagotin see Yahotyn
78 G12 **Yagoua** Extrême-Nord, NE Cameroon
159 Q11 **Yagradagzê Shan** ▲ C China
Yaguachi see Yaguachi Nuevo
56 B7 **Yaguachi Nuevo** var. Yaguachi. Guayas, W Ecuador
Yaguarón, Río see Jaguarão, Rio
117 Q11 **Yahorlyts'kyy Lyman** bay S Ukraine
117 Q5 **Yahotyn** Rus. Yagotin. Kyyivs'ka Oblast', N Ukraine
40 L12 **Yahualica** Jalisco, SW Mexico
79 L17 **Yahuma** Orientale, N Dem. Rep. Congo
136 K15 **Yahyalı** Kayseri, C Turkey
167 N15 **Yai, Khao** ▲ SW Thailand
164 M14 **Yaizu** Shizuoka, Honshū, S Japan
160 G9 **Yajiang** var. Hekou, Tib. Nyagquka. Sichuan, C China
119 O14 **Yakawlyevichi** Rus. Yakovlevichi. Vitsyebskaya Voblasts', NE Belarus
163 S6 **Yakeshi** Nei Mongol Zizhiqu, N China
32 I9 **Yakima** Washington, NW USA
32 J10 **Yakima River** ≈ Washington, NW USA
114 G7 **Yakimovo** Montana, NW Bulgaria
Yakkabag see Yakkabogʻ
147 N12 **Yakkabogʻ** Rus. Yakkabag. Qashqadaryo Viloyati, S Uzbekistan
148 L12 **Yakmach** Baluchistān, SW Pakistan
77 O12 **Yako** W Burkina
39 W13 **Yakobi Island** island Alexander Archipelago, Alaska, USA
79 K16 **Yakoma** Equateur, N Dem. Rep. Congo
114 H11 **Yakoruda** Blagoevgrad, SW Bulgaria
Yakovlevichi see Yakawlyevichi
127 T2 **Yakshur-Bod'ya** Udmurtskaya Respublika, NW Russian Federation
165 Q5 **Yakumo** Hokkaidō, NE Japan
164 B17 **Yaku-shima** island Nansei-shotō, SW Japan
39 V12 **Yakutat** Alaska, USA
39 U12 **Yakutat Bay** inlet Alaska, USA
Yakutia/Yakutiya, Respublika see Sakha (Yakutiya), Respublika
123 Q10 **Yakutsk** Respublika Sakha (Yakutiya), NE Russian Federation
167 O17 **Yala** Yala, SW Thailand
182 D6 **Yalata** South Australia
31 S9 **Yale** Michigan, N USA
180 I11 **Yalgoo** Western Australia
114 O12 **Yalıköy** İstanbul, NW Turkey
79 L14 **Yalinga** Haute-Kotto, C Central African Republic
119 M17 **Yalizava** Rus. Yelizovo. Mahilyowskaya Voblasts', E Belarus
44 L13 **Yallahs Hill** ▲ E Jamaica
22 L3 **Yalobusha River** ≈ Mississippi, S USA
79 H15 **Yaloké** Ombella-Mpoko, W Central African Republic
160 E7 **Yalong Jiang** ≈ C China
136 E11 **Yalova** Yalova, NW Turkey
136 E11 **Yalova** ◈ province NW Turkey
Yaloveny see Ialoveni
Yalpug see Ialpug
Yalpug, Ozero see Yalpuh, Ozero
117 N12 **Yalpuh, Ozero** Rus. Ozero Yalpug. ◎ SW Ukraine
117 T14 **Yalta** Respublika Krym, S Ukraine
163 W12 **Yalu** Chin. Yalu Jiang, Jap. Oryokko, Kor. Amnok-kang. ≈ China/North Korea
Yalu Jiang see Yalu
136 F14 **Yalvaç** Isparta, SW Turkey
165 R9 **Yamada** Iwate, Honshū, C Japan
165 D14 **Yamaga** Kumamoto, Kyūshū, SW Japan
165 P10 **Yamagata** Yamagata, Honshū, C Japan
165 P9 **Yamagata** off. Yamagata-ken. ◈ prefecture Honshū, C Japan
Yamagata-ken see Yamagata
164 C16 **Yamagawa** Kagoshima, Kyūshū, SW Japan
164 E13 **Yamaguchi** var. Yamaguti. Yamaguchi, Honshū, SW Japan
164 E13 **Yamaguchi** off. Yamaguchi-ken, var. Yamaguti. ◈ prefecture Honshū, SW Japan
Yamaguchi-ken see Yamaguchi
Yamaguti see Yamaguchi
125 X5 **Yamalo-Nenetskiy Avtonomnyy Okrug** ◈ autonomous district N Russian Federation
122 J7 **Yamal, Poluostrov** peninsula N Russian Federation
165 N13 **Yamanashi** off. Yamanashi-ken, var. Yamanasi. ◈ prefecture Honshū, S Japan
Yamanashi-ken see Yamanashi
Yamanasi see Yamanashi
Yamanīyah, Al Jumhūrīyah al see Yemen
127 W5 **Yamantau** ▲ W Russian Federation
Yamasaki see Yamazaki
15 P12 **Yamaska** ≈ Québec, SE Canada
192 G4 **Yamato Ridge** undersea feature S Sea of Japan
164 I13 **Yamazaki** var. Yamasaki. Hyōgo, Honshū, SW Japan
183 V5 **Yamba** New South Wales, SE Australia
81 D16 **Yambio** var. Yambiyo. Western Equatoria, S Sudan
Yambiyo see Yambio
114 L10 **Yambol** Turk. Yanboli. Yambol, E Bulgaria
114 M11 **Yambol** ◈ province E Bulgaria
79 M17 **Yambuya** Orientale, N Dem. Rep. Congo
171 T15 **Yamdena, Pulau** prev. Jamdena. island Kepulauan Tanimbar, E Indonesia
165 O14 **Yame** Fukuoka, Kyūshū, SW Japan
166 M6 **Yamethin** Mandalay, C Myanmar (Burma)
186 C6 **Yaminbot** East Sepik, NW Papua New Guinea
181 U9 **Yamma Yamma, Lake** ◎ Queensland, C Australia
76 M16 **Yamoussoukro** ● (Ivory Coast) C Ivory Coast
37 P3 **Yampa River** ≈ Colorado, C USA
117 S2 **Yampil'** Sums'ka Oblast', NE Ukraine
116 M8 **Yampil'** Vinnyts'ka Oblast', C Ukraine
123 T9 **Yamsk** Magadanskaya Oblast', E Russian Federation
152 J8 **Yamuna** prev. Jumna. ≈ N India
152 I9 **Yamunānagar** Haryāna, N India
Yamundá see Nhamundá, Rio
145 U8 **Yamyshevo** Pavlodar, NE Kazakhstan
159 N16 **Yamzho Yumco** ◎ W China
123 Q8 **Yana** ≈ NE Russian Federation
186 H9 **Yanaba Island** island SE Papua New Guinea
155 L16 **Yanam** var. Yanaon. Pondicherry, E India
160 L5 **Yan'an** var. Yanan. Shaanxi, C China
Yanaon see Yanam
127 U3 **Yanaul** Respublika Bashkortostan, W Russian Federation
118 O12 **Yanavichy** Rus. Yanovichi. Vitsyebskaya Voblasts', NE Belarus
Yanboli see Yambol
140 K8 **Yanbu 'al Baḩr** Al Madīnah, W Saudi Arabia
21 T8 **Yanceyville** North Carolina, SE USA
161 R7 **Yancheng** Jiangsu, E China
159 W8 **Yanchi** Ningxia, N China
160 L5 **Yanchuan** Shaanxi, C China
183 O10 **Yanco Creek** seasonal river New South Wales, SE Australia
183 O6 **Yanda Creek** seasonal river New South Wales, SE Australia
182 K4 **Yandama Creek** seasonal river New South Wales/South Australia
161 S11 **Yandang Shan** ▲▲ SE China
159 O6 **Yandun** Xinjiang Uygur Zizhiqu, W China
76 L13 **Yanfolila** Sikasso, SW Mali
79 M18 **Yangambi** Orientale, N Dem. Rep. Congo
158 M15 **Yangbajain** Xizang Zizhiqu, W China
Yangchow see Yangzhou
160 M15 **Yangchun** var. Chuncheng. Guangdong, S China
161 N2 **Yanggao** Shanxi, C China
Yanggeta see Yaqeta
Yangiabad see Yangiobod
Yangibazar see Dzhany-Bazar
Yangi-Bazar see Kofarnihon
Yangiklshak see Yangiqishloq
146 M13 **Yangi-Nishon** Rus. Yangi-Nishan. Qashqadaryo Viloyati, S Uzbekistan
147 Q9 **Yangiobod** Rus. Yangiabad. Toshkent Viloyati, E Uzbekistan
147 O10 **Yangiqishloq** Rus. Yangiklshak. Jizzax Viloyati, C Uzbekistan
147 P11 **Yangiyer** Sirdaryo Viloyati, E Uzbekistan
147 P9 **Yangiyoʻl** Rus. Yangiyul'. Toshkent Viloyati, E Uzbekistan
Yangiyul' see Yangiyoʻl
160 M15 **Yangjiang** Guangdong, S China
Yangku see Taiyuan
Yang-Nishan see Yangi-Nishon
166 L8 **Yangon** Eng. Rangoon. ● (Myanmar (Burma)) Yangon, S Myanmar (Burma)
166 M8 **Yangon** Eng. Rangoon. ◈ division SW Myanmar (Burma)
161 N4 **Yangquan** Shanxi, C China
161 N13 **Yangshan** Guangdong, S China
167 U12 **Yang Sin, Chu** ▲ S Vietnam
Yangtze see Chang Jiang
Yangtze see Chang Jiang/Jinsha Jiang
Yangtze see Jinsha Jiang
Yangtze Kiang see Chang Jiang
Yangtze Kiang see Chang Jiang
161 R7 **Yangzhou** var. Yangchow. Jiangsu, E China
160 L5 **Yan He** ≈ C China
163 Y10 **Yanji** Jilin, NE China
Yanji see Longjing
Yanjing see Yangyuan
29 Q12 **Yankton** South Dakota, N USA
161 O12 **Yanling** prev. Lingxian, Ling Xian. Hunan, S China
Yannina see Ioánnina
123 Q7 **Yano-Indigirskaya Nizmennost'** plain NE Russian Federation
Yanovichi see Yanavichy
155 K24 **Yan Oya** ≈ N Sri Lanka
158 K6 **Yanqi** var. Yanqi Huizu Zizhixian. Xinjiang Uygur Zizhiqu, NW China
Yanqi Huizu Zizhixian see Yanqi
161 Q10 **Yanshan** var. Hekou. Jiangxi, S China
160 H14 **Yanshan** var. Jiangna. Yunnan, SW China
161 P2 **Yan Shan** ▲▲ E China
163 X8 **Yanshou** Heilongjiang, NE China
123 Q7 **Yanskiy Zaliv** bay N Russian Federation
183 O4 **Yantabulla** New South Wales, SE Australia
161 R4 **Yantai** var. Yan-t'ai; prev. Chefoo, Chih-fu. Shandong, E China
118 A13 **Yantarnyy** Ger. Palmnicken. Kaliningradskaya Oblast', W Russian Federation
114 J9 **Yantra** Gabrovo, N Bulgaria
114 K9 **Yantra** ≈ N Bulgaria
160 G11 **Yanyuan** var. Yanjing. Sichuan, C China
161 P5 **Yanzhou** Shandong, E China
79 E16 **Yaoundé** var. Yaunde. ● (Cameroon) Centre, S Cameroon
188 I14 **Yap** ◈ state W Micronesia
188 F16 **Yap** island Caroline Islands, W Micronesia
57 M18 **Yapacani, Rio** ≈ C Bolivia
171 W14 **Yapa Kopra** Papua, E Indonesia
Yapan see Yapen, Selat
Yapanskoye More East Sea/Japan, Sea of
77 P15 **Yapei** N Ghana
12 M10 **Yapeitso, Mont** ▲ Québec, E Canada
171 W12 **Yapen, Pulau** prev. Japen. island E Indonesia
171 W12 **Yapen, Selat** var. Yapan. strait Papua, E Indonesia
61 E15 **Yapeyú** Corrientes, NE Argentina
136 I11 **Yapraklı** Çankırı, N Turkey
174 M3 **Yap Trench** var. Yap Trough. undersea feature SE Philippine Sea
Yap Trough see Yap Trench
Yapurá see Caquetá, Río, Brazil/Colombia
Yapurá see Japurá, Rio, Brazil/Colombia
197 I12 **Yaqaga** island N Fiji
197 H12 **Yaqeta** prev. Yanggeta. island Yasawa Group, NW Fiji
40 G6 **Yaqui** Sonora, NW Mexico
32 E12 **Yaquina Bay** bay Oregon, NW USA
40 G6 **Yaqui, Río** ≈ NW Mexico
54 K5 **Yaracuy** off. Estado Yaracuy. ◈ state NW Venezuela
Yaracuy, Estado see Yaracuy
146 E13 **Yarajy** Rus. Yaradzhi. Ahal Welaýaty, C Turkmenistan
Yaradzhi see Yarajy
125 Q15 **Yaransk** Kirovskaya Oblast', NW Russian Federation
136 F17 **Yardımcı Burnu** headland SW Turkey
97 Q19 **Yare** ≈ E England, UK
125 S9 **Yarega** Respublika Komi, NW Russian Federation
116 I7 **Yaremcha** Ivano-Frankivs'ka Oblast', W Ukraine
189 Q9 **Yaren** SW Nauru
125 Q10 **Yarensk** Arkhangel'skaya Oblast', NW Russian Federation
155 F16 **Yargatti** Karnātaka, W India
164 M12 **Yariga-take** ▲ Honshū, S Japan
141 O15 **Yarīm** W Yemen
54 F14 **Yarí, Río** ≈ SW Colombia
54 K5 **Yaritagua** Yaracuy, N Venezuela
Yarkand see Yarkant He
Yarkant see Shache
158 E9 **Yarkant He** var. Yarkand. ≈ NW China
149 U3 **Yarkhūn** ≈ NW Pakistan
Yarlung Zangbo Jiang see Brahmaputra
116 L6 **Yarmolyntsi** Khmel'nyts'ka Oblast', W Ukraine
163 T11 **Yar Moron** ≈ N China
13 O16 **Yarmouth** Nova Scotia, SE Canada
Yarmouth see Great Yarmouth
Yaroslav see Jarosław
124 L15 **Yaroslavl'** Yaroslavskaya Oblast', W Russian Federation
124 K14 **Yaroslavskaya Oblast'** ◈ province W Russian Federation
123 N11 **Yaroslavskiy** Respublika Sakha (Yakutiya), NE Russian Federation
183 P13 **Yarram** Victoria, SE Australia
183 O11 **Yarrawonga** Victoria, SE Australia
182 L4 **Yarriarraburra Swamp** wetland New South Wales, SE Australia
122 I8 **Yar-Sale** Yamalo-Nenetskiy Avtonomnyy Okrug, N Russian Federation
122 K11 **Yartsevo** Krasnoyarskiy Kray, C Russian Federation
126 I4 **Yartsevo** Smolenskaya Oblast', W Russian Federation
54 E8 **Yarumal** Antioquia, NW Colombia
187 W14 **Yasawa Group** island group NW Fiji
77 V12 **Yashi** Katsina, N Nigeria
77 S14 **Yashikera** Kwara, W Nigeria
147 T14 **Yashilkŭl** Rus. Ozero Yashil'kul'. ◎ SE Tajikistan
Yashil'kul', Ozero see Yashilkŭl
165 P9 **Yashima** Akita, Honshū, C Japan
127 P13 **Yashkul'** Respublika Kalmykiya, SW Russian Federation
146 F13 **Yashlyk** Ahal Welaýaty, C Turkmenistan
Yasinovataya see Yasynuvata
114 N10 **Yasna Polyana** Burgas, E Bulgaria
167 R10 **Yasothon** Yasothon, E Thailand
183 R10 **Yass** New South Wales, SE Australia
Yassy see Iaşi
164 H12 **Yasugi** Shimane, Honshū, SW Japan
143 N10 **Yāsūj** var. Yesuj; prev. Tal-e Khosravī. Kohkīlūyeh va Būyer AHmad, C Iran
136 M11 **Yasun Burnu** headland N Turkey
117 X8 **Yasynuvata** Rus. Yasinovataya. Donets'ka Oblast', SE Ukraine
136 C15 **Yatağan** Muğla, SW Turkey
165 Q7 **Yatate-tōge** pass Honshū, C Japan
187 Q17 **Yaté** Province Sud, S New Caledonia
27 P6 **Yates Center** Kansas, C USA
185 B21 **Yates Point** headland South Island, New Zealand
9 N9 **Yathkyed Lake** ◎ Nunavut, NE Canada
171 T16 **Yatoke** Pulau Babar, E Indonesia
79 M18 **Yatolema** Orientale, N Dem. Rep. Congo
164 C15 **Yatsushiro** var. Yatusiro. Kumamoto, Kyūshū, SW Japan
164 C15 **Yatsushiro-kai** bay SW Japan
138 F11 **Yatta** var. Yuta. S West Bank
81 J20 **Yatta Plateau** plateau SE Kenya
Yatusiro see Yatsushiro
57 F17 **Yauca, Río** ≈ SW Peru
45 S6 **Yauco** W Puerto Rico
Yaunde see Yaoundé
Yavan see Yovon
Yavarí see Javari, Rio
56 G9 **Yavari Mirim, Río** ≈ NE Peru
40 G7 **Yavaros** Sonora, NW Mexico
154 I13 **Yavatmāl** Mahārāshtra, C India
54 M9 **Yaví, Cerro** ▲ C Venezuela
43 W16 **Yaviza** Darién, SE Panama
138 F10 **Yavne** Central, W Israel
116 H5 **Yavoriv** Pol. Jaworów, Rus. Yavorov. L'vivs'ka Oblast', NW Ukraine
Yavorov see Yavoriv
164 F14 **Yawatahama** Ehime, Shikoku, SW Japan
Ya Xian see Sanya
136 L17 **Yayladaǧı** Hatay, S Turkey
125 V13 **Yayva** Permskaya Oblast', NW Russian Federation
125 V12 **Yayva** ≈ NW Russian Federation
143 Q9 **Yazd** var. Yezd. Yazd, C Iran
143 Q8 **Yazd** off. Ostān-e Yazd, var. Yezd. ◈ province C Iran
Yazd, Ostān-e see Yazd
Yazgulemskiy Khrebet see Yazgulom, Qatorkŭhi
147 S13 **Yazgulom, Qatorkŭhi** Rus. Yazgulemskiy Khrebet. ▲▲ S Tajikistan
22 K5 **Yazoo City** Mississippi, S USA
22 K5 **Yazoo River** ≈ Mississippi, S USA
127 Q5 **Yazykovo** Ul'yanovskaya Oblast', W Russian Federation
109 U4 **Ybbs** Niederösterreich, NE Austria
109 U4 **Ybbs** ≈ C Austria
95 G22 **Yding Skovhøj** hill C Denmark
115 G20 **Ýdra** var. Ídhra, Idra. Ýdra, S Greece
115 G21 **Ýdra** var. Ídhra. island Ýdra, S Greece
115 G20 **Ýdras, Kólpos** strait S Greece
167 N10 **Ye** Mon State, S Myanmar (Burma)
183 O12 **Yea** Victoria, SE Australia
Yebaishou see Jianping
78 I5 **Yebbi-Bou** Borkou-Ennedi-Tibesti, N Chad
158 F9 **Yecheng** var. Kargilik. Xinjiang Uygur Zizhiqu, NW China
105 R11 **Yecla** Murcia, SE Spain
40 H6 **Yécora** Sonora, NW Mexico
Yedintsy see Edineţ
124 J13 **Yefimovskiy** Leningradskaya Oblast', NW Russian Federation
126 K6 **Yefremov** Tul'skaya Oblast', W Russian Federation
Yêgainnyin see Henan
137 U12 **Yeghegis** Rus. Yekhegis. ≈ C Armenia
137 U12 **Yeghegnadzor** C Armenia
145 T10 **Yegindybulak** Kaz. Egindibulaq. Karaganda, C Kazakhstan
126 L4 **Yegor'yevsk** Moskovskaya Oblast', W Russian Federation
Yehuda, Haré see Judaean Hills
81 E15 **Yei** ≈ S Sudan
161 P8 **Yeji** var. Yejiaji. Anhui, E China
Yejiaji see Yeji
122 G10 **Yekaterinburg** prev. Sverdlovsk. Sverdlovskaya Oblast', C Russian Federation
Yekaterinodar see Krasnodar
Yekaterinoslav see Dnipropetrovs'k
123 R13 **Yekaterinoslavka** Amurskaya Oblast', SE Russian Federation
127 O7 **Yekaterinovka** Saratovskaya Oblast', W Russian Federation
76 K16 **Yekepa** NE Liberia
Yekhegis see Yeghegis
127 T3 **Yelabuga** Respublika Tatarstan, W Russian Federation
Yela Island see Rossel Island
127 O8 **Yelan'** Volgogradskaya Oblast', SW Russian Federation
117 Q9 **Yelanets'** Rus. Yelanets. Mykolayivs'ka Oblast', S Ukraine
126 L7 **Yelets** Lipetskaya Oblast', W Russian Federation
125 W4 **Yeletskiy** Respublika Komi, NW Russian Federation
76 J11 **Yélimané** Kayes, W Mali
Yelisavetpol see Gäncä
Yelizavetgrad see Kirovohrad
123 T12 **Yelizavety, Mys** cape SE Russian Federation
Yelizovo see Yalizava
127 S5 **Yelkhovka** Samarskaya Oblast', W Russian Federation
96 M1 **Yell** island NE Scotland, UK
155 E17 **Yellāpur** Karnātaka, W India
9 U17 **Yellow Grass** Saskatchewan, S Canada
Yellowhammer State see Alabama
9 O15 **Yellowhead Pass** pass Alberta/British Columbia, SW Canada
8 K10 **Yellowknife** territory capital Northwest Territories, W Canada
8 K9 **Yellowknife** ≈ Northwest Territories, NW Canada
23 P8 **Yellow River** ≈ Alabama/Florida, SE USA
30 K7 **Yellow River** ≈ Wisconsin, N USA
30 I4 **Yellow River** ≈ Wisconsin, N USA
30 J6 **Yellow River** ≈ Wisconsin, N USA
Yellow River see Huang He
157 V8 **Yellow Sea** Chin. Huang Hai, Kor. Hwang-Hae. sea E Asia

◆ Country ● Country Capital ◇ Dependent Territory ○ Dependent Territory Capital ◈ Administrative Regions ✈ International Airport ▲ Mountain ▲▲ Mountain Range Volcano ≈ River ◎ Lake ▣ Reservoir

33 S13 **Yellowstone Lake** ◎ Wyoming, C USA
33 T13 **Yellowstone National Park** *national park* Wyoming, NW USA
33 Y8 **Yellowstone River** ≈ Montana/Wyoming, NW USA
96 L1 **Yell Sound** *strait* N Scotland, UK
27 U9 **Yellville** Arkansas, C USA
122 K10 **Yeloguy** ≈ C Russian Federation
Yëloten *see* Ýolöten
119 M20 **Yel'sk** *Rus.* Yel'sk. Homyel'skaya Voblasts', SE Belarus
77 T13 **Yelwa** Kebbi, W Nigeria
21 R15 **Yemassee** South Carolina, SE USA
141 O15 **Yemen** *off.* Republic of Yemen, *Ar.* Al Jumhuriyah al Yamaniyah, Al Yaman. ◆ *republic* SW Asia
Yemen, Republic of *see* Yemen
116 M4 **Yemil'chyne** Zhytomyrs'ka Oblast', N Ukraine
124 M10 **Yemtsa** Arkhangel'skaya Oblast', NW Russian Federation
124 M10 **Yemtsa** ≈ NW Russian Federation
125 R10 **Yemva** *prev.* Zheleznodorozhnyy. Respublika Komi, NW Russian Federation
77 U17 **Yenagoa** Bayelsa, S Nigeria
117 X7 **Yenakiyeve** *Rus.* Yenakiyevo; *prev.* Ordzhonikidze, Rykovo. Donets'ka Oblast', E Ukraine
Yenakiyevo *see* Yenakiyeve
166 L6 **Yenangyaung** Magwe, W Myanmar (Burma)
167 S5 **Yên Bai** Yên Bai, N Vietnam
183 P9 **Yenda** New South Wales, SE Australia
77 Q14 **Yendi** NE Ghana
Yêndum *see* Zhag'yab
158 E8 **Yengisar** Xinjiang Uygur Zizhiqu, NW China
121 R1 **Yenierenköy** *var.* Yialousa, *Gk.* Agialoúsa. NE Cyprus
Yenipazar *see* Novi Pazar
136 E12 **Yenişehir** Bursa, NW Turkey
Yenisei Bay *see* Yeniseyskiy Zaliv
122 K12 **Yeniseysk** Krasnoyarskiy Kray, C Russian Federation
197 W10 **Yeniseyskiy Zaliv** *var.* Yenisei Bay. *bay* N Russian Federation
127 Q12 **Yenotayevka** Astrakhanskaya Oblast', SW Russian Federation
124 L4 **Yenozero, Ozero** ◎ NW Russian Federation
Yenping *see* Nanping
39 Q11 **Yentna River** ≈ Alaska, USA
180 M10 **Yeo, Lake** *salt lake* Western Australia
183 R7 **Yeoval** New South Wales, SE Australia
97 K23 **Yeovil** SW England, UK
40 H6 **Yepachic** Chihuahua, N Mexico
181 Y8 **Yeppoon** Queensland, E Australia
126 M5 **Yeraktur** Ryazanskaya Oblast', W Russian Federation
Yeraliyev *see* Kuryk
146 F12 **Yerbent** Ahal Welaýaty, C Turkmenistan
123 N11 **Yerbogachen** Irkutskaya Oblast', C Russian Federation
137 T12 **Yerevan** *Eng.* Erivan. ● (Armenia) C Armenia
137 U12 **Yerevan** ✈ C Armenia
127 O12 **Yergeni** *hill range* SW Russian Federation
Yeriho *see* Jericho
35 R6 **Yerington** Nevada, W USA
136 J13 **Yerköy** Yozgat, C Turkey
114 L13 **Yerlisu** Edirne, NW Turkey
Yermak *see* Aksu
145 R9 **Yermentau** *var.* Jermentau, *Kaz.* Ereymentaū. Akmola, C Kazakhstan
145 R9 **Yermentau, Gory** ▲▲ C Kazakhstan
125 R5 **Yermitsa** Respublika Komi, NW Russian Federation
35 V14 **Yermo** California, W USA
123 P13 **Yerofey Pavlovich** Amurskaya Oblast', SE Russian Federation
99 F15 **Yerseke** Zeeland, SW Netherlands
127 Q8 **Yershov** Saratovskaya Oblast', W Russian Federation
125 P9 **Yërtom** Respublika Komi, NW Russian Federation
56 D13 **Yerupaja, Nevado** ▲ C Peru
Yerushalayim *see* Jerusalem
105 R4 **Yesa, Embalse de** ⊟ NE Spain
144 F9 **Yesensay** Zapadnyy Kazakhstan, NW Kazakhstan
145 V15 **Yesik** *Kaz.* Esik; *prev.* Issyk. Almaty, SE Kazakhstan
145 O8 **Yesil'** *Kaz.* Esil. Akmola, C Kazakhstan
136 K15 **Yeşilhisar** Kayseri, C Turkey
136 L11 **Yeşilırmak** *var.* Iris. ≈ N Turkey
37 U12 **Yeso** New Mexico, SW USA
Yeso *see* Hokkaidō
127 N15 **Yessentuki** Stavropol'skiy Kray, SW Russian Federation
122 M9 **Yessey** Evenkiyskiy Avtonomnyy Okrug, N Russian Federation
105 P12 **Yeste** Castilla-La Mancha, C Spain
Yesuj *see* Yāsūj
183 T4 **Yetman** New South Wales, SE Australia
76 L4 **Yetti** *physical region* N Mauritania
166 M4 **Ye-u** Sagaing, C Myanmar (Burma)
102 H9 **Yeu, Île d'** *island* NW France
Yevlakh *see* Yevlax
137 W11 **Yevlax** *Rus.* Yevlakh. C Azerbaijan
117 S13 **Yevpatoriya** Respublika Krym, S Ukraine
Ye Xian *see* Laizhou
126 K12 **Yeya** ≈ SW Russian Federation
158 I10 **Yeyik** Xinjiang Uygur Zizhiqu, W China
126 K12 **Yeysk** Krasnodarskiy Kray, SW Russian Federation
Yezd *see* Yazd
Yezerishche *see* Yezyaryshcha
Yezhou *see* Jianshi
Yezo *see* Hokkaidō
118 N11 **Yezyaryshcha** *Rus.* Yezerishche. Vitsyebskaya Voblasts', NE Belarus
Yialí *see* Gyalí
Yialousa *see* Yenierenköy
163 V7 **Yi'an** Heilongjiang, NE China
Yiannitsá *see* Giannitsá
160 I10 **Yibin** Sichuan, C China
158 K13 **Yibug Caka** ◎ W China
160 M9 **Yichang** Hubei, C China
160 L5 **Yichuan** *var.* Danzhou. Shaanxi, C China
163 X6 **Yichun** *var.* I-ch'un. Heilongjiang, NE China
157 W3 **Yichun** Heilongjiang, NE China
161 O11 **Yichun** Jiangxi, S China
160 M9 **Yidu** *prev.* Zhicheng. Hubei, C China
Yidu *see* Qingzhou
188 C15 **Yigo** NE Guam
161 Q5 **Yi He** ≈ E China
163 X8 **Yilan** Heilongjiang, NE China
136 C9 **Yıldız Dağları** ▲▲ NW Turkey
136 L13 **Yıldızeli** Sivas, N Turkey
163 U4 **Yilehuli Shan** ▲▲ NE China
163 S7 **Yimin He** ≈ NE China
159 W8 **Yinchuan** *var.* Yinch'uan, Yin-ch'uan, Yinchwan. *province capital* Ningxia, N China
Yin-ch'uan/Yinch'uan *see* Yinchuan
Yinchwan *see* Yinchuan
Yindu He *see* Indus
Yingcheng *see* Yingde
161 N14 **Yingde** *var.* Yingcheng. Guangdong, S China
161 O7 **Ying He** ≈ C China
163 U13 **Yingkou** *var.* Ying-k'ou, Yingkow; *prev.* Newchwang, Niuchwang. Liaoning, NE China
Ying-k'ou *see* Yingkou
Yingkow *see* Yingkou
161 P9 **Yingshan** *var.* Wenquan. Hubei, C China
Yingshan *see* Guangshui
161 Q10 **Yingtan** Jiangxi, S China
Yin-hsien *see* Ningbo
158 H5 **Yining** *var.* I-ning, *Uigh.* Gulja, Kuldja. Xinjiang Uygur Zizhiqu, NW China
160 K11 **Yinjiang** *var.* Yinjiang Tujiazu Miaozu Zizhixian. Guizhou, S China
Yinjiang Tujiazu Miaozu Zizhixian *see* Yinjiang
166 L4 **Yinmabin** Sagaing, C Myanmar (Burma)
163 N13 **Yin Shan** ▲▲ N China
Yin-tu Ho *see* Indus
159 P15 **Yi'ong Zangbo** ≈ W China
Yioúra *see* Gyáros
81 J14 **Yirga 'Alem** *It.* Irgalem. Southern, S Ethiopia
61 E19 **Yí, Río** ≈ C Uruguay
81 E14 **Yirol** El Buhayrat, S Sudan
163 S8 **Yirshi** *var.* Yirxie. Nei Mongol Zizhiqu, N China
Yirxie *see* Yirshi
Yishan *see* Guanyun
161 Q5 **Yishui** Shandong, E China
Yisrael/Yisra'el *see* Israel
Yíthion *see* Gýtheio
Yitiaoshan *see* Jingtai
163 W10 **Yitong** *var.* Yitong Manzu Zizhixian. Jilin, NE China
Yitong Manzu Zizhixian *see* Yitong
159 P5 **Yiwu** *var.* Aratürük. Xinjiang Uygur Zizhiqu, NW China
163 U12 **Yiwulü Shan** ▲▲ N China
163 T12 **Yixian** *var.* Yizhou. Liaoning, NE China
161 N10 **Yiyang** Hunan, S China
161 Q10 **Yiyang** Jiangxi, S China
161 N13 **Yizhang** Hunan, S China
Yizhou *see* Yixian
93 K19 **Yläne** Länsi-Soumi, SW Finland
93 L14 **Yli-Ii** Oulu, C Finland
93 L14 **Ylikiiminki** Oulu, C Finland
92 N13 **Yli-Kitka** ◎ NE Finland
93 K17 **Ylistaro** Länsi-Soumi, W Finland
92 K13 **Ylitornio** Lappi, NW Finland
93 L15 **Ylivieska** Oulu, W Finland
93 L18 **Ylöjärvi** Länsi-Suomi, W Finland
95 N17 **Yngaren** ◎ C Sweden
25 T12 **Yoakum** Texas, SW USA
77 X13 **Yobe** ◈ *state* NE Nigeria
165 R3 **Yobetsu-dake** ⋀ Hokkaidō, NE Japan
80 L11 **Yoboki** C Djibouti
22 M4 **Yockanookany River** ≈ Mississippi, S USA
22 L2 **Yocona River** ≈ Mississippi, S USA
171 Y15 **Yodom** Papua, E Indonesia
169 Q16 **Yogyakarta** *prev.* Djokjakarta, Jogjakarta, Jokyakarta. Jawa, C Indonesia
169 P17 **Yogyakarta** *off.* Daerah Istimewa Yogyakarta, *var.* Djokjakarta, Jogjakarta, Jokyakarta. ◈ *autonomous district* S Indonesia
Yogyakarta, Daerah Istimewa *see* Yogyakarta
165 Q3 **Yoichi** Hokkaidō, NE Japan
42 G6 **Yojoa, Lago de** ◎ NW Honduras
79 G16 **Yokadouma** Est, SE Cameroon
164 K13 **Yokkaichi** *var.* Yokkaiti. Mie, Honshū, SW Japan
Yokkaiti *see* Yokkaichi
79 E15 **Yoko** Centre, C Cameroon
165 V15 **Yokoate-jima** *island* Nansei-shotō, SW Japan
165 R6 **Yokohama** Aomori, Honshū, C Japan
165 O14 **Yokosuka** Kanagawa, Honshū, S Japan
164 G12 **Yokota** Shimane, Honshū, SW Japan
165 Q9 **Yokote** Akita, Honshū, C Japan
77 Y14 **Yola** Adamawa, E Nigeria
79 L19 **Yolombo** Equateur, C Dem. Rep. Congo
146 J14 **Ýolöten** *Rus.* Yëloten; *prev.* Iolotan'. Mary Welaýaty, S Turkmenistan
165 Y15 **Yome-jima** *island* Ogasawara-shotō, SE Japan
76 K16 **Yomou** SE Guinea
171 Y15 **Yomuka** Papua, E Indonesia
188 C16 **Yona** E Guam
164 H12 **Yonago** Tottori, Honshū, SW Japan
165 N16 **Yonaguni** Okinawa, SW Japan
165 N16 **Yonaguni-jima** *island* Nansei-shotō, SW Japan
165 T16 **Yonaha-dake** ▲ Okinawa, SW Japan
163 X14 **Yonan** SW North Korea
165 P10 **Yonezawa** Yamagata, Honshū, C Japan
161 Q12 **Yong'an** *var.* Yongan. Fujian, SE China
Yong'an *see* Fengjie
159 T9 **Yongchang** Gansu, N China
161 P7 **Yongcheng** Henan, C China
163 Z15 **Yŏngch'ŏn** *Jap.* Eisen. SE South Korea
160 J10 **Yongchuan** Chongqing Shi, C China
159 U10 **Yongdeng** Gansu, C China
Yongding *see* Yongren
129 W9 **Yongding He** ≈ E China
161 P11 **Yongfeng** *var.* Enjiang. Jiangxi, S China
158 L5 **Yongfengqu** Xinjiang Uygur Zizhiqu, W China
160 L13 **Yongfu** Guangxi Zhuangzu Ziziqu
163 X13 **Yŏnghŭng** E North Korea
159 U10 **Yongjing** Gansu, C China
Yongjing *see* Xifeng
163 Y15 **Yŏngju** *Jap.* Eishū. C South Korea
Yongning *see* Xuyong
160 E12 **Yongping** Yunnan, SW China
160 G12 **Yongren** *var.* Yongding. Yunnan, SW China
160 L10 **Yongshun** *var.* Lingxi. Hunan, S China
161 P10 **Yongxiu** *var.* Tujiabu. Jiangxi, S China
160 M12 **Yongzhou** *var.* Lengshuitan. Hunan, S China
Yongzhou *see* Zhishan
18 K14 **Yonkers** New York, NE USA
103 Q7 **Yonne** ◈ *department* C France
103 P6 **Yonne** ≈ C France
54 H9 **Yopal** *var.* El Yopal. Casanare, C Colombia
158 E8 **Yopurga** *var.* Yukuriawat. Xinjiang Uygur Zizhiqu, NW China
147 S11 **Yordan** *var.* Iordan, *Rus.* Jardan. Farg'ona Viloyati, E Uzbekistan
180 J12 **York** Western Australia
97 M16 **York** *anc.* Eboracum, Eburacum. N England, UK
23 N5 **York** Alabama, S USA
29 Q15 **York** Nebraska, C USA
18 G16 **York** Pennsylvania, NE USA
21 R11 **York** South Carolina, SE USA
14 J13 **York** ≈ Ontario, SE Canada
15 X6 **York** ≈ Québec, SE Canada
181 V1 **York, Cape** *headland* Queensland, NE Australia
182 I9 **Yorke Peninsula** *peninsula* South Australia
182 I9 **Yorketown** South Australia
19 P9 **York Harbor** Maine, NE USA
York, Kap *see* Innaanganeq
21 X6 **York River** ≈ Virginia, NE USA
97 M16 **Yorkshire** *cultural region* N England, UK
97 L16 **Yorkshire Dales** *physical region* N England, UK
9 V16 **Yorkton** Saskatchewan, S Canada
25 T12 **Yorktown** Texas, SW USA
21 X6 **Yorktown** Virginia, NE USA
30 M11 **Yorkville** Illinois, N USA
42 I5 **Yoro** Yoro, C Honduras
42 H5 **Yoro** ◈ *department* N Honduras
165 T16 **Yoron-jima** *island* Nansei-shotō, SW Japan
77 N13 **Yorosso** Sikasso, S Mali
35 R8 **Yosemite National Park** *national park* California, W USA
127 Q3 **Yoshkar-Ola** Respublika Mariy El, W Russian Federation
Yösönbulag *see* Altay
162 K8 **Yösöndzüyl** *var.* Mönhbulag. Övörhangay, C Mongolia
171 Y16 **Yos Sudarso, Pulau** *var.* Pulau Dolak, Pulau Kolepom; *prev.* Jos Sudarso. *island* E Indonesia
163 Y17 **Yŏsu** *Jap.* Reisui. S South Korea
165 R4 **Yotei-zan** ▲ Hokkaidō, NE Japan
97 D21 **Youghal** *Ir.* Eochaill. Cork, S Ireland
97 D21 **Youghal Bay** *Ir.* Cuan Eochaille. *inlet* S Ireland
18 C15 **Youghiogheny River** ≈ Pennsylvania, NE USA
160 K14 **You Jiang** ≈ S China
183 Q9 **Young** New South Wales, SE Australia
9 T15 **Young** Saskatchewan, S Canada
61 E18 **Young** Río Negro, W Uruguay
182 G5 **Younghusband, Lake** *salt lake* South Australia
182 J10 **Younghusband Peninsula** *peninsula* South Australia
184 Q10 **Young Nicks Head** *headland* North Island, New Zealand
185 D20 **Young Range** ▲▲ South Island, New Zealand
191 Q15 **Young's Rock** *island* Pitcairn Island, Pitcairn Islands
9 R16 **Youngstown** Alberta, SW Canada
31 V12 **Youngstown** Ohio, N USA
159 N9 **Youshashan** Qinghai, C China
Youth, Isle of *see* Juventud, Isla de la
77 N11 **Youvarou** Mopti, C Mali
160 K10 **Youyang** *var.* Zhongduo. Chongqing Shi, C China
163 Y7 **Youyi** Heilongjiang, NE China
147 P13 **Yovon** *Rus.* Yavan. SW Tajikistan
136 J13 **Yozgat** Yozgat, C Turkey
136 K13 **Yozgat** ◈ *province* C Turkey
62 O6 **Ypacaraí** *var.* Ypacaray. Central, S Paraguay
Ypacaray *see* Ypacaraí
62 P5 **Ypané, Río** ≈ C Paraguay
Ypres *see* Ieper
114 I13 **Ypsário** *var.* Ipsario. ▲ Thásos, E Greece
31 R10 **Ypsilanti** Michigan, N USA
34 M1 **Yreka** California, W USA
Yrendagüé *see* General Eugenio A. Garay
186 G5 **Ysabel Channel** *channel* N Papua New Guinea
14 K8 **Yser, Lac** ◎ Québec, SE Canada
147 Y8 **Yshtyk** Issyk-Kul'skaya Oblast', E Kyrgyzstan
Yssel *see* IJssel
103 Q12 **Yssingeaux** Haute-Loire, C France
95 K23 **Ystad** Skåne, S Sweden
Ysyk-Köl *see* Balykchy
Ysyk-Köl *see* Issyk-Kul', Ozero
Ysyk-Köl Oblasty *see* Issyk-Kul'skaya Oblast'
96 L8 **Ythan** ≈ NE Scotland, UK
Y Trallwng *see* Welshpool
94 C13 **Ytre Arna** Hordaland, S Norway
94 B12 **Ytre Sula** *island* S Norway
93 G17 **Ytterhogdal** Jämtland, C Sweden
Yu *see* Henan
Yuan *see* Red River
Yuan Jiang *see* Red River
161 S13 **Yüanlin** *Jap.* Inrin. C Taiwan
161 N3 **Yuanping** Shanxi, C China
Yuanquan *see* Anxi
Yuanshan *see* Lianping
161 O11 **Yuan Shui** ≈ S China
35 O6 **Yuba City** California, W USA
35 O6 **Yuba River** ≈ California, W USA
80 H13 **Yubdo** Oromo, C Ethiopia
126 L3 **Yubileynyy** Moskovskaya Oblast', W Russian Federation
41 X12 **Yucatán** ◈ *state* SE Mexico
47 O3 **Yucatan Basin** *var.* Yucatan Deep. *undersea feature* N Caribbean Sea
Yucatán, Canal de *see* Yucatan Channel
41 Y10 **Yucatan Channel** *Sp.* Canal de Yucatán. *channel* Cuba/Mexico
Yucatan Deep *see* Yucatan Basin
Yucatan Peninsula *see* Yucatán, Península de
41 X13 **Yucatán, Península de** *Eng.* Yucatan Peninsula. *peninsula* Guatemala/Mexico
36 I11 **Yucca** Arizona, SW USA
35 V15 **Yucca Valley** California, W USA
161 P4 **Yucheng** Shandong, E China
Yuci *see* Jinzhong
129 X5 **Yudoma** ≈ E Russian Federation
161 P12 **Yudu** *var.* Gaongjiang. Jiangxi, C China
Yue *see* Guangdong
Yuecheng *see* Yuexi
160 M12 **Yuecheng Ling** ▲▲ S China
Yuegaitan *see* Qumarlêb
181 P7 **Yuendumu** Northern Territory, N Australia
Yue Shan, Tai *see* Lantau Island
160 H10 **Yuexi** *var.* Yuecheng. Sichuan, C China
161 N10 **Yueyang** Hunan, S China
125 U14 **Yug** Permskaya Oblast', NW Russian Federation
125 P13 **Yug** ≈ NW Russian Federation
123 R10 **Yugorenok** Respublika Sakha (Yakutiya), NE Russian Federation
122 H9 **Yugorsk** Khanty-Mansiyskiy Avtonomnyy Okrug, C Russian Federation
122 H7 **Yugorskiy Poluostrov** *peninsula* NW Russian Federation
Yugoslavia *see* Serbia
146 K14 **Yugo-Vostochnyye Garagumy** *prev.* Yugo-Vostochnyye Karakumy. *desert* E Turkmenistan
Yugo-Vostochnyye Karakumy *see* Yugo-Vostochnyye Garagumy
Yuhu *see* Eryuan
161 S10 **Yuhuan Dao** *island* SE China
160 L14 **Yu Jiang** ≈ S China
Yujin *see* Qianwei
123 S7 **Yukagirskoye Ploskogor'ye** *plateau* NE Russian Federation
118 L11 **Yukhavichy** *Rus.* Yukhovichi. Vitsyebskaya Voblasts', N Belarus
126 J4 **Yukhnov** Kaluzhskaya Oblast', W Russian Federation
Yukhovichi *see* Yukhavichy
79 J20 **Yuki** *var.* Yuki Kengunda. Bandundu, W Dem. Rep. Congo
Yuki Kengunda *see* Yuki
26 M10 **Yukon** Oklahoma, C USA
0 F4 **Yukon** ≈ Canada/USA
Yukon *see* Yukon Territory
39 S7 **Yukon Flats** *salt flat* Alaska, USA
Yukon, Territoire du *see* Yukon Territory
10 I5 **Yukon Territory** *var.* Yukon, *Fr.* Territoire du Yukon. ◈ *territory* NW Canada
137 T16 **Yüksekova** Hakkâri, SE Turkey
123 N10 **Yukta** Evenkiyskiy Avtonomnyy Okrug, C Russian Federation
165 O13 **Yukuhashi** *var.* Yukuhasi. Fukuoka, Kyūshū, SW Japan
Yukuhasi *see* Yukuhashi
Yukuriawat *see* Yopurga
125 O9 **Yula** ≈ NW Russian Federation
181 P8 **Yulara** Northern Territory, N Australia
127 W6 **Yuldybayevo** Respublika Bashkortostan, W Russian Federation
23 W8 **Yulee** Florida, SE USA
158 K7 **Yuli** *var.* Lopnur. Xinjiang Uygur Zizhiqu, NW China
161 T14 **Yüli** C Taiwan
160 L15 **Yulin** Guangxi Zhuangzu Zizhiqu, S China
160 L4 **Yulin** Shaanxi, C China
161 T14 **Yüli Shan** ▲ E Taiwan
160 F11 **Yulong Xueshan** ▲ SW China
36 H14 **Yuma** Arizona, SW USA
37 W3 **Yuma** Colorado, C USA
54 K5 **Yumare** Yaracuy, N Venezuela
63 G14 **Yumbel** Bío Bío, C Chile
79 N19 **Yumbi** Maniema, E Dem. Rep. Congo
159 R8 **Yumen** *var.* Laojunmiao, Yümen. Gansu, N China
159 Q7 **Yumenzhen** Gansu, N China
158 J3 **Yumin** Xinjiang Uygur Zizhiqu, NW China
Yun *see* Yunnan
136 G14 **Yunak** Konya, W Turkey
45 O8 **Yuna, Río** ≈ E Dominican Republic
38 I17 **Yunaska Island** *island* Aleutian Islands, Alaska, USA
160 M6 **Yuncheng** Shanxi, C China
161 N14 **Yunfu** Guangdong, S China
57 L18 **Yungas** *physical region* E Bolivia
Yungki *see* Jilin
Yung-ning *see* Nanning
160 I12 **Yungui Gaoyuan** *plateau* SW China
Yunjinghong *see* Jinghong
160 M15 **Yunkai Dashan** ▲▲ S China
Yunki *see* Jilin
160 E11 **Yun Ling** ▲▲ SW China
161 N9 **Yunmeng** Hubei, C China
157 N14 **Yunnan** *var.* Yun, Yunnan Sheng, Yünnan, Yun-nan. ◈ *province* SW China
Yunnan *see* Kunming
Yunnan Sheng *see* Yunnan
Yünnan/Yun-nan *see* Yunnan
165 P15 **Yunomae** Kumamoto, Kyūshū, SW Japan
161 N8 **Yun Shui** ≈ C China
182 J7 **Yunta** South Australia
161 Q14 **Yunxiao** Fujian, SE China
160 K9 **Yunyang** Sichuan, C China
193 S9 **Yupanqui Basin** *undersea feature* E Pacific Ocean
Yuping *see* Libo
Yuping *see* Pingbian
Yuratishki *see* Yuratsishki
119 I15 **Yuratsishki** *Pol.* Juraciszki, *Rus.* Yuratishki. Hrodzyenskaya Voblasts', W Belarus
Yurev *see* Tartu
122 J12 **Yurga** Kemerovskaya Oblast', S Russian Federation
56 E10 **Yurimaguas** Loreto, N Peru
127 P3 **Yurino** Respublika Mariy El, W Russian Federation
41 N13 **Yuriria** Guanajuato, C Mexico
125 T13 **Yurla** Permskaya Oblast', NW Russian Federation
Yuruá, Río *see* Juruá, Rio
114 M13 **Yürük** Tekirdağ, NW Turkey
158 G10 **Yurungkax He** ≈ W China
125 Q14 **Yur'ya** *var.* Jarja. Kirovskaya Oblast', NW Russian Federation
Yury'ev *see* Tartu
125 N16 **Yur'yevets** Ivanovskaya Oblast', W Russian Federation
126 M3 **Yur'yev-Pol'skiy** Vladimirskaya Oblast', W Russian Federation
117 V7 **Yur"yivka** Dnipropetrovs'ka Oblast', E Ukraine
42 I7 **Yuscarán** El Paraíso, S Honduras
161 P12 **Yu Shan** ▲ S China
159 R13 **Yushu** *var.* Gyêgu. Qinghai, C China
127 P12 **Yusta** Respublika Kalmykiya, SW Russian Federation
124 I10 **Yustozero** Respublika Kareliya, NW Russian Federation
137 Q11 **Yusufeli** Artvin, NE Turkey
164 F14 **Yusuhara** Kōchi, Shikoku, SW Japan
125 T14 **Yus'va** Permskaya Oblast', NW Russian Federation
Yuta *see* Yatta
161 P2 **Yutian** Hebei, E China
158 H10 **Yutian** *var.* Keriya. Xinjiang Uygur Zizhiqu, NW China
62 K5 **Yuto** Jujuy, NW Argentina
62 P7 **Yuty** Caazapá, S Paraguay
160 G13 **Yuxi** Yunnan, SW China
161 O2 **Yuxian** *prev.* Yu Xian. Hebei, E China
Yu Xian *see* Yuxian
165 Q9 **Yuzawa** Akita, Honshū, C Japan
125 N16 **Yuzha** Ivanovskaya Oblast', W Russian Federation
Yuzhno-Alichurskiy Khrebet *see* Alichuri Janubí, Qatorkŭhi
Yuzhno-Kazakhstanskaya Oblast' *see* Yuzhnyy Kazakhstan
123 T13 **Yuzhno-Sakhalinsk** *Jap.* Toyohara; *prev.* Vladimirovka. Ostrov Sakhalin, Sakhalinskaya Oblast', SE Russian Federation
127 P14 **Yuzhno-Sukhokumsk** Respublika Dagestan, SW Russian Federation
145 Z10 **Yuzhnyy Altay, Khrebet** ▲▲ E Kazakhstan
Yuzhnyy Bug *see* Pivdennyy Buh
145 O15 **Yuzhnyy Kazakhstan** *off.* Yuzhno-Kazakhstanskaya Oblast', *Eng.* South Kazakhstan, *Kaz.* Ongtüstik Qazaqstan Oblysy; *prev.* Chimkentskaya Oblast'. ◈ *province* S Kazakhstan
123 U10 **Yuzhnyy, Mys** *cape* E Russian Federation
127 W6 **Yuzhnyy Ural** *var.* Southern Urals. ▲▲ W Russian Federation
159 V10 **Yuzhong** Gansu, C China
Yuzhou *see* Chongqing
103 N5 **Yvelines** ◈ *department* N France
108 B9 **Yverdon** *var.* Yverdon-les-Bains, *Ger.* Iferten; *anc.* Eborodunum. Vaud, W Switzerland
Yverdon-les-Bains *see* Yverdon
102 M3 **Yvetot** Seine-Maritime, N France
Ýylanly *see* Gurbansoltan Eje
Ýylanly *see* Gurbansoltan Eje

Z

147 T12 **Zaalayskiy Khrebet** *Taj.* Qatorkŭhi Pasi Oloy. ▲▲ Kyrgyzstan/Tajikistan
Zaamin *see* Zomin
Zaandam *see* Zaanstad
98 I10 **Zaanstad** *prev.* Zaandam. Noord-Holland, C Netherlands
Zabadani *see* Az Zabdānī
119 L18 **Zabalatstsye** *Rus.* Zabolot'ye. Homyel'skaya Voblasts', SE Belarus
112 L9 **Žabalj** *Ger.* Josefsdorf, *Hung.* Zsablya; *prev.* Józseffalva. Vojvodina, N Serbia
Zāb aş Şaghīr, Nahraz *see* Little Zab
123 P14 **Zabaykal'sk** Chitinskaya Oblast', S Russian Federation
Zāb-e Kūchek, Rūdkhāneh-ye *see* Little Zab
Zabeln *see* Sabile
Zabéré *see* Zabré
Zabern *see* Saverne
141 N16 **Zabīd** W Yemen
141 O16 **Zabīd, Wādī** *dry watercourse* SW Yemen
Żabinka *see* Zhabinka
Ząbkowice *see* Ząbkowice Śląskie
111 G15 **Ząbkowice Śląskie** *var.* Ząbkowice, *Ger.* Frankenstein, Frankenstein in Schlesien. Dolnośląskie, SW Poland
110 P10 **Zabłudów** Podlaskie, NE Poland
112 D8 **Zabok** Krapina-Zagorje, N Croatia
143 W9 **Zābol** *var.* Shahr-i-Zabul, Zabul; *prev.* Nasratabad. Sīstān va Balūchestān, E Iran
149 O7 **Zābol** *Pash.* Zābul. ◈ *province* SE Afghanistan
143 W13 **Zāboli** Sīstān va Balūchestān, SE Iran
Zabolot'ye *see* Zabalatstsye
77 Q13 **Zabré** *var.* Zabéré. S Burkina
111 G17 **Zábřeh** *Ger.* Hohenstadt. Olomoucký Kraj, E Czech Republic
111 J16 **Zabrze** *Ger.* Hindenburg, Hindenburg in Oberschlesien. Śląskie, S Poland
Zābul *see* Zābol
Zabul/Zābul *see* Zābol
42 E6 **Zacapa** Zacapa, E Guatemala
42 A3 **Zacapa** *off.* Departamento de Zacapa. ◈ *department* E Guatemala
Zacapa, Departamento de *see* Zacapa
40 M14 **Zacapú** Michoacán de Ocampo, SW Mexico
41 V14 **Zacatal** Campeche, SE Mexico
40 M11 **Zacatecas** Zacatecas, C Mexico
40 L10 **Zacatecas** ◈ *state* C Mexico
42 F8 **Zacatecoluca** La Paz, S El Salvador
41 P15 **Zacatepec** Morelos, S Mexico
41 Q13 **Zacatlán** Puebla, S Mexico
144 F8 **Zachagansk** Zapadnyy Kazakhstan, NW Kazakhstan
115 D20 **Zacháro** *var.* Zaharo, Zakháro. Dytikí Ellás, S Greece
22 J8 **Zachary** Louisiana, S USA
117 U6 **Zachepylivka** Kharkivs'ka Oblast', E Ukraine
Zachist'ye *see* Zachystsye
110 E9 **Zachodnio-pomorskie** ◈ *province* NW Poland
119 L14 **Zachystsye** *Rus.* Zachist'ye. Minskaya Voblasts', NW Belarus
40 L13 **Zacoalco** *var.* Zacoalco de Torres. Jalisco, SW Mexico
Zacoalco de Torres *see* Zacoalco
41 P13 **Zacualtipán** Hidalgo, C Mexico
112 C12 **Zadar** *It.* Zara; *anc.* Iader. Zadar, SW Croatia
112 C12 **Zadar** *off.* Zadarsko-Kninska Županija, Zadar-Knin. ◈ *province* SW Croatia
Zadar-Knin *see* Zadar
Zadarsko-Kninska Županija *see* Zadar
166 M14 **Zadetkyi Kyun** *var.* St.Matthew's Island. *island* Mergui Archipelago, S Myanmar (Burma)
67 Q9 **Zadié** *var.* Djadié. ≈ NE Gabon
159 Q13 **Zadoi** *var.* Qapugtang. Qinghai, C China
126 L7 **Zadonsk** Lipetskaya Oblast', W Russian Federation
75 X8 **Za'farâna** E Egypt
149 W7 **Zafarwāl** Punjab, E Pakistan
121 Q1 **Zafer Burnu** *var.* Cape Andreas, Cape Apostolas Andreas, *Gk.* Akrotíri Apostólou Andréa. *cape* NE Cyprus
107 J23 **Zafferano, Capo** *headland* Sicilia, Italy, C Mediterranean Sea
114 M7 **Zafirovo** Silistra, NE Bulgaria
Záfora *see* Sofraná
104 J12 **Zafra** Extremadura, W Spain
110 E13 **Żagań** *var.* Zagań, Żegań, *Ger.* Sagan. Lubuskie, W Poland
118 F10 **Žagarė** *Pol.* Żagory. Šiaulai, N Lithuania
75 W7 **Zagazig** *var.* Az Zaqāzīq. N Egypt
74 M5 **Zaghouan** *var.* Zaghwān. NE Tunisia
Zaghwān *see* Zaghouan
115 G16 **Zagorá** Thessalía, C Greece
Zagorod'ye *see* Zaharoddzye
Żagory *see* Žagarė
Zágráb *see* Zagreb
112 E8 **Zagreb** *Ger.* Agram, *Hung.* Zágráb. ● (Croatia) Zagreb, N Croatia
112 E8 **Zagreb** *prev.* Grad Zagreb. ◈ *province* N Croatia
142 L7 **Zāgros, Kūhhā-ye** *Eng.* Zagros Mountains. ▲▲ W Iran
Zagros Mountains *see* Zāgros, Kūhhā-ye
112 O12 **Žagubica** Serbia, E Serbia
Zagunao *see* Lixian

◆ Country
● Country Capital
◇ Dependent Territory
○ Dependent Territory Capital
◈ Administrative Regions
✈ International Airport
▲ Mountain
▲▲ Mountain Range
⋀ Volcano
≈ River
◎ Lake
⊟ Reservoir

111 *L22* **Zagyva** ~ N Hungary
Zaharo *see* Zacháro
119 *G19* **Zaharoddzye** *Rus.* Zagorod'ye. *physical region* SW Belarus
143 *W11* **Zāhedān** *var.* Zahidan; *prev.* Duzdab. Sīstān va Balūchestān, SE Iran
Zahidan *see* Zāhedān
Zaḥlah *see* Zahlé
138 *H7* **Zahlé** *var.* Zaḥlah. C Lebanon
146 *J14* **Zähmet** *Rus.* Zakhmet. Mary Welaýaty, C Turkmenistan
111 *O20* **Záhony** Szabolcs-Szatmár-Bereg, NE Hungary
141 *N13* **Ẓahrān** 'Asīr, S Saudi Arabia
139 *R12* **Ẓahrat al Baṭn** *hill range* S Iraq
120 *H11* **Zahrez Chergui** *var.* Zahrez Chergúi. *marsh* N Algeria
Zainlha *see* Xinjin
127 *S4* **Zainsk** Respublika Tatarstan, W Russian Federation
82 *A10* **Zaire** *prev.* Congo. ◐ *province* NW Angola
Zaire *see* Congo (river)
Zaire *see* Congo (Democratic Republic of)
112 *P13* **Zaječar** Serbia, E Serbia
83 *L18* **Zaka** Masvingo, E Zimbabwe
122 *M14* **Zakamensk** Respublika Buryatiya, S Russian Federation
116 *G7* **Zakarpats'ka Oblast'** *Eng.* Transcarpathian Oblast, *Rus.* Zakarpatskaya Oblast'. ◐ *province* W Ukraine
Zakarpatskaya Oblast' *see* Zakarpats'ka Oblast'
Zakataly *see* Zaqatala
Zakháro *see* Zacháro
Zakhidnyy Buh/Zakhodni Buh *see* Bug
Zakhmet *see* Zähmet
139 *Q1* **Zākhō** *var.* Zākhū. N Iraq
Zākhū *see* Zākhō
Zákinthos *see* Zákynthos
111 *L18* **Zakopane** Małopolskie, S Poland
78 *J12* **Zakouma** Salamat, S Chad
115 *L25* **Zákros** Kríti, Greece, E Mediterranean Sea
115 *C19* **Zákynthos** *var.* Zákinthos. Zákynthos, W Greece
115 *C20* **Zákynthos** *var.* Zákinthos, *It.* Zante. *island* Iónia Nísoi, Greece, C Mediterranean Sea
115 *C19* **Zakýnthou, Porthmós** *strait* SW Greece
111 *G24* **Zala** *off.* Zala Megye. ◐ *county* W Hungary
111 *G24* **Zala** ~ W Hungary
138 *M4* **Zalābiyah** Dayr az Zawr, C Syria
111 *G24* **Zalaegerszeg** Zala, W Hungary
104 *K11* **Zalamea de la Serena** Extremadura, W Spain
104 *J13* **Zalamea la Real** Andalucía, S Spain
Zala Megye *see* Zala
163 *U7* **Zalantun** *var.* Butha Qi. Nei Mongol Zizhiqu, N China
111 *G23* **Zalaszentgrót** Zala, SW Hungary
Zalatna *see* Zlatna
116 *G9* **Zalău** *Ger.* Waltenberg, *Hung.* Zilah; *prev. Ger.* Zillenmarkt. Sălaj, NW Romania
109 *V10* **Žalec** *Ger.* Sachsenfeld. C Slovenia
117 *S9* **Zalenodol's'k** Dnipropetrovs'ka Oblast', E Ukraine
110 *K8* **Zalewo** *Ger.* Saalfeld. Warmińsko-Mazurskie, NE Poland
141 *N9* **Ẓalim** Makkah, W Saudi Arabia
80 *A11* **Zalingei** *var.* Zalinje. Western Darfur, W Sudan
Zalinje *see* Zalingei
116 *K7* **Zalishchyky** Ternopil's'ka Oblast', W Ukraine
Zallah *see* Zillah
98 *J13* **Zaltbommel** Gelderland, C Netherlands
124 *H15* **Zaluch'ye** Novgorodskaya Oblast', NW Russian Federation
Zamak *see* Zamakh
141 *Q14* **Zamakh** *var.* Zamak. N Yemen
136 *K15* **Zamantı Irmağı** ~ C Turkey
Zambesi/Zambeze *see* Zambezi
83 *G14* **Zambezi** North Western, W Zambia
83 *K15* **Zambezi** *var.* Zambesi, *Port.* Zambeze. ~ S Africa
83 *O15* **Zambézia** *off.* Província da Zambézia. ◐ *province* C Mozambique
Zambézia, Província da *see* Zambézia
83 *I14* **Zambia** *off.* Republic of Zambia; *prev.* Northern Rhodesia. ◆ *republic* S Africa
Zambia, Republic of *see* Zambia
171 *O8* **Zamboanga** *off.* Zamboanga City. Mindanao, S Philippines
Zamboanga City *see* Zamboanga
54 *E5* **Zambrano** Bolívar, N Colombia
110 *N10* **Zambrów** Łomża, E Poland
83 *L14* **Zambué** Tete, NW Mozambique
77 *T13* **Zamfara** ~ NW Nigeria
Zamkog *see* Zamtang
56 *C9* **Zamora** Zamora Chinchipe, S Ecuador
104 *K6* **Zamora** Castilla-León, NW Spain
104 *K5* **Zamora** ◐ *province* Castilla-León, NW Spain
Zamora *see* Barinas
56 *A13* **Zamora Chinchipe** ◐ *province* S Ecuador
40 *M13* **Zamora de Hidalgo** Michoacán de Ocampo, SW Mexico
111 *P15* **Zamość** *Rus.* Zamoste. Lubelskie, E Poland
Zamoste *see* Zamość
160 *G7* **Zamtang** *var.* Zamkog; *prev.* Gamba. Sichuan, C China
75 *O8* **Zamzam, Wādī** *dry watercourse* NW Libya
79 *F20* **Zanaga** La Lékoumou, S Congo
41 *T16* **Zanatepec** Oaxaca, SE Mexico
105 *P9* **Záncara** ~ C Spain
Zancle *see* Messina
158 *G14* **Zanda** Xizang Zizhiqu, W China
98 *H10* **Zandvoort** Noord-Holland, W Netherlands
39 *P8* **Zane Hills** *hill range* Alaska, USA
31 *T13* **Zanesville** Ohio, N USA
142 *L4* **Zanjān** *var.* Zenjan, Zinjan. Zanjān, NW Iran
142 *L4* **Zanjān** *off.* Ostān-e Zanjān, *var.* Zenjan, Zinjan. ◐ *province* NW Iran
Zanjān, Ostān-e *see* Zanjān
Zante *see* Zákynthos
81 *J22* **Zanzibar** Zanzibar, E Tanzania
81 *J22* **Zanzibar** ◐ *region* E Tanzania
81 *J22* **Zanzibar** *Swa.* Unguja. *island* E Tanzania
81 *J22* **Zanzibar Channel** *channel* E Tanzania
165 *P10* **Zaō-san** ▲ Honshū, C Japan
161 *N8* **Zaoyang** Hubei, C China
124 *J2* **Zaozërsk** Murmanskaya Oblast', NW Russian Federation
161 *Q6* **Zaozhuang** Shandong, E China
28 *L4* **Zap** North Dakota, N USA
112 *L13* **Zapadna Morava** *Ger.* Westliche Morava. ~ C Serbia
124 *H16* **Zapadnaya Dvina** Tverskaya Oblast', W Russian Federation
Zapadnaya Dvina *see* Western Dvina
Zapadno-Kazakhstanskaya Oblast' *see* Zapadnyy Kazakhstan
122 *I9* **Zapadno-Sibirskaya Ravnina** *Eng.* West Siberian Plain. *plain* C Russian Federation
Zapadnyy Bug *see* Bug
144 *E9* **Zapadnyy Kazakhstan** *off.* Zapadno-Kazakhstanskaya Oblast', *Eng.* West Kazakhstan, *Kaz.* Batys Qazaqstan Oblysy; *prev.* Ural'skaya Oblast'. ◐ *province* NW Kazakhstan
122 *K13* **Zapadnyy Sayan** *Eng.* Western Sayans. ▲▲ S Russian Federation
63 *H15* **Zapala** Neuquén, W Argentina
62 *I4* **Zapaleri, Cerro** *var.* Cerro Sapaleri. ▲ N Chile
25 *Q16* **Zapata** Texas, SW USA
44 *D5* **Zapata, Península de** *peninsula* W Cuba
61 *G19* **Zapicán** Lavalleja, S Uruguay
65 *J19* **Zapiola Ridge** *undersea feature* SW Atlantic Ocean
65 *L19* **Zapiola Seamount** *undersea feature* S Atlantic Ocean
124 *I2* **Zapolyarnyy** Murmanskaya Oblast', NW Russian Federation
117 *U8* **Zaporizhzhya** *Rus.* Zaporozh'ye; *prev.* Aleksandrovsk. Zaporiz'ka Oblast', SE Ukraine
Zaporizhzhya *see* Zaporiz'ka Oblast'
117 *U9* **Zaporiz'ka Oblast'** *var.* Zaporizhzhya, *Rus.* Zaporozhskaya Oblast'. ◐ *province* SE Ukraine
Zaporozhskaya Oblast' *see* Zaporiz'ka Oblast'
Zaporozh'ye *see* Zaporizhzhya
40 *L14* **Zapotiltic** Jalisco, SW Mexico
158 *G13* **Zapug** Xizang Zizhiqu, W China
137 *V10* **Zaqatala** *Rus.* Zakataly. NW Azerbaijan
159 *P13* **Zaqên** Qinghai, W China
159 *Q13* **Za Qu** ~ C China
136 *M13* **Zara** Sivas, C Turkey
Zara *see* Zadar
Zarafshan *see* Zarafshon
147 *P12* **Zarafshon** *Rus.* Zeravshan. W Tajikistan
146 *L9* **Zarafshon** *Rus.* Zarafshan. Navoiy Viloyati, N Uzbekistan
Zarafshon *see* Zeravshan
147 *O12* **Zarafshon, Qatorkŭhi** *Rus.* Zeravshanskiy Khrebet, *Uzb.* Zarafshon Tizmasi. ▲▲ Tajikistan/Uzbekistan
Zarafshon Tizmasi *see* Zarafshon, Qatorkŭhi
54 *E7* **Zaragoza** Antioquia, N Colombia
40 *I5* **Zaragoza** Chihuahua, N Mexico
41 *N6* **Zaragoza** Coahuila de Zaragoza, NE Mexico
41 *O10* **Zaragoza** Nuevo León, NE Mexico
105 *R5* **Zaragoza** *Eng.* Saragossa; *anc.* Caesaraugusta, Salduba. Aragón, NE Spain
105 *R6* **Zaragoza** ◐ *province* Aragón, NE Spain
105 *R5* **Zaragoza** ✕ Aragón, NE Spain
143 *S10* **Zarand** Kermān, C Iran
148 *J9* **Zaranj** Nīmrūz, SW Afghanistan
118 *I11* **Zarasai** Utena, E Lithuania
62 *N12* **Zárate** *prev.* General José F.Uriburu. Buenos Aires, E Argentina
105 *Q2* **Zarautz** *var.* Zarauz. País Vasco, N Spain
Zarauz *see* Zarautz
Zaravecchia *see* Biograd na Moru
Zarāyīn *see* Zarēn
126 *L4* **Zaraysk** Moskovskaya Oblast', W Russian Federation
55 *N6* **Zaraza** Guárico, N Venezuela
Zarbdar *see* Zarbdor
147 *P11* **Zarbdor** *Rus.* Zarbdar. Jizzax Viloyati, C Uzbekistan
142 *M8* **Zard Kūh** ▲ SW Iran
124 *I5* **Zarechensk** Murmanskaya Oblast', NW Russian Federation
127 *P6* **Zarechnyy** Penzenskaya Oblast', W Russian Federation
Zareh Sharan *see* Sharan
39 *Y14* **Zarembo Island** *island* Alexander Archipelago, Alaska, USA
139 *V4* **Zarēn** *var.* Zarāyīn. E Iraq
149 *Q7* **Zarghūn Shahr** *var.* Katawaz. Paktīkā, SE Afghanistan
77 *V13* **Zaria** Kaduna, C Nigeria
116 *K2* **Zarichne** Rivnens'ka Oblast', NW Ukraine
122 *J13* **Zarinsk** Altayskiy Kray, S Russian Federation
116 *J12* **Zărnești** *Hung.* Zernest. Brașov, C Romania
115 *J25* **Zarós** Kríti, Greece, E Mediterranean Sea
100 *O9* **Zarow** ~ NE Germany
Zarqa *see* Az Zarqā'
Zarqa/Muḥāfazat az Zarqā' *see* Az Zarqā'
111 *G20* **Záruby** ▲ W Slovakia
56 *B8* **Zaruma** El Oro, SW Ecuador
110 *E13* **Żary** *Ger.* Sorau, Sorau in der Niederlausitz. Lubuskie, W Poland
54 *D10* **Zarzal** Valle del Cauca, W Colombia
42 *I7* **Zarzalar, Cerro** ▲ S Honduras
152 *I5* **Zāskār** ~ NE India
152 *I5* **Zāskār Range** ▲▲ NE India
119 *K15* **Zaslawye** Minskaya Voblasts', C Belarus
116 *K7* **Zastavna** Chernivets'ka Oblast', W Ukraine
111 *B16* **Žatec** *Ger.* Saaz. Ústecký Kraj, NW Czech Republic
Zaumgarten *see* Chrzanów
Zaunguzskiye Garagumy *see* Üngüz Angyrsyndaky Garagum
25 *X9* **Zavalla** Texas, SW USA
99 *H18* **Zaventem** Vlaams Brabant, C Belgium
99 *H18* **Zaventem** ✕ (Brussel/Bruxelles) Vlaams Brabant, C Belgium
Zavertse *see* Zawiercie
114 *L7* **Zavet** Razgrad, NE Bulgaria
127 *O12* **Zavetnoye** Rostovskaya Oblast', SW Russian Federation
156 *M3* **Zavhan Gol** ~ W Mongolia
112 *H12* **Zavidoviči** ◐ Federacija Bosna I Hercegovina, N Bosnia and Herzegovina
123 *R13* **Zavitinsk** Amurskaya Oblast', SE Russian Federation
Zawia *see* Az Zāwiyah
111 *K15* **Zawiercie** *Rus.* Zavertse. Śląskie, S Poland
75 *P11* **Zawīlah** *var.* Zuwaylah, *It.* Zueila. C Libya
138 *I4* **Zāwiyah, Jabal az** ▲▲ NW Syria
109 *Y3* **Zaya** ~ NE Austria
166 *M8* **Zayatkyi** Pegu, C Myanmar (Burma)
145 *Y11* **Zaysan** Vostochnyy Kazakhstan, E Kazakhstan
Zaysan Köl *see* Zaysan, Ozero
145 *Y11* **Zaysan, Ozero** *Kaz.* Zaysan Köl. ◎ E Kazakhstan
159 *R16* **Zayü** *var.* Gyigang. Xizang Zizhiqu, W China
Zayyq *see* Ural
44 *F6* **Zaza** ~ C Cuba
116 *K5* **Zbarazh** Ternopil's'ka Oblast', W Ukraine
116 *J5* **Zboriv** Ternopil's'ka Oblast', W Ukraine
111 *F18* **Zbraslav** Jihomoravský Kraj, SE Czech Republic
116 *K6* **Zbruch** ~ W Ukraine
Žďár *see* Žďár nad Sázavou
111 *F17* **Žďár nad Sázavou** *Ger.* Saar in Mähren; *prev.* Žďár. Vysočina, C Czech Republic
116 *K4* **Zdolbuniv** *Pol.* Zdolbunów, *Rus.* Zdolbunov. Rivnens'ka Oblast', NW Ukraine
Zdolbunov/Zdolbunów *see* Zdolbuniv
110 *J13* **Zduńska Wola** Sieradz, C Poland
117 *O4* **Zdvizh** ~ N Ukraine
Zdzięciół *see* Dzyatlava
111 *I16* **Zdzieszowice** *Ger.* Odertal. Opolskie, SW Poland
Zealand *see* Sjælland
188 *K6* **Zealandia Bank** *undersea feature* C Pacific Ocean
63 *H20* **Zeballos, Monte** ▲ S Argentina
83 *K20* **Zebediela** Limpopo, NE South Africa
113 *L18* **Zebë, Mal** *var.* Mali i Zebës. ▲ NE Albania
Zebës, Mali i *see* Zebë, Mal
21 *V9* **Zebulon** North Carolina, SE USA
112 *K8* **Žednik** *Hung.* Bácsjózseffalva. Vojvodina, N Serbia
99 *C15* **Zeebrugge** West-Vlaanderen, NW Belgium
183 *N16* **Zeehan** Tasmania, SE Australia
99 *L14* **Zeeland** Noord-Brabant, SE Netherlands
29 *N7* **Zeeland** North Dakota, N USA
99 *E14* **Zeeland** ◐ *province* SW Netherlands
83 *I21* **Zeerust** North-West, N South Africa
98 *K10* **Zeewolde** Flevoland, C Netherlands
138 *G8* **Ẓefat** *var.* Safed, Tsefat, *Ar.* Safad. Northern, N Israel
Zegań *see* Żagań
Zehden *see* Cedynia
100 *O11* **Zehdenick** Brandenburg, NE Germany
Zē-i Bādīnān *see* Great Zab
Zeiden *see* Codlea
146 *M14* **Zeidskoye Vodokhranilishche** ⊠ E Turkmenistan
Zē-i Kōya *see* Little Zab
181 *P7* **Zeil, Mount** ▲ Northern Territory, C Australia
98 *J12* **Zeist** Utrecht, C Netherlands
101 *M16* **Zeitz** Sachsen-Anhalt, E Germany
159 *T11* **Zêkog** *var.* Sonag. Qinghai, C China
Zelaya Norte *see* Atlántico Norte, Región Autónoma
Zelaya Sur *see* Atlántico Sur, Región Autónoma
99 *F17* **Zele** Oost-Vlaanderen, NW Belgium
110 *N12* **Żelechów** Lubelskie, E Poland
113 *H14* **Zelena Glava** ▲ SE Bosnia and Herzegovina
113 *I14* **Zelengora** ▲▲ S Bosnia and Herzegovina
124 *I5* **Zelenoborskiy** Murmanskaya Oblast', NW Russian Federation
127 *R3* **Zelenodol'sk** Respublika Tatarstan, W Russian Federation
122 *J12* **Zelenogorsk** Krasnoyarskiy Kray, C Russian Federation
124 *G12* **Zelenogorsk** *Fin.* Terijoki. Leningradskaya Oblast', NW Russian Federation
126 *K3* **Zelenograd** Moskovskaya Oblast', W Russian Federation
118 *B13* **Zelenogradsk** *Ger.* Cranz, Kranz. Kaliningradskaya Oblast', W Russian Federation
127 *O15* **Zelenokumsk** Stavropol'skiy Kray, SW Russian Federation
165 *X4* **Zelënyy, Ostrov** *var.* Shibotsu-jima. *island* NE Russian Federation
Železna Kapela *see* Eisenkappel
Železna Vrata *see* Demir Kapija
112 *L11* **Železniki** Serbia, N Serbia
98 *N12* **Zelhem** Gelderland, E Netherlands
113 *N18* **Želino** NW FYR Macedonia
113 *M14* **Željin** ▲ C Serbia
101 *K17* **Zella-Mehlis** Thüringen, C Germany
109 *P7* **Zell am See** *var.* Zell-am-See. Salzburg, S Austria
Zell-am-See *see* Zell am See
109 *N7* **Zell am Ziller** Tirol, W Austria
Zelle *see* Celle
109 *W2* **Zellerndorf** Niederösterreich, NE Austria
109 *U7* **Zeltweg** Steiermark, S Austria
119 *G17* **Zel'va** *Pol.* Zelwa. Hrodzyenskaya Voblasts', W Belarus
118 *H13* **Želva** Vilnius, C Lithuania
Zelwa *see* Zel'va
99 *E16* **Zelzate** *var.* Selzaete. Oost-Vlaanderen, NW Belgium
118 *E11* **Žemaičių Aukštumas** *physical region* W Lithuania
118 *C12* **Žemaičių Naumiestis** Klaipėda, SW Lithuania
119 *L14* **Zembin** *var.* Zyembin. Minskaya Voblasts', C Belarus
127 *N6* **Zemetchino** Penzenskaya Oblast', W Russian Federation
79 *M15* **Zémio** Haut-Mbomou, E Central African Republic
41 *R16* **Zempoaltepec, Cerro** ▲ SE Mexico
99 *G17* **Zemst** Vlaams Brabant, C Belgium
112 *L11* **Zemun** Serbia, N Serbia
Zendajan *see* Zendeh Jan
148 *J5* **Zendeh Jan** *var.* Zendajan, Zindajān. Herāt, NW Afghanistan
Zengg *see* Senj
112 *H12* **Zenica** ◐ Federacija Bosna I Hercegovina, C Bosnia and Herzegovina
Zenjan *see* Zanjān
Zen'kov *see* Zin'kiv
Zenshū *see* Chŏnju
Zenta *see* Senta
82 *B11* **Zenza do Itombe** Cuanza Norte, NW Angola
112 *H12* **Žepče** ◐ Federacija Bosna I Hercegovina, N Bosnia and Herzegovina
23 *W12* **Zephyrhills** Florida, SE USA
158 *F9* **Zepu** *var.* Poskam. Xinjiang Uygur Zizhiqu, NW China
147 *Q12* **Zeravshan** *Taj./Uzb.* Zarafshon. ~ Tajikistan/Uzbekistan
Zeravshan *see* Zarafshon
Zeravshanskiy Khrebet *see* Zarafshon, Qatorkŭhi
101 *M14* **Zerbst** Sachsen-Anhalt, E Germany
145 *P8* **Zerenda** Akmola, N Kazakhstan
110 *H12* **Żerków** Wielkopolskie, C Poland
108 *E11* **Zermatt** Valais, SW Switzerland
Zernest *see* Zărnești
108 *J9* **Zernez** Graubünden, SE Switzerland
126 *L12* **Zernograd** Rostovskaya Oblast', SW Russian Federation
Zestafoni *see* Zestap'oni
137 *S9* **Zestap'oni** *Rus.* Zestafoni. C Georgia
98 *H12* **Zestienhoven** ✕ (Rotterdam) Zuid-Holland, SW Netherlands
113 *J16* **Zeta** ~ C Montenegro
8 *L6* **Zeta Lake** ◎ Victoria Island, Northwest Territories, N Canada
98 *L12* **Zetten** Gelderland, SE Netherlands
101 *M17* **Zeulenroda** Thüringen, C Germany
100 *H10* **Zeven** Niedersachsen, NW Germany
98 *M12* **Zevenaar** Gelderland, SE Netherlands
99 *H14* **Zevenbergen** Noord-Brabant, S Netherlands
129 *X6* **Zeya** ~ SE Russian Federation
Zeya Reservoir *see* Zeyskoye Vodokhranilishche
143 *T11* **Zeynalābād** Kermān, C Iran
123 *R12* **Zeyskoye Vodokhranilishche** *Eng.* Zeya Reservoir. ⊠ SE Russian Federation
104 *H8* **Zêzere, Rio** ~ C Portugal
Zgerzh *see* Zgierz
138 *H6* **Zgharta** N Lebanon
110 *K12* **Zgierz** *Ger.* Neuhof, *Rus.* Zgerzh. Łódź, C Poland
111 *E14* **Zgorzelec** *Ger.* Görlitz. Dolnośląskie, SW Poland
158 *I15* **Zhabdün** Xizang Zizhiqu, W China
119 *F19* **Zhabinka** *Pol.* Żabinka, *Rus.* Zhabinka. Brestskaya Voblasts', SW Belarus
Zhaggo *see* Luhuo
159 *R15* **Zhag'yab** *var.* Yêndum. Xizang Zizhiqu, W China
144 *L9* **Zhailma** *Kaz.* Zhayylma. Kostanay, N Kazakhstan
145 *V16* **Zhalanash** Almaty, SE Kazakhstan
Zhalashash *see* Dzhalagash
145 *S7* **Zhalauly, Ozero** ◎ NE Kazakhstan
144 *E9* **Zhalpaktal** *prev.* Furmanovo. Zapadnyy Kazakhstan, W Kazakhstan
119 *G16* **Zhaludok** *Rus.* Zheludok. Hrodzyenskaya Voblasts', W Belarus
Zhaman-Akkol', Ozero *see* Akkol', Ozero
145 *Q14* **Zhambyl** *off.* Zhambylskaya Oblast', *Kaz.* Zhambyl Oblysy; *prev.* Dzhambulskaya Oblast'. ◐ *province* S Kazakhstan
Zhambyl *see* Taraz
Zhambyl Oblysy/Zhambylskaya Oblast' *see* Zhambyl
Zhamo *see* Bomi
145 *S12* **Zhamshy** ~ C Kazakhstan
144 *M15* **Zhanadar'ya** Kzylorda, S Kazakhstan
145 *O15* **Zhanakorgan** *Kaz.* Zhangaqorghan. Kzylorda, S Kazakhstan
159 *N16* **Zhanang** *var.* Chatang. Xizang Zizhiqu, W China
145 *T12* **Zhanatortalyk** Karaganda, C Kazakhstan
144 *F15* **Zhanaozen** *Kaz.* Zhangaözen; *prev.* Novyy Uzen'. Mangistau, W Kazakhstan
145 *Q16* **Zhanatas** Zhambyl, S Kazakhstan
Zhangaözen *see* Zhanaozen
Zhangaqazaly *see* Ayteke Bi
Zhangaqorghan *see* Zhanakorgan
161 *O2* **Zhangbei** Hebei, E China
Zhang-chia-k'ou *see* Zhangjiakou
Zhangdian *see* Zibo
Zhanggu *see* Danba
163 *X9* **Zhangguangcai Ling** ▲▲ NE China
145 *W10* **Zhangiztobe** Vostochnyy Kazakhstan, E Kazakhstan
159 *W11* **Zhangjiachuan** Gansu, N China
160 *L10* **Zhangjiajie** *var.* Dayong. Hunan, S China
161 *O2* **Zhangjiakou** *var.* Changkiakow, Zhang-chia-k'ou, *Eng.* Kalgan; *prev.* Wanchuan. Hebei, E China
161 *Q13* **Zhangping** Fujian, SE China
161 *Q13* **Zhangpu** *var.* Sui'an. Fujian, SE China
163 *U11* **Zhangwu** Liaoning, NE China
159 *S8* **Zhangye** *var.* Ganzhou. Gansu, N China
161 *Q13* **Zhangzhou** Fujian, SE China
163 *W6* **Zhan He** ~ NE China
144 *D9* **Zhanibek** *var.* Zhänibek, *Rus.* Dzhanibek, Dzhanybek. Zapadnyy Kazakhstan, W Kazakhstan
160 *L16* **Zhanjiang** *var.* Chanchiang, Chan-chiang, *Cant.* Tsamkong, *Fr.* Fort-Bayard. Guangdong, S China
Zhansügirov *see* Dzhansugurov
163 *V8* **Zhaodong** Heilongjiang, NE China
Zhaoge *see* Qixian
160 *H11* **Zhaojue** *var.* Xincheng. Sichuan, C China
161 *N14* **Zhaoqing** Guangdong, S China
Zhaoren *see* Changwu
158 *H5* **Zhaosu** *var.* Mongolküre. Xinjiang Uygur Zizhiqu, NW China
160 *H11* **Zhaotong** Yunnan, SW China
163 *V9* **Zhaoyuan** Heilongjiang, NE China
163 *V9* **Zhaozhou** Heilongjiang, NE China
145 *X13* **Zharbulak** Vostochnyy Kazakhstan, E Kazakhstan
158 *J15* **Zhari Namco** ◎ W China
144 *I12* **Zharkamys** *Kaz.* Zharqamys. Aktyubinsk, W Kazakhstan
145 *W15* **Zharkent** *prev.* Panfilov. Taldykorgan, SE Kazakhstan
124 *H17* **Zharkovskiy** Tverskaya Oblast', W Russian Federation
145 *W11* **Zharma** Vostochnyy Kazakhstan, E Kazakhstan
144 *F14* **Zharmysh** Mangistau, SW Kazakhstan
Zharqamys *see* Zharkamys
118 *L13* **Zhary** *Rus.* Zhary. Vitsyebskaya Voblasts', N Belarus
Zhaslyk *see* Jaslıq
158 *J14* **Zhaxi Co** ◎ W China
Zhayylma *see* Zhailma
Zhdanov *see* Beyläqan
Zhdanov *see* Mariupol'
Zhe *see* Zhejiang
161 *R10* **Zhejiang** *var.* Che-chiang, Chekiang, Zhe, Zhejiang Sheng. ◐ *province* SE China
Zhejiang Sheng *see* Zhejiang
145 *S7* **Zhelezinka** Pavlodar, N Kazakhstan
119 *C14* **Zheleznodorozhnyy** *Ger.* Gerdauen. Kaliningradskaya Oblast', W Russian Federation
Zheleznodorozhnyy *see* Yemva
122 *K12* **Zheleznogorsk** Krasnoyarskiy Kray, C Russian Federation
126 *J7* **Zheleznogorsk** Kurskaya Oblast', W Russian Federation
127 *N15* **Zheleznovodsk** Stavropol'skiy Kray, SW Russian Federation
Zhëltyye Vody *see* Zhovti Vody
Zheludok *see* Zhaludok
Zhem *see* Emba
160 *K7* **Zhenba** Shaanxi, C China
160 *I13* **Zhenfeng** Guizhou, S China
Zhengjiatun *see* Shuangliao
159 *X10* **Zhengning** *var.* Shanhe. Gansu, N China
Zhengxiangbai Qi *see* Qagan Nur
161 *N6* **Zhengzhou** *var.* Ch'eng-chou, Chengchow; *prev.* Chenghsien. *province capital* Henan, C China
161 *R8* **Zhenjiang** *var.* Chenkiang. Jiangsu, E China
163 *U9* **Zhenlai** Jilin, NE China
160 *I11* **Zhenxiong** Yunnan, SW China
160 *K11* **Zhenyuan** *var.* Wuyang. Guizhou, S China
161 *R11* **Zherong** *var.* Shuangcheng. Fujian, SE China
145 *U15* **Zhetigen** *prev.* Nikolayevka. Almaty, SE Kazakhstan
Zhetiqara *see* Zhitikara
Zhetiqara *see* Zhitikara
144 *F15* **Zhetybay** Mangistau, SW Kazakhstan
145 *P17* **Zhetysay** *var.* Dzhetysay. Yuzhnyy Kazakhstan, S Kazakhstan
160 *M11* **Zhexi Shuiku** ⊠ C China
145 *O12* **Zhezdy** Karaganda, C Kazakhstan
145 *O12* **Zhezkazgan** *Kaz.* Zhezqazghan; *prev.* Dzhezkazgan. Karaganda, C Kazakhstan
Zhezqazghan *see* Zhezkazgan
Zhicheng *see* Yidu
Zhidachov *see* Zhydachiv
159 *Q12* **Zhidoi** *var.* Gyaijêpozhanggê. Qinghai, C China
122 *M13* **Zhigalovo** Irkutskaya Oblast', S Russian Federation
127 *R6* **Zhigulevsk** Samarskaya Oblast', W Russian Federation
118 *D13* **Zhilino** *Ger.* Schillen. Kaliningradskaya Oblast', W Russian Federation
Zhiloy, Ostrov *see* Çiloy Adası
127 *O8* **Zhirnovsk** Volgogradskaya Oblast', SW Russian Federation
160 *M12* **Zhishan** *prev.* Yongzhou. Hunan, S China
Zhitarovo *see* Vetren
144 *L8* **Zhitikara** *Kaz.* Zhetiqara; *prev.* Dzhetygara. Kostanay, NW Kazakhstan
144 *L8* **Zhitikara** *Kaz.* Zhetiqara; *prev.* Džetygara. Kostanay, NW Kazakhstan
Zhitkovichi *see* Zhytkavichy
127 *P10* **Zhitkur** Volgogradskaya Oblast', SW Russian Federation
Zhitomir *see* Zhytomyr
Zhitomirskaya Oblast' *see* Zhytomyrs'ka Oblast'
126 *J5* **Zhizdra** Kaluzhskaya Oblast', W Russian Federation
119 *N18* **Zhlobin** Homyel'skaya Voblasts', SE Belarus
Zhmerinka *see* Zhmerynka
116 *M7* **Zhmerynka** *Rus.* Zhmerinka. Vinnyts'ka Oblast', C Ukraine
149 *R9* **Zhob** *var.* Fort Sandeman. Baluchistān, SW Pakistan
149 *R8* **Zhob** ~ C Pakistan
Zhodino *see* Zhodzina
119 *L15* **Zhodzina** *Rus.* Zhodino. Minskaya Voblasts', C Belarus
123 *Q5* **Zhokhova, Ostrov** *island* Novosibirskiye Ostrova, NE Russian Federation
Zholkev/Zholkva *see* Zhovkva
Zholsaly *see* Dzhusaly
Zhondor *see* Jondor
158 *I15* **Zhongba** *var.* Tuoji. Xizang Zizhiqu, W China
Zhongba *see* Jiangyou
160 *F11* **Zhongdian** Yunnan, SW China
Zhongduo *see* Youyang
Zhonghe *see* Xiushan
Zhonghua Renmin Gongheguo *see* China
159 *V9* **Zhongning** Ningxia, N China
Zhongping *see* Huize
161 *N15* **Zhongshan** Guangdong, S China
195 *X7* **Zhongshan** *Chinese research station* Antarctica
160 *M6* **Zhongtiao Shan** ▲ C China
159 *V9* **Zhongwei** Ningxia, N China
160 *K9* **Zhongxian** *var.* Zhongzhou. Chongqing Shi, C China
161 *N9* **Zhongxiang** Hubei, C China
Zhongzhou *see* Zhongxian
161 *O7* **Zhoukou** *var.* Zhoukouzhen. Henan, C China
Zhoukouzhen *see* Zhoukou
161 *S9* **Zhoushan** Zhejiang, S China
Zhoushan Islands *see* Zhoushan Qundao
161 *S9* **Zhoushan Qundao** *Eng.* Zhoushan Islands. *island group* SE China
116 *I5* **Zhovkva** *Pol.* Żółkiew, *Rus.* Zholkev, Zholkva; *prev.* Nesterov. L'vivs'ka Oblast', NW Ukraine
117 *S7* **Zhovti Vody** *Rus.* Zhëltyye Vody. Dnipropetrovs'ka Oblast', E Ukraine
117 *Q10* **Zhovtneve** *Rus.* Zhovtnevoye. Mykolayivs'ka Oblast', S Ukraine
Zhovtnevoye *see* Zhovtneve
114 *K9* **Zhrebchevo, Yazovir** ⊠ C Bulgaria
163 *V13* **Zhuanghe** Liaoning, NE China
159 *W11* **Zhuanglang** *var.* Shuilocheng. Gansu, C China
145 *P15* **Zhuantobe** *Kaz.* Zhūantöbe. Yuzhnyy Kazakhstan, S Kazakhstan
161 *Q5* **Zhucheng** Shandong, E China
159 *V12* **Zhugqu** Gansu, C China
161 *N15* **Zhuhai** Guangdong, S China
Zhuizishan *see* Weichang
Zhuji *see* Shangqiu
126 *I5* **Zhukovka** Bryanskaya Oblast', W Russian Federation
161 *N7* **Zhumadian** Henan, C China
Zhuo Xian *see* Zhuozhou
161 *O3* **Zhuozhou** *prev.* Zhuo Xian. Hebei, E China
162 *L14* **Zhuozi Shan** ▲ N China
Zhuravichi *see* Zhuravichy
119 *O17* **Zhuravichy** *Rus.* Zhuravichi. Homyel'skaya Voblasts', SE Belarus
145 *Q8* **Zhuravlevka** Akmola, N Kazakhstan
117 *Q4* **Zhurivka** Kyyivs'ka Oblast', N Ukraine
144 *J11* **Zhuryn** Aktyubinsk, W Kazakhstan
145 *T15* **Zhusandala, Step'** *grassland* SE Kazakhstan
160 *L8* **Zhushan** Hubei, C China
Zhushan *see* Xuan'en
Zhuyang *see* Dazhu
161 *N11* **Zhuzhou** Hunan, S China

◆ Country ● Country Capital ◇ Dependent Territory ○ Dependent Territory Capital ◐ Administrative Regions ✕ International Airport ▲ Mountain ▲▲ Mountain Range ⚠ Volcano ~ River ◎ Lake ⊠ Reservoir

116 *I6* **Zhydachiv** *Pol.* Żydaczów, *Rus.* Zhidachov. L'vivs'ka Oblast', NW Ukraine
144 *G9* **Zhympity** *Kaz.* Zhympīty; *prev.* Dzhambeyty. Zapadnyy, W Kazakhstan
119 *K19* **Zhytkavichy** *Rus.* Zhitkovichi. Homyel'skaya Voblasts', SE Belarus
117 *N4* **Zhytomyr** *Rus.* Zhitomir. Zhytomyrs'ka Oblast', NW Ukraine
Zhytomyr *see* Zhytomyrs'ka Oblast'
116 *M4* **Zhytomyrs'ka Oblast'** *var.* Zhytomyr, *Rus.* Zhitomirskaya Oblast'. ◐ *province* N Ukraine
153 *U15* **Zia** ✈ (Dhaka) Dhaka, C Bangladesh
111 *J20* **Žiar nad Hronom** *var.* Sväty Kríž nad Hronom, *Ger.* Heiligenkreuz, *Hung.* Garamszentkereszt. Banskobystrický Kraj, C Slovakia
161 *Q4* **Zibo** *var.* Zhangdian. Shandong, E China
160 *L4* **Zichang** *prev.* Wayaobu. Shaanxi, C China
Zichenau *see* Ciechanów
111 *G15* **Ziębice** *Ger.* Münsterberg in Schlesien. Dolnośląskie, SW Poland
Ziebingen *see* Cybinka
Ziegenhais *see* Głuchołazy
110 *E12* **Zielona Góra** *Ger.* Grünberg, Grünberg in Schlesien, Grüneberg. Lubuskie, W Poland
99 *F14* **Zierikzee** Zeeland, SW Netherlands
160 *I10* **Zigong** *var.* Tzekung. Sichuan, C China
76 *G12* **Ziguinchor** SW Senegal
41 *N16* **Zihuatanejo** Guerrero, S Mexico
Ziketan *see* Xinghai
Zilah *see* Zalău
127 *W7* **Zilair** Respublika Bashkortostan, W Russian Federation
136 *L12* **Zile** Tokat, N Turkey
111 *J18* **Žilina** *Ger.* Sillein, *Hung.* Zsolna. Zlínský Kraj, N Slovakia
111 *J19* **Žilinský Kraj** ◐ *region* N Slovakia
75 *Q9* **Zillah** *var.* Zallah. C Libya
Zillenmarkt *see* Zalău
109 *N7* **Ziller** ≈ W Austria
Zillertal Alps *see* Zillertaler Alpen
109 *N8* **Zillertaler Alpen** *Eng.* Zillertal Alps, *It.* Alpi Aurine. ▲▲ Austria/Italy
118 *K10* **Zilupe** *Ger.* Rosenhof. Ludza, E Latvia
41 *O13* **Zimapán** Hidalgo, C Mexico
83 *I16* **Zimba** Southern, S Zambia
83 *J17* **Zimbabwe** *off.* Republic of Zimbabwe; *prev.* Rhodesia. ◆ *republic* S Africa
Zimbabwe, Republic of *see* Zimbabwe
116 *H10* **Zimbor** *Hung.* Magyarzsombor. Sălaj, NW Romania
Zimmerbude *see* Svetlyy
116 *J15* **Zimnicea** Teleorman, S Romania
114 *L9* **Zimnitsa** Yambol, E Bulgaria
127 *N12* **Zimovniki** Rostovskaya Oblast', SW Russian Federation
Zindajān *see* Zendeh Jan
77 *V12* **Zinder** Zinder, S Niger
77 *W11* **Zinder** ◐ *department* S Niger
77 *P12* **Ziniaré** C Burkina
Zinjan *see* Zanjān
141 *P16* **Zinjibār** SW Yemen
117 *T4* **Zin'kiv** *var.* Zen'kov. Poltavs'ka Oblast', NE Ukraine
Zinov'yevsk *see* Kirovohrad
Zintenhof *see* Sindi
31 *N10* **Zion** Illinois, N USA
54 *F10* **Zipaquirá** Cundinamarca, C Colombia
Zipser Neudorf *see* Spišská Nová Ves
111 *H23* **Zirc** Veszprém, W Hungary
113 *D14* **Žirje** *It.* Zuri. *island* S Croatia
Zirknitz *see* Cerknica
108 *M7* **Zirl** Tirol, W Austria
101 *K20* **Zirndorf** Bayern, SE Germany
160 *M11* **Zi Shui** ≈ C China
109 *Y3* **Zistersdorf** Niederösterreich, NE Austria
41 *O14* **Zitácuaro** Michoacán de Ocampo, SW Mexico
Zito *see* Lhorong
101 *Q16* **Zittau** Sachsen, E Germany
112 *I12* **Živinice** ◐ Federacija Bosna I Hercegovina, E Bosnia and Herzegovina
Ziwa Magharibi *see* Kagera
81 *J14* **Ziway Hāyk'** ◎ C Ethiopia
161 *N12* **Zixing** Hunan, S China
127 *W7* **Ziyanchurino** Orenburgskaya Oblast', W Russian Federation
160 *K8* **Ziyang** Shaanxi, C China
111 *I20* **Zlaté Moravce** *Hung.* Aranyosmarót. Nitriansky Kraj, SW Slovakia
112 *K13* **Zlatibor** ▲▲ W Serbia
114 *L9* **Zlati Voyvoda** Sliven, C Bulgaria
116 *G11* **Zlatna** *Ger.* Kleinschlatten, *Hung.* Zalatna; *prev. Ger.* Goldmarkt. Alba, C Romania
114 *I8* **Zlatna Panega** Lovech, N Bulgaria
114 *N8* **Zlatni Pyasŭtsi** Dobrich, NE Bulgaria
122 *F11* **Zlatoust** Chelyabinskaya Oblast', C Russian Federation
111 *M19* **Zlatý Stôl** *Ger.* Goldener Tisch, *Hung.* Aranyosasztal. ▲ C Slovakia
113 *P18* **Zletovo** NE FYR Macedonia
111 *H18* **Zlín** *prev.* Gottwaldov. Zlínský Kraj, E Czech Republic
111 *H19* **Zlínský Kraj** ◐ *region* E Czech Republic
75 *O7* **Zlīṭan** W Libya
110 *F9* **Złocieniec** *Ger.* Falkenburg in Pommern. Zachodnio-pomorskie, NW Poland
110 *J13* **Złoczew** Sieradz, S Poland
Złoczów *see* Zolochiv
111 *F14* **Złotoryja** *Ger.* Goldberg. Dolnośląskie, W Poland
110 *G9* **Złotów** Wielkopolskie, C Poland
110 *G13* **Żmigród** *Ger.* Trachenberg. Dolnośląskie, SW Poland
126 *J6* **Zmiyevka** Orlovskaya Oblast', W Russian Federation
117 *V5* **Zmiyiv** Kharkivs'ka Oblast', E Ukraine
Zna *see* Tsna
Znaim *see* Znojmo
126 *M7* **Znamenka** Tambovskaya Oblast', W Russian Federation
Znamenka *see* Znam"yanka
119 *C14* **Znamens** Astrakhanskaya Oblast', W Russian Federation
127 *P10* **Znamensk** *Ger.* Wehlau. Kaliningradskaya Oblast', W Russian Federation
117 *R7* **Znam"yanka** *Rus.* Znamenka. Kirovohrads'ka Oblast', C Ukraine
110 *H10* **Żnin** Kujawsko-pomorskie, C Poland
111 *F19* **Znojmo** *Ger.* Znaim. Jihomoravský Kraj, SE Czech Republic
79 *N16* **Zobia** Orientale, N Dem. Rep. Congo
83 *N15* **Zóbuè** Tete, NW Mozambique
98 *G12* **Zoetermeer** Zuid-Holland, W Netherlands
108 *E7* **Zofingen** Aargau, N Switzerland
159 *R15* **Zogang** *var.* Wangda. Xizang Zizhiqu, W China
106 *E7* **Zogno** Lombardia, N Italy
142 *M10* **Zohreh, Rūd-e** ≈ SW Iran
160 *H7* **Zoigê** *var.* Dagcagoin. Sichuan, C China
Zółkiew *see* Zhovkva
108 *D8* **Zollikofen** Bern, W Switzerland
Zolochev *see* Zolochiv
117 *U4* **Zolochiv** *Rus.* Zolochev. Kharkivs'ka Oblast', E Ukraine
116 *J5* **Zolochiv** *Pol.* Złoczów, *Rus.* Zolochev. L'vivs'ka Oblast', W Ukraine
117 *X7* **Zolote** *Rus.* Zolotoye. Luhans'ka Oblast', E Ukraine
117 *Q6* **Zolotonosha** Cherkas'ka Oblast', C Ukraine
Zolotoye *see* Zolote
Zólyom *see* Zvolen
83 *N15* **Zomba** Southern, S Malawi
Zombor *see* Sombor
99 *D17* **Zomergem** Oost-Vlaanderen, NW Belgium
147 *P11* **Zomin** *Rus.* Zaamin. Jizzax Viloyati, C Uzbekistan
79 *I15* **Zongo** Equateur, N Dem. Rep. Congo
136 *G10* **Zonguldak** Zonguldak, NW Turkey
136 *H10* **Zonguldak** ◐ *province* NW Turkey
99 *K17* **Zonhoven** Limburg, NE Belgium
142 *J2* **Zonūz** Āžarbāyjān-e Khāvarī, NW Iran
103 *Y16* **Zonza** Corse, France, C Mediterranean Sea
Zoppot *see* Sopot
Zorgho *see* Zorgo
77 *Q13* **Zorgo** *var.* Zorgho. C Burkina
104 *K10* **Zorita** Extremadura, W Spain
147 *U14* **Zorkŭl** *Rus.* Ozero Zorkul'. ◎ SE Tajikistan
Zorkul', Ozero *see* Zorkŭl
56 *A8* **Zorritos** Tumbes, N Peru
111 *J16* **Żory** *var.* Zory, *Ger.* Sohrau. Śląskie, S Poland
76 *K15* **Zorzor** N Liberia
99 *E18* **Zottegem** Oost-Vlaanderen, NW Belgium
77 *R15* **Zou** ≈ S Benin
78 *H6* **Zouar** Borkou-Ennedi-Tibesti, N Chad
76 *J6* **Zouérat** *var.* Zouérate, Zouîrât. Tiris Zemmour, N Mauritania
Zouérate *see* Zouérat
Zoug *see* Zug
Zouîrât *see* Zouérat
76 *M16* **Zoukougbeu** C Ivory Coast
98 *M5* **Zoutkamp** Groningen, NE Netherlands
99 *J18* **Zoutleeuw** *Fr.* Leau. Vlaams Brabant, C Belgium
112 *L9* **Zrenjanin** *prev.* Petrovgrad, Veliki Bečkerek, *Ger.* Grossbetschkerek, *Hung.* Nagybecskerek. Vojvodina, N Serbia
112 *E10* **Zrinska Gora** ▲▲ C Croatia
Zsablya *see* Žabalj
101 *N16* **Zschopau** ≈ E Germany
Zsebely *see* Jebel
Zsibó *see* Jibou
Zsilyvajdevulkán *see* Vulcan
Zsil/Zsily *see* Jiu
Zsolna *see* Žilina
Zsombolya *see* Jimbolia
Zsupanya *see* Županja
55 *N7* **Zuata** Anzoátegui, NE Venezuela
105 *N14* **Zubia** Andalucía, S Spain
65 *P16* **Zubov Seamount** *undersea feature* E Atlantic Ocean
124 *I16* **Zubtsov** Tverskaya Oblast', W Russian Federation
108 *M8* **Zuckerhütl** ▲ SW Austria
Zueila *see* Zawīlah
76 *M16* **Zuénoula** C Ivory Coast
105 *S5* **Zuera** Aragón, NE Spain
141 *V13* **Ẓufār** *Eng.* Dhofar. *physical region* SW Oman
108 *G8* **Zug** *Fr.* Zoug. Zug, C Switzerland
108 *G8* **Zug** *Fr.* Zoug. ◐ *canton* C Switzerland
137 *R9* **Zugdidi** W Georgia
108 *G8* **Zuger See** ◎ NW Switzerland
101 *K25* **Zugspitze** ▲ S Germany
99 *E15* **Zuid-Beveland** *var.* South Beveland. *island* SW Netherlands
98 *K10* **Zuidelijk-Flevoland** *polder* C Netherlands
Zuider Zee *see* IJsselmeer
98 *G12* **Zuid-Holland** *Eng.* South Holland. ◐ *province* W Netherlands
98 *N5* **Zuidhorn** Groningen, NE Netherlands
98 *O6* **Zuidlaardermeer** ◎ NE Netherlands
98 *O6* **Zuidlaren** Drenthe, NE Netherlands
99 *K14* **Zuid-Willemsvaart Kanaal** *canal* S Netherlands
98 *N8* **Zuidwolde** Drenthe, NE Netherlands
Zuitai/Zuitaizi *see* Kangxian
105 *O14* **Zújar** Andalucía, S Spain
104 *L11* **Zújar** ≈ W Spain
104 *L11* **Zújar, Embalse del** ⊠ W Spain
80 *J9* **Zula** E Eritrea
54 *G6* **Zulia** *off.* Estado Zulia. ◐ *state* NW Venezuela
Zulia, Estado *see* Zulia
Zullapara *see* Sinchaingbyin
Züllichau *see* Sulechów
105 *P3* **Zumárraga** País Vasco, N Spain
112 *D8* **Žumberačko Gorje** *var.* Gorjanči, Uskocke Planine, Žumberak, *Ger.* Uskokengebirge; *prev.* Sichelburger Gerbirge. ▲ Croatia/Slovenia ***see also*** Gorjanci
Žumberak *see* Žumberačko Gorje
Žumberak *see* Gorjanci/Žumberačko Gorje
194 *K7* **Zumberge Coast** *coastal feature* Antarctica
Zumbo *see* Vila do Zumbo
29 *W10* **Zumbro Falls** Minnesota, N USA
29 *W10* **Zumbro River** ≈ Minnesota, N USA
29 *W10* **Zumbrota** Minnesota, N USA
99 *H15* **Zundert** Noord-Brabant, S Netherlands
Zungaria *see* Dzungaria
77 *U14* **Zungeru** Niger, C Nigeria
161 *P2* **Zunhua** Hebei, E China
37 *O11* **Zuni** New Mexico, SW USA
37 *P11* **Zuni Mountains** ▲▲ New Mexico, SW USA
160 *J11* **Zunyi** Guizhou, S China
160 *J15* **Zuo Jiang** ≈ China/Vietnam
108 *J9* **Zuoz** Graubünden, SE Switzerland
112 *I10* **Županja** *Hung.* Zsupanya. Vukovar-Srijem, E Croatia
113 *M17* **Žur** Kosovo, S Serbia
127 *T2* **Zura** Udmurtskaya Respublika, NW Russian Federation
139 *V8* **Zurbāṭīyah** E Iraq
Zuri *see* Žirje
108 *F7* **Zürich** *Eng./Fr.* Zurich, *It.* Zurigo. Zürich, N Switzerland
108 *G6* **Zürich** *Eng./Fr.* Zurich. ◐ *canton* N Switzerland
Zurich, Lake *see* Zürichsee
108 *G7* **Zürichsee** *Eng.* Lake Zurich. ◎ NE Switzerland
Zurigo *see* Zürich
149 *V1* **Zŭrkŭl** *Pash.* Sarī Qūl, *Rus.* Ozero Zurkul'. ◎ Afghanistan/Tajikistan ***see also*** Sarī Qūl
Zŭrkŭl *see* Sarī Qūl
Zurkul', Ozero *see* Sarī Qūl/Zŭrkŭl
110 *K10* **Żuromin** Mazowieckie, C Poland
108 *J8* **Zürs** Vorarlberg, W Austria
77 *T13* **Zuru** Kebbi, W Nigeria
108 *F6* **Zurzach** Aargau, N Switzerland
101 *J22* **Zusam** ≈ S Germany
98 *M11* **Zutphen** Gelderland, E Netherlands
75 *N7* **Zuwārah** NW Libya
Zuwaylah *see* Zawīlah
125 *R14* **Zuyevka** Kirovskaya Oblast', NW Russian Federation
161 *N10* **Zuzhou** Hunan, S China
Zvenigorodka *see* Zvenyhorodka
117 *P6* **Zvenyhorodka** *Rus.* Zvenigorodka. Cherkas'ka Oblast', C Ukraine
123 *N12* **Zvezdnyy** Irkutskaya Oblast', C Russian Federation
125 *U14* **Zvëzdnyy** Permskaya Oblast', NW Russian Federation
83 *K18* **Zvishavane** *prev.* Shabani. Matabeleland South, S Zimbabwe
111 *J20* **Zvolen** *Ger.* Altsohl, *Hung.* Zólyom. Banskobystrický Kraj, C Slovakia
112 *J12* **Zvornik** E Bosnia and Herzegovina
98 *M5* **Zwaagwesteinde** *Fris.* De Westerein. Friesland, N Netherlands
98 *H10* **Zwanenburg** Noord-Holland, C Netherlands
98 *L8* **Zwarte Meer** ◎ N Netherlands
98 *M9* **Zwarte Water** ≈ N Netherlands
98 *M8* **Zwartsluis** Overijssel, E Netherlands
76 *L17* **Zwedru** *var.* Tchien. E Liberia
98 *O8* **Zweeloo** Drenthe, NE Netherlands
101 *E20* **Zweibrücken** *Fr.* Deux-Ponts, *Lat.* Bipontium. Rheinland-Pfalz, SW Germany
108 *D9* **Zweisimmen** Fribourg, W Switzerland
101 *M15* **Zwenkau** Sachsen, E Germany
109 *V3* **Zwettl** Wien, NE Austria
109 *T3* **Zwettl an der Rodl** Oberösterreich, N Austria
99 *D18* **Zwevegem** West-Vlaanderen, W Belgium
101 *M17* **Zwickau** Sachsen, E Germany
101 *N16* **Zwikauer Mulde** ≈ E Germany
101 *O21* **Zwiesel** Bayern, SE Germany
98 *H13* **Zwijndrecht** Zuid-Holland, SW Netherlands
Zwischenwässern *see* Medvode
Zwittau *see* Svitavy
110 *N13* **Zwoleń** Mazowieckie, SE Poland
98 *M9* **Zwolle** Overijssel, E Netherlands
22 *G6* **Zwolle** Louisiana, S USA
110 *K12* **Żychlin** Łódzkie, C Poland
Żydaczów *see* Zhydachiv
Zyembin *see* Zembin
Zyôetu *see* Jōetsu
110 *L12* **Żyrardów** Mazowieckie, C Poland
123 *S8* **Zyryanka** Respublika Sakha (Yakutiya), NE Russian Federation
145 *Y9* **Zyryanovsk** Vostochnyy Kazakhstan, E Kazakhstan
111 *J17* **Żywiec** *Ger.* Bäckermühle Schulzenmühle. Śląskie, S Poland

◆ Country
● Country Capital
◇ Dependent Territory
○ Dependent Territory Capital
◐ Administrative Regions
✈ International Airport
▲ Mountain
▲▲ Mountain Range
Volcano
≈ River
◎ Lake
⊠ Reservoir

PICTURE CREDITS

DORLING KINDERSLEY *would like to express their thanks to the following individuals, companies, and institutions for their help in preparing this atlas.*

Earth Resource Mapping Ltd., Egham, Surrey
Brian Groombridge, World Conservation Monitoring Centre, Cambridge
The British Library, London
British Library of Political and Economic Science, London
The British Museum, London
The City Business Library, London
King's College, London
National Meteorological Library and Archive, Bracknell
The Printed Word, London
The Royal Geographical Society, London
University of London Library
Paul Beardmore
Philip Boyes
Hayley Crockford
Alistair Dougal
Reg Grant
Louise Keane
Zoe Livesley
Laura Porter
Jeff Eidenshink
Chris Hornby
Rachelle Smith
Ray Pinchard
Robert Meisner
Fiona Strawbridge

Every effort has been made to trace the copyright holders and we apologize in advance for any unintentional omissions. We would be pleased to insert the appropriate acknowledgment in any subsequent edition of this publication.

Adams Picture Library: 86CLA; **G Andrews:** 186CR; **Ardea London Ltd:** K Ghana 150C; M Iljima 132TC; R Waller 148TR; Art Directors **Aspect Picture Library:** P Carmichael 160TR; 131CR(below); G Tompkinson 190TRB; **Axiom:** C Bradley 148CA, 158CA; J Holmes xivCRA, xxivBCR, xxviiCRB, 150TCR, 165C(below), 166TL, J Morris 75TL, 77CRB, J Spaull 134BL; **Bridgeman Art Library, London / New York:** Collection of the Earl of Pembroke, Wilton House xxBC; **The J. Allan Cash Photolibrary:** xlBR, xliiCLA, xlivCL, 10BC, 60CL, 69CLB, 70CL, 72CLB, 75BR, 76BC, 87BL, 109BR, 138BCL, 141TL, 154CR, 178BR, 181TR; **Bruce Coleman Ltd:** 86BC, 98CL, 100TC; S Alden 192BC(below); Atlantide xxviTCR, 138BR; E Bjurstrom 141BR; S Bond 96CRB; T Buchholz xvCL, 92TR, 123TCL; J Burton xxiiiC; J Cancalosi 181TRB; B J Coates xxvBL, 192CL; B Coleman 63TL; B & C Colhoun 2TR, 36CB; A Compost xxiiiCBR; Dr S Coyne 45TL; G Cubitt xviTCL, 169BR, 178TR, 184TR; P Davey xxviiCLB, 121TL(below); N Devore 189CBL; S J Doylee xxiiCRR; H Flygare xviiCRA; M P L Fogden 17C(above) ; Jeff Foott Productions xxiiiCRB, 11CRA; M Freeman 91BRA; P van Gaalen 86TR; G Gualco 140C; B Henderson 194CR; Dr C Henneghien 69C; HPH Photography, H Van den Berg 69CR; C Hughes 69BCL; C James xxxixTC; J Johnson 39CR, 197TR; J Jurka 91CA; S C Kaufman 28C; S J Krasemann 33TR; H Lange 10TRB, 68CA; C Lockwood 32BC; L C Marigo xxiiBC, xxviiCLA, 49CRA, 59BR; M McCoy 187TR; D Meredith 3CR; J Murray xvCR, 179BR; Orion Press 165CR(above); Orion Services & Trading Co. Inc. 164CR; C Ott 17BL; Dr E Pott 9TR, 40CL, 87C, 93TL, 194CLB; F Prenzel 186BC, 193BC; M Read 42BR, 43CRB; H Reinhard xxiiCR, xxviiTR, 194BR; L Lee Rue III 151BCL; J Shaw xixTL; K N Swenson 194BC; P Terry 115CR; N Tomalin 54BCL; P Ward 78TC; S Widstrand 57TR; K Wothe 91C, 173TCL; J T Wright 127BR; **Colorific:** Black Star / L Mulvehil 156CL; Black Star / R Rogers 57BR; Black Star / J Rupp 161BCR; Camera Tres / C. Meyer 59BRA; R Caputo / Matrix 78CL; J. Hill 117CLB; M Koene 55TR; G Satterley xliiCLAR; M Yamashita 156BL, 167CR(above); **Comstock:** 108CRB; Corbis UK Ltd: 170TR, 170BL; **D Cousens:** 147 CRA; **Sue Cunningham Photographic:** 51CR; S Alden 192BC(below) **James Davis Travel Photography:** xxxviTCB, xxxviTR, xxxviCL, 13CA, 19BC, 49TLB, 56BCR, 57CLA, 61BCL, 93BC, 94TC, 102TR, 120CB, 158BC, 179CRA, 191BR; **G Dunnet:** 124CA; **Environmental Picture Library:** Chris Westwood 126C; **Eye Ubiquitous:** xlCA; L. Fordyce 12CLA; L Johnstone 6CRA, 28BLA, 30CB; S. Miller xxiCA; M Southern 73BLA; **Chris Fairclough Colour Library:** xliBR; **Ffotograff:** N. Tapsell 158CL **FLPA -Images of nature:** 123TR; **Geoscience Features:** xviBCR, xviBR, 102CL, 108BC, 122BR; Solar Film 64TC; **gettyone stone**: 131BC, 133BR, 164CR(above); G Johnson 130BL; R Passmore 120TR; D Austen 187CL; G Allison 186CL; L Ulrich 17TL; M Vines 17BL; R Wells 193BL; **Robert Harding Picture Library:** xviiTC, xxivCR, xxxC, xxxvTC, 2TLB, 3CA, 15CRB, 15CR, 37BC, 38CRA, 50BL, 95BR, 99CR, 114CR, 122BL, 131CLA, 142CB, 143TL, 147TR, 168TR, 168CA, 166BR; P G. Adam 13TCB; D Atchison-Jones 70BLA; J Bayne 72BCL; B Schuster 80CR; C Bowman 50BR, 53CA, 62CL, 70CRL; C Campbell xxiBC; G Corrigan 159CRB, 161CRB; P Craven xxxvBL; R Cundy 69BR; Delu 79BC; A Durand 111BR; Financial Times 142BR; R Frerck 51BL; T Gervis 3BCL, 7CR; I Griffiths xxxCL, 77TL; T Hall 166CRA; D Harney 142CA; S Harris xliiiBCL; G Hellier xvCRB, 135BL; F Jackson 137BCR; Jacobs xxxviiTL; P Koch 139TR; F Joseph Land 122TR; Y Marcoux 9BR; S Massif xvBC; A Mills 88CLB; L Murray 114TR; R Rainford xlivBL; G Renner 74CB, 194C; C Rennie 48CL, 116BR; R Richardson 118CL; P Van Riel 48BR; E Rooney 124TR; Sassoon xxivCL, 148CLB; P Scholey 176TR; M Short 137TL; E Simanor xxviiCR; V Southwell 139CR; J Strachan 42TR, 111BL, 132BCR; C Tokeley 131CLA; A C Waltham 161C; T Waltham xviiBL, xxiiCLLL, 138CRB; Westlight 37CR; N Wheeler 139BL; A Williams xxxviiiBR, xlTR; A Woolfitt 95BRA; Paul Harris: 168TC; **Hutchison Library:** 131CR (above) 6BL; P. Collomb 137CR; C. Dodwell 130TR; S Errington 70BCL; P. Hellyer 142BC; J. Horner xxxiTC; R. Ian Lloyd 134CRA; N. Durrell McKenna xxviBCR; J.Nowell 135CLB, 143TC; A Zvoznikov xxiiCL; **Image Bank:** 87BR; J Banagan 190BCA; A Becker xxivBCL; M Khansa 121CR, M Isy-Schwart 193CR(above), 191CL; Khansa K Forest 163TR; Lomeo xxivTCR; T Madison 170TL(below); C Molyneux xxiiCRRR; C Navajas xviiiTR; Ocean Images Inc. 192CLB; J van Os xviiTCR; S Proehl 6CL; T Rakke xixTC, 64CL; M Reitz 196CA; M Romanelli 166CL(below); G A Rossi 151BCR, 176BLA; B Roussel 109TL; S Satushek xviiBCR; Stock Photos / J M Spielman xxivTRL; **Images Colour Library:** xxiiCLL, xxxixTR, xliCR, xliiiBL, 3BR, 19BR, 37TL, 44TL, 62TC, 91BR, 102CLB, 103CR, 150CL, 180CA; 164BC, 165TL; **Impact Photos:** J & G Andrews 186BL; C. Bluntzer 156BR; Cosmos / G. Buthaud 65BC; S Franklin 126BL; A. le Garsmeur 131C; A Indge xxviiTC; C Jones xxxiCB, 70BL; V. Nemirousky 137BR; J Nicholl 76TCR; C. Penn 187C(below); G Sweeney xviiBR, 196CB, 196TR, J & G Andrews 186TR; **JVZ Picture Library:** T Nilson 135TC; **Frank Lane Picture Agency:** xxiTCR, xxiiiBL, 93TR; A Christiansen 58CRA; J Holmes xivBL; S. McCutcheon 3C; Silvestris 173TCR; D Smith xxiiBCL; W Wisniewsli 195BR; **Leeds Castle Foundation:** xxxviiBC; **Magnum:** Abbas 83CR, 136CA; S Franklin 134CRB; D Hurn 4BCL; P. Jones-Griffiths 191BL; H Kubota xviBCL, 156CLB; F Maver xviBL; S McCurry 73CL, 133BCR; G. Rodger 74TR; C Steele Perkins 72BL; **Mountain Camera / John Cleare:** 153TR; C Monteath 153CR; **Nature Photographers:** E.A. Janes 112CL; **Natural Science Photos:** M Andera 110C; **Network Photographers Ltd.:** C Sappa / Rapho 119BL; **N.H.P.A.:** N. J. Dennis xxiiiCL; D Heuchlin xxiiiCLA; S Krasemann 15BL, 25BR, 38TC; K Schafer 49CB; R Tidman 160CLB; D Tomlinson 145CR; M Wendler 48TR; **Nottingham Trent University:** T Waltham xivCL, xvBR; **Novosti:** 144BLA; **Oxford Scientific Films:** D Allan xxiiTR; H R Bardarson xviiiBC; D Bown xxiiiCBLL; M Brown 140BL; M Colbeck 147CAR; W Faidley 3TL; L Gould xxiiiTRB; D Guravich xxiiiTR; P Hammerschmidy / Okapia 87CLA; M Hill 57TL, 195TR; C Menteath ; J Netherton 2CRB; S Osolinski 82CA; R Packwood 72CA; M Pitts 179TC; N Rosing xxiiiCBL, 9TR, 197BR; D Simonson 57C; Survival Anglia / C Catton 137TR; R Toms xxiiiBR; K Wothe xxiBL, xviiCLA; **Panos Pictures:** B Aris 133C; P Barker xxivBR; T Bolstao 153BR; N Cooper 82CB, 153TC; J-L Dugast 166C(below), 167BR; J Hartley 73CA, 90CL; J Holmes 149BC; J Morris 76CLB; M Rose 146TR; D Sansoni 155CL; C Stowers 163TL; **Edward Parker:** 49TL, 49CLB; **Pictor International:** xivBR, xvBRA, xixTCL, xxCL, 3CLA, 17BR, 20TR, 20CRB, 23BCA, 23CL, 26CB, 27BC, 30CA, 33TRB, 34BC, 34BR, 34CR, 38CB, 38CL, 43CL, 63BR, 65TC, 82CL, 83CLB, 99BR, 107CLA, 166TR, 171CL(above), 180CLB, 185TL; **Pictures Colour Library:** xxiBCL, xxiiBR, xxviBCL, 6BR, 15TR, 8TR, 16CL(above), 19TL, 20BL, 24C, 24CLA, 27TR, 32TRB, 36BC, 41CA, 43CRA, 68BL, 90TCB, 94BL, 99BL, 106CA, 107CLB, 107CR, 107BR, 117BL, 164BC, 192BL, K Forest 165TL(below); **Planet Earth Pictures:** 193CR(below); D Barrett 148CB, 184CA; R Coomber 16BL; G Douwma 172BR; E Edmonds 173BR; J Lythgoe 196BL; A Mounter 172CR; M Potts 6CA; P Scoones xxTR; J Walencik 110TR; J Waters 53BCL; **Popperfoto:** Reuters / J Drake xxxiiCLA; **Rex Features:** 165CR; Antelope xxxiiCLB; M Friedel xxiCR; I McIlgorm xxxCBR; J Shelley xxxCR; Sipa Press xxxCR; Sipa Press / Alix xxxCBL; Sipa Press / Chamussy 176BL; **Robert Harding Picture Library:** C. Tokeley 131TL; J Strachan 132BL; Franz Joseph Land 122TR; Franz Joseph Land 364/7088 123BL, 169C(above), 170C(above), 168CL, Tony Waltham 186CR(below), Y Marcoux 9BR; **Russia & Republics Photolibrary:** M Wadlow 118CR, 119CL, 124BC, 124CL, 125TL, 125BR, 126TCR; **Science Photo Library:** Earth Satellite Corporation xixTRB, xxxiCR, 49BCL; F Gohier xiCR; J Heseltine xviTCB; K Kent xvBLA; P Menzell xvBL; N.A.S.A. xBC; D Parker xivBC; University of Cambridge Collection Air Pictures 87CLB; RJ Wainscoat / P Arnold, Inc. xiBC; D Weintraub xiBL; **South American Pictures:** 57BL, 62TR; R Francis 52BL; Guyana Space Centre 50TR; T Morrison 49CRB, 49BL, 50CR, 52TR, 54TR, 60BL, 61C; **Southampton Oceanography:** xviiiBL; **Sovofoto / Eastfoto:** xxxiiCBR; **Spectrum Colour Library:** 50BC, 160BC; J King 145BR; **Frank Spooner Pictures:** Gamma-Liason/Vogel 131CL(above); 26CRB; E. Baitel xxxiiBC; Bernstein xxxiCL; Contrast 112CR; Diard / Photo News 113CL; Liaison / C. Hires xxxiiTCB; Liaison / Nickelsberg xxxiiTR; Marleen 113TL; Novosti 116CA; P. Piel xxxCA; N Quidu 135CL; H Stucke 188CLB, 190CA; Torrengo / Figaro 78BR; A Zamur 113BL; **Still Pictures:** C Caldicott 77TC; A Crump 189CL; M & C Denis-Huot xxiiBL, 78CR, 81BL; M Edwards xxiCRL, 53BL, 64CR, 69BLA, 155BR; J Frebet 53CLB; H Giradet 53TC; E Parker 52CL; M Gunther 121BC; **Tony Stone Images:** xxviTR, 4CA, 7BL, 7CL, 13CRB, 39BR, 58C, 97BC, 101BR, 106TR, 109CL, 109CRB, 164CLB, 165C,180CB, 181BR, 188BC, 192TR; G Allison 18TR, 31CRB, 187CRB; D Armand 14TCB; D Austen 180TR, 186CL, 187CL; J Beatty 74CL; O Benn xxviBR; K Biggs xxiTL; R Bradbury 44BR; R A Butcher xxviTL; J Callahan xxviiCRA; P Chesley 185BCL, 188C; W Clay 30BL, 31CRA; J Cornish 96BL, 107TL; C Condina 41CB; T Craddock xxivTR; P Degginger 36CLB; Demetrio 5BR; N DeVore xxivBC; A Diesendruck 60BR; S Egan 87CRA, 96BR; R Elliot xxiiBCR; S Elmore 19C; J Garrett 73CR; S Grandadam 14BR; R Grosskopf 28BL; D Hanson 104BC; C Harvey 69TL; G Hellier 110BL, 165CR; S Huber 103CRB; D Hughs xxxiBR; A Husmo 91TR; G Irvine 31BC; J Jangoux 58CL; D Johnston xviiTR; A Kehr 113C; R Koskas xviTR; J Lamb 96CRA; J Lawrence 75CRA; L Lefkowitz 7CA; M Lewis 45CLA; S Mayman 55BR; Murray & Associates 45CR; G Norways 104CA; N Parfitt xxviiCL, 68TCR, 81TL; R Passmore 121TR; N Press xviBCA; E Pritchard 88CA, 90CLR; T Raymond 21BL, 29TR; L Resnick 74BR; M Rogers 80BR; A Sacks 28TCB; C Saule 90CR; S Schulhof xxivTC; P Seaward 34CL; M Segal 32BL; V Shenai 152CL; R Sherman 26CL; H Sitton 136CR; R Smith xxvBLA, 56C; S Studd 108CLA; H Strand 49BR, 63TR; P Tweedie 177CR; L Ulrich 17BL; M Vines 17TC; A B Wadham 60CR; J Warden 63CLB; R Wells 23CRA, 193BL; G Yeowell 34BL; **Telegraph Colour Library:** 61CRB, 61TCR, 157TL; R Antrobus xxxixBR; J Sims 26BR; **Topham Picturepoint:** xxxiCBL, 162BR, 168TR, 168BC; **Travel Ink:** A Cowin 88TR; **Trip:** 140BR, 144CA, 155CRA; B Ashe 159TR; D Cole 190BCL, 190CR; D Davis 89BL; I Deineko xxxiTR; J Dennis 22BL; Dinodia 154CL; Eye Ubiquitous / L Fordyce 2CLB; A Gasson 149CR; W Jacobs 43TL, 54BL, 177BC, 178CLA, 185BCR, 186BL; P Kingsbury 112C; K Knight 177BR; V Kolpakov 147BL; T Noorits 87TL, 119BR, 146CL; R Power 41TR; N Ray 166BL, 168TC; C Rennie 116CLB; V Sidoropolev 145TR; E Smith 183BC, 183TL; **Woodfin Camp & Associates:** 92BLR; **World Pictures:** xvCRA, xviiCRA, 9CRB, 22CL, 23BC, 24BL, 35BL, 40TR, 51TR, 71BR, 80TCR, 82TR, 83BL, 86BCR, 96TC, 98BL, 100CR, 101CR, 103BC, 105TC, 157BL, 161BCL, 162CLB, 172CLB, 172BC, 179BL, 182CB, 183C, 184CL, 185CR; 121BR, 121TT; **Zefa Picture Library:** xviBLR, xviiBCL, xviiiCL, 3CL, 8BC, 8CT, 9CR, 13BC, 14TC, 16TR, 21TL, 22CRB, 25BL, 32TCR, 36BCR, 59BCL, 65TCL, 69CLA, 79TL, 81BR, 87CRB, 92C, 98C, 99TL, 100BL, 107TR, 118CRB, 120BL; 122C(below), 124CLA, 164BR, 183TR; Anatol 113BR; Barone 114BL; Brandenburg 5C; A J Brown 44TR; H J Clauss 55CLB; Damm 71BC; Evert 92BL; W Felger 3BL; J Fields 189CRA; R Frerck 4BL; G Heil 56BR; K Heibig 115BR; Heilman 28BC; Hunter 8C; Kitchen 10TR, 8CL, 8BL, 9TR; Dr H Kramarz 7BLA, 123CR(below); Mehlio 155BL; J F Raga 24TR; Rossenbach 105BR; Streichan 89TL; T Stewart 13TR, 19CR; Sunak 54BR, 162TR; D H Teuffen 95TL; B Zaunders 40BC. **Additional Photography:** Geoff Dann; Rob Reichenfeld; H Taylor; Jerry Young.

NORTH AMERICA

CANADA
PAGES 8–15

UNITED STATES OF AMERICA
PAGES 16–39

MEXICO
PAGES 40–41

BELIZE
PAGES 42–43

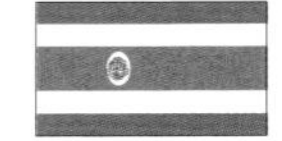
COSTA RICA
PAGES 42–43

EL SALVADOR
PAGES 42–43

GUATEMALA
PAGES 42–43

HONDURAS
PAGES 42–43

GRENADA
PAGES 44–45

HAITI
PAGES 44–45

JAMAICA
PAGES 44–45

ST KITTS & NEVIS
PAGES 44–45

ST LUCIA
PAGES 44–45

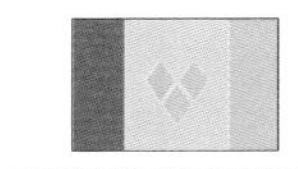
ST VINCENT & THE GRENADINES
PAGES 44–45

TRINIDAD & TOBAGO
PAGES 44–45

SOUTH AMERICA

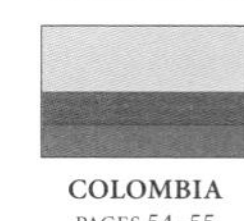
COLOMBIA
PAGES 54–55

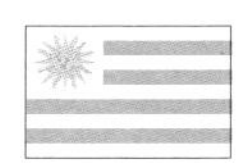
URUGUAY
PAGES 60–61

CHILE
PAGES 62–63

PARAGUAY
PAGES 62–63

AFRICA

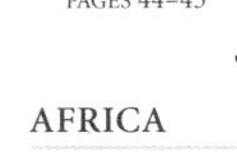
ALGERIA
PAGES 74–75

EGYPT
PAGES 74–75

LIBYA
PAGES 74–75

MOROCCO
PAGES 74–75

TUNISIA
PAGES 74–75

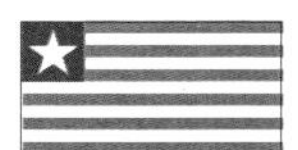
LIBERIA
PAGES 76–77

MALI
PAGES 76–77

MAURITANIA
PAGES 76–77

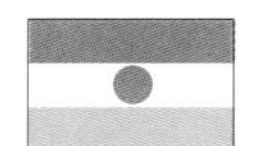
NIGER
PAGES 76–77

NIGERIA
PAGES 76–77

SENEGAL
PAGES 76–77

SIERRA LEONE
PAGES 76–77

TOGO
PAGES 76–77

BURUNDI
PAGES 80–81

DJIBOUTI
PAGES 80–81

ERITREA
PAGES 80–81

ETHIOPIA
PAGES 80–81

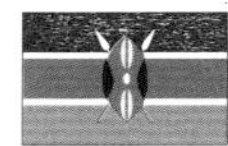
KENYA
PAGES 80–81

RWANDA
PAGES 80–81

SOMALIA
PAGES 80–81

SUDAN
PAGES 80–81

SOUTH AFRICA
PAGES 82–83

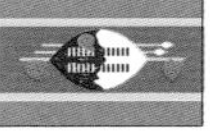
SWAZILAND
PAGES 82–83

ZAMBIA
PAGES 82–83

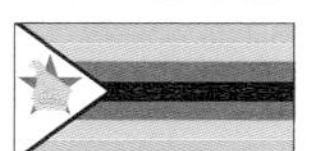
ZIMBABWE
PAGES 82–83

EUROPE

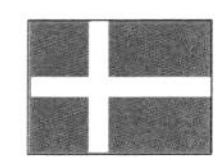
DENMARK
PAGES 92–93

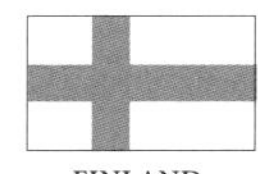
FINLAND
PAGES 92–93

ICELAND
PAGES 92–93

NORWAY
PAGES 92–95

MONACO
PAGES 102–103

ANDORRA
PAGES 104–105

PORTUGAL
PAGES 104–105

SPAIN
PAGES 104–105

ITALY
PAGES 106–107

SAN MARINO
PAGES 106–107

VATICAN CITY
PAGES 106–107

AUSTRIA
PAGES 108–109

BOSNIA & HERZEGOVINA
PAGES 112–113

CROATIA
PAGES 112–113

MACEDONIA
PAGES 112–113

MONTENEGRO
PAGES 112–113

SERBIA
PAGES 112–113

BULGARIA
PAGES 114–115

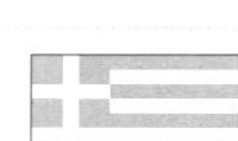
GREECE
PAGES 114–115

MOLDOVA
PAGES 116–117

ASIA

ARMENIA
PAGES 136–137

AZERBAIJAN
PAGES 136–137

GEORGIA
PAGES 136–137

TURKEY
PAGES 136–137/114–115

IRAQ
PAGES 138–139

ISRAEL
PAGES 138–139

JORDAN
PAGES 138–139

LEBANON
PAGES 138–139

IRAN
PAGES 142–143

KAZAKHSTAN
PAGES 144–145

KYRGYZSTAN
PAGES 146–147

TAJIKISTAN
PAGES 146–147

TURKMENISTAN
PAGES 146–147

UZBEKISTAN
PAGES 146–147

AFGHANISTAN
PAGES 148–149

PAKISTAN
PAGES 148–151

TAIWAN
PAGES 160–161

JAPAN
PAGES 164–165

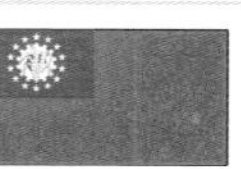
MYANMAR
PAGES 166–167

CAMBODIA
PAGES 166–167

LAOS
PAGES 166–167

PHILIPPINES
PAGES 166–167

THAILAND
PAGES 166–167

VIETNAM
PAGES 166–167

MAURITIUS
PAGES 172–173

SEYCHELLES
PAGES 172–173

AUSTRALASIA & OCEANIA

AUSTRALIA
PAGES 180–183

NEW ZEALAND
PAGES 184–185

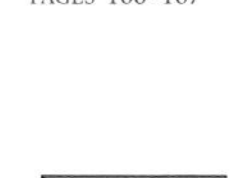

PAPUA NEW GUINEA
PAGES 186–187

FIJI
PAGES 186–187

SOLOMON ISLANDS
PAGES 186–187

VANUATU
PAGES 186–187

ML 12/08